Presented to Chris Martin
on June 18, 2017
by Sandy Bell

The Jesus Bible

sixty-six books. one story. all about one name.

ZONDERVAN®

The Jesus Bible, NIV Edition

Published by Zondervan
Zondervan, *Grand Rapids, Michigan 49546*

www.zondervan.com

Library of Congress Catalog Card Number 2016944211

Printed in China

N120712

---

16 17 18 19 20 21 22 23 24 25 /DSC/ 20 19 18 17 16 15 14 13 12 11 10 9 8 7 6 5 4 3 2 1

A portion of the purchase price of your NIV® Bible is provided to Biblica so together we support the mission of *Transforming lives through God's Word.*

Biblica provides God's Word to people through translation, publishing and Bible engagement in Africa, Asia Pacific, Europe, Latin America, Middle East, and North America. Through its worldwide reach, Biblica engages people with God's Word so that their lives are transformed through a relationship with Jesus Christ.

TABLE OF CONTENTS

THE OLD TESTAMENT

THE NEW TESTAMENT

PREFACE

The goal of the New International Version (NIV) is to enable English-speaking people from around the world to read and hear God's eternal Word in their own language. Our work as translators is motivated by our conviction that the Bible is God's Word in written form. We believe that the Bible contains the divine answer to the deepest needs of humanity, sheds unique light on our path in a dark world and sets forth the way to our eternal well-being. Out of these deep convictions, we have sought to recreate as far as possible the experience of the original audience — blending transparency to the original text with accessibility for the millions of English speakers around the world. We have prioritized accuracy, clarity and literary quality with the goal of creating a translation suitable for public and private reading, evangelism, teaching, preaching, memorizing and liturgical use. We have also sought to preserve a measure of continuity with the long tradition of translating the Scriptures into English.

The complete NIV Bible was first published in 1978. It was a completely new translation made by over a hundred scholars working directly from the best available Hebrew, Aramaic and Greek texts. The translators came from the United States, Great Britain, Canada, Australia and New Zealand, giving the translation an international scope. They were from many denominations and churches — including Anglican, Assemblies of God, Baptist, Brethren, Christian Reformed, Church of Christ, Evangelical Covenant, Evangelical Free, Lutheran, Mennonite, Methodist, Nazarene, Presbyterian, Wesleyan and others. This breadth of denominational and theological perspective helped to safeguard the translation from sectarian bias. For these reasons, and by the grace of God, the NIV has gained a wide readership in all parts of the English-speaking world.

The work of translating the Bible is never finished. As good as they are, English translations must be regularly updated so that they will continue to communicate accurately the meaning of God's Word. Updates are needed in order to reflect the latest developments in our understanding of the biblical world and its languages and to keep pace with changes in English usage. Recognizing, then, that the NIV would retain its ability to communicate God's Word accurately only if it were regularly updated, the original translators established the Committee on Bible Translation (CBT). The Committee is a self-perpetuating group of biblical scholars charged with keeping abreast of advances in biblical scholarship and changes in English and issuing periodic updates to the NIV. The CBT is an independent, self-governing body and has sole responsibility for the NIV text. The Committee mirrors the original group of translators in its diverse international and denominational makeup and in its unifying commitment to the Bible as God's inspired Word.

In obedience to its mandate, the Committee has issued periodic updates to the NIV. An initial revision was released in 1984. A more thorough revision process was completed in 2005, resulting in the separately published TNIV. The updated NIV you now have in your hands builds on both the original NIV and the TNIV and represents the latest effort of the Committee to articulate God's unchanging Word in the way the original authors might have said it had they been speaking in English to the global English-speaking audience today.

Translation Philosophy

The Committee's translating work has been governed by three widely accepted principles about the way people use words and about the way we understand them.

First, the meaning of words is determined by the way that users of the language actually use them at any given time. For the biblical languages, therefore, the Committee utilizes the best and most recent scholarship on the way Hebrew, Aramaic and Greek words were being used in biblical times. At the same time, the Committee carefully studies the state of modern English. Good translation is like good communication: one must know the target audience so that the appropriate choices can be made about which English words to use to represent the original words of Scripture. From its inception, the NIV has had as its target the general English-speaking population all over the world, the "International" in its title reflecting this concern. The aim of the Committee is to put the Scriptures into natural English that will communicate effectively with the broadest possible audience of English speakers.

Modern technology has enhanced the Committee's ability to choose the right English words to convey the meaning of the original text. The field of computational linguistics harnesses the power of computers to provide broadly applicable and current data about the state of the language. Translators can now access huge databases of modern English to better understand the current meaning and usage of key words. The Committee utilized this resource in preparing the

2011 edition of the NIV. An area of especially rapid and significant change in English is the way certain nouns and pronouns are used to refer to human beings. The Committee therefore requested experts in computational linguistics at Collins Dictionaries to pose some key questions about this usage to its database of English — the largest in the world, with over 4.4 billion words, gathered from several English-speaking countries and including both spoken and written English. (The Collins Study, called "The Development and Use of Gender Language in Contemporary English," can be accessed at *http://www.thenivbible.com/about-the-niv/about-the-2011-edition/*.) The study revealed that the most popular words to describe the human race in modern U.S. English were "humanity," "man" and "mankind." The Committee then used this data in the updated NIV, choosing from among these three words (and occasionally others also) depending on the context.

A related issue creates a larger problem for modern translations: the move away from using the third-person masculine singular pronouns — "he/him/his" — to refer to men and women equally. This usage does persist in some forms of English, and this revision therefore occasionally uses these pronouns in a generic sense. But the tendency, recognized in day-to-day usage and confirmed by the Collins study, is away from the generic use of "he," "him" and "his." In recognition of this shift in language and in an effort to translate into the natural English that people are actually using, this revision of the NIV generally uses other constructions when the biblical text is plainly addressed to men and women equally. The reader will encounter especially frequently a "they," "their" or "them" to express a generic singular idea. Thus, for instance, Mark 8:36 reads: "What good is it for someone to gain the whole world, yet forfeit their soul?" This generic use of the "distributive" or "singular" "they/them/their" has been used for many centuries by respected writers of English and has now become established as standard English, spoken and written, all over the world.

A second linguistic principle that feeds into the Committee's translation work is that meaning is found not in individual words, as vital as they are, but in larger clusters: phrases, clauses, sentences, discourses. Translation is not, as many people think, a matter of word substitution: English word *x* in place of Hebrew word *y*. Translators must first determine the meaning of the words of the biblical languages in the context of the passage and then select English words that accurately communicate that meaning to modern listeners and readers. This means that accurate translation will not always reflect the exact structure of the original language. To be sure, there is debate over the degree to which translators should try to preserve the "form" of the original text in English. From the beginning, the NIV has taken a mediating position on this issue. The manual produced when the translation that became the NIV was first being planned states: "If the Greek or Hebrew syntax has a good parallel in modern English, it should be used. But if there is no good parallel, the English syntax appropriate to the meaning of the original is to be chosen." It is fine, in other words, to carry over the form of the biblical languages into English — but not at the expense of natural expression. The principle that meaning resides in larger clusters of words means that the Committee has not insisted on a "word-for-word" approach to translation. We certainly believe that every word of Scripture is inspired by God and therefore to be carefully studied to determine what God is saying to us. It is for this reason that the Committee labors over every single word of the original texts, working hard to determine how each of those words contributes to what the text is saying. Ultimately, however, it is how these individual words function in combination with other words that determines meaning.

A third linguistic principle guiding the Committee in its translation work is the recognition that words have a spectrum of meaning. It is popular to define a word by using another word, or "gloss," to substitute for it. This substitute word is then sometimes called the "literal" meaning of a word. In fact, however, words have a range of possible meanings. Those meanings will vary depending on the context, and words in one language will usually not occupy the same semantic range as words in another language. The Committee therefore studies each original word of Scripture in its context to identify its meaning in a particular verse and then chooses an appropriate English word (or phrase) to represent it. It is impossible, then, to translate any given Hebrew, Aramaic or Greek word with the same English word all the time. The Committee does try to translate related occurrences of a word in the original languages with the same English word in order to preserve the connection for the English reader. But the Committee generally privileges clear natural meaning over a concern with consistency in rendering particular words.

Textual Basis

For the Old Testament the standard Hebrew text, the Masoretic Text as published in the latest edition of *Biblia Hebraica*, has been used throughout. The Masoretic Text tradition contains marginal notations that offer variant readings. These have sometimes been followed instead of the text itself. Because such instances involve variants within the Masoretic tradition, they have not been indicated in the textual notes. In a few cases, words in the basic consonantal text have been divided differently than in the Masoretic Text. Such cases are usually indicated in the textual footnotes. The Dead Sea Scrolls contain biblical texts that represent an earlier stage of the transmission of the Hebrew text. They have been consulted, as have been the Samaritan Pentateuch and the ancient scribal traditions concerning deliberate textual changes. The translators also consulted the more important early versions. Readings from these versions, the Dead Sea Scrolls and the scribal traditions were occasionally followed where the Masoretic Text seemed doubtful and where accepted principles of textual criticism showed that one or more of these textual witnesses appeared to provide the correct reading. In rare cases, the translators have emended the Hebrew text where it appears to have become corrupted at an even earlier stage of its transmission. These departures from the Masoretic Text are also indicated in the textual footnotes. Sometimes the vowel indicators (which are later additions to the basic consonantal text) found in the Masoretic Text did not, in the judgment of the translators, represent the correct vowels for the original text. Accordingly, some words have been read with a different set of vowels. These instances are usually not indicated in the footnotes.

The Greek text used in translating the New Testament has been an eclectic one, based on the latest editions of the Nestle-Aland/United Bible Societies' Greek New Testament. The translators have made their choices among the variant readings in accordance with widely accepted principles of New Testament textual criticism. Footnotes call attention to places where uncertainty remains.

The New Testament authors, writing in Greek, often quote the Old Testament from its ancient Greek version, the Septuagint. This is one reason why some of the Old Testament quotations in the NIV New Testament are not identical to the corresponding passages in the NIV Old Testament. Such quotations in the New Testament are indicated with the footnote "(see Septuagint)."

Footnotes and Formatting

Footnotes in this version are of several kinds, most of which need no explanation. Those giving alternative translations begin with "Or" and generally introduce the alternative with the last word preceding it in the text, except when it is a single-word alternative. When poetry is quoted in a footnote a slash mark indicates a line division.

It should be noted that references to diseases, minerals, flora and fauna, architectural details, clothing, jewelry, musical instruments and other articles cannot always be identified with precision. Also, linear measurements and measures of capacity can only be approximated (see the Table of Weights and Measures). Although *Selah*, used mainly in the Psalms, is probably a musical term, its meaning is uncertain. Since it may interrupt reading and distract the reader, this word has not been kept in the English text, but every occurrence has been signaled by a footnote.

As an aid to the reader, sectional headings have been inserted. They are not to be regarded as part of the biblical text and are not intended for oral reading. It is the Committee's hope that these headings may prove more helpful to the reader than the traditional chapter divisions, which were introduced long after the Bible was written.

Sometimes the chapter and/or verse numbering in English translations of the Old Testament differs from that found in published Hebrew texts. This is particularly the case in the Psalms, where the traditional titles are included in the Hebrew verse numbering. Such differences are indicated in the footnotes at the bottom of the page. In the New Testament, verse numbers that marked off portions of the traditional English text not supported by the best Greek manuscripts now appear in brackets, with a footnote indicating the text that has been omitted (see, for example, Matthew 17:[21]).

Mark 16:9–20 and John 7:53—8:11, although long accorded virtually equal status with the rest of the Gospels in which they stand, have a questionable standing in the textual history of the New Testament, as noted in the bracketed annotations with which they are set off. A different typeface has been chosen for these passages to indicate their uncertain status.

Basic formatting of the text, such as lining the poetry, paragraphing (both prose and poetry), setting up of (administrative-like) lists, indenting letters and lengthy prayers within narratives and the insertion of sectional headings, has been the work of the Committee. However, the choice between single-column and double-column formats has been left to the publishers. Also the issuing of "red-letter" editions is a publisher's choice—one that the Committee does not endorse.

The Committee has again been reminded that every human effort is flawed—including this revision of the NIV. We trust, however, that many will find in it an improved representation of the Word of God, through which they hear his call to faith in our Lord Jesus Christ and to service in his kingdom. We offer this version of the Bible to him in whose name and for whose glory it has been made.

The Committee on Bible Translation

CONTRIBUTORS

EDITOR IN CHIEF
Louie Giglio

GENERAL EDITOR
Aaron B. Coe, PhD

FEATURE ARTICLES
Randy Alcorn
Louie Giglio
Max Lucado
John Piper, PhD
Ravi Zacharias, PhD

LEAD WRITER
Matthew A. Rogers, PhD

CONTENT ARCHITECT
John Kramp

LEAD EDITOR
Carol Postma

EDITORIAL TEAM, PASSION PUBLISHING
Aaron B. Coe, PhD
Kevin Marks
Emily Vogeltanz

EDITORIAL TEAM, ZONDERVAN
Melinda Bouma
John Kramp
Daniel Marrs
Carol Postma
Mike Vander Klipp

CONTRIBUTING WRITERS
Jon Akin, PhD
Carmen Coe
Jason Dees, PhD
Kyle Dunn
Jeni Fobart
Lindsay Guerin
Jonathan Hansen
Jake Jelinek
Michael Kelley
John Kramp
Will McGee
Tobin Perry
Joe Rice
Ben Roberts
Matt Sliger, PhD
Ben Stuart
Ryan West, PhD
Thomas West
Jonny Wills
Karen Woodall
Don Wooley
Freddy T. Wyatt
Aynsley Younker
Brett Younker

WELCOME
TO THE STORY OF GOD!
—LOUIE GIGLIO

No book on earth has been talked about, debated, revered or hated more than the one you hold in your hands. This single book has revolutionized cultures and ignited revolutions.

It's not uncommon for people to approach the Bible with preconceived notions about where it came from or what it has to say. Some assert it is fable, created by men. Others view it as just another religious manual, while some see it simply as a helpful roadmap for those seeking spiritual guidance.

But ultimately the Bible defines itself, claiming to be a book like no other. The Bible declares that it is altogether different — the holy, sacred, inspired, alive and active Word of God. It is the unique story of God from beginning to end, with one central character — Jesus Christ.

From the beginning of time, oral tradition (story) has played a crucial role in human development, serving as the vehicle by which communities bonded, history was understood and culture was transferred from one generation to the next. In places where the written word has yet to emerge, the singular force of story remains.

Yet everywhere on earth, no matter how advanced the civilization, people are attracted to well-told stories. Every great film, novel, song, video game and art form — even the recounting of a recent vacation or the marketing muscle of the best corporate brand — is rooted in the power of story.

Why are we so attracted to story? Could it be because we are made in the image of a story-creating God, born into the already-in-motion story of the One who has always been, yet chose to make himself known to you and me? The story is undoubtedly his story, yet, miraculously, he weaves us into its pages as those prized and pursued by him.

Theologian N.T. Wright says that Scripture reveals that Christianity is the true story of the whole world. That's a beautiful thought when you consider the idea of story is woven into the fabric of humanity.

Speaking of and for itself, the Bible says, "All Scripture is God-breathed" (2Ti 3:16). While penned by human writers under the inspiration of the Holy Spirit, the Bible is comprised of God-breathed words. What you are holding is not simply ink on a page. It is breath on a page! It is the revelation of the holiness, mercy and grace of God to everyone.

Front and center in the story is Jesus. He is the God-man who created everything, yet he entered history to redeem sinful man and raise us by grace to everlasting life. Not only carefully chronicled by eyewitness Gospel accounts, Jesus' life was acknowledged by the leading historians of his day. His death and resurrection are the defining moments in human history, the latter being one of the most investigated events of all time. As Jesus' death and resurrection are proclaimed, their power brings men and women from spiritual death to life on every continent every single day.

But Jesus' role in the story is not confined to the accounts of Matthew, Mark, Luke and John. Jesus is as visible on the first page as the last. He is as present in the Garden of Eden as he is in the garden tomb. The entire story points to him. Jesus himself affirms this when he said, "You study the Scriptures diligently because you think that in them you have eternal life. These are the very Scriptures that testify about me" (Jn 5:39).

That's why we have created *The Jesus Bible*. Filled with relevant notes and pertinent articles, *The Jesus Bible* will help you follow the thread of Jesus from cover to cover to discover a new depth to the Bible's meaning as you see him in every chapter of the story.

You may be asking, "How do I get my head around such a massive story? Where do I start in gaining a better grasp of the full story of the Bible?"

The Bible is best understood when it's viewed as one story in six acts:

As we take a quick look at each act, we see traces of Jesus at every turn.

BEGINNINGS

Every story has a beginning.

Every philosopher, scientist, civilization, poet, religion and everyday person has a story of beginnings.

As Jesus people, our story begins with a creating God. The text underscores that you are created in the image of God. Thus, your origination was in the mind of a majestic God. Everything beautiful, spiritual, wonderful and eternal about you is the result of his divine image woven into your spirit from the start.

The triune God ("Let *us* make mankind in *our* image," Ge 1:26) works through the Son to bring about the creation of everything. "For in him

WELCOME

(CONTINUED)

[Jesus] all things were created: things in heaven and on earth, visible and invisible, whether thrones or powers or rulers or authorities; all things have been created through him and for him" (Col 1:16).

In the beginning Jesus created everything.

REVOLT

Every story has a problem. The problem for humanity is sin.

Though welcomed into paradise, Adam and Eve had free will. Choosing to attempt to become like God, they fell into physical and spiritual death. The consequences were severe and humankind was separated from their Creator. Yet, in mercy, God sacrificed an animal and made a covering for the man and woman. This covering was a picture of what was to come — forgiveness and righteousness through the sacrifice of Jesus Christ.

When people revolted, God had already set in motion a plan of salvation through Jesus Christ.

PEOPLE

Every story has participants — those who are going to be impacted by the unfolding drama.

The fall resulted in mankind's struggles with hardship of every kind. But God was not silent. Through Abraham, God commissioned a people to be his — a special chosen people who would be a witness on earth of his faithfulness. God showered them in blessing, yet they constantly reverted to sinful ways. Time and time again the people rejected God, their decisions ultimately leading them to oppression and loss. Invariably, they called out to the God they had forgotten, and God, in turn, always showed mercy.

At each turn of this vicious cycle of death and destruction, God would announce through a prophet a coming Savior, Jesus Christ.

SAVIOR

Every story has a hero. In this story his name is Jesus.

The Bible says that in the fullness of time, God's promised Savior was born in a stable. Jesus did what no other could do, by bringing an end to the system of sacrifice and ritual. Once and for all, Jesus appeased God's wrath through his death on the cross, opening the way for rebels to come home to a peace-making Father.

A star led the shepherds to the place of Christ's birth, but history has been pointing to Jesus since time began. Jesus is God's appointed and God's anointed. He is the way, the truth and the life. All come to the Father through him (Jn 14:6).

CHURCH

Every story has an effect.

The church is made up of a people who have been redeemed by Jesus and have been formed to live on mission with him.

Once Jesus was raised from the dead and ascended into heaven, he sent the Holy Spirit to give birth to his Church. While churches come in all shapes and sizes, the true Church of Jesus is comprised of all who have confessed him as Savior and Lord. A living organism, his body, the church, serves to extend his grace and truth on earth. Powered by that same Spirit, the church exists to proclaim Jesus' glory to all people.

FOREVER

Every story has a resolution.

At a time only the Father knows, everything in heaven and earth will be put right once and for all. Those opposed to Jesus will get what they have asked for — an eternity without his goodness and glory. The redeemed will gather in his presence from every race and nation, singing the song of Jesus who rescued them from death and brought them into unending life.

As you open these pages, you step into the greatest story of all. Rich in historical accuracy, this biblical story, written over thousands of years by dozens of authors, is stunning in its symmetry and cohesiveness. Contrary to what some may think, this story isn't designed to limit mankind. The story of Jesus liberates us in his light, saving us from the perilous paths of our limited understanding and leading us to the most vibrant life imaginable.

Through the Scripture, God makes extraordinary promises to you and me. The Bible claims it can make us wise, bring life to our souls, open our eyes to see who and whose we are, fill our hearts with joy, make us purposeful, give our lives meaning, restore what has been lost and protect us from a shipwrecked life.

If you approach the Bible with an open mind, I am confident you will be met by the Spirit of God who breathed these words into existence. He promises that "he will guide you into all the truth" (Jn 16:13). Ultimately, you will come face to face with the One who appears on each page and in every act. You will soon discover that it is Jesus whom the story is all about.

And that's the goal. For as precious and enduring as the Bible is, you were not made for information alone, but for a relationship with Jesus. He is the One who helps us see that truth is not simply a thing; rather, truth is a person. Truth is in Jesus and Jesus is truth. He alone is the one who ends death and gives life to all who hope in Him.

Welcome to the story of God. More specifically, welcome to the story of how Jesus creates and restores all things.

OLD TESTAMENT

JESUS: OUR GLORIOUS CREATOR

GENESIS

GENESIS

CREATION *Unknown*	ABRAM GOES TO CANAAN *c. 2091 BC*	JACOB AND HIS FAMILY GO TO EGYPT *c. 1876 BC*

The book of beginnings starts with the most significant words of all time: "In the beginning God." With these words, the story of God's grand and glorious plan for humanity commences. The opening book of the Bible is about God's created design for his world, humankind's fall into sin and rebellion, and God's gracious plan to rescue his beloved people from the terrible implications of their sin. The stories of famous people such as Abram/Abraham, Isaac, Jacob and Joseph fill the book and trace the story of God's grace toward his chosen people. At the outset of the Bible, right after the first sin, God promised to send One who would defeat Satan and sin forever. Jesus, the creative Word by which God spoke all things into being (Jn 1:1) would one day make his dwelling in a fallen world in order to save sinful humanity.

God, through Moses, prepared these documents to present a unified picture of the nature and character of himself and his work in the world to the second generation of those freed from slavery in Egypt — those who were poised to take the land of promise. This record of God's dealings with humanity, starting with his created design, connected this generation to God's continued grace, mercy and guidance.

The first few chapters of Genesis introduce the God of creation and his goal for his created image-bearers. Human sin contaminated and marred God's created world, but it has not thwarted his purposes. He will still be known and worshiped, and his glory will fill the earth. In order to demonstrate his holiness and hatred of sin, God acted in judgment (Ge 3:16 – 19). This judgment, however, did not obscure the abundance of grace seen throughout Genesis. He pledged to send a child, an offspring of the woman, who would one day crush the head of Satan forever (Ge 3:15). In this way, God declared that he had a plan to reclaim rebellious image-bearers from their sin. Throughout Genesis, God repeatedly made these promises in the form of a series of covenants in which he pledged his loyalty, faithfulness and grace to humans, who were then called to respond to this grace with worshipful obedience.

God's created design and mission in the world have not changed. He is still intent on filling the earth with his glory and using his created image-bearers to accomplish that goal. Christ, in his wrath-bearing death and life-giving resurrection, allows people to fulfill the very purpose for which they were created. His death fulfilled the covenant promises of God to make a way for people to have a right relationship with God in spite of human sin. Jesus' perfect obedience demonstrated the values of the kingdom of God and defined the hope that we look for — the coming day when sin and death will be eradicated forever.

IN THE BEGINNING GOD CREATED THE HEAVENS AND THE EARTH.

Genesis 1:1

GENESIS

The Beginning

1 In the beginning God created the heavens and the earth. 2 Now the earth
was formless and empty, darkness was over the surface of the deep, and the
Spirit of God was hovering over the waters.

3 And God said, "Let there be light," and there was light. 4 God saw that the light
was good, and he separated the light from the darkness. 5 God called the
light "day," and the darkness he called "night." And there was evening, and
there was morning — the first day.
6 And God said, "Let there be a vault between the waters to separate water from
water." 7 So God made the vault and separated the water under the vault
from the water above it. And it was so. 8 God called the vault "sky." And
there was evening, and there was morning — the second day.
9 And God said, "Let the water under the sky be gathered to one place, and let
dry ground appear." And it was so. 10 God called the dry ground "land," and
the gathered waters he called "seas." And God saw that it was good.
11 Then God said, "Let the land produce vegetation: seed-bearing plants
and trees on the land that bear fruit with seed in it, according to their various kinds." And it was so. 12 The land produced vegetation: plants bearing
seed according to their kinds and trees bearing fruit with seed in it according to their kinds. And God saw that it was good. 13 And there was evening,
and there was morning — the third day.
14 And God said, "Let there be lights in the vault of the sky to separate the day
from the night, and let them serve as signs to mark sacred times, and days
and years, 15 and let them be lights in the vault of the sky to give light on
the earth." And it was so. 16 God made two great lights — the greater light
to govern the day and the lesser light to govern the night. He also made
the stars. 17 God set them in the vault of the sky to give light on the earth,
18 to govern the day and the night, and to separate light from darkness. And
God saw that it was good. 19 And there was evening, and there was morning — the fourth day.
20 And God said, "Let the water teem with living creatures, and let birds fly
above the earth across the vault of the sky." 21 So God created the great creatures of the sea and every living thing with which the water teems and that
moves about in it, according to their kinds, and every winged bird according to its kind. And God saw that it was good. 22 God blessed them and said,
"Be fruitful and increase in number and fill the water in the seas, and let
the birds increase on the earth." 23 And there was evening, and there was
morning — the fifth day.
24 And God said, "Let the land produce living creatures according to their kinds:
the livestock, the creatures that move along the ground, and the wild animals, each according to its kind." And it was so. 25 God made the wild animals according to their kinds, the livestock according to their kinds, and
all the creatures that move along the ground according to their kinds. And
God saw that it was good.
26 Then God said, "Let us make mankind in our image, in our likeness,
so that they may rule over the fish in the sea and the birds in the sky, over
the livestock and all the wild animals,[a] and over all the creatures that move
along the ground."

[a] *26* Probable reading of the original Hebrew text (see Syriac); Masoretic Text *the earth*

GENESIS 1:3

LET THERE BE LIGHT

God brings light into darkness. That is a recurring theme throughout the Bible, and it begins here. In this verse, the spoken words of God create physical light to brighten a dark world. The New Testament records God sending his Son, Jesus, to be the light of the world (Jn 1:1 – 14). And Paul wrote to the church in Corinth that salvation occurs when God commands the light of his own glory "displayed in the face of Christ" to shine on the darkness of sinful hearts (2Co 4:6). Light represents the glory and salvation of God as it is expressed in Jesus Christ. Jesus is the exact representation of God, and he revealed God to a world sitting in darkness. Those who trust in Jesus are brought from the darkness of sin into God's light — where there is joy, peace and hope forever. In the end, there will be no more darkness, and the light of God's glory will shine brightly in God's eternal kingdom (Rev 21:23).

GENESIS 1:26 – 27

MADE IN GOD'S IMAGE

Human beings are uniquely created in the image of God. When the rest of creation was being birthed, it was "good." God created the birds, fish, plants and stars to display his splendor and oh, how amazing they are.

(continued on page 6)

JESUS CREATED EVERYTHING AND HOLDS IT ALL TOGETHER

Jesus has been from the beginning. We live in a pluralist society where many people believe in some type of "god." Therefore you probably would not get a whole lot of pushback when you say, "God created the heavens and the earth." However, understanding that Jesus created everything changes how one views the whole of Scripture. Colossians 1:15 – 17 says that, "The Son [Jesus] is the image of the invisible God, the firstborn over all creation. For in him all things were created: things in heaven and on earth, visible and invisible, whether thrones or powers or rulers or authorities; all things have been created through him and for him. He is before all things, and in him all things hold together." Paul writes that all things were created by, through and for Jesus.

John makes a similar claim at the outset of his Gospel. The New Testament was written in Greek to a largely Greco-Roman audience. The Greeks believed that there was a unifying force that holds the entire world together. They defined that force as the *Logos*. The Gospel of John defines the *Logos* as Jesus. John 1:1 – 2 says, "In the beginning was the Word [*Logos*], and the Word [*Logos*] was with God, and the Word [*Logos*] was God. He was with God in the beginning." The Word of God — the very agent God used to create all things — took on flesh and made his dwelling on earth in the person of Jesus Christ.

John and Paul affirm this is the agent of creation — the eternal Word of God who was used by God to make something out of nothing. Understanding that Jesus created everything and holds everything together should shape how we read the whole of Scripture. Jesus does not make his first appearance in the book of Matthew. God's Trinitarian nature is on display from the outset of the Scriptures. And, in many ways, the various stories found throughout the Old Testament help explain the nature, character and work of Jesus Christ. Time and time again, God sets the stage for the sending of the Son to fulfill his eternal plan to save those who were dead in their sins.

(Made in God's Image, continued)

God said these creations were good. However, when it came to humans, the tone changed. He said that the creation of humans was "very good." Human beings are an extra-special creation for at least three reasons. First, it is clear that humans have an identity that is rooted in God. When God said, "Let us make mankind in our image," he reiterated the presence of Jesus and the Holy Spirit in the act of creation (see article on Ge 1:1). Humans are special because Jesus, as a part of the Trinity, created them in his image. Second, humans are special because they were created for a unique purpose. No two humans are the same. Other aspects of creation serve general functions, but only humans have a unique, individual purpose. Third, humans are designed to have a one-on-one relationship with God through Jesus, powered by the Holy Spirit. As a right of being created in the image of their Creator, humans can relate directly to him. It is through Jesus that this relationship is made possible. He came and tore down the dividing wall of hostility that separated his special creation from God (Ro 8:34–39).

GENESIS 1:28

GOD'S CREATED MISSION

Adam and Eve lived on mission. This is seen in a couple of ways. First, they were to multiply and fill the earth. As created image-bearers, were it not for sin, they would naturally multiply and fill the earth with more and more image-bearing worshipers of God. As worshipers spread, the glory of God

(continued on next page)

27 So God created mankind in his own image,
in the image of God he created them;
male and female he created them.

28 God blessed them and said to them, "Be fruitful and increase in number; fill the earth and subdue it. Rule over the fish in the sea and the birds
in the sky and over every living creature that moves on the ground."
29 Then God said, "I give you every seed-bearing plant on the face of the
whole earth and every tree that has fruit with seed in it. They will be yours
for food. 30 And to all the beasts of the earth and all the birds in the sky
and all the creatures that move along the ground—everything that has the
breath of life in it—I give every green plant for food." And it was so.
31 God saw all that he had made, and it was very good. And there was
evening, and there was morning—the sixth day.

2 Thus the heavens and the earth were completed in all their vast array.

2 By the seventh day God had finished the work he had been doing; so on the
seventh day he rested from all his work. 3 Then God blessed the seventh day
and made it holy, because on it he rested from all the work of creating that
he had done.

Adam and Eve

4 This is the account of the heavens and the earth when they were created,
when the LORD God made the earth and the heavens.
5 Now no shrub had yet appeared on the earth[a] and no plant had yet sprung
up, for the LORD God had not sent rain on the earth and there was no one to
work the ground, 6 but streams[b] came up from the earth and watered the whole
surface of the ground. 7 Then the LORD God formed a man[c] from the dust of the
ground and breathed into his nostrils the breath of life, and the man became a
living being.
8 Now the LORD God had planted a garden in the east, in Eden; and there he
put the man he had formed. 9 The LORD God made all kinds of trees grow out of
the ground—trees that were pleasing to the eye and good for food. In the middle
of the garden were the tree of life and the tree of the knowledge of good and evil.
10 A river watering the garden flowed from Eden; from there it was separated
into four headwaters. 11 The name of the first is the Pishon; it winds through the
entire land of Havilah, where there is gold. 12 (The gold of that land is good; aro-
matic resin[d] and onyx are also there.) 13 The name of the second river is the Gihon; it winds through the entire land of Cush.[e] 14 The name of the third river is the
Tigris; it runs along the east side of Ashur. And the fourth river is the Euphrates.
15 The LORD God took the man and put him in the Garden of Eden to work it
and take care of it. 16 And the LORD God commanded the man, "You are free to
eat from any tree in the garden; 17 but you must not eat from the tree of the knowledge of good and evil, for when you eat from it you will certainly die."
18 The LORD God said, "It is not good for the man to be alone. I will make a
helper suitable for him."
19 Now the LORD God had formed out of the ground all the wild animals and
all the birds in the sky. He brought them to the man to see what he would name
them; and whatever the man called each living creature, that was its name. 20 So
the man gave names to all the livestock, the birds in the sky and all the wild
animals.

But for Adam[f] no suitable helper was found. 21 So the LORD God caused the
man to fall into a deep sleep; and while he was sleeping, he took one of the man's

---

[a] 5 Or *land*; also in verse 6 [b] 6 Or *mist* [c] 7 The Hebrew for *man (adam)* sounds like and may be related to the Hebrew for *ground (adamah)*; it is also the name *Adam* (see verse 20). [d] 12 Or *good; pearls* [e] 13 Possibly southeast Mesopotamia [f] 20 Or *the man*

ribs[a] and then closed up the place with flesh. 22 Then the LORD God made a woman from the rib[b] he had taken out of the man, and he brought her to the man.
23 The man said,

"This is now bone of my bones
  and flesh of my flesh;
she shall be called 'woman,'
  for she was taken out of man."

24 That is why a man leaves his father and mother and is united to his wife, and
they become one flesh.
25 Adam and his wife were both naked, and they felt no shame.

The Fall

3 Now the serpent was more crafty than any of the wild animals the LORD God
had made. He said to the woman, "Did God really say, 'You must not eat from
any tree in the garden'?"
2 The woman said to the serpent, "We may eat fruit from the trees in the garden, 3 but God did say, 'You must not eat fruit from the tree that is in the middle
of the garden, and you must not touch it, or you will die.' "
4 "You will not certainly die," the serpent said to the woman. 5 "For God knows
that when you eat from it your eyes will be opened, and you will be like God,
knowing good and evil."
6 When the woman saw that the fruit of the tree was good for food and pleasing
to the eye, and also desirable for gaining wisdom, she took some and ate it. She
also gave some to her husband, who was with her, and he ate it. 7 Then the eyes
of both of them were opened, and they realized they were naked; so they sewed
fig leaves together and made coverings for themselves.
8 Then the man and his wife heard the sound of the LORD God as he was walking in the garden in the cool of the day, and they hid from the LORD God among
the trees of the garden. 9 But the LORD God called to the man, "Where are you?"
10 He answered, "I heard you in the garden, and I was afraid because I was
naked; so I hid."
11 And he said, "Who told you that you were naked? Have you eaten from the
tree that I commanded you not to eat from?"
12 The man said, "The woman you put here with me — she gave me some fruit
from the tree, and I ate it."
13 Then the LORD God said to the woman, "What is this you have done?"
The woman said, "The serpent deceived me, and I ate."
14 So the LORD God said to the serpent, "Because you have done this,

"Cursed are you above all livestock
  and all wild animals!
You will crawl on your belly
  and you will eat dust
  all the days of your life.
15 And I will put enmity
  between you and the woman,
  and between your offspring[c] and hers;
he will crush[d] your head,
  and you will strike his heel."

16 To the woman he said,

"I will make your pains in childbearing very severe;
  with painful labor you will give birth to children.
Your desire will be for your husband,
  and he will rule over you."

---

[a] 21 Or *took part of the man's side* [b] 22 Or *part* [c] 15 Or *seed* [d] 15 Or *strike*

(God's Created Mission, continued)

would be seen throughout the world God had created. Second, people were to exercise dominion over God's world. They were to do more than simply care for the world — they were to harness the latent potential built into God's very good created design in order to magnify the order, beauty and capabilities inherent in all things made by God. Sin changed all that God created, but it did not obliterate this mandate. In Christ, men and women can fulfill their God-given mission to fill the earth with worshipers and develop the world in such a way as to bring God great glory.

GENESIS 3:15 – 17

THE PROMISED ONE

God's judgment of sin is interrupted by a stunning picture of his grace. Because of human sin, there are vast implications — from men and women to the very creation itself. But God promises that sin will not have the final word. This first reference to the plan of God to save fallen sinners, sometimes referred to as the protoevangelium (the first gospel), declares God's commitment to his creation. He will not abandon it to destruction but will pursue it in love. His promise is clear — a descendant of the woman will crush the head of the serpent. The heel of this male heir of the first parents will be struck, though the child will emerge victorious by crushing the head of the evil one. The exact nature of the plan is yet to be explained, but the plan is already in place. Jesus, the promised seed of the woman, would leave no doubt as to the fulfillment of this promise. It would appear that Satan

(continued on page 14)

BEGINNINGS

JESUS AS THE SUPREME DISPLAY OF THE GLORY OF GOD

—JOHN PIPER

GENESIS 1–2

After the question "Does God exist?" (to which God answers, "I Am," Ex 3:14), the next question that can shape your life most deeply is "Why did God create the world?"

The short answer that resounds through the whole Bible like rolling thunder is this: *God created the world for his glory*. We'll see what that means below, but first let's establish the fact. "Bring my sons from afar and my daughters from the ends of the earth — everyone who is called by my name, whom *I created for my glory*, whom I formed and made" (Isa 43:6–7). Even if the narrower meaning here is "I brought Israel into being for my glory," the use of the words "created," "formed," and "made" are pointing us back to the original act of creation. This is why Israel *ultimately* exists. Because this is why *all things* ultimately exist — for the glory of God.

THE BIBLE IS CLEAR

When the first chapter of the Bible says, "God created mankind *in his own image*, in the *image of God* he created them; male and female he created them" (Ge 1:27), what is the point? The point of an image is to image. Images are erected in public to display the original. Point to the original. Glorify the original.

God made humans in his image so that the world would be filled with reflectors of God. Images of God. Billions of statues of God. So that nobody would miss the point of creation. Nobody (unless they were spiritually blind) could miss the point of humanity, namely, God! Knowing, loving, showing God.

The angels cry, "Holy, holy, holy is the Lord Almighty; *the whole earth is full of his glory*" (Isa 6:3). It's full of human image-bearers. Glorious ruins. But not only humans. Also nature! Why such a breathtaking world for us to live in? Why such a vast universe? Scientists now say (I can't verify it!) that there are more stars in the universe than there are words and sounds that all humans of all time have ever spoken. Why is it so gigantic?

The Bible is crystal clear about this: "The heavens declare the glory of God" (Ps 19:1). If someone asks, "If earth is the only inhabited planet in the universe, and man the only rational inhabitant among the stars, why is there such a large and empty universe?" The answer is: It's not about us. It's about God. Which means it's not an overstatement; it's an understatement. God created us to know him and love him and show him. And then he gave us a hint of what he is like — the universe.

We can see the purpose of creation even where the apostle Paul describes how we have fallen short of it. He says in Romans 1:20 – 21:

"God's invisible qualities — his eternal power and divine nature — have been clearly seen, being understood from what has been made, so that people are without excuse. For although they knew God, they neither glorified him as God nor gave thanks to him."

The great tragedy of the universe is that, while human beings were made to glorify God, we have all fallen short of this purpose and "exchanged the glory of the immortal God for images made to look like a mortal human being" (Ro 1:23).

GOD HELPS US FEEL THIS TRUTH

So, resounding through the whole Bible — from eternity to eternity — like rolling thunder is God's great purpose for all things: *He created the world for his glory.* Besides Isaiah 43:7 ("created for my glory"), Isaiah presses home the reality over and over to help us feel it and make it part of the fabric of our thinking:

"Every valley shall be raised up, every mountain and hill made low ... And *the glory of the* L*ORD* *will be revealed,* and all people will see it together" (Isa 40:4 – 5).

"I am the LORD; that is my name! I will not yield my glory to another" (Isa 42:8).

"The LORD has redeemed Jacob, he displays his glory in Israel" (Isa 44:23).

""For my own name"s sake I delay my wrath; for the sake of my praise I hold it back from you ... I have tested you in the furnace of affliction. For my own sake, for my own sake, I do this. How can I let myself be defamed? I will not yield my glory to another" (Isa 48:9 – 11).

"He said to me, 'You are my servant, Israel, in whom *I will display my splendor*'" (Isa 49:3).

"The Spirit of the Sovereign LORD is on me, because the LORD has anointed me to proclaim good news to the poor ... They will be called oaks of righteousness, a planting of the LORD *for the display of his splendor*" (Isa 61:1 – 3).

GLORIFY IS DIFFERENT FROM BEAUTIFY

This is why God created the world — that he may be glorified. Which does not mean that he may be *made* glorious. Don't take the word *glorify* and treat it like the word *beautify.* To beautify means to take something plain and make it beautiful. We don't take a plain God and make him beautiful. That is not what glorifying God means.

BEGINNINGS

(CONTINUED)

GENESIS 1–2

When God created the world, he did not create out of any need or any weakness or any deficiency. He created out of fullness and strength and complete sufficiency. As Jonathan Edwards said, "Tis no argument of the emptiness or deficiency of a fountain that it is inclined to overflow."

Or switch to the word *magnify*. We magnify his glory like a *telescope*, not a microscope. Microscopes make small things look bigger than they are. Telescopes make unimaginably big things look more like what they really are. Our lives are to be telescopes for the glory of God.

WHY THIS PARTICULAR WORLD?

But we can't leave it here. It's too general. It's too disconnected from the specific persons of the Trinity and from the flow of history the way God is guiding it. The question is not just, "Why did God create the world?" but why *this* world? Why these thousands of years of human history with a glorious beginning, and a horrible fall into sin, and a history of Israel, and the coming of the Son of God into the world, a substitutionary death, a triumphant resurrection, the founding of the church and the history of global missions to where we are today? Why *this* world? This history?

And the short answer to that question is for the glory of God''s grace displayed supremely in the death of Jesus. Or to say it more fully, this world — this history as it is unfolding — was created and is guided and sustained by God so that the grace of God, supremely displayed in the death and resurrection of Jesus for sinners, would be glorified throughout all eternity in the Christ-exalting joys of the redeemed.

Or let's just keep it short: This world exists for the glory of God's grace revealed in the saving work of Jesus. There is an unbreakable connection between the glory of God, the glory of grace, the glory of Christ, the glory of the cross.

THE GLORY OF GOD AND THE CROSS OF CHRIST

Let me show you this from God's Word in five steps.

1. The apex — the highpoint — of God's display of his own glory is the display of his grace.

"God predestined us for adoption to sonship through Jesus Christ, in accordance with his pleasure and will — *to the praise of his glorious grace*" (Eph 1:5 – 6). In other words, the glory of God's *grace* — what Paul calls "the incomparable riches of his grace, expressed in his kindness to us in Christ Jesus" (Eph 2:7) — is the highpoint and endpoint in the revelation of God's glory. And the aim of predestination is that we live "to the praise of his glorious grace" forever.

This is the endpoint of his glory, and everything else — even God's wrath — serves this. So Paul said, "Choosing to show his *wrath* and make his power known, bore with great patience the objects of his wrath ... *to make the riches of his glory known to the objects of his mercy*" (Ro 9:22–23). Wrath is penultimate. The glory of grace on the objects of mercy is ultimate.

2. God planned this — the praise of the glory of his grace — before creation.

God "chose us in him before the creation of the world ... to the praise of his glorious grace" (Eph 1:4,6).

Grace was not an afterthought in response to the fall of man. It was planned before creation. It was the plan, because grace is the summit of the mountain of his glory. And he created the world for his glory. He planned the world for the glory of *his grace*.

3. God's plan was that the praise of the glory of his grace would come about through the Son of God, Jesus Christ.

"He predestined us for adoption to sonship *through Jesus Christ* ... to the praise of his glorious grace" (Eph 1:5–6). This predestination to the praise of the glory of God's grace happened "through Jesus Christ." In the eternal fellowship of the Trinity, the Father and the Son planned that God's grace would be supremely revealed through the saving work of the Son.

4. From eternity, God's plan was that the glory of God's grace would reach its highpoint in the saving work of Jesus on the cross.

We see this in the title that was already on the book of the redeemed before the creation of the world. Before there was any human sin to die for, God planned that his Son would be slain for sinners. We know this because of the name given to the book of life before creation. "All inhabitants of the earth will worship the beast — all whose names have not been written in the Lamb's book of life, the Lamb who was slain from the creation of the world" (Rev 13:8).

The name of the book before creation was "the Lamb's book of life, the Lamb *who was slain from the creation of the world*." The plan was glory. The plan was grace. The plan was Christ. And the plan was *death*. And that death for sinners like us is the heart of the gospel, which is why Paul calls it "the *gospel that displays the glory of Christ*" (2Co 4:4).

5. Therefore, the ultimate purpose of creating and guiding and sustaining this world — this history — is the praise of the glory of the grace of God in the crucifixion of his Son for sinners.

This is why Revelation 5:9 and 13 show that for all eternity we will sing the song *of the*

BEGINNINGS

(CONTINUED)

GENESIS 1–2

Lamb. We will say with white-hot admiration and praise, "You are worthy to take the scroll and to open its seals, *because you were slain*, and with your blood you purchased for God persons from every tribe and language and people and nation" (Rev 5:9).

YOUR BRIGHTEST TREASURE

So we ask again, in conclusion, "Why did God create the world?" And we answer with the Scriptures: *God created the world for his glory*. God did not create out of need. He did not create the world out of a deficiency. He was not lonely. He was supremely happy in the fellowship of the Trinity — Father, Son and Holy Spirit. He created the world to put his glory on display that his people might know him, and enjoy him and show him.

And why did he create a world that would become like this world? A world that fell into sin? A world that exchanged his glory for the glory of images? Why would he permit and guide and sustain such a world? And we answer: for *the praise of the glory of the grace of God displayed supremely in the death of Jesus*.

I ask:

- Is the glory of God the brightest treasure on the horizon of your future? Paul expressed the Christian heart in Romans 5:2, "We boast in the hope of the glory of God."
- Is the glory of grace the sweetest news to your guilty soul?
- Is the glory of Christ in your life the present, personal embodiment of the grace of God?
- Is the glory of the cross the saddest and happiest beauty to your redeemed soul?

Note: When italics are used in the Scripture references above, they have been added by the author to show emphasis.

THE FIRST ADAM AND THE RUIN OF HUMANITY

Adam and Eve represent a profound paradox. They are simultaneously the crowning achievement of God's creation, created in his very image, and the symbol of mankind's greatest failure. In verse 1 the serpent appeared in Paradise with no introduction. The serpent symbolizes something both fascinating and loathsome. Yet neither Adam nor Eve saw the danger embodied in the serpent. The danger of this creature was quickly realized in verse 8 after Adam and Eve were enticed by its suggestion and drawn into the depth of sin. According to his custom, God came walking through the garden in the cool of the day, and for the first time Adam and Eve hid from him in shame because of their sinful disobedience.

In Romans 5:12 – 21 Paul takes his readers back to this very moment in history and offers a divinely inspired interpretation. He explains that Adam's sin led to the downfall and death of the entire human race. Through one man (Adam), death came. Yet through one Man (Jesus Christ), grace and the gift of God (eternal life) was given.

The works of these two men, Adam and Jesus, are not merely opposites of one another. Christ's work — the work of redemption accomplished on the cross — is far greater, for it brings God's life and redemption to those who are spiritually dead. The death of Adam spread to all, but the life of Christ overcame it. Through Adam's disobedience, death reigned and the world stood condemned before God.

In the face of this condemnation, Jesus offered humanity the free gift of salvation by faith that resulted in justification. That is to say, the aim of this gift is to justify (remove condemnation) from those who stood condemned. This glorious promise provides remarkable hope for those who are "in Christ." They have been reborn, by the power of God, and their status is transferred from being "in Adam" to "in Christ." In turn, they receive the inheritance promised to all those who are "in Christ" and avoid the wrath of those who are "in Adam." So much greater is the work of Jesus than the sin of Adam!

(The Promised One, continued)

had done far more than strike the heel of the Son of God as Jesus hung lifeless on a cross. But God would have the final word. Through Jesus' victorious resurrection, he would crush the head of Satan — permanently declaring victory over sin and death and fulfilling the promise made at the outset of the Bible.

17 To Adam he said, "Because you listened to your wife and ate fruit from the
tree about which I commanded you, 'You must not eat from it,'

"Cursed is the ground because of you;
through painful toil you will eat food from it
all the days of your life.
18 It will produce thorns and thistles for you,
and you will eat the plants of the field.
19 By the sweat of your brow
you will eat your food
until you return to the ground,
since from it you were taken;
for dust you are
and to dust you will return."

20 Adam[a] named his wife Eve,[b] because she would become the mother of all
the living.
21 The LORD God made garments of skin for Adam and his wife and clothed
them. 22 And the LORD God said, "The man has now become like one of us, knowing good and evil. He must not be allowed to reach out his hand and take also
from the tree of life and eat, and live forever." 23 So the LORD God banished him
from the Garden of Eden to work the ground from which he had been taken.
24 After he drove the man out, he placed on the east side[c] of the Garden of Eden
cherubim and a flaming sword flashing back and forth to guard the way to the
tree of life.

Cain and Abel

4 Adam[a] made love to his wife Eve, and she became pregnant and gave birth
to Cain.[d] She said, "With the help of the LORD I have brought forth[e] a man."
2 Later she gave birth to his brother Abel.
Now Abel kept flocks, and Cain worked the soil. 3 In the course of time Cain
brought some of the fruits of the soil as an offering to the LORD. 4 And Abel also
brought an offering — fat portions from some of the firstborn of his flock. The
LORD looked with favor on Abel and his offering, 5 but on Cain and his offering
he did not look with favor. So Cain was very angry, and his face was downcast.
6 Then the LORD said to Cain, "Why are you angry? Why is your face downcast? 7 If you do what is right, will you not be accepted? But if you do not do what
is right, sin is crouching at your door; it desires to have you, but you must rule
over it."
8 Now Cain said to his brother Abel, "Let's go out to the field."[f] While they were
in the field, Cain attacked his brother Abel and killed him.
9 Then the LORD said to Cain, "Where is your brother Abel?"
"I don't know," he replied. "Am I my brother's keeper?"
10 The LORD said, "What have you done? Listen! Your brother's blood cries out
to me from the ground. 11 Now you are under a curse and driven from the ground,
which opened its mouth to receive your brother's blood from your hand. 12 When
you work the ground, it will no longer yield its crops for you. You will be a restless
wanderer on the earth."
13 Cain said to the LORD, "My punishment is more than I can bear. 14 Today you
are driving me from the land, and I will be hidden from your presence; I will be a
restless wanderer on the earth, and whoever finds me will kill me."
15 But the LORD said to him, "Not so[g]; anyone who kills Cain will suffer vengeance seven times over." Then the LORD put a mark on Cain so that no one who

[a] *20,1* Or *The man* [b] *20* *Eve* probably means *living.* [c] *24* Or *placed in front* [d] *1* *Cain* sounds like the Hebrew for *brought forth* or *acquired.* [e] *1* Or *have acquired* [f] *8* Samaritan Pentateuch, Septuagint, Vulgate and Syriac; Masoretic Text does not have *"Let's go out to the field."* [g] *15* Septuagint, Vulgate and Syriac; Hebrew *Very well*

found him would kill him. [16]So Cain went out from the LORD's presence and lived in the land of Nod,[a] east of Eden.

[17]Cain made love to his wife, and she became pregnant and gave birth to Enoch. Cain was then building a city, and he named it after his son Enoch. [18]To Enoch was born Irad, and Irad was the father of Mehujael, and Mehujael was the father of Methushael, and Methushael was the father of Lamech.

[19]Lamech married two women, one named Adah and the other Zillah. [20]Adah gave birth to Jabal; he was the father of those who live in tents and raise livestock. [21]His brother's name was Jubal; he was the father of all who play stringed instruments and pipes. [22]Zillah also had a son, Tubal-Cain, who forged all kinds of tools out of[b] bronze and iron. Tubal-Cain's sister was Naamah.

[23]Lamech said to his wives,

"Adah and Zillah, listen to me;
  wives of Lamech, hear my words.
I have killed a man for wounding me,
  a young man for injuring me.
[24]If Cain is avenged seven times,
  then Lamech seventy-seven times."

[25]Adam made love to his wife again, and she gave birth to a son and named him Seth,[c] saying, "God has granted me another child in place of Abel, since Cain killed him." [26]Seth also had a son, and he named him Enosh.

At that time people began to call on[d] the name of the LORD.

From Adam to Noah

5 This is the written account of Adam's family line.

When God created mankind, he made them in the likeness of God. [2]He created them male and female and blessed them. And he named them "Mankind"[e] when they were created.

[3]When Adam had lived 130 years, he had a son in his own likeness, in his own image; and he named him Seth. [4]After Seth was born, Adam lived 800 years and had other sons and daughters. [5]Altogether, Adam lived a total of 930 years, and then he died.

[6]When Seth had lived 105 years, he became the father[f] of Enosh. [7]After he became the father of Enosh, Seth lived 807 years and had other sons and daughters. [8]Altogether, Seth lived a total of 912 years, and then he died.

[9]When Enosh had lived 90 years, he became the father of Kenan. [10]After he became the father of Kenan, Enosh lived 815 years and had other sons and daughters. [11]Altogether, Enosh lived a total of 905 years, and then he died.

[12]When Kenan had lived 70 years, he became the father of Mahalalel. [13]After he became the father of Mahalalel, Kenan lived 840 years and had other sons and daughters. [14]Altogether, Kenan lived a total of 910 years, and then he died.

[15]When Mahalalel had lived 65 years, he became the father of Jared. [16]After he became the father of Jared, Mahalalel lived 830 years and had other sons and daughters. [17]Altogether, Mahalalel lived a total of 895 years, and then he died.

[18]When Jared had lived 162 years, he became the father of Enoch. [19]After he became the father of Enoch, Jared lived 800 years and had other sons and daughters. [20]Altogether, Jared lived a total of 962 years, and then he died.

[21]When Enoch had lived 65 years, he became the father of Methuselah. [22]After he became the father of Methuselah, Enoch walked faithfully with God 300 years and had other sons and daughters. [23]Altogether, Enoch lived a total of 365 years. [24]Enoch walked faithfully with God; then he was no more, because God took him away.

---

[a] 16 *Nod* means *wandering* (see verses 12 and 14). [b] 22 Or *who instructed all who work in* [c] 25 *Seth* probably means *granted.* [d] 26 Or *to proclaim* [e] 2 Hebrew *adam* [f] 6 *Father* may mean *ancestor*; also in verses 7-26.

GENESIS 5:5

DEATH REIGNS UNTIL CHRIST

The pace of chapter 5 demonstrates the tragedy of human sin. Person after person appears and then is gone. The repetition of the phrase "and then he died" reminds the reader of the implications of the curse. No longer can people live forever; they appear for a moment and then return to the ground (Ge 3:19). There is no escaping this reality. The just and the unjust, the righteous and the unrighteous, all die. From Adam to Noah, death reigns universally. Jesus, knowing and experiencing this reality personally when confronted with the death of his friend Lazarus, makes a remarkable claim. Those who believe in him, even though their physical bodies will die, will be raised to new life forever (Jn 11:25–26). Like Christ, they will pass through death only to emerge victorious. Belief in Christ is the only antidote to the lineage of death recounted in Genesis and seen throughout all subsequent generations.

25When Methuselah had lived 187 years, he became the father of Lamech.
26After he became the father of Lamech, Methuselah lived 782 years and had
other sons and daughters. 27Altogether, Methuselah lived a total of 969 years,
and then he died.
28When Lamech had lived 182 years, he had a son. 29He named him Noah[a]
and said, "He will comfort us in the labor and painful toil of our hands caused
by the ground the LORD has cursed." 30After Noah was born, Lamech lived 595
years and had other sons and daughters. 31Altogether, Lamech lived a total of
777 years, and then he died.
32After Noah was 500 years old, he became the father of Shem, Ham and Japheth.

Wickedness in the World

6 When human beings began to increase in number on the earth and daughters were born to them, 2the sons of God saw that the daughters of humans
were beautiful, and they married any of them they chose. 3Then the LORD said,
"My Spirit will not contend with[b] humans forever, for they are mortal[c]; their days
will be a hundred and twenty years."
4The Nephilim were on the earth in those days — and also afterward — when
the sons of God went to the daughters of humans and had children by them.
They were the heroes of old, men of renown.
5The LORD saw how great the wickedness of the human race had become on
the earth, and that every inclination of the thoughts of the human heart was only
evil all the time. 6The LORD regretted that he had made human beings on the
earth, and his heart was deeply troubled. 7So the LORD said, "I will wipe from the
face of the earth the human race I have created — and with them the animals,
the birds and the creatures that move along the ground — for I regret that I have
made them." 8But Noah found favor in the eyes of the LORD.

Noah and the Flood

9This is the account of Noah and his family.
Noah was a righteous man, blameless among the people of his time, and he
walked faithfully with God. 10Noah had three sons: Shem, Ham and Japheth.
11Now the earth was corrupt in God's sight and was full of violence. 12God saw
how corrupt the earth had become, for all the people on earth had corrupted
their ways. 13So God said to Noah, "I am going to put an end to all people, for the
earth is filled with violence because of them. I am surely going to destroy both
them and the earth. 14So make yourself an ark of cypress[d] wood; make rooms in
it and coat it with pitch inside and out. 15This is how you are to build it: The ark is
to be three hundred cubits long, fifty cubits wide and thirty cubits high.[e] 16Make
a roof for it, leaving below the roof an opening one cubit[f] high all around.[g] Put a
door in the side of the ark and make lower, middle and upper decks. 17I am going to bring floodwaters on the earth to destroy all life under the heavens, every
creature that has the breath of life in it. Everything on earth will perish. 18But I
will establish my covenant with you, and you will enter the ark — you and your
sons and your wife and your sons' wives with you. 19You are to bring into the ark
two of all living creatures, male and female, to keep them alive with you. 20Two
of every kind of bird, of every kind of animal and of every kind of creature that
moves along the ground will come to you to be kept alive. 21You are to take every
kind of food that is to be eaten and store it away as food for you and for them."
22Noah did everything just as God commanded him.

GENESIS 6:18

NOAH AND THE FLOOD

The story of Noah offers a clear picture of the saving mercy of God. In the midst of humanity's sin and rebellion, God made a way for the salvation of the human race through Noah and the ark. Were there not a man and a family who by God's grace stood out from the wickedness of their day, there would have been a new beginning on the part of God that would have omitted all of us! Mercifully, God provided Noah and his family with the ark to escape the floodwaters. The ark is a powerful picture of Jesus Christ in whom salvation would come to everyone who believed in him. Jesus, like the ark, would one day be lifted high above the floodwaters of our sin to endure the full wrath of God. By putting our hope in Jesus, we are rescued like Noah and his family.

[a] 29 *Noah* sounds like the Hebrew for *comfort.* [b] 3 Or *My spirit will not remain in* [c] 3 Or *corrupt* [d] 14 The meaning of the Hebrew for this word is uncertain. [e] 15 That is, about 450 feet long, 75 feet wide and 45 feet high or about 135 meters long, 23 meters wide and 14 meters high [f] 16 That is, about 18 inches or about 45 centimeters [g] 16 The meaning of the Hebrew for this clause is uncertain.

SIN

The exact nature of the sin described in these verses is perplexing to most readers. While the actions are somewhat unclear, what is abundantly evident is the fact that God's good, created order has been corrupted by human rebellion. The people have done the very thing God commanded them to do in the garden — they have been fruitful and multiplied and filled the earth (Ge 1:28). Sadly, rather than filling the earth with image-bearers who reflect God's glory, they have instead filled the earth with brokenness.

Interestingly, the sin recounted here describes the people seeing something as beautiful and pursuing that thing in rebellion to God's command, as did Adam and Eve. Rather than submitting to the command of God and trusting the goodness of his dictates, the first couple chose to trust their eyes and follow the lusts of their hearts (Ge 3:1 – 7). At its core, this is the nature of all sin.

God, the Creator of all things, knows best how the human life should be lived. He provides clear guidance on his good and gracious plans for humanity, which are ultimately for good. Sin is rooted in unbelief in the promises of God. Rather than trusting in the ways of God, all people choose to follow the desires of their own hearts and, in so doing, elevate themselves to the position of God. People believe they know better than God; therefore, they run after the lusts of their hearts and the desires of their eyes. John warns, however, that these things are passing away and so are those who live their lives in pursuit of them. Only those who do "the will of God" can live (1Jn 2:16 – 17).

But, how does one do the will of God? The implications of Adam's sin and the fall are not merely that all people make bad decisions, yet if they try hard enough they can keep God's law. Rather, sin renders all people unable to keep God's law and trapped in the shackles of their sin. Jesus perfectly and completely lived the life they could not live, no matter how hard they tried. Those who are aware of their inability to keep God's law can turn to Christ in repentance and faith and be given the free gift of righteousness. By grace, God credits the perfection of Jesus to men and women who could never earn it by their own merit (2Co 5:21).

7 The LORD then said to Noah, "Go into the ark, you and your whole family, because I have found you righteous in this generation. 2Take with you seven pairs of every kind of clean animal, a male and its mate, and one pair of every kind of unclean animal, a male and its mate, 3and also seven pairs of every kind of bird, male and female, to keep their various kinds alive throughout the earth. 4Seven days from now I will send rain on the earth for forty days and forty nights, and I will wipe from the face of the earth every living creature I have made."

5And Noah did all that the LORD commanded him.

6Noah was six hundred years old when the floodwaters came on the earth. 7And Noah and his sons and his wife and his sons' wives entered the ark to escape the waters of the flood. 8Pairs of clean and unclean animals, of birds and of all creatures that move along the ground, 9male and female, came to Noah and entered the ark, as God had commanded Noah. 10And after the seven days the floodwaters came on the earth.

11In the six hundredth year of Noah's life, on the seventeenth day of the second month — on that day all the springs of the great deep burst forth, and the floodgates of the heavens were opened. 12And rain fell on the earth forty days and forty nights.

13On that very day Noah and his sons, Shem, Ham and Japheth, together with his wife and the wives of his three sons, entered the ark. 14They had with them every wild animal according to its kind, all livestock according to their kinds, every creature that moves along the ground according to its kind and every bird according to its kind, everything with wings. 15Pairs of all creatures that have the breath of life in them came to Noah and entered the ark. 16The animals going in were male and female of every living thing, as God had commanded Noah. Then the LORD shut him in.

17For forty days the flood kept coming on the earth, and as the waters increased they lifted the ark high above the earth. 18The waters rose and increased greatly on the earth, and the ark floated on the surface of the water. 19They rose greatly on the earth, and all the high mountains under the entire heavens were covered. 20The waters rose and covered the mountains to a depth of more than fifteen cubits.[a,b] 21Every living thing that moved on land perished — birds, livestock, wild animals, all the creatures that swarm over the earth, and all mankind. 22Everything on dry land that had the breath of life in its nostrils died. 23Every living thing on the face of the earth was wiped out; people and animals and the creatures that move along the ground and the birds were wiped from the earth. Only Noah was left, and those with him in the ark.

24The waters flooded the earth for a hundred and fifty days.

8 But God remembered Noah and all the wild animals and the livestock that were with him in the ark, and he sent a wind over the earth, and the waters receded. 2Now the springs of the deep and the floodgates of the heavens had been closed, and the rain had stopped falling from the sky. 3The water receded steadily from the earth. At the end of the hundred and fifty days the water had gone down, 4and on the seventeenth day of the seventh month the ark came to rest on the mountains of Ararat. 5The waters continued to recede until the tenth month, and on the first day of the tenth month the tops of the mountains became visible.

6After forty days Noah opened a window he had made in the ark 7and sent out a raven, and it kept flying back and forth until the water had dried up from the earth. 8Then he sent out a dove to see if the water had receded from the surface of the ground. 9But the dove could find nowhere to perch because there was water over all the surface of the earth; so it returned to Noah in the ark. He reached out his hand and took the dove and brought it back to himself in the ark. 10He waited seven more days and again sent out the dove from the ark. 11When the dove

[a] *20* That is, about 23 feet or about 6.8 meters [b] *20* Or *rose more than fifteen cubits, and the mountains were covered*

GENESIS 7:23

THE REALITY OF NOAH AND THE FLOOD

In the days of Noah, the wickedness of mankind had reached a breaking point. The sin that started with Adam and Eve in the garden had spread throughout the entire world and "every inclination of the thoughts of the human heart was only evil all the time" (Ge 6:5). In response to the rebellion of humanity, God sent a flood to destroy every living creature on the earth. People died — old people and young, beautiful and brave along with the grisly and gray. Only Noah and those with him escaped the terrible, universal death of the wicked. Even the survival of Noah and his family was the result of undeserved mercy, because they were broken and sinful like everyone else (Ge 9:20 – 27). Many people have rejected the story of Noah and the flood as folklore without any historical merit. However, Jesus affirmed the reality of the "days of Noah" when he compared them to the last days (Mt 24:37 – 38; Lk 17:26 – 27). Peter also used the story of Noah and the flood as a pattern for the final judgment (1Pe 3:20; 2Pe 2:5; 3:5 – 6).

returned to him in the evening, there in its beak was a freshly plucked olive leaf!
Then Noah knew that the water had receded from the earth. 12He waited seven
more days and sent the dove out again, but this time it did not return to him.
13By the first day of the first month of Noah's six hundred and first year, the
water had dried up from the earth. Noah then removed the covering from the ark
and saw that the surface of the ground was dry. 14By the twenty-seventh day of
the second month the earth was completely dry.
15Then God said to Noah, 16"Come out of the ark, you and your wife and your
sons and their wives. 17Bring out every kind of living creature that is with you—
the birds, the animals, and all the creatures that move along the ground—so
they can multiply on the earth and be fruitful and increase in number on it."
18So Noah came out, together with his sons and his wife and his sons' wives.
19All the animals and all the creatures that move along the ground and all the
birds—everything that moves on land—came out of the ark, one kind after another.
20Then Noah built an altar to the LORD and, taking some of all the clean animals and clean birds, he sacrificed burnt offerings on it. 21The LORD smelled the
pleasing aroma and said in his heart: "Never again will I curse the ground because of humans, even though[a] every inclination of the human heart is evil from
childhood. And never again will I destroy all living creatures, as I have done.

22"As long as the earth endures,
seedtime and harvest,
cold and heat,
summer and winter,
day and night
will never cease."

God's Covenant With Noah

9 Then God blessed Noah and his sons, saying to them, "Be fruitful and increase in number and fill the earth. 2The fear and dread of you will fall on
all the beasts of the earth, and on all the birds in the sky, on every creature that
moves along the ground, and on all the fish in the sea; they are given into your
hands. 3Everything that lives and moves about will be food for you. Just as I gave
you the green plants, I now give you everything.
4"But you must not eat meat that has its lifeblood still in it. 5And for your lifeblood I will surely demand an accounting. I will demand an accounting from
every animal. And from each human being, too, I will demand an accounting
for the life of another human being.

6"Whoever sheds human blood,
by humans shall their blood be shed;
for in the image of God
has God made mankind.

7As for you, be fruitful and increase in number; multiply on the earth and increase upon it."
8Then God said to Noah and to his sons with him: 9"I now establish my covenant with you and with your descendants after you 10and with every living
creature that was with you—the birds, the livestock and all the wild animals,
all those that came out of the ark with you—every living creature on earth. 11I
establish my covenant with you: Never again will all life be destroyed by the waters of a flood; never again will there be a flood to destroy the earth."
12And God said, "This is the sign of the covenant I am making between me
and you and every living creature with you, a covenant for all generations to
come: 13I have set my rainbow in the clouds, and it will be the sign of the covenant between me and the earth. 14Whenever I bring clouds over the earth and

---

[a] 21 Or *humans, for*

THE BOW IN THE HEAVENS

The rainbow is a symbol of God's promise never to destroy the earth again with a flood. More importantly, it serves as a tangible reminder of the faithfulness of God to fulfill his promises to his people. To modern ears, the notion of God "remembering" something may sound strange. How can an all-knowing God forget anything? Rather, the text points out that God would consistently call to mind his covenant promises, even when the people's rebellion seemingly knew no end.

These promises stem from the task given to Adam and Eve in the garden (Ge 1:26–31). They were not merely to relax and enjoy their home. They were to represent God by exercising dominion and rule over the world in which they were placed. They were also to multiply and fill the earth with image-bearing worshipers.

Sin holistically altered the nature of this task, but it did not change the mission. The mission continues even after the systemic nature of sin was demonstrated in unthinkable ways, causing God to lament his work of creation (Ge 6:6). God acted in judgment, though he sustained a chosen remnant from the flood. Following their deliverance in the ark, God reinstated his mission with Noah and his family (Ge 9:1). They were called to multiply and fill the earth — a task made possible by the grace of God.

God affirmed his role in their lives and mission through a covenant. Throughout the ancient world, covenants were often used to describe the relationship of a king to his subjects. In it, the nature of the relationship was described along with the subjects' responsibilities for obedience and life in the kingdom. This was certainly the case with Noah.

The foundation of God's covenant with Noah and his family was grace and mercy. He called them, protected them and pledged his faithfulness to them. The death of Jesus fulfilled God's covenant to Noah. As the pointed spear of a Roman soldier pierced Jesus' side while he hung on a criminal's cross, God's wrath was directed at God's only Son (Jn 19:34). In that climactic moment, the wrath of God and the grace of God met, and all of God's promises found their fulfillment in Jesus (2Co 1:20).

the rainbow appears in the clouds, [15]I will remember my covenant between me
and you and all living creatures of every kind. Never again will the waters become a flood to destroy all life. [16]Whenever the rainbow appears in the clouds,
I will see it and remember the everlasting covenant between God and all living
creatures of every kind on the earth."

[17]So God said to Noah, "This is the sign of the covenant I have established between me and all life on the earth."

The Sons of Noah

[18]The sons of Noah who came out of the ark were Shem, Ham and Japheth.
(Ham was the father of Canaan.) [19]These were the three sons of Noah, and from
them came the people who were scattered over the whole earth.

[20]Noah, a man of the soil, proceeded[a] to plant a vineyard. [21]When he drank
some of its wine, he became drunk and lay uncovered inside his tent. [22]Ham,
the father of Canaan, saw his father naked and told his two brothers outside.
[23]But Shem and Japheth took a garment and laid it across their shoulders; then
they walked in backward and covered their father's naked body. Their faces were
turned the other way so that they would not see their father naked.

[24]When Noah awoke from his wine and found out what his youngest son had
done to him, [25]he said,

"Cursed be Canaan!
  The lowest of slaves
  will he be to his brothers."

[26]He also said,

"Praise be to the LORD, the God of Shem!
  May Canaan be the slave of Shem.
[27]May God extend Japheth's[b] territory;
  may Japheth live in the tents of Shem,
  and may Canaan be the slave of Japheth."

[28]After the flood Noah lived 350 years. [29]Noah lived a total of 950 years, and
then he died.

The Table of Nations

10 This is the account of Shem, Ham and Japheth, Noah's sons, who themselves had sons after the flood.

The Japhethites

[2]The sons[c] of Japheth:
  Gomer, Magog, Madai, Javan, Tubal, Meshek and Tiras.
[3]The sons of Gomer:
  Ashkenaz, Riphath and Togarmah.
[4]The sons of Javan:
  Elishah, Tarshish, the Kittites and the Rodanites.[d] [5](From these the
  maritime peoples spread out into their territories by their clans within
  their nations, each with its own language.)

The Hamites

[6]The sons of Ham:
  Cush, Egypt, Put and Canaan.
[7]The sons of Cush:
  Seba, Havilah, Sabtah, Raamah and Sabteka.

[a] 20 Or *soil, was the first* [b] 27 *Japheth* sounds like the Hebrew for *extend.* [c] 2 *Sons* may mean *descendants* or *successors* or *nations*; also in verses 3, 4, 6, 7, 20-23, 29 and 31.
[d] 4 Some manuscripts of the Masoretic Text and Samaritan Pentateuch (see also Septuagint and 1 Chron. 1:7); most manuscripts of the Masoretic Text *Dodanites*

GENESIS 10:1

JESUS FROM THE FAMILY OF NOAH

Though not every ancient people group is listed in this chapter, it is seen here that all of the people of the earth, regardless of locale or language, descended from Noah. From this line Abraham and ultimately Jesus will emerge. It was Abraham with whom God made an everlasting covenant, promising that kings would come from his line (Ge 17:6). In the first line of the New Testament, Jesus is introduced as Messiah and "the son of Abraham" (Mt 1:1). It is clear to see, even this early on in Scripture, that God had a plan that was ultimately revealed in Jesus. The coming of Jesus as the Promised One in the line of Abraham established the continuity of the promise and plan of God from Genesis to Revelation.

The sons of Raamah:
Sheba and Dedan.
8 Cush was the father[a] of Nimrod, who became a mighty warrior on the earth.
9 He was a mighty hunter before the LORD; that is why it is said, "Like Nimrod, a
mighty hunter before the LORD." 10 The first centers of his kingdom were Babylon,
Uruk, Akkad and Kalneh, in[b] Shinar.[c] 11 From that land he went to Assyria, where
he built Nineveh, Rehoboth Ir,[d] Calah 12 and Resen, which is between Nineveh
and Calah — which is the great city.

13 Egypt was the father of
the Ludites, Anamites, Lehabites, Naphtuhites, 14 Pathrusites, Kaslu-
hites (from whom the Philistines came) and Caphtorites.
15 Canaan was the father of
Sidon his firstborn,[e] and of the Hittites, 16 Jebusites, Amorites, Girgashites, 17 Hivites, Arkites, Sinites, 18 Arvadites, Zemarites and Hamathites.

Later the Canaanite clans scattered 19 and the borders of Canaan reached
from Sidon toward Gerar as far as Gaza, and then toward Sodom, Gomorrah,
Admah and Zeboyim, as far as Lasha.
20 These are the sons of Ham by their clans and languages, in their territories
and nations.

The Semites

21 Sons were also born to Shem, whose older brother was[f] Japheth; Shem was
the ancestor of all the sons of Eber.

22 The sons of Shem:
Elam, Ashur, Arphaxad, Lud and Aram.
23 The sons of Aram:
Uz, Hul, Gether and Meshek.[g]
24 Arphaxad was the father of[h] Shelah,
and Shelah the father of Eber.
25 Two sons were born to Eber:
One was named Peleg,[i] because in his time the earth was divided; his
brother was named Joktan.
26 Joktan was the father of
Almodad, Sheleph, Hazarmaveth, Jerah, 27 Hadoram, Uzal, Diklah,
28 Obal, Abimael, Sheba, 29 Ophir, Havilah and Jobab. All these were sons
of Joktan.

30 The region where they lived stretched from Mesha toward Sephar, in the eastern hill country.
31 These are the sons of Shem by their clans and languages, in their territories
and nations.

32 These are the clans of Noah's sons, according to their lines of descent, within their nations. From these the nations spread out over the earth after the flood.

The Tower of Babel

11 Now the whole world had one language and a common speech. 2 As people
moved eastward,[j] they found a plain in Shinar[c] and settled there.
3 They said to each other, "Come, let's make bricks and bake them thoroughly."

[a] 8 *Father* may mean *ancestor* or *predecessor* or *founder*; also in verses 13, 15, 24 and 26.
[b] 10 Or *Uruk and Akkad — all of them in* [c] 10,2 That is, Babylonia [d] 11 Or *Nineveh with its city squares* [e] 15 Or *of the Sidonians, the foremost* [f] 21 Or *Shem, the older brother of* [g] 23 See Septuagint and 1 Chron. 1:17; Hebrew *Mash.* [h] 24 Hebrew; Septuagint *father of Cainan, and Cainan was the father of* [i] 25 *Peleg* means *division.* [j] 2 Or *from the east*; or *in the east*

They used brick instead of stone, and tar for mortar. 4Then they said, “Come,
let us build ourselves a city, with a tower that reaches to the heavens, so that we
may make a name for ourselves; otherwise we will be scattered over the face of
the whole earth.”
5But the LORD came down to see the city and the tower the people were
building. 6The LORD said, “If as one people speaking the same language they
have begun to do this, then nothing they plan to do will be impossible for them.
7Come, let us go down and confuse their language so they will not understand
each other.”
8So the LORD scattered them from there over all the earth, and they stopped
building the city. 9That is why it was called Babel[a]—because there the LORD
confused the language of the whole world. From there the LORD scattered them
over the face of the whole earth.

From Shem to Abram

10This is the account of Shem’s family line.

Two years after the flood, when Shem was 100 years old, he became the father[b] of Arphaxad. 11And after he became the father of Arphaxad, Shem lived 500
years and had other sons and daughters.
12When Arphaxad had lived 35 years, he became the father of Shelah. 13And
after he became the father of Shelah, Arphaxad lived 403 years and had other
sons and daughters.[c]
14When Shelah had lived 30 years, he became the father of Eber. 15And after
he became the father of Eber, Shelah lived 403 years and had other sons and
daughters.
16When Eber had lived 34 years, he became the father of Peleg. 17And after he
became the father of Peleg, Eber lived 430 years and had other sons and daughters.
18When Peleg had lived 30 years, he became the father of Reu. 19And after he
became the father of Reu, Peleg lived 209 years and had other sons and daughters.
20When Reu had lived 32 years, he became the father of Serug. 21And after he
became the father of Serug, Reu lived 207 years and had other sons and daughters.
22When Serug had lived 30 years, he became the father of Nahor. 23And after
he became the father of Nahor, Serug lived 200 years and had other sons and
daughters.
24When Nahor had lived 29 years, he became the father of Terah. 25And after
he became the father of Terah, Nahor lived 119 years and had other sons and
daughters.
26After Terah had lived 70 years, he became the father of Abram, Nahor and
Haran.

Abram’s Family

27This is the account of Terah’s family line.

Terah became the father of Abram, Nahor and Haran. And Haran became
the father of Lot. 28While his father Terah was still alive, Haran died in Ur of the
Chaldeans, in the land of his birth. 29Abram and Nahor both married. The name
of Abram’s wife was Sarai, and the name of Nahor’s wife was Milkah; she was the
daughter of Haran, the father of both Milkah and Iskah. 30Now Sarai was childless because she was not able to conceive.

---

[a] 9 That is, Babylon; *Babel* sounds like the Hebrew for *confused*. [b] *10 Father* may mean *ancestor*; also in verses 11-25. [c] *12,13* Hebrew; Septuagint (see also Luke 3:35, 36 and note at Gen. 10:24) *35 years, he became the father of Cainan. 13And after he became the father of Cainan, Arphaxad lived 430 years and had other sons and daughters, and then he died. When Cainan had lived 130 years, he became the father of Shelah. And after he became the father of Shelah, Cainan lived 330 years and had other sons and daughters*

REVOLT

—*LOUIE GIGLIO*

GENESIS 3–11

Something is wrong with humanity. While we might try to put on our best face for the world, evil lurks deep inside us all. To deny this reality is to close our eyes to history, for the checkered past of humankind is a monument to the fallen nature we all bear.

Should we ever think otherwise, we need only visit the gas chambers of Auschwitz, where haunted walls recount unspeakable murderous acts; the Edmund Pettus Bridge in Selma, Alabama, where blacks were brutalized because of the color of their skin; the jungle of the Congo, where child soldiers were forced to maim or kill their families; or the brothels of Delhi, where innocent young girls are bought and sold to appease twisted cravings. A brief stop in any of these places should jar us back to grim reality again.

We are capable of committing outrageous wrongs. Those sins, both the ones we act out and those we harbor in our thoughts, are equal in the eyes of God.

So it was in the beginning, starting with Adam and Eve in the Garden of Eden.

REBELLIOUS FROM THE START

Since that time, humankind's capacity to rebel against God has not diminished. We are born with a propensity to go our own way. The first humans arrived on earth with a choice: the free will to follow God toward abundant life or to do things their own way and come face-to-face with death. Adam and Eve chose death, and we all bear the consequences of their fall (Ro 5:12).

How easy it is for us to condemn the first couple for their derelict behavior. God himself walked with them in the cool of the day, and everything about their world was perfect. They were naked, yet unashamed; free from sickness, weariness, brokenness, pain and death. Before them were trees of every kind, gifts of God for their enjoyment. Adam and Eve's purpose was to manage and care for the plants and creatures on the earth. Their very being was fashioned in the image of God. Among the trees of the garden, God placed the tree of life and the tree of the knowledge of good *and* evil in the center. He instructed Adam to steer clear of the fruit of the latter lest he die. One tree to avoid versus countless trees to enjoy, all set in paradise. An easy choice, right?

However, another voice, the voice of a serpent personifying Satan himself, entered God's story and blurred the lines between good and evil. Satan, like humankind, at one time also had a choice. He could have worshiped God in the company of the angels or revolted. Foolishly, Satan chose his own glory and was jolted from heaven like a falling star. In his rebellion, God granted him limited freedom on earth. With that freedom he sold a lie to Adam and Eve, convincing them that God was trying to rob them of a greater joy by keeping them from this one tree.

The serpent called God's trustworthiness into question, undermining God's character and goodwill toward his creation. Adam and Eve took the bait and turned their backs on God, reaching for the heights of God-like status, yet falling to the depths of futility, rebellion and death.

Immediately, paradise was shattered into a billion tiny pieces. Guilt ended innocence. The couple hid from the presence of God. Judgment fell. Death entered the scene. Adam and Eve's perfectly harmonious tenure in the Garden of Eden was over.

I WILL DO IT MY WAY

What happened in the garden is called sin. But there is no better way to characterize it than using the word *revolt*. Humankind said on that day what we still say every day. I WILL DO IT MY WAY!

It's hard to imagine anyone spitting in the face of a friend, tracking mud through the home of a neighbor on a rainy day, cutting off a funeral procession in traffic, or mocking a person with a disability. Common human decency causes us to recoil at the thought. Yet, we casually ignore the Almighty, rebuff his counsel, laugh at his wisdom, pursue our own pleasure, and straight-up say no when he calls us to his path and plan.

If the word *revolt* sounds too strong, consider that God is the originator and owner of us all. Yet, we attempt to dismiss and belittle the One who formed us from the dust. We spit in God's face and slam the door on his love. Often without a thought or even a twinge of regret, we treat God worse than we treat most of our friends and neighbors. We repeatedly say toward heaven, "No, thanks, I'm doing just fine without you!"

God has graciously invited us into his story, breathed into us the very breath that gives us life, and invited us to know and walk with him. To do less, to choose less, is to shove our will in the face of the Almighty. And every time we do, we turn his best for us upside down.

In God's eyes all people are in the same predicament. That's what Scripture indicates when the New Testament writer Paul says, "All have sinned and fall short of the glory of God" (Ro 3:23). The prophet Isaiah amplified our plight when he wrote, "We all, like sheep, have gone astray, each of us has turned to our own way" (Isa 53:6). The psalmist wrote, "All have turned away, all have become corrupt; there is no one who does good, not even one" (Ps 14:3).

Like Adam and Eve, we seek to elevate ourselves to God's status, free ourselves from his authority

REVOLT

(CONTINUED)

GENESIS 3 – 11

and define for ourselves what is wrong and what is right.

Comparing our behavior against someone else's in an attempt to make ourselves look more desirable does us no good. Revolt has never been about the magnitude of our sin but the fact that we are willing to look into the face of a good and loving God and turn and run the other way.

TRADING TRUTH FOR LIES

Left to ourselves, we will do what Adam and Eve did in the garden. We exchange "the glory of the immortal God for images made to look like a mortal human being" (Ro 1:23). God promised life and sought to protect people from destruction and death. The serpent twisted God's words, and the world around us does the same. We often discard what is best for us from God's perspective for what is easiest. We ditch what is good for what is convenient. Our culture scoffs at what is innocent and pure while it celebrates what is perverse and immoral. More and more, honesty, decency and modesty are marginalized and even vilified.

This exchange of truth for lies does not happen without consequences. Once jettisoned from Eden, humankind did not cease to worship (which we were created to do); humans just exchanged the true worship of holy God for something else. Scripture says, "They exchanged the truth about God for a lie, and worshiped and served created things rather than the Creator" (Ro 1:25).

When we turn our God-intended worship toward a person or pleasure or thing, we break ranks with God and violate the first of his Ten Commandments (Ex 20:3).

Sin shatters God's perfect plan for us and leaves us with powerless idols that soak up our affection while returning nothing of spiritual benefit to our lives.

But that's not all. It gets worse.

Like we see in Eden, a holy, righteous and just God cannot turn a blind eye toward our revolt. He cannot simply wink and magically make it disappear. While we rationalize away our sin, God cannot deny his own character.

Our sin derailed our worship, separated us from God, introduced us to hardship and toil, put hostility between us and others, filled our hearts with selfish intentions, brought pain into childbirth, and spawned a global epidemic of hatred and war and injustice that marches on in full force today.

Even creation itself was rocked by humankind's sinful revolt. Natural disasters continue to mar our world, and nothing in creation on this earth is as it was meant to be (Ro 8:19 – 22). Everything has been broken because of sin. Decay and death now mark every inch of human existence.

Families fracture. Marriages fail. Litigations flourish. Deception darkens. Addiction crushes. Complacency numbs. Violence escalates. Insanity imprisons. Pleasures disappoint. Riches disappear. Prejudice blinds. Insecurity mars. Jealousy rots. Power corrupts.

GOD'S WRATH

Yet, our sin does something more. Our revolt places us in the crosshairs of God's wrath — his righteous indignation that is set on eradicating all wrong from the face of the earth.

While God's wrath gets a bad rap, any of us, if we thought it through, would act in the same way. We want the weight of justice to fall on those who abuse and injure us or others. In the same way, yet on a much grander scale, God's wrath will fall on every rebel heart. Humankind is without excuse, guilty before a holy God and deserving of eternal punishment.

Revolt didn't simply make us bad. It left us spiritually dead (Ro 6:23). But, fortunately this is God's story and not ours. The story does not end in death; rather, the seeds of salvation are sown in Eden's soil. The God of mercy trumped revolt with redemption in an outrageous plan to buy back the rebels at the cost of his one and only Son. While judgment rained down on Adam and Eve and the earth and the serpent, grace was on the horizon. The first sign of grace was God's banishment of Adam and Eve from the Garden of Eden. In this act of kindness, he prevented those he loved from eating from the tree of life, thus saving them from living forever in their state of death. Outside Eden, a heavenly mission could ensue, one foreshadowed as God made coverings for the man and the woman.

Once sin smashed Eden's innocence, Adam and Eve were filled with shame. No one told them to be ashamed, as if guilt is a human-induced effect meant to give control of the people to religious higher-ups. Adam and Eve were convinced on their own that something was amiss. Their consciences shouted "run and hide" as the Spirit of God brought conviction to their hearts.

GOD'S MERCY AND GRACE

Though God judged their actions, his mercy intervened to cover their shame. Using fig leaves from a nearby tree, Adam and Eve tried to hide their nakedness. But God went a step further by clothing them with animal skin. This was a picture of the sacrifice of the One who would ultimately shed his blood so that all people could have an opportunity to be saved.

This kind of grace is staggering, especially in light of the fact that there is no record of so much as an

REVOLT

(CONTINUED)

GENESIS 3 – 11

"I'm sorry" from Adam or Eve. Once their deed was exposed, Adam danced the dance we often dance as well, passing the blame to Eve in a weak attempt to deflect God's attention from his disobedience and the responsibility only he himself bore.

One would think Adam would have quickly blurted out, "Please forgive me, God! I am a fool and I cannot believe what I've done." But Adam couldn't bring himself to confess, so he blamed someone else.

Yet, God's redemption plan was undeterred.

Not only did he make a covering for their nakedness, God promised that a descendant of Adam and Eve would one day crush the serpent's head, though he would be harmed in the process (Ge 3:15). This promise and plan, while far from clear in Genesis 3, would define the story that unfolds in the rest of the Bible. God fulfilled his promise by seeing to it that Jesus Christ, a descendant of the woman, would crush Satan, sin and death forever.

God wasn't going to turn his back on those who were made to bear his image in the world. While humankind chose their own way, Jesus yielded to the Father's plan. Taking on flesh, Jesus was tempted like every other human, yet Jesus did not sin. Jesus exchanged his life for every rebel who turns to him to accept the price he paid for their sin and trust in him for salvation.

The final sacrifice for sin was made as Jesus took our blows, carried our sin, bore our shame and was crushed by the wrath of God in our place. In the process, "God made him who had no sin to be sin for us, so that in him we might become the righteousness of God" (2Co 5:21). Rebels could now be forgiven. Sinners could be made clean. And all those who drifted far from their heavenly Father could come home again.

The key to this brand-new life is our willingness to end the revolt. To be forgiven, we must admit our sin. To say that we have no sin is to make God a liar and seal our fate (1Jn 1:10). But to admit our wrongs and raise the white flag of surrender is to truly find freedom and enjoy life in God's presence that will never end.

THE SIN AT BABEL

At the heart of sin is the desire for humanity to believe that they know better than God. In the garden Satan tempted Eve by asking her, "Did God really say . . . ?" in regards to his admonition to not eat the fruit from the tree. When it comes to Babel, the same reality is in play; the people believe they have come up with a better way than what God commanded.

After human beings had been wiped from the planet by the flood, God made a covenant with the lone survivors, Noah and his family, to "fill the earth" (Ge 9:1). However, by the time we get to the story of Babel, the people have concocted a plan that would keep them from having to keep this command (Ge 11:4).

In Babel we see a combination of arrogance and insecurity. The tower demonstrates mankind taking matters into their own hands, in essence showing God that they know better than he does. Their actions show that they are not relying on God for their well-being; they can handle life on their own. The reality is that the people, by seeking to make a name for themselves, were in competition with God.

In not wanting to scatter over the earth, the people again were showing that they did not trust God for their security. They felt that scattering included too many unknowns, thus leading them to believe that they would be better off staying in one place. This insecurity paralyzed them into believing they needed their own plan. Ultimately God came and shattered the selfish plans of the people by confusing their language and scattering them throughout the earth.

In Acts 1:8, Jesus says his followers are to be his witnesses to the "ends of the earth." However, once the power of the Holy Spirit came in Acts 2, the result was not a scattering to the ends of the earth, but a staying in one place, Jerusalem. This all changed when Stephen was stoned to death in Acts 7 and persecution came against the church. This tyranny resulted in the church spreading throughout the known world.

Ultimately what Babel and the early church in Jerusalem show us is that God is asking us to trust him. However, in the face of human pride and disobedience, he will choose to allow calamities to occur in order for his plans to move forward.

31 Terah took his son Abram, his grandson Lot son of Haran, and his daughter-in-law Sarai, the wife of his son Abram, and together they set out from Ur of the Chaldeans to go to Canaan. But when they came to Harran, they settled there.
32 Terah lived 205 years, and he died in Harran.

The Call of Abram

12 The LORD had said to Abram, "Go from your country, your people and your father's household to the land I will show you.

2 "I will make you into a great nation,
and I will bless you;
I will make your name great,
and you will be a blessing.[a]
3 I will bless those who bless you,
and whoever curses you I will curse;
and all peoples on earth
will be blessed through you."[b]

4 So Abram went, as the LORD had told him; and Lot went with him. Abram was seventy-five years old when he set out from Harran. 5 He took his wife Sarai, his nephew Lot, all the possessions they had accumulated and the people they had acquired in Harran, and they set out for the land of Canaan, and they arrived there.

6 Abram traveled through the land as far as the site of the great tree of Moreh at Shechem. At that time the Canaanites were in the land. 7 The LORD appeared to Abram and said, "To your offspring[c] I will give this land." So he built an altar there to the LORD, who had appeared to him.

8 From there he went on toward the hills east of Bethel and pitched his tent, with Bethel on the west and Ai on the east. There he built an altar to the LORD and called on the name of the LORD.

9 Then Abram set out and continued toward the Negev.

Abram in Egypt

10 Now there was a famine in the land, and Abram went down to Egypt to live there for a while because the famine was severe. 11 As he was about to enter Egypt, he said to his wife Sarai, "I know what a beautiful woman you are. 12 When the Egyptians see you, they will say, 'This is his wife.' Then they will kill me but will let you live. 13 Say you are my sister, so that I will be treated well for your sake and my life will be spared because of you."

14 When Abram came to Egypt, the Egyptians saw that Sarai was a very beautiful woman. 15 And when Pharaoh's officials saw her, they praised her to Pharaoh, and she was taken into his palace. 16 He treated Abram well for her sake, and Abram acquired sheep and cattle, male and female donkeys, male and female servants, and camels.

17 But the LORD inflicted serious diseases on Pharaoh and his household because of Abram's wife Sarai. 18 So Pharaoh summoned Abram. "What have you done to me?" he said. "Why didn't you tell me she was your wife? 19 Why did you say, 'She is my sister,' so that I took her to be my wife? Now then, here is your wife. Take her and go!" 20 Then Pharaoh gave orders about Abram to his men, and they sent him on his way, with his wife and everything he had.

Abram and Lot Separate

13 So Abram went up from Egypt to the Negev, with his wife and everything he had, and Lot went with him. 2 Abram had become very wealthy in livestock and in silver and gold.

---

[a] 2 Or *be seen as blessed* [b] 3 Or *earth / will use your name in blessings* (see 48:20)
[c] 7 Or *seed*

ONGOING PROMISES OF A FAITHFUL GOD

The covenant between God and Abraham (often referred to as the Abrahamic covenant) occupies the central focus of the next several chapters of the Bible. Genesis 12 begins with a vital prologue that sets the stage for the promises and ceremonies that would follow. They testify to the irrevocable nature of the promises of God.

The passage begins with a task given to Abram. He was called to leave all that he had known — his home, most of his family and his country of origin — and travel to an unknown location that God would reveal in due time. While the passage begins with an act of obedience, it is clear that the covenant is based on the promises of God.

Seven promises follow in rapid succession. (1) God promised to make Abram into a great nation — a pledge that would find fulfillment in the birth of the Hebrew nation. (2) God promised to bless Abram, his family and the nation that would emerge with his loving care and continued provision. (3) Abram, later renamed Abraham, would be given a name that would live on long after his earthly life concluded. (4) The nation would be a blessing to other nations as they modeled conformity to God's law and demonstrated proper worship of the awe-inspiring God. (5) God would bless those who blessed the nation. (6) God would stand in judgment against those who oppressed his people. (7) All people would be blessed through Abram and the generations that followed him.

These grand and glorious promises were rooted in the nature and character of God. In spite of the people's unbelief, rebellion, idolatry and spiritual adultery, God remained faithful to his promises because the covenant was based on grace and not on law. Paul writes that God gave Abraham these promises long before the law was given on Mount Sinai (Gal 3:16 – 17).

As one born in the line of Abraham, Jesus was the means by which these promises could be fulfilled. All those in Christ, born again by the grace of God, are children of Abraham and recipients of the promises of God that were fulfilled in Jesus. Paul testified to this reality when he claimed that all those who respond in faith to the good news of Jesus are heirs of the promises given to Abraham (Gal 3:28 – 29).

[3]From the Negev he went from place to place until he came to Bethel, to the place between Bethel and Ai where his tent had been earlier [4]and where he had first built an altar. There Abram called on the name of the LORD.

[5]Now Lot, who was moving about with Abram, also had flocks and herds and tents. [6]But the land could not support them while they stayed together, for their possessions were so great that they were not able to stay together. [7]And quarreling arose between Abram's herders and Lot's. The Canaanites and Perizzites were also living in the land at that time.

[8]So Abram said to Lot, "Let's not have any quarreling between you and me, or between your herders and mine, for we are close relatives. [9]Is not the whole land before you? Let's part company. If you go to the left, I'll go to the right; if you go to the right, I'll go to the left."

[10]Lot looked around and saw that the whole plain of the Jordan toward Zoar was well watered, like the garden of the LORD, like the land of Egypt. (This was before the LORD destroyed Sodom and Gomorrah.) [11]So Lot chose for himself the whole plain of the Jordan and set out toward the east. The two men parted company: [12]Abram lived in the land of Canaan, while Lot lived among the cities of the plain and pitched his tents near Sodom. [13]Now the people of Sodom were wicked and were sinning greatly against the LORD.

[14]The LORD said to Abram after Lot had parted from him, "Look around from where you are, to the north and south, to the east and west. [15]All the land that you see I will give to you and your offspring[a] forever. [16]I will make your offspring like the dust of the earth, so that if anyone could count the dust, then your offspring could be counted. [17]Go, walk through the length and breadth of the land, for I am giving it to you."

[18]So Abram went to live near the great trees of Mamre at Hebron, where he pitched his tents. There he built an altar to the LORD.

Abram Rescues Lot

14 At the time when Amraphel was king of Shinar,[b] Arioch king of Ellasar, Kedorlaomer king of Elam and Tidal king of Goyim, [2]these kings went to war against Bera king of Sodom, Birsha king of Gomorrah, Shinab king of Admah, Shemeber king of Zeboyim, and the king of Bela (that is, Zoar). [3]All these latter kings joined forces in the Valley of Siddim (that is, the Dead Sea Valley). [4]For twelve years they had been subject to Kedorlaomer, but in the thirteenth year they rebelled.

[5]In the fourteenth year, Kedorlaomer and the kings allied with him went out and defeated the Rephaites in Ashteroth Karnaim, the Zuzites in Ham, the Emites in Shaveh Kiriathaim [6]and the Horites in the hill country of Seir, as far as El Paran near the desert. [7]Then they turned back and went to En Mishpat (that is, Kadesh), and they conquered the whole territory of the Amalekites, as well as the Amorites who were living in Hazezon Tamar.

[8]Then the king of Sodom, the king of Gomorrah, the king of Admah, the king of Zeboyim and the king of Bela (that is, Zoar) marched out and drew up their battle lines in the Valley of Siddim [9]against Kedorlaomer king of Elam, Tidal king of Goyim, Amraphel king of Shinar and Arioch king of Ellasar—four kings against five. [10]Now the Valley of Siddim was full of tar pits, and when the kings of Sodom and Gomorrah fled, some of the men fell into them and the rest fled to the hills. [11]The four kings seized all the goods of Sodom and Gomorrah and all their food; then they went away. [12]They also carried off Abram's nephew Lot and his possessions, since he was living in Sodom.

[13]A man who had escaped came and reported this to Abram the Hebrew. Now Abram was living near the great trees of Mamre the Amorite, a brother[c] of Eshkol and Aner, all of whom were allied with Abram. [14]When Abram heard that his

---

[a] *15* Or *seed*; also in verse 16 [b] *1* That is, Babylonia; also in verse 9 [c] *13* Or *a relative*; or *an ally*

relative had been taken captive, he called out the 318 trained men born in his
household and went in pursuit as far as Dan. 15During the night Abram divided his men to attack them and he routed them, pursuing them as far as Hobah,
north of Damascus. 16He recovered all the goods and brought back his relative
Lot and his possessions, together with the women and the other people.
17After Abram returned from defeating Kedorlaomer and the kings allied with
him, the king of Sodom came out to meet him in the Valley of Shaveh (that is,
the King's Valley).
18Then Melchizedek king of Salem brought out bread and wine. He was priest
of God Most High, 19and he blessed Abram, saying,

"Blessed be Abram by God Most High,
Creator of heaven and earth.
20And praise be to God Most High,
who delivered your enemies into your hand."

Then Abram gave him a tenth of everything.
21The king of Sodom said to Abram, "Give me the people and keep the goods
for yourself."
22But Abram said to the king of Sodom, "With raised hand I have sworn an
oath to the LORD, God Most High, Creator of heaven and earth, 23that I will accept nothing belonging to you, not even a thread or the strap of a sandal, so that
you will never be able to say, 'I made Abram rich.' 24I will accept nothing but
what my men have eaten and the share that belongs to the men who went with
me — to Aner, Eshkol and Mamre. Let them have their share."

The LORD's Covenant With Abram

15 After this, the word of the LORD came to Abram in a vision:

"Do not be afraid, Abram.
I am your shield,[a]
your very great reward.[b]"

2But Abram said, "Sovereign LORD, what can you give me since I remain
childless and the one who will inherit[c] my estate is Eliezer of Damascus?" 3And
Abram said, "You have given me no children; so a servant in my household will
be my heir."
4Then the word of the LORD came to him: "This man will not be your heir,
but a son who is your own flesh and blood will be your heir." 5He took him outside and said, "Look up at the sky and count the stars — if indeed you can count
them." Then he said to him, "So shall your offspring[d] be."
6Abram believed the LORD, and he credited it to him as righteousness.
7He also said to him, "I am the LORD, who brought you out of Ur of the Chaldeans to give you this land to take possession of it."
8But Abram said, "Sovereign LORD, how can I know that I will gain possession of it?"
9So the LORD said to him, "Bring me a heifer, a goat and a ram, each three
years old, along with a dove and a young pigeon."
10Abram brought all these to him, cut them in two and arranged the halves
opposite each other; the birds, however, he did not cut in half. 11Then birds of
prey came down on the carcasses, but Abram drove them away.
12As the sun was setting, Abram fell into a deep sleep, and a thick and dreadful darkness came over him. 13Then the LORD said to him, "Know for certain
that for four hundred years your descendants will be strangers in a country not
their own and that they will be enslaved and mistreated there. 14But I will punish the nation they serve as slaves, and afterward they will come out with great

[a] 1 Or *sovereign* [b] 1 Or *shield; / your reward will be very great* [c] 2 The meaning of the Hebrew for this phrase is uncertain. [d] 5 Or *seed*

GENESIS 15:6

FAITH AND OBEDIENCE

Faith and obedience were hallmarks of Abram's life (Heb 11:18 – 19). When God made Abram promises, he believed. And when he was commanded, Abram obeyed (Ge 12:4; 22:3). At times this faith required great risk on Abram's part. Abram left what was known to him in order to step out into what God was calling him to. It is faith like Abram's — faith in the only living God — that saves sinners (Eph 2:8). It was Abram's faith in God's promise to give him many descendants that caused God to count him as righteous (Ge 15:1 – 6). Abram's faith was well founded in the God who always keeps his promises. It's important to note that it wasn't Abram's own righteous living nor good deeds that made him righteous in God's eyes; it was simply faith.

possessions. 15You, however, will go to your ancestors in peace and be buried at
a good old age. 16In the fourth generation your descendants will come back here,
for the sin of the Amorites has not yet reached its full measure."
17When the sun had set and darkness had fallen, a smoking firepot with a
blazing torch appeared and passed between the pieces. 18On that day the LORD
made a covenant with Abram and said, "To your descendants I give this land,
from the Wadi[a] of Egypt to the great river, the Euphrates — 19the land of the Kenites, Kenizzites, Kadmonites, 20Hittites, Perizzites, Rephaites, 21Amorites, Canaanites, Girgashites and Jebusites."

Hagar and Ishmael

16 Now Sarai, Abram's wife, had borne him no children. But she had an
Egyptian slave named Hagar; 2so she said to Abram, "The LORD has kept
me from having children. Go, sleep with my slave; perhaps I can build a family
through her."
Abram agreed to what Sarai said. 3So after Abram had been living in Canaan
ten years, Sarai his wife took her Egyptian slave Hagar and gave her to her husband to be his wife. 4He slept with Hagar, and she conceived.
When she knew she was pregnant, she began to despise her mistress. 5Then
Sarai said to Abram, "You are responsible for the wrong I am suffering. I put my
slave in your arms, and now that she knows she is pregnant, she despises me.
May the LORD judge between you and me."
6"Your slave is in your hands," Abram said. "Do with her whatever you think
best." Then Sarai mistreated Hagar; so she fled from her.
7The angel of the LORD found Hagar near a spring in the desert; it was the
spring that is beside the road to Shur. 8And he said, "Hagar, slave of Sarai, where
have you come from, and where are you going?"
"I'm running away from my mistress Sarai," she answered.
9Then the angel of the LORD told her, "Go back to your mistress and submit to
her." 10The angel added, "I will increase your descendants so much that they will
be too numerous to count."
11The angel of the LORD also said to her:

"You are now pregnant
 and you will give birth to a son.
You shall name him Ishmael,[b]
 for the LORD has heard of your misery.
12He will be a wild donkey of a man;
 his hand will be against everyone
 and everyone's hand against him,
and he will live in hostility
 toward[c] all his brothers."

13She gave this name to the LORD who spoke to her: "You are the God who sees
me," for she said, "I have now seen[d] the One who sees me." 14That is why the well
was called Beer Lahai Roi[e]; it is still there, between Kadesh and Bered.
15So Hagar bore Abram a son, and Abram gave the name Ishmael to the son
she had borne. 16Abram was eighty-six years old when Hagar bore him Ishmael.

The Covenant of Circumcision

17 When Abram was ninety-nine years old, the LORD appeared to him and
said, "I am God Almighty[f]; walk before me faithfully and be blameless.
2Then I will make my covenant between me and you and will greatly increase
your numbers."
3Abram fell facedown, and God said to him, 4"As for me, this is my covenant

GENESIS 16:15

VISITATION FROM GOD

Hagar, a slave, got caught up in Abram and Sarai's attempt to bear the son that God had promised them. Though Hagar became pregnant with a son, the conception was not according to the Lord's plan and she grew dismayed (Ge 16:4 – 5). After being mistreated by Sarai, Hagar ran away and was met by the angel of the Lord. The site and outcome of Hagar's visitation from the angel of the Lord are beautiful. She was found by a spring of water in the desert, which closely represents her situation — pregnant with a child, yet feeling abandoned and hopeless. She was comforted by this visitation (Ge 16:13) despite being told that her son, Ishmael, would not be the son of promise but would experience hostility in all of his relationships and that he would roam the desert like a wild donkey (Ge 16:11 – 12; Gal 4:22 – 23).

[a] *18* Or *river* [b] *11* *Ishmael* means *God hears.* [c] *12* Or *live to the east / of* [d] *13* Or *seen the back of* [e] *14* *Beer Lahai Roi* means *well of the Living One who sees me.* [f] *1* Hebrew *El-Shaddai*

with you: You will be the father of many nations. 5No longer will you be called Abram[a]; your name will be Abraham,[b] for I have made you a father of many nations. 6I will make you very fruitful; I will make nations of you, and kings will come from you. 7I will establish my covenant as an everlasting covenant between me and you and your descendants after you for the generations to come, to be your God and the God of your descendants after you. 8The whole land of Canaan, where you now reside as a foreigner, I will give as an everlasting possession to you and your descendants after you; and I will be their God."

9Then God said to Abraham, "As for you, you must keep my covenant, you and your descendants after you for the generations to come. 10This is my covenant with you and your descendants after you, the covenant you are to keep: Every male among you shall be circumcised. 11You are to undergo circumcision, and it will be the sign of the covenant between me and you. 12For the generations to come every male among you who is eight days old must be circumcised, including those born in your household or bought with money from a foreigner — those who are not your offspring. 13Whether born in your household or bought with your money, they must be circumcised. My covenant in your flesh is to be an everlasting covenant. 14Any uncircumcised male, who has not been circumcised in the flesh, will be cut off from his people; he has broken my covenant."

15God also said to Abraham, "As for Sarai your wife, you are no longer to call her Sarai; her name will be Sarah. 16I will bless her and will surely give you a son by her. I will bless her so that she will be the mother of nations; kings of peoples will come from her."

17Abraham fell facedown; he laughed and said to himself, "Will a son be born to a man a hundred years old? Will Sarah bear a child at the age of ninety?" 18And Abraham said to God, "If only Ishmael might live under your blessing!"

19Then God said, "Yes, but your wife Sarah will bear you a son, and you will call him Isaac.[c] I will establish my covenant with him as an everlasting covenant for his descendants after him. 20And as for Ishmael, I have heard you: I will surely bless him; I will make him fruitful and will greatly increase his numbers. He will be the father of twelve rulers, and I will make him into a great nation. 21But my covenant I will establish with Isaac, whom Sarah will bear to you by this time next year." 22When he had finished speaking with Abraham, God went up from him.

23On that very day Abraham took his son Ishmael and all those born in his household or bought with his money, every male in his household, and circumcised them, as God told him. 24Abraham was ninety-nine years old when he was circumcised, 25and his son Ishmael was thirteen; 26Abraham and his son Ishmael were both circumcised on that very day. 27And every male in Abraham's household, including those born in his household or bought from a foreigner, was circumcised with him.

The Three Visitors

18 The LORD appeared to Abraham near the great trees of Mamre while he was sitting at the entrance to his tent in the heat of the day. 2Abraham looked up and saw three men standing nearby. When he saw them, he hurried from the entrance of his tent to meet them and bowed low to the ground.

3He said, "If I have found favor in your eyes, my lord,[d] do not pass your servant by. 4Let a little water be brought, and then you may all wash your feet and rest under this tree. 5Let me get you something to eat, so you can be refreshed and then go on your way — now that you have come to your servant."

"Very well," they answered, "do as you say."

6So Abraham hurried into the tent to Sarah. "Quick," he said, "get three seahs[e] of the finest flour and knead it and bake some bread."

---

[a] 5 *Abram* means *exalted father.* [b] 5 *Abraham* probably means *father of many.*
[c] 19 *Isaac* means *he laughs.* [d] 3 Or *eyes, Lord* [e] 6 That is, probably about 36 pounds or about 16 kilograms

---

GENESIS 18:1–2

A KNOWABLE GOD

God's tender affection for his people is shown by his willingness to reveal himself, often through his spoken word, to his people. It is clear that the people of God were stunned that God would even speak to them. They often stood at a distance, in fear and awe, at the revelation of God to his people (Ex 20:21). These appearances in the Old Testament find perfect fulfillment in the incarnation of Jesus Christ. In his birth, Jesus willingly laid aside the glories of heaven to take the form of a servant in order to make a way for sinful people to come to the Father (Php 2:1 – 11). In his deity, Jesus demonstrated and declared to the world the nature and character of God in a way that allowed humanity to see not only a temporary glimpse of his glory but the exact imprint of God's glory in a permanent, ongoing fashion (Heb 1:3). Jesus made himself known so that fallen men and women can know God.

FATHER OF MANY NATIONS

God's grand mission to restore his rebellious worshipers, as broad as it seems, was as narrow as a single man — Abram. But the scope of that mission was about to become much broader. God told Abram that he was going to make him the father of many nations and accordingly renamed him "Abraham." The Lord would indeed make Abram into Abraham, and he would do it in two ways.

In a purely physical sense, Abraham's sons Ishmael and Isaac would become the fathers of nations. Ishmael, in spite of his shame and rejection, would father a great nation (Ge 17:20). His children would go on to become the Ishmaelites (25:13 – 16; 37:27 – 28). Isaac's two sons, Esau and Jacob, were both the source of nations. Esau would become the father of the Edomites (36:9), who lived on the borders of Canaan. Abraham's grandson Jacob was renamed "Israel" by God — the name of the great nation he would father (35:10 – 11).

In a spiritual sense, Abraham's descendants would form a massive number of individuals from many nations. God used Abraham as a father of many spiritual descendants who, like him, entered into a relationship with God by faith. This cross-national, interracial people group was what God was working to establish through Abraham.

God's promise to make Abraham the father of many nations involved two major campaigns into the hostile territory of the rebellious Gentile nations, drawing worshipers who would place their faith in God. The first campaign to reach the nations occurred as God called Israel to be his witness to the Gentiles (Isa 42:5 – 7). While limited in success, many representatives from other nations were reached during this time; Israel's witness to the Gentiles included unique missionaries like Jonah and memorable converts such as Rahab and Ruth.

God's second campaign to bring his promise to completion involves his new cross-national, interracial people — the church. From its very onset, the church was intended to finish the work of reaching the nations (Ac 2:5 – 11). As the church expands, bringing the message of Abrahamic faith to the nations, God's promise to Abraham is slowly coming to fruition.

[7]Then he ran to the herd and selected a choice, tender calf and gave it to a servant, who hurried to prepare it. [8]He then brought some curds and milk and the calf that had been prepared, and set these before them. While they ate, he stood near them under a tree.

[9]"Where is your wife Sarah?" they asked him.

"There, in the tent," he said.

[10]Then one of them said, "I will surely return to you about this time next year, and Sarah your wife will have a son."

Now Sarah was listening at the entrance to the tent, which was behind him.
[11]Abraham and Sarah were already very old, and Sarah was past the age of childbearing. [12]So Sarah laughed to herself as she thought, "After I am worn out and my lord is old, will I now have this pleasure?"

[13]Then the LORD said to Abraham, "Why did Sarah laugh and say, 'Will I really have a child, now that I am old?' [14]Is anything too hard for the LORD? I will return to you at the appointed time next year, and Sarah will have a son."

[15]Sarah was afraid, so she lied and said, "I did not laugh."

But he said, "Yes, you did laugh."

Abraham Pleads for Sodom

[16]When the men got up to leave, they looked down toward Sodom, and Abraham walked along with them to see them on their way. [17]Then the LORD said, "Shall I hide from Abraham what I am about to do? [18]Abraham will surely become a great and powerful nation, and all nations on earth will be blessed through him.[a] [19]For I have chosen him, so that he will direct his children and his household after him to keep the way of the LORD by doing what is right and just, so that the LORD will bring about for Abraham what he has promised him."

[20]Then the LORD said, "The outcry against Sodom and Gomorrah is so great and their sin so grievous [21]that I will go down and see if what they have done is as bad as the outcry that has reached me. If not, I will know."

[22]The men turned away and went toward Sodom, but Abraham remained standing before the LORD.[b] [23]Then Abraham approached him and said: "Will you sweep away the righteous with the wicked? [24]What if there are fifty righteous people in the city? Will you really sweep it away and not spare[c] the place for the sake of the fifty righteous people in it? [25]Far be it from you to do such a thing—to kill the righteous with the wicked, treating the righteous and the wicked alike. Far be it from you! Will not the Judge of all the earth do right?"

[26]The LORD said, "If I find fifty righteous people in the city of Sodom, I will spare the whole place for their sake."

[27]Then Abraham spoke up again: "Now that I have been so bold as to speak to the Lord, though I am nothing but dust and ashes, [28]what if the number of the righteous is five less than fifty? Will you destroy the whole city for lack of five people?"

"If I find forty-five there," he said, "I will not destroy it."

[29]Once again he spoke to him, "What if only forty are found there?"

He said, "For the sake of forty, I will not do it."

[30]Then he said, "May the Lord not be angry, but let me speak. What if only thirty can be found there?"

He answered, "I will not do it if I find thirty there."

[31]Abraham said, "Now that I have been so bold as to speak to the Lord, what if only twenty can be found there?"

He said, "For the sake of twenty, I will not destroy it."

[32]Then he said, "May the Lord not be angry, but let me speak just once more. What if only ten can be found there?"

He answered, "For the sake of ten, I will not destroy it."

---

[a] *18* Or *will use his name in blessings* (see 48:20) [b] *22* Masoretic Text; an ancient Hebrew scribal tradition *but the LORD remained standing before Abraham* [c] *24* Or *forgive*; also in verse 26

33 When the LORD had finished speaking with Abraham, he left, and Abraham returned home.

Sodom and Gomorrah Destroyed

19 The two angels arrived at Sodom in the evening, and Lot was sitting in the gateway of the city. When he saw them, he got up to meet them and bowed down with his face to the ground. 2 "My lords," he said, "please turn aside to your servant's house. You can wash your feet and spend the night and then go on your way early in the morning."

"No," they answered, "we will spend the night in the square."

3 But he insisted so strongly that they did go with him and entered his house. He prepared a meal for them, baking bread without yeast, and they ate. 4 Before they had gone to bed, all the men from every part of the city of Sodom — both young and old — surrounded the house. 5 They called to Lot, "Where are the men who came to you tonight? Bring them out to us so that we can have sex with them."

6 Lot went outside to meet them and shut the door behind him 7 and said, "No, my friends. Don't do this wicked thing. 8 Look, I have two daughters who have never slept with a man. Let me bring them out to you, and you can do what you like with them. But don't do anything to these men, for they have come under the protection of my roof."

9 "Get out of our way," they replied. "This fellow came here as a foreigner, and now he wants to play the judge! We'll treat you worse than them." They kept bringing pressure on Lot and moved forward to break down the door.

10 But the men inside reached out and pulled Lot back into the house and shut the door. 11 Then they struck the men who were at the door of the house, young and old, with blindness so that they could not find the door.

12 The two men said to Lot, "Do you have anyone else here — sons-in-law, sons or daughters, or anyone else in the city who belongs to you? Get them out of here, 13 because we are going to destroy this place. The outcry to the LORD against its people is so great that he has sent us to destroy it."

14 So Lot went out and spoke to his sons-in-law, who were pledged to marry[a] his daughters. He said, "Hurry and get out of this place, because the LORD is about to destroy the city!" But his sons-in-law thought he was joking.

15 With the coming of dawn, the angels urged Lot, saying, "Hurry! Take your wife and your two daughters who are here, or you will be swept away when the city is punished."

16 When he hesitated, the men grasped his hand and the hands of his wife and of his two daughters and led them safely out of the city, for the LORD was merciful to them. 17 As soon as they had brought them out, one of them said, "Flee for your lives! Don't look back, and don't stop anywhere in the plain! Flee to the mountains or you will be swept away!"

18 But Lot said to them, "No, my lords,[b] please! 19 Your[c] servant has found favor in your[c] eyes, and you[c] have shown great kindness to me in sparing my life. But I can't flee to the mountains; this disaster will overtake me, and I'll die. 20 Look, here is a town near enough to run to, and it is small. Let me flee to it — it is very small, isn't it? Then my life will be spared."

21 He said to him, "Very well, I will grant this request too; I will not overthrow the town you speak of. 22 But flee there quickly, because I cannot do anything until you reach it." (That is why the town was called Zoar.[d])

23 By the time Lot reached Zoar, the sun had risen over the land. 24 Then the LORD rained down burning sulfur on Sodom and Gomorrah — from the LORD out of the heavens. 25 Thus he overthrew those cities and the entire plain, destroying all those living in the cities — and also the vegetation in the land. 26 But Lot's wife looked back, and she became a pillar of salt.

[a] *14* Or *were married to* [b] *18* Or *No, Lord;* or *No, my lord* [c] *19* The Hebrew is singular.
[d] *22* *Zoar* means *small.*

GENESIS 19:24

SODOM AND GOMORRAH

Sodom and Gomorrah stand as testimony to the judgment of God. Though the inhabitants of these cities shared the common depravity that has reigned since Adam, their sin was uniquely and justly condemned by God and judged in a most memorable way. The very names Sodom and Gomorrah are known to this day to be marks of heinous sin and immorality. God's judgment was not the act of a vindictive or capricious deity; rather, it followed his gracious allowance of time and space to repent. Peter writes that this episode should serve as a warning to all those who rebel against God and fail to repent of their sin (2Pe 2:6,9 – 10). He will surely and rightly judge those who live in disobedience. But he will do so after granting them space and time to repent, lest they suffer the same fate as Sodom and Gomorrah. Our God is a gracious judge, who will one day perfectly condemn sin.

[27]Early the next morning Abraham got up and returned to the place where
he had stood before the LORD. [28]He looked down toward Sodom and Gomorrah,
toward all the land of the plain, and he saw dense smoke rising from the land,
like smoke from a furnace.

[29]So when God destroyed the cities of the plain, he remembered Abraham,
and he brought Lot out of the catastrophe that overthrew the cities where Lot
had lived.

Lot and His Daughters

[30]Lot and his two daughters left Zoar and settled in the mountains, for he
was afraid to stay in Zoar. He and his two daughters lived in a cave. [31]One day
the older daughter said to the younger, "Our father is old, and there is no man
around here to give us children — as is the custom all over the earth. [32]Let's get
our father to drink wine and then sleep with him and preserve our family line
through our father."

[33]That night they got their father to drink wine, and the older daughter went in
and slept with him. He was not aware of it when she lay down or when she got up.

[34]The next day the older daughter said to the younger, "Last night I slept with
my father. Let's get him to drink wine again tonight, and you go in and sleep with
him so we can preserve our family line through our father." [35]So they got their
father to drink wine that night also, and the younger daughter went in and slept
with him. Again he was not aware of it when she lay down or when she got up.

[36]So both of Lot's daughters became pregnant by their father. [37]The older
daughter had a son, and she named him Moab[a]; he is the father of the Moabites of today. [38]The younger daughter also had a son, and she named him Ben-
Ammi[b]; he is the father of the Ammonites[c] of today.

Abraham and Abimelek

20 Now Abraham moved on from there into the region of the Negev and
lived between Kadesh and Shur. For a while he stayed in Gerar, [2]and there
Abraham said of his wife Sarah, "She is my sister." Then Abimelek king of Gerar
sent for Sarah and took her.

[3]But God came to Abimelek in a dream one night and said to him, "You are as
good as dead because of the woman you have taken; she is a married woman."

[4]Now Abimelek had not gone near her, so he said, "Lord, will you destroy an
innocent nation? [5]Did he not say to me, 'She is my sister,' and didn't she also say,
'He is my brother'? I have done this with a clear conscience and clean hands."

[6]Then God said to him in the dream, "Yes, I know you did this with a clear
conscience, and so I have kept you from sinning against me. That is why I did
not let you touch her. [7]Now return the man's wife, for he is a prophet, and he will
pray for you and you will live. But if you do not return her, you may be sure that
you and all who belong to you will die."

[8]Early the next morning Abimelek summoned all his officials, and when he
told them all that had happened, they were very much afraid. [9]Then Abimelek
called Abraham in and said, "What have you done to us? How have I wronged
you that you have brought such great guilt upon me and my kingdom? You have
done things to me that should never be done." [10]And Abimelek asked Abraham,
"What was your reason for doing this?"

[11]Abraham replied, "I said to myself, 'There is surely no fear of God in this
place, and they will kill me because of my wife.' [12]Besides, she really is my sister,
the daughter of my father though not of my mother; and she became my wife.
[13]And when God had me wander from my father's household, I said to her, 'This
is how you can show your love to me: Everywhere we go, say of me, "He is my
brother." ' "

[14]Then Abimelek brought sheep and cattle and male and female slaves and

---

[a] *37 Moab* sounds like the Hebrew for *from father.* [b] *38 Ben-Ammi* means *son of my father's people.* [c] *38* Hebrew *Bene-Ammon*

gave them to Abraham, and he returned Sarah his wife to him. 15And Abimelek said, "My land is before you; live wherever you like."

16To Sarah he said, "I am giving your brother a thousand shekels[a] of silver. This is to cover the offense against you before all who are with you; you are completely vindicated."

17Then Abraham prayed to God, and God healed Abimelek, his wife and his female slaves so they could have children again, 18for the LORD had kept all the women in Abimelek's household from conceiving because of Abraham's wife Sarah.

The Birth of Isaac

21 Now the LORD was gracious to Sarah as he had said, and the LORD did for Sarah what he had promised. 2Sarah became pregnant and bore a son to Abraham in his old age, at the very time God had promised him. 3Abraham gave the name Isaac[b] to the son Sarah bore him. 4When his son Isaac was eight days old, Abraham circumcised him, as God commanded him. 5Abraham was a hundred years old when his son Isaac was born to him.

6Sarah said, "God has brought me laughter, and everyone who hears about this will laugh with me." 7And she added, "Who would have said to Abraham that Sarah would nurse children? Yet I have borne him a son in his old age."

Hagar and Ishmael Sent Away

8The child grew and was weaned, and on the day Isaac was weaned Abraham held a great feast. 9But Sarah saw that the son whom Hagar the Egyptian had borne to Abraham was mocking, 10and she said to Abraham, "Get rid of that slave woman and her son, for that woman's son will never share in the inheritance with my son Isaac."

11The matter distressed Abraham greatly because it concerned his son. 12But God said to him, "Do not be so distressed about the boy and your slave woman. Listen to whatever Sarah tells you, because it is through Isaac that your offspring[c] will be reckoned. 13I will make the son of the slave into a nation also, because he is your offspring."

14Early the next morning Abraham took some food and a skin of water and gave them to Hagar. He set them on her shoulders and then sent her off with the boy. She went on her way and wandered in the Desert of Beersheba.

15When the water in the skin was gone, she put the boy under one of the bushes. 16Then she went off and sat down about a bowshot away, for she thought, "I cannot watch the boy die." And as she sat there, she[d] began to sob.

17God heard the boy crying, and the angel of God called to Hagar from heaven and said to her, "What is the matter, Hagar? Do not be afraid; God has heard the boy crying as he lies there. 18Lift the boy up and take him by the hand, for I will make him into a great nation."

19Then God opened her eyes and she saw a well of water. So she went and filled the skin with water and gave the boy a drink.

20God was with the boy as he grew up. He lived in the desert and became an archer. 21While he was living in the Desert of Paran, his mother got a wife for him from Egypt.

The Treaty at Beersheba

22At that time Abimelek and Phicol the commander of his forces said to Abraham, "God is with you in everything you do. 23Now swear to me here before God that you will not deal falsely with me or my children or my descendants. Show to me and the country where you now reside as a foreigner the same kindness I have shown to you."

[a] 16 That is, about 25 pounds or about 12 kilograms [b] 3 *Isaac* means *he laughs.*
[c] 12 Or *seed* [d] 16 Hebrew; Septuagint *the child*

GENESIS 21:1–7

GOD IS FAITHFUL

Isaac's birth previews the coming of Jesus. Isaac was born because God is faithful and promised Abraham a son, just as he promised sinners a Savior. The birth of Isaac came as a demonstration of God's grace, just as it was demonstrated at the coming of Christ. Abraham and Sarah were quite elderly when Isaac was born—so far beyond the years of child bearing that Sarah laughed at God's plan (Ge 18:9–12)—yet God often does the humanly impossible to fulfill his purposes. Jesus, after all, was born of a virgin, conceived by the Holy Spirit (Mt 1:18). Though Abraham and Sarah devised what they thought to be a more practical plan to fulfill God's promise by using Hagar as a surrogate (Ge 16:1–4), it was ultimately God's faithfulness—not human effort—which brought forth Isaac. In a similar way, Jesus came to earth because God is faithful and fulfills all of his promises. After Isaac was born, Sarah laughed once again, but this time it was not out of unbelief and mockery but out of astonishment and joy (Ge 21:5–6). Today, believers should also be filled with joy and astonishment at the faithfulness of God to keep his promises.

24Abraham said, "I swear it."
25Then Abraham complained to Abimelek about a well of water that Abimelek's servants had seized. 26But Abimelek said, "I don't know who has done this.
You did not tell me, and I heard about it only today."
27So Abraham brought sheep and cattle and gave them to Abimelek, and the
two men made a treaty. 28Abraham set apart seven ewe lambs from the flock,
29and Abimelek asked Abraham, "What is the meaning of these seven ewe lambs
you have set apart by themselves?"
30He replied, "Accept these seven lambs from my hand as a witness that I dug
this well."
31So that place was called Beersheba,[a] because the two men swore an oath
there.
32After the treaty had been made at Beersheba, Abimelek and Phicol the commander of his forces returned to the land of the Philistines. 33Abraham planted
a tamarisk tree in Beersheba, and there he called on the name of the LORD, the
Eternal God. 34And Abraham stayed in the land of the Philistines for a long time.

Abraham Tested

22 Some time later God tested Abraham. He said to him, "Abraham!"
"Here I am," he replied.
2Then God said, "Take your son, your only son, whom you love — Isaac — and
go to the region of Moriah. Sacrifice him there as a burnt offering on a mountain
I will show you."
3Early the next morning Abraham got up and loaded his donkey. He took with
him two of his servants and his son Isaac. When he had cut enough wood for the
burnt offering, he set out for the place God had told him about. 4On the third day
Abraham looked up and saw the place in the distance. 5He said to his servants,
"Stay here with the donkey while I and the boy go over there. We will worship
and then we will come back to you."
6Abraham took the wood for the burnt offering and placed it on his son Isaac,
and he himself carried the fire and the knife. As the two of them went on together, 7Isaac spoke up and said to his father Abraham, "Father?"
"Yes, my son?" Abraham replied.
"The fire and wood are here," Isaac said, "but where is the lamb for the burnt
offering?"
8Abraham answered, "God himself will provide the lamb for the burnt offering, my son." And the two of them went on together.
9When they reached the place God had told him about, Abraham built an altar there and arranged the wood on it. He bound his son Isaac and laid him on
the altar, on top of the wood. 10Then he reached out his hand and took the knife
to slay his son. 11But the angel of the LORD called out to him from heaven, "Abraham! Abraham!"
"Here I am," he replied.
12"Do not lay a hand on the boy," he said. "Do not do anything to him. Now I
know that you fear God, because you have not withheld from me your son, your
only son."
13Abraham looked up and there in a thicket he saw a ram[b] caught by its horns.
He went over and took the ram and sacrificed it as a burnt offering instead of his
son. 14So Abraham called that place The LORD Will Provide. And to this day it is
said, "On the mountain of the LORD it will be provided."
15The angel of the LORD called to Abraham from heaven a second time 16and
said, "I swear by myself, declares the LORD, that because you have done this and
have not withheld your son, your only son, 17I will surely bless you and make
your descendants as numerous as the stars in the sky and as the sand on the

[a] 31 *Beersheba* can mean *well of seven* and *well of the oath.* [b] 13 Many manuscripts of the Masoretic Text, Samaritan Pentateuch, Septuagint and Syriac; most manuscripts of the Masoretic Text *a ram behind him*

GENESIS 22:5

CONFIDENCE IN GOD

Abraham's confidence in light of his impending task testifies to a deeper confidence — his profound confidence in God. Not only had God asked him to do this startling task, but Abraham was certain that God would provide a means of deliverance. He told his servants to wait while he and Isaac, his son, went to worship God on the mountain. Knowing that God commanded him to sacrifice his son, Abraham told the servants that he and the boy would come back soon. "We will worship and then we will come back to you," he said. He knew that God had promised to create a great nation through Isaac (Ge 12:1 – 3; 13:14 – 16; 15:1 – 21; 17:1 – 22; 18:1 – 15). For this reason, Abraham knew that God would either deliver Isaac from death or resurrect him following his death (Heb 11:19). Either way, God would keep his word. Jesus also trusted God in the face of impending death. The ultimate son of the promise, Jesus asked that God take away the cup of his suffering (Lk 22:42). Yet Jesus knew that God would be faithful — either by providing deliverance from death or through his subsequent, victorious resurrection. Unlike Isaac, Jesus would willingly and confidently walk not only to the brink of death but through death itself and once again demonstrate the faithfulness of God to his promises.

GENESIS 22:17 – 18

BLESSED TO BLESS

God promised Abraham that he and his descendants would be a blessing to all people (see also Ge 12:2 – 3).

(continued on page 43)

THE SACRIFICIAL SON

Without question, this story of Abraham and Isaac is one of the most shocking and memorable narratives in all of Scripture. And yet in its outcome, it is one of the greatest stories describing the loyalty of God to his covenant and the foreshadowing of his plan to save the world. In Genesis 3:15, God made a promise to destroy evil and redeem humanity through the offspring of the woman.

In this story God puts Abraham's faithfulness to the test by asking him to do the unthinkable, to sacrifice his son Isaac as a burnt offering. Abraham had another son, Ishmael, but Isaac was the "only son" (Ge 22:2) in which all of God's promises resided because he was born of Sarah. Isaac represented the continuation of God's promise to bless all the nations of the earth through Abraham's descendants (Ge 12:1 – 3), and the ultimate promise to destroy evil in the world (Ge 3:15). Everything about Isaac's life was the result of God's supernatural plan and provision. Against all odds Sarah, Abraham's wife, became pregnant with Isaac despite being 90 years old (Ge 17:17). And now, in spite of all that Isaac represented, God asked Abraham to surrender his beloved son.

The toll of this command on Abraham and Sarah must have been enormous. What a powerful picture of what God did to his only Son for us! Little is said of Abraham's thoughts, or the thoughts of the boy's mother. All we read is the account of the father's complete obedience to God's command (Ge 22:3). Abraham laid the wood for the offering on his son's back, and Isaac carried it to the altar. Isaac was confused, "The fire and wood are here … but where is the lamb for the burnt offering?" Then Abraham offers a glimpse of his faith in God's provision by saying, "God *himself* will provide the lamb" (Ge 22:7 – 8, emphasis added). Abraham understood, like the apostle Paul after him, that God must keep his promises in order to uphold his *own* righteousness. The sacrifice of Jesus not only fulfilled God's promise to destroy evil and save the world, but it also proved God's righteousness by providing a punishment for the sin of the whole world. Just as God provided Jesus *himself* to demonstrate *his* righteousness and take the punishment we deserved, so also he provided a ram *himself* to uphold his promise by keeping Isaac alive.

seashore. Your descendants will take possession of the cities of their enemies,
18and through your offspring[a] all nations on earth will be blessed,[b] because you
have obeyed me."
19Then Abraham returned to his servants, and they set off together for Beersheba. And Abraham stayed in Beersheba.

Nahor's Sons

20Some time later Abraham was told, "Milkah is also a mother; she has borne
sons to your brother Nahor: 21Uz the firstborn, Buz his brother, Kemuel (the father of Aram), 22Kesed, Hazo, Pildash, Jidlaph and Bethuel." 23Bethuel became
the father of Rebekah. Milkah bore these eight sons to Abraham's brother Nahor. 24His concubine, whose name was Reumah, also had sons: Tebah, Gaham,
Tahash and Maakah.

The Death of Sarah

23 Sarah lived to be a hundred and twenty-seven years old. 2She died at Kiriath Arba (that is, Hebron) in the land of Canaan, and Abraham went to
mourn for Sarah and to weep over her.
3Then Abraham rose from beside his dead wife and spoke to the Hittites.[c] He
said, 4"I am a foreigner and stranger among you. Sell me some property for a
burial site here so I can bury my dead."
5The Hittites replied to Abraham, 6"Sir, listen to us. You are a mighty prince
among us. Bury your dead in the choicest of our tombs. None of us will refuse you
his tomb for burying your dead."
7Then Abraham rose and bowed down before the people of the land, the Hittites. 8He said to them, "If you are willing to let me bury my dead, then listen to
me and intercede with Ephron son of Zohar on my behalf 9so he will sell me the
cave of Machpelah, which belongs to him and is at the end of his field. Ask him
to sell it to me for the full price as a burial site among you."
10Ephron the Hittite was sitting among his people and he replied to Abraham
in the hearing of all the Hittites who had come to the gate of his city. 11"No, my
lord," he said. "Listen to me; I give[d] you the field, and I give[d] you the cave that is
in it. I give[d] it to you in the presence of my people. Bury your dead."
12Again Abraham bowed down before the people of the land 13and he said to
Ephron in their hearing, "Listen to me, if you will. I will pay the price of the field.
Accept it from me so I can bury my dead there."
14Ephron answered Abraham, 15"Listen to me, my lord; the land is worth
four hundred shekels[e] of silver, but what is that between you and me? Bury your
dead."
16Abraham agreed to Ephron's terms and weighed out for him the price he had
named in the hearing of the Hittites: four hundred shekels of silver, according to
the weight current among the merchants.
17So Ephron's field in Machpelah near Mamre — both the field and the cave
in it, and all the trees within the borders of the field — was deeded 18to Abraham
as his property in the presence of all the Hittites who had come to the gate of the
city. 19Afterward Abraham buried his wife Sarah in the cave in the field of Machpelah near Mamre (which is at Hebron) in the land of Canaan. 20So the field and
the cave in it were deeded to Abraham by the Hittites as a burial site.

Isaac and Rebekah

24 Abraham was now very old, and the LORD had blessed him in every way.
2He said to the senior servant in his household, the one in charge of all
that he had, "Put your hand under my thigh. 3I want you to swear by the LORD,

[a] *18* Or *seed* [b] *18* Or *and all nations on earth will use the name of your offspring in blessings* (see 48:20) [c] *3* Or *the descendants of Heth*; also in verses 5, 7, 10, 16, 18 and 20 [d] *11* Or *sell* [e] *15* That is, about 10 pounds or about 4.6 kilograms

(Blessed to Bless, continued)

The obedience of God's people would lead to this blessing of the nations. This promise demonstrated the vast mission of the nation of Israel. They were a chosen nation, not merely for their own blessing, but so that through them God would declare and demonstrate his glory to every other nation as well. God affirmed this promise once again to Abraham and declared the means by which the blessing would happen — the obedience of God's people. Likewise, in God's church, Jew and Gentile alike are called by God to be a blessing to the nations. As God's chosen people, a new and holy nation purchased by Christ's blood, the church serves as a light to the nations by obeying God (1Pe 2:9 – 10).

GENESIS 24:1 – 53

FINDING A BRIDE

Abraham's servant was commissioned to undertake a difficult journey to find a bride for Isaac. After a journey of about three weeks, this man arrived with impressive gifts but an unlikely task — find a woman in a distant land, who is of a particular family, and who will respond in faith to leave her land and become Isaac's wife. Despite the seeming impossibility of the mission, the servant cried out to God for help and God orchestrated the events to ensure that Isaac received a wife and the promise of a descendant who would bring universal blessing to mankind.

In a similar sense, Jesus carried out a mission to bring his bride to himself. No distance or cost or improbability would keep him from getting his bride. He came from heaven to earth

(continued on next page)

(Finding a Bride, continued)

in order to rescue his church. He paid a price for his bride that exceeded the greatest kingly riches imaginable; his blood secured her as his own. Moreover, the sovereign hand of God orchestrated the events of the gospel and the plans of people's lives so that the improbable — rebels becoming worshipers of God — would become a reality.

the God of heaven and the God of earth, that you will not get a wife for my son
from the daughters of the Canaanites, among whom I am living, 4but will go to
my country and my own relatives and get a wife for my son Isaac."
5The servant asked him, "What if the woman is unwilling to come back with
me to this land? Shall I then take your son back to the country you came from?"
6"Make sure that you do not take my son back there," Abraham said. 7"The
LORD, the God of heaven, who brought me out of my father's household and my
native land and who spoke to me and promised me on oath, saying, 'To your offspring[a] I will give this land' — he will send his angel before you so that you can
get a wife for my son from there. 8If the woman is unwilling to come back with
you, then you will be released from this oath of mine. Only do not take my son
back there." 9So the servant put his hand under the thigh of his master Abraham
and swore an oath to him concerning this matter.
10Then the servant left, taking with him ten of his master's camels loaded
with all kinds of good things from his master. He set out for Aram Naharaim[b]
and made his way to the town of Nahor. 11He had the camels kneel down near
the well outside the town; it was toward evening, the time the women go out to
draw water.
12Then he prayed, "LORD, God of my master Abraham, make me successful
today, and show kindness to my master Abraham. 13See, I am standing beside
this spring, and the daughters of the townspeople are coming out to draw water.
14May it be that when I say to a young woman, 'Please let down your jar that I may
have a drink,' and she says, 'Drink, and I'll water your camels too' — let her be
the one you have chosen for your servant Isaac. By this I will know that you have
shown kindness to my master."
15Before he had finished praying, Rebekah came out with her jar on her shoulder. She was the daughter of Bethuel son of Milkah, who was the wife of Abraham's brother Nahor. 16The woman was very beautiful, a virgin; no man had ever
slept with her. She went down to the spring, filled her jar and came up again.
17The servant hurried to meet her and said, "Please give me a little water from
your jar."
18"Drink, my lord," she said, and quickly lowered the jar to her hands and
gave him a drink.
19After she had given him a drink, she said, "I'll draw water for your camels
too, until they have had enough to drink." 20So she quickly emptied her jar into
the trough, ran back to the well to draw more water, and drew enough for all his
camels. 21Without saying a word, the man watched her closely to learn whether
or not the LORD had made his journey successful.
22When the camels had finished drinking, the man took out a gold nose ring
weighing a beka[c] and two gold bracelets weighing ten shekels.[d] 23Then he asked,
"Whose daughter are you? Please tell me, is there room in your father's house for
us to spend the night?"
24She answered him, "I am the daughter of Bethuel, the son that Milkah bore
to Nahor." 25And she added, "We have plenty of straw and fodder, as well as room
for you to spend the night."
26Then the man bowed down and worshiped the LORD, 27saying, "Praise be to
the LORD, the God of my master Abraham, who has not abandoned his kindness
and faithfulness to my master. As for me, the LORD has led me on the journey to
the house of my master's relatives."
28The young woman ran and told her mother's household about these things.
29Now Rebekah had a brother named Laban, and he hurried out to the man at
the spring. 30As soon as he had seen the nose ring, and the bracelets on his sister's arms, and had heard Rebekah tell what the man said to her, he went out to
the man and found him standing by the camels near the spring. 31"Come, you

[a] *7* Or *seed* [b] *10* That is, Northwest Mesopotamia [c] *22* That is, about 1/5 ounce or about 5.7 grams [d] *22* That is, about 4 ounces or about 115 grams

who are blessed by the LORD," he said. "Why are you standing out here? I have
prepared the house and a place for the camels."
[32]So the man went to the house, and the camels were unloaded. Straw and
fodder were brought for the camels, and water for him and his men to wash their
feet. [33]Then food was set before him, but he said, "I will not eat until I have told
you what I have to say."
"Then tell us," Laban said.
[34]So he said, "I am Abraham's servant. [35]The LORD has blessed my master
abundantly, and he has become wealthy. He has given him sheep and cattle, silver and gold, male and female servants, and camels and donkeys. [36]My master's
wife Sarah has borne him a son in her old age, and he has given him everything
he owns. [37]And my master made me swear an oath, and said, 'You must not get a
wife for my son from the daughters of the Canaanites, in whose land I live, [38]but
go to my father's family and to my own clan, and get a wife for my son.'
[39]"Then I asked my master, 'What if the woman will not come back with me?'
[40]"He replied, 'The LORD, before whom I have walked faithfully, will send his
angel with you and make your journey a success, so that you can get a wife for my
son from my own clan and from my father's family. [41]You will be released from
my oath if, when you go to my clan, they refuse to give her to you — then you will
be released from my oath.'
[42]"When I came to the spring today, I said, 'LORD, God of my master Abraham,
if you will, please grant success to the journey on which I have come. [43]See, I am
standing beside this spring. If a young woman comes out to draw water and I say
to her, "Please let me drink a little water from your jar," [44]and if she says to me,
"Drink, and I'll draw water for your camels too," let her be the one the LORD has
chosen for my master's son.'
[45]"Before I finished praying in my heart, Rebekah came out, with her jar on
her shoulder. She went down to the spring and drew water, and I said to her,
'Please give me a drink.'
[46]"She quickly lowered her jar from her shoulder and said, 'Drink, and I'll water your camels too.' So I drank, and she watered the camels also.
[47]"I asked her, 'Whose daughter are you?'
"She said, 'The daughter of Bethuel son of Nahor, whom Milkah bore to him.'
"Then I put the ring in her nose and the bracelets on her arms, [48]and I bowed
down and worshiped the LORD. I praised the LORD, the God of my master Abraham, who had led me on the right road to get the granddaughter of my master's
brother for his son. [49]Now if you will show kindness and faithfulness to my master, tell me; and if not, tell me, so I may know which way to turn."
[50]Laban and Bethuel answered, "This is from the LORD; we can say nothing to
you one way or the other. [51]Here is Rebekah; take her and go, and let her become
the wife of your master's son, as the LORD has directed."
[52]When Abraham's servant heard what they said, he bowed down to the
ground before the LORD. [53]Then the servant brought out gold and silver jewelry
and articles of clothing and gave them to Rebekah; he also gave costly gifts to her
brother and to her mother. [54]Then he and the men who were with him ate and
drank and spent the night there.
When they got up the next morning, he said, "Send me on my way to my master."
[55]But her brother and her mother replied, "Let the young woman remain with
us ten days or so; then you[a] may go."
[56]But he said to them, "Do not detain me, now that the LORD has granted success to my journey. Send me on my way so I may go to my master."
[57]Then they said, "Let's call the young woman and ask her about it." [58]So they
called Rebekah and asked her, "Will you go with this man?"
"I will go," she said.

[a] 55 Or *she*

[59]So they sent their sister Rebekah on her way, along with her nurse and Abraham's servant and his men. [60]And they blessed Rebekah and said to her,

"Our sister, may you increase
  to thousands upon thousands;
may your offspring possess
  the cities of their enemies."

[61]Then Rebekah and her attendants got ready and mounted the camels and went back with the man. So the servant took Rebekah and left.

[62]Now Isaac had come from Beer Lahai Roi, for he was living in the Negev. [63]He went out to the field one evening to meditate,[a] and as he looked up, he saw camels approaching. [64]Rebekah also looked up and saw Isaac. She got down from her camel [65]and asked the servant, "Who is that man in the field coming to meet us?"

"He is my master," the servant answered. So she took her veil and covered herself.

[66]Then the servant told Isaac all he had done. [67]Isaac brought her into the tent of his mother Sarah, and he married Rebekah. So she became his wife, and he loved her; and Isaac was comforted after his mother's death.

The Death of Abraham

25 Abraham had taken another wife, whose name was Keturah. [2]She bore him Zimran, Jokshan, Medan, Midian, Ishbak and Shuah. [3]Jokshan was the father of Sheba and Dedan; the descendants of Dedan were the Ashurites, the Letushites and the Leummites. [4]The sons of Midian were Ephah, Epher, Hanok, Abida and Eldaah. All these were descendants of Keturah.

[5]Abraham left everything he owned to Isaac. [6]But while he was still living, he gave gifts to the sons of his concubines and sent them away from his son Isaac to the land of the east.

[7]Abraham lived a hundred and seventy-five years. [8]Then Abraham breathed his last and died at a good old age, an old man and full of years; and he was gathered to his people. [9]His sons Isaac and Ishmael buried him in the cave of Machpelah near Mamre, in the field of Ephron son of Zohar the Hittite, [10]the field Abraham had bought from the Hittites.[b] There Abraham was buried with his wife Sarah. [11]After Abraham's death, God blessed his son Isaac, who then lived near Beer Lahai Roi.

Ishmael's Sons

[12]This is the account of the family line of Abraham's son Ishmael, whom Sarah's slave, Hagar the Egyptian, bore to Abraham.

[13]These are the names of the sons of Ishmael, listed in the order of their birth: Nebaioth the firstborn of Ishmael, Kedar, Adbeel, Mibsam, [14]Mishma, Dumah, Massa, [15]Hadad, Tema, Jetur, Naphish and Kedemah. [16]These were the sons of Ishmael, and these are the names of the twelve tribal rulers according to their settlements and camps. [17]Ishmael lived a hundred and thirty-seven years. He breathed his last and died, and he was gathered to his people. [18]His descendants settled in the area from Havilah to Shur, near the eastern border of Egypt, as you go toward Ashur. And they lived in hostility toward[c] all the tribes related to them.

Jacob and Esau

[19]This is the account of the family line of Abraham's son Isaac.

Abraham became the father of Isaac, [20]and Isaac was forty years old when he married Rebekah daughter of Bethuel the Aramean from Paddan Aram[d] and sister of Laban the Aramean.

---

[a] *63* The meaning of the Hebrew for this word is uncertain. [b] *10* Or *the descendants of Heth*
[c] *18* Or *lived to the east of* [d] *20* That is, Northwest Mesopotamia

21 Isaac prayed to the LORD on behalf of his wife, because she was childless.
The LORD answered his prayer, and his wife Rebekah became pregnant. 22 The
babies jostled each other within her, and she said, "Why is this happening to
me?" So she went to inquire of the LORD.
23 The LORD said to her,

"Two nations are in your womb,
  and two peoples from within you will be separated;
one people will be stronger than the other,
  and the older will serve the younger."

24 When the time came for her to give birth, there were twin boys in her womb.
25 The first to come out was red, and his whole body was like a hairy garment; so
they named him Esau.[a] 26 After this, his brother came out, with his hand grasping Esau's heel; so he was named Jacob.[b] Isaac was sixty years old when Rebekah
gave birth to them.
27 The boys grew up, and Esau became a skillful hunter, a man of the open
country, while Jacob was content to stay at home among the tents. 28 Isaac, who
had a taste for wild game, loved Esau, but Rebekah loved Jacob.
29 Once when Jacob was cooking some stew, Esau came in from the open country, famished. 30 He said to Jacob, "Quick, let me have some of that red stew! I'm
famished!" (That is why he was also called Edom.[c])
31 Jacob replied, "First sell me your birthright."
32 "Look, I am about to die," Esau said. "What good is the birthright to me?"
33 But Jacob said, "Swear to me first." So he swore an oath to him, selling his
birthright to Jacob.
34 Then Jacob gave Esau some bread and some lentil stew. He ate and drank,
and then got up and left.
So Esau despised his birthright.

Isaac and Abimelek

26 Now there was a famine in the land — besides the previous famine
in Abraham's time — and Isaac went to Abimelek king of the Philistines
in Gerar. 2 The LORD appeared to Isaac and said, "Do not go down to Egypt; live in
the land where I tell you to live. 3 Stay in this land for a while, and I will be with
you and will bless you. For to you and your descendants I will give all these lands
and will confirm the oath I swore to your father Abraham. 4 I will make your
descendants as numerous as the stars in the sky and will give them all these
lands, and through your offspring[d] all nations on earth will be blessed,[e] 5 because Abraham obeyed me and did everything I required of him, keeping my
commands, my decrees and my instructions." 6 So Isaac stayed in Gerar.
7 When the men of that place asked him about his wife, he said, "She is my sister," because he was afraid to say, "She is my wife." He thought, "The men of this
place might kill me on account of Rebekah, because she is beautiful."
8 When Isaac had been there a long time, Abimelek king of the Philistines
looked down from a window and saw Isaac caressing his wife Rebekah. 9 So
Abimelek summoned Isaac and said, "She is really your wife! Why did you say,
'She is my sister'?"
Isaac answered him, "Because I thought I might lose my life on account of
her."
10 Then Abimelek said, "What is this you have done to us? One of the men
might well have slept with your wife, and you would have brought guilt upon us."
11 So Abimelek gave orders to all the people: "Anyone who harms this man or
his wife shall surely be put to death."

[a] 25 *Esau* may mean *hairy.* [b] 26 *Jacob* means *he grasps the heel,* a Hebrew idiom for *he deceives.* [c] 30 *Edom* means *red.* [d] 4 Or *seed* [e] 4 Or *and all nations on earth will use the name of your offspring in blessings* (see 48:20)

GENESIS 26:2 – 5

HEIR OF THE PROMISE

God designed a world for his created image-bearers to multiply and fill. His covenant with Abraham established the ongoing validity of this goal, even in the face of human sin (Ge 12:1 – 3). In this passage, God reiterates his promise to Isaac and pledges to be faithful to his promise by multiplying Isaac's descendants, giving them a great land and blessing all the earth through his family. Peter demonstrates that these promises find their fulfillment in the birth of the New Testament church and the sending of God's Spirit (Ac 3:25). In the church, all those who bear Jesus' name, both Jews and Gentiles alike, can be grafted into one heavenly family (Gal 3:8). As Abraham's offspring, the church is now the heir of the promises of God and entrusted with the mission of filling the earth with image-bearing worshipers who are a blessing to the nations.

FINGERPRINTS OF GRACE

What a scandalous claim! In the original readers' culture, the claim that an older brother would serve a younger brother was outrageous and disgraceful. But in God's dealings with people, this sort of role reversal is just the opposite; it is a work of grace (Ro 9:10 – 13). Grace turns the natural order of things on their head. Time and again throughout the book of Genesis, the headlines to these narratives seemed shocking to their original audience. Perhaps in the mind of the modern reader this wonder is lost, but the implications for Christians are gigantic. God seeks to restore worshipers to himself by graciously pouring out his favor upon them. Consider the following headlines in light of God's scandalous grace:

God gave animal skins to Adam and Eve instead of retribution (Ge 3:21). Adam and Eve deserved death for their rebellion (2:17), but God gave them grace instead.

Abel gained favor with God over Cain (Ge 4:4 – 5). In another example of the younger sibling receiving the grace of God, Abel was granted God's favor because he brought a simple sacrifice out of faith (Heb 11:4), while Cain only revealed his sinful heart in the encounter (Ge 4:5 – 7).

God spared a flawed man and his family by means of an ark. It would be easy to skim over or avoid Genesis 9:20 – 27 due to its awkward and uncomfortable content. It serves as a contradistinction to the man who the writer first introduced as having "found favor in the eyes of the LORD" (Ge 6:8). The fact remains that Noah's favor with God was not because he was or would always be a perfect man.

Abraham received a unilateral covenant from God. The ramifications of God's pledge to Abram in Genesis 15 are vast. From this fountainhead, the rest of the Scriptures pour out. But the history of this blessed man was far from pristine. Joshua wrote that Abram's father worshiped other gods (Jos 24:2) and Abram lied to protect himself (Ge 12:10 – 20; 20:2). God's grace turns Abram into the father of many nations and a source of everlasting blessing to the whole world.

Every narrative of the book of Genesis is covered in the fingerprints of grace. All of these upheavals and role reversals are the handiwork of a gracious God who pours out his favor in order to bring maximum glory to himself.

12Isaac planted crops in that land and the same year reaped a hundredfold, because the LORD blessed him. 13The man became rich, and his wealth continued to grow until he became very wealthy. 14He had so many flocks and herds and servants that the Philistines envied him. 15So all the wells that his father's servants had dug in the time of his father Abraham, the Philistines stopped up, filling them with earth.

16Then Abimelek said to Isaac, "Move away from us; you have become too powerful for us."

17So Isaac moved away from there and encamped in the Valley of Gerar, where he settled. 18Isaac reopened the wells that had been dug in the time of his father Abraham, which the Philistines had stopped up after Abraham died, and he gave them the same names his father had given them.

19Isaac's servants dug in the valley and discovered a well of fresh water there. 20But the herders of Gerar quarreled with those of Isaac and said, "The water is ours!" So he named the well Esek,[a] because they disputed with him. 21Then they dug another well, but they quarreled over that one also; so he named it Sitnah.[b] 22He moved on from there and dug another well, and no one quarreled over it. He named it Rehoboth,[c] saying, "Now the LORD has given us room and we will flourish in the land."

23From there he went up to Beersheba. 24That night the LORD appeared to him and said, "I am the God of your father Abraham. Do not be afraid, for I am with you; I will bless you and will increase the number of your descendants for the sake of my servant Abraham."

25Isaac built an altar there and called on the name of the LORD. There he pitched his tent, and there his servants dug a well.

26Meanwhile, Abimelek had come to him from Gerar, with Ahuzzath his personal adviser and Phicol the commander of his forces. 27Isaac asked them, "Why have you come to me, since you were hostile to me and sent me away?"

28They answered, "We saw clearly that the LORD was with you; so we said, 'There ought to be a sworn agreement between us' — between us and you. Let us make a treaty with you 29that you will do us no harm, just as we did not harm you but always treated you well and sent you away peacefully. And now you are blessed by the LORD."

30Isaac then made a feast for them, and they ate and drank. 31Early the next morning the men swore an oath to each other. Then Isaac sent them on their way, and they went away peacefully.

32That day Isaac's servants came and told him about the well they had dug. They said, "We've found water!" 33He called it Shibah,[d] and to this day the name of the town has been Beersheba.[e]

Jacob Takes Esau's Blessing

34When Esau was forty years old, he married Judith daughter of Beeri the Hittite, and also Basemath daughter of Elon the Hittite. 35They were a source of grief to Isaac and Rebekah.

27 When Isaac was old and his eyes were so weak that he could no longer see, he called for Esau his older son and said to him, "My son."

"Here I am," he answered.

2Isaac said, "I am now an old man and don't know the day of my death. 3Now then, get your equipment — your quiver and bow — and go out to the open country to hunt some wild game for me. 4Prepare me the kind of tasty food I like and bring it to me to eat, so that I may give you my blessing before I die."

5Now Rebekah was listening as Isaac spoke to his son Esau. When Esau left for the open country to hunt game and bring it back, 6Rebekah said to her son Jacob, "Look, I overheard your father say to your brother Esau, 7'Bring me some game

[a] 20 *Esek* means *dispute.* [b] 21 *Sitnah* means *opposition.* [c] 22 *Rehoboth* means *room.* [d] 33 *Shibah* can mean *oath* or *seven.* [e] 33 *Beersheba* can mean *well of the oath* and *well of seven.*

and prepare me some tasty food to eat, so that I may give you my blessing in the
presence of the LORD before I die.' 8Now, my son, listen carefully and do what I
tell you: 9Go out to the flock and bring me two choice young goats, so I can prepare some tasty food for your father, just the way he likes it. 10Then take it to your
father to eat, so that he may give you his blessing before he dies."

11Jacob said to Rebekah his mother, "But my brother Esau is a hairy man while
I have smooth skin. 12What if my father touches me? I would appear to be trick-
ing him and would bring down a curse on myself rather than a blessing."

13His mother said to him, "My son, let the curse fall on me. Just do what I say;
go and get them for me."

14So he went and got them and brought them to his mother, and she prepared
some tasty food, just the way his father liked it. 15Then Rebekah took the best
clothes of Esau her older son, which she had in the house, and put them on her
younger son Jacob. 16She also covered his hands and the smooth part of his neck
with the goatskins. 17Then she handed to her son Jacob the tasty food and the
bread she had made.

18He went to his father and said, "My father."

"Yes, my son," he answered. "Who is it?"

19Jacob said to his father, "I am Esau your firstborn. I have done as you told me.
Please sit up and eat some of my game, so that you may give me your blessing."

20Isaac asked his son, "How did you find it so quickly, my son?"

"The LORD your God gave me success," he replied.

21Then Isaac said to Jacob, "Come near so I can touch you, my son, to know
whether you really are my son Esau or not."

22Jacob went close to his father Isaac, who touched him and said, "The voice is
the voice of Jacob, but the hands are the hands of Esau." 23He did not recognize
him, for his hands were hairy like those of his brother Esau; so he proceeded to
bless him. 24"Are you really my son Esau?" he asked.

"I am," he replied.

25Then he said, "My son, bring me some of your game to eat, so that I may give
you my blessing."

Jacob brought it to him and he ate; and he brought some wine and he drank.
26Then his father Isaac said to him, "Come here, my son, and kiss me."

27So he went to him and kissed him. When Isaac caught the smell of his
clothes, he blessed him and said,

"Ah, the smell of my son
    is like the smell of a field
    that the LORD has blessed.
28May God give you heaven's dew
    and earth's richness—
    an abundance of grain and new wine.
29May nations serve you
    and peoples bow down to you.
Be lord over your brothers,
    and may the sons of your mother bow down to you.
May those who curse you be cursed
    and those who bless you be blessed."

30After Isaac finished blessing him, and Jacob had scarcely left his father's
presence, his brother Esau came in from hunting. 31He too prepared some tasty
food and brought it to his father. Then he said to him, "My father, please sit up
and eat some of my game, so that you may give me your blessing."

32His father Isaac asked him, "Who are you?"

"I am your son," he answered, "your firstborn, Esau."

33Isaac trembled violently and said, "Who was it, then, that hunted game and
brought it to me? I ate it just before you came and I blessed him—and indeed he
will be blessed!"

34 When Esau heard his father's words, he burst out with a loud and bitter cry
and said to his father, "Bless me — me too, my father!"
35 But he said, "Your brother came deceitfully and took your blessing."
36 Esau said, "Isn't he rightly named Jacob[a]? This is the second time he has
taken advantage of me: He took my birthright, and now he's taken my blessing!"
Then he asked, "Haven't you reserved any blessing for me?"
37 Isaac answered Esau, "I have made him lord over you and have made all his
relatives his servants, and I have sustained him with grain and new wine. So
what can I possibly do for you, my son?"
38 Esau said to his father, "Do you have only one blessing, my father? Bless me
too, my father!" Then Esau wept aloud.
39 His father Isaac answered him,

"Your dwelling will be
away from the earth's richness,
away from the dew of heaven above.
40 You will live by the sword
and you will serve your brother.
But when you grow restless,
you will throw his yoke
from off your neck."

41 Esau held a grudge against Jacob because of the blessing his father had giv-
en him. He said to himself, "The days of mourning for my father are near; then I
will kill my brother Jacob."
42 When Rebekah was told what her older son Esau had said, she sent for her
younger son Jacob and said to him, "Your brother Esau is planning to avenge
himself by killing you. 43 Now then, my son, do what I say: Flee at once to my
brother Laban in Harran. 44 Stay with him for a while until your brother's fury
subsides. 45 When your brother is no longer angry with you and forgets what you
did to him, I'll send word for you to come back from there. Why should I lose both
of you in one day?"
46 Then Rebekah said to Isaac, "I'm disgusted with living because of these Hittite women. If Jacob takes a wife from among the women of this land, from Hittite
women like these, my life will not be worth living."

28 So Isaac called for Jacob and blessed him. Then he commanded him:
"Do not marry a Canaanite woman. 2 Go at once to Paddan Aram,[b] to the
house of your mother's father Bethuel. Take a wife for yourself there, from among
the daughters of Laban, your mother's brother. 3 May God Almighty[c] bless you
and make you fruitful and increase your numbers until you become a community of peoples. 4 May he give you and your descendants the blessing given to
Abraham, so that you may take possession of the land where you now reside as
a foreigner, the land God gave to Abraham." 5 Then Isaac sent Jacob on his way,
and he went to Paddan Aram, to Laban son of Bethuel the Aramean, the brother
of Rebekah, who was the mother of Jacob and Esau.
6 Now Esau learned that Isaac had blessed Jacob and had sent him to Paddan
Aram to take a wife from there, and that when he blessed him he commanded
him, "Do not marry a Canaanite woman," 7 and that Jacob had obeyed his father
and mother and had gone to Paddan Aram. 8 Esau then realized how displeasing
the Canaanite women were to his father Isaac; 9 so he went to Ishmael and married Mahalath, the sister of Nebaioth and daughter of Ishmael son of Abraham,
in addition to the wives he already had.

Jacob's Dream at Bethel

10 Jacob left Beersheba and set out for Harran. 11 When he reached a certain
place, he stopped for the night because the sun had set. Taking one of the stones

[a] 36 *Jacob* means *he grasps the heel*, a Hebrew idiom for *he takes advantage of* or *he deceives.*
[b] 2 That is, Northwest Mesopotamia; also in verses 5, 6 and 7 [c] 3 Hebrew *El-Shaddai*

GENESIS 28:10 – 22

A STAIRWAY FROM HEAVEN

Fleeing to Harran to escape his brother's wrath, Jacob stopped for the night. Jacob dreamed that a stairway stretched from heaven to earth, with angels ascending and descending the heavenly staircase. The picture portrayed the grand, cosmic reality of life on this earth. While it may seem that all that is real is that which can be seen, there is an eternal, heavenly world closely connected to this one. The heavenly realm is consistently interacting with this world in ways that lie beyond what the human mind can comprehend and the human eye can see.

Jesus' birth would bring this reality into greater focus. The fully divine and human Son of God would serve as the ladder between heaven and earth (Jn 1:51). At his baptism, the heavens were opened and the Spirit of God descended on the Son of God, indicating his divine status and God-ordained mission (Mt 3:13 – 17). In Jesus, heaven met earth, and with him came glimpses of the coming kingdom as the lame walked, the blind regained sight and prisoners gained freedom (Lk 4:18). At the incarnation, the Son of God descended the heavenly staircase in order to usher sinful humanity into the kingdom of God.

there, he put it under his head and lay down to sleep. 12 He had a dream in which
he saw a stairway resting on the earth, with its top reaching to heaven, and the
angels of God were ascending and descending on it. 13 There above it[a] stood the
LORD, and he said: "I am the LORD, the God of your father Abraham and the God
of Isaac. I will give you and your descendants the land on which you are lying.
14 Your descendants will be like the dust of the earth, and you will spread out to
the west and to the east, to the north and to the south. All peoples on earth will
be blessed through you and your offspring.[b] 15 I am with you and will watch over
you wherever you go, and I will bring you back to this land. I will not leave you
until I have done what I have promised you."

16 When Jacob awoke from his sleep, he thought, "Surely the LORD is in this
place, and I was not aware of it." 17 He was afraid and said, "How awesome is
this place! This is none other than the house of God; this is the gate of heaven."

18 Early the next morning Jacob took the stone he had placed under his head
and set it up as a pillar and poured oil on top of it. 19 He called that place Bethel,[c]
though the city used to be called Luz.

20 Then Jacob made a vow, saying, "If God will be with me and will watch over
me on this journey I am taking and will give me food to eat and clothes to wear
21 so that I return safely to my father's household, then the LORD[d] will be my God
22 and[e] this stone that I have set up as a pillar will be God's house, and of all that
you give me I will give you a tenth."

Jacob Arrives in Paddan Aram

29 Then Jacob continued on his journey and came to the land of the eastern
peoples. 2 There he saw a well in the open country, with three flocks of
sheep lying near it because the flocks were watered from that well. The stone
over the mouth of the well was large. 3 When all the flocks were gathered there,
the shepherds would roll the stone away from the well's mouth and water the
sheep. Then they would return the stone to its place over the mouth of the well.

4 Jacob asked the shepherds, "My brothers, where are you from?"

"We're from Harran," they replied.

5 He said to them, "Do you know Laban, Nahor's grandson?"

"Yes, we know him," they answered.

6 Then Jacob asked them, "Is he well?"

"Yes, he is," they said, "and here comes his daughter Rachel with the sheep."

7 "Look," he said, "the sun is still high; it is not time for the flocks to be gathered. Water the sheep and take them back to pasture."

8 "We can't," they replied, "until all the flocks are gathered and the stone has
been rolled away from the mouth of the well. Then we will water the sheep."

9 While he was still talking with them, Rachel came with her father's sheep,
for she was a shepherd. 10 When Jacob saw Rachel daughter of his uncle Laban,
and Laban's sheep, he went over and rolled the stone away from the mouth of
the well and watered his uncle's sheep. 11 Then Jacob kissed Rachel and began to
weep aloud. 12 He had told Rachel that he was a relative of her father and a son of
Rebekah. So she ran and told her father.

13 As soon as Laban heard the news about Jacob, his sister's son, he hurried to
meet him. He embraced him and kissed him and brought him to his home, and
there Jacob told him all these things. 14 Then Laban said to him, "You are my own
flesh and blood."

Jacob Marries Leah and Rachel

After Jacob had stayed with him for a whole month, 15 Laban said to him, "Just
because you are a relative of mine, should you work for me for nothing? Tell me
what your wages should be."

---

[a] 13 Or *There beside him* [b] 14 Or *will use your name and the name of your offspring in blessings* (see 48:20) [c] 19 *Bethel* means *house of God.* [d] 20,21 Or *Since God . . . father's household, the LORD* [e] 21,22 Or *household, and the LORD will be my God,* 22 *then*

16Now Laban had two daughters; the name of the older was Leah, and the
name of the younger was Rachel. 17Leah had weak[a] eyes, but Rachel had a lovely
figure and was beautiful. 18Jacob was in love with Rachel and said, "I'll work for
you seven years in return for your younger daughter Rachel."

19Laban said, "It's better that I give her to you than to some other man. Stay
here with me." 20So Jacob served seven years to get Rachel, but they seemed like
only a few days to him because of his love for her.

21Then Jacob said to Laban, "Give me my wife. My time is completed, and I
want to make love to her."

22So Laban brought together all the people of the place and gave a feast. 23But
when evening came, he took his daughter Leah and brought her to Jacob, and
Jacob made love to her. 24And Laban gave his servant Zilpah to his daughter as
her attendant.

25When morning came, there was Leah! So Jacob said to Laban, "What is
this you have done to me? I served you for Rachel, didn't I? Why have you deceived me?"

26Laban replied, "It is not our custom here to give the younger daughter in
marriage before the older one. 27Finish this daughter's bridal week; then we will
give you the younger one also, in return for another seven years of work."

28And Jacob did so. He finished the week with Leah, and then Laban gave
him his daughter Rachel to be his wife. 29Laban gave his servant Bilhah to his
daughter Rachel as her attendant. 30Jacob made love to Rachel also, and his love
for Rachel was greater than his love for Leah. And he worked for Laban another
seven years.

Jacob's Children

31When the LORD saw that Leah was not loved, he enabled her to conceive, but
Rachel remained childless. 32Leah became pregnant and gave birth to a son. She
named him Reuben,[b] for she said, "It is because the LORD has seen my misery.
Surely my husband will love me now."

33She conceived again, and when she gave birth to a son she said, "Because
the LORD heard that I am not loved, he gave me this one too." So she named him
Simeon.[c]

34Again she conceived, and when she gave birth to a son she said, "Now at last
my husband will become attached to me, because I have borne him three sons."
So he was named Levi.[d]

35She conceived again, and when she gave birth to a son she said, "This time I
will praise the LORD." So she named him Judah.[e] Then she stopped having children.

30 When Rachel saw that she was not bearing Jacob any children, she became
jealous of her sister. So she said to Jacob, "Give me children, or I'll die!"

2Jacob became angry with her and said, "Am I in the place of God, who has
kept you from having children?"

3Then she said, "Here is Bilhah, my servant. Sleep with her so that she can
bear children for me and I too can build a family through her."

4So she gave him her servant Bilhah as a wife. Jacob slept with her, 5and she
became pregnant and bore him a son. 6Then Rachel said, "God has vindicated
me; he has listened to my plea and given me a son." Because of this she named
him Dan.[f]

7Rachel's servant Bilhah conceived again and bore Jacob a second son. 8Then
Rachel said, "I have had a great struggle with my sister, and I have won." So she
named him Naphtali.[g]

---

[a] 17 Or *delicate* [b] 32 *Reuben* sounds like the Hebrew for *he has seen my misery*; the name means *see, a son.* [c] 33 *Simeon* probably means *one who hears.* [d] 34 *Levi* sounds like and may be derived from the Hebrew for *attached.* [e] 35 *Judah* sounds like and may be derived from the Hebrew for *praise.* [f] 6 *Dan* here means *he has vindicated.* [g] 8 *Naphtali* means *my struggle.*

9When Leah saw that she had stopped having children, she took her servant
Zilpah and gave her to Jacob as a wife. 10Leah's servant Zilpah bore Jacob a son.
11Then Leah said, "What good fortune!"[a] So she named him Gad.[b]

12Leah's servant Zilpah bore Jacob a second son. 13Then Leah said, "How happy I am! The women will call me happy." So she named him Asher.[c]

14During wheat harvest, Reuben went out into the fields and found some
mandrake plants, which he brought to his mother Leah. Rachel said to Leah,
"Please give me some of your son's mandrakes."

15But she said to her, "Wasn't it enough that you took away my husband? Will
you take my son's mandrakes too?"

"Very well," Rachel said, "he can sleep with you tonight in return for your son's
mandrakes."

16So when Jacob came in from the fields that evening, Leah went out to meet
him. "You must sleep with me," she said. "I have hired you with my son's mandrakes." So he slept with her that night.

17God listened to Leah, and she became pregnant and bore Jacob a fifth son.
18Then Leah said, "God has rewarded me for giving my servant to my husband."
So she named him Issachar.[d]

19Leah conceived again and bore Jacob a sixth son. 20Then Leah said, "God
has presented me with a precious gift. This time my husband will treat me with
honor, because I have borne him six sons." So she named him Zebulun.[e]

21Some time later she gave birth to a daughter and named her Dinah.

22Then God remembered Rachel; he listened to her and enabled her to conceive. 23She became pregnant and gave birth to a son and said, "God has taken
away my disgrace." 24She named him Joseph,[f] and said, "May the LORD add to
me another son."

Jacob's Flocks Increase

25After Rachel gave birth to Joseph, Jacob said to Laban, "Send me on my way
so I can go back to my own homeland. 26Give me my wives and children, for
whom I have served you, and I will be on my way. You know how much work I've
done for you."

27But Laban said to him, "If I have found favor in your eyes, please stay. I have
learned by divination that the LORD has blessed me because of you." 28He added,
"Name your wages, and I will pay them."

29Jacob said to him, "You know how I have worked for you and how your livestock has fared under my care. 30The little you had before I came has increased
greatly, and the LORD has blessed you wherever I have been. But now, when may
I do something for my own household?"

31"What shall I give you?" he asked.

"Don't give me anything," Jacob replied. "But if you will do this one thing for
me, I will go on tending your flocks and watching over them: 32Let me go through
all your flocks today and remove from them every speckled or spotted sheep,
every dark-colored lamb and every spotted or speckled goat. They will be my
wages. 33And my honesty will testify for me in the future, whenever you check
on the wages you have paid me. Any goat in my possession that is not speckled or
spotted, or any lamb that is not dark-colored, will be considered stolen."

34"Agreed," said Laban. "Let it be as you have said." 35That same day he removed all the male goats that were streaked or spotted, and all the speckled
or spotted female goats (all that had white on them) and all the dark-colored
lambs, and he placed them in the care of his sons. 36Then he put a three-day
journey between himself and Jacob, while Jacob continued to tend the rest of
Laban's flocks.

---

[a] *11* Or *"A troop is coming!"* [b] *11 Gad* can mean *good fortune* or *a troop.* [c] *13 Asher* means *happy.* [d] *18 Issachar* sounds like the Hebrew for *reward.* [e] *20 Zebulun* probably means *honor.* [f] *24 Joseph* means *may he add.*

[37]Jacob, however, took fresh-cut branches from poplar, almond and plane trees and made white stripes on them by peeling the bark and exposing the white inner wood of the branches. [38]Then he placed the peeled branches in all the watering troughs, so that they would be directly in front of the flocks when they came to drink. When the flocks were in heat and came to drink, [39]they mated in front of the branches. And they bore young that were streaked or speckled or spotted. [40]Jacob set apart the young of the flock by themselves, but made the rest face the streaked and dark-colored animals that belonged to Laban. Thus he made separate flocks for himself and did not put them with Laban's animals. [41]Whenever the stronger females were in heat, Jacob would place the branches in the troughs in front of the animals so they would mate near the branches, [42]but if the animals were weak, he would not place them there. So the weak animals went to Laban and the strong ones to Jacob. [43]In this way the man grew exceedingly prosperous and came to own large flocks, and female and male servants, and camels and donkeys.

Jacob Flees From Laban

31 Jacob heard that Laban's sons were saying, "Jacob has taken everything our father owned and has gained all this wealth from what belonged to our father." [2]And Jacob noticed that Laban's attitude toward him was not what it had been.

[3]Then the LORD said to Jacob, "Go back to the land of your fathers and to your relatives, and I will be with you."

[4]So Jacob sent word to Rachel and Leah to come out to the fields where his flocks were. [5]He said to them, "I see that your father's attitude toward me is not what it was before, but the God of my father has been with me. [6]You know that I've worked for your father with all my strength, [7]yet your father has cheated me by changing my wages ten times. However, God has not allowed him to harm me. [8]If he said, 'The speckled ones will be your wages,' then all the flocks gave birth to speckled young; and if he said, 'The streaked ones will be your wages,' then all the flocks bore streaked young. [9]So God has taken away your father's livestock and has given them to me.

[10]"In breeding season I once had a dream in which I looked up and saw that the male goats mating with the flock were streaked, speckled or spotted. [11]The angel of God said to me in the dream, 'Jacob.' I answered, 'Here I am.' [12]And he said, 'Look up and see that all the male goats mating with the flock are streaked, speckled or spotted, for I have seen all that Laban has been doing to you. [13]I am the God of Bethel, where you anointed a pillar and where you made a vow to me. Now leave this land at once and go back to your native land.' "

[14]Then Rachel and Leah replied, "Do we still have any share in the inheritance of our father's estate? [15]Does he not regard us as foreigners? Not only has he sold us, but he has used up what was paid for us. [16]Surely all the wealth that God took away from our father belongs to us and our children. So do whatever God has told you."

[17]Then Jacob put his children and his wives on camels, [18]and he drove all his livestock ahead of him, along with all the goods he had accumulated in Paddan Aram,[a] to go to his father Isaac in the land of Canaan.

[19]When Laban had gone to shear his sheep, Rachel stole her father's household gods. [20]Moreover, Jacob deceived Laban the Aramean by not telling him he was running away. [21]So he fled with all he had, crossed the Euphrates River, and headed for the hill country of Gilead.

Laban Pursues Jacob

[22]On the third day Laban was told that Jacob had fled. [23]Taking his relatives with him, he pursued Jacob for seven days and caught up with him in the hill

[a] *18* That is, Northwest Mesopotamia

GENESIS 31:22–24

RESTORING PEACE IN A BROKEN WORLD

God's rescue operation for humanity integrally involved the descendants of Jacob. God had promised to Jacob, as his father and grandfather before him, that his grand plan for restoring *shalom* back to the universe was via a massive blessing in and through his descendants (Ge 28:13–15). Hope for blessing rested in the safety and expansion of this fledgling family. And God would ensure that Jacob would move forward under divine protection and multiplication. In this passage, Jacob risked his life and the Messiah's line. His aggressive business relationship with Laban and ensuing flight from his father-in-law put him in a dangerous spot. God continued to demonstrate his faithfulness to Jacob, in spite of the seeming chaos. Ultimately, the potential risks that threatened to short circuit God's plan in Jesus were also overcome in his sovereignty and power. This story of the protection and progress of God's plan for the redemptive Messiah plays out again and again in the pages of Scripture.

country of Gilead. 24Then God came to Laban the Aramean in a dream at night and said to him, "Be careful not to say anything to Jacob, either good or bad."

25Jacob had pitched his tent in the hill country of Gilead when Laban overtook him, and Laban and his relatives camped there too. 26Then Laban said to Jacob, "What have you done? You've deceived me, and you've carried off my daughters like captives in war. 27Why did you run off secretly and deceive me? Why didn't you tell me, so I could send you away with joy and singing to the music of timbrels and harps? 28You didn't even let me kiss my grandchildren and my daughters goodbye. You have done a foolish thing. 29I have the power to harm you; but last night the God of your father said to me, 'Be careful not to say anything to Jacob, either good or bad.' 30Now you have gone off because you longed to return to your father's household. But why did you steal my gods?"

31Jacob answered Laban, "I was afraid, because I thought you would take your daughters away from me by force. 32But if you find anyone who has your gods, that person shall not live. In the presence of our relatives, see for yourself whether there is anything of yours here with me; and if so, take it." Now Jacob did not know that Rachel had stolen the gods.

33So Laban went into Jacob's tent and into Leah's tent and into the tent of the two female servants, but he found nothing. After he came out of Leah's tent, he entered Rachel's tent. 34Now Rachel had taken the household gods and put them inside her camel's saddle and was sitting on them. Laban searched through everything in the tent but found nothing.

35Rachel said to her father, "Don't be angry, my lord, that I cannot stand up in your presence; I'm having my period." So he searched but could not find the household gods.

36Jacob was angry and took Laban to task. "What is my crime?" he asked Laban. "How have I wronged you that you hunt me down? 37Now that you have searched through all my goods, what have you found that belongs to your household? Put it here in front of your relatives and mine, and let them judge between the two of us.

38"I have been with you for twenty years now. Your sheep and goats have not miscarried, nor have I eaten rams from your flocks. 39I did not bring you animals torn by wild beasts; I bore the loss myself. And you demanded payment from me for whatever was stolen by day or night. 40This was my situation: The heat consumed me in the daytime and the cold at night, and sleep fled from my eyes. 41It was like this for the twenty years I was in your household. I worked for you fourteen years for your two daughters and six years for your flocks, and you changed my wages ten times. 42If the God of my father, the God of Abraham and the Fear of Isaac, had not been with me, you would surely have sent me away empty-handed. But God has seen my hardship and the toil of my hands, and last night he rebuked you."

43Laban answered Jacob, "The women are my daughters, the children are my children, and the flocks are my flocks. All you see is mine. Yet what can I do today about these daughters of mine, or about the children they have borne? 44Come now, let's make a covenant, you and I, and let it serve as a witness between us."

45So Jacob took a stone and set it up as a pillar. 46He said to his relatives, "Gather some stones." So they took stones and piled them in a heap, and they ate there by the heap. 47Laban called it Jegar Sahadutha, and Jacob called it Galeed.[a]

48Laban said, "This heap is a witness between you and me today." That is why it was called Galeed. 49It was also called Mizpah,[b] because he said, "May the LORD keep watch between you and me when we are away from each other. 50If you mistreat my daughters or if you take any wives besides my daughters, even though no one is with us, remember that God is a witness between you and me."

[a] 47 The Aramaic *Jegar Sahadutha* and the Hebrew *Galeed* both mean *witness heap.*
[b] 49 *Mizpah* means *watchtower.*

51 Laban also said to Jacob, "Here is this heap, and here is this pillar I have set
up between you and me. 52 This heap is a witness, and this pillar is a witness, that
I will not go past this heap to your side to harm you and that you will not go past
this heap and pillar to my side to harm me. 53 May the God of Abraham and the
God of Nahor, the God of their father, judge between us."
So Jacob took an oath in the name of the Fear of his father Isaac. 54 He offered
a sacrifice there in the hill country and invited his relatives to a meal. After they
had eaten, they spent the night there.
55 Early the next morning Laban kissed his grandchildren and his daughters
and blessed them. Then he left and returned home.[a]

Jacob Prepares to Meet Esau

32[b] Jacob also went on his way, and the angels of God met him. 2 When Jacob
saw them, he said, "This is the camp of God!" So he named that place
Mahanaim.[c]
3 Jacob sent messengers ahead of him to his brother Esau in the land of Seir,
the country of Edom. 4 He instructed them: "This is what you are to say to my
lord Esau: 'Your servant Jacob says, I have been staying with Laban and have
remained there till now. 5 I have cattle and donkeys, sheep and goats, male and
female servants. Now I am sending this message to my lord, that I may find favor
in your eyes.'"
6 When the messengers returned to Jacob, they said, "We went to your brother
Esau, and now he is coming to meet you, and four hundred men are with him."
7 In great fear and distress Jacob divided the people who were with him into
two groups,[d] and the flocks and herds and camels as well. 8 He thought, "If Esau
comes and attacks one group,[e] the group[e] that is left may escape."
9 Then Jacob prayed, "O God of my father Abraham, God of my father Isaac,
LORD, you who said to me, 'Go back to your country and your relatives, and I
will make you prosper,' 10 I am unworthy of all the kindness and faithfulness
you have shown your servant. I had only my staff when I crossed this Jordan, but
now I have become two camps. 11 Save me, I pray, from the hand of my brother
Esau, for I am afraid he will come and attack me, and also the mothers with their
children. 12 But you have said, 'I will surely make you prosper and will make your
descendants like the sand of the sea, which cannot be counted.'"
13 He spent the night there, and from what he had with him he selected a gift
for his brother Esau: 14 two hundred female goats and twenty male goats, two
hundred ewes and twenty rams, 15 thirty female camels with their young, forty
cows and ten bulls, and twenty female donkeys and ten male donkeys. 16 He put
them in the care of his servants, each herd by itself, and said to his servants, "Go
ahead of me, and keep some space between the herds."
17 He instructed the one in the lead: "When my brother Esau meets you and
asks, 'Who do you belong to, and where are you going, and who owns all these
animals in front of you?' 18 then you are to say, 'They belong to your servant Jacob.
They are a gift sent to my lord Esau, and he is coming behind us.'"
19 He also instructed the second, the third and all the others who followed the
herds: "You are to say the same thing to Esau when you meet him. 20 And be sure
to say, 'Your servant Jacob is coming behind us.'" For he thought, "I will pacify
him with these gifts I am sending on ahead; later, when I see him, perhaps he
will receive me." 21 So Jacob's gifts went on ahead of him, but he himself spent
the night in the camp.

Jacob Wrestles With God

22 That night Jacob got up and took his two wives, his two female servants
and his eleven sons and crossed the ford of the Jabbok. 23 After he had sent them

---

[a] *55* In Hebrew texts this verse (31:55) is numbered 32:1. [b] In Hebrew texts 32:1-32 is numbered 32:2-33. [c] *2* *Mahanaim* means *two camps.* [d] *7* Or *camps* [e] *8* Or *camp*

across the stream, he sent over all his possessions. [24]So Jacob was left alone, and
a man wrestled with him till daybreak. [25]When the man saw that he could not
overpower him, he touched the socket of Jacob's hip so that his hip was wrenched
as he wrestled with the man. [26]Then the man said, "Let me go, for it is daybreak."

But Jacob replied, "I will not let you go unless you bless me."

[27]The man asked him, "What is your name?"

"Jacob," he answered.

[28]Then the man said, "Your name will no longer be Jacob, but Israel,[a] because
you have struggled with God and with humans and have overcome."

[29]Jacob said, "Please tell me your name."

But he replied, "Why do you ask my name?" Then he blessed him there.

[30]So Jacob called the place Peniel,[b] saying, "It is because I saw God face to
face, and yet my life was spared."

[31]The sun rose above him as he passed Peniel,[c] and he was limping because of
his hip. [32]Therefore to this day the Israelites do not eat the tendon attached to the
socket of the hip, because the socket of Jacob's hip was touched near the tendon.

Jacob Meets Esau

33 Jacob looked up and there was Esau, coming with his four hundred men;
so he divided the children among Leah, Rachel and the two female servants. [2]He put the female servants and their children in front, Leah and her children next, and Rachel and Joseph in the rear. [3]He himself went on ahead and
bowed down to the ground seven times as he approached his brother.

[4]But Esau ran to meet Jacob and embraced him; he threw his arms around his
neck and kissed him. And they wept. [5]Then Esau looked up and saw the women
and children. "Who are these with you?" he asked.

Jacob answered, "They are the children God has graciously given your servant."

[6]Then the female servants and their children approached and bowed down.
[7]Next, Leah and her children came and bowed down. Last of all came Joseph and
Rachel, and they too bowed down.

[8]Esau asked, "What's the meaning of all these flocks and herds I met?"

"To find favor in your eyes, my lord," he said.

[9]But Esau said, "I already have plenty, my brother. Keep what you have for
yourself."

[10]"No, please!" said Jacob. "If I have found favor in your eyes, accept this gift
from me. For to see your face is like seeing the face of God, now that you have
received me favorably. [11]Please accept the present that was brought to you, for
God has been gracious to me and I have all I need." And because Jacob insisted,
Esau accepted it.

[12]Then Esau said, "Let us be on our way; I'll accompany you."

[13]But Jacob said to him, "My lord knows that the children are tender and that
I must care for the ewes and cows that are nursing their young. If they are driv-
en hard just one day, all the animals will die. [14]So let my lord go on ahead of his
servant, while I move along slowly at the pace of the flocks and herds before me
and the pace of the children, until I come to my lord in Seir."

[15]Esau said, "Then let me leave some of my men with you."

"But why do that?" Jacob asked. "Just let me find favor in the eyes of my lord."

[16]So that day Esau started on his way back to Seir. [17]Jacob, however, went to
Sukkoth, where he built a place for himself and made shelters for his livestock.
That is why the place is called Sukkoth.[d]

[18]After Jacob came from Paddan Aram,[e] he arrived safely at the city of Shechem in Canaan and camped within sight of the city. [19]For a hundred pieces

---

[a] *28 Israel* probably means *he struggles with God.* [b] *30 Peniel* means *face of God.*
[c] *31* Hebrew *Penuel,* a variant of *Peniel* [d] *17 Sukkoth* means *shelters.* [e] *18* That is,
Northwest Mesopotamia

A NEW NAME

God gave Jacob a new name. Throughout the Old Testament, a name carried an identity. For example, God changed Abram's name to Abraham to indicate that he would be "a father of many nations" (Ge 17:5). The new name indicated the favor of God and pointed forward to the coming promise of God.

In a similar fashion, after wrestling with God, Jacob was renamed Israel. This name was then used to refer to the entire nation that derived from his family lineage. This name was not chosen by Jacob but was given to him by God as a gift and a promise. For the rest of his life, this new name reminded Jacob of the favor of God in allowing him to wrestle with God and live, and of his privileged place within God's redemptive plan. God's chosen people throughout the Old Testament would be reminded of their status as God's people when anyone referred to them by the name Israel.

The New Testament church is no longer defined by an ethnic heritage like the nation of Israel. Now, Jews and Gentiles alike are grafted into one diverse family with God as their Father. God grants all those who are saved by faith in Jesus the glorious privilege of being called a child of God (Jn 1:12). As children, they are granted a unique identity given to them by virtue of their relationship with God. In fact, within the church, God's people are called Christians because of their relationship with Jesus Christ. This name denotes far more than mere proximity to Jesus. God's people are those who are "in Christ" — called into relationship with him and given a role to play in his redemptive mission.

This new identity also indicates the changes that are brought by God's Spirit in the life of his children. "If anyone is in Christ, the new creation has come: The old has gone, the new is here!" (2Co 5:17). The saving work of God fundamentally changes the identity of those saved by faith. No longer dead in trespasses and sins, God's people are declared holy and blameless and are given a right relationship with God. Like the change of a name, this change of identity should produce radical transformation in the worship, life and mission of God's children.

ENEMIES MADE FRIENDS

Genesis 33 recounts the unthinkable reconciliation between Jacob and Esau. These estranged brothers had seemingly insurmountable odds stacked against the restoration of their relationship. Their history had been marked by strife, deceit and mutual harm. The relationship between these two men was ravished by sin, and they became bitter enemies. But Esau, in an act of love and mercy, pursued his brother and received him back into fellowship with lavish generosity.

Like Jacob, all of humanity is guilty of rebellion and sin against God, thus altering their relationship with their Creator. Image-bearers, created to walk with God in fellowship, find themselves estranged from God and unable to right the relationship by their own choosing. This broken fellowship takes those who were created to be friends of God and makes them his enemies (Ro 5:10). All people, like Jacob, should rightfully cower in fear and shame because of the judgment they surely deserve.

God's mercy is seen in the restorative act that he works on behalf of his enemies. Rather than expecting them to grovel in his presence or clean themselves up through obedience, God pursues his enemies in love. The biblical notion of reconciliation captures this profound image. God takes those who were his enemies and works on their behalf to bring them back into a right relationship with himself (Col 1:21 – 22). Like Esau, God pursues his enemies, recognizes their need and blesses them with a restored relationship as an act of mercy.

Jesus elaborates on this work of reconciliation in his parable of a loving father and his wayward son (Lk 15:11 – 32). The son requested his inheritance early, only to squander everything and end up longing to eat from the trough of the pigs he fed. Only then did the young man realize his sin. The son expected to meet his father's displeasure and anticipated taking the posture of a hired servant. As the son returned, his dad saw him while he was a long way off and ran to meet him. Rather than shame or condemnation, the son was greeted by his father's loving embrace. The father gave him a hero's welcome — killing the fattened calf in order to throw a party and celebrate the return of his son. Like Esau and the loving father, God is pictured as a merciful heavenly Father who pursues his enemies in love and invites them into a restored relationship made possible through Jesus' death.

of silver,[a] he bought from the sons of Hamor, the father of Shechem, the plot
of ground where he pitched his tent. 20There he set up an altar and called it El
Elohe Israel.[b]

Dinah and the Shechemites

34 Now Dinah, the daughter Leah had borne to Jacob, went out to visit the
women of the land. 2When Shechem son of Hamor the Hivite, the ruler
of that area, saw her, he took her and raped her. 3His heart was drawn to Dinah
daughter of Jacob; he loved the young woman and spoke tenderly to her. 4And
Shechem said to his father Hamor, "Get me this girl as my wife."

5When Jacob heard that his daughter Dinah had been defiled, his sons were
in the fields with his livestock; so he did nothing about it until they came home.

6Then Shechem's father Hamor went out to talk with Jacob. 7Meanwhile, Jacob's sons had come in from the fields as soon as they heard what had happened.
They were shocked and furious, because Shechem had done an outrageous thing
in[c] Israel by sleeping with Jacob's daughter — a thing that should not be done.

8But Hamor said to them, "My son Shechem has his heart set on your daughter. Please give her to him as his wife. 9Intermarry with us; give us your daughters and take our daughters for yourselves. 10You can settle among us; the land is
open to you. Live in it, trade[d] in it, and acquire property in it."

11Then Shechem said to Dinah's father and brothers, "Let me find favor in
your eyes, and I will give you whatever you ask. 12Make the price for the bride
and the gift I am to bring as great as you like, and I'll pay whatever you ask me.
Only give me the young woman as my wife."

13Because their sister Dinah had been defiled, Jacob's sons replied deceitfully
as they spoke to Shechem and his father Hamor. 14They said to them, "We can't
do such a thing; we can't give our sister to a man who is not circumcised. That
would be a disgrace to us. 15We will enter into an agreement with you on one
condition only: that you become like us by circumcising all your males. 16Then
we will give you our daughters and take your daughters for ourselves. We'll settle among you and become one people with you. 17But if you will not agree to be
circumcised, we'll take our sister and go."

18Their proposal seemed good to Hamor and his son Shechem. 19The young
man, who was the most honored of all his father's family, lost no time in doing
what they said, because he was delighted with Jacob's daughter. 20So Hamor and
his son Shechem went to the gate of their city to speak to the men of their city.
21"These men are friendly toward us," they said. "Let them live in our land and
trade in it; the land has plenty of room for them. We can marry their daughters
and they can marry ours. 22But the men will agree to live with us as one people
only on the condition that our males be circumcised, as they themselves are.
23Won't their livestock, their property and all their other animals become ours?
So let us agree to their terms, and they will settle among us."

24All the men who went out of the city gate agreed with Hamor and his son
Shechem, and every male in the city was circumcised.

25Three days later, while all of them were still in pain, two of Jacob's sons, Simeon and Levi, Dinah's brothers, took their swords and attacked the unsuspecting
city, killing every male. 26They put Hamor and his son Shechem to the sword
and took Dinah from Shechem's house and left. 27The sons of Jacob came upon
the dead bodies and looted the city where[e] their sister had been defiled. 28They
seized their flocks and herds and donkeys and everything else of theirs in the
city and out in the fields. 29They carried off all their wealth and all their women
and children, taking as plunder everything in the houses.

30Then Jacob said to Simeon and Levi, "You have brought trouble on me by

---

[a] 19 Hebrew *hundred kesitahs*; a kesitah was a unit of money of unknown weight and value. [b] 20 *El Elohe Israel* can mean *El is the God of Israel* or *mighty is the God of Israel.* [c] 7 Or *against* [d] 10 Or *move about freely*; also in verse 21 [e] 27 Or *because*

making me obnoxious to the Canaanites and Perizzites, the people living in this land. We are few in number, and if they join forces against me and attack me, I and my household will be destroyed."

31 But they replied, "Should he have treated our sister like a prostitute?"

Jacob Returns to Bethel

35 Then God said to Jacob, "Go up to Bethel and settle there, and build an altar there to God, who appeared to you when you were fleeing from your brother Esau."

2 So Jacob said to his household and to all who were with him, "Get rid of the foreign gods you have with you, and purify yourselves and change your clothes. 3 Then come, let us go up to Bethel, where I will build an altar to God, who answered me in the day of my distress and who has been with me wherever I have gone." 4 So they gave Jacob all the foreign gods they had and the rings in their ears, and Jacob buried them under the oak at Shechem. 5 Then they set out, and the terror of God fell on the towns all around them so that no one pursued them.

6 Jacob and all the people with him came to Luz (that is, Bethel) in the land of Canaan. 7 There he built an altar, and he called the place El Bethel,[a] because it was there that God revealed himself to him when he was fleeing from his brother.

8 Now Deborah, Rebekah's nurse, died and was buried under the oak outside Bethel. So it was named Allon Bakuth.[b]

9 After Jacob returned from Paddan Aram,[c] God appeared to him again and blessed him. 10 God said to him, "Your name is Jacob,[d] but you will no longer be called Jacob; your name will be Israel.[e]" So he named him Israel.

11 And God said to him, "I am God Almighty[f]; be fruitful and increase in number. A nation and a community of nations will come from you, and kings will be among your descendants. 12 The land I gave to Abraham and Isaac I also give to you, and I will give this land to your descendants after you." 13 Then God went up from him at the place where he had talked with him.

14 Jacob set up a stone pillar at the place where God had talked with him, and he poured out a drink offering on it; he also poured oil on it. 15 Jacob called the place where God had talked with him Bethel.[g]

The Deaths of Rachel and Isaac

16 Then they moved on from Bethel. While they were still some distance from Ephrath, Rachel began to give birth and had great difficulty. 17 And as she was having great difficulty in childbirth, the midwife said to her, "Don't despair, for you have another son." 18 As she breathed her last—for she was dying—she named her son Ben-Oni.[h] But his father named him Benjamin.[i]

19 So Rachel died and was buried on the way to Ephrath (that is, Bethlehem). 20 Over her tomb Jacob set up a pillar, and to this day that pillar marks Rachel's tomb.

21 Israel moved on again and pitched his tent beyond Migdal Eder. 22 While Israel was living in that region, Reuben went in and slept with his father's concubine Bilhah, and Israel heard of it.

Jacob had twelve sons:

23 The sons of Leah:
Reuben the firstborn of Jacob,
Simeon, Levi, Judah, Issachar and Zebulun.

24 The sons of Rachel:
Joseph and Benjamin.

GENESIS 35:1–7

A PLACE FOR WORSHIP

God told Jacob to return to the place where he first saw God's glory (Ge 28:10–19). The rationale behind this command was unclear at the time. All Jacob knew was that God told him to return to Bethel, and once he arrived, he must worship God on an altar that he must build. Like his grandfather, Abraham, Jacob heard God and obeyed. His actions were predicated on his knowledge of God's past faithfulness and his awareness of the Lord's continued care. Jacob's obedience positioned him to receive the blessing of God.

Like Jacob, Jesus' followers obey the commands of God based on his faithfulness in their lives and their desire to worship him as he deserves (Jn 15:14). Obedience positions God's people to fulfill his purposes for their lives and receive the blessing he has promised—perhaps not in this life, but certainly in the life to come (Jn 10:10).

---

[a] *7 El Bethel* means *God of Bethel.* [b] *8 Allon Bakuth* means *oak of weeping.* [c] *9* That is, Northwest Mesopotamia; also in verse 26 [d] *10 Jacob* means *he grasps the heel,* a Hebrew idiom for *he deceives.* [e] *10 Israel* probably means *he struggles with God.* [f] *11* Hebrew *El-Shaddai* [g] *15 Bethel* means *house of God.* [h] *18 Ben-Oni* means *son of my trouble.* [i] *18 Benjamin* means *son of my right hand.*

[25]The sons of Rachel's servant Bilhah:
Dan and Naphtali.
[26]The sons of Leah's servant Zilpah:
Gad and Asher.
These were the sons of Jacob, who were born to him in Paddan Aram.

[27]Jacob came home to his father Isaac in Mamre, near Kiriath Arba (that is,
Hebron), where Abraham and Isaac had stayed. [28]Isaac lived a hundred and
eighty years. [29]Then he breathed his last and died and was gathered to his people, old and full of years. And his sons Esau and Jacob buried him.

Esau's Descendants

36 This is the account of the family line of Esau (that is, Edom).

[2]Esau took his wives from the women of Canaan: Adah daughter of Elon
the Hittite, and Oholibamah daughter of Anah and granddaughter of Zibeon the Hivite— [3]also Basemath daughter of Ishmael and sister of Nebaioth.
[4]Adah bore Eliphaz to Esau, Basemath bore Reuel, [5]and Oholibamah
bore Jeush, Jalam and Korah. These were the sons of Esau, who were born
to him in Canaan.
[6]Esau took his wives and sons and daughters and all the members of
his household, as well as his livestock and all his other animals and all
the goods he had acquired in Canaan, and moved to a land some distance
from his brother Jacob. [7]Their possessions were too great for them to remain together; the land where they were staying could not support them
both because of their livestock. [8]So Esau (that is, Edom) settled in the hill
country of Seir.

[9]This is the account of the family line of Esau the father of the Edomites in the
hill country of Seir.

[10]These are the names of Esau's sons:
Eliphaz, the son of Esau's wife Adah, and Reuel, the son of Esau's wife Basemath.
[11]The sons of Eliphaz:
Teman, Omar, Zepho, Gatam and Kenaz.
[12]Esau's son Eliphaz also had a concubine named Timna, who bore him Amalek. These were grandsons of Esau's wife Adah.
[13]The sons of Reuel:
Nahath, Zerah, Shammah and Mizzah. These were grandsons of Esau's wife Basemath.
[14]The sons of Esau's wife Oholibamah daughter of Anah and granddaughter of Zibeon, whom she bore to Esau:
Jeush, Jalam and Korah.

[15]These were the chiefs among Esau's descendants:
The sons of Eliphaz the firstborn of Esau:
Chiefs Teman, Omar, Zepho, Kenaz, [16]Korah,[a] Gatam and Amalek.
These were the chiefs descended from Eliphaz in Edom; they were grandsons of Adah.
[17]The sons of Esau's son Reuel:
Chiefs Nahath, Zerah, Shammah and Mizzah. These were the chiefs descended from Reuel in Edom; they were grandsons of Esau's wife Basemath.
[18]The sons of Esau's wife Oholibamah:
Chiefs Jeush, Jalam and Korah. These were the chiefs descended from Esau's wife Oholibamah daughter of Anah.
[19]These were the sons of Esau (that is, Edom), and these were their chiefs.

[a] *16* Masoretic Text; Samaritan Pentateuch (also verse 11 and 1 Chron. 1:36) does not have *Korah*.

[20]These were the sons of Seir the Horite, who were living in the region:
Lotan, Shobal, Zibeon, Anah, [21]Dishon, Ezer and Dishan. These sons of
Seir in Edom were Horite chiefs.
[22]The sons of Lotan:
Hori and Homam.[a] Timna was Lotan's sister.
[23]The sons of Shobal:
Alvan, Manahath, Ebal, Shepho and Onam.
[24]The sons of Zibeon:
Aiah and Anah. This is the Anah who discovered the hot springs[b] in the
desert while he was grazing the donkeys of his father Zibeon.
[25]The children of Anah:
Dishon and Oholibamah daughter of Anah.
[26]The sons of Dishon[c]:
Hemdan, Eshban, Ithran and Keran.
[27]The sons of Ezer:
Bilhan, Zaavan and Akan.
[28]The sons of Dishan:
Uz and Aran.
[29]These were the Horite chiefs:
Lotan, Shobal, Zibeon, Anah, [30]Dishon, Ezer and Dishan. These were
the Horite chiefs, according to their divisions, in the land of Seir.

The Rulers of Edom

[31]These were the kings who reigned in Edom before any Israelite king reigned:
[32]Bela son of Beor became king of Edom. His city was named Dinhabah.
[33]When Bela died, Jobab son of Zerah from Bozrah succeeded him as king.
[34]When Jobab died, Husham from the land of the Temanites succeeded him
as king.
[35]When Husham died, Hadad son of Bedad, who defeated Midian in the
country of Moab, succeeded him as king. His city was named Avith.
[36]When Hadad died, Samlah from Masrekah succeeded him as king.
[37]When Samlah died, Shaul from Rehoboth on the river succeeded him as
king.
[38]When Shaul died, Baal-Hanan son of Akbor succeeded him as king.
[39]When Baal-Hanan son of Akbor died, Hadad[d] succeeded him as king. His
city was named Pau, and his wife's name was Mehetabel daughter of
Matred, the daughter of Me-Zahab.

[40]These were the chiefs descended from Esau, by name, according to their
clans and regions:
Timna, Alvah, Jetheth, [41]Oholibamah, Elah, Pinon, [42]Kenaz, Teman,
Mibzar, [43]Magdiel and Iram. These were the chiefs of Edom, according
to their settlements in the land they occupied.

This is the family line of Esau, the father of the Edomites.

Joseph's Dreams

37 Jacob lived in the land where his father had stayed, the land of Canaan.

[2]This is the account of Jacob's family line.

Joseph, a young man of seventeen, was tending the flocks with his brothers, the sons of Bilhah and the sons of Zilpah, his father's wives, and he brought their father a bad report about them.

---

[a] *22* Hebrew *Hemam,* a variant of *Homam* (see 1 Chron. 1:39) [b] *24* Vulgate; Syriac *discovered water;* the meaning of the Hebrew for this word is uncertain. [c] *26* Hebrew *Dishan,* a variant of *Dishon* [d] *39* Many manuscripts of the Masoretic Text, Samaritan Pentateuch and Syriac (see also 1 Chron. 1:50); most manuscripts of the Masoretic Text *Hadar*

3Now Israel loved Joseph more than any of his other sons, because he had been born to him in his old age; and he made an ornate[a] robe for him. 4When his brothers saw that their father loved him more than any of them, they hated him and could not speak a kind word to him.

5Joseph had a dream, and when he told it to his brothers, they hated him all the more. 6He said to them, "Listen to this dream I had: 7We were binding sheaves of grain out in the field when suddenly my sheaf rose and stood upright, while your sheaves gathered around mine and bowed down to it."

8His brothers said to him, "Do you intend to reign over us? Will you actually rule us?" And they hated him all the more because of his dream and what he had said.

9Then he had another dream, and he told it to his brothers. "Listen," he said, "I had another dream, and this time the sun and moon and eleven stars were bowing down to me."

10When he told his father as well as his brothers, his father rebuked him and said, "What is this dream you had? Will your mother and I and your brothers actually come and bow down to the ground before you?" 11His brothers were jealous of him, but his father kept the matter in mind.

Joseph Sold by His Brothers

12Now his brothers had gone to graze their father's flocks near Shechem, 13and Israel said to Joseph, "As you know, your brothers are grazing the flocks near Shechem. Come, I am going to send you to them."

"Very well," he replied.

14So he said to him, "Go and see if all is well with your brothers and with the flocks, and bring word back to me." Then he sent him off from the Valley of Hebron.

When Joseph arrived at Shechem, 15a man found him wandering around in the fields and asked him, "What are you looking for?"

16He replied, "I'm looking for my brothers. Can you tell me where they are grazing their flocks?"

17"They have moved on from here," the man answered. "I heard them say, 'Let's go to Dothan.' "

So Joseph went after his brothers and found them near Dothan. 18But they saw him in the distance, and before he reached them, they plotted to kill him.

19"Here comes that dreamer!" they said to each other. 20"Come now, let's kill him and throw him into one of these cisterns and say that a ferocious animal devoured him. Then we'll see what comes of his dreams."

21When Reuben heard this, he tried to rescue him from their hands. "Let's not take his life," he said. 22"Don't shed any blood. Throw him into this cistern here in the wilderness, but don't lay a hand on him." Reuben said this to rescue him from them and take him back to his father.

23So when Joseph came to his brothers, they stripped him of his robe — the ornate robe he was wearing — 24and they took him and threw him into the cistern. The cistern was empty; there was no water in it.

25As they sat down to eat their meal, they looked up and saw a caravan of Ishmaelites coming from Gilead. Their camels were loaded with spices, balm and myrrh, and they were on their way to take them down to Egypt.

26Judah said to his brothers, "What will we gain if we kill our brother and cover up his blood? 27Come, let's sell him to the Ishmaelites and not lay our hands on him; after all, he is our brother, our own flesh and blood." His brothers agreed.

28So when the Midianite merchants came by, his brothers pulled Joseph up out of the cistern and sold him for twenty shekels[b] of silver to the Ishmaelites, who took him to Egypt.

---

[a] *3* The meaning of the Hebrew for this word is uncertain; also in verses 23 and 32.
[b] *28* That is, about 8 ounces or about 230 grams

29When Reuben returned to the cistern and saw that Joseph was not there, he tore his clothes. 30He went back to his brothers and said, "The boy isn't there! Where can I turn now?"

31Then they got Joseph's robe, slaughtered a goat and dipped the robe in the blood. 32They took the ornate robe back to their father and said, "We found this. Examine it to see whether it is your son's robe."

33He recognized it and said, "It is my son's robe! Some ferocious animal has devoured him. Joseph has surely been torn to pieces."

34Then Jacob tore his clothes, put on sackcloth and mourned for his son many days. 35All his sons and daughters came to comfort him, but he refused to be comforted. "No," he said, "I will continue to mourn until I join my son in the grave." So his father wept for him.

36Meanwhile, the Midianites[a] sold Joseph in Egypt to Potiphar, one of Pharaoh's officials, the captain of the guard.

Judah and Tamar

38 At that time, Judah left his brothers and went down to stay with a man of Adullam named Hirah. 2There Judah met the daughter of a Canaanite man named Shua. He married her and made love to her; 3she became pregnant and gave birth to a son, who was named Er. 4She conceived again and gave birth to a son and named him Onan. 5She gave birth to still another son and named him Shelah. It was at Kezib that she gave birth to him.

6Judah got a wife for Er, his firstborn, and her name was Tamar. 7But Er, Judah's firstborn, was wicked in the LORD's sight; so the LORD put him to death.

8Then Judah said to Onan, "Sleep with your brother's wife and fulfill your duty to her as a brother-in-law to raise up offspring for your brother." 9But Onan knew that the child would not be his; so whenever he slept with his brother's wife, he spilled his semen on the ground to keep from providing offspring for his brother. 10What he did was wicked in the LORD's sight; so the LORD put him to death also.

11Judah then said to his daughter-in-law Tamar, "Live as a widow in your father's household until my son Shelah grows up." For he thought, "He may die too, just like his brothers." So Tamar went to live in her father's household.

12After a long time Judah's wife, the daughter of Shua, died. When Judah had recovered from his grief, he went up to Timnah, to the men who were shearing his sheep, and his friend Hirah the Adullamite went with him.

13When Tamar was told, "Your father-in-law is on his way to Timnah to shear his sheep," 14she took off her widow's clothes, covered herself with a veil to disguise herself, and then sat down at the entrance to Enaim, which is on the road to Timnah. For she saw that, though Shelah had now grown up, she had not been given to him as his wife.

15When Judah saw her, he thought she was a prostitute, for she had covered her face. 16Not realizing that she was his daughter-in-law, he went over to her by the roadside and said, "Come now, let me sleep with you."

"And what will you give me to sleep with you?" she asked.

17"I'll send you a young goat from my flock," he said.

"Will you give me something as a pledge until you send it?" she asked.

18He said, "What pledge should I give you?"

"Your seal and its cord, and the staff in your hand," she answered. So he gave them to her and slept with her, and she became pregnant by him. 19After she left, she took off her veil and put on her widow's clothes again.

20Meanwhile Judah sent the young goat by his friend the Adullamite in order to get his pledge back from the woman, but he did not find her. 21He asked the men who lived there, "Where is the shrine prostitute who was beside the road at Enaim?"

---

[a] *36* Samaritan Pentateuch, Septuagint, Vulgate and Syriac (see also verse 28); Masoretic Text *Medanites*

"There hasn't been any shrine prostitute here," they said.
[22]So he went back to Judah and said, "I didn't find her. Besides, the men who
lived there said, 'There hasn't been any shrine prostitute here.' "
[23]Then Judah said, "Let her keep what she has, or we will become a laughingstock. After all, I did send her this young goat, but you didn't find her."
[24]About three months later Judah was told, "Your daughter-in-law Tamar is
guilty of prostitution, and as a result she is now pregnant."
Judah said, "Bring her out and have her burned to death!"
[25]As she was being brought out, she sent a message to her father-in-law. "I am
pregnant by the man who owns these," she said. And she added, "See if you recognize whose seal and cord and staff these are."
[26]Judah recognized them and said, "She is more righteous than I, since I
wouldn't give her to my son Shelah." And he did not sleep with her again.
[27]When the time came for her to give birth, there were twin boys in her womb.
[28]As she was giving birth, one of them put out his hand; so the midwife took a
scarlet thread and tied it on his wrist and said, "This one came out first." [29]But
when he drew back his hand, his brother came out, and she said, "So this is how
you have broken out!" And he was named Perez.[a] [30]Then his brother, who had
the scarlet thread on his wrist, came out. And he was named Zerah.[b]

Joseph and Potiphar's Wife

39 Now Joseph had been taken down to Egypt. Potiphar, an Egyptian who
was one of Pharaoh's officials, the captain of the guard, bought him from
the Ishmaelites who had taken him there.
[2]The LORD was with Joseph so that he prospered, and he lived in the house of
his Egyptian master. [3]When his master saw that the LORD was with him and that
the LORD gave him success in everything he did, [4]Joseph found favor in his eyes
and became his attendant. Potiphar put him in charge of his household, and he
entrusted to his care everything he owned. [5]From the time he put him in charge
of his household and of all that he owned, the LORD blessed the household of
the Egyptian because of Joseph. The blessing of the LORD was on everything
Potiphar had, both in the house and in the field. [6]So Potiphar left everything
he had in Joseph's care; with Joseph in charge, he did not concern himself with
anything except the food he ate.
Now Joseph was well-built and handsome, [7]and after a while his master's wife
took notice of Joseph and said, "Come to bed with me!"
[8]But he refused. "With me in charge," he told her, "my master does not concern himself with anything in the house; everything he owns he has entrusted
to my care. [9]No one is greater in this house than I am. My master has withheld
nothing from me except you, because you are his wife. How then could I do such
a wicked thing and sin against God?" [10]And though she spoke to Joseph day after
day, he refused to go to bed with her or even be with her.
[11]One day he went into the house to attend to his duties, and none of the
household servants was inside. [12]She caught him by his cloak and said, "Come
to bed with me!" But he left his cloak in her hand and ran out of the house.
[13]When she saw that he had left his cloak in her hand and had run out of the
house, [14]she called her household servants. "Look," she said to them, "this Hebrew has been brought to us to make sport of us! He came in here to sleep with
me, but I screamed. [15]When he heard me scream for help, he left his cloak beside
me and ran out of the house."
[16]She kept his cloak beside her until his master came home. [17]Then she told
him this story: "That Hebrew slave you brought us came to me to make sport of
me. [18]But as soon as I screamed for help, he left his cloak beside me and ran out
of the house."
[19]When his master heard the story his wife told him, saying, "This is how your

[a] 29 *Perez* means *breaking out.* [b] 30 *Zerah* can mean *scarlet* or *brightness.*

GENESIS 38:30

AN UNLIKELY FAMILY

Perez and Zerah were unexpected recipients of the blessing of God. These twin children of the licentious relationship between Judah and his daughter-in-law Tamar established families within the house of Judah (1Ch 2:3 – 9). Though Tamar displayed suspicious behavior and was probably a Canaanite, she was grafted into the people of God and became a member of the family of promise (Ru 4:12,18 – 22). Her name is mentioned again in a most unlikely place — the lineage of Jesus Christ, the Messiah (Mt 1:3).

While recounting the Jewish origins of the Messiah, Matthew included the names of scores of unlikely people who became the recipients of God's grace and were a part of ushering in the birth of the promised Son of God. God's family is defined, not by ethnicity or morality, but by the grace of God. He uses all sorts of people, even those with questionable pasts, to demonstrate the stunning riches of his grace in kindness to all people in Christ Jesus (Eph 2:7).

GENESIS 39:1 – 23

TRUST AND TEMPTATION

Joseph's resistance to temptation is a testimony to his trust in God's work on his behalf. Not only would giving in to the temptation have catered to his masculine desires, but also it would have surely secured the favor of a powerful woman. Still Joseph rejected the advances of Potiphar's wife and entrusted himself to the care of God.

(continued on next page)

(Trust and Temptation, continued)

In a similar way, at the beginning of his earthly ministry, Jesus faced temptation by Satan himself. Had he capitulated to Satan's ploy, he could have attained glory and power in a moment. However, knowing this was not the plan of God, he rejected Satan and entrusted himself to God's grand purposes (Mt 4:1 – 11). Like Joseph, Jesus rested in the faithfulness of God. Jesus sets an example for Christians seeking victory over temptation. God's people are to entrust themselves to God, knowing that "In all things God works for the good of those who love him, who have been called according to his purpose" (Ro 8:28).

slave treated me," he burned with anger. 20Joseph's master took him and put him in prison, the place where the king's prisoners were confined.

But while Joseph was there in the prison, 21the LORD was with him; he showed him kindness and granted him favor in the eyes of the prison warden. 22So the warden put Joseph in charge of all those held in the prison, and he was made responsible for all that was done there. 23The warden paid no attention to anything under Joseph's care, because the LORD was with Joseph and gave him success in whatever he did.

The Cupbearer and the Baker

40 Some time later, the cupbearer and the baker of the king of Egypt offended their master, the king of Egypt. 2Pharaoh was angry with his two officials, the chief cupbearer and the chief baker, 3and put them in custody in the house of the captain of the guard, in the same prison where Joseph was confined. 4The captain of the guard assigned them to Joseph, and he attended them.

After they had been in custody for some time, 5each of the two men — the cupbearer and the baker of the king of Egypt, who were being held in prison — had a dream the same night, and each dream had a meaning of its own.

6When Joseph came to them the next morning, he saw that they were dejected. 7So he asked Pharaoh's officials who were in custody with him in his master's house, "Why do you look so sad today?"

8"We both had dreams," they answered, "but there is no one to interpret them."

Then Joseph said to them, "Do not interpretations belong to God? Tell me your dreams."

9So the chief cupbearer told Joseph his dream. He said to him, "In my dream I saw a vine in front of me, 10and on the vine were three branches. As soon as it budded, it blossomed, and its clusters ripened into grapes. 11Pharaoh's cup was in my hand, and I took the grapes, squeezed them into Pharaoh's cup and put the cup in his hand."

12"This is what it means," Joseph said to him. "The three branches are three days. 13Within three days Pharaoh will lift up your head and restore you to your position, and you will put Pharaoh's cup in his hand, just as you used to do when you were his cupbearer. 14But when all goes well with you, remember me and show me kindness; mention me to Pharaoh and get me out of this prison. 15I was forcibly carried off from the land of the Hebrews, and even here I have done nothing to deserve being put in a dungeon."

16When the chief baker saw that Joseph had given a favorable interpretation, he said to Joseph, "I too had a dream: On my head were three baskets of bread.[a] 17In the top basket were all kinds of baked goods for Pharaoh, but the birds were eating them out of the basket on my head."

18"This is what it means," Joseph said. "The three baskets are three days. 19Within three days Pharaoh will lift off your head and impale your body on a pole. And the birds will eat away your flesh."

20Now the third day was Pharaoh's birthday, and he gave a feast for all his officials. He lifted up the heads of the chief cupbearer and the chief baker in the presence of his officials: 21He restored the chief cupbearer to his position, so that he once again put the cup into Pharaoh's hand — 22but he impaled the chief baker, just as Joseph had said to them in his interpretation.

23The chief cupbearer, however, did not remember Joseph; he forgot him.

Pharaoh's Dreams

41 When two full years had passed, Pharaoh had a dream: He was standing by the Nile, 2when out of the river there came up seven cows, sleek and fat, and they grazed among the reeds. 3After them, seven other cows, ugly

---

[a] *16* Or *three wicker baskets*

and gaunt, came up out of the Nile and stood beside those on the riverbank.
4And the cows that were ugly and gaunt ate up the seven sleek, fat cows. Then
Pharaoh woke up.
5He fell asleep again and had a second dream: Seven heads of grain, healthy
and good, were growing on a single stalk. 6After them, seven other heads of grain
sprouted — thin and scorched by the east wind. 7The thin heads of grain swallowed up the seven healthy, full heads. Then Pharaoh woke up; it had been a
dream.
8In the morning his mind was troubled, so he sent for all the magicians and
wise men of Egypt. Pharaoh told them his dreams, but no one could interpret
them for him.
9Then the chief cupbearer said to Pharaoh, "Today I am reminded of my
shortcomings. 10Pharaoh was once angry with his servants, and he imprisoned
me and the chief baker in the house of the captain of the guard. 11Each of us had a
dream the same night, and each dream had a meaning of its own. 12Now a young
Hebrew was there with us, a servant of the captain of the guard. We told him our
dreams, and he interpreted them for us, giving each man the interpretation of
his dream. 13And things turned out exactly as he interpreted them to us: I was
restored to my position, and the other man was impaled."
14So Pharaoh sent for Joseph, and he was quickly brought from the dungeon.
When he had shaved and changed his clothes, he came before Pharaoh.
15Pharaoh said to Joseph, "I had a dream, and no one can interpret it. But I
have heard it said of you that when you hear a dream you can interpret it."
16"I cannot do it," Joseph replied to Pharaoh, "but God will give Pharaoh the
answer he desires."
17Then Pharaoh said to Joseph, "In my dream I was standing on the bank of
the Nile, 18when out of the river there came up seven cows, fat and sleek, and they
grazed among the reeds. 19After them, seven other cows came up — scrawny and
very ugly and lean. I had never seen such ugly cows in all the land of Egypt. 20The
lean, ugly cows ate up the seven fat cows that came up first. 21But even after they
ate them, no one could tell that they had done so; they looked just as ugly as before. Then I woke up.
22"In my dream I saw seven heads of grain, full and good, growing on a single stalk. 23After them, seven other heads sprouted — withered and thin and
scorched by the east wind. 24The thin heads of grain swallowed up the seven
good heads. I told this to the magicians, but none of them could explain it to me."
25Then Joseph said to Pharaoh, "The dreams of Pharaoh are one and the
same. God has revealed to Pharaoh what he is about to do. 26The seven good
cows are seven years, and the seven good heads of grain are seven years; it is one
and the same dream. 27The seven lean, ugly cows that came up afterward are
seven years, and so are the seven worthless heads of grain scorched by the east
wind: They are seven years of famine.
28"It is just as I said to Pharaoh: God has shown Pharaoh what he is about to
do. 29Seven years of great abundance are coming throughout the land of Egypt,
30but seven years of famine will follow them. Then all the abundance in Egypt
will be forgotten, and the famine will ravage the land. 31The abundance in the
land will not be remembered, because the famine that follows it will be so severe. 32The reason the dream was given to Pharaoh in two forms is that the matter has been firmly decided by God, and God will do it soon.
33"And now let Pharaoh look for a discerning and wise man and put him in
charge of the land of Egypt. 34Let Pharaoh appoint commissioners over the
land to take a fifth of the harvest of Egypt during the seven years of abundance.
35They should collect all the food of these good years that are coming and store
up the grain under the authority of Pharaoh, to be kept in the cities for food.
36This food should be held in reserve for the country, to be used during the sev-
en years of famine that will come upon Egypt, so that the country may not be
ruined by the famine."

37The plan seemed good to Pharaoh and to all his officials. 38So Pharaoh asked them, "Can we find anyone like this man, one in whom is the spirit of God[a]?"

39Then Pharaoh said to Joseph, "Since God has made all this known to you, there is no one so discerning and wise as you. 40You shall be in charge of my palace, and all my people are to submit to your orders. Only with respect to the throne will I be greater than you."

Joseph in Charge of Egypt

41So Pharaoh said to Joseph, "I hereby put you in charge of the whole land of Egypt." 42Then Pharaoh took his signet ring from his finger and put it on Joseph's finger. He dressed him in robes of fine linen and put a gold chain around his neck. 43He had him ride in a chariot as his second-in-command,[b] and people shouted before him, "Make way[c]!" Thus he put him in charge of the whole land of Egypt.

44Then Pharaoh said to Joseph, "I am Pharaoh, but without your word no one will lift hand or foot in all Egypt." 45Pharaoh gave Joseph the name Zaphenath-Paneah and gave him Asenath daughter of Potiphera, priest of On,[d] to be his wife. And Joseph went throughout the land of Egypt.

46Joseph was thirty years old when he entered the service of Pharaoh king of Egypt. And Joseph went out from Pharaoh's presence and traveled throughout Egypt. 47During the seven years of abundance the land produced plentifully. 48Joseph collected all the food produced in those seven years of abundance in Egypt and stored it in the cities. In each city he put the food grown in the fields surrounding it. 49Joseph stored up huge quantities of grain, like the sand of the sea; it was so much that he stopped keeping records because it was beyond measure.

50Before the years of famine came, two sons were born to Joseph by Asenath daughter of Potiphera, priest of On. 51Joseph named his firstborn Manasseh[e] and said, "It is because God has made me forget all my trouble and all my father's household." 52The second son he named Ephraim[f] and said, "It is because God has made me fruitful in the land of my suffering."

53The seven years of abundance in Egypt came to an end, 54and the seven years of famine began, just as Joseph had said. There was famine in all the other lands, but in the whole land of Egypt there was food. 55When all Egypt began to feel the famine, the people cried to Pharaoh for food. Then Pharaoh told all the Egyptians, "Go to Joseph and do what he tells you."

56When the famine had spread over the whole country, Joseph opened all the storehouses and sold grain to the Egyptians, for the famine was severe throughout Egypt. 57And all the world came to Egypt to buy grain from Joseph, because the famine was severe everywhere.

Joseph's Brothers Go to Egypt

42 When Jacob learned that there was grain in Egypt, he said to his sons, "Why do you just keep looking at each other?" 2He continued, "I have heard that there is grain in Egypt. Go down there and buy some for us, so that we may live and not die."

3Then ten of Joseph's brothers went down to buy grain from Egypt. 4But Jacob did not send Benjamin, Joseph's brother, with the others, because he was afraid that harm might come to him. 5So Israel's sons were among those who went to buy grain, for there was famine in the land of Canaan also.

6Now Joseph was the governor of the land, the person who sold grain to all its people. So when Joseph's brothers arrived, they bowed down to him with their faces to the ground. 7As soon as Joseph saw his brothers, he recognized them,

---

[a] 38 Or *of the gods* [b] 43 Or *in the chariot of his second-in-command*; or *in his second chariot* [c] 43 Or *Bow down* [d] 45 That is, Heliopolis; also in verse 50 [e] 51 *Manasseh* sounds like and may be derived from the Hebrew for *forget.* [f] 52 *Ephraim* sounds like the Hebrew for *twice fruitful.*

but he pretended to be a stranger and spoke harshly to them. "Where do you come from?" he asked.

"From the land of Canaan," they replied, "to buy food."

8Although Joseph recognized his brothers, they did not recognize him. 9Then he remembered his dreams about them and said to them, "You are spies! You have come to see where our land is unprotected."

10"No, my lord," they answered. "Your servants have come to buy food. 11We are all the sons of one man. Your servants are honest men, not spies."

12"No!" he said to them. "You have come to see where our land is unprotected."

13But they replied, "Your servants were twelve brothers, the sons of one man, who lives in the land of Canaan. The youngest is now with our father, and one is no more."

14Joseph said to them, "It is just as I told you: You are spies! 15And this is how you will be tested: As surely as Pharaoh lives, you will not leave this place unless your youngest brother comes here. 16Send one of your number to get your brother; the rest of you will be kept in prison, so that your words may be tested to see if you are telling the truth. If you are not, then as surely as Pharaoh lives, you are spies!" 17And he put them all in custody for three days.

18On the third day, Joseph said to them, "Do this and you will live, for I fear God: 19If you are honest men, let one of your brothers stay here in prison, while the rest of you go and take grain back for your starving households. 20But you must bring your youngest brother to me, so that your words may be verified and that you may not die." This they proceeded to do.

21They said to one another, "Surely we are being punished because of our brother. We saw how distressed he was when he pleaded with us for his life, but we would not listen; that's why this distress has come on us."

22Reuben replied, "Didn't I tell you not to sin against the boy? But you wouldn't listen! Now we must give an accounting for his blood." 23They did not realize that Joseph could understand them, since he was using an interpreter.

24He turned away from them and began to weep, but then came back and spoke to them again. He had Simeon taken from them and bound before their eyes.

25Joseph gave orders to fill their bags with grain, to put each man's silver back in his sack, and to give them provisions for their journey. After this was done for them, 26they loaded their grain on their donkeys and left.

27At the place where they stopped for the night one of them opened his sack to get feed for his donkey, and he saw his silver in the mouth of his sack. 28"My silver has been returned," he said to his brothers. "Here it is in my sack."

Their hearts sank and they turned to each other trembling and said, "What is this that God has done to us?"

29When they came to their father Jacob in the land of Canaan, they told him all that had happened to them. They said, 30"The man who is lord over the land spoke harshly to us and treated us as though we were spying on the land. 31But we said to him, 'We are honest men; we are not spies. 32We were twelve brothers, sons of one father. One is no more, and the youngest is now with our father in Canaan.'

33"Then the man who is lord over the land said to us, 'This is how I will know whether you are honest men: Leave one of your brothers here with me, and take food for your starving households and go. 34But bring your youngest brother to me so I will know that you are not spies but honest men. Then I will give your brother back to you, and you can trade[a] in the land.'"

35As they were emptying their sacks, there in each man's sack was his pouch of silver! When they and their father saw the money pouches, they were frightened. 36Their father Jacob said to them, "You have deprived me of my children. Joseph is no more and Simeon is no more, and now you want to take Benjamin. Everything is against me!"

---

[a] 34 Or *move about freely*

[37]Then Reuben said to his father, "You may put both of my sons to death if I do
not bring him back to you. Entrust him to my care, and I will bring him back."
[38]But Jacob said, "My son will not go down there with you; his brother is dead
and he is the only one left. If harm comes to him on the journey you are taking,
you will bring my gray head down to the grave in sorrow."

The Second Journey to Egypt

43 Now the famine was still severe in the land. [2]So when they had eaten all
the grain they had brought from Egypt, their father said to them, "Go back
and buy us a little more food."
[3]But Judah said to him, "The man warned us solemnly, 'You will not see my
face again unless your brother is with you.' [4]If you will send our brother along
with us, we will go down and buy food for you. [5]But if you will not send him, we
will not go down, because the man said to us, 'You will not see my face again
unless your brother is with you.'"
[6]Israel asked, "Why did you bring this trouble on me by telling the man you
had another brother?"
[7]They replied, "The man questioned us closely about ourselves and our family. 'Is your father still living?' he asked us. 'Do you have another brother?' We
simply answered his questions. How were we to know he would say, 'Bring your
brother down here'?"
[8]Then Judah said to Israel his father, "Send the boy along with me and we will
go at once, so that we and you and our children may live and not die. [9]I myself
will guarantee his safety; you can hold me personally responsible for him. If I
do not bring him back to you and set him here before you, I will bear the blame
before you all my life. [10]As it is, if we had not delayed, we could have gone and
returned twice."
[11]Then their father Israel said to them, "If it must be, then do this: Put some
of the best products of the land in your bags and take them down to the man as
a gift — a little balm and a little honey, some spices and myrrh, some pistachio
nuts and almonds. [12]Take double the amount of silver with you, for you must return the silver that was put back into the mouths of your sacks. Perhaps it was a
mistake. [13]Take your brother also and go back to the man at once. [14]And may God
Almighty[a] grant you mercy before the man so that he will let your other brother
and Benjamin come back with you. As for me, if I am bereaved, I am bereaved."
[15]So the men took the gifts and double the amount of silver, and Benjamin
also. They hurried down to Egypt and presented themselves to Joseph. [16]When
Joseph saw Benjamin with them, he said to the steward of his house, "Take these
men to my house, slaughter an animal and prepare a meal; they are to eat with
me at noon."
[17]The man did as Joseph told him and took the men to Joseph's house. [18]Now
the men were frightened when they were taken to his house. They thought, "We
were brought here because of the silver that was put back into our sacks the first
time. He wants to attack us and overpower us and seize us as slaves and take
our donkeys."
[19]So they went up to Joseph's steward and spoke to him at the entrance to the
house. [20]"We beg your pardon, our lord," they said, "we came down here the first
time to buy food. [21]But at the place where we stopped for the night we opened
our sacks and each of us found his silver — the exact weight — in the mouth of his
sack. So we have brought it back with us. [22]We have also brought additional silver
with us to buy food. We don't know who put our silver in our sacks."
[23]"It's all right," he said. "Don't be afraid. Your God, the God of your father,
has given you treasure in your sacks; I received your silver." Then he brought
Simeon out to them.
[24]The steward took the men into Joseph's house, gave them water to wash

[a] *14* Hebrew *El-Shaddai*

GENESIS 43:8 – 9

BECOMING A SLAVE SO A SLAVE COULD GO FREE

Judah makes a risky and bold move in this passage in complete contrast to his cowardly and unrighteous behavior earlier (Ge 37:26 – 27; 38:11 – 26). When Judah was forced to act on this pledge (44:33 – 34), he remained faithful to his promise, offering himself as a slave so that his brother could avoid a similar fate (44:17). His substitutionary act would have allowed Benjamin to return to his father as a free man.

Centuries later, one of Judah's descendants would offer himself in the place of sinners so that they might be freed from their penalty and slavery. Judah's pledge of his life as the substitute for his younger brother is a striking parallel to Jesus' substitutionary sacrifice of his life for his adopted brothers and sisters — the church (Ro 8:17,29). Unlike Judah, however (Ge 37:26 – 27), Jesus did not contribute to the slavery of the church. Instead, Jesus graciously pledged himself as a substitute so that he might bring home his redeemed ones, right into the heavenly Father's very presence.

their feet and provided fodder for their donkeys. [25]They prepared their gifts for
Joseph's arrival at noon, because they had heard that they were to eat there.
[26]When Joseph came home, they presented to him the gifts they had brought
into the house, and they bowed down before him to the ground. [27]He asked them
how they were, and then he said, "How is your aged father you told me about?
Is he still living?"
[28]They replied, "Your servant our father is still alive and well." And they
bowed down, prostrating themselves before him.
[29]As he looked about and saw his brother Benjamin, his own mother's son, he
asked, "Is this your youngest brother, the one you told me about?" And he said,
"God be gracious to you, my son." [30]Deeply moved at the sight of his brother, Joseph hurried out and looked for a place to weep. He went into his private room
and wept there.
[31]After he had washed his face, he came out and, controlling himself, said,
"Serve the food."
[32]They served him by himself, the brothers by themselves, and the Egyptians
who ate with him by themselves, because Egyptians could not eat with Hebrews,
for that is detestable to Egyptians. [33]The men had been seated before him in the
order of their ages, from the firstborn to the youngest; and they looked at each
other in astonishment. [34]When portions were served to them from Joseph's table, Benjamin's portion was five times as much as anyone else's. So they feasted
and drank freely with him.

A Silver Cup in a Sack

44 Now Joseph gave these instructions to the steward of his house: "Fill the
men's sacks with as much food as they can carry, and put each man's silver in the mouth of his sack. [2]Then put my cup, the silver one, in the mouth of
the youngest one's sack, along with the silver for his grain." And he did as Joseph
said.
[3]As morning dawned, the men were sent on their way with their donkeys.
[4]They had not gone far from the city when Joseph said to his steward, "Go after
those men at once, and when you catch up with them, say to them, 'Why have
you repaid good with evil? [5]Isn't this the cup my master drinks from and also
uses for divination? This is a wicked thing you have done.'"
[6]When he caught up with them, he repeated these words to them. [7]But they
said to him, "Why does my lord say such things? Far be it from your servants to
do anything like that! [8]We even brought back to you from the land of Canaan the
silver we found inside the mouths of our sacks. So why would we steal silver or
gold from your master's house? [9]If any of your servants is found to have it, he will
die; and the rest of us will become my lord's slaves."
[10]"Very well, then," he said, "let it be as you say. Whoever is found to have it
will become my slave; the rest of you will be free from blame."
[11]Each of them quickly lowered his sack to the ground and opened it. [12]Then
the steward proceeded to search, beginning with the oldest and ending with the
youngest. And the cup was found in Benjamin's sack. [13]At this, they tore their
clothes. Then they all loaded their donkeys and returned to the city.
[14]Joseph was still in the house when Judah and his brothers came in, and they
threw themselves to the ground before him. [15]Joseph said to them, "What is this
you have done? Don't you know that a man like me can find things out by divination?"
[16]"What can we say to my lord?" Judah replied. "What can we say? How can
we prove our innocence? God has uncovered your servants' guilt. We are now
my lord's slaves—we ourselves and the one who was found to have the cup."
[17]But Joseph said, "Far be it from me to do such a thing! Only the man who
was found to have the cup will become my slave. The rest of you, go back to your
father in peace."
[18]Then Judah went up to him and said: "Pardon your servant, my lord, let

me speak a word to my lord. Do not be angry with your servant, though you are equal to Pharaoh himself. [19]My lord asked his servants, 'Do you have a father or a brother?' [20]And we answered, 'We have an aged father, and there is a young son born to him in his old age. His brother is dead, and he is the only one of his mother's sons left, and his father loves him.'

[21]"Then you said to your servants, 'Bring him down to me so I can see him for myself.' [22]And we said to my lord, 'The boy cannot leave his father; if he leaves him, his father will die.' [23]But you told your servants, 'Unless your youngest brother comes down with you, you will not see my face again.' [24]When we went back to your servant my father, we told him what my lord had said.

[25]"Then our father said, 'Go back and buy a little more food.' [26]But we said, 'We cannot go down. Only if our youngest brother is with us will we go. We cannot see the man's face unless our youngest brother is with us.'

[27]"Your servant my father said to us, 'You know that my wife bore me two sons. [28]One of them went away from me, and I said, "He has surely been torn to pieces." And I have not seen him since. [29]If you take this one from me too and harm comes to him, you will bring my gray head down to the grave in misery.'

[30]"So now, if the boy is not with us when I go back to your servant my father, and if my father, whose life is closely bound up with the boy's life, [31]sees that the boy isn't there, he will die. Your servants will bring the gray head of our father down to the grave in sorrow. [32]Your servant guaranteed the boy's safety to my father. I said, 'If I do not bring him back to you, I will bear the blame before you, my father, all my life!'

[33]"Now then, please let your servant remain here as my lord's slave in place of the boy, and let the boy return with his brothers. [34]How can I go back to my father if the boy is not with me? No! Do not let me see the misery that would come on my father."

Joseph Makes Himself Known

45 Then Joseph could no longer control himself before all his attendants, and he cried out, "Have everyone leave my presence!" So there was no one with Joseph when he made himself known to his brothers. [2]And he wept so loudly that the Egyptians heard him, and Pharaoh's household heard about it.

[3]Joseph said to his brothers, "I am Joseph! Is my father still living?" But his brothers were not able to answer him, because they were terrified at his presence.

[4]Then Joseph said to his brothers, "Come close to me." When they had done so, he said, "I am your brother Joseph, the one you sold into Egypt! [5]And now, do not be distressed and do not be angry with yourselves for selling me here, because it was to save lives that God sent me ahead of you. [6]For two years now there has been famine in the land, and for the next five years there will be no plowing and reaping. [7]But God sent me ahead of you to preserve for you a remnant on earth and to save your lives by a great deliverance.[a]

[8]"So then, it was not you who sent me here, but God. He made me father to Pharaoh, lord of his entire household and ruler of all Egypt. [9]Now hurry back to my father and say to him, 'This is what your son Joseph says: God has made me lord of all Egypt. Come down to me; don't delay. [10]You shall live in the region of Goshen and be near me—you, your children and grandchildren, your flocks and herds, and all you have. [11]I will provide for you there, because five years of famine are still to come. Otherwise you and your household and all who belong to you will become destitute.'

[12]"You can see for yourselves, and so can my brother Benjamin, that it is really I who am speaking to you. [13]Tell my father about all the honor accorded me in Egypt and about everything you have seen. And bring my father down here quickly."

GENESIS 45:4–7

AN APPOINTED TIME

Joseph beautifully summed up his experience for his brothers, declaring the providence of God in the face of their evil actions. Joseph stated his confidence in the timing of God, the love of God and the grace of God. God's timing put Joseph in the right position at the right time to save the lives of his family. The providential care of God was still at work behind all the chaos—providing for his chosen ones in the coming drought. And God's grace gave hope and forgiveness in spite of the hurt and sin that Joseph had experienced through the ordeal.

Similarly, Jesus was sent by the Father at the appointed time (Gal 4:4–5). God precisely ordained the time of Christ's coming so that the events would properly unfold, resulting in the salvation of many lives (Ro 5:10). His love was the grand motive for his coming (Jn 3:16), and his grace even offered hope for those who had put him to death (Lk 23:34; Ac 2:22–24,36–38).

---

[a] 7 Or *save you as a great band of survivors*

GENESIS 45:1 – 28

A DWELLING PLACE FOREVER

While Joseph did not know it, his work in Egypt was preparing a place for a provision for his family. God had seen fit to bring Joseph to Egypt, bestowing wisdom upon him, and positioning him to prepare the nation for the impending famine. Joseph gave himself to the work of developing a strategy, building facilities and preparing the people to store massive amounts of grain. Though they did not recognize Joseph, his hungry brothers asked for his gracious provision of food. Joseph revealed his identity to his brothers who reported the stunning news to their aging father. Joseph's work through his years in Egypt had prepared a blessing for those in his family.

Jesus also indicates that he is preparing a place of blessing for his people. Like Joseph, the path to this position is unexpected. He would suffer and die on a Roman cross, be raised to life by the power of God and ascend to the right hand of the Father. There he works to prepare a place of blessing for the people of God. God pictures the heavenly dwelling like a house with many rooms (Jn 14:2 – 3). He will work to prepare this place for his people between the resurrection and the coming day when God will make all things new.

It is difficult to fathom the splendor of this dwelling place. Creator God made all things that exist in the span of six days. The vast mountain ranges, breathtaking beaches and sprawling forests demonstrate the handiwork of God at the dawn of creation. Now, thousands of years later, God is working to prepare a new dwelling in which his people will live forever. Quoting the prophet Isaiah, Paul exclaimed that no eye has seen, no ear has heard, and no mind has conceived what God has prepared for his people (1Co 2:9).

The biblical images of heaven seem to make people grapple for words to describe the glory of this place. The heavenly dwelling, free from the implications of sin, is described as containing streets made of gold and seas as beautiful as crystal. There, God's people will be given the bountiful provision of God's blessing. Free from sin, they will be able to worship God by enjoying fellowship with God, loving one another, giving of themselves in meaningful work and feasting on the storehouse of God's good gifts that he has prepared for them to enjoy.

[14]Then he threw his arms around his brother Benjamin and wept, and Benjamin embraced him, weeping. [15]And he kissed all his brothers and wept over them. Afterward his brothers talked with him.

[16]When the news reached Pharaoh's palace that Joseph's brothers had come, Pharaoh and all his officials were pleased. [17]Pharaoh said to Joseph, "Tell your brothers, 'Do this: Load your animals and return to the land of Canaan, [18]and bring your father and your families back to me. I will give you the best of the land of Egypt and you can enjoy the fat of the land.'

[19]"You are also directed to tell them, 'Do this: Take some carts from Egypt for your children and your wives, and get your father and come. [20]Never mind about your belongings, because the best of all Egypt will be yours.'"

[21]So the sons of Israel did this. Joseph gave them carts, as Pharaoh had commanded, and he also gave them provisions for their journey. [22]To each of them he gave new clothing, but to Benjamin he gave three hundred shekels[a] of silver and five sets of clothes. [23]And this is what he sent to his father: ten donkeys loaded with the best things of Egypt, and ten female donkeys loaded with grain and bread and other provisions for his journey. [24]Then he sent his brothers away, and as they were leaving he said to them, "Don't quarrel on the way!"

[25]So they went up out of Egypt and came to their father Jacob in the land of Canaan. [26]They told him, "Joseph is still alive! In fact, he is ruler of all Egypt." Jacob was stunned; he did not believe them. [27]But when they told him everything Joseph had said to them, and when he saw the carts Joseph had sent to carry him back, the spirit of their father Jacob revived. [28]And Israel said, "I'm convinced! My son Joseph is still alive. I will go and see him before I die."

Jacob Goes to Egypt

46 So Israel set out with all that was his, and when he reached Beersheba, he offered sacrifices to the God of his father Isaac.

[2]And God spoke to Israel in a vision at night and said, "Jacob! Jacob!"

"Here I am," he replied.

[3]"I am God, the God of your father," he said. "Do not be afraid to go down to Egypt, for I will make you into a great nation there. [4]I will go down to Egypt with you, and I will surely bring you back again. And Joseph's own hand will close your eyes."

[5]Then Jacob left Beersheba, and Israel's sons took their father Jacob and their children and their wives in the carts that Pharaoh had sent to transport him. [6]So Jacob and all his offspring went to Egypt, taking with them their livestock and the possessions they had acquired in Canaan. [7]Jacob brought with him to Egypt his sons and grandsons and his daughters and granddaughters — all his offspring.

[8]These are the names of the sons of Israel (Jacob and his descendants) who went to Egypt:

Reuben the firstborn of Jacob.

[9]The sons of Reuben:
  Hanok, Pallu, Hezron and Karmi.

[10]The sons of Simeon:
  Jemuel, Jamin, Ohad, Jakin, Zohar and Shaul the son of a Canaanite woman.

[11]The sons of Levi:
  Gershon, Kohath and Merari.

[12]The sons of Judah:
  Er, Onan, Shelah, Perez and Zerah (but Er and Onan had died in the land of Canaan).
  The sons of Perez:
    Hezron and Hamul.

---

[a] *22* That is, about 7 1/2 pounds or about 3.5 kilograms

13 The sons of Issachar:
Tola, Puah,[a] Jashub[b] and Shimron.
14 The sons of Zebulun:
Sered, Elon and Jahleel.
15 These were the sons Leah bore to Jacob in Paddan Aram,[c] besides his daughter Dinah. These sons and daughters of his were thirty-three in all.

16 The sons of Gad:
Zephon,[d] Haggi, Shuni, Ezbon, Eri, Arodi and Areli.
17 The sons of Asher:
Imnah, Ishvah, Ishvi and Beriah.
Their sister was Serah.
The sons of Beriah:
Heber and Malkiel.
18 These were the children born to Jacob by Zilpah, whom Laban had given to
his daughter Leah — sixteen in all.

19 The sons of Jacob's wife Rachel:
Joseph and Benjamin. 20 In Egypt, Manasseh and Ephraim were born to
Joseph by Asenath daughter of Potiphera, priest of On.[e]
21 The sons of Benjamin:
Bela, Beker, Ashbel, Gera, Naaman, Ehi, Rosh, Muppim, Huppim and Ard.
22 These were the sons of Rachel who were born to Jacob — fourteen in all.

23 The son of Dan:
Hushim.
24 The sons of Naphtali:
Jahziel, Guni, Jezer and Shillem.
25 These were the sons born to Jacob by Bilhah, whom Laban had given to his
daughter Rachel — seven in all.

26 All those who went to Egypt with Jacob — those who were his direct descendants, not counting his sons' wives — numbered sixty-six persons. 27 With the
two sons[f] who had been born to Joseph in Egypt, the members of Jacob's family,
which went to Egypt, were seventy[g] in all.

28 Now Jacob sent Judah ahead of him to Joseph to get directions to Goshen.
When they arrived in the region of Goshen, 29 Joseph had his chariot made ready
and went to Goshen to meet his father Israel. As soon as Joseph appeared before
him, he threw his arms around his father[h] and wept for a long time.
30 Israel said to Joseph, "Now I am ready to die, since I have seen for myself
that you are still alive."
31 Then Joseph said to his brothers and to his father's household, "I will go up
and speak to Pharaoh and will say to him, 'My brothers and my father's household, who were living in the land of Canaan, have come to me. 32 The men are
shepherds; they tend livestock, and they have brought along their flocks and
herds and everything they own.' 33 When Pharaoh calls you in and asks, 'What
is your occupation?' 34 you should answer, 'Your servants have tended livestock
from our boyhood on, just as our fathers did.' Then you will be allowed to settle
in the region of Goshen, for all shepherds are detestable to the Egyptians."

47 Joseph went and told Pharaoh, "My father and brothers, with their flocks
and herds and everything they own, have come from the land of Canaan
and are now in Goshen." 2 He chose five of his brothers and presented them before Pharaoh.

---

[a] *13* Samaritan Pentateuch and Syriac (see also 1 Chron. 7:1); Masoretic Text *Puvah*
[b] *13* Samaritan Pentateuch and some Septuagint manuscripts (see also Num. 26:24 and 1 Chron. 7:1); Masoretic Text *Iob*
[c] *15* That is, Northwest Mesopotamia
[d] *16* Samaritan Pentateuch and Septuagint (see also Num. 26:15); Masoretic Text *Ziphion*
[e] *20* That is, Heliopolis
[f] *27* Hebrew; Septuagint *the nine children*
[g] *27* Hebrew (see also Exodus 1:5 and note); Septuagint (see also Acts 7:14) *seventy-five*
[h] *29* Hebrew *around him*

3 Pharaoh asked the brothers, "What is your occupation?"

"Your servants are shepherds," they replied to Pharaoh, "just as our fathers were." 4 They also said to him, "We have come to live here for a while, because the famine is severe in Canaan and your servants' flocks have no pasture. So now, please let your servants settle in Goshen."

5 Pharaoh said to Joseph, "Your father and your brothers have come to you, 6 and the land of Egypt is before you; settle your father and your brothers in the best part of the land. Let them live in Goshen. And if you know of any among them with special ability, put them in charge of my own livestock."

7 Then Joseph brought his father Jacob in and presented him before Pharaoh. After Jacob blessed[a] Pharaoh, 8 Pharaoh asked him, "How old are you?"

9 And Jacob said to Pharaoh, "The years of my pilgrimage are a hundred and thirty. My years have been few and difficult, and they do not equal the years of the pilgrimage of my fathers." 10 Then Jacob blessed[b] Pharaoh and went out from his presence.

11 So Joseph settled his father and his brothers in Egypt and gave them property in the best part of the land, the district of Rameses, as Pharaoh directed. 12 Joseph also provided his father and his brothers and all his father's household with food, according to the number of their children.

Joseph and the Famine

13 There was no food, however, in the whole region because the famine was severe; both Egypt and Canaan wasted away because of the famine. 14 Joseph collected all the money that was to be found in Egypt and Canaan in payment for the grain they were buying, and he brought it to Pharaoh's palace. 15 When the money of the people of Egypt and Canaan was gone, all Egypt came to Joseph and said, "Give us food. Why should we die before your eyes? Our money is all gone."

16 "Then bring your livestock," said Joseph. "I will sell you food in exchange for your livestock, since your money is gone." 17 So they brought their livestock to Joseph, and he gave them food in exchange for their horses, their sheep and goats, their cattle and donkeys. And he brought them through that year with food in exchange for all their livestock.

18 When that year was over, they came to him the following year and said, "We cannot hide from our lord the fact that since our money is gone and our livestock belongs to you, there is nothing left for our lord except our bodies and our land. 19 Why should we perish before your eyes—we and our land as well? Buy us and our land in exchange for food, and we with our land will be in bondage to Pharaoh. Give us seed so that we may live and not die, and that the land may not become desolate."

20 So Joseph bought all the land in Egypt for Pharaoh. The Egyptians, one and all, sold their fields, because the famine was too severe for them. The land became Pharaoh's, 21 and Joseph reduced the people to servitude,[c] from one end of Egypt to the other. 22 However, he did not buy the land of the priests, because they received a regular allotment from Pharaoh and had food enough from the allotment Pharaoh gave them. That is why they did not sell their land.

23 Joseph said to the people, "Now that I have bought you and your land today for Pharaoh, here is seed for you so you can plant the ground. 24 But when the crop comes in, give a fifth of it to Pharaoh. The other four-fifths you may keep as seed for the fields and as food for yourselves and your households and your children."

25 "You have saved our lives," they said. "May we find favor in the eyes of our lord; we will be in bondage to Pharaoh."

26 So Joseph established it as a law concerning land in Egypt—still in force

---

[a] 7 Or *greeted* [b] 10 Or *said farewell to* [c] 21 Samaritan Pentateuch and Septuagint (see also Vulgate); Masoretic Text *and he moved the people into the cities*

today — that a fifth of the produce belongs to Pharaoh. It was only the land of the
priests that did not become Pharaoh's.
27 Now the Israelites settled in Egypt in the region of Goshen. They acquired
property there and were fruitful and increased greatly in number.
28 Jacob lived in Egypt seventeen years, and the years of his life were a hundred
and forty-seven. 29 When the time drew near for Israel to die, he called for his son
Joseph and said to him, "If I have found favor in your eyes, put your hand under
my thigh and promise that you will show me kindness and faithfulness. Do not
bury me in Egypt, 30 but when I rest with my fathers, carry me out of Egypt and
bury me where they are buried."
"I will do as you say," he said.
31 "Swear to me," he said. Then Joseph swore to him, and Israel worshiped as
he leaned on the top of his staff.[a]

Manasseh and Ephraim

48 Some time later Joseph was told, "Your father is ill." So he took his two sons
Manasseh and Ephraim along with him. 2 When Jacob was told, "Your son
Joseph has come to you," Israel rallied his strength and sat up on the bed.
3 Jacob said to Joseph, "God Almighty[b] appeared to me at Luz in the land of
Canaan, and there he blessed me 4 and said to me, 'I am going to make you fruitful and increase your numbers. I will make you a community of peoples, and I
will give this land as an everlasting possession to your descendants after you.'
5 "Now then, your two sons born to you in Egypt before I came to you here will
be reckoned as mine; Ephraim and Manasseh will be mine, just as Reuben and
Simeon are mine. 6 Any children born to you after them will be yours; in the territory they inherit they will be reckoned under the names of their brothers. 7 As
I was returning from Paddan,[c] to my sorrow Rachel died in the land of Canaan
while we were still on the way, a little distance from Ephrath. So I buried her
there beside the road to Ephrath" (that is, Bethlehem).
8 When Israel saw the sons of Joseph, he asked, "Who are these?"
9 "They are the sons God has given me here," Joseph said to his father.
Then Israel said, "Bring them to me so I may bless them."
10 Now Israel's eyes were failing because of old age, and he could hardly see.
So Joseph brought his sons close to him, and his father kissed them and embraced them.
11 Israel said to Joseph, "I never expected to see your face again, and now God
has allowed me to see your children too."
12 Then Joseph removed them from Israel's knees and bowed down with his
face to the ground. 13 And Joseph took both of them, Ephraim on his right toward Israel's left hand and Manasseh on his left toward Israel's right hand, and
brought them close to him. 14 But Israel reached out his right hand and put it on
Ephraim's head, though he was the younger, and crossing his arms, he put his
left hand on Manasseh's head, even though Manasseh was the firstborn.
15 Then he blessed Joseph and said,

"May the God before whom my fathers
 Abraham and Isaac walked faithfully,
the God who has been my shepherd
 all my life to this day,
16 the Angel who has delivered me from all harm
 — may he bless these boys.
May they be called by my name
 and the names of my fathers Abraham and Isaac,
and may they increase greatly
 on the earth."

---

[a] 31 Or *Israel bowed down at the head of his bed* [b] 3 Hebrew *El-Shaddai* [c] 7 That is, Northwest Mesopotamia

17When Joseph saw his father placing his right hand on Ephraim's head he was
displeased; so he took hold of his father's hand to move it from Ephraim's head to
Manasseh's head. 18Joseph said to him, "No, my father, this one is the firstborn;
put your right hand on his head."
19But his father refused and said, "I know, my son, I know. He too will become
a people, and he too will become great. Nevertheless, his younger brother will
be greater than he, and his descendants will become a group of nations." 20He
blessed them that day and said,

"In your[a] name will Israel pronounce this blessing:
'May God make you like Ephraim and Manasseh.'"

So he put Ephraim ahead of Manasseh.
21Then Israel said to Joseph, "I am about to die, but God will be with you[b] and
take you[b] back to the land of your[b] fathers. 22And to you I give one more ridge of
land[c] than to your brothers, the ridge I took from the Amorites with my sword
and my bow."

Jacob Blesses His Sons

49 Then Jacob called for his sons and said: "Gather around so I can tell you
what will happen to you in days to come.

2"Assemble and listen, sons of Jacob;
listen to your father Israel.

3"Reuben, you are my firstborn,
my might, the first sign of my strength,
excelling in honor, excelling in power.
4Turbulent as the waters, you will no longer excel,
for you went up onto your father's bed,
onto my couch and defiled it.

5"Simeon and Levi are brothers —
their swords[d] are weapons of violence.
6Let me not enter their council,
let me not join their assembly,
for they have killed men in their anger
and hamstrung oxen as they pleased.
7Cursed be their anger, so fierce,
and their fury, so cruel!
I will scatter them in Jacob
and disperse them in Israel.

8"Judah,[e] your brothers will praise you;
your hand will be on the neck of your enemies;
your father's sons will bow down to you.
9You are a lion's cub, Judah;
you return from the prey, my son.
Like a lion he crouches and lies down,
like a lioness — who dares to rouse him?
10The scepter will not depart from Judah,
nor the ruler's staff from between his feet,[f]
until he to whom it belongs[g] shall come
and the obedience of the nations shall be his.
11He will tether his donkey to a vine,
his colt to the choicest branch;

---

[a] *20* The Hebrew is singular. [b] *21* The Hebrew is plural. [c] *22* The Hebrew for *ridge of land* is identical with the place name Shechem. [d] *5* The meaning of the Hebrew for this word is uncertain. [e] *8* *Judah* sounds like and may be derived from the Hebrew for *praise.* [f] *10* Or *from his descendants* [g] *10* Or *to whom tribute belongs;* the meaning of the Hebrew for this phrase is uncertain.

GENESIS 49:10

THE RULING KING FROM JUDAH

The royal lineage of Jesus is foreshadowed in the images of this text. The scepter was an ornate rod used by kings to communicate their authoritative dictates. Those in power could grant laws and enact judgment should one fail to submit to their rule. "He to whom it belongs" is an obscure phrase, likely referring to the divine King and lawgiver who would come from the line of Judah to fulfill the promises of this passage. To this King, all people, not simply those of a certain earthly kingdom, would owe their allegiance.

Jesus, the King from the tribe of Judah, ushers in the kingdom of God and announces the rule and reign of God through his incarnation. One day, all people (in heaven, on earth and under the earth) will bow at his very name (Php 2:9–11). As the great suffering servant, his earthly ministry and his execution via a criminal's death seem to undermine his cosmic rule. But his victorious resurrection and glorious ascension vindicate his claim to deity and establish him as the King of kings and Lord of lords and the one to whom all people owe their worship (Ro 1:4).

he will wash his garments in wine,
his robes in the blood of grapes.
12 His eyes will be darker than wine,
his teeth whiter than milk.[a]

13 "Zebulun will live by the seashore
and become a haven for ships;
his border will extend toward Sidon.

14 "Issachar is a rawboned[b] donkey
lying down among the sheep pens.[c]
15 When he sees how good is his resting place
and how pleasant is his land,
he will bend his shoulder to the burden
and submit to forced labor.

16 "Dan[d] will provide justice for his people
as one of the tribes of Israel.
17 Dan will be a snake by the roadside,
a viper along the path,
that bites the horse's heels
so that its rider tumbles backward.

18 "I look for your deliverance, LORD.

19 "Gad[e] will be attacked by a band of raiders,
but he will attack them at their heels.

20 "Asher's food will be rich;
he will provide delicacies fit for a king.

21 "Naphtali is a doe set free
that bears beautiful fawns.[f]

22 "Joseph is a fruitful vine,
a fruitful vine near a spring,
whose branches climb over a wall.[g]
23 With bitterness archers attacked him;
they shot at him with hostility.
24 But his bow remained steady,
his strong arms stayed[h] limber,
because of the hand of the Mighty One of Jacob,
because of the Shepherd, the Rock of Israel,
25 because of your father's God, who helps you,
because of the Almighty,[i] who blesses you
with blessings of the skies above,
blessings of the deep springs below,
blessings of the breast and womb.
26 Your father's blessings are greater
than the blessings of the ancient mountains,
than[j] the bounty of the age-old hills.
Let all these rest on the head of Joseph,
on the brow of the prince among[k] his brothers.

27 "Benjamin is a ravenous wolf;
in the morning he devours the prey,
in the evening he divides the plunder."

---

[a] 12 Or *will be dull from wine, / his teeth white from milk* [b] 14 Or *strong* [c] 14 Or *the campfires*; or *the saddlebags* [d] 16 *Dan* here means *he provides justice.* [e] 19 *Gad* sounds like the Hebrew for *attack* and also for *band of raiders.* [f] 21 Or *free; / he utters beautiful words* [g] 22 Or *Joseph is a wild colt, / a wild colt near a spring, / a wild donkey on a terraced hill* [h] 23,24 Or *archers will attack . . . will shoot . . . will remain . . . will stay* [i] 25 Hebrew *Shaddai* [j] 26 Or *of my progenitors, / as great as* [k] 26 Or *of the one separated from*

[28]All these are the twelve tribes of Israel, and this is what their father said to them when he blessed them, giving each the blessing appropriate to him.

The Death of Jacob

[29]Then he gave them these instructions: "I am about to be gathered to my people. Bury me with my fathers in the cave in the field of Ephron the Hittite, [30]the cave in the field of Machpelah, near Mamre in Canaan, which Abraham bought along with the field as a burial place from Ephron the Hittite. [31]There Abraham and his wife Sarah were buried, there Isaac and his wife Rebekah were buried, and there I buried Leah. [32]The field and the cave in it were bought from the Hittites.[a]"

[33]When Jacob had finished giving instructions to his sons, he drew his feet up into the bed, breathed his last and was gathered to his people.

50 Joseph threw himself on his father and wept over him and kissed him. [2]Then Joseph directed the physicians in his service to embalm his father Israel. So the physicians embalmed him, [3]taking a full forty days, for that was the time required for embalming. And the Egyptians mourned for him seventy days.

[4]When the days of mourning had passed, Joseph said to Pharaoh's court, "If I have found favor in your eyes, speak to Pharaoh for me. Tell him, [5]'My father made me swear an oath and said, "I am about to die; bury me in the tomb I dug for myself in the land of Canaan." Now let me go up and bury my father; then I will return.'"

[6]Pharaoh said, "Go up and bury your father, as he made you swear to do."

[7]So Joseph went up to bury his father. All Pharaoh's officials accompanied him—the dignitaries of his court and all the dignitaries of Egypt— [8]besides all the members of Joseph's household and his brothers and those belonging to his father's household. Only their children and their flocks and herds were left in Goshen. [9]Chariots and horsemen[b] also went up with him. It was a very large company.

[10]When they reached the threshing floor of Atad, near the Jordan, they lamented loudly and bitterly; and there Joseph observed a seven-day period of mourning for his father. [11]When the Canaanites who lived there saw the mourning at the threshing floor of Atad, they said, "The Egyptians are holding a solemn ceremony of mourning." That is why that place near the Jordan is called Abel Mizraim.[c]

[12]So Jacob's sons did as he had commanded them: [13]They carried him to the land of Canaan and buried him in the cave in the field of Machpelah, near Mamre, which Abraham had bought along with the field as a burial place from Ephron the Hittite. [14]After burying his father, Joseph returned to Egypt, together with his brothers and all the others who had gone with him to bury his father.

Joseph Reassures His Brothers

[15]When Joseph's brothers saw that their father was dead, they said, "What if Joseph holds a grudge against us and pays us back for all the wrongs we did to him?" [16]So they sent word to Joseph, saying, "Your father left these instructions before he died: [17]'This is what you are to say to Joseph: I ask you to forgive your brothers the sins and the wrongs they committed in treating you so badly.' Now please forgive the sins of the servants of the God of your father." When their message came to him, Joseph wept.

[18]His brothers then came and threw themselves down before him. "We are your slaves," they said.

[19]But Joseph said to them, "Don't be afraid. Am I in the place of God? [20]You intended to harm me, but God intended it for good to accomplish what is now being done, the saving of many lives. [21]So then, don't be afraid. I will provide for you and your children." And he reassured them and spoke kindly to them.

---

[a] 32 Or *the descendants of Heth* [b] 9 Or *charioteers* [c] 11 *Abel Mizraim* means *mourning of the Egyptians.*

MEANT FOR EVIL, USED FOR GOOD

God rules and reigns over all things and orchestrates the events of this world to perfectly fulfill his good intentions for his creation. This hope is magnified in light of the depth of human sin and the systemic evil at work in the world. God is capable of taking every facet of life, even great evil, and working it together to accomplish his will.

This truth is demonstrated profoundly in Joseph's life. The outcast brother, sold into slavery and forgotten in prison, finds himself second in command in all of Egypt. His brothers' actions, though malicious, were used by God in order to position Joseph to save his brothers and his family when they needed food in order to escape the famine. While Joseph may never have chosen the path his life took, he could look back at the course of his life and see the ever-present hand of God. Joseph affirmed the grand scope of the sovereignty of God when he reassured his brothers that the things they meant for evil were ultimately under the authority of God. No evil plan of humans could thwart the purposes of a sovereign God.

God demonstrates his sovereign hand throughout the continued history of his people. He takes all things, even their rebellion, and uses them to accomplish even greater good. The greatest experience of human depravity is seen in the brutal murder of the perfect Son of God. At the cross, it would seem that the religious leaders, Roman authorities and Satan himself had emerged victorious. Yet, as with the life of Joseph, God was orchestrating these unthinkable acts in order to accomplish the great good of satisfying the wrath of God through the death of his Son.

Believers can find hope to face the complex, and often tumultuous, circumstances of life in a fallen world with the knowledge of the sovereign rule and reign of God. Paul reminds the church in Rome that in all things, even suffering and sin, "God works for the good of those who love him, who have been called according to his purpose" (Ro 8:28). God is not surprised by evil. He is not at a loss for how to respond. His plans cannot be defeated, and he will accomplish everything exactly as he intends.

The Death of Joseph

22 Joseph stayed in Egypt, along with all his father's family. He lived a hundred and ten years 23 and saw the third generation of Ephraim's children. Also
the children of Makir son of Manasseh were placed at birth on Joseph's knees.[a]
24 Then Joseph said to his brothers, "I am about to die. But God will surely
come to your aid and take you up out of this land to the land he promised on oath
to Abraham, Isaac and Jacob." 25 And Joseph made the Israelites swear an oath
and said, "God will surely come to your aid, and then you must carry my bones
up from this place."
26 So Joseph died at the age of a hundred and ten. And after they embalmed
him, he was placed in a coffin in Egypt.

GENESIS 50:24

THE GOD OF ABRAHAM, ISAAC AND JACOB

Approaching death, Joseph reassured his family of the covenant faithfulness of God. The threefold repetition of the names Abraham, Isaac and Jacob is used through the Pentateuch to describe the recipients of the promises God made to Abram in Genesis 12:1 – 3 (Ge 48:15; 49:29 – 31; Ex 2:24; 3:16). Joseph recognized that his death was not the culmination of the work of God on behalf of the people of God. This work did not depend on Joseph; rather it rested on the faithfulness of God. Joseph knew that God was always faithful to his promises and would surely bring the nation of Israel into the good land that he had pledged to them as their inheritance. God's covenantal faithfulness led him to send Jesus as the fulfillment of the promises he made to Abraham, Isaac and Jacob. The hope of Joseph's life found its fulfillment in the sending of the Savior.

[a] *23* That is, were counted as his

JESUS: OUR MIRACULOUS DELIVERER

EXODUS

EXODUS

ISRAELITES ENSLAVED IN EGYPT *c. 1600 BC*	MOSES IS BORN *c. 1526 BC*	EXODUS FROM EGYPT *c. 1446 BC*

The book of Exodus describes a climactic moment in the life of the people of God — their deliverance from slavery in Egypt by the mighty hand of the Lord. The population of Israel in Exodus is the fulfillment of God's promise to Abram/Abraham in Genesis 12:1 – 3; these people, whom God had called as his chosen ones, and their descendants serve as a central focus throughout the remainder of the Old Testament.

God called Moses, the main character in Exodus, to lead the people out of Egypt. In spite of Moses' initial protests to God, Moses approached the hard-hearted Pharaoh and implored him to release God's people from slavery. When Pharaoh refused, God began his process of deliverance, demonstrating the scope of his might and power. Following his work of deliverance, God gave his people the Law so they could understand how they should respond to God's grace and fulfill their calling to be "a kingdom of priests and a holy nation" (19:6).

The first section of Exodus (chs. 1 – 18) describes in glorious detail the way that God prevailed over the greatest world power at that time — the nation of Egypt. Through his miraculous might, God demonstrated his supremacy over the false gods of the nations and the sinful hearts of kings. The Hebrew people continually recounted the wonders of God's might throughout the book of Exodus, and, in fact, still celebrate this deliverance today.

The second section (chs. 19 – 40) outlines the Law of God, given as a benevolent gift of grace by a personal God to his chosen people. They represent his unique nature and character, demonstrating that God is righteous, holy in all things and rightly deserving of the worship of those whom he has saved. The book ends with the completion of the tabernacle, which stands as the center point of their encampment and the central place of worship for God's people throughout their journey in the wilderness.

The book of Exodus portrays Moses as a God-ordained redeemer of the people of God. For this reason he serves as a type of messiah, a precursor to the One who was to come, Jesus Christ. Like Moses, Jesus would serve in three roles: as a prophet — communicating God's word to the people; as a priest — making it possible for humankind to worship God rightly; and as a king — leading the people from slavery into safety. The historical events of this book, such as the Passover (ch. 12) prefigure the atoning work of Christ for the sins of his people (Jn 1:29,36; 1Co 5:7). Christ is the perfect sacrifice, the fulfillment of the Old Testament law (Mt 5:17), and the One who breaks the shackles of sin and delivers his people forever.

DO NOT BE AFRAID. STAND FIRM AND YOU WILL SEE THE DELIVERANCE THE LORD WILL BRING YOU TODAY.

Exodus 14:13

EXODUS

EXODUS 1:6 – 7

MULTIPLICATION

In spite of the sin of humanity, God was faithful to allow people to fulfill their created design. They were fruitful, multiplied and filled the earth (Ge 1:26 – 28). God's promise to Abraham was proven true. His children were as numerous as the stars in the sky (Ge 15:5) and the sand on the shore (Ge 22:17). These promises, made to the patriarch and his barren wife, were seemingly hopeless. But God acted by providing a son for Abraham and Sarah and greatly multiplied subsequent generations in spite of their sin and rebellion.

The abundance of the people of Israel is only a small microcosm of the people whom God would call to himself across the span of the centuries. Paul wrote in Galatians 3:26 – 29 that all those who place their faith in Christ are heirs of the promise made to Abraham and seen at the outset of the book of Exodus. Now God's people, by virtue of the grace of God, fill the globe testifying to the faithfulness of God to sustain his people forever.

EXODUS 2:1 – 10

DRAWN OUT OF THE WATER

Moses was born to parents from the house of Levi, which eventually became the priestly family for Israel.

(continued on next page)

The Israelites Oppressed

1 These are the names of the sons of Israel who went to Egypt with Jacob, each with his family: 2Reuben, Simeon, Levi and Judah; 3Issachar, Zebulun and Benjamin; 4Dan and Naphtali; Gad and Asher. 5The descendants of Jacob numbered seventy[a] in all; Joseph was already in Egypt.

6Now Joseph and all his brothers and all that generation died, 7but the Israelites were exceedingly fruitful; they multiplied greatly, increased in numbers and became so numerous that the land was filled with them.

8Then a new king, to whom Joseph meant nothing, came to power in Egypt. 9"Look," he said to his people, "the Israelites have become far too numerous for us. 10Come, we must deal shrewdly with them or they will become even more numerous and, if war breaks out, will join our enemies, fight against us and leave the country."

11So they put slave masters over them to oppress them with forced labor, and they built Pithom and Rameses as store cities for Pharaoh. 12But the more they were oppressed, the more they multiplied and spread; so the Egyptians came to dread the Israelites 13and worked them ruthlessly. 14They made their lives bitter with harsh labor in brick and mortar and with all kinds of work in the fields; in all their harsh labor the Egyptians worked them ruthlessly.

15The king of Egypt said to the Hebrew midwives, whose names were Shiphrah and Puah, 16"When you are helping the Hebrew women during childbirth on the delivery stool, if you see that the baby is a boy, kill him; but if it is a girl, let her live." 17The midwives, however, feared God and did not do what the king of Egypt had told them to do; they let the boys live. 18Then the king of Egypt summoned the midwives and asked them, "Why have you done this? Why have you let the boys live?"

19The midwives answered Pharaoh, "Hebrew women are not like Egyptian women; they are vigorous and give birth before the midwives arrive."

20So God was kind to the midwives and the people increased and became even more numerous. 21And because the midwives feared God, he gave them families of their own.

22Then Pharaoh gave this order to all his people: "Every Hebrew boy that is born you must throw into the Nile, but let every girl live."

The Birth of Moses

2 Now a man of the tribe of Levi married a Levite woman, 2and she became pregnant and gave birth to a son. When she saw that he was a fine child, she hid him for three months. 3But when she could hide him no longer, she got a papyrus basket[b] for him and coated it with tar and pitch. Then she placed the child in it and put it among the reeds along the bank of the Nile. 4His sister stood at a distance to see what would happen to him.

5Then Pharaoh's daughter went down to the Nile to bathe, and her attendants were walking along the riverbank. She saw the basket among the reeds and sent her female slave to get it. 6She opened it and saw the baby. He was crying, and she felt sorry for him. "This is one of the Hebrew babies," she said.

7Then his sister asked Pharaoh's daughter, "Shall I go and get one of the Hebrew women to nurse the baby for you?"

8"Yes, go," she answered. So the girl went and got the baby's mother. 9Pharaoh's

---

[a] 5 Masoretic Text (see also Gen. 46:27); Dead Sea Scrolls and Septuagint (see also Acts 7:14 and note at Gen. 46:27) *seventy-five* [b] 3 The Hebrew can also mean *ark*, as in Gen. 6:14.

daughter said to her, "Take this baby and nurse him for me, and I will pay you." So the woman took the baby and nursed him. 10When the child grew older, she took him to Pharaoh's daughter and he became her son. She named him Moses,[a] saying, "I drew him out of the water."

Moses Flees to Midian

11One day, after Moses had grown up, he went out to where his own people were and watched them at their hard labor. He saw an Egyptian beating a Hebrew, one of his own people. 12Looking this way and that and seeing no one, he killed the Egyptian and hid him in the sand. 13The next day he went out and saw two Hebrews fighting. He asked the one in the wrong, "Why are you hitting your fellow Hebrew?"

14The man said, "Who made you ruler and judge over us? Are you thinking of killing me as you killed the Egyptian?" Then Moses was afraid and thought, "What I did must have become known."

15When Pharaoh heard of this, he tried to kill Moses, but Moses fled from Pharaoh and went to live in Midian, where he sat down by a well. 16Now a priest of Midian had seven daughters, and they came to draw water and fill the troughs to water their father's flock. 17Some shepherds came along and drove them away, but Moses got up and came to their rescue and watered their flock.

18When the girls returned to Reuel their father, he asked them, "Why have you returned so early today?"

19They answered, "An Egyptian rescued us from the shepherds. He even drew water for us and watered the flock."

20"And where is he?" Reuel asked his daughters. "Why did you leave him? Invite him to have something to eat."

21Moses agreed to stay with the man, who gave his daughter Zipporah to Moses in marriage. 22Zipporah gave birth to a son, and Moses named him Gershom,[b] saying, "I have become a foreigner in a foreign land."

23During that long period, the king of Egypt died. The Israelites groaned in their slavery and cried out, and their cry for help because of their slavery went up to God. 24God heard their groaning and he remembered his covenant with Abraham, with Isaac and with Jacob. 25So God looked on the Israelites and was concerned about them.

Moses and the Burning Bush

3 Now Moses was tending the flock of Jethro his father-in-law, the priest of Midian, and he led the flock to the far side of the wilderness and came to Horeb, the mountain of God. 2There the angel of the LORD appeared to him in flames of fire from within a bush. Moses saw that though the bush was on fire it did not burn up. 3So Moses thought, "I will go over and see this strange sight—why the bush does not burn up."

4When the LORD saw that he had gone over to look, God called to him from within the bush, "Moses! Moses!"

And Moses said, "Here I am."

5"Do not come any closer," God said. "Take off your sandals, for the place where you are standing is holy ground." 6Then he said, "I am the God of your father,[c] the God of Abraham, the God of Isaac and the God of Jacob." At this, Moses hid his face, because he was afraid to look at God.

7The LORD said, "I have indeed seen the misery of my people in Egypt. I have heard them crying out because of their slave drivers, and I am concerned about their suffering. 8So I have come down to rescue them from the hand of the Egyptians and to bring them up out of that land into a good and spacious land, a land flowing with milk and honey—the home of the Canaanites, Hittites, Amorites,

[a] *10* *Moses* sounds like the Hebrew for *draw out.* [b] *22* *Gershom* sounds like the Hebrew for *a foreigner there.* [c] *6* Masoretic Text; Samaritan Pentateuch (see Acts 7:32) *fathers*

(Drawn Out of the Water, continued)

After three months, Moses' mother placed him in a basket to protect him from murder at the hands of Pharaoh. Like the ark that protected Noah, this small basket sustained Moses until Pharaoh's daughter found him. The daughter was ill equipped to nurse a baby, so she called a Hebrew woman, the mother of Moses, to nurse the child. Miraculously, God provided deliverance for the baby, but he did so through the very one who tried to destroy him. Moses was adopted by Pharaoh's daughter and was raised in Pharaoh's house. Moses' Egyptian name means "is born," which sounds like the Hebrew for "draw out," thus testifying to God's deliverance of his ordained leader from the waters of the Nile.

In a similar fashion, God protected Jesus at the outset of his ministry from the hand of Herod, who wanted to destroy any threat to his throne by killing all Jewish boys two years old and under (Mt 2:13–16). Like Moses, Jesus was delivered by God from the enemy and was positioned to fulfill God's appointed plan for his life.

Perizzites, Hivites and Jebusites. 9And now the cry of the Israelites has reached
me, and I have seen the way the Egyptians are oppressing them. 10So now, go. I
am sending you to Pharaoh to bring my people the Israelites out of Egypt."
11But Moses said to God, "Who am I that I should go to Pharaoh and bring the
Israelites out of Egypt?"
12And God said, "I will be with you. And this will be the sign to you that it is
I who have sent you: When you have brought the people out of Egypt, you[a] will
worship God on this mountain."
13Moses said to God, "Suppose I go to the Israelites and say to them, 'The God
of your fathers has sent me to you,' and they ask me, 'What is his name?' Then
what shall I tell them?"
14God said to Moses, "I AM WHO I AM.[b] This is what you are to say to the Israelites: 'I AM has sent me to you.'"
15God also said to Moses, "Say to the Israelites, 'The LORD,[c] the God of your
fathers — the God of Abraham, the God of Isaac and the God of Jacob — has sent
me to you.'

"This is my name forever,
the name you shall call me
from generation to generation.

16"Go, assemble the elders of Israel and say to them, 'The LORD, the God of
your fathers — the God of Abraham, Isaac and Jacob — appeared to me and said:
I have watched over you and have seen what has been done to you in Egypt.
17And I have promised to bring you up out of your misery in Egypt into the land
of the Canaanites, Hittites, Amorites, Perizzites, Hivites and Jebusites — a land
flowing with milk and honey.'
18"The elders of Israel will listen to you. Then you and the elders are to go to
the king of Egypt and say to him, 'The LORD, the God of the Hebrews, has met
with us. Let us take a three-day journey into the wilderness to offer sacrifices
to the LORD our God.' 19But I know that the king of Egypt will not let you go unless a mighty hand compels him. 20So I will stretch out my hand and strike the
Egyptians with all the wonders that I will perform among them. After that, he
will let you go.
21"And I will make the Egyptians favorably disposed toward this people, so
that when you leave you will not go empty-handed. 22Every woman is to ask her
neighbor and any woman living in her house for articles of silver and gold and
for clothing, which you will put on your sons and daughters. And so you will
plunder the Egyptians."

Signs for Moses

4 Moses answered, "What if they do not believe me or listen to me and say, 'The
LORD did not appear to you'?"
2Then the LORD said to him, "What is that in your hand?"
"A staff," he replied.
3The LORD said, "Throw it on the ground."
Moses threw it on the ground and it became a snake, and he ran from it. 4Then
the LORD said to him, "Reach out your hand and take it by the tail." So Moses
reached out and took hold of the snake and it turned back into a staff in his hand.
5"This," said the LORD, "is so that they may believe that the LORD, the God of
their fathers — the God of Abraham, the God of Isaac and the God of Jacob — has
appeared to you."
6Then the LORD said, "Put your hand inside your cloak." So Moses put his
hand into his cloak, and when he took it out, the skin was leprous[d] — it had become as white as snow.

[a] 12 The Hebrew is plural. [b] 14 Or *I WILL BE WHAT I WILL BE* [c] 15 The Hebrew for *LORD* sounds like and may be related to the Hebrew for *I AM* in verse 14. [d] 6 The Hebrew word for *leprous* was used for various diseases affecting the skin.

EXODUS 3:14

"I AM"

God provided his people with a name that denotes his uncaused, independent and eternal character. Moses, faced with the unenviable task of asking Pharaoh for the freedom of the Israelites, asked God for his name. He knew that the Israelites would ask for the name of the one who gave Moses these instructions. God told Moses to call him, "I AM." He is and will always be. He owes nothing and no one for his existence. Rather, he is the supreme, uncreated, sovereign and sole God of the universe. All things owe their being to him.

Jesus used this same name to declare his identity during his earthly ministry. While the people argued about the relationship of Jesus to the promises God made to Abraham, Jesus defied their understanding by declaring that he is not merely one in a long line of those whom God uses. Rather, he is the "I am" (Jn 8:58). The immense nature of this claim caused many to attempt to stone Jesus because they knew the implications of this term. By using this term Jesus announced himself to be God, committing the ultimate sin of blasphemy in the minds of his Jewish audience. They simply could not comprehend that this carpenter from Nazareth could be the very Son of God, in human form, to whom all people owe their allegiance and worship.

7"Now put it back into your cloak," he said. So Moses put his hand back into his cloak, and when he took it out, it was restored, like the rest of his flesh.

8Then the LORD said, "If they do not believe you or pay attention to the first sign, they may believe the second. 9But if they do not believe these two signs or listen to you, take some water from the Nile and pour it on the dry ground. The water you take from the river will become blood on the ground."

10Moses said to the LORD, "Pardon your servant, Lord. I have never been eloquent, neither in the past nor since you have spoken to your servant. I am slow of speech and tongue."

11The LORD said to him, "Who gave human beings their mouths? Who makes them deaf or mute? Who gives them sight or makes them blind? Is it not I, the LORD? 12Now go; I will help you speak and will teach you what to say."

13But Moses said, "Pardon your servant, Lord. Please send someone else."

14Then the LORD's anger burned against Moses and he said, "What about your brother, Aaron the Levite? I know he can speak well. He is already on his way to meet you, and he will be glad to see you. 15You shall speak to him and put words in his mouth; I will help both of you speak and will teach you what to do. 16He will speak to the people for you, and it will be as if he were your mouth and as if you were God to him. 17But take this staff in your hand so you can perform the signs with it."

Moses Returns to Egypt

18Then Moses went back to Jethro his father-in-law and said to him, "Let me return to my own people in Egypt to see if any of them are still alive."

Jethro said, "Go, and I wish you well."

19Now the LORD had said to Moses in Midian, "Go back to Egypt, for all those who wanted to kill you are dead." 20So Moses took his wife and sons, put them on a donkey and started back to Egypt. And he took the staff of God in his hand.

21The LORD said to Moses, "When you return to Egypt, see that you perform before Pharaoh all the wonders I have given you the power to do. But I will harden his heart so that he will not let the people go. 22Then say to Pharaoh, 'This is what the LORD says: Israel is my firstborn son, 23and I told you, "Let my son go, so he may worship me." But you refused to let him go; so I will kill your firstborn son.'"

24At a lodging place on the way, the LORD met Moses[a] and was about to kill him. 25But Zipporah took a flint knife, cut off her son's foreskin and touched Moses' feet with it.[b] "Surely you are a bridegroom of blood to me," she said. 26So the LORD let him alone. (At that time she said "bridegroom of blood," referring to circumcision.)

27The LORD said to Aaron, "Go into the wilderness to meet Moses." So he met Moses at the mountain of God and kissed him. 28Then Moses told Aaron everything the LORD had sent him to say, and also about all the signs he had commanded him to perform.

29Moses and Aaron brought together all the elders of the Israelites, 30and Aaron told them everything the LORD had said to Moses. He also performed the signs before the people, 31and they believed. And when they heard that the LORD was concerned about them and had seen their misery, they bowed down and worshiped.

Bricks Without Straw

5 Afterward Moses and Aaron went to Pharaoh and said, "This is what the LORD, the God of Israel, says: 'Let my people go, so that they may hold a festival to me in the wilderness.'"

2Pharaoh said, "Who is the LORD, that I should obey him and let Israel go? I do not know the LORD and I will not let Israel go."

---

[a] *24* Hebrew *him* [b] *25* The meaning of the Hebrew for this clause is uncertain.

[3]Then they said, "The God of the Hebrews has met with us. Now let us take a three-day journey into the wilderness to offer sacrifices to the LORD our God, or he may strike us with plagues or with the sword."

[4]But the king of Egypt said, "Moses and Aaron, why are you taking the people away from their labor? Get back to your work!" [5]Then Pharaoh said, "Look, the people of the land are now numerous, and you are stopping them from working."

[6]That same day Pharaoh gave this order to the slave drivers and overseers in charge of the people: [7]"You are no longer to supply the people with straw for making bricks; let them go and gather their own straw. [8]But require them to make the same number of bricks as before; don't reduce the quota. They are lazy; that is why they are crying out, 'Let us go and sacrifice to our God.' [9]Make the work harder for the people so that they keep working and pay no attention to lies."

[10]Then the slave drivers and the overseers went out and said to the people, "This is what Pharaoh says: 'I will not give you any more straw. [11]Go and get your own straw wherever you can find it, but your work will not be reduced at all.' " [12]So the people scattered all over Egypt to gather stubble to use for straw. [13]The slave drivers kept pressing them, saying, "Complete the work required of you for each day, just as when you had straw." [14]And Pharaoh's slave drivers beat the Israelite overseers they had appointed, demanding, "Why haven't you met your quota of bricks yesterday or today, as before?"

[15]Then the Israelite overseers went and appealed to Pharaoh: "Why have you treated your servants this way? [16]Your servants are given no straw, yet we are told, 'Make bricks!' Your servants are being beaten, but the fault is with your own people."

[17]Pharaoh said, "Lazy, that's what you are—lazy! That is why you keep saying, 'Let us go and sacrifice to the LORD.' [18]Now get to work. You will not be given any straw, yet you must produce your full quota of bricks."

[19]The Israelite overseers realized they were in trouble when they were told, "You are not to reduce the number of bricks required of you for each day." [20]When they left Pharaoh, they found Moses and Aaron waiting to meet them, [21]and they said, "May the LORD look on you and judge you! You have made us obnoxious to Pharaoh and his officials and have put a sword in their hand to kill us."

God Promises Deliverance

[22]Moses returned to the LORD and said, "Why, Lord, why have you brought trouble on this people? Is this why you sent me? [23]Ever since I went to Pharaoh to speak in your name, he has brought trouble on this people, and you have not rescued your people at all."

6 Then the LORD said to Moses, "Now you will see what I will do to Pharaoh: Because of my mighty hand he will let them go; because of my mighty hand he will drive them out of his country."

[2]God also said to Moses, "I am the LORD. [3]I appeared to Abraham, to Isaac and to Jacob as God Almighty,[a] but by my name the LORD[b] I did not make myself fully known to them. [4]I also established my covenant with them to give them the land of Canaan, where they resided as foreigners. [5]Moreover, I have heard the groaning of the Israelites, whom the Egyptians are enslaving, and I have remembered my covenant.

[6]"Therefore, say to the Israelites: 'I am the LORD, and I will bring you out from under the yoke of the Egyptians. I will free you from being slaves to them, and I will redeem you with an outstretched arm and with mighty acts of judgment. [7]I will take you as my own people, and I will be your God. Then you will know that I am the LORD your God, who brought you out from under the yoke of the Egyptians. [8]And I will bring you to the land I swore with uplifted hand to give to Abraham, to Isaac and to Jacob. I will give it to you as a possession. I am the LORD.' "

[a] 3 Hebrew *El-Shaddai* [b] 3 See note at 3:15.

EXODUS 6:1 – 8

I AM THE LORD

The patriarchs had known God Almighty, but they had never heard the unique name of God. God revealed himself to Moses with intimate clarity, connecting his personal name with the wonders that he had done for the people up to this point in their story. He is the one who called Abraham, initiated a covenant with him and inaugurated a great nation through a child promised to him and his then-barren wife (Ge 12; 15). He is the God who used what man intended for evil to promote Joseph to second-in-command in Egypt (Ge 50:20). He is the one who led his people to seek refuge in the land of Egypt to escape a dire famine. And he is the one who promised to deliver the people from slavery through Moses' leadership. The people were urged to avoid worry — the God who promised to act on their behalf is the God who had always come through on the behalf of his people.

This personal revelation is distinct to Christians. The God of the Bible is not some disengaged deity, unconcerned with the plight of his people. Rather, he is the God who is both omnipotent and sovereignly in charge of all things and the God who is intimately concerned and engaged with the affairs of his children.

This personal care is best demonstrated in the way Jesus humbled himself, leaving the right hand of the Father and taking the place of a servant on the cross (Php 2:5 – 11). Paul wrote that God was intent on redeeming his people, so Jesus laid aside equality with God and humbled himself to take on human flesh. While, in the age to come, every knee will bow and every tongue will confess that Jesus is Lord, the early ministry of Jesus demonstrated how far God would stoop to show his personal love for his children. Jesus is the perfect Son of God, yet one who loved his enemies and called them his friends (Ro 5:10). He is the radiance of the glory of God, yet willing to love those who show even a childlike faith (Lk 18:16). God is the King of the universe, yet one who allows frail humans to approach him as their father (Ro 8:15). He is *Yahweh*, the Lord God Almighty.

9Moses reported this to the Israelites, but they did not listen to him because
of their discouragement and harsh labor.
10Then the LORD said to Moses, 11"Go, tell Pharaoh king of Egypt to let the Israelites go out of his country."
12But Moses said to the LORD, "If the Israelites will not listen to me, why would
Pharaoh listen to me, since I speak with faltering lips[a]?"

Family Record of Moses and Aaron

13Now the LORD spoke to Moses and Aaron about the Israelites and Pharaoh
king of Egypt, and he commanded them to bring the Israelites out of Egypt.
14These were the heads of their families[b]:

The sons of Reuben the firstborn son of Israel were Hanok and Pallu,
Hezron and Karmi. These were the clans of Reuben.
15The sons of Simeon were Jemuel, Jamin, Ohad, Jakin, Zohar and Shaul
the son of a Canaanite woman. These were the clans of Simeon.
16These were the names of the sons of Levi according to their records:
Gershon, Kohath and Merari. Levi lived 137 years.
17The sons of Gershon, by clans, were Libni and Shimei.
18The sons of Kohath were Amram, Izhar, Hebron and Uzziel. Kohath
lived 133 years.
19The sons of Merari were Mahli and Mushi.
These were the clans of Levi according to their records.
20Amram married his father's sister Jochebed, who bore him Aaron and
Moses. Amram lived 137 years.
21The sons of Izhar were Korah, Nepheg and Zikri.
22The sons of Uzziel were Mishael, Elzaphan and Sithri.
23Aaron married Elisheba, daughter of Amminadab and sister of Nahshon, and she bore him Nadab and Abihu, Eleazar and Ithamar.
24The sons of Korah were Assir, Elkanah and Abiasaph. These were the
Korahite clans.
25Eleazar son of Aaron married one of the daughters of Putiel, and she
bore him Phinehas.

These were the heads of the Levite families, clan by clan.

26It was this Aaron and Moses to whom the LORD said, "Bring the Israelites out
of Egypt by their divisions." 27They were the ones who spoke to Pharaoh king of
Egypt about bringing the Israelites out of Egypt — this same Moses and Aaron.

Aaron to Speak for Moses

28Now when the LORD spoke to Moses in Egypt, 29he said to him, "I am the
LORD. Tell Pharaoh king of Egypt everything I tell you."
30But Moses said to the LORD, "Since I speak with faltering lips, why would
Pharaoh listen to me?"

7 Then the LORD said to Moses, "See, I have made you like God to Pharaoh,
and your brother Aaron will be your prophet. 2You are to say everything I
command you, and your brother Aaron is to tell Pharaoh to let the Israelites go
out of his country. 3But I will harden Pharaoh's heart, and though I multiply my
signs and wonders in Egypt, 4he will not listen to you. Then I will lay my hand on
Egypt and with mighty acts of judgment I will bring out my divisions, my people
the Israelites. 5And the Egyptians will know that I am the LORD when I stretch
out my hand against Egypt and bring the Israelites out of it."
6Moses and Aaron did just as the LORD commanded them. 7Moses was eighty
years old and Aaron eighty-three when they spoke to Pharaoh.

---

[a] *12* Hebrew *I am uncircumcised of lips*; also in verse 30 [b] *14* The Hebrew for *families* here and in verse 25 refers to units larger than clans.

Aaron's Staff Becomes a Snake

8 The LORD said to Moses and Aaron, 9 "When Pharaoh says to you, 'Perform a miracle,' then say to Aaron, 'Take your staff and throw it down before Pharaoh,' and it will become a snake."

10 So Moses and Aaron went to Pharaoh and did just as the LORD commanded. Aaron threw his staff down in front of Pharaoh and his officials, and it became a snake. 11 Pharaoh then summoned wise men and sorcerers, and the Egyptian magicians also did the same things by their secret arts: 12 Each one threw down his staff and it became a snake. But Aaron's staff swallowed up their staffs. 13 Yet Pharaoh's heart became hard and he would not listen to them, just as the LORD had said.

The Plague of Blood

14 Then the LORD said to Moses, "Pharaoh's heart is unyielding; he refuses to let the people go. 15 Go to Pharaoh in the morning as he goes out to the river. Confront him on the bank of the Nile, and take in your hand the staff that was changed into a snake. 16 Then say to him, 'The LORD, the God of the Hebrews, has sent me to say to you: Let my people go, so that they may worship me in the wilderness. But until now you have not listened. 17 This is what the LORD says: By this you will know that I am the LORD: With the staff that is in my hand I will strike the water of the Nile, and it will be changed into blood. 18 The fish in the Nile will die, and the river will stink; the Egyptians will not be able to drink its water.' "

19 The LORD said to Moses, "Tell Aaron, 'Take your staff and stretch out your hand over the waters of Egypt—over the streams and canals, over the ponds and all the reservoirs—and they will turn to blood.' Blood will be everywhere in Egypt, even in vessels[a] of wood and stone."

20 Moses and Aaron did just as the LORD had commanded. He raised his staff in the presence of Pharaoh and his officials and struck the water of the Nile, and all the water was changed into blood. 21 The fish in the Nile died, and the river smelled so bad that the Egyptians could not drink its water. Blood was everywhere in Egypt.

22 But the Egyptian magicians did the same things by their secret arts, and Pharaoh's heart became hard; he would not listen to Moses and Aaron, just as the LORD had said. 23 Instead, he turned and went into his palace, and did not take even this to heart. 24 And all the Egyptians dug along the Nile to get drinking water, because they could not drink the water of the river.

The Plague of Frogs

8[b] 25 Seven days passed after the LORD struck the Nile. 1 Then the LORD said to Moses, "Go to Pharaoh and say to him, 'This is what the LORD says: Let my people go, so that they may worship me. 2 If you refuse to let them go, I will send a plague of frogs on your whole country. 3 The Nile will teem with frogs. They will come up into your palace and your bedroom and onto your bed, into the houses of your officials and on your people, and into your ovens and kneading troughs. 4 The frogs will come up on you and your people and all your officials.' "

5 Then the LORD said to Moses, "Tell Aaron, 'Stretch out your hand with your staff over the streams and canals and ponds, and make frogs come up on the land of Egypt.' "

6 So Aaron stretched out his hand over the waters of Egypt, and the frogs came up and covered the land. 7 But the magicians did the same things by their secret arts; they also made frogs come up on the land of Egypt.

8 Pharaoh summoned Moses and Aaron and said, "Pray to the LORD to take

---

[a] 19 Or *even on their idols* [b] In Hebrew texts 8:1-4 is numbered 7:26-29, and 8:5-32 is numbered 8:1-28.

the frogs away from me and my people, and I will let your people go to offer sacrifices to the LORD."

9Moses said to Pharaoh, "I leave to you the honor of setting the time for me to pray for you and your officials and your people that you and your houses may be rid of the frogs, except for those that remain in the Nile."

10"Tomorrow," Pharaoh said.

Moses replied, "It will be as you say, so that you may know there is no one like the LORD our God. 11The frogs will leave you and your houses, your officials and your people; they will remain only in the Nile."

12After Moses and Aaron left Pharaoh, Moses cried out to the LORD about the frogs he had brought on Pharaoh. 13And the LORD did what Moses asked. The frogs died in the houses, in the courtyards and in the fields. 14They were piled into heaps, and the land reeked of them. 15But when Pharaoh saw that there was relief, he hardened his heart and would not listen to Moses and Aaron, just as the LORD had said.

The Plague of Gnats

16Then the LORD said to Moses, "Tell Aaron, 'Stretch out your staff and strike the dust of the ground,' and throughout the land of Egypt the dust will become gnats." 17They did this, and when Aaron stretched out his hand with the staff and struck the dust of the ground, gnats came on people and animals. All the dust throughout the land of Egypt became gnats. 18But when the magicians tried to produce gnats by their secret arts, they could not.

Since the gnats were on people and animals everywhere, 19the magicians said to Pharaoh, "This is the finger of God." But Pharaoh's heart was hard and he would not listen, just as the LORD had said.

The Plague of Flies

20Then the LORD said to Moses, "Get up early in the morning and confront Pharaoh as he goes to the river and say to him, 'This is what the LORD says: Let my people go, so that they may worship me. 21If you do not let my people go, I will send swarms of flies on you and your officials, on your people and into your houses. The houses of the Egyptians will be full of flies; even the ground will be covered with them.

22" 'But on that day I will deal differently with the land of Goshen, where my people live; no swarms of flies will be there, so that you will know that I, the LORD, am in this land. 23I will make a distinction[a] between my people and your people. This sign will occur tomorrow.' "

24And the LORD did this. Dense swarms of flies poured into Pharaoh's palace and into the houses of his officials; throughout Egypt the land was ruined by the flies.

25Then Pharaoh summoned Moses and Aaron and said, "Go, sacrifice to your God here in the land."

26But Moses said, "That would not be right. The sacrifices we offer the LORD our God would be detestable to the Egyptians. And if we offer sacrifices that are detestable in their eyes, will they not stone us? 27We must take a three-day journey into the wilderness to offer sacrifices to the LORD our God, as he commands us."

28Pharaoh said, "I will let you go to offer sacrifices to the LORD your God in the wilderness, but you must not go very far. Now pray for me."

29Moses answered, "As soon as I leave you, I will pray to the LORD, and tomorrow the flies will leave Pharaoh and his officials and his people. Only let Pharaoh be sure that he does not act deceitfully again by not letting the people go to offer sacrifices to the LORD."

30Then Moses left Pharaoh and prayed to the LORD, 31and the LORD did what

[a] 23 Septuagint and Vulgate; Hebrew *will put a deliverance*

EXODUS 8:22

SET APART

In the fourth plague, God explicitly singled out the land of Goshen, the dwelling place of the Israelites, for protection from his judgment, making his people the recipients of his gracious mercy. God demonstrated his power through his ability to withhold a judgment, such as a swarm of flies, from a certain location while flies wreaked havoc on the rest of the surrounding region. No one could deny that the people of God were uniquely set apart to him.

In a similar fashion, God's people are uniquely set apart from God's judgment and for his use. Authors of the New Testament, such as Paul, used an astounding word to speak of Christians — they called believers "holy" (1Co 1:2; Eph 1:1). This word denotes a special type of person, not by virtue of their perfect conformity to God's law but because of the imputed righteousness provided through Christ's death. God's people are chosen by God to be holy, uniquely set apart for God's purposes and protected from his judgment (Col 3:12). In the coming age, those who trust in Jesus will be protected from the ultimate judgment of God, while many others will face eternal destruction.

Moses asked. The flies left Pharaoh and his officials and his people; not a fly remained. 32But this time also Pharaoh hardened his heart and would not let the people go.

The Plague on Livestock

9 Then the LORD said to Moses, "Go to Pharaoh and say to him, 'This is what the LORD, the God of the Hebrews, says: "Let my people go, so that they may worship me." 2If you refuse to let them go and continue to hold them back, 3the hand of the LORD will bring a terrible plague on your livestock in the field — on your horses, donkeys and camels and on your cattle, sheep and goats. 4But the LORD will make a distinction between the livestock of Israel and that of Egypt, so that no animal belonging to the Israelites will die.'"

5The LORD set a time and said, "Tomorrow the LORD will do this in the land." 6And the next day the LORD did it: All the livestock of the Egyptians died, but not one animal belonging to the Israelites died. 7Pharaoh investigated and found that not even one of the animals of the Israelites had died. Yet his heart was unyielding and he would not let the people go.

The Plague of Boils

8Then the LORD said to Moses and Aaron, "Take handfuls of soot from a furnace and have Moses toss it into the air in the presence of Pharaoh. 9It will become fine dust over the whole land of Egypt, and festering boils will break out on people and animals throughout the land."

10So they took soot from a furnace and stood before Pharaoh. Moses tossed it into the air, and festering boils broke out on people and animals. 11The magicians could not stand before Moses because of the boils that were on them and on all the Egyptians. 12But the LORD hardened Pharaoh's heart and he would not listen to Moses and Aaron, just as the LORD had said to Moses.

The Plague of Hail

13Then the LORD said to Moses, "Get up early in the morning, confront Pharaoh and say to him, 'This is what the LORD, the God of the Hebrews, says: Let my people go, so that they may worship me, 14or this time I will send the full force of my plagues against you and against your officials and your people, so you may know that there is no one like me in all the earth. 15For by now I could have stretched out my hand and struck you and your people with a plague that would have wiped you off the earth. 16But I have raised you up[a] for this very purpose, that I might show you my power and that my name might be proclaimed in all the earth. 17You still set yourself against my people and will not let them go. 18Therefore, at this time tomorrow I will send the worst hailstorm that has ever fallen on Egypt, from the day it was founded till now. 19Give an order now to bring your livestock and everything you have in the field to a place of shelter, because the hail will fall on every person and animal that has not been brought in and is still out in the field, and they will die.'"

20Those officials of Pharaoh who feared the word of the LORD hurried to bring their slaves and their livestock inside. 21But those who ignored the word of the LORD left their slaves and livestock in the field.

22Then the LORD said to Moses, "Stretch out your hand toward the sky so that hail will fall all over Egypt — on people and animals and on everything growing in the fields of Egypt." 23When Moses stretched out his staff toward the sky, the LORD sent thunder and hail, and lightning flashed down to the ground. So the LORD rained hail on the land of Egypt; 24hail fell and lightning flashed back and forth. It was the worst storm in all the land of Egypt since it had become a nation. 25Throughout Egypt hail struck everything in the fields — both people and animals; it beat down everything growing in the fields and stripped every

[a] 16 Or *have spared you*

EXODUS 9:13 – 16

PHARAOH

Pharaoh's vindictive rule contrasted sharply with the goodness of God. Pharaoh was an evil ruler of a powerful nation, setting himself up as the supreme object of his people's worship and obedience. God rightly judged Pharaoh's treachery in order to free his chosen people, demonstrate his power and declare his glory to the world. God hardened Pharaoh in his sin and demonstrated that he can, and will, use the disobedience of fallen humanity in order to accomplish his sovereign purposes.

Pilate fulfilled the same role in relation to God's mission to reclaim his wayward people. Facing death, Jesus stood before a ruler who failed to act justly. Fearing the wrath of the people, Pilate condemned Jesus to death. Jesus warned Pilate that only God granted him the power to hand down the death sentence. In the death of his Son, God used the hardness of heart of rebellious leaders to accomplish his good purposes (Jn 19:8 – 11). Though Pilate attempted to rid himself of the guilt of his crime (Mt 27:24 – 26), God will ultimately hold wayward leaders guilty for their sin. In time, all rulers, no matter how powerful, will face a far greater King who will execute his righteous judgment.

tree. 26The only place it did not hail was the land of Goshen, where the Israelites were.
27Then Pharaoh summoned Moses and Aaron. "This time I have sinned," he
said to them. "The LORD is in the right, and I and my people are in the wrong.
28Pray to the LORD, for we have had enough thunder and hail. I will let you go;
you don't have to stay any longer."
29Moses replied, "When I have gone out of the city, I will spread out my hands
in prayer to the LORD. The thunder will stop and there will be no more hail, so
you may know that the earth is the LORD's. 30But I know that you and your officials still do not fear the LORD God."
31(The flax and barley were destroyed, since the barley had headed and the
flax was in bloom. 32The wheat and spelt, however, were not destroyed, because
they ripen later.)
33Then Moses left Pharaoh and went out of the city. He spread out his hands
toward the LORD; the thunder and hail stopped, and the rain no longer poured
down on the land. 34When Pharaoh saw that the rain and hail and thunder had
stopped, he sinned again: He and his officials hardened their hearts. 35So Pharaoh's heart was hard and he would not let the Israelites go, just as the LORD had
said through Moses.

The Plague of Locusts

10 Then the LORD said to Moses, "Go to Pharaoh, for I have hardened his
heart and the hearts of his officials so that I may perform these signs of
mine among them 2that you may tell your children and grandchildren how I
dealt harshly with the Egyptians and how I performed my signs among them,
and that you may know that I am the LORD."
3So Moses and Aaron went to Pharaoh and said to him, "This is what the
LORD, the God of the Hebrews, says: 'How long will you refuse to humble yourself before me? Let my people go, so that they may worship me. 4If you refuse to
let them go, I will bring locusts into your country tomorrow. 5They will cover the
face of the ground so that it cannot be seen. They will devour what little you have
left after the hail, including every tree that is growing in your fields. 6They will
fill your houses and those of all your officials and all the Egyptians — something
neither your parents nor your ancestors have ever seen from the day they settled
in this land till now.' " Then Moses turned and left Pharaoh.
7Pharaoh's officials said to him, "How long will this man be a snare to us? Let
the people go, so that they may worship the LORD their God. Do you not yet realize that Egypt is ruined?"
8Then Moses and Aaron were brought back to Pharaoh. "Go, worship the
LORD your God," he said. "But tell me who will be going."
9Moses answered, "We will go with our young and our old, with our sons and
our daughters, and with our flocks and herds, because we are to celebrate a festival to the LORD."
10Pharaoh said, "The LORD be with you — if I let you go, along with your wom-
en and children! Clearly you are bent on evil.[a] 11No! Have only the men go and
worship the LORD, since that's what you have been asking for." Then Moses and
Aaron were driven out of Pharaoh's presence.
12And the LORD said to Moses, "Stretch out your hand over Egypt so that locusts swarm over the land and devour everything growing in the fields, everything left by the hail."
13So Moses stretched out his staff over Egypt, and the LORD made an east wind
blow across the land all that day and all that night. By morning the wind had
brought the locusts; 14they invaded all Egypt and settled down in every area of
the country in great numbers. Never before had there been such a plague of locusts, nor will there ever be again. 15They covered all the ground until it was

[a] 10 Or *Be careful, trouble is in store for you!*

black. They devoured all that was left after the hail — everything growing in the
fields and the fruit on the trees. Nothing green remained on tree or plant in all
the land of Egypt.
16Pharaoh quickly summoned Moses and Aaron and said, "I have sinned
against the LORD your God and against you. 17Now forgive my sin once more
and pray to the LORD your God to take this deadly plague away from me."
18Moses then left Pharaoh and prayed to the LORD. 19And the LORD changed
the wind to a very strong west wind, which caught up the locusts and carried
them into the Red Sea.[a] Not a locust was left anywhere in Egypt. 20But the LORD
hardened Pharaoh's heart, and he would not let the Israelites go.

The Plague of Darkness

21Then the LORD said to Moses, "Stretch out your hand toward the sky so that
darkness spreads over Egypt — darkness that can be felt." 22So Moses stretched
out his hand toward the sky, and total darkness covered all Egypt for three days.
23No one could see anyone else or move about for three days. Yet all the Israelites
had light in the places where they lived.
24Then Pharaoh summoned Moses and said, "Go, worship the LORD. Even your
women and children may go with you; only leave your flocks and herds behind."
25But Moses said, "You must allow us to have sacrifices and burnt offerings to
present to the LORD our God. 26Our livestock too must go with us; not a hoof is
to be left behind. We have to use some of them in worshiping the LORD our God,
and until we get there we will not know what we are to use to worship the LORD."
27But the LORD hardened Pharaoh's heart, and he was not willing to let them
go. 28Pharaoh said to Moses, "Get out of my sight! Make sure you do not appear
before me again! The day you see my face you will die."
29"Just as you say," Moses replied. "I will never appear before you again."

The Plague on the Firstborn

11 Now the LORD had said to Moses, "I will bring one more plague on Pharaoh
and on Egypt. After that, he will let you go from here, and when he does,
he will drive you out completely. 2Tell the people that men and women alike
are to ask their neighbors for articles of silver and gold." 3(The LORD made the
Egyptians favorably disposed toward the people, and Moses himself was highly
regarded in Egypt by Pharaoh's officials and by the people.)
4So Moses said, "This is what the LORD says: 'About midnight I will go throughout Egypt. 5Every firstborn son in Egypt will die, from the firstborn son of Pharaoh,
who sits on the throne, to the firstborn son of the female slave, who is at her hand
mill, and all the firstborn of the cattle as well. 6There will be loud wailing throughout Egypt — worse than there has ever been or ever will be again. 7But among the
Israelites not a dog will bark at any person or animal.' Then you will know that the
LORD makes a distinction between Egypt and Israel. 8All these officials of yours
will come to me, bowing down before me and saying, 'Go, you and all the people
who follow you!' After that I will leave." Then Moses, hot with anger, left Pharaoh.
9The LORD had said to Moses, "Pharaoh will refuse to listen to you — so that
my wonders may be multiplied in Egypt." 10Moses and Aaron performed all
these wonders before Pharaoh, but the LORD hardened Pharaoh's heart, and he
would not let the Israelites go out of his country.

The Passover and the Festival of Unleavened Bread

12 The LORD said to Moses and Aaron in Egypt, 2"This month is to be for you
the first month, the first month of your year. 3Tell the whole community of
Israel that on the tenth day of this month each man is to take a lamb[b] for his family,
one for each household. 4If any household is too small for a whole lamb, they must
share one with their nearest neighbor, having taken into account the number of

[a] *19* Or *the Sea of Reeds* [b] *3* The Hebrew word can mean *lamb* or *kid*; also in verse 4.

people there are. You are to determine the amount of lamb needed in accordance
with what each person will eat. 5The animals you choose must be year-old males
without defect, and you may take them from the sheep or the goats. 6Take care of
them until the fourteenth day of the month, when all the members of the community of Israel must slaughter them at twilight. 7Then they are to take some of
the blood and put it on the sides and tops of the doorframes of the houses where
they eat the lambs. 8That same night they are to eat the meat roasted over the fire,
along with bitter herbs, and bread made without yeast. 9Do not eat the meat raw
or boiled in water, but roast it over a fire—with the head, legs and internal organs.
10Do not leave any of it till morning; if some is left till morning, you must burn it.
11This is how you are to eat it: with your cloak tucked into your belt, your sandals
on your feet and your staff in your hand. Eat it in haste; it is the LORD's Passover.

12"On that same night I will pass through Egypt and strike down every firstborn of both people and animals, and I will bring judgment on all the gods of
Egypt. I am the LORD. 13The blood will be a sign for you on the houses where you
are, and when I see the blood, I will pass over you. No destructive plague will
touch you when I strike Egypt.

14"This is a day you are to commemorate; for the generations to come you shall
celebrate it as a festival to the LORD—a lasting ordinance. 15For seven days you
are to eat bread made without yeast. On the first day remove the yeast from your
houses, for whoever eats anything with yeast in it from the first day through the
seventh must be cut off from Israel. 16On the first day hold a sacred assembly,
and another one on the seventh day. Do no work at all on these days, except to
prepare food for everyone to eat; that is all you may do.

17"Celebrate the Festival of Unleavened Bread, because it was on this very
day that I brought your divisions out of Egypt. Celebrate this day as a lasting
ordinance for the generations to come. 18In the first month you are to eat bread
made without yeast, from the evening of the fourteenth day until the evening
of the twenty-first day. 19For seven days no yeast is to be found in your houses.
And anyone, whether foreigner or native-born, who eats anything with yeast in
it must be cut off from the community of Israel. 20Eat nothing made with yeast.
Wherever you live, you must eat unleavened bread."

21Then Moses summoned all the elders of Israel and said to them, "Go at once
and select the animals for your families and slaughter the Passover lamb. 22Take
a bunch of hyssop, dip it into the blood in the basin and put some of the blood on
the top and on both sides of the doorframe. None of you shall go out of the door
of your house until morning. 23When the LORD goes through the land to strike
down the Egyptians, he will see the blood on the top and sides of the doorframe
and will pass over that doorway, and he will not permit the destroyer to enter
your houses and strike you down.

24"Obey these instructions as a lasting ordinance for you and your descendants. 25When you enter the land that the LORD will give you as he promised, observe this ceremony. 26And when your children ask you, 'What does this ceremony mean to you?' 27then tell them, 'It is the Passover sacrifice to the LORD, who
passed over the houses of the Israelites in Egypt and spared our homes when
he struck down the Egyptians.'" Then the people bowed down and worshiped.
28The Israelites did just what the LORD commanded Moses and Aaron.

29At midnight the LORD struck down all the firstborn in Egypt, from the firstborn of Pharaoh, who sat on the throne, to the firstborn of the prisoner, who was
in the dungeon, and the firstborn of all the livestock as well. 30Pharaoh and all
his officials and all the Egyptians got up during the night, and there was loud
wailing in Egypt, for there was not a house without someone dead.

The Exodus

31During the night Pharaoh summoned Moses and Aaron and said, "Up! Leave
my people, you and the Israelites! Go, worship the LORD as you have requested.
32Take your flocks and herds, as you have said, and go. And also bless me."

EXODUS 12:1 – 30

THE PASSOVER LAMB

The Passover celebrates God's miraculous deliverance of his people from slavery in Egypt. The focal point of the ceremony was the sacrifice of a Passover lamb whose blood was placed on the doorframes of the houses of the Israelites. While God enacted his final plague, the killing of the firstborn of the nation of Egypt, those living in homes marked by blood were spared death.

God provided clear specifications for the lamb that could be used at Passover — the lamb had to be a young male, without blemish or defect. In order to ensure its purity, the lamb was examined for four days following its selection. Those animals meeting God's requirements were sacrificed in public, and none of the animal's bones could be broken (Ex 12:46). The severity of the coming judgment required that the people of God observe this sacrifice with the utmost care. The annual commemoration of the Passover reminded the people both of the faithfulness of God to provide deliverance for his people and of their ongoing need for a substitute to pay the price their sin deserved.

The Passover sacrifice is one of the clearest pictures in the Old Testament of the coming work of Jesus. At the beginning of his earthly ministry, John the Baptist called Jesus "the Lamb of God, who takes away the sin of the world" (Jn 1:29). His life met the requirements for a Passover sacrifice. He too was a young male, perfect in all ways. He would die a heinous, public death, though none of his bones were broken in the process (Jn 19:36). Because of Jesus' death, those covered by his blood are spared the coming judgment (Ro 5:9; Eph 2:13).

New Testament authors refer to Jesus' work using the imagery of the Passover because of the exact way in which Jesus fulfills the divinely orchestrated image of the Passover lamb (1Pe 1:19). Paul calls Jesus the Passover lamb who was sacrificed for his church (1Co 5:7). His perfect purity and substitutionary death uniquely qualified him to play this role. As the one and only Son of God, he could do what no animal could ever do — he could permanently satisfy the wrath of God on behalf of his people.

33The Egyptians urged the people to hurry and leave the country. "For otherwise," they said, "we will all die!" 34So the people took their dough before the yeast was added, and carried it on their shoulders in kneading troughs wrapped in clothing. 35The Israelites did as Moses instructed and asked the Egyptians for articles of silver and gold and for clothing. 36The LORD had made the Egyptians favorably disposed toward the people, and they gave them what they asked for; so they plundered the Egyptians.

37The Israelites journeyed from Rameses to Sukkoth. There were about six hundred thousand men on foot, besides women and children. 38Many other people went up with them, and also large droves of livestock, both flocks and herds. 39With the dough the Israelites had brought from Egypt, they baked loaves of unleavened bread. The dough was without yeast because they had been driven out of Egypt and did not have time to prepare food for themselves.

40Now the length of time the Israelite people lived in Egypt[a] was 430 years. 41At the end of the 430 years, to the very day, all the LORD's divisions left Egypt. 42Because the LORD kept vigil that night to bring them out of Egypt, on this night all the Israelites are to keep vigil to honor the LORD for the generations to come.

Passover Restrictions

43The LORD said to Moses and Aaron, "These are the regulations for the Passover meal:

"No foreigner may eat it. 44Any slave you have bought may eat it after you have circumcised him, 45but a temporary resident or a hired worker may not eat it.

46"It must be eaten inside the house; take none of the meat outside the house. Do not break any of the bones. 47The whole community of Israel must celebrate it.

48"A foreigner residing among you who wants to celebrate the LORD's Passover must have all the males in his household circumcised; then he may take part like one born in the land. No uncircumcised male may eat it. 49The same law applies both to the native-born and to the foreigner residing among you."

50All the Israelites did just what the LORD had commanded Moses and Aaron. 51And on that very day the LORD brought the Israelites out of Egypt by their divisions.

Consecration of the Firstborn

13 The LORD said to Moses, 2"Consecrate to me every firstborn male. The first offspring of every womb among the Israelites belongs to me, whether human or animal."

3Then Moses said to the people, "Commemorate this day, the day you came out of Egypt, out of the land of slavery, because the LORD brought you out of it with a mighty hand. Eat nothing containing yeast. 4Today, in the month of Aviv, you are leaving. 5When the LORD brings you into the land of the Canaanites, Hittites, Amorites, Hivites and Jebusites — the land he swore to your ancestors to give you, a land flowing with milk and honey — you are to observe this ceremony in this month: 6For seven days eat bread made without yeast and on the seventh day hold a festival to the LORD. 7Eat unleavened bread during those seven days; nothing with yeast in it is to be seen among you, nor shall any yeast be seen anywhere within your borders. 8On that day tell your son, 'I do this because of what the LORD did for me when I came out of Egypt.' 9This observance will be for you like a sign on your hand and a reminder on your forehead that this law of the LORD is to be on your lips. For the LORD brought you out of Egypt with his mighty hand. 10You must keep this ordinance at the appointed time year after year.

11"After the LORD brings you into the land of the Canaanites and gives it to you, as he promised on oath to you and your ancestors, 12you are to give over to the LORD the first offspring of every womb. All the firstborn males of your

[a] 40 Masoretic Text; Samaritan Pentateuch and Septuagint *Egypt and Canaan*

livestock belong to the LORD. [13]Redeem with a lamb every firstborn donkey, but if you do not redeem it, break its neck. Redeem every firstborn among your sons.

[14]"In days to come, when your son asks you, 'What does this mean?' say to him, 'With a mighty hand the LORD brought us out of Egypt, out of the land of slavery. [15]When Pharaoh stubbornly refused to let us go, the LORD killed the firstborn of both people and animals in Egypt. This is why I sacrifice to the LORD the first male offspring of every womb and redeem each of my firstborn sons.' [16]And it will be like a sign on your hand and a symbol on your forehead that the LORD brought us out of Egypt with his mighty hand."

Crossing the Sea

[17]When Pharaoh let the people go, God did not lead them on the road through the Philistine country, though that was shorter. For God said, "If they face war, they might change their minds and return to Egypt." [18]So God led the people around by the desert road toward the Red Sea.[a] The Israelites went up out of Egypt ready for battle.

[19]Moses took the bones of Joseph with him because Joseph had made the Israelites swear an oath. He had said, "God will surely come to your aid, and then you must carry my bones up with you from this place."[b]

[20]After leaving Sukkoth they camped at Etham on the edge of the desert. [21]By day the LORD went ahead of them in a pillar of cloud to guide them on their way and by night in a pillar of fire to give them light, so that they could travel by day or night. [22]Neither the pillar of cloud by day nor the pillar of fire by night left its place in front of the people.

14 Then the LORD said to Moses, [2]"Tell the Israelites to turn back and encamp near Pi Hahiroth, between Migdol and the sea. They are to encamp by the sea, directly opposite Baal Zephon. [3]Pharaoh will think, 'The Israelites are wandering around the land in confusion, hemmed in by the desert.' [4]And I will harden Pharaoh's heart, and he will pursue them. But I will gain glory for myself through Pharaoh and all his army, and the Egyptians will know that I am the LORD." So the Israelites did this.

[5]When the king of Egypt was told that the people had fled, Pharaoh and his officials changed their minds about them and said, "What have we done? We have let the Israelites go and have lost their services!" [6]So he had his chariot made ready and took his army with him. [7]He took six hundred of the best chariots, along with all the other chariots of Egypt, with officers over all of them. [8]The LORD hardened the heart of Pharaoh king of Egypt, so that he pursued the Israelites, who were marching out boldly. [9]The Egyptians — all Pharaoh's horses and chariots, horsemen[c] and troops — pursued the Israelites and overtook them as they camped by the sea near Pi Hahiroth, opposite Baal Zephon.

[10]As Pharaoh approached, the Israelites looked up, and there were the Egyptians, marching after them. They were terrified and cried out to the LORD. [11]They said to Moses, "Was it because there were no graves in Egypt that you brought us to the desert to die? What have you done to us by bringing us out of Egypt? [12]Didn't we say to you in Egypt, 'Leave us alone; let us serve the Egyptians'? It would have been better for us to serve the Egyptians than to die in the desert!"

[13]Moses answered the people, "Do not be afraid. Stand firm and you will see the deliverance the LORD will bring you today. The Egyptians you see today you will never see again. [14]The LORD will fight for you; you need only to be still."

[15]Then the LORD said to Moses, "Why are you crying out to me? Tell the Israelites to move on. [16]Raise your staff and stretch out your hand over the sea to divide the water so that the Israelites can go through the sea on dry ground. [17]I will harden the hearts of the Egyptians so that they will go in after them. And I will gain glory through Pharaoh and all his army, through his chariots and

---

[a] *18* Or *the Sea of Reeds* [b] *19* See Gen. 50:25. [c] *9* Or *charioteers*; also in verses 17, 18, 23, 26 and 28

EXODUS 13:21 – 22

THE LIGHT

As night fell, the darkness of the desert made travel virtually impossible. The movement of thousands of people across a rugged terrain was not easy in the day, much less at night. Light was a practical necessity for survival in the wilderness. Without it, the people would be left to stumble in the darkness, face the constant fear of unforeseen attacks by their enemies and struggle to accomplish the basic actions necessary for living in a harsh land.

Once again, God provided for his people in a unique way. Rather than asking the people to create light, he provided it for them in the form of a pillar of fire. Often a mark of judgment, here the fire of God was a means of his provision. Even more, the fire embodied the presence of God among his people. The Israelites simply looked out at night, saw the pillar of fire and were reminded that God was their God and they were his people. He had broken into the darkness of human history and chosen them to be his. Even in the wilderness, they were reminded that God had worked mighty deeds of deliverance on their behalf and was leading them to the land of promise.

God's very being is characterized by light. The apostle John wrote, "God is light; in him there is no darkness at all" (1Jn 1:5). His holiness is described as a perfect light, without the darkness of sin. Jesus, as the perfect Son of God, was sent on a mission to a dark world. His birth was the embodiment of God's light (Jn 1:5). He came to a sin-darkened world and overcame that darkness by his all-consuming light.

He lights the path by which all those who know him can follow him. God's children no longer have to cower in the darkness; they can come into the light where they will discover newfound safety, peace and joy. In fact, a central mark of God's people is that they love the light. Sin festers and grows in the darkness, so those who long to obey God renounce the darkness and drag their sin into the light of God's grace. There they find fellowship with God and fellowship with one another (1Jn 1:6 – 7). In God's light, sin is hated, repentance is ongoing and holiness is pursued.

his horsemen. 18The Egyptians will know that I am the LORD when I gain glory
through Pharaoh, his chariots and his horsemen."
19Then the angel of God, who had been traveling in front of Israel's army, withdrew and went behind them. The pillar of cloud also moved from in front and
stood behind them, 20coming between the armies of Egypt and Israel. Throughout the night the cloud brought darkness to the one side and light to the other
side; so neither went near the other all night long.
21Then Moses stretched out his hand over the sea, and all that night the LORD
drove the sea back with a strong east wind and turned it into dry land. The waters were divided, 22and the Israelites went through the sea on dry ground, with
a wall of water on their right and on their left.
23The Egyptians pursued them, and all Pharaoh's horses and chariots and
horsemen followed them into the sea. 24During the last watch of the night the
LORD looked down from the pillar of fire and cloud at the Egyptian army and
threw it into confusion. 25He jammed[a] the wheels of their chariots so that they
had difficulty driving. And the Egyptians said, "Let's get away from the Israelites! The LORD is fighting for them against Egypt."
26Then the LORD said to Moses, "Stretch out your hand over the sea so that
the waters may flow back over the Egyptians and their chariots and horsemen."
27Moses stretched out his hand over the sea, and at daybreak the sea went back
to its place. The Egyptians were fleeing toward[b] it, and the LORD swept them into
the sea. 28The water flowed back and covered the chariots and horsemen — the
entire army of Pharaoh that had followed the Israelites into the sea. Not one of
them survived.
29But the Israelites went through the sea on dry ground, with a wall of water on their right and on their left. 30That day the LORD saved Israel from the
hands of the Egyptians, and Israel saw the Egyptians lying dead on the shore.
31And when the Israelites saw the mighty hand of the LORD displayed against
the Egyptians, the people feared the LORD and put their trust in him and in Moses his servant.

The Song of Moses and Miriam

15 Then Moses and the Israelites sang this song to the LORD:

"I will sing to the LORD,
for he is highly exalted.
Both horse and driver
he has hurled into the sea.

2 "The LORD is my strength and my defense[c];
he has become my salvation.
He is my God, and I will praise him,
my father's God, and I will exalt him.
3 The LORD is a warrior;
the LORD is his name.
4 Pharaoh's chariots and his army
he has hurled into the sea.
The best of Pharaoh's officers
are drowned in the Red Sea.[d]
5 The deep waters have covered them;
they sank to the depths like a stone.
6 Your right hand, LORD,
was majestic in power.
Your right hand, LORD,
shattered the enemy.

[a] 25 See Samaritan Pentateuch, Septuagint and Syriac; Masoretic Text *removed*
[b] 27 Or *from* [c] 2 Or *song* [d] 4 Or *the Sea of Reeds*; also in verse 22

EXODUS 14:21 – 31

THE GREAT ONE

The great work of deliverance is attributed to God and God alone. Literally, the passage refers to "the mighty hand of the LORD" (v. 31), which powerfully acted on behalf of his people and broke the shackles of their slavery. The people clearly understood the might of God displayed in this act because they responded in awestruck fear. The great work of a great God propelled Israel into their subsequent journey toward the promised land.

Throughout human history the strong arm of the Lord has worked on behalf of his people. He gave them victory and delivered them from the dire circumstances caused by their sinful rebellion (Ps 89:13; 118:15 – 24), foreshadowing the climactic moment when God broke into human history through the person of Jesus Christ. Jesus' perfect life, substitutionary death and victorious resurrection accomplish a far greater work of deliverance than the exodus from Egypt. Christ's work accomplished a "great" salvation for all his people (Heb 2:3). Like the nation of Israel responded, our proper response to the great work accomplished by this great God is awestruck worship.

EXODUS 15:1 – 21

VICTORY SONG

The juxtaposition of "strength" and "song" portrays the basis for the song found in Exodus 15. This entire passage reflects a victory cry from the people of God recounting the profound strength and power of

(continued on page 107)

PATH OF DELIVERANCE

Moses' command to not be afraid must have sounded foolish as the Israelites watched as Pharaoh and his army drew near. Yet, the Lord promised to provide salvation by accomplishing a deed so vast, so incredible and so unheard of that only God could do it.

The people stood on the brink of the Red Sea, unable to cross, with the sound of six hundred chariots barreling down upon them. At best, they would be hauled off to return to slavery in Egypt where they would be forced to work even harder than before. At worst, they would be killed for their insurrection. The hardness of Pharaoh's heart proved that the latter was the more likely outcome.

God promised, however, that he would provide a way of escape — the people must simply trust in him. After commanding Moses to lift up his staff and stretch out his hand, God told him to divide the water and instruct the people to walk forward in God's path of deliverance. The vast Red Sea obeyed the command of the Lord and formed a wall of water on either side of the Israelites, allowing them to walk forward on dry ground. After safely arriving on the other bank, the nation of God turned around to watch the waters consume the army of Pharaoh.

These types of scenes are all too common for the people of God. Their sin places them in situations where, unless God acts and delivers them, they will be crushed and consumed. The angelic announcement on the night of Jesus' birth demonstrated that he had come to deliver his people. "Do not be afraid," the angel said to the shepherds. "I bring you good news that will cause great joy for all the people" (Lk 2:10).

This good news follows a similar blueprint as God's deliverance of his people at the Red Sea. Jesus' work provides a singular way of deliverance (Jn 14:6). He is, in fact, the only way in which sinful mankind can be delivered from the plight of sin. This path is not easy, however. It is a narrow path, and only those who trust God and spurn the ways of this world will be led to safety (Mt 7:13 – 14). Like Israel before, the church today must trust that God will deliver his people, but only through the path that he has made in Christ.

[7] "In the greatness of your majesty
you threw down those who opposed you.
You unleashed your burning anger;
it consumed them like stubble.
[8] By the blast of your nostrils
the waters piled up.
The surging waters stood up like a wall;
the deep waters congealed in the heart of the sea.
[9] The enemy boasted,
'I will pursue, I will overtake them.
I will divide the spoils;
I will gorge myself on them.
I will draw my sword
and my hand will destroy them.'
[10] But you blew with your breath,
and the sea covered them.
They sank like lead
in the mighty waters.
[11] Who among the gods
is like you, LORD?
Who is like you —
majestic in holiness,
awesome in glory,
working wonders?
[12] "You stretch out your right hand,
and the earth swallows your enemies.
[13] In your unfailing love you will lead
the people you have redeemed.
In your strength you will guide them
to your holy dwelling.
[14] The nations will hear and tremble;
anguish will grip the people of Philistia.
[15] The chiefs of Edom will be terrified,
the leaders of Moab will be seized with trembling,
the people[a] of Canaan will melt away;
16 terror and dread will fall on them.
By the power of your arm
they will be as still as a stone —
until your people pass by, LORD,
until the people you bought[b] pass by.
[17] You will bring them in and plant them
on the mountain of your inheritance —
the place, LORD, you made for your dwelling,
the sanctuary, Lord, your hands established.
[18] "The LORD reigns
for ever and ever."

[19] When Pharaoh's horses, chariots and horsemen[c] went into the sea, the LORD
brought the waters of the sea back over them, but the Israelites walked through
the sea on dry ground. [20] Then Miriam the prophet, Aaron's sister, took a timbrel
in her hand, and all the women followed her, with timbrels and dancing. [21] Miriam sang to them:

"Sing to the LORD,
for he is highly exalted.

[a] 15 Or *rulers* [b] 16 Or *created* [c] 19 Or *charioteers*

(Victory Song, continued)

the Lord shown in their deliverance. They sang as a redeemed people, confidently relishing the powerful kindness God had shown them. The divine, sovereign and omnipotent God acted to deliver his beloved people. This work was not motivated by the inherent righteousness of the people of God. In fact, the case is just the opposite. God's strength is seen in his action toward a depraved, wayward and stiff-necked people whom he knew would be unfaithful to their covenant promises.

God continued to act strongly on behalf of his people through Jesus, who defeats Satan, sin and death forever. As a result, Paul could taunt death in his letter to the church at Corinth, mocking the fact that the sting of sin and death has been revoked through Christ's redemptive work (1Co 15:54 – 57). The church can sing a strong, victorious and joyful cry of deliverance to God.

EXODUS 16:4–5

GOD PROVIDES

With the Passover and mighty works of God at the forefront of their minds, Moses led the nation of Israel across a body of water into the wilderness and up to a mountain. Along the way, the massive, hungry gaggle of people had to trust God for the provision of bread from heaven as they divided into their allotted encampments each night, trusting that they could skip collecting bread on the Sabbath and survive the harsh desert conditions.

In John's Gospel, Jesus engaged the people in a similar drama. As the Passover season was immediately at hand and because of the mighty works of God done by Jesus, a large crowd of people followed him across a body of water and up to a mountain in the wilderness (Jn 6:1–4). Jesus then proceeded to sustain them with bread and meat in the wilderness (Jn 6:5–13).

Ultimately, Jesus offered the people the opportunity to participate in a second exodus—a spiritual exodus. In this exodus, he wanted them to do more than eat the physical bread which would sustain them for a day, but to trust in him so that they might eat and live forever (Jn 6:47–51).

Both horse and driver
  he has hurled into the sea."

The Waters of Marah and Elim

[22]Then Moses led Israel from the Red Sea and they went into the Desert of
Shur. For three days they traveled in the desert without finding water. [23]When
they came to Marah, they could not drink its water because it was bitter. (That is
why the place is called Marah.[a]) [24]So the people grumbled against Moses, saying, "What are we to drink?"

[25]Then Moses cried out to the LORD, and the LORD showed him a piece of
wood. He threw it into the water, and the water became fit to drink.

There the LORD issued a ruling and instruction for them and put them to the
test. [26]He said, "If you listen carefully to the LORD your God and do what is right
in his eyes, if you pay attention to his commands and keep all his decrees, I will
not bring on you any of the diseases I brought on the Egyptians, for I am the
LORD, who heals you."

[27]Then they came to Elim, where there were twelve springs and seventy palm
trees, and they camped there near the water.

Manna and Quail

16 The whole Israelite community set out from Elim and came to the Desert
of Sin, which is between Elim and Sinai, on the fifteenth day of the second
month after they had come out of Egypt. [2]In the desert the whole community
grumbled against Moses and Aaron. [3]The Israelites said to them, "If only we had
died by the LORD's hand in Egypt! There we sat around pots of meat and ate all
the food we wanted, but you have brought us out into this desert to starve this
entire assembly to death."

[4]Then the LORD said to Moses, "I will rain down bread from heaven for you.
The people are to go out each day and gather enough for that day. In this way I
will test them and see whether they will follow my instructions. [5]On the sixth
day they are to prepare what they bring in, and that is to be twice as much as they
gather on the other days."

[6]So Moses and Aaron said to all the Israelites, "In the evening you will know
that it was the LORD who brought you out of Egypt, [7]and in the morning you
will see the glory of the LORD, because he has heard your grumbling against
him. Who are we, that you should grumble against us?" [8]Moses also said, "You
will know that it was the LORD when he gives you meat to eat in the evening
and all the bread you want in the morning, because he has heard your grumbling against him. Who are we? You are not grumbling against us, but against
the LORD."

[9]Then Moses told Aaron, "Say to the entire Israelite community, 'Come before
the LORD, for he has heard your grumbling.' "

[10]While Aaron was speaking to the whole Israelite community, they looked
toward the desert, and there was the glory of the LORD appearing in the cloud.

[11]The LORD said to Moses, [12]"I have heard the grumbling of the Israelites. Tell
them, 'At twilight you will eat meat, and in the morning you will be filled with
bread. Then you will know that I am the LORD your God.' "

[13]That evening quail came and covered the camp, and in the morning there
was a layer of dew around the camp. [14]When the dew was gone, thin flakes like
frost on the ground appeared on the desert floor. [15]When the Israelites saw it,
they said to each other, "What is it?" For they did not know what it was.

Moses said to them, "It is the bread the LORD has given you to eat. [16]This is
what the LORD has commanded: 'Everyone is to gather as much as they need.
Take an omer[b] for each person you have in your tent.' "

---

[a] *23* *Marah* means *bitter*. [b] *16* That is, possibly about 3 pounds or about 1.4 kilograms; also in verses 18, 32, 33 and 36

[17]The Israelites did as they were told; some gathered much, some little. [18]And when they measured it by the omer, the one who gathered much did not have too much, and the one who gathered little did not have too little. Everyone had gathered just as much as they needed.

[19]Then Moses said to them, "No one is to keep any of it until morning."

[20]However, some of them paid no attention to Moses; they kept part of it until morning, but it was full of maggots and began to smell. So Moses was angry with them.

[21]Each morning everyone gathered as much as they needed, and when the sun grew hot, it melted away. [22]On the sixth day, they gathered twice as much — two omers[a] for each person — and the leaders of the community came and reported this to Moses. [23]He said to them, "This is what the LORD commanded: 'Tomorrow is to be a day of sabbath rest, a holy sabbath to the LORD. So bake what you want to bake and boil what you want to boil. Save whatever is left and keep it until morning.'"

[24]So they saved it until morning, as Moses commanded, and it did not stink or get maggots in it. [25]"Eat it today," Moses said, "because today is a sabbath to the LORD. You will not find any of it on the ground today. [26]Six days you are to gather it, but on the seventh day, the Sabbath, there will not be any."

[27]Nevertheless, some of the people went out on the seventh day to gather it, but they found none. [28]Then the LORD said to Moses, "How long will you[b] refuse to keep my commands and my instructions? [29]Bear in mind that the LORD has given you the Sabbath; that is why on the sixth day he gives you bread for two days. Everyone is to stay where they are on the seventh day; no one is to go out." [30]So the people rested on the seventh day.

[31]The people of Israel called the bread manna.[c] It was white like coriander seed and tasted like wafers made with honey. [32]Moses said, "This is what the LORD has commanded: 'Take an omer of manna and keep it for the generations to come, so they can see the bread I gave you to eat in the wilderness when I brought you out of Egypt.'"

[33]So Moses said to Aaron, "Take a jar and put an omer of manna in it. Then place it before the LORD to be kept for the generations to come."

[34]As the LORD commanded Moses, Aaron put the manna with the tablets of the covenant law, so that it might be preserved. [35]The Israelites ate manna forty years, until they came to a land that was settled; they ate manna until they reached the border of Canaan.

[36](An omer is one-tenth of an ephah.)

Water From the Rock

17 The whole Israelite community set out from the Desert of Sin, traveling from place to place as the LORD commanded. They camped at Rephidim, but there was no water for the people to drink. [2]So they quarreled with Moses and said, "Give us water to drink."

Moses replied, "Why do you quarrel with me? Why do you put the LORD to the test?"

[3]But the people were thirsty for water there, and they grumbled against Moses. They said, "Why did you bring us up out of Egypt to make us and our children and livestock die of thirst?"

[4]Then Moses cried out to the LORD, "What am I to do with these people? They are almost ready to stone me."

[5]The LORD answered Moses, "Go out in front of the people. Take with you some of the elders of Israel and take in your hand the staff with which you struck the Nile, and go. [6]I will stand there before you by the rock at Horeb. Strike the rock, and water will come out of it for the people to drink." So Moses did this in

[a] *22* That is, possibly about 6 pounds or about 2.8 kilograms [b] *28* The Hebrew is plural.
[c] *31* *Manna* sounds like the Hebrew for *What is it?* (see verse 15).

EXODUS 17:6

STRIKING THE ROCK

Despite Israel's faithlessness, God continued to provide for his people. In this particular instance, God sustained the people by having Moses strike the rock, from which water miraculously began to flow. While this provision was a startling way to provide water, the water itself was normal. The people of Israel would need water again in the future, and God would certainly provide.

In John 4:13 – 14, Jesus responded to a request for water by claiming that he could provide water that would cause a person never to be thirsty again. Jesus would indeed provide this water, but he was not speaking of literal water. Instead, Jesus was referencing the way in which God would provide salvation from sin. In the same way that Moses struck the rock to provide the life-saving water, Jesus was stricken and afflicted on the cross in order to provide the life-giving water of salvation. God struck one rock to provide for the temporary, physical needs of his people, but he struck the second Rock to provide for the spiritual needs of his people.

BREAD FROM HEAVEN

God fed his people with bread from heaven. This act of kindness was magnified by the fact that God's people seemed to be filled with unending complaints against God and the leaders he had appointed. They foolishly longed for the days of slavery in Egypt, where they recalled eating pots of meat and all the food they wanted. Now they feared that they would starve in the wilderness. Only one chapter removed from the miraculous deliverance at the Red Sea and their song of victory, the people now blamed God and mourned their seemingly dire circumstances.

God faithfully feeds his faithless children. His motive for providing this food is clear — God wanted his people to see his glory and remember that he was working on their behalf. Each day, they awakened to fresh evidence of God's generosity. And this blessing was specific, not just to the nation of Israel as a whole, but also to each of the families of the people of God.

Jesus compared his mission on this earth to the provision of manna in the desert. After demonstrating his miraculous power by feeding 5,000 on a hillside and walking on water, he describes himself as "the bread of life" (Jn 6:35). Those who know him discover a source of nourishment far greater than any meal can provide. Jesus satisfies the craving of all those longing for a source of satisfaction in life and hope in the life to come. Like manna in the wilderness, Jesus provides food for a hungry soul. His provision is sufficient to meet the needs of all those who, by faith, feast on him. In shocking imagery, Jesus said that those who eat his flesh and drink his blood will have eternal life (Jn 6:53 – 54). Many, upon hearing these words, turned back and no longer followed Jesus (Jn 6:66).

On the night he was betrayed, these startling words would have profound significance. In an upper room, Jesus would celebrate the Passover with his disciples. There he would break a loaf of bread as a picture of his soon-to-be-broken body. From that time on, those who know Jesus celebrate the Lord's Supper by eating the bread as a reminder of the Lord's great sacrifice. They are reminded that true fulfillment, satisfaction and nourishment are found by feasting on the bread from heaven, broken for his followers.

the sight of the elders of Israel. 7And he called the place Massah[a] and Meribah[b]
because the Israelites quarreled and because they tested the LORD saying, "Is
the LORD among us or not?"

The Amalekites Defeated

8The Amalekites came and attacked the Israelites at Rephidim. 9Moses said to
Joshua, "Choose some of our men and go out to fight the Amalekites. Tomorrow I
will stand on top of the hill with the staff of God in my hands."

10So Joshua fought the Amalekites as Moses had ordered, and Moses, Aaron
and Hur went to the top of the hill. 11As long as Moses held up his hands, the Israelites were winning, but whenever he lowered his hands, the Amalekites were
winning. 12When Moses' hands grew tired, they took a stone and put it under
him and he sat on it. Aaron and Hur held his hands up — one on one side, one on
the other — so that his hands remained steady till sunset. 13So Joshua overcame
the Amalekite army with the sword.

14Then the LORD said to Moses, "Write this on a scroll as something to be remembered and make sure that Joshua hears it, because I will completely blot out
the name of Amalek from under heaven."

15Moses built an altar and called it The LORD is my Banner. 16He said, "Because hands were lifted up against[c] the throne of the LORD,[d] the LORD will be at
war against the Amalekites from generation to generation."

Jethro Visits Moses

18 Now Jethro, the priest of Midian and father-in-law of Moses, heard of everything God had done for Moses and for his people Israel, and how the
LORD had brought Israel out of Egypt.

2After Moses had sent away his wife Zipporah, his father-in-law Jethro received her 3and her two sons. One son was named Gershom,[e] for Moses said,
"I have become a foreigner in a foreign land"; 4and the other was named Eliezer,[f] for he said, "My father's God was my helper; he saved me from the sword
of Pharaoh."

5Jethro, Moses' father-in-law, together with Moses' sons and wife, came to
him in the wilderness, where he was camped near the mountain of God. 6Jethro
had sent word to him, "I, your father-in-law Jethro, am coming to you with your
wife and her two sons."

7So Moses went out to meet his father-in-law and bowed down and kissed
him. They greeted each other and then went into the tent. 8Moses told his father-in-law about everything the LORD had done to Pharaoh and the Egyptians
for Israel's sake and about all the hardships they had met along the way and how
the LORD had saved them.

9Jethro was delighted to hear about all the good things the LORD had done for
Israel in rescuing them from the hand of the Egyptians. 10He said, "Praise be to
the LORD, who rescued you from the hand of the Egyptians and of Pharaoh, and
who rescued the people from the hand of the Egyptians. 11Now I know that the
LORD is greater than all other gods, for he did this to those who had treated Israel arrogantly." 12Then Jethro, Moses' father-in-law, brought a burnt offering and
other sacrifices to God, and Aaron came with all the elders of Israel to eat a meal
with Moses' father-in-law in the presence of God.

13The next day Moses took his seat to serve as judge for the people, and they
stood around him from morning till evening. 14When his father-in-law saw all
that Moses was doing for the people, he said, "What is this you are doing for the
people? Why do you alone sit as judge, while all these people stand around you
from morning till evening?"

---

[a] 7 *Massah* means *testing.* [b] 7 *Meribah* means *quarreling.* [c] 16 Or *to* [d] 16 The meaning of the Hebrew for this clause is uncertain. [e] 3 *Gershom* sounds like the Hebrew for *a foreigner there.* [f] 4 *Eliezer* means *my God is helper.*

WATER FROM THE ROCK

The people demanded that Moses provide water to satiate their thirst. God provided Moses with instructions for how to provide water for their needs. God told Moses to take the rod and strike a rock. From this unlikely source, God provided water to meet the people's need. The faithless Israelites were reminded that the Lord would take care of them by bringing water from a rock.

The rock of God continues to nourish God's people throughout all of redemptive history. Centuries after God's miraculous provision from a rock in the wilderness, Jesus faced another group of contentious people. This time the Pharisees and the Sadducees asked him to show them a sign to validate his authority. Jesus, knowing their hearts, refused to entertain their demands. Rather, he took his disciples to a remote, mountainous location at Caesarea Philippi and there gave them a vivid object lesson.

He asked his followers to describe the public opinion regarding his identity. Peter, as the outspoken leader of Jesus' inner circle, declared that Jesus is "the Messiah, the Son of the living God" (Mt 16:16). These titles were not mere flattery, but demonstrated that Peter understood Jesus to be the long-awaited King in the line of David. Jesus responded to Peter, whose name means "rock," telling him that this confession would be the basis for the foundation of his church. Jesus will build his church on this truth, and nothing, not even the gates of hell, will be able to destroy his church (Mt 16:17 – 18).

This rock will provide water for God's people for days without end. Jesus himself will provide streams of living water to his people in the church. Those who recognize their thirst can come to Jesus and be satisfied. Not only that, but the Spirit of God will fill them with streams of living water to quench their thirst forever (Jn 7:38 – 39).

15Moses answered him, "Because the people come to me to seek God's will.
16Whenever they have a dispute, it is brought to me, and I decide between the
parties and inform them of God's decrees and instructions."
17Moses' father-in-law replied, "What you are doing is not good. 18You and
these people who come to you will only wear yourselves out. The work is too
heavy for you; you cannot handle it alone. 19Listen now to me and I will give
you some advice, and may God be with you. You must be the people's representative before God and bring their disputes to him. 20Teach them his decrees
and instructions, and show them the way they are to live and how they are to
behave. 21But select capable men from all the people — men who fear God, trustworthy men who hate dishonest gain — and appoint them as officials over thousands, hundreds, fifties and tens. 22Have them serve as judges for the people at
all times, but have them bring every difficult case to you; the simple cases they
can decide themselves. That will make your load lighter, because they will share
it with you. 23If you do this and God so commands, you will be able to stand the
strain, and all these people will go home satisfied."
24Moses listened to his father-in-law and did everything he said. 25He chose
capable men from all Israel and made them leaders of the people, officials over
thousands, hundreds, fifties and tens. 26They served as judges for the people at
all times. The difficult cases they brought to Moses, but the simple ones they
decided themselves.
27Then Moses sent his father-in-law on his way, and Jethro returned to his
own country.

At Mount Sinai

19 On the first day of the third month after the Israelites left Egypt — on that
very day — they came to the Desert of Sinai. 2After they set out from Rephidim, they entered the Desert of Sinai, and Israel camped there in the desert in
front of the mountain.
3Then Moses went up to God, and the LORD called to him from the mountain
and said, "This is what you are to say to the descendants of Jacob and what you
are to tell the people of Israel: 4'You yourselves have seen what I did to Egypt, and
how I carried you on eagles' wings and brought you to myself. 5Now if you obey
me fully and keep my covenant, then out of all nations you will be my treasured
possession. Although the whole earth is mine, 6you[a] will be for me a kingdom of
priests and a holy nation.' These are the words you are to speak to the Israelites."
7So Moses went back and summoned the elders of the people and set before
them all the words the LORD had commanded him to speak. 8The people all responded together, "We will do everything the LORD has said." So Moses brought
their answer back to the LORD.
9The LORD said to Moses, "I am going to come to you in a dense cloud, so that
the people will hear me speaking with you and will always put their trust in you."
Then Moses told the LORD what the people had said.
10And the LORD said to Moses, "Go to the people and consecrate them today
and tomorrow. Have them wash their clothes 11and be ready by the third day,
because on that day the LORD will come down on Mount Sinai in the sight of all
the people. 12Put limits for the people around the mountain and tell them, 'Be
careful that you do not approach the mountain or touch the foot of it. Whoever
touches the mountain is to be put to death. 13They are to be stoned or shot with
arrows; not a hand is to be laid on them. No person or animal shall be permitted
to live.' Only when the ram's horn sounds a long blast may they approach the
mountain."
14After Moses had gone down the mountain to the people, he consecrated
them, and they washed their clothes. 15Then he said to the people, "Prepare
yourselves for the third day. Abstain from sexual relations."

---

[a] 5,6 Or *possession, for the whole earth is mine.* 6*You*

EXODUS 19:12

APPROACHING GOD

God's people were forbidden from approaching God. Graciously, God dwelt among the people at his appointed mountain. This location, however, was protected lest the sinful people came near to a holy God. The all-consuming holiness of God would consume those who came into his presence. Only the priests at certain appointed times and in clearly defined ways could enter the presence of God. God was so concerned about protecting his dwelling that he instructed Moses to set boundaries around the mountain to keep the people at a safe distance. If the people failed to honor the boundaries, they were harshly judged by God.

The book of Hebrews demonstrates a stark transition that occurred as a result of Christ's work. Since Jesus perfectly and finally provided the sacrifice for the sins of his people, the dividing walls between God and man have been removed. A new and living way has now been opened whereby God's people can have confidence to draw near to him through the blood of Christ (Heb 10:19–22). Rather than finding safety by maintaining distance from God, those who know Christ can find safety by drawing near to God.

[16]On the morning of the third day there was thunder and lightning, with a
thick cloud over the mountain, and a very loud trumpet blast. Everyone in the
camp trembled. [17]Then Moses led the people out of the camp to meet with God,
and they stood at the foot of the mountain. [18]Mount Sinai was covered with
smoke, because the LORD descended on it in fire. The smoke billowed up from
it like smoke from a furnace, and the whole mountain[a] trembled violently. [19]As
the sound of the trumpet grew louder and louder, Moses spoke and the voice of
God answered him.[b]

[20]The LORD descended to the top of Mount Sinai and called Moses to the top
of the mountain. So Moses went up [21]and the LORD said to him, "Go down and
warn the people so they do not force their way through to see the LORD and many
of them perish. [22]Even the priests, who approach the LORD, must consecrate
themselves, or the LORD will break out against them."

[23]Moses said to the LORD, "The people cannot come up Mount Sinai, because
you yourself warned us, 'Put limits around the mountain and set it apart as holy.'"

[24]The LORD replied, "Go down and bring Aaron up with you. But the priests
and the people must not force their way through to come up to the LORD, or he
will break out against them."

[25]So Moses went down to the people and told them.

The Ten Commandments

20 And God spoke all these words:

[2]"I am the LORD your God, who brought you out of Egypt, out of the
land of slavery.

[3]"You shall have no other gods before[c] me.

[4]"You shall not make for yourself an image in the form of anything in heaven
above or on the earth beneath or in the waters below. [5]You shall not
bow down to them or worship them; for I, the LORD your God, am a
jealous God, punishing the children for the sin of the parents to the
third and fourth generation of those who hate me, [6]but showing love
to a thousand generations of those who love me and keep my commandments.

[7]"You shall not misuse the name of the LORD your God, for the LORD will not
hold anyone guiltless who misuses his name.

[8]"Remember the Sabbath day by keeping it holy. [9]Six days you shall labor
and do all your work, [10]but the seventh day is a sabbath to the LORD
your God. On it you shall not do any work, neither you, nor your son or
daughter, nor your male or female servant, nor your animals, nor any
foreigner residing in your towns. [11]For in six days the LORD made the
heavens and the earth, the sea, and all that is in them, but he rested
on the seventh day. Therefore the LORD blessed the Sabbath day and
made it holy.

[12]"Honor your father and your mother, so that you may live long in the land
the LORD your God is giving you.

[13]"You shall not murder.

[14]"You shall not commit adultery.

[15]"You shall not steal.

[16]"You shall not give false testimony against your neighbor.

[17]"You shall not covet your neighbor's house. You shall not covet your neighbor's wife, or his male or female servant, his ox or donkey, or anything
that belongs to your neighbor."

[18]When the people saw the thunder and lightning and heard the trumpet and
saw the mountain in smoke, they trembled with fear. They stayed at a distance

[a] 18 Most Hebrew manuscripts; a few Hebrew manuscripts and Septuagint *and all the people*
[b] 19 Or *and God answered him with thunder* [c] 3 Or *besides*

EXODUS 20:1–17

THE LAW OF GOD

The role of the law is a hotly debated question among Bible scholars. One thing is certain: at the outset, the law was never designed as a means by which people could earn a right relationship with God. The preamble to the law in Exodus 20 bases the dictates of God on his character and work. He is the one who established a relationship with his people and showed his might by delivering them from slavery in Egypt. As a result of God's gracious initiative, the people were to respond through worshipful obedience.

Though Israel was never able to keep the law perfectly, the law showed the nature of obedience and highlighted the inability of fallen humanity to obey God (Ro 7:7–12). Their failure only served to demonstrate their need for a Savior to atone for their sins. God's work to make propitiation for the sins of his people prompts a desire to obey, not in order to earn his favor, but as a proper response to his unilateral work. A life of obedience is a work of God's grace by the power of his Spirit in those whom he has already adopted as his children.

THE TWO GREATEST COMMANDMENTS

The law was given as a gift of God's grace. God made a covenant with the entire nation of Israel while they were encamped at Mount Sinai. This covenant, often known as the Mosaic covenant because God gave the law through Moses, formalized the relationship that God would have with his people. In keeping with the form of ancient treaties, the law expounded the type of relationship that a superior (God) would have with his subjects (the nation of Israel). At the outset of the law, God reminded the people of his faithful character and the way he had cared for them.

Through obedience to the law, God's people could live out their identity as a holy people in contrast to their pagan neighbors. They were the object of God's relentless love and had become his special treasure (Ex 19:5 – 6). Through the law, they were given unique insight into the way God designed his people to function, relate to one another and approach him. Their distinctive way of life would also serve to expose the surrounding nations to the glory of God. Other nations were meant to look at the nation of Israel and be drawn to know their God.

The instructions given in chapter 20 outline the path of righteousness that God desires for his people to follow. These first ten laws begin with the supremacy of God in all things and the type of worship he is due. From there, the people of God were given instructions on how their love for God should inform their love for other people made in the image of God.

Jesus distilled the law to these two chief pillars as well. When asked what the greatest commandment in the law is, he summarized the law as love for God and love for others. All of the law and the prophets' instructions hang on these two great commands, according to Jesus (Mt 22:37 – 40). This simplicity need not minimize the grand scope of the law but is meant to demonstrate the intended focus of obedience. A heart filled with love for God and for others will spill over into innumerable actions that embody this love. As God's beloved people, the church is to model the sacrificial work of Jesus himself, give themselves to the good work of loving God and others, and, in so doing, fulfill the law of Christ.

19 and said to Moses, "Speak to us yourself and we will listen. But do not have God speak to us or we will die."

20 Moses said to the people, "Do not be afraid. God has come to test you, so that the fear of God will be with you to keep you from sinning."

21 The people remained at a distance, while Moses approached the thick darkness where God was.

Idols and Altars

22 Then the LORD said to Moses, "Tell the Israelites this: 'You have seen for yourselves that I have spoken to you from heaven: 23 Do not make any gods to be alongside me; do not make for yourselves gods of silver or gods of gold.

24 " 'Make an altar of earth for me and sacrifice on it your burnt offerings and fellowship offerings, your sheep and goats and your cattle. Wherever I cause my name to be honored, I will come to you and bless you. 25 If you make an altar of stones for me, do not build it with dressed stones, for you will defile it if you use a tool on it. 26 And do not go up to my altar on steps, or your private parts may be exposed.'

21

"These are the laws you are to set before them:

Hebrew Servants

2 "If you buy a Hebrew servant, he is to serve you for six years. But in the seventh year, he shall go free, without paying anything. 3 If he comes alone, he is to go free alone; but if he has a wife when he comes, she is to go with him. 4 If his master gives him a wife and she bears him sons or daughters, the woman and her children shall belong to her master, and only the man shall go free.

5 "But if the servant declares, 'I love my master and my wife and children and do not want to go free,' 6 then his master must take him before the judges.[a] He shall take him to the door or the doorpost and pierce his ear with an awl. Then he will be his servant for life.

7 "If a man sells his daughter as a servant, she is not to go free as male servants do. 8 If she does not please the master who has selected her for himself,[b] he must let her be redeemed. He has no right to sell her to foreigners, because he has broken faith with her. 9 If he selects her for his son, he must grant her the rights of a daughter. 10 If he marries another woman, he must not deprive the first one of her food, clothing and marital rights. 11 If he does not provide her with these three things, she is to go free, without any payment of money.

Personal Injuries

12 "Anyone who strikes a person with a fatal blow is to be put to death. 13 However, if it is not done intentionally, but God lets it happen, they are to flee to a place I will designate. 14 But if anyone schemes and kills someone deliberately, that person is to be taken from my altar and put to death.

15 "Anyone who attacks[c] their father or mother is to be put to death.

16 "Anyone who kidnaps someone is to be put to death, whether the victim has been sold or is still in the kidnapper's possession.

17 "Anyone who curses their father or mother is to be put to death.

18 "If people quarrel and one person hits another with a stone or with their fist[d] and the victim does not die but is confined to bed, 19 the one who struck the blow will not be held liable if the other can get up and walk around outside with a staff; however, the guilty party must pay the injured person for any loss of time and see that the victim is completely healed.

20 "Anyone who beats their male or female slave with a rod must be punished if the slave dies as a direct result, 21 but they are not to be punished if the slave recovers after a day or two, since the slave is their property.

EXODUS 21:2–4

FREEDOM

The law of Israel contained a provision for granting freedom to fellow Israelites who sold themselves as indentured servants. After a period of six years, indentured servants were set free and allowed to return to their former lives. This process ensured that the ongoing practice of granting freedom was built into the fabric of the people of God.

Jesus taught that this practice modeled a far greater heavenly reality. The nature of sin enslaves all mankind by virtue of their common relationship with Adam's sin and their ongoing sinful actions (Jn 8:34–36). Jesus' work proclaimed freedom to spiritual slaves (Ro 6:22). Now free from the penalty and power of sin, Christians are free to submit to a far greater Master, one whose yoke is easy and whose burden is light (Mt 11:30).

---

[a] 6 Or *before God* [b] 8 Or *master so that he does not choose her* [c] 15 Or *kills*
[d] 18 Or *with a tool*

22“If people are fighting and hit a pregnant woman and she gives birth prematurely[a] but there is no serious injury, the offender must be fined whatever the woman’s husband demands and the court allows. 23But if there is serious injury, you are to take life for life, 24eye for eye, tooth for tooth, hand for hand, foot for foot, 25burn for burn, wound for wound, bruise for bruise.

26“An owner who hits a male or female slave in the eye and destroys it must let the slave go free to compensate for the eye. 27And an owner who knocks out the tooth of a male or female slave must let the slave go free to compensate for the tooth.

28“If a bull gores a man or woman to death, the bull is to be stoned to death, and its meat must not be eaten. But the owner of the bull will not be held responsible. 29If, however, the bull has had the habit of goring and the owner has been warned but has not kept it penned up and it kills a man or woman, the bull is to be stoned and its owner also is to be put to death. 30However, if payment is demanded, the owner may redeem his life by the payment of whatever is demanded. 31This law also applies if the bull gores a son or daughter. 32If the bull gores a male or female slave, the owner must pay thirty shekels[b] of silver to the master of the slave, and the bull is to be stoned to death.

33“If anyone uncovers a pit or digs one and fails to cover it and an ox or a donkey falls into it, 34the one who opened the pit must pay the owner for the loss and take the dead animal in exchange.

35“If anyone’s bull injures someone else’s bull and it dies, the two parties are to sell the live one and divide both the money and the dead animal equally. 36However, if it was known that the bull had the habit of goring, yet the owner did not keep it penned up, the owner must pay, animal for animal, and take the dead animal in exchange.

Protection of Property

22[c] “Whoever steals an ox or a sheep and slaughters it or sells it must pay back five head of cattle for the ox and four sheep for the sheep.

2“If a thief is caught breaking in at night and is struck a fatal blow, the defender is not guilty of bloodshed; 3but if it happens after sunrise, the defender is guilty of bloodshed.

“Anyone who steals must certainly make restitution, but if they have nothing, they must be sold to pay for their theft. 4If the stolen animal is found alive in their possession—whether ox or donkey or sheep—they must pay back double.

5“If anyone grazes their livestock in a field or vineyard and lets them stray and they graze in someone else’s field, the offender must make restitution from the best of their own field or vineyard.

6“If a fire breaks out and spreads into thornbushes so that it burns shocks of grain or standing grain or the whole field, the one who started the fire must make restitution.

7“If anyone gives a neighbor silver or goods for safekeeping and they are stolen from the neighbor’s house, the thief, if caught, must pay back double. 8But if the thief is not found, the owner of the house must appear before the judges, and they must[d] determine whether the owner of the house has laid hands on the other person’s property. 9In all cases of illegal possession of an ox, a donkey, a sheep, a garment, or any other lost property about which somebody says, ‘This is mine,’ both parties are to bring their cases before the judges.[e] The one whom the judges declare[f] guilty must pay back double to the other.

10“If anyone gives a donkey, an ox, a sheep or any other animal to their neighbor for safekeeping and it dies or is injured or is taken away while no one is looking, 11the issue between them will be settled by the taking of an oath before the

---

[a] 22 Or *she has a miscarriage* [b] 32 That is, about 12 ounces or about 345 grams [c] In Hebrew texts 22:1 is numbered 21:37, and 22:2-31 is numbered 22:1-30. [d] 8 Or *before God, and he will* [e] 9 Or *before God* [f] 9 Or *whom God declares*

LORD that the neighbor did not lay hands on the other person's property. The owner is to accept this, and no restitution is required. 12But if the animal was stolen from the neighbor, restitution must be made to the owner. 13If it was torn to pieces by a wild animal, the neighbor shall bring in the remains as evidence and shall not be required to pay for the torn animal.

14"If anyone borrows an animal from their neighbor and it is injured or dies while the owner is not present, they must make restitution. 15But if the owner is with the animal, the borrower will not have to pay. If the animal was hired, the money paid for the hire covers the loss.

Social Responsibility

16"If a man seduces a virgin who is not pledged to be married and sleeps with her, he must pay the bride-price, and she shall be his wife. 17If her father absolutely refuses to give her to him, he must still pay the bride-price for virgins.

18"Do not allow a sorceress to live.

19"Anyone who has sexual relations with an animal is to be put to death.

20"Whoever sacrifices to any god other than the LORD must be destroyed.[a]

21"Do not mistreat or oppress a foreigner, for you were foreigners in Egypt.

22"Do not take advantage of the widow or the fatherless. 23If you do and they cry out to me, I will certainly hear their cry. 24My anger will be aroused, and I will kill you with the sword; your wives will become widows and your children fatherless.

25"If you lend money to one of my people among you who is needy, do not treat it like a business deal; charge no interest. 26If you take your neighbor's cloak as a pledge, return it by sunset, 27because that cloak is the only covering your neighbor has. What else can they sleep in? When they cry out to me, I will hear, for I am compassionate.

28"Do not blaspheme God[b] or curse the ruler of your people.

29"Do not hold back offerings from your granaries or your vats.[c]

"You must give me the firstborn of your sons. 30Do the same with your cattle and your sheep. Let them stay with their mothers for seven days, but give them to me on the eighth day.

31"You are to be my holy people. So do not eat the meat of an animal torn by wild beasts; throw it to the dogs.

Laws of Justice and Mercy

23 "Do not spread false reports. Do not help a guilty person by being a malicious witness.

2"Do not follow the crowd in doing wrong. When you give testimony in a lawsuit, do not pervert justice by siding with the crowd, 3and do not show favoritism to a poor person in a lawsuit.

4"If you come across your enemy's ox or donkey wandering off, be sure to return it. 5If you see the donkey of someone who hates you fallen down under its load, do not leave it there; be sure you help them with it.

6"Do not deny justice to your poor people in their lawsuits. 7Have nothing to do with a false charge and do not put an innocent or honest person to death, for I will not acquit the guilty.

8"Do not accept a bribe, for a bribe blinds those who see and twists the words of the innocent.

9"Do not oppress a foreigner; you yourselves know how it feels to be foreigners, because you were foreigners in Egypt.

Sabbath Laws

10"For six years you are to sow your fields and harvest the crops, 11but during the seventh year let the land lie unplowed and unused. Then the poor among

---

[a] *20* The Hebrew term refers to the irrevocable giving over of things or persons to the LORD, often by totally destroying them. [b] *28* Or *Do not revile the judges* [c] *29* The meaning of the Hebrew for this phrase is uncertain.

your people may get food from it, and the wild animals may eat what is left. Do
the same with your vineyard and your olive grove.
[12]"Six days do your work, but on the seventh day do not work, so that your ox
and your donkey may rest, and so that the slave born in your household and the
foreigner living among you may be refreshed.
[13]"Be careful to do everything I have said to you. Do not invoke the names of
other gods; do not let them be heard on your lips.

The Three Annual Festivals

[14]"Three times a year you are to celebrate a festival to me.
[15]"Celebrate the Festival of Unleavened Bread; for seven days eat bread made
without yeast, as I commanded you. Do this at the appointed time in the month
of Aviv, for in that month you came out of Egypt.
"No one is to appear before me empty-handed.
[16]"Celebrate the Festival of Harvest with the firstfruits of the crops you sow
in your field.
"Celebrate the Festival of Ingathering at the end of the year, when you gather
in your crops from the field.
[17]"Three times a year all the men are to appear before the Sovereign LORD.
[18]"Do not offer the blood of a sacrifice to me along with anything containing
yeast.
"The fat of my festival offerings must not be kept until morning.
[19]"Bring the best of the firstfruits of your soil to the house of the LORD your God.
"Do not cook a young goat in its mother's milk.

God's Angel to Prepare the Way

[20]"See, I am sending an angel ahead of you to guard you along the way and to
bring you to the place I have prepared. [21]Pay attention to him and listen to what he
says. Do not rebel against him; he will not forgive your rebellion, since my Name
is in him. [22]If you listen carefully to what he says and do all that I say, I will be an
enemy to your enemies and will oppose those who oppose you. [23]My angel will go
ahead of you and bring you into the land of the Amorites, Hittites, Perizzites, Canaanites, Hivites and Jebusites, and I will wipe them out. [24]Do not bow down before their gods or worship them or follow their practices. You must demolish them
and break their sacred stones to pieces. [25]Worship the LORD your God, and his
blessing will be on your food and water. I will take away sickness from among you,
[26]and none will miscarry or be barren in your land. I will give you a full life span.
[27]"I will send my terror ahead of you and throw into confusion every nation
you encounter. I will make all your enemies turn their backs and run. [28]I will
send the hornet ahead of you to drive the Hivites, Canaanites and Hittites out
of your way. [29]But I will not drive them out in a single year, because the land
would become desolate and the wild animals too numerous for you. [30]Little by
little I will drive them out before you, until you have increased enough to take
possession of the land.
[31]"I will establish your borders from the Red Sea[a] to the Mediterranean Sea,[b]
and from the desert to the Euphrates River. I will give into your hands the people who live in the land, and you will drive them out before you. [32]Do not make
a covenant with them or with their gods. [33]Do not let them live in your land or
they will cause you to sin against me, because the worship of their gods will certainly be a snare to you."

The Covenant Confirmed

24 Then the LORD said to Moses, "Come up to the LORD, you and Aaron, Nadab and Abihu, and seventy of the elders of Israel. You are to worship at
a distance, [2]but Moses alone is to approach the LORD; the others must not come
near. And the people may not come up with him."

---

[a] 31 Or *the Sea of Reeds* [b] 31 Hebrew *to the Sea of the Philistines*

EXODUS 23:20 – 26

GOD'S ANGEL

God, on occasion, tangibly manifested himself among the nation of Israel in the form of an angel. The phrase "my angel" can refer either to a supernatural being or to a God-appointed messenger. For example, the prophet Malachi's name itself means "my messenger." The connection between the angel of the Lord and the messenger of God highlights the focus of these types of appearances of God in the Old Testament. The angel of the Lord was given the assignment to communicate God's word to his people, often at critical junctures in their journey. The angel led the people of God as the cloud and fire did in their wilderness journey (Ex 13:21 – 22; 14:19 – 24; 16:10; 19:9,16; 24:15 – 18; 33:9 – 11; 34:5; 40:34 – 38).

The special role of the angels and their sudden appearances lead some to question whether these angels are the pre-incarnate form of Jesus himself. Theophanies, or appearances of God among his people, occur on rare occasions in the Old Testament. This angel appears to Hagar and Ishmael in the wilderness (Ge 16:7 – 14), to Abraham by the trees of Mamre (Ge 18:1 – 3), to Jacob in a dream (Ge 31:11 – 13) and to Moses in the flame of a burning bush (Ex 3:2 – 4).

In each of these occasions, the angel appears to have unique insight, even personal knowledge, of the nature, character and plan of God. Some suppose him to be the second member of the Trinity, making a brief appearance on the earth before the God-ordained time of his birth had arrived (Gal 4:4 – 7). The Scriptures do not clearly state that this is the case, so firm conclusions are impossible.

What is clear is that God, in tangible form, consistently breaks into human history in order to care for his people, communicate his message to them and lead them from harm and to safety. The incarnation of Jesus would represent far more than a mere theophany in the Old Testament. His birth brought with it the in-breaking of the kingdom of God, the revelation of God's eternal plan of redemption and the process by which humanity could be made right with God through faith in this promise.

3When Moses went and told the people all the LORD's words and laws, they
responded with one voice, "Everything the LORD has said we will do." 4Moses
then wrote down everything the LORD had said.

He got up early the next morning and built an altar at the foot of the mountain
and set up twelve stone pillars representing the twelve tribes of Israel. 5Then he
sent young Israelite men, and they offered burnt offerings and sacrificed young
bulls as fellowship offerings to the LORD. 6Moses took half of the blood and put
it in bowls, and the other half he splashed against the altar. 7Then he took the
Book of the Covenant and read it to the people. They responded, "We will do everything the LORD has said; we will obey."

8Moses then took the blood, sprinkled it on the people and said, "This is the
blood of the covenant that the LORD has made with you in accordance with all
these words."

9Moses and Aaron, Nadab and Abihu, and the seventy elders of Israel went up
10and saw the God of Israel. Under his feet was something like a pavement made
of lapis lazuli, as bright blue as the sky. 11But God did not raise his hand against
these leaders of the Israelites; they saw God, and they ate and drank.

12The LORD said to Moses, "Come up to me on the mountain and stay here,
and I will give you the tablets of stone with the law and commandments I have
written for their instruction."

13Then Moses set out with Joshua his aide, and Moses went up on the mountain of God. 14He said to the elders, "Wait here for us until we come back to you.
Aaron and Hur are with you, and anyone involved in a dispute can go to them."

15When Moses went up on the mountain, the cloud covered it, 16and the glory
of the LORD settled on Mount Sinai. For six days the cloud covered the mountain,
and on the seventh day the LORD called to Moses from within the cloud. 17To the
Israelites the glory of the LORD looked like a consuming fire on top of the mountain. 18Then Moses entered the cloud as he went on up the mountain. And he
stayed on the mountain forty days and forty nights.

Offerings for the Tabernacle

25 The LORD said to Moses, 2"Tell the Israelites to bring me an offering. You
are to receive the offering for me from everyone whose heart prompts
them to give. 3These are the offerings you are to receive from them: gold, silver
and bronze; 4blue, purple and scarlet yarn and fine linen; goat hair; 5ram skins
dyed red and another type of durable leather[a]; acacia wood; 6olive oil for the
light; spices for the anointing oil and for the fragrant incense; 7and onyx stones
and other gems to be mounted on the ephod and breastpiece.

8"Then have them make a sanctuary for me, and I will dwell among them.
9Make this tabernacle and all its furnishings exactly like the pattern I will show
you.

The Ark

10"Have them make an ark[b] of acacia wood — two and a half cubits long, a cubit and a half wide, and a cubit and a half high.[c] 11Overlay it with pure gold, both
inside and out, and make a gold molding around it. 12Cast four gold rings for it
and fasten them to its four feet, with two rings on one side and two rings on the
other. 13Then make poles of acacia wood and overlay them with gold. 14Insert the
poles into the rings on the sides of the ark to carry it. 15The poles are to remain in
the rings of this ark; they are not to be removed. 16Then put in the ark the tablets
of the covenant law, which I will give you.

17"Make an atonement cover of pure gold — two and a half cubits long and a
cubit and a half wide. 18And make two cherubim out of hammered gold at the

[a] *5* Possibly the hides of large aquatic mammals [b] *10* That is, a chest [c] *10* That is, about 3 3/4 feet long and 2 1/4 feet wide and high or about 1.1 meters long and 68 centimeters wide and high; similarly in verse 17

EXODUS 24:5–8

SPRINKLED WITH BLOOD

God's covenant relationship with his people was made possible by the blood of a sacrifice. At the Passover, the Israelites placed blood over the doors of their houses. Here the individual members of the nation of Israel were sprinkled with the blood of the covenant. The people understood that their relationship with God was predicated on the substitutionary death of something else. The sin of the people was transmitted to the animal, and the animal died the death the people deserved, temporarily restoring their relationship with God.

Whereas the people of God in the Old Testament were marked with the blood of a sacrificial animal, the people of God in the church are permanently covered with the blood of the perfect sacrifice — Jesus Christ. Peter, writing to Christians scattered throughout Asia Minor, noted that they also were sprinkled with the blood of Jesus Christ (1Pe 1:2). Though they are dispersed among the nations, God still marks his people by blood.

EXODUS 25:17–22

ATONEMENT

The atonement cover was the place for sacrifices within the tabernacle on the Day of Atonement. The title, derived from the verb meaning "to cover over," "to atone for" or "to make propitiation," was the place of offering on this day. This symbol refers to the cover placed on top of the ark and was the base on which

(continued on page 123)

A HEAVENLY PATTERN

To a modern reader, the exact specifications for the construction of the ark of the testimony may seem like a strange matter to include in God's written Word. Paul reminded the church, however, that there is no portion of the Scriptures which is not profitable for their edification (2Ti 3:16). Not only did God provide these instructions to the nation of Israel, but he also preserved them throughout the centuries for the instruction of his church. Thus, this passage (and the many others like it in the Old Testament) is important for understanding how God dwells among his people.

Creation itself was arranged in a particular order, with rivers marking the outmost boundaries of the Garden of Eden (Ge 2:10 – 14). Though the dimensions are not specified, it is clear there was a pattern for the organization of the dwelling of God among his first created image bearers. Sin exiled the first couple from the garden and banished them from the intimacy of God's presence.

Years later, Moses was shown a pattern for the ongoing dwelling of God among his people. This dwelling would not be in a garden but in an intricately designed tabernacle, filled with furniture designed to symbolize the way in which humanity could again commune with God. Moses was not simply asked to build a dwelling for God, but he was given the exact specifications for the shape, size and structure of this gathering place and was commanded to follow the exact pattern that he was shown by God. This pattern indicated that there is a heavenly form to which the earthly tabernacle corresponds and reflects (Heb 8:5 – 6). The tabernacle, and later the temple, served as the physical location for the dwelling of God among the people until he would dwell among them perfectly in the form of his incarnate Son, Jesus Christ (Jn 1:1 – 14). Through Christ's work, the dwelling of God would move among the people, no longer confined to a dwelling made by human hands (Ac 17:24).

His second coming will one day usher in a day when the dwelling of God will once again be among his people (Rev 21:1 – 4). The prophet Habakkuk pictures a day when "the earth will be filled with the knowledge of the glory of the LORD as the waters cover the sea" (Hab 2:14). No longer will there be boundaries separating humanity from God, but the entire cosmos will resound with his fame.

ends of the cover. [19]Make one cherub on one end and the second cherub on the other; make the cherubim of one piece with the cover, at the two ends. [20]The cherubim are to have their wings spread upward, overshadowing the cover with them. The cherubim are to face each other, looking toward the cover. [21]Place the cover on top of the ark and put in the ark the tablets of the covenant law that I will give you. [22]There, above the cover between the two cherubim that are over the ark of the covenant law, I will meet with you and give you all my commands for the Israelites.

The Table

[23]"Make a table of acacia wood — two cubits long, a cubit wide and a cubit and a half high.[a] [24]Overlay it with pure gold and make a gold molding around it. [25]Also make around it a rim a handbreadth[b] wide and put a gold molding on the rim. [26]Make four gold rings for the table and fasten them to the four corners, where the four legs are. [27]The rings are to be close to the rim to hold the poles used in carrying the table. [28]Make the poles of acacia wood, overlay them with gold and carry the table with them. [29]And make its plates and dishes of pure gold, as well as its pitchers and bowls for the pouring out of offerings. [30]Put the bread of the Presence on this table to be before me at all times.

The Lampstand

[31]"Make a lampstand of pure gold. Hammer out its base and shaft, and make its flowerlike cups, buds and blossoms of one piece with them. [32]Six branches are to extend from the sides of the lampstand — three on one side and three on the other. [33]Three cups shaped like almond flowers with buds and blossoms are to be on one branch, three on the next branch, and the same for all six branches extending from the lampstand. [34]And on the lampstand there are to be four cups shaped like almond flowers with buds and blossoms. [35]One bud shall be under the first pair of branches extending from the lampstand, a second bud under the second pair, and a third bud under the third pair — six branches in all. [36]The buds and branches shall all be of one piece with the lampstand, hammered out of pure gold.

[37]"Then make its seven lamps and set them up on it so that they light the space in front of it. [38]Its wick trimmers and trays are to be of pure gold. [39]A talent[c] of pure gold is to be used for the lampstand and all these accessories. [40]See that you make them according to the pattern shown you on the mountain.

The Tabernacle

26 "Make the tabernacle with ten curtains of finely twisted linen and blue, purple and scarlet yarn, with cherubim woven into them by a skilled worker. [2]All the curtains are to be the same size — twenty-eight cubits long and four cubits wide.[d] [3]Join five of the curtains together, and do the same with the other five. [4]Make loops of blue material along the edge of the end curtain in one set, and do the same with the end curtain in the other set. [5]Make fifty loops on one curtain and fifty loops on the end curtain of the other set, with the loops opposite each other. [6]Then make fifty gold clasps and use them to fasten the curtains together so that the tabernacle is a unit.

[7]"Make curtains of goat hair for the tent over the tabernacle — eleven altogether. [8]All eleven curtains are to be the same size — thirty cubits long and four cubits wide.[e] [9]Join five of the curtains together into one set and the other six into another set. Fold the sixth curtain double at the front of the tent. [10]Make fifty loops along the edge of the end curtain in one set and also along the edge of the

[a] *23* That is, about 3 feet long, 1 1/2 feet wide and 2 1/4 feet high or about 90 centimeters long, 45 centimeters wide and 68 centimeters high [b] *25* That is, about 3 inches or about 7.5 centimeters [c] *39* That is, about 75 pounds or about 34 kilograms [d] *2* That is, about 42 feet long and 6 feet wide or about 13 meters long and 1.8 meters wide [e] *8* That is, about 45 feet long and 6 feet wide or about 13.5 meters long and 1.8 meters wide

(Atonement, continued)

the cherubim were placed (Heb 9:5). There, sacrificial animals were offered to the Lord and, by God's mercy, peace between God and humanity was established. The atonement cover served as the physical location at which the mercy and judgment of God met, and the sins of mankind were atoned for.

At the cross, God's mercy and judgment met as they did at the atonement cover. There, God's judgment was placed upon his Son, and his mercy is freely given. His death atones, or covers over, the sins of his people, making peace by the blood of the cross (Col 1:20; 1Jn 4:10). The ongoing significance of the cross as a symbol for Christians testifies to the profound way in which this peace with God is possible.

end curtain in the other set. 11Then make fifty bronze clasps and put them in the
loops to fasten the tent together as a unit. 12As for the additional length of the tent
curtains, the half curtain that is left over is to hang down at the rear of the tabernacle. 13The tent curtains will be a cubit[a] longer on both sides; what is left will
hang over the sides of the tabernacle so as to cover it. 14Make for the tent a covering of ram skins dyed red, and over that a covering of the other durable leather.[b]
15"Make upright frames of acacia wood for the tabernacle. 16Each frame is to
be ten cubits long and a cubit and a half wide,[c] 17with two projections set parallel
to each other. Make all the frames of the tabernacle in this way. 18Make twenty
frames for the south side of the tabernacle 19and make forty silver bases to go
under them — two bases for each frame, one under each projection. 20For the
other side, the north side of the tabernacle, make twenty frames 21and forty silver bases — two under each frame. 22Make six frames for the far end, that is, the
west end of the tabernacle, 23and make two frames for the corners at the far end.
24At these two corners they must be double from the bottom all the way to the
top and fitted into a single ring; both shall be like that. 25So there will be eight
frames and sixteen silver bases — two under each frame.
26"Also make crossbars of acacia wood: five for the frames on one side of the
tabernacle, 27five for those on the other side, and five for the frames on the west,
at the far end of the tabernacle. 28The center crossbar is to extend from end to
end at the middle of the frames. 29Overlay the frames with gold and make gold
rings to hold the crossbars. Also overlay the crossbars with gold.
30"Set up the tabernacle according to the plan shown you on the mountain.
31"Make a curtain of blue, purple and scarlet yarn and finely twisted linen,
with cherubim woven into it by a skilled worker. 32Hang it with gold hooks on
four posts of acacia wood overlaid with gold and standing on four silver bases.
33Hang the curtain from the clasps and place the ark of the covenant law behind
the curtain. The curtain will separate the Holy Place from the Most Holy Place.
34Put the atonement cover on the ark of the covenant law in the Most Holy Place.
35Place the table outside the curtain on the north side of the tabernacle and put
the lampstand opposite it on the south side.
36"For the entrance to the tent make a curtain of blue, purple and scarlet yarn
and finely twisted linen — the work of an embroiderer. 37Make gold hooks for this
curtain and five posts of acacia wood overlaid with gold. And cast five bronze
bases for them.

The Altar of Burnt Offering

27 "Build an altar of acacia wood, three cubits[d] high; it is to be square, five
cubits long and five cubits wide.[e] 2Make a horn at each of the four corners,
so that the horns and the altar are of one piece, and overlay the altar with bronze.
3Make all its utensils of bronze — its pots to remove the ashes, and its shovels,
sprinkling bowls, meat forks and firepans. 4Make a grating for it, a bronze network, and make a bronze ring at each of the four corners of the network. 5Put
it under the ledge of the altar so that it is halfway up the altar. 6Make poles of
acacia wood for the altar and overlay them with bronze. 7The poles are to be
inserted into the rings so they will be on two sides of the altar when it is carried.
8Make the altar hollow, out of boards. It is to be made just as you were shown on
the mountain.

The Courtyard

9"Make a courtyard for the tabernacle. The south side shall be a hundred cubits[f] long and is to have curtains of finely twisted linen, 10with twenty posts and

[a] *13* That is, about 18 inches or about 45 centimeters [b] *14* Possibly the hides of large aquatic mammals (see 25:5) [c] *16* That is, about 15 feet long and 2 1/4 feet wide or about 4.5 meters long and 68 centimeters wide [d] *1* That is, about 4 1/2 feet or about 1.4 meters [e] *1* That is, about 7 1/2 feet or about 2.3 meters long and wide [f] *9* That is, about 150 feet or about 45 meters; also in verse 11

EXODUS 26:31 – 33

DRAW NEAR

Even within the tabernacle, the priests were separated from God by a curtain. The two chambers of the tabernacle were divided by a beautiful, intricately made curtain, which was hung from posts. The innermost area, the Most Holy Place, was the site of the offering made by the high priest on the annual Day of Atonement to atone for the sins of the people. The high priest could not enter the area behind the curtain into the Most Holy Place whenever he wanted, but only at the God-appointed time and by following a carefully outlined protocol. To transgress this process and enter God's presence in another way would lead to certain death.

The division between man and God was forever obliterated at the cross. In essence, Christ entered the Most Holy Place and offered himself there as a sacrifice for the sins of the world. He did not enter with the blood of bulls and goats, but rather with his own blood, offering a perfect sacrifice once and for all. The symbolic rending of the temple curtain, from top to bottom, indicated that access to God has been granted because of what Christ has accomplished (Mt 27:51). Those with faith in Jesus can, with confidence, draw near to his presence at any time (Heb 4:16).

twenty bronze bases and with silver hooks and bands on the posts. 11The north side shall also be a hundred cubits long and is to have curtains, with twenty posts and twenty bronze bases and with silver hooks and bands on the posts.

12"The west end of the courtyard shall be fifty cubits[a] wide and have curtains, with ten posts and ten bases. 13On the east end, toward the sunrise, the courtyard shall also be fifty cubits wide. 14Curtains fifteen cubits[b] long are to be on one side of the entrance, with three posts and three bases, 15and curtains fifteen cubits long are to be on the other side, with three posts and three bases.

16"For the entrance to the courtyard, provide a curtain twenty cubits[c] long, of blue, purple and scarlet yarn and finely twisted linen — the work of an embroiderer — with four posts and four bases. 17All the posts around the courtyard are to have silver bands and hooks, and bronze bases. 18The courtyard shall be a hundred cubits long and fifty cubits wide,[d] with curtains of finely twisted linen five cubits[e] high, and with bronze bases. 19All the other articles used in the service of the tabernacle, whatever their function, including all the tent pegs for it and those for the courtyard, are to be of bronze.

Oil for the Lampstand

20"Command the Israelites to bring you clear oil of pressed olives for the light so that the lamps may be kept burning. 21In the tent of meeting, outside the curtain that shields the ark of the covenant law, Aaron and his sons are to keep the lamps burning before the LORD from evening till morning. This is to be a lasting ordinance among the Israelites for the generations to come.

The Priestly Garments

28 "Have Aaron your brother brought to you from among the Israelites, along with his sons Nadab and Abihu, Eleazar and Ithamar, so they may serve me as priests. 2Make sacred garments for your brother Aaron to give him dignity and honor. 3Tell all the skilled workers to whom I have given wisdom in such matters that they are to make garments for Aaron, for his consecration, so he may serve me as priest. 4These are the garments they are to make: a breastpiece, an ephod, a robe, a woven tunic, a turban and a sash. They are to make these sacred garments for your brother Aaron and his sons, so they may serve me as priests. 5Have them use gold, and blue, purple and scarlet yarn, and fine linen.

The Ephod

6"Make the ephod of gold, and of blue, purple and scarlet yarn, and of finely twisted linen — the work of skilled hands. 7It is to have two shoulder pieces attached to two of its corners, so it can be fastened. 8Its skillfully woven waistband is to be like it — of one piece with the ephod and made with gold, and with blue, purple and scarlet yarn, and with finely twisted linen.

9"Take two onyx stones and engrave on them the names of the sons of Israel 10in the order of their birth — six names on one stone and the remaining six on the other. 11Engrave the names of the sons of Israel on the two stones the way a gem cutter engraves a seal. Then mount the stones in gold filigree settings 12and fasten them on the shoulder pieces of the ephod as memorial stones for the sons of Israel. Aaron is to bear the names on his shoulders as a memorial before the LORD. 13Make gold filigree settings 14and two braided chains of pure gold, like a rope, and attach the chains to the settings.

The Breastpiece

15"Fashion a breastpiece for making decisions — the work of skilled hands. Make it like the ephod: of gold, and of blue, purple and scarlet yarn, and of finely

---

[a] *12* That is, about 75 feet or about 23 meters; also in verse 13 [b] *14* That is, about 23 feet or about 6.8 meters; also in verse 15 [c] *16* That is, about 30 feet or about 9 meters [d] *18* That is, about 150 feet long and 75 feet wide or about 45 meters long and 23 meters wide
[e] *18* That is, about 7 1/2 feet or about 2.3 meters

twisted linen. [16]It is to be square — a span[a] long and a span wide — and folded double. [17]Then mount four rows of precious stones on it. The first row shall be carnelian, chrysolite and beryl; [18]the second row shall be turquoise, lapis lazuli and emerald; [19]the third row shall be jacinth, agate and amethyst; [20]the fourth row shall be topaz, onyx and jasper.[b] Mount them in gold filigree settings. [21]There are to be twelve stones, one for each of the names of the sons of Israel, each engraved like a seal with the name of one of the twelve tribes.

[22]"For the breastpiece make braided chains of pure gold, like a rope. [23]Make two gold rings for it and fasten them to two corners of the breastpiece. [24]Fasten the two gold chains to the rings at the corners of the breastpiece, [25]and the other ends of the chains to the two settings, attaching them to the shoulder pieces of the ephod at the front. [26]Make two gold rings and attach them to the other two corners of the breastpiece on the inside edge next to the ephod. [27]Make two more gold rings and attach them to the bottom of the shoulder pieces on the front of the ephod, close to the seam just above the waistband of the ephod. [28]The rings of the breastpiece are to be tied to the rings of the ephod with blue cord, connecting it to the waistband, so that the breastpiece will not swing out from the ephod.

[29]"Whenever Aaron enters the Holy Place, he will bear the names of the sons of Israel over his heart on the breastpiece of decision as a continuing memorial before the LORD. [30]Also put the Urim and the Thummim in the breastpiece, so they may be over Aaron's heart whenever he enters the presence of the LORD. Thus Aaron will always bear the means of making decisions for the Israelites over his heart before the LORD.

Other Priestly Garments

[31]"Make the robe of the ephod entirely of blue cloth, [32]with an opening for the head in its center. There shall be a woven edge like a collar[c] around this opening, so that it will not tear. [33]Make pomegranates of blue, purple and scarlet yarn around the hem of the robe, with gold bells between them. [34]The gold bells and the pomegranates are to alternate around the hem of the robe. [35]Aaron must wear it when he ministers. The sound of the bells will be heard when he enters the Holy Place before the LORD and when he comes out, so that he will not die.

[36]"Make a plate of pure gold and engrave on it as on a seal: HOLY TO THE LORD. [37]Fasten a blue cord to it to attach it to the turban; it is to be on the front of the turban. [38]It will be on Aaron's forehead, and he will bear the guilt involved in the sacred gifts the Israelites consecrate, whatever their gifts may be. It will be on Aaron's forehead continually so that they will be acceptable to the LORD.

[39]"Weave the tunic of fine linen and make the turban of fine linen. The sash is to be the work of an embroiderer. [40]Make tunics, sashes and caps for Aaron's sons to give them dignity and honor. [41]After you put these clothes on your brother Aaron and his sons, anoint and ordain them. Consecrate them so they may serve me as priests.

[42]"Make linen undergarments as a covering for the body, reaching from the waist to the thigh. [43]Aaron and his sons must wear them whenever they enter the tent of meeting or approach the altar to minister in the Holy Place, so that they will not incur guilt and die.

"This is to be a lasting ordinance for Aaron and his descendants.

Consecration of the Priests

29 "This is what you are to do to consecrate them, so they may serve me as priests: Take a young bull and two rams without defect. [2]And from the finest wheat flour make round loaves without yeast, thick loaves without yeast and with olive oil mixed in, and thin loaves without yeast and brushed with olive oil. [3]Put them in a basket and present them along with the bull and the two rams.

---

[a] *16* That is, about 9 inches or about 23 centimeters [b] *20* The precise identification of some of these precious stones is uncertain. [c] *32* The meaning of the Hebrew for this word is uncertain.

[4]Then bring Aaron and his sons to the entrance to the tent of meeting and wash them with water. [5]Take the garments and dress Aaron with the tunic, the robe of the ephod, the ephod itself and the breastpiece. Fasten the ephod on him by its skillfully woven waistband. [6]Put the turban on his head and attach the sacred emblem to the turban. [7]Take the anointing oil and anoint him by pouring it on his head. [8]Bring his sons and dress them in tunics [9]and fasten caps on them. Then tie sashes on Aaron and his sons.[a] The priesthood is theirs by a lasting ordinance.

"Then you shall ordain Aaron and his sons.

[10]"Bring the bull to the front of the tent of meeting, and Aaron and his sons shall lay their hands on its head. [11]Slaughter it in the LORD's presence at the entrance to the tent of meeting. [12]Take some of the bull's blood and put it on the horns of the altar with your finger, and pour out the rest of it at the base of the altar. [13]Then take all the fat on the internal organs, the long lobe of the liver, and both kidneys with the fat on them, and burn them on the altar. [14]But burn the bull's flesh and its hide and its intestines outside the camp. It is a sin offering.[b]

[15]"Take one of the rams, and Aaron and his sons shall lay their hands on its head. [16]Slaughter it and take the blood and splash it against the sides of the altar. [17]Cut the ram into pieces and wash the internal organs and the legs, putting them with the head and the other pieces. [18]Then burn the entire ram on the altar. It is a burnt offering to the LORD, a pleasing aroma, a food offering presented to the LORD.

[19]"Take the other ram, and Aaron and his sons shall lay their hands on its head. [20]Slaughter it, take some of its blood and put it on the lobes of the right ears of Aaron and his sons, on the thumbs of their right hands, and on the big toes of their right feet. Then splash blood against the sides of the altar. [21]And take some blood from the altar and some of the anointing oil and sprinkle it on Aaron and his garments and on his sons and their garments. Then he and his sons and their garments will be consecrated.

[22]"Take from this ram the fat, the fat tail, the fat on the internal organs, the long lobe of the liver, both kidneys with the fat on them, and the right thigh. (This is the ram for the ordination.) [23]From the basket of bread made without yeast, which is before the LORD, take one round loaf, one thick loaf with olive oil mixed in, and one thin loaf. [24]Put all these in the hands of Aaron and his sons and have them wave them before the LORD as a wave offering. [25]Then take them from their hands and burn them on the altar along with the burnt offering for a pleasing aroma to the LORD, a food offering presented to the LORD. [26]After you take the breast of the ram for Aaron's ordination, wave it before the LORD as a wave offering, and it will be your share.

[27]"Consecrate those parts of the ordination ram that belong to Aaron and his sons: the breast that was waved and the thigh that was presented. [28]This is always to be the perpetual share from the Israelites for Aaron and his sons. It is the contribution the Israelites are to make to the LORD from their fellowship offerings.

[29]"Aaron's sacred garments will belong to his descendants so that they can be anointed and ordained in them. [30]The son who succeeds him as priest and comes to the tent of meeting to minister in the Holy Place is to wear them seven days.

[31]"Take the ram for the ordination and cook the meat in a sacred place. [32]At the entrance to the tent of meeting, Aaron and his sons are to eat the meat of the ram and the bread that is in the basket. [33]They are to eat these offerings by which atonement was made for their ordination and consecration. But no one else may eat them, because they are sacred. [34]And if any of the meat of the ordination ram or any bread is left over till morning, burn it up. It must not be eaten, because it is sacred.

---

[a] 9 Hebrew; Septuagint *on them* [b] *14* Or *purification offering*; also in verse 36

[35]“Do for Aaron and his sons everything I have commanded you, taking seven days to ordain them. [36]Sacrifice a bull each day as a sin offering to make atonement. Purify the altar by making atonement for it, and anoint it to consecrate it. [37]For seven days make atonement for the altar and consecrate it. Then the altar will be most holy, and whatever touches it will be holy.

[38]“This is what you are to offer on the altar regularly each day: two lambs a year old. [39]Offer one in the morning and the other at twilight. [40]With the first lamb offer a tenth of an ephah[a] of the finest flour mixed with a quarter of a hin[b] of oil from pressed olives, and a quarter of a hin of wine as a drink offering. [41]Sacrifice the other lamb at twilight with the same grain offering and its drink offering as in the morning — a pleasing aroma, a food offering presented to the LORD.

[42]“For the generations to come this burnt offering is to be made regularly at the entrance to the tent of meeting, before the LORD. There I will meet you and speak to you; [43]there also I will meet with the Israelites, and the place will be consecrated by my glory.

[44]“So I will consecrate the tent of meeting and the altar and will consecrate Aaron and his sons to serve me as priests. [45]Then I will dwell among the Israelites and be their God. [46]They will know that I am the LORD their God, who brought them out of Egypt so that I might dwell among them. I am the LORD their God.

The Altar of Incense

30 “Make an altar of acacia wood for burning incense. [2]It is to be square, a cubit long and a cubit wide, and two cubits high[c] — its horns of one piece with it. [3]Overlay the top and all the sides and the horns with pure gold, and make a gold molding around it. [4]Make two gold rings for the altar below the molding — two on each of the opposite sides — to hold the poles used to carry it. [5]Make the poles of acacia wood and overlay them with gold. [6]Put the altar in front of the curtain that shields the ark of the covenant law — before the atonement cover that is over the tablets of the covenant law — where I will meet with you.

[7]“Aaron must burn fragrant incense on the altar every morning when he tends the lamps. [8]He must burn incense again when he lights the lamps at twilight so incense will burn regularly before the LORD for the generations to come. [9]Do not offer on this altar any other incense or any burnt offering or grain offering, and do not pour a drink offering on it. [10]Once a year Aaron shall make atonement on its horns. This annual atonement must be made with the blood of the atoning sin offering[d] for the generations to come. It is most holy to the LORD.”

Atonement Money

[11]Then the LORD said to Moses, [12]“When you take a census of the Israelites to count them, each one must pay the LORD a ransom for his life at the time he is counted. Then no plague will come on them when you number them. [13]Each one who crosses over to those already counted is to give a half shekel,[e] according to the sanctuary shekel, which weighs twenty gerahs. This half shekel is an offering to the LORD. [14]All who cross over, those twenty years old or more, are to give an offering to the LORD. [15]The rich are not to give more than a half shekel and the poor are not to give less when you make the offering to the LORD to atone for your lives. [16]Receive the atonement money from the Israelites and use it for the service of the tent of meeting. It will be a memorial for the Israelites before the LORD, making atonement for your lives.”

Basin for Washing

[17]Then the LORD said to Moses, [18]“Make a bronze basin, with its bronze stand, for washing. Place it between the tent of meeting and the altar, and put water

---

[a] *40* That is, probably about 3 1/2 pounds or about 1.6 kilograms [b] *40* That is, probably about 1 quart or about 1 liter [c] *2* That is, about 1 1/2 feet long and wide and 3 feet high or about 45 centimeters long and wide and 90 centimeters high [d] *10* Or *purification offering* [e] *13* That is, about 1/5 ounce or about 5.8 grams; also in verse 15

PRIESTS

Aaron and his sons were uniquely set apart by God to serve as priests among the people of God. They played a mediator function between the people and God in that they represented the people before God. They had unique access to God because they oversaw the people's worship of God, making sacrifices on behalf of the people and representing their needs before a holy God. Like Noah and Abraham before them (Ge 8:20; 22:13), the priests were to worship God in the manner and location prescribed by him alone. Their work was not what most might think of when they imagine the holy leaders of the people of God. Rather than sterile worship, the priests gave themselves to the ongoing slaughter of animal after animal on behalf of the sins of the people. Their work was bloody and grotesque. In the desert heat, the ongoing sacrifice of animals would have created a nauseating concoction of animal waste, blood, sweat and rotting flesh.

The imagery of the priesthood is central to the language the New Testament authors used to describe Jesus' work (Heb 7). Like Aaron and his sons, Jesus is appointed by God to the office of priest. He is given the task of facilitating the worship of God by his people and representing them before God. However, unlike the ancient priests who would offer an animal sacrifice, Jesus offered himself (Heb 7:27). The God-appointed priest and the very Son of God became the lamb of sacrifice on behalf of the sins of his people. His brutal execution embodied the nature of the priest's work. His beaten and bloodied body hung naked on a Roman cross in the heat of the day for all to see. Passersby would turn their faces in revulsion at this repulsive sight. Few would believe that on the cross the great high priest accomplished his greatest priestly work.

His once-for-all sacrifice finally and forever accomplished the work of the priesthood. This act completed, he sits now at the right hand of the Father, knowing that there will never again be the need for another sacrifice for sin (Heb 10:12). Now those who worship God do so, not by means of a human priesthood and an animal sacrifice, but through faith in Jesus, the One who was both the great high priest and the perfect Lamb of God.

in it. [19]Aaron and his sons are to wash their hands and feet with water from it. [20]Whenever they enter the tent of meeting, they shall wash with water so that they will not die. Also, when they approach the altar to minister by presenting a food offering to the LORD, [21]they shall wash their hands and feet so that they will not die. This is to be a lasting ordinance for Aaron and his descendants for the generations to come."

Anointing Oil

[22]Then the LORD said to Moses, [23]"Take the following fine spices: 500 shekels[a] of liquid myrrh, half as much (that is, 250 shekels) of fragrant cinnamon, 250 shekels[b] of fragrant calamus, [24]500 shekels of cassia—all according to the sanctuary shekel—and a hin[c] of olive oil. [25]Make these into a sacred anointing oil, a fragrant blend, the work of a perfumer. It will be the sacred anointing oil. [26]Then use it to anoint the tent of meeting, the ark of the covenant law, [27]the table and all its articles, the lampstand and its accessories, the altar of incense, [28]the altar of burnt offering and all its utensils, and the basin with its stand. [29]You shall consecrate them so they will be most holy, and whatever touches them will be holy.

[30]"Anoint Aaron and his sons and consecrate them so they may serve me as priests. [31]Say to the Israelites, 'This is to be my sacred anointing oil for the generations to come. [32]Do not pour it on anyone else's body and do not make any other oil using the same formula. It is sacred, and you are to consider it sacred. [33]Whoever makes perfume like it and puts it on anyone other than a priest must be cut off from their people.' "

Incense

[34]Then the LORD said to Moses, "Take fragrant spices—gum resin, onycha and galbanum—and pure frankincense, all in equal amounts, [35]and make a fragrant blend of incense, the work of a perfumer. It is to be salted and pure and sacred. [36]Grind some of it to powder and place it in front of the ark of the covenant law in the tent of meeting, where I will meet with you. It shall be most holy to you. [37]Do not make any incense with this formula for yourselves; consider it holy to the LORD. [38]Whoever makes incense like it to enjoy its fragrance must be cut off from their people."

Bezalel and Oholiab

31 Then the LORD said to Moses, [2]"See, I have chosen Bezalel son of Uri, the son of Hur, of the tribe of Judah, [3]and I have filled him with the Spirit of God, with wisdom, with understanding, with knowledge and with all kinds of skills— [4]to make artistic designs for work in gold, silver and bronze, [5]to cut and set stones, to work in wood, and to engage in all kinds of crafts. [6]Moreover, I have appointed Oholiab son of Ahisamak, of the tribe of Dan, to help him. Also I have given ability to all the skilled workers to make everything I have commanded you: [7]the tent of meeting, the ark of the covenant law with the atonement cover on it, and all the other furnishings of the tent— [8]the table and its articles, the pure gold lampstand and all its accessories, the altar of incense, [9]the altar of burnt offering and all its utensils, the basin with its stand— [10]and also the woven garments, both the sacred garments for Aaron the priest and the garments for his sons when they serve as priests, [11]and the anointing oil and fragrant incense for the Holy Place. They are to make them just as I commanded you."

The Sabbath

[12]Then the LORD said to Moses, [13]"Say to the Israelites, 'You must observe my Sabbaths. This will be a sign between me and you for the generations to come, so you may know that I am the LORD, who makes you holy.

[a] *23* That is, about 12 1/2 pounds or about 5.8 kilograms; also in verse 24 [b] *23* That is, about 6 1/4 pounds or about 2.9 kilograms [c] *24* That is, probably about 1 gallon or about 3.8 liters

EXODUS 31:1–11

WORKMANSHIP

Bezalel son of Uri is not a household name for most people. However, at the beginning of the construction of the tabernacle he is singled out as uniquely filled with God's Spirit and instrumental in building a house of worship for the people of God. Bezalel, whose name means "in the shadow of God," reflects God's glory by serving as the lead artisan for the tabernacle. The result of the Spirit's work is seen in Bezalel's wisdom, understanding, knowledge and workmanship. The twice-repeated phrase "all kinds of skills" (Ex 31:3; 35:31) portrays Bezalel as being one with a multitude of gifts uniquely suited for his calling to build the tabernacle.

Paul would later use the same concept to speak of all those who are brought from death to life by virtue of Jesus' work. They are then "God's handiwork, created in Christ Jesus to do good works" (Eph 2:10). Certainly these works will differ from person to person, yet all people are endowed with gifts by the Spirit and given a vital role to play in God's mission in the world (Ro 12:3–8).

14“ ‘Observe the Sabbath, because it is holy to you. Anyone who desecrates it is
to be put to death; those who do any work on that day must be cut off from their
people. 15For six days work is to be done, but the seventh day is a day of sabbath
rest, holy to the LORD. Whoever does any work on the Sabbath day is to be put
to death. 16The Israelites are to observe the Sabbath, celebrating it for the generations to come as a lasting covenant. 17It will be a sign between me and the
Israelites forever, for in six days the LORD made the heavens and the earth, and
on the seventh day he rested and was refreshed.’ ”
18When the LORD finished speaking to Moses on Mount Sinai, he gave him the
two tablets of the covenant law, the tablets of stone inscribed by the finger of God.

The Golden Calf

32 When the people saw that Moses was so long in coming down from the
mountain, they gathered around Aaron and said, “Come, make us gods[a]
who will go before us. As for this fellow Moses who brought us up out of Egypt,
we don’t know what has happened to him.”
2Aaron answered them, “Take off the gold earrings that your wives, your sons
and your daughters are wearing, and bring them to me.” 3So all the people took
off their earrings and brought them to Aaron. 4He took what they handed him
and made it into an idol cast in the shape of a calf, fashioning it with a tool. Then
they said, “These are your gods,[b] Israel, who brought you up out of Egypt.”
5When Aaron saw this, he built an altar in front of the calf and announced,
“Tomorrow there will be a festival to the LORD.” 6So the next day the people rose
early and sacrificed burnt offerings and presented fellowship offerings. Afterward they sat down to eat and drink and got up to indulge in revelry.
7Then the LORD said to Moses, “Go down, because your people, whom you
brought up out of Egypt, have become corrupt. 8They have been quick to turn
away from what I commanded them and have made themselves an idol cast in
the shape of a calf. They have bowed down to it and sacrificed to it and have said,
‘These are your gods, Israel, who brought you up out of Egypt.’
9“I have seen these people,” the LORD said to Moses, “and they are a
stiff-necked people. 10Now leave me alone so that my anger may burn against
them and that I may destroy them. Then I will make you into a great nation.”
11But Moses sought the favor of the LORD his God. “LORD,” he said, “why
should your anger burn against your people, whom you brought out of Egypt
with great power and a mighty hand? 12Why should the Egyptians say, ‘It was
with evil intent that he brought them out, to kill them in the mountains and to
wipe them off the face of the earth’? Turn from your fierce anger; relent and do
not bring disaster on your people. 13Remember your servants Abraham, Isaac
and Israel, to whom you swore by your own self: ‘I will make your descendants
as numerous as the stars in the sky and I will give your descendants all this land
I promised them, and it will be their inheritance forever.’ ” 14Then the LORD relented and did not bring on his people the disaster he had threatened.
15Moses turned and went down the mountain with the two tablets of the covenant law in his hands. They were inscribed on both sides, front and back. 16The
tablets were the work of God; the writing was the writing of God, engraved on
the tablets.
17When Joshua heard the noise of the people shouting, he said to Moses,
“There is the sound of war in the camp.”
18Moses replied:

“It is not the sound of victory,
  it is not the sound of defeat;
  it is the sound of singing that I hear.”

19When Moses approached the camp and saw the calf and the dancing, his
anger burned and he threw the tablets out of his hands, breaking them to pieces

[a] *1* Or *a god;* also in verses 23 and 31 [b] *4* Or *This is your god;* also in verse 8

EXODUS 32:11 – 13

PERFECT INTERCESSION

Moses interceded before God on behalf of the people in a priestly prayer, asking him to relent from destroying the nation based on three factors. First, God had just delivered the nation of Israel from Egypt, and he could not abandon them now. Second, Pharaoh would learn of the destruction of the nation and believe that Egypt had, in fact, been victorious and that God’s plan was to bring them out of Egypt in order to kill them. Third, God had promised to uphold his covenant to his people, and he could not turn back on his promises. Moses’ prayer demonstrated his understanding of the severity of the sin of the people, his knowledge of the glory of the Lord and his zeal for his people.

Jesus’ intercessory prayer in the garden on the night he was betrayed follows this same pattern (Jn 17). Knowing the reality of life in a fallen world, he asked God to guard his people, protect them from the enemy, demonstrate his love to them and transform them by means of his Word. The author of Hebrews stated that Jesus, as the sinless intercessor and Son of God, has been resurrected and has ascended to the right hand of the Father so he can plead for the needs of his people (Heb 7:23 – 25).

at the foot of the mountain. [20]And he took the calf the people had made and burned it in the fire; then he ground it to powder, scattered it on the water and made the Israelites drink it.

[21]He said to Aaron, "What did these people do to you, that you led them into such great sin?"

[22]"Do not be angry, my lord," Aaron answered. "You know how prone these people are to evil. [23]They said to me, 'Make us gods who will go before us. As for this fellow Moses who brought us up out of Egypt, we don't know what has happened to him.' [24]So I told them, 'Whoever has any gold jewelry, take it off.' Then they gave me the gold, and I threw it into the fire, and out came this calf!"

[25]Moses saw that the people were running wild and that Aaron had let them get out of control and so become a laughingstock to their enemies. [26]So he stood at the entrance to the camp and said, "Whoever is for the LORD, come to me." And all the Levites rallied to him.

[27]Then he said to them, "This is what the LORD, the God of Israel, says: 'Each man strap a sword to his side. Go back and forth through the camp from one end to the other, each killing his brother and friend and neighbor.' " [28]The Levites did as Moses commanded, and that day about three thousand of the people died. [29]Then Moses said, "You have been set apart to the LORD today, for you were against your own sons and brothers, and he has blessed you this day."

[30]The next day Moses said to the people, "You have committed a great sin. But now I will go up to the LORD; perhaps I can make atonement for your sin."

[31]So Moses went back to the LORD and said, "Oh, what a great sin these people have committed! They have made themselves gods of gold. [32]But now, please forgive their sin—but if not, then blot me out of the book you have written."

[33]The LORD replied to Moses, "Whoever has sinned against me I will blot out of my book. [34]Now go, lead the people to the place I spoke of, and my angel will go before you. However, when the time comes for me to punish, I will punish them for their sin."

[35]And the LORD struck the people with a plague because of what they did with the calf Aaron had made.

33 Then the LORD said to Moses, "Leave this place, you and the people you brought up out of Egypt, and go up to the land I promised on oath to Abraham, Isaac and Jacob, saying, 'I will give it to your descendants.' [2]I will send an angel before you and drive out the Canaanites, Amorites, Hittites, Perizzites, Hivites and Jebusites. [3]Go up to the land flowing with milk and honey. But I will not go with you, because you are a stiff-necked people and I might destroy you on the way."

[4]When the people heard these distressing words, they began to mourn and no one put on any ornaments. [5]For the LORD had said to Moses, "Tell the Israelites, 'You are a stiff-necked people. If I were to go with you even for a moment, I might destroy you. Now take off your ornaments and I will decide what to do with you.' " [6]So the Israelites stripped off their ornaments at Mount Horeb.

The Tent of Meeting

[7]Now Moses used to take a tent and pitch it outside the camp some distance away, calling it the "tent of meeting." Anyone inquiring of the LORD would go to the tent of meeting outside the camp. [8]And whenever Moses went out to the tent, all the people rose and stood at the entrances to their tents, watching Moses until he entered the tent. [9]As Moses went into the tent, the pillar of cloud would come down and stay at the entrance, while the LORD spoke with Moses. [10]Whenever the people saw the pillar of cloud standing at the entrance to the tent, they all stood and worshiped, each at the entrance to their tent. [11]The LORD would speak to Moses face to face, as one speaks to a friend. Then Moses would return to the camp, but his young aide Joshua son of Nun did not leave the tent.

EXODUS 32:32

MY LIFE FOR THEIR LIVES

Moses begged God to forgive the sin of the people, offering to give his life as a substitute for theirs should God so desire. The inexcusable sin of making and worshiping the golden calf prompted the righteous judgment of God. How could a people who had so recently been the recipients of the might and power of God decide to do such a thing? The inexplicable nature of this sin highlights the foolishness of all sin and the necessity of God's judgment.

Yet, as always, God's grace shone through. He did not blot Israel from the face of the earth, though he would have been justified in doing so. He was faithful to his covenant and sustained the nation, though he judged those who sinned against him. In his request, Moses recognized that someone must die for these sins, and he asked God to allow a substitute. But what they needed was a perfect substitute—one who was without sin and capable of offering himself to God as an unblemished sacrifice. They needed Jesus, the one who could do what Moses could not—namely, offer himself for sin, not merely for Israel, but for all of God's people forever.

Moses and the Glory of the Lord

[12]Moses said to the LORD, "You have been telling me, 'Lead these people,' but
you have not let me know whom you will send with me. You have said, 'I know
you by name and you have found favor with me.' [13]If you are pleased with me,
teach me your ways so I may know you and continue to find favor with you. Remember that this nation is your people."
[14]The LORD replied, "My Presence will go with you, and I will give you rest."
[15]Then Moses said to him, "If your Presence does not go with us, do not send
us up from here. [16]How will anyone know that you are pleased with me and with
your people unless you go with us? What else will distinguish me and your people from all the other people on the face of the earth?"
[17]And the LORD said to Moses, "I will do the very thing you have asked, because I am pleased with you and I know you by name."
[18]Then Moses said, "Now show me your glory."
[19]And the LORD said, "I will cause all my goodness to pass in front of you, and
I will proclaim my name, the LORD, in your presence. I will have mercy on whom
I will have mercy, and I will have compassion on whom I will have compassion.
[20]But," he said, "you cannot see my face, for no one may see me and live."
[21]Then the LORD said, "There is a place near me where you may stand on a
rock. [22]When my glory passes by, I will put you in a cleft in the rock and cover
you with my hand until I have passed by. [23]Then I will remove my hand and you
will see my back; but my face must not be seen."

The New Stone Tablets

34 The LORD said to Moses, "Chisel out two stone tablets like the first ones,
and I will write on them the words that were on the first tablets, which
you broke. [2]Be ready in the morning, and then come up on Mount Sinai. Present
yourself to me there on top of the mountain. [3]No one is to come with you or be
seen anywhere on the mountain; not even the flocks and herds may graze in
front of the mountain."
[4]So Moses chiseled out two stone tablets like the first ones and went up Mount
Sinai early in the morning, as the LORD had commanded him; and he carried
the two stone tablets in his hands. [5]Then the LORD came down in the cloud and
stood there with him and proclaimed his name, the LORD. [6]And he passed in
front of Moses, proclaiming, "The LORD, the LORD, the compassionate and gracious God, slow to anger, abounding in love and faithfulness, [7]maintaining love
to thousands, and forgiving wickedness, rebellion and sin. Yet he does not leave
the guilty unpunished; he punishes the children and their children for the sin of
the parents to the third and fourth generation."
[8]Moses bowed to the ground at once and worshiped. [9]"Lord," he said, "if I
have found favor in your eyes, then let the Lord go with us. Although this is a
stiff-necked people, forgive our wickedness and our sin, and take us as your inheritance."
[10]Then the LORD said: "I am making a covenant with you. Before all your people I will do wonders never before done in any nation in all the world. The people
you live among will see how awesome is the work that I, the LORD, will do for
you. [11]Obey what I command you today. I will drive out before you the Amorites,
Canaanites, Hittites, Perizzites, Hivites and Jebusites. [12]Be careful not to make a
treaty with those who live in the land where you are going, or they will be a snare
among you. [13]Break down their altars, smash their sacred stones and cut down
their Asherah poles.[a] [14]Do not worship any other god, for the LORD, whose name
is Jealous, is a jealous God.
[15]"Be careful not to make a treaty with those who live in the land; for when
they prostitute themselves to their gods and sacrifice to them, they will invite you and you will eat their sacrifices. [16]And when you choose some of their

[a] *13* That is, wooden symbols of the goddess Asherah

EXODUS 33:18–23

GLORY

Moses made an astounding request. He asked God to show him his glory. The word "glory" conveys the idea of weight, significance or importance. In short, God's glory is the sum total of all the things that make him God. God, in an act of grace, agreed to Moses' request and provided him a brief and passing glimpse of his eternal worth and majesty, demonstrating his power, his love to his chosen servant and his calling for Moses to lead Israel into the promised land.

One would think that this type of exposure to the glory of God would be reserved only for the great leaders of the Bible—people like Abraham, Joseph, Moses or David. Yet God actually provides all Christians with an ever-increasing display of his glory (2Co 4:6). But this glimpse of glory is not physically observable now. Instead, the Spirit of God captivates believers' hearts with the glory of God, flooding them with the light of Christ and allowing them to see the majesty of God demonstrated in the person and work of Jesus Christ. This glimpse of glory is the basis for loving God, renouncing sin and serving in God's mission in the world.

daughters as wives for your sons and those daughters prostitute themselves to
their gods, they will lead your sons to do the same.
17“Do not make any idols.
18“Celebrate the Festival of Unleavened Bread. For seven days eat bread made
without yeast, as I commanded you. Do this at the appointed time in the month
of Aviv, for in that month you came out of Egypt.
19“The first offspring of every womb belongs to me, including all the firstborn
males of your livestock, whether from herd or flock. 20Redeem the firstborn donkey with a lamb, but if you do not redeem it, break its neck. Redeem all your
firstborn sons.
“No one is to appear before me empty-handed.
21“Six days you shall labor, but on the seventh day you shall rest; even during
the plowing season and harvest you must rest.
22“Celebrate the Festival of Weeks with the firstfruits of the wheat harvest,
and the Festival of Ingathering at the turn of the year.[a] 23Three times a year all
your men are to appear before the Sovereign LORD, the God of Israel. 24I will
drive out nations before you and enlarge your territory, and no one will covet
your land when you go up three times each year to appear before the LORD your
God.
25“Do not offer the blood of a sacrifice to me along with anything containing
yeast, and do not let any of the sacrifice from the Passover Festival remain until
morning.
26“Bring the best of the firstfruits of your soil to the house of the LORD your
God.
“Do not cook a young goat in its mother’s milk.”
27Then the LORD said to Moses, “Write down these words, for in accordance
with these words I have made a covenant with you and with Israel.” 28Moses was
there with the LORD forty days and forty nights without eating bread or drinking
water. And he wrote on the tablets the words of the covenant—the Ten Commandments.

The Radiant Face of Moses

29When Moses came down from Mount Sinai with the two tablets of the covenant law in his hands, he was not aware that his face was radiant because he
had spoken with the LORD. 30When Aaron and all the Israelites saw Moses, his
face was radiant, and they were afraid to come near him. 31But Moses called to
them; so Aaron and all the leaders of the community came back to him, and he
spoke to them. 32Afterward all the Israelites came near him, and he gave them
all the commands the LORD had given him on Mount Sinai.
33When Moses finished speaking to them, he put a veil over his face. 34But
whenever he entered the LORD’s presence to speak with him, he removed the
veil until he came out. And when he came out and told the Israelites what he had
been commanded, 35they saw that his face was radiant. Then Moses would put
the veil back over his face until he went in to speak with the LORD.

Sabbath Regulations

35 Moses assembled the whole Israelite community and said to them,
“These are the things the LORD has commanded you to do: 2For six days,
work is to be done, but the seventh day shall be your holy day, a day of sabbath
rest to the LORD. Whoever does any work on it is to be put to death. 3Do not light
a fire in any of your dwellings on the Sabbath day.”

Materials for the Tabernacle

4Moses said to the whole Israelite community, “This is what the LORD has
commanded: 5From what you have, take an offering for the LORD. Everyone who

[a] *22* That is, in the autumn

UNVEILED FACES

Moses' proximity to God's glory caused his face to radiate with light. The fact that a sinful man like Moses was allowed to see a glimpse of the glory of God demonstrates the sacrifice of God and his willingness — in fact, his desire — to be known by those whom he has created. As Moses descended from the mountain, the glow on his face proved that he had been in the presence of God.

The veil separating mankind from the glory of God was symbolic of a far greater divide. The holy, blameless God could no longer commune with his broken image-bearers due to their sin. Without a sacrifice, mankind would never again be able to walk with God in the cool of the garden and talk with him as a friend. Instead, all people were cast out of his presence, shown by the distance the people had to maintain between themselves and the mountain on which God dwelled. Even Moses could not partake of the full radiance of the glory of God, nor could he communicate that glory to the people without a veil of separation.

Paul claimed that the entire Old Testament law and sacrificial system functioned as a preventative veil that hindered the ability of the Jewish nation to properly respond to the person and work of Jesus Christ (2Co 3:7 – 18). Rather than serving as a tutor to show people their need for Christ, the law caused people to stumble and miss their need for Christ's redemptive work. The veil was far more than something they wore on their faces, but it was something that surrounded their hearts and prevented them from faith in Jesus. They wrongly believed that they could be made right with God by keeping the law rather than repenting and trusting in Christ.

Paul pointed out that this type of veil can only be removed by Christ himself. He, by the work of his Spirit, is capable of removing the veil that separates humanity from God. This freedom from the burden of the law allows mankind to see and respond to the glory of God with unveiled faces. And, as people see the glory of God, they are transformed to reflect that glory, from one degree to another, until the great and glorious day when all of his people see him face to face.

A FOREVER REST

Sabbath rest followed the model God established in creation, when, after creating the world in six days, he rested on the seventh day and called it holy. This rhythm of work and rest was built into the way God designed humanity to function and thrive. All believers are to give themselves to meaningful work that cares for and enhances God's world in order to give him glory. Then, as an act of faith and trust, believers must rest, showing their dependence on God and finding satisfaction in intimacy with their Creator.

The hope of the promised land served as a picture of Sabbath rest. After enslavement in Egypt and an arduous journey in the wilderness, the people found rest in a land that was free from war and flowing with milk and honey. There they could dwell in safety and worship God rightly — or so they thought. The story of the nation of Israel proves that such rest was short-lived, at best. The people were never willing to drive out the inhabitants of the land completely, thus they were constantly facing the threat of enemy attacks. Their inconsistent obedience meant that the judgment of God was never far off. The hope of rest remained, but it likely seemed like a long-forgotten dream.

The author of Hebrews reminded a scattered church, long after Israel's failure and exile, that the hope of rest still stands (Heb 4). This time, however, the promise of rest is not found in a day of the week or a location on a map. Instead, the promise of rest is found by being united with Christ, free from the tyranny of sin. This rest frees humanity from the laborious and impossible process of trying to secure God's blessing by means of their righteous deeds. Since Christ has fulfilled the law for his people and given them his righteousness through faith, they can rest, knowing that the work is finished and their standing before God is secure. They can find rest at any time and at any place by coming to Christ whose yoke is easy and whose burden is light (Mt 11:30). In him, weary souls can find refreshment, and broken hearts can be made whole.

is willing is to bring to the LORD an offering of gold, silver and bronze; 6blue,
purple and scarlet yarn and fine linen; goat hair; 7ram skins dyed red and another type of durable leather[a]; acacia wood; 8olive oil for the light; spices for the
anointing oil and for the fragrant incense; 9and onyx stones and other gems to
be mounted on the ephod and breastpiece.

10"All who are skilled among you are to come and make everything the LORD
has commanded: 11the tabernacle with its tent and its covering, clasps, frames,
crossbars, posts and bases; 12the ark with its poles and the atonement cover
and the curtain that shields it; 13the table with its poles and all its articles and
the bread of the Presence; 14the lampstand that is for light with its accessories,
lamps and oil for the light; 15the altar of incense with its poles, the anointing
oil and the fragrant incense; the curtain for the doorway at the entrance to the
tabernacle; 16the altar of burnt offering with its bronze grating, its poles and
all its utensils; the bronze basin with its stand; 17the curtains of the courtyard
with its posts and bases, and the curtain for the entrance to the courtyard;
18the tent pegs for the tabernacle and for the courtyard, and their ropes; 19the
woven garments worn for ministering in the sanctuary—both the sacred garments for Aaron the priest and the garments for his sons when they serve as
priests."

20Then the whole Israelite community withdrew from Moses' presence, 21and
everyone who was willing and whose heart moved them came and brought an
offering to the LORD for the work on the tent of meeting, for all its service, and for
the sacred garments. 22All who were willing, men and women alike, came and
brought gold jewelry of all kinds: brooches, earrings, rings and ornaments. They
all presented their gold as a wave offering to the LORD. 23Everyone who had blue,
purple or scarlet yarn or fine linen, or goat hair, ram skins dyed red or the other
durable leather brought them. 24Those presenting an offering of silver or bronze
brought it as an offering to the LORD, and everyone who had acacia wood for
any part of the work brought it. 25Every skilled woman spun with her hands and
brought what she had spun—blue, purple or scarlet yarn or fine linen. 26And all
the women who were willing and had the skill spun the goat hair. 27The leaders
brought onyx stones and other gems to be mounted on the ephod and breastpiece. 28They also brought spices and olive oil for the light and for the anointing
oil and for the fragrant incense. 29All the Israelite men and women who were
willing brought to the LORD freewill offerings for all the work the LORD through
Moses had commanded them to do.

Bezalel and Oholiab

30Then Moses said to the Israelites, "See, the LORD has chosen Bezalel son of
Uri, the son of Hur, of the tribe of Judah, 31and he has filled him with the Spirit
of God, with wisdom, with understanding, with knowledge and with all kinds
of skills— 32to make artistic designs for work in gold, silver and bronze, 33to cut
and set stones, to work in wood and to engage in all kinds of artistic crafts. 34And
he has given both him and Oholiab son of Ahisamak, of the tribe of Dan, the ability to teach others. 35He has filled them with skill to do all kinds of work as en-
gravers, designers, embroiderers in blue, purple and scarlet yarn and fine linen,
36 and weavers—all of them skilled workers and designers. 1So Bezalel,
Oholiab and every skilled person to whom the LORD has given skill and
ability to know how to carry out all the work of constructing the sanctuary are to
do the work just as the LORD has commanded."

2Then Moses summoned Bezalel and Oholiab and every skilled person to
whom the LORD had given ability and who was willing to come and do the work.
3They received from Moses all the offerings the Israelites had brought to carry
out the work of constructing the sanctuary. And the people continued to bring
freewill offerings morning after morning. 4So all the skilled workers who were

---

[a] 7 Possibly the hides of large aquatic mammals; also in verse 23

doing all the work on the sanctuary left what they were doing [5]and said to Moses, "The people are bringing more than enough for doing the work the LORD commanded to be done."

[6]Then Moses gave an order and they sent this word throughout the camp: "No man or woman is to make anything else as an offering for the sanctuary." And so the people were restrained from bringing more, [7]because what they already had was more than enough to do all the work.

The Tabernacle

[8]All those who were skilled among the workers made the tabernacle with ten curtains of finely twisted linen and blue, purple and scarlet yarn, with cherubim woven into them by expert hands. [9]All the curtains were the same size — twenty-eight cubits long and four cubits wide.[a] [10]They joined five of the curtains together and did the same with the other five. [11]Then they made loops of blue material along the edge of the end curtain in one set, and the same was done with the end curtain in the other set. [12]They also made fifty loops on one curtain and fifty loops on the end curtain of the other set, with the loops opposite each other. [13]Then they made fifty gold clasps and used them to fasten the two sets of curtains together so that the tabernacle was a unit.

[14]They made curtains of goat hair for the tent over the tabernacle — eleven altogether. [15]All eleven curtains were the same size — thirty cubits long and four cubits wide.[b] [16]They joined five of the curtains into one set and the other six into another set. [17]Then they made fifty loops along the edge of the end curtain in one set and also along the edge of the end curtain in the other set. [18]They made fifty bronze clasps to fasten the tent together as a unit. [19]Then they made for the tent a covering of ram skins dyed red, and over that a covering of the other durable leather.[c]

[20]They made upright frames of acacia wood for the tabernacle. [21]Each frame was ten cubits long and a cubit and a half wide,[d] [22]with two projections set parallel to each other. They made all the frames of the tabernacle in this way. [23]They made twenty frames for the south side of the tabernacle [24]and made forty silver bases to go under them — two bases for each frame, one under each projection. [25]For the other side, the north side of the tabernacle, they made twenty frames [26]and forty silver bases — two under each frame. [27]They made six frames for the far end, that is, the west end of the tabernacle, [28]and two frames were made for the corners of the tabernacle at the far end. [29]At these two corners the frames were double from the bottom all the way to the top and fitted into a single ring; both were made alike. [30]So there were eight frames and sixteen silver bases — two under each frame.

[31]They also made crossbars of acacia wood: five for the frames on one side of the tabernacle, [32]five for those on the other side, and five for the frames on the west, at the far end of the tabernacle. [33]They made the center crossbar so that it extended from end to end at the middle of the frames. [34]They overlaid the frames with gold and made gold rings to hold the crossbars. They also overlaid the crossbars with gold.

[35]They made the curtain of blue, purple and scarlet yarn and finely twisted linen, with cherubim woven into it by a skilled worker. [36]They made four posts of acacia wood for it and overlaid them with gold. They made gold hooks for them and cast their four silver bases. [37]For the entrance to the tent they made a curtain of blue, purple and scarlet yarn and finely twisted linen — the work of an embroiderer; [38]and they made five posts with hooks for them. They overlaid the tops of the posts and their bands with gold and made their five bases of bronze.

---

[a] *9* That is, about 42 feet long and 6 feet wide or about 13 meters long and 1.8 meters wide
[b] *15* That is, about 45 feet long and 6 feet wide or about 14 meters long and 1.8 meters wide
[c] *19* Possibly the hides of large aquatic mammals (see 35:7)
[d] *21* That is, about 15 feet long and 2 1/4 feet wide or about 4.5 meters long and 68 centimeters wide

The Ark

37 Bezalel made the ark of acacia wood—two and a half cubits long, a cubit
and a half wide, and a cubit and a half high.[a] 2He overlaid it with pure
gold, both inside and out, and made a gold molding around it. 3He cast four gold
rings for it and fastened them to its four feet, with two rings on one side and two
rings on the other. 4Then he made poles of acacia wood and overlaid them with
gold. 5And he inserted the poles into the rings on the sides of the ark to carry it.
6He made the atonement cover of pure gold—two and a half cubits long and
a cubit and a half wide. 7Then he made two cherubim out of hammered gold at
the ends of the cover. 8He made one cherub on one end and the second cherub
on the other; at the two ends he made them of one piece with the cover. 9The
cherubim had their wings spread upward, overshadowing the cover with them.
The cherubim faced each other, looking toward the cover.

The Table

10They[b] made the table of acacia wood—two cubits long, a cubit wide and a
cubit and a half high.[c] 11Then they overlaid it with pure gold and made a gold
molding around it. 12They also made around it a rim a handbreadth[d] wide and
put a gold molding on the rim. 13They cast four gold rings for the table and fastened them to the four corners, where the four legs were. 14The rings were put
close to the rim to hold the poles used in carrying the table. 15The poles for carrying the table were made of acacia wood and were overlaid with gold. 16And they
made from pure gold the articles for the table—its plates and dishes and bowls
and its pitchers for the pouring out of drink offerings.

The Lampstand

17They made the lampstand of pure gold. They hammered out its base and
shaft, and made its flowerlike cups, buds and blossoms of one piece with them.
18Six branches extended from the sides of the lampstand—three on one side
and three on the other. 19Three cups shaped like almond flowers with buds and
blossoms were on one branch, three on the next branch and the same for all six
branches extending from the lampstand. 20And on the lampstand were four cups
shaped like almond flowers with buds and blossoms. 21One bud was under the
first pair of branches extending from the lampstand, a second bud under the
second pair, and a third bud under the third pair—six branches in all. 22The
buds and the branches were all of one piece with the lampstand, hammered out
of pure gold.
23They made its seven lamps, as well as its wick trimmers and trays, of pure
gold. 24They made the lampstand and all its accessories from one talent[e] of pure
gold.

The Altar of Incense

25They made the altar of incense out of acacia wood. It was square, a cubit
long and a cubit wide and two cubits high[f]—its horns of one piece with it. 26They
overlaid the top and all the sides and the horns with pure gold, and made a gold
molding around it. 27They made two gold rings below the molding—two on each
of the opposite sides—to hold the poles used to carry it. 28They made the poles
of acacia wood and overlaid them with gold.
29They also made the sacred anointing oil and the pure, fragrant incense—
the work of a perfumer.

---

[a] *1* That is, about 3 3/4 feet long and 2 1/4 feet wide and high or about 1.1 meters long and 68 centimeters wide and high; similarly in verse 6 [b] *10* Or *He*; also in verses 11-29
[c] *10* That is, about 3 feet long, 1 1/2 feet wide and 2 1/4 feet high or about 90 centimeters long, 45 centimeters wide and 68 centimeters high [d] *12* That is, about 3 inches or about 7.5 centimeters [e] *24* That is, about 75 pounds or about 34 kilograms [f] *25* That is, about 1 1/2 feet long and wide and 3 feet high or about 45 centimeters long and wide and 90 centimeters high

The Altar of Burnt Offering

38 They[a] built the altar of burnt offering of acacia wood, three cubits[b] high; it was square, five cubits long and five cubits wide.[c] 2They made a horn at each of the four corners, so that the horns and the altar were of one piece, and they overlaid the altar with bronze. 3They made all its utensils of bronze — its pots, shovels, sprinkling bowls, meat forks and firepans. 4They made a grating for the altar, a bronze network, to be under its ledge, halfway up the altar. 5They cast bronze rings to hold the poles for the four corners of the bronze grating. 6They made the poles of acacia wood and overlaid them with bronze. 7They inserted the poles into the rings so they would be on the sides of the altar for carrying it. They made it hollow, out of boards.

The Basin for Washing

8They made the bronze basin and its bronze stand from the mirrors of the women who served at the entrance to the tent of meeting.

The Courtyard

9Next they made the courtyard. The south side was a hundred cubits[d] long and had curtains of finely twisted linen, 10with twenty posts and twenty bronze bases, and with silver hooks and bands on the posts. 11The north side was also a hundred cubits long and had twenty posts and twenty bronze bases, with silver hooks and bands on the posts.

12The west end was fifty cubits[e] wide and had curtains, with ten posts and ten bases, with silver hooks and bands on the posts. 13The east end, toward the sunrise, was also fifty cubits wide. 14Curtains fifteen cubits[f] long were on one side of the entrance, with three posts and three bases, 15and curtains fifteen cubits long were on the other side of the entrance to the courtyard, with three posts and three bases. 16All the curtains around the courtyard were of finely twisted linen. 17The bases for the posts were bronze. The hooks and bands on the posts were silver, and their tops were overlaid with silver; so all the posts of the courtyard had silver bands.

18The curtain for the entrance to the courtyard was made of blue, purple and scarlet yarn and finely twisted linen — the work of an embroiderer. It was twenty cubits[g] long and, like the curtains of the courtyard, five cubits[h] high, 19with four posts and four bronze bases. Their hooks and bands were silver, and their tops were overlaid with silver. 20All the tent pegs of the tabernacle and of the surrounding courtyard were bronze.

The Materials Used

21These are the amounts of the materials used for the tabernacle, the tabernacle of the covenant law, which were recorded at Moses' command by the Levites under the direction of Ithamar son of Aaron, the priest. 22(Bezalel son of Uri, the son of Hur, of the tribe of Judah, made everything the LORD commanded Moses; 23with him was Oholiab son of Ahisamak, of the tribe of Dan — an engraver and designer, and an embroiderer in blue, purple and scarlet yarn and fine linen.) 24The total amount of the gold from the wave offering used for all the work on the sanctuary was 29 talents and 730 shekels,[i] according to the sanctuary shekel.

25The silver obtained from those of the community who were counted in the census was 100 talents[j] and 1,775 shekels,[k] according to the sanctuary shekel — 26one beka per person, that is, half a shekel,[l] according to the sanctuary shekel, from everyone who had crossed over to those counted, twenty years old or more,

[a] *1* Or *He*; also in verses 2-9 [b] *1* That is, about 4 1/2 feet or about 1.4 meters [c] *1* That is, about 7 1/2 feet or about 2.3 meters long and wide [d] *9* That is, about 150 feet or about 45 meters [e] *12* That is, about 75 feet or about 23 meters [f] *14* That is, about 22 feet or about 6.8 meters [g] *18* That is, about 30 feet or about 9 meters [h] *18* That is, about 7 1/2 feet or about 2.3 meters [i] *24* The weight of the gold was a little over a ton or about 1 metric ton. [j] *25* That is, about 3 3/4 tons or about 3.4 metric tons; also in verse 27 [k] *25* That is, about 44 pounds or about 20 kilograms; also in verse 28 [l] *26* That is, about 1/5 ounce or about 5.7 grams

a total of 603,550 men. 27The 100 talents of silver were used to cast the bases for
the sanctuary and for the curtain — 100 bases from the 100 talents, one talent
for each base. 28They used the 1,775 shekels to make the hooks for the posts, to
overlay the tops of the posts, and to make their bands.

29The bronze from the wave offering was 70 talents and 2,400 shekels.[a] 30They
used it to make the bases for the entrance to the tent of meeting, the bronze altar
with its bronze grating and all its utensils, 31the bases for the surrounding courtyard and those for its entrance and all the tent pegs for the tabernacle and those
for the surrounding courtyard.

The Priestly Garments

39 From the blue, purple and scarlet yarn they made woven garments for
ministering in the sanctuary. They also made sacred garments for Aaron,
as the LORD commanded Moses.

The Ephod

2They[b] made the ephod of gold, and of blue, purple and scarlet yarn, and of
finely twisted linen. 3They hammered out thin sheets of gold and cut strands
to be worked into the blue, purple and scarlet yarn and fine linen — the work of
skilled hands. 4They made shoulder pieces for the ephod, which were attached
to two of its corners, so it could be fastened. 5Its skillfully woven waistband was
like it — of one piece with the ephod and made with gold, and with blue, purple
and scarlet yarn, and with finely twisted linen, as the LORD commanded Moses.

6They mounted the onyx stones in gold filigree settings and engraved them
like a seal with the names of the sons of Israel. 7Then they fastened them on the
shoulder pieces of the ephod as memorial stones for the sons of Israel, as the
LORD commanded Moses.

The Breastpiece

8They fashioned the breastpiece — the work of a skilled craftsman. They
made it like the ephod: of gold, and of blue, purple and scarlet yarn, and of finely
twisted linen. 9It was square — a span[c] long and a span wide — and folded double. 10Then they mounted four rows of precious stones on it. The first row was
carnelian, chrysolite and beryl; 11the second row was turquoise, lapis lazuli and
emerald; 12the third row was jacinth, agate and amethyst; 13the fourth row was
topaz, onyx and jasper.[d] They were mounted in gold filigree settings. 14There
were twelve stones, one for each of the names of the sons of Israel, each engraved
like a seal with the name of one of the twelve tribes.

15For the breastpiece they made braided chains of pure gold, like a rope. 16They
made two gold filigree settings and two gold rings, and fastened the rings to two of
the corners of the breastpiece. 17They fastened the two gold chains to the rings at the
corners of the breastpiece, 18and the other ends of the chains to the two settings, attaching them to the shoulder pieces of the ephod at the front. 19They made two gold
rings and attached them to the other two corners of the breastpiece on the inside
edge next to the ephod. 20Then they made two more gold rings and attached them
to the bottom of the shoulder pieces on the front of the ephod, close to the seam just
above the waistband of the ephod. 21They tied the rings of the breastpiece to the
rings of the ephod with blue cord, connecting it to the waistband so that the breastpiece would not swing out from the ephod — as the LORD commanded Moses.

Other Priestly Garments

22They made the robe of the ephod entirely of blue cloth — the work of a weaver — 23with an opening in the center of the robe like the opening of a collar,[e] and

---

[a] *29* The weight of the bronze was about 2 1/2 tons or about 2.4 metric tons. [b] *2* Or *He*; also in verses 7, 8 and 22 [c] *9* That is, about 9 inches or about 23 centimeters [d] *13* The precise identification of some of these precious stones is uncertain. [e] *23* The meaning of the Hebrew for this word is uncertain.

a band around this opening, so that it would not tear. [24]They made pomegranates of blue, purple and scarlet yarn and finely twisted linen around the hem of the robe. [25]And they made bells of pure gold and attached them around the hem between the pomegranates. [26]The bells and pomegranates alternated around the hem of the robe to be worn for ministering, as the LORD commanded Moses.

[27]For Aaron and his sons, they made tunics of fine linen — the work of a weaver — [28]and the turban of fine linen, the linen caps and the undergarments of finely twisted linen. [29]The sash was made of finely twisted linen and blue, purple and scarlet yarn — the work of an embroiderer — as the LORD commanded Moses.

[30]They made the plate, the sacred emblem, out of pure gold and engraved on it, like an inscription on a seal: HOLY TO THE LORD. [31]Then they fastened a blue cord to it to attach it to the turban, as the LORD commanded Moses.

Moses Inspects the Tabernacle

[32]So all the work on the tabernacle, the tent of meeting, was completed. The Israelites did everything just as the LORD commanded Moses. [33]Then they brought the tabernacle to Moses: the tent and all its furnishings, its clasps, frames, crossbars, posts and bases; [34]the covering of ram skins dyed red and the covering of another durable leather[a] and the shielding curtain; [35]the ark of the covenant law with its poles and the atonement cover; [36]the table with all its articles and the bread of the Presence; [37]the pure gold lampstand with its row of lamps and all its accessories, and the olive oil for the light; [38]the gold altar, the anointing oil, the fragrant incense, and the curtain for the entrance to the tent; [39]the bronze altar with its bronze grating, its poles and all its utensils; the basin with its stand; [40]the curtains of the courtyard with its posts and bases, and the curtain for the entrance to the courtyard; the ropes and tent pegs for the courtyard; all the furnishings for the tabernacle, the tent of meeting; [41]and the woven garments worn for ministering in the sanctuary, both the sacred garments for Aaron the priest and the garments for his sons when serving as priests.

[42]The Israelites had done all the work just as the LORD had commanded Moses. [43]Moses inspected the work and saw that they had done it just as the LORD had commanded. So Moses blessed them.

Setting Up the Tabernacle

40 Then the LORD said to Moses: [2]"Set up the tabernacle, the tent of meeting, on the first day of the first month. [3]Place the ark of the covenant law in it and shield the ark with the curtain. [4]Bring in the table and set out what belongs on it. Then bring in the lampstand and set up its lamps. [5]Place the gold altar of incense in front of the ark of the covenant law and put the curtain at the entrance to the tabernacle.

[6]"Place the altar of burnt offering in front of the entrance to the tabernacle, the tent of meeting; [7]place the basin between the tent of meeting and the altar and put water in it. [8]Set up the courtyard around it and put the curtain at the entrance to the courtyard.

[9]"Take the anointing oil and anoint the tabernacle and everything in it; consecrate it and all its furnishings, and it will be holy. [10]Then anoint the altar of burnt offering and all its utensils; consecrate the altar, and it will be most holy. [11]Anoint the basin and its stand and consecrate them.

[12]"Bring Aaron and his sons to the entrance to the tent of meeting and wash them with water. [13]Then dress Aaron in the sacred garments, anoint him and consecrate him so he may serve me as priest. [14]Bring his sons and dress them in tunics. [15]Anoint them just as you anointed their father, so they may serve me as priests. Their anointing will be to a priesthood that will continue throughout their generations." [16]Moses did everything just as the LORD commanded him.

[a] *34* Possibly the hides of large aquatic mammals

EXODUS 39:32

FINALLY FINISHED

The place of worship was finally finished. After what was surely a grueling process, the Israelites were now able to celebrate the completion of the means by which they could worship God on their journey to the promised land. God's house, though, would not last forever. Once in the promised land, the people of God would construct a stationary dwelling for God — the temple. On its completion, the temple was thought to be a permanent structure (2Ch 8:16). The rebellion of the people and their exile from the land proved that the temple would not last forever either. The people were carried away from the land, and the temple was destroyed. The impermanence of the tabernacle and temple demonstrated the need for a dwelling place for God that would last.

Jesus' incarnation was the means by which God "tabernacled," or dwelt among, his people once again (Jn 1:14). His cry from the cross, "It is finished" was finally true (Jn 19:30). The dwelling of God among people was permanently and irrevocably established through Christ's work. The Holy Spirit has filled his people and will never be taken away.

17 So the tabernacle was set up on the first day of the first month in the second
year. 18 When Moses set up the tabernacle, he put the bases in place, erected the
frames, inserted the crossbars and set up the posts. 19 Then he spread the tent
over the tabernacle and put the covering over the tent, as the LORD commanded him.

20 He took the tablets of the covenant law and placed them in the ark, attached
the poles to the ark and put the atonement cover over it. 21 Then he brought the
ark into the tabernacle and hung the shielding curtain and shielded the ark of
the covenant law, as the LORD commanded him.

22 Moses placed the table in the tent of meeting on the north side of the tabernacle outside the curtain 23 and set out the bread on it before the LORD, as the
LORD commanded him.

24 He placed the lampstand in the tent of meeting opposite the table on the
south side of the tabernacle 25 and set up the lamps before the LORD, as the LORD
commanded him.

26 Moses placed the gold altar in the tent of meeting in front of the curtain
27 and burned fragrant incense on it, as the LORD commanded him.

28 Then he put up the curtain at the entrance to the tabernacle. 29 He set the altar of burnt offering near the entrance to the tabernacle, the tent of meeting, and
offered on it burnt offerings and grain offerings, as the LORD commanded him.

30 He placed the basin between the tent of meeting and the altar and put water in it for washing, 31 and Moses and Aaron and his sons used it to wash their
hands and feet. 32 They washed whenever they entered the tent of meeting or
approached the altar, as the LORD commanded Moses.

33 Then Moses set up the courtyard around the tabernacle and altar and put
up the curtain at the entrance to the courtyard. And so Moses finished the work.

The Glory of the LORD

34 Then the cloud covered the tent of meeting, and the glory of the LORD filled
the tabernacle. 35 Moses could not enter the tent of meeting because the cloud
had settled on it, and the glory of the LORD filled the tabernacle.

36 In all the travels of the Israelites, whenever the cloud lifted from above the
tabernacle, they would set out; 37 but if the cloud did not lift, they did not set
out—until the day it lifted. 38 So the cloud of the LORD was over the tabernacle
by day, and fire was in the cloud by night, in the sight of all the Israelites during
all their travels.

JESUS: OUR SACRIFICIAL SUBSTITUTE

LEVITICUS

LEVITICUS

EXODUS FROM EGYPT *c. 1446 BC*	AARON AND SONS CONSECRATED AS PRIESTS *c. 1445 BC*	FORTY YEARS IN THE WILDERNESS ENDS *c. 1406 BC*

The recently redeemed nation of Israel received instructions on proper worship throughout the book of Leviticus. God's love for his people is demonstrated in his unrelenting drive for fellowship with them. By giving these detailed instructions, God established the way that these fallen people would approach a holy God during their journey from Egypt to their final dwelling in the promised land. These instructions were clearly not a means by which people earned favor with God; rather, they outlined the path of worship for those who had already experienced God's gracious, redemptive work.

This book outlines the nature of that worship and details many of the responsibilities of those who served as priestly mediators between God and the nation itself. The instructions provided in the book describe how impure people can approach a holy God and can be forgiven of their sins. For this reason, Leviticus was not simply a manual for the priests. Its instructions helped all of God's people to understand how to approach God on his terms and offer him the worship he rightly deserves.

The book of Leviticus was written to describe the way that God's people could live in ritual and moral purity in spite of their sin. If they did so, God could dwell among the people and demonstrate his glory to them, and they could fulfill their mission of serving as a light to the surrounding nations. The consistent theme of sacrifice throughout the book demonstrates that sin has drastic implications — someone or something had to die to cover personal and communal sin before people could worship God rightly. The sacrificial death of a substitute was meant to remind the nation that they lived and worshiped under God's gracious permission in spite of their sinfulness. Leviticus, therefore, describes two main themes that are vital to understanding God's great work of salvation: first, the consequence of sin is death; second, the only way for people to avoid death is through the sacrifice of a substitute.

Leviticus, while often thought of as an archaic book filled with outdated rituals, directly foreshadows the work of Christ. Jesus serves as the perfect Lamb of God who takes away the sin of the world (Jn 1:29). In his substitutionary death, Christ fulfills the sacrifices called for throughout the book. He also serves as the great high priest — the one who makes it possible for fallen humanity to have a right relationship with God. Jesus was, and still is, the mediator between God and humanity, making human worship of a holy God possible.

IN THIS WAY THE PRIEST WILL MAKE ATONEMENT FOR THEM BEFORE THE LORD, AND THEY WILL BE FORGIVEN FOR ANY OF THE THINGS THEY DID THAT MADE THEM GUILTY.

Leviticus 6:7

LEVITICUS

The Burnt Offering

1 The LORD called to Moses and spoke to him from the tent of meeting. He said,
2“Speak to the Israelites and say to them: ‘When anyone among you brings
an offering to the LORD, bring as your offering an animal from either the herd
or the flock.
3“ ‘If the offering is a burnt offering from the herd, you are to offer a male without defect. You must present it at the entrance to the tent of meeting so that it will
be acceptable to the LORD. 4You are to lay your hand on the head of the burnt
offering, and it will be accepted on your behalf to make atonement for you. 5You
are to slaughter the young bull before the LORD, and then Aaron’s sons the priests
shall bring the blood and splash it against the sides of the altar at the entrance
to the tent of meeting. 6You are to skin the burnt offering and cut it into pieces.
7The sons of Aaron the priest are to put fire on the altar and arrange wood on the
fire. 8Then Aaron’s sons the priests shall arrange the pieces, including the head
and the fat, on the wood that is burning on the altar. 9You are to wash the internal
organs and the legs with water, and the priest is to burn all of it on the altar. It is
a burnt offering, a food offering, an aroma pleasing to the LORD.
10“ ‘If the offering is a burnt offering from the flock, from either the sheep or
the goats, you are to offer a male without defect. 11You are to slaughter it at the
north side of the altar before the LORD, and Aaron’s sons the priests shall splash
its blood against the sides of the altar. 12You are to cut it into pieces, and the
priest shall arrange them, including the head and the fat, on the wood that is
burning on the altar. 13You are to wash the internal organs and the legs with water, and the priest is to bring all of them and burn them on the altar. It is a burnt
offering, a food offering, an aroma pleasing to the LORD.
14“ ‘If the offering to the LORD is a burnt offering of birds, you are to offer a dove
or a young pigeon. 15The priest shall bring it to the altar, wring off the head and
burn it on the altar; its blood shall be drained out on the side of the altar. 16He
is to remove the crop and the feathers[a] and throw them down east of the altar
where the ashes are. 17He shall tear it open by the wings, not dividing it completely, and then the priest shall burn it on the wood that is burning on the altar.
It is a burnt offering, a food offering, an aroma pleasing to the LORD.

The Grain Offering

2 “ ‘When anyone brings a grain offering to the LORD, their offering is to be of
the finest flour. They are to pour olive oil on it, put incense on it 2and take it
to Aaron’s sons the priests. The priest shall take a handful of the flour and oil,
together with all the incense, and burn this as a memorial[b] portion on the altar,
a food offering, an aroma pleasing to the LORD. 3The rest of the grain offering
belongs to Aaron and his sons; it is a most holy part of the food offerings presented to the LORD.
4“ ‘If you bring a grain offering baked in an oven, it is to consist of the finest
flour: either thick loaves made without yeast and with olive oil mixed in or thin
loaves made without yeast and brushed with olive oil. 5If your grain offering is
prepared on a griddle, it is to be made of the finest flour mixed with oil, and
without yeast. 6Crumble it and pour oil on it; it is a grain offering. 7If your grain
offering is cooked in a pan, it is to be made of the finest flour and some olive
oil. 8Bring the grain offering made of these things to the LORD; present it to the

---

[a] 16 Or *crop with its contents*; the meaning of the Hebrew for this word is uncertain.
[b] 2 Or *representative*; also in verses 9 and 16

OFFERINGS OF SACRIFICE

The first offerings recorded in Scripture were made by Cain and Abel. In the book of Leviticus, Israel's priests managed the transaction between God and mankind. They ensured God's instructions for offerings were carefully followed. Blood was splashed on the holy altar, specific parts of the sacrifice were burned and an aroma pleasing to the Lord rose from the fire. The offerings were not made to the Lord because he had needs. They were careful acts of thanksgiving and repentance, acknowledging Israel's covenant God as Creator and Judge.

Burnt offerings required the slaughter of an unblemished animal as atonement — a bull, sheep, goat or bird. Blood and death were offered as substitutionary payment for the person who sinned.

Grain offerings accompanied all burnt offerings. Raw, roasted or baked grain was given in gratitude to God for the fruitfulness of the land.

Fellowship offerings were given out of gratitude, expressing fellowship between the worshiper and God. Unblemished cattle, sheep and goats were sacrificed in response to blessings or as unprompted offerings of thanksgiving.

Sin offerings involved the occasion of sin committed unintentionally, but no restitution was possible since the violation was against God. Different types of sacrifices were prescribed for different people within Israelite society — from high priest down to common citizen.

Guilt offerings atoned for sins committed unintentionally, where restitution could be made to the one offended. A guilt offering would be made when there was either a mistreatment of the Lord's holy things or an offense against a neighbor. In both cases, the priests calculated restitution.

Atonement was gruesome work — the noise of animals dying, the scene of blood splashed on an altar, the smoky smell of cooked flesh. In Leviticus, we see this was also intensely personal work. When the one who sinned brought an offering, they were required to place a hand on the animal's head as it was killed. The up-close experience reminded the sinner of personal guilt and the cost to regain right standing with God.

At an appointed time, God made a new and final way for dealing with sin. Jesus offered himself as the once-for-all sacrifice for our guilt (Heb 10:10). The cross became a holy altar for Christ's worthy blood. Jesus became our sacrificial lamb. Jesus suffered a terrible death he did not deserve — absorbing wrath we could never withstand, to give us hope for forgiveness. When Jesus died, the Levitical system of sacrifice became obsolete. Jesus, now alive forever, remains the only offering sufficient to cancel sin. The Lord no longer requires or accepts the blood of animals. Now, he only accepts personal faith in the death and resurrection of Jesus (Ro 10:9 – 10).

LEVITICUS 3:1

WITHOUT DEFECT

Only the best of flock or herd or crop was fit for sacrifice to God, who is infinitely worthy. Each offering had to be free of anything objectionable — a standard that mattered enormously to the Lord (Mal 1:6 – 14). The repeated instruction for a sacrifice "without defect" challenged the giver to consider what best honored God, reflecting a sincere and reverent sacrifice of worship.

When God graced the world with a Savior, he gave us the best — his own Son. Jesus is perfect in every way. In him there is no evil or weakness or fault or flaw. Our redemption has been accomplished through Christ who is precious, a lamb without blemish or defect (1Pe 1:19). The quality of God's offering on the cross shows his great love for people and confirms that only Jesus, who never sinned, could be a sufficient sacrifice. Jesus is worthy and without defect. Faith in him reconciles us to the Lord — making us holy and without blemish, fully acceptable to God (Col 1:22).

LEVITICUS 4:1 – 12

OFFERINGS

For the people of Israel, an offering was something a person brought to God to secure cleansing from sin or to express thanksgiving and devotion (see article on Lev 1:1 – 2). The system of exact procedures, though bloody and complex, was a gift of divine mercy. God created ways for sinners to cancel guilt. And he arranged rituals so the people could respond to his many works with gratitude

(continued on next page)

priest, who shall take it to the altar. [9]He shall take out the memorial portion from
the grain offering and burn it on the altar as a food offering, an aroma pleasing
to the LORD. [10]The rest of the grain offering belongs to Aaron and his sons; it is a
most holy part of the food offerings presented to the LORD.
[11]" 'Every grain offering you bring to the LORD must be made without yeast, for
you are not to burn any yeast or honey in a food offering presented to the LORD.
[12]You may bring them to the LORD as an offering of the firstfruits, but they are
not to be offered on the altar as a pleasing aroma. [13]Season all your grain offerings with salt. Do not leave the salt of the covenant of your God out of your grain
offerings; add salt to all your offerings.
[14]" 'If you bring a grain offering of firstfruits to the LORD, offer crushed heads
of new grain roasted in the fire. [15]Put oil and incense on it; it is a grain offering.
[16]The priest shall burn the memorial portion of the crushed grain and the oil,
together with all the incense, as a food offering presented to the LORD.

The Fellowship Offering

3 " 'If your offering is a fellowship offering, and you offer an animal from the
herd, whether male or female, you are to present before the LORD an animal
without defect. [2]You are to lay your hand on the head of your offering and slaughter it at the entrance to the tent of meeting. Then Aaron's sons the priests shall
splash the blood against the sides of the altar. [3]From the fellowship offering you
are to bring a food offering to the LORD: the internal organs and all the fat that
is connected to them, [4]both kidneys with the fat on them near the loins, and the
long lobe of the liver, which you will remove with the kidneys. [5]Then Aaron's
sons are to burn it on the altar on top of the burnt offering that is lying on the
burning wood; it is a food offering, an aroma pleasing to the LORD.
[6]" 'If you offer an animal from the flock as a fellowship offering to the LORD,
you are to offer a male or female without defect. [7]If you offer a lamb, you are to
present it before the LORD, [8]lay your hand on its head and slaughter it in front of
the tent of meeting. Then Aaron's sons shall splash its blood against the sides
of the altar. [9]From the fellowship offering you are to bring a food offering to the
LORD: its fat, the entire fat tail cut off close to the backbone, the internal organs
and all the fat that is connected to them, [10]both kidneys with the fat on them
near the loins, and the long lobe of the liver, which you will remove with the
kidneys. [11]The priest shall burn them on the altar as a food offering presented
to the LORD.
[12]" 'If your offering is a goat, you are to present it before the LORD, [13]lay your
hand on its head and slaughter it in front of the tent of meeting. Then Aaron's
sons shall splash its blood against the sides of the altar. [14]From what you offer
you are to present this food offering to the LORD: the internal organs and all the
fat that is connected to them, [15]both kidneys with the fat on them near the loins,
and the long lobe of the liver, which you will remove with the kidneys. [16]The
priest shall burn them on the altar as a food offering, a pleasing aroma. All the
fat is the LORD's.
[17]" 'This is a lasting ordinance for the generations to come, wherever you live:
You must not eat any fat or any blood.' "

The Sin Offering

4 The LORD said to Moses, [2]"Say to the Israelites: 'When anyone sins unintentionally and does what is forbidden in any of the LORD's commands —
[3]" 'If the anointed priest sins, bringing guilt on the people, he must bring to
the LORD a young bull without defect as a sin offering[a] for the sin he has committed. [4]He is to present the bull at the entrance to the tent of meeting before the
LORD. He is to lay his hand on its head and slaughter it there before the LORD.
[5]Then the anointed priest shall take some of the bull's blood and carry it into

[a] 3 Or *purification offering*; here and throughout this chapter

the tent of meeting. 6He is to dip his finger into the blood and sprinkle some of it seven times before the LORD, in front of the curtain of the sanctuary. 7The priest shall then put some of the blood on the horns of the altar of fragrant incense that is before the LORD in the tent of meeting. The rest of the bull's blood he shall pour out at the base of the altar of burnt offering at the entrance to the tent of meeting. 8He shall remove all the fat from the bull of the sin offering—all the fat that is connected to the internal organs, 9both kidneys with the fat on them near the loins, and the long lobe of the liver, which he will remove with the kidneys— 10just as the fat is removed from the ox[a] sacrificed as a fellowship offering. Then the priest shall burn them on the altar of burnt offering. 11But the hide of the bull and all its flesh, as well as the head and legs, the internal organs and the intestines— 12that is, all the rest of the bull—he must take outside the camp to a place ceremonially clean, where the ashes are thrown, and burn it there in a wood fire on the ash heap.

13" 'If the whole Israelite community sins unintentionally and does what is forbidden in any of the LORD's commands, even though the community is unaware of the matter, when they realize their guilt 14and the sin they committed becomes known, the assembly must bring a young bull as a sin offering and present it before the tent of meeting. 15The elders of the community are to lay their hands on the bull's head before the LORD, and the bull shall be slaughtered before the LORD. 16Then the anointed priest is to take some of the bull's blood into the tent of meeting. 17He shall dip his finger into the blood and sprinkle it before the LORD seven times in front of the curtain. 18He is to put some of the blood on the horns of the altar that is before the LORD in the tent of meeting. The rest of the blood he shall pour out at the base of the altar of burnt offering at the entrance to the tent of meeting. 19He shall remove all the fat from it and burn it on the altar, 20and do with this bull just as he did with the bull for the sin offering. In this way the priest will make atonement for the community, and they will be forgiven. 21Then he shall take the bull outside the camp and burn it as he burned the first bull. This is the sin offering for the community.

22" 'When a leader sins unintentionally and does what is forbidden in any of the commands of the LORD his God, when he realizes his guilt 23and the sin he has committed becomes known, he must bring as his offering a male goat without defect. 24He is to lay his hand on the goat's head and slaughter it at the place where the burnt offering is slaughtered before the LORD. It is a sin offering. 25Then the priest shall take some of the blood of the sin offering with his finger and put it on the horns of the altar of burnt offering and pour out the rest of the blood at the base of the altar. 26He shall burn all the fat on the altar as he burned the fat of the fellowship offering. In this way the priest will make atonement for the leader's sin, and he will be forgiven.

27" 'If any member of the community sins unintentionally and does what is forbidden in any of the LORD's commands, when they realize their guilt 28and the sin they have committed becomes known, they must bring as their offering for the sin they committed a female goat without defect. 29They are to lay their hand on the head of the sin offering and slaughter it at the place of the burnt offering. 30Then the priest is to take some of the blood with his finger and put it on the horns of the altar of burnt offering and pour out the rest of the blood at the base of the altar. 31They shall remove all the fat, just as the fat is removed from the fellowship offering, and the priest shall burn it on the altar as an aroma pleasing to the LORD. In this way the priest will make atonement for them, and they will be forgiven.

32" 'If someone brings a lamb as their sin offering, they are to bring a female without defect. 33They are to lay their hand on its head and slaughter it for a sin offering at the place where the burnt offering is slaughtered. 34Then the priest

[a] *10* The Hebrew word can refer to either male or female.

(Offerings, continued)

and praise. The sacrificial system ensured that God's people could have hope that their sin would be forgiven by a holy God and that they could, in turn, joyfully worship him with all of life.

Jesus' death on the cross was the ultimate offering, a final sacrifice that ended the need for any others. Jesus gave himself up for us all as the perfect sacrifice for sin (Eph 5:2). While offerings for sin are no longer required, the Lord delights in people giving themselves as sacrifices of praise and service to him (Ro 12:1).

shall take some of the blood of the sin offering with his finger and put it on the horns of the altar of burnt offering and pour out the rest of the blood at the base of the altar. 35They shall remove all the fat, just as the fat is removed from the lamb of the fellowship offering, and the priest shall burn it on the altar on top of the food offerings presented to the LORD. In this way the priest will make atonement for them for the sin they have committed, and they will be forgiven.

5 " 'If anyone sins because they do not speak up when they hear a public charge to testify regarding something they have seen or learned about, they will be held responsible.

2" 'If anyone becomes aware that they are guilty — if they unwittingly touch anything ceremonially unclean (whether the carcass of an unclean animal, wild or domestic, or of any unclean creature that moves along the ground) and they are unaware that they have become unclean, but then they come to realize their guilt; 3or if they touch human uncleanness (anything that would make them unclean) even though they are unaware of it, but then they learn of it and realize their guilt; 4or if anyone thoughtlessly takes an oath to do anything, whether good or evil (in any matter one might carelessly swear about) even though they are unaware of it, but then they learn of it and realize their guilt — 5when anyone becomes aware that they are guilty in any of these matters, they must confess in what way they have sinned. 6As a penalty for the sin they have committed, they must bring to the LORD a female lamb or goat from the flock as a sin offering[a]; and the priest shall make atonement for them for their sin.

7" 'Anyone who cannot afford a lamb is to bring two doves or two young pigeons to the LORD as a penalty for their sin — one for a sin offering and the other for a burnt offering. 8They are to bring them to the priest, who shall first offer the one for the sin offering. He is to wring its head from its neck, not dividing it completely, 9and is to splash some of the blood of the sin offering against the side of the altar; the rest of the blood must be drained out at the base of the altar. It is a sin offering. 10The priest shall then offer the other as a burnt offering in the prescribed way and make atonement for them for the sin they have committed, and they will be forgiven.

11" 'If, however, they cannot afford two doves or two young pigeons, they are to bring as an offering for their sin a tenth of an ephah[b] of the finest flour for a sin offering. They must not put olive oil or incense on it, because it is a sin offering. 12They are to bring it to the priest, who shall take a handful of it as a memorial[c] portion and burn it on the altar on top of the food offerings presented to the LORD. It is a sin offering. 13In this way the priest will make atonement for them for any of these sins they have committed, and they will be forgiven. The rest of the offering will belong to the priest, as in the case of the grain offering.' "

The Guilt Offering

14The LORD said to Moses: 15"When anyone is unfaithful to the LORD by sinning unintentionally in regard to any of the LORD's holy things, they are to bring to the LORD as a penalty a ram from the flock, one without defect and of the proper value in silver, according to the sanctuary shekel.[d] It is a guilt offering. 16They must make restitution for what they have failed to do in regard to the holy things, pay an additional penalty of a fifth of its value and give it all to the priest. The priest will make atonement for them with the ram as a guilt offering, and they will be forgiven.

17"If anyone sins and does what is forbidden in any of the LORD's commands, even though they do not know it, they are guilty and will be held responsible. 18They are to bring to the priest as a guilt offering a ram from the flock, one without defect and of the proper value. In this way the priest will make atonement for

[a] 6 Or *purification offering*; here and throughout this chapter [b] *11* That is, probably about 3 1/2 pounds or about 1.6 kilograms [c] *12* Or *representative* [d] *15* That is, about 2/5 ounce or about 12 grams

them for the wrong they have committed unintentionally, and they will be forgiv-
en. 19It is a guilt offering; they have been guilty of[a] wrongdoing against the LORD."
6[b] The LORD said to Moses: 2"If anyone sins and is unfaithful to the LORD by
deceiving a neighbor about something entrusted to them or left in their care
or about something stolen, or if they cheat their neighbor, 3or if they find lost
property and lie about it, or if they swear falsely about any such sin that people
may commit— 4when they sin in any of these ways and realize their guilt, they
must return what they have stolen or taken by extortion, or what was entrusted
to them, or the lost property they found, 5or whatever it was they swore falsely
about. They must make restitution in full, add a fifth of the value to it and give
it all to the owner on the day they present their guilt offering. 6And as a penalty
they must bring to the priest, that is, to the LORD, their guilt offering, a ram from
the flock, one without defect and of the proper value. 7In this way the priest will
make atonement for them before the LORD, and they will be forgiven for any of
the things they did that made them guilty."

The Burnt Offering

8The LORD said to Moses: 9"Give Aaron and his sons this command: 'These
are the regulations for the burnt offering: The burnt offering is to remain on the
altar hearth throughout the night, till morning, and the fire must be kept burning on the altar. 10The priest shall then put on his linen clothes, with linen undergarments next to his body, and shall remove the ashes of the burnt offering
that the fire has consumed on the altar and place them beside the altar. 11Then
he is to take off these clothes and put on others, and carry the ashes outside the
camp to a place that is ceremonially clean. 12The fire on the altar must be kept
burning; it must not go out. Every morning the priest is to add firewood and arrange the burnt offering on the fire and burn the fat of the fellowship offerings on
it. 13The fire must be kept burning on the altar continuously; it must not go out.

The Grain Offering

14" 'These are the regulations for the grain offering: Aaron's sons are to bring it
before the LORD, in front of the altar. 15The priest is to take a handful of the finest
flour and some olive oil, together with all the incense on the grain offering, and
burn the memorial[c] portion on the altar as an aroma pleasing to the LORD. 16Aaron
and his sons shall eat the rest of it, but it is to be eaten without yeast in the sanctuary area; they are to eat it in the courtyard of the tent of meeting. 17It must not be
baked with yeast; I have given it as their share of the food offerings presented to
me. Like the sin offering[d] and the guilt offering, it is most holy. 18Any male descendant of Aaron may eat it. For all generations to come it is his perpetual share of the
food offerings presented to the LORD. Whatever touches them will become holy.[e]' "
19The LORD also said to Moses, 20"This is the offering Aaron and his sons are
to bring to the LORD on the day he[f] is anointed: a tenth of an ephah[g] of the finest
flour as a regular grain offering, half of it in the morning and half in the evening.
21It must be prepared with oil on a griddle; bring it well-mixed and present the
grain offering broken[h] in pieces as an aroma pleasing to the LORD. 22The son who
is to succeed him as anointed priest shall prepare it. It is the LORD's perpetual
share and is to be burned completely. 23Every grain offering of a priest shall be
burned completely; it must not be eaten."

The Sin Offering

24The LORD said to Moses, 25"Say to Aaron and his sons: 'These are the regulations for the sin offering: The sin offering is to be slaughtered before the LORD in

[a] *19* Or *offering; atonement has been made for their* [b] In Hebrew texts 6:1-7 is numbered 5:20-26, and 6:8-30 is numbered 6:1-23. [c] *15* Or *representative* [d] *17* Or *purification offering*; also in verses 25 and 30 [e] *18* Or *Whoever touches them must be holy*; similarly in verse 27 [f] *20* Or *each* [g] *20* That is, probably about 3 1/2 pounds or about 1.6 kilograms [h] *21* The meaning of the Hebrew for this word is uncertain.

LEVITICUS 6:8–13

FIRE AND ASH

Maintaining the altar fire was the daily work of Aaron and his sons. Ashes from previous sacrifices had to be removed each day. The priests were instructed to always keep the fire burning on the altar—it must not go out. Perpetual fire symbolized the perpetual worship of God and the continual need for atonement and reconciliation.

Jesus came from heaven to fulfill the Law and to finish, by his death, the work of atonement for sin. He died on the cross, but unlike the sacrifices before, Jesus was not destroyed—becoming like ash. He triumphed over the grave by rising from the dead and he is alive forever (Ro 6:9–10; Rev 1:18).

Today there is no need for maintaining a connection to God through fire. We have all that we need through Christ. Jesus the Son is our Savior from sin, our access to adoption by the Father and the one who secured the continual presence of the Spirit in our lives.

the place the burnt offering is slaughtered; it is most holy. [26]The priest who offers it shall eat it; it is to be eaten in the sanctuary area, in the courtyard of the tent of meeting. [27]Whatever touches any of the flesh will become holy, and if any of the blood is spattered on a garment, you must wash it in the sanctuary area. [28]The clay pot the meat is cooked in must be broken; but if it is cooked in a bronze pot, the pot is to be scoured and rinsed with water. [29]Any male in a priest's family may eat it; it is most holy. [30]But any sin offering whose blood is brought into the tent of meeting to make atonement in the Holy Place must not be eaten; it must be burned up.

The Guilt Offering

7 " 'These are the regulations for the guilt offering, which is most holy: [2]The guilt offering is to be slaughtered in the place where the burnt offering is slaughtered, and its blood is to be splashed against the sides of the altar. [3]All its fat shall be offered: the fat tail and the fat that covers the internal organs, [4]both kidneys with the fat on them near the loins, and the long lobe of the liver, which is to be removed with the kidneys. [5]The priest shall burn them on the altar as a food offering presented to the LORD. It is a guilt offering. [6]Any male in a priest's family may eat it, but it must be eaten in the sanctuary area; it is most holy.

[7]" 'The same law applies to both the sin offering[a] and the guilt offering: They belong to the priest who makes atonement with them. [8]The priest who offers a burnt offering for anyone may keep its hide for himself. [9]Every grain offering baked in an oven or cooked in a pan or on a griddle belongs to the priest who offers it, [10]and every grain offering, whether mixed with olive oil or dry, belongs equally to all the sons of Aaron.

The Fellowship Offering

[11]" 'These are the regulations for the fellowship offering anyone may present to the LORD:

[12]" 'If they offer it as an expression of thankfulness, then along with this thank offering they are to offer thick loaves made without yeast and with olive oil mixed in, thin loaves made without yeast and brushed with oil, and thick loaves of the finest flour well-kneaded and with oil mixed in. [13]Along with their fellowship offering of thanksgiving they are to present an offering with thick loaves of bread made with yeast. [14]They are to bring one of each kind as an offering, a contribution to the LORD; it belongs to the priest who splashes the blood of the fellowship offering against the altar. [15]The meat of their fellowship offering of thanksgiving must be eaten on the day it is offered; they must leave none of it till morning.

[16]" 'If, however, their offering is the result of a vow or is a freewill offering, the sacrifice shall be eaten on the day they offer it, but anything left over may be eaten on the next day. [17]Any meat of the sacrifice left over till the third day must be burned up. [18]If any meat of the fellowship offering is eaten on the third day, the one who offered it will not be accepted. It will not be reckoned to their credit, for it has become impure; the person who eats any of it will be held responsible.

[19]" 'Meat that touches anything ceremonially unclean must not be eaten; it must be burned up. As for other meat, anyone ceremonially clean may eat it. [20]But if anyone who is unclean eats any meat of the fellowship offering belonging to the LORD, they must be cut off from their people. [21]Anyone who touches something unclean—whether human uncleanness or an unclean animal or any unclean creature that moves along the ground[b]—and then eats any of the meat of the fellowship offering belonging to the LORD must be cut off from their people.' "

Eating Fat and Blood Forbidden

[22]The LORD said to Moses, [23]"Say to the Israelites: 'Do not eat any of the fat of cattle, sheep or goats. [24]The fat of an animal found dead or torn by wild animals

LEVITICUS 7:13

YEAST

Yeast added to bread dough has an expanding and multiplying effect. The dough rises, often doubling its original size. Yeast is the difference between leavened and unleavened bread—the two types specified for the various offerings and festivals in the Israelite community. Since the bread with yeast mentioned here was not burned on the altar, the prohibition in Leviticus 2:11 and Exodus 23:18 did not apply.

In the New Testament, yeast is usually referenced in a negative connotation as an agent of corruption. Symbolizing evil, yeast is something to get rid of because a small amount can have a big impact. Jesus gave a warning against the yeast of the Pharisees and Sadducees—pointing to the corrupting influence of legalism and hypocrisy (Mt 16:6). Only in Matthew 13:33 is yeast used as a positive symbol of the permeating power of the gospel. Jesus compared the kingdom of heaven to yeast, which once added, changes the entire batch of dough. When a person moves from death to life through the gospel, their entire life is changed by the power of Christ.

---

[a] *7* Or *purification offering;* also in verse 37 [b] *21* A few Hebrew manuscripts, Samaritan Pentateuch, Syriac and Targum (see 5:2); most Hebrew manuscripts *any unclean, detestable thing*

may be used for any other purpose, but you must not eat it. [25]Anyone who eats the fat of an animal from which a food offering may be[a] presented to the Lord must be cut off from their people. [26]And wherever you live, you must not eat the blood of any bird or animal. [27]Anyone who eats blood must be cut off from their people.' "

The Priests' Share

[28]The Lord said to Moses, [29]"Say to the Israelites: 'Anyone who brings a fellowship offering to the Lord is to bring part of it as their sacrifice to the Lord. [30]With their own hands they are to present the food offering to the Lord; they are to bring the fat, together with the breast, and wave the breast before the Lord as a wave offering. [31]The priest shall burn the fat on the altar, but the breast belongs to Aaron and his sons. [32]You are to give the right thigh of your fellowship offerings to the priest as a contribution. [33]The son of Aaron who offers the blood and the fat of the fellowship offering shall have the right thigh as his share. [34]From the fellowship offerings of the Israelites, I have taken the breast that is waved and the thigh that is presented and have given them to Aaron the priest and his sons as their perpetual share from the Israelites.' "

[35]This is the portion of the food offerings presented to the Lord that were allotted to Aaron and his sons on the day they were presented to serve the Lord as priests. [36]On the day they were anointed, the Lord commanded that the Israelites give this to them as their perpetual share for the generations to come.

[37]These, then, are the regulations for the burnt offering, the grain offering, the sin offering, the guilt offering, the ordination offering and the fellowship offering, [38]which the Lord gave Moses at Mount Sinai in the Desert of Sinai on the day he commanded the Israelites to bring their offerings to the Lord.

The Ordination of Aaron and His Sons

8 The Lord said to Moses, [2]"Bring Aaron and his sons, their garments, the anointing oil, the bull for the sin offering,[b] the two rams and the basket containing bread made without yeast, [3]and gather the entire assembly at the entrance to the tent of meeting." [4]Moses did as the Lord commanded him, and the assembly gathered at the entrance to the tent of meeting.

[5]Moses said to the assembly, "This is what the Lord has commanded to be done." [6]Then Moses brought Aaron and his sons forward and washed them with water. [7]He put the tunic on Aaron, tied the sash around him, clothed him with the robe and put the ephod on him. He also fastened the ephod with a decorative waistband, which he tied around him. [8]He placed the breastpiece on him and put the Urim and Thummim in the breastpiece. [9]Then he placed the turban on Aaron's head and set the gold plate, the sacred emblem, on the front of it, as the Lord commanded Moses.

[10]Then Moses took the anointing oil and anointed the tabernacle and everything in it, and so consecrated them. [11]He sprinkled some of the oil on the altar seven times, anointing the altar and all its utensils and the basin with its stand, to consecrate them. [12]He poured some of the anointing oil on Aaron's head and anointed him to consecrate him. [13]Then he brought Aaron's sons forward, put tunics on them, tied sashes around them and fastened caps on them, as the Lord commanded Moses.

[14]He then presented the bull for the sin offering, and Aaron and his sons laid their hands on its head. [15]Moses slaughtered the bull and took some of the blood, and with his finger he put it on all the horns of the altar to purify the altar. He poured out the rest of the blood at the base of the altar. So he consecrated it to make atonement for it. [16]Moses also took all the fat around the internal organs, the long lobe of the liver, and both kidneys and their fat, and burned it on the altar. [17]But the bull with its hide and its flesh and its intestines he burned up outside the camp, as the Lord commanded Moses.

[a] 25 Or *offering is* [b] 2 Or *purification offering*; also in verse 14

LEVITICUS 8:12

ANOINTING

God chose and set apart the descendants of Abraham from all the peoples of the earth. They were holy in their identity as the children of God and holy in their vocation as the people of God (Lev 20:26). Among the Israelites, God designated the tribe of Levi to serve in the tabernacle. And within this tribe, Aaron and his sons were appointed priests. They were not perfect men. They were sinful and in need of the same ongoing cleansing and covering which their service facilitated for others.

In Leviticus 8:12, Moses anointed Aaron with oil to consecrate him like the kings of Israel (1Sa 10:1) and some of God's prophets (1Ki 19:16). Aaron was inaugurated as a mediator to instruct and facilitate worship, sacrifices and the yearly observances God required.

Aaron's position was a foreshadowing of God's permanent high priest, Jesus Christ. Aaron was anointed with oil, but "God anointed Jesus of Nazareth with the Holy Spirit and power" (Ac 10:38). Jesus combines in his person the offices of high priest, king and prophet, so he is *the* anointed one, which is the meaning of the names Messiah and Christ.

THE LAW

The Law of God came to the people of Israel through Moses (Ex 21:1). In decrees, commands, instructions and statutes, the Lord declared how their relationship with him would work. The Law gave glimpses into the nature and character of God — revealing his preferences and methods. It gave boundaries and much-needed clarity for how to approach and relate to God.

Having heard from the Lord in the fire and smoke atop Mount Sinai, Moses went down and told the people all the Lord's words and laws before writing everything down (Ex 24:3 – 4). Eventually, God inscribed his laws on stone tablets and gave them to Moses (Ex 24:12).

It is common to think of the Law as limited to the Ten Commandments. Actually, it was comprised of regulations for worship, instructions on legal matters, principles for society, edicts for sexual conduct and more. When obeyed, the Law was a path to fruitful life (Lev 18:4 – 5). The Lord made it clear that his laws were not negotiable — he expected unconditional obedience. Those refusing to listen to him and carry out all of his commands would be met with divine terror, overwhelming cost and the realization that God would always get his way (Lev 26:14 – 39).

The Law is much more than a set of restrictions — it gives guidance about the destructiveness of sin and it highlights habits leading to contentment and joy. The benefits of following God's laws are passionately extolled by the writer of Psalm 119, who learned to take delight in the Lord's commands.

The Law governed the Old Testament system of sacrifices — the mechanisms for maintaining a right standing with God. Yet it was only a shadow of the superior sacrifice Jesus made when he came to earth to redeem us from the guilt of our sins. In his death, Jesus set aside the first way and paved a new way by providing the perfect, ultimate sacrifice of himself once and for all. Men and women are now made holy through faith in his sacrifice and resurrection (Heb 10:1 – 10). This helps us understand Jesus' words when he said that he did not come to abolish the Law but to complete it (Mt 5:17).

18He then presented the ram for the burnt offering, and Aaron and his sons laid their hands on its head. 19Then Moses slaughtered the ram and splashed the blood against the sides of the altar. 20He cut the ram into pieces and burned the head, the pieces and the fat. 21He washed the internal organs and the legs with water and burned the whole ram on the altar. It was a burnt offering, a pleasing aroma, a food offering presented to the LORD, as the LORD commanded Moses.

22He then presented the other ram, the ram for the ordination, and Aaron and his sons laid their hands on its head. 23Moses slaughtered the ram and took some of its blood and put it on the lobe of Aaron's right ear, on the thumb of his right hand and on the big toe of his right foot. 24Moses also brought Aaron's sons forward and put some of the blood on the lobes of their right ears, on the thumbs of their right hands and on the big toes of their right feet. Then he splashed blood against the sides of the altar. 25After that, he took the fat, the fat tail, all the fat around the internal organs, the long lobe of the liver, both kidneys and their fat and the right thigh. 26And from the basket of bread made without yeast, which was before the LORD, he took one thick loaf, one thick loaf with olive oil mixed in, and one thin loaf, and he put these on the fat portions and on the right thigh. 27He put all these in the hands of Aaron and his sons, and they waved them before the LORD as a wave offering. 28Then Moses took them from their hands and burned them on the altar on top of the burnt offering as an ordination offering, a pleasing aroma, a food offering presented to the LORD. 29Moses also took the breast, which was his share of the ordination ram, and waved it before the LORD as a wave offering, as the LORD commanded Moses.

30Then Moses took some of the anointing oil and some of the blood from the altar and sprinkled them on Aaron and his garments and on his sons and their garments. So he consecrated Aaron and his garments and his sons and their garments.

31Moses then said to Aaron and his sons, "Cook the meat at the entrance to the tent of meeting and eat it there with the bread from the basket of ordination offerings, as I was commanded: 'Aaron and his sons are to eat it.' 32Then burn up the rest of the meat and the bread. 33Do not leave the entrance to the tent of meeting for seven days, until the days of your ordination are completed, for your ordination will last seven days. 34What has been done today was commanded by the LORD to make atonement for you. 35You must stay at the entrance to the tent of meeting day and night for seven days and do what the LORD requires, so you will not die; for that is what I have been commanded."

36So Aaron and his sons did everything the LORD commanded through Moses.

The Priests Begin Their Ministry

9 On the eighth day Moses summoned Aaron and his sons and the elders of Israel. 2He said to Aaron, "Take a bull calf for your sin offering[a] and a ram for your burnt offering, both without defect, and present them before the LORD. 3Then say to the Israelites: 'Take a male goat for a sin offering, a calf and a lamb—both a year old and without defect—for a burnt offering, 4and an ox[b] and a ram for a fellowship offering to sacrifice before the LORD, together with a grain offering mixed with olive oil. For today the LORD will appear to you.'"

5They took the things Moses commanded to the front of the tent of meeting, and the entire assembly came near and stood before the LORD. 6Then Moses said, "This is what the LORD has commanded you to do, so that the glory of the LORD may appear to you."

7Moses said to Aaron, "Come to the altar and sacrifice your sin offering and your burnt offering and make atonement for yourself and the people; sacrifice the offering that is for the people and make atonement for them, as the LORD has commanded."

[a] 2 Or *purification offering*; here and throughout this chapter [b] 4 The Hebrew word can refer to either male or female; also in verses 18 and 19.

LEVITICUS 9:7

ATONEMENT

In the Scriptures, *atonement* refers to payment for sin. Offerings were made to gain God's favor so that he would remove a worshiper's guilt. The sacrifice was presented as a substitute for the offender. An animal died in the offender's place, and the wrath of God was turned aside. The imagery was clear—because of sin someone had to die. It would either be the sinner or a substitute.

Like the animals offered to atone for the sins of the Israelites, Jesus' life was offered as a substitute for ours. His death satisfied God's wrath and covered our sin (Ro 3:25). This concept is captured in the lyrics of the hymn, "Jesus Paid It All": "Oh praise the one who paid my debt and raised this life up from the dead!" Jesus, as the great substitute, paid the price of death on behalf of his people. The one who paid our penalty is worthy of glory and honor both now and forever.

[8]So Aaron came to the altar and slaughtered the calf as a sin offering for himself. [9]His sons brought the blood to him, and he dipped his finger into the blood and put it on the horns of the altar; the rest of the blood he poured out at the base of the altar. [10]On the altar he burned the fat, the kidneys and the long lobe of the liver from the sin offering, as the LORD commanded Moses; [11]the flesh and the hide he burned up outside the camp.

[12]Then he slaughtered the burnt offering. His sons handed him the blood, and he splashed it against the sides of the altar. [13]They handed him the burnt offering piece by piece, including the head, and he burned them on the altar. [14]He washed the internal organs and the legs and burned them on top of the burnt offering on the altar.

[15]Aaron then brought the offering that was for the people. He took the goat for the people's sin offering and slaughtered it and offered it for a sin offering as he did with the first one.

[16]He brought the burnt offering and offered it in the prescribed way. [17]He also brought the grain offering, took a handful of it and burned it on the altar in addition to the morning's burnt offering.

[18]He slaughtered the ox and the ram as the fellowship offering for the people. His sons handed him the blood, and he splashed it against the sides of the altar. [19]But the fat portions of the ox and the ram—the fat tail, the layer of fat, the kidneys and the long lobe of the liver— [20]these they laid on the breasts, and then Aaron burned the fat on the altar. [21]Aaron waved the breasts and the right thigh before the LORD as a wave offering, as Moses commanded.

[22]Then Aaron lifted his hands toward the people and blessed them. And having sacrificed the sin offering, the burnt offering and the fellowship offering, he stepped down.

[23]Moses and Aaron then went into the tent of meeting. When they came out, they blessed the people; and the glory of the LORD appeared to all the people. [24]Fire came out from the presence of the LORD and consumed the burnt offering and the fat portions on the altar. And when all the people saw it, they shouted for joy and fell facedown.

The Death of Nadab and Abihu

10 Aaron's sons Nadab and Abihu took their censers, put fire in them and added incense; and they offered unauthorized fire before the LORD, contrary to his command. [2]So fire came out from the presence of the LORD and consumed them, and they died before the LORD. [3]Moses then said to Aaron, "This is what the LORD spoke of when he said:

"'Among those who approach me
I will be proved holy;
in the sight of all the people
I will be honored.'"

Aaron remained silent.

[4]Moses summoned Mishael and Elzaphan, sons of Aaron's uncle Uzziel, and said to them, "Come here; carry your cousins outside the camp, away from the front of the sanctuary." [5]So they came and carried them, still in their tunics, outside the camp, as Moses ordered.

[6]Then Moses said to Aaron and his sons Eleazar and Ithamar, "Do not let your hair become unkempt[a] and do not tear your clothes, or you will die and the LORD will be angry with the whole community. But your relatives, all the Israelites, may mourn for those the LORD has destroyed by fire. [7]Do not leave the entrance to the tent of meeting or you will die, because the LORD's anointing oil is on you." So they did as Moses said.

[8]Then the LORD said to Aaron, [9]"You and your sons are not to drink wine or other fermented drink whenever you go into the tent of meeting, or you will die.

LEVITICUS 10:1–2

APPROACHING GOD

Aaron's sons Nadab and Abihu were sanctuary priests who inappropriately approached God, offering "unauthorized fire before the LORD" in some unspecified way. As a result, they were consumed by fire from the Lord. God gave specific instructions for how priests were to come before him. These instructions were as much for their protection as they were for God's honor (Ex 19:22).

Fire was a daily part of Israel's worship of God—offerings were burned and lamps held a flame. The death of Aaron's sons reveals that access to God's presence required strict adherence to his methods and protocols. Yet God's plan from the beginning was to make a way to draw near to him with confidence and assurance without fear. That method is no longer through careful ritual but through faith in the life, death and resurrection of Jesus Christ. All are invited to approach him with repentance and faith (Eph 3:12). In John 14:6, Jesus confirms that he is the exclusive way for entering God's presence: "No one comes to the Father except through me."

[a] 6 Or *Do not uncover your heads*

LEVITICUS 9:1 – 24

THE SINFUL PRIEST AND THE SINLESS PRIEST

Aaron (the high priest of Israel) and Jesus (the great high priest) have a few things in common — yet they are profoundly different.

They are the same in the following features:

- Aaron exercised his office by carefully following the Lord's commands (Lev 8:36). Though he was imperfect, his example is noteworthy. Jesus, on the other hand, came to do perfectly what Aaron fell short of. Jesus is the ultimate example of honoring God — as he always yielded to his Father's leadership (Jn 8:28).
- Aaron served so that the glory of the Lord would appear to the people (Lev 9:6). Jesus came to enable mankind to see and know God (Jn 1:18). In fact, anyone who has seen Jesus has seen the Father (Jn 14:8 – 11). Jesus came to earth as the exact image of the invisible God (Col 1:15).

However, they were different in a number of ways:

- Aaron was an appointed mediator between the people and God. Eventually, he and his successors were made obsolete by Jesus. Jesus Christ is the one and only mediator between God and mankind (1Ti 2:5 – 6). And because Christ's work on the cross enabled our righteousness, we are invited to approach God on our own with confidence (Heb 4:16).
- Aaron arranged for atonement for all of Israel (Lev 9:7). Jesus purchased atonement for the whole world, for all who would come to him by faith (1Jn 2:2). Jesus came to Israel as the promised Messiah, but salvation in his name is available for people of every nation (Ro 3:29).
- Aaron needed to make atonement for his own sins (Lev 9:8). Jesus never sinned. He was and is perfect in word, thought and deed. Jesus died on the cross as an unblemished substitute. His sinless perfection made him a worthy sacrifice and makes him a worthy priest in heaven (Heb 7:26 – 27).
- Aaron was a priest over Israel because he was ordained and anointed by Moses (Lev 8:1 – 12). Jesus the Son is our great high priest, unique and eternal — because God the Father designated him for that honor (Heb 5:1 – 5). While Aaron stood *before* God, Jesus *is* God (Col 1:15 – 17).

This is a lasting ordinance for the generations to come, 10so that you can distinguish between the holy and the common, between the unclean and the clean,
11and so you can teach the Israelites all the decrees the LORD has given them
through Moses."

12Moses said to Aaron and his remaining sons, Eleazar and Ithamar, "Take
the grain offering left over from the food offerings prepared without yeast and
presented to the LORD and eat it beside the altar, for it is most holy. 13Eat it in the
sanctuary area, because it is your share and your sons' share of the food offerings
presented to the LORD; for so I have been commanded. 14But you and your sons
and your daughters may eat the breast that was waved and the thigh that was presented. Eat them in a ceremonially clean place; they have been given to you and
your children as your share of the Israelites' fellowship offerings. 15The thigh that
was presented and the breast that was waved must be brought with the fat portions
of the food offerings, to be waved before the LORD as a wave offering. This will
be the perpetual share for you and your children, as the LORD has commanded."

16When Moses inquired about the goat of the sin offering[a] and found that it
had been burned up, he was angry with Eleazar and Ithamar, Aaron's remaining sons, and asked, 17"Why didn't you eat the sin offering in the sanctuary area?
It is most holy; it was given to you to take away the guilt of the community by
making atonement for them before the LORD. 18Since its blood was not taken
into the Holy Place, you should have eaten the goat in the sanctuary area, as I
commanded."

19Aaron replied to Moses, "Today they sacrificed their sin offering and their
burnt offering before the LORD, but such things as this have happened to me.
Would the LORD have been pleased if I had eaten the sin offering today?" 20When
Moses heard this, he was satisfied.

Clean and Unclean Food

11 The LORD said to Moses and Aaron, 2"Say to the Israelites: 'Of all the animals that live on land, these are the ones you may eat: 3You may eat any
animal that has a divided hoof and that chews the cud.

4" 'There are some that only chew the cud or only have a divided hoof, but you
must not eat them. The camel, though it chews the cud, does not have a divided
hoof; it is ceremonially unclean for you. 5The hyrax, though it chews the cud,
does not have a divided hoof; it is unclean for you. 6The rabbit, though it chews
the cud, does not have a divided hoof; it is unclean for you. 7And the pig, though
it has a divided hoof, does not chew the cud; it is unclean for you. 8You must not
eat their meat or touch their carcasses; they are unclean for you.

9" 'Of all the creatures living in the water of the seas and the streams you may
eat any that have fins and scales. 10But all creatures in the seas or streams that
do not have fins and scales—whether among all the swarming things or among
all the other living creatures in the water—you are to regard as unclean. 11And
since you are to regard them as unclean, you must not eat their meat; you must
regard their carcasses as unclean. 12Anything living in the water that does not
have fins and scales is to be regarded as unclean by you.

13" 'These are the birds you are to regard as unclean and not eat because they
are unclean: the eagle,[b] the vulture, the black vulture, 14the red kite, any kind of
black kite, 15any kind of raven, 16the horned owl, the screech owl, the gull, any
kind of hawk, 17the little owl, the cormorant, the great owl, 18the white owl, the
desert owl, the osprey, 19the stork, any kind of heron, the hoopoe and the bat.

20" 'All flying insects that walk on all fours are to be regarded as unclean by
you. 21There are, however, some flying insects that walk on all fours that you
may eat: those that have jointed legs for hopping on the ground. 22Of these you
may eat any kind of locust, katydid, cricket or grasshopper. 23But all other flying
insects that have four legs you are to regard as unclean.

---

[a] *16* Or *purification offering*; also in verses 17 and 19 [b] *13* The precise identification of some of the birds, insects and animals in this chapter is uncertain.

24" 'You will make yourselves unclean by these; whoever touches their carcasses will be unclean till evening. 25Whoever picks up one of their carcasses
must wash their clothes, and they will be unclean till evening.
26" 'Every animal that does not have a divided hoof or that does not chew the
cud is unclean for you; whoever touches the carcass of any of them will be unclean. 27Of all the animals that walk on all fours, those that walk on their paws
are unclean for you; whoever touches their carcasses will be unclean till evening. 28Anyone who picks up their carcasses must wash their clothes, and they
will be unclean till evening. These animals are unclean for you.
29" 'Of the animals that move along the ground, these are unclean for you:
the weasel, the rat, any kind of great lizard, 30the gecko, the monitor lizard, the
wall lizard, the skink and the chameleon. 31Of all those that move along the
ground, these are unclean for you. Whoever touches them when they are dead
will be unclean till evening. 32When one of them dies and falls on something,
that article, whatever its use, will be unclean, whether it is made of wood,
cloth, hide or sackcloth. Put it in water; it will be unclean till evening, and
then it will be clean. 33If one of them falls into a clay pot, everything in it will
be unclean, and you must break the pot. 34Any food you are allowed to eat that
has come into contact with water from any such pot is unclean, and any liquid
that is drunk from such a pot is unclean. 35Anything that one of their carcasses
falls on becomes unclean; an oven or cooking pot must be broken up. They are
unclean, and you are to regard them as unclean. 36A spring, however, or a cistern for collecting water remains clean, but anyone who touches one of these
carcasses is unclean. 37If a carcass falls on any seeds that are to be planted,
they remain clean. 38But if water has been put on the seed and a carcass falls
on it, it is unclean for you.
39" 'If an animal that you are allowed to eat dies, anyone who touches its carcass will be unclean till evening. 40Anyone who eats some of its carcass must
wash their clothes, and they will be unclean till evening. Anyone who picks up
the carcass must wash their clothes, and they will be unclean till evening.
41" 'Every creature that moves along the ground is to be regarded as unclean; it
is not to be eaten. 42You are not to eat any creature that moves along the ground,
whether it moves on its belly or walks on all fours or on many feet; it is unclean.
43Do not defile yourselves by any of these creatures. Do not make yourselves unclean by means of them or be made unclean by them. 44I am the LORD your God;
consecrate yourselves and be holy, because I am holy. Do not make yourselves
unclean by any creature that moves along the ground. 45I am the LORD, who
brought you up out of Egypt to be your God; therefore be holy, because I am holy.
46" 'These are the regulations concerning animals, birds, every living thing
that moves about in the water and every creature that moves along the ground.
47You must distinguish between the unclean and the clean, between living creatures that may be eaten and those that may not be eaten.' "

Purification After Childbirth

12 The LORD said to Moses, 2"Say to the Israelites: 'A woman who becomes
pregnant and gives birth to a son will be ceremonially unclean for seven
days, just as she is unclean during her monthly period. 3On the eighth day the
boy is to be circumcised. 4Then the woman must wait thirty-three days to be purified from her bleeding. She must not touch anything sacred or go to the sanctuary until the days of her purification are over. 5If she gives birth to a daughter,
for two weeks the woman will be unclean, as during her period. Then she must
wait sixty-six days to be purified from her bleeding.
6" 'When the days of her purification for a son or daughter are over, she is to
bring to the priest at the entrance to the tent of meeting a year-old lamb for a
burnt offering and a young pigeon or a dove for a sin offering.[a] 7He shall offer

---

[a] 6 Or *purification offering*; also in verse 8

HOLINESS

There is no one like our God. He is holy and perfect in motive and action, the essence of a clean, pure light of love and glory. He is absolutely unique from the lifeless gods of the nations.

God chose to put his greatness and goodness on display through a special relationship with the people of Israel. With the blessings of his care and provision came an expectation that the people would consecrate themselves and be holy as he is — not divine, but separate and unique in the ways of worship and daily conduct. The call to be holy was not simply to make Israel look different from other peoples — they were to be holy by association, because God is holy. In other words, their holiness spoke something about him. The careful life they lived in accordance with God's requirements helped identify them as belonging to him.

God gave laws for appropriate interaction with the people and things around them. His commands were connected to the goal of remaining clean and undefiled. Some laws listed what should not be touched or eaten — these things would render a person unclean. The letter of these laws applied only to ancient Israel, but the spirit of them continues to apply to God's people today. Like the Hebrews, we are called to holiness in every area of life (1Pe 1:14 – 16).

Jesus brought new clarity to what it means to be clean. He taught that what defiles us comes from the inside — from the heart — not from external things we touch or eat (Mt 15:1 – 11). Christians live under the covering of God's grace. Our forgiveness is full and permanent — we do not fear defilement leading to a loss of the righteousness given to us by Christ. We touch and eat in a careful freedom built upon the Holy Spirit living in us and our discernment of sin.

We are holy because of Jesus (Heb 10:10) — and yet the Bible calls us to keep growing in holiness as we separate ourselves from sin (1Th 4:1 – 8). Christians are purchased people. God has every right to expect our obedience to his preferences for how we live out our days on the earth. When we live holy lives, we distinguish ourselves as God's people and honor him through happy obedience.

them before the LORD to make atonement for her, and then she will be ceremonially clean from her flow of blood.

7"'These are the regulations for the woman who gives birth to a boy or a girl. 8But if she cannot afford a lamb, she is to bring two doves or two young pigeons, one for a burnt offering and the other for a sin offering. In this way the priest will make atonement for her, and she will be clean.'"

Regulations About Defiling Skin Diseases

13 The LORD said to Moses and Aaron, 2"When anyone has a swelling or a rash or a shiny spot on their skin that may be a defiling skin disease,[a] they must be brought to Aaron the priest or to one of his sons[b] who is a priest. 3The priest is to examine the sore on the skin, and if the hair in the sore has turned white and the sore appears to be more than skin deep, it is a defiling skin disease. When the priest examines that person, he shall pronounce them ceremonially unclean. 4If the shiny spot on the skin is white but does not appear to be more than skin deep and the hair in it has not turned white, the priest is to isolate the affected person for seven days. 5On the seventh day the priest is to examine them, and if he sees that the sore is unchanged and has not spread in the skin, he is to isolate them for another seven days. 6On the seventh day the priest is to examine them again, and if the sore has faded and has not spread in the skin, the priest shall pronounce them clean; it is only a rash. They must wash their clothes, and they will be clean. 7But if the rash does spread in their skin after they have shown themselves to the priest to be pronounced clean, they must appear before the priest again. 8The priest is to examine that person, and if the rash has spread in the skin, he shall pronounce them unclean; it is a defiling skin disease.

9"When anyone has a defiling skin disease, they must be brought to the priest. 10The priest is to examine them, and if there is a white swelling in the skin that has turned the hair white and if there is raw flesh in the swelling, 11it is a chronic skin disease and the priest shall pronounce them unclean. He is not to isolate them, because they are already unclean.

12"If the disease breaks out all over their skin and, so far as the priest can see, it covers all the skin of the affected person from head to foot, 13the priest is to examine them, and if the disease has covered their whole body, he shall pronounce them clean. Since it has all turned white, they are clean. 14But whenever raw flesh appears on them, they will be unclean. 15When the priest sees the raw flesh, he shall pronounce them unclean. The raw flesh is unclean; they have a defiling disease. 16If the raw flesh changes and turns white, they must go to the priest. 17The priest is to examine them, and if the sores have turned white, the priest shall pronounce the affected person clean; then they will be clean.

18"When someone has a boil on their skin and it heals, 19and in the place where the boil was, a white swelling or reddish-white spot appears, they must present themselves to the priest. 20The priest is to examine it, and if it appears to be more than skin deep and the hair in it has turned white, the priest shall pronounce that person unclean. It is a defiling skin disease that has broken out where the boil was. 21But if, when the priest examines it, there is no white hair in it and it is not more than skin deep and has faded, then the priest is to isolate them for seven days. 22If it is spreading in the skin, the priest shall pronounce them unclean; it is a defiling disease. 23But if the spot is unchanged and has not spread, it is only a scar from the boil, and the priest shall pronounce them clean.

24"When someone has a burn on their skin and a reddish-white or white spot appears in the raw flesh of the burn, 25the priest is to examine the spot, and if the hair in it has turned white, and it appears to be more than skin deep, it is a defiling disease that has broken out in the burn. The priest shall pronounce them

---

[a] *2* The Hebrew word for *defiling skin disease,* traditionally translated "leprosy," was used for various diseases affecting the skin; here and throughout verses 3-46. [b] *2* Or *descendants*

unclean; it is a defiling skin disease. 26But if the priest examines it and there is no white hair in the spot and if it is not more than skin deep and has faded, then the priest is to isolate them for seven days. 27On the seventh day the priest is to examine that person, and if it is spreading in the skin, the priest shall pronounce them unclean; it is a defiling skin disease. 28If, however, the spot is unchanged and has not spread in the skin but has faded, it is a swelling from the burn, and the priest shall pronounce them clean; it is only a scar from the burn.

29"If a man or woman has a sore on their head or chin, 30the priest is to examine the sore, and if it appears to be more than skin deep and the hair in it is yellow and thin, the priest shall pronounce them unclean; it is a defiling skin disease on the head or chin. 31But if, when the priest examines the sore, it does not seem to be more than skin deep and there is no black hair in it, then the priest is to isolate the affected person for seven days. 32On the seventh day the priest is to examine the sore, and if it has not spread and there is no yellow hair in it and it does not appear to be more than skin deep, 33then the man or woman must shave themselves, except for the affected area, and the priest is to keep them isolated another seven days. 34On the seventh day the priest is to examine the sore, and if it has not spread in the skin and appears to be no more than skin deep, the priest shall pronounce them clean. They must wash their clothes, and they will be clean. 35But if the sore does spread in the skin after they are pronounced clean, 36the priest is to examine them, and if he finds that the sore has spread in the skin, he does not need to look for yellow hair; they are unclean. 37If, however, the sore is unchanged so far as the priest can see, and if black hair has grown in it, the affected person is healed. They are clean, and the priest shall pronounce them clean.

38"When a man or woman has white spots on the skin, 39the priest is to examine them, and if the spots are dull white, it is a harmless rash that has broken out on the skin; they are clean.

40"A man who has lost his hair and is bald is clean. 41If he has lost his hair from the front of his scalp and has a bald forehead, he is clean. 42But if he has a reddish-white sore on his bald head or forehead, it is a defiling disease breaking out on his head or forehead. 43The priest is to examine him, and if the swollen sore on his head or forehead is reddish-white like a defiling skin disease, 44the man is diseased and is unclean. The priest shall pronounce him unclean because of the sore on his head.

45"Anyone with such a defiling disease must wear torn clothes, let their hair be unkempt,[a] cover the lower part of their face and cry out, 'Unclean! Unclean!' 46As long as they have the disease they remain unclean. They must live alone; they must live outside the camp.

Regulations About Defiling Molds

47"As for any fabric that is spoiled with a defiling mold — any woolen or linen clothing, 48any woven or knitted material of linen or wool, any leather or anything made of leather — 49if the affected area in the fabric, the leather, the woven or knitted material, or any leather article, is greenish or reddish, it is a defiling mold and must be shown to the priest. 50The priest is to examine the affected area and isolate the article for seven days. 51On the seventh day he is to examine it, and if the mold has spread in the fabric, the woven or knitted material, or the leather, whatever its use, it is a persistent defiling mold; the article is unclean. 52He must burn the fabric, the woven or knitted material of wool or linen, or any leather article that has been spoiled; because the defiling mold is persistent, the article must be burned.

53"But if, when the priest examines it, the mold has not spread in the fabric, the woven or knitted material, or the leather article, 54he shall order that the spoiled article be washed. Then he is to isolate it for another seven days. 55After

---

[a] 45 Or *clothes, uncover their head*

the article has been washed, the priest is to examine it again, and if the mold has
not changed its appearance, even though it has not spread, it is unclean. Burn
it, no matter which side of the fabric has been spoiled. 56If, when the priest examines it, the mold has faded after the article has been washed, he is to tear the
spoiled part out of the fabric, the leather, or the woven or knitted material. 57But
if it reappears in the fabric, in the woven or knitted material, or in the leather article, it is a spreading mold; whatever has the mold must be burned. 58Any fabric,
woven or knitted material, or any leather article that has been washed and is rid
of the mold, must be washed again. Then it will be clean."

59These are the regulations concerning defiling molds in woolen or linen
clothing, woven or knitted material, or any leather article, for pronouncing them
clean or unclean.

Cleansing From Defiling Skin Diseases

14 The LORD said to Moses, 2"These are the regulations for any diseased person at the time of their ceremonial cleansing, when they are brought to
the priest: 3The priest is to go outside the camp and examine them. If they have
been healed of their defiling skin disease,[a] 4the priest shall order that two live
clean birds and some cedar wood, scarlet yarn and hyssop be brought for the
person to be cleansed. 5Then the priest shall order that one of the birds be killed
over fresh water in a clay pot. 6He is then to take the live bird and dip it, together
with the cedar wood, the scarlet yarn and the hyssop, into the blood of the bird
that was killed over the fresh water. 7Seven times he shall sprinkle the one to be
cleansed of the defiling disease, and then pronounce them clean. After that, he
is to release the live bird in the open fields.

8"The person to be cleansed must wash their clothes, shave off all their hair
and bathe with water; then they will be ceremonially clean. After this they may
come into the camp, but they must stay outside their tent for seven days. 9On the
seventh day they must shave off all their hair; they must shave their head, their
beard, their eyebrows and the rest of their hair. They must wash their clothes
and bathe themselves with water, and they will be clean.

10"On the eighth day they must bring two male lambs and one ewe lamb a year
old, each without defect, along with three-tenths of an ephah[b] of the finest flour
mixed with olive oil for a grain offering, and one log[c] of oil. 11The priest who pronounces them clean shall present both the one to be cleansed and their offerings
before the LORD at the entrance to the tent of meeting.

12"Then the priest is to take one of the male lambs and offer it as a guilt offering, along with the log of oil; he shall wave them before the LORD as a wave
offering. 13He is to slaughter the lamb in the sanctuary area where the sin offering[d] and the burnt offering are slaughtered. Like the sin offering, the guilt
offering belongs to the priest; it is most holy. 14The priest is to take some of the
blood of the guilt offering and put it on the lobe of the right ear of the one to
be cleansed, on the thumb of their right hand and on the big toe of their right
foot. 15The priest shall then take some of the log of oil, pour it in the palm of his
own left hand, 16dip his right forefinger into the oil in his palm, and with his
finger sprinkle some of it before the LORD seven times. 17The priest is to put
some of the oil remaining in his palm on the lobe of the right ear of the one to
be cleansed, on the thumb of their right hand and on the big toe of their right
foot, on top of the blood of the guilt offering. 18The rest of the oil in his palm the
priest shall put on the head of the one to be cleansed and make atonement for
them before the LORD.

19"Then the priest is to sacrifice the sin offering and make atonement for the
one to be cleansed from their uncleanness. After that, the priest shall slaughter

[a] *3* The Hebrew word for *defiling skin disease,* traditionally translated "leprosy," was used for various diseases affecting the skin; also in verses 7, 32, 54 and 57. [b] *10* That is, probably about 11 pounds or about 5 kilograms [c] *10* That is, about 1/3 quart or about 0.3 liter; also in verses 12, 15, 21 and 24 [d] *13* Or *purification offering;* also in verses 19, 22 and 31

LEVITICUS 14:1–3

EXAMINATION

To be required to live outside the camp meant removal from the community because something made a person unclean. There, far off from family and friends, an awkward society of the defiled waited for permission to return. For the leper, seeing a priest walk his or her way was an anxious moment. They desperately needed the spiritual leader's pronouncement of "clean." Once a positive determination was made, proper rituals were carried out, giving thanks to God for healing and restoration.

The priest of Leviticus 14:3 prefigures Christ in the act of moving toward untouchables. In Luke 5:12–14, Jesus encounters a leper who falls on the ground begging to be made clean — a plea born of a desperate existence in crushing isolation. Jesus did more than examine the leper. He touched him and spoke a command that instantly made him clean. Jesus is full of compassion and power. He brings near those who were once far off, enabling them to know love and community through his name.

the burnt offering [20]and offer it on the altar, together with the grain offering, and
make atonement for them, and they will be clean.

[21]"If, however, they are poor and cannot afford these, they must take one male
lamb as a guilt offering to be waved to make atonement for them, together with
a tenth of an ephah[a] of the finest flour mixed with olive oil for a grain offering, a
log of oil, [22]and two doves or two young pigeons, such as they can afford, one for
a sin offering and the other for a burnt offering.

[23]"On the eighth day they must bring them for their cleansing to the priest at
the entrance to the tent of meeting, before the LORD. [24]The priest is to take the
lamb for the guilt offering, together with the log of oil, and wave them before
the LORD as a wave offering. [25]He shall slaughter the lamb for the guilt offering
and take some of its blood and put it on the lobe of the right ear of the one to be
cleansed, on the thumb of their right hand and on the big toe of their right foot.
[26]The priest is to pour some of the oil into the palm of his own left hand, [27]and
with his right forefinger sprinkle some of the oil from his palm seven times before the LORD. [28]Some of the oil in his palm he is to put on the same places he
put the blood of the guilt offering — on the lobe of the right ear of the one to be
cleansed, on the thumb of their right hand and on the big toe of their right foot.
[29]The rest of the oil in his palm the priest shall put on the head of the one to be
cleansed, to make atonement for them before the LORD. [30]Then he shall sacrifice the doves or the young pigeons, such as the person can afford, [31]one as a sin
offering and the other as a burnt offering, together with the grain offering. In
this way the priest will make atonement before the LORD on behalf of the one
to be cleansed."

[32]These are the regulations for anyone who has a defiling skin disease and
who cannot afford the regular offerings for their cleansing.

Cleansing From Defiling Molds

[33]The LORD said to Moses and Aaron, [34]"When you enter the land of Canaan,
which I am giving you as your possession, and I put a spreading mold in a house
in that land, [35]the owner of the house must go and tell the priest, 'I have seen
something that looks like a defiling mold in my house.' [36]The priest is to order
the house to be emptied before he goes in to examine the mold, so that nothing
in the house will be pronounced unclean. After this the priest is to go in and inspect the house. [37]He is to examine the mold on the walls, and if it has greenish
or reddish depressions that appear to be deeper than the surface of the wall,
[38]the priest shall go out the doorway of the house and close it up for seven days.
[39]On the seventh day the priest shall return to inspect the house. If the mold has
spread on the walls, [40]he is to order that the contaminated stones be torn out and
thrown into an unclean place outside the town. [41]He must have all the inside
walls of the house scraped and the material that is scraped off dumped into an
unclean place outside the town. [42]Then they are to take other stones to replace
these and take new clay and plaster the house.

[43]"If the defiling mold reappears in the house after the stones have been torn
out and the house scraped and plastered, [44]the priest is to go and examine it and,
if the mold has spread in the house, it is a persistent defiling mold; the house is
unclean. [45]It must be torn down — its stones, timbers and all the plaster — and
taken out of the town to an unclean place.

[46]"Anyone who goes into the house while it is closed up will be unclean till
evening. [47]Anyone who sleeps or eats in the house must wash their clothes.

[48]"But if the priest comes to examine it and the mold has not spread after the
house has been plastered, he shall pronounce the house clean, because the defiling mold is gone. [49]To purify the house he is to take two birds and some cedar
wood, scarlet yarn and hyssop. [50]He shall kill one of the birds over fresh water in
a clay pot. [51]Then he is to take the cedar wood, the hyssop, the scarlet yarn and

---

[a] 21 That is, probably about 3 1/2 pounds or about 1.6 kilograms

the live bird, dip them into the blood of the dead bird and the fresh water, and sprinkle the house seven times. [52]He shall purify the house with the bird's blood, the fresh water, the live bird, the cedar wood, the hyssop and the scarlet yarn. [53]Then he is to release the live bird in the open fields outside the town. In this way he will make atonement for the house, and it will be clean."

[54]These are the regulations for any defiling skin disease, for a sore, [55]for defiling molds in fabric or in a house, [56]and for a swelling, a rash or a shiny spot, [57]to determine when something is clean or unclean.

These are the regulations for defiling skin diseases and defiling molds.

Discharges Causing Uncleanness

15 The LORD said to Moses and Aaron, [2]"Speak to the Israelites and say to them: 'When any man has an unusual bodily discharge, such a discharge is unclean. [3]Whether it continues flowing from his body or is blocked, it will make him unclean. This is how his discharge will bring about uncleanness:

[4]" 'Any bed the man with a discharge lies on will be unclean, and anything he sits on will be unclean. [5]Anyone who touches his bed must wash their clothes and bathe with water, and they will be unclean till evening. [6]Whoever sits on anything that the man with a discharge sat on must wash their clothes and bathe with water, and they will be unclean till evening.

[7]" 'Whoever touches the man who has a discharge must wash their clothes and bathe with water, and they will be unclean till evening.

[8]" 'If the man with the discharge spits on anyone who is clean, they must wash their clothes and bathe with water, and they will be unclean till evening.

[9]" 'Everything the man sits on when riding will be unclean, [10]and whoever touches any of the things that were under him will be unclean till evening; whoever picks up those things must wash their clothes and bathe with water, and they will be unclean till evening.

[11]" 'Anyone the man with a discharge touches without rinsing his hands with water must wash their clothes and bathe with water, and they will be unclean till evening.

[12]" 'A clay pot that the man touches must be broken, and any wooden article is to be rinsed with water.

[13]" 'When a man is cleansed from his discharge, he is to count off seven days for his ceremonial cleansing; he must wash his clothes and bathe himself with fresh water, and he will be clean. [14]On the eighth day he must take two doves or two young pigeons and come before the LORD to the entrance to the tent of meeting and give them to the priest. [15]The priest is to sacrifice them, the one for a sin offering[a] and the other for a burnt offering. In this way he will make atonement before the LORD for the man because of his discharge.

[16]" 'When a man has an emission of semen, he must bathe his whole body with water, and he will be unclean till evening. [17]Any clothing or leather that has semen on it must be washed with water, and it will be unclean till evening. [18]When a man has sexual relations with a woman and there is an emission of semen, both of them must bathe with water, and they will be unclean till evening.

[19]" 'When a woman has her regular flow of blood, the impurity of her monthly period will last seven days, and anyone who touches her will be unclean till evening.

[20]" 'Anything she lies on during her period will be unclean, and anything she sits on will be unclean. [21]Anyone who touches her bed will be unclean; they must wash their clothes and bathe with water, and they will be unclean till evening. [22]Anyone who touches anything she sits on will be unclean; they must wash their clothes and bathe with water, and they will be unclean till evening. [23]Whether it is the bed or anything she was sitting on, when anyone touches it, they will be unclean till evening.

[a] *15* Or *purification offering*; also in verse 30

24“ ‘If a man has sexual relations with her and her monthly flow touches him, he will be unclean for seven days; any bed he lies on will be unclean.

25“ ‘When a woman has a discharge of blood for many days at a time other than her monthly period or has a discharge that continues beyond her period, she will be unclean as long as she has the discharge, just as in the days of her period. 26Any bed she lies on while her discharge continues will be unclean, as is her bed during her monthly period, and anything she sits on will be unclean, as during her period. 27Anyone who touches them will be unclean; they must wash their clothes and bathe with water, and they will be unclean till evening.

28“ ‘When she is cleansed from her discharge, she must count off seven days, and after that she will be ceremonially clean. 29On the eighth day she must take two doves or two young pigeons and bring them to the priest at the entrance to the tent of meeting. 30The priest is to sacrifice one for a sin offering and the other for a burnt offering. In this way he will make atonement for her before the LORD for the uncleanness of her discharge.

31“ ‘You must keep the Israelites separate from things that make them unclean, so they will not die in their uncleanness for defiling my dwelling place,[a] which is among them.’ ”

32These are the regulations for a man with a discharge, for anyone made unclean by an emission of semen, 33for a woman in her monthly period, for a man or a woman with a discharge, and for a man who has sexual relations with a woman who is ceremonially unclean.

The Day of Atonement

16 The LORD spoke to Moses after the death of the two sons of Aaron who died when they approached the LORD. 2The LORD said to Moses: “Tell your brother Aaron that he is not to come whenever he chooses into the Most Holy Place behind the curtain in front of the atonement cover on the ark, or else he will die. For I will appear in the cloud over the atonement cover.

3“This is how Aaron is to enter the Most Holy Place: He must first bring a young bull for a sin offering[b] and a ram for a burnt offering. 4He is to put on the sacred linen tunic, with linen undergarments next to his body; he is to tie the linen sash around him and put on the linen turban. These are sacred garments; so he must bathe himself with water before he puts them on. 5From the Israelite community he is to take two male goats for a sin offering and a ram for a burnt offering.

6“Aaron is to offer the bull for his own sin offering to make atonement for himself and his household. 7Then he is to take the two goats and present them before the LORD at the entrance to the tent of meeting. 8He is to cast lots for the two goats — one lot for the LORD and the other for the scapegoat.[c] 9Aaron shall bring the goat whose lot falls to the LORD and sacrifice it for a sin offering. 10But the goat chosen by lot as the scapegoat shall be presented alive before the LORD to be used for making atonement by sending it into the wilderness as a scapegoat.

11“Aaron shall bring the bull for his own sin offering to make atonement for himself and his household, and he is to slaughter the bull for his own sin offering. 12He is to take a censer full of burning coals from the altar before the LORD and two handfuls of finely ground fragrant incense and take them behind the curtain. 13He is to put the incense on the fire before the LORD, and the smoke of the incense will conceal the atonement cover above the tablets of the covenant law, so that he will not die. 14He is to take some of the bull’s blood and with his finger sprinkle it on the front of the atonement cover; then he shall sprinkle some of it with his finger seven times before the atonement cover.

15“He shall then slaughter the goat for the sin offering for the people and take its blood behind the curtain and do with it as he did with the bull’s blood: He shall sprinkle it on the atonement cover and in front of it. 16In this way he will make atonement for the Most Holy Place because of the uncleanness and

---

[a] *31* Or *my tabernacle* [b] *3* Or *purification offering*; here and throughout this chapter
[c] *8* The meaning of the Hebrew for this word is uncertain; also in verses 10 and 26.

JESUS AND THE DAY OF ATONEMENT

Atonement is the process of restoring right standing with God once sin has occurred. In the Old Testament, an elaborate ceremony took place every year to atone for Israel's sins. In accordance with God's instructions, their guilt had to be covered over — their offenses had to be paid for through the shedding of blood.

Before entering the Most Holy Place, the high priest had to carefully wash himself and put on special garments. A bull was killed to cover the sins of the priest and his household. Then the priest cast lots over two goats — one to be sacrificed and one to become the scapegoat, carrying the people's sins away from the community. Incense was burned over the ark so that smoke concealed the holiest place, protecting the priest. The blood of the sacrificed bull and goat were sprinkled on the atonement cover, the tent of meeting and the altar. Then the scapegoat was sent off with all of Israel's sins on its head. Then the priest washed himself and changed his clothes before exiting the tent to burn portions of the offering on the altar. Finally, the remains of the animals were removed and the attendants who removed them — along with the man who led the scapegoat away — had to wash their clothes and bathe themselves. All of this happened every year so that people could be cleansed from all their sins (Lev 16:1 – 30).

The main feature of the ceremony, the shedding of blood, taught that atonement symbolizes the substitution of life for life. In that way, the Old Testament points forward to the atoning sacrifice of Christ on the cross for our sins. God presented Jesus as a sacrifice of atonement (Ro 3:25 – 26). He gave his only Son as a payment for the sins of the world. Jesus had no guilt of his own, so he was worthy to be our substitute upon the altar of the cross.

God did this to demonstrate his righteousness. Sin was never waved off, disregarded or left unaccounted for. God upheld his righteousness and the worth of his name by requiring blood atonement for cleansing from sin. Justice shines in the way God kept his word to punish sin. Grace shines in the way God placed all of our sins on Christ. Salvation is a free gift to those with faith (Eph 2:8 – 9), but the gift itself was not free — atonement was purchased with the precious blood of Christ (1Pe 1:18 – 19).

rebellion of the Israelites, whatever their sins have been. He is to do the same for the tent of meeting, which is among them in the midst of their uncleanness. 17No one is to be in the tent of meeting from the time Aaron goes in to make atonement in the Most Holy Place until he comes out, having made atonement for himself, his household and the whole community of Israel.

18"Then he shall come out to the altar that is before the LORD and make atonement for it. He shall take some of the bull's blood and some of the goat's blood and put it on all the horns of the altar. 19He shall sprinkle some of the blood on it with his finger seven times to cleanse it and to consecrate it from the uncleanness of the Israelites.

20"When Aaron has finished making atonement for the Most Holy Place, the tent of meeting and the altar, he shall bring forward the live goat. 21He is to lay both hands on the head of the live goat and confess over it all the wickedness and rebellion of the Israelites — all their sins — and put them on the goat's head. He shall send the goat away into the wilderness in the care of someone appointed for the task. 22The goat will carry on itself all their sins to a remote place; and the man shall release it in the wilderness.

23"Then Aaron is to go into the tent of meeting and take off the linen garments he put on before he entered the Most Holy Place, and he is to leave them there. 24He shall bathe himself with water in the sanctuary area and put on his regular garments. Then he shall come out and sacrifice the burnt offering for himself and the burnt offering for the people, to make atonement for himself and for the people. 25He shall also burn the fat of the sin offering on the altar.

26"The man who releases the goat as a scapegoat must wash his clothes and bathe himself with water; afterward he may come into the camp. 27The bull and the goat for the sin offerings, whose blood was brought into the Most Holy Place to make atonement, must be taken outside the camp; their hides, flesh and intestines are to be burned up. 28The man who burns them must wash his clothes and bathe himself with water; afterward he may come into the camp.

29"This is to be a lasting ordinance for you: On the tenth day of the seventh month you must deny yourselves[a] and not do any work — whether native-born or a foreigner residing among you — 30because on this day atonement will be made for you, to cleanse you. Then, before the LORD, you will be clean from all your sins. 31It is a day of sabbath rest, and you must deny yourselves; it is a lasting ordinance. 32The priest who is anointed and ordained to succeed his father as high priest is to make atonement. He is to put on the sacred linen garments 33and make atonement for the Most Holy Place, for the tent of meeting and the altar, and for the priests and all the members of the community.

34"This is to be a lasting ordinance for you: Atonement is to be made once a year for all the sins of the Israelites."

And it was done, as the LORD commanded Moses.

Eating Blood Forbidden

17 The LORD said to Moses, 2"Speak to Aaron and his sons and to all the Israelites and say to them: 'This is what the LORD has commanded: 3Any Israelite who sacrifices an ox,[b] a lamb or a goat in the camp or outside of it 4instead of bringing it to the entrance to the tent of meeting to present it as an offering to the LORD in front of the tabernacle of the LORD — that person shall be considered guilty of bloodshed; they have shed blood and must be cut off from their people. 5This is so the Israelites will bring to the LORD the sacrifices they are now making in the open fields. They must bring them to the priest, that is, to the LORD, at the entrance to the tent of meeting and sacrifice them as fellowship offerings. 6The priest is to splash the blood against the altar of the LORD at the entrance to the tent of meeting and burn the fat as an aroma pleasing to the LORD. 7They must no longer offer any of their sacrifices to the goat

[a] 29 Or *must fast;* also in verse 31 [b] 3 The Hebrew word can refer to either male or female.

LEVITICUS 16:20–22

BEARING OUR SIN

There are two goats in the stages of the Day of Atonement ritual described in Leviticus 16. One goat served its purpose by dying and the other by remaining alive. The first goat was killed as a sacrifice, its blood sprinkled on the atonement cover, tent of meeting and altar. The second goat bore the sins of the nation on its head. Aaron laid both hands on this beast while confessing all of Israel's sins. This is the origin of the term *scapegoat*. The animal was led away — carrying all of their sins — and was released in a remote place where it could not return to the Israelite camp.

When Jesus made atonement on the cross, he bore the sins of the human race (1Jn 2:2). For the Christian, all guilt has been removed — and it will not return. Jesus died under the weight of our sins and God's righteous wrath so that we might have forgiveness and have new life in him (1Pe 2:24).

idols[a] to whom they prostitute themselves. This is to be a lasting ordinance for
them and for the generations to come.'
8"Say to them: 'Any Israelite or any foreigner residing among them who offers
a burnt offering or sacrifice 9and does not bring it to the entrance to the tent of
meeting to sacrifice it to the LORD must be cut off from the people of Israel.
10" 'I will set my face against any Israelite or any foreigner residing among
them who eats blood, and I will cut them off from the people. 11For the life of a
creature is in the blood, and I have given it to you to make atonement for yourselves on the altar; it is the blood that makes atonement for one's life.[b] 12There-
fore I say to the Israelites, "None of you may eat blood, nor may any foreigner
residing among you eat blood."
13" 'Any Israelite or any foreigner residing among you who hunts any animal
or bird that may be eaten must drain out the blood and cover it with earth, 14be-
cause the life of every creature is its blood. That is why I have said to the Israelites, "You must not eat the blood of any creature, because the life of every creature is its blood; anyone who eats it must be cut off."
15" 'Anyone, whether native-born or foreigner, who eats anything found dead
or torn by wild animals must wash their clothes and bathe with water, and they
will be ceremonially unclean till evening; then they will be clean. 16But if they
do not wash their clothes and bathe themselves, they will be held responsible.' "

Unlawful Sexual Relations

18 The LORD said to Moses, 2"Speak to the Israelites and say to them: 'I am
the LORD your God. 3You must not do as they do in Egypt, where you used
to live, and you must not do as they do in the land of Canaan, where I am bringing you. Do not follow their practices. 4You must obey my laws and be careful to
follow my decrees. I am the LORD your God. 5Keep my decrees and laws, for the
person who obeys them will live by them. I am the LORD.
6" 'No one is to approach any close relative to have sexual relations. I am the
LORD.
7" 'Do not dishonor your father by having sexual relations with your mother.
She is your mother; do not have relations with her.
8" 'Do not have sexual relations with your father's wife; that would dishonor
your father.
9" 'Do not have sexual relations with your sister, either your father's daughter or your mother's daughter, whether she was born in the same home or elsewhere.
10" 'Do not have sexual relations with your son's daughter or your daughter's
daughter; that would dishonor you.
11" 'Do not have sexual relations with the daughter of your father's wife, born
to your father; she is your sister.
12" 'Do not have sexual relations with your father's sister; she is your father's
close relative.
13" 'Do not have sexual relations with your mother's sister, because she is your
mother's close relative.
14" 'Do not dishonor your father's brother by approaching his wife to have sexual relations; she is your aunt.
15" 'Do not have sexual relations with your daughter-in-law. She is your son's
wife; do not have relations with her.
16" 'Do not have sexual relations with your brother's wife; that would dishonor
your brother.
17" 'Do not have sexual relations with both a woman and her daughter. Do not
have sexual relations with either her son's daughter or her daughter's daughter;
they are her close relatives. That is wickedness.
18" 'Do not take your wife's sister as a rival wife and have sexual relations with
her while your wife is living.

[a] 7 Or *the demons* [b] 11 Or *atonement by the life in the blood*

LEVITICUS 18:1–5

OBEY AND BE DIFFERENT

Moses relayed God's command to reject the practices of the Egyptians and Canaanites especially in the area of sexual ethics. God's people were to obey his laws and decrees even if the culture gave permission for something different. His commands were more than distinguishing markers for his unique people—they were a means to life. God pointed his people on paths of joy and satisfaction, leading them to avoid paths of regret and destruction.

Jesus calls us to keep his commands just as he obeyed the commands of the Father. Christians seek to obey because we are submitted to the authority of God over all of life—no matter what others around us do. The primacy given to sexual ethics applies to the church, as well. This is a clear distinguishing mark for God's church to this day. Concurrently, we seek to obey because it keeps us close to Jesus and results in great joy (Jn 15:10–11).

LEVITICUS 17:11

NOTHING BUT THE BLOOD OF JESUS

Atonement required blood. God explained that the life of a creature is in its blood — so the life-liquid must be treated with respect. It is the blood that effected atonement, but the substance had no power in itself. The power to cancel sin resides in God, who ordained the method.

Jesus did not secure our pardon by simply living a sinless life. He bled so we could be free. Without the shedding of blood there is no forgiveness of sin (Heb 9:22). Take note of the multiple New Testament references to the power of the blood of Jesus:

"This is my blood of the covenant, which is poured out for many" (Mk 14:24).

"God presented Christ as a sacrifice of atonement, through the shedding of his blood — to be received by faith. He did this to demonstrate his righteousness, because in his forbearance he had left the sins committed beforehand unpunished" (Ro 3:25).

"In the same way, after supper he took the cup, saying, 'This cup is the new covenant in my blood; do this, whenever you drink it, in remembrance of me.' For whenever you eat this bread and drink this cup, you proclaim the Lord's death until he comes" (1Co 11:25 – 26).

"In him we have redemption through his blood, the forgiveness of sins, in accordance with the riches of God's grace" (Eph 1:7).

"But now in Christ Jesus you who once were far away have been brought near by the blood of Christ" (Eph 2:13).

"And through him to reconcile to himself all things, whether things on earth or things in heaven, by making peace through his blood, shed on the cross" (Col 1:20).

"Therefore, brothers and sisters, since we have confidence to enter the Most Holy Place by the blood of Jesus, by a new and living way opened for us through the curtain, that is, his body" (Heb 10:19 – 20).

"For you know that it was not with perishable things such as silver or gold that you were redeemed from the empty way of life handed down to you from your ancestors, but with the precious blood of Christ, a lamb without blemish or defect" (1Pe 1:18 – 19).

"But if we walk in the light, as he is in the light, we have fellowship with one another, and the blood of Jesus, his Son, purifies us from all sin" (1Jn 1:7).

"To him who loves us and has freed us from our sins by his blood" (Rev 1:5).

"These are they who have come out of the great tribulation; they have washed their robes and made them white in the blood of the Lamb" (Rev 7:14).

"They triumphed over him by the blood of the Lamb" (Rev 12:11).

All who want their sins forgiven must be purified by the blood of Jesus Christ (1Jn 1:7). There is no other way — atonement is in the blood. Good works do not cancel the debt of sin. Great knowledge does not move people from death to life. The only hope for salvation is faith in the shed blood of Jesus.

19“ ‘Do not approach a woman to have sexual relations during the uncleanness of her monthly period.
20“ ‘Do not have sexual relations with your neighbor’s wife and defile yourself
with her.
21“ ‘Do not give any of your children to be sacrificed to Molek, for you must not
profane the name of your God. I am the LORD.
22“ ‘Do not have sexual relations with a man as one does with a woman; that
is detestable.
23“ ‘Do not have sexual relations with an animal and defile yourself with it.
A woman must not present herself to an animal to have sexual relations with it;
that is a perversion.
24“ ‘Do not defile yourselves in any of these ways, because this is how the nations that I am going to drive out before you became defiled. 25Even the land
was defiled; so I punished it for its sin, and the land vomited out its inhabitants.
26But you must keep my decrees and my laws. The native-born and the foreigners residing among you must not do any of these detestable things, 27for all these
things were done by the people who lived in the land before you, and the land
became defiled. 28And if you defile the land, it will vomit you out as it vomited
out the nations that were before you.
29“ ‘Everyone who does any of these detestable things — such persons must be
cut off from their people. 30Keep my requirements and do not follow any of the
detestable customs that were practiced before you came and do not defile yourselves with them. I am the LORD your God.’ ”

Various Laws

19 The LORD said to Moses, 2“Speak to the entire assembly of Israel and say
to them: ‘Be holy because I, the LORD your God, am holy.
3“ ‘Each of you must respect your mother and father, and you must observe my
Sabbaths. I am the LORD your God.
4“ ‘Do not turn to idols or make metal gods for yourselves. I am the LORD your
God.
5“ ‘When you sacrifice a fellowship offering to the LORD, sacrifice it in such a
way that it will be accepted on your behalf. 6It shall be eaten on the day you sacrifice it or on the next day; anything left over until the third day must be burned
up. 7If any of it is eaten on the third day, it is impure and will not be accepted.
8Whoever eats it will be held responsible because they have desecrated what is
holy to the LORD; they must be cut off from their people.
9“ ‘When you reap the harvest of your land, do not reap to the very edges of
your field or gather the gleanings of your harvest. 10Do not go over your vineyard
a second time or pick up the grapes that have fallen. Leave them for the poor and
the foreigner. I am the LORD your God.
11“ ‘Do not steal.
“ ‘Do not lie.
“ ‘Do not deceive one another.
12“ ‘Do not swear falsely by my name and so profane the name of your God. I
am the LORD.
13“ ‘Do not defraud or rob your neighbor.
“ ‘Do not hold back the wages of a hired worker overnight.
14“ ‘Do not curse the deaf or put a stumbling block in front of the blind, but fear
your God. I am the LORD.
15“ ‘Do not pervert justice; do not show partiality to the poor or favoritism to
the great, but judge your neighbor fairly.
16“ ‘Do not go about spreading slander among your people.
“ ‘Do not do anything that endangers your neighbor’s life. I am the LORD.
17“ ‘Do not hate a fellow Israelite in your heart. Rebuke your neighbor frankly
so you will not share in their guilt.
18“ ‘Do not seek revenge or bear a grudge against anyone among your people,
but love your neighbor as yourself. I am the LORD.

LEVITICUS 19:18

REVENGE

When wronged and wounded by others, Christians face the option to seek revenge or to love as Jesus taught. Someone once asked him about the greatest commandment and his reply was to love God with all your heart, soul and mind. He then added, “Love your neighbor as yourself,” quoting this section of Leviticus (Mt 22:39). Jesus loved fully and freely, showing us how to love others — even those who hurt us.

Bearing a grudge — scheming for the opportunity to strike back — is one of the easiest things to do. Refusing to take revenge is one of the hardest. It is the courageous and God-honoring choice; trusting him to accomplish justice while dispensing mercy and grace.

Revenge-seeking keeps anger fanned into flame and keeps open the wound of offense. Withholding forgiveness supports a sense of self-importance and entitlement, looking to win some invisible competition. Most importantly, it is contrary to the instruction and example of Christ. Facing the cross, a most horrific display of hatred and torture, Jesus did not call down heaven against mankind. His response was, “Father, forgive them” (Lk 23:34). No grudge, no desire for revenge, only love — full and free.

19“ ‘Keep my decrees.
“ ‘Do not mate different kinds of animals.
“ ‘Do not plant your field with two kinds of seed.
“ ‘Do not wear clothing woven of two kinds of material.
20“ ‘If a man sleeps with a female slave who is promised to another man but
who has not been ransomed or given her freedom, there must be due punishment.[a] Yet they are not to be put to death, because she had not been freed. 21The
man, however, must bring a ram to the entrance to the tent of meeting for a guilt
offering to the LORD. 22With the ram of the guilt offering the priest is to make
atonement for him before the LORD for the sin he has committed, and his sin
will be forgiven.

23“ ‘When you enter the land and plant any kind of fruit tree, regard its fruit
as forbidden.[b] For three years you are to consider it forbidden[b]; it must not be
eaten. 24In the fourth year all its fruit will be holy, an offering of praise to the
LORD. 25But in the fifth year you may eat its fruit. In this way your harvest will be
increased. I am the LORD your God.

26“ ‘Do not eat any meat with the blood still in it.
“ ‘Do not practice divination or seek omens.
27“ ‘Do not cut the hair at the sides of your head or clip off the edges of your
beard.
28“ ‘Do not cut your bodies for the dead or put tattoo marks on yourselves. I
am the LORD.
29“ ‘Do not degrade your daughter by making her a prostitute, or the land will
turn to prostitution and be filled with wickedness.
30“ ‘Observe my Sabbaths and have reverence for my sanctuary. I am the LORD.
31“ ‘Do not turn to mediums or seek out spiritists, for you will be defiled by
them. I am the LORD your God.
32“ ‘Stand up in the presence of the aged, show respect for the elderly and revere your God. I am the LORD.
33“ ‘When a foreigner resides among you in your land, do not mistreat them.
34The foreigner residing among you must be treated as your native-born. Love
them as yourself, for you were foreigners in Egypt. I am the LORD your God.
35“ ‘Do not use dishonest standards when measuring length, weight or quantity. 36Use honest scales and honest weights, an honest ephah[c] and an honest hin.[d]
I am the LORD your God, who brought you out of Egypt.
37“ ‘Keep all my decrees and all my laws and follow them. I am the LORD.’ ”

Punishments for Sin

20 The LORD said to Moses, 2“Say to the Israelites: ‘Any Israelite or any foreigner residing in Israel who sacrifices any of his children to Molek is to
be put to death. The members of the community are to stone him. 3I myself will
set my face against him and will cut him off from his people; for by sacrificing
his children to Molek, he has defiled my sanctuary and profaned my holy name.
4If the members of the community close their eyes when that man sacrifices one
of his children to Molek and if they fail to put him to death, 5I myself will set my
face against him and his family and will cut them off from their people together
with all who follow him in prostituting themselves to Molek.

6“ ‘I will set my face against anyone who turns to mediums and spiritists
to prostitute themselves by following them, and I will cut them off from their
people.
7“ ‘Consecrate yourselves and be holy, because I am the LORD your God. 8Keep
my decrees and follow them. I am the LORD, who makes you holy.
9“ ‘Anyone who curses their father or mother is to be put to death. Because
they have cursed their father or mother, their blood will be on their own head.

[a] 20 Or *be an inquiry* [b] 23 Hebrew *uncircumcised* [c] 36 An ephah was a dry measure having the capacity of about 3/5 of a bushel or about 22 liters. [d] 36 A hin was a liquid measure having the capacity of about 1 gallon or about 3.8 liters.

10“ ‘If a man commits adultery with another man’s wife—with the wife of his
neighbor—both the adulterer and the adulteress are to be put to death.
11“ ‘If a man has sexual relations with his father’s wife, he has dishonored his
father. Both the man and the woman are to be put to death; their blood will be
on their own heads.
12“ ‘If a man has sexual relations with his daughter-in-law, both of them are
to be put to death. What they have done is a perversion; their blood will be on
their own heads.
13“ ‘If a man has sexual relations with a man as one does with a woman, both
of them have done what is detestable. They are to be put to death; their blood
will be on their own heads.
14“ ‘If a man marries both a woman and her mother, it is wicked. Both he and
they must be burned in the fire, so that no wickedness will be among you.
15“ ‘If a man has sexual relations with an animal, he is to be put to death, and
you must kill the animal.
16“ ‘If a woman approaches an animal to have sexual relations with it, kill both
the woman and the animal. They are to be put to death; their blood will be on
their own heads.
17“ ‘If a man marries his sister, the daughter of either his father or his mother,
and they have sexual relations, it is a disgrace. They are to be publicly removed
from their people. He has dishonored his sister and will be held responsible.
18“ ‘If a man has sexual relations with a woman during her monthly period, he
has exposed the source of her flow, and she has also uncovered it. Both of them
are to be cut off from their people.
19“ ‘Do not have sexual relations with the sister of either your mother or your
father, for that would dishonor a close relative; both of you would be held responsible.
20“ ‘If a man has sexual relations with his aunt, he has dishonored his uncle.
They will be held responsible; they will die childless.
21“ ‘If a man marries his brother’s wife, it is an act of impurity; he has dishonored his brother. They will be childless.
22“ ‘Keep all my decrees and laws and follow them, so that the land where I am
bringing you to live may not vomit you out. 23You must not live according to the
customs of the nations I am going to drive out before you. Because they did all
these things, I abhorred them. 24But I said to you, “You will possess their land;
I will give it to you as an inheritance, a land flowing with milk and honey.” I am
the LORD your God, who has set you apart from the nations.
25“ ‘You must therefore make a distinction between clean and unclean animals and between unclean and clean birds. Do not defile yourselves by any
animal or bird or anything that moves along the ground—those that I have set
apart as unclean for you. 26You are to be holy to me because I, the LORD, am holy,
and I have set you apart from the nations to be my own.
27“ ‘A man or woman who is a medium or spiritist among you must be put to
death. You are to stone them; their blood will be on their own heads.’ ”

Rules for Priests

21 The LORD said to Moses, “Speak to the priests, the sons of Aaron, and say
to them: ‘A priest must not make himself ceremonially unclean for any
of his people who die, 2except for a close relative, such as his mother or father,
his son or daughter, his brother, 3or an unmarried sister who is dependent on
him since she has no husband—for her he may make himself unclean. 4He must
not make himself unclean for people related to him by marriage,[a] and so defile
himself.
5“ ‘Priests must not shave their heads or shave off the edges of their beards or
cut their bodies. 6They must be holy to their God and must not profane the name

[a] 4 Or *unclean as a leader among his people*

PUNISHMENTS FOR SIN

When parents respond to misbehavior with appropriate and measured discipline, the child is likely to think their parents are cruel and lacking grace. For many readers, God's plan of discipline for sinners — spelled out in Leviticus 20 — seems cruel, harsh and even extreme. In most cases, all parties in the sinful activity were to be put to death by the community.

The promised punishments were actually generous warnings, shedding light on God's desire that his people live and not die. His explicit commands helped the people know what conduct to avoid. The Lord, who is always just, repeatedly noted that offenders who disregarded his warnings would die — but their blood would be on their own heads (Lev 20:9,11,12,13,16,27).

The list of behaviors and consequences also served to train the Israelites to obey their God while staying away from the dark practices of other nations. God wanted them anchored to his concept of holiness before they entered the new land he was about to give them (Lev 20:22 – 24).

In the New Testament, Jesus gave the community new instructions for responding to friends and family members in sin. He taught that the offender should be pursued with the goal of repentance. Jesus even outlined different scenarios and responses (Mt 18:15 – 17). Paul the apostle instructed that churches should remove sinners claiming to be Christians if they refused to repent from wickedness (1Co 5:9 – 13).

There is evidence that death as a consequence of defiance occurred beyond the Old Testament context. Paul explained to the Corinthian church that some of their people had become sick or died because they mistreated the occasion of the Lord's Supper (1Co 11:27 – 32). Elsewhere in the New Testament we are reminded that the Lord disciplines us as a father disciplines the children he loves (Heb 12:5 – 11).

God requires holiness from his people and promises to assist us in the process. He will, through our obedience and close association with him — together with occasional necessary discipline — make his people holy (Lev 20:7 – 8). He will do this for his glory and for our good.

of their God. Because they present the food offerings to the LORD, the food of
their God, they are to be holy.
7“ ‘They must not marry women defiled by prostitution or divorced from their
husbands, because priests are holy to their God. 8Regard them as holy, because
they offer up the food of your God. Consider them holy, because I the LORD am
holy — I who make you holy.
9“ ‘If a priest’s daughter defiles herself by becoming a prostitute, she disgraces
her father; she must be burned in the fire.
10“ ‘The high priest, the one among his brothers who has had the anointing oil
poured on his head and who has been ordained to wear the priestly garments,
must not let his hair become unkempt[a] or tear his clothes. 11He must not enter a
place where there is a dead body. He must not make himself unclean, even for his
father or mother, 12nor leave the sanctuary of his God or desecrate it, because he
has been dedicated by the anointing oil of his God. I am the LORD.
13“ ‘The woman he marries must be a virgin. 14He must not marry a widow, a
divorced woman, or a woman defiled by prostitution, but only a virgin from his
own people, 15so that he will not defile his offspring among his people. I am the
LORD, who makes him holy.’ ”
16The LORD said to Moses, 17“Say to Aaron: ‘For the generations to come none
of your descendants who has a defect may come near to offer the food of his God.
18No man who has any defect may come near: no man who is blind or lame, disfigured or deformed; 19no man with a crippled foot or hand, 20or who is a hunch-
back or a dwarf, or who has any eye defect, or who has festering or running sores
or damaged testicles. 21No descendant of Aaron the priest who has any defect is
to come near to present the food offerings to the LORD. He has a defect; he must
not come near to offer the food of his God. 22He may eat the most holy food of his
God, as well as the holy food; 23yet because of his defect, he must not go near the
curtain or approach the altar, and so desecrate my sanctuary. I am the LORD,
who makes them holy.’ ”
24So Moses told this to Aaron and his sons and to all the Israelites.
22 The LORD said to Moses, 2“Tell Aaron and his sons to treat with respect
the sacred offerings the Israelites consecrate to me, so they will not profane my holy name. I am the LORD.
3“Say to them: ‘For the generations to come, if any of your descendants is ceremonially unclean and yet comes near the sacred offerings that the Israelites
consecrate to the LORD, that person must be cut off from my presence. I am the
LORD.
4“ ‘If a descendant of Aaron has a defiling skin disease[b] or a bodily discharge,
he may not eat the sacred offerings until he is cleansed. He will also be unclean
if he touches something defiled by a corpse or by anyone who has an emission of
semen, 5or if he touches any crawling thing that makes him unclean, or any person who makes him unclean, whatever the uncleanness may be. 6The one who
touches any such thing will be unclean till evening. He must not eat any of the
sacred offerings unless he has bathed himself with water. 7When the sun goes
down, he will be clean, and after that he may eat the sacred offerings, for they
are his food. 8He must not eat anything found dead or torn by wild animals, and
so become unclean through it. I am the LORD.
9“ ‘The priests are to perform my service in such a way that they do not become guilty and die for treating it with contempt. I am the LORD, who makes
them holy.
10“ ‘No one outside a priest’s family may eat the sacred offering, nor may
the guest of a priest or his hired worker eat it. 11But if a priest buys a slave
with money, or if slaves are born in his household, they may eat his food. 12If
a priest’s daughter marries anyone other than a priest, she may not eat any of

[a] *10* Or *not uncover his head* [b] *4* The Hebrew word for *defiling skin disease,* traditionally
translated “leprosy,” was used for various diseases affecting the skin.

the sacred contributions. 13But if a priest's daughter becomes a widow or is
divorced, yet has no children, and she returns to live in her father's household
as in her youth, she may eat her father's food. No unauthorized person, however, may eat it.
14" 'Anyone who eats a sacred offering by mistake must make restitution to the
priest for the offering and add a fifth of the value to it. 15The priests must not desecrate the sacred offerings the Israelites present to the LORD 16by allowing them
to eat the sacred offerings and so bring upon them guilt requiring payment. I am
the LORD, who makes them holy.' "

Unacceptable Sacrifices

17The LORD said to Moses, 18"Speak to Aaron and his sons and to all the Israelites and say to them: 'If any of you — whether an Israelite or a foreigner residing
in Israel — presents a gift for a burnt offering to the LORD, either to fulfill a vow
or as a freewill offering, 19you must present a male without defect from the cattle, sheep or goats in order that it may be accepted on your behalf. 20Do not bring
anything with a defect, because it will not be accepted on your behalf. 21When
anyone brings from the herd or flock a fellowship offering to the LORD to fulfill
a special vow or as a freewill offering, it must be without defect or blemish to be
acceptable. 22Do not offer to the LORD the blind, the injured or the maimed, or
anything with warts or festering or running sores. Do not place any of these on
the altar as a food offering presented to the LORD. 23You may, however, present
as a freewill offering an ox[a] or a sheep that is deformed or stunted, but it will not
be accepted in fulfillment of a vow. 24You must not offer to the LORD an animal
whose testicles are bruised, crushed, torn or cut. You must not do this in your
own land, 25and you must not accept such animals from the hand of a foreigner
and offer them as the food of your God. They will not be accepted on your behalf,
because they are deformed and have defects.' "
26The LORD said to Moses, 27"When a calf, a lamb or a goat is born, it is to remain with its mother for seven days. From the eighth day on, it will be acceptable
as a food offering presented to the LORD. 28Do not slaughter a cow or a sheep and
its young on the same day.
29"When you sacrifice a thank offering to the LORD, sacrifice it in such a way
that it will be accepted on your behalf. 30It must be eaten that same day; leave
none of it till morning. I am the LORD.
31"Keep my commands and follow them. I am the LORD. 32Do not profane my
holy name, for I must be acknowledged as holy by the Israelites. I am the LORD,
who made you holy 33and who brought you out of Egypt to be your God. I am
the LORD."

The Appointed Festivals

23 The LORD said to Moses, 2"Speak to the Israelites and say to them: 'These
are my appointed festivals, the appointed festivals of the LORD, which you
are to proclaim as sacred assemblies.

The Sabbath

3" 'There are six days when you may work, but the seventh day is a day of sabbath rest, a day of sacred assembly. You are not to do any work; wherever you live,
it is a sabbath to the LORD.

The Passover and the Festival of Unleavened Bread

4" 'These are the LORD's appointed festivals, the sacred assemblies you are to
proclaim at their appointed times: 5The LORD's Passover begins at twilight on
the fourteenth day of the first month. 6On the fifteenth day of that month the
LORD's Festival of Unleavened Bread begins; for seven days you must eat bread

[a] *23* The Hebrew word can refer to either male or female.

LEVITICUS 23:5

THE PASSOVER

The Passover is a religious commemoration that all Jewish people are familiar with as they celebrate liberation by God from the tyranny of the Egyptians. The last plague God unleashed upon the Egyptians was one of death — the death of the firstborn in every family. Yet the Lord made a way to go through this judgment untouched by death. Any family who killed a lamb and painted its blood over the doorpost of their home would be *passed over* by the Lord (Ex 12:13). Long after their deliverance, the Israelites understood the significance in the annual day of remembrance: a lamb was sacrificed so that by its death others would be spared.

On the night Jesus was betrayed and handed over for trial and execution, he gathered with his disciples to celebrate the Passover (Mt 26:17 – 19). But Jesus took this religious ceremony and breathed life into it in a way his disciples never expected. "This is *my* body ... This is *my* blood ... poured out for many" (Mt 26:26 – 28, emphasis added). Jesus is "the Lamb of God, who takes away the sin of the world" (Jn 1:29). His innocent blood was shed so that by his death and resurrection others could have life (Mt 20:28).

made without yeast. [7]On the first day hold a sacred assembly and do no regular work. [8]For seven days present a food offering to the LORD. And on the seventh day hold a sacred assembly and do no regular work.' "

Offering the Firstfruits

[9]The LORD said to Moses, [10]"Speak to the Israelites and say to them: 'When you enter the land I am going to give you and you reap its harvest, bring to the priest a sheaf of the first grain you harvest. [11]He is to wave the sheaf before the LORD so it will be accepted on your behalf; the priest is to wave it on the day after the Sabbath. [12]On the day you wave the sheaf, you must sacrifice as a burnt offering to the LORD a lamb a year old without defect, [13]together with its grain offering of two-tenths of an ephah[a] of the finest flour mixed with olive oil — a food offering presented to the LORD, a pleasing aroma — and its drink offering of a quarter of a hin[b] of wine. [14]You must not eat any bread, or roasted or new grain, until the very day you bring this offering to your God. This is to be a lasting ordinance for the generations to come, wherever you live.

The Festival of Weeks

[15]" 'From the day after the Sabbath, the day you brought the sheaf of the wave offering, count off seven full weeks. [16]Count off fifty days up to the day after the seventh Sabbath, and then present an offering of new grain to the LORD. [17]From wherever you live, bring two loaves made of two-tenths of an ephah of the finest flour, baked with yeast, as a wave offering of firstfruits to the LORD. [18]Present with this bread seven male lambs, each a year old and without defect, one young bull and two rams. They will be a burnt offering to the LORD, together with their grain offerings and drink offerings — a food offering, an aroma pleasing to the LORD. [19]Then sacrifice one male goat for a sin offering[c] and two lambs, each a year old, for a fellowship offering. [20]The priest is to wave the two lambs before the LORD as a wave offering, together with the bread of the firstfruits. They are a sacred offering to the LORD for the priest. [21]On that same day you are to proclaim a sacred assembly and do no regular work. This is to be a lasting ordinance for the generations to come, wherever you live.

[22]" 'When you reap the harvest of your land, do not reap to the very edges of your field or gather the gleanings of your harvest. Leave them for the poor and for the foreigner residing among you. I am the LORD your God.' "

The Festival of Trumpets

[23]The LORD said to Moses, [24]"Say to the Israelites: 'On the first day of the seventh month you are to have a day of sabbath rest, a sacred assembly commemorated with trumpet blasts. [25]Do no regular work, but present a food offering to the LORD.' "

The Day of Atonement

[26]The LORD said to Moses, [27]"The tenth day of this seventh month is the Day of Atonement. Hold a sacred assembly and deny yourselves,[d] and present a food offering to the LORD. [28]Do not do any work on that day, because it is the Day of Atonement, when atonement is made for you before the LORD your God. [29]Those who do not deny themselves on that day must be cut off from their people. [30]I will destroy from among their people anyone who does any work on that day. [31]You shall do no work at all. This is to be a lasting ordinance for the generations to come, wherever you live. [32]It is a day of sabbath rest for you, and you must deny yourselves. From the evening of the ninth day of the month until the following evening you are to observe your sabbath."

---

[a] *13* That is, probably about 7 pounds or about 3.2 kilograms; also in verse 17 [b] *13* That is, about 1 quart or about 1 liter [c] *19* Or *purification offering* [d] *27* Or *and fast*; similarly in verses 29 and 32

LEVITICUS 23:15–22

THE FESTIVAL OF WEEKS AND PENTECOST

The Lord commanded a summer Festival of Weeks exactly seven Sabbaths after the Offering of Firstfruits, which celebrated the beginning of the barley harvest. Wherever they were, Israelites were required to come together for a sacred assembly. They rested from work and offered various sacrifices to God, reflecting on his goodness at the onset of the wheat harvest. This national gathering eventually became known as *Pentecost*— a name containing the Greek word for *fifty*, the number of days between the Firstfruits and Weeks celebrations.

Jesus promised his disciples that when he finished his earthly work and ascended to be with the Father, he would send the Holy Spirit (Jn 16:4 – 14). On the day of Pentecost, the Holy Spirit came with fire and power — giving birth to the church (Ac 2:1 – 11). The Holy Spirit came to bear witness to Jesus, to outfit the church with gifts, to unite all believers and to empower Christian ministry. Jews from every nation were gathered in Jerusalem for the festival when the Spirit descended from heaven. God seized this moment to demonstrate that the gospel of Jesus is for people of every tribe and tongue.

The Festival of Tabernacles

33The LORD said to Moses, 34"Say to the Israelites: 'On the fifteenth day of the seventh month the LORD's Festival of Tabernacles begins, and it lasts for seven days. 35The first day is a sacred assembly; do no regular work. 36For seven days present food offerings to the LORD, and on the eighth day hold a sacred assembly and present a food offering to the LORD. It is the closing special assembly; do no regular work.

37(" 'These are the LORD's appointed festivals, which you are to proclaim as sacred assemblies for bringing food offerings to the LORD — the burnt offerings and grain offerings, sacrifices and drink offerings required for each day. 38These offerings are in addition to those for the LORD's Sabbaths and[a] in addition to your gifts and whatever you have vowed and all the freewill offerings you give to the LORD.)

39" 'So beginning with the fifteenth day of the seventh month, after you have gathered the crops of the land, celebrate the festival to the LORD for seven days; the first day is a day of sabbath rest, and the eighth day also is a day of sabbath rest. 40On the first day you are to take branches from luxuriant trees — from palms, willows and other leafy trees — and rejoice before the LORD your God for seven days. 41Celebrate this as a festival to the LORD for seven days each year. This is to be a lasting ordinance for the generations to come; celebrate it in the seventh month. 42Live in temporary shelters for seven days: All native-born Israelites are to live in such shelters 43so your descendants will know that I had the Israelites live in temporary shelters when I brought them out of Egypt. I am the LORD your God.' "

44So Moses announced to the Israelites the appointed festivals of the LORD.

Olive Oil and Bread Set Before the LORD

24 The LORD said to Moses, 2"Command the Israelites to bring you clear oil of pressed olives for the light so that the lamps may be kept burning continually. 3Outside the curtain that shields the ark of the covenant law in the tent of meeting, Aaron is to tend the lamps before the LORD from evening till morning, continually. This is to be a lasting ordinance for the generations to come. 4The lamps on the pure gold lampstand before the LORD must be tended continually.

5"Take the finest flour and bake twelve loaves of bread, using two-tenths of an ephah[b] for each loaf. 6Arrange them in two stacks, six in each stack, on the table of pure gold before the LORD. 7By each stack put some pure incense as a memorial[c] portion to represent the bread and to be a food offering presented to the LORD. 8This bread is to be set out before the LORD regularly, Sabbath after Sabbath, on behalf of the Israelites, as a lasting covenant. 9It belongs to Aaron and his sons, who are to eat it in the sanctuary area, because it is a most holy part of their perpetual share of the food offerings presented to the LORD."

A Blasphemer Put to Death

10Now the son of an Israelite mother and an Egyptian father went out among the Israelites, and a fight broke out in the camp between him and an Israelite. 11The son of the Israelite woman blasphemed the Name with a curse; so they brought him to Moses. (His mother's name was Shelomith, the daughter of Dibri the Danite.) 12They put him in custody until the will of the LORD should be made clear to them.

13Then the LORD said to Moses: 14"Take the blasphemer outside the camp. All those who heard him are to lay their hands on his head, and the entire assembly is to stone him. 15Say to the Israelites: 'Anyone who curses their God will be held responsible; 16anyone who blasphemes the name of the LORD is to be put to death. The entire assembly must stone them. Whether foreigner or native-born, when they blaspheme the Name they are to be put to death.

---

[a] 38 Or *These festivals are in addition to the LORD's Sabbaths, and these offerings are*
[b] 5 That is, probably about 7 pounds or about 3.2 kilograms [c] 7 Or *representative*

LEVITICUS 23:1–44

FESTIVALS

The majority of the laws in Leviticus deal with matters of *worship*: legislation concerning offerings and sacrifices, priests, the Day of Atonement and the annual religious festivals. God's people followed a calendar of carefully directed observances. Weekly, the *Sabbath* was celebrated as a day of solemn rest from all work. On the first day of each month, the *New Moon* feast featured a day of rest, specific sacrifices and the blowing of trumpets. A series of special celebrations and rituals occurred once each year:

Passover. On the fourteenth day of the first month, this festival commemorated God's deliverance of Israel from bondage in Egypt.

The Festival of Unleavened Bread. This festival, which marked the beginning of the barley harvest, immediately followed Passover and lasted until the twenty-first day of the month.

The Offering of Firstfruits. This offering was to be a portion, the "firstfruits," of the harvest. In giving this offering, the people demonstrated their dependence and trust in God for their provision.

The Festival of Weeks (Pentecost). This festival took place fifty days after the barley harvest, and involved new grain offerings from the wheat harvest to the Lord, together with animal sacrifices and a wave offering of bread.

The Festival of Trumpets (Rosh Hashanah). The first day of the seventh month marked this occasion which involved a Sabbath-rest, the blowing of trumpets and a holy convocation.

The Day of Atonement (Yom Kippur). Observed on the tenth day of the seventh month, this was a day of fasting and rest for the purpose of atoning for the sins of the past year.

The Festival of Tabernacles (Booths). This seven-day celebration lasted from the fifteenth to the twenty-first day of the seventh month. The people lived in booths for seven days to remember the exodus from Egypt.

Beyond these annual observances, Israelites celebrated the *sabbath year* every seventh year. It was designated as a "year of release" to allow the land to lie fallow.

Every fiftieth year was the *Year of Jubilee*. This followed seven sabbath years, with liberty proclaimed to those who were servants because of debt. It also returned land to the former owners.

17"'Anyone who takes the life of a human being is to be put to death. 18Anyone who takes the life of someone's animal must make restitution—life for life. 19Anyone who injures their neighbor is to be injured in the same manner: 20fracture for fracture, eye for eye, tooth for tooth. The one who has inflicted the injury must suffer the same injury. 21Whoever kills an animal must make restitution, but whoever kills a human being is to be put to death. 22You are to have the same law for the foreigner and the native-born. I am the LORD your God.'"

23Then Moses spoke to the Israelites, and they took the blasphemer outside the camp and stoned him. The Israelites did as the LORD commanded Moses.

The Sabbath Year

25 The LORD said to Moses at Mount Sinai, 2"Speak to the Israelites and say to them: 'When you enter the land I am going to give you, the land itself must observe a sabbath to the LORD. 3For six years sow your fields, and for six years prune your vineyards and gather their crops. 4But in the seventh year the land is to have a year of sabbath rest, a sabbath to the LORD. Do not sow your fields or prune your vineyards. 5Do not reap what grows of itself or harvest the grapes of your untended vines. The land is to have a year of rest. 6Whatever the land yields during the sabbath year will be food for you—for yourself, your male and female servants, and the hired worker and temporary resident who live among you, 7as well as for your livestock and the wild animals in your land. Whatever the land produces may be eaten.

The Year of Jubilee

8"'Count off seven sabbath years—seven times seven years—so that the seven sabbath years amount to a period of forty-nine years. 9Then have the trumpet sounded everywhere on the tenth day of the seventh month; on the Day of Atonement sound the trumpet throughout your land. 10Consecrate the fiftieth year and proclaim liberty throughout the land to all its inhabitants. It shall be a jubilee for you; each of you is to return to your family property and to your own clan. 11The fiftieth year shall be a jubilee for you; do not sow and do not reap what grows of itself or harvest the untended vines. 12For it is a jubilee and is to be holy for you; eat only what is taken directly from the fields.

13"'In this Year of Jubilee everyone is to return to their own property.

14"'If you sell land to any of your own people or buy land from them, do not take advantage of each other. 15You are to buy from your own people on the basis of the number of years since the Jubilee. And they are to sell to you on the basis of the number of years left for harvesting crops. 16When the years are many, you are to increase the price, and when the years are few, you are to decrease the price, because what is really being sold to you is the number of crops. 17Do not take advantage of each other, but fear your God. I am the LORD your God.

18"'Follow my decrees and be careful to obey my laws, and you will live safely in the land. 19Then the land will yield its fruit, and you will eat your fill and live there in safety. 20You may ask, "What will we eat in the seventh year if we do not plant or harvest our crops?" 21I will send you such a blessing in the sixth year that the land will yield enough for three years. 22While you plant during the eighth year, you will eat from the old crop and will continue to eat from it until the harvest of the ninth year comes in.

23"'The land must not be sold permanently, because the land is mine and you reside in my land as foreigners and strangers. 24Throughout the land that you hold as a possession, you must provide for the redemption of the land.

25"'If one of your fellow Israelites becomes poor and sells some of their property, their nearest relative is to come and redeem what they have sold. 26If, however, there is no one to redeem it for them but later on they prosper and acquire sufficient means to redeem it themselves, 27they are to determine the value for the years since they sold it and refund the balance to the one to whom they sold it; they can then go back to their own property. 28But if they do not acquire the

---

LEVITICUS 25:10

JUBILEE

The word *jubilee* means "ram's horn" or "trumpet," but the concept is rooted in liberation. Every fiftieth year, a trumpet would blow throughout the land to announce a special season of God's favor. By decree, each person returned to their family property—even if that property now belonged to another. Ownership reverted to the original family, restoring what had been lost to crop failure, illness or some other financial hardship. The jubilee reversed the string of events that forced family land-owners to become land-sellers, then people of no land, usually hiring themselves out as servants. The sound of the fiftieth year trumpet was a happy signal of a reset to life and community—debts were canceled, hardships were erased and families long scattered were reconnected in the land of their fathers and mothers.

Jesus had his own trumpeting moment (Lk 4:16–21). Reading from the scroll of Isaiah, he announced a perpetual jubilee for people, not property. Jesus came into the world to reverse the effects of sin, restore lost things, forgive debts, liberate prisoners and reconcile people to God.

means to repay, what was sold will remain in the possession of the buyer until
the Year of Jubilee. It will be returned in the Jubilee, and they can then go back
to their property.
29" 'Anyone who sells a house in a walled city retains the right of redemption
a full year after its sale. During that time the seller may redeem it. 30If it is not
redeemed before a full year has passed, the house in the walled city shall belong
permanently to the buyer and the buyer's descendants. It is not to be returned
in the Jubilee. 31But houses in villages without walls around them are to be considered as belonging to the open country. They can be redeemed, and they are
to be returned in the Jubilee.
32" 'The Levites always have the right to redeem their houses in the Levitical
towns, which they possess. 33So the property of the Levites is redeemable — that
is, a house sold in any town they hold — and is to be returned in the Jubilee, because the houses in the towns of the Levites are their property among the Israelites. 34But the pastureland belonging to their towns must not be sold; it is their
permanent possession.
35" 'If any of your fellow Israelites become poor and are unable to support themselves among you, help them as you would a foreigner and stranger, so they can
continue to live among you. 36Do not take interest or any profit from them, but
fear your God, so that they may continue to live among you. 37You must not lend
them money at interest or sell them food at a profit. 38I am the LORD your God,
who brought you out of Egypt to give you the land of Canaan and to be your God.
39" 'If any of your fellow Israelites become poor and sell themselves to you, do
not make them work as slaves. 40They are to be treated as hired workers or temporary residents among you; they are to work for you until the Year of Jubilee.
41Then they and their children are to be released, and they will go back to their
own clans and to the property of their ancestors. 42Because the Israelites are my
servants, whom I brought out of Egypt, they must not be sold as slaves. 43Do not
rule over them ruthlessly, but fear your God.
44" 'Your male and female slaves are to come from the nations around you;
from them you may buy slaves. 45You may also buy some of the temporary residents living among you and members of their clans born in your country, and
they will become your property. 46You can bequeath them to your children as
inherited property and can make them slaves for life, but you must not rule over
your fellow Israelites ruthlessly.
47" 'If a foreigner residing among you becomes rich and any of your fellow
Israelites become poor and sell themselves to the foreigner or to a member of
the foreigner's clan, 48they retain the right of redemption after they have sold
themselves. One of their relatives may redeem them: 49An uncle or a cousin or
any blood relative in their clan may redeem them. Or if they prosper, they may
redeem themselves. 50They and their buyer are to count the time from the year
they sold themselves up to the Year of Jubilee. The price for their release is to
be based on the rate paid to a hired worker for that number of years. 51If many
years remain, they must pay for their redemption a larger share of the price paid
for them. 52If only a few years remain until the Year of Jubilee, they are to com-
pute that and pay for their redemption accordingly. 53They are to be treated as
workers hired from year to year; you must see to it that those to whom they owe
service do not rule over them ruthlessly.
54" 'Even if someone is not redeemed in any of these ways, they and their children are to be released in the Year of Jubilee, 55for the Israelites belong to me
as servants. They are my servants, whom I brought out of Egypt. I am the LORD
your God.

Reward for Obedience

26 " 'Do not make idols or set up an image or a sacred stone for yourselves,
and do not place a carved stone in your land to bow down before it. I am
the LORD your God.

2" 'Observe my Sabbaths and have reverence for my sanctuary. I am the LORD.
3" 'If you follow my decrees and are careful to obey my commands, 4I will
send you rain in its season, and the ground will yield its crops and the trees their
fruit. 5Your threshing will continue until grape harvest and the grape harvest
will continue until planting, and you will eat all the food you want and live in
safety in your land.
6" 'I will grant peace in the land, and you will lie down and no one will make
you afraid. I will remove wild beasts from the land, and the sword will not pass
through your country. 7You will pursue your enemies, and they will fall by the
sword before you. 8Five of you will chase a hundred, and a hundred of you will
chase ten thousand, and your enemies will fall by the sword before you.
9" 'I will look on you with favor and make you fruitful and increase your numbers, and I will keep my covenant with you. 10You will still be eating last year's
harvest when you will have to move it out to make room for the new. 11I will put
my dwelling place[a] among you, and I will not abhor you. 12I will walk among
you and be your God, and you will be my people. 13I am the LORD your God, who
brought you out of Egypt so that you would no longer be slaves to the Egyptians;
I broke the bars of your yoke and enabled you to walk with heads held high.

Punishment for Disobedience

14" 'But if you will not listen to me and carry out all these commands, 15and if
you reject my decrees and abhor my laws and fail to carry out all my commands
and so violate my covenant, 16then I will do this to you: I will bring on you sudden terror, wasting diseases and fever that will destroy your sight and sap your
strength. You will plant seed in vain, because your enemies will eat it. 17I will
set my face against you so that you will be defeated by your enemies; those who
hate you will rule over you, and you will flee even when no one is pursuing you.
18" 'If after all this you will not listen to me, I will punish you for your sins sev-
en times over. 19I will break down your stubborn pride and make the sky above
you like iron and the ground beneath you like bronze. 20Your strength will be
spent in vain, because your soil will not yield its crops, nor will the trees of your
land yield their fruit.
21" 'If you remain hostile toward me and refuse to listen to me, I will multiply
your afflictions seven times over, as your sins deserve. 22I will send wild animals
against you, and they will rob you of your children, destroy your cattle and make
you so few in number that your roads will be deserted.
23" 'If in spite of these things you do not accept my correction but continue to
be hostile toward me, 24I myself will be hostile toward you and will afflict you
for your sins seven times over. 25And I will bring the sword on you to avenge
the breaking of the covenant. When you withdraw into your cities, I will send
a plague among you, and you will be given into enemy hands. 26When I cut off
your supply of bread, ten women will be able to bake your bread in one oven, and
they will dole out the bread by weight. You will eat, but you will not be satisfied.
27" 'If in spite of this you still do not listen to me but continue to be hostile
toward me, 28then in my anger I will be hostile toward you, and I myself will
punish you for your sins seven times over. 29You will eat the flesh of your sons
and the flesh of your daughters. 30I will destroy your high places, cut down your
incense altars and pile your dead bodies[b] on the lifeless forms of your idols, and
I will abhor you. 31I will turn your cities into ruins and lay waste your sanctuaries, and I will take no delight in the pleasing aroma of your offerings. 32I myself
will lay waste the land, so that your enemies who live there will be appalled. 33I
will scatter you among the nations and will draw out my sword and pursue you.
Your land will be laid waste, and your cities will lie in ruins. 34Then the land will
enjoy its sabbath years all the time that it lies desolate and you are in the country of your enemies; then the land will rest and enjoy its sabbaths. 35All the time

[a] 11 Or *my tabernacle* [b] 30 Or *your funeral offerings*

that it lies desolate, the land will have the rest it did not have during the sabbaths
you lived in it.
36“ ‘As for those of you who are left, I will make their hearts so fearful in the
lands of their enemies that the sound of a windblown leaf will put them to flight.
They will run as though fleeing from the sword, and they will fall, even though
no one is pursuing them. 37They will stumble over one another as though fleeing
from the sword, even though no one is pursuing them. So you will not be able
to stand before your enemies. 38You will perish among the nations; the land of
your enemies will devour you. 39Those of you who are left will waste away in the
lands of their enemies because of their sins; also because of their ancestors' sins
they will waste away.
40“ ‘But if they will confess their sins and the sins of their ancestors — their
unfaithfulness and their hostility toward me, 41which made me hostile toward
them so that I sent them into the land of their enemies — then when their uncircumcised hearts are humbled and they pay for their sin, 42I will remember my
covenant with Jacob and my covenant with Isaac and my covenant with Abraham, and I will remember the land. 43For the land will be deserted by them and
will enjoy its sabbaths while it lies desolate without them. They will pay for their
sins because they rejected my laws and abhorred my decrees. 44Yet in spite of
this, when they are in the land of their enemies, I will not reject them or abhor
them so as to destroy them completely, breaking my covenant with them. I am
the LORD their God. 45But for their sake I will remember the covenant with their
ancestors whom I brought out of Egypt in the sight of the nations to be their God.
I am the LORD.' ”
46These are the decrees, the laws and the regulations that the LORD established at Mount Sinai between himself and the Israelites through Moses.

Redeeming What Is the LORD's

27 The LORD said to Moses, 2“Speak to the Israelites and say to them: 'If anyone makes a special vow to dedicate a person to the LORD by giving the
equivalent value, 3set the value of a male between the ages of twenty and sixty at
fifty shekels[a] of silver, according to the sanctuary shekel[b]; 4for a female, set her
value at thirty shekels[c]; 5for a person between the ages of five and twenty, set the
value of a male at twenty shekels[d] and of a female at ten shekels[e]; 6for a person
between one month and five years, set the value of a male at five shekels[f] of silver and that of a female at three shekels[g] of silver; 7for a person sixty years old
or more, set the value of a male at fifteen shekels[h] and of a female at ten shekels.
8If anyone making the vow is too poor to pay the specified amount, the person
being dedicated is to be presented to the priest, who will set the value according
to what the one making the vow can afford.
9“ ‘If what they vowed is an animal that is acceptable as an offering to the
LORD, such an animal given to the LORD becomes holy. 10They must not exchange it or substitute a good one for a bad one, or a bad one for a good one; if
they should substitute one animal for another, both it and the substitute become
holy. 11If what they vowed is a ceremonially unclean animal — one that is not acceptable as an offering to the LORD — the animal must be presented to the priest,
12who will judge its quality as good or bad. Whatever value the priest then sets,
that is what it will be. 13If the owner wishes to redeem the animal, a fifth must
be added to its value.
14“ ‘If anyone dedicates their house as something holy to the LORD, the priest
will judge its quality as good or bad. Whatever value the priest then sets, so it will

---

[a] *3* That is, about 1 1/4 pounds or about 575 grams; also in verse 16 [b] *3* That is, about 2/5 ounce or about 12 grams; also in verse 25 [c] *4* That is, about 12 ounces or about 345 grams [d] *5* That is, about 8 ounces or about 230 grams [e] *5* That is, about 4 ounces or about 115 grams; also in verse 7 [f] *6* That is, about 2 ounces or about 58 grams [g] *6* That is, about 1 1/4 ounces or about 35 grams [h] *7* That is, about 6 ounces or about 175 grams

REDEMPTION THROUGH JESUS

The Israelites occasionally made vows for giving themselves, their animals, houses and land to serve the purposes of the tabernacle. These people and things were dedicated to the Lord. If someone wished to reclaim their devoted object, it had to be *redeemed* — bought back. By redeeming at a certain price that which had been dedicated to the sanctuary, the Israelite gave the value of the gift they had vowed. Leviticus 27 established value amounts for redemption. Some items were given a fixed price. Other items such as houses and property received a value amount only after a priest inspected their worth. In many cases, an additional percentage was added to the redemption value in order to make up for any loss incurred by the sanctuary.

As unsavory as it may seem to modern readers, monetary values were assigned for the redemption of individual people. Amounts were set according to age and gender, in relation to a person's potential for work or child-bearing. The highest values were placed on men between the ages of twenty and sixty. The lowest values were placed on females in the age range of one month to five years. However, when the one making a vow was too poor to pay prescribed amounts, the priest could set a price according to what the person could afford.

Redemption is a treasured concept in our salvation through Jesus Christ. We have been justified by grace — only because Jesus *redeemed* us (Ro 3:24). He bought us back from the curse of the law (Gal 3:13). And through his redemption, we have received adoption as sons and daughters of God (Gal 4:4 – 5). The payment made was neither cheap nor common. We were purchased with the precious blood of Christ — something of infinite value and worth (1Pe 1:18 – 19). Our redemption speaks to the scope of God's outrageous love. And it reveals his desire to liberate us from the law which left us without hope. In the fulfillment of a glorious plan made before the foundation of the world, God both judged sin and paid for sin on the cross. He chose to redeem rebels through the life and blood of his Son.

remain. 15If the one who dedicates their house wishes to redeem it, they must
add a fifth to its value, and the house will again become theirs.

16“ ‘If anyone dedicates to the LORD part of their family land, its value is to be
set according to the amount of seed required for it — fifty shekels of silver to a
homer[a] of barley seed. 17If they dedicate a field during the Year of Jubilee, the
value that has been set remains. 18But if they dedicate a field after the Jubilee,
the priest will determine the value according to the number of years that remain
until the next Year of Jubilee, and its set value will be reduced. 19If the one who
dedicates the field wishes to redeem it, they must add a fifth to its value, and the
field will again become theirs. 20If, however, they do not redeem the field, or if
they have sold it to someone else, it can never be redeemed. 21When the field is
released in the Jubilee, it will become holy, like a field devoted to the LORD; it will
become priestly property.

22“ ‘If anyone dedicates to the LORD a field they have bought, which is not part
of their family land, 23the priest will determine its value up to the Year of Jubilee,
and the owner must pay its value on that day as something holy to the LORD. 24In
the Year of Jubilee the field will revert to the person from whom it was bought,
the one whose land it was. 25Every value is to be set according to the sanctuary
shekel, twenty gerahs to the shekel.

26“ ‘No one, however, may dedicate the firstborn of an animal, since the firstborn already belongs to the LORD; whether an ox[b] or a sheep, it is the LORD’s. 27If
it is one of the unclean animals, it may be bought back at its set value, adding a
fifth of the value to it. If it is not redeemed, it is to be sold at its set value.

28“ ‘But nothing that a person owns and devotes[c] to the LORD — whether a human being or an animal or family land — may be sold or redeemed; everything
so devoted is most holy to the LORD.

29“ ‘No person devoted to destruction[d] may be ransomed; they are to be put
to death.

30“ ‘A tithe of everything from the land, whether grain from the soil or fruit
from the trees, belongs to the LORD; it is holy to the LORD. 31Whoever would redeem any of their tithe must add a fifth of the value to it. 32Every tithe of the herd
and flock — every tenth animal that passes under the shepherd’s rod — will be
holy to the LORD. 33No one may pick out the good from the bad or make any substitution. If anyone does make a substitution, both the animal and its substitute
become holy and cannot be redeemed.’ ”

34These are the commands the LORD gave Moses at Mount Sinai for the Israelites.

---

[a] *16* That is, probably about 300 pounds or about 135 kilograms [b] *26* The Hebrew word can refer to either male or female. [c] *28* The Hebrew term refers to the irrevocable giving over of things or persons to the LORD. [d] *29* The Hebrew term refers to the irrevocable giving over of things or persons to the LORD, often by totally destroying them.

JESUS: OUR GRACIOUS PROVISION

NUMBERS

NUMBERS

CENSUS, TRIBES, DUTIES GIVEN *c. 1445 BC*	AARON DIES *c. 1407 BC*	ISRAEL ENTERS PROMISED LAND *c. 1406 BC*

The book of Numbers stands as a testimony of God's faithfulness in leading his people through the wilderness to the brink of the promised land. This journey was not a straightforward path toward triumph: the people were both the recipients of God's gracious blessings and the rebellious agents of idolatry. Through discipline and instruction, God trained the hearts of the people to worship him as they prepared to enter the land.

Many of the names and places mentioned throughout this book are unknown to the modern reader, which leads many to assume that the book of Numbers lacks relevance for today. Israel's journey is, however, an ongoing testimony to the faithfulness of God. Each name is a person God had redeemed from slavery in Egypt. Each place is evidence of God's provision. Each movement is an indication of God's military might and his faithfulness to his promises.

The book of Numbers begins in the wilderness of Sinai in the second month of the second year after God rescued Israel from slavery in Egypt. The journey stretched across nearly another 39 years in the wilderness as the people moved toward the promised land. The first census listed the men who were the first generation of those redeemed from Israel and who were prepared to lead the advance of the people of God. Instead of obedience to God, however, this first generation consistently murmured against the Lord, failed to trust his provision and committed heinous sins of disobedience against his instructions.

The Lord judged this generation by preventing them from entering the promised land; however, he continued to sustain their lives and provide for their needs in the wilderness. He graciously communicated his word to this generation so that they could prepare their sons and daughters to take the land. After 40 years of wandering, Moses and Aaron counted the second generation (Nu 26). They were prepared to enter the land. The question remained: Would this generation succeed where their parents had failed?

This book, like all of the Old Testament, stands as a testimony to God's promise to deliver his people from the consequences of their sin. In Numbers, God demonstrated his divine forbearance and benevolence to a wayward and stubborn people. In spite of their sin, God accomplished his good purposes in their lives and on behalf of the surrounding nations. These good purposes ultimately came to a crescendo in the provision of the Messiah, Jesus Christ, who perfectly and finally dealt with Satan, sin and death. The book foreshadows God's sovereign intention to accomplish these purposes against the backdrop of human sin. Nothing can stop God's plan — not even human sin. His grace is sufficient to lead his people lovingly into his presence — then, now and forever.

GOD IS NOT HUMAN, THAT HE SHOULD LIE,
NOT A HUMAN BEING, THAT HE SHOULD
CHANGE HIS MIND. DOES HE SPEAK AND THEN NOT ACT?
DOES HE PROMISE AND NOT FULFILL?

Numbers 23:19

NUMBERS

The Census

1 The LORD spoke to Moses in the tent of meeting in the Desert of Sinai on the
first day of the second month of the second year after the Israelites came
out of Egypt. He said: 2 "Take a census of the whole Israelite community by their
clans and families, listing every man by name, one by one. 3 You and Aaron are
to count according to their divisions all the men in Israel who are twenty years
old or more and able to serve in the army. 4 One man from each tribe, each of
them the head of his family, is to help you. 5 These are the names of the men who
are to assist you:

from Reuben, Elizur son of Shedeur;
6 from Simeon, Shelumiel son of Zurishaddai;
7 from Judah, Nahshon son of Amminadab;
8 from Issachar, Nethanel son of Zuar;
9 from Zebulun, Eliab son of Helon;
10 from the sons of Joseph:
from Ephraim, Elishama son of Ammihud;
from Manasseh, Gamaliel son of Pedahzur;
11 from Benjamin, Abidan son of Gideoni;
12 from Dan, Ahiezer son of Ammishaddai;
13 from Asher, Pagiel son of Okran;
14 from Gad, Eliasaph son of Deuel;
15 from Naphtali, Ahira son of Enan."

16 These were the men appointed from the community, the leaders of their
ancestral tribes. They were the heads of the clans of Israel.

17 Moses and Aaron took these men whose names had been specified, 18 and
they called the whole community together on the first day of the second month.
The people registered their ancestry by their clans and families, and the men
twenty years old or more were listed by name, one by one, 19 as the LORD commanded Moses. And so he counted them in the Desert of Sinai:

20 From the descendants of Reuben the firstborn son of Israel:
All the men twenty years old or more who were able to serve in the army
were listed by name, one by one, according to the records of their clans
and families. 21 The number from the tribe of Reuben was 46,500.

22 From the descendants of Simeon:
All the men twenty years old or more who were able to serve in the army
were counted and listed by name, one by one, according to the records
of their clans and families. 23 The number from the tribe of Simeon was
59,300.

24 From the descendants of Gad:
All the men twenty years old or more who were able to serve in the army
were listed by name, according to the records of their clans and families.
25 The number from the tribe of Gad was 45,650.

26 From the descendants of Judah:
All the men twenty years old or more who were able to serve in the army
were listed by name, according to the records of their clans and families.
27 The number from the tribe of Judah was 74,600.

28 From the descendants of Issachar:
All the men twenty years old or more who were able to serve in the army

were listed by name, according to the records of their clans and families.
[29]The number from the tribe of Issachar was 54,400.

30 From the descendants of Zebulun:
All the men twenty years old or more who were able to serve in the army were listed by name, according to the records of their clans and families.
31 The number from the tribe of Zebulun was 57,400.

32 From the sons of Joseph:
From the descendants of Ephraim:
All the men twenty years old or more who were able to serve in the army were listed by name, according to the records of their clans and families.
33 The number from the tribe of Ephraim was 40,500.

34 From the descendants of Manasseh:
All the men twenty years old or more who were able to serve in the army were listed by name, according to the records of their clans and families.
35 The number from the tribe of Manasseh was 32,200.

36 From the descendants of Benjamin:
All the men twenty years old or more who were able to serve in the army were listed by name, according to the records of their clans and families.
37 The number from the tribe of Benjamin was 35,400.

38 From the descendants of Dan:
All the men twenty years old or more who were able to serve in the army were listed by name, according to the records of their clans and families.
39 The number from the tribe of Dan was 62,700.

40 From the descendants of Asher:
All the men twenty years old or more who were able to serve in the army were listed by name, according to the records of their clans and families.
41 The number from the tribe of Asher was 41,500.

42 From the descendants of Naphtali:
All the men twenty years old or more who were able to serve in the army were listed by name, according to the records of their clans and families.
43 The number from the tribe of Naphtali was 53,400.

44 These were the men counted by Moses and Aaron and the twelve leaders
of Israel, each one representing his family. 45 All the Israelites twenty years old
or more who were able to serve in Israel's army were counted according to their
families. 46 The total number was 603,550.
47 The ancestral tribe of the Levites, however, was not counted along with the
others. 48 The LORD had said to Moses: 49 "You must not count the tribe of Levi or
include them in the census of the other Israelites. 50 Instead, appoint the Levites
to be in charge of the tabernacle of the covenant law — over all its furnishings
and everything belonging to it. They are to carry the tabernacle and all its furnishings; they are to take care of it and encamp around it. 51 Whenever the tabernacle is to move, the Levites are to take it down, and whenever the tabernacle is
to be set up, the Levites shall do it. Anyone else who approaches it is to be put to
death. 52 The Israelites are to set up their tents by divisions, each of them in their
own camp under their standard. 53 The Levites, however, are to set up their tents around the tabernacle of the covenant law so that my wrath will not fall on the Israelite community. The Levites are to be responsible for the care of the tabernacle of the covenant law."
54 The Israelites did all this just as the LORD commanded Moses.

The Arrangement of the Tribal Camps

2 The LORD said to Moses and Aaron: 2 "The Israelites are to camp around the
tent of meeting some distance from it, each of them under their standard and holding the banners of their family."

NUMBERS 2:1–2

DISTANCE

The intricate order and arrangement of the people of God made it clear that they were to maintain a considerable distance between themselves and the presence of God. In his grace, God dwelled among the people via the tent of meeting, or tabernacle. But they camped "some distance" from the tabernacle, and they were only able to approach the Lord's presence at certain times and in carefully prescribed ways. Due to the sinfulness of the people, they dared not approach the holy dwelling of God in their own way or by their own merit.

In the New Testament, Paul wrote that the substitutionary death of Jesus makes it possible for those who were once far off to be brought near to God (Eph 2:13). They would still not approach him on their own merit, but through faith in Christ's work. Those who are in Christ no longer must stand far off, distant from the presence of God, but they can freely and confidently enter his presence at any time (Eph 3:12).

NUMBERS 2:3–34

ENCAMPMENT

The tribe of Judah, leading Issachar and Zebulun, occupied the preferred position on the east side of the camp. From this position, they marched first when Israel was called by God. Reuben, Simeon and Gad departed second. God's presence remained at the center of his people—with the Levites as they carried the tent of meeting—as their formation marched through the wilderness. The final six tribes followed behind, so that the nation on the move directly mirrored the encampment. Judah was uniquely equipped to lead Israel because God provided them with the largest number of military men. The tribe's unique role extended to the coming Messiah. Through them, One came as a ruling lion, bringing the obedience of the nations and reigning with the eternal scepter (Ge 49:10). The Lord Jesus Christ descended from Judah as the king, a sovereign and great high priest despite not being a Levite. He ushered in a change in the law and offered hope through his death and resurrection (Heb 7:11,14). He is the Judaic leader of his people, and the one his people follow at all times.

3 On the east, toward the sunrise, the divisions of the camp of Judah are
to encamp under their standard. The leader of the people of Judah is Nahshon son of Amminadab. 4 His division numbers 74,600.
5 The tribe of Issachar will camp next to them. The leader of the people of
Issachar is Nethanel son of Zuar. 6 His division numbers 54,400.
7 The tribe of Zebulun will be next. The leader of the people of Zebulun
is Eliab son of Helon. 8 His division numbers 57,400.
9 All the men assigned to the camp of Judah, according to their divisions,
number 186,400. They will set out first.

10 On the south will be the divisions of the camp of Reuben under their
standard. The leader of the people of Reuben is Elizur son of Shedeur. 11 His
division numbers 46,500.
12 The tribe of Simeon will camp next to them. The leader of the people
of Simeon is Shelumiel son of Zurishaddai. 13 His division numbers 59,300.
14 The tribe of Gad will be next. The leader of the people of Gad is Eliasaph son of Deuel.[a] 15 His division numbers 45,650.
16 All the men assigned to the camp of Reuben, according to their divisions, number 151,450. They will set out second.

17 Then the tent of meeting and the camp of the Levites will set out in the
middle of the camps. They will set out in the same order as they encamp,
each in their own place under their standard.

18 On the west will be the divisions of the camp of Ephraim under their
standard. The leader of the people of Ephraim is Elishama son of Ammihud. 19 His division numbers 40,500.
20 The tribe of Manasseh will be next to them. The leader of the people
of Manasseh is Gamaliel son of Pedahzur. 21 His division numbers 32,200.
22 The tribe of Benjamin will be next. The leader of the people of Benjamin is Abidan son of Gideoni. 23 His division numbers 35,400.
24 All the men assigned to the camp of Ephraim, according to their divisions, number 108,100. They will set out third.

25 On the north will be the divisions of the camp of Dan under their standard. The leader of the people of Dan is Ahiezer son of Ammishaddai. 26 His
division numbers 62,700.
27 The tribe of Asher will camp next to them. The leader of the people of
Asher is Pagiel son of Okran. 28 His division numbers 41,500.
29 The tribe of Naphtali will be next. The leader of the people of Naphtali
is Ahira son of Enan. 30 His division numbers 53,400.
31 All the men assigned to the camp of Dan number 157,600. They will set
out last, under their standards.

32 These are the Israelites, counted according to their families. All the
men in the camps, by their divisions, number 603,550. 33 The Levites, however, were not counted along with the other Israelites, as the LORD commanded Moses.

34 So the Israelites did everything the LORD commanded Moses; that is the
way they encamped under their standards, and that is the way they set out, each
of them with their clan and family.

The Levites

3 This is the account of the family of Aaron and Moses at the time the LORD
spoke to Moses at Mount Sinai.
2 The names of the sons of Aaron were Nadab the firstborn and Abihu, Eleazar
and Ithamar. 3 Those were the names of Aaron's sons, the anointed priests, who

[a] *14* Many manuscripts of the Masoretic Text, Samaritan Pentateuch and Vulgate (see also 1:14); most manuscripts of the Masoretic Text *Reuel*

REVOLVING AROUND WORSHIP

God prescribed a specific arrangement for the people of God as they lived in the wilderness. The central point around which all the people were encamped was the tent of meeting — that is, the tabernacle. In this tent, God dwelled among his people, and they worshiped him by means of the sacrificial system. The members of the tribe of Levi who oversaw Israelite worship encircled the tent. From there, the twelve tribes of the people of God were broken into four groups with three tribes in each group. The tribes of Dan, Asher and Naphtali camped to the north of the tent; Issachar, Judah and Zebulun to the east; Gad, Reuben and Simeon to the south; and Benjamin, Ephraim and Manasseh to the west. This alignment demonstrated that the focal point for the life of the people of God was the worship of the God of Abraham, Isaac and Jacob. Worship was not an arbitrary, additional task to which the people of God were required to attend to from time to time. Rather, their whole lives and, in fact, their entire community revolved around worship. Also, any other nation which observed the camp of the people of God immediately understood that God was central to their identity and mission.

John, the author of the book of Revelation, pictured a similar reality in heaven when all things will be made new; however, John wrote, "a great multitude that no one could count, from every nation, tribe, people and language" will gather around the throne and declare, "Salvation belongs to our God, who sits on the throne, and to the Lamb" (Rev 7:9 – 10). God's people will one day gather around the presence of God in all-consuming worship.

The Christian life, as a foretaste of this coming reality, is meant to center on the worship of the true and living God. Worship, as described by the New Testament authors, is to be the hub around which all of life revolves. In fact, Paul wrote that Christians are to give their entire lives to God as an act of "true and proper worship" (Ro 12:1). Whole-life worship is made possible through the finished work of Jesus and empowered by the Spirit of God. The beauty of Jesus' work should prompt believers to organize their lives around worship. As they do, others will be able to see the centrality of God among the people of God.

were ordained to serve as priests. 4Nadab and Abihu, however, died before the LORD when they made an offering with unauthorized fire before him in the Desert of Sinai. They had no sons, so Eleazar and Ithamar served as priests during the lifetime of their father Aaron.

5The LORD said to Moses, 6"Bring the tribe of Levi and present them to Aaron the priest to assist him. 7They are to perform duties for him and for the whole community at the tent of meeting by doing the work of the tabernacle. 8They are to take care of all the furnishings of the tent of meeting, fulfilling the obligations of the Israelites by doing the work of the tabernacle. 9Give the Levites to Aaron and his sons; they are the Israelites who are to be given wholly to him.[a] 10Appoint Aaron and his sons to serve as priests; anyone else who approaches the sanctuary is to be put to death."

11The LORD also said to Moses, 12"I have taken the Levites from among the Israelites in place of the first male offspring of every Israelite woman. The Levites are mine, 13for all the firstborn are mine. When I struck down all the firstborn in Egypt, I set apart for myself every firstborn in Israel, whether human or animal. They are to be mine. I am the LORD."

14The LORD said to Moses in the Desert of Sinai, 15"Count the Levites by their families and clans. Count every male a month old or more." 16So Moses counted them, as he was commanded by the word of the LORD.

17These were the names of the sons of Levi:
  Gershon, Kohath and Merari.
18These were the names of the Gershonite clans:
  Libni and Shimei.
19The Kohathite clans:
  Amram, Izhar, Hebron and Uzziel.
20The Merarite clans:
  Mahli and Mushi.
These were the Levite clans, according to their families.

21To Gershon belonged the clans of the Libnites and Shimeites; these were the Gershonite clans. 22The number of all the males a month old or more who were counted was 7,500. 23The Gershonite clans were to camp on the west, behind the tabernacle. 24The leader of the families of the Gershonites was Eliasaph son of Lael. 25At the tent of meeting the Gershonites were responsible for the care of the tabernacle and tent, its coverings, the curtain at the entrance to the tent of meeting, 26the curtains of the courtyard, the curtain at the entrance to the courtyard surrounding the tabernacle and altar, and the ropes — and everything related to their use.

27To Kohath belonged the clans of the Amramites, Izharites, Hebronites and Uzzielites; these were the Kohathite clans. 28The number of all the males a month old or more was 8,600.[b] The Kohathites were responsible for the care of the sanctuary. 29The Kohathite clans were to camp on the south side of the tabernacle. 30The leader of the families of the Kohathite clans was Elizaphan son of Uzziel. 31They were responsible for the care of the ark, the table, the lampstand, the altars, the articles of the sanctuary used in ministering, the curtain, and everything related to their use. 32The chief leader of the Levites was Eleazar son of Aaron, the priest. He was appointed over those who were responsible for the care of the sanctuary.

33To Merari belonged the clans of the Mahlites and the Mushites; these were the Merarite clans. 34The number of all the males a month old or more who were counted was 6,200. 35The leader of the families of the Merarite clans was

---

[a] 9 Most manuscripts of the Masoretic Text; some manuscripts of the Masoretic Text, Samaritan Pentateuch and Septuagint (see also 8:16) *to me* [b] 28 Hebrew; some Septuagint manuscripts *8,300*

Zuriel son of Abihail; they were to camp on the north side of the tabernacle.
36 The Merarites were appointed to take care of the frames of the tabernacle,
its crossbars, posts, bases, all its equipment, and everything related to their
use, 37 as well as the posts of the surrounding courtyard with their bases, tent
pegs and ropes.

38 Moses and Aaron and his sons were to camp to the east of the tabernacle,
toward the sunrise, in front of the tent of meeting. They were responsible for the
care of the sanctuary on behalf of the Israelites. Anyone else who approached
the sanctuary was to be put to death.

39 The total number of Levites counted at the LORD's command by Moses and
Aaron according to their clans, including every male a month old or more, was
22,000.

40 The LORD said to Moses, "Count all the firstborn Israelite males who are a
month old or more and make a list of their names. 41 Take the Levites for me in
place of all the firstborn of the Israelites, and the livestock of the Levites in place
of all the firstborn of the livestock of the Israelites. I am the LORD."
42 So Moses counted all the firstborn of the Israelites, as the LORD commanded
him. 43 The total number of firstborn males a month old or more, listed by name,
was 22,273.

44 The LORD also said to Moses, 45 "Take the Levites in place of all the firstborn
of Israel, and the livestock of the Levites in place of their livestock. The Levites
are to be mine. I am the LORD. 46 To redeem the 273 firstborn Israelites who exceed the number of the Levites, 47 collect five shekels[a] for each one, according
to the sanctuary shekel, which weighs twenty gerahs. 48 Give the money for the
redemption of the additional Israelites to Aaron and his sons."
49 So Moses collected the redemption money from those who exceeded the
number redeemed by the Levites. 50 From the firstborn of the Israelites he collected silver weighing 1,365 shekels,[b] according to the sanctuary shekel. 51 Moses
gave the redemption money to Aaron and his sons, as he was commanded by the
word of the LORD.

The Kohathites

4 The LORD said to Moses and Aaron: 2 "Take a census of the Kohathite branch
of the Levites by their clans and families. 3 Count all the men from thirty to
fifty years of age who come to serve in the work at the tent of meeting.

4 "This is the work of the Kohathites at the tent of meeting: the care of the most
holy things. 5 When the camp is to move, Aaron and his sons are to go in and take
down the shielding curtain and put it over the ark of the covenant law. 6 Then
they are to cover the curtain with a durable leather,[c] spread a cloth of solid blue
over that and put the poles in place.

7 "Over the table of the Presence they are to spread a blue cloth and put on it
the plates, dishes and bowls, and the jars for drink offerings; the bread that is
continually there is to remain on it. 8 They are to spread a scarlet cloth over them,
cover that with the durable leather and put the poles in place.

9 "They are to take a blue cloth and cover the lampstand that is for light, together with its lamps, its wick trimmers and trays, and all its jars for the olive oil
used to supply it. 10 Then they are to wrap it and all its accessories in a covering
of the durable leather and put it on a carrying frame.

11 "Over the gold altar they are to spread a blue cloth and cover that with the
durable leather and put the poles in place.

---

[a] *47* That is, about 2 ounces or about 58 grams [b] *50* That is, about 35 pounds or about 16 kilograms [c] *6* Possibly the hides of large aquatic mammals; also in verses 8, 10, 11, 12, 14 and 25

12“They are to take all the articles used for ministering in the sanctuary, wrap them in a blue cloth, cover that with the durable leather and put them on a carrying frame.

13“They are to remove the ashes from the bronze altar and spread a purple cloth over it. 14Then they are to place on it all the utensils used for ministering at the altar, including the firepans, meat forks, shovels and sprinkling bowls. Over it they are to spread a covering of the durable leather and put the poles in place.

15“After Aaron and his sons have finished covering the holy furnishings and all the holy articles, and when the camp is ready to move, only then are the Kohathites to come and do the carrying. But they must not touch the holy things or they will die. The Kohathites are to carry those things that are in the tent of meeting.

16“Eleazar son of Aaron, the priest, is to have charge of the oil for the light, the fragrant incense, the regular grain offering and the anointing oil. He is to be in charge of the entire tabernacle and everything in it, including its holy furnishings and articles.”

17The LORD said to Moses and Aaron, 18“See that the Kohathite tribal clans are not destroyed from among the Levites. 19So that they may live and not die when they come near the most holy things, do this for them: Aaron and his sons are to go into the sanctuary and assign to each man his work and what he is to carry. 20But the Kohathites must not go in to look at the holy things, even for a moment, or they will die.”

The Gershonites

21The LORD said to Moses, 22“Take a census also of the Gershonites by their families and clans. 23Count all the men from thirty to fifty years of age who come to serve in the work at the tent of meeting.

24“This is the service of the Gershonite clans in their carrying and their other work: 25They are to carry the curtains of the tabernacle, that is, the tent of meeting, its covering and its outer covering of durable leather, the curtains for the entrance to the tent of meeting, 26the curtains of the courtyard surrounding the tabernacle and altar, the curtain for the entrance to the courtyard, the ropes and all the equipment used in the service of the tent. The Gershonites are to do all that needs to be done with these things. 27All their service, whether carrying or doing other work, is to be done under the direction of Aaron and his sons. You shall assign to them as their responsibility all they are to carry. 28This is the service of the Gershonite clans at the tent of meeting. Their duties are to be under the direction of Ithamar son of Aaron, the priest.

The Merarites

29“Count the Merarites by their clans and families. 30Count all the men from thirty to fifty years of age who come to serve in the work at the tent of meeting. 31As part of all their service at the tent, they are to carry the frames of the tabernacle, its crossbars, posts and bases, 32as well as the posts of the surrounding courtyard with their bases, tent pegs, ropes, all their equipment and everything related to their use. Assign to each man the specific things he is to carry. 33This is the service of the Merarite clans as they work at the tent of meeting under the direction of Ithamar son of Aaron, the priest.”

The Numbering of the Levite Clans

34Moses, Aaron and the leaders of the community counted the Kohathites by their clans and families. 35All the men from thirty to fifty years of age who came to serve in the work at the tent of meeting, 36counted by clans, were 2,750. 37This was the total of all those in the Kohathite clans who served at the tent of meeting. Moses and Aaron counted them according to the LORD’s command through Moses.

38The Gershonites were counted by their clans and families. 39All the men

SEPARATION

Since Adam and Eve's sin in the garden, the people of God are separated from the presence of God. This division between mankind and God is first marked by "cherubim and a flaming sword" that kept sinful humanity from the tree of life (Ge 3:24).

Subsequently, the presence of God dwelled among the people in the tent of meeting. There, too, God's people had symbolic dividing walls between themselves and the holy things of God. Inside the tabernacle, curtains were used to mark the boundaries past which the people were not allowed to enter. Only certain people were permitted to go past the curtains — and then only in carefully prescribed ways and at designated times. These verses describe the different layers of curtains that marked divisions between the Most Holy Place and everything outside of that. The Gershonites were responsible for carrying these curtains and putting them in place. Once in place, these curtains marked the fact that God was set apart. Furthermore, the curtains represented the fact that there were many different layers that the people had to go through before they were able to come before God, and it was a long process before they were able to experience his presence. The curtains made it clear that God was distinct, holy and — without a sacrificial offering — altogether unapproachable by fallen humanity.

These divisions were rendered obsolete as a result of Jesus' work on the cross. The moment of Jesus' death was marked by a stunning occurrence. The immense curtain in the temple was torn in two from top to bottom (Mk 15:38), demonstrating that God had opened the way for people to enter God's presence. No longer do God's image-bearers need to stand at a distance, separated by dividing walls, but by virtue of Christ's work they can dwell in God's presence again. In addition, Paul wrote that Christ's work tears down the "dividing wall of hostility" that has separated different types of people from one another (Eph 2:14). Now all people, regardless of gender, race or other distinguishing marks, can enter the presence of God as one people. There they will find not walls that divide but a Savior who welcomes sinners and invites them to enter his presence in worship.

from thirty to fifty years of age who came to serve in the work at the tent of meeting, 40counted by their clans and families, were 2,630. 41This was the total of those in the Gershonite clans who served at the tent of meeting. Moses and Aaron counted them according to the LORD's command.

42The Merarites were counted by their clans and families. 43All the men from thirty to fifty years of age who came to serve in the work at the tent of meeting, 44counted by their clans, were 3,200. 45This was the total of those in the Merarite clans. Moses and Aaron counted them according to the LORD's command through Moses.

46So Moses, Aaron and the leaders of Israel counted all the Levites by their clans and families. 47All the men from thirty to fifty years of age who came to do the work of serving and carrying the tent of meeting 48numbered 8,580. 49At the LORD's command through Moses, each was assigned his work and told what to carry.

Thus they were counted, as the LORD commanded Moses.

The Purity of the Camp

5 The LORD said to Moses, 2"Command the Israelites to send away from the camp anyone who has a defiling skin disease[a] or a discharge of any kind, or who is ceremonially unclean because of a dead body. 3Send away male and female alike; send them outside the camp so they will not defile their camp, where I dwell among them." 4The Israelites did so; they sent them outside the camp. They did just as the LORD had instructed Moses.

Restitution for Wrongs

5The LORD said to Moses, 6"Say to the Israelites: 'Any man or woman who wrongs another in any way[b] and so is unfaithful to the LORD is guilty 7and must confess the sin they have committed. They must make full restitution for the wrong they have done, add a fifth of the value to it and give it all to the person they have wronged. 8But if that person has no close relative to whom restitution can be made for the wrong, the restitution belongs to the LORD and must be given to the priest, along with the ram with which atonement is made for the wrongdoer. 9All the sacred contributions the Israelites bring to a priest will belong to him. 10Sacred things belong to their owners, but what they give to the priest will belong to the priest.' "

The Test for an Unfaithful Wife

11Then the LORD said to Moses, 12"Speak to the Israelites and say to them: 'If a man's wife goes astray and is unfaithful to him 13so that another man has sexual relations with her, and this is hidden from her husband and her impurity is undetected (since there is no witness against her and she has not been caught in the act), 14and if feelings of jealousy come over her husband and he suspects his wife and she is impure — or if he is jealous and suspects her even though she is not impure — 15then he is to take his wife to the priest. He must also take an offering of a tenth of an ephah[c] of barley flour on her behalf. He must not pour olive oil on it or put incense on it, because it is a grain offering for jealousy, a reminder-offering to draw attention to wrongdoing.

16" 'The priest shall bring her and have her stand before the LORD. 17Then he shall take some holy water in a clay jar and put some dust from the tabernacle floor into the water. 18After the priest has had the woman stand before the LORD, he shall loosen her hair and place in her hands the reminder-offering, the grain offering for jealousy, while he himself holds the bitter water that brings a curse. 19Then the priest shall put the woman under oath and say to her, "If no other man

---

[a] *2* The Hebrew word for *defiling skin disease,* traditionally translated "leprosy," was used for various diseases affecting the skin. [b] *6* Or *woman who commits any wrong common to mankind* [c] *15* That is, probably about 3 1/2 pounds or about 1.6 kilograms

has had sexual relations with you and you have not gone astray and become impure while married to your husband, may this bitter water that brings a curse not harm you. [20]But if you have gone astray while married to your husband and you have made yourself impure by having sexual relations with a man other than your husband" — [21]here the priest is to put the woman under this curse — "may the LORD cause you to become a curse[a] among your people when he makes your womb miscarry and your abdomen swell. [22]May this water that brings a curse enter your body so that your abdomen swells or your womb miscarries."

" 'Then the woman is to say, "Amen. So be it."

[23]" 'The priest is to write these curses on a scroll and then wash them off into the bitter water. [24]He shall make the woman drink the bitter water that brings a curse, and this water that brings a curse and causes bitter suffering will enter her. [25]The priest is to take from her hands the grain offering for jealousy, wave it before the LORD and bring it to the altar. [26]The priest is then to take a handful of the grain offering as a memorial[b] offering and burn it on the altar; after that, he is to have the woman drink the water. [27]If she has made herself impure and been unfaithful to her husband, this will be the result: When she is made to drink the water that brings a curse and causes bitter suffering, it will enter her, her abdomen will swell and her womb will miscarry, and she will become a curse. [28]If, however, the woman has not made herself impure, but is clean, she will be cleared of guilt and will be able to have children.

[29]" 'This, then, is the law of jealousy when a woman goes astray and makes herself impure while married to her husband, [30]or when feelings of jealousy come over a man because he suspects his wife. The priest is to have her stand before the LORD and is to apply this entire law to her. [31]The husband will be innocent of any wrongdoing, but the woman will bear the consequences of her sin.' "

The Nazirite

6 The LORD said to Moses, [2]"Speak to the Israelites and say to them: 'If a man or woman wants to make a special vow, a vow of dedication to the LORD as a Nazirite, [3]they must abstain from wine and other fermented drink and must not drink vinegar made from wine or other fermented drink. They must not drink grape juice or eat grapes or raisins. [4]As long as they remain under their Nazirite vow, they must not eat anything that comes from the grapevine, not even the seeds or skins.

[5]" 'During the entire period of their Nazirite vow, no razor may be used on their head. They must be holy until the period of their dedication to the LORD is over; they must let their hair grow long.

[6]" 'Throughout the period of their dedication to the LORD, the Nazirite must not go near a dead body. [7]Even if their own father or mother or brother or sister dies, they must not make themselves ceremonially unclean on account of them, because the symbol of their dedication to God is on their head. [8]Throughout the period of their dedication, they are consecrated to the LORD.

[9]" 'If someone dies suddenly in the Nazirite's presence, thus defiling the hair that symbolizes their dedication, they must shave their head on the seventh day — the day of their cleansing. [10]Then on the eighth day they must bring two doves or two young pigeons to the priest at the entrance to the tent of meeting. [11]The priest is to offer one as a sin offering[c] and the other as a burnt offering to make atonement for the Nazirite because they sinned by being in the presence of the dead body. That same day they are to consecrate their head again. [12]They must rededicate themselves to the LORD for the same period of dedication and must bring a year-old male lamb as a guilt offering. The previous days do not count, because they became defiled during their period of dedication.

[a] *21* That is, may he cause your name to be used in cursing (see Jer. 29:22); or, may others see that you are cursed; similarly in verse 27. [b] *26* Or *representative* [c] *11* Or *purification offering*; also in verses 14 and 16

NUMBERS 6:2 – 15

NAZIRITE

Any Israelite who desired to make a special promise or commitment to God would make a Nazirite vow. The vow was intended to mark these individuals as holy — uniquely set apart for God for a prescribed period of time (v. 8). The person who made this vow committed to abstain from eating or drinking "anything that comes from the grapevine" (vv. 3 – 4), cutting their hair (v. 5) and going near a dead body (vv. 6 – 7). If someone died suddenly in a Nazirite's presence, the Nazirite became defiled and had to bring a sacrifice to the priest (vv. 9 – 15). These procedures were marks of holiness among the people of God.

Jesus, however, did not commit himself to such practices. He was known for touching the diseased and the dead and associating himself with tax collectors and other notorious sinners (Lk 5:13; 7:34). Association with brokenness, not asceticism, marked the way the Son of God demonstrated extreme commitment to the Father. Similarly, the church is meant to live on a mission to the margins of society, caring for the broken and wounded. In doing so, the church models the holiness demonstrated by Jesus himself.

13“ ‘Now this is the law of the Nazirite when the period of their dedication is over. They are to be brought to the entrance to the tent of meeting. 14There they are to present their offerings to the LORD: a year-old male lamb without defect for a burnt offering, a year-old ewe lamb without defect for a sin offering, a ram without defect for a fellowship offering, 15together with their grain offerings and drink offerings, and a basket of bread made with the finest flour and without yeast—thick loaves with olive oil mixed in, and thin loaves brushed with olive oil.

16“ ‘The priest is to present all these before the LORD and make the sin offering and the burnt offering. 17He is to present the basket of unleavened bread and is to sacrifice the ram as a fellowship offering to the LORD, together with its grain offering and drink offering.

18“ ‘Then at the entrance to the tent of meeting, the Nazirite must shave off the hair that symbolizes their dedication. They are to take the hair and put it in the fire that is under the sacrifice of the fellowship offering.

19“ ‘After the Nazirite has shaved off the hair that symbolizes their dedication, the priest is to place in their hands a boiled shoulder of the ram, and one thick loaf and one thin loaf from the basket, both made without yeast. 20The priest shall then wave these before the LORD as a wave offering; they are holy and belong to the priest, together with the breast that was waved and the thigh that was presented. After that, the Nazirite may drink wine.

21“ ‘This is the law of the Nazirite who vows offerings to the LORD in accordance with their dedication, in addition to whatever else they can afford. They must fulfill the vows they have made, according to the law of the Nazirite.’ ”

The Priestly Blessing

22The LORD said to Moses, 23“Tell Aaron and his sons, ‘This is how you are to bless the Israelites. Say to them:

24“ ‘ “The LORD bless you
and keep you;
25the LORD make his face shine on you
and be gracious to you;
26the LORD turn his face toward you
and give you peace.” ’

27“So they will put my name on the Israelites, and I will bless them.”

Offerings at the Dedication of the Tabernacle

7 When Moses finished setting up the tabernacle, he anointed and consecrated it and all its furnishings. He also anointed and consecrated the altar and all its utensils. 2Then the leaders of Israel, the heads of families who were the tribal leaders in charge of those who were counted, made offerings. 3They brought as their gifts before the LORD six covered carts and twelve oxen—an ox from each leader and a cart from every two. These they presented before the tabernacle.

4The LORD said to Moses, 5“Accept these from them, that they may be used in the work at the tent of meeting. Give them to the Levites as each man’s work requires.”

6So Moses took the carts and oxen and gave them to the Levites. 7He gave two carts and four oxen to the Gershonites, as their work required, 8and he gave four carts and eight oxen to the Merarites, as their work required. They were all under the direction of Ithamar son of Aaron, the priest. 9But Moses did not give any to the Kohathites, because they were to carry on their shoulders the holy things, for which they were responsible.

10When the altar was anointed, the leaders brought their offerings for its dedication and presented them before the altar. 11For the LORD had said to Moses, “Each day one leader is to bring his offering for the dedication of the altar.”

NUMBERS 7:1

ANOINTED

The symbolic anointing with oil was a critical, outward mark that indicated God had selected a person or object to fulfill a unique role in his plan for the community. Priests, like Aaron, received this anointing, as did prophets and kings (Ex 30:30; 1Ki 19:16). The anointing usually came from an important leader and was often given to the next-generation leader at the outset of his ministry.

At the opening of Jesus’ ministry, he was also anointed by God the Father, who poured out nothing less than the Holy Spirit on Jesus’ life and work on earth (Ac 10:37–38). This unique anointing was beyond any anointing witnessed thus far in Scripture. God himself proclaimed the blessing over Jesus (Mt 3:17), emphasizing his pleasure in the Son as Moses alluded to in the Aaronic benediction (Nu 6:22–27). Thus Jesus is the archetypal anointed one—the Christ. This anointing of Christ still has lasting effects for the people of God today. Christians, because of their relationship with Jesus, also receive anointing for their commission to spread the fame of God to the nations. Just as the Holy Spirit descended on Christ, so he dwells within believers today (2Co 1:21–22).

THREE BLESSINGS

God's people received innumerable blessings from the hand of God. In this passage, the Lord instructed Moses to tell Aaron and his sons to say a blessing on the people. This famous Aaronic benediction declared the blessing that would rest on all of the people by virtue of God's care. This blessing, which immediately followed a lengthy description of the Nazirite vow, made it clear that the people would receive God's blessings through his benevolence and not through outstanding acts of devotion on their part. The recounted actions provide vivid images of God's goodness. He promised to bless and keep his people. He assured them that he would accomplish his good purposes and plans and would make his face shine on them, allowing them to have an intimate sense of the presence of his glory — splendor and beauty akin to what Moses experienced when he talked with God on Mount Sinai (Ex 34:29 – 35). God would be gracious to the people, allowing them access to his presence (in spite of their sin). His countenance would be lifted up toward the people. Rather than a scornful expression of wrath, God would smile upon the people in love. And he would give them peace with himself and with one another.

Jesus offered a similar priestly prayer in the Garden of Gethsemane prior to his crucifixion (Jn 17:1 – 26). He first prayed for himself (v. 2). Then he asked the Father to protect his disciples from the evil one and his schemes in the world (vv. 11,15). Jesus prayed that the Father would give them grace to be transformed by God's Word so that they could be sent on a mission into the world (vv. 17 – 18). He longed for believers to experience the peace found in the perfect unity of the Godhead and to reflect this peace in oneness with those whom God came to save (vv. 22 – 23). Finally, he asked that they would see the glory of God and find delight in his presence (v. 24). These prayers would come to pass in Christ's death, burial and resurrection as the great high priest and perfect Lamb of God.

12 The one who brought his offering on the first day was Nahshon son of Amminadab of the tribe of Judah.

13 His offering was one silver plate weighing a hundred and thirty shekels[a] and one silver sprinkling bowl weighing seventy shekels,[b] both according to the sanctuary shekel, each filled with the finest flour mixed with olive oil as a grain offering; 14 one gold dish weighing ten shekels,[c] filled with incense; 15 one young bull, one ram and one male lamb a year old for a burnt offering; 16 one male goat for a sin offering[d]; 17 and two oxen, five rams, five male goats and five male lambs a year old to be sacrificed as a fellowship offering. This was the offering of Nahshon son of Amminadab.

18 On the second day Nethanel son of Zuar, the leader of Issachar, brought his offering.

19 The offering he brought was one silver plate weighing a hundred and thirty shekels and one silver sprinkling bowl weighing seventy shekels, both according to the sanctuary shekel, each filled with the finest flour mixed with olive oil as a grain offering; 20 one gold dish weighing ten shekels, filled with incense; 21 one young bull, one ram and one male lamb a year old for a burnt offering; 22 one male goat for a sin offering; 23 and two oxen, five rams, five male goats and five male lambs a year old to be sacrificed as a fellowship offering. This was the offering of Nethanel son of Zuar.

24 On the third day, Eliab son of Helon, the leader of the people of Zebulun, brought his offering.

25 His offering was one silver plate weighing a hundred and thirty shekels and one silver sprinkling bowl weighing seventy shekels, both according to the sanctuary shekel, each filled with the finest flour mixed with olive oil as a grain offering; 26 one gold dish weighing ten shekels, filled with incense; 27 one young bull, one ram and one male lamb a year old for a burnt offering; 28 one male goat for a sin offering; 29 and two oxen, five rams, five male goats and five male lambs a year old to be sacrificed as a fellowship offering. This was the offering of Eliab son of Helon.

30 On the fourth day Elizur son of Shedeur, the leader of the people of Reuben, brought his offering.

31 His offering was one silver plate weighing a hundred and thirty shekels and one silver sprinkling bowl weighing seventy shekels, both according to the sanctuary shekel, each filled with the finest flour mixed with olive oil as a grain offering; 32 one gold dish weighing ten shekels, filled with incense; 33 one young bull, one ram and one male lamb a year old for a burnt offering; 34 one male goat for a sin offering; 35 and two oxen, five rams, five male goats and five male lambs a year old to be sacrificed as a fellowship offering. This was the offering of Elizur son of Shedeur.

36 On the fifth day Shelumiel son of Zurishaddai, the leader of the people of Simeon, brought his offering.

37 His offering was one silver plate weighing a hundred and thirty shekels and one silver sprinkling bowl weighing seventy shekels, both according to the sanctuary shekel, each filled with the finest flour mixed with olive oil as a grain offering; 38 one gold dish weighing ten shekels, filled with incense; 39 one young bull, one ram and one male lamb a year old for a burnt offering; 40 one male goat for a sin offering; 41 and two oxen, five rams, five male goats and five male lambs a year old to be sacrificed as a fellowship offering. This was the offering of Shelumiel son of Zurishaddai.

---

[a] *13* That is, about 3 1/4 pounds or about 1.5 kilograms; also elsewhere in this chapter
[b] *13* That is, about 1 3/4 pounds or about 800 grams; also elsewhere in this chapter
[c] *14* That is, about 4 ounces or about 115 grams; also elsewhere in this chapter [d] *16* Or *purification offering*; also elsewhere in this chapter

[42]On the sixth day Eliasaph son of Deuel, the leader of the people of Gad, brought
his offering.
[43]His offering was one silver plate weighing a hundred and thirty shekels
and one silver sprinkling bowl weighing seventy shekels, both according
to the sanctuary shekel, each filled with the finest flour mixed with olive
oil as a grain offering; [44]one gold dish weighing ten shekels, filled with incense; [45]one young bull, one ram and one male lamb a year old for a burnt
offering; [46]one male goat for a sin offering; [47]and two oxen, five rams, five
male goats and five male lambs a year old to be sacrificed as a fellowship
offering. This was the offering of Eliasaph son of Deuel.

[48]On the seventh day Elishama son of Ammihud, the leader of the people of
Ephraim, brought his offering.
[49]His offering was one silver plate weighing a hundred and thirty shekels
and one silver sprinkling bowl weighing seventy shekels, both according
to the sanctuary shekel, each filled with the finest flour mixed with olive
oil as a grain offering; [50]one gold dish weighing ten shekels, filled with incense; [51]one young bull, one ram and one male lamb a year old for a burnt
offering; [52]one male goat for a sin offering; [53]and two oxen, five rams, five
male goats and five male lambs a year old to be sacrificed as a fellowship
offering. This was the offering of Elishama son of Ammihud.

[54]On the eighth day Gamaliel son of Pedahzur, the leader of the people of Manasseh, brought his offering.
[55]His offering was one silver plate weighing a hundred and thirty shekels
and one silver sprinkling bowl weighing seventy shekels, both according
to the sanctuary shekel, each filled with the finest flour mixed with olive
oil as a grain offering; [56]one gold dish weighing ten shekels, filled with incense; [57]one young bull, one ram and one male lamb a year old for a burnt
offering; [58]one male goat for a sin offering; [59]and two oxen, five rams, five
male goats and five male lambs a year old to be sacrificed as a fellowship
offering. This was the offering of Gamaliel son of Pedahzur.

[60]On the ninth day Abidan son of Gideoni, the leader of the people of Benjamin,
brought his offering.
[61]His offering was one silver plate weighing a hundred and thirty shekels
and one silver sprinkling bowl weighing seventy shekels, both according
to the sanctuary shekel, each filled with the finest flour mixed with olive
oil as a grain offering; [62]one gold dish weighing ten shekels, filled with incense; [63]one young bull, one ram and one male lamb a year old for a burnt
offering; [64]one male goat for a sin offering; [65]and two oxen, five rams, five
male goats and five male lambs a year old to be sacrificed as a fellowship
offering. This was the offering of Abidan son of Gideoni.

[66]On the tenth day Ahiezer son of Ammishaddai, the leader of the people of Dan,
brought his offering.
[67]His offering was one silver plate weighing a hundred and thirty shekels
and one silver sprinkling bowl weighing seventy shekels, both according
to the sanctuary shekel, each filled with the finest flour mixed with olive
oil as a grain offering; [68]one gold dish weighing ten shekels, filled with incense; [69]one young bull, one ram and one male lamb a year old for a burnt
offering; [70]one male goat for a sin offering; [71]and two oxen, five rams, five
male goats and five male lambs a year old to be sacrificed as a fellowship
offering. This was the offering of Ahiezer son of Ammishaddai.

[72]On the eleventh day Pagiel son of Okran, the leader of the people of Asher,
brought his offering.
[73]His offering was one silver plate weighing a hundred and thirty shekels
and one silver sprinkling bowl weighing seventy shekels, both according
to the sanctuary shekel, each filled with the finest flour mixed with olive

oil as a grain offering; [74]one gold dish weighing ten shekels, filled with incense; [75]one young bull, one ram and one male lamb a year old for a burnt
offering; [76]one male goat for a sin offering; [77]and two oxen, five rams, five
male goats and five male lambs a year old to be sacrificed as a fellowship
offering. This was the offering of Pagiel son of Okran.

[78]On the twelfth day Ahira son of Enan, the leader of the people of Naphtali,
brought his offering.

[79]His offering was one silver plate weighing a hundred and thirty shekels
and one silver sprinkling bowl weighing seventy shekels, both according
to the sanctuary shekel, each filled with the finest flour mixed with olive
oil as a grain offering; [80]one gold dish weighing ten shekels, filled with incense; [81]one young bull, one ram and one male lamb a year old for a burnt
offering; [82]one male goat for a sin offering; [83]and two oxen, five rams, five
male goats and five male lambs a year old to be sacrificed as a fellowship
offering. This was the offering of Ahira son of Enan.

[84]These were the offerings of the Israelite leaders for the dedication of the altar when it was anointed: twelve silver plates, twelve silver sprinkling bowls and
twelve gold dishes. [85]Each silver plate weighed a hundred and thirty shekels,
and each sprinkling bowl seventy shekels. Altogether, the silver dishes weighed
two thousand four hundred shekels,[a] according to the sanctuary shekel. [86]The
twelve gold dishes filled with incense weighed ten shekels each, according to
the sanctuary shekel. Altogether, the gold dishes weighed a hundred and twenty shekels.[b] [87]The total number of animals for the burnt offering came to twelve
young bulls, twelve rams and twelve male lambs a year old, together with their
grain offering. Twelve male goats were used for the sin offering. [88]The total number of animals for the sacrifice of the fellowship offering came to twenty-four
oxen, sixty rams, sixty male goats and sixty male lambs a year old. These were
the offerings for the dedication of the altar after it was anointed.

[89]When Moses entered the tent of meeting to speak with the LORD, he heard
the voice speaking to him from between the two cherubim above the atonement
cover on the ark of the covenant law. In this way the LORD spoke to him.

Setting Up the Lamps

8 The LORD said to Moses, [2]"Speak to Aaron and say to him, 'When you set up
the lamps, see that all seven light up the area in front of the lampstand.' "

[3]Aaron did so; he set up the lamps so that they faced forward on the lampstand, just as the LORD commanded Moses. [4]This is how the lampstand was
made: It was made of hammered gold—from its base to its blossoms. The lampstand was made exactly like the pattern the LORD had shown Moses.

The Setting Apart of the Levites

[5]The LORD said to Moses: [6]"Take the Levites from among all the Israelites and
make them ceremonially clean. [7]To purify them, do this: Sprinkle the water of
cleansing on them; then have them shave their whole bodies and wash their
clothes. And so they will purify themselves. [8]Have them take a young bull with
its grain offering of the finest flour mixed with olive oil; then you are to take a
second young bull for a sin offering.[c] [9]Bring the Levites to the front of the tent of
meeting and assemble the whole Israelite community. [10]You are to bring the Levites before the LORD, and the Israelites are to lay their hands on them. [11]Aaron
is to present the Levites before the LORD as a wave offering from the Israelites, so
that they may be ready to do the work of the LORD.

[12]"Then the Levites are to lay their hands on the heads of the bulls, using one
for a sin offering to the LORD and the other for a burnt offering, to make atonement for the Levites. [13]Have the Levites stand in front of Aaron and his sons and

NUMBERS 8:5–22

PURIFICATION OF THE LEVITES

The purification and dedication of the Levites is a drama that acted out the love of the Father and the sacrifice of the Son. First, in order to bring the Levites into God's presence, a sacrifice was necessary (vv. 12–14). In the second act, the Levites were dedicated to God's service as living sacrifices in order to bring the whole nation into fellowship with God (vv. 15–19). They became a firstborn sacrifice—the best the nation had to offer to satisfy the demand of God's Law. As a Levite, their lives were to be marked by a distinctive holiness.

In a similar drama, Jesus gave himself as the great sacrifice for sin (Col 1:14,20). He is the one who restores, not just a tribe or nation, but the entire cosmos to a relationship with God. And he is God's firstborn—the best God has to satisfy the demand of his Law (v. 15).

[a] *85* That is, about 60 pounds or about 28 kilograms [b] *86* That is, about 3 pounds or about 1.4 kilograms [c] *8* Or *purification offering*; also in verse 12

then present them as a wave offering to the LORD. 14In this way you are to set the
Levites apart from the other Israelites, and the Levites will be mine.
15"After you have purified the Levites and presented them as a wave offering,
they are to come to do their work at the tent of meeting. 16They are the Israelites
who are to be given wholly to me. I have taken them as my own in place of the
firstborn, the first male offspring from every Israelite woman. 17Every firstborn
male in Israel, whether human or animal, is mine. When I struck down all the
firstborn in Egypt, I set them apart for myself. 18And I have taken the Levites in
place of all the firstborn sons in Israel. 19From among all the Israelites, I have giv-
en the Levites as gifts to Aaron and his sons to do the work at the tent of meeting
on behalf of the Israelites and to make atonement for them so that no plague will
strike the Israelites when they go near the sanctuary."
20Moses, Aaron and the whole Israelite community did with the Levites just
as the LORD commanded Moses. 21The Levites purified themselves and washed
their clothes. Then Aaron presented them as a wave offering before the LORD
and made atonement for them to purify them. 22After that, the Levites came to
do their work at the tent of meeting under the supervision of Aaron and his sons.
They did with the Levites just as the LORD commanded Moses.
23The LORD said to Moses, 24"This applies to the Levites: Men twenty-five
years old or more shall come to take part in the work at the tent of meeting, 25but
at the age of fifty, they must retire from their regular service and work no longer.
26They may assist their brothers in performing their duties at the tent of meeting,
but they themselves must not do the work. This, then, is how you are to assign the
responsibilities of the Levites."

The Passover

9 The LORD spoke to Moses in the Desert of Sinai in the first month of the second year after they came out of Egypt. He said, 2"Have the Israelites celebrate the Passover at the appointed time. 3Celebrate it at the appointed time,
at twilight on the fourteenth day of this month, in accordance with all its rules
and regulations."
4So Moses told the Israelites to celebrate the Passover, 5and they did so in the
Desert of Sinai at twilight on the fourteenth day of the first month. The Israelites
did everything just as the LORD commanded Moses.
6But some of them could not celebrate the Passover on that day because they
were ceremonially unclean on account of a dead body. So they came to Moses
and Aaron that same day 7and said to Moses, "We have become unclean because
of a dead body, but why should we be kept from presenting the LORD's offering
with the other Israelites at the appointed time?"
8Moses answered them, "Wait until I find out what the LORD commands concerning you."
9Then the LORD said to Moses, 10"Tell the Israelites: 'When any of you or your
descendants are unclean because of a dead body or are away on a journey, they are
still to celebrate the LORD's Passover, 11but they are to do it on the fourteenth day of
the second month at twilight. They are to eat the lamb, together with unleavened
bread and bitter herbs. 12They must not leave any of it till morning or break any of
its bones. When they celebrate the Passover, they must follow all the regulations.
13But if anyone who is ceremonially clean and not on a journey fails to celebrate
the Passover, they must be cut off from their people for not presenting the LORD's
offering at the appointed time. They will bear the consequences of their sin.
14" 'A foreigner residing among you is also to celebrate the LORD's Passover in
accordance with its rules and regulations. You must have the same regulations
for both the foreigner and the native-born.' "

The Cloud Above the Tabernacle

15On the day the tabernacle, the tent of the covenant law, was set up, the cloud
covered it. From evening till morning the cloud above the tabernacle looked like

---

NUMBERS 9:1 – 14

THE PASSOVER

The Passover was a particularly poignant time in the life of the people of God. It served as an ongoing reminder of the Lord's protection and stood as a lasting reminder that the Lord had delivered his people and that he would surely fulfill his promises on their behalf. Here, at the base of Mount Sinai, the people celebrated the Passover before their journey to the land of Canaan.

In the New Testament, Jesus celebrated the Passover with his disciples before his journey to the cross. The significance of Jesus celebrating the Passover with his disciples is that he acknowledged the Lord's provision both throughout history and through what was about to occur in his crucifixion. Jesus knew that his death on the cross and resurrection from the dead was a fulfillment of God's promises to his people. A festival that had been celebrated throughout Israel's history completely changed when Jesus offered his body as an eternal sacrifice.

fire. 16That is how it continued to be; the cloud covered it, and at night it looked like fire. 17Whenever the cloud lifted from above the tent, the Israelites set out; wherever the cloud settled, the Israelites encamped. 18At the LORD's command the Israelites set out, and at his command they encamped. As long as the cloud stayed over the tabernacle, they remained in camp. 19When the cloud remained over the tabernacle a long time, the Israelites obeyed the LORD's order and did not set out. 20Sometimes the cloud was over the tabernacle only a few days; at the LORD's command they would encamp, and then at his command they would set out. 21Sometimes the cloud stayed only from evening till morning, and when it lifted in the morning, they set out. Whether by day or by night, whenever the cloud lifted, they set out. 22Whether the cloud stayed over the tabernacle for two days or a month or a year, the Israelites would remain in camp and not set out; but when it lifted, they would set out. 23At the LORD's command they encamped, and at the LORD's command they set out. They obeyed the LORD's order, in accordance with his command through Moses.

The Silver Trumpets

10 The LORD said to Moses: 2"Make two trumpets of hammered silver, and use them for calling the community together and for having the camps set out. 3When both are sounded, the whole community is to assemble before you at the entrance to the tent of meeting. 4If only one is sounded, the leaders — the heads of the clans of Israel — are to assemble before you. 5When a trumpet blast is sounded, the tribes camping on the east are to set out. 6At the sounding of a second blast, the camps on the south are to set out. The blast will be the signal for setting out. 7To gather the assembly, blow the trumpets, but not with the signal for setting out.

8"The sons of Aaron, the priests, are to blow the trumpets. This is to be a lasting ordinance for you and the generations to come. 9When you go into battle in your own land against an enemy who is oppressing you, sound a blast on the trumpets. Then you will be remembered by the LORD your God and rescued from your enemies. 10Also at your times of rejoicing — your appointed festivals and New Moon feasts — you are to sound the trumpets over your burnt offerings and fellowship offerings, and they will be a memorial for you before your God. I am the LORD your God."

The Israelites Leave Sinai

11On the twentieth day of the second month of the second year, the cloud lifted from above the tabernacle of the covenant law. 12Then the Israelites set out from the Desert of Sinai and traveled from place to place until the cloud came to rest in the Desert of Paran. 13They set out, this first time, at the LORD's command through Moses.

14The divisions of the camp of Judah went first, under their standard. Nahshon son of Amminadab was in command. 15Nethanel son of Zuar was over the division of the tribe of Issachar, 16and Eliab son of Helon was over the division of the tribe of Zebulun. 17Then the tabernacle was taken down, and the Gershonites and Merarites, who carried it, set out.

18The divisions of the camp of Reuben went next, under their standard. Elizur son of Shedeur was in command. 19Shelumiel son of Zurishaddai was over the division of the tribe of Simeon, 20and Eliasaph son of Deuel was over the division of the tribe of Gad. 21Then the Kohathites set out, carrying the holy things. The tabernacle was to be set up before they arrived.

22The divisions of the camp of Ephraim went next, under their standard. Elishama son of Ammihud was in command. 23Gamaliel son of Pedahzur was over the division of the tribe of Manasseh, 24and Abidan son of Gideoni was over the division of the tribe of Benjamin.

25Finally, as the rear guard for all the units, the divisions of the camp of Dan set out under their standard. Ahiezer son of Ammishaddai was in command.

NUMBERS 10:1 – 10

TRUMPET CALLS

The sound of the trumpet served as a rallying call for the people of Israel, as a sign of advancement and as a declaration of military action. This instrument, a straight horn with a flaring hammered silver bell at the end, was used primarily to signal the movement of the nation of Israel. Whenever the trumpet sounded the people began their march to wherever God was leading them. At the sound of the trumpet declaring military action, the people of God broke camp, moved toward the land in their God-ordained arrangement and fought in the power God supplied.

Jesus secured a greater victory over an oppressive enemy through his death, burial and resurrection, yet little fanfare accompanied this first victory. However, a day is coming when the "last trumpet" will sound, Jesus will return and he will declare to the entire world that he is the victor (1Co 15:50 – 57). Until that day, believers fight a spiritual opponent in the power supplied by God's Spirit (Eph 6:10 – 17), fully trusting that Jesus has already won the battle on their behalf.

FOLLOWING JESUS

God made it clear how the people were to follow him in their journey from the wilderness to the promised land. They would not have to guess as to where God wanted them to dwell and when he wanted them to move. During the day, a cloud covered the dwelling of God in the tabernacle. There, God communed with his people. At night, this cloud turned to fire, and the entire nation saw the all-consuming presence of the Lord. When God was ready for the people to break camp and set out to a new location, the cloud moved, traveling ahead of the people to the place God wanted them to go next. God's instructions were simple: Stay put as long as the cloud and fire are there. When they move, you move. When the people did this, they could rest assured that they were following God and moving in the path he ordained.

The same simple message inaugurates Jesus' earthly ministry. "Come, follow me," he says to his newly commissioned disciples (Mt 4:19). Over the next three years, they accompanied the Son of God as he boldly proclaimed the availability of the kingdom of God and performed many miraculous signs that demonstrated the dawning of a new age. Following Jesus had much in common with the way in which the nation of Israel followed God in the wilderness. Where Jesus went, the disciples went, and there they received the blessing of his presence and provision.

Following his death and resurrection, Jesus sent the Holy Spirit to provide all subsequent believers with guidance for how they can also follow Jesus. As believers are filled with God's Spirit (Eph 5:18) and refrain from those practices that may quench his Spirit, they can follow the path that God has purposed for their lives. This path may seem less clear than following a cloud and fire in the wilderness or walking the earth following the Son of God. However, believers are now indwelt with God's Spirit — meaning that the power to obey and follow Jesus now comes from within. Rather than following external signs, God's people have the Spirit of God living within them and directing their steps to follow his ways.

26Pagiel son of Okran was over the division of the tribe of Asher, 27and Ahira son
of Enan was over the division of the tribe of Naphtali. 28This was the order of
march for the Israelite divisions as they set out.

29Now Moses said to Hobab son of Reuel the Midianite, Moses' father-in-law,
"We are setting out for the place about which the LORD said, 'I will give it to you.'
Come with us and we will treat you well, for the LORD has promised good things
to Israel."

30He answered, "No, I will not go; I am going back to my own land and my
own people."

31But Moses said, "Please do not leave us. You know where we should camp
in the wilderness, and you can be our eyes. 32If you come with us, we will share
with you whatever good things the LORD gives us."

33So they set out from the mountain of the LORD and traveled for three days.
The ark of the covenant of the LORD went before them during those three days
to find them a place to rest. 34The cloud of the LORD was over them by day when
they set out from the camp.

35Whenever the ark set out, Moses said,

"Rise up, LORD!
  May your enemies be scattered;
  may your foes flee before you."

36Whenever it came to rest, he said,

"Return, LORD,
  to the countless thousands of Israel."

Fire From the LORD

11 Now the people complained about their hardships in the hearing of the
LORD, and when he heard them his anger was aroused. Then fire from the
LORD burned among them and consumed some of the outskirts of the camp.
2When the people cried out to Moses, he prayed to the LORD and the fire died
down. 3So that place was called Taberah,[a] because fire from the LORD had
burned among them.

Quail From the LORD

4The rabble with them began to crave other food, and again the Israelites
started wailing and said, "If only we had meat to eat! 5We remember the fish we
ate in Egypt at no cost—also the cucumbers, melons, leeks, onions and garlic.
6But now we have lost our appetite; we never see anything but this manna!"

7The manna was like coriander seed and looked like resin. 8The people went
around gathering it, and then ground it in a hand mill or crushed it in a mortar.
They cooked it in a pot or made it into loaves. And it tasted like something made
with olive oil. 9When the dew settled on the camp at night, the manna also came
down.

10Moses heard the people of every family wailing at the entrance to their tents.
The LORD became exceedingly angry, and Moses was troubled. 11He asked the
LORD, "Why have you brought this trouble on your servant? What have I done to
displease you that you put the burden of all these people on me? 12Did I conceive
all these people? Did I give them birth? Why do you tell me to carry them in my
arms, as a nurse carries an infant, to the land you promised on oath to their ancestors? 13Where can I get meat for all these people? They keep wailing to me,
'Give us meat to eat!' 14I cannot carry all these people by myself; the burden is too
heavy for me. 15If this is how you are going to treat me, please go ahead and kill
me—if I have found favor in your eyes—and do not let me face my own ruin."

16The LORD said to Moses: "Bring me seventy of Israel's elders who are known
to you as leaders and officials among the people. Have them come to the tent of

---

[a] 3 *Taberah* means *burning.*

THE FIRE FROM THE LORD

The Israelites were prone to complain against the Lord and his anointed leaders. At an earlier stage, only three days after their miraculous deliverance from the Egyptian army at the Red Sea, they murmured against God because they lacked water (Ex 15:22 – 24). Here, after another three-day journey, they complained again (for unspecified reasons). Their complaints demonstrated a failure to trust God to meet the needs of his people, even though he had always cared for them. This act of rebellion necessitated the judgment of God, which came in the form of fire from the Lord that consumed some of the people. The dual attributes of God's judgment and his mercy are on display. *Some* of the people on the *outskirts* of the camp were destroyed, but not *all* of the people *throughout* the camp. The fire from the Lord is both an act of judgment and a warning to the entire nation.

Fire is symbolic of the judgment of God against the contamination of sin (Ge 19:24). During his earthly ministry, two of Jesus' disciples asked him if they should call down fire from heaven to consume an inhospitable Samaritan village. Jesus, however, rebuked the disciples (Lk 9:51 – 55).

The coming day of the Lord, at the end of this age, will be marked by the same fire of judgment (2Pe 3:10). This fire will purge the earth and all created things from the contamination brought about by sin. Those who remain hostile to God will be destroyed and thrown "into the blazing furnace, where there will be weeping and gnashing of teeth" (Mt 13:49 – 50).

These dire warnings function like the fire seen in Numbers 11. They demonstrate the unrivaled holiness of God and his utter hatred of the sins that deface his good, created order. However, God in his goodness allows time for those who do not know him to believe. His Word urges people to turn to him while it is still "Today" (Heb 3:12 – 13). Additionally, an urgency is placed on believers to make Jesus known to those who do not know him. The Lord desires that no one on earth would perish (Jn 3:16; 2Pe 3:9).

meeting, that they may stand there with you. 17 I will come down and speak with
you there, and I will take some of the power of the Spirit that is on you and put it
on them. They will share the burden of the people with you so that you will not
have to carry it alone.

18 "Tell the people: 'Consecrate yourselves in preparation for tomorrow, when
you will eat meat. The LORD heard you when you wailed, "If only we had meat to
eat! We were better off in Egypt!" Now the LORD will give you meat, and you will
eat it. 19 You will not eat it for just one day, or two days, or five, ten or twenty days,
20 but for a whole month — until it comes out of your nostrils and you loathe it —
because you have rejected the LORD, who is among you, and have wailed before
him, saying, "Why did we ever leave Egypt?"'"

21 But Moses said, "Here I am among six hundred thousand men on foot, and
you say, 'I will give them meat to eat for a whole month!' 22 Would they have
enough if flocks and herds were slaughtered for them? Would they have enough
if all the fish in the sea were caught for them?"

23 The LORD answered Moses, "Is the LORD's arm too short? Now you will see
whether or not what I say will come true for you."

24 So Moses went out and told the people what the LORD had said. He brought
together seventy of their elders and had them stand around the tent. 25 Then the
LORD came down in the cloud and spoke with him, and he took some of the power of the Spirit that was on him and put it on the seventy elders. When the Spirit
rested on them, they prophesied — but did not do so again.

26 However, two men, whose names were Eldad and Medad, had remained in
the camp. They were listed among the elders, but did not go out to the tent. Yet
the Spirit also rested on them, and they prophesied in the camp. 27 A young man
ran and told Moses, "Eldad and Medad are prophesying in the camp."

28 Joshua son of Nun, who had been Moses' aide since youth, spoke up and
said, "Moses, my lord, stop them!"

29 But Moses replied, "Are you jealous for my sake? I wish that all the LORD's
people were prophets and that the LORD would put his Spirit on them!" 30 Then
Moses and the elders of Israel returned to the camp.

31 Now a wind went out from the LORD and drove quail in from the sea. It scattered them up to two cubits[a] deep all around the camp, as far as a day's walk in
any direction. 32 All that day and night and all the next day the people went out
and gathered quail. No one gathered less than ten homers.[b] Then they spread
them out all around the camp. 33 But while the meat was still between their teeth
and before it could be consumed, the anger of the LORD burned against the people, and he struck them with a severe plague. 34 Therefore the place was named
Kibroth Hattaavah,[c] because there they buried the people who had craved other
food.

35 From Kibroth Hattaavah the people traveled to Hazeroth and stayed there.

Miriam and Aaron Oppose Moses

12 Miriam and Aaron began to talk against Moses because of his Cushite
wife, for he had married a Cushite. 2 "Has the LORD spoken only through
Moses?" they asked. "Hasn't he also spoken through us?" And the LORD heard
this.

3 (Now Moses was a very humble man, more humble than anyone else on the
face of the earth.)

4 At once the LORD said to Moses, Aaron and Miriam, "Come out to the tent of
meeting, all three of you." So the three of them went out. 5 Then the LORD came
down in a pillar of cloud; he stood at the entrance to the tent and summoned
Aaron and Miriam. When the two of them stepped forward, 6 he said, "Listen to
my words:

[a] 31 That is, about 3 feet or about 90 centimeters [b] 32 That is, possibly about 1 3/4 tons or about 1.6 metric tons [c] 34 *Kibroth Hattaavah* means *graves of craving.*

NUMBERS 12:3

HUMILITY

Moses' leadership of the people of God was characterized by unrivaled humility. This parenthetical note, added within the story of the conflict between Miriam, Aaron and Moses, demonstrated the way in which Old Testament leaders exemplified God's character. Much about Moses' life could have resulted in pride — he was chosen by God, called to lead the people, and saw firsthand God's glory. Yet his humility was singled out as a distinctive characteristic that allowed him to faithfully lead God's people. He was not, however, without fault. Like Noah and Abraham before him, his sin clouded his judgment, and this ultimately disqualified him from leading the people into the promised land (Nu 20:12).

All people, like Moses, are mere shadows of the perfection that is Jesus Christ. Jesus' humility was demonstrated by his willingness to leave the glories of heaven, take on the form of a servant, and suffer and die at the hands of the very ones he came to save (Php 2:5 – 11).

"When there is a prophet among you,
I, the LORD, reveal myself to them in visions,
I speak to them in dreams.
7 But this is not true of my servant Moses;
he is faithful in all my house.
8 With him I speak face to face,
clearly and not in riddles;
he sees the form of the LORD.
Why then were you not afraid
to speak against my servant Moses?"

9 The anger of the LORD burned against them, and he left them.
10 When the cloud lifted from above the tent, Miriam's skin was leprous[a]—
it became as white as snow. Aaron turned toward her and saw that she had a
defiling skin disease, 11 and he said to Moses, "Please, my lord, I ask you not to
hold against us the sin we have so foolishly committed. 12 Do not let her be like a
stillborn infant coming from its mother's womb with its flesh half eaten away."
13 So Moses cried out to the LORD, "Please, God, heal her!"
14 The LORD replied to Moses, "If her father had spit in her face, would she not
have been in disgrace for seven days? Confine her outside the camp for seven
days; after that she can be brought back." 15 So Miriam was confined outside the
camp for seven days, and the people did not move on till she was brought back.
16 After that, the people left Hazeroth and encamped in the Desert of Paran.

Exploring Canaan

13 The LORD said to Moses, 2 "Send some men to explore the land of Canaan,
which I am giving to the Israelites. From each ancestral tribe send one of
its leaders."
3 So at the LORD's command Moses sent them out from the Desert of Paran. All
of them were leaders of the Israelites. 4 These are their names:

from the tribe of Reuben, Shammua son of Zakkur;
5 from the tribe of Simeon, Shaphat son of Hori;
6 from the tribe of Judah, Caleb son of Jephunneh;
7 from the tribe of Issachar, Igal son of Joseph;
8 from the tribe of Ephraim, Hoshea son of Nun;
9 from the tribe of Benjamin, Palti son of Raphu;
10 from the tribe of Zebulun, Gaddiel son of Sodi;
11 from the tribe of Manasseh (a tribe of Joseph), Gaddi son of Susi;
12 from the tribe of Dan, Ammiel son of Gemalli;
13 from the tribe of Asher, Sethur son of Michael;
14 from the tribe of Naphtali, Nahbi son of Vophsi;
15 from the tribe of Gad, Geuel son of Maki.

16 These are the names of the men Moses sent to explore the land. (Moses gave
Hoshea son of Nun the name Joshua.)
17 When Moses sent them to explore Canaan, he said, "Go up through the Negev and on into the hill country. 18 See what the land is like and whether the people who live there are strong or weak, few or many. 19 What kind of land do they
live in? Is it good or bad? What kind of towns do they live in? Are they unwalled
or fortified? 20 How is the soil? Is it fertile or poor? Are there trees in it or not? Do
your best to bring back some of the fruit of the land." (It was the season for the
first ripe grapes.)
21 So they went up and explored the land from the Desert of Zin as far as Rehob,
toward Lebo Hamath. 22 They went up through the Negev and came to Hebron,
where Ahiman, Sheshai and Talmai, the descendants of Anak, lived. (Hebron
had been built seven years before Zoan in Egypt.) 23 When they reached the

[a] 10 The Hebrew for *leprous* was used for various diseases affecting the skin.

Valley of Eshkol,[a] they cut off a branch bearing a single cluster of grapes. Two of them carried it on a pole between them, along with some pomegranates and figs. 24That place was called the Valley of Eshkol because of the cluster of grapes the Israelites cut off there. 25At the end of forty days they returned from exploring the land.

Report on the Exploration

26They came back to Moses and Aaron and the whole Israelite community at Kadesh in the Desert of Paran. There they reported to them and to the whole assembly and showed them the fruit of the land. 27They gave Moses this account: "We went into the land to which you sent us, and it does flow with milk and honey! Here is its fruit. 28But the people who live there are powerful, and the cities are fortified and very large. We even saw descendants of Anak there. 29The Amalekites live in the Negev; the Hittites, Jebusites and Amorites live in the hill country; and the Canaanites live near the sea and along the Jordan."

30Then Caleb silenced the people before Moses and said, "We should go up and take possession of the land, for we can certainly do it."

31But the men who had gone up with him said, "We can't attack those people; they are stronger than we are." 32And they spread among the Israelites a bad report about the land they had explored. They said, "The land we explored devours those living in it. All the people we saw there are of great size. 33We saw the Nephilim there (the descendants of Anak come from the Nephilim). We seemed like grasshoppers in our own eyes, and we looked the same to them."

The People Rebel

14 That night all the members of the community raised their voices and wept aloud. 2All the Israelites grumbled against Moses and Aaron, and the whole assembly said to them, "If only we had died in Egypt! Or in this wilderness! 3Why is the LORD bringing us to this land only to let us fall by the sword? Our wives and children will be taken as plunder. Wouldn't it be better for us to go back to Egypt?" 4And they said to each other, "We should choose a leader and go back to Egypt."

5Then Moses and Aaron fell facedown in front of the whole Israelite assembly gathered there. 6Joshua son of Nun and Caleb son of Jephunneh, who were among those who had explored the land, tore their clothes 7and said to the entire Israelite assembly, "The land we passed through and explored is exceedingly good. 8If the LORD is pleased with us, he will lead us into that land, a land flowing with milk and honey, and will give it to us. 9Only do not rebel against the LORD. And do not be afraid of the people of the land, because we will devour them. Their protection is gone, but the LORD is with us. Do not be afraid of them."

10But the whole assembly talked about stoning them. Then the glory of the LORD appeared at the tent of meeting to all the Israelites. 11The LORD said to Moses, "How long will these people treat me with contempt? How long will they refuse to believe in me, in spite of all the signs I have performed among them? 12I will strike them down with a plague and destroy them, but I will make you into a nation greater and stronger than they."

13Moses said to the LORD, "Then the Egyptians will hear about it! By your power you brought these people up from among them. 14And they will tell the inhabitants of this land about it. They have already heard that you, LORD, are with these people and that you, LORD, have been seen face to face, that your cloud stays over them, and that you go before them in a pillar of cloud by day and a pillar of fire by night. 15If you put all these people to death, leaving none alive, the nations who have heard this report about you will say, 16'The LORD was not able to bring these people into the land he promised them on oath, so he slaughtered them in the wilderness.'

[a] 23 *Eshkol* means *cluster*; also in verse 24.

NUMBERS 14:9

THE SIN OF REBELLION

The word *rebel* poignantly describes an aspect of the nature of sin. Rebels are those who willingly disregard and disobey the directives of an established authority. The Israelites were instructed to follow the directives of God and, in so doing, take the land God had promised. However, if the people rebelled, they would face the judgment of the Lord. The stiff-necked people often failed to heed these warnings, choosing to usurp the authority of God and go their own way (Dt 1:26,43; 9:23–24). The consequences for such rebellion often involved physical destruction and divine chastisement. Paul warned the church at Corinth that "these things occurred as examples to keep us from setting our hearts on evil things as they did" (1Co 10:6). The negative example of the rebellious nature of the people of God is meant to warn all sinful rebels of the implications of such rebellion, both in this life and in the age to come.

CONFIDENCE IN THE LORD

The Israelites were instructed to take a land that was already inhabited. This was surely a daunting challenge for a nation that had been wandering in the wilderness for the last forty years. In order to discern the challenge these inhabitants would present, the Israelites sent twelve spies into the land. These men all acknowledged that the land was indeed a good land — flowing with milk, honey and other examples of God's exceeding kindness. But rather than being emboldened with courage, the spies shuddered in fear at the power of the people and the fortifications of their cities. As a result, the Israelites were tempted to turn back. Caleb and Joshua were the exception. They recognized the scope of the mission and the obstacles that they would face, but they had confidence in the Lord. They knew that he had always been faithful to his people. He had delivered them from slavery in Egypt and protected them through the treacherous wilderness. He would never abandon them. He is a God who always fulfills his promises, even in the face of seemingly insurmountable odds.

Most onlookers would have assumed that Jesus' victory would be unlikely as well. Few things about his life communicated that he would be the victorious King of the universe. In fact, it seemed quite the opposite. He was born in a lowly stable, was raised in obscurity, ministered as an itinerant teacher and died the death of a common criminal. The men responsible for his crucifixion, in a grand, cosmic irony, mocked him with a sign declaring him to be the king of the Jews (Mt 27:37). Yet God is always faithful to his promise. He used the sacrifice of his Son, against all odds, to overthrow a far greater enemy than the nation of Israel would ever face — Satan, sin and death.

Believers today may also find themselves cowering in fear at the power and might of the forces arrayed against them. It may seem that the enemy is powerful and the world is winning. Yet those who know Jesus can take heart knowing that "the one who is in you is greater than the one who is in the world" (1Jn 4:4). Christians can live with confidence knowing that they are indwelt by an all-powerful God, and this God will always fulfill his good promises.

RESISTING GOD DESPITE HIS WORK

The contemptuous Israelites turned their scorn toward Moses and Aaron. Longing to return to Egypt, they blamed these God-ordained leaders and even talked about stoning them. The irony is stark. Moses and Aaron were the human means by which God accomplished his miraculous deliverance of the people from slavery in Egypt. There, God had enacted signs and wonders to demonstrate his glory and power. No one could deny that this deliverance was from the Lord. Yet not long after observing God's might and being the recipients of his favor, the people of God blamed God for bringing them into the wilderness to die. Moses and Aaron, as the leaders of the people, were the objects of the nation's accusations; however, the people clearly believed that the fault actually lay with God himself (v. 3). In the New Testament, Stephen, in his speech to the Sanhedrin, said that the failure of the people to obey God should be attributed to their rejection of him and their disbelief in his promises (Ac 7:39).

Jesus suffered a similar fate. Throughout his earthly ministry, he provided countless signs and wonders, demonstrating himself to be the Son of God and the one through whom the kingdom of God would come. In spite of these clear manifestations of the power of God, many still did not believe (Jn 12:37).

A foreshadowing of his own subsequent resurrection, Jesus raised his friend Lazarus from the dead to life in the plain sight of all those watching (Jn 11). This miraculous act was soon reported to the Jewish religious leaders who, rather than believing that he was the Son of God, concocted a plan to kill him for fear that all of the people would follow Jesus. Their sin was evidenced by their disbelief.

Today, people are prone to resist the clear work of God as well. All around are abundant evidences of his goodness, and he still performs mighty signs and wonders to demonstrate his power. Yet many do not believe. Their hard-hearted resistance to these acts of God is evidence of their pride. Like the Israelites before them, many will be judged for their disbelief in God's goodness and grace. Those who recognize God's work can, by the power of his Spirit, humble themselves and believe in him.

17“Now may the Lord’s strength be displayed, just as you have declared: 18‘The
LORD is slow to anger, abounding in love and forgiving sin and rebellion. Yet he
does not leave the guilty unpunished; he punishes the children for the sin of the
parents to the third and fourth generation.’ 19In accordance with your great love,
forgive the sin of these people, just as you have pardoned them from the time
they left Egypt until now.”

20The LORD replied, “I have forgiven them, as you asked. 21Nevertheless, as
surely as I live and as surely as the glory of the LORD fills the whole earth, 22not
one of those who saw my glory and the signs I performed in Egypt and in the wilderness but who disobeyed me and tested me ten times — 23not one of them will
ever see the land I promised on oath to their ancestors. No one who has treated
me with contempt will ever see it. 24But because my servant Caleb has a different
spirit and follows me wholeheartedly, I will bring him into the land he went to,
and his descendants will inherit it. 25Since the Amalekites and the Canaanites
are living in the valleys, turn back tomorrow and set out toward the desert along
the route to the Red Sea.[a]”

26The LORD said to Moses and Aaron: 27“How long will this wicked community grumble against me? I have heard the complaints of these grumbling Israelites. 28So tell them, ‘As surely as I live, declares the LORD, I will do to you the
very thing I heard you say: 29In this wilderness your bodies will fall — every one
of you twenty years old or more who was counted in the census and who has
grumbled against me. 30Not one of you will enter the land I swore with uplifted
hand to make your home, except Caleb son of Jephunneh and Joshua son of Nun.
31As for your children that you said would be taken as plunder, I will bring them
in to enjoy the land you have rejected. 32But as for you, your bodies will fall in
this wilderness. 33Your children will be shepherds here for forty years, suffering
for your unfaithfulness, until the last of your bodies lies in the wilderness. 34For
forty years — one year for each of the forty days you explored the land — you will
suffer for your sins and know what it is like to have me against you.’ 35I, the LORD,
have spoken, and I will surely do these things to this whole wicked community,
which has banded together against me. They will meet their end in this wilderness; here they will die.”

36So the men Moses had sent to explore the land, who returned and made the
whole community grumble against him by spreading a bad report about it —
37these men who were responsible for spreading the bad report about the land
were struck down and died of a plague before the LORD. 38Of the men who went to
explore the land, only Joshua son of Nun and Caleb son of Jephunneh survived.

39When Moses reported this to all the Israelites, they mourned bitterly. 40Early
the next morning they set out for the highest point in the hill country, saying, “Now
we are ready to go up to the land the LORD promised. Surely we have sinned!”

41But Moses said, “Why are you disobeying the LORD’s command? This will
not succeed! 42Do not go up, because the LORD is not with you. You will be defeated by your enemies, 43for the Amalekites and the Canaanites will face you
there. Because you have turned away from the LORD, he will not be with you and
you will fall by the sword.”

44Nevertheless, in their presumption they went up toward the highest point
in the hill country, though neither Moses nor the ark of the LORD’s covenant
moved from the camp. 45Then the Amalekites and the Canaanites who lived in
that hill country came down and attacked them and beat them down all the way
to Hormah.

Supplementary Offerings

15 The LORD said to Moses, 2“Speak to the Israelites and say to them: ‘After
you enter the land I am giving you as a home 3and you present to the LORD
food offerings from the herd or the flock, as an aroma pleasing to the LORD —

[a] 25 Or *the Sea of Reeds*

whether burnt offerings or sacrifices, for special vows or freewill offerings or festival offerings — [4]then the person who brings an offering shall present to the LORD a grain offering of a tenth of an ephah[a] of the finest flour mixed with a quarter of a hin[b] of olive oil. [5]With each lamb for the burnt offering or the sacrifice, prepare a quarter of a hin of wine as a drink offering.

[6]" 'With a ram prepare a grain offering of two-tenths of an ephah[c] of the finest flour mixed with a third of a hin[d] of olive oil, [7]and a third of a hin of wine as a drink offering. Offer it as an aroma pleasing to the LORD.

[8]" 'When you prepare a young bull as a burnt offering or sacrifice, for a special vow or a fellowship offering to the LORD, [9]bring with the bull a grain offering of three-tenths of an ephah[e] of the finest flour mixed with half a hin[f] of olive oil, [10]and also bring half a hin of wine as a drink offering. This will be a food offering, an aroma pleasing to the LORD. [11]Each bull or ram, each lamb or young goat, is to be prepared in this manner. [12]Do this for each one, for as many as you prepare.

[13]" 'Everyone who is native-born must do these things in this way when they present a food offering as an aroma pleasing to the LORD. [14]For the generations to come, whenever a foreigner or anyone else living among you presents a food offering as an aroma pleasing to the LORD, they must do exactly as you do. [15]The community is to have the same rules for you and for the foreigner residing among you; this is a lasting ordinance for the generations to come. You and the foreigner shall be the same before the LORD: [16]The same laws and regulations will apply both to you and to the foreigner residing among you.' "

[17]The LORD said to Moses, [18]"Speak to the Israelites and say to them: 'When you enter the land to which I am taking you [19]and you eat the food of the land, present a portion as an offering to the LORD. [20]Present a loaf from the first of your ground meal and present it as an offering from the threshing floor. [21]Throughout the generations to come you are to give this offering to the LORD from the first of your ground meal.

Offerings for Unintentional Sins

[22]" 'Now if you as a community unintentionally fail to keep any of these commands the LORD gave Moses — [23]any of the LORD's commands to you through him, from the day the LORD gave them and continuing through the generations to come — [24]and if this is done unintentionally without the community being aware of it, then the whole community is to offer a young bull for a burnt offering as an aroma pleasing to the LORD, along with its prescribed grain offering and drink offering, and a male goat for a sin offering.[g] [25]The priest is to make atonement for the whole Israelite community, and they will be forgiven, for it was not intentional and they have presented to the LORD for their wrong a food offering and a sin offering. [26]The whole Israelite community and the foreigners residing among them will be forgiven, because all the people were involved in the unintentional wrong.

[27]" 'But if just one person sins unintentionally, that person must bring a year-old female goat for a sin offering. [28]The priest is to make atonement before the LORD for the one who erred by sinning unintentionally, and when atonement has been made, that person will be forgiven. [29]One and the same law applies to everyone who sins unintentionally, whether a native-born Israelite or a foreigner residing among you.

[30]" 'But anyone who sins defiantly, whether native-born or foreigner, blasphemes the LORD and must be cut off from the people of Israel. [31]Because they have despised the LORD's word and broken his commands, they must surely be cut off; their guilt remains on them.' "

---

[a] *4* That is, probably about 3 1/2 pounds or about 1.6 kilograms [b] *4* That is, about 1 quart or about 1 liter; also in verse 5 [c] *6* That is, probably about 7 pounds or about 3.2 kilograms [d] *6* That is, about 1 1/3 quarts or about 1.3 liters; also in verse 7 [e] *9* That is, probably about 11 pounds or about 5 kilograms [f] *9* That is, about 2 quarts or about 1.9 liters; also in verse 10 [g] *24* Or *purification offering;* also in verses 25 and 27

The Sabbath-Breaker Put to Death

32While the Israelites were in the wilderness, a man was found gathering
wood on the Sabbath day. 33Those who found him gathering wood brought him
to Moses and Aaron and the whole assembly, 34and they kept him in custody, because it was not clear what should be done to him. 35Then the LORD said to Moses, "The man must die. The whole assembly must stone him outside the camp."
36So the assembly took him outside the camp and stoned him to death, as the
LORD commanded Moses.

Tassels on Garments

37The LORD said to Moses, 38"Speak to the Israelites and say to them:
'Throughout the generations to come you are to make tassels on the corners of
your garments, with a blue cord on each tassel. 39You will have these tassels to
look at and so you will remember all the commands of the LORD, that you may
obey them and not prostitute yourselves by chasing after the lusts of your own
hearts and eyes. 40Then you will remember to obey all my commands and will
be consecrated to your God. 41I am the LORD your God, who brought you out of
Egypt to be your God. I am the LORD your God.'"

Korah, Dathan and Abiram

16 Korah son of Izhar, the son of Kohath, the son of Levi, and certain Reubenites — Dathan and Abiram, sons of Eliab, and On son of Peleth — became
insolent[a] 2and rose up against Moses. With them were 250 Israelite men, well-
known community leaders who had been appointed members of the council.
3They came as a group to oppose Moses and Aaron and said to them, "You have
gone too far! The whole community is holy, every one of them, and the LORD is
with them. Why then do you set yourselves above the LORD's assembly?"
4When Moses heard this, he fell facedown. 5Then he said to Korah and all his
followers: "In the morning the LORD will show who belongs to him and who is
holy, and he will have that person come near him. The man he chooses he will
cause to come near him. 6You, Korah, and all your followers are to do this: Take
censers 7and tomorrow put burning coals and incense in them before the LORD.
The man the LORD chooses will be the one who is holy. You Levites have gone
too far!"
8Moses also said to Korah, "Now listen, you Levites! 9Isn't it enough for you
that the God of Israel has separated you from the rest of the Israelite community and brought you near himself to do the work at the LORD's tabernacle and to
stand before the community and minister to them? 10He has brought you and all
your fellow Levites near himself, but now you are trying to get the priesthood
too. 11It is against the LORD that you and all your followers have banded together.
Who is Aaron that you should grumble against him?"
12Then Moses summoned Dathan and Abiram, the sons of Eliab. But they
said, "We will not come! 13Isn't it enough that you have brought us up out of a
land flowing with milk and honey to kill us in the wilderness? And now you also
want to lord it over us! 14Moreover, you haven't brought us into a land flowing
with milk and honey or given us an inheritance of fields and vineyards. Do you
want to treat these men like slaves[b]? No, we will not come!"
15Then Moses became very angry and said to the LORD, "Do not accept their
offering. I have not taken so much as a donkey from them, nor have I wronged
any of them."
16Moses said to Korah, "You and all your followers are to appear before the LORD
tomorrow — you and they and Aaron. 17Each man is to take his censer and put incense in it — 250 censers in all — and present it before the LORD. You and Aaron
are to present your censers also." 18So each of them took his censer, put burning

---

[a] 1 Or *Peleth — took men* [b] 14 Or *to deceive these men*; Hebrew *Will you gouge out the eyes of these men*

coals and incense in it, and stood with Moses and Aaron at the entrance to the tent of meeting. 19When Korah had gathered all his followers in opposition to them at the entrance to the tent of meeting, the glory of the LORD appeared to the entire assembly. 20The LORD said to Moses and Aaron, 21"Separate yourselves from this assembly so I can put an end to them at once."

22But Moses and Aaron fell facedown and cried out, "O God, the God who gives breath to all living things, will you be angry with the entire assembly when only one man sins?"

23Then the LORD said to Moses, 24"Say to the assembly, 'Move away from the tents of Korah, Dathan and Abiram.' "

25Moses got up and went to Dathan and Abiram, and the elders of Israel followed him. 26He warned the assembly, "Move back from the tents of these wicked men! Do not touch anything belonging to them, or you will be swept away because of all their sins." 27So they moved away from the tents of Korah, Dathan and Abiram. Dathan and Abiram had come out and were standing with their wives, children and little ones at the entrances to their tents.

28Then Moses said, "This is how you will know that the LORD has sent me to do all these things and that it was not my idea: 29If these men die a natural death and suffer the fate of all mankind, then the LORD has not sent me. 30But if the LORD brings about something totally new, and the earth opens its mouth and swallows them, with everything that belongs to them, and they go down alive into the realm of the dead, then you will know that these men have treated the LORD with contempt."

31As soon as he finished saying all this, the ground under them split apart 32and the earth opened its mouth and swallowed them and their households, and all those associated with Korah, together with their possessions. 33They went down alive into the realm of the dead, with everything they owned; the earth closed over them, and they perished and were gone from the community. 34At their cries, all the Israelites around them fled, shouting, "The earth is going to swallow us too!"

35And fire came out from the LORD and consumed the 250 men who were offering the incense.

36The LORD said to Moses, 37"Tell Eleazar son of Aaron, the priest, to remove the censers from the charred remains and scatter the coals some distance away, for the censers are holy — 38the censers of the men who sinned at the cost of their lives. Hammer the censers into sheets to overlay the altar, for they were presented before the LORD and have become holy. Let them be a sign to the Israelites."

39So Eleazar the priest collected the bronze censers brought by those who had been burned to death, and he had them hammered out to overlay the altar, 40as the LORD directed him through Moses. This was to remind the Israelites that no one except a descendant of Aaron should come to burn incense before the LORD, or he would become like Korah and his followers.

41The next day the whole Israelite community grumbled against Moses and Aaron. "You have killed the LORD's people," they said.

42But when the assembly gathered in opposition to Moses and Aaron and turned toward the tent of meeting, suddenly the cloud covered it and the glory of the LORD appeared. 43Then Moses and Aaron went to the front of the tent of meeting, 44and the LORD said to Moses, 45"Get away from this assembly so I can put an end to them at once." And they fell facedown.

46Then Moses said to Aaron, "Take your censer and put incense in it, along with burning coals from the altar, and hurry to the assembly to make atonement for them. Wrath has come out from the LORD; the plague has started." 47So Aaron did as Moses said, and ran into the midst of the assembly. The plague had already started among the people, but Aaron offered the incense and made atonement for them. 48He stood between the living and the dead, and the plague stopped. 49But 14,700 people died from the plague, in addition to those who had

GRUMBLING INSTEAD OF SERVING

Korah's rebellion stands as a testament to the disastrous results of arrogant leadership. In Numbers 16, Korah asserted that his family deserved just as much privilege as was given to Aaron and his descendants (v. 3). Korah demanded that Moses and Aaron level the playing field for priestly service. Dissatisfied with caring for the mundane aspects of the tabernacle, the upstarts saw the Aaronic priesthood as a position of prestige and unfair advantage (vv. 8 – 11). But as Korah seized the next rung, God brought his efforts to nothing. The rebellion of Korah and those who banded with him against God was quickly brought to a dramatic end (vv. 31 – 35).

The destruction of Korah is so memorable that Jude's critique of the prideful behavior of the false teachers of his day distinctly reminded him of Korah's behavior (Jude 11). Jude underscored the pride of false teachers by combining the stories of Cain, Balaam and Korah to make his point. The pride of leaders like Korah is just as dangerous and unfulfilling today as it was when the children of Israel were wandering in the desert (vv. 12 – 13).

Jesus and Korah stand in stark contrast. Korah used his influence in his pursuit of authority. Recognizing his status in the community, Korah made a tactical move against Moses and Aaron (Nu 16:1 – 2). In contrast, Paul described the ministry of Jesus as a rejection of significance (Php 2:6 – 8). Jesus could have drawn together the elite of society in order to stage a coup, but he opted to follow the Father's will and serve and die instead.

Korah assumed that roles of service are actually positions of power. Korah's claim that Moses and Aaron had set themselves above the rest of the nation revealed his view of leadership. To Korah, leadership was an opportunity to exert one's power — controlling the weak for self-serving ends. Jesus modeled the opposite view of leadership. Leadership is primarily an opportunity to serve (Jn 13:15 – 16).

Korah saw success also as a path of upward mobility. Moses rebuked Korah's dissatisfaction with menial and mundane service (Nu 16:9 – 11), highlighting his upward ambitions. Jesus served as the opposite example. Korah took up his censor, but Jesus took up a towel (Jn 13:1 – 17). Korah's attempted climb caused many to fall (Nu 16:31 – 35); Jesus' descent caused many to rise (Ro 5:18 – 21).

died because of Korah. 50Then Aaron returned to Moses at the entrance to the tent of meeting, for the plague had stopped.[a]

The Budding of Aaron's Staff

17[b] The LORD said to Moses, 2"Speak to the Israelites and get twelve staffs from them, one from the leader of each of their ancestral tribes. Write the name of each man on his staff. 3On the staff of Levi write Aaron's name, for there must be one staff for the head of each ancestral tribe. 4Place them in the tent of meeting in front of the ark of the covenant law, where I meet with you. 5The staff belonging to the man I choose will sprout, and I will rid myself of this constant grumbling against you by the Israelites."

6So Moses spoke to the Israelites, and their leaders gave him twelve staffs, one for the leader of each of their ancestral tribes, and Aaron's staff was among them. 7Moses placed the staffs before the LORD in the tent of the covenant law.

8The next day Moses entered the tent and saw that Aaron's staff, which represented the tribe of Levi, had not only sprouted but had budded, blossomed and produced almonds. 9Then Moses brought out all the staffs from the LORD's presence to all the Israelites. They looked at them, and each of the leaders took his own staff.

10The LORD said to Moses, "Put back Aaron's staff in front of the ark of the covenant law, to be kept as a sign to the rebellious. This will put an end to their grumbling against me, so that they will not die." 11Moses did just as the LORD commanded him.

12The Israelites said to Moses, "We will die! We are lost, we are all lost! 13Anyone who even comes near the tabernacle of the LORD will die. Are we all going to die?"

Duties of Priests and Levites

18 The LORD said to Aaron, "You, your sons and your family are to bear the responsibility for offenses connected with the sanctuary, and you and your sons alone are to bear the responsibility for offenses connected with the priesthood. 2Bring your fellow Levites from your ancestral tribe to join you and assist you when you and your sons minister before the tent of the covenant law. 3They are to be responsible to you and are to perform all the duties of the tent, but they must not go near the furnishings of the sanctuary or the altar. Otherwise both they and you will die. 4They are to join you and be responsible for the care of the tent of meeting—all the work at the tent—and no one else may come near where you are.

5"You are to be responsible for the care of the sanctuary and the altar, so that my wrath will not fall on the Israelites again. 6I myself have selected your fellow Levites from among the Israelites as a gift to you, dedicated to the LORD to do the work at the tent of meeting. 7But only you and your sons may serve as priests in connection with everything at the altar and inside the curtain. I am giving you the service of the priesthood as a gift. Anyone else who comes near the sanctuary is to be put to death."

Offerings for Priests and Levites

8Then the LORD said to Aaron, "I myself have put you in charge of the offerings presented to me; all the holy offerings the Israelites give me I give to you and your sons as your portion, your perpetual share. 9You are to have the part of the most holy offerings that is kept from the fire. From all the gifts they bring me as most holy offerings, whether grain or sin[c] or guilt offerings, that part belongs to you and your sons. 10Eat it as something most holy; every male shall eat it. You must regard it as holy.

[a] *50* In Hebrew texts 16:36-50 is numbered 17:1-15. [b] In Hebrew texts 17:1-13 is numbered 17:16-28. [c] *9* Or *purification*

11“This also is yours: whatever is set aside from the gifts of all the wave offerings of the Israelites. I give this to you and your sons and daughters as your perpetual share. Everyone in your household who is ceremonially clean may eat it.
12“I give you all the finest olive oil and all the finest new wine and grain they
give the LORD as the firstfruits of their harvest. 13All the land’s firstfruits that
they bring to the LORD will be yours. Everyone in your household who is ceremonially clean may eat it.
14“Everything in Israel that is devoted[a] to the LORD is yours. 15The first offspring of every womb, both human and animal, that is offered to the LORD is
yours. But you must redeem every firstborn son and every firstborn male of unclean animals. 16When they are a month old, you must redeem them at the redemption price set at five shekels[b] of silver, according to the sanctuary shekel,
which weighs twenty gerahs.
17“But you must not redeem the firstborn of a cow, a sheep or a goat; they are
holy. Splash their blood against the altar and burn their fat as a food offering,
an aroma pleasing to the LORD. 18Their meat is to be yours, just as the breast of
the wave offering and the right thigh are yours. 19Whatever is set aside from the
holy offerings the Israelites present to the LORD I give to you and your sons and
daughters as your perpetual share. It is an everlasting covenant of salt before the
LORD for both you and your offspring.”
20The LORD said to Aaron, “You will have no inheritance in their land, nor will
you have any share among them; I am your share and your inheritance among
the Israelites.
21“I give to the Levites all the tithes in Israel as their inheritance in return for
the work they do while serving at the tent of meeting. 22From now on the Israelites must not go near the tent of meeting, or they will bear the consequences
of their sin and will die. 23It is the Levites who are to do the work at the tent of
meeting and bear the responsibility for any offenses they commit against it. This
is a lasting ordinance for the generations to come. They will receive no inheritance among the Israelites. 24Instead, I give to the Levites as their inheritance
the tithes that the Israelites present as an offering to the LORD. That is why I said
concerning them: ‘They will have no inheritance among the Israelites.’ ”
25The LORD said to Moses, 26“Speak to the Levites and say to them: ‘When you
receive from the Israelites the tithe I give you as your inheritance, you must present a tenth of that tithe as the LORD’s offering. 27Your offering will be reckoned
to you as grain from the threshing floor or juice from the winepress. 28In this
way you also will present an offering to the LORD from all the tithes you receive
from the Israelites. From these tithes you must give the LORD’s portion to Aaron
the priest. 29You must present as the LORD’s portion the best and holiest part of
everything given to you.’
30“Say to the Levites: ‘When you present the best part, it will be reckoned to
you as the product of the threshing floor or the winepress. 31You and your households may eat the rest of it anywhere, for it is your wages for your work at the tent
of meeting. 32By presenting the best part of it you will not be guilty in this matter;
then you will not defile the holy offerings of the Israelites, and you will not die.’ ”

The Water of Cleansing

19 The LORD said to Moses and Aaron: 2“This is a requirement of the law
that the LORD has commanded: Tell the Israelites to bring you a red heifer
without defect or blemish and that has never been under a yoke. 3Give it to Eleazar the priest; it is to be taken outside the camp and slaughtered in his presence.
4Then Eleazar the priest is to take some of its blood on his finger and sprinkle it
seven times toward the front of the tent of meeting. 5While he watches, the heifer
is to be burned — its hide, flesh, blood and intestines. 6The priest is to take some

[a] *14* The Hebrew term refers to the irrevocable giving over of things or persons to the LORD.
[b] *16* That is, about 2 ounces or about 58 grams

NUMBERS 19:1 – 6

THE RED HEIFER

The pervasive images of death throughout the Old Testament demonstrate the stark consequences of sin. In grace, God made it possible for the death of a red heifer to be used in the act of ceremonial cleansing. The ashes of the heifer were mixed with water to provide a means of cleansing after contact with dead bodies. The death of the red heifer merely prefigured a much greater substitute, the Lord Jesus Christ. His death did not simply cover the sins of his people; his death bore the wrath of the curse forever. The author of Hebrews used this image to contrast the external cleansing brought about by “the ashes of a heifer sprinkled on those who are ceremonially unclean” and the internal transformation wrought by the “blood of Christ” (Heb 9:13 – 14). He bore the wrath of God in order to purge his people from the consequences of sin and empower them to throw off sin and pursue obedience with a clear conscience.

cedar wood, hyssop and scarlet wool and throw them onto the burning heifer. 7After that, the priest must wash his clothes and bathe himself with water. He may then come into the camp, but he will be ceremonially unclean till evening. 8The man who burns it must also wash his clothes and bathe with water, and he too will be unclean till evening.

9"A man who is clean shall gather up the ashes of the heifer and put them in a ceremonially clean place outside the camp. They are to be kept by the Israelite community for use in the water of cleansing; it is for purification from sin. 10The man who gathers up the ashes of the heifer must also wash his clothes, and he too will be unclean till evening. This will be a lasting ordinance both for the Israelites and for the foreigners residing among them.

11"Whoever touches a human corpse will be unclean for seven days. 12They must purify themselves with the water on the third day and on the seventh day; then they will be clean. But if they do not purify themselves on the third and seventh days, they will not be clean. 13If they fail to purify themselves after touching a human corpse, they defile the LORD's tabernacle. They must be cut off from Israel. Because the water of cleansing has not been sprinkled on them, they are unclean; their uncleanness remains on them.

14"This is the law that applies when a person dies in a tent: Anyone who enters the tent and anyone who is in it will be unclean for seven days, 15and every open container without a lid fastened on it will be unclean.

16"Anyone out in the open who touches someone who has been killed with a sword or someone who has died a natural death, or anyone who touches a human bone or a grave, will be unclean for seven days.

17"For the unclean person, put some ashes from the burned purification offering into a jar and pour fresh water over them. 18Then a man who is ceremonially clean is to take some hyssop, dip it in the water and sprinkle the tent and all the furnishings and the people who were there. He must also sprinkle anyone who has touched a human bone or a grave or anyone who has been killed or anyone who has died a natural death. 19The man who is clean is to sprinkle those who are unclean on the third and seventh days, and on the seventh day he is to purify them. Those who are being cleansed must wash their clothes and bathe with water, and that evening they will be clean. 20But if those who are unclean do not purify themselves, they must be cut off from the community, because they have defiled the sanctuary of the LORD. The water of cleansing has not been sprinkled on them, and they are unclean. 21This is a lasting ordinance for them.

"The man who sprinkles the water of cleansing must also wash his clothes, and anyone who touches the water of cleansing will be unclean till evening. 22Anything that an unclean person touches becomes unclean, and anyone who touches it becomes unclean till evening."

Water From the Rock

20 In the first month the whole Israelite community arrived at the Desert of Zin, and they stayed at Kadesh. There Miriam died and was buried.

2Now there was no water for the community, and the people gathered in opposition to Moses and Aaron. 3They quarreled with Moses and said, "If only we had died when our brothers fell dead before the LORD! 4Why did you bring the LORD's community into this wilderness, that we and our livestock should die here? 5Why did you bring us up out of Egypt to this terrible place? It has no grain or figs, grapevines or pomegranates. And there is no water to drink!"

6Moses and Aaron went from the assembly to the entrance to the tent of meeting and fell facedown, and the glory of the LORD appeared to them. 7The LORD said to Moses, 8"Take the staff, and you and your brother Aaron gather the assembly together. Speak to that rock before their eyes and it will pour out its water. You will bring water out of the rock for the community so they and their livestock can drink."

9So Moses took the staff from the LORD's presence, just as he commanded him. 10He and Aaron gathered the assembly together in front of the rock and

---

NUMBERS 20:1 – 13

BANISHED FROM THE PROMISED LAND

The sin of ingratitude raised its ugly head again, as it did when the Israelite people first left Egypt forty years earlier (Ex 17). The same issue, a lack of water, provoked the people to blame God and their leadership. God was not angry with the hostile people; instead, he lovingly desired to provide the nurture they needed. In contrast to God's kindness, Moses responded in unrighteous anger and disobeyed by striking the rock (as God had instructed him to in Ex 17) and losing the opportunity to enter into the promised land.

Similarly, Adam and Eve in the garden had a lapse of judgment and ate from the tree of the knowledge of good and evil. This deliberate disobedience caused their ejection from the Garden of Eden. Their sin demanded that someone come and remedy the sinful state in which mankind was entrenched.

God's providence and grace are evident in the gushing of the rock to provide for the people and the livestock in spite of Moses' actions. God demonstrated his benevolent nature to supply the needs of his people. This grace is manifested richly to all mankind, even while they were (and are) still sinners (Ro 5:8), through the death of Christ on the cross.

Moses said to them, "Listen, you rebels, must we bring you water out of this rock?" 11Then Moses raised his arm and struck the rock twice with his staff. Water gushed out, and the community and their livestock drank.

12But the LORD said to Moses and Aaron, "Because you did not trust in me enough to honor me as holy in the sight of the Israelites, you will not bring this community into the land I give them."

13These were the waters of Meribah,[a] where the Israelites quarreled with the LORD and where he was proved holy among them.

Edom Denies Israel Passage

14Moses sent messengers from Kadesh to the king of Edom, saying:

"This is what your brother Israel says: You know about all the hardships that have come on us. 15Our ancestors went down into Egypt, and we lived there many years. The Egyptians mistreated us and our ancestors, 16but when we cried out to the LORD, he heard our cry and sent an angel and brought us out of Egypt.

"Now we are here at Kadesh, a town on the edge of your territory. 17Please let us pass through your country. We will not go through any field or vineyard, or drink water from any well. We will travel along the King's Highway and not turn to the right or to the left until we have passed through your territory."

18But Edom answered:

"You may not pass through here; if you try, we will march out and attack you with the sword."

19The Israelites replied:

"We will go along the main road, and if we or our livestock drink any of your water, we will pay for it. We only want to pass through on foot — nothing else."

20Again they answered:

"You may not pass through."

Then Edom came out against them with a large and powerful army. 21Since Edom refused to let them go through their territory, Israel turned away from them.

The Death of Aaron

22The whole Israelite community set out from Kadesh and came to Mount Hor. 23At Mount Hor, near the border of Edom, the LORD said to Moses and Aaron, 24"Aaron will be gathered to his people. He will not enter the land I give the Israelites, because both of you rebelled against my command at the waters of Meribah. 25Get Aaron and his son Eleazar and take them up Mount Hor. 26Remove Aaron's garments and put them on his son Eleazar, for Aaron will be gathered to his people; he will die there."

27Moses did as the LORD commanded: They went up Mount Hor in the sight of the whole community. 28Moses removed Aaron's garments and put them on his son Eleazar. And Aaron died there on top of the mountain. Then Moses and Eleazar came down from the mountain, 29and when the whole community learned that Aaron had died, all the Israelites mourned for him thirty days.

Arad Destroyed

21 When the Canaanite king of Arad, who lived in the Negev, heard that Israel was coming along the road to Atharim, he attacked the Israelites and captured some of them. 2Then Israel made this vow to the LORD: "If you will

---

[a] *13 Meribah* means *quarreling.*

JESUS IS THE LIVING WATER

God's patience and provision for his people is memorably demonstrated in the two passages where the Lord brought water out of a rock to refresh a thirsty nation (Ex 17; Nu 20). On these occasions, God chose to bless his murmuring and rebellious people rather than punish them. He nourished and satisfied them when they were least deserving of his gift. Through the story of redemption found throughout the Bible, this theme surfaces, culminating in the life and ministry of Jesus.

The psalms are full of allusions to God's blessing as water, even directly referencing God's miraculous provision in the wilderness (Ps 78:15; 105:41). In a frequently referenced passage, the psalmist compared passion for God to the desire of an exhausted, wild animal for water (Ps 42:1 – 2). The psalmist also recognized that God's blessing is the only drink that will truly satisfy the needy soul (Ps 63:1 – 5).

By Jeremiah's time, the nation had walked away from God, and the exile was rapidly closing in. The impending destruction gave the weeping prophet an opportunity to issue an urgent call for repentance. The Lord wanted to be a fresh fountain of water for the Israelites (Jer 2:13). He desired to flood their souls with blessing, but they wanted to satisfy their own needs, a futile attempt that only resulted in a deeper emptiness than ever before (17:13).

Another prophet, Isaiah, frequently relied upon water imagery to focus the attention of the nation on a coming blessing of God which would bring hydration to their parched souls and desolate land (Isa 12:3; 41:17 – 18; 44:3; 58:11). In an impassioned plea, Isaiah called upon not merely the nation of Israel but everyone who thirsts to partake of the abundance of God's water supply (55:1 – 2).

Jesus' use of water imagery for God's blessing — a blessing that flows out from him — relied heavily upon the Old Testament echoes in the Pentateuch, psalms and prophets. On two occasions in John's Gospel, Jesus called on people to drink the life-giving supply of blessing that only he can offer. His offer applied to the Samaritan woman who was distant from God (Jn 4:1 – 30) and to the dutifully religious crowd gathered at the Jewish temple (7:37 – 38). The blessing of God in the person of Christ is available free of charge to every thirsty soul who relinquishes their attempts at self-satisfaction and turns to Jesus for living water.

deliver these people into our hands, we will totally destroy[a] their cities." 3The
LORD listened to Israel's plea and gave the Canaanites over to them. They completely destroyed them and their towns; so the place was named Hormah.[b]

The Bronze Snake

4They traveled from Mount Hor along the route to the Red Sea,[c] to go around
Edom. But the people grew impatient on the way; 5they spoke against God and
against Moses, and said, "Why have you brought us up out of Egypt to die in the
wilderness? There is no bread! There is no water! And we detest this miserable
food!"

6Then the LORD sent venomous snakes among them; they bit the people and
many Israelites died. 7The people came to Moses and said, "We sinned when we
spoke against the LORD and against you. Pray that the LORD will take the snakes
away from us." So Moses prayed for the people.

8The LORD said to Moses, "Make a snake and put it up on a pole; anyone who
is bitten can look at it and live." 9So Moses made a bronze snake and put it up on
a pole. Then when anyone was bitten by a snake and looked at the bronze snake,
they lived.

The Journey to Moab

10The Israelites moved on and camped at Oboth. 11Then they set out from
Oboth and camped in Iye Abarim, in the wilderness that faces Moab toward the
sunrise. 12From there they moved on and camped in the Zered Valley. 13They set
out from there and camped alongside the Arnon, which is in the wilderness extending into Amorite territory. The Arnon is the border of Moab, between Moab
and the Amorites. 14That is why the Book of the Wars of the LORD says:

". . . Zahab[d] in Suphah and the ravines,
the Arnon 15and[e] the slopes of the ravines
that lead to the settlement of Ar
and lie along the border of Moab."

16From there they continued on to Beer, the well where the LORD said to Moses,
"Gather the people together and I will give them water."

17Then Israel sang this song:

"Spring up, O well!
Sing about it,
18about the well that the princes dug,
that the nobles of the people sank—
the nobles with scepters and staffs."

Then they went from the wilderness to Mattanah, 19from Mattanah to Nahaliel,
from Nahaliel to Bamoth, 20and from Bamoth to the valley in Moab where the
top of Pisgah overlooks the wasteland.

Defeat of Sihon and Og

21Israel sent messengers to say to Sihon king of the Amorites:

22"Let us pass through your country. We will not turn aside into any field
or vineyard, or drink water from any well. We will travel along the King's
Highway until we have passed through your territory."

23But Sihon would not let Israel pass through his territory. He mustered his entire army and marched out into the wilderness against Israel. When he reached
Jahaz, he fought with Israel. 24Israel, however, put him to the sword and took

NUMBERS 21:7–9

ALLEVIATION OF THE CURSE

The poisonous snakes represented God's judgment of the people for their proclivity to sin. The people cried out to Moses for help. God instructed Moses to craft a unique source of deliverance—an image of a snake placed on a pole and lifted up among the people. Those who looked at this symbol lived. Jesus used this image to instruct Nicodemus about the way he would provide true and lasting healing from the work of the enemy. Jesus said that those who look in faith upon his death on a cross will live (Jn 3:14–15). The Roman cross is a far more grotesque image than a snake, as heinous criminals and scoundrels died horrific deaths in plain view of everyone. Soon, Jesus said, his death on a cross would alleviate the curse brought about by the sin in the garden (Ge 3:15). Those who look to him in repentance and faith will live—in this life and in the age to come.

[a] 2 The Hebrew term refers to the irrevocable giving over of things or persons to the LORD, often by totally destroying them; also in verse 3. [b] 3 *Hormah* means *destruction*.
[c] 4 Or *the Sea of Reeds* [d] 14 Septuagint; Hebrew *Waheb* [e] 14,15 Or *"I have been given from Suphah and the ravines / of the Arnon* 15*to*

NUMBERS 21:4 – 9

DRAWING ALL PEOPLE

The people of Israel had a tendency to have short memories. When they were hungry or thirsty, they forgot that God had provided food and water in the past. When they learned of their strong enemies, they forgot that God had delivered them from Egypt with no need for an army (Nu 14:1 – 4). In Numbers 21, the people of Israel began to loath the miraculous manna and started to complain once again about their food. In previous occurrences, God responded to complaints with miraculous provision (Ex 15:22 – 27; 16:1 – 17). However, on this occasion God responded with a miraculous judgment — venomous snakes. This judgment remained even after the people of Israel realized their sin. Rather than removing the venomous snakes, God commanded Moses to fashion a bronze snake. Moses then placed that snake on a pole, and all Israel gathered before the snake to receive healing. Though Israel had a tendency to forget God's provision, the people did not soon forget how they were healed from the snakes.

Sometimes people need examples to remind them that God is faithful. Israel was not unique in this tendency to forget God's past actions and seek comfort elsewhere. Just as Israel's sin in Numbers 21 had consequences, everyone's sin has consequences, and the result is death and separation from God. These consequences do not disappear when people realize their sin, just as God did not simply remove the snakes when Israel repented. However, Jesus stated that he too would be lifted up as Moses lifted up the bronze snake (Jn 3:14 – 15; 12:32 – 33). Jesus intercedes on behalf of his people, and he made the payment for their sin on the cross. In order for people to be healed from the sting of sin and death, they must first draw near and look on Jesus in faith, just as the people of Israel drew near and looked upon the snake to be healed.

When life is difficult, people need reminders that God is active and righting the world of the effects of sin. Jesus is that reminder. He has already healed his people from the sting of sin, just as the bronze snake healed the people of Israel from the bites of snakes.

over his land from the Arnon to the Jabbok, but only as far as the Ammonites,
because their border was fortified. 25 Israel captured all the cities of the Amorites
and occupied them, including Heshbon and all its surrounding settlements.
26 Heshbon was the city of Sihon king of the Amorites, who had fought against
the former king of Moab and had taken from him all his land as far as the Arnon.
27 That is why the poets say:

"Come to Heshbon and let it be rebuilt;
let Sihon's city be restored.
28 "Fire went out from Heshbon,
a blaze from the city of Sihon.
It consumed Ar of Moab,
the citizens of Arnon's heights.
29 Woe to you, Moab!
You are destroyed, people of Chemosh!
He has given up his sons as fugitives
and his daughters as captives
to Sihon king of the Amorites.
30 "But we have overthrown them;
Heshbon's dominion has been destroyed all the way to Dibon.
We have demolished them as far as Nophah,
which extends to Medeba."

31 So Israel settled in the land of the Amorites.
32 After Moses had sent spies to Jazer, the Israelites captured its surrounding
settlements and drove out the Amorites who were there. 33 Then they turned and
went up along the road toward Bashan, and Og king of Bashan and his whole
army marched out to meet them in battle at Edrei.
34 The LORD said to Moses, "Do not be afraid of him, for I have delivered him
into your hands, along with his whole army and his land. Do to him what you did
to Sihon king of the Amorites, who reigned in Heshbon."
35 So they struck him down, together with his sons and his whole army, leaving
them no survivors. And they took possession of his land.

Balak Summons Balaam

22 Then the Israelites traveled to the plains of Moab and camped along the
Jordan across from Jericho.
2 Now Balak son of Zippor saw all that Israel had done to the Amorites, 3 and
Moab was terrified because there were so many people. Indeed, Moab was filled
with dread because of the Israelites.
4 The Moabites said to the elders of Midian, "This horde is going to lick up everything around us, as an ox licks up the grass of the field."
So Balak son of Zippor, who was king of Moab at that time, 5 sent messengers
to summon Balaam son of Beor, who was at Pethor, near the Euphrates River, in
his native land. Balak said:

"A people has come out of Egypt; they cover the face of the land and have
settled next to me. 6 Now come and put a curse on these people, because
they are too powerful for me. Perhaps then I will be able to defeat them and
drive them out of the land. For I know that whoever you bless is blessed,
and whoever you curse is cursed."

7 The elders of Moab and Midian left, taking with them the fee for divination.
When they came to Balaam, they told him what Balak had said.
8 "Spend the night here," Balaam said to them, "and I will report back to you
with the answer the LORD gives me." So the Moabite officials stayed with him.
9 God came to Balaam and asked, "Who are these men with you?"
10 Balaam said to God, "Balak son of Zippor, king of Moab, sent me this message: 11 'A people that has come out of Egypt covers the face of the land. Now

NUMBERS 22:1–35

LYING PROPHETS

God used key figures throughout the Old Testament to declare his word to the nation of Israel. Since these individuals spoke on behalf of God himself, it was vital that they rightly represent his message. Lying came with a stark consequence and evoked the divine displeasure of God. He uses any instrument, even a talking donkey, to arrest those who lead God's people astray. This prophetic role was embodied by Jesus during his early ministry. The words he spoke were given to him by the Father and served as a clarion call to his disciples, those whom the Father had called out of the world (Jn 8:28; 12:49; 17:13–18). Because Jesus is God's Son, he can be trusted to only and always speak what is true. These words serve as both a foundation for obedience by God's people and a wall of protection from the assaults of the evil one.

come and put a curse on them for me. Perhaps then I will be able to fight them
and drive them away.' "
12But God said to Balaam, "Do not go with them. You must not put a curse on
those people, because they are blessed."
13The next morning Balaam got up and said to Balak's officials, "Go back to
your own country, for the LORD has refused to let me go with you."
14So the Moabite officials returned to Balak and said, "Balaam refused to
come with us."
15Then Balak sent other officials, more numerous and more distinguished
than the first. 16They came to Balaam and said:

> "This is what Balak son of Zippor says: Do not let anything keep you
> from coming to me, 17because I will reward you handsomely and do what-
> ever you say. Come and put a curse on these people for me."

18But Balaam answered them, "Even if Balak gave me all the silver and gold
in his palace, I could not do anything great or small to go beyond the command
of the LORD my God. 19Now spend the night here so that I can find out what else
the LORD will tell me."
20That night God came to Balaam and said, "Since these men have come to
summon you, go with them, but do only what I tell you."

Balaam's Donkey

21Balaam got up in the morning, saddled his donkey and went with the Moabite officials. 22But God was very angry when he went, and the angel of the LORD
stood in the road to oppose him. Balaam was riding on his donkey, and his two
servants were with him. 23When the donkey saw the angel of the LORD standing
in the road with a drawn sword in his hand, it turned off the road into a field.
Balaam beat it to get it back on the road.
24Then the angel of the LORD stood in a narrow path through the vineyards,
with walls on both sides. 25When the donkey saw the angel of the LORD, it pressed
close to the wall, crushing Balaam's foot against it. So he beat the donkey again.
26Then the angel of the LORD moved on ahead and stood in a narrow place
where there was no room to turn, either to the right or to the left. 27When the
donkey saw the angel of the LORD, it lay down under Balaam, and he was angry
and beat it with his staff. 28Then the LORD opened the donkey's mouth, and it said
to Balaam, "What have I done to you to make you beat me these three times?"
29Balaam answered the donkey, "You have made a fool of me! If only I had a
sword in my hand, I would kill you right now."
30The donkey said to Balaam, "Am I not your own donkey, which you have always ridden, to this day? Have I been in the habit of doing this to you?"
"No," he said.
31Then the LORD opened Balaam's eyes, and he saw the angel of the LORD
standing in the road with his sword drawn. So he bowed low and fell facedown.
32The angel of the LORD asked him, "Why have you beaten your donkey these
three times? I have come here to oppose you because your path is a reckless one
before me.[a] 33The donkey saw me and turned away from me these three times.
If it had not turned away, I would certainly have killed you by now, but I would
have spared it."
34Balaam said to the angel of the LORD, "I have sinned. I did not realize you
were standing in the road to oppose me. Now if you are displeased, I will go back."
35The angel of the LORD said to Balaam, "Go with the men, but speak only
what I tell you." So Balaam went with Balak's officials.
36When Balak heard that Balaam was coming, he went out to meet him at the
Moabite town on the Arnon border, at the edge of his territory. 37Balak said to
Balaam, "Did I not send you an urgent summons? Why didn't you come to me?
Am I really not able to reward you?"

---

[a] *32* The meaning of the Hebrew for this clause is uncertain.

[38]"Well, I have come to you now," Balaam replied. "But I can't say whatever I
please. I must speak only what God puts in my mouth."
[39]Then Balaam went with Balak to Kiriath Huzoth. [40]Balak sacrificed cattle
and sheep, and gave some to Balaam and the officials who were with him. [41]The
next morning Balak took Balaam up to Bamoth Baal, and from there he could see
the outskirts of the Israelite camp.

Balaam's First Message

23 Balaam said, "Build me seven altars here, and prepare seven bulls and
seven rams for me." [2]Balak did as Balaam said, and the two of them offered a bull and a ram on each altar.
[3]Then Balaam said to Balak, "Stay here beside your offering while I go aside.
Perhaps the LORD will come to meet with me. Whatever he reveals to me I will
tell you." Then he went off to a barren height.
[4]God met with him, and Balaam said, "I have prepared seven altars, and on
each altar I have offered a bull and a ram."
[5]The LORD put a word in Balaam's mouth and said, "Go back to Balak and give
him this word."
[6]So he went back to him and found him standing beside his offering, with all
the Moabite officials. [7]Then Balaam spoke his message:

"Balak brought me from Aram,
  the king of Moab from the eastern mountains.
'Come,' he said, 'curse Jacob for me;
  come, denounce Israel.'
[8]How can I curse
  those whom God has not cursed?
How can I denounce
  those whom the LORD has not denounced?
[9]From the rocky peaks I see them,
  from the heights I view them.
I see a people who live apart
  and do not consider themselves one of the nations.
[10]Who can count the dust of Jacob
  or number even a fourth of Israel?
Let me die the death of the righteous,
  and may my final end be like theirs!"

[11]Balak said to Balaam, "What have you done to me? I brought you to curse my
enemies, but you have done nothing but bless them!"
[12]He answered, "Must I not speak what the LORD puts in my mouth?"

Balaam's Second Message

[13]Then Balak said to him, "Come with me to another place where you can see
them; you will not see them all but only the outskirts of their camp. And from
there, curse them for me." [14]So he took him to the field of Zophim on the top of
Pisgah, and there he built seven altars and offered a bull and a ram on each altar.
[15]Balaam said to Balak, "Stay here beside your offering while I meet with him
over there."
[16]The LORD met with Balaam and put a word in his mouth and said, "Go back
to Balak and give him this word."
[17]So he went to him and found him standing beside his offering, with the Moabite officials. Balak asked him, "What did the LORD say?"
[18]Then he spoke his message:

"Arise, Balak, and listen;
  hear me, son of Zippor.
[19]God is not human, that he should lie,
  not a human being, that he should change his mind.

Does he speak and then not act?
Does he promise and not fulfill?
20 I have received a command to bless;
he has blessed, and I cannot change it.

21 "No misfortune is seen in Jacob,
no misery observed[a] in Israel.
The LORD their God is with them;
the shout of the King is among them.
22 God brought them out of Egypt;
they have the strength of a wild ox.
23 There is no divination against[b] Jacob,
no evil omens against[b] Israel.
It will now be said of Jacob
and of Israel, 'See what God has done!'
24 The people rise like a lioness;
they rouse themselves like a lion
that does not rest till it devours its prey
and drinks the blood of its victims."

25 Then Balak said to Balaam, "Neither curse them at all nor bless them at all!"
26 Balaam answered, "Did I not tell you I must do whatever the LORD says?"

Balaam's Third Message

27 Then Balak said to Balaam, "Come, let me take you to another place. Perhaps it will please God to let you curse them for me from there." 28 And Balak took
Balaam to the top of Peor, overlooking the wasteland.

29 Balaam said, "Build me seven altars here, and prepare seven bulls and sev-
en rams for me." 30 Balak did as Balaam had said, and offered a bull and a ram
on each altar.

24 Now when Balaam saw that it pleased the LORD to bless Israel, he did not
resort to divination as at other times, but turned his face toward the wilderness. 2 When Balaam looked out and saw Israel encamped tribe by tribe, the
Spirit of God came on him 3 and he spoke his message:

"The prophecy of Balaam son of Beor,
the prophecy of one whose eye sees clearly,
4 the prophecy of one who hears the words of God,
who sees a vision from the Almighty,[c]
who falls prostrate, and whose eyes are opened:

5 "How beautiful are your tents, Jacob,
your dwelling places, Israel!

6 "Like valleys they spread out,
like gardens beside a river,
like aloes planted by the LORD,
like cedars beside the waters.
7 Water will flow from their buckets;
their seed will have abundant water.

"Their king will be greater than Agag;
their kingdom will be exalted.

8 "God brought them out of Egypt;
they have the strength of a wild ox.
They devour hostile nations
and break their bones in pieces;
with their arrows they pierce them.

---

[a] 21 Or *He has not looked on Jacob's offenses / or on the wrongs found* [b] 23 Or *in*
[c] 4 Hebrew *Shaddai*; also in verse 16

9 Like a lion they crouch and lie down,
like a lioness — who dares to rouse them?

"May those who bless you be blessed
and those who curse you be cursed!"

10 Then Balak's anger burned against Balaam. He struck his hands together
and said to him, "I summoned you to curse my enemies, but you have blessed
them these three times. 11 Now leave at once and go home! I said I would reward
you handsomely, but the LORD has kept you from being rewarded."
12 Balaam answered Balak, "Did I not tell the messengers you sent me, 13 'Even
if Balak gave me all the silver and gold in his palace, I could not do anything of my
own accord, good or bad, to go beyond the command of the LORD — and I must
say only what the LORD says'? 14 Now I am going back to my people, but come, let
me warn you of what this people will do to your people in days to come."

Balaam's Fourth Message

15 Then he spoke his message:

"The prophecy of Balaam son of Beor,
the prophecy of one whose eye sees clearly,
16 the prophecy of one who hears the words of God,
who has knowledge from the Most High,
who sees a vision from the Almighty,
who falls prostrate, and whose eyes are opened:

17 "I see him, but not now;
I behold him, but not near.
A star will come out of Jacob;
a scepter will rise out of Israel.
He will crush the foreheads of Moab,
the skulls[a] of[b] all the people of Sheth.[c]
18 Edom will be conquered;
Seir, his enemy, will be conquered,
but Israel will grow strong.
19 A ruler will come out of Jacob
and destroy the survivors of the city."

Balaam's Fifth Message

20 Then Balaam saw Amalek and spoke his message:

"Amalek was first among the nations,
but their end will be utter destruction."

Balaam's Sixth Message

21 Then he saw the Kenites and spoke his message:

"Your dwelling place is secure,
your nest is set in a rock;
22 yet you Kenites will be destroyed
when Ashur takes you captive."

Balaam's Seventh Message

23 Then he spoke his message:

"Alas! Who can live when God does this?[d]
24 Ships will come from the shores of Cyprus;

---

[a] *17* Samaritan Pentateuch (see also Jer. 48:45); the meaning of the word in the Masoretic Text is uncertain. [b] *17* Or possibly *Moab, / batter* [c] *17* Or *all the noisy boasters*
[d] *23* Masoretic Text; with a different word division of the Hebrew *The people from the islands will gather from the north.*

A STAR AND A SCEPTER

This is the fourth message proclaimed by the pagan prophet Balaam. God's use of Balaam, a non-Jewish outsider, proves that God's ways and thoughts are truly above human intentions (Isa 55:8). God used a prophet who was on the payroll of an enemy nation, which was the antithesis of what would have been expected. However, God utilizes whatever and whomever he desires to reveal himself and his plan to his people.

Balaam's poetic prophecy offered a ray of hope to the reader, reminding them of a coming Messiah. The coming of the Messiah had been anticipated since the revolt of Adam (Ge 3:15) and promised through the line of Abraham (22:18). Additionally, Jacob prophesied that his son, Judah, would be heir to the royal lineage of the nation through his offspring (49:10).

Balaam pictured the Messiah-king using imagery of a "star" and a "scepter" (Nu 24:17). The Messiah would be like a star, bright and radiant. Upon the birth of the Messiah, Jesus, there was a star marking the place of his birth (Mt 2:1 – 10). In the book of Revelation, Jesus refers to himself as "the Root and the Offspring of David, and the bright Morning Star" (Rev 22:16).

The scepter evokes thoughts of royalty. A king would normally hold a scepter as a symbol of his power. The king's responsibility was not solely to rule over his people but also to care for them. Subsequently, the Messiah came not merely to usher in a new kingdom but also to take care of and shepherd the people of that kingdom. This is what sets apart the Messiah-king from the kings of the day.

Balaam's prophecy concluded with the future Messiah bringing victory over the enemies of God (Nu 24:17 – 19). Moab, the nation that hired Balaam, was proclaimed as the one who would be destroyed and become a possession of Israel. Edom denied Israel safe passage (20:14 – 21) and ultimately caused their own destruction. The Messiah, who came from the line of Jacob, will call every created thing to do what they were created to do — worship the God of creation through the power of the Spirit. The Messiah will bid all people to come and worship him (Php 2:10 – 11).

they will subdue Ashur and Eber,
but they too will come to ruin."

25Then Balaam got up and returned home, and Balak went his own way.

Moab Seduces Israel

25 While Israel was staying in Shittim, the men began to indulge in sexual
immorality with Moabite women, 2who invited them to the sacrifices to
their gods. The people ate the sacrificial meal and bowed down before these
gods. 3So Israel yoked themselves to the Baal of Peor. And the LORD's anger
burned against them.
4The LORD said to Moses, "Take all the leaders of these people, kill them and
expose them in broad daylight before the LORD, so that the LORD's fierce anger
may turn away from Israel."
5So Moses said to Israel's judges, "Each of you must put to death those of your
people who have yoked themselves to the Baal of Peor."
6Then an Israelite man brought into the camp a Midianite woman right before the eyes of Moses and the whole assembly of Israel while they were weeping at the entrance to the tent of meeting. 7When Phinehas son of Eleazar, the
son of Aaron, the priest, saw this, he left the assembly, took a spear in his hand
8and followed the Israelite into the tent. He drove the spear into both of them,
right through the Israelite man and into the woman's stomach. Then the plague
against the Israelites was stopped; 9but those who died in the plague numbered
24,000.
10The LORD said to Moses, 11"Phinehas son of Eleazar, the son of Aaron, the
priest, has turned my anger away from the Israelites. Since he was as zealous for
my honor among them as I am, I did not put an end to them in my zeal. 12There-
fore tell him I am making my covenant of peace with him. 13He and his descendants will have a covenant of a lasting priesthood, because he was zealous for
the honor of his God and made atonement for the Israelites."
14The name of the Israelite who was killed with the Midianite woman was
Zimri son of Salu, the leader of a Simeonite family. 15And the name of the Midianite woman who was put to death was Kozbi daughter of Zur, a tribal chief of
a Midianite family.
16The LORD said to Moses, 17"Treat the Midianites as enemies and kill them.
18They treated you as enemies when they deceived you in the Peor incident involving their sister Kozbi, the daughter of a Midianite leader, the woman who
was killed when the plague came as a result of that incident."

The Second Census

26 After the plague the LORD said to Moses and Eleazar son of Aaron, the
priest, 2"Take a census of the whole Israelite community by families — all
those twenty years old or more who are able to serve in the army of Israel." 3So
on the plains of Moab by the Jordan across from Jericho, Moses and Eleazar the
priest spoke with them and said, 4"Take a census of the men twenty years old or
more, as the LORD commanded Moses."

These were the Israelites who came out of Egypt:

5The descendants of Reuben, the firstborn son of Israel, were:
through Hanok, the Hanokite clan;
through Pallu, the Palluite clan;
6through Hezron, the Hezronite clan;
through Karmi, the Karmite clan.
7These were the clans of Reuben; those numbered were 43,730.
8The son of Pallu was Eliab, 9and the sons of Eliab were Nemuel, Dathan and
Abiram. The same Dathan and Abiram were the community officials who rebelled against Moses and Aaron and were among Korah's followers when they
rebelled against the LORD. 10The earth opened its mouth and swallowed them

along with Korah, whose followers died when the fire devoured the 250 men.
And they served as a warning sign. 11The line of Korah, however, did not die out.

12The descendants of Simeon by their clans were:
through Nemuel, the Nemuelite clan;
through Jamin, the Jaminite clan;
through Jakin, the Jakinite clan;
13 through Zerah, the Zerahite clan;
through Shaul, the Shaulite clan.
14These were the clans of Simeon; those numbered were 22,200.

15The descendants of Gad by their clans were:
through Zephon, the Zephonite clan;
through Haggi, the Haggite clan;
through Shuni, the Shunite clan;
16 through Ozni, the Oznite clan;
through Eri, the Erite clan;
17 through Arodi,[a] the Arodite clan;
through Areli, the Arelite clan.
18These were the clans of Gad; those numbered were 40,500.

19Er and Onan were sons of Judah, but they died in Canaan.
20The descendants of Judah by their clans were:
through Shelah, the Shelanite clan;
through Perez, the Perezite clan;
through Zerah, the Zerahite clan.
21 The descendants of Perez were:
through Hezron, the Hezronite clan;
through Hamul, the Hamulite clan.
22These were the clans of Judah; those numbered were 76,500.

23The descendants of Issachar by their clans were:
through Tola, the Tolaite clan;
through Puah, the Puite[b] clan;
24 through Jashub, the Jashubite clan;
through Shimron, the Shimronite clan.
25These were the clans of Issachar; those numbered were 64,300.

26The descendants of Zebulun by their clans were:
through Sered, the Seredite clan;
through Elon, the Elonite clan;
through Jahleel, the Jahleelite clan.
27These were the clans of Zebulun; those numbered were 60,500.
28The descendants of Joseph by their clans through Manasseh and Ephraim were:
29The descendants of Manasseh:
through Makir, the Makirite clan (Makir was the father of Gilead);
through Gilead, the Gileadite clan.
30 These were the descendants of Gilead:
through Iezer, the Iezerite clan;
through Helek, the Helekite clan;
31 through Asriel, the Asrielite clan;
through Shechem, the Shechemite clan;
32 through Shemida, the Shemidaite clan;
through Hepher, the Hepherite clan.

---

[a] 17 Samaritan Pentateuch and Syriac (see also Gen. 46:16); Masoretic Text *Arod*
[b] 23 Samaritan Pentateuch, Septuagint, Vulgate and Syriac (see also 1 Chron. 7:1); Masoretic Text *through Puvah, the Punite*

33 (Zelophehad son of Hepher had no sons; he had only daughters, whose
names were Mahlah, Noah, Hoglah, Milkah and Tirzah.)
34 These were the clans of Manasseh; those numbered were 52,700.

35 These were the descendants of Ephraim by their clans:
through Shuthelah, the Shuthelahite clan;
through Beker, the Bekerite clan;
through Tahan, the Tahanite clan.
36 These were the descendants of Shuthelah:
through Eran, the Eranite clan.
37 These were the clans of Ephraim; those numbered were 32,500.

These were the descendants of Joseph by their clans.

38 The descendants of Benjamin by their clans were:
through Bela, the Belaite clan;
through Ashbel, the Ashbelite clan;
through Ahiram, the Ahiramite clan;
39 through Shupham,[a] the Shuphamite clan;
through Hupham, the Huphamite clan.
40 The descendants of Bela through Ard and Naaman were:
through Ard,[b] the Ardite clan;
through Naaman, the Naamite clan.
41 These were the clans of Benjamin; those numbered were 45,600.

42 These were the descendants of Dan by their clans:
through Shuham, the Shuhamite clan.
These were the clans of Dan: 43 All of them were Shuhamite clans; and those
numbered were 64,400.

44 The descendants of Asher by their clans were:
through Imnah, the Imnite clan;
through Ishvi, the Ishvite clan;
through Beriah, the Beriite clan;
45 and through the descendants of Beriah:
through Heber, the Heberite clan;
through Malkiel, the Malkielite clan.
46 (Asher had a daughter named Serah.)
47 These were the clans of Asher; those numbered were 53,400.

48 The descendants of Naphtali by their clans were:
through Jahzeel, the Jahzeelite clan;
through Guni, the Gunite clan;
49 through Jezer, the Jezerite clan;
through Shillem, the Shillemite clan.
50 These were the clans of Naphtali; those numbered were 45,400.
51 The total number of the men of Israel was 601,730.

52 The LORD said to Moses, 53 "The land is to be allotted to them as an inheritance based on the number of names. 54 To a larger group give a larger inheritance,
and to a smaller group a smaller one; each is to receive its inheritance according
to the number of those listed. 55 Be sure that the land is distributed by lot. What
each group inherits will be according to the names for its ancestral tribe. 56 Each
inheritance is to be distributed by lot among the larger and smaller groups."

57 These were the Levites who were counted by their clans:
through Gershon, the Gershonite clan;

---

[a] *39* A few manuscripts of the Masoretic Text, Samaritan Pentateuch, Vulgate and Syriac (see also Septuagint); most manuscripts of the Masoretic Text *Shephupham* [b] *40* Samaritan Pentateuch and Vulgate (see also Septuagint); Masoretic Text does not have *through Ard.*

NUMBERS 26:53

A NEW LAND

Central to the promises of God was the gift of land. Reminiscent of the Garden of Eden, the people were promised that they would dwell with God in a good land overflowing with the provision of the Lord. The Israelites were not merely inhabitants in this land; they were each given a portion of the land as a bountiful inheritance. They were reminded that God was not merely a God of the nation but a personal God who cared for each of them individually. Jesus demonstrated the same personal care when he promised an inheritance in heaven to all of his children (Jn 14:1 – 4). He is now preparing this dwelling place for each of those who have trusted in him by faith and repentance. There they will receive the inheritance of those who are in Christ Jesus as they rule and reign forever with him in a new land, the new heaven and new earth (2Pe 3:13; Rev 21:1).

through Kohath, the Kohathite clan;
through Merari, the Merarite clan.
58These also were Levite clans:
the Libnite clan,
the Hebronite clan,
the Mahlite clan,
the Mushite clan,
the Korahite clan.
(Kohath was the forefather of Amram; 59the name of Amram's wife was
Jochebed, a descendant of Levi, who was born to the Levites[a] in Egypt.
To Amram she bore Aaron, Moses and their sister Miriam. 60Aaron was
the father of Nadab and Abihu, Eleazar and Ithamar. 61But Nadab and
Abihu died when they made an offering before the LORD with unauthorized fire.)

62All the male Levites a month old or more numbered 23,000. They were not
counted along with the other Israelites because they received no inheritance
among them.

63These are the ones counted by Moses and Eleazar the priest when they
counted the Israelites on the plains of Moab by the Jordan across from Jericho.
64Not one of them was among those counted by Moses and Aaron the priest
when they counted the Israelites in the Desert of Sinai. 65For the LORD had told
those Israelites they would surely die in the wilderness, and not one of them was
left except Caleb son of Jephunneh and Joshua son of Nun.

Zelophehad's Daughters

27 The daughters of Zelophehad son of Hepher, the son of Gilead, the son of
Makir, the son of Manasseh, belonged to the clans of Manasseh son of Joseph. The names of the daughters were Mahlah, Noah, Hoglah, Milkah and Tirzah. They came forward 2and stood before Moses, Eleazar the priest, the leaders
and the whole assembly at the entrance to the tent of meeting and said, 3"Our
father died in the wilderness. He was not among Korah's followers, who banded
together against the LORD, but he died for his own sin and left no sons. 4Why
should our father's name disappear from his clan because he had no son? Give
us property among our father's relatives."

5So Moses brought their case before the LORD, 6and the LORD said to him,
7"What Zelophehad's daughters are saying is right. You must certainly give them
property as an inheritance among their father's relatives and give their father's
inheritance to them.

8"Say to the Israelites, 'If a man dies and leaves no son, give his inheritance to
his daughter. 9If he has no daughter, give his inheritance to his brothers. 10If he
has no brothers, give his inheritance to his father's brothers. 11If his father had
no brothers, give his inheritance to the nearest relative in his clan, that he may
possess it. This is to have the force of law for the Israelites, as the LORD commanded Moses.'"

Joshua to Succeed Moses

12Then the LORD said to Moses, "Go up this mountain in the Abarim Range
and see the land I have given the Israelites. 13After you have seen it, you too will
be gathered to your people, as your brother Aaron was, 14for when the community rebelled at the waters in the Desert of Zin, both of you disobeyed my command to honor me as holy before their eyes." (These were the waters of Meribah
Kadesh, in the Desert of Zin.)

15Moses said to the LORD, 16"May the LORD, the God who gives breath to all living things, appoint someone over this community 17to go out and come in before

[a] 59 Or *Jochebed, a daughter of Levi, who was born to Levi*

NUMBERS 27:15–17

SHEEP WITHOUT A SHEPHERD

Moses recognized that sinful people were doomed to destruction without a godly leader. The people of God are pictured here as wayward and helpless sheep without the care of a benevolent shepherd. Knowing of his impending death, Moses interceded on behalf of the people and asked God to provide a shepherd who could lead the people into God's promised land. God anointed Joshua for this role; however, like all subsequent leaders, he proved inadequate to fully provide the leadership and care that the people required.

Israel needed more than any sinful human leader could provide. This need prompted Jesus, like Moses, to lament over the condition of God's flock (Mk 6:34). He knew that they needed a Good Shepherd who would not only lead them to safety but also ultimately lay down his life for the sheep he so dearly loved (Jn 10:1–18). Jesus provided the type of care Moses longed for in this passage—a kind of leadership that is impossible for a fallen person to provide. Only the Son of God could be the Good Shepherd the people so desperately needed.

them, one who will lead them out and bring them in, so the LORD's people will
not be like sheep without a shepherd."
[18]So the LORD said to Moses, "Take Joshua son of Nun, a man in whom is the
spirit of leadership,[a] and lay your hand on him. [19]Have him stand before Eleazar the priest and the entire assembly and commission him in their presence.
[20]Give him some of your authority so the whole Israelite community will obey
him. [21]He is to stand before Eleazar the priest, who will obtain decisions for him
by inquiring of the Urim before the LORD. At his command he and the entire
community of the Israelites will go out, and at his command they will come in."
[22]Moses did as the LORD commanded him. He took Joshua and had him stand
before Eleazar the priest and the whole assembly. [23]Then he laid his hands on
him and commissioned him, as the LORD instructed through Moses.

Daily Offerings

28 The LORD said to Moses, [2]"Give this command to the Israelites and say to
them: 'Make sure that you present to me at the appointed time my food
offerings, as an aroma pleasing to me.' [3]Say to them: 'This is the food offering you
are to present to the LORD: two lambs a year old without defect, as a regular burnt
offering each day. [4]Offer one lamb in the morning and the other at twilight, [5]to-
gether with a grain offering of a tenth of an ephah[b] of the finest flour mixed with
a quarter of a hin[c] of oil from pressed olives. [6]This is the regular burnt offering
instituted at Mount Sinai as a pleasing aroma, a food offering presented to the
LORD. [7]The accompanying drink offering is to be a quarter of a hin of fermented
drink with each lamb. Pour out the drink offering to the LORD at the sanctuary.
[8]Offer the second lamb at twilight, along with the same kind of grain offering
and drink offering that you offer in the morning. This is a food offering, an aroma pleasing to the LORD.

Sabbath Offerings

[9]" 'On the Sabbath day, make an offering of two lambs a year old without defect, together with its drink offering and a grain offering of two-tenths of an
ephah[d] of the finest flour mixed with olive oil. [10]This is the burnt offering for
every Sabbath, in addition to the regular burnt offering and its drink offering.

Monthly Offerings

[11]" 'On the first of every month, present to the LORD a burnt offering of two
young bulls, one ram and seven male lambs a year old, all without defect. [12]With
each bull there is to be a grain offering of three-tenths of an ephah[e] of the finest
flour mixed with oil; with the ram, a grain offering of two-tenths of an ephah
of the finest flour mixed with oil; [13]and with each lamb, a grain offering of a
tenth of an ephah of the finest flour mixed with oil. This is for a burnt offering,
a pleasing aroma, a food offering presented to the LORD. [14]With each bull there
is to be a drink offering of half a hin[f] of wine; with the ram, a third of a hin[g]; and
with each lamb, a quarter of a hin. This is the monthly burnt offering to be made
at each new moon during the year. [15]Besides the regular burnt offering with its
drink offering, one male goat is to be presented to the LORD as a sin offering.[h]

The Passover

[16]" 'On the fourteenth day of the first month the LORD's Passover is to be held.
[17]On the fifteenth day of this month there is to be a festival; for seven days eat
bread made without yeast. [18]On the first day hold a sacred assembly and do no

[a] *18* Or *the Spirit* [b] *5* That is, probably about 3 1/2 pounds or about 1.6 kilograms; also in verses 13, 21 and 29 [c] *5* That is, about 1 quart or about 1 liter; also in verses 7 and 14
[d] *9* That is, probably about 7 pounds or about 3.2 kilograms; also in verses 12, 20 and 28
[e] *12* That is, probably about 11 pounds or about 5 kilograms; also in verses 20 and 28
[f] *14* That is, about 2 quarts or about 1.9 liters [g] *14* That is, about 1 1/3 quarts or about 1.3 liters [h] *15* Or *purification offering*; also in verse 22

NUMBERS 28:1–8

ONGOING DAILY OFFERINGS

God commanded his people to carefully make the proper offerings for sin—offerings that took place every day. The frequency of these sacrifices filled the wilderness with the blood of slaughtered animals, vividly reminding Israel that sin demanded a blood sacrifice. The sheer volume of people, combined with the heat of the wilderness, made this a stark reality for all to see. The people longed for the day when these seemingly unending sacrifices would cease and they could permanently and unalterably be made right with God.

Jesus, as the pure and spotless Lamb of God, did just that. The writer of Hebrews demonstrated that Jesus' sacrificial death fully and finally made atonement for the sins of his people. No longer are daily sacrifices necessary because believers "have been made holy through the sacrifice of the body of Jesus Christ once for all" (Heb 10:1–10).

regular work. 19 Present to the LORD a food offering consisting of a burnt offering of two young bulls, one ram and seven male lambs a year old, all without defect. 20 With each bull offer a grain offering of three-tenths of an ephah of the finest flour mixed with oil; with the ram, two-tenths; 21 and with each of the seven lambs, one-tenth. 22 Include one male goat as a sin offering to make atonement for you. 23 Offer these in addition to the regular morning burnt offering. 24 In this way present the food offering every day for seven days as an aroma pleasing to the LORD; it is to be offered in addition to the regular burnt offering and its drink offering. 25 On the seventh day hold a sacred assembly and do no regular work.

The Festival of Weeks

26 " 'On the day of firstfruits, when you present to the LORD an offering of new grain during the Festival of Weeks, hold a sacred assembly and do no regular work. 27 Present a burnt offering of two young bulls, one ram and seven male lambs a year old as an aroma pleasing to the LORD. 28 With each bull there is to be a grain offering of three-tenths of an ephah of the finest flour mixed with oil; with the ram, two-tenths; 29 and with each of the seven lambs, one-tenth. 30 Include one male goat to make atonement for you. 31 Offer these together with their drink offerings, in addition to the regular burnt offering and its grain offering. Be sure the animals are without defect.

The Festival of Trumpets

29 " 'On the first day of the seventh month hold a sacred assembly and do no regular work. It is a day for you to sound the trumpets. 2 As an aroma pleasing to the LORD, offer a burnt offering of one young bull, one ram and seven male lambs a year old, all without defect. 3 With the bull offer a grain offering of three-tenths of an ephah[a] of the finest flour mixed with olive oil; with the ram, two-tenths[b]; 4 and with each of the seven lambs, one-tenth.[c] 5 Include one male goat as a sin offering[d] to make atonement for you. 6 These are in addition to the monthly and daily burnt offerings with their grain offerings and drink offerings as specified. They are food offerings presented to the LORD, a pleasing aroma.

The Day of Atonement

7 " 'On the tenth day of this seventh month hold a sacred assembly. You must deny yourselves[e] and do no work. 8 Present as an aroma pleasing to the LORD a burnt offering of one young bull, one ram and seven male lambs a year old, all without defect. 9 With the bull offer a grain offering of three-tenths of an ephah of the finest flour mixed with oil; with the ram, two-tenths; 10 and with each of the seven lambs, one-tenth. 11 Include one male goat as a sin offering, in addition to the sin offering for atonement and the regular burnt offering with its grain offering, and their drink offerings.

The Festival of Tabernacles

12 " 'On the fifteenth day of the seventh month, hold a sacred assembly and do no regular work. Celebrate a festival to the LORD for seven days. 13 Present as an aroma pleasing to the LORD a food offering consisting of a burnt offering of thirteen young bulls, two rams and fourteen male lambs a year old, all without defect. 14 With each of the thirteen bulls offer a grain offering of three-tenths of an ephah of the finest flour mixed with oil; with each of the two rams, two-tenths; 15 and with each of the fourteen lambs, one-tenth. 16 Include one male goat as a sin offering, in addition to the regular burnt offering with its grain offering and drink offering.

17 " 'On the second day offer twelve young bulls, two rams and fourteen male

---

[a] *3* That is, probably about 11 pounds or about 5 kilograms; also in verses 9 and 14 [b] *3* That is, probably about 7 pounds or about 3.2 kilograms; also in verses 9 and 14 [c] *4* That is, probably about 3 1/2 pounds or about 1.6 kilograms; also in verses 10 and 15 [d] *5* Or *purification offering*; also elsewhere in this chapter [e] *7* Or *must fast*

NUMBERS 29:1–6

OFFERINGS OF JOY

The Old Testament sacrificial system was complex and costly. God provided instructions that required hundreds and hundreds of bulls, rams, lambs and goats to be killed every year (not to mention the use of massive amounts of grain, oil and wine). The altar of the tabernacle became messy and bloody—much like the hearts of God's people. But these instructions concerning worship were given to a people who were already in relationship with God—they are his people and he is their God. These sacrifices were never meant to be a means whereby people, by their own merit, could procure a relationship with God. They were meant to be offerings of joy, acts of worship, an outpouring of praise to the God who had already redeemed them. This is true for all of God's people throughout redemptive history. Sacrifices, whether of time, money, obedience or praise, are not meant to make one right before God. Only Jesus can do that. His death redeemed a people, called them to himself and made them right with God. The response to that grace is seen in the sacrifices of praise offered by the people of God.

lambs a year old, all without defect. [18]With the bulls, rams and lambs, offer their
grain offerings and drink offerings according to the number specified. [19]Include
one male goat as a sin offering, in addition to the regular burnt offering with its
grain offering, and their drink offerings.
[20]" 'On the third day offer eleven bulls, two rams and fourteen male lambs a
year old, all without defect. [21]With the bulls, rams and lambs, offer their grain
offerings and drink offerings according to the number specified. [22]Include one
male goat as a sin offering, in addition to the regular burnt offering with its grain
offering and drink offering.
[23]" 'On the fourth day offer ten bulls, two rams and fourteen male lambs a
year old, all without defect. [24]With the bulls, rams and lambs, offer their grain
offerings and drink offerings according to the number specified. [25]Include one
male goat as a sin offering, in addition to the regular burnt offering with its grain
offering and drink offering.
[26]" 'On the fifth day offer nine bulls, two rams and fourteen male lambs a year
old, all without defect. [27]With the bulls, rams and lambs, offer their grain offerings and drink offerings according to the number specified. [28]Include one male
goat as a sin offering, in addition to the regular burnt offering with its grain offering and drink offering.
[29]" 'On the sixth day offer eight bulls, two rams and fourteen male lambs a
year old, all without defect. [30]With the bulls, rams and lambs, offer their grain
offerings and drink offerings according to the number specified. [31]Include one
male goat as a sin offering, in addition to the regular burnt offering with its grain
offering and drink offering.
[32]" 'On the seventh day offer seven bulls, two rams and fourteen male lambs
a year old, all without defect. [33]With the bulls, rams and lambs, offer their grain
offerings and drink offerings according to the number specified. [34]Include one
male goat as a sin offering, in addition to the regular burnt offering with its grain
offering and drink offering.
[35]" 'On the eighth day hold a closing special assembly and do no regular work.
[36]Present as an aroma pleasing to the LORD a food offering consisting of a burnt
offering of one bull, one ram and seven male lambs a year old, all without defect. [37]With the bull, the ram and the lambs, offer their grain offerings and drink
offerings according to the number specified. [38]Include one male goat as a sin offering, in addition to the regular burnt offering with its grain offering and drink
offering.
[39]" 'In addition to what you vow and your freewill offerings, offer these to the
LORD at your appointed festivals: your burnt offerings, grain offerings, drink offerings and fellowship offerings.' "
[40]Moses told the Israelites all that the LORD commanded him.[a]

Vows

30 [b] Moses said to the heads of the tribes of Israel: "This is what the LORD
commands: [2]When a man makes a vow to the LORD or takes an oath to
obligate himself by a pledge, he must not break his word but must do everything
he said.
[3]"When a young woman still living in her father's household makes a vow to
the LORD or obligates herself by a pledge [4]and her father hears about her vow or
pledge but says nothing to her, then all her vows and every pledge by which she
obligated herself will stand. [5]But if her father forbids her when he hears about
it, none of her vows or the pledges by which she obligated herself will stand; the
LORD will release her because her father has forbidden her.
[6]"If she marries after she makes a vow or after her lips utter a rash promise
by which she obligates herself [7]and her husband hears about it but says nothing

---

[a] *40* In Hebrew texts this verse (29:40) is numbered 30:1. [b] In Hebrew texts 30:1-16 is numbered 30:2-17.

to her, then her vows or the pledges by which she obligated herself will stand. 8But if her husband forbids her when he hears about it, he nullifies the vow that obligates her or the rash promise by which she obligates herself, and the LORD will release her.

9"Any vow or obligation taken by a widow or divorced woman will be binding on her.

10"If a woman living with her husband makes a vow or obligates herself by a pledge under oath 11and her husband hears about it but says nothing to her and does not forbid her, then all her vows or the pledges by which she obligated herself will stand. 12But if her husband nullifies them when he hears about them, then none of the vows or pledges that came from her lips will stand. Her husband has nullified them, and the LORD will release her. 13Her husband may confirm or nullify any vow she makes or any sworn pledge to deny herself.[a] 14But if her husband says nothing to her about it from day to day, then he confirms all her vows or the pledges binding on her. He confirms them by saying nothing to her when he hears about them. 15If, however, he nullifies them some time after he hears about them, then he must bear the consequences of her wrongdoing."

16These are the regulations the LORD gave Moses concerning relationships between a man and his wife, and between a father and his young daughter still living at home.

Vengeance on the Midianites

31 The LORD said to Moses, 2"Take vengeance on the Midianites for the Israelites. After that, you will be gathered to your people."

3So Moses said to the people, "Arm some of your men to go to war against the Midianites so that they may carry out the LORD's vengeance on them. 4Send into battle a thousand men from each of the tribes of Israel." 5So twelve thousand men armed for battle, a thousand from each tribe, were supplied from the clans of Israel. 6Moses sent them into battle, a thousand from each tribe, along with Phinehas son of Eleazar, the priest, who took with him articles from the sanctuary and the trumpets for signaling.

7They fought against Midian, as the LORD commanded Moses, and killed every man. 8Among their victims were Evi, Rekem, Zur, Hur and Reba — the five kings of Midian. They also killed Balaam son of Beor with the sword. 9The Israelites captured the Midianite women and children and took all the Midianite herds, flocks and goods as plunder. 10They burned all the towns where the Midianites had settled, as well as all their camps. 11They took all the plunder and spoils, including the people and animals, 12and brought the captives, spoils and plunder to Moses and Eleazar the priest and the Israelite assembly at their camp on the plains of Moab, by the Jordan across from Jericho.

13Moses, Eleazar the priest and all the leaders of the community went to meet them outside the camp. 14Moses was angry with the officers of the army — the commanders of thousands and commanders of hundreds — who returned from the battle.

15"Have you allowed all the women to live?" he asked them. 16"They were the ones who followed Balaam's advice and enticed the Israelites to be unfaithful to the LORD in the Peor incident, so that a plague struck the LORD's people. 17Now kill all the boys. And kill every woman who has slept with a man, 18but save for yourselves every girl who has never slept with a man.

19"Anyone who has killed someone or touched someone who was killed must stay outside the camp seven days. On the third and seventh days you must purify yourselves and your captives. 20Purify every garment as well as everything made of leather, goat hair or wood."

21Then Eleazar the priest said to the soldiers who had gone into battle, "This is what is required by the law that the LORD gave Moses: 22Gold, silver, bronze,

---

[a] 13 Or *to fast*

iron, tin, lead 23and anything else that can withstand fire must be put through
the fire, and then it will be clean. But it must also be purified with the water of
cleansing. And whatever cannot withstand fire must be put through that water.
24On the seventh day wash your clothes and you will be clean. Then you may
come into the camp."

Dividing the Spoils

25The LORD said to Moses, 26"You and Eleazar the priest and the family heads
of the community are to count all the people and animals that were captured.
27Divide the spoils equally between the soldiers who took part in the battle and
the rest of the community. 28From the soldiers who fought in the battle, set apart
as tribute for the LORD one out of every five hundred, whether people, cattle,
donkeys or sheep. 29Take this tribute from their half share and give it to Eleazar
the priest as the LORD's part. 30From the Israelites' half, select one out of every
fifty, whether people, cattle, donkeys, sheep or other animals. Give them to the
Levites, who are responsible for the care of the LORD's tabernacle." 31So Moses
and Eleazar the priest did as the LORD commanded Moses.

32The plunder remaining from the spoils that the soldiers took was 675,000
sheep, 3372,000 cattle, 3461,000 donkeys 35and 32,000 women who had never
slept with a man.

36The half share of those who fought in the battle was:

337,500 sheep, 37of which the tribute for the LORD was 675;
38 36,000 cattle, of which the tribute for the LORD was 72;
39 30,500 donkeys, of which the tribute for the LORD was 61;
40 16,000 people, of whom the tribute for the LORD was 32.

41Moses gave the tribute to Eleazar the priest as the LORD's part, as the LORD
commanded Moses.

42The half belonging to the Israelites, which Moses set apart from that of the
fighting men— 43the community's half—was 337,500 sheep, 4436,000 cattle,
4530,500 donkeys 46and 16,000 people. 47From the Israelites' half, Moses selected one out of every fifty people and animals, as the LORD commanded him, and
gave them to the Levites, who were responsible for the care of the LORD's tabernacle.

48Then the officers who were over the units of the army—the commanders
of thousands and commanders of hundreds—went to Moses 49and said to him,
"Your servants have counted the soldiers under our command, and not one is
missing. 50So we have brought as an offering to the LORD the gold articles each of
us acquired—armlets, bracelets, signet rings, earrings and necklaces—to make
atonement for ourselves before the LORD."

51Moses and Eleazar the priest accepted from them the gold—all the crafted
articles. 52All the gold from the commanders of thousands and commanders of
hundreds that Moses and Eleazar presented as a gift to the LORD weighed 16,750
shekels.[a] 53Each soldier had taken plunder for himself. 54Moses and Eleazar the
priest accepted the gold from the commanders of thousands and commanders
of hundreds and brought it into the tent of meeting as a memorial for the Israelites before the LORD.

The Transjordan Tribes

32 The Reubenites and Gadites, who had very large herds and flocks, saw
that the lands of Jazer and Gilead were suitable for livestock. 2So they
came to Moses and Eleazar the priest and to the leaders of the community, and
said, 3"Ataroth, Dibon, Jazer, Nimrah, Heshbon, Elealeh, Sebam, Nebo and
Beon— 4the land the LORD subdued before the people of Israel—are suitable
for livestock, and your servants have livestock. 5If we have found favor in your

[a] 52 That is, about 420 pounds or about 190 kilograms

eyes," they said, "let this land be given to your servants as our possession. Do not make us cross the Jordan."

[6]Moses said to the Gadites and Reubenites, "Should your fellow Israelites go to war while you sit here? [7]Why do you discourage the Israelites from crossing over into the land the LORD has given them? [8]This is what your fathers did when I sent them from Kadesh Barnea to look over the land. [9]After they went up to the Valley of Eshkol and viewed the land, they discouraged the Israelites from entering the land the LORD had given them. [10]The LORD's anger was aroused that day and he swore this oath: [11]'Because they have not followed me wholeheartedly, not one of those who were twenty years old or more when they came up out of Egypt will see the land I promised on oath to Abraham, Isaac and Jacob — [12]not one except Caleb son of Jephunneh the Kenizzite and Joshua son of Nun, for they followed the LORD wholeheartedly.' [13]The LORD's anger burned against Israel and he made them wander in the wilderness forty years, until the whole generation of those who had done evil in his sight was gone.

[14]"And here you are, a brood of sinners, standing in the place of your fathers and making the LORD even more angry with Israel. [15]If you turn away from following him, he will again leave all this people in the wilderness, and you will be the cause of their destruction."

[16]Then they came up to him and said, "We would like to build pens here for our livestock and cities for our women and children. [17]But we will arm ourselves for battle[a] and go ahead of the Israelites until we have brought them to their place. Meanwhile our women and children will live in fortified cities, for protection from the inhabitants of the land. [18]We will not return to our homes until each of the Israelites has received their inheritance. [19]We will not receive any inheritance with them on the other side of the Jordan, because our inheritance has come to us on the east side of the Jordan."

[20]Then Moses said to them, "If you will do this — if you will arm yourselves before the LORD for battle [21]and if all of you who are armed cross over the Jordan before the LORD until he has driven his enemies out before him — [22]then when the land is subdued before the LORD, you may return and be free from your obligation to the LORD and to Israel. And this land will be your possession before the LORD.

[23]"But if you fail to do this, you will be sinning against the LORD; and you may be sure that your sin will find you out. [24]Build cities for your women and children, and pens for your flocks, but do what you have promised."

[25]The Gadites and Reubenites said to Moses, "We your servants will do as our lord commands. [26]Our children and wives, our flocks and herds will remain here in the cities of Gilead. [27]But your servants, every man who is armed for battle, will cross over to fight before the LORD, just as our lord says."

[28]Then Moses gave orders about them to Eleazar the priest and Joshua son of Nun and to the family heads of the Israelite tribes. [29]He said to them, "If the Gadites and Reubenites, every man armed for battle, cross over the Jordan with you before the LORD, then when the land is subdued before you, you must give them the land of Gilead as their possession. [30]But if they do not cross over with you armed, they must accept their possession with you in Canaan."

[31]The Gadites and Reubenites answered, "Your servants will do what the LORD has said. [32]We will cross over before the LORD into Canaan armed, but the property we inherit will be on this side of the Jordan."

[33]Then Moses gave to the Gadites, the Reubenites and the half-tribe of Manasseh son of Joseph the kingdom of Sihon king of the Amorites and the kingdom of Og king of Bashan — the whole land with its cities and the territory around them.

[34]The Gadites built up Dibon, Ataroth, Aroer, [35]Atroth Shophan, Jazer, Jogbehah, [36]Beth Nimrah and Beth Haran as fortified cities, and built pens for their

[a] *17* Septuagint; Hebrew *will be quick to arm ourselves*

flocks. [37]And the Reubenites rebuilt Heshbon, Elealeh and Kiriathaim, [38]as well
as Nebo and Baal Meon (these names were changed) and Sibmah. They gave
names to the cities they rebuilt.

[39]The descendants of Makir son of Manasseh went to Gilead, captured it and
drove out the Amorites who were there. [40]So Moses gave Gilead to the Makirites, the descendants of Manasseh, and they settled there. [41]Jair, a descendant
of Manasseh, captured their settlements and called them Havvoth Jair.[a] [42]And
Nobah captured Kenath and its surrounding settlements and called it Nobah
after himself.

Stages in Israel's Journey

33 Here are the stages in the journey of the Israelites when they came out
of Egypt by divisions under the leadership of Moses and Aaron. [2]At the
LORD's command Moses recorded the stages in their journey. This is their journey by stages:

[3]The Israelites set out from Rameses on the fifteenth day of the first
month, the day after the Passover. They marched out defiantly in full view
of all the Egyptians, [4]who were burying all their firstborn, whom the LORD
had struck down among them; for the LORD had brought judgment on their
gods.

[5]The Israelites left Rameses and camped at Sukkoth.

[6]They left Sukkoth and camped at Etham, on the edge of the desert.

[7]They left Etham, turned back to Pi Hahiroth, to the east of Baal Zephon,
and camped near Migdol.

[8]They left Pi Hahiroth[b] and passed through the sea into the desert, and
when they had traveled for three days in the Desert of Etham, they camped
at Marah.

[9]They left Marah and went to Elim, where there were twelve springs and
seventy palm trees, and they camped there.

[10]They left Elim and camped by the Red Sea.[c]

[11]They left the Red Sea and camped in the Desert of Sin.

[12]They left the Desert of Sin and camped at Dophkah.

[13]They left Dophkah and camped at Alush.

[14]They left Alush and camped at Rephidim, where there was no water
for the people to drink.

[15]They left Rephidim and camped in the Desert of Sinai.

[16]They left the Desert of Sinai and camped at Kibroth Hattaavah.

[17]They left Kibroth Hattaavah and camped at Hazeroth.

[18]They left Hazeroth and camped at Rithmah.

[19]They left Rithmah and camped at Rimmon Perez.

[20]They left Rimmon Perez and camped at Libnah.

[21]They left Libnah and camped at Rissah.

[22]They left Rissah and camped at Kehelathah.

[23]They left Kehelathah and camped at Mount Shepher.

[24]They left Mount Shepher and camped at Haradah.

[25]They left Haradah and camped at Makheloth.

[26]They left Makheloth and camped at Tahath.

[27]They left Tahath and camped at Terah.

[28]They left Terah and camped at Mithkah.

[29]They left Mithkah and camped at Hashmonah.

[30]They left Hashmonah and camped at Moseroth.

[31]They left Moseroth and camped at Bene Jaakan.

[32]They left Bene Jaakan and camped at Hor Haggidgad.

---

[a] 41 Or *them the settlements of Jair* [b] 8 Many manuscripts of the Masoretic Text, Samaritan Pentateuch and Vulgate; most manuscripts of the Masoretic Text *left from before Hahiroth*
[c] 10 Or *the Sea of Reeds*; also in verse 11

33 They left Hor Haggidgad and camped at Jotbathah.

34 They left Jotbathah and camped at Abronah.

35 They left Abronah and camped at Ezion Geber.

36 They left Ezion Geber and camped at Kadesh, in the Desert of Zin.

37 They left Kadesh and camped at Mount Hor, on the border of Edom.

38 At the LORD's command Aaron the priest went up Mount Hor, where he died on the first day of the fifth month of the fortieth year after the Israelites came out of Egypt. 39 Aaron was a hundred and twenty-three years old when he died on Mount Hor.

40 The Canaanite king of Arad, who lived in the Negev of Canaan, heard that the Israelites were coming.

41 They left Mount Hor and camped at Zalmonah.

42 They left Zalmonah and camped at Punon.

43 They left Punon and camped at Oboth.

44 They left Oboth and camped at Iye Abarim, on the border of Moab.

45 They left Iye Abarim and camped at Dibon Gad.

46 They left Dibon Gad and camped at Almon Diblathaim.

47 They left Almon Diblathaim and camped in the mountains of Abarim, near Nebo.

48 They left the mountains of Abarim and camped on the plains of Moab by the Jordan across from Jericho. 49 There on the plains of Moab they camped along the Jordan from Beth Jeshimoth to Abel Shittim.

50 On the plains of Moab by the Jordan across from Jericho the LORD said to Moses, 51 "Speak to the Israelites and say to them: 'When you cross the Jordan into Canaan, 52 drive out all the inhabitants of the land before you. Destroy all their carved images and their cast idols, and demolish all their high places. 53 Take possession of the land and settle in it, for I have given you the land to possess. 54 Distribute the land by lot, according to your clans. To a larger group give a larger inheritance, and to a smaller group a smaller one. Whatever falls to them by lot will be theirs. Distribute it according to your ancestral tribes.

55 " 'But if you do not drive out the inhabitants of the land, those you allow to remain will become barbs in your eyes and thorns in your sides. They will give you trouble in the land where you will live. 56 And then I will do to you what I plan to do to them.' "

Boundaries of Canaan

34 The LORD said to Moses, 2 "Command the Israelites and say to them: 'When you enter Canaan, the land that will be allotted to you as an inheritance is to have these boundaries:

3 " 'Your southern side will include some of the Desert of Zin along the border of Edom. Your southern boundary will start in the east from the southern end of the Dead Sea, 4 cross south of Scorpion Pass, continue on to Zin and go south of Kadesh Barnea. Then it will go to Hazar Addar and over to Azmon, 5 where it will turn, join the Wadi of Egypt and end at the Mediterranean Sea.

6 " 'Your western boundary will be the coast of the Mediterranean Sea. This will be your boundary on the west.

7 " 'For your northern boundary, run a line from the Mediterranean Sea to Mount Hor 8 and from Mount Hor to Lebo Hamath. Then the boundary will go to Zedad, 9 continue to Ziphron and end at Hazar Enan. This will be your boundary on the north.

10 " 'For your eastern boundary, run a line from Hazar Enan to Shepham. 11 The boundary will go down from Shepham to Riblah on the east side of Ain and continue along the slopes east of the Sea of Galilee.[a] 12 Then the boundary will go down along the Jordan and end at the Dead Sea.

[a] 11 Hebrew *Kinnereth*

NUMBERS 34:1 – 13

INHERITANCE

At the culmination of the book of Numbers, God's people were given a detailed description of where God was leading them after all the years of wandering. There they received the inheritance that God had promised and had been faithful to fulfill. God's people throughout the Bible are promised such an inheritance. Unlike the children of Israel, however, Christians do not receive an inheritance because of a national identity but because of an adoption effected through the blood of the Son of God (Col 1:12). Because of the gift of Jesus, the Father qualifies believers to participate in an inheritance that they could never deserve. In addition, unlike the children of Israel, the church does not receive an earthly inheritance of tangible significance. The earthly inheritance is found in the hope, joy and peace that comes through knowing they have a right relationship with God and a secure eternal destiny. The church is granted a heavenly and eternal inheritance — Jesus Christ himself.

" 'This will be your land, with its boundaries on every side.' "
[13]Moses commanded the Israelites: "Assign this land by lot as an inheritance.
The LORD has ordered that it be given to the nine and a half tribes, [14]because the
families of the tribe of Reuben, the tribe of Gad and the half-tribe of Manasseh
have received their inheritance. [15]These two and a half tribes have received their
inheritance east of the Jordan across from Jericho, toward the sunrise."
[16]The LORD said to Moses, [17]"These are the names of the men who are to assign the land for you as an inheritance: Eleazar the priest and Joshua son of Nun.
[18]And appoint one leader from each tribe to help assign the land. [19]These are
their names:

Caleb son of Jephunneh,
  from the tribe of Judah;
[20]Shemuel son of Ammihud,
  from the tribe of Simeon;
[21]Elidad son of Kislon,
  from the tribe of Benjamin;
[22]Bukki son of Jogli,
  the leader from the tribe of Dan;
[23]Hanniel son of Ephod,
  the leader from the tribe of Manasseh son of Joseph;
[24]Kemuel son of Shiphtan,
  the leader from the tribe of Ephraim son of Joseph;
[25]Elizaphan son of Parnak,
  the leader from the tribe of Zebulun;
[26]Paltiel son of Azzan,
  the leader from the tribe of Issachar;
[27]Ahihud son of Shelomi,
  the leader from the tribe of Asher;
[28]Pedahel son of Ammihud,
  the leader from the tribe of Naphtali."

[29]These are the men the LORD commanded to assign the inheritance to the
Israelites in the land of Canaan.

Towns for the Levites

35 On the plains of Moab by the Jordan across from Jericho, the LORD said to
Moses, [2]"Command the Israelites to give the Levites towns to live in from
the inheritance the Israelites will possess. And give them pasturelands around
the towns. [3]Then they will have towns to live in and pasturelands for the cattle
they own and all their other animals.
[4]"The pasturelands around the towns that you give the Levites will extend a
thousand cubits[a] from the town wall. [5]Outside the town, measure two thousand
cubits[b] on the east side, two thousand on the south side, two thousand on the
west and two thousand on the north, with the town in the center. They will have
this area as pastureland for the towns.

Cities of Refuge

[6]"Six of the towns you give the Levites will be cities of refuge, to which a person who has killed someone may flee. In addition, give them forty-two other
towns. [7]In all you must give the Levites forty-eight towns, together with their
pasturelands. [8]The towns you give the Levites from the land the Israelites possess are to be given in proportion to the inheritance of each tribe: Take many
towns from a tribe that has many, but few from one that has few."
[9]Then the LORD said to Moses: [10]"Speak to the Israelites and say to them:
'When you cross the Jordan into Canaan, [11]select some towns to be your cities of

[a] 4 That is, about 1,500 feet or about 450 meters [b] 5 That is, about 3,000 feet or about 900 meters

NUMBERS 35:6–34

CITIES OF REFUGE

As God's people made their final preparations to enter the promised land, God commanded Moses to establish six cities of refuge from the towns given to the tribe of Levi, where both Israelites and foreigners living among them who were accused of murder could seek sanctuary. The Old Testament Law allowed for the closest male relative of a person who was killed to seek vengeance for their deceased family member. But if the death was perhaps accidental, the "manslayer" could flee to a city of refuge where the accused would stand trial and, if found guilty of intentional murder by the judges, faced the death penalty. God refused to allow injustice to go unpunished because it would pollute both the people and their land; God's justice demanded that sin be punished.

But the cities of refuge also pointed forward to Christ, an even better sanctuary and means of dealing with the sins of God's people. All are guilty of sin and, if forced to stand trial before God alone, would be condemned to eternal punishment; however, God's people can take hold of Christ as their refuge. He offers them forgiveness from their sins and escape from the death they all deserve (Jn 8:51).

refuge, to which a person who has killed someone accidentally may flee. 12They
will be places of refuge from the avenger, so that anyone accused of murder may
not die before they stand trial before the assembly. 13These six towns you give
will be your cities of refuge. 14Give three on this side of the Jordan and three in
Canaan as cities of refuge. 15These six towns will be a place of refuge for Israelites
and for foreigners residing among them, so that anyone who has killed another
accidentally can flee there.

16" 'If anyone strikes someone a fatal blow with an iron object, that person
is a murderer; the murderer is to be put to death. 17Or if anyone is holding a
stone and strikes someone a fatal blow with it, that person is a murderer; the
murderer is to be put to death. 18Or if anyone is holding a wooden object and
strikes someone a fatal blow with it, that person is a murderer; the murderer is
to be put to death. 19The avenger of blood shall put the murderer to death; when
the avenger comes upon the murderer, the avenger shall put the murderer to
death. 20If anyone with malice aforethought shoves another or throws something at them intentionally so that they die 21or if out of enmity one person hits
another with their fist so that the other dies, that person is to be put to death;
that person is a murderer. The avenger of blood shall put the murderer to death
when they meet.

22" 'But if without enmity someone suddenly pushes another or throws something at them unintentionally 23or, without seeing them, drops on them a stone
heavy enough to kill them, and they die, then since that other person was not an
enemy and no harm was intended, 24the assembly must judge between the accused and the avenger of blood according to these regulations. 25The assembly
must protect the one accused of murder from the avenger of blood and send the
accused back to the city of refuge to which they fled. The accused must stay there
until the death of the high priest, who was anointed with the holy oil.

26" 'But if the accused ever goes outside the limits of the city of refuge to which
they fled 27and the avenger of blood finds them outside the city, the avenger of
blood may kill the accused without being guilty of murder. 28The accused must
stay in the city of refuge until the death of the high priest; only after the death of
the high priest may they return to their own property.

29" 'This is to have the force of law for you throughout the generations to come,
wherever you live.

30" 'Anyone who kills a person is to be put to death as a murderer only on the
testimony of witnesses. But no one is to be put to death on the testimony of only
one witness.

31" 'Do not accept a ransom for the life of a murderer, who deserves to die.
They are to be put to death.

32" 'Do not accept a ransom for anyone who has fled to a city of refuge and so
allow them to go back and live on their own land before the death of the high
priest.

33" 'Do not pollute the land where you are. Bloodshed pollutes the land, and
atonement cannot be made for the land on which blood has been shed, except
by the blood of the one who shed it. 34Do not defile the land where you live and
where I dwell, for I, the LORD, dwell among the Israelites.' "

Inheritance of Zelophehad's Daughters

36 The family heads of the clan of Gilead son of Makir, the son of Manasseh, who were from the clans of the descendants of Joseph, came and
spoke before Moses and the leaders, the heads of the Israelite families. 2They
said, "When the LORD commanded my lord to give the land as an inheritance
to the Israelites by lot, he ordered you to give the inheritance of our brother Zelophehad to his daughters. 3Now suppose they marry men from other Israelite
tribes; then their inheritance will be taken from our ancestral inheritance and
added to that of the tribe they marry into. And so part of the inheritance allotted
to us will be taken away. 4When the Year of Jubilee for the Israelites comes, their

inheritance will be added to that of the tribe into which they marry, and their
property will be taken from the tribal inheritance of our ancestors."
[5]Then at the LORD's command Moses gave this order to the Israelites: "What
the tribe of the descendants of Joseph is saying is right. [6]This is what the LORD
commands for Zelophehad's daughters: They may marry anyone they please as
long as they marry within their father's tribal clan. [7]No inheritance in Israel is
to pass from one tribe to another, for every Israelite shall keep the tribal inheritance of their ancestors. [8]Every daughter who inherits land in any Israelite tribe
must marry someone in her father's tribal clan, so that every Israelite will possess the inheritance of their ancestors. [9]No inheritance may pass from one tribe
to another, for each Israelite tribe is to keep the land it inherits."
[10]So Zelophehad's daughters did as the LORD commanded Moses. [11]Zelophe-
had's daughters — Mahlah, Tirzah, Hoglah, Milkah and Noah — married their
cousins on their father's side. [12]They married within the clans of the descendants of Manasseh son of Joseph, and their inheritance remained in their father's tribe and clan.

[13]These are the commands and regulations the LORD gave through Moses to
the Israelites on the plains of Moab by the Jordan across from Jericho.

JESUS: OUR PROMISED HOPE

DEUTERONOMY

DEUTERONOMY

EXODUS FROM EGYPT *c. 1446 BC*	MOSES ADDRESSES ISRAEL IN MOAB *c. 1406 BC*	ISRAEL ENTERS PROMISED LAND *c. 1406 BC*

The fifth and final book of Moses recounts Moses' last statements to the people of God as they camped on the plains of Moab prior to entering the promised land. Moses, in his old age, knew that he would not enter the land as a result of his sin in the wilderness (Nu 20:1 – 12). But God graciously allowed Moses to see the land and to speak words of hope, grace and encouragement to the nation prior to their crossing the Jordan River and entering the land of promise.

Inspired by God, Deuteronomy serves as a testimony of God's grace written by those who had experienced God's miraculous favor firsthand. In it Moses recounts the national history of God's people — from their deliverance from Egypt, to their rebellion on the brink of the promised land, to their subsequent sojourn in the wilderness for nearly 40 years. He reminds the nation of their sin and rebellion, while consistently affirming God's covenantal faithfulness. Not only had God judged their sin, but he had also protected them in the wilderness and taught them to depend only on him for their daily survival.

This historical backdrop contrasts with the future promises of God to the new generation. The people did not have to wallow in shame and self-pity; rather, they could learn from the lessons of the past and trust God to fulfill his promises to them. The repetition of the word "today" throughout the book testifies to the forward-facing nature of Moses' exhortations (Dt 4:40).

In this way, this book is about grace. God freely gave a stiff-necked people a relationship with him and the gift of the promised land apart from anything they had done — in fact, in *spite* of all that they had done. As Moses looked over the people and toward the promised land on the horizon, he could die knowing that God was, is, and will always be faithful to his promises.

The covenantal structure of the book reminded the people of God's covenant commitments and their subsequent responsibilities. For this reason, Deuteronomy is a foundational document on which the subsequent history of God's people rests.

Moses knew full well that the people would prove incapable once again of keeping their covenant promises. That's why he pledged that God would raise up a future prophet from their midst to lead the people by his Word (Dt 18:15). This future prophet, the Messiah, would declare the new covenant promises whereby God's people, Jew and Gentile alike, could claim the inheritance promised to Abraham long ago. Moses' prophecy was perfectly fulfilled by Jesus (Lk 22:20).

SEE, THE LORD YOUR GOD HAS GIVEN YOU THE LAND. GO UP AND TAKE POSSESSION OF IT AS THE LORD, THE GOD OF YOUR ANCESTORS, TOLD YOU. DO NOT BE AFRAID; DO NOT BE DISCOURAGED.

Deuteronomy 1:21

DEUTERONOMY

The Command to Leave Horeb

1 These are the words Moses spoke to all Israel in the wilderness east of the Jordan — that is, in the Arabah — opposite Suph, between Paran and Tophel, Laban, Hazeroth and Dizahab. 2(It takes eleven days to go from Horeb to Kadesh Barnea by the Mount Seir road.)

3In the fortieth year, on the first day of the eleventh month, Moses proclaimed to the Israelites all that the LORD had commanded him concerning them. 4This was after he had defeated Sihon king of the Amorites, who reigned in Heshbon, and at Edrei had defeated Og king of Bashan, who reigned in Ashtaroth.

5East of the Jordan in the territory of Moab, Moses began to expound this law, saying:

6The LORD our God said to us at Horeb, "You have stayed long enough at this mountain. 7Break camp and advance into the hill country of the Amorites; go to all the neighboring peoples in the Arabah, in the mountains, in the western foothills, in the Negev and along the coast, to the land of the Canaanites and to Lebanon, as far as the great river, the Euphrates. 8See, I have given you this land. Go in and take possession of the land the LORD swore he would give to your fathers — to Abraham, Isaac and Jacob — and to their descendants after them."

The Appointment of Leaders

9At that time I said to you, "You are too heavy a burden for me to carry alone. 10The LORD your God has increased your numbers so that today you are as numerous as the stars in the sky. 11May the LORD, the God of your ancestors, increase you a thousand times and bless you as he has promised! 12But how can I bear your problems and your burdens and your disputes all by myself? 13Choose some wise, understanding and respected men from each of your tribes, and I will set them over you."

14You answered me, "What you propose to do is good."

15So I took the leading men of your tribes, wise and respected men, and appointed them to have authority over you — as commanders of thousands, of hundreds, of fifties and of tens and as tribal officials. 16And I charged your judges at that time, "Hear the disputes between your people and judge fairly, whether the case is between two Israelites or between an Israelite and a foreigner residing among you. 17Do not show partiality in judging; hear both small and great alike. Do not be afraid of anyone, for judgment belongs to God. Bring me any case too hard for you, and I will hear it." 18And at that time I told you everything you were to do.

Spies Sent Out

19Then, as the LORD our God commanded us, we set out from Horeb and went toward the hill country of the Amorites through all that vast and dreadful wilderness that you have seen, and so we reached Kadesh Barnea. 20Then I said to you, "You have reached the hill country of the Amorites, which the LORD our God is giving us. 21See, the LORD your God has given you the land. Go up and take possession of it as the LORD, the God of your ancestors, told you. Do not be afraid; do not be discouraged."

22Then all of you came to me and said, "Let us send men ahead to spy out the land for us and bring back a report about the route we are to take and the towns we will come to."

23The idea seemed good to me; so I selected twelve of you, one man from each tribe. 24They left and went up into the hill country, and came to the Valley of

---

DEUTERONOMY 1:1

LOOK TO THE WORD

In the Jewish tradition, the book of Deuteronomy is called "words" (*debarim*), meaning the words of Moses to the people of God. Moses' goal in this book was to restate and explain the law of God found in Exodus. Therefore, our English title of the book — from the Greek *deuteros* + *nomos* — means "second law" or the second accumulation of God's law for his people. In this book, Moses emphasized the covenant between God and Israel and the requirements God placed on his people to ensure ongoing blessings. Do not overlook the importance of the covenantal requirements of keeping the law throughout the pages of Deuteronomy. The Old Testament reveals a cyclical pattern of Israel being unable to keep the law, falling into sin and needing to make continuous sacrificial offerings to atone for their failures — thus, the need for Jesus, who kept the law perfectly and went to the cross as a perfect, unblemished sacrifice on our behalf.

Eshkol and explored it. 25 Taking with them some of the fruit of the land, they brought it down to us and reported, "It is a good land that the LORD our God is giving us."

Rebellion Against the LORD

26 But you were unwilling to go up; you rebelled against the command of the LORD your God. 27 You grumbled in your tents and said, "The LORD hates us; so he brought us out of Egypt to deliver us into the hands of the Amorites to destroy us. 28 Where can we go? Our brothers have made our hearts melt in fear. They say, 'The people are stronger and taller than we are; the cities are large, with walls up to the sky. We even saw the Anakites there.' "

29 Then I said to you, "Do not be terrified; do not be afraid of them. 30 The LORD your God, who is going before you, will fight for you, as he did for you in Egypt, before your very eyes, 31 and in the wilderness. There you saw how the LORD your God carried you, as a father carries his son, all the way you went until you reached this place."

32 In spite of this, you did not trust in the LORD your God, 33 who went ahead of you on your journey, in fire by night and in a cloud by day, to search out places for you to camp and to show you the way you should go.

34 When the LORD heard what you said, he was angry and solemnly swore: 35 "No one from this evil generation shall see the good land I swore to give your ancestors, 36 except Caleb son of Jephunneh. He will see it, and I will give him and his descendants the land he set his feet on, because he followed the LORD wholeheartedly."

37 Because of you the LORD became angry with me also and said, "You shall not enter it, either. 38 But your assistant, Joshua son of Nun, will enter it. Encourage him, because he will lead Israel to inherit it. 39 And the little ones that you said would be taken captive, your children who do not yet know good from bad—they will enter the land. I will give it to them and they will take possession of it. 40 But as for you, turn around and set out toward the desert along the route to the Red Sea.[a]"

41 Then you replied, "We have sinned against the LORD. We will go up and fight, as the LORD our God commanded us." So every one of you put on his weapons, thinking it easy to go up into the hill country.

42 But the LORD said to me, "Tell them, 'Do not go up and fight, because I will not be with you. You will be defeated by your enemies.' "

43 So I told you, but you would not listen. You rebelled against the LORD's command and in your arrogance you marched up into the hill country. 44 The Amorites who lived in those hills came out against you; they chased you like a swarm of bees and beat you down from Seir all the way to Hormah. 45 You came back and wept before the LORD, but he paid no attention to your weeping and turned a deaf ear to you. 46 And so you stayed in Kadesh many days—all the time you spent there.

Wanderings in the Wilderness

2 Then we turned back and set out toward the wilderness along the route to the Red Sea,[a] as the LORD had directed me. For a long time we made our way around the hill country of Seir.

2 Then the LORD said to me, 3 "You have made your way around this hill country long enough; now turn north. 4 Give the people these orders: 'You are about to pass through the territory of your relatives the descendants of Esau, who live in Seir. They will be afraid of you, but be very careful. 5 Do not provoke them to war, for I will not give you any of their land, not even enough to put your foot on. I have given Esau the hill country of Seir as his own. 6 You are to pay them in silver for the food you eat and the water you drink.' "

---

[a] *40,1* Or *the Sea of Reeds*

DEUTERONOMY 2:24

CHRIST, THE VICTOR OVER SIN

Sihon the Amorite, king of Heshbon, refused Israel peaceful passage through his land during their wilderness wanderings and attacked the vulnerable Israelites (Nu 21:21 – 26; Dt 2:26 – 37). As a new generation prepared to enter the land, God spoke through Moses, declaring, "See, I have given into your hand Sihon the Amorite, king of Heshbon, and his country." This is likely a subtle reminder that the previous generation had accused God of bringing them from Egypt only to be handed to the Amorites (Dt 1:27). So God extended the same command (and promise) to the new generation that the previous generation had ignored. God made it clear that he would fulfill his promise, and as Israel obeyed they experienced the victory of God who led them into battle and delivered them. Israel's strength was insufficient for the battle, but by placing their faith in God to lead them, they enjoyed the victory by God's saving right hand.

Just as God led Israel through the sea, out of the wilderness and into the promised land, he delivered them from their chief threat — sin — and continued to act on behalf of his people against the worst enemy. God's ultimate saving activity came through his Son, Jesus. Rather than Jesus rallying Israel together to lead them in battle, he came to seek and save the lost and to redeem the people of God by removing the separation sin created. Through Jesus, God won the victory over humanity's chief enemy.

7The LORD your God has blessed you in all the work of your hands. He has watched over your journey through this vast wilderness. These forty years the LORD your God has been with you, and you have not lacked anything.

8So we went on past our relatives the descendants of Esau, who live in Seir. We turned from the Arabah road, which comes up from Elath and Ezion Geber, and traveled along the desert road of Moab.

9Then the LORD said to me, "Do not harass the Moabites or provoke them to war, for I will not give you any part of their land. I have given Ar to the descendants of Lot as a possession."

10(The Emites used to live there — a people strong and numerous, and as tall as the Anakites. 11Like the Anakites, they too were considered Rephaites, but the Moabites called them Emites. 12Horites used to live in Seir, but the descendants of Esau drove them out. They destroyed the Horites from before them and settled in their place, just as Israel did in the land the LORD gave them as their possession.)

13And the LORD said, "Now get up and cross the Zered Valley." So we crossed the valley.

14Thirty-eight years passed from the time we left Kadesh Barnea until we crossed the Zered Valley. By then, that entire generation of fighting men had perished from the camp, as the LORD had sworn to them. 15The LORD's hand was against them until he had completely eliminated them from the camp.

16Now when the last of these fighting men among the people had died, 17the LORD said to me, 18"Today you are to pass by the region of Moab at Ar. 19When you come to the Ammonites, do not harass them or provoke them to war, for I will not give you possession of any land belonging to the Ammonites. I have given it as a possession to the descendants of Lot."

20(That too was considered a land of the Rephaites, who used to live there; but the Ammonites called them Zamzummites. 21They were a people strong and numerous, and as tall as the Anakites. The LORD destroyed them from before the Ammonites, who drove them out and settled in their place. 22The LORD had done the same for the descendants of Esau, who lived in Seir, when he destroyed the Horites from before them. They drove them out and have lived in their place to this day. 23And as for the Avvites who lived in villages as far as Gaza, the Caphtorites coming out from Caphtor[a] destroyed them and settled in their place.)

Defeat of Sihon King of Heshbon

24"Set out now and cross the Arnon Gorge. See, I have given into your hand Sihon the Amorite, king of Heshbon, and his country. Begin to take possession of it and engage him in battle. 25This very day I will begin to put the terror and fear of you on all the nations under heaven. They will hear reports of you and will tremble and be in anguish because of you."

26From the Desert of Kedemoth I sent messengers to Sihon king of Heshbon offering peace and saying, 27"Let us pass through your country. We will stay on the main road; we will not turn aside to the right or to the left. 28Sell us food to eat and water to drink for their price in silver. Only let us pass through on foot — 29as the descendants of Esau, who live in Seir, and the Moabites, who live in Ar, did for us — until we cross the Jordan into the land the LORD our God is giving us." 30But Sihon king of Heshbon refused to let us pass through. For the LORD your God had made his spirit stubborn and his heart obstinate in order to give him into your hands, as he has now done.

31The LORD said to me, "See, I have begun to deliver Sihon and his country over to you. Now begin to conquer and possess his land."

32When Sihon and all his army came out to meet us in battle at Jahaz, 33the LORD our God delivered him over to us and we struck him down, together with his sons and his whole army. 34At that time we took all his towns and

[a] *23* That is, Crete

completely destroyed[a] them — men, women and children. We left no survivors.
35But the livestock and the plunder from the towns we had captured we carried
off for ourselves. 36From Aroer on the rim of the Arnon Gorge, and from the
town in the gorge, even as far as Gilead, not one town was too strong for us. The
LORD our God gave us all of them. 37But in accordance with the command of
the LORD our God, you did not encroach on any of the land of the Ammonites,
neither the land along the course of the Jabbok nor that around the towns in
the hills.

Defeat of Og King of Bashan

3 Next we turned and went up along the road toward Bashan, and Og king of
Bashan with his whole army marched out to meet us in battle at Edrei. 2The
LORD said to me, "Do not be afraid of him, for I have delivered him into your
hands, along with his whole army and his land. Do to him what you did to Sihon
king of the Amorites, who reigned in Heshbon."
3So the LORD our God also gave into our hands Og king of Bashan and all his
army. We struck them down, leaving no survivors. 4At that time we took all his
cities. There was not one of the sixty cities that we did not take from them — the
whole region of Argob, Og's kingdom in Bashan. 5All these cities were fortified
with high walls and with gates and bars, and there were also a great many unwalled villages. 6We completely destroyed[a] them, as we had done with Sihon
king of Heshbon, destroying[a] every city — men, women and children. 7But all
the livestock and the plunder from their cities we carried off for ourselves.
8So at that time we took from these two kings of the Amorites the territory east
of the Jordan, from the Arnon Gorge as far as Mount Hermon. 9(Hermon is called
Sirion by the Sidonians; the Amorites call it Senir.) 10We took all the towns on
the plateau, and all Gilead, and all Bashan as far as Salekah and Edrei, towns of
Og's kingdom in Bashan. 11(Og king of Bashan was the last of the Rephaites. His
bed was decorated with iron and was more than nine cubits long and four cubits
wide.[b] It is still in Rabbah of the Ammonites.)

Division of the Land

12Of the land that we took over at that time, I gave the Reubenites and the
Gadites the territory north of Aroer by the Arnon Gorge, including half the hill
country of Gilead, together with its towns. 13The rest of Gilead and also all of
Bashan, the kingdom of Og, I gave to the half-tribe of Manasseh. (The whole
region of Argob in Bashan used to be known as a land of the Rephaites. 14Jair, a
descendant of Manasseh, took the whole region of Argob as far as the border of
the Geshurites and the Maakathites; it was named after him, so that to this day
Bashan is called Havvoth Jair.[c]) 15And I gave Gilead to Makir. 16But to the Reubenites and the Gadites I gave the territory extending from Gilead down to the
Arnon Gorge (the middle of the gorge being the border) and out to the Jabbok
River, which is the border of the Ammonites. 17Its western border was the Jordan
in the Arabah, from Kinnereth to the Sea of the Arabah (that is, the Dead Sea),
below the slopes of Pisgah.
18I commanded you at that time: "The LORD your God has given you this land
to take possession of it. But all your able-bodied men, armed for battle, must
cross over ahead of the other Israelites. 19However, your wives, your children
and your livestock (I know you have much livestock) may stay in the towns I
have given you, 20until the LORD gives rest to your fellow Israelites as he has to
you, and they too have taken over the land that the LORD your God is giving
them across the Jordan. After that, each of you may go back to the possession I
have given you."

---

[a] *34,6* The Hebrew term refers to the irrevocable giving over of things or persons to the LORD, often by totally destroying them. [b] *11* That is, about 14 feet long and 6 feet wide or about 4 meters long and 1.8 meters wide [c] *14* Or *called the settlements of Jair*

Moses Forbidden to Cross the Jordan

[21]At that time I commanded Joshua: "You have seen with your own eyes all that the LORD your God has done to these two kings. The LORD will do the same to all the kingdoms over there where you are going. [22]Do not be afraid of them; the LORD your God himself will fight for you."

[23]At that time I pleaded with the LORD: [24]"Sovereign LORD, you have begun to show to your servant your greatness and your strong hand. For what god is there in heaven or on earth who can do the deeds and mighty works you do? [25]Let me go over and see the good land beyond the Jordan — that fine hill country and Lebanon."

[26]But because of you the LORD was angry with me and would not listen to me. "That is enough," the LORD said. "Do not speak to me anymore about this matter. [27]Go up to the top of Pisgah and look west and north and south and east. Look at the land with your own eyes, since you are not going to cross this Jordan. [28]But commission Joshua, and encourage and strengthen him, for he will lead this people across and will cause them to inherit the land that you will see." [29]So we stayed in the valley near Beth Peor.

Obedience Commanded

4 Now, Israel, hear the decrees and laws I am about to teach you. Follow them so that you may live and may go in and take possession of the land the LORD, the God of your ancestors, is giving you. [2]Do not add to what I command you and do not subtract from it, but keep the commands of the LORD your God that I give you.

[3]You saw with your own eyes what the LORD did at Baal Peor. The LORD your God destroyed from among you everyone who followed the Baal of Peor, [4]but all of you who held fast to the LORD your God are still alive today.

[5]See, I have taught you decrees and laws as the LORD my God commanded me, so that you may follow them in the land you are entering to take possession of it. [6]Observe them carefully, for this will show your wisdom and understanding to the nations, who will hear about all these decrees and say, "Surely this great nation is a wise and understanding people." [7]What other nation is so great as to have their gods near them the way the LORD our God is near us whenever we pray to him? [8]And what other nation is so great as to have such righteous decrees and laws as this body of laws I am setting before you today?

[9]Only be careful, and watch yourselves closely so that you do not forget the things your eyes have seen or let them fade from your heart as long as you live. Teach them to your children and to their children after them. [10]Remember the day you stood before the LORD your God at Horeb, when he said to me, "Assemble the people before me to hear my words so that they may learn to revere me as long as they live in the land and may teach them to their children." [11]You came near and stood at the foot of the mountain while it blazed with fire to the very heavens, with black clouds and deep darkness. [12]Then the LORD spoke to you out of the fire. You heard the sound of words but saw no form; there was only a voice. [13]He declared to you his covenant, the Ten Commandments, which he commanded you to follow and then wrote them on two stone tablets. [14]And the LORD directed me at that time to teach you the decrees and laws you are to follow in the land that you are crossing the Jordan to possess.

Idolatry Forbidden

[15]You saw no form of any kind the day the LORD spoke to you at Horeb out of the fire. Therefore watch yourselves very carefully, [16]so that you do not become corrupt and make for yourselves an idol, an image of any shape, whether formed like a man or a woman, [17]or like any animal on earth or any bird that flies in the air, [18]or like any creature that moves along the ground or any fish in the waters below. [19]And when you look up to the sky and see the sun, the moon and the stars — all the heavenly array — do not be enticed into bowing down to

A SURE STANDING AS GOD'S PEOPLE

The history of God's people in the Old Testament shows how unsure their standing was before God. The Israelites were people chosen by God, called to be his people. Additionally, God established clear requirements for the covenant relationship between himself and his people, requirements to atone for their human fallibility in light of his perfect holiness. He even appointed Moses to lead his people out of slavery in Egypt and to serve as a mediator between himself and his people lest their sins cause his displeasure to negate this covenant relationship. Yet these clear requirements, means of atoning for unholiness and an appointed mediator, were not sufficient.

Much like the Israelites, how tremendous are the sins of all people. No person can keep the covenant requirements of relationship with God. As the Israelites' sins and unbelief led to judgment from God, all people's failure to have perfect faith and obedience makes them deserving of his displeasure as well. But Christians have a mediator who is far superior to Moses, one who keeps God's standard of perfection on their behalf (Jer 31:31 – 34; Heb 9:14 – 15). Whereas Moses was unable to ensure the Lord's favor as the leader of his people, Jesus enables believers to enter the presence of God with confidence as their numerous sins were cast on him and his perfect righteousness was bestowed to them (Heb 10:19 – 22).

Believers do not have to live in fear — afraid that one day God's promises will not come to pass — because, in Jesus, God will not condemn those he calls to be his people (Ro 8:1 – 4). Through Jesus the righteous requirements of the law are fulfilled. Jesus provides a sure standing before God, one that entails unending blessings as his people now and for all of eternity.

them and worshiping things the LORD your God has apportioned to all the nations under heaven. [20]But as for you, the LORD took you and brought you out of the iron-smelting furnace, out of Egypt, to be the people of his inheritance, as you now are.

[21]The LORD was angry with me because of you, and he solemnly swore that I would not cross the Jordan and enter the good land the LORD your God is giving you as your inheritance. [22]I will die in this land; I will not cross the Jordan; but you are about to cross over and take possession of that good land. [23]Be careful not to forget the covenant of the LORD your God that he made with you; do not make for yourselves an idol in the form of anything the LORD your God has forbidden. [24]For the LORD your God is a consuming fire, a jealous God.

[25]After you have had children and grandchildren and have lived in the land a long time — if you then become corrupt and make any kind of idol, doing evil in the eyes of the LORD your God and arousing his anger, [26]I call the heavens and the earth as witnesses against you this day that you will quickly perish from the land that you are crossing the Jordan to possess. You will not live there long but will certainly be destroyed. [27]The LORD will scatter you among the peoples, and only a few of you will survive among the nations to which the LORD will drive you. [28]There you will worship man-made gods of wood and stone, which cannot see or hear or eat or smell. [29]But if from there you seek the LORD your God, you will find him if you seek him with all your heart and with all your soul. [30]When you are in distress and all these things have happened to you, then in later days you will return to the LORD your God and obey him. [31]For the LORD your God is a merciful God; he will not abandon or destroy you or forget the covenant with your ancestors, which he confirmed to them by oath.

The LORD Is God

[32]Ask now about the former days, long before your time, from the day God created human beings on the earth; ask from one end of the heavens to the other. Has anything so great as this ever happened, or has anything like it ever been heard of? [33]Has any other people heard the voice of God[a] speaking out of fire, as you have, and lived? [34]Has any god ever tried to take for himself one nation out of another nation, by testings, by signs and wonders, by war, by a mighty hand and an outstretched arm, or by great and awesome deeds, like all the things the LORD your God did for you in Egypt before your very eyes?

[35]You were shown these things so that you might know that the LORD is God; besides him there is no other. [36]From heaven he made you hear his voice to discipline you. On earth he showed you his great fire, and you heard his words from out of the fire. [37]Because he loved your ancestors and chose their descendants after them, he brought you out of Egypt by his Presence and his great strength, [38]to drive out before you nations greater and stronger than you and to bring you into their land to give it to you for your inheritance, as it is today.

[39]Acknowledge and take to heart this day that the LORD is God in heaven above and on the earth below. There is no other. [40]Keep his decrees and commands, which I am giving you today, so that it may go well with you and your children after you and that you may live long in the land the LORD your God gives you for all time.

Cities of Refuge

[41]Then Moses set aside three cities east of the Jordan, [42]to which anyone who had killed a person could flee if they had unintentionally killed a neighbor without malice aforethought. They could flee into one of these cities and save their life. [43]The cities were these: Bezer in the wilderness plateau, for the Reubenites; Ramoth in Gilead, for the Gadites; and Golan in Bashan, for the Manassites.

[a] *33* Or *of a god*

DEUTERONOMY 4:32 – 40

THE LORD IS GOD

God's approach to establish a relationship with Israel at Sinai represents a significant moment in human history. Until Sinai, gods were considered territorially constrained and without obligation to peoples. However, God chose to deliver Israel from bondage in Egypt in such spectacular fashion in order to demonstrate his love for Israel so they might know God's magnificence over and above the gods of other nations. As highlighted in other texts, the book of Deuteronomy was written to help Israel understand and remember God's power to deliver them, his sovereignty over heaven and earth (not a corner of land) and his love for them over other nations. Toward that end, Moses consistently reminded each generation of what God had done for their ancestors by calling them to remember the story of their deliverance.

John 1 narrates another monumental moment in human history, one that is worthy of being consistently remembered: the incarnation. When God took on human flesh and "made his dwelling" (literally, "tabernacled"; v. 14) among God's people, they were provided greater access to God throughout Jesus' public ministry. It is through Jesus that God has proven his power to deliver his people from the power of sin, shown us his absolute love and provided a way for all nations of the earth to have a relationship with the one, true God.

THE IMPORTANCE OF REMEMBERING

Throughout Scripture, remembering is a major theme. Authors constantly reminded God's people to remember his faithfulness. The nations were admonished to remember the Lord and turn to him (Ps 22:27). In contrast, the Lord was petitioned to not remember sins and show instead his goodness and pour out his blessing (Ps 25:6 – 7). Among God's people the failure to remember results in cyclical patterns of sin and rebellion (Isa 57:11). When the people forgot God — both his character and his past faithfulness to the nation — they were prone to a host of sins. Most specifically, the people of God pursued the idolatry of the surrounding nations. False gods seemed more tangible, more concrete and more immediate. One could see and touch these false gods. Ironically, though these gods had a material substance, they could not speak or act on behalf of the people. Yahweh, in contrast, was not made by human hands but could act mightily on behalf of his people. The nation of Israel was reminded, time and time again, not to forget this.

How forgetful God's people are concerning the truths of Scripture, thus finding themselves unable to stand firm on God's promises (1Co 15:1). They forget the goodness of the Lord and his Word. They forget the frailty of human limitations and their propensity to live according to their own way. They forget their former longings for the Lord and the blessed experience of walking closely with him. God knows his people's limitations and sees their forgetfulness as another way in which they need his gracious mercy. Therefore, he reminds them again and again to remember him, and he supplies the means to overcome their human inability to remember the things of God by providing the Spirit of Christ (Jn 14:26).

The Good News of the gospel is that Jesus remembers the covenant that God made with his people and intercedes in the midst of unfaithful moments (Heb 7:24 – 25). Without fail, Jesus is remembering and reminding the Father of his promises to his children. Jesus remembers and applies his death and resurrection as payment. Jesus remembers and sends the Spirit to strengthen his children during their journey of faith and to remind them of the goodness of God and walking in his ways. The triune God remembers because of Jesus' intercession and oversight of continued sanctification (Ro 8:26 – 30).

DEUTERONOMY 5:4–5

A BETTER MEDIATOR

A mediator is a person who seeks to resolve conflicts, bringing about a negotiated peace between two parties who are at odds with one another. The conflict between God and mankind is not one that a mediator can simply negotiate away. Something deep — God's holiness — has been transgressed and the required mediation involves the offending party to make it right. The enmity between God and humanity calls for something much more significant than a typical negotiation. Something supernatural needs to occur to bring about a resolution in the conflict between God's holiness and fallen human beings.

Though we see Moses functioning as a mediator in Deuteronomy 5:5, Christians have a mediator who is far superior to him. In fact, this mediator satisfied the terms of the negotiation himself by taking the punishment required to bring about peace and right the wrongs caused by our unrighteousness (Jer 31:31–34; Heb 9:14–15). Whereas Moses was unable to ensure the Lord's continued favor as the leader of the Israelites, Jesus secured eternal blessing for those who find righteousness in him. Whereas the people of Israel feared the presence of God because of their sin (Dt 5:5), Christians may enter the presence of God boldly because of a perfect standing before the Lord through Jesus (Eph 3:12). In Jesus and through faith in him, believers may approach God with freedom and confidence that they will not be rejected or judged for shortcomings. His righteous perfection covers imperfection and provides admission into the presence of God. What a mediator is Christ Jesus!

Introduction to the Law

44 This is the law Moses set before the Israelites. 45 These are the stipulations,
decrees and laws Moses gave them when they came out of Egypt 46 and were in the
valley near Beth Peor east of the Jordan, in the land of Sihon king of the Amorites,
who reigned in Heshbon and was defeated by Moses and the Israelites as they
came out of Egypt. 47 They took possession of his land and the land of Og king of Bashan, the two Amorite kings east of the Jordan. 48 This land extended from Aroer on
the rim of the Arnon Gorge to Mount Sirion[a] (that is, Hermon), 49 and included all
the Arabah east of the Jordan, as far as the Dead Sea,[b] below the slopes of Pisgah.

The Ten Commandments

5 Moses summoned all Israel and said:
Hear, Israel, the decrees and laws I declare in your hearing today. Learn
them and be sure to follow them. 2 The LORD our God made a covenant with us
at Horeb. 3 It was not with our ancestors[c] that the LORD made this covenant, but
with us, with all of us who are alive here today. 4 The LORD spoke to you face to
face out of the fire on the mountain. 5 (At that time I stood between the LORD and
you to declare to you the word of the LORD, because you were afraid of the fire
and did not go up the mountain.) And he said:

6 "I am the LORD your God, who brought you out of Egypt, out of the land of slavery.

7 "You shall have no other gods before[d] me.

8 "You shall not make for yourself an image in the form of anything in heaven
above or on the earth beneath or in the waters below. 9 You shall not
bow down to them or worship them; for I, the LORD your God, am a
jealous God, punishing the children for the sin of the parents to the
third and fourth generation of those who hate me, 10 but showing love
to a thousand generations of those who love me and keep my commandments.

11 "You shall not misuse the name of the LORD your God, for the LORD will not hold anyone guiltless who misuses his name.

12 "Observe the Sabbath day by keeping it holy, as the LORD your God has
commanded you. 13 Six days you shall labor and do all your work,
14 but the seventh day is a sabbath to the LORD your God. On it you
shall not do any work, neither you, nor your son or daughter, nor your
male or female servant, nor your ox, your donkey or any of your animals, nor any foreigner residing in your towns, so that your male and
female servants may rest, as you do. 15 Remember that you were slaves
in Egypt and that the LORD your God brought you out of there with a
mighty hand and an outstretched arm. Therefore the LORD your God
has commanded you to observe the Sabbath day.

16 "Honor your father and your mother, as the LORD your God has commanded you, so that you may live long and that it may go well with you in the land the LORD your God is giving you.

17 "You shall not murder.

18 "You shall not commit adultery.

19 "You shall not steal.

20 "You shall not give false testimony against your neighbor.

21 "You shall not covet your neighbor's wife. You shall not set your desire on your neighbor's house or land, his male or female servant, his ox or donkey, or anything that belongs to your neighbor."

22 These are the commandments the LORD proclaimed in a loud voice to your
whole assembly there on the mountain from out of the fire, the cloud and the

---

[a] 48 Syriac (see also 3:9); Hebrew *Siyon* [b] 49 Hebrew *the Sea of the Arabah* [c] 3 Or *not only with our parents* [d] 7 Or *besides*

deep darkness; and he added nothing more. Then he wrote them on two stone
tablets and gave them to me.
[23]When you heard the voice out of the darkness, while the mountain was
ablaze with fire, all the leaders of your tribes and your elders came to me. [24]And
you said, "The LORD our God has shown us his glory and his majesty, and we
have heard his voice from the fire. Today we have seen that a person can live
even if God speaks with them. [25]But now, why should we die? This great fire will
consume us, and we will die if we hear the voice of the LORD our God any longer. [26]For what mortal has ever heard the voice of the living God speaking out of
fire, as we have, and survived? [27]Go near and listen to all that the LORD our God
says. Then tell us whatever the LORD our God tells you. We will listen and obey."
[28]The LORD heard you when you spoke to me, and the LORD said to me, "I have
heard what this people said to you. Everything they said was good. [29]Oh, that
their hearts would be inclined to fear me and keep all my commands always, so
that it might go well with them and their children forever!
[30]"Go, tell them to return to their tents. [31]But you stay here with me so that I
may give you all the commands, decrees and laws you are to teach them to follow
in the land I am giving them to possess."
[32]So be careful to do what the LORD your God has commanded you; do not
turn aside to the right or to the left. [33]Walk in obedience to all that the LORD your
God has commanded you, so that you may live and prosper and prolong your
days in the land that you will possess.

Love the LORD Your God

6 These are the commands, decrees and laws the LORD your God directed me
to teach you to observe in the land that you are crossing the Jordan to possess, [2]so that you, your children and their children after them may fear the LORD
your God as long as you live by keeping all his decrees and commands that I give
you, and so that you may enjoy long life. [3]Hear, Israel, and be careful to obey so
that it may go well with you and that you may increase greatly in a land flowing
with milk and honey, just as the LORD, the God of your ancestors, promised you.
[4]Hear, O Israel: The LORD our God, the LORD is one.[a] [5]Love the LORD your
God with all your heart and with all your soul and with all your strength. [6]These
commandments that I give you today are to be on your hearts. [7]Impress them on
your children. Talk about them when you sit at home and when you walk along
the road, when you lie down and when you get up. [8]Tie them as symbols on your
hands and bind them on your foreheads. [9]Write them on the doorframes of your
houses and on your gates.
[10]When the LORD your God brings you into the land he swore to your fathers,
to Abraham, Isaac and Jacob, to give you — a land with large, flourishing cities
you did not build, [11]houses filled with all kinds of good things you did not provide, wells you did not dig, and vineyards and olive groves you did not plant —
then when you eat and are satisfied, [12]be careful that you do not forget the LORD,
who brought you out of Egypt, out of the land of slavery.
[13]Fear the LORD your God, serve him only and take your oaths in his name.
[14]Do not follow other gods, the gods of the peoples around you; [15]for the LORD
your God, who is among you, is a jealous God and his anger will burn against
you, and he will destroy you from the face of the land. [16]Do not put the LORD
your God to the test as you did at Massah. [17]Be sure to keep the commands of the
LORD your God and the stipulations and decrees he has given you. [18]Do what is
right and good in the LORD's sight, so that it may go well with you and you may
go in and take over the good land the LORD promised on oath to your ancestors,
[19]thrusting out all your enemies before you, as the LORD said.
[20]In the future, when your son asks you, "What is the meaning of the stipulations, decrees and laws the LORD our God has commanded you?" [21]tell him:

[a] 4 Or *The LORD our God is one LORD*; or *The LORD is our God, the LORD is one*; or *The LORD is our God, the LORD alone*

DEUTERONOMY 6:1 – 25

THE TRIUNE GOD MERCIFULLY BLESSES HIS CHILDREN

Knowing God, keeping the decrees of God, loving God alone without serving other gods — the commands within Deuteronomy can be a bit overwhelming, even to the point of feeling the weight of works-based righteousness. A reader of the Bible must ask why God wanted Moses to emphasize these themes over and over again throughout this book, particularly in chapter 6. As verses 1 – 3 and 6 – 9 teach, the exhortations in this chapter are for the people's own good and the good of their children. Moses calls Israel to love the Lord with all of one's heart, soul and strength (vv. 4 – 5). Total love is the ideal. Why? It is for his people's good. There is no better place to be than centering one's life around the law — or teachings — of God because they exist to show us the path to blessing and deep joy in knowing the Father. Yet, all people know that they often pursue other things as their ultimate desire. Why is it so impossible to follow God's way if we know that it leads to blessing and not doing so leads to sorrow?

Just as the Israelites were enslaved in Egypt, unable to alter their circumstances, all people are enslaved to sin apart from God interjecting his merciful grace in their lives (Eph 2:1 – 10). As this chapter of Deuteronomy progresses, it is evident that any commands from God to his people are tied closely to the mercy he has shown to them (Dt 6:20 – 25). God's glorious mercy takes human sin, placing it on Jesus as the atonement for humanity's inability to love God completely as commanded in Deuteronomy 6:5. Jesus has kept the law — a requirement to be righteous before God according to Deuteronomy 6:25 — and given us the righteousness of Jesus himself (Ro 3:21 – 22). This is true because the Father draws believers to himself (Jn 6:44), Jesus offers the perfect life and sacrifice for sin, and the Spirit guides believers in truth (Jn 16:13). The triune God works mercifully on Christians' behalf to ensure that they will experience the blessed experience of living in his favor. They do not follow the law of God in order to earn his favor but because he has shown favor in his mercy. God's children are freed by God's gracious mercy through Christ to experience the blessing of following God's desires for us found in the Bible.

"We were slaves of Pharaoh in Egypt, but the LORD brought us out of Egypt with a mighty hand. [22]Before our eyes the LORD sent signs and wonders — great and terrible — on Egypt and Pharaoh and his whole household. [23]But he brought us out from there to bring us in and give us the land he promised on oath to our ancestors. [24]The LORD commanded us to obey all these decrees and to fear the LORD our God, so that we might always prosper and be kept alive, as is the case today. [25]And if we are careful to obey all this law before the LORD our God, as he has commanded us, that will be our righteousness."

Driving Out the Nations

7 When the LORD your God brings you into the land you are entering to possess and drives out before you many nations — the Hittites, Girgashites, Amorites, Canaanites, Perizzites, Hivites and Jebusites, seven nations larger and stronger than you — [2]and when the LORD your God has delivered them over to you and you have defeated them, then you must destroy them totally.[a] Make no treaty with them, and show them no mercy. [3]Do not intermarry with them. Do not give your daughters to their sons or take their daughters for your sons, [4]for they will turn your children away from following me to serve other gods, and the LORD's anger will burn against you and will quickly destroy you. [5]This is what you are to do to them: Break down their altars, smash their sacred stones, cut down their Asherah poles[b] and burn their idols in the fire. [6]For you are a people holy to the LORD your God. The LORD your God has chosen you out of all the peoples on the face of the earth to be his people, his treasured possession.

[7]The LORD did not set his affection on you and choose you because you were more numerous than other peoples, for you were the fewest of all peoples. [8]But it was because the LORD loved you and kept the oath he swore to your ancestors that he brought you out with a mighty hand and redeemed you from the land of slavery, from the power of Pharaoh king of Egypt. [9]Know therefore that the LORD your God is God; he is the faithful God, keeping his covenant of love to a thousand generations of those who love him and keep his commandments. [10]But

those who hate him he will repay to their face by destruction;
he will not be slow to repay to their face those who hate him.

[11]Therefore, take care to follow the commands, decrees and laws I give you today.

[12]If you pay attention to these laws and are careful to follow them, then the LORD your God will keep his covenant of love with you, as he swore to your ancestors. [13]He will love you and bless you and increase your numbers. He will bless the fruit of your womb, the crops of your land — your grain, new wine and olive oil — the calves of your herds and the lambs of your flocks in the land he swore to your ancestors to give you. [14]You will be blessed more than any other people; none of your men or women will be childless, nor will any of your livestock be without young. [15]The LORD will keep you free from every disease. He will not inflict on you the horrible diseases you knew in Egypt, but he will inflict them on all who hate you. [16]You must destroy all the peoples the LORD your God gives over to you. Do not look on them with pity and do not serve their gods, for that will be a snare to you.

[17]You may say to yourselves, "These nations are stronger than we are. How can we drive them out?" [18]But do not be afraid of them; remember well what the LORD your God did to Pharaoh and to all Egypt. [19]You saw with your own eyes the great trials, the signs and wonders, the mighty hand and outstretched arm, with which the LORD your God brought you out. The LORD your God will do the same to all the peoples you now fear. [20]Moreover, the LORD your God will send the hornet among them until even the survivors who hide from you have perished.

[a] 2 The Hebrew term refers to the irrevocable giving over of things or persons to the LORD, often by totally destroying them; also in verse 26. [b] 5 That is, wooden symbols of the goddess Asherah; here and elsewhere in Deuteronomy

PEOPLE

— *LOUIE GIGLIO*

GENESIS 12 TO MALACHI

All of us constantly find ourselves in a vicious cycle with God, a pattern we see clearly throughout this act of Scripture. The stages are familiar: God initiates a relationship and blesses us, God calls us to honor him, and we promise to serve and worship him alone, yet we soon drift into complacency. We are easily enticed by the flickering lights of temptation, so we wander and stray. Ultimately, we defy our Creator, falling into dark pits of sin with dreadful consequences. We hit rock bottom, we get fed up, we long for change, we cry out for mercy, God hears and restores, we promise to never leave him again ... but, in time the cycle begins again.

Yet, even when we are faithless, God remains faithful.

The consequence of the *revolt* in Eden was that mankind eventually scattered across the earth. And as they spread far and wide, their sin followed them. When they moved on, the fruit of their brokenness went with them. Relationships were torn apart. Hope dimmed and the earth was filled with rebellion as God's people continued to cultivate their fallen nature and direct their sin into ever-increasing forms of disobedience (Ge 11:1 – 9).

Yet in the midst of unrest and devastation, God chose a people — a people who would be set apart and "holy to the LORD." Out of all the people groups on earth, God chose Israel "to be his people, his treasured possession" (Dt 7:6). God chose Abram to be the ancestor and leader of this people, promising to make him "into a great nation." And ultimately, all people of the world would be blessed through him (Ge 12:2 – 3). God was on a mission for all of humanity. He would redeem people, through a *people!*

God's plan was to bless, prosper and guide his people as a demonstration of his goodness in a self-destructing world where people worshiped everything but the one true God. But God's chosen people were incessantly rebellious, constantly doing things their own way.

However, God's mission never changed. God was not caught off-guard by humanity's decision. Because he is sovereign (ruling over all things) and omniscient (knowing all things) God had already factored humanity's revolt into the equation. God ordained a rescue mission to restore fallen people to his original intention for their lives. Though one mission had stalled (humankind's opportunity to purely reflect God's glory), God's supreme mission (exalting his love, grace and mercy by the renewal of all things through the gift of his Son) was now underway.

Where people were (and are) unable to invent sufficient ways to draw near to a perfect God (through religion), God was building a bridge by which the Almighty could span the gap from heaven to mankind (through grace). Thus, grace reverses normal thinking — that we have to find a way to God — and ushers in the inconceivable: God makes a way to us.

So, you might be asking, if salvation is coming in the next act of the story, why don't we just skip this act called *people* and get right to the life and times of Jesus? Why not just get straight to his salvation work on the cross? Why keep re-reading the sin-filled cycle of God's chosen people? The answer is because the section called *people* is in fact about one *person,* and in studying the Old Testament account of God's relationship with his chosen people we see at least seven key things about God:

1. The Old Testament gives us a glimpse into God's glory.

God is not like mankind. Though he created us in his image, God alone is holy. He is *other.* He is altogether on an entirely different plane than humans — not just a little bigger. Mankind does not look at God eye-to-eye. God stoops from the heights of heaven to make himself known to humanity. And when he reaches down to show us who he is, he leads with his glory.

The Hebrew word for *glory* in much of the Old Testament can be translated as *weight.* To put it mildly and a bit figuratively, God is *heavy.* His righteousness, perfection, brilliance and radiant beauty span galaxies and cause the earth to shudder. Lightning and thunder proceed from his throne. To see him in full would be the end of any mortal.

Thus, God reveals glimpses of himself to fallen mankind. Knowing sinful people could never find God on their own, God initiates a relationship and reveals himself to his created ones. And when God shows up to engage mankind, his glory follows. Whether a burning bush through which he spoke to Moses, a cloud by day and a fiery pillar at night to lead them, or a cloud that descended from heaven to envelop the place where Moses encountered God on behalf of the people, God displayed his glory to the Israelites.

Even as God gave the law, he did it through his glory. As Moses was on Mount Sinai receiving the stone tablets containing the Ten Commandments, he asked to see God's glory (Ex 33:18). God tucked him into a craggy place. Then God covered Moses with his hand and only allowed him to see his back after he had passed by (Ex 33:18 – 23). Moses' face shone in the aftermath as he came down from the mountain, and the Israelites were "afraid to come near him" (Ex 29 – 30). God's glory is no small thing. It is not something to be taken lightly.

PEOPLE

(CONTINUED)

GENESIS 12 TO MALACHI

The people failed to grasp the *weight,* but God could not disregard his glory. He dwells in unapproachable light (1Ti 6:16). And, he fiercely defends his glory — his name (Isa 42:8).

2. The Old Testament gives us a glimpse into God's mercy.

God would have been without fault if he had simply said "goodbye and good luck" to Adam and Eve when he expelled them from the garden. Instead, he watched over his people and later came to Abram with a blessing and a promise.

God's call of Abram was a decisive juncture in the story (Ge 12:1 – 3). Were it not for God's initiative, humans would have been lost in sin forever and doomed to destruction. Yet God made a covenant with Abram in which he promised that his children would be the recipients of God's gracious salvation. Establishing covenants was a common practice in the ancient Near East, a means by which a king would establish a relationship between himself and his subjects. In these agreements, the parties would initiate the terms of the relationship, the responsibilities of both parties, the blessings that would come to those who kept the covenant, and the curses that would result from disobedience. God, in a breathtaking act of love, entered into this kind of relationship with his sin-stained people.

God selected Abram and called him to leave his pagan city and to travel to the land of God's choosing where he would receive God's blessing and become the father of a great nation. Abram believed God and was counted righteous as a result (Ge 15:6). God pledged his covenant faithfulness and bountiful love to Abram and his heirs (Ge 17). More astounding is the fact that God's promises were not predicated on Abram's obedience; rather, the covenant promises were based solely on the character and generosity of God. God made promises to Abram, even changing his name to "Abraham," which means "father of many nations" (Ge 17:5). God does not break his promises, since "his love endures forever" (Ps 136:3).

From Abraham onward, God began gathering his people. Abraham's descendants, the Israelites, were the recipients of a multitude of blessings from God. God delivered them from slavery in Egypt in a miraculous demonstration of his power. And God made an extraordinary offer to them: You will be my people and I will be your God. Through you I will show all the inhabitants of the earth that I am the One true God (Ge 17:7 – 8, Ex 6:7).

3. The Old Testament gives us a glimpse into God's provision.

Once God delivered his people from Egyptian bondage, he led them by an arduous route toward the promised land. He did this to protect and lead them through salvation's waters at the Red Sea and into a desert land that would teach them that God provides no matter what circumstances his people face.

In the desert he showed them his provision by giving them manna to eat (Ex 16:31); he showed his protecting presence by giving them a cloud by day and fire by night to guide their way (Ex 13:21); and he showed them his faithfulness as a promise-keeping God by never leaving or forsaking them (Ex 13 – 17).

4. The Old Testament gives us a glimpse into the fact that religion is not enough.

In the wilderness, God gave the people of Israel his law, which was never intended to institute a means by which people could merit their own salvation. Rather, God gave them the law to expose their sinful nature.

The sacrificial system God established made it clear that sin required punishment (Ge 3:21). The people brought a sacrificial substitute — an animal that bore the sin of the people in their place. The wrath of God for sin was ceremonially placed on the substitute; in turn, the people were able to avoid God's wrath for their rebellion and sin. The ongoing practice of sacrifice ensured that the people would never forget that the only way to placate God's fury over sin was through the blood sacrifice of a substitute.

This system pointed the way to a promised hope — a Messiah — who would fulfill the intent of the sacrificial system once and for all (Mt 5:17).

5. The Old Testament gives us a glimpse into God's eternal plan.

God ultimately led his people to the promised land. Like the garden of old, the promised land was a place of God's choosing where the people were to live while they enjoyed God's bountiful provision.

God used forty years in the wilderness to humble his people and teach them to depend on him. He then allowed them to conquer the pagan inhabitants of the land, and he set them there to reflect his glory to the world once more. More astounding, God lived among his people in the tabernacle. There his presence would reside, and his people could continually worship him through their sacrifices. Yet this land of promise was only a preview

PEOPLE

(CONTINUED)

GENESIS 12 TO MALACHI

of *forever* — the final act in God's story — in which his people will permanently live with him and enjoy eternal freedom from sin, death and shame in heaven.

6. The Old Testament gives us a glimpse into the dreadful state of humanity apart from God.

God's people had so much going for them. Not only did they have a relationship with God (though partial), they also had the law, which told them how to obey God; the sacrificial system that allowed them to worship God; the tabernacle where they could experience the presence of God; and the land where they could enjoy the provision of God. These gifts of grace should have allowed them to fill the earth with the knowledge of God's glory. His fame was not meant to be limited to the nation of Israel; through them, all nations would hear about the One true God and see his glory reflected in his people.

The people, however, proved to be utter failures in this mission. They embraced the idolatrous practices of the surrounding nations rather than living a distinctive, holy life as God had required. They looked toward human leaders — like Saul, David and Solomon — to usher in God's promised blessings while they turned away from God himself. As a result, God's people began to unravel at the seams, splintering into two separate nations and facing continual threats of war.

God had no choice but to judge his rebellious people. As a result, God's people were defeated by their pagan enemies and exiled from their land to become servants of ruthless masters who mocked and hated Jehovah God. Through the prophets, God called the people back home again, and the cycle continued.

For centuries Israel's defiance led to collapse, and collapse led to contrition. Contrition always birthed a cry for mercy, and that cry was always heard by a merciful God. Enemies, whom God used as instruments of judgment for his people, were dispatched and defeated in one heavenly gesture. Even when his rebellious people were helpless, God would seek them out and draw them to himself.

But every generation seemed to take Israel further from Eden's paradise. The scene at the end of the Old Testament is bleak. God's remnant people were broken and in need of deliverance from their cycle of death. Thankfully, God's mission never changed. The prophets continued to remind God's people of the coming promised One — the Messiah who would fulfill God's promises, reclaim God's people as worshipers, and establish his rule and reign forever. He would give his people a new heart, pulsating with the new life of his Spirit (Eze 36:26). God would not abandon his people; rather, he would save them in his time and in his way.

7. The Old Testament gives us a glimpse into God's invitation to know him as sons and daughters.

Where people proved to be faithless, God was faithful, never once denying his own character. So while it might be tempting to skim over the Old Testament account and get to the good news of the New Testament, we find in the Old Testament a helpful mirror for ourselves. We are challenged to take seriously our inclination towards the deceptive but deadly spiral of sin's cycle. It is a picture of our depravity that keeps us humbly dependent on his Spirit's leading every step of the way, and it contains the promise of heaven's beauty and our true home. We also find a constant reminder of God's mercy, mercies that are new every day (La 3:22 – 23). We are encouraged by his provision as we see over and over a God who is able to be more than we need in every situation. While the Old Testament serves as a reminder that our effort will never be enough to make us acceptable to God, it still invites us to draw near to God.

In the end, through a relationship made possible by the death and resurrection of Jesus Christ, we not only become God's people but are actually born again as God's adopted sons and daughters, made alive by faith to become all that he always dreamed we would be. His Spirit dwells within us, affording us a fellowship (relationship) with God that the people living in the time of the Old Testament could only dream of. In Christ, the Almighty God becomes our perfect Father, and we humbly walk with him forever.

THE BLESSINGS AND RESPONSIBILITY OF THE ELECT

These verses show the wondrous grace of God toward his people. Having done nothing of note nor being special in any way, the Israelites were selected by God out of all the existing nations to be a chosen people upon whom he would bestow his covenant blessings (vv. 7 – 8). The history of Israel is full of examples of their continuous inability to remain faithful to the Lord and keep his law — yet God was faithful to keep his oath to the nation (v. 9). This text contains what theologians call the doctrine of election: God choosing people upon whom he bestows his unmerited favor without end, even when those people prove to be unfaithful to him.

Moses was referring to the covenant that God made with Abraham in Genesis 12. In the establishment of this covenant between God and the descendants of Abraham, being God's chosen people was a great privilege for the Israelites. But there were also tremendous implications associated with that privilege that benefited other nations (Ge 12:3). In the first few chapters of Scripture, God took action on behalf of his image-bearers as he refused to abandon humanity to live in the effects of the fall brought about by Adam and Eve. He began a plan of redemption by making a sacrifice to cover their sin and nakedness, an animal sacrifice that prefigured the killing of Jesus to cover sin and shame (Ge 3:21). In Genesis 12, God unfolded another aspect of his plan of redemption hinted at in Genesis 3:15. By redeeming Israel to be his people, God chose them to be a holy nation set apart as a picture of humanity restored to a right relationship with its Creator, the one true and living God. They, in turn, would be the vehicle through which he would bring about redemption and restoration from sin, sorrow and death to their fellow human beings — to be a blessing to the nations. Ultimately, through the lineage of the Hebrew nation the Christ came, extending God's chosen race beyond ethnic lines.

To this day, God's story of redemption continues. He continues to elect people, bringing them from sin and darkness to himself (Jn 6:44; Eph 2:1 – 10). The means that God uses to spread his story of redemption is through his people sharing the gospel (Ro 10:14). Truly, believers receive tremendous blessing as God's children, as he knows our every need and will never leave us nor forsake us (Dt 31:6; Heb 13:5). This blessing, however, is not simply one in which privileges associated with being a child of the King are received, but rather a privileged status of being set apart for service is declared (Mt 28:19 – 20).

21Do not be terrified by them, for the LORD your God, who is among you, is a great
and awesome God. 22The LORD your God will drive out those nations before you,
little by little. You will not be allowed to eliminate them all at once, or the wild
animals will multiply around you. 23But the LORD your God will deliver them
over to you, throwing them into great confusion until they are destroyed. 24He
will give their kings into your hand, and you will wipe out their names from under heaven. No one will be able to stand up against you; you will destroy them.
25The images of their gods you are to burn in the fire. Do not covet the silver and
gold on them, and do not take it for yourselves, or you will be ensnared by it, for
it is detestable to the LORD your God. 26Do not bring a detestable thing into your
house or you, like it, will be set apart for destruction. Regard it as vile and utterly
detest it, for it is set apart for destruction.

Do Not Forget the LORD

8 Be careful to follow every command I am giving you today, so that you may
live and increase and may enter and possess the land the LORD promised on
oath to your ancestors. 2Remember how the LORD your God led you all the way
in the wilderness these forty years, to humble and test you in order to know what
was in your heart, whether or not you would keep his commands. 3He humbled
you, causing you to hunger and then feeding you with manna, which neither
you nor your ancestors had known, to teach you that man does not live on bread
alone but on every word that comes from the mouth of the LORD. 4Your clothes
did not wear out and your feet did not swell during these forty years. 5Know then
in your heart that as a man disciplines his son, so the LORD your God disciplines
you.

6Observe the commands of the LORD your God, walking in obedience to him
and revering him. 7For the LORD your God is bringing you into a good land—a
land with brooks, streams, and deep springs gushing out into the valleys and
hills; 8a land with wheat and barley, vines and fig trees, pomegranates, olive oil
and honey; 9a land where bread will not be scarce and you will lack nothing; a
land where the rocks are iron and you can dig copper out of the hills.

10When you have eaten and are satisfied, praise the LORD your God for the
good land he has given you. 11Be careful that you do not forget the LORD your
God, failing to observe his commands, his laws and his decrees that I am giving you this day. 12Otherwise, when you eat and are satisfied, when you build
fine houses and settle down, 13and when your herds and flocks grow large and
your silver and gold increase and all you have is multiplied, 14then your heart
will become proud and you will forget the LORD your God, who brought you out
of Egypt, out of the land of slavery. 15He led you through the vast and dreadful
wilderness, that thirsty and waterless land, with its venomous snakes and scorpions. He brought you water out of hard rock. 16He gave you manna to eat in the
wilderness, something your ancestors had never known, to humble and test you
so that in the end it might go well with you. 17You may say to yourself, "My power
and the strength of my hands have produced this wealth for me." 18But remember the LORD your God, for it is he who gives you the ability to produce wealth,
and so confirms his covenant, which he swore to your ancestors, as it is today.

19If you ever forget the LORD your God and follow other gods and worship and
bow down to them, I testify against you today that you will surely be destroyed.
20Like the nations the LORD destroyed before you, so you will be destroyed for
not obeying the LORD your God.

Not Because of Israel's Righteousness

9 Hear, Israel: You are now about to cross the Jordan to go in and dispossess
nations greater and stronger than you, with large cities that have walls up to
the sky. 2The people are strong and tall—Anakites! You know about them and
have heard it said: "Who can stand up against the Anakites?" 3But be assured
today that the LORD your God is the one who goes across ahead of you like a

DEUTERONOMY 8:2–3

TRUE SATISFACTION FOR HUNGER AND THIRST

As Israel wandered through the wilderness, they were humbled and tested by God in order to reveal the true condition of their hearts, especially whether or not they trusted the Lord's promise when provisions were lacking and they grew hungry. God saw their need and responded to it, using the occasion to refine his people's faith in him yet again. His proclamation reminded them that life is not supported by physical sustenance alone—people require more than bread and water to live and thrive on earth. In this incident, God taught the Israelites that their spiritual life was sustained in the same way their physical bodies were sustained: with daily faith.

During his temptation in the wilderness Jesus referenced this verse when Satan enticed him to "tell these stones to become bread" to prove himself to be the Son of God (Mt 4:3). But Jesus trusted that God would supply all that he needed physically, spiritually, emotionally and otherwise. Also, by drawing upon this text, Jesus linked himself to the Lord God of Israel and strengthened his self-identification as the living bread of heaven (Jn 6:33–51). By contrasting himself with the manna given to Israel, which only met temporary physical needs, he revealed the superiority of the eternal nourishment found in him as opposed to physical sustenance alone.

devouring fire. He will destroy them; he will subdue them before you. And you will drive them out and annihilate them quickly, as the LORD has promised you.

4After the LORD your God has driven them out before you, do not say to yourself, "The LORD has brought me here to take possession of this land because of my righteousness." No, it is on account of the wickedness of these nations that the LORD is going to drive them out before you. 5It is not because of your righteousness or your integrity that you are going in to take possession of their land; but on account of the wickedness of these nations, the LORD your God will drive them out before you, to accomplish what he swore to your fathers, to Abraham, Isaac and Jacob. 6Understand, then, that it is not because of your righteousness that the LORD your God is giving you this good land to possess, for you are a stiff-necked people.

The Golden Calf

7Remember this and never forget how you aroused the anger of the LORD your God in the wilderness. From the day you left Egypt until you arrived here, you have been rebellious against the LORD. 8At Horeb you aroused the LORD's wrath so that he was angry enough to destroy you. 9When I went up on the mountain to receive the tablets of stone, the tablets of the covenant that the LORD had made with you, I stayed on the mountain forty days and forty nights; I ate no bread and drank no water. 10The LORD gave me two stone tablets inscribed by the finger of God. On them were all the commandments the LORD proclaimed to you on the mountain out of the fire, on the day of the assembly.

11At the end of the forty days and forty nights, the LORD gave me the two stone tablets, the tablets of the covenant. 12Then the LORD told me, "Go down from here at once, because your people whom you brought out of Egypt have become corrupt. They have turned away quickly from what I commanded them and have made an idol for themselves."

13And the LORD said to me, "I have seen this people, and they are a stiff-necked people indeed! 14Let me alone, so that I may destroy them and blot out their name from under heaven. And I will make you into a nation stronger and more numerous than they."

15So I turned and went down from the mountain while it was ablaze with fire. And the two tablets of the covenant were in my hands. 16When I looked, I saw that you had sinned against the LORD your God; you had made for yourselves an idol cast in the shape of a calf. You had turned aside quickly from the way that the LORD had commanded you. 17So I took the two tablets and threw them out of my hands, breaking them to pieces before your eyes.

18Then once again I fell prostrate before the LORD for forty days and forty nights; I ate no bread and drank no water, because of all the sin you had committed, doing what was evil in the LORD's sight and so arousing his anger. 19I feared the anger and wrath of the LORD, for he was angry enough with you to destroy you. But again the LORD listened to me. 20And the LORD was angry enough with Aaron to destroy him, but at that time I prayed for Aaron too. 21Also I took that sinful thing of yours, the calf you had made, and burned it in the fire. Then I crushed it and ground it to powder as fine as dust and threw the dust into a stream that flowed down the mountain.

22You also made the LORD angry at Taberah, at Massah and at Kibroth Hattaavah.

23And when the LORD sent you out from Kadesh Barnea, he said, "Go up and take possession of the land I have given you." But you rebelled against the command of the LORD your God. You did not trust him or obey him. 24You have been rebellious against the LORD ever since I have known you.

25I lay prostrate before the LORD those forty days and forty nights because the LORD had said he would destroy you. 26I prayed to the LORD and said, "Sovereign LORD, do not destroy your people, your own inheritance that you redeemed by your great power and brought out of Egypt with a mighty hand. 27Remember your servants Abraham, Isaac and Jacob. Overlook the stubbornness of this

DEUTERONOMY 9:25–29

THE NEED FOR ONE TO INTERCEDE

After Israel sinned against God by making a golden calf and worshiping it while Moses was in the presence of God on Mount Sinai, God approached Moses to disown his people and begin again with Moses. The book of Deuteronomy intensifies the nature of Israel's sin in the incident with the golden calf by putting it in the context of Israel's recent reception of the Ten Commandments and the saving activity of God who brought them out of bondage in Egypt "with a mighty hand" (v. 26). However, Moses countered God's plan to disassociate from Israel by interceding on their behalf. He pleaded with God to remember his promises to the patriarchs and overlook the people's sin. He also argued that by destroying the people of God's own inheritance, God's saving power and the authenticity of God's love for his treasured possession would be called into question.

Just as Moses interceded on behalf of Israel, so also Jesus Christ intercedes on behalf of believers who approach God through him. The salvation Jesus offers through the new covenant is a complete salvation that endures for all time and extends to all of life. Those who place their faith in the finished work of Jesus are saved by virtue of his sinless life, sacrificial death and glorious resurrection.

people, their wickedness and their sin. 28 Otherwise, the country from which you
brought us will say, 'Because the LORD was not able to take them into the land
he had promised them, and because he hated them, he brought them out to put
them to death in the wilderness.' 29 But they are your people, your inheritance
that you brought out by your great power and your outstretched arm."

Tablets Like the First Ones

10 At that time the LORD said to me, "Chisel out two stone tablets like the first
ones and come up to me on the mountain. Also make a wooden ark.[a] 2 I
will write on the tablets the words that were on the first tablets, which you broke.
Then you are to put them in the ark."

3 So I made the ark out of acacia wood and chiseled out two stone tablets like
the first ones, and I went up on the mountain with the two tablets in my hands.
4 The LORD wrote on these tablets what he had written before, the Ten Commandments he had proclaimed to you on the mountain, out of the fire, on the
day of the assembly. And the LORD gave them to me. 5 Then I came back down
the mountain and put the tablets in the ark I had made, as the LORD commanded
me, and they are there now.

6 (The Israelites traveled from the wells of Bene Jaakan to Moserah. There Aaron died and was buried, and Eleazar his son succeeded him as priest. 7 From
there they traveled to Gudgodah and on to Jotbathah, a land with streams of
water. 8 At that time the LORD set apart the tribe of Levi to carry the ark of the
covenant of the LORD, to stand before the LORD to minister and to pronounce
blessings in his name, as they still do today. 9 That is why the Levites have no
share or inheritance among their fellow Israelites; the LORD is their inheritance,
as the LORD your God told them.)

10 Now I had stayed on the mountain forty days and forty nights, as I did the
first time, and the LORD listened to me at this time also. It was not his will to
destroy you. 11 "Go," the LORD said to me, "and lead the people on their way, so
that they may enter and possess the land I swore to their ancestors to give them."

Fear the LORD

12 And now, Israel, what does the LORD your God ask of you but to fear the
LORD your God, to walk in obedience to him, to love him, to serve the LORD your
God with all your heart and with all your soul, 13 and to observe the LORD's com-
mands and decrees that I am giving you today for your own good?

14 To the LORD your God belong the heavens, even the highest heavens, the earth
and everything in it. 15 Yet the LORD set his affection on your ancestors and loved
them, and he chose you, their descendants, above all the nations — as it is today.
16 Circumcise your hearts, therefore, and do not be stiff-necked any longer. 17 For
the LORD your God is God of gods and Lord of lords, the great God, mighty and
awesome, who shows no partiality and accepts no bribes. 18 He defends the cause
of the fatherless and the widow, and loves the foreigner residing among you, giving them food and clothing. 19 And you are to love those who are foreigners, for
you yourselves were foreigners in Egypt. 20 Fear the LORD your God and serve him.
Hold fast to him and take your oaths in his name. 21 He is the one you praise; he
is your God, who performed for you those great and awesome wonders you saw
with your own eyes. 22 Your ancestors who went down into Egypt were seventy in
all, and now the LORD your God has made you as numerous as the stars in the sky.

Love and Obey the LORD

11 Love the LORD your God and keep his requirements, his decrees, his laws
and his commands always. 2 Remember today that your children were
not the ones who saw and experienced the discipline of the LORD your God: his
majesty, his mighty hand, his outstretched arm; 3 the signs he performed and

[a] *1* That is, a chest

DEUTERONOMY 10:16

SPIRITUAL RENEWAL THROUGH JESUS ALONE

Moses commanded the Israelites to circumcise their hearts rather than being rebellious. Circumcision carried tremendous significance in the minds of the Israelites as it was a physical sign of the covenant between them and God. Living in close proximity to the Canaanites whose worship system involved sexual promiscuity, circumcision of a Hebrew male was a reminder to avoid such cultural rituals. But circumcision was much more than a physical act. A person's heart must reflect the physical sign. God is concerned not merely with the outward marks of holiness but with the posture of the human heart. The covenant of God required a spiritual change to love God as he desires: with all of one's heart, soul and strength (Dt 10:12 – 13; 30:6). Such a necessary change only comes through Jesus (Col 2:11 – 12). In Christ our debt was canceled; our flesh which ruled us was buried, and we were raised from death to life.

THE PURPOSE OF THE LAW

Moses addressed the heart of the moral law given by God to the nation of Israel (v. 12). Incidentally, the heart of the law is intended to address the hearts of sinful men and women. Based on God's majestic work of redemption, a feat that proved him to be the one true God, the people were to respond in wholehearted worship. This worship would spring from a deep love for God and a desire to please him.

Moses revealed another motive for keeping the law. Not only is the law a response to the grace of God, but it is also the best way to live life. As Moses said here in the text, the law is for the good of the people (v. 13). Many times people are prone to assume that God's laws are foolish or a barrier to human joy and fulfillment.

This could not be further from the truth. The law of God is true because it is based on the nature of God who made all things. Who else would know how best to live than the one who created all things in the first place? The law of God is wise — it counteracts human folly and instructs men and women on the mind of God. Finally, obedience to the law is the path to human joy and flourishing. Sin, not God's law, is the barrier to joy.

The pages of Scripture repeatedly attest to this reality. They demonstrate that God is all-wise and his law is the path to true life (Ps 19:7 – 9; 119:1 – 176). But time and time again, the people demonstrated that they were incapable of keeping the law (Ro 7:7 – 12). Moses pointed forward to the need for heart transformation rather than mere external obedience to the law (Dt 10:16). He knew that their obedience would be short-lived. What they needed was circumcised hearts instead of hearts of stone. God, through the prophet Ezekiel, declared that a day would come when God would remove the heart of stone and put a heart of flesh in its place (Eze 36:26). This new heart is a gift of God's grace given to those who place their faith in Jesus Christ and are reborn by his Spirit (Jn 3:3 – 5).

the things he did in the heart of Egypt, both to Pharaoh king of Egypt and to his
whole country; 4what he did to the Egyptian army, to its horses and chariots, how
he overwhelmed them with the waters of the Red Sea[a] as they were pursuing
you, and how the LORD brought lasting ruin on them. 5It was not your children
who saw what he did for you in the wilderness until you arrived at this place,
6and what he did to Dathan and Abiram, sons of Eliab the Reubenite, when the
earth opened its mouth right in the middle of all Israel and swallowed them up
with their households, their tents and every living thing that belonged to them.
7But it was your own eyes that saw all these great things the LORD has done.

8Observe therefore all the commands I am giving you today, so that you may
have the strength to go in and take over the land that you are crossing the Jordan to possess, 9and so that you may live long in the land the LORD swore to your
ancestors to give to them and their descendants, a land flowing with milk and
honey. 10The land you are entering to take over is not like the land of Egypt, from
which you have come, where you planted your seed and irrigated it by foot as in
a vegetable garden. 11But the land you are crossing the Jordan to take possession
of is a land of mountains and valleys that drinks rain from heaven. 12It is a land
the LORD your God cares for; the eyes of the LORD your God are continually on it
from the beginning of the year to its end.

13So if you faithfully obey the commands I am giving you today—to love the
LORD your God and to serve him with all your heart and with all your soul—
14then I will send rain on your land in its season, both autumn and spring rains,
so that you may gather in your grain, new wine and olive oil. 15I will provide grass
in the fields for your cattle, and you will eat and be satisfied.

16Be careful, or you will be enticed to turn away and worship other gods and
bow down to them. 17Then the LORD's anger will burn against you, and he will
shut up the heavens so that it will not rain and the ground will yield no produce,
and you will soon perish from the good land the LORD is giving you. 18Fix these
words of mine in your hearts and minds; tie them as symbols on your hands and
bind them on your foreheads. 19Teach them to your children, talking about them
when you sit at home and when you walk along the road, when you lie down and
when you get up. 20Write them on the doorframes of your houses and on your
gates, 21so that your days and the days of your children may be many in the land
the LORD swore to give your ancestors, as many as the days that the heavens are
above the earth.

22If you carefully observe all these commands I am giving you to follow—to
love the LORD your God, to walk in obedience to him and to hold fast to him—
23then the LORD will drive out all these nations before you, and you will dispossess nations larger and stronger than you. 24Every place where you set your foot
will be yours: Your territory will extend from the desert to Lebanon, and from the
Euphrates River to the Mediterranean Sea. 25No one will be able to stand against
you. The LORD your God, as he promised you, will put the terror and fear of you
on the whole land, wherever you go.

26See, I am setting before you today a blessing and a curse— 27the blessing
if you obey the commands of the LORD your God that I am giving you today;
28the curse if you disobey the commands of the LORD your God and turn from
the way that I command you today by following other gods, which you have not
known. 29When the LORD your God has brought you into the land you are entering to possess, you are to proclaim on Mount Gerizim the blessings, and on
Mount Ebal the curses. 30As you know, these mountains are across the Jordan,
westward, toward the setting sun, near the great trees of Moreh, in the territory
of those Canaanites living in the Arabah in the vicinity of Gilgal. 31You are about
to cross the Jordan to enter and take possession of the land the LORD your God is
giving you. When you have taken it over and are living there, 32be sure that you
obey all the decrees and laws I am setting before you today.

[a] 4 Or *the Sea of Reeds*

The One Place of Worship

12 These are the decrees and laws you must be careful to follow in the land that the LORD, the God of your ancestors, has given you to possess—as long as you live in the land. 2Destroy completely all the places on the high mountains, on the hills and under every spreading tree, where the nations you are dispossessing worship their gods. 3Break down their altars, smash their sacred stones and burn their Asherah poles in the fire; cut down the idols of their gods and wipe out their names from those places.

4You must not worship the LORD your God in their way. 5But you are to seek the place the LORD your God will choose from among all your tribes to put his Name there for his dwelling. To that place you must go; 6there bring your burnt offerings and sacrifices, your tithes and special gifts, what you have vowed to give and your freewill offerings, and the firstborn of your herds and flocks. 7There, in the presence of the LORD your God, you and your families shall eat and shall rejoice in everything you have put your hand to, because the LORD your God has blessed you.

8You are not to do as we do here today, everyone doing as they see fit, 9since you have not yet reached the resting place and the inheritance the LORD your God is giving you. 10But you will cross the Jordan and settle in the land the LORD your God is giving you as an inheritance, and he will give you rest from all your enemies around you so that you will live in safety. 11Then to the place the LORD your God will choose as a dwelling for his Name—there you are to bring everything I command you: your burnt offerings and sacrifices, your tithes and special gifts, and all the choice possessions you have vowed to the LORD. 12And there rejoice before the LORD your God—you, your sons and daughters, your male and female servants, and the Levites from your towns who have no allotment or inheritance of their own. 13Be careful not to sacrifice your burnt offerings anywhere you please. 14Offer them only at the place the LORD will choose in one of your tribes, and there observe everything I command you.

15Nevertheless, you may slaughter your animals in any of your towns and eat as much of the meat as you want, as if it were gazelle or deer, according to the blessing the LORD your God gives you. Both the ceremonially unclean and the clean may eat it. 16But you must not eat the blood; pour it out on the ground like water. 17You must not eat in your own towns the tithe of your grain and new wine and olive oil, or the firstborn of your herds and flocks, or whatever you have vowed to give, or your freewill offerings or special gifts. 18Instead, you are to eat them in the presence of the LORD your God at the place the LORD your God will choose—you, your sons and daughters, your male and female servants, and the Levites from your towns—and you are to rejoice before the LORD your God in everything you put your hand to. 19Be careful not to neglect the Levites as long as you live in your land.

20When the LORD your God has enlarged your territory as he promised you, and you crave meat and say, "I would like some meat," then you may eat as much of it as you want. 21If the place where the LORD your God chooses to put his Name is too far away from you, you may slaughter animals from the herds and flocks the LORD has given you, as I have commanded you, and in your own towns you may eat as much of them as you want. 22Eat them as you would gazelle or deer. Both the ceremonially unclean and the clean may eat. 23But be sure you do not eat the blood, because the blood is the life, and you must not eat the life with the meat. 24You must not eat the blood; pour it out on the ground like water. 25Do not eat it, so that it may go well with you and your children after you, because you will be doing what is right in the eyes of the LORD.

26But take your consecrated things and whatever you have vowed to give, and go to the place the LORD will choose. 27Present your burnt offerings on the altar of the LORD your God, both the meat and the blood. The blood of your sacrifices must be poured beside the altar of the LORD your God, but you may eat the meat. 28Be careful to obey all these regulations I am giving you, so that it may always

---

DEUTERONOMY 12:1–7

JESUS EXPANDS THE PLACE OF TRUE WORSHIP

The place of worship in the Old Testament was extremely important. The presence of God rested on the place he chose. Unlike the false places of worship—that were creations of cultures surrounding the Israelites—God commanded that true worship would occur only in the place he designated. In these verses, Moses contrasted the false places of worship so prevalent at that time with the place of true worship chosen by God. The preeminent means of access to God was found in the tabernacle while Israel wandered in the wilderness and for many years after settling in the promise land, and later in the temple in Jerusalem.

The place of true worship is just as important today as it was at that time, but God has expanded the reality of "place." In Jesus, the place of worship is no longer limited to a specific physical location (Jn 2:18–22). Now the Spirit of God dwells within believers, and our bodies serve as the temple of God (1Co 6:19). This is why Christians are able to "pray continually," meaning, worship God wherever they are, at all times (1Th 5:17).

go well with you and your children after you, because you will be doing what is
good and right in the eyes of the LORD your God.
29The LORD your God will cut off before you the nations you are about to invade
and dispossess. But when you have driven them out and settled in their land, 30and
after they have been destroyed before you, be careful not to be ensnared by inquiring about their gods, saying, "How do these nations serve their gods? We will
do the same." 31You must not worship the LORD your God in their way, because in
worshiping their gods, they do all kinds of detestable things the LORD hates. They
even burn their sons and daughters in the fire as sacrifices to their gods.
32See that you do all I command you; do not add to it or take away from it.[a]

Worshiping Other Gods

13[b] If a prophet, or one who foretells by dreams, appears among you and announces to you a sign or wonder, 2and if the sign or wonder spoken of takes
place, and the prophet says, "Let us follow other gods" (gods you have not known)
"and let us worship them," 3you must not listen to the words of that prophet or
dreamer. The LORD your God is testing you to find out whether you love him with
all your heart and with all your soul. 4It is the LORD your God you must follow, and
him you must revere. Keep his commands and obey him; serve him and hold fast to
him. 5That prophet or dreamer must be put to death for inciting rebellion against
the LORD your God, who brought you out of Egypt and redeemed you from the land
of slavery. That prophet or dreamer tried to turn you from the way the LORD your
God commanded you to follow. You must purge the evil from among you.
6If your very own brother, or your son or daughter, or the wife you love, or your
closest friend secretly entices you, saying, "Let us go and worship other gods"
(gods that neither you nor your ancestors have known, 7gods of the peoples
around you, whether near or far, from one end of the land to the other), 8do not
yield to them or listen to them. Show them no pity. Do not spare them or shield
them. 9You must certainly put them to death. Your hand must be the first in putting them to death, and then the hands of all the people. 10Stone them to death,
because they tried to turn you away from the LORD your God, who brought you
out of Egypt, out of the land of slavery. 11Then all Israel will hear and be afraid,
and no one among you will do such an evil thing again.
12If you hear it said about one of the towns the LORD your God is giving you to
live in 13that troublemakers have arisen among you and have led the people of
their town astray, saying, "Let us go and worship other gods" (gods you have not
known), 14then you must inquire, probe and investigate it thoroughly. And if it is
true and it has been proved that this detestable thing has been done among you,
15you must certainly put to the sword all who live in that town. You must destroy
it completely,[c] both its people and its livestock. 16You are to gather all the plunder
of the town into the middle of the public square and completely burn the town
and all its plunder as a whole burnt offering to the LORD your God. That town
is to remain a ruin forever, never to be rebuilt, 17and none of the condemned
things[c] are to be found in your hands. Then the LORD will turn from his fierce
anger, will show you mercy, and will have compassion on you. He will increase
your numbers, as he promised on oath to your ancestors— 18because you obey
the LORD your God by keeping all his commands that I am giving you today and
doing what is right in his eyes.

Clean and Unclean Food

14 You are the children of the LORD your God. Do not cut yourselves or shave
the front of your heads for the dead, 2for you are a people holy to the LORD
your God. Out of all the peoples on the face of the earth, the LORD has chosen you
to be his treasured possession.

[a] *32* In Hebrew texts this verse (12:32) is numbered 13:1. [b] In Hebrew texts 13:1-18 is numbered 13:2-19. [c] *15,17* The Hebrew term refers to the irrevocable giving over of things or persons to the LORD, often by totally destroying them.

DEUTERONOMY 15:1–6

RELIEF FROM MISERY

Financial poverty and debt is a crushing experience, making the indebted person or family feel that there is little to no hope for escape. So binding is financial poverty that the Lord inspired the authors of Scripture to include instructions on how to properly handle finances (Lev 25:25–28; Ps 37:21; Pr 28:8; Mt 25:27; Ro 13:8). In cases where Israelites owed a debt to a fellow countryman, Moses commanded that the creditor release the debtor after seven years, offering relief to the oppressive realities of being in debt. How great was this news to those crushed by unending financial obligations!

This financial relief points to the proclamation of Jesus bringing good news to the poor, offering freedom from various forms of intense suffering (Lk 4:18–19). While we do not have the same legal statutes in place to offer freedom from debt every seven years, Jesus offers the Lord's favor in the midst of human sorrow. Our physical circumstances may not change, but Jesus provides relief and comfort to those struggling under oppression or crushing experiences. He offers the kingdom of God to his followers: a sure blessing that will include a wonderful and worshipful exchange of our current suffering for blessing without end in the eternal presence of God.

3Do not eat any detestable thing. 4These are the animals you may eat: the ox, the sheep, the goat, 5the deer, the gazelle, the roe deer, the wild goat, the ibex, the antelope and the mountain sheep.[a] 6You may eat any animal that has a divided hoof and that chews the cud. 7However, of those that chew the cud or that have a divided hoof you may not eat the camel, the rabbit or the hyrax. Although they chew the cud, they do not have a divided hoof; they are ceremonially unclean for you. 8The pig is also unclean; although it has a divided hoof, it does not chew the cud. You are not to eat their meat or touch their carcasses.

9Of all the creatures living in the water, you may eat any that has fins and scales. 10But anything that does not have fins and scales you may not eat; for you it is unclean.

11You may eat any clean bird. 12But these you may not eat: the eagle, the vulture, the black vulture, 13the red kite, the black kite, any kind of falcon, 14any kind of raven, 15the horned owl, the screech owl, the gull, any kind of hawk, 16the little owl, the great owl, the white owl, 17the desert owl, the osprey, the cormorant, 18the stork, any kind of heron, the hoopoe and the bat.

19All flying insects are unclean to you; do not eat them. 20But any winged creature that is clean you may eat.

21Do not eat anything you find already dead. You may give it to the foreigner residing in any of your towns, and they may eat it, or you may sell it to any other foreigner. But you are a people holy to the LORD your God.

Do not cook a young goat in its mother's milk.

Tithes

22Be sure to set aside a tenth of all that your fields produce each year. 23Eat the tithe of your grain, new wine and olive oil, and the firstborn of your herds and flocks in the presence of the LORD your God at the place he will choose as a dwelling for his Name, so that you may learn to revere the LORD your God always. 24But if that place is too distant and you have been blessed by the LORD your God and cannot carry your tithe (because the place where the LORD will choose to put his Name is so far away), 25then exchange your tithe for silver, and take the silver with you and go to the place the LORD your God will choose. 26Use the silver to buy whatever you like: cattle, sheep, wine or other fermented drink, or anything you wish. Then you and your household shall eat there in the presence of the LORD your God and rejoice. 27And do not neglect the Levites living in your towns, for they have no allotment or inheritance of their own.

28At the end of every three years, bring all the tithes of that year's produce and store it in your towns, 29so that the Levites (who have no allotment or inheritance of their own) and the foreigners, the fatherless and the widows who live in your towns may come and eat and be satisfied, and so that the LORD your God may bless you in all the work of your hands.

The Year for Canceling Debts

15 At the end of every seven years you must cancel debts. 2This is how it is to be done: Every creditor shall cancel any loan they have made to a fellow Israelite. They shall not require payment from anyone among their own people, because the LORD's time for canceling debts has been proclaimed. 3You may require payment from a foreigner, but you must cancel any debt your fellow Israelite owes you. 4However, there need be no poor people among you, for in the land the LORD your God is giving you to possess as your inheritance, he will richly bless you, 5if only you fully obey the LORD your God and are careful to follow all these commands I am giving you today. 6For the LORD your God will bless you as he has promised, and you will lend to many nations but will borrow from none. You will rule over many nations but none will rule over you.

[a] 5 The precise identification of some of the birds and animals in this chapter is uncertain.

7If anyone is poor among your fellow Israelites in any of the towns of the
land the LORD your God is giving you, do not be hardhearted or tightfisted toward them. 8Rather, be openhanded and freely lend them whatever they need.
9Be careful not to harbor this wicked thought: "The seventh year, the year for
canceling debts, is near," so that you do not show ill will toward the needy
among your fellow Israelites and give them nothing. They may then appeal to
the LORD against you, and you will be found guilty of sin. 10Give generously to
them and do so without a grudging heart; then because of this the LORD your
God will bless you in all your work and in everything you put your hand to.
11There will always be poor people in the land. Therefore I command you to
be openhanded toward your fellow Israelites who are poor and needy in your
land.

Freeing Servants

12If any of your people—Hebrew men or women—sell themselves to you and
serve you six years, in the seventh year you must let them go free. 13And when
you release them, do not send them away empty-handed. 14Supply them liberal-
ly from your flock, your threshing floor and your winepress. Give to them as the
LORD your God has blessed you. 15Remember that you were slaves in Egypt and
the LORD your God redeemed you. That is why I give you this command today.
16But if your servant says to you, "I do not want to leave you," because he
loves you and your family and is well off with you, 17then take an awl and push
it through his earlobe into the door, and he will become your servant for life. Do
the same for your female servant.
18Do not consider it a hardship to set your servant free, because their service
to you these six years has been worth twice as much as that of a hired hand. And
the LORD your God will bless you in everything you do.

The Firstborn Animals

19Set apart for the LORD your God every firstborn male of your herds and
flocks. Do not put the firstborn of your cows to work, and do not shear the firstborn of your sheep. 20Each year you and your family are to eat them in the presence of the LORD your God at the place he will choose. 21If an animal has a defect,
is lame or blind, or has any serious flaw, you must not sacrifice it to the LORD
your God. 22You are to eat it in your own towns. Both the ceremonially unclean
and the clean may eat it, as if it were gazelle or deer. 23But you must not eat the
blood; pour it out on the ground like water.

The Passover

16 Observe the month of Aviv and celebrate the Passover of the LORD your
God, because in the month of Aviv he brought you out of Egypt by night.
2Sacrifice as the Passover to the LORD your God an animal from your flock or
herd at the place the LORD will choose as a dwelling for his Name. 3Do not eat it
with bread made with yeast, but for seven days eat unleavened bread, the bread
of affliction, because you left Egypt in haste—so that all the days of your life you
may remember the time of your departure from Egypt. 4Let no yeast be found in
your possession in all your land for seven days. Do not let any of the meat you
sacrifice on the evening of the first day remain until morning.
5You must not sacrifice the Passover in any town the LORD your God gives you
6except in the place he will choose as a dwelling for his Name. There you must
sacrifice the Passover in the evening, when the sun goes down, on the anniver-
sary[a] of your departure from Egypt. 7Roast it and eat it at the place the LORD
your God will choose. Then in the morning return to your tents. 8For six days eat
unleavened bread and on the seventh day hold an assembly to the LORD your
God and do no work.

[a] 6 Or *down, at the time of day*

JESUS, OUR JUBILEE

To be released from an overwhelming debt is a tremendous experience. In this chapter, the Lord wanted his people to see this concept within the larger framework of his mercy to them. The primary theme in this chapter is "Jubilee," which started on the Day of Atonement to symbolize that Israel's sin had been paid for (Lev 25). This celebratory concept was intended to remind the Israelites of God's act to rescue them from Egyptian bondage (v. 15) with applications for contemporary considerations such as releasing people from their debts (vv. 1 – 6) and being generous to the poor (vv. 7 – 11). Ultimately, the Israelites were expected to cancel various bondages — indentured servants, debts or liens on land — based on God's gracious mercy toward them as a people.

This practice prefigured the ultimate jubilee offered by God through Christ's atonement for our debt to sin (Ro 6:17 – 18). In the same way that the Israelites were enslaved to the Egyptians and were unable to free themselves, all people are hopelessly bound to sin apart from Christ's act on their behalf to offer them freedom (Ro 5:6 – 8). His death and resurrection, as payment for the debt of sin, is the only means that God the Father has provided for people to be reconciled to God (Jn 14:6). He gives people the credit needed to be free from sin and death. He became the benefactor, willing to make a payment and release them from a line of credit that proved to be beyond their capability to pay for (Dt 15:2). Whereas all people were dead through Adam, Christ has brought life to all who believe the gospel and are redeemed by the Lord (Ro 5:12 – 21).

Theologians refer to this transaction as the "great exchange," meaning what was due to mankind — because of our sin — was transferred to Jesus, and what was due to him — because of his perfection — was transferred to believers. He took the wrath of God on our behalf and transferred to us the blessings of the Father which we had absolutely no right to claim. Indeed, Christians have a reason to shout to the nations that we have "jubilee" in Jesus!

The Festival of Weeks

9Count off seven weeks from the time you begin to put the sickle to the standing grain. 10Then celebrate the Festival of Weeks to the LORD your God by giving
a freewill offering in proportion to the blessings the LORD your God has given
you. 11And rejoice before the LORD your God at the place he will choose as a
dwelling for his Name—you, your sons and daughters, your male and female
servants, the Levites in your towns, and the foreigners, the fatherless and the
widows living among you. 12Remember that you were slaves in Egypt, and follow
carefully these decrees.

The Festival of Tabernacles

13Celebrate the Festival of Tabernacles for seven days after you have gathered
the produce of your threshing floor and your winepress. 14Be joyful at your festival—you, your sons and daughters, your male and female servants, and the Levites, the foreigners, the fatherless and the widows who live in your towns. 15For
seven days celebrate the festival to the LORD your God at the place the LORD will
choose. For the LORD your God will bless you in all your harvest and in all the
work of your hands, and your joy will be complete.

16Three times a year all your men must appear before the LORD your God
at the place he will choose: at the Festival of Unleavened Bread, the Festival of
Weeks and the Festival of Tabernacles. No one should appear before the LORD
empty-handed: 17Each of you must bring a gift in proportion to the way the LORD
your God has blessed you.

Judges

18Appoint judges and officials for each of your tribes in every town the LORD
your God is giving you, and they shall judge the people fairly. 19Do not pervert
justice or show partiality. Do not accept a bribe, for a bribe blinds the eyes of the
wise and twists the words of the innocent. 20Follow justice and justice alone, so
that you may live and possess the land the LORD your God is giving you.

Worshiping Other Gods

21Do not set up any wooden Asherah pole beside the altar you build to the
LORD your God, 22and do not erect a sacred stone, for these the LORD your God
hates.

17 Do not sacrifice to the LORD your God an ox or a sheep that has any defect
or flaw in it, for that would be detestable to him.

2If a man or woman living among you in one of the towns the LORD gives you
is found doing evil in the eyes of the LORD your God in violation of his covenant,
3and contrary to my command has worshiped other gods, bowing down to them
or to the sun or the moon or the stars in the sky, 4and this has been brought to
your attention, then you must investigate it thoroughly. If it is true and it has
been proved that this detestable thing has been done in Israel, 5take the man
or woman who has done this evil deed to your city gate and stone that person to
death. 6On the testimony of two or three witnesses a person is to be put to death,
but no one is to be put to death on the testimony of only one witness. 7The hands
of the witnesses must be the first in putting that person to death, and then the
hands of all the people. You must purge the evil from among you.

Law Courts

8If cases come before your courts that are too difficult for you to judge—
whether bloodshed, lawsuits or assaults—take them to the place the LORD your
God will choose. 9Go to the Levitical priests and to the judge who is in office
at that time. Inquire of them and they will give you the verdict. 10You must act
according to the decisions they give you at the place the LORD will choose. Be
careful to do everything they instruct you to do. 11Act according to whatever
they teach you and the decisions they give you. Do not turn aside from what they

DEUTERONOMY 16:21—17:7

JESUS, THE CENTER OF SCRIPTURE AND TRUE RELIGION

There are so many options, so many ways that people try to worship God. From Eastern meditation and yoga to other world religions, mankind seeks to communicate with a higher being and satisfy the requirements of various religious systems. Yet we must ask the question, what does all of this activity actually accomplish? According to this passage, it does not accomplish anything more than stir up God's anger when his people carry out religious practices that are not aligned with Scripture. Jesus taught us that not all religious activity is equal or even valid and that God expects his creatures to worship him in specific ways (Jn 4:22–24). God's people, however, often drift to religious practices that are not satisfying to God, reflecting pagan values or the imaginations of religious leaders rather than Scripture. Valid religion is found in Jesus alone (Jn 14:6–7). He is the capstone of God's revelation in the Bible and through him we worship God according to his standard. All of Scripture points to Jesus as the perfect revelation of God, his ideals and his desires for us as his created beings (Heb 1:1–3).

tell you, to the right or to the left. 12Anyone who shows contempt for the judge
or for the priest who stands ministering there to the LORD your God is to be put
to death. You must purge the evil from Israel. 13All the people will hear and be
afraid, and will not be contemptuous again.

The King

14When you enter the land the LORD your God is giving you and have taken
possession of it and settled in it, and you say, "Let us set a king over us like all
the nations around us," 15be sure to appoint over you a king the LORD your God
chooses. He must be from among your fellow Israelites. Do not place a foreigner over you, one who is not an Israelite. 16The king, moreover, must not acquire
great numbers of horses for himself or make the people return to Egypt to get
more of them, for the LORD has told you, "You are not to go back that way again."
17He must not take many wives, or his heart will be led astray. He must not accumulate large amounts of silver and gold.

18When he takes the throne of his kingdom, he is to write for himself on a
scroll a copy of this law, taken from that of the Levitical priests. 19It is to be with
him, and he is to read it all the days of his life so that he may learn to revere the
LORD his God and follow carefully all the words of this law and these decrees
20and not consider himself better than his fellow Israelites and turn from the
law to the right or to the left. Then he and his descendants will reign a long time
over his kingdom in Israel.

DEUTERONOMY 17:14–20

JESUS, THE PERFECT KING

Here are instructions from the Lord to Israel concerning their desire to have a king reign over them. God laid out in detail (through Moses) the type of a person who should be their king, setting a standard for the leader of the Israelites. Throughout the remainder of the Old Testament, however, the kings of Israel proved to be lacking in major ways — although Moses clearly stated the requirements. Saul turned out to be an evil man, seeking ungodly pursuits rather than the way of the Lord. David committed murder and adultery, operating as a scandalous and selfish leader. Although he was considered extremely wise, Solomon had numerous wives and concubines, thus violating God's instructions for a king (v. 17). As great as these men were, they were fallible human beings and left much to be desired. Ultimately, Jesus proved to be the king that Israel always wanted (Isa 9:6 – 7). Jesus fulfilled the ideals expressed in these verses of Deuteronomy 17, without blemish, moral failure or selfish ambition. He is a stark contrast to the imperfect kings of Israel in the Old Testament.

Offerings for Priests and Levites

18 The Levitical priests — indeed, the whole tribe of Levi — are to have no allotment or inheritance with Israel. They shall live on the food offerings
presented to the LORD, for that is their inheritance. 2They shall have no inheritance among their fellow Israelites; the LORD is their inheritance, as he promised
them.

3This is the share due the priests from the people who sacrifice a bull or a sheep:
the shoulder, the internal organs and the meat from the head. 4You are to give
them the firstfruits of your grain, new wine and olive oil, and the first wool from
the shearing of your sheep, 5for the LORD your God has chosen them and their descendants out of all your tribes to stand and minister in the LORD's name always.

6If a Levite moves from one of your towns anywhere in Israel where he is living, and comes in all earnestness to the place the LORD will choose, 7he may
minister in the name of the LORD his God like all his fellow Levites who serve
there in the presence of the LORD. 8He is to share equally in their benefits, even
though he has received money from the sale of family possessions.

Occult Practices

9When you enter the land the LORD your God is giving you, do not learn to
imitate the detestable ways of the nations there. 10Let no one be found among
you who sacrifices their son or daughter in the fire, who practices divination
or sorcery, interprets omens, engages in witchcraft, 11or casts spells, or who is a
medium or spiritist or who consults the dead. 12Anyone who does these things
is detestable to the LORD; because of these same detestable practices the LORD
your God will drive out those nations before you. 13You must be blameless before
the LORD your God.

The Prophet

14The nations you will dispossess listen to those who practice sorcery or divination. But as for you, the LORD your God has not permitted you to do so. 15The
LORD your God will raise up for you a prophet like me from among you, from your
fellow Israelites. You must listen to him. 16For this is what you asked of the LORD
your God at Horeb on the day of the assembly when you said, "Let us not hear
the voice of the LORD our God nor see this great fire anymore, or we will die."

17The LORD said to me: "What they say is good. 18I will raise up for them a prophet like you from among their fellow Israelites, and I will put my words in his mouth. He will tell them everything I command him. 19I myself will call to account anyone who does not listen to my words that the prophet speaks in my name. 20But a prophet who presumes to speak in my name anything I have not commanded, or a prophet who speaks in the name of other gods, is to be put to death."

21You may say to yourselves, "How can we know when a message has not been spoken by the LORD?" 22If what a prophet proclaims in the name of the LORD does not take place or come true, that is a message the LORD has not spoken. That prophet has spoken presumptuously, so do not be alarmed.

Cities of Refuge

19 When the LORD your God has destroyed the nations whose land he is giving you, and when you have driven them out and settled in their towns and houses, 2then set aside for yourselves three cities in the land the LORD your God is giving you to possess. 3Determine the distances involved and divide into three parts the land the LORD your God is giving you as an inheritance, so that a person who kills someone may flee for refuge to one of these cities.

4This is the rule concerning anyone who kills a person and flees there for safety — anyone who kills a neighbor unintentionally, without malice aforethought. 5For instance, a man may go into the forest with his neighbor to cut wood, and as he swings his ax to fell a tree, the head may fly off and hit his neighbor and kill him. That man may flee to one of these cities and save his life. 6Otherwise, the avenger of blood might pursue him in a rage, overtake him if the distance is too great, and kill him even though he is not deserving of death, since he did it to his neighbor without malice aforethought. 7This is why I command you to set aside for yourselves three cities.

8If the LORD your God enlarges your territory, as he promised on oath to your ancestors, and gives you the whole land he promised them, 9because you carefully follow all these laws I command you today — to love the LORD your God and to walk always in obedience to him — then you are to set aside three more cities. 10Do this so that innocent blood will not be shed in your land, which the LORD your God is giving you as your inheritance, and so that you will not be guilty of bloodshed.

11But if out of hate someone lies in wait, assaults and kills a neighbor, and then flees to one of these cities, 12the killer shall be sent for by the town elders, be brought back from the city, and be handed over to the avenger of blood to die. 13Show no pity. You must purge from Israel the guilt of shedding innocent blood, so that it may go well with you.

14Do not move your neighbor's boundary stone set up by your predecessors in the inheritance you receive in the land the LORD your God is giving you to possess.

Witnesses

15One witness is not enough to convict anyone accused of any crime or offense they may have committed. A matter must be established by the testimony of two or three witnesses.

16If a malicious witness takes the stand to accuse someone of a crime, 17the two people involved in the dispute must stand in the presence of the LORD before the priests and the judges who are in office at the time. 18The judges must make a thorough investigation, and if the witness proves to be a liar, giving false testimony against a fellow Israelite, 19then do to the false witness as that witness intended to do to the other party. You must purge the evil from among you. 20The rest of the people will hear of this and be afraid, and never again will such an evil thing be done among you. 21Show no pity: life for life, eye for eye, tooth for tooth, hand for hand, foot for foot.

CHRIST, THE PROMISED PROPHET

Throughout the first five books of the Bible (the Pentateuch), Moses served the people of Israel in three primary offices or ways: prophet (Dt 34:10 – 12), priest (Ex 32:31 – 35) and as a type of king or ruler (Ex 18:24 – 26). The people of God relied on Moses to lead them as a forming nation and in religious practices according to God's Word, as well as petitioning the Lord on their behalf. Moses foretold of another prophet that God would raise up to serve Israel in the same vein. Deuteronomy 18:15 states, "The LORD your God will raise up for you a prophet like me from among you, from your fellow Israelites. You must listen to him." This verse established a culture of anticipation that went unfulfilled for hundreds of years. The people of Israel longed for the next great leader, one who would lead them as a king, priest and prophet. Moses foreshadowed the one for whom Israel waited. He was a type of Christ, looking forward to the Messiah who was yet to come.

Jesus proved to be the long-anticipated prophet, following in the offices of Moses and fulfilling the anticipation of Israel recorded in the Old Testament (Mt 4:12 – 17; Lk 4:16 – 21). Although many Israelites looked for a military leader, Jesus came as a humble servant, even willing to face the most humiliating form of execution within the Roman Empire (Php 2:5 – 8). He is a king — whose kingdom is not of this world — who came to serve his people by atoning for their sin on a cross to rescue them from the judgment of God. He is a prophet who proclaimed the commands of God and showed his followers the right path to please the Lord (Jn 14:15,23). Finally, he is a priest, going before the Father on behalf of the people of God, an office he currently fulfills at the right hand of the Father without ceasing (Heb 7:23 – 25).

Ultimately, all of the Old Testament authors — from Moses to David and the other prophets — looked forward to the day when the Messiah would come and bring finality to their anticipation, a day when they would see their ultimate Prophet, Priest and King.

Going to War

20 When you go to war against your enemies and see horses and chariots and an army greater than yours, do not be afraid of them, because the LORD your God, who brought you up out of Egypt, will be with you. 2When you are about to go into battle, the priest shall come forward and address the army. 3He shall say: "Hear, Israel: Today you are going into battle against your enemies. Do not be fainthearted or afraid; do not panic or be terrified by them. 4For the LORD your God is the one who goes with you to fight for you against your enemies to give you victory."

5The officers shall say to the army: "Has anyone built a new house and not yet begun to live in it? Let him go home, or he may die in battle and someone else may begin to live in it. 6Has anyone planted a vineyard and not begun to enjoy it? Let him go home, or he may die in battle and someone else enjoy it. 7Has anyone become pledged to a woman and not married her? Let him go home, or he may die in battle and someone else marry her." 8Then the officers shall add, "Is anyone afraid or fainthearted? Let him go home so that his fellow soldiers will not become disheartened too." 9When the officers have finished speaking to the army, they shall appoint commanders over it.

10When you march up to attack a city, make its people an offer of peace. 11If they accept and open their gates, all the people in it shall be subject to forced labor and shall work for you. 12If they refuse to make peace and they engage you in battle, lay siege to that city. 13When the LORD your God delivers it into your hand, put to the sword all the men in it. 14As for the women, the children, the livestock and everything else in the city, you may take these as plunder for yourselves. And you may use the plunder the LORD your God gives you from your enemies. 15This is how you are to treat all the cities that are at a distance from you and do not belong to the nations nearby.

16However, in the cities of the nations the LORD your God is giving you as an inheritance, do not leave alive anything that breathes. 17Completely destroy[a] them—the Hittites, Amorites, Canaanites, Perizzites, Hivites and Jebusites—as the LORD your God has commanded you. 18Otherwise, they will teach you to follow all the detestable things they do in worshiping their gods, and you will sin against the LORD your God.

19When you lay siege to a city for a long time, fighting against it to capture it, do not destroy its trees by putting an ax to them, because you can eat their fruit. Do not cut them down. Are the trees people, that you should besiege them?[b] 20However, you may cut down trees that you know are not fruit trees and use them to build siege works until the city at war with you falls.

Atonement for an Unsolved Murder

21 If someone is found slain, lying in a field in the land the LORD your God is giving you to possess, and it is not known who the killer was, 2your elders and judges shall go out and measure the distance from the body to the neighboring towns. 3Then the elders of the town nearest the body shall take a heifer that has never been worked and has never worn a yoke 4and lead it down to a valley that has not been plowed or planted and where there is a flowing stream. There in the valley they are to break the heifer's neck. 5The Levitical priests shall step forward, for the LORD your God has chosen them to minister and to pronounce blessings in the name of the LORD and to decide all cases of dispute and assault. 6Then all the elders of the town nearest the body shall wash their hands over the heifer whose neck was broken in the valley, 7and they shall declare: "Our hands did not shed this blood, nor did our eyes see it done. 8Accept this atonement for your people Israel, whom you have redeemed, LORD, and do not hold your people

---

[a] *17* The Hebrew term refers to the irrevocable giving over of things or persons to the LORD, often by totally destroying them. [b] *19* Or *down to use in the siege, for the fruit trees are for the benefit of people.*

guilty of the blood of an innocent person." Then the bloodshed will be atoned
for, [9]and you will have purged from yourselves the guilt of shedding innocent
blood, since you have done what is right in the eyes of the LORD.

Marrying a Captive Woman

[10]When you go to war against your enemies and the LORD your God delivers
them into your hands and you take captives, [11]if you notice among the captives a
beautiful woman and are attracted to her, you may take her as your wife. [12]Bring
her into your home and have her shave her head, trim her nails [13]and put aside
the clothes she was wearing when captured. After she has lived in your house
and mourned her father and mother for a full month, then you may go to her and
be her husband and she shall be your wife. [14]If you are not pleased with her, let
her go wherever she wishes. You must not sell her or treat her as a slave, since
you have dishonored her.

The Right of the Firstborn

[15]If a man has two wives, and he loves one but not the other, and both bear
him sons but the firstborn is the son of the wife he does not love, [16]when he wills
his property to his sons, he must not give the rights of the firstborn to the son of
the wife he loves in preference to his actual firstborn, the son of the wife he does
not love. [17]He must acknowledge the son of his unloved wife as the firstborn by
giving him a double share of all he has. That son is the first sign of his father's
strength. The right of the firstborn belongs to him.

A Rebellious Son

[18]If someone has a stubborn and rebellious son who does not obey his father
and mother and will not listen to them when they discipline him, [19]his father and
mother shall take hold of him and bring him to the elders at the gate of his town.
[20]They shall say to the elders, "This son of ours is stubborn and rebellious. He
will not obey us. He is a glutton and a drunkard." [21]Then all the men of his town
are to stone him to death. You must purge the evil from among you. All Israel will
hear of it and be afraid.

Various Laws

[22]If someone guilty of a capital offense is put to death and their body is exposed on a pole, [23]you must not leave the body hanging on the pole overnight.
Be sure to bury it that same day, because anyone who is hung on a pole is under
God's curse. You must not desecrate the land the LORD your God is giving you
as an inheritance.

22 If you see your fellow Israelite's ox or sheep straying, do not ignore it but
be sure to take it back to its owner. [2]If they do not live near you or if you do
not know who owns it, take it home with you and keep it until they come looking
for it. Then give it back. [3]Do the same if you find their donkey or cloak or anything else they have lost. Do not ignore it.

[4]If you see your fellow Israelite's donkey or ox fallen on the road, do not ignore
it. Help the owner get it to its feet.

[5]A woman must not wear men's clothing, nor a man wear women's clothing,
for the LORD your God detests anyone who does this.

[6]If you come across a bird's nest beside the road, either in a tree or on the
ground, and the mother is sitting on the young or on the eggs, do not take the
mother with the young. [7]You may take the young, but be sure to let the mother
go, so that it may go well with you and you may have a long life.

[8]When you build a new house, make a parapet around your roof so that you
may not bring the guilt of bloodshed on your house if someone falls from the roof.

[9]Do not plant two kinds of seed in your vineyard; if you do, not only the crops
you plant but also the fruit of the vineyard will be defiled.[a]

---

[a] 9 Or *be forfeited to the sanctuary*

A CURSED MAN

The promised land was of such value that God made provisions to ensure that its splendor was protected. God knew that his people would rebel from his law and kill one another, as the story of Cain and Abel demonstrates (Ge 4:8). This sin, and others like it, tarnished the people of God and the land itself. God instructed the people to punish the evildoer with death, as a sign of God's divine judgment against sins of this magnitude. At times those who were put to death by stoning, the ordinary form of capital punishment prescribed by the law, would be impaled on a pole as a testimony to all bystanders of the implications of sin. God, however, instructed the nation to take down those bodies which were exposed in this fashion and bury them right away. They were cursed by God, and the bodies should not remain overnight.

Centuries later the Romans invented a far more notorious form of exposure. Rather than executing criminals first, they would nail them to a wooden cross. This punishment was reserved for the worst of the worst, particularly those who undermined the Roman government. The Romans wanted to teach onlookers a lesson, and crucifixion on a wooden cross was a sure sign that they had better not offend Rome. They killed in the most excruciating way and made sure everyone saw the agony.

The Romans intended Jesus' crucifixion to make this same point. Not only had he supposedly usurped the rule of Rome, but also he had claimed to be God — a claim the Jews thought was blasphemous since Jesus was a Jewish carpenter from Nazareth (Jn 10:30 – 33). His brutal torture and execution were designed to show that he was not a king and certainly not God.

God used Jesus' crucifixion to communicate a far greater message, one rooted in Deuteronomy 21. As he hung on the cross, Jesus was cursed by God. His curse was not based on his sin, however. He was the pure and spotless Son of God. He was cursed by God for the sin of his people. Jesus willingly became a cursed man, submitting himself to death on a cross in order to save men and women from having to bear the wrath of God themselves (Gal 3:10 – 14). He was cursed so that his people could be blessed.

[10]Do not plow with an ox and a donkey yoked together.
[11]Do not wear clothes of wool and linen woven together.
[12]Make tassels on the four corners of the cloak you wear.

Marriage Violations

[13]If a man takes a wife and, after sleeping with her, dislikes her [14]and slanders her and gives her a bad name, saying, "I married this woman, but when I
approached her, I did not find proof of her virginity," [15]then the young woman's
father and mother shall bring to the town elders at the gate proof that she was a
virgin. [16]Her father will say to the elders, "I gave my daughter in marriage to this
man, but he dislikes her. [17]Now he has slandered her and said, 'I did not find your
daughter to be a virgin.' But here is the proof of my daughter's virginity." Then
her parents shall display the cloth before the elders of the town, [18]and the elders
shall take the man and punish him. [19]They shall fine him a hundred shekels[a] of
silver and give them to the young woman's father, because this man has given an
Israelite virgin a bad name. She shall continue to be his wife; he must not divorce
her as long as he lives.
[20]If, however, the charge is true and no proof of the young woman's virginity
can be found, [21]she shall be brought to the door of her father's house and there
the men of her town shall stone her to death. She has done an outrageous thing
in Israel by being promiscuous while still in her father's house. You must purge
the evil from among you.
[22]If a man is found sleeping with another man's wife, both the man who slept
with her and the woman must die. You must purge the evil from Israel.
[23]If a man happens to meet in a town a virgin pledged to be married and
he sleeps with her, [24]you shall take both of them to the gate of that town and
stone them to death — the young woman because she was in a town and did not
scream for help, and the man because he violated another man's wife. You must
purge the evil from among you.
[25]But if out in the country a man happens to meet a young woman pledged to
be married and rapes her, only the man who has done this shall die. [26]Do nothing to the woman; she has committed no sin deserving death. This case is like
that of someone who attacks and murders a neighbor, [27]for the man found the
young woman out in the country, and though the betrothed woman screamed,
there was no one to rescue her.
[28]If a man happens to meet a virgin who is not pledged to be married and
rapes her and they are discovered, [29]he shall pay her father fifty shekels[b] of silver.
He must marry the young woman, for he has violated her. He can never divorce
her as long as he lives.
[30]A man is not to marry his father's wife; he must not dishonor his father's bed.[c]

Exclusion From the Assembly

23[d] No one who has been emasculated by crushing or cutting may enter the
assembly of the LORD.
[2]No one born of a forbidden marriage[e] nor any of their descendants may enter
the assembly of the LORD, not even in the tenth generation.
[3]No Ammonite or Moabite or any of their descendants may enter the assembly of the LORD, not even in the tenth generation. [4]For they did not come to meet
you with bread and water on your way when you came out of Egypt, and they
hired Balaam son of Beor from Pethor in Aram Naharaim[f] to pronounce a curse
on you. [5]However, the LORD your God would not listen to Balaam but turned the
curse into a blessing for you, because the LORD your God loves you. [6]Do not seek
a treaty of friendship with them as long as you live.

---

[a] *19* That is, about 2 1/2 pounds or about 1.2 kilograms [b] *29* That is, about 1 1/4 pounds or about 575 grams [c] *30* In Hebrew texts this verse (22:30) is numbered 23:1. [d] In Hebrew texts 23:1-25 is numbered 23:2-26. [e] *2* Or *one of illegitimate birth* [f] *4* That is, Northwest Mesopotamia

7Do not despise an Edomite, for the Edomites are related to you. Do not despise an Egyptian, because you resided as foreigners in their country. 8The third generation of children born to them may enter the assembly of the LORD.

Uncleanness in the Camp

9When you are encamped against your enemies, keep away from everything impure. 10If one of your men is unclean because of a nocturnal emission, he is to go outside the camp and stay there. 11But as evening approaches he is to wash himself, and at sunset he may return to the camp.

12Designate a place outside the camp where you can go to relieve yourself. 13As part of your equipment have something to dig with, and when you relieve yourself, dig a hole and cover up your excrement. 14For the LORD your God moves about in your camp to protect you and to deliver your enemies to you. Your camp must be holy, so that he will not see among you anything indecent and turn away from you.

Miscellaneous Laws

15If a slave has taken refuge with you, do not hand them over to their master. 16Let them live among you wherever they like and in whatever town they choose. Do not oppress them.

17No Israelite man or woman is to become a shrine prostitute. 18You must not bring the earnings of a female prostitute or of a male prostitute[a] into the house of the LORD your God to pay any vow, because the LORD your God detests them both.

19Do not charge a fellow Israelite interest, whether on money or food or anything else that may earn interest. 20You may charge a foreigner interest, but not a fellow Israelite, so that the LORD your God may bless you in everything you put your hand to in the land you are entering to possess.

21If you make a vow to the LORD your God, do not be slow to pay it, for the LORD your God will certainly demand it of you and you will be guilty of sin. 22But if you refrain from making a vow, you will not be guilty. 23Whatever your lips utter you must be sure to do, because you made your vow freely to the LORD your God with your own mouth.

24If you enter your neighbor's vineyard, you may eat all the grapes you want, but do not put any in your basket. 25If you enter your neighbor's grainfield, you may pick kernels with your hands, but you must not put a sickle to their standing grain.

24 If a man marries a woman who becomes displeasing to him because he finds something indecent about her, and he writes her a certificate of divorce, gives it to her and sends her from his house, 2and if after she leaves his house she becomes the wife of another man, 3and her second husband dislikes her and writes her a certificate of divorce, gives it to her and sends her from his house, or if he dies, 4then her first husband, who divorced her, is not allowed to marry her again after she has been defiled. That would be detestable in the eyes of the LORD. Do not bring sin upon the land the LORD your God is giving you as an inheritance.

5If a man has recently married, he must not be sent to war or have any other duty laid on him. For one year he is to be free to stay at home and bring happiness to the wife he has married.

6Do not take a pair of millstones — not even the upper one — as security for a debt, because that would be taking a person's livelihood as security.

7If someone is caught kidnapping a fellow Israelite and treating or selling them as a slave, the kidnapper must die. You must purge the evil from among you.

8In cases of defiling skin diseases,[b] be very careful to do exactly as the Levitical priests instruct you. You must follow carefully what I have commanded

[a] *18* Hebrew *of a dog* [b] *8* The Hebrew word for *defiling skin diseases*, traditionally translated "leprosy," was used for various diseases affecting the skin.

DEUTERONOMY 24:1 – 4

GOD'S COVENANT AND DIVORCE

Divorce among the people of God was never advocated or promoted, though it was granted on occasion as a concession to human sin. Jesus said that it was because of the hardness of the human heart that Moses permitted divorce (Mk 10:2 – 5). Jesus then pointed to God's created design in the beginning, while warning people not to tear apart that which God had joined together (Mk 10:6 – 9). The covenantal nature of marriage is meant to model the way in which God loves, pursues and sacrifices on behalf of adulterous people (Eph 5:22 – 33). Therefore any act, especially divorce, which violates the marriage covenant fails to model the faithfulness of God demonstrated throughout redemptive history. While scholars may debate whether or not Jesus grants exceptions for divorce, one thing is clear — divorce is a result of human sin and fails to model the covenant faithfulness of God to his people.

them. [9]Remember what the LORD your God did to Miriam along the way after you came out of Egypt.

[10]When you make a loan of any kind to your neighbor, do not go into their house to get what is offered to you as a pledge. [11]Stay outside and let the neighbor to whom you are making the loan bring the pledge out to you. [12]If the neighbor is poor, do not go to sleep with their pledge in your possession. [13]Return their cloak by sunset so that your neighbor may sleep in it. Then they will thank you, and it will be regarded as a righteous act in the sight of the LORD your God.

[14]Do not take advantage of a hired worker who is poor and needy, whether that worker is a fellow Israelite or a foreigner residing in one of your towns. [15]Pay them their wages each day before sunset, because they are poor and are counting on it. Otherwise they may cry to the LORD against you, and you will be guilty of sin.

[16]Parents are not to be put to death for their children, nor children put to death for their parents; each will die for their own sin.

[17]Do not deprive the foreigner or the fatherless of justice, or take the cloak of the widow as a pledge. [18]Remember that you were slaves in Egypt and the LORD your God redeemed you from there. That is why I command you to do this.

[19]When you are harvesting in your field and you overlook a sheaf, do not go back to get it. Leave it for the foreigner, the fatherless and the widow, so that the LORD your God may bless you in all the work of your hands. [20]When you beat the olives from your trees, do not go over the branches a second time. Leave what remains for the foreigner, the fatherless and the widow. [21]When you harvest the grapes in your vineyard, do not go over the vines again. Leave what remains for the foreigner, the fatherless and the widow. [22]Remember that you were slaves in Egypt. That is why I command you to do this.

25 When people have a dispute, they are to take it to court and the judges will decide the case, acquitting the innocent and condemning the guilty. [2]If the guilty person deserves to be beaten, the judge shall make them lie down and have them flogged in his presence with the number of lashes the crime deserves, [3]but the judge must not impose more than forty lashes. If the guilty party is flogged more than that, your fellow Israelite will be degraded in your eyes.

[4]Do not muzzle an ox while it is treading out the grain.

[5]If brothers are living together and one of them dies without a son, his widow must not marry outside the family. Her husband's brother shall take her and marry her and fulfill the duty of a brother-in-law to her. [6]The first son she bears shall carry on the name of the dead brother so that his name will not be blotted out from Israel.

[7]However, if a man does not want to marry his brother's wife, she shall go to the elders at the town gate and say, "My husband's brother refuses to carry on his brother's name in Israel. He will not fulfill the duty of a brother-in-law to me." [8]Then the elders of his town shall summon him and talk to him. If he persists in saying, "I do not want to marry her," [9]his brother's widow shall go up to him in the presence of the elders, take off one of his sandals, spit in his face and say, "This is what is done to the man who will not build up his brother's family line." [10]That man's line shall be known in Israel as The Family of the Unsandaled.

[11]If two men are fighting and the wife of one of them comes to rescue her husband from his assailant, and she reaches out and seizes him by his private parts, [12]you shall cut off her hand. Show her no pity.

[13]Do not have two differing weights in your bag — one heavy, one light. [14]Do not have two differing measures in your house — one large, one small. [15]You must have accurate and honest weights and measures, so that you may live long in the land the LORD your God is giving you. [16]For the LORD your God detests anyone who does these things, anyone who deals dishonestly.

[17]Remember what the Amalekites did to you along the way when you came out of Egypt. [18]When you were weary and worn out, they met you on your journey and attacked all who were lagging behind; they had no fear of God. [19]When the

LORD your God gives you rest from all the enemies around you in the land he is
giving you to possess as an inheritance, you shall blot out the name of Amalek
from under heaven. Do not forget!

Firstfruits and Tithes

26 When you have entered the land the LORD your God is giving you as an
inheritance and have taken possession of it and settled in it, [2]take some
of the firstfruits of all that you produce from the soil of the land the LORD your
God is giving you and put them in a basket. Then go to the place the LORD your
God will choose as a dwelling for his Name [3]and say to the priest in office at the
time, "I declare today to the LORD your God that I have come to the land the
LORD swore to our ancestors to give us." [4]The priest shall take the basket from
your hands and set it down in front of the altar of the LORD your God. [5]Then you
shall declare before the LORD your God: "My father was a wandering Aramean,
and he went down into Egypt with a few people and lived there and became
a great nation, powerful and numerous. [6]But the Egyptians mistreated us and
made us suffer, subjecting us to harsh labor. [7]Then we cried out to the LORD,
the God of our ancestors, and the LORD heard our voice and saw our misery, toil
and oppression. [8]So the LORD brought us out of Egypt with a mighty hand and
an outstretched arm, with great terror and with signs and wonders. [9]He brought
us to this place and gave us this land, a land flowing with milk and honey; [10]and
now I bring the firstfruits of the soil that you, LORD, have given me." Place the
basket before the LORD your God and bow down before him. [11]Then you and the
Levites and the foreigners residing among you shall rejoice in all the good things
the LORD your God has given to you and your household.

[12]When you have finished setting aside a tenth of all your produce in the third
year, the year of the tithe, you shall give it to the Levite, the foreigner, the fatherless and the widow, so that they may eat in your towns and be satisfied. [13]Then
say to the LORD your God: "I have removed from my house the sacred portion
and have given it to the Levite, the foreigner, the fatherless and the widow, according to all you commanded. I have not turned aside from your commands
nor have I forgotten any of them. [14]I have not eaten any of the sacred portion
while I was in mourning, nor have I removed any of it while I was unclean, nor
have I offered any of it to the dead. I have obeyed the LORD my God; I have done
everything you commanded me. [15]Look down from heaven, your holy dwelling
place, and bless your people Israel and the land you have given us as you promised on oath to our ancestors, a land flowing with milk and honey."

Follow the LORD's Commands

[16]The LORD your God commands you this day to follow these decrees and
laws; carefully observe them with all your heart and with all your soul. [17]You
have declared this day that the LORD is your God and that you will walk in obedience to him, that you will keep his decrees, commands and laws — that you
will listen to him. [18]And the LORD has declared this day that you are his people,
his treasured possession as he promised, and that you are to keep all his commands. [19]He has declared that he will set you in praise, fame and honor high
above all the nations he has made and that you will be a people holy to the LORD
your God, as he promised.

The Altar on Mount Ebal

27 Moses and the elders of Israel commanded the people: "Keep all these
commands that I give you today. [2]When you have crossed the Jordan into
the land the LORD your God is giving you, set up some large stones and coat them
with plaster. [3]Write on them all the words of this law when you have crossed over
to enter the land the LORD your God is giving you, a land flowing with milk and
honey, just as the LORD, the God of your ancestors, promised you. [4]And when you
have crossed the Jordan, set up these stones on Mount Ebal, as I command you

DEUTERONOMY 26:1 – 11

FIRSTFRUITS OFFERING

When God's people entered the promised land, they were instructed to give an offering of the firstfruits of their harvest to God. This first portion was placed in a basket, brought to the tabernacle and offered to God as an act of worship. The offering demonstrated that the people remembered that God had graciously given them a good land and that all things were a gift from his hand. Though the offering described here only occurred once, the Israelites were also instructed to offer their firstfruits annually (Lev 23:10 – 11).

Paul spoke of Jesus as a firstfruits offering. His victory over death served as a precursor to the resurrection of all those who are in Christ Jesus (1Co 15:20 – 23). Christians celebrate the firstfruits offering when they reflect upon and trust in the finished work of Jesus Christ. They also offer their lives as a living sacrifice to God — knowing that all good things they are given are a gift from God and a testimony to his faithfulness (Ro 12:1 – 2; Heb 13:15).

JESUS, HIS FOLLOWERS AND THE POOR

A trend in evangelical circles is the emphasis on being socially conscious, which includes caring for the weak and vulnerable. This trend, however, is nothing new.

The Old Testament leaves little room to doubt God's perspective on this issue: he cares about human suffering and calls his people to do the same. In these verses, Moses tied an Israelite's holiness before the Lord to a faithful tithe and providing for the foreigner, fatherless and widow (along with the Levite) according to the command of God (v. 13). Without doubt, the Hebrews could not claim to live a satisfactory life according to God's Word without caring for the vulnerable people around them. The consistent theme evident throughout Deuteronomy is this: righteousness is not the result of works performed, but rather works are an expected outcome of the faith of persons within the covenant community. God expected his people to care about the hurting and disadvantaged among them because renewed and circumcised hearts gave them a love for such people.

The New Testament, much like the Old Testament, is straightforward in teaching that God cares about human suffering and calls his people to do the same. The life and teachings of Jesus, the ministry of the early church in Acts (Ac 4:34 – 35) and the exhortations of Paul (Ro 12:13) all point to this fact: God wants his people to care for the weak and vulnerable around them.

Christ taught his followers to be compassionate and merciful to those who are weary and heavy laden. There is a clear connection between righteousness and good works in caring for the weak and vulnerable (Lk 10:29 – 37). Christ assumed that his followers would assist the needy in meeting their physical needs (Mt 6:2 – 3). In the vein of Jesus' teachings and actions, believers are to clothe and feed the homeless, care for the neglected, and love all people. Jesus made an obvious connection that should propel all Christians to action — that is, those who have true righteousness in Christ will care for the "least of these" among us (Mt 25:34 – 40).

today, and coat them with plaster. 5Build there an altar to the LORD your God,
an altar of stones. Do not use any iron tool on them. 6Build the altar of the LORD
your God with fieldstones and offer burnt offerings on it to the LORD your God.
7Sacrifice fellowship offerings there, eating them and rejoicing in the presence
of the LORD your God. 8And you shall write very clearly all the words of this law
on these stones you have set up."

Curses From Mount Ebal

9Then Moses and the Levitical priests said to all Israel, "Be silent, Israel, and
listen! You have now become the people of the LORD your God. 10Obey the LORD
your God and follow his commands and decrees that I give you today."
11On the same day Moses commanded the people:
12When you have crossed the Jordan, these tribes shall stand on Mount Gerizim to bless the people: Simeon, Levi, Judah, Issachar, Joseph and Benjamin.
13And these tribes shall stand on Mount Ebal to pronounce curses: Reuben, Gad,
Asher, Zebulun, Dan and Naphtali.
14The Levites shall recite to all the people of Israel in a loud voice:
15"Cursed is anyone who makes an idol—a thing detestable to the LORD,
the work of skilled hands—and sets it up in secret."
Then all the people shall say, "Amen!"
16"Cursed is anyone who dishonors their father or mother."
Then all the people shall say, "Amen!"
17"Cursed is anyone who moves their neighbor's boundary stone."
Then all the people shall say, "Amen!"
18"Cursed is anyone who leads the blind astray on the road."
Then all the people shall say, "Amen!"
19"Cursed is anyone who withholds justice from the foreigner, the fatherless or the widow."
Then all the people shall say, "Amen!"
20"Cursed is anyone who sleeps with his father's wife, for he dishonors
his father's bed."
Then all the people shall say, "Amen!"
21"Cursed is anyone who has sexual relations with any animal."
Then all the people shall say, "Amen!"
22"Cursed is anyone who sleeps with his sister, the daughter of his father
or the daughter of his mother."
Then all the people shall say, "Amen!"
23"Cursed is anyone who sleeps with his mother-in-law."
Then all the people shall say, "Amen!"
24"Cursed is anyone who kills their neighbor secretly."
Then all the people shall say, "Amen!"
25"Cursed is anyone who accepts a bribe to kill an innocent person."
Then all the people shall say, "Amen!"
26"Cursed is anyone who does not uphold the words of this law by carrying them out."
Then all the people shall say, "Amen!"

Blessings for Obedience

28 If you fully obey the LORD your God and carefully follow all his commands I give you today, the LORD your God will set you high above all the
nations on earth. 2All these blessings will come on you and accompany you if
you obey the LORD your God:
3You will be blessed in the city and blessed in the country.
4The fruit of your womb will be blessed, and the crops of your land and
the young of your livestock—the calves of your herds and the lambs of your
flocks.

DEUTERONOMY 28:1–19

PERFECTION ENSURES BLESSING, IMPERFECTION BRINGS CURSES

Who can be perfect? Who can keep the rules all the time without failing, even one little bit? No one! Yet the book of Deuteronomy clearly shows the connection between covenant blessings and the requirement to keep the law of God carefully. There is no room for negotiation. God established his covenant requirements—if Israel wanted to be a holy nation, set apart as the blessed people of the one true God, they had to do what he wanted. What he demanded of them was to "carefully follow all his commands" (v. 1). And Moses stated clearly the consequences of not keeping all his commands: curses come to those who do not keep all of God's commands perfectly (v. 15). What an overwhelming predicament! Keep the commands of God and be blessed. Fail to do so and you, your family, your land and your work will be cursed. It seems cruel because of the impossibility to meet God's mandatory flawlessness. The Israelites knew their deficiencies and need for intercession and sacrifices to atone for their imperfections.

The people of God are no different today. No one is able to perfectly keep God's requirements to be in a covenant relationship with him; therefore, all are in danger of receiving a curse from the Lord. But God, in a gracious act of mercy, sent Jesus to bear the curse, redeeming the elect from the consequences of unrighteousness (Gal 3:10–14).

5Your basket and your kneading trough will be blessed.
6You will be blessed when you come in and blessed when you go out.

7The LORD will grant that the enemies who rise up against you will be defeated before you. They will come at you from one direction but flee from you
in seven.
8The LORD will send a blessing on your barns and on everything you put your
hand to. The LORD your God will bless you in the land he is giving you.
9The LORD will establish you as his holy people, as he promised you on oath,
if you keep the commands of the LORD your God and walk in obedience to him.
10Then all the peoples on earth will see that you are called by the name of the
LORD, and they will fear you. 11The LORD will grant you abundant prosperity — in the fruit of your womb, the young of your livestock and the crops of your
ground — in the land he swore to your ancestors to give you.
12The LORD will open the heavens, the storehouse of his bounty, to send rain
on your land in season and to bless all the work of your hands. You will lend to
many nations but will borrow from none. 13The LORD will make you the head,
not the tail. If you pay attention to the commands of the LORD your God that I
give you this day and carefully follow them, you will always be at the top, never
at the bottom. 14Do not turn aside from any of the commands I give you today, to
the right or to the left, following other gods and serving them.

Curses for Disobedience

15However, if you do not obey the LORD your God and do not carefully follow
all his commands and decrees I am giving you today, all these curses will come
on you and overtake you:

16You will be cursed in the city and cursed in the country.
17Your basket and your kneading trough will be cursed.
18The fruit of your womb will be cursed, and the crops of your land, and
the calves of your herds and the lambs of your flocks.
19You will be cursed when you come in and cursed when you go out.

20The LORD will send on you curses, confusion and rebuke in everything you
put your hand to, until you are destroyed and come to sudden ruin because of
the evil you have done in forsaking him.[a] 21The LORD will plague you with diseases until he has destroyed you from the land you are entering to possess. 22The
LORD will strike you with wasting disease, with fever and inflammation, with
scorching heat and drought, with blight and mildew, which will plague you until you perish. 23The sky over your head will be bronze, the ground beneath you
iron. 24The LORD will turn the rain of your country into dust and powder; it will
come down from the skies until you are destroyed.
25The LORD will cause you to be defeated before your enemies. You will come
at them from one direction but flee from them in seven, and you will become a
thing of horror to all the kingdoms on earth. 26Your carcasses will be food for
all the birds and the wild animals, and there will be no one to frighten them
away. 27The LORD will afflict you with the boils of Egypt and with tumors, festering sores and the itch, from which you cannot be cured. 28The LORD will afflict
you with madness, blindness and confusion of mind. 29At midday you will grope
about like a blind person in the dark. You will be unsuccessful in everything you
do; day after day you will be oppressed and robbed, with no one to rescue you.
30You will be pledged to be married to a woman, but another will take her and
rape her. You will build a house, but you will not live in it. You will plant a vineyard, but you will not even begin to enjoy its fruit. 31Your ox will be slaughtered
before your eyes, but you will eat none of it. Your donkey will be forcibly taken
from you and will not be returned. Your sheep will be given to your enemies,
and no one will rescue them. 32Your sons and daughters will be given to another

[a] 20 Hebrew *me*

nation, and you will wear out your eyes watching for them day after day, powerless to lift a hand. 33A people that you do not know will eat what your land and
labor produce, and you will have nothing but cruel oppression all your days.
34The sights you see will drive you mad. 35The LORD will afflict your knees and
legs with painful boils that cannot be cured, spreading from the soles of your
feet to the top of your head.

36The LORD will drive you and the king you set over you to a nation unknown
to you or your ancestors. There you will worship other gods, gods of wood and
stone. 37You will become a thing of horror, a byword and an object of ridicule
among all the peoples where the LORD will drive you.

38You will sow much seed in the field but you will harvest little, because locusts will devour it. 39You will plant vineyards and cultivate them but you will
not drink the wine or gather the grapes, because worms will eat them. 40You will
have olive trees throughout your country but you will not use the oil, because
the olives will drop off. 41You will have sons and daughters but you will not keep
them, because they will go into captivity. 42Swarms of locusts will take over all
your trees and the crops of your land.

43The foreigners who reside among you will rise above you higher and higher,
but you will sink lower and lower. 44They will lend to you, but you will not lend to
them. They will be the head, but you will be the tail.

45All these curses will come on you. They will pursue you and overtake you
until you are destroyed, because you did not obey the LORD your God and observe the commands and decrees he gave you. 46They will be a sign and a wonder to you and your descendants forever. 47Because you did not serve the LORD
your God joyfully and gladly in the time of prosperity, 48therefore in hunger and
thirst, in nakedness and dire poverty, you will serve the enemies the LORD sends
against you. He will put an iron yoke on your neck until he has destroyed you.

49The LORD will bring a nation against you from far away, from the ends of
the earth, like an eagle swooping down, a nation whose language you will not
understand, 50a fierce-looking nation without respect for the old or pity for the
young. 51They will devour the young of your livestock and the crops of your land
until you are destroyed. They will leave you no grain, new wine or olive oil, nor
any calves of your herds or lambs of your flocks until you are ruined. 52They will
lay siege to all the cities throughout your land until the high fortified walls in
which you trust fall down. They will besiege all the cities throughout the land
the LORD your God is giving you.

53Because of the suffering your enemy will inflict on you during the siege, you
will eat the fruit of the womb, the flesh of the sons and daughters the LORD your
God has given you. 54Even the most gentle and sensitive man among you will
have no compassion on his own brother or the wife he loves or his surviving children, 55and he will not give to one of them any of the flesh of his children that he
is eating. It will be all he has left because of the suffering your enemy will inflict
on you during the siege of all your cities. 56The most gentle and sensitive woman among you — so sensitive and gentle that she would not venture to touch the
ground with the sole of her foot — will begrudge the husband she loves and her
own son or daughter 57the afterbirth from her womb and the children she bears.
For in her dire need she intends to eat them secretly because of the suffering
your enemy will inflict on you during the siege of your cities.

58If you do not carefully follow all the words of this law, which are written in
this book, and do not revere this glorious and awesome name — the LORD your
God — 59the LORD will send fearful plagues on you and your descendants, harsh
and prolonged disasters, and severe and lingering illnesses. 60He will bring on
you all the diseases of Egypt that you dreaded, and they will cling to you. 61The
LORD will also bring on you every kind of sickness and disaster not recorded in
this Book of the Law, until you are destroyed. 62You who were as numerous as
the stars in the sky will be left but few in number, because you did not obey the
LORD your God. 63Just as it pleased the LORD to make you prosper and increase in

number, so it will please him to ruin and destroy you. You will be uprooted from the land you are entering to possess.

[64]Then the LORD will scatter you among all nations, from one end of the earth to the other. There you will worship other gods — gods of wood and stone, which neither you nor your ancestors have known. [65]Among those nations you will find no repose, no resting place for the sole of your foot. There the LORD will give you an anxious mind, eyes weary with longing, and a despairing heart. [66]You will live in constant suspense, filled with dread both night and day, never sure of your life. [67]In the morning you will say, "If only it were evening!" and in the evening, "If only it were morning!" — because of the terror that will fill your hearts and the sights that your eyes will see. [68]The LORD will send you back in ships to Egypt on a journey I said you should never make again. There you will offer yourselves for sale to your enemies as male and female slaves, but no one will buy you.

Renewal of the Covenant

29[a] These are the terms of the covenant the LORD commanded Moses to make with the Israelites in Moab, in addition to the covenant he had made with them at Horeb.

[2]Moses summoned all the Israelites and said to them:

Your eyes have seen all that the LORD did in Egypt to Pharaoh, to all his officials and to all his land. [3]With your own eyes you saw those great trials, those signs and great wonders. [4]But to this day the LORD has not given you a mind that understands or eyes that see or ears that hear. [5]Yet the LORD says, "During the forty years that I led you through the wilderness, your clothes did not wear out, nor did the sandals on your feet. [6]You ate no bread and drank no wine or other fermented drink. I did this so that you might know that I am the LORD your God."

[7]When you reached this place, Sihon king of Heshbon and Og king of Bashan came out to fight against us, but we defeated them. [8]We took their land and gave it as an inheritance to the Reubenites, the Gadites and the half-tribe of Manasseh.

[9]Carefully follow the terms of this covenant, so that you may prosper in everything you do. [10]All of you are standing today in the presence of the LORD your God — your leaders and chief men, your elders and officials, and all the other men of Israel, [11]together with your children and your wives, and the foreigners living in your camps who chop your wood and carry your water. [12]You are standing here in order to enter into a covenant with the LORD your God, a covenant the LORD is making with you this day and sealing with an oath, [13]to confirm you this day as his people, that he may be your God as he promised you and as he swore to your fathers, Abraham, Isaac and Jacob. [14]I am making this covenant, with its oath, not only with you [15]who are standing here with us today in the presence of the LORD our God but also with those who are not here today.

[16]You yourselves know how we lived in Egypt and how we passed through the countries on the way here. [17]You saw among them their detestable images and idols of wood and stone, of silver and gold. [18]Make sure there is no man or woman, clan or tribe among you today whose heart turns away from the LORD our God to go and worship the gods of those nations; make sure there is no root among you that produces such bitter poison.

[19]When such a person hears the words of this oath and they invoke a blessing on themselves, thinking, "I will be safe, even though I persist in going my own way," they will bring disaster on the watered land as well as the dry. [20]The LORD will never be willing to forgive them; his wrath and zeal will burn against them. All the curses written in this book will fall on them, and the LORD will blot out their names from under heaven. [21]The LORD will single them out from all the tribes of Israel for disaster, according to all the curses of the covenant written in this Book of the Law.

[22]Your children who follow you in later generations and foreigners who come

[a] In Hebrew texts 29:1 is numbered 28:69, and 29:2-29 is numbered 29:1-28.

DEUTERONOMY 29:1 – 6

THE NEED FOR A NEW HEART

Moses traced the Israelites' inability to keep the terms of the covenant of God to a root problem. According to verse 4, the Lord had not given them the ability to understand, see and hear. Immediately following chapter 28, which contrasts the blessings for keeping God's covenant commands with curses for not doing so, Moses connected their potential inability to uphold their end of the covenant requirements with the fact that they were unable to appreciate all the Lord had done for them. Elsewhere, it is clear that their inadequacies are connected to needing a new or changed heart (Dt 10:16; 30:6; Eze 36:26). Being an ethnic Israelite had limitations. Physical connection to a genealogical line did not equate to blessings from the Lord. Therefore, the Old Testament authors offered a consistent message: the people of God were unable to keep God's law, thus they needed spiritual renewal. This message prefigured the new heart to come in Christ (Jer 31:31 – 34). Apart from renewal in Christ Jesus, no one can come to God by pleasing him and keeping all his commands (Ro 3:10 – 12,21 – 26).

from distant lands will see the calamities that have fallen on the land and the
diseases with which the LORD has afflicted it. 23The whole land will be a burning waste of salt and sulfur — nothing planted, nothing sprouting, no vegetation
growing on it. It will be like the destruction of Sodom and Gomorrah, Admah
and Zeboyim, which the LORD overthrew in fierce anger. 24All the nations will
ask: "Why has the LORD done this to this land? Why this fierce, burning anger?"
25And the answer will be: "It is because this people abandoned the covenant
of the LORD, the God of their ancestors, the covenant he made with them when
he brought them out of Egypt. 26They went off and worshiped other gods and
bowed down to them, gods they did not know, gods he had not given them.
27Therefore the LORD's anger burned against this land, so that he brought on it
all the curses written in this book. 28In furious anger and in great wrath the LORD
uprooted them from their land and thrust them into another land, as it is now."
29The secret things belong to the LORD our God, but the things revealed belong to us and to our children forever, that we may follow all the words of this law.

Prosperity After Turning to the LORD

30 When all these blessings and curses I have set before you come on you
and you take them to heart wherever the LORD your God disperses you
among the nations, 2and when you and your children return to the LORD your
God and obey him with all your heart and with all your soul according to everything I command you today, 3then the LORD your God will restore your fortunes[a]
and have compassion on you and gather you again from all the nations where he
scattered you. 4Even if you have been banished to the most distant land under
the heavens, from there the LORD your God will gather you and bring you back.
5He will bring you to the land that belonged to your ancestors, and you will take
possession of it. He will make you more prosperous and numerous than your ancestors. 6The LORD your God will circumcise your hearts and the hearts of your
descendants, so that you may love him with all your heart and with all your soul,
and live. 7The LORD your God will put all these curses on your enemies who hate
and persecute you. 8You will again obey the LORD and follow all his commands
I am giving you today. 9Then the LORD your God will make you most prosperous
in all the work of your hands and in the fruit of your womb, the young of your
livestock and the crops of your land. The LORD will again delight in you and make
you prosperous, just as he delighted in your ancestors, 10if you obey the LORD your
God and keep his commands and decrees that are written in this Book of the Law
and turn to the LORD your God with all your heart and with all your soul.

The Offer of Life or Death

11Now what I am commanding you today is not too difficult for you or beyond
your reach. 12It is not up in heaven, so that you have to ask, "Who will ascend
into heaven to get it and proclaim it to us so we may obey it?" 13Nor is it beyond
the sea, so that you have to ask, "Who will cross the sea to get it and proclaim it
to us so we may obey it?" 14No, the word is very near you; it is in your mouth and
in your heart so you may obey it.
15See, I set before you today life and prosperity, death and destruction. 16For I
command you today to love the LORD your God, to walk in obedience to him, and
to keep his commands, decrees and laws; then you will live and increase, and the
LORD your God will bless you in the land you are entering to possess.
17But if your heart turns away and you are not obedient, and if you are drawn
away to bow down to other gods and worship them, 18I declare to you this day
that you will certainly be destroyed. You will not live long in the land you are
crossing the Jordan to enter and possess.
19This day I call the heavens and the earth as witnesses against you that I have
set before you life and death, blessings and curses. Now choose life, so that you

[a] 3 Or *will bring you back from captivity*

DEUTERONOMY 30:11 – 14

THE NEAR WORD

Moses did not claim that God's word, or message, is easy to obey but that his word is near. No one has traveled to the heavens or to a remote part of the world, but God has given his law to his people in a form they can understand. Like God himself, his word is near to the people (Ro 10:6 – 8). They could hear it, memorize it and talk about it with others. God does not stand far off and require that humans come to him through their own moral efforts or that they wander in darkness trying to discern his plan and purpose for life. Instead, he comes near — first in the form of his revealed Word given to Moses and then in the form of God's Son, Jesus, who would dwell among the people in the flesh (Jn 1:1 – 14). The nearness of God demonstrates the great length that God goes to save his people from their sins.

DEUTERONOMY 30:11–20

CHOOSE LIFE

At the end of his life, knowing that he would die without ever entering the promised land, Moses once again held out the covenant promises of God to the nation of Israel. In many ways, the challenge to "choose life, so that you … may live" (v. 19) is as old as mankind. In the garden, God held out the same promise to Adam and Eve (Ge 2:15–17), though they made the foolish choice and pursued death. Ever since, all people have been trapped in a cycle of sin. Certainly there have been times when people returned to God, but these seasons have been short-lived.

Moses, at this point the leader of God's people for forty years, knew full well the inability of the people to choose life that they could live. Throughout their journey, they had consistently murmured against God, doubted Moses' leadership and been given over to death and destruction. Moses began his final sermons to the people of God on the plains of Moab with a vivid recounting of the gory details of their rebellion in chapter 1 of this very book. Even Moses, the great deliverer, had been unable to consistently choose life; therefore he died without ever stepping foot on the ground that he had been pursuing for forty years (3:21–29).

Yet, he again reminded the people of their need to choose life. By this point, the entire generation that scorned the promises of God and were forced to wander in the wilderness had died. This new generation could vividly remember the death of their parents in these wilderness years. They now were faced with a decision: Would they follow in the path of their ancestors, disobey God and die — or would they be a new generation who trusted God, walked in his ways and lived bountifully in the land of promise?

Jesus' life and ministry ushered in hope for all those trapped in the cyclical pattern of sin and death. He fulfilled God's promises to the people by giving them a path to life. John wrote that Jesus claimed to be "the way and the truth and the life" (Jn 14:6). By coming to him, people can find the path to life, not through conformity to a system of rules, but by submission to the person of Christ. In him is life and life to the full (Jn 10:10).

and your children may live 20and that you may love the LORD your God, listen to
his voice, and hold fast to him. For the LORD is your life, and he will give you many
years in the land he swore to give to your fathers, Abraham, Isaac and Jacob.

Joshua to Succeed Moses

31 Then Moses went out and spoke these words to all Israel: 2"I am now a
hundred and twenty years old and I am no longer able to lead you. The
LORD has said to me, 'You shall not cross the Jordan.' 3The LORD your God himself will cross over ahead of you. He will destroy these nations before you, and
you will take possession of their land. Joshua also will cross over ahead of you,
as the LORD said. 4And the LORD will do to them what he did to Sihon and Og, the
kings of the Amorites, whom he destroyed along with their land. 5The LORD will
deliver them to you, and you must do to them all that I have commanded you.
6Be strong and courageous. Do not be afraid or terrified because of them, for the
LORD your God goes with you; he will never leave you nor forsake you."
7Then Moses summoned Joshua and said to him in the presence of all Israel,
"Be strong and courageous, for you must go with this people into the land that the
LORD swore to their ancestors to give them, and you must divide it among them
as their inheritance. 8The LORD himself goes before you and will be with you; he
will never leave you nor forsake you. Do not be afraid; do not be discouraged."

Public Reading of the Law

9So Moses wrote down this law and gave it to the Levitical priests, who carried
the ark of the covenant of the LORD, and to all the elders of Israel. 10Then Moses
commanded them: "At the end of every seven years, in the year for canceling
debts, during the Festival of Tabernacles, 11when all Israel comes to appear before the LORD your God at the place he will choose, you shall read this law before
them in their hearing. 12Assemble the people — men, women and children, and
the foreigners residing in your towns — so they can listen and learn to fear the
LORD your God and follow carefully all the words of this law. 13Their children,
who do not know this law, must hear it and learn to fear the LORD your God as
long as you live in the land you are crossing the Jordan to possess."

Israel's Rebellion Predicted

14The LORD said to Moses, "Now the day of your death is near. Call Joshua and
present yourselves at the tent of meeting, where I will commission him." So Moses and Joshua came and presented themselves at the tent of meeting.
15Then the LORD appeared at the tent in a pillar of cloud, and the cloud stood
over the entrance to the tent. 16And the LORD said to Moses: "You are going to
rest with your ancestors, and these people will soon prostitute themselves to the
foreign gods of the land they are entering. They will forsake me and break the
covenant I made with them. 17And in that day I will become angry with them and
forsake them; I will hide my face from them, and they will be destroyed. Many disasters and calamities will come on them, and in that day they will ask, 'Have not
these disasters come on us because our God is not with us?' 18And I will certainly
hide my face in that day because of all their wickedness in turning to other gods.
19"Now write down this song and teach it to the Israelites and have them sing
it, so that it may be a witness for me against them. 20When I have brought them
into the land flowing with milk and honey, the land I promised on oath to their
ancestors, and when they eat their fill and thrive, they will turn to other gods and
worship them, rejecting me and breaking my covenant. 21And when many disasters and calamities come on them, this song will testify against them, because
it will not be forgotten by their descendants. I know what they are disposed to
do, even before I bring them into the land I promised them on oath." 22So Moses
wrote down this song that day and taught it to the Israelites.
23The LORD gave this command to Joshua son of Nun: "Be strong and courageous, for you will bring the Israelites into the land I promised them on oath, and
I myself will be with you."

DEUTERONOMY 31:1 – 6

AN EVER-PRESENT GOD

Moses commanded the people to take heart, be courageous and take the land God had promised to give them as an inheritance. The basis for their courage was found in the fact that God would surely go before them into the land. His ever-present protection and guidance was meant to bolster the confidence of the people as they ventured into a land filled with imposing nations and idolatrous worship. As with the pillar of fire and the cloud in the wilderness, God pledged to go before the people on this journey, and if they would simply trust him, he would grant them victory and bountiful blessing in the land.

In much the same way, Jesus gave his followers a mission grand in scope. Go into all the world, he said, and declare and demonstrate the hope of the gospel and call people to repentance and faith. This mission would be impossible were it not for the promise of God to go with his church and supply it with all the power, protection and provision needed to accomplish the mission to which it is entrusted (Mt 28:20). The presence of God, going both before and with the church, should provide it with confidence and encouragement to embark on the mission of filling the earth "with the knowledge of the glory of the LORD" (Hab 2:14).

24 After Moses finished writing in a book the words of this law from beginning
to end, 25 he gave this command to the Levites who carried the ark of the covenant of the LORD: 26 "Take this Book of the Law and place it beside the ark of the
covenant of the LORD your God. There it will remain as a witness against you.
27 For I know how rebellious and stiff-necked you are. If you have been rebellious
against the LORD while I am still alive and with you, how much more will you
rebel after I die! 28 Assemble before me all the elders of your tribes and all your
officials, so that I can speak these words in their hearing and call the heavens
and the earth to testify against them. 29 For I know that after my death you are
sure to become utterly corrupt and to turn from the way I have commanded you.
In days to come, disaster will fall on you because you will do evil in the sight of
the LORD and arouse his anger by what your hands have made."

The Song of Moses

30 And Moses recited the words of this song from beginning to end in the hearing of the whole assembly of Israel:

32 Listen, you heavens, and I will speak;
hear, you earth, the words of my mouth.
2 Let my teaching fall like rain
and my words descend like dew,
like showers on new grass,
like abundant rain on tender plants.

3 I will proclaim the name of the LORD.
Oh, praise the greatness of our God!
4 He is the Rock, his works are perfect,
and all his ways are just.
A faithful God who does no wrong,
upright and just is he.

5 They are corrupt and not his children;
to their shame they are a warped and crooked
generation.
6 Is this the way you repay the LORD,
you foolish and unwise people?
Is he not your Father, your Creator,[a]
who made you and formed you?

7 Remember the days of old;
consider the generations long past.
Ask your father and he will tell you,
your elders, and they will explain to you.
8 When the Most High gave the nations their inheritance,
when he divided all mankind,
he set up boundaries for the peoples
according to the number of the sons of Israel.[b]
9 For the LORD's portion is his people,
Jacob his allotted inheritance.

10 In a desert land he found him,
in a barren and howling waste.
He shielded him and cared for him;
he guarded him as the apple of his eye,
11 like an eagle that stirs up its nest
and hovers over its young,
that spreads its wings to catch them
and carries them aloft.

[a] 6 Or *Father, who bought you* [b] 8 Masoretic Text; Dead Sea Scrolls (see also Septuagint) *sons of God*

[12] The LORD alone led him;
no foreign god was with him.

[13] He made him ride on the heights of the land
and fed him with the fruit of the fields.
He nourished him with honey from the rock,
and with oil from the flinty crag,
[14] with curds and milk from herd and flock
and with fattened lambs and goats,
with choice rams of Bashan
and the finest kernels of wheat.
You drank the foaming blood of the grape.

[15] Jeshurun[a] grew fat and kicked;
filled with food, they became heavy and sleek.
They abandoned the God who made them
and rejected the Rock their Savior.
[16] They made him jealous with their foreign gods
and angered him with their detestable idols.
[17] They sacrificed to false gods, which are not God—
gods they had not known,
gods that recently appeared,
gods your ancestors did not fear.
[18] You deserted the Rock, who fathered you;
you forgot the God who gave you birth.

[19] The LORD saw this and rejected them
because he was angered by his sons and daughters.
[20] "I will hide my face from them," he said,
"and see what their end will be;
for they are a perverse generation,
children who are unfaithful.
[21] They made me jealous by what is no god
and angered me with their worthless idols.
I will make them envious by those who are not a people;
I will make them angry by a nation that has no understanding.
[22] For a fire will be kindled by my wrath,
one that burns down to the realm of the dead below.
It will devour the earth and its harvests
and set afire the foundations of the mountains.

[23] "I will heap calamities on them
and spend my arrows against them.
[24] I will send wasting famine against them,
consuming pestilence and deadly plague;
I will send against them the fangs of wild beasts,
the venom of vipers that glide in the dust.
[25] In the street the sword will make them childless;
in their homes terror will reign.
The young men and young women will perish,
the infants and those with gray hair.
[26] I said I would scatter them
and erase their name from human memory,
[27] but I dreaded the taunt of the enemy,
lest the adversary misunderstand
and say, 'Our hand has triumphed;
the LORD has not done all this.'"

---

[a] 15 *Jeshurun* means *the upright one*, that is, Israel.

28 They are a nation without sense,
there is no discernment in them.
29 If only they were wise and would understand this
and discern what their end will be!
30 How could one man chase a thousand,
or two put ten thousand to flight,
unless their Rock had sold them,
unless the LORD had given them up?
31 For their rock is not like our Rock,
as even our enemies concede.
32 Their vine comes from the vine of Sodom
and from the fields of Gomorrah.
Their grapes are filled with poison,
and their clusters with bitterness.
33 Their wine is the venom of serpents,
the deadly poison of cobras.

34 "Have I not kept this in reserve
and sealed it in my vaults?
35 It is mine to avenge; I will repay.
In due time their foot will slip;
their day of disaster is near
and their doom rushes upon them."

36 The LORD will vindicate his people
and relent concerning his servants
when he sees their strength is gone
and no one is left, slave or free.[a]
37 He will say: "Now where are their gods,
the rock they took refuge in,
38 the gods who ate the fat of their sacrifices
and drank the wine of their drink offerings?
Let them rise up to help you!
Let them give you shelter!

39 "See now that I myself am he!
There is no god besides me.
I put to death and I bring to life,
I have wounded and I will heal,
and no one can deliver out of my hand.
40 I lift my hand to heaven and solemnly swear:
As surely as I live forever,
41 when I sharpen my flashing sword
and my hand grasps it in judgment,
I will take vengeance on my adversaries
and repay those who hate me.
42 I will make my arrows drunk with blood,
while my sword devours flesh:
the blood of the slain and the captives,
the heads of the enemy leaders."

43 Rejoice, you nations, with his people,[b,c]
for he will avenge the blood of his servants;
he will take vengeance on his enemies
and make atonement for his land and people.

---

[a] *36* Or *and they are without a ruler or leader* [b] *43* Or *Make his people rejoice, you nations* [c] *43* Masoretic Text; Dead Sea Scrolls (see also Septuagint) *people, / and let all the angels worship him, /*

44 Moses came with Joshua[a] son of Nun and spoke all the words of this song in
the hearing of the people. 45 When Moses finished reciting all these words to all
Israel, 46 he said to them, "Take to heart all the words I have solemnly declared
to you this day, so that you may command your children to obey carefully all
the words of this law. 47 They are not just idle words for you — they are your life.
By them you will live long in the land you are crossing the Jordan to possess."

Moses to Die on Mount Nebo

48 On that same day the LORD told Moses, 49 "Go up into the Abarim Range to
Mount Nebo in Moab, across from Jericho, and view Canaan, the land I am giving the Israelites as their own possession. 50 There on the mountain that you have
climbed you will die and be gathered to your people, just as your brother Aaron
died on Mount Hor and was gathered to his people. 51 This is because both of
you broke faith with me in the presence of the Israelites at the waters of Meribah
Kadesh in the Desert of Zin and because you did not uphold my holiness among
the Israelites. 52 Therefore, you will see the land only from a distance; you will not
enter the land I am giving to the people of Israel."

Moses Blesses the Tribes

33 This is the blessing that Moses the man of God pronounced on the Israelites before his death. 2 He said:

"The LORD came from Sinai
    and dawned over them from Seir;
    he shone forth from Mount Paran.
He came with[b] myriads of holy ones
    from the south, from his mountain slopes.[c]
3 Surely it is you who love the people;
    all the holy ones are in your hand.
At your feet they all bow down,
    and from you receive instruction,
4 the law that Moses gave us,
    the possession of the assembly of Jacob.
5 He was king over Jeshurun[d]
    when the leaders of the people assembled,
    along with the tribes of Israel.

6 "Let Reuben live and not die,
    nor[e] his people be few."

7 And this he said about Judah:

"Hear, LORD, the cry of Judah;
    bring him to his people.
With his own hands he defends his cause.
    Oh, be his help against his foes!"

8 About Levi he said:

"Your Thummim and Urim belong
    to your faithful servant.
You tested him at Massah;
    you contended with him at the waters of Meribah.
9 He said of his father and mother,
    'I have no regard for them.'
He did not recognize his brothers
    or acknowledge his own children,

[a] 44 Hebrew *Hoshea,* a variant of *Joshua* [b] 2 Or *from* [c] 2 The meaning of the Hebrew for this phrase is uncertain. [d] 5 *Jeshurun* means *the upright one,* that is, Israel; also in verse 26. [e] 6 Or *but let*

DEUTERONOMY 32:48 – 52

THE GOD OF SECOND CHANCES

God's grace is evident in Moses' death. Moses had experienced the highs and lows of the universal human experience. But he also had been the mouthpiece of God before Pharaoh, led the miraculous deliverance of the people from Egypt, seen the glory of God firsthand and received the very law of God. Yet he had rebelled against God, "broke faith" with God, and failed to "uphold [God's] holiness" (Nu 20:24; Dt 32:51). His sinful choice resulted in his inability to go into the land of promise; but God, in his kindness, did allow him to see the land. It is as if God was saying, "Moses, have a look. See my faithfulness. I told you that I would bring my people here. There was never a reason to doubt me. I always keep my promises."

At the end of his life, Moses could die with the assurance that God would lead his people into the land and his work had not been in vain. In a similar fashion, God provides grace-filled second chances to all those who, like Moses, David, Paul and a host of others, have a questionable past. Jesus' work assures believers that, no matter what mistakes they have made, God will surely keep his promises and lead them into the eternal rest he has secured for his people (Heb 4:1 – 11).

but he watched over your word
and guarded your covenant.
10 He teaches your precepts to Jacob
and your law to Israel.
He offers incense before you
and whole burnt offerings on your altar.
11 Bless all his skills, LORD,
and be pleased with the work of his hands.
Strike down those who rise against him,
his foes till they rise no more."

12 About Benjamin he said:

"Let the beloved of the LORD rest secure in him,
for he shields him all day long,
and the one the LORD loves rests between his shoulders."

13 About Joseph he said:

"May the LORD bless his land
with the precious dew from heaven above
and with the deep waters that lie below;
14 with the best the sun brings forth
and the finest the moon can yield;
15 with the choicest gifts of the ancient mountains
and the fruitfulness of the everlasting hills;
16 with the best gifts of the earth and its fullness
and the favor of him who dwelt in the burning bush.
Let all these rest on the head of Joseph,
on the brow of the prince among[a] his brothers.
17 In majesty he is like a firstborn bull;
his horns are the horns of a wild ox.
With them he will gore the nations,
even those at the ends of the earth.
Such are the ten thousands of Ephraim;
such are the thousands of Manasseh."

18 About Zebulun he said:

"Rejoice, Zebulun, in your going out,
and you, Issachar, in your tents.
19 They will summon peoples to the mountain
and there offer the sacrifices of the righteous;
they will feast on the abundance of the seas,
on the treasures hidden in the sand."

20 About Gad he said:

"Blessed is he who enlarges Gad's domain!
Gad lives there like a lion,
tearing at arm or head.
21 He chose the best land for himself;
the leader's portion was kept for him.
When the heads of the people assembled,
he carried out the LORD's righteous will,
and his judgments concerning Israel."

22 About Dan he said:

"Dan is a lion's cub,
springing out of Bashan."

---

[a] 16 Or *of the one separated from*

[23]About Naphtali he said:

"Naphtali is abounding with the favor of the LORD
and is full of his blessing;
he will inherit southward to the lake."

[24]About Asher he said:

"Most blessed of sons is Asher;
let him be favored by his brothers,
and let him bathe his feet in oil.
[25]The bolts of your gates will be iron and bronze,
and your strength will equal your days.

[26]"There is no one like the God of Jeshurun,
who rides across the heavens to help you
and on the clouds in his majesty.
[27]The eternal God is your refuge,
and underneath are the everlasting arms.
He will drive out your enemies before you,
saying, 'Destroy them!'
[28]So Israel will live in safety;
Jacob will dwell[a] secure
in a land of grain and new wine,
where the heavens drop dew.
[29]Blessed are you, Israel!
Who is like you,
a people saved by the LORD?
He is your shield and helper
and your glorious sword.
Your enemies will cower before you,
and you will tread on their heights."

The Death of Moses

34 Then Moses climbed Mount Nebo from the plains of Moab to the top
of Pisgah, across from Jericho. There the LORD showed him the whole
land—from Gilead to Dan, [2]all of Naphtali, the territory of Ephraim and Manasseh, all the land of Judah as far as the Mediterranean Sea, [3]the Negev and the
whole region from the Valley of Jericho, the City of Palms, as far as Zoar. [4]Then
the LORD said to him, "This is the land I promised on oath to Abraham, Isaac and
Jacob when I said, 'I will give it to your descendants.' I have let you see it with
your eyes, but you will not cross over into it."
[5]And Moses the servant of the LORD died there in Moab, as the LORD had said.
[6]He buried him[b] in Moab, in the valley opposite Beth Peor, but to this day no one
knows where his grave is. [7]Moses was a hundred and twenty years old when he
died, yet his eyes were not weak nor his strength gone. [8]The Israelites grieved for
Moses in the plains of Moab thirty days, until the time of weeping and mourning was over.
[9]Now Joshua son of Nun was filled with the spirit[c] of wisdom because Moses
had laid his hands on him. So the Israelites listened to him and did what the
LORD had commanded Moses.
[10]Since then, no prophet has risen in Israel like Moses, whom the LORD knew
face to face, [11]who did all those signs and wonders the LORD sent him to do in
Egypt—to Pharaoh and to all his officials and to his whole land. [12]For no one has
ever shown the mighty power or performed the awesome deeds that Moses did
in the sight of all Israel.

DEUTERONOMY 34:10–12

A PROPHET LIKE MOSES

Interestingly, Deuteronomy ends with three verses that express an extreme void within the nation of Israel. After the death of Moses, there was no one like him to fill his leadership position at the same level of quality that the Israelites came to expect from him. There is a felt emptiness created by the death of Moses. During his time as the leader of this people, he interacted with God face to face, led a nation out of Egyptian slavery, performed miracles and exhibited unrivaled wisdom. While Moses was not without fault, it is clear that he was a gift of God to the people of God. The people looked to him as a mediator between them and God and as a leader who helped them to follow God's ways. Following his death, the people of Israel continued to anticipate a prophet who would be like Moses, a longing that was left unfulfilled until the birth of Jesus (Ac 3:22–26).

[a] 28 Septuagint; Hebrew *Jacob's spring is* [b] 6 Or *He was buried* [c] 9 Or *Spirit*

JESUS: OUR PERFECT LEADER

JOSHUA

JOSHUA

EXODUS FROM EGYPT	CONQUEST OF CANAAN	PERIOD OF JUDGES BEGINS
c. 1446 BC	*c. 1406 – 1400 BC*	*c. 1375 BC*

The book of Joshua describes Israel's conquest of the promised land from the initial invasion across the Jordan River to the final division of the land among the twelve tribes. This historical narrative highlights God's might, power and faithfulness as Israel's commander-in-chief. He is the one who fulfills his promises, wins the victories and gives good land as a gift to his children. This reality is seen clearly in the battle of Jericho (Jos 6), in which God unequivocally demonstrates that he is the One who fights on behalf of his people.

The events in the book of Joshua recount the various tactics God used to give Israel victory over the inhabitants of Canaan. The descriptions do not suggest that Israel advanced due to their superior strength or military savvy. In fact, when they acted apart from God's will, three thousand of Israel's troops were routed by a small contingent of enemy soldiers (Jos 7:2 – 5). Throughout the book, God demonstrates that Israel's victories were because of his power at work in the people and not because of their skill.

Though the book describes the possession of the land, the focus is on the fact that this land is a fulfillment of God's covenant promises to Abraham (Ge 12:7; 13:14 – 17; 15:18 – 21; 17:8; 22:17), to Isaac (Ge 26:3 – 4), to Jacob (Ge 28:4,13; 35:12) and to the succeeding generations (Ge 48:4 – 22; 50:24). The land they receive is a good and fertile land, flowing with milk and honey; but more importantly it is the promised land — the fulfillment of God's promises and a concrete demonstration of his covenant faithfulness.

The book is named for the human leader who takes center stage throughout the book. Joshua's name, which means "the LORD saves" or "the LORD gives victory," demonstrates that his leadership was representative of God's guidance. God's strength and might, seen throughout the book of Joshua, are emblematic of a far greater victory won by Jesus Christ. Joshua's name, in fact, is the Hebrew equivalent of the name "Jesus" (which is a Greek name). When Joshua led God's people into the land, he foreshadowed the One who would ultimately bring "many sons and daughters to glory" (Heb 2:10) and "gives us the victory" through his own work on the cross (1Co 15:57).

Though Joshua proved to be a good and worthy leader, every human leader pales in comparison to Jesus. While on earth, Jesus was the perfect embodiment of humility and action. He confronted the injustices of corrupt religious leaders and government officials, yet led with gentleness when interacting with society's most vulnerable people. Though we can learn much from looking at the lives of great leaders like Joshua, we must always judge each one in light of Jesus, who was and remains our perfect leader (Rev 21:1 – 7).

HAVE I NOT COMMANDED YOU? BE STRONG
AND COURAGEOUS. DO NOT BE AFRAID;
DO NOT BE DISCOURAGED, FOR THE LORD YOUR GOD
WILL BE WITH YOU WHEREVER YOU GO.

Joshua 1:9

JOSHUA

Joshua Installed as Leader

1 After the death of Moses the servant of the LORD, the LORD said to Joshua son of Nun, Moses' aide: 2"Moses my servant is dead. Now then, you and all these people, get ready to cross the Jordan River into the land I am about to give to them — to the Israelites. 3I will give you every place where you set your foot, as I promised Moses. 4Your territory will extend from the desert to Lebanon, and from the great river, the Euphrates — all the Hittite country — to the Mediterranean Sea in the west. 5No one will be able to stand against you all the days of your life. As I was with Moses, so I will be with you; I will never leave you nor forsake you. 6Be strong and courageous, because you will lead these people to inherit the land I swore to their ancestors to give them.

7"Be strong and very courageous. Be careful to obey all the law my servant Moses gave you; do not turn from it to the right or to the left, that you may be successful wherever you go. 8Keep this Book of the Law always on your lips; meditate on it day and night, so that you may be careful to do everything written in it. Then you will be prosperous and successful. 9Have I not commanded you? Be strong and courageous. Do not be afraid; do not be discouraged, for the LORD your God will be with you wherever you go."

10So Joshua ordered the officers of the people: 11"Go through the camp and tell the people, 'Get your provisions ready. Three days from now you will cross the Jordan here to go in and take possession of the land the LORD your God is giving you for your own.' "

12But to the Reubenites, the Gadites and the half-tribe of Manasseh, Joshua said, 13"Remember the command that Moses the servant of the LORD gave you after he said, 'The LORD your God will give you rest by giving you this land.' 14Your wives, your children and your livestock may stay in the land that Moses gave you east of the Jordan, but all your fighting men, ready for battle, must cross over ahead of your fellow Israelites. You are to help them 15until the LORD gives them rest, as he has done for you, and until they too have taken possession of the land the LORD your God is giving them. After that, you may go back and occupy your own land, which Moses the servant of the LORD gave you east of the Jordan toward the sunrise."

16Then they answered Joshua, "Whatever you have commanded us we will do, and wherever you send us we will go. 17Just as we fully obeyed Moses, so we will obey you. Only may the LORD your God be with you as he was with Moses. 18Whoever rebels against your word and does not obey it, whatever you may command them, will be put to death. Only be strong and courageous!"

Rahab and the Spies

2 Then Joshua son of Nun secretly sent two spies from Shittim. "Go, look over the land," he said, "especially Jericho." So they went and entered the house of a prostitute named Rahab and stayed there.

2The king of Jericho was told, "Look, some of the Israelites have come here tonight to spy out the land." 3So the king of Jericho sent this message to Rahab: "Bring out the men who came to you and entered your house, because they have come to spy out the whole land."

4But the woman had taken the two men and hidden them. She said, "Yes, the men came to me, but I did not know where they had come from. 5At dusk, when it was time to close the city gate, they left. I don't know which way they went. Go after them quickly. You may catch up with them." 6(But she had taken them up to the roof and hidden them under the stalks of flax she had laid out on the roof.)

JOSHUA 1:6 – 7,9,18

COURAGE

Strength and courage are not found naturally in fallen humanity. Sin renders people frail, broken, shameful and fearful — though they may mask these feelings with all sorts of actions. Joshua demonstrated the basis for true strength and courage both for the nation of Israel and for all Christians throughout history. Joshua reminded the people of the ever-present faithfulness of God. God keeps his word, so people can have confidence that God will do what he promises regardless of the odds. God has given the Bible, which provides authoritative guidance into the plans and purposes of God. When people conform their lives to God's standards by the power of his Spirit, they can have boldness, courage and strength knowing they are walking faithfully with God. The faithfulness of God and the Word of God were the God-ordained means of providing strength and courage to the people as they entered the promised land. In the same way, today's church is a testimony of God's faithfulness and his written Word. As Christians reflect on the faithfulness of God and the Word of God, they will develop the strength and courage that they could never find in themselves.

THE BEAUTY OF THE LAW

The Lord called Joshua to be strong and courageous as Joshua replaced Moses as Israel's leader and led the people into the promised land. This calling was based on his obedience and submission to the Word of God. As the Creator, God knows how life is meant to be lived and the way for people to experience life to the full (Jn 10:10). The gift of the law was a gracious act of God to instruct his people in his ways. It was never intended to be a moralistic plan to earn God's favor. Rather, the law was given to those who had already experienced God's redeeming grace. In the law, God provided instructions for how his children can love him and other people. This law is not a collection of arbitrary dictates from a malevolent deity, but instead it is the wisdom of God distilled in human language. It is a path to joy and life — the way people were meant to live.

The Bible continually portrays the law of God in this fashion. For example, in the longest psalm in the Bible, Psalm 119, the author says that he loves, treasures, delights in and longs for the law. It is a source of hope, peace, joy and direction. In Psalm 19, the psalmist says the law refreshes the soul, makes wise the simple, gives joy to the heart and gives light to the eyes (Ps 19:7 – 8). The law is a beautiful gift from a gracious God.

Jesus testified to the lasting value of the law when he said that he did not come to abolish the law (Mt 5:17). Instead, Jesus amplified the law, explaining the transformation that should result as a proper response to his work. In his masterful Sermon on the Mount in Matthew 5 through 7, Jesus called people to a far greater standard of obedience than mere conformity to external regulations. Instead of simply condemning murder, Jesus unmasked the anger that fueled this act. Adultery is not the prime culprit, but lust rooted in the human heart is the real problem. Jesus methodically outlined the heart-level change that the law relied upon. Rather than rendering the law obsolete, Jesus showed that the law continued to provide an authoritative standard and guidance for God's people. Now, because of the finished work of Christ, believers have hope that the price for their disobedience of the law has been paid and that they have God's Spirit dwelling within them, providing them the power to live the life God intends.

[7]So the men set out in pursuit of the spies on the road that leads to the fords of the Jordan, and as soon as the pursuers had gone out, the gate was shut.

[8]Before the spies lay down for the night, she went up on the roof [9]and said to them, "I know that the LORD has given you this land and that a great fear of you has fallen on us, so that all who live in this country are melting in fear because of you. [10]We have heard how the LORD dried up the water of the Red Sea[a] for you when you came out of Egypt, and what you did to Sihon and Og, the two kings of the Amorites east of the Jordan, whom you completely destroyed.[b] [11]When we heard of it, our hearts melted in fear and everyone's courage failed because of you, for the LORD your God is God in heaven above and on the earth below.

[12]"Now then, please swear to me by the LORD that you will show kindness to my family, because I have shown kindness to you. Give me a sure sign [13]that you will spare the lives of my father and mother, my brothers and sisters, and all who belong to them — and that you will save us from death."

[14]"Our lives for your lives!" the men assured her. "If you don't tell what we are doing, we will treat you kindly and faithfully when the LORD gives us the land."

[15]So she let them down by a rope through the window, for the house she lived in was part of the city wall. [16]She said to them, "Go to the hills so the pursuers will not find you. Hide yourselves there three days until they return, and then go on your way."

[17]Now the men had said to her, "This oath you made us swear will not be binding on us [18]unless, when we enter the land, you have tied this scarlet cord in the window through which you let us down, and unless you have brought your father and mother, your brothers and all your family into your house. [19]If any of them go outside your house into the street, their blood will be on their own heads; we will not be responsible. As for those who are in the house with you, their blood will be on our head if a hand is laid on them. [20]But if you tell what we are doing, we will be released from the oath you made us swear."

[21]"Agreed," she replied. "Let it be as you say."

So she sent them away, and they departed. And she tied the scarlet cord in the window.

[22]When they left, they went into the hills and stayed there three days, until the pursuers had searched all along the road and returned without finding them. [23]Then the two men started back. They went down out of the hills, forded the river and came to Joshua son of Nun and told him everything that had happened to them. [24]They said to Joshua, "The LORD has surely given the whole land into our hands; all the people are melting in fear because of us."

Crossing the Jordan

3 Early in the morning Joshua and all the Israelites set out from Shittim and went to the Jordan, where they camped before crossing over. [2]After three days the officers went throughout the camp, [3]giving orders to the people: "When you see the ark of the covenant of the LORD your God, and the Levitical priests carrying it, you are to move out from your positions and follow it. [4]Then you will know which way to go, since you have never been this way before. But keep a distance of about two thousand cubits[c] between you and the ark; do not go near it."

[5]Joshua told the people, "Consecrate yourselves, for tomorrow the LORD will do amazing things among you."

[6]Joshua said to the priests, "Take up the ark of the covenant and pass on ahead of the people." So they took it up and went ahead of them.

[7]And the LORD said to Joshua, "Today I will begin to exalt you in the eyes of all Israel, so they may know that I am with you as I was with Moses. [8]Tell the priests who carry the ark of the covenant: 'When you reach the edge of the Jordan's waters, go and stand in the river.'"

JOSHUA 2:8 – 11

RAHAB AND FAITH

Rahab's claim was an amazing expression of faith from the lips of a Gentile prostitute. Not only had she heard of the God of Israel — the one true and living God — but she also believed the power and promises of God. She affirmed that God would indeed give the land in which she lived to the nation of Israel. This affirmation of faith was a life-altering claim for Rahab. With it, she set herself apart from her people, her land and the pagan gods her people worshiped. Her faith radically changed her future, and within a short period, her faith was confirmed as she witnessed the destruction of her people and her city. Rahab was saved by faith. This truth sets the paradigm for God's saving work throughout all history. Down through the ages believers are saved not based on their righteous deeds but by their faith in God's faithfulness. Faith has the power to save God's people from life in a fallen world and from the judgment of God.

[a] *10* Or *the Sea of Reeds* [b] *10* The Hebrew term refers to the irrevocable giving over of things or persons to the LORD, often by totally destroying them. [c] *4* That is, about 3,000 feet or about 900 meters

[9]Joshua said to the Israelites, "Come here and listen to the words of the LORD your God. [10]This is how you will know that the living God is among you and that he will certainly drive out before you the Canaanites, Hittites, Hivites, Perizzites, Girgashites, Amorites and Jebusites. [11]See, the ark of the covenant of the Lord of all the earth will go into the Jordan ahead of you. [12]Now then, choose twelve men from the tribes of Israel, one from each tribe. [13]And as soon as the priests who carry the ark of the LORD — the Lord of all the earth — set foot in the Jordan, its waters flowing downstream will be cut off and stand up in a heap."

[14]So when the people broke camp to cross the Jordan, the priests carrying the ark of the covenant went ahead of them. [15]Now the Jordan is at flood stage all during harvest. Yet as soon as the priests who carried the ark reached the Jordan and their feet touched the water's edge, [16]the water from upstream stopped flowing. It piled up in a heap a great distance away, at a town called Adam in the vicinity of Zarethan, while the water flowing down to the Sea of the Arabah (that is, the Dead Sea) was completely cut off. So the people crossed over opposite Jericho. [17]The priests who carried the ark of the covenant of the LORD stopped in the middle of the Jordan and stood on dry ground, while all Israel passed by until the whole nation had completed the crossing on dry ground.

4 When the whole nation had finished crossing the Jordan, the LORD said to Joshua, [2]"Choose twelve men from among the people, one from each tribe, [3]and tell them to take up twelve stones from the middle of the Jordan, from right where the priests are standing, and carry them over with you and put them down at the place where you stay tonight."

[4]So Joshua called together the twelve men he had appointed from the Israelites, one from each tribe, [5]and said to them, "Go over before the ark of the LORD your God into the middle of the Jordan. Each of you is to take up a stone on his shoulder, according to the number of the tribes of the Israelites, [6]to serve as a sign among you. In the future, when your children ask you, 'What do these stones mean?' [7]tell them that the flow of the Jordan was cut off before the ark of the covenant of the LORD. When it crossed the Jordan, the waters of the Jordan were cut off. These stones are to be a memorial to the people of Israel forever."

[8]So the Israelites did as Joshua commanded them. They took twelve stones from the middle of the Jordan, according to the number of the tribes of the Israelites, as the LORD had told Joshua; and they carried them over with them to their camp, where they put them down. [9]Joshua set up the twelve stones that had been[a] in the middle of the Jordan at the spot where the priests who carried the ark of the covenant had stood. And they are there to this day.

[10]Now the priests who carried the ark remained standing in the middle of the Jordan until everything the LORD had commanded Joshua was done by the people, just as Moses had directed Joshua. The people hurried over, [11]and as soon as all of them had crossed, the ark of the LORD and the priests came to the other side while the people watched. [12]The men of Reuben, Gad and the half-tribe of Manasseh crossed over, ready for battle, in front of the Israelites, as Moses had directed them. [13]About forty thousand armed for battle crossed over before the LORD to the plains of Jericho for war.

[14]That day the LORD exalted Joshua in the sight of all Israel; and they stood in awe of him all the days of his life, just as they had stood in awe of Moses.

[15]Then the LORD said to Joshua, [16]"Command the priests carrying the ark of the covenant law to come up out of the Jordan."

[17]So Joshua commanded the priests, "Come up out of the Jordan."

[18]And the priests came up out of the river carrying the ark of the covenant of the LORD. No sooner had they set their feet on the dry ground than the waters of the Jordan returned to their place and ran at flood stage as before.

[19]On the tenth day of the first month the people went up from the Jordan and camped at Gilgal on the eastern border of Jericho. [20]And Joshua set up at Gilgal

[a] 9 Or *Joshua also set up twelve stones*

SEEN AND UNSEEN

Joshua had a memorial built to remind the people of God's faithfulness in giving them the land of promise. This external marker served to remind the nation of God's power to do the unthinkable — lead a band of former slaves to obtain a good land inhabited by giants in walled cities. The presence of two and a half tribes on the eastern side of the Jordan meant that the people would continue to traverse the Jordan and see these memorial stones. As early as Noah in Genesis 8:20, God's people built such visible altars or memorials to remind them to worship God for his character and actions.

Sadly, these external markers often became a source of idolatrous worship for the people. For example, the Samaritan woman in John 4 asked Jesus for the location where true worship was to happen (Jn 4:20). Would it be on the mountain where her ancestors worshiped or would it be in Jerusalem? Jesus, knowing the deep-seated brokenness of this woman, beckoned her to a deeper form of worship — one that would not be marked by an external location but one that would happen by the Spirit of God dwelling within a person.

The radical grace shown by Jesus to this woman demonstrated the ongoing faithfulness of God to his promises. He gives an inheritance far greater than physical land to all those who trust in him. This woman, in spite of her checkered past, could inherit the great and glorious promises made to Abraham. One wonders whether that well in Samaria continued to function as a memorial for her in the days, weeks, months and years to follow. Like the memorial stones in the Jordan, every time this woman saw the ordinary well — one she likely visited every day — she was reminded of the day that her life changed forever. Certainly an old well was not meant to be an object of worship, but it could have served as a valuable memorial of God's grace and kindness. Even more, John recorded that many in the city believed in the good news of Jesus because of this woman's testimony (Jn 4:39).

the twelve stones they had taken out of the Jordan. 21 He said to the Israelites,
“In the future when your descendants ask their parents, ‘What do these stones
mean?’ 22 tell them, ‘Israel crossed the Jordan on dry ground.’ 23 For the LORD
your God dried up the Jordan before you until you had crossed over. The LORD
your God did to the Jordan what he had done to the Red Sea[a] when he dried it up
before us until we had crossed over. 24 He did this so that all the peoples of the
earth might know that the hand of the LORD is powerful and so that you might
always fear the LORD your God.”

5 Now when all the Amorite kings west of the Jordan and all the Canaanite
kings along the coast heard how the LORD had dried up the Jordan before
the Israelites until they[b] had crossed over, their hearts melted in fear and they
no longer had the courage to face the Israelites.

Circumcision and Passover at Gilgal

2 At that time the LORD said to Joshua, “Make flint knives and circumcise the
Israelites again.” 3 So Joshua made flint knives and circumcised the Israelites at
Gibeath Haaraloth.[c]

4 Now this is why he did so: All those who came out of Egypt — all the men of
military age — died in the wilderness on the way after leaving Egypt. 5 All the
people that came out had been circumcised, but all the people born in the wilderness during the journey from Egypt had not. 6 The Israelites had moved about
in the wilderness forty years until all the men who were of military age when
they left Egypt had died, since they had not obeyed the LORD. For the LORD had
sworn to them that they would not see the land he had solemnly promised their
ancestors to give us, a land flowing with milk and honey. 7 So he raised up their
sons in their place, and these were the ones Joshua circumcised. They were still
uncircumcised because they had not been circumcised on the way. 8 And after the whole nation had been circumcised, they remained where they were in
camp until they were healed.

9 Then the LORD said to Joshua, “Today I have rolled away the reproach of
Egypt from you.” So the place has been called Gilgal[d] to this day.

10 On the evening of the fourteenth day of the month, while camped at Gilgal
on the plains of Jericho, the Israelites celebrated the Passover. 11 The day after
the Passover, that very day, they ate some of the produce of the land: unleavened
bread and roasted grain. 12 The manna stopped the day after[e] they ate this food
from the land; there was no longer any manna for the Israelites, but that year
they ate the produce of Canaan.

The Fall of Jericho

13 Now when Joshua was near Jericho, he looked up and saw a man standing in
front of him with a drawn sword in his hand. Joshua went up to him and asked,
“Are you for us or for our enemies?”

14 “Neither,” he replied, “but as commander of the army of the LORD I have now
come.” Then Joshua fell facedown to the ground in reverence, and asked him,
“What message does my Lord[f] have for his servant?”

15 The commander of the LORD’s army replied, “Take off your sandals, for the
place where you are standing is holy.” And Joshua did so.

6 Now the gates of Jericho were securely barred because of the Israelites. No
one went out and no one came in.

2 Then the LORD said to Joshua, “See, I have delivered Jericho into your hands,
along with its king and its fighting men. 3 March around the city once with all
the armed men. Do this for six days. 4 Have seven priests carry trumpets of rams’
horns in front of the ark. On the seventh day, march around the city seven times,
with the priests blowing the trumpets. 5 When you hear them sound a long blast

---

JOSHUA 5:13 – 14

WORTHY OF WORSHIP

People behave differently when they are in the presence of someone they truly believe to be significant or important. Joshua’s response to the man in this passage demonstrated the significance of this enigmatic figure, who some scholars believe to be the pre-incarnate Christ. Joshua did what many will one day do when they meet Jesus — he fell on his face in reverence. Much about the figure in this passage is unclear — his name, his background and the way in which he appeared. He disclosed his identity in a similar cryptic form by saying that he was the commander of the Lord’s army. Joshua’s subsequent response also affirmed the greatness of this man. He humbled himself and awaited the instructions of one to whom honor is clearly due. Joshua demonstrated his submission and faithfulness to the appearance of God here near Jericho. One day, all people will give similar honor to God, as every knee will bow and every tongue will acknowledge that Jesus is Lord (Php 2:10 – 11). Some will bow in judgment and be cast away from God’s presence forever. Others will bow in worship of the one true King forever (Rev 1:17; 4:10; 7:11; 11:16).

---

[a] 23 Or *the Sea of Reeds* [b] 1 Another textual tradition *we* [c] 3 *Gibeath Haaraloth* means *the hill of foreskins.* [d] 9 *Gilgal* sounds like the Hebrew for *roll.* [e] 12 Or *the day* [f] 14 Or *lord*

JOSHUA 5:2–9

A FRESH START

The scene at Gilgal is far from pleasant to the modern reader. The mass circumcision undertaken in this passage was a stunning, public testimony of both the failure and the future hope of the people of God. The Israelites had abandoned the practice of circumcision during their wilderness wanderings. The absence of circumcision seemed to be a mark of shame on the nation.

Now, on the brink of the promised land, the people made a bold statement that was meant to signify their commitment to keep the covenant once again. The external mark of circumcision was meant to communicate a heart change to allow the new generation to inherit the land and remain faithful to God in it. The Lord blessed this act, saying that the mark of shame had been taken away.

The continued hard-heartedness and rebellion of the people necessitated something far greater to take away the shame of sin. The author of Hebrews wrote that Jesus scorned the cross — though he endured it and completely overcame it through his victorious resurrection (Heb 12:2). The inglorious nature of his brutal death was a public means by which God took on himself the shame of sin. In this act, the full wrath of God toward sin was poured out on Jesus and, as a result, believers are forever forgiven, clean, holy and pure.

For those who know him, Christ removes the shamefulness that sin brings. Like Adam and Eve in the garden, all people are prone to hide in shame because of the foolish choices they have made (Ge 3:7). Shame causes people to try to cover for their sin with all sorts of flimsy fig leaves such as good behavior, community service or religious performance. Jesus offers a better way. By accepting his free gift of salvation, men and women can embrace the good news that he has taken away their shame forever. In spite of sin, they are loved, accepted and declared holy, and this declaration is based on the work of God on their behalf and not their moral goodness. Christians experience a far greater act of circumcision, one not done with human hands to the external body but one done by God to the heart (Ro 2:28–29).

on the trumpets, have the whole army give a loud shout; then the wall of the city
will collapse and the army will go up, everyone straight in."
6 So Joshua son of Nun called the priests and said to them, "Take up the ark
of the covenant of the LORD and have seven priests carry trumpets in front of
it." 7 And he ordered the army, "Advance! March around the city, with an armed
guard going ahead of the ark of the LORD."
8 When Joshua had spoken to the people, the seven priests carrying the seven
trumpets before the LORD went forward, blowing their trumpets, and the ark of
the LORD's covenant followed them. 9 The armed guard marched ahead of the
priests who blew the trumpets, and the rear guard followed the ark. All this time
the trumpets were sounding. 10 But Joshua had commanded the army, "Do not
give a war cry, do not raise your voices, do not say a word until the day I tell you
to shout. Then shout!" 11 So he had the ark of the LORD carried around the city,
circling it once. Then the army returned to camp and spent the night there.
12 Joshua got up early the next morning and the priests took up the ark of the
LORD. 13 The seven priests carrying the seven trumpets went forward, marching before the ark of the LORD and blowing the trumpets. The armed men went
ahead of them and the rear guard followed the ark of the LORD, while the trumpets kept sounding. 14 So on the second day they marched around the city once
and returned to the camp. They did this for six days.
15 On the seventh day, they got up at daybreak and marched around the city
seven times in the same manner, except that on that day they circled the city
seven times. 16 The seventh time around, when the priests sounded the trumpet blast, Joshua commanded the army, "Shout! For the LORD has given you the
city! 17 The city and all that is in it are to be devoted[a] to the LORD. Only Rahab the
prostitute and all who are with her in her house shall be spared, because she
hid the spies we sent. 18 But keep away from the devoted things, so that you will
not bring about your own destruction by taking any of them. Otherwise you will
make the camp of Israel liable to destruction and bring trouble on it. 19 All the
silver and gold and the articles of bronze and iron are sacred to the LORD and
must go into his treasury."
20 When the trumpets sounded, the army shouted, and at the sound of the
trumpet, when the men gave a loud shout, the wall collapsed; so everyone
charged straight in, and they took the city. 21 They devoted the city to the LORD
and destroyed with the sword every living thing in it — men and women, young
and old, cattle, sheep and donkeys.
22 Joshua said to the two men who had spied out the land, "Go into the prostitute's house and bring her out and all who belong to her, in accordance with your
oath to her." 23 So the young men who had done the spying went in and brought
out Rahab, her father and mother, her brothers and sisters and all who belonged
to her. They brought out her entire family and put them in a place outside the
camp of Israel.
24 Then they burned the whole city and everything in it, but they put the silver and gold and the articles of bronze and iron into the treasury of the LORD's
house. 25 But Joshua spared Rahab the prostitute, with her family and all who belonged to her, because she hid the men Joshua had sent as spies to Jericho — and
she lives among the Israelites to this day.
26 At that time Joshua pronounced this solemn oath: "Cursed before the LORD
is the one who undertakes to rebuild this city, Jericho:

"At the cost of his firstborn son
  he will lay its foundations;
at the cost of his youngest
  he will set up its gates."

27 So the LORD was with Joshua, and his fame spread throughout the land.

---

[a] *17* The Hebrew term refers to the irrevocable giving over of things or persons to the LORD, often by totally destroying them; also in verses 18 and 21.

JOSHUA 6:22 – 25

AN UNLIKELY ANCESTOR OF JESUS

The story of Rahab serves as a glimmer of hope in the midst of the destruction of the pagan nations who inhabited the land God had promised to give his children. News of God's might and power had long ago reached the nations, though they continued to harden their hearts in unbelief. As a result, God's judgment was poured out on the people for their sin. At this point in redemptive history, that judgment was enacted primarily through God's people, the nation of Israel, who were told to destroy these pagan nations.

Rahab proved to be an exception. Although a pagan and a prostitute, this woman had protected the Hebrew spies as they entered the land and, as a result, was given the promise of protection. Now that the people were finally laying claim to the land, the spies remained true to their promise and allowed Rahab and all of her family to escape the destruction that fell on the city.

Rahab stands in a long line of unlikely recipients of God's mercy. Matthew, in his Gospel account, begins with a lengthy genealogy, which was meant to demonstrate to his Jewish audience that Jesus Christ was the long-awaited, promised descendant of Abraham and David. This genealogy is not what one might expect, however. Matthew did not simply list the fathers of the faith — such as Abraham or David. The list prominently included a wide assortment of unlikely or unheard of characters, such as Tamar, Bathsheba, Ahaz, Eliud, Mary and Rahab. Some of these are only mentioned briefly in the annals of Scripture; some are not mentioned at all. Others such as Bathsheba and Rahab are known for their sin. But there they are listed, called by name and linked to the coming of Jesus.

The ancestry of Jesus may be one of the greatest testaments to the grace of God recorded in all of the Scripture. Not only was Rahab spared from death, but she also was brought into the family of God and given a share of the inheritance promised to his people. Her story serves as a great encouragement to all subsequent generations of outcasts, no-names and sinners of all sorts. God's grace extends to all types of people. In fact, the grace of God is seen most clearly when he saves and transforms those, like Rahab, who otherwise have no hope.

Achan's Sin

7 But the Israelites were unfaithful in regard to the devoted things[a]; Achan son
of Karmi, the son of Zimri,[b] the son of Zerah, of the tribe of Judah, took some
of them. So the LORD's anger burned against Israel.
2Now Joshua sent men from Jericho to Ai, which is near Beth Aven to the east
of Bethel, and told them, "Go up and spy out the region." So the men went up
and spied out Ai.
3When they returned to Joshua, they said, "Not all the army will have to go
up against Ai. Send two or three thousand men to take it and do not weary the
whole army, for only a few people live there." 4So about three thousand went up;
but they were routed by the men of Ai, 5who killed about thirty-six of them. They
chased the Israelites from the city gate as far as the stone quarries and struck
them down on the slopes. At this the hearts of the people melted in fear and
became like water.
6Then Joshua tore his clothes and fell facedown to the ground before the ark
of the LORD, remaining there till evening. The elders of Israel did the same, and
sprinkled dust on their heads. 7And Joshua said, "Alas, Sovereign LORD, why did
you ever bring this people across the Jordan to deliver us into the hands of the
Amorites to destroy us? If only we had been content to stay on the other side of
the Jordan! 8Pardon your servant, Lord. What can I say, now that Israel has been
routed by its enemies? 9The Canaanites and the other people of the country will
hear about this and they will surround us and wipe out our name from the earth.
What then will you do for your own great name?"
10The LORD said to Joshua, "Stand up! What are you doing down on your face?
11Israel has sinned; they have violated my covenant, which I commanded them
to keep. They have taken some of the devoted things; they have stolen, they have
lied, they have put them with their own possessions. 12That is why the Israelites
cannot stand against their enemies; they turn their backs and run because they
have been made liable to destruction. I will not be with you anymore unless you
destroy whatever among you is devoted to destruction.
13"Go, consecrate the people. Tell them, 'Consecrate yourselves in preparation for tomorrow; for this is what the LORD, the God of Israel, says: There are
devoted things among you, Israel. You cannot stand against your enemies until
you remove them.
14" 'In the morning, present yourselves tribe by tribe. The tribe the LORD
chooses shall come forward clan by clan; the clan the LORD chooses shall come
forward family by family; and the family the LORD chooses shall come forward
man by man. 15Whoever is caught with the devoted things shall be destroyed by
fire, along with all that belongs to him. He has violated the covenant of the LORD
and has done an outrageous thing in Israel!' "
16Early the next morning Joshua had Israel come forward by tribes, and Judah
was chosen. 17The clans of Judah came forward, and the Zerahites were chosen.
He had the clan of the Zerahites come forward by families, and Zimri was chosen. 18Joshua had his family come forward man by man, and Achan son of Karmi, the son of Zimri, the son of Zerah, of the tribe of Judah, was chosen.
19Then Joshua said to Achan, "My son, give glory to the LORD, the God of Israel, and honor him. Tell me what you have done; do not hide it from me."
20Achan replied, "It is true! I have sinned against the LORD, the God of Israel.
This is what I have done: 21When I saw in the plunder a beautiful robe from Babylonia,[c] two hundred shekels[d] of silver and a bar of gold weighing fifty shekels,[e]
I coveted them and took them. They are hidden in the ground inside my tent,
with the silver underneath."

---

[a] *1* The Hebrew term refers to the irrevocable giving over of things or persons to the LORD, often by totally destroying them; also in verses 11, 12, 13 and 15. [b] *1* See Septuagint and 1 Chron. 2:6; Hebrew *Zabdi*; also in verses 17 and 18. [c] *21* Hebrew *Shinar* [d] *21* That is, about 5 pounds or about 2.3 kilograms [e] *21* That is, about 1 1/4 pounds or about 575 grams

JOSHUA 7:1 – 26

DISOBEDIENCE: THE DESTRUCTIVE PATTERN

The book of Joshua began on a high note. Finally, after years of wandering in the wilderness, the people took the land. The fall of Jericho, recorded in chapter 6, served as a foreshadowing of the way God would grant the nation victory over the pagan nations. They would prevail, not because of military might, political shrewdness or sheer force but simply because God would demonstrate his power and give them the land as a gift of grace. He intended to teach them that these battles and, in fact, all the challenges of life, are not won by human might nor power, but by the Spirit of God (Zec 4:6).

The juxtaposition of Joshua 7 against the extraordinary story of God's power in chapter 6 demonstrates the folly of the human heart and the diabolical implication of sin. Achan, a random Israelite in the tribe of Judah, sinned in secret — or so he thought. He took some of the spoils of war, which were meant to be devoted to God, and kept them for himself. The result of Achan's sin was disastrous, both for Achan and for the entire nation.

Like Achan, all people are prone to harbor secret sin in their hearts even in the face of the amazing faithfulness and power of God actively at work in their lives. Secret sin is never secret in the presence of an all-knowing God. And, like Achan's sin, those hidden actions have far-reaching implications for families, communities and even nations. Therefore, Paul implored people to relinquish those sins done in secret and bring them out into the light of Christ, where true and lasting transformation can be found (Eph 5:8 – 16). His counsel is driven by a stark reality: time is fleeting, and the judgment of God is imminent. The judgment of sin, seen acutely in the story of Achan, will fall on all those who fail to repent and trust in Christ. God will ultimately bring into the light all things that are done in secret (1Co 4:5). Christians, having placed their faith in Christ, can bring their sin out from the shadows and into the light. They, of all people, know the catastrophic implications of hidden sin and the freedom found by bringing sin into the light.

22So Joshua sent messengers, and they ran to the tent, and there it was, hidden in his tent, with the silver underneath. 23They took the things from the tent,
brought them to Joshua and all the Israelites and spread them out before the
LORD.
24Then Joshua, together with all Israel, took Achan son of Zerah, the silver, the
robe, the gold bar, his sons and daughters, his cattle, donkeys and sheep, his tent
and all that he had, to the Valley of Achor. 25Joshua said, "Why have you brought
this trouble on us? The LORD will bring trouble on you today."

Then all Israel stoned him, and after they had stoned the rest, they burned
them. 26Over Achan they heaped up a large pile of rocks, which remains to this
day. Then the LORD turned from his fierce anger. Therefore that place has been
called the Valley of Achor[a] ever since.

Ai Destroyed

8 Then the LORD said to Joshua, "Do not be afraid; do not be discouraged. Take
the whole army with you, and go up and attack Ai. For I have delivered into
your hands the king of Ai, his people, his city and his land. 2You shall do to Ai
and its king as you did to Jericho and its king, except that you may carry off their
plunder and livestock for yourselves. Set an ambush behind the city."
3So Joshua and the whole army moved out to attack Ai. He chose thirty thousand of his best fighting men and sent them out at night 4with these orders: "Listen carefully. You are to set an ambush behind the city. Don't go very far from it.
All of you be on the alert. 5I and all those with me will advance on the city, and
when the men come out against us, as they did before, we will flee from them.
6They will pursue us until we have lured them away from the city, for they will
say, 'They are running away from us as they did before.' So when we flee from
them, 7you are to rise up from ambush and take the city. The LORD your God will
give it into your hand. 8When you have taken the city, set it on fire. Do what the
LORD has commanded. See to it; you have my orders."
9Then Joshua sent them off, and they went to the place of ambush and lay in
wait between Bethel and Ai, to the west of Ai—but Joshua spent that night with
the people.
10Early the next morning Joshua mustered his army, and he and the leaders of
Israel marched before them to Ai. 11The entire force that was with him marched
up and approached the city and arrived in front of it. They set up camp north
of Ai, with the valley between them and the city. 12Joshua had taken about five
thousand men and set them in ambush between Bethel and Ai, to the west of
the city. 13So the soldiers took up their positions—with the main camp to the
north of the city and the ambush to the west of it. That night Joshua went into
the valley.
14When the king of Ai saw this, he and all the men of the city hurried out early in
the morning to meet Israel in battle at a certain place overlooking the Arabah. But
he did not know that an ambush had been set against him behind the city. 15Josh-
ua and all Israel let themselves be driven back before them, and they fled toward
the wilderness. 16All the men of Ai were called to pursue them, and they pursued
Joshua and were lured away from the city. 17Not a man remained in Ai or Bethel
who did not go after Israel. They left the city open and went in pursuit of Israel.
18Then the LORD said to Joshua, "Hold out toward Ai the javelin that is in your
hand, for into your hand I will deliver the city." So Joshua held out toward the city
the javelin that was in his hand. 19As soon as he did this, the men in the ambush
rose quickly from their position and rushed forward. They entered the city and
captured it and quickly set it on fire.
20The men of Ai looked back and saw the smoke of the city rising up into the
sky, but they had no chance to escape in any direction; the Israelites who had
been fleeing toward the wilderness had turned back against their pursuers.

[a] 26 *Achor* means *trouble.*

[21]For when Joshua and all Israel saw that the ambush had taken the city and that smoke was going up from it, they turned around and attacked the men of Ai. [22]Those in the ambush also came out of the city against them, so that they were caught in the middle, with Israelites on both sides. Israel cut them down, leaving them neither survivors nor fugitives. [23]But they took the king of Ai alive and brought him to Joshua.

[24]When Israel had finished killing all the men of Ai in the fields and in the wilderness where they had chased them, and when every one of them had been put to the sword, all the Israelites returned to Ai and killed those who were in it. [25]Twelve thousand men and women fell that day—all the people of Ai. [26]For Joshua did not draw back the hand that held out his javelin until he had destroyed[a] all who lived in Ai. [27]But Israel did carry off for themselves the livestock and plunder of this city, as the LORD had instructed Joshua.

[28]So Joshua burned Ai[b] and made it a permanent heap of ruins, a desolate place to this day. [29]He impaled the body of the king of Ai on a pole and left it there until evening. At sunset, Joshua ordered them to take the body from the pole and throw it down at the entrance of the city gate. And they raised a large pile of rocks over it, which remains to this day.

The Covenant Renewed at Mount Ebal

[30]Then Joshua built on Mount Ebal an altar to the LORD, the God of Israel, [31]as Moses the servant of the LORD had commanded the Israelites. He built it according to what is written in the Book of the Law of Moses—an altar of uncut stones, on which no iron tool had been used. On it they offered to the LORD burnt offerings and sacrificed fellowship offerings. [32]There, in the presence of the Israelites, Joshua wrote on stones a copy of the law of Moses. [33]All the Israelites, with their elders, officials and judges, were standing on both sides of the ark of the covenant of the LORD, facing the Levitical priests who carried it. Both the foreigners living among them and the native-born were there. Half of the people stood in front of Mount Gerizim and half of them in front of Mount Ebal, as Moses the servant of the LORD had formerly commanded when he gave instructions to bless the people of Israel.

[34]Afterward, Joshua read all the words of the law—the blessings and the curses—just as it is written in the Book of the Law. [35]There was not a word of all that Moses had commanded that Joshua did not read to the whole assembly of Israel, including the women and children, and the foreigners who lived among them.

The Gibeonite Deception

9 Now when all the kings west of the Jordan heard about these things—the kings in the hill country, in the western foothills, and along the entire coast of the Mediterranean Sea as far as Lebanon (the kings of the Hittites, Amorites, Canaanites, Perizzites, Hivites and Jebusites)— [2]they came together to wage war against Joshua and Israel.

[3]However, when the people of Gibeon heard what Joshua had done to Jericho and Ai, [4]they resorted to a ruse: They went as a delegation whose donkeys were loaded[c] with worn-out sacks and old wineskins, cracked and mended. [5]They put worn and patched sandals on their feet and wore old clothes. All the bread of their food supply was dry and moldy. [6]Then they went to Joshua in the camp at Gilgal and said to him and the Israelites, "We have come from a distant country; make a treaty with us."

[7]The Israelites said to the Hivites, "But perhaps you live near us, so how can we make a treaty with you?"

[8]"We are your servants," they said to Joshua.

JOSHUA 8:30–35

OLD AND NEW COVENANTS

Joshua recounted the law of God given to Moses and established it as the ongoing standard response of God's people to his grace as they entered the land. This law, written on tablets of stone, was a God-given gift of grace to provide former slaves with the keys to the blessing and freedom found in obedience to God.

Paul later said that something far more incredible happened through the gift of salvation. The law is no longer contained on tablets of stone—now it is written on the human heart (2Co 3:3). The transformation brought about by God's saving grace should be demonstrated by those who claim to follow Jesus. This change is not the result of following an abstract set of external, moral principles but the working of the Spirit of God dwelling in the hearts of God's people. God, through the work of salvation, takes out a person's heart of stone and puts in its place a heart of flesh that pulsates with new life. On this new heart is written God's law—a miracle far greater than the Law given at Mount Sinai.

[a] *26* The Hebrew term refers to the irrevocable giving over of things or persons to the LORD, often by totally destroying them. [b] *28* *Ai* means *the ruin.* [c] *4* Most Hebrew manuscripts; some Hebrew manuscripts, Vulgate and Syriac (see also Septuagint) *They prepared provisions and loaded their donkeys*

But Joshua asked, "Who are you and where do you come from?"

9They answered: "Your servants have come from a very distant country because of the fame of the LORD your God. For we have heard reports of him: all that he did in Egypt, 10and all that he did to the two kings of the Amorites east of the Jordan — Sihon king of Heshbon, and Og king of Bashan, who reigned in Ashtaroth. 11And our elders and all those living in our country said to us, 'Take provisions for your journey; go and meet them and say to them, "We are your servants; make a treaty with us."' 12This bread of ours was warm when we packed it at home on the day we left to come to you. But now see how dry and moldy it is. 13And these wineskins that we filled were new, but see how cracked they are. And our clothes and sandals are worn out by the very long journey."

14The Israelites sampled their provisions but did not inquire of the LORD. 15Then Joshua made a treaty of peace with them to let them live, and the leaders of the assembly ratified it by oath.

16Three days after they made the treaty with the Gibeonites, the Israelites heard that they were neighbors, living near them. 17So the Israelites set out and on the third day came to their cities: Gibeon, Kephirah, Beeroth and Kiriath Jearim. 18But the Israelites did not attack them, because the leaders of the assembly had sworn an oath to them by the LORD, the God of Israel.

The whole assembly grumbled against the leaders, 19but all the leaders answered, "We have given them our oath by the LORD, the God of Israel, and we cannot touch them now. 20This is what we will do to them: We will let them live, so that God's wrath will not fall on us for breaking the oath we swore to them." 21They continued, "Let them live, but let them be woodcutters and water carriers in the service of the whole assembly." So the leaders' promise to them was kept.

22Then Joshua summoned the Gibeonites and said, "Why did you deceive us by saying, 'We live a long way from you,' while actually you live near us? 23You are now under a curse: You will never be released from service as woodcutters and water carriers for the house of my God."

24They answered Joshua, "Your servants were clearly told how the LORD your God had commanded his servant Moses to give you the whole land and to wipe out all its inhabitants from before you. So we feared for our lives because of you, and that is why we did this. 25We are now in your hands. Do to us whatever seems good and right to you."

26So Joshua saved them from the Israelites, and they did not kill them. 27That day he made the Gibeonites woodcutters and water carriers for the assembly, to provide for the needs of the altar of the LORD at the place the LORD would choose. And that is what they are to this day.

The Sun Stands Still

10

Now Adoni-Zedek king of Jerusalem heard that Joshua had taken Ai and totally destroyed[a] it, doing to Ai and its king as he had done to Jericho and its king, and that the people of Gibeon had made a treaty of peace with Israel and had become their allies. 2He and his people were very much alarmed at this, because Gibeon was an important city, like one of the royal cities; it was larger than Ai, and all its men were good fighters. 3So Adoni-Zedek king of Jerusalem appealed to Hoham king of Hebron, Piram king of Jarmuth, Japhia king of Lachish and Debir king of Eglon. 4"Come up and help me attack Gibeon," he said, "because it has made peace with Joshua and the Israelites."

5Then the five kings of the Amorites — the kings of Jerusalem, Hebron, Jarmuth, Lachish and Eglon — joined forces. They moved up with all their troops and took up positions against Gibeon and attacked it.

6The Gibeonites then sent word to Joshua in the camp at Gilgal: "Do not abandon your servants. Come up to us quickly and save us! Help us, because all the Amorite kings from the hill country have joined forces against us."

[a] *1* The Hebrew term refers to the irrevocable giving over of things or persons to the LORD, often by totally destroying them; also in verses 28, 35, 37, 39 and 40.

7So Joshua marched up from Gilgal with his entire army, including all the best fighting men. 8The LORD said to Joshua, "Do not be afraid of them; I have given them into your hand. Not one of them will be able to withstand you."

9After an all-night march from Gilgal, Joshua took them by surprise. 10The LORD threw them into confusion before Israel, so Joshua and the Israelites defeated them completely at Gibeon. Israel pursued them along the road going up to Beth Horon and cut them down all the way to Azekah and Makkedah. 11As they fled before Israel on the road down from Beth Horon to Azekah, the LORD hurled large hailstones down on them, and more of them died from the hail than were killed by the swords of the Israelites.

12On the day the LORD gave the Amorites over to Israel, Joshua said to the LORD in the presence of Israel:

"Sun, stand still over Gibeon,
  and you, moon, over the Valley of Aijalon."
13So the sun stood still,
  and the moon stopped,
  till the nation avenged itself on[a] its enemies,

as it is written in the Book of Jashar.

The sun stopped in the middle of the sky and delayed going down about a full day. 14There has never been a day like it before or since, a day when the LORD listened to a human being. Surely the LORD was fighting for Israel!

15Then Joshua returned with all Israel to the camp at Gilgal.

Five Amorite Kings Killed

16Now the five kings had fled and hidden in the cave at Makkedah. 17When Joshua was told that the five kings had been found hiding in the cave at Makkedah, 18he said, "Roll large rocks up to the mouth of the cave, and post some men there to guard it. 19But don't stop; pursue your enemies! Attack them from the rear and don't let them reach their cities, for the LORD your God has given them into your hand."

20So Joshua and the Israelites defeated them completely, but a few survivors managed to reach their fortified cities. 21The whole army then returned safely to Joshua in the camp at Makkedah, and no one uttered a word against the Israelites.

22Joshua said, "Open the mouth of the cave and bring those five kings out to me." 23So they brought the five kings out of the cave — the kings of Jerusalem, Hebron, Jarmuth, Lachish and Eglon. 24When they had brought these kings to Joshua, he summoned all the men of Israel and said to the army commanders who had come with him, "Come here and put your feet on the necks of these kings." So they came forward and placed their feet on their necks.

25Joshua said to them, "Do not be afraid; do not be discouraged. Be strong and courageous. This is what the LORD will do to all the enemies you are going to fight." 26Then Joshua put the kings to death and exposed their bodies on five poles, and they were left hanging on the poles until evening.

27At sunset Joshua gave the order and they took them down from the poles and threw them into the cave where they had been hiding. At the mouth of the cave they placed large rocks, which are there to this day.

Southern Cities Conquered

28That day Joshua took Makkedah. He put the city and its king to the sword and totally destroyed everyone in it. He left no survivors. And he did to the king of Makkedah as he had done to the king of Jericho.

29Then Joshua and all Israel with him moved on from Makkedah to Libnah and attacked it. 30The LORD also gave that city and its king into Israel's hand. The

[a] 13 Or *nation triumphed over*

THE SUN AND THE SON

God's continued control over creation was demonstrated by his ability to make the "sun stand still," v. 12. At Joshua's request, God showed his continued control over creation by extending daylight in order to aid Israel's victory in battle. Though we don't know exactly what happened, these miraculous events displayed God's ability to overcome darkness.

Not only can God overcome darkness in his created order, but he also has the power to banish the darkness of sin from the human heart (Eph 1:18). God overcame human blindness and grants his children the ability to see the light of his glory, seen most clearly in the person of Jesus (2Co 4:4). Those who see Jesus and respond in faith are transformed to reflect his image before the world.

John began his Gospel by claiming that Jesus was the light of God in human form — a light that came to push back the darkness of a world blinded by sin (Jn 1:1 – 14). John wrote, however, that people — because of sin — are unable or unwilling to see the light of Jesus; as a result, they choose to remain in the darkness.

So what did Jesus do? He entered the darkness and experienced it in order to overcome it. The scene at the cross testified to this reality. For three hours in the middle of the day while Jesus hung beaten and naked on a Roman cross, darkness filled the land (Mt 27:45; Lk 23:44). The entire cosmos testified to the fact that the wrath of God against human sin was being poured out on Jesus. At this point, few would have thought that this work was a means of ushering in the light of the glory of the kingdom of God as a crucified Savior hung on a Roman cross in darkness. But God knew that this was the only way to bring those trapped in darkness into the light. The Son of God had to endure darkness for them so that they could come with him into his kingdom of light (Col 1:13). After three days in a dark tomb, Jesus emerged into the light demonstrating that he overcame the darkness of sin. His resurrection was the firstfruits of all those who, like Jesus, will experience the joy of life in the light and the glory of the resurrection (1Co 15:20).

city and everyone in it Joshua put to the sword. He left no survivors there. And he
did to its king as he had done to the king of Jericho.
31Then Joshua and all Israel with him moved on from Libnah to Lachish; he
took up positions against it and attacked it. 32The LORD gave Lachish into Israel's
hands, and Joshua took it on the second day. The city and everyone in it he put
to the sword, just as he had done to Libnah. 33Meanwhile, Horam king of Gezer
had come up to help Lachish, but Joshua defeated him and his army — until no
survivors were left.
34Then Joshua and all Israel with him moved on from Lachish to Eglon; they
took up positions against it and attacked it. 35They captured it that same day and
put it to the sword and totally destroyed everyone in it, just as they had done to
Lachish.
36Then Joshua and all Israel with him went up from Eglon to Hebron and attacked it. 37They took the city and put it to the sword, together with its king, its
villages and everyone in it. They left no survivors. Just as at Eglon, they totally
destroyed it and everyone in it.
38Then Joshua and all Israel with him turned around and attacked Debir.
39They took the city, its king and its villages, and put them to the sword. Everyone in it they totally destroyed. They left no survivors. They did to Debir and its
king as they had done to Libnah and its king and to Hebron.
40So Joshua subdued the whole region, including the hill country, the Negev,
the western foothills and the mountain slopes, together with all their kings. He
left no survivors. He totally destroyed all who breathed, just as the LORD, the
God of Israel, had commanded. 41Joshua subdued them from Kadesh Barnea to
Gaza and from the whole region of Goshen to Gibeon. 42All these kings and their
lands Joshua conquered in one campaign, because the LORD, the God of Israel,
fought for Israel.
43Then Joshua returned with all Israel to the camp at Gilgal.

Northern Kings Defeated

11 When Jabin king of Hazor heard of this, he sent word to Jobab king of Ma-
don, to the kings of Shimron and Akshaph, 2and to the northern kings who
were in the mountains, in the Arabah south of Kinnereth, in the western foothills and in Naphoth Dor on the west; 3to the Canaanites in the east and west;
to the Amorites, Hittites, Perizzites and Jebusites in the hill country; and to the
Hivites below Hermon in the region of Mizpah. 4They came out with all their
troops and a large number of horses and chariots — a huge army, as numerous as
the sand on the seashore. 5All these kings joined forces and made camp together
at the Waters of Merom to fight against Israel.
6The LORD said to Joshua, "Do not be afraid of them, because by this time tomorrow I will hand all of them, slain, over to Israel. You are to hamstring their
horses and burn their chariots."
7So Joshua and his whole army came against them suddenly at the Waters
of Merom and attacked them, 8and the LORD gave them into the hand of Israel.
They defeated them and pursued them all the way to Greater Sidon, to Misre-
photh Maim, and to the Valley of Mizpah on the east, until no survivors were
left. 9Joshua did to them as the LORD had directed: He hamstrung their horses
and burned their chariots.
10At that time Joshua turned back and captured Hazor and put its king to the
sword. (Hazor had been the head of all these kingdoms.) 11Everyone in it they put
to the sword. They totally destroyed[a] them, not sparing anyone that breathed,
and he burned Hazor itself.
12Joshua took all these royal cities and their kings and put them to the sword.
He totally destroyed them, as Moses the servant of the LORD had commanded.

[a] *11* The Hebrew term refers to the irrevocable giving over of things or persons to the LORD, often by totally destroying them; also in verses 12, 20 and 21.

13 Yet Israel did not burn any of the cities built on their mounds — except Hazor, which Joshua burned. 14 The Israelites carried off for themselves all the plunder and livestock of these cities, but all the people they put to the sword until they completely destroyed them, not sparing anyone that breathed. 15 As the LORD commanded his servant Moses, so Moses commanded Joshua, and Joshua did it; he left nothing undone of all that the LORD commanded Moses.

16 So Joshua took this entire land: the hill country, all the Negev, the whole region of Goshen, the western foothills, the Arabah and the mountains of Israel with their foothills, 17 from Mount Halak, which rises toward Seir, to Baal Gad in the Valley of Lebanon below Mount Hermon. He captured all their kings and put them to death. 18 Joshua waged war against all these kings for a long time. 19 Except for the Hivites living in Gibeon, not one city made a treaty of peace with the Israelites, who took them all in battle. 20 For it was the LORD himself who hardened their hearts to wage war against Israel, so that he might destroy them totally, exterminating them without mercy, as the LORD had commanded Moses.

21 At that time Joshua went and destroyed the Anakites from the hill country: from Hebron, Debir and Anab, from all the hill country of Judah, and from all the hill country of Israel. Joshua totally destroyed them and their towns. 22 No Anakites were left in Israelite territory; only in Gaza, Gath and Ashdod did any survive.

23 So Joshua took the entire land, just as the LORD had directed Moses, and he gave it as an inheritance to Israel according to their tribal divisions. Then the land had rest from war.

List of Defeated Kings

12 These are the kings of the land whom the Israelites had defeated and whose territory they took over east of the Jordan, from the Arnon Gorge to Mount Hermon, including all the eastern side of the Arabah:

2 Sihon king of the Amorites, who reigned in Heshbon.
He ruled from Aroer on the rim of the Arnon Gorge — from the middle of the gorge — to the Jabbok River, which is the border of the Ammonites. This included half of Gilead. 3 He also ruled over the eastern Arabah from the Sea of Galilee[a] to the Sea of the Arabah (that is, the Dead Sea), to Beth Jeshimoth, and then southward below the slopes of Pisgah.

4 And the territory of Og king of Bashan, one of the last of the Rephaites, who reigned in Ashtaroth and Edrei.
5 He ruled over Mount Hermon, Salekah, all of Bashan to the border of the people of Geshur and Maakah, and half of Gilead to the border of Sihon king of Heshbon.

6 Moses, the servant of the LORD, and the Israelites conquered them. And Moses the servant of the LORD gave their land to the Reubenites, the Gadites and the half-tribe of Manasseh to be their possession.

7 Here is a list of the kings of the land that Joshua and the Israelites conquered on the west side of the Jordan, from Baal Gad in the Valley of Lebanon to Mount Halak, which rises toward Seir. Joshua gave their lands as an inheritance to the tribes of Israel according to their tribal divisions. 8 The lands included the hill country, the western foothills, the Arabah, the mountain slopes, the wilderness and the Negev. These were the lands of the Hittites, Amorites, Canaanites, Perizzites, Hivites and Jebusites. These were the kings:

9 the king of Jericho	one
the king of Ai (near Bethel)	one
10 the king of Jerusalem	one
the king of Hebron	one

[a] 3 Hebrew *Kinnereth*

JOSHUA 12:1 – 24

TRIUMPH

Joshua 12 recounts a list of kings that Israel has defeated. The list goes into great detail by not only giving the names of the defeated kings, but also going to great length to describe the land over which the defeated kings previously ruled. The vast size of this territory is a testament to God's ability to conquer great kings and great lands.

These victories are minor in comparison to the far greater victory won by Jesus himself. He did not simply win a battle against a pagan king, but he defeated Satan, sin and the principalities of darkness. He did not merely conquer a portion of land, but he secured his rule and reign over all the earth (Eph 1:21 – 22). While the list of kings and land in Joshua 12 may appear large and valuable to people, Jesus was not inclined to accept temporal kingdoms as his victory (Mt 4:8 – 10). By virtue of Jesus' work, he is worthy of all honor, fame and glory forever. All things, both in heaven and on earth, both temporal and cosmic, both now and forever, are placed under his kingly rule. This list of victories may be "great," but it pales in comparison to the ultimate victory of Jesus.

[11] the king of Jarmuth	one
the king of Lachish	one
[12] the king of Eglon	one
the king of Gezer	one
[13] the king of Debir	one
the king of Geder	one
[14] the king of Hormah	one
the king of Arad	one
[15] the king of Libnah	one
the king of Adullam	one
[16] the king of Makkedah	one
the king of Bethel	one
[17] the king of Tappuah	one
the king of Hepher	one
[18] the king of Aphek	one
the king of Lasharon	one
[19] the king of Madon	one
the king of Hazor	one
[20] the king of Shimron Meron	one
the king of Akshaph	one
[21] the king of Taanach	one
the king of Megiddo	one
[22] the king of Kedesh	one
the king of Jokneam in Carmel	one
[23] the king of Dor (in Naphoth Dor)	one
the king of Goyim in Gilgal	one
[24] the king of Tirzah	one
	thirty-one kings in all.

Land Still to Be Taken

13 When Joshua had grown old, the LORD said to him, "You are now very old,
and there are still very large areas of land to be taken over.

[2] "This is the land that remains: all the regions of the Philistines and Geshurites, [3] from the Shihor River on the east of Egypt to the territory of Ekron
on the north, all of it counted as Canaanite though held by the five Philistine rulers in Gaza, Ashdod, Ashkelon, Gath and Ekron; the territory of
the Avvites [4] on the south; all the land of the Canaanites, from Arah of the
Sidonians as far as Aphek and the border of the Amorites; [5] the area of Byblos; and all Lebanon to the east, from Baal Gad below Mount Hermon to
Lebo Hamath.

[6] "As for all the inhabitants of the mountain regions from Lebanon to Misre-
photh Maim, that is, all the Sidonians, I myself will drive them out before the
Israelites. Be sure to allocate this land to Israel for an inheritance, as I have instructed you, [7] and divide it as an inheritance among the nine tribes and half of
the tribe of Manasseh."

Division of the Land East of the Jordan

[8] The other half of Manasseh,[a] the Reubenites and the Gadites had received the
inheritance that Moses had given them east of the Jordan, as he, the servant of
the LORD, had assigned it to them.

[9] It extended from Aroer on the rim of the Arnon Gorge, and from the town
in the middle of the gorge, and included the whole plateau of Medeba as far
as Dibon, [10] and all the towns of Sihon king of the Amorites, who ruled in
Heshbon, out to the border of the Ammonites. [11] It also included Gilead, the

[a] 8 Hebrew *With it* (that is, with the other half of Manasseh)

JOSHUA 13:8

INHERITANCE

The word *inheritance* refers to a possession or property that is given to an heir. Throughout the Old Testament, the word was linked to God's faithfulness to give the people the things he had promised them. Specifically here, Joshua referred to the giving of a parcel of land that God had long ago pledged to the descendants of Abraham. God, as the owner of all things, can bequeath anything he desires to his children as a gift of his grace.

The nature of the promised inheritance extends far beyond a piece of land. The inheritance of God is most clearly seen in him giving of himself to his people (Ps 16:5–6; Jer 10:16). He is the real gift of grace. In his kindness, God allows his people to know him and fellowship with him in spite of their sin. The gift of God makes every gift the fallen world can offer pale in comparison. Those who know the nature of the glorious inheritance in Christ (Col 1:12; 2:3) can relinquish the promises of a fallen world and treasure the far greater gift of knowing God (1Pe 1:4).

territory of the people of Geshur and Maakah, all of Mount Hermon and all
Bashan as far as Salekah— 12that is, the whole kingdom of Og in Bashan,
who had reigned in Ashtaroth and Edrei. (He was the last of the Rephaites.)
Moses had defeated them and taken over their land. 13But the Israelites did
not drive out the people of Geshur and Maakah, so they continue to live
among the Israelites to this day.

14But to the tribe of Levi he gave no inheritance, since the food offerings presented to the LORD, the God of Israel, are their inheritance, as he promised them.

15This is what Moses had given to the tribe of Reuben, according to its clans:

16The territory from Aroer on the rim of the Arnon Gorge, and from the
town in the middle of the gorge, and the whole plateau past Medeba 17to
Heshbon and all its towns on the plateau, including Dibon, Bamoth Baal,
Beth Baal Meon, 18Jahaz, Kedemoth, Mephaath, 19Kiriathaim, Sibmah, Zereth Shahar on the hill in the valley, 20Beth Peor, the slopes of Pisgah, and
Beth Jeshimoth— 21all the towns on the plateau and the entire realm of Sihon king of the Amorites, who ruled at Heshbon. Moses had defeated him
and the Midianite chiefs, Evi, Rekem, Zur, Hur and Reba—princes allied
with Sihon—who lived in that country. 22In addition to those slain in battle, the Israelites had put to the sword Balaam son of Beor, who practiced
divination. 23The boundary of the Reubenites was the bank of the Jordan.
These towns and their villages were the inheritance of the Reubenites, according to their clans.

24This is what Moses had given to the tribe of Gad, according to its clans:

25The territory of Jazer, all the towns of Gilead and half the Ammonite
country as far as Aroer, near Rabbah; 26and from Heshbon to Ramath Mizpah and Betonim, and from Mahanaim to the territory of Debir; 27and in
the valley, Beth Haram, Beth Nimrah, Sukkoth and Zaphon with the rest of
the realm of Sihon king of Heshbon (the east side of the Jordan, the territory
up to the end of the Sea of Galilee[a]). 28These towns and their villages were
the inheritance of the Gadites, according to their clans.

29This is what Moses had given to the half-tribe of Manasseh, that is, to half the
family of the descendants of Manasseh, according to its clans:

30The territory extending from Mahanaim and including all of Bashan, the
entire realm of Og king of Bashan—all the settlements of Jair in Bashan,
sixty towns, 31half of Gilead, and Ashtaroth and Edrei (the royal cities of Og
in Bashan). This was for the descendants of Makir son of Manasseh—for
half of the sons of Makir, according to their clans.

32This is the inheritance Moses had given when he was in the plains of Moab
across the Jordan east of Jericho. 33But to the tribe of Levi, Moses had given no inheritance; the LORD, the God of Israel, is their inheritance, as he promised them.

Division of the Land West of the Jordan

14 Now these are the areas the Israelites received as an inheritance in the
land of Canaan, which Eleazar the priest, Joshua son of Nun and the heads
of the tribal clans of Israel allotted to them. 2Their inheritances were assigned
by lot to the nine and a half tribes, as the LORD had commanded through Moses.
3Moses had granted the two and a half tribes their inheritance east of the Jordan but had not granted the Levites an inheritance among the rest, 4for Joseph's
descendants had become two tribes—Manasseh and Ephraim. The Levites received no share of the land but only towns to live in, with pasturelands for their
flocks and herds. 5So the Israelites divided the land, just as the LORD had commanded Moses.

[a] 27 Hebrew *Kinnereth*

CANAAN

The biblical authors portrayed the land of Canaan with a vast array of imagery. The land flowed "with milk and honey," symbolic of the lavish provision of God for his people (Ex 33:3). The land was also a land of peace (*shalom*). In the land of the promise and in contrast to the effects of the curse of sin, the people were meant to live free from the destruction caused by war. Finally, the land allowed the people to worship God, live under his rule and experience fellowship with him. Whereas Adam and Eve walked with God in the cool of the day in the garden, now God's people could walk with him and experience his grace once again. For these reasons the land of Canaan served as a type of Garden of Eden.

Not only did Canaan point backward to the Garden of Eden, but it also pointed forward to a far greater reality. The blessing, peace and fellowship meant to be experienced in the land would be a fleeting reality. Sin hampered Israel's experience of the land's beauty and ultimately caused the people to be banished from the land at the hands of the Assyrians and Babylonians. The people were forced to look forward to a better day, a day when these realities could be experienced fully and finally.

John's vision in Revelation 21 points forward to the hope of the coming kingdom of God for those who have experienced the grace of God. John pictured "a new heaven and a new earth" using similar themes. The blessings of God will be experienced in previously unknown ways. The greatest images the human mind can conjure — streets made of gold and walls made of precious stones — were used by John to describe this coming reality. In addition, the peace of God will also reign over all. No longer will war and disease contaminate God's world. There will be lasting peace, and, as a result, there will be no more tears, no more division and no more pain. Finally, God's rule and reign will be perfectly experienced on earth as it is in heaven. Christians today cry, "Come, Lord Jesus" knowing that this is the only hope for experiencing God's blessing, peace and presence perfectly and forever (Rev 22:20).

Allotment for Caleb

6 Now the people of Judah approached Joshua at Gilgal, and Caleb son of Jephunneh the Kenizzite said to him, "You know what the LORD said to Moses the
man of God at Kadesh Barnea about you and me. 7 I was forty years old when Moses the servant of the LORD sent me from Kadesh Barnea to explore the land. And
I brought him back a report according to my convictions, 8 but my fellow Israelites
who went up with me made the hearts of the people melt in fear. I, however, followed the LORD my God wholeheartedly. 9 So on that day Moses swore to me, 'The
land on which your feet have walked will be your inheritance and that of your
children forever, because you have followed the LORD my God wholeheartedly.'[a]
10 "Now then, just as the LORD promised, he has kept me alive for forty-five
years since the time he said this to Moses, while Israel moved about in the wilderness. So here I am today, eighty-five years old! 11 I am still as strong today as
the day Moses sent me out; I'm just as vigorous to go out to battle now as I was
then. 12 Now give me this hill country that the LORD promised me that day. You
yourself heard then that the Anakites were there and their cities were large and
fortified, but, the LORD helping me, I will drive them out just as he said."
13 Then Joshua blessed Caleb son of Jephunneh and gave him Hebron as his
inheritance. 14 So Hebron has belonged to Caleb son of Jephunneh the Kenizzite ever since, because he followed the LORD, the God of Israel, wholeheartedly.
15 (Hebron used to be called Kiriath Arba after Arba, who was the greatest man
among the Anakites.)

Then the land had rest from war.

Allotment for Judah

15 The allotment for the tribe of Judah, according to its clans, extended down
to the territory of Edom, to the Desert of Zin in the extreme south.
2 Their southern boundary started from the bay at the southern end of
the Dead Sea, 3 crossed south of Scorpion Pass, continued on to Zin and
went over to the south of Kadesh Barnea. Then it ran past Hezron up to
Addar and curved around to Karka. 4 It then passed along to Azmon and
joined the Wadi of Egypt, ending at the Mediterranean Sea. This is their[b]
southern boundary.
5 The eastern boundary is the Dead Sea as far as the mouth of the Jordan.

The northern boundary started from the bay of the sea at the mouth of
the Jordan, 6 went up to Beth Hoglah and continued north of Beth Arabah
to the Stone of Bohan son of Reuben. 7 The boundary then went up to Debir
from the Valley of Achor and turned north to Gilgal, which faces the Pass
of Adummim south of the gorge. It continued along to the waters of En Shemesh and came out at En Rogel. 8 Then it ran up the Valley of Ben Hinnom
along the southern slope of the Jebusite city (that is, Jerusalem). From there
it climbed to the top of the hill west of the Hinnom Valley at the northern
end of the Valley of Rephaim. 9 From the hilltop the boundary headed toward the spring of the waters of Nephtoah, came out at the towns of Mount
Ephron and went down toward Baalah (that is, Kiriath Jearim). 10 Then it
curved westward from Baalah to Mount Seir, ran along the northern slope
of Mount Jearim (that is, Kesalon), continued down to Beth Shemesh and
crossed to Timnah. 11 It went to the northern slope of Ekron, turned toward Shikkeron, passed along to Mount Baalah and reached Jabneel. The
boundary ended at the sea.
12 The western boundary is the coastline of the Mediterranean Sea.

These are the boundaries around the people of Judah by their clans.

13 In accordance with the LORD's command to him, Joshua gave to Caleb son
of Jephunneh a portion in Judah—Kiriath Arba, that is, Hebron. (Arba was the

[a] 9 Deut. 1:36 [b] 4 Septuagint; Hebrew *your*

JOSHUA 14:6–9

CALEB

Caleb, because of his faithfulness and obedience to God, was given entrance into the land and the glorious inheritance God pledged to his people—a gift that was squandered by those of Caleb's generation. Over the ensuing decades, Caleb watched as all of his contemporaries died in the wilderness. Surely Caleb doubted the promise of God as he wandered in the wilderness, observed the hard-heartedness of the people and watched person after person die under the judgment of God. Would God be faithful to give the people this long-awaited land? If so, would he remember Caleb and grant him an inheritance among the people?

Like Caleb, Christians today await the fulfillment of God's promises. In a fallen world, it can be easy to question whether God's plan is unfolding as intended, whether Christ will return and whether he will remember his children when he does. The faithfulness of God to remember Caleb serves as an encouragement of God's care for every person who longs for his coming (2Pe 3:11–13).

forefather of Anak.) [14]From Hebron Caleb drove out the three Anakites — Sheshai, Ahiman and Talmai, the sons of Anak. [15]From there he marched against the people living in Debir (formerly called Kiriath Sepher). [16]And Caleb said, "I will give my daughter Aksah in marriage to the man who attacks and captures Kiriath Sepher." [17]Othniel son of Kenaz, Caleb's brother, took it; so Caleb gave his daughter Aksah to him in marriage.

[18]One day when she came to Othniel, she urged him[a] to ask her father for a field. When she got off her donkey, Caleb asked her, "What can I do for you?"

[19]She replied, "Do me a special favor. Since you have given me land in the Negev, give me also springs of water." So Caleb gave her the upper and lower springs.

[20]This is the inheritance of the tribe of Judah, according to its clans:

[21]The southernmost towns of the tribe of Judah in the Negev toward the boundary of Edom were:

Kabzeel, Eder, Jagur, [22]Kinah, Dimonah, Adadah, [23]Kedesh, Hazor, Ithnan, [24]Ziph, Telem, Bealoth, [25]Hazor Hadattah, Kerioth Hezron (that is, Hazor), [26]Amam, Shema, Moladah, [27]Hazar Gaddah, Heshmon, Beth Pelet, [28]Hazar Shual, Beersheba, Biziothiah, [29]Baalah, Iyim, Ezem, [30]Eltolad, Kesil, Hormah, [31]Ziklag, Madmannah, Sansannah, [32]Lebaoth, Shilhim, Ain and Rimmon — a total of twenty-nine towns and their villages.

[33]In the western foothills:

Eshtaol, Zorah, Ashnah, [34]Zanoah, En Gannim, Tappuah, Enam, [35]Jarmuth, Adullam, Sokoh, Azekah, [36]Shaaraim, Adithaim and Gederah (or Gederothaim)[b] — fourteen towns and their villages.

[37]Zenan, Hadashah, Migdal Gad, [38]Dilean, Mizpah, Joktheel, [39]Lachish, Bozkath, Eglon, [40]Kabbon, Lahmas, Kitlish, [41]Gederoth, Beth Dagon, Naamah and Makkedah — sixteen towns and their villages.

[42]Libnah, Ether, Ashan, [43]Iphtah, Ashnah, Nezib, [44]Keilah, Akzib and Mareshah — nine towns and their villages.

[45]Ekron, with its surrounding settlements and villages; [46]west of Ekron, all that were in the vicinity of Ashdod, together with their villages; [47]Ashdod, its surrounding settlements and villages; and Gaza, its settlements and villages, as far as the Wadi of Egypt and the coastline of the Mediterranean Sea.

[48]In the hill country:

Shamir, Jattir, Sokoh, [49]Dannah, Kiriath Sannah (that is, Debir), [50]Anab, Eshtemoh, Anim, [51]Goshen, Holon and Giloh — eleven towns and their villages.

[52]Arab, Dumah, Eshan, [53]Janim, Beth Tappuah, Aphekah, [54]Humtah, Kiriath Arba (that is, Hebron) and Zior — nine towns and their villages.

[55]Maon, Carmel, Ziph, Juttah, [56]Jezreel, Jokdeam, Zanoah, [57]Kain, Gibeah and Timnah — ten towns and their villages.

[58]Halhul, Beth Zur, Gedor, [59]Maarath, Beth Anoth and Eltekon — six towns and their villages.[c]

[60]Kiriath Baal (that is, Kiriath Jearim) and Rabbah — two towns and their villages.

[61]In the wilderness:

Beth Arabah, Middin, Sekakah, [62]Nibshan, the City of Salt and En Gedi — six towns and their villages.

[63]Judah could not dislodge the Jebusites, who were living in Jerusalem; to this day the Jebusites live there with the people of Judah.

---

[a] *18* Hebrew and some Septuagint manuscripts; other Septuagint manuscripts (see also note at Judges 1:14) *Othniel, he urged her* [b] *36* Or *Gederah and Gederothaim* [c] *59* The Septuagint adds another district of eleven towns, including Tekoa and Ephrathah (Bethlehem).

Allotment for Ephraim and Manasseh

16 The allotment for Joseph began at the Jordan, east of the springs
of Jericho, and went up from there through the desert into the hill
country of Bethel. 2It went on from Bethel (that is, Luz),[a] crossed over to the
territory of the Arkites in Ataroth, 3descended westward to the territory of
the Japhletites as far as the region of Lower Beth Horon and on to Gezer,
ending at the Mediterranean Sea.
4So Manasseh and Ephraim, the descendants of Joseph, received their inheritance.

5This was the territory of Ephraim, according to its clans:

The boundary of their inheritance went from Ataroth Addar in the east
to Upper Beth Horon 6and continued to the Mediterranean Sea. From Mikmethath on the north it curved eastward to Taanath Shiloh, passing by it
to Janoah on the east. 7Then it went down from Janoah to Ataroth and Naarah, touched Jericho and came out at the Jordan. 8From Tappuah the border went west to the Kanah Ravine and ended at the Mediterranean Sea.
This was the inheritance of the tribe of the Ephraimites, according to its
clans. 9It also included all the towns and their villages that were set aside
for the Ephraimites within the inheritance of the Manassites.
10They did not dislodge the Canaanites living in Gezer; to this day the Canaanites live among the people of Ephraim but are required to do forced labor.

17 This was the allotment for the tribe of Manasseh as Joseph's firstborn, that
is, for Makir, Manasseh's firstborn. Makir was the ancestor of the Gileadites, who had received Gilead and Bashan because the Makirites were great soldiers. 2So this allotment was for the rest of the people of Manasseh — the clans of
Abiezer, Helek, Asriel, Shechem, Hepher and Shemida. These are the other male
descendants of Manasseh son of Joseph by their clans.

3Now Zelophehad son of Hepher, the son of Gilead, the son of Makir, the
son of Manasseh, had no sons but only daughters, whose names were Mahlah,
Noah, Hoglah, Milkah and Tirzah. 4They went to Eleazar the priest, Joshua son
of Nun, and the leaders and said, "The LORD commanded Moses to give us an
inheritance among our relatives." So Joshua gave them an inheritance along
with the brothers of their father, according to the LORD's command. 5Manas-
seh's share consisted of ten tracts of land besides Gilead and Bashan east of the
Jordan, 6because the daughters of the tribe of Manasseh received an inheritance among the sons. The land of Gilead belonged to the rest of the descendants of Manasseh.

7The territory of Manasseh extended from Asher to Mikmethath east of
Shechem. The boundary ran southward from there to include the people
living at En Tappuah. 8(Manasseh had the land of Tappuah, but Tappuah
itself, on the boundary of Manasseh, belonged to the Ephraimites.) 9Then
the boundary continued south to the Kanah Ravine. There were towns belonging to Ephraim lying among the towns of Manasseh, but the boundary
of Manasseh was the northern side of the ravine and ended at the Mediterranean Sea. 10On the south the land belonged to Ephraim, on the north to
Manasseh. The territory of Manasseh reached the Mediterranean Sea and
bordered Asher on the north and Issachar on the east.

11Within Issachar and Asher, Manasseh also had Beth Shan, Ibleam and
the people of Dor, Endor, Taanach and Megiddo, together with their surrounding settlements (the third in the list is Naphoth[b]).
12Yet the Manassites were not able to occupy these towns, for the Canaanites
were determined to live in that region. 13However, when the Israelites grew
stronger, they subjected the Canaanites to forced labor but did not drive them
out completely.

[a] 2 Septuagint; Hebrew *Bethel to Luz* [b] 11 That is, Naphoth Dor

---

JOSHUA 16:1–4

PROVISION FOR THE TRIBES

God fulfilled his promise by giving an allotment of the land to each of the tribes of Israel (Nu 33:54). Among a huge mass of humanity, God took care to provide for each of the tribes and, consequently, each of the families making up these tribes. The sovereign King of the universe takes personal care of each person who is the recipient of his promise. Two and a half tribes were given land on the east side of the Jordan, while the remaining nine and a half tribes were given territory west of the Jordan.

Jesus also made a remarkable claim recorded in John's Gospel. He compared himself to a Good Shepherd who would ultimately lay down his life to demonstrate his love and care for his sheep. This shepherding care is seen in the personal attention he gives to each of his sheep. The sheep's ability to hear and respond to the shepherd's voice demonstrates their knowledge of him. He calls his sheep, not as a group, but individually — by name. God also keeps those whom he calls, and he will not let any enemy snatch them from his hand (Jn 10:1–29).

[14]The people of Joseph said to Joshua, "Why have you given us only one allotment and one portion for an inheritance? We are a numerous people, and the LORD has blessed us abundantly."

[15]"If you are so numerous," Joshua answered, "and if the hill country of Ephraim is too small for you, go up into the forest and clear land for yourselves there in the land of the Perizzites and Rephaites."

[16]The people of Joseph replied, "The hill country is not enough for us, and all the Canaanites who live in the plain have chariots fitted with iron, both those in Beth Shan and its settlements and those in the Valley of Jezreel."

[17]But Joshua said to the tribes of Joseph — to Ephraim and Manasseh — "You are numerous and very powerful. You will have not only one allotment [18]but the forested hill country as well. Clear it, and its farthest limits will be yours; though the Canaanites have chariots fitted with iron and though they are strong, you can drive them out."

Division of the Rest of the Land

18 The whole assembly of the Israelites gathered at Shiloh and set up the tent of meeting there. The country was brought under their control, [2]but there were still seven Israelite tribes who had not yet received their inheritance.

[3]So Joshua said to the Israelites: "How long will you wait before you begin to take possession of the land that the LORD, the God of your ancestors, has given you? [4]Appoint three men from each tribe. I will send them out to make a survey of the land and to write a description of it, according to the inheritance of each. Then they will return to me. [5]You are to divide the land into seven parts. Judah is to remain in its territory on the south and the tribes of Joseph in their territory on the north. [6]After you have written descriptions of the seven parts of the land, bring them here to me and I will cast lots for you in the presence of the LORD our God. [7]The Levites, however, do not get a portion among you, because the priestly service of the LORD is their inheritance. And Gad, Reuben and the half-tribe of Manasseh have already received their inheritance on the east side of the Jordan. Moses the servant of the LORD gave it to them."

[8]As the men started on their way to map out the land, Joshua instructed them, "Go and make a survey of the land and write a description of it. Then return to me, and I will cast lots for you here at Shiloh in the presence of the LORD." [9]So the men left and went through the land. They wrote its description on a scroll, town by town, in seven parts, and returned to Joshua in the camp at Shiloh. [10]Joshua then cast lots for them in Shiloh in the presence of the LORD, and there he distributed the land to the Israelites according to their tribal divisions.

Allotment for Benjamin

[11]The first lot came up for the tribe of Benjamin according to its clans. Their allotted territory lay between the tribes of Judah and Joseph:

[12]On the north side their boundary began at the Jordan, passed the northern slope of Jericho and headed west into the hill country, coming out at the wilderness of Beth Aven. [13]From there it crossed to the south slope of Luz (that is, Bethel) and went down to Ataroth Addar on the hill south of Lower Beth Horon.

[14]From the hill facing Beth Horon on the south the boundary turned south along the western side and came out at Kiriath Baal (that is, Kiriath Jearim), a town of the people of Judah. This was the western side.

[15]The southern side began at the outskirts of Kiriath Jearim on the west, and the boundary came out at the spring of the waters of Nephtoah. [16]The boundary went down to the foot of the hill facing the Valley of Ben Hinnom, north of the Valley of Rephaim. It continued down the Hinnom Valley along the southern slope of the Jebusite city and so to En Rogel. [17]It then curved north, went to En Shemesh, continued to Geliloth, which faces the

---

JOSHUA 18:1 – 10

BLESSINGS OF FAITHFULNESS

This scene was eerily reminiscent of the sending of the spies in Numbers 13, except this time the result was more favorable. This time emissaries of the nation went throughout the promised land to map out the territory allotted to the seven tribes who had not yet received their land. There they saw the glorious inheritance that God would give to the nation. The land would testify to the faithfulness of God and demonstrate that he was continuing to accomplish his mission.

The church functions in the same way today. As believers gather in local churches around the world, they see a tangible picture of the grace of God. He is still at work, granting salvation to the lost and uniting them together into his family. Local churches, filled with believers, put the manifold wisdom of God on display for a watching world. The mystery of his grace, hidden for generations yet revealed in the person of Jesus, is evident for all to see (Eph 3:8 – 11). He is indeed faithful to bless his people, on earth and ultimately in heaven.

Pass of Adummim, and ran down to the Stone of Bohan son of Reuben. [18]It
continued to the northern slope of Beth Arabah[a] and on down into the Arabah. [19]It then went to the northern slope of Beth Hoglah and came out at
the northern bay of the Dead Sea, at the mouth of the Jordan in the south.
This was the southern boundary.

[20]The Jordan formed the boundary on the eastern side.

These were the boundaries that marked out the inheritance of the clans of Benjamin on all sides.

[21]The tribe of Benjamin, according to its clans, had the following towns:
Jericho, Beth Hoglah, Emek Keziz, [22]Beth Arabah, Zemaraim, Bethel,
[23]Avvim, Parah, Ophrah, [24]Kephar Ammoni, Ophni and Geba—twelve
towns and their villages.

[25]Gibeon, Ramah, Beeroth, [26]Mizpah, Kephirah, Mozah, [27]Rekem, Irpe-
el, Taralah, [28]Zelah, Haeleph, the Jebusite city (that is, Jerusalem), Gibeah
and Kiriath—fourteen towns and their villages.

This was the inheritance of Benjamin for its clans.

Allotment for Simeon

19 The second lot came out for the tribe of Simeon according to its clans.
Their inheritance lay within the territory of Judah. [2]It included:
Beersheba (or Sheba),[b] Moladah, [3]Hazar Shual, Balah, Ezem, [4]Eltolad,
Bethul, Hormah, [5]Ziklag, Beth Markaboth, Hazar Susah, [6]Beth Lebaoth
and Sharuhen—thirteen towns and their villages;

[7]Ain, Rimmon, Ether and Ashan—four towns and their villages— [8]and
all the villages around these towns as far as Baalath Beer (Ramah in the
Negev).

This was the inheritance of the tribe of the Simeonites, according to its clans.
[9]The inheritance of the Simeonites was taken from the share of Judah, because
Judah's portion was more than they needed. So the Simeonites received their
inheritance within the territory of Judah.

Allotment for Zebulun

[10]The third lot came up for Zebulun according to its clans:
The boundary of their inheritance went as far as Sarid. [11]Going west
it ran to Maralah, touched Dabbesheth, and extended to the ravine near
Jokneam. [12]It turned east from Sarid toward the sunrise to the territory of
Kisloth Tabor and went on to Daberath and up to Japhia. [13]Then it contin-
ued eastward to Gath Hepher and Eth Kazin; it came out at Rimmon and
turned toward Neah. [14]There the boundary went around on the north to
Hannathon and ended at the Valley of Iphtah El. [15]Included were Kattath,
Nahalal, Shimron, Idalah and Bethlehem. There were twelve towns and
their villages.

[16]These towns and their villages were the inheritance of Zebulun, according to
its clans.

Allotment for Issachar

[17]The fourth lot came out for Issachar according to its clans. [18]Their territory
included:
Jezreel, Kesulloth, Shunem, [19]Hapharaim, Shion, Anaharath, [20]Rabbith,
Kishion, Ebez, [21]Remeth, En Gannim, En Haddah and Beth Pazzez. [22]The
boundary touched Tabor, Shahazumah and Beth Shemesh, and ended at
the Jordan. There were sixteen towns and their villages.

[23]These towns and their villages were the inheritance of the tribe of Issachar,
according to its clans.

---

[a] *18* Septuagint; Hebrew *slope facing the Arabah* [b] *2* Or *Beersheba, Sheba*; 1 Chron. 4:28 does not have *Sheba*.

Allotment for Asher

24 The fifth lot came out for the tribe of Asher according to its clans. 25 Their territory included:

Helkath, Hali, Beten, Akshaph, 26 Allammelek, Amad and Mishal. On the west the boundary touched Carmel and Shihor Libnath. 27 It then turned east toward Beth Dagon, touched Zebulun and the Valley of Iphtah El, and went north to Beth Emek and Neiel, passing Kabul on the left. 28 It went to Abdon,[a] Rehob, Hammon and Kanah, as far as Greater Sidon. 29 The boundary then turned back toward Ramah and went to the fortified city of Tyre, turned toward Hosah and came out at the Mediterranean Sea in the region of Akzib, 30 Ummah, Aphek and Rehob. There were twenty-two towns and their villages.

31 These towns and their villages were the inheritance of the tribe of Asher, according to its clans.

Allotment for Naphtali

32 The sixth lot came out for Naphtali according to its clans:

33 Their boundary went from Heleph and the large tree in Zaanannim, passing Adami Nekeb and Jabneel to Lakkum and ending at the Jordan. 34 The boundary ran west through Aznoth Tabor and came out at Hukkok. It touched Zebulun on the south, Asher on the west and the Jordan[b] on the east. 35 The fortified towns were Ziddim, Zer, Hammath, Rakkath, Kinnereth, 36 Adamah, Ramah, Hazor, 37 Kedesh, Edrei, En Hazor, 38 Iron, Migdal El, Horem, Beth Anath and Beth Shemesh. There were nineteen towns and their villages.

39 These towns and their villages were the inheritance of the tribe of Naphtali, according to its clans.

Allotment for Dan

40 The seventh lot came out for the tribe of Dan according to its clans. 41 The territory of their inheritance included:

Zorah, Eshtaol, Ir Shemesh, 42 Shaalabbin, Aijalon, Ithlah, 43 Elon, Timnah, Ekron, 44 Eltekeh, Gibbethon, Baalath, 45 Jehud, Bene Berak, Gath Rimmon, 46 Me Jarkon and Rakkon, with the area facing Joppa.

47 (When the territory of the Danites was lost to them, they went up and attacked Leshem, took it, put it to the sword and occupied it. They settled in Leshem and named it Dan after their ancestor.)

48 These towns and their villages were the inheritance of the tribe of Dan, according to its clans.

Allotment for Joshua

49 When they had finished dividing the land into its allotted portions, the Israelites gave Joshua son of Nun an inheritance among them, 50 as the LORD had commanded. They gave him the town he asked for — Timnath Serah[c] in the hill country of Ephraim. And he built up the town and settled there.

51 These are the territories that Eleazar the priest, Joshua son of Nun and the heads of the tribal clans of Israel assigned by lot at Shiloh in the presence of the LORD at the entrance to the tent of meeting. And so they finished dividing the land.

Cities of Refuge

20 Then the LORD said to Joshua: 2 "Tell the Israelites to designate the cities of refuge, as I instructed you through Moses, 3 so that anyone who kills a person accidentally and unintentionally may flee there and find protection from

[a] 28 Some Hebrew manuscripts (see also 21:30); most Hebrew manuscripts *Ebron*
[b] 34 Septuagint; Hebrew *west, and Judah, the Jordan,*
[c] 50 Also known as *Timnath Heres* (see Judges 2:9)

JOSHUA 20:1 – 3

CITIES OF REFUGE

The first three verses of Joshua 20 provide a description of cities intended as safe zones for people who had accidentally killed someone. If someone was killed, that person's family and loved ones were likely to seek out the killer and avenge the dead person. The goal of these cities was to provide a place of refuge for people who had unintentionally killed someone, and the cities were also to provide a place for the cases of both sides to be heard.

These cities typify Christ and the refuge that he is for believers. Every person has sinned against another person in one way or another, and though this sin may not be murder, everyone needs a place of refuge. For believers, Christ is that refuge. He provides a place for people to come when they are guilty, and he acts as a representative before the judgment of God to all who come to him. However, when the trial is held and the sins of believers are to be accounted for, Jesus has already taken all punishment on behalf of those who trust in him. These cities of refuge were meant to temporarily keep people safe while they waited for a fair trial, but Jesus provides believers with an eternal refuge and a fair trial in which their guilt has already been accounted for.

the avenger of blood. 4When they flee to one of these cities, they are to stand in
the entrance of the city gate and state their case before the elders of that city.
Then the elders are to admit the fugitive into their city and provide a place to
live among them. 5If the avenger of blood comes in pursuit, the elders must not
surrender the fugitive, because the fugitive killed their neighbor unintentionally and without malice aforethought. 6They are to stay in that city until they
have stood trial before the assembly and until the death of the high priest who is
serving at that time. Then they may go back to their own home in the town from
which they fled."

7So they set apart Kedesh in Galilee in the hill country of Naphtali, Shechem
in the hill country of Ephraim, and Kiriath Arba (that is, Hebron) in the hill
country of Judah. 8East of the Jordan (on the other side from Jericho) they designated Bezer in the wilderness on the plateau in the tribe of Reuben, Ramoth in
Gilead in the tribe of Gad, and Golan in Bashan in the tribe of Manasseh. 9Any
of the Israelites or any foreigner residing among them who killed someone accidentally could flee to these designated cities and not be killed by the avenger of
blood prior to standing trial before the assembly.

Towns for the Levites

21 Now the family heads of the Levites approached Eleazar the priest, Joshua
son of Nun, and the heads of the other tribal families of Israel 2at Shiloh in
Canaan and said to them, "The LORD commanded through Moses that you give
us towns to live in, with pasturelands for our livestock." 3So, as the LORD had
commanded, the Israelites gave the Levites the following towns and pasturelands out of their own inheritance:

4The first lot came out for the Kohathites, according to their clans. The Levites
who were descendants of Aaron the priest were allotted thirteen towns from the
tribes of Judah, Simeon and Benjamin. 5The rest of Kohath's descendants were
allotted ten towns from the clans of the tribes of Ephraim, Dan and half of Manasseh.

6The descendants of Gershon were allotted thirteen towns from the clans of
the tribes of Issachar, Asher, Naphtali and the half-tribe of Manasseh in Bashan.

7The descendants of Merari, according to their clans, received twelve towns
from the tribes of Reuben, Gad and Zebulun.

8So the Israelites allotted to the Levites these towns and their pasturelands,
as the LORD had commanded through Moses.

9From the tribes of Judah and Simeon they allotted the following towns by name
10(these towns were assigned to the descendants of Aaron who were from the Kohathite clans of the Levites, because the first lot fell to them):

11They gave them Kiriath Arba (that is, Hebron), with its surrounding
pastureland, in the hill country of Judah. (Arba was the forefather of Anak.)
12But the fields and villages around the city they had given to Caleb son of
Jephunneh as his possession.

13So to the descendants of Aaron the priest they gave Hebron (a city of
refuge for one accused of murder), Libnah, 14Jattir, Eshtemoa, 15Holon, Debir, 16Ain, Juttah and Beth Shemesh, together with their pasturelands—
nine towns from these two tribes.

17And from the tribe of Benjamin they gave them Gibeon, Geba, 18Ana-
thoth and Almon, together with their pasturelands—four towns.

19The total number of towns for the priests, the descendants of Aaron, came to
thirteen, together with their pasturelands.

20The rest of the Kohathite clans of the Levites were allotted towns from the tribe
of Ephraim:

21In the hill country of Ephraim they were given Shechem (a city of refuge for one accused of murder) and Gezer, 22Kibzaim and Beth Horon, together with their pasturelands—four towns.

[23]Also from the tribe of Dan they received Eltekeh, Gibbethon, [24]Aijalon
and Gath Rimmon, together with their pasturelands — four towns.
[25]From half the tribe of Manasseh they received Taanach and Gath Rimmon, together with their pasturelands — two towns.
[26]All these ten towns and their pasturelands were given to the rest of the Kohathite clans.

[27]The Levite clans of the Gershonites were given:
from the half-tribe of Manasseh,
Golan in Bashan (a city of refuge for one accused of murder) and Be Eshte-
rah, together with their pasturelands — two towns;
[28]from the tribe of Issachar,
Kishion, Daberath, [29]Jarmuth and En Gannim, together with their pasturelands — four towns;
[30]from the tribe of Asher,
Mishal, Abdon, [31]Helkath and Rehob, together with their pasturelands —
four towns;
[32]from the tribe of Naphtali,
Kedesh in Galilee (a city of refuge for one accused of murder), Hammoth
Dor and Kartan, together with their pasturelands — three towns.
[33]The total number of towns of the Gershonite clans came to thirteen, together
with their pasturelands.

[34]The Merarite clans (the rest of the Levites) were given:
from the tribe of Zebulun,
Jokneam, Kartah, [35]Dimnah and Nahalal, together with their pasturelands — four towns;
[36]from the tribe of Reuben,
Bezer, Jahaz, [37]Kedemoth and Mephaath, together with their pasturelands — four towns;
[38]from the tribe of Gad,
Ramoth in Gilead (a city of refuge for one accused of murder), Mahanaim,
[39]Heshbon and Jazer, together with their pasturelands — four towns in all.
[40]The total number of towns allotted to the Merarite clans, who were the rest of
the Levites, came to twelve.

[41]The towns of the Levites in the territory held by the Israelites were forty-
eight in all, together with their pasturelands. [42]Each of these towns had pasturelands surrounding it; this was true for all these towns.

[43]So the LORD gave Israel all the land he had sworn to give their ancestors,
and they took possession of it and settled there. [44]The LORD gave them rest on
every side, just as he had sworn to their ancestors. Not one of their enemies withstood them; the LORD gave all their enemies into their hands. [45]Not one of all the
LORD's good promises to Israel failed; every one was fulfilled.

Eastern Tribes Return Home

22 Then Joshua summoned the Reubenites, the Gadites and the half-tribe of
Manasseh [2]and said to them, "You have done all that Moses the servant
of the LORD commanded, and you have obeyed me in everything I commanded.
[3]For a long time now — to this very day — you have not deserted your fellow Israelites but have carried out the mission the LORD your God gave you. [4]Now that
the LORD your God has given them rest as he promised, return to your homes in
the land that Moses the servant of the LORD gave you on the other side of the Jordan. [5]But be very careful to keep the commandment and the law that Moses the
servant of the LORD gave you: to love the LORD your God, to walk in obedience
to him, to keep his commands, to hold fast to him and to serve him with all your
heart and with all your soul."

[6]Then Joshua blessed them and sent them away, and they went to their homes.
[7](To the half-tribe of Manasseh Moses had given land in Bashan, and to the other

half of the tribe Joshua gave land on the west side of the Jordan along with their
fellow Israelites.) When Joshua sent them home, he blessed them, 8saying, “Return to your homes with your great wealth — with large herds of livestock, with
silver, gold, bronze and iron, and a great quantity of clothing — and divide the
plunder from your enemies with your fellow Israelites.”
9So the Reubenites, the Gadites and the half-tribe of Manasseh left the Israelites at Shiloh in Canaan to return to Gilead, their own land, which they had
acquired in accordance with the command of the LORD through Moses.
10When they came to Geliloth near the Jordan in the land of Canaan, the Reubenites, the Gadites and the half-tribe of Manasseh built an imposing altar there
by the Jordan. 11And when the Israelites heard that they had built the altar on the
border of Canaan at Geliloth near the Jordan on the Israelite side, 12the whole
assembly of Israel gathered at Shiloh to go to war against them.
13So the Israelites sent Phinehas son of Eleazar, the priest, to the land of Gilead — to Reuben, Gad and the half-tribe of Manasseh. 14With him they sent ten
of the chief men, one from each of the tribes of Israel, each the head of a family
division among the Israelite clans.
15When they went to Gilead — to Reuben, Gad and the half-tribe of Manasseh — they said to them: 16“The whole assembly of the LORD says: ‘How could
you break faith with the God of Israel like this? How could you turn away from
the LORD and build yourselves an altar in rebellion against him now? 17Was not
the sin of Peor enough for us? Up to this very day we have not cleansed ourselves
from that sin, even though a plague fell on the community of the LORD! 18And are
you now turning away from the LORD?
“ ‘If you rebel against the LORD today, tomorrow he will be angry with the
whole community of Israel. 19If the land you possess is defiled, come over to the
LORD’s land, where the LORD’s tabernacle stands, and share the land with us. But
do not rebel against the LORD or against us by building an altar for yourselves,
other than the altar of the LORD our God. 20When Achan son of Zerah was unfaithful in regard to the devoted things,[a] did not wrath come on the whole community of Israel? He was not the only one who died for his sin.’ ”
21Then Reuben, Gad and the half-tribe of Manasseh replied to the heads of
the clans of Israel: 22“The Mighty One, God, the LORD! The Mighty One, God,
the LORD! He knows! And let Israel know! If this has been in rebellion or disobedience to the LORD, do not spare us this day. 23If we have built our own altar
to turn away from the LORD and to offer burnt offerings and grain offerings, or
to sacrifice fellowship offerings on it, may the LORD himself call us to account.
24“No! We did it for fear that some day your descendants might say to ours,
‘What do you have to do with the LORD, the God of Israel? 25The LORD has made
the Jordan a boundary between us and you — you Reubenites and Gadites! You
have no share in the LORD.’ So your descendants might cause ours to stop fearing the LORD.
26“That is why we said, ‘Let us get ready and build an altar — but not for burnt
offerings or sacrifices.’ 27On the contrary, it is to be a witness between us and you
and the generations that follow, that we will worship the LORD at his sanctuary
with our burnt offerings, sacrifices and fellowship offerings. Then in the future
your descendants will not be able to say to ours, ‘You have no share in the LORD.’
28“And we said, ‘If they ever say this to us, or to our descendants, we will answer: Look at the replica of the LORD’s altar, which our ancestors built, not for
burnt offerings and sacrifices, but as a witness between us and you.’
29“Far be it from us to rebel against the LORD and turn away from him today
by building an altar for burnt offerings, grain offerings and sacrifices, other than
the altar of the LORD our God that stands before his tabernacle.”
30When Phinehas the priest and the leaders of the community — the heads of
the clans of the Israelites — heard what Reuben, Gad and Manasseh had to say,

[a] *20* The Hebrew term refers to the irrevocable giving over of things or persons to the LORD, often by totally destroying them.

JOSHUA 22:10 – 34

TRIBES ON THE OTHER SIDE OF THE JORDAN

The tribes of Reuben, Gad and half of the tribe of Manasseh were allotted an inheritance on the east side of the Jordan River. There they constructed an imposing altar to declare their faithfulness to God and to demonstrate their ongoing loyalty to the other tribes who crossed the Jordan and settled in Canaan. In fact, they went with these tribes into the land and fought to secure and rid it of its pagan inhabitants before returning back to their portion of the land on the other side of the Jordan. The tribes to the west of the Jordan questioned this altar because they wrongly assumed that the people intended to worship at that altar and not with the rest of the nation at the altar in the tabernacle. The rest of the nation relented of their questioning after learning that the altar — rather than being a location for aberrant worship — was meant to be a witness to future generations of the commitment of the Transjordan tribes to remain faithful to the Lord. John, in the book of Revelation, pictures Jesus as “the faithful witness” who, like this altar, would prove to be a faithful and credible witness throughout all generations (Rev 1:5).

they were pleased. 31And Phinehas son of Eleazar, the priest, said to Reuben, Gad
and Manasseh, "Today we know that the LORD is with us, because you have not
been unfaithful to the LORD in this matter. Now you have rescued the Israelites
from the LORD's hand."
32Then Phinehas son of Eleazar, the priest, and the leaders returned to Canaan from their meeting with the Reubenites and Gadites in Gilead and reported to the Israelites. 33They were glad to hear the report and praised God. And
they talked no more about going to war against them to devastate the country
where the Reubenites and the Gadites lived.
34And the Reubenites and the Gadites gave the altar this name: A Witness Between Us—that the LORD is God.

Joshua's Farewell to the Leaders

23 After a long time had passed and the LORD had given Israel rest from all
their enemies around them, Joshua, by then a very old man, 2summoned
all Israel—their elders, leaders, judges and officials—and said to them: "I am
very old. 3You yourselves have seen everything the LORD your God has done to
all these nations for your sake; it was the LORD your God who fought for you. 4Re-
member how I have allotted as an inheritance for your tribes all the land of the
nations that remain—the nations I conquered—between the Jordan and the
Mediterranean Sea in the west. 5The LORD your God himself will push them out
for your sake. He will drive them out before you, and you will take possession of
their land, as the LORD your God promised you.
6"Be very strong; be careful to obey all that is written in the Book of the Law
of Moses, without turning aside to the right or to the left. 7Do not associate with
these nations that remain among you; do not invoke the names of their gods or
swear by them. You must not serve them or bow down to them. 8But you are to
hold fast to the LORD your God, as you have until now.
9"The LORD has driven out before you great and powerful nations; to this day
no one has been able to withstand you. 10One of you routs a thousand, because
the LORD your God fights for you, just as he promised. 11So be very careful to love
the LORD your God.
12"But if you turn away and ally yourselves with the survivors of these nations that remain among you and if you intermarry with them and associate with
them, 13then you may be sure that the LORD your God will no longer drive out
these nations before you. Instead, they will become snares and traps for you,
whips on your backs and thorns in your eyes, until you perish from this good
land, which the LORD your God has given you.
14"Now I am about to go the way of all the earth. You know with all your heart
and soul that not one of all the good promises the LORD your God gave you has
failed. Every promise has been fulfilled; not one has failed. 15But just as all the
good things the LORD your God has promised you have come to you, so he will
bring on you all the evil things he has threatened, until the LORD your God has
destroyed you from this good land he has given you. 16If you violate the covenant
of the LORD your God, which he commanded you, and go and serve other gods
and bow down to them, the LORD's anger will burn against you, and you will
quickly perish from the good land he has given you."

The Covenant Renewed at Shechem

24 Then Joshua assembled all the tribes of Israel at Shechem. He summoned
the elders, leaders, judges and officials of Israel, and they presented
themselves before God.
2Joshua said to all the people, "This is what the LORD, the God of Israel, says:
'Long ago your ancestors, including Terah the father of Abraham and Nahor,
lived beyond the Euphrates River and worshiped other gods. 3But I took your
father Abraham from the land beyond the Euphrates and led him throughout
Canaan and gave him many descendants. I gave him Isaac, 4and to Isaac I gave

JOSHUA 23:6–8

JOSHUA'S CHALLENGE

Joshua reminded the people of the necessity of obedience as they fully possessed the land. Faithful obedience serves two key functions both now and then. First, it demonstrates that a person has experienced the grace of God. The fact of God's faithfulness fuels the fires of obedience. Second, it allows people to realize the blessings of God. The Israelites would live long in the land that God had given them if they obeyed his law and shunned the worship of the idols of the land.

The New Testament authors exhorted the church to obedience based on the same foundations. The love of God, seen in the grace of God, empowers the people of God to obey the Word of God. Jesus said that those who love him will demonstrate this love through their obedience to his commands (Jn 14:15). Because God knows the best way to live, obedience to his commands is a path to life, freedom, joy and peace (Ps 119:105).

JESUS: THE PROMISE OF GOD

Joshua finished his life with an astounding observation about God's work. He claimed that God had been faithful to fulfill every one of his promises to the nation of Israel. In spite of the sin of the people and the vast scope of God's redemptive work, God had proven the covenant-keeping nature of his character. He is always faithful to his promises. He always keeps his word. He will never break a promise.

While this claim comes at the culmination of Joshua's life and mission, it continues throughout all subsequent generations. In fact, God's promises were meant to extend throughout all generations. His promise in Genesis 3:15, that one would come who would "crush" Satan forever, was not merely a promise to the nation of Israel but to all those who would suffer under the implications of life in a sin-drenched world. His promises to the nation of Israel, fulfilled in their taking of the land, represent only a portion of the great and glorious promises made by God throughout all history.

Paul, at the beginning of his letter to the church at Rome, claimed that Jesus was the pinnacle of the fulfillment of the promises of God (Ro 1:1 – 4). Jesus' sacrificial death was not a knee-jerk reaction by God to address human sin but was the plan of God before the foundation of the world. Paul traced the details of the coming of Christ — from his lineage, to the timing of his birth, to the manner of his death — and identified them as a fulfillment of God's plan. The writings of the prophets validate this claim, as they make repeated promises about intricate details of Jesus' life that are ultimately fulfilled hundreds of years later. This confidence led Paul to conclude, in 2 Corinthians 1:18 – 20, that all of God's promises are answered in Christ. Both the specific promises regarding the Messiah and the general promises regarding God's plan for dealing with human sin are fulfilled by Jesus.

God's faithfulness to his promises provides hope for his people. Not only has he done what he said he would do, but he will continue to perfectly execute his plan. In spite of the seeming chaos of life in a fallen world, Christians can take heart that he has overcome the world and will perfectly accomplish all he set out to do (Jn 16:33).

Jacob and Esau. I assigned the hill country of Seir to Esau, but Jacob and his family went down to Egypt.

5"'Then I sent Moses and Aaron, and I afflicted the Egyptians by what I did there, and I brought you out. 6When I brought your people out of Egypt, you came to the sea, and the Egyptians pursued them with chariots and horsemen[a] as far as the Red Sea.[b] 7But they cried to the LORD for help, and he put darkness between you and the Egyptians; he brought the sea over them and covered them. You saw with your own eyes what I did to the Egyptians. Then you lived in the wilderness for a long time.

8"'I brought you to the land of the Amorites who lived east of the Jordan. They fought against you, but I gave them into your hands. I destroyed them from before you, and you took possession of their land. 9When Balak son of Zippor, the king of Moab, prepared to fight against Israel, he sent for Balaam son of Beor to put a curse on you. 10But I would not listen to Balaam, so he blessed you again and again, and I delivered you out of his hand.

11"'Then you crossed the Jordan and came to Jericho. The citizens of Jericho fought against you, as did also the Amorites, Perizzites, Canaanites, Hittites, Girgashites, Hivites and Jebusites, but I gave them into your hands. 12I sent the hornet ahead of you, which drove them out before you—also the two Amorite kings. You did not do it with your own sword and bow. 13So I gave you a land on which you did not toil and cities you did not build; and you live in them and eat from vineyards and olive groves that you did not plant.'

14"Now fear the LORD and serve him with all faithfulness. Throw away the gods your ancestors worshiped beyond the Euphrates River and in Egypt, and serve the LORD. 15But if serving the LORD seems undesirable to you, then choose for yourselves this day whom you will serve, whether the gods your ancestors served beyond the Euphrates, or the gods of the Amorites, in whose land you are living. But as for me and my household, we will serve the LORD."

16Then the people answered, "Far be it from us to forsake the LORD to serve other gods! 17It was the LORD our God himself who brought us and our parents up out of Egypt, from that land of slavery, and performed those great signs before our eyes. He protected us on our entire journey and among all the nations through which we traveled. 18And the LORD drove out before us all the nations, including the Amorites, who lived in the land. We too will serve the LORD, because he is our God."

19Joshua said to the people, "You are not able to serve the LORD. He is a holy God; he is a jealous God. He will not forgive your rebellion and your sins. 20If you forsake the LORD and serve foreign gods, he will turn and bring disaster on you and make an end of you, after he has been good to you."

21But the people said to Joshua, "No! We will serve the LORD."

22Then Joshua said, "You are witnesses against yourselves that you have chosen to serve the LORD."

"Yes, we are witnesses," they replied.

23"Now then," said Joshua, "throw away the foreign gods that are among you and yield your hearts to the LORD, the God of Israel."

24And the people said to Joshua, "We will serve the LORD our God and obey him."

25On that day Joshua made a covenant for the people, and there at Shechem he reaffirmed for them decrees and laws. 26And Joshua recorded these things in the Book of the Law of God. Then he took a large stone and set it up there under the oak near the holy place of the LORD.

27"See!" he said to all the people. "This stone will be a witness against us. It has heard all the words the LORD has said to us. It will be a witness against you if you are untrue to your God."

28Then Joshua dismissed the people, each to their own inheritance.

JOSHUA 24:14–15

MAKE A CHOICE

Joshua continued to remind the nation of the life-altering choice that each person must make. Either they would serve the false gods worshiped by their ancestors and the pagan people in the land, or they would fear the one true God and serve him alone. Joshua then publicly made his choice: he and his household would serve the Lord. Like Joshua and the nation of Israel, all people today face a similar choice—a decision of what to do with Jesus Christ.

Jesus continually held out the divisive nature of his claim to be God and the only path to salvation (Ac 4:12). Not only would those who worship him as the one true God have to flee the idolatry of the world, but they may also have to choose loyalty to God over loyalty to their family, friends or any other thing or person that hindered their walk with God. This choice, for all God's people, is a path of self-denial and self-sacrifice. But those who choose this path have been promised to ultimately find life in God's kingdom forever.

[a] 6 Or *charioteers* [b] 6 Or *the Sea of Reeds*

Buried in the Promised Land

[29]After these things, Joshua son of Nun, the servant of the LORD, died at the
age of a hundred and ten. [30]And they buried him in the land of his inheritance, at
Timnath Serah[a] in the hill country of Ephraim, north of Mount Gaash.
[31]Israel served the LORD throughout the lifetime of Joshua and of the elders
who outlived him and who had experienced everything the LORD had done for
Israel.
[32]And Joseph's bones, which the Israelites had brought up from Egypt, were
buried at Shechem in the tract of land that Jacob bought for a hundred pieces of
silver[b] from the sons of Hamor, the father of Shechem. This became the inheritance of Joseph's descendants.
[33]And Eleazar son of Aaron died and was buried at Gibeah, which had been
allotted to his son Phinehas in the hill country of Ephraim.

---

[a] *30* Also known as *Timnath Heres* (see Judges 2:9) [b] *32* Hebrew *hundred kesitahs*; a kesitah was a unit of money of unknown weight and value.

JESUS: OUR RIGHTEOUS RULER

JUDGES

JUDGES

DEBORAH, BARAK DEFEAT CANAANITES	GIDEON DEFEATS MIDIANITES	SAMSON OPPOSES THE PHILISTINES
c. 1209 – 1169 BC	*c. 1162 BC*	*c. 1075 – 1055 BC*

The book of Judges demonstrates God's continued faithfulness to his persistently wayward people. The cyclical pattern of the people's sin and God's rescue is the steady refrain throughout the book. Often God demonstrated his love through judgment, purging the filth of sin from among the people and teaching them to fear him alone. Yet despite their sin, God continued to send human deliverers — namely, the judges — whom he empowered to remind the people of God's ways and call them to repentance and obedience.

Judges demonstrates the depravity of humankind and the necessity of God's judgment. God did not turn his back to Israel's sin; rather, he turned toward his beloved people in loving pursuit. God's redemptive mission necessitated that he allow Israel to feel the weight of their choices because sin has earthly consequences as well as heavenly ones. Israel suffered consistent internal strife and external turmoil with foreign nations. Through it all, God was always faithful to the covenant promises he made to Abraham and his descendants. Then as now, salvation happens by God's sheer grace: There is no question that the people don't merit God's mercy through their own moral uprightness or their willingness to turn from their sin. God acts because he is faithful. This same covenant faithfulness provides the only hope of God's people throughout time and eternity.

The pattern of rebellion, judgment and deliverance dominates each subsequent event in Israel's life. Over time, this pattern devolved as the Israelites found increasingly heinous ways to rebel against God's decrees and their faithlessness necessitated God's judgment. The book consistently demonstrates Israel's corrupt nature throughout the time of the judges, beginning with the generation that followed Joshua's (2:6 – 15). In contrast to the preceding book of Joshua, this book sounds a depressing, hopeless tone that indicates just how far and how quickly the people of God had fallen.

By the end of the book, there is no question as to whether a human leader would ever be capable of delivering the people from their sin. As we see from the cycles in Judges, only God is capable of rescuing such a wayward people.

Today, all believers understand this reality. Broken and battered by sin, people long for the true deliverer, the One of whom the judges were a mere shadow. Jesus, the incarnate Son of God, has provided this deliverance by taking God's judgment on himself and fulfilling for all time God's promise to always be faithful to his people.

HE SENT THEM A PROPHET, WHO SAID, "THIS IS WHAT THE LORD, THE GOD OF ISRAEL, SAYS: I BROUGHT YOU UP OUT OF EGYPT, OUT OF THE LAND OF SLAVERY."

Judges 6:8

JUDGES

Israel Fights the Remaining Canaanites

1 After the death of Joshua, the Israelites asked the LORD, "Who of us is to go up first to fight against the Canaanites?"

2The LORD answered, "Judah shall go up; I have given the land into their hands."

3The men of Judah then said to the Simeonites their fellow Israelites, "Come up with us into the territory allotted to us, to fight against the Canaanites. We in turn will go with you into yours." So the Simeonites went with them.

4When Judah attacked, the LORD gave the Canaanites and Perizzites into their hands, and they struck down ten thousand men at Bezek. 5It was there that they found Adoni-Bezek and fought against him, putting to rout the Canaanites and Perizzites. 6Adoni-Bezek fled, but they chased him and caught him, and cut off his thumbs and big toes.

7Then Adoni-Bezek said, "Seventy kings with their thumbs and big toes cut off have picked up scraps under my table. Now God has paid me back for what I did to them." They brought him to Jerusalem, and he died there.

8The men of Judah attacked Jerusalem also and took it. They put the city to the sword and set it on fire.

9After that, Judah went down to fight against the Canaanites living in the hill country, the Negev and the western foothills. 10They advanced against the Canaanites living in Hebron (formerly called Kiriath Arba) and defeated Sheshai, Ahiman and Talmai. 11From there they advanced against the people living in Debir (formerly called Kiriath Sepher).

12And Caleb said, "I will give my daughter Aksah in marriage to the man who attacks and captures Kiriath Sepher." 13Othniel son of Kenaz, Caleb's younger brother, took it; so Caleb gave his daughter Aksah to him in marriage.

14One day when she came to Othniel, she urged him[a] to ask her father for a field. When she got off her donkey, Caleb asked her, "What can I do for you?"

15She replied, "Do me a special favor. Since you have given me land in the Negev, give me also springs of water." So Caleb gave her the upper and lower springs.

16The descendants of Moses' father-in-law, the Kenite, went up from the City of Palms[b] with the people of Judah to live among the inhabitants of the Desert of Judah in the Negev near Arad.

17Then the men of Judah went with the Simeonites their fellow Israelites and attacked the Canaanites living in Zephath, and they totally destroyed[c] the city. Therefore it was called Hormah.[d] 18Judah also took[e] Gaza, Ashkelon and Ekron — each city with its territory.

19The LORD was with the men of Judah. They took possession of the hill country, but they were unable to drive the people from the plains, because they had chariots fitted with iron. 20As Moses had promised, Hebron was given to Caleb, who drove from it the three sons of Anak. 21The Benjamites, however, did not drive out the Jebusites, who were living in Jerusalem; to this day the Jebusites live there with the Benjamites.

22Now the tribes of Joseph attacked Bethel, and the LORD was with them. 23When they sent men to spy out Bethel (formerly called Luz), 24the spies saw

JUDGES 1:1 – 2

NEEDING A LEADER

Joshua had just passed away, leaving Israel's leadership role vacant. The main question for the Israelites was inescapable: Who was going to lead them into battle? God had promised Israel a land that was inhabited by the Canaanites, but with the death of Joshua and the lack of a king, no clear military leader existed to conquer the land. The Lord himself boldly proclaimed that Judah would lead the people into the land. Previously, the scepter and ruler's staff were promised to never depart from Judah, revealing the line of kings to come (Ge 49:10). The first true king of Judah and the great king of Israel came in the form of a shepherd boy, King David, with the final culmination of the line of Judah being a carpenter, Jesus, the promised Messiah and everlasting King (Mt 1:1 – 16).

---

[a] 14 Hebrew; Septuagint and Vulgate *Othniel, he urged her* [b] 16 That is, Jericho
[c] 17 The Hebrew term refers to the irrevocable giving over of things or persons to the LORD, often by totally destroying them. [d] 17 *Hormah* means *destruction.* [e] 18 Hebrew; Septuagint *Judah did not take*

LEADERS IN MISSION

God was faithful to his promise to give the descendants of Abraham a land overflowing with his blessing and provision. Since the time when Adam lived in the garden, God gave his image-bearers a significant role in leading his people. Abraham, Isaac, Jacob, Joseph, Moses and Joshua are examples of individuals God used. These leaders, though fallen and marred by the consequences of sin, were instrumental in stewarding God's work in the world. Yet as children of the curse, these leaders all died.

The book of Judges opens with the death of a great leader of Israel. Joshua mobilized the people of God to conquer the land of Canaan following Moses' death. He exhorted the people to be obedient, emboldened them with confidence and led them to take the land God had provided. This land, however, was still littered with God's enemies. God commanded his people to rid the land of any nation who stood opposed to the one true God and his people. At the time of Joshua's death, much work remained undone and the mission needed to be completed.

Now the God-ordained leaders — the tribe of Judah — needed to take up the mantle of leadership. Empowered by God's Spirit, they led God's people to face their bitter opponents. God's promise was clear — he would go before them and remain with them so they had nothing to fear. It was God, and God alone, who would win the victory and give the opponents over to destruction. All the nation of Israel needed to do was trust and obey.

God's faithfulness to his mission continues today. Leaders come and go, but God remains sovereign to work according to his good purposes. This work will continue based on the power and presence of God — not the ingenuity or strength of human leaders.

Jesus demonstrated this reality following his resurrection. He told his followers to wait on the power of the Holy Spirit before they moved out in mission with him (Ac 1:4). For them, the task would not be occupying a territory by military might but filling the entire earth with the knowledge and glory of God. This mission is one that will happen " 'not by might nor by power, but by my Spirit,' says the LORD Almighty" (Zec 4:6).

a man coming out of the city and they said to him, "Show us how to get into the city and we will see that you are treated well." 25So he showed them, and they put the city to the sword but spared the man and his whole family. 26He then went to the land of the Hittites, where he built a city and called it Luz, which is its name to this day.

27But Manasseh did not drive out the people of Beth Shan or Taanach or Dor or Ibleam or Megiddo and their surrounding settlements, for the Canaanites were determined to live in that land. 28When Israel became strong, they pressed the Canaanites into forced labor but never drove them out completely. 29Nor did Ephraim drive out the Canaanites living in Gezer, but the Canaanites continued to live there among them. 30Neither did Zebulun drive out the Canaanites living in Kitron or Nahalol, so these Canaanites lived among them, but Zebulun did subject them to forced labor. 31Nor did Asher drive out those living in Akko or Sidon or Ahlab or Akzib or Helbah or Aphek or Rehob. 32The Asherites lived among the Canaanite inhabitants of the land because they did not drive them out. 33Neither did Naphtali drive out those living in Beth Shemesh or Beth Anath; but the Naphtalites too lived among the Canaanite inhabitants of the land, and those living in Beth Shemesh and Beth Anath became forced laborers for them. 34The Amorites confined the Danites to the hill country, not allowing them to come down into the plain. 35And the Amorites were determined also to hold out in Mount Heres, Aijalon and Shaalbim, but when the power of the tribes of Joseph increased, they too were pressed into forced labor. 36The boundary of the Amorites was from Scorpion Pass to Sela and beyond.

The Angel of the LORD at Bokim

2 The angel of the LORD went up from Gilgal to Bokim and said, "I brought you up out of Egypt and led you into the land I swore to give to your ancestors. I said, 'I will never break my covenant with you, 2and you shall not make a covenant with the people of this land, but you shall break down their altars.' Yet you have disobeyed me. Why have you done this? 3And I have also said, 'I will not drive them out before you; they will become traps for you, and their gods will become snares to you.'"

4When the angel of the LORD had spoken these things to all the Israelites, the people wept aloud, 5and they called that place Bokim.[a] There they offered sacrifices to the LORD.

Disobedience and Defeat

6After Joshua had dismissed the Israelites, they went to take possession of the land, each to their own inheritance. 7The people served the LORD throughout the lifetime of Joshua and of the elders who outlived him and who had seen all the great things the LORD had done for Israel.

8Joshua son of Nun, the servant of the LORD, died at the age of a hundred and ten. 9And they buried him in the land of his inheritance, at Timnath Heres[b] in the hill country of Ephraim, north of Mount Gaash.

10After that whole generation had been gathered to their ancestors, another generation grew up who knew neither the LORD nor what he had done for Israel. 11Then the Israelites did evil in the eyes of the LORD and served the Baals. 12They forsook the LORD, the God of their ancestors, who had brought them out of Egypt. They followed and worshiped various gods of the peoples around them. They aroused the LORD's anger 13because they forsook him and served Baal and the Ashtoreths. 14In his anger against Israel the LORD gave them into the hands of raiders who plundered them. He sold them into the hands of their enemies all around, whom they were no longer able to resist. 15Whenever Israel went out to fight, the hand of the LORD was against them to defeat them, just as he had sworn to them. They were in great distress.

[a] 5 *Bokim* means *weepers.* [b] 9 Also known as *Timnath Serah* (see Joshua 19:50 and 24:30)

JUDGES 2:1 – 3

WARNINGS TO A WAYWARD PEOPLE

God in his grace gives all people an opportunity to turn from their sin and follow him. In the Old Testament, God appeared to his people in visible form. The "angel of the LORD" is not specifically named, though it is clear that the angel represents God by declaring a message of warning and impending judgment. Sadly, the cyclical pattern of rebellion continued until Jesus' birth.

Jesus, in similar fashion, inaugurated his earthly ministry by proclaiming, "Repent, for the kingdom of heaven has come near" (Mt 4:17). Like the angel, he warned the people to turn from their sin lest they face the wrath of God. Little did they know that the very One who spoke these words would soon bear the weight of the wrath and judgment of God to deliver God's people from the consequences of their sin forever. In Jesus, God not only warns people about the effects of their sin, but he gives them an opportunity for everlasting atonement for those sins.

[16]Then the LORD raised up judges,[a] who saved them out of the hands of these raiders. [17]Yet they would not listen to their judges but prostituted themselves to other gods and worshiped them. They quickly turned from the ways of their ancestors, who had been obedient to the LORD's commands. [18]Whenever the LORD raised up a judge for them, he was with the judge and saved them out of the hands of their enemies as long as the judge lived; for the LORD relented because of their groaning under those who oppressed and afflicted them. [19]But when the judge died, the people returned to ways even more corrupt than those of their ancestors, following other gods and serving and worshiping them. They refused to give up their evil practices and stubborn ways.

[20]Therefore the LORD was very angry with Israel and said, "Because this nation has violated the covenant I ordained for their ancestors and has not listened to me, [21]I will no longer drive out before them any of the nations Joshua left when he died. [22]I will use them to test Israel and see whether they will keep the way of the LORD and walk in it as their ancestors did." [23]The LORD had allowed those nations to remain; he did not drive them out at once by giving them into the hands of Joshua.

3 These are the nations the LORD left to test all those Israelites who had not experienced any of the wars in Canaan [2](he did this only to teach warfare to the descendants of the Israelites who had not had previous battle experience): [3]the five rulers of the Philistines, all the Canaanites, the Sidonians, and the Hivites living in the Lebanon mountains from Mount Baal Hermon to Lebo Hamath. [4]They were left to test the Israelites to see whether they would obey the LORD's commands, which he had given their ancestors through Moses.

[5]The Israelites lived among the Canaanites, Hittites, Amorites, Perizzites, Hivites and Jebusites. [6]They took their daughters in marriage and gave their own daughters to their sons, and served their gods.

Othniel

[7]The Israelites did evil in the eyes of the LORD; they forgot the LORD their God and served the Baals and the Asherahs. [8]The anger of the LORD burned against Israel so that he sold them into the hands of Cushan-Rishathaim king of Aram Naharaim,[b] to whom the Israelites were subject for eight years. [9]But when they cried out to the LORD, he raised up for them a deliverer, Othniel son of Kenaz, Caleb's younger brother, who saved them. [10]The Spirit of the LORD came on him, so that he became Israel's judge[c] and went to war. The LORD gave Cushan-Rishathaim king of Aram into the hands of Othniel, who overpowered him. [11]So the land had peace for forty years, until Othniel son of Kenaz died.

Ehud

[12]Again the Israelites did evil in the eyes of the LORD, and because they did this evil the LORD gave Eglon king of Moab power over Israel. [13]Getting the Ammonites and Amalekites to join him, Eglon came and attacked Israel, and they took possession of the City of Palms.[d] [14]The Israelites were subject to Eglon king of Moab for eighteen years.

[15]Again the Israelites cried out to the LORD, and he gave them a deliverer—Ehud, a left-handed man, the son of Gera the Benjamite. The Israelites sent him with tribute to Eglon king of Moab. [16]Now Ehud had made a double-edged sword about a cubit[e] long, which he strapped to his right thigh under his clothing. [17]He presented the tribute to Eglon king of Moab, who was a very fat man. [18]After Ehud had presented the tribute, he sent on their way those who had carried it. [19]But on reaching the stone images near Gilgal he himself went back to Eglon and said, "Your Majesty, I have a secret message for you."

The king said to his attendants, "Leave us!" And they all left.

[a] *16* Or *leaders;* similarly in verses 17-19 [b] *8* That is, Northwest Mesopotamia
[c] *10* Or *leader* [d] *13* That is, Jericho [e] *16* That is, about 18 inches or about 45 centimeters

JUDGES 2:16–19

A TUTOR TO THE GOSPEL

Even at the beginning, the author made it clear that the judges failed to produce lasting change in the people. In fact, the death of a judge seemingly fueled the rebellion of the people. With each successive judge, the people's rebellion continued to escalate. The leadership of the judges functioned to expose the nation to the depravity of their sin and inability to keep God's righteous law. Paul, in the New Testament, wrote that this is a primary function of the Old Testament law and sacrificial system. It was meant to serve as a "guardian" to teach the people what God commands and to show them that they were altogether unable to obey his law (Gal 3:24). This inability is meant to cause people to long for a true and lasting deliverer who will accomplish what the judges could not. Jesus' work provides hope for people who, acknowledging their inability to keep God's law, place their faith in his finished work on their behalf.

A FAITHFUL GOD AND AN UNFAITHFUL PEOPLE

The book of Judges presents a stark contrast between the faithfulness of God and the unfaithfulness of his people. It is astounding to consider that so soon after their miraculous deliverance from Egypt, a generation arrived on the scene that neither knew the Lord nor the works that he had done for them. The very same nation who was an eyewitness to the stunning might of God had now forgotten him altogether. Their forgetfulness is seen in their ever-increasing propensity toward rebellion.

One would anticipate that their sin would prompt God to abandon his people forever. Yet, time and time again, an avalanche of God's grace meets the faithlessness of the people. In fact, the text records God's pity on the people and his attentiveness to their cries. Previously, Moses recounted how the people of God groaned because of their slavery and cried out to the Lord (Ex 2:23 – 25). These cries for deliverance were met by responses from the Lord. He heard their cries. He remembered the promises he had made in his covenant with them. He saw their need, and he knew their pain. This is the nature of the faithfulness of God — he hears, remembers, sees and knows.

Now, generations later, God heard the cries of his people and provided judges to lead them to victory. He did this despite the fact that they had demonstrated a perpetual inability to obey, even for a generation. God's faithfulness is clearly not predicated on the goodness of his people. Rather, God's faithfulness is founded on his character. He is a faithful God who always keeps his promises.

The faithfulness of God is the hope on which the Christian life is built. Those who know Jesus through repentance and faith can rest assured that God is faithful to his promises (1Co 1:9). He will not abandon his people, nor will he turn his back on them when they are unfaithful. Instead he hears, remembers, sees and knows. He hears the cry for mercy from those who know they are broken. He remembers his covenant, made long ago to Abraham, to save his people. He knows the needs of his people and, by virtue of Christ's work, has made provision to meet those needs and restore them to a right relationship with him forever.

[20]Ehud then approached him while he was sitting alone in the upper room of
his palace[a] and said, "I have a message from God for you." As the king rose from
his seat, [21]Ehud reached with his left hand, drew the sword from his right thigh
and plunged it into the king's belly. [22]Even the handle sank in after the blade,
and his bowels discharged. Ehud did not pull the sword out, and the fat closed in
over it. [23]Then Ehud went out to the porch[b]; he shut the doors of the upper room
behind him and locked them.

[24]After he had gone, the servants came and found the doors of the upper room
locked. They said, "He must be relieving himself in the inner room of the palace." [25]They waited to the point of embarrassment, but when he did not open
the doors of the room, they took a key and unlocked them. There they saw their
lord fallen to the floor, dead.

[26]While they waited, Ehud got away. He passed by the stone images and escaped to Seirah. [27]When he arrived there, he blew a trumpet in the hill country of Ephraim, and the Israelites went down with him from the hills, with him
leading them.

[28]"Follow me," he ordered, "for the LORD has given Moab, your enemy, into
your hands." So they followed him down and took possession of the fords of the
Jordan that led to Moab; they allowed no one to cross over. [29]At that time they
struck down about ten thousand Moabites, all vigorous and strong; not one escaped. [30]That day Moab was made subject to Israel, and the land had peace for
eighty years.

Shamgar

[31]After Ehud came Shamgar son of Anath, who struck down six hundred Philistines with an oxgoad. He too saved Israel.

Deborah

4 Again the Israelites did evil in the eyes of the LORD, now that Ehud was dead.
[2]So the LORD sold them into the hands of Jabin king of Canaan, who reigned
in Hazor. Sisera, the commander of his army, was based in Harosheth Haggoyim. [3]Because he had nine hundred chariots fitted with iron and had cruelly oppressed the Israelites for twenty years, they cried to the LORD for help.

[4]Now Deborah, a prophet, the wife of Lappidoth, was leading[c] Israel at that
time. [5]She held court under the Palm of Deborah between Ramah and Bethel in
the hill country of Ephraim, and the Israelites went up to her to have their disputes decided. [6]She sent for Barak son of Abinoam from Kedesh in Naphtali and
said to him, "The LORD, the God of Israel, commands you: 'Go, take with you ten
thousand men of Naphtali and Zebulun and lead them up to Mount Tabor. [7]I will
lead Sisera, the commander of Jabin's army, with his chariots and his troops to
the Kishon River and give him into your hands.'"

[8]Barak said to her, "If you go with me, I will go; but if you don't go with me, I
won't go."

[9]"Certainly I will go with you," said Deborah. "But because of the course you
are taking, the honor will not be yours, for the LORD will deliver Sisera into the
hands of a woman." So Deborah went with Barak to Kedesh. [10]There Barak summoned Zebulun and Naphtali, and ten thousand men went up under his command. Deborah also went up with him.

[11]Now Heber the Kenite had left the other Kenites, the descendants of Hobab,
Moses' brother-in-law,[d] and pitched his tent by the great tree in Zaanannim near
Kedesh.

[12]When they told Sisera that Barak son of Abinoam had gone up to Mount Tabor, [13]Sisera summoned from Harosheth Haggoyim to the Kishon River all his
men and his nine hundred chariots fitted with iron.

[a] *20* The meaning of the Hebrew for this word is uncertain; also in verse 24.
[b] *23* The meaning of the Hebrew for this word is uncertain. [c] *4* Traditionally *judging*
[d] *11* Or *father-in-law*

JUDGES 4:1 – 10

A BRIEF RAY OF HOPE

The story of Deborah and Barak provides a brief respite in an otherwise depressing decline of the nation of Israel. Their faithfulness is seen in their willingness to hear the Lord and obey his commands. Their responsiveness to God stands in stark contrast to the stiff-necked rebellion and hard-heartedness demonstrated by God's people throughout most of the remainder of the book.

These glimmers of hope are short-lived throughout the Old Testament. The brief faithfulness of certain individuals or leaders was rapidly followed by the onslaught of rebellion and sin. This pattern continued until the time of Christ. Jesus obeyed where all others fell, not just once, but through the entirety of his life. Peter wrote that Jesus never sinned, completely obeying the law of God down to the very last detail (1Pe 2:22). This perfect righteousness demonstrated that he is the Son of God who was given as a gift to those who place their faith in his work on the cross. Those who are in Christ can look forward to a coming day when a permanent break from sin will take place and the earth itself will be forever purified from the impediments of sin.

[14]Then Deborah said to Barak, "Go! This is the day the LORD has given Sisera
into your hands. Has not the LORD gone ahead of you?" So Barak went down
Mount Tabor, with ten thousand men following him. [15]At Barak's advance, the
LORD routed Sisera and all his chariots and army by the sword, and Sisera got
down from his chariot and fled on foot.
[16]Barak pursued the chariots and army as far as Harosheth Haggoyim, and all
Sisera's troops fell by the sword; not a man was left. [17]Sisera, meanwhile, fled on
foot to the tent of Jael, the wife of Heber the Kenite, because there was an alliance
between Jabin king of Hazor and the family of Heber the Kenite.
[18]Jael went out to meet Sisera and said to him, "Come, my lord, come right
in. Don't be afraid." So he entered her tent, and she covered him with a blanket.
[19]"I'm thirsty," he said. "Please give me some water." She opened a skin of
milk, gave him a drink, and covered him up.
[20]"Stand in the doorway of the tent," he told her. "If someone comes by and
asks you, 'Is anyone in there?' say 'No.'"
[21]But Jael, Heber's wife, picked up a tent peg and a hammer and went quietly
to him while he lay fast asleep, exhausted. She drove the peg through his temple
into the ground, and he died.
[22]Just then Barak came by in pursuit of Sisera, and Jael went out to meet him.
"Come," she said, "I will show you the man you're looking for." So he went in with
her, and there lay Sisera with the tent peg through his temple — dead.
[23]On that day God subdued Jabin king of Canaan before the Israelites. [24]And
the hand of the Israelites pressed harder and harder against Jabin king of Canaan until they destroyed him.

The Song of Deborah

5 On that day Deborah and Barak son of Abinoam sang this song:

[2] "When the princes in Israel take the lead,
when the people willingly offer themselves —
praise the LORD!

[3] "Hear this, you kings! Listen, you rulers!
I, even I, will sing to[a] the LORD;
I will praise the LORD, the God of Israel, in song.

[4] "When you, LORD, went out from Seir,
when you marched from the land of Edom,
the earth shook, the heavens poured,
the clouds poured down water.
[5] The mountains quaked before the LORD, the One of Sinai,
before the LORD, the God of Israel.

[6] "In the days of Shamgar son of Anath,
in the days of Jael, the highways were abandoned;
travelers took to winding paths.
[7] Villagers in Israel would not fight;
they held back until I, Deborah, arose,
until I arose, a mother in Israel.
[8] God chose new leaders
when war came to the city gates,
but not a shield or spear was seen
among forty thousand in Israel.
[9] My heart is with Israel's princes,
with the willing volunteers among the people.
Praise the LORD!

[a] 3 Or *of*

JUDGES 5:1 – 31

SONGS OF DELIVERANCE

Singing was a distinctive feature of worship for the nation of Israel. This musical praise, sometimes accompanied by an instrument, was meant to be a way for the people to exalt God and his faithfulness throughout all generations. Following their miraculous deliverance from the hand of Pharaoh, Moses and the children of God sang praise declaring, "The LORD reigns for ever and ever" (Ex 15:18). Now years later and living in the land of promise, Deborah and Barak sang a song to bless the Lord for his mighty work. Songs are found throughout the pages of Scripture and are often a means by which people declare praise to God for something he has done for the worshiper (Ps 98:5; 101:1; 149:3) or for his faithful character (Ps 9:11; 105:2). Often the singing of praise was accompanied by a call to worship, in which the people were summoned to offer their praise to God (Jdg 5:3; Isa 12:5). The singing of praise to God continues to be a distinctive feature in the life of the church (Col 3:16). The church is to declare God's wondrous deeds in providing salvation through Christ and his faithful character throughout all generations.

10 "You who ride on white donkeys,
sitting on your saddle blankets,
and you who walk along the road,
consider 11 the voice of the singers[a] at the watering places.
They recite the victories of the LORD,
the victories of his villagers in Israel.

"Then the people of the LORD
went down to the city gates.
12 'Wake up, wake up, Deborah!
Wake up, wake up, break out in song!
Arise, Barak!
Take captive your captives, son of Abinoam.'

13 "The remnant of the nobles came down;
the people of the LORD came down to me against the mighty.
14 Some came from Ephraim, whose roots were in Amalek;
Benjamin was with the people who followed you.
From Makir captains came down,
from Zebulun those who bear a commander's[a] staff.
15 The princes of Issachar were with Deborah;
yes, Issachar was with Barak,
sent under his command into the valley.
In the districts of Reuben
there was much searching of heart.
16 Why did you stay among the sheep pens[b]
to hear the whistling for the flocks?
In the districts of Reuben
there was much searching of heart.
17 Gilead stayed beyond the Jordan.
And Dan, why did he linger by the ships?
Asher remained on the coast
and stayed in his coves.
18 The people of Zebulun risked their very lives;
so did Naphtali on the terraced fields.

19 "Kings came, they fought,
the kings of Canaan fought.
At Taanach, by the waters of Megiddo,
they took no plunder of silver.
20 From the heavens the stars fought,
from their courses they fought against Sisera.
21 The river Kishon swept them away,
the age-old river, the river Kishon.
March on, my soul; be strong!
22 Then thundered the horses' hooves —
galloping, galloping go his mighty steeds.
23 'Curse Meroz,' said the angel of the LORD.
'Curse its people bitterly,
because they did not come to help the LORD,
to help the LORD against the mighty.'

24 "Most blessed of women be Jael,
the wife of Heber the Kenite,
most blessed of tent-dwelling women.

[a] *11,14* The meaning of the Hebrew for this word is uncertain. [b] *16* Or *the campfires*; or *the saddlebags*

JUDGES 6:13

THE LORD

The two uses of the word "lord" in this passage are illustrative of the supreme worth of God alone. Gideon first referred to the angel of God as "my lord." This usage indicates a polite address to a person worthy of respect. When Gideon speaks of God, however, he referred to him as "the LORD." This title declares the personal name of God (Yahweh), which was the name God used when speaking to Moses at Mount Horeb at the burning bush (Ex 3:13 – 16; 6:2 – 8). When the Israelites spoke of "Yahweh," they were referring to the nature and character of the One who had called them to himself and executed marvelous acts to deliver them and give them a land. Much more, he was the God whom they had sinned against, yet he had provided them with a means of fellowship with himself. God is not merely a person worthy of respect, but he is the One to whom all people owe their ultimate allegiance.

Jesus embodied the title of "Lord" during his earthly ministry, substitutionary death and victorious resurrection. As the ruler of all creation, he is to be preeminent in all things — including every facet of the lives of his children (Col 1:15 – 20).

25 He asked for water, and she gave him milk;
in a bowl fit for nobles she brought him curdled milk.
26 Her hand reached for the tent peg,
her right hand for the workman's hammer.
She struck Sisera, she crushed his head,
she shattered and pierced his temple.
27 At her feet he sank,
he fell; there he lay.
At her feet he sank, he fell;
where he sank, there he fell — dead.
28 "Through the window peered Sisera's mother;
behind the lattice she cried out,
'Why is his chariot so long in coming?
Why is the clatter of his chariots delayed?'
29 The wisest of her ladies answer her;
indeed, she keeps saying to herself,
30 'Are they not finding and dividing the spoils:
a woman or two for each man,
colorful garments as plunder for Sisera,
colorful garments embroidered,
highly embroidered garments for my neck —
all this as plunder?'

31 "So may all your enemies perish, LORD!
But may all who love you be like the sun
when it rises in its strength."

Then the land had peace forty years.

Gideon

6 The Israelites did evil in the eyes of the LORD, and for seven years he gave
them into the hands of the Midianites. 2Because the power of Midian was
so oppressive, the Israelites prepared shelters for themselves in mountain
clefts, caves and strongholds. 3Whenever the Israelites planted their crops, the
Midianites, Amalekites and other eastern peoples invaded the country. 4They
camped on the land and ruined the crops all the way to Gaza and did not spare a
living thing for Israel, neither sheep nor cattle nor donkeys. 5They came up with
their livestock and their tents like swarms of locusts. It was impossible to count
them or their camels; they invaded the land to ravage it. 6Midian so impoverished the Israelites that they cried out to the LORD for help.
7When the Israelites cried out to the LORD because of Midian, 8he sent them
a prophet, who said, "This is what the LORD, the God of Israel, says: I brought
you up out of Egypt, out of the land of slavery. 9I rescued you from the hand of
the Egyptians. And I delivered you from the hand of all your oppressors; I drove
them out before you and gave you their land. 10I said to you, 'I am the LORD your
God; do not worship the gods of the Amorites, in whose land you live.' But you
have not listened to me."
11The angel of the LORD came and sat down under the oak in Ophrah that
belonged to Joash the Abiezrite, where his son Gideon was threshing wheat in a
winepress to keep it from the Midianites. 12When the angel of the LORD appeared
to Gideon, he said, "The LORD is with you, mighty warrior."
13"Pardon me, my lord," Gideon replied, "but if the LORD is with us, why has all
this happened to us? Where are all his wonders that our ancestors told us about
when they said, 'Did not the LORD bring us up out of Egypt?' But now the LORD
has abandoned us and given us into the hand of Midian."
14The LORD turned to him and said, "Go in the strength you have and save
Israel out of Midian's hand. Am I not sending you?"

15“Pardon me, my lord,” Gideon replied, “but how can I save Israel? My clan is
the weakest in Manasseh, and I am the least in my family.”
16The LORD answered, “I will be with you, and you will strike down all the
Midianites, leaving none alive.”
17Gideon replied, “If now I have found favor in your eyes, give me a sign that
it is really you talking to me. 18Please do not go away until I come back and bring
my offering and set it before you.”
And the LORD said, “I will wait until you return.”
19Gideon went inside, prepared a young goat, and from an ephah[a] of flour he
made bread without yeast. Putting the meat in a basket and its broth in a pot, he
brought them out and offered them to him under the oak.
20The angel of God said to him, “Take the meat and the unleavened bread,
place them on this rock, and pour out the broth.” And Gideon did so. 21Then the
angel of the LORD touched the meat and the unleavened bread with the tip of
the staff that was in his hand. Fire flared from the rock, consuming the meat and
the bread. And the angel of the LORD disappeared. 22When Gideon realized that
it was the angel of the LORD, he exclaimed, “Alas, Sovereign LORD! I have seen
the angel of the LORD face to face!”
23But the LORD said to him, “Peace! Do not be afraid. You are not going to die.”
24So Gideon built an altar to the LORD there and called it The LORD Is Peace.
To this day it stands in Ophrah of the Abiezrites.
25That same night the LORD said to him, “Take the second bull from your father’s herd, the one seven years old.[b] Tear down your father’s altar to Baal and
cut down the Asherah pole[c] beside it. 26Then build a proper kind of[d] altar to the
LORD your God on the top of this height. Using the wood of the Asherah pole that
you cut down, offer the second[e] bull as a burnt offering.”
27So Gideon took ten of his servants and did as the LORD told him. But because
he was afraid of his family and the townspeople, he did it at night rather than in
the daytime.
28In the morning when the people of the town got up, there was Baal’s altar,
demolished, with the Asherah pole beside it cut down and the second bull sacrificed on the newly built altar!
29They asked each other, “Who did this?”
When they carefully investigated, they were told, “Gideon son of Joash did it.”
30The people of the town demanded of Joash, “Bring out your son. He must
die, because he has broken down Baal’s altar and cut down the Asherah pole
beside it.”
31But Joash replied to the hostile crowd around him, “Are you going to plead
Baal’s cause? Are you trying to save him? Whoever fights for him shall be put to
death by morning! If Baal really is a god, he can defend himself when someone
breaks down his altar.” 32So because Gideon broke down Baal’s altar, they gave
him the name Jerub-Baal[f] that day, saying, “Let Baal contend with him.”
33Now all the Midianites, Amalekites and other eastern peoples joined forces and crossed over the Jordan and camped in the Valley of Jezreel. 34Then the
Spirit of the LORD came on Gideon, and he blew a trumpet, summoning the Abiezrites to follow him. 35He sent messengers throughout Manasseh, calling them
to arms, and also into Asher, Zebulun and Naphtali, so that they too went up to
meet them.
36Gideon said to God, “If you will save Israel by my hand as you have promised — 37look, I will place a wool fleece on the threshing floor. If there is dew
only on the fleece and all the ground is dry, then I will know that you will save
Israel by my hand, as you said.” 38And that is what happened. Gideon rose early
the next day; he squeezed the fleece and wrung out the dew — a bowlful of water.

---

[a] *19* That is, probably about 36 pounds or about 16 kilograms [b] *25* Or *Take a full-grown, mature bull from your father’s herd* [c] *25* That is, a wooden symbol of the goddess Asherah; also in verses 26, 28 and 30 [d] *26* Or *build with layers of stone an* [e] *26* Or *full-grown*; also in verse 28 [f] *32* *Jerub-Baal* probably means *let Baal contend.*

PUTTING GOD TO THE TEST

Gideon put God to the test. Gideon, by placing a fleece on the floor, took matters into his own hands and showed that he did not fully trust God. God had already told him that he would fight on the behalf of his people. Gideon's practice, however, confirmed that he was reluctant to simply take God at his word. The tangible symbol of the wet fleece was a secondary sign of God's faithfulness to confirm his word to the leader he had chosen.

Faced with a far more daunting challenge, Jesus, at the beginning of his earthly ministry, was placed in a situation in which his trust in God's word was challenged (Mt 4:1 – 11). Satan tempted Jesus to circumvent God's plan and take matters into his own hands. First, after fasting for forty days, Jesus was challenged to turn stones into bread. Jesus, who would soon multiply a meager amount of fish and bread to feed the multitudes, surely had the ability to turn a stone into a piece of bread. But this action would have amounted to a failure to trust that God the Father, in his time and ways, would supply Jesus' needs. Second, Satan tempted Jesus to throw himself off the highest point of the temple, citing that angels would protect him. This temptation would have bypassed the God-ordained path for his life, death and victorious resurrection. Third, the King of the universe was tempted to doubt God's word and procure his own path to power and glory.

At each juncture, Jesus refused to test God's word and faithfulness. Instead, relying on the power of God's promises, he rejected Satan and continued to walk in confidence that God would provide. Throughout Jesus' earthly ministry, religious leaders continued to place tests before Jesus in an effort to discount his claims to being the Son of God (Mt 16:1; Mk 10:2). Jesus refused to cater to their demands, while indicating that his public words and deeds were more than enough to show them who he was.

God's Word and his proven faithfulness are a strong foundation for the faith of his people today. Met with the challenges of life in a fallen world, the church need not test God with trivial exercises like Gideon did here. God's people, following the pattern set by Jesus, can stand securely on his Word and his character even in an uncertain future.

[39]Then Gideon said to God, "Do not be angry with me. Let me make just one more request. Allow me one more test with the fleece, but this time make the fleece dry and let the ground be covered with dew." [40]That night God did so. Only the fleece was dry; all the ground was covered with dew.

Gideon Defeats the Midianites

7 Early in the morning, Jerub-Baal (that is, Gideon) and all his men camped at the spring of Harod. The camp of Midian was north of them in the valley near the hill of Moreh. [2]The LORD said to Gideon, "You have too many men. I cannot deliver Midian into their hands, or Israel would boast against me, 'My own strength has saved me.' [3]Now announce to the army, 'Anyone who trembles with fear may turn back and leave Mount Gilead.' " So twenty-two thousand men left, while ten thousand remained.

[4]But the LORD said to Gideon, "There are still too many men. Take them down to the water, and I will thin them out for you there. If I say, 'This one shall go with you,' he shall go; but if I say, 'This one shall not go with you,' he shall not go."

[5]So Gideon took the men down to the water. There the LORD told him, "Separate those who lap the water with their tongues as a dog laps from those who kneel down to drink." [6]Three hundred of them drank from cupped hands, lapping like dogs. All the rest got down on their knees to drink.

[7]The LORD said to Gideon, "With the three hundred men that lapped I will save you and give the Midianites into your hands. Let all the others go home." [8]So Gideon sent the rest of the Israelites home but kept the three hundred, who took over the provisions and trumpets of the others.

Now the camp of Midian lay below him in the valley. [9]During that night the LORD said to Gideon, "Get up, go down against the camp, because I am going to give it into your hands. [10]If you are afraid to attack, go down to the camp with your servant Purah [11]and listen to what they are saying. Afterward, you will be encouraged to attack the camp." So he and Purah his servant went down to the outposts of the camp. [12]The Midianites, the Amalekites and all the other eastern peoples had settled in the valley, thick as locusts. Their camels could no more be counted than the sand on the seashore.

[13]Gideon arrived just as a man was telling a friend his dream. "I had a dream," he was saying. "A round loaf of barley bread came tumbling into the Midianite camp. It struck the tent with such force that the tent overturned and collapsed."

[14]His friend responded, "This can be nothing other than the sword of Gideon son of Joash, the Israelite. God has given the Midianites and the whole camp into his hands."

[15]When Gideon heard the dream and its interpretation, he bowed down and worshiped. He returned to the camp of Israel and called out, "Get up! The LORD has given the Midianite camp into your hands." [16]Dividing the three hundred men into three companies, he placed trumpets and empty jars in the hands of all of them, with torches inside.

[17]"Watch me," he told them. "Follow my lead. When I get to the edge of the camp, do exactly as I do. [18]When I and all who are with me blow our trumpets, then from all around the camp blow yours and shout, 'For the LORD and for Gideon.' "

[19]Gideon and the hundred men with him reached the edge of the camp at the beginning of the middle watch, just after they had changed the guard. They blew their trumpets and broke the jars that were in their hands. [20]The three companies blew the trumpets and smashed the jars. Grasping the torches in their left hands and holding in their right hands the trumpets they were to blow, they shouted, "A sword for the LORD and for Gideon!" [21]While each man held his position around the camp, all the Midianites ran, crying out as they fled.

[22]When the three hundred trumpets sounded, the LORD caused the men throughout the camp to turn on each other with their swords. The army fled to

Beth Shittah toward Zererah as far as the border of Abel Meholah near Tabbath. [23]Israelites from Naphtali, Asher and all Manasseh were called out, and they pursued the Midianites. [24]Gideon sent messengers throughout the hill country of Ephraim, saying, "Come down against the Midianites and seize the waters of the Jordan ahead of them as far as Beth Barah."

So all the men of Ephraim were called out and they seized the waters of the Jordan as far as Beth Barah. [25]They also captured two of the Midianite leaders, Oreb and Zeeb. They killed Oreb at the rock of Oreb, and Zeeb at the winepress of Zeeb. They pursued the Midianites and brought the heads of Oreb and Zeeb to Gideon, who was by the Jordan.

Zebah and Zalmunna

8 Now the Ephraimites asked Gideon, "Why have you treated us like this? Why didn't you call us when you went to fight Midian?" And they challenged him vigorously.

[2]But he answered them, "What have I accomplished compared to you? Aren't the gleanings of Ephraim's grapes better than the full grape harvest of Abiezer? [3]God gave Oreb and Zeeb, the Midianite leaders, into your hands. What was I able to do compared to you?" At this, their resentment against him subsided.

[4]Gideon and his three hundred men, exhausted yet keeping up the pursuit, came to the Jordan and crossed it. [5]He said to the men of Sukkoth, "Give my troops some bread; they are worn out, and I am still pursuing Zebah and Zalmunna, the kings of Midian."

[6]But the officials of Sukkoth said, "Do you already have the hands of Zebah and Zalmunna in your possession? Why should we give bread to your troops?"

[7]Then Gideon replied, "Just for that, when the LORD has given Zebah and Zalmunna into my hand, I will tear your flesh with desert thorns and briers."

[8]From there he went up to Peniel[a] and made the same request of them, but they answered as the men of Sukkoth had. [9]So he said to the men of Peniel, "When I return in triumph, I will tear down this tower."

[10]Now Zebah and Zalmunna were in Karkor with a force of about fifteen thousand men, all that were left of the armies of the eastern peoples; a hundred and twenty thousand swordsmen had fallen. [11]Gideon went up by the route of the nomads east of Nobah and Jogbehah and attacked the unsuspecting army. [12]Zebah and Zalmunna, the two kings of Midian, fled, but he pursued them and captured them, routing their entire army.

[13]Gideon son of Joash then returned from the battle by the Pass of Heres. [14]He caught a young man of Sukkoth and questioned him, and the young man wrote down for him the names of the seventy-seven officials of Sukkoth, the elders of the town. [15]Then Gideon came and said to the men of Sukkoth, "Here are Zebah and Zalmunna, about whom you taunted me by saying, 'Do you already have the hands of Zebah and Zalmunna in your possession? Why should we give bread to your exhausted men?' " [16]He took the elders of the town and taught the men of Sukkoth a lesson by punishing them with desert thorns and briers. [17]He also pulled down the tower of Peniel and killed the men of the town.

[18]Then he asked Zebah and Zalmunna, "What kind of men did you kill at Tabor?"

"Men like you," they answered, "each one with the bearing of a prince."

[19]Gideon replied, "Those were my brothers, the sons of my own mother. As surely as the LORD lives, if you had spared their lives, I would not kill you." [20]Turning to Jether, his oldest son, he said, "Kill them!" But Jether did not draw his sword, because he was only a boy and was afraid.

[21]Zebah and Zalmunna said, "Come, do it yourself. 'As is the man, so is his strength.' " So Gideon stepped forward and killed them, and took the ornaments off their camels' necks.

---

[a] 8 Hebrew *Penuel,* a variant of *Peniel*; also in verses 9 and 17

Gideon's Ephod

22The Israelites said to Gideon, "Rule over us — you, your son and your grandson — because you have saved us from the hand of Midian."
23But Gideon told them, "I will not rule over you, nor will my son rule over you.
The LORD will rule over you." 24And he said, "I do have one request, that each of
you give me an earring from your share of the plunder." (It was the custom of the
Ishmaelites to wear gold earrings.)
25They answered, "We'll be glad to give them." So they spread out a garment,
and each of them threw a ring from his plunder onto it. 26The weight of the gold
rings he asked for came to seventeen hundred shekels,[a] not counting the ornaments, the pendants and the purple garments worn by the kings of Midian or the
chains that were on their camels' necks. 27Gideon made the gold into an ephod,
which he placed in Ophrah, his town. All Israel prostituted themselves by worshiping it there, and it became a snare to Gideon and his family.

Gideon's Death

28Thus Midian was subdued before the Israelites and did not raise its head
again. During Gideon's lifetime, the land had peace forty years.
29Jerub-Baal son of Joash went back home to live. 30He had seventy sons of his
own, for he had many wives. 31His concubine, who lived in Shechem, also bore
him a son, whom he named Abimelek. 32Gideon son of Joash died at a good old
age and was buried in the tomb of his father Joash in Ophrah of the Abiezrites.
33No sooner had Gideon died than the Israelites again prostituted themselves
to the Baals. They set up Baal-Berith as their god 34and did not remember the
LORD their God, who had rescued them from the hands of all their enemies on
every side. 35They also failed to show any loyalty to the family of Jerub-Baal (that
is, Gideon) in spite of all the good things he had done for them.

Abimelek

9 Abimelek son of Jerub-Baal went to his mother's brothers in Shechem and
said to them and to all his mother's clan, 2"Ask all the citizens of Shechem,
'Which is better for you: to have all seventy of Jerub-Baal's sons rule over you, or
just one man?' Remember, I am your flesh and blood."
3When the brothers repeated all this to the citizens of Shechem, they were
inclined to follow Abimelek, for they said, "He is related to us." 4They gave him
seventy shekels[b] of silver from the temple of Baal-Berith, and Abimelek used it
to hire reckless scoundrels, who became his followers. 5He went to his father's
home in Ophrah and on one stone murdered his seventy brothers, the sons of
Jerub-Baal. But Jotham, the youngest son of Jerub-Baal, escaped by hiding.
6Then all the citizens of Shechem and Beth Millo gathered beside the great tree
at the pillar in Shechem to crown Abimelek king.
7When Jotham was told about this, he climbed up on the top of Mount Gerizim and shouted to them, "Listen to me, citizens of Shechem, so that God may
listen to you. 8One day the trees went out to anoint a king for themselves. They
said to the olive tree, 'Be our king.'
9"But the olive tree answered, 'Should I give up my oil, by which both gods and
humans are honored, to hold sway over the trees?'
10"Next, the trees said to the fig tree, 'Come and be our king.'
11"But the fig tree replied, 'Should I give up my fruit, so good and sweet, to
hold sway over the trees?'
12"Then the trees said to the vine, 'Come and be our king.'
13"But the vine answered, 'Should I give up my wine, which cheers both gods
and humans, to hold sway over the trees?'
14"Finally all the trees said to the thornbush, 'Come and be our king.'

---

[a] *26* That is, about 43 pounds or about 20 kilograms [b] *4* That is, about 1 3/4 pounds or about 800 grams

15 “The thornbush said to the trees, ‘If you really want to anoint me king over you, come and take refuge in my shade; but if not, then let fire come out of the thornbush and consume the cedars of Lebanon!’

16 “Have you acted honorably and in good faith by making Abimelek king? Have you been fair to Jerub-Baal and his family? Have you treated him as he deserves? 17 Remember that my father fought for you and risked his life to rescue you from the hand of Midian. 18 But today you have revolted against my father’s family. You have murdered his seventy sons on a single stone and have made Abimelek, the son of his female slave, king over the citizens of Shechem because he is related to you. 19 So have you acted honorably and in good faith toward Jerub-Baal and his family today? If you have, may Abimelek be your joy, and may you be his, too! 20 But if you have not, let fire come out from Abimelek and consume you, the citizens of Shechem and Beth Millo, and let fire come out from you, the citizens of Shechem and Beth Millo, and consume Abimelek!”

21 Then Jotham fled, escaping to Beer, and he lived there because he was afraid of his brother Abimelek.

22 After Abimelek had governed Israel three years, 23 God stirred up animosity between Abimelek and the citizens of Shechem so that they acted treacherously against Abimelek. 24 God did this in order that the crime against Jerub-Baal’s seventy sons, the shedding of their blood, might be avenged on their brother Abimelek and on the citizens of Shechem, who had helped him murder his brothers. 25 In opposition to him these citizens of Shechem set men on the hilltops to ambush and rob everyone who passed by, and this was reported to Abimelek.

26 Now Gaal son of Ebed moved with his clan into Shechem, and its citizens put their confidence in him. 27 After they had gone out into the fields and gathered the grapes and trodden them, they held a festival in the temple of their god. While they were eating and drinking, they cursed Abimelek. 28 Then Gaal son of Ebed said, “Who is Abimelek, and why should we Shechemites be subject to him? Isn’t he Jerub-Baal’s son, and isn’t Zebul his deputy? Serve the family of Hamor, Shechem’s father! Why should we serve Abimelek? 29 If only this people were under my command! Then I would get rid of him. I would say to Abimelek, ‘Call out your whole army!’ ”[a]

30 When Zebul the governor of the city heard what Gaal son of Ebed said, he was very angry. 31 Under cover he sent messengers to Abimelek, saying, “Gaal son of Ebed and his clan have come to Shechem and are stirring up the city against you. 32 Now then, during the night you and your men should come and lie in wait in the fields. 33 In the morning at sunrise, advance against the city. When Gaal and his men come out against you, seize the opportunity to attack them.”

34 So Abimelek and all his troops set out by night and took up concealed positions near Shechem in four companies. 35 Now Gaal son of Ebed had gone out and was standing at the entrance of the city gate just as Abimelek and his troops came out from their hiding place.

36 When Gaal saw them, he said to Zebul, “Look, people are coming down from the tops of the mountains!”

Zebul replied, “You mistake the shadows of the mountains for men.”

37 But Gaal spoke up again: “Look, people are coming down from the central hill,[b] and a company is coming from the direction of the diviners’ tree.”

38 Then Zebul said to him, “Where is your big talk now, you who said, ‘Who is Abimelek that we should be subject to him?’ Aren’t these the men you ridiculed? Go out and fight them!”

39 So Gaal led out[c] the citizens of Shechem and fought Abimelek. 40 Abimelek chased him all the way to the entrance of the gate, and many were killed as they fled. 41 Then Abimelek stayed in Arumah, and Zebul drove Gaal and his clan out of Shechem.

---

[a] 29 Septuagint; Hebrew *him.” Then he said to Abimelek, “Call out your whole army!”*

[b] 37 The Hebrew for this phrase means *the navel of the earth.* [c] 39 Or *Gaal went out in the sight of*

HUMAN LEADERSHIP AFTER THE FALL

The nation of Israel was meant to be a theocracy — a people living under the sovereign rule and reign of God. The story of the people of God demonstrated their consistent desire to elevate human leaders to dignified, and often aberrant, positions of power. The people of God never seemed to be satisfied with what God had established for them.

Human government is the locus of the cumulative power of people which has been entrusted to leaders in unique ways throughout the history of God's people. At times, human leaders walk faithfully with God and lead the people to repentance and obedience. These leaders can be valuable means of restraining evil, judging wickedness and instructing the nation in the ways of God.

More often, human government provides an outlet for pride and rebellion. The book of Judges details the destruction that resulted from human leaders who were unwilling to submit to God and who were absorbed with their own authority. Not only were these leaders prone to lead people to rebel, but they also persecuted those seeking to walk faithfully with God.

The failure of human leaders and the persecution of God's people were addressed by Jesus in what is referred to as the Sermon on the Mount (Mt 5 – 7). Jesus cautioned his followers against defensiveness or retaliation for persecution. Instead, he said that people are blessed when they are persecuted by virtue of their association with him. Those who are persecuted can rest assured that they will receive a reward in heaven.

Broken human government is an ongoing reality of life in a fallen world, and it can drive the church to either cower in fear or persevere through God-honoring submission to human leaders, praying on their behalf and honoring the office these leaders hold (Ro 13:1 – 7). God, in his grand sovereignty, holds the destiny of the world and the hearts of the leaders in his ever-capable hands. Even in the midst of the rebellion of leaders, God's people can trust that he is working all things together for their good and his glory.

42The next day the people of Shechem went out to the fields, and this was reported to Abimelek. 43So he took his men, divided them into three companies and set an ambush in the fields. When he saw the people coming out of the city, he rose to attack them. 44Abimelek and the companies with him rushed forward to a position at the entrance of the city gate. Then two companies attacked those in the fields and struck them down. 45All that day Abimelek pressed his attack against the city until he had captured it and killed its people. Then he destroyed the city and scattered salt over it.

46On hearing this, the citizens in the tower of Shechem went into the stronghold of the temple of El-Berith. 47When Abimelek heard that they had assembled there, 48he and all his men went up Mount Zalmon. He took an ax and cut off some branches, which he lifted to his shoulders. He ordered the men with him, "Quick! Do what you have seen me do!" 49So all the men cut branches and followed Abimelek. They piled them against the stronghold and set it on fire with the people still inside. So all the people in the tower of Shechem, about a thousand men and women, also died.

50Next Abimelek went to Thebez and besieged it and captured it. 51Inside the city, however, was a strong tower, to which all the men and women — all the people of the city — had fled. They had locked themselves in and climbed up on the tower roof. 52Abimelek went to the tower and attacked it. But as he approached the entrance to the tower to set it on fire, 53a woman dropped an upper millstone on his head and cracked his skull.

54Hurriedly he called to his armor-bearer, "Draw your sword and kill me, so that they can't say, 'A woman killed him.'" So his servant ran him through, and he died. 55When the Israelites saw that Abimelek was dead, they went home.

56Thus God repaid the wickedness that Abimelek had done to his father by murdering his seventy brothers. 57God also made the people of Shechem pay for all their wickedness. The curse of Jotham son of Jerub-Baal came on them.

Tola

10 After the time of Abimelek, a man of Issachar named Tola son of Puah, the son of Dodo, rose to save Israel. He lived in Shamir, in the hill country of Ephraim. 2He led[a] Israel twenty-three years; then he died, and was buried in Shamir.

Jair

3He was followed by Jair of Gilead, who led Israel twenty-two years. 4He had thirty sons, who rode thirty donkeys. They controlled thirty towns in Gilead, which to this day are called Havvoth Jair.[b] 5When Jair died, he was buried in Kamon.

Jephthah

6Again the Israelites did evil in the eyes of the LORD. They served the Baals and the Ashtoreths, and the gods of Aram, the gods of Sidon, the gods of Moab, the gods of the Ammonites and the gods of the Philistines. And because the Israelites forsook the LORD and no longer served him, 7he became angry with them. He sold them into the hands of the Philistines and the Ammonites, 8who that year shattered and crushed them. For eighteen years they oppressed all the Israelites on the east side of the Jordan in Gilead, the land of the Amorites. 9The Ammonites also crossed the Jordan to fight against Judah, Benjamin and Ephraim; Israel was in great distress. 10Then the Israelites cried out to the LORD, "We have sinned against you, forsaking our God and serving the Baals."

11The LORD replied, "When the Egyptians, the Amorites, the Ammonites, the Philistines, 12the Sidonians, the Amalekites and the Maonites[c] oppressed you and you cried to me for help, did I not save you from their hands? 13But you have

[a] 2 Traditionally *judged*; also in verse 3 [b] 4 Or *called the settlements of Jair* [c] 12 Hebrew; some Septuagint manuscripts *Midianites*

JUDGES 9:50 – 56

LONGING FOR A KING

Abimelek, who was the son of Gideon by his Shechemite slave woman turned concubine (Jdg 8:11; 9:18), suffered the just consequences for his sin. The actions of the woman and Abimelek's armor-bearer are clearly the execution of the judgment of God. Though Abimelek schemed to have himself crowned king, it quickly became evident that his kingdom would only harness the violent depravity of humanity (9:1 – 6,42 – 49). People need leaders to lead them, but human kings, like Abimelek, are incapable of ushering people into the *shalom* of God. The Israelites' deep-seated longing for a king and the constant disappointment in human kings left a void, which King Jesus eventually filled. His life demonstrated that only the sinless Son of God would be capable of leading people to follow God rightly. John, in his apocalyptic visions in the book of Revelation, declares Jesus to be the "Lord of lords and King of kings" (Rev 17:14; 19:16). All human leadership pales in comparison to the majesty of Jesus' rule and reign. By submitting to him, men and women can be led into a true and lasting kingdom not marked by death and depravity, but filled with love, peace and joy. And his great kingdom will have no end.

forsaken me and served other gods, so I will no longer save you. [14]Go and cry out
to the gods you have chosen. Let them save you when you are in trouble!"
[15]But the Israelites said to the LORD, "We have sinned. Do with us whatever
you think best, but please rescue us now." [16]Then they got rid of the foreign gods
among them and served the LORD. And he could bear Israel's misery no longer.
[17]When the Ammonites were called to arms and camped in Gilead, the Israelites assembled and camped at Mizpah. [18]The leaders of the people of Gilead
said to each other, "Whoever will take the lead in attacking the Ammonites will
be head over all who live in Gilead."

11 Jephthah the Gileadite was a mighty warrior. His father was Gilead; his
mother was a prostitute. [2]Gilead's wife also bore him sons, and when they
were grown up, they drove Jephthah away. "You are not going to get any inheritance in our family," they said, "because you are the son of another woman." [3]So
Jephthah fled from his brothers and settled in the land of Tob, where a gang of
scoundrels gathered around him and followed him.
[4]Some time later, when the Ammonites were fighting against Israel, [5]the elders of Gilead went to get Jephthah from the land of Tob. [6]"Come," they said, "be
our commander, so we can fight the Ammonites."
[7]Jephthah said to them, "Didn't you hate me and drive me from my father's
house? Why do you come to me now, when you're in trouble?"
[8]The elders of Gilead said to him, "Nevertheless, we are turning to you now;
come with us to fight the Ammonites, and you will be head over all of us who
live in Gilead."
[9]Jephthah answered, "Suppose you take me back to fight the Ammonites and
the LORD gives them to me — will I really be your head?"
[10]The elders of Gilead replied, "The LORD is our witness; we will certainly do
as you say." [11]So Jephthah went with the elders of Gilead, and the people made
him head and commander over them. And he repeated all his words before the
LORD in Mizpah.
[12]Then Jephthah sent messengers to the Ammonite king with the question:
"What do you have against me that you have attacked my country?"
[13]The king of the Ammonites answered Jephthah's messengers, "When Israel
came up out of Egypt, they took away my land from the Arnon to the Jabbok, all
the way to the Jordan. Now give it back peaceably."
[14]Jephthah sent back messengers to the Ammonite king, [15]saying:

"This is what Jephthah says: Israel did not take the land of Moab or the
land of the Ammonites. [16]But when they came up out of Egypt, Israel went
through the wilderness to the Red Sea[a] and on to Kadesh. [17]Then Israel sent
messengers to the king of Edom, saying, 'Give us permission to go through
your country,' but the king of Edom would not listen. They sent also to the
king of Moab, and he refused. So Israel stayed at Kadesh.
[18]"Next they traveled through the wilderness, skirted the lands of Edom
and Moab, passed along the eastern side of the country of Moab, and
camped on the other side of the Arnon. They did not enter the territory of
Moab, for the Arnon was its border.
[19]"Then Israel sent messengers to Sihon king of the Amorites, who ruled
in Heshbon, and said to him, 'Let us pass through your country to our own
place.' [20]Sihon, however, did not trust Israel[b] to pass through his territory.
He mustered all his troops and encamped at Jahaz and fought with Israel.
[21]"Then the LORD, the God of Israel, gave Sihon and his whole army into
Israel's hands, and they defeated them. Israel took over all the land of the
Amorites who lived in that country, [22]capturing all of it from the Arnon to
the Jabbok and from the desert to the Jordan.
[23]"Now since the LORD, the God of Israel, has driven the Amorites out
before his people Israel, what right have you to take it over? [24]Will you not

[a] *16* Or *the Sea of Reeds* [b] *20* Or *however, would not make an agreement for Israel*

JUDGES 11:1 – 3

MIGHTY IN FAITH

The author of Judges refers to Jephthah, who became one of Israel's judges, as "a mighty warrior." Jephthah was from Gilead, located east of the Jordan River. Jephthah's might distinguished him from other men. Because he was the son of an illegitimate relationship, his half brothers expelled him from the family. As a result, he fled to the land of Tob, and there he became the leader of a "gang of scoundrels" — likely roaming mercenaries. Centuries later, in the book of Hebrews, Jephthah appeared in another list. This time he is singled out, not for his might, his illegitimate birth or his wayward relationships, but for his faith (Heb 11:32). He is listed alongside greats such as Abraham, Moses and David as one who modeled the type of faith that all Christians should possess. Jephthah demonstrated that faith is the distinguishing mark of greatness in the economy of the kingdom of God.

take what your god Chemosh gives you? Likewise, whatever the LORD our God has given us, we will possess. [25]Are you any better than Balak son of Zippor, king of Moab? Did he ever quarrel with Israel or fight with them? [26]For three hundred years Israel occupied Heshbon, Aroer, the surrounding settlements and all the towns along the Arnon. Why didn't you retake them during that time? [27]I have not wronged you, but you are doing me wrong by waging war against me. Let the LORD, the Judge, decide the dispute this day between the Israelites and the Ammonites."

[28]The king of Ammon, however, paid no attention to the message Jephthah sent him.

[29]Then the Spirit of the LORD came on Jephthah. He crossed Gilead and Manasseh, passed through Mizpah of Gilead, and from there he advanced against the Ammonites. [30]And Jephthah made a vow to the LORD: "If you give the Ammonites into my hands, [31]whatever comes out of the door of my house to meet me when I return in triumph from the Ammonites will be the LORD's, and I will sacrifice it as a burnt offering."

[32]Then Jephthah went over to fight the Ammonites, and the LORD gave them into his hands. [33]He devastated twenty towns from Aroer to the vicinity of Minnith, as far as Abel Keramim. Thus Israel subdued Ammon.

[34]When Jephthah returned to his home in Mizpah, who should come out to meet him but his daughter, dancing to the sound of timbrels! She was an only child. Except for her he had neither son nor daughter. [35]When he saw her, he tore his clothes and cried, "Oh no, my daughter! You have brought me down and I am devastated. I have made a vow to the LORD that I cannot break."

[36]"My father," she replied, "you have given your word to the LORD. Do to me just as you promised, now that the LORD has avenged you of your enemies, the Ammonites. [37]But grant me this one request," she said. "Give me two months to roam the hills and weep with my friends, because I will never marry."

[38]"You may go," he said. And he let her go for two months. She and her friends went into the hills and wept because she would never marry. [39]After the two months, she returned to her father, and he did to her as he had vowed. And she was a virgin.

From this comes the Israelite tradition [40]that each year the young women of Israel go out for four days to commemorate the daughter of Jephthah the Gileadite.

Jephthah and Ephraim

12 The Ephraimite forces were called out, and they crossed over to Zaphon. They said to Jephthah, "Why did you go to fight the Ammonites without calling us to go with you? We're going to burn down your house over your head."

[2]Jephthah answered, "I and my people were engaged in a great struggle with the Ammonites, and although I called, you didn't save me out of their hands. [3]When I saw that you wouldn't help, I took my life in my hands and crossed over to fight the Ammonites, and the LORD gave me the victory over them. Now why have you come up today to fight me?"

[4]Jephthah then called together the men of Gilead and fought against Ephraim. The Gileadites struck them down because the Ephraimites had said, "You Gileadites are renegades from Ephraim and Manasseh." [5]The Gileadites captured the fords of the Jordan leading to Ephraim, and whenever a survivor of Ephraim said, "Let me cross over," the men of Gilead asked him, "Are you an Ephraimite?" If he replied, "No," [6]they said, "All right, say 'Shibboleth.'" If he said, "Sibboleth," because he could not pronounce the word correctly, they seized him and killed him at the fords of the Jordan. Forty-two thousand Ephraimites were killed at that time.

[7]Jephthah led[a] Israel six years. Then Jephthah the Gileadite died and was buried in a town in Gilead.

---

[a] 7 Traditionally *judged*; also in verses 8-14

Ibzan, Elon and Abdon

8After him, Ibzan of Bethlehem led Israel. 9He had thirty sons and thirty
daughters. He gave his daughters away in marriage to those outside his clan, and
for his sons he brought in thirty young women as wives from outside his clan.
Ibzan led Israel seven years. 10Then Ibzan died and was buried in Bethlehem.
11After him, Elon the Zebulunite led Israel ten years. 12Then Elon died and
was buried in Aijalon in the land of Zebulun.
13After him, Abdon son of Hillel, from Pirathon, led Israel. 14He had forty sons
and thirty grandsons, who rode on seventy donkeys. He led Israel eight years.
15Then Abdon son of Hillel died and was buried at Pirathon in Ephraim, in the
hill country of the Amalekites.

The Birth of Samson

13 Again the Israelites did evil in the eyes of the LORD, so the LORD delivered
them into the hands of the Philistines for forty years.
2A certain man of Zorah, named Manoah, from the clan of the Danites, had
a wife who was childless, unable to give birth. 3The angel of the LORD appeared
to her and said, "You are barren and childless, but you are going to become
pregnant and give birth to a son. 4Now see to it that you drink no wine or other
fermented drink and that you do not eat anything unclean. 5You will become
pregnant and have a son whose head is never to be touched by a razor because
the boy is to be a Nazirite, dedicated to God from the womb. He will take the lead
in delivering Israel from the hands of the Philistines."
6Then the woman went to her husband and told him, "A man of God came
to me. He looked like an angel of God, very awesome. I didn't ask him where he
came from, and he didn't tell me his name. 7But he said to me, 'You will become
pregnant and have a son. Now then, drink no wine or other fermented drink and
do not eat anything unclean, because the boy will be a Nazirite of God from the
womb until the day of his death.' "
8Then Manoah prayed to the LORD: "Pardon your servant, Lord. I beg you to
let the man of God you sent to us come again to teach us how to bring up the boy
who is to be born."
9God heard Manoah, and the angel of God came again to the woman while
she was out in the field; but her husband Manoah was not with her. 10The woman hurried to tell her husband, "He's here! The man who appeared to me the
other day!"
11Manoah got up and followed his wife. When he came to the man, he said,
"Are you the man who talked to my wife?"
"I am," he said.
12So Manoah asked him, "When your words are fulfilled, what is to be the rule
that governs the boy's life and work?"
13The angel of the LORD answered, "Your wife must do all that I have told her.
14She must not eat anything that comes from the grapevine, nor drink any wine
or other fermented drink nor eat anything unclean. She must do everything I
have commanded her."
15Manoah said to the angel of the LORD, "We would like you to stay until we
prepare a young goat for you."
16The angel of the LORD replied, "Even though you detain me, I will not eat any
of your food. But if you prepare a burnt offering, offer it to the LORD." (Manoah
did not realize that it was the angel of the LORD.)
17Then Manoah inquired of the angel of the LORD, "What is your name, so that
we may honor you when your word comes true?"
18He replied, "Why do you ask my name? It is beyond understanding.[a]" 19Then
Manoah took a young goat, together with the grain offering, and sacrificed it on
a rock to the LORD. And the LORD did an amazing thing while Manoah and his

---

[a] *18* Or *is wonderful*

wife watched: [20]As the flame blazed up from the altar toward heaven, the angel
of the LORD ascended in the flame. Seeing this, Manoah and his wife fell with
their faces to the ground. [21]When the angel of the LORD did not show himself
again to Manoah and his wife, Manoah realized that it was the angel of the LORD.
[22]"We are doomed to die!" he said to his wife. "We have seen God!"
[23]But his wife answered, "If the LORD had meant to kill us, he would not have
accepted a burnt offering and grain offering from our hands, nor shown us all
these things or now told us this."
[24]The woman gave birth to a boy and named him Samson. He grew and the
LORD blessed him, [25]and the Spirit of the LORD began to stir him while he was in
Mahaneh Dan, between Zorah and Eshtaol.

Samson's Marriage

14 Samson went down to Timnah and saw there a young Philistine woman.
[2]When he returned, he said to his father and mother, "I have seen a Philistine woman in Timnah; now get her for me as my wife."
[3]His father and mother replied, "Isn't there an acceptable woman among your
relatives or among all our people? Must you go to the uncircumcised Philistines
to get a wife?"
But Samson said to his father, "Get her for me. She's the right one for me." [4](His
parents did not know that this was from the LORD, who was seeking an occasion
to confront the Philistines; for at that time they were ruling over Israel.)
[5]Samson went down to Timnah together with his father and mother. As they
approached the vineyards of Timnah, suddenly a young lion came roaring toward him. [6]The Spirit of the LORD came powerfully upon him so that he tore the
lion apart with his bare hands as he might have torn a young goat. But he told
neither his father nor his mother what he had done. [7]Then he went down and
talked with the woman, and he liked her.
[8]Some time later, when he went back to marry her, he turned aside to look at
the lion's carcass, and in it he saw a swarm of bees and some honey. [9]He scooped
out the honey with his hands and ate as he went along. When he rejoined his
parents, he gave them some, and they too ate it. But he did not tell them that he
had taken the honey from the lion's carcass.
[10]Now his father went down to see the woman. And there Samson held a feast,
as was customary for young men. [11]When the people saw him, they chose thirty
men to be his companions.
[12]"Let me tell you a riddle," Samson said to them. "If you can give me the answer within the seven days of the feast, I will give you thirty linen garments and
thirty sets of clothes. [13]If you can't tell me the answer, you must give me thirty
linen garments and thirty sets of clothes."
"Tell us your riddle," they said. "Let's hear it."
[14]He replied,

"Out of the eater, something to eat;
out of the strong, something sweet."

For three days they could not give the answer.
[15]On the fourth[a] day, they said to Samson's wife, "Coax your husband into
explaining the riddle for us, or we will burn you and your father's household to
death. Did you invite us here to steal our property?"
[16]Then Samson's wife threw herself on him, sobbing, "You hate me! You don't
really love me. You've given my people a riddle, but you haven't told me the answer."
"I haven't even explained it to my father or mother," he replied, "so why should
I explain it to you?" [17]She cried the whole seven days of the feast. So on the seventh day he finally told her, because she continued to press him. She in turn
explained the riddle to her people.

JUDGES 14:6–19

THE SPIRIT'S POWER

The Holy Spirit played an active role in the Old Testament. In the book of Judges, the Holy Spirit empowered numerous individuals. The Holy Spirit "came on Gideon" when Gideon fought against the Midianites and Amalekites (Jdg 6:34); the Spirit "came on Jephthah" (11:29) when he went to fight against the Ammonites; the Spirit also "came powerfully upon" Samson and enabled him to defeat his adversary (14:6). When the Holy Spirit moved, amazing things happened.

While the Holy Spirit used people in the Old Testament to perform mighty deeds, the Spirit is still doing great things today. Jesus told his disciples that it was to their benefit that he would leave them, for after he left, "the Advocate" would come (Jn 16:5–15). Jesus promised that the Holy Spirit would convict the world of sin and guide the disciples into all truth. Though Christians today may not have the physical strength to tear apart a lion like Samson did, they have an even greater power to stand against sin and take the gospel to the nations.

[a] 15 Some Septuagint manuscripts and Syriac; Hebrew *seventh*

A COMING REDEEMER

Samson and Jesus brought Spirit-empowered redemption to God's people in remarkably similar ways. Just consider the contours of Samson's life. Even before his miraculous birth, an angel appeared to Samson's parents, preparing them for his ministry (Jdg 13:2 – 3; Lk 1:26 – 27,34) and explaining that their child would act as a savior of his people (Jdg 13:5; Mt 1:21). Samson was consecrated to live a life of marked devotion to God by following the Nazirite vow, underscoring the importance of fulfilling the Law (Jdg 13:7; Mt 5:17). Samson's mission in life was uniquely empowered by the Spirit (Jdg 14:6,19; Mt 3:16). During this mission, Samson served as the sole agent of God's work to redeem his people. While Deborah had Barak, and Gideon had his soldiers, Samson bore God-given responsibilities alone. In the course of Samson's work, God ordained that he be handed over to the Gentile occupiers by his fellow Israelites (Jdg 15:9 – 13; Mt 27:1 – 2), ultimately experiencing painful betrayal at the hands of one whom he loved (Jdg 16:15,18 – 21; Mt 26:47 – 50) and mockery from his oppressors (Jdg 16:23 – 27; Mt 26:67 – 68; 27:27 – 31). At the end of all this, the epitaph of Samson was that he achieved more in his death than he did in his life (Jdg 16:30; Jn 12:31 – 32; Heb 2:14; 1Jn 3:8). These shocking parallels between Samson and Jesus are no accident!

In spite of the similarity in their life narratives, Jesus and Samson stand in stark contrast. Samson caved to the morals of his society while Jesus confronted the norms of his culture. One slept with a prostitute (Jdg 16:1), while the other brings life-change to prostitutes and sinners (Lk 7:36 – 39; Jn 8:11). They evidence vastly different levels of commitment to the plan of God. Samson risked his mission in the arms of a prostitute, but Jesus remained committed even when faced with a cross. When Jesus could have asserted his own will or sought his own comfort, he chose the Father's will instead (Lk 22:42). Samson pursued a physical deliverance of God's people through the slaughter of their enemies on the battlefield. Jesus secured the spiritual deliverance of God's people through his own slaughter on the cross.

18Before sunset on the seventh day the men of the town said to him,

"What is sweeter than honey?
What is stronger than a lion?"

Samson said to them,

"If you had not plowed with my heifer,
you would not have solved my riddle."

19Then the Spirit of the LORD came powerfully upon him. He went down to
Ashkelon, struck down thirty of their men, stripped them of everything and gave
their clothes to those who had explained the riddle. Burning with anger, he returned to his father's home. 20And Samson's wife was given to one of his companions who had attended him at the feast.

Samson's Vengeance on the Philistines

15 Later on, at the time of wheat harvest, Samson took a young goat and went
to visit his wife. He said, "I'm going to my wife's room." But her father
would not let him go in.
2"I was so sure you hated her," he said, "that I gave her to your companion.
Isn't her younger sister more attractive? Take her instead."
3Samson said to them, "This time I have a right to get even with the Philistines; I will really harm them." 4So he went out and caught three hundred foxes
and tied them tail to tail in pairs. He then fastened a torch to every pair of tails,
5lit the torches and let the foxes loose in the standing grain of the Philistines.
He burned up the shocks and standing grain, together with the vineyards and
olive groves.
6When the Philistines asked, "Who did this?" they were told, "Samson, the
Timnite's son-in-law, because his wife was given to his companion."
So the Philistines went up and burned her and her father to death. 7Samson
said to them, "Since you've acted like this, I swear that I won't stop until I get my
revenge on you." 8He attacked them viciously and slaughtered many of them.
Then he went down and stayed in a cave in the rock of Etam.
9The Philistines went up and camped in Judah, spreading out near Lehi. 10The
people of Judah asked, "Why have you come to fight us?"
"We have come to take Samson prisoner," they answered, "to do to him as he
did to us."
11Then three thousand men from Judah went down to the cave in the rock of
Etam and said to Samson, "Don't you realize that the Philistines are rulers over
us? What have you done to us?"
He answered, "I merely did to them what they did to me."
12They said to him, "We've come to tie you up and hand you over to the Philistines."
Samson said, "Swear to me that you won't kill me yourselves."
13"Agreed," they answered. "We will only tie you up and hand you over to
them. We will not kill you." So they bound him with two new ropes and led
him up from the rock. 14As he approached Lehi, the Philistines came toward
him shouting. The Spirit of the LORD came powerfully upon him. The ropes on
his arms became like charred flax, and the bindings dropped from his hands.
15Finding a fresh jawbone of a donkey, he grabbed it and struck down a thousand men.
16Then Samson said,

"With a donkey's jawbone
I have made donkeys of them.[a]
With a donkey's jawbone
I have killed a thousand men."

---

[a] 16 Or *made a heap or two*; the Hebrew for *donkey* sounds like the Hebrew for *heap*.

[17]When he finished speaking, he threw away the jawbone; and the place was called Ramath Lehi.[a]

[18]Because he was very thirsty, he cried out to the LORD, "You have given your servant this great victory. Must I now die of thirst and fall into the hands of the uncircumcised?" [19]Then God opened up the hollow place in Lehi, and water came out of it. When Samson drank, his strength returned and he revived. So the spring was called En Hakkore,[b] and it is still there in Lehi.

[20]Samson led[c] Israel for twenty years in the days of the Philistines.

Samson and Delilah

16 One day Samson went to Gaza, where he saw a prostitute. He went in to spend the night with her. [2]The people of Gaza were told, "Samson is here!" So they surrounded the place and lay in wait for him all night at the city gate. They made no move during the night, saying, "At dawn we'll kill him."

[3]But Samson lay there only until the middle of the night. Then he got up and took hold of the doors of the city gate, together with the two posts, and tore them loose, bar and all. He lifted them to his shoulders and carried them to the top of the hill that faces Hebron.

[4]Some time later, he fell in love with a woman in the Valley of Sorek whose name was Delilah. [5]The rulers of the Philistines went to her and said, "See if you can lure him into showing you the secret of his great strength and how we can overpower him so we may tie him up and subdue him. Each one of us will give you eleven hundred shekels[d] of silver."

[6]So Delilah said to Samson, "Tell me the secret of your great strength and how you can be tied up and subdued."

[7]Samson answered her, "If anyone ties me with seven fresh bowstrings that have not been dried, I'll become as weak as any other man."

[8]Then the rulers of the Philistines brought her seven fresh bowstrings that had not been dried, and she tied him with them. [9]With men hidden in the room, she called to him, "Samson, the Philistines are upon you!" But he snapped the bowstrings as easily as a piece of string snaps when it comes close to a flame. So the secret of his strength was not discovered.

[10]Then Delilah said to Samson, "You have made a fool of me; you lied to me. Come now, tell me how you can be tied."

[11]He said, "If anyone ties me securely with new ropes that have never been used, I'll become as weak as any other man."

[12]So Delilah took new ropes and tied him with them. Then, with men hidden in the room, she called to him, "Samson, the Philistines are upon you!" But he snapped the ropes off his arms as if they were threads.

[13]Delilah then said to Samson, "All this time you have been making a fool of me and lying to me. Tell me how you can be tied."

He replied, "If you weave the seven braids of my head into the fabric on the loom and tighten it with the pin, I'll become as weak as any other man." So while he was sleeping, Delilah took the seven braids of his head, wove them into the fabric [14]and[e] tightened it with the pin.

Again she called to him, "Samson, the Philistines are upon you!" He awoke from his sleep and pulled up the pin and the loom, with the fabric.

[15]Then she said to him, "How can you say, 'I love you,' when you won't confide in me? This is the third time you have made a fool of me and haven't told me the secret of your great strength." [16]With such nagging she prodded him day after day until he was sick to death of it.

[17]So he told her everything. "No razor has ever been used on my head," he said, "because I have been a Nazirite dedicated to God from my mother's womb.

---

[a] *17 Ramath Lehi* means *jawbone hill.* [b] *19 En Hakkore* means *caller's spring.*
[c] *20* Traditionally *judged* [d] *5* That is, about 28 pounds or about 13 kilograms
[e] *13,14* Some Septuagint manuscripts; Hebrew *replied, "I can if you weave the seven braids of my head into the fabric on the loom."* [14]*So she*

If my head were shaved, my strength would leave me, and I would become as weak as any other man."
[18]When Delilah saw that he had told her everything, she sent word to the rulers of the Philistines, "Come back once more; he has told me everything." So the rulers of the Philistines returned with the silver in their hands. [19]After putting him to sleep on her lap, she called for someone to shave off the seven braids of his hair, and so began to subdue him.[a] And his strength left him.

[20]Then she called, "Samson, the Philistines are upon you!"

He awoke from his sleep and thought, "I'll go out as before and shake myself free." But he did not know that the LORD had left him.

[21]Then the Philistines seized him, gouged out his eyes and took him down to Gaza. Binding him with bronze shackles, they set him to grinding grain in the prison. [22]But the hair on his head began to grow again after it had been shaved.

The Death of Samson

[23]Now the rulers of the Philistines assembled to offer a great sacrifice to Dagon their god and to celebrate, saying, "Our god has delivered Samson, our enemy, into our hands."
[24]When the people saw him, they praised their god, saying,

"Our god has delivered our enemy
  into our hands,
the one who laid waste our land
  and multiplied our slain."

[25]While they were in high spirits, they shouted, "Bring out Samson to entertain us." So they called Samson out of the prison, and he performed for them.

When they stood him among the pillars, [26]Samson said to the servant who held his hand, "Put me where I can feel the pillars that support the temple, so that I may lean against them." [27]Now the temple was crowded with men and women; all the rulers of the Philistines were there, and on the roof were about three thousand men and women watching Samson perform. [28]Then Samson prayed to the LORD, "Sovereign LORD, remember me. Please, God, strengthen me just once more, and let me with one blow get revenge on the Philistines for my two eyes." [29]Then Samson reached toward the two central pillars on which the temple stood. Bracing himself against them, his right hand on the one and his left hand on the other, [30]Samson said, "Let me die with the Philistines!" Then he pushed with all his might, and down came the temple on the rulers and all the people in it. Thus he killed many more when he died than while he lived.

[31]Then his brothers and his father's whole family went down to get him. They brought him back and buried him between Zorah and Eshtaol in the tomb of Manoah his father. He had led[b] Israel twenty years.

Micah's Idols

17 Now a man named Micah from the hill country of Ephraim [2]said to his mother, "The eleven hundred shekels[c] of silver that were taken from you and about which I heard you utter a curse—I have that silver with me; I took it."

Then his mother said, "The LORD bless you, my son!"

[3]When he returned the eleven hundred shekels of silver to his mother, she said, "I solemnly consecrate my silver to the LORD for my son to make an image overlaid with silver. I will give it back to you."

[4]So after he returned the silver to his mother, she took two hundred shekels[d] of silver and gave them to a silversmith, who used them to make the idol. And it was put in Micah's house.

[5]Now this man Micah had a shrine, and he made an ephod and some

---

[a] *19* Hebrew; some Septuagint manuscripts *and he began to weaken* [b] *31* Traditionally *judged* [c] *2* That is, about 28 pounds or about 13 kilograms [d] *4* That is, about 5 pounds or about 2.3 kilograms

household gods and installed one of his sons as his priest. 6In those days Israel
had no king; everyone did as they saw fit.

7A young Levite from Bethlehem in Judah, who had been living within the
clan of Judah, 8left that town in search of some other place to stay. On his way[a]
he came to Micah's house in the hill country of Ephraim.

9Micah asked him, "Where are you from?"

"I'm a Levite from Bethlehem in Judah," he said, "and I'm looking for a place
to stay."

10Then Micah said to him, "Live with me and be my father and priest, and I'll
give you ten shekels[b] of silver a year, your clothes and your food." 11So the Levite
agreed to live with him, and the young man became like one of his sons to him.
12Then Micah installed the Levite, and the young man became his priest and
lived in his house. 13And Micah said, "Now I know that the LORD will be good to
me, since this Levite has become my priest."

The Danites Settle in Laish

18 In those days Israel had no king.
And in those days the tribe of the Danites was seeking a place of their
own where they might settle, because they had not yet come into an inheritance
among the tribes of Israel. 2So the Danites sent five of their leading men from
Zorah and Eshtaol to spy out the land and explore it. These men represented all
the Danites. They told them, "Go, explore the land."

So they entered the hill country of Ephraim and came to the house of Micah,
where they spent the night. 3When they were near Micah's house, they recognized the voice of the young Levite; so they turned in there and asked him, "Who
brought you here? What are you doing in this place? Why are you here?"

4He told them what Micah had done for him, and said, "He has hired me and
I am his priest."

5Then they said to him, "Please inquire of God to learn whether our journey
will be successful."

6The priest answered them, "Go in peace. Your journey has the LORD's approval."

7So the five men left and came to Laish, where they saw that the people were
living in safety, like the Sidonians, at peace and secure. And since their land
lacked nothing, they were prosperous.[c] Also, they lived a long way from the Sidonians and had no relationship with anyone else.[d]

8When they returned to Zorah and Eshtaol, their fellow Danites asked them,
"How did you find things?"

9They answered, "Come on, let's attack them! We have seen the land, and it is
very good. Aren't you going to do something? Don't hesitate to go there and take
it over. 10When you get there, you will find an unsuspecting people and a spacious land that God has put into your hands, a land that lacks nothing whatever."

11Then six hundred men of the Danites, armed for battle, set out from Zorah and Eshtaol. 12On their way they set up camp near Kiriath Jearim in Judah.
This is why the place west of Kiriath Jearim is called Mahaneh Dan[e] to this day.
13From there they went on to the hill country of Ephraim and came to Micah's
house.

14Then the five men who had spied out the land of Laish said to their fellow
Danites, "Do you know that one of these houses has an ephod, some household
gods and an image overlaid with silver? Now you know what to do." 15So they
turned in there and went to the house of the young Levite at Micah's place and
greeted him. 16The six hundred Danites, armed for battle, stood at the entrance
of the gate. 17The five men who had spied out the land went inside and took the

[a] 8 Or *To carry on his profession* [b] 10 That is, about 4 ounces or about 115 grams
[c] 7 The meaning of the Hebrew for this clause is uncertain. [d] 7 Hebrew; some Septuagint
manuscripts *with the Arameans* [e] 12 *Mahaneh Dan* means *Dan's camp.*

idol, the ephod and the household gods while the priest and the six hundred
armed men stood at the entrance of the gate.
18When the five men went into Micah's house and took the idol, the ephod and
the household gods, the priest said to them, "What are you doing?"
19They answered him, "Be quiet! Don't say a word. Come with us, and be our
father and priest. Isn't it better that you serve a tribe and clan in Israel as priest
rather than just one man's household?" 20The priest was very pleased. He took
the ephod, the household gods and the idol and went along with the people.
21Putting their little children, their livestock and their possessions in front of
them, they turned away and left.
22When they had gone some distance from Micah's house, the men who lived
near Micah were called together and overtook the Danites. 23As they shouted
after them, the Danites turned and said to Micah, "What's the matter with you
that you called out your men to fight?"
24He replied, "You took the gods I made, and my priest, and went away. What
else do I have? How can you ask, 'What's the matter with you?'"
25The Danites answered, "Don't argue with us, or some of the men may get
angry and attack you, and you and your family will lose your lives." 26So the Danites went their way, and Micah, seeing that they were too strong for him, turned
around and went back home.
27Then they took what Micah had made, and his priest, and went on to Laish,
against a people at peace and secure. They attacked them with the sword and
burned down their city. 28There was no one to rescue them because they lived a
long way from Sidon and had no relationship with anyone else. The city was in
a valley near Beth Rehob.
The Danites rebuilt the city and settled there. 29They named it Dan after their
ancestor Dan, who was born to Israel — though the city used to be called Laish.
30There the Danites set up for themselves the idol, and Jonathan son of Gershom,
the son of Moses,[a] and his sons were priests for the tribe of Dan until the time
of the captivity of the land. 31They continued to use the idol Micah had made,
all the time the house of God was in Shiloh.

A Levite and His Concubine

19 In those days Israel had no king.
Now a Levite who lived in a remote area in the hill country of Ephraim
took a concubine from Bethlehem in Judah. 2But she was unfaithful to him. She
left him and went back to her parents' home in Bethlehem, Judah. After she had
been there four months, 3her husband went to her to persuade her to return. He
had with him his servant and two donkeys. She took him into her parents' home,
and when her father saw him, he gladly welcomed him. 4His father-in-law, the
woman's father, prevailed on him to stay; so he remained with him three days,
eating and drinking, and sleeping there.
5On the fourth day they got up early and he prepared to leave, but the woman's father said to his son-in-law, "Refresh yourself with something to eat; then
you can go." 6So the two of them sat down to eat and drink together. Afterward
the woman's father said, "Please stay tonight and enjoy yourself." 7And when the
man got up to go, his father-in-law persuaded him, so he stayed there that night.
8On the morning of the fifth day, when he rose to go, the woman's father said,
"Refresh yourself. Wait till afternoon!" So the two of them ate together.
9Then when the man, with his concubine and his servant, got up to leave, his
father-in-law, the woman's father, said, "Now look, it's almost evening. Spend
the night here; the day is nearly over. Stay and enjoy yourself. Early tomorrow
morning you can get up and be on your way home." 10But, unwilling to stay another night, the man left and went toward Jebus (that is, Jerusalem), with his two
saddled donkeys and his concubine.

[a] *30* Many Hebrew manuscripts, some Septuagint manuscripts and Vulgate; many other Hebrew manuscripts and some other Septuagint manuscripts *Manasseh*

JUDGES 19:1 – 30

THE CYCLE OF SIN

Sin is never satisfied — it festers, grows, spreads and destroys all things in its path. The unnamed Levite and the people of Gibeah illustrate the depth of depravity of which humans are capable. There seemed to be no end to the self-centeredness of mankind apart from God's gracious intervention. This reality was compounded in the seasons when the nation was without human leaders; though, even when they had leaders they proved to be incapable of consistent obedience. They needed a deliverer, a Savior, to break the cycle of sin, condemnation and death.

Paul declared that Jesus' once-for-all sacrifice breaks the death-grip of sin and sets believers free to live a righteous life (Ro 6:15 – 23). Whereas the just outcome of sin is death, the fruit of Jesus' work is freedom, joy and holiness. Jesus' victory is the only power great enough to break the power of sin within the nation of Israel and all of humanity.

11When they were near Jebus and the day was almost gone, the servant said to his master, "Come, let's stop at this city of the Jebusites and spend the night."

12His master replied, "No. We won't go into any city whose people are not Israelites. We will go on to Gibeah." 13He added, "Come, let's try to reach Gibeah or Ramah and spend the night in one of those places." 14So they went on, and the sun set as they neared Gibeah in Benjamin. 15There they stopped to spend the night. They went and sat in the city square, but no one took them in for the night.

16That evening an old man from the hill country of Ephraim, who was living in Gibeah (the inhabitants of the place were Benjamites), came in from his work in the fields. 17When he looked and saw the traveler in the city square, the old man asked, "Where are you going? Where did you come from?"

18He answered, "We are on our way from Bethlehem in Judah to a remote area in the hill country of Ephraim where I live. I have been to Bethlehem in Judah and now I am going to the house of the LORD.[a] No one has taken me in for the night. 19We have both straw and fodder for our donkeys and bread and wine for ourselves your servants — me, the woman and the young man with us. We don't need anything."

20"You are welcome at my house," the old man said. "Let me supply whatever you need. Only don't spend the night in the square." 21So he took him into his house and fed his donkeys. After they had washed their feet, they had something to eat and drink.

22While they were enjoying themselves, some of the wicked men of the city surrounded the house. Pounding on the door, they shouted to the old man who owned the house, "Bring out the man who came to your house so we can have sex with him."

23The owner of the house went outside and said to them, "No, my friends, don't be so vile. Since this man is my guest, don't do this outrageous thing. 24Look, here is my virgin daughter, and his concubine. I will bring them out to you now, and you can use them and do to them whatever you wish. But as for this man, don't do such an outrageous thing."

25But the men would not listen to him. So the man took his concubine and sent her outside to them, and they raped her and abused her throughout the night, and at dawn they let her go. 26At daybreak the woman went back to the house where her master was staying, fell down at the door and lay there until daylight.

27When her master got up in the morning and opened the door of the house and stepped out to continue on his way, there lay his concubine, fallen in the doorway of the house, with her hands on the threshold. 28He said to her, "Get up; let's go." But there was no answer. Then the man put her on his donkey and set out for home.

29When he reached home, he took a knife and cut up his concubine, limb by limb, into twelve parts and sent them into all the areas of Israel. 30Everyone who saw it was saying to one another, "Such a thing has never been seen or done, not since the day the Israelites came up out of Egypt. Just imagine! We must do something! So speak up!"

The Israelites Punish the Benjamites

20 Then all Israel from Dan to Beersheba and from the land of Gilead came together as one and assembled before the LORD in Mizpah. 2The leaders of all the people of the tribes of Israel took their places in the assembly of God's people, four hundred thousand men armed with swords. 3(The Benjamites heard that the Israelites had gone up to Mizpah.) Then the Israelites said, "Tell us how this awful thing happened."

4So the Levite, the husband of the murdered woman, said, "I and my concubine came to Gibeah in Benjamin to spend the night. 5During the night the men

[a] 18 Hebrew, Vulgate, Syriac and Targum; Septuagint *going home*

of Gibeah came after me and surrounded the house, intending to kill me. They raped my concubine, and she died. 6I took my concubine, cut her into pieces and sent one piece to each region of Israel's inheritance, because they committed this lewd and outrageous act in Israel. 7Now, all you Israelites, speak up and tell me what you have decided to do."

8All the men rose up together as one, saying, "None of us will go home. No, not one of us will return to his house. 9But now this is what we'll do to Gibeah: We'll go up against it in the order decided by casting lots. 10We'll take ten men out of every hundred from all the tribes of Israel, and a hundred from a thousand, and a thousand from ten thousand, to get provisions for the army. Then, when the army arrives at Gibeah[a] in Benjamin, it can give them what they deserve for this outrageous act done in Israel." 11So all the Israelites got together and united as one against the city.

12The tribes of Israel sent messengers throughout the tribe of Benjamin, saying, "What about this awful crime that was committed among you? 13Now turn those wicked men of Gibeah over to us so that we may put them to death and purge the evil from Israel."

But the Benjamites would not listen to their fellow Israelites. 14From their towns they came together at Gibeah to fight against the Israelites. 15At once the Benjamites mobilized twenty-six thousand swordsmen from their towns, in addition to seven hundred able young men from those living in Gibeah. 16Among all these soldiers there were seven hundred select troops who were left-handed, each of whom could sling a stone at a hair and not miss.

17Israel, apart from Benjamin, mustered four hundred thousand swordsmen, all of them fit for battle.

18The Israelites went up to Bethel[b] and inquired of God. They said, "Who of us is to go up first to fight against the Benjamites?"

The LORD replied, "Judah shall go first."

19The next morning the Israelites got up and pitched camp near Gibeah. 20The Israelites went out to fight the Benjamites and took up battle positions against them at Gibeah. 21The Benjamites came out of Gibeah and cut down twenty-two thousand Israelites on the battlefield that day. 22But the Israelites encouraged one another and again took up their positions where they had stationed themselves the first day. 23The Israelites went up and wept before the LORD until evening, and they inquired of the LORD. They said, "Shall we go up again to fight against the Benjamites, our fellow Israelites?"

The LORD answered, "Go up against them."

24Then the Israelites drew near to Benjamin the second day. 25This time, when the Benjamites came out from Gibeah to oppose them, they cut down another eighteen thousand Israelites, all of them armed with swords.

26Then all the Israelites, the whole army, went up to Bethel, and there they sat weeping before the LORD. They fasted that day until evening and presented burnt offerings and fellowship offerings to the LORD. 27And the Israelites inquired of the LORD. (In those days the ark of the covenant of God was there, 28with Phinehas son of Eleazar, the son of Aaron, ministering before it.) They asked, "Shall we go up again to fight against the Benjamites, our fellow Israelites, or not?"

The LORD responded, "Go, for tomorrow I will give them into your hands."

29Then Israel set an ambush around Gibeah. 30They went up against the Benjamites on the third day and took up positions against Gibeah as they had done before. 31The Benjamites came out to meet them and were drawn away from the city. They began to inflict casualties on the Israelites as before, so that about thirty men fell in the open field and on the roads — the one leading to Bethel and the other to Gibeah. 32While the Benjamites were saying, "We are defeating

---

[a] *10* One Hebrew manuscript; most Hebrew manuscripts *Geba,* a variant of *Gibeah*

[b] *18* Or *to the house of God;* also in verse 26

them as before," the Israelites were saying, "Let's retreat and draw them away
from the city to the roads."
33All the men of Israel moved from their places and took up positions at Baal
Tamar, and the Israelite ambush charged out of its place on the west[a] of Gibeah.[b]
34Then ten thousand of Israel's able young men made a frontal attack on Gibeah.
The fighting was so heavy that the Benjamites did not realize how near disaster
was. 35The LORD defeated Benjamin before Israel, and on that day the Israelites
struck down 25,100 Benjamites, all armed with swords. 36Then the Benjamites
saw that they were beaten.

Now the men of Israel had given way before Benjamin, because they relied on
the ambush they had set near Gibeah. 37Those who had been in ambush made a
sudden dash into Gibeah, spread out and put the whole city to the sword. 38The
Israelites had arranged with the ambush that they should send up a great cloud
of smoke from the city, 39and then the Israelites would counterattack.

The Benjamites had begun to inflict casualties on the Israelites (about thirty), and they said, "We are defeating them as in the first battle." 40But when the
column of smoke began to rise from the city, the Benjamites turned and saw
the whole city going up in smoke. 41Then the Israelites counterattacked, and
the Benjamites were terrified, because they realized that disaster had come on
them. 42So they fled before the Israelites in the direction of the wilderness, but
they could not escape the battle. And the Israelites who came out of the towns
cut them down there. 43They surrounded the Benjamites, chased them and easily[c] overran them in the vicinity of Gibeah on the east. 44Eighteen thousand Benjamites fell, all of them valiant fighters. 45As they turned and fled toward the
wilderness to the rock of Rimmon, the Israelites cut down five thousand men
along the roads. They kept pressing after the Benjamites as far as Gidom and
struck down two thousand more.

46On that day twenty-five thousand Benjamite swordsmen fell, all of them
valiant fighters. 47But six hundred of them turned and fled into the wilderness
to the rock of Rimmon, where they stayed four months. 48The men of Israel went
back to Benjamin and put all the towns to the sword, including the animals and
everything else they found. All the towns they came across they set on fire.

Wives for the Benjamites

21 The men of Israel had taken an oath at Mizpah: "Not one of us will give his
daughter in marriage to a Benjamite."

2The people went to Bethel,[d] where they sat before God until evening, raising
their voices and weeping bitterly. 3"LORD, God of Israel," they cried, "why has
this happened to Israel? Why should one tribe be missing from Israel today?"

4Early the next day the people built an altar and presented burnt offerings
and fellowship offerings.

5Then the Israelites asked, "Who from all the tribes of Israel has failed to assemble before the LORD?" For they had taken a solemn oath that anyone who
failed to assemble before the LORD at Mizpah was to be put to death.

6Now the Israelites grieved for the tribe of Benjamin, their fellow Israelites.
"Today one tribe is cut off from Israel," they said. 7"How can we provide wives
for those who are left, since we have taken an oath by the LORD not to give them
any of our daughters in marriage?" 8Then they asked, "Which one of the tribes
of Israel failed to assemble before the LORD at Mizpah?" They discovered that
no one from Jabesh Gilead had come to the camp for the assembly. 9For when
they counted the people, they found that none of the people of Jabesh Gilead
were there.

10So the assembly sent twelve thousand fighting men with instructions to go
to Jabesh Gilead and put to the sword those living there, including the women

---

[a] *33* Some Septuagint manuscripts and Vulgate; the meaning of the Hebrew for this word is uncertain. [b] *33* Hebrew *Geba,* a variant of *Gibeah* [c] *43* The meaning of the Hebrew for this word is uncertain. [d] *2* Or *to the house of God*

JUDGES 21:25

NOT JUST ANY KING

The anticlimactic ending of the book of Judges portrays a hopeless nation. Throughout the book, the author noted a correlation between the evil of the people and the absence of a king (17:6; 18:1; 19:1; 21:25). Each time, though, it appears that the sin of the people advanced in terms of its scope and destructive impact. Here the people who were meant to dwell in an amazing land and delight in fellowship with God are presented as a divided people living in constant fear.

The blame is placed squarely on the shoulders of the people. They did what was right in their own eyes and, in so doing, failed to do what was right in the eyes of God. Like Adam and Eve in the garden, they disregarded the wisdom of God and trusted in their own discernment.

Over and over again, God's people fall prey to the temptation of Satan to trust in themselves and follow after their own desires. The apostle John explained that "everything in the world — the lust of the flesh, the lust of the eyes, and the pride of life" — comes from the world and is doomed for destruction (1Jn 2:16). Time after time people chase after desires that were never meant to fully satisfy their soul.

The path to life is found through a king. Not just any king, but *the* King. King Jesus invites people to follow a better leader who both models a life of total obedience to God and invites others to follow this path. Jesus, as the truer and better Adam, would do what Adam could not do. Jesus obeyed where Adam failed. Jesus led his people to obey God (Ro 5:12 – 21). He did far more than any earthly, human king could ever do — he took the judgment of God. Through his death and resurrection, he grants his people the gift of a perfect, righteous standing before God. In his presence, they find acceptance, love and forgiveness. Jesus' perfect kingship is the type of leadership that the people at the conclusion of the book of Judges — and people today — desperately need.

and children. [11]"This is what you are to do," they said. "Kill every male and every woman who is not a virgin." [12]They found among the people living in Jabesh Gilead four hundred young women who had never slept with a man, and they took them to the camp at Shiloh in Canaan.

[13]Then the whole assembly sent an offer of peace to the Benjamites at the rock of Rimmon. [14]So the Benjamites returned at that time and were given the women of Jabesh Gilead who had been spared. But there were not enough for all of them.

[15]The people grieved for Benjamin, because the LORD had made a gap in the tribes of Israel. [16]And the elders of the assembly said, "With the women of Benjamin destroyed, how shall we provide wives for the men who are left? [17]The Benjamite survivors must have heirs," they said, "so that a tribe of Israel will not be wiped out. [18]We can't give them our daughters as wives, since we Israelites have taken this oath: 'Cursed be anyone who gives a wife to a Benjamite.' [19]But look, there is the annual festival of the LORD in Shiloh, which lies north of Bethel, east of the road that goes from Bethel to Shechem, and south of Lebonah."

[20]So they instructed the Benjamites, saying, "Go and hide in the vineyards [21]and watch. When the young women of Shiloh come out to join in the dancing, rush from the vineyards and each of you seize one of them to be your wife. Then return to the land of Benjamin. [22]When their fathers or brothers complain to us, we will say to them, 'Do us the favor of helping them, because we did not get wives for them during the war. You will not be guilty of breaking your oath because you did not give your daughters to them.' "

[23]So that is what the Benjamites did. While the young women were dancing, each man caught one and carried her off to be his wife. Then they returned to their inheritance and rebuilt the towns and settled in them.

[24]At that time the Israelites left that place and went home to their tribes and clans, each to his own inheritance.

[25]In those days Israel had no king; everyone did as they saw fit.

JESUS: OUR GUARDIAN-REDEEMER

RUTH

RUTH

PERIOD OF THE JUDGES *c. 1375 – 1050 BC*	SAUL BECOMES KING OF ISRAEL *c. 1050 BC*	DAVID'S REIGN BEGINS *c. 1010 BC*

The book of Ruth poignantly describes a story of redemption and love. Ruth, a Moabite woman and one of the main characters of the book, was saved by the sovereign care of God. Through her relationship with her late husband and her mother-in-law, Naomi, Ruth learned about the God of Israel, became his devoted follower and faithfully followed his leading. Undoubtedly this decision did not come without cost for Ruth, though through obedience to Yahweh she found greater blessing — both the provision she needed to survive and a central role in the family line of Jesus Christ (Ru 4:18 – 22; Mt 1:5).

The story of Ruth takes place during the time when a series of judges led the people of God. This period is known to have been a time of extreme moral decline and spiritual poverty. The story of Ruth and Boaz provides a glimpse of the hope of redemption that can come even in the midst of overwhelming cultural chaos and immorality.

The loyalty that Ruth demonstrates toward Naomi throughout the book is emblematic of the type of covenant love that God shows to his people. Even though Ruth was originally unfamiliar with the Law of God, she was a recipient of God's gracious blessings to his people.

God's sovereign work is seen throughout the story of Ruth and Boaz. The odds seemed stacked against their relationship from the outset — Ruth was an outsider who, after suffering great loss, followed her mother-in-law to Bethlehem. She had every reason to feel discouraged and defeated. Without a husband or a family, Ruth's future prospects were dim. She was a poverty-stricken widow scraping out a meager existence by gleaning what the harvesters left in the wheat fields. What she could not see is clear to the modern reader — God was orchestrating all the seemingly isolated events of her life to bring her to the knowledge of the one true and living God and into the blessing that he had promised to his children.

A central concept of the book, and the role played by Boaz, Ruth's eventual husband, is that of a guardian-redeemer. In ancient Israel, a man's nearest relative was expected to marry a widow and provide for her needs to fulfill the obligations of her husband, including providing an heir. Boaz claimed that responsibility for Naomi's deceased husband and sons, dramatically changing the lives and the futures of both Ruth and Naomi. Like Boaz, Jesus was a guardian-redeemer. He paid the ultimate price for humanity's redemption — his own blood — and claimed his people by the power of his love, changing their eternal futures. Boaz's love for Ruth is a picture of the way that God loves his church. He takes notice of her, redeems her, lavishes grace upon her and places her within the community of faith as her guardian-redeemer. God blessed the marriage of Ruth and Boaz with a child who would become an ancestor to King David and later a part of the earthly line of the promised Messiah.

MAY THE LORD REPAY YOU FOR WHAT YOU HAVE DONE. MAY YOU BE RICHLY REWARDED BY THE LORD, THE GOD OF ISRAEL, UNDER WHOSE WINGS YOU HAVE COME TO TAKE REFUGE.

Ruth 2:12

RUTH

RUTH 1:1 – 2

BETHLEHEM AND THE STORY OF RUTH

Even the smallest details in Scripture matter. Bethlehem means "house of food" or "house of bread" and is the place where the Messiah was prophesied to come from (Mic 5:2). When the Israelites were wandering in the desert, God gave them manna from heaven (Ex 16:31). He provided for his people, foreshadowing the ultimate and final provision they would have in Jesus Christ. Jesus called himself the bread of life (Jn 6:35). Through the story of Ruth, God preserved and protected the line of David, thus protecting the lineage of Jesus (Mt 1:1 – 17). The symbolism of food found in the story of Ruth is a reminder that even the smallest details matter in the story of God.

RUTH 1:14 – 17

RUTH'S CHOICE

As the story unfolds, the character of Ruth takes shape as she swears an oath to stay with her mother-in-law after her husband's untimely death. She had to choose between her old life and the gods of her people or her husband's family and their God. She chose the latter. Ruth must have seen something different in her mother-in-law, and Ruth began to serve the one true God. Throughout the book of Ruth, God honored that choice in many ways, with the most

(continued on page 388)

Naomi Loses Her Husband and Sons

1 In the days when the judges ruled,[a] there was a famine in the land. So a man
from Bethlehem in Judah, together with his wife and two sons, went to live for
a while in the country of Moab. 2 The man's name was Elimelek, his wife's name
was Naomi, and the names of his two sons were Mahlon and Kilion. They were
Ephrathites from Bethlehem, Judah. And they went to Moab and lived there.
3 Now Elimelek, Naomi's husband, died, and she was left with her two sons.
4 They married Moabite women, one named Orpah and the other Ruth. After
they had lived there about ten years, 5 both Mahlon and Kilion also died, and
Naomi was left without her two sons and her husband.

Naomi and Ruth Return to Bethlehem

6 When Naomi heard in Moab that the LORD had come to the aid of his people by
providing food for them, she and her daughters-in-law prepared to return home
from there. 7 With her two daughters-in-law she left the place where she had been
living and set out on the road that would take them back to the land of Judah.
8 Then Naomi said to her two daughters-in-law, "Go back, each of you, to your
mother's home. May the LORD show you kindness, as you have shown kindness
to your dead husbands and to me. 9 May the LORD grant that each of you will find
rest in the home of another husband."
Then she kissed them goodbye and they wept aloud 10 and said to her, "We will
go back with you to your people."
11 But Naomi said, "Return home, my daughters. Why would you come with
me? Am I going to have any more sons, who could become your husbands?
12 Return home, my daughters; I am too old to have another husband. Even if I
thought there was still hope for me — even if I had a husband tonight and then
gave birth to sons — 13 would you wait until they grew up? Would you remain
unmarried for them? No, my daughters. It is more bitter for me than for you, because the LORD's hand has turned against me!"
14 At this they wept aloud again. Then Orpah kissed her mother-in-law goodbye, but Ruth clung to her.
15 "Look," said Naomi, "your sister-in-law is going back to her people and her
gods. Go back with her."
16 But Ruth replied, "Don't urge me to leave you or to turn back from you.
Where you go I will go, and where you stay I will stay. Your people will be my
people and your God my God. 17 Where you die I will die, and there I will be buried. May the LORD deal with me, be it ever so severely, if even death separates
you and me." 18 When Naomi realized that Ruth was determined to go with her,
she stopped urging her.
19 So the two women went on until they came to Bethlehem. When they arrived in Bethlehem, the whole town was stirred because of them, and the women
exclaimed, "Can this be Naomi?"
20 "Don't call me Naomi,[b]" she told them. "Call me Mara,[c] because the Almighty[d] has made my life very bitter. 21 I went away full, but the LORD has brought
me back empty. Why call me Naomi? The LORD has afflicted[e] me; the Almighty
has brought misfortune upon me."
22 So Naomi returned from Moab accompanied by Ruth the Moabite, her
daughter-in-law, arriving in Bethlehem as the barley harvest was beginning.

[a] *1* Traditionally *judged* [b] *20 Naomi* means *pleasant.* [c] *20 Mara* means *bitter.*
[d] *20* Hebrew *Shaddai*; also in verse 21 [e] *21* Or *has testified against*

GOD AND THE WORLD

Ruth was determined to remain by her mother-in-law's side. This was important since her assertion that Naomi's God would be her God is an affirmation of her faith in the one true God of Israel. She was choosing to cling to God, to Naomi and to Naomi's people, forsaking all that she had ever known to follow God. Ruth had an opportunity to choose between making a new life with God or returning to her old way of life and the idols of her people. She decided to fervently and stubbornly remain by her mother-in-law's side to serve God and stay true to the faith she had come to know.

It is amazing that God chose someone (a woman no less) outside of the Jewish faith to not only follow the God of Israel but also to become a part of the lineage of the Messiah (Mt 1:5). This was a shadow of the reality that would be the redemption of the entire world first for the Jew and then for the Gentile (Ro 1:16). Jesus would not only be the Savior of the Jews but of the whole world. He actually had Gentile (non-Jewish) blood running through his human veins, thanks to "outsiders" in his family line such as Ruth. When he came to earth, he made it abundantly clear that salvation was offered for the whole world.

Similar to Ruth, who was brought into the family of God through her Jewish family and her faith, followers of Jesus are brought into the family of God through faith in Christ and grace given by God. "Consequently, you are no longer foreigners and strangers, but fellow citizens with God's people and also members of his household, built on the foundation of the apostles and prophets, with Christ Jesus himself as the chief cornerstone" (Eph 2:19 – 20). John writes in John 3:16, which has become an epic anthem for the worldwide church epitomizing the gospel message, "For God so loved the world that he gave his one and only Son, that whoever believes in him shall not perish but have eternal life."

(Ruth's Choice, continued)

incredible one being that Ruth, a woman and foreigner from humble beginnings, ultimately became part of the lineage of the Messiah (4:18–22; Mt 1:5). She walked with the wise (Naomi) and became wise (Pr 13:20). She honored God and he brought her into his story. Similarly, those who follow Christ can choose to honor God with their choices and come near to him, and he will, in turn, come near to them (Jas 4:8).

RUTH 2:8–12

KINDNESS TO A FOREIGNER

Kindness and family are strong themes throughout the book of Ruth. The word "kindness" in Ruth 1:8 means "loyal love" and refers to the loyalty of God to the covenant of his people. Naomi expressed the hope that the Lord's love would extend to her daughters-in-law, who were not Jewish. It is mentioned repeatedly that Ruth was a Moabite, a foreigner, but she was brought into the family of God through her earthly family.

Boaz reached out to Ruth with great kindness and respect. He allowed her to gather barley in his field and eat with the harvesters, providing protection and provision for her needs. Boaz showed his great faith and integrity in this small act. Based upon Levitical law, harvesting was to be done with only one pass, leaving behind some for the poor and foreigner (of which Ruth was both) to gather for their needs. The heart of this law was to allow God's people to respond to his provision by being generous to those with less.

Ruth Meets Boaz in the Grain Field

2 Now Naomi had a relative on her husband's side, a man of standing from the
clan of Elimelek, whose name was Boaz.
2And Ruth the Moabite said to Naomi, "Let me go to the fields and pick up the
leftover grain behind anyone in whose eyes I find favor."
Naomi said to her, "Go ahead, my daughter." 3So she went out, entered a field
and began to glean behind the harvesters. As it turned out, she was working in a
field belonging to Boaz, who was from the clan of Elimelek.
4Just then Boaz arrived from Bethlehem and greeted the harvesters, "The
LORD be with you!"
"The LORD bless you!" they answered.
5Boaz asked the overseer of his harvesters, "Who does that young woman belong to?"
6The overseer replied, "She is the Moabite who came back from Moab with
Naomi. 7She said, 'Please let me glean and gather among the sheaves behind the
harvesters.' She came into the field and has remained here from morning till
now, except for a short rest in the shelter."
8So Boaz said to Ruth, "My daughter, listen to me. Don't go and glean in another field and don't go away from here. Stay here with the women who work for me.
9Watch the field where the men are harvesting, and follow along after the wom-
en. I have told the men not to lay a hand on you. And whenever you are thirsty,
go and get a drink from the water jars the men have filled."
10At this, she bowed down with her face to the ground. She asked him, "Why
have I found such favor in your eyes that you notice me—a foreigner?"
11Boaz replied, "I've been told all about what you have done for your mother-
in-law since the death of your husband—how you left your father and mother
and your homeland and came to live with a people you did not know before.
12May the LORD repay you for what you have done. May you be richly rewarded
by the LORD, the God of Israel, under whose wings you have come to take refuge."
13"May I continue to find favor in your eyes, my lord," she said. "You have put
me at ease by speaking kindly to your servant—though I do not have the standing of one of your servants."
14At mealtime Boaz said to her, "Come over here. Have some bread and dip it
in the wine vinegar."
When she sat down with the harvesters, he offered her some roasted grain.
She ate all she wanted and had some left over. 15As she got up to glean, Boaz gave
orders to his men, "Let her gather among the sheaves and don't reprimand her.
16Even pull out some stalks for her from the bundles and leave them for her to
pick up, and don't rebuke her."
17So Ruth gleaned in the field until evening. Then she threshed the barley she
had gathered, and it amounted to about an ephah.[a] 18She carried it back to town,
and her mother-in-law saw how much she had gathered. Ruth also brought out
and gave her what she had left over after she had eaten enough.
19Her mother-in-law asked her, "Where did you glean today? Where did you
work? Blessed be the man who took notice of you!"
Then Ruth told her mother-in-law about the one at whose place she had been
working. "The name of the man I worked with today is Boaz," she said.
20"The LORD bless him!" Naomi said to her daughter-in-law. "He has not
stopped showing his kindness to the living and the dead." She added, "That man
is our close relative; he is one of our guardian-redeemers.[b]"
21Then Ruth the Moabite said, "He even said to me, 'Stay with my workers until they finish harvesting all my grain.' "
22Naomi said to Ruth her daughter-in-law, "It will be good for you, my daughter,

---

[a] *17* That is, probably about 30 pounds or about 13 kilograms [b] *20* The Hebrew word for *guardian-redeemer* is a legal term for one who has the obligation to redeem a relative in serious difficulty (see Lev. 25:25-55).

to go with the women who work for him, because in someone else's field you might be harmed."

[23]So Ruth stayed close to the women of Boaz to glean until the barley and wheat harvests were finished. And she lived with her mother-in-law.

Ruth and Boaz at the Threshing Floor

3 One day Ruth's mother-in-law Naomi said to her, "My daughter, I must find a home[a] for you, where you will be well provided for. [2]Now Boaz, with whose women you have worked, is a relative of ours. Tonight he will be winnowing barley on the threshing floor. [3]Wash, put on perfume, and get dressed in your best clothes. Then go down to the threshing floor, but don't let him know you are there until he has finished eating and drinking. [4]When he lies down, note the place where he is lying. Then go and uncover his feet and lie down. He will tell you what to do."

[5]"I will do whatever you say," Ruth answered. [6]So she went down to the threshing floor and did everything her mother-in-law told her to do.

[7]When Boaz had finished eating and drinking and was in good spirits, he went over to lie down at the far end of the grain pile. Ruth approached quietly, uncovered his feet and lay down. [8]In the middle of the night something startled the man; he turned—and there was a woman lying at his feet!

[9]"Who are you?" he asked.

"I am your servant Ruth," she said. "Spread the corner of your garment over me, since you are a guardian-redeemer[b] of our family."

[10]"The LORD bless you, my daughter," he replied. "This kindness is greater than that which you showed earlier: You have not run after the younger men, whether rich or poor. [11]And now, my daughter, don't be afraid. I will do for you all you ask. All the people of my town know that you are a woman of noble character. [12]Although it is true that I am a guardian-redeemer of our family, there is another who is more closely related than I. [13]Stay here for the night, and in the morning if he wants to do his duty as your guardian-redeemer, good; let him redeem you. But if he is not willing, as surely as the LORD lives I will do it. Lie here until morning."

[14]So she lay at his feet until morning, but got up before anyone could be recognized; and he said, "No one must know that a woman came to the threshing floor."

[15]He also said, "Bring me the shawl you are wearing and hold it out." When she did so, he poured into it six measures of barley and placed the bundle on her. Then he[c] went back to town.

[16]When Ruth came to her mother-in-law, Naomi asked, "How did it go, my daughter?"

Then she told her everything Boaz had done for her [17]and added, "He gave me these six measures of barley, saying, 'Don't go back to your mother-in-law empty-handed.'"

[18]Then Naomi said, "Wait, my daughter, until you find out what happens. For the man will not rest until the matter is settled today."

Boaz Marries Ruth

4 Meanwhile Boaz went up to the town gate and sat down there just as the guardian-redeemer[d] he had mentioned came along. Boaz said, "Come over here, my friend, and sit down." So he went over and sat down.

[2]Boaz took ten of the elders of the town and said, "Sit here," and they did so.

[a] *1* Hebrew *find rest* (see 1:9) [b] *9* The Hebrew word for *guardian-redeemer* is a legal term for one who has the obligation to redeem a relative in serious difficulty (see Lev. 25:25-55); also in verses 12 and 13. [c] *15* Most Hebrew manuscripts; many Hebrew manuscripts, Vulgate and Syriac *she* [d] *1* The Hebrew word for *guardian-redeemer* is a legal term for one who has the obligation to redeem a relative in serious difficulty (see Lev. 25:25-55); also in verses 3, 6, 8 and 14.

RUTH 3:11

RUTH: AN UNLIKELY CHOICE

When Boaz acknowledged that Ruth was a "woman of noble character," he used the same Hebrew phrase as is found in Proverbs 31:10. In this time period, it would be considered outrageous, even absurd, that a woman who was not of Jewish descent would be the star of a book situated in the original Hebrew Bible. The Jewish audience reading Ruth would immediately recognize this embodiment of a noble woman as that used in Proverbs 31. The same Hebrew phrasing is used in both places, and it is astounding that verses famously written to depict a highly honored, godly woman would also be used to describe Ruth. God chose an unlikely person to show his love and mercy to his people. In the same way, God has chosen to show his love to his people through what Jesus has done, choosing them in him before the foundation of the world (Eph 1:4), thus enabling them to choose a new life with him despite their sin and rebellion.

JESUS: OUR GUARDIAN-REDEEMER

The book of Ruth is a beautiful picture of God's plan for redemption that was ultimately realized in Jesus. A clear picture of Jesus can be seen through Boaz's relationship with Ruth as her "guardian-redeemer." Upon the death of her husband, Ruth had only her mother-in-law, Naomi. Both were poor and dependent on the kindness of others for their well-being. Naomi sent Ruth to gather grain in a nearby field, and a series of events led to Boaz acting as a possible "guardian-redeemer" and eventually a marriage, ultimately redeeming Ruth's family name and securing her place in the lineage of Jesus.

A guardian-redeemer, or *ga'al* (*go'el*) in the Hebrew, refers to a close relative who acts as a protector of the family rights. He could be called upon to perform a number of duties including buying back property the family had sold, providing an heir for a deceased relative, releasing a family member from slavery or avenging a relative's murder. God calls himself the "Redeemer" or close relative of Israel in Isaiah 60:16, and Jesus is referred to as a redeemer in 1 Peter 1:18 – 19.

By becoming human, Jesus became humanity's own Guardian-Redeemer. He came from heaven and walked the earth, bringing with him restoration and making it available to all people through the cross and a relationship with him. Just as Boaz made it possible for Naomi and Ruth's lineage to live on, now through Christ all believers are made holy, invited into the family of God (Heb 2:11) and become heirs of God and co-heirs with Christ (Ro 8:17). Just as Boaz preserved and protected Ruth's family and their future, in the most perfect way Christ preserves his people, restores dignity and gives hope for the future. Reading and studying Ruth in light of what has now been revealed in Jesus shows not only the glorious stamp of God and his work in Ruth's day, but also the undeniable way that redemption in Christ was being prepared before the foundation of time. Jesus was and is now the true Guardian-Redeemer, always the ultimate protector, the One who continues to preserve the very lives of his people today, as they continue to follow him day by day.

[3]Then he said to the guardian-redeemer, "Naomi, who has come back from
Moab, is selling the piece of land that belonged to our relative Elimelek. [4]I
thought I should bring the matter to your attention and suggest that you buy it in
the presence of these seated here and in the presence of the elders of my people.
If you will redeem it, do so. But if you[a] will not, tell me, so I will know. For no one
has the right to do it except you, and I am next in line."

"I will redeem it," he said.

[5]Then Boaz said, "On the day you buy the land from Naomi, you also acquire
Ruth the Moabite, the[b] dead man's widow, in order to maintain the name of the
dead with his property."

[6]At this, the guardian-redeemer said, "Then I cannot redeem it because I
might endanger my own estate. You redeem it yourself. I cannot do it."

[7](Now in earlier times in Israel, for the redemption and transfer of property to
become final, one party took off his sandal and gave it to the other. This was the
method of legalizing transactions in Israel.)

[8]So the guardian-redeemer said to Boaz, "Buy it yourself." And he removed
his sandal.

[9]Then Boaz announced to the elders and all the people, "Today you are witnesses that I have bought from Naomi all the property of Elimelek, Kilion and
Mahlon. [10]I have also acquired Ruth the Moabite, Mahlon's widow, as my wife,
in order to maintain the name of the dead with his property, so that his name
will not disappear from among his family or from his hometown. Today you are
witnesses!"

[11]Then the elders and all the people at the gate said, "We are witnesses. May
the LORD make the woman who is coming into your home like Rachel and Leah,
who together built up the family of Israel. May you have standing in Ephrathah
and be famous in Bethlehem. [12]Through the offspring the LORD gives you by
this young woman, may your family be like that of Perez, whom Tamar bore to
Judah."

Naomi Gains a Son

[13]So Boaz took Ruth and she became his wife. When he made love to her, the
LORD enabled her to conceive, and she gave birth to a son. [14]The women said to
Naomi: "Praise be to the LORD, who this day has not left you without a guardian-
redeemer. May he become famous throughout Israel! [15]He will renew your life
and sustain you in your old age. For your daughter-in-law, who loves you and
who is better to you than seven sons, has given him birth."

[16]Then Naomi took the child in her arms and cared for him. [17]The women living there said, "Naomi has a son!" And they named him Obed. He was the father
of Jesse, the father of David.

The Genealogy of David

[18]This, then, is the family line of Perez:

Perez was the father of Hezron,
[19]Hezron the father of Ram,
Ram the father of Amminadab,
[20]Amminadab the father of Nahshon,
Nahshon the father of Salmon,[c]
[21]Salmon the father of Boaz,
Boaz the father of Obed,
[22]Obed the father of Jesse,
and Jesse the father of David.

---

[a] *4* Many Hebrew manuscripts, Septuagint, Vulgate and Syriac; most Hebrew manuscripts *he*
[b] *5* Vulgate and Syriac; Hebrew (see also Septuagint) *Naomi and from Ruth the Moabite, you acquire the*
[c] *20* A few Hebrew manuscripts, some Septuagint manuscripts and Vulgate (see also verse 21 and Septuagint of 1 Chron. 2:11); most Hebrew manuscripts *Salma*

RUTH 4:13 – 17

A GOD OF ABUNDANCE

At the beginning of the book of Ruth, Naomi said the Lord had "afflicted" and "brought misfortune" on her. By the end of the book of Ruth, God had not only restored Ruth through her guardian-redeemer Boaz, but he had also provided for Naomi. This is a beautiful restoration of her life. God took Naomi's emptiness and bitterness (1:20 – 21) and replaced it with abundance and blessing through Ruth and Boaz and their child Obed.

Fullness can be experienced when people come to know Jesus and become part of the church. They go from emptiness to abundance in Christ. Boaz gave Ruth an overabundance of food to take back to Naomi, and Naomi immediately blessed Boaz for his kindness (2:14 – 20). Her emptiness began to turn into fullness. God provided for Ruth and her mother-in-law through Boaz, and in the same way, he has provided for all of our needs through Christ.

JESUS: OUR TRUE KING

1 SAMUEL

1 SAMUEL

SAMUEL IS BORN	SAMUEL ANOINTS DAVID	REIGN OF DAVID BEGINS
c. 1105 BC	*c. 1025 BC*	*c. 1010 BC*

The book of 1 Samuel opens at a spiritual low point in the nation of Israel. The judges were still ruling over Israel, and the people had continued to fall prey to idolatry. Even some of the priests had been corrupted by heinous sin. The failure of Israel's leaders accentuated the people's moral perversion; they showed open disdain for God and his word. In the face of such rebellion, however, God protected a remnant of faithful Israelites who loved God and kept his word.

The moral chaos prompted infighting among the people of God and rebellion against the rule of the judges. The nation longed for a king to lead them — a desire they developed through watching the surrounding nations. They were under constant threat and harassment by neighboring powers, and they wanted a king to unify them so that they could protect themselves. Despite Samuel's warnings (1Sa 8:6 – 20) the people persisted in their request, and God granted it. He called a man who seemed to possess all of the marks of a king — he was handsome, tall and early on in his reign showed signs of strong military prowess. The people appointed Saul by lot, and he led God's people for forty years (1Sa 10). His ultimately fatal flaw was his repeated disregard for God's commands late in his reign. His rebellion incurred God's judgment; God rejected him as king and allowed him to suffer the consequences of his folly.

God prompted Samuel to anoint David as king over Israel while Saul was still in power. As young David's reputation for following God's direction with courage and conviction grew, Saul even brought him on as a leader in the Israelite military. David's fame grew and Saul quickly lost heart, became jealous of David's victories and eventually tried to kill David. In the wake of Saul's failure to obey him, God raised up King David, who obeyed God's commands and led Israel in a way Saul never could.

The united monarchy in Israel demonstrated how God led his people through human agents. These leaders were entrusted with the task of speaking God's word and modeling God's character to lead the people of Israel to obey him in all things. Sin effectively hamstrung these men in their attempt to provide the type of leadership God desired, exposing the fact that no human leader can provide perfect leadership for his people. Only the true King, Jesus Christ, can ever provide the kind of leadership that faithfully represents God and his will for humanity.

THERE IS NO ONE HOLY LIKE THE LORD;
THERE IS NO ONE BESIDES YOU;
THERE IS NO ROCK LIKE OUR GOD.

---

1 Samuel 2:2

1 SAMUEL

The Birth of Samuel

1 There was a certain man from Ramathaim, a Zuphite[a] from the hill country of Ephraim, whose name was Elkanah son of Jeroham, the son of Elihu, the son of Tohu, the son of Zuph, an Ephraimite. 2He had two wives; one was called Hannah and the other Peninnah. Peninnah had children, but Hannah had none.

3Year after year this man went up from his town to worship and sacrifice to the LORD Almighty at Shiloh, where Hophni and Phinehas, the two sons of Eli, were priests of the LORD. 4Whenever the day came for Elkanah to sacrifice, he would give portions of the meat to his wife Peninnah and to all her sons and daughters. 5But to Hannah he gave a double portion because he loved her, and the LORD had closed her womb. 6Because the LORD had closed Hannah's womb, her rival kept provoking her in order to irritate her. 7This went on year after year. Whenever Hannah went up to the house of the LORD, her rival provoked her till she wept and would not eat. 8Her husband Elkanah would say to her, "Hannah, why are you weeping? Why don't you eat? Why are you downhearted? Don't I mean more to you than ten sons?"

9Once when they had finished eating and drinking in Shiloh, Hannah stood up. Now Eli the priest was sitting on his chair by the doorpost of the LORD's house. 10In her deep anguish Hannah prayed to the LORD, weeping bitterly. 11And she made a vow, saying, "LORD Almighty, if you will only look on your servant's misery and remember me, and not forget your servant but give her a son, then I will give him to the LORD for all the days of his life, and no razor will ever be used on his head."

12As she kept on praying to the LORD, Eli observed her mouth. 13Hannah was praying in her heart, and her lips were moving but her voice was not heard. Eli thought she was drunk 14and said to her, "How long are you going to stay drunk? Put away your wine."

15"Not so, my lord," Hannah replied, "I am a woman who is deeply troubled. I have not been drinking wine or beer; I was pouring out my soul to the LORD. 16Do not take your servant for a wicked woman; I have been praying here out of my great anguish and grief."

17Eli answered, "Go in peace, and may the God of Israel grant you what you have asked of him."

18She said, "May your servant find favor in your eyes." Then she went her way and ate something, and her face was no longer downcast.

19Early the next morning they arose and worshiped before the LORD and then went back to their home at Ramah. Elkanah made love to his wife Hannah, and the LORD remembered her. 20So in the course of time Hannah became pregnant and gave birth to a son. She named him Samuel,[b] saying, "Because I asked the LORD for him."

Hannah Dedicates Samuel

21When her husband Elkanah went up with all his family to offer the annual sacrifice to the LORD and to fulfill his vow, 22Hannah did not go. She said to her husband, "After the boy is weaned, I will take him and present him before the LORD, and he will live there always."[c]

---

[a] *1* See Septuagint and 1 Chron. 6:26-27,33-35; or *from Ramathaim Zuphim.* [b] *20* *Samuel* sounds like the Hebrew for *heard by God.* [c] *22* Masoretic Text; Dead Sea Scrolls *always. I have dedicated him as a Nazirite—all the days of his life."*

23“Do what seems best to you,” her husband Elkanah told her. “Stay here until
you have weaned him; only may the LORD make good his[a] word.” So the woman
stayed at home and nursed her son until she had weaned him.
24After he was weaned, she took the boy with her, young as he was, along with
a three-year-old bull,[b] an ephah[c] of flour and a skin of wine, and brought him
to the house of the LORD at Shiloh. 25When the bull had been sacrificed, they
brought the boy to Eli, 26and she said to him, “Pardon me, my lord. As surely
as you live, I am the woman who stood here beside you praying to the LORD. 27I
prayed for this child, and the LORD has granted me what I asked of him. 28So now
I give him to the LORD. For his whole life he will be given over to the LORD.” And
he worshiped the LORD there.

Hannah’s Prayer

2 Then Hannah prayed and said:

“My heart rejoices in the LORD;
  in the LORD my horn[d] is lifted high.
My mouth boasts over my enemies,
  for I delight in your deliverance.

2“There is no one holy like the LORD;
  there is no one besides you;
  there is no Rock like our God.

3“Do not keep talking so proudly
  or let your mouth speak such arrogance,
for the LORD is a God who knows,
  and by him deeds are weighed.

4“The bows of the warriors are broken,
  but those who stumbled are armed with strength.
5Those who were full hire themselves out for food,
  but those who were hungry are hungry no more.
She who was barren has borne seven children,
  but she who has had many sons pines away.

6“The LORD brings death and makes alive;
  he brings down to the grave and raises up.
7The LORD sends poverty and wealth;
  he humbles and he exalts.
8He raises the poor from the dust
  and lifts the needy from the ash heap;
he seats them with princes
  and has them inherit a throne of honor.

“For the foundations of the earth are the LORD’s;
  on them he has set the world.
9He will guard the feet of his faithful servants,
  but the wicked will be silenced in the place of darkness.

“It is not by strength that one prevails;
10 those who oppose the LORD will be broken.
The Most High will thunder from heaven;
  the LORD will judge the ends of the earth.

“He will give strength to his king
  and exalt the horn of his anointed.”

---

[a] *23* Masoretic Text; Dead Sea Scrolls, Septuagint and Syriac *your* [b] *24* Dead Sea Scrolls, Septuagint and Syriac; Masoretic Text *with three bulls* [c] *24* That is, probably about 36 pounds or about 16 kilograms [d] *1* *Horn* here symbolizes strength; also in verse 10.

---

1 SAMUEL 2:9–10

HANNAH’S PRAYER

Hannah’s prayer echoed the longing of God’s people. They were waiting for a king who would reign with power and bring stability and safety to Israel. Hannah’s prayer demonstrated the characteristics of a world under the rule and reign of God. It will be a world where God delivers his people, silences his enemies and brings justice to the entire world. The longing for a king like this is expressed in Hannah’s final words. She prayed with anticipation for a king that would be strengthened and anointed by God. Hannah directed the reader toward a messianic figure, a savior of God’s people, who would bring justice and peace to the world.

Years later, Mary, the mother of Jesus, offered a prayer similar to Hannah’s (Lk 1:46–55). Mary’s prayer anticipated the arrival of a far greater King who would do what no Old Testament king could do—usher in the rule and reign of God.

[11]Then Elkanah went home to Ramah, but the boy ministered before the LORD under Eli the priest.

Eli's Wicked Sons

[12]Eli's sons were scoundrels; they had no regard for the LORD. [13]Now it was the practice of the priests that, whenever any of the people offered a sacrifice, the priest's servant would come with a three-pronged fork in his hand while the meat was being boiled [14]and would plunge the fork into the pan or kettle or caldron or pot. Whatever the fork brought up the priest would take for himself. This is how they treated all the Israelites who came to Shiloh. [15]But even before the fat was burned, the priest's servant would come and say to the person who was sacrificing, "Give the priest some meat to roast; he won't accept boiled meat from you, but only raw."

[16]If the person said to him, "Let the fat be burned first, and then take whatever you want," the servant would answer, "No, hand it over now; if you don't, I'll take it by force."

[17]This sin of the young men was very great in the LORD's sight, for they[a] were treating the LORD's offering with contempt.

[18]But Samuel was ministering before the LORD—a boy wearing a linen ephod.
[19]Each year his mother made him a little robe and took it to him when she went up with her husband to offer the annual sacrifice. [20]Eli would bless Elkanah and his wife, saying, "May the LORD give you children by this woman to take the place of the one she prayed for and gave to[b] the LORD." Then they would go home.
[21]And the LORD was gracious to Hannah; she gave birth to three sons and two daughters. Meanwhile, the boy Samuel grew up in the presence of the LORD.

[22]Now Eli, who was very old, heard about everything his sons were doing to all Israel and how they slept with the women who served at the entrance to the tent of meeting. [23]So he said to them, "Why do you do such things? I hear from all the people about these wicked deeds of yours. [24]No, my sons; the report I hear spreading among the LORD's people is not good. [25]If one person sins against another, God[c] may mediate for the offender; but if anyone sins against the LORD, who will intercede for them?" His sons, however, did not listen to their father's rebuke, for it was the LORD's will to put them to death.

[26]And the boy Samuel continued to grow in stature and in favor with the LORD and with people.

Prophecy Against the House of Eli

[27]Now a man of God came to Eli and said to him, "This is what the LORD says: 'Did I not clearly reveal myself to your ancestor's family when they were in Egypt under Pharaoh? [28]I chose your ancestor out of all the tribes of Israel to be my priest, to go up to my altar, to burn incense, and to wear an ephod in my presence. I also gave your ancestor's family all the food offerings presented by the Israelites. [29]Why do you[d] scorn my sacrifice and offering that I prescribed for my dwelling? Why do you honor your sons more than me by fattening yourselves on the choice parts of every offering made by my people Israel?'

[30]"Therefore the LORD, the God of Israel, declares: 'I promised that members of your family would minister before me forever.' But now the LORD declares: 'Far be it from me! Those who honor me I will honor, but those who despise me will be disdained. [31]The time is coming when I will cut short your strength and the strength of your priestly house, so that no one in it will reach old age, [32]and you will see distress in my dwelling. Although good will be done to Israel, no one in your family line will ever reach old age. [33]Every one of you that I do not cut off from serving at my altar I will spare only to destroy your sight and sap your strength, and all your descendants will die in the prime of life.

[34]" 'And what happens to your two sons, Hophni and Phinehas, will be a sign

---

[a] *17* Dead Sea Scrolls and Septuagint; Masoretic Text *people* [b] *20* Dead Sea Scrolls; Masoretic Text *and asked from* [c] *25* Or *the judges* [d] *29* The Hebrew is plural.

to you — they will both die on the same day. 35I will raise up for myself a faithful
priest, who will do according to what is in my heart and mind. I will firmly establish his priestly house, and they will minister before my anointed one always.
36Then everyone left in your family line will come and bow down before him for
a piece of silver and a loaf of bread and plead, "Appoint me to some priestly office
so I can have food to eat." ' "

The LORD Calls Samuel

3 The boy Samuel ministered before the LORD under Eli. In those days the
word of the LORD was rare; there were not many visions.
2One night Eli, whose eyes were becoming so weak that he could barely see,
was lying down in his usual place. 3The lamp of God had not yet gone out, and
Samuel was lying down in the house of the LORD, where the ark of God was.
4Then the LORD called Samuel.
Samuel answered, "Here I am." 5And he ran to Eli and said, "Here I am; you
called me."
But Eli said, "I did not call; go back and lie down." So he went and lay down.
6Again the LORD called, "Samuel!" And Samuel got up and went to Eli and
said, "Here I am; you called me."
"My son," Eli said, "I did not call; go back and lie down."
7Now Samuel did not yet know the LORD: The word of the LORD had not yet
been revealed to him.
8A third time the LORD called, "Samuel!" And Samuel got up and went to Eli
and said, "Here I am; you called me."
Then Eli realized that the LORD was calling the boy. 9So Eli told Samuel, "Go
and lie down, and if he calls you, say, 'Speak, LORD, for your servant is listening.' " So Samuel went and lay down in his place.
10The LORD came and stood there, calling as at the other times, "Samuel!
Samuel!"
Then Samuel said, "Speak, for your servant is listening."
11And the LORD said to Samuel: "See, I am about to do something in Israel
that will make the ears of everyone who hears about it tingle. 12At that time I will
carry out against Eli everything I spoke against his family — from beginning to
end. 13For I told him that I would judge his family forever because of the sin he
knew about; his sons blasphemed God,[a] and he failed to restrain them. 14There-
fore I swore to the house of Eli, 'The guilt of Eli's house will never be atoned for
by sacrifice or offering.' "
15Samuel lay down until morning and then opened the doors of the house
of the LORD. He was afraid to tell Eli the vision, 16but Eli called him and said,
"Samuel, my son."
Samuel answered, "Here I am."
17"What was it he said to you?" Eli asked. "Do not hide it from me. May God
deal with you, be it ever so severely, if you hide from me anything he told you."
18So Samuel told him everything, hiding nothing from him. Then Eli said, "He is
the LORD; let him do what is good in his eyes."
19The LORD was with Samuel as he grew up, and he let none of Samuel's words
fall to the ground. 20And all Israel from Dan to Beersheba recognized that Samuel was attested as a prophet of the LORD. 21The LORD continued to appear at
Shiloh, and there he revealed himself to Samuel through his word.

4 And Samuel's word came to all Israel.

The Philistines Capture the Ark

Now the Israelites went out to fight against the Philistines. The Israelites
camped at Ebenezer, and the Philistines at Aphek. 2The Philistines deployed

---

[a] *13* An ancient Hebrew scribal tradition (see also Septuagint); Masoretic Text *sons made themselves contemptible*

1 SAMUEL 3:19 – 21

THE CALL OF SAMUEL

Israel was in a desperate time in history. Their priests were tarnished and doomed by the wickedness of Eli's sons and Eli's failure to restrain or remove them (1Sa 2:12 – 36) and were without a prophet because no one was speaking the word of the Lord (1Sa 3:1). They were experiencing moral anarchy, as "everyone did as they saw fit" (Jdg 21:25). It was a time when Israel was in dire need of a priest to serve the people faithfully, a prophet to speak the word of the Lord and a judge to lead the people in the pursuit of justice and righteousness. God called Samuel to fill these roles. The Lord was with Samuel as he grew up, and Samuel fulfilled these roles for the sake of Israel.

Samuel's faithfulness directs attention to the one who would serve as an even greater prophet, priest and judge. Jesus would be the ultimate prophet, preaching with authority (Mk 1:27). He would be the ultimate priest, offering himself as the atoning sacrifice for the sins of the world (Heb 9:11 – 14). He would stand before his Father, the ultimate judge (Jn 5:27 – 30), completely innocent but offering himself in the place of sinners.

SPEAK, FOR YOUR SERVANT IS LISTENING

Samuel served as the assistant to the high priest Eli. One evening Samuel heard a voice calling to him. Assuming it was Eli calling, he asked what the high priest wanted from him. But Eli had not called. This happened three times when Eli realized that it must be God calling out to Samuel. Eli instructed Samuel to answer, "Speak, LORD, for your servant is listening" (v. 9). Eli realized that when God speaks, one must take the time to listen. God was calling Samuel to become his prophet at a time when Israel desperately needed someone to speak the word of the Lord. Samuel was the one whom God would use to move his people from leadership by judges to rule by a king. Samuel would become a great prophet and priest for his people and would ultimately anoint Israel's first two kings, Saul and David. The Bible says that "the LORD was with Samuel as he grew up, and he let none of Samuel's words fall to the ground" (v. 19). God called Samuel to a great task, but it had to begin with Samuel listening to God's voice.

This is a theme that runs throughout the Scriptures. When God calls someone to lead his people, he often calls them first to a time of hearing his voice. David was anointed to be king, but before taking the throne, he first spent many years as a shepherd listening to God. The apostle Paul was called by God to become a great missionary, but before going to work, he spent three years listening to God (Gal 1:16 – 17). Likewise, Jesus taught that he did nothing without first hearing from the Father (Jn 5:19; 8:28; 12:49). Jesus would go on to tell his disciples that they could hear from God through the Holy Spirit and that he would guide them in the way that they should live (Lk 12:12; Jn 16:13). When a person becomes a disciple of Jesus, they are given the Spirit as a gift that takes up residence in their heart. Then the process of learning to identify the Spirit's voice begins, to become attuned to the call of God. The task of the Christian is to listen to God's voice through the Spirit and the Word and like Samuel to confess, "Speak, LORD, for your servant is listening."

their forces to meet Israel, and as the battle spread, Israel was defeated by the Philistines, who killed about four thousand of them on the battlefield. [3]When the soldiers returned to camp, the elders of Israel asked, "Why did the LORD bring defeat on us today before the Philistines? Let us bring the ark of the LORD's covenant from Shiloh, so that he may go with us and save us from the hand of our enemies."

[4]So the people sent men to Shiloh, and they brought back the ark of the covenant of the LORD Almighty, who is enthroned between the cherubim. And Eli's two sons, Hophni and Phinehas, were there with the ark of the covenant of God.

[5]When the ark of the LORD's covenant came into the camp, all Israel raised such a great shout that the ground shook. [6]Hearing the uproar, the Philistines asked, "What's all this shouting in the Hebrew camp?"

When they learned that the ark of the LORD had come into the camp, [7]the Philistines were afraid. "A god has[a] come into the camp," they said. "Oh no! Nothing like this has happened before. [8]We're doomed! Who will deliver us from the hand of these mighty gods? They are the gods who struck the Egyptians with all kinds of plagues in the wilderness. [9]Be strong, Philistines! Be men, or you will be subject to the Hebrews, as they have been to you. Be men, and fight!"

[10]So the Philistines fought, and the Israelites were defeated and every man fled to his tent. The slaughter was very great; Israel lost thirty thousand foot soldiers. [11]The ark of God was captured, and Eli's two sons, Hophni and Phinehas, died.

Death of Eli

[12]That same day a Benjamite ran from the battle line and went to Shiloh with his clothes torn and dust on his head. [13]When he arrived, there was Eli sitting on his chair by the side of the road, watching, because his heart feared for the ark of God. When the man entered the town and told what had happened, the whole town sent up a cry.

[14]Eli heard the outcry and asked, "What is the meaning of this uproar?"

The man hurried over to Eli, [15]who was ninety-eight years old and whose eyes had failed so that he could not see. [16]He told Eli, "I have just come from the battle line; I fled from it this very day."

Eli asked, "What happened, my son?"

[17]The man who brought the news replied, "Israel fled before the Philistines, and the army has suffered heavy losses. Also your two sons, Hophni and Phinehas, are dead, and the ark of God has been captured."

[18]When he mentioned the ark of God, Eli fell backward off his chair by the side of the gate. His neck was broken and he died, for he was an old man, and he was heavy. He had led[b] Israel forty years.

[19]His daughter-in-law, the wife of Phinehas, was pregnant and near the time of delivery. When she heard the news that the ark of God had been captured and that her father-in-law and her husband were dead, she went into labor and gave birth, but was overcome by her labor pains. [20]As she was dying, the women attending her said, "Don't despair; you have given birth to a son." But she did not respond or pay any attention.

[21]She named the boy Ichabod,[c] saying, "The Glory has departed from Israel"—because of the capture of the ark of God and the deaths of her father-in-law and her husband. [22]She said, "The Glory has departed from Israel, for the ark of God has been captured."

The Ark in Ashdod and Ekron

5 After the Philistines had captured the ark of God, they took it from Ebenezer to Ashdod. [2]Then they carried the ark into Dagon's temple and set it beside Dagon. [3]When the people of Ashdod rose early the next day, there was Dagon,

[a] 7 Or *"Gods have* (see Septuagint) [b] 18 Traditionally *judged* [c] 21 *Ichabod* means *no glory.*

1 SAMUEL 5:1–5

VICTORY OVER FALSE GODS

Dagon was the chief god of the Philistines and was thought to control the weather and the fertility of the land. Worship of Dagon was thought to ensure a good crop and bring blessing. The Philistines placed their hope for a blessing and a secure future in the hands of Dagon. But in the presence of the ark of God, Dagon fell on his face—as if he were worshiping the one true God—and was ultimately left in broken pieces.

This story shows that before the true God, all false gods are exposed for the frauds that they are. When people place their hope for the future in the hands of something other than God, they have created an idol. People often make idols out of success, popularity or wealth, hoping that these things will provide ultimate joy and security. But it is only God who offers complete joy. The apostle John explained that there is coming a day when all people will be exposed as they are judged before the throne of the one true God (Rev 20:11–15).

fallen on his face on the ground before the ark of the LORD! They took Dagon and
put him back in his place. 4But the following morning when they rose, there was
Dagon, fallen on his face on the ground before the ark of the LORD! His head and
hands had been broken off and were lying on the threshold; only his body remained. 5That is why to this day neither the priests of Dagon nor any others who
enter Dagon's temple at Ashdod step on the threshold.

6The LORD's hand was heavy on the people of Ashdod and its vicinity; he
brought devastation on them and afflicted them with tumors.[a] 7When the people of Ashdod saw what was happening, they said, "The ark of the god of Israel
must not stay here with us, because his hand is heavy on us and on Dagon our
god." 8So they called together all the rulers of the Philistines and asked them,
"What shall we do with the ark of the god of Israel?"

They answered, "Have the ark of the god of Israel moved to Gath." So they
moved the ark of the God of Israel.

9But after they had moved it, the LORD's hand was against that city, throwing
it into a great panic. He afflicted the people of the city, both young and old, with
an outbreak of tumors.[b] 10So they sent the ark of God to Ekron.

As the ark of God was entering Ekron, the people of Ekron cried out, "They
have brought the ark of the god of Israel around to us to kill us and our people."
11So they called together all the rulers of the Philistines and said, "Send the ark
of the god of Israel away; let it go back to its own place, or it[c] will kill us and our
people." For death had filled the city with panic; God's hand was very heavy on
it. 12Those who did not die were afflicted with tumors, and the outcry of the city
went up to heaven.

The Ark Returned to Israel

6 When the ark of the LORD had been in Philistine territory seven months, 2the
Philistines called for the priests and the diviners and said, "What shall we do
with the ark of the LORD? Tell us how we should send it back to its place."

3They answered, "If you return the ark of the god of Israel, do not send it back
to him without a gift; by all means send a guilt offering to him. Then you will be
healed, and you will know why his hand has not been lifted from you."

4The Philistines asked, "What guilt offering should we send to him?"

They replied, "Five gold tumors and five gold rats, according to the number
of the Philistine rulers, because the same plague has struck both you and your
rulers. 5Make models of the tumors and of the rats that are destroying the country, and give glory to Israel's god. Perhaps he will lift his hand from you and your
gods and your land. 6Why do you harden your hearts as the Egyptians and Pharaoh did? When Israel's god dealt harshly with them, did they not send the Israelites out so they could go on their way?

7"Now then, get a new cart ready, with two cows that have calved and have
never been yoked. Hitch the cows to the cart, but take their calves away and pen
them up. 8Take the ark of the LORD and put it on the cart, and in a chest beside
it put the gold objects you are sending back to him as a guilt offering. Send it
on its way, 9but keep watching it. If it goes up to its own territory, toward Beth
Shemesh, then the LORD has brought this great disaster on us. But if it does not,
then we will know that it was not his hand that struck us but that it happened to
us by chance."

10So they did this. They took two such cows and hitched them to the cart and
penned up their calves. 11They placed the ark of the LORD on the cart and along
with it the chest containing the gold rats and the models of the tumors. 12Then
the cows went straight up toward Beth Shemesh, keeping on the road and lowing
all the way; they did not turn to the right or to the left. The rulers of the Philistines followed them as far as the border of Beth Shemesh.

[a] 6 Hebrew; Septuagint and Vulgate *tumors. And rats appeared in their land, and there was death and destruction throughout the city* [b] 9 Or *with tumors in the groin* (see Septuagint)
[c] 11 Or *he*

1 SAMUEL 6:1 – 12

RELIGION: MAKING UP A RESPONSE TO GOD

After taking possession of the ark of the Lord, the Philistines began experiencing trouble. Their possession of the ark caused the god Dagon to topple and brought about a plague of tumors on the Philistines. It was clear that God's judgment was on them. They assumed the solution was to simply return the ark along with a guilt offering. This proved to be more difficult than imagined because they did not know the proper requirements for such a task.

Often, when people experience guilt they attempt to conjure up ways to appease God's judgment. They do this because they don't have a clear understanding of God's pathways of forgiveness. But Jesus came to make God's way and requirements clear. Jesus is the ultimate sacrifice for sins, and his death is the only offering that is acceptable to God (Jn 3:16; Ro 3:25). The way to forgiveness and grace is not through empty sacrifices but only through belief in Jesus.

13 Now the people of Beth Shemesh were harvesting their wheat in the valley, and when they looked up and saw the ark, they rejoiced at the sight. 14 The cart came to the field of Joshua of Beth Shemesh, and there it stopped beside a large rock. The people chopped up the wood of the cart and sacrificed the cows as a burnt offering to the LORD. 15 The Levites took down the ark of the LORD, together with the chest containing the gold objects, and placed them on the large rock. On that day the people of Beth Shemesh offered burnt offerings and made sacrifices to the LORD. 16 The five rulers of the Philistines saw all this and then returned that same day to Ekron.

17 These are the gold tumors the Philistines sent as a guilt offering to the LORD—one each for Ashdod, Gaza, Ashkelon, Gath and Ekron. 18 And the number of the gold rats was according to the number of Philistine towns belonging to the five rulers—the fortified towns with their country villages. The large rock on which the Levites set the ark of the LORD is a witness to this day in the field of Joshua of Beth Shemesh.

19 But God struck down some of the inhabitants of Beth Shemesh, putting seventy[a] of them to death because they looked into the ark of the LORD. The people mourned because of the heavy blow the LORD had dealt them. 20 And the people of Beth Shemesh asked, "Who can stand in the presence of the LORD, this holy God? To whom will the ark go up from here?"

21 Then they sent messengers to the people of Kiriath Jearim, saying, "The Philistines have returned the ark of the LORD. Come down and take it up to your town."

7 1 So the men of Kiriath Jearim came and took up the ark of the LORD. They brought it to Abinadab's house on the hill and consecrated Eleazar his son to guard the ark of the LORD. 2 The ark remained at Kiriath Jearim a long time—twenty years in all.

Samuel Subdues the Philistines at Mizpah

Then all the people of Israel turned back to the LORD. 3 So Samuel said to all the Israelites, "If you are returning to the LORD with all your hearts, then rid yourselves of the foreign gods and the Ashtoreths and commit yourselves to the LORD and serve him only, and he will deliver you out of the hand of the Philistines." 4 So the Israelites put away their Baals and Ashtoreths, and served the LORD only.

5 Then Samuel said, "Assemble all Israel at Mizpah, and I will intercede with the LORD for you." 6 When they had assembled at Mizpah, they drew water and poured it out before the LORD. On that day they fasted and there they confessed, "We have sinned against the LORD." Now Samuel was serving as leader[b] of Israel at Mizpah.

7 When the Philistines heard that Israel had assembled at Mizpah, the rulers of the Philistines came up to attack them. When the Israelites heard of it, they were afraid because of the Philistines. 8 They said to Samuel, "Do not stop crying out to the LORD our God for us, that he may rescue us from the hand of the Philistines." 9 Then Samuel took a suckling lamb and sacrificed it as a whole burnt offering to the LORD. He cried out to the LORD on Israel's behalf, and the LORD answered him.

10 While Samuel was sacrificing the burnt offering, the Philistines drew near to engage Israel in battle. But that day the LORD thundered with loud thunder against the Philistines and threw them into such a panic that they were routed before the Israelites. 11 The men of Israel rushed out of Mizpah and pursued the Philistines, slaughtering them along the way to a point below Beth Kar.

12 Then Samuel took a stone and set it up between Mizpah and Shen. He named it Ebenezer,[c] saying, "Thus far the LORD has helped us."

13 So the Philistines were subdued and they stopped invading Israel's territory. Throughout Samuel's lifetime, the hand of the LORD was against the

---

[a] *19* A few Hebrew manuscripts; most Hebrew manuscripts and Septuagint *50,070*

[b] *6* Traditionally *judge*; also in verse 15 [c] *12* *Ebenezer* means *stone of help.*

FAITHFUL LEADERSHIP

Samuel was a faithful leader. At a time when Israel lacked trustworthy leadership, Samuel proved himself to be an honorable prophet, priest and judge. In this passage, he demonstrated his leadership in each of these roles. He used his prophetic voice to call the people to repent of their idolatry (v. 3). He acted as a priest and interceded on behalf of the nation (v. 9). He was declared as a faithful judge (or leader) over Israel all the days of his life (v. 15). Samuel lived in obedience to the Lord and called his nation to turn from their idols and seek God. This God-centered leadership brought great blessing for the people. But in spite of this, the Israelites wanted to go their own way.

This is the last story about Samuel in the Bible before the people ask for a king. God had been faithful to Israel under Samuel's leadership because he feared the Lord and recognized that the Lord alone was the true king of the people. But the people wanted to be like other nations and have an earthly king they could see. Under Samuel's leadership and God's rule, the people were protected from the Philistines (v. 13). God kept them safe because Samuel was faithful to the Lord. But under the rule of Saul, they lived in fear of their enemies. Faithful leadership is crucial for the prospering of God's people.

Samuel's faithfulness pointed the people of Israel toward what they truly needed. They needed a savior who would stand as a prophet, priest and king — one who would call people to repentance, intercede for them on behalf of their sins, and rule and reign with justice and grace. Samuel's life prefigures Jesus. In the past, God spoke through prophets but now has spoken through his Son Jesus — creator and heir of all things (Heb 1:1 – 3). He is hailed as the great high priest who provides purification for sins. He sits at the throne of God and reigns as the true king that God's people have always longed for. God's people experienced peace and safety under the leadership of Samuel, but under the rule and reign of Jesus, believers will experience the fullness of the kingdom of God where all things will be made right for all of eternity.

Philistines. 14The towns from Ekron to Gath that the Philistines had captured
from Israel were restored to Israel, and Israel delivered the neighboring territory from the hands of the Philistines. And there was peace between Israel and
the Amorites.
15Samuel continued as Israel's leader all the days of his life. 16From year to
year he went on a circuit from Bethel to Gilgal to Mizpah, judging Israel in all
those places. 17But he always went back to Ramah, where his home was, and
there he also held court for Israel. And he built an altar there to the LORD.

Israel Asks for a King

8 When Samuel grew old, he appointed his sons as Israel's leaders.[a] 2The name
of his firstborn was Joel and the name of his second was Abijah, and they
served at Beersheba. 3But his sons did not follow his ways. They turned aside
after dishonest gain and accepted bribes and perverted justice.
4So all the elders of Israel gathered together and came to Samuel at Ramah.
5They said to him, "You are old, and your sons do not follow your ways; now appoint a king to lead[b] us, such as all the other nations have."
6But when they said, "Give us a king to lead us," this displeased Samuel; so he
prayed to the LORD. 7And the LORD told him: "Listen to all that the people are
saying to you; it is not you they have rejected, but they have rejected me as their
king. 8As they have done from the day I brought them up out of Egypt until this
day, forsaking me and serving other gods, so they are doing to you. 9Now listen to
them; but warn them solemnly and let them know what the king who will reign
over them will claim as his rights."
10Samuel told all the words of the LORD to the people who were asking him for
a king. 11He said, "This is what the king who will reign over you will claim as his
rights: He will take your sons and make them serve with his chariots and horses,
and they will run in front of his chariots. 12Some he will assign to be commanders of thousands and commanders of fifties, and others to plow his ground and
reap his harvest, and still others to make weapons of war and equipment for his
chariots. 13He will take your daughters to be perfumers and cooks and bakers.
14He will take the best of your fields and vineyards and olive groves and give
them to his attendants. 15He will take a tenth of your grain and of your vintage
and give it to his officials and attendants. 16Your male and female servants and
the best of your cattle[c] and donkeys he will take for his own use. 17He will take a
tenth of your flocks, and you yourselves will become his slaves. 18When that day
comes, you will cry out for relief from the king you have chosen, but the LORD
will not answer you in that day."
19But the people refused to listen to Samuel. "No!" they said. "We want a king
over us. 20Then we will be like all the other nations, with a king to lead us and to
go out before us and fight our battles."
21When Samuel heard all that the people said, he repeated it before the LORD.
22The LORD answered, "Listen to them and give them a king."
Then Samuel said to the Israelites, "Everyone go back to your own town."

Samuel Anoints Saul

9 There was a Benjamite, a man of standing, whose name was Kish son of Abiel, the son of Zeror, the son of Bekorath, the son of Aphiah of Benjamin. 2Kish
had a son named Saul, as handsome a young man as could be found anywhere
in Israel, and he was a head taller than anyone else.
3Now the donkeys belonging to Saul's father Kish were lost, and Kish said to
his son Saul, "Take one of the servants with you and go and look for the donkeys."
4So he passed through the hill country of Ephraim and through the area around
Shalisha, but they did not find them. They went on into the district of Shaalim,

[a] *1* Traditionally *judges* [b] *5* Traditionally *judge*; also in verses 6 and 20 [c] *16* Septuagint; Hebrew *young men*

CHANGING KINGS

The Israelites' request that Samuel establish a king to rule over Israel was an act of faithlessness that led to serious negative consequences. Kingship itself is not necessarily an evil institution. However, for the Israelites it demonstrated a lack of trust in God to provide for their needs. Deuteronomy 17:14 – 20 anticipates a kingship by outlining God's rules for a king of Israel. So why is Israel's request for a king an act of faithlessness?

Israel's request was a desire to be like "all the other nations" (1Sa 8:5,20). God had chosen and redeemed Israel so that they would be different than the nations around them. What differentiated Israel from other nations was the fact that God was their king. This eliminated the need for a human king. Their desire to be like everyone else was an act of disobedience to what God had called them to be — set apart. By deciding to become more like the cultures around them, Israel was denying the purposes for which God had created and saved them. Samuel warned the people that this sinful act would cause all kinds of grief to the nation. The Israelites opened themselves up to a king who would exploit and suppress them rather than love and protect them. This king would be far from the picture God outlined for Israel in Deuteronomy 17. There would indeed be serious consequences to Israel's rebellion. What they thought would bring them peace and security would instead bring them destruction and harm.

But even in spite of their disobedience, God honored their request for a king. He told Samuel to surrender to their evil desire. God even demonstrated his grace in their request. Israel's first king, Saul, would be a disappointment and would do exactly what Samuel warned. But their second king, David, would lead them well, and through his offspring would come Jesus, the Messiah. Jesus would ultimately remove the guilt of the people by dying on the cross for their sins. While Israel would still have to suffer for the consequences of their decision, God would be gracious to provide for them even in their disobedience.

In Jesus, God's provision is not conditional. His gift of grace is not based on humanity's righteousness or unrighteousness, but solely on his mercy for people. The heart of the gospel is that "God demonstrates his own love for us in this: While we were still sinners, Christ died for us" (Ro 5:8).

but the donkeys were not there. Then he passed through the territory of Benjamin, but they did not find them.
5When they reached the district of Zuph, Saul said to the servant who was
with him, "Come, let's go back, or my father will stop thinking about the donkeys
and start worrying about us."
6But the servant replied, "Look, in this town there is a man of God; he is highly respected, and everything he says comes true. Let's go there now. Perhaps he
will tell us what way to take."
7Saul said to his servant, "If we go, what can we give the man? The food in
our sacks is gone. We have no gift to take to the man of God. What do we have?"
8The servant answered him again. "Look," he said, "I have a quarter of a shekel[a] of silver. I will give it to the man of God so that he will tell us what way to take."
9(Formerly in Israel, if someone went to inquire of God, they would say, "Come,
let us go to the seer," because the prophet of today used to be called a seer.)
10"Good," Saul said to his servant. "Come, let's go." So they set out for the town
where the man of God was.
11As they were going up the hill to the town, they met some young women
coming out to draw water, and they asked them, "Is the seer here?"
12"He is," they answered. "He's ahead of you. Hurry now; he has just come to
our town today, for the people have a sacrifice at the high place. 13As soon as you
enter the town, you will find him before he goes up to the high place to eat. The
people will not begin eating until he comes, because he must bless the sacrifice;
afterward, those who are invited will eat. Go up now; you should find him about
this time."
14They went up to the town, and as they were entering it, there was Samuel,
coming toward them on his way up to the high place.
15Now the day before Saul came, the LORD had revealed this to Samuel:
16"About this time tomorrow I will send you a man from the land of Benjamin.
Anoint him ruler over my people Israel; he will deliver them from the hand of the
Philistines. I have looked on my people, for their cry has reached me."
17When Samuel caught sight of Saul, the LORD said to him, "This is the man I
spoke to you about; he will govern my people."
18Saul approached Samuel in the gateway and asked, "Would you please tell
me where the seer's house is?"
19"I am the seer," Samuel replied. "Go up ahead of me to the high place, for
today you are to eat with me, and in the morning I will send you on your way and
will tell you all that is in your heart. 20As for the donkeys you lost three days ago,
do not worry about them; they have been found. And to whom is all the desire of
Israel turned, if not to you and your whole family line?"
21Saul answered, "But am I not a Benjamite, from the smallest tribe of Israel,
and is not my clan the least of all the clans of the tribe of Benjamin? Why do you
say such a thing to me?"
22Then Samuel brought Saul and his servant into the hall and seated them
at the head of those who were invited — about thirty in number. 23Samuel said
to the cook, "Bring the piece of meat I gave you, the one I told you to lay aside."
24So the cook took up the thigh with what was on it and set it in front of Saul.
Samuel said, "Here is what has been kept for you. Eat, because it was set aside
for you for this occasion from the time I said, 'I have invited guests.'" And Saul
dined with Samuel that day.
25After they came down from the high place to the town, Samuel talked with
Saul on the roof of his house. 26They rose about daybreak, and Samuel called
to Saul on the roof, "Get ready, and I will send you on your way." When Saul got
ready, he and Samuel went outside together. 27As they were going down to the
edge of the town, Samuel said to Saul, "Tell the servant to go on ahead of us" —
and the servant did so — "but you stay here for a while, so that I may give you a
message from God."

[a] 8 That is, about 1/10 ounce or about 3 grams

10 Then Samuel took a flask of olive oil and poured it on Saul's head and
kissed him, saying, "Has not the LORD anointed you ruler over his inheritance?[a] 2When you leave me today, you will meet two men near Rachel's tomb,
at Zelzah on the border of Benjamin. They will say to you, 'The donkeys you set
out to look for have been found. And now your father has stopped thinking about
them and is worried about you. He is asking, "What shall I do about my son?"'
3"Then you will go on from there until you reach the great tree of Tabor. Three
men going up to worship God at Bethel will meet you there. One will be carrying
three young goats, another three loaves of bread, and another a skin of wine.
4They will greet you and offer you two loaves of bread, which you will accept
from them.
5"After that you will go to Gibeah of God, where there is a Philistine outpost.
As you approach the town, you will meet a procession of prophets coming down
from the high place with lyres, timbrels, pipes and harps being played before
them, and they will be prophesying. 6The Spirit of the LORD will come powerfully upon you, and you will prophesy with them; and you will be changed into
a different person. 7Once these signs are fulfilled, do whatever your hand finds
to do, for God is with you.
8"Go down ahead of me to Gilgal. I will surely come down to you to sacrifice
burnt offerings and fellowship offerings, but you must wait seven days until I
come to you and tell you what you are to do."

Saul Made King

9As Saul turned to leave Samuel, God changed Saul's heart, and all these signs
were fulfilled that day. 10When he and his servant arrived at Gibeah, a procession of prophets met him; the Spirit of God came powerfully upon him, and he
joined in their prophesying. 11When all those who had formerly known him saw
him prophesying with the prophets, they asked each other, "What is this that has
happened to the son of Kish? Is Saul also among the prophets?"
12A man who lived there answered, "And who is their father?" So it became a
saying: "Is Saul also among the prophets?" 13After Saul stopped prophesying, he
went to the high place.
14Now Saul's uncle asked him and his servant, "Where have you been?"
"Looking for the donkeys," he said. "But when we saw they were not to be
found, we went to Samuel."
15Saul's uncle said, "Tell me what Samuel said to you."
16Saul replied, "He assured us that the donkeys had been found." But he did
not tell his uncle what Samuel had said about the kingship.
17Samuel summoned the people of Israel to the LORD at Mizpah 18and said to
them, "This is what the LORD, the God of Israel, says: 'I brought Israel up out of
Egypt, and I delivered you from the power of Egypt and all the kingdoms that
oppressed you.' 19But you have now rejected your God, who saves you out of all
your disasters and calamities. And you have said, 'No, appoint a king over us.' So
now present yourselves before the LORD by your tribes and clans."
20When Samuel had all Israel come forward by tribes, the tribe of Benjamin
was taken by lot. 21Then he brought forward the tribe of Benjamin, clan by clan,
and Matri's clan was taken. Finally Saul son of Kish was taken. But when they
looked for him, he was not to be found. 22So they inquired further of the LORD,
"Has the man come here yet?"
And the LORD said, "Yes, he has hidden himself among the supplies."
23They ran and brought him out, and as he stood among the people he was a
head taller than any of the others. 24Samuel said to all the people, "Do you see
the man the LORD has chosen? There is no one like him among all the people."
Then the people shouted, "Long live the king!"

[a] *1* Hebrew; Septuagint and Vulgate *over his people Israel? You will reign over the LORD's people and save them from the power of their enemies round about. And this will be a sign to you that the LORD has anointed you ruler over his inheritance:*

---

1 SAMUEL 10:1–10

CHANGE OF HEART

In this account, God changed Saul's heart. In Hebrew this expression literally reads, "God changed him for another heart." It may seem that Saul's subsequent attitudes and behavior did not reflect a genuine spiritual life. Yet, Saul seemed to have struggled with his sin and experienced times where he desired to worship God (14:34–35; 15:24–31). Nevertheless, for Saul to embrace the life God was calling him to live, he needed God to change his heart.

This theme of a need for inner transformation and a new heart runs throughout the Scriptures (Eze 36:26). The New Testament demonstrates that complete inner transformation comes through Jesus and is empowered by the Holy Spirit (Jn 3:5). Jesus' transforming work changes lives from the inside out (2Co 5:17). Therefore, believers can receive the same heart that David asked for in Psalm 51. God works to change the hearts of those who follow him, and Saul and David are examples of what believers today can experience.

[25]Samuel explained to the people the rights and duties of kingship. He wrote them down on a scroll and deposited it before the LORD. Then Samuel dismissed the people to go to their own homes.

[26]Saul also went to his home in Gibeah, accompanied by valiant men whose hearts God had touched. [27]But some scoundrels said, "How can this fellow save us?" They despised him and brought him no gifts. But Saul kept silent.

Saul Rescues the City of Jabesh

11 Nahash[a] the Ammonite went up and besieged Jabesh Gilead. And all the men of Jabesh said to him, "Make a treaty with us, and we will be subject to you."

[2]But Nahash the Ammonite replied, "I will make a treaty with you only on the condition that I gouge out the right eye of every one of you and so bring disgrace on all Israel."

[3]The elders of Jabesh said to him, "Give us seven days so we can send messengers throughout Israel; if no one comes to rescue us, we will surrender to you."

[4]When the messengers came to Gibeah of Saul and reported these terms to the people, they all wept aloud. [5]Just then Saul was returning from the fields, behind his oxen, and he asked, "What is wrong with everyone? Why are they weeping?" Then they repeated to him what the men of Jabesh had said.

[6]When Saul heard their words, the Spirit of God came powerfully upon him, and he burned with anger. [7]He took a pair of oxen, cut them into pieces, and sent the pieces by messengers throughout Israel, proclaiming, "This is what will be done to the oxen of anyone who does not follow Saul and Samuel." Then the terror of the LORD fell on the people, and they came out together as one. [8]When Saul mustered them at Bezek, the men of Israel numbered three hundred thousand and those of Judah thirty thousand.

[9]They told the messengers who had come, "Say to the men of Jabesh Gilead, 'By the time the sun is hot tomorrow, you will be rescued.'" When the messengers went and reported this to the men of Jabesh, they were elated. [10]They said to the Ammonites, "Tomorrow we will surrender to you, and you can do to us whatever you like."

[11]The next day Saul separated his men into three divisions; during the last watch of the night they broke into the camp of the Ammonites and slaughtered them until the heat of the day. Those who survived were scattered, so that no two of them were left together.

Saul Confirmed as King

[12]The people then said to Samuel, "Who was it that asked, 'Shall Saul reign over us?' Turn these men over to us so that we may put them to death."

[13]But Saul said, "No one will be put to death today, for this day the LORD has rescued Israel."

[14]Then Samuel said to the people, "Come, let us go to Gilgal and there renew the kingship." [15]So all the people went to Gilgal and made Saul king in the presence of the LORD. There they sacrificed fellowship offerings before the LORD, and Saul and all the Israelites held a great celebration.

Samuel's Farewell Speech

12 Samuel said to all Israel, "I have listened to everything you said to me and have set a king over you. [2]Now you have a king as your leader. As for me, I am old and gray, and my sons are here with you. I have been your leader from my youth until this day. [3]Here I stand. Testify against me in the presence of the LORD

---

[a] 1 Masoretic Text; Dead Sea Scrolls *gifts. Now Nahash king of the Ammonites oppressed the Gadites and Reubenites severely. He gouged out all their right eyes and struck terror and dread in Israel. Not a man remained among the Israelites beyond the Jordan whose right eye was not gouged out by Nahash king of the Ammonites, except that seven thousand men fled from the Ammonites and entered Jabesh Gilead. About a month later,* [1]*Nahash*

and his anointed. Whose ox have I taken? Whose donkey have I taken? Whom have I cheated? Whom have I oppressed? From whose hand have I accepted a bribe to make me shut my eyes? If I have done any of these things, I will make it right."

4 "You have not cheated or oppressed us," they replied. "You have not taken anything from anyone's hand."

5 Samuel said to them, "The LORD is witness against you, and also his anointed is witness this day, that you have not found anything in my hand."

"He is witness," they said.

6 Then Samuel said to the people, "It is the LORD who appointed Moses and Aaron and brought your ancestors up out of Egypt. 7 Now then, stand here, because I am going to confront you with evidence before the LORD as to all the righteous acts performed by the LORD for you and your ancestors.

8 "After Jacob entered Egypt, they cried to the LORD for help, and the LORD sent Moses and Aaron, who brought your ancestors out of Egypt and settled them in this place.

9 "But they forgot the LORD their God; so he sold them into the hand of Sisera, the commander of the army of Hazor, and into the hands of the Philistines and the king of Moab, who fought against them. 10 They cried out to the LORD and said, 'We have sinned; we have forsaken the LORD and served the Baals and the Ashtoreths. But now deliver us from the hands of our enemies, and we will serve you.' 11 Then the LORD sent Jerub-Baal,[a] Barak,[b] Jephthah and Samuel,[c] and he delivered you from the hands of your enemies all around you, so that you lived in safety.

12 "But when you saw that Nahash king of the Ammonites was moving against you, you said to me, 'No, we want a king to rule over us' — even though the LORD your God was your king. 13 Now here is the king you have chosen, the one you asked for; see, the LORD has set a king over you. 14 If you fear the LORD and serve and obey him and do not rebel against his commands, and if both you and the king who reigns over you follow the LORD your God — good! 15 But if you do not obey the LORD, and if you rebel against his commands, his hand will be against you, as it was against your ancestors.

16 "Now then, stand still and see this great thing the LORD is about to do before your eyes! 17 Is it not wheat harvest now? I will call on the LORD to send thunder and rain. And you will realize what an evil thing you did in the eyes of the LORD when you asked for a king."

18 Then Samuel called on the LORD, and that same day the LORD sent thunder and rain. So all the people stood in awe of the LORD and of Samuel.

19 The people all said to Samuel, "Pray to the LORD your God for your servants so that we will not die, for we have added to all our other sins the evil of asking for a king."

20 "Do not be afraid," Samuel replied. "You have done all this evil; yet do not turn away from the LORD, but serve the LORD with all your heart. 21 Do not turn away after useless idols. They can do you no good, nor can they rescue you, because they are useless. 22 For the sake of his great name the LORD will not reject his people, because the LORD was pleased to make you his own. 23 As for me, far be it from me that I should sin against the LORD by failing to pray for you. And I will teach you the way that is good and right. 24 But be sure to fear the LORD and serve him faithfully with all your heart; consider what great things he has done for you. 25 Yet if you persist in doing evil, both you and your king will perish."

Samuel Rebukes Saul

13 Saul was thirty[d] years old when he became king, and he reigned over Israel forty-[e] two years.

2 Saul chose three thousand men from Israel; two thousand were with him at

---

1 SAMUEL 12:22

HIS NAME'S SAKE

In this chapter, Samuel delivered his farewell speech to the Israelites and reminded the people of God's faithfulness to them throughout history. He retold their journey from deliverance in Egypt and to the promised land (vv. 6 – 8). But he also reminded them of their faithlessness and the times they turned their backs on God (vv. 9 – 10). He explained that because they had now asked for a human king, they were once again demonstrating their lack of trust in God to provide for their needs. As they began to wise up about what they had done, they became afraid. But Samuel encouraged them by telling them that while they may have been faithless, God was still faithful. God would continue to love and accept them "for the sake of his great name."

In ancient times, one's name stood for one's character. The name of God speaks of his reputation and attributes. For God to abandon his people would be inconsistent with his reputation for faithfulness. He would remain faithful to them by delivering on his promise to send a Messiah to redeem and restore his people. In the New Testament, the apostle Paul writes of Jesus, "If we are faithless, he remains faithful, for he cannot disown himself" (2Ti 2:13). By sending Jesus, God the Father demonstrated that he never gives up on those he loves because he cannot disown his own character.

---

[a] *11* Also called *Gideon* [b] *11* Some Septuagint manuscripts and Syriac; Hebrew *Bedan* [c] *11* Hebrew; some Septuagint manuscripts and Syriac *Samson* [d] *1* A few late manuscripts of the Septuagint; Hebrew does not have *thirty.* [e] *1* Probable reading of the original Hebrew text (see Acts 13:21); Masoretic Text does not have *forty-*.

1 SAMUEL 12:14–15

OBEDIENCE AND BLESSING

First Samuel demonstrates the blessing that comes when one is obedient to God versus the destruction that comes when one chooses to live their own way. This is a key biblical theme that runs throughout the Old Testament. This principle is seen very clearly in 1 Samuel 12:14–15: Obedience to God leads one into a blessed life while disobedience to God's ways often brings troubles. The examples are numerous: The disobedience of Eli's sons disqualified them from becoming judges in Israel. The same was true of Samuel's sons.

The life of Saul demonstrates this principle even more clearly. Saul disobeyed God on a number of occasions. Saul was impatient with God's timing when he offered a sacrifice before the Lord's commanded time (13:7–14). He was rash and foolish when he made an oath he was unable to honor (14:24–44). He disobeyed the Lord's instructions to totally destroy the Amalekites and their possessions (15:1–34). He was greatly jealous when the people praised David for his heroics and virtue (18:8). On many occasions he sought to kill David (18:10–11,20–25; 19:7–10; 22:6–19; 23:7–8; 24:1–2; 26:1–3; 27:1). He dishonored the Lord by consulting with a medium (28:3–25). Saul's kingship was marked by disobedience to God, and the consequences were serious: God's Spirit departed from Saul and left him to his own destruction. As a result, Saul would lose the approval of his people and forfeit his kingship.

David, on the other hand, showed himself to be obedient to God. God looked beyond his appearance and named him the king of Israel. David was a man after God's own heart (13:14), and God blessed him for it. However, even David would fail to be fully obedient to God's commands (2Sa 11:1–27). His life was not without flaws, and there were consequences. Israel's greatest hope was in a king who would never let them down and would always obey God's ways.

Jesus' life was marked by full obedience to the will of the Father. Even when obedience cost him his life, Jesus never took the path of disobedience. He proclaimed, "Not my will, but yours be done" (Lk 22:42). Jesus' obedience would bring the ultimate blessing. Although he would be crucified, he made a way for all of God's people to experience ultimate blessing and access to the kingdom of God by removing sins.

Mikmash and in the hill country of Bethel, and a thousand were with Jonathan at Gibeah in Benjamin. The rest of the men he sent back to their homes.

[3]Jonathan attacked the Philistine outpost at Geba, and the Philistines heard about it. Then Saul had the trumpet blown throughout the land and said, "Let the Hebrews hear!" [4]So all Israel heard the news: "Saul has attacked the Philistine outpost, and now Israel has become obnoxious to the Philistines." And the people were summoned to join Saul at Gilgal.

[5]The Philistines assembled to fight Israel, with three thousand[a] chariots, six thousand charioteers, and soldiers as numerous as the sand on the seashore. They went up and camped at Mikmash, east of Beth Aven. [6]When the Israelites saw that their situation was critical and that their army was hard pressed, they hid in caves and thickets, among the rocks, and in pits and cisterns. [7]Some Hebrews even crossed the Jordan to the land of Gad and Gilead.

Saul remained at Gilgal, and all the troops with him were quaking with fear. [8]He waited seven days, the time set by Samuel; but Samuel did not come to Gilgal, and Saul's men began to scatter. [9]So he said, "Bring me the burnt offering and the fellowship offerings." And Saul offered up the burnt offering. [10]Just as he finished making the offering, Samuel arrived, and Saul went out to greet him.

[11]"What have you done?" asked Samuel.

Saul replied, "When I saw that the men were scattering, and that you did not come at the set time, and that the Philistines were assembling at Mikmash, [12]I thought, 'Now the Philistines will come down against me at Gilgal, and I have not sought the LORD's favor.' So I felt compelled to offer the burnt offering."

[13]"You have done a foolish thing," Samuel said. "You have not kept the command the LORD your God gave you; if you had, he would have established your kingdom over Israel for all time. [14]But now your kingdom will not endure; the LORD has sought out a man after his own heart and appointed him ruler of his people, because you have not kept the LORD's command."

[15]Then Samuel left Gilgal[b] and went up to Gibeah in Benjamin, and Saul counted the men who were with him. They numbered about six hundred.

Israel Without Weapons

[16]Saul and his son Jonathan and the men with them were staying in Gibeah[c] in Benjamin, while the Philistines camped at Mikmash. [17]Raiding parties went out from the Philistine camp in three detachments. One turned toward Ophrah in the vicinity of Shual, [18]another toward Beth Horon, and the third toward the borderland overlooking the Valley of Zeboyim facing the wilderness.

[19]Not a blacksmith could be found in the whole land of Israel, because the Philistines had said, "Otherwise the Hebrews will make swords or spears!" [20]So all Israel went down to the Philistines to have their plow points, mattocks, axes and sickles[d] sharpened. [21]The price was two-thirds of a shekel[e] for sharpening plow points and mattocks, and a third of a shekel[f] for sharpening forks and axes and for repointing goads.

[22]So on the day of the battle not a soldier with Saul and Jonathan had a sword or spear in his hand; only Saul and his son Jonathan had them.

Jonathan Attacks the Philistines

[23]Now a detachment of Philistines had gone out to the pass at Mikmash.

14 [1]One day Jonathan son of Saul said to his young armor-bearer, "Come, let's go over to the Philistine outpost on the other side." But he did not tell his father.

[2]Saul was staying on the outskirts of Gibeah under a pomegranate tree in Migron. With him were about six hundred men, [3]among whom was Ahijah, who

---

[a] 5 Some Septuagint manuscripts and Syriac; Hebrew *thirty thousand* [b] 15 Hebrew; Septuagint *Gilgal and went his way; the rest of the people went after Saul to meet the army, and they went out of Gilgal* [c] 16 Two Hebrew manuscripts; most Hebrew manuscripts *Geba,* a variant of *Gibeah* [d] 20 Septuagint; Hebrew *plow points* [e] 21 That is, about 1/4 ounce or about 8 grams [f] 21 That is, about 1/8 ounce or about 4 grams

was wearing an ephod. He was a son of Ichabod's brother Ahitub son of Phinehas, the son of Eli, the LORD's priest in Shiloh. No one was aware that Jonathan had left.

[4]On each side of the pass that Jonathan intended to cross to reach the Philistine outpost was a cliff; one was called Bozez and the other Seneh. [5]One cliff stood to the north toward Mikmash, the other to the south toward Geba.

[6]Jonathan said to his young armor-bearer, "Come, let's go over to the outpost of those uncircumcised men. Perhaps the LORD will act in our behalf. Nothing can hinder the LORD from saving, whether by many or by few."

[7]"Do all that you have in mind," his armor-bearer said. "Go ahead; I am with you heart and soul."

[8]Jonathan said, "Come on, then; we will cross over toward them and let them see us. [9]If they say to us, 'Wait there until we come to you,' we will stay where we are and not go up to them. [10]But if they say, 'Come up to us,' we will climb up, because that will be our sign that the LORD has given them into our hands."

[11]So both of them showed themselves to the Philistine outpost. "Look!" said the Philistines. "The Hebrews are crawling out of the holes they were hiding in." [12]The men of the outpost shouted to Jonathan and his armor-bearer, "Come up to us and we'll teach you a lesson."

So Jonathan said to his armor-bearer, "Climb up after me; the LORD has given them into the hand of Israel."

[13]Jonathan climbed up, using his hands and feet, with his armor-bearer right behind him. The Philistines fell before Jonathan, and his armor-bearer followed and killed behind him. [14]In that first attack Jonathan and his armor-bearer killed some twenty men in an area of about half an acre.

Israel Routs the Philistines

[15]Then panic struck the whole army—those in the camp and field, and those in the outposts and raiding parties—and the ground shook. It was a panic sent by God.[a]

[16]Saul's lookouts at Gibeah in Benjamin saw the army melting away in all directions. [17]Then Saul said to the men who were with him, "Muster the forces and see who has left us." When they did, it was Jonathan and his armor-bearer who were not there.

[18]Saul said to Ahijah, "Bring the ark of God." (At that time it was with the Israelites.)[b] [19]While Saul was talking to the priest, the tumult in the Philistine camp increased more and more. So Saul said to the priest, "Withdraw your hand."

[20]Then Saul and all his men assembled and went to the battle. They found the Philistines in total confusion, striking each other with their swords. [21]Those Hebrews who had previously been with the Philistines and had gone up with them to their camp went over to the Israelites who were with Saul and Jonathan. [22]When all the Israelites who had hidden in the hill country of Ephraim heard that the Philistines were on the run, they joined the battle in hot pursuit. [23]So on that day the LORD saved Israel, and the battle moved on beyond Beth Aven.

Jonathan Eats Honey

[24]Now the Israelites were in distress that day, because Saul had bound the people under an oath, saying, "Cursed be anyone who eats food before evening comes, before I have avenged myself on my enemies!" So none of the troops tasted food.

[25]The entire army entered the woods, and there was honey on the ground. [26]When they went into the woods, they saw the honey oozing out; yet no one put his hand to his mouth, because they feared the oath. [27]But Jonathan had not heard that his father had bound the people with the oath, so he reached out the

[a] 15 Or *a terrible panic* [b] 18 Hebrew; Septuagint *"Bring the ephod." (At that time he wore the ephod before the Israelites.)*

---

1 SAMUEL 14:24–46

FOOLISH OATHS

By declaring, "Cursed be anyone who eats food before evening comes," Saul foolishly ordered that none of his soldiers should eat until he had taken vengeance on his enemies (v. 24). Unlike Jonathan, Saul did not view the battle as the Lord's (v. 12). Saul made another foolish oath (v. 39) when he proclaimed that whoever was guilty must die. The recklessness with which Saul made these oaths placed him in a situation in which his credibility as a leader was called into question. By failing to honor his oaths, Saul proved himself to be rash and unworthy of trust.

In contrast, Jesus told his disciples in the Sermon on the Mount to avoid making oaths. He said, "All you need to say is simply 'Yes' or 'No'; anything beyond this comes from the evil one" (Mt 5:37). Saul's inability to keep his word showed that ultimately he was not the king that Israel hoped for. Only Jesus, the true king of Israel, would keep his word to the end. He is the king who can be trusted and worshiped.

end of the staff that was in his hand and dipped it into the honeycomb. He raised his hand to his mouth, and his eyes brightened.[a] 28 Then one of the soldiers told him, "Your father bound the army under a strict oath, saying, 'Cursed be anyone who eats food today!' That is why the men are faint."

29 Jonathan said, "My father has made trouble for the country. See how my eyes brightened when I tasted a little of this honey. 30 How much better it would have been if the men had eaten today some of the plunder they took from their enemies. Would not the slaughter of the Philistines have been even greater?"

31 That day, after the Israelites had struck down the Philistines from Mikmash to Aijalon, they were exhausted. 32 They pounced on the plunder and, taking sheep, cattle and calves, they butchered them on the ground and ate them, together with the blood. 33 Then someone said to Saul, "Look, the men are sinning against the LORD by eating meat that has blood in it."

"You have broken faith," he said. "Roll a large stone over here at once." 34 Then he said, "Go out among the men and tell them, 'Each of you bring me your cattle and sheep, and slaughter them here and eat them. Do not sin against the LORD by eating meat with blood still in it.'"

So everyone brought his ox that night and slaughtered it there. 35 Then Saul built an altar to the LORD; it was the first time he had done this.

36 Saul said, "Let us go down and pursue the Philistines by night and plunder them till dawn, and let us not leave one of them alive."

"Do whatever seems best to you," they replied.

But the priest said, "Let us inquire of God here."

37 So Saul asked God, "Shall I go down and pursue the Philistines? Will you give them into Israel's hand?" But God did not answer him that day.

38 Saul therefore said, "Come here, all you who are leaders of the army, and let us find out what sin has been committed today. 39 As surely as the LORD who rescues Israel lives, even if the guilt lies with my son Jonathan, he must die." But not one of them said a word.

40 Saul then said to all the Israelites, "You stand over there; I and Jonathan my son will stand over here."

"Do what seems best to you," they replied.

41 Then Saul prayed to the LORD, the God of Israel, "Why have you not answered your servant today? If the fault is in me or my son Jonathan, respond with Urim, but if the men of Israel are at fault,[b] respond with Thummim." Jonathan and Saul were taken by lot, and the men were cleared. 42 Saul said, "Cast the lot between me and Jonathan my son." And Jonathan was taken.

43 Then Saul said to Jonathan, "Tell me what you have done."

So Jonathan told him, "I tasted a little honey with the end of my staff. And now I must die!"

44 Saul said, "May God deal with me, be it ever so severely, if you do not die, Jonathan."

45 But the men said to Saul, "Should Jonathan die — he who has brought about this great deliverance in Israel? Never! As surely as the LORD lives, not a hair of his head will fall to the ground, for he did this today with God's help." So the men rescued Jonathan, and he was not put to death.

46 Then Saul stopped pursuing the Philistines, and they withdrew to their own land.

47 After Saul had assumed rule over Israel, he fought against their enemies on every side: Moab, the Ammonites, Edom, the kings[c] of Zobah, and the Philistines. Wherever he turned, he inflicted punishment on them.[d] 48 He fought valiantly and defeated the Amalekites, delivering Israel from the hands of those who had plundered them.

---

[a] *27* Or *his strength was renewed*; similarly in verse 29 [b] *41* Septuagint; Hebrew does not have *"Why . . . at fault.* [c] *47* Masoretic Text; Dead Sea Scrolls and Septuagint *king*
[d] *47* Hebrew; Septuagint *he was victorious*

Saul's Family

49 Saul's sons were Jonathan, Ishvi and Malki-Shua. The name of his older daughter was Merab, and that of the younger was Michal. 50 His wife's name was Ahinoam daughter of Ahimaaz. The name of the commander of Saul's army was Abner son of Ner, and Ner was Saul's uncle. 51 Saul's father Kish and Abner's father Ner were sons of Abiel.

52 All the days of Saul there was bitter war with the Philistines, and whenever Saul saw a mighty or brave man, he took him into his service.

The LORD Rejects Saul as King

15 Samuel said to Saul, "I am the one the LORD sent to anoint you king over his people Israel; so listen now to the message from the LORD. 2 This is what the LORD Almighty says: 'I will punish the Amalekites for what they did to Israel when they waylaid them as they came up from Egypt. 3 Now go, attack the Amalekites and totally destroy[a] all that belongs to them. Do not spare them; put to death men and women, children and infants, cattle and sheep, camels and donkeys.' "

4 So Saul summoned the men and mustered them at Telaim — two hundred thousand foot soldiers and ten thousand from Judah. 5 Saul went to the city of Amalek and set an ambush in the ravine. 6 Then he said to the Kenites, "Go away, leave the Amalekites so that I do not destroy you along with them; for you showed kindness to all the Israelites when they came up out of Egypt." So the Kenites moved away from the Amalekites.

7 Then Saul attacked the Amalekites all the way from Havilah to Shur, near the eastern border of Egypt. 8 He took Agag king of the Amalekites alive, and all his people he totally destroyed with the sword. 9 But Saul and the army spared Agag and the best of the sheep and cattle, the fat calves[b] and lambs — everything that was good. These they were unwilling to destroy completely, but everything that was despised and weak they totally destroyed.

10 Then the word of the LORD came to Samuel: 11 "I regret that I have made Saul king, because he has turned away from me and has not carried out my instructions." Samuel was angry, and he cried out to the LORD all that night.

12 Early in the morning Samuel got up and went to meet Saul, but he was told, "Saul has gone to Carmel. There he has set up a monument in his own honor and has turned and gone on down to Gilgal."

13 When Samuel reached him, Saul said, "The LORD bless you! I have carried out the LORD's instructions."

14 But Samuel said, "What then is this bleating of sheep in my ears? What is this lowing of cattle that I hear?"

15 Saul answered, "The soldiers brought them from the Amalekites; they spared the best of the sheep and cattle to sacrifice to the LORD your God, but we totally destroyed the rest."

16 "Enough!" Samuel said to Saul. "Let me tell you what the LORD said to me last night."

"Tell me," Saul replied.

17 Samuel said, "Although you were once small in your own eyes, did you not become the head of the tribes of Israel? The LORD anointed you king over Israel. 18 And he sent you on a mission, saying, 'Go and completely destroy those wicked people, the Amalekites; wage war against them until you have wiped them out.' 19 Why did you not obey the LORD? Why did you pounce on the plunder and do evil in the eyes of the LORD?"

20 "But I did obey the LORD," Saul said. "I went on the mission the LORD assigned me. I completely destroyed the Amalekites and brought back Agag their

---

[a] 3 The Hebrew term refers to the irrevocable giving over of things or persons to the LORD, often by totally destroying them; also in verses 8, 9, 15, 18, 20 and 21. [b] 9 Or *the grown bulls*; the meaning of the Hebrew for this phrase is uncertain.

OBEDIENCE AND SACRIFICE

First Samuel 15 tells the tragic story of the Lord rejecting Saul as Israel's king. This account serves as a warning that the Lord values obedience to his commands over religious practices. Saul and his army were commanded by the Lord to destroy the Amalekites and to leave nothing behind. But when Saul returned from the battle, the Lord was displeased. By bringing the Amalekites' king and the best of their cattle home from the battle, rather than destroying them, Saul had failed to honor the entirety of the Lord's command. God spoke to Samuel and expressed his regret for making Saul king (v. 11). Samuel was upset, and he cried out to God all that night. The next morning he brought a message to Saul. "Why did you not obey the LORD?" he asked (v. 19). Saul replied, "But I did obey the LORD," explaining that his men brought home the cattle for offering a sacrifice to the Lord (vv. 20 – 21). Then Samuel explained a core principle: "To obey is better than sacrifice" (v. 22). This assertion runs throughout the Old Testament, that God desires our obedience more than our religious rituals (Ps 40:6 – 8; 50:8 – 15; 51:16 – 17; Pr 15:8; 21:3; 28:9; Isa 1:11 – 15; Jer 6:19 – 20; Hos 6:6; Am 5:21).

This is a puzzling principle because on the surface it seems that Saul was doing an honorable thing to please the Lord. But the Lord showed Samuel and Saul that formal religious worship is no substitute for an obedient life. God was offering a glimpse of what was to come in the anointing of David as Israel's new king — God is concerned with the heart rather than the external appearance (1Sa 16:7). In the lives of believers today, the principle still applies. Church attendance, Bible studies and Christian conferences are great, but they are no substitute for genuine obedience to God.

In the New Testament, Jesus demonstrated what a life of obedience to the Father looked like in practice. Jesus upset the religious leaders of the day because he disobeyed the external religious laws and customs. But Jesus was not concerned with impressing those around him. He was only concerned with pleasing his Father. Jesus' obedience was what God wanted — for him to lay down his life for sinners. Jesus demonstrated costly obedience to the Father throughout his life (Jn 10:18; Ro 5:19; Heb 5:8; 1Jn 3:16). Ultimately, Jesus was obedient to death on a cross (Php 2:8). Jesus' obedience was the most pleasing sacrifice to the Lord. By his obedience, sinners can now be free from sin.

king. 21The soldiers took sheep and cattle from the plunder, the best of what was
devoted to God, in order to sacrifice them to the LORD your God at Gilgal."
22But Samuel replied:

"Does the LORD delight in burnt offerings and sacrifices
as much as in obeying the LORD?
To obey is better than sacrifice,
and to heed is better than the fat of rams.
23 For rebellion is like the sin of divination,
and arrogance like the evil of idolatry.
Because you have rejected the word of the LORD,
he has rejected you as king."

24Then Saul said to Samuel, "I have sinned. I violated the LORD's command
and your instructions. I was afraid of the men and so I gave in to them. 25Now I
beg you, forgive my sin and come back with me, so that I may worship the LORD."
26But Samuel said to him, "I will not go back with you. You have rejected the
word of the LORD, and the LORD has rejected you as king over Israel!"
27As Samuel turned to leave, Saul caught hold of the hem of his robe, and it
tore. 28Samuel said to him, "The LORD has torn the kingdom of Israel from you
today and has given it to one of your neighbors — to one better than you. 29He
who is the Glory of Israel does not lie or change his mind; for he is not a human
being, that he should change his mind."
30Saul replied, "I have sinned. But please honor me before the elders of my
people and before Israel; come back with me, so that I may worship the LORD
your God." 31So Samuel went back with Saul, and Saul worshiped the LORD.
32Then Samuel said, "Bring me Agag king of the Amalekites."
Agag came to him in chains.[a] And he thought, "Surely the bitterness of death
is past."
33But Samuel said,

"As your sword has made women childless,
so will your mother be childless among women."

And Samuel put Agag to death before the LORD at Gilgal.
34Then Samuel left for Ramah, but Saul went up to his home in Gibeah of
Saul. 35Until the day Samuel died, he did not go to see Saul again, though Samuel
mourned for him. And the LORD regretted that he had made Saul king over Israel.

Samuel Anoints David

16 The LORD said to Samuel, "How long will you mourn for Saul, since I have
rejected him as king over Israel? Fill your horn with oil and be on your way;
I am sending you to Jesse of Bethlehem. I have chosen one of his sons to be king."
2But Samuel said, "How can I go? If Saul hears about it, he will kill me."
The LORD said, "Take a heifer with you and say, 'I have come to sacrifice to
the LORD.' 3Invite Jesse to the sacrifice, and I will show you what to do. You are to
anoint for me the one I indicate."
4Samuel did what the LORD said. When he arrived at Bethlehem, the elders
of the town trembled when they met him. They asked, "Do you come in peace?"
5Samuel replied, "Yes, in peace; I have come to sacrifice to the LORD. Consecrate yourselves and come to the sacrifice with me." Then he consecrated Jesse
and his sons and invited them to the sacrifice.
6When they arrived, Samuel saw Eliab and thought, "Surely the LORD's
anointed stands here before the LORD."
7But the LORD said to Samuel, "Do not consider his appearance or his height,
for I have rejected him. The LORD does not look at the things people look at. People look at the outward appearance, but the LORD looks at the heart."
8Then Jesse called Abinadab and had him pass in front of Samuel. But Samuel

[a] 32 The meaning of the Hebrew for this phrase is uncertain.

1 SAMUEL 16:1 – 13

ANOINTED ONE

Anointing with oil signified the act of placing a person into a special office or setting them apart for sacred rites. The word *messiah* means "anointed one" and refers to a king or priest set apart by God for a high position of service. This passage tells how God chose David to be Israel's king after Saul's refusal to remain true to God. David was anointed to become the king that Israel needed — one who would be faithful to God. While Saul and David both served as an "anointed one," they were ultimately paving the way for Jesus, the true Messiah and the ultimate Anointed One.

In the Old Testament, the Messiah is referred to as David's son (Isa 9:6 – 7), the "Root of Jesse" (Isa 11:10) and the servant of the Lord (Isa 42:1 – 4). God's people have always been in need of the salvation that the Messiah would bring through his personal suffering and death, and it is clear that he would eventually rule over the nations (Zec 9:9 – 10; Ro 15:12). In the New Testament, Jesus is clearly recognized as that Messiah, and he himself claimed to be God's anointed one (Mt 3:17; Jn 4:25 – 26).

LOOKING AT THE HEART

With all the drama of an "unlikely hero" story, 1 Samuel 16 introduces the reader to David, a shepherd boy from Bethlehem. King Saul had just recently been stripped of his kingship because of his disobedience, and Samuel went on the search for Israel's next king. God sent Samuel to meet Jesse in Bethlehem, where God instructed him to anoint one of Jesse's sons.

When Jesse's sons arrived, Samuel had an immediate assumption about whom God had in mind for king. Samuel remembered Saul's impressive appearance (9:1 – 2) as he saw Eliab, Jesse's oldest son. But God reminded Samuel that he is not concerned with one's appearance but rather their heart. In the end, God instructed Samuel to anoint David, the youngest of Jesse's sons. Samuel failed to see David's potential because he was only looking at his outward appearance. But God knew David's heart. He knew that David was different than Saul and that David was a man who desired the heart of God (1Sa 13:14; Ac 13:22). David may not have been impressive to those around him, but God knew what was inside him and saw that he would lead Israel in a way that glorified God.

David was an unlikely king. He was not the king that Israel expected, but he was the king that God wanted for them. Similarly, Jesus was not what many of the religious leaders expected the Messiah to be. Jesus — born in Bethlehem to a virgin mother and an earthly family of humble means — seemed nothing like the savior Israel imagined. They expected a warrior king, but God gave them a suffering servant who humbly gave himself for the sake of others (Isa 53:2 – 6; Php 2:1 – 11). Many people failed to recognize him for who he was, and in the end they put him to death (Isa 52:14; 53:2). They imagined a messiah who would destroy their enemies, but God gave them Jesus, who came to save their enemies by inviting them into his kingdom. Jesus was God in the flesh; his heart was completely pure. He may not have been externally impressive, but he embodied the perfect love and grace of God here on this earth.

said, "The LORD has not chosen this one either." [9]Jesse then had Shammah pass by, but Samuel said, "Nor has the LORD chosen this one." [10]Jesse had seven of his sons pass before Samuel, but Samuel said to him, "The LORD has not chosen these." [11]So he asked Jesse, "Are these all the sons you have?"

"There is still the youngest," Jesse answered. "He is tending the sheep."

Samuel said, "Send for him; we will not sit down until he arrives."
[12]So he sent for him and had him brought in. He was glowing with health and had a fine appearance and handsome features.

Then the LORD said, "Rise and anoint him; this is the one."
[13]So Samuel took the horn of oil and anointed him in the presence of his brothers, and from that day on the Spirit of the LORD came powerfully upon David. Samuel then went to Ramah.

David in Saul's Service

[14]Now the Spirit of the LORD had departed from Saul, and an evil[a] spirit from the LORD tormented him.

[15]Saul's attendants said to him, "See, an evil spirit from God is tormenting
you. [16]Let our lord command his servants here to search for someone who can play the lyre. He will play when the evil spirit from God comes on you, and you will feel better."

[17]So Saul said to his attendants, "Find someone who plays well and bring him to me."

[18]One of the servants answered, "I have seen a son of Jesse of Bethlehem who knows how to play the lyre. He is a brave man and a warrior. He speaks well and is a fine-looking man. And the LORD is with him."

[19]Then Saul sent messengers to Jesse and said, "Send me your son David, who
is with the sheep." [20]So Jesse took a donkey loaded with bread, a skin of wine and a young goat and sent them with his son David to Saul.

[21]David came to Saul and entered his service. Saul liked him very much, and
David became one of his armor-bearers. [22]Then Saul sent word to Jesse, saying, "Allow David to remain in my service, for I am pleased with him."

[23]Whenever the spirit from God came on Saul, David would take up his lyre and play. Then relief would come to Saul; he would feel better, and the evil spirit would leave him.

David and Goliath

17 Now the Philistines gathered their forces for war and assembled at Sokoh in Judah. They pitched camp at Ephes Dammim, between Sokoh and Azekah. [2]Saul and the Israelites assembled and camped in the Valley of Elah and
drew up their battle line to meet the Philistines. [3]The Philistines occupied one hill and the Israelites another, with the valley between them.

[4]A champion named Goliath, who was from Gath, came out of the Philistine
camp. His height was six cubits and a span.[b] [5]He had a bronze helmet on his head and wore a coat of scale armor of bronze weighing five thousand shekels[c];
[6]on his legs he wore bronze greaves, and a bronze javelin was slung on his back.
[7]His spear shaft was like a weaver's rod, and its iron point weighed six hundred shekels.[d] His shield bearer went ahead of him.

[8]Goliath stood and shouted to the ranks of Israel, "Why do you come out and line up for battle? Am I not a Philistine, and are you not the servants of Saul?
Choose a man and have him come down to me. [9]If he is able to fight and kill me, we will become your subjects; but if I overcome him and kill him, you will
become our subjects and serve us." [10]Then the Philistine said, "This day I defy the armies of Israel! Give me a man and let us fight each other." [11]On hearing
the Philistine's words, Saul and all the Israelites were dismayed and terrified.

---

[a] *14* Or *and a harmful*; similarly in verses 15, 16 and 23 [b] *4* That is, about 9 feet 9 inches or about 3 meters [c] *5* That is, about 125 pounds or about 58 kilograms [d] *7* That is, about 15 pounds or about 6.9 kilograms

[12]Now David was the son of an Ephrathite named Jesse, who was from Bethlehem in Judah. Jesse had eight sons, and in Saul's time he was very old. [13]Jesse's three oldest sons had followed Saul to the war: The firstborn was Eliab; the second, Abinadab; and the third, Shammah. [14]David was the youngest. The three oldest followed Saul, [15]but David went back and forth from Saul to tend his father's sheep at Bethlehem.

[16]For forty days the Philistine came forward every morning and evening and took his stand.

[17]Now Jesse said to his son David, "Take this ephah[a] of roasted grain and these ten loaves of bread for your brothers and hurry to their camp. [18]Take along these ten cheeses to the commander of their unit. See how your brothers are and bring back some assurance[b] from them. [19]They are with Saul and all the men of Israel in the Valley of Elah, fighting against the Philistines."

[20]Early in the morning David left the flock in the care of a shepherd, loaded up and set out, as Jesse had directed. He reached the camp as the army was going out to its battle positions, shouting the war cry. [21]Israel and the Philistines were drawing up their lines facing each other. [22]David left his things with the keeper of supplies, ran to the battle lines and asked his brothers how they were. [23]As he was talking with them, Goliath, the Philistine champion from Gath, stepped out from his lines and shouted his usual defiance, and David heard it. [24]Whenever the Israelites saw the man, they all fled from him in great fear.

[25]Now the Israelites had been saying, "Do you see how this man keeps coming out? He comes out to defy Israel. The king will give great wealth to the man who kills him. He will also give him his daughter in marriage and will exempt his family from taxes in Israel."

[26]David asked the men standing near him, "What will be done for the man who kills this Philistine and removes this disgrace from Israel? Who is this uncircumcised Philistine that he should defy the armies of the living God?"

[27]They repeated to him what they had been saying and told him, "This is what will be done for the man who kills him."

[28]When Eliab, David's oldest brother, heard him speaking with the men, he burned with anger at him and asked, "Why have you come down here? And with whom did you leave those few sheep in the wilderness? I know how conceited you are and how wicked your heart is; you came down only to watch the battle."

[29]"Now what have I done?" said David. "Can't I even speak?" [30]He then turned away to someone else and brought up the same matter, and the men answered him as before. [31]What David said was overheard and reported to Saul, and Saul sent for him.

[32]David said to Saul, "Let no one lose heart on account of this Philistine; your servant will go and fight him."

[33]Saul replied, "You are not able to go out against this Philistine and fight him; you are only a young man, and he has been a warrior from his youth."

[34]But David said to Saul, "Your servant has been keeping his father's sheep. When a lion or a bear came and carried off a sheep from the flock, [35]I went after it, struck it and rescued the sheep from its mouth. When it turned on me, I seized it by its hair, struck it and killed it. [36]Your servant has killed both the lion and the bear; this uncircumcised Philistine will be like one of them, because he has defied the armies of the living God. [37]The LORD who rescued me from the paw of the lion and the paw of the bear will rescue me from the hand of this Philistine."

Saul said to David, "Go, and the LORD be with you."

[38]Then Saul dressed David in his own tunic. He put a coat of armor on him and a bronze helmet on his head. [39]David fastened on his sword over the tunic and tried walking around, because he was not used to them.

"I cannot go in these," he said to Saul, "because I am not used to them." So he took them off. [40]Then he took his staff in his hand, chose five smooth stones from

---

[a] *17* That is, probably about 36 pounds or about 16 kilograms [b] *18* Or *some token*; or *some pledge of spoils*

the stream, put them in the pouch of his shepherd's bag and, with his sling in his
hand, approached the Philistine.
41 Meanwhile, the Philistine, with his shield bearer in front of him, kept coming closer to David. 42 He looked David over and saw that he was little more than
a boy, glowing with health and handsome, and he despised him. 43 He said to
David, "Am I a dog, that you come at me with sticks?" And the Philistine cursed
David by his gods. 44 "Come here," he said, "and I'll give your flesh to the birds
and the wild animals!"
45 David said to the Philistine, "You come against me with sword and spear
and javelin, but I come against you in the name of the LORD Almighty, the God
of the armies of Israel, whom you have defied. 46 This day the LORD will deliver
you into my hands, and I'll strike you down and cut off your head. This very day
I will give the carcasses of the Philistine army to the birds and the wild animals,
and the whole world will know that there is a God in Israel. 47 All those gathered
here will know that it is not by sword or spear that the LORD saves; for the battle
is the LORD's, and he will give all of you into our hands."
48 As the Philistine moved closer to attack him, David ran quickly toward the
battle line to meet him. 49 Reaching into his bag and taking out a stone, he slung it
and struck the Philistine on the forehead. The stone sank into his forehead, and
he fell facedown on the ground.
50 So David triumphed over the Philistine with a sling and a stone; without a
sword in his hand he struck down the Philistine and killed him.
51 David ran and stood over him. He took hold of the Philistine's sword and
drew it from the sheath. After he killed him, he cut off his head with the sword.
When the Philistines saw that their hero was dead, they turned and ran.
52 Then the men of Israel and Judah surged forward with a shout and pursued
the Philistines to the entrance of Gath[a] and to the gates of Ekron. Their dead
were strewn along the Shaaraim road to Gath and Ekron. 53 When the Israelites
returned from chasing the Philistines, they plundered their camp.
54 David took the Philistine's head and brought it to Jerusalem; he put the Philistine's weapons in his own tent.
55 As Saul watched David going out to meet the Philistine, he said to Abner,
commander of the army, "Abner, whose son is that young man?"
Abner replied, "As surely as you live, Your Majesty, I don't know."
56 The king said, "Find out whose son this young man is."
57 As soon as David returned from killing the Philistine, Abner took him and
brought him before Saul, with David still holding the Philistine's head.
58 "Whose son are you, young man?" Saul asked him.
David said, "I am the son of your servant Jesse of Bethlehem."

Saul's Growing Fear of David

18 After David had finished talking with Saul, Jonathan became one in spirit
with David, and he loved him as himself. 2 From that day Saul kept David
with him and did not let him return home to his family. 3 And Jonathan made a
covenant with David because he loved him as himself. 4 Jonathan took off the
robe he was wearing and gave it to David, along with his tunic, and even his
sword, his bow and his belt.
5 Whatever mission Saul sent him on, David was so successful that Saul gave
him a high rank in the army. This pleased all the troops, and Saul's officers as well.
6 When the men were returning home after David had killed the Philistine,
the women came out from all the towns of Israel to meet King Saul with singing
and dancing, with joyful songs and with timbrels and lyres. 7 As they danced,
they sang:

"Saul has slain his thousands,
and David his tens of thousands."

[a] 52 Some Septuagint manuscripts; Hebrew *of a valley*

1 SAMUEL 18:1–4

SACRIFICIAL FRIENDSHIP

This covenant between Jonathan and David was a mutual agreement in which the two men were bound to care for the needs and attend the interests of each other. This is a beautiful picture of friendship. Jonathan had little to gain by entering into a covenant with David. As Saul's son, Jonathan was next in line to the throne. Instead, Jonathan took off his robe, armor and sword (symbols of his kingly authority) and gave them to David. He honored David by giving up his rights. This is a great picture of friendship.

Jesus later told his disciples, "Greater love has no one than this: to lay down one's life for one's friends" (Jn 15:13). Like Jonathan gave up his rights to enter into a covenant with David, Jesus gave up his rights by laying down his life for sinners so that they could be called his friends. He laid aside his kingly robes and died the death of a sinner, so that sinners could have eternal life.

[8]Saul was very angry; this refrain displeased him greatly. "They have credited David with tens of thousands," he thought, "but me with only thousands. What more can he get but the kingdom?" [9]And from that time on Saul kept a close eye on David.

[10]The next day an evil[a] spirit from God came forcefully on Saul. He was prophesying in his house, while David was playing the lyre, as he usually did. Saul had a spear in his hand [11]and he hurled it, saying to himself, "I'll pin David to the wall." But David eluded him twice.

[12]Saul was afraid of David, because the LORD was with David but had departed from Saul. [13]So he sent David away from him and gave him command over a thousand men, and David led the troops in their campaigns. [14]In everything he did he had great success, because the LORD was with him. [15]When Saul saw how successful he was, he was afraid of him. [16]But all Israel and Judah loved David, because he led them in their campaigns.

[17]Saul said to David, "Here is my older daughter Merab. I will give her to you in marriage; only serve me bravely and fight the battles of the LORD." For Saul said to himself, "I will not raise a hand against him. Let the Philistines do that!"

[18]But David said to Saul, "Who am I, and what is my family or my clan in Israel, that I should become the king's son-in-law?" [19]So[b] when the time came for Merab, Saul's daughter, to be given to David, she was given in marriage to Adriel of Meholah.

[20]Now Saul's daughter Michal was in love with David, and when they told Saul about it, he was pleased. [21]"I will give her to him," he thought, "so that she may be a snare to him and so that the hand of the Philistines may be against him." So Saul said to David, "Now you have a second opportunity to become my son-in-law."

[22]Then Saul ordered his attendants: "Speak to David privately and say, 'Look, the king likes you, and his attendants all love you; now become his son-in-law.' "

[23]They repeated these words to David. But David said, "Do you think it is a small matter to become the king's son-in-law? I'm only a poor man and little known."

[24]When Saul's servants told him what David had said, [25]Saul replied, "Say to David, 'The king wants no other price for the bride than a hundred Philistine foreskins, to take revenge on his enemies.' " Saul's plan was to have David fall by the hands of the Philistines.

[26]When the attendants told David these things, he was pleased to become the king's son-in-law. So before the allotted time elapsed, [27]David took his men with him and went out and killed two hundred Philistines and brought back their foreskins. They counted out the full number to the king so that David might become the king's son-in-law. Then Saul gave him his daughter Michal in marriage.

[28]When Saul realized that the LORD was with David and that his daughter Michal loved David, [29]Saul became still more afraid of him, and he remained his enemy the rest of his days.

[30]The Philistine commanders continued to go out to battle, and as often as they did, David met with more success than the rest of Saul's officers, and his name became well known.

1 SAMUEL 19:1

PERSECUTING AN INNOCENT ONE

Saul realized that the people loved David more than him. He became enraged and jealous and began plotting to kill David. When his more indirect plans to ensnare David crumbled (18:17 – 30), he clearly announced his plans to kill David. David was completely innocent according to the law, yet Saul wanted to kill him because he was a threat to Saul's power and control.

Jesus also posed a threat to the religious leaders of his day — so much so that they wanted him killed (Mt 12:14; Mk 3:6; Jn 11:53). Before Jesus' crucifixion, Pontius Pilate could not find any fault in Jesus but still sent him to be crucified because he feared losing his own power (Jn 19:1 – 16). If Jesus is indeed the King of kings, then only he is worthy to lead. In order to follow Jesus, control must be surrendered to him. Many people reject Jesus because they fear losing their own sense of power and control over their lives. But Jesus is a good king and can be trusted. Instead of trying to silence him, believers are invited to walk in faith and know that he is trustworthy to follow.

Saul Tries to Kill David

19 Saul told his son Jonathan and all the attendants to kill David. But Jonathan had taken a great liking to David [2]and warned him, "My father Saul is looking for a chance to kill you. Be on your guard tomorrow morning; go into hiding and stay there. [3]I will go out and stand with my father in the field where you are. I'll speak to him about you and will tell you what I find out."

[4]Jonathan spoke well of David to Saul his father and said to him, "Let not the

[a] *10* Or *a harmful* [b] *19* Or *However,*

king do wrong to his servant David; he has not wronged you, and what he has
done has benefited you greatly. 5He took his life in his hands when he killed the
Philistine. The LORD won a great victory for all Israel, and you saw it and were
glad. Why then would you do wrong to an innocent man like David by killing
him for no reason?"

6Saul listened to Jonathan and took this oath: "As surely as the LORD lives,
David will not be put to death."

7So Jonathan called David and told him the whole conversation. He brought
him to Saul, and David was with Saul as before.

8Once more war broke out, and David went out and fought the Philistines. He
struck them with such force that they fled before him.

9But an evil[a] spirit from the LORD came on Saul as he was sitting in his house
with his spear in his hand. While David was playing the lyre, 10Saul tried to pin
him to the wall with his spear, but David eluded him as Saul drove the spear into
the wall. That night David made good his escape.

11Saul sent men to David's house to watch it and to kill him in the morning.
But Michal, David's wife, warned him, "If you don't run for your life tonight, tomorrow you'll be killed." 12So Michal let David down through a window, and he
fled and escaped. 13Then Michal took an idol and laid it on the bed, covering it
with a garment and putting some goats' hair at the head.

14When Saul sent the men to capture David, Michal said, "He is ill."

15Then Saul sent the men back to see David and told them, "Bring him up to
me in his bed so that I may kill him." 16But when the men entered, there was the
idol in the bed, and at the head was some goats' hair.

17Saul said to Michal, "Why did you deceive me like this and send my enemy
away so that he escaped?"

Michal told him, "He said to me, 'Let me get away. Why should I kill you?'"

18When David had fled and made his escape, he went to Samuel at Ramah and
told him all that Saul had done to him. Then he and Samuel went to Naioth and
stayed there. 19Word came to Saul: "David is in Naioth at Ramah"; 20so he sent
men to capture him. But when they saw a group of prophets prophesying, with
Samuel standing there as their leader, the Spirit of God came on Saul's men, and
they also prophesied. 21Saul was told about it, and he sent more men, and they
prophesied too. Saul sent men a third time, and they also prophesied. 22Finally,
he himself left for Ramah and went to the great cistern at Seku. And he asked,
"Where are Samuel and David?"

"Over in Naioth at Ramah," they said.

23So Saul went to Naioth at Ramah. But the Spirit of God came even on him,
and he walked along prophesying until he came to Naioth. 24He stripped off his
garments, and he too prophesied in Samuel's presence. He lay naked all that day
and all that night. This is why people say, "Is Saul also among the prophets?"

David and Jonathan

20 Then David fled from Naioth at Ramah and went to Jonathan and asked,
"What have I done? What is my crime? How have I wronged your father,
that he is trying to kill me?"

2"Never!" Jonathan replied. "You are not going to die! Look, my father doesn't
do anything, great or small, without letting me know. Why would he hide this
from me? It isn't so!"

3But David took an oath and said, "Your father knows very well that I have
found favor in your eyes, and he has said to himself, 'Jonathan must not know
this or he will be grieved.' Yet as surely as the LORD lives and as you live, there is
only a step between me and death."

4Jonathan said to David, "Whatever you want me to do, I'll do for you."

5So David said, "Look, tomorrow is the New Moon feast, and I am supposed

---

[a] 9 Or *But a harmful*

to dine with the king; but let me go and hide in the field until the evening of the
day after tomorrow. [6]If your father misses me at all, tell him, 'David earnestly
asked my permission to hurry to Bethlehem, his hometown, because an annual
sacrifice is being made there for his whole clan.' [7]If he says, 'Very well,' then your
servant is safe. But if he loses his temper, you can be sure that he is determined to
harm me. [8]As for you, show kindness to your servant, for you have brought him
into a covenant with you before the LORD. If I am guilty, then kill me yourself!
Why hand me over to your father?"

[9]"Never!" Jonathan said. "If I had the least inkling that my father was determined to harm you, wouldn't I tell you?"

[10]David asked, "Who will tell me if your father answers you harshly?"

[11]"Come," Jonathan said, "let's go out into the field." So they went there together.

[12]Then Jonathan said to David, "I swear by the LORD, the God of Israel, that I
will surely sound out my father by this time the day after tomorrow! If he is favorably disposed toward you, will I not send you word and let you know? [13]But
if my father intends to harm you, may the LORD deal with Jonathan, be it ever so
severely, if I do not let you know and send you away in peace. May the LORD be
with you as he has been with my father. [14]But show me unfailing kindness like
the LORD's kindness as long as I live, so that I may not be killed, [15]and do not ever
cut off your kindness from my family — not even when the LORD has cut off every
one of David's enemies from the face of the earth."

[16]So Jonathan made a covenant with the house of David, saying, "May the
LORD call David's enemies to account." [17]And Jonathan had David reaffirm his
oath out of love for him, because he loved him as he loved himself.

[18]Then Jonathan said to David, "Tomorrow is the New Moon feast. You will
be missed, because your seat will be empty. [19]The day after tomorrow, toward
evening, go to the place where you hid when this trouble began, and wait by the
stone Ezel. [20]I will shoot three arrows to the side of it, as though I were shooting
at a target. [21]Then I will send a boy and say, 'Go, find the arrows.' If I say to him,
'Look, the arrows are on this side of you; bring them here,' then come, because,
as surely as the LORD lives, you are safe; there is no danger. [22]But if I say to the
boy, 'Look, the arrows are beyond you,' then you must go, because the LORD
has sent you away. [23]And about the matter you and I discussed — remember, the
LORD is witness between you and me forever."

[24]So David hid in the field, and when the New Moon feast came, the king sat
down to eat. [25]He sat in his customary place by the wall, opposite Jonathan,[a] and
Abner sat next to Saul, but David's place was empty. [26]Saul said nothing that day,
for he thought, "Something must have happened to David to make him ceremonially unclean — surely he is unclean." [27]But the next day, the second day of the
month, David's place was empty again. Then Saul said to his son Jonathan, "Why
hasn't the son of Jesse come to the meal, either yesterday or today?"

[28]Jonathan answered, "David earnestly asked me for permission to go to
Bethlehem. [29]He said, 'Let me go, because our family is observing a sacrifice
in the town and my brother has ordered me to be there. If I have found favor in
your eyes, let me get away to see my brothers.' That is why he has not come to
the king's table."

[30]Saul's anger flared up at Jonathan and he said to him, "You son of a perverse
and rebellious woman! Don't I know that you have sided with the son of Jesse to
your own shame and to the shame of the mother who bore you? [31]As long as the
son of Jesse lives on this earth, neither you nor your kingdom will be established.
Now send someone to bring him to me, for he must die!"

[32]"Why should he be put to death? What has he done?" Jonathan asked his
father. [33]But Saul hurled his spear at him to kill him. Then Jonathan knew that
his father intended to kill David.

---

[a] 25 Septuagint; Hebrew *wall. Jonathan arose*

[34]Jonathan got up from the table in fierce anger; on that second day of the
feast he did not eat, because he was grieved at his father's shameful treatment
of David.
[35]In the morning Jonathan went out to the field for his meeting with David.
He had a small boy with him, [36]and he said to the boy, "Run and find the arrows I
shoot." As the boy ran, he shot an arrow beyond him. [37]When the boy came to the
place where Jonathan's arrow had fallen, Jonathan called out after him, "Isn't the
arrow beyond you?" [38]Then he shouted, "Hurry! Go quickly! Don't stop!" The boy
picked up the arrow and returned to his master. [39](The boy knew nothing about
all this; only Jonathan and David knew.) [40]Then Jonathan gave his weapons to
the boy and said, "Go, carry them back to town."
[41]After the boy had gone, David got up from the south side of the stone and
bowed down before Jonathan three times, with his face to the ground. Then they
kissed each other and wept together — but David wept the most.
[42]Jonathan said to David, "Go in peace, for we have sworn friendship with
each other in the name of the LORD, saying, 'The LORD is witness between you
and me, and between your descendants and my descendants forever.'" Then
David left, and Jonathan went back to the town.[a]

David at Nob

21 [b] David went to Nob, to Ahimelek the priest. Ahimelek trembled when he
met him, and asked, "Why are you alone? Why is no one with you?"
[2]David answered Ahimelek the priest, "The king sent me on a mission and
said to me, 'No one is to know anything about the mission I am sending you on.'
As for my men, I have told them to meet me at a certain place. [3]Now then, what
do you have on hand? Give me five loaves of bread, or whatever you can find."
[4]But the priest answered David, "I don't have any ordinary bread on hand;
however, there is some consecrated bread here — provided the men have kept
themselves from women."
[5]David replied, "Indeed women have been kept from us, as usual whenever[c] I
set out. The men's bodies are holy even on missions that are not holy. How much
more so today!" [6]So the priest gave him the consecrated bread, since there was
no bread there except the bread of the Presence that had been removed from before the LORD and replaced by hot bread on the day it was taken away.
[7]Now one of Saul's servants was there that day, detained before the LORD; he
was Doeg the Edomite, Saul's chief shepherd.
[8]David asked Ahimelek, "Don't you have a spear or a sword here? I haven't
brought my sword or any other weapon, because the king's mission was urgent."
[9]The priest replied, "The sword of Goliath the Philistine, whom you killed in
the Valley of Elah, is here; it is wrapped in a cloth behind the ephod. If you want
it, take it; there is no sword here but that one."
David said, "There is none like it; give it to me."

David at Gath

[10]That day David fled from Saul and went to Achish king of Gath. [11]But the
servants of Achish said to him, "Isn't this David, the king of the land? Isn't he the
one they sing about in their dances:

"'Saul has slain his thousands,
and David his tens of thousands'?"

[12]David took these words to heart and was very much afraid of Achish king
of Gath. [13]So he pretended to be insane in their presence; and while he was in
their hands he acted like a madman, making marks on the doors of the gate and
letting saliva run down his beard.
[14]Achish said to his servants, "Look at the man! He is insane! Why bring him

[a] *42* In Hebrew texts this sentence (20:42b) is numbered 21:1. [b] In Hebrew texts 21:1-15 is numbered 21:2-16. [c] *5* Or *from us in the past few days since*

1 SAMUEL 21:3–6

HOLY BREAD

In response to David's request for provisions, Ahimelek explained that there was no ordinary bread. The only bread available was the sacred or consecrated bread, sometimes called the "bread of the Presence," which had been displayed before the Lord in the tabernacle (v. 6; see also Ex 25:30; Lev 24:5–9). According to God's law, this bread could be eaten only by priests. David explained to Ahimelek that his men had avoided ritual impurity, having had no recent sexual contact with women (Ex 19:15; Lev 15:16–18). And this consecrated bread had been replaced with new bread before the Lord.

The Talmud, the Jewish collection of laws and doctrines, explains this apparent breach of the law on the basis that the preservation of life takes precedence over nearly all other commandments in the law. Jesus referred to this incident in his discussion with the Pharisees concerning the Sabbath (Mt 12:2–4; Mk 2:25–26). The spirit of the law was kept by Ahimelek's compassionate act.

to me? [15]Am I so short of madmen that you have to bring this fellow here to carry
on like this in front of me? Must this man come into my house?"

David at Adullam and Mizpah

22 David left Gath and escaped to the cave of Adullam. When his brothers
and his father's household heard about it, they went down to him there.
[2]All those who were in distress or in debt or discontented gathered around him,
and he became their commander. About four hundred men were with him.
[3]From there David went to Mizpah in Moab and said to the king of Moab,
"Would you let my father and mother come and stay with you until I learn what
God will do for me?" [4]So he left them with the king of Moab, and they stayed with
him as long as David was in the stronghold.
[5]But the prophet Gad said to David, "Do not stay in the stronghold. Go into the
land of Judah." So David left and went to the forest of Hereth.

Saul Kills the Priests of Nob

[6]Now Saul heard that David and his men had been discovered. And Saul was
seated, spear in hand, under the tamarisk tree on the hill at Gibeah, with all his
officials standing at his side. [7]He said to them, "Listen, men of Benjamin! Will
the son of Jesse give all of you fields and vineyards? Will he make all of you commanders of thousands and commanders of hundreds? [8]Is that why you have all
conspired against me? No one tells me when my son makes a covenant with the
son of Jesse. None of you is concerned about me or tells me that my son has incited my servant to lie in wait for me, as he does today."
[9]But Doeg the Edomite, who was standing with Saul's officials, said, "I saw
the son of Jesse come to Ahimelek son of Ahitub at Nob. [10]Ahimelek inquired
of the LORD for him; he also gave him provisions and the sword of Goliath the
Philistine."
[11]Then the king sent for the priest Ahimelek son of Ahitub and all the men of
his family, who were the priests at Nob, and they all came to the king. [12]Saul said,
"Listen now, son of Ahitub."
"Yes, my lord," he answered.
[13]Saul said to him, "Why have you conspired against me, you and the son of
Jesse, giving him bread and a sword and inquiring of God for him, so that he has
rebelled against me and lies in wait for me, as he does today?"
[14]Ahimelek answered the king, "Who of all your servants is as loyal as David,
the king's son-in-law, captain of your bodyguard and highly respected in your
household? [15]Was that day the first time I inquired of God for him? Of course not!
Let not the king accuse your servant or any of his father's family, for your servant
knows nothing at all about this whole affair."
[16]But the king said, "You will surely die, Ahimelek, you and your whole family."
[17]Then the king ordered the guards at his side: "Turn and kill the priests of
the LORD, because they too have sided with David. They knew he was fleeing,
yet they did not tell me."
But the king's officials were unwilling to raise a hand to strike the priests of
the LORD.
[18]The king then ordered Doeg, "You turn and strike down the priests." So
Doeg the Edomite turned and struck them down. That day he killed eighty-five
men who wore the linen ephod. [19]He also put to the sword Nob, the town of the
priests, with its men and women, its children and infants, and its cattle, donkeys
and sheep.
[20]But one son of Ahimelek son of Ahitub, named Abiathar, escaped and fled
to join David. [21]He told David that Saul had killed the priests of the LORD. [22]Then
David said to Abiathar, "That day, when Doeg the Edomite was there, I knew he
would be sure to tell Saul. I am responsible for the death of your whole family.
[23]Stay with me; don't be afraid. The man who wants to kill you is trying to kill me
too. You will be safe with me."

1 SAMUEL 22:1–2

AN UNIMPRESSIVE TEAM

While David was on the run from Saul, many men began to form around him offering protection, and he rose to become their commander. What a ragtag crowd assembled around David! These were primarily men who were oppressed and discontented with Saul's rule. Many were distressed. Others were in considerable debt—meaning they were in danger of being sold into slavery by their creditors (2Ki 4:1). The four hundred men soon grew to six hundred (1Sa 23:13). They were a group of drifters and debtors, troublemakers and those who were troubled. But many of them would ultimately become David's "mighty warriors" (2Sa 23:8–39).

In the New Testament, Jesus assembled a team consisting of tax collectors, fishermen and zealots. Jesus' group of disciples would not be impressive, but the apostle Paul would say, "Not many of you were wise by human standards . . . But God chose the foolish things of the world to shame the wise; God chose the weak things of the world to shame the strong" (1Co 1:26–27).

David Saves Keilah

23 When David was told, "Look, the Philistines are fighting against Keilah
and are looting the threshing floors," 2he inquired of the LORD, saying,
"Shall I go and attack these Philistines?"
The LORD answered him, "Go, attack the Philistines and save Keilah."
3But David's men said to him, "Here in Judah we are afraid. How much more,
then, if we go to Keilah against the Philistine forces!"
4Once again David inquired of the LORD, and the LORD answered him, "Go
down to Keilah, for I am going to give the Philistines into your hand." 5So David
and his men went to Keilah, fought the Philistines and carried off their livestock.
He inflicted heavy losses on the Philistines and saved the people of Keilah.
6(Now Abiathar son of Ahimelek had brought the ephod down with him when
he fled to David at Keilah.)

Saul Pursues David

7Saul was told that David had gone to Keilah, and he said, "God has delivered
him into my hands, for David has imprisoned himself by entering a town with
gates and bars." 8And Saul called up all his forces for battle, to go down to Keilah
to besiege David and his men.
9When David learned that Saul was plotting against him, he said to Abiathar
the priest, "Bring the ephod." 10David said, "LORD, God of Israel, your servant
has heard definitely that Saul plans to come to Keilah and destroy the town on
account of me. 11Will the citizens of Keilah surrender me to him? Will Saul come
down, as your servant has heard? LORD, God of Israel, tell your servant."
And the LORD said, "He will."
12Again David asked, "Will the citizens of Keilah surrender me and my men
to Saul?"
And the LORD said, "They will."
13So David and his men, about six hundred in number, left Keilah and kept
moving from place to place. When Saul was told that David had escaped from
Keilah, he did not go there.
14David stayed in the wilderness strongholds and in the hills of the Desert of
Ziph. Day after day Saul searched for him, but God did not give David into his hands.
15While David was at Horesh in the Desert of Ziph, he learned that[a] Saul had
come out to take his life. 16And Saul's son Jonathan went to David at Horesh and
helped him find strength in God. 17"Don't be afraid," he said. "My father Saul will
not lay a hand on you. You will be king over Israel, and I will be second to you.
Even my father Saul knows this." 18The two of them made a covenant before the
LORD. Then Jonathan went home, but David remained at Horesh.
19The Ziphites went up to Saul at Gibeah and said, "Is not David hiding among
us in the strongholds at Horesh, on the hill of Hakilah, south of Jeshimon? 20Now,
Your Majesty, come down whenever it pleases you to do so, and we will be responsible for giving him into your hands."
21Saul replied, "The LORD bless you for your concern for me. 22Go and get
more information. Find out where David usually goes and who has seen him
there. They tell me he is very crafty. 23Find out about all the hiding places he uses
and come back to me with definite information. Then I will go with you; if he is
in the area, I will track him down among all the clans of Judah."
24So they set out and went to Ziph ahead of Saul. Now David and his men were
in the Desert of Maon, in the Arabah south of Jeshimon. 25Saul and his men began the search, and when David was told about it, he went down to the rock and
stayed in the Desert of Maon. When Saul heard this, he went into the Desert of
Maon in pursuit of David.
26Saul was going along one side of the mountain, and David and his men were
on the other side, hurrying to get away from Saul. As Saul and his forces were

---

[a] 15 Or *he was afraid because*

closing in on David and his men to capture them, [27]a messenger came to Saul, saying, "Come quickly! The Philistines are raiding the land." [28]Then Saul broke off his pursuit of David and went to meet the Philistines. That is why they call this place Sela Hammahlekoth.[a] [29]And David went up from there and lived in the strongholds of En Gedi.[b]

David Spares Saul's Life

24 [c] After Saul returned from pursuing the Philistines, he was told, "David is in the Desert of En Gedi." [2]So Saul took three thousand able young men from all Israel and set out to look for David and his men near the Crags of the Wild Goats.

[3]He came to the sheep pens along the way; a cave was there, and Saul went in to relieve himself. David and his men were far back in the cave. [4]The men said, "This is the day the LORD spoke of when he said[d] to you, 'I will give your enemy into your hands for you to deal with as you wish.'" Then David crept up unnoticed and cut off a corner of Saul's robe.

[5]Afterward, David was conscience-stricken for having cut off a corner of his robe. [6]He said to his men, "The LORD forbid that I should do such a thing to my master, the LORD's anointed, or lay my hand on him; for he is the anointed of the LORD." [7]With these words David sharply rebuked his men and did not allow them to attack Saul. And Saul left the cave and went his way.

[8]Then David went out of the cave and called out to Saul, "My lord the king!" When Saul looked behind him, David bowed down and prostrated himself with his face to the ground. [9]He said to Saul, "Why do you listen when men say, 'David is bent on harming you'? [10]This day you have seen with your own eyes how the LORD delivered you into my hands in the cave. Some urged me to kill you, but I spared you; I said, 'I will not lay my hand on my lord, because he is the LORD's anointed.' [11]See, my father, look at this piece of your robe in my hand! I cut off the corner of your robe but did not kill you. See that there is nothing in my hand to indicate that I am guilty of wrongdoing or rebellion. I have not wronged you, but you are hunting me down to take my life. [12]May the LORD judge between you and me. And may the LORD avenge the wrongs you have done to me, but my hand will not touch you. [13]As the old saying goes, 'From evildoers come evil deeds,' so my hand will not touch you.

[14]"Against whom has the king of Israel come out? Who are you pursuing? A dead dog? A flea? [15]May the LORD be our judge and decide between us. May he consider my cause and uphold it; may he vindicate me by delivering me from your hand."

[16]When David finished saying this, Saul asked, "Is that your voice, David my son?" And he wept aloud. [17]"You are more righteous than I," he said. "You have treated me well, but I have treated you badly. [18]You have just now told me about the good you did to me; the LORD delivered me into your hands, but you did not kill me. [19]When a man finds his enemy, does he let him get away unharmed? May the LORD reward you well for the way you treated me today. [20]I know that you will surely be king and that the kingdom of Israel will be established in your hands. [21]Now swear to me by the LORD that you will not kill off my descendants or wipe out my name from my father's family."

[22]So David gave his oath to Saul. Then Saul returned home, but David and his men went up to the stronghold.

David, Nabal and Abigail

25 Now Samuel died, and all Israel assembled and mourned for him; and they buried him at his home in Ramah. Then David moved down into the Desert of Paran.[e]

---

1 SAMUEL 25:1–31

ABIGAIL INTERCEDES

When Abigail discovered that her husband, Nabal, had foolishly rejected David's request for food and water, she realized that her entire household was in danger. She collected and brought a large amount of food for David and his men, and she begged David for mercy. David was so affected by Abigail's words and actions that he extended mercy on her household and sent her home in peace.

This story offers an interesting parallel for understanding the work of Jesus. Mankind is like Nabal by foolishly rejecting God's goodness and consequently deserving his judgment. Like David, God holds all accountable for their disobedience. The only hope for humanity is someone to intercede like Abigail interceded for Nabal. She demonstrated how Jesus bridges the gap between sinful humanity and a holy God. Jesus intercedes on behalf of people and accepts the penalty for our sin so that we can receive mercy.

---

[a] 28 *Sela Hammahlekoth* means *rock of parting.* [b] 29 In Hebrew texts this verse (23:29) is numbered 24:1. [c] In Hebrew texts 24:1-22 is numbered 24:2-23. [d] 4 Or *"Today the LORD is saying* [e] 1 Hebrew and some Septuagint manuscripts; other Septuagint manuscripts *Maon*

1 SAMUEL 24:1 – 22

THE LORD'S ANOINTED

At this point in Israel's history, a civil war threatened to divide the nation as Saul was trying to kill David. David had ascended to great popularity while Saul had fallen out of favor with the people. While David was out slaying giants and winning battles, Saul's jealousy eroded the health of the kingdom. Blinded by his own insecurities, Saul lost the support of his people. Saul tried to kill David on numerous occasions until David finally fled to the wilderness.

For years, David had been running from Saul and his men. But something unexpected happened inside this cave. Saul found himself in a vulnerable position and at the mercy of David. Of course, David's men encouraged him to take advantage of the situation and end Saul's life. In this moment, David had the chance to end Saul's terror over his life and take the throne that God had ordained for him years earlier. David had the political power, the public's support and the right from God to the throne, but he used this opportunity to reinforce Saul and his kingship instead of destroy him.

To cut off a piece of Saul's robe (24:4,11) would have been a symbolic act that discredited Saul's authority as king. It may have looked as if David was going to listen to the encouragements of his friends and kill Saul. Despite the fact that killing Saul would have seemed like the logical thing to do, David knew he could not kill God's anointed king no matter the circumstances. David refused to touch Saul because he was showing his allegiance to "the LORD's anointed" (24:6,10). David realized that all of his popularity and status had been given to him by God. Therefore, David trusted that God would protect him and give him the throne at the right time.

In the New Testament, Jesus demonstrated that he was truly the anointed Son of God. Yet the people used opportunities to disobey God's ways — and they struck the Anointed One. Still, Jesus demonstrated great mercy. He did not strike back but instead forgave them and prayed for them (Lk 23:34). After his crucifixion, death and burial, Jesus rose from the dead and took his rightful place on the throne in heaven, establishing his kingdom once and forever.

2A certain man in Maon, who had property there at Carmel, was very wealthy. He had a thousand goats and three thousand sheep, which he was shearing in Carmel. 3His name was Nabal and his wife's name was Abigail. She was an intelligent and beautiful woman, but her husband was surly and mean in his dealings — he was a Calebite.

4While David was in the wilderness, he heard that Nabal was shearing sheep. 5So he sent ten young men and said to them, "Go up to Nabal at Carmel and greet him in my name. 6Say to him: 'Long life to you! Good health to you and your household! And good health to all that is yours!

7" 'Now I hear that it is sheep-shearing time. When your shepherds were with us, we did not mistreat them, and the whole time they were at Carmel nothing of theirs was missing. 8Ask your own servants and they will tell you. Therefore be favorable toward my men, since we come at a festive time. Please give your servants and your son David whatever you can find for them.' "

9When David's men arrived, they gave Nabal this message in David's name. Then they waited.

10Nabal answered David's servants, "Who is this David? Who is this son of Jesse? Many servants are breaking away from their masters these days. 11Why should I take my bread and water, and the meat I have slaughtered for my shearers, and give it to men coming from who knows where?"

12David's men turned around and went back. When they arrived, they reported every word. 13David said to his men, "Each of you strap on your sword!" So they did, and David strapped his on as well. About four hundred men went up with David, while two hundred stayed with the supplies.

14One of the servants told Abigail, Nabal's wife, "David sent messengers from the wilderness to give our master his greetings, but he hurled insults at them. 15Yet these men were very good to us. They did not mistreat us, and the whole time we were out in the fields near them nothing was missing. 16Night and day they were a wall around us the whole time we were herding our sheep near them. 17Now think it over and see what you can do, because disaster is hanging over our master and his whole household. He is such a wicked man that no one can talk to him."

18Abigail acted quickly. She took two hundred loaves of bread, two skins of wine, five dressed sheep, five seahs[a] of roasted grain, a hundred cakes of raisins and two hundred cakes of pressed figs, and loaded them on donkeys. 19Then she told her servants, "Go on ahead; I'll follow you." But she did not tell her husband Nabal.

20As she came riding her donkey into a mountain ravine, there were David and his men descending toward her, and she met them. 21David had just said, "It's been useless — all my watching over this fellow's property in the wilderness so that nothing of his was missing. He has paid me back evil for good. 22May God deal with David,[b] be it ever so severely, if by morning I leave alive one male of all who belong to him!"

23When Abigail saw David, she quickly got off her donkey and bowed down before David with her face to the ground. 24She fell at his feet and said: "Pardon your servant, my lord, and let me speak to you; hear what your servant has to say. 25Please pay no attention, my lord, to that wicked man Nabal. He is just like his name — his name means Fool, and folly goes with him. And as for me, your servant, I did not see the men my lord sent. 26And now, my lord, as surely as the LORD your God lives and as you live, since the LORD has kept you from bloodshed and from avenging yourself with your own hands, may your enemies and all who are intent on harming my lord be like Nabal. 27And let this gift, which your servant has brought to my lord, be given to the men who follow you.

28"Please forgive your servant's presumption. The LORD your God will certainly make a lasting dynasty for my lord, because you fight the LORD's battles,

[a] *18* That is, probably about 60 pounds or about 27 kilograms [b] *22* Some Septuagint manuscripts; Hebrew *with David's enemies*

and no wrongdoing will be found in you as long as you live. 29Even though someone is pursuing you to take your life, the life of my lord will be bound securely in
the bundle of the living by the LORD your God, but the lives of your enemies he
will hurl away as from the pocket of a sling. 30When the LORD has fulfilled for my
lord every good thing he promised concerning him and has appointed him ruler
over Israel, 31my lord will not have on his conscience the staggering burden of
needless bloodshed or of having avenged himself. And when the LORD your God
has brought my lord success, remember your servant."

32David said to Abigail, "Praise be to the LORD, the God of Israel, who has
sent you today to meet me. 33May you be blessed for your good judgment and
for keeping me from bloodshed this day and from avenging myself with my own
hands. 34Otherwise, as surely as the LORD, the God of Israel, lives, who has kept
me from harming you, if you had not come quickly to meet me, not one male belonging to Nabal would have been left alive by daybreak."

35Then David accepted from her hand what she had brought him and said,
"Go home in peace. I have heard your words and granted your request."

36When Abigail went to Nabal, he was in the house holding a banquet like that
of a king. He was in high spirits and very drunk. So she told him nothing at all
until daybreak. 37Then in the morning, when Nabal was sober, his wife told him
all these things, and his heart failed him and he became like a stone. 38About ten
days later, the LORD struck Nabal and he died.

39When David heard that Nabal was dead, he said, "Praise be to the LORD,
who has upheld my cause against Nabal for treating me with contempt. He has
kept his servant from doing wrong and has brought Nabal's wrongdoing down
on his own head."

Then David sent word to Abigail, asking her to become his wife. 40His servants went to Carmel and said to Abigail, "David has sent us to you to take you
to become his wife."

41She bowed down with her face to the ground and said, "I am your servant
and am ready to serve you and wash the feet of my lord's servants." 42Abigail
quickly got on a donkey and, attended by her five female servants, went with
David's messengers and became his wife. 43David had also married Ahinoam of
Jezreel, and they both were his wives. 44But Saul had given his daughter Michal,
David's wife, to Paltiel[a] son of Laish, who was from Gallim.

David Again Spares Saul's Life

26 The Ziphites went to Saul at Gibeah and said, "Is not David hiding on the
hill of Hakilah, which faces Jeshimon?"

2So Saul went down to the Desert of Ziph, with his three thousand select Israelite troops, to search there for David. 3Saul made his camp beside the road on
the hill of Hakilah facing Jeshimon, but David stayed in the wilderness. When he
saw that Saul had followed him there, 4he sent out scouts and learned that Saul
had definitely arrived.

5Then David set out and went to the place where Saul had camped. He saw
where Saul and Abner son of Ner, the commander of the army, had lain down.
Saul was lying inside the camp, with the army encamped around him.

6David then asked Ahimelek the Hittite and Abishai son of Zeruiah, Joab's
brother, "Who will go down into the camp with me to Saul?"

"I'll go with you," said Abishai.

7So David and Abishai went to the army by night, and there was Saul, lying
asleep inside the camp with his spear stuck in the ground near his head. Abner
and the soldiers were lying around him.

8Abishai said to David, "Today God has delivered your enemy into your
hands. Now let me pin him to the ground with one thrust of the spear; I won't
strike him twice."

[a] 44 Hebrew *Palti*, a variant of *Paltiel*

1 SAMUEL 26:17–25

REPENTANCE AND ACTION

Saul considered David's popularity to be a threat to his power and authority. He wanted nothing more than for David to be out of the picture. For years, Saul pursued David hoping to kill him. David was understandably distressed as he constantly feared for his life, but God always protected him. On this particular occasion, David found Saul in a vulnerable position and had the opportunity to kill him—which would have ended David's struggle and gained him the kingship. When Saul realized his situation, he admitted that he had acted like a fool and even promised David that he would never again try to harm him. David was skeptical—he sensed that Saul had not truly repented or experienced a real change in character (27:1).

In the New Testament, when Jesus spoke of repentance he was speaking about something more than a mere apology. Repentance is a change in character, a turning and walking the other direction. Jesus began his ministry by proclaiming, "Repent, for the kingdom of heaven has come near" (Mt 4:17). Turning to God and following Jesus are the genuine demonstrations of a new life.

1 SAMUEL 27:1

FEAR OF THE FUTURE

David confessed his greatest fear: "One of these days I will be destroyed by the hand of Saul." He had been running for his life from Saul for so long that he felt uncertain of his

(continued on next page)

9But David said to Abishai, "Don't destroy him! Who can lay a hand on the
LORD's anointed and be guiltless? 10As surely as the LORD lives," he said, "the
LORD himself will strike him, or his time will come and he will die, or he will
go into battle and perish. 11But the LORD forbid that I should lay a hand on the
LORD's anointed. Now get the spear and water jug that are near his head, and
let's go."
12So David took the spear and water jug near Saul's head, and they left. No one
saw or knew about it, nor did anyone wake up. They were all sleeping, because
the LORD had put them into a deep sleep.
13Then David crossed over to the other side and stood on top of the hill some
distance away; there was a wide space between them. 14He called out to the army
and to Abner son of Ner, "Aren't you going to answer me, Abner?"
Abner replied, "Who are you who calls to the king?"
15David said, "You're a man, aren't you? And who is like you in Israel? Why
didn't you guard your lord the king? Someone came to destroy your lord the king.
16What you have done is not good. As surely as the LORD lives, you and your men
must die, because you did not guard your master, the LORD's anointed. Look
around you. Where are the king's spear and water jug that were near his head?"
17Saul recognized David's voice and said, "Is that your voice, David my son?"
David replied, "Yes it is, my lord the king." 18And he added, "Why is my lord
pursuing his servant? What have I done, and what wrong am I guilty of? 19Now
let my lord the king listen to his servant's words. If the LORD has incited you
against me, then may he accept an offering. If, however, people have done it,
may they be cursed before the LORD! They have driven me today from my share
in the LORD's inheritance and have said, 'Go, serve other gods.' 20Now do not let
my blood fall to the ground far from the presence of the LORD. The king of Israel has come out to look for a flea—as one hunts a partridge in the mountains."
21Then Saul said, "I have sinned. Come back, David my son. Because you considered my life precious today, I will not try to harm you again. Surely I have
acted like a fool and have been terribly wrong."
22"Here is the king's spear," David answered. "Let one of your young men
come over and get it. 23The LORD rewards everyone for their righteousness and
faithfulness. The LORD delivered you into my hands today, but I would not lay a
hand on the LORD's anointed. 24As surely as I valued your life today, so may the
LORD value my life and deliver me from all trouble."
25Then Saul said to David, "May you be blessed, David my son; you will do
great things and surely triumph."
So David went on his way, and Saul returned home.

David Among the Philistines

27 But David thought to himself, "One of these days I will be destroyed by
the hand of Saul. The best thing I can do is to escape to the land of the
Philistines. Then Saul will give up searching for me anywhere in Israel, and I
will slip out of his hand."
2So David and the six hundred men with him left and went over to Achish son
of Maok king of Gath. 3David and his men settled in Gath with Achish. Each man
had his family with him, and David had his two wives: Ahinoam of Jezreel and
Abigail of Carmel, the widow of Nabal. 4When Saul was told that David had fled
to Gath, he no longer searched for him.
5Then David said to Achish, "If I have found favor in your eyes, let a place be
assigned to me in one of the country towns, that I may live there. Why should
your servant live in the royal city with you?"
6So on that day Achish gave him Ziklag, and it has belonged to the kings of Judah ever since. 7David lived in Philistine territory a year and four months.
8Now David and his men went up and raided the Geshurites, the Girzites
and the Amalekites. (From ancient times these peoples had lived in the land
extending to Shur and Egypt.) 9Whenever David attacked an area, he did not

leave a man or woman alive, but took sheep and cattle, donkeys and camels, and
clothes. Then he returned to Achish.
10When Achish asked, "Where did you go raiding today?" David would say,
"Against the Negev of Judah" or "Against the Negev of Jerahmeel" or "Against
the Negev of the Kenites." 11He did not leave a man or woman alive to be
brought to Gath, for he thought, "They might inform on us and say, 'This is what
David did.' " And such was his practice as long as he lived in Philistine territory.
12Achish trusted David and said to himself, "He has become so obnoxious to his
people, the Israelites, that he will be my servant for life."

28 In those days the Philistines gathered their forces to fight against Israel.
Achish said to David, "You must understand that you and your men will
accompany me in the army."
2David said, "Then you will see for yourself what your servant can do."
Achish replied, "Very well, I will make you my bodyguard for life."

Saul and the Medium at Endor

3Now Samuel was dead, and all Israel had mourned for him and buried him
in his own town of Ramah. Saul had expelled the mediums and spiritists from
the land.
4The Philistines assembled and came and set up camp at Shunem, while Saul
gathered all Israel and set up camp at Gilboa. 5When Saul saw the Philistine
army, he was afraid; terror filled his heart. 6He inquired of the LORD, but the
LORD did not answer him by dreams or Urim or prophets. 7Saul then said to his
attendants, "Find me a woman who is a medium, so I may go and inquire of her."
"There is one in Endor," they said.
8So Saul disguised himself, putting on other clothes, and at night he and two
men went to the woman. "Consult a spirit for me," he said, "and bring up for me
the one I name."
9But the woman said to him, "Surely you know what Saul has done. He has cut
off the mediums and spiritists from the land. Why have you set a trap for my life
to bring about my death?"
10Saul swore to her by the LORD, "As surely as the LORD lives, you will not be
punished for this."
11Then the woman asked, "Whom shall I bring up for you?"
"Bring up Samuel," he said.
12When the woman saw Samuel, she cried out at the top of her voice and said
to Saul, "Why have you deceived me? You are Saul!"
13The king said to her, "Don't be afraid. What do you see?"
The woman said, "I see a ghostly figure[a] coming up out of the earth."
14"What does he look like?" he asked.
"An old man wearing a robe is coming up," she said.
Then Saul knew it was Samuel, and he bowed down and prostrated himself
with his face to the ground.
15Samuel said to Saul, "Why have you disturbed me by bringing me up?"
"I am in great distress," Saul said. "The Philistines are fighting against me,
and God has departed from me. He no longer answers me, either by prophets or
by dreams. So I have called on you to tell me what to do."
16Samuel said, "Why do you consult me, now that the LORD has departed from
you and become your enemy? 17The LORD has done what he predicted through
me. The LORD has torn the kingdom out of your hands and given it to one of your
neighbors — to David. 18Because you did not obey the LORD or carry out his fierce
wrath against the Amalekites, the LORD has done this to you today. 19The LORD
will deliver both Israel and you into the hands of the Philistines, and tomorrow
you and your sons will be with me. The LORD will also give the army of Israel into
the hands of the Philistines."

[a] 13 Or *see spirits*; or *see gods*

(Fear of the Future, continued)

future. Perhaps David dreamed of his life before God had anointed him. Being a shepherd was hard work, but as a keeper of sheep he would not have to live in constant fear for his life. As it was, it seemed like following God's will for his life was the scariest possible future.

In the New Testament, Jesus' disciples must have felt the same fear. Thomas said, "Let us also go, that we may die with him" (Jn 11:16). The disciples did not know the future, but they knew Jesus was trustworthy; they had seen him perform signs and wonders and had sat under his teaching. As Peter said, "Lord, to whom shall we go? You have the words of eternal life" (Jn 6:68). We do not know what the future holds, but we do know the one who holds the future: Jesus.

[20]Immediately Saul fell full length on the ground, filled with fear because of
Samuel's words. His strength was gone, for he had eaten nothing all that day
and all that night.
[21]When the woman came to Saul and saw that he was greatly shaken, she said,
"Look, your servant has obeyed you. I took my life in my hands and did what you
told me to do. [22]Now please listen to your servant and let me give you some food
so you may eat and have the strength to go on your way."
[23]He refused and said, "I will not eat."
But his men joined the woman in urging him, and he listened to them. He got
up from the ground and sat on the couch.
[24]The woman had a fattened calf at the house, which she butchered at once.
She took some flour, kneaded it and baked bread without yeast. [25]Then she set
it before Saul and his men, and they ate. That same night they got up and left.

Achish Sends David Back to Ziklag

29 The Philistines gathered all their forces at Aphek, and Israel camped by the
spring in Jezreel. [2]As the Philistine rulers marched with their units of hundreds and thousands, David and his men were marching at the rear with Achish.
[3]The commanders of the Philistines asked, "What about these Hebrews?"
Achish replied, "Is this not David, who was an officer of Saul king of Israel? He
has already been with me for over a year, and from the day he left Saul until now,
I have found no fault in him."
[4]But the Philistine commanders were angry with Achish and said, "Send the
man back, that he may return to the place you assigned him. He must not go with
us into battle, or he will turn against us during the fighting. How better could he
regain his master's favor than by taking the heads of our own men? [5]Isn't this the
David they sang about in their dances:

"'Saul has slain his thousands,
and David his tens of thousands'?"

[6]So Achish called David and said to him, "As surely as the LORD lives, you have
been reliable, and I would be pleased to have you serve with me in the army.
From the day you came to me until today, I have found no fault in you, but the
rulers don't approve of you. [7]Now turn back and go in peace; do nothing to displease the Philistine rulers."
[8]"But what have I done?" asked David. "What have you found against your
servant from the day I came to you until now? Why can't I go and fight against
the enemies of my lord the king?"
[9]Achish answered, "I know that you have been as pleasing in my eyes as an
angel of God; nevertheless, the Philistine commanders have said, 'He must not
go up with us into battle.' [10]Now get up early, along with your master's servants
who have come with you, and leave in the morning as soon as it is light."
[11]So David and his men got up early in the morning to go back to the land of
the Philistines, and the Philistines went up to Jezreel.

David Destroys the Amalekites

30 David and his men reached Ziklag on the third day. Now the Amalekites
had raided the Negev and Ziklag. They had attacked Ziklag and burned it,
[2]and had taken captive the women and everyone else in it, both young and old.
They killed none of them, but carried them off as they went on their way.
[3]When David and his men reached Ziklag, they found it destroyed by fire and
their wives and sons and daughters taken captive. [4]So David and his men wept
aloud until they had no strength left to weep. [5]David's two wives had been captured — Ahinoam of Jezreel and Abigail, the widow of Nabal of Carmel. [6]David
was greatly distressed because the men were talking of stoning him; each one
was bitter in spirit because of his sons and daughters. But David found strength
in the LORD his God.

1 SAMUEL 30:3–6

FINDING STRENGTH THROUGH PRAYER

David found himself in a difficult situation. He was greatly distressed because he was grieving the capture of his family. He also feared for his life because his men wanted to stone him to death. They were angry and felt that David, as their leader, was the one responsible for the situation they were in. David felt hopeless, so he turned to the giver of hope and "found strength in the LORD his God" (v. 6). David served as an example of how to respond in the midst of fear.

Likewise, Jesus demonstrated where our true source of strength is found. When Jesus felt the pressures of life, he would take time to pull away from his public ministry and seek solitude with God. When the crowds became too large, he would retreat to spend time with his Father (Mk 1:35). When the fear of the future was painful to bear, he communed with the Father to find the strength to continue (Mt 26:36). If even Jesus himself needed time alone with God to find strength, how much more so do we need to find strength in him? "Come near to God and he will come near to you" (Jas 4:8).

SAUL AND THE MEDIUM AT ENDOR

First Samuel 28 tells the story of Saul's final disobedience to the Lord. On the eve of the battle with the Philistines, Saul knew the outcome. When God refused to speak to him, Saul sought advice from a medium at Endor. A "medium" was one who consulted the dead on behalf of the living. It was a form of witchcraft that was prevalent in the nations surrounding Israel. God, however, had condemned all forms of witchcraft (Ex 22:18; Lev 19:31; 20:6,27; Dt 18:10–12,14). The Israelites were not to associate with mediums as it would have been in direct disobedience to God. Once again, Saul went his own way rather than submitting to the way of the Lord.

The medium was aware of God's commands and was skeptical of Saul inquiring of her, thinking it was a trap. Saul assured her of her safety, and she obliged, bringing up Samuel. Samuel informed Saul that his days were numbered. Saul, the once-anointed king of Israel, was seeing the result of his disobedient life.

The story of Saul's disobedience should serve as a warning to all people; there are consequences to blatant and continued sin. Saul had gotten to the point where he felt as if he was above God's commands. He assumed the rules did not apply to him. By God's grace, the Holy Spirit is given to believers to help lead in God's ways (Jn 14:26–27). The Spirit illuminates the truth of the Scriptures in our life and helps us apply God's Word. God has also provided the church to help when seeking counsel. When looking for wisdom, the Scriptures encourage people to seek counsel from godly friends who will help us live obedient to the ways of the Lord (Pr 11:14). Saul's life is a cautionary tale of trying to find wisdom apart from the Holy Spirit and godly counsel. Saul's attempt at wisdom apart from God led him on a downward slope into spiritual darkness. The wisdom of the Spirit, on the other hand, leads us into all truth (Jn 16:13).

7 Then David said to Abiathar the priest, the son of Ahimelek, "Bring me the
ephod." Abiathar brought it to him, 8 and David inquired of the LORD, "Shall I
pursue this raiding party? Will I overtake them?"

"Pursue them," he answered. "You will certainly overtake them and succeed
in the rescue."

9 David and the six hundred men with him came to the Besor Valley, where
some stayed behind. 10 Two hundred of them were too exhausted to cross the
valley, but David and the other four hundred continued the pursuit.

11 They found an Egyptian in a field and brought him to David. They gave him
water to drink and food to eat— 12 part of a cake of pressed figs and two cakes of
raisins. He ate and was revived, for he had not eaten any food or drunk any water
for three days and three nights.

13 David asked him, "Who do you belong to? Where do you come from?"

He said, "I am an Egyptian, the slave of an Amalekite. My master abandoned
me when I became ill three days ago. 14 We raided the Negev of the Kerethites,
some territory belonging to Judah and the Negev of Caleb. And we burned Ziklag."

15 David asked him, "Can you lead me down to this raiding party?"

He answered, "Swear to me before God that you will not kill me or hand me
over to my master, and I will take you down to them."

16 He led David down, and there they were, scattered over the countryside,
eating, drinking and reveling because of the great amount of plunder they had
taken from the land of the Philistines and from Judah. 17 David fought them from
dusk until the evening of the next day, and none of them got away, except four
hundred young men who rode off on camels and fled. 18 David recovered everything the Amalekites had taken, including his two wives. 19 Nothing was missing:
young or old, boy or girl, plunder or anything else they had taken. David brought
everything back. 20 He took all the flocks and herds, and his men drove them
ahead of the other livestock, saying, "This is David's plunder."

21 Then David came to the two hundred men who had been too exhausted to
follow him and who were left behind at the Besor Valley. They came out to meet
David and the men with him. As David and his men approached, he asked them
how they were. 22 But all the evil men and troublemakers among David's followers
said, "Because they did not go out with us, we will not share with them the plunder
we recovered. However, each man may take his wife and children and go."

23 David replied, "No, my brothers, you must not do that with what the LORD
has given us. He has protected us and delivered into our hands the raiding party
that came against us. 24 Who will listen to what you say? The share of the man
who stayed with the supplies is to be the same as that of him who went down to
the battle. All will share alike." 25 David made this a statute and ordinance for
Israel from that day to this.

26 When David reached Ziklag, he sent some of the plunder to the elders of
Judah, who were his friends, saying, "Here is a gift for you from the plunder of
the LORD's enemies."

27 David sent it to those who were in Bethel, Ramoth Negev and Jattir; 28 to
those in Aroer, Siphmoth, Eshtemoa 29 and Rakal; to those in the towns of the
Jerahmeelites and the Kenites; 30 to those in Hormah, Bor Ashan, Athak 31 and
Hebron; and to those in all the other places where he and his men had roamed.

Saul Takes His Life

31 Now the Philistines fought against Israel; the Israelites fled before them,
and many fell dead on Mount Gilboa. 2 The Philistines were in hot pursuit of Saul and his sons, and they killed his sons Jonathan, Abinadab and Malki-Shua. 3 The fighting grew fierce around Saul, and when the archers overtook
him, they wounded him critically.

4 Saul said to his armor-bearer, "Draw your sword and run me through, or
these uncircumcised fellows will come and run me through and abuse me."

But his armor-bearer was terrified and would not do it; so Saul took his own
sword and fell on it. [5]When the armor-bearer saw that Saul was dead, he too fell
on his sword and died with him. [6]So Saul and his three sons and his armor-bearer
and all his men died together that same day.

[7]When the Israelites along the valley and those across the Jordan saw that
the Israelite army had fled and that Saul and his sons had died, they abandoned
their towns and fled. And the Philistines came and occupied them.

[8]The next day, when the Philistines came to strip the dead, they found Saul
and his three sons fallen on Mount Gilboa. [9]They cut off his head and stripped
off his armor, and they sent messengers throughout the land of the Philistines
to proclaim the news in the temple of their idols and among their people. [10]They
put his armor in the temple of the Ashtoreths and fastened his body to the wall
of Beth Shan.

[11]When the people of Jabesh Gilead heard what the Philistines had done to
Saul, [12]all their valiant men marched through the night to Beth Shan. They took
down the bodies of Saul and his sons from the wall of Beth Shan and went to Jabesh, where they burned them. [13]Then they took their bones and buried them
under a tamarisk tree at Jabesh, and they fasted seven days.

JESUS: OUR ETERNAL ONE

2 SAMUEL

REIGN OF DAVID BEGINS	ABSALOM REVOLTS AGAINST DAVID	DAVID DIES/SOLOMON BECOMES KING
c. 1010 BC	*c. 980 BC*	*c. 970 BC*

Second Samuel provides a biography of the life of one of history's greatest human leaders. God called and appointed King David, a man of unremarkable pedigree, to lead the nation of Israel following Saul's extended, but ultimately failed, reign. David inherited a fractured nation that, under God's direction, he built into a prominent, powerful, united nation. The book of 2 Samuel, like most political biographies, describes the character traits that enabled David to lead the people — traits such as his courage, faith, daily reliance on God, and wisdom. David's failures are also chronicled throughout the book, as his lust and pride ultimately hindered his leadership and resulted in tragic consequences for David, his family and the nation.

Second Samuel describes the time from the death of Saul to the latter part of David's reign. With God's leading, David united the people and led this young nation to become a military power able to dominate the other, much more established nations of his day. After capturing the Jebusite fortress of Jerusalem, David made this fortified city the capital of the nation and organized Israel's worship of God at this key location. From there, David led the people to drive out the inhabitants of the land in all of the surrounding region. Israel's burgeoning military power combined with the waning influence of the pagan nations allowed David to eventually control territory from the border of Egypt to the Euphrates River. God's leadership over Israel and their submission to his rule allowed them to appropriate the blessings found in the promised land. God had not only proven faithful to give them the land, but he also was faithful to provide his promised blessings for their obedience.

The account of David's reign maintains a consistently hopeful tone in contrast to the failure seen at the end of Saul's rule. Even after his well-publicized personal failures, David's humility and leadership served as the embodiment of God's leadership among the people. Yet David himself would not be the eternal king; that king would come through David's line and would rule in a way far superior to David — without the sin that ultimately hampered David's reign. God reiterated his covenant commitment to his people and provided David with a unique glimpse into the way in which he would ultimately fulfill his promises in the Davidic covenant, where God promised David an eternal throne, an eternal reign and an eternal dynasty (2Sa 7:12 – 16). God fulfilled this threefold promise to David by sending Jesus, the Messiah who had been promised for centuries. This perfect King would perfectly establish God's eternal throne, reign and dynasty (Lk 1:32 – 33). It's this perfect reign that believers both enjoy today through the power of the Holy Spirit and look forward to in the future, when Jesus will return on the clouds to bring justice to the nations and to restore all of creation (Mt 24:30; 26:64).

AS FOR GOD, HIS WAY IS PERFECT: THE LORD'S WORD IS FLAWLESS; HE SHIELDS ALL WHO TAKE REFUGE IN HIM.

---

2 Samuel 22:31

2 SAMUEL

David Hears of Saul's Death

1 After the death of Saul, David returned from striking down the Amalekites
and stayed in Ziklag two days. 2On the third day a man arrived from Saul's
camp with his clothes torn and dust on his head. When he came to David, he fell
to the ground to pay him honor.
3"Where have you come from?" David asked him.
He answered, "I have escaped from the Israelite camp."
4"What happened?" David asked. "Tell me."
"The men fled from the battle," he replied. "Many of them fell and died. And
Saul and his son Jonathan are dead."
5Then David said to the young man who brought him the report, "How do you
know that Saul and his son Jonathan are dead?"
6"I happened to be on Mount Gilboa," the young man said, "and there was
Saul, leaning on his spear, with the chariots and their drivers in hot pursuit.
7When he turned around and saw me, he called out to me, and I said, 'What can
I do?'
8"He asked me, 'Who are you?'
" 'An Amalekite,' I answered.
9"Then he said to me, 'Stand here by me and kill me! I'm in the throes of death,
but I'm still alive.'
10"So I stood beside him and killed him, because I knew that after he had fall-
en he could not survive. And I took the crown that was on his head and the band
on his arm and have brought them here to my lord."
11Then David and all the men with him took hold of their clothes and tore
them. 12They mourned and wept and fasted till evening for Saul and his son Jonathan, and for the army of the LORD and for the nation of Israel, because they
had fallen by the sword.
13David said to the young man who brought him the report, "Where are you
from?"
"I am the son of a foreigner, an Amalekite," he answered.
14David asked him, "Why weren't you afraid to lift your hand to destroy the
LORD's anointed?"
15Then David called one of his men and said, "Go, strike him down!" So he
struck him down, and he died. 16For David had said to him, "Your blood be on
your own head. Your own mouth testified against you when you said, 'I killed
the LORD's anointed.' "

David's Lament for Saul and Jonathan

17David took up this lament concerning Saul and his son Jonathan, 18and he
ordered that the people of Judah be taught this lament of the bow (it is written
in the Book of Jashar):

19 "A gazelle[a] lies slain on your heights, Israel.
How the mighty have fallen!

20 "Tell it not in Gath,
proclaim it not in the streets of Ashkelon,
lest the daughters of the Philistines be glad,
lest the daughters of the uncircumcised rejoice.

[a] 19 *Gazelle* here symbolizes a human dignitary.

2 SAMUEL 1:17 – 27

GRACE AND FORGIVENESS

Some of the most amazing storylines throughout Scripture involve grace and forgiveness. Typically, when human reasoning would say that bitterness is warranted, God shows that his grace is enough. In this passage, David was extremely gracious regarding Saul. Rather than recount Saul's shortcomings, David chose to honor him in this song. In spite of all that Saul had done to harm David, he did not hold these things against him following his death.

Likewise, through Jesus, God does not hold the sins of believers against them. When he sees them, he does not see the sin, but he sees Jesus. "As far as the east is from the west, so far has he removed our transgressions from us" (Ps 103:12). In many respects, David prefigured the grace and forgiveness of Christ, foreshadowing Jesus' gracious response to people through all time. Even while suffering under the hands of his oppressors, Jesus responded with grace and forgiveness rather than employing the powerful wrath of God (Mt 26:53).

21 "Mountains of Gilboa,
may you have neither dew nor rain,
may no showers fall on your terraced fields.[a]
For there the shield of the mighty was despised,
the shield of Saul — no longer rubbed with oil.

22 "From the blood of the slain,
from the flesh of the mighty,
the bow of Jonathan did not turn back,
the sword of Saul did not return unsatisfied.
23 Saul and Jonathan —
in life they were loved and admired,
and in death they were not parted.
They were swifter than eagles,
they were stronger than lions.
24 "Daughters of Israel,
weep for Saul,
who clothed you in scarlet and finery,
who adorned your garments with ornaments of gold.

25 "How the mighty have fallen in battle!
Jonathan lies slain on your heights.
26 I grieve for you, Jonathan my brother;
you were very dear to me.
Your love for me was wonderful,
more wonderful than that of women.

27 "How the mighty have fallen!
The weapons of war have perished!"

David Anointed King Over Judah

2 In the course of time, David inquired of the LORD. "Shall I go up to one of the
towns of Judah?" he asked.
The LORD said, "Go up."
David asked, "Where shall I go?"
"To Hebron," the LORD answered.
2 So David went up there with his two wives, Ahinoam of Jezreel and Abigail,
the widow of Nabal of Carmel. 3 David also took the men who were with him,
each with his family, and they settled in Hebron and its towns. 4 Then the men
of Judah came to Hebron, and there they anointed David king over the tribe of
Judah.
When David was told that it was the men from Jabesh Gilead who had buried
Saul, 5 he sent messengers to them to say to them, "The LORD bless you for showing this kindness to Saul your master by burying him. 6 May the LORD now show
you kindness and faithfulness, and I too will show you the same favor because
you have done this. 7 Now then, be strong and brave, for Saul your master is dead,
and the people of Judah have anointed me king over them."

War Between the Houses of David and Saul

8 Meanwhile, Abner son of Ner, the commander of Saul's army, had taken Ish-
Bosheth son of Saul and brought him over to Mahanaim. 9 He made him king
over Gilead, Ashuri and Jezreel, and also over Ephraim, Benjamin and all Israel.
10 Ish-Bosheth son of Saul was forty years old when he became king over Israel,
and he reigned two years. The tribe of Judah, however, remained loyal to David.
11 The length of time David was king in Hebron over Judah was seven years and
six months.
12 Abner son of Ner, together with the men of Ish-Bosheth son of Saul, left

[a] 21 Or / *nor fields that yield grain for offerings*

2 SAMUEL 2:8 – 17

A GUARANTEED KINGDOM

David's security, as king over the people of Israel, proved to be in question throughout this book. In the natural order of things, it would not be uncommon for the son of the deceased king to ascend to the throne. However, that was not God's plan. David's kingdom was guaranteed and never in question from the perspective of God's sovereign oversight of his life.

Jesus was born as a proclaimed king, one whose reign would be without end, the one for whom Israel longed. Zechariah 9:9 states, "Rejoice greatly, Daughter Zion! Shout, Daughter Jerusalem! See, your king comes to you, righteous and victorious, lowly and riding on a donkey, on a colt, the foal of a donkey." Although it seemed that his rule was insecure to his disciples at times, Jesus' kingdom was promised. Even today, when believers look around them and feel that the world has gone awry, God's plan of final redemption has not changed. He is working all things to his glory and moving all things toward a final conclusion when Jesus will have final victory over all ungodliness (Rev 21:6 – 8). His is a kingdom that is guaranteed.

Mahanaim and went to Gibeon. [13]Joab son of Zeruiah and David's men went out
and met them at the pool of Gibeon. One group sat down on one side of the pool
and one group on the other side.
[14]Then Abner said to Joab, "Let's have some of the young men get up and fight
hand to hand in front of us."
"All right, let them do it," Joab said.
[15]So they stood up and were counted off — twelve men for Benjamin and Ish-
Bosheth son of Saul, and twelve for David. [16]Then each man grabbed his opponent by the head and thrust his dagger into his opponent's side, and they fell
down together. So that place in Gibeon was called Helkath Hazzurim.[a]
[17]The battle that day was very fierce, and Abner and the Israelites were defeated by David's men.
[18]The three sons of Zeruiah were there: Joab, Abishai and Asahel. Now Asahel
was as fleet-footed as a wild gazelle. [19]He chased Abner, turning neither to the
right nor to the left as he pursued him. [20]Abner looked behind him and asked,
"Is that you, Asahel?"
"It is," he answered.
[21]Then Abner said to him, "Turn aside to the right or to the left; take on one of
the young men and strip him of his weapons." But Asahel would not stop chasing him.
[22]Again Abner warned Asahel, "Stop chasing me! Why should I strike you
down? How could I look your brother Joab in the face?"
[23]But Asahel refused to give up the pursuit; so Abner thrust the butt of his
spear into Asahel's stomach, and the spear came out through his back. He fell
there and died on the spot. And every man stopped when he came to the place
where Asahel had fallen and died.
[24]But Joab and Abishai pursued Abner, and as the sun was setting, they came
to the hill of Ammah, near Giah on the way to the wasteland of Gibeon. [25]Then
the men of Benjamin rallied behind Abner. They formed themselves into a group
and took their stand on top of a hill.
[26]Abner called out to Joab, "Must the sword devour forever? Don't you realize
that this will end in bitterness? How long before you order your men to stop pursuing their fellow Israelites?"
[27]Joab answered, "As surely as God lives, if you had not spoken, the men would
have continued pursuing them until morning."
[28]So Joab blew the trumpet, and all the troops came to a halt; they no longer
pursued Israel, nor did they fight anymore.
[29]All that night Abner and his men marched through the Arabah. They
crossed the Jordan, continued through the morning hours[b] and came to Mahanaim.
[30]Then Joab stopped pursuing Abner and assembled the whole army. Besides
Asahel, nineteen of David's men were found missing. [31]But David's men had
killed three hundred and sixty Benjamites who were with Abner. [32]They took
Asahel and buried him in his father's tomb at Bethlehem. Then Joab and his men
marched all night and arrived at Hebron by daybreak.

3 The war between the house of Saul and the house of David lasted a long time.
David grew stronger and stronger, while the house of Saul grew weaker and
weaker.
[2]Sons were born to David in Hebron:
His firstborn was Amnon the son of Ahinoam of Jezreel;
[3]his second, Kileab the son of Abigail the widow of Nabal of Carmel;
the third, Absalom the son of Maakah daughter of Talmai king of Geshur;
[4]the fourth, Adonijah the son of Haggith;
the fifth, Shephatiah the son of Abital;

---

[a] 16 *Helkath Hazzurim* means *field of daggers* or *field of hostilities.* [b] 29 See Septuagint; the meaning of the Hebrew for this phrase is uncertain.

5 and the sixth, Ithream the son of David's wife Eglah.
These were born to David in Hebron.

Abner Goes Over to David

6During the war between the house of Saul and the house of David, Abner had
been strengthening his own position in the house of Saul. 7Now Saul had had
a concubine named Rizpah daughter of Aiah. And Ish-Bosheth said to Abner,
"Why did you sleep with my father's concubine?"
8Abner was very angry because of what Ish-Bosheth said. So he answered,
"Am I a dog's head — on Judah's side? This very day I am loyal to the house of your
father Saul and to his family and friends. I haven't handed you over to David.
Yet now you accuse me of an offense involving this woman! 9May God deal with
Abner, be it ever so severely, if I do not do for David what the LORD promised him
on oath 10and transfer the kingdom from the house of Saul and establish David's
throne over Israel and Judah from Dan to Beersheba." 11Ish-Bosheth did not dare
to say another word to Abner, because he was afraid of him.
12Then Abner sent messengers on his behalf to say to David, "Whose land is
it? Make an agreement with me, and I will help you bring all Israel over to you."
13"Good," said David. "I will make an agreement with you. But I demand one
thing of you: Do not come into my presence unless you bring Michal daughter of
Saul when you come to see me." 14Then David sent messengers to Ish-Bosheth
son of Saul, demanding, "Give me my wife Michal, whom I betrothed to myself
for the price of a hundred Philistine foreskins."
15So Ish-Bosheth gave orders and had her taken away from her husband Paltiel son of Laish. 16Her husband, however, went with her, weeping behind her all
the way to Bahurim. Then Abner said to him, "Go back home!" So he went back.
17Abner conferred with the elders of Israel and said, "For some time you have
wanted to make David your king. 18Now do it! For the LORD promised David, 'By
my servant David I will rescue my people Israel from the hand of the Philistines
and from the hand of all their enemies.'"
19Abner also spoke to the Benjamites in person. Then he went to Hebron to
tell David everything that Israel and the whole tribe of Benjamin wanted to do.
20When Abner, who had twenty men with him, came to David at Hebron, David
prepared a feast for him and his men. 21Then Abner said to David, "Let me go at
once and assemble all Israel for my lord the king, so that they may make a covenant with you, and that you may rule over all that your heart desires." So David
sent Abner away, and he went in peace.

Joab Murders Abner

22Just then David's men and Joab returned from a raid and brought with them
a great deal of plunder. But Abner was no longer with David in Hebron, because
David had sent him away, and he had gone in peace. 23When Joab and all the soldiers with him arrived, he was told that Abner son of Ner had come to the king
and that the king had sent him away and that he had gone in peace.
24So Joab went to the king and said, "What have you done? Look, Abner came
to you. Why did you let him go? Now he is gone! 25You know Abner son of Ner;
he came to deceive you and observe your movements and find out everything
you are doing."
26Joab then left David and sent messengers after Abner, and they brought him
back from the cistern at Sirah. But David did not know it. 27Now when Abner returned to Hebron, Joab took him aside into an inner chamber, as if to speak with
him privately. And there, to avenge the blood of his brother Asahel, Joab stabbed
him in the stomach, and he died.
28Later, when David heard about this, he said, "I and my kingdom are forever
innocent before the LORD concerning the blood of Abner son of Ner. 29May his
blood fall on the head of Joab and on his whole family! May Joab's family never

be without someone who has a running sore or leprosy[a] or who leans on a crutch
or who falls by the sword or who lacks food."
30 (Joab and his brother Abishai murdered Abner because he had killed their
brother Asahel in the battle at Gibeon.)
31 Then David said to Joab and all the people with him, "Tear your clothes and
put on sackcloth and walk in mourning in front of Abner." King David himself
walked behind the bier. 32 They buried Abner in Hebron, and the king wept aloud
at Abner's tomb. All the people wept also.
33 The king sang this lament for Abner:

"Should Abner have died as the lawless die?
34 Your hands were not bound,
your feet were not fettered.
You fell as one falls before the wicked."

And all the people wept over him again.
35 Then they all came and urged David to eat something while it was still day;
but David took an oath, saying, "May God deal with me, be it ever so severely, if
I taste bread or anything else before the sun sets!"
36 All the people took note and were pleased; indeed, everything the king did
pleased them. 37 So on that day all the people there and all Israel knew that the
king had no part in the murder of Abner son of Ner.
38 Then the king said to his men, "Do you not realize that a commander and
a great man has fallen in Israel this day? 39 And today, though I am the anointed
king, I am weak, and these sons of Zeruiah are too strong for me. May the LORD
repay the evildoer according to his evil deeds!"

Ish-Bosheth Murdered

4 When Ish-Bosheth son of Saul heard that Abner had died in Hebron, he lost
courage, and all Israel became alarmed. 2 Now Saul's son had two men who
were leaders of raiding bands. One was named Baanah and the other Rekab;
they were sons of Rimmon the Beerothite from the tribe of Benjamin — Beeroth
is considered part of Benjamin, 3 because the people of Beeroth fled to Gittaim
and have resided there as foreigners to this day.
4 (Jonathan son of Saul had a son who was lame in both feet. He was five years
old when the news about Saul and Jonathan came from Jezreel. His nurse picked
him up and fled, but as she hurried to leave, he fell and became disabled. His
name was Mephibosheth.)
5 Now Rekab and Baanah, the sons of Rimmon the Beerothite, set out for the
house of Ish-Bosheth, and they arrived there in the heat of the day while he was
taking his noonday rest. 6 They went into the inner part of the house as if to get
some wheat, and they stabbed him in the stomach. Then Rekab and his brother
Baanah slipped away.
7 They had gone into the house while he was lying on the bed in his bedroom.
After they stabbed and killed him, they cut off his head. Taking it with them, they
traveled all night by way of the Arabah. 8 They brought the head of Ish-Bosheth
to David at Hebron and said to the king, "Here is the head of Ish-Bosheth son of
Saul, your enemy, who tried to kill you. This day the LORD has avenged my lord
the king against Saul and his offspring."
9 David answered Rekab and his brother Baanah, the sons of Rimmon the Beerothite, "As surely as the LORD lives, who has delivered me out of every trouble,
10 when someone told me, 'Saul is dead,' and thought he was bringing good news,
I seized him and put him to death in Ziklag. That was the reward I gave him for
his news! 11 How much more — when wicked men have killed an innocent man
in his own house and on his own bed — should I not now demand his blood from
your hand and rid the earth of you!"

[a] 29 The Hebrew for *leprosy* was used for various diseases affecting the skin.

---

2 SAMUEL 4:1 – 12

RETRIBUTION AND GRACE

The deaths of Saul, Abner and Ish-Bosheth removed major obstacles from David's path to be king over Israel. David secured power in both the northern and southern territories as a result of Rimmon's two merciless sons, Baanah and Rekab. After murdering Ish-Bosheth, these men expected a reward because they believed themselves to be agents acting on David's behalf and the Lord. But they misread the situation, revealing that they did not know David's values as king and were mistaken concerning the judgment and purposes of God. Ultimately, David understood that men like Baanah and Rekab could not grasp that the Lord redeems life and brings judgment on the wrongdoer.

Another example of this is found in Luke 9:51 – 56. Jesus was on his way to Jerusalem and opted to go through Samaria, where he did not receive a warm reception. The disciples were incensed, particularly James and John, so they asked Jesus if they should call down fire from heaven to consume the Samaritans. Jesus rebuked the disciples, whose understanding of retribution was mistaken. Jesus, like David, embraced even bitter rivals in love and forgiveness — an embrace that he continues to offer to this day to those who deserve nothing other than retribution.

FORGIVENESS VERSUS RETALIATION

As Saul's chief military leader and head of his protection unit, Abner had no doubt made David's life miserable, seeking to kill him as Saul directed and desired. Yet David forgave Abner and formed a constructive alliance with him. In contrast, Joab hated Abner because Abner had killed his brother. As a result, Joab killed Abner. While Joab's desire to avenge his brother's death might be understandable, David too had reason to seek revenge. But he didn't. Instead he wept because of Abner's death. David, in a sign of mourning, put on sackcloth and wept at Abner's grave (vv. 31 – 32). The people of Israel were stunned by David's response and urged him to eat (v. 35). Instead, David reminded the people that a great man had died, and they too should honor him (vv. 36 – 39). In spite of Abner's sin, David did not treat him as his sin deserved but chose to esteem his life.

How much more astounding is the grace of God in the face of human sin. God knows all things — every aspect of the rebellious hearts of all people. Nothing is hidden from God (Heb 4:13). All sins that people try to hide are known fully by God. Yet God willingly forgives sin — blotting it out forever for those who place their faith in Jesus (Isa 43:25). This forgiveness does not mean that God turns a blind eye to human failures. He knows full well the treachery of his people, yet he forgives anyway. He removes sin as far as the east is from the west as an intentional act of his grace (Ps 103:12). How can a just God forgive in this way? Paul answered this in Romans 3:25 – 26. God is just because he did not simply ignore sin, but he placed the penalty for sin on his Son, Jesus. Because Jesus satisfied the wrath of God, those who know Jesus can be made right with God. In this way, God does not treat his children as their sin deserves but instead lavishes mercy and grace on them.

[12]So David gave an order to his men, and they killed them. They cut off their
hands and feet and hung the bodies by the pool in Hebron. But they took the
head of Ish-Bosheth and buried it in Abner's tomb at Hebron.

David Becomes King Over Israel

5 All the tribes of Israel came to David at Hebron and said, "We are your own
flesh and blood. [2]In the past, while Saul was king over us, you were the one
who led Israel on their military campaigns. And the LORD said to you, 'You will
shepherd my people Israel, and you will become their ruler.' "
[3]When all the elders of Israel had come to King David at Hebron, the king
made a covenant with them at Hebron before the LORD, and they anointed David king over Israel.
[4]David was thirty years old when he became king, and he reigned forty years.
[5]In Hebron he reigned over Judah seven years and six months, and in Jerusalem
he reigned over all Israel and Judah thirty-three years.

David Conquers Jerusalem

[6]The king and his men marched to Jerusalem to attack the Jebusites, who
lived there. The Jebusites said to David, "You will not get in here; even the blind
and the lame can ward you off." They thought, "David cannot get in here." [7]Nev-
ertheless, David captured the fortress of Zion—which is the City of David.
[8]On that day David had said, "Anyone who conquers the Jebusites will have to
use the water shaft to reach those 'lame and blind' who are David's enemies.[a]"
That is why they say, "The 'blind and lame' will not enter the palace."
[9]David then took up residence in the fortress and called it the City of David.
He built up the area around it, from the terraces[b] inward. [10]And he became more
and more powerful, because the LORD God Almighty was with him.
[11]Now Hiram king of Tyre sent envoys to David, along with cedar logs and
carpenters and stonemasons, and they built a palace for David. [12]Then David
knew that the LORD had established him as king over Israel and had exalted his
kingdom for the sake of his people Israel.
[13]After he left Hebron, David took more concubines and wives in Jerusalem,
and more sons and daughters were born to him. [14]These are the names of the
children born to him there: Shammua, Shobab, Nathan, Solomon, [15]Ibhar, Elishua, Nepheg, Japhia, [16]Elishama, Eliada and Eliphelet.

David Defeats the Philistines

[17]When the Philistines heard that David had been anointed king over Israel,
they went up in full force to search for him, but David heard about it and went
down to the stronghold. [18]Now the Philistines had come and spread out in the
Valley of Rephaim; [19]so David inquired of the LORD, "Shall I go and attack the
Philistines? Will you deliver them into my hands?"
The LORD answered him, "Go, for I will surely deliver the Philistines into your
hands."
[20]So David went to Baal Perazim, and there he defeated them. He said, "As waters break out, the LORD has broken out against my enemies before me." So that
place was called Baal Perazim.[c] [21]The Philistines abandoned their idols there,
and David and his men carried them off.
[22]Once more the Philistines came up and spread out in the Valley of Rephaim;
[23]so David inquired of the LORD, and he answered, "Do not go straight up, but
circle around behind them and attack them in front of the poplar trees. [24]As soon
as you hear the sound of marching in the tops of the poplar trees, move quickly,
because that will mean the LORD has gone out in front of you to strike the Philistine army." [25]So David did as the LORD commanded him, and he struck down
the Philistines all the way from Gibeon[d] to Gezer.

---

[a] 8 Or *are hated by David* [b] 9 Or *the Millo* [c] 20 *Baal Perazim* means *the lord who breaks out.* [d] 25 Septuagint (see also 1 Chron. 14:16); Hebrew *Geba*

JERUSALEM, THE CITY OF GOD

The city of Jerusalem has held a place of significance in Scripture for thousands of years. In one of his first acts as king over all the tribes of Israel, David assailed the Jebusites in Jerusalem, taking the city as his royal seat. He was able to do these things not by his own might but rather by the power of almighty God (v. 10). David and his army were mocked as weak (v. 6), but God enabled them to overpower the Jebusite warriors and gain control of the city. God established David's city as a physical manifestation of his goodness to his people. For years to come, it was described in Scripture with the utmost regard: the city of God (Ps 87:1 – 3), the place where God put his Name (2Ki 21:4), a place of salvation (Isa 46:13), "The Throne of the LORD" (Jer 3:17) and the holy city (Isa 52:1). This city, however, fell from prominence as the people of God faced hardships and exile at the hands of neighboring nations in the days to come.

Many years later, Jerusalem would again become central to the redemptive story of God. It was outside of this city where Jesus' sacrifice took place, establishing the promise of a future forever in the presence of God for those who repent of their sins while believing and calling on the name of Jesus for forgiveness. The promise of salvation from God was established through David at a physical location, and that location became the central place in which Jesus expanded God's kingdom through another victory — a victory over death.

In Christ, believers also look to Jerusalem with historical and spiritual significance as well as with hope of a beautiful promise associated with salvation. Revelation 21:1 – 5 reads, "Then I saw 'a new heaven and a new earth,' ... I saw the Holy City, the new Jerusalem, coming down out of heaven from God, prepared as a bride beautifully dressed for her husband. And I heard a loud voice from the throne saying, 'Look! God's dwelling place is now among the people, and he will dwell with them. They will be his people, and God himself will be with them and be their God. "He will wipe every tear from their eyes. There will be no more death" or mourning or crying or pain, for the old order of things has passed away.' He who was seated on the throne said, 'I am making everything new!'"

The Ark Brought to Jerusalem

6 David again brought together all the able young men of Israel — thirty thousand. [2]He and all his men went to Baalah[a] in Judah to bring up from there the ark of God, which is called by the Name,[b] the name of the LORD Almighty, who is enthroned between the cherubim on the ark. [3]They set the ark of God on a new cart and brought it from the house of Abinadab, which was on the hill. Uzzah and Ahio, sons of Abinadab, were guiding the new cart [4]with the ark of God on it,[c] and Ahio was walking in front of it. [5]David and all Israel were celebrating with all their might before the LORD, with castanets,[d] harps, lyres, timbrels, sistrums and cymbals.

[6]When they came to the threshing floor of Nakon, Uzzah reached out and took hold of the ark of God, because the oxen stumbled. [7]The LORD's anger burned against Uzzah because of his irreverent act; therefore God struck him down, and he died there beside the ark of God.

[8]Then David was angry because the LORD's wrath had broken out against Uzzah, and to this day that place is called Perez Uzzah.[e]

[9]David was afraid of the LORD that day and said, "How can the ark of the LORD ever come to me?" [10]He was not willing to take the ark of the LORD to be with him in the City of David. Instead, he took it to the house of Obed-Edom the Gittite. [11]The ark of the LORD remained in the house of Obed-Edom the Gittite for three months, and the LORD blessed him and his entire household.

[12]Now King David was told, "The LORD has blessed the household of Obed-Edom and everything he has, because of the ark of God." So David went to bring up the ark of God from the house of Obed-Edom to the City of David with rejoicing. [13]When those who were carrying the ark of the LORD had taken six steps, he sacrificed a bull and a fattened calf. [14]Wearing a linen ephod, David was dancing before the LORD with all his might, [15]while he and all Israel were bringing up the ark of the LORD with shouts and the sound of trumpets.

[16]As the ark of the LORD was entering the City of David, Michal daughter of Saul watched from a window. And when she saw King David leaping and dancing before the LORD, she despised him in her heart.

[17]They brought the ark of the LORD and set it in its place inside the tent that David had pitched for it, and David sacrificed burnt offerings and fellowship offerings before the LORD. [18]After he had finished sacrificing the burnt offerings and fellowship offerings, he blessed the people in the name of the LORD Almighty. [19]Then he gave a loaf of bread, a cake of dates and a cake of raisins to each person in the whole crowd of Israelites, both men and women. And all the people went to their homes.

[20]When David returned home to bless his household, Michal daughter of Saul came out to meet him and said, "How the king of Israel has distinguished himself today, going around half-naked in full view of the slave girls of his servants as any vulgar fellow would!"

[21]David said to Michal, "It was before the LORD, who chose me rather than your father or anyone from his house when he appointed me ruler over the LORD's people Israel — I will celebrate before the LORD. [22]I will become even more undignified than this, and I will be humiliated in my own eyes. But by these slave girls you spoke of, I will be held in honor."

[23]And Michal daughter of Saul had no children to the day of her death.

God's Promise to David

7 After the king was settled in his palace and the LORD had given him rest from all his enemies around him, [2]he said to Nathan the prophet, "Here I am, living in a house of cedar, while the ark of God remains in a tent."

[a] *2* That is, Kiriath Jearim (see 1 Chron. 13:6) [b] *2* Hebrew; Septuagint and Vulgate do not have *the Name.* [c] *3,4* Dead Sea Scrolls and some Septuagint manuscripts; Masoretic Text *cart* [4]*and they brought it with the ark of God from the house of Abinadab, which was on the hill* [d] *5* Masoretic Text; Dead Sea Scrolls and Septuagint (see also 1 Chron. 13:8) *songs* [e] *8* *Perez Uzzah* means *outbreak against Uzzah.*

2 SAMUEL 6:1 – 10

VIOLATING THE HOLINESS OF GOD

For Israel, the ark represented God's awe-inspiring presence, and it unified the twelve tribes as one people. For this pilgrimage David had men set the ark on a new cart pulled by oxen. When the oxen stumbled, Uzzah reached out to stabilize it. Immediately, the anger of the Lord burned against him and he died.

The Lord had given strict instructions concerning the transportation of the ark (Ex 25:13 – 14; Nu 4:15; 7:7 – 9; 2Ch 15:13 – 15). It was only to be transported by poles carried on the shoulders of Levites. When these commands were violated, the Lord defended his holiness. This zeal frightened David. All in the procession were reminded that when the fear of the Lord fades, the community is at risk. When sinful man encroaches upon the holiness of God, a price must be paid.

Because of Christ's atoning death and resurrection, believers now have access to boldly approach God in prayer with confidence and a clean conscience (Heb 10:19 – 22). Jesus paid the price for encroaching upon the holiness of God. On the cross, Jesus died in our place as payment. Therefore, Jesus opened a new and living way to enter the holy sanctuary of God.

3Nathan replied to the king, "Whatever you have in mind, go ahead and do it,
for the LORD is with you."
4But that night the word of the LORD came to Nathan, saying:

5"Go and tell my servant David, 'This is what the LORD says: Are you the
one to build me a house to dwell in? 6I have not dwelt in a house from the
day I brought the Israelites up out of Egypt to this day. I have been moving
from place to place with a tent as my dwelling. 7Wherever I have moved
with all the Israelites, did I ever say to any of their rulers whom I commanded to shepherd my people Israel, "Why have you not built me a house
of cedar?"'

8"Now then, tell my servant David, 'This is what the LORD Almighty says:
I took you from the pasture, from tending the flock, and appointed you
ruler over my people Israel. 9I have been with you wherever you have gone,
and I have cut off all your enemies from before you. Now I will make your
name great, like the names of the greatest men on earth. 10And I will provide a place for my people Israel and will plant them so that they can have
a home of their own and no longer be disturbed. Wicked people will not
oppress them anymore, as they did at the beginning 11and have done ever
since the time I appointed leaders[a] over my people Israel. I will also give
you rest from all your enemies.

"'The LORD declares to you that the LORD himself will establish a
house for you: 12When your days are over and you rest with your ancestors, I will raise up your offspring to succeed you, your own flesh and
blood, and I will establish his kingdom. 13He is the one who will build a
house for my Name, and I will establish the throne of his kingdom forever. 14I will be his father, and he will be my son. When he does wrong, I
will punish him with a rod wielded by men, with floggings inflicted by
human hands. 15But my love will never be taken away from him, as I took
it away from Saul, whom I removed from before you. 16Your house and
your kingdom will endure forever before me[b]; your throne will be established forever.'"

17Nathan reported to David all the words of this entire revelation.

David's Prayer

18Then King David went in and sat before the LORD, and he said:

"Who am I, Sovereign LORD, and what is my family, that you have
brought me this far? 19And as if this were not enough in your sight, Sovereign LORD, you have also spoken about the future of the house of your
servant—and this decree, Sovereign LORD, is for a mere human![c]

20"What more can David say to you? For you know your servant, Sovereign LORD. 21For the sake of your word and according to your will, you have
done this great thing and made it known to your servant.

22"How great you are, Sovereign LORD! There is no one like you, and
there is no God but you, as we have heard with our own ears. 23And who
is like your people Israel—the one nation on earth that God went out to
redeem as a people for himself, and to make a name for himself, and to
perform great and awesome wonders by driving out nations and their gods
from before your people, whom you redeemed from Egypt?[d] 24You have established your people Israel as your very own forever, and you, LORD, have
become their God.

25"And now, LORD God, keep forever the promise you have made

[a] 11 Traditionally *judges* [b] 16 Some Hebrew manuscripts and Septuagint; most Hebrew manuscripts *you* [c] 19 Or *for the human race* [d] 23 See Septuagint and 1 Chron. 17:21; Hebrew *wonders for your land and before your people, whom you redeemed from Egypt, from the nations and their gods.*

2 SAMUEL 7:8

THE GOOD SHEPHERD

From David's childhood, he was tasked with watching over a flock, playing an important role in his family's source of income. He was to guard the livestock from predators and thieves alike. Taking David from his humble beginnings as a lowly shepherd, God gave him the responsibility to rule over his chosen nation. The skills David learned during his early years translated into his oversight of God's people as he led and protected them throughout his time as king.

Jesus, in turn, would prove to be the chosen shepherd of God's people. It is significant how often Jesus used this same imagery as he taught about his life and ministry when he called himself the good shepherd and his followers his sheep (Jn 10:11,14). Jesus saw himself as one designated to protect and lead the people of God and—as a faithful shepherd—give his own life for the sake of the sheep.

concerning your servant and his house. Do as you promised, [26]so that your name will be great forever. Then people will say, 'The LORD Almighty is God over Israel!' And the house of your servant David will be established in your sight.

[27]"LORD Almighty, God of Israel, you have revealed this to your servant, saying, 'I will build a house for you.' So your servant has found courage to pray this prayer to you. [28]Sovereign LORD, you are God! Your covenant is trustworthy, and you have promised these good things to your servant. [29]Now be pleased to bless the house of your servant, that it may continue forever in your sight; for you, Sovereign LORD, have spoken, and with your blessing the house of your servant will be blessed forever."

David's Victories

8 In the course of time, David defeated the Philistines and subdued them, and he took Metheg Ammah from the control of the Philistines.

[2]David also defeated the Moabites. He made them lie down on the ground and measured them off with a length of cord. Every two lengths of them were put to death, and the third length was allowed to live. So the Moabites became subject to David and brought him tribute.

[3]Moreover, David defeated Hadadezer son of Rehob, king of Zobah, when he went to restore his monument at[a] the Euphrates River. [4]David captured a thousand of his chariots, seven thousand charioteers[b] and twenty thousand foot soldiers. He hamstrung all but a hundred of the chariot horses.

[5]When the Arameans of Damascus came to help Hadadezer king of Zobah, David struck down twenty-two thousand of them. [6]He put garrisons in the Aramean kingdom of Damascus, and the Arameans became subject to him and brought tribute. The LORD gave David victory wherever he went.

[7]David took the gold shields that belonged to the officers of Hadadezer and brought them to Jerusalem. [8]From Tebah[c] and Berothai, towns that belonged to Hadadezer, King David took a great quantity of bronze.

[9]When Tou[d] king of Hamath heard that David had defeated the entire army of Hadadezer, [10]he sent his son Joram[e] to King David to greet him and congratulate him on his victory in battle over Hadadezer, who had been at war with Tou. Joram brought with him articles of silver, of gold and of bronze.

[11]King David dedicated these articles to the LORD, as he had done with the silver and gold from all the nations he had subdued: [12]Edom[f] and Moab, the Ammonites and the Philistines, and Amalek. He also dedicated the plunder taken from Hadadezer son of Rehob, king of Zobah.

[13]And David became famous after he returned from striking down eighteen thousand Edomites[g] in the Valley of Salt.

[14]He put garrisons throughout Edom, and all the Edomites became subject to David. The LORD gave David victory wherever he went.

David's Officials

[15]David reigned over all Israel, doing what was just and right for all his people. [16]Joab son of Zeruiah was over the army; Jehoshaphat son of Ahilud was recorder; [17]Zadok son of Ahitub and Ahimelek son of Abiathar were priests; Seraiah was secretary; [18]Benaiah son of Jehoiada was over the Kerethites and Pelethites; and David's sons were priests.[h]

---

[a] *3* Or *his control along* [b] *4* Septuagint (see also Dead Sea Scrolls and 1 Chron. 18:4); Masoretic Text *captured seventeen hundred of his charioteers* [c] *8* See some Septuagint manuscripts (see also 1 Chron. 18:8); Hebrew *Betah.* [d] *9* Hebrew *Toi,* a variant of *Tou;* also in verse 10 [e] *10* A variant of *Hadoram* [f] *12* Some Hebrew manuscripts, Septuagint and Syriac (see also 1 Chron. 18:11); most Hebrew manuscripts *Aram* [g] *13* A few Hebrew manuscripts, Septuagint and Syriac (see also 1 Chron. 18:12); most Hebrew manuscripts *Aram* (that is, Arameans) [h] *18* Or *were chief officials* (see Septuagint and Targum; see also 1 Chron. 18:17)

---

2 SAMUEL 8:15

THE KING: JUST AND RIGHT

David is described as doing what was "just" and "right," which are two of the primary attributes of the character of God (Ps 33:5; Jer 9:24) and virtues of people that pleased the Lord (Ps 106:3; Eze 18:5). By executing justice and doing righteousness, one could expect to continue in the covenant promises and blessings between God and his people. As king, David's godly leadership brought blessing upon the land and people. His administration enforced and fostered authentic worship, and he led military campaigns according to the word of the Lord. He kept records and commands with such competency that future generations could remember all the wonders that the Lord had done.

As great as David's reign was, a greater king would come. Isaiah 9:6–7 pointed to an expected king whose reign would be much greater than David's glorious rule. It drew upon David's kingship and pointed Israel toward the hope of a future ideal king who would rule as God himself, over all the earth and in righteousness and peace for all time. In this way, Isaiah applied 2 Samuel 8:15 to Jesus, the Son of God. The connection offered by Isaiah shows that Jesus is the Davidic King, the Messiah for whom all of Israel longed!

JESUS, THE PROMISED KING

David's life is one of great triumphs mixed with personal failures, reoccurring political and military uncertainty, and betrayal by his son, Absalom (2Sa 15:1 – 37). All of these aspects of his life were events and developments within the larger narrative of God's grace. The Lord established David's kingdom, using him to band together God's people to form the strongest military power in the Middle East at that time. It was through David that God settled his people as a nation among the Middle Eastern nations, spreading the Israelites' territory from Egypt to the Euphrates River. Eventually God gave David rest from his military conquests (2Sa 7:1), affording the war-hardened king the opportunity to look to the future. David's desire was to build a temple for the Lord, yet this was not God's plan (vv. 2 – 7).

Rather than implementing David's good intentions, God made it clear to Nathan that his desire was much larger. He had positioned his people, through David's leadership, to be established forever. God's vision was to establish and fulfill promises that he had made to his people as they came out of Egypt through a covenant with David's heirs (vv. 8 – 17). David's son, Solomon, would solidify the Jewish nation forever, as well as build a house for God's Name (v. 13).

David's prayer in verses 18 – 29 concludes by showing his response to the Lord. David expressed his humble response to God's promises to David — which ultimately unfolded fully in the New Testament through the birth, life, death and resurrection of Jesus. These promises revealed God's larger acts of redemption as recounted by David (vv. 22 – 24). It was here that David realized his significant contribution to the Lord's grander scheme. God had used David's life and work as a piece of a much larger puzzle which is revealed over the course of the entirety of Scripture: God's story of redemption.

God enabled David to see his glorious plan to establish a kingdom for himself that, through David's heirs, would be unending. Those promises were fulfilled initially during Jesus' earthly ministry and established finally when Jesus was crucified and defeated death (Lk 2:4; 20:41; Rev 3:7; 5:5; 22:16). Jesus was called the Son of the Most High, given the throne of his forefather David and promised a kingdom with no end (Lk 1:32 – 33). Clearly, Jesus was the One through whom God finalized his covenant promises to David. Whereas other heirs of David sinned, failed and eventually died, Jesus proved to be the ultimate Heir — living a perfect life and defeating sin and death.

David and Mephibosheth

9 David asked, "Is there anyone still left of the house of Saul to whom I can
show kindness for Jonathan's sake?"
2Now there was a servant of Saul's household named Ziba. They summoned
him to appear before David, and the king said to him, "Are you Ziba?"
"At your service," he replied.
3The king asked, "Is there no one still alive from the house of Saul to whom I
can show God's kindness?"
Ziba answered the king, "There is still a son of Jonathan; he is lame in both
feet."
4"Where is he?" the king asked.
Ziba answered, "He is at the house of Makir son of Ammiel in Lo Debar."
5So King David had him brought from Lo Debar, from the house of Makir son
of Ammiel.
6When Mephibosheth son of Jonathan, the son of Saul, came to David, he
bowed down to pay him honor.
David said, "Mephibosheth!"
"At your service," he replied.
7"Don't be afraid," David said to him, "for I will surely show you kindness for
the sake of your father Jonathan. I will restore to you all the land that belonged
to your grandfather Saul, and you will always eat at my table."
8Mephibosheth bowed down and said, "What is your servant, that you should
notice a dead dog like me?"
9Then the king summoned Ziba, Saul's steward, and said to him, "I have given
your master's grandson everything that belonged to Saul and his family. 10You
and your sons and your servants are to farm the land for him and bring in the
crops, so that your master's grandson may be provided for. And Mephibosheth,
grandson of your master, will always eat at my table." (Now Ziba had fifteen sons
and twenty servants.)
11Then Ziba said to the king, "Your servant will do whatever my lord the king
commands his servant to do." So Mephibosheth ate at David's[a] table like one of
the king's sons.
12Mephibosheth had a young son named Mika, and all the members of Ziba's
household were servants of Mephibosheth. 13And Mephibosheth lived in Jerusalem, because he always ate at the king's table; he was lame in both feet.

David Defeats the Ammonites

10 In the course of time, the king of the Ammonites died, and his son Hanun
succeeded him as king. 2David thought, "I will show kindness to Hanun
son of Nahash, just as his father showed kindness to me." So David sent a delegation to express his sympathy to Hanun concerning his father.
When David's men came to the land of the Ammonites, 3the Ammonite commanders said to Hanun their lord, "Do you think David is honoring your father
by sending envoys to you to express sympathy? Hasn't David sent them to you
only to explore the city and spy it out and overthrow it?" 4So Hanun seized David's envoys, shaved off half of each man's beard, cut off their garments at the
buttocks, and sent them away.
5When David was told about this, he sent messengers to meet the men, for
they were greatly humiliated. The king said, "Stay at Jericho till your beards have
grown, and then come back."
6When the Ammonites realized that they had become obnoxious to David,
they hired twenty thousand Aramean foot soldiers from Beth Rehob and Zobah,
as well as the king of Maakah with a thousand men, and also twelve thousand
men from Tob.
7On hearing this, David sent Joab out with the entire army of fighting men.

[a] 11 Septuagint; Hebrew *my*

---

2 SAMUEL 9:7 – 11

UNMERITED MERCY

Mephibosheth had a justified reason to fear King David. Typically when founding a new dynasty, kings in the Middle East killed all surviving heirs of a deposed monarch to keep them from trying to regain power. David's response to Mephibosheth is a picture of God's work in Christ: no longer considering people his enemies, but considering them his friends and "children of God." For example, the apostle Paul wrote, "You see, at just the right time, when we were still powerless, Christ died for the ungodly. Very rarely will anyone die for a righteous person, though for a good person someone might possibly dare to die. But God demonstrates his own love for us in this: While we were still sinners, Christ died for us" (Ro 5:6 – 8). Whereas those without Christ were once children of darkness — deserving the displeasure of the King of light — they have now received unmerited mercy from God through Jesus' sacrifice (Eph 5:8). Like David, God chose to not vanquish humanity, as was deserved for being children of his great enemy, but rather gave mercy and favor to people, making them his very own children. Like Mephibosheth, people who are followers of Jesus have no reason to fear because God has adopted them into his forever family.

2 SAMUEL 10:1 – 4

REJECTING A GRACIOUS OFFER

After David had established Israel's supremacy in the region, he was

(continued on next page)

8The Ammonites came out and drew up in battle formation at the entrance of their city gate, while the Arameans of Zobah and Rehob and the men of Tob and Maakah were by themselves in the open country.

9Joab saw that there were battle lines in front of him and behind him; so he selected some of the best troops in Israel and deployed them against the Arameans. 10He put the rest of the men under the command of Abishai his brother and deployed them against the Ammonites. 11Joab said, "If the Arameans are too strong for me, then you are to come to my rescue; but if the Ammonites are too strong for you, then I will come to rescue you. 12Be strong, and let us fight bravely for our people and the cities of our God. The LORD will do what is good in his sight."

13Then Joab and the troops with him advanced to fight the Arameans, and they fled before him. 14When the Ammonites realized that the Arameans were fleeing, they fled before Abishai and went inside the city. So Joab returned from fighting the Ammonites and came to Jerusalem.

15After the Arameans saw that they had been routed by Israel, they regrouped. 16Hadadezer had Arameans brought from beyond the Euphrates River; they went to Helam, with Shobak the commander of Hadadezer's army leading them.

17When David was told of this, he gathered all Israel, crossed the Jordan and went to Helam. The Arameans formed their battle lines to meet David and fought against him. 18But they fled before Israel, and David killed seven hundred of their charioteers and forty thousand of their foot soldiers.[a] He also struck down Shobak the commander of their army, and he died there. 19When all the kings who were vassals of Hadadezer saw that they had been routed by Israel, they made peace with the Israelites and became subject to them.

So the Arameans were afraid to help the Ammonites anymore.

David and Bathsheba

11 In the spring, at the time when kings go off to war, David sent Joab out with the king's men and the whole Israelite army. They destroyed the Ammonites and besieged Rabbah. But David remained in Jerusalem.

2One evening David got up from his bed and walked around on the roof of the palace. From the roof he saw a woman bathing. The woman was very beautiful, 3and David sent someone to find out about her. The man said, "She is Bathsheba, the daughter of Eliam and the wife of Uriah the Hittite." 4Then David sent messengers to get her. She came to him, and he slept with her. (Now she was purifying herself from her monthly uncleanness.) Then she went back home. 5The woman conceived and sent word to David, saying, "I am pregnant."

6So David sent this word to Joab: "Send me Uriah the Hittite." And Joab sent him to David. 7When Uriah came to him, David asked him how Joab was, how the soldiers were and how the war was going. 8Then David said to Uriah, "Go down to your house and wash your feet." So Uriah left the palace, and a gift from the king was sent after him. 9But Uriah slept at the entrance to the palace with all his master's servants and did not go down to his house.

10David was told, "Uriah did not go home." So he asked Uriah, "Haven't you just come from a military campaign? Why didn't you go home?"

11Uriah said to David, "The ark and Israel and Judah are staying in tents,[b] and my commander Joab and my lord's men are camped in the open country. How could I go to my house to eat and drink and make love to my wife? As surely as you live, I will not do such a thing!"

12Then David said to him, "Stay here one more day, and tomorrow I will send you back." So Uriah remained in Jerusalem that day and the next. 13At David's invitation, he ate and drank with him, and David made him drunk. But in the evening Uriah went out to sleep on his mat among his master's servants; he did not go home.

[a] 18 Some Septuagint manuscripts (see also 1 Chron. 19:18); Hebrew *horsemen*

[b] 11 Or *staying at Sukkoth*

(Rejecting a Gracious Offer, continued)

determined to demonstrate covenant faithfulness, or "kindness," to one inside the covenant nation (Mephibosheth; 2Sa 9:7) and to one outside the covenantal people of God (Hanun; 2Sa 10:2). David was a king willing to put self-interest at risk in order to uphold justice and righteousness with friend and rival alike. He sent a delegation to the new Ammonite king, Hanun, in order to offer condolences on the death of his father. Rather than receive the men graciously, Hanun shaved off half their beards and cut off their garments to utterly humiliate David's messengers.

In response to humanity's propensity to repeat the patterns established by Hanun and the Israelites, God sent his only Son in order to save the people. He came preaching, performing miracles and signs, and proclaiming the good news that God's kingdom had come. How did Israel receive Jesus? The Jewish leaders responded by advocating the beating, stripping and crucifying of him on the cross.

14In the morning David wrote a letter to Joab and sent it with Uriah. 15In it he wrote, "Put Uriah out in front where the fighting is fiercest. Then withdraw from him so he will be struck down and die."

16So while Joab had the city under siege, he put Uriah at a place where he knew the strongest defenders were. 17When the men of the city came out and fought against Joab, some of the men in David's army fell; moreover, Uriah the Hittite died.

18Joab sent David a full account of the battle. 19He instructed the messenger: "When you have finished giving the king this account of the battle, 20the king's anger may flare up, and he may ask you, 'Why did you get so close to the city to fight? Didn't you know they would shoot arrows from the wall? 21Who killed Abimelek son of Jerub-Besheth[a]? Didn't a woman drop an upper millstone on him from the wall, so that he died in Thebez? Why did you get so close to the wall?' If he asks you this, then say to him, 'Moreover, your servant Uriah the Hittite is dead.'"

22The messenger set out, and when he arrived he told David everything Joab had sent him to say. 23The messenger said to David, "The men overpowered us and came out against us in the open, but we drove them back to the entrance of the city gate. 24Then the archers shot arrows at your servants from the wall, and some of the king's men died. Moreover, your servant Uriah the Hittite is dead."

25David told the messenger, "Say this to Joab: 'Don't let this upset you; the sword devours one as well as another. Press the attack against the city and destroy it.' Say this to encourage Joab."

26When Uriah's wife heard that her husband was dead, she mourned for him. 27After the time of mourning was over, David had her brought to his house, and she became his wife and bore him a son. But the thing David had done displeased the LORD.

Nathan Rebukes David

12 The LORD sent Nathan to David. When he came to him, he said, "There were two men in a certain town, one rich and the other poor. 2The rich man had a very large number of sheep and cattle, 3but the poor man had nothing except one little ewe lamb he had bought. He raised it, and it grew up with him and his children. It shared his food, drank from his cup and even slept in his arms. It was like a daughter to him.

4"Now a traveler came to the rich man, but the rich man refrained from taking one of his own sheep or cattle to prepare a meal for the traveler who had come to him. Instead, he took the ewe lamb that belonged to the poor man and prepared it for the one who had come to him."

5David burned with anger against the man and said to Nathan, "As surely as the LORD lives, the man who did this must die! 6He must pay for that lamb four times over, because he did such a thing and had no pity."

7Then Nathan said to David, "You are the man! This is what the LORD, the God of Israel, says: 'I anointed you king over Israel, and I delivered you from the hand of Saul. 8I gave your master's house to you, and your master's wives into your arms. I gave you all Israel and Judah. And if all this had been too little, I would have given you even more. 9Why did you despise the word of the LORD by doing what is evil in his eyes? You struck down Uriah the Hittite with the sword and took his wife to be your own. You killed him with the sword of the Ammonites. 10Now, therefore, the sword will never depart from your house, because you despised me and took the wife of Uriah the Hittite to be your own.'

11"This is what the LORD says: 'Out of your own household I am going to bring calamity on you. Before your very eyes I will take your wives and give them to one who is close to you, and he will sleep with your wives in broad daylight. 12You did it in secret, but I will do this thing in broad daylight before all Israel.'"

---

[a] *21* Also known as *Jerub-Baal* (that is, Gideon)

BETRAYAL LEADING TO DEATH

Decisions matter. David's sin with Bathsheba was preceded by a decision he made to stay at home versus going off to war with his men. This choice afforded him the circumstances to take what was not his, having sex with a woman whose husband was off at war. Committing adultery with Bathsheba clearly violated God's standard for righteous sexuality in passages such as Genesis 2:22 – 24 and Exodus 20:14. Both of these decisions led to a truly terrible decision: David trying to hide his actions through the murder of an innocent man. Bathsheba's husband, Uriah, was one of David's "mighty warriors" and a purely innocent victim of David's horrible choices (2Sa 11:15). David betrayed Uriah, an act that led to the death of his faithful comrade.

In this account of David's betrayal of Uriah, there is a parallel to the life of Jesus. Like Uriah, Jesus was betrayed by a friend — Judas — and sent to his death because of Judas' actions. But, more importantly, this story of David's act reflects all of humankind's betrayal of Jesus. Through our personal sin, each person has contributed to the collective sin for which Jesus died. First Peter 2:22 – 24 demonstrates that Jesus, who was completely innocent of any wrongdoing, suffered a wrongful death: " 'He committed no sin, and no deceit was found in his mouth.' When they hurled their insults at him, he did not retaliate; when he suffered, he made no threats. Instead, he entrusted himself to him, who judges justly. 'He himself bore our sins' in his body on the cross, so that we might die to sins and live for righteousness; 'by his wounds you have been healed.' " Quoting Isaiah 53, Peter tells his readers that Jesus was betrayed and sentenced to death unjustly for the sake of taking away the sins of believers. In the same way that Uriah was an innocent party in David's deceptive schemes, Jesus was an innocent recipient of the penalty due for mankind's sins.

2 SAMUEL 12:15–23

HOPE OF THE RESURRECTION

The death of a child is a terribly tragic experience. Indeed, anytime a loved one or a close friend dies, deep anguish follows—as is the case here with the death of David's son. In the midst of sorrow associated with death, Christians have complete confidence to believe they will be reunited with a deceased loved one. The story of the death of David's son suggests that David believed he and his child would be reunited. David said, "I will go to him, but he will not return to me." Christian believers can hold to the same hope that Old Testament believers understood faintly—that death is inevitable, but God's people will have life after death. Jesus said: "I am the resurrection and the life. The one who believes in me will live, even though they die; and whoever lives by believing in me will never die" (Jn 11:25–26). Jesus' words were not empty but rather were validated through his own resurrection. Truly, Jesus has power over death—the greatest and most feared inevitability in the human experience—and has promised to apply that power to his followers (1Pe 1:3–7).

2 SAMUEL 13:1–15

THE CORROSIVE NATURE OF SIN

The story of Amnon and Tamar is the first in a trilogy of narratives (the other two relating to Absalom's murder of Amnon and Absalom's return from exile) that take the book

(continued on next page)

13Then David said to Nathan, "I have sinned against the LORD."
Nathan replied, "The LORD has taken away your sin. You are not going to die.
14But because by doing this you have shown utter contempt for[a] the LORD, the
son born to you will die."
15After Nathan had gone home, the LORD struck the child that Uriah's wife
had borne to David, and he became ill. 16David pleaded with God for the child.
He fasted and spent the nights lying in sackcloth[b] on the ground. 17The elders of
his household stood beside him to get him up from the ground, but he refused,
and he would not eat any food with them.
18On the seventh day the child died. David's attendants were afraid to tell him
that the child was dead, for they thought, "While the child was still living, he
wouldn't listen to us when we spoke to him. How can we now tell him the child
is dead? He may do something desperate."
19David noticed that his attendants were whispering among themselves, and
he realized the child was dead. "Is the child dead?" he asked.
"Yes," they replied, "he is dead."
20Then David got up from the ground. After he had washed, put on lotions and
changed his clothes, he went into the house of the LORD and worshiped. Then
he went to his own house, and at his request they served him food, and he ate.
21His attendants asked him, "Why are you acting this way? While the child
was alive, you fasted and wept, but now that the child is dead, you get up and
eat!"
22He answered, "While the child was still alive, I fasted and wept. I thought,
'Who knows? The LORD may be gracious to me and let the child live.' 23But now
that he is dead, why should I go on fasting? Can I bring him back again? I will go
to him, but he will not return to me."
24Then David comforted his wife Bathsheba, and he went to her and made
love to her. She gave birth to a son, and they named him Solomon. The LORD
loved him; 25and because the LORD loved him, he sent word through Nathan the
prophet to name him Jedidiah.[c]
26Meanwhile Joab fought against Rabbah of the Ammonites and captured
the royal citadel. 27Joab then sent messengers to David, saying, "I have fought
against Rabbah and taken its water supply. 28Now muster the rest of the troops
and besiege the city and capture it. Otherwise I will take the city, and it will be
named after me."
29So David mustered the entire army and went to Rabbah, and attacked and
captured it. 30David took the crown from their king's[d] head, and it was placed
on his own head. It weighed a talent[e] of gold, and it was set with precious stones.
David took a great quantity of plunder from the city 31and brought out the people who were there, consigning them to labor with saws and with iron picks and
axes, and he made them work at brickmaking.[f] David did this to all the Ammonite towns. Then he and his entire army returned to Jerusalem.

Amnon and Tamar

13 In the course of time, Amnon son of David fell in love with Tamar, the
beautiful sister of Absalom son of David.
2Amnon became so obsessed with his sister Tamar that he made himself ill.
She was a virgin, and it seemed impossible for him to do anything to her.
3Now Amnon had an adviser named Jonadab son of Shimeah, David's brother. Jonadab was a very shrewd man. 4He asked Amnon, "Why do you, the king's
son, look so haggard morning after morning? Won't you tell me?"
Amnon said to him, "I'm in love with Tamar, my brother Absalom's sister."
5"Go to bed and pretend to be ill," Jonadab said. "When your father comes to

[a] *14* An ancient Hebrew scribal tradition; Masoretic Text *for the enemies of* [b] *16* Dead Sea Scrolls and Septuagint; Masoretic Text does not have *in sackcloth.* [c] *25* *Jedidiah* means *loved by the LORD.* [d] *30* Or *from Milkom's* (that is, Molek's) [e] *30* That is, about 75 pounds or about 34 kilograms [f] *31* The meaning of the Hebrew for this clause is uncertain.

see you, say to him, 'I would like my sister Tamar to come and give me something to eat. Let her prepare the food in my sight so I may watch her and then eat it from her hand.'"

6So Amnon lay down and pretended to be ill. When the king came to see him, Amnon said to him, "I would like my sister Tamar to come and make some special bread in my sight, so I may eat from her hand."

7David sent word to Tamar at the palace: "Go to the house of your brother Amnon and prepare some food for him."
8So Tamar went to the house of her brother Amnon, who was lying down. She took some dough, kneaded it, made the bread in his sight and baked it.
9Then she took the pan and served him the bread, but he refused to eat.

"Send everyone out of here," Amnon said. So everyone left him.
10Then Amnon said to Tamar, "Bring the food here into my bedroom so I may eat from your hand." And Tamar took the bread she had prepared and brought it to her brother Amnon in his bedroom.
11But when she took it to him to eat, he grabbed her and said, "Come to bed with me, my sister."

12"No, my brother!" she said to him. "Don't force me! Such a thing should not be done in Israel! Don't do this wicked thing.
13What about me? Where could I get rid of my disgrace? And what about you? You would be like one of the wicked fools in Israel. Please speak to the king; he will not keep me from being married to you."
14But he refused to listen to her, and since he was stronger than she, he raped her.

15Then Amnon hated her with intense hatred. In fact, he hated her more than he had loved her. Amnon said to her, "Get up and get out!"

16"No!" she said to him. "Sending me away would be a greater wrong than what you have already done to me."

But he refused to listen to her.
17He called his personal servant and said, "Get this woman out of my sight and bolt the door after her."
18So his servant put her out and bolted the door after her. She was wearing an ornate[a] robe, for this was the kind of garment the virgin daughters of the king wore.
19Tamar put ashes on her head and tore the ornate robe she was wearing. She put her hands on her head and went away, weeping aloud as she went.

20Her brother Absalom said to her, "Has that Amnon, your brother, been with you? Be quiet for now, my sister; he is your brother. Don't take this thing to heart." And Tamar lived in her brother Absalom's house, a desolate woman.

21When King David heard all this, he was furious.
22And Absalom never said a word to Amnon, either good or bad; he hated Amnon because he had disgraced his sister Tamar.

Absalom Kills Amnon

23Two years later, when Absalom's sheepshearers were at Baal Hazor near the border of Ephraim, he invited all the king's sons to come there.
24Absalom went to the king and said, "Your servant has had shearers come. Will the king and his attendants please join me?"

25"No, my son," the king replied. "All of us should not go; we would only be a burden to you." Although Absalom urged him, he still refused to go but gave him his blessing.

26Then Absalom said, "If not, please let my brother Amnon come with us."

The king asked him, "Why should he go with you?"
27But Absalom urged him, so he sent with him Amnon and the rest of the king's sons.

28Absalom ordered his men, "Listen! When Amnon is in high spirits from drinking wine and I say to you, 'Strike Amnon down,' then kill him. Don't be afraid. Haven't I given you this order? Be strong and brave."
29So Absalom's men did to Amnon what Absalom had ordered. Then all the king's sons got up, mounted their mules and fled.

[a] *18* The meaning of the Hebrew for this word is uncertain; also in verse 19.

(The Corrosive Nature of Sin, continued)

of Samuel in a dark direction. They also correspond to David's adultery with Bathsheba and the murder of Uriah the Hittite. The nature of sin was on full display here, especially 2 Samuel 13:15, where the false promises of sin that fueled Amnon's lust led him toward destruction. "He hated her more than he had loved her." Here is a powerful description of the destructive nature of sin and the expected consequences when sin is brought into the light.

The question becomes how to overcome the power of sin that leads to death. "All have sinned and fall short of the glory of God, and all are justified freely by his grace through the redemption that came by Christ Jesus" (Ro 3:23). Sin is a human condition that is universal and terminal. But God provided Jesus, whose death accomplished the redemption of all who believe in him. Sin is corrosive, creating sorrow and bitterness that permeates all of life apart from the grace and redemption of God through Christ Jesus.

2 SAMUEL 14:1,23–33

LOVE AND JUSTICE

David's love for Absalom, his son, was admirable, but in his love, he set aside justice. Absalom had murdered his half brother Amnon, a sin that required consequences. David's actions, as the king of Israel tasked with protecting the people and ensuring that godliness permeated the land, thus fell far short of God's standards in the case of his son. By focusing on love at the expense of justice, David failed to deal adequately with either justice or love. The law made it clear that murder deserved death (Nu 35:31–34). Yet David allowed his love for his son to become paramount, causing him to overlook a clear biblical precedent in this case.

In contrast, God the Father loved his Son, Jesus, but allowed his wrath against sin to fall on Jesus to provide a way for people to come to God. The Trinitarian God—Father, Son and Holy Spirit—carried out the ultimate act of love in order to uphold justice and extend the love of forgiveness to all who believe. God would not, like David, simply overlook sin. Rather, he required the consequence of death for mankind's sin. This was a payment initiated by the Father, made by Jesus and applied by the Holy Spirit (Jn 14:16–17; Ro 3:21–26). Truly, God has offered love, while upholding justice, to his chosen children.

30 While they were on their way, the report came to David: "Absalom has
struck down all the king's sons; not one of them is left." 31 The king stood up, tore
his clothes and lay down on the ground; and all his attendants stood by with
their clothes torn.
32 But Jonadab son of Shimeah, David's brother, said, "My lord should not
think that they killed all the princes; only Amnon is dead. This has been Absalom's express intention ever since the day Amnon raped his sister Tamar. 33 My
lord the king should not be concerned about the report that all the king's sons
are dead. Only Amnon is dead."
34 Meanwhile, Absalom had fled.
Now the man standing watch looked up and saw many people on the road
west of him, coming down the side of the hill. The watchman went and told the
king, "I see men in the direction of Horonaim, on the side of the hill."[a]
35 Jonadab said to the king, "See, the king's sons have come; it has happened
just as your servant said."
36 As he finished speaking, the king's sons came in, wailing loudly. The king,
too, and all his attendants wept very bitterly.
37 Absalom fled and went to Talmai son of Ammihud, the king of Geshur. But
King David mourned many days for his son.
38 After Absalom fled and went to Geshur, he stayed there three years. 39 And
King David longed to go to Absalom, for he was consoled concerning Amnon's
death.

Absalom Returns to Jerusalem

14 Joab son of Zeruiah knew that the king's heart longed for Absalom. 2 So
Joab sent someone to Tekoa and had a wise woman brought from there. He
said to her, "Pretend you are in mourning. Dress in mourning clothes, and don't
use any cosmetic lotions. Act like a woman who has spent many days grieving
for the dead. 3 Then go to the king and speak these words to him." And Joab put
the words in her mouth.
4 When the woman from Tekoa went[b] to the king, she fell with her face to the
ground to pay him honor, and she said, "Help me, Your Majesty!"
5 The king asked her, "What is troubling you?"
She said, "I am a widow; my husband is dead. 6 I your servant had two sons.
They got into a fight with each other in the field, and no one was there to separate them. One struck the other and killed him. 7 Now the whole clan has risen up
against your servant; they say, 'Hand over the one who struck his brother down,
so that we may put him to death for the life of his brother whom he killed; then
we will get rid of the heir as well.' They would put out the only burning coal I have
left, leaving my husband neither name nor descendant on the face of the earth."
8 The king said to the woman, "Go home, and I will issue an order in your behalf."
9 But the woman from Tekoa said to him, "Let my lord the king pardon me and
my family, and let the king and his throne be without guilt."
10 The king replied, "If anyone says anything to you, bring them to me, and
they will not bother you again."
11 She said, "Then let the king invoke the LORD his God to prevent the avenger
of blood from adding to the destruction, so that my son will not be destroyed."
"As surely as the LORD lives," he said, "not one hair of your son's head will fall
to the ground."
12 Then the woman said, "Let your servant speak a word to my lord the king."
"Speak," he replied.
13 The woman said, "Why then have you devised a thing like this against the
people of God? When the king says this, does he not convict himself, for the king
has not brought back his banished son? 14 Like water spilled on the ground, which

[a] 34 Septuagint; Hebrew does not have this sentence. [b] 4 Many Hebrew manuscripts, Septuagint, Vulgate and Syriac; most Hebrew manuscripts *spoke*

cannot be recovered, so we must die. But that is not what God desires; rather,
he devises ways so that a banished person does not remain banished from him.
15"And now I have come to say this to my lord the king because the people
have made me afraid. Your servant thought, 'I will speak to the king; perhaps
he will grant his servant's request. 16Perhaps the king will agree to deliver his
servant from the hand of the man who is trying to cut off both me and my son
from God's inheritance.'

17"And now your servant says, 'May the word of my lord the king secure my
inheritance, for my lord the king is like an angel of God in discerning good and
evil. May the LORD your God be with you.' "

18Then the king said to the woman, "Don't keep from me the answer to what
I am going to ask you."

"Let my lord the king speak," the woman said.

19The king asked, "Isn't the hand of Joab with you in all this?"

The woman answered, "As surely as you live, my lord the king, no one can
turn to the right or to the left from anything my lord the king says. Yes, it was
your servant Joab who instructed me to do this and who put all these words into
the mouth of your servant. 20Your servant Joab did this to change the present situation. My lord has wisdom like that of an angel of God—he knows everything
that happens in the land."

21The king said to Joab, "Very well, I will do it. Go, bring back the young man
Absalom."

22Joab fell with his face to the ground to pay him honor, and he blessed the
king. Joab said, "Today your servant knows that he has found favor in your eyes,
my lord the king, because the king has granted his servant's request."

23Then Joab went to Geshur and brought Absalom back to Jerusalem. 24But
the king said, "He must go to his own house; he must not see my face." So Absalom went to his own house and did not see the face of the king.

25In all Israel there was not a man so highly praised for his handsome appearance as Absalom. From the top of his head to the sole of his foot there was
no blemish in him. 26Whenever he cut the hair of his head—he used to cut his
hair once a year because it became too heavy for him—he would weigh it, and
its weight was two hundred shekels[a] by the royal standard.

27Three sons and a daughter were born to Absalom. His daughter's name was
Tamar, and she became a beautiful woman.

28Absalom lived two years in Jerusalem without seeing the king's face. 29Then
Absalom sent for Joab in order to send him to the king, but Joab refused to come
to him. So he sent a second time, but he refused to come. 30Then he said to his
servants, "Look, Joab's field is next to mine, and he has barley there. Go and set
it on fire." So Absalom's servants set the field on fire.

31Then Joab did go to Absalom's house, and he said to him, "Why have your
servants set my field on fire?"

32Absalom said to Joab, "Look, I sent word to you and said, 'Come here so I can
send you to the king to ask, "Why have I come from Geshur? It would be better for
me if I were still there!" ' Now then, I want to see the king's face, and if I am guilty
of anything, let him put me to death."

33So Joab went to the king and told him this. Then the king summoned Absalom, and he came in and bowed down with his face to the ground before the
king. And the king kissed Absalom.

Absalom's Conspiracy

15 In the course of time, Absalom provided himself with a chariot and horses
and with fifty men to run ahead of him. 2He would get up early and stand
by the side of the road leading to the city gate. Whenever anyone came with a
complaint to be placed before the king for a decision, Absalom would call out

[a] 26 That is, about 5 pounds or about 2.3 kilograms

to him, "What town are you from?" He would answer, "Your servant is from one
of the tribes of Israel." 3Then Absalom would say to him, "Look, your claims are
valid and proper, but there is no representative of the king to hear you." 4And
Absalom would add, "If only I were appointed judge in the land! Then everyone
who has a complaint or case could come to me and I would see that they receive
justice."

5Also, whenever anyone approached him to bow down before him, Absalom
would reach out his hand, take hold of him and kiss him. 6Absalom behaved in
this way toward all the Israelites who came to the king asking for justice, and so
he stole the hearts of the people of Israel.

7At the end of four[a] years, Absalom said to the king, "Let me go to Hebron
and fulfill a vow I made to the LORD. 8While your servant was living at Geshur in
Aram, I made this vow: 'If the LORD takes me back to Jerusalem, I will worship
the LORD in Hebron.[b]'"

9The king said to him, "Go in peace." So he went to Hebron.

10Then Absalom sent secret messengers throughout the tribes of Israel to say,
"As soon as you hear the sound of the trumpets, then say, 'Absalom is king in Hebron.'" 11Two hundred men from Jerusalem had accompanied Absalom. They
had been invited as guests and went quite innocently, knowing nothing about
the matter. 12While Absalom was offering sacrifices, he also sent for Ahithophel
the Gilonite, David's counselor, to come from Giloh, his hometown. And so the
conspiracy gained strength, and Absalom's following kept on increasing.

David Flees

13A messenger came and told David, "The hearts of the people of Israel are
with Absalom."

14Then David said to all his officials who were with him in Jerusalem, "Come!
We must flee, or none of us will escape from Absalom. We must leave immediately, or he will move quickly to overtake us and bring ruin on us and put the
city to the sword."

15The king's officials answered him, "Your servants are ready to do whatever
our lord the king chooses."

16The king set out, with his entire household following him; but he left ten
concubines to take care of the palace. 17So the king set out, with all the people
following him, and they halted at the edge of the city. 18All his men marched past
him, along with all the Kerethites and Pelethites; and all the six hundred Gittites
who had accompanied him from Gath marched before the king.

19The king said to Ittai the Gittite, "Why should you come along with us? Go
back and stay with King Absalom. You are a foreigner, an exile from your homeland. 20You came only yesterday. And today shall I make you wander about with
us, when I do not know where I am going? Go back, and take your people with
you. May the LORD show you kindness and faithfulness."[c]

21But Ittai replied to the king, "As surely as the LORD lives, and as my lord the
king lives, wherever my lord the king may be, whether it means life or death,
there will your servant be."

22David said to Ittai, "Go ahead, march on." So Ittai the Gittite marched on
with all his men and the families that were with him.

23The whole countryside wept aloud as all the people passed by. The king also
crossed the Kidron Valley, and all the people moved on toward the wilderness.

24Zadok was there, too, and all the Levites who were with him were carrying
the ark of the covenant of God. They set down the ark of God, and Abiathar offered sacrifices until all the people had finished leaving the city.

25Then the king said to Zadok, "Take the ark of God back into the city. If I find

---

[a] *7* Some Septuagint manuscripts, Syriac and Josephus; Hebrew *forty* [b] *8* Some Septuagint manuscripts; Hebrew does not have *in Hebron.* [c] *20* Septuagint; Hebrew *May kindness and faithfulness be with you*

favor in the LORD's eyes, he will bring me back and let me see it and his dwelling
place again. 26But if he says, 'I am not pleased with you,' then I am ready; let him
do to me whatever seems good to him."
27The king also said to Zadok the priest, "Do you understand? Go back to the
city with my blessing. Take your son Ahimaaz with you, and also Abiathar's son
Jonathan. You and Abiathar return with your two sons. 28I will wait at the fords
in the wilderness until word comes from you to inform me." 29So Zadok and Abiathar took the ark of God back to Jerusalem and stayed there.
30But David continued up the Mount of Olives, weeping as he went; his head
was covered and he was barefoot. All the people with him covered their heads
too and were weeping as they went up. 31Now David had been told, "Ahithophel
is among the conspirators with Absalom." So David prayed, "LORD, turn Ahithophel's counsel into foolishness."
32When David arrived at the summit, where people used to worship God, Hushai the Arkite was there to meet him, his robe torn and dust on his head. 33David
said to him, "If you go with me, you will be a burden to me. 34But if you return
to the city and say to Absalom, 'Your Majesty, I will be your servant; I was your
father's servant in the past, but now I will be your servant,' then you can help
me by frustrating Ahithophel's advice. 35Won't the priests Zadok and Abiathar
be there with you? Tell them anything you hear in the king's palace. 36Their two
sons, Ahimaaz son of Zadok and Jonathan son of Abiathar, are there with them.
Send them to me with anything you hear."
37So Hushai, David's confidant, arrived at Jerusalem as Absalom was entering the city.

David and Ziba

16 When David had gone a short distance beyond the summit, there was
Ziba, the steward of Mephibosheth, waiting to meet him. He had a string
of donkeys saddled and loaded with two hundred loaves of bread, a hundred
cakes of raisins, a hundred cakes of figs and a skin of wine.
2The king asked Ziba, "Why have you brought these?"
Ziba answered, "The donkeys are for the king's household to ride on, the
bread and fruit are for the men to eat, and the wine is to refresh those who become exhausted in the wilderness."
3The king then asked, "Where is your master's grandson?"
Ziba said to him, "He is staying in Jerusalem, because he thinks, 'Today the
Israelites will restore to me my grandfather's kingdom.'"
4Then the king said to Ziba, "All that belonged to Mephibosheth is now yours."
"I humbly bow," Ziba said. "May I find favor in your eyes, my lord the king."

Shimei Curses David

5As King David approached Bahurim, a man from the same clan as Saul's
family came out from there. His name was Shimei son of Gera, and he cursed as
he came out. 6He pelted David and all the king's officials with stones, though all
the troops and the special guard were on David's right and left. 7As he cursed,
Shimei said, "Get out, get out, you murderer, you scoundrel! 8The LORD has repaid you for all the blood you shed in the household of Saul, in whose place you
have reigned. The LORD has given the kingdom into the hands of your son Absalom. You have come to ruin because you are a murderer!"
9Then Abishai son of Zeruiah said to the king, "Why should this dead dog
curse my lord the king? Let me go over and cut off his head."
10But the king said, "What does this have to do with you, you sons of Zeruiah?
If he is cursing because the LORD said to him, 'Curse David,' who can ask, 'Why
do you do this?'"
11David then said to Abishai and all his officials, "My son, my own flesh and
blood, is trying to kill me. How much more, then, this Benjamite! Leave him
alone; let him curse, for the LORD has told him to. 12It may be that the LORD will

2 SAMUEL 15:30–32

THE MOUNT OF OLIVES

David and Jesus each had a unique connection with the Mount of Olives. When Absalom rose up as usurper of his father, David fled Jerusalem via the Mount of Olives. It was David's chosen path away from his son, perhaps so that he could worship God as he left the safety of his palace to an unknown future and the wilderness before him. Second Samuel 15:32 notes that the Mount of Olives was a well-known place of worship for the people of God. After celebrating the Passover feast with his disciples and instituting the Lord's Supper, Jesus and his disciples went out to the Mount of Olives (Mt 26:30). At a particular spot on the mountain—Gethsemane—Jesus prayed to the Father in a way that David would not. Unlike David, Jesus made it clear that he would not seek to escape the hand of his oppressor. Rather, he accepted the Father's will (Mt 26:39).

2 SAMUEL 16:5–14

GODLY RESPONSE TO FALSE ACCUSATION

With the threat of Absalom's coup budding, David fled Jerusalem for his life, encountering an enduring threat on his way out of town. During this vulnerable flight, David was assaulted by stones and curses from Shimei, who vocalized an undercurrent of thought in Israel—that David was reaping what he had sown by replacing the house of Saul. David

(continued on next page)

(Godly Response to False Accusation, continued)

did not express his own innocence, engage Shimei or ask God to interfere, but rather he waited on God's vindication.

Jesus reacted in a similar way: "When they hurled their insults at him, he did not retaliate; when he suffered, he made no threats. Instead, he entrusted himself to him who judges justly" (1Pe 2:23). Like David, Jesus did not retreat in the face of intimidation, but he trusted God in the midst of his trials. Jesus' example shows believers how they should respond to difficulties even when facing false accusations: "Consider him who endured such opposition from sinners, so that you will not grow weary and lose heart" (Heb 12:3). Believers can draw courage from Jesus' faithful and enduring example of glorifying God by trusting him to provide justification and vindication at the right time.

2 SAMUEL 16:15–22

THE CHAIN OF SIN'S CONSEQUENCES

Absalom's behavior fulfilled God's prophecy to David in 2 Samuel 12:11–12. David understood his exile, the acts of Absalom, and the curses heaped on him by Shimei as punishment from the Lord (2Sa 16:10–12). This passage illustrates the foundational principle of sin that humanity reaps what is sown and what is sown has long-term, unanticipated negative consequences. David believed he had fallen out of favor with the Lord and expected nothing other than a future of consequences for his sins. After all, he

(continued on next page)

look upon my misery and restore to me his covenant blessing instead of his curse
today."
13 So David and his men continued along the road while Shimei was going
along the hillside opposite him, cursing as he went and throwing stones at him
and showering him with dirt. 14 The king and all the people with him arrived at
their destination exhausted. And there he refreshed himself.

The Advice of Ahithophel and Hushai

15 Meanwhile, Absalom and all the men of Israel came to Jerusalem, and
Ahithophel was with him. 16 Then Hushai the Arkite, David's confidant, went to
Absalom and said to him, "Long live the king! Long live the king!"
17 Absalom said to Hushai, "So this is the love you show your friend? If he's
your friend, why didn't you go with him?"
18 Hushai said to Absalom, "No, the one chosen by the LORD, by these people,
and by all the men of Israel—his I will be, and I will remain with him. 19 Furthermore, whom should I serve? Should I not serve the son? Just as I served your
father, so I will serve you."
20 Absalom said to Ahithophel, "Give us your advice. What should we do?"
21 Ahithophel answered, "Sleep with your father's concubines whom he left
to take care of the palace. Then all Israel will hear that you have made yourself
obnoxious to your father, and the hands of everyone with you will be more res-
olute." 22 So they pitched a tent for Absalom on the roof, and he slept with his
father's concubines in the sight of all Israel.
23 Now in those days the advice Ahithophel gave was like that of one who in-
quires of God. That was how both David and Absalom regarded all of Ahithophel's advice.

17 Ahithophel said to Absalom, "I would[a] choose twelve thousand men and
set out tonight in pursuit of David. 2 I would attack him while he is weary
and weak. I would strike him with terror, and then all the people with him will
flee. I would strike down only the king 3 and bring all the people back to you.
The death of the man you seek will mean the return of all; all the people will be
unharmed." 4 This plan seemed good to Absalom and to all the elders of Israel.
5 But Absalom said, "Summon also Hushai the Arkite, so we can hear what
he has to say as well." 6 When Hushai came to him, Absalom said, "Ahithophel
has given this advice. Should we do what he says? If not, give us your opinion."
7 Hushai replied to Absalom, "The advice Ahithophel has given is not good
this time. 8 You know your father and his men; they are fighters, and as fierce as
a wild bear robbed of her cubs. Besides, your father is an experienced fighter;
he will not spend the night with the troops. 9 Even now, he is hidden in a cave
or some other place. If he should attack your troops first,[b] whoever hears about
it will say, 'There has been a slaughter among the troops who follow Absalom.'
10 Then even the bravest soldier, whose heart is like the heart of a lion, will melt
with fear, for all Israel knows that your father is a fighter and that those with
him are brave.
11 "So I advise you: Let all Israel, from Dan to Beersheba—as numerous as the
sand on the seashore—be gathered to you, with you yourself leading them into
battle. 12 Then we will attack him wherever he may be found, and we will fall on
him as dew settles on the ground. Neither he nor any of his men will be left alive.
13 If he withdraws into a city, then all Israel will bring ropes to that city, and we
will drag it down to the valley until not so much as a pebble is left."
14 Absalom and all the men of Israel said, "The advice of Hushai the Arkite is
better than that of Ahithophel." For the LORD had determined to frustrate the
good advice of Ahithophel in order to bring disaster on Absalom.
15 Hushai told Zadok and Abiathar, the priests, "Ahithophel has advised Absalom and the elders of Israel to do such and such, but I have advised them to do so

[a] 1 Or *Let me* [b] 9 Or *When some of the men fall at the first attack*

and so. 16 Now send a message at once and tell David, 'Do not spend the night at the fords in the wilderness; cross over without fail, or the king and all the people with him will be swallowed up.' "

17 Jonathan and Ahimaaz were staying at En Rogel. A female servant was to go and inform them, and they were to go and tell King David, for they could not risk being seen entering the city. 18 But a young man saw them and told Absalom. So the two of them left at once and went to the house of a man in Bahurim. He had a well in his courtyard, and they climbed down into it. 19 His wife took a covering and spread it out over the opening of the well and scattered grain over it. No one knew anything about it.

20 When Absalom's men came to the woman at the house, they asked, "Where are Ahimaaz and Jonathan?"

The woman answered them, "They crossed over the brook."[a] The men searched but found no one, so they returned to Jerusalem.

21 After they had gone, the two climbed out of the well and went to inform King David. They said to him, "Set out and cross the river at once; Ahithophel has advised such and such against you." 22 So David and all the people with him set out and crossed the Jordan. By daybreak, no one was left who had not crossed the Jordan.

23 When Ahithophel saw that his advice had not been followed, he saddled his donkey and set out for his house in his hometown. He put his house in order and then hanged himself. So he died and was buried in his father's tomb.

Absalom's Death

24 David went to Mahanaim, and Absalom crossed the Jordan with all the men of Israel. 25 Absalom had appointed Amasa over the army in place of Joab. Amasa was the son of Jether,[b] an Ishmaelite[c] who had married Abigail,[d] the daughter of Nahash and sister of Zeruiah the mother of Joab. 26 The Israelites and Absalom camped in the land of Gilead.

27 When David came to Mahanaim, Shobi son of Nahash from Rabbah of the Ammonites, and Makir son of Ammiel from Lo Debar, and Barzillai the Gileadite from Rogelim 28 brought bedding and bowls and articles of pottery. They also brought wheat and barley, flour and roasted grain, beans and lentils,[e] 29 honey and curds, sheep, and cheese from cows' milk for David and his people to eat. For they said, "The people have become exhausted and hungry and thirsty in the wilderness."

18 David mustered the men who were with him and appointed over them commanders of thousands and commanders of hundreds. 2 David sent out his troops, a third under the command of Joab, a third under Joab's brother Abishai son of Zeruiah, and a third under Ittai the Gittite. The king told the troops, "I myself will surely march out with you."

3 But the men said, "You must not go out; if we are forced to flee, they won't care about us. Even if half of us die, they won't care; but you are worth ten thousand of us.[f] It would be better now for you to give us support from the city."

4 The king answered, "I will do whatever seems best to you."

So the king stood beside the gate while all his men marched out in units of hundreds and of thousands. 5 The king commanded Joab, Abishai and Ittai, "Be gentle with the young man Absalom for my sake." And all the troops heard the king giving orders concerning Absalom to each of the commanders.

6 David's army marched out of the city to fight Israel, and the battle took place in the forest of Ephraim. 7 There Israel's troops were routed by David's men, and

---

[a] 20 Or *"They passed by the sheep pen toward the water."* [b] 25 Hebrew *Ithra*, a variant of *Jether* [c] 25 Some Septuagint manuscripts (see also 1 Chron. 2:17); Hebrew and other Septuagint manuscripts *Israelite* [d] 25 Hebrew *Abigal*, a variant of *Abigail* [e] 28 Most Septuagint manuscripts and Syriac; Hebrew *lentils, and roasted grain* [f] 3 Two Hebrew manuscripts, some Septuagint manuscripts and Vulgate; most Hebrew manuscripts *care; for now there are ten thousand like us*

(The Chain of Sin's Consequences, continued)

had seen his predecessor Saul suffer the same fate.

One should expect a growing chain of consequences for previous poor decisions and ungodly actions. Sin can spread over a lifetime, and even over generations, before we appreciate fully the "good news" of the gospel about Jesus' life, death and resurrection. While there are certainly consequences to sin, Jesus unconditionally loves all of humanity in spite of their offenses toward him. Unlike David, who had an insecure hope that God would restore favor on him, all people who follow Jesus have an assurance that God will never leave nor forsake his own (Heb 13:5 – 6). Even the seemingly worst of sins, such as Peter's denial of Jesus, do not warrant an insecure standing before God.

2 SAMUEL 17:1 – 14

VANQUISHING SIN'S CONSEQUENCES

As Absalom was plotting to attack and kill David, counterforces were already coming into place to block his progress. God used the "advice" of Hushai to give David and his men an advantage and an opportunity to prevail over Absalom's wicked schemes. Although Absalom thought he was in control of the situation, God was already working against him to fulfill his promises to David and to David's other descendants. In the same way, those who resist God and pursue sin are laying up trouble for themselves (Ro 2:4 – 9). This life is filled with events shaped by sinful human actions. For believers, Jesus has applied his grace to cover sin. Yet, Christians

(continued on next page)

the casualties that day were great — twenty thousand men. 8The battle spread out over the whole countryside, and the forest swallowed up more men that day than the sword.

9Now Absalom happened to meet David's men. He was riding his mule, and as the mule went under the thick branches of a large oak, Absalom's hair got caught in the tree. He was left hanging in midair, while the mule he was riding kept on going.

10When one of the men saw what had happened, he told Joab, "I just saw Absalom hanging in an oak tree."

11Joab said to the man who had told him this, "What! You saw him? Why didn't you strike him to the ground right there? Then I would have had to give you ten shekels[a] of silver and a warrior's belt."

12But the man replied, "Even if a thousand shekels[b] were weighed out into my hands, I would not lay a hand on the king's son. In our hearing the king commanded you and Abishai and Ittai, 'Protect the young man Absalom for my sake.'[c] 13And if I had put my life in jeopardy[d] — and nothing is hidden from the king — you would have kept your distance from me."

14Joab said, "I'm not going to wait like this for you." So he took three javelins in his hand and plunged them into Absalom's heart while Absalom was still alive in the oak tree. 15And ten of Joab's armor-bearers surrounded Absalom, struck him and killed him.

16Then Joab sounded the trumpet, and the troops stopped pursuing Israel, for Joab halted them. 17They took Absalom, threw him into a big pit in the forest and piled up a large heap of rocks over him. Meanwhile, all the Israelites fled to their homes.

18During his lifetime Absalom had taken a pillar and erected it in the King's Valley as a monument to himself, for he thought, "I have no son to carry on the memory of my name." He named the pillar after himself, and it is called Absalom's Monument to this day.

David Mourns

19Now Ahimaaz son of Zadok said, "Let me run and take the news to the king that the LORD has vindicated him by delivering him from the hand of his enemies."

20"You are not the one to take the news today," Joab told him. "You may take the news another time, but you must not do so today, because the king's son is dead."

21Then Joab said to a Cushite, "Go, tell the king what you have seen." The Cushite bowed down before Joab and ran off.

22Ahimaaz son of Zadok again said to Joab, "Come what may, please let me run behind the Cushite."

But Joab replied, "My son, why do you want to go? You don't have any news that will bring you a reward."

23He said, "Come what may, I want to run."

So Joab said, "Run!" Then Ahimaaz ran by way of the plain[e] and outran the Cushite.

24While David was sitting between the inner and outer gates, the watchman went up to the roof of the gateway by the wall. As he looked out, he saw a man running alone. 25The watchman called out to the king and reported it.

The king said, "If he is alone, he must have good news." And the runner came closer and closer.

26Then the watchman saw another runner, and he called down to the gatekeeper, "Look, another man running alone!"

The king said, "He must be bringing good news, too."

[a] *11* That is, about 4 ounces or about 115 grams [b] *12* That is, about 25 pounds or about 12 kilograms [c] *12* A few Hebrew manuscripts, Septuagint, Vulgate and Syriac; most Hebrew manuscripts may be translated *Absalom, whoever you may be.* [d] *13* Or *Otherwise, if I had acted treacherously toward him* [e] *23* That is, the plain of the Jordan

(Vanquishing Sin's Consequences, continued)

still experience the implications of the wrong actions of others. Part of the "good news" of the gospel is that eventually the world will see how God has conquered sin's effects in our world once and for all. One day, believers will experience the beautiful reality expressed in Revelation 21:4: " 'He will wipe every tear from their eyes. There will be no more death' or mourning or crying or pain, for the old order of things has passed away." Even now, God is at work to set things right, to work against evil and bring peace through Christ. And there is a much greater day in the future, one that is no longer marred by sin's consequences.

27The watchman said, "It seems to me that the first one runs like Ahimaaz
son of Zadok."
"He's a good man," the king said. "He comes with good news."
28Then Ahimaaz called out to the king, "All is well!" He bowed down before
the king with his face to the ground and said, "Praise be to the LORD your God!
He has delivered up those who lifted their hands against my lord the king."
29The king asked, "Is the young man Absalom safe?"
Ahimaaz answered, "I saw great confusion just as Joab was about to send the
king's servant and me, your servant, but I don't know what it was."
30The king said, "Stand aside and wait here." So he stepped aside and stood
there.
31Then the Cushite arrived and said, "My lord the king, hear the good news!
The LORD has vindicated you today by delivering you from the hand of all who
rose up against you."
32The king asked the Cushite, "Is the young man Absalom safe?"
The Cushite replied, "May the enemies of my lord the king and all who rise up
to harm you be like that young man."
33The king was shaken. He went up to the room over the gateway and wept. As
he went, he said: "O my son Absalom! My son, my son Absalom! If only I had died
instead of you — O Absalom, my son, my son!"[a]
19[b] Joab was told, "The king is weeping and mourning for Absalom." 2And for
the whole army the victory that day was turned into mourning, because
on that day the troops heard it said, "The king is grieving for his son." 3The men
stole into the city that day as men steal in who are ashamed when they flee from
battle. 4The king covered his face and cried aloud, "O my son Absalom! O Absalom, my son, my son!"
5Then Joab went into the house to the king and said, "Today you have humiliated all your men, who have just saved your life and the lives of your sons and
daughters and the lives of your wives and concubines. 6You love those who hate
you and hate those who love you. You have made it clear today that the commanders and their men mean nothing to you. I see that you would be pleased if
Absalom were alive today and all of us were dead. 7Now go out and encourage
your men. I swear by the LORD that if you don't go out, not a man will be left with
you by nightfall. This will be worse for you than all the calamities that have come
on you from your youth till now."
8So the king got up and took his seat in the gateway. When the men were told,
"The king is sitting in the gateway," they all came before him.
Meanwhile, the Israelites had fled to their homes.

David Returns to Jerusalem

9Throughout the tribes of Israel, all the people were arguing among themselves, saying, "The king delivered us from the hand of our enemies; he is the
one who rescued us from the hand of the Philistines. But now he has fled the
country to escape from Absalom; 10and Absalom, whom we anointed to rule over
us, has died in battle. So why do you say nothing about bringing the king back?"
11King David sent this message to Zadok and Abiathar, the priests: "Ask the
elders of Judah, 'Why should you be the last to bring the king back to his palace,
since what is being said throughout Israel has reached the king at his quarters?
12You are my relatives, my own flesh and blood. So why should you be the last to
bring back the king?' 13And say to Amasa, 'Are you not my own flesh and blood?
May God deal with me, be it ever so severely, if you are not the commander of my
army for life in place of Joab.' "
14He won over the hearts of the men of Judah so that they were all of one mind.
They sent word to the king, "Return, you and all your men." 15Then the king returned and went as far as the Jordan.

---

[a] *33* In Hebrew texts this verse (18:33) is numbered 19:1. [b] In Hebrew texts 19:1-43 is numbered 19:2-44.

A BROKEN HEART

In spite of Absalom's treachery, David grieved at the death of his son. Absalom's conspiracy, beginning in chapter 15, led to greater divisiveness and suffering among the nation. Not only did David suffer harm at the hands of these enemies, but also he continually wept because of the situation they found themselves in (15:30). It surely broke his heart to consider that his son Absalom had abandoned him. David also understood that this rebellion would lead to harm for those who remained loyal to him. In spite of these factors, David urged his men to be gentle with Absalom — not because he deserved it but because of David's deep love for him (18:5).

News of Absalom's death was overwhelming for King David. Upon hearing the news, David mourned for his loss and wept bitter tears (18:33). His heartfelt desire was that he would have died in Absalom's place.

Many years later, Jesus would also weep over the people whom he loved. Jesus, looking over the city of Jerusalem, repeated his longing for the people to turn to him (Mt 23:37; Lk 19:41 – 44). His desire was to care for them as a hen does baby chicks, but the people chose to disregard his care and run into their own destruction. Jesus demonstrated his tender love for his enemies, which would be shown fully by his sacrificial death on their behalf (Ro 5:8).

The great apostle Paul also modeled this heart of compassion for enemies of God. Writing to the church in Rome, Paul made a bold claim. He said that he wished that he were cut off from the mercy of God if that meant that God's people would understand and respond to the grace offered through Christ (Ro 9:3).

God's people, moved by love for those who do not know Jesus, should long for them to be reconciled to God. This longing should produce a broken heart, passionate prayer and bold witness.

Now the men of Judah had come to Gilgal to go out and meet the king and
bring him across the Jordan. 16Shimei son of Gera, the Benjamite from Bahurim, hurried down with the men of Judah to meet King David. 17With him were
a thousand Benjamites, along with Ziba, the steward of Saul's household, and
his fifteen sons and twenty servants. They rushed to the Jordan, where the king
was. 18They crossed at the ford to take the king's household over and to do whatever he wished.

When Shimei son of Gera crossed the Jordan, he fell prostrate before the king
19and said to him, "May my lord not hold me guilty. Do not remember how your
servant did wrong on the day my lord the king left Jerusalem. May the king put
it out of his mind. 20For I your servant know that I have sinned, but today I have
come here as the first from the tribes of Joseph to come down and meet my lord
the king."

21Then Abishai son of Zeruiah said, "Shouldn't Shimei be put to death for this?
He cursed the LORD's anointed."

22David replied, "What does this have to do with you, you sons of Zeruiah?
What right do you have to interfere? Should anyone be put to death in Israel to-
day? Don't I know that today I am king over Israel?" 23So the king said to Shimei,
"You shall not die." And the king promised him on oath.

24Mephibosheth, Saul's grandson, also went down to meet the king. He had
not taken care of his feet or trimmed his mustache or washed his clothes from
the day the king left until the day he returned safely. 25When he came from Jerusalem to meet the king, the king asked him, "Why didn't you go with me, Mephibosheth?"

26He said, "My lord the king, since I your servant am lame, I said, 'I will have
my donkey saddled and will ride on it, so I can go with the king.' But Ziba my
servant betrayed me. 27And he has slandered your servant to my lord the king.
My lord the king is like an angel of God; so do whatever you wish. 28All my grandfather's descendants deserved nothing but death from my lord the king, but you
gave your servant a place among those who eat at your table. So what right do I
have to make any more appeals to the king?"

29The king said to him, "Why say more? I order you and Ziba to divide the land."

30Mephibosheth said to the king, "Let him take everything, now that my lord
the king has returned home safely."

31Barzillai the Gileadite also came down from Rogelim to cross the Jordan
with the king and to send him on his way from there. 32Now Barzillai was very
old, eighty years of age. He had provided for the king during his stay in Mahanaim, for he was a very wealthy man. 33The king said to Barzillai, "Cross over with
me and stay with me in Jerusalem, and I will provide for you."

34But Barzillai answered the king, "How many more years will I live, that I
should go up to Jerusalem with the king? 35I am now eighty years old. Can I tell
the difference between what is enjoyable and what is not? Can your servant taste
what he eats and drinks? Can I still hear the voices of male and female singers?
Why should your servant be an added burden to my lord the king? 36Your servant
will cross over the Jordan with the king for a short distance, but why should the
king reward me in this way? 37Let your servant return, that I may die in my own
town near the tomb of my father and mother. But here is your servant Kimham.
Let him cross over with my lord the king. Do for him whatever you wish."

38The king said, "Kimham shall cross over with me, and I will do for him whatever you wish. And anything you desire from me I will do for you."

39So all the people crossed the Jordan, and then the king crossed over. The
king kissed Barzillai and bid him farewell, and Barzillai returned to his home.

40When the king crossed over to Gilgal, Kimham crossed with him. All the
troops of Judah and half the troops of Israel had taken the king over.

41Soon all the men of Israel were coming to the king and saying to him, "Why
did our brothers, the men of Judah, steal the king away and bring him and his
household across the Jordan, together with all his men?"

2 SAMUEL 20:1–2

UNFAITHFUL DESERTION AND UNCOMPROMISING LOYALTY

In the midst of difficult times, loyalty is at a premium. Those who are loyal to a leader, despite the current circumstances or potential outcomes, are worth their weight in gold. The majority of David's reign over the Hebrews required great loyalty from his followers. In the incident recorded here, the king interacts with men who have been disloyal and those who stayed faithful. The ones who remained faithful did so in spite of the overarching uncertainty of the situation. This incident very much resembles the experience of Jesus several centuries later. Not only did one of his inner circle betray him to the authorities (Mt 26:46–47), leading to his death, but all of his followers left him out of fear for their own lives (Mt 26:56). Jesus suffered the awful experience of a Roman crucifixion with none of his closest followers being willing to suffer with him. Denial and fear were the responses of his close disciples. Yet even they experienced forgiveness from the resurrected Jesus (Jn 21:17). Although we may prove disloyal to the Lord at times, he always proves faithful. Jesus is loyal without compromise.

[42]All the men of Judah answered the men of Israel, "We did this because the king is closely related to us. Why are you angry about it? Have we eaten any of the king's provisions? Have we taken anything for ourselves?"

[43]Then the men of Israel answered the men of Judah, "We have ten shares in the king; so we have a greater claim on David than you have. Why then do you treat us with contempt? Weren't we the first to speak of bringing back our king?"

But the men of Judah pressed their claims even more forcefully than the men of Israel.

Sheba Rebels Against David

20 Now a troublemaker named Sheba son of Bikri, a Benjamite, happened to be there. He sounded the trumpet and shouted,

"We have no share in David,
  no part in Jesse's son!
Every man to his tent, Israel!"

[2]So all the men of Israel deserted David to follow Sheba son of Bikri. But the men of Judah stayed by their king all the way from the Jordan to Jerusalem.

[3]When David returned to his palace in Jerusalem, he took the ten concubines he had left to take care of the palace and put them in a house under guard. He provided for them but had no sexual relations with them. They were kept in confinement till the day of their death, living as widows.

[4]Then the king said to Amasa, "Summon the men of Judah to come to me within three days, and be here yourself." [5]But when Amasa went to summon Judah, he took longer than the time the king had set for him.

[6]David said to Abishai, "Now Sheba son of Bikri will do us more harm than Absalom did. Take your master's men and pursue him, or he will find fortified cities and escape from us."[a] [7]So Joab's men and the Kerethites and Pelethites and all the mighty warriors went out under the command of Abishai. They marched out from Jerusalem to pursue Sheba son of Bikri.

[8]While they were at the great rock in Gibeon, Amasa came to meet them. Joab was wearing his military tunic, and strapped over it at his waist was a belt with a dagger in its sheath. As he stepped forward, it dropped out of its sheath.

[9]Joab said to Amasa, "How are you, my brother?" Then Joab took Amasa by the beard with his right hand to kiss him. [10]Amasa was not on his guard against the dagger in Joab's hand, and Joab plunged it into his belly, and his intestines spilled out on the ground. Without being stabbed again, Amasa died. Then Joab and his brother Abishai pursued Sheba son of Bikri.

[11]One of Joab's men stood beside Amasa and said, "Whoever favors Joab, and whoever is for David, let him follow Joab!" [12]Amasa lay wallowing in his blood in the middle of the road, and the man saw that all the troops came to a halt there. When he realized that everyone who came up to Amasa stopped, he dragged him from the road into a field and threw a garment over him. [13]After Amasa had been removed from the road, everyone went on with Joab to pursue Sheba son of Bikri.

[14]Sheba passed through all the tribes of Israel to Abel Beth Maakah and through the entire region of the Bikrites,[b] who gathered together and followed him. [15]All the troops with Joab came and besieged Sheba in Abel Beth Maakah. They built a siege ramp up to the city, and it stood against the outer fortifications. While they were battering the wall to bring it down, [16]a wise woman called from the city, "Listen! Listen! Tell Joab to come here so I can speak to him." [17]He went toward her, and she asked, "Are you Joab?"

"I am," he answered.

She said, "Listen to what your servant has to say."

"I'm listening," he said.

[a] 6 Or *and do us serious injury* [b] 14 See Septuagint and Vulgate; Hebrew *Berites.*

[18]She continued, "Long ago they used to say, 'Get your answer at Abel,' and
that settled it. [19]We are the peaceful and faithful in Israel. You are trying to destroy a city that is a mother in Israel. Why do you want to swallow up the LORD's
inheritance?"
[20]"Far be it from me!" Joab replied, "Far be it from me to swallow up or destroy!
[21]That is not the case. A man named Sheba son of Bikri, from the hill country of
Ephraim, has lifted up his hand against the king, against David. Hand over this
one man, and I'll withdraw from the city."

The woman said to Joab, "His head will be thrown to you from the wall."
[22]Then the woman went to all the people with her wise advice, and they cut off
the head of Sheba son of Bikri and threw it to Joab. So he sounded the trumpet,
and his men dispersed from the city, each returning to his home. And Joab went
back to the king in Jerusalem.

David's Officials

[23]Joab was over Israel's entire army; Benaiah son of Jehoiada was over the
Kerethites and Pelethites; [24]Adoniram[a] was in charge of forced labor; Jehoshaphat son of Ahilud was recorder; [25]Sheva was secretary; Zadok and Abiathar
were priests; [26]and Ira the Jairite[b] was David's priest.

The Gibeonites Avenged

21 During the reign of David, there was a famine for three successive years;
so David sought the face of the LORD. The LORD said, "It is on account of
Saul and his blood-stained house; it is because he put the Gibeonites to death."
[2]The king summoned the Gibeonites and spoke to them. (Now the Gibeonites
were not a part of Israel but were survivors of the Amorites; the Israelites had
sworn to spare them, but Saul in his zeal for Israel and Judah had tried to annihilate them.) [3]David asked the Gibeonites, "What shall I do for you? How shall I
make atonement so that you will bless the LORD's inheritance?"
[4]The Gibeonites answered him, "We have no right to demand silver or gold
from Saul or his family, nor do we have the right to put anyone in Israel to death."

"What do you want me to do for you?" David asked.
[5]They answered the king, "As for the man who destroyed us and plotted
against us so that we have been decimated and have no place anywhere in Israel, [6]let seven of his male descendants be given to us to be killed and their bodies
exposed before the LORD at Gibeah of Saul — the LORD's chosen one."

So the king said, "I will give them to you."
[7]The king spared Mephibosheth son of Jonathan, the son of Saul, because
of the oath before the LORD between David and Jonathan son of Saul. [8]But the
king took Armoni and Mephibosheth, the two sons of Aiah's daughter Rizpah,
whom she had borne to Saul, together with the five sons of Saul's daughter Merab,[c] whom she had borne to Adriel son of Barzillai the Meholathite. [9]He handed
them over to the Gibeonites, who killed them and exposed their bodies on a hill
before the LORD. All seven of them fell together; they were put to death during
the first days of the harvest, just as the barley harvest was beginning.
[10]Rizpah daughter of Aiah took sackcloth and spread it out for herself on a
rock. From the beginning of the harvest till the rain poured down from the heavens on the bodies, she did not let the birds touch them by day or the wild animals
by night. [11]When David was told what Aiah's daughter Rizpah, Saul's concubine,
had done, [12]he went and took the bones of Saul and his son Jonathan from the
citizens of Jabesh Gilead. (They had stolen their bodies from the public square at
Beth Shan, where the Philistines had hung them after they struck Saul down on

[a] 24 Some Septuagint manuscripts (see also 1 Kings 4:6 and 5:14); Hebrew *Adoram*
[b] 26 Hebrew; some Septuagint manuscripts and Syriac (see also 23:38) *Ithrite*
[c] 8 Two Hebrew manuscripts, some Septuagint manuscripts and Syriac (see also 1 Samuel 18:19); most Hebrew and Septuagint manuscripts *Michal*

2 SAMUEL 21:1 – 14

ATONEMENT: DEATH IS REQUIRED

Often times the life of a follower of Jesus demands something radical. God's standard for his people is perfection (Mt 5:48). He requires absolute surrender. However, no one is able to live up to that standard, which is what makes God's restorative work throughout Scripture such a miracle. When God restores people to a right relationship with himself, he removes the barrier that sin creates between himself and humanity. This is a radical thought!

God's standard — perfection — is not just overwhelming; it is impossible. In this passage, the Gibeonites asked for an outrageous payment from David to atone for Saul's sins against them. But in the New Testament, Jesus becomes the once and for all payment for the sin of humanity. No longer would individual sin require individual and unique sacrifices, but Jesus covers all sin — past, present and future. There is nothing more radical than a perfect man, dying once and for all for humanity's indiscretions and failures.

Gilboa.) 13 David brought the bones of Saul and his son Jonathan from there, and
the bones of those who had been killed and exposed were gathered up.
14 They buried the bones of Saul and his son Jonathan in the tomb of Saul's father Kish, at Zela in Benjamin, and did everything the king commanded. After
that, God answered prayer in behalf of the land.

Wars Against the Philistines

15 Once again there was a battle between the Philistines and Israel. David
went down with his men to fight against the Philistines, and he became exhausted. 16 And Ishbi-Benob, one of the descendants of Rapha, whose bronze spear-
head weighed three hundred shekels[a] and who was armed with a new sword,
said he would kill David. 17 But Abishai son of Zeruiah came to David's rescue;
he struck the Philistine down and killed him. Then David's men swore to him,
saying, "Never again will you go out with us to battle, so that the lamp of Israel
will not be extinguished."
18 In the course of time, there was another battle with the Philistines, at Gob. At
that time Sibbekai the Hushathite killed Saph, one of the descendants of Rapha.
19 In another battle with the Philistines at Gob, Elhanan son of Jair[b] the Beth-
lehemite killed the brother of[c] Goliath the Gittite, who had a spear with a shaft
like a weaver's rod.
20 In still another battle, which took place at Gath, there was a huge man with
six fingers on each hand and six toes on each foot—twenty-four in all. He also
was descended from Rapha. 21 When he taunted Israel, Jonathan son of Shimeah,
David's brother, killed him.
22 These four were descendants of Rapha in Gath, and they fell at the hands of
David and his men.

David's Song of Praise

22 David sang to the LORD the words of this song when the LORD delivered
him from the hand of all his enemies and from the hand of Saul. 2 He said:

"The LORD is my rock, my fortress and my deliverer;
3 my God is my rock, in whom I take refuge,
my shield[d] and the horn[e] of my salvation.
He is my stronghold, my refuge and my savior—
from violent people you save me.

4 "I called to the LORD, who is worthy of praise,
and have been saved from my enemies.
5 The waves of death swirled about me;
the torrents of destruction overwhelmed me.
6 The cords of the grave coiled around me;
the snares of death confronted me.

7 "In my distress I called to the LORD;
I called out to my God.
From his temple he heard my voice;
my cry came to his ears.
8 The earth trembled and quaked,
the foundations of the heavens[f] shook;
they trembled because he was angry.
9 Smoke rose from his nostrils;
consuming fire came from his mouth,
burning coals blazed out of it.

---

[a] 16 That is, about 7 1/2 pounds or about 3.5 kilograms [b] 19 See 1 Chron. 20:5; Hebrew *Jaare-Oregim.* [c] 19 See 1 Chron. 20:5; Hebrew does not have *the brother of.* [d] 3 Or *sovereign* [e] 3 *Horn* here symbolizes strength. [f] 8 Hebrew; Vulgate and Syriac (see also Psalm 18:7) *mountains*

---

2 SAMUEL 22:1–51

HEAD OF NATIONS

According to verse 1 of this chapter, David wrote this song of praise as he reflected on how God had delivered him from his enemies. After years of hardship at the hands of various enemies—whether it was the unjust envy of Saul (1Sa 18:8–9) or the warring Philistines—David now experienced peace and authored this song, having seen the evidence that God was his rock, fortress and deliverer (2Sa 22:2). Although generated out of the personal deliverance experience of David, this song was included in the book of Psalms (Ps 18) because it has broader applications for those who experience God's love and protection. Also noteworthy are the parts of this song that speak of David as the "head of nations" (2Sa 22:44; Ps 18:43). In a limited sense, this applied to David in his day, but it would apply ultimately to Jesus as discussed in 2 Samuel 7. David closed his song of praise by highlighting God's faithfulness to him and his descendants forever. Clearly, God had faithfully honored his promise to David by preserving his place as the head of nations, a promise that David remembered and was applied to Jesus in Luke 1:32–33.

10 He parted the heavens and came down;
dark clouds were under his feet.
11 He mounted the cherubim and flew;
he soared[a] on the wings of the wind.
12 He made darkness his canopy around him —
the dark[b] rain clouds of the sky.
13 Out of the brightness of his presence
bolts of lightning blazed forth.
14 The LORD thundered from heaven;
the voice of the Most High resounded.
15 He shot his arrows and scattered the enemy,
with great bolts of lightning he routed them.
16 The valleys of the sea were exposed
and the foundations of the earth laid bare
at the rebuke of the LORD,
at the blast of breath from his nostrils.

17 "He reached down from on high and took hold of me;
he drew me out of deep waters.
18 He rescued me from my powerful enemy,
from my foes, who were too strong for me.
19 They confronted me in the day of my disaster,
but the LORD was my support.
20 He brought me out into a spacious place;
he rescued me because he delighted in me.

21 "The LORD has dealt with me according to my
righteousness;
according to the cleanness of my hands he has
rewarded me.
22 For I have kept the ways of the LORD;
I am not guilty of turning from my God.
23 All his laws are before me;
I have not turned away from his decrees.
24 I have been blameless before him
and have kept myself from sin.
25 The LORD has rewarded me according to my righteousness,
according to my cleanness[c] in his sight.

26 "To the faithful you show yourself faithful,
to the blameless you show yourself blameless,
27 to the pure you show yourself pure,
but to the devious you show yourself shrewd.
28 You save the humble,
but your eyes are on the haughty to bring them low.
29 You, LORD, are my lamp;
the LORD turns my darkness into light.
30 With your help I can advance against a troop[d];
with my God I can scale a wall.

31 "As for God, his way is perfect:
The LORD's word is flawless;
he shields all who take refuge in him.
32 For who is God besides the LORD?
And who is the Rock except our God?

[a] 11 Many Hebrew manuscripts (see also Psalm 18:10); most Hebrew manuscripts *appeared*
[b] 12 Septuagint (see also Psalm 18:11); Hebrew *massed* [c] 25 Hebrew; Septuagint and Vulgate (see also Psalm 18:24) *to the cleanness of my hands* [d] 30 Or *can run through a barricade*

33 It is God who arms me with strength[a]
and keeps my way secure.
34 He makes my feet like the feet of a deer;
he causes me to stand on the heights.
35 He trains my hands for battle;
my arms can bend a bow of bronze.
36 You make your saving help my shield;
your help has made[b] me great.
37 You provide a broad path for my feet,
so that my ankles do not give way.

38 "I pursued my enemies and crushed them;
I did not turn back till they were destroyed.
39 I crushed them completely, and they could not rise;
they fell beneath my feet.
40 You armed me with strength for battle;
you humbled my adversaries before me.
41 You made my enemies turn their backs in flight,
and I destroyed my foes.
42 They cried for help, but there was no one to save them —
to the LORD, but he did not answer.
43 I beat them as fine as the dust of the earth;
I pounded and trampled them like mud in the streets.

44 "You have delivered me from the attacks of the peoples;
you have preserved me as the head of nations.
People I did not know now serve me,
45 foreigners cower before me;
as soon as they hear of me, they obey me.
46 They all lose heart;
they come trembling[c] from their strongholds.

47 "The LORD lives! Praise be to my Rock!
Exalted be my God, the Rock, my Savior!
48 He is the God who avenges me,
who puts the nations under me,
49 who sets me free from my enemies.
You exalted me above my foes;
from a violent man you rescued me.
50 Therefore I will praise you, LORD, among the nations;
I will sing the praises of your name.

51 "He gives his king great victories;
he shows unfailing kindness to his anointed,
to David and his descendants forever."

David's Last Words

23 These are the last words of David:

"The inspired utterance of David son of Jesse,
the utterance of the man exalted by the Most High,
the man anointed by the God of Jacob,
the hero of Israel's songs:

2 "The Spirit of the LORD spoke through me;
his word was on my tongue.

---

[a] *33* Dead Sea Scrolls, some Septuagint manuscripts, Vulgate and Syriac (see also Psalm 18:32); Masoretic Text *who is my strong refuge* [b] *36* Dead Sea Scrolls; Masoretic Text *shield; / you stoop down to make* [c] *46* Some Septuagint manuscripts and Vulgate (see also Psalm 18:45); Masoretic Text *they arm themselves*

3 The God of Israel spoke,
the Rock of Israel said to me:
'When one rules over people in righteousness,
when he rules in the fear of God,
4 he is like the light of morning at sunrise
on a cloudless morning,
like the brightness after rain
that brings grass from the earth.'

5 "If my house were not right with God,
surely he would not have made with me an everlasting covenant,
arranged and secured in every part;
surely he would not bring to fruition my salvation
and grant me my every desire.
6 But evil men are all to be cast aside like thorns,
which are not gathered with the hand.
7 Whoever touches thorns
uses a tool of iron or the shaft of a spear;
they are burned up where they lie."

David's Mighty Warriors

8 These are the names of David's mighty warriors:
Josheb-Basshebeth,[a] a Tahkemonite,[b] was chief of the Three; he raised his
spear against eight hundred men, whom he killed[c] in one encounter.
9 Next to him was Eleazar son of Dodai the Ahohite. As one of the three mighty
warriors, he was with David when they taunted the Philistines gathered at Pas
Dammim[d] for battle. Then the Israelites retreated, 10 but Eleazar stood his
ground and struck down the Philistines till his hand grew tired and froze to the
sword. The LORD brought about a great victory that day. The troops returned to
Eleazar, but only to strip the dead.
11 Next to him was Shammah son of Agee the Hararite. When the Philistines
banded together at a place where there was a field full of lentils, Israel's troops
fled from them. 12 But Shammah took his stand in the middle of the field. He defended it and struck the Philistines down, and the LORD brought about a great
victory.
13 During harvest time, three of the thirty chief warriors came down to David
at the cave of Adullam, while a band of Philistines was encamped in the Valley
of Rephaim. 14 At that time David was in the stronghold, and the Philistine garrison was at Bethlehem. 15 David longed for water and said, "Oh, that someone
would get me a drink of water from the well near the gate of Bethlehem!" 16 So the
three mighty warriors broke through the Philistine lines, drew water from the
well near the gate of Bethlehem and carried it back to David. But he refused to
drink it; instead, he poured it out before the LORD. 17 "Far be it from me, LORD, to
do this!" he said. "Is it not the blood of men who went at the risk of their lives?"
And David would not drink it.
Such were the exploits of the three mighty warriors.
18 Abishai the brother of Joab son of Zeruiah was chief of the Three.[e] He raised
his spear against three hundred men, whom he killed, and so he became as famous as the Three. 19 Was he not held in greater honor than the Three? He became their commander, even though he was not included among them.
20 Benaiah son of Jehoiada, a valiant fighter from Kabzeel, performed great
exploits. He struck down Moab's two mightiest warriors. He also went down into

---

[a] *8* Hebrew; some Septuagint manuscripts suggest *Ish-Bosheth,* that is, *Esh-Baal* (see also 1 Chron. 11:11 *Jashobeam*). [b] *8* Probably a variant of *Hakmonite* (see 1 Chron. 11:11) [c] *8* Some Septuagint manuscripts (see also 1 Chron. 11:11); Hebrew and other Septuagint manuscripts *Three; it was Adino the Eznite who killed eight hundred men* [d] *9* See 1 Chron. 11:13; Hebrew *gathered there.* [e] *18* Most Hebrew manuscripts (see also 1 Chron. 11:20); two Hebrew manuscripts and Syriac *Thirty*

COVENANTS MADE AND RENEWED

David's final poetic words revealed the supreme trust he had in God's faithfulness to fulfill his promises. He reaffirmed the "everlasting covenant" God made with David long ago (v. 5). These promises, first made in 2 Samuel 7:12 – 16, were a firm foundation for David's trust, even in the face of his impending death. God's covenant pledged that someone from David's lineage would reign as God's anointed king. In the short term, this promise was fulfilled in David's son, Solomon, who built the temple and established the worship of God among the people. But this would not be the end of God's covenant promises. David reminded Solomon that if he walked faithfully before God, he would not lack a successor on the throne of Israel (1Ki 2:4). Solomon knew the promise of God's anointed king was still to come. Neither David nor Solomon could fully understand or comprehend the person of Jesus Christ, but their hope was clearly set on a coming king who would, unlike them, be able to usher in the rule and reign of God over his people. The prophet Isaiah looked forward to this day when he wrote:

> "For to us a child is born,
> to us a son is given,
> and the government will be on his shoulders.
> And he will be called
> Wonderful Counselor, Mighty God,
> Everlasting Father, Prince of Peace.
> Of the greatness of his government and peace
> there will be no end.
> He will reign on David's throne
> and over his kingdom,
> establishing and upholding it
> with justice and righteousness
> from that time on and forever.
> The zeal of the LORD Almighty
> will accomplish this" (Isa 9:6 – 7).

God would fulfill his promises, just as David believed. Though the people would continue to turn from God, God would not abandon his people. The zeal of God and not the faithfulness of humanity would establish the throne of David. And this throne, unlike David's, will have no end.

a pit on a snowy day and killed a lion. 21 And he struck down a huge Egyptian. Although the Egyptian had a spear in his hand, Benaiah went against him with a
club. He snatched the spear from the Egyptian's hand and killed him with his own
spear. 22 Such were the exploits of Benaiah son of Jehoiada; he too was as famous
as the three mighty warriors. 23 He was held in greater honor than any of the Thirty, but he was not included among the Three. And David put him in charge of his
bodyguard.

24 Among the Thirty were:
Asahel the brother of Joab,
Elhanan son of Dodo from Bethlehem,
25 Shammah the Harodite,
Elika the Harodite,
26 Helez the Paltite,
Ira son of Ikkesh from Tekoa,
27 Abiezer from Anathoth,
Sibbekai[a] the Hushathite,
28 Zalmon the Ahohite,
Maharai the Netophathite,
29 Heled[b] son of Baanah the Netophathite,
Ithai son of Ribai from Gibeah in Benjamin,
30 Benaiah the Pirathonite,
Hiddai[c] from the ravines of Gaash,
31 Abi-Albon the Arbathite,
Azmaveth the Barhumite,
32 Eliahba the Shaalbonite,
the sons of Jashen,
Jonathan 33 son of[d] Shammah the Hararite,
Ahiam son of Sharar[e] the Hararite,
34 Eliphelet son of Ahasbai the Maakathite,
Eliam son of Ahithophel the Gilonite,
35 Hezro the Carmelite,
Paarai the Arbite,
36 Igal son of Nathan from Zobah,
the son of Hagri,[f]
37 Zelek the Ammonite,
Naharai the Beerothite, the armor-bearer of Joab son of Zeruiah,
38 Ira the Ithrite,
Gareb the Ithrite
39 and Uriah the Hittite.
There were thirty-seven in all.

David Enrolls the Fighting Men

24 Again the anger of the LORD burned against Israel, and he incited David
against them, saying, "Go and take a census of Israel and Judah."
2 So the king said to Joab and the army commanders[g] with him, "Go throughout the tribes of Israel from Dan to Beersheba and enroll the fighting men, so
that I may know how many there are."
3 But Joab replied to the king, "May the LORD your God multiply the troops a
hundred times over, and may the eyes of my lord the king see it. But why does my
lord the king want to do such a thing?"

---

[a] *27* Some Septuagint manuscripts (see also 21:18; 1 Chron. 11:29); Hebrew *Mebunnai*
[b] *29* Some Hebrew manuscripts and Vulgate (see also 1 Chron. 11:30); most Hebrew manuscripts *Heleb*
[c] *30* Hebrew; some Septuagint manuscripts (see also 1 Chron. 11:32) *Hurai*
[d] *33* Some Septuagint manuscripts (see also 1 Chron. 11:34); Hebrew does not have *son of.*
[e] *33* Hebrew; some Septuagint manuscripts (see also 1 Chron. 11:35) *Sakar*
[f] *36* Some Septuagint manuscripts (see also 1 Chron. 11:38); Hebrew *Haggadi*
[g] *2* Septuagint (see also verse 4 and 1 Chron. 21:2); Hebrew *Joab the army commander*

THE NEED FOR ATONEMENT

There are consequences for sin. This has been the overarching story in the life of David. David's saga entails acts of disobedience and then moments of repentance and reconciliation with God. However, the impact of his sin was evident. In this episode, the result of David's sin was that over seventy thousand people lost their lives in a plague (24:15). Again, the consequences of sin are real!

Ultimately, David found atonement for his sin by God's grace and mercy. Out of this tragic scene comes the site for the future temple of Solomon, which became a central location for the future of the Jewish people (1Ch 21:28 — 22:1). God's promises of grace to his people thus come together in this instance of David atoning for his sin (2Sa 24:18 – 25). God is able to take the ugliness of a person's disobedience and turn it into a beautiful picture of his redeeming grace.

This location and the future temple point to a much greater atonement, offered by the grace and mercy of God through a much greater temple. This entire narrative of worship that develops through the stories of David and Solomon prefigures Christ as the final temple where atonement was accomplished once for all believers (Jn 2:19 – 21). The atonement for sin required a perfect sacrifice. Jesus was that sacrifice. According to 1 Peter 1:18 – 21, Jesus was the perfect, spotless Lamb of God, who offered himself as a payment to God for the offenses of believers. The Jewish people could inherit eternal salvation, not by their ethnic heritage, but by believing in the gospel secured by the atonement of Jesus, the spotless Lamb. As Luke wrote, "And beginning with Moses and all the Prophets, he explained to them what was said in all the Scriptures concerning himself" (Lk 24:27). These authors had a rich understanding of who Jesus is. He is the atonement. He is the temple. He is what David needed as well as what we need: the once for all offering for sins.

4 The king's word, however, overruled Joab and the army commanders; so they left the presence of the king to enroll the fighting men of Israel.

5 After crossing the Jordan, they camped near Aroer, south of the town in the gorge, and then went through Gad and on to Jazer. 6 They went to Gilead and the region of Tahtim Hodshi, and on to Dan Jaan and around toward Sidon. 7 Then they went toward the fortress of Tyre and all the towns of the Hivites and Canaanites. Finally, they went on to Beersheba in the Negev of Judah.

8 After they had gone through the entire land, they came back to Jerusalem at the end of nine months and twenty days.

9 Joab reported the number of the fighting men to the king: In Israel there were eight hundred thousand able-bodied men who could handle a sword, and in Judah five hundred thousand.

10 David was conscience-stricken after he had counted the fighting men, and he said to the LORD, "I have sinned greatly in what I have done. Now, LORD, I beg you, take away the guilt of your servant. I have done a very foolish thing."

11 Before David got up the next morning, the word of the LORD had come to Gad the prophet, David's seer: 12 "Go and tell David, 'This is what the LORD says: I am giving you three options. Choose one of them for me to carry out against you.' "

13 So Gad went to David and said to him, "Shall there come on you three[a] years of famine in your land? Or three months of fleeing from your enemies while they pursue you? Or three days of plague in your land? Now then, think it over and decide how I should answer the one who sent me."

14 David said to Gad, "I am in deep distress. Let us fall into the hands of the LORD, for his mercy is great; but do not let me fall into human hands."

15 So the LORD sent a plague on Israel from that morning until the end of the time designated, and seventy thousand of the people from Dan to Beersheba died. 16 When the angel stretched out his hand to destroy Jerusalem, the LORD relented concerning the disaster and said to the angel who was afflicting the people, "Enough! Withdraw your hand." The angel of the LORD was then at the threshing floor of Araunah the Jebusite.

17 When David saw the angel who was striking down the people, he said to the LORD, "I have sinned; I, the shepherd,[b] have done wrong. These are but sheep. What have they done? Let your hand fall on me and my family."

David Builds an Altar

18 On that day Gad went to David and said to him, "Go up and build an altar to the LORD on the threshing floor of Araunah the Jebusite." 19 So David went up, as the LORD had commanded through Gad. 20 When Araunah looked and saw the king and his officials coming toward him, he went out and bowed down before the king with his face to the ground.

21 Araunah said, "Why has my lord the king come to his servant?"

"To buy your threshing floor," David answered, "so I can build an altar to the LORD, that the plague on the people may be stopped."

22 Araunah said to David, "Let my lord the king take whatever he wishes and offer it up. Here are oxen for the burnt offering, and here are threshing sledges and ox yokes for the wood. 23 Your Majesty, Araunah[c] gives all this to the king." Araunah also said to him, "May the LORD your God accept you."

24 But the king replied to Araunah, "No, I insist on paying you for it. I will not sacrifice to the LORD my God burnt offerings that cost me nothing."

So David bought the threshing floor and the oxen and paid fifty shekels[d] of silver for them. 25 David built an altar to the LORD there and sacrificed burnt offerings and fellowship offerings. Then the LORD answered his prayer in behalf of the land, and the plague on Israel was stopped.

---

[a] *13* Septuagint (see also 1 Chron. 21:12); Hebrew *seven*

[b] *17* Dead Sea Scrolls and Septuagint; Masoretic Text does not have *the shepherd*.

[c] *23* Some Hebrew manuscripts and Septuagint; most Hebrew manuscripts *King Araunah*

[d] *24* That is, about 1 1/4 pounds or about 575 grams

JESUS: OUR ONLY HOPE

1 KINGS

1 KINGS

REIGN OF SOLOMON *c. 970 – 930 BC*	ISRAEL DIVIDED *c. 930 BC*	ELIJAH BEGINS MINISTRY *c. 875 BC*

The book of 1 Kings portrays the lives of both godly and ungodly individuals during a defining period in the life of the nation of Israel. People such as King David (1Ki 1:24 – 30), King Solomon (1Ki 3:1 – 15) and the Queen of Sheba (1Ki 10:1 – 13) sought after God, though they were far from perfect in this quest. Others such as Ahab and Jezebel notoriously rebelled against God's commands and suffered the just consequences for their actions (2Ki 9:30 – 37; 10:1 – 10). As a whole, the book demonstrates the implications of choosing between these two paths through the lives of good and bad kings, true and false prophets and an assortment of others whose lives shaped Israel's spiritual odyssey. The ever-present backdrop of God's unchanging faithfulness provides hope and confidence to those who seek him.

The unknown author of this book recounts Israel's history beginning with the death of the great King David in the tenth century and concluding in 2 Kings, nearly 400 years later, with Jerusalem's destruction and the bitter exile of God's divided people. The author highlights the spiritual successes and failures that defined the nation, including Solomon's demise and the nation's successive, nearly immediate splintering — with ten tribes in the north aligning under Jeroboam and two tribes in the south under the rule of Solomon's son Rehoboam. From that time forward, the author juxtaposes the spiritual apostasy of the two kingdoms against the small glimmers of faithfulness still seen among the people.

Though 1 Kings is a historical narrative, it is much more than a mere recounting of factual events. Rather, the author's purpose was theological — he wanted to demonstrate that obedience to God was, and is, the proper response to God's consistent and grace-filled faithfulness. The people had been warned — both before they entered the promised land and throughout their time in the land — that those who failed to honor God and obey his word would face stark consequences. And, time and again, the people of Israel learned the truth of this lesson the hard way. The continued inability of the people to obey points forward to humanity's need for the long-awaited Messiah.

Jesus Christ would do what the nation of Israel was unable to do — he would perfectly obey the law of God. His wisdom, miracles and faithfulness are foreshadowed, though imperfectly, through exemplary figures such as Solomon, Elijah and Elisha. The stories of God's grace seen in these godly individuals provide believers today with a model of the worshipful obedience that should still be seen among God's people today.

LORD, THE GOD OF ISRAEL, THERE IS NO GOD LIKE YOU IN HEAVEN ABOVE OR ON EARTH BELOW — YOU WHO KEEP YOUR COVENANT OF LOVE WITH YOUR SERVANTS WHO CONTINUE WHOLEHEARTEDLY IN YOUR WAY.

1 Kings 8:23

1 KINGS

Adonijah Sets Himself Up as King

1 When King David was very old, he could not keep warm even when they put covers over him. 2So his attendants said to him, "Let us look for a young virgin to serve the king and take care of him. She can lie beside him so that our lord the king may keep warm."

3Then they searched throughout Israel for a beautiful young woman and found Abishag, a Shunammite, and brought her to the king. 4The woman was very beautiful; she took care of the king and waited on him, but the king had no sexual relations with her.

5Now Adonijah, whose mother was Haggith, put himself forward and said, "I will be king." So he got chariots and horses[a] ready, with fifty men to run ahead of him. 6(His father had never rebuked him by asking, "Why do you behave as you do?" He was also very handsome and was born next after Absalom.)

7Adonijah conferred with Joab son of Zeruiah and with Abiathar the priest, and they gave him their support. 8But Zadok the priest, Benaiah son of Jehoiada, Nathan the prophet, Shimei and Rei and David's special guard did not join Adonijah. 9Adonijah then sacrificed sheep, cattle and fattened calves at the Stone of Zoheleth near En Rogel. He invited all his brothers, the king's sons, and all the royal officials of Judah, 10but he did not invite Nathan the prophet or Benaiah or the special guard or his brother Solomon.

11Then Nathan asked Bathsheba, Solomon's mother, "Have you not heard that Adonijah, the son of Haggith, has become king, and our lord David knows nothing about it? 12Now then, let me advise you how you can save your own life and the life of your son Solomon. 13Go in to King David and say to him, 'My lord the king, did you not swear to me your servant: "Surely Solomon your son shall be king after me, and he will sit on my throne"? Why then has Adonijah become king?' 14While you are still there talking to the king, I will come in and add my word to what you have said."

15So Bathsheba went to see the aged king in his room, where Abishag the Shunammite was attending him. 16Bathsheba bowed down, prostrating herself before the king.

"What is it you want?" the king asked.

17She said to him, "My lord, you yourself swore to me your servant by the LORD your God: 'Solomon your son shall be king after me, and he will sit on my throne.' 18But now Adonijah has become king, and you, my lord the king, do not know about it. 19He has sacrificed great numbers of cattle, fattened calves, and sheep, and has invited all the king's sons, Abiathar the priest and Joab the commander of the army, but he has not invited Solomon your servant. 20My lord the king, the eyes of all Israel are on you, to learn from you who will sit on the throne of my lord the king after him. 21Otherwise, as soon as my lord the king is laid to rest with his ancestors, I and my son Solomon will be treated as criminals."

22While she was still speaking with the king, Nathan the prophet arrived. 23And the king was told, "Nathan the prophet is here." So he went before the king and bowed with his face to the ground.

24Nathan said, "Have you, my lord the king, declared that Adonijah shall be king after you, and that he will sit on your throne? 25Today he has gone down and sacrificed great numbers of cattle, fattened calves, and sheep. He has invited all the king's sons, the commanders of the army and Abiathar the priest. Right now they are eating and drinking with him and saying, 'Long live King Adonijah!'

1 KINGS 1:28–39

PROTECTING THE LINE OF DAVID

Throughout the reign of the Davidic dynasty, God faithfully preserved the promises he had made to David. Adonijah, Solomon's older brother, vied to sit on the throne of his father David. As Bathsheba pointed out, had Adonijah gained the throne, she and Solomon would have been counted as criminals (v. 21). God's promises, however, were stronger than Adonijah's schemes. The line of David would be carried on through Solomon, not Adonijah, because the Lord had appointed Solomon ruler over Israel and Judah. God's faithfulness to protect the kingly line of David would usher in the birth of the King of kings, Jesus Christ, a descendant of David and the one to whom the promises pointed (Mt 1:1). Through Christ, the Davidic throne was perfectly established and was secured forever.

[a] 5 Or *charioteers*

26But me your servant, and Zadok the priest, and Benaiah son of Jehoiada, and
your servant Solomon he did not invite. 27Is this something my lord the king has
done without letting his servants know who should sit on the throne of my lord
the king after him?"

David Makes Solomon King

28Then King David said, "Call in Bathsheba." So she came into the king's presence and stood before him.
29The king then took an oath: "As surely as the LORD lives, who has delivered
me out of every trouble, 30I will surely carry out this very day what I swore to you
by the LORD, the God of Israel: Solomon your son shall be king after me, and he
will sit on my throne in my place."
31Then Bathsheba bowed down with her face to the ground, prostrating herself before the king, and said, "May my lord King David live forever!"
32King David said, "Call in Zadok the priest, Nathan the prophet and Benaiah
son of Jehoiada." When they came before the king, 33he said to them: "Take your
lord's servants with you and have Solomon my son mount my own mule and
take him down to Gihon. 34There have Zadok the priest and Nathan the prophet
anoint him king over Israel. Blow the trumpet and shout, 'Long live King Solomon!' 35Then you are to go up with him, and he is to come and sit on my throne
and reign in my place. I have appointed him ruler over Israel and Judah."
36Benaiah son of Jehoiada answered the king, "Amen! May the LORD, the God
of my lord the king, so declare it. 37As the LORD was with my lord the king, so
may he be with Solomon to make his throne even greater than the throne of my
lord King David!"
38So Zadok the priest, Nathan the prophet, Benaiah son of Jehoiada, the Kerethites and the Pelethites went down and had Solomon mount King David's
mule, and they escorted him to Gihon. 39Zadok the priest took the horn of oil
from the sacred tent and anointed Solomon. Then they sounded the trumpet
and all the people shouted, "Long live King Solomon!" 40And all the people went
up after him, playing pipes and rejoicing greatly, so that the ground shook with
the sound.
41Adonijah and all the guests who were with him heard it as they were finishing their feast. On hearing the sound of the trumpet, Joab asked, "What's the
meaning of all the noise in the city?"
42Even as he was speaking, Jonathan son of Abiathar the priest arrived. Adonijah said, "Come in. A worthy man like you must be bringing good news."
43"Not at all!" Jonathan answered. "Our lord King David has made Solomon
king. 44The king has sent with him Zadok the priest, Nathan the prophet, Benaiah son of Jehoiada, the Kerethites and the Pelethites, and they have put him on
the king's mule, 45and Zadok the priest and Nathan the prophet have anointed him king at Gihon. From there they have gone up cheering, and the city resounds with it. That's the noise you hear. 46Moreover, Solomon has taken his
seat on the royal throne. 47Also, the royal officials have come to congratulate
our lord King David, saying, 'May your God make Solomon's name more famous
than yours and his throne greater than yours!' And the king bowed in worship
on his bed 48and said, 'Praise be to the LORD, the God of Israel, who has allowed
my eyes to see a successor on my throne today.'"
49At this, all Adonijah's guests rose in alarm and dispersed. 50But Adonijah,
in fear of Solomon, went and took hold of the horns of the altar. 51Then Solomon
was told, "Adonijah is afraid of King Solomon and is clinging to the horns of the
altar. He says, 'Let King Solomon swear to me today that he will not put his servant to death with the sword.'"
52Solomon replied, "If he shows himself to be worthy, not a hair of his head
will fall to the ground; but if evil is found in him, he will die." 53Then King Solomon sent men, and they brought him down from the altar. And Adonijah came
and bowed down to King Solomon, and Solomon said, "Go to your home."

David's Charge to Solomon

2 When the time drew near for David to die, he gave a charge to Solomon his
son.
2“I am about to go the way of all the earth,” he said. “So be strong, act like a
man, 3and observe what the LORD your God requires: Walk in obedience to him,
and keep his decrees and commands, his laws and regulations, as written in the
Law of Moses. Do this so that you may prosper in all you do and wherever you go
4and that the LORD may keep his promise to me: ‘If your descendants watch how
they live, and if they walk faithfully before me with all their heart and soul, you
will never fail to have a successor on the throne of Israel.’
5“Now you yourself know what Joab son of Zeruiah did to me—what he did
to the two commanders of Israel's armies, Abner son of Ner and Amasa son of
Jether. He killed them, shedding their blood in peacetime as if in battle, and
with that blood he stained the belt around his waist and the sandals on his feet.
6Deal with him according to your wisdom, but do not let his gray head go down
to the grave in peace.
7“But show kindness to the sons of Barzillai of Gilead and let them be among
those who eat at your table. They stood by me when I fled from your brother
Absalom.
8“And remember, you have with you Shimei son of Gera, the Benjamite from
Bahurim, who called down bitter curses on me the day I went to Mahanaim.
When he came down to meet me at the Jordan, I swore to him by the LORD: ‘I will
not put you to death by the sword.’ 9But now, do not consider him innocent. You
are a man of wisdom; you will know what to do to him. Bring his gray head down
to the grave in blood.”
10Then David rested with his ancestors and was buried in the City of David.
11He had reigned forty years over Israel—seven years in Hebron and thirty-three
in Jerusalem. 12So Solomon sat on the throne of his father David, and his rule was
firmly established.

Solomon's Throne Established

13Now Adonijah, the son of Haggith, went to Bathsheba, Solomon's mother.
Bathsheba asked him, “Do you come peacefully?”
He answered, “Yes, peacefully.” 14Then he added, “I have something to say
to you.”
“You may say it,” she replied.
15“As you know,” he said, “the kingdom was mine. All Israel looked to me as
their king. But things changed, and the kingdom has gone to my brother; for it
has come to him from the LORD. 16Now I have one request to make of you. Do
not refuse me.”
“You may make it,” she said.
17So he continued, “Please ask King Solomon—he will not refuse you—to
give me Abishag the Shunammite as my wife.”
18“Very well,” Bathsheba replied, “I will speak to the king for you.”
19When Bathsheba went to King Solomon to speak to him for Adonijah, the
king stood up to meet her, bowed down to her and sat down on his throne. He
had a throne brought for the king's mother, and she sat down at his right hand.
20“I have one small request to make of you,” she said. “Do not refuse me.”
The king replied, “Make it, my mother; I will not refuse you.”
21So she said, “Let Abishag the Shunammite be given in marriage to your
brother Adonijah.”
22King Solomon answered his mother, “Why do you request Abishag the Shunammite for Adonijah? You might as well request the kingdom for him—after
all, he is my older brother—yes, for him and for Abiathar the priest and Joab son
of Zeruiah!”
23Then King Solomon swore by the LORD: “May God deal with me, be it ever
so severely, if Adonijah does not pay with his life for this request! 24And now, as

---

1 KINGS 2:1–4

A LESS-THAN-PERFECT KING

It seems that David's charge to Solomon required him to do the impossible—perfectly keep the law of God. In similar fashion, often the nation of Israel was given the command to walk in God's ways, and, in so doing, enjoy the favor and blessing of God. But here that command was uniquely directed at King Solomon alone. As God's chosen king, he was to exemplify godliness for the nation. The subsequent cycle of failure in Solomon's life soon demonstrated that he, like the nation as a whole, was incapable of keeping these lofty instructions. No one, not even the wise king, could keep the law without faltering.

Jesus accomplished what Solomon and every other figure in the Old Testament could not. Jesus perfectly fulfilled the law of God. Peter said that Jesus “committed no sin, and no deceit was found in his mouth” (1Pe 2:22). As the perfect king, Jesus did what Solomon could not do and secured the blessing of God for those who place their faith in his completed work.

surely as the LORD lives — he who has established me securely on the throne of
my father David and has founded a dynasty for me as he promised — Adonijah
shall be put to death today!" 25So King Solomon gave orders to Benaiah son of
Jehoiada, and he struck down Adonijah and he died.
26To Abiathar the priest the king said, "Go back to your fields in Anathoth. You
deserve to die, but I will not put you to death now, because you carried the ark
of the Sovereign LORD before my father David and shared all my father's hardships." 27So Solomon removed Abiathar from the priesthood of the LORD, fulfilling the word the LORD had spoken at Shiloh about the house of Eli.
28When the news reached Joab, who had conspired with Adonijah though not
with Absalom, he fled to the tent of the LORD and took hold of the horns of the altar.
29King Solomon was told that Joab had fled to the tent of the LORD and was beside
the altar. Then Solomon ordered Benaiah son of Jehoiada, "Go, strike him down!"
30So Benaiah entered the tent of the LORD and said to Joab, "The king says,
'Come out!' "
But he answered, "No, I will die here."
Benaiah reported to the king, "This is how Joab answered me."
31Then the king commanded Benaiah, "Do as he says. Strike him down and
bury him, and so clear me and my whole family of the guilt of the innocent blood
that Joab shed. 32The LORD will repay him for the blood he shed, because without
my father David knowing it he attacked two men and killed them with the sword.
Both of them — Abner son of Ner, commander of Israel's army, and Amasa son
of Jether, commander of Judah's army — were better men and more upright than
he. 33May the guilt of their blood rest on the head of Joab and his descendants
forever. But on David and his descendants, his house and his throne, may there
be the LORD's peace forever."
34So Benaiah son of Jehoiada went up and struck down Joab and killed him, and
he was buried at his home out in the country. 35The king put Benaiah son of Jehoiada over the army in Joab's position and replaced Abiathar with Zadok the priest.
36Then the king sent for Shimei and said to him, "Build yourself a house in
Jerusalem and live there, but do not go anywhere else. 37The day you leave and
cross the Kidron Valley, you can be sure you will die; your blood will be on your
own head."
38Shimei answered the king, "What you say is good. Your servant will do as my
lord the king has said." And Shimei stayed in Jerusalem for a long time.
39But three years later, two of Shimei's slaves ran off to Achish son of Maakah,
king of Gath, and Shimei was told, "Your slaves are in Gath." 40At this, he saddled
his donkey and went to Achish at Gath in search of his slaves. So Shimei went
away and brought the slaves back from Gath.
41When Solomon was told that Shimei had gone from Jerusalem to Gath and
had returned, 42the king summoned Shimei and said to him, "Did I not make
you swear by the LORD and warn you, 'On the day you leave to go anywhere else,
you can be sure you will die'? At that time you said to me, 'What you say is good.
I will obey.' 43Why then did you not keep your oath to the LORD and obey the
command I gave you?"
44The king also said to Shimei, "You know in your heart all the wrong you
did to my father David. Now the LORD will repay you for your wrongdoing. 45But
King Solomon will be blessed, and David's throne will remain secure before the
LORD forever."
46Then the king gave the order to Benaiah son of Jehoiada, and he went out
and struck Shimei down and he died.
The kingdom was now established in Solomon's hands.

Solomon Asks for Wisdom

3 Solomon made an alliance with Pharaoh king of Egypt and married his
daughter. He brought her to the City of David until he finished building his
palace and the temple of the LORD, and the wall around Jerusalem. 2The people,

however, were still sacrificing at the high places, because a temple had not yet
been built for the Name of the LORD. [3]Solomon showed his love for the LORD by
walking according to the instructions given him by his father David, except that
he offered sacrifices and burned incense on the high places.
[4]The king went to Gibeon to offer sacrifices, for that was the most important
high place, and Solomon offered a thousand burnt offerings on that altar. [5]At
Gibeon the LORD appeared to Solomon during the night in a dream, and God
said, "Ask for whatever you want me to give you."
[6]Solomon answered, "You have shown great kindness to your servant, my father David, because he was faithful to you and righteous and upright in heart.
You have continued this great kindness to him and have given him a son to sit
on his throne this very day.
[7]"Now, LORD my God, you have made your servant king in place of my father
David. But I am only a little child and do not know how to carry out my duties.
[8]Your servant is here among the people you have chosen, a great people, too numerous to count or number. [9]So give your servant a discerning heart to govern
your people and to distinguish between right and wrong. For who is able to govern this great people of yours?"
[10]The Lord was pleased that Solomon had asked for this. [11]So God said to him,
"Since you have asked for this and not for long life or wealth for yourself, nor
have asked for the death of your enemies but for discernment in administering
justice, [12]I will do what you have asked. I will give you a wise and discerning
heart, so that there will never have been anyone like you, nor will there ever be.
[13]Moreover, I will give you what you have not asked for — both wealth and hon-
or — so that in your lifetime you will have no equal among kings. [14]And if you
walk in obedience to me and keep my decrees and commands as David your
father did, I will give you a long life." [15]Then Solomon awoke — and he realized
it had been a dream.
He returned to Jerusalem, stood before the ark of the Lord's covenant and
sacrificed burnt offerings and fellowship offerings. Then he gave a feast for all
his court.

A Wise Ruling

[16]Now two prostitutes came to the king and stood before him. [17]One of them said,
"Pardon me, my lord. This woman and I live in the same house, and I had a baby
while she was there with me. [18]The third day after my child was born, this woman
also had a baby. We were alone; there was no one in the house but the two of us.
[19]"During the night this woman's son died because she lay on him. [20]So she got
up in the middle of the night and took my son from my side while I your servant
was asleep. She put him by her breast and put her dead son by my breast. [21]The
next morning, I got up to nurse my son — and he was dead! But when I looked at
him closely in the morning light, I saw that it wasn't the son I had borne."
[22]The other woman said, "No! The living one is my son; the dead one is yours."
But the first one insisted, "No! The dead one is yours; the living one is mine."
And so they argued before the king.
[23]The king said, "This one says, 'My son is alive and your son is dead,' while
that one says, 'No! Your son is dead and mine is alive.'"
[24]Then the king said, "Bring me a sword." So they brought a sword for the
king. [25]He then gave an order: "Cut the living child in two and give half to one
and half to the other."
[26]The woman whose son was alive was deeply moved out of love for her son
and said to the king, "Please, my lord, give her the living baby! Don't kill him!"
But the other said, "Neither I nor you shall have him. Cut him in two!"
[27]Then the king gave his ruling: "Give the living baby to the first woman. Do
not kill him; she is his mother."
[28]When all Israel heard the verdict the king had given, they held the king in
awe, because they saw that he had wisdom from God to administer justice.

THE VALUE OF WISDOM

God made Solomon an offer that anyone would envy. Solomon could ask God for anything — wealth, honor, a long life (v. 5). The God of all creation and owner of everything extended an offer for any provision Solomon desired. Solomon's request was both unexpected and remarkable. He asked for a discerning heart to distinguish right from wrong, which uniquely equipped him to lead the people of God (v. 9). God responded by granting this request, but he also gave Solomon the wealth and honor he had not requested (v. 13). Solomon is credited with more than 3,000 proverbs and 1,000 songs, and his wisdom eventually made him the most famous man of his day (1Ki 4:33 – 34).

Wisdom serves as a valuable precursor to wealth and power. Either of these gifts, when given to a fool, leads to great harm; however, wisdom allows a person to utilize God's provision of wealth or power in a manner that causes God's people to thrive. This is why Solomon claimed that wisdom is "more profitable than silver" and "yields better returns than gold" (Pr 3:13 – 14).

Jesus knew the profitability of wisdom. As the incarnate Son of God, he did not merely possess insight into the mind of God; rather, he actually possessed the mind of God. Wisdom was not personified in Christ; it was perfected in Christ.

God's people continue to find wisdom in Jesus. Solomon's counsel in the book of Proverbs to seek wisdom (Pr 4:7) finds its fulfillment in seeking after Christ. As Christians abide in Christ, they are given insight into the very wisdom of God. For example, the apostles, following Christ's death, burial and resurrection, began to speak the words given to them by Christ concerning his kingdom. This courageous teaching and perseverance in the face of suffering demonstrated that Peter and John had, in fact, been with Jesus (Ac 4:13). God's Spirit allows Christians today to ascertain the wisdom of God through Jesus. God's children are graciously given "the mind of Christ," allowing them to have Solomon-like insight into God's will and ways (1Co 2:16).

Solomon's Officials and Governors

4 So King Solomon ruled over all Israel. 2And these were his chief officials:

Azariah son of Zadok — the priest;
3 Elihoreph and Ahijah, sons of Shisha — secretaries;
Jehoshaphat son of Ahilud — recorder;
4 Benaiah son of Jehoiada — commander in chief;
Zadok and Abiathar — priests;
5 Azariah son of Nathan — in charge of the district governors;
Zabud son of Nathan — a priest and adviser to the king;
6 Ahishar — palace administrator;
Adoniram son of Abda — in charge of forced labor.

7Solomon had twelve district governors over all Israel, who supplied provisions for the king and the royal household. Each one had to provide supplies for
one month in the year. 8These are their names:

Ben-Hur — in the hill country of Ephraim;
9 Ben-Deker — in Makaz, Shaalbim, Beth Shemesh and Elon Bethhanan;
10 Ben-Hesed — in Arubboth (Sokoh and all the land of Hepher were his);
11 Ben-Abinadab — in Naphoth Dor (he was married to Taphath daughter of Solomon);
12 Baana son of Ahilud — in Taanach and Megiddo, and in all of Beth Shan next to Zarethan below Jezreel, from Beth Shan to Abel Meholah across to Jokmeam;
13 Ben-Geber — in Ramoth Gilead (the settlements of Jair son of Manasseh in Gilead were his, as well as the region of Argob in Bashan and its sixty large walled cities with bronze gate bars);
14 Ahinadab son of Iddo — in Mahanaim;
15 Ahimaaz — in Naphtali (he had married Basemath daughter of Solomon);
16 Baana son of Hushai — in Asher and in Aloth;
17 Jehoshaphat son of Paruah — in Issachar;
18 Shimei son of Ela — in Benjamin;
19 Geber son of Uri — in Gilead (the country of Sihon king of the Amorites and the country of Og king of Bashan). He was the only governor over the district.

Solomon's Daily Provisions

20The people of Judah and Israel were as numerous as the sand on the seashore; they ate, they drank and they were happy. 21And Solomon ruled over all
the kingdoms from the Euphrates River to the land of the Philistines, as far as
the border of Egypt. These countries brought tribute and were Solomon's subjects all his life.

22Solomon's daily provisions were thirty cors[a] of the finest flour and sixty
cors[b] of meal, 23ten head of stall-fed cattle, twenty of pasture-fed cattle and a
hundred sheep and goats, as well as deer, gazelles, roebucks and choice fowl.
24For he ruled over all the kingdoms west of the Euphrates River, from Tiphsah
to Gaza, and had peace on all sides. 25During Solomon's lifetime Judah and Israel, from Dan to Beersheba, lived in safety, everyone under their own vine and
under their own fig tree.

26Solomon had four[c] thousand stalls for chariot horses, and twelve thousand
horses.[d]

27The district governors, each in his month, supplied provisions for King
Solomon and all who came to the king's table. They saw to it that nothing was

[a] 22 That is, probably about 5 1/2 tons or about 5 metric tons [b] 22 That is, probably about 11 tons or about 10 metric tons [c] 26 Some Septuagint manuscripts (see also 2 Chron. 9:25); Hebrew *forty* [d] 26 Or *charioteers*

lacking. 28They also brought to the proper place their quotas of barley and straw for the chariot horses and the other horses.

Solomon's Wisdom

29God gave Solomon wisdom and very great insight, and a breadth of understanding as measureless as the sand on the seashore. 30Solomon's wisdom was greater than the wisdom of all the people of the East, and greater than all the wisdom of Egypt. 31He was wiser than anyone else, including Ethan the Ezrahite — wiser than Heman, Kalkol and Darda, the sons of Mahol. And his fame spread to all the surrounding nations. 32He spoke three thousand proverbs and his songs numbered a thousand and five. 33He spoke about plant life, from the cedar of Lebanon to the hyssop that grows out of walls. He also spoke about animals and birds, reptiles and fish. 34From all nations people came to listen to Solomon's wisdom, sent by all the kings of the world, who had heard of his wisdom.[a]

Preparations for Building the Temple

5 [b] When Hiram king of Tyre heard that Solomon had been anointed king to succeed his father David, he sent his envoys to Solomon, because he had always been on friendly terms with David. 2Solomon sent back this message to Hiram:

> 3"You know that because of the wars waged against my father David from all sides, he could not build a temple for the Name of the LORD his God until the LORD put his enemies under his feet. 4But now the LORD my God has given me rest on every side, and there is no adversary or disaster. 5I intend, therefore, to build a temple for the Name of the LORD my God, as the LORD told my father David, when he said, 'Your son whom I will put on the throne in your place will build the temple for my Name.'
>
> 6"So give orders that cedars of Lebanon be cut for me. My men will work with yours, and I will pay you for your men whatever wages you set. You know that we have no one so skilled in felling timber as the Sidonians."

7When Hiram heard Solomon's message, he was greatly pleased and said, "Praise be to the LORD today, for he has given David a wise son to rule over this great nation."

8So Hiram sent word to Solomon:

> "I have received the message you sent me and will do all you want in providing the cedar and juniper logs. 9My men will haul them down from Lebanon to the Mediterranean Sea, and I will float them as rafts by sea to the place you specify. There I will separate them and you can take them away. And you are to grant my wish by providing food for my royal household."

10In this way Hiram kept Solomon supplied with all the cedar and juniper logs he wanted, 11and Solomon gave Hiram twenty thousand cors[c] of wheat as food for his household, in addition to twenty thousand baths[d,e] of pressed olive oil. Solomon continued to do this for Hiram year after year. 12The LORD gave Solomon wisdom, just as he had promised him. There were peaceful relations between Hiram and Solomon, and the two of them made a treaty.

13King Solomon conscripted laborers from all Israel — thirty thousand men. 14He sent them off to Lebanon in shifts of ten thousand a month, so that they spent one month in Lebanon and two months at home. Adoniram was in charge of the forced labor. 15Solomon had seventy thousand carriers and eighty thousand stonecutters in the hills, 16as well as thirty-three hundred[f] foremen who

[a] *34* In Hebrew texts 4:21-34 is numbered 5:1-14. [b] In Hebrew texts 5:1-18 is numbered 5:15-32. [c] *11* That is, probably about 3,600 tons or about 3,250 metric tons [d] *11* Septuagint (see also 2 Chron. 2:10); Hebrew *twenty cors* [e] *11* That is, about 120,000 gallons or about 440,000 liters [f] *16* Hebrew; some Septuagint manuscripts (see also 2 Chron. 2:2,18) *thirty-six hundred*

1 KINGS 4:29–34

A WISE LEADER

The attribute of wisdom allows worldly rulers to discern critical military strategy and apply the appropriate leadership principles required to rule rightly. History records that the wisdom of Solomon surpassed the wisdom of all his contemporaries — among those known for their wisdom, none could match him. Even pagan kings were attracted to the wisdom of Solomon and traveled from far and wide to learn from his God-given insight. Jesus also was known for his unique wisdom. The crowds and his disciples marveled at his teaching and insight (Mt 7:28). His words were words of life, which provided people with knowledge of the mind of God and the nature of his kingdom. The drastic nature of his teaching prompted many to turn back and no longer follow him (Jn 6:66). Peter, however, demonstrated that some recognized that Jesus possessed unparalleled wisdom. There was no one else, Peter said, who had the words of life; therefore, the disciples would continue to follow even when the teaching they received was hard (Jn 6:68–69). As the unique Son of God, Jesus had the mind of God. And his followers, both then and now, draw near to him in order to understand God's character, will and ways.

1 KINGS 5:5

FULFILLING A PROMISE

The construction of the temple fulfilled the long-awaited promise of a permanent dwelling place for God

(continued on next page)

(Fulfilling a Promise, continued)

among the people (2Sa 7:13). During their wilderness sojourn, the tabernacle served as a temporary residence for God. Long after the people had taken the land of promise, God pledged to allow Solomon to build a long-term location for the worship of God among his sinful people. In spite of the intimate care God took in establishing the temple, the subsequent failure of the people would lead to its destruction.

Jesus, however, claimed that his resurrection body serves as the true and lasting temple (Jn 2:19–22). No longer would God confine his place of worship to a geographic locale. Rather, he would free people everywhere to live a life of worship before their Creator (Jn 4:20–24). In Christ, God would dwell among his people and then send his Spirit to build those people — his church — into a lasting dwelling place for himself (1Pe 2:4–5).

supervised the project and directed the workers. 17At the king's command they removed from the quarry large blocks of high-grade stone to provide a foundation of dressed stone for the temple. 18The craftsmen of Solomon and Hiram and workers from Byblos cut and prepared the timber and stone for the building of the temple.

Solomon Builds the Temple

6 In the four hundred and eightieth[a] year after the Israelites came out of Egypt, in the fourth year of Solomon's reign over Israel, in the month of Ziv, the second month, he began to build the temple of the LORD.

2The temple that King Solomon built for the LORD was sixty cubits long, twenty wide and thirty high.[b] 3The portico at the front of the main hall of the temple extended the width of the temple, that is twenty cubits,[c] and projected ten cubits[d] from the front of the temple. 4He made narrow windows high up in the temple walls. 5Against the walls of the main hall and inner sanctuary he built a structure around the building, in which there were side rooms. 6The lowest floor was five cubits[e] wide, the middle floor six cubits[f] and the third floor seven.[g] He made offset ledges around the outside of the temple so that nothing would be inserted into the temple walls.

7In building the temple, only blocks dressed at the quarry were used, and no hammer, chisel or any other iron tool was heard at the temple site while it was being built.

8The entrance to the lowest[h] floor was on the south side of the temple; a stairway led up to the middle level and from there to the third. 9So he built the temple and completed it, roofing it with beams and cedar planks. 10And he built the side rooms all along the temple. The height of each was five cubits, and they were attached to the temple by beams of cedar.

11The word of the LORD came to Solomon: 12"As for this temple you are building, if you follow my decrees, observe my laws and keep all my commands and obey them, I will fulfill through you the promise I gave to David your father. 13And I will live among the Israelites and will not abandon my people Israel."

14So Solomon built the temple and completed it. 15He lined its interior walls with cedar boards, paneling them from the floor of the temple to the ceiling, and covered the floor of the temple with planks of juniper. 16He partitioned off twenty cubits at the rear of the temple with cedar boards from floor to ceiling to form within the temple an inner sanctuary, the Most Holy Place. 17The main hall in front of this room was forty cubits[i] long. 18The inside of the temple was cedar, carved with gourds and open flowers. Everything was cedar; no stone was to be seen.

19He prepared the inner sanctuary within the temple to set the ark of the covenant of the LORD there. 20The inner sanctuary was twenty cubits long, twenty wide and twenty high. He overlaid the inside with pure gold, and he also overlaid the altar of cedar. 21Solomon covered the inside of the temple with pure gold, and he extended gold chains across the front of the inner sanctuary, which was overlaid with gold. 22So he overlaid the whole interior with gold. He also overlaid with gold the altar that belonged to the inner sanctuary.

23For the inner sanctuary he made a pair of cherubim out of olive wood, each ten cubits high. 24One wing of the first cherub was five cubits long, and the other wing five cubits — ten cubits from wing tip to wing tip. 25The second cherub also measured ten cubits, for the two cherubim were identical in size and shape.

---

[a] *1* Hebrew; Septuagint *four hundred and fortieth* [b] *2* That is, about 90 feet long, 30 feet wide and 45 feet high or about 27 meters long, 9 meters wide and 14 meters high [c] *3* That is, about 30 feet or about 9 meters; also in verses 16 and 20 [d] *3* That is, about 15 feet or about 4.5 meters; also in verses 23-26 [e] *6* That is, about 7 1/2 feet or about 2.3 meters; also in verses 10 and 24 [f] *6* That is, about 9 feet or about 2.7 meters [g] *6* That is, about 11 feet or about 3.2 meters [h] *8* Septuagint; Hebrew *middle* [i] *17* That is, about 60 feet or about 18 meters

26 The height of each cherub was ten cubits. 27 He placed the cherubim inside the innermost room of the temple, with their wings spread out. The wing of one cherub touched one wall, while the wing of the other touched the other wall, and their wings touched each other in the middle of the room. 28 He overlaid the cherubim with gold.

29 On the walls all around the temple, in both the inner and outer rooms, he carved cherubim, palm trees and open flowers. 30 He also covered the floors of both the inner and outer rooms of the temple with gold.

31 For the entrance to the inner sanctuary he made doors out of olive wood that were one fifth of the width of the sanctuary. 32 And on the two olive-wood doors he carved cherubim, palm trees and open flowers, and overlaid the cherubim and palm trees with hammered gold. 33 In the same way, for the entrance to the main hall he made doorframes out of olive wood that were one fourth of the width of the hall. 34 He also made two doors out of juniper wood, each having two leaves that turned in sockets. 35 He carved cherubim, palm trees and open flowers on them and overlaid them with gold hammered evenly over the carvings.

36 And he built the inner courtyard of three courses of dressed stone and one course of trimmed cedar beams.

37 The foundation of the temple of the LORD was laid in the fourth year, in the month of Ziv. 38 In the eleventh year in the month of Bul, the eighth month, the temple was finished in all its details according to its specifications. He had spent seven years building it.

Solomon Builds His Palace

7 It took Solomon thirteen years, however, to complete the construction of his palace. 2 He built the Palace of the Forest of Lebanon a hundred cubits long, fifty wide and thirty high,[a] with four rows of cedar columns supporting trimmed cedar beams. 3 It was roofed with cedar above the beams that rested on the columns — forty-five beams, fifteen to a row. 4 Its windows were placed high in sets of three, facing each other. 5 All the doorways had rectangular frames; they were in the front part in sets of three, facing each other.[b]

6 He made a colonnade fifty cubits long and thirty wide.[c] In front of it was a portico, and in front of that were pillars and an overhanging roof.

7 He built the throne hall, the Hall of Justice, where he was to judge, and he covered it with cedar from floor to ceiling.[d] 8 And the palace in which he was to live, set farther back, was similar in design. Solomon also made a palace like this hall for Pharaoh's daughter, whom he had married.

9 All these structures, from the outside to the great courtyard and from foundation to eaves, were made of blocks of high-grade stone cut to size and smoothed on their inner and outer faces. 10 The foundations were laid with large stones of good quality, some measuring ten cubits[e] and some eight.[f] 11 Above were high-grade stones, cut to size, and cedar beams. 12 The great courtyard was surrounded by a wall of three courses of dressed stone and one course of trimmed cedar beams, as was the inner courtyard of the temple of the LORD with its portico.

The Temple's Furnishings

13 King Solomon sent to Tyre and brought Huram,[g] 14 whose mother was a widow from the tribe of Naphtali and whose father was from Tyre and a skilled craftsman in bronze. Huram was filled with wisdom, with understanding and with knowledge to do all kinds of bronze work. He came to King Solomon and did all the work assigned to him.

1 KINGS 7:13–51

THE TEMPLE

Solomon's temple had much in common with its precursor — the tabernacle. Both contained a host of ornate furnishings and implements that allowed sinful people to worship a holy God. The slaughter of animals to atone for the sins of the people was the ongoing routine in each. However, the temple differed from the tabernacle in terms of its permanence and its size. The temporary tabernacle was replaced with a building meant to communicate the grandeur of God's glory. This progressive development of God's dwelling is amplified by the prophet Ezekiel's vision of a heavenly temple that would eclipse both the tabernacle and the temple (Eze 40 – 43).

The church, God's new temple built with the living stones of those who place their faith in Christ, expands the scope of the dwelling of God all the more. Christians now take the dwelling of God with them to the ends of the earth (Mt 28:18 – 20). Finally, the coming dwelling of God with humanity, pictured by the apostle John, will one day fill the entire cosmos with the presence of God (Rev 21:3; 22:5).

---

[a] *2* That is, about 150 feet long, 75 feet wide and 45 feet high or about 45 meters long, 23 meters wide and 14 meters high [b] *5* The meaning of the Hebrew for this verse is uncertain. [c] *6* That is, about 75 feet long and 45 feet wide or about 23 meters long and 14 meters wide [d] *7* Vulgate and Syriac; Hebrew *floor* [e] *10* That is, about 15 feet or about 4.5 meters; also in verse 23 [f] *10* That is, about 12 feet or about 3.6 meters [g] *13* Hebrew *Hiram,* a variant of *Huram;* also in verses 40 and 45

GOD AMONG HIS PEOPLE

The intricate physical layout of the temple contained spiritual significance. It revealed a pattern for the worship practices of God's people — from the nation of Israel to the church today. The temple consisted of three main sections: the outer courtyard, the Holy Place and the Most Holy Place (Ex 26:33). In the Most Holy Place, God dwelled among his people and made it possible for their sins to be forgiven.

Since the fall, the fellowship between God and his created image-bearers had been broken. Following their sin, Adam and Eve were banished from the Garden of Eden, and angels guarded the way back into the presence of God. No longer could they simply walk with God in the cool of the day. They were now outsiders, barred from communion with their Creator.

God graciously intervened in humanity's sinful predicament. Rather than requiring the people to prove themselves pure and capable of communing with their holy Creator, God determined to invade their sin-drenched world with his glorious presence. First, he dwelled in a tabernacle that moved with the people throughout their time in the wilderness. Later, God dwelled in the temple, where he communed with people through the sacrifice of substitutionary animals. The temple modeled the original garden, with the entrance to the Most Holy Place guarded by imposing angelic figures carved in olive wood and overlaid with gold, just as angels had once blocked reentry into God's presence (Ge 3:24; 1Ki 6:23 – 28).

Then the dwelling of God among his people took a startling turn. The very Son of God, Jesus Christ, came to dwell among his people (Jn 1:1 – 14). The glory of God became flesh and blood. All people — including tax collectors, prostitutes, Pharisees — could see the glory of God, hear him speak and see him work wonders. The physical proximity to the glory of God did not mean that all people understood or worshiped God. Many people had eyes but failed to see; they had ears but did not hear (Mk 8:18). However, true worshipers coming to God in faith and repentance see and respond to the glory of God in the person of Christ — a reality that the tabernacle and temple could merely foreshadow.

[15]He cast two bronze pillars, each eighteen cubits high and twelve cubits in circumference.[a] [16]He also made two capitals of cast bronze to set on the tops of the pillars; each capital was five cubits[b] high. [17]A network of interwoven chains adorned the capitals on top of the pillars, seven for each capital. [18]He made pomegranates in two rows[c] encircling each network to decorate the capitals on top of the pillars.[d] He did the same for each capital. [19]The capitals on top of the pillars in the portico were in the shape of lilies, four cubits[e] high. [20]On the capitals of both pillars, above the bowl-shaped part next to the network, were the two hundred pomegranates in rows all around. [21]He erected the pillars at the portico of the temple. The pillar to the south he named Jakin[f] and the one to the north Boaz.[g] [22]The capitals on top were in the shape of lilies. And so the work on the pillars was completed.

[23]He made the Sea of cast metal, circular in shape, measuring ten cubits from rim to rim and five cubits high. It took a line of thirty cubits[h] to measure around it. [24]Below the rim, gourds encircled it—ten to a cubit. The gourds were cast in two rows in one piece with the Sea.

[25]The Sea stood on twelve bulls, three facing north, three facing west, three facing south and three facing east. The Sea rested on top of them, and their hindquarters were toward the center. [26]It was a handbreadth[i] in thickness, and its rim was like the rim of a cup, like a lily blossom. It held two thousand baths.[j]

[27]He also made ten movable stands of bronze; each was four cubits long, four wide and three high.[k] [28]This is how the stands were made: They had side panels attached to uprights. [29]On the panels between the uprights were lions, bulls and cherubim—and on the uprights as well. Above and below the lions and bulls were wreaths of hammered work. [30]Each stand had four bronze wheels with bronze axles, and each had a basin resting on four supports, cast with wreaths on each side. [31]On the inside of the stand there was an opening that had a circular frame one cubit[l] deep. This opening was round, and with its basework it measured a cubit and a half.[m] Around its opening there was engraving. The panels of the stands were square, not round. [32]The four wheels were under the panels, and the axles of the wheels were attached to the stand. The diameter of each wheel was a cubit and a half. [33]The wheels were made like chariot wheels; the axles, rims, spokes and hubs were all of cast metal.

[34]Each stand had four handles, one on each corner, projecting from the stand. [35]At the top of the stand there was a circular band half a cubit[n] deep. The supports and panels were attached to the top of the stand. [36]He engraved cherubim, lions and palm trees on the surfaces of the supports and on the panels, in every available space, with wreaths all around. [37]This is the way he made the ten stands. They were all cast in the same molds and were identical in size and shape.

[38]He then made ten bronze basins, each holding forty baths[o] and measuring four cubits across, one basin to go on each of the ten stands. [39]He placed five of the stands on the south side of the temple and five on the north. He placed the Sea on the south side, at the southeast corner of the temple. [40]He also made the pots[p] and shovels and sprinkling bowls.

---

[a] *15* That is, about 27 feet high and 18 feet in circumference or about 8.1 meters high and 5.4 meters in circumference [b] *16* That is, about 7 1/2 feet or about 2.3 meters; also in verse 23 [c] *18* Two Hebrew manuscripts and Septuagint; most Hebrew manuscripts *made the pillars, and there were two rows* [d] *18* Many Hebrew manuscripts and Syriac; most Hebrew manuscripts *pomegranates* [e] *19* That is, about 6 feet or about 1.8 meters; also in verse 38 [f] *21* *Jakin* probably means *he establishes.* [g] *21* *Boaz* probably means *in him is strength.* [h] *23* That is, about 45 feet or about 14 meters [i] *26* That is, about 3 inches or about 7.5 centimeters [j] *26* That is, about 12,000 gallons or about 44,000 liters; the Septuagint does not have this sentence. [k] *27* That is, about 6 feet long and wide and about 4 1/2 feet high or about 1.8 meters long and wide and 1.4 meters high [l] *31* That is, about 18inches or about 45 centimeters [m] *31* That is, about 2 1/4 feet or about 68 centimeters; also in verse 32 [n] *35* That is, about 9 inches or about 23 centimeters [o] *38* That is, about 240 gallons or about 880 liters [p] *40* Many Hebrew manuscripts, Septuagint, Syriac and Vulgate (see also verse 45 and 2 Chron. 4:11); many other Hebrew manuscripts *basins*

So Huram finished all the work he had undertaken for King Solomon in the
temple of the LORD:

41 the two pillars;
the two bowl-shaped capitals on top of the pillars;
the two sets of network decorating the two bowl-shaped capitals on top of
the pillars;
42 the four hundred pomegranates for the two sets of network (two rows of
pomegranates for each network decorating the bowl-shaped capitals on
top of the pillars);
43 the ten stands with their ten basins;
44 the Sea and the twelve bulls under it;
45 the pots, shovels and sprinkling bowls.

All these objects that Huram made for King Solomon for the temple of the
LORD were of burnished bronze. 46 The king had them cast in clay molds in the
plain of the Jordan between Sukkoth and Zarethan. 47 Solomon left all these
things unweighed, because there were so many; the weight of the bronze was
not determined.
48 Solomon also made all the furnishings that were in the LORD's temple:

the golden altar;
the golden table on which was the bread of the Presence;
49 the lampstands of pure gold (five on the right and five on the left, in front of
the inner sanctuary);
the gold floral work and lamps and tongs;
50 the pure gold basins, wick trimmers, sprinkling bowls, dishes and censers;
and the gold sockets for the doors of the innermost room, the Most Holy
Place, and also for the doors of the main hall of the temple.

51 When all the work King Solomon had done for the temple of the LORD was
finished, he brought in the things his father David had dedicated — the silver
and gold and the furnishings — and he placed them in the treasuries of the
LORD's temple.

The Ark Brought to the Temple

8 Then King Solomon summoned into his presence at Jerusalem the elders
of Israel, all the heads of the tribes and the chiefs of the Israelite families,
to bring up the ark of the LORD's covenant from Zion, the City of David. 2 All the
Israelites came together to King Solomon at the time of the festival in the month
of Ethanim, the seventh month.
3 When all the elders of Israel had arrived, the priests took up the ark, 4 and
they brought up the ark of the LORD and the tent of meeting and all the sacred
furnishings in it. The priests and Levites carried them up, 5 and King Solomon
and the entire assembly of Israel that had gathered about him were before the
ark, sacrificing so many sheep and cattle that they could not be recorded or
counted.
6 The priests then brought the ark of the LORD's covenant to its place in the
inner sanctuary of the temple, the Most Holy Place, and put it beneath the wings
of the cherubim. 7 The cherubim spread their wings over the place of the ark and
overshadowed the ark and its carrying poles. 8 These poles were so long that their
ends could be seen from the Holy Place in front of the inner sanctuary, but not
from outside the Holy Place; and they are still there today. 9 There was nothing in
the ark except the two stone tablets that Moses had placed in it at Horeb, where
the LORD made a covenant with the Israelites after they came out of Egypt.
10 When the priests withdrew from the Holy Place, the cloud filled the temple
of the LORD. 11 And the priests could not perform their service because of the
cloud, for the glory of the LORD filled his temple.
12 Then Solomon said, "The LORD has said that he would dwell in a dark cloud;

1 KINGS 8:10–11

THE GLORY OF GOD IN THE TEMPLE

The completion of the temple culminated in the glory of God filling the newly constructed dwelling. It is astounding to consider that the sum total of God's attributes could be located in a structure made with human hands. Yet, this is the nature of God's humility — he stooped to earth to be known by his people. The tangible sign of a cloud, sometimes referred to as the "shekinah glory," signified God's presence within the nation of Israel. With God among them, the people of God had a motive for worship and obedience.

Long before Jesus' day, this first temple, built by Solomon, was destroyed. The second temple, built by the returning Babylonian exiles, was undergoing a massive rebuilding project that had begun under Herod's direction. Jesus stunned his Jewish audience when he claimed that this ever-expanding temple — which by then had been under construction for nearly 50 years and displayed astonishing levels of beauty and opulence — would be destroyed and rebuilt in three days. They failed to discern that Jesus was not talking about a physical structure made by human hands, but about his very body, which would be destroyed on a Roman cross only to be resurrected three days later (Jn 2:19–22).

Paul added to Jesus' identification of his physical body as the true temple where God dwelled among his people. Writing to the church in Corinth which was made up of people saved by Christ, Paul reminded them that they were God's temple (1Co 3:16). The Spirit of God, which once filled the temple, now fills believers with the power and presence of the glory of God.

As with the ancient temple, the awareness of the glory of God dwelling within Christians should prompt worship and obedience. In the church, God's people should be reminded of the holiness of God every time they see one another — fellow image-bearers in whom the Spirit of God dwells. The gathering of the church — whether in small groups, Bible study classes or in corporate worship — should prompt reverential awe at the fact that God dwells in his people. Not only that, but the ongoing reality of the dwelling of God within his people should cause them to desire to use their bodies in a holy manner. Paul used this logic to urge sexual purity on the part of those indwelled by God's Spirit (1Co 6:19). Since God dwells in his people in all of his glory, sin should be shunned and holiness pursued as an act of worship in the new temple of God.

[13]I have indeed built a magnificent temple for you, a place for you to dwell forever."

[14]While the whole assembly of Israel was standing there, the king turned around and blessed them. [15]Then he said:

> "Praise be to the LORD, the God of Israel, who with his own hand has fulfilled what he promised with his own mouth to my father David. For he said, [16]'Since the day I brought my people Israel out of Egypt, I have not chosen a city in any tribe of Israel to have a temple built so that my Name might be there, but I have chosen David to rule my people Israel.'
>
> [17]"My father David had it in his heart to build a temple for the Name of the LORD, the God of Israel. [18]But the LORD said to my father David, 'You did well to have it in your heart to build a temple for my Name. [19]Nevertheless, you are not the one to build the temple, but your son, your own flesh and blood—he is the one who will build the temple for my Name.'
>
> [20]"The LORD has kept the promise he made: I have succeeded David my father and now I sit on the throne of Israel, just as the LORD promised, and I have built the temple for the Name of the LORD, the God of Israel. [21]I have provided a place there for the ark, in which is the covenant of the LORD that he made with our ancestors when he brought them out of Egypt."

Solomon's Prayer of Dedication

[22]Then Solomon stood before the altar of the LORD in front of the whole assembly of Israel, spread out his hands toward heaven [23]and said:

> "LORD, the God of Israel, there is no God like you in heaven above or on earth below—you who keep your covenant of love with your servants who continue wholeheartedly in your way. [24]You have kept your promise to your servant David my father; with your mouth you have promised and with your hand you have fulfilled it—as it is today.
>
> [25]"Now LORD, the God of Israel, keep for your servant David my father the promises you made to him when you said, 'You shall never fail to have a successor to sit before me on the throne of Israel, if only your descendants are careful in all they do to walk before me faithfully as you have done.' [26]And now, God of Israel, let your word that you promised your servant David my father come true.
>
> [27]"But will God really dwell on earth? The heavens, even the highest heaven, cannot contain you. How much less this temple I have built! [28]Yet give attention to your servant's prayer and his plea for mercy, LORD my God. Hear the cry and the prayer that your servant is praying in your presence this day. [29]May your eyes be open toward this temple night and day, this place of which you said, 'My Name shall be there,' so that you will hear the prayer your servant prays toward this place. [30]Hear the supplication of your servant and of your people Israel when they pray toward this place. Hear from heaven, your dwelling place, and when you hear, forgive.
>
> [31]"When anyone wrongs their neighbor and is required to take an oath and they come and swear the oath before your altar in this temple, [32]then hear from heaven and act. Judge between your servants, condemning the guilty by bringing down on their heads what they have done, and vindicating the innocent by treating them in accordance with their innocence.
>
> [33]"When your people Israel have been defeated by an enemy because they have sinned against you, and when they turn back to you and give praise to your name, praying and making supplication to you in this temple, [34]then hear from heaven and forgive the sin of your people Israel and bring them back to the land you gave to their ancestors.
>
> [35]"When the heavens are shut up and there is no rain because your people have sinned against you, and when they pray toward this place and give praise to your name and turn from their sin because you have afflicted

them, 36then hear from heaven and forgive the sin of your servants, your
people Israel. Teach them the right way to live, and send rain on the land
you gave your people for an inheritance.

37"When famine or plague comes to the land, or blight or mildew, locusts or grasshoppers, or when an enemy besieges them in any of their cities, whatever disaster or disease may come, 38and when a prayer or plea is
made by anyone among your people Israel — being aware of the afflictions
of their own hearts, and spreading out their hands toward this temple —
39then hear from heaven, your dwelling place. Forgive and act; deal with
everyone according to all they do, since you know their hearts (for you
alone know every human heart), 40so that they will fear you all the time
they live in the land you gave our ancestors.

41"As for the foreigner who does not belong to your people Israel but
has come from a distant land because of your name — 42for they will hear
of your great name and your mighty hand and your outstretched arm —
when they come and pray toward this temple, 43then hear from heaven,
your dwelling place. Do whatever the foreigner asks of you, so that all the
peoples of the earth may know your name and fear you, as do your own
people Israel, and may know that this house I have built bears your Name.

44"When your people go to war against their enemies, wherever you
send them, and when they pray to the LORD toward the city you have chosen and the temple I have built for your Name, 45then hear from heaven
their prayer and their plea, and uphold their cause.

46"When they sin against you — for there is no one who does not sin —
and you become angry with them and give them over to their enemies, who
take them captive to their own lands, far away or near; 47and if they have
a change of heart in the land where they are held captive, and repent and
plead with you in the land of their captors and say, 'We have sinned, we
have done wrong, we have acted wickedly'; 48and if they turn back to you
with all their heart and soul in the land of their enemies who took them
captive, and pray to you toward the land you gave their ancestors, toward
the city you have chosen and the temple I have built for your Name; 49then
from heaven, your dwelling place, hear their prayer and their plea, and uphold their cause. 50And forgive your people, who have sinned against you;
forgive all the offenses they have committed against you, and cause their
captors to show them mercy; 51for they are your people and your inheritance, whom you brought out of Egypt, out of that iron-smelting furnace.

52"May your eyes be open to your servant's plea and to the plea of your
people Israel, and may you listen to them whenever they cry out to you.
53For you singled them out from all the nations of the world to be your own
inheritance, just as you declared through your servant Moses when you,
Sovereign LORD, brought our ancestors out of Egypt."

54When Solomon had finished all these prayers and supplications to the
LORD, he rose from before the altar of the LORD, where he had been kneeling
with his hands spread out toward heaven. 55He stood and blessed the whole assembly of Israel in a loud voice, saying:

56"Praise be to the LORD, who has given rest to his people Israel just as he
promised. Not one word has failed of all the good promises he gave through
his servant Moses. 57May the LORD our God be with us as he was with our
ancestors; may he never leave us nor forsake us. 58May he turn our hearts
to him, to walk in obedience to him and keep the commands, decrees and
laws he gave our ancestors. 59And may these words of mine, which I have
prayed before the LORD, be near to the LORD our God day and night, that he
may uphold the cause of his servant and the cause of his people Israel according to each day's need, 60so that all the peoples of the earth may know
that the LORD is God and that there is no other. 61And may your hearts be

fully committed to the LORD our God, to live by his decrees and obey his
commands, as at this time."

The Dedication of the Temple

[62]Then the king and all Israel with him offered sacrifices before the LORD.
[63]Solomon offered a sacrifice of fellowship offerings to the LORD: twenty-two
thousand cattle and a hundred and twenty thousand sheep and goats. So the
king and all the Israelites dedicated the temple of the LORD.
[64]On that same day the king consecrated the middle part of the courtyard in
front of the temple of the LORD, and there he offered burnt offerings, grain offerings and the fat of the fellowship offerings, because the bronze altar that stood
before the LORD was too small to hold the burnt offerings, the grain offerings and
the fat of the fellowship offerings.
[65]So Solomon observed the festival at that time, and all Israel with him — a
vast assembly, people from Lebo Hamath to the Wadi of Egypt. They celebrated
it before the LORD our God for seven days and seven days more, fourteen days in
all. [66]On the following day he sent the people away. They blessed the king and
then went home, joyful and glad in heart for all the good things the LORD had
done for his servant David and his people Israel.

The LORD Appears to Solomon

9 When Solomon had finished building the temple of the LORD and the royal
palace, and had achieved all he had desired to do, [2]the LORD appeared to
him a second time, as he had appeared to him at Gibeon. [3]The LORD said to him:

"I have heard the prayer and plea you have made before me; I have consecrated this temple, which you have built, by putting my Name there forever. My eyes and my heart will always be there.
[4]"As for you, if you walk before me faithfully with integrity of heart and
uprightness, as David your father did, and do all I command and observe
my decrees and laws, [5]I will establish your royal throne over Israel forever,
as I promised David your father when I said, 'You shall never fail to have a
successor on the throne of Israel.'
[6]"But if you[a] or your descendants turn away from me and do not observe
the commands and decrees I have given you[a] and go off to serve other gods
and worship them, [7]then I will cut off Israel from the land I have given them
and will reject this temple I have consecrated for my Name. Israel will then
become a byword and an object of ridicule among all peoples. [8]This temple
will become a heap of rubble. All[b] who pass by will be appalled and will
scoff and say, 'Why has the LORD done such a thing to this land and to this
temple?' [9]People will answer, 'Because they have forsaken the LORD their
God, who brought their ancestors out of Egypt, and have embraced other
gods, worshiping and serving them — that is why the LORD brought all this
disaster on them.' "

Solomon's Other Activities

[10]At the end of twenty years, during which Solomon built these two buildings — the temple of the LORD and the royal palace — [11]King Solomon gave
twenty towns in Galilee to Hiram king of Tyre, because Hiram had supplied him
with all the cedar and juniper and gold he wanted. [12]But when Hiram went from
Tyre to see the towns that Solomon had given him, he was not pleased with them.
[13]"What kind of towns are these you have given me, my brother?" he asked. And
he called them the Land of Kabul,[c] a name they have to this day. [14]Now Hiram
had sent to the king 120 talents[d] of gold.

[a] *6* The Hebrew is plural. [b] *8* See some Septuagint manuscripts, Old Latin, Syriac, Arabic and Targum; Hebrew *And though this temple is now imposing, all* [c] *13* *Kabul* sounds like the Hebrew for *good-for-nothing.* [d] *14* That is, about 4 1/2 tons or about 4 metric tons

1 KINGS 9:10 – 13

CAN ANYTHING GOOD COME FROM THERE?

Solomon gave King Hiram twenty towns in the northern region of the promised land in return for his provision for the people of God. Though the nation surely resented losing a portion of the promised land, it is clear that this region was less than desirable. Even King Hiram, upon seeing the land, named it the Land of Kabul, which sounds like the Hebrew for "good-for-nothing." This area around the Sea of Galilee was still considered undesirable at the time of Jesus' life. Many refused to acknowledge that Jesus could be the Messiah because he was from this region (Jn 1:46; 7:41). It was thought that nothing good could come from this worthless land — certainly not the Messiah. God, however, specializes in taking that which is deemed undesirable and using it for his purposes. The epicenter of Jesus' ministry took place in this "good-for-nothing" land, and he would prove that something of little value can be transformed by God into an object of great worth. Jesus' great act of salvation transforms fallen, broken and undesirable people into trophies of his grace (Eph 2:4 – 7).

THE CLEAR CHOICES OF DISCIPLESHIP

God's charge to Solomon, though it came at a critical juncture in the national identity of the nation of Israel, was far from original. Moses had ended his instructions to the nation on the brink of the promised land with a similar challenge (Dt 30:11 – 20). Joshua, after leading the people to possess the land and nearing his death, had repeated these instructions (Jos 24:14 – 28). The message was simple: God had given the people his presence and his promises and the people should respond with worship and obedience. In each case, the great leaders explained that the people must make a critical choice between living a life of obedience to God and experiencing his blessings or following the path of disobedience and idolatry and facing pain, discipline and destruction. The choice between life and death was not a means of securing God's love; rather, the decision to pursue life is the proper response of those who have experienced the love of God in their salvation.

Echoing the leaders before him, Jesus ended his Sermon on the Mount by presenting two ways to live (Mt 7:13 – 14). On the one hand, there is the wide gate that opens to an easy path that Jesus said many will take. Those who choose this path, following the ways of the world and rebelling against God, will find death and destruction. On the other hand, there is the path leading to life and blessing. This path is hard and its entrance narrow. As a result, few find it. These two paths demonstrate the choice confronting all people, both in the nation of Israel and in the world today.

The consistent pattern of the Old Testament people of God reveals that people naturally choose the path to destruction. Jesus is the only one who has ever walked through the narrow gate and perfectly followed the path to life. Through faith, his followers can receive the gift of the righteous life of Christ — meaning that God sees them living the life they could not live, consistently choosing the path to life (2Co 5:16 – 21). He then sent his Spirit to empower his children to walk the narrow path that leads to fullness of life now and an eternal life of glory with God forever (Jn 16:13 – 15).

15 Here is the account of the forced labor King Solomon conscripted to build the LORD's temple, his own palace, the terraces,[a] the wall of Jerusalem, and Hazor, Megiddo and Gezer. 16 (Pharaoh king of Egypt had attacked and captured Gezer. He had set it on fire. He killed its Canaanite inhabitants and then gave it as a wedding gift to his daughter, Solomon's wife. 17 And Solomon rebuilt Gezer.) He built up Lower Beth Horon, 18 Baalath, and Tadmor[b] in the desert, within his land, 19 as well as all his store cities and the towns for his chariots and for his horses[c] — whatever he desired to build in Jerusalem, in Lebanon and throughout all the territory he ruled.

20 There were still people left from the Amorites, Hittites, Perizzites, Hivites and Jebusites (these peoples were not Israelites). 21 Solomon conscripted the descendants of all these peoples remaining in the land — whom the Israelites could not exterminate[d] — to serve as slave labor, as it is to this day. 22 But Solomon did not make slaves of any of the Israelites; they were his fighting men, his government officials, his officers, his captains, and the commanders of his chariots and charioteers. 23 They were also the chief officials in charge of Solomon's projects — 550 officials supervising those who did the work.

24 After Pharaoh's daughter had come up from the City of David to the palace Solomon had built for her, he constructed the terraces.

25 Three times a year Solomon sacrificed burnt offerings and fellowship offerings on the altar he had built for the LORD, burning incense before the LORD along with them, and so fulfilled the temple obligations.

26 King Solomon also built ships at Ezion Geber, which is near Elath in Edom, on the shore of the Red Sea.[e] 27 And Hiram sent his men — sailors who knew the sea — to serve in the fleet with Solomon's men. 28 They sailed to Ophir and brought back 420 talents[f] of gold, which they delivered to King Solomon.

The Queen of Sheba Visits Solomon

10 When the queen of Sheba heard about the fame of Solomon and his relationship to the LORD, she came to test Solomon with hard questions. 2 Arriving at Jerusalem with a very great caravan — with camels carrying spices, large quantities of gold, and precious stones — she came to Solomon and talked with him about all that she had on her mind. 3 Solomon answered all her questions; nothing was too hard for the king to explain to her. 4 When the queen of Sheba saw all the wisdom of Solomon and the palace he had built, 5 the food on his table, the seating of his officials, the attending servants in their robes, his cupbearers, and the burnt offerings he made at[g] the temple of the LORD, she was overwhelmed.

6 She said to the king, "The report I heard in my own country about your achievements and your wisdom is true. 7 But I did not believe these things until I came and saw with my own eyes. Indeed, not even half was told me; in wisdom and wealth you have far exceeded the report I heard. 8 How happy your people must be! How happy your officials, who continually stand before you and hear your wisdom! 9 Praise be to the LORD your God, who has delighted in you and placed you on the throne of Israel. Because of the LORD's eternal love for Israel, he has made you king to maintain justice and righteousness."

10 And she gave the king 120 talents[h] of gold, large quantities of spices, and precious stones. Never again were so many spices brought in as those the queen of Sheba gave to King Solomon.

11 (Hiram's ships brought gold from Ophir; and from there they brought great cargoes of almugwood[i] and precious stones. 12 The king used the almugwood to

---

[a] *15* Or *the Millo*; also in verse 24 [b] *18* The Hebrew may also be read *Tamar.* [c] *19* Or *charioteers* [d] *21* The Hebrew term refers to the irrevocable giving over of things or persons to the LORD, often by totally destroying them. [e] *26* Or *the Sea of Reeds* [f] *28* That is, about 16 tons or about 14 metric tons [g] *5* Or *the ascent by which he went up to* [h] *10* That is, about 4 1/2 tons or about 4 metric tons [i] *11* Probably a variant of *algumwood*; also in verse 12

make supports[a] for the temple of the LORD and for the royal palace, and to make harps and lyres for the musicians. So much almugwood has never been imported or seen since that day.)

13King Solomon gave the queen of Sheba all she desired and asked for, besides what he had given her out of his royal bounty. Then she left and returned with her retinue to her own country.

Solomon's Splendor

14The weight of the gold that Solomon received yearly was 666 talents,[b] 15not including the revenues from merchants and traders and from all the Arabian kings and the governors of the territories.

16King Solomon made two hundred large shields of hammered gold; six hundred shekels[c] of gold went into each shield. 17He also made three hundred small shields of hammered gold, with three minas[d] of gold in each shield. The king put them in the Palace of the Forest of Lebanon.

18Then the king made a great throne covered with ivory and overlaid with fine gold. 19The throne had six steps, and its back had a rounded top. On both sides of the seat were armrests, with a lion standing beside each of them. 20Twelve lions stood on the six steps, one at either end of each step. Nothing like it had ever been made for any other kingdom. 21All King Solomon's goblets were gold, and all the household articles in the Palace of the Forest of Lebanon were pure gold. Nothing was made of silver, because silver was considered of little value in Solomon's days. 22The king had a fleet of trading ships[e] at sea along with the ships of Hiram. Once every three years it returned, carrying gold, silver and ivory, and apes and baboons.

23King Solomon was greater in riches and wisdom than all the other kings of the earth. 24The whole world sought audience with Solomon to hear the wisdom God had put in his heart. 25Year after year, everyone who came brought a gift—articles of silver and gold, robes, weapons and spices, and horses and mules.

26Solomon accumulated chariots and horses; he had fourteen hundred chariots and twelve thousand horses,[f] which he kept in the chariot cities and also with him in Jerusalem. 27The king made silver as common in Jerusalem as stones, and cedar as plentiful as sycamore-fig trees in the foothills. 28Solomon's horses were imported from Egypt and from Kue[g]—the royal merchants purchased them from Kue at the current price. 29They imported a chariot from Egypt for six hundred shekels of silver, and a horse for a hundred and fifty.[h] They also exported them to all the kings of the Hittites and of the Arameans.

Solomon's Wives

11 King Solomon, however, loved many foreign women besides Pharaoh's daughter—Moabites, Ammonites, Edomites, Sidonians and Hittites. 2They were from nations about which the LORD had told the Israelites, "You must not intermarry with them, because they will surely turn your hearts after their gods." Nevertheless, Solomon held fast to them in love. 3He had seven hundred wives of royal birth and three hundred concubines, and his wives led him astray. 4As Solomon grew old, his wives turned his heart after other gods, and his heart was not fully devoted to the LORD his God, as the heart of David his father had been. 5He followed Ashtoreth the goddess of the Sidonians, and Molek the detestable god of the Ammonites. 6So Solomon did evil in the eyes of the LORD; he did not follow the LORD completely, as David his father had done.

7On a hill east of Jerusalem, Solomon built a high place for Chemosh the

---

[a] *12* The meaning of the Hebrew for this word is uncertain. [b] *14* That is, about 25 tons or about 23 metric tons [c] *16* That is, about 15 pounds or about 6.9 kilograms; also in verse 29 [d] *17* That is, about 3 3/4 pounds or about 1.7 kilograms; or perhaps reference is to double minas, that is, about 7 1/2 pounds or about 3.5 kilograms. [e] *22* Hebrew *of ships of Tarshish* [f] *26* Or *charioteers* [g] *28* Probably *Cilicia* [h] *29* That is, about 3 3/4 pounds or about 1.7 kilograms

detestable god of Moab, and for Molek the detestable god of the Ammonites. [8]He
did the same for all his foreign wives, who burned incense and offered sacrifices
to their gods.
[9]The LORD became angry with Solomon because his heart had turned away
from the LORD, the God of Israel, who had appeared to him twice. [10]Although he
had forbidden Solomon to follow other gods, Solomon did not keep the LORD's
command. [11]So the LORD said to Solomon, "Since this is your attitude and you
have not kept my covenant and my decrees, which I commanded you, I will most
certainly tear the kingdom away from you and give it to one of your subordi-
nates. [12]Nevertheless, for the sake of David your father, I will not do it during
your lifetime. I will tear it out of the hand of your son. [13]Yet I will not tear the
whole kingdom from him, but will give him one tribe for the sake of David my
servant and for the sake of Jerusalem, which I have chosen."

Solomon's Adversaries

[14]Then the LORD raised up against Solomon an adversary, Hadad the Edomite,
from the royal line of Edom. [15]Earlier when David was fighting with Edom, Joab
the commander of the army, who had gone up to bury the dead, had struck down
all the men in Edom. [16]Joab and all the Israelites stayed there for six months,
until they had destroyed all the men in Edom. [17]But Hadad, still only a boy, fled
to Egypt with some Edomite officials who had served his father. [18]They set out
from Midian and went to Paran. Then taking people from Paran with them, they
went to Egypt, to Pharaoh king of Egypt, who gave Hadad a house and land and
provided him with food.
[19]Pharaoh was so pleased with Hadad that he gave him a sister of his own wife,
Queen Tahpenes, in marriage. [20]The sister of Tahpenes bore him a son named
Genubath, whom Tahpenes brought up in the royal palace. There Genubath
lived with Pharaoh's own children.
[21]While he was in Egypt, Hadad heard that David rested with his ancestors
and that Joab the commander of the army was also dead. Then Hadad said to
Pharaoh, "Let me go, that I may return to my own country."
[22]"What have you lacked here that you want to go back to your own country?"
Pharaoh asked.
"Nothing," Hadad replied, "but do let me go!"
[23]And God raised up against Solomon another adversary, Rezon son of Eliada, who had fled from his master, Hadadezer king of Zobah. [24]When David destroyed Zobah's army, Rezon gathered a band of men around him and became
their leader; they went to Damascus, where they settled and took control. [25]Re-
zon was Israel's adversary as long as Solomon lived, adding to the trouble caused
by Hadad. So Rezon ruled in Aram and was hostile toward Israel.

Jeroboam Rebels Against Solomon

[26]Also, Jeroboam son of Nebat rebelled against the king. He was one of Solomon's officials, an Ephraimite from Zeredah, and his mother was a widow
named Zeruah.
[27]Here is the account of how he rebelled against the king: Solomon had built
the terraces[a] and had filled in the gap in the wall of the city of David his father.
[28]Now Jeroboam was a man of standing, and when Solomon saw how well the
young man did his work, he put him in charge of the whole labor force of the
tribes of Joseph.
[29]About that time Jeroboam was going out of Jerusalem, and Ahijah the
prophet of Shiloh met him on the way, wearing a new cloak. The two of them
were alone out in the country, [30]and Ahijah took hold of the new cloak he was
wearing and tore it into twelve pieces. [31]Then he said to Jeroboam, "Take ten
pieces for yourself, for this is what the LORD, the God of Israel, says: 'See, I am

[a] *27* Or *the Millo*

THE WISE FOOL VERSUS THE WISE SAVIOR

Solomon's wisdom was legendary. God granted his request, bestowing upon him the ability to perfectly distinguish right from wrong, and this unique ability garnered him the attention of the nations of his day (1Ki 4:29 – 34). Throughout history, the name of Solomon has been associated with unparalleled wisdom.

In spite of his great wisdom, Solomon's life testifies to the nature of human sin. He proved repeatedly to be incapable of living in conformity with the wisdom he was given. Though he was unrivaled in his wisdom, he lived like a fool. For example, in the book of Proverbs, Solomon discussed the folly of sexual immorality (Pr 5:1 – 14). He showed that the path of the adulterer was the path to destruction (Pr 7:21 – 23). He exhorted each husband to find satisfaction in his wife and to be captivated by her love (Pr 5:18 – 19). These wise instructions and warnings demonstrate the God-given insight Solomon possessed.

However, Solomon did not live up to his words. During his life, he had 700 wives and 300 concubines. These women led his heart away from the one true God, causing him to build altars to pagan gods on a hill outside of Jerusalem. He lived his life in opposition to the things he knew to be true and, in so doing, demonstrated that he was the wisest fool who has ever lived.

Solomon's life highlights the contrast between great leaders in the Bible and Jesus Christ. Jesus possessed perfect insight into the wisdom of God. He consistently demonstrated that this wisdom was far deeper than mere outward obedience. For example, he commanded people not only to avoid adultery but to flee from lust as well (Mt 5:27 – 30). What makes Jesus' wisdom astounding is not that he said these things, but also that he could live a life that conformed to these standards. Unlike Solomon, the Son of God was always able to live up to his message. He spoke not only of the wisdom of God but also modeled a life of conformity to that very message. The consistency between the wisdom and actions of Jesus proves, once again, that he is who he says he is — the perfect Son of God.

going to tear the kingdom out of Solomon's hand and give you ten tribes. [32]But for the sake of my servant David and the city of Jerusalem, which I have chosen out of all the tribes of Israel, he will have one tribe. [33]I will do this because they have[a] forsaken me and worshiped Ashtoreth the goddess of the Sidonians, Chemosh the god of the Moabites, and Molek the god of the Ammonites, and have not walked in obedience to me, nor done what is right in my eyes, nor kept my decrees and laws as David, Solomon's father, did.

[34]" 'But I will not take the whole kingdom out of Solomon's hand; I have made him ruler all the days of his life for the sake of David my servant, whom I chose and who obeyed my commands and decrees. [35]I will take the kingdom from his son's hands and give you ten tribes. [36]I will give one tribe to his son so that David my servant may always have a lamp before me in Jerusalem, the city where I chose to put my Name. [37]However, as for you, I will take you, and you will rule over all that your heart desires; you will be king over Israel. [38]If you do whatever I command you and walk in obedience to me and do what is right in my eyes by obeying my decrees and commands, as David my servant did, I will be with you. I will build you a dynasty as enduring as the one I built for David and will give Israel to you. [39]I will humble David's descendants because of this, but not forever.' "

[40]Solomon tried to kill Jeroboam, but Jeroboam fled to Egypt, to Shishak the king, and stayed there until Solomon's death.

Solomon's Death

[41]As for the other events of Solomon's reign — all he did and the wisdom he displayed — are they not written in the book of the annals of Solomon? [42]Solomon reigned in Jerusalem over all Israel forty years. [43]Then he rested with his ancestors and was buried in the city of David his father. And Rehoboam his son succeeded him as king.

Israel Rebels Against Rehoboam

12 Rehoboam went to Shechem, for all Israel had gone there to make him king. [2]When Jeroboam son of Nebat heard this (he was still in Egypt, where he had fled from King Solomon), he returned from[b] Egypt. [3]So they sent for Jeroboam, and he and the whole assembly of Israel went to Rehoboam and said to him: [4]"Your father put a heavy yoke on us, but now lighten the harsh labor and the heavy yoke he put on us, and we will serve you."

[5]Rehoboam answered, "Go away for three days and then come back to me." So the people went away.

[6]Then King Rehoboam consulted the elders who had served his father Solomon during his lifetime. "How would you advise me to answer these people?" he asked.

[7]They replied, "If today you will be a servant to these people and serve them and give them a favorable answer, they will always be your servants."

[8]But Rehoboam rejected the advice the elders gave him and consulted the young men who had grown up with him and were serving him. [9]He asked them, "What is your advice? How should we answer these people who say to me, 'Lighten the yoke your father put on us'?"

[10]The young men who had grown up with him replied, "These people have said to you, 'Your father put a heavy yoke on us, but make our yoke lighter.' Now tell them, 'My little finger is thicker than my father's waist. [11]My father laid on you a heavy yoke; I will make it even heavier. My father scourged you with whips; I will scourge you with scorpions.' "

[12]Three days later Jeroboam and all the people returned to Rehoboam, as the king had said, "Come back to me in three days." [13]The king answered the people harshly. Rejecting the advice given him by the elders, [14]he followed the advice of the young men and said, "My father made your yoke heavy; I will make it even

---

1 KINGS 12:1 – 17

LASTING REPERCUSSIONS OF DIVISION

The arrogance and harshness of Solomon's son Rehoboam sparked the division of the nation of God's people. The northern kingdom, called Israel, consisted of ten tribes led by Jeroboam, formerly in charge of the labor force under Solomon. The southern kingdom, called Judah, retained Rehoboam as their king. The prophecy of 1 Kings 11:29 – 33 was fulfilled, and the unified monarchy was ripped apart. Infighting, division, turmoil and strife henceforth marked the people who were established to be a light to the nations and a testimony to the glory of God. No earthly king would be able to unite the people of God ever again. The people needed a better king to fix the problems created by their sin.

The great unifier of the people of God eventually came in the person of Christ. He broke down the dividing walls separating humankind from one another and formed in himself one new, united people of God (Eph 2:11 – 22; 4:1 – 6). This new people, including both Jews and Gentiles, would be grafted together as God's church, a community uniquely marked by unity and sacrificial love.

---

[a] 33 Hebrew; Septuagint, Vulgate and Syriac *because he has* [b] 2 Or *he remained in*

heavier. My father scourged you with whips; I will scourge you with scorpions."
15 So the king did not listen to the people, for this turn of events was from the
LORD, to fulfill the word the LORD had spoken to Jeroboam son of Nebat through
Ahijah the Shilonite.
16 When all Israel saw that the king refused to listen to them, they answered
the king:

"What share do we have in David,
  what part in Jesse's son?
To your tents, Israel!
  Look after your own house, David!"

So the Israelites went home. 17 But as for the Israelites who were living in the
towns of Judah, Rehoboam still ruled over them.
18 King Rehoboam sent out Adoniram,[a] who was in charge of forced labor, but
all Israel stoned him to death. King Rehoboam, however, managed to get into
his chariot and escape to Jerusalem. 19 So Israel has been in rebellion against the
house of David to this day.
20 When all the Israelites heard that Jeroboam had returned, they sent and
called him to the assembly and made him king over all Israel. Only the tribe of
Judah remained loyal to the house of David.
21 When Rehoboam arrived in Jerusalem, he mustered all Judah and the tribe
of Benjamin — a hundred and eighty thousand able young men — to go to war
against Israel and to regain the kingdom for Rehoboam son of Solomon.
22 But this word of God came to Shemaiah the man of God: 23 "Say to Rehoboam son of Solomon king of Judah, to all Judah and Benjamin, and to the rest
of the people, 24 'This is what the LORD says: Do not go up to fight against your
brothers, the Israelites. Go home, every one of you, for this is my doing.' " So they
obeyed the word of the LORD and went home again, as the LORD had ordered.

Golden Calves at Bethel and Dan

25 Then Jeroboam fortified Shechem in the hill country of Ephraim and lived
there. From there he went out and built up Peniel.[b]
26 Jeroboam thought to himself, "The kingdom will now likely revert to the
house of David. 27 If these people go up to offer sacrifices at the temple of the
LORD in Jerusalem, they will again give their allegiance to their lord, Rehoboam
king of Judah. They will kill me and return to King Rehoboam."
28 After seeking advice, the king made two golden calves. He said to the people, "It is too much for you to go up to Jerusalem. Here are your gods, Israel, who
brought you up out of Egypt." 29 One he set up in Bethel, and the other in Dan.
30 And this thing became a sin; the people came to worship the one at Bethel and
went as far as Dan to worship the other.[c]
31 Jeroboam built shrines on high places and appointed priests from all sorts
of people, even though they were not Levites. 32 He instituted a festival on the
fifteenth day of the eighth month, like the festival held in Judah, and offered sacrifices on the altar. This he did in Bethel, sacrificing to the calves he had made.
And at Bethel he also installed priests at the high places he had made. 33 On the
fifteenth day of the eighth month, a month of his own choosing, he offered sacrifices on the altar he had built at Bethel. So he instituted the festival for the
Israelites and went up to the altar to make offerings.

The Man of God From Judah

13 By the word of the LORD a man of God came from Judah to Bethel, as Jeroboam was standing by the altar to make an offering. 2 By the word of the
LORD he cried out against the altar: "Altar, altar! This is what the LORD says:

---

[a] 18 Some Septuagint manuscripts and Syriac (see also 4:6 and 5:14); Hebrew *Adoram*
[b] 25 Hebrew *Penuel,* a variant of *Peniel* [c] 30 Probable reading of the original Hebrew text;
Masoretic Text *people went to the one as far as Dan*

THE DIVIDED KINGDOM (930 – 586 BC)

God's people fractured into northern and southern kingdoms following the reign of King Solomon. At one level, the division of the kingdom was a judgment on the Davidic line for specific failures (1Ki 11:9 – 11; 12:12 – 15). Additionally, the northern tribes found their center of politics and trade facing Phoenicia and underwent massive rifts as indicated toward the end of the book of Judges. All of these changes made it easy for them to reject the kingdom and the religion that had once drawn them to the distant, higher elevation of Jerusalem.

While the northern kingdom valued their trade routes to the north, their greatest enemy crouched to the north as well. Syria could wreak havoc on Israel by surging down the trade routes that bisected the nation. Implementing the siege warfare tactics of Tiglath-Pileser III, the Assyrians were able to place the northern kingdom under tribute by 732 BC and brought the capital city of Samaria to ruins in 722/721 BC. As typical for the Assyrian campaigns, the remaining people of the northern kingdom were deported, and new inhabitants were brought in.

The rift between the northern and southern kingdoms resulted in a number of territorial conflicts between the two brother nations. This border region south of Bethel was established following clashes between Asa and Baasha. The northern kingdom was often militarily superior and suited to fighting on the plains with many chariots. Their impressive array of chariots is even referenced in the Assyrian records. But Judah, by contrast, needed a substantially smaller force due to its elevation and natural fortification.

Judah's primary source of conflict lay to the west — the land of the Philistines. The artery of trade and the avenue for conquering armies flowed north from Lachish to Hebron and then to Jerusalem. Both the Assyrians (in 701 BC) and the Babylonians (in 597 and 586 BC) laid siege to the city, ultimately turning the city and temple to rubble and bringing a seeming end to the Messianic line of David.

While the northern and southern kingdoms were the same in terms of where they began (descendants of the same man — Abraham) and where they ended up (destroyed and deported), they also exhibited vast differences. The south, despite oscillating between idolatry and faithfulness, remained committed to the line of David. The north descended into idolatry without reprieve under a series of capricious and bloodthirsty dynasties.

'A son named Josiah will be born to the house of David. On you he will sacrifice
the priests of the high places who make offerings here, and human bones will be
burned on you.' " 3That same day the man of God gave a sign: "This is the sign
the LORD has declared: The altar will be split apart and the ashes on it will be
poured out."

4When King Jeroboam heard what the man of God cried out against the altar
at Bethel, he stretched out his hand from the altar and said, "Seize him!" But the
hand he stretched out toward the man shriveled up, so that he could not pull it
back. 5Also, the altar was split apart and its ashes poured out according to the
sign given by the man of God by the word of the LORD.

6Then the king said to the man of God, "Intercede with the LORD your God
and pray for me that my hand may be restored." So the man of God interceded
with the LORD, and the king's hand was restored and became as it was before.

7The king said to the man of God, "Come home with me for a meal, and I will
give you a gift."

8But the man of God answered the king, "Even if you were to give me half your
possessions, I would not go with you, nor would I eat bread or drink water here.
9For I was commanded by the word of the LORD: 'You must not eat bread or drink
water or return by the way you came.' " 10So he took another road and did not return by the way he had come to Bethel.

11Now there was a certain old prophet living in Bethel, whose sons came and
told him all that the man of God had done there that day. They also told their
father what he had said to the king. 12Their father asked them, "Which way did
he go?" And his sons showed him which road the man of God from Judah had
taken. 13So he said to his sons, "Saddle the donkey for me." And when they had
saddled the donkey for him, he mounted it 14and rode after the man of God. He
found him sitting under an oak tree and asked, "Are you the man of God who
came from Judah?"

"I am," he replied.

15So the prophet said to him, "Come home with me and eat."

16The man of God said, "I cannot turn back and go with you, nor can I eat
bread or drink water with you in this place. 17I have been told by the word of
the LORD: 'You must not eat bread or drink water there or return by the way you
came.' "

18The old prophet answered, "I too am a prophet, as you are. And an angel said
to me by the word of the LORD: 'Bring him back with you to your house so that he
may eat bread and drink water.' " (But he was lying to him.) 19So the man of God
returned with him and ate and drank in his house.

20While they were sitting at the table, the word of the LORD came to the old
prophet who had brought him back. 21He cried out to the man of God who had
come from Judah, "This is what the LORD says: 'You have defied the word of the
LORD and have not kept the command the LORD your God gave you. 22You came
back and ate bread and drank water in the place where he told you not to eat or
drink. Therefore your body will not be buried in the tomb of your ancestors.' "

23When the man of God had finished eating and drinking, the prophet who
had brought him back saddled his donkey for him. 24As he went on his way, a lion
met him on the road and killed him, and his body was left lying on the road, with
both the donkey and the lion standing beside it. 25Some people who passed by
saw the body lying there, with the lion standing beside the body, and they went
and reported it in the city where the old prophet lived.

26When the prophet who had brought him back from his journey heard of it,
he said, "It is the man of God who defied the word of the LORD. The LORD has
given him over to the lion, which has mauled him and killed him, as the word of
the LORD had warned him."

27The prophet said to his sons, "Saddle the donkey for me," and they did so.
28Then he went out and found the body lying on the road, with the donkey and
the lion standing beside it. The lion had neither eaten the body nor mauled the

GOD'S WORD IN THE MIDST OF SIN

The nation of Israel was prone to idolatry. The worship of pagan gods practiced by the surrounding nations was a regular source of temptation for God's people. The kings of the people of God even set up altars to these foreign gods, thus fostering further sin on the part of the people.

God promised to destroy the pagan altar constructed by Jeroboam, reducing it to rubble and thereby demonstrating its futility. Josiah, a descendant of David, fulfilled this prophecy in 2 Kings 23:15 – 18 when he pulled down the altar and the associated implements of worship and burned them all.

This action proves that, in spite of the sin of the people, God graciously protected them from their folly. Rather than letting their idolatry run amok, he raised up godly leaders who destroyed the altars and hindered the idolatrous worship of the nation. In many ways, the history of the people of God proves the depths of sin that people are capable of practicing. Yet, it could have been far worse without God's ongoing intervention.

God's goal was not simply to destroy the altar of pagan worship but to arrest the people in their sin. The dust heap of an altar was meant to expose the impotence of the pagan gods and the foolishness of the people in worshiping them.

God has always acted to expose the folly of people trapped in cycles of idolatry. Whether their false gods are represented by carved images or embodied in the misdirected pursuits of sex or power, God shatters those gods' illusory attraction. In his grace, God thwarts the worship of these gods by exposing them as false. The goal is the same as that found here in 1 Kings — to prove that false gods are not deserving of worship and to point people to the one, true and living God who does deserve that worship. God is the only proper object of worship, and God will use any means necessary — including the destruction of false gods — to cause people to see their need for him.

donkey. [29]So the prophet picked up the body of the man of God, laid it on the donkey, and brought it back to his own city to mourn for him and bury him. [30]Then he laid the body in his own tomb, and they mourned over him and said, "Alas, my brother!"

[31]After burying him, he said to his sons, "When I die, bury me in the grave where the man of God is buried; lay my bones beside his bones. [32]For the message he declared by the word of the LORD against the altar in Bethel and against all the shrines on the high places in the towns of Samaria will certainly come true."

[33]Even after this, Jeroboam did not change his evil ways, but once more appointed priests for the high places from all sorts of people. Anyone who wanted to become a priest he consecrated for the high places. [34]This was the sin of the house of Jeroboam that led to its downfall and to its destruction from the face of the earth.

Ahijah's Prophecy Against Jeroboam

14 At that time Abijah son of Jeroboam became ill, [2]and Jeroboam said to his wife, "Go, disguise yourself, so you won't be recognized as the wife of Jeroboam. Then go to Shiloh. Ahijah the prophet is there—the one who told me I would be king over this people. [3]Take ten loaves of bread with you, some cakes and a jar of honey, and go to him. He will tell you what will happen to the boy." [4]So Jeroboam's wife did what he said and went to Ahijah's house in Shiloh.

Now Ahijah could not see; his sight was gone because of his age. [5]But the LORD had told Ahijah, "Jeroboam's wife is coming to ask you about her son, for he is ill, and you are to give her such and such an answer. When she arrives, she will pretend to be someone else."

[6]So when Ahijah heard the sound of her footsteps at the door, he said, "Come in, wife of Jeroboam. Why this pretense? I have been sent to you with bad news. [7]Go, tell Jeroboam that this is what the LORD, the God of Israel, says: 'I raised you up from among the people and appointed you ruler over my people Israel. [8]I tore the kingdom away from the house of David and gave it to you, but you have not been like my servant David, who kept my commands and followed me with all his heart, doing only what was right in my eyes. [9]You have done more evil than all who lived before you. You have made for yourself other gods, idols made of metal; you have aroused my anger and turned your back on me.

[10]" 'Because of this, I am going to bring disaster on the house of Jeroboam. I will cut off from Jeroboam every last male in Israel—slave or free.[a] I will burn up the house of Jeroboam as one burns dung, until it is all gone. [11]Dogs will eat those belonging to Jeroboam who die in the city, and the birds will feed on those who die in the country. The LORD has spoken!'

[12]"As for you, go back home. When you set foot in your city, the boy will die. [13]All Israel will mourn for him and bury him. He is the only one belonging to Jeroboam who will be buried, because he is the only one in the house of Jeroboam in whom the LORD, the God of Israel, has found anything good.

[14]"The LORD will raise up for himself a king over Israel who will cut off the family of Jeroboam. Even now this is beginning to happen.[b] [15]And the LORD will strike Israel, so that it will be like a reed swaying in the water. He will uproot Israel from this good land that he gave to their ancestors and scatter them beyond the Euphrates River, because they aroused the LORD's anger by making Asherah poles.[c] [16]And he will give Israel up because of the sins Jeroboam has committed and has caused Israel to commit."

[17]Then Jeroboam's wife got up and left and went to Tirzah. As soon as she stepped over the threshold of the house, the boy died. [18]They buried him, and

[a] *10* Or *Israel—every ruler or leader* [b] *14* The meaning of the Hebrew for this sentence is uncertain. [c] *15* That is, wooden symbols of the goddess Asherah; here and elsewhere in 1 Kings

1 KINGS 14:1–18

PROPHECY FULFILLED

The sin of Jeroboam caused God to stir the prophet Ahijah to prophesy Jeroboam's impending destruction, the collapse of his kingdom and the extermination of his household. A short time later, these promises were fulfilled with exacting precision (1Ki 14:17–18; 15:29–30). He and his entire family were destroyed because he provoked the Lord to anger by fostering the rebellion of the nation against God. The immediate fulfillment of God's promises demonstrated that he was faithful to his word and would not leave the guilty unpunished. In this and similar cases, God promised to act and fulfilled his promise in that generation. This quick fulfillment allowed the same people who heard the promise to see it fulfilled before their very eyes, providing a clear confirmation of God's word. However, on other occasions, the fulfillment of biblical prophecy happened following a lengthy span of time. The consistency of God's promises across generations attests to his faithfulness. Prophecy proves that God is faithful, in both the short term and long term, to fulfill his promises to save his people from their sin.

all Israel mourned for him, as the LORD had said through his servant the prophet Ahijah.

19The other events of Jeroboam's reign, his wars and how he ruled, are written in the book of the annals of the kings of Israel. 20He reigned for twenty-two years and then rested with his ancestors. And Nadab his son succeeded him as king.

Rehoboam King of Judah

21Rehoboam son of Solomon was king in Judah. He was forty-one years old when he became king, and he reigned seventeen years in Jerusalem, the city the LORD had chosen out of all the tribes of Israel in which to put his Name. His mother's name was Naamah; she was an Ammonite.

22Judah did evil in the eyes of the LORD. By the sins they committed they stirred up his jealous anger more than those who were before them had done. 23They also set up for themselves high places, sacred stones and Asherah poles on every high hill and under every spreading tree. 24There were even male shrine prostitutes in the land; the people engaged in all the detestable practices of the nations the LORD had driven out before the Israelites.

25In the fifth year of King Rehoboam, Shishak king of Egypt attacked Jerusalem. 26He carried off the treasures of the temple of the LORD and the treasures of the royal palace. He took everything, including all the gold shields Solomon had made. 27So King Rehoboam made bronze shields to replace them and assigned these to the commanders of the guard on duty at the entrance to the royal palace. 28Whenever the king went to the LORD's temple, the guards bore the shields, and afterward they returned them to the guardroom.

29As for the other events of Rehoboam's reign, and all he did, are they not written in the book of the annals of the kings of Judah? 30There was continual warfare between Rehoboam and Jeroboam. 31And Rehoboam rested with his ancestors and was buried with them in the City of David. His mother's name was Naamah; she was an Ammonite. And Abijah[a] his son succeeded him as king.

Abijah King of Judah

15 In the eighteenth year of the reign of Jeroboam son of Nebat, Abijah[b] became king of Judah, 2and he reigned in Jerusalem three years. His mother's name was Maakah daughter of Abishalom.[c]

3He committed all the sins his father had done before him; his heart was not fully devoted to the LORD his God, as the heart of David his forefather had been. 4Nevertheless, for David's sake the LORD his God gave him a lamp in Jerusalem by raising up a son to succeed him and by making Jerusalem strong. 5For David had done what was right in the eyes of the LORD and had not failed to keep any of the LORD's commands all the days of his life — except in the case of Uriah the Hittite.

6There was war between Abijah[d] and Jeroboam throughout Abijah's lifetime. 7As for the other events of Abijah's reign, and all he did, are they not written in the book of the annals of the kings of Judah? There was war between Abijah and Jeroboam. 8And Abijah rested with his ancestors and was buried in the City of David. And Asa his son succeeded him as king.

Asa King of Judah

9In the twentieth year of Jeroboam king of Israel, Asa became king of Judah, 10and he reigned in Jerusalem forty-one years. His grandmother's name was Maakah daughter of Abishalom.

11Asa did what was right in the eyes of the LORD, as his father David had done.

---

[a] *31* Some Hebrew manuscripts and Septuagint (see also 2 Chron. 12:16); most Hebrew manuscripts *Abijam* [b] *1* Some Hebrew manuscripts and Septuagint (see also 2 Chron. 12:16); most Hebrew manuscripts *Abijam*; also in verses 7 and 8 [c] *2* A variant of *Absalom*; also in verse 10 [d] *6* Some Hebrew manuscripts and Syriac *Abijam* (that is, Abijah); most Hebrew manuscripts *Rehoboam*

12He expelled the male shrine prostitutes from the land and got rid of all the idols
his ancestors had made. 13He even deposed his grandmother Maakah from her
position as queen mother, because she had made a repulsive image for the worship of Asherah. Asa cut it down and burned it in the Kidron Valley. 14Although
he did not remove the high places, Asa's heart was fully committed to the LORD
all his life. 15He brought into the temple of the LORD the silver and gold and the
articles that he and his father had dedicated.

16There was war between Asa and Baasha king of Israel throughout their
reigns. 17Baasha king of Israel went up against Judah and fortified Ramah to prevent anyone from leaving or entering the territory of Asa king of Judah.

18Asa then took all the silver and gold that was left in the treasuries of the
LORD's temple and of his own palace. He entrusted it to his officials and sent
them to Ben-Hadad son of Tabrimmon, the son of Hezion, the king of Aram, who
was ruling in Damascus. 19"Let there be a treaty between me and you," he said,
"as there was between my father and your father. See, I am sending you a gift
of silver and gold. Now break your treaty with Baasha king of Israel so he will
withdraw from me."

20Ben-Hadad agreed with King Asa and sent the commanders of his forces
against the towns of Israel. He conquered Ijon, Dan, Abel Beth Maakah and all
Kinnereth in addition to Naphtali. 21When Baasha heard this, he stopped building Ramah and withdrew to Tirzah. 22Then King Asa issued an order to all Judah—no one was exempt—and they carried away from Ramah the stones and
timber Baasha had been using there. With them King Asa built up Geba in Benjamin, and also Mizpah.

23As for all the other events of Asa's reign, all his achievements, all he did and
the cities he built, are they not written in the book of the annals of the kings of
Judah? In his old age, however, his feet became diseased. 24Then Asa rested with
his ancestors and was buried with them in the city of his father David. And Jehoshaphat his son succeeded him as king.

Nadab King of Israel

25Nadab son of Jeroboam became king of Israel in the second year of Asa king
of Judah, and he reigned over Israel two years. 26He did evil in the eyes of the
LORD, following the ways of his father and committing the same sin his father
had caused Israel to commit.

27Baasha son of Ahijah from the tribe of Issachar plotted against him, and
he struck him down at Gibbethon, a Philistine town, while Nadab and all Israel
were besieging it. 28Baasha killed Nadab in the third year of Asa king of Judah
and succeeded him as king.

29As soon as he began to reign, he killed Jeroboam's whole family. He did not
leave Jeroboam anyone that breathed, but destroyed them all, according to the
word of the LORD given through his servant Ahijah the Shilonite. 30This happened because of the sins Jeroboam had committed and had caused Israel to
commit, and because he aroused the anger of the LORD, the God of Israel.

31As for the other events of Nadab's reign, and all he did, are they not written
in the book of the annals of the kings of Israel? 32There was war between Asa and
Baasha king of Israel throughout their reigns.

Baasha King of Israel

33In the third year of Asa king of Judah, Baasha son of Ahijah became king of
all Israel in Tirzah, and he reigned twenty-four years. 34He did evil in the eyes of
the LORD, following the ways of Jeroboam and committing the same sin Jeroboam had caused Israel to commit.

16 Then the word of the LORD came to Jehu son of Hanani concerning Baasha: 2"I lifted you up from the dust and appointed you ruler over my people
Israel, but you followed the ways of Jeroboam and caused my people Israel to sin
and to arouse my anger by their sins. 3So I am about to wipe out Baasha and his

house, and I will make your house like that of Jeroboam son of Nebat. 4Dogs will
eat those belonging to Baasha who die in the city, and birds will feed on those
who die in the country."
5As for the other events of Baasha's reign, what he did and his achievements,
are they not written in the book of the annals of the kings of Israel? 6Baasha
rested with his ancestors and was buried in Tirzah. And Elah his son succeeded
him as king.
7Moreover, the word of the LORD came through the prophet Jehu son of Hanani to Baasha and his house, because of all the evil he had done in the eyes of
the LORD, arousing his anger by the things he did, becoming like the house of
Jeroboam — and also because he destroyed it.

Elah King of Israel

8In the twenty-sixth year of Asa king of Judah, Elah son of Baasha became
king of Israel, and he reigned in Tirzah two years.
9Zimri, one of his officials, who had command of half his chariots, plotted
against him. Elah was in Tirzah at the time, getting drunk in the home of Arza,
the palace administrator at Tirzah. 10Zimri came in, struck him down and killed
him in the twenty-seventh year of Asa king of Judah. Then he succeeded him
as king.
11As soon as he began to reign and was seated on the throne, he killed off Baasha's whole family. He did not spare a single male, whether relative or friend.
12So Zimri destroyed the whole family of Baasha, in accordance with the word
of the LORD spoken against Baasha through the prophet Jehu — 13because of
all the sins Baasha and his son Elah had committed and had caused Israel to
commit, so that they aroused the anger of the LORD, the God of Israel, by their
worthless idols.
14As for the other events of Elah's reign, and all he did, are they not written in
the book of the annals of the kings of Israel?

Zimri King of Israel

15In the twenty-seventh year of Asa king of Judah, Zimri reigned in Tirzah
seven days. The army was encamped near Gibbethon, a Philistine town. 16When
the Israelites in the camp heard that Zimri had plotted against the king and murdered him, they proclaimed Omri, the commander of the army, king over Israel that very day there in the camp. 17Then Omri and all the Israelites with him
withdrew from Gibbethon and laid siege to Tirzah. 18When Zimri saw that the
city was taken, he went into the citadel of the royal palace and set the palace on
fire around him. So he died, 19because of the sins he had committed, doing evil
in the eyes of the LORD and following the ways of Jeroboam and committing the
same sin Jeroboam had caused Israel to commit.
20As for the other events of Zimri's reign, and the rebellion he carried out, are
they not written in the book of the annals of the kings of Israel?

Omri King of Israel

21Then the people of Israel were split into two factions; half supported Tibni
son of Ginath for king, and the other half supported Omri. 22But Omri's followers proved stronger than those of Tibni son of Ginath. So Tibni died and Omri
became king.
23In the thirty-first year of Asa king of Judah, Omri became king of Israel, and
he reigned twelve years, six of them in Tirzah. 24He bought the hill of Samaria
from Shemer for two talents[a] of silver and built a city on the hill, calling it Samaria, after Shemer, the name of the former owner of the hill.
25But Omri did evil in the eyes of the LORD and sinned more than all those
before him. 26He followed completely the ways of Jeroboam son of Nebat,

[a] *24* That is, about 150 pounds or about 68 kilograms

committing the same sin Jeroboam had caused Israel to commit, so that they
aroused the anger of the LORD, the God of Israel, by their worthless idols.
27 As for the other events of Omri's reign, what he did and the things he
achieved, are they not written in the book of the annals of the kings of Israel?
28 Omri rested with his ancestors and was buried in Samaria. And Ahab his son
succeeded him as king.

Ahab Becomes King of Israel

29 In the thirty-eighth year of Asa king of Judah, Ahab son of Omri became king
of Israel, and he reigned in Samaria over Israel twenty-two years. 30 Ahab son of
Omri did more evil in the eyes of the LORD than any of those before him. 31 He not
only considered it trivial to commit the sins of Jeroboam son of Nebat, but he also
married Jezebel daughter of Ethbaal king of the Sidonians, and began to serve
Baal and worship him. 32 He set up an altar for Baal in the temple of Baal that he
built in Samaria. 33 Ahab also made an Asherah pole and did more to arouse the
anger of the LORD, the God of Israel, than did all the kings of Israel before him.
34 In Ahab's time, Hiel of Bethel rebuilt Jericho. He laid its foundations at the
cost of his firstborn son Abiram, and he set up its gates at the cost of his youngest son Segub, in accordance with the word of the LORD spoken by Joshua son
of Nun.

Elijah Announces a Great Drought

17 Now Elijah the Tishbite, from Tishbe[a] in Gilead, said to Ahab, "As the
LORD, the God of Israel, lives, whom I serve, there will be neither dew nor
rain in the next few years except at my word."

Elijah Fed by Ravens

2 Then the word of the LORD came to Elijah: 3 "Leave here, turn eastward and
hide in the Kerith Ravine, east of the Jordan. 4 You will drink from the brook, and
I have directed the ravens to supply you with food there."
5 So he did what the LORD had told him. He went to the Kerith Ravine, east of
the Jordan, and stayed there. 6 The ravens brought him bread and meat in the
morning and bread and meat in the evening, and he drank from the brook.

Elijah and the Widow at Zarephath

7 Some time later the brook dried up because there had been no rain in the
land. 8 Then the word of the LORD came to him: 9 "Go at once to Zarephath in the
region of Sidon and stay there. I have directed a widow there to supply you with
food." 10 So he went to Zarephath. When he came to the town gate, a widow was
there gathering sticks. He called to her and asked, "Would you bring me a little
water in a jar so I may have a drink?" 11 As she was going to get it, he called, "And
bring me, please, a piece of bread."
12 "As surely as the LORD your God lives," she replied, "I don't have any bread—
only a handful of flour in a jar and a little olive oil in a jug. I am gathering a few
sticks to take home and make a meal for myself and my son, that we may eat
it—and die."
13 Elijah said to her, "Don't be afraid. Go home and do as you have said. But
first make a small loaf of bread for me from what you have and bring it to me, and
then make something for yourself and your son. 14 For this is what the LORD, the
God of Israel, says: 'The jar of flour will not be used up and the jug of oil will not
run dry until the day the LORD sends rain on the land.'"
15 She went away and did as Elijah had told her. So there was food every day
for Elijah and for the woman and her family. 16 For the jar of flour was not used
up and the jug of oil did not run dry, in keeping with the word of the LORD spoken by Elijah.

[a] 1 Or *Tishbite, of the settlers*

1 KINGS 16:29–33

THE BAD ROAD DOWNWARD

The downward trajectory of the northern kingdom reached new depths in the appointment of Ahab as king over Israel. While the list of sins recounted here is far from unique to Ahab, the extent of his rebellion eclipsed all of those who ruled prior to him. The unraveling of the nation and the continued spread of sin among the people reveal a simple fact—sin is never static. It grows, expands and contaminates all that it touches. No person or nation, even the nation of Israel, is immune to its destructive nature.

Jesus entered a culture that continued to bear the marks of the impact and spread of sin. Human government is unable to rid itself from the effects of sin and the implications of the fall. Into this broken world, Jesus ushered a new kingdom marked by his perfect rule and reign (Mt 3:2). Submission to Jesus breaks the cycle of sin and provides the hope and peace no human king could ever bring.

[17]Some time later the son of the woman who owned the house became ill.
He grew worse and worse, and finally stopped breathing. [18]She said to Elijah,
"What do you have against me, man of God? Did you come to remind me of my
sin and kill my son?"
[19]"Give me your son," Elijah replied. He took him from her arms, carried him
to the upper room where he was staying, and laid him on his bed. [20]Then he cried
out to the LORD, "LORD my God, have you brought tragedy even on this widow I
am staying with, by causing her son to die?" [21]Then he stretched himself out on
the boy three times and cried out to the LORD, "LORD my God, let this boy's life
return to him!"
[22]The LORD heard Elijah's cry, and the boy's life returned to him, and he lived.
[23]Elijah picked up the child and carried him down from the room into the house.
He gave him to his mother and said, "Look, your son is alive!"
[24]Then the woman said to Elijah, "Now I know that you are a man of God and
that the word of the LORD from your mouth is the truth."

Elijah and Obadiah

18 After a long time, in the third year, the word of the LORD came to Elijah:
"Go and present yourself to Ahab, and I will send rain on the land." [2]So
Elijah went to present himself to Ahab.
Now the famine was severe in Samaria, [3]and Ahab had summoned Obadiah,
his palace administrator. (Obadiah was a devout believer in the LORD. [4]While
Jezebel was killing off the LORD's prophets, Obadiah had taken a hundred prophets and hidden them in two caves, fifty in each, and had supplied them with food
and water.) [5]Ahab had said to Obadiah, "Go through the land to all the springs
and valleys. Maybe we can find some grass to keep the horses and mules alive so
we will not have to kill any of our animals." [6]So they divided the land they were
to cover, Ahab going in one direction and Obadiah in another.
[7]As Obadiah was walking along, Elijah met him. Obadiah recognized him,
bowed down to the ground, and said, "Is it really you, my lord Elijah?"
[8]"Yes," he replied. "Go tell your master, 'Elijah is here.'"
[9]"What have I done wrong," asked Obadiah, "that you are handing your servant
over to Ahab to be put to death? [10]As surely as the LORD your God lives, there is not
a nation or kingdom where my master has not sent someone to look for you. And
whenever a nation or kingdom claimed you were not there, he made them swear
they could not find you. [11]But now you tell me to go to my master and say, 'Elijah is
here.' [12]I don't know where the Spirit of the LORD may carry you when I leave you.
If I go and tell Ahab and he doesn't find you, he will kill me. Yet I your servant have
worshiped the LORD since my youth. [13]Haven't you heard, my lord, what I did while
Jezebel was killing the prophets of the LORD? I hid a hundred of the LORD's prophets in two caves, fifty in each, and supplied them with food and water. [14]And now
you tell me to go to my master and say, 'Elijah is here.' He will kill me!"
[15]Elijah said, "As the LORD Almighty lives, whom I serve, I will surely present
myself to Ahab today."

Elijah on Mount Carmel

[16]So Obadiah went to meet Ahab and told him, and Ahab went to meet Elijah.
[17]When he saw Elijah, he said to him, "Is that you, you troubler of Israel?"
[18]"I have not made trouble for Israel," Elijah replied. "But you and your father's
family have. You have abandoned the LORD's commands and have followed the
Baals. [19]Now summon the people from all over Israel to meet me on Mount Carmel. And bring the four hundred and fifty prophets of Baal and the four hundred
prophets of Asherah, who eat at Jezebel's table."
[20]So Ahab sent word throughout all Israel and assembled the prophets on
Mount Carmel. [21]Elijah went before the people and said, "How long will you waver between two opinions? If the LORD is God, follow him; but if Baal is God,
follow him."

THE BREAD OF LIFE

Elijah's actions in chapter 17 are a demonstration of the power of God to provide for people and overcome the disastrous effects of sin and death. Through power given to him by God, Elijah multiplied a small amount of flour and oil in order to provide bread for the widow and her son for many days. God also worked through Elijah to bring the widow's son back to life after he became sick and died. These miracles marked Elijah as God's appointed messenger at that stage in history.

However, Elijah's two miracles recounted in this text have additional significance: they prefigure the person and work of Jesus Christ. Jesus, as God's Son and appointed messenger, was personally able to turn a meager meal into a feast for multitudes (Mt 14:13 – 21). The feeding of the 5,000 boldly proclaimed that Jesus was capable of abundantly providing for people. Jesus' provision was not limited to mere physical bread, though. He claimed to be the true bread from heaven, sent to provide for all those who would feast on him (Jn 6:26 – 51).

Jesus also performed other miracles, proving him to be God in the flesh and one who possessed ultimate power over sin and death. Like Elijah, Jesus brought the dead son of a widow back to life. Seeing the woman and having compassion on her, Jesus spoke to the son and he sat up and began to speak (Lk 7:11 – 15). Jesus said that acts like these demonstrated that he was the Messiah who would bring healing and restoration to those broken by sin's consequences (Lk 7:18 – 23).

The death of Jesus' friend Lazarus provided another opportunity for him to demonstrate the power he possessed. Unlike the widow's son, Lazarus had been dead for several days and his body had been wrapped in funeral linens and placed in a tomb. Jesus prayed to the Father and then spoke to the corpse, calling it to life. Jesus attested to the fact that raising Lazarus served as a testimony to the glory of God (Jn 11:1 – 44).

Soon this glory was seen in a far greater resurrection — that of Jesus himself. The power of God over Satan, sin and death was fully demonstrated by Christ's victorious emergence from the grave. His resurrected life would serve as a firstfruits of the resurrection promised to all those who place their faith in him. By God's power, all those longing for provision and broken by death can be restored to new life, now and forevermore.

But the people said nothing.

22 Then Elijah said to them, "I am the only one of the LORD's prophets left, but Baal has four hundred and fifty prophets. 23 Get two bulls for us. Let Baal's prophets choose one for themselves, and let them cut it into pieces and put it on the wood but not set fire to it. I will prepare the other bull and put it on the wood but not set fire to it. 24 Then you call on the name of your god, and I will call on the name of the LORD. The god who answers by fire — he is God."

Then all the people said, "What you say is good."

25 Elijah said to the prophets of Baal, "Choose one of the bulls and prepare it first, since there are so many of you. Call on the name of your god, but do not light the fire." 26 So they took the bull given them and prepared it.

Then they called on the name of Baal from morning till noon. "Baal, answer us!" they shouted. But there was no response; no one answered. And they danced around the altar they had made.

27 At noon Elijah began to taunt them. "Shout louder!" he said. "Surely he is a god! Perhaps he is deep in thought, or busy, or traveling. Maybe he is sleeping and must be awakened." 28 So they shouted louder and slashed themselves with swords and spears, as was their custom, until their blood flowed. 29 Midday passed, and they continued their frantic prophesying until the time for the evening sacrifice. But there was no response, no one answered, no one paid attention.

30 Then Elijah said to all the people, "Come here to me." They came to him, and he repaired the altar of the LORD, which had been torn down. 31 Elijah took twelve stones, one for each of the tribes descended from Jacob, to whom the word of the LORD had come, saying, "Your name shall be Israel." 32 With the stones he built an altar in the name of the LORD, and he dug a trench around it large enough to hold two seahs[a] of seed. 33 He arranged the wood, cut the bull into pieces and laid it on the wood. Then he said to them, "Fill four large jars with water and pour it on the offering and on the wood."

34 "Do it again," he said, and they did it again.

"Do it a third time," he ordered, and they did it the third time. 35 The water ran down around the altar and even filled the trench.

36 At the time of sacrifice, the prophet Elijah stepped forward and prayed: "LORD, the God of Abraham, Isaac and Israel, let it be known today that you are God in Israel and that I am your servant and have done all these things at your command. 37 Answer me, LORD, answer me, so these people will know that you, LORD, are God, and that you are turning their hearts back again."

38 Then the fire of the LORD fell and burned up the sacrifice, the wood, the stones and the soil, and also licked up the water in the trench.

39 When all the people saw this, they fell prostrate and cried, "The LORD — he is God! The LORD — he is God!"

40 Then Elijah commanded them, "Seize the prophets of Baal. Don't let anyone get away!" They seized them, and Elijah had them brought down to the Kishon Valley and slaughtered there.

41 And Elijah said to Ahab, "Go, eat and drink, for there is the sound of a heavy rain." 42 So Ahab went off to eat and drink, but Elijah climbed to the top of Carmel, bent down to the ground and put his face between his knees.

43 "Go and look toward the sea," he told his servant. And he went up and looked.

"There is nothing there," he said.

Seven times Elijah said, "Go back."

44 The seventh time the servant reported, "A cloud as small as a man's hand is rising from the sea."

So Elijah said, "Go and tell Ahab, 'Hitch up your chariot and go down before the rain stops you.' "

---

[a] *32* That is, probably about 24 pounds or about 11 kilograms

TURNING HEARTS TO GOD

The confrontation between Elijah and the prophets of Baal on Mount Carmel is one of the most well-known stories in the book of 1 Kings. As God's messenger, Elijah boldly confronted the pagan worship that not only filled the surrounding nations but also had become rampant among the people of God. Elijah mocked the inability of the pagan gods to prove their power by consuming the offering on the altar. Elijah seemingly stacked the odds against his God; however, in a mighty display of power, the Lord consumed not only the sacrificial offering but also the wood, the stones and the water Elijah had poured on the altar.

After this miraculous episode, threatened by Jezebel and fearing for his life, Elijah ran into the desert, wanting to end it all (1Ki 19:4). His mountaintop testimony to the glory of God had not turned the hearts of the people back to God or halted the nation's headlong course toward destruction — a course that even the greatest leaders in the nation's history had seemed powerless to stop.

In spite of the nation's failure to return to God in a meaningful way, God continued to display his glorious might through history. At each juncture, the goal was not merely to correct the behavior of people but to redirect their hearts toward proper worship. His glory was meant to turn the hearts of people. This work was necessary due to the fact that sin positions all human hearts in opposition to God, leading them to turn their backs on him and harden their hearts in rebellion. Like Pharaoh in Egypt, no matter what mighty acts humans observe, they staunchly refuse to acknowledge the truthfulness of the claims of Christ and the depravity of their own hearts. God could rightly give people over to their sin and let them run from him forever. But in his grace he continues to demonstrate his glory in order to turn their hearts back to him in worship.

When humans turn from their sin and turn to Christ, they display the fact that God has replaced their hearts of stone with soft and pliable hearts (Eze 36:26). These new hearts, pulsating with life given by the power of God, are drawn to the awe-inspiring glory of God.

45 Meanwhile, the sky grew black with clouds, the wind rose, a heavy rain started falling and Ahab rode off to Jezreel. 46 The power of the LORD came on Elijah and, tucking his cloak into his belt, he ran ahead of Ahab all the way to Jezreel.

Elijah Flees to Horeb

19 Now Ahab told Jezebel everything Elijah had done and how he had killed all the prophets with the sword. 2 So Jezebel sent a messenger to Elijah to say, "May the gods deal with me, be it ever so severely, if by this time tomorrow I do not make your life like that of one of them."

3 Elijah was afraid[a] and ran for his life. When he came to Beersheba in Judah, he left his servant there, 4 while he himself went a day's journey into the wilderness. He came to a broom bush, sat down under it and prayed that he might die. "I have had enough, LORD," he said. "Take my life; I am no better than my ancestors." 5 Then he lay down under the bush and fell asleep.

All at once an angel touched him and said, "Get up and eat." 6 He looked around, and there by his head was some bread baked over hot coals, and a jar of water. He ate and drank and then lay down again.

7 The angel of the LORD came back a second time and touched him and said, "Get up and eat, for the journey is too much for you." 8 So he got up and ate and drank. Strengthened by that food, he traveled forty days and forty nights until he reached Horeb, the mountain of God. 9 There he went into a cave and spent the night.

The LORD Appears to Elijah

And the word of the LORD came to him: "What are you doing here, Elijah?"

10 He replied, "I have been very zealous for the LORD God Almighty. The Israelites have rejected your covenant, torn down your altars, and put your prophets to death with the sword. I am the only one left, and now they are trying to kill me too."

11 The LORD said, "Go out and stand on the mountain in the presence of the LORD, for the LORD is about to pass by."

Then a great and powerful wind tore the mountains apart and shattered the rocks before the LORD, but the LORD was not in the wind. After the wind there was an earthquake, but the LORD was not in the earthquake. 12 After the earthquake came a fire, but the LORD was not in the fire. And after the fire came a gentle whisper. 13 When Elijah heard it, he pulled his cloak over his face and went out and stood at the mouth of the cave.

Then a voice said to him, "What are you doing here, Elijah?"

14 He replied, "I have been very zealous for the LORD God Almighty. The Israelites have rejected your covenant, torn down your altars, and put your prophets to death with the sword. I am the only one left, and now they are trying to kill me too."

15 The LORD said to him, "Go back the way you came, and go to the Desert of Damascus. When you get there, anoint Hazael king over Aram. 16 Also, anoint Jehu son of Nimshi king over Israel, and anoint Elisha son of Shaphat from Abel Meholah to succeed you as prophet. 17 Jehu will put to death any who escape the sword of Hazael, and Elisha will put to death any who escape the sword of Jehu. 18 Yet I reserve seven thousand in Israel — all whose knees have not bowed down to Baal and whose mouths have not kissed him."

The Call of Elisha

19 So Elijah went from there and found Elisha son of Shaphat. He was plowing with twelve yoke of oxen, and he himself was driving the twelfth pair. Elijah went up to him and threw his cloak around him. 20 Elisha then left his oxen and

1 KINGS 19:1 – 18

GOD'S PROVISION FOR HIS SERVANTS

God provided for Elijah by meeting his needs, protecting his life and speaking to him in a gentle whisper. Although Elijah was running for his life and lacked the basic provisions required to survive, God provided for his messenger. In a similar way, when Jesus sent out his new messengers, the disciples, to declare and demonstrate the good news message, he ensured that they had the necessary resources. Jesus instructed them not to worry about carrying sufficient provision for their journey. They were not to take a staff, a bag, bread, money or even a change of clothes (Lk 9:1 – 6). God would provide for these needs as he had for the nation of Israel in the wilderness and for messengers like Elijah. They only needed to trust him.

Christians today can live with the same bold confidence in the care of God, who promises to go with them as they go to make disciples of all nations (Mt 28:19 – 20). Though they may face suffering, encounter harm or even be put to death, God's children can trust that he will allow them to accomplish the mission he has placed before them and will forever meet their needs according to the glorious riches of his grace toward them in Christ Jesus (Php 4:19).

[a] 3 Or *Elijah saw*

ran after Elijah. "Let me kiss my father and mother goodbye," he said, "and then
I will come with you."
"Go back," Elijah replied. "What have I done to you?"
21 So Elisha left him and went back. He took his yoke of oxen and slaughtered
them. He burned the plowing equipment to cook the meat and gave it to the
people, and they ate. Then he set out to follow Elijah and became his servant.

Ben-Hadad Attacks Samaria

20 Now Ben-Hadad king of Aram mustered his entire army. Accompanied by
thirty-two kings with their horses and chariots, he went up and besieged
Samaria and attacked it. 2 He sent messengers into the city to Ahab king of Israel,
saying, "This is what Ben-Hadad says: 3 'Your silver and gold are mine, and the
best of your wives and children are mine.' "
4 The king of Israel answered, "Just as you say, my lord the king. I and all I have
are yours."
5 The messengers came again and said, "This is what Ben-Hadad says: 'I sent
to demand your silver and gold, your wives and your children. 6 But about this
time tomorrow I am going to send my officials to search your palace and the
houses of your officials. They will seize everything you value and carry it away.' "
7 The king of Israel summoned all the elders of the land and said to them, "See
how this man is looking for trouble! When he sent for my wives and my children,
my silver and my gold, I did not refuse him."
8 The elders and the people all answered, "Don't listen to him or agree to his
demands."
9 So he replied to Ben-Hadad's messengers, "Tell my lord the king, 'Your servant will do all you demanded the first time, but this demand I cannot meet.' "
They left and took the answer back to Ben-Hadad.
10 Then Ben-Hadad sent another message to Ahab: "May the gods deal with
me, be it ever so severely, if enough dust remains in Samaria to give each of my
men a handful."
11 The king of Israel answered, "Tell him: 'One who puts on his armor should
not boast like one who takes it off.' "
12 Ben-Hadad heard this message while he and the kings were drinking in
their tents,[a] and he ordered his men: "Prepare to attack." So they prepared to
attack the city.

Ahab Defeats Ben-Hadad

13 Meanwhile a prophet came to Ahab king of Israel and announced, "This is
what the LORD says: 'Do you see this vast army? I will give it into your hand today,
and then you will know that I am the LORD.' "
14 "But who will do this?" asked Ahab.
The prophet replied, "This is what the LORD says: 'The junior officers under
the provincial commanders will do it.' "
"And who will start the battle?" he asked.
The prophet answered, "You will."
15 So Ahab summoned the 232 junior officers under the provincial commanders. Then he assembled the rest of the Israelites, 7,000 in all. 16 They set out at
noon while Ben-Hadad and the 32 kings allied with him were in their tents getting drunk. 17 The junior officers under the provincial commanders went out first.
Now Ben-Hadad had dispatched scouts, who reported, "Men are advancing
from Samaria."
18 He said, "If they have come out for peace, take them alive; if they have come
out for war, take them alive."
19 The junior officers under the provincial commanders marched out of the
city with the army behind them 20 and each one struck down his opponent. At

[a] 12 Or *in Sukkoth*; also in verse 16

that, the Arameans fled, with the Israelites in pursuit. But Ben-Hadad king of Aram escaped on horseback with some of his horsemen. [21]The king of Israel advanced and overpowered the horses and chariots and inflicted heavy losses on the Arameans.

[22]Afterward, the prophet came to the king of Israel and said, "Strengthen your position and see what must be done, because next spring the king of Aram will attack you again."

[23]Meanwhile, the officials of the king of Aram advised him, "Their gods are gods of the hills. That is why they were too strong for us. But if we fight them on the plains, surely we will be stronger than they. [24]Do this: Remove all the kings from their commands and replace them with other officers. [25]You must also raise an army like the one you lost—horse for horse and chariot for chariot—so we can fight Israel on the plains. Then surely we will be stronger than they." He agreed with them and acted accordingly.

[26]The next spring Ben-Hadad mustered the Arameans and went up to Aphek to fight against Israel. [27]When the Israelites were also mustered and given provisions, they marched out to meet them. The Israelites camped opposite them like two small flocks of goats, while the Arameans covered the countryside.

[28]The man of God came up and told the king of Israel, "This is what the LORD says: 'Because the Arameans think the LORD is a god of the hills and not a god of the valleys, I will deliver this vast army into your hands, and you will know that I am the LORD.'"

[29]For seven days they camped opposite each other, and on the seventh day the battle was joined. The Israelites inflicted a hundred thousand casualties on the Aramean foot soldiers in one day. [30]The rest of them escaped to the city of Aphek, where the wall collapsed on twenty-seven thousand of them. And Ben-Hadad fled to the city and hid in an inner room.

[31]His officials said to him, "Look, we have heard that the kings of Israel are merciful. Let us go to the king of Israel with sackcloth around our waists and ropes around our heads. Perhaps he will spare your life."

[32]Wearing sackcloth around their waists and ropes around their heads, they went to the king of Israel and said, "Your servant Ben-Hadad says: 'Please let me live.'"

The king answered, "Is he still alive? He is my brother."

[33]The men took this as a good sign and were quick to pick up his word. "Yes, your brother Ben-Hadad!" they said.

"Go and get him," the king said. When Ben-Hadad came out, Ahab had him come up into his chariot.

[34]"I will return the cities my father took from your father," Ben-Hadad offered. "You may set up your own market areas in Damascus, as my father did in Samaria."

Ahab said, "On the basis of a treaty I will set you free." So he made a treaty with him, and let him go.

A Prophet Condemns Ahab

[35]By the word of the LORD one of the company of the prophets said to his companion, "Strike me with your weapon," but he refused.

[36]So the prophet said, "Because you have not obeyed the LORD, as soon as you leave me a lion will kill you." And after the man went away, a lion found him and killed him.

[37]The prophet found another man and said, "Strike me, please." So the man struck him and wounded him. [38]Then the prophet went and stood by the road waiting for the king. He disguised himself with his headband down over his eyes. [39]As the king passed by, the prophet called out to him, "Your servant went into the thick of the battle, and someone came to me with a captive and said, 'Guard this man. If he is missing, it will be your life for his life, or you must pay a talent[a] of silver.' [40]While your servant was busy here and there, the man disappeared."

1 KINGS 20:28

GOD OF THE HILLS AND THE VALLEYS

The Arameans embarked on their second campaign in the Jordan Valley from Aphek, a city east of the Sea of Galilee. The hills had long provided a prime advantage for the military of the northern kingdom of Israel. The Arameans assumed the reason the Israelites had been victorious in the past was that their god held power in the hill country. They would soon learn, however, that the Lord was not merely "a god of the hills" but also the God of the valleys. Israel's military position was not what allowed them to be victorious; rather, it was the power of God at work, both in the hills and in the valleys, or plains (1Ki 20:23–25). The same is true for every aspect of the lives of God's people. Whether in the high places of life or in the valleys, God is faithful to his people. As the well-loved psalm recounts, "Even though I walk through the darkest valley, I will fear no evil, for you are with me" (Ps 23:4). The ever-present reality of God's Spirit allows believers to have hope, even in the deepest valleys of life.

[a] 39 That is, about 75 pounds or about 34 kilograms

"That is your sentence," the king of Israel said. "You have pronounced it yourself."
41 Then the prophet quickly removed the headband from his eyes, and the
king of Israel recognized him as one of the prophets. 42 He said to the king, "This
is what the LORD says: 'You have set free a man I had determined should die.[a]
Therefore it is your life for his life, your people for his people.' " 43 Sullen and angry, the king of Israel went to his palace in Samaria.

Naboth's Vineyard

21 Some time later there was an incident involving a vineyard belonging to
Naboth the Jezreelite. The vineyard was in Jezreel, close to the palace of
Ahab king of Samaria. 2 Ahab said to Naboth, "Let me have your vineyard to use
for a vegetable garden, since it is close to my palace. In exchange I will give you a
better vineyard or, if you prefer, I will pay you whatever it is worth."
3 But Naboth replied, "The LORD forbid that I should give you the inheritance
of my ancestors."
4 So Ahab went home, sullen and angry because Naboth the Jezreelite had
said, "I will not give you the inheritance of my ancestors." He lay on his bed sulking and refused to eat.
5 His wife Jezebel came in and asked him, "Why are you so sullen? Why won't
you eat?"
6 He answered her, "Because I said to Naboth the Jezreelite, 'Sell me your vineyard; or if you prefer, I will give you another vineyard in its place.' But he said, 'I
will not give you my vineyard.' "
7 Jezebel his wife said, "Is this how you act as king over Israel? Get up and eat!
Cheer up. I'll get you the vineyard of Naboth the Jezreelite."
8 So she wrote letters in Ahab's name, placed his seal on them, and sent them
to the elders and nobles who lived in Naboth's city with him. 9 In those letters
she wrote:

> "Proclaim a day of fasting and seat Naboth in a prominent place among
> the people. 10 But seat two scoundrels opposite him and have them bring
> charges that he has cursed both God and the king. Then take him out and
> stone him to death."

11 So the elders and nobles who lived in Naboth's city did as Jezebel directed
in the letters she had written to them. 12 They proclaimed a fast and seated Naboth in a prominent place among the people. 13 Then two scoundrels came and
sat opposite him and brought charges against Naboth before the people, saying,
"Naboth has cursed both God and the king." So they took him outside the city
and stoned him to death. 14 Then they sent word to Jezebel: "Naboth has been
stoned to death."
15 As soon as Jezebel heard that Naboth had been stoned to death, she said
to Ahab, "Get up and take possession of the vineyard of Naboth the Jezreelite
that he refused to sell you. He is no longer alive, but dead." 16 When Ahab heard
that Naboth was dead, he got up and went down to take possession of Naboth's
vineyard.
17 Then the word of the LORD came to Elijah the Tishbite: 18 "Go down to meet
Ahab king of Israel, who rules in Samaria. He is now in Naboth's vineyard, where
he has gone to take possession of it. 19 Say to him, 'This is what the LORD says:
Have you not murdered a man and seized his property?' Then say to him, 'This
is what the LORD says: In the place where dogs licked up Naboth's blood, dogs
will lick up your blood—yes, yours!' "
20 Ahab said to Elijah, "So you have found me, my enemy!"
"I have found you," he answered, "because you have sold yourself to do evil in
the eyes of the LORD. 21 He says, 'I am going to bring disaster on you. I will wipe

[a] *42* The Hebrew term refers to the irrevocable giving over of things or persons to the LORD, often by totally destroying them.

1 KINGS 21:17–19

BLOOD POURED OUT

The Lord's graphic and decisive judgment on King Ahab corresponded to the king's blatant disregard for the commandments of God. Dogs licked up the blood of this once-mighty king by the pool in Samaria (22:37–38). Ahab's death stands as a stark testimony to the dire consequences of abandoning God's law. In taking Naboth's vineyard (cf. Dt 19:14), Ahab revealed that he loved neither God nor his neighbor—the totality of the law of God.

King Jesus lived and died for rebels who fail to love God and their neighbor. His blood was poured out, like King Ahab, as a result of human sin. Jesus, however, was not guilty of sin himself. Rather, he willingly gave his life so that his blood would satisfy the wrath of God, which all of humanity deserved. By faith and repentance, sinful rebels like Ahab can avoid the terrible fate that they deserve.

out your descendants and cut off from Ahab every last male in Israel — slave or
free.[a] 22I will make your house like that of Jeroboam son of Nebat and that of
Baasha son of Ahijah, because you have aroused my anger and have caused Israel to sin.'

23"And also concerning Jezebel the LORD says: 'Dogs will devour Jezebel by
the wall of[b] Jezreel.'

24"Dogs will eat those belonging to Ahab who die in the city, and the birds will
feed on those who die in the country."

25(There was never anyone like Ahab, who sold himself to do evil in the eyes
of the LORD, urged on by Jezebel his wife. 26He behaved in the vilest manner by
going after idols, like the Amorites the LORD drove out before Israel.)

27When Ahab heard these words, he tore his clothes, put on sackcloth and
fasted. He lay in sackcloth and went around meekly.

28Then the word of the LORD came to Elijah the Tishbite: 29"Have you noticed
how Ahab has humbled himself before me? Because he has humbled himself, I
will not bring this disaster in his day, but I will bring it on his house in the days
of his son."

Micaiah Prophesies Against Ahab

22 For three years there was no war between Aram and Israel. 2But in the
third year Jehoshaphat king of Judah went down to see the king of Israel.
3The king of Israel had said to his officials, "Don't you know that Ramoth Gilead
belongs to us and yet we are doing nothing to retake it from the king of Aram?"

4So he asked Jehoshaphat, "Will you go with me to fight against Ramoth Gilead?"

Jehoshaphat replied to the king of Israel, "I am as you are, my people as your
people, my horses as your horses." 5But Jehoshaphat also said to the king of Israel, "First seek the counsel of the LORD."

6So the king of Israel brought together the prophets — about four hundred
men — and asked them, "Shall I go to war against Ramoth Gilead, or shall I refrain?"

"Go," they answered, "for the Lord will give it into the king's hand."

7But Jehoshaphat asked, "Is there no longer a prophet of the LORD here whom
we can inquire of?"

8The king of Israel answered Jehoshaphat, "There is still one prophet through
whom we can inquire of the LORD, but I hate him because he never prophesies
anything good about me, but always bad. He is Micaiah son of Imlah."

"The king should not say such a thing," Jehoshaphat replied.

9So the king of Israel called one of his officials and said, "Bring Micaiah son
of Imlah at once."

10Dressed in their royal robes, the king of Israel and Jehoshaphat king of Judah were sitting on their thrones at the threshing floor by the entrance of the
gate of Samaria, with all the prophets prophesying before them. 11Now Zedekiah
son of Kenaanah had made iron horns and he declared, "This is what the LORD
says: 'With these you will gore the Arameans until they are destroyed.'"

12All the other prophets were prophesying the same thing. "Attack Ramoth
Gilead and be victorious," they said, "for the LORD will give it into the king's
hand."

13The messenger who had gone to summon Micaiah said to him, "Look, the
other prophets without exception are predicting success for the king. Let your
word agree with theirs, and speak favorably."

14But Micaiah said, "As surely as the LORD lives, I can tell him only what the
LORD tells me."

15When he arrived, the king asked him, "Micaiah, shall we go to war against
Ramoth Gilead, or not?"

---

[a] *21* Or *Israel — every ruler or leader* [b] *23* Most Hebrew manuscripts; a few Hebrew manuscripts, Vulgate and Syriac (see also 2 Kings 9:26) *the plot of ground at*

"Attack and be victorious," he answered, "for the LORD will give it into the
king's hand."
16The king said to him, "How many times must I make you swear to tell me
nothing but the truth in the name of the LORD?"
17Then Micaiah answered, "I saw all Israel scattered on the hills like sheep
without a shepherd, and the LORD said, 'These people have no master. Let each
one go home in peace.' "
18The king of Israel said to Jehoshaphat, "Didn't I tell you that he never prophesies anything good about me, but only bad?"
19Micaiah continued, "Therefore hear the word of the LORD: I saw the LORD
sitting on his throne with all the multitudes of heaven standing around him on
his right and on his left. 20And the LORD said, 'Who will entice Ahab into attacking Ramoth Gilead and going to his death there?'
"One suggested this, and another that. 21Finally, a spirit came forward, stood
before the LORD and said, 'I will entice him.'
22" 'By what means?' the LORD asked.
" 'I will go out and be a deceiving spirit in the mouths of all his prophets,' he
said.
" 'You will succeed in enticing him,' said the LORD. 'Go and do it.'
23"So now the LORD has put a deceiving spirit in the mouths of all these prophets of yours. The LORD has decreed disaster for you."
24Then Zedekiah son of Kenaanah went up and slapped Micaiah in the face.
"Which way did the spirit from[a] the LORD go when he went from me to speak to
you?" he asked.
25Micaiah replied, "You will find out on the day you go to hide in an inner
room."
26The king of Israel then ordered, "Take Micaiah and send him back to Amon
the ruler of the city and to Joash the king's son 27and say, 'This is what the king
says: Put this fellow in prison and give him nothing but bread and water until I
return safely.' "
28Micaiah declared, "If you ever return safely, the LORD has not spoken
through me." Then he added, "Mark my words, all you people!"

Ahab Killed at Ramoth Gilead

29So the king of Israel and Jehoshaphat king of Judah went up to Ramoth Gilead. 30The king of Israel said to Jehoshaphat, "I will enter the battle in disguise,
but you wear your royal robes." So the king of Israel disguised himself and went
into battle.
31Now the king of Aram had ordered his thirty-two chariot commanders, "Do
not fight with anyone, small or great, except the king of Israel." 32When the chariot commanders saw Jehoshaphat, they thought, "Surely this is the king of Israel." So they turned to attack him, but when Jehoshaphat cried out, 33the chariot
commanders saw that he was not the king of Israel and stopped pursuing him.
34But someone drew his bow at random and hit the king of Israel between the
sections of his armor. The king told his chariot driver, "Wheel around and get
me out of the fighting. I've been wounded." 35All day long the battle raged, and
the king was propped up in his chariot facing the Arameans. The blood from his
wound ran onto the floor of the chariot, and that evening he died. 36As the sun
was setting, a cry spread through the army: "Every man to his town. Every man
to his land!"
37So the king died and was brought to Samaria, and they buried him there.
38They washed the chariot at a pool in Samaria (where the prostitutes bathed),[b]
and the dogs licked up his blood, as the word of the LORD had declared.
39As for the other events of Ahab's reign, including all he did, the palace he
built and adorned with ivory, and the cities he fortified, are they not written in

---

[a] 24 Or *Spirit of* [b] 38 Or *Samaria and cleaned the weapons*

A PROPHET'S WARNING

Jehoshaphat, the good king of Judah, and Ahab, the wicked king of Israel, agreed to work together to fight the king of Aram and take back Ramoth Gilead. Jehoshaphat sought counsel from the Lord before going into battle. Ahab, desiring to secure military victory, was willing to seek God's direction as well, so long as that direction corresponded with what he wanted to hear. The 400 prophets Ahab gathered did just that — they told Ahab to go into battle and that God would give the land into his hand.

At Jehoshaphat's urging, Ahab sent for the prophet Micaiah. Complaining that Micaiah never prophesied anything good concerning him, Ahab assumed that Micaiah's words would contradict that of the other prophets. At first, it appeared as if God's prophet agreed with the pagan prophets who had spoken beforehand. Ahab continued his inquiry, suspecting that the prophet had more to reveal. His second message, though cryptic, sounded a clear note of warning. The Lord, in fact, had decreed disaster against the armies of Israel and Judah, which would result in the death of King Ahab. In spite of the warning, Jehoshaphat and Ahab rode off into battle and were soundly defeated. The seemingly random death of Ahab was a sure testimony to the truthfulness of God's message through the prophet Micaiah.

Throughout history, the Word of God has elicited a wide range of reactions. Some people, seeking to honor God and walk in his ways, respond to the Word of God with humility, repentance and obedience. Others, like the religious leaders of Jesus' day, demonstrate their hardness of heart by turning a deaf ear to the commands and warnings of God. Jesus continually denounced the leadership of these "blind guides." He claimed that not only were they deceived but they were also leading others into rebellion (Mt 15:14; 23:16,24). Like the 400 false prophets, the religious leaders of Jesus' day were leading people to follow a system that would result in their condemnation and ultimate death. Jesus, as the truer and better prophet, declared to them the futility of their behavior and pointed them to the path to life. But like King Ahab before them, many turned a deaf ear to these words.

the book of the annals of the kings of Israel? [40]Ahab rested with his ancestors.
And Ahaziah his son succeeded him as king.

Jehoshaphat King of Judah

[41]Jehoshaphat son of Asa became king of Judah in the fourth year of Ahab king
of Israel. [42]Jehoshaphat was thirty-five years old when he became king, and he
reigned in Jerusalem twenty-five years. His mother's name was Azubah daughter of Shilhi. [43]In everything he followed the ways of his father Asa and did not
stray from them; he did what was right in the eyes of the LORD. The high places,
however, were not removed, and the people continued to offer sacrifices and
burn incense there.[a] [44]Jehoshaphat was also at peace with the king of Israel.

[45]As for the other events of Jehoshaphat's reign, the things he achieved and
his military exploits, are they not written in the book of the annals of the kings of
Judah? [46]He rid the land of the rest of the male shrine prostitutes who remained
there even after the reign of his father Asa. [47]There was then no king in Edom; a
provincial governor ruled.

[48]Now Jehoshaphat built a fleet of trading ships[b] to go to Ophir for gold, but
they never set sail—they were wrecked at Ezion Geber. [49]At that time Ahaziah
son of Ahab said to Jehoshaphat, "Let my men sail with yours," but Jehoshaphat
refused.

[50]Then Jehoshaphat rested with his ancestors and was buried with them in
the city of David his father. And Jehoram his son succeeded him as king.

Ahaziah King of Israel

[51]Ahaziah son of Ahab became king of Israel in Samaria in the seventeenth
year of Jehoshaphat king of Judah, and he reigned over Israel two years. [52]He
did evil in the eyes of the LORD, because he followed the ways of his father and
mother and of Jeroboam son of Nebat, who caused Israel to sin. [53]He served and
worshiped Baal and aroused the anger of the LORD, the God of Israel, just as his
father had done.

---

[a] *43* In Hebrew texts this sentence (22:43b) is numbered 22:44, and 22:44-53 is numbered 22:45-54. [b] *48* Hebrew *of ships of Tarshish*

JESUS: OUR PERFECT PROPHET

2 KINGS

2 KINGS

ELISHA SUCCEEDS ELIJAH *c. 848 BC*	FALL OF ISRAEL *c. 722 BC*	FALL OF JUDAH *c. 586 BC*

The book of 2 Kings continues the narrative of the people of God as they divide into a northern and southern kingdom. It follows a timeline from the ascension of the prophet Elijah until the ultimate destruction and exile of the divided nations of Israel (722 BC) and Judah (586 BC). This story of the people of God emphasizes the cyclical pattern of sin — both among the leaders of the two nations and the people themselves. The leaders and the people rebelled against God, incurred his judgment, repented and promised to be faithful, only to fall into greater and greater forms of evil.

The book continues the chronological outline of the leaders of the two nations found in 1 Kings, beginning with the reigns of Ahaziah in the northern kingdom (853 – 852 BC) and Jehoshaphat in the southern kingdom (872 – 848 BC). The narrative follows two vibrant prophetic voices of the time — Elijah and Elisha — and recounts the stories of those shaped by their extended ministries (Elijah ministered for 27 years; Elisha for 51). These prophets provide insight into the role of Jesus, who would invade a spiritually dark world and call people to return to the one true and living God, to live under his rule and reign forever.

At one critical juncture in Israel's history, Jehu, the king of the northern kingdom, purged the rampant Baal worship that consistently plagued Israel (2Ki 10:18 – 28). Unfortunately, rather than leading the people to worship the one true God, Jehu continued to allow the worship of the golden calves set up by Jeroboam I (2Ki 10:29). During this time the southern kingdom did not fare much better, languishing under the leadership of the idolatrous king Ahaziah and his wicked mother, Queen Athaliah (2Ki 8:25 – 27; 11:1 – 3).

The death of King Zechariah in 752 BC marked the beginning of a period of rapid decline in the northern kingdom, mirroring its spiritual status. Foolish military and political alliances, combined with the people's spiritual lethargy and moral debauchery, led to their defeat at the hands of the Assyrians in 722 BC. Meanwhile, King Ahaz led the southern kingdom to a similar fate due to his idolatry and rebellion. A large portion of the book of 2 Kings describes the devolution of the nation from the righteous king Hezekiah to the wicked sons and grandsons of Josiah. Under their leadership, the nation faced three invasions and deportations — the last of which happened in 586 BC. Though the book ends tragically with each kingdom cast out of the land, Jehoiachin's release from prison at the end of the book provides a glimmer of hope (25:27 – 30). The Lord would remain faithful to his people and once again restore them to the land.

Throughout the Old Testament, Israel's experience serves as a template for the larger group of people of God throughout history. God's steadfast faithfulness never fails; those who follow him experience his blessing, and those who rebel against him experience trouble (Jn 3:36). The hopeful passages at the end of this book point forward to a time when all peoples will recognize Jesus' just and perfect reign and rule (Php 2:9 – 11) and when his followers will enjoy being in his presence forever.

NOW, LORD OUR GOD, DELIVER US FROM HIS HAND,
SO THAT ALL THE KINGDOMS OF THE EARTH
MAY KNOW THAT YOU ALONE, LORD, ARE GOD.

---

2 Kings 19:19

2 KINGS

The LORD's Judgment on Ahaziah

1 After Ahab's death, Moab rebelled against Israel. [2]Now Ahaziah had fallen
through the lattice of his upper room in Samaria and injured himself. So he
sent messengers, saying to them, "Go and consult Baal-Zebub, the god of Ekron,
to see if I will recover from this injury."
[3]But the angel of the LORD said to Elijah the Tishbite, "Go up and meet the
messengers of the king of Samaria and ask them, 'Is it because there is no God in
Israel that you are going off to consult Baal-Zebub, the god of Ekron?' [4]Therefore
this is what the LORD says: 'You will not leave the bed you are lying on. You will
certainly die!' " So Elijah went.
[5]When the messengers returned to the king, he asked them, "Why have you
come back?"
[6]"A man came to meet us," they replied. "And he said to us, 'Go back to the
king who sent you and tell him, "This is what the LORD says: Is it because there
is no God in Israel that you are sending messengers to consult Baal-Zebub, the
god of Ekron? Therefore you will not leave the bed you are lying on. You will
certainly die!" ' "
[7]The king asked them, "What kind of man was it who came to meet you and
told you this?"
[8]They replied, "He had a garment of hair[a] and had a leather belt around his
waist."
The king said, "That was Elijah the Tishbite."
[9]Then he sent to Elijah a captain with his company of fifty men. The captain
went up to Elijah, who was sitting on the top of a hill, and said to him, "Man of
God, the king says, 'Come down!' "
[10]Elijah answered the captain, "If I am a man of God, may fire come down
from heaven and consume you and your fifty men!" Then fire fell from heaven
and consumed the captain and his men.
[11]At this the king sent to Elijah another captain with his fifty men. The captain said to him, "Man of God, this is what the king says, 'Come down at once!' "
[12]"If I am a man of God," Elijah replied, "may fire come down from heaven
and consume you and your fifty men!" Then the fire of God fell from heaven and
consumed him and his fifty men.
[13]So the king sent a third captain with his fifty men. This third captain went
up and fell on his knees before Elijah. "Man of God," he begged, "please have
respect for my life and the lives of these fifty men, your servants! [14]See, fire has
fallen from heaven and consumed the first two captains and all their men. But
now have respect for my life!"
[15]The angel of the LORD said to Elijah, "Go down with him; do not be afraid of
him." So Elijah got up and went down with him to the king.
[16]He told the king, "This is what the LORD says: Is it because there is no God
in Israel for you to consult that you have sent messengers to consult Baal-Zebub,
the god of Ekron? Because you have done this, you will never leave the bed you
are lying on. You will certainly die!" [17]So he died, according to the word of the
LORD that Elijah had spoken.

Because Ahaziah had no son, Joram[b] succeeded him as king in the second
year of Jehoram son of Jehoshaphat king of Judah. [18]As for all the other events of
Ahaziah's reign, and what he did, are they not written in the book of the annals
of the kings of Israel?

---

[a] 8 Or *He was a hairy man* [b] 17 Hebrew *Jehoram*, a variant of *Joram*

Elijah Taken Up to Heaven

2 When the LORD was about to take Elijah up to heaven in a whirlwind, Elijah
and Elisha were on their way from Gilgal. 2Elijah said to Elisha, "Stay here;
the LORD has sent me to Bethel."
But Elisha said, "As surely as the LORD lives and as you live, I will not leave
you." So they went down to Bethel.
3The company of the prophets at Bethel came out to Elisha and asked, "Do you
know that the LORD is going to take your master from you today?"
"Yes, I know," Elisha replied, "so be quiet."
4Then Elijah said to him, "Stay here, Elisha; the LORD has sent me to Jericho."
And he replied, "As surely as the LORD lives and as you live, I will not leave
you." So they went to Jericho.
5The company of the prophets at Jericho went up to Elisha and asked him, "Do
you know that the LORD is going to take your master from you today?"
"Yes, I know," he replied, "so be quiet."
6Then Elijah said to him, "Stay here; the LORD has sent me to the Jordan."
And he replied, "As surely as the LORD lives and as you live, I will not leave
you." So the two of them walked on.
7Fifty men from the company of the prophets went and stood at a distance,
facing the place where Elijah and Elisha had stopped at the Jordan. 8Elijah took
his cloak, rolled it up and struck the water with it. The water divided to the right
and to the left, and the two of them crossed over on dry ground.
9When they had crossed, Elijah said to Elisha, "Tell me, what can I do for you
before I am taken from you?"
"Let me inherit a double portion of your spirit," Elisha replied.
10"You have asked a difficult thing," Elijah said, "yet if you see me when I am
taken from you, it will be yours—otherwise, it will not."
11As they were walking along and talking together, suddenly a chariot of fire
and horses of fire appeared and separated the two of them, and Elijah went up
to heaven in a whirlwind. 12Elisha saw this and cried out, "My father! My father!
The chariots and horsemen of Israel!" And Elisha saw him no more. Then he took
hold of his garment and tore it in two.
13Elisha then picked up Elijah's cloak that had fallen from him and went back
and stood on the bank of the Jordan. 14He took the cloak that had fallen from
Elijah and struck the water with it. "Where now is the LORD, the God of Elijah?"
he asked. When he struck the water, it divided to the right and to the left, and he
crossed over.
15The company of the prophets from Jericho, who were watching, said, "The
spirit of Elijah is resting on Elisha." And they went to meet him and bowed to the
ground before him. 16"Look," they said, "we your servants have fifty able men.
Let them go and look for your master. Perhaps the Spirit of the LORD has picked
him up and set him down on some mountain or in some valley."
"No," Elisha replied, "do not send them."
17But they persisted until he was too embarrassed to refuse. So he said, "Send
them." And they sent fifty men, who searched for three days but did not find
him. 18When they returned to Elisha, who was staying in Jericho, he said to them,
"Didn't I tell you not to go?"

Healing of the Water

19The people of the city said to Elisha, "Look, our lord, this town is well situated, as you can see, but the water is bad and the land is unproductive."
20"Bring me a new bowl," he said, "and put salt in it." So they brought it to him.
21Then he went out to the spring and threw the salt into it, saying, "This is
what the LORD says: 'I have healed this water. Never again will it cause death or
make the land unproductive.' " 22And the water has remained pure to this day,
according to the word Elisha had spoken.

2 KINGS 2:1–16

DIVIDING THE WATERS

The parting of the waters of the Jordan confirmed the succession of the prophets from Elijah to Elisha. This was certainly not the first time that a God-ordained leader had miraculously parted water—Moses did it at the Red Sea (Ex 14:21–22), and Joshua did it at the Jordan (Jos 3:7–17). In the minds of the original readers, water was a symbol of death and chaos due to its seemingly uncontrollable and unexplainable power. The parting of the waters on each occasion not only allowed the people to pass safely, but it also symbolized that God had the power over death and destruction. Chaos was rendered impotent by the all-surpassing greatness and might of God. In its place, the almighty God of Israel provided safety and a sure passage for his people. In a far greater way, Jesus' baptism (Mt 3:13–17) and his miraculous resurrection from the dead (Lk 24:1–8) demonstrate that he has overcome the powers of this broken world and provides his people with a way of escape.

AN ASCENSION PREVIEW

Elijah's unique ascension into heaven testified to his vital role as a prophet to the people of God at a very critical stage in their history. Elijah shared many similarities with John the Baptist, who would come later to help prepare the way for Jesus. Both John and Elijah lived in the desert, confronted the sinfulness of their day and urged the people to turn back to God. Jesus himself even pointed out the close association between these two mighty prophets (Mt 17:9 – 13). By his ascension into heaven, Elijah foreshadowed what Jesus would one day do (Lk 24:51). Luke records that those who witnessed Jesus' ascension reacted in worship. Surely, those who witnessed Elijah's miraculous ascension had a similar feeling of awe, fear and worship — not on account of Elijah, but on account of the glory of God.

Paul encouraged the church at Thessalonica as people raised questions about Jesus' return. Believers at that time expected Jesus to return during their lifetime. As some of the believers died, other believers began to question what would happen to those who died before the second coming of Jesus. Paul told the church to encourage each other with reminders of their future with Christ (1Th 4:17 – 18). The ascension of Jesus is a precursor to what will happen to all who trust in Christ's finished work. Jesus will return, and the dead will rise, join with those who are alive physically and in Christ, and be called up to the Lord (1Th 4:13 – 18). The ascensions of Elijah and Jesus provide a preview for what will happen to all those who have placed their faith in Jesus.

This hope and promise gives all followers of Jesus confidence and strength to endure life in this fallen and broken world. Following Elijah's ascension, Elisha demonstrated the power of God on earth by working a host of miracles (2Ki 2:13 – 22; 4:1 — 6:23). Jesus' disciples, following his ascension and the outpouring of the Holy Spirit at Pentecost, also performed miracles which demonstrated the power of God (Ac 2:43). Today, believers know the power of God and the future hope that awaits all who are in Christ, and they can fully trust that God can and will use them to accomplish great things as well. Since believers know that they will one day join with Jesus, they can live out their days without fear. By the power of God's Spirit, believers can live confidently and courageously, trusting that death does not have the final say.

Elisha Is Jeered

23From there Elisha went up to Bethel. As he was walking along the road, some
boys came out of the town and jeered at him. "Get out of here, baldy!" they said.
"Get out of here, baldy!" 24He turned around, looked at them and called down a
curse on them in the name of the LORD. Then two bears came out of the woods
and mauled forty-two of the boys. 25And he went on to Mount Carmel and from
there returned to Samaria.

Moab Revolts

3 Joram[a] son of Ahab became king of Israel in Samaria in the eighteenth year
of Jehoshaphat king of Judah, and he reigned twelve years. 2He did evil in
the eyes of the LORD, but not as his father and mother had done. He got rid of
the sacred stone of Baal that his father had made. 3Nevertheless he clung to the
sins of Jeroboam son of Nebat, which he had caused Israel to commit; he did not
turn away from them.

4Now Mesha king of Moab raised sheep, and he had to pay the king of Israel a
tribute of a hundred thousand lambs and the wool of a hundred thousand rams.
5But after Ahab died, the king of Moab rebelled against the king of Israel. 6So
at that time King Joram set out from Samaria and mobilized all Israel. 7He also
sent this message to Jehoshaphat king of Judah: "The king of Moab has rebelled
against me. Will you go with me to fight against Moab?"

"I will go with you," he replied. "I am as you are, my people as your people, my
horses as your horses."

8"By what route shall we attack?" he asked.

"Through the Desert of Edom," he answered.

9So the king of Israel set out with the king of Judah and the king of Edom. After
a roundabout march of seven days, the army had no more water for themselves
or for the animals with them.

10"What!" exclaimed the king of Israel. "Has the LORD called us three kings
together only to deliver us into the hands of Moab?"

11But Jehoshaphat asked, "Is there no prophet of the LORD here, through
whom we may inquire of the LORD?"

An officer of the king of Israel answered, "Elisha son of Shaphat is here. He
used to pour water on the hands of Elijah.[b]"

12Jehoshaphat said, "The word of the LORD is with him." So the king of Israel
and Jehoshaphat and the king of Edom went down to him.

13Elisha said to the king of Israel, "Why do you want to involve me? Go to the
prophets of your father and the prophets of your mother."

"No," the king of Israel answered, "because it was the LORD who called us
three kings together to deliver us into the hands of Moab."

14Elisha said, "As surely as the LORD Almighty lives, whom I serve, if I did not
have respect for the presence of Jehoshaphat king of Judah, I would not pay any
attention to you. 15But now bring me a harpist."

While the harpist was playing, the hand of the LORD came on Elisha 16and he
said, "This is what the LORD says: I will fill this valley with pools of water. 17For
this is what the LORD says: You will see neither wind nor rain, yet this valley
will be filled with water, and you, your cattle and your other animals will drink.
18This is an easy thing in the eyes of the LORD; he will also deliver Moab into
your hands. 19You will overthrow every fortified city and every major town. You
will cut down every good tree, stop up all the springs, and ruin every good field
with stones."

20The next morning, about the time for offering the sacrifice, there it was—
water flowing from the direction of Edom! And the land was filled with water.

21Now all the Moabites had heard that the kings had come to fight against

[a] *1* Hebrew *Jehoram,* a variant of *Joram;* also in verse 6 [b] *11* That is, he was Elijah's personal servant.

2 KINGS 3:1–20

THE GIFT OF WATER

Joram was the king of Israel in Samaria, and though he did not worship the false god Baal like his father, Ahab, he was still an evil king. Joram went to war with Moab over lambs and wool, and to bolster his chances of military success he organized an alliance with Judah and Edom. Despite Joram's reputation, Jehoshaphat, king of Judah, still joined the alliance without seeking God's wisdom or consulting with the prophet Elisha. Only after the coalition wandered lost in the wilderness of Edom for seven days and almost died of thirst did they seek God's help through the prophet. Elisha told them that God would miraculously provide. Overnight, without wind or rain, God filled the dry valley with water and brought confusion and ultimately defeat to the Moabites. This provision echoed an earlier incident in the wilderness at Horeb when God had miraculously rescued his people by causing water to flow where there was none (Ex 17:6).

Many years later, he provided life-sustaining water of an even better kind through his Son. Jesus offers living water to God's people. In Christ, thirsty souls can be satisfied and sins can be cleansed (Jn 4:7–14). In him, a wellspring forever flows with life (Rev 22:1).

them; so every man, young and old, who could bear arms was called up and
stationed on the border. 22When they got up early in the morning, the sun was
shining on the water. To the Moabites across the way, the water looked red — like
blood. 23"That's blood!" they said. "Those kings must have fought and slaughtered each other. Now to the plunder, Moab!"

24But when the Moabites came to the camp of Israel, the Israelites rose up and
fought them until they fled. And the Israelites invaded the land and slaughtered
the Moabites. 25They destroyed the towns, and each man threw a stone on every
good field until it was covered. They stopped up all the springs and cut down every good tree. Only Kir Hareseth was left with its stones in place, but men armed
with slings surrounded it and attacked it.

26When the king of Moab saw that the battle had gone against him, he took
with him seven hundred swordsmen to break through to the king of Edom, but
they failed. 27Then he took his firstborn son, who was to succeed him as king,
and offered him as a sacrifice on the city wall. The fury against Israel was great;
they withdrew and returned to their own land.

The Widow's Olive Oil

4 The wife of a man from the company of the prophets cried out to Elisha,
"Your servant my husband is dead, and you know that he revered the LORD.
But now his creditor is coming to take my two boys as his slaves."

2Elisha replied to her, "How can I help you? Tell me, what do you have in your
house?"

"Your servant has nothing there at all," she said, "except a small jar of olive
oil."

3Elisha said, "Go around and ask all your neighbors for empty jars. Don't ask
for just a few. 4Then go inside and shut the door behind you and your sons. Pour
oil into all the jars, and as each is filled, put it to one side."

5She left him and shut the door behind her and her sons. They brought the
jars to her and she kept pouring. 6When all the jars were full, she said to her son,
"Bring me another one."

But he replied, "There is not a jar left." Then the oil stopped flowing.

7She went and told the man of God, and he said, "Go, sell the oil and pay your
debts. You and your sons can live on what is left."

The Shunammite's Son Restored to Life

8One day Elisha went to Shunem. And a well-to-do woman was there, who
urged him to stay for a meal. So whenever he came by, he stopped there to eat.
9She said to her husband, "I know that this man who often comes our way is a
holy man of God. 10Let's make a small room on the roof and put in it a bed and
a table, a chair and a lamp for him. Then he can stay there whenever he comes
to us."

11One day when Elisha came, he went up to his room and lay down there. 12He
said to his servant Gehazi, "Call the Shunammite." So he called her, and she
stood before him. 13Elisha said to him, "Tell her, 'You have gone to all this trouble
for us. Now what can be done for you? Can we speak on your behalf to the king or
the commander of the army?' "

She replied, "I have a home among my own people."

14"What can be done for her?" Elisha asked.

Gehazi said, "She has no son, and her husband is old."

15Then Elisha said, "Call her." So he called her, and she stood in the doorway.
16"About this time next year," Elisha said, "you will hold a son in your arms."

"No, my lord!" she objected. "Please, man of God, don't mislead your servant!"

17But the woman became pregnant, and the next year about that same time
she gave birth to a son, just as Elisha had told her.

18The child grew, and one day he went out to his father, who was with the reapers. 19He said to his father, "My head! My head!"

His father told a servant, "Carry him to his mother." 20After the servant had
lifted him up and carried him to his mother, the boy sat on her lap until noon,
and then he died. 21She went up and laid him on the bed of the man of God, then
shut the door and went out.

22She called her husband and said, "Please send me one of the servants and a
donkey so I can go to the man of God quickly and return."

23"Why go to him today?" he asked. "It's not the New Moon or the Sabbath."

"That's all right," she said.

24She saddled the donkey and said to her servant, "Lead on; don't slow down
for me unless I tell you." 25So she set out and came to the man of God at Mount
Carmel.

When he saw her in the distance, the man of God said to his servant Gehazi,
"Look! There's the Shunammite! 26Run to meet her and ask her, 'Are you all right?
Is your husband all right? Is your child all right?' "

"Everything is all right," she said.

27When she reached the man of God at the mountain, she took hold of his
feet. Gehazi came over to push her away, but the man of God said, "Leave her
alone! She is in bitter distress, but the LORD has hidden it from me and has not
told me why."

28"Did I ask you for a son, my lord?" she said. "Didn't I tell you, 'Don't raise
my hopes'?"

29Elisha said to Gehazi, "Tuck your cloak into your belt, take my staff in your
hand and run. Don't greet anyone you meet, and if anyone greets you, do not
answer. Lay my staff on the boy's face."

30But the child's mother said, "As surely as the LORD lives and as you live, I will
not leave you." So he got up and followed her.

31Gehazi went on ahead and laid the staff on the boy's face, but there was no
sound or response. So Gehazi went back to meet Elisha and told him, "The boy
has not awakened."

32When Elisha reached the house, there was the boy lying dead on his couch.
33He went in, shut the door on the two of them and prayed to the LORD. 34Then
he got on the bed and lay on the boy, mouth to mouth, eyes to eyes, hands to
hands. As he stretched himself out on him, the boy's body grew warm. 35Elisha
turned away and walked back and forth in the room and then got on the bed
and stretched out on him once more. The boy sneezed seven times and opened
his eyes.

36Elisha summoned Gehazi and said, "Call the Shunammite." And he did.
When she came, he said, "Take your son." 37She came in, fell at his feet and
bowed to the ground. Then she took her son and went out.

Death in the Pot

38Elisha returned to Gilgal and there was a famine in that region. While the
company of the prophets was meeting with him, he said to his servant, "Put on
the large pot and cook some stew for these prophets."

39One of them went out into the fields to gather herbs and found a wild vine
and picked as many of its gourds as his garment could hold. When he returned,
he cut them up into the pot of stew, though no one knew what they were. 40The
stew was poured out for the men, but as they began to eat it, they cried out, "Man
of God, there is death in the pot!" And they could not eat it.

41Elisha said, "Get some flour." He put it into the pot and said, "Serve it to the
people to eat." And there was nothing harmful in the pot.

Feeding of a Hundred

42A man came from Baal Shalishah, bringing the man of God twenty loaves of
barley bread baked from the first ripe grain, along with some heads of new grain.
"Give it to the people to eat," Elisha said.

43"How can I set this before a hundred men?" his servant asked.

THE LIMITED POWER OF A MIRACLE

Elisha, like his predecessor Elijah (1Ki 17:17 – 24), performed the miracle of raising a child from death to life by the power of God. The mother was rightly distraught about the loss of her loved one. She had begged God for a child for many years, and now the boy that God had given to her had died. Upon arriving at the home, Elisha stretched himself over the lifeless boy's body, bringing him back to life and restoring him back to his grieving mother. Overwhelming joy must have flooded the mother at the sight of her son alive and breathing.

But sometimes even the most astonishing signs and wonders are not sufficient to turn hearts toward God. One day Jesus told the parable of the rich man and Lazarus. The rich man begged Abraham to send Lazarus back to his family so that his own brothers might avoid the torment that he was facing. Abraham reminded the rich man that the Law and the Prophets should be sufficient; if they rejected those, they would reject a man raised from the dead as well (Lk 16:19 – 31). Those listening to Jesus' parable that day needed to understand that witnessing a miracle — even a resurrection — does not create faith in God. Even when Jesus raised Mary and Martha's brother (who happened to be named Lazarus) from the dead, some of those who watched the miracle immediately left and told the Jewish religious leaders what Jesus had done, and they began plotting ways to kill Jesus (Jn 11).

These miracles and parables foreshadowed the day when Jesus forever defeated death. Without Jesus' resurrection, there would be no purpose for his death. His resurrection is what differentiates Jesus from every other prophet, teacher or so-called god. Jesus is the resurrected Messiah. The miracles performed in Scripture all relied on God to intervene, thereby providing evidence for his power. But in Jesus, death itself was overcome.

The miracles and resurrection of Jesus display God's power over the grave and his care for the lost and the hurting. These signs and wonders also teach that God's people are to be ambassadors of mercy and compassion to those in need. Most importantly, each miracle and parable ultimately points people to Jesus — and the hope of sharing in Jesus' resurrection. That hope is offered freely to anyone who places their trust in him (Ro 6:4,8 – 11; 8:10 – 11; Col 3:1 – 4).

But Elisha answered, "Give it to the people to eat. For this is what the LORD
says: 'They will eat and have some left over.' " 44Then he set it before them, and
they ate and had some left over, according to the word of the LORD.

Naaman Healed of Leprosy

5 Now Naaman was commander of the army of the king of Aram. He was a
great man in the sight of his master and highly regarded, because through
him the LORD had given victory to Aram. He was a valiant soldier, but he had
leprosy.[a]
2Now bands of raiders from Aram had gone out and had taken captive a young
girl from Israel, and she served Naaman's wife. 3She said to her mistress, "If only
my master would see the prophet who is in Samaria! He would cure him of his
leprosy."
4Naaman went to his master and told him what the girl from Israel had said.
5"By all means, go," the king of Aram replied. "I will send a letter to the king of
Israel." So Naaman left, taking with him ten talents[b] of silver, six thousand shekels[c] of gold and ten sets of clothing. 6The letter that he took to the king of Israel
read: "With this letter I am sending my servant Naaman to you so that you may
cure him of his leprosy."
7As soon as the king of Israel read the letter, he tore his robes and said, "Am I
God? Can I kill and bring back to life? Why does this fellow send someone to me
to be cured of his leprosy? See how he is trying to pick a quarrel with me!"
8When Elisha the man of God heard that the king of Israel had torn his robes,
he sent him this message: "Why have you torn your robes? Have the man come
to me and he will know that there is a prophet in Israel." 9So Naaman went with
his horses and chariots and stopped at the door of Elisha's house. 10Elisha sent a
messenger to say to him, "Go, wash yourself seven times in the Jordan, and your
flesh will be restored and you will be cleansed."
11But Naaman went away angry and said, "I thought that he would surely
come out to me and stand and call on the name of the LORD his God, wave his
hand over the spot and cure me of my leprosy. 12Are not Abana and Pharpar, the
rivers of Damascus, better than all the waters of Israel? Couldn't I wash in them
and be cleansed?" So he turned and went off in a rage.
13Naaman's servants went to him and said, "My father, if the prophet had told
you to do some great thing, would you not have done it? How much more, then,
when he tells you, 'Wash and be cleansed'!" 14So he went down and dipped himself in the Jordan seven times, as the man of God had told him, and his flesh was
restored and became clean like that of a young boy.
15Then Naaman and all his attendants went back to the man of God. He stood
before him and said, "Now I know that there is no God in all the world except in
Israel. So please accept a gift from your servant."
16The prophet answered, "As surely as the LORD lives, whom I serve, I will not
accept a thing." And even though Naaman urged him, he refused.
17"If you will not," said Naaman, "please let me, your servant, be given as
much earth as a pair of mules can carry, for your servant will never again make
burnt offerings and sacrifices to any other god but the LORD. 18But may the LORD
forgive your servant for this one thing: When my master enters the temple of
Rimmon to bow down and he is leaning on my arm and I have to bow there
also—when I bow down in the temple of Rimmon, may the LORD forgive your
servant for this."
19"Go in peace," Elisha said.
After Naaman had traveled some distance, 20Gehazi, the servant of Elisha the
man of God, said to himself, "My master was too easy on Naaman, this Aramean,

[a] *1* The Hebrew for *leprosy* was used for various diseases affecting the skin; also in verses 3, 6, 7, 11 and 27. [b] *5* That is, about 750 pounds or about 340 kilograms [c] *5* That is, about 150 pounds or about 69 kilograms

2 KINGS 5:1–3

FAITH IN GOD'S CLEANSING POWER

The young servant girl displayed astounding trust in the power of God to heal her master, an Aramean commander named Naaman. She boldly declared that Elisha could heal Naaman and urged him to seek the prophet's help. Her faith was well founded, as the leprous Naaman was cleansed by the power of God through the prophet's words.

This cleansing prefigured the far greater cleansing that Jesus brings to those who place their trust and faith in him. The cleansing that Christ offers washes away the guilt of sin and ultimately provides a new body, freed from the brokenness of sin. Just as God's gracious healing power extended to Naaman, a non-Israelite, the cleansing power of Christ extends to those of the nation of Israel and beyond—to all tribes, tongues and nations. The hope of salvation is founded not upon an abstract wish but upon the person of Christ himself. The object of believers' faith, the same God whom the servant girl believed could heal Naaman, is worthy of supreme trust.

by not accepting from him what he brought. As surely as the LORD lives, I will run
after him and get something from him."
[21]So Gehazi hurried after Naaman. When Naaman saw him running toward
him, he got down from the chariot to meet him. "Is everything all right?" he
asked.
[22]"Everything is all right," Gehazi answered. "My master sent me to say, 'Two
young men from the company of the prophets have just come to me from the hill
country of Ephraim. Please give them a talent[a] of silver and two sets of clothing.'"
[23]"By all means, take two talents," said Naaman. He urged Gehazi to accept
them, and then tied up the two talents of silver in two bags, with two sets of
clothing. He gave them to two of his servants, and they carried them ahead of
Gehazi. [24]When Gehazi came to the hill, he took the things from the servants
and put them away in the house. He sent the men away and they left.
[25]When he went in and stood before his master, Elisha asked him, "Where
have you been, Gehazi?"
"Your servant didn't go anywhere," Gehazi answered.
[26]But Elisha said to him, "Was not my spirit with you when the man got
down from his chariot to meet you? Is this the time to take money or to accept
clothes — or olive groves and vineyards, or flocks and herds, or male and female
slaves? [27]Naaman's leprosy will cling to you and to your descendants forever."
Then Gehazi went from Elisha's presence and his skin was leprous — it had become as white as snow.

An Axhead Floats

6 The company of the prophets said to Elisha, "Look, the place where we meet
with you is too small for us. [2]Let us go to the Jordan, where each of us can get
a pole; and let us build a place there for us to meet."
And he said, "Go."
[3]Then one of them said, "Won't you please come with your servants?"
"I will," Elisha replied. [4]And he went with them.
They went to the Jordan and began to cut down trees. [5]As one of them was cutting down a tree, the iron axhead fell into the water. "Oh no, my lord!" he cried
out. "It was borrowed!"
[6]The man of God asked, "Where did it fall?" When he showed him the place,
Elisha cut a stick and threw it there, and made the iron float. [7]"Lift it out," he said.
Then the man reached out his hand and took it.

Elisha Traps Blinded Arameans

[8]Now the king of Aram was at war with Israel. After conferring with his officers, he said, "I will set up my camp in such and such a place."
[9]The man of God sent word to the king of Israel: "Beware of passing that place,
because the Arameans are going down there." [10]So the king of Israel checked on
the place indicated by the man of God. Time and again Elisha warned the king,
so that he was on his guard in such places.
[11]This enraged the king of Aram. He summoned his officers and demanded of
them, "Tell me! Which of us is on the side of the king of Israel?"
[12]"None of us, my lord the king," said one of his officers, "but Elisha, the
prophet who is in Israel, tells the king of Israel the very words you speak in your
bedroom."
[13]"Go, find out where he is," the king ordered, "so I can send men and capture him." The report came back: "He is in Dothan." [14]Then he sent horses and
chariots and a strong force there. They went by night and surrounded the city.
[15]When the servant of the man of God got up and went out early the next
morning, an army with horses and chariots had surrounded the city. "Oh no,
my lord! What shall we do?" the servant asked.

---

[a] *22* That is, about 75 pounds or about 34 kilograms

16“Don’t be afraid,” the prophet answered. “Those who are with us are more
than those who are with them.”
17And Elisha prayed, “Open his eyes, LORD, so that he may see.” Then the
LORD opened the servant’s eyes, and he looked and saw the hills full of horses
and chariots of fire all around Elisha.
18As the enemy came down toward him, Elisha prayed to the LORD, “Strike this
army with blindness.” So he struck them with blindness, as Elisha had asked.
19Elisha told them, “This is not the road and this is not the city. Follow me,
and I will lead you to the man you are looking for.” And he led them to Samaria.
20After they entered the city, Elisha said, “LORD, open the eyes of these men
so they can see.” Then the LORD opened their eyes and they looked, and there
they were, inside Samaria.
21When the king of Israel saw them, he asked Elisha, “Shall I kill them, my
father? Shall I kill them?”
22“Do not kill them,” he answered. “Would you kill those you have captured
with your own sword or bow? Set food and water before them so that they may
eat and drink and then go back to their master.” 23So he prepared a great feast
for them, and after they had finished eating and drinking, he sent them away,
and they returned to their master. So the bands from Aram stopped raiding Israel’s territory.

Famine in Besieged Samaria

24Some time later, Ben-Hadad king of Aram mobilized his entire army and
marched up and laid siege to Samaria. 25There was a great famine in the city; the
siege lasted so long that a donkey’s head sold for eighty shekels[a] of silver, and a
quarter of a cab[b] of seed pods[c] for five shekels.[d]
26As the king of Israel was passing by on the wall, a woman cried to him, “Help
me, my lord the king!”
27The king replied, “If the LORD does not help you, where can I get help for
you? From the threshing floor? From the winepress?” 28Then he asked her,
“What’s the matter?”
She answered, “This woman said to me, ‘Give up your son so we may eat him
today, and tomorrow we’ll eat my son.’ 29So we cooked my son and ate him. The
next day I said to her, ‘Give up your son so we may eat him,’ but she had hidden
him.”
30When the king heard the woman’s words, he tore his robes. As he went along
the wall, the people looked, and they saw that, under his robes, he had sackcloth
on his body. 31He said, “May God deal with me, be it ever so severely, if the head
of Elisha son of Shaphat remains on his shoulders today!”
32Now Elisha was sitting in his house, and the elders were sitting with him.
The king sent a messenger ahead, but before he arrived, Elisha said to the elders,
“Don’t you see how this murderer is sending someone to cut off my head? Look,
when the messenger comes, shut the door and hold it shut against him. Is not
the sound of his master’s footsteps behind him?” 33While he was still talking to
them, the messenger came down to him.
The king said, “This disaster is from the LORD. Why should I wait for the LORD
any longer?”
7 Elisha replied, “Hear the word of the LORD. This is what the LORD says: About
this time tomorrow, a seah[e] of the finest flour will sell for a shekel[f] and two
seahs[g] of barley for a shekel at the gate of Samaria.”
2The officer on whose arm the king was leaning said to the man of God, “Look,
even if the LORD should open the floodgates of the heavens, could this happen?”

---

[a] *25* That is, about 2 pounds or about 920 grams [b] *25* That is, probably about 1/4 pound or about 100 grams [c] *25* Or *of doves’ dung* [d] *25* That is, about 2 ounces or about 58 grams
[e] *1* That is, probably about 12 pounds or about 5.5 kilograms of flour; also in verses 16 and 18
[f] *1* That is, about 2/5 ounce or about 12 grams; also in verses 16 and 18 [g] *1* That is, probably about 20 pounds or about 9 kilograms of barley; also in verses 16 and 18

GREATER ARE THOSE WITH US

Naaman was a valiant soldier, but his strength could not save him from the disease of leprosy. His miraculous healing demonstrated God's power to overcome physical sickness and suffering. The healing of Naaman's physical leprosy is a fitting picture of the work of Jesus to heal those afflicted by the far greater leprosy of a sin-sick heart.

This miracle revealed at a personal level that God is constantly at work. The story told in 2 Kings 6 broadens this claim. Israel was once again embroiled in conflict with a rival nation — this time with the king of Aram — but the Israelite army had a secret weapon. Elisha, the prophet of God, warned Israel and their king of the movements of their enemy. Every time Aram devised a new tactic, Elisha's warning allowed them to take preemptive measures and avoid defeat. After discovering Israel's secret, the king of Aram sought to capture Elisha. In the dead of night, his forces surrounded the city in which Elisha was staying.

The next morning, Elisha's servant observed the strong force encamped around the city. Answering his servant's alarm, Elisha answered with a word of encouragement: "Those who are with us are more than those who are with them" (6:16). Considering the size of each side's army, Elisha's encouraging words seemed to make no sense. Then Elisha prayed that the servant would see what he saw. Lifting up his eyes, the servant could then see the stunning spiritual reality — the hills were teeming with horses and chariots of fire ready to fight on Israel's behalf.

God still fights for his people, even when they cannot see the full picture. In the book of Revelation, John described Jesus as the Warrior King who will one day return to fight for his people and defeat Satan, sin and death once and for all (Rev 19:11 – 21). This coming reality provides hope for the people of God: Christ alone is the victorious King who will rid the world of all suffering and pain. In the meantime, this same Warrior King is with his people by the power of the Spirit. Jesus promises that he will go with his people as they seek to take the gospel to the ends of the world (Mt 28:18 – 20). As John reminded the church, "The one who is in you is greater than the one who is in the world" (1Jn 4:4). Though Satan is taking aim at the people of God, believers can have full confidence. God is at work in ways they cannot see or comprehend, preparing them spiritually for every challenge (Eph 6:10 – 17).

"You will see it with your own eyes," answered Elisha, "but you will not eat
any of it!"

The Siege Lifted

3Now there were four men with leprosy[a] at the entrance of the city gate. They
said to each other, "Why stay here until we die? 4If we say, 'We'll go into the
city' — the famine is there, and we will die. And if we stay here, we will die. So
let's go over to the camp of the Arameans and surrender. If they spare us, we live;
if they kill us, then we die."
5At dusk they got up and went to the camp of the Arameans. When they reached
the edge of the camp, no one was there, 6for the Lord had caused the Arameans
to hear the sound of chariots and horses and a great army, so that they said to one
another, "Look, the king of Israel has hired the Hittite and Egyptian kings to attack
us!" 7So they got up and fled in the dusk and abandoned their tents and their horses and donkeys. They left the camp as it was and ran for their lives.
8The men who had leprosy reached the edge of the camp, entered one of the
tents and ate and drank. Then they took silver, gold and clothes, and went off and
hid them. They returned and entered another tent and took some things from it
and hid them also.
9Then they said to each other, "What we're doing is not right. This is a day of
good news and we are keeping it to ourselves. If we wait until daylight, punishment will overtake us. Let's go at once and report this to the royal palace."
10So they went and called out to the city gatekeepers and told them, "We went
into the Aramean camp and no one was there — not a sound of anyone — only
tethered horses and donkeys, and the tents left just as they were." 11The gatekeepers shouted the news, and it was reported within the palace.
12The king got up in the night and said to his officers, "I will tell you what
the Arameans have done to us. They know we are starving; so they have left the
camp to hide in the countryside, thinking, 'They will surely come out, and then
we will take them alive and get into the city.'"
13One of his officers answered, "Have some men take five of the horses that
are left in the city. Their plight will be like that of all the Israelites left here — yes,
they will only be like all these Israelites who are doomed. So let us send them to
find out what happened."
14So they selected two chariots with their horses, and the king sent them after the Aramean army. He commanded the drivers, "Go and find out what has
happened." 15They followed them as far as the Jordan, and they found the whole
road strewn with the clothing and equipment the Arameans had thrown away
in their headlong flight. So the messengers returned and reported to the king.
16Then the people went out and plundered the camp of the Arameans. So a seah
of the finest flour sold for a shekel, and two seahs of barley sold for a shekel, as
the LORD had said.
17Now the king had put the officer on whose arm he leaned in charge of the gate,
and the people trampled him in the gateway, and he died, just as the man of God
had foretold when the king came down to his house. 18It happened as the man of
God had said to the king: "About this time tomorrow, a seah of the finest flour will
sell for a shekel and two seahs of barley for a shekel at the gate of Samaria."
19The officer had said to the man of God, "Look, even if the LORD should open the
floodgates of the heavens, could this happen?" The man of God had replied, "You
will see it with your own eyes, but you will not eat any of it!" 20And that is exactly
what happened to him, for the people trampled him in the gateway, and he died.

The Shunammite's Land Restored

8 Now Elisha had said to the woman whose son he had restored to life, "Go
away with your family and stay for a while wherever you can, because the
LORD has decreed a famine in the land that will last seven years." 2The woman

[a] 3 The Hebrew for *leprosy* was used for various diseases affecting the skin; also in verse 8.

2 KINGS 7:3 – 9

SHARING GOOD NEWS

Aram's siege of Samaria in Israel resulted in economic disaster and famine, but hope was not lost. God was still in control. Elisha prophesied a message of hope: God would reverse his people's suffering (2Ki 7:1). And that is exactly what happened. Four lepers who sat outside the city's gates, knowing that Samaria had nothing to offer them but famine and death, decided to take their chances with the Arameans. At twilight, they made their way to the Aramean camp, but God caused the sound of their approach to be as loud as a great army, and the entire Aramean camp fled in fear. The lepers entered a tent and filled their stomachs with food and their pockets with food, silver and gold. They entered another tent, taking more and hiding it. Then they were convicted about not sharing the good news, food and wealth with the rest of Samaria.

God's Son, Jesus, once visited a man ostracized and pushed to the fringes of society and gave him something far more valuable than silver or gold. Like the Israelites in the Old Testament story, this man lived under siege — the spiritual siege of demonic possession — but Jesus saved him. Despite the man's pleas to go with his Savior, Jesus refused. Instead, Jesus sent this man back to his home to tell his family and friends what had happened. Even more than silver and gold, the good news of salvation is a treasure meant to be shared (Mk 5:1 – 20).

proceeded to do as the man of God said. She and her family went away and
stayed in the land of the Philistines seven years.
[3]At the end of the seven years she came back from the land of the Philistines
and went to appeal to the king for her house and land. [4]The king was talking to
Gehazi, the servant of the man of God, and had said, "Tell me about all the great
things Elisha has done." [5]Just as Gehazi was telling the king how Elisha had restored the dead to life, the woman whose son Elisha had brought back to life
came to appeal to the king for her house and land.

Gehazi said, "This is the woman, my lord the king, and this is her son whom
Elisha restored to life." [6]The king asked the woman about it, and she told him.

Then he assigned an official to her case and said to him, "Give back everything that belonged to her, including all the income from her land from the day
she left the country until now."

Hazael Murders Ben-Hadad

[7]Elisha went to Damascus, and Ben-Hadad king of Aram was ill. When the
king was told, "The man of God has come all the way up here," [8]he said to Hazael,
"Take a gift with you and go to meet the man of God. Consult the LORD through
him; ask him, 'Will I recover from this illness?' "
[9]Hazael went to meet Elisha, taking with him as a gift forty camel-loads of
all the finest wares of Damascus. He went in and stood before him, and said,
"Your son Ben-Hadad king of Aram has sent me to ask, 'Will I recover from this
illness?' "
[10]Elisha answered, "Go and say to him, 'You will certainly recover.' Nevertheless,[a] the LORD has revealed to me that he will in fact die." [11]He stared at him
with a fixed gaze until Hazael was embarrassed. Then the man of God began
to weep.
[12]"Why is my lord weeping?" asked Hazael.

"Because I know the harm you will do to the Israelites," he answered. "You
will set fire to their fortified places, kill their young men with the sword, dash
their little children to the ground, and rip open their pregnant women."
[13]Hazael said, "How could your servant, a mere dog, accomplish such a feat?"

"The LORD has shown me that you will become king of Aram," answered Elisha.
[14]Then Hazael left Elisha and returned to his master. When Ben-Hadad asked,
"What did Elisha say to you?" Hazael replied, "He told me that you would certainly recover." [15]But the next day he took a thick cloth, soaked it in water and
spread it over the king's face, so that he died. Then Hazael succeeded him as
king.

Jehoram King of Judah

[16]In the fifth year of Joram son of Ahab king of Israel, when Jehoshaphat was
king of Judah, Jehoram son of Jehoshaphat began his reign as king of Judah.
[17]He was thirty-two years old when he became king, and he reigned in Jerusalem eight years. [18]He followed the ways of the kings of Israel, as the house of
Ahab had done, for he married a daughter of Ahab. He did evil in the eyes of
the LORD. [19]Nevertheless, for the sake of his servant David, the LORD was not
willing to destroy Judah. He had promised to maintain a lamp for David and his
descendants forever.
[20]In the time of Jehoram, Edom rebelled against Judah and set up its own king.
[21]So Jehoram[b] went to Zair with all his chariots. The Edomites surrounded him
and his chariot commanders, but he rose up and broke through by night; his
army, however, fled back home. [22]To this day Edom has been in rebellion against
Judah. Libnah revolted at the same time.
[23]As for the other events of Jehoram's reign, and all he did, are they not written in the book of the annals of the kings of Judah? [24]Jehoram rested with his

[a] *10* The Hebrew may also be read *Go and say, 'You will certainly not recover,' for.*
[b] *21* Hebrew *Joram,* a variant of *Jehoram;* also in verses 23 and 24

2 KINGS 8:7–15

FULFILLING THE PROPHETIC WORD

The king of Aram, Ben-Hadad, was ill and uncertain if he would survive. Word reached him that the prophet Elisha had come to Damascus, so he sent his servant Hazael with forty camels loaded with gifts and asked the prophet whether he would live or die. Hazael did as he was instructed, but he could have never imagined what Elisha would tell him. According to Elisha, God decreed that the king would die and that Hazael would rule over Aram. Earlier God had told this same truth to Elijah, Elisha's predecessor (1Ki 19:15). God's words create and shape reality; they can topple empires and replace kings with servants. At one time, God chose to speak his reality-shaping words through the prophets, people like Elisha and Elijah. Now he has chosen to speak uniquely through his Son, Jesus (Heb 1:1–2). And with ultimate authority and power, Jesus' words pierce the innermost parts of people, revealing their secret thoughts and intentions (Heb 4:12–13). By his word, judgment falls upon the unrepentant and mercy comes to those with a contrite heart.

ancestors and was buried with them in the City of David. And Ahaziah his son succeeded him as king.

Ahaziah King of Judah

[25]In the twelfth year of Joram son of Ahab king of Israel, Ahaziah son of Jehoram king of Judah began to reign. [26]Ahaziah was twenty-two years old when he became king, and he reigned in Jerusalem one year. His mother's name was Athaliah, a granddaughter of Omri king of Israel. [27]He followed the ways of the house of Ahab and did evil in the eyes of the LORD, as the house of Ahab had done, for he was related by marriage to Ahab's family.

[28]Ahaziah went with Joram son of Ahab to war against Hazael king of Aram at Ramoth Gilead. The Arameans wounded Joram; [29]so King Joram returned to Jezreel to recover from the wounds the Arameans had inflicted on him at Ramoth[a] in his battle with Hazael king of Aram.

Then Ahaziah son of Jehoram king of Judah went down to Jezreel to see Joram son of Ahab, because he had been wounded.

Jehu Anointed King of Israel

9 The prophet Elisha summoned a man from the company of the prophets and said to him, "Tuck your cloak into your belt, take this flask of olive oil with you and go to Ramoth Gilead. [2]When you get there, look for Jehu son of Jehoshaphat, the son of Nimshi. Go to him, get him away from his companions and take him into an inner room. [3]Then take the flask and pour the oil on his head and declare, 'This is what the LORD says: I anoint you king over Israel.' Then open the door and run; don't delay!"

[4]So the young prophet went to Ramoth Gilead. [5]When he arrived, he found the army officers sitting together. "I have a message for you, commander," he said.

"For which of us?" asked Jehu.

"For you, commander," he replied.

[6]Jehu got up and went into the house. Then the prophet poured the oil on Jehu's head and declared, "This is what the LORD, the God of Israel, says: 'I anoint you king over the LORD's people Israel. [7]You are to destroy the house of Ahab your master, and I will avenge the blood of my servants the prophets and the blood of all the LORD's servants shed by Jezebel. [8]The whole house of Ahab will perish. I will cut off from Ahab every last male in Israel — slave or free.[b] [9]I will make the house of Ahab like the house of Jeroboam son of Nebat and like the house of Baasha son of Ahijah. [10]As for Jezebel, dogs will devour her on the plot of ground at Jezreel, and no one will bury her.'" Then he opened the door and ran.

[11]When Jehu went out to his fellow officers, one of them asked him, "Is everything all right? Why did this maniac come to you?"

"You know the man and the sort of things he says," Jehu replied.

[12]"That's not true!" they said. "Tell us."

Jehu said, "Here is what he told me: 'This is what the LORD says: I anoint you king over Israel.'"

[13]They quickly took their cloaks and spread them under him on the bare steps. Then they blew the trumpet and shouted, "Jehu is king!"

Jehu Kills Joram and Ahaziah

[14]So Jehu son of Jehoshaphat, the son of Nimshi, conspired against Joram. (Now Joram and all Israel had been defending Ramoth Gilead against Hazael king of Aram, [15]but King Joram[c] had returned to Jezreel to recover from the wounds the Arameans had inflicted on him in the battle with Hazael king of Aram.) Jehu said, "If you desire to make me king, don't let anyone slip out of the city to go and tell the news in Jezreel." [16]Then he got into his chariot and rode to

---

[a] *29* Hebrew *Ramah,* a variant of *Ramoth* [b] *8* Or *Israel — every ruler or leader*
[c] *15* Hebrew *Jehoram,* a variant of *Joram;* also in verses 17 and 21-24

Jezreel, because Joram was resting there and Ahaziah king of Judah had gone down to see him.

17 When the lookout standing on the tower in Jezreel saw Jehu's troops approaching, he called out, "I see some troops coming."

"Get a horseman," Joram ordered. "Send him to meet them and ask, 'Do you come in peace?' "

18 The horseman rode off to meet Jehu and said, "This is what the king says: 'Do you come in peace?' "

"What do you have to do with peace?" Jehu replied. "Fall in behind me."

The lookout reported, "The messenger has reached them, but he isn't coming back."

19 So the king sent out a second horseman. When he came to them he said, "This is what the king says: 'Do you come in peace?' "

Jehu replied, "What do you have to do with peace? Fall in behind me."

20 The lookout reported, "He has reached them, but he isn't coming back either. The driving is like that of Jehu son of Nimshi—he drives like a maniac."

21 "Hitch up my chariot," Joram ordered. And when it was hitched up, Joram king of Israel and Ahaziah king of Judah rode out, each in his own chariot, to meet Jehu. They met him at the plot of ground that had belonged to Naboth the Jezreelite. 22 When Joram saw Jehu he asked, "Have you come in peace, Jehu?"

"How can there be peace," Jehu replied, "as long as all the idolatry and witchcraft of your mother Jezebel abound?"

23 Joram turned about and fled, calling out to Ahaziah, "Treachery, Ahaziah!"

24 Then Jehu drew his bow and shot Joram between the shoulders. The arrow pierced his heart and he slumped down in his chariot. 25 Jehu said to Bidkar, his chariot officer, "Pick him up and throw him on the field that belonged to Naboth the Jezreelite. Remember how you and I were riding together in chariots behind Ahab his father when the LORD spoke this prophecy against him: 26 'Yesterday I saw the blood of Naboth and the blood of his sons, declares the LORD, and I will surely make you pay for it on this plot of ground, declares the LORD.'[a] Now then, pick him up and throw him on that plot, in accordance with the word of the LORD."

27 When Ahaziah king of Judah saw what had happened, he fled up the road to Beth Haggan.[b] Jehu chased him, shouting, "Kill him too!" They wounded him in his chariot on the way up to Gur near Ibleam, but he escaped to Megiddo and died there. 28 His servants took him by chariot to Jerusalem and buried him with his ancestors in his tomb in the City of David. 29 (In the eleventh year of Joram son of Ahab, Ahaziah had become king of Judah.)

Jezebel Killed

30 Then Jehu went to Jezreel. When Jezebel heard about it, she put on eye makeup, arranged her hair and looked out of a window. 31 As Jehu entered the gate, she asked, "Have you come in peace, you Zimri, you murderer of your master?"[c]

32 He looked up at the window and called out, "Who is on my side? Who?" Two or three eunuchs looked down at him. 33 "Throw her down!" Jehu said. So they threw her down, and some of her blood spattered the wall and the horses as they trampled her underfoot.

34 Jehu went in and ate and drank. "Take care of that cursed woman," he said, "and bury her, for she was a king's daughter." 35 But when they went out to bury her, they found nothing except her skull, her feet and her hands. 36 They went back and told Jehu, who said, "This is the word of the LORD that he spoke through his servant Elijah the Tishbite: On the plot of ground at Jezreel dogs will devour Jezebel's flesh.[d] 37 Jezebel's body will be like dung on the ground in the plot at Jezreel, so that no one will be able to say, 'This is Jezebel.' "

---

[a] 26 See 1 Kings 21:19. [b] 27 Or *fled by way of the garden house* [c] 31 Or *"Was there peace for Zimri, who murdered his master?"* [d] 36 See 1 Kings 21:23.

Ahab's Family Killed

10 Now there were in Samaria seventy sons of the house of Ahab. So Jehu
wrote letters and sent them to Samaria: to the officials of Jezreel,[a] to the
elders and to the guardians of Ahab's children. He said, 2“You have your master's
sons with you and you have chariots and horses, a fortified city and weapons.
Now as soon as this letter reaches you, 3choose the best and most worthy of your
master's sons and set him on his father's throne. Then fight for your master's
house.”
4But they were terrified and said, “If two kings could not resist him, how
can we?”
5So the palace administrator, the city governor, the elders and the guardians
sent this message to Jehu: “We are your servants and we will do anything you say.
We will not appoint anyone as king; you do whatever you think best.”
6Then Jehu wrote them a second letter, saying, “If you are on my side and will
obey me, take the heads of your master's sons and come to me in Jezreel by this
time tomorrow.”
Now the royal princes, seventy of them, were with the leading men of the city,
who were rearing them. 7When the letter arrived, these men took the princes
and slaughtered all seventy of them. They put their heads in baskets and sent
them to Jehu in Jezreel. 8When the messenger arrived, he told Jehu, “They have
brought the heads of the princes.”
Then Jehu ordered, “Put them in two piles at the entrance of the city gate until
morning.”
9The next morning Jehu went out. He stood before all the people and said,
“You are innocent. It was I who conspired against my master and killed him, but
who killed all these? 10Know, then, that not a word the LORD has spoken against
the house of Ahab will fail. The LORD has done what he announced through his
servant Elijah.” 11So Jehu killed everyone in Jezreel who remained of the house
of Ahab, as well as all his chief men, his close friends and his priests, leaving
him no survivor.
12Jehu then set out and went toward Samaria. At Beth Eked of the Shepherds,
13he met some relatives of Ahaziah king of Judah and asked, “Who are you?”
They said, “We are relatives of Ahaziah, and we have come down to greet the
families of the king and of the queen mother.”
14“Take them alive!” he ordered. So they took them alive and slaughtered
them by the well of Beth Eked — forty-two of them. He left no survivor.
15After he left there, he came upon Jehonadab son of Rekab, who was on his
way to meet him. Jehu greeted him and said, “Are you in accord with me, as I
am with you?”
“I am,” Jehonadab answered.
“If so,” said Jehu, “give me your hand.” So he did, and Jehu helped him up into
the chariot. 16Jehu said, “Come with me and see my zeal for the LORD.” Then he
had him ride along in his chariot.
17When Jehu came to Samaria, he killed all who were left there of Ahab's family; he destroyed them, according to the word of the LORD spoken to Elijah.

Servants of Baal Killed

18Then Jehu brought all the people together and said to them, “Ahab served
Baal a little; Jehu will serve him much. 19Now summon all the prophets of Baal,
all his servants and all his priests. See that no one is missing, because I am going
to hold a great sacrifice for Baal. Anyone who fails to come will no longer live.”
But Jehu was acting deceptively in order to destroy the servants of Baal.
20Jehu said, “Call an assembly in honor of Baal.” So they proclaimed it. 21Then
he sent word throughout Israel, and all the servants of Baal came; not one stayed
away. They crowded into the temple of Baal until it was full from one end to the

[a] *1* Hebrew; some Septuagint manuscripts and Vulgate *of the city*

2 KINGS 10:1 – 17

JUDGMENT ON FALSE WORSHIP

The destruction of the house of Ahab fulfilled God's prophetic words of judgment (1Ki 21:21 – 22). God hates idolatry because it distorts human worship and causes people to direct their passions, sacrifices, affections and loyalties to created things instead of to God. Ahab and Jezebel were guilty not only of personal idolatry but also of leading others to sin against God in this fashion, and their lives illustrate idolatry's destructive effects. Years of pursuing false gods eventually warped Ahab's very identity as king. Instead of caring for his people, he used his position of power to take advantage of them, eventually murdering one of his own subjects and stealing his vineyard (1Ki 21). This sin finally prompted God's terrible punishment. God's judgment comes against all those who exchange the glory of God for worship of created things (Ro 1:18 – 32).

Throughout Jesus' earthly ministry, he issued similarly strong warnings about the destruction that will surely come to those who fail to worship God. Ironically, Jesus often reserved this condemnation for religious leaders who had turned their religious performance into a source of false worship. Jesus warned these leaders of the temporal judgment they will face as well as the fact that they would one day be judged by the one to whom all worship is due (Mt 23:13 – 39; Rev 20:11 – 15).

other. 22And Jehu said to the keeper of the wardrobe, "Bring robes for all the servants of Baal." So he brought out robes for them.

23Then Jehu and Jehonadab son of Rekab went into the temple of Baal. Jehu said to the servants of Baal, "Look around and see that no one who serves the LORD is here with you — only servants of Baal." 24So they went in to make sacrifices and burnt offerings. Now Jehu had posted eighty men outside with this warning: "If one of you lets any of the men I am placing in your hands escape, it will be your life for his life."

25As soon as Jehu had finished making the burnt offering, he ordered the guards and officers: "Go in and kill them; let no one escape." So they cut them down with the sword. The guards and officers threw the bodies out and then entered the inner shrine of the temple of Baal. 26They brought the sacred stone out of the temple of Baal and burned it. 27They demolished the sacred stone of Baal and tore down the temple of Baal, and people have used it for a latrine to this day.

28So Jehu destroyed Baal worship in Israel. 29However, he did not turn away from the sins of Jeroboam son of Nebat, which he had caused Israel to commit — the worship of the golden calves at Bethel and Dan.

30The LORD said to Jehu, "Because you have done well in accomplishing what is right in my eyes and have done to the house of Ahab all I had in mind to do, your descendants will sit on the throne of Israel to the fourth generation." 31Yet Jehu was not careful to keep the law of the LORD, the God of Israel, with all his heart. He did not turn away from the sins of Jeroboam, which he had caused Israel to commit.

32In those days the LORD began to reduce the size of Israel. Hazael overpowered the Israelites throughout their territory 33east of the Jordan in all the land of Gilead (the region of Gad, Reuben and Manasseh), from Aroer by the Arnon Gorge through Gilead to Bashan.

34As for the other events of Jehu's reign, all he did, and all his achievements, are they not written in the book of the annals of the kings of Israel?

35Jehu rested with his ancestors and was buried in Samaria. And Jehoahaz his son succeeded him as king. 36The time that Jehu reigned over Israel in Samaria was twenty-eight years.

Athaliah and Joash

11 When Athaliah the mother of Ahaziah saw that her son was dead, she proceeded to destroy the whole royal family. 2But Jehosheba, the daughter of King Jehoram[a] and sister of Ahaziah, took Joash son of Ahaziah and stole him away from among the royal princes, who were about to be murdered. She put him and his nurse in a bedroom to hide him from Athaliah; so he was not killed. 3He remained hidden with his nurse at the temple of the LORD for six years while Athaliah ruled the land.

4In the seventh year Jehoiada sent for the commanders of units of a hundred, the Carites and the guards and had them brought to him at the temple of the LORD. He made a covenant with them and put them under oath at the temple of the LORD. Then he showed them the king's son. 5He commanded them, saying, "This is what you are to do: You who are in the three companies that are going on duty on the Sabbath — a third of you guarding the royal palace, 6a third at the Sur Gate, and a third at the gate behind the guard, who take turns guarding the temple — 7and you who are in the other two companies that normally go off Sabbath duty are all to guard the temple for the king. 8Station yourselves around the king, each of you with weapon in hand. Anyone who approaches your ranks[b] is to be put to death. Stay close to the king wherever he goes."

9The commanders of units of a hundred did just as Jehoiada the priest ordered. Each one took his men — those who were going on duty on the Sabbath and those who were going off duty — and came to Jehoiada the priest. 10Then

[a] 2 Hebrew *Joram,* a variant of *Jehoram* [b] 8 Or *approaches the precincts*

2 KINGS 11:1–3

GUARD THE KING

Athaliah, whose name means "the LORD is exalted," did not live up to her name. As the nation unraveled, she continued the murderous pattern of many of the previous pagan leaders. When her son (King Ahaziah) died, she murdered every remaining royal heir and took the throne for herself. But she missed one heir: young Joash, her grandson and the son of Ahaziah. Jehosheba, Ahaziah's half sister, was married to the high priest and stood in a perfect location to rescue and hide Joash. Athaliah may not have even known of Joash's existence, which protected him from her rampage. The Lord protected Joash, ensuring that he would inherit the promises God made to David. Once again, David's royal line endured against all human odds through God's covenant faithfulness (2Sa 7:16).

In the same way, God protected the infant Jesus from death at the hands of King Herod and allowed him to secure the Davidic throne forever (Mt 2:13–20). The entire story of the Bible testifies to God's faithfulness to fulfill his promises and establish his rule and reign.

he gave the commanders the spears and shields that had belonged to King David and that were in the temple of the LORD. [11]The guards, each with weapon in hand, stationed themselves around the king—near the altar and the temple, from the south side to the north side of the temple.

[12]Jehoiada brought out the king's son and put the crown on him; he presented him with a copy of the covenant and proclaimed him king. They anointed him, and the people clapped their hands and shouted, "Long live the king!"

[13]When Athaliah heard the noise made by the guards and the people, she went to the people at the temple of the LORD. [14]She looked and there was the king, standing by the pillar, as the custom was. The officers and the trumpeters were beside the king, and all the people of the land were rejoicing and blowing trumpets. Then Athaliah tore her robes and called out, "Treason! Treason!"

[15]Jehoiada the priest ordered the commanders of units of a hundred, who were in charge of the troops: "Bring her out between the ranks[a] and put to the sword anyone who follows her." For the priest had said, "She must not be put to death in the temple of the LORD." [16]So they seized her as she reached the place where the horses enter the palace grounds, and there she was put to death.

[17]Jehoiada then made a covenant between the LORD and the king and people that they would be the LORD's people. He also made a covenant between the king and the people. [18]All the people of the land went to the temple of Baal and tore it down. They smashed the altars and idols to pieces and killed Mattan the priest of Baal in front of the altars.

Then Jehoiada the priest posted guards at the temple of the LORD. [19]He took with him the commanders of hundreds, the Carites, the guards and all the people of the land, and together they brought the king down from the temple of the LORD and went into the palace, entering by way of the gate of the guards. The king then took his place on the royal throne. [20]All the people of the land rejoiced, and the city was calm, because Athaliah had been slain with the sword at the palace.

[21]Joash[b] was seven years old when he began to reign.[c]

Joash Repairs the Temple

12[d] In the seventh year of Jehu, Joash[e] became king, and he reigned in Jerusalem forty years. His mother's name was Zibiah; she was from Beersheba. [2]Joash did what was right in the eyes of the LORD all the years Jehoiada the priest instructed him. [3]The high places, however, were not removed; the people continued to offer sacrifices and burn incense there.

[4]Joash said to the priests, "Collect all the money that is brought as sacred offerings to the temple of the LORD—the money collected in the census, the money received from personal vows and the money brought voluntarily to the temple. [5]Let every priest receive the money from one of the treasurers, then use it to repair whatever damage is found in the temple."

[6]But by the twenty-third year of King Joash the priests still had not repaired the temple. [7]Therefore King Joash summoned Jehoiada the priest and the other priests and asked them, "Why aren't you repairing the damage done to the temple? Take no more money from your treasurers, but hand it over for repairing the temple." [8]The priests agreed that they would not collect any more money from the people and that they would not repair the temple themselves.

[9]Jehoiada the priest took a chest and bored a hole in its lid. He placed it beside the altar, on the right side as one enters the temple of the LORD. The priests who guarded the entrance put into the chest all the money that was brought to the temple of the LORD. [10]Whenever they saw that there was a large amount of money in the chest, the royal secretary and the high priest came, counted the money

2 KINGS 12:1–16

THE TEMPLE IN DISREPAIR

The Old Testament records a number of leaders who, like a ray of light breaking through the clouds, did right in the eyes of the Lord. Although Joash's reforms were only partial, he did seek to repair the dilapidated temple. The broken condition of the temple mirrored the people's broken spiritual condition. Joash led the people once again to prioritize the temple and bring about much needed repairs.

In Jesus' day, the disciples were enamored by the beautiful majesty of Herod's temple. While the outward appearance suggested commitment to God, Jesus warned that God's judgment was coming and that the temple would be demolished (Mt 24:1–2). That prophesied destruction occurred in AD 70, when the Romans sacked Jerusalem. Throughout his ministry, Jesus warned against assuming that outward appearances—of people or structures—provide a trustworthy indication of the spiritual state within.

[a] *15* Or *out from the precincts* [b] *21* Hebrew *Jehoash,* a variant of *Joash* [c] *21* In Hebrew texts this verse (11:21) is numbered 12:1. [d] In Hebrew texts 12:1-21 is numbered 12:2-22.
[e] *1* Hebrew *Jehoash,* a variant of *Joash;* also in verses 2, 4, 6, 7 and 18

that had been brought into the temple of the LORD and put it into bags. 11When the amount had been determined, they gave the money to the men appointed to supervise the work on the temple. With it they paid those who worked on the temple of the LORD — the carpenters and builders, 12the masons and stonecutters. They purchased timber and blocks of dressed stone for the repair of the temple of the LORD, and met all the other expenses of restoring the temple.

13The money brought into the temple was not spent for making silver basins, wick trimmers, sprinkling bowls, trumpets or any other articles of gold or silver for the temple of the LORD; 14it was paid to the workers, who used it to repair the temple. 15They did not require an accounting from those to whom they gave the money to pay the workers, because they acted with complete honesty. 16The money from the guilt offerings and sin offerings[a] was not brought into the temple of the LORD; it belonged to the priests.

17About this time Hazael king of Aram went up and attacked Gath and captured it. Then he turned to attack Jerusalem. 18But Joash king of Judah took all the sacred objects dedicated by his predecessors — Jehoshaphat, Jehoram and Ahaziah, the kings of Judah — and the gifts he himself had dedicated and all the gold found in the treasuries of the temple of the LORD and of the royal palace, and he sent them to Hazael king of Aram, who then withdrew from Jerusalem.

19As for the other events of the reign of Joash, and all he did, are they not written in the book of the annals of the kings of Judah? 20His officials conspired against him and assassinated him at Beth Millo, on the road down to Silla. 21The officials who murdered him were Jozabad son of Shimeath and Jehozabad son of Shomer. He died and was buried with his ancestors in the City of David. And Amaziah his son succeeded him as king.

Jehoahaz King of Israel

13 In the twenty-third year of Joash son of Ahaziah king of Judah, Jehoahaz son of Jehu became king of Israel in Samaria, and he reigned seventeen years. 2He did evil in the eyes of the LORD by following the sins of Jeroboam son of Nebat, which he had caused Israel to commit, and he did not turn away from them. 3So the LORD's anger burned against Israel, and for a long time he kept them under the power of Hazael king of Aram and Ben-Hadad his son.

4Then Jehoahaz sought the LORD's favor, and the LORD listened to him, for he saw how severely the king of Aram was oppressing Israel. 5The LORD provided a deliverer for Israel, and they escaped from the power of Aram. So the Israelites lived in their own homes as they had before. 6But they did not turn away from the sins of the house of Jeroboam, which he had caused Israel to commit; they continued in them. Also, the Asherah pole[b] remained standing in Samaria.

7Nothing had been left of the army of Jehoahaz except fifty horsemen, ten chariots and ten thousand foot soldiers, for the king of Aram had destroyed the rest and made them like the dust at threshing time.

8As for the other events of the reign of Jehoahaz, all he did and his achievements, are they not written in the book of the annals of the kings of Israel? 9Jehoahaz rested with his ancestors and was buried in Samaria. And Jehoash[c] his son succeeded him as king.

Jehoash King of Israel

10In the thirty-seventh year of Joash king of Judah, Jehoash son of Jehoahaz became king of Israel in Samaria, and he reigned sixteen years. 11He did evil in the eyes of the LORD and did not turn away from any of the sins of Jeroboam son of Nebat, which he had caused Israel to commit; he continued in them.

12As for the other events of the reign of Jehoash, all he did and his achievements, including his war against Amaziah king of Judah, are they not written in the book of the annals of the kings of Israel? 13Jehoash rested with his ancestors,

---

[a] 16 Or *purification offerings* [b] 6 That is, a wooden symbol of the goddess Asherah; here and elsewhere in 2 Kings [c] 9 Hebrew *Joash,* a variant of *Jehoash*; also in verses 12-14 and 25

and Jeroboam succeeded him on the throne. Jehoash was buried in Samaria
with the kings of Israel.
[14]Now Elisha had been suffering from the illness from which he died. Jehoash
king of Israel went down to see him and wept over him. "My father! My father!"
he cried. "The chariots and horsemen of Israel!"
[15]Elisha said, "Get a bow and some arrows," and he did so. [16]"Take the bow in
your hands," he said to the king of Israel. When he had taken it, Elisha put his
hands on the king's hands.
[17]"Open the east window," he said, and he opened it. "Shoot!" Elisha said, and
he shot. "The LORD's arrow of victory, the arrow of victory over Aram!" Elisha
declared. "You will completely destroy the Arameans at Aphek."
[18]Then he said, "Take the arrows," and the king took them. Elisha told him,
"Strike the ground." He struck it three times and stopped. [19]The man of God was
angry with him and said, "You should have struck the ground five or six times;
then you would have defeated Aram and completely destroyed it. But now you
will defeat it only three times."
[20]Elisha died and was buried.
Now Moabite raiders used to enter the country every spring. [21]Once while
some Israelites were burying a man, suddenly they saw a band of raiders; so they
threw the man's body into Elisha's tomb. When the body touched Elisha's bones,
the man came to life and stood up on his feet.
[22]Hazael king of Aram oppressed Israel throughout the reign of Jehoahaz.
[23]But the LORD was gracious to them and had compassion and showed concern
for them because of his covenant with Abraham, Isaac and Jacob. To this day he
has been unwilling to destroy them or banish them from his presence.
[24]Hazael king of Aram died, and Ben-Hadad his son succeeded him as king.
[25]Then Jehoash son of Jehoahaz recaptured from Ben-Hadad son of Hazael the
towns he had taken in battle from his father Jehoahaz. Three times Jehoash defeated him, and so he recovered the Israelite towns.

Amaziah King of Judah

14 In the second year of Jehoash[a] son of Jehoahaz king of Israel, Amaziah son
of Joash king of Judah began to reign. [2]He was twenty-five years old when
he became king, and he reigned in Jerusalem twenty-nine years. His mother's
name was Jehoaddan; she was from Jerusalem. [3]He did what was right in the
eyes of the LORD, but not as his father David had done. In everything he followed
the example of his father Joash. [4]The high places, however, were not removed;
the people continued to offer sacrifices and burn incense there.
[5]After the kingdom was firmly in his grasp, he executed the officials who had
murdered his father the king. [6]Yet he did not put the children of the assassins to
death, in accordance with what is written in the Book of the Law of Moses where
the LORD commanded: "Parents are not to be put to death for their children, nor
children put to death for their parents; each will die for their own sin."[b]
[7]He was the one who defeated ten thousand Edomites in the Valley of Salt and
captured Sela in battle, calling it Joktheel, the name it has to this day.
[8]Then Amaziah sent messengers to Jehoash son of Jehoahaz, the son of Jehu,
king of Israel, with the challenge: "Come, let us face each other in battle."
[9]But Jehoash king of Israel replied to Amaziah king of Judah: "A thistle in Lebanon sent a message to a cedar in Lebanon, 'Give your daughter to my son in
marriage.' Then a wild beast in Lebanon came along and trampled the thistle
underfoot. [10]You have indeed defeated Edom and now you are arrogant. Glory in
your victory, but stay at home! Why ask for trouble and cause your own downfall
and that of Judah also?"
[11]Amaziah, however, would not listen, so Jehoash king of Israel attacked. He
and Amaziah king of Judah faced each other at Beth Shemesh in Judah. [12]Judah

[a] *1* Hebrew *Joash,* a variant of *Jehoash*; also in verses 13, 23 and 27 [b] *6* Deut. 24:16

2 KINGS 13:22–23

GLIMMERS OF GRACE

The kings and people of Israel continued to walk in sin (2Ki 13:2,11). Yet God provided a glimmer of grace and compassion to his elect by turning toward them and not destroying them — all because of his loyalty to his covenant promises with Abraham, Isaac and Jacob. God's covenants are indissoluble and eternal. His love pours out on his people even in the midst of their sin. God shows his faithfulness to his people by reminding them of the promises he made and fulfilled in the past.

When Jesus came, he made his relationship to past covenants crystal clear: He had come to fulfill the Law and the Prophets (Mt 5:17). Jesus told Zacchaeus that salvation had come to Zacchaeus' house due to him being a true "son of Abraham" and, thus, a recipient of the covenant promises. And Jesus proclaimed that he came for the lost — those who like the Old Testament Israelites live in sin and need salvation (Lk 19:9–10). God always keeps his promises, ultimately offering grace and mercy to those who turn from their sin and put their faith in Jesus.

was routed by Israel, and every man fled to his home. [13]Jehoash king of Israel captured Amaziah king of Judah, the son of Joash, the son of Ahaziah, at Beth Shemesh. Then Jehoash went to Jerusalem and broke down the wall of Jerusalem from the Ephraim Gate to the Corner Gate — a section about four hundred cubits long.[a] [14]He took all the gold and silver and all the articles found in the temple of the LORD and in the treasuries of the royal palace. He also took hostages and returned to Samaria.

[15]As for the other events of the reign of Jehoash, what he did and his achievements, including his war against Amaziah king of Judah, are they not written in the book of the annals of the kings of Israel? [16]Jehoash rested with his ancestors and was buried in Samaria with the kings of Israel. And Jeroboam his son succeeded him as king.

[17]Amaziah son of Joash king of Judah lived for fifteen years after the death of Jehoash son of Jehoahaz king of Israel. [18]As for the other events of Amaziah's reign, are they not written in the book of the annals of the kings of Judah?

[19]They conspired against him in Jerusalem, and he fled to Lachish, but they sent men after him to Lachish and killed him there. [20]He was brought back by horse and was buried in Jerusalem with his ancestors, in the City of David.

[21]Then all the people of Judah took Azariah,[b] who was sixteen years old, and made him king in place of his father Amaziah. [22]He was the one who rebuilt Elath and restored it to Judah after Amaziah rested with his ancestors.

Jeroboam II King of Israel

[23]In the fifteenth year of Amaziah son of Joash king of Judah, Jeroboam son of Jehoash king of Israel became king in Samaria, and he reigned forty-one years. [24]He did evil in the eyes of the LORD and did not turn away from any of the sins of Jeroboam son of Nebat, which he had caused Israel to commit. [25]He was the one who restored the boundaries of Israel from Lebo Hamath to the Dead Sea,[c] in accordance with the word of the LORD, the God of Israel, spoken through his servant Jonah son of Amittai, the prophet from Gath Hepher.

[26]The LORD had seen how bitterly everyone in Israel, whether slave or free, was suffering;[d] there was no one to help them. [27]And since the LORD had not said he would blot out the name of Israel from under heaven, he saved them by the hand of Jeroboam son of Jehoash.

[28]As for the other events of Jeroboam's reign, all he did, and his military achievements, including how he recovered for Israel both Damascus and Hamath, which had belonged to Judah, are they not written in the book of the annals of the kings of Israel? [29]Jeroboam rested with his ancestors, the kings of Israel. And Zechariah his son succeeded him as king.

Azariah King of Judah

15 In the twenty-seventh year of Jeroboam king of Israel, Azariah[e] son of Amaziah king of Judah began to reign. [2]He was sixteen years old when he became king, and he reigned in Jerusalem fifty-two years. His mother's name was Jekoliah; she was from Jerusalem. [3]He did what was right in the eyes of the LORD, just as his father Amaziah had done. [4]The high places, however, were not removed; the people continued to offer sacrifices and burn incense there.

[5]The LORD afflicted the king with leprosy[f] until the day he died, and he lived in a separate house.[g] Jotham the king's son had charge of the palace and governed the people of the land.

[6]As for the other events of Azariah's reign, and all he did, are they not written in the book of the annals of the kings of Judah? [7]Azariah rested with his

[a] *13* That is, about 600 feet or about 180 meters [b] *21* Also called *Uzziah* [c] *25* Hebrew *the Sea of the Arabah* [d] *26* Or *Israel was suffering. They were without a ruler or leader, and* [e] *1* Also called *Uzziah;* also in verses 6, 7, 8, 17, 23 and 27 [f] *5* The Hebrew for *leprosy* was used for various diseases affecting the skin. [g] *5* Or *in a house where he was relieved of responsibilities*

A FALSE VISION OF GREATNESS

The people of Judah, under King Amaziah, walked more faithfully with God than the people of Israel did under their king, Jehoash. God allowed Judah and King Amaziah to conquer a rival nation, but this victory fostered pride in the heart of the king. His pride caused him to think more highly of himself and his actions than he ought, which led him to take reckless action that resulted in devastating consequences for him and his nation. Amaziah challenged Jehoash to battle, and Jehoash replied to him in the form of a fable. By comparing King Amaziah to a thistle in contrast to the cedars of Lebanon, King Jehoash attempted to help him have a more realistic picture of his status and accomplishments. Blinded by pride, Amaziah would not listen. He was soundly defeated in battle by Jehoash's army.

Pride is an ever-present temptation for all people, including those who have received the gift of God's grace. Scripture notes that even Jesus' disciples struggled with pride. For example, immediately following the Lord's Supper, the disciples debated over which one of them was the greatest. They, like Amaziah, had witnessed God doing amazing things in and through their lives. This success fueled their pride. Jesus redirected them, teaching them that his followers would be marked by humility and service (Lk 22:24 – 30). Greatness in the kingdom of God is not found in elevating oneself, but in lowering oneself and modeling the servant-nature of Christ (Php 2:1 – 11).

Jesus also warned his followers about the danger of approaching God with a spirit of pride and self-righteousness. He told the parable of two people, a notorious sinner and a noted religious leader (Lk 18:9 – 14). The religious leader, confident in himself, came to God and thanked him that he was not like the sinful man. The notorious sinner, in contrast, stood at a distance, bowed his head and begged God to be merciful to him in spite of his sin.

Jesus' followers should be marked by a dependence on God for his mercy and grace, knowing that in and of themselves they have nothing to offer. Pride will ultimately lead to destruction, while humility leads to the mercy of God.

ancestors and was buried near them in the City of David. And Jotham his son
succeeded him as king.

Zechariah King of Israel

[8]In the thirty-eighth year of Azariah king of Judah, Zechariah son of Jeroboam became king of Israel in Samaria, and he reigned six months. [9]He did evil in
the eyes of the LORD, as his predecessors had done. He did not turn away from
the sins of Jeroboam son of Nebat, which he had caused Israel to commit.
[10]Shallum son of Jabesh conspired against Zechariah. He attacked him in
front of the people,[a] assassinated him and succeeded him as king. [11]The other
events of Zechariah's reign are written in the book of the annals of the kings of
Israel. [12]So the word of the LORD spoken to Jehu was fulfilled: "Your descendants
will sit on the throne of Israel to the fourth generation."[b]

Shallum King of Israel

[13]Shallum son of Jabesh became king in the thirty-ninth year of Uzziah king
of Judah, and he reigned in Samaria one month. [14]Then Menahem son of Gadi
went from Tirzah up to Samaria. He attacked Shallum son of Jabesh in Samaria,
assassinated him and succeeded him as king.
[15]The other events of Shallum's reign, and the conspiracy he led, are written
in the book of the annals of the kings of Israel.
[16]At that time Menahem, starting out from Tirzah, attacked Tiphsah and everyone in the city and its vicinity, because they refused to open their gates. He
sacked Tiphsah and ripped open all the pregnant women.

Menahem King of Israel

[17]In the thirty-ninth year of Azariah king of Judah, Menahem son of Gadi became king of Israel, and he reigned in Samaria ten years. [18]He did evil in the
eyes of the LORD. During his entire reign he did not turn away from the sins of
Jeroboam son of Nebat, which he had caused Israel to commit.
[19]Then Pul[c] king of Assyria invaded the land, and Menahem gave him a thousand talents[d] of silver to gain his support and strengthen his own hold on the
kingdom. [20]Menahem exacted this money from Israel. Every wealthy person had
to contribute fifty shekels[e] of silver to be given to the king of Assyria. So the king
of Assyria withdrew and stayed in the land no longer.
[21]As for the other events of Menahem's reign, and all he did, are they not written in the book of the annals of the kings of Israel? [22]Menahem rested with his
ancestors. And Pekahiah his son succeeded him as king.

Pekahiah King of Israel

[23]In the fiftieth year of Azariah king of Judah, Pekahiah son of Menahem became king of Israel in Samaria, and he reigned two years. [24]Pekahiah did evil
in the eyes of the LORD. He did not turn away from the sins of Jeroboam son of
Nebat, which he had caused Israel to commit. [25]One of his chief officers, Pekah
son of Remaliah, conspired against him. Taking fifty men of Gilead with him, he
assassinated Pekahiah, along with Argob and Arieh, in the citadel of the royal
palace at Samaria. So Pekah killed Pekahiah and succeeded him as king.
[26]The other events of Pekahiah's reign, and all he did, are written in the book
of the annals of the kings of Israel.

Pekah King of Israel

[27]In the fifty-second year of Azariah king of Judah, Pekah son of Remaliah became king of Israel in Samaria, and he reigned twenty years. [28]He did evil in the

[a] *10* Hebrew; some Septuagint manuscripts *in Ibleam* [b] *12* 2 Kings 10:30 [c] *19* Also called *Tiglath-Pileser* [d] *19* That is, about 38 tons or about 34 metric tons [e] *20* That is, about 1 1/4 pounds or about 575 grams

---

2 KINGS 15:8–31

THE DOWNWARD SLOPE

Israel's freedom from foreign oppression was short-lived because the leadership of the northern kingdom continued to spiral downward into ungodliness. Israel suffered through a progression of weak kings who largely came to power through conspiracy and assassination. God was at work judging the previous 200 years of rebellion against him. This pattern of wickedness in the kings of Israel was one of the ways by which the judgment of God came upon his people.

Jesus came to the remnant of this nation under the oppression of Rome. They lived in fear of the capricious government and under a deafening silence from their God. There had been no prophets to call them back to God in a long time. Jesus arrived into this world and proclaimed that God's kingdom had come. Liberation and freedom were now available for his people. The wickedness of the religious leaders drove him to call them to repentance (Mt 9:13; Mk 2:17; Lk 5:32). God displays his love for his people in his judgment and his calls for them to repent. It is in this call to repentance that people have the opportunity to cease following wicked leadership and acknowledge God's leadership in their lives.

eyes of the LORD. He did not turn away from the sins of Jeroboam son of Nebat,
which he had caused Israel to commit.
[29]In the time of Pekah king of Israel, Tiglath-Pileser king of Assyria came and
took Ijon, Abel Beth Maakah, Janoah, Kedesh and Hazor. He took Gilead and
Galilee, including all the land of Naphtali, and deported the people to Assyria. [30]Then Hoshea son of Elah conspired against Pekah son of Remaliah. He attacked and assassinated him, and then succeeded him as king in the twentieth
year of Jotham son of Uzziah.
[31]As for the other events of Pekah's reign, and all he did, are they not written
in the book of the annals of the kings of Israel?

Jotham King of Judah

[32]In the second year of Pekah son of Remaliah king of Israel, Jotham son of
Uzziah king of Judah began to reign. [33]He was twenty-five years old when he became king, and he reigned in Jerusalem sixteen years. His mother's name was
Jerusha daughter of Zadok. [34]He did what was right in the eyes of the LORD, just
as his father Uzziah had done. [35]The high places, however, were not removed; the
people continued to offer sacrifices and burn incense there. Jotham rebuilt the
Upper Gate of the temple of the LORD.
[36]As for the other events of Jotham's reign, and what he did, are they not written in the book of the annals of the kings of Judah? [37](In those days the LORD
began to send Rezin king of Aram and Pekah son of Remaliah against Judah.)
[38]Jotham rested with his ancestors and was buried with them in the City of David, the city of his father. And Ahaz his son succeeded him as king.

Ahaz King of Judah

16 In the seventeenth year of Pekah son of Remaliah, Ahaz son of Jotham
king of Judah began to reign. [2]Ahaz was twenty years old when he became
king, and he reigned in Jerusalem sixteen years. Unlike David his father, he did
not do what was right in the eyes of the LORD his God. [3]He followed the ways of
the kings of Israel and even sacrificed his son in the fire, engaging in the detestable practices of the nations the LORD had driven out before the Israelites.
[4]He offered sacrifices and burned incense at the high places, on the hilltops and
under every spreading tree.
[5]Then Rezin king of Aram and Pekah son of Remaliah king of Israel marched
up to fight against Jerusalem and besieged Ahaz, but they could not overpower
him. [6]At that time, Rezin king of Aram recovered Elath for Aram by driving out
the people of Judah. Edomites then moved into Elath and have lived there to
this day.
[7]Ahaz sent messengers to say to Tiglath-Pileser king of Assyria, "I am your
servant and vassal. Come up and save me out of the hand of the king of Aram
and of the king of Israel, who are attacking me." [8]And Ahaz took the silver and
gold found in the temple of the LORD and in the treasuries of the royal palace
and sent it as a gift to the king of Assyria. [9]The king of Assyria complied by attacking Damascus and capturing it. He deported its inhabitants to Kir and put
Rezin to death.
[10]Then King Ahaz went to Damascus to meet Tiglath-Pileser king of Assyria. He saw an altar in Damascus and sent to Uriah the priest a sketch of the altar, with detailed plans for its construction. [11]So Uriah the priest built an altar
in accordance with all the plans that King Ahaz had sent from Damascus and
finished it before King Ahaz returned. [12]When the king came back from Damascus and saw the altar, he approached it and presented offerings[a] on it. [13]He
offered up his burnt offering and grain offering, poured out his drink offering,
and splashed the blood of his fellowship offerings against the altar. [14]As for
the bronze altar that stood before the LORD, he brought it from the front of the

[a] 12 Or *and went up*

2 KINGS 16:10–16

FALSE WORSHIP IN THE TEMPLE

King Ahaz observed a pagan altar while visiting Damascus and purposed to construct a similar altar in the temple of God in Jerusalem, which would have been a further sign of submission to the Assyrians. After he commanded Uriah to construct an altar following the pattern of the one in Damascus, Ahaz offered worship upon the pagan altar in the temple of God. This act demonstrated the profound moral perversion of the nation of Judah. The king himself, who functioned as the people's leader and representative, offered false worship on the site where God was meant to be worshiped.

Jesus faced a similar situation when he observed the money changers and merchants in the temple of God. Jesus drove the people from the temple because he was angered that his house was turned into a den of robbers (Mt 21:12–13). Judah's moral decline did not stop with King Ahaz. Repeatedly the people demonstrated an impoverished view of God by practicing false worship.

The church throughout all generations must guard itself at all costs against twisting God's good gifts into a means of false worship. They must work to protect God's church from those who would lead them to worship something other than God.

temple — from between the new altar and the temple of the LORD — and put it on
the north side of the new altar.
15King Ahaz then gave these orders to Uriah the priest: "On the large new altar, offer the morning burnt offering and the evening grain offering, the king's
burnt offering and his grain offering, and the burnt offering of all the people of
the land, and their grain offering and their drink offering. Splash against this
altar the blood of all the burnt offerings and sacrifices. But I will use the bronze
altar for seeking guidance." 16And Uriah the priest did just as King Ahaz had
ordered.
17King Ahaz cut off the side panels and removed the basins from the movable
stands. He removed the Sea from the bronze bulls that supported it and set it on a
stone base. 18He took away the Sabbath canopy[a] that had been built at the temple
and removed the royal entryway outside the temple of the LORD, in deference to
the king of Assyria.
19As for the other events of the reign of Ahaz, and what he did, are they not
written in the book of the annals of the kings of Judah? 20Ahaz rested with his
ancestors and was buried with them in the City of David. And Hezekiah his son
succeeded him as king.

Hoshea Last King of Israel

17 In the twelfth year of Ahaz king of Judah, Hoshea son of Elah became king
of Israel in Samaria, and he reigned nine years. 2He did evil in the eyes of
the LORD, but not like the kings of Israel who preceded him.
3Shalmaneser king of Assyria came up to attack Hoshea, who had been Shalmaneser's vassal and had paid him tribute. 4But the king of Assyria discovered
that Hoshea was a traitor, for he had sent envoys to So[b] king of Egypt, and he no
longer paid tribute to the king of Assyria, as he had done year by year. Therefore
Shalmaneser seized him and put him in prison. 5The king of Assyria invaded
the entire land, marched against Samaria and laid siege to it for three years. 6In
the ninth year of Hoshea, the king of Assyria captured Samaria and deported the
Israelites to Assyria. He settled them in Halah, in Gozan on the Habor River and
in the towns of the Medes.

Israel Exiled Because of Sin

7All this took place because the Israelites had sinned against the LORD their
God, who had brought them up out of Egypt from under the power of Pharaoh
king of Egypt. They worshiped other gods 8and followed the practices of the nations the LORD had driven out before them, as well as the practices that the kings
of Israel had introduced. 9The Israelites secretly did things against the LORD
their God that were not right. From watchtower to fortified city they built themselves high places in all their towns. 10They set up sacred stones and Asherah
poles on every high hill and under every spreading tree. 11At every high place
they burned incense, as the nations whom the LORD had driven out before them
had done. They did wicked things that aroused the LORD's anger. 12They worshiped idols, though the LORD had said, "You shall not do this."[c] 13The LORD
warned Israel and Judah through all his prophets and seers: "Turn from your evil
ways. Observe my commands and decrees, in accordance with the entire Law
that I commanded your ancestors to obey and that I delivered to you through my
servants the prophets."
14But they would not listen and were as stiff-necked as their ancestors, who
did not trust in the LORD their God. 15They rejected his decrees and the covenant
he had made with their ancestors and the statutes he had warned them to keep.
They followed worthless idols and themselves became worthless. They imitat-
ed the nations around them although the LORD had ordered them, "Do not do
as they do."

[a] *18* Or *the dais of his throne* (see Septuagint) [b] *4* *So* is probably an abbreviation for *Osorkon.* [c] *12* Exodus 20:4,5

2 KINGS 17:7–20

THE CONSEQUENCES OF SIN

The Israelites were often referred to as "stiff-necked" (2Ki 17:14). This title is an apt description of the consistent, deep-seated rebellion that plagued the people at every turn. Like an animal stiffens its neck in protest rather than submitting to its master's guidance, so the nations of Israel and Judah refused to submit to God. They had been warned repeatedly that such insubordination would incur the judgment of God. Specifically, they had been told that if they would not obey, God would kick them out of the land in order to protect the honor of his name. God saw their continued rebellion, and he enacted his just judgment.

John the Baptist warned of the impending doom the people in his day too were sure to face. "Repent!" he cried (Mt 3:2). Jesus' consistent call was for people to turn from their sin and to turn to him in faith. Those who are unwilling to turn from sin and toward him will face the sure judgment of God that sin deserves. The good news is that all who do repent will be spared the wrath of God, and by his grace they will be granted fellowship with him forever.

16They forsook all the commands of the LORD their God and made for themselves two idols cast in the shape of calves, and an Asherah pole. They bowed
down to all the starry hosts, and they worshiped Baal. 17They sacrificed their
sons and daughters in the fire. They practiced divination and sought omens and
sold themselves to do evil in the eyes of the LORD, arousing his anger.

18So the LORD was very angry with Israel and removed them from his presence. Only the tribe of Judah was left, 19and even Judah did not keep the commands of the LORD their God. They followed the practices Israel had introduced.
20Therefore the LORD rejected all the people of Israel; he afflicted them and gave
them into the hands of plunderers, until he thrust them from his presence.

21When he tore Israel away from the house of David, they made Jeroboam
son of Nebat their king. Jeroboam enticed Israel away from following the LORD
and caused them to commit a great sin. 22The Israelites persisted in all the sins
of Jeroboam and did not turn away from them 23until the LORD removed them
from his presence, as he had warned through all his servants the prophets. So
the people of Israel were taken from their homeland into exile in Assyria, and
they are still there.

Samaria Resettled

24The king of Assyria brought people from Babylon, Kuthah, Avva, Hamath
and Sepharvaim and settled them in the towns of Samaria to replace the Israelites. They took over Samaria and lived in its towns. 25When they first lived there,
they did not worship the LORD; so he sent lions among them and they killed some
of the people. 26It was reported to the king of Assyria: "The people you deported
and resettled in the towns of Samaria do not know what the god of that country
requires. He has sent lions among them, which are killing them off, because the
people do not know what he requires."

27Then the king of Assyria gave this order: "Have one of the priests you took
captive from Samaria go back to live there and teach the people what the god
of the land requires." 28So one of the priests who had been exiled from Samaria
came to live in Bethel and taught them how to worship the LORD.

29Nevertheless, each national group made its own gods in the several towns
where they settled, and set them up in the shrines the people of Samaria had
made at the high places. 30The people from Babylon made Sukkoth Benoth,
those from Kuthah made Nergal, and those from Hamath made Ashima; 31the
Avvites made Nibhaz and Tartak, and the Sepharvites burned their children in
the fire as sacrifices to Adrammelek and Anammelek, the gods of Sepharvaim.
32They worshiped the LORD, but they also appointed all sorts of their own people
to officiate for them as priests in the shrines at the high places. 33They worshiped
the LORD, but they also served their own gods in accordance with the customs of
the nations from which they had been brought.

34To this day they persist in their former practices. They neither worship the
LORD nor adhere to the decrees and regulations, the laws and commands that
the LORD gave the descendants of Jacob, whom he named Israel. 35When the
LORD made a covenant with the Israelites, he commanded them: "Do not worship any other gods or bow down to them, serve them or sacrifice to them. 36But
the LORD, who brought you up out of Egypt with mighty power and outstretched
arm, is the one you must worship. To him you shall bow down and to him offer
sacrifices. 37You must always be careful to keep the decrees and regulations, the
laws and commands he wrote for you. Do not worship other gods. 38Do not forget the covenant I have made with you, and do not worship other gods. 39Rather,
worship the LORD your God; it is he who will deliver you from the hand of all
your enemies."

40They would not listen, however, but persisted in their former practices.
41Even while these people were worshiping the LORD, they were serving their
idols. To this day their children and grandchildren continue to do as their ancestors did.

Hezekiah King of Judah

18 In the third year of Hoshea son of Elah king of Israel, Hezekiah son of Ahaz king of Judah began to reign. 2He was twenty-five years old when he became king, and he reigned in Jerusalem twenty-nine years. His mother's name was Abijah[a] daughter of Zechariah. 3He did what was right in the eyes of the LORD, just as his father David had done. 4He removed the high places, smashed the sacred stones and cut down the Asherah poles. He broke into pieces the bronze snake Moses had made, for up to that time the Israelites had been burning incense to it. (It was called Nehushtan.[b])

5Hezekiah trusted in the LORD, the God of Israel. There was no one like him among all the kings of Judah, either before him or after him. 6He held fast to the LORD and did not stop following him; he kept the commands the LORD had given Moses. 7And the LORD was with him; he was successful in whatever he undertook. He rebelled against the king of Assyria and did not serve him. 8From watchtower to fortified city, he defeated the Philistines, as far as Gaza and its territory.

9In King Hezekiah's fourth year, which was the seventh year of Hoshea son of Elah king of Israel, Shalmaneser king of Assyria marched against Samaria and laid siege to it. 10At the end of three years the Assyrians took it. So Samaria was captured in Hezekiah's sixth year, which was the ninth year of Hoshea king of Israel. 11The king of Assyria deported Israel to Assyria and settled them in Halah, in Gozan on the Habor River and in towns of the Medes. 12This happened because they had not obeyed the LORD their God, but had violated his covenant—all that Moses the servant of the LORD commanded. They neither listened to the commands nor carried them out.

13In the fourteenth year of King Hezekiah's reign, Sennacherib king of Assyria attacked all the fortified cities of Judah and captured them. 14So Hezekiah king of Judah sent this message to the king of Assyria at Lachish: "I have done wrong. Withdraw from me, and I will pay whatever you demand of me." The king of Assyria exacted from Hezekiah king of Judah three hundred talents[c] of silver and thirty talents[d] of gold. 15So Hezekiah gave him all the silver that was found in the temple of the LORD and in the treasuries of the royal palace.

16At this time Hezekiah king of Judah stripped off the gold with which he had covered the doors and doorposts of the temple of the LORD, and gave it to the king of Assyria.

Sennacherib Threatens Jerusalem

17The king of Assyria sent his supreme commander, his chief officer and his field commander with a large army, from Lachish to King Hezekiah at Jerusalem. They came up to Jerusalem and stopped at the aqueduct of the Upper Pool, on the road to the Washerman's Field. 18They called for the king; and Eliakim son of Hilkiah the palace administrator, Shebna the secretary, and Joah son of Asaph the recorder went out to them.

19The field commander said to them, "Tell Hezekiah:

"'This is what the great king, the king of Assyria, says: On what are you basing this confidence of yours? 20You say you have the counsel and the might for war—but you speak only empty words. On whom are you depending, that you rebel against me? 21Look, I know you are depending on Egypt, that splintered reed of a staff, which pierces the hand of anyone who leans on it! Such is Pharaoh king of Egypt to all who depend on him. 22But if you say to me, "We are depending on the LORD our God"—isn't he the one whose high places and altars Hezekiah removed, saying to Judah and Jerusalem, "You must worship before this altar in Jerusalem"?

23"'Come now, make a bargain with my master, the king of Assyria: I will

---

[a] *2* Hebrew *Abi,* a variant of *Abijah* [b] *4 Nehushtan* sounds like the Hebrew for both *bronze* and *snake.* [c] *14* That is, about 11 tons or about 10 metric tons [d] *14* That is, about 1 ton or about 1 metric ton

THE RELICS OF WORSHIP

Throughout the Old Testament, God gave specific commands to his people regarding the high places on which pagans worshiped a host of false gods. Knowing that the presence of these high places would provide a steady temptation for his people, God commanded them to destroy entirely the worship sites (Nu 33:52; Dt 12:2). Ironically, Israelites who worshiped at these locations sometimes maintained traditions of worship of the one true God while also integrating the perverse worship of a wide array of gods including Baal and Asherah.

King Hezekiah knew that the removal of these locations would not render idolatry obsolete, but it would aid in the return of the people to the worship of the one true God. He also destroyed the objects of worship used by the pagan cults — many of which had been introduced during the reign of his apostate father, Ahaz. One such object of false worship was the bronze snake that had been preserved since the time of Moses (2Ki 18:4). This bronze snake was originally intended by God to provide a tangible symbol of salvation. At some point, however, this God-ordained object became venerated in and of itself — an example of the gift overshadowing the Giver. The snake was never meant to be an object of worship, but, like many symbols, it became something different from what God intended it to be.

Paul argued in the book of Romans that misdirected worship is at the heart of all human sin. People, by virtue of their sin nature, take God's created handiwork and elevate it to a place of worship (Ro 1:23). As a result, the worship of the one true God is overshadowed, devalued or excluded completely. All things created by God are good, yet they can be turned into a source of sin when given a more prominent place in the human heart than they deserve. Even objects used in worship, such as a church building, style of music or various programmatic structures in the church can become idolatrous if they cause the people of God to stumble and turn from the worship of the true God. Like the bronze snake, these objects often have great spiritual significance; however, they can become packed with idolatrous potential. All people must guard their hearts from the worship of relics and redirect their hearts, by the power of the Spirit, to worship the only one worthy of all worship: Jesus.

give you two thousand horses — if you can put riders on them! 24How can you repulse one officer of the least of my master's officials, even though you are depending on Egypt for chariots and horsemen[a]? 25Furthermore, have I come to attack and destroy this place without word from the LORD? The LORD himself told me to march against this country and destroy it.' "

26Then Eliakim son of Hilkiah, and Shebna and Joah said to the field commander, "Please speak to your servants in Aramaic, since we understand it. Don't speak to us in Hebrew in the hearing of the people on the wall."

27But the commander replied, "Was it only to your master and you that my master sent me to say these things, and not to the people sitting on the wall — who, like you, will have to eat their own excrement and drink their own urine?"

28Then the commander stood and called out in Hebrew, "Hear the word of the great king, the king of Assyria! 29This is what the king says: Do not let Hezekiah deceive you. He cannot deliver you from my hand. 30Do not let Hezekiah persuade you to trust in the LORD when he says, 'The LORD will surely deliver us; this city will not be given into the hand of the king of Assyria.'

31"Do not listen to Hezekiah. This is what the king of Assyria says: Make peace with me and come out to me. Then each of you will eat fruit from your own vine and fig tree and drink water from your own cistern, 32until I come and take you to a land like your own — a land of grain and new wine, a land of bread and vineyards, a land of olive trees and honey. Choose life and not death!

"Do not listen to Hezekiah, for he is misleading you when he says, 'The LORD will deliver us.' 33Has the god of any nation ever delivered his land from the hand of the king of Assyria? 34Where are the gods of Hamath and Arpad? Where are the gods of Sepharvaim, Hena and Ivvah? Have they rescued Samaria from my hand? 35Who of all the gods of these countries has been able to save his land from me? How then can the LORD deliver Jerusalem from my hand?"

36But the people remained silent and said nothing in reply, because the king had commanded, "Do not answer him."

37Then Eliakim son of Hilkiah the palace administrator, Shebna the secretary, and Joah son of Asaph the recorder went to Hezekiah, with their clothes torn, and told him what the field commander had said.

Jerusalem's Deliverance Foretold

19 When King Hezekiah heard this, he tore his clothes and put on sackcloth and went into the temple of the LORD. 2He sent Eliakim the palace administrator, Shebna the secretary and the leading priests, all wearing sackcloth, to the prophet Isaiah son of Amoz. 3They told him, "This is what Hezekiah says: This day is a day of distress and rebuke and disgrace, as when children come to the moment of birth and there is no strength to deliver them. 4It may be that the LORD your God will hear all the words of the field commander, whom his master, the king of Assyria, has sent to ridicule the living God, and that he will rebuke him for the words the LORD your God has heard. Therefore pray for the remnant that still survives."

5When King Hezekiah's officials came to Isaiah, 6Isaiah said to them, "Tell your master, 'This is what the LORD says: Do not be afraid of what you have heard — those words with which the underlings of the king of Assyria have blasphemed me. 7Listen! When he hears a certain report, I will make him want to return to his own country, and there I will have him cut down with the sword.' "

8When the field commander heard that the king of Assyria had left Lachish, he withdrew and found the king fighting against Libnah.

9Now Sennacherib received a report that Tirhakah, the king of Cush,[b] was marching out to fight against him. So he again sent messengers to Hezekiah with this word: 10"Say to Hezekiah king of Judah: Do not let the god you depend on deceive you when he says, 'Jerusalem will not be given into the hands of the king

2 KINGS 18:28 – 37

GOD'S VINDICATION

Many of the greatest failures in history seemed like prudent decisions at the time. King Sennacherib's mockery of Judah and their God, delivered by his field commander, seemed appropriate based on the situation. God's chosen people had diminished as Assyria sacked the northern kingdom during Hezekiah's reign. Now the remainder of God's special nation was holed up in cities, besieged and starving. The evidence seemed to support Sennacherib's assertion: the God of Judah was powerless in the face of the massive Assyrian army. But despite the military odds, the Lord of armies brought mighty Assyria to its knees. God vindicated his name against the mockers.

At Jesus' trial and execution, many mocked him. The soldiers shamed him (Mt 27:31). Passersby, religious leaders and even one of those executed alongside him demonstrated their contempt for Jesus by deriding him as he died (Mt 27:38 – 44). But in the end it was God who emerged victorious (Ps 2:1 – 4). Jesus rose from the dead and defeated the plans of the religious and political rulers of his day as well as the spiritual powers of darkness that drove them to their wicked schemes (Col 2:15).

[a] 24 Or *charioteers* [b] 9 That is, the upper Nile region

of Assyria.' [11]Surely you have heard what the kings of Assyria have done to all
the countries, destroying them completely. And will you be delivered? [12]Did the
gods of the nations that were destroyed by my predecessors deliver them — the
gods of Gozan, Harran, Rezeph and the people of Eden who were in Tel Assar?
[13]Where is the king of Hamath or the king of Arpad? Where are the kings of Lair,
Sepharvaim, Hena and Ivvah?"

Hezekiah's Prayer

[14]Hezekiah received the letter from the messengers and read it. Then he went
up to the temple of the LORD and spread it out before the LORD. [15]And Hezekiah
prayed to the LORD: "LORD, the God of Israel, enthroned between the cherubim,
you alone are God over all the kingdoms of the earth. You have made heaven and
earth. [16]Give ear, LORD, and hear; open your eyes, LORD, and see; listen to the
words Sennacherib has sent to ridicule the living God.

[17]"It is true, LORD, that the Assyrian kings have laid waste these nations and
their lands. [18]They have thrown their gods into the fire and destroyed them, for
they were not gods but only wood and stone, fashioned by human hands. [19]Now,
LORD our God, deliver us from his hand, so that all the kingdoms of the earth
may know that you alone, LORD, are God."

Isaiah Prophesies Sennacherib's Fall

[20]Then Isaiah son of Amoz sent a message to Hezekiah: "This is what the
LORD, the God of Israel, says: I have heard your prayer concerning Sennacherib
king of Assyria. [21]This is the word that the LORD has spoken against him:

"'Virgin Daughter Zion
despises you and mocks you.
Daughter Jerusalem
tosses her head as you flee.
[22]Who is it you have ridiculed and blasphemed?
Against whom have you raised your voice
and lifted your eyes in pride?
Against the Holy One of Israel!
[23]By your messengers
you have ridiculed the Lord.
And you have said,
"With my many chariots
I have ascended the heights of the mountains,
the utmost heights of Lebanon.
I have cut down its tallest cedars,
the choicest of its junipers.
I have reached its remotest parts,
the finest of its forests.
[24]I have dug wells in foreign lands
and drunk the water there.
With the soles of my feet
I have dried up all the streams of Egypt."
[25]"'Have you not heard?
Long ago I ordained it.
In days of old I planned it;
now I have brought it to pass,
that you have turned fortified cities
into piles of stone.
[26]Their people, drained of power,
are dismayed and put to shame.
They are like plants in the field,
like tender green shoots,

like grass sprouting on the roof,
scorched before it grows up.

27 " 'But I know where you are
and when you come and go
and how you rage against me.
28 Because you rage against me
and because your insolence has reached my ears,
I will put my hook in your nose
and my bit in your mouth,
and I will make you return
by the way you came.'

29 "This will be the sign for you, Hezekiah:

"This year you will eat what grows by itself,
and the second year what springs from that.
But in the third year sow and reap,
plant vineyards and eat their fruit.
30 Once more a remnant of the kingdom of Judah
will take root below and bear fruit above.
31 For out of Jerusalem will come a remnant,
and out of Mount Zion a band of survivors.

"The zeal of the LORD Almighty will accomplish this.

32 "Therefore this is what the LORD says concerning the king of Assyria:

" 'He will not enter this city
or shoot an arrow here.
He will not come before it with shield
or build a siege ramp against it.
33 By the way that he came he will return;
he will not enter this city,
declares the LORD.

34 I will defend this city and save it,
for my sake and for the sake of David my servant.' "

35 That night the angel of the LORD went out and put to death a hundred and
eighty-five thousand in the Assyrian camp. When the people got up the next
morning — there were all the dead bodies! 36 So Sennacherib king of Assyria
broke camp and withdrew. He returned to Nineveh and stayed there.
37 One day, while he was worshiping in the temple of his god Nisrok, his sons
Adrammelek and Sharezer killed him with the sword, and they escaped to the
land of Ararat. And Esarhaddon his son succeeded him as king.

Hezekiah's Illness

20 In those days Hezekiah became ill and was at the point of death. The
prophet Isaiah son of Amoz went to him and said, "This is what the LORD
says: Put your house in order, because you are going to die; you will not recover."
2 Hezekiah turned his face to the wall and prayed to the LORD, 3 "Remember,
LORD, how I have walked before you faithfully and with wholehearted devotion
and have done what is good in your eyes." And Hezekiah wept bitterly.
4 Before Isaiah had left the middle court, the word of the LORD came to him:
5 "Go back and tell Hezekiah, the ruler of my people, 'This is what the LORD, the
God of your father David, says: I have heard your prayer and seen your tears;
I will heal you. On the third day from now you will go up to the temple of the
LORD. 6 I will add fifteen years to your life. And I will deliver you and this city from
the hand of the king of Assyria. I will defend this city for my sake and for the sake
of my servant David.' "

7 Then Isaiah said, "Prepare a poultice of figs." They did so and applied it to
the boil, and he recovered.
8 Hezekiah had asked Isaiah, "What will be the sign that the LORD will heal
me and that I will go up to the temple of the LORD on the third day from now?"
9 Isaiah answered, "This is the LORD's sign to you that the LORD will do what he
has promised: Shall the shadow go forward ten steps, or shall it go back ten steps?"
10 "It is a simple matter for the shadow to go forward ten steps," said Hezekiah.
"Rather, have it go back ten steps."
11 Then the prophet Isaiah called on the LORD, and the LORD made the shadow
go back the ten steps it had gone down on the stairway of Ahaz.

Envoys From Babylon

12 At that time Marduk-Baladan son of Baladan king of Babylon sent Hezekiah letters and a gift, because he had heard of Hezekiah's illness. 13 Hezekiah
received the envoys and showed them all that was in his storehouses — the silver, the gold, the spices and the fine olive oil — his armory and everything found
among his treasures. There was nothing in his palace or in all his kingdom that
Hezekiah did not show them.
14 Then Isaiah the prophet went to King Hezekiah and asked, "What did those
men say, and where did they come from?"
"From a distant land," Hezekiah replied. "They came from Babylon."
15 The prophet asked, "What did they see in your palace?"
"They saw everything in my palace," Hezekiah said. "There is nothing among
my treasures that I did not show them."
16 Then Isaiah said to Hezekiah, "Hear the word of the LORD: 17 The time will
surely come when everything in your palace, and all that your predecessors have
stored up until this day, will be carried off to Babylon. Nothing will be left, says
the LORD. 18 And some of your descendants, your own flesh and blood who will
be born to you, will be taken away, and they will become eunuchs in the palace
of the king of Babylon."
19 "The word of the LORD you have spoken is good," Hezekiah replied. For he
thought, "Will there not be peace and security in my lifetime?"
20 As for the other events of Hezekiah's reign, all his achievements and how he
made the pool and the tunnel by which he brought water into the city, are they
not written in the book of the annals of the kings of Judah? 21 Hezekiah rested
with his ancestors. And Manasseh his son succeeded him as king.

Manasseh King of Judah

21 Manasseh was twelve years old when he became king, and he reigned
in Jerusalem fifty-five years. His mother's name was Hephzibah. 2 He did
evil in the eyes of the LORD, following the detestable practices of the nations the
LORD had driven out before the Israelites. 3 He rebuilt the high places his father
Hezekiah had destroyed; he also erected altars to Baal and made an Asherah
pole, as Ahab king of Israel had done. He bowed down to all the starry hosts and
worshiped them. 4 He built altars in the temple of the LORD, of which the LORD
had said, "In Jerusalem I will put my Name." 5 In the two courts of the temple of
the LORD, he built altars to all the starry hosts. 6 He sacrificed his own son in the
fire, practiced divination, sought omens, and consulted mediums and spiritists.
He did much evil in the eyes of the LORD, arousing his anger.
7 He took the carved Asherah pole he had made and put it in the temple, of
which the LORD had said to David and to his son Solomon, "In this temple and in
Jerusalem, which I have chosen out of all the tribes of Israel, I will put my Name
forever. 8 I will not again make the feet of the Israelites wander from the land I
gave their ancestors, if only they will be careful to do everything I commanded
them and will keep the whole Law that my servant Moses gave them." 9 But the
people did not listen. Manasseh led them astray, so that they did more evil than
the nations the LORD had destroyed before the Israelites.

2 KINGS 20:1 – 21

FAITHFULNESS REWARDED

In contrast to many of the kings in ancient Judah, Hezekiah was a great and faithful king. He trusted God and held fast to his commandments (2Ki 18:5 – 6). Faced with his impending death, Hezekiah wept before the Lord and asked that God would extend his life. God, in kindness, granted Hezekiah's request and added fifteen years to his life. While Hezekiah could have easily used this extra fifteen years to his own selfish advantage, he remained faithful to God by living in obedience. However, the verses following Hezekiah's healing describe a rare, unwise decision made by Hezekiah. He hosted envoys from the king of Babylon and revealed to them the vast provision that the Lord had entrusted to him and to the nation.

Isaiah responded to Hezekiah's actions by warning him of a day when invaders from Babylon would return to the land of the people of God only to steal the very riches Hezekiah had shown off. The silver, gold and even some of Hezekiah's own descendants would be hauled off to that foreign land. Isaiah told Hezekiah that, in the final analysis, nothing would be left of his vast riches. It is easy to read Hezekiah's reaction as selfish and smug. He appeared to be grateful that any negative consequences for his actions would be experienced after his death, so he would not have to deal with his own mistake. However, a more accurate interpretation that is in line with Hezekiah's character is that he humbly accepted the word of the prophet. Hezekiah seemed to resign himself to the consequences of his mistake, and he may have been relieved that what Isaiah said would not happen during his lifetime.

In contrast, Jesus willingly took on the consequences of everyone's mistakes. Jesus knew that, like Hezekiah, everyone has made bad decisions that will one day have consequences — consequences like death and separation from God (Ro 6:23). However, Jesus' death frees believers from these consequences and gives them eternal life with God. Believers should respond to this news with Hezekiah-like humility and gratefulness, knowing that the Word of God is true. It is now the responsibility of Christians to share the great news that Jesus came and paid for everyone's sins.

[10]The LORD said through his servants the prophets: [11]"Manasseh king of Judah has committed these detestable sins. He has done more evil than the Amorites who preceded him and has led Judah into sin with his idols. [12]Therefore
this is what the LORD, the God of Israel, says: I am going to bring such disaster
on Jerusalem and Judah that the ears of everyone who hears of it will tingle. [13]I
will stretch out over Jerusalem the measuring line used against Samaria and
the plumb line used against the house of Ahab. I will wipe out Jerusalem as one
wipes a dish, wiping it and turning it upside down. [14]I will forsake the remnant
of my inheritance and give them into the hands of enemies. They will be looted
and plundered by all their enemies; [15]they have done evil in my eyes and have
aroused my anger from the day their ancestors came out of Egypt until this day."

[16]Moreover, Manasseh also shed so much innocent blood that he filled Jerusalem from end to end — besides the sin that he had caused Judah to commit, so
that they did evil in the eyes of the LORD.

[17]As for the other events of Manasseh's reign, and all he did, including the sin
he committed, are they not written in the book of the annals of the kings of Judah? [18]Manasseh rested with his ancestors and was buried in his palace garden,
the garden of Uzza. And Amon his son succeeded him as king.

Amon King of Judah

[19]Amon was twenty-two years old when he became king, and he reigned in
Jerusalem two years. His mother's name was Meshullemeth daughter of Haruz;
she was from Jotbah. [20]He did evil in the eyes of the LORD, as his father Manasseh
had done. [21]He followed completely the ways of his father, worshiping the idols
his father had worshiped, and bowing down to them. [22]He forsook the LORD, the
God of his ancestors, and did not walk in obedience to him.

[23]Amon's officials conspired against him and assassinated the king in his palace. [24]Then the people of the land killed all who had plotted against King Amon,
and they made Josiah his son king in his place.

[25]As for the other events of Amon's reign, and what he did, are they not written
in the book of the annals of the kings of Judah? [26]He was buried in his tomb in the
garden of Uzza. And Josiah his son succeeded him as king.

The Book of the Law Found

22 Josiah was eight years old when he became king, and he reigned in Jerusalem thirty-one years. His mother's name was Jedidah daughter of Adaiah; she was from Bozkath. [2]He did what was right in the eyes of the LORD and
followed completely the ways of his father David, not turning aside to the right
or to the left.

[3]In the eighteenth year of his reign, King Josiah sent the secretary, Shaphan
son of Azaliah, the son of Meshullam, to the temple of the LORD. He said: [4]"Go
up to Hilkiah the high priest and have him get ready the money that has been
brought into the temple of the LORD, which the doorkeepers have collected from
the people. [5]Have them entrust it to the men appointed to supervise the work on
the temple. And have these men pay the workers who repair the temple of the
LORD — [6]the carpenters, the builders and the masons. Also have them purchase
timber and dressed stone to repair the temple. [7]But they need not account for the
money entrusted to them, because they are honest in their dealings."

[8]Hilkiah the high priest said to Shaphan the secretary, "I have found the Book
of the Law in the temple of the LORD." He gave it to Shaphan, who read it. [9]Then
Shaphan the secretary went to the king and reported to him: "Your officials have
paid out the money that was in the temple of the LORD and have entrusted it to
the workers and supervisors at the temple." [10]Then Shaphan the secretary informed the king, "Hilkiah the priest has given me a book." And Shaphan read
from it in the presence of the king.

[11]When the king heard the words of the Book of the Law, he tore his robes.
[12]He gave these orders to Hilkiah the priest, Ahikam son of Shaphan, Akbor son

of Micaiah, Shaphan the secretary and Asaiah the king's attendant: [13]"Go and inquire of the LORD for me and for the people and for all Judah about what is written in this book that has been found. Great is the LORD's anger that burns against us because those who have gone before us have not obeyed the words of this book; they have not acted in accordance with all that is written there concerning us."

[14]Hilkiah the priest, Ahikam, Akbor, Shaphan and Asaiah went to speak to the prophet Huldah, who was the wife of Shallum son of Tikvah, the son of Harhas, keeper of the wardrobe. She lived in Jerusalem, in the New Quarter.

[15]She said to them, "This is what the LORD, the God of Israel, says: Tell the man who sent you to me, [16]'This is what the LORD says: I am going to bring disaster on this place and its people, according to everything written in the book the king of Judah has read. [17]Because they have forsaken me and burned incense to other gods and aroused my anger by all the idols their hands have made,[a] my anger will burn against this place and will not be quenched.' [18]Tell the king of Judah, who sent you to inquire of the LORD, 'This is what the LORD, the God of Israel, says concerning the words you heard: [19]Because your heart was responsive and you humbled yourself before the LORD when you heard what I have spoken against this place and its people — that they would become a curse[b] and be laid waste — and because you tore your robes and wept in my presence, I also have heard you, declares the LORD. [20]Therefore I will gather you to your ancestors, and you will be buried in peace. Your eyes will not see all the disaster I am going to bring on this place.' "

So they took her answer back to the king.

Josiah Renews the Covenant

23 Then the king called together all the elders of Judah and Jerusalem. [2]He went up to the temple of the LORD with the people of Judah, the inhabitants of Jerusalem, the priests and the prophets — all the people from the least to the greatest. He read in their hearing all the words of the Book of the Covenant, which had been found in the temple of the LORD. [3]The king stood by the pillar and renewed the covenant in the presence of the LORD — to follow the LORD and keep his commands, statutes and decrees with all his heart and all his soul, thus confirming the words of the covenant written in this book. Then all the people pledged themselves to the covenant.

[4]The king ordered Hilkiah the high priest, the priests next in rank and the doorkeepers to remove from the temple of the LORD all the articles made for Baal and Asherah and all the starry hosts. He burned them outside Jerusalem in the fields of the Kidron Valley and took the ashes to Bethel. [5]He did away with the idolatrous priests appointed by the kings of Judah to burn incense on the high places of the towns of Judah and on those around Jerusalem — those who burned incense to Baal, to the sun and moon, to the constellations and to all the starry hosts. [6]He took the Asherah pole from the temple of the LORD to the Kidron Valley outside Jerusalem and burned it there. He ground it to powder and scattered the dust over the graves of the common people. [7]He also tore down the quarters of the male shrine prostitutes that were in the temple of the LORD, the quarters where women did weaving for Asherah.

[8]Josiah brought all the priests from the towns of Judah and desecrated the high places, from Geba to Beersheba, where the priests had burned incense. He broke down the gateway at the entrance of the Gate of Joshua, the city governor, which was on the left of the city gate. [9]Although the priests of the high places did not serve at the altar of the LORD in Jerusalem, they ate unleavened bread with their fellow priests.

[10]He desecrated Topheth, which was in the Valley of Ben Hinnom, so no one

---

[a] 17 Or *by everything they have done* [b] 19 That is, their names would be used in cursing (see Jer. 29:22); or, others would see that they are cursed.

MARKS OF REVIVAL

The physical and spiritual reforms under King Josiah marked a critical time of revival among the people of God. Josiah was only eight years old when he began his reign, which lasted 31 years. During that time, he played a central role in the recovery of the spiritual vitality of God's people and, in doing so, provided a lasting testimony to the marks of revival among the people of God.

First, revival begins with a personal commitment to worship and obedience. From an early age, Josiah displayed this commitment, resolving to do what was right in the eyes of God rather than following in the ways of his pagan predecessors. Scripture records that Josiah walked with God and did not turn aside to the right or to the left (v. 2). Like Josiah, God's people must commit to follow him regardless of the cost.

Second, for revival to happen, God's people must prioritize the Word of God. Hilkiah made a remarkable discovery in 2 Kings 22; he found the Book of the Law (some or all of the Pentateuch) in the temple. One would think that there would be no way that the Word of God could be lost in the very dwelling place of God, but this is just what had happened. Once discovered, the king listened to the book being read and came to understand the purposes and plans of God for his people. Believers today must be careful not to lose the Word of God through neglect or apathy. Instead, they must meditate on the Word day and night so that they can be careful to do all that is written in it. The Word is a light and compass.

Third, when God's people long for revival, they must recognize and confess their sins and plead with God for mercy. During the revival under Josiah, the reading of God's Word prompted repentance, first in Josiah's life, and then within the nation. They quickly realized that they had not acted in accordance with the law. Josiah wept at this revelation and tore his clothes as a sign of mourning. He confessed his sins and the sins of the nation before God and vowed to live obediently from that time forward.

Finally, those hoping for revival must decisively turn away from everything that competes with God for their worship. Josiah began an aggressive campaign to rid the land of idols (2Ki 23:4 – 25). He knew that if idolatry was left unchecked, the people would soon be drawn back into their former patterns of life. Like Josiah, God's people must ruthlessly eliminate anything that would draw their hearts away from God — particularly those things that shaped their former lives of sin (Eph 4:20 – 24).

could use it to sacrifice their son or daughter in the fire to Molek. [11]He removed
from the entrance to the temple of the LORD the horses that the kings of Judah
had dedicated to the sun. They were in the court[a] near the room of an official
named Nathan-Melek. Josiah then burned the chariots dedicated to the sun.
[12]He pulled down the altars the kings of Judah had erected on the roof near
the upper room of Ahaz, and the altars Manasseh had built in the two courts of
the temple of the LORD. He removed them from there, smashed them to pieces
and threw the rubble into the Kidron Valley. [13]The king also desecrated the high
places that were east of Jerusalem on the south of the Hill of Corruption — the
ones Solomon king of Israel had built for Ashtoreth the vile goddess of the Sidonians, for Chemosh the vile god of Moab, and for Molek the detestable god of the
people of Ammon. [14]Josiah smashed the sacred stones and cut down the Asherah poles and covered the sites with human bones.
[15]Even the altar at Bethel, the high place made by Jeroboam son of Nebat,
who had caused Israel to sin — even that altar and high place he demolished. He
burned the high place and ground it to powder, and burned the Asherah pole
also. [16]Then Josiah looked around, and when he saw the tombs that were there
on the hillside, he had the bones removed from them and burned on the altar to
defile it, in accordance with the word of the LORD proclaimed by the man of God
who foretold these things.
[17]The king asked, "What is that tombstone I see?"
The people of the city said, "It marks the tomb of the man of God who came
from Judah and pronounced against the altar of Bethel the very things you have
done to it."
[18]"Leave it alone," he said. "Don't let anyone disturb his bones." So they
spared his bones and those of the prophet who had come from Samaria.
[19]Just as he had done at Bethel, Josiah removed all the shrines at the high places that the kings of Israel had built in the towns of Samaria and that had aroused
the LORD's anger. [20]Josiah slaughtered all the priests of those high places on the
altars and burned human bones on them. Then he went back to Jerusalem.
[21]The king gave this order to all the people: "Celebrate the Passover to the
LORD your God, as it is written in this Book of the Covenant." [22]Neither in
the days of the judges who led Israel nor in the days of the kings of Israel and the
kings of Judah had any such Passover been observed. [23]But in the eighteenth
year of King Josiah, this Passover was celebrated to the LORD in Jerusalem.
[24]Furthermore, Josiah got rid of the mediums and spiritists, the household
gods, the idols and all the other detestable things seen in Judah and Jerusalem.
This he did to fulfill the requirements of the law written in the book that Hilkiah
the priest had discovered in the temple of the LORD. [25]Neither before nor after
Josiah was there a king like him who turned to the LORD as he did — with all his
heart and with all his soul and with all his strength, in accordance with all the
Law of Moses.
[26]Nevertheless, the LORD did not turn away from the heat of his fierce anger,
which burned against Judah because of all that Manasseh had done to arouse
his anger. [27]So the LORD said, "I will remove Judah also from my presence as I removed Israel, and I will reject Jerusalem, the city I chose, and this temple, about
which I said, 'My Name shall be there.'[b]"
[28]As for the other events of Josiah's reign, and all he did, are they not written
in the book of the annals of the kings of Judah?
[29]While Josiah was king, Pharaoh Necho king of Egypt went up to the Euphrates River to help the king of Assyria. King Josiah marched out to meet him
in battle, but Necho faced him and killed him at Megiddo. [30]Josiah's servants
brought his body in a chariot from Megiddo to Jerusalem and buried him in his
own tomb. And the people of the land took Jehoahaz son of Josiah and anointed
him and made him king in place of his father.

---

2 KINGS 23:21–25

TURNING TO GOD

Josiah turned his affections toward God. He attempted to restore a nation that had lost its foundation and roots back to its covenant fellowship with God. Josiah was a king who followed after the Lord with all his heart, soul and strength (v. 25). Similar to Moses, whose covenant he was trying to uphold, Josiah served God even though the nation was doomed. Moses and Josiah attempted to display to their people that God was worthy of their service, regardless of the circumstances.

Josiah's rediscovery of the Book of the Law (2Ki 22:8–13) was instrumental in calling the nation to follow the Lord with all of their hearts, souls and strength. Similarly, in Luke 10:25–28, Jesus questioned an expert in the law regarding a summation of the Law. The expert responded by saying he believed it could be summed up this way: " 'Love the Lord your God with all your heart and with all your soul and with all your strength and with all your mind'; and, 'Love your neighbor as yourself' " (Lk 10:27). Jesus agreed, and in Matthew 22:35–40 he identified these two commandments as the first and second most important laws, upon which "all the Law and the Prophets hang" (Mt 22:40). The life of Josiah displayed his unwavering allegiance to the Law — an allegiance grounded in his love for God.

---

[a] *11* The meaning of the Hebrew for this word is uncertain. [b] *27* 1 Kings 8:29

Jehoahaz King of Judah

31 Jehoahaz was twenty-three years old when he became king, and he reigned
in Jerusalem three months. His mother's name was Hamutal daughter of Jeremiah; she was from Libnah. 32 He did evil in the eyes of the LORD, just as his
predecessors had done. 33 Pharaoh Necho put him in chains at Riblah in the land
of Hamath so that he might not reign in Jerusalem, and he imposed on Judah a
levy of a hundred talents[a] of silver and a talent[b] of gold. 34 Pharaoh Necho made
Eliakim son of Josiah king in place of his father Josiah and changed Eliakim's
name to Jehoiakim. But he took Jehoahaz and carried him off to Egypt, and there
he died. 35 Jehoiakim paid Pharaoh Necho the silver and gold he demanded. In
order to do so, he taxed the land and exacted the silver and gold from the people
of the land according to their assessments.

Jehoiakim King of Judah

36 Jehoiakim was twenty-five years old when he became king, and he reigned
in Jerusalem eleven years. His mother's name was Zebidah daughter of Pedaiah;
she was from Rumah. 37 And he did evil in the eyes of the LORD, just as his predecessors had done.

24 During Jehoiakim's reign, Nebuchadnezzar king of Babylon invaded the
land, and Jehoiakim became his vassal for three years. But then he turned
against Nebuchadnezzar and rebelled. 2 The LORD sent Babylonian,[c] Aramean,
Moabite and Ammonite raiders against him to destroy Judah, in accordance
with the word of the LORD proclaimed by his servants the prophets. 3 Surely these
things happened to Judah according to the LORD's command, in order to remove
them from his presence because of the sins of Manasseh and all he had done,
4 including the shedding of innocent blood. For he had filled Jerusalem with innocent blood, and the LORD was not willing to forgive.

5 As for the other events of Jehoiakim's reign, and all he did, are they not written in the book of the annals of the kings of Judah? 6 Jehoiakim rested with his
ancestors. And Jehoiachin his son succeeded him as king.

7 The king of Egypt did not march out from his own country again, because
the king of Babylon had taken all his territory, from the Wadi of Egypt to the
Euphrates River.

Jehoiachin King of Judah

8 Jehoiachin was eighteen years old when he became king, and he reigned in
Jerusalem three months. His mother's name was Nehushta daughter of Elnathan; she was from Jerusalem. 9 He did evil in the eyes of the LORD, just as his
father had done.

10 At that time the officers of Nebuchadnezzar king of Babylon advanced on
Jerusalem and laid siege to it, 11 and Nebuchadnezzar himself came up to the city
while his officers were besieging it. 12 Jehoiachin king of Judah, his mother, his
attendants, his nobles and his officials all surrendered to him.

In the eighth year of the reign of the king of Babylon, he took Jehoiachin prisoner. 13 As the LORD had declared, Nebuchadnezzar removed the treasures from
the temple of the LORD and from the royal palace, and cut up the gold articles
that Solomon king of Israel had made for the temple of the LORD. 14 He carried all
Jerusalem into exile: all the officers and fighting men, and all the skilled workers and artisans — a total of ten thousand. Only the poorest people of the land
were left.

15 Nebuchadnezzar took Jehoiachin captive to Babylon. He also took from Jerusalem to Babylon the king's mother, his wives, his officials and the prominent
people of the land. 16 The king of Babylon also deported to Babylon the entire
force of seven thousand fighting men, strong and fit for war, and a thousand

---

[a] *33* That is, about 3 3/4 tons or about 3.4 metric tons [b] *33* That is, about 75 pounds or
about 34 kilograms [c] *2* Or *Chaldean*

skilled workers and artisans. 17He made Mattaniah, Jehoiachin's uncle, king in
his place and changed his name to Zedekiah.

Zedekiah King of Judah

18Zedekiah was twenty-one years old when he became king, and he reigned in
Jerusalem eleven years. His mother's name was Hamutal daughter of Jeremiah;
she was from Libnah. 19He did evil in the eyes of the LORD, just as Jehoiakim had
done. 20It was because of the LORD's anger that all this happened to Jerusalem
and Judah, and in the end he thrust them from his presence.

The Fall of Jerusalem

Now Zedekiah rebelled against the king of Babylon.

25 So in the ninth year of Zedekiah's reign, on the tenth day of the tenth
month, Nebuchadnezzar king of Babylon marched against Jerusalem
with his whole army. He encamped outside the city and built siege works all
around it. 2The city was kept under siege until the eleventh year of King Zedekiah.

3By the ninth day of the fourth[a] month the famine in the city had become so
severe that there was no food for the people to eat. 4Then the city wall was broken through, and the whole army fled at night through the gate between the two
walls near the king's garden, though the Babylonians[b] were surrounding the
city. They fled toward the Arabah,[c] 5but the Babylonian[d] army pursued the king
and overtook him in the plains of Jericho. All his soldiers were separated from
him and scattered, 6and he was captured.

He was taken to the king of Babylon at Riblah, where sentence was pronounced on him. 7They killed the sons of Zedekiah before his eyes. Then they
put out his eyes, bound him with bronze shackles and took him to Babylon.

8On the seventh day of the fifth month, in the nineteenth year of Nebuchadnezzar king of Babylon, Nebuzaradan commander of the imperial guard, an official of the king of Babylon, came to Jerusalem. 9He set fire to the temple of the
LORD, the royal palace and all the houses of Jerusalem. Every important building he burned down. 10The whole Babylonian army under the commander of
the imperial guard broke down the walls around Jerusalem. 11Nebuzaradan the
commander of the guard carried into exile the people who remained in the city,
along with the rest of the populace and those who had deserted to the king of
Babylon. 12But the commander left behind some of the poorest people of the
land to work the vineyards and fields.

13The Babylonians broke up the bronze pillars, the movable stands and the
bronze Sea that were at the temple of the LORD and they carried the bronze to
Babylon. 14They also took away the pots, shovels, wick trimmers, dishes and all
the bronze articles used in the temple service. 15The commander of the imperial guard took away the censers and sprinkling bowls — all that were made of
pure gold or silver.

16The bronze from the two pillars, the Sea and the movable stands, which
Solomon had made for the temple of the LORD, was more than could be weighed.
17Each pillar was eighteen cubits[e] high. The bronze capital on top of one pillar
was three cubits[f] high and was decorated with a network and pomegranates of
bronze all around. The other pillar, with its network, was similar.

18The commander of the guard took as prisoners Seraiah the chief priest,
Zephaniah the priest next in rank and the three doorkeepers. 19Of those still in
the city, he took the officer in charge of the fighting men, and five royal advisers. He also took the secretary who was chief officer in charge of conscripting
the people of the land and sixty of the conscripts who were found in the city.

---

[a] *3* Probable reading of the original Hebrew text (see Jer. 52:6); Masoretic Text does not have *fourth.* [b] *4* Or *Chaldeans*; also in verses 13, 25 and 26 [c] *4* Or *the Jordan Valley*
[d] *5* Or *Chaldean*; also in verses 10 and 24 [e] *17* That is, about 27 feet or about 8.1 meters
[f] *17* That is, about 4 1/2 feet or about 1.4 meters

GOD'S CLEAR WARNING

God used the prophets to warn the people of their moral bankruptcy and their need to repent and return to God. The exile of the people of Judah, recounted in 2 Kings 24 – 25, had long ago been prophesied to the people (Dt 28:49 – 52). Even before the Israelites inherited the land, they were warned that they would be driven from the land if they did not obey God and keep his commands. Interestingly, the Israelites' fate was foreshadowed by their own conquest of the promised land. God told his people to drive out the nations in order to inherit the land, warning that Israel would face a similar fate themselves if they disobeyed (Dt 4:25 – 27).

Prophets such as Isaiah and Jeremiah foresaw the disaster that awaited the people of God due to their sin. Years earlier, Isaiah prophesied that God would use the Babylonian nation to purge his people from the land (Isa 39:5 – 8). Likewise, Jeremiah warned the nation of their impending time in captivity and later summarized the process by which the people were carried into exile (Jer 25:8 – 14; 52:1 – 30).

These prophetic warnings served two purposes. First, they demonstrated that God was providentially in control of all things. As an all-knowing and all-powerful God, he gave the prophets insight into the exact details that would not be fulfilled until much later. Second, they showed that God had left his people clear warnings. God did not simply let his people pursue the wayward longings of their hearts, but he continually raised up individuals who would urge them to return to him before it was too late. Sadly, they did not listen.

The same is true today. God is still perfectly in charge of all things and will accomplish his good purpose in this world (Ro 8:28). This purpose will include the judgment of God against sin. However, God has not left people without warning or without hope. The Word of God, the people of God and the Spirit of God are all at work in the world, reminding people to turn to God before they have to face his judgment (Mt 3:2; Lk 5:32; Jn 16:8; 1Jn 1:8 – 9).

2 KINGS 25:27–30

PRESERVING THE LINE TO JESUS

God used kings like Hezekiah and Josiah to prompt revival in Judah. The revivals were short-lived, however, and the kings following Josiah led the nation toward spiritual unfaithfulness once again. Zedekiah, Judah's last king, dismissed the prophet Jeremiah's warning and rebelled against Nebuchadnezzar, king of Babylon (Jer 38:17–18; 52:3). This prompted a sequence of events that culminated with the Babylonians destroying Jerusalem and the temple in 586 BC. The people of Judah were carried into captivity and their homes were destroyed. It seemed as if the people had finally gone too far—forever and irrevocably severing any hope of a relationship with God. In the midst of this destruction, Jehoiachin, Zedekiah's nephew and the former king of Judah, survived. The line of the Messiah was protected, even as the people of God suffered the just consequences for their idolatry. Once again, God proved that he would be faithful to the promises he made long ago, protecting the Davidic line from which his Son, Jesus Christ, would one day come.

20Nebuzaradan the commander took them all and brought them to the king of
Babylon at Riblah. 21There at Riblah, in the land of Hamath, the king had them
executed.

So Judah went into captivity, away from her land.

22Nebuchadnezzar king of Babylon appointed Gedaliah son of Ahikam, the
son of Shaphan, to be over the people he had left behind in Judah. 23When all the
army officers and their men heard that the king of Babylon had appointed Gedaliah as governor, they came to Gedaliah at Mizpah—Ishmael son of Nethaniah,
Johanan son of Kareah, Seraiah son of Tanhumeth the Netophathite, Jaazaniah
the son of the Maakathite, and their men. 24Gedaliah took an oath to reassure
them and their men. "Do not be afraid of the Babylonian officials," he said. "Settle down in the land and serve the king of Babylon, and it will go well with you."

25In the seventh month, however, Ishmael son of Nethaniah, the son of Elishama, who was of royal blood, came with ten men and assassinated Gedaliah and
also the men of Judah and the Babylonians who were with him at Mizpah. 26At
this, all the people from the least to the greatest, together with the army officers,
fled to Egypt for fear of the Babylonians.

Jehoiachin Released

27In the thirty-seventh year of the exile of Jehoiachin king of Judah, in the
year Awel-Marduk became king of Babylon, he released Jehoiachin king of Judah
from prison. He did this on the twenty-seventh day of the twelfth month. 28He
spoke kindly to him and gave him a seat of honor higher than those of the other
kings who were with him in Babylon. 29So Jehoiachin put aside his prison clothes
and for the rest of his life ate regularly at the king's table. 30Day by day the king
gave Jehoiachin a regular allowance as long as he lived.

JESUS: OUR PERFECT RESTORER

1 CHRONICLES

1 CHRONICLES

DAVID'S REIGN OVER JUDAH BEGINS *c. 1010 BC*	DAVID'S REIGN OVER ALL ISRAEL BEGINS *c. 1003 BC*	ARK BROUGHT TO JERUSALEM *c. 997 BC*

About a century after God's people were allowed to return home from exile, the author of 1 and 2 Chronicles (perhaps Ezra) sought to inspire the Jews living in Judah to remain faithful to their covenant-keeping God. He did this by reminding them of their unique spiritual heritage and the faithfulness of God, which spanned generations.

The book focuses on the spiritual highlights of the nation's history, thus detailing in great length the reign of King David. As king, David sought to restore the worship of God to the epicenter of Israel's life. He brought the ark of the covenant into Jerusalem amidst great celebration and appointed priests and Levites to lead the people to worship God in the God-ordained pattern. David longed for the people to give God the glory he rightly deserves (1Ch 16:29) — a desire echoed by the Chronicler to the postexilic people.

The book of 1 Chronicles also reminded the restored community of their familial heritage, substantiated by the lengthy genealogy at the outset of this book. The initial audience for the book understood from the genealogy that they were connected to the great heroes of the faith; specifically, the genealogy connected them to King David through the line of Judah's son Perez.

The remnant had returned and sought to rebuild the temple, which had been ravaged by the pagan Babylonians who took Judah into exile. But God would still be faithful to fulfill the promises he made to Abraham, Isaac and Jacob — and most recently to King David. Through these men, God would carry forth his plan to redeem his people by the establishment of the Davidic kingdom and the eternal royal reign that he had promised to

David. The focus on the great triumphs of David's life — such as his conquest of Jerusalem (11:4 – 9), his relocating the ark to Jerusalem (15:25 – 29) and his victories over Israel's enemies (18:1 – 12) — emboldened the people with strength and hope in the promises they were sure to inherit.

The promises were meant to prompt the people to worship God. David, during his reign, had done just that. His focus on the tabernacle and temple underscored his desire to see the people worship an ever-faithful God. First Chronicles, in a similar fashion, sought to remind the postexilic people of the central importance of proper worship.

God's covenant promises to David were a prelude to what the Messiah would one day bring about. King Jesus walked with God, like David, and now draws the hearts of his people to the proper worship of God. In so doing, he is fulfilling the promises made to David and establishing his royal throne forever.

SING TO THE LORD, ALL THE EARTH;
PROCLAIM HIS SALVATION DAY AFTER DAY.
DECLARE HIS GLORY AMONG THE NATIONS,
HIS MARVELOUS DEEDS AMONG ALL PEOPLES.

---

1 Chronicles 16:23 – 24

1 CHRONICLES

Historical Records From Adam to Abraham

To Noah's Sons

1 Adam, Seth, Enosh, 2 Kenan, Mahalalel, Jared, 3 Enoch, Methuselah, Lamech,
Noah.

4 The sons of Noah:[a]
Shem, Ham and Japheth.

The Japhethites

5 The sons[b] of Japheth:
Gomer, Magog, Madai, Javan, Tubal, Meshek and Tiras.
6 The sons of Gomer:
Ashkenaz, Riphath[c] and Togarmah.
7 The sons of Javan:
Elishah, Tarshish, the Kittites and the Rodanites.

The Hamites

8 The sons of Ham:
Cush, Egypt, Put and Canaan.
9 The sons of Cush:
Seba, Havilah, Sabta, Raamah and Sabteka.
The sons of Raamah:
Sheba and Dedan.
10 Cush was the father[d] of
Nimrod, who became a mighty warrior on earth.
11 Egypt was the father of
the Ludites, Anamites, Lehabites, Naphtuhites, 12 Pathrusites, Kaslu-
hites (from whom the Philistines came) and Caphtorites.
13 Canaan was the father of
Sidon his firstborn,[e] and of the Hittites, 14 Jebusites, Amorites, Girgashites,
15 Hivites, Arkites, Sinites, 16 Arvadites, Zemarites and Hamathites.

The Semites

17 The sons of Shem:
Elam, Ashur, Arphaxad, Lud and Aram.
The sons of Aram:[f]
Uz, Hul, Gether and Meshek.
18 Arphaxad was the father of Shelah,
and Shelah the father of Eber.
19 Two sons were born to Eber:
One was named Peleg,[g] because in his time the earth was divided; his
brother was named Joktan.
20 Joktan was the father of
Almodad, Sheleph, Hazarmaveth, Jerah, 21 Hadoram, Uzal, Diklah,

---

[a] *4* Septuagint; Hebrew does not have this line. [b] *5* *Sons* may mean *descendants* or *successors* or *nations*; also in verses 6-9, 17 and 23. [c] *6* Many Hebrew manuscripts and Vulgate (see also Septuagint and Gen. 10:3); most Hebrew manuscripts *Diphath*
[d] *10* *Father* may mean *ancestor* or *predecessor* or *founder*; also in verses 11, 13, 18 and 20.
[e] *13* Or *of the Sidonians, the foremost* [f] *17* One Hebrew manuscript and some Septuagint manuscripts (see also Gen. 10:23); most Hebrew manuscripts do not have this line.
[g] *19* *Peleg* means *division*.

[22]Obal,[a] Abimael, Sheba, [23]Ophir, Havilah and Jobab. All these were
sons of Joktan.

[24]Shem, Arphaxad,[b] Shelah,
[25]Eber, Peleg, Reu,
[26]Serug, Nahor, Terah
[27]and Abram (that is, Abraham).

The Family of Abraham

[28]The sons of Abraham:
Isaac and Ishmael.

Descendants of Hagar

[29]These were their descendants:
Nebaioth the firstborn of Ishmael, Kedar, Adbeel, Mibsam, [30]Mishma,
Dumah, Massa, Hadad, Tema, [31]Jetur, Naphish and Kedemah. These
were the sons of Ishmael.

Descendants of Keturah

[32]The sons born to Keturah, Abraham's concubine:
Zimran, Jokshan, Medan, Midian, Ishbak and Shuah.
The sons of Jokshan:
Sheba and Dedan.
[33]The sons of Midian:
Ephah, Epher, Hanok, Abida and Eldaah.
All these were descendants of Keturah.

Descendants of Sarah

[34]Abraham was the father of Isaac.
The sons of Isaac:
Esau and Israel.

Esau's Sons

[35]The sons of Esau:
Eliphaz, Reuel, Jeush, Jalam and Korah.
[36]The sons of Eliphaz:
Teman, Omar, Zepho,[c] Gatam and Kenaz;
by Timna: Amalek.[d]
[37]The sons of Reuel:
Nahath, Zerah, Shammah and Mizzah.

The People of Seir in Edom

[38]The sons of Seir:
Lotan, Shobal, Zibeon, Anah, Dishon, Ezer and Dishan.
[39]The sons of Lotan:
Hori and Homam. Timna was Lotan's sister.
[40]The sons of Shobal:
Alvan,[e] Manahath, Ebal, Shepho and Onam.
The sons of Zibeon:
Aiah and Anah.
[41]The son of Anah:
Dishon.

---

[a] *22* Some Hebrew manuscripts and Syriac (see also Gen. 10:28); most Hebrew manuscripts *Ebal* [b] *24* Hebrew; some Septuagint manuscripts *Arphaxad, Cainan* (see also note at Gen. 11:10) [c] *36* Many Hebrew manuscripts, some Septuagint manuscripts and Syriac (see also Gen. 36:11); most Hebrew manuscripts *Zephi* [d] *36* Some Septuagint manuscripts (see also Gen. 36:12); Hebrew *Gatam, Kenaz, Timna and Amalek* [e] *40* Many Hebrew manuscripts and some Septuagint manuscripts (see also Gen. 36:23); most Hebrew manuscripts *Alian*

The sons of Dishon:
Hemdan,[a] Eshban, Ithran and Keran.
42 The sons of Ezer:
Bilhan, Zaavan and Akan.[b]
The sons of Dishan[c]:
Uz and Aran.

The Rulers of Edom

43 These were the kings who reigned in Edom before any Israelite king reigned:
Bela son of Beor, whose city was named Dinhabah.
44 When Bela died, Jobab son of Zerah from Bozrah succeeded him as king.
45 When Jobab died, Husham from the land of the Temanites succeeded him as king.
46 When Husham died, Hadad son of Bedad, who defeated Midian in the country of Moab, succeeded him as king. His city was named Avith.
47 When Hadad died, Samlah from Masrekah succeeded him as king.
48 When Samlah died, Shaul from Rehoboth on the river[d] succeeded him as king.
49 When Shaul died, Baal-Hanan son of Akbor succeeded him as king.
50 When Baal-Hanan died, Hadad succeeded him as king. His city was named Pau,[e] and his wife's name was Mehetabel daughter of Matred, the daughter of Me-Zahab.
51 Hadad also died.

The chiefs of Edom were:
Timna, Alvah, Jetheth,
52 Oholibamah, Elah, Pinon,
53 Kenaz, Teman, Mibzar,
54 Magdiel and Iram. These were the chiefs of Edom.

Israel's Sons

2 These were the sons of Israel:
Reuben, Simeon, Levi, Judah, Issachar, Zebulun,
2 Dan, Joseph, Benjamin, Naphtali, Gad and Asher.

Judah

To Hezron's Sons

3 The sons of Judah:
Er, Onan and Shelah. These three were born to him by a Canaanite woman, the daughter of Shua. Er, Judah's firstborn, was wicked in the LORD's sight; so the LORD put him to death.
4 Judah's daughter-in-law Tamar bore Perez and Zerah to Judah. He had five sons in all.

5 The sons of Perez:
Hezron and Hamul.
6 The sons of Zerah:
Zimri, Ethan, Heman, Kalkol and Darda[f]—five in all.
7 The son of Karmi:
Achar,[g] who brought trouble on Israel by violating the ban on taking devoted things.[h]
8 The son of Ethan:
Azariah.

---

[a] *41* Many Hebrew manuscripts and some Septuagint manuscripts (see also Gen. 36:26); most Hebrew manuscripts *Hamran* [b] *42* Many Hebrew and Septuagint manuscripts (see also Gen. 36:27); most Hebrew manuscripts *Zaavan, Jaakan* [c] *42* See Gen. 36:28; Hebrew *Dishon,* a variant of *Dishan* [d] *48* Possibly the Euphrates [e] *50* Many Hebrew manuscripts, some Septuagint manuscripts, Vulgate and Syriac (see also Gen. 36:39); most Hebrew manuscripts *Pai* [f] *6* Many Hebrew manuscripts, some Septuagint manuscripts and Syriac (see also 1 Kings 4:31); most Hebrew manuscripts *Dara* [g] *7* *Achar* means *trouble; Achar* is called *Achan* in Joshua. [h] *7* The Hebrew term refers to the irrevocable giving over of things or persons to the LORD, often by totally destroying them.

[9] The sons born to Hezron were:
Jerahmeel, Ram and Caleb.[a]

From Ram Son of Hezron

[10] Ram was the father of
Amminadab, and Amminadab the father of Nahshon, the leader of the
people of Judah. [11] Nahshon was the father of Salmon,[b] Salmon the father of Boaz, [12] Boaz the father of Obed and Obed the father of Jesse.
[13] Jesse was the father of
Eliab his firstborn; the second son was Abinadab, the third Shimea,
[14] the fourth Nethanel, the fifth Raddai, [15] the sixth Ozem and the seventh David. [16] Their sisters were Zeruiah and Abigail. Zeruiah's three
sons were Abishai, Joab and Asahel. [17] Abigail was the mother of Amasa,
whose father was Jether the Ishmaelite.

Caleb Son of Hezron

[18] Caleb son of Hezron had children by his wife Azubah (and by Jerioth).
These were her sons: Jesher, Shobab and Ardon. [19] When Azubah died,
Caleb married Ephrath, who bore him Hur. [20] Hur was the father of Uri,
and Uri the father of Bezalel.
[21] Later, Hezron, when he was sixty years old, married the daughter of Makir
the father of Gilead. He made love to her, and she bore him Segub. [22] Segub was the father of Jair, who controlled twenty-three towns in Gilead.
[23] (But Geshur and Aram captured Havvoth Jair,[c] as well as Kenath with
its surrounding settlements — sixty towns.) All these were descendants
of Makir the father of Gilead.
[24] After Hezron died in Caleb Ephrathah, Abijah the wife of Hezron bore him
Ashhur the father[d] of Tekoa.

Jerahmeel Son of Hezron

[25] The sons of Jerahmeel the firstborn of Hezron:
Ram his firstborn, Bunah, Oren, Ozem and[e] Ahijah. [26] Jerahmeel had an-
other wife, whose name was Atarah; she was the mother of Onam.
[27] The sons of Ram the firstborn of Jerahmeel:
Maaz, Jamin and Eker.
[28] The sons of Onam:
Shammai and Jada.
The sons of Shammai:
Nadab and Abishur.
[29] Abishur's wife was named Abihail, who bore him Ahban and Molid.
[30] The sons of Nadab:
Seled and Appaim. Seled died without children.
[31] The son of Appaim:
Ishi, who was the father of Sheshan.
Sheshan was the father of Ahlai.
[32] The sons of Jada, Shammai's brother:
Jether and Jonathan. Jether died without children.
[33] The sons of Jonathan:
Peleth and Zaza.
These were the descendants of Jerahmeel.
[34] Sheshan had no sons — only daughters.
He had an Egyptian servant named Jarha. [35] Sheshan gave his daughter
in marriage to his servant Jarha, and she bore him Attai.

[a] 9 Hebrew *Kelubai,* a variant of *Caleb* [b] *11* Septuagint (see also Ruth 4:21); Hebrew *Salma* [c] *23* Or *captured the settlements of Jair* [d] *24* *Father* may mean *civic leader* or *military leader*; also in verses 42, 45, 49-52 and possibly elsewhere. [e] *25* Or *Oren and Ozem, by*

36 Attai was the father of Nathan,
Nathan the father of Zabad,
37 Zabad the father of Ephlal,
Ephlal the father of Obed,
38 Obed the father of Jehu,
Jehu the father of Azariah,
39 Azariah the father of Helez,
Helez the father of Eleasah,
40 Eleasah the father of Sismai,
Sismai the father of Shallum,
41 Shallum the father of Jekamiah,
and Jekamiah the father of Elishama.

The Clans of Caleb

42 The sons of Caleb the brother of Jerahmeel:
Mesha his firstborn, who was the father of Ziph, and his son Mareshah,[a]
who was the father of Hebron.
43 The sons of Hebron:
Korah, Tappuah, Rekem and Shema. 44 Shema was the father of Raham,
and Raham the father of Jorkeam. Rekem was the father of Shammai.
45 The son of Shammai was Maon, and Maon was the father of Beth Zur.
46 Caleb's concubine Ephah was the mother of Haran, Moza and Gazez. Haran was the father of Gazez.
47 The sons of Jahdai:
Regem, Jotham, Geshan, Pelet, Ephah and Shaaph.
48 Caleb's concubine Maakah was the mother of Sheber and Tirhanah. 49 She
also gave birth to Shaaph the father of Madmannah and to Sheva the father of Makbenah and Gibea. Caleb's daughter was Aksah. 50 These were
the descendants of Caleb.

The sons of Hur the firstborn of Ephrathah:
Shobal the father of Kiriath Jearim, 51 Salma the father of Bethlehem,
and Hareph the father of Beth Gader.
52 The descendants of Shobal the father of Kiriath Jearim were:
Haroeh, half the Manahathites, 53 and the clans of Kiriath Jearim: the
Ithrites, Puthites, Shumathites and Mishraites. From these descended
the Zorathites and Eshtaolites.
54 The descendants of Salma:
Bethlehem, the Netophathites, Atroth Beth Joab, half the Manahathites,
the Zorites, 55 and the clans of scribes[b] who lived at Jabez: the Tirath-
ites, Shimeathites and Sucathites. These are the Kenites who came from
Hammath, the father of the Rekabites.[c]

The Sons of David

3 These were the sons of David born to him in Hebron:
The firstborn was Amnon the son of Ahinoam of Jezreel;
the second, Daniel the son of Abigail of Carmel;
2 the third, Absalom the son of Maakah daughter of Talmai king of Geshur;
the fourth, Adonijah the son of Haggith;
3 the fifth, Shephatiah the son of Abital;
and the sixth, Ithream, by his wife Eglah.
4 These six were born to David in Hebron, where he reigned seven years
and six months.
David reigned in Jerusalem thirty-three years, 5 and these were the children
born to him there:

---

[a] 42 The meaning of the Hebrew for this phrase is uncertain. [b] 55 Or *of the Sopherites*
[c] 55 Or *father of Beth Rekab*

---

1 CHRONICLES 3:1–9

COMPARE AND CONTRAST

The two books of Chronicles repeat much of the information found in the two books of Kings. Yet there are several ways the two histories differ. The books of Kings had a purpose of *indictment*—documenting the failures of God's people. The books of Chronicles had a purpose of *incitement*—encouraging the Jews returning from captivity. In terms of focus, the two books of Kings give attention to both the northern and southern kingdoms of Israel, including all of their kings whether good or evil. The two books of Chronicles focus on the southern kingdom of Judah—highlighting King David, King Solomon and their godly successors. On matters of the temple and worship, a sharp contrast is evident—1 and 2 Kings devote only five chapters to these details while 1 and 2 Chronicles devote twenty chapters. In general, the books of Kings offer a civil and political perspective while the books of Chronicles were written from a moral and spiritual point of view.

1 CHRONICLES 1:1 — 2:55

WHY GENEALOGIES?

First Chronicles comprises a history of God's people from Adam through the time of King David. It demonstrates how God had plans for his people from the beginning of human history.

The genealogies remind the church that the Bible is about *real* people in *real* places facing *real* circumstances — some of triumph and some of tragedy. Noah was a real man who built an ark under God's direction so he and his family could be delivered from the flood (Ge 6:13 – 18). Job actually endured the loss of all of his children when a storm caused his oldest son's house to collapse (Job 1:18 – 21). Joseph found himself abandoned at the bottom of a literal pit (Ge 37:24). Deborah was a real prophetess who sang a real song after the defeat of a Canaanite king (Jdg 4:23 — 5:31). Peter actually walked on the Sea of Galilee (Mt 14:22 – 33). Jesus literally died on a cross and actually came back to life again (Mt 27:32 — 28:10).

Some of those named in the genealogical record of 1 Chronicles are people about whom very little is known — people such as Onam, Shammai, Jada, Nadab, Abishur and Molid. While the details of their stories remain unknown to succeeding generations, they hold a significant place in the line of faith and each of them matters to God. This should be an encouragement to the majority of Christians who will never be famous — the details of their stories will likely dissolve into history. But during their years on earth they play a necessary part in the grand epic of God. One day, when they stand before the Lord at the consummation of all things, they will know the impact of their less-than-famous lives. By faith, God's people live now for the purpose of magnifying Christ, bearing fruit to his eternal glory — caring more about his fame than their own.

The New Testament begins with a beautiful and impressive genealogy in the book of Matthew, following Jesus' lineage back to Abraham (Mt 1:1 – 16). The book of Luke follows the trail all the way back to Adam (Lk 3:23 – 38). The family trees trace Jesus' ancestral line, confirming that he is God's promised Messiah.

Those with saving faith in Jesus stand in a line of spiritual genealogy — a heritage of the gospel passed down from person to person. Believers today have a responsibility. Someone in their past explained the gospel to them, and they now have the privilege to add to that genealogy by helping others respond to Jesus with faith.

Shammua,[a] Shobab, Nathan and Solomon. These four were by Bathsheba[b] daughter of Ammiel. 6 There were also Ibhar, Elishua,[c] Eliphelet,
7 Nogah, Nepheg, Japhia, 8 Elishama, Eliada and Eliphelet — nine in all.
9 All these were the sons of David, besides his sons by his concubines.
And Tamar was their sister.

The Kings of Judah

10 Solomon's son was Rehoboam,
Abijah his son,
Asa his son,
Jehoshaphat his son,
11 Jehoram[d] his son,
Ahaziah his son,
Joash his son,
12 Amaziah his son,
Azariah his son,
Jotham his son,
13 Ahaz his son,
Hezekiah his son,
Manasseh his son,
14 Amon his son,
Josiah his son.
15 The sons of Josiah:
Johanan the firstborn,
Jehoiakim the second son,
Zedekiah the third,
Shallum the fourth.
16 The successors of Jehoiakim:
Jehoiachin[e] his son,
and Zedekiah.

The Royal Line After the Exile

17 The descendants of Jehoiachin the captive:
Shealtiel his son, 18 Malkiram, Pedaiah, Shenazzar, Jekamiah, Hoshama
and Nedabiah.
19 The sons of Pedaiah:
Zerubbabel and Shimei.
The sons of Zerubbabel:
Meshullam and Hananiah.
Shelomith was their sister.
20 There were also five others:
Hashubah, Ohel, Berekiah, Hasadiah and Jushab-Hesed.
21 The descendants of Hananiah:
Pelatiah and Jeshaiah, and the sons of Rephaiah, of Arnan, of Obadiah
and of Shekaniah.
22 The descendants of Shekaniah:
Shemaiah and his sons:
Hattush, Igal, Bariah, Neariah and Shaphat — six in all.
23 The sons of Neariah:
Elioenai, Hizkiah and Azrikam — three in all.
24 The sons of Elioenai:
Hodaviah, Eliashib, Pelaiah, Akkub, Johanan, Delaiah and Anani —
seven in all.

---

[a] 5 Hebrew *Shimea,* a variant of *Shammua* [b] 5 One Hebrew manuscript and Vulgate (see also Septuagint and 2 Samuel 11:3); most Hebrew manuscripts *Bathshua* [c] 6 Two Hebrew manuscripts (see also 2 Samuel 5:15 and 1 Chron. 14:5); most Hebrew manuscripts *Elishama* [d] 11 Hebrew *Joram,* a variant of *Jehoram* [e] 16 Hebrew *Jeconiah,* a variant of *Jehoiachin;* also in verse 17

Other Clans of Judah

4 The descendants of Judah:
Perez, Hezron, Karmi, Hur and Shobal.
2 Reaiah son of Shobal was the father of Jahath, and Jahath the father of Ahumai and Lahad. These were the clans of the Zorathites.
3 These were the sons[a] of Etam:
Jezreel, Ishma and Idbash. Their sister was named Hazzelelponi. 4 Penuel was the father of Gedor, and Ezer the father of Hushah.
These were the descendants of Hur, the firstborn of Ephrathah and father[b] of Bethlehem.
5 Ashhur the father of Tekoa had two wives, Helah and Naarah.
6 Naarah bore him Ahuzzam, Hepher, Temeni and Haahashtari. These were the descendants of Naarah.
7 The sons of Helah:
Zereth, Zohar, Ethnan, 8 and Koz, who was the father of Anub and Hazzobebah and of the clans of Aharhel son of Harum.

9 Jabez was more honorable than his brothers. His mother had named him Jabez,[c] saying, "I gave birth to him in pain." 10 Jabez cried out to the God of Israel,
"Oh, that you would bless me and enlarge my territory! Let your hand be with me, and keep me from harm so that I will be free from pain." And God granted his request.

11 Kelub, Shuhah's brother, was the father of Mehir, who was the father of
Eshton. 12 Eshton was the father of Beth Rapha, Paseah and Tehinnah the father of Ir Nahash.[d] These were the men of Rekah.
13 The sons of Kenaz:
Othniel and Seraiah.
The sons of Othniel:
Hathath and Meonothai.[e] 14 Meonothai was the father of Ophrah.
Seraiah was the father of Joab, the father of Ge Harashim.[f] It was called this because its people were skilled workers.
15 The sons of Caleb son of Jephunneh:
Iru, Elah and Naam.
The son of Elah:
Kenaz.
16 The sons of Jehallelel:
Ziph, Ziphah, Tiria and Asarel.
17 The sons of Ezrah:
Jether, Mered, Epher and Jalon. One of Mered's wives gave birth to Miriam, Shammai and Ishbah the father of Eshtemoa. 18 (His wife from the
tribe of Judah gave birth to Jered the father of Gedor, Heber the father of Soko, and Jekuthiel the father of Zanoah.) These were the children of Pharaoh's daughter Bithiah, whom Mered had married.
19 The sons of Hodiah's wife, the sister of Naham:
the father of Keilah the Garmite, and Eshtemoa the Maakathite.
20 The sons of Shimon:
Amnon, Rinnah, Ben-Hanan and Tilon.
The descendants of Ishi:
Zoheth and Ben-Zoheth.
21 The sons of Shelah son of Judah:

[a] 3 Some Septuagint manuscripts (see also Vulgate); Hebrew *father* [b] 4 *Father* may mean *civic leader* or *military leader*; also in verses 12, 14, 17, 18 and possibly elsewhere. [c] 9 *Jabez* sounds like the Hebrew for *pain*. [d] 12 Or *of the city of Nahash* [e] 13 Some Septuagint manuscripts and Vulgate; Hebrew does not have *and Meonothai*. [f] 14 *Ge Harashim* means *valley of skilled workers*.

1 CHRONICLES 4:24–43

HIGHLIGHTING HISTORY

The Chronicles were written to provide the most important elements of Israel's history to those who lived in Judah in the era after the exile. The books provide a selective history of God's people, omitting many of the unsavory incidents recorded in the books of Samuel and Kings — such as those involving Bathsheba, Absalom and Tamar.

The New Testament presents a different sort of history than the one offered in Chronicles. It openly describes the weaknesses and failures of men and women — pointing out the need all people have for God's grace. Luke revealed Zacchaeus to be a corrupt tax collector, exploiting his own people for profit (Lk 19:1–10). Jesus encountered a woman who had been caught in the act of adultery (Jn 8:1–11). Peter, a key disciple who had many great moments with the Savior, also had episodes of arrogance and even denied knowing Jesus. Nor did Luke sanitize the apostle Paul's history: before meeting Christ on the road to Damascus, Paul was a fierce opponent of the church (Ac 8:1–3).

Every person found by Christ was at one time lost. And after a person follows Jesus they will occasionally stumble in sin. Reading about the failures of ancient disciples gives encouragement to modern followers and connects believers in a kind of camaraderie of grace. Because God preserved these and other accounts of the flawed, God's people today glimpse portraits of themselves — ordinary people in desperate need of salvation that comes through Jesus Christ (Titus 2:11–14).

Er the father of Lekah, Laadah the father of Mareshah and the clans of
the linen workers at Beth Ashbea, 22Jokim, the men of Kozeba, and Joash
and Saraph, who ruled in Moab and Jashubi Lehem. (These records are
from ancient times.) 23They were the potters who lived at Netaim and
Gederah; they stayed there and worked for the king.

Simeon

24The descendants of Simeon:
Nemuel, Jamin, Jarib, Zerah and Shaul;
25Shallum was Shaul's son, Mibsam his son and Mishma his son.
26The descendants of Mishma:
Hammuel his son, Zakkur his son and Shimei his son.
27Shimei had sixteen sons and six daughters, but his brothers did not have
many children; so their entire clan did not become as numerous as the people
of Judah. 28They lived in Beersheba, Moladah, Hazar Shual, 29Bilhah, Ezem, To-
lad, 30Bethuel, Hormah, Ziklag, 31Beth Markaboth, Hazar Susim, Beth Biri and
Shaaraim. These were their towns until the reign of David. 32Their surrounding
villages were Etam, Ain, Rimmon, Token and Ashan — five towns — 33and all
the villages around these towns as far as Baalath.[a] These were their settlements.
And they kept a genealogical record.

34Meshobab, Jamlech, Joshah son of Amaziah, 35Joel, Jehu son of Joshibiah,
the son of Seraiah, the son of Asiel, 36also Elioenai, Jaakobah, Jeshohaiah,
Asaiah, Adiel, Jesimiel, Benaiah, 37and Ziza son of Shiphi, the son of Allon,
the son of Jedaiah, the son of Shimri, the son of Shemaiah.

38The men listed above by name were leaders of their clans. Their families
increased greatly, 39and they went to the outskirts of Gedor to the east of the valley in search of pasture for their flocks. 40They found rich, good pasture, and the
land was spacious, peaceful and quiet. Some Hamites had lived there formerly.
41The men whose names were listed came in the days of Hezekiah king of Judah. They attacked the Hamites in their dwellings and also the Meunites who
were there and completely destroyed[b] them, as is evident to this day. Then they
settled in their place, because there was pasture for their flocks. 42And five hundred of these Simeonites, led by Pelatiah, Neariah, Rephaiah and Uzziel, the
sons of Ishi, invaded the hill country of Seir. 43They killed the remaining Amalekites who had escaped, and they have lived there to this day.

Reuben

5 The sons of Reuben the firstborn of Israel (he was the firstborn, but when
he defiled his father's marriage bed, his rights as firstborn were given to the
sons of Joseph son of Israel; so he could not be listed in the genealogical record
in accordance with his birthright, 2and though Judah was the strongest of his
brothers and a ruler came from him, the rights of the firstborn belonged to Joseph) — 3the sons of Reuben the firstborn of Israel:
Hanok, Pallu, Hezron and Karmi.
4The descendants of Joel:
Shemaiah his son, Gog his son,
Shimei his son, 5Micah his son,
Reaiah his son, Baal his son,
6and Beerah his son, whom Tiglath-Pileser[c] king of Assyria took into exile. Beerah was a leader of the Reubenites.
7Their relatives by clans, listed according to their genealogical records:
Jeiel the chief, Zechariah, 8and Bela son of Azaz, the son of Shema, the
son of Joel. They settled in the area from Aroer to Nebo and Baal Meon.

---

[a] *33* Some Septuagint manuscripts (see also Joshua 19:8); Hebrew *Baal* [b] *41* The Hebrew term refers to the irrevocable giving over of things or persons to the LORD, often by totally destroying them. [c] *6* Hebrew *Tilgath-Pilneser,* a variant of *Tiglath-Pileser;* also in verse 26

[9]To the east they occupied the land up to the edge of the desert that extends to the Euphrates River, because their livestock had increased in
Gilead.
[10]During Saul's reign they waged war against the Hagrites, who were defeated at their hands; they occupied the dwellings of the Hagrites throughout the entire region east of Gilead.

Gad

[11] The Gadites lived next to them in Bashan, as far as Salekah:
[12] Joel was the chief, Shapham the second, then Janai and Shaphat, in Bashan.
[13] Their relatives, by families, were:
Michael, Meshullam, Sheba, Jorai, Jakan, Zia and Eber — seven in all.
[14] These were the sons of Abihail son of Huri, the son of Jaroah, the son of Gilead, the son of Michael, the son of Jeshishai, the son of Jahdo, the son of Buz.
[15] Ahi son of Abdiel, the son of Guni, was head of their family.
[16] The Gadites lived in Gilead, in Bashan and its outlying villages, and on all the pasturelands of Sharon as far as they extended.
[17]All these were entered in the genealogical records during the reigns of Jo-
tham king of Judah and Jeroboam king of Israel.

[18]The Reubenites, the Gadites and the half-tribe of Manasseh had 44,760
men ready for military service — able-bodied men who could handle shield and
sword, who could use a bow, and who were trained for battle. [19]They waged war
against the Hagrites, Jetur, Naphish and Nodab. [20]They were helped in fighting
them, and God delivered the Hagrites and all their allies into their hands, because they cried out to him during the battle. He answered their prayers, because
they trusted in him. [21]They seized the livestock of the Hagrites — fifty thousand
camels, two hundred fifty thousand sheep and two thousand donkeys. They also
took one hundred thousand people captive, [22]and many others fell slain, because
the battle was God's. And they occupied the land until the exile.

The Half-Tribe of Manasseh

[23]The people of the half-tribe of Manasseh were numerous; they settled in the
land from Bashan to Baal Hermon, that is, to Senir (Mount Hermon).
[24]These were the heads of their families: Epher, Ishi, Eliel, Azriel, Jeremiah, Hodaviah and Jahdiel. They were brave warriors, famous men, and heads
of their families. [25]But they were unfaithful to the God of their ancestors and
prostituted themselves to the gods of the peoples of the land, whom God had
destroyed before them. [26]So the God of Israel stirred up the spirit of Pul king of
Assyria (that is, Tiglath-Pileser king of Assyria), who took the Reubenites, the
Gadites and the half-tribe of Manasseh into exile. He took them to Halah, Habor,
Hara and the river of Gozan, where they are to this day.

Levi

6[a] The sons of Levi:
Gershon, Kohath and Merari.
[2] The sons of Kohath:
Amram, Izhar, Hebron and Uzziel.
[3] The children of Amram:
Aaron, Moses and Miriam.
The sons of Aaron:
Nadab, Abihu, Eleazar and Ithamar.
[4] Eleazar was the father of Phinehas,
Phinehas the father of Abishua,

[a] In Hebrew texts 6:1-15 is numbered 5:27-41, and 6:16-81 is numbered 6:1-66.

1 CHRONICLES 5:1 – 26

GENERATIONS

Ancient Hebrew culture depended on detailed genealogical lists to determine questions of inheritance and land-use rights. After the conquest of Canaan, each tribe received its portion of the promised land (Jos 13 – 21). Ownership and land rights were passed from father to oldest son, or daughter if there was no son (Nu 27:1 – 11). Other matters such as service in the temple and royal succession were also determined by genealogy. Old Testament genealogies attest to God's faithfulness — across generations — in honoring his promise to make Israel a great nation (Ge 12:1 – 3).

The genealogy of Jesus (Mt 1:1 – 17) reflects the promises of God kept since the days of Abraham, Isaac and Jacob (Ac 13:32 – 33). It shows Christ as the legitimate heir in the line of David. In Jesus, God fulfilled his promise to establish the ultimate king on David's throne (Isa 9:6 – 7; Ro 1:2 – 3).

[5]Abishua the father of Bukki,
Bukki the father of Uzzi,
[6]Uzzi the father of Zerahiah,
Zerahiah the father of Meraioth,
[7]Meraioth the father of Amariah,
Amariah the father of Ahitub,
[8]Ahitub the father of Zadok,
Zadok the father of Ahimaaz,
[9]Ahimaaz the father of Azariah,
Azariah the father of Johanan,
[10]Johanan the father of Azariah (it was he who served as priest in the temple Solomon built in Jerusalem),
[11]Azariah the father of Amariah,
Amariah the father of Ahitub,
[12]Ahitub the father of Zadok,
Zadok the father of Shallum,
[13]Shallum the father of Hilkiah,
Hilkiah the father of Azariah,
[14]Azariah the father of Seraiah,
and Seraiah the father of Jozadak.[a]
[15]Jozadak was deported when the LORD sent Judah and Jerusalem into exile by the hand of Nebuchadnezzar.
[16]The sons of Levi:
Gershon,[b] Kohath and Merari.
[17]These are the names of the sons of Gershon:
Libni and Shimei.
[18]The sons of Kohath:
Amram, Izhar, Hebron and Uzziel.
[19]The sons of Merari:
Mahli and Mushi.
These are the clans of the Levites listed according to their fathers:
[20]Of Gershon:
Libni his son, Jahath his son,
Zimmah his son, [21]Joah his son,
Iddo his son, Zerah his son
and Jeatherai his son.
[22]The descendants of Kohath:
Amminadab his son, Korah his son,
Assir his son, [23]Elkanah his son,
Ebiasaph his son, Assir his son,
[24]Tahath his son, Uriel his son,
Uzziah his son and Shaul his son.
[25]The descendants of Elkanah:
Amasai, Ahimoth,
[26]Elkanah his son,[c] Zophai his son,
Nahath his son, [27]Eliab his son,
Jeroham his son, Elkanah his son
and Samuel his son.[d]
[28]The sons of Samuel:
Joel[e] the firstborn
and Abijah the second son.

---

[a] *14* Hebrew *Jehozadak*, a variant of *Jozadak*; also in verse 15 [b] *16* Hebrew *Gershom*, a variant of *Gershon*; also in verses 17, 20, 43, 62 and 71 [c] *26* Some Hebrew manuscripts, Septuagint and Syriac; most Hebrew manuscripts *Ahimoth [26]and Elkanah. The sons of Elkanah:* [d] *27* Some Septuagint manuscripts (see also 1 Samuel 1:19,20 and 1 Chron. 6:33,34); Hebrew does not have *and Samuel his son.* [e] *28* Some Septuagint manuscripts and Syriac (see also 1 Samuel 8:2 and 1 Chron. 6:33); Hebrew does not have *Joel.*

[29] The descendants of Merari:
Mahli, Libni his son,
Shimei his son, Uzzah his son,
[30] Shimea his son, Haggiah his son
and Asaiah his son.

The Temple Musicians

[31] These are the men David put in charge of the music in the house of the LORD
after the ark came to rest there. [32] They ministered with music before the tabernacle, the tent of meeting, until Solomon built the temple of the LORD in Jerusalem. They performed their duties according to the regulations laid down for
them.
[33] Here are the men who served, together with their sons:
From the Kohathites:
Heman, the musician,
the son of Joel, the son of Samuel,
[34] the son of Elkanah, the son of Jeroham,
the son of Eliel, the son of Toah,
[35] the son of Zuph, the son of Elkanah,
the son of Mahath, the son of Amasai,
[36] the son of Elkanah, the son of Joel,
the son of Azariah, the son of Zephaniah,
[37] the son of Tahath, the son of Assir,
the son of Ebiasaph, the son of Korah,
[38] the son of Izhar, the son of Kohath,
the son of Levi, the son of Israel;
[39] and Heman's associate Asaph, who served at his right hand:
Asaph son of Berekiah, the son of Shimea,
[40] the son of Michael, the son of Baaseiah,[a]
the son of Malkijah, [41] the son of Ethni,
the son of Zerah, the son of Adaiah,
[42] the son of Ethan, the son of Zimmah,
the son of Shimei, [43] the son of Jahath,
the son of Gershon, the son of Levi;
[44] and from their associates, the Merarites, at his left hand:
Ethan son of Kishi, the son of Abdi,
the son of Malluk, [45] the son of Hashabiah,
the son of Amaziah, the son of Hilkiah,
[46] the son of Amzi, the son of Bani,
the son of Shemer, [47] the son of Mahli,
the son of Mushi, the son of Merari,
the son of Levi.

[48] Their fellow Levites were assigned to all the other duties of the tabernacle,
the house of God. [49] But Aaron and his descendants were the ones who presented
offerings on the altar of burnt offering and on the altar of incense in connection
with all that was done in the Most Holy Place, making atonement for Israel, in
accordance with all that Moses the servant of God had commanded.

[50] These were the descendants of Aaron:
Eleazar his son, Phinehas his son,
Abishua his son, [51] Bukki his son,
Uzzi his son, Zerahiah his son,
[52] Meraioth his son, Amariah his son,
Ahitub his son, [53] Zadok his son
and Ahimaaz his son.

---

[a] *40* Most Hebrew manuscripts; some Hebrew manuscripts, one Septuagint manuscript and Syriac *Maaseiah*

THE CENTRAL ROLE OF MUSIC IN WORSHIP

Music is a marvelous gift from God — a rhythmic and melodic combination of beauty, art and emotion. Without a doubt, music enhances the worship experience for God's people. Moses and the Israelites played instruments and sang a song of worship after God ended the pursuit of Pharaoh and his army (Ex 15:1 – 21). King David composed and commissioned many songs for the Lord — the book of Psalms is full of prayers set to music to be utilized on various occasions of worship. Here, David assigned three men — Heman, Asaph and Ethan — to lead music at the tabernacle until the completion of Solomon's temple. Many years after the exile, instrumentalists and singers celebrated the rebuilding of Jerusalem's wall with joyful songs of thanksgiving (Ne 12:27). Affection, praise and gratitude — music carries these from the human soul to the heart of God.

Many of the best-loved songs sung in churches everywhere direct the attention of God's people to Jesus — celebrating his divinity, his power, his love, his sacrifice and his promised return. Music was evidently meaningful to Christ in the last days before going to the cross. Following the solemn occasion of the Last Supper, Jesus and his disciples crowned the evening with the singing of a hymn before going out to the Mount of Olives (Mt 26:26 – 30). Worship is a response to God where his "worth" is declared. When Jesus and his followers sang on that night, they were declaring that God was worthy in the midst of trial. Underneath their worship was a belief that God was going to come through in the end.

Scholars believe some New Testament Scripture passages were actually hymns sung by the early church. One example is a section of Paul's letter to the Philippians. Imagine the first-century believers gathered to sing of Jesus with reverence and joy: "God exalted him to the highest place and gave him the name that is above every name, that at the name of Jesus every knee should bow, in heaven and on earth and under the earth, and every tongue acknowledge that Jesus Christ is Lord, to the glory of God the Father" (Php 2:9 – 11).

[54]These were the locations of their settlements allotted as their territory (they were assigned to the descendants of Aaron who were from the Kohathite clan, because the first lot was for them):

[55]They were given Hebron in Judah with its surrounding pasturelands.
[56]But the fields and villages around the city were given to Caleb son of Jephunneh.

[57]So the descendants of Aaron were given Hebron (a city of refuge), and
Libnah,[a] Jattir, Eshtemoa, [58]Hilen, Debir, [59]Ashan, Juttah[b] and Beth Shemesh, together with their pasturelands. [60]And from the tribe of Benjamin
they were given Gibeon,[c] Geba, Alemeth and Anathoth, together with their pasturelands.

The total number of towns distributed among the Kohathite clans came to thirteen.

[61]The rest of Kohath's descendants were allotted ten towns from the clans of half the tribe of Manasseh.

[62]The descendants of Gershon, clan by clan, were allotted thirteen towns from the tribes of Issachar, Asher and Naphtali, and from the part of the tribe of Manasseh that is in Bashan.

[63]The descendants of Merari, clan by clan, were allotted twelve towns from the tribes of Reuben, Gad and Zebulun.

[64]So the Israelites gave the Levites these towns and their pasturelands.
[65]From the tribes of Judah, Simeon and Benjamin they allotted the previously named towns.

[66]Some of the Kohathite clans were given as their territory towns from the tribe of Ephraim.

[67]In the hill country of Ephraim they were given Shechem (a city of refuge), and Gezer,[d] [68]Jokmeam, Beth Horon, [69]Aijalon and Gath Rimmon, together with their pasturelands.

[70]And from half the tribe of Manasseh the Israelites gave Aner and Bileam, together with their pasturelands, to the rest of the Kohathite clans.

[71]The Gershonites received the following:
From the clan of the half-tribe of Manasseh
they received Golan in Bashan and also Ashtaroth, together with their pasturelands;
[72]from the tribe of Issachar
they received Kedesh, Daberath, [73]Ramoth and Anem, together with their pasturelands;
[74]from the tribe of Asher
they received Mashal, Abdon, [75]Hukok and Rehob, together with their pasturelands;
[76]and from the tribe of Naphtali
they received Kedesh in Galilee, Hammon and Kiriathaim, together with their pasturelands.

[77]The Merarites (the rest of the Levites) received the following:
From the tribe of Zebulun
they received Jokneam, Kartah,[e] Rimmono and Tabor, together with their pasturelands;
[78]from the tribe of Reuben across the Jordan east of Jericho
they received Bezer in the wilderness, Jahzah, [79]Kedemoth and Mephaath, together with their pasturelands;
[80]and from the tribe of Gad

---

[a] 57 See Joshua 21:13; Hebrew *given the cities of refuge: Hebron, Libnah.* [b] 59 Syriac (see also Septuagint and Joshua 21:16); Hebrew does not have *Juttah.* [c] 60 See Joshua 21:17; Hebrew does not have *Gibeon.* [d] 67 See Joshua 21:21; Hebrew *given the cities of refuge: Shechem, Gezer.* [e] 77 See Septuagint and Joshua 21:34; Hebrew does not have *Jokneam, Kartah.*

they received Ramoth in Gilead, Mahanaim, [81]Heshbon and Jazer, together with their pasturelands.

Issachar

7 The sons of Issachar:
Tola, Puah, Jashub and Shimron — four in all.
[2]The sons of Tola:
Uzzi, Rephaiah, Jeriel, Jahmai, Ibsam and Samuel — heads of their families. During the reign of David, the descendants of Tola listed as fighting men in their genealogy numbered 22,600.
[3]The son of Uzzi:
Izrahiah.
The sons of Izrahiah:
Michael, Obadiah, Joel and Ishiah. All five of them were chiefs. [4]According to their family genealogy, they had 36,000 men ready for battle, for they had many wives and children.
[5]The relatives who were fighting men belonging to all the clans of Issachar, as listed in their genealogy, were 87,000 in all.

Benjamin

[6]Three sons of Benjamin:
Bela, Beker and Jediael.
[7]The sons of Bela:
Ezbon, Uzzi, Uzziel, Jerimoth and Iri, heads of families — five in all. Their genealogical record listed 22,034 fighting men.
[8]The sons of Beker:
Zemirah, Joash, Eliezer, Elioenai, Omri, Jeremoth, Abijah, Anathoth and Alemeth. All these were the sons of Beker. [9]Their genealogical record listed the heads of families and 20,200 fighting men.
[10]The son of Jediael:
Bilhan.
The sons of Bilhan:
Jeush, Benjamin, Ehud, Kenaanah, Zethan, Tarshish and Ahishahar.
[11]All these sons of Jediael were heads of families. There were 17,200 fighting men ready to go out to war.
[12]The Shuppites and Huppites were the descendants of Ir, and the Hushites[a] the descendants of Aher.

Naphtali

[13]The sons of Naphtali:
Jahziel, Guni, Jezer and Shillem[b] — the descendants of Bilhah.

Manasseh

[14]The descendants of Manasseh:
Asriel was his descendant through his Aramean concubine. She gave birth to Makir the father of Gilead. [15]Makir took a wife from among the Huppites and Shuppites. His sister's name was Maakah.
Another descendant was named Zelophehad, who had only daughters.
[16]Makir's wife Maakah gave birth to a son and named him Peresh. His brother was named Sheresh, and his sons were Ulam and Rakem.
[17]The son of Ulam:
Bedan.
These were the sons of Gilead son of Makir, the son of Manasseh. [18]His sister Hammoleketh gave birth to Ishhod, Abiezer and Mahlah.

---

[a] *12* Or *Ir. The sons of Dan: Hushim,* (see Gen. 46:23); Hebrew does not have *The sons of Dan.*
[b] *13* Some Hebrew and Septuagint manuscripts (see also Gen. 46:24 and Num. 26:49); most Hebrew manuscripts *Shallum*

[19] The sons of Shemida were:
Ahian, Shechem, Likhi and Aniam.

Ephraim

[20] The descendants of Ephraim:
Shuthelah, Bered his son,
Tahath his son, Eleadah his son,
Tahath his son, [21] Zabad his son
and Shuthelah his son.
Ezer and Elead were killed by the native-born men of Gath, when they went
down to seize their livestock. [22] Their father Ephraim mourned for them many
days, and his relatives came to comfort him. [23] Then he made love to his wife
again, and she became pregnant and gave birth to a son. He named him Beriah,[a] because there had been misfortune in his family. [24] His daughter was
Sheerah, who built Lower and Upper Beth Horon as well as Uzzen Sheerah.

[25] Rephah was his son, Resheph his son,[b]
Telah his son, Tahan his son,
[26] Ladan his son, Ammihud his son,
Elishama his son, [27] Nun his son
and Joshua his son.

[28] Their lands and settlements included Bethel and its surrounding villages,
Naaran to the east, Gezer and its villages to the west, and Shechem and its villages all the way to Ayyah and its villages. [29] Along the borders of Manasseh were
Beth Shan, Taanach, Megiddo and Dor, together with their villages. The descendants of Joseph son of Israel lived in these towns.

Asher

[30] The sons of Asher:
Imnah, Ishvah, Ishvi and Beriah. Their sister was Serah.
[31] The sons of Beriah:
Heber and Malkiel, who was the father of Birzaith.
[32] Heber was the father of Japhlet, Shomer and Hotham and of their sister Shua.
[33] The sons of Japhlet:
Pasak, Bimhal and Ashvath.
These were Japhlet's sons.
[34] The sons of Shomer:
Ahi, Rohgah,[c] Hubbah and Aram.
[35] The sons of his brother Helem:
Zophah, Imna, Shelesh and Amal.
[36] The sons of Zophah:
Suah, Harnepher, Shual, Beri, Imrah, [37] Bezer, Hod, Shamma, Shilshah,
Ithran[d] and Beera.
[38] The sons of Jether:
Jephunneh, Pispah and Ara.
[39] The sons of Ulla:
Arah, Hanniel and Rizia.

[40] All these were descendants of Asher—heads of families, choice men, brave
warriors and outstanding leaders. The number of men ready for battle, as listed
in their genealogy, was 26,000.

The Genealogy of Saul the Benjamite

8 Benjamin was the father of Bela his firstborn,
Ashbel the second son, Aharah the third,
[2] Nohah the fourth and Rapha the fifth.

---

[a] 23 *Beriah* sounds like the Hebrew for *misfortune*. [b] 25 Some Septuagint manuscripts; Hebrew does not have *his son*. [c] 34 Or *of his brother Shomer: Rohgah* [d] 37 Possibly a variant of *Jether*

1 CHRONICLES 8:1–40

CHOOSING SAUL RATHER THAN GOD

The book of 1 Chronicles includes the genealogy of Saul, Israel's first king. Saul came to power when the elders of Israel demanded that Samuel, the Lord's man in leadership, appoint a king to lead them like the other nations. Samuel resisted, but the Lord instructed him to carry out their request—noting that asking for a national king was a rejection of God, not of Samuel (1Sa 8:1–9). From the nation's founding, the people had the opportunity to serve God as their true king. Yet arrogance, impatience and envy caused Israel to believe the Lord's kingship was insufficient. Saul reigned forty-two years (1Sa 13:1), but his eventual rebellion against God led to a bitter end (1Ch 10:13–14).

With the appearance of Jesus, Israel and the world once again have the opportunity to serve God as their king. Humankind is limited and corrupt, but God knows all things and always does what is right. He is the ultimate, all-sufficient King. Those who believe in Jesus become more than subjects in God's kingdom—they become his sons and daughters (Jn 1:12).

3 The sons of Bela were:
Addar, Gera, Abihud,[a] 4 Abishua, Naaman, Ahoah, 5 Gera, Shephuphan
and Huram.
6 These were the descendants of Ehud, who were heads of families of those
living in Geba and were deported to Manahath:
7 Naaman, Ahijah, and Gera, who deported them and who was the father
of Uzza and Ahihud.
8 Sons were born to Shaharaim in Moab after he had divorced his wives Hushim and Baara. 9 By his wife Hodesh he had Jobab, Zibia, Mesha, Malkam, 10 Jeuz, Sakia and Mirmah. These were his sons, heads of families.
11 By Hushim he had Abitub and Elpaal.
12 The sons of Elpaal:
Eber, Misham, Shemed (who built Ono and Lod with its surrounding
villages), 13 and Beriah and Shema, who were heads of families of those
living in Aijalon and who drove out the inhabitants of Gath.
14 Ahio, Shashak, Jeremoth, 15 Zebadiah, Arad, Eder, 16 Michael, Ishpah and
Joha were the sons of Beriah.
17 Zebadiah, Meshullam, Hizki, Heber, 18 Ishmerai, Izliah and Jobab were the
sons of Elpaal.
19 Jakim, Zikri, Zabdi, 20 Elienai, Zillethai, Eliel, 21 Adaiah, Beraiah and Shim-
rath were the sons of Shimei.
22 Ishpan, Eber, Eliel, 23 Abdon, Zikri, Hanan, 24 Hananiah, Elam, Anthothi-
jah, 25 Iphdeiah and Penuel were the sons of Shashak.
26 Shamsherai, Shehariah, Athaliah, 27 Jaareshiah, Elijah and Zikri were the
sons of Jeroham.
28 All these were heads of families, chiefs as listed in their genealogy, and they
lived in Jerusalem.

29 Jeiel[b] the father[c] of Gibeon lived in Gibeon.
His wife's name was Maakah, 30 and his firstborn son was Abdon, followed by Zur, Kish, Baal, Ner,[d] Nadab, 31 Gedor, Ahio, Zeker 32 and Mikloth, who was the father of Shimeah. They too lived near their relatives
in Jerusalem.
33 Ner was the father of Kish, Kish the father of Saul, and Saul the father of
Jonathan, Malki-Shua, Abinadab and Esh-Baal.[e]
34 The son of Jonathan:
Merib-Baal,[f] who was the father of Micah.
35 The sons of Micah:
Pithon, Melek, Tarea and Ahaz.
36 Ahaz was the father of Jehoaddah, Jehoaddah was the father of Alemeth,
Azmaveth and Zimri, and Zimri was the father of Moza. 37 Moza was the
father of Binea; Raphah was his son, Eleasah his son and Azel his son.
38 Azel had six sons, and these were their names:
Azrikam, Bokeru, Ishmael, Sheariah, Obadiah and Hanan. All these
were the sons of Azel.
39 The sons of his brother Eshek:
Ulam his firstborn, Jeush the second son and Eliphelet the third. 40 The
sons of Ulam were brave warriors who could handle the bow. They had
many sons and grandsons — 150 in all.
All these were the descendants of Benjamin.

9 All Israel was listed in the genealogies recorded in the book of the kings of
Israel and Judah. They were taken captive to Babylon because of their unfaithfulness.

[a] 3 Or *Gera the father of Ehud* [b] 29 Some Septuagint manuscripts (see also 9:35); Hebrew does not have *Jeiel.* [c] 29 *Father* may mean *civic leader* or *military leader.* [d] 30 Some Septuagint manuscripts (see also 9:36); Hebrew does not have *Ner.* [e] 33 Also known as *Ish-Bosheth* [f] 34 Also known as *Mephibosheth*

The People in Jerusalem

2 Now the first to resettle on their own property in their own towns were some
Israelites, priests, Levites and temple servants.
3 Those from Judah, from Benjamin, and from Ephraim and Manasseh who
lived in Jerusalem were:
4 Uthai son of Ammihud, the son of Omri, the son of Imri, the son of Bani, a
descendant of Perez son of Judah.
5 Of the Shelanites[a]:
Asaiah the firstborn and his sons.
6 Of the Zerahites:
Jeuel.
The people from Judah numbered 690.
7 Of the Benjamites:
Sallu son of Meshullam, the son of Hodaviah, the son of Hassenuah;
8 Ibneiah son of Jeroham; Elah son of Uzzi, the son of Mikri; and Meshullam son of Shephatiah, the son of Reuel, the son of Ibnijah.
9 The people from Benjamin, as listed in their genealogy, numbered 956.
All these men were heads of their families.
10 Of the priests:
Jedaiah; Jehoiarib; Jakin;
11 Azariah son of Hilkiah, the son of Meshullam, the son of Zadok, the son
of Meraioth, the son of Ahitub, the official in charge of the house of God;
12 Adaiah son of Jeroham, the son of Pashhur, the son of Malkijah; and
Maasai son of Adiel, the son of Jahzerah, the son of Meshullam, the son
of Meshillemith, the son of Immer.
13 The priests, who were heads of families, numbered 1,760. They were able
men, responsible for ministering in the house of God.
14 Of the Levites:
Shemaiah son of Hasshub, the son of Azrikam, the son of Hashabiah, a
Merarite; 15 Bakbakkar, Heresh, Galal and Mattaniah son of Mika, the
son of Zikri, the son of Asaph; 16 Obadiah son of Shemaiah, the son of
Galal, the son of Jeduthun; and Berekiah son of Asa, the son of Elkanah,
who lived in the villages of the Netophathites.
17 The gatekeepers:
Shallum, Akkub, Talmon, Ahiman and their fellow Levites, Shallum
their chief 18 being stationed at the King's Gate on the east, up to the
present time. These were the gatekeepers belonging to the camp of the
Levites. 19 Shallum son of Kore, the son of Ebiasaph, the son of Korah,
and his fellow gatekeepers from his family (the Korahites) were responsible for guarding the thresholds of the tent just as their ancestors had
been responsible for guarding the entrance to the dwelling of the LORD.
20 In earlier times Phinehas son of Eleazar was the official in charge of
the gatekeepers, and the LORD was with him. 21 Zechariah son of Meshelemiah was the gatekeeper at the entrance to the tent of meeting.
22 Altogether, those chosen to be gatekeepers at the thresholds numbered
212. They were registered by genealogy in their villages. The gatekeepers had
been assigned to their positions of trust by David and Samuel the seer. 23 They
and their descendants were in charge of guarding the gates of the house of the
LORD — the house called the tent of meeting. 24 The gatekeepers were on the four
sides: east, west, north and south. 25 Their fellow Levites in their villages had to
come from time to time and share their duties for seven-day periods. 26 But the
four principal gatekeepers, who were Levites, were entrusted with the responsibility for the rooms and treasuries in the house of God. 27 They would spend the
night stationed around the house of God, because they had to guard it; and they
had charge of the key for opening it each morning.

---

[a] 5 See Num. 26:20; Hebrew *Shilonites.*

[28]Some of them were in charge of the articles used in the temple service; they counted them when they were brought in and when they were taken out. [29]Others were assigned to take care of the furnishings and all the other articles of the sanctuary, as well as the special flour and wine, and the olive oil, incense and spices. [30]But some of the priests took care of mixing the spices. [31]A Levite named Mattithiah, the firstborn son of Shallum the Korahite, was entrusted with the responsibility for baking the offering bread. [32]Some of the Kohathites, their fellow Levites, were in charge of preparing for every Sabbath the bread set out on the table.

[33]Those who were musicians, heads of Levite families, stayed in the rooms of the temple and were exempt from other duties because they were responsible for the work day and night.

[34]All these were heads of Levite families, chiefs as listed in their genealogy, and they lived in Jerusalem.

The Genealogy of Saul

[35]Jeiel the father[a] of Gibeon lived in Gibeon.

His wife's name was Maakah, [36]and his firstborn son was Abdon, followed by Zur, Kish, Baal, Ner, Nadab, [37]Gedor, Ahio, Zechariah and Mikloth. [38]Mikloth was the father of Shimeam. They too lived near their relatives in Jerusalem.

[39]Ner was the father of Kish, Kish the father of Saul, and Saul the father of Jonathan, Malki-Shua, Abinadab and Esh-Baal.[b]

[40]The son of Jonathan:

Merib-Baal,[c] who was the father of Micah.

[41]The sons of Micah:

Pithon, Melek, Tahrea and Ahaz.[d]

[42]Ahaz was the father of Jadah, Jadah[e] was the father of Alemeth, Azmaveth and Zimri, and Zimri was the father of Moza. [43]Moza was the father of Binea; Rephaiah was his son, Eleasah his son and Azel his son.

[44]Azel had six sons, and these were their names:

Azrikam, Bokeru, Ishmael, Sheariah, Obadiah and Hanan. These were the sons of Azel.

Saul Takes His Life

10 Now the Philistines fought against Israel; the Israelites fled before them, and many fell dead on Mount Gilboa. [2]The Philistines were in hot pursuit of Saul and his sons, and they killed his sons Jonathan, Abinadab and Malki-Shua. [3]The fighting grew fierce around Saul, and when the archers overtook him, they wounded him.

[4]Saul said to his armor-bearer, "Draw your sword and run me through, or these uncircumcised fellows will come and abuse me."

But his armor-bearer was terrified and would not do it; so Saul took his own sword and fell on it. [5]When the armor-bearer saw that Saul was dead, he too fell on his sword and died. [6]So Saul and his three sons died, and all his house died together.

[7]When all the Israelites in the valley saw that the army had fled and that Saul and his sons had died, they abandoned their towns and fled. And the Philistines came and occupied them.

[8]The next day, when the Philistines came to strip the dead, they found Saul and his sons fallen on Mount Gilboa. [9]They stripped him and took his head and his armor, and sent messengers throughout the land of the Philistines to

[a] *35 Father* may mean *civic leader* or *military leader.* [b] *39* Also known as *Ish-Bosheth* [c] *40* Also known as *Mephibosheth* [d] *41* Vulgate and Syriac (see also Septuagint and 8:35); Hebrew does not have *and Ahaz.* [e] *42* Some Hebrew manuscripts and Septuagint (see also 8:36); most Hebrew manuscripts *Jarah, Jarah*

proclaim the news among their idols and their people. 10They put his armor in the temple of their gods and hung up his head in the temple of Dagon.

11When all the inhabitants of Jabesh Gilead heard what the Philistines had done to Saul, 12all their valiant men went and took the bodies of Saul and his sons and brought them to Jabesh. Then they buried their bones under the great tree in Jabesh, and they fasted seven days.

13Saul died because he was unfaithful to the LORD; he did not keep the word of the LORD and even consulted a medium for guidance, 14and did not inquire of the LORD. So the LORD put him to death and turned the kingdom over to David son of Jesse.

David Becomes King Over Israel

11 All Israel came together to David at Hebron and said, "We are your own flesh and blood. 2In the past, even while Saul was king, you were the one who led Israel on their military campaigns. And the LORD your God said to you, 'You will shepherd my people Israel, and you will become their ruler.' "

3When all the elders of Israel had come to King David at Hebron, he made a covenant with them at Hebron before the LORD, and they anointed David king over Israel, as the LORD had promised through Samuel.

David Conquers Jerusalem

4David and all the Israelites marched to Jerusalem (that is, Jebus). The Jebusites who lived there 5said to David, "You will not get in here." Nevertheless, David captured the fortress of Zion — which is the City of David.

6David had said, "Whoever leads the attack on the Jebusites will become commander-in-chief." Joab son of Zeruiah went up first, and so he received the command.

7David then took up residence in the fortress, and so it was called the City of David. 8He built up the city around it, from the terraces[a] to the surrounding wall, while Joab restored the rest of the city. 9And David became more and more powerful, because the LORD Almighty was with him.

David's Mighty Warriors

10These were the chiefs of David's mighty warriors — they, together with all Israel, gave his kingship strong support to extend it over the whole land, as the LORD had promised — 11this is the list of David's mighty warriors:

Jashobeam,[b] a Hakmonite, was chief of the officers[c]; he raised his spear against three hundred men, whom he killed in one encounter.

12Next to him was Eleazar son of Dodai the Ahohite, one of the three mighty warriors. 13He was with David at Pas Dammim when the Philistines gathered there for battle. At a place where there was a field full of barley, the troops fled from the Philistines. 14But they took their stand in the middle of the field. They defended it and struck the Philistines down, and the LORD brought about a great victory.

15Three of the thirty chiefs came down to David to the rock at the cave of Adullam, while a band of Philistines was encamped in the Valley of Rephaim. 16At that time David was in the stronghold, and the Philistine garrison was at Bethlehem. 17David longed for water and said, "Oh, that someone would get me a drink of water from the well near the gate of Bethlehem!" 18So the Three broke through the Philistine lines, drew water from the well near the gate of Bethlehem and carried it back to David. But he refused to drink it; instead, he poured it out to the LORD. 19"God forbid that I should do this!" he said. "Should I drink the blood of these men who went at the risk of their lives?" Because they risked their lives to bring it back, David would not drink it.

[a] 8 Or *the Millo* [b] 11 Possibly a variant of *Jashob-Baal* [c] 11 Or *Thirty*; some Septuagint manuscripts *Three* (see also 2 Samuel 23:8)

1 CHRONICLES 11:1 – 9

JERUSALEM

One of David's first acts as king was to march to and capture the city of Jerusalem, making it his national capital. This marked the beginning of Jerusalem's significant role in history. About a thousand years later, Jesus rode into the same city astride a donkey, welcomed with cheers: "Hosanna to the Son of David!" "Blessed is he who comes in the name of the Lord!" (Mt 21:1 – 11). King David entered Jerusalem with force, determined to conquer the city and its people. Jesus, the King of kings, entered Jerusalem with humility as the Messiah, intent on offering salvation to the whole world. This city has witnessed astounding, world-changing events in its tumultuous history. The book of Revelation hints at significant events in Jerusalem's future, in the time leading up to the consummation of all things (Rev 11:2,8). Ultimately, God will establish a "new Jerusalem" on the earth as a place where his people will dwell in peace forever (Rev 21:1 — 22:5).

1 CHRONICLES 11:10 – 47

TRANSFORMATION

The group known as David's mighty men first joined his ranks at the cave of Adullam — where David hid to evade Saul (1Sa 22:1 – 2). The men, numbered among the distressed, indebted and discontented, were nothing like the fierce warriors they would become. But when they put themselves under David's command they soon accumulated impressive victories and legendary reputations.

(continued on page 597)

SAUL, DAVID AND JESUS

Saul had the throne of all Israel and the blessing of God, but turning away from the Lord resulted in the loss of everything. Following Saul's death, God gave Israel's throne to David.

Saul faltered in obedience when he failed to destroy the Amalekites completely (1Sa 15:1 – 23). God had instructed that none of the Amalekites — including their livestock — were to survive the attack. God rejected Saul as king because Saul disregarded the instructions in favor of sparing the Amalekite king and keeping the best animals for himself. On another occasion, he chose to disobey God and consulted a medium before going into his final battle with the Philistines (1Sa 28:3 – 20). Even though Saul sought wisdom, he did so in a manner that was clearly forbidden. In his early days, Saul had walked with God and listened to his words. But by the end of his life, he habitually ignored God and tried to forge his own path through the situations he faced.

Before Saul, Israel had been led by judges raised up by God to guide and protect the people. God alone was their King. When Israel demanded that Samuel give them a human king like the other nations, God allowed it. But God also warned that the monarchy would be a mixed blessing, resulting eventually in hardship for the people (1Sa 8:10 – 18). Israel's first two kings illustrate both the blessings and the limits of human kingship. They also provide an object lesson on the relationship between divine and human authority. Only when human leaders submit in faith and obedience to God can they provide genuine leadership for God's people. As Saul's failures mounted, God chose to put the kingdom in the hands of David. David outshone Saul in leadership, wisdom and fidelity to the ways of the Lord. He prospered during his reign — conquering Jerusalem, constructing a palace in the newly named "City of David" and earning the respect of neighboring nations. But for all of David's good qualities, he was a sinner like every other mere human.

Jesus, the King of kings, lived an earthly life far above the examples of Saul and David. Jesus never sinned. He treated all people with compassion and fairness. He exercised authority with humility while standing for justice with unwavering conviction. At all times, he honored God, living in perfect obedience. In love, he gave his life on the cross as a sacrifice for the world's sin. This selfless act — taking on a penalty he did not deserve (2Co 5:21) — is history's greatest act of a King serving the people he loves.

Such were the exploits of the three mighty warriors.
[20]Abishai the brother of Joab was chief of the Three. He raised his spear
against three hundred men, whom he killed, and so he became as famous as the
Three. [21]He was doubly honored above the Three and became their commander,
even though he was not included among them.
[22]Benaiah son of Jehoiada, a valiant fighter from Kabzeel, performed great
exploits. He struck down Moab's two mightiest warriors. He also went down into
a pit on a snowy day and killed a lion. [23]And he struck down an Egyptian who
was five cubits[a] tall. Although the Egyptian had a spear like a weaver's rod in
his hand, Benaiah went against him with a club. He snatched the spear from the
Egyptian's hand and killed him with his own spear. [24]Such were the exploits of
Benaiah son of Jehoiada; he too was as famous as the three mighty warriors. [25]He
was held in greater honor than any of the Thirty, but he was not included among
the Three. And David put him in charge of his bodyguard.

[26]The mighty warriors were:
Asahel the brother of Joab,
Elhanan son of Dodo from Bethlehem,
[27]Shammoth the Harorite,
Helez the Pelonite,
[28]Ira son of Ikkesh from Tekoa,
Abiezer from Anathoth,
[29]Sibbekai the Hushathite,
Ilai the Ahohite,
[30]Maharai the Netophathite,
Heled son of Baanah the Netophathite,
[31]Ithai son of Ribai from Gibeah in Benjamin,
Benaiah the Pirathonite,
[32]Hurai from the ravines of Gaash,
Abiel the Arbathite,
[33]Azmaveth the Baharumite,
Eliahba the Shaalbonite,
[34]the sons of Hashem the Gizonite,
Jonathan son of Shagee the Hararite,
[35]Ahiam son of Sakar the Hararite,
Eliphal son of Ur,
[36]Hepher the Mekerathite,
Ahijah the Pelonite,
[37]Hezro the Carmelite,
Naarai son of Ezbai,
[38]Joel the brother of Nathan,
Mibhar son of Hagri,
[39]Zelek the Ammonite,
Naharai the Berothite, the armor-bearer of Joab son of Zeruiah,
[40]Ira the Ithrite,
Gareb the Ithrite,
[41]Uriah the Hittite,
Zabad son of Ahlai,
[42]Adina son of Shiza the Reubenite, who was chief of the Reubenites, and
the thirty with him,
[43]Hanan son of Maakah,
Joshaphat the Mithnite,
[44]Uzzia the Ashterathite,
Shama and Jeiel the sons of Hotham the Aroerite,
[45]Jediael son of Shimri,
his brother Joha the Tizite,

[a] *23* That is, about 7 feet 6 inches or about 2.3 meters

(Transformation, continued)

When the group destined to become the twelve disciples first followed Jesus they were ordinary people untrained for the adventures ahead. Several of them were simple fishermen and one was a tax collector. Under Christ's leadership, they became partners in his ministry and eventually leaders of the church. God can use anyone in his kingdom work. Things such as talent, family connections, wealth or experience are not prerequisites for serving the Lord. Jesus has the power to transform ordinary men and women for accomplishing extraordinary, even eternal things. When average, everyday people follow Jesus, he will accomplish unimaginable things through them!

[46]Eliel the Mahavite,
Jeribai and Joshaviah the sons of Elnaam,
Ithmah the Moabite,
[47]Eliel, Obed and Jaasiel the Mezobaite.

Warriors Join David

12 These were the men who came to David at Ziklag, while he was banished from the presence of Saul son of Kish (they were among the warriors who helped him in battle; [2]they were armed with bows and were able to shoot arrows or to sling stones right-handed or left-handed; they were relatives of Saul from the tribe of Benjamin):

[3]Ahiezer their chief and Joash the sons of Shemaah the Gibeathite; Jeziel and Pelet the sons of Azmaveth; Berakah, Jehu the Anathothite, [4]and Ishmaiah the Gibeonite, a mighty warrior among the Thirty, who was a leader of the Thirty; Jeremiah, Jahaziel, Johanan, Jozabad the Gederathite,[a] [5]Eluzai, Jerimoth, Bealiah, Shemariah and Shephatiah the Haruphite; [6]Elkanah, Ishiah, Azarel, Joezer and Jashobeam the Korahites; [7]and Joelah and Zebadiah the sons of Jeroham from Gedor.

[8]Some Gadites defected to David at his stronghold in the wilderness. They were brave warriors, ready for battle and able to handle the shield and spear. Their faces were the faces of lions, and they were as swift as gazelles in the mountains.

[9]Ezer was the chief,
Obadiah the second in command, Eliab the third,
[10]Mishmannah the fourth, Jeremiah the fifth,
[11]Attai the sixth, Eliel the seventh,
[12]Johanan the eighth, Elzabad the ninth,
[13]Jeremiah the tenth and Makbannai the eleventh.

[14]These Gadites were army commanders; the least was a match for a hundred, and the greatest for a thousand. [15]It was they who crossed the Jordan in the first month when it was overflowing all its banks, and they put to flight everyone living in the valleys, to the east and to the west.

[16]Other Benjamites and some men from Judah also came to David in his stronghold. [17]David went out to meet them and said to them, "If you have come to me in peace to help me, I am ready for you to join me. But if you have come to betray me to my enemies when my hands are free from violence, may the God of our ancestors see it and judge you."

[18]Then the Spirit came on Amasai, chief of the Thirty, and he said:

"We are yours, David!
  We are with you, son of Jesse!
Success, success to you,
  and success to those who help you,
    for your God will help you."

So David received them and made them leaders of his raiding bands.

[19]Some of the tribe of Manasseh defected to David when he went with the Philistines to fight against Saul. (He and his men did not help the Philistines because, after consultation, their rulers sent him away. They said, "It will cost us our heads if he deserts to his master Saul.") [20]When David went to Ziklag, these were the men of Manasseh who defected to him: Adnah, Jozabad, Jediael, Michael, Jozabad, Elihu and Zillethai, leaders of units of a thousand in Manasseh. [21]They helped David against raiding bands, for all of them were brave warriors, and they were commanders in his army. [22]Day after day men came to help David, until he had a great army, like the army of God.[b]

---

[a] *4* In Hebrew texts the second half of this verse (*Jeremiah . . . Gederathite*) is numbered 12:5, and 12:5-40 is numbered 12:6-41. [b] *22* Or *a great and mighty army*

Others Join David at Hebron

[23]These are the numbers of the men armed for battle who came to David at
Hebron to turn Saul's kingdom over to him, as the LORD had said:
[24]from Judah, carrying shield and spear — 6,800 armed for battle;
[25]from Simeon, warriors ready for battle — 7,100;
[26]from Levi — 4,600, [27]including Jehoiada, leader of the family of Aaron, with
3,700 men, [28]and Zadok, a brave young warrior, with 22 officers from his
family;
[29]from Benjamin, Saul's tribe — 3,000, most of whom had remained loyal to
Saul's house until then;
[30]from Ephraim, brave warriors, famous in their own clans — 20,800;
[31]from half the tribe of Manasseh, designated by name to come and make
David king — 18,000;
[32]from Issachar, men who understood the times and knew what Israel should
do — 200 chiefs, with all their relatives under their command;
[33]from Zebulun, experienced soldiers prepared for battle with every type of
weapon, to help David with undivided loyalty — 50,000;
[34]from Naphtali — 1,000 officers, together with 37,000 men carrying shields
and spears;
[35]from Dan, ready for battle — 28,600;
[36]from Asher, experienced soldiers prepared for battle — 40,000;
[37]and from east of the Jordan, from Reuben, Gad and the half-tribe of Manasseh, armed with every type of weapon — 120,000.
[38]All these were fighting men who volunteered to serve in the ranks. They
came to Hebron fully determined to make David king over all Israel. All the rest
of the Israelites were also of one mind to make David king. [39]The men spent three
days there with David, eating and drinking, for their families had supplied provisions for them. [40]Also, their neighbors from as far away as Issachar, Zebulun
and Naphtali came bringing food on donkeys, camels, mules and oxen. There
were plentiful supplies of flour, fig cakes, raisin cakes, wine, olive oil, cattle and
sheep, for there was joy in Israel.

Bringing Back the Ark

13 David conferred with each of his officers, the commanders of thousands
and commanders of hundreds. [2]He then said to the whole assembly of Israel, "If it seems good to you and if it is the will of the LORD our God, let us send
word far and wide to the rest of our people throughout the territories of Israel,
and also to the priests and Levites who are with them in their towns and pasturelands, to come and join us. [3]Let us bring the ark of our God back to us, for we did
not inquire of[a] it[b] during the reign of Saul." [4]The whole assembly agreed to do
this, because it seemed right to all the people.
[5]So David assembled all Israel, from the Shihor River in Egypt to Lebo Hamath, to bring the ark of God from Kiriath Jearim. [6]David and all Israel went to
Baalah of Judah (Kiriath Jearim) to bring up from there the ark of God the LORD,
who is enthroned between the cherubim — the ark that is called by the Name.
[7]They moved the ark of God from Abinadab's house on a new cart, with Uzzah and Ahio guiding it. [8]David and all the Israelites were celebrating with all
their might before God, with songs and with harps, lyres, timbrels, cymbals and
trumpets.
[9]When they came to the threshing floor of Kidon, Uzzah reached out his hand
to steady the ark, because the oxen stumbled. [10]The LORD's anger burned against
Uzzah, and he struck him down because he had put his hand on the ark. So he
died there before God.
[11]Then David was angry because the LORD's wrath had broken out against
Uzzah, and to this day that place is called Perez Uzzah.[c]

1 CHRONICLES 13:1 – 11

CONFRONTING HOLINESS

David was angry about the death of Uzzah. It seemed harsh that the man should lose his life for reaching to steady and protect the ark of God. Yet the Lord had been clear about protocols for handling holy things (Nu 4:15). The only way to transfer the ark was by using long poles (Ex 25:13 – 15) and only the Levites were authorized to carry it (1Ch 15:13 – 15). Despite Uzzah's good intentions, his actions still violated God's law.

In Jesus' ministry, he often confronted religious leaders who assumed they knew how to approach God. In their self-confidence, they missed the gracious nature of Jesus' confrontations with them about their error and their sin. Jesus' stern words for the religious leaders were gracious because God in the flesh did not take their lives — rather, he invited them to change, to go a better way. Just as Uzzah could not touch the ark, so people cannot approach God apart from the way that was established through Christ (Heb 10:19 – 22). Jesus invites all men and women — no matter what they've done — to find life and forgiveness through faith in him (Jn 14:6).

[a] 3 Or *we neglected* [b] 3 Or *him* [c] 11 *Perez Uzzah* means *outbreak against Uzzah.*

1 CHRONICLES 12:32

THE ISSACHAR MINDSET

The men of Issachar joined with David, offering their swords and unique set of skills. They understood the times and they knew what the Israelites should do. These talents would give a strong advantage to any king.

Knowing details about history and profiles of past leaders can only help to a point — a historian is not as valuable as one who understands the current times and circumstances. The chiefs of Issachar operated in wisdom and discernment, perceiving things such as national momentum, community morale and the people's capacity for religious and military endeavors. David may well have taken advantage of their counsel when he conferred with his officers before bringing the ark to Jerusalem (1Ch 13:1).

In Jesus' day, he engaged people with a perfect version of the Issachar mindset. Jesus understood the times perfectly, having complete knowledge of all things political, social and religious. He considered discernment of the times an important ability — even chastising those lacking it (Lk 12:54 – 56). More importantly, he knew what people needed to do. For that reason, Jesus spoke the truth with authority (Mk 1:21 – 22).

Discernment is a valuable skill for followers of Christ. Some situations call for bold action while others require patient observation. At times, a fight must be engaged to preserve old ways, and at other times a fight is needed to revolutionize systems that have become stagnant or corrupt. Knowing what is called for in a given season and identifying the best steps of response is a significant discipleship challenge. It is made more difficult because of humanity's limited knowledge and tendencies toward sin.

As a source of help, Jesus gave the Holy Spirit to counsel the hearts of his people in wisdom and truth. The Holy Spirit reminds them of what Jesus said, guides them away from sin and enables them to glorify Christ (Jn 16:7 – 15). The power that comes through the Holy Spirit gives believers the power to live with strength and conviction. Jesus does not ask his followers to make their way through life on their own; he provides the source for living!

12David was afraid of God that day and asked, "How can I ever bring the ark of
God to me?" 13He did not take the ark to be with him in the City of David. Instead,
he took it to the house of Obed-Edom the Gittite. 14The ark of God remained with
the family of Obed-Edom in his house for three months, and the LORD blessed
his household and everything he had.

David's House and Family

14 Now Hiram king of Tyre sent messengers to David, along with cedar logs,
stonemasons and carpenters to build a palace for him. 2And David knew
that the LORD had established him as king over Israel and that his kingdom had
been highly exalted for the sake of his people Israel.
3In Jerusalem David took more wives and became the father of more sons and
daughters. 4These are the names of the children born to him there: Shammua,
Shobab, Nathan, Solomon, 5Ibhar, Elishua, Elpelet, 6Nogah, Nepheg, Japhia,
7Elishama, Beeliada[a] and Eliphelet.

David Defeats the Philistines

8When the Philistines heard that David had been anointed king over all Israel,
they went up in full force to search for him, but David heard about it and went
out to meet them. 9Now the Philistines had come and raided the Valley of Rephaim; 10so David inquired of God: "Shall I go and attack the Philistines? Will you
deliver them into my hands?"
The LORD answered him, "Go, I will deliver them into your hands."
11So David and his men went up to Baal Perazim, and there he defeated them.
He said, "As waters break out, God has broken out against my enemies by my
hand." So that place was called Baal Perazim.[b] 12The Philistines had abandoned
their gods there, and David gave orders to burn them in the fire.
13Once more the Philistines raided the valley; 14so David inquired of God
again, and God answered him, "Do not go directly after them, but circle around
them and attack them in front of the poplar trees. 15As soon as you hear the
sound of marching in the tops of the poplar trees, move out to battle, because
that will mean God has gone out in front of you to strike the Philistine army." 16So
David did as God commanded him, and they struck down the Philistine army,
all the way from Gibeon to Gezer.
17So David's fame spread throughout every land, and the LORD made all the
nations fear him.

The Ark Brought to Jerusalem

15 After David had constructed buildings for himself in the City of David, he
prepared a place for the ark of God and pitched a tent for it. 2Then David
said, "No one but the Levites may carry the ark of God, because the LORD chose
them to carry the ark of the LORD and to minister before him forever."
3David assembled all Israel in Jerusalem to bring up the ark of the LORD to
the place he had prepared for it. 4He called together the descendants of Aaron
and the Levites:

5From the descendants of Kohath,
Uriel the leader and 120 relatives;
6from the descendants of Merari,
Asaiah the leader and 220 relatives;
7from the descendants of Gershon,[c]
Joel the leader and 130 relatives;
8from the descendants of Elizaphan,
Shemaiah the leader and 200 relatives;
9from the descendants of Hebron,
Eliel the leader and 80 relatives;

---

[a] 7 A variant of *Eliada* [b] 11 *Baal Perazim* means *the lord who breaks out.* [c] 7 Hebrew *Gershom,* a variant of *Gershon*

1 CHRONICLES 14:8–17

WHEN GOD JOINS THE FIGHT

David's army defeated the Philistines in two phases of battle. In both confrontations, the deciding factor was God's intervention — not Israel's military might. David inquired of the Lord both times, yielding to his divine pleasure and will. God accomplished victory for his people and increased his fame among the nations. Even then, God was on a mission to redeem his people and set a precedent for what he would do in the future.

Often, the physical battles of the Old Testament illustrate the spiritual battles between the forces of good and evil. In overview, the life and ministry of Jesus outline the cosmic fight in which Christ defeats Satan and his hosts. Jesus drove out demons (Mt 12:22) and gave his disciples the authority to overcome Satan's power (Lk 10:18–19). The enemy was disarmed and defeated on the cross (Col 2:15), but Satan's ultimate demise won't come until the consummation of history (Rev 20:7–10).

1 CHRONICLES 15:1–29

A DAY OF GLORY

The ark of the covenant's arrival in Jerusalem was a joyous spectacle. All Israel assembled to witness the moment. The Levites appointed singers and musicians to make jubilant sounds with all kinds of instruments — adding to the dancing and shouts of celebration. The people and their king were elated to have the symbol of God's presence at home in their city. And the glory that

(continued on next page)

(A Day of Glory, continued)

rested on the ark was God's way of making himself visibly present to his people. The day David brought the ark to Jerusalem was the day when God's glory—his presence and power—was manifest in the city in a new way. In the beginning of Luke's Gospel we read of Simeon, a faithful son of Israel, who longed for the appearance of God's promised Messiah. Simeon encountered Mary, Joseph and the Christ-child in the temple and burst into praise for God—salvation for the world had finally come (Lk 2:22–32)! With far less fanfare than the arrival of the ark, Jesus entered the world planning to make his home in the hearts of men and women. When Jesus was born, God's glory came to humanity once again—this time as more than a symbol. When the beloved Son of God took on human nature and was born in Bethlehem, God himself entered history (Jn 1:14).

1 CHRONICLES 16:1

WHERE TO WORSHIP

For a number of years, Israel had, in effect, *two* tabernacles: David constructed a new tent for the ark of the covenant when he moved it to Jerusalem (1Ch 16:1), and in the meantime the old tabernacle remained at Gibeon (1Ch 16:39–40). During David's reign, priests were assigned to both locations. Then, during Solomon's reign, the temple was built on Mount Moriah in Jerusalem (2Ch 3:1—5:1). Throughout Israel's history, various rival locations emerged as locations for the worship of God, including sites in Dan, Bethel and Samaria.

(continued on next page)

10 from the descendants of Uzziel,
Amminadab the leader and 112 relatives.
11 Then David summoned Zadok and Abiathar the priests, and Uriel, Asaiah,
Joel, Shemaiah, Eliel and Amminadab the Levites. 12 He said to them, "You are
the heads of the Levitical families; you and your fellow Levites are to consecrate
yourselves and bring up the ark of the LORD, the God of Israel, to the place I have
prepared for it. 13 It was because you, the Levites, did not bring it up the first time
that the LORD our God broke out in anger against us. We did not inquire of him
about how to do it in the prescribed way." 14 So the priests and Levites consecrated themselves in order to bring up the ark of the LORD, the God of Israel. 15 And
the Levites carried the ark of God with the poles on their shoulders, as Moses had
commanded in accordance with the word of the LORD.
16 David told the leaders of the Levites to appoint their fellow Levites as musicians to make a joyful sound with musical instruments: lyres, harps and cymbals.
17 So the Levites appointed Heman son of Joel; from his relatives, Asaph son of
Berekiah; and from their relatives the Merarites, Ethan son of Kushaiah; 18 and
with them their relatives next in rank: Zechariah,[a] Jaaziel, Shemiramoth, Jehiel,
Unni, Eliab, Benaiah, Maaseiah, Mattithiah, Eliphelehu, Mikneiah, Obed-Edom
and Jeiel,[b] the gatekeepers.
19 The musicians Heman, Asaph and Ethan were to sound the bronze cymbals; 20 Zechariah, Jaaziel,[c] Shemiramoth, Jehiel, Unni, Eliab, Maaseiah and Benaiah were to play the lyres according to *alamoth*,[d] 21 and Mattithiah, Eliphelehu, Mikneiah, Obed-Edom, Jeiel and Azaziah were to play the harps, directing
according to *sheminith*.[d] 22 Kenaniah the head Levite was in charge of the singing; that was his responsibility because he was skillful at it.
23 Berekiah and Elkanah were to be doorkeepers for the ark. 24 Shebaniah,
Joshaphat, Nethanel, Amasai, Zechariah, Benaiah and Eliezer the priests were
to blow trumpets before the ark of God. Obed-Edom and Jehiah were also to be
doorkeepers for the ark.
25 So David and the elders of Israel and the commanders of units of a thousand
went to bring up the ark of the covenant of the LORD from the house of Obed-
Edom, with rejoicing. 26 Because God had helped the Levites who were carrying
the ark of the covenant of the LORD, seven bulls and seven rams were sacrificed.
27 Now David was clothed in a robe of fine linen, as were all the Levites who were
carrying the ark, and as were the musicians, and Kenaniah, who was in charge
of the singing of the choirs. David also wore a linen ephod. 28 So all Israel brought
up the ark of the covenant of the LORD with shouts, with the sounding of rams'
horns and trumpets, and of cymbals, and the playing of lyres and harps.
29 As the ark of the covenant of the LORD was entering the City of David, Michal
daughter of Saul watched from a window. And when she saw King David dancing
and celebrating, she despised him in her heart.

Ministering Before the Ark

16 They brought the ark of God and set it inside the tent that David had
pitched for it, and they presented burnt offerings and fellowship offerings before God. 2 After David had finished sacrificing the burnt offerings and
fellowship offerings, he blessed the people in the name of the LORD. 3 Then he
gave a loaf of bread, a cake of dates and a cake of raisins to each Israelite man
and woman.
4 He appointed some of the Levites to minister before the ark of the LORD,
to extol,[e] thank, and praise the LORD, the God of Israel: 5 Asaph was the chief,
and next to him in rank were Zechariah, then Jaaziel,[f] Shemiramoth, Jehiel,

[a] *18* Three Hebrew manuscripts and most Septuagint manuscripts (see also verse 20 and 16:5); most Hebrew manuscripts *Zechariah son and* or *Zechariah, Ben and* [b] *18* Hebrew; Septuagint (see also verse 21) *Jeiel and Azaziah* [c] *20* See verse 18; Hebrew *Aziel*, a variant of *Jaaziel*. [d] *20,21* Probably a musical term [e] *4* Or *petition*; or *invoke* [f] *5* See 15:18,20; Hebrew *Jeiel*, possibly another name for *Jaaziel*.

Mattithiah, Eliab, Benaiah, Obed-Edom and Jeiel. They were to play the lyres
and harps, Asaph was to sound the cymbals, [6]and Benaiah and Jahaziel the
priests were to blow the trumpets regularly before the ark of the covenant of
God.

[7]That day David first appointed Asaph and his associates to give praise to the
LORD in this manner:

[8]Give praise to the LORD, proclaim his name;
make known among the nations what he has done.
[9]Sing to him, sing praise to him;
tell of all his wonderful acts.
[10]Glory in his holy name;
let the hearts of those who seek the LORD rejoice.
[11]Look to the LORD and his strength;
seek his face always.

[12]Remember the wonders he has done,
his miracles, and the judgments he pronounced,
[13]you his servants, the descendants of Israel,
his chosen ones, the children of Jacob.
[14]He is the LORD our God;
his judgments are in all the earth.
[15]He remembers[a] his covenant forever,
the promise he made, for a thousand generations,
[16]the covenant he made with Abraham,
the oath he swore to Isaac.
[17]He confirmed it to Jacob as a decree,
to Israel as an everlasting covenant:
[18]"To you I will give the land of Canaan
as the portion you will inherit."

[19]When they were but few in number,
few indeed, and strangers in it,
[20]they[b] wandered from nation to nation,
from one kingdom to another.
[21]He allowed no one to oppress them;
for their sake he rebuked kings:
[22]"Do not touch my anointed ones;
do my prophets no harm."
[23]Sing to the LORD, all the earth;
proclaim his salvation day after day.
[24]Declare his glory among the nations,
his marvelous deeds among all peoples.

[25]For great is the LORD and most worthy of praise;
he is to be feared above all gods.
[26]For all the gods of the nations are idols,
but the LORD made the heavens.
[27]Splendor and majesty are before him;
strength and joy are in his dwelling place.

[28]Ascribe to the LORD, all you families of nations,
ascribe to the LORD glory and strength.
[29]Ascribe to the LORD the glory due his name;
bring an offering and come before him.

[a] *15* Some Septuagint manuscripts (see also Psalm 105:8); Hebrew *Remember* [b] *18-20* One Hebrew manuscript, Septuagint and Vulgate (see also Psalm 105:12); most Hebrew manuscripts *inherit, / [19]though you are but few in number, / few indeed, and strangers in it." / [20]They*

(Where to Worship, continued)

In Jesus' conversation with a Samaritan woman — many generations after the time of David — she expressed confusion about this issue (Jn 4:19 – 24). Jesus clarified that the location of worship is less important than the inward dispositions of those worshiping him — the Father seeks those who worship "in the Spirit and in truth" (Jn 4:24). Because God is Spirit, he is not confined to any particular place of worship. God's people can worship the Father in the name of the Son, in the power of the Spirit with reverence and joy — at any time and in any place.

Worship the LORD in the splendor of his[a] holiness.
30 Tremble before him, all the earth!
The world is firmly established; it cannot be moved.

31 Let the heavens rejoice, let the earth be glad;
let them say among the nations, "The LORD reigns!"
32 Let the sea resound, and all that is in it;
let the fields be jubilant, and everything in them!
33 Let the trees of the forest sing,
let them sing for joy before the LORD,
for he comes to judge the earth.

34 Give thanks to the LORD, for he is good;
his love endures forever.
35 Cry out, "Save us, God our Savior;
gather us and deliver us from the nations,
that we may give thanks to your holy name,
and glory in your praise."
36 Praise be to the LORD, the God of Israel,
from everlasting to everlasting.

Then all the people said "Amen" and "Praise the LORD."

37 David left Asaph and his associates before the ark of the covenant of the
LORD to minister there regularly, according to each day's requirements. 38 He
also left Obed-Edom and his sixty-eight associates to minister with them. Obed-Edom son of Jeduthun, and also Hosah, were gatekeepers.

39 David left Zadok the priest and his fellow priests before the tabernacle of
the LORD at the high place in Gibeon 40 to present burnt offerings to the LORD on
the altar of burnt offering regularly, morning and evening, in accordance with
everything written in the Law of the LORD, which he had given Israel. 41 With
them were Heman and Jeduthun and the rest of those chosen and designated
by name to give thanks to the LORD, "for his love endures forever." 42 Heman and
Jeduthun were responsible for the sounding of the trumpets and cymbals and for the playing of the other instruments for sacred song. The sons of Jeduthun were stationed at the gate.

43 Then all the people left, each for their own home, and David returned home to bless his family.

God's Promise to David

17 After David was settled in his palace, he said to Nathan the prophet, "Here I am, living in a house of cedar, while the ark of the covenant of the LORD is under a tent."

2 Nathan replied to David, "Whatever you have in mind, do it, for God is with you."

3 But that night the word of God came to Nathan, saying:

> 4 "Go and tell my servant David, 'This is what the LORD says: You are not
> the one to build me a house to dwell in. 5 I have not dwelt in a house from
> the day I brought Israel up out of Egypt to this day. I have moved from one
> tent site to another, from one dwelling place to another. 6 Wherever I have
> moved with all the Israelites, did I ever say to any of their leaders[b] whom I commanded to shepherd my people, "Why have you not built me a house of cedar?"'
>
> 7 "Now then, tell my servant David, 'This is what the LORD Almighty says:
> I took you from the pasture, from tending the flock, and appointed you ruler
> over my people Israel. 8 I have been with you wherever you have gone, and I
> have cut off all your enemies from before you. Now I will make your name

[a] 29 Or *LORD with the splendor of* [b] 6 Traditionally *judges*; also in verse 10

like the names of the greatest men on earth. 9And I will provide a place for my
people Israel and will plant them so that they can have a home of their own
and no longer be disturbed. Wicked people will not oppress them anymore,
as they did at the beginning 10and have done ever since the time I appointed
leaders over my people Israel. I will also subdue all your enemies.
"'I declare to you that the LORD will build a house for you: 11When your
days are over and you go to be with your ancestors, I will raise up your offspring to succeed you, one of your own sons, and I will establish his kingdom. 12He is the one who will build a house for me, and I will establish his
throne forever. 13I will be his father, and he will be my son. I will never take
my love away from him, as I took it away from your predecessor. 14I will set
him over my house and my kingdom forever; his throne will be established
forever.'"

15Nathan reported to David all the words of this entire revelation.

David's Prayer

16Then King David went in and sat before the LORD, and he said:

"Who am I, LORD God, and what is my family, that you have brought me
this far? 17And as if this were not enough in your sight, my God, you have
spoken about the future of the house of your servant. You, LORD God, have
looked on me as though I were the most exalted of men.
18"What more can David say to you for honoring your servant? For you
know your servant, 19LORD. For the sake of your servant and according to
your will, you have done this great thing and made known all these great
promises.
20"There is no one like you, LORD, and there is no God but you, as we
have heard with our own ears. 21And who is like your people Israel—the
one nation on earth whose God went out to redeem a people for himself,
and to make a name for yourself, and to perform great and awesome wonders by driving out nations from before your people, whom you redeemed
from Egypt? 22You made your people Israel your very own forever, and you,
LORD, have become their God.
23"And now, LORD, let the promise you have made concerning your servant and his house be established forever. Do as you promised, 24so that it
will be established and that your name will be great forever. Then people
will say, 'The LORD Almighty, the God over Israel, is Israel's God!' And the
house of your servant David will be established before you.
25"You, my God, have revealed to your servant that you will build a
house for him. So your servant has found courage to pray to you. 26You,
LORD, are God! You have promised these good things to your servant.
27Now you have been pleased to bless the house of your servant, that it may
continue forever in your sight; for you, LORD, have blessed it, and it will be
blessed forever."

David's Victories

18 In the course of time, David defeated the Philistines and subdued them,
and he took Gath and its surrounding villages from the control of the Philistines.
2David also defeated the Moabites, and they became subject to him and
brought him tribute.
3Moreover, David defeated Hadadezer king of Zobah, in the vicinity of Hamath, when he went to set up his monument at[a] the Euphrates River. 4David
captured a thousand of his chariots, seven thousand charioteers and twenty
thousand foot soldiers. He hamstrung all but a hundred of the chariot horses.

---

1 CHRONICLES 17:16–27

SUBMITTING TO GOD'S WILL

Despite David's success as a warrior, he was truly humble. He never forgot his modest background as a shepherd and credited his victories to God rather than his own military prowess. In David's heart, there lived a strong desire to build a house for the Lord—a temple for his presence and name (1Ch 22:6–10; Ac 7:45–46). When God told David he would not get to build the temple but that the honor would fall to one of his sons, David remained humble and yielded to God's will. David trusted God's plan even though his dream was denied.

Jesus' human will remained perfectly submitted to the Father's will (Jn 6:38). When faced with drinking the cup of God's wrath—taking on the world's sin at the cross—Jesus remained surrendered, trusting the Father's plan. Though he could have claimed his right as God at any time, he "did not consider equality with God something to be used to his own advantage" (Php 2:6).

---

[a] 3 Or *to restore his control over*

CHRONICLING DAVID'S LIFE

The name of King David stirs so many dramatic associations — a shepherd boy tending flocks while singing songs in the night, a young man anointed by Samuel, a stone launched from a sling to kill the giant Goliath, an enviable friendship with Jonathan, the capture of Jerusalem, a half-dressed king dancing for joy over the ark of the covenant, lust-driven adultery and a murder to cover it up, confrontation from the prophet Nathan, the death of an infant while the king begged God for mercy, Absalom's revolt and efforts to kill his own father, preparations for the temple of the Lord and the rise of an heir named Solomon. David's story in Scripture is without rival, apart from that of Jesus.

First Chronicles focuses primarily on David's active leadership — his public administration, planning for the temple and military victories. The book does not include David's sin with Bathsheba and the many family problems documented so thoroughly in the books of Samuel and the first two chapters of 1 Kings. First Chronicles attends instead to the highlights of David's forty-year reign. David came to the throne only after Saul's unfaithfulness led to his death (1Ch 10:13 — 11:3). The newly crowned king then took Jerusalem as his capital (1Ch 11:4 – 9). Soon after, warriors from all over Israel rallied to join David's army (1Ch 11:10 — 12:38). The middle chapters of the book record David's many royal accomplishments. And the book ends with the report that David "died at a good old age, having enjoyed long life, wealth and honor" (1Ch 29:28).

But no highlight from David's highly impressive biography is more important than the covenant God made with him. The Lord promised David a descendant who would reign forever over an eternal kingdom (1Ch 17:11 – 14). God fulfilled this promise in Christ. "After removing Saul, he made David their king. God testified concerning him: 'I have found David son of Jesse, a man after my own heart; he will do everything I want him to do.' From this man's descendants God has brought to Israel the Savior Jesus, as he promised" (Ac 13:22 – 23). In the book of Revelation, Jesus identifies himself as "the Root and the Offspring of David" (Rev 22:16).

[5]When the Arameans of Damascus came to help Hadadezer king of Zobah,
David struck down twenty-two thousand of them. [6]He put garrisons in the Aramean kingdom of Damascus, and the Arameans became subject to him and
brought him tribute. The LORD gave David victory wherever he went.
[7]David took the gold shields carried by the officers of Hadadezer and brought
them to Jerusalem. [8]From Tebah[a] and Kun, towns that belonged to Hadadezer,
David took a great quantity of bronze, which Solomon used to make the bronze
Sea, the pillars and various bronze articles.
[9]When Tou king of Hamath heard that David had defeated the entire army of
Hadadezer king of Zobah, [10]he sent his son Hadoram to King David to greet him
and congratulate him on his victory in battle over Hadadezer, who had been
at war with Tou. Hadoram brought all kinds of articles of gold, of silver and of
bronze.
[11]King David dedicated these articles to the LORD, as he had done with the
silver and gold he had taken from all these nations: Edom and Moab, the Ammonites and the Philistines, and Amalek.
[12]Abishai son of Zeruiah struck down eighteen thousand Edomites in the Valley of Salt. [13]He put garrisons in Edom, and all the Edomites became subject to
David. The LORD gave David victory wherever he went.

David's Officials

[14]David reigned over all Israel, doing what was just and right for all his people.
[15]Joab son of Zeruiah was over the army; Jehoshaphat son of Ahilud was recorder; [16]Zadok son of Ahitub and Ahimelek[b] son of Abiathar were priests; Shavsha
was secretary; [17]Benaiah son of Jehoiada was over the Kerethites and Pelethites;
and David's sons were chief officials at the king's side.

David Defeats the Ammonites

19 In the course of time, Nahash king of the Ammonites died, and his son
succeeded him as king. [2]David thought, "I will show kindness to Hanun
son of Nahash, because his father showed kindness to me." So David sent a delegation to express his sympathy to Hanun concerning his father.
When David's envoys came to Hanun in the land of the Ammonites to express
sympathy to him, [3]the Ammonite commanders said to Hanun, "Do you think
David is honoring your father by sending envoys to you to express sympathy?
Haven't his envoys come to you only to explore and spy out the country and overthrow it?" [4]So Hanun seized David's envoys, shaved them, cut off their garments
at the buttocks, and sent them away.
[5]When someone came and told David about the men, he sent messengers to
meet them, for they were greatly humiliated. The king said, "Stay at Jericho till
your beards have grown, and then come back."
[6]When the Ammonites realized that they had become obnoxious to David,
Hanun and the Ammonites sent a thousand talents[c] of silver to hire chariots and
charioteers from Aram Naharaim,[d] Aram Maakah and Zobah. [7]They hired thirty-two thousand chariots and charioteers, as well as the king of Maakah with his
troops, who came and camped near Medeba, while the Ammonites were mustered from their towns and moved out for battle.
[8]On hearing this, David sent Joab out with the entire army of fighting men.
[9]The Ammonites came out and drew up in battle formation at the entrance to
their city, while the kings who had come were by themselves in the open country.
[10]Joab saw that there were battle lines in front of him and behind him; so he
selected some of the best troops in Israel and deployed them against the Arameans. [11]He put the rest of the men under the command of Abishai his brother, and
they were deployed against the Ammonites. [12]Joab said, "If the Arameans are too

[a] *8* Hebrew *Tibhath,* a variant of *Tebah* [b] *16* Some Hebrew manuscripts, Vulgate and Syriac (see also 2 Samuel 8:17); most Hebrew manuscripts *Abimelek* [c] *6* That is, about 38 tons or about 34 metric tons [d] *6* That is, Northwest Mesopotamia

1 CHRONICLES 18:14

ADMINISTERING JUSTICE

King David led many military campaigns to protect and serve his people in the course of securing the kingdom's borders. Once the borders were established, he led and served his people in a different way — he dispensed justice. Ruling on disputes and punishing crime is a necessary function within any nation. People will sin. The weak are violated or exploited. David administered justice for all his people with both firmness and fairness. It is no wonder Israel looked upon him as the ideal king.

The prophet Isaiah foretold of Jesus, the perfect king — who would bring justice to all nations (Isa 42:1 – 4). Jesus lived on the earth with compassion for the weak and appropriate rebuke for hypocrites and oppressors. When he returns, Jesus will judge all people according to what they have done. Anyone whose name is in his book of life will be saved (Rev 20:11 – 15). His desire is that all people would have eternal life, which is found only in himself.

1 CHRONICLES 19:1 – 18

BECOMING ENEMIES

David sent a delegation to the Ammonites, a people who were grieving the death of their king. Paranoia and terrible advice led the new Ammonite king to reject the show of sympathy — resulting in a severe offense against David. Israel, like a disturbed hornet's nest, assembled for battle and won a lopsided victory over the Ammonites and their allies. It is

(continued on next page)

(Becoming Enemies, continued)

astonishing to observe how quickly the Ammonites reverted from friendship with Israel to renewing longtime hostilities.

All people have sinned, making themselves enemies of God. But Jesus gave his life to reconcile rebels. Through faith in Christ's death and resurrection, believers are transferred from the kingdom of darkness into the kingdom of the Son (Col 1:13). Believing in Jesus—in an instant of awakening—moves a person from death to life, from being God's enemy to being God's child (Ro 5:10). The gift of salvation that comes through Jesus is a miracle and sign of his mercy.

1 CHRONICLES 20:1–3

THE FRUIT OF FORGIVENESS

First Chronicles 20:1–3 differs from its companion passage in 2 Samuel 11. This account, written after the exile, omits mention of David's sin with Bathsheba, the low point of his life. This omission provides a beautiful illustration of full forgiveness through Jesus Christ. While sin always has consequences, God's grace ensures his people are not permanently marked by the worst days of their lives or the worst thing they have done.

In Christ, the guilt of sin is not simply waved off or disregarded. Jesus purchased forgiveness on the cross. Redemption and pardon are never free—they are bought with the precious blood of Christ and then offered to men and women as gifts of grace (Eph 1:7). One of the great benefits

(continued on next page)

strong for me, then you are to rescue me; but if the Ammonites are too strong for
you, then I will rescue you. 13Be strong, and let us fight bravely for our people and
the cities of our God. The LORD will do what is good in his sight."
14Then Joab and the troops with him advanced to fight the Arameans, and
they fled before him. 15When the Ammonites realized that the Arameans were
fleeing, they too fled before his brother Abishai and went inside the city. So Joab
went back to Jerusalem.
16After the Arameans saw that they had been routed by Israel, they sent messengers and had Arameans brought from beyond the Euphrates River, with Shophak the commander of Hadadezer's army leading them.
17When David was told of this, he gathered all Israel and crossed the Jordan;
he advanced against them and formed his battle lines opposite them. David
formed his lines to meet the Arameans in battle, and they fought against him.
18But they fled before Israel, and David killed seven thousand of their charioteers and forty thousand of their foot soldiers. He also killed Shophak the commander of their army.
19When the vassals of Hadadezer saw that they had been routed by Israel, they
made peace with David and became subject to him.
So the Arameans were not willing to help the Ammonites anymore.

The Capture of Rabbah

20 In the spring, at the time when kings go off to war, Joab led out the armed
forces. He laid waste the land of the Ammonites and went to Rabbah and
besieged it, but David remained in Jerusalem. Joab attacked Rabbah and left it in
ruins. 2David took the crown from the head of their king[a]—its weight was found
to be a talent[b] of gold, and it was set with precious stones—and it was placed on
David's head. He took a great quantity of plunder from the city 3and brought out
the people who were there, consigning them to labor with saws and with iron
picks and axes. David did this to all the Ammonite towns. Then David and his
entire army returned to Jerusalem.

War With the Philistines

4In the course of time, war broke out with the Philistines, at Gezer. At that
time Sibbekai the Hushathite killed Sippai, one of the descendants of the Rephaites, and the Philistines were subjugated.
5In another battle with the Philistines, Elhanan son of Jair killed Lahmi the
brother of Goliath the Gittite, who had a spear with a shaft like a weaver's rod.
6In still another battle, which took place at Gath, there was a huge man with
six fingers on each hand and six toes on each foot—twenty-four in all. He also
was descended from Rapha. 7When he taunted Israel, Jonathan son of Shimea,
David's brother, killed him.
8These were descendants of Rapha in Gath, and they fell at the hands of David
and his men.

David Counts the Fighting Men

21 Satan rose up against Israel and incited David to take a census of Israel.
2So David said to Joab and the commanders of the troops, "Go and count
the Israelites from Beersheba to Dan. Then report back to me so that I may know
how many there are."
3But Joab replied, "May the LORD multiply his troops a hundred times over.
My lord the king, are they not all my lord's subjects? Why does my lord want to
do this? Why should he bring guilt on Israel?"
4The king's word, however, overruled Joab; so Joab left and went throughout
Israel and then came back to Jerusalem. 5Joab reported the number of the fighting men to David: In all Israel there were one million one hundred thousand

[a] 2 Or *of Milkom,* that is, Molek [b] 2 That is, about 75 pounds or about 34 kilograms

men who could handle a sword, including four hundred and seventy thousand
in Judah.
[6]But Joab did not include Levi and Benjamin in the numbering, because the
king's command was repulsive to him. [7]This command was also evil in the sight
of God; so he punished Israel.
[8]Then David said to God, "I have sinned greatly by doing this. Now, I beg you,
take away the guilt of your servant. I have done a very foolish thing."
[9]The LORD said to Gad, David's seer, [10]"Go and tell David, 'This is what the
LORD says: I am giving you three options. Choose one of them for me to carry
out against you.' "
[11]So Gad went to David and said to him, "This is what the LORD says: 'Take
your choice: [12]three years of famine, three months of being swept away[a] before
your enemies, with their swords overtaking you, or three days of the sword of
the LORD — days of plague in the land, with the angel of the LORD ravaging every part of Israel.' Now then, decide how I should answer the one who sent me."
[13]David said to Gad, "I am in deep distress. Let me fall into the hands of the
LORD, for his mercy is very great; but do not let me fall into human hands."
[14]So the LORD sent a plague on Israel, and seventy thousand men of Israel fell
dead. [15]And God sent an angel to destroy Jerusalem. But as the angel was doing
so, the LORD saw it and relented concerning the disaster and said to the angel
who was destroying the people, "Enough! Withdraw your hand." The angel of the
LORD was then standing at the threshing floor of Araunah[b] the Jebusite.
[16]David looked up and saw the angel of the LORD standing between heaven
and earth, with a drawn sword in his hand extended over Jerusalem. Then David
and the elders, clothed in sackcloth, fell facedown.
[17]David said to God, "Was it not I who ordered the fighting men to be counted?
I, the shepherd,[c] have sinned and done wrong. These are but sheep. What have
they done? LORD my God, let your hand fall on me and my family, but do not let
this plague remain on your people."

David Builds an Altar

[18]Then the angel of the LORD ordered Gad to tell David to go up and build
an altar to the LORD on the threshing floor of Araunah the Jebusite. [19]So David
went up in obedience to the word that Gad had spoken in the name of the LORD.
[20]While Araunah was threshing wheat, he turned and saw the angel; his four
sons who were with him hid themselves. [21]Then David approached, and when
Araunah looked and saw him, he left the threshing floor and bowed down before
David with his face to the ground.
[22]David said to him, "Let me have the site of your threshing floor so I can build
an altar to the LORD, that the plague on the people may be stopped. Sell it to me
at the full price."
[23]Araunah said to David, "Take it! Let my lord the king do whatever pleases
him. Look, I will give the oxen for the burnt offerings, the threshing sledges for
the wood, and the wheat for the grain offering. I will give all this."
[24]But King David replied to Araunah, "No, I insist on paying the full price. I
will not take for the LORD what is yours, or sacrifice a burnt offering that costs
me nothing."
[25]So David paid Araunah six hundred shekels[d] of gold for the site. [26]David
built an altar to the LORD there and sacrificed burnt offerings and fellowship
offerings. He called on the LORD, and the LORD answered him with fire from
heaven on the altar of burnt offering.
[27]Then the LORD spoke to the angel, and he put his sword back into its sheath.
[28]At that time, when David saw that the LORD had answered him on the threshing

(The Fruit of Forgiveness, continued)

of salvation through Jesus is that his people become new creations in him — the old life disappears and a new one begins (2Co 5:17). The stains from old sins and the regrets from ungodly choices — marks of disgrace on the lives of those adopted into his family — are erased forever, thanks to Christ's work on the cross (Isa 1:18).

---

[a] *12* Hebrew; Septuagint and Vulgate (see also 2 Samuel 24:13) *of fleeing* [b] *15* Hebrew *Ornan,* a variant of *Araunah*; also in verses 18-28 [c] *17* Probable reading of the original Hebrew text (see 2 Samuel 24:17 and note); Masoretic Text does not have *the shepherd.*
[d] *25* That is, about 15 pounds or about 6.9 kilograms

THE PLACE OF SACRIFICE

The site King David purchased from Araunah is a sacred piece of real estate in the history of Israel — significant in both the Old and New Testaments. Known as Mount Moriah (2Ch 3:1), it was there that Abraham brought Isaac with the intention of sacrificing him to the Lord (Ge 22:2). At the last moment, God intervened in the test of faith and provided a ram as a substitute. Abraham called the place "The LORD Will Provide" (Ge 22:14). David needed Araunah's threshing floor for the site of a sacrificial altar. The Lord's angel instructed the king to make offerings following his sin, repentance and punishment. God accepted David's burnt offerings and fellowship offerings — compelling him to add more offerings in thanksgiving (1Ch 21:28). This location was so meaningful to David that he declared it to be the location for the house of the Lord, the much anticipated temple of Solomon (1Ch 22:1).

When Jesus died on the cross at the hill called Golgotha, Mount Moriah was involved once again. He was crucified outside of the city gates across the valley from the temple. At the moment of Jesus' death, the veil of the temple — the curtain separating the Most Holy Place from the common areas — ripped in two from top to bottom (Mk 15:37 – 38). This signified that God's presence was finally open to all people. The book of Hebrews describes the access Jesus created by giving himself to ransom mankind: "Therefore, brothers and sisters, since we have confidence to enter the Most Holy Place by the blood of Jesus, by a new and living way opened for us through the curtain, that is, his body, and since we have a great high priest over the house of God, let us draw near to God with a sincere heart and with the full assurance that faith brings, having our hearts sprinkled to cleanse us from a guilty conscience and having our bodies washed with pure water" (Heb 10:19 – 22).

The area around Mount Moriah has been marked by incredible events. The greatest of these is the sacrifice of Jesus as the substitute payment for humanity's sin. Just as God was pleased with Abraham's act of faith and David's offerings, God accepted the death of Jesus as complete atonement. The Father then offered the world the opportunity to be made righteous through faith in the Son (Ro 5:18 – 19).

The location of these sacrifices did not make them special or powerful. They were effective because they were offered in humility to the one true God — and he found them pleasing and acceptable.

floor of Araunah the Jebusite, he offered sacrifices there. 29The tabernacle of the
LORD, which Moses had made in the wilderness, and the altar of burnt offering
were at that time on the high place at Gibeon. 30But David could not go before it
to inquire of God, because he was afraid of the sword of the angel of the LORD.
22 Then David said, "The house of the LORD God is to be here, and also the
altar of burnt offering for Israel."

Preparations for the Temple

2So David gave orders to assemble the foreigners residing in Israel, and from
among them he appointed stonecutters to prepare dressed stone for building the
house of God. 3He provided a large amount of iron to make nails for the doors of
the gateways and for the fittings, and more bronze than could be weighed. 4He
also provided more cedar logs than could be counted, for the Sidonians and Tyr-
ians had brought large numbers of them to David.

5David said, "My son Solomon is young and inexperienced, and the house to
be built for the LORD should be of great magnificence and fame and splendor in
the sight of all the nations. Therefore I will make preparations for it." So David
made extensive preparations before his death.

6Then he called for his son Solomon and charged him to build a house for the
LORD, the God of Israel. 7David said to Solomon: "My son, I had it in my heart
to build a house for the Name of the LORD my God. 8But this word of the LORD
came to me: 'You have shed much blood and have fought many wars. You are not
to build a house for my Name, because you have shed much blood on the earth
in my sight. 9But you will have a son who will be a man of peace and rest, and I
will give him rest from all his enemies on every side. His name will be Solomon,[a]
and I will grant Israel peace and quiet during his reign. 10He is the one who will
build a house for my Name. He will be my son, and I will be his father. And I will
establish the throne of his kingdom over Israel forever.'

11"Now, my son, the LORD be with you, and may you have success and build
the house of the LORD your God, as he said you would. 12May the LORD give you
discretion and understanding when he puts you in command over Israel, so that
you may keep the law of the LORD your God. 13Then you will have success if you
are careful to observe the decrees and laws that the LORD gave Moses for Israel.
Be strong and courageous. Do not be afraid or discouraged.

14"I have taken great pains to provide for the temple of the LORD a hundred
thousand talents[b] of gold, a million talents[c] of silver, quantities of bronze and
iron too great to be weighed, and wood and stone. And you may add to them.
15You have many workers: stonecutters, masons and carpenters, as well as those
skilled in every kind of work 16in gold and silver, bronze and iron — craftsmen
beyond number. Now begin the work, and the LORD be with you."

17Then David ordered all the leaders of Israel to help his son Solomon. 18He
said to them, "Is not the LORD your God with you? And has he not granted you
rest on every side? For he has given the inhabitants of the land into my hands,
and the land is subject to the LORD and to his people. 19Now devote your heart
and soul to seeking the LORD your God. Begin to build the sanctuary of the LORD
God, so that you may bring the ark of the covenant of the LORD and the sacred
articles belonging to God into the temple that will be built for the Name of the
LORD."

The Levites

23 When David was old and full of years, he made his son Solomon king over
Israel.

2He also gathered together all the leaders of Israel, as well as the priests
and Levites. 3The Levites thirty years old or more were counted, and the total

[a] 9 *Solomon* sounds like and may be derived from the Hebrew for *peace*. [b] 14 That is,
about 3,750 tons or about 3,400 metric tons [c] 14 That is, about 37,500 tons or about
34,000 metric tons

PREPARING A TEMPLE

King David longed to build the temple, but the Lord chose Solomon to oversee its completion (vv. 7 – 10). God was glad about this house for his Name — it was not merely some human indulgence. The temple would be magnificent and massive and impressive, because God is all of those things (v. 5).

David took care to ready his young and inexperienced son for the daunting task of leading the temple project. He did this by making extensive preparations for finances, materials and manpower (v. 5). Many thousand talents of gold — along with silver, bronze, iron, wood and stone — were stockpiled for construction (v. 14). Stonecutters, masons, carpenters and other skilled craftsmen were recruited for Solomon's use (vv. 15 – 16). And King David ordered all the leaders of Israel to help in the monumental effort (v. 17).

Beyond these material provisions, David issued a charge and spoke a blessing to his son — wishing him success and praying to God for the future leader's discretion and understanding. He also admonished Solomon to observe the laws of the Lord at all times and to go forward in the work without fear: "Be strong and courageous. Do not be afraid or discouraged" (vv. 11 – 13). This blessing is reminiscent of Moses transferring leadership and authority to Joshua near the time of the great deliverer's death (Dt 31:1 – 8).

David spent several years strategizing for the building of the temple. These preparations seem impressive until one considers that God established his plan to reconcile sinful humankind through Jesus before the creation of the world (1Pe 1:19 – 20). Before there was earth or sky or day or night, God chose his future people in Christ to be made holy and to become adopted members of his family (Eph 1:3 – 5).

God's plans are higher and more intricate than finite human plans. His purposes are far beyond anything that the human mind can conceive: "As the heavens are higher than the earth, so are my ways higher than your ways and my thoughts than your thoughts" (Isa 55:9).

number of men was thirty-eight thousand. [4]David said, "Of these, twenty-four
thousand are to be in charge of the work of the temple of the LORD and six thousand are to be officials and judges. [5]Four thousand are to be gatekeepers and
four thousand are to praise the LORD with the musical instruments I have provided for that purpose."
[6]David separated the Levites into divisions corresponding to the sons of Levi:
Gershon, Kohath and Merari.

Gershonites

[7]Belonging to the Gershonites:
Ladan and Shimei.
[8]The sons of Ladan:
Jehiel the first, Zetham and Joel—three in all.
[9]The sons of Shimei:
Shelomoth, Haziel and Haran—three in all.
These were the heads of the families of Ladan.
[10]And the sons of Shimei:
Jahath, Ziza,[a] Jeush and Beriah.
These were the sons of Shimei—four in all.
[11]Jahath was the first and Ziza the second, but Jeush and Beriah did not
have many sons; so they were counted as one family with one assignment.

Kohathites

[12]The sons of Kohath:
Amram, Izhar, Hebron and Uzziel—four in all.
[13]The sons of Amram:
Aaron and Moses.
Aaron was set apart, he and his descendants forever, to consecrate the
most holy things, to offer sacrifices before the LORD, to minister before
him and to pronounce blessings in his name forever. [14]The sons of Moses the man of God were counted as part of the tribe of Levi.
[15]The sons of Moses:
Gershom and Eliezer.
[16]The descendants of Gershom:
Shubael was the first.
[17]The descendants of Eliezer:
Rehabiah was the first.
Eliezer had no other sons, but the sons of Rehabiah were very numerous.
[18]The sons of Izhar:
Shelomith was the first.
[19]The sons of Hebron:
Jeriah the first, Amariah the second, Jahaziel the third and Jekameam
the fourth.
[20]The sons of Uzziel:
Micah the first and Ishiah the second.

Merarites

[21]The sons of Merari:
Mahli and Mushi.
The sons of Mahli:
Eleazar and Kish.
[22]Eleazar died without having sons: he had only daughters. Their cousins,
the sons of Kish, married them.

---

[a] *10* One Hebrew manuscript, Septuagint and Vulgate (see also verse 11); most Hebrew manuscripts *Zina*

[23] The sons of Mushi:
Mahli, Eder and Jerimoth — three in all.

[24] These were the descendants of Levi by their families — the heads of families as they were registered under their names and counted individually, that
is, the workers twenty years old or more who served in the temple of the LORD.
[25] For David had said, "Since the LORD, the God of Israel, has granted rest to his
people and has come to dwell in Jerusalem forever, [26] the Levites no longer need
to carry the tabernacle or any of the articles used in its service." [27] According to
the last instructions of David, the Levites were counted from those twenty years
old or more.
[28] The duty of the Levites was to help Aaron's descendants in the service of the
temple of the LORD: to be in charge of the courtyards, the side rooms, the purification of all sacred things and the performance of other duties at the house of
God. [29] They were in charge of the bread set out on the table, the special flour for
the grain offerings, the thin loaves made without yeast, the baking and the mixing, and all measurements of quantity and size. [30] They were also to stand every
morning to thank and praise the LORD. They were to do the same in the evening
[31] and whenever burnt offerings were presented to the LORD on the Sabbaths, at
the New Moon feasts and at the appointed festivals. They were to serve before
the LORD regularly in the proper number and in the way prescribed for them.
[32] And so the Levites carried out their responsibilities for the tent of meeting,
for the Holy Place and, under their relatives the descendants of Aaron, for the
service of the temple of the LORD.

---

1 CHRONICLES 23:24 – 32

ASSIGNED FOR SERVICE

For centuries, the Levites served in and around the tabernacle — the portable tent of meeting that housed the ark of the covenant and the many accessories used in worship (Nu 4:5 – 15). Israel's priests managed the sacrificial system and took responsibility for disassembling and reassembling the tent each time the camp relocated. When the Lord arranged for Israel to rest from the threat of war in the last years of David's reign, the king seized the opportunity to reassign the Levites to new responsibilities. This coincided with plans for building a permanent temple in Jerusalem — the portable tent would no longer be necessary. With forethought and care, David managed Israel's leaders for optimum effectiveness in service to the Lord (1Ch 23:2 – 6).

This is similar to how Jesus loves and serves the church. He assigns various spiritual gifts as needed, for the good of the body of Christ (Ro 12:4 – 8). Just as national changes in the era of King David called for adjustments in the use of leaders, so Christ manages the church's changing needs — assigning specific gifts to empower ministry. Spiritual gifts are meant to serve the church body, enable it to perform its mission to the world and glorify God through Jesus (1Pe 4:10 – 11).

The Divisions of Priests

24 These were the divisions of the descendants of Aaron:
The sons of Aaron were Nadab, Abihu, Eleazar and Ithamar. [2] But Nadab
and Abihu died before their father did, and they had no sons; so Eleazar and
Ithamar served as the priests. [3] With the help of Zadok a descendant of Eleazar
and Ahimelek a descendant of Ithamar, David separated them into divisions for
their appointed order of ministering. [4] A larger number of leaders were found
among Eleazar's descendants than among Ithamar's, and they were divided accordingly: sixteen heads of families from Eleazar's descendants and eight heads
of families from Ithamar's descendants. [5] They divided them impartially by casting lots, for there were officials of the sanctuary and officials of God among the
descendants of both Eleazar and Ithamar.
[6] The scribe Shemaiah son of Nethanel, a Levite, recorded their names in the
presence of the king and of the officials: Zadok the priest, Ahimelek son of Abiathar and the heads of families of the priests and of the Levites — one family being
taken from Eleazar and then one from Ithamar.

[7] The first lot fell to Jehoiarib,
the second to Jedaiah,
[8] the third to Harim,
the fourth to Seorim,
[9] the fifth to Malkijah,
the sixth to Mijamin,
[10] the seventh to Hakkoz,
the eighth to Abijah,
[11] the ninth to Jeshua,
the tenth to Shekaniah,
[12] the eleventh to Eliashib,
the twelfth to Jakim,
[13] the thirteenth to Huppah,
the fourteenth to Jeshebeab,
[14] the fifteenth to Bilgah,
the sixteenth to Immer,

[15]the seventeenth to Hezir,
the eighteenth to Happizzez,
[16]the nineteenth to Pethahiah,
the twentieth to Jehezkel,
[17]the twenty-first to Jakin,
the twenty-second to Gamul,
[18]the twenty-third to Delaiah
and the twenty-fourth to Maaziah.

[19]This was their appointed order of ministering when they entered the temple of the LORD, according to the regulations prescribed for them by their ancestor Aaron, as the LORD, the God of Israel, had commanded him.

The Rest of the Levites

[20]As for the rest of the descendants of Levi:
from the sons of Amram: Shubael;
from the sons of Shubael: Jehdeiah.
[21]As for Rehabiah, from his sons:
Ishiah was the first.
[22]From the Izharites: Shelomoth;
from the sons of Shelomoth: Jahath.
[23]The sons of Hebron: Jeriah the first,[a] Amariah the second, Jahaziel the third and Jekameam the fourth.
[24]The son of Uzziel: Micah;
from the sons of Micah: Shamir.
[25]The brother of Micah: Ishiah;
from the sons of Ishiah: Zechariah.
[26]The sons of Merari: Mahli and Mushi.
The son of Jaaziah: Beno.
[27]The sons of Merari:
from Jaaziah: Beno, Shoham, Zakkur and Ibri.
[28]From Mahli: Eleazar, who had no sons.
[29]From Kish: the son of Kish:
Jerahmeel.
[30]And the sons of Mushi: Mahli, Eder and Jerimoth.

These were the Levites, according to their families. [31]They also cast lots, just as their relatives the descendants of Aaron did, in the presence of King David and of Zadok, Ahimelek, and the heads of families of the priests and of the Levites. The families of the oldest brother were treated the same as those of the youngest.

The Musicians

25 David, together with the commanders of the army, set apart some of the sons of Asaph, Heman and Jeduthun for the ministry of prophesying, accompanied by harps, lyres and cymbals. Here is the list of the men who performed this service:

[2]From the sons of Asaph:
Zakkur, Joseph, Nethaniah and Asarelah. The sons of Asaph were under the supervision of Asaph, who prophesied under the king's supervision.
[3]As for Jeduthun, from his sons:
Gedaliah, Zeri, Jeshaiah, Shimei,[b] Hashabiah and Mattithiah, six in all, under the supervision of their father Jeduthun, who prophesied, using the harp in thanking and praising the LORD.

[a] *23* Two Hebrew manuscripts and some Septuagint manuscripts (see also 23:19); most Hebrew manuscripts *The sons of Jeriah:* [b] *3* One Hebrew manuscript and some Septuagint manuscripts (see also verse 17); most Hebrew manuscripts do not have *Shimei.*

1 CHRONICLES 25:1 – 31

PROCLAMATION THROUGH MUSIC

King David knew the importance of proclaiming the wonders of God to increase the Lord's fame on the earth. He assigned 288 people the task of recounting God's works through singing and playing instruments. It was their full-time job to praise the Lord and to prophesy — to proclaim truths about who God is, what he had done and what he could do. Their music possessed weight; it was much more than a pleasant fanfare or simple song. It was intended to be heard, contemplated and absorbed. David's music leaders crafted anthems that carried the name of the Lord — creatively reminding people about their God and his care for them.

While Scripture does not depict Jesus using music for creative truth-speaking during his earthly ministry, he acted in ways similar to David as he taught the crowds — often telling parables to connect people to God. These stories spoke of God's character, addressed issues of the day and illustrated the Father in accessible, easily remembered ways. Christ's parables are full of truth about God and truth about people. They were difficult to ignore, often leaving listeners questioning and thinking about what they had heard. Jesus used as many as forty creative and poignant parables to paint pictures of the kingdom and its King (e.g., Mt 13:1 – 52).

4 As for Heman, from his sons:
Bukkiah, Mattaniah, Uzziel, Shubael and Jerimoth; Hananiah, Hanani,
Eliathah, Giddalti and Romamti-Ezer; Joshbekashah, Mallothi, Hothir and
Mahazioth. 5 (All these were sons of Heman the king's seer. They were given
him through the promises of God to exalt him. God gave Heman fourteen
sons and three daughters.)

6 All these men were under the supervision of their father for the music of the
temple of the LORD, with cymbals, lyres and harps, for the ministry at the house
of God.
Asaph, Jeduthun and Heman were under the supervision of the king. 7 Along
with their relatives — all of them trained and skilled in music for the LORD —
they numbered 288. 8 Young and old alike, teacher as well as student, cast lots
for their duties.

9 The first lot, which was for Asaph, fell to Joseph,
his sons and relatives[a] 12[b]
the second to Gedaliah,
him and his relatives and sons 12
10 the third to Zakkur,
his sons and relatives 12
11 the fourth to Izri,[c]
his sons and relatives 12
12 the fifth to Nethaniah,
his sons and relatives 12
13 the sixth to Bukkiah,
his sons and relatives 12
14 the seventh to Jesarelah,[d]
his sons and relatives 12
15 the eighth to Jeshaiah,
his sons and relatives 12
16 the ninth to Mattaniah,
his sons and relatives 12
17 the tenth to Shimei,
his sons and relatives 12
18 the eleventh to Azarel,[e]
his sons and relatives 12
19 the twelfth to Hashabiah,
his sons and relatives 12
20 the thirteenth to Shubael,
his sons and relatives 12
21 the fourteenth to Mattithiah,
his sons and relatives 12
22 the fifteenth to Jerimoth,
his sons and relatives 12
23 the sixteenth to Hananiah,
his sons and relatives 12
24 the seventeenth to Joshbekashah,
his sons and relatives 12
25 the eighteenth to Hanani,
his sons and relatives 12
26 the nineteenth to Mallothi,
his sons and relatives 12
27 the twentieth to Eliathah,
his sons and relatives 12

[a] *9* See Septuagint; Hebrew does not have *his sons and relatives.* [b] *9* See the total in verse 7; Hebrew does not have *twelve.* [c] *11* A variant of *Zeri* [d] *14* A variant of *Asarelah* [e] *18* A variant of *Uzziel*

[28] the twenty-first to Hothir,
his sons and relatives 12
[29] the twenty-second to Giddalti,
his sons and relatives 12
[30] the twenty-third to Mahazioth,
his sons and relatives 12
[31] the twenty-fourth to Romamti-Ezer,
his sons and relatives 12.

The Gatekeepers

26 The divisions of the gatekeepers:

From the Korahites: Meshelemiah son of Kore, one of the sons of Asaph.
[2] Meshelemiah had sons:
Zechariah the firstborn,
Jediael the second,
Zebadiah the third,
Jathniel the fourth,
[3] Elam the fifth,
Jehohanan the sixth
and Eliehoenai the seventh.
[4] Obed-Edom also had sons:
Shemaiah the firstborn,
Jehozabad the second,
Joah the third,
Sakar the fourth,
Nethanel the fifth,
[5] Ammiel the sixth,
Issachar the seventh
and Peullethai the eighth.
(For God had blessed Obed-Edom.)

[6] Obed-Edom's son Shemaiah also had sons, who were leaders in their
father's family because they were very capable men. [7] The sons of Shemaiah: Othni, Rephael, Obed and Elzabad; his relatives Elihu and Sem-
akiah were also able men. [8] All these were descendants of Obed-Edom;
they and their sons and their relatives were capable men with the
strength to do the work — descendants of Obed-Edom, 62 in all.
[9] Meshelemiah had sons and relatives, who were able men — 18 in all.

[10] Hosah the Merarite had sons: Shimri the first (although he was not the
firstborn, his father had appointed him the first), [11] Hilkiah the second,
Tabaliah the third and Zechariah the fourth. The sons and relatives of
Hosah were 13 in all.

[12] These divisions of the gatekeepers, through their leaders, had duties for
ministering in the temple of the LORD, just as their relatives had. [13] Lots were
cast for each gate, according to their families, young and old alike.
[14] The lot for the East Gate fell to Shelemiah.[a] Then lots were cast for his son
Zechariah, a wise counselor, and the lot for the North Gate fell to him. [15] The lot
for the South Gate fell to Obed-Edom, and the lot for the storehouse fell to his
sons. [16] The lots for the West Gate and the Shalleketh Gate on the upper road fell
to Shuppim and Hosah.

Guard was alongside of guard: [17] There were six Levites a day on the east, four a
day on the north, four a day on the south and two at a time at the storehouse. [18] As
for the court[b] to the west, there were four at the road and two at the court[b] itself.
[19] These were the divisions of the gatekeepers who were descendants of Korah
and Merari.

---

[a] *14* A variant of *Meshelemiah* [b] *18* The meaning of the Hebrew for this word is uncertain.

The Treasurers and Other Officials

20 Their fellow Levites were[a] in charge of the treasuries of the house of God
and the treasuries for the dedicated things.
21 The descendants of Ladan, who were Gershonites through Ladan and who
were heads of families belonging to Ladan the Gershonite, were Jehieli, 22 the
sons of Jehieli, Zetham and his brother Joel. They were in charge of the treasuries of the temple of the LORD.
23 From the Amramites, the Izharites, the Hebronites and the Uzzielites:

24 Shubael, a descendant of Gershom son of Moses, was the official in charge
of the treasuries. 25 His relatives through Eliezer: Rehabiah his son,
Jeshaiah his son, Joram his son, Zikri his son and Shelomith his son.
26 Shelomith and his relatives were in charge of all the treasuries for the
things dedicated by King David, by the heads of families who were
the commanders of thousands and commanders of hundreds, and by
the other army commanders. 27 Some of the plunder taken in battle they
dedicated for the repair of the temple of the LORD. 28 And everything
dedicated by Samuel the seer and by Saul son of Kish, Abner son of Ner
and Joab son of Zeruiah, and all the other dedicated things were in the
care of Shelomith and his relatives.
29 From the Izharites: Kenaniah and his sons were assigned duties away from
the temple, as officials and judges over Israel.
30 From the Hebronites: Hashabiah and his relatives — seventeen hundred
able men — were responsible in Israel west of the Jordan for all the work
of the LORD and for the king's service. 31 As for the Hebronites, Jeriah
was their chief according to the genealogical records of their families.
In the fortieth year of David's reign a search was made in the records,
and capable men among the Hebronites were found at Jazer in Gilead.
32 Jeriah had twenty-seven hundred relatives, who were able men and
heads of families, and King David put them in charge of the Reubenites,
the Gadites and the half-tribe of Manasseh for every matter pertaining
to God and for the affairs of the king.

Army Divisions

27 This is the list of the Israelites — heads of families, commanders of thousands and commanders of hundreds, and their officers, who served the
king in all that concerned the army divisions that were on duty month by month
throughout the year. Each division consisted of 24,000 men.

2 In charge of the first division, for the first month, was Jashobeam son of Zabdiel. There were 24,000 men in his division. 3 He was a descendant of Perez
and chief of all the army officers for the first month.
4 In charge of the division for the second month was Dodai the Ahohite; Mikloth was the leader of his division. There were 24,000 men in his division.
5 The third army commander, for the third month, was Benaiah son of Jehoiada
the priest. He was chief and there were 24,000 men in his division. 6 This
was the Benaiah who was a mighty warrior among the Thirty and was over
the Thirty. His son Ammizabad was in charge of his division.
7 The fourth, for the fourth month, was Asahel the brother of Joab; his son Zebadiah was his successor. There were 24,000 men in his division.
8 The fifth, for the fifth month, was the commander Shamhuth the Izrahite.
There were 24,000 men in his division.
9 The sixth, for the sixth month, was Ira the son of Ikkesh the Tekoite. There
were 24,000 men in his division.
10 The seventh, for the seventh month, was Helez the Pelonite, an Ephraimite.
There were 24,000 men in his division.

[a] 20 Septuagint; Hebrew *As for the Levites, Ahijah was*

1 CHRONICLES 26:20 – 32

DEDICATED TO THE LORD

The Levites in charge of the treasury were responsible for receiving, storing and protecting the people's offerings and the plunder accumulated from war victories. Over time, the storehouse acquired large amounts of gold, silver and other valuables. When civil war broke out between Israel and Judah, the kingdom was divided. Eventually both Israel and Judah were overthrown by other nations, the storehouse was destroyed and objects of worship were hauled off by foreigners.

In what has been called Jesus' Sermon on the Mount, Jesus taught people the ultimate value of storing up treasures in heaven — such spiritual treasures cannot be stolen or ruined (Mt 6:19 – 21). All material things treasured by this world will one day meet destruction. But the love God's people show in Christ's name and the works they do to serve his kingdom will endure forever. Those who labor for the Lord will someday receive an eternal reward from him (Col 3:23 – 24).

11 The eighth, for the eighth month, was Sibbekai the Hushathite, a Zerahite. There were 24,000 men in his division.
12 The ninth, for the ninth month, was Abiezer the Anathothite, a Benjamite. There were 24,000 men in his division.
13 The tenth, for the tenth month, was Maharai the Netophathite, a Zerahite. There were 24,000 men in his division.
14 The eleventh, for the eleventh month, was Benaiah the Pirathonite, an Ephraimite. There were 24,000 men in his division.
15 The twelfth, for the twelfth month, was Heldai the Netophathite, from the family of Othniel. There were 24,000 men in his division.

Leaders of the Tribes

16 The leaders of the tribes of Israel:
over the Reubenites: Eliezer son of Zikri;
over the Simeonites: Shephatiah son of Maakah;
17 over Levi: Hashabiah son of Kemuel;
over Aaron: Zadok;
18 over Judah: Elihu, a brother of David;
over Issachar: Omri son of Michael;
19 over Zebulun: Ishmaiah son of Obadiah;
over Naphtali: Jerimoth son of Azriel;
20 over the Ephraimites: Hoshea son of Azaziah;
over half the tribe of Manasseh: Joel son of Pedaiah;
21 over the half-tribe of Manasseh in Gilead: Iddo son of Zechariah;
over Benjamin: Jaasiel son of Abner;
22 over Dan: Azarel son of Jeroham.
These were the leaders of the tribes of Israel.

23 David did not take the number of the men twenty years old or less, because
the LORD had promised to make Israel as numerous as the stars in the sky. 24 Joab
son of Zeruiah began to count the men but did not finish. God's wrath came on
Israel on account of this numbering, and the number was not entered in the
book[a] of the annals of King David.

The King's Overseers

25 Azmaveth son of Adiel was in charge of the royal storehouses.
Jonathan son of Uzziah was in charge of the storehouses in the outlying districts, in the towns, the villages and the watchtowers.
26 Ezri son of Kelub was in charge of the workers who farmed the land.
27 Shimei the Ramathite was in charge of the vineyards.
Zabdi the Shiphmite was in charge of the produce of the vineyards for the wine vats.
28 Baal-Hanan the Gederite was in charge of the olive and sycamore-fig trees in the western foothills.
Joash was in charge of the supplies of olive oil.
29 Shitrai the Sharonite was in charge of the herds grazing in Sharon.
Shaphat son of Adlai was in charge of the herds in the valleys.
30 Obil the Ishmaelite was in charge of the camels.
Jehdeiah the Meronothite was in charge of the donkeys.
31 Jaziz the Hagrite was in charge of the flocks.
All these were the officials in charge of King David's property.

32 Jonathan, David's uncle, was a counselor, a man of insight and a scribe. Jehiel son of Hakmoni took care of the king's sons.
33 Ahithophel was the king's counselor.

[a] 24 Septuagint; Hebrew *number*

Hushai the Arkite was the king's confidant. 34Ahithophel was succeeded by Jehoiada son of Benaiah and by Abiathar.

Joab was the commander of the royal army.

David's Plans for the Temple

28 David summoned all the officials of Israel to assemble at Jerusalem: the officers over the tribes, the commanders of the divisions in the service of the king, the commanders of thousands and commanders of hundreds, and the officials in charge of all the property and livestock belonging to the king and his sons, together with the palace officials, the warriors and all the brave fighting men.

2King David rose to his feet and said: "Listen to me, my fellow Israelites, my people. I had it in my heart to build a house as a place of rest for the ark of the covenant of the LORD, for the footstool of our God, and I made plans to build it. 3But God said to me, 'You are not to build a house for my Name, because you are a warrior and have shed blood.'

4"Yet the LORD, the God of Israel, chose me from my whole family to be king over Israel forever. He chose Judah as leader, and from the tribe of Judah he chose my family, and from my father's sons he was pleased to make me king over all Israel. 5Of all my sons — and the LORD has given me many — he has chosen my son Solomon to sit on the throne of the kingdom of the LORD over Israel. 6He said to me: 'Solomon your son is the one who will build my house and my courts, for I have chosen him to be my son, and I will be his father. 7I will establish his kingdom forever if he is unswerving in carrying out my commands and laws, as is being done at this time.'

8"So now I charge you in the sight of all Israel and of the assembly of the LORD, and in the hearing of our God: Be careful to follow all the commands of the LORD your God, that you may possess this good land and pass it on as an inheritance to your descendants forever.

9"And you, my son Solomon, acknowledge the God of your father, and serve him with wholehearted devotion and with a willing mind, for the LORD searches every heart and understands every desire and every thought. If you seek him, he will be found by you; but if you forsake him, he will reject you forever. 10Consider now, for the LORD has chosen you to build a house as the sanctuary. Be strong and do the work."

11Then David gave his son Solomon the plans for the portico of the temple, its buildings, its storerooms, its upper parts, its inner rooms and the place of atonement. 12He gave him the plans of all that the Spirit had put in his mind for the courts of the temple of the LORD and all the surrounding rooms, for the treasuries of the temple of God and for the treasuries for the dedicated things. 13He gave him instructions for the divisions of the priests and Levites, and for all the work of serving in the temple of the LORD, as well as for all the articles to be used in its service. 14He designated the weight of gold for all the gold articles to be used in various kinds of service, and the weight of silver for all the silver articles to be used in various kinds of service: 15the weight of gold for the gold lampstands and their lamps, with the weight for each lampstand and its lamps; and the weight of silver for each silver lampstand and its lamps, according to the use of each lampstand; 16the weight of gold for each table for consecrated bread; the weight of silver for the silver tables; 17the weight of pure gold for the forks, sprinkling bowls and pitchers; the weight of gold for each gold dish; the weight of silver for each silver dish; 18and the weight of the refined gold for the altar of incense. He also gave him the plan for the chariot, that is, the cherubim of gold that spread their wings and overshadow the ark of the covenant of the LORD.

19"All this," David said, "I have in writing as a result of the LORD's hand on me, and he enabled me to understand all the details of the plan."

20David also said to Solomon his son, "Be strong and courageous, and do the work. Do not be afraid or discouraged, for the LORD God, my God, is with you.

---

1 CHRONICLES 28:2

GOD'S FOOTSTOOL

David realized that a mere building could never house the eternal, all-powerful God of the universe. He planned to construct the temple as the Lord's footstool — a metaphor describing the earthly base of activity for God, who sits enthroned in heaven, high above all things. Elsewhere in Scripture, the whole earth is depicted as God's footstool (Isa 66:1). No physical place of worship — even Solomon's temple — could capture the grandeur and glory of God. He cannot be contained (Ac 7:48 – 50).

In kindness to the people of the earth, God sent Jesus to disclose his character and power (Jn 1:18). God came down to us from on high — to dwell in hearts, not religious buildings (Eph 3:16 – 17). God's people do not need to go into a church to be with God — he is Spirit, simultaneously inhabiting all places. Jesus, in whom the fullness of God dwells, is ever-present in the life of the believer (Col 1:19 – 27).

He will not fail you or forsake you until all the work for the service of the temple of the LORD is finished. 21The divisions of the priests and Levites are ready for all the work on the temple of God, and every willing person skilled in any craft will help you in all the work. The officials and all the people will obey your every command."

Gifts for Building the Temple

29 Then King David said to the whole assembly: "My son Solomon, the one whom God has chosen, is young and inexperienced. The task is great, because this palatial structure is not for man but for the LORD God. 2With all my resources I have provided for the temple of my God — gold for the gold work, silver for the silver, bronze for the bronze, iron for the iron and wood for the wood, as well as onyx for the settings, turquoise,[a] stones of various colors, and all kinds of fine stone and marble — all of these in large quantities. 3Besides, in my devotion to the temple of my God I now give my personal treasures of gold and silver for the temple of my God, over and above everything I have provided for this holy temple: 4three thousand talents[b] of gold (gold of Ophir) and seven thousand talents[c] of refined silver, for the overlaying of the walls of the buildings, 5for the gold work and the silver work, and for all the work to be done by the craftsmen. Now, who is willing to consecrate themselves to the LORD today?"

6Then the leaders of families, the officers of the tribes of Israel, the commanders of thousands and commanders of hundreds, and the officials in charge of the king's work gave willingly. 7They gave toward the work on the temple of God five thousand talents[d] and ten thousand darics[e] of gold, ten thousand talents[f] of silver, eighteen thousand talents[g] of bronze and a hundred thousand talents[h] of iron. 8Anyone who had precious stones gave them to the treasury of the temple of the LORD in the custody of Jehiel the Gershonite. 9The people rejoiced at the willing response of their leaders, for they had given freely and wholeheartedly to the LORD. David the king also rejoiced greatly.

David's Prayer

10David praised the LORD in the presence of the whole assembly, saying,

"Praise be to you, LORD,
the God of our father Israel,
from everlasting to everlasting.
11 Yours, LORD, is the greatness and the power
and the glory and the majesty and the splendor,
for everything in heaven and earth is yours.
Yours, LORD, is the kingdom;
you are exalted as head over all.
12 Wealth and honor come from you;
you are the ruler of all things.
In your hands are strength and power
to exalt and give strength to all.
13 Now, our God, we give you thanks,
and praise your glorious name.

14"But who am I, and who are my people, that we should be able to give as generously as this? Everything comes from you, and we have given you only what comes from your hand. 15We are foreigners and strangers in your sight, as were all our ancestors. Our days on earth are like a shadow, without hope. 16LORD our God, all this abundance that we have provided for building you a temple for

[a] 2 The meaning of the Hebrew for this word is uncertain. [b] 4 That is, about 110 tons or about 100 metric tons [c] 4 That is, about 260 tons or about 235 metric tons [d] 7 That is, about 190 tons or about 170 metric tons [e] 7 That is, about 185 pounds or about 84 kilograms [f] 7 That is, about 380 tons or about 340 metric tons [g] 7 That is, about 675 tons or about 610 metric tons [h] 7 That is, about 3,800 tons or about 3,400 metric tons

THE QUEST FOR TRUE WORSHIP

Worship can be thought of as affection, attention, obedience, awe or credit given to God — inwardly or outwardly — in recognition of his worth or works. This practice has always been central to the people of God. When King David neared death, he called the Israelites together and reminded them of the implications of their status as God's people. They were a people formed around a specific purpose: praising the Lord (1Ch 29:10 – 20). What does it really mean to worship God?

Worship is first and foremost a response. When God's people glimpse the majesty and beauty of God's supreme worth, they do not pause to calculate whether the lyrics or melody fit the sight — they just respond. True worship bursts from a heart that has seen the Lord (Isa 6:1 – 5). He is surrounded by praise at all times. The creatures surrounding him react and respond to his glory — the radiance of his collective perfections — and they never stop speaking praise (Rev 4:8 – 11). Of all the people and things that humans treasure, God is infinitely greater and infinitely more satisfying. He is the ultimate object of awe.

Worship involves much more than music — it includes how God's people live every day. Recognizing God's glorious nature has an impact on the choices made. God desires a lifestyle of worship integrity — a *wholeness,* a seamless quality between what his people profess to believe and the way they live (1Ch 29:17). Obedience is the fruit of true worship. God's people attend church services on Sundays and sing with enthusiasm and intensity. Yet it is Monday that will prove whether or not it was worship. If the end of the songs on Sunday marks the end of their worship, something is wrong. In the New Testament, Paul reminded the church in Rome that offering their very bodies to the service of Jesus constituted their spiritual service of worship (Ro 12:1 – 2).

True worship expresses gratitude for God's provisions and works. Who is faithful like God? His kindness can be seen in the memory of last year, last month and last night. He is good to his people! He gives breath today. He provided for every need in the past. He answered prayers. For his name's sake and for the good of his people, he has unlocked, opened, diverted, thwarted, arranged, rearranged and removed — all as blessings to his beloved daughters and sons. "Sing the praises of the LORD, you his faithful people; praise his holy name" (Ps 30:4).

your Holy Name comes from your hand, and all of it belongs to you. [17]I know, my God, that you test the heart and are pleased with integrity. All these things I have given willingly and with honest intent. And now I have seen with joy how willingly your people who are here have given to you. [18]LORD, the God of our fathers Abraham, Isaac and Israel, keep these desires and thoughts in the hearts of your people forever, and keep their hearts loyal to you. [19]And give my son Solomon the wholehearted devotion to keep your commands, statutes and decrees and to do everything to build the palatial structure for which I have provided."

[20]Then David said to the whole assembly, "Praise the LORD your God." So they all praised the LORD, the God of their fathers; they bowed down, prostrating themselves before the LORD and the king.

Solomon Acknowledged as King

[21]The next day they made sacrifices to the LORD and presented burnt offerings to him: a thousand bulls, a thousand rams and a thousand male lambs, together with their drink offerings, and other sacrifices in abundance for all Israel. [22]They ate and drank with great joy in the presence of the LORD that day.

Then they acknowledged Solomon son of David as king a second time, anointing him before the LORD to be ruler and Zadok to be priest. [23]So Solomon sat on the throne of the LORD as king in place of his father David. He prospered and all Israel obeyed him. [24]All the officers and warriors, as well as all of King David's sons, pledged their submission to King Solomon.

[25]The LORD highly exalted Solomon in the sight of all Israel and bestowed on him royal splendor such as no king over Israel ever had before.

The Death of David

[26]David son of Jesse was king over all Israel. [27]He ruled over Israel forty years — seven in Hebron and thirty-three in Jerusalem. [28]He died at a good old age, having enjoyed long life, wealth and honor. His son Solomon succeeded him as king.

[29]As for the events of King David's reign, from beginning to end, they are written in the records of Samuel the seer, the records of Nathan the prophet and the records of Gad the seer, [30]together with the details of his reign and power, and the circumstances that surrounded him and Israel and the kingdoms of all the other lands.

JESUS: OUR TRUE WORSHIP

2 CHRONICLES

2 CHRONICLES

SOLOMON BEGINS TEMPLE CONSTRUCTION *c. 966 BC*	ISRAEL DIVIDED *c. 930 BC*	FALL OF JUDAH *c. 586 BC*

The book of 2 Chronicles follows the pattern established in 1 Chronicles. The author wrote to remind a people in need of encouragement that God had not revoked his promises or forgotten his people. Even though the Israelites had demonstrated their consistent inability to remain faithful, God would do what he had always done — show himself faithful to his gracious promises to his people.

The storied history of the nations of Israel and Judah demonstrates the remarkable power of God's grace to redeem a sinful people. Second Chronicles traces the theme of redemption from David's death (at the end of 1 Chronicles) through the reign of his son Solomon and his successors. Though rulers would come and go, the focus of the book is on how God's actions are consistent with his promises to King David.

Solomon fulfilled David's longing to build a temple for the worship of God. Second Chronicles describes the construction of the temple and the worship that it facilitated for the nation.

This book focuses nearly all of its attention on Judah's history rather than on Israel's. Since the nation divided into two kingdoms, Judah had inherited the promises of the Davidic kingdom. Though David's successors who led Judah ruled only a portion of the overall nation, God remained faithful to his promises to this small remnant. Judah became the core population through which God would accomplish his work of redemption and send the Messiah.

David commissioned and gathered materials so that Solomon could build the temple as God's dwelling place among his people (1Ch 22:5 – 13). Since the first sin in the garden, humanity had been incapable of coming into the presence of a holy God. God, in his grace, provided a way for the people to approach him in the tabernacle and the temple through the sacrificial system. Solomon himself recognized that this temple was incapable of containing God (2Ch 6:18). While God would humble himself to meet with the people in the temple, there was a resounding need for a far greater dwelling of God among his people.

Jesus' incarnation did what the temple could never do — it invaded the cosmos with the dwelling of God in human form. Jesus came as Immanuel, "God with us" (Mt 1:23), and lived among fallen humanity in a sin-darkened world (Jn 1:1 – 14). Jesus likened his body to the temple, showing that, while it would be destroyed on the cross, God would rebuild it again through his glorious resurrection (Jn 2:19). Ultimately, in God's eternal kingdom, there will be no need for the temple because the presence of God will pervade the new Jerusalem and his worship will fill the Holy City once more (Rev 21:22).

THE TRUMPETERS AND MUSICIANS JOINED IN UNISON TO GIVE PRAISE AND THANKS TO THE LORD. ACCOMPANIED BY TRUMPETS, CYMBALS AND OTHER INSTRUMENTS, THE SINGERS RAISED THEIR VOICES IN PRAISE TO THE LORD AND SANG: "HE IS GOOD; HIS LOVE ENDURES FOREVER" THEN THE TEMPLE OF THE LORD WAS FILLED WITH THE CLOUD.

2 Chronicles 5:13

2 CHRONICLES

Solomon Asks for Wisdom

1 Solomon son of David established himself firmly over his kingdom, for the
LORD his God was with him and made him exceedingly great.
[2]Then Solomon spoke to all Israel — to the commanders of thousands and
commanders of hundreds, to the judges and to all the leaders in Israel, the heads
of families — [3]and Solomon and the whole assembly went to the high place at
Gibeon, for God's tent of meeting was there, which Moses the LORD's servant had
made in the wilderness. [4]Now David had brought up the ark of God from Kiriath
Jearim to the place he had prepared for it, because he had pitched a tent for it in
Jerusalem. [5]But the bronze altar that Bezalel son of Uri, the son of Hur, had made
was in Gibeon in front of the tabernacle of the LORD; so Solomon and the assembly inquired of him there. [6]Solomon went up to the bronze altar before the LORD
in the tent of meeting and offered a thousand burnt offerings on it.
[7]That night God appeared to Solomon and said to him, "Ask for whatever you
want me to give you."
[8]Solomon answered God, "You have shown great kindness to David my father
and have made me king in his place. [9]Now, LORD God, let your promise to my
father David be confirmed, for you have made me king over a people who are as
numerous as the dust of the earth. [10]Give me wisdom and knowledge, that I may
lead this people, for who is able to govern this great people of yours?"
[11]God said to Solomon, "Since this is your heart's desire and you have not
asked for wealth, possessions or honor, nor for the death of your enemies, and
since you have not asked for a long life but for wisdom and knowledge to govern
my people over whom I have made you king, [12]therefore wisdom and knowledge
will be given you. And I will also give you wealth, possessions and honor, such as
no king who was before you ever had and none after you will have."
[13]Then Solomon went to Jerusalem from the high place at Gibeon, from before
the tent of meeting. And he reigned over Israel.
[14]Solomon accumulated chariots and horses; he had fourteen hundred chariots and twelve thousand horses,[a] which he kept in the chariot cities and also
with him in Jerusalem. [15]The king made silver and gold as common in Jerusalem
as stones, and cedar as plentiful as sycamore-fig trees in the foothills. [16]Solo-
mon's horses were imported from Egypt and from Kue[b] — the royal merchants
purchased them from Kue at the current price. [17]They imported a chariot from
Egypt for six hundred shekels[c] of silver, and a horse for a hundred and fifty.[d]
They also exported them to all the kings of the Hittites and of the Arameans.

Preparations for Building the Temple

2[e] Solomon gave orders to build a temple for the Name of the LORD and a royal
palace for himself. [2]He conscripted 70,000 men as carriers and 80,000 as
stonecutters in the hills and 3,600 as foremen over them.
[3]Solomon sent this message to Hiram[f] king of Tyre:

"Send me cedar logs as you did for my father David when you sent him
cedar to build a palace to live in. [4]Now I am about to build a temple for the
Name of the LORD my God and to dedicate it to him for burning fragrant
incense before him, for setting out the consecrated bread regularly, and for

[a] 14 Or *charioteers* [b] 16 Probably Cilicia [c] 17 That is, about 15 pounds or about 6.9 kilograms [d] 17 That is, about 3 3/4 pounds or about 1.7 kilograms [e] In Hebrew texts 2:1 is numbered 1:18, and 2:2-18 is numbered 2:1-17. [f] 3 Hebrew *Huram,* a variant of *Hiram;* also in verses 11 and 12

---

2 CHRONICLES 1:7 – 12

ONE GREATER THAN SOLOMON

Solomon was exalted to the throne of Israel in Jerusalem, and that night God appeared and said to him, "Ask for whatever you want me to give you." Solomon knew the promise to David his father — that he would never fail to have a son on the throne of Israel (cf. 2Sa 7:4 – 16). But Solomon also recognized that God had fulfilled his promise to Abraham by making the nation "as numerous as the dust of the earth" (2Ch 1:9; cf. Ge 13:16). Therefore, in order for Solomon to rule well over such a great people, he requested wisdom and knowledge from God to govern the people (2Ch 1:10). God granted Solomon's request.

While Solomon started his reign well, ruling in wisdom, his reign ended in colossal failure (1Ki 11:1 – 13). Israel needed a truly wise king who not only understood the wisdom that Solomon laid out in the Proverbs but who lived in accord with that wisdom to the end. Isaiah 11:1 – 3 promised such a king, and the New Testament revealed that this promise was fulfilled in Jesus. He is the Son of David who "grew in wisdom and stature, and in favor with God and man" (Lk 2:52). And he is the one who is "greater than Solomon" (Mt 12:42).

THE PURPOSE OF THE CHRONICLER

The purpose of those who recorded the books of 1 and 2 Chronicles was different from the purpose of the author of 1 and 2 Kings. The author of 1 and 2 Kings arranged the historical material in those books for the purpose of showing Israel why they had been carried off into exile. The books of Kings were an indictment on Israel for their sin and their breach of the covenant with the Lord. On the other hand, the historical material in the books of Chronicles was arranged with the purpose of showing Israel that God would keep his promises to David. Of all the historical material which could have been included in these books, the writer selected and arranged historical episodes that reaffirmed particular promises: a descendant of David would ultimately reign on the throne forever and a new temple would be built.

So, the author of Kings had an essentially pessimistic purpose while the author of Chronicles had an optimistic purpose. Therefore, Chronicles passes over certain negative events from that time period. It passes over David's sin with Bathsheba and Solomon's sin with his foreign wives. The purpose was not to produce a revisionist history but rather to assure the returned remnant after the Babylonian exile that God would fulfill his promises to David. Chronicles revealed to them that despite the fact that David and all of his sons failed in the past, God would remain merciful and faithful to his promises that a Messiah — specifically a descendant of David — would come to establish an eternal kingdom on earth. These promises would ultimately be fulfilled in Jesus of Nazareth. He is the Son of David who received the promises made to his ancestor. That is why Paul preached, "God raised him from the dead so that he will never be subject to decay. As God has said, 'I will give you the holy and sure blessings promised to David.' So it is also stated elsewhere: 'You will not let your holy one see decay.' Now when David had served God's purpose in his own generation, he fell asleep; he was buried with his ancestors and his body decayed. But the one whom God raised from the dead did not see decay" (Ac 13:34 – 37).

making burnt offerings every morning and evening and on the Sabbaths, at the New Moons and at the appointed festivals of the Lord our God. This is a lasting ordinance for Israel.

5“The temple I am going to build will be great, because our God is greater than all other gods. 6But who is able to build a temple for him, since the heavens, even the highest heavens, cannot contain him? Who then am I to build a temple for him, except as a place to burn sacrifices before him?

7“Send me, therefore, a man skilled to work in gold and silver, bronze and iron, and in purple, crimson and blue yarn, and experienced in the art of engraving, to work in Judah and Jerusalem with my skilled workers, whom my father David provided.

8“Send me also cedar, juniper and algum[a] logs from Lebanon, for I know that your servants are skilled in cutting timber there. My servants will work with yours 9to provide me with plenty of lumber, because the temple I build must be large and magnificent. 10I will give your servants, the woodsmen who cut the timber, twenty thousand cors[b] of ground wheat, twenty thousand cors[c] of barley, twenty thousand baths[d] of wine and twenty thousand baths of olive oil.”

11Hiram king of Tyre replied by letter to Solomon:

“Because the Lord loves his people, he has made you their king.”

12And Hiram added:

“Praise be to the Lord, the God of Israel, who made heaven and earth! He has given King David a wise son, endowed with intelligence and discernment, who will build a temple for the Lord and a palace for himself.

13“I am sending you Huram-Abi, a man of great skill, 14whose mother was from Dan and whose father was from Tyre. He is trained to work in gold and silver, bronze and iron, stone and wood, and with purple and blue and crimson yarn and fine linen. He is experienced in all kinds of engraving and can execute any design given to him. He will work with your skilled workers and with those of my lord, David your father.

15“Now let my lord send his servants the wheat and barley and the olive oil and wine he promised, 16and we will cut all the logs from Lebanon that you need and will float them as rafts by sea down to Joppa. You can then take them up to Jerusalem.”

17Solomon took a census of all the foreigners residing in Israel, after the census his father David had taken; and they were found to be 153,600. 18He assigned 70,000 of them to be carriers and 80,000 to be stonecutters in the hills, with 3,600 foremen over them to keep the people working.

Solomon Builds the Temple

3 Then Solomon began to build the temple of the Lord in Jerusalem on Mount Moriah, where the Lord had appeared to his father David. It was on the threshing floor of Araunah[e] the Jebusite, the place provided by David. 2He began building on the second day of the second month in the fourth year of his reign.

3The foundation Solomon laid for building the temple of God was sixty cubits long and twenty cubits wide[f] (using the cubit of the old standard). 4The portico at the front of the temple was twenty cubits[g] long across the width of the building and twenty[h] cubits high.

He overlaid the inside with pure gold. 5He paneled the main hall with juniper

[a] *8* Probably a variant of *almug* [b] *10* That is, probably about 3,600 tons or about 3,200 metric tons of wheat [c] *10* That is, probably about 3,000 tons or about 2,700 metric tons of barley [d] *10* That is, about 120,000 gallons or about 440,000 liters [e] *1* Hebrew *Ornan,* a variant of *Araunah* [f] *3* That is, about 90 feet long and 30 feet wide or about 27 meters long and 9 meters wide [g] *4* That is, about 30 feet or about 9 meters; also in verses 8, 11 and 13 [h] *4* Some Septuagint and Syriac manuscripts; Hebrew *and a hundred and twenty*

2 CHRONICLES 2:1

JESUS IS THE TRUE TEMPLE

The temple, like the tabernacle, was the place where God lived with his people. The temple was the place where God's people could draw near to worship him. The problem was that it was located in Jerusalem, and many had to travel great distances in order to come before God. The New Testament reveals something far greater. Yes, kings—like Solomon—are the ones who build temples. But, King Jesus built a different kind of temple. He said that the true temple was his body (Jn 2:21). With the coming of that temple, worship is no longer relegated to one place (Jn 4:21–23). People can come near to God wherever they are. Jesus is the true temple because he is God in human flesh, living among his people (Jn 1:14).

Believers can draw near to God through Jesus because he has torn down the curtain in the old temple that separated them from God—a feat he accomplished by means of his death on the cross (Mt 27:51). Additionally, God's people are now the temple of God—the church is Christ's body, and the Spirit of God dwells in them (1Co 3:16–17; Eph 2:19–22). King Jesus is building a temple made of living stones (1Pe 2:5). And someday the true temple will be "the Lord God Almighty and the Lamb" (Rev 21:22). Then, God will forever live among his people with no barriers separating us!

and covered it with fine gold and decorated it with palm tree and chain designs.
[6]He adorned the temple with precious stones. And the gold he used was gold of
Parvaim. [7]He overlaid the ceiling beams, doorframes, walls and doors of the
temple with gold, and he carved cherubim on the walls.
[8]He built the Most Holy Place, its length corresponding to the width of the
temple — twenty cubits long and twenty cubits wide. He overlaid the inside with
six hundred talents[a] of fine gold. [9]The gold nails weighed fifty shekels.[b] He also
overlaid the upper parts with gold.
[10]For the Most Holy Place he made a pair of sculptured cherubim and overlaid them with gold. [11]The total wingspan of the cherubim was twenty cubits.
One wing of the first cherub was five cubits[c] long and touched the temple wall,
while its other wing, also five cubits long, touched the wing of the other cherub.
[12]Similarly one wing of the second cherub was five cubits long and touched the
other temple wall, and its other wing, also five cubits long, touched the wing of
the first cherub. [13]The wings of these cherubim extended twenty cubits. They
stood on their feet, facing the main hall.[d]
[14]He made the curtain of blue, purple and crimson yarn and fine linen, with
cherubim worked into it.
[15]For the front of the temple he made two pillars, which together were thirty-five cubits[e] long, each with a capital five cubits high. [16]He made interwoven
chains[f] and put them on top of the pillars. He also made a hundred pomegranates and attached them to the chains. [17]He erected the pillars in the front of the
temple, one to the south and one to the north. The one to the south he named
Jakin[g] and the one to the north Boaz.[h]

The Temple's Furnishings

4 He made a bronze altar twenty cubits long, twenty cubits wide and ten cubits high.[i] [2]He made the Sea of cast metal, circular in shape, measuring ten
cubits from rim to rim and five cubits[j] high. It took a line of thirty cubits[k] to
measure around it. [3]Below the rim, figures of bulls encircled it — ten to a cubit.[l]
The bulls were cast in two rows in one piece with the Sea.
[4]The Sea stood on twelve bulls, three facing north, three facing west, three
facing south and three facing east. The Sea rested on top of them, and their hindquarters were toward the center. [5]It was a handbreadth[m] in thickness, and its
rim was like the rim of a cup, like a lily blossom. It held three thousand baths.[n]
[6]He then made ten basins for washing and placed five on the south side and
five on the north. In them the things to be used for the burnt offerings were
rinsed, but the Sea was to be used by the priests for washing.
[7]He made ten gold lampstands according to the specifications for them and
placed them in the temple, five on the south side and five on the north.
[8]He made ten tables and placed them in the temple, five on the south side and
five on the north. He also made a hundred gold sprinkling bowls.
[9]He made the courtyard of the priests, and the large court and the doors for
the court, and overlaid the doors with bronze. [10]He placed the Sea on the south
side, at the southeast corner.
[11]And Huram also made the pots and shovels and sprinkling bowls.
So Huram finished the work he had undertaken for King Solomon in the temple of God:

[a] *8* That is, about 23 tons or about 21 metric tons [b] *9* That is, about 1 1/4 pounds or about 575 grams [c] *11* That is, about 7 1/2 feet or about 2.3 meters; also in verse 15 [d] *13* Or *facing inward* [e] *15* That is, about 53 feet or about 16 meters [f] *16* Or possibly *made chains in the inner sanctuary*; the meaning of the Hebrew for this phrase is uncertain. [g] *17* *Jakin* probably means *he establishes.* [h] *17* *Boaz* probably means *in him is strength.* [i] *1* That is, about 30 feet long and wide and 15 feet high or about 9 meters long and wide and 4.5 meters high [j] *2* That is, about 7 1/2 feet or about 2.3 meters [k] *2* That is, about 45 feet or about 14 meters [l] *3* That is, about 18 inches or about 45 centimeters [m] *5* That is, about 3 inches or about 7.5 centimeters [n] *5* That is, about 18,000 gallons or about 66,000 liters

2 CHRONICLES 3:1

THE SUBSTITUTE SACRIFICE

Solomon built the temple in Jerusalem on Mount Moriah, a location that had great significance for the people of Israel. God had commanded Abraham to take his son Isaac to Mount Moriah and sacrifice him there (Ge 22:2). Abraham trusted and obeyed God — reasoning that God could raise Isaac from the dead (Heb 11:19). However, God provided a substitute for Isaac, Abraham's only son of the promise. Instead of Isaac, Abraham sacrificed the ram that was caught by its horns in a nearby thicket (Ge 22:13). Solomon built the temple on the same spot, and in the temple animals were offered up as sacrifices in the place of the people to bring forgiveness for their sins. God graciously poured out his judgment on the substitute instead of the sinner.

Years later, God would offer up the ultimate sacrifice — his only Son whom he loved. Jesus is the Lamb of God who takes away the sin of the world (Jn 1:29). Jesus is the sacrifice who took humanity's place on the cross. The story of Isaac and the location of the temple point forward to the offering of God's one and only Son who offers eternal life (Jn 3:16).

ACCESS TO GOD

The Most Holy Place was the inner room of the temple where God dwelled among his people. A veil separated the inner room from mankind, and sinful humanity could not approach a holy God in that inner room without dying. Only the high priest could enter the room without dying, and only once a year under very special conditions on the Day of Atonement. The veil covering the entrance to the Most Holy Place had cherubim woven into it, recalling the events of Genesis 3. When Adam and Eve sinned against God, they were exiled east of the garden so that they could not eat from the tree of life and live forever in their sinful state. Cherubim were placed outside the garden with a flaming sword to keep people out. The Most Holy Place was like a new Garden of Eden — a place of communion with God with an entrance symbolically blocked by cherubim. When the high priest entered the Most Holy Place once a year, it was like a brief return to Paradise, made temporarily possible through a blood sacrifice (Heb 9:7). An animal died so that the priest did not.

When Jesus breathed his last breath on the cross, the veil in the temple was torn in two from top to bottom (Mt 27:51). Jesus' death reopened humankind's access to God. People are no longer separated from him because of their sin. They can be reconciled to God and live with him forever by virtue of Christ's death on the cross. They can now come boldly into his presence in worship. As Scripture says, "Since we have confidence to enter the Most Holy Place by the blood of Jesus, by a new and living way opened for us through the curtain, that is, his body, and since we have a great priest over the house of God, let us draw near to God with a sincere heart and with the full assurance that faith brings" (Heb 10:19 – 22). Better yet, Christ's work of reconciliation not only creates fellowship with God now, but grants believers the hope of heaven, where God will live in perfect, unbroken communion with his people forever (Rev 21:3).

[12]the two pillars;
the two bowl-shaped capitals on top of the pillars;
the two sets of network decorating the two bowl-shaped capitals on top of the pillars;
[13]the four hundred pomegranates for the two sets of network (two rows of pomegranates for each network, decorating the bowl-shaped capitals on top of the pillars);
[14]the stands with their basins;
[15]the Sea and the twelve bulls under it;
[16]the pots, shovels, meat forks and all related articles.

All the objects that Huram-Abi made for King Solomon for the temple of the
LORD were of polished bronze. [17]The king had them cast in clay molds in the
plain of the Jordan between Sukkoth and Zarethan.[a] [18]All these things that Solomon made amounted to so much that the weight of the bronze could not be calculated.

[19]Solomon also made all the furnishings that were in God's temple:
the golden altar;
the tables on which was the bread of the Presence;
[20]the lampstands of pure gold with their lamps, to burn in front of the inner sanctuary as prescribed;
[21]the gold floral work and lamps and tongs (they were solid gold);
[22]the pure gold wick trimmers, sprinkling bowls, dishes and censers; and the gold doors of the temple: the inner doors to the Most Holy Place and the doors of the main hall.

5 When all the work Solomon had done for the temple of the LORD was finished, he brought in the things his father David had dedicated — the silver
and gold and all the furnishings — and he placed them in the treasuries of God's temple.

The Ark Brought to the Temple

[2]Then Solomon summoned to Jerusalem the elders of Israel, all the heads of
the tribes and the chiefs of the Israelite families, to bring up the ark of the LORD's
covenant from Zion, the City of David. [3]And all the Israelites came together to
the king at the time of the festival in the seventh month.
[4]When all the elders of Israel had arrived, the Levites took up the ark, [5]and
they brought up the ark and the tent of meeting and all the sacred furnishings in
it. The Levitical priests carried them up; [6]and King Solomon and the entire assembly of Israel that had gathered about him were before the ark, sacrificing so
many sheep and cattle that they could not be recorded or counted.
[7]The priests then brought the ark of the LORD's covenant to its place in the
inner sanctuary of the temple, the Most Holy Place, and put it beneath the
wings of the cherubim. [8]The cherubim spread their wings over the place of
the ark and covered the ark and its carrying poles. [9]These poles were so long
that their ends, extending from the ark, could be seen from in front of the inner
sanctuary, but not from outside the Holy Place; and they are still there today.
[10]There was nothing in the ark except the two tablets that Moses had placed
in it at Horeb, where the LORD made a covenant with the Israelites after they came out of Egypt.
[11]The priests then withdrew from the Holy Place. All the priests who were
there had consecrated themselves, regardless of their divisions. [12]All the Levites
who were musicians — Asaph, Heman, Jeduthun and their sons and relatives —
stood on the east side of the altar, dressed in fine linen and playing cymbals,
harps and lyres. They were accompanied by 120 priests sounding trumpets.
[13]The trumpeters and musicians joined in unison to give praise and thanks to

[a] 17 Hebrew *Zeredatha,* a variant of *Zarethan*

2 CHRONICLES 5:2 – 10

GOD LIVES WITH HIS PEOPLE

Once the temple was finished, Solomon had the ark of the covenant brought in and placed in the Most Holy Place. The ark symbolized the presence of God, and its position in the Most Holy Place represented the fact that God lived among his people.

The ark was only temporary though, because God's intention from the beginning was to eventually live among his people as one of them. God took on human flesh in the incarnation of Jesus Christ and "made his dwelling among us" (Jn 1:14). In fact, all of history is leading up to the moment when God makes his dwelling permanently with his people in the new Jerusalem. Revelation 21:3 – 4 describes that day: "And I heard a loud voice from the throne saying, 'Look! God's dwelling place is now among the people, and he will dwell with them. They will be his people, and God himself will be with them and be their God. "He will wipe every tear from their eyes. There will be no more death" or mourning or crying or pain, for the old order of things has passed away.' "

2 CHRONICLES 5:13 – 14

THE GLORY OF THE LORD

Once the temple was finished and the ark of the covenant was in the Most Holy Place, the glory cloud of the Lord filled the temple, showing that God lived among his people. His very presence was with them.

(continued on next page)

(The Glory of the Lord, continued)

Despite God's presence, Israel's sin and unfaithfulness toward God continued. When the people of Judah were exiled to Babylon for their sin, the glory of God departed from the temple and the temple was destroyed. In fact, Ezekiel saw a vision of the glory of God leaving the temple (Eze 10:3–19). Once the people returned to the land after the exile, they began to rebuild the temple. Yet, as Haggai revealed, the rebuilt temple did not come close to the glory of the previous temple (Hag 2:3). Isaiah prophesied that the Lord's return to Zion would be visible (Isa 52:8)—Israel would visibly see the glory of God return to the land. It is in this context that God's people read the words of John 1:14: "The Word became flesh and made his dwelling among us. We have seen his glory." God's glory lived among his people as one of them. And in the new Jerusalem there will be no temple building or sun because Jesus will be the temple and his glory will shine brightly (Rev 21:22–23).

2 CHRONICLES 6:19–40

PRAYER AND FORGIVENESS

Solomon made a prayer of dedication after he completed the temple. In the prayer, he asked God to keep his eyes continually open toward the temple. The idea was that the temple was a place where God's people could meet with him in prayer—he would see them and hear their requests when they faced the temple. Solomon's main request was that when Israel sinned and fell into judgment, they could pray toward the temple, and

(continued on next page)

the LORD. Accompanied by trumpets, cymbals and other instruments, the singers raised their voices in praise to the LORD and sang:

"He is good;
his love endures forever."

Then the temple of the LORD was filled with the cloud,
14and the priests could not perform their service because of the cloud, for the glory of the LORD filled the temple of God.

6 Then Solomon said, "The LORD has said that he would dwell in a dark cloud;
2I have built a magnificent temple for you, a place for you to dwell forever."
3While the whole assembly of Israel was standing there, the king turned around and blessed them.
4Then he said:

"Praise be to the LORD, the God of Israel, who with his hands has fulfilled what he promised with his mouth to my father David. For he said,
5'Since the day I brought my people out of Egypt, I have not chosen a city in any tribe of Israel to have a temple built so that my Name might be there, nor have I chosen anyone to be ruler over my people Israel.
6But now I have chosen Jerusalem for my Name to be there, and I have chosen David to rule my people Israel.'

7"My father David had it in his heart to build a temple for the Name of the LORD, the God of Israel.
8But the LORD said to my father David, 'You did well to have it in your heart to build a temple for my Name.
9Nevertheless, you are not the one to build the temple, but your son, your own flesh and blood—he is the one who will build the temple for my Name.'

10"The LORD has kept the promise he made. I have succeeded David my father and now I sit on the throne of Israel, just as the LORD promised, and I have built the temple for the Name of the LORD, the God of Israel.
11There I have placed the ark, in which is the covenant of the LORD that he made with the people of Israel."

Solomon's Prayer of Dedication

12Then Solomon stood before the altar of the LORD in front of the whole assembly of Israel and spread out his hands.
13Now he had made a bronze platform, five cubits long, five cubits wide and three cubits high,[a] and had placed it in the center of the outer court. He stood on the platform and then knelt down before the whole assembly of Israel and spread out his hands toward heaven.
14He said:

"LORD, the God of Israel, there is no God like you in heaven or on earth—you who keep your covenant of love with your servants who continue wholeheartedly in your way.
15You have kept your promise to your servant David my father; with your mouth you have promised and with your hand you have fulfilled it—as it is today.

16"Now, LORD, the God of Israel, keep for your servant David my father the promises you made to him when you said, 'You shall never fail to have a successor to sit before me on the throne of Israel, if only your descendants are careful in all they do to walk before me according to my law, as you have done.'
17And now, LORD, the God of Israel, let your word that you promised your servant David come true.

18"But will God really dwell on earth with humans? The heavens, even the highest heavens, cannot contain you. How much less this temple I have built!
19Yet, LORD my God, give attention to your servant's prayer and his plea for mercy. Hear the cry and the prayer that your servant is praying in your presence.
20May your eyes be open toward this temple day and night, this place of which you said you would put your Name there. May you hear the prayer your servant prays toward this place.
21Hear the supplications

[a] *13* That is, about 7 1/2 feet long and wide and 4 1/2 feet high or about 2.3 meters long and wide and 1.4 meters high

of your servant and of your people Israel when they pray toward this place.
Hear from heaven, your dwelling place; and when you hear, forgive.
22 "When anyone wrongs their neighbor and is required to take an oath
and they come and swear the oath before your altar in this temple, 23 then
hear from heaven and act. Judge between your servants, condemning the
guilty and bringing down on their heads what they have done, and vindi-
cating the innocent by treating them in accordance with their innocence.
24 "When your people Israel have been defeated by an enemy because
they have sinned against you and when they turn back and give praise to
your name, praying and making supplication before you in this temple,
25 then hear from heaven and forgive the sin of your people Israel and bring
them back to the land you gave to them and their ancestors.
26 "When the heavens are shut up and there is no rain because your people have sinned against you, and when they pray toward this place and
give praise to your name and turn from their sin because you have afflicted
them, 27 then hear from heaven and forgive the sin of your servants, your
people Israel. Teach them the right way to live, and send rain on the land
you gave your people for an inheritance.
28 "When famine or plague comes to the land, or blight or mildew, locusts or grasshoppers, or when enemies besiege them in any of their cities, whatever disaster or disease may come, 29 and when a prayer or plea
is made by anyone among your people Israel—being aware of their afflictions and pains, and spreading out their hands toward this temple—
30 then hear from heaven, your dwelling place. Forgive, and deal with everyone according to all they do, since you know their hearts (for you alone
know the human heart), 31 so that they will fear you and walk in obedience
to you all the time they live in the land you gave our ancestors.
32 "As for the foreigner who does not belong to your people Israel but has
come from a distant land because of your great name and your mighty
hand and your outstretched arm—when they come and pray toward this
temple, 33 then hear from heaven, your dwelling place. Do whatever the foreigner asks of you, so that all the peoples of the earth may know your name
and fear you, as do your own people Israel, and may know that this house I
have built bears your Name.
34 "When your people go to war against their enemies, wherever you
send them, and when they pray to you toward this city you have chosen
and the temple I have built for your Name, 35 then hear from heaven their
prayer and their plea, and uphold their cause.
36 "When they sin against you—for there is no one who does not sin—
and you become angry with them and give them over to the enemy, who
takes them captive to a land far away or near; 37 and if they have a change
of heart in the land where they are held captive, and repent and plead with
you in the land of their captivity and say, 'We have sinned, we have done
wrong and acted wickedly'; 38 and if they turn back to you with all their
heart and soul in the land of their captivity where they were taken, and
pray toward the land you gave their ancestors, toward the city you have
chosen and toward the temple I have built for your Name; 39 then from
heaven, your dwelling place, hear their prayer and their pleas, and uphold
their cause. And forgive your people, who have sinned against you.
40 "Now, my God, may your eyes be open and your ears attentive to the
prayers offered in this place.

41 "Now arise, LORD God, and come to your resting place,
you and the ark of your might.
May your priests, LORD God, be clothed with salvation,
may your faithful people rejoice in your goodness.
42 LORD God, do not reject your anointed one.
Remember the great love promised to David your servant."

(Prayer and Forgiveness, continued)

God would hear their prayers and forgive them. In fact, Solomon prayed that even foreigners who were not part of Israel could pray toward the temple and have their prayers heard (vv. 32–33). He prayed that in exile the people could pray toward the temple and that God would hear them, forgive them and return them to the land (vv. 24–25). These verses, written after the exile, would have been incredibly encouraging to the returned exiles because they show that God keeps his promises!

In the New Testament, Jesus is the temple. Anyone, no matter their circumstances or national identity, can pray to him for forgiveness (1Jn 1:9). Solomon confessed, "There is no one who does not sin" (2Ch 6:36). The good news is that there is no one whose sins Jesus will not forgive if they repent.

The Dedication of the Temple

7 When Solomon finished praying, fire came down from heaven and consumed the burnt offering and the sacrifices, and the glory of the LORD filled the temple. [2]The priests could not enter the temple of the LORD because the glory of the LORD filled it. [3]When all the Israelites saw the fire coming down and the glory of the LORD above the temple, they knelt on the pavement with their faces to the ground, and they worshiped and gave thanks to the LORD, saying,

"He is good;
his love endures forever."

[4]Then the king and all the people offered sacrifices before the LORD. [5]And King Solomon offered a sacrifice of twenty-two thousand head of cattle and a hundred and twenty thousand sheep and goats. So the king and all the people dedicated the temple of God. [6]The priests took their positions, as did the Levites with the LORD's musical instruments, which King David had made for praising the LORD and which were used when he gave thanks, saying, "His love endures forever." Opposite the Levites, the priests blew their trumpets, and all the Israelites were standing.

[7]Solomon consecrated the middle part of the courtyard in front of the temple of the LORD, and there he offered burnt offerings and the fat of the fellowship offerings, because the bronze altar he had made could not hold the burnt offerings, the grain offerings and the fat portions.

[8]So Solomon observed the festival at that time for seven days, and all Israel with him — a vast assembly, people from Lebo Hamath to the Wadi of Egypt. [9]On the eighth day they held an assembly, for they had celebrated the dedication of the altar for seven days and the festival for seven days more. [10]On the twenty-third day of the seventh month he sent the people to their homes, joyful and glad in heart for the good things the LORD had done for David and Solomon and for his people Israel.

The LORD Appears to Solomon

[11]When Solomon had finished the temple of the LORD and the royal palace, and had succeeded in carrying out all he had in mind to do in the temple of the LORD and in his own palace, [12]the LORD appeared to him at night and said:

"I have heard your prayer and have chosen this place for myself as a temple for sacrifices.

[13]"When I shut up the heavens so that there is no rain, or command locusts to devour the land or send a plague among my people, [14]if my people, who are called by my name, will humble themselves and pray and seek my face and turn from their wicked ways, then I will hear from heaven, and I will forgive their sin and will heal their land. [15]Now my eyes will be open and my ears attentive to the prayers offered in this place. [16]I have chosen and consecrated this temple so that my Name may be there forever. My eyes and my heart will always be there.

[17]"As for you, if you walk before me faithfully as David your father did, and do all I command, and observe my decrees and laws, [18]I will establish your royal throne, as I covenanted with David your father when I said, 'You shall never fail to have a successor to rule over Israel.'

[19]"But if you[a] turn away and forsake the decrees and commands I have given you[a] and go off to serve other gods and worship them, [20]then I will uproot Israel from my land, which I have given them, and will reject this temple I have consecrated for my Name. I will make it a byword and an object of ridicule among all peoples. [21]This temple will become a heap of rubble. All[b] who pass by will be appalled and say, 'Why has the LORD done such

---

[a] *19* The Hebrew is plural. [b] *21* See some Septuagint manuscripts, Old Latin, Syriac, Arabic and Targum; Hebrew *And though this temple is now so imposing, all*

PRAYER FOR REVIVAL

One of the challenges in approaching Scripture is the temptation to allow one's own biases to drive interpretation. It can be tempting, particularly in this specific text, to see a formula of revival for one's own place and time. However, as with any portion of Scripture, it is important to understand the context before attempting to apply it.

A careful reading of 2 Chronicles 7:14 reveals that it is part of a larger sequence that starts in verse 13. This sequence is, in turn, a part of the larger narrative of chapters 6 and 7. Solomon completed building the temple and prayed a grand prayer of dedication (2Ch 6:14 – 42). Solomon specifically prayed that when Israel faced divine judgment for particular sins, they could pray toward the temple in repentance and receive restoration (2Ch 6:36 – 39). Then God appeared to Solomon and granted his earlier request, assuring Solomon that when the people of Israel rebelled, a prayer of repentance would "heal their land" (2Ch 7:11 – 14). Linguistic similarities between Solomon's prayer in chapter 6 and God's words to Solomon in chapter 7 signal a connection between the two passages (e.g., 2Ch 6:26; 7:13). God's promises in 2 Chronicles 7:13 – 14 applied specifically to the people and situations addressed in Solomon's prayer.

Although this passage is not a particular prescription for today, believers can find joy in knowing that the promises of forgiveness and restoration given here have been fulfilled in Jesus Christ — in a manner that far exceeds the scope of the original promises to Solomon. Those who believe in Jesus find true revival. When people come to faith in Christ, they are moving from death to life (Eph 2:1 – 5). They are moving from a state of spiritual blindness to a state of seeing life the way that God intended. Therefore, when people today long for revival in their land, they should ultimately be longing for people to see Jesus for who he really is. Rather than relying on a formula based on a promise made to Solomon, believers should pray that people find new life in Christ. Those individual transformations have the power to change the trajectory of any nation.

a thing to this land and to this temple?' [22]People will answer, 'Because they have forsaken the LORD, the God of their ancestors, who brought them out of Egypt, and have embraced other gods, worshiping and serving them — that is why he brought all this disaster on them.' "

Solomon's Other Activities

8 At the end of twenty years, during which Solomon built the temple of the LORD and his own palace, [2]Solomon rebuilt the villages that Hiram[a] had given him, and settled Israelites in them. [3]Solomon then went to Hamath Zobah and captured it. [4]He also built up Tadmor in the desert and all the store cities he had built in Hamath. [5]He rebuilt Upper Beth Horon and Lower Beth Horon as fortified cities, with walls and with gates and bars, [6]as well as Baalath and all his store cities, and all the cities for his chariots and for his horses[b] — whatever he desired to build in Jerusalem, in Lebanon and throughout all the territory he ruled.

[7]There were still people left from the Hittites, Amorites, Perizzites, Hivites and Jebusites (these people were not Israelites). [8]Solomon conscripted the descendants of all these people remaining in the land — whom the Israelites had not destroyed — to serve as slave labor, as it is to this day. [9]But Solomon did not make slaves of the Israelites for his work; they were his fighting men, commanders of his captains, and commanders of his chariots and charioteers. [10]They were also King Solomon's chief officials — two hundred and fifty officials supervising the men.

[11]Solomon brought Pharaoh's daughter up from the City of David to the palace he had built for her, for he said, "My wife must not live in the palace of David king of Israel, because the places the ark of the LORD has entered are holy."

[12]On the altar of the LORD that he had built in front of the portico, Solomon sacrificed burnt offerings to the LORD, [13]according to the daily requirement for offerings commanded by Moses for the Sabbaths, the New Moons and the three annual festivals — the Festival of Unleavened Bread, the Festival of Weeks and the Festival of Tabernacles. [14]In keeping with the ordinance of his father David, he appointed the divisions of the priests for their duties, and the Levites to lead the praise and to assist the priests according to each day's requirement. He also appointed the gatekeepers by divisions for the various gates, because this was what David the man of God had ordered. [15]They did not deviate from the king's commands to the priests or to the Levites in any matter, including that of the treasuries.

[16]All Solomon's work was carried out, from the day the foundation of the temple of the LORD was laid until its completion. So the temple of the LORD was finished.

[17]Then Solomon went to Ezion Geber and Elath on the coast of Edom. [18]And Hiram sent him ships commanded by his own men, sailors who knew the sea. These, with Solomon's men, sailed to Ophir and brought back four hundred and fifty talents[c] of gold, which they delivered to King Solomon.

The Queen of Sheba Visits Solomon

9 When the queen of Sheba heard of Solomon's fame, she came to Jerusalem to test him with hard questions. Arriving with a very great caravan — with camels carrying spices, large quantities of gold, and precious stones — she came to Solomon and talked with him about all she had on her mind. [2]Solomon answered all her questions; nothing was too hard for him to explain to her. [3]When the queen of Sheba saw the wisdom of Solomon, as well as the palace he had built, [4]the food on his table, the seating of his officials, the attending servants in their robes, the cupbearers in their robes and the burnt offerings he made at[d] the temple of the LORD, she was overwhelmed.

2 CHRONICLES 9:1 – 4

THE NATIONS COME TO JESUS

When the queen of Sheba visited Solomon to be blessed by his wisdom, she brought gifts for him. The theme of the nations streaming to Israel and bringing gifts to the king is repeated often in Scripture, and it is fulfilled in Jesus Christ. Isaiah prophesied that the nations would stream to Zion, and that they would bring gifts like gold and incense (Isa 2:3 – 4; 60:6).

In Matthew 2, the wise men came to Israel bringing these very gifts to the newborn King. Throughout Jesus' ministry, people from the nations came to him, such as the Canaanite woman from the region of Tyre and Sidon (Mt 15:21 – 22) and the centurion whose servant was paralyzed (Mt 8:5 – 6). This pattern continues with the church. A partial fulfillment of the theme occurred when Gentile churches took up a collection to send to the church in Jerusalem (Ro 15:25 – 27; 1Co 16:1 – 4; 2Co 8:1 – 15). And the pattern will be fulfilled completely when the kings of the earth bring their "splendor" to the new Jerusalem (Rev 21:24).

[a] *2* Hebrew *Huram,* a variant of *Hiram*; also in verse 18 [b] *6* Or *charioteers* [c] *18* That is, about 17 tons or about 15 metric tons [d] *4* Or *and the ascent by which he went up to*

5 She said to the king, "The report I heard in my own country about your
achievements and your wisdom is true. 6 But I did not believe what they said until I came and saw with my own eyes. Indeed, not even half the greatness of your
wisdom was told me; you have far exceeded the report I heard. 7 How happy your
people must be! How happy your officials, who continually stand before you and
hear your wisdom! 8 Praise be to the LORD your God, who has delighted in you
and placed you on his throne as king to rule for the LORD your God. Because of
the love of your God for Israel and his desire to uphold them forever, he has made
you king over them, to maintain justice and righteousness."
9 Then she gave the king 120 talents[a] of gold, large quantities of spices, and
precious stones. There had never been such spices as those the queen of Sheba
gave to King Solomon.
10 (The servants of Hiram and the servants of Solomon brought gold from
Ophir; they also brought algumwood[b] and precious stones. 11 The king used the
algumwood to make steps for the temple of the LORD and for the royal palace,
and to make harps and lyres for the musicians. Nothing like them had ever been
seen in Judah.)
12 King Solomon gave the queen of Sheba all she desired and asked for; he gave
her more than she had brought to him. Then she left and returned with her retinue to her own country.

Solomon's Splendor

13 The weight of the gold that Solomon received yearly was 666 talents,[c] 14 not
including the revenues brought in by merchants and traders. Also all the kings
of Arabia and the governors of the territories brought gold and silver to Solomon.
15 King Solomon made two hundred large shields of hammered gold; six hundred shekels[d] of hammered gold went into each shield. 16 He also made three
hundred small shields of hammered gold, with three hundred shekels[e] of gold in
each shield. The king put them in the Palace of the Forest of Lebanon.
17 Then the king made a great throne covered with ivory and overlaid with
pure gold. 18 The throne had six steps, and a footstool of gold was attached to
it. On both sides of the seat were armrests, with a lion standing beside each
of them. 19 Twelve lions stood on the six steps, one at either end of each step.
Nothing like it had ever been made for any other kingdom. 20 All King Solomon's
goblets were gold, and all the household articles in the Palace of the Forest of
Lebanon were pure gold. Nothing was made of silver, because silver was considered of little value in Solomon's day. 21 The king had a fleet of trading ships[f]
manned by Hiram's[g] servants. Once every three years it returned, carrying gold,
silver and ivory, and apes and baboons.
22 King Solomon was greater in riches and wisdom than all the other kings of
the earth. 23 All the kings of the earth sought audience with Solomon to hear the
wisdom God had put in his heart. 24 Year after year, everyone who came brought
a gift — articles of silver and gold, and robes, weapons and spices, and horses
and mules.
25 Solomon had four thousand stalls for horses and chariots, and twelve
thousand horses,[h] which he kept in the chariot cities and also with him in Jerusalem. 26 He ruled over all the kings from the Euphrates River to the land of
the Philistines, as far as the border of Egypt. 27 The king made silver as common in Jerusalem as stones, and cedar as plentiful as sycamore-fig trees in
the foothills. 28 Solomon's horses were imported from Egypt and from all other
countries.

[a] *9* That is, about 4 1/2 tons or about 4 metric tons [b] *10* Probably a variant of *almugwood* [c] *13* That is, about 25 tons or about 23 metric tons [d] *15* That is, about 15 pounds or about 6.9 kilograms [e] *16* That is, about 7 1/2 pounds or about 3.5 kilograms [f] *21* Hebrew *of ships that could go to Tarshish* [g] *21* Hebrew *Huram,* a variant of *Hiram* [h] *25* Or *charioteers*

2 CHRONICLES 9:17 – 19

THE LION OF THE TRIBE OF JUDAH

Perhaps the most stunning feature of Solomon's magnificent throne were the statues of lions that surrounded it — located beside each armrest and flanking each of the six steps leading up to the golden footstool. Lions were a fitting symbol for Solomon's kingship. Not only were lions commonly thought of as the kings of the beasts, but Solomon was a king from the tribe of Judah. The lions surrounding the throne recalled the prophecy that God made through Jacob concerning Judah. Jacob called Judah a "lion" who would rule as a king with a scepter, prophesying that he would rule over "the nations" (Ge 49:9 – 10). The lions surrounding Solomon's throne called back to Jacob's prophecy about Judah and pointed forward to "the Lion of the tribe of Judah" — Jesus Christ (Rev 5:5). Due to this King's victory on the cross, he now rules over "persons from every tribe and language and people and nation" (Rev 5:9).

Solomon's Death

29As for the other events of Solomon's reign, from beginning to end, are they
not written in the records of Nathan the prophet, in the prophecy of Ahijah the
Shilonite and in the visions of Iddo the seer concerning Jeroboam son of Nebat?
30Solomon reigned in Jerusalem over all Israel forty years. 31Then he rested with
his ancestors and was buried in the city of David his father. And Rehoboam his
son succeeded him as king.

Israel Rebels Against Rehoboam

10 Rehoboam went to Shechem, for all Israel had gone there to make him
king. 2When Jeroboam son of Nebat heard this (he was in Egypt, where he
had fled from King Solomon), he returned from Egypt. 3So they sent for Jeroboam, and he and all Israel went to Rehoboam and said to him: 4"Your father put a
heavy yoke on us, but now lighten the harsh labor and the heavy yoke he put on
us, and we will serve you."

5Rehoboam answered, "Come back to me in three days." So the people went
away.

6Then King Rehoboam consulted the elders who had served his father Solomon during his lifetime. "How would you advise me to answer these people?"
he asked.

7They replied, "If you will be kind to these people and please them and give
them a favorable answer, they will always be your servants."

8But Rehoboam rejected the advice the elders gave him and consulted the
young men who had grown up with him and were serving him. 9He asked them,
"What is your advice? How should we answer these people who say to me, 'Light-
en the yoke your father put on us'?"

10The young men who had grown up with him replied, "The people have said
to you, 'Your father put a heavy yoke on us, but make our yoke lighter.' Now tell
them, 'My little finger is thicker than my father's waist. 11My father laid on you a
heavy yoke; I will make it even heavier. My father scourged you with whips; I will
scourge you with scorpions.' "

12Three days later Jeroboam and all the people returned to Rehoboam, as
the king had said, "Come back to me in three days." 13The king answered them
harshly. Rejecting the advice of the elders, 14he followed the advice of the young
men and said, "My father made your yoke heavy; I will make it even heavier.
My father scourged you with whips; I will scourge you with scorpions." 15So the
king did not listen to the people, for this turn of events was from God, to fulfill
the word the LORD had spoken to Jeroboam son of Nebat through Ahijah the
Shilonite.

16When all Israel saw that the king refused to listen to them, they answered
the king:

"What share do we have in David,
  what part in Jesse's son?
To your tents, Israel!
  Look after your own house, David!"

So all the Israelites went home. 17But as for the Israelites who were living in the
towns of Judah, Rehoboam still ruled over them.

18King Rehoboam sent out Adoniram,[a] who was in charge of forced labor, but
the Israelites stoned him to death. King Rehoboam, however, managed to get
into his chariot and escape to Jerusalem. 19So Israel has been in rebellion against
the house of David to this day.

11 When Rehoboam arrived in Jerusalem, he mustered Judah and Benjamin — a hundred and eighty thousand able young men — to go to war
against Israel and to regain the kingdom for Rehoboam.

---

[a] *18* Hebrew *Hadoram,* a variant of *Adoniram*

LISTENING TO WRONG VOICES

The people of Israel asked King Rehoboam to lighten the burden of harsh labor that his father Solomon had placed on them. Rehoboam said he would take three days to come up with an answer. The elders counseled Rehoboam to do as the people requested and thereby win their support. Instead, Rehoboam listened to the counsel of his peers who had grown up with him. They told him to make the labor even harsher and bring the people to their knees. They even used an inappropriate euphemism to suggest that Rehoboam was a bigger and mightier man than his father Solomon. Rehoboam listened to the wrong voices and made a foolish decision. His decision led to the division of Israel into two separate kingdoms — the southern kingdom of Judah and the northern kingdom of Israel.

Rehoboam was the son of the wisest man who had ever lived in Israel, and yet he foolishly listened to his peers rather than his elders. His foolishness not only led to a divided nation but would ultimately lead to the exile itself. Solomon had sought throughout his life to instruct his son in wisdom in Proverbs (Pr 5:1,7; 7:1,24). Solomon wanted to set his son up to rule wisely, but Rehoboam was a fool.

This tragedy points to the need for a new king — a better king — who would rule in wisdom and reunite Israel. That king's name is Jesus of Nazareth. He is the Messiah who is the embodiment of all the wisdom of Proverbs (Pr 1:1 – 7; Isa 11:1 – 3). His wisdom is greater than Solomon's (Mt 12:42). He is the Son who grew in wisdom and stature and favor with God and man (Lk 2:52). And as Ezekiel prophesied, God will someday reunite his scattered and divided people as one nation under one King — a new David who shepherds the people of God (Eze 37:15 – 28). These prophecies form the context for Jesus' words: "I am the good shepherd. The good shepherd lays down his life for the sheep"; and "Holy Father, protect them by the power of your name, the name you gave me, so that they may be one as we are one" (Jn 10:11; 17:11).

[2]But this word of the LORD came to Shemaiah the man of God: [3]"Say to Rehoboam son of Solomon king of Judah and to all Israel in Judah and Benjamin, [4]'This is what the LORD says: Do not go up to fight against your fellow Israelites. Go home, every one of you, for this is my doing.' " So they obeyed the words of the LORD and turned back from marching against Jeroboam.

Rehoboam Fortifies Judah

[5]Rehoboam lived in Jerusalem and built up towns for defense in Judah: [6]Bethlehem, Etam, Tekoa, [7]Beth Zur, Soko, Adullam, [8]Gath, Mareshah, Ziph, [9]Adoraim, Lachish, Azekah, [10]Zorah, Aijalon and Hebron. These were fortified cities in Judah and Benjamin. [11]He strengthened their defenses and put commanders in them, with supplies of food, olive oil and wine. [12]He put shields and spears in all the cities, and made them very strong. So Judah and Benjamin were his.

[13]The priests and Levites from all their districts throughout Israel sided with him. [14]The Levites even abandoned their pasturelands and property and came to Judah and Jerusalem, because Jeroboam and his sons had rejected them as priests of the LORD [15]when he appointed his own priests for the high places and for the goat and calf idols he had made. [16]Those from every tribe of Israel who set their hearts on seeking the LORD, the God of Israel, followed the Levites to Jerusalem to offer sacrifices to the LORD, the God of their ancestors. [17]They strengthened the kingdom of Judah and supported Rehoboam son of Solomon three years, following the ways of David and Solomon during this time.

Rehoboam's Family

[18]Rehoboam married Mahalath, who was the daughter of David's son Jerimoth and of Abihail, the daughter of Jesse's son Eliab. [19]She bore him sons: Jeush, Shemariah and Zaham. [20]Then he married Maakah daughter of Absalom, who bore him Abijah, Attai, Ziza and Shelomith. [21]Rehoboam loved Maakah daughter of Absalom more than any of his other wives and concubines. In all, he had eighteen wives and sixty concubines, twenty-eight sons and sixty daughters.

[22]Rehoboam appointed Abijah son of Maakah as crown prince among his brothers, in order to make him king. [23]He acted wisely, dispersing some of his sons throughout the districts of Judah and Benjamin, and to all the fortified cities. He gave them abundant provisions and took many wives for them.

Shishak Attacks Jerusalem

12 After Rehoboam's position as king was established and he had become strong, he and all Israel[a] with him abandoned the law of the LORD. [2]Because they had been unfaithful to the LORD, Shishak king of Egypt attacked Jerusalem in the fifth year of King Rehoboam. [3]With twelve hundred chariots and sixty thousand horsemen and the innumerable troops of Libyans, Sukkites and Cushites[b] that came with him from Egypt, [4]he captured the fortified cities of Judah and came as far as Jerusalem.

[5]Then the prophet Shemaiah came to Rehoboam and to the leaders of Judah who had assembled in Jerusalem for fear of Shishak, and he said to them, "This is what the LORD says, 'You have abandoned me; therefore, I now abandon you to Shishak.' "

[6]The leaders of Israel and the king humbled themselves and said, "The LORD is just."

[7]When the LORD saw that they humbled themselves, this word of the LORD came to Shemaiah: "Since they have humbled themselves, I will not destroy them but will soon give them deliverance. My wrath will not be poured out on Jerusalem through Shishak. [8]They will, however, become subject to him, so that they may learn the difference between serving me and serving the kings of other lands."

[a] *1* That is, Judah, as frequently in 2 Chronicles [b] *3* That is, people from the upper Nile region

2 CHRONICLES 11:13–17

CORRUPTED RELIGIOUS SYSTEMS

Jeroboam, the newly appointed king of the northern tribes of Israel, refused to allow the priests and Levites who lived in the north to fulfill their ministry. This act was clearly a violation of the law that gave the priests and Levites their duties in Israel (Nu 18:1–7). Instead, Jeroboam constructed goat and calf idols. Jeroboam also set up his own priests. Therefore, the priests and Levites, along with all the people of the northern kingdom who had set their hearts to seek the Lord, returned to Judah and Jerusalem to worship the true God, Yahweh, in the temple.

During the time of Jesus, the religious system had become so corrupted that the leaders of the Pharisees and other groups had, in effect, stopped worshiping the true God. They elevated their traditions above the truth God had revealed in his law. Jesus highlighted the religious leaders' prioritization of human tradition over obedience to God's law, noting that they neglected caring for their elderly parents in favor of donating funds to the temple (Mk 7:9–13). However, there were leaders whose hearts God stirred, such as Nicodemus who came to seek truth from Jesus (Jn 3:1–2). In order to understand Jesus' person and work, it is vital to recognize that part of Jesus' mission included confronting a religious system that had been completely corrupted.

9When Shishak king of Egypt attacked Jerusalem, he carried off the treasures of the temple of the LORD and the treasures of the royal palace. He took everything, including the gold shields Solomon had made. 10So King Rehoboam made bronze shields to replace them and assigned these to the commanders of the guard on duty at the entrance to the royal palace. 11Whenever the king went to the LORD's temple, the guards went with him, bearing the shields, and afterward they returned them to the guardroom.

12Because Rehoboam humbled himself, the LORD's anger turned from him, and he was not totally destroyed. Indeed, there was some good in Judah.

13King Rehoboam established himself firmly in Jerusalem and continued as king. He was forty-one years old when he became king, and he reigned seventeen years in Jerusalem, the city the LORD had chosen out of all the tribes of Israel in which to put his Name. His mother's name was Naamah; she was an Ammonite. 14He did evil because he had not set his heart on seeking the LORD.

15As for the events of Rehoboam's reign, from beginning to end, are they not written in the records of Shemaiah the prophet and of Iddo the seer that deal with genealogies? There was continual warfare between Rehoboam and Jeroboam. 16Rehoboam rested with his ancestors and was buried in the City of David. And Abijah his son succeeded him as king.

Abijah King of Judah

13 In the eighteenth year of the reign of Jeroboam, Abijah became king of Judah, 2and he reigned in Jerusalem three years. His mother's name was Maakah,[a] a daughter[b] of Uriel of Gibeah.

There was war between Abijah and Jeroboam. 3Abijah went into battle with an army of four hundred thousand able fighting men, and Jeroboam drew up a battle line against him with eight hundred thousand able troops.

4Abijah stood on Mount Zemaraim, in the hill country of Ephraim, and said, "Jeroboam and all Israel, listen to me! 5Don't you know that the LORD, the God of Israel, has given the kingship of Israel to David and his descendants forever by a covenant of salt? 6Yet Jeroboam son of Nebat, an official of Solomon son of David, rebelled against his master. 7Some worthless scoundrels gathered around him and opposed Rehoboam son of Solomon when he was young and indecisive and not strong enough to resist them.

8"And now you plan to resist the kingdom of the LORD, which is in the hands of David's descendants. You are indeed a vast army and have with you the golden calves that Jeroboam made to be your gods. 9But didn't you drive out the priests of the LORD, the sons of Aaron, and the Levites, and make priests of your own as the peoples of other lands do? Whoever comes to consecrate himself with a young bull and seven rams may become a priest of what are not gods.

10"As for us, the LORD is our God, and we have not forsaken him. The priests who serve the LORD are sons of Aaron, and the Levites assist them. 11Every morning and evening they present burnt offerings and fragrant incense to the LORD. They set out the bread on the ceremonially clean table and light the lamps on the gold lampstand every evening. We are observing the requirements of the LORD our God. But you have forsaken him. 12God is with us; he is our leader. His priests with their trumpets will sound the battle cry against you. People of Israel, do not fight against the LORD, the God of your ancestors, for you will not succeed."

13Now Jeroboam had sent troops around to the rear, so that while he was in front of Judah the ambush was behind them. 14Judah turned and saw that they were being attacked at both front and rear. Then they cried out to the LORD. The priests blew their trumpets 15and the men of Judah raised the battle cry. At the sound of their battle cry, God routed Jeroboam and all Israel before Abijah and Judah. 16The Israelites fled before Judah, and God delivered them into their

[a] 2 Most Septuagint manuscripts and Syriac (see also 11:20 and 1 Kings 15:2); Hebrew *Micaiah* [b] 2 Or *granddaughter*

---

2 CHRONICLES 12:1–8

NATIONS AS JUDGMENT

Solomon's son Rehoboam abandoned the laws of God, and in response, God raised up a foreign enemy against him—Shishak, the king of Egypt. Rehoboam and his fellow leaders humbled themselves before the Lord. He gave them a measure of relief but they still faced the consequences of their disobedience: servitude to Egypt. God often used foreign armies to judge his people for their sin: Egypt, Assyria, Babylon, Persia and more. Deuteronomy made clear that the punishment for forsaking the Lord would be captivity to a foreign army and exile (Dt 28:49–68). The exile would end when the people sought the Lord with their whole hearts (Dt 30:1–3).

In the time of Jesus, Israel was captive to Rome. God used Rome in his plan for Jesus to die for the sins of Israel and the sins of the whole world (Jn 11:49–53). Jesus took humanity's place on the cross. It is only through Jesus that people's hearts can be cleansed of sins and be turned wholly toward the Lord.

2 CHRONICLES 14:2 – 15

THE SAVING KING

The background to the life and reign of King Asa is the covenant that God made with David. God promised David an eternal dynasty with rest and peace from his enemies (2Sa 7:8 – 16). But, there was a condition to the covenant. If David's sons would be faithful, then they would be blessed, but if they were unfaithful, then God would punish them (2Sa 7:14). Because Asa walked in the ways of the Lord, the Lord blessed him. Asa began his reign by ridding the land of idolatry, so the Lord granted him victory over his enemies and many years of peace. Zerah the Cushite marched against King Asa and Judah with "an army of thousands upon thousands" (2Ch 14:9). But even though they were outnumbered, Asa humbly relied upon the Lord, and the Lord granted them victory. The Lord used Asa as a warrior-king to save his people from a marauding enemy. The Bible presents Jesus as the Warrior-King who defeats his people's enemies — Satan, sin and death — and rescues them (cf. Ge 3:15; Rev 19:11 – 21).

2 CHRONICLES 15:1 – 19

REVIVAL AND THE WORD

The Spirit of God came upon the prophet Azariah, and he preached the word of God to King Asa. Asa applied the preaching of God's prophet, and it led to an incredible revival. Asa implemented everything the prophet said. He put away the idols and he renewed the covenant with the Lord.

(continued on next page)

hands. 17Abijah and his troops inflicted heavy losses on them, so that there were
five hundred thousand casualties among Israel's able men. 18The Israelites were
subdued on that occasion, and the people of Judah were victorious because they
relied on the LORD, the God of their ancestors.
19Abijah pursued Jeroboam and took from him the towns of Bethel, Jeshanah
and Ephron, with their surrounding villages. 20Jeroboam did not regain power
during the time of Abijah. And the LORD struck him down and he died.
21But Abijah grew in strength. He married fourteen wives and had twenty-two
sons and sixteen daughters.
22The other events of Abijah's reign, what he did and what he said, are written
in the annotations of the prophet Iddo.

14 [a] And Abijah rested with his ancestors and was buried in the City of David.
Asa his son succeeded him as king, and in his days the country was at
peace for ten years.

Asa King of Judah

2Asa did what was good and right in the eyes of the LORD his God. 3He removed the foreign altars and the high places, smashed the sacred stones and
cut down the Asherah poles.[b] 4He commanded Judah to seek the LORD, the God
of their ancestors, and to obey his laws and commands. 5He removed the high
places and incense altars in every town in Judah, and the kingdom was at peace
under him. 6He built up the fortified cities of Judah, since the land was at peace.
No one was at war with him during those years, for the LORD gave him rest.
7"Let us build up these towns," he said to Judah, "and put walls around them,
with towers, gates and bars. The land is still ours, because we have sought the
LORD our God; we sought him and he has given us rest on every side." So they
built and prospered.
8Asa had an army of three hundred thousand men from Judah, equipped with
large shields and with spears, and two hundred and eighty thousand from Benjamin, armed with small shields and with bows. All these were brave fighting
men.
9Zerah the Cushite marched out against them with an army of thousands
upon thousands and three hundred chariots, and came as far as Mareshah.
10Asa went out to meet him, and they took up battle positions in the Valley of
Zephathah near Mareshah.
11Then Asa called to the LORD his God and said, "LORD, there is no one like
you to help the powerless against the mighty. Help us, LORD our God, for we rely
on you, and in your name we have come against this vast army. LORD, you are
our God; do not let mere mortals prevail against you."
12The LORD struck down the Cushites before Asa and Judah. The Cushites
fled, 13and Asa and his army pursued them as far as Gerar. Such a great number
of Cushites fell that they could not recover; they were crushed before the LORD
and his forces. The men of Judah carried off a large amount of plunder. 14They
destroyed all the villages around Gerar, for the terror of the LORD had fallen on
them. They looted all these villages, since there was much plunder there. 15They
also attacked the camps of the herders and carried off droves of sheep and goats
and camels. Then they returned to Jerusalem.

Asa's Reform

15 The Spirit of God came on Azariah son of Oded. 2He went out to meet Asa
and said to him, "Listen to me, Asa and all Judah and Benjamin. The LORD
is with you when you are with him. If you seek him, he will be found by you, but
if you forsake him, he will forsake you. 3For a long time Israel was without the
true God, without a priest to teach and without the law. 4But in their distress

[a] In Hebrew texts 14:1 is numbered 13:23, and 14:2-15 is numbered 14:1-14. [b] 3 That is, wooden symbols of the goddess Asherah; here and elsewhere in 2 Chronicles

they turned to the LORD, the God of Israel, and sought him, and he was found by
them. [5]In those days it was not safe to travel about, for all the inhabitants of the
lands were in great turmoil. [6]One nation was being crushed by another and one
city by another, because God was troubling them with every kind of distress.
[7]But as for you, be strong and do not give up, for your work will be rewarded."
[8]When Asa heard these words and the prophecy of Azariah son of[a] Oded the
prophet, he took courage. He removed the detestable idols from the whole land
of Judah and Benjamin and from the towns he had captured in the hills of Ephraim. He repaired the altar of the LORD that was in front of the portico of the LORD's
temple.
[9]Then he assembled all Judah and Benjamin and the people from Ephraim,
Manasseh and Simeon who had settled among them, for large numbers had
come over to him from Israel when they saw that the LORD his God was with him.
[10]They assembled at Jerusalem in the third month of the fifteenth year of Asa's
reign. [11]At that time they sacrificed to the LORD seven hundred head of cattle and
seven thousand sheep and goats from the plunder they had brought back. [12]They
entered into a covenant to seek the LORD, the God of their ancestors, with all
their heart and soul. [13]All who would not seek the LORD, the God of Israel, were
to be put to death, whether small or great, man or woman. [14]They took an oath
to the LORD with loud acclamation, with shouting and with trumpets and horns.
[15]All Judah rejoiced about the oath because they had sworn it wholeheartedly.
They sought God eagerly, and he was found by them. So the LORD gave them rest
on every side.
[16]King Asa also deposed his grandmother Maakah from her position as queen
mother, because she had made a repulsive image for the worship of Asherah. Asa
cut it down, broke it up and burned it in the Kidron Valley. [17]Although he did not
remove the high places from Israel, Asa's heart was fully committed to the LORD
all his life. [18]He brought into the temple of God the silver and gold and the articles that he and his father had dedicated.
[19]There was no more war until the thirty-fifth year of Asa's reign.

Asa's Last Years

16 In the thirty-sixth year of Asa's reign Baasha king of Israel went up against
Judah and fortified Ramah to prevent anyone from leaving or entering the
territory of Asa king of Judah.
[2]Asa then took the silver and gold out of the treasuries of the LORD's temple
and of his own palace and sent it to Ben-Hadad king of Aram, who was ruling in
Damascus. [3]"Let there be a treaty between me and you," he said, "as there was
between my father and your father. See, I am sending you silver and gold. Now
break your treaty with Baasha king of Israel so he will withdraw from me."
[4]Ben-Hadad agreed with King Asa and sent the commanders of his forces
against the towns of Israel. They conquered Ijon, Dan, Abel Maim[b] and all the
store cities of Naphtali. [5]When Baasha heard this, he stopped building Ramah
and abandoned his work. [6]Then King Asa brought all the men of Judah, and they
carried away from Ramah the stones and timber Baasha had been using. With
them he built up Geba and Mizpah.
[7]At that time Hanani the seer came to Asa king of Judah and said to him: "Because you relied on the king of Aram and not on the LORD your God, the army of
the king of Aram has escaped from your hand. [8]Were not the Cushites[c] and Libyans a mighty army with great numbers of chariots and horsemen[d]? Yet when you
relied on the LORD, he delivered them into your hand. [9]For the eyes of the LORD
range throughout the earth to strengthen those whose hearts are fully committed to him. You have done a foolish thing, and from now on you will be at war."

[a] 8 Vulgate and Syriac (see also Septuagint and verse 1); Hebrew does not have *Azariah son of.*
[b] 4 Also known as *Abel Beth Maakah* [c] 8 That is, people from the upper Nile region
[d] 8 Or *charioteers*

(Revival and the Word, continued)

He also began to reunify Israel: many people from the northern tribes came down to join with Judah because they saw that God was with Asa (15:9). As a part of this spiritual renewal, Asa even "deposed his grandmother Maakah from her position as queen mother, because she had made a repulsive image for the worship of Asherah" (v. 16).

All of this points to Jesus. Jesus was the one anointed by the Spirit of God (Mt 3:16). Jesus was the final prophet and the final word from God (Heb 1:1–2). Jesus inaugurated the new covenant (Jer 31:31–33; Mt 26:28). And renewal by Jesus may mean severing ties with family members. Jesus said, "If anyone comes to me and does not hate father and mother, wife and children, brothers and sisters—yes, even their own life—such a person cannot be my disciple" (Lk 14:26).

2 CHRONICLES 16:9

HEARTS FULLY COMMITTED TO GOD

King Asa began his reign fully relying on God, and God granted him victory over his enemies as a result. However, Asa ended his reign relying on humans instead of God. That sad fact ultimately ruined his kingdom. King Baasha of Israel (the northern kingdom) came against Asa and Judah (the southern kingdom). Instead of relying on God for the victory, Asa made a treaty with Aram—giving the treasures of the temple to King Ben-Hadad. Hanani the prophet condemned Asa for his actions, pointing out that when Asa had relied on

(continued on next page)

10 Asa was angry with the seer because of this; he was so enraged that he put
him in prison. At the same time Asa brutally oppressed some of the people.
11 The events of Asa's reign, from beginning to end, are written in the book
of the kings of Judah and Israel. 12 In the thirty-ninth year of his reign Asa was
afflicted with a disease in his feet. Though his disease was severe, even in his
illness he did not seek help from the LORD, but only from the physicians. 13 Then
in the forty-first year of his reign Asa died and rested with his ancestors. 14 They
buried him in the tomb that he had cut out for himself in the City of David. They
laid him on a bier covered with spices and various blended perfumes, and they
made a huge fire in his honor.

Jehoshaphat King of Judah

17 Jehoshaphat his son succeeded him as king and strengthened himself
against Israel. 2 He stationed troops in all the fortified cities of Judah and
put garrisons in Judah and in the towns of Ephraim that his father Asa had captured.
3 The LORD was with Jehoshaphat because he followed the ways of his father
David before him. He did not consult the Baals 4 but sought the God of his father
and followed his commands rather than the practices of Israel. 5 The LORD established the kingdom under his control; and all Judah brought gifts to Jehoshaphat, so that he had great wealth and honor. 6 His heart was devoted to the ways
of the LORD; furthermore, he removed the high places and the Asherah poles
from Judah.
7 In the third year of his reign he sent his officials Ben-Hail, Obadiah, Zechariah, Nethanel and Micaiah to teach in the towns of Judah. 8 With them were
certain Levites — Shemaiah, Nethaniah, Zebadiah, Asahel, Shemiramoth, Jehonathan, Adonijah, Tobijah and Tob-Adonijah — and the priests Elishama and
Jehoram. 9 They taught throughout Judah, taking with them the Book of the Law
of the LORD; they went around to all the towns of Judah and taught the people.
10 The fear of the LORD fell on all the kingdoms of the lands surrounding Judah,
so that they did not go to war against Jehoshaphat. 11 Some Philistines brought
Jehoshaphat gifts and silver as tribute, and the Arabs brought him flocks: seven
thousand seven hundred rams and seven thousand seven hundred goats.
12 Jehoshaphat became more and more powerful; he built forts and store cities
in Judah 13 and had large supplies in the towns of Judah. He also kept experienced fighting men in Jerusalem. 14 Their enrollment by families was as follows:

From Judah, commanders of units of 1,000:
Adnah the commander, with 300,000 fighting men;
15 next, Jehohanan the commander, with 280,000;
16 next, Amasiah son of Zikri, who volunteered himself for the service of
the LORD, with 200,000.
17 From Benjamin:
Eliada, a valiant soldier, with 200,000 men armed with bows and shields;
18 next, Jehozabad, with 180,000 men armed for battle.

19 These were the men who served the king, besides those he stationed in the
fortified cities throughout Judah.

Micaiah Prophesies Against Ahab

18 Now Jehoshaphat had great wealth and honor, and he allied himself with
Ahab by marriage. 2 Some years later he went down to see Ahab in Samaria. Ahab slaughtered many sheep and cattle for him and the people with him and
urged him to attack Ramoth Gilead. 3 Ahab king of Israel asked Jehoshaphat king
of Judah, "Will you go with me against Ramoth Gilead?"
Jehoshaphat replied, "I am as you are, and my people as your people; we will
join you in the war." 4 But Jehoshaphat also said to the king of Israel, "First seek
the counsel of the LORD."

(Hearts Fully Committed to God, continued)

the Lord, Asa had defeated a much mightier Cushite army. Hanani, after reminding Asa that the all-seeing God looks for those who rely fully on him and strengthens them, gave this judgment: "You have done a foolish thing, and from now on you will be at war" (v. 9). Because of Asa's sin, he would no longer have rest and peace. Believers today, no less than ancient Israel, need a King whose heart is fully reliant on God and thus brings lasting peace. In contrast to Asa and every other person, Jesus lived on earth as a man fully committed to God, remaining obedient at every point. As a result, he is the King who is the Prince of Peace (Isa 9:6).

2 CHRONICLES 16:11 – 14

A BETTER KING

Because Asa had rejected God, his reign ended with disease and death. His reign began with such promise, but ended in failure. Every descendant of David failed at some point, but that strengthened the hope for a King who did not end up rotting in a tomb under the curse of sin (cf. Ps 16:9 – 11). When Asa's life ended, he was buried, along with spices and perfumes, "in the tomb that he had cut out for himself" (2Ch 16:14). However, one Son of David did not need to prepare a tomb for himself; he merely borrowed one for three days. When women came to anoint him with spices as had been done with previous kings, they found only his grave clothes.

Jesus could have relied on the flesh when he was tempted to eat in the wilderness after forty days of fasting

(continued on page 648)

THE STREAMING NATIONS

King Jehoshaphat began his reign by ridding the land of idolatry and reestablishing instruction in God's Word. As a result, the fear of the Lord fell on the nations that surrounded Judah so that they did not make war with Jehoshaphat. These foreign peoples came bringing treasure to King Jehoshaphat. Philistines and Arabs brought tribute gifts to him. Something similar had happened during the reign of Solomon. The nations were in awe of Solomon's wisdom and wanted to be associated with God's blessings in Solomon's life, so they brought tribute gifts to him (1Ki 10:23 – 25).

The Old Testament promised that what happened with Solomon and Jehoshaphat would happen in a greater way in the future. Isaiah prophesied that the nations would stream to Zion in order to learn the ways of God (Isa 2:2 – 3). Psalm 72:10 – 11 foretold that foreign kings would bring gifts to the Messiah and bow down before him, and Isaiah said those gifts would include incense and gold (Isa 60:6). According to Zechariah 8:23, "In those days ten people from all languages and nations will take firm hold of one Jew by the hem of his robe and say, 'Let us go with you, because we have heard that God is with you.' "

Matthew 2:11 shows the fulfillment of these prophecies when the wise men brought gold, frankincense and myrrh to the young king. Matthew 8:5 – 13 also shows the fulfillment of these prophecies when Jesus blessed a Gentile centurion because of his faith. And Revelation 21:24 predicts the final fulfillment of these promises when the kings of the earth bring their splendor into the new Jerusalem. What happened in the reign of King Jehoshaphat was just a preview — a glimpse — of what will happen when Jesus reigns once and for all! Right now nations are streaming to King Jesus as the gospel is preached among the previously unreached through the church's obedience to the Great Commission (Mt 28:18 – 20). The nations bow to Jesus, and they offer more than just their gifts — they offer their lives (Ro 12:1).

(A Better King, continued)

or escape the cross's suffering. But he fully relied on God, and three days later he walked away from death as David's descendant who reigns eternally. So Peter preached, "I can tell you confidently that the patriarch David died and was buried, and his tomb is here to this day. But he was a prophet and knew that God had promised him on oath that he would place one of his descendants on his throne. Seeing what was to come, he spoke of the resurrection of the Messiah, that he was not abandoned to the realm of the dead, nor did his body see decay" (Ac 2:29 – 31).

---

2 CHRONICLES 17:7 – 9

THE WORD PREACHED

The Lord was with King Jehoshaphat because he followed the example of his father David (v. 3). Not only did Jehoshaphat refuse to follow the Baals, but he was also a man of the law — the Word of God. The ideal king — like David early on — was a man who committed himself to God's law (cf. Dt 17:18 – 19). One of the ways that Jehoshaphat ordered and established his kingdom was by sending out officials, Levites and priests to every town in Judah to teach the law of God. King Jesus did the same thing in his ministry. Luke 10:1 says, "After this the Lord appointed seventy-two others and sent them two by two ahead of him to every town and place where he was about to go." They were sent out to teach about the kingdom of God (Lk 10:9). The teaching of the Word of God is critical to the kingdom of Christ and its advancement. As the Word spreads, the church grows (Ac 6:7; 12:24; 19:20).

5 So the king of Israel brought together the prophets — four hundred men —
and asked them, "Shall we go to war against Ramoth Gilead, or shall I not?"
"Go," they answered, "for God will give it into the king's hand."
6 But Jehoshaphat asked, "Is there no longer a prophet of the LORD here whom
we can inquire of?"
7 The king of Israel answered Jehoshaphat, "There is still one prophet through
whom we can inquire of the LORD, but I hate him because he never prophesies
anything good about me, but always bad. He is Micaiah son of Imlah."
"The king should not say such a thing," Jehoshaphat replied.
8 So the king of Israel called one of his officials and said, "Bring Micaiah son
of Imlah at once."
9 Dressed in their royal robes, the king of Israel and Jehoshaphat king of Judah
were sitting on their thrones at the threshing floor by the entrance of the gate of
Samaria, with all the prophets prophesying before them. 10 Now Zedekiah son of
Kenaanah had made iron horns, and he declared, "This is what the LORD says:
'With these you will gore the Arameans until they are destroyed.' "
11 All the other prophets were prophesying the same thing. "Attack Ramoth
Gilead and be victorious," they said, "for the LORD will give it into the king's
hand."
12 The messenger who had gone to summon Micaiah said to him, "Look, the
other prophets without exception are predicting success for the king. Let your
word agree with theirs, and speak favorably."
13 But Micaiah said, "As surely as the LORD lives, I can tell him only what my
God says."
14 When he arrived, the king asked him, "Micaiah, shall we go to war against
Ramoth Gilead, or shall I not?"
"Attack and be victorious," he answered, "for they will be given into your
hand."
15 The king said to him, "How many times must I make you swear to tell me
nothing but the truth in the name of the LORD?"
16 Then Micaiah answered, "I saw all Israel scattered on the hills like sheep
without a shepherd, and the LORD said, 'These people have no master. Let each
one go home in peace.' "
17 The king of Israel said to Jehoshaphat, "Didn't I tell you that he never prophesies anything good about me, but only bad?"
18 Micaiah continued, "Therefore hear the word of the LORD: I saw the LORD
sitting on his throne with all the multitudes of heaven standing on his right and
on his left. 19 And the LORD said, 'Who will entice Ahab king of Israel into attacking Ramoth Gilead and going to his death there?'
"One suggested this, and another that. 20 Finally, a spirit came forward, stood
before the LORD and said, 'I will entice him.'
" 'By what means?' the LORD asked.
21 " 'I will go and be a deceiving spirit in the mouths of all his prophets,' he said.
" 'You will succeed in enticing him,' said the LORD. 'Go and do it.'
22 "So now the LORD has put a deceiving spirit in the mouths of these prophets
of yours. The LORD has decreed disaster for you."
23 Then Zedekiah son of Kenaanah went up and slapped Micaiah in the face.
"Which way did the spirit from[a] the LORD go when he went from me to speak to
you?" he asked.
24 Micaiah replied, "You will find out on the day you go to hide in an inner
room."
25 The king of Israel then ordered, "Take Micaiah and send him back to Amon
the ruler of the city and to Joash the king's son, 26 and say, 'This is what the king
says: Put this fellow in prison and give him nothing but bread and water until I
return safely.' "

---

[a] 23 Or *Spirit of*

[27]Micaiah declared, "If you ever return safely, the LORD has not spoken
through me." Then he added, "Mark my words, all you people!"

Ahab Killed at Ramoth Gilead

[28]So the king of Israel and Jehoshaphat king of Judah went up to Ramoth Gilead. [29]The king of Israel said to Jehoshaphat, "I will enter the battle in disguise,
but you wear your royal robes." So the king of Israel disguised himself and went
into battle.
[30]Now the king of Aram had ordered his chariot commanders, "Do not fight
with anyone, small or great, except the king of Israel." [31]When the chariot commanders saw Jehoshaphat, they thought, "This is the king of Israel." So they
turned to attack him, but Jehoshaphat cried out, and the LORD helped him. God
drew them away from him, [32]for when the chariot commanders saw that he was
not the king of Israel, they stopped pursuing him.
[33]But someone drew his bow at random and hit the king of Israel between
the breastplate and the scale armor. The king told the chariot driver, "Wheel
around and get me out of the fighting. I've been wounded." [34]All day long the
battle raged, and the king of Israel propped himself up in his chariot facing the
Arameans until evening. Then at sunset he died.

19 When Jehoshaphat king of Judah returned safely to his palace in Jerusalem, [2]Jehu the seer, the son of Hanani, went out to meet him and said to
the king, "Should you help the wicked and love[a] those who hate the LORD? Because of this, the wrath of the LORD is on you. [3]There is, however, some good in
you, for you have rid the land of the Asherah poles and have set your heart on
seeking God."

Jehoshaphat Appoints Judges

[4]Jehoshaphat lived in Jerusalem, and he went out again among the people
from Beersheba to the hill country of Ephraim and turned them back to the
LORD, the God of their ancestors. [5]He appointed judges in the land, in each of the
fortified cities of Judah. [6]He told them, "Consider carefully what you do, because
you are not judging for mere mortals but for the LORD, who is with you whenever
you give a verdict. [7]Now let the fear of the LORD be on you. Judge carefully, for
with the LORD our God there is no injustice or partiality or bribery."
[8]In Jerusalem also, Jehoshaphat appointed some of the Levites, priests and
heads of Israelite families to administer the law of the LORD and to settle disputes. And they lived in Jerusalem. [9]He gave them these orders: "You must serve
faithfully and wholeheartedly in the fear of the LORD. [10]In every case that comes
before you from your people who live in the cities — whether bloodshed or other
concerns of the law, commands, decrees or regulations — you are to warn them
not to sin against the LORD; otherwise his wrath will come on you and your people. Do this, and you will not sin.
[11]"Amariah the chief priest will be over you in any matter concerning the
LORD, and Zebadiah son of Ishmael, the leader of the tribe of Judah, will be over
you in any matter concerning the king, and the Levites will serve as officials
before you. Act with courage, and may the LORD be with those who do well."

Jehoshaphat Defeats Moab and Ammon

20 After this, the Moabites and Ammonites with some of the Meunites[b]
came to wage war against Jehoshaphat.
[2]Some people came and told Jehoshaphat, "A vast army is coming against you
from Edom,[c] from the other side of the Dead Sea. It is already in Hazezon Tamar"
(that is, En Gedi). [3]Alarmed, Jehoshaphat resolved to inquire of the LORD, and
he proclaimed a fast for all Judah. [4]The people of Judah came together to seek
help from the LORD; indeed, they came from every town in Judah to seek him.

[a] 2 Or *and make alliances with* [b] 1 Some Septuagint manuscripts; Hebrew *Ammonites*
[c] 2 One Hebrew manuscript; most Hebrew manuscripts, Septuagint and Vulgate *Aram*

2 CHRONICLES 18:1 – 27

THE REJECTED PROPHET

It could be easy to get caught up in the details of this passage, confused about the mention of an enticing spirit, and miss the point. King Jehoshaphat entered an unholy alliance with the wicked King Ahab of Israel, and they decided to go to battle against the Arameans. However, Jehoshaphat at least had enough sense to request counsel from a true prophet of Yahweh before they went to war. Ahab didn't like the prophet Micaiah because Micaiah always spoke against Ahab. True to form, Micaiah prophesied for God that Ahab would die in battle. In response, Zedekiah, one of Ahab's four hundred prophets, struck Micaiah on the cheek and mocked him. Finally, Ahab had Micaiah thrown in jail.

Micaiah's ministry points to Jesus' ministry as the true but rejected prophet of the Lord. Like Micaiah, Jesus was struck on the cheek and mocked (Mt 26:67 – 68). Like Micaiah, Jesus was seized for his message and put in captivity. And yet, God's rejected prophets are always vindicated. Micaiah was vindicated when Ahab fell on the battlefield. And Jesus' words that his opponents would see him coming on the clouds of heaven will be vindicated at his second coming — with power and glory (Mt 24:30; Mt 26:64).

[5]Then Jehoshaphat stood up in the assembly of Judah and Jerusalem at the
temple of the LORD in the front of the new courtyard [6]and said:

"LORD, the God of our ancestors, are you not the God who is in heav-
en? You rule over all the kingdoms of the nations. Power and might are in
your hand, and no one can withstand you. [7]Our God, did you not drive out
the inhabitants of this land before your people Israel and give it forever to
the descendants of Abraham your friend? [8]They have lived in it and have
built in it a sanctuary for your Name, saying, [9]'If calamity comes upon us,
whether the sword of judgment, or plague or famine, we will stand in your
presence before this temple that bears your Name and will cry out to you
in our distress, and you will hear us and save us.'
[10]"But now here are men from Ammon, Moab and Mount Seir, whose
territory you would not allow Israel to invade when they came from Egypt;
so they turned away from them and did not destroy them. [11]See how they
are repaying us by coming to drive us out of the possession you gave us as
an inheritance. [12]Our God, will you not judge them? For we have no power
to face this vast army that is attacking us. We do not know what to do, but
our eyes are on you."

[13]All the men of Judah, with their wives and children and little ones, stood
there before the LORD.
[14]Then the Spirit of the LORD came on Jahaziel son of Zechariah, the son of Benaiah, the son of Jeiel, the son of Mattaniah, a Levite and descendant of Asaph,
as he stood in the assembly.
[15]He said: "Listen, King Jehoshaphat and all who live in Judah and Jerusalem!
This is what the LORD says to you: 'Do not be afraid or discouraged because of
this vast army. For the battle is not yours, but God's. [16]Tomorrow march down
against them. They will be climbing up by the Pass of Ziz, and you will find them
at the end of the gorge in the Desert of Jeruel. [17]You will not have to fight this
battle. Take up your positions; stand firm and see the deliverance the LORD will
give you, Judah and Jerusalem. Do not be afraid; do not be discouraged. Go out
to face them tomorrow, and the LORD will be with you.'"
[18]Jehoshaphat bowed down with his face to the ground, and all the people of
Judah and Jerusalem fell down in worship before the LORD. [19]Then some Levites
from the Kohathites and Korahites stood up and praised the LORD, the God of
Israel, with a very loud voice.
[20]Early in the morning they left for the Desert of Tekoa. As they set out, Jehoshaphat stood and said, "Listen to me, Judah and people of Jerusalem! Have faith
in the LORD your God and you will be upheld; have faith in his prophets and you
will be successful." [21]After consulting the people, Jehoshaphat appointed men to
sing to the LORD and to praise him for the splendor of his[a] holiness as they went
out at the head of the army, saying:

"Give thanks to the LORD,
for his love endures forever."

[22]As they began to sing and praise, the LORD set ambushes against the men
of Ammon and Moab and Mount Seir who were invading Judah, and they were
defeated. [23]The Ammonites and Moabites rose up against the men from Mount
Seir to destroy and annihilate them. After they finished slaughtering the men
from Seir, they helped to destroy one another.
[24]When the men of Judah came to the place that overlooks the desert and
looked toward the vast army, they saw only dead bodies lying on the ground;
no one had escaped. [25]So Jehoshaphat and his men went to carry off their plunder, and they found among them a great amount of equipment and clothing[b]
and also articles of value — more than they could take away. There was so much

2 CHRONICLES 20:5 – 12

PRAYER FOR DELIVERANCE

When the Moabites and the Ammonites came against Judah, the people gathered for prayer. This action displayed trust in promises God had given to Solomon in response to Solomon's temple dedication prayer (2Ch 7:11 – 16). In that prayer, Solomon had prayed that God would hear the cries of his people when they faced the temple (2Ch 6:14 – 42). In fact, Solomon had specifically prayed that whenever disaster or a foreign army came against Israel, the people should stand before God at the temple and cry to him for salvation.

In his prayer (known as the Lord's Prayer), Jesus similarly trained his disciples to pray that they would be "deliver[ed] ... from the evil one" (Mt 6:9 – 13). The New Testament reminds believers that the enemy is not "flesh and blood" (Eph 6:12) and that they can place their hope in Christ since he is in control and has placed all enemies under his feet (1Co 15:25; Eph 1:22).

[a] 21 Or *him with the splendor of* [b] 25 Some Hebrew manuscripts and Vulgate; most Hebrew manuscripts *corpses*

plunder that it took three days to collect it. [26]On the fourth day they assembled in the Valley of Berakah, where they praised the LORD. This is why it is called the Valley of Berakah[a] to this day.

[27]Then, led by Jehoshaphat, all the men of Judah and Jerusalem returned joyfully to Jerusalem, for the LORD had given them cause to rejoice over their enemies. [28]They entered Jerusalem and went to the temple of the LORD with harps and lyres and trumpets.

[29]The fear of God came on all the surrounding kingdoms when they heard how the LORD had fought against the enemies of Israel. [30]And the kingdom of Jehoshaphat was at peace, for his God had given him rest on every side.

The End of Jehoshaphat's Reign

[31]So Jehoshaphat reigned over Judah. He was thirty-five years old when he became king of Judah, and he reigned in Jerusalem twenty-five years. His mother's name was Azubah daughter of Shilhi. [32]He followed the ways of his father Asa and did not stray from them; he did what was right in the eyes of the LORD. [33]The high places, however, were not removed, and the people still had not set their hearts on the God of their ancestors.

[34]The other events of Jehoshaphat's reign, from beginning to end, are written in the annals of Jehu son of Hanani, which are recorded in the book of the kings of Israel.

[35]Later, Jehoshaphat king of Judah made an alliance with Ahaziah king of Israel, whose ways were wicked. [36]He agreed with him to construct a fleet of trading ships.[b] After these were built at Ezion Geber, [37]Eliezer son of Dodavahu of Mareshah prophesied against Jehoshaphat, saying, "Because you have made an alliance with Ahaziah, the LORD will destroy what you have made." The ships were wrecked and were not able to set sail to trade.[c]

21 Then Jehoshaphat rested with his ancestors and was buried with them in the City of David. And Jehoram his son succeeded him as king. [2]Jehoram's brothers, the sons of Jehoshaphat, were Azariah, Jehiel, Zechariah, Azariahu, Michael and Shephatiah. All these were sons of Jehoshaphat king of Israel.[d] [3]Their father had given them many gifts of silver and gold and articles of value, as well as fortified cities in Judah, but he had given the kingdom to Jehoram because he was his firstborn son.

Jehoram King of Judah

[4]When Jehoram established himself firmly over his father's kingdom, he put all his brothers to the sword along with some of the officials of Israel. [5]Jehoram was thirty-two years old when he became king, and he reigned in Jerusalem eight years. [6]He followed the ways of the kings of Israel, as the house of Ahab had done, for he married a daughter of Ahab. He did evil in the eyes of the LORD. [7]Nevertheless, because of the covenant the LORD had made with David, the LORD was not willing to destroy the house of David. He had promised to maintain a lamp for him and his descendants forever.

[8]In the time of Jehoram, Edom rebelled against Judah and set up its own king. [9]So Jehoram went there with his officers and all his chariots. The Edomites surrounded him and his chariot commanders, but he rose up and broke through by night. [10]To this day Edom has been in rebellion against Judah.

Libnah revolted at the same time, because Jehoram had forsaken the LORD, the God of his ancestors. [11]He had also built high places on the hills of Judah and had caused the people of Jerusalem to prostitute themselves and had led Judah astray.

[12]Jehoram received a letter from Elijah the prophet, which said:

"This is what the LORD, the God of your father David, says: 'You have not followed the ways of your father Jehoshaphat or of Asa king of Judah. [13]But

---

[a] 26 *Berakah* means *praise.* [b] 36 Hebrew *of ships that could go to Tarshish* [c] 37 Hebrew *sail for Tarshish* [d] 2 That is, Judah, as frequently in 2 Chronicles

WORSHIP AS WARFARE

Armies from Moab and Ammon came against King Jehoshaphat and Judah. The Spirit came on a Levite named Jahaziel. He told the people not to be afraid because the Lord would deliver them in battle, and the people would not have to lift a weapon. Instead, they were to stand still and watch God save them. Then, something amazing happened. The army held a worship service where singers went out in front of the army praising God for the splendor of his holiness. As they sang praises, God destroyed the enemy army! When Judah's army finally got to the spot, they found only dead bodies, and it took three days to carry away all of the plunder.

This victory pointed forward to Jesus Christ. Jesus defeated his people's enemies on their behalf (Heb 2:14–15; 10:13). And, like the Old Testament saints, believers today engage in worship as warfare against the enemies — "not against flesh and blood, but ... against the powers of this dark world and against the spiritual forces of evil in the heavenly realms" (Eph 6:12). Worship was seen as warfare throughout the Bible. Worship is described in the Old Testament as "appearing before God," which gave the imagery of an army assembling for inspection by the commanding officer. After all, God responded to the prayers of his people by defeating Egypt (Ex 3:7–10). And, the trumpet-led worship service at Jericho caused the walls to fall down (Jos 6:20).

In worship gatherings today, the people do not gather at Mount Sinai, but rather they gather spiritually at Mount Zion, surrounded by innumerable angels and the redeemed of all the ages (Heb 12:22–23). And as they worship the Lord he thunders from heaven, promising that he is in the process of establishing a kingdom that cannot be shaken. When God talked about his judgment at the end of the age, he pointed to the story of Jehoshaphat (Joel 3:1–2,12–13). The book of Hebrews further confirms the connection between worship and that day of judgment. God — a consuming fire who devours the enemy and rescues his people — will someday go to war in the final judgment in response to the church's worship (Heb 12:25–29; cf. Rev 8:3–5).

you have followed the ways of the kings of Israel, and you have led Judah
and the people of Jerusalem to prostitute themselves, just as the house of
Ahab did. You have also murdered your own brothers, members of your
own family, men who were better than you. 14So now the LORD is about to
strike your people, your sons, your wives and everything that is yours, with
a heavy blow. 15You yourself will be very ill with a lingering disease of the
bowels, until the disease causes your bowels to come out.' "

16The LORD aroused against Jehoram the hostility of the Philistines and of the
Arabs who lived near the Cushites. 17They attacked Judah, invaded it and carried
off all the goods found in the king's palace, together with his sons and wives. Not
a son was left to him except Ahaziah,[a] the youngest.
18After all this, the LORD afflicted Jehoram with an incurable disease of the
bowels. 19In the course of time, at the end of the second year, his bowels came
out because of the disease, and he died in great pain. His people made no funeral
fire in his honor, as they had for his predecessors.
20Jehoram was thirty-two years old when he became king, and he reigned in
Jerusalem eight years. He passed away, to no one's regret, and was buried in the
City of David, but not in the tombs of the kings.

Ahaziah King of Judah

22 The people of Jerusalem made Ahaziah, Jehoram's youngest son, king in
his place, since the raiders, who came with the Arabs into the camp, had
killed all the older sons. So Ahaziah son of Jehoram king of Judah began to reign.
2Ahaziah was twenty-two[b] years old when he became king, and he reigned in
Jerusalem one year. His mother's name was Athaliah, a granddaughter of Omri.
3He too followed the ways of the house of Ahab, for his mother encouraged
him to act wickedly. 4He did evil in the eyes of the LORD, as the house of Ahab
had done, for after his father's death they became his advisers, to his undoing.
5He also followed their counsel when he went with Joram[c] son of Ahab king of
Israel to wage war against Hazael king of Aram at Ramoth Gilead. The Arameans
wounded Joram; 6so he returned to Jezreel to recover from the wounds they had
inflicted on him at Ramoth[d] in his battle with Hazael king of Aram.
Then Ahaziah[e] son of Jehoram king of Judah went down to Jezreel to see Joram son of Ahab because he had been wounded.
7Through Ahaziah's visit to Joram, God brought about Ahaziah's downfall.
When Ahaziah arrived, he went out with Joram to meet Jehu son of Nimshi, whom
the LORD had anointed to destroy the house of Ahab. 8While Jehu was executing
judgment on the house of Ahab, he found the officials of Judah and the sons of
Ahaziah's relatives, who had been attending Ahaziah, and he killed them. 9He
then went in search of Ahaziah, and his men captured him while he was hiding
in Samaria. He was brought to Jehu and put to death. They buried him, for they
said, "He was a son of Jehoshaphat, who sought the LORD with all his heart." So
there was no one in the house of Ahaziah powerful enough to retain the kingdom.

Athaliah and Joash

10When Athaliah the mother of Ahaziah saw that her son was dead, she proceeded to destroy the whole royal family of the house of Judah. 11But Jehosheba,[f]
the daughter of King Jehoram, took Joash son of Ahaziah and stole him away
from among the royal princes who were about to be murdered and put him and
his nurse in a bedroom. Because Jehosheba,[f] the daughter of King Jehoram and
wife of the priest Jehoiada, was Ahaziah's sister, she hid the child from Athaliah

---

[a] *17* Hebrew *Jehoahaz,* a variant of *Ahaziah* [b] *2* Some Septuagint manuscripts and Syriac (see also 2 Kings 8:26); Hebrew *forty-two* [c] *5* Hebrew *Jehoram,* a variant of *Joram*; also in verses 6 and 7 [d] *6* Hebrew *Ramah,* a variant of *Ramoth* [e] *6* Some Hebrew manuscripts, Septuagint, Vulgate and Syriac (see also 2 Kings 8:29); most Hebrew manuscripts *Azariah*
[f] *11* Hebrew *Jehoshabeath,* a variant of *Jehosheba*

THE HIDDEN SAVIOR

When the wicked Athaliah saw that her son Ahaziah was dead, she attempted to murder all of his sons, but Joash was hidden away. The background to this story was the promise of offspring. In Genesis 3:15, God promised a war between the serpent's offspring and the woman's offspring. That meant there would be a great cosmic war throughout history where Satan would attempt to wipe out the line of the Messiah before the Savior came. He moved Cain to murder Abel (Ge 4:1 – 16), Pharaoh to kill the Hebrew males (Ex 1:8 – 22), Haman to attempt to exterminate the Jews in the book of Esther, and Herod to attempt to kill Jesus (Mt 2:13 – 18). This passage in 2 Chronicles would have seemed familiar to the post-exilic Jews. The account of a wicked tyrant attempting to kill many sons, one of whom was hidden and preserved, reminded the text's original audience of the ongoing war between the serpent's offspring and the woman's. And it pointed forward to Jesus who was hidden from Herod and who later saved the world from its sin.

Athaliah attempted to kill all of David's royal descendants, which would have put an end to God's promise that a descendant of David would establish an eternal kingdom (2Sa 7:4 – 17). Her attempt seemed successful, and the promises to David looked dead in Jerusalem tombs. But God has a way of resurrecting seemingly dead promises. When Joash was finally revealed as alive, a coup was staged, Athaliah was killed and David's offspring once again assumed the throne. The Lord brought life out of what seemed like death.

God so loved the world that he would not allow the line of the Messiah to be wiped out — and when the time was right, he brought forth a son of David who brings everlasting life to all who believe in him. Joash's story points forward to Christ in yet another way. The number seven is highly significant in the Bible. It is the number of the Sabbath — the number of rest. Joash, the son of David, was hidden from a murderous tyrant, assumed the throne and brought Sabbath rest to the land after six years under Athaliah's burdensome rule. Jesus, the son of David, would be hidden from a murderous tyrant. Jesus would defeat the enemies. Jesus would assume the throne. And one day, Jesus will bring his people the final rest (Heb 4:3).

so she could not kill him. 12He remained hidden with them at the temple of God
for six years while Athaliah ruled the land.

23 In the seventh year Jehoiada showed his strength. He made a covenant
with the commanders of units of a hundred: Azariah son of Jeroham,
Ishmael son of Jehohanan, Azariah son of Obed, Maaseiah son of Adaiah, and
Elishaphat son of Zikri. 2They went throughout Judah and gathered the Levites
and the heads of Israelite families from all the towns. When they came to Jerusalem, 3the whole assembly made a covenant with the king at the temple of God.

Jehoiada said to them, "The king's son shall reign, as the LORD promised concerning the descendants of David. 4Now this is what you are to do: A third of you
priests and Levites who are going on duty on the Sabbath are to keep watch at
the doors, 5a third of you at the royal palace and a third at the Foundation Gate,
and all the others are to be in the courtyards of the temple of the LORD. 6No one is
to enter the temple of the LORD except the priests and Levites on duty; they may
enter because they are consecrated, but all the others are to observe the LORD's
command not to enter.[a] 7The Levites are to station themselves around the king,
each with weapon in hand. Anyone who enters the temple is to be put to death.
Stay close to the king wherever he goes."

8The Levites and all the men of Judah did just as Jehoiada the priest ordered.
Each one took his men — those who were going on duty on the Sabbath and those
who were going off duty — for Jehoiada the priest had not released any of the
divisions. 9Then he gave the commanders of units of a hundred the spears and
the large and small shields that had belonged to King David and that were in the
temple of God. 10He stationed all the men, each with his weapon in his hand,
around the king — near the altar and the temple, from the south side to the north
side of the temple.

11Jehoiada and his sons brought out the king's son and put the crown on him;
they presented him with a copy of the covenant and proclaimed him king. They
anointed him and shouted, "Long live the king!"

12When Athaliah heard the noise of the people running and cheering the
king, she went to them at the temple of the LORD. 13She looked, and there was
the king, standing by his pillar at the entrance. The officers and the trumpeters
were beside the king, and all the people of the land were rejoicing and blowing
trumpets, and musicians with their instruments were leading the praises. Then
Athaliah tore her robes and shouted, "Treason! Treason!"

14Jehoiada the priest sent out the commanders of units of a hundred, who were
in charge of the troops, and said to them: "Bring her out between the ranks[b] and
put to the sword anyone who follows her." For the priest had said, "Do not put her
to death at the temple of the LORD." 15So they seized her as she reached the entrance of the Horse Gate on the palace grounds, and there they put her to death.

16Jehoiada then made a covenant that he, the people and the king[c] would be
the LORD's people. 17All the people went to the temple of Baal and tore it down.
They smashed the altars and idols and killed Mattan the priest of Baal in front
of the altars.

18Then Jehoiada placed the oversight of the temple of the LORD in the hands
of the Levitical priests, to whom David had made assignments in the temple, to
present the burnt offerings of the LORD as written in the Law of Moses, with rejoicing and singing, as David had ordered. 19He also stationed gatekeepers at the
gates of the LORD's temple so that no one who was in any way unclean might enter.

20He took with him the commanders of hundreds, the nobles, the rulers of the
people and all the people of the land and brought the king down from the temple
of the LORD. They went into the palace through the Upper Gate and seated the
king on the royal throne. 21All the people of the land rejoiced, and the city was
calm, because Athaliah had been slain with the sword.

---

[a] 6 Or *are to stand guard where the LORD has assigned them* [b] 14 Or *out from the precincts*
[c] 16 Or *covenant between the LORD and the people and the king that they* (see 2 Kings 11:17)

2 CHRONICLES 24:17–22

KILLING GOD'S MESSENGER

King Joash only did good things as long as he was under the authority of God's priest Jehoiada. As soon as Jehoiada died, Joash failed. He began to listen to the wrong advisors and became an idolater. God empowered Jehoiada's son Zechariah with the Spirit to prophesy against Joash for his evil. However, Joash rejected Zechariah's words and had him killed. Worse yet, Zechariah was stoned to death in the temple courtyard.

This scene points forward to a parable that Jesus told about tenants who were renting a vineyard (Mt 21:33–46). When the landowner sent servants to collect the harvest from the tenants, the tenants killed the servants and eventually murdered the owner's son. One of the servants was stoned to death. Jesus told that parable to indict the nation of Israel and its leaders for the way they treated God's messengers, and he predicted that this habit of murdering God's prophets would culminate in the murder of God's Son. Jesus again referenced that sweep of Old Testament history in Matthew 23:35 when he said they would be held responsible for all the righteous blood shed on earth, from Abel to Zechariah. Jesus' murder on the cross was the climax of Israel's bloody history of rejecting and killing the messengers that God sent to them.

Joash Repairs the Temple

24 Joash was seven years old when he became king, and he reigned in Jerusalem forty years. His mother's name was Zibiah; she was from Beersheba. 2Joash did what was right in the eyes of the LORD all the years of Jehoiada the priest. 3Jehoiada chose two wives for him, and he had sons and daughters.

4Some time later Joash decided to restore the temple of the LORD. 5He called together the priests and Levites and said to them, "Go to the towns of Judah and collect the money due annually from all Israel, to repair the temple of your God. Do it now." But the Levites did not act at once.

6Therefore the king summoned Jehoiada the chief priest and said to him, "Why haven't you required the Levites to bring in from Judah and Jerusalem the tax imposed by Moses the servant of the LORD and by the assembly of Israel for the tent of the covenant law?"

7Now the sons of that wicked woman Athaliah had broken into the temple of God and had used even its sacred objects for the Baals.

8At the king's command, a chest was made and placed outside, at the gate of the temple of the LORD. 9A proclamation was then issued in Judah and Jerusalem that they should bring to the LORD the tax that Moses the servant of God had required of Israel in the wilderness. 10All the officials and all the people brought their contributions gladly, dropping them into the chest until it was full. 11Whenever the chest was brought in by the Levites to the king's officials and they saw that there was a large amount of money, the royal secretary and the officer of the chief priest would come and empty the chest and carry it back to its place. They did this regularly and collected a great amount of money. 12The king and Jehoiada gave it to those who carried out the work required for the temple of the LORD. They hired masons and carpenters to restore the LORD's temple, and also workers in iron and bronze to repair the temple.

13The men in charge of the work were diligent, and the repairs progressed under them. They rebuilt the temple of God according to its original design and reinforced it. 14When they had finished, they brought the rest of the money to the king and Jehoiada, and with it were made articles for the LORD's temple: articles for the service and for the burnt offerings, and also dishes and other objects of gold and silver. As long as Jehoiada lived, burnt offerings were presented continually in the temple of the LORD.

15Now Jehoiada was old and full of years, and he died at the age of a hundred and thirty. 16He was buried with the kings in the City of David, because of the good he had done in Israel for God and his temple.

The Wickedness of Joash

17After the death of Jehoiada, the officials of Judah came and paid homage to the king, and he listened to them. 18They abandoned the temple of the LORD, the God of their ancestors, and worshiped Asherah poles and idols. Because of their guilt, God's anger came on Judah and Jerusalem. 19Although the LORD sent prophets to the people to bring them back to him, and though they testified against them, they would not listen.

20Then the Spirit of God came on Zechariah son of Jehoiada the priest. He stood before the people and said, "This is what God says: 'Why do you disobey the LORD's commands? You will not prosper. Because you have forsaken the LORD, he has forsaken you.'"

21But they plotted against him, and by order of the king they stoned him to death in the courtyard of the LORD's temple. 22King Joash did not remember the kindness Zechariah's father Jehoiada had shown him but killed his son, who said as he lay dying, "May the LORD see this and call you to account."

23At the turn of the year,[a] the army of Aram marched against Joash; it invaded Judah and Jerusalem and killed all the leaders of the people. They sent all the

[a] 23 Probably in the spring

2 CHRONICLES 24:4 – 14

THE NEW TEMPLE

Joash was a good king who did what was right as long as he was under the authority of God's priest. He decided to repair and rebuild the temple because its sacred objects had been used blasphemously to worship Baal. Therefore, Joash commanded the Levites to take up a collection to fund the repairs. When they resisted, Joash had a chest made and called on the people to put money in that chest to fund the repairs. The people joyfully brought their gifts, and the temple was restored.

Many have looked to passages like this to justify giving campaigns for their churches. They might even put together a "Chest of Joash" that people can fill with money dedicated to repairing the roof of the church. But that is not how to apply this passage to our times. Today, the temple is not a building made with bricks and mortar; it is the body of Christ. Joash repaired the temple because kings were temple-builders. The original temple built by King Solomon was torn down by the Babylonians, and the rebuilt temple of Jesus' day was destroyed by the Romans. But the prophets prophesied that a greater temple would be built by a king (Zec 6:12 – 15).

In the New Testament, King Jesus identified his own body as the temple when he equated the rebuilding of the temple with his resurrection from the dead: "Destroy this temple, and I will raise it again in three days" (Jn 2:19). The new temple is Christ's body, and God's people are incorporated into the body of Christ through the unifying work of the Spirit. The church, as the body of Christ, is the new temple where God dwells (Eph 2:19 – 22). The Spirit of God which fell on the tabernacle and later fell on Solomon's temple and which descended on Jesus like a dove has now fallen on the church of God (Ac 2:1 – 21). Money donated for a construction project does not build the new temple. Rather, the spiritually gifted people of the church build it up in Christ Jesus (Eph 4:11 – 16).

plunder to their king in Damascus. 24Although the Aramean army had come
with only a few men, the LORD delivered into their hands a much larger army.
Because Judah had forsaken the LORD, the God of their ancestors, judgment was
executed on Joash. 25When the Arameans withdrew, they left Joash severely
wounded. His officials conspired against him for murdering the son of Jehoiada
the priest, and they killed him in his bed. So he died and was buried in the City
of David, but not in the tombs of the kings.

26Those who conspired against him were Zabad,[a] son of Shimeath an Ammonite woman, and Jehozabad, son of Shimrith[b] a Moabite woman. 27The
account of his sons, the many prophecies about him, and the record of the restoration of the temple of God are written in the annotations on the book of the
kings. And Amaziah his son succeeded him as king.

Amaziah King of Judah

25 Amaziah was twenty-five years old when he became king, and he reigned
in Jerusalem twenty-nine years. His mother's name was Jehoaddan; she
was from Jerusalem. 2He did what was right in the eyes of the LORD, but not
wholeheartedly. 3After the kingdom was firmly in his control, he executed the
officials who had murdered his father the king. 4Yet he did not put their children
to death, but acted in accordance with what is written in the Law, in the Book
of Moses, where the LORD commanded: "Parents shall not be put to death for
their children, nor children be put to death for their parents; each will die for
their own sin."[c]

5Amaziah called the people of Judah together and assigned them according
to their families to commanders of thousands and commanders of hundreds for
all Judah and Benjamin. He then mustered those twenty years old or more and
found that there were three hundred thousand men fit for military service, able
to handle the spear and shield. 6He also hired a hundred thousand fighting men
from Israel for a hundred talents[d] of silver.

7But a man of God came to him and said, "Your Majesty, these troops from
Israel must not march with you, for the LORD is not with Israel—not with any of
the people of Ephraim. 8Even if you go and fight courageously in battle, God will
overthrow you before the enemy, for God has the power to help or to overthrow."

9Amaziah asked the man of God, "But what about the hundred talents I paid
for these Israelite troops?"

The man of God replied, "The LORD can give you much more than that."

10So Amaziah dismissed the troops who had come to him from Ephraim and
sent them home. They were furious with Judah and left for home in a great rage.

11Amaziah then marshaled his strength and led his army to the Valley of Salt,
where he killed ten thousand men of Seir. 12The army of Judah also captured ten
thousand men alive, took them to the top of a cliff and threw them down so that
all were dashed to pieces.

13Meanwhile the troops that Amaziah had sent back and had not allowed to
take part in the war raided towns belonging to Judah from Samaria to Beth Horon. They killed three thousand people and carried off great quantities of plunder.

14When Amaziah returned from slaughtering the Edomites, he brought back
the gods of the people of Seir. He set them up as his own gods, bowed down to
them and burned sacrifices to them. 15The anger of the LORD burned against
Amaziah, and he sent a prophet to him, who said, "Why do you consult this people's gods, which could not save their own people from your hand?"

16While he was still speaking, the king said to him, "Have we appointed you
an adviser to the king? Stop! Why be struck down?"

So the prophet stopped but said, "I know that God has determined to destroy
you, because you have done this and have not listened to my counsel."

---

[a] *26* A variant of *Jozabad* [b] *26* A variant of *Shomer* [c] *4* Deut. 24:16 [d] *6* That is, about
3 3/4 tons or about 3.4 metric tons; also in verse 9

[17]After Amaziah king of Judah consulted his advisers, he sent this challenge to Jehoash[a] son of Jehoahaz, the son of Jehu, king of Israel: "Come, let us face each other in battle."

[18]But Jehoash king of Israel replied to Amaziah king of Judah: "A thistle in Lebanon sent a message to a cedar in Lebanon, 'Give your daughter to my son in marriage.' Then a wild beast in Lebanon came along and trampled the thistle underfoot. [19]You say to yourself that you have defeated Edom, and now you are arrogant and proud. But stay at home! Why ask for trouble and cause your own downfall and that of Judah also?"

[20]Amaziah, however, would not listen, for God so worked that he might deliver them into the hands of Jehoash, because they sought the gods of Edom. [21]So Jehoash king of Israel attacked. He and Amaziah king of Judah faced each other at Beth Shemesh in Judah. [22]Judah was routed by Israel, and every man fled to his home. [23]Jehoash king of Israel captured Amaziah king of Judah, the son of Joash, the son of Ahaziah,[b] at Beth Shemesh. Then Jehoash brought him to Jerusalem and broke down the wall of Jerusalem from the Ephraim Gate to the Corner Gate — a section about four hundred cubits[c] long. [24]He took all the gold and silver and all the articles found in the temple of God that had been in the care of Obed-Edom, together with the palace treasures and the hostages, and returned to Samaria.

[25]Amaziah son of Joash king of Judah lived for fifteen years after the death of Jehoash son of Jehoahaz king of Israel. [26]As for the other events of Amaziah's reign, from beginning to end, are they not written in the book of the kings of Judah and Israel? [27]From the time that Amaziah turned away from following the LORD, they conspired against him in Jerusalem and he fled to Lachish, but they sent men after him to Lachish and killed him there. [28]He was brought back by horse and was buried with his ancestors in the City of Judah.[d]

Uzziah King of Judah

26 Then all the people of Judah took Uzziah,[e] who was sixteen years old, and made him king in place of his father Amaziah. [2]He was the one who rebuilt Elath and restored it to Judah after Amaziah rested with his ancestors.

[3]Uzziah was sixteen years old when he became king, and he reigned in Jerusalem fifty-two years. His mother's name was Jekoliah; she was from Jerusalem. [4]He did what was right in the eyes of the LORD, just as his father Amaziah had done. [5]He sought God during the days of Zechariah, who instructed him in the fear[f] of God. As long as he sought the LORD, God gave him success.

[6]He went to war against the Philistines and broke down the walls of Gath, Jabneh and Ashdod. He then rebuilt towns near Ashdod and elsewhere among the Philistines. [7]God helped him against the Philistines and against the Arabs who lived in Gur Baal and against the Meunites. [8]The Ammonites brought tribute to Uzziah, and his fame spread as far as the border of Egypt, because he had become very powerful.

[9]Uzziah built towers in Jerusalem at the Corner Gate, at the Valley Gate and at the angle of the wall, and he fortified them. [10]He also built towers in the wilderness and dug many cisterns, because he had much livestock in the foothills and in the plain. He had people working his fields and vineyards in the hills and in the fertile lands, for he loved the soil.

[11]Uzziah had a well-trained army, ready to go out by divisions according to their numbers as mustered by Jeiel the secretary and Maaseiah the officer under the direction of Hananiah, one of the royal officials. [12]The total number of family leaders over the fighting men was 2,600. [13]Under their command was an army

---

[a] *17* Hebrew *Joash,* a variant of *Jehoash;* also in verses 18, 21, 23 and 25 [b] *23* Hebrew *Jehoahaz,* a variant of *Ahaziah* [c] *23* That is, about 600 feet or about 180 meters
[d] *28* Most Hebrew manuscripts; some Hebrew manuscripts, Septuagint, Vulgate and Syriac (see also 2 Kings 14:20) *David* [e] *1* Also called *Azariah* [f] *5* Many Hebrew manuscripts, Septuagint and Syriac; other Hebrew manuscripts *vision*

of 307,500 men trained for war, a powerful force to support the king against his enemies. [14]Uzziah provided shields, spears, helmets, coats of armor, bows and slingstones for the entire army. [15]In Jerusalem he made devices invented for use on the towers and on the corner defenses so that soldiers could shoot arrows and hurl large stones from the walls. His fame spread far and wide, for he was greatly helped until he became powerful.

[16]But after Uzziah became powerful, his pride led to his downfall. He was unfaithful to the LORD his God, and entered the temple of the LORD to burn incense on the altar of incense. [17]Azariah the priest with eighty other courageous priests of the LORD followed him in. [18]They confronted King Uzziah and said, "It is not right for you, Uzziah, to burn incense to the LORD. That is for the priests, the descendants of Aaron, who have been consecrated to burn incense. Leave the sanctuary, for you have been unfaithful; and you will not be honored by the LORD God."

[19]Uzziah, who had a censer in his hand ready to burn incense, became angry. While he was raging at the priests in their presence before the incense altar in the LORD's temple, leprosy[a] broke out on his forehead. [20]When Azariah the chief priest and all the other priests looked at him, they saw that he had leprosy on his forehead, so they hurried him out. Indeed, he himself was eager to leave, because the LORD had afflicted him.

[21]King Uzziah had leprosy until the day he died. He lived in a separate house[b]—leprous, and banned from the temple of the LORD. Jotham his son had charge of the palace and governed the people of the land.

[22]The other events of Uzziah's reign, from beginning to end, are recorded by the prophet Isaiah son of Amoz. [23]Uzziah rested with his ancestors and was buried near them in a cemetery that belonged to the kings, for people said, "He had leprosy." And Jotham his son succeeded him as king.

Jotham King of Judah

27 Jotham was twenty-five years old when he became king, and he reigned in Jerusalem sixteen years. His mother's name was Jerusha daughter of Zadok. [2]He did what was right in the eyes of the LORD, just as his father Uzziah had done, but unlike him he did not enter the temple of the LORD. The people, however, continued their corrupt practices. [3]Jotham rebuilt the Upper Gate of the temple of the LORD and did extensive work on the wall at the hill of Ophel. [4]He built towns in the hill country of Judah and forts and towers in the wooded areas.

[5]Jotham waged war against the king of the Ammonites and conquered them. That year the Ammonites paid him a hundred talents[c] of silver, ten thousand cors[d] of wheat and ten thousand cors[e] of barley. The Ammonites brought him the same amount also in the second and third years.

[6]Jotham grew powerful because he walked steadfastly before the LORD his God.

[7]The other events in Jotham's reign, including all his wars and the other things he did, are written in the book of the kings of Israel and Judah. [8]He was twenty-five years old when he became king, and he reigned in Jerusalem sixteen years. [9]Jotham rested with his ancestors and was buried in the City of David. And Ahaz his son succeeded him as king.

Ahaz King of Judah

28 Ahaz was twenty years old when he became king, and he reigned in Jerusalem sixteen years. Unlike David his father, he did not do what was right in the eyes of the LORD. [2]He followed the ways of the kings of Israel and also made

[a] *19* The Hebrew for *leprosy* was used for various diseases affecting the skin; also in verses 20, 21 and 23. [b] *21* Or *in a house where he was relieved of responsibilities* [c] *5* That is, about 3 3/4 tons or about 3.4 metric tons [d] *5* That is, probably about 1,800 tons or about 1,600 metric tons of wheat [e] *5* That is, probably about 1,500 tons or about 1,350 metric tons of barley

2 CHRONICLES 26:16–21

UZZIAH'S PRIDE

Uzziah was a good king who had started out his reign well (v. 5), and as a result he experienced God's blessing. But his successes caused him to swell up with pride, and he began to take prerogatives that did not belong to him. He usurped the authority of the priests and attempted to burn incense in the temple. God judged Uzziah's pride and presumptuousness by striking him with leprosy. His reign ended in great failure, but it revealed that God's people needed a humble king.

Jesus is the antithesis of Uzziah. Jesus did not get struck with leprosy; he went around healing lepers (Lk 17:11–19). Jesus did not pridefully take privileges that did not belong to him; rather he humbly and voluntarily gave up privileges and rights that did belong to him (Php 2:5–11). Jesus is equal with God, and yet he laid aside the free exercise of his rights by humbling himself in becoming a man and dying on the cross. Therefore, God has exalted him to the throne!

idols for worshiping the Baals. [3]He burned sacrifices in the Valley of Ben Hinnom
and sacrificed his children in the fire, engaging in the detestable practices of the
nations the LORD had driven out before the Israelites. [4]He offered sacrifices and
burned incense at the high places, on the hilltops and under every spreading tree.

[5]Therefore the LORD his God delivered him into the hands of the king of
Aram. The Arameans defeated him and took many of his people as prisoners
and brought them to Damascus.

He was also given into the hands of the king of Israel, who inflicted heavy casualties on him. [6]In one day Pekah son of Remaliah killed a hundred and twenty
thousand soldiers in Judah — because Judah had forsaken the LORD, the God of
their ancestors. [7]Zikri, an Ephraimite warrior, killed Maaseiah the king's son,
Azrikam the officer in charge of the palace, and Elkanah, second to the king.
[8]The men of Israel took captive from their fellow Israelites who were from Judah
two hundred thousand wives, sons and daughters. They also took a great deal of
plunder, which they carried back to Samaria.

[9]But a prophet of the LORD named Oded was there, and he went out to meet the
army when it returned to Samaria. He said to them, "Because the LORD, the God
of your ancestors, was angry with Judah, he gave them into your hand. But you
have slaughtered them in a rage that reaches to heaven. [10]And now you intend to
make the men and women of Judah and Jerusalem your slaves. But aren't you also
guilty of sins against the LORD your God? [11]Now listen to me! Send back your fellow
Israelites you have taken as prisoners, for the LORD's fierce anger rests on you."

[12]Then some of the leaders in Ephraim — Azariah son of Jehohanan, Berekiah son of Meshillemoth, Jehizkiah son of Shallum, and Amasa son of Had-
lai — confronted those who were arriving from the war. [13]"You must not bring
those prisoners here," they said, "or we will be guilty before the LORD. Do you
intend to add to our sin and guilt? For our guilt is already great, and his fierce
anger rests on Israel."

[14]So the soldiers gave up the prisoners and plunder in the presence of the officials and all the assembly. [15]The men designated by name took the prisoners,
and from the plunder they clothed all who were naked. They provided them with
clothes and sandals, food and drink, and healing balm. All those who were weak
they put on donkeys. So they took them back to their fellow Israelites at Jericho,
the City of Palms, and returned to Samaria.

[16]At that time King Ahaz sent to the kings[a] of Assyria for help. [17]The Edomites had again come and attacked Judah and carried away prisoners, [18]while the
Philistines had raided towns in the foothills and in the Negev of Judah. They
captured and occupied Beth Shemesh, Aijalon and Gederoth, as well as Soko,
Timnah and Gimzo, with their surrounding villages. [19]The LORD had humbled
Judah because of Ahaz king of Israel,[b] for he had promoted wickedness in Judah and had been most unfaithful to the LORD. [20]Tiglath-Pileser[c] king of Assyria
came to him, but he gave him trouble instead of help. [21]Ahaz took some of the
things from the temple of the LORD and from the royal palace and from the officials and presented them to the king of Assyria, but that did not help him.

[22]In his time of trouble King Ahaz became even more unfaithful to the LORD.
[23]He offered sacrifices to the gods of Damascus, who had defeated him; for he
thought, "Since the gods of the kings of Aram have helped them, I will sacrifice
to them so they will help me." But they were his downfall and the downfall of
all Israel.

[24]Ahaz gathered together the furnishings from the temple of God and cut
them in pieces. He shut the doors of the LORD's temple and set up altars at every street corner in Jerusalem. [25]In every town in Judah he built high places to
burn sacrifices to other gods and aroused the anger of the LORD, the God of his
ancestors.

---

[a] *16* Most Hebrew manuscripts; one Hebrew manuscript, Septuagint and Vulgate (see also 2 Kings 16:7) *king* [b] *19* That is, Judah, as frequently in 2 Chronicles [c] *20* Hebrew *Tilgath-Pilneser,* a variant of *Tiglath-Pileser*

26The other events of his reign and all his ways, from beginning to end, are written in the book of the kings of Judah and Israel. 27Ahaz rested with his ancestors and was buried in the city of Jerusalem, but he was not placed in the tombs of the kings of Israel. And Hezekiah his son succeeded him as king.

Hezekiah Purifies the Temple

29 Hezekiah was twenty-five years old when he became king, and he reigned in Jerusalem twenty-nine years. His mother's name was Abijah daughter of Zechariah. 2He did what was right in the eyes of the LORD, just as his father David had done.

3In the first month of the first year of his reign, he opened the doors of the temple of the LORD and repaired them. 4He brought in the priests and the Levites, assembled them in the square on the east side 5and said: "Listen to me, Levites! Consecrate yourselves now and consecrate the temple of the LORD, the God of your ancestors. Remove all defilement from the sanctuary. 6Our parents were unfaithful; they did evil in the eyes of the LORD our God and forsook him. They turned their faces away from the LORD's dwelling place and turned their backs on him. 7They also shut the doors of the portico and put out the lamps. They did not burn incense or present any burnt offerings at the sanctuary to the God of Israel. 8Therefore, the anger of the LORD has fallen on Judah and Jerusalem; he has made them an object of dread and horror and scorn, as you can see with your own eyes. 9This is why our fathers have fallen by the sword and why our sons and daughters and our wives are in captivity. 10Now I intend to make a covenant with the LORD, the God of Israel, so that his fierce anger will turn away from us. 11My sons, do not be negligent now, for the LORD has chosen you to stand before him and serve him, to minister before him and to burn incense."

12Then these Levites set to work:
from the Kohathites,
  Mahath son of Amasai and Joel son of Azariah;
from the Merarites,
  Kish son of Abdi and Azariah son of Jehallelel;
from the Gershonites,
  Joah son of Zimmah and Eden son of Joah;
13from the descendants of Elizaphan,
  Shimri and Jeiel;
from the descendants of Asaph,
  Zechariah and Mattaniah;
14from the descendants of Heman,
  Jehiel and Shimei;
from the descendants of Jeduthun,
  Shemaiah and Uzziel.

15When they had assembled their fellow Levites and consecrated themselves, they went in to purify the temple of the LORD, as the king had ordered, following the word of the LORD. 16The priests went into the sanctuary of the LORD to purify it. They brought out to the courtyard of the LORD's temple everything unclean that they found in the temple of the LORD. The Levites took it and carried it out to the Kidron Valley. 17They began the consecration on the first day of the first month, and by the eighth day of the month they reached the portico of the LORD. For eight more days they consecrated the temple of the LORD itself, finishing on the sixteenth day of the first month.

18Then they went in to King Hezekiah and reported: "We have purified the entire temple of the LORD, the altar of burnt offering with all its utensils, and the table for setting out the consecrated bread, with all its articles. 19We have prepared and consecrated all the articles that King Ahaz removed in his unfaithfulness while he was king. They are now in front of the LORD's altar."

20Early the next morning King Hezekiah gathered the city officials together and went up to the temple of the LORD. 21They brought seven bulls, seven rams,

---

2 CHRONICLES 29:3–19

THE KING CLEANSES THE TEMPLE

King Hezekiah ordered that the priests and Levites should enter the temple and cleanse it from its defilements. The temple had been greatly defiled under King Ahaz (2Ki 16:10–16), but now King Hezekiah took measures to dedicate it to the Lord once again. The priests and Levites removed all the unholy objects of pagan worship and carried them to the Kidron Valley. Then, the ritually purified priests and Levites led the nation in renewed worship, offering hundreds of sacrifices and singing praises to God in the temple (2Ch 29:20–36).

Many years later, a descendant of Hezekiah walked into the temple and saw it defiled by the money changers. Jesus drove them out and cleansed the temple (Mt 21:12–13; Jn 2:13–17). He told them that the temple was to be a house of prayer, but they had turned it into a den of robbers. Like King Hezekiah, King Jesus cleaned out the temple, which was the house of God, so that people could rightly and appropriately worship the one true God. Now Jesus is the new temple—and believers can worship God in spirit and in truth wherever they are if they come to God through Jesus.

seven male lambs and seven male goats as a sin offering[a] for the kingdom, for the sanctuary and for Judah. The king commanded the priests, the descendants of Aaron, to offer these on the altar of the LORD. [22]So they slaughtered the bulls, and the priests took the blood and splashed it against the altar; next they slaughtered the rams and splashed their blood against the altar; then they slaughtered the lambs and splashed their blood against the altar. [23]The goats for the sin offering were brought before the king and the assembly, and they laid their hands on them. [24]The priests then slaughtered the goats and presented their blood on the altar for a sin offering to atone for all Israel, because the king had ordered the burnt offering and the sin offering for all Israel.

[25]He stationed the Levites in the temple of the LORD with cymbals, harps and lyres in the way prescribed by David and Gad the king's seer and Nathan the prophet; this was commanded by the LORD through his prophets. [26]So the Levites stood ready with David's instruments, and the priests with their trumpets.

[27]Hezekiah gave the order to sacrifice the burnt offering on the altar. As the offering began, singing to the LORD began also, accompanied by trumpets and the instruments of David king of Israel. [28]The whole assembly bowed in worship, while the musicians played and the trumpets sounded. All this continued until the sacrifice of the burnt offering was completed.

[29]When the offerings were finished, the king and everyone present with him knelt down and worshiped. [30]King Hezekiah and his officials ordered the Levites to praise the LORD with the words of David and of Asaph the seer. So they sang praises with gladness and bowed down and worshiped.

[31]Then Hezekiah said, "You have now dedicated yourselves to the LORD. Come and bring sacrifices and thank offerings to the temple of the LORD." So the assembly brought sacrifices and thank offerings, and all whose hearts were willing brought burnt offerings.

[32]The number of burnt offerings the assembly brought was seventy bulls, a hundred rams and two hundred male lambs — all of them for burnt offerings to the LORD. [33]The animals consecrated as sacrifices amounted to six hundred bulls and three thousand sheep and goats. [34]The priests, however, were too few to skin all the burnt offerings; so their relatives the Levites helped them until the task was finished and until other priests had been consecrated, for the Levites had been more conscientious in consecrating themselves than the priests had been. [35]There were burnt offerings in abundance, together with the fat of the fellowship offerings and the drink offerings that accompanied the burnt offerings.

So the service of the temple of the LORD was reestablished. [36]Hezekiah and all the people rejoiced at what God had brought about for his people, because it was done so quickly.

Hezekiah Celebrates the Passover

30 Hezekiah sent word to all Israel and Judah and also wrote letters to Ephraim and Manasseh, inviting them to come to the temple of the LORD in Jerusalem and celebrate the Passover to the LORD, the God of Israel. [2]The king and his officials and the whole assembly in Jerusalem decided to celebrate the Passover in the second month. [3]They had not been able to celebrate it at the regular time because not enough priests had consecrated themselves and the people had not assembled in Jerusalem. [4]The plan seemed right both to the king and to the whole assembly. [5]They decided to send a proclamation throughout Israel, from Beersheba to Dan, calling the people to come to Jerusalem and celebrate the Passover to the LORD, the God of Israel. It had not been celebrated in large numbers according to what was written.

[6]At the king's command, couriers went throughout Israel and Judah with letters from the king and from his officials, which read:

[a] *21* Or *purification offering*; also in verses 23 and 24

2 CHRONICLES 30:1 – 20

HEZEKIAH AND THE PASSOVER

King Hezekiah arranged for the people to celebrate the Passover because they had not always observed it as they should. Not only did he arrange for the southern tribes to eat the meal, but he also brought a degree of unity by arranging for the northern tribes to be involved if they desired. The Passover celebrated how God had saved the people of Israel while they were slaves in Egypt (Ex 11:1 — 12:42). God defeated the Egyptians and rescued his people from slavery. The Hebrews were saved from the plague because they killed a lamb and smeared its blood on the doorposts of their houses. The lamb substituted for the firstborn of the house. When the Lord saw the blood on the doorpost he passed over it.

This meal pointed forward to the full and final salvation of God's people through Jesus — the Lamb who takes away the sin of the world (Jn 1:29). He is the Passover Lamb for all God's people (1Co 5:7). He died in humanity's place so that eternal death will pass by.

"People of Israel, return to the LORD, the God of Abraham, Isaac and
Israel, that he may return to you who are left, who have escaped from the
hand of the kings of Assyria. 7 Do not be like your parents and your fellow
Israelites, who were unfaithful to the LORD, the God of their ancestors, so
that he made them an object of horror, as you see. 8 Do not be stiff-necked,
as your ancestors were; submit to the LORD. Come to his sanctuary, which
he has consecrated forever. Serve the LORD your God, so that his fierce anger will turn away from you. 9 If you return to the LORD, then your fellow
Israelites and your children will be shown compassion by their captors and
will return to this land, for the LORD your God is gracious and compassionate. He will not turn his face from you if you return to him."

10 The couriers went from town to town in Ephraim and Manasseh, as far as
Zebulun, but people scorned and ridiculed them. 11 Nevertheless, some from
Asher, Manasseh and Zebulun humbled themselves and went to Jerusalem.
12 Also in Judah the hand of God was on the people to give them unity of mind
to carry out what the king and his officials had ordered, following the word of
the LORD.

13 A very large crowd of people assembled in Jerusalem to celebrate the Fes-
tival of Unleavened Bread in the second month. 14 They removed the altars in
Jerusalem and cleared away the incense altars and threw them into the Kidron
Valley.

15 They slaughtered the Passover lamb on the fourteenth day of the second
month. The priests and the Levites were ashamed and consecrated themselves
and brought burnt offerings to the temple of the LORD. 16 Then they took up their
regular positions as prescribed in the Law of Moses the man of God. The priests
splashed against the altar the blood handed to them by the Levites. 17 Since many
in the crowd had not consecrated themselves, the Levites had to kill the Passover lambs for all those who were not ceremonially clean and could not consecrate their lambs[a] to the LORD. 18 Although most of the many people who came
from Ephraim, Manasseh, Issachar and Zebulun had not purified themselves,
yet they ate the Passover, contrary to what was written. But Hezekiah prayed
for them, saying, "May the LORD, who is good, pardon everyone 19 who sets their
heart on seeking God — the LORD, the God of their ancestors — even if they are
not clean according to the rules of the sanctuary." 20 And the LORD heard Hezekiah and healed the people.

21 The Israelites who were present in Jerusalem celebrated the Festival of
Unleavened Bread for seven days with great rejoicing, while the Levites and
priests praised the LORD every day with resounding instruments dedicated to
the LORD.[b]

22 Hezekiah spoke encouragingly to all the Levites, who showed good understanding of the service of the LORD. For the seven days they ate their assigned
portion and offered fellowship offerings and praised[c] the LORD, the God of their
ancestors.

23 The whole assembly then agreed to celebrate the festival seven more days;
so for another seven days they celebrated joyfully. 24 Hezekiah king of Judah provided a thousand bulls and seven thousand sheep and goats for the assembly,
and the officials provided them with a thousand bulls and ten thousand sheep
and goats. A great number of priests consecrated themselves. 25 The entire assembly of Judah rejoiced, along with the priests and Levites and all who had
assembled from Israel, including the foreigners who had come from Israel and
also those who resided in Judah. 26 There was great joy in Jerusalem, for since the
days of Solomon son of David king of Israel there had been nothing like this in Jerusalem. 27 The priests and the Levites stood to bless the people, and God heard
them, for their prayer reached heaven, his holy dwelling place.

---

[a] 17 Or *consecrate themselves* [b] 21 Or *priests sang to the LORD every day, accompanied by the LORD's instruments of praise* [c] 22 Or *and confessed their sins to*

31 When all this had ended, the Israelites who were there went out to the towns of Judah, smashed the sacred stones and cut down the Asherah poles. They destroyed the high places and the altars throughout Judah and Benjamin and in Ephraim and Manasseh. After they had destroyed all of them, the Israelites returned to their own towns and to their own property.

Contributions for Worship

[2]Hezekiah assigned the priests and Levites to divisions — each of them according to their duties as priests or Levites — to offer burnt offerings and fellowship offerings, to minister, to give thanks and to sing praises at the gates of the LORD's dwelling. [3]The king contributed from his own possessions for the morning and evening burnt offerings and for the burnt offerings on the Sabbaths, at the New Moons and at the appointed festivals as written in the Law of the LORD. [4]He ordered the people living in Jerusalem to give the portion due the priests and Levites so they could devote themselves to the Law of the LORD. [5]As soon as the order went out, the Israelites generously gave the firstfruits of their grain, new wine, olive oil and honey and all that the fields produced. They brought a great amount, a tithe of everything. [6]The people of Israel and Judah who lived in the towns of Judah also brought a tithe of their herds and flocks and a tithe of the holy things dedicated to the LORD their God, and they piled them in heaps. [7]They began doing this in the third month and finished in the seventh month. [8]When Hezekiah and his officials came and saw the heaps, they praised the LORD and blessed his people Israel.

[9]Hezekiah asked the priests and Levites about the heaps; [10]and Azariah the chief priest, from the family of Zadok, answered, "Since the people began to bring their contributions to the temple of the LORD, we have had enough to eat and plenty to spare, because the LORD has blessed his people, and this great amount is left over."

[11]Hezekiah gave orders to prepare storerooms in the temple of the LORD, and this was done. [12]Then they faithfully brought in the contributions, tithes and dedicated gifts. Konaniah, a Levite, was the overseer in charge of these things, and his brother Shimei was next in rank. [13]Jehiel, Azaziah, Nahath, Asahel, Jerimoth, Jozabad, Eliel, Ismakiah, Mahath and Benaiah were assistants of Konaniah and Shimei his brother. All these served by appointment of King Hezekiah and Azariah the official in charge of the temple of God.

[14]Kore son of Imnah the Levite, keeper of the East Gate, was in charge of the freewill offerings given to God, distributing the contributions made to the LORD and also the consecrated gifts. [15]Eden, Miniamin, Jeshua, Shemaiah, Amariah and Shekaniah assisted him faithfully in the towns of the priests, distributing to their fellow priests according to their divisions, old and young alike.

[16]In addition, they distributed to the males three years old or more whose names were in the genealogical records — all who would enter the temple of the LORD to perform the daily duties of their various tasks, according to their responsibilities and their divisions. [17]And they distributed to the priests enrolled by their families in the genealogical records and likewise to the Levites twenty years old or more, according to their responsibilities and their divisions. [18]They included all the little ones, the wives, and the sons and daughters of the whole community listed in these genealogical records. For they were faithful in consecrating themselves.

[19]As for the priests, the descendants of Aaron, who lived on the farmlands around their towns or in any other towns, men were designated by name to distribute portions to every male among them and to all who were recorded in the genealogies of the Levites.

[20]This is what Hezekiah did throughout Judah, doing what was good and right and faithful before the LORD his God. [21]In everything that he undertook in the service of God's temple and in obedience to the law and the commands, he sought his God and worked wholeheartedly. And so he prospered.

Sennacherib Threatens Jerusalem

32 After all that Hezekiah had so faithfully done, Sennacherib king of Assyria came and invaded Judah. He laid siege to the fortified cities, thinking to conquer them for himself. 2When Hezekiah saw that Sennacherib had come and that he intended to wage war against Jerusalem, 3he consulted with his officials and military staff about blocking off the water from the springs outside the city, and they helped him. 4They gathered a large group of people who blocked all the springs and the stream that flowed through the land. "Why should the kings[a] of Assyria come and find plenty of water?" they said. 5Then he worked hard repairing all the broken sections of the wall and building towers on it. He built another wall outside that one and reinforced the terraces[b] of the City of David. He also made large numbers of weapons and shields.

6He appointed military officers over the people and assembled them before him in the square at the city gate and encouraged them with these words: 7"Be strong and courageous. Do not be afraid or discouraged because of the king of Assyria and the vast army with him, for there is a greater power with us than with him. 8With him is only the arm of flesh, but with us is the LORD our God to help us and to fight our battles." And the people gained confidence from what Hezekiah the king of Judah said.

9Later, when Sennacherib king of Assyria and all his forces were laying siege to Lachish, he sent his officers to Jerusalem with this message for Hezekiah king of Judah and for all the people of Judah who were there:

> 10"This is what Sennacherib king of Assyria says: On what are you basing your confidence, that you remain in Jerusalem under siege? 11When Hezekiah says, 'The LORD our God will save us from the hand of the king of Assyria,' he is misleading you, to let you die of hunger and thirst. 12Did not Hezekiah himself remove this god's high places and altars, saying to Judah and Jerusalem, 'You must worship before one altar and burn sacrifices on it'?
>
> 13"Do you not know what I and my predecessors have done to all the peoples of the other lands? Were the gods of those nations ever able to deliver their land from my hand? 14Who of all the gods of these nations that my predecessors destroyed has been able to save his people from me? How then can your god deliver you from my hand? 15Now do not let Hezekiah deceive you and mislead you like this. Do not believe him, for no god of any nation or kingdom has been able to deliver his people from my hand or the hand of my predecessors. How much less will your god deliver you from my hand!"

16Sennacherib's officers spoke further against the LORD God and against his servant Hezekiah. 17The king also wrote letters ridiculing the LORD, the God of Israel, and saying this against him: "Just as the gods of the peoples of the other lands did not rescue their people from my hand, so the god of Hezekiah will not rescue his people from my hand." 18Then they called out in Hebrew to the people of Jerusalem who were on the wall, to terrify them and make them afraid in order to capture the city. 19They spoke about the God of Jerusalem as they did about the gods of the other peoples of the world — the work of human hands.

20King Hezekiah and the prophet Isaiah son of Amoz cried out in prayer to heaven about this. 21And the LORD sent an angel, who annihilated all the fighting men and the commanders and officers in the camp of the Assyrian king. So he withdrew to his own land in disgrace. And when he went into the temple of his god, some of his sons, his own flesh and blood, cut him down with the sword.

22So the LORD saved Hezekiah and the people of Jerusalem from the hand of Sennacherib king of Assyria and from the hand of all others. He took care of them[c] on every side. 23Many brought offerings to Jerusalem for the LORD and

[a] *4* Hebrew; Septuagint and Syriac *king* [b] *5* Or *the Millo* [c] *22* Hebrew; Septuagint and Vulgate *He gave them rest*

valuable gifts for Hezekiah king of Judah. From then on he was highly regarded
by all the nations.

Hezekiah's Pride, Success and Death

[24]In those days Hezekiah became ill and was at the point of death. He prayed
to the LORD, who answered him and gave him a miraculous sign. [25]But Hezekiah's heart was proud and he did not respond to the kindness shown him; therefore the LORD's wrath was on him and on Judah and Jerusalem. [26]Then Hezekiah
repented of the pride of his heart, as did the people of Jerusalem; therefore the
LORD's wrath did not come on them during the days of Hezekiah.

[27]Hezekiah had very great wealth and honor, and he made treasuries for his
silver and gold and for his precious stones, spices, shields and all kinds of valuables. [28]He also made buildings to store the harvest of grain, new wine and olive
oil; and he made stalls for various kinds of cattle, and pens for the flocks. [29]He
built villages and acquired great numbers of flocks and herds, for God had given
him very great riches.

[30]It was Hezekiah who blocked the upper outlet of the Gihon spring and chan-
neled the water down to the west side of the City of David. He succeeded in everything he undertook. [31]But when envoys were sent by the rulers of Babylon to
ask him about the miraculous sign that had occurred in the land, God left him
to test him and to know everything that was in his heart.

[32]The other events of Hezekiah's reign and his acts of devotion are written in
the vision of the prophet Isaiah son of Amoz in the book of the kings of Judah and
Israel. [33]Hezekiah rested with his ancestors and was buried on the hill where the
tombs of David's descendants are. All Judah and the people of Jerusalem honored him when he died. And Manasseh his son succeeded him as king.

Manasseh King of Judah

33 Manasseh was twelve years old when he became king, and he reigned in
Jerusalem fifty-five years. [2]He did evil in the eyes of the LORD, following
the detestable practices of the nations the LORD had driven out before the Israelites. [3]He rebuilt the high places his father Hezekiah had demolished; he also
erected altars to the Baals and made Asherah poles. He bowed down to all the
starry hosts and worshiped them. [4]He built altars in the temple of the LORD, of
which the LORD had said, "My Name will remain in Jerusalem forever." [5]In both
courts of the temple of the LORD, he built altars to all the starry hosts. [6]He sacrificed his children in the fire in the Valley of Ben Hinnom, practiced divination
and witchcraft, sought omens, and consulted mediums and spiritists. He did
much evil in the eyes of the LORD, arousing his anger.

[7]He took the image he had made and put it in God's temple, of which God had
said to David and to his son Solomon, "In this temple and in Jerusalem, which I
have chosen out of all the tribes of Israel, I will put my Name forever. [8]I will not
again make the feet of the Israelites leave the land I assigned to your ancestors, if
only they will be careful to do everything I commanded them concerning all the
laws, decrees and regulations given through Moses." [9]But Manasseh led Judah
and the people of Jerusalem astray, so that they did more evil than the nations
the LORD had destroyed before the Israelites.

[10]The LORD spoke to Manasseh and his people, but they paid no attention.
[11]So the LORD brought against them the army commanders of the king of Assyria, who took Manasseh prisoner, put a hook in his nose, bound him with bronze
shackles and took him to Babylon. [12]In his distress he sought the favor of the
LORD his God and humbled himself greatly before the God of his ancestors.
[13]And when he prayed to him, the LORD was moved by his entreaty and listened
to his plea; so he brought him back to Jerusalem and to his kingdom. Then Manasseh knew that the LORD is God.

[14]Afterward he rebuilt the outer wall of the City of David, west of the Gihon
spring in the valley, as far as the entrance of the Fish Gate and encircling the hill

of Ophel; he also made it much higher. He stationed military commanders in all
the fortified cities in Judah.
[15]He got rid of the foreign gods and removed the image from the temple of the
LORD, as well as all the altars he had built on the temple hill and in Jerusalem;
and he threw them out of the city. [16]Then he restored the altar of the LORD and
sacrificed fellowship offerings and thank offerings on it, and told Judah to serve
the LORD, the God of Israel. [17]The people, however, continued to sacrifice at the
high places, but only to the LORD their God.
[18]The other events of Manasseh's reign, including his prayer to his God and
the words the seers spoke to him in the name of the LORD, the God of Israel, are
written in the annals of the kings of Israel.[a] [19]His prayer and how God was moved
by his entreaty, as well as all his sins and unfaithfulness, and the sites where he
built high places and set up Asherah poles and idols before he humbled himself — all these are written in the records of the seers.[b] [20]Manasseh rested with
his ancestors and was buried in his palace. And Amon his son succeeded him
as king.

Amon King of Judah

[21]Amon was twenty-two years old when he became king, and he reigned in
Jerusalem two years. [22]He did evil in the eyes of the LORD, as his father Manasseh
had done. Amon worshiped and offered sacrifices to all the idols Manasseh had
made. [23]But unlike his father Manasseh, he did not humble himself before the
LORD; Amon increased his guilt.
[24]Amon's officials conspired against him and assassinated him in his palace.
[25]Then the people of the land killed all who had plotted against King Amon, and
they made Josiah his son king in his place.

Josiah's Reforms

34 Josiah was eight years old when he became king, and he reigned in Jerusalem thirty-one years. [2]He did what was right in the eyes of the LORD and
followed the ways of his father David, not turning aside to the right or to the left.
[3]In the eighth year of his reign, while he was still young, he began to seek the
God of his father David. In his twelfth year he began to purge Judah and Jerusalem of high places, Asherah poles and idols. [4]Under his direction the altars
of the Baals were torn down; he cut to pieces the incense altars that were above
them, and smashed the Asherah poles and the idols. These he broke to pieces
and scattered over the graves of those who had sacrificed to them. [5]He burned
the bones of the priests on their altars, and so he purged Judah and Jerusalem.
[6]In the towns of Manasseh, Ephraim and Simeon, as far as Naphtali, and in the
ruins around them, [7]he tore down the altars and the Asherah poles and crushed
the idols to powder and cut to pieces all the incense altars throughout Israel.
Then he went back to Jerusalem.
[8]In the eighteenth year of Josiah's reign, to purify the land and the temple, he
sent Shaphan son of Azaliah and Maaseiah the ruler of the city, with Joah son of
Joahaz, the recorder, to repair the temple of the LORD his God.
[9]They went to Hilkiah the high priest and gave him the money that had been
brought into the temple of God, which the Levites who were the gatekeepers
had collected from the people of Manasseh, Ephraim and the entire remnant
of Israel and from all the people of Judah and Benjamin and the inhabitants of
Jerusalem. [10]Then they entrusted it to the men appointed to supervise the work
on the LORD's temple. These men paid the workers who repaired and restored
the temple. [11]They also gave money to the carpenters and builders to purchase
dressed stone, and timber for joists and beams for the buildings that the kings of
Judah had allowed to fall into ruin.

---

[a] *18* That is, Judah, as frequently in 2 Chronicles [b] *19* One Hebrew manuscript and Septuagint; most Hebrew manuscripts *of Hozai*

EXILE AND RESTORATION

The inclusion of the story of Manasseh's sin, exile in Babylon, repentance and return to the land fits perfectly with Chronicles' purpose. Unlike 1 and 2 Kings which justified the exile, the books of Chronicles were intended to highlight the reality of the Lord's faithfulness to his covenant with David so as to strengthen the people's hope that a descendant of David would reign and the promises would be fulfilled. Manasseh's story is a great example of God's mercy and faithfulness to those who had returned from exile. If the worst king in David's line could be restored to the throne before the exile, then surely the Lord would be gracious and restore the Davidic line after the exile.

Manasseh's story strengthened the hope of the post-exilic Jews that God would one day establish David's dynasty, defeat their enemies and finally save them. In fact, Manasseh's story was a picture in miniature of God's dealings with his people. Manasseh had sinned, been taken in exile to Babylon, repented while in Babylon, and then returned to the land. Just as God restored the king when he repented in exile, so God also restored the nation itself after its exile to Babylon. God was faithful to his promise to David and to the nation, despite all that had happened.

The inadequacy of David's sons as described in Chronicles anticipated David's great Son who would come — Jesus Christ. None of the sons had lived up to the ideal, and yet despite their failings, God remained faithful to his promise that one day a son of David would establish an eternal kingdom. Long after the restoration from exile, Jesus sits on the throne forever with all of his enemies under his feet. He fulfills all of the good qualities of David, Solomon and the others with none of their bad qualities. Chronicles began with a genealogy, and it ended with exile and an invitation to return. Chronicles was the last book of the Hebrew canon, and the very next words in the Bible after the end of Chronicles are these: "This is the genealogy of Jesus the Messiah the son of David" (Mt 1:1).

[12]The workers labored faithfully. Over them to direct them were Jahath and Obadiah, Levites descended from Merari, and Zechariah and Meshullam, descended from Kohath. The Levites — all who were skilled in playing musical instruments — [13]had charge of the laborers and supervised all the workers from job to job. Some of the Levites were secretaries, scribes and gatekeepers.

2 CHRONICLES 34:14 – 33

JOSIAH'S REFORMS

During King Josiah's reign, the high priest found the Book of the Law in the temple. A messenger took it and read it to the king, and Josiah ripped his robes because he was convicted about his nation's disobedience to God's Word. He repented and cried out in confession to the Lord. The Lord indicated that all of the curses of Deuteronomy 28:15 – 68 would come upon the people, but because of their repentance, God would not exile them during Josiah's reign.

The first readers of this passage in Chronicles were the Jews who lived in Judah some years after the exile. While this account may seem like bad news, it was actually good news to the restored community. If God kept his word by exiling the people, and if God kept his word by bringing them back to the land, then God would certainly keep his word to circumcise their hearts so that they could wholeheartedly follow him. Daniel and Jeremiah prophesied about the complete fulfillment of this promise of inner transformation and salvation, which would come when the Messiah was put to death (Jer 31:31 – 34; Da 9:24 – 27). Jesus, in his death, inaugurated a new covenant and brought full and lasting transformation to his people.

The Book of the Law Found

[14]While they were bringing out the money that had been taken into the temple of the LORD, Hilkiah the priest found the Book of the Law of the LORD that had been given through Moses. [15]Hilkiah said to Shaphan the secretary, "I have found the Book of the Law in the temple of the LORD." He gave it to Shaphan.

[16]Then Shaphan took the book to the king and reported to him: "Your officials are doing everything that has been committed to them. [17]They have paid out the money that was in the temple of the LORD and have entrusted it to the supervisors and workers." [18]Then Shaphan the secretary informed the king, "Hilkiah the priest has given me a book." And Shaphan read from it in the presence of the king.

[19]When the king heard the words of the Law, he tore his robes. [20]He gave these orders to Hilkiah, Ahikam son of Shaphan, Abdon son of Micah,[a] Shaphan the secretary and Asaiah the king's attendant: [21]"Go and inquire of the LORD for me and for the remnant in Israel and Judah about what is written in this book that has been found. Great is the LORD's anger that is poured out on us because those who have gone before us have not kept the word of the LORD; they have not acted in accordance with all that is written in this book."

[22]Hilkiah and those the king had sent with him[b] went to speak to the prophet Huldah, who was the wife of Shallum son of Tokhath,[c] the son of Hasrah,[d] keeper of the wardrobe. She lived in Jerusalem, in the New Quarter.

[23]She said to them, "This is what the LORD, the God of Israel, says: Tell the man who sent you to me, [24]'This is what the LORD says: I am going to bring disaster on this place and its people — all the curses written in the book that has been read in the presence of the king of Judah. [25]Because they have forsaken me and burned incense to other gods and aroused my anger by all that their hands have made,[e] my anger will be poured out on this place and will not be quenched.' [26]Tell the king of Judah, who sent you to inquire of the LORD, 'This is what the LORD, the God of Israel, says concerning the words you heard: [27]Because your heart was responsive and you humbled yourself before God when you heard what he spoke against this place and its people, and because you humbled yourself before me and tore your robes and wept in my presence, I have heard you, declares the LORD. [28]Now I will gather you to your ancestors, and you will be buried in peace. Your eyes will not see all the disaster I am going to bring on this place and on those who live here.'"

So they took her answer back to the king.

[29]Then the king called together all the elders of Judah and Jerusalem. [30]He went up to the temple of the LORD with the people of Judah, the inhabitants of Jerusalem, the priests and the Levites — all the people from the least to the greatest. He read in their hearing all the words of the Book of the Covenant, which had been found in the temple of the LORD. [31]The king stood by his pillar and renewed the covenant in the presence of the LORD — to follow the LORD and keep his commands, statutes and decrees with all his heart and all his soul, and to obey the words of the covenant written in this book.

[32]Then he had everyone in Jerusalem and Benjamin pledge themselves to it; the people of Jerusalem did this in accordance with the covenant of God, the God of their ancestors.

[33]Josiah removed all the detestable idols from all the territory belonging to the

[a] *20* Also called *Akbor son of Micaiah* [b] *22* One Hebrew manuscript, Vulgate and Syriac; most Hebrew manuscripts do not have *had sent with him.* [c] *22* Also called *Tikvah* [d] *22* Also called *Harhas* [e] *25* Or *by everything they have done*

Israelites, and he had all who were present in Israel serve the LORD their God. As long as he lived, they did not fail to follow the LORD, the God of their ancestors.

Josiah Celebrates the Passover

35 Josiah celebrated the Passover to the LORD in Jerusalem, and the Passover lamb was slaughtered on the fourteenth day of the first month. 2He appointed the priests to their duties and encouraged them in the service of the LORD's temple. 3He said to the Levites, who instructed all Israel and who had been consecrated to the LORD: "Put the sacred ark in the temple that Solomon son of David king of Israel built. It is not to be carried about on your shoulders. Now serve the LORD your God and his people Israel. 4Prepare yourselves by families in your divisions, according to the instructions written by David king of Israel and by his son Solomon.

5"Stand in the holy place with a group of Levites for each subdivision of the families of your fellow Israelites, the lay people. 6Slaughter the Passover lambs, consecrate yourselves and prepare the lambs for your fellow Israelites, doing what the LORD commanded through Moses."

7Josiah provided for all the lay people who were there a total of thirty thousand lambs and goats for the Passover offerings, and also three thousand cattle—all from the king's own possessions.

8His officials also contributed voluntarily to the people and the priests and Levites. Hilkiah, Zechariah and Jehiel, the officials in charge of God's temple, gave the priests twenty-six hundred Passover offerings and three hundred cattle. 9Also Konaniah along with Shemaiah and Nethanel, his brothers, and Hashabiah, Jeiel and Jozabad, the leaders of the Levites, provided five thousand Passover offerings and five hundred head of cattle for the Levites.

10The service was arranged and the priests stood in their places with the Levites in their divisions as the king had ordered. 11The Passover lambs were slaughtered, and the priests splashed against the altar the blood handed to them, while the Levites skinned the animals. 12They set aside the burnt offerings to give them to the subdivisions of the families of the people to offer to the LORD, as it is written in the Book of Moses. They did the same with the cattle. 13They roasted the Passover animals over the fire as prescribed, and boiled the holy offerings in pots, caldrons and pans and served them quickly to all the people. 14After this, they made preparations for themselves and for the priests, because the priests, the descendants of Aaron, were sacrificing the burnt offerings and the fat portions until nightfall. So the Levites made preparations for themselves and for the Aaronic priests.

15The musicians, the descendants of Asaph, were in the places prescribed by David, Asaph, Heman and Jeduthun the king's seer. The gatekeepers at each gate did not need to leave their posts, because their fellow Levites made the preparations for them.

16So at that time the entire service of the LORD was carried out for the celebration of the Passover and the offering of burnt offerings on the altar of the LORD, as King Josiah had ordered. 17The Israelites who were present celebrated the Passover at that time and observed the Festival of Unleavened Bread for seven days. 18The Passover had not been observed like this in Israel since the days of the prophet Samuel; and none of the kings of Israel had ever celebrated such a Passover as did Josiah, with the priests, the Levites and all Judah and Israel who were there with the people of Jerusalem. 19This Passover was celebrated in the eighteenth year of Josiah's reign.

The Death of Josiah

20After all this, when Josiah had set the temple in order, Necho king of Egypt went up to fight at Carchemish on the Euphrates, and Josiah marched out to meet him in battle. 21But Necho sent messengers to him, saying, "What quarrel is there, king of Judah, between you and me? It is not you I am attacking at this

time, but the house with which I am at war. God has told me to hurry; so stop
opposing God, who is with me, or he will destroy you."
22Josiah, however, would not turn away from him, but disguised himself to
engage him in battle. He would not listen to what Necho had said at God's command but went to fight him on the plain of Megiddo.
23Archers shot King Josiah, and he told his officers, "Take me away; I am badly wounded." 24So they took him out of his chariot, put him in his other chariot
and brought him to Jerusalem, where he died. He was buried in the tombs of his
ancestors, and all Judah and Jerusalem mourned for him.
25Jeremiah composed laments for Josiah, and to this day all the male and female singers commemorate Josiah in the laments. These became a tradition in
Israel and are written in the Laments.
26The other events of Josiah's reign and his acts of devotion in accordance with
what is written in the Law of the LORD — 27all the events, from beginning to end,
36 are written in the book of the kings of Israel and Judah. 1And the people
of the land took Jehoahaz son of Josiah and made him king in Jerusalem
in place of his father.

Jehoahaz King of Judah

2Jehoahaz[a] was twenty-three years old when he became king, and he reigned
in Jerusalem three months. 3The king of Egypt dethroned him in Jerusalem and
imposed on Judah a levy of a hundred talents[b] of silver and a talent[c] of gold.
4The king of Egypt made Eliakim, a brother of Jehoahaz, king over Judah and
Jerusalem and changed Eliakim's name to Jehoiakim. But Necho took Eliakim's
brother Jehoahaz and carried him off to Egypt.

Jehoiakim King of Judah

5Jehoiakim was twenty-five years old when he became king, and he reigned
in Jerusalem eleven years. He did evil in the eyes of the LORD his God. 6Nebu-
chadnezzar king of Babylon attacked him and bound him with bronze shackles
to take him to Babylon. 7Nebuchadnezzar also took to Babylon articles from the
temple of the LORD and put them in his temple[d] there.
8The other events of Jehoiakim's reign, the detestable things he did and all
that was found against him, are written in the book of the kings of Israel and
Judah. And Jehoiachin his son succeeded him as king.

Jehoiachin King of Judah

9Jehoiachin was eighteen[e] years old when he became king, and he reigned in
Jerusalem three months and ten days. He did evil in the eyes of the LORD. 10In the
spring, King Nebuchadnezzar sent for him and brought him to Babylon, together with articles of value from the temple of the LORD, and he made Jehoiachin's
uncle,[f] Zedekiah, king over Judah and Jerusalem.

Zedekiah King of Judah

11Zedekiah was twenty-one years old when he became king, and he reigned in
Jerusalem eleven years. 12He did evil in the eyes of the LORD his God and did not
humble himself before Jeremiah the prophet, who spoke the word of the LORD.
13He also rebelled against King Nebuchadnezzar, who had made him take an
oath in God's name. He became stiff-necked and hardened his heart and would
not turn to the LORD, the God of Israel. 14Furthermore, all the leaders of the
priests and the people became more and more unfaithful, following all the detestable practices of the nations and defiling the temple of the LORD, which he
had consecrated in Jerusalem.

---

[a] *2* Hebrew *Joahaz,* a variant of *Jehoahaz;* also in verse 4 [b] *3* That is, about 3 3/4 tons or about 3.4 metric tons [c] *3* That is, about 75 pounds or about 34 kilograms [d] *7* Or *palace*
[e] *9* One Hebrew manuscript, some Septuagint manuscripts and Syriac (see also 2 Kings 24:8); most Hebrew manuscripts *eight* [f] *10* Hebrew *brother,* that is, relative (see 2 Kings 24:17)

The Fall of Jerusalem

15The LORD, the God of their ancestors, sent word to them through his messengers again and again, because he had pity on his people and on his dwelling
place. 16But they mocked God's messengers, despised his words and scoffed at
his prophets until the wrath of the LORD was aroused against his people and
there was no remedy. 17He brought up against them the king of the Babylonians,[a] who killed their young men with the sword in the sanctuary, and did not
spare young men or young women, the elderly or the infirm. God gave them all
into the hands of Nebuchadnezzar. 18He carried to Babylon all the articles from
the temple of God, both large and small, and the treasures of the LORD's temple
and the treasures of the king and his officials. 19They set fire to God's temple and
broke down the wall of Jerusalem; they burned all the palaces and destroyed
everything of value there.

20He carried into exile to Babylon the remnant, who escaped from the sword,
and they became servants to him and his successors until the kingdom of Persia
came to power. 21The land enjoyed its sabbath rests; all the time of its desolation
it rested, until the seventy years were completed in fulfillment of the word of the
LORD spoken by Jeremiah.

22In the first year of Cyrus king of Persia, in order to fulfill the word of the
LORD spoken by Jeremiah, the LORD moved the heart of Cyrus king of Persia to
make a proclamation throughout his realm and also to put it in writing:

> 23"This is what Cyrus king of Persia says:
>
> "'The LORD, the God of heaven, has given me all the kingdoms of the earth and he has appointed me to build a temple for him at Jerusalem in Judah. Any of his people among you may go up, and may the LORD their God be with them.'"

---

[a] 17 Or *Chaldeans*

JESUS: OUR HOPE FOR RETURN

EZRA

EZRA

TEMPLE DESTROYED	TEMPLE REBUILT	EZRA ARRIVES IN JERUSALEM
c. 586 BC	*c. 536 – 516 BC*	*c. 458 BC*

The book of Ezra tells the story of the return of the remnant of Jews back to the promised land from captivity in Babylon. There this remnant would seek to rebuild the temple and reestablish themselves as a community marked by God as his treasured possession. This small band of Jews faced a host of obstacles and impediments along the way, but through it all God once again showed that he was faithful to his promises.

In 539 BC, King Cyrus of Persia defeated the once-mighty Babylonian Empire. Once in power, Cyrus did what the Babylonian kings had been unwilling to do — he allowed the captive peoples to return to their homelands and to worship their respective gods. Among those exiles were this small band of Israelites who were allowed to return to Jerusalem while remaining subject to the Persian emperor.

The return took place in two stages, the first of which was led by Zerubbabel in about 538 BC. He led a group back to the promised land and began the work of rebuilding the temple (chs. 1 – 6). This daunting work took two decades to complete — the people finally finished in the sixth year of the reign of Darius (c. 516 BC). Ezra led a second group back in 458 BC and instituted a number of reforms during that time, calling the people to account for their practice of intermarriage with their pagan neighbors and leading them to confess their sins.

The story told in Ezra portrays the grand scope of the task of rebuilding the temple as well as rebuilding the nation as a worshiping people of God. Through his gracious acts on their behalf, God fulfilled his promise to the people to allow them to dwell in the land of promise and worship him in the temple. The words of earlier prophets rang in the people's ears as they faced the overwhelming task of rebuilding the life of the people of God in the land of God. Their hope was not simply that God would rebuild the temple; they trusted that God could rebuild their hearts as well.

Zerubbabel, as a descendant of David, is found in the genealogy of Jesus Christ at the outset of Matthew's Gospel (Mt 1:12 – 13). Perhaps more important, when God returned his people to the land of promise, he took another step toward setting the stage for the advent of Jesus Christ, who was to be born in this land in the city of Bethlehem (Mic 5:2). Through Christ, God now calls his people to repent and return to him, and grants them forgiveness and restoration when they do.

NOW HONOR THE LORD, THE GOD OF YOUR ANCESTORS, AND DO HIS WILL.

Ezra 10:11

EZRA

EZRA 1:2–4

CYRUS POINTS TO THE MESSIAH

About 150 years beforehand, Isaiah prophesied the events described in the book of Ezra. He foretold that Cyrus would be the Lord's "shepherd" and would rebuild Jerusalem and its temple (Isa 44:28). This prophecy was fulfilled in Ezra 1:2–4 when Cyrus proclaimed that he would rebuild the Lord's temple and he released the Israelites to return to their homeland for the construction project. This pagan king can be viewed as a foreshadowing of the Messiah.

Like Cyrus but much better, the true Messiah is a king-shepherd who rules with the Lord's authority (Eze 34:23–24; 37:24–25; Jn 10:11). Like Cyrus, Jesus Christ would build God's house. Jesus said that his body was the temple, which would be destroyed and then raised up again in three days (Jn 2:19–22). Also, the church is the new "holy temple in the Lord" which Jesus built by his death and resurrection (Eph 2:19–22). Finally, like Cyrus, the Messiah would bring about a new exodus. The original exodus—when the Lord saved his people from slavery in Egypt—was the premier salvation event in the Old Testament. However, a promise was made that a new exodus would occur in the future, with the Lord freeing his people from slavery forever and living among them. Passages like Isaiah 11 and Ezekiel 37 prophesied that the Messiah would accomplish

(continued on next page)

Cyrus Helps the Exiles to Return

1 In the first year of Cyrus king of Persia, in order to fulfill the word of the LORD
spoken by Jeremiah, the LORD moved the heart of Cyrus king of Persia to
make a proclamation throughout his realm and also to put it in writing:

2 "This is what Cyrus king of Persia says:
" 'The LORD, the God of heaven, has given me all the kingdoms of the
earth and he has appointed me to build a temple for him at Jerusalem in
Judah. 3 Any of his people among you may go up to Jerusalem in Judah and
build the temple of the LORD, the God of Israel, the God who is in Jerusalem, and may their God be with them. 4 And in any locality where survivors
may now be living, the people are to provide them with silver and gold,
with goods and livestock, and with freewill offerings for the temple of God
in Jerusalem.' "

5 Then the family heads of Judah and Benjamin, and the priests and Levites—
everyone whose heart God had moved—prepared to go up and build the house
of the LORD in Jerusalem. 6 All their neighbors assisted them with articles of silver and gold, with goods and livestock, and with valuable gifts, in addition to all
the freewill offerings.
7 Moreover, King Cyrus brought out the articles belonging to the temple of the
LORD, which Nebuchadnezzar had carried away from Jerusalem and had placed
in the temple of his god.[a] 8 Cyrus king of Persia had them brought by Mithredath
the treasurer, who counted them out to Sheshbazzar the prince of Judah.
9 This was the inventory:

gold dishes	30
silver dishes	1,000
silver pans[b]	29
10 gold bowls	30
matching silver bowls	410
other articles	1,000

11 In all, there were 5,400 articles of gold and of silver. Sheshbazzar brought
all these along with the exiles when they came up from Babylon to Jerusalem.

The List of the Exiles Who Returned

2 Now these are the people of the province who came up from the captivity of
the exiles, whom Nebuchadnezzar king of Babylon had taken captive to Babylon (they returned to Jerusalem and Judah, each to their own town, 2 in company with Zerubbabel, Joshua, Nehemiah, Seraiah, Reelaiah, Mordecai, Bilshan,
Mispar, Bigvai, Rehum and Baanah):

The list of the men of the people of Israel:

3 the descendants of Parosh	2,172
4 of Shephatiah	372
5 of Arah	775
6 of Pahath-Moab (through the line of Jeshua and Joab)	2,812
7 of Elam	1,254
8 of Zattu	945
9 of Zakkai	760
10 of Bani	642

[a] 7 Or *gods* [b] 9 The meaning of the Hebrew for this word is uncertain.

[11] of Bebai 623
[12] of Azgad 1,222
[13] of Adonikam 666
[14] of Bigvai 2,056
[15] of Adin 454
[16] of Ater (through Hezekiah) 98
[17] of Bezai 323
[18] of Jorah 112
[19] of Hashum 223
[20] of Gibbar 95

[21] the men of Bethlehem 123
[22] of Netophah 56
[23] of Anathoth 128
[24] of Azmaveth 42
[25] of Kiriath Jearim,[a] Kephirah and Beeroth 743
[26] of Ramah and Geba 621
[27] of Mikmash 122
[28] of Bethel and Ai 223
[29] of Nebo 52
[30] of Magbish 156
[31] of the other Elam 1,254
[32] of Harim 320
[33] of Lod, Hadid and Ono 725
[34] of Jericho 345
[35] of Senaah 3,630

[36] The priests:

the descendants of Jedaiah (through the family of Jeshua) 973
[37] of Immer 1,052
[38] of Pashhur 1,247
[39] of Harim 1,017

[40] The Levites:

the descendants of Jeshua and Kadmiel (of the line of Hodaviah) 74

[41] The musicians:

the descendants of Asaph 128

[42] The gatekeepers of the temple:

the descendants of
Shallum, Ater, Talmon,
Akkub, Hatita and Shobai 139

[43] The temple servants:

the descendants of
Ziha, Hasupha, Tabbaoth,
[44] Keros, Siaha, Padon,
[45] Lebanah, Hagabah, Akkub,
[46] Hagab, Shalmai, Hanan,
[47] Giddel, Gahar, Reaiah,
[48] Rezin, Nekoda, Gazzam,
[49] Uzza, Paseah, Besai,
[50] Asnah, Meunim, Nephusim,
[51] Bakbuk, Hakupha, Harhur,

[a] 25 See Septuagint (see also Neh. 7:29); Hebrew *Kiriath Arim.*

(Cyrus Points to the Messiah, continued)

this new and final salvation, and the New Testament describes the fulfillment of these prophecies in Jesus of Nazareth (cf. Rev 21:1–5).

EZRA 2:1–2

THE DAVIDIC PROMISE

Ezra 2 lists those that returned to Israel from captivity. What is most important about this passage is that David's family returned from captivity through his descendant Zerubbabel. In 2 Samuel 7:16, God promised an eternal dynasty to David—David would never fail to have a son on the throne of Israel. The keeping of that promise looked bleak when Nebuchadnezzar razed Jerusalem to the ground and took David's descendants as captives to Babylon. However, Amos foretold that the fallen house of David would be restored (Am 9:11). This prophecy began to be realized in Ezra 2 when Zerubbabel returned to Jerusalem. God would finally fulfill this prophecy by raising David's descendant—Jesus of Nazareth—from the dead and seating him on an eternal throne (Ac 2:29–36; 13:32–37). The fact that Zerubbabel, from the royal line of David, was one of the returning exiles must have given great hope to the restored community that God keeps his promises no matter the situation. This truth should give God's people hope today as well.

EZRA 3:8

KINGS, PRIESTS AND TEMPLES

Ezra 3:8 notified its readers that Zerubbabel and Joshua oversaw the building of the new temple. This was significant because Zerubbabel was a descendant of King David and Joshua was the high priest. It makes good sense that these two men would oversee the project since kings are temple-builders and priests are temple-workers. After all, King David wanted to build the original temple (2Sa 7:1–13), and his son Solomon ended up building it (1Ki 5–8). It was fitting that for the second temple, David's offspring, Zerubbabel, oversaw its construction. And it was also fitting that Joshua the high priest took up the priestly duty of interceding for the people by offering sacrifices to the Lord in the temple for the people's sins (Ezr 6:15–18; cf. Lev 1–9; 16).

Both of these roles—king and priest—point forward to Jesus Christ, who is both the greater King and the greater Priest. He built God's temple—the church (Eph 2:19–22). He offered the final sacrifice to God that once and for all dealt with humanity's sin problem (Heb 10:11–14). And Jesus is the risen High Priest who "is able to save completely those who come to God through him, because he always lives to intercede for them" (Heb 7:25). He is the one who gives true and lasting access to God and his house!

52 Bazluth, Mehida, Harsha,
53 Barkos, Sisera, Temah,
54 Neziah and Hatipha

55 The descendants of the servants of Solomon:

the descendants of
Sotai, Hassophereth, Peruda,
56 Jaala, Darkon, Giddel,
57 Shephatiah, Hattil,
Pokereth-Hazzebaim and Ami

58 The temple servants and the descendants of the servants
of Solomon 392

59 The following came up from the towns of Tel Melah, Tel Harsha, Kerub, Addon and Immer, but they could not show that their families were descended from Israel:

60 The descendants of
Delaiah, Tobiah and Nekoda 652

61 And from among the priests:

The descendants of
Hobaiah, Hakkoz and Barzillai (a man who had married a daughter of Barzillai the Gileadite and was called by that name).

62 These searched for their family records, but they could not find them and so were excluded from the priesthood as unclean.
63 The governor ordered them not to eat any of the most sacred food until there was a priest ministering with the Urim and Thummim.

64 The whole company numbered 42,360,
65 besides their 7,337 male and female slaves; and they also had 200 male and female singers.
66 They had 736 horses, 245 mules,
67 435 camels and 6,720 donkeys.

68 When they arrived at the house of the LORD in Jerusalem, some of the heads of the families gave freewill offerings toward the rebuilding of the house of God on its site.
69 According to their ability they gave to the treasury for this work 61,000 darics[a] of gold, 5,000 minas[b] of silver and 100 priestly garments.
70 The priests, the Levites, the musicians, the gatekeepers and the temple servants settled in their own towns, along with some of the other people, and the rest of the Israelites settled in their towns.

Rebuilding the Altar

3 When the seventh month came and the Israelites had settled in their towns, the people assembled together as one in Jerusalem.
2 Then Joshua son of Jozadak and his fellow priests and Zerubbabel son of Shealtiel and his associates began to build the altar of the God of Israel to sacrifice burnt offerings on it, in accordance with what is written in the Law of Moses the man of God.
3 Despite their fear of the peoples around them, they built the altar on its foundation and sacrificed burnt offerings on it to the LORD, both the morning and evening sacrifices.
4 Then in accordance with what is written, they celebrated the Festival of Tabernacles with the required number of burnt offerings prescribed for each day.
5 After that, they presented the regular burnt offerings, the New Moon sacrifices and the sacrifices for all the appointed sacred festivals of the LORD, as well as those brought as freewill offerings to the LORD.
6 On the first day of the seventh month they began to offer burnt offerings to the LORD, though the foundation of the LORD's temple had not yet been laid.

[a] *69* That is, about 1,100 pounds or about 500 kilograms [b] *69* That is, about 3 tons or about 2.8 metric tons

Rebuilding the Temple

7Then they gave money to the masons and carpenters, and gave food and
drink and olive oil to the people of Sidon and Tyre, so that they would bring cedar logs by sea from Lebanon to Joppa, as authorized by Cyrus king of Persia.
8In the second month of the second year after their arrival at the house of
God in Jerusalem, Zerubbabel son of Shealtiel, Joshua son of Jozadak and the
rest of the people (the priests and the Levites and all who had returned from the
captivity to Jerusalem) began the work. They appointed Levites twenty years
old and older to supervise the building of the house of the LORD. 9Joshua and his
sons and brothers and Kadmiel and his sons (descendants of Hodaviah[a]) and
the sons of Henadad and their sons and brothers — all Levites — joined together
in supervising those working on the house of God.
10When the builders laid the foundation of the temple of the LORD, the priests
in their vestments and with trumpets, and the Levites (the sons of Asaph) with
cymbals, took their places to praise the LORD, as prescribed by David king of Israel. 11With praise and thanksgiving they sang to the LORD:

"He is good;
his love toward Israel endures forever."

And all the people gave a great shout of praise to the LORD, because the foundation of the house of the LORD was laid. 12But many of the older priests and
Levites and family heads, who had seen the former temple, wept aloud when
they saw the foundation of this temple being laid, while many others shouted
for joy. 13No one could distinguish the sound of the shouts of joy from the sound
of weeping, because the people made so much noise. And the sound was heard
far away.

Opposition to the Rebuilding

4 When the enemies of Judah and Benjamin heard that the exiles were building a temple for the LORD, the God of Israel, 2they came to Zerubbabel and to
the heads of the families and said, "Let us help you build because, like you, we
seek your God and have been sacrificing to him since the time of Esarhaddon
king of Assyria, who brought us here."
3But Zerubbabel, Joshua and the rest of the heads of the families of Israel answered, "You have no part with us in building a temple to our God. We alone
will build it for the LORD, the God of Israel, as King Cyrus, the king of Persia,
commanded us."
4Then the peoples around them set out to discourage the people of Judah
and make them afraid to go on building.[b] 5They bribed officials to work against
them and frustrate their plans during the entire reign of Cyrus king of Persia and
down to the reign of Darius king of Persia.

Later Opposition Under Xerxes and Artaxerxes

6At the beginning of the reign of Xerxes,[c] they lodged an accusation against
the people of Judah and Jerusalem.
7And in the days of Artaxerxes king of Persia, Bishlam, Mithredath, Tabeel
and the rest of his associates wrote a letter to Artaxerxes. The letter was written
in Aramaic script and in the Aramaic language.[d,e]
8Rehum the commanding officer and Shimshai the secretary wrote a letter
against Jerusalem to Artaxerxes the king as follows:
9Rehum the commanding officer and Shimshai the secretary, together
with the rest of their associates — the judges, officials and administrators
over the people from Persia, Uruk and Babylon, the Elamites of Susa, 10and

[a] 9 Hebrew *Yehudah,* a variant of *Hodaviah* [b] 4 Or *and troubled them as they built*
[c] 6 Hebrew *Ahasuerus* [d] 7 Or *written in Aramaic and translated* [e] 7 The text of 4:8 – 6:18
is in Aramaic.

EZRA 3:12 – 13

THE GREATER, MORE GLORIOUS TEMPLE

When the workers laid the foundation of the new temple, the older people who had seen Solomon's temple wept loudly — apparently realizing from the outset that the second temple was not going to be as glorious as the first. Yet, several years later the Lord promised, through the prophet Haggai, that the future glory of this temple would far outshine the glory of Solomon's temple, and the Lord would fill the new temple with his glory (Hag 2:7 – 9). The first temple had occasionally been enveloped by the glory of God in a way that all Israel could see that God was with them (1Ki 8:10 – 11), just as the tabernacle had been previously (Ex 40:34). Just before the exile, God gave Ezekiel a vision, in chapter 10, of his glory departing from the temple. However, Ezekiel also received a vision, in chapter 43, promising that the glory of the Lord would return to a perfect new temple.

John's Gospel describes, in part, the fulfillment of that prophecy: the Word (Jesus) became flesh and "made his dwelling among us," and "we have seen his glory" (Jn 1:14). Revelation says there will be no temple in the new Jerusalem because "the Lord God Almighty and the Lamb" are its temple, and no sun will be needed there because God's glory will provide the light (Rev 21:22 – 23). The rebuilt temple in Ezra's day did not hold a candle to the glory of the future temple — where God himself lives with his people forever as their God (Rev 21:3).

the other people whom the great and honorable Ashurbanipal deported and settled in the city of Samaria and elsewhere in Trans-Euphrates.

11(This is a copy of the letter they sent him.)

To King Artaxerxes,

From your servants in Trans-Euphrates:

12The king should know that the people who came up to us from you have gone to Jerusalem and are rebuilding that rebellious and wicked city. They are restoring the walls and repairing the foundations.
13Furthermore, the king should know that if this city is built and its walls are restored, no more taxes, tribute or duty will be paid, and eventually the royal revenues will suffer.[a] 14Now since we are under obligation to the
palace and it is not proper for us to see the king dishonored, we are sending this message to inform the king, 15so that a search may be made in the archives of your predecessors. In these records you will find that this city is a rebellious city, troublesome to kings and provinces, a place with a long history of sedition. That is why this city was destroyed. 16We inform the
king that if this city is built and its walls are restored, you will be left with nothing in Trans-Euphrates.

17The king sent this reply:

To Rehum the commanding officer, Shimshai the secretary and the rest of their associates living in Samaria and elsewhere in Trans-Euphrates:

Greetings.

18The letter you sent us has been read and translated in my presence.
19I issued an order and a search was made, and it was found that this city has a long history of revolt against kings and has been a place of rebellion and sedition. 20Jerusalem has had powerful kings ruling over the whole
of Trans-Euphrates, and taxes, tribute and duty were paid to them. 21Now
issue an order to these men to stop work, so that this city will not be rebuilt until I so order. 22Be careful not to neglect this matter. Why let this threat
grow, to the detriment of the royal interests?

23As soon as the copy of the letter of King Artaxerxes was read to Rehum and Shimshai the secretary and their associates, they went immediately to the Jews in Jerusalem and compelled them by force to stop.

24Thus the work on the house of God in Jerusalem came to a standstill until the second year of the reign of Darius king of Persia.

Tattenai's Letter to Darius

5 Now Haggai the prophet and Zechariah the prophet, a descendant of Iddo, prophesied to the Jews in Judah and Jerusalem in the name of the God of Israel, who was over them. 2Then Zerubbabel son of Shealtiel and Joshua son of
Jozadak set to work to rebuild the house of God in Jerusalem. And the prophets of God were with them, supporting them.
3At that time Tattenai, governor of Trans-Euphrates, and Shethar-Bozenai and their associates went to them and asked, "Who authorized you to rebuild this temple and to finish it?" 4They[b] also asked, "What are the names of those
who are constructing this building?" 5But the eye of their God was watching over the elders of the Jews, and they were not stopped until a report could go to Darius and his written reply be received.
6This is a copy of the letter that Tattenai, governor of Trans-Euphrates, and

---

[a] *13* The meaning of the Aramaic for this clause is uncertain. [b] *4* See Septuagint; Aramaic *We.*

Shethar-Bozenai and their associates, the officials of Trans-Euphrates, sent to King Darius. 7 The report they sent him read as follows:

To King Darius:

Cordial greetings.

8 The king should know that we went to the district of Judah, to the temple of the great God. The people are building it with large stones and placing the timbers in the walls. The work is being carried on with diligence and is making rapid progress under their direction.

9 We questioned the elders and asked them, "Who authorized you to rebuild this temple and to finish it?" 10 We also asked them their names, so that we could write down the names of their leaders for your information.
11 This is the answer they gave us:

"We are the servants of the God of heaven and earth, and we are rebuilding the temple that was built many years ago, one that a great king of Israel built and finished. 12 But because our ancestors angered the God of heaven, he gave them into the hands of Nebuchadnezzar the Chaldean, king of Babylon, who destroyed this temple and deported the people to Babylon.

13 "However, in the first year of Cyrus king of Babylon, King Cyrus issued a decree to rebuild this house of God. 14 He even removed from the temple[a] of Babylon the gold and silver articles of the house of God, which Nebuchadnezzar had taken from the temple in Jerusalem and brought to the temple[a] in Babylon. Then King Cyrus gave them to a man named Sheshbazzar, whom he had appointed governor, 15 and he told him, 'Take these articles and go and deposit them in the temple in Jerusalem. And rebuild the house of God on its site.'

16 "So this Sheshbazzar came and laid the foundations of the house of God in Jerusalem. From that day to the present it has been under construction but is not yet finished."

17 Now if it pleases the king, let a search be made in the royal archives of Babylon to see if King Cyrus did in fact issue a decree to rebuild this house of God in Jerusalem. Then let the king send us his decision in this matter.

The Decree of Darius

6 King Darius then issued an order, and they searched in the archives stored in the treasury at Babylon. 2 A scroll was found in the citadel of Ecbatana in the province of Media, and this was written on it:

Memorandum:

3 In the first year of King Cyrus, the king issued a decree concerning the temple of God in Jerusalem:

Let the temple be rebuilt as a place to present sacrifices, and let its foundations be laid. It is to be sixty cubits[b] high and sixty cubits wide, 4 with three courses of large stones and one of timbers. The costs are to be paid by the royal treasury. 5 Also, the gold and silver articles of the house of God, which Nebuchadnezzar took from the temple in Jerusalem and brought to Babylon, are to be returned to their places in the temple in Jerusalem; they are to be deposited in the house of God.

6 Now then, Tattenai, governor of Trans-Euphrates, and Shethar-Bozenai and you other officials of that province, stay away from there. 7 Do not interfere with the work on this temple of God. Let the governor of the Jews and the Jewish elders rebuild this house of God on its site.

---

[a] *14* Or *palace* [b] *3* That is, about 90 feet or about 27 meters

[8]Moreover, I hereby decree what you are to do for these elders of the Jews in the construction of this house of God:

Their expenses are to be fully paid out of the royal treasury, from the revenues of Trans-Euphrates, so that the work will not stop. [9]Whatever is needed — young bulls, rams, male lambs for burnt offerings to the God of heaven, and wheat, salt, wine and olive oil, as requested by the priests in Jerusalem — must be given them daily without fail, [10]so that they may offer sacrifices pleasing to the God of heaven and pray for the well-being of the king and his sons.

[11]Furthermore, I decree that if anyone defies this edict, a beam is to be pulled from their house and they are to be impaled on it. And for this crime their house is to be made a pile of rubble. [12]May God, who has caused his Name to dwell there, overthrow any king or people who lifts a hand to change this decree or to destroy this temple in Jerusalem.

I Darius have decreed it. Let it be carried out with diligence.

Completion and Dedication of the Temple

[13]Then, because of the decree King Darius had sent, Tattenai, governor of Trans-Euphrates, and Shethar-Bozenai and their associates carried it out with diligence. [14]So the elders of the Jews continued to build and prosper under the preaching of Haggai the prophet and Zechariah, a descendant of Iddo. They finished building the temple according to the command of the God of Israel and the decrees of Cyrus, Darius and Artaxerxes, kings of Persia. [15]The temple was completed on the third day of the month Adar, in the sixth year of the reign of King Darius.

[16]Then the people of Israel — the priests, the Levites and the rest of the exiles — celebrated the dedication of the house of God with joy. [17]For the dedication of this house of God they offered a hundred bulls, two hundred rams, four hundred male lambs and, as a sin offering[a] for all Israel, twelve male goats, one for each of the tribes of Israel. [18]And they installed the priests in their divisions and the Levites in their groups for the service of God at Jerusalem, according to what is written in the Book of Moses.

The Passover

[19]On the fourteenth day of the first month, the exiles celebrated the Passover. [20]The priests and Levites had purified themselves and were all ceremonially clean. The Levites slaughtered the Passover lamb for all the exiles, for their relatives the priests and for themselves. [21]So the Israelites who had returned from the exile ate it, together with all who had separated themselves from the unclean practices of their Gentile neighbors in order to seek the LORD, the God of Israel. [22]For seven days they celebrated with joy the Festival of Unleavened Bread, because the LORD had filled them with joy by changing the attitude of the king of Assyria so that he assisted them in the work on the house of God, the God of Israel.

Ezra Comes to Jerusalem

7 After these things, during the reign of Artaxerxes king of Persia, Ezra son of Seraiah, the son of Azariah, the son of Hilkiah, [2]the son of Shallum, the son of Zadok, the son of Ahitub, [3]the son of Amariah, the son of Azariah, the son of Meraioth, [4]the son of Zerahiah, the son of Uzzi, the son of Bukki, [5]the son of Abishua, the son of Phinehas, the son of Eleazar, the son of Aaron the chief priest — [6]this Ezra came up from Babylon. He was a teacher well versed in the Law of Moses, which the LORD, the God of Israel, had given. The king had granted him everything he asked, for the hand of the LORD his God was on him. [7]Some of the Israelites, including priests, Levites, musicians, gatekeepers and temple servants, also came up to Jerusalem in the seventh year of King Artaxerxes.

[a] 17 Or *purification offering*

EZRA 6:16–20

THE LAMB WHO REMOVES THE WORLD'S SIN

At the dedication of the new temple, the Israelites offered hundreds of sin offerings to atone for their sins, including twelve goats to atone for each of the twelve tribes. Atonement means that these sacrifices received the judgment of God that the people of Israel deserved because of their sin. Then, in connection with the dedication of the new temple, the returned exiles celebrated the Passover. The Passover recalled how the Lord passed over the Israelite houses in Egypt and did not kill their firstborn. Death had already happened in that house when a lamb was killed in the firstborn's place (Ex 12). However, these activities — sacrifice and Passover — were merely provisional because they could not deal with the people's sin problem once for all. All of these slaughtered animals pointed forward to the final Passover Lamb — Jesus Christ — who takes away the sin of the world (Jn 1:29; 1Co 5:7).

[8]Ezra arrived in Jerusalem in the fifth month of the seventh year of the king.
[9]He had begun his journey from Babylon on the first day of the first month, and
he arrived in Jerusalem on the first day of the fifth month, for the gracious hand
of his God was on him. [10]For Ezra had devoted himself to the study and observance of the Law of the LORD, and to teaching its decrees and laws in Israel.

King Artaxerxes' Letter to Ezra

[11]This is a copy of the letter King Artaxerxes had given to Ezra the priest, a
teacher of the Law, a man learned in matters concerning the commands and
decrees of the LORD for Israel:

[12]Artaxerxes, king of kings,

To Ezra the priest, teacher of the Law of the God of heaven:

Greetings.

[13]Now I decree that any of the Israelites in my kingdom, including priests
and Levites, who volunteer to go to Jerusalem with you, may go. [14]You are
sent by the king and his seven advisers to inquire about Judah and Jerusalem with regard to the Law of your God, which is in your hand. [15]Moreover,
you are to take with you the silver and gold that the king and his advisers
have freely given to the God of Israel, whose dwelling is in Jerusalem, [16]to-
gether with all the silver and gold you may obtain from the province of
Babylon, as well as the freewill offerings of the people and priests for the
temple of their God in Jerusalem. [17]With this money be sure to buy bulls,
rams and male lambs, together with their grain offerings and drink offerings, and sacrifice them on the altar of the temple of your God in Jerusalem.

[18]You and your fellow Israelites may then do whatever seems best with
the rest of the silver and gold, in accordance with the will of your God.
[19]Deliver to the God of Jerusalem all the articles entrusted to you for worship in the temple of your God. [20]And anything else needed for the temple
of your God that you are responsible to supply, you may provide from the
royal treasury.

[21]Now I, King Artaxerxes, decree that all the treasurers of Trans-Euphrates are to provide with diligence whatever Ezra the priest, the teacher of the Law of the God of heaven, may ask of you— [22]up to a hundred
talents[a] of silver, a hundred cors[b] of wheat, a hundred baths[c] of wine, a
hundred baths[c] of olive oil, and salt without limit. [23]Whatever the God of
heaven has prescribed, let it be done with diligence for the temple of the
God of heaven. Why should his wrath fall on the realm of the king and of
his sons? [24]You are also to know that you have no authority to impose taxes,
tribute or duty on any of the priests, Levites, musicians, gatekeepers, temple servants or other workers at this house of God.

[25]And you, Ezra, in accordance with the wisdom of your God, which
you possess, appoint magistrates and judges to administer justice to all
the people of Trans-Euphrates—all who know the laws of your God. And
you are to teach any who do not know them. [26]Whoever does not obey the
law of your God and the law of the king must surely be punished by death,
banishment, confiscation of property, or imprisonment.[d]

[27]Praise be to the LORD, the God of our ancestors, who has put it into the king's
heart to bring honor to the house of the LORD in Jerusalem in this way [28]and who
has extended his good favor to me before the king and his advisers and all the
king's powerful officials. Because the hand of the LORD my God was on me, I took
courage and gathered leaders from Israel to go up with me.

---

[a] *22* That is, about 3 3/4 tons or about 3.4 metric tons [b] *22* That is, probably about 18 tons or about 16 metric tons [c] *22* That is, about 600 gallons or about 2,200 liters [d] *26* The text of 7:12-26 is in Aramaic.

List of the Family Heads Returning With Ezra

8 These are the family heads and those registered with them who came up
with me from Babylon during the reign of King Artaxerxes:
2 of the descendants of Phinehas, Gershom;
of the descendants of Ithamar, Daniel;
of the descendants of David, Hattush 3 of the descendants of Shekaniah;

of the descendants of Parosh, Zechariah, and with him were registered 150
men;
4 of the descendants of Pahath-Moab, Eliehoenai son of Zerahiah, and with
him 200 men;
5 of the descendants of Zattu,[a] Shekaniah son of Jahaziel, and with him 300
men;
6 of the descendants of Adin, Ebed son of Jonathan, and with him 50 men;
7 of the descendants of Elam, Jeshaiah son of Athaliah, and with him 70 men;
8 of the descendants of Shephatiah, Zebadiah son of Michael, and with him
80 men;
9 of the descendants of Joab, Obadiah son of Jehiel, and with him 218 men;
10 of the descendants of Bani,[b] Shelomith son of Josiphiah, and with him 160
men;
11 of the descendants of Bebai, Zechariah son of Bebai, and with him 28 men;
12 of the descendants of Azgad, Johanan son of Hakkatan, and with him 110
men;
13 of the descendants of Adonikam, the last ones, whose names were Eliphelet, Jeuel and Shemaiah, and with them 60 men;
14 of the descendants of Bigvai, Uthai and Zakkur, and with them 70 men.

The Return to Jerusalem

15 I assembled them at the canal that flows toward Ahava, and we camped
there three days. When I checked among the people and the priests, I found no
Levites there. 16 So I summoned Eliezer, Ariel, Shemaiah, Elnathan, Jarib, Elnathan, Nathan, Zechariah and Meshullam, who were leaders, and Joiarib and Elnathan, who were men of learning, 17 and I ordered them to go to Iddo, the leader
in Kasiphia. I told them what to say to Iddo and his fellow Levites, the temple
servants in Kasiphia, so that they might bring attendants to us for the house of
our God. 18 Because the gracious hand of our God was on us, they brought us
Sherebiah, a capable man, from the descendants of Mahli son of Levi, the son of
Israel, and Sherebiah's sons and brothers, 18 in all; 19 and Hashabiah, together
with Jeshaiah from the descendants of Merari, and his brothers and nephews,
20 in all. 20 They also brought 220 of the temple servants — a body that David and
the officials had established to assist the Levites. All were registered by name.
21 There, by the Ahava Canal, I proclaimed a fast, so that we might humble
ourselves before our God and ask him for a safe journey for us and our children,
with all our possessions. 22 I was ashamed to ask the king for soldiers and horsemen to protect us from enemies on the road, because we had told the king, "The
gracious hand of our God is on everyone who looks to him, but his great anger is
against all who forsake him." 23 So we fasted and petitioned our God about this,
and he answered our prayer.
24 Then I set apart twelve of the leading priests, namely, Sherebiah, Hashabiah and ten of their brothers, 25 and I weighed out to them the offering of silver
and gold and the articles that the king, his advisers, his officials and all Israel
present there had donated for the house of our God. 26 I weighed out to them 650
talents[c] of silver, silver articles weighing 100 talents,[d] 100 talents[d] of gold, 27 20

---

[a] *5* Some Septuagint manuscripts (also 1 Esdras 8:32); Hebrew does not have *Zattu.*
[b] *10* Some Septuagint manuscripts (also 1 Esdras 8:36); Hebrew does not have *Bani.*
[c] *26* That is, about 24 tons or about 22 metric tons [d] *26* That is, about 3 3/4 tons or about 3.4 metric tons

bowls of gold valued at 1,000 darics,[a] and two fine articles of polished bronze, as precious as gold.

[28]I said to them, "You as well as these articles are consecrated to the LORD. The silver and gold are a freewill offering to the LORD, the God of your ancestors. [29]Guard them carefully until you weigh them out in the chambers of the house of the LORD in Jerusalem before the leading priests and the Levites and the family heads of Israel." [30]Then the priests and Levites received the silver and gold and sacred articles that had been weighed out to be taken to the house of our God in Jerusalem.

[31]On the twelfth day of the first month we set out from the Ahava Canal to go to Jerusalem. The hand of our God was on us, and he protected us from enemies and bandits along the way. [32]So we arrived in Jerusalem, where we rested three days.

[33]On the fourth day, in the house of our God, we weighed out the silver and gold and the sacred articles into the hands of Meremoth son of Uriah, the priest. Eleazar son of Phinehas was with him, and so were the Levites Jozabad son of Jeshua and Noadiah son of Binnui. [34]Everything was accounted for by number and weight, and the entire weight was recorded at that time.

[35]Then the exiles who had returned from captivity sacrificed burnt offerings to the God of Israel: twelve bulls for all Israel, ninety-six rams, seventy-seven male lambs and, as a sin offering,[b] twelve male goats. All this was a burnt offering to the LORD. [36]They also delivered the king's orders to the royal satraps and to the governors of Trans-Euphrates, who then gave assistance to the people and to the house of God.

Ezra's Prayer About Intermarriage

9 After these things had been done, the leaders came to me and said, "The people of Israel, including the priests and the Levites, have not kept themselves separate from the neighboring peoples with their detestable practices, like those of the Canaanites, Hittites, Perizzites, Jebusites, Ammonites, Moabites, Egyptians and Amorites. [2]They have taken some of their daughters as wives for themselves and their sons, and have mingled the holy race with the peoples around them. And the leaders and officials have led the way in this unfaithfulness."

[3]When I heard this, I tore my tunic and cloak, pulled hair from my head and beard and sat down appalled. [4]Then everyone who trembled at the words of the God of Israel gathered around me because of this unfaithfulness of the exiles. And I sat there appalled until the evening sacrifice.

[5]Then, at the evening sacrifice, I rose from my self-abasement, with my tunic and cloak torn, and fell on my knees with my hands spread out to the LORD my God [6]and prayed:

> "I am too ashamed and disgraced, my God, to lift up my face to you, because our sins are higher than our heads and our guilt has reached to the heavens. [7]From the days of our ancestors until now, our guilt has been great. Because of our sins, we and our kings and our priests have been subjected to the sword and captivity, to pillage and humiliation at the hand of foreign kings, as it is today.
>
> [8]"But now, for a brief moment, the LORD our God has been gracious in leaving us a remnant and giving us a firm place[c] in his sanctuary, and so our God gives light to our eyes and a little relief in our bondage. [9]Though we are slaves, our God has not forsaken us in our bondage. He has shown us kindness in the sight of the kings of Persia: He has granted us new life to rebuild the house of our God and repair its ruins, and he has given us a wall of protection in Judah and Jerusalem.
>
> [10]"But now, our God, what can we say after this? For we have forsaken

[a] 27 That is, about 19 pounds or about 8.4 kilograms [b] 35 Or *purification offering*
[c] 8 Or *a foothold*

THE BACKDROP OF EZRA

God, in Deuteronomy 30, had prophesied that Israel would disobey God's law and go into exile. Once in exile, they would seek the Lord with all their hearts and the Lord would restore them to the land. God also promised that he would one day circumcise the hearts of his people so that they would be fully devoted to him (Dt 30:1 – 6). At first glance, Ezra might seem to depict the fulfillment of this prophecy. After all, the people had forsaken the Lord, gone into exile and then returned to the land. But while God's promises to Israel were starting to come true, they were not fully realized. The people's hearts had not been transformed, which was evident in the fact that they intermarried with the pagans in the land just as they had done when they entered the land after the exodus from Egypt (Jdg 3:5 – 6; Ezr 9:1 – 2). The Israelites did not separate themselves from the neighboring peoples and their sinful practices. The issue was one of religion, not race — being unequally yoked to unbelievers.

To understand what happened in Ezra, one must realize that Daniel's prayer in Daniel 9 forms the backdrop to the two books known as Ezra and Nehemiah. As Daniel read Jeremiah's prophecy in Jeremiah 29:10 – 14, he realized that the exile in Babylon would last seventy years (Da 9:2). So, in accordance with Deuteronomy and 1 Kings 8, Daniel prayed to the Lord confessing the sins of Israel in order to prepare them for the return to the land. He understood that repentance had to precede the return. Ezra reveals that God stirred up King Cyrus to return the Israelites to their land in order to fulfill God's word spoken through Jeremiah (Ezr 1:1).

However, the angel Gabriel came to Daniel at the end of his prayer and prophesied that the exile would not just last seventy years. Rather, the exile would last seventy times seven years — not truly coming to an end until the Anointed One, the Messiah, was put to death (Da 9:20 – 27).

So Ezra is an "already but not yet" book. God's promises were already partially coming true but had not yet fully come true. God kept his promise to bring them back to the land, but the transformation promised in Deuteronomy and other places had not happened. They were, in a sense, exiles in their own land (a situation that remained in effect at the time of Jesus, at which point Judea was under Roman rule). Therefore, Ezra pointed to the need for Israel to be truly rescued from exile and truly transformed. Ezra pointed forward to the need for the Messiah. Not until Jesus was separated from God the Father as he hung on the cross (Da 9:26) would the people's separation from God truly end and their transformation be fully accomplished.

the commands [11]you gave through your servants the prophets when you
said: 'The land you are entering to possess is a land polluted by the corruption of its peoples. By their detestable practices they have filled it with their
impurity from one end to the other. [12]Therefore, do not give your daughters
in marriage to their sons or take their daughters for your sons. Do not seek
a treaty of friendship with them at any time, that you may be strong and eat
the good things of the land and leave it to your children as an everlasting
inheritance.'

[13]"What has happened to us is a result of our evil deeds and our great
guilt, and yet, our God, you have punished us less than our sins deserved
and have given us a remnant like this. [14]Shall we then break your commands again and intermarry with the peoples who commit such detestable
practices? Would you not be angry enough with us to destroy us, leaving us
no remnant or survivor? [15]LORD, the God of Israel, you are righteous! We
are left this day as a remnant. Here we are before you in our guilt, though
because of it not one of us can stand in your presence."

The People's Confession of Sin

10 While Ezra was praying and confessing, weeping and throwing himself
down before the house of God, a large crowd of Israelites—men, women
and children—gathered around him. They too wept bitterly. [2]Then Shekaniah
son of Jehiel, one of the descendants of Elam, said to Ezra, "We have been unfaithful to our God by marrying foreign women from the peoples around us. But
in spite of this, there is still hope for Israel. [3]Now let us make a covenant before
our God to send away all these women and their children, in accordance with
the counsel of my lord and of those who fear the commands of our God. Let it be
done according to the Law. [4]Rise up; this matter is in your hands. We will support
you, so take courage and do it."

[5]So Ezra rose up and put the leading priests and Levites and all Israel under
oath to do what had been suggested. And they took the oath. [6]Then Ezra withdrew from before the house of God and went to the room of Jehohanan son of
Eliashib. While he was there, he ate no food and drank no water, because he
continued to mourn over the unfaithfulness of the exiles.

[7]A proclamation was then issued throughout Judah and Jerusalem for all the
exiles to assemble in Jerusalem. [8]Anyone who failed to appear within three days
would forfeit all his property, in accordance with the decision of the officials and
elders, and would himself be expelled from the assembly of the exiles.

[9]Within the three days, all the men of Judah and Benjamin had gathered in
Jerusalem. And on the twentieth day of the ninth month, all the people were
sitting in the square before the house of God, greatly distressed by the occasion
and because of the rain. [10]Then Ezra the priest stood up and said to them, "You
have been unfaithful; you have married foreign women, adding to Israel's guilt.
[11]Now honor[a] the LORD, the God of your ancestors, and do his will. Separate
yourselves from the peoples around you and from your foreign wives."

[12]The whole assembly responded with a loud voice: "You are right! We must do
as you say. [13]But there are many people here and it is the rainy season; so we cannot stand outside. Besides, this matter cannot be taken care of in a day or two,
because we have sinned greatly in this thing. [14]Let our officials act for the whole
assembly. Then let everyone in our towns who has married a foreign woman
come at a set time, along with the elders and judges of each town, until the fierce
anger of our God in this matter is turned away from us." [15]Only Jonathan son of
Asahel and Jahzeiah son of Tikvah, supported by Meshullam and Shabbethai
the Levite, opposed this.

[16]So the exiles did as was proposed. Ezra the priest selected men who were
family heads, one from each family division, and all of them designated by

[a] 11 Or *Now make confession to*

EZRA 9:13

THE REMNANT

The Lord promised Abraham that his offspring would be an uncountable multitude as numerous as the stars in the sky and the sand on the beach (Ge 22:17). After Israel's rebellion against the Lord and his judgment on them in the Babylonian exile, only a remnant—a small number of people—returned to the land. But as Isaiah had prophesied—using the example of a tree that is cut down to a stump but sprouts new growth—from the broken stump of the returned exiles the Messiah would sprout and bring forth new life (Isa 6:11–13; 11:1). During the time of Ezra, Israel was a small stump, but in the future it would once again sprout into an uncountable multitude. God would keep his promise that the offspring of Abraham would be as numerous as the stars and the sand. How did God keep his promise? Through the offspring of Abraham who is Jesus Christ (Gal 3:16). All who believe in Jesus—regardless of ethnicity—are the offspring of Abraham (Gal 3:28–29), and no one will be able to count that multitude on the last day (Rev 7:9).

EZRA 10:1

THE MERCY OF GOD

Ezra gave an outward sign of repentance by tearing his clothes and pulling hair from his head and beard (Ezr 9:3). He then offered a prayer of repentance by recounting the faithless history of Israel. But he also acknowledged that despite their sin, God had shown favor in more recent events, particularly the return of the

(continued on next page)

(The Mercy of God, continued)

remnant and the reconstruction of the temple. Despite God's favor, the returned exiles sinned by intermarrying with the inhabitants of the land, just as the people of Israel had done when they first entered the promised land after the exodus from Egypt (Ezr 9:1–2; Jdg 3:5–6). Even some of the priests had married foreign women (Ezr 10:18). The problem with the marriages was not race; it was religion. God's chosen people had married idolaters who did not worship the true God. And yet, following Ezra's prayer of confession, the people followed Ezra's lead and began to confess their sins in front of the temple (10:1).

This scene of repentance reflected a request Solomon had made of God long ago: that God would be merciful and forgive his rebellious, exiled people if they turned toward the temple and confessed their sins (1Ki 8:46–51). Despite the Israelites' continual disobedience, God remained incredibly merciful to them. The situation for believers today is different from ancient Israel. The church does not pray toward a temple made with bricks and mortar. Rather, God's people pray to the new temple—Jesus of Nazareth (Jn 2:21). And when they do, he is faithful to forgive their sins (1Jn 1:9).

name. On the first day of the tenth month they sat down to investigate the cases,
17 and by the first day of the first month they finished dealing with all the men
who had married foreign women.

Those Guilty of Intermarriage

18 Among the descendants of the priests, the following had married foreign women:

From the descendants of Joshua son of Jozadak, and his brothers: Maaseiah, Eliezer, Jarib and Gedaliah.
19 (They all gave their hands in pledge to put away their wives, and for their guilt they each presented a ram from the flock as a guilt offering.)

20 From the descendants of Immer:
Hanani and Zebadiah.
21 From the descendants of Harim:
Maaseiah, Elijah, Shemaiah, Jehiel and Uzziah.
22 From the descendants of Pashhur:
Elioenai, Maaseiah, Ishmael, Nethanel, Jozabad and Elasah.

23 Among the Levites:

Jozabad, Shimei, Kelaiah (that is, Kelita), Pethahiah, Judah and Eliezer.
24 From the musicians:
Eliashib.
From the gatekeepers:
Shallum, Telem and Uri.

25 And among the other Israelites:

From the descendants of Parosh:
Ramiah, Izziah, Malkijah, Mijamin, Eleazar, Malkijah and Benaiah.
26 From the descendants of Elam:
Mattaniah, Zechariah, Jehiel, Abdi, Jeremoth and Elijah.
27 From the descendants of Zattu:
Elioenai, Eliashib, Mattaniah, Jeremoth, Zabad and Aziza.
28 From the descendants of Bebai:
Jehohanan, Hananiah, Zabbai and Athlai.
29 From the descendants of Bani:
Meshullam, Malluk, Adaiah, Jashub, Sheal and Jeremoth.
30 From the descendants of Pahath-Moab:
Adna, Kelal, Benaiah, Maaseiah, Mattaniah, Bezalel, Binnui and Manasseh.
31 From the descendants of Harim:
Eliezer, Ishijah, Malkijah, Shemaiah, Shimeon,
32 Benjamin, Malluk and Shemariah.
33 From the descendants of Hashum:
Mattenai, Mattattah, Zabad, Eliphelet, Jeremai, Manasseh and Shimei.
34 From the descendants of Bani:
Maadai, Amram, Uel,
35 Benaiah, Bedeiah, Keluhi,
36 Vaniah, Meremoth, Eliashib,
37 Mattaniah, Mattenai and Jaasu.
38 From the descendants of Binnui:[a]
Shimei,
39 Shelemiah, Nathan, Adaiah,
40 Maknadebai, Shashai, Sharai,
41 Azarel, Shelemiah, Shemariah,
42 Shallum, Amariah and Joseph.
43 From the descendants of Nebo:
Jeiel, Mattithiah, Zabad, Zebina, Jaddai, Joel and Benaiah.

44 All these had married foreign women, and some of them had children by these wives.[b]

---

[a] 37,38 See Septuagint (also 1 Esdras 9:34); Hebrew *Jaasu* [38] *and Bani and Binnui,*
[b] 44 Or *and they sent them away with their children*

JESUS: OUR REBUILDER OF THE BROKEN

NEHEMIAH

NEHEMIAH

EZRA ARRIVES IN JERUSALEM	NEHEMIAH ARRIVES IN JERUSALEM	NEHEMIAH REBUILDS THE WALL
c. 458 BC	*c. 444 BC*	*c. 444 BC*

The book of Nehemiah tells the story of a God-ordained leader and his work to aid the restored community to rebuild the wall around the city of Jerusalem. But, more than that, the book recounts God's faithfulness to his promise to restore the fortunes of his people and grant them the joy that comes through worshiping him.

In 444 BC, the Persian emperor Artaxerxes granted Nehemiah the freedom to relocate to the Jewish homeland, even appointing him to be the governor of Judah. Once there, Nehemiah led the people, descendants of the remnant that had returned from exile a century earlier, to rebuild the wall around Jerusalem. Under his direction, this task took only 52 days. In about 432 BC, Nehemiah was recalled to Persia for approximately a year before returning to Judah for a second term (5:14; 13:6 – 7).

Nehemiah's inclusion of Ezra's spiritual reforms in this book makes clear that his goal was to restore the spiritual health of the people along with rebuilding the wall. The earlier exile to Babylon and the temple's destruction vividly portrayed the consequence of sin. The fact that Jerusalem was in shambles was a picture of the spiritual state of the people, and God would not allow his people to tarnish his name and make a mockery of his dwelling place. Rebuilding the temple (which happened a century before Nehemiah's return) and the wall around the city demonstrated that God had not forgotten his people; he would help his people rebuild, and would be worshiped once again.

The people that Nehemiah came back to, however, continued in their lackadaisical spiritual stupor, even after having been in the land for many years. They had faced ongoing opposition since their return, which exposed their spiritual lethargy and coldhearted indifference to the Lord. In light of God's mercies, God anointed leaders like Nehemiah and prophets like Malachi to continue to remind the people of their need to repent. The latter half of the book of Nehemiah portrays the spiritual revival that followed their rebuilding of the wall around the city. Not only was the city rebuilt, but the people were rebuilt as well.

One theme of the book is clear — God will see to it that his name is glorified. In spite of the people's sin and the brokenness of life in a fallen world, he would, time and time again, see to it that his people were restored so that the world would know the greatness of his name. The spiritual restoration led by Nehemiah is a picture of the hope offered by the good news of Jesus. To those broken and destroyed by sin, Jesus' work offers the ever-present hope of restoration.

YOU ARE A FORGIVING GOD, GRACIOUS AND COMPASSIONATE, SLOW TO ANGER AND ABOUNDING IN LOVE.

Nehemiah 9:17

NEHEMIAH

NEHEMIAH 2:4 – 5

WHAT IS IT YOU WANT?

Four months after Nehemiah heard of the conditions in Jerusalem, the king asked him a blunt question: "What is it you want?" It was within the king's power to grant Nehemiah almost anything or to punish him as he wished. The moment was ripe with potential and danger. Nehemiah prayed to God, then answered with an extravagant request. He desired to leave the service of the king, the most powerful person in the world, to go and rebuild the wall of Jerusalem. The king could have received this as an insult and responded accordingly, but God answered Nehemiah's prayers and the audacious request was granted.

In the New Testament, Jesus asked two blind men, "What do you want me to do for you?" (Mt 20:32). Full of faith, the men asked for the impossible — that their eyes might be opened. Jesus, full of power, granted the request and gave them sight. A contrasting story appears in Acts 3:1 – 10. A man lame from birth asked Peter and John for money. His request was much too small. Instead of giving him silver or gold, Peter healed him "in the name of Jesus Christ of Nazareth." The man stood, walked, then leaped into the air praising God. Jesus reminded his followers that all authority in heaven and on earth had been given to him (Mt 28:18). Jesus is the King of all kings, and, by his grace, believers can boldly ask for blessings that accord with his will and bring glory to his name.

Nehemiah's Prayer

1 The words of Nehemiah son of Hakaliah:

In the month of Kislev in the twentieth year, while I was in the citadel of
Susa, 2Hanani, one of my brothers, came from Judah with some other men, and
I questioned them about the Jewish remnant that had survived the exile, and
also about Jerusalem.

3They said to me, "Those who survived the exile and are back in the province
are in great trouble and disgrace. The wall of Jerusalem is broken down, and its
gates have been burned with fire."

4When I heard these things, I sat down and wept. For some days I mourned
and fasted and prayed before the God of heaven. 5Then I said:

> "LORD, the God of heaven, the great and awesome God, who keeps his
> covenant of love with those who love him and keep his commandments,
> 6let your ear be attentive and your eyes open to hear the prayer your ser-
> vant is praying before you day and night for your servants, the people of
> Israel. I confess the sins we Israelites, including myself and my father's
> family, have committed against you. 7We have acted very wickedly toward
> you. We have not obeyed the commands, decrees and laws you gave your
> servant Moses.
>
> 8"Remember the instruction you gave your servant Moses, saying, 'If
> you are unfaithful, I will scatter you among the nations, 9but if you return
> to me and obey my commands, then even if your exiled people are at the
> farthest horizon, I will gather them from there and bring them to the place
> I have chosen as a dwelling for my Name.'
>
> 10"They are your servants and your people, whom you redeemed by your
> great strength and your mighty hand. 11Lord, let your ear be attentive to the
> prayer of this your servant and to the prayer of your servants who delight in
> revering your name. Give your servant success today by granting him favor
> in the presence of this man."
>
> I was cupbearer to the king.

Artaxerxes Sends Nehemiah to Jerusalem

2 In the month of Nisan in the twentieth year of King Artaxerxes, when wine
was brought for him, I took the wine and gave it to the king. I had not been
sad in his presence before, 2so the king asked me, "Why does your face look so
sad when you are not ill? This can be nothing but sadness of heart."

I was very much afraid, 3but I said to the king, "May the king live forever! Why
should my face not look sad when the city where my ancestors are buried lies in
ruins, and its gates have been destroyed by fire?"

4The king said to me, "What is it you want?"

Then I prayed to the God of heaven, 5and I answered the king, "If it pleases the
king and if your servant has found favor in his sight, let him send me to the city
in Judah where my ancestors are buried so that I can rebuild it."

6Then the king, with the queen sitting beside him, asked me, "How long will
your journey take, and when will you get back?" It pleased the king to send me;
so I set a time.

7I also said to him, "If it pleases the king, may I have letters to the governors
of Trans-Euphrates, so that they will provide me safe-conduct until I arrive in
Judah? 8And may I have a letter to Asaph, keeper of the royal park, so he will give

REALITY-CHANGING PRAYER

The gap between "what was" and "what should be" led Nehemiah to many days of tearful mourning. The first Israelites had returned from exile to the holy city of Jerusalem nearly a century earlier. In spite of these years and all that *should* have been accomplished, God's people remained "in great trouble and disgrace" (v. 3). The personal condition of its inhabitants mirrored the physical condition of Jerusalem. Collectively, they were broken, humiliated, vulnerable to their enemies and seemingly incapable of moving into the future God intended. Though a thousand miles away and living in great luxury, Nehemiah was shattered by the news. His response was to take action, and his first action was prayer. The remainder of the book of Nehemiah is really the record of history-changing events set in motion by one man's prayer.

Nehemiah offers a practical case study of God-honoring prayer. He began by declaring the greatness of God and God's faithfulness to his covenant. Nehemiah understood that the current conditions in Jerusalem were not God's will. He also understood the conditions in Jerusalem to be the result of sin. Nehemiah openly confessed the collective sins of Israel, and also his own. Though he had never been to Jerusalem himself, he shared an identity as one of the "children of Israel," and likewise shared in their guilt. Though God's people had broken covenant with God, he had not left them without hope. Nehemiah did not wallow helplessly in despair but declared his belief in God's promise of restoration for those who would return to him. Nehemiah's prayer of confession and declaration marked such a returning to God. It was a pivotal moment of change that decisively transformed the trajectory of Nehemiah's life and the life of all Israel.

The idea of "confession," or "declaration," is central to the gospel. In Romans 10:9 – 10, the apostle Paul wrote, "If you declare with your mouth, 'Jesus is Lord,' and believe in your heart that God raised him from the dead, you will be saved. For it is with your heart that you believe and are justified, and it is with your mouth that you profess your faith and are saved." The greatest change any human being can experience is that of salvation. This change is marked by confessing Jesus as Lord (the one to whom every aspect of our lives is to be submitted) and believing the truth of his resurrection (a demonstration of God's love and God's power even over death). Such a confession dramatically alters the course of one's life. Moreover, as Jesus lives in the believer and accomplishes his will through those who obey him, the world is transformed as well.

me timber to make beams for the gates of the citadel by the temple and for the
city wall and for the residence I will occupy?" And because the gracious hand of
my God was on me, the king granted my requests. 9So I went to the governors of
Trans-Euphrates and gave them the king's letters. The king had also sent army
officers and cavalry with me.

10When Sanballat the Horonite and Tobiah the Ammonite official heard
about this, they were very much disturbed that someone had come to promote
the welfare of the Israelites.

Nehemiah Inspects Jerusalem's Walls

11I went to Jerusalem, and after staying there three days 12I set out during the
night with a few others. I had not told anyone what my God had put in my heart to
do for Jerusalem. There were no mounts with me except the one I was riding on.

13By night I went out through the Valley Gate toward the Jackal[a] Well and the
Dung Gate, examining the walls of Jerusalem, which had been broken down, and
its gates, which had been destroyed by fire. 14Then I moved on toward the Fountain Gate and the King's Pool, but there was not enough room for my mount to get
through; 15so I went up the valley by night, examining the wall. Finally, I turned
back and reentered through the Valley Gate. 16The officials did not know where I
had gone or what I was doing, because as yet I had said nothing to the Jews or the
priests or nobles or officials or any others who would be doing the work.

17Then I said to them, "You see the trouble we are in: Jerusalem lies in ruins,
and its gates have been burned with fire. Come, let us rebuild the wall of Jerusalem, and we will no longer be in disgrace." 18I also told them about the gracious
hand of my God on me and what the king had said to me.

They replied, "Let us start rebuilding." So they began this good work.

19But when Sanballat the Horonite, Tobiah the Ammonite official and Geshem the Arab heard about it, they mocked and ridiculed us. "What is this you
are doing?" they asked. "Are you rebelling against the king?"

20I answered them by saying, "The God of heaven will give us success. We his
servants will start rebuilding, but as for you, you have no share in Jerusalem or
any claim or historic right to it."

Builders of the Wall

3 Eliashib the high priest and his fellow priests went to work and rebuilt the
Sheep Gate. They dedicated it and set its doors in place, building as far as
the Tower of the Hundred, which they dedicated, and as far as the Tower of Hananel. 2The men of Jericho built the adjoining section, and Zakkur son of Imri
built next to them.

3The Fish Gate was rebuilt by the sons of Hassenaah. They laid its beams and
put its doors and bolts and bars in place. 4Meremoth son of Uriah, the son of
Hakkoz, repaired the next section. Next to him Meshullam son of Berekiah, the
son of Meshezabel, made repairs, and next to him Zadok son of Baana also made
repairs. 5The next section was repaired by the men of Tekoa, but their nobles
would not put their shoulders to the work under their supervisors.[b]

6The Jeshanah[c] Gate was repaired by Joiada son of Paseah and Meshullam
son of Besodeiah. They laid its beams and put its doors with their bolts and bars
in place. 7Next to them, repairs were made by men from Gibeon and Mizpah—
Melatiah of Gibeon and Jadon of Meronoth—places under the authority of the
governor of Trans-Euphrates. 8Uzziel son of Harhaiah, one of the goldsmiths,
repaired the next section; and Hananiah, one of the perfume-makers, made repairs next to that. They restored Jerusalem as far as the Broad Wall. 9Repha-
iah son of Hur, ruler of a half-district of Jerusalem, repaired the next section.
10Adjoining this, Jedaiah son of Harumaph made repairs opposite his house, and

---

[a] *13* Or *Serpent* or *Fig* [b] *5* Or *their Lord* or *the governor* [c] *6* Or *Old*

Hattush son of Hashabneiah made repairs next to him. 11 Malkijah son of Harim and Hasshub son of Pahath-Moab repaired another section and the Tower of the Ovens. 12 Shallum son of Hallohesh, ruler of a half-district of Jerusalem, repaired the next section with the help of his daughters.

13 The Valley Gate was repaired by Hanun and the residents of Zanoah. They rebuilt it and put its doors with their bolts and bars in place. They also repaired a thousand cubits[a] of the wall as far as the Dung Gate.

14 The Dung Gate was repaired by Malkijah son of Rekab, ruler of the district of Beth Hakkerem. He rebuilt it and put its doors with their bolts and bars in place.

15 The Fountain Gate was repaired by Shallun son of Kol-Hozeh, ruler of the district of Mizpah. He rebuilt it, roofing it over and putting its doors and bolts and bars in place. He also repaired the wall of the Pool of Siloam,[b] by the King's Garden, as far as the steps going down from the City of David. 16 Beyond him, Nehemiah son of Azbuk, ruler of a half-district of Beth Zur, made repairs up to a point opposite the tombs[c] of David, as far as the artificial pool and the House of the Heroes.

17 Next to him, the repairs were made by the Levites under Rehum son of Bani. Beside him, Hashabiah, ruler of half the district of Keilah, carried out repairs for his district. 18 Next to him, the repairs were made by their fellow Levites under Binnui[d] son of Henadad, ruler of the other half-district of Keilah. 19 Next to him, Ezer son of Jeshua, ruler of Mizpah, repaired another section, from a point facing the ascent to the armory as far as the angle of the wall. 20 Next to him, Baruch son of Zabbai zealously repaired another section, from the angle to the entrance of the house of Eliashib the high priest. 21 Next to him, Meremoth son of Uriah, the son of Hakkoz, repaired another section, from the entrance of Eliashib's house to the end of it.

22 The repairs next to him were made by the priests from the surrounding region. 23 Beyond them, Benjamin and Hasshub made repairs in front of their house; and next to them, Azariah son of Maaseiah, the son of Ananiah, made repairs beside his house. 24 Next to him, Binnui son of Henadad repaired another section, from Azariah's house to the angle and the corner, 25 and Palal son of Uzai worked opposite the angle and the tower projecting from the upper palace near the court of the guard. Next to him, Pedaiah son of Parosh 26 and the temple servants living on the hill of Ophel made repairs up to a point opposite the Water Gate toward the east and the projecting tower. 27 Next to them, the men of Tekoa repaired another section, from the great projecting tower to the wall of Ophel.

28 Above the Horse Gate, the priests made repairs, each in front of his own house. 29 Next to them, Zadok son of Immer made repairs opposite his house. Next to him, Shemaiah son of Shekaniah, the guard at the East Gate, made repairs. 30 Next to him, Hananiah son of Shelemiah, and Hanun, the sixth son of Zalaph, repaired another section. Next to them, Meshullam son of Berekiah made repairs opposite his living quarters. 31 Next to him, Malkijah, one of the goldsmiths, made repairs as far as the house of the temple servants and the merchants, opposite the Inspection Gate, and as far as the room above the corner; 32 and between the room above the corner and the Sheep Gate the goldsmiths and merchants made repairs.

Opposition to the Rebuilding

4 [e] When Sanballat heard that we were rebuilding the wall, he became angry and was greatly incensed. He ridiculed the Jews, 2 and in the presence of his associates and the army of Samaria, he said, "What are those feeble Jews doing?

[a] *13* That is, about 1,500 feet or about 450 meters [b] *15* Hebrew *Shelah,* a variant of *Shiloah,* that is, Siloam [c] *16* Hebrew; Septuagint, some Vulgate manuscripts and Syriac *tomb* [d] *18* Two Hebrew manuscripts and Syriac (see also Septuagint and verse 24); most Hebrew manuscripts *Bavvai* [e] In Hebrew texts 4:1-6 is numbered 3:33-38, and 4:7-23 is numbered 4:1-17.

NEHEMIAH 4:1 – 18

ESCALATING OPPOSITION

The rebuilding of the wall of Jerusalem was met with opposition from the beginning. Others had a vested interest in keeping the restored community weak. They were protecting their own power and influence in the area, and they saw the rise of Jerusalem as a threat. As the work of rebuilding continued, the threats against the people of Judah multiplied. In the first verses of chapter 4, the opposition consisted of mocking words from Sanballat and Tobiah. By the seventh verse, the list of enemies had grown to include the Arabs, the Ammonites and the people of Ashdod, all of whom threatened violence. Nehemiah's response? He prayed, took preventive measures and continued working. Once again, he urged the people not to be afraid, but to "remember the Lord, who is great and awesome" (v. 14).

Opposition to Jesus' ministry followed a similar pattern. Initially, the religious and national leaders were eager to hear Jesus and to witness his miracles. They soon realized, however, that Jesus represented a threat to every power structure and political agenda. The more Jesus was embraced by the general population, the more he was opposed by the leaders of Israel's factions. The more he accomplished God's will, the more his enemies conspired to kill him. Like Nehemiah, Jesus responded with prayer and perseverance.

BUILDING TOGETHER

Jerusalem's wall had lain in disrepair for more than 140 years, since its destruction by the Babylonians in 586 BC. Eventually, Cyrus of Persia, who had conquered Babylon in 539 BC, allowed the Jews to return to their homeland shortly thereafter. Nehemiah's party, with the permission of King Artaxerxes, arrived in Jerusalem approximately 94 years after the first returnees. Through all the prior years, the rubble of the city's walls and the burned timbers of its gates had been a constant reminder of Judah's shame and weakness. The Jews had attempted to rebuild the walls earlier in the reign of Artaxerxes I; but after some protests, the king ordered the Jews to stop the work (Ezr 4:21 – 23). This likely led to the report made to Nehemiah (Ne 1:3) and his efforts to once again rebuild the walls.

Nehemiah did not encourage them to trust in themselves for this work. Instead, Nehemiah told them how *God* had already acted for their good (2:18). With this news, they accepted the invitation. Rather than briefly summarizing the construction work, chapter 3 offers a remarkably detailed account of how many different people — from different families, of different cities, with different vocations, both men and women — came together to restore Jerusalem's walls and reset its gates. They were an unlikely team, but they shared a common purpose. As each did his or her part, the work was completed.

Centuries later, Jesus invited an even more disparate group to the all-encompassing task of rebuilding Israel spiritually. The twelve disciples included fishermen, a tax collector and likely an anti-government zealot. As Jesus' followers grew in number, the level of diversity only increased. They had little in common except Jesus himself, and he was enough. Through these first believers, Jesus established and spread his church. As was true with the rebuilding of the wall in Nehemiah's time, the church is built only as believers fulfill their individual roles in humble cooperation with others. The apostle Paul refers to the church as the body of Christ (Ro 12:3 – 8; 1Co 12; Eph 4:1 – 16). The body is made up of many parts. While each part is different, all are critically important. Each believer possesses different spiritual gifts, but the body is only complete when each is present to share those gifts. Every believer has a function, but the mission of the church can only be completed when each is faithful to fulfill that function.

Will they restore their wall? Will they offer sacrifices? Will they finish in a day?
Can they bring the stones back to life from those heaps of rubble — burned as
they are?"
[3]Tobiah the Ammonite, who was at his side, said, "What they are building —
even a fox climbing up on it would break down their wall of stones!"

[4]Hear us, our God, for we are despised. Turn their insults back on their own
heads. Give them over as plunder in a land of captivity. [5]Do not cover up their
guilt or blot out their sins from your sight, for they have thrown insults in the
face of[a] the builders.

[6]So we rebuilt the wall till all of it reached half its height, for the people worked
with all their heart.
[7]But when Sanballat, Tobiah, the Arabs, the Ammonites and the people of
Ashdod heard that the repairs to Jerusalem's walls had gone ahead and that the
gaps were being closed, they were very angry. [8]They all plotted together to come
and fight against Jerusalem and stir up trouble against it. [9]But we prayed to our
God and posted a guard day and night to meet this threat.
[10]Meanwhile, the people in Judah said, "The strength of the laborers is giving
out, and there is so much rubble that we cannot rebuild the wall."
[11]Also our enemies said, "Before they know it or see us, we will be right there
among them and will kill them and put an end to the work."
[12]Then the Jews who lived near them came and told us ten times over, "Wherever you turn, they will attack us."
[13]Therefore I stationed some of the people behind the lowest points of the wall
at the exposed places, posting them by families, with their swords, spears and
bows. [14]After I looked things over, I stood up and said to the nobles, the officials
and the rest of the people, "Don't be afraid of them. Remember the Lord, who is
great and awesome, and fight for your families, your sons and your daughters,
your wives and your homes."
[15]When our enemies heard that we were aware of their plot and that God had
frustrated it, we all returned to the wall, each to our own work.
[16]From that day on, half of my men did the work, while the other half were
equipped with spears, shields, bows and armor. The officers posted themselves
behind all the people of Judah [17]who were building the wall. Those who carried
materials did their work with one hand and held a weapon in the other, [18]and
each of the builders wore his sword at his side as he worked. But the man who
sounded the trumpet stayed with me.
[19]Then I said to the nobles, the officials and the rest of the people, "The work
is extensive and spread out, and we are widely separated from each other along
the wall. [20]Wherever you hear the sound of the trumpet, join us there. Our God
will fight for us!"
[21]So we continued the work with half the men holding spears, from the first
light of dawn till the stars came out. [22]At that time I also said to the people, "Have
every man and his helper stay inside Jerusalem at night, so they can serve us as
guards by night and as workers by day." [23]Neither I nor my brothers nor my men
nor the guards with me took off our clothes; each had his weapon, even when he
went for water.[b]

Nehemiah Helps the Poor

5 Now the men and their wives raised a great outcry against their fellow Jews.
[2]Some were saying, "We and our sons and daughters are numerous; in order
for us to eat and stay alive, we must get grain."
[3]Others were saying, "We are mortgaging our fields, our vineyards and our
homes to get grain during the famine."
[4]Still others were saying, "We have had to borrow money to pay the king's

---

[a] 5 Or *have aroused your anger before* [b] 23 The meaning of the Hebrew for this clause is uncertain.

NEHEMIAH 6:1 – 19

DEVIOUS CRITICS

Having failed to stop Nehemiah from rebuilding the wall by open opposition, his enemies changed tactics. They attempted to distract him with invitations for dialogue. To provoke fear, they said Nehemiah intended to have himself declared king of Judah — an act that would have represented revolt against Artaxerxes and would likely lead to the destruction of all they had built. Finally, they tried to trick Nehemiah into discrediting himself by cowardly seeking safety in the Holy Place inside the temple, a place where only priests were allowed. In this last ploy, Shemaiah, a fellow Israelite, was a coconspirator. Nehemiah maintained his righteousness in the face of these temptations and kept his focus on the work of God.

The enemies of Jesus, even Satan himself, used many of these same tactics. In the wilderness the devil tempted Jesus to betray God for his own gain (Mt 4:1 – 11). Jesus remained steadfast. Throughout Jesus' ministry, religious leaders tried to trick him in order to discredit him. Their attempts to trap Jesus with politically and religiously charged riddles met with failure every time. In the end, as was the case with Nehemiah, the enemies of Jesus engaged someone on the inside, Judas, in their efforts. Even this, however, served God's purpose of salvation. In spite of the most severe temptations, and in spite of having the power to spare himself, Jesus remained faithful to the end. "He humbled himself by becoming obedient to death — even death on a cross!" (Php 2:8).

tax on our fields and vineyards. 5Although we are of the same flesh and blood
as our fellow Jews and though our children are as good as theirs, yet we have to
subject our sons and daughters to slavery. Some of our daughters have already
been enslaved, but we are powerless, because our fields and our vineyards belong to others."
6When I heard their outcry and these charges, I was very angry. 7I pondered
them in my mind and then accused the nobles and officials. I told them, "You are
charging your own people interest!" So I called together a large meeting to deal
with them 8and said: "As far as possible, we have bought back our fellow Jews who
were sold to the Gentiles. Now you are selling your own people, only for them to
be sold back to us!" They kept quiet, because they could find nothing to say.
9So I continued, "What you are doing is not right. Shouldn't you walk in the
fear of our God to avoid the reproach of our Gentile enemies? 10I and my brothers and my men are also lending the people money and grain. But let us stop
charging interest! 11Give back to them immediately their fields, vineyards, olive
groves and houses, and also the interest you are charging them — one percent of
the money, grain, new wine and olive oil."
12"We will give it back," they said. "And we will not demand anything more
from them. We will do as you say."
Then I summoned the priests and made the nobles and officials take an oath
to do what they had promised. 13I also shook out the folds of my robe and said,
"In this way may God shake out of their house and possessions anyone who does
not keep this promise. So may such a person be shaken out and emptied!"
At this the whole assembly said, "Amen," and praised the LORD. And the people did as they had promised.
14Moreover, from the twentieth year of King Artaxerxes, when I was appointed to be their governor in the land of Judah, until his thirty-second year — twelve
years — neither I nor my brothers ate the food allotted to the governor. 15But the
earlier governors — those preceding me — placed a heavy burden on the people
and took forty shekels[a] of silver from them in addition to food and wine. Their
assistants also lorded it over the people. But out of reverence for God I did not act
like that. 16Instead, I devoted myself to the work on this wall. All my men were
assembled there for the work; we[b] did not acquire any land.
17Furthermore, a hundred and fifty Jews and officials ate at my table, as well
as those who came to us from the surrounding nations. 18Each day one ox, six
choice sheep and some poultry were prepared for me, and every ten days an
abundant supply of wine of all kinds. In spite of all this, I never demanded the
food allotted to the governor, because the demands were heavy on these people.
19Remember me with favor, my God, for all I have done for these people.

Further Opposition to the Rebuilding

6 When word came to Sanballat, Tobiah, Geshem the Arab and the rest of our
enemies that I had rebuilt the wall and not a gap was left in it — though up to
that time I had not set the doors in the gates — 2Sanballat and Geshem sent me this
message: "Come, let us meet together in one of the villages[c] on the plain of Ono."
But they were scheming to harm me; 3so I sent messengers to them with this
reply: "I am carrying on a great project and cannot go down. Why should the
work stop while I leave it and go down to you?" 4Four times they sent me the same
message, and each time I gave them the same answer.
5Then, the fifth time, Sanballat sent his aide to me with the same message,
and in his hand was an unsealed letter 6in which was written:

"It is reported among the nations — and Geshem[d] says it is true — that
you and the Jews are plotting to revolt, and therefore you are building the

[a] *15* That is, about 1 pound or about 460 grams [b] *16* Most Hebrew manuscripts; some Hebrew manuscripts, Septuagint, Vulgate and Syriac *I* [c] *2* Or *in Kephirim* [d] *6* Hebrew *Gashmu*, a variant of *Geshem*

GOOD NEWS FOR THE POOR

In Nehemiah 5, the focus shifts from external opposition to internal strife. The wealthy of Judah had taken advantage of the poor, whose needs had reached a critical level. Without adequate food and money to pay their taxes, the poor had mortgaged their land, borrowed money at interest and had even been reduced to selling their children to their fellow Jews as slaves. Loaning money at interest and enslaving a fellow Jew were both violations of Jewish law and an egregious failure to love and care for one's neighbor. Upon learning of these travesties, Nehemiah confronted the guilty. True to form, his actions were grounded in his understanding of God and God's will. The behavior of the wealthy indicated a lack of reverence for God and an indifference to how their actions against the poor dishonored God.

Nehemiah's own conduct toward those in need was exemplary. It was within his legal rights as governor to tax the people to cover his own expenses. It was also customary for a man in his position to burden those under his rule for his own benefit. Like other members of the wealthy class, Nehemiah could have enriched himself through acquiring and selling real estate or loaning money at interest. But he did none of these things. He understood that true reverence for God requires treating others with compassion, confronting oppressors and caring for the poor.

Jesus, teaching in a synagogue many years later, read from the book of Isaiah: "The Spirit of the Lord is on me, because he has anointed me to proclaim good news to the poor. He has sent me to proclaim freedom for the prisoners and recovery of sight for the blind, to set the oppressed free" (Lk 4:18). Jesus then made clear to his listeners that he was the fulfillment of Isaiah's prophecy. Jesus' ministry centered on the gospel, the ultimate expression of which is Jesus' atoning death on the cross and his defeat of death in the resurrection. His sacrifice makes salvation possible for all who repent and believe. But Jesus also made it clear that repentance and belief lead a true follower of Christ to genuine concern and action on behalf of the poor, the suffering and the oppressed. Jesus did not mince words when it came to those who profited at the expense of others or were indifferent to their needs. He warned his disciples to beware of the teachers of the law who *appeared* pious but loved privilege and money and cheated widows of their property in pursuit of these things. Though these religious leaders enjoyed an elevated status in Jewish culture, Jesus said they would receive especially severe punishment (Lk 20:46 – 47).

NEHEMIAH 7:1–3

BUILDING PEOPLE AND A CITY

The rebuilding of Jerusalem was primarily a venture of spiritual restoration. This spiritual goal was achieved, however, with physical work. Likewise, the ongoing spiritual vitality of this rebuilt city would require the never-ending work of meeting practical needs. To that end, Nehemiah appointed gatekeepers to guard the city gates, as well as the temple, and musicians to lead worship in the temple (v. 1). To ensure the city's security, Nehemiah appointed two officials, each with responsibility for half of Jerusalem (v. 2; cf. 3:9,12). Additionally, citizens were to take turns standing guard near their own homes. Nehemiah, managing the details, ordered that the gates remain closed until well into the day (7:3). This would prevent sneak attacks at sunrise, the normal time for a city's gates to be opened.

Jesus promised to build his church (Mt 16:18). Whereas the walls and gates of Jerusalem represented a defense against enemies, Jesus depicts his church as on offense, storming enemy territory. In this spiritual venture of building the church, Jesus' strategy was to send his disciples out in pairs. The spiritual ministry of preaching and healing required dirty, well-traveled feet, as well as considering the physical necessities of food and lodging. Addressing these practical details, Jesus instructed them to stay in a home where they were welcomed and to eat and drink whatever was offered (Lk 10:1–12). Jesus' practical strategy was used by the apostles and the early church as well, resulting in the expansion of the Christian faith throughout the known world.

wall. Moreover, according to these reports you are about to become their
king [7]and have even appointed prophets to make this proclamation about
you in Jerusalem: 'There is a king in Judah!' Now this report will get back
to the king; so come, let us meet together."

[8]I sent him this reply: "Nothing like what you are saying is happening; you are
just making it up out of your head."

[9]They were all trying to frighten us, thinking, "Their hands will get too weak
for the work, and it will not be completed."

But I prayed, "Now strengthen my hands."

[10]One day I went to the house of Shemaiah son of Delaiah, the son of Mehetabel, who was shut in at his home. He said, "Let us meet in the house of God,
inside the temple, and let us close the temple doors, because men are coming to
kill you — by night they are coming to kill you."

[11]But I said, "Should a man like me run away? Or should someone like me go
into the temple to save his life? I will not go!" [12]I realized that God had not sent
him, but that he had prophesied against me because Tobiah and Sanballat had
hired him. [13]He had been hired to intimidate me so that I would commit a sin by
doing this, and then they would give me a bad name to discredit me.

[14]Remember Tobiah and Sanballat, my God, because of what they have done;
remember also the prophet Noadiah and how she and the rest of the prophets
have been trying to intimidate me. [15]So the wall was completed on the twenty-
fifth of Elul, in fifty-two days.

Opposition to the Completed Wall

[16]When all our enemies heard about this, all the surrounding nations were
afraid and lost their self-confidence, because they realized that this work had
been done with the help of our God.

[17]Also, in those days the nobles of Judah were sending many letters to Tobiah,
and replies from Tobiah kept coming to them. [18]For many in Judah were under
oath to him, since he was son-in-law to Shekaniah son of Arah, and his son Jehohanan had married the daughter of Meshullam son of Berekiah. [19]Moreover,
they kept reporting to me his good deeds and then telling him what I said. And
Tobiah sent letters to intimidate me.

7 After the wall had been rebuilt and I had set the doors in place, the gatekeepers,
the musicians and the Levites were appointed. [2]I put in charge of Jerusalem my
brother Hanani, along with Hananiah the commander of the citadel, because he
was a man of integrity and feared God more than most people do. [3]I said to them,
"The gates of Jerusalem are not to be opened until the sun is hot. While the gatekeepers are still on duty, have them shut the doors and bar them. Also appoint residents of Jerusalem as guards, some at their posts and some near their own houses."

The List of the Exiles Who Returned

[4]Now the city was large and spacious, but there were few people in it, and the
houses had not yet been rebuilt. [5]So my God put it into my heart to assemble the
nobles, the officials and the common people for registration by families. I found
the genealogical record of those who had been the first to return. This is what I
found written there:

[6]These are the people of the province who came up from the captivity of
the exiles whom Nebuchadnezzar king of Babylon had taken captive (they
returned to Jerusalem and Judah, each to his own town, [7]in company with
Zerubbabel, Joshua, Nehemiah, Azariah, Raamiah, Nahamani, Mordecai,
Bilshan, Mispereth, Bigvai, Nehum and Baanah):

The list of the men of Israel:

[8]the descendants of Parosh	2,172
[9]of Shephatiah	372

10 of Arah	652
11 of Pahath-Moab (through the line of Jeshua and Joab)	2,818
12 of Elam	1,254
13 of Zattu	845
14 of Zakkai	760
15 of Binnui	648
16 of Bebai	628
17 of Azgad	2,322
18 of Adonikam	667
19 of Bigvai	2,067
20 of Adin	655
21 of Ater (through Hezekiah)	98
22 of Hashum	328
23 of Bezai	324
24 of Hariph	112
25 of Gibeon	95
26 the men of Bethlehem and Netophah	188
27 of Anathoth	128
28 of Beth Azmaveth	42
29 of Kiriath Jearim, Kephirah and Beeroth	743
30 of Ramah and Geba	621
31 of Mikmash	122
32 of Bethel and Ai	123
33 of the other Nebo	52
34 of the other Elam	1,254
35 of Harim	320
36 of Jericho	345
37 of Lod, Hadid and Ono	721
38 of Senaah	3,930

39 The priests:

the descendants of Jedaiah (through the family of Jeshua)	973
40 of Immer	1,052
41 of Pashhur	1,247
42 of Harim	1,017

43 The Levites:

the descendants of Jeshua (through Kadmiel through the line of Hodaviah)	74

44 The musicians:

the descendants of Asaph	148

45 The gatekeepers:

the descendants of Shallum, Ater, Talmon, Akkub, Hatita and Shobai	138

46 The temple servants:

the descendants of
Ziha, Hasupha, Tabbaoth,
47 Keros, Sia, Padon,
48 Lebana, Hagaba, Shalmai,
49 Hanan, Giddel, Gahar,
50 Reaiah, Rezin, Nekoda,
51 Gazzam, Uzza, Paseah,
52 Besai, Meunim, Nephusim,
53 Bakbuk, Hakupha, Harhur,

54 Bazluth, Mehida, Harsha,
55 Barkos, Sisera, Temah,
56 Neziah and Hatipha

57 The descendants of the servants of Solomon:

the descendants of
Sotai, Sophereth, Perida,
58 Jaala, Darkon, Giddel,
59 Shephatiah, Hattil,
Pokereth-Hazzebaim and Amon

60 The temple servants and the descendants of the servants
of Solomon 392

61 The following came up from the towns of Tel Melah, Tel Harsha, Kerub, Addon and Immer, but they could not show that their families were
descended from Israel:

62 the descendants of
Delaiah, Tobiah and Nekoda 642

63 And from among the priests:

the descendants of
Hobaiah, Hakkoz and Barzillai (a man who had married a daughter
of Barzillai the Gileadite and was called by that name).

64 These searched for their family records, but they could not find them
and so were excluded from the priesthood as unclean. 65 The governor,
therefore, ordered them not to eat any of the most sacred food until there
should be a priest ministering with the Urim and Thummim.

66 The whole company numbered 42,360, 67 besides their 7,337 male and
female slaves; and they also had 245 male and female singers. 68 There were
736 horses, 245 mules,[a] 69 435 camels and 6,720 donkeys.

70 Some of the heads of the families contributed to the work. The governor gave to the treasury 1,000 darics[b] of gold, 50 bowls and 530 garments
for priests. 71 Some of the heads of the families gave to the treasury for the
work 20,000 darics[c] of gold and 2,200 minas[d] of silver. 72 The total given by
the rest of the people was 20,000 darics of gold, 2,000 minas[e] of silver and
67 garments for priests.

73 The priests, the Levites, the gatekeepers, the musicians and the temple servants, along with certain of the people and the rest of the Israelites,
settled in their own towns.

Ezra Reads the Law

8 When the seventh month came and the Israelites had settled in their towns, 1 all
the people came together as one in the square before the Water Gate. They
told Ezra the teacher of the Law to bring out the Book of the Law of Moses, which
the LORD had commanded for Israel.

2 So on the first day of the seventh month Ezra the priest brought the Law before the assembly, which was made up of men and women and all who were able
to understand. 3 He read it aloud from daybreak till noon as he faced the square
before the Water Gate in the presence of the men, women and others who could
understand. And all the people listened attentively to the Book of the Law.

4 Ezra the teacher of the Law stood on a high wooden platform built for the occasion. Beside him on his right stood Mattithiah, Shema, Anaiah, Uriah, Hilkiah

---

[a] *68* Some Hebrew manuscripts (see also Ezra 2:66); most Hebrew manuscripts do not have this verse. [b] *70* That is, about 19 pounds or about 8.4 kilograms [c] *71* That is, about 375 pounds or about 170 kilograms; also in verse 72 [d] *71* That is, about 1 1/3 tons or about 1.2 metric tons [e] *72* That is, about 1 1/4 tons or about 1.1 metric tons

and Maaseiah; and on his left were Pedaiah, Mishael, Malkijah, Hashum, Hash-
baddanah, Zechariah and Meshullam.
5Ezra opened the book. All the people could see him because he was standing above them; and as he opened it, the people all stood up. 6Ezra praised
the LORD, the great God; and all the people lifted their hands and responded,
"Amen! Amen!" Then they bowed down and worshiped the LORD with their faces to the ground.
7The Levites — Jeshua, Bani, Sherebiah, Jamin, Akkub, Shabbethai, Hodiah,
Maaseiah, Kelita, Azariah, Jozabad, Hanan and Pelaiah — instructed the people
in the Law while the people were standing there. 8They read from the Book of the
Law of God, making it clear[a] and giving the meaning so that the people understood what was being read.
9Then Nehemiah the governor, Ezra the priest and teacher of the Law, and the
Levites who were instructing the people said to them all, "This day is holy to the
LORD your God. Do not mourn or weep." For all the people had been weeping as
they listened to the words of the Law.
10Nehemiah said, "Go and enjoy choice food and sweet drinks, and send some
to those who have nothing prepared. This day is holy to our Lord. Do not grieve,
for the joy of the LORD is your strength."
11The Levites calmed all the people, saying, "Be still, for this is a holy day. Do
not grieve."
12Then all the people went away to eat and drink, to send portions of food and
to celebrate with great joy, because they now understood the words that had
been made known to them.
13On the second day of the month, the heads of all the families, along with
the priests and the Levites, gathered around Ezra the teacher to give attention
to the words of the Law. 14They found written in the Law, which the LORD had
commanded through Moses, that the Israelites were to live in temporary shelters during the festival of the seventh month 15and that they should proclaim
this word and spread it throughout their towns and in Jerusalem: "Go out into
the hill country and bring back branches from olive and wild olive trees, and
from myrtles, palms and shade trees, to make temporary shelters" — as it is
written.[b]
16So the people went out and brought back branches and built themselves
temporary shelters on their own roofs, in their courtyards, in the courts of the
house of God and in the square by the Water Gate and the one by the Gate of
Ephraim. 17The whole company that had returned from exile built temporary
shelters and lived in them. From the days of Joshua son of Nun until that day, the
Israelites had not celebrated it like this. And their joy was very great.
18Day after day, from the first day to the last, Ezra read from the Book of the
Law of God. They celebrated the festival for seven days, and on the eighth day,
in accordance with the regulation, there was an assembly.

The Israelites Confess Their Sins

9 On the twenty-fourth day of the same month, the Israelites gathered together, fasting and wearing sackcloth and putting dust on their heads. 2Those of
Israelite descent had separated themselves from all foreigners. They stood in
their places and confessed their sins and the sins of their ancestors. 3They stood
where they were and read from the Book of the Law of the LORD their God for a
quarter of the day, and spent another quarter in confession and in worshiping
the LORD their God. 4Standing on the stairs of the Levites were Jeshua, Bani,
Kadmiel, Shebaniah, Bunni, Sherebiah, Bani and Kenani. They cried out with
loud voices to the LORD their God. 5And the Levites — Jeshua, Kadmiel, Bani,
Hashabneiah, Sherebiah, Hodiah, Shebaniah and Pethahiah — said: "Stand up
and praise the LORD your God, who is from everlasting to everlasting.[c]"

---

[a] 8 Or *God, translating it* [b] 15 See Lev. 23:37-40. [c] 5 Or *God for ever and ever*

GRACE THROUGH THE WORD

In Nehemiah 8, physical rebuilding and the practicalities of sustaining a city gave way to the greater work of spiritual revival. Importantly, this revival was launched by the reading of God's Word. The priest Ezra had brought the Book of the Law to Jerusalem some 14 years earlier. Now, just six days after the completion of the wall, the Book of the Law was being made public to everyone. It was a remarkable scene. Everyone was included — men, women and children. For five or six hours, they heard words written to the people of Israel in an era long-since forgotten. As they listened, they were overwhelmed by how far they had fallen short of who they were meant to be. As Nehemiah had grieved the conditions of Jerusalem (1:3 – 4), they grieved over their sins and those of their ancestors. They mourned and wept, evidence of conviction and sorrow. This was a natural response, but the reaction of Nehemiah and the Levites is instructive. This was not a time to dwell on the mistakes of the past, but to embrace a new reality marked by obedience and faithfulness. The reading of the Law was not to produce mourning for what was, but to celebrate the victory of the present and a joyful hope for the future.

The Gospels recount the story of Jesus. His perfect love and unblemished faithfulness stand in stark contrast to our sinfulness. In reading about and hearing of Jesus, people are confronted with the magnitude of their failures. Humans have become so much less than they were created to be. Yet, Jesus did not die so that sinful humans would wallow in their sinful past. The writings of the New Testament are not given to produce mourning but repentance which leads to rejoicing. Conviction *is* overwhelming apart from the grace of Christ.

Among New Testament writers, the apostle Paul was unparalleled in his recognition of sin's terrible power. But this recognition fueled his appreciation for the beauty and power of grace. Writing to the church at Corinth, Paul said, "Therefore, if anyone is in Christ, the new creation has come: The old has gone, the new is here!" (2Co 5:17). As one who had violently persecuted Christians only to become the faith's greatest evangelist, Paul had seen the reality of these words in his own life. Since the time of Paul, for two thousand years, these words have been passed down from generation to generation. Like all of Scripture, they are an invitation to celebrate what Christ has done and to embrace with confidence a future filled with hope.

"Blessed be your glorious name, and may it be exalted above all blessing and praise. [6]You alone are the LORD. You made the heavens, even the highest heavens, and all their starry host, the earth and all that is on it, the seas and all that is in them. You give life to everything, and the multitudes of heaven worship you.

[7]"You are the LORD God, who chose Abram and brought him out of Ur of the Chaldeans and named him Abraham. [8]You found his heart faithful to you, and you made a covenant with him to give to his descendants the land of the Canaanites, Hittites, Amorites, Perizzites, Jebusites and Girgashites. You have kept your promise because you are righteous.

[9]"You saw the suffering of our ancestors in Egypt; you heard their cry at the Red Sea.[a] [10]You sent signs and wonders against Pharaoh, against all his officials and all the people of his land, for you knew how arrogantly the Egyptians treated them. You made a name for yourself, which remains to this day. [11]You divided the sea before them, so that they passed through it on dry ground, but you hurled their pursuers into the depths, like a stone into mighty waters. [12]By day you led them with a pillar of cloud, and by night with a pillar of fire to give them light on the way they were to take.

[13]"You came down on Mount Sinai; you spoke to them from heaven. You gave them regulations and laws that are just and right, and decrees and commands that are good. [14]You made known to them your holy Sabbath and gave them commands, decrees and laws through your servant Moses. [15]In their hunger you gave them bread from heaven and in their thirst you brought them water from the rock; you told them to go in and take possession of the land you had sworn with uplifted hand to give them.

[16]"But they, our ancestors, became arrogant and stiff-necked, and they did not obey your commands. [17]They refused to listen and failed to remember the miracles you performed among them. They became stiff-necked and in their rebellion appointed a leader in order to return to their slavery. But you are a forgiving God, gracious and compassionate, slow to anger and abounding in love. Therefore you did not desert them, [18]even when they cast for themselves an image of a calf and said, 'This is your god, who brought you up out of Egypt,' or when they committed awful blasphemies.

[19]"Because of your great compassion you did not abandon them in the wilderness. By day the pillar of cloud did not fail to guide them on their path, nor the pillar of fire by night to shine on the way they were to take. [20]You gave your good Spirit to instruct them. You did not withhold your manna from their mouths, and you gave them water for their thirst. [21]For forty years you sustained them in the wilderness; they lacked nothing, their clothes did not wear out nor did their feet become swollen.

[22]"You gave them kingdoms and nations, allotting to them even the remotest frontiers. They took over the country of Sihon[b] king of Heshbon and the country of Og king of Bashan. [23]You made their children as numerous as the stars in the sky, and you brought them into the land that you told their parents to enter and possess. [24]Their children went in and took possession of the land. You subdued before them the Canaanites, who lived in the land; you gave the Canaanites into their hands, along with their kings and the peoples of the land, to deal with them as they pleased. [25]They captured fortified cities and fertile land; they took possession of houses filled with all kinds of good things, wells already dug, vineyards, olive groves and fruit trees in abundance. They ate to the full and were well-nourished; they reveled in your great goodness.

[26]"But they were disobedient and rebelled against you; they turned their backs on your law. They killed your prophets, who had warned them in

[a] 9 Or *the Sea of Reeds* [b] 22 One Hebrew manuscript and Septuagint; most Hebrew manuscripts *Sihon, that is, the country of the*

order to turn them back to you; they committed awful blasphemies. 27So
you delivered them into the hands of their enemies, who oppressed them.
But when they were oppressed they cried out to you. From heaven you
heard them, and in your great compassion you gave them deliverers, who
rescued them from the hand of their enemies.

28"But as soon as they were at rest, they again did what was evil in your
sight. Then you abandoned them to the hand of their enemies so that they
ruled over them. And when they cried out to you again, you heard from
heaven, and in your compassion you delivered them time after time.

29"You warned them in order to turn them back to your law, but they became arrogant and disobeyed your commands. They sinned against your
ordinances, of which you said, 'The person who obeys them will live by
them.' Stubbornly they turned their backs on you, became stiff-necked and
refused to listen. 30For many years you were patient with them. By your
Spirit you warned them through your prophets. Yet they paid no attention,
so you gave them into the hands of the neighboring peoples. 31But in your
great mercy you did not put an end to them or abandon them, for you are a
gracious and merciful God.

32"Now therefore, our God, the great God, mighty and awesome, who
keeps his covenant of love, do not let all this hardship seem trifling in your
eyes — the hardship that has come on us, on our kings and leaders, on our
priests and prophets, on our ancestors and all your people, from the days
of the kings of Assyria until today. 33In all that has happened to us, you
have remained righteous; you have acted faithfully, while we acted wickedly. 34Our kings, our leaders, our priests and our ancestors did not follow
your law; they did not pay attention to your commands or the statutes you
warned them to keep. 35Even while they were in their kingdom, enjoying
your great goodness to them in the spacious and fertile land you gave them,
they did not serve you or turn from their evil ways.

36"But see, we are slaves today, slaves in the land you gave our ancestors
so they could eat its fruit and the other good things it produces. 37Because
of our sins, its abundant harvest goes to the kings you have placed over
us. They rule over our bodies and our cattle as they please. We are in great
distress.

The Agreement of the People

38"In view of all this, we are making a binding agreement, putting it in writing, and our leaders, our Levites and our priests are affixing their seals to it."[a]

10[b] Those who sealed it were:

Nehemiah the governor, the son of Hakaliah.

Zedekiah, 2Seraiah, Azariah, Jeremiah,
3Pashhur, Amariah, Malkijah,
4Hattush, Shebaniah, Malluk,
5Harim, Meremoth, Obadiah,
6Daniel, Ginnethon, Baruch,
7Meshullam, Abijah, Mijamin,
8Maaziah, Bilgai and Shemaiah.
These were the priests.

9The Levites:

Jeshua son of Azaniah, Binnui of the sons of Henadad, Kadmiel,
10and their associates: Shebaniah,
Hodiah, Kelita, Pelaiah, Hanan,

[a] *38* In Hebrew texts this verse (9:38) is numbered 10:1. [b] In Hebrew texts 10:1-39 is numbered 10:2-40.

REMEMBERING WITH A PURPOSE

The story of Israel is marked by critical moments of transition. In these moments, the leader of Israel sometimes gathered the people to hear and remember together their collective history. Both Moses (Dt 32:1 – 43) and Joshua (Jos 24:1 – 28) initiated such gatherings just before their deaths. Similarly, upon finding the Book of the Law, King Josiah gathered all the people of Judah and read it to them (2Ki 23:1 – 3). Remembering the past gave them a focus for the future. Having heard their own story, God's people faced a decision. They could renew their covenant and continue on with God, or choose a different future, dedicated to other "gods."

In Nehemiah 9, the people had been engaged in public worship for more than three weeks. Their days were filled with listening to the Book of the Law, followed by confession and worship. Spiritually they were being prepared to renew their covenant with God. This covenant was not defined by a code of behavior or a list of intellectual truths. The covenant was framed by the narrative of God's gracious acts toward a rebellious people. After praising the greatness of God and acknowledging him as the Creator and Sustainer of all things, the Levites retold the story. Beginning with the Lord's call of Abraham and covenant with him, they remembered God's faithfulness and lamented their ancestors' sins. These sins had ultimately led to the punishment of exile. In spite of having returned physically to their homeland, it is clear that the people understood they were still under God's judgment. They recognized that they were not fully restored — a truth made painfully clear in the fact that they lived as "slaves" in their own land, under the rule of the pagan Persian Empire (vv. 36 – 37). From Abraham to their present moment, all was remembered. And this remembering had the desired result.

In the New Testament, Stephen followed the tradition of his ancestors in publicly recounting Israel's history (Ac 7:2 – 53). His purpose was to confront his persecutors with God's goodness and the fact of their sin. Though they imagined themselves to be the most righteous of their kinsmen, Stephen painted a very different picture. They were actually guilty of *opposing* God. They had rejected the new covenant established by Christ, betraying and murdering him instead. Throughout Israel's history, when the story of Israel was retold, the people of Israel had renewed their commitment to God. Stephen's speech proved to be an exception; the leaders of Israel tragically chose a different path.

[11] Mika, Rehob, Hashabiah,
[12] Zakkur, Sherebiah, Shebaniah,
[13] Hodiah, Bani and Beninu.

[14] The leaders of the people:

Parosh, Pahath-Moab, Elam, Zattu, Bani,
[15] Bunni, Azgad, Bebai,
[16] Adonijah, Bigvai, Adin,
[17] Ater, Hezekiah, Azzur,
[18] Hodiah, Hashum, Bezai,
[19] Hariph, Anathoth, Nebai,
[20] Magpiash, Meshullam, Hezir,
[21] Meshezabel, Zadok, Jaddua,
[22] Pelatiah, Hanan, Anaiah,
[23] Hoshea, Hananiah, Hasshub,
[24] Hallohesh, Pilha, Shobek,
[25] Rehum, Hashabnah, Maaseiah,
[26] Ahiah, Hanan, Anan,
[27] Malluk, Harim and Baanah.

[28] "The rest of the people — priests, Levites, gatekeepers, musicians,
temple servants and all who separated themselves from the neighboring
peoples for the sake of the Law of God, together with their wives and all
their sons and daughters who are able to understand — [29] all these now
join their fellow Israelites the nobles, and bind themselves with a curse
and an oath to follow the Law of God given through Moses the servant of
God and to obey carefully all the commands, regulations and decrees of
the LORD our Lord.
[30] "We promise not to give our daughters in marriage to the peoples
around us or take their daughters for our sons.
[31] "When the neighboring peoples bring merchandise or grain to sell on
the Sabbath, we will not buy from them on the Sabbath or on any holy day.
Every seventh year we will forgo working the land and will cancel all debts.
[32] "We assume the responsibility for carrying out the commands to give
a third of a shekel[a] each year for the service of the house of our God: [33] for
the bread set out on the table; for the regular grain offerings and burnt offerings;
for the offerings on the Sabbaths, at the New Moon feasts and at the
appointed festivals; for the holy offerings; for sin offerings[b] to make atonement
for Israel; and for all the duties of the house of our God.
[34] "We — the priests, the Levites and the people — have cast lots to determine
when each of our families is to bring to the house of our God at set
times each year a contribution of wood to burn on the altar of the LORD our
God, as it is written in the Law.
[35] "We also assume responsibility for bringing to the house of the LORD
each year the firstfruits of our crops and of every fruit tree.
[36] "As it is also written in the Law, we will bring the firstborn of our sons
and of our cattle, of our herds and of our flocks to the house of our God, to
the priests ministering there.
[37] "Moreover, we will bring to the storerooms of the house of our God, to
the priests, the first of our ground meal, of our grain offerings, of the fruit of
all our trees and of our new wine and olive oil. And we will bring a tithe of
our crops to the Levites, for it is the Levites who collect the tithes in all the
towns where we work. [38] A priest descended from Aaron is to accompany
the Levites when they receive the tithes, and the Levites are to bring a tenth
of the tithes up to the house of our God, to the storerooms of the treasury.

[a] *32* That is, about 1/8 ounce or about 4 grams [b] *33* Or *purification offerings*

NEHEMIAH 10:28 – 39

GOOD INTENTIONS TO OBEY

In this passage, the people collectively entered into a covenant to keep God's law. This involved the practical move of taxing themselves to ensure the temple's activities were sufficiently funded. Additionally, they made laws that required giving of their "firstfruits" to the house of the Lord, including their sons, livestock, produce, wine and oil. Their enthusiasm for the things of God is awe-inspiring, their self-sacrificing intentions laudable. Good intentions, however, were not sufficient to ensure obedience. Like their ancestors and their descendants, they failed to keep their covenant with God.

In the early church, a dispute arose about what parts of the Jewish law were binding on Christians. Some insisted that new believers had to be circumcised in order to be saved and should be required to keep the Law of Moses (Ac 15:5). As the leaders of the church gathered to resolve this conflict, the apostle Peter stood and reminded them that in spite of their best intentions neither they nor their ancestors had proven capable of obedience to the law. Then, he pointed them to Christianity's central, life-changing truths. God purifies hearts through *faith*. The hope of a Christian is founded in *grace*. In their fallen state, human beings are simply unable to obey God and are unable to save themselves. But Peter's conclusion is reassuring and confident: "We believe it is through the grace of our Lord Jesus that we are saved, just as they are" (Ac 15:11).

[39]The people of Israel, including the Levites, are to bring their contributions of grain, new wine and olive oil to the storerooms, where the articles for the sanctuary and for the ministering priests, the gatekeepers and the musicians are also kept.

"We will not neglect the house of our God."

The New Residents of Jerusalem

11 Now the leaders of the people settled in Jerusalem. The rest of the people cast lots to bring one out of every ten of them to live in Jerusalem, the holy city, while the remaining nine were to stay in their own towns. [2]The people commended all who volunteered to live in Jerusalem.

[3]These are the provincial leaders who settled in Jerusalem (now some Israelites, priests, Levites, temple servants and descendants of Solomon's servants lived in the towns of Judah, each on their own property in the various towns, [4]while other people from both Judah and Benjamin lived in Jerusalem):

From the descendants of Judah:

Athaiah son of Uzziah, the son of Zechariah, the son of Amariah, the son of Shephatiah, the son of Mahalalel, a descendant of Perez; [5]and Maaseiah son of Baruch, the son of Kol-Hozeh, the son of Hazaiah, the son of Adaiah, the son of Joiarib, the son of Zechariah, a descendant of Shelah. [6]The descendants of Perez who lived in Jerusalem totaled 468 men of standing.

[7]From the descendants of Benjamin:

Sallu son of Meshullam, the son of Joed, the son of Pedaiah, the son of Kolaiah, the son of Maaseiah, the son of Ithiel, the son of Jeshaiah, [8]and his followers, Gabbai and Sallai—928 men. [9]Joel son of Zikri was their chief officer, and Judah son of Hassenuah was over the New Quarter of the city.

[10]From the priests:

Jedaiah; the son of Joiarib; Jakin; [11]Seraiah son of Hilkiah, the son of Meshullam, the son of Zadok, the son of Meraioth, the son of Ahitub, the official in charge of the house of God, [12]and their associates, who carried on work for the temple—822 men; Adaiah son of Jeroham, the son of Pelaliah, the son of Amzi, the son of Zechariah, the son of Pashhur, the son of Malkijah, [13]and his associates, who were heads of families—242 men; Amashsai son of Azarel, the son of Ahzai, the son of Meshillemoth, the son of Immer, [14]and his[a] associates, who were men of standing—128. Their chief officer was Zabdiel son of Haggedolim.

[15]From the Levites:

Shemaiah son of Hasshub, the son of Azrikam, the son of Hashabiah, the son of Bunni; [16]Shabbethai and Jozabad, two of the heads of the Levites, who had charge of the outside work of the house of God; [17]Mattaniah son of Mika, the son of Zabdi, the son of Asaph, the director who led in thanksgiving and prayer; Bakbukiah, second among his associates; and Abda son of Shammua, the son of Galal, the son of Jeduthun. [18]The Levites in the holy city totaled 284.

[19]The gatekeepers:

Akkub, Talmon and their associates, who kept watch at the gates—172 men.

[20]The rest of the Israelites, with the priests and Levites, were in all the towns of Judah, each on their ancestral property.

[21]The temple servants lived on the hill of Ophel, and Ziha and Gishpa were in charge of them.

---

[a] *14* Most Septuagint manuscripts; Hebrew *their*

[22]The chief officer of the Levites in Jerusalem was Uzzi son of Bani, the son
of Hashabiah, the son of Mattaniah, the son of Mika. Uzzi was one of Asaph's
descendants, who were the musicians responsible for the service of the house of
God. [23]The musicians were under the king's orders, which regulated their daily
activity.

[24]Pethahiah son of Meshezabel, one of the descendants of Zerah son of Judah,
was the king's agent in all affairs relating to the people.

[25]As for the villages with their fields, some of the people of Judah lived in Kiriath Arba and its surrounding settlements, in Dibon and its settlements, in Jekabzeel and its villages, [26]in Jeshua, in Moladah, in Beth Pelet, [27]in Hazar Shual,
in Beersheba and its settlements, [28]in Ziklag, in Mekonah and its settlements,
[29]in En Rimmon, in Zorah, in Jarmuth, [30]Zanoah, Adullam and their villages, in
Lachish and its fields, and in Azekah and its settlements. So they were living all
the way from Beersheba to the Valley of Hinnom.

[31]The descendants of the Benjamites from Geba lived in Mikmash, Aija, Bethel
and its settlements, [32]in Anathoth, Nob and Ananiah, [33]in Hazor, Ramah and Gittaim, [34]in Hadid, Zeboim and Neballat, [35]in Lod and Ono, and in Ge Harashim.

[36]Some of the divisions of the Levites of Judah settled in Benjamin.

Priests and Levites

12 These were the priests and Levites who returned with Zerubbabel son of Shealtiel and with Joshua:

Seraiah, Jeremiah, Ezra,
[2]Amariah, Malluk, Hattush,
[3]Shekaniah, Rehum, Meremoth,
[4]Iddo, Ginnethon,[a] Abijah,
[5]Mijamin,[b] Moadiah, Bilgah,
[6]Shemaiah, Joiarib, Jedaiah,
[7]Sallu, Amok, Hilkiah and Jedaiah.

These were the leaders of the priests and their associates in the days of Joshua.

[8]The Levites were Jeshua, Binnui, Kadmiel, Sherebiah, Judah, and also Mattaniah, who, together with his associates, was in charge of the songs of thanksgiving. [9]Bakbukiah and Unni, their associates, stood opposite them in the services.

[10]Joshua was the father of Joiakim, Joiakim the father of Eliashib, Eliashib the
father of Joiada, [11]Joiada the father of Jonathan, and Jonathan the father of Jaddua.

[12]In the days of Joiakim, these were the heads of the priestly families:
of Seraiah's family, Meraiah;
of Jeremiah's, Hananiah;
[13]of Ezra's, Meshullam;
of Amariah's, Jehohanan;
[14]of Malluk's, Jonathan;
of Shekaniah's,[c] Joseph;
[15]of Harim's, Adna;
of Meremoth's,[d] Helkai;
[16]of Iddo's, Zechariah;
of Ginnethon's, Meshullam;
[17]of Abijah's, Zikri;
of Miniamin's and of Moadiah's, Piltai;
[18]of Bilgah's, Shammua;
of Shemaiah's, Jehonathan;
[19]of Joiarib's, Mattenai;
of Jedaiah's, Uzzi;

---

[a] *4* Many Hebrew manuscripts and Vulgate (see also verse 16); most Hebrew manuscripts *Ginnethoi* [b] *5* A variant of *Miniamin* [c] *14* Very many Hebrew manuscripts, some Septuagint manuscripts and Syriac (see also verse 3); most Hebrew manuscripts *Shebaniah's* [d] *15* Some Septuagint manuscripts (see also verse 3); Hebrew *Meraioth's*

[20] of Sallu's, Kallai;
of Amok's, Eber;
[21] of Hilkiah's, Hashabiah;
of Jedaiah's, Nethanel.
[22] The family heads of the Levites in the days of Eliashib, Joiada, Johanan and
Jaddua, as well as those of the priests, were recorded in the reign of Darius the
Persian. [23] The family heads among the descendants of Levi up to the time of Johanan son of Eliashib were recorded in the book of the annals. [24] And the leaders
of the Levites were Hashabiah, Sherebiah, Jeshua son of Kadmiel, and their associates, who stood opposite them to give praise and thanksgiving, one section
responding to the other, as prescribed by David the man of God.
[25] Mattaniah, Bakbukiah, Obadiah, Meshullam, Talmon and Akkub were
gatekeepers who guarded the storerooms at the gates. [26] They served in the days
of Joiakim son of Joshua, the son of Jozadak, and in the days of Nehemiah the
governor and of Ezra the priest, the teacher of the Law.

Dedication of the Wall of Jerusalem

[27] At the dedication of the wall of Jerusalem, the Levites were sought out from
where they lived and were brought to Jerusalem to celebrate joyfully the dedication with songs of thanksgiving and with the music of cymbals, harps and
lyres. [28] The musicians also were brought together from the region around Jerusalem — from the villages of the Netophathites, [29] from Beth Gilgal, and from the
area of Geba and Azmaveth, for the musicians had built villages for themselves
around Jerusalem. [30] When the priests and Levites had purified themselves ceremonially, they purified the people, the gates and the wall.
[31] I had the leaders of Judah go up on top of[a] the wall. I also assigned two large
choirs to give thanks. One was to proceed on top of[b] the wall to the right, toward
the Dung Gate. [32] Hoshaiah and half the leaders of Judah followed them, [33] along
with Azariah, Ezra, Meshullam, [34] Judah, Benjamin, Shemaiah, Jeremiah, [35] as
well as some priests with trumpets, and also Zechariah son of Jonathan, the son
of Shemaiah, the son of Mattaniah, the son of Micaiah, the son of Zakkur, the
son of Asaph, [36] and his associates — Shemaiah, Azarel, Milalai, Gilalai, Maai,
Nethanel, Judah and Hanani — with musical instruments prescribed by David
the man of God. Ezra the teacher of the Law led the procession. [37] At the Fountain Gate they continued directly up the steps of the City of David on the ascent
to the wall and passed above the site of David's palace to the Water Gate on the
east.
[38] The second choir proceeded in the opposite direction. I followed them on
top of[c] the wall, together with half the people — past the Tower of the Ovens to
the Broad Wall, [39] over the Gate of Ephraim, the Jeshanah[d] Gate, the Fish Gate,
the Tower of Hananel and the Tower of the Hundred, as far as the Sheep Gate. At
the Gate of the Guard they stopped.
[40] The two choirs that gave thanks then took their places in the house of God;
so did I, together with half the officials, [41] as well as the priests — Eliakim, Maaseiah, Miniamin, Micaiah, Elioenai, Zechariah and Hananiah with their trumpets — [42] and also Maaseiah, Shemaiah, Eleazar, Uzzi, Jehohanan, Malkijah,
Elam and Ezer. The choirs sang under the direction of Jezrahiah. [43] And on that
day they offered great sacrifices, rejoicing because God had given them great
joy. The women and children also rejoiced. The sound of rejoicing in Jerusalem
could be heard far away.
[44] At that time men were appointed to be in charge of the storerooms for the
contributions, firstfruits and tithes. From the fields around the towns they were
to bring into the storerooms the portions required by the Law for the priests
and the Levites, for Judah was pleased with the ministering priests and Levites.
[45] They performed the service of their God and the service of purification, as did

[a] 31 Or *go alongside* [b] 31 Or *proceed alongside* [c] 38 Or *them alongside* [d] 39 Or *Old*

NEHEMIAH 12:27 – 43

JOYFUL PRAISE AND WORSHIP

Conditions in Jerusalem were dramatically better than when Nehemiah had arrived. Separated individuals had become a true people who, by God's grace, had achieved what had seemed impossible. Strong walls and protective gates had replaced rubble and burned timbers. Encouragement had overcome despair. It was a time to celebrate what God had accomplished through their faithfulness. Tobiah the Ammonite had mocked them, saying even the weight of a fox would cause their wall to crumble (Ne 4:3). Now the leaders of the people and two large choirs, accompanied by musicians, stood atop the walls playing instruments, singing loudly and offering thanksgiving. It was an incredible time of rejoicing. Such joy-filled celebration honors God and encourages even greater faith.

This celebration, like the book of Psalms, underscores the importance of worship, singing and praise in the Old Testament, but these were no less important in the New Testament. One example is found in Philippians 2:5 – 11, seen by many as an early Christian hymn. These poetic words recounted and celebrated the example of Jesus' humility and obedience, even to the point of dying on the cross. Paul makes clear his purpose in sharing the hymn. It is not just remembrance but a call to action. The celebration of Jesus is also a call to follow Jesus' example. God-honoring celebration has the effect of encouraging greater obedience and a deeper faith.

also the musicians and gatekeepers, according to the commands of David and his son Solomon. 46For long ago, in the days of David and Asaph, there had been directors for the musicians and for the songs of praise and thanksgiving to God. 47So in the days of Zerubbabel and of Nehemiah, all Israel contributed the daily portions for the musicians and the gatekeepers. They also set aside the portion for the other Levites, and the Levites set aside the portion for the descendants of Aaron.

Nehemiah's Final Reforms

13 On that day the Book of Moses was read aloud in the hearing of the people and there it was found written that no Ammonite or Moabite should ever be admitted into the assembly of God, 2because they had not met the Israelites with food and water but had hired Balaam to call a curse down on them. (Our God, however, turned the curse into a blessing.) 3When the people heard this law, they excluded from Israel all who were of foreign descent.

4Before this, Eliashib the priest had been put in charge of the storerooms of the house of our God. He was closely associated with Tobiah, 5and he had provided him with a large room formerly used to store the grain offerings and incense and temple articles, and also the tithes of grain, new wine and olive oil prescribed for the Levites, musicians and gatekeepers, as well as the contributions for the priests.

6But while all this was going on, I was not in Jerusalem, for in the thirty-second year of Artaxerxes king of Babylon I had returned to the king. Some time later I asked his permission 7and came back to Jerusalem. Here I learned about the evil thing Eliashib had done in providing Tobiah a room in the courts of the house of God. 8I was greatly displeased and threw all Tobiah's household goods out of the room. 9I gave orders to purify the rooms, and then I put back into them the equipment of the house of God, with the grain offerings and the incense.

10I also learned that the portions assigned to the Levites had not been given to them, and that all the Levites and musicians responsible for the service had gone back to their own fields. 11So I rebuked the officials and asked them, "Why is the house of God neglected?" Then I called them together and stationed them at their posts.

12All Judah brought the tithes of grain, new wine and olive oil into the storerooms. 13I put Shelemiah the priest, Zadok the scribe, and a Levite named Pedaiah in charge of the storerooms and made Hanan son of Zakkur, the son of Mattaniah, their assistant, because they were considered trustworthy. They were made responsible for distributing the supplies to their fellow Levites.

14Remember me for this, my God, and do not blot out what I have so faithfully done for the house of my God and its services.

15In those days I saw people in Judah treading winepresses on the Sabbath and bringing in grain and loading it on donkeys, together with wine, grapes, figs and all other kinds of loads. And they were bringing all this into Jerusalem on the Sabbath. Therefore I warned them against selling food on that day. 16People from Tyre who lived in Jerusalem were bringing in fish and all kinds of merchandise and selling them in Jerusalem on the Sabbath to the people of Judah. 17I rebuked the nobles of Judah and said to them, "What is this wicked thing you are doing — desecrating the Sabbath day? 18Didn't your ancestors do the same things, so that our God brought all this calamity on us and on this city? Now you are stirring up more wrath against Israel by desecrating the Sabbath."

19When evening shadows fell on the gates of Jerusalem before the Sabbath, I ordered the doors to be shut and not opened until the Sabbath was over. I stationed some of my own men at the gates so that no load could be brought in on the Sabbath day. 20Once or twice the merchants and sellers of all kinds of goods spent the night outside Jerusalem. 21But I warned them and said, "Why do you spend the night by the wall? If you do this again, I will arrest you." From that time

NEHEMIAH 13:4 – 28

CORRUPTION THROUGH COMPROMISE

Sometime after the dedication of the wall, Nehemiah returned to Persia. Arriving again in Jerusalem, he found the walls intact but the spiritual health of its inhabitants in ruin. Evidence of their compromised faith was everywhere. Tobiah the Ammonite, with the help of Jewish allies, had taken up residence in one of the temple's storerooms. The Levites and musicians had returned to their fields because the people had not honored their pledge to support them. The Sabbath had been utterly defiled, in spite of the people's agreement to keep it holy. Instead of a day of rest dedicated to God, work and commerce continued as if it were any other day. The people's compromise had driven them further from God, which angered Nehemiah.

Over 400 years later, Jesus, too, was angry at the spiritual corruption of God's people. The most vivid displays of this anger are Jesus' cleansing of the temple — apparently once at the beginning of his ministry (Jn 2:13 – 17) and once at the end of his ministry (Mt 21:12 – 13). The temple was meant to be a place of prayer. Instead God's house had become a place where the poor were defrauded, as merchants sold animals for sacrifice, and money changers charged a fee for converting currency. Jesus' response to their compromise and corruption is much like Nehemiah's and, like Nehemiah's, is not limited to words of admonition. Jesus flipped over the tables of the money changers and drove both them and the merchants out of the temple.

on they no longer came on the Sabbath. [22]Then I commanded the Levites to purify themselves and go and guard the gates in order to keep the Sabbath day holy.

Remember me for this also, my God, and show mercy to me according to your great love.

[23]Moreover, in those days I saw men of Judah who had married women from
Ashdod, Ammon and Moab. [24]Half of their children spoke the language of Ashdod or the language of one of the other peoples, and did not know how to speak
the language of Judah. [25]I rebuked them and called curses down on them. I beat
some of the men and pulled out their hair. I made them take an oath in God's
name and said: "You are not to give your daughters in marriage to their sons,
nor are you to take their daughters in marriage for your sons or for yourselves.
[26]Was it not because of marriages like these that Solomon king of Israel sinned?
Among the many nations there was no king like him. He was loved by his God,
and God made him king over all Israel, but even he was led into sin by foreign
women. [27]Must we hear now that you too are doing all this terrible wickedness
and are being unfaithful to our God by marrying foreign women?"

[28]One of the sons of Joiada son of Eliashib the high priest was son-in-law to
Sanballat the Horonite. And I drove him away from me.

[29]Remember them, my God, because they defiled the priestly office and the
covenant of the priesthood and of the Levites.

[30]So I purified the priests and the Levites of everything foreign, and assigned
them duties, each to his own task. [31]I also made provision for contributions of
wood at designated times, and for the firstfruits.

Remember me with favor, my God.

JESUS: OUR DIVINE ADVOCATE

ESTHER

ESTHER

FIRST JEWS RETURN TO JUDAH FROM EXILE *c. 538 BC*	XERXES REIGNS IN PERSIA *c. 486 – 465 BC*	THE JEWS TRIUMPH OVER THEIR ENEMIES (PURIM) *c. 473 BC*

The book of Esther, one of only two books in the Bible named after a woman, recounts the story of the rise of a beautiful young orphan girl from obscurity to royalty. The story has all of the action, romance, power and deceit often found in a great novel. Through it all, the main character of the book is never actually mentioned; God himself is at work to protect his people and save them from clear destruction, yet we never hear any of the characters, even the Jewish ones, mention him.

The events described in Esther span the years in which Xerxes ruled over Persia. He continued his father Darius's campaign against Greece, and around 483 BC he threw a magnificent feast to celebrate his accomplishments and to prepare the population for further military incursions.

Esther is not mentioned in historical writings outside of the Bible, so little is known about her background or position. The word "queen" may refer merely to a principal wife rather than to someone who ruled alongside the king. Esther was a Jew, though she originally hid this fact from her Persian rulers. She even chose to use her Persian name, Esther, instead of her Jewish name, Hadassah, even in the final, climactic moment in the book when she revealed her true identity.

God's sovereign work is seen throughout the book of Esther. Though some people balk at admitting this book's significance, noting that the name of God is never mentioned, it is clear that the unnamed author was well aware of God's providence from start to finish. As God has always done, he proves that no situation, no matter how broken, is beyond his reach or his influence. God is always at work, orchestrating with his providential hand and turning hopelessness into hopefulness.

At a time when God seemed distant, even absent, from his people, the author reveals that God was still at work. Even in the very center of the Persian kingdom, he protected a remnant of people whom he would use to accomplish his purpose of bringing glory to his name. God did not forget those Israelites who remained in foreign lands. They too knew God's gracious protection, experienced his mercy, and testified to his greatness among the nations.

God sent Jesus, like Esther, at a particular point in history to accomplish his sovereign plan. Paul revealed that God sent Jesus at just the right time to redeem fallen humanity (Gal 4:4 – 5). Though both Esther and Jesus were put in harm's way, God used them both to fulfill his masterful plan in spite of opposition and danger. Esther's boldness and courage are emblematic of the faith that comes to those who trust in Jesus and rest in the sure fact that God will always accomplish his mission.

AND WHO KNOWS BUT THAT YOU HAVE COME TO YOUR ROYAL POSITION FOR SUCH A TIME AS THIS?

Esther 4:14

ESTHER

Queen Vashti Deposed

1 This is what happened during the time of Xerxes,[a] the Xerxes who ruled
over 127 provinces stretching from India to Cush[b]: [2]At that time King Xerxes reigned from his royal throne in the citadel of Susa, [3]and in the third year of
his reign he gave a banquet for all his nobles and officials. The military leaders
of Persia and Media, the princes, and the nobles of the provinces were present.
[4]For a full 180 days he displayed the vast wealth of his kingdom and the splendor and glory of his majesty. [5]When these days were over, the king gave a banquet, lasting seven days, in the enclosed garden of the king's palace, for all the
people from the least to the greatest who were in the citadel of Susa. [6]The garden
had hangings of white and blue linen, fastened with cords of white linen and
purple material to silver rings on marble pillars. There were couches of gold and
silver on a mosaic pavement of porphyry, marble, mother-of-pearl and other
costly stones. [7]Wine was served in goblets of gold, each one different from the
other, and the royal wine was abundant, in keeping with the king's liberality.
[8]By the king's command each guest was allowed to drink with no restrictions,
for the king instructed all the wine stewards to serve each man what he wished.
[9]Queen Vashti also gave a banquet for the women in the royal palace of King
Xerxes.
[10]On the seventh day, when King Xerxes was in high spirits from wine, he
commanded the seven eunuchs who served him — Mehuman, Biztha, Harbona, Bigtha, Abagtha, Zethar and Karkas — [11]to bring before him Queen Vashti,
wearing her royal crown, in order to display her beauty to the people and nobles, for she was lovely to look at. [12]But when the attendants delivered the king's
command, Queen Vashti refused to come. Then the king became furious and
burned with anger.
[13]Since it was customary for the king to consult experts in matters of law and
justice, he spoke with the wise men who understood the times [14]and were closest
to the king — Karshena, Shethar, Admatha, Tarshish, Meres, Marsena and Memukan, the seven nobles of Persia and Media who had special access to the king
and were highest in the kingdom.
[15]"According to law, what must be done to Queen Vashti?" he asked. "She has
not obeyed the command of King Xerxes that the eunuchs have taken to her."
[16]Then Memukan replied in the presence of the king and the nobles, "Queen
Vashti has done wrong, not only against the king but also against all the nobles
and the peoples of all the provinces of King Xerxes. [17]For the queen's conduct
will become known to all the women, and so they will despise their husbands
and say, 'King Xerxes commanded Queen Vashti to be brought before him, but
she would not come.' [18]This very day the Persian and Median women of the nobility who have heard about the queen's conduct will respond to all the king's
nobles in the same way. There will be no end of disrespect and discord.
[19]"Therefore, if it pleases the king, let him issue a royal decree and let it be
written in the laws of Persia and Media, which cannot be repealed, that Vashti is
never again to enter the presence of King Xerxes. Also let the king give her royal
position to someone else who is better than she. [20]Then when the king's edict is
proclaimed throughout all his vast realm, all the women will respect their husbands, from the least to the greatest."
[21]The king and his nobles were pleased with this advice, so the king did as
Memukan proposed. [22]He sent dispatches to all parts of the kingdom, to each

[a] *1* Hebrew *Ahasuerus*; here and throughout Esther   [b] *1* That is, the upper Nile region

THE IMPOSSIBLE MADE POSSIBLE

The book of Esther records a terrifying situation for the chosen people of God. King Xerxes had a vast kingdom. He had amassed 127 provinces stretching from India to Egypt. People of numerous ethnicities, languages, customs and religions were under his command. The Jews were one of many minorities immersed in Persian daily life. But even though they had been exiled from their homeland many years earlier, God still had his hand of protection on them. At the climax of this story, an irrevocable law was passed legalizing the genocide of the Jewish people. This seemed like an impossible situation, but God proved to be in control the whole time.

The book of Esther opens with six months of festivities, likely a war council held to plan the Persian invasion of Greece. After that, everyone in Susa — from the greatest to the least — was invited to an opulent garden party that lasted a week. Sadly, at the end of this feast, when the king and all his guests were intoxicated and irrational, he called for his queen to parade around for the pleasure of everyone to see. However, the queen refused. When she didn't expose herself to all the partiers, the king asked his advisors what should be done. It was decided that her royal position was to be given to another who was more worthy. In the midst of this challenging set of circumstances, the door was opened for Esther to step into the story. One queen had to be removed so that another could step in to what God had planned. Esther stepped in so that ultimately her people could be saved.

Jesus said in Matthew 5:48, "Be perfect … as your heavenly Father is perfect." That is an impossible standard! Thank goodness Jesus makes believers worthy. Jesus stepped into the story of humanity so that the will of God could be accomplished. No one is worthy to carry out the story of God on their own, but Jesus makes the way, "so that you may live a life worthy of the Lord and please him in every way: bearing fruit in every good work, growing in the knowledge of God" (Col 1:10).

Even though King Xerxes' feast ended with the dismissal of a queen, it provided an open door for God to put someone in place who would have influence over the king and save God's people — a provision so dramatic that the Jewish people still celebrate it today.

province in its own script and to each people in their own language, proclaiming
that every man should be ruler over his own household, using his native tongue.

Esther Made Queen

2 Later when King Xerxes' fury had subsided, he remembered Vashti and what
she had done and what he had decreed about her. [2]Then the king's personal attendants proposed, "Let a search be made for beautiful young virgins for
the king. [3]Let the king appoint commissioners in every province of his realm
to bring all these beautiful young women into the harem at the citadel of Susa.
Let them be placed under the care of Hegai, the king's eunuch, who is in charge
of the women; and let beauty treatments be given to them. [4]Then let the young
woman who pleases the king be queen instead of Vashti." This advice appealed
to the king, and he followed it.

[5]Now there was in the citadel of Susa a Jew of the tribe of Benjamin, named
Mordecai son of Jair, the son of Shimei, the son of Kish, [6]who had been carried
into exile from Jerusalem by Nebuchadnezzar king of Babylon, among those taken
captive with Jehoiachin[a] king of Judah. [7]Mordecai had a cousin named Hadassah,
whom he had brought up because she had neither father nor mother. This young
woman, who was also known as Esther, had a lovely figure and was beautiful. Mordecai had taken her as his own daughter when her father and mother died.

[8]When the king's order and edict had been proclaimed, many young women
were brought to the citadel of Susa and put under the care of Hegai. Esther also
was taken to the king's palace and entrusted to Hegai, who had charge of the harem. [9]She pleased him and won his favor. Immediately he provided her with her
beauty treatments and special food. He assigned to her seven female attendants
selected from the king's palace and moved her and her attendants into the best
place in the harem.

[10]Esther had not revealed her nationality and family background, because
Mordecai had forbidden her to do so. [11]Every day he walked back and forth near
the courtyard of the harem to find out how Esther was and what was happening
to her.

[12]Before a young woman's turn came to go in to King Xerxes, she had to complete twelve months of beauty treatments prescribed for the women, six months
with oil of myrrh and six with perfumes and cosmetics. [13]And this is how she
would go to the king: Anything she wanted was given her to take with her from
the harem to the king's palace. [14]In the evening she would go there and in the
morning return to another part of the harem to the care of Shaashgaz, the king's
eunuch who was in charge of the concubines. She would not return to the king
unless he was pleased with her and summoned her by name.

[15]When the turn came for Esther (the young woman Mordecai had adopted,
the daughter of his uncle Abihail) to go to the king, she asked for nothing other
than what Hegai, the king's eunuch who was in charge of the harem, suggested. And Esther won the favor of everyone who saw her. [16]She was taken to King
Xerxes in the royal residence in the tenth month, the month of Tebeth, in the
seventh year of his reign.

[17]Now the king was attracted to Esther more than to any of the other women,
and she won his favor and approval more than any of the other virgins. So he
set a royal crown on her head and made her queen instead of Vashti. [18]And the
king gave a great banquet, Esther's banquet, for all his nobles and officials. He
proclaimed a holiday throughout the provinces and distributed gifts with royal
liberality.

Mordecai Uncovers a Conspiracy

[19]When the virgins were assembled a second time, Mordecai was sitting at the
king's gate. [20]But Esther had kept secret her family background and nationality

ESTHER 2:8–9

THE SEARCH

A search was made across all of the Persian Empire for a new queen. Esther was gathered with many other young women in the palace. The competition was fierce, and Esther probably felt inadequate. However, out of all of the potential choices, she was the one chosen by the king!

Jesus once told several parables demonstrating how God the Father will search for his loved ones. The Lost Sheep in Luke 15:4–6, and the Lost Coin in Luke 15:8–9 both tell of a great search. Each child of God is valuable to him. Esther was searched for and chosen out of all the young women of a massive kingdom. What were the odds?! The same search will be made for each believer. Out of all the people on earth, God the Father won't stop till his chosen know and walk in the love of their Savior.

[a] 6 Hebrew *Jeconiah,* a variant of *Jehoiachin*

just as Mordecai had told her to do, for she continued to follow Mordecai's instructions as she had done when he was bringing her up.
[21]During the time Mordecai was sitting at the king's gate, Bigthana[a] and Teresh, two of the king's officers who guarded the doorway, became angry and conspired to assassinate King Xerxes.
[22]But Mordecai found out about the plot and told Queen Esther, who in turn reported it to the king, giving credit to Mordecai.
[23]And when the report was investigated and found to be true, the two officials were impaled on poles. All this was recorded in the book of the annals in the presence of the king.

Haman's Plot to Destroy the Jews

3 After these events, King Xerxes honored Haman son of Hammedatha, the Agagite, elevating him and giving him a seat of honor higher than that of all the other nobles.
[2]All the royal officials at the king's gate knelt down and paid honor to Haman, for the king had commanded this concerning him. But Mordecai would not kneel down or pay him honor.
[3]Then the royal officials at the king's gate asked Mordecai, "Why do you disobey the king's command?"
[4]Day after day they spoke to him but he refused to comply. Therefore they told Haman about it to see whether Mordecai's behavior would be tolerated, for he had told them he was a Jew.
[5]When Haman saw that Mordecai would not kneel down or pay him honor, he was enraged.
[6]Yet having learned who Mordecai's people were, he scorned the idea of killing only Mordecai. Instead Haman looked for a way to destroy all Mordecai's people, the Jews, throughout the whole kingdom of Xerxes.
[7]In the twelfth year of King Xerxes, in the first month, the month of Nisan, the *pur* (that is, the lot) was cast in the presence of Haman to select a day and month. And the lot fell on[b] the twelfth month, the month of Adar.
[8]Then Haman said to King Xerxes, "There is a certain people dispersed among the peoples in all the provinces of your kingdom who keep themselves separate. Their customs are different from those of all other people, and they do not obey the king's laws; it is not in the king's best interest to tolerate them.
[9]If it pleases the king, let a decree be issued to destroy them, and I will give ten thousand talents[c] of silver to the king's administrators for the royal treasury."
[10]So the king took his signet ring from his finger and gave it to Haman son of Hammedatha, the Agagite, the enemy of the Jews.
[11]"Keep the money," the king said to Haman, "and do with the people as you please."
[12]Then on the thirteenth day of the first month the royal secretaries were summoned. They wrote out in the script of each province and in the language of each people all Haman's orders to the king's satraps, the governors of the various provinces and the nobles of the various peoples. These were written in the name of King Xerxes himself and sealed with his own ring.
[13]Dispatches were sent by couriers to all the king's provinces with the order to destroy, kill and annihilate all the Jews — young and old, women and children — on a single day, the thirteenth day of the twelfth month, the month of Adar, and to plunder their goods.
[14]A copy of the text of the edict was to be issued as law in every province and made known to the people of every nationality so they would be ready for that day.
[15]The couriers went out, spurred on by the king's command, and the edict was issued in the citadel of Susa. The king and Haman sat down to drink, but the city of Susa was bewildered.

Mordecai Persuades Esther to Help

4 When Mordecai learned of all that had been done, he tore his clothes, put on sackcloth and ashes, and went out into the city, wailing loudly and bitterly.
[2]But he went only as far as the king's gate, because no one clothed in sackcloth

[a] *21* Hebrew *Bigthan,* a variant of *Bigthana* [b] *7* Septuagint; Hebrew does not have *And the lot fell on.* [c] *9* That is, about 375 tons or about 340 metric tons

---

ESTHER 3:5–6

HATRED

At the close of chapter 2, Mordecai saved King Xerxes' life by exposing a plot to take his life. But nothing was done to reward Mordecai for his good deed (2:21–23; 6:3). The next recorded events are the rise and promotion of Haman. Haman was no friend of Mordecai. "When Haman saw that Mordecai would not kneel down or pay him honor, he was enraged" (3:5). His rage consumed him so much that he not only wanted to kill Mordecai, but all of his people too (3:6).

Jesus felt the same sting of hatred. Luke 6:11 says that "the Pharisees and the teachers of the law were furious and began to discuss with one another what they might do to Jesus." There is a striking parallel between Haman's directive to "destroy, kill and annihilate" (Est 3:13) and Jesus' description of the thief who "comes only to steal and kill and destroy" (Jn 10:10).

was allowed to enter it. 3In every province to which the edict and order of the
king came, there was great mourning among the Jews, with fasting, weeping and
wailing. Many lay in sackcloth and ashes.
4When Esther's eunuchs and female attendants came and told her about Mordecai, she was in great distress. She sent clothes for him to put on instead of his
sackcloth, but he would not accept them. 5Then Esther summoned Hathak, one
of the king's eunuchs assigned to attend her, and ordered him to find out what
was troubling Mordecai and why.
6So Hathak went out to Mordecai in the open square of the city in front of the
king's gate. 7Mordecai told him everything that had happened to him, including
the exact amount of money Haman had promised to pay into the royal treasury
for the destruction of the Jews. 8He also gave him a copy of the text of the edict
for their annihilation, which had been published in Susa, to show to Esther and
explain it to her, and he told him to instruct her to go into the king's presence to
beg for mercy and plead with him for her people.
9Hathak went back and reported to Esther what Mordecai had said. 10Then
she instructed him to say to Mordecai, 11"All the king's officials and the people
of the royal provinces know that for any man or woman who approaches the king
in the inner court without being summoned the king has but one law: that they
be put to death unless the king extends the gold scepter to them and spares their
lives. But thirty days have passed since I was called to go to the king."
12When Esther's words were reported to Mordecai, 13he sent back this answer:
"Do not think that because you are in the king's house you alone of all the Jews will
escape. 14For if you remain silent at this time, relief and deliverance for the Jews
will arise from another place, but you and your father's family will perish. And
who knows but that you have come to your royal position for such a time as this?"
15Then Esther sent this reply to Mordecai: 16"Go, gather together all the Jews
who are in Susa, and fast for me. Do not eat or drink for three days, night or day.
I and my attendants will fast as you do. When this is done, I will go to the king,
even though it is against the law. And if I perish, I perish."
17So Mordecai went away and carried out all of Esther's instructions.

Esther's Request to the King

5 On the third day Esther put on her royal robes and stood in the inner court of
the palace, in front of the king's hall. The king was sitting on his royal throne
in the hall, facing the entrance. 2When he saw Queen Esther standing in the
court, he was pleased with her and held out to her the gold scepter that was in his
hand. So Esther approached and touched the tip of the scepter.
3Then the king asked, "What is it, Queen Esther? What is your request? Even
up to half the kingdom, it will be given you."
4"If it pleases the king," replied Esther, "let the king, together with Haman,
come today to a banquet I have prepared for him."
5"Bring Haman at once," the king said, "so that we may do what Esther asks."
So the king and Haman went to the banquet Esther had prepared. 6As they
were drinking wine, the king again asked Esther, "Now what is your petition?
It will be given you. And what is your request? Even up to half the kingdom, it
will be granted."
7Esther replied, "My petition and my request is this: 8If the king regards me
with favor and if it pleases the king to grant my petition and fulfill my request,
let the king and Haman come tomorrow to the banquet I will prepare for them.
Then I will answer the king's question."

Haman's Rage Against Mordecai

9Haman went out that day happy and in high spirits. But when he saw Mordecai at the king's gate and observed that he neither rose nor showed fear in his
presence, he was filled with rage against Mordecai. 10Nevertheless, Haman restrained himself and went home.

ESTHER 5:1–2

CLOSING THE GAP

The walk toward the king's hall in the inner court must have been terrifying for Queen Esther. Approaching the king without being summoned could easily be punishable by death. In this moment there is a "gap" created—where action is taken in obedience before the result is known. Believers can find courage in Esther's actions. When steps are taken in obedience, this can leave a gap for the Holy Spirit to move and even exceed expectations.

Before Jesus' sacrifice, access to God was not available to everyone. Paul connected the pieces in Ephesians 2:18: "For through him we both have access to the Father by one Spirit." In this gap, the Holy Spirit meets the believer's obedience and delivers God-sized results.

Ultimately the king replied to Esther, "What is your request? Even up to half the kingdom, it will be granted" (Est 5:6). Our heavenly Father has given us an even better response, "You may ask me for anything in my name, and I will do it" (Jn 14:14). Jesus stands in the gap for those who believe in him and follow him.

GOD PROTECTS HIS PEOPLE

Mordecai trusted God to protect his people. Since Mordecai was a devout Jew, we can be sure that his faith and resolve stood on the firm foundation of what the prophets of God proclaimed. God had previously said through the prophet Isaiah, "Since you are precious and honored in my sight, and because I love you, I will give people in exchange for you, nations in exchange for your life. Do not be afraid, for I am with you" (Isa 43:4 – 5). Mordecai could see how God had allowed Esther to become queen so she could be used by God to save her people and fulfill the promises of God.

As her adoptive father, Mordecai would have taught Esther how to put her trust in God, take a step of faith and believe God would give her favor. Mordecai advised Queen Esther to "go into the king's presence to beg for mercy and plead with him for her people" (Est 4:8). Likewise, in each struggle, trial and pain, believers "have an advocate with the Father — Jesus Christ, the Righteous One" (1Jn 2:1). Every presented request is an opportunity for Jesus to intercede.

Believers can be sure that God wants to use his children to do great things. The words of the prophet Isaiah are a rallying cry: "For Zion's sake I will not keep silent, for Jerusalem's sake I will not remain quiet, till her vindication shines out like the dawn, her salvation like a blazing torch" (Isa 62:1). If Esther kept silent, Mordecai was sure that deliverance would "arise from another place" (Est 4:14).

Queen Esther undoubtedly found courage in the promises of God. Her faith became greater than her doubt. "I will go to the king, even though it is against the law. And if I perish, I perish" (4:16). Ultimately, she was willing to sacrifice her own life, foreshadowing the willingness of Jesus to die for us (Lk 22:42; Ro 5:6 – 11). As the body of Christ, the church has the assurance that whatever the circumstances, no matter how awful it seems, nothing will be able to separate us from God's love (Ro 8:38 – 39).

Calling together his friends and Zeresh, his wife, 11Haman boasted to them
about his vast wealth, his many sons, and all the ways the king had honored him
and how he had elevated him above the other nobles and officials. 12"And that's
not all," Haman added. "I'm the only person Queen Esther invited to accompany
the king to the banquet she gave. And she has invited me along with the king tomorrow. 13But all this gives me no satisfaction as long as I see that Jew Mordecai
sitting at the king's gate."
14His wife Zeresh and all his friends said to him, "Have a pole set up, reaching to a height of fifty cubits,[a] and ask the king in the morning to have Mordecai
impaled on it. Then go with the king to the banquet and enjoy yourself." This
suggestion delighted Haman, and he had the pole set up.

Mordecai Honored

6 That night the king could not sleep; so he ordered the book of the chronicles,
the record of his reign, to be brought in and read to him. 2It was found recorded there that Mordecai had exposed Bigthana and Teresh, two of the king's officers who guarded the doorway, who had conspired to assassinate King Xerxes.
3"What honor and recognition has Mordecai received for this?" the king
asked.
"Nothing has been done for him," his attendants answered.
4The king said, "Who is in the court?" Now Haman had just entered the outer
court of the palace to speak to the king about impaling Mordecai on the pole he
had set up for him.
5His attendants answered, "Haman is standing in the court."
"Bring him in," the king ordered.
6When Haman entered, the king asked him, "What should be done for the
man the king delights to honor?"
Now Haman thought to himself, "Who is there that the king would rather
honor than me?" 7So he answered the king, "For the man the king delights to
honor, 8have them bring a royal robe the king has worn and a horse the king has
ridden, one with a royal crest placed on its head. 9Then let the robe and horse
be entrusted to one of the king's most noble princes. Let them robe the man
the king delights to honor, and lead him on the horse through the city streets,
proclaiming before him, 'This is what is done for the man the king delights to
honor!'"
10"Go at once," the king commanded Haman. "Get the robe and the horse and
do just as you have suggested for Mordecai the Jew, who sits at the king's gate. Do
not neglect anything you have recommended."
11So Haman got the robe and the horse. He robed Mordecai, and led him on
horseback through the city streets, proclaiming before him, "This is what is done
for the man the king delights to honor!"
12Afterward Mordecai returned to the king's gate. But Haman rushed home,
with his head covered in grief, 13and told Zeresh his wife and all his friends everything that had happened to him.
His advisers and his wife Zeresh said to him, "Since Mordecai, before whom
your downfall has started, is of Jewish origin, you cannot stand against him —
you will surely come to ruin!" 14While they were still talking with him, the king's
eunuchs arrived and hurried Haman away to the banquet Esther had prepared.

Haman Impaled

7 So the king and Haman went to Queen Esther's banquet, 2and as they were
drinking wine on the second day, the king again asked, "Queen Esther, what
is your petition? It will be given you. What is your request? Even up to half the
kingdom, it will be granted."
3Then Queen Esther answered, "If I have found favor with you, Your Majesty,

ESTHER 6:4 – 10

PRIDE VERSUS HUMILITY

It's not hard to see the irony in this turn of events. Haman was on his way to recommend that Mordecai be hanged, yet he unknowingly is recommending that Mordecai be honored and given the royal treatment. "Pride goes before destruction, a haughty spirit before a fall" (Pr 16:18). Exhibit A: Haman.

Even after Mordecai saved the king's life, Mordecai was humble enough not to demand recognition or a reward. Jesus said, "For those who exalt themselves will be humbled, and those who humble themselves will be exalted" (Mt 23:12).

God's timing is perfect, and he knows where to find his followers when he is ready to honor them. Believers don't have to manipulate or force their position anywhere . . . at work . . . in the church . . . among friends and family. But "your Father, who sees what is done in secret, will reward you" (Mt 6:18).

Jesus is the ultimate model and inspiration. Not only did Jesus model humility (Php 2:8), his followers also are to be marked by humility. "Be completely humble and gentle; be patient, bearing with one another in love. Make every effort to keep the unity of the Spirit through the bond of peace" (Eph 4:2 – 3).

[a] *14* That is, about 75 feet or about 23 meters

and if it pleases you, grant me my life — this is my petition. And spare my people —
this is my request. 4For I and my people have been sold to be destroyed, killed and
annihilated. If we had merely been sold as male and female slaves, I would have
kept quiet, because no such distress would justify disturbing the king.[a]"

5King Xerxes asked Queen Esther, "Who is he? Where is he — the man who has
dared to do such a thing?"

6Esther said, "An adversary and enemy! This vile Haman!"

Then Haman was terrified before the king and queen. 7The king got up in a
rage, left his wine and went out into the palace garden. But Haman, realizing
that the king had already decided his fate, stayed behind to beg Queen Esther
for his life.

8Just as the king returned from the palace garden to the banquet hall, Haman
was falling on the couch where Esther was reclining.

The king exclaimed, "Will he even molest the queen while she is with me in
the house?"

As soon as the word left the king's mouth, they covered Haman's face. 9Then
Harbona, one of the eunuchs attending the king, said, "A pole reaching to a
height of fifty cubits[b] stands by Haman's house. He had it set up for Mordecai,
who spoke up to help the king."

The king said, "Impale him on it!" 10So they impaled Haman on the pole he
had set up for Mordecai. Then the king's fury subsided.

The King's Edict in Behalf of the Jews

8 That same day King Xerxes gave Queen Esther the estate of Haman, the enemy of the Jews. And Mordecai came into the presence of the king, for Esther
had told how he was related to her. 2The king took off his signet ring, which he
had reclaimed from Haman, and presented it to Mordecai. And Esther appointed him over Haman's estate.

3Esther again pleaded with the king, falling at his feet and weeping. She
begged him to put an end to the evil plan of Haman the Agagite, which he had
devised against the Jews. 4Then the king extended the gold scepter to Esther and
she arose and stood before him.

5"If it pleases the king," she said, "and if he regards me with favor and thinks
it the right thing to do, and if he is pleased with me, let an order be written over-
ruling the dispatches that Haman son of Hammedatha, the Agagite, devised and
wrote to destroy the Jews in all the king's provinces. 6For how can I bear to see
disaster fall on my people? How can I bear to see the destruction of my family?"

7King Xerxes replied to Queen Esther and to Mordecai the Jew, "Because Haman attacked the Jews, I have given his estate to Esther, and they have impaled
him on the pole he set up. 8Now write another decree in the king's name in behalf
of the Jews as seems best to you, and seal it with the king's signet ring — for no
document written in the king's name and sealed with his ring can be revoked."

9At once the royal secretaries were summoned — on the twenty-third day of
the third month, the month of Sivan. They wrote out all Mordecai's orders to the
Jews, and to the satraps, governors and nobles of the 127 provinces stretching
from India to Cush.[c] These orders were written in the script of each province
and the language of each people and also to the Jews in their own script and language. 10Mordecai wrote in the name of King Xerxes, sealed the dispatches with
the king's signet ring, and sent them by mounted couriers, who rode fast horses
especially bred for the king.

11The king's edict granted the Jews in every city the right to assemble and
protect themselves; to destroy, kill and annihilate the armed men of any nationality or province who might attack them and their women and children,[d] and to
plunder the property of their enemies. 12The day appointed for the Jews to do this

[a] 4 Or *quiet, but the compensation our adversary offers cannot be compared with the loss the king would suffer* [b] 9 That is, about 75 feet or about 23 meters [c] 9 That is, the upper Nile region [d] 11 Or *province, together with their women and children, who might attack them;*

ESTHER 7:10

PARADOX

Haman gave full vent to his anger, and it made him a fool (Pr 29:11). He listened to the advice of his wife and friends, and in a great paradox, Haman was impaled on the very pole they had advised him to set up for Mordecai. Jesus said, "There is nothing hidden that will not be disclosed, and nothing concealed that will not be known or brought out into the open" (Lk 8:17).

Believers also wrestle with the paradox of Paul's great proclamation, "For to me, to live is Christ and to die is gain" (Php 1:21). Paul reasoned that if he survived his imprisonment, he would be able to continue preaching the gospel and see lives transformed. But he also knew that if he died, God could also use his death to further the kingdom, *and* he would be with Jesus! Paul clearly saw the advantages of both life and death. Jesus' death gave us life. Because of Jesus' death and resurrection, death is swallowed up in victory (1Co 15:54).

ESTHER 8:1–8

WRITE A NEW CHAPTER

Up until this point, Queen Esther had to approach the king and confront Haman alone. The closest Mordecai had gotten was the king's gate. But finally Mordecai had an audience with the king after the queen revealed they were related. Mordecai was given Haman's position as second in rank to the king (10:3) and the king's signet ring. The same ring King Xerxes had given to Haman, he

(continued on next page)

(Write a New Chapter, continued)

now placed on Mordecai's finger. The ring on Haman's hand brought great mourning, fasting and tears (4:3). But on Mordecai's hand, it brought happiness, joy and honor (8:16).

Because of his newfound favor with the king, Mordecai and Queen Esther were asked to write a new decree that would allow the Jews to defend themselves. Mordecai could have requested an audience with the king after he saved his life or later when he was publicly honored for doing so. But he waited for God to move on his behalf. "Wealth and honor come from you; you are the ruler of all things. In your hands are strength and power to exalt and give strength to all" (1Ch 29:12).

in all the provinces of King Xerxes was the thirteenth day of the twelfth month, the month of Adar. [13]A copy of the text of the edict was to be issued as law in every province and made known to the people of every nationality so that the Jews would be ready on that day to avenge themselves on their enemies.

[14]The couriers, riding the royal horses, went out, spurred on by the king's command, and the edict was issued in the citadel of Susa.

The Triumph of the Jews

[15]When Mordecai left the king's presence, he was wearing royal garments of blue and white, a large crown of gold and a purple robe of fine linen. And the city of Susa held a joyous celebration. [16]For the Jews it was a time of happiness and joy, gladness and honor. [17]In every province and in every city to which the edict of the king came, there was joy and gladness among the Jews, with feasting and celebrating. And many people of other nationalities became Jews because fear of the Jews had seized them.

9 On the thirteenth day of the twelfth month, the month of Adar, the edict commanded by the king was to be carried out. On this day the enemies of the Jews had hoped to overpower them, but now the tables were turned and the Jews got the upper hand over those who hated them. [2]The Jews assembled in their cities in all the provinces of King Xerxes to attack those determined to destroy them. No one could stand against them, because the people of all the other nationalities were afraid of them. [3]And all the nobles of the provinces, the satraps, the governors and the king's administrators helped the Jews, because fear of Mordecai had seized them. [4]Mordecai was prominent in the palace; his reputation spread throughout the provinces, and he became more and more powerful.

[5]The Jews struck down all their enemies with the sword, killing and destroying them, and they did what they pleased to those who hated them. [6]In the citadel of Susa, the Jews killed and destroyed five hundred men. [7]They also killed Parshandatha, Dalphon, Aspatha, [8]Poratha, Adalia, Aridatha, [9]Parmashta, Arisai, Aridai and Vaizatha, [10]the ten sons of Haman son of Hammedatha, the enemy of the Jews. But they did not lay their hands on the plunder.

[11]The number of those killed in the citadel of Susa was reported to the king that same day. [12]The king said to Queen Esther, "The Jews have killed and destroyed five hundred men and the ten sons of Haman in the citadel of Susa. What have they done in the rest of the king's provinces? Now what is your petition? It will be given you. What is your request? It will also be granted."

[13]"If it pleases the king," Esther answered, "give the Jews in Susa permission to carry out this day's edict tomorrow also, and let Haman's ten sons be impaled on poles."

[14]So the king commanded that this be done. An edict was issued in Susa, and they impaled the ten sons of Haman. [15]The Jews in Susa came together on the fourteenth day of the month of Adar, and they put to death in Susa three hundred men, but they did not lay their hands on the plunder.

[16]Meanwhile, the remainder of the Jews who were in the king's provinces also assembled to protect themselves and get relief from their enemies. They killed seventy-five thousand of them but did not lay their hands on the plunder. [17]This happened on the thirteenth day of the month of Adar, and on the fourteenth they rested and made it a day of feasting and joy.

[18]The Jews in Susa, however, had assembled on the thirteenth and fourteenth, and then on the fifteenth they rested and made it a day of feasting and joy.

[19]That is why rural Jews — those living in villages — observe the fourteenth of the month of Adar as a day of joy and feasting, a day for giving presents to each other.

Purim Established

[20]Mordecai recorded these events, and he sent letters to all the Jews throughout the provinces of King Xerxes, near and far, [21]to have them celebrate annually

THE PRINCIPLE OF THE SEED

Almost 12 months had passed since the couriers had taken Haman's edict throughout the Persian Empire (3:7 – 14). On the day God's people were to be annihilated, they were given the right to defend themselves and overpowered their enemies instead. God's people had seen deliverance from the hands of their enemies many times before, but memories are short.

God established the principle of the seed. He governs over the rules and economy of sowing, planting, feeding, producing, pruning, reaping, harvesting and gleaning. As his people, all believers are led through each of these phases with the utmost love and care. Lean in. Keep in close conversation with the heavenly Father. Esther used several occasions to plant a seed and implore her king's favor, and his response was always, "What is your petition? It will be given you. What is your request? It will also be granted" (9:12).

Esther was even willing for her seed to die so others would live. In John 12:24,27 Jesus said about his own life, "Very truly I tell you, unless a kernel of wheat falls to the ground and dies, it remains only a single seed. But if it dies, it produces many seeds … Now my soul is troubled, and what shall I say? 'Father, save me from this hour'? No, it was for this very reason I came to this hour." The hopes and dreams and treasures of a Christ follower are counted as loss and sown in the ground to ultimately produce a harvest greater than one can imagine. Whatever is given up in trust to Jesus, God uses as seed to produce a large crop.

Jesus longs for us to see his overarching story. In the midst of tragedy, there is purpose. Suffering offers a closeness and intimacy with Jesus. As his beloved, we are in a position to ask and keep asking to see his name glorified. "Ask and it will be given to you; seek and you will find; knock and the door will be opened to you" (Mt 7:7).

Jesus' followers can rest in the promise of God that in all things — including present suffering — "God works for the good of those who love him, who have been called according to his purpose" (Ro 8:28). God is writing an overarching story of redemption across all time until Christ's return. Believers can entrust their "seed" — families, businesses, dreams, health and their very lives — into the hands of God. There is assurance that with the planting of a seed, a great harvest is coming when Jesus returns.

the fourteenth and fifteenth days of the month of Adar [22]as the time when the Jews got relief from their enemies, and as the month when their sorrow was turned into joy and their mourning into a day of celebration. He wrote them to observe the days as days of feasting and joy and giving presents of food to one another and gifts to the poor.

[23]So the Jews agreed to continue the celebration they had begun, doing what Mordecai had written to them. [24]For Haman son of Hammedatha, the Agagite, the enemy of all the Jews, had plotted against the Jews to destroy them and had cast the *pur* (that is, the lot) for their ruin and destruction. [25]But when the plot came to the king's attention,[a] he issued written orders that the evil scheme Haman had devised against the Jews should come back onto his own head, and that he and his sons should be impaled on poles. [26](Therefore these days were called Purim, from the word *pur*.) Because of everything written in this letter and because of what they had seen and what had happened to them, [27]the Jews took it on themselves to establish the custom that they and their descendants and all who join them should without fail observe these two days every year, in the way prescribed and at the time appointed. [28]These days should be remembered and observed in every generation by every family, and in every province and in every city. And these days of Purim should never fail to be celebrated by the Jews — nor should the memory of these days die out among their descendants.

[29]So Queen Esther, daughter of Abihail, along with Mordecai the Jew, wrote with full authority to confirm this second letter concerning Purim. [30]And Mordecai sent letters to all the Jews in the 127 provinces of Xerxes' kingdom — words of goodwill and assurance — [31]to establish these days of Purim at their designated times, as Mordecai the Jew and Queen Esther had decreed for them, and as they had established for themselves and their descendants in regard to their times of fasting and lamentation. [32]Esther's decree confirmed these regulations about Purim, and it was written down in the records.

The Greatness of Mordecai

10 King Xerxes imposed tribute throughout the empire, to its distant shores. [2]And all his acts of power and might, together with a full account of the greatness of Mordecai, whom the king had promoted, are they not written in the book of the annals of the kings of Media and Persia? [3]Mordecai the Jew was second in rank to King Xerxes, preeminent among the Jews, and held in high esteem by his many fellow Jews, because he worked for the good of his people and spoke up for the welfare of all the Jews.

ESTHER 10:1–4

A DAY TO REMEMBER

Mordecai left a legacy. For the rest of his life, Mordecai was well known and respected by his people for his greatness. He was known for seeking good for the Jewish people. Purim is still celebrated among the Jewish people today in remembrance of how God delivered the Jews from a day marked for their destruction. Nothing would thwart the plans of God for the promised Messiah. Throughout Scripture, God has always had a purpose to reconcile the world to himself (2Co 5:19). Believers should remember these days and God's ways "so the next generation would know them, even the children yet to be born, and they in turn would tell their children. Then they would put their trust in God and would not forget his deeds but would keep his commands" (Ps 78:6–7).

[a] 25 Or *when Esther came before the king*

JESUS: OUR SUFFERING SAVIOR

JOB

JOB

ABRAHAM IS BORN	ISAAC IS BORN	ABRAHAM DIES
c. 2166 BC	*c. 2066 BC*	*c. 1991 BC*

Job probably lived in the second millennium BC (2000 – 1000), and his story is one of the most famous stories in all the Bible. Christians and non-Christians alike are likely to know this tale of suffering and pain. The book begins and ends with a prose description of Job's life, comparing the suffering Satan inflicted on him over against God's care, protection and ultimate blessing (chs. 1 – 2; 42:7 – 17). The majority of the book is made up of a series of speeches, spoken by men who were Job's early supporters (Job 2:13), but quickly became his greatest critics (chs. 3 – 37).

This book tackles massive questions that have loomed in the minds of sufferers throughout all time. How can a good God allow righteous people to suffer? Doesn't this either make God unloving or unjust? Why doesn't God stop human suffering, and the suffering of all creation, if he is in control of all things?

These questions are posed throughout the book, though the answers seem to evade the grasp of Job, his wife and his friends. Ultimately, God speaks and reminds Job that his knowledge is very limited when compared to the inexplicable wisdom of God. God is good and he is in control — though his people may wonder where he is at certain times. God cautions Job, and the readers of this book, against trying to make a simplistic correlation between their blessing or suffering on this earth and God's goodness, care or control. God is always at work and is capable of using great pain and suffering to fulfill his good purposes for this world.

Jesus' death on the cross is the ultimate example of God's control over evil. On the surface, it seems like the cross was the greatest evil that could have been perpetrated against God's Son. Jesus' body, beaten and broken, hung on a Roman cross — to the horror of his followers. It seemed that Jesus' battle against evil was lost. Yet all the while, God was working to perfectly accomplish his glorious mission to save fallen sinners. His mission required that his Son go *through* suffering, not around it. Three days later, Jesus' empty tomb shouted victory to all creation. Jesus Christ, the promised Messiah, had defeated Satan, sin and death through the most unlikely path: by experiencing death himself.

Christians today can take heart in the fact that, while they will surely suffer, God is at work and he can be trusted. He has already won the war.

THE LORD GAVE AND THE LORD HAS TAKEN AWAY; MAY THE NAME OF THE LORD BE PRAISED.

Job 1:21

JOB

Prologue

1 In the land of Uz there lived a man whose name was Job. This man was blameless and upright; he feared God and shunned evil. 2He had seven sons and three daughters, 3and he owned seven thousand sheep, three thousand camels, five hundred yoke of oxen and five hundred donkeys, and had a large number of servants. He was the greatest man among all the people of the East.

4His sons used to hold feasts in their homes on their birthdays, and they would invite their three sisters to eat and drink with them. 5When a period of feasting had run its course, Job would make arrangements for them to be purified. Early in the morning he would sacrifice a burnt offering for each of them, thinking, "Perhaps my children have sinned and cursed God in their hearts." This was Job's regular custom.

6One day the angels[a] came to present themselves before the LORD, and Satan[b] also came with them. 7The LORD said to Satan, "Where have you come from?"

Satan answered the LORD, "From roaming throughout the earth, going back and forth on it."

8Then the LORD said to Satan, "Have you considered my servant Job? There is no one on earth like him; he is blameless and upright, a man who fears God and shuns evil."

9"Does Job fear God for nothing?" Satan replied. 10"Have you not put a hedge around him and his household and everything he has? You have blessed the work of his hands, so that his flocks and herds are spread throughout the land. 11But now stretch out your hand and strike everything he has, and he will surely curse you to your face."

12The LORD said to Satan, "Very well, then, everything he has is in your power, but on the man himself do not lay a finger."

Then Satan went out from the presence of the LORD.

13One day when Job's sons and daughters were feasting and drinking wine at the oldest brother's house, 14a messenger came to Job and said, "The oxen were plowing and the donkeys were grazing nearby, 15and the Sabeans attacked and made off with them. They put the servants to the sword, and I am the only one who has escaped to tell you!"

16While he was still speaking, another messenger came and said, "The fire of God fell from the heavens and burned up the sheep and the servants, and I am the only one who has escaped to tell you!"

17While he was still speaking, another messenger came and said, "The Chaldeans formed three raiding parties and swept down on your camels and made off with them. They put the servants to the sword, and I am the only one who has escaped to tell you!"

18While he was still speaking, yet another messenger came and said, "Your sons and daughters were feasting and drinking wine at the oldest brother's house, 19when suddenly a mighty wind swept in from the desert and struck the four corners of the house. It collapsed on them and they are dead, and I am the only one who has escaped to tell you!"

20At this, Job got up and tore his robe and shaved his head. Then he fell to the ground in worship 21and said:

"Naked I came from my mother's womb,
and naked I will depart.[c]

[a] 6 Hebrew *the sons of God* [b] 6 Hebrew *satan* means *adversary.* [c] 21 Or *will return there*

JOB 1:6–12

GOD HAS NO EQUAL

The first two chapters of Job provide a rare glimpse into the activity in heaven. The living God, the ruling and reigning sovereign Lord, sits at the center of the divine throne room, surrounded and served by celestial "sons of God" (see NIV text note on v. 6), or angels (1Ki 22:19; Ps 89:5–7). Satan, numbered among these created beings, is in no way the Lord's equal in power, majesty or knowledge. Though he has some degree of control over the earth at the present time (1Jn 5:19), he remains a subservient creature subject to the authority of the one supreme ruler (Rev 17:14). The book of Job teaches that God is sovereign over all of life's activities and circumstances. The New Testament reveals that Jesus himself is this incomparable God, without equal: Jesus is "far above all rule and authority, power and dominion, and every name that is invoked, not only in the present age but also in the one to come" (Eph 1:21). All of Scripture — including the difficult book of Job — demonstrates that even in the difficult times, Jesus remains the sovereign God.

The LORD gave and the LORD has taken away;
may the name of the LORD be praised."

22In all this, Job did not sin by charging God with wrongdoing.

2 On another day the angels[a] came to present themselves before the LORD, and
Satan also came with them to present himself before him. 2And the LORD
said to Satan, "Where have you come from?"
Satan answered the LORD, "From roaming throughout the earth, going back
and forth on it."
3Then the LORD said to Satan, "Have you considered my servant Job? There is
no one on earth like him; he is blameless and upright, a man who fears God and
shuns evil. And he still maintains his integrity, though you incited me against
him to ruin him without any reason."
4"Skin for skin!" Satan replied. "A man will give all he has for his own life.
5But now stretch out your hand and strike his flesh and bones, and he will surely
curse you to your face."
6The LORD said to Satan, "Very well, then, he is in your hands; but you must
spare his life."
7So Satan went out from the presence of the LORD and afflicted Job with painful sores from the soles of his feet to the crown of his head. 8Then Job took a piece
of broken pottery and scraped himself with it as he sat among the ashes.
9His wife said to him, "Are you still maintaining your integrity? Curse God
and die!"
10He replied, "You are talking like a foolish[b] woman. Shall we accept good
from God, and not trouble?"
In all this, Job did not sin in what he said.

11When Job's three friends, Eliphaz the Temanite, Bildad the Shuhite and Zophar the Naamathite, heard about all the troubles that had come upon him, they
set out from their homes and met together by agreement to go and sympathize with
him and comfort him. 12When they saw him from a distance, they could hardly recognize him; they began to weep aloud, and they tore their robes and sprinkled dust
on their heads. 13Then they sat on the ground with him for seven days and seven
nights. No one said a word to him, because they saw how great his suffering was.

Job Speaks

3 After this, Job opened his mouth and cursed the day of his birth. 2He said:

3"May the day of my birth perish,
and the night that said, 'A boy is conceived!'
4That day — may it turn to darkness;
may God above not care about it;
may no light shine on it.
5May gloom and utter darkness claim it once more;
may a cloud settle over it;
may blackness overwhelm it.
6That night — may thick darkness seize it;
may it not be included among the days of the year
nor be entered in any of the months.
7May that night be barren;
may no shout of joy be heard in it.
8May those who curse days[c] curse that day,
those who are ready to rouse Leviathan.
9May its morning stars become dark;
may it wait for daylight in vain
and not see the first rays of dawn,

JOB 2:11 – 13

TRUSTING GOD THROUGH PAIN

Satan's malicious work brought about a perfect storm of calamity in Job's life. Gone were his children and his property, and his physical suffering had left him barely recognizable. In the void of God's silence concerning his situation, Job sought solace in the company of his companions. For a time, they sat in silence with him, sharing in his sufferings. But in subsequent chapters, Job only found more agony as his friends speculated aloud that all these terrible events were the fruit of Job's unfaithfulness and sin. Adversity often leaves people asking why. When answers do not come, believers should not necessarily assume God is ignoring or punishing them for wrongdoing. Scripture promises that God hears prayers (Pr 15:29) and actively works in the most desperate situations to bring about good (Ro 8:28).

The Gospels record the incredible torment Jesus endured as the supreme example of trusting God in the midst of suffering. Blinded by his pain but quoting Psalm 22, Jesus exclaimed, "My God, my God why have you forsaken me?" (Mt 27:46). Though he could not sense his Father's presence through the unimaginable anguish, Jesus trusted enough to place his life into the Almighty's hands (Lk 23:46). His model graphically reminds believers that faith in God's unseen work is possible — and profitable — even when they do not feel anything but agony and sorrow.

[a] *1* Hebrew *the sons of God* [b] *10* The Hebrew word rendered *foolish* denotes moral deficiency. [c] *8* Or *curse the sea*

JOB 4:7–9

SUFFERING AS PUNISHMENT?

Strength to endure affliction often comes through the company of supporting and encouraging companions (1Th 5:11). However, when Eliphaz spoke, his distorted beliefs only added to Job's suffering. His counsel echoed the persistent human conviction that God brings blessing to the righteous and only allows tragedy to fall on sinners, thus concluding that Job must have received just punishment for his sin. Jesus soundly refuted this kind of thinking in the New Testament. In one instance, citing two separate events that resulted in the deaths of a number of innocent citizens, Christ made it clear that unrighteousness does not always result in personal calamity. "Do you think that these Galileans were worse sinners than all the other Galileans because they suffered this way?" Jesus asked; then he quickly responded to his own question with an emphatic, "I tell you, no!" (Lk 13:1–5; cf. Jn 9:1–3). His concluding remark—"But unless you repent, you too will all perish"—warned that all people are sinful from birth, and in need of repentance and forgiveness (Lk 13:3,5; Ac 2:38; Ro 3:10,23). Such salvation—the kind that saves us from the wrath of God—comes only through a relationship with Christ (Jn 3:36).

10 for it did not shut the doors of the womb on me
to hide trouble from my eyes.

11 "Why did I not perish at birth,
and die as I came from the womb?
12 Why were there knees to receive me
and breasts that I might be nursed?
13 For now I would be lying down in peace;
I would be asleep and at rest
14 with kings and rulers of the earth,
who built for themselves places now lying in ruins,
15 with princes who had gold,
who filled their houses with silver.
16 Or why was I not hidden away in the ground like a stillborn child,
like an infant who never saw the light of day?
17 There the wicked cease from turmoil,
and there the weary are at rest.
18 Captives also enjoy their ease;
they no longer hear the slave driver's shout.
19 The small and the great are there,
and the slaves are freed from their owners.

20 "Why is light given to those in misery,
and life to the bitter of soul,
21 to those who long for death that does not come,
who search for it more than for hidden treasure,
22 who are filled with gladness
and rejoice when they reach the grave?
23 Why is life given to a man
whose way is hidden,
whom God has hedged in?
24 For sighing has become my daily food;
my groans pour out like water.
25 What I feared has come upon me;
what I dreaded has happened to me.
26 I have no peace, no quietness;
I have no rest, but only turmoil."

Eliphaz

4 Then Eliphaz the Temanite replied:

2 "If someone ventures a word with you, will you be impatient?
But who can keep from speaking?
3 Think how you have instructed many,
how you have strengthened feeble hands.
4 Your words have supported those who stumbled;
you have strengthened faltering knees.
5 But now trouble comes to you, and you are discouraged;
it strikes you, and you are dismayed.
6 Should not your piety be your confidence
and your blameless ways your hope?

7 "Consider now: Who, being innocent, has ever perished?
Where were the upright ever destroyed?
8 As I have observed, those who plow evil
and those who sow trouble reap it.
9 At the breath of God they perish;
at the blast of his anger they are no more.

[10]The lions may roar and growl,
yet the teeth of the great lions are broken.
[11]The lion perishes for lack of prey,
and the cubs of the lioness are scattered.

[12]"A word was secretly brought to me,
my ears caught a whisper of it.
[13]Amid disquieting dreams in the night,
when deep sleep falls on people,
[14]fear and trembling seized me
and made all my bones shake.
[15]A spirit glided past my face,
and the hair on my body stood on end.
[16]It stopped,
but I could not tell what it was.
A form stood before my eyes,
and I heard a hushed voice:
[17]'Can a mortal be more righteous than God?
Can even a strong man be more pure than his Maker?
[18]If God places no trust in his servants,
if he charges his angels with error,
[19]how much more those who live in houses of clay,
whose foundations are in the dust,
who are crushed more readily than a moth!
[20]Between dawn and dusk they are broken to pieces;
unnoticed, they perish forever.
[21]Are not the cords of their tent pulled up,
so that they die without wisdom?'

5 "Call if you will, but who will answer you?
To which of the holy ones will you turn?
[2]Resentment kills a fool,
and envy slays the simple.
[3]I myself have seen a fool taking root,
but suddenly his house was cursed.
[4]His children are far from safety,
crushed in court without a defender.
[5]The hungry consume his harvest,
taking it even from among thorns,
and the thirsty pant after his wealth.
[6]For hardship does not spring from the soil,
nor does trouble sprout from the ground.
[7]Yet man is born to trouble
as surely as sparks fly upward.

[8]"But if I were you, I would appeal to God;
I would lay my cause before him.
[9]He performs wonders that cannot be fathomed,
miracles that cannot be counted.
[10]He provides rain for the earth;
he sends water on the countryside.
[11]The lowly he sets on high,
and those who mourn are lifted to safety.
[12]He thwarts the plans of the crafty,
so that their hands achieve no success.
[13]He catches the wise in their craftiness,
and the schemes of the wily are swept away.
[14]Darkness comes upon them in the daytime;
at noon they grope as in the night.

JOB 5:1 – 8

TO JUDGE OR NOT TO JUDGE

Eliphaz made broad and sweeping judgments about Job's character based chiefly on the intensity of his friend's suffering. He also insinuated that the demise of Job's children was due to Job's foolishness (vv. 2 – 4), questioned the depth of Job's faith (v. 8), and since "hardship does not spring from the soil" (v. 6), implied that Job was essentially the cause of his own suffering. These flawed accusations were based solely in Eliphaz's own assumptions (vv. 3,8) and served only to intensify Job's anguish.

While Jesus warned against passing judgments like this (Mt 7:1), Scripture still charges believers to "test [or judge] the spirits" of those who claim to have a word from God (1Jn 4:1) and to make wise "judgments about all things" (1Co 2:15). The surface contradiction between these verses and the Matthew passage can be resolved by looking at the Greek terms. The words *dokimazô* (1Jn 4:1) and *anakrinô* (1Co 2:15) carry subtle differences in meaning from the word *krinô* (Mt 7:1), which Jesus used when he warned against judging other people. The first two words encourage believers to evaluate all things carefully and wisely and to exercise spiritual discernment. The word in Matthew 7:1, *krinô*, indicates a type of legal judgment that pronounces condemnation. Jesus went on to warn that "the measure you use" to judge others will be "measured to you" (Mt 7:2). This should stand as a powerful reminder to remain generous at all times, extending great grace, mercy and forgiveness.

15 He saves the needy from the sword in their mouth;
he saves them from the clutches of the powerful.
16 So the poor have hope,
and injustice shuts its mouth.

17 "Blessed is the one whom God corrects;
so do not despise the discipline of the Almighty.[a]
18 For he wounds, but he also binds up;
he injures, but his hands also heal.
19 From six calamities he will rescue you;
in seven no harm will touch you.
20 In famine he will deliver you from death,
and in battle from the stroke of the sword.
21 You will be protected from the lash of the tongue,
and need not fear when destruction comes.
22 You will laugh at destruction and famine,
and need not fear the wild animals.
23 For you will have a covenant with the stones of the field,
and the wild animals will be at peace with you.
24 You will know that your tent is secure;
you will take stock of your property and find nothing missing.
25 You will know that your children will be many,
and your descendants like the grass of the earth.
26 You will come to the grave in full vigor,
like sheaves gathered in season.

27 "We have examined this, and it is true.
So hear it and apply it to yourself."

Job

6 Then Job replied:

2 "If only my anguish could be weighed
and all my misery be placed on the scales!
3 It would surely outweigh the sand of the seas—
no wonder my words have been impetuous.
4 The arrows of the Almighty are in me,
my spirit drinks in their poison;
God's terrors are marshaled against me.
5 Does a wild donkey bray when it has grass,
or an ox bellow when it has fodder?
6 Is tasteless food eaten without salt,
or is there flavor in the sap of the mallow[b]?
7 I refuse to touch it;
such food makes me ill.

8 "Oh, that I might have my request,
that God would grant what I hope for,
9 that God would be willing to crush me,
to let loose his hand and cut off my life!
10 Then I would still have this consolation—
my joy in unrelenting pain—
that I had not denied the words of the Holy One.

11 "What strength do I have, that I should still hope?
What prospects, that I should be patient?
12 Do I have the strength of stone?
Is my flesh bronze?

[a] 17 Hebrew *Shaddai*; here and throughout Job
[b] 6 The meaning of the Hebrew for this phrase is uncertain.

13 Do I have any power to help myself,
now that success has been driven from me?

14 "Anyone who withholds kindness from a friend
forsakes the fear of the Almighty.
15 But my brothers are as undependable as intermittent
streams,
as the streams that overflow
16 when darkened by thawing ice
and swollen with melting snow,
17 but that stop flowing in the dry season,
and in the heat vanish from their channels.
18 Caravans turn aside from their routes;
they go off into the wasteland and perish.
19 The caravans of Tema look for water,
the traveling merchants of Sheba look in hope.
20 They are distressed, because they had been confident;
they arrive there, only to be disappointed.
21 Now you too have proved to be of no help;
you see something dreadful and are afraid.
22 Have I ever said, 'Give something on my behalf,
pay a ransom for me from your wealth,
23 deliver me from the hand of the enemy,
rescue me from the clutches of the ruthless'?

24 "Teach me, and I will be quiet;
show me where I have been wrong.
25 How painful are honest words!
But what do your arguments prove?
26 Do you mean to correct what I say,
and treat my desperate words as wind?
27 You would even cast lots for the fatherless
and barter away your friend.

28 "But now be so kind as to look at me.
Would I lie to your face?
29 Relent, do not be unjust;
reconsider, for my integrity is at stake.[a]
30 Is there any wickedness on my lips?
Can my mouth not discern malice?

7 "Do not mortals have hard service on earth?
Are not their days like those of hired laborers?
2 Like a slave longing for the evening shadows,
or a hired laborer waiting to be paid,
3 so I have been allotted months of futility,
and nights of misery have been assigned to me.
4 When I lie down I think, 'How long before I get up?'
The night drags on, and I toss and turn until dawn.
5 My body is clothed with worms and scabs,
my skin is broken and festering.

6 "My days are swifter than a weaver's shuttle,
and they come to an end without hope.
7 Remember, O God, that my life is but a breath;
my eyes will never see happiness again.
8 The eye that now sees me will see me no longer;
you will look for me, but I will be no more.

[a] 29 Or *my righteousness still stands*

JOB 7:17–21

GOD, WHERE ARE YOU?

"God, where are you?" It would seem reasonable and normal for a person in Job's situation to ask that very common question. However, despite his intense level of suffering and lack of knowledge regarding the divine purpose for his adversity, Job never questioned God's presence or activity. Certain of God's involvement, he instead uttered a desperate plea for the Lord to simply leave him alone. But these sputtering statements from the lips of a man pressed by unrelenting despair remind readers that everything that touches their lives is ultimately under the watchful eye of God (Ps 33:18; 34:15; 139:7–12; Pr 15:3).

Centuries later, David's poetic writing gave new meaning to Job's anguished plea. Overwhelmed by the vastness and majesty of the heavens compared to humankind, David was humbled and awed by God's constant presence and care (Ps 8:3–4). Much of the glory and honor ascribed to humanity by the Lord at creation was lost when Adam chose to disobey (Ro 5:12–18), but what was obscured by sin has been restored through the power of the death and resurrection of Jesus (Ro 6:23). Christ was willing to be "made lower than the angels for a little while" in his incarnation (Heb 2:9), so that through faith, it became possible for believers to be once again "crowned ... with glory and honor" (Ps 8:5).

9 As a cloud vanishes and is gone,
so one who goes down to the grave does not return.
10 He will never come to his house again;
his place will know him no more.

11 "Therefore I will not keep silent;
I will speak out in the anguish of my spirit,
I will complain in the bitterness of my soul.
12 Am I the sea, or the monster of the deep,
that you put me under guard?
13 When I think my bed will comfort me
and my couch will ease my complaint,
14 even then you frighten me with dreams
and terrify me with visions,
15 so that I prefer strangling and death,
rather than this body of mine.
16 I despise my life; I would not live forever.
Let me alone; my days have no meaning.

17 "What is mankind that you make so much of them,
that you give them so much attention,
18 that you examine them every morning
and test them every moment?
19 Will you never look away from me,
or let me alone even for an instant?
20 If I have sinned, what have I done to you,
you who see everything we do?
Why have you made me your target?
Have I become a burden to you?[a]
21 Why do you not pardon my offenses
and forgive my sins?
For I will soon lie down in the dust;
you will search for me, but I will be no more."

Bildad

8 Then Bildad the Shuhite replied:

2 "How long will you say such things?
Your words are a blustering wind.
3 Does God pervert justice?
Does the Almighty pervert what is right?
4 When your children sinned against him,
he gave them over to the penalty of their sin.
5 But if you will seek God earnestly
and plead with the Almighty,
6 if you are pure and upright,
even now he will rouse himself on your behalf
and restore you to your prosperous state.
7 Your beginnings will seem humble,
so prosperous will your future be.

8 "Ask the former generation
and find out what their ancestors learned,
9 for we were born only yesterday and know nothing,
and our days on earth are but a shadow.

[a] *20* A few manuscripts of the Masoretic Text, an ancient Hebrew scribal tradition and Septuagint; most manuscripts of the Masoretic Text *I have become a burden to myself.*

[10] Will they not instruct you and tell you?
Will they not bring forth words from their understanding?
[11] Can papyrus grow tall where there is no marsh?
Can reeds thrive without water?
[12] While still growing and uncut,
they wither more quickly than grass.
[13] Such is the destiny of all who forget God;
so perishes the hope of the godless.
[14] What they trust in is fragile[a];
what they rely on is a spider's web.
[15] They lean on the web, but it gives way;
they cling to it, but it does not hold.
[16] They are like a well-watered plant in the sunshine,
spreading its shoots over the garden;
[17] it entwines its roots around a pile of rocks
and looks for a place among the stones.
[18] But when it is torn from its spot,
that place disowns it and says, 'I never saw you.'
[19] Surely its life withers away,
and[b] from the soil other plants grow.

[20] "Surely God does not reject one who is blameless
or strengthen the hands of evildoers.
[21] He will yet fill your mouth with laughter
and your lips with shouts of joy.
[22] Your enemies will be clothed in shame,
and the tents of the wicked will be no more."

Job

9 Then Job replied:

[2] "Indeed, I know that this is true.
But how can mere mortals prove their innocence before God?
[3] Though they wished to dispute with him,
they could not answer him one time out of a thousand.
[4] His wisdom is profound, his power is vast.
Who has resisted him and come out unscathed?
[5] He moves mountains without their knowing it
and overturns them in his anger.
[6] He shakes the earth from its place
and makes its pillars tremble.
[7] He speaks to the sun and it does not shine;
he seals off the light of the stars.
[8] He alone stretches out the heavens
and treads on the waves of the sea.
[9] He is the Maker of the Bear[c] and Orion,
the Pleiades and the constellations of the south.
[10] He performs wonders that cannot be fathomed,
miracles that cannot be counted.
[11] When he passes me, I cannot see him;
when he goes by, I cannot perceive him.
[12] If he snatches away, who can stop him?
Who can say to him, 'What are you doing?'
[13] God does not restrain his anger;
even the cohorts of Rahab cowered at his feet.

---

[a] *14* The meaning of the Hebrew for this word is uncertain. [b] *19* Or *Surely all the joy it has / is that* [c] *9* Or *of Leo*

14 "How then can I dispute with him?
How can I find words to argue with him?
15 Though I were innocent, I could not answer him;
I could only plead with my Judge for mercy.
16 Even if I summoned him and he responded,
I do not believe he would give me a hearing.
17 He would crush me with a storm
and multiply my wounds for no reason.
18 He would not let me catch my breath
but would overwhelm me with misery.
19 If it is a matter of strength, he is mighty!
And if it is a matter of justice, who can challenge him[a]?
20 Even if I were innocent, my mouth would condemn me;
if I were blameless, it would pronounce me guilty.

21 "Although I am blameless,
I have no concern for myself;
I despise my own life.
22 It is all the same; that is why I say,
'He destroys both the blameless and the wicked.'
23 When a scourge brings sudden death,
he mocks the despair of the innocent.
24 When a land falls into the hands of the wicked,
he blindfolds its judges.
If it is not he, then who is it?

25 "My days are swifter than a runner;
they fly away without a glimpse of joy.
26 They skim past like boats of papyrus,
like eagles swooping down on their prey.
27 If I say, 'I will forget my complaint,
I will change my expression, and smile,'
28 I still dread all my sufferings,
for I know you will not hold me innocent.
29 Since I am already found guilty,
why should I struggle in vain?
30 Even if I washed myself with soap
and my hands with cleansing powder,
31 you would plunge me into a slime pit
so that even my clothes would detest me.

32 "He is not a mere mortal like me that I might answer him,
that we might confront each other in court.
33 If only there were someone to mediate between us,
someone to bring us together,
34 someone to remove God's rod from me,
so that his terror would frighten me no more.
35 Then I would speak up without fear of him,
but as it now stands with me, I cannot.

10 "I loathe my very life;
therefore I will give free rein to my complaint
and speak out in the bitterness of my soul.
2 I say to God: Do not declare me guilty,
but tell me what charges you have against me.
3 Does it please you to oppress me,
to spurn the work of your hands,
while you smile on the plans of the wicked?

[a] *19* See Septuagint; Hebrew *me.*

[4]Do you have eyes of flesh?
Do you see as a mortal sees?
[5]Are your days like those of a mortal
or your years like those of a strong man,
[6]that you must search out my faults
and probe after my sin —
[7]though you know that I am not guilty
and that no one can rescue me from your hand?

[8]"Your hands shaped me and made me.
Will you now turn and destroy me?
[9]Remember that you molded me like clay.
Will you now turn me to dust again?
[10]Did you not pour me out like milk
and curdle me like cheese,
[11]clothe me with skin and flesh
and knit me together with bones and sinews?
[12]You gave me life and showed me kindness,
and in your providence watched over my spirit.

[13]"But this is what you concealed in your heart,
and I know that this was in your mind:
[14]If I sinned, you would be watching me
and would not let my offense go unpunished.
[15]If I am guilty — woe to me!
Even if I am innocent, I cannot lift my head,
for I am full of shame
and drowned in[a] my affliction.
[16]If I hold my head high, you stalk me like a lion
and again display your awesome power against me.
[17]You bring new witnesses against me
and increase your anger toward me;
your forces come against me wave upon wave.

[18]"Why then did you bring me out of the womb?
I wish I had died before any eye saw me.
[19]If only I had never come into being,
or had been carried straight from the womb to the grave!
[20]Are not my few days almost over?
Turn away from me so I can have a moment's joy
[21]before I go to the place of no return,
to the land of gloom and utter darkness,
[22]to the land of deepest night,
of utter darkness and disorder,
where even the light is like darkness."

Zophar

11 Then Zophar the Naamathite replied:

[2]"Are all these words to go unanswered?
Is this talker to be vindicated?
[3]Will your idle talk reduce others to silence?
Will no one rebuke you when you mock?
[4]You say to God, 'My beliefs are flawless
and I am pure in your sight.'
[5]Oh, how I wish that God would speak,
that he would open his lips against you

[a] 15 Or *and aware of*

JOB 11:1 – 11

BLIND ADVICE

People often make the mistake of giving simplistic answers to those who are in difficult situations. Such was the case with Job's friend, Zophar. Regardless of Job's insistence that he was innocent of wrongdoing (6:24; 9:21; 10:2,7), this third companion began his analysis of Job's situation based on the flawed assumption that his friend's great torment was clear evidence of his hidden moral guilt. Citing God's infinite wisdom, he insinuated that not only was Job receiving his due penalty, but that if the full depth of Job's sin were revealed, it would be just for him to receive even greater punishment than he had thus far experienced (11:5 – 6). However, this insensitive friend evidently missed his own hypocrisy. Since no one can be judged faultless compared to the perfection of God, Zophar also merited the same penalty he thought Job deserved.

In the Sermon on the Mount, Jesus used an exaggerated contrast to warn his followers of well-intentioned but damaging double standards. "Why do you look at the speck of sawdust in your brother's eye and pay no attention to the plank in your own eye? . . . You hypocrite, first take the plank out of your own eye, and then you will see clearly to remove the speck from your brother's eye" (Mt 7:3,5). Scripture encourages believers to help and guide others as they deal with wrongdoing (Gal 6:2; Col 3:13,16), but not before serious self-examination and dealing honestly with personal failures.

JOB 12:7 – 10

OBVIOUSLY

In his longest response to the criticism of his friends, Job continued to reject allegations that his sin was to blame for his suffering. Instead, he reminded them that their self-righteous analysis failed to account for calamities that befall faithful followers of God (Job 12:4) as well as for the prosperity of those who purposefully carry out evil (Job 12:6). With biting sarcasm, Job challenged his tactless companions to consult the creatures of the earth who were obviously more aware than them that the Lord ultimately rules over all that transpires on the earth (vv. 7 – 10; Ps 103:19).

In Romans, Paul agreed with Job's supposition about creation's ability to reveal God, reminding New Testament readers that the truth about God's "eternal power and divine nature" can be understood from nature (Ro 1:20). The complexity and arrangement of each component in the cosmos as well as the order and intricacy of the smallest atom attest to the controlling hand of a purposeful and loving Creator. So clear are his fingerprints that those who claim ignorance of God are "without excuse." With this knowledge also comes the certainty that no one can approach the Lord since humanity's flawed nature is starkly inferior to the one whose glory is declared by the heavens (Ps 19:1). While everyone can learn about God's characteristics from the natural world, the separation caused by sin necessitated the sacrifice of Christ to build the foundational bridge which makes knowing God possible at all (Jn 1:18; 3:16; 10:30; 14:6 – 10).

6 and disclose to you the secrets of wisdom,
for true wisdom has two sides.
Know this: God has even forgotten some of your sin.

7 "Can you fathom the mysteries of God?
Can you probe the limits of the Almighty?
8 They are higher than the heavens above — what can you do?
They are deeper than the depths below — what can you know?
9 Their measure is longer than the earth
and wider than the sea.

10 "If he comes along and confines you in prison
and convenes a court, who can oppose him?
11 Surely he recognizes deceivers;
and when he sees evil, does he not take note?
12 But the witless can no more become wise
than a wild donkey's colt can be born human.[a]

13 "Yet if you devote your heart to him
and stretch out your hands to him,
14 if you put away the sin that is in your hand
and allow no evil to dwell in your tent,
15 then, free of fault, you will lift up your face;
you will stand firm and without fear.
16 You will surely forget your trouble,
recalling it only as waters gone by.
17 Life will be brighter than noonday,
and darkness will become like morning.
18 You will be secure, because there is hope;
you will look about you and take your rest in safety.
19 You will lie down, with no one to make you afraid,
and many will court your favor.
20 But the eyes of the wicked will fail,
and escape will elude them;
their hope will become a dying gasp."

Job

12 Then Job replied:

2 "Doubtless you are the only people who matter,
and wisdom will die with you!
3 But I have a mind as well as you;
I am not inferior to you.
Who does not know all these things?

4 "I have become a laughingstock to my friends,
though I called on God and he answered —
a mere laughingstock, though righteous and blameless!
5 Those who are at ease have contempt for misfortune
as the fate of those whose feet are slipping.
6 The tents of marauders are undisturbed,
and those who provoke God are secure —
those God has in his hand.[b]

7 "But ask the animals, and they will teach you,
or the birds in the sky, and they will tell you;
8 or speak to the earth, and it will teach you,
or let the fish in the sea inform you.

[a] 12 Or *wild donkey can be born tame* [b] 6 Or *those whose god is in their own hand*

[9] Which of all these does not know
that the hand of the LORD has done this?
[10] In his hand is the life of every creature
and the breath of all mankind.
[11] Does not the ear test words
as the tongue tastes food?
[12] Is not wisdom found among the aged?
Does not long life bring understanding?

[13] "To God belong wisdom and power;
counsel and understanding are his.
[14] What he tears down cannot be rebuilt;
those he imprisons cannot be released.
[15] If he holds back the waters, there is drought;
if he lets them loose, they devastate the land.
[16] To him belong strength and insight;
both deceived and deceiver are his.
[17] He leads rulers away stripped
and makes fools of judges.
[18] He takes off the shackles put on by kings
and ties a loincloth[a] around their waist.
[19] He leads priests away stripped
and overthrows officials long established.
[20] He silences the lips of trusted advisers
and takes away the discernment of elders.
[21] He pours contempt on nobles
and disarms the mighty.
[22] He reveals the deep things of darkness
and brings utter darkness into the light.
[23] He makes nations great, and destroys them;
he enlarges nations, and disperses them.
[24] He deprives the leaders of the earth of their reason;
he makes them wander in a trackless waste.
[25] They grope in darkness with no light;
he makes them stagger like drunkards.

13 "My eyes have seen all this,
my ears have heard and understood it.
[2] What you know, I also know;
I am not inferior to you.
[3] But I desire to speak to the Almighty
and to argue my case with God.
[4] You, however, smear me with lies;
you are worthless physicians, all of you!
[5] If only you would be altogether silent!
For you, that would be wisdom.
[6] Hear now my argument;
listen to the pleas of my lips.
[7] Will you speak wickedly on God's behalf?
Will you speak deceitfully for him?
[8] Will you show him partiality?
Will you argue the case for God?
[9] Would it turn out well if he examined you?
Could you deceive him as you might deceive a mortal?
[10] He would surely call you to account
if you secretly showed partiality.

[a] *18* Or *shackles of kings / and ties a belt*

11 Would not his splendor terrify you?
Would not the dread of him fall on you?
12 Your maxims are proverbs of ashes;
your defenses are defenses of clay.

13 "Keep silent and let me speak;
then let come to me what may.
14 Why do I put myself in jeopardy
and take my life in my hands?
15 Though he slay me, yet will I hope in him;
I will surely[a] defend my ways to his face.
16 Indeed, this will turn out for my deliverance,
for no godless person would dare come before him!
17 Listen carefully to what I say;
let my words ring in your ears.
18 Now that I have prepared my case,
I know I will be vindicated.
19 Can anyone bring charges against me?
If so, I will be silent and die.

20 "Only grant me these two things, God,
and then I will not hide from you:
21 Withdraw your hand far from me,
and stop frightening me with your terrors.
22 Then summon me and I will answer,
or let me speak, and you reply to me.
23 How many wrongs and sins have I committed?
Show me my offense and my sin.
24 Why do you hide your face
and consider me your enemy?
25 Will you torment a windblown leaf?
Will you chase after dry chaff?
26 For you write down bitter things against me
and make me reap the sins of my youth.
27 You fasten my feet in shackles;
you keep close watch on all my paths
by putting marks on the soles of my feet.

28 "So man wastes away like something rotten,
like a garment eaten by moths.

14 "Mortals, born of woman,
are of few days and full of trouble.
2 They spring up like flowers and wither away;
like fleeting shadows, they do not endure.
3 Do you fix your eye on them?
Will you bring them[b] before you for judgment?
4 Who can bring what is pure from the impure?
No one!
5 A person's days are determined;
you have decreed the number of his months
and have set limits he cannot exceed.
6 So look away from him and let him alone,
till he has put in his time like a hired laborer.

7 "At least there is hope for a tree:
If it is cut down, it will sprout again,
and its new shoots will not fail.

---

[a] 15 Or *He will surely slay me; I have no hope — / yet I will* [b] 3 Septuagint, Vulgate and Syriac; Hebrew *me*

[8] Its roots may grow old in the ground
and its stump die in the soil,
[9] yet at the scent of water it will bud
and put forth shoots like a plant.
[10] But a man dies and is laid low;
he breathes his last and is no more.
[11] As the water of a lake dries up
or a riverbed becomes parched and dry,
[12] so he lies down and does not rise;
till the heavens are no more, people will not awake
or be roused from their sleep.

[13] "If only you would hide me in the grave
and conceal me till your anger has passed!
If only you would set me a time
and then remember me!
[14] If someone dies, will they live again?
All the days of my hard service
I will wait for my renewal[a] to come.
[15] You will call and I will answer you;
you will long for the creature your hands have made.
[16] Surely then you will count my steps
but not keep track of my sin.
[17] My offenses will be sealed up in a bag;
you will cover over my sin.

[18] "But as a mountain erodes and crumbles
and as a rock is moved from its place,
[19] as water wears away stones
and torrents wash away the soil,
so you destroy a person's hope.
[20] You overpower them once for all, and they are gone;
you change their countenance and send them
away.
[21] If their children are honored, they do not know it;
if their offspring are brought low, they do not see it.
[22] They feel but the pain of their own bodies
and mourn only for themselves."

Eliphaz

15 Then Eliphaz the Temanite replied:

[2] "Would a wise person answer with empty notions
or fill their belly with the hot east wind?
[3] Would they argue with useless words,
with speeches that have no value?
[4] But you even undermine piety
and hinder devotion to God.
[5] Your sin prompts your mouth;
you adopt the tongue of the crafty.
[6] Your own mouth condemns you, not mine;
your own lips testify against you.

[7] "Are you the first man ever born?
Were you brought forth before the hills?
[8] Do you listen in on God's council?
Do you have a monopoly on wisdom?

[a] 14 Or *release*

JOB 15:4–6

IN YOUR OWN WORDS

The second phase of the conversation between Job and his three friends opened with Eliphaz disputing Job's claim of innocence before God. Twisting Job's words, this companion rejected his desire for a rightful "day in court" by insisting that his own words testified against him (v. 6). While his conclusions seemed plausible from his own flawed point of view, Eliphaz lacked the proper spiritual vantage point to identify the true source of Job's suffering (1:6–12; 2:1–7).

The Jewish leaders expressed a similar lack of spiritual understanding when they attempted to use Jesus' own words to incriminate him. Searching for a credible reason to indict him of treason, they demanded Jesus publicly validate or deny his claim to be the Messiah (Lk 22:67). Refusing to be manipulated, Jesus instead laid claim to sovereignty over a more wide-ranging kingdom than they could comprehend (Mk 14:62). At this, the teachers of the Law believed they had sufficient grounds to condemn Jesus of blasphemy. However, being more concerned about advancing their own agenda than discovering the truth, the accusing leaders missed the crucial spiritual reality: Jesus truly is God.

While people may believe they are pursuing God, like Job's friends or the Jewish council, it is possible they are missing the most obvious truths. Though God loves everyone immensely, he often has priorities that are not easily understood. Sometimes the finite sufferings of God's people fall within a much larger divine plan.

THE CONDITION OF HUMANITY

Job described life's misery and brevity through two vivid metaphors: a fading flower and a fleeing shadow. In the midst of suffering, the fragility and temporariness of life comes to the forefront. The sufferer's life sometimes feels like a cut flower whose petals are beginning to wilt, or like a shadow at sunset growing dimmer by the moment until it slips away.

If all anyone had was Job's sad assessment of reality, then life would be hopeless. But there is a perfect sufferer, who graciously entered into humanity's suffering! The Son of God, a heaven-dwelling member of the Trinity, chose to enter the lives and pain of people.

Suffering taught Job to understand the reality of this sin-marred world: it can be fleeting, painful and brutal. Knowing this reality, it is incredible that Jesus humbled himself to enter into humankind's condition. Scripture says, "In your relationships with one another, have the same mindset as Christ Jesus: Who, being in very nature God, did not consider equality with God something to be used to his own advantage; rather, he made himself nothing by taking the very nature of a servant, being made in human likeness" (Php 2:5 – 7).

Jesus knows what people face on a daily basis, and he entered into it — because of his great love. Jesus' life was not easy. He faced the same hardships and temptations that everyone faces. He endured this life with perfect humility and never once questioned the greatness and goodness of God. His commitment to live for God led him all the way to the cross: "And being found in appearance as a man, he humbled himself by becoming obedient to death — even death on a cross" (Php 2:8).

In the midst of suffering, humans can lean on Jesus. Although lamenting and complaining when life is hard is natural for humans, Jesus provides an opportunity to rise above suffering and trust that his ways are perfect. Not only has Jesus joined humanity in their suffering, providing comfort through his presence, he also brings hope of the final defeat of sin and suffering. Scripture shows that because of the life, death and resurrection of Christ, the difficulties of life are temporary: "For while we are in this tent, we groan and are burdened, because we do not wish to be unclothed but to be clothed instead with our heavenly dwelling, so that what is mortal may be swallowed up by life" (2Co 5:4). In his return, Jesus will make a new creation where the flowers never fade and the shadows never grow dim.

9 What do you know that we do not know?
What insights do you have that we do not have?
10 The gray-haired and the aged are on our side,
men even older than your father.
11 Are God's consolations not enough for you,
words spoken gently to you?
12 Why has your heart carried you away,
and why do your eyes flash,
13 so that you vent your rage against God
and pour out such words from your mouth?

14 "What are mortals, that they could be pure,
or those born of woman, that they could be righteous?
15 If God places no trust in his holy ones,
if even the heavens are not pure in his eyes,
16 how much less mortals, who are vile and corrupt,
who drink up evil like water!

17 "Listen to me and I will explain to you;
let me tell you what I have seen,
18 what the wise have declared,
hiding nothing received from their ancestors
19 (to whom alone the land was given
when no foreigners moved among them):
20 All his days the wicked man suffers torment,
the ruthless man through all the years stored up for him.
21 Terrifying sounds fill his ears;
when all seems well, marauders attack him.
22 He despairs of escaping the realm of darkness;
he is marked for the sword.
23 He wanders about for food like a vulture;
he knows the day of darkness is at hand.
24 Distress and anguish fill him with terror;
troubles overwhelm him, like a king poised to attack,
25 because he shakes his fist at God
and vaunts himself against the Almighty,
26 defiantly charging against him
with a thick, strong shield.

27 "Though his face is covered with fat
and his waist bulges with flesh,
28 he will inhabit ruined towns
and houses where no one lives,
houses crumbling to rubble.
29 He will no longer be rich and his wealth will not endure,
nor will his possessions spread over the land.
30 He will not escape the darkness;
a flame will wither his shoots,
and the breath of God's mouth will carry him away.
31 Let him not deceive himself by trusting what is worthless,
for he will get nothing in return.
32 Before his time he will wither,
and his branches will not flourish.
33 He will be like a vine stripped of its unripe grapes,
like an olive tree shedding its blossoms.
34 For the company of the godless will be barren,
and fire will consume the tents of those who love bribes.
35 They conceive trouble and give birth to evil;
their womb fashions deceit."

JOB 16:6 – 14

ASSESSING GOD'S LOVE

When put into difficult situations, even committed believers understandably question God's actions. Job was no exception. Though he was certain he was guilty of no wrongdoing, he still wondered if God was angry at him or seeking some kind of vengeance. Often, as in the case of Job, external circumstances fail as reliable indicators of God's attitude toward us.

Romans 5:8 says, "God demonstrates his own love for us in this: While we were still sinners, Christ died for us." This verse states plainly that Christ's death ultimately *proved* God's love. Believers do not have to depend on comfortable circumstances as a barometer indicating right standing with the Lord. All that was necessary to demonstrate God's unwavering love has already been done. While questions about the purpose for adversity and pain persist, the New Testament points to the crucifixion and resurrection of Jesus Christ as the ultimate, objective, steadfast and concrete proof of the love of God.

Job

16 Then Job replied:

2 "I have heard many things like these;
you are miserable comforters, all of you!
3 Will your long-winded speeches never end?
What ails you that you keep on arguing?
4 I also could speak like you,
if you were in my place;
I could make fine speeches against you
and shake my head at you.
5 But my mouth would encourage you;
comfort from my lips would bring you relief.

6 "Yet if I speak, my pain is not relieved;
and if I refrain, it does not go away.
7 Surely, God, you have worn me out;
you have devastated my entire household.
8 You have shriveled me up — and it has become a witness;
my gauntness rises up and testifies against me.
9 God assails me and tears me in his anger
and gnashes his teeth at me;
my opponent fastens on me his piercing eyes.
10 People open their mouths to jeer at me;
they strike my cheek in scorn
and unite together against me.
11 God has turned me over to the ungodly
and thrown me into the clutches of the wicked.
12 All was well with me, but he shattered me;
he seized me by the neck and crushed me.
He has made me his target;
13 his archers surround me.
Without pity, he pierces my kidneys
and spills my gall on the ground.
14 Again and again he bursts upon me;
he rushes at me like a warrior.

15 "I have sewed sackcloth over my skin
and buried my brow in the dust.
16 My face is red with weeping,
dark shadows ring my eyes;
17 yet my hands have been free of violence
and my prayer is pure.

18 "Earth, do not cover my blood;
may my cry never be laid to rest!
19 Even now my witness is in heaven;
my advocate is on high.
20 My intercessor is my friend[a]
as my eyes pour out tears to God;
21 on behalf of a man he pleads with God
as one pleads for a friend.

22 "Only a few years will pass
before I take the path of no return.

17 1 My spirit is broken,
my days are cut short,
the grave awaits me.

[a] 20 Or *My friends treat me with scorn*

[2] Surely mockers surround me;
my eyes must dwell on their hostility.

[3] "Give me, O God, the pledge you demand.
Who else will put up security for me?
[4] You have closed their minds to understanding;
therefore you will not let them triumph.
[5] If anyone denounces their friends for reward,
the eyes of their children will fail.

[6] "God has made me a byword to everyone,
a man in whose face people spit.
[7] My eyes have grown dim with grief;
my whole frame is but a shadow.
[8] The upright are appalled at this;
the innocent are aroused against the ungodly.
[9] Nevertheless, the righteous will hold to their ways,
and those with clean hands will grow stronger.

[10] "But come on, all of you, try again!
I will not find a wise man among you.
[11] My days have passed, my plans are shattered.
Yet the desires of my heart
[12] turn night into day;
in the face of the darkness light is near.
[13] If the only home I hope for is the grave,
if I spread out my bed in the realm of darkness,
[14] if I say to corruption, 'You are my father,'
and to the worm, 'My mother' or 'My sister,'
[15] where then is my hope—
who can see any hope for me?
[16] Will it go down to the gates of death?
Will we descend together into the dust?"

Bildad

18 Then Bildad the Shuhite replied:

[2] "When will you end these speeches?
Be sensible, and then we can talk.
[3] Why are we regarded as cattle
and considered stupid in your sight?
[4] You who tear yourself to pieces in your anger,
is the earth to be abandoned for your sake?
Or must the rocks be moved from their place?

[5] "The lamp of a wicked man is snuffed out;
the flame of his fire stops burning.
[6] The light in his tent becomes dark;
the lamp beside him goes out.
[7] The vigor of his step is weakened;
his own schemes throw him down.
[8] His feet thrust him into a net;
he wanders into its mesh.
[9] A trap seizes him by the heel;
a snare holds him fast.
[10] A noose is hidden for him on the ground;
a trap lies in his path.
[11] Terrors startle him on every side
and dog his every step.

[12] Calamity is hungry for him;
disaster is ready for him when he falls.
[13] It eats away parts of his skin;
death's firstborn devours his limbs.
[14] He is torn from the security of his tent
and marched off to the king of terrors.
[15] Fire resides[a] in his tent;
burning sulfur is scattered over his dwelling.
[16] His roots dry up below
and his branches wither above.
[17] The memory of him perishes from the earth;
he has no name in the land.
[18] He is driven from light into the realm of darkness
and is banished from the world.
[19] He has no offspring or descendants among his people,
no survivor where once he lived.
[20] People of the west are appalled at his fate;
those of the east are seized with horror.
[21] Surely such is the dwelling of an evil man;
such is the place of one who does not know God."

Job

19 Then Job replied:

[2] "How long will you torment me
and crush me with words?
[3] Ten times now you have reproached me;
shamelessly you attack me.
[4] If it is true that I have gone astray,
my error remains my concern alone.
[5] If indeed you would exalt yourselves above me
and use my humiliation against me,
[6] then know that God has wronged me
and drawn his net around me.

[7] "Though I cry, 'Violence!' I get no response;
though I call for help, there is no justice.
[8] He has blocked my way so I cannot pass;
he has shrouded my paths in darkness.
[9] He has stripped me of my honor
and removed the crown from my head.
[10] He tears me down on every side till I am gone;
he uproots my hope like a tree.
[11] His anger burns against me;
he counts me among his enemies.
[12] His troops advance in force;
they build a siege ramp against me
and encamp around my tent.

[13] "He has alienated my family from me;
my acquaintances are completely estranged from me.
[14] My relatives have gone away;
my closest friends have forgotten me.
[15] My guests and my female servants count me a foreigner;
they look on me as on a stranger.
[16] I summon my servant, but he does not answer,
though I beg him with my own mouth.

---

[a] 15 Or *Nothing he had remains*

THE MYSTERY OF HUMAN SUFFERING

Job's friends were harsh toward Job. Bildad's speech can be summed up in five searing words: "You got what you deserved." Bildad, along with Job's other two friends, concluded that Job's suffering was evidence of sin in his life (Job 4:7 – 9; 8:1 – 19).

Job's friends' theology was not entirely incorrect, but their perspective was limited. They were right to think that Scripture, especially parts like Deuteronomy 27 and 28, teaches that the righteous person can expect God's blessing and the wicked can expect God's curse. Both Eliphaz (Job 15:27 – 35) and Zophar (Job 20:4 – 29) mentioned that sometimes the wicked will enjoy temporary prosperity as Job had. They believed that the wicked would be punished eventually, as the book of Proverbs teaches (Pr 1:17 – 19; 6:12 – 15). Their theology was an oversimplified combination of multiple truths: Bad things are going to happen to bad people, good things are going to happen to good people and everyone will get what they deserve in the end.

The problem with their theology was that it was too narrow in its scope — and therefore it was not flexible enough to accommodate real life experiences. The three friends made a mistake in how they applied abstract truths to real life experiences. They were right to believe that in the end God rewards the righteous and punishes the wicked. But Job's friends did not have God's perspective on the situation.

Good theology accounts for the complexities of Scripture and the huge range of life experiences. The truth is this: human suffering or happiness in this life is not proportional to people's sins or good works. Sometimes the wicked seem to get away with wrongs; sometimes the righteous experience terrible things that they do not deserve.

The author of Hebrews offered a reminder that God does good things in unexpected ways: "In bringing many sons and daughters to glory, it was fitting that God, for whom and through whom everything exists, should make the pioneer of their salvation perfect through what he suffered" (Heb 2:10). God used Jesus' sufferings to bring about the ultimate blessing. He is always at work in the suffering of his people. The exact manner in which God is working may remain a mystery for now. Yet, eternity will show that he was always good, he was always in control and he was always working to show his glory.

[17] My breath is offensive to my wife;
I am loathsome to my own family.
[18] Even the little boys scorn me;
when I appear, they ridicule me.
[19] All my intimate friends detest me;
those I love have turned against me.
[20] I am nothing but skin and bones;
I have escaped only by the skin of my teeth.[a]

[21] "Have pity on me, my friends, have pity,
for the hand of God has struck me.
[22] Why do you pursue me as God does?
Will you never get enough of my flesh?
[23] "Oh, that my words were recorded,
that they were written on a scroll,
[24] that they were inscribed with an iron tool on[b] lead,
or engraved in rock forever!
[25] I know that my redeemer[c] lives,
and that in the end he will stand on the earth.[d]
[26] And after my skin has been destroyed,
yet[e] in[f] my flesh I will see God;
[27] I myself will see him
with my own eyes—I, and not another.
How my heart yearns within me!

[28] "If you say, 'How we will hound him,
since the root of the trouble lies in him,[g]'
[29] you should fear the sword yourselves;
for wrath will bring punishment by the sword,
and then you will know that there is judgment.[h]"

JOB 20:3–9

WHEN THE WICKED THRIVE

Zophar attempted to sidestep Job's rebuke with a caustic reminder that evil people only thrive and succeed for a little while. His skewed perspective led him to the conclusion that Job's suffering was the natural consequence of a wicked life exposed at last. Jesus presented a contrasting view that reminds believers to keep an eternal perspective on reward and judgment (Mt 13:24–30). While Scripture assures that the wicked will receive a just punishment for their defiance and rejection of the Lord (Ps 145:20; Jn 3:36; Gal 6:7–8), often that verdict does not come until the end of this earthly life. God's judgment is not hasty, but he promises an eventual day when he will separate good from evil (Mt 25:31–46). While waiting for justice to be served, it is tempting to suppose that the abundance of the unrighteous person is a sign of God's lack of justice. In reality, the delay in judgment is an expression of God's abundant patience and grace, granting unbelievers more time to respond to the mercy and forgiveness extended to them through Jesus Christ (2Pe 3:9).

Zophar

20 Then Zophar the Naamathite replied:

[2] "My troubled thoughts prompt me to answer
because I am greatly disturbed.
[3] I hear a rebuke that dishonors me,
and my understanding inspires me to reply.

[4] "Surely you know how it has been from of old,
ever since mankind[i] was placed on the earth,
[5] that the mirth of the wicked is brief,
the joy of the godless lasts but a moment.
[6] Though the pride of the godless person reaches to the heavens
and his head touches the clouds,
[7] he will perish forever, like his own dung;
those who have seen him will say, 'Where is he?'
[8] Like a dream he flies away, no more to be found,
banished like a vision of the night.
[9] The eye that saw him will not see him again;
his place will look on him no more.
[10] His children must make amends to the poor;
his own hands must give back his wealth.

[a] 20 Or *only by my gums* [b] 24 Or *and* [c] 25 Or *vindicator* [d] 25 Or *on my grave* [e] 26 Or *And after I awake, / though this body has been destroyed, / then* [f] 26 Or *destroyed, / apart from* [g] 28 Many Hebrew manuscripts, Septuagint and Vulgate; most Hebrew manuscripts *me* [h] 29 Or *sword, / that you may come to know the Almighty* [i] 4 Or *Adam*

MY REDEEMER LIVES

Job's belief in God is amazing. Even more striking is how God allowed Job to get to the place where he could trust in God, even though his circumstances looked hopeless. God delivered Job not *from* his sufferings, but *through* his sufferings. In the midst of battling his ignorant friends, something clicked. Through his resistance against bad advice from friends and through his persistent battle for belief, a new insight emerged. Job was able to confess and believe that God was with him.

When faced with intense pain, God's people may not learn "why" as much as they come to know "Who." Job never received answers to all of his questions. What he really needed to learn was that God is the "Who" he could depend on. In life there is so much that happens that cannot be explained. In the midst of life's uncertainties, God knows what people need (La 3:55 – 57). Jesus is holding on to his people, and this relationship allows them to endure to the end (Jn 10:28).

God was not risking Job's faith; God was refining his faith. Only when everything is stripped away can a person evaluate what truly matters. After suffering unimaginable loss, Job was able to confess, "After my skin has been destroyed, yet in my flesh I will see God; I myself will see him with my own eyes — I, and not another. How my heart yearns within me!" (Job 19:26 – 27). Oftentimes God's people do not learn that God is all they need until God is all they have.

Without God, this life and the eternity that follows will be full of pain. But when someone trusts in Jesus Christ, God promises that all the sad things will one day be healed and redeemed: "We know that in all things God works for the good of those who love him, who have been called according to his purpose" (Ro 8:28).

Job's faith in the midst of the fight is a model for life. "Without faith it is impossible to please God, because anyone who comes to him must believe that he exists and that he rewards those who earnestly seek him" (Heb 11:6). When people put their faith in Jesus, they can have hope that the way things are in the world is not the way they will always be. Suffering and pain can be seen as temporary in light of eternity with Jesus!

11 The youthful vigor that fills his bones
will lie with him in the dust.

12 "Though evil is sweet in his mouth
and he hides it under his tongue,
13 though he cannot bear to let it go
and lets it linger in his mouth,
14 yet his food will turn sour in his stomach;
it will become the venom of serpents within him.
15 He will spit out the riches he swallowed;
God will make his stomach vomit them up.
16 He will suck the poison of serpents;
the fangs of an adder will kill him.
17 He will not enjoy the streams,
the rivers flowing with honey and cream.
18 What he toiled for he must give back uneaten;
he will not enjoy the profit from his trading.
19 For he has oppressed the poor and left them destitute;
he has seized houses he did not build.

20 "Surely he will have no respite from his craving;
he cannot save himself by his treasure.
21 Nothing is left for him to devour;
his prosperity will not endure.
22 In the midst of his plenty, distress will overtake him;
the full force of misery will come upon him.
23 When he has filled his belly,
God will vent his burning anger against him
and rain down his blows on him.
24 Though he flees from an iron weapon,
a bronze-tipped arrow pierces him.
25 He pulls it out of his back,
the gleaming point out of his liver.
Terrors will come over him;
26 total darkness lies in wait for his treasures.
A fire unfanned will consume him
and devour what is left in his tent.
27 The heavens will expose his guilt;
the earth will rise up against him.
28 A flood will carry off his house,
rushing waters[a] on the day of God's wrath.
29 Such is the fate God allots the wicked,
the heritage appointed for them by God."

Job

21 Then Job replied:

2 "Listen carefully to my words;
let this be the consolation you give me.
3 Bear with me while I speak,
and after I have spoken, mock on.

4 "Is my complaint directed to a human being?
Why should I not be impatient?
5 Look at me and be appalled;
clap your hand over your mouth.
6 When I think about this, I am terrified;
trembling seizes my body.

[a] 28 Or *The possessions in his house will be carried off, / washed away*

[7] Why do the wicked live on,
growing old and increasing in power?
[8] They see their children established around them,
their offspring before their eyes.
[9] Their homes are safe and free from fear;
the rod of God is not on them.
[10] Their bulls never fail to breed;
their cows calve and do not miscarry.
[11] They send forth their children as a flock;
their little ones dance about.
[12] They sing to the music of timbrel and lyre;
they make merry to the sound of the pipe.
[13] They spend their years in prosperity
and go down to the grave in peace.[a]
[14] Yet they say to God, 'Leave us alone!
We have no desire to know your ways.
[15] Who is the Almighty, that we should serve him?
What would we gain by praying to him?'
[16] But their prosperity is not in their own hands,
so I stand aloof from the plans of the wicked.

[17] "Yet how often is the lamp of the wicked snuffed out?
How often does calamity come upon them,
the fate God allots in his anger?
[18] How often are they like straw before the wind,
like chaff swept away by a gale?
[19] It is said, 'God stores up the punishment of the wicked for their children.'
Let him repay the wicked, so that they themselves will experience it!
[20] Let their own eyes see their destruction;
let them drink the cup of the wrath of the Almighty.
[21] For what do they care about the families they leave behind
when their allotted months come to an end?

[22] "Can anyone teach knowledge to God,
since he judges even the highest?
[23] One person dies in full vigor,
completely secure and at ease,
[24] well nourished in body,[b]
bones rich with marrow.
[25] Another dies in bitterness of soul,
never having enjoyed anything good.
[26] Side by side they lie in the dust,
and worms cover them both.

[27] "I know full well what you are thinking,
the schemes by which you would wrong me.
[28] You say, 'Where now is the house of the great,
the tents where the wicked lived?'
[29] Have you never questioned those who travel?
Have you paid no regard to their accounts—
[30] that the wicked are spared from the day of calamity,
that they are delivered from[c] the day of wrath?
[31] Who denounces their conduct to their face?
Who repays them for what they have done?
[32] They are carried to the grave,
and watch is kept over their tombs.

---

[a] 13 Or *in an instant* [b] 24 The meaning of the Hebrew for this word is uncertain.
[c] 30 Or *wicked are reserved for the day of calamity, / that they are brought forth to*

THE NARROW PATH

Job's response to his friends' foolish words and accusations was simple: the facts did not support their theology. The facts showed that many wicked people live a life that looks fairly comfortable. They seem not to suffer. They seem free from struggles. They actually seem to enjoy themselves. At the same time, many righteous people struggle in this world. They try to live for God, but life remains difficult. They give generously but experience seasons when they do not have as much as they need.

The theology of Job's friends broke under the weight of reality. The facts did not add up to their simplistic theological outlook. Many wicked people are not punished in this life, while many righteous people suffer from the cradle to the grave. It did not make sense to accuse Job of secret sin while so many other people who were clearly more wicked than Job did not suffer for their sins.

The world is unfair. Often, the righteous suffer and the wicked prosper. When people fail to realize this reality, they become rigid and uptight in every way. Their counsel sounds much like the words of "comfort" that Job received. They fail to grasp the harsh reality of life in a fallen world, accusing innocent people of harboring hidden sin.

Jesus' life and ministry revealed how mixed up the world is. Contrary to the way of the world, Jesus demonstrated that the heights of true glory can be found only in the depths of humility (Php 2:5 – 11). He taught that the way to attain a full and meaningful life is to give one's life over entirely to Christ and the gospel (Mk 8:34 – 38).

Many people reject the way of Jesus. Jesus contrasted the two ways people look at life by talking about a broad and a narrow path: "Enter through the narrow gate. For wide is the gate and broad is the road that leads to destruction, and many enter through it. But small is the gate and narrow the road that leads to life, and only a few find it" (Mt 7:13 – 14). Many people think that the meaning of life is found here and now. They desperately avoid all difficulties and focus entirely on getting as much pleasure or happiness as possible before they die. But there is another way — the way of Jesus. This world is not all there is. This life is only the prelude to a glorious, divine reality that will be fully revealed in eternity.

[33]The soil in the valley is sweet to them;
everyone follows after them,
and a countless throng goes[a] before them.

[34]"So how can you console me with your nonsense?
Nothing is left of your answers but falsehood!"

Eliphaz

22 Then Eliphaz the Temanite replied:

[2]"Can a man be of benefit to God?
Can even a wise person benefit him?
[3]What pleasure would it give the Almighty if you were righteous?
What would he gain if your ways were blameless?

[4]"Is it for your piety that he rebukes you
and brings charges against you?
[5]Is not your wickedness great?
Are not your sins endless?
[6]You demanded security from your relatives for no reason;
you stripped people of their clothing, leaving them naked.
[7]You gave no water to the weary
and you withheld food from the hungry,
[8]though you were a powerful man, owning land—
an honored man, living on it.
[9]And you sent widows away empty-handed
and broke the strength of the fatherless.
[10]That is why snares are all around you,
why sudden peril terrifies you,
[11]why it is so dark you cannot see,
and why a flood of water covers you.

[12]"Is not God in the heights of heaven?
And see how lofty are the highest stars!
[13]Yet you say, 'What does God know?
Does he judge through such darkness?
[14]Thick clouds veil him, so he does not see us
as he goes about in the vaulted heavens.'
[15]Will you keep to the old path
that the wicked have trod?
[16]They were carried off before their time,
their foundations washed away by a flood.
[17]They said to God, 'Leave us alone!
What can the Almighty do to us?'
[18]Yet it was he who filled their houses with good things,
so I stand aloof from the plans of the wicked.
[19]The righteous see their ruin and rejoice;
the innocent mock them, saying,
[20]'Surely our foes are destroyed,
and fire devours their wealth.'

[21]"Submit to God and be at peace with him;
in this way prosperity will come to you.
[22]Accept instruction from his mouth
and lay up his words in your heart.
[23]If you return to the Almighty, you will be restored:
If you remove wickedness far from your tent

[a] 33 Or *them, / as a countless throng went*

JOB 22:6–11

JUDGED FALSELY BY OTHERS

It is impossible to know everything. But that does not stop many people from entering into conversations or casting accusations as if they do. That is exactly what Eliphaz did to Job. Eliphaz assumed that Job was suffering because Job was wicked—even though Job was suffering because God was in a contest with Satan. The Bible teaches as a general principle that the righteous will always experience God's blessing and the wicked will always experience God's judgment—the life of Job proves that this principle does not always hold true within the limited context of earthly life. Eliphaz accused Job of acquiring his wealth through greed and exploitation of the poor. Yet God's own witness to Satan reveals to the reader that these charges were false (Job 1:8; 2:3). Eliphaz's accusations were baseless; his only proof for Job's alleged wickedness was Job's suffering (Job 22:10–11).

All of this is a great reminder that people should hesitate to cast accusations—they may not have all the pertinent facts. Eliphaz's approach to Job's innocent sufferings foreshadows the manner in which the Pharisees would look at Jesus' actions, even his miracles, and attribute them to Satan (Mt 12:22–28). On the surface, it looked like Eliphaz and the religious leaders could be right—but they did not know all the information. They judged, and they judged falsely. Jesus gave a warning that remains relevant today: "Do not judge, or you too will be judged" (Mt 7:1).

JOB 23:1–12

THE DEPTHS OF DESPAIR

Job was honest about his pain and frustration. He cried out to God from the depths of his heart. He felt abandoned, he felt like he did not have the answers to his questions, but he kept holding on to God. Even though God did not seem to be near to Job at all, Job still expressed an unshaken confidence in God. Job knew that God was refining him through this process. Gold must be heated to 1,063 degrees Celsius in order to melt. The impurities in the gold only come out when the gold melts down. Job trusted God when life was hard. He trusted that God was purifying him (v. 10).

Job's sufferings foreshadow the experience of Jesus on the cross as he cried out, "My God, my God, why have you forsaken me?" (Mt 27:46). Job's sufferings were terrible, but they do not compare to the depth of agony that Jesus experienced on the cross as he died for us. God's best for the world is not going around pain and suffering, but through it. Job went through these unthinkable circumstances in order to be refined. Jesus went through the ordeal of the cross in order to create the only way to God.

JOB 24:1

WHEN GOD IS SILENT

Sometimes God's people feel he is nowhere to be found in their moments of greatest need. Jesus' own disciples felt this way while they were

(continued on next page)

24 and assign your nuggets to the dust,
your gold of Ophir to the rocks in the ravines,
25 then the Almighty will be your gold,
the choicest silver for you.
26 Surely then you will find delight in the Almighty
and will lift up your face to God.
27 You will pray to him, and he will hear you,
and you will fulfill your vows.
28 What you decide on will be done,
and light will shine on your ways.
29 When people are brought low and you say, 'Lift them up!'
then he will save the downcast.
30 He will deliver even one who is not innocent,
who will be delivered through the cleanness of your hands."

Job

23 Then Job replied:

2 "Even today my complaint is bitter;
his hand[a] is heavy in spite of[b] my groaning.
3 If only I knew where to find him;
if only I could go to his dwelling!
4 I would state my case before him
and fill my mouth with arguments.
5 I would find out what he would answer me,
and consider what he would say to me.
6 Would he vigorously oppose me?
No, he would not press charges against me.
7 There the upright can establish their innocence before him,
and there I would be delivered forever from my judge.

8 "But if I go to the east, he is not there;
if I go to the west, I do not find him.
9 When he is at work in the north, I do not see him;
when he turns to the south, I catch no glimpse of him.
10 But he knows the way that I take;
when he has tested me, I will come forth as gold.
11 My feet have closely followed his steps;
I have kept to his way without turning aside.
12 I have not departed from the commands of his lips;
I have treasured the words of his mouth more than my daily bread.

13 "But he stands alone, and who can oppose him?
He does whatever he pleases.
14 He carries out his decree against me,
and many such plans he still has in store.
15 That is why I am terrified before him;
when I think of all this, I fear him.
16 God has made my heart faint;
the Almighty has terrified me.
17 Yet I am not silenced by the darkness,
by the thick darkness that covers my face.

24 "Why does the Almighty not set times for judgment?
Why must those who know him look in vain for such days?
2 There are those who move boundary stones;
they pasture flocks they have stolen.

[a] 2 Septuagint and Syriac; Hebrew / *the hand on me* [b] 2 Or *heavy on me in*

[3] They drive away the orphan's donkey
and take the widow's ox in pledge.
[4] They thrust the needy from the path
and force all the poor of the land into hiding.
[5] Like wild donkeys in the desert,
the poor go about their labor of foraging food;
the wasteland provides food for their children.
[6] They gather fodder in the fields
and glean in the vineyards of the wicked.
[7] Lacking clothes, they spend the night naked;
they have nothing to cover themselves in the cold.
[8] They are drenched by mountain rains
and hug the rocks for lack of shelter.
[9] The fatherless child is snatched from the breast;
the infant of the poor is seized for a debt.
[10] Lacking clothes, they go about naked;
they carry the sheaves, but still go hungry.
[11] They crush olives among the terraces[a];
they tread the winepresses, yet suffer thirst.
[12] The groans of the dying rise from the city,
and the souls of the wounded cry out for help.
But God charges no one with wrongdoing.

[13] "There are those who rebel against the light,
who do not know its ways
or stay in its paths.
[14] When daylight is gone, the murderer rises up,
kills the poor and needy,
and in the night steals forth like a thief.
[15] The eye of the adulterer watches for dusk;
he thinks, 'No eye will see me,'
and he keeps his face concealed.
[16] In the dark, thieves break into houses,
but by day they shut themselves in;
they want nothing to do with the light.
[17] For all of them, midnight is their morning;
they make friends with the terrors of darkness.

[18] "Yet they are foam on the surface of the water;
their portion of the land is cursed,
so that no one goes to the vineyards.
[19] As heat and drought snatch away the melted snow,
so the grave snatches away those who have sinned.
[20] The womb forgets them,
the worm feasts on them;
the wicked are no longer remembered
but are broken like a tree.
[21] They prey on the barren and childless woman,
and to the widow they show no kindness.
[22] But God drags away the mighty by his power;
though they become established, they have no assurance of life.
[23] He may let them rest in a feeling of security,
but his eyes are on their ways.
[24] For a little while they are exalted, and then they are gone;
they are brought low and gathered up like all others;
they are cut off like heads of grain.

[a] 11 The meaning of the Hebrew for this word is uncertain.

(When God Is Silent, continued)

with him. In the midst of a terrible storm, they woke Jesus with the complaint, "Teacher, don't you care if we drown?" (Mk 4:38). Job felt this way, too. In the darkest times, no amount of human companionship is sufficient. The soul was made for God, and humans need divine revelation more than philosophical arguments when facing suffering. God has a plan for the good of his people, even though they cannot always see or understand how it is all coming together.

At the heart of God's plan is Jesus—Jesus is how people come to know God and how everything can be made right. Jesus took the worst of humanity's sufferings upon himself. Job wished that someone would step in to mediate between himself and God (Job 9:33). Praise God that he has provided the best mediator for us: "For there is one God and one mediator between God and mankind, the man Christ Jesus, who gave himself as a ransom for all people. This has now been witnessed to at the proper time" (1Ti 2:5–6). God sent Jesus at the proper time to defeat sin and make humans right with God; God's people can trust his timing and his provision.

[25] "If this is not so, who can prove me false
and reduce my words to nothing?"

Bildad

25 Then Bildad the Shuhite replied:

[2] "Dominion and awe belong to God;
he establishes order in the heights of heaven.
[3] Can his forces be numbered?
On whom does his light not rise?
[4] How then can a mortal be righteous before God?
How can one born of woman be pure?
[5] If even the moon is not bright
and the stars are not pure in his eyes,
[6] how much less a mortal, who is but a maggot—
a human being, who is only a worm!"

Job

26 Then Job replied:

[2] "How you have helped the powerless!
How you have saved the arm that is feeble!
[3] What advice you have offered to one without wisdom!
And what great insight you have displayed!
[4] Who has helped you utter these words?
And whose spirit spoke from your mouth?

[5] "The dead are in deep anguish,
those beneath the waters and all that live in them.
[6] The realm of the dead is naked before God;
Destruction[a] lies uncovered.
[7] He spreads out the northern skies over empty space;
he suspends the earth over nothing.
[8] He wraps up the waters in his clouds,
yet the clouds do not burst under their weight.
[9] He covers the face of the full moon,
spreading his clouds over it.
[10] He marks out the horizon on the face of the waters
for a boundary between light and darkness.
[11] The pillars of the heavens quake,
aghast at his rebuke.
[12] By his power he churned up the sea;
by his wisdom he cut Rahab to pieces.
[13] By his breath the skies became fair;
his hand pierced the gliding serpent.
[14] And these are but the outer fringe of his works;
how faint the whisper we hear of him!
Who then can understand the thunder of his power?"

Job's Final Word to His Friends

27 And Job continued his discourse:

[2] "As surely as God lives, who has denied me justice,
the Almighty, who has made my life bitter,
[3] as long as I have life within me,
the breath of God in my nostrils,

[a] 6 Hebrew *Abaddon*

JOB 26:7

A NEW EARTH

Job's universe seemed broken beyond repair, and he must have longed for a fresh start, a complete fix or even an all-new earth. The longing for a new earth is actually a good longing to have, and a longing that all followers of Jesus should experience. God created the earth (Ac 14:15), but the earth has been cursed because of humanity's rebellion, beginning with Adam and Eve's sin in the Garden of Eden. Jesus died to reconcile not only people, but the very world back to himself (Col 1:20). Followers of Jesus have now been given the ministry of spreading that reconciliation (2Co 5:11–21). God's people are his ambassadors on this earth, and God is making his appeal through them for the world to be reconciled with the Creator. Christians personally participate by fighting sin, pursuing holiness, doing their jobs in a distinctly Christian way, and most importantly, telling people the good news about what God has done. A day is coming when the new heavens and new earth will descend from heaven and God will live with his people forever (Rev 21:1–5). Life is not about going "up" to heaven as much as it is about heaven coming "down" to earth. Jesus already came as a glimpse of what it will be like when his people live with him forever.

THE QUESTION OF RIGHTEOUSNESS

One of Job's friends, Bildad, asked a penetrating question: "How then can a mortal be righteous before God?" (Job 25:4). This vital question operates at several levels, cutting to the heart of the human condition and pointing to the great hope God's people have in Christ.

The question also looks for a solution. Here, Job's friend simply wondered whether righteousness before God was a possibility. From cover to cover, the Bible is absolutely clear that no human being can ever be righteous before God on his or her own. But in Christ, it is possible for sinful people to be made right with God.

The question reveals the complex relationship between sin and suffering. Bildad was clinging to the false idea that Job was suffering because he had unconfessed sin in his life. Job was not sinless, but he was forgiven. He confessed his sins (Job 7:21) and made the sacrifices God demanded (Job 1:5) — and those sacrifices pointed to the ultimate sacrifice of Jesus on the cross.

Lastly, the question highlights a common misunderstanding. No one is righteous before God; this is certain. But Bildad inferred that human beings cannot be righteous because they are the equivalent of a "maggot" or "worm" — and this is entirely misleading (Job 25:6). God never belittles humans like this. God sees people as creatures of worth and value, made in his image and precious enough to send Jesus to die for — even when they are in the depths of sin and rebellion.

Righteousness cannot be attained, but it can be received. Jesus pointed out that it is a mistake to try to justify oneself before God like the Pharisees (Mt 5:20). Only God is righteous (Ps 119:142; cf. Ro 3:10). For humans to be righteous, they need God to give his righteousness to them. This is why people need Jesus! Jesus' perfect life made his sacrificial death a means of righteousness for those who respond to him in faith (Ro 1:17).

All throughout Scripture, righteousness before God is found in trusting God's promises — that is what it means to have faith. This pattern is seen with Abraham, who believed God and it was credited to him as righteousness (Ge 15:6; cf. Ro 4:3). The only way for a person to be right before God is for God to give that person right standing based on Jesus' perfection. What Abraham believed, Jesus accomplished.

JOB 27:6

RIGHTEOUSNESS

Job's three friends were convinced that Job's sufferings were the result of some sin he must have committed. They were wrong. God was not punishing Job — instead, God was displaying his glory to Satan and the entire world by sustaining Job's faith in the midst of suffering. Yet, through the process of enduring suffering, Job was tempted to sin; he was tempted to justify himself (Job 32:2). It seems that Job revealed some pride and self-righteousness. Righteousness means being right with God. Righteousness is not something people can earn or claim for themselves; it is a title and name that God grants through his grace. Deep down inside, Job knew that his trial was not the result of some specific sin he committed. But he could easily drift into the thinking that he had no sin at all — and that would be a terrible mistake.

The Bible is clear that Jesus is the only person who ever lived who can claim a perfect life (Heb 4:15). Jesus is the standard, and from God's perspective, everyone has fallen short of the standard (Ro 3:9 – 18). Becoming right with God is never based on what people do, or how good or kind they are or how they compare with others. Becoming righteous begins by agreeing with God in his assessment of humanity's sinful nature and looking to the only perfect person, Jesus Christ, to be the perfect One on behalf of sinful humanity. Jesus' righteousness is credited to his people when they call upon him in faith (1Co 1:30).

4 my lips will not say anything wicked,
and my tongue will not utter lies.
5 I will never admit you are in the right;
till I die, I will not deny my integrity.
6 I will maintain my innocence and never let go of it;
my conscience will not reproach me as long as I live.

7 "May my enemy be like the wicked,
my adversary like the unjust!
8 For what hope have the godless when they are cut off,
when God takes away their life?
9 Does God listen to their cry
when distress comes upon them?
10 Will they find delight in the Almighty?
Will they call on God at all times?

11 "I will teach you about the power of God;
the ways of the Almighty I will not conceal.
12 You have all seen this yourselves.
Why then this meaningless talk?

13 "Here is the fate God allots to the wicked,
the heritage a ruthless man receives from the Almighty:
14 However many his children, their fate is the sword;
his offspring will never have enough to eat.
15 The plague will bury those who survive him,
and their widows will not weep for them.
16 Though he heaps up silver like dust
and clothes like piles of clay,
17 what he lays up the righteous will wear,
and the innocent will divide his silver.
18 The house he builds is like a moth's cocoon,
like a hut made by a watchman.
19 He lies down wealthy, but will do so no more;
when he opens his eyes, all is gone.
20 Terrors overtake him like a flood;
a tempest snatches him away in the night.
21 The east wind carries him off, and he is gone;
it sweeps him out of his place.
22 It hurls itself against him without mercy
as he flees headlong from its power.
23 It claps its hands in derision
and hisses him out of his place."

Interlude: Where Wisdom Is Found

28 There is a mine for silver
and a place where gold is refined.
2 Iron is taken from the earth,
and copper is smelted from ore.
3 Mortals put an end to the darkness;
they search out the farthest recesses
for ore in the blackest darkness.
4 Far from human dwellings they cut a shaft,
in places untouched by human feet;
far from other people they dangle and sway.
5 The earth, from which food comes,
is transformed below as by fire;
6 lapis lazuli comes from its rocks,
and its dust contains nuggets of gold.

[7] No bird of prey knows that hidden path,
no falcon's eye has seen it.
[8] Proud beasts do not set foot on it,
and no lion prowls there.
[9] People assault the flinty rock with their hands
and lay bare the roots of the mountains.
[10] They tunnel through the rock;
their eyes see all its treasures.
[11] They search[a] the sources of the rivers
and bring hidden things to light.

[12] But where can wisdom be found?
Where does understanding dwell?
[13] No mortal comprehends its worth;
it cannot be found in the land of the living.
[14] The deep says, "It is not in me";
the sea says, "It is not with me."
[15] It cannot be bought with the finest gold,
nor can its price be weighed out in silver.
[16] It cannot be bought with the gold of Ophir,
with precious onyx or lapis lazuli.
[17] Neither gold nor crystal can compare with it,
nor can it be had for jewels of gold.
[18] Coral and jasper are not worthy of mention;
the price of wisdom is beyond rubies.
[19] The topaz of Cush cannot compare with it;
it cannot be bought with pure gold.

[20] Where then does wisdom come from?
Where does understanding dwell?
[21] It is hidden from the eyes of every living thing,
concealed even from the birds in the sky.
[22] Destruction[b] and Death say,
"Only a rumor of it has reached our ears."
[23] God understands the way to it
and he alone knows where it dwells,
[24] for he views the ends of the earth
and sees everything under the heavens.
[25] When he established the force of the wind
and measured out the waters,
[26] when he made a decree for the rain
and a path for the thunderstorm,
[27] then he looked at wisdom and appraised it;
he confirmed it and tested it.
[28] And he said to the human race,
"The fear of the Lord—that is wisdom,
and to shun evil is understanding."

Job's Final Defense

29 Job continued his discourse:

[2] "How I long for the months gone by,
for the days when God watched over me,
[3] when his lamp shone on my head
and by his light I walked through darkness!
[4] Oh, for the days when I was in my prime,
when God's intimate friendship blessed my house,

[a] *11* Septuagint, Aquila and Vulgate; Hebrew *They dam up* [b] *22* Hebrew *Abaddon*

JOB 28:1–28

TRUE WISDOM

The search for wisdom is like a search for hidden treasure. Job 28, a poetic interlude in the book, compares the one who searches for wisdom to a miner searching for something valuable that is buried and hidden in the dark. People will take great risks, brave great depths and heights, and push back darkness in order to find treasure; the search for wisdom is no less strenuous. Simply put, wisdom is knowing and doing the will of God—which is a hard thing to do in the midst of suffering. The book of Proverbs is all about wisdom, and it begins with a thesis statement of sorts about wisdom: "The fear of the LORD is the beginning of knowledge, but fools despise wisdom and instruction" (Pr 1:7).

All people fit into one of two categories: those who pursue wisdom, and those who despise wisdom. Jesus taught that true wisdom was to obey his words (Mt 7:24). Jesus also thanked his Father for hiding spiritual truths from people who were wise in their own eyes (Mt 11:25). Wisdom is about seeing that this world does not get it right all the time. Sometimes bad things happen to people who do not deserve it. Sometimes the wicked thrive while the righteous struggle. Wisdom teaches that the way up to glory is to go low in humility; the way to save one's life is to lose it following Jesus. Jesus came to turn the values of the world upside down, through divine wisdom.

[5] when the Almighty was still with me
and my children were around me,
[6] when my path was drenched with cream
and the rock poured out for me streams of olive oil.

[7] "When I went to the gate of the city
and took my seat in the public square,
[8] the young men saw me and stepped aside
and the old men rose to their feet;
[9] the chief men refrained from speaking
and covered their mouths with their hands;
[10] the voices of the nobles were hushed,
and their tongues stuck to the roof of their mouths.
[11] Whoever heard me spoke well of me,
and those who saw me commended me,
[12] because I rescued the poor who cried for help,
and the fatherless who had none to assist them.
[13] The one who was dying blessed me;
I made the widow's heart sing.
[14] I put on righteousness as my clothing;
justice was my robe and my turban.
[15] I was eyes to the blind
and feet to the lame.
[16] I was a father to the needy;
I took up the case of the stranger.
[17] I broke the fangs of the wicked
and snatched the victims from their teeth.

[18] "I thought, 'I will die in my own house,
my days as numerous as the grains of sand.
[19] My roots will reach to the water,
and the dew will lie all night on my branches.
[20] My glory will not fade;
the bow will be ever new in my hand.'

[21] "People listened to me expectantly,
waiting in silence for my counsel.
[22] After I had spoken, they spoke no more;
my words fell gently on their ears.
[23] They waited for me as for showers
and drank in my words as the spring rain.
[24] When I smiled at them, they scarcely believed it;
the light of my face was precious to them.[a]
[25] I chose the way for them and sat as their chief;
I dwelt as a king among his troops;
I was like one who comforts mourners.

30 "But now they mock me,
men younger than I,
whose fathers I would have disdained
to put with my sheep dogs.
[2] Of what use was the strength of their hands to me,
since their vigor had gone from them?
[3] Haggard from want and hunger,
they roamed[b] the parched land
in desolate wastelands at night.
[4] In the brush they gathered salt herbs,
and their food[c] was the root of the broom bush.

JOB 30:1–31

DAYS OF SUFFERING

Affliction is a terrible thing—just ask Job. The word carries nuances of misery and poverty. It contains the idea of being trapped under a heavy burden. It means suffering. The Bible teaches that God cares about our afflictions. He hears the cries of his people (Ex 2:23–25). The notion of affliction in the Old Testament appears again in the New Testament: Peter tells the suffering Christian, "Cast all your anxiety on him because he cares for you" (1Pe 5:7). The God who controls the universe is the God who cares for you—that is a real comfort. Since he controls all things, we can be assured that he is working in every situation to bring about what is good for his people (Ro 8:28). This is true in our stories, and it is true for Job as well.

Jesus encouraged people to give him their burdens and receive the blessing of being his followers; in doing this, they would find that his burdens were completely different than the afflictions and suffering they carried (Mt 11:28–30). The apostle Paul, who knew suffering all too well, was able to conclude, "That is why, for Christ's sake, I delight in weaknesses, in insults, in hardships, in persecutions, in difficulties. For when I am weak, then I am strong" (2Co 12:10; see also Ro 12:12).

[a] *24* The meaning of the Hebrew for this clause is uncertain. [b] *3* Or *gnawed* [c] *4* Or *fuel*

LONGING FOR FORMER GLORY

The Christian life contains mountains and valleys. There are moments when the experience of God feels so high, real and tangible. Then there are moments in which God feels distant and far away. Expecting only mountaintop experiences with God reveals a misunderstanding of the Christian life. The God who people worship on the mountain is the same one who walks with them through the valleys (Ps 23:4).

Job found himself in a low valley. A death valley. God seemed so far away. The times that he had spent on the mountain with God seemed like another lifetime. Job longed for past glory, a time when he had experienced good things. He was tired of his present condition and simply wanted to move on. He was heartbroken as he remembered how good his life had been.

God's people can always trust that he is with them. God has promised never to leave or forsake his people (Heb 13:5). When Jesus' followers find themselves at a low point in their journey with God, they need not lose heart. God is with them on the mountains and in the valleys.

Job's longing for the past foreshadows Jesus' prayer to the Father the night before he was betrayed and killed. Jesus expressed his longing for the glory he had experienced in eternity (Jn 17:5). Jesus found himself in a valley lower than Job's. Jesus had known a glory that was much greater than Job's. His heart truly broke as he faced suffering. But Jesus died to make the glory of eternity past into the future hope of everyone who would trust him in faith.

Philippians 2:5 – 11 teaches that Jesus had true glory with God. The Son was sent by the Father to come down off the mountain of glory and to suffer in the valley. God's way of bringing Jesus out of the valley was not *around* suffering, but *through* suffering. God sent Jesus up the hill of Golgotha where Jesus experienced the ultimate loss — loss of the love of his Father. In that moment, God made Jesus to be sin so that his people could become the righteousness of God (2Co 5:21). Jesus endured all this for his glory and for the good of his people. Remembering Christ in the low valleys of life provides sustenance and comfort for the journey back up the mountain.

5 They were banished from human society,
shouted at as if they were thieves.
6 They were forced to live in the dry stream beds,
among the rocks and in holes in the ground.
7 They brayed among the bushes
and huddled in the undergrowth.
8 A base and nameless brood,
they were driven out of the land.

9 "And now those young men mock me in song;
I have become a byword among them.
10 They detest me and keep their distance;
they do not hesitate to spit in my face.
11 Now that God has unstrung my bow and afflicted me,
they throw off restraint in my presence.
12 On my right the tribe[a] attacks;
they lay snares for my feet,
they build their siege ramps against me.
13 They break up my road;
they succeed in destroying me.
'No one can help him,' they say.
14 They advance as through a gaping breach;
amid the ruins they come rolling in.
15 Terrors overwhelm me;
my dignity is driven away as by the wind,
my safety vanishes like a cloud.

16 "And now my life ebbs away;
days of suffering grip me.
17 Night pierces my bones;
my gnawing pains never rest.
18 In his great power God becomes like clothing to me[b];
he binds me like the neck of my garment.
19 He throws me into the mud,
and I am reduced to dust and ashes.

20 "I cry out to you, God, but you do not answer;
I stand up, but you merely look at me.
21 You turn on me ruthlessly;
with the might of your hand you attack me.
22 You snatch me up and drive me before the wind;
you toss me about in the storm.
23 I know you will bring me down to death,
to the place appointed for all the living.

24 "Surely no one lays a hand on a broken man
when he cries for help in his distress.
25 Have I not wept for those in trouble?
Has not my soul grieved for the poor?
26 Yet when I hoped for good, evil came;
when I looked for light, then came darkness.
27 The churning inside me never stops;
days of suffering confront me.
28 I go about blackened, but not by the sun;
I stand up in the assembly and cry for help.
29 I have become a brother of jackals,
a companion of owls.

---

[a] *12* The meaning of the Hebrew for this word is uncertain. [b] *18* Hebrew; Septuagint *power he grasps my clothing*

30 My skin grows black and peels;
my body burns with fever.
31 My lyre is tuned to mourning,
and my pipe to the sound of wailing.

31 "I made a covenant with my eyes
not to look lustfully at a young woman.
2 For what is our lot from God above,
our heritage from the Almighty on high?
3 Is it not ruin for the wicked,
disaster for those who do wrong?
4 Does he not see my ways
and count my every step?

5 "If I have walked with falsehood
or my foot has hurried after deceit—
6 let God weigh me in honest scales
and he will know that I am blameless—
7 if my steps have turned from the path,
if my heart has been led by my eyes,
or if my hands have been defiled,
8 then may others eat what I have sown,
and may my crops be uprooted.

9 "If my heart has been enticed by a woman,
or if I have lurked at my neighbor's door,
10 then may my wife grind another man's grain,
and may other men sleep with her.
11 For that would have been wicked,
a sin to be judged.
12 It is a fire that burns to Destruction[a];
it would have uprooted my harvest.

13 "If I have denied justice to any of my servants,
whether male or female,
when they had a grievance against me,
14 what will I do when God confronts me?
What will I answer when called to account?
15 Did not he who made me in the womb make them?
Did not the same one form us both within our
mothers?

16 "If I have denied the desires of the poor
or let the eyes of the widow grow weary,
17 if I have kept my bread to myself,
not sharing it with the fatherless—
18 but from my youth I reared them as a father would,
and from my birth I guided the widow—
19 if I have seen anyone perishing for lack of clothing,
or the needy without garments,
20 and their hearts did not bless me
for warming them with the fleece from my sheep,
21 if I have raised my hand against the fatherless,
knowing that I had influence in court,
22 then let my arm fall from the shoulder,
let it be broken off at the joint.
23 For I dreaded destruction from God,
and for fear of his splendor I could not do such things.

[a] 12 Hebrew *Abaddon*

JOB 31:1–8

THE HEART BEHIND THE ACTION

Job believed that he was innocent. Innocent is a strong word because it means sinless. Yet the Bible is clear that no mere human is sinless: "Indeed, there is no one on earth who is righteous, no one who does what is right and never sins" (Ecc 7:20). Job claimed not only that he had done the right things, but that he had acted from a right heart. The heart functions like the throne of our lives—whatever lives and rules in the heart will eventually reign in our lives. Jesus said, "A good man brings good things out of the good stored up in his heart, and an evil man brings evil things out of the evil stored up in his heart. For the mouth speaks what the heart is full of" (Lk 6:45).

Amazingly, Job responded by focusing on the outward actions and the inward motivations he had in his heart (Job 31:5–8). Jesus would come along and highlight the important connection between actions and heart motives in the Sermon on the Mount (Mt 5–7). Yet, it is impossible for people to justify themselves completely before God. Isaiah teaches that all people are ultimately unclean; their best works are like filthy rags (Isa 64:6). By the conclusion of the book, Job saw and understood his helpless state before a sovereign God and repented in dust and ashes (Job 42:6).

24 "If I have put my trust in gold
or said to pure gold, 'You are my security,'
25 if I have rejoiced over my great wealth,
the fortune my hands had gained,
26 if I have regarded the sun in its radiance
or the moon moving in splendor,
27 so that my heart was secretly enticed
and my hand offered them a kiss of homage,
28 then these also would be sins to be judged,
for I would have been unfaithful to God on high.

29 "If I have rejoiced at my enemy's misfortune
or gloated over the trouble that came to him—
30 I have not allowed my mouth to sin
by invoking a curse against their life—
31 if those of my household have never said,
'Who has not been filled with Job's meat?'—
32 but no stranger had to spend the night in the street,
for my door was always open to the traveler—
33 if I have concealed my sin as people do,[a]
by hiding my guilt in my heart
34 because I so feared the crowd
and so dreaded the contempt of the clans
that I kept silent and would not go outside—

35 ("Oh, that I had someone to hear me!
I sign now my defense—let the Almighty answer me;
let my accuser put his indictment in writing.
36 Surely I would wear it on my shoulder,
I would put it on like a crown.
37 I would give him an account of my every step;
I would present it to him as to a ruler.)—

38 "if my land cries out against me
and all its furrows are wet with tears,
39 if I have devoured its yield without payment
or broken the spirit of its tenants,
40 then let briers come up instead of wheat
and stinkweed instead of barley."

The words of Job are ended.

Elihu

32 So these three men stopped answering Job, because he was righteous in
his own eyes. 2 But Elihu son of Barakel the Buzite, of the family of Ram,
became very angry with Job for justifying himself rather than God. 3 He was also
angry with the three friends, because they had found no way to refute Job, and
yet had condemned him.[b] 4 Now Elihu had waited before speaking to Job because they were older than he. 5 But when he saw that the three men had nothing
more to say, his anger was aroused.

6 So Elihu son of Barakel the Buzite said:

"I am young in years,
and you are old;
that is why I was fearful,
not daring to tell you what I know.
7 I thought, 'Age should speak;
advanced years should teach wisdom.'

[a] 33 Or *as Adam did* [b] 3 Masoretic Text; an ancient Hebrew scribal tradition *Job, and so had condemned God*

JOB 32:2

JUSTIFICATION

Self-justification. The theme is faint but present nonetheless in Job's reasoning in the previous chapters. Clearly, God did not allow these things to happen to Job because Job was proud. Instead, God allowed these things to happen in order to bring transformation to Job's life. God wanted Job. In Job's suffering, God proved himself to be extremely kind. It is a kind God who causes a cold to fall upon a person in order to get the person to a doctor—a doctor who then discovers a hidden cancer in time to cure it. In a similar sense, God was good to allow Job's suffering, which exposed that hint of dangerous pride in order to deal with it. Job was more righteous than most of the people of his day were, but he was still far below God's standard of righteousness. God does not save people because they are good, but in order to make them good. Salvation comes before good works. Consider what God said to his people after the exodus: "I am the LORD, who brought you up out of Egypt to be your God; therefore be holy, because I am holy" (Lev 11:45). No matter how "good" people can be, they still fall short of God's standard of holiness and remain in need of a Savior.

8 But it is the spirit[a] in a person,
the breath of the Almighty, that gives them understanding.
9 It is not only the old[b] who are wise,
not only the aged who understand what is right.

10 "Therefore I say: Listen to me;
I too will tell you what I know.
11 I waited while you spoke,
I listened to your reasoning;
while you were searching for words,
12 I gave you my full attention.
But not one of you has proved Job wrong;
none of you has answered his arguments.
13 Do not say, 'We have found wisdom;
let God, not a man, refute him.'
14 But Job has not marshaled his words against me,
and I will not answer him with your arguments.

15 "They are dismayed and have no more to say;
words have failed them.
16 Must I wait, now that they are silent,
now that they stand there with no reply?
17 I too will have my say;
I too will tell what I know.
18 For I am full of words,
and the spirit within me compels me;
19 inside I am like bottled-up wine,
like new wineskins ready to burst.
20 I must speak and find relief;
I must open my lips and reply.
21 I will show no partiality,
nor will I flatter anyone;
22 for if I were skilled in flattery,
my Maker would soon take me away.

33 "But now, Job, listen to my words;
pay attention to everything I say.
2 I am about to open my mouth;
my words are on the tip of my tongue.
3 My words come from an upright heart;
my lips sincerely speak what I know.
4 The Spirit of God has made me;
the breath of the Almighty gives me life.
5 Answer me then, if you can;
stand up and argue your case before me.
6 I am the same as you in God's sight;
I too am a piece of clay.
7 No fear of me should alarm you,
nor should my hand be heavy on you.

8 "But you have said in my hearing—
I heard the very words—
9 'I am pure, I have done no wrong;
I am clean and free from sin.
10 Yet God has found fault with me;
he considers me his enemy.
11 He fastens my feet in shackles;
he keeps close watch on all my paths.'

[a] 8 Or *Spirit*; also in verse 18 [b] 9 Or *many*; or *great*

12 "But I tell you, in this you are not right,
for God is greater than any mortal.
13 Why do you complain to him
that he responds to no one's words[a]?
14 For God does speak — now one way, now another —
though no one perceives it.
15 In a dream, in a vision of the night,
when deep sleep falls on people
as they slumber in their beds,
16 he may speak in their ears
and terrify them with warnings,
17 to turn them from wrongdoing
and keep them from pride,
18 to preserve them from the pit,
their lives from perishing by the sword.[b]

19 "Or someone may be chastened on a bed of pain
with constant distress in their bones,
20 so that their body finds food repulsive
and their soul loathes the choicest meal.
21 Their flesh wastes away to nothing,
and their bones, once hidden, now stick out.
22 They draw near to the pit,
and their life to the messengers of death.[c]
23 Yet if there is an angel at their side,
a messenger, one out of a thousand,
sent to tell them how to be upright,
24 and he is gracious to that person and says to God,
'Spare them from going down to the pit;
I have found a ransom for them —
25 let their flesh be renewed like a child's;
let them be restored as in the days of their youth' —
26 then that person can pray to God and find favor with him,
they will see God's face and shout for joy;
he will restore them to full well-being.
27 And they will go to others and say,
'I have sinned, I have perverted what is right,
but I did not get what I deserved.
28 God has delivered me from going down to the pit,
and I shall live to enjoy the light of life.'

29 "God does all these things to a person —
twice, even three times —
30 to turn them back from the pit,
that the light of life may shine on them.

31 "Pay attention, Job, and listen to me;
be silent, and I will speak.
32 If you have anything to say, answer me;
speak up, for I want to vindicate you.
33 But if not, then listen to me;
be silent, and I will teach you wisdom."

34 Then Elihu said:

2 "Hear my words, you wise men;
listen to me, you men of learning.

[a] 13 Or *that he does not answer for any of his actions* [b] 18 Or *from crossing the river*
[c] 22 Or *to the place of the dead*

TRICKED BY PRIDE?

Job's suffering was not due to his sin. The reader can understand the greater things that are at stake. Job was not being punished. Rather, Job's life was the battleground on which God's glory was being proven supreme against the threats of the enemy.

Even so, sinful attitudes in Job's heart were exposed through the trials he experienced. Elihu's words pierced right to the heart of the problem: Job had been acting as if he was God's equal. Job was wrong to think of God as a mere human who could be held accountable. Elihu later concluded that Job had become proud, even though he sat dejected in ashes (Job 36:8 – 9; 37:14 – 24). It is prideful to demand an audience with God to present one's own case: it implies that a mere human can judge whether God has been just (Job 35:2).

The consistent humility of Jesus stands in stark contrast to the pride of Job. Job presumed upon God's kindness and blessings. Jesus knew that all people ultimately deserved to suffer and that everything outside of hell was grace. Jesus was humble at all points in spite of the fact that he is God. Job grew proud and sought to question God even though he was sinful.

Grace is receiving something undeserved. God gives grace to help people in their many struggles. James, the half brother of Jesus, said it like this: "But he gives us more grace. That is why Scripture says: 'God opposes the proud but shows favor to the humble' " (Jas 4:6; cf. Pr 3:34). Pursuing a life of humility begins with a clear picture of God's glory. The humble realize their place is low in comparison to God's majesty. When God comes into focus, everything in their lives is seen for what it really is. Focusing on the glory of God is the only anchor that will keep a heart humble — and God loves the humble in heart. God loves the humble, the meek and the lowly so much that he promises they will inherit the earth (Mt 5:5).

JOB 34:5

BETTER THAN WHAT WE DESERVE

Job had overstated his case. Yes, Job was more righteous than his friends and many people of his day. Elihu, whose words serve as a transition between the speeches of the three friends and God's upcoming speech, was different than Job's three friends. He was young, yet wise. He was patient, yet passionate. And he was truthful, but caring. Elihu spoke with incredible wisdom about the situation. Job had claimed that he was innocent and had not done anything wrong, suggesting that God had denied him justice. People get this distorted view of God when they come to God for what they can get from God, instead of coming to God for God himself. Elihu explained that this kind of thinking is foolishness (34:31 – 37). God later confirmed that Job spoke without knowledge (38:2). It is dangerous to come to God seeking only the blessings he can give. During Jesus' ministry, his disciples sacrificed much to follow him. Yet Peter asked the question in Matthew 19:27, "We have left everything to follow you! What then will there be for us?" Jesus confirmed that his disciples would receive rewards upon his return, but Peter's question revealed questionable motives and a misunderstanding about the relationship between God and his people. That relationship, thankfully, is not based on a calculation of behaviors meriting rewards or punishments. Instead, God rewards his people for what Christ has done.

3 For the ear tests words
as the tongue tastes food.
4 Let us discern for ourselves what is right;
let us learn together what is good.

5 "Job says, 'I am innocent,
but God denies me justice.
6 Although I am right,
I am considered a liar;
although I am guiltless,
his arrow inflicts an incurable wound.'
7 Is there anyone like Job,
who drinks scorn like water?
8 He keeps company with evildoers;
he associates with the wicked.
9 For he says, 'There is no profit
in trying to please God.'

10 "So listen to me, you men of understanding.
Far be it from God to do evil,
from the Almighty to do wrong.
11 He repays everyone for what they have done;
he brings on them what their conduct deserves.
12 It is unthinkable that God would do wrong,
that the Almighty would pervert justice.
13 Who appointed him over the earth?
Who put him in charge of the whole world?
14 If it were his intention
and he withdrew his spirit[a] and breath,
15 all humanity would perish together
and mankind would return to the dust.

16 "If you have understanding, hear this;
listen to what I say.
17 Can someone who hates justice govern?
Will you condemn the just and mighty One?
18 Is he not the One who says to kings, 'You are worthless,'
and to nobles, 'You are wicked,'
19 who shows no partiality to princes
and does not favor the rich over the poor,
for they are all the work of his hands?
20 They die in an instant, in the middle of the night;
the people are shaken and they pass away;
the mighty are removed without human hand.

21 "His eyes are on the ways of mortals;
he sees their every step.
22 There is no deep shadow, no utter darkness,
where evildoers can hide.
23 God has no need to examine people further,
that they should come before him for judgment.
24 Without inquiry he shatters the mighty
and sets up others in their place.
25 Because he takes note of their deeds,
he overthrows them in the night and they are
crushed.
26 He punishes them for their wickedness
where everyone can see them,

[a] *14* Or *Spirit*

[27] because they turned from following him
and had no regard for any of his ways.
[28] They caused the cry of the poor to come before him,
so that he heard the cry of the needy.
[29] But if he remains silent, who can condemn him?
If he hides his face, who can see him?
Yet he is over individual and nation alike,
30 to keep the godless from ruling,
from laying snares for the people.

[31] "Suppose someone says to God,
'I am guilty but will offend no more.
[32] Teach me what I cannot see;
if I have done wrong, I will not do so again.'
[33] Should God then reward you on your terms,
when you refuse to repent?
You must decide, not I;
so tell me what you know.

[34] "Men of understanding declare,
wise men who hear me say to me,
[35] 'Job speaks without knowledge;
his words lack insight.'
[36] Oh, that Job might be tested to the utmost
for answering like a wicked man!
[37] To his sin he adds rebellion;
scornfully he claps his hands among us
and multiplies his words against God."

35 Then Elihu said:

[2] "Do you think this is just?
You say, 'I am in the right, not God.'
[3] Yet you ask him, 'What profit is it to me,[a]
and what do I gain by not sinning?'

[4] "I would like to reply to you
and to your friends with you.
[5] Look up at the heavens and see;
gaze at the clouds so high above you.
[6] If you sin, how does that affect him?
If your sins are many, what does that do to him?
[7] If you are righteous, what do you give to him,
or what does he receive from your hand?
[8] Your wickedness only affects humans like yourself,
and your righteousness only other people.

[9] "People cry out under a load of oppression;
they plead for relief from the arm of the powerful.
[10] But no one says, 'Where is God my Maker,
who gives songs in the night,
[11] who teaches us more than he teaches[b] the beasts of the earth
and makes us wiser than[c] the birds in the sky?'
[12] He does not answer when people cry out
because of the arrogance of the wicked.
[13] Indeed, God does not listen to their empty plea;
the Almighty pays no attention to it.

[a] 3 Or *you* [b] 10,11 Or *night,* / [11] *who teaches us by* [c] 11 Or *us wise by*

JOB 35:1–3

MISUNDERSTANDING GOD

Job's story is challenging to many who assume that God rewards those who live a righteous life by allowing them to avoid suffering. But that is not how God works. God does not treat his people on the basis of their own lives, but on the basis of the life that Jesus lived for them. God does not have to do this. He chooses to do this—that is why it is called grace. It is undeserved and unearned. God did not owe Job an explanation for anything that had taken place. Furthermore, God had not wronged Job in any way through all of this. And yet, Job asked to argue his case before God in court. Job misunderstood God because God was not under obligation to Job for anything. God does not need people, but he loves them. He is not in debt to people; they are in debt to him. Therefore, the foundational attitude of people in a relationship with God ought to be worship: knowing God and making him known through their lives.

Jesus drove home this point in his own life. In John 17:5, he prayed that God would glorify himself in all that Jesus did. Likewise, God's people should not serve God in order to attain a reward. Rather they should seek to please God with their lives because God is worthy of all honor. And those who devote their lives to God in this way discover that the very act of worshiping God is the greatest reward imaginable.

14 How much less, then, will he listen
when you say that you do not see him,
that your case is before him
and you must wait for him,
15 and further, that his anger never punishes
and he does not take the least notice of wickedness.[a]
16 So Job opens his mouth with empty talk;
without knowledge he multiplies words."

36

Elihu continued:

2 "Bear with me a little longer and I will show you
that there is more to be said in God's behalf.
3 I get my knowledge from afar;
I will ascribe justice to my Maker.
4 Be assured that my words are not false;
one who has perfect knowledge is with you.

5 "God is mighty, but despises no one;
he is mighty, and firm in his purpose.
6 He does not keep the wicked alive
but gives the afflicted their rights.
7 He does not take his eyes off the righteous;
he enthrones them with kings
and exalts them forever.
8 But if people are bound in chains,
held fast by cords of affliction,
9 he tells them what they have done—
that they have sinned arrogantly.
10 He makes them listen to correction
and commands them to repent of their evil.
11 If they obey and serve him,
they will spend the rest of their days in prosperity
and their years in contentment.
12 But if they do not listen,
they will perish by the sword[b]
and die without knowledge.

13 "The godless in heart harbor resentment;
even when he fetters them, they do not cry for help.
14 They die in their youth,
among male prostitutes of the shrines.
15 But those who suffer he delivers in their suffering;
he speaks to them in their affliction.

16 "He is wooing you from the jaws of distress
to a spacious place free from restriction,
to the comfort of your table laden with choice food.
17 But now you are laden with the judgment due the wicked;
judgment and justice have taken hold of you.
18 Be careful that no one entices you by riches;
do not let a large bribe turn you aside.
19 Would your wealth or even all your mighty efforts
sustain you so you would not be in distress?
20 Do not long for the night,
to drag people away from their homes.[c]

---

[a] *15* Symmachus, Theodotion and Vulgate; the meaning of the Hebrew for this word is uncertain. [b] *12* Or *will cross the river* [c] *20* The meaning of the Hebrew for verses 18-20 is uncertain.

21 Beware of turning to evil,
which you seem to prefer to affliction.

22 "God is exalted in his power.
Who is a teacher like him?
23 Who has prescribed his ways for him,
or said to him, 'You have done wrong'?
24 Remember to extol his work,
which people have praised in song.
25 All humanity has seen it;
mortals gaze on it from afar.
26 How great is God — beyond our understanding!
The number of his years is past finding out.

27 "He draws up the drops of water,
which distill as rain to the streams[a];
28 the clouds pour down their moisture
and abundant showers fall on mankind.
29 Who can understand how he spreads out the clouds,
how he thunders from his pavilion?
30 See how he scatters his lightning about him,
bathing the depths of the sea.
31 This is the way he governs[b] the nations
and provides food in abundance.
32 He fills his hands with lightning
and commands it to strike its mark.
33 His thunder announces the coming storm;
even the cattle make known its approach.[c]

37 "At this my heart pounds
and leaps from its place.
2 Listen! Listen to the roar of his voice,
to the rumbling that comes from his mouth.
3 He unleashes his lightning beneath the whole heaven
and sends it to the ends of the earth.
4 After that comes the sound of his roar;
he thunders with his majestic voice.
When his voice resounds,
he holds nothing back.
5 God's voice thunders in marvelous ways;
he does great things beyond our understanding.
6 He says to the snow, 'Fall on the earth,'
and to the rain shower, 'Be a mighty downpour.'
7 So that everyone he has made may know his work,
he stops all people from their labor.[d]
8 The animals take cover;
they remain in their dens.
9 The tempest comes out from its chamber,
the cold from the driving winds.
10 The breath of God produces ice,
and the broad waters become frozen.
11 He loads the clouds with moisture;
he scatters his lightning through them.
12 At his direction they swirl around
over the face of the whole earth
to do whatever he commands them.

[a] 27 Or *distill from the mist as rain* [b] 31 Or *nourishes* [c] 33 Or *announces his coming — / the One zealous against evil* [d] 7 Or *work, / he fills all people with fear by his power*

JOB 36:22 – 33

PROCLAIMING GOD'S MAJESTY

Warning labels are helpful — they communicate the right way to handle something that is powerful. Elihu gave Job a word of warning and caution. He told Job the right way to make sense of what had taken place. According to Elihu, God intended to teach Job something through his affliction. Rather than trying to correct the teacher, Job was to remember and magnify God as the maker of all things. God's best for Job did not mean going around a tough season of life, but going through it. God's ways are higher than humanity can understand. They cannot know all the reasons God has for doing what he does. God is majestic in all of his ways. He is holy, high above and so much wiser than humans. And yet, God has come near to people in Jesus. Jesus lived as an ordinary man, and yet with majesty (2Pe 1:16). God has thousands of reasons for doing what he does. If he acts in a way that seems unexplainable, it must be remembered that he is always acting for his glory and in a way that is consistent with his majestic character.

JOB 37:1 – 24

AWESOME GOD

Thinking about God should always lead to worship. God has revealed himself in his Word so that people may know him and worship him. Conversations about God should have the ultimate goal of pointing people to God and helping them love God. Elihu's speech ends with praise for

(continued on next page)

(Awesome God, continued)

God. Elihu points out that no human can control the weather, the storm or the lightning, but God does. God puts the sky in place and sets the clouds wherever he likes. No human can look into the sun without becoming blurry-eyed for a few minutes, but God's golden splendor is brighter than the sun. He is exalted. He is glorious. He has great power and many other attributes too numerous to name. He could rule over people as a tyrant with power and might, and yet, he chooses to rule with love.

Jesus left the people he encountered with a sense of awe as he exercised his authority humbly (Mt 9:8). His actions inspired people to praise God (Lk 5:26). He lived in such a way that people recognized him as a great prophet and helper sent by God (Lk 7:16). Jesus is majestic. He is the gift that can never be taken away and that leads to a life of worship that never ends. "Therefore, since we are receiving a kingdom that cannot be shaken, let us be thankful, and so worship God acceptably with reverence and awe" (Heb 12:28).

13 He brings the clouds to punish people,
or to water his earth and show his love.

14 "Listen to this, Job;
stop and consider God's wonders.
15 Do you know how God controls the clouds
and makes his lightning flash?
16 Do you know how the clouds hang poised,
those wonders of him who has perfect knowledge?
17 You who swelter in your clothes
when the land lies hushed under the south wind,
18 can you join him in spreading out the skies,
hard as a mirror of cast bronze?

19 "Tell us what we should say to him;
we cannot draw up our case because of our darkness.
20 Should he be told that I want to speak?
Would anyone ask to be swallowed up?
21 Now no one can look at the sun,
bright as it is in the skies
after the wind has swept them clean.
22 Out of the north he comes in golden splendor;
God comes in awesome majesty.
23 The Almighty is beyond our reach and exalted in power;
in his justice and great righteousness, he does not oppress.
24 Therefore, people revere him,
for does he not have regard for all the wise in heart?[a]"

The LORD Speaks

38 Then the LORD spoke to Job out of the storm. He said:

2 "Who is this that obscures my plans
with words without knowledge?
3 Brace yourself like a man;
I will question you,
and you shall answer me.

4 "Where were you when I laid the earth's foundation?
Tell me, if you understand.
5 Who marked off its dimensions? Surely you know!
Who stretched a measuring line across it?
6 On what were its footings set,
or who laid its cornerstone—
7 while the morning stars sang together
and all the angels[b] shouted for joy?

8 "Who shut up the sea behind doors
when it burst forth from the womb,
9 when I made the clouds its garment
and wrapped it in thick darkness,
10 when I fixed limits for it
and set its doors and bars in place,
11 when I said, 'This far you may come and no farther;
here is where your proud waves halt'?

12 "Have you ever given orders to the morning,
or shown the dawn its place,

---

[a] 24 Or *for he does not have regard for any who think they are wise.* [b] 7 Hebrew *the sons of God*

[13]that it might take the earth by the edges
and shake the wicked out of it?
[14]The earth takes shape like clay under a seal;
its features stand out like those of a garment.
[15]The wicked are denied their light,
and their upraised arm is broken.

[16]"Have you journeyed to the springs of the sea
or walked in the recesses of the deep?
[17]Have the gates of death been shown to you?
Have you seen the gates of the deepest darkness?
[18]Have you comprehended the vast expanses of the earth?
Tell me, if you know all this.

[19]"What is the way to the abode of light?
And where does darkness reside?
[20]Can you take them to their places?
Do you know the paths to their dwellings?
[21]Surely you know, for you were already born!
You have lived so many years!

[22]"Have you entered the storehouses of the snow
or seen the storehouses of the hail,
[23]which I reserve for times of trouble,
for days of war and battle?
[24]What is the way to the place where the lightning is dispersed,
or the place where the east winds are scattered over
the earth?
[25]Who cuts a channel for the torrents of rain,
and a path for the thunderstorm,
[26]to water a land where no one lives,
an uninhabited desert,
[27]to satisfy a desolate wasteland
and make it sprout with grass?
[28]Does the rain have a father?
Who fathers the drops of dew?
[29]From whose womb comes the ice?
Who gives birth to the frost from the heavens
[30]when the waters become hard as stone,
when the surface of the deep is frozen?

[31]"Can you bind the chains[a] of the Pleiades?
Can you loosen Orion's belt?
[32]Can you bring forth the constellations in their seasons[b]
or lead out the Bear[c] with its cubs?
[33]Do you know the laws of the heavens?
Can you set up God's[d] dominion over the earth?

[34]"Can you raise your voice to the clouds
and cover yourself with a flood of water?
[35]Do you send the lightning bolts on their way?
Do they report to you, 'Here we are'?
[36]Who gives the ibis wisdom[e]
or gives the rooster understanding?[f]
[37]Who has the wisdom to count the clouds?
Who can tip over the water jars of the heavens

[a] *31* Septuagint; Hebrew *beauty* [b] *32* Or *the morning star in its season* [c] *32* Or *out Leo*
[d] *33* Or *their* [e] *36* That is, wisdom about the flooding of the Nile [f] *36* That is, understanding of when to crow; the meaning of the Hebrew for this verse is uncertain.

GOD'S POSITION AND OURS

People do not need answers to their questions and arguments as much as they need to be overwhelmed by the fact that they do not understand everything as well as they think they do. This is precisely what Job 38 (and 39) teaches. Job was full of questions and concerns. God's response was not to provide answers, but instead to point Job to everything that he did not understand. God knows people infinitely better than they know themselves.

God's questions to Job are focused on the world in which Job lived. These questions reveal Job's presumption in expecting God to line up with his understanding, when he did not even understand the world around him. As the questions continue throughout Job 38 and 39, it becomes more and more apparent that God is so much higher and wiser than humanity. His words point to the magnitude of his works in creation. When humans open their eyes to those works, they are humbled before God.

This is God's world, and God can and will do what he wants. God has used the weather to bless his people and even help his people in battle. God has also used the weather to judge his people by sending a flood or withholding rain (Ge 7:4; 1Ki 17:1). God's ability to use the weather however he likes proves that he is in control of the weather. In reminding Job of this truth, God also illustrated his character through the weather. Thunder and lightning symbolize God's power and majesty. The falling of rain and snow on the earth, which results in the watering of the ground and nurturing of vegetation, pictures the way the Word works on the hearts of his people and points to the gracious God who gives life. God compares his judgment to raging storms and likens his blessings to refreshing showers.

God contrasts Job's feeble questions with his infinite power to create and manage the world. The way that God questions Job points back to Genesis 1:1 – 10 and John 1:1 – 13 as Jesus, the Word of God, participated in the act of creation. Jesus' power, strength, purpose and oversight in creation should be the overarching framework that Christians use when viewing or experiencing suffering. This is who Jesus is — the Creator. All thanks be to Jesus. In his grace and mercy he has chosen to be the Savior. All people are utterly dependent on him for life in this world and eternal life with him in the world to come.

38 when the dust becomes hard
and the clods of earth stick together?

39 "Do you hunt the prey for the lioness
and satisfy the hunger of the lions
40 when they crouch in their dens
or lie in wait in a thicket?
41 Who provides food for the raven
when its young cry out to God
and wander about for lack of food?

39 "Do you know when the mountain goats give birth?
Do you watch when the doe bears her fawn?
2 Do you count the months till they bear?
Do you know the time they give birth?
3 They crouch down and bring forth their young;
their labor pains are ended.
4 Their young thrive and grow strong in the wilds;
they leave and do not return.

5 "Who let the wild donkey go free?
Who untied its ropes?
6 I gave it the wasteland as its home,
the salt flats as its habitat.
7 It laughs at the commotion in the town;
it does not hear a driver's shout.
8 It ranges the hills for its pasture
and searches for any green thing.

9 "Will the wild ox consent to serve you?
Will it stay by your manger at night?
10 Can you hold it to the furrow with a harness?
Will it till the valleys behind you?
11 Will you rely on it for its great strength?
Will you leave your heavy work to it?
12 Can you trust it to haul in your grain
and bring it to your threshing floor?

13 "The wings of the ostrich flap joyfully,
though they cannot compare
with the wings and feathers of the stork.
14 She lays her eggs on the ground
and lets them warm in the sand,
15 unmindful that a foot may crush them,
that some wild animal may trample them.
16 She treats her young harshly, as if they were not hers;
she cares not that her labor was in vain,
17 for God did not endow her with wisdom
or give her a share of good sense.
18 Yet when she spreads her feathers to run,
she laughs at horse and rider.

19 "Do you give the horse its strength
or clothe its neck with a flowing mane?
20 Do you make it leap like a locust,
striking terror with its proud snorting?
21 It paws fiercely, rejoicing in its strength,
and charges into the fray.
22 It laughs at fear, afraid of nothing;
it does not shy away from the sword.

[23] The quiver rattles against its side,
along with the flashing spear and lance.
[24] In frenzied excitement it eats up the ground;
it cannot stand still when the trumpet sounds.
[25] At the blast of the trumpet it snorts, 'Aha!
It catches the scent of battle from afar,
the shout of commanders and the battle cry.

[26] "Does the hawk take flight by your wisdom
and spread its wings toward the south?
[27] Does the eagle soar at your command
and build its nest on high?
[28] It dwells on a cliff and stays there at night;
a rocky crag is its stronghold.
[29] From there it looks for food;
its eyes detect it from afar.
[30] Its young ones feast on blood,
and where the slain are, there it is."

40 The LORD said to Job:

[2] "Will the one who contends with the Almighty correct him?
Let him who accuses God answer him!"

[3] Then Job answered the LORD:

[4] "I am unworthy—how can I reply to you?
I put my hand over my mouth.
[5] I spoke once, but I have no answer—
twice, but I will say no more."

[6] Then the LORD spoke to Job out of the storm:

[7] "Brace yourself like a man;
I will question you,
and you shall answer me.

[8] "Would you discredit my justice?
Would you condemn me to justify yourself?
[9] Do you have an arm like God's,
and can your voice thunder like his?
[10] Then adorn yourself with glory and splendor,
and clothe yourself in honor and majesty.
[11] Unleash the fury of your wrath,
look at all who are proud and bring them low,
[12] look at all who are proud and humble them,
crush the wicked where they stand.
[13] Bury them all in the dust together;
shroud their faces in the grave.
[14] Then I myself will admit to you
that your own right hand can save you.

[15] "Look at Behemoth,
which I made along with you
and which feeds on grass like an ox.
[16] What strength it has in its loins,
what power in the muscles of its belly!
[17] Its tail sways like a cedar;
the sinews of its thighs are close-knit.
[18] Its bones are tubes of bronze,
its limbs like rods of iron.

JOB 40:8

REAP WHAT YOU SOW?

God asked Job questions which were intended to overwhelm Job—in a good way. The questions all point to God's goodness, power and freedom. The freedom of God might not seem like good news at first, but as the idea makes itself at home in the hearts of God's people, it becomes more and more beautiful. God's freedom means that God is under no obligation to do anything for anyone. God is only responsible to do what he says he will do.

Job's four friends maintained a general principle that can be found in various forms throughout Scripture: "A man reaps what he sows" (Gal 6:7). That is a true statement; people generally receive what they put out. One of the many reasons Job is in the Bible is to show that God may choose to bypass this general rule from time to time and not communicate why—because God is not accountable to people. There may be some comfort in knowing that despite short-term variations, the "law of the harvest" applies in the long term (Gal 6:8–10). But at an even more fundamental level, God has transformed the general "you reap what you sow" principle in Jesus Christ. Sinless and undeserving of death, Jesus was crucified on a cross so that sinful humans might have life. In Jesus' death and resurrection, God transformed the standard system of retribution and reward. God is free to do whatever he wills; God decided to send Jesus to save us.

[19] It ranks first among the works of God,
yet its Maker can approach it with his sword.
[20] The hills bring it their produce,
and all the wild animals play nearby.
[21] Under the lotus plants it lies,
hidden among the reeds in the marsh.
[22] The lotuses conceal it in their shadow;
the poplars by the stream surround it.
[23] A raging river does not alarm it;
it is secure, though the Jordan should surge against its mouth.
[24] Can anyone capture it by the eyes,
or trap it and pierce its nose?

41 [a] "Can you pull in Leviathan with a fishhook
or tie down its tongue with a rope?
[2] Can you put a cord through its nose
or pierce its jaw with a hook?
[3] Will it keep begging you for mercy?
Will it speak to you with gentle words?
[4] Will it make an agreement with you
for you to take it as your slave for life?
[5] Can you make a pet of it like a bird
or put it on a leash for the young women in your house?
[6] Will traders barter for it?
Will they divide it up among the merchants?
[7] Can you fill its hide with harpoons
or its head with fishing spears?
[8] If you lay a hand on it,
you will remember the struggle and never do it again!
[9] Any hope of subduing it is false;
the mere sight of it is overpowering.
[10] No one is fierce enough to rouse it.
Who then is able to stand against me?
[11] Who has a claim against me that I must pay?
Everything under heaven belongs to me.

[12] "I will not fail to speak of Leviathan's limbs,
its strength and its graceful form.
[13] Who can strip off its outer coat?
Who can penetrate its double coat of armor[b]?
[14] Who dares open the doors of its mouth,
ringed about with fearsome teeth?
[15] Its back has[c] rows of shields
tightly sealed together;
[16] each is so close to the next
that no air can pass between.
[17] They are joined fast to one another;
they cling together and cannot be parted.
[18] Its snorting throws out flashes of light;
its eyes are like the rays of dawn.
[19] Flames stream from its mouth;
sparks of fire shoot out.
[20] Smoke pours from its nostrils
as from a boiling pot over burning reeds.
[21] Its breath sets coals ablaze,
and flames dart from its mouth.

[a] In Hebrew texts 41:1-8 is numbered 40:25-32, and 41:9-34 is numbered 41:1-26.
[b] *13* Septuagint; Hebrew *double bridle* [c] *15* Or *Its pride is its*

22 Strength resides in its neck;
dismay goes before it.
23 The folds of its flesh are tightly joined;
they are firm and immovable.
24 Its chest is hard as rock,
hard as a lower millstone.
25 When it rises up, the mighty are terrified;
they retreat before its thrashing.
26 The sword that reaches it has no effect,
nor does the spear or the dart or the javelin.
27 Iron it treats like straw
and bronze like rotten wood.
28 Arrows do not make it flee;
slingstones are like chaff to it.
29 A club seems to it but a piece of straw;
it laughs at the rattling of the lance.
30 Its undersides are jagged potsherds,
leaving a trail in the mud like a threshing sledge.
31 It makes the depths churn like a boiling caldron
and stirs up the sea like a pot of ointment.
32 It leaves a glistening wake behind it;
one would think the deep had white hair.
33 Nothing on earth is its equal —
a creature without fear.
34 It looks down on all that are haughty;
it is king over all that are proud."

Job

42 Then Job replied to the LORD:

2 "I know that you can do all things;
no purpose of yours can be thwarted.
3 You asked, 'Who is this that obscures my plans without knowledge?'
Surely I spoke of things I did not understand,
things too wonderful for me to know.

4 "You said, 'Listen now, and I will speak;
I will question you,
and you shall answer me.'
5 My ears had heard of you
but now my eyes have seen you.
6 Therefore I despise myself
and repent in dust and ashes."

Epilogue

7 After the LORD had said these things to Job, he said to Eliphaz the Temanite,
"I am angry with you and your two friends, because you have not spoken the
truth about me, as my servant Job has. 8 So now take seven bulls and seven rams
and go to my servant Job and sacrifice a burnt offering for yourselves. My servant
Job will pray for you, and I will accept his prayer and not deal with you according
to your folly. You have not spoken the truth about me, as my servant Job has." 9 So
Eliphaz the Temanite, Bildad the Shuhite and Zophar the Naamathite did what
the LORD told them; and the LORD accepted Job's prayer.
10 After Job had prayed for his friends, the LORD restored his fortunes and gave
him twice as much as he had before. 11 All his brothers and sisters and everyone
who had known him before came and ate with him in his house. They comforted

RESTORED BY GRACE ALONE

God treats people in ways they do not deserve — and this is a good thing. All people deserve punishment from God for the sins they have committed against him. Instead of punishment, God decided to draw near to humanity in grace. His grace is a gift that people do not deserve to receive — and it can only be received with the surrendered hands of faith.

God had already displayed grace throughout Job's sufferings. When Satan wanted to tempt and test Job, it was God who limited the extent of Satan's attacks. That was grace. And Job's past fortunes and eventual restoration were all by grace alone. His prosperity was not a reward for his integrity but a gift from God, who "restored his fortunes and gave him twice as much as he had before" and "blessed the latter part of Job's life more than the former part" (Job 42:10,12).

Job encountered God. It was only after the intense season of suffering, prayer and waiting that a transformed Job got to see God for who he really is (Job 42:5). Job's response of humility and repentance should serve as an example for every person who encounters God (Job 42:1 – 6). After all of Job's questions and frustrations, he was left with the one phrase that he could confess in confidence: "I know that you can do all things" (Job 42:2).

When Job saw God more clearly, he also began to see himself more clearly. When people discover the reality of God, they find the reality of themselves. Job only discovered these things through an intense season that seemed unbearable at times. But God knows from the beginning what he intends in the end. God knew the journey that he needed to take Job through, so God did it. And for Job to arrive at the destination of a transformed view of God was sheer grace.

The ultimate way God has shown his grace is by sending Jesus Christ to die for sinners. The cross leaves people with limitless reasons for repenting of their rebellion against God, and it should lead them to walk, live and love more like Jesus.

and consoled him over all the trouble the LORD had brought on him, and each
one gave him a piece of silver[a] and a gold ring.
12The LORD blessed the latter part of Job's life more than the former part. He
had fourteen thousand sheep, six thousand camels, a thousand yoke of oxen
and a thousand donkeys. 13And he also had seven sons and three daughters.
14The first daughter he named Jemimah, the second Keziah and the third Ker-
en-Happuch. 15Nowhere in all the land were there found women as beautiful as
Job's daughters, and their father granted them an inheritance along with their
brothers.
16After this, Job lived a hundred and forty years; he saw his children and their
children to the fourth generation. 17And so Job died, an old man and full of years.

[a] 11 Hebrew *him a kesitah*; a kesitah was a unit of money of unknown weight and value.

JESUS: OUR PRAISE-WORTHY KING

PSALMS

PSALMS

DEATH OF MOSES, TO WHOM PSALM 90 IS ASCRIBED *c. 1406 BC*	DEATH OF DAVID, TO WHOM MANY PSALMS ARE ASCRIBED *c. 970 BC*	BOOK OF PSALMS COMPILED IN FINAL FORM *c. 400 – 300 BC*

God's people are a worshiping people. The psalms are a collection of praise songs written by King David and many of Israel's other worship leaders. Often referred to as "wisdom literature," the books of Job, Psalms, Proverbs, Ecclesiastes and Song of Songs provide insight into God's plans and purposes for his people. While other portions of Scripture include praise to God, the 150 psalms reflect a worshipful, poetic tone that is unique among the books of the Bible. The hope-filled, worship-fueled writings found in Psalms provide a wide array of memorable passages that have inspired the praise of God's people throughout history.

The psalms describe the highs and lows of humanity's plight in a fallen world. At times the psalmists languish under the burden of their sin and the sin of others (Ps 51). The writers cry out to God for deliverance and plead with him for forgiveness. They profess their deep belief that God does indeed hear their prayers, respond to their brokenness and meet their needs (43:5). In the face of the depths of human pain, God is ever-present to provide a source of refuge for those who love him (46:1).

At other times, the writers of the psalms declare their unceasing joy and praise to God. They sing of his greatness and shout for joy at his works (100:1). He is the God of history who has shown his might and power; he is the God of the people who has graciously given himself to them in covenant relationship (105:8 – 11). The people's repeated refrain of praise to God serves as the psalmists' hope and the ultimate goal of humankind (Ps 103).

Behind the joy and sadness, brokenness and blessedness of the book of Psalms is the future hope of the coming of God's promised One (Ps 2; 22; 110). This One, pictured throughout the book as God's anointed Messiah, will be a true King who will usher in God's kingdom (Ps 89). Numerous psalms point forward to a day when God will answer the longing of his people by sending the One who will deliver his people from the burden of their sin. Many of these psalms are quoted by the Gospel writers or by Jesus himself to show the ways in which Jesus' life, death and resurrection fulfill God's promise. Jesus declares that God's kingdom is near, and he invites broken sinners to find hope, joy and love in his kingdom. Unlike earthly kingdoms, however, the coming kingdom of God will have no end.

PRAISE THE LORD, MY SOUL;
ALL MY INMOST BEING,
PRAISE HIS HOLY NAME.

Psalm 103:1

PSALMS

BOOK I

Psalms 1–41

Psalm 1

[1] Blessed is the one
who does not walk in step with the wicked
or stand in the way that sinners take
or sit in the company of mockers,
[2] but whose delight is in the law of the LORD,
and who meditates on his law day and night.
[3] That person is like a tree planted by streams of water,
which yields its fruit in season
and whose leaf does not wither—
whatever they do prospers.

[4] Not so the wicked!
They are like chaff
that the wind blows away.
[5] Therefore the wicked will not stand in the judgment,
nor sinners in the assembly of the righteous.

[6] For the LORD watches over the way of the righteous,
but the way of the wicked leads to destruction.

Psalm 2

[1] Why do the nations conspire[a]
and the peoples plot in vain?
[2] The kings of the earth rise up
and the rulers band together
against the LORD and against his anointed, saying,
[3] "Let us break their chains
and throw off their shackles."

[4] The One enthroned in heaven laughs;
the Lord scoffs at them.
[5] He rebukes them in his anger
and terrifies them in his wrath, saying,
[6] "I have installed my king
on Zion, my holy mountain."

[7] I will proclaim the LORD's decree:

He said to me, "You are my son;
today I have become your father.
[8] Ask me,
and I will make the nations your inheritance,
the ends of the earth your possession.
[9] You will break them with a rod of iron[b];
you will dash them to pieces like pottery."

PSALM 2:6

THE HOLY MOUNTAIN

Generally speaking, "Zion" refers to the city of Jerusalem and, on occasion, serves as a metaphor for God's people (e.g., Isa 3:16; La 4:2). In this case, Zion is pictured as the prominent mountain or hill in Jerusalem, an image that suggests the supremacy and kingship of God as well as the meeting of God with his people. In the ancient Near East, making contact with a deity was widely thought to occur in the highest places of a region, since that's where a heavenly deity could easily reach down to earthly humans. Thus, for the people of Israel and their surrounding neighbors, a mountain was an understandable and expected place to meet with a god. High up in Zion (Jerusalem) the one true God consistently condescended from his throne to reach out to his people (Isa 8:18). In the sacrificial offering of his own Son (Mt 27:45–56), God did not just reach down to a mountaintop. He reached down into the very depths of human existence—to the point of suffering and death—to bring his people back to himself.

[a] *1* Hebrew; Septuagint *rage* [b] *9* Or *will rule them with an iron scepter* (see Septuagint and Syriac)

MEDITATING ON GOD'S WORD

Psalm 1 serves as a significant foundation for the entire book and encourages its readers to live a life that finds its pleasures solely in God. Here it becomes clear that there are two paths — or rather, two types of people: the wicked and the righteous. This dichotomy is found throughout the wisdom literature of the Bible. According to the psalmist, in order to be counted among the "righteous" one must love God's Word (i.e., Hebrew *torah*, or law), meditate on God's instruction, and follow in the way of the Lord.

Learning the way of the Lord is one of the chief priorities of the Christian life, and this can be accomplished only through Christ and through Scripture. In the Gospel of John, Jesus told his listeners that *he* is "the way and the truth and the life" (Jn 14:6). *He* is the image of the invisible God (Col 1:15) and in him humanity sees the ultimate picture of righteousness. Knowing Jesus is of first importance as believers move toward becoming "the righteous" men or women described by the psalmist. Following Jesus' example is the next step.

Jesus knew God's words through and through. He knew them well enough to quote Scripture with ease, to speak with surety about his Father's heart and to live the perfect life. Christians must likewise find their way, truth and life in the person of Christ and in the breadth of God's words. To that end, they must spend time reading and listening to Scripture so that they can get to know God, understand his likes and dislikes, discern the difference between God's voice and that of the world and become like deep-rooted trees that yield fruit (Ps 1:3).

Psalm 1 points to one practical way to start and continue on the path of righteousness: "meditate" on God's Word. Interestingly, the Hebrew word used for "meditate" here in Psalm 1 actually means "to utter, to speak, to soliloquize." Meditating on Scripture thus can be thought of as making God's words one's own — either by reading Scripture or recalling it from memory. This is worth noting since the idea of meditation can feel a bit foreign (and somewhat impractical) to many people. It is simply a practical way for Christians to let Scripture permeate their minds, hearts and lives as they seek to follow the way of Christ.

GOD'S ADDRESS TO HIS SON

Psalm 2 was likely used in the coronation ceremonies of Israel's kings in which the Davidic ruler was declared to be God's son through God's initiative to adopt him as such (2Sa 7:12 – 16). Other songs that served as coronation anthems can be found in Psalms 18, 20, 45, 72, 89 and 110. Each time one of David's descendants was crowned, the words like those found in Psalm 2:7 affirmed both the king's adoption and his authority.

The king's adoption meant that he now looked to God as his "Father" and it signified an intimate, familial relationship. His task was thus to honor his Father by caring for God's people — a task that would be enabled by God himself and would bring glory to his name (2Sa 7:23). Furthermore, the king would be installed as an authoritative mediator of God's promise to make Israel into God's covenant people (2Sa 7:24) who are called to be a blessing to all the nations (Ge 12:1 – 3) — a relevant reflection that must still inform the lives of God's people today.

Finally, the divine decree of "You are my son" foreshadowed the coming of God's only begotten Son, Jesus — the ultimate mediator and King. The New Testament acknowledges Jesus as the dearly loved Son of God (Mt 3:17), the long-anticipated Davidic Messiah (Mt 16:15 – 17; Mk 8:29; Jn 4:25 – 26; 7:28 – 42) and the eternal King (Rev 3:20 – 21; 11:15). Jesus was declared to be king at his birth (Mt 2:1 – 2), and his coronation, as Paul says in Acts 13:33, was accomplished at his resurrection.

Because of Jesus, people can be adopted into the family of God. Paul quoted Psalm 2:7 in Acts 13:33, assuring those who believe in and follow Jesus that Jesus is still alive and able to offer both the forgiveness of and freedom from sin (Ac 13:28,34,39). Above all, and as previously noted, adoption into God's kingdom means that Christians, like their King, are now set apart to worship God and to be a blessing to all the nations.

10 Therefore, you kings, be wise;
be warned, you rulers of the earth.
11 Serve the LORD with fear
and celebrate his rule with trembling.
12 Kiss his son, or he will be angry
and your way will lead to your destruction,
for his wrath can flare up in a moment.
Blessed are all who take refuge in him.

Psalm 3[a]

A psalm of David. When he fled from his son Absalom.

1 LORD, how many are my foes!
How many rise up against me!
2 Many are saying of me,
"God will not deliver him."[b]

3 But you, LORD, are a shield around me,
my glory, the One who lifts my head high.
4 I call out to the LORD,
and he answers me from his holy mountain.

5 I lie down and sleep;
I wake again, because the LORD sustains me.
6 I will not fear though tens of thousands
assail me on every side.

7 Arise, LORD!
Deliver me, my God!
Strike all my enemies on the jaw;
break the teeth of the wicked.

8 From the LORD comes deliverance.
May your blessing be on your people.

Psalm 4[c]

For the director of music. With stringed instruments. A psalm of David.

1 Answer me when I call to you,
my righteous God.
Give me relief from my distress;
have mercy on me and hear my prayer.

2 How long will you people turn my glory into shame?
How long will you love delusions and seek false gods[d]?[e]
3 Know that the LORD has set apart his faithful servant for himself;
the LORD hears when I call to him.

4 Tremble and[f] do not sin;
when you are on your beds,
search your hearts and be silent.
5 Offer the sacrifices of the righteous
and trust in the LORD.

6 Many, LORD, are asking, "Who will bring us prosperity?"
Let the light of your face shine on us.

[a] In Hebrew texts 3:1-8 is numbered 3:2-9. [b] 2 The Hebrew has *Selah* (a word of uncertain meaning) here and at the end of verses 4 and 8. [c] In Hebrew texts 4:1-8 is numbered 4:2-9. [d] 2 Or *seek lies* [e] 2 The Hebrew has *Selah* (a word of uncertain meaning) here and at the end of verse 4. [f] 4 Or *In your anger* (see Septuagint)

PSALM 3:1 – 8

FINDING JUSTICE IN THE MIDST OF INJUSTICE

The superscription of Psalm 3 establishes the context for David's words — a context of desperation. David's own son had stolen his kingdom and now sought to kill him. While most readers probably cannot relate to the exact circumstances described, they can recall events in their own lives when people have wounded them deeply. They can identify with David's request for divine justice. Although David's words may appear harsh since he compared his enemies to wild animals (i.e., "break the teeth of the wicked" in v. 7), they are the heartfelt pleas of a man who has been hurt. Further, his words must be understood in light of the cross. The punishment requested by David pales in comparison to the ultimate punishment for sin — a punishment that Jesus bore when he took humanity's sins upon himself and died a gruesome death of torture and crucifixion. Psalms like this remind readers that God does not turn a blind eye to injustice and sweep it under the cosmic carpet. Instead, he chose to unleash his wrath against sin on his own Son and, in so doing, make right all wrongs, pay all debts and free all captives. This psalm shows that God is the one people should cry out to in the midst of unfair pain, because it is God who makes war on sin in order to make peace for all humankind.

PSALM 4:4

TREMBLE AND DO NOT SIN

David described circumstances here that warrant feelings of trembling or anger. He had been personally injured because of wicked people who had actively sought to hear and tell lies. His angst is thus a natural, understandable and even commendable response to malice and slander. Jesus himself expressed appropriate anger when he made a whip and cleared out the temple courts in order to protect the true purpose of his Father's house (Mt 21:12–13; Jn 2:13–17). Therefore, God's people must learn to express anger over the things that anger God, yet do so in a manner that does not "give the devil a foothold" nor give way to prolonged bitterness (Eph 4:26–27). Too often, the balances are tipped, and anger is either dishonestly suppressed or abusively expressed. Very rarely do people strike the balance that exemplifies David's command not to sin despite the injustice he felt. Perhaps God's people would do well to follow David's example: to be quiet and ponder the reason for feeling angry. Then, having trusted that vengeance is the Lord's and that his approval is sufficient, speak openly to God about the offense instead of looking for personal revenge.

PSALM 6:1–10

LAMENTS AND THE JUDGMENT THAT BRINGS HOPE

David's lament in Psalm 6 expresses extreme discomfort and concern

(continued on next page)

7 Fill my heart with joy
when their grain and new wine abound.

8 In peace I will lie down and sleep,
for you alone, LORD,
make me dwell in safety.

Psalm 5[a]

For the director of music. For pipes. A psalm of David.

1 Listen to my words, LORD,
consider my lament.
2 Hear my cry for help,
my King and my God,
for to you I pray.

3 In the morning, LORD, you hear my voice;
in the morning I lay my requests before you
and wait expectantly.
4 For you are not a God who is pleased with wickedness;
with you, evil people are not welcome.
5 The arrogant cannot stand
in your presence.
You hate all who do wrong;
6 you destroy those who tell lies.
The bloodthirsty and deceitful
you, LORD, detest.
7 But I, by your great love,
can come into your house;
in reverence I bow down
toward your holy temple.

8 Lead me, LORD, in your righteousness
because of my enemies—
make your way straight before me.
9 Not a word from their mouth can be trusted;
their heart is filled with malice.
Their throat is an open grave;
with their tongues they tell lies.
10 Declare them guilty, O God!
Let their intrigues be their downfall.
Banish them for their many sins,
for they have rebelled against you.
11 But let all who take refuge in you be glad;
let them ever sing for joy.
Spread your protection over them,
that those who love your name may rejoice in you.

12 Surely, LORD, you bless the righteous;
you surround them with your favor as with a shield.

Psalm 6[b]

For the director of music. With stringed instruments.
According to sheminith.[c] *A psalm of David.*

1 LORD, do not rebuke me in your anger
or discipline me in your wrath.

[a] In Hebrew texts 5:1-12 is numbered 5:2-13. [b] In Hebrew texts 6:1-10 is numbered 6:2-11.
[c] Title: Probably a musical term

2 Have mercy on me, LORD, for I am faint;
heal me, LORD, for my bones are in agony.
3 My soul is in deep anguish.
How long, LORD, how long?

4 Turn, LORD, and deliver me;
save me because of your unfailing love.
5 Among the dead no one proclaims your name.
Who praises you from the grave?

6 I am worn out from my groaning.

All night long I flood my bed with weeping
and drench my couch with tears.
7 My eyes grow weak with sorrow;
they fail because of all my foes.

8 Away from me, all you who do evil,
for the LORD has heard my weeping.
9 The LORD has heard my cry for mercy;
the LORD accepts my prayer.
10 All my enemies will be overwhelmed with shame and anguish;
they will turn back and suddenly be put to shame.

Psalm 7[a]

A shiggaion[b] *of David, which he sang to the LORD concerning Cush, a Benjamite.*

1 LORD my God, I take refuge in you;
save and deliver me from all who pursue me,
2 or they will tear me apart like a lion
and rip me to pieces with no one to rescue me.

3 LORD my God, if I have done this
and there is guilt on my hands —
4 if I have repaid my ally with evil
or without cause have robbed my foe —
5 then let my enemy pursue and overtake me;
let him trample my life to the ground
and make me sleep in the dust.[c]

6 Arise, LORD, in your anger;
rise up against the rage of my enemies.
Awake, my God; decree justice.
7 Let the assembled peoples gather around you,
while you sit enthroned over them on high.
8 Let the LORD judge the peoples.
Vindicate me, LORD, according to my righteousness,
according to my integrity, O Most High.
9 Bring to an end the violence of the wicked
and make the righteous secure —
you, the righteous God
who probes minds and hearts.

10 My shield[d] is God Most High,
who saves the upright in heart.
11 God is a righteous judge,
a God who displays his wrath every day.

(Laments and the Judgment That Brings Hope, continued)

about his circumstances. Though the exact nature of David's situation is unclear, David nevertheless called out to God, pleading for mercy and for deliverance from both his pain and his enemies. The Gospel accounts similarly describe Jesus as one who suffered at the hands of his enemies, as one who lamented and as one who prayed (e.g., Mk 14:32 – 35; Lk 23:20 – 25). Moreover, Luke was keen to point out that Jesus himself will deal with the problem of suffering as well as with the problem of evildoers. Hence, David's words in Psalm 6:8 are reasserted in Jesus' declaration, "Away from me, all you evildoers!" (Lk 13:27). These words appear in a context where Jesus promised to bring judgment to those who persist in their evil actions. Thus, as God's people read this psalm and, at times, resonate with David's plea for mercy and judgment in verses 9 – 10, they are reminded that Jesus has come in response to their laments and will bring mercy and judgment (Lk 17:26 – 30).

[a] In Hebrew texts 7:1-17 is numbered 7:2-18. [b] Title: Probably a literary or musical term
[c] 5 The Hebrew has *Selah* (a word of uncertain meaning) here. [d] 10 Or *sovereign*

[12] If he does not relent,
he[a] will sharpen his sword;
he will bend and string his bow.
[13] He has prepared his deadly weapons;
he makes ready his flaming arrows.

[14] Whoever is pregnant with evil
conceives trouble and gives birth to disillusionment.
[15] Whoever digs a hole and scoops it out
falls into the pit they have made.
[16] The trouble they cause recoils on them;
their violence comes down on their own heads.

[17] I will give thanks to the LORD because of his righteousness;
I will sing the praises of the name of the LORD Most High.

Psalm 8[b]

For the director of music. According to gittith.[c] *A psalm of David.*

[1] LORD, our Lord,
how majestic is your name in all the earth!

You have set your glory
in the heavens.
[2] Through the praise of children and infants
you have established a stronghold against your enemies,
to silence the foe and the avenger.
[3] When I consider your heavens,
the work of your fingers,
the moon and the stars,
which you have set in place,
[4] what is mankind that you are mindful of them,
human beings that you care for them?[d]

[5] You have made them[e] a little lower than the angels[f]
and crowned them[e] with glory and honor.
[6] You made them rulers over the works of your hands;
you put everything under their[g] feet:
[7] all flocks and herds,
and the animals of the wild,
[8] the birds in the sky,
and the fish in the sea,
all that swim the paths of the seas.

[9] LORD, our Lord,
how majestic is your name in all the earth!

Psalm 9[h,i]

For the director of music. To the tune of "The Death of the Son." A psalm of David.

[1] I will give thanks to you, LORD, with all my heart;
I will tell of all your wonderful deeds.
[2] I will be glad and rejoice in you;
I will sing the praises of your name, O Most High.

---

[a] 12 Or *If anyone does not repent, / God* [b] In Hebrew texts 8:1-9 is numbered 8:2-10. [c] Title: Probably a musical term [d] 4 Or *what is a human being that you are mindful of him, / a son of man that you care for him?* [e] 5 Or *him* [f] 5 Or *than God* [g] 6 Or *made him ruler . . . ; / . . . his* [h] Psalms 9 and 10 may originally have been a single acrostic poem in which alternating lines began with the successive letters of the Hebrew alphabet. In the Septuagint they constitute one psalm. [i] In Hebrew texts 9:1-20 is numbered 9:2-21.

GOD USES THE WEAK TO DISPLAY HIS STRENGTH

One reason why God is worthy of praise is because of *how* he accomplishes his will. He uses the weakest voices of the earth — "the praise of children and infants" — to show off his glory and to prevail. Surely this is good news for any and all who have ever felt weak, unsure or afraid.

The New Testament follows this counterintuitive thread and teaches that weakness is the way of the Christian life. God's people are called "children of God" (1Jn 3:1). Jesus himself invites the little children to come to him (Lk 18:16), and Christians are affectionately referred to as "dear children" and "dearly loved children" (Eph 5:1; 1Jn 2:1). All of this "children" language simply reaffirms the truth that the kingdom of God is upside down. It is the weak who God uses to shame the strong; it is the children who are able to enter into his presence; it is the lowly who will be raised up (Ps 18:27; 1Co 1:27).

Jesus highlighted the choice to embrace the role of God's child when he said, "Truly I tell you, unless you change and become like little children, you will never enter the kingdom of heaven. Therefore, whoever takes the lowly position of this child is the greatest in the kingdom of heaven" (Mt 18:3 – 4). To become like a child then, one must do what children do: ask for help, think highly of others, express wonder and awe, submit to the Father's authority, etc. After all, God is committed to caring for his children, and he is ever mindful of their needs (Mt 6:26; 7:11).

This psalm reveals that God's mindfulness is unmerited. He *chooses* to see his people, to think about them, to give them the good gift of glory and to empower them when they are weak. God knows that humanity is frail, yet he delights to pour out his grace by giving his people a position of honor in his creation (Ps 8:5). And he does this because he is truly "majestic" and worthy of acclaim. That God would work in such a manner makes him easy to worship and to be praised. This is why David ended with the refrain "Lord, our Lord, how majestic is your name in all the earth!" (v. 9). God is happy to use those who are weak, and he is doing it for the glory of his name.

PSALM 9:7–10

THE THRONE FOR JUDGMENT

In society today, the idea of judgment is widely misunderstood and really quite unpopular. Yet the Bible talks about God's judgment as the means for making all things right. In God's economy, judgment is what it costs to bring about *restoration*, which is the central hope of all humanity. The "whole creation has been groaning" to be redeemed (Ro 8:22–23). Thus when David celebrated God's "throne for judgment," he was picturing the end goals of justice meted out: refuge for the oppressed, remembrance of the needy and hopes fulfilled for the afflicted (Ps 9:7,9,18).

The longing for judgment and the cry for justice are dealt with at God's throne, and it is Jesus who will act as judge. The New Testament speaks frequently about Jesus' rightful role as judge (Mt 19:28; Jn 5:22–30; Ac 10:42; Ro 2:16). For those who are in Christ, the day that Jesus judges the world is a day to pray for and a day for which to give thanks (2Ti 4:8; 1Jn 4:17; Rev 19–21)—just like David. This is the day when all debts will be paid, tears will be wiped away and death will be forever conquered because Jesus has assumed the throne!

PSALM 10:1–18

GOD IS IN CONTROL

In light of the brazen abuses committed by wicked people, the psalmist wondered aloud, "Why, LORD, do you stand far off?" (v. 1). At first glance, it would seem that the perennial question of the problem of evil has

(continued on next page)

[3] My enemies turn back;
they stumble and perish before you.
[4] For you have upheld my right and my cause,
sitting enthroned as the righteous judge.
[5] You have rebuked the nations and destroyed the wicked;
you have blotted out their name for ever and ever.
[6] Endless ruin has overtaken my enemies,
you have uprooted their cities;
even the memory of them has perished.

[7] The LORD reigns forever;
he has established his throne for judgment.
[8] He rules the world in righteousness
and judges the peoples with equity.
[9] The LORD is a refuge for the oppressed,
a stronghold in times of trouble.
[10] Those who know your name trust in you,
for you, LORD, have never forsaken those who
seek you.

[11] Sing the praises of the LORD, enthroned in Zion;
proclaim among the nations what he has done.
[12] For he who avenges blood remembers;
he does not ignore the cries of the afflicted.
[13] LORD, see how my enemies persecute me!
Have mercy and lift me up from the gates of death,
[14] that I may declare your praises
in the gates of Daughter Zion,
and there rejoice in your salvation.

[15] The nations have fallen into the pit they have dug;
their feet are caught in the net they have hidden.
[16] The LORD is known by his acts of justice;
the wicked are ensnared by the work of their hands.[a]
[17] The wicked go down to the realm of the dead,
all the nations that forget God.
[18] But God will never forget the needy;
the hope of the afflicted will never perish.

[19] Arise, LORD, do not let mortals triumph;
let the nations be judged in your presence.
[20] Strike them with terror, LORD;
let the nations know they are only mortal.

Psalm 10[b]

[1] Why, LORD, do you stand far off?
Why do you hide yourself in times of trouble?
[2] In his arrogance the wicked man hunts down the weak,
who are caught in the schemes he devises.
[3] He boasts about the cravings of his heart;
he blesses the greedy and reviles the LORD.
[4] In his pride the wicked man does not seek him;
in all his thoughts there is no room for God.

[a] *16* The Hebrew has *Higgaion* and *Selah* (words of uncertain meaning) here; *Selah* occurs also at the end of verse 20. [b] Psalms 9 and 10 may originally have been a single acrostic poem in which alternating lines began with the successive letters of the Hebrew alphabet. In the Septuagint they constitute one psalm.

[5] His ways are always prosperous;
your laws are rejected by[a] him;
he sneers at all his enemies.
[6] He says to himself, "Nothing will ever shake me."
He swears, "No one will ever do me harm."

[7] His mouth is full of lies and threats;
trouble and evil are under his tongue.
[8] He lies in wait near the villages;
from ambush he murders the innocent.
His eyes watch in secret for his victims;
[9] like a lion in cover he lies in wait.
He lies in wait to catch the helpless;
he catches the helpless and drags them off in his net.
[10] His victims are crushed, they collapse;
they fall under his strength.
[11] He says to himself, "God will never notice;
he covers his face and never sees."

[12] Arise, LORD! Lift up your hand, O God.
Do not forget the helpless.
[13] Why does the wicked man revile God?
Why does he say to himself,
"He won't call me to account"?
[14] But you, God, see the trouble of the afflicted;
you consider their grief and take it in hand.
The victims commit themselves to you;
you are the helper of the fatherless.
[15] Break the arm of the wicked man;
call the evildoer to account for his wickedness
that would not otherwise be found out.

[16] The LORD is King for ever and ever;
the nations will perish from his land.
[17] You, LORD, hear the desire of the afflicted;
you encourage them, and you listen to their cry,
[18] defending the fatherless and the oppressed,
so that mere earthly mortals
will never again strike terror.

Psalm 11

For the director of music. Of David.

[1] In the LORD I take refuge.
How then can you say to me:
"Flee like a bird to your mountain.
[2] For look, the wicked bend their bows;
they set their arrows against the strings
to shoot from the shadows
at the upright in heart.
[3] When the foundations are being destroyed,
what can the righteous do?"

[4] The LORD is in his holy temple;
the LORD is on his heavenly throne.
He observes everyone on earth;
his eyes examine them.

[a] 5 See Septuagint; Hebrew / *they are haughty, and your laws are far from*

(God Is in Control, continued)

again stolen the spotlight and remained unanswered. Yet, the psalmist's conclusion suggests not only an answer, but also an entirely different emphasis — *a faith-filled focus on the trustworthiness and action of God*. Consider the psalmist's proclamation that "the LORD is King for ever and ever" (v. 16)! Clearly he believed that God hears, God sees, God acts and God defends "the fatherless and the oppressed"; and God promises that the wicked, ultimately, "will never again strike terror" (v. 18). The truth is that God *is* in control. God's kingdom is now, and it is coming. God will reign as King. The bottom line is that the reality of God's authority and actions come to bear on today's injustices — if not now, then in the future. Because of this, God's people can take heart in the good news that Jesus is coming, and he is "coming soon" (Rev 22:20).

PSALM 11:3 – 4

IF THE FOUNDATIONS ARE DESTROYED

Sometimes it looks like the battle is being lost. Evil appears to triumph daily and the moorings of societal morality are further undone. No matter how impossible the circumstances may seem, the truth is that God is still in control. Knowing that "the LORD is in his holy temple" (v. 4) gave David confidence as he looked forward to the day where the upright would "see [God's] face" (v. 7). That same knowledge continues to give God's people confidence today. Even though it may feel as though nothing can be done and that "the foundations are being destroyed" (v. 3), the truth is

(continued on next page)

(If the Foundations Are Destroyed, continued)

that there is always a proven course of action: *trust*. Because God refuses to forsake his people and because he is still in charge, the foundations are *never* truly destroyed. Yes, the foundations may shake, but the shaking itself is an opportunity for the upright to have their faith tested and proven (v. 5). So when the ground feels like it is giving way, believers must seize the moment to put their confidence in God — the One who is on the throne and whose face they shall very soon see (Rev 22:3 – 4).

PSALM 12:1 – 8

THE FLAWLESS WORD OF GOD

Faithlessness. Flattery. Lies. Deception. In this psalm, David lamented the dishonest words of the wicked and contrasted them with the trustworthy words of the Lord. Not only are God's words portrayed as truthful, but also they are described as completely flawless — signified by the number seven (v. 6), which indicates completion in Hebrew. So what does it mean for God's words to be completely flawless? It means that he speaks at the right time in the right way with the right words for the right reason. Imagining this type of perfection is difficult to do in the midst of the world's dishonest and unkind language. Yet, the idea of God's words being flawless is significant. It means that what he says is trustworthy and is worth believing and affirming. As for the world's words, on the other hand, David reminds readers to identify the lies they hear and to reject them, choosing to

(continued on next page)

5 The LORD examines the righteous,
but the wicked, those who love violence,
he hates with a passion.
6 On the wicked he will rain
fiery coals and burning sulfur;
a scorching wind will be their lot.

7 For the LORD is righteous,
he loves justice;
the upright will see his face.

Psalm 12[a]

For the director of music. According to sheminith.[b]
A psalm of David.

1 Help, LORD, for no one is faithful anymore;
those who are loyal have vanished from the human race.
2 Everyone lies to their neighbor;
they flatter with their lips
but harbor deception in their hearts.

3 May the LORD silence all flattering lips
and every boastful tongue —
4 those who say,
"By our tongues we will prevail;
our own lips will defend us — who is lord over us?"

5 "Because the poor are plundered and the needy groan,
I will now arise," says the LORD.
"I will protect them from those who malign them."
6 And the words of the LORD are flawless,
like silver purified in a crucible,
like gold[c] refined seven times.

7 You, LORD, will keep the needy safe
and will protect us forever from the wicked,
8 who freely strut about
when what is vile is honored by the human race.

Psalm 13[d]

For the director of music. A psalm of David.

1 How long, LORD? Will you forget me forever?
How long will you hide your face from me?
2 How long must I wrestle with my thoughts
and day after day have sorrow in my heart?
How long will my enemy triumph over me?

3 Look on me and answer, LORD my God.
Give light to my eyes, or I will sleep in death,
4 and my enemy will say, "I have overcome him,"
and my foes will rejoice when I fall.

5 But I trust in your unfailing love;
my heart rejoices in your salvation.
6 I will sing the LORD's praise,
for he has been good to me.

[a] In Hebrew texts 12:1-8 is numbered 12:2-9. [b] Title: Probably a musical term
[c] 6 Probable reading of the original Hebrew text; Masoretic Text *earth* [d] In Hebrew texts 13:1-6 is numbered 13:2-6.

Psalm 14

For the director of music. Of David.

1 The fool[a] says in his heart,
"There is no God."
They are corrupt, their deeds are vile;
there is no one who does good.

2 The LORD looks down from heaven
on all mankind
to see if there are any who understand,
any who seek God.
3 All have turned away, all have become corrupt;
there is no one who does good,
not even one.

4 Do all these evildoers know nothing?

They devour my people as though eating bread;
they never call on the LORD.
5 But there they are, overwhelmed with dread,
for God is present in the company of the righteous.
6 You evildoers frustrate the plans of the poor,
but the LORD is their refuge.

7 Oh, that salvation for Israel would come out of Zion!
When the LORD restores his people,
let Jacob rejoice and Israel be glad!

Psalm 15

A psalm of David.

1 LORD, who may dwell in your sacred tent?
Who may live on your holy mountain?

2 The one whose walk is blameless,
who does what is righteous,
who speaks the truth from their heart;
3 whose tongue utters no slander,
who does no wrong to a neighbor,
and casts no slur on others;
4 who despises a vile person
but honors those who fear the LORD;
who keeps an oath even when it hurts,
and does not change their mind;
5 who lends money to the poor without interest;
who does not accept a bribe against the innocent.

Whoever does these things
will never be shaken.

Psalm 16

A miktam[b] of David.

1 Keep me safe, my God,
for in you I take refuge.

2 I say to the LORD, "You are my Lord;
apart from you I have no good thing."

[a] *1* The Hebrew words rendered *fool* in Psalms denote one who is morally deficient. [b] Title: Probably a literary or musical term

(The Flawless Word of God, continued)

hold on to God's promises instead. After all, Jesus himself is the guarantee. Paul said, "For no matter how many promises God has made, they are 'Yes' in Christ. And so through him the 'Amen' is spoken by us to the glory of God. Now it is God who makes both us and you stand firm in Christ. He anointed us, set his seal of ownership on us, and put his Spirit in our hearts as a deposit, guaranteeing what is to come" (2Co 1:20–22).

PSALM 13:1–6

HOW LONG?

The psalms are songs, not theological essays, and they express the psalmists' honest thoughts and heartfelt emotions. In this song, David expressed his anguish to God as he repeatedly asked, "How long?" Exhausted and weary, David's questions represent more of a tearful plea than a search for informational answers. Similarly, Jesus called out to God in his desperation. After telling his disciples that his soul was "overwhelmed with sorrow to the point of death," he went away to pray alone: "My Father, if it is possible, may this cup be taken from me. Yet not as I will, but as you will" (Mt 26:38–39). These historic accounts not only validate the human need to express oneself openly to God, but also they teach an important lesson. *Both David and Jesus did more than lament.* They asked God for help and they declared their willingness to trust in him. David spoke of God's love and works while Jesus readily surrendered to his Father's will. How often are God's people guilty of lamenting without trusting or, conversely, of

(continued on next page)

(How Long? continued)

declaring faith without honest expressions of the heart? The holistic expression of this psalm — lament, ask and trust — is a model worth emulating.

PSALM 15:1 – 5

RELATIVE RIGHTEOUSNESS

Books such as Psalms and Proverbs refer frequently to righteousness in order to draw a contrast between the righteous and the wicked, while much of the New Testament speaks of righteousness in a different sense: perfection. This distinction is important to note as the former expresses "relative righteousness" which compares humans to humans, whereas the latter expresses "absolute righteousness" which compares humans to God. When David asked, "Who may live on [God's] holy mountain?" he was describing what the people of God should look like (v. 1). "Relative righteousness" looks like doing good, telling the truth, keeping oaths, ethical lending and more (vv. 2 – 5). Of course, the expression of relative righteousness (in comparison with those who are not God's people) is an outworking of the imputed "absolute righteousness" of Christ. Romans 10:4 says, "Christ is the culmination of the law so that there may be righteousness for everyone who believes." For those who are in Christ then, God's righteousness has been freely given to them through faith and can now be joyfully manifested by living a righteous life that looks like David's description in Psalm 15 and is empowered by God himself (Eph 3:20; Php 1:6).

3 I say of the holy people who are in the land,
"They are the noble ones in whom is all my delight."
4 Those who run after other gods will suffer more and more.
I will not pour out libations of blood to such gods
or take up their names on my lips.

5 LORD, you alone are my portion and my cup;
you make my lot secure.
6 The boundary lines have fallen for me in pleasant places;
surely I have a delightful inheritance.
7 I will praise the LORD, who counsels me;
even at night my heart instructs me.
8 I keep my eyes always on the LORD.
With him at my right hand, I will not be shaken.

9 Therefore my heart is glad and my tongue rejoices;
my body also will rest secure,
10 because you will not abandon me to the realm of the dead,
nor will you let your faithful[a] one see decay.
11 You make known to me the path of life;
you will fill me with joy in your presence,
with eternal pleasures at your right hand.

Psalm 17

A prayer of David.

1 Hear me, LORD, my plea is just;
listen to my cry.
Hear my prayer —
it does not rise from deceitful lips.
2 Let my vindication come from you;
may your eyes see what is right.

3 Though you probe my heart,
though you examine me at night and test me,
you will find that I have planned no evil;
my mouth has not transgressed.
4 Though people tried to bribe me,
I have kept myself from the ways of the violent
through what your lips have commanded.
5 My steps have held to your paths;
my feet have not stumbled.

6 I call on you, my God, for you will answer me;
turn your ear to me and hear my prayer.
7 Show me the wonders of your great love,
you who save by your right hand
those who take refuge in you from their foes.
8 Keep me as the apple of your eye;
hide me in the shadow of your wings
9 from the wicked who are out to destroy me,
from my mortal enemies who surround me.

10 They close up their callous hearts,
and their mouths speak with arrogance.
11 They have tracked me down, they now surround me,
with eyes alert, to throw me to the ground.

[a] *10* Or *holy*

[12] They are like a lion hungry for prey,
like a fierce lion crouching in cover.

[13] Rise up, LORD, confront them, bring them down;
with your sword rescue me from the wicked.
[14] By your hand save me from such people, LORD,
from those of this world whose reward is in this life.
May what you have stored up for the wicked fill their bellies;
may their children gorge themselves on it,
and may there be leftovers for their little ones.

[15] As for me, I will be vindicated and will see your face;
when I awake, I will be satisfied with seeing your likeness.

Psalm 18[a]

For the director of music. Of David the servant of the LORD. He sang to the LORD the words of this song when the LORD delivered him from the hand of all his enemies and from the hand of Saul. He said:

[1] I love you, LORD, my strength.

[2] The LORD is my rock, my fortress and my deliverer;
my God is my rock, in whom I take refuge,
my shield[b] and the horn[c] of my salvation, my stronghold.

[3] I called to the LORD, who is worthy of praise,
and I have been saved from my enemies.
[4] The cords of death entangled me;
the torrents of destruction overwhelmed me.
[5] The cords of the grave coiled around me;
the snares of death confronted me.

[6] In my distress I called to the LORD;
I cried to my God for help.
From his temple he heard my voice;
my cry came before him, into his ears.
[7] The earth trembled and quaked,
and the foundations of the mountains shook;
they trembled because he was angry.
[8] Smoke rose from his nostrils;
consuming fire came from his mouth,
burning coals blazed out of it.
[9] He parted the heavens and came down;
dark clouds were under his feet.
[10] He mounted the cherubim and flew;
he soared on the wings of the wind.
[11] He made darkness his covering, his canopy around him—
the dark rain clouds of the sky.
[12] Out of the brightness of his presence clouds advanced,
with hailstones and bolts of lightning.
[13] The LORD thundered from heaven;
the voice of the Most High resounded.[d]
[14] He shot his arrows and scattered the enemy,
with great bolts of lightning he routed them.
[15] The valleys of the sea were exposed
and the foundations of the earth laid bare

[a] In Hebrew texts 18:1-50 is numbered 18:2-51. [b] *2* Or *sovereign* [c] *2* *Horn* here symbolizes strength. [d] *13* Some Hebrew manuscripts and Septuagint (see also 2 Samuel 22:14); most Hebrew manuscripts *resounded, / amid hailstones and bolts of lightning*

PSALM 16:9–11

TODAY'S LIFE AND THE AFTERLIFE

Although the concept of an afterlife was largely undeveloped in ancient Israel, the idea of *Sheol* was loosely equated with death (49:15; Job 11:8; Pr 15:24), from which the righteous could be delivered. David thus expressed his trust in God to protect him from this place of death as he celebrated the joy of finding lasting pleasures in God's presence. This initial aspect of David's view offers a practical counter to today's propensity to think too much about the promise of heaven and not enough about the reality of God's transformative presence. Thus David's psalm, in part, encourages God's people to become well acquainted with the goodness of God now, not later!

It was not until Peter's speech at Pentecost, in Acts 2, that people were encouraged to see the wider application of this psalm—the hope of the resurrection. While on the surface of things it seems as though David primarily pointed out the immediate benefits of knowing God, Peter explained that David *also* envisaged the coming Messiah. After quoting Psalm 16:8–11 in Acts 2:25–28, Peter declared, "Seeing what was to come, [David] spoke of the resurrection of the Messiah, that he was not abandoned to the realm of the dead, nor did his body see decay. God has raised this Jesus to life" (Ac 2:31–32). This psalm celebrates the life-changing nature of God's current presence as well as the future hope of eternal life because of the resurrection of Jesus.

PSALM 17:1–15

SAFE IN THE MIDST OF SLANDER

Desperate for vindication, David cried out to God in this prayer. The repeated references to "lips," "mouths" and "deceit" suggest David was suffering because of the words of his enemies, possibly through false accusations. Regardless of the exact situation, this psalm presents a particular mindset to employ when facing unfair circumstances, especially when the nature of the challenge is slander or misrepresentation. It's amazing how other people's words can cut to the very heart of a person, leaving them feeling maligned, misunderstood and destroyed. Yet David — one who knew the infuriating unfairness of slander — chose to focus on more than just vindication. This "something more" had to do with seeing God's face (v. 15); it had to do with his love (v. 7); and it had to do with perspective. God already knows the truth about his people, the truth about the times when they have been wronged and chosen the high road, the truth that their enemies' claims were false. The relief of looking into God's eyes and seeing that *he already knows* will be more satisfying than a certified retraction from an accuser published for all to see. It is God's opinion that counts. It is God's love that matters. It is God's face that makes everyone else's pale in comparison. This is the perspective David brought to bear to be freed from falsehood and lies.

at your rebuke, LORD,
at the blast of breath from your nostrils.

16 He reached down from on high and took hold of me;
he drew me out of deep waters.
17 He rescued me from my powerful enemy,
from my foes, who were too strong for me.
18 They confronted me in the day of my disaster,
but the LORD was my support.
19 He brought me out into a spacious place;
he rescued me because he delighted in me.

20 The LORD has dealt with me according to my righteousness;
according to the cleanness of my hands he has
rewarded me.
21 For I have kept the ways of the LORD;
I am not guilty of turning from my God.
22 All his laws are before me;
I have not turned away from his decrees.
23 I have been blameless before him
and have kept myself from sin.
24 The LORD has rewarded me according to my righteousness,
according to the cleanness of my hands in his sight.

25 To the faithful you show yourself faithful,
to the blameless you show yourself blameless,
26 to the pure you show yourself pure,
but to the devious you show yourself shrewd.
27 You save the humble
but bring low those whose eyes are haughty.
28 You, LORD, keep my lamp burning;
my God turns my darkness into light.
29 With your help I can advance against a troop[a];
with my God I can scale a wall.

30 As for God, his way is perfect:
The LORD's word is flawless;
he shields all who take refuge in him.
31 For who is God besides the LORD?
And who is the Rock except our God?
32 It is God who arms me with strength
and keeps my way secure.
33 He makes my feet like the feet of a deer;
he causes me to stand on the heights.
34 He trains my hands for battle;
my arms can bend a bow of bronze.
35 You make your saving help my shield,
and your right hand sustains me;
your help has made me great.
36 You provide a broad path for my feet,
so that my ankles do not give way.

37 I pursued my enemies and overtook them;
I did not turn back till they were destroyed.
38 I crushed them so that they could not rise;
they fell beneath my feet.
39 You armed me with strength for battle;
you humbled my adversaries before me.

[a] 29 Or *can run through a barricade*

[40] You made my enemies turn their backs in flight,
and I destroyed my foes.
[41] They cried for help, but there was no one to save them—
to the LORD, but he did not answer.
[42] I beat them as fine as windblown dust;
I trampled them[a] like mud in the streets.
[43] You have delivered me from the attacks of the people;
you have made me the head of nations.
People I did not know now serve me,
44 foreigners cower before me;
as soon as they hear of me, they obey me.
[45] They all lose heart;
they come trembling from their strongholds.
[46] The LORD lives! Praise be to my Rock!
Exalted be God my Savior!
[47] He is the God who avenges me,
who subdues nations under me,
48 who saves me from my enemies.
You exalted me above my foes;
from a violent man you rescued me.
[49] Therefore I will praise you, LORD, among the nations;
I will sing the praises of your name.
[50] He gives his king great victories;
he shows unfailing love to his anointed,
to David and to his descendants forever.

Psalm 19[b]

For the director of music. A psalm of David.

[1] The heavens declare the glory of God;
the skies proclaim the work of his hands.
[2] Day after day they pour forth speech;
night after night they reveal knowledge.
[3] They have no speech, they use no words;
no sound is heard from them.
[4] Yet their voice[c] goes out into all the earth,
their words to the ends of the world.
In the heavens God has pitched a tent for the sun.
5 It is like a bridegroom coming out of his chamber,
like a champion rejoicing to run his course.
[6] It rises at one end of the heavens
and makes its circuit to the other;
nothing is deprived of its warmth.

[7] The law of the LORD is perfect,
refreshing the soul.
The statutes of the LORD are trustworthy,
making wise the simple.
[8] The precepts of the LORD are right,
giving joy to the heart.
The commands of the LORD are radiant,
giving light to the eyes.
[9] The fear of the LORD is pure,
enduring forever.

[a] *42* Many Hebrew manuscripts, Septuagint, Syriac and Targum (see also 2 Samuel 22:43); Masoretic Text *I poured them out* [b] In Hebrew texts 19:1-14 is numbered 19:2-15.
[c] *4* Septuagint, Jerome and Syriac; Hebrew *measuring line*

PSALM 18:43

THE HEAD OF NATIONS

Much of the text of this psalm is also found in 2 Samuel 22, as David recounted how the Lord delivered him from Saul and many other enemies so that he could reign as king and, in turn, sing praises to God (Ps 18:49). David even went so far as to say that God had made him "the head of nations" (v. 43). There is a prophetic expectation in this psalm of the coming Messiah and King, an expectation that Paul highlighted in Romans 15. Paul alluded to the backdrop of Psalm 18 and even quoted directly from verse 49: "Therefore I will praise you among the Gentiles; I will sing the praises of your name" (Ro 15:9). In reminding his audience of David's song, of David's deliverance from his enemies so that he could reign for the purpose of making known the glory of God to the nations, Paul effectively set up the argument that Jesus is the fulfillment of the "promises made to the patriarchs" (Ro 15:8), that he is the Messiah, that he will include the Gentiles so that they can "glorify God for his mercy" (Ro 15:9) and that he is, ultimately, the "head of nations."

PSALM 20:1 – 9

WELL-PLACED TRUST

Horse-drawn chariots were one of the primary weapons of warfare in the ancient Near East. Yet David knew that the determining factor of victory was not military might, but rather the name of God (Ps 20:7). Having God on his side meant that the Israelites could "lift up [their] banners," signifying triumph over their enemies (v. 5). This is the kind of confidence David had in God's commitment to save "his anointed" (v. 6). Similarly, Jesus trusted in his Father to bring victory over sin and death by giving "his life as a ransom for many" (Mt 20:28). Consider Jesus' admonishment of the disciples as they drew their swords to prevent his arrest: "Do you think I cannot call on my Father, and he will at once put at my disposal more than twelve legions of angels?" (Mt 26:53). Jesus showed perfect confidence in his Father's power when he forewarned his disciples of his death while encouraging them that "on the third day he [would] be raised to life" (Mt 20:19). Scripture teaches that God is able and willing to save (Zep 3:17). It is the reason why so much of his Word reminds his people that they need not fear, for the battle belongs to the Lord (Dt 31:6; Isa 41:10; Ro 8:15; Heb 13:5 – 6).

PSALM 21:1 – 7

GOD BLESS THE KING

Psalm 21 is a royal psalm, meaning that it focuses on the king and his reign. While the subject matter may feel a bit foreign to today's readers,

(continued on next page)

The decrees of the LORD are firm,
and all of them are righteous.
10 They are more precious than gold,
than much pure gold;
they are sweeter than honey,
than honey from the honeycomb.
11 By them your servant is warned;
in keeping them there is great reward.
12 But who can discern their own errors?
Forgive my hidden faults.
13 Keep your servant also from willful sins;
may they not rule over me.
Then I will be blameless,
innocent of great transgression.

14 May these words of my mouth and this meditation of my heart
be pleasing in your sight,
LORD, my Rock and my Redeemer.

Psalm 20[a]

For the director of music. A psalm of David.

1 May the LORD answer you when you are in distress;
may the name of the God of Jacob protect you.
2 May he send you help from the sanctuary
and grant you support from Zion.
3 May he remember all your sacrifices
and accept your burnt offerings.[b]
4 May he give you the desire of your heart
and make all your plans succeed.
5 May we shout for joy over your victory
and lift up our banners in the name of our God.

May the LORD grant all your requests.

6 Now this I know:
The LORD gives victory to his anointed.
He answers him from his heavenly sanctuary
with the victorious power of his right hand.
7 Some trust in chariots and some in horses,
but we trust in the name of the LORD our God.
8 They are brought to their knees and fall,
but we rise up and stand firm.
9 LORD, give victory to the king!
Answer us when we call!

Psalm 21[c]

For the director of music. A psalm of David.

1 The king rejoices in your strength, LORD.
How great is his joy in the victories you give!
2 You have granted him his heart's desire
and have not withheld the request of his lips.[b]
3 You came to greet him with rich blessings
and placed a crown of pure gold on his head.

[a] In Hebrew texts 20:1-9 is numbered 20:2-10. [b] *3,2* The Hebrew has *Selah* (a word of uncertain meaning) here. [c] In Hebrew texts 21:1-13 is numbered 21:2-14.

[4] He asked you for life, and you gave it to him—
length of days, for ever and ever.
[5] Through the victories you gave, his glory is great;
you have bestowed on him splendor and majesty.
[6] Surely you have granted him unending blessings
and made him glad with the joy of your presence.
[7] For the king trusts in the LORD;
through the unfailing love of the Most High
he will not be shaken.

[8] Your hand will lay hold on all your enemies;
your right hand will seize your foes.
[9] When you appear for battle,
you will burn them up as in a blazing furnace.
The LORD will swallow them up in his wrath,
and his fire will consume them.
[10] You will destroy their descendants from the earth,
their posterity from mankind.
[11] Though they plot evil against you
and devise wicked schemes, they cannot succeed.
[12] You will make them turn their backs
when you aim at them with drawn bow.

[13] Be exalted in your strength, LORD;
we will sing and praise your might.

Psalm 22[a]

For the director of music. To the tune of "The Doe of the Morning." A psalm of David.

[1] My God, my God, why have you forsaken me?
Why are you so far from saving me,
so far from my cries of anguish?
[2] My God, I cry out by day, but you do not answer,
by night, but I find no rest.[b]

[3] Yet you are enthroned as the Holy One;
you are the one Israel praises.[c]
[4] In you our ancestors put their trust;
they trusted and you delivered them.
[5] To you they cried out and were saved;
in you they trusted and were not put to shame.

[6] But I am a worm and not a man,
scorned by everyone, despised by the people.
[7] All who see me mock me;
they hurl insults, shaking their heads.
[8] "He trusts in the LORD," they say,
"let the LORD rescue him.
Let him deliver him,
since he delights in him."

[9] Yet you brought me out of the womb;
you made me trust in you, even at my mother's
breast.
[10] From birth I was cast on you;
from my mother's womb you have been my God.

[a] In Hebrew texts 22:1-31 is numbered 22:2-32. [b] 2 Or *night, and am not silent* [c] 3 Or *Yet you are holy, / enthroned on the praises of Israel*

(God Bless the King, continued)

it is yet a crucial concept within the Christian faith. God's people were ruled by a king during Israel's monarchical period, and the king was responsible for bringing God's will to pass. The king held the highest calling of bringing justice and righteousness to bear in a way that blessed his people and the surrounding nations. Looking forward to Christ's coming reign then, God's people can relate to the expression of eager anticipation found in Psalm 21:6—anticipation that the king will be granted "unending blessings." Indeed, the deepest longing of humanity is for the perfect leader, the discerning judge, the ultimate provider, the champion of peace and the king of love. Thus, the church today likewise must pray for Christ to come as King over all. After all, "God placed all things under [Jesus'] feet and appointed him to be head over everything for the church, which is his body, the fullness of him who fills everything in every way" (Eph 1:22–23).

PSALM 22:1 – 2

FORSAKEN BY GOD?

Historically, Psalm 22 is attributed to David and is an individual lament of his suffering. He described the utmost feelings of forsakenness and despair yet chose to proclaim God's faithfulness and to believe that deliverance was forthcoming. In its immediate context, this psalm brings perspective to life, particularly to the dark nights of the soul. It reflects the common human experience of suffering and crying out to God, only to be met with God's apparent silence. Reflecting on the stories of God's faithfulness in the past, however, gives God's people reason to believe that he will speak again, he will come through and he will again rescue his children. In these moments, God's children may cry out in pain while fully expecting to be vindicated. They can choose to worship in the midst of waiting.

The New Testament Gospel writers make use of Psalm 22 in another manner. Alluding to and quoting directly from this psalm, the writers focused on the Messianic concept of the innocent sufferer, one who experiences affliction and scorn only to be vindicated for the purposes of atonement and praise. This expectation of redemption must have couched the cries of Jesus in the context of hope as the first-century audience recalled the psalmist's triumphant conclusion. After the resurrection, it became clear that Jesus' cry of despair had not been the end.

What did Jesus experience in his anguished moments? While the precise details remain unknown, Scripture speaks about Jesus' suffering, crucifixion and death as something that brought him deep sorrow that he hoped to avoid if at all possible (Mt 26:38 – 39). No one, not even the Savior himself, wants to endure the dark nights of the soul, much less be tortured to death. Furthermore, Christ became "a curse for us" (Gal 3:13) and "'bore our sins' in his body on the cross" (1Pe 2:24). This type of suffering is interpreted by many evangelical theologians to mean that Jesus endured the very wrath of God to its end, and with it his terrible hatred for sin. Such relational trauma, physical pain and spiritual torment is beyond our imagination and experience, yet Jesus managed to choose to endure all this for the "joy set before him" (Heb 12:2). This is why Christ quoted Psalm 22 (Mt 27:46; Mk 15:34), because he knew that God *would* deliver him from death, just as David believed and as Isaiah prophesied: "After he has suffered, he will see the light of life and be satisfied" (Isa 53:11). Forsaken for a moment, yes, but only for a short time and for the greater good that God had promised.

[11]Do not be far from me,
for trouble is near
and there is no one to help.

[12]Many bulls surround me;
strong bulls of Bashan encircle me.
[13]Roaring lions that tear their prey
open their mouths wide against me.
[14]I am poured out like water,
and all my bones are out of joint.
My heart has turned to wax;
it has melted within me.
[15]My mouth[a] is dried up like a potsherd,
and my tongue sticks to the roof of my mouth;
you lay me in the dust of death.

[16]Dogs surround me,
a pack of villains encircles me;
they pierce[b] my hands and my feet.
[17]All my bones are on display;
people stare and gloat over me.
[18]They divide my clothes among them
and cast lots for my garment.

[19]But you, LORD, do not be far from me.
You are my strength; come quickly to help me.
[20]Deliver me from the sword,
my precious life from the power of the dogs.
[21]Rescue me from the mouth of the lions;
save me from the horns of the wild oxen.

[22]I will declare your name to my people;
in the assembly I will praise you.
[23]You who fear the LORD, praise him!
All you descendants of Jacob, honor him!
Revere him, all you descendants of Israel!
[24]For he has not despised or scorned
the suffering of the afflicted one;
he has not hidden his face from him
but has listened to his cry for help.

[25]From you comes the theme of my praise in the great assembly;
before those who fear you[c] I will fulfill my vows.
[26]The poor will eat and be satisfied;
those who seek the LORD will praise him—
may your hearts live forever!

[27]All the ends of the earth
will remember and turn to the LORD,
and all the families of the nations
will bow down before him,
[28]for dominion belongs to the LORD
and he rules over the nations.

[29]All the rich of the earth will feast and worship;
all who go down to the dust will kneel before him—
those who cannot keep themselves alive.

---

[a] *15* Probable reading of the original Hebrew text; Masoretic Text *strength* [b] *16* Dead Sea Scrolls and some manuscripts of the Masoretic Text, Septuagint and Syriac; most manuscripts of the Masoretic Text *me, / like a lion* [c] *25* Hebrew *him*

[30] Posterity will serve him;
future generations will be told about the Lord.
[31] They will proclaim his righteousness,
declaring to a people yet unborn:
He has done it!

Psalm 23

A psalm of David.

[1] The LORD is my shepherd, I lack nothing.
[2] He makes me lie down in green pastures,
he leads me beside quiet waters,
[3] he refreshes my soul.
He guides me along the right paths
for his name's sake.
[4] Even though I walk
through the darkest valley,[a]
I will fear no evil,
for you are with me;
your rod and your staff,
they comfort me.

[5] You prepare a table before me
in the presence of my enemies.
You anoint my head with oil;
my cup overflows.
[6] Surely your goodness and love will follow me
all the days of my life,
and I will dwell in the house of the LORD
forever.

PSALM 24:1–10

GATES OF ZION

While the exact event is not specified, some scholars theorize that a procession involving the ark of the covenant was the occasion for writing Psalm 24. The superscription indicates that it was composed by David, and it may have been written when he first brought the ark into Jerusalem (2Sa 6). It's easy to imagine the ark being carried high as David called out to the people gathered near one of Jerusalem's gates. The very presence of God had come to Israel's capital city, and the people responded with an energetic chorus of praises about his glory. Regardless of the exact circumstance, this psalm clearly celebrated God's presence and might!

The New Testament carries on the themes of Psalm 24 as it describes Jesus as the "King of kings and Lord of lords" (Rev 19:16) who will return to rule his kingdom (Ac 1:11). Jesus will come "on the clouds of heaven, with power and great glory" (Mt 24:30) and will gather his people to himself. Christians look forward to his coming: "For the Lord himself will come down from heaven, with a loud command, with the voice of the archangel and with the trumpet call of God, and the dead in Christ will rise first. After that, we who are still alive and are left will be caught up together with them in the clouds to meet the Lord in the air. And so we will be with the Lord forever" (1Th 4:16–17).

Psalm 24

Of David. A psalm.

[1] The earth is the LORD's, and everything in it,
the world, and all who live in it;
[2] for he founded it on the seas
and established it on the waters.
[3] Who may ascend the mountain of the LORD?
Who may stand in his holy place?
[4] The one who has clean hands and a pure heart,
who does not trust in an idol
or swear by a false god.[b]
[5] They will receive blessing from the LORD
and vindication from God their Savior.
[6] Such is the generation of those who seek him,
who seek your face, God of Jacob.[c,d]

[7] Lift up your heads, you gates;
be lifted up, you ancient doors,
that the King of glory may come in.
[8] Who is this King of glory?
The LORD strong and mighty,
the LORD mighty in battle.

[a] 4 Or *the valley of the shadow of death* [b] 4 Or *swear falsely* [c] 6 Two Hebrew manuscripts and Syriac (see also Septuagint); most Hebrew manuscripts *face, Jacob* [d] 6 The Hebrew has *Selah* (a word of uncertain meaning) here and at the end of verse 10.

OUR SHEPHERD

Psalm 23 describes God as a caring shepherd. Yet the job of "shepherd" is relatively unknown to the average person today. What exactly does a shepherd do? Why is God depicted as such? A cursory study of shepherds and sheep seems necessary to unpack the riches of the imagery in Psalm 23 as well as the psalm's relevance to the New Testament's depiction of Christ as the "good shepherd" (Jn 10:1 – 18).

One of the primary responsibilities of a shepherd is guarding his flock. Thieves, wild animals and the wandering inclinations of the sheep themselves mean that a shepherd must actively work to keep his sheep safe from harm (1Sa 17:34 – 35). Every night, a shepherd counts his sheep to ensure none have strayed or been stolen (Jer 33:13). If any of the sheep are missing, he goes out to look for them, discontent to lose any of those under his care (Eze 34:11). Not only does the shepherd tend to their wounds when they have been attacked, but he also "bind[s] up the injured and strengthen[s] the weak" even when their injuries or weaknesses are of their own doing (Eze 34:16).

A shepherd also meets his flock's basic needs for food and water by traveling far and wide to locate viable sources. What may appear to be a simple provision is, in actuality, a strenuous undertaking. Leading masses of sheep to food and water often involves trekking across difficult terrain and enduring harsh climates (Ge 31:40). Shepherding requires fortitude, endurance and skill.

God is depicted in Scripture as the kind of shepherd who does more than provide food, shelter and safety; he even goes so far as to *bless* his flock. The entire thirty-fourth chapter of Ezekiel describes God as a good shepherd who will "send down showers in season … showers of blessing" (Eze 34:26). Truly the "cup overflows" for those who are shepherded by God himself (Ps 23:5).

Likewise, Jesus refers to himself as the "good shepherd" who "lays down his life for the sheep" (Jn 10:11). He is the Messianic shepherd hoped for by God's people, foreshadowed by the psalmist David and foretold by the prophets. Jesus is the Good Shepherd worth listening to and worth following (Jn 10:3 – 5), the Good Shepherd who knows the name of every sheep and who died to give them life "to the full" (vv. 10 – 11).

[9] Lift up your heads, you gates;
lift them up, you ancient doors,
that the King of glory may come in.
[10] Who is he, this King of glory?
The LORD Almighty—
he is the King of glory.

PSALM 25:1–3

UNASHAMED

Honor and shame were of the utmost consequence in ancient Near Eastern culture. It is no surprise then that David felt strongly about avoiding shame (vv. 1–3,20). What is unexpected, however, particularly in a cultural context that bilaterally contrasts honor with shame, is David's choice to bring trust into the equation. Psalm 25 thus highlights the truth that putting one's hopes and trust in God is the only effective deterrent to shame. After all, God promises to guide "the humble in what is right" (Ps 25:9), and a righteous life, trusting in the Lord, is worthy of honor. Trusting God, quite simply, brings honor and spurns shame.

Jesus expanded on this idea when he warned his disciples of his imminent death and of Peter's denial. In light of this, Jesus urged them to trust in him: "Do not let your hearts be troubled. You believe in God; believe also in me" (Jn 14:1). He even went so far as to say, "Whoever is ashamed of me and my words, the Son of Man will be ashamed of them when he comes in his glory and in the glory of the Father and of the holy angels" (Lk 9:26). Jesus unequivocally calls his followers to trust in him and, in doing so, they will be unashamed and bring honor to God.

Psalm 25[a]

Of David.

[1] In you, LORD my God,
I put my trust.
[2] I trust in you;
do not let me be put to shame,
nor let my enemies triumph over me.
[3] No one who hopes in you
will ever be put to shame,
but shame will come on those
who are treacherous without cause.
[4] Show me your ways, LORD,
teach me your paths.
[5] Guide me in your truth and teach me,
for you are God my Savior,
and my hope is in you all day long.
[6] Remember, LORD, your great mercy and love,
for they are from of old.
[7] Do not remember the sins of my youth
and my rebellious ways;
according to your love remember me,
for you, LORD, are good.
[8] Good and upright is the LORD;
therefore he instructs sinners in his ways.
[9] He guides the humble in what is right
and teaches them his way.
[10] All the ways of the LORD are loving and faithful
toward those who keep the demands of his covenant.
[11] For the sake of your name, LORD,
forgive my iniquity, though it is great.
[12] Who, then, are those who fear the LORD?
He will instruct them in the ways they should choose.[b]
[13] They will spend their days in prosperity,
and their descendants will inherit the land.
[14] The LORD confides in those who fear him;
he makes his covenant known to them.
[15] My eyes are ever on the LORD,
for only he will release my feet from the snare.
[16] Turn to me and be gracious to me,
for I am lonely and afflicted.
[17] Relieve the troubles of my heart
and free me from my anguish.
[18] Look on my affliction and my distress
and take away all my sins.

[a] This psalm is an acrostic poem, the verses of which begin with the successive letters of the Hebrew alphabet. [b] *12* Or *ways he chooses*

WHO IS THIS KING OF GLORY?

Psalm 24 is a song about the glory of God. But what exactly *is* God's glory? David asked the question, "Who is this King of glory?" and answered with a resounding declaration about God's strength and might. Psalm 96 likewise describes strength as an aspect of God's glory; however, the list goes on to include his "marvelous deeds" (96:3), his "majesty" (96:6), his "holiness" (96:9), his "righteousness" and his "faithfulness" (96:13). When Moses asked to see God's glory, God said that that he would allow his "goodness" to pass before him (Ex 33:18 – 19). The point is that just a sampling of the texts about God's glory confirms that it is the sum of every amazing attribute God possesses and every perfect action he does. All of these things comprise its weight, its essence, its brightness and light!

God's glory is further revealed to the world in the person of Christ. He claimed to possess this glory when he prayed, "Father, glorify me in your presence with the glory I had with you before the world began" (Jn 17:5). John likewise attested to Christ's glory when he wrote, "The Word became flesh and made his dwelling among us. We have seen his glory, the glory of the one and only Son, who came from the Father, full of grace and truth" (Jn 1:14). Matthew describes Jesus' glory in his account of the transfiguration, saying, "[Jesus'] face shone like the sun, and his clothes became as white as the light" (Mt 17:2). And Peter wrote, "We were eyewitnesses of [Jesus'] majesty. He received honor and glory from God the Father when the voice came to him from the Majestic Glory, saying, 'This is my Son, whom I love; with him I am well pleased.' We ourselves heard this voice that came from heaven when we were with him on the sacred mountain" (2Pe 1:16 – 18).

In summary, Jesus is "the Lord of glory" (1Co 2:8). And, since he is continually being revealed to the church through Scripture and by the Holy Spirit, Christians have the unbelievable privilege of seeing the very glory of God through "the face of Christ" (2Co 4:6). Furthermore, God's people were made to reflect his glory to the world as they grow in their relationship with Christ. There should be a certain radiance about the people who claim to know him, for, as Paul says, they "are being transformed into his image with ever-increasing glory, which comes from the Lord, who is the Spirit" (2Co 3:18).

PSALM 26:1

VINDICATION

David used the word "vindicate" to ask God for a declaration of righteousness. Claiming to have "led a blameless life" and to have "trusted in the LORD," David requested that God bring justice and deliverance. Interestingly, the remainder of the psalm reveals that this declaration of vindication is not meant for David's own psychological satisfaction, but rather as a qualification for praising God with integrity. David said, "I wash my hands in innocence, and go about your altar, LORD, proclaiming aloud your praise and telling of all your wonderful deeds" (vv. 6–7). What greater testimony to the character of God than the righteousness of those who have been transformed by him? Their righteousness comes by being "mindful of [his] unfailing love" and by living "in reliance on [his] faithfulness" (v. 3). It comes by trusting in the Lord (v. 1) and by avoiding evil (vv. 4–5). Through faith, a life of righteousness is possible, and it is meant to legitimate one's testimony about and praises to God through the person of Jesus Christ!

PSALM 27:1

FEAR NO MORE

Fear has no place in the heart of God's children. Even if the "wicked advance" or an "army besiege[s]" or "war break[s] out," the people of God can remain confident and unafraid (vv. 2–3). While this mentality is much easier said than done, it is possible. David outlined the way forward in the face of such fearsome trials: "Wait for the LORD; be strong and take

(continued on next page)

19 See how numerous are my enemies
and how fiercely they hate me!

20 Guard my life and rescue me;
do not let me be put to shame,
for I take refuge in you.
21 May integrity and uprightness protect me,
because my hope, LORD,[a] is in you.

22 Deliver Israel, O God,
from all their troubles!

Psalm 26

Of David.

1 Vindicate me, LORD,
for I have led a blameless life;
I have trusted in the LORD
and have not faltered.
2 Test me, LORD, and try me,
examine my heart and my mind;
3 for I have always been mindful of your unfailing love
and have lived in reliance on your faithfulness.
4 I do not sit with the deceitful,
nor do I associate with hypocrites.
5 I abhor the assembly of evildoers
and refuse to sit with the wicked.
6 I wash my hands in innocence,
and go about your altar, LORD,
7 proclaiming aloud your praise
and telling of all your wonderful deeds.
8 LORD, I love the house where you live,
the place where your glory dwells.
9 Do not take away my soul along with sinners,
my life with those who are bloodthirsty,
10 in whose hands are wicked schemes,
whose right hands are full of bribes.
11 I lead a blameless life;
deliver me and be merciful to me.

12 My feet stand on level ground;
in the great congregation I will praise the LORD.

Psalm 27

Of David.

1 The LORD is my light and my salvation—
whom shall I fear?
The LORD is the stronghold of my life—
of whom shall I be afraid?
2 When the wicked advance against me
to devour[b] me,
it is my enemies and my foes
who will stumble and fall.
3 Though an army besiege me,
my heart will not fear;

[a] *21* Septuagint; Hebrew does not have *LORD.* [b] *2* Or *slander*

though war break out against me,
even then I will be confident.
4 One thing I ask from the LORD,
this only do I seek:
that I may dwell in the house of the LORD
all the days of my life,
to gaze on the beauty of the LORD
and to seek him in his temple.
5 For in the day of trouble
he will keep me safe in his dwelling;
he will hide me in the shelter of his sacred tent
and set me high upon a rock.

6 Then my head will be exalted
above the enemies who surround me;
at his sacred tent I will sacrifice with shouts of joy;
I will sing and make music to the LORD.

7 Hear my voice when I call, LORD;
be merciful to me and answer me.
8 My heart says of you, "Seek his face!"
Your face, LORD, I will seek.
9 Do not hide your face from me,
do not turn your servant away in anger;
you have been my helper.
Do not reject me or forsake me,
God my Savior.
10 Though my father and mother forsake me,
the LORD will receive me.
11 Teach me your way, LORD;
lead me in a straight path
because of my oppressors.
12 Do not turn me over to the desire of my foes,
for false witnesses rise up against me,
spouting malicious accusations.

13 I remain confident of this:
I will see the goodness of the LORD
in the land of the living.
14 Wait for the LORD;
be strong and take heart
and wait for the LORD.

Psalm 28

Of David.

1 To you, LORD, I call;
you are my Rock,
do not turn a deaf ear to me.
For if you remain silent,
I will be like those who go down to the pit.
2 Hear my cry for mercy
as I call to you for help,
as I lift up my hands
toward your Most Holy Place.

3 Do not drag me away with the wicked,
with those who do evil,
who speak cordially with their neighbors
but harbor malice in their hearts.

(Fear No More, continued)

heart and wait for the LORD" (v. 14). Sometimes fighting for faith looks like waiting on God to come through, standing in the strength he has provided for that moment. Jesus offered this reasoning for fighting fear when he said, "Do not be afraid of those who kill the body but cannot kill the soul. Rather, be afraid of the One who can destroy both soul and body in hell. Are not two sparrows sold for a penny? Yet not one of them will fall to the ground outside your Father's care. And even the very hairs of your head are all numbered. So don't be afraid; you are worth more than many sparrows" (Mt 10:28 – 31). Jesus promises his presence and with it his peace: "I have told you these things, so that in me you may have peace. In this world you will have trouble. But take heart! I have overcome the world" (Jn 16:33).

PSALM 28:6 – 9

GOD HEARS

In his hour of need, the psalmist prayed to God for help because he believed that God listens and responds. The psalmist's hope was not disappointed. The psalmist thanked the Lord with praises in the remainder of his song. Jesus likewise expressed confidence in the truth that God hears when he raised Lazarus from the dead: "Then Jesus looked up and said, 'Father, I thank you that you have heard me. I knew that you always hear me, but I said this for the benefit of the people standing here, that they may believe that you sent me.' When he had said this, Jesus called in a loud voice, 'Lazarus, come out!' The dead man came out" (Jn 11:41 – 44). Notice that Jesus expressed thanks to God *before* God had even answered because he was so sure that his Father would hear and respond. Throughout the Bible, God urges his people to pray with confidence that he will listen and respond (Pr 15:29; Jer 29:12; Mk 11:24; 1Jn 5:14). Once they ask, he faithfully answers, and their appropriate response (like that of the psalmist and of Christ) should be thankful praise!

PSALM 29:1 – 11

THE GLORY DUE HIS NAME

Psalm 29 calls upon the "heavenly beings" (presumably angels) to acknowledge and attest to the awesomeness of God (vv. 1 – 2). This style was common among the Canaanites who envisioned heavenly beings as a council of gods worshiping Baal.

(continued on next page)

4 Repay them for their deeds
and for their evil work;
repay them for what their hands have done
and bring back on them what they deserve.

5 Because they have no regard for the deeds of the LORD
and what his hands have done,
he will tear them down
and never build them up again.

6 Praise be to the LORD,
for he has heard my cry for mercy.
7 The LORD is my strength and my shield;
my heart trusts in him, and he helps me.
My heart leaps for joy,
and with my song I praise him.

8 The LORD is the strength of his people,
a fortress of salvation for his anointed one.
9 Save your people and bless your inheritance;
be their shepherd and carry them forever.

Psalm 29

A psalm of David.

1 Ascribe to the LORD, you heavenly beings,
ascribe to the LORD glory and strength.
2 Ascribe to the LORD the glory due his name;
worship the LORD in the splendor of his[a] holiness.

3 The voice of the LORD is over the waters;
the God of glory thunders,
the LORD thunders over the mighty waters.
4 The voice of the LORD is powerful;
the voice of the LORD is majestic.
5 The voice of the LORD breaks the cedars;
the LORD breaks in pieces the cedars of Lebanon.
6 He makes Lebanon leap like a calf,
Sirion[b] like a young wild ox.
7 The voice of the LORD strikes
with flashes of lightning.
8 The voice of the LORD shakes the desert;
the LORD shakes the Desert of Kadesh.
9 The voice of the LORD twists the oaks[c]
and strips the forests bare.
And in his temple all cry, "Glory!"

10 The LORD sits enthroned over the flood;
the LORD is enthroned as King forever.
11 The LORD gives strength to his people;
the LORD blesses his people with peace.

Psalm 30[d]

A psalm. A song. For the dedication of the temple.[e] Of David.

1 I will exalt you, LORD,
for you lifted me out of the depths
and did not let my enemies gloat over me.

[a] 2 Or *LORD with the splendor of* [b] 6 That is, Mount Hermon [c] 9 Or *LORD makes the deer give birth* [d] In Hebrew texts 30:1-12 is numbered 30:2-13. [e] Title: Or *palace*

[2] LORD my God, I called to you for help,
and you healed me.
[3] You, LORD, brought me up from the realm of the dead;
you spared me from going down to the pit.

[4] Sing the praises of the LORD, you his faithful people;
praise his holy name.
[5] For his anger lasts only a moment,
but his favor lasts a lifetime;
weeping may stay for the night,
but rejoicing comes in the morning.

[6] When I felt secure, I said,
"I will never be shaken."
[7] LORD, when you favored me,
you made my royal mountain[a] stand firm;
but when you hid your face,
I was dismayed.
[8] To you, LORD, I called;
to the Lord I cried for mercy:
[9] "What is gained if I am silenced,
if I go down to the pit?
Will the dust praise you?
Will it proclaim your faithfulness?
[10] Hear, LORD, and be merciful to me;
LORD, be my help."

[11] You turned my wailing into dancing;
you removed my sackcloth and clothed me
with joy,
[12] that my heart may sing your praises and not be
silent.
LORD my God, I will praise you forever.

Psalm 31[b]

For the director of music. A psalm of David.

[1] In you, LORD, I have taken refuge;
let me never be put to shame;
deliver me in your righteousness.
[2] Turn your ear to me,
come quickly to my rescue;
be my rock of refuge,
a strong fortress to save me.
[3] Since you are my rock and my fortress,
for the sake of your name lead and guide me.
[4] Keep me free from the trap that is set for me,
for you are my refuge.
[5] Into your hands I commit my spirit;
deliver me, LORD, my faithful God.

[6] I hate those who cling to worthless idols;
as for me, I trust in the LORD.
[7] I will be glad and rejoice in your love,
for you saw my affliction
and knew the anguish of my soul.

[a] 7 That is, Mount Zion [b] In Hebrew texts 31:1-24 is numbered 31:2-25.

(The Glory Due His Name, continued)

It is likely that the psalmist used this form in order to subvert the pagan concept and thus set the Lord apart from all other gods. The Lord, as the psalmist declared, is worthy of praise because of his power and majesty, and no other god is like him (v. 4). Ascribing glory to God involves reveling in his many attributes and actions, admiring them and agreeing with the truths about God. Here the psalmist focused on "the voice of the LORD" and used the refrain seven times to paint a complete picture of God's power (vv. 3–9). Furthermore, he proclaimed the unique omnipotence of the Lord who created the flood and who is King of the world (v. 10). This is the God who alone is able to give strength to his people and bless them with peace (v. 11), a God to whom the ascription of glory is surely due!

The New Testament paints a similar picture of Jesus commanding angels and receiving honor and glory and power (Mt 24:31; Rev 5:13). Jesus is the one to whom the final glory is given as he is seated at God's "right hand in the heavenly realms, far above all rule and authority, power and dominion" (Eph 1:20–21). It is to Jesus that the church now cries, "Glory!"

JOY IN THE STORM

When people encounter unexpected hardship or difficulty, they often respond with a familiar list of questions: Why is this happening? Who's responsible? What happens now? Though loved by the Father, believers are not exempted from terrible tragedies or the messy situations and consequences of living in a sin-contaminated world. Nor are they freed from the questions that naturally follow distressing events. However, those who know Christ as Savior need to redirect how they respond to their circumstances and move away from demanding answers or pointing fingers. They need to be intentional about seeking God's perspective and trusting him in times of adversity.

In Psalm 30, David's encounter with an undisclosed difficulty left him feeling as if he was in the "depths" and oppressed by his enemies. But instead of surrendering to the intense emotional pain, he deliberately chose to exalt the Lord (v. 1). That purposeful shift in focus helped David to experience God's presence with him in his circumstances and to rest in the surety of the Lord's control.

Jesus demonstrated this principle to his disciples in a tangible way as they struggled mightily through a fierce storm as their boat was battered by unrelenting wind and waves, and Jesus was asleep in the stern. As the storm raged and anxiety and fear seemed to be winning, the disciples woke Jesus. He calmed the wind and the waves and then asked the disciples, "Why are you so afraid? Do you still have no faith?" (Mk 4:40). Instead of simply removing his followers from the raging gale, Christ was with the disciples in the midst of the storm, teaching the disciples a deeper truth than they were expecting: that he is Lord over all things. As his resurrection from the dead later proved, not even death could overpower him (1Co 15:55–57). Through his sacrifice and triumph over sin, he imparts to believers the certain hope of resurrection and eternal life.

Though this life may be filled with the pain of loss, the confusion of disappointment and the sting of rejection, Christians can be assured that through faith in Jesus, God is always present in their current difficulties. They can faithfully trust in the certainty of their eternal destination, knowing that "weeping may stay for the night, but rejoicing comes in the morning" (Ps 30:5).

PSALM 31:5

INTO YOUR HANDS

It is not hard to imagine that, in the first century, many Jewish families would practice giving thanks to God at the end of each day. The father might pray Psalm 31:5 with his family as the curtain of night closed over the household: "Into your hands I commit my spirit." These words spoken then are the same words that Jesus spoke as his death drew near on the cross. The knowledge that this was also a prayer that a Hebrew child might have offered up deepens the meaning of these words, subtly but dramatically. And with the addition of one word, Christ shifted his cry from simply an Old Testament quotation to a personal statement: "Father, into your hands I commit my spirit" (Lk 23:46).

Only moments before, Christ had expressed his inability to feel the presence of the Almighty as the weight of the world's sin pressed down on him. "My God, my God, why have you forsaken me?" he exclaimed (Mt 27:46). Yet, in those final seconds as his physical agony likely reached its peak, Jesus called out to his Father with no formality. It was personal, a desperate plea that only a father would understand from his son. Though unimaginable pain racked his body, this intimate connection was the basis of his trust and gave him the ability to place his life in his Father's hands.

In this, Christ modeled the kind of relationship believers need to cultivate if they are to dispel the fear of the unknown and push back the frightening specter of death. It begins with faith in Jesus (Ro 10:9 – 10) and over time (through Scripture, prayer, worship and other disciplines) can develop into a relationship that slowly alters a person's core being, providing a sure foundation that will give sustenance through the worst of life's storms.

But until Christ-followers understand the fundamental difference between truly knowing the Father and just obeying a set of religious rules, they will always sense something missing in their lives and struggle with anxiety about the future. Knowing the Lord in a deep, life-altering way is attainable for those who seek him (Jas 4:8).

8 You have not given me into the hands of the enemy
but have set my feet in a spacious place.

9 Be merciful to me, LORD, for I am in distress;
my eyes grow weak with sorrow,
my soul and body with grief.
10 My life is consumed by anguish
and my years by groaning;
my strength fails because of my affliction,[a]
and my bones grow weak.
11 Because of all my enemies,
I am the utter contempt of my neighbors
and an object of dread to my closest friends—
those who see me on the street flee from me.
12 I am forgotten as though I were dead;
I have become like broken pottery.
13 For I hear many whispering,
"Terror on every side!"
They conspire against me
and plot to take my life.

14 But I trust in you, LORD;
I say, "You are my God."
15 My times are in your hands;
deliver me from the hands of my enemies,
from those who pursue me.
16 Let your face shine on your servant;
save me in your unfailing love.
17 Let me not be put to shame, LORD,
for I have cried out to you;
but let the wicked be put to shame
and be silent in the realm of the dead.
18 Let their lying lips be silenced,
for with pride and contempt
they speak arrogantly against the righteous.

19 How abundant are the good things
that you have stored up for those who fear you,
that you bestow in the sight of all,
on those who take refuge in you.
20 In the shelter of your presence you hide them
from all human intrigues;
you keep them safe in your dwelling
from accusing tongues.

21 Praise be to the LORD,
for he showed me the wonders of his love
when I was in a city under siege.
22 In my alarm I said,
"I am cut off from your sight!"
Yet you heard my cry for mercy
when I called to you for help.

23 Love the LORD, all his faithful people!
The LORD preserves those who are true to him,
but the proud he pays back in full.
24 Be strong and take heart,
all you who hope in the LORD.

---

[a] *10* Or *guilt*

Psalm 32

Of David. A maskil.[a]

[1] Blessed is the one
whose transgressions are forgiven,
whose sins are covered.
[2] Blessed is the one
whose sin the LORD does not count against them
and in whose spirit is no deceit.

[3] When I kept silent,
my bones wasted away
through my groaning all day long.
[4] For day and night
your hand was heavy on me;
my strength was sapped
as in the heat of summer.[b]

[5] Then I acknowledged my sin to you
and did not cover up my iniquity.
I said, "I will confess
my transgressions to the LORD."
And you forgave
the guilt of my sin.

[6] Therefore let all the faithful pray to you
while you may be found;
surely the rising of the mighty waters
will not reach them.
[7] You are my hiding place;
you will protect me from trouble
and surround me with songs of deliverance.

[8] I will instruct you and teach you in the way you should go;
I will counsel you with my loving eye on you.
[9] Do not be like the horse or the mule,
which have no understanding
but must be controlled by bit and bridle
or they will not come to you.
[10] Many are the woes of the wicked,
but the LORD's unfailing love
surrounds the one who trusts in him.

[11] Rejoice in the LORD and be glad, you righteous;
sing, all you who are upright in heart!

Psalm 33

[1] Sing joyfully to the LORD, you righteous;
it is fitting for the upright to praise him.
[2] Praise the LORD with the harp;
make music to him on the ten-stringed lyre.
[3] Sing to him a new song;
play skillfully, and shout for joy.

[4] For the word of the LORD is right and true;
he is faithful in all he does.
[5] The LORD loves righteousness and justice;
the earth is full of his unfailing love.

[a] Title: Probably a literary or musical term [b] *4* The Hebrew has *Selah* (a word of uncertain meaning) here and at the end of verses 5 and 7.

PSALM 32:1 – 2

COVERED

Throughout Scripture, David is hailed as the greatest king in the history of Israel. After rescuing the army of Saul from the tyranny of Goliath and the Philistine army, this simple shepherd boy rocketed from obscurity to national celebrity in an instant (1Sa 17 – 18). Years later, after ascending to the throne, he drew unparalleled loyalty as the collective hopes and aspirations of the people rested on him (2Sa 5:1 – 5). Though David exhibited supreme devotion to the Lord and led the nation well, he monumentally failed as well. The sordid details of his adultery with Bathsheba, the elaborate but failed attempt to cover it up and the premeditated murder of her husband Uriah were exposed when God sent Nathan the prophet to confront the king with his wrongdoing (2Sa 11 – 12). Realizing his transgression was fundamentally against God, David responded with mournful brokenness and genuine repentance (Ps 51). Some commentators believe that the forgiveness and restoration David received from the Lord (2Sa 12:13) prompted him to pen Psalm 32, which extols the magnitude of God's pardon and the resulting freedom received by the one "whose sins are covered" (Ps 32:1). Centuries later, Paul quoted verses 1 and 2 as he explained the total forgiveness and perfect righteousness believers receive from God as a result of Christ's sacrifice on the cross (Ro 4:6 – 8). The perfection he offers in exchange for sin is not deserved and cannot be earned by good works or right behavior but is imparted solely to God's followers by grace through faith (Eph 2:8).

THE GREATEST NEED

Poverty, disease and oppression are just a few of the issues that plague the world's population. But none of those can supersede humanity's most basic need: the forgiveness of sin. When Adam and Eve disobeyed their Creator in the Garden of Eden, sin tainted the entire human race, and Adam's legacy of spiritual death was passed on to all of his descendants (Ro 5:12). Since then, all people have been born with a corrupted nature and cannot please God. Ephesians 2:1 describes this condition as being "dead in your transgressions and sins." People are not just sick. A little help or a little more effort will not suffice. The undeniable fact is that without Christ, a person's spirit is dead, and no person can pass from death back to life alone. Because of God's compassion for the helpless state of the world, he sent Jesus Christ to pay the price for sin (Ro 4:25; 6:23 – 24). Second Corinthians 5:21 explains the purpose of Christ's death: "God made him who had no sin to be sin for us, so that in him we might become the righteousness of God." He stood in the place of those who were dead in sin so that they could be made spiritually alive.

The apostle Paul helped Christians understand the radical change that takes place at the time of their salvation and grasp the enormity of their new standing with God by reminding them of verses from Psalm 32 (Ro 4:6 – 8). Through faith, sin is removed and righteousness is credited to all those "who believe in him who raised Jesus our Lord from the dead" (Ro 4:23 – 25). Simply put, that means Jesus received the just punishment for the sins of humanity, and as a result, those who believe in him receive the righteousness of Christ and are reconciled to God.

This great exchange is offered to all people through God's grace and mercy and is received through faith (Eph 2:8 – 9). Once a person acknowledges his or her desperate need for a savior (Ro 10:9 – 10), God delights in forgiving their guilt (Ps 32:5) and in so doing, meeting humanity's greatest need through the person of Jesus Christ.

6 By the word of the LORD the heavens were made,
their starry host by the breath of his mouth.
7 He gathers the waters of the sea into jars[a];
he puts the deep into storehouses.
8 Let all the earth fear the LORD;
let all the people of the world revere him.
9 For he spoke, and it came to be;
he commanded, and it stood firm.

10 The LORD foils the plans of the nations;
he thwarts the purposes of the peoples.
11 But the plans of the LORD stand firm forever,
the purposes of his heart through all generations.

12 Blessed is the nation whose God is the LORD,
the people he chose for his inheritance.
13 From heaven the LORD looks down
and sees all mankind;
14 from his dwelling place he watches
all who live on earth—
15 he who forms the hearts of all,
who considers everything they do.

16 No king is saved by the size of his army;
no warrior escapes by his great strength.
17 A horse is a vain hope for deliverance;
despite all its great strength it cannot save.
18 But the eyes of the LORD are on those who fear him,
on those whose hope is in his unfailing love,
19 to deliver them from death
and keep them alive in famine.

20 We wait in hope for the LORD;
he is our help and our shield.
21 In him our hearts rejoice,
for we trust in his holy name.
22 May your unfailing love be with us, LORD,
even as we put our hope in you.

Psalm 34[b,c]

Of David. When he pretended to be insane before Abimelek, who drove him away, and he left.

1 I will extol the LORD at all times;
his praise will always be on my lips.
2 I will glory in the LORD;
let the afflicted hear and rejoice.
3 Glorify the LORD with me;
let us exalt his name together.

4 I sought the LORD, and he answered me;
he delivered me from all my fears.
5 Those who look to him are radiant;
their faces are never covered with shame.
6 This poor man called, and the LORD heard him;
he saved him out of all his troubles.

[a] 7 Or *sea as into a heap* [b] This psalm is an acrostic poem, the verses of which begin with the successive letters of the Hebrew alphabet. [c] In Hebrew texts 34:1-22 is numbered 34:2-23.

PSALM 33:1–9

SING AND MAKE MUSIC

The first biblical reference to music appears in Genesis 4 where Jubal, a descendant of Cain, is identified as "the father of all who play stringed instruments and pipes" (v. 21). By the time music is specifically mentioned again in the story of Jacob and Laban, it had become an integral part of societal and family activity (Ge 31:27). Scripture indicates that Moses, Miriam, and Joshua employed songs and instruments to commemorate great victories and interventions by God (Ex 15:1; Nu 21:17; Jos 6:4). Women were active in celebratory praise, often leading in dancing, singing and the playing of melodies to mark important occasions (Ex 15:20–21; Jdg 5:1–3; 11:34; 1Sa 18:6). Music was woven so tightly into the fabric of Hebrew culture that even when the text does not mention it explicitly, readers can rightly assume that it accompanied virtually every significant occasion in public and private activity. However, it was not until the time of King David that instrumental music became a decreed part of worship in the tabernacle and temple (1Ch 15:22; 16:4; 25:1–3). And as an accomplished musician himself (1Sa 16:15–23), David actively encouraged, endorsed and participated in public worship celebrations (1Ch 15:15–29; 16:1–6). Indeed, he wrote many of the psalms in the book of Psalms. Following this rich heritage guides modern believers to embrace music as an indispensable means of honoring the Lord, celebrating his attributes and exalting him as the only trustworthy King (Ps 33:4–5,8).

PSALM 34:20

NO BROKEN BONES

Provision was made in the Law of Moses for a variety of forms of capital punishment for persons found guilty of a rather lengthy list of crimes (Ex 21:12–36; Lev 20; 24:10–23). The method of execution was stoning, except for burning in the case of grave sexual sins (Lev 20:14; 21:9). Included in these regulations were also some directions about the proper treatment of the bodies of the executed. Though it was acceptable to display the bodies of deceased criminals on a pole, the Law forbade the exposure of dead bodies overnight (Dt 21:22–23). However, with the Romans' introduction of crucifixion, it became difficult to adhere to this stipulation. The gruesome process often required several days, so if a victim ended up dying on the Sabbath, Jewish people faced a dilemma: either break the Sabbath to perform the work of removing and burying the body, or break the law forbidding the overnight suspension of dead bodies. In cases where such an untenable outcome seemed likely, Jewish leaders endorsed the practice of breaking the criminal's legs, which increased pain but hastened death because the victim then could not put any weight on his legs and breathing would be difficult (Jn 19:31).

With the Passover Sabbath approaching, the Jewish leaders asked for this practice to be applied to Jesus, yet found it to be unnecessary; Christ had already died (Jn 19:33). Keeping his bones intact fulfilled the prophecy of Psalm 34:20, quoted in John 19:36, and identified Jesus with the sacrificial Passover lamb (Ex 12:46). He vividly demonstrated his overwhelming love by voluntarily surrendering his life for the world's sins (Jn 10:18; 15:13; 19:30).

7 The angel of the LORD encamps around those who fear him,
and he delivers them.

8 Taste and see that the LORD is good;
blessed is the one who takes refuge in him.
9 Fear the LORD, you his holy people,
for those who fear him lack nothing.
10 The lions may grow weak and hungry,
but those who seek the LORD lack no good thing.
11 Come, my children, listen to me;
I will teach you the fear of the LORD.
12 Whoever of you loves life
and desires to see many good days,
13 keep your tongue from evil
and your lips from telling lies.
14 Turn from evil and do good;
seek peace and pursue it.

15 The eyes of the LORD are on the righteous,
and his ears are attentive to their cry;
16 but the face of the LORD is against those who do evil,
to blot out their name from the earth.

17 The righteous cry out, and the LORD hears them;
he delivers them from all their troubles.
18 The LORD is close to the brokenhearted
and saves those who are crushed in spirit.

19 The righteous person may have many troubles,
but the LORD delivers him from them all;
20 he protects all his bones,
not one of them will be broken.

21 Evil will slay the wicked;
the foes of the righteous will be condemned.
22 The LORD will rescue his servants;
no one who takes refuge in him will be condemned.

Psalm 35

Of David.

1 Contend, LORD, with those who contend with me;
fight against those who fight against me.
2 Take up shield and armor;
arise and come to my aid.
3 Brandish spear and javelin[a]
against those who pursue me.
Say to me,
"I am your salvation."

4 May those who seek my life
be disgraced and put to shame;
may those who plot my ruin
be turned back in dismay.
5 May they be like chaff before the wind,
with the angel of the LORD driving them away;
6 may their path be dark and slippery,
with the angel of the LORD pursuing them.

[a] 3 Or *and block the way*

[7] Since they hid their net for me without cause
and without cause dug a pit for me,
[8] may ruin overtake them by surprise—
may the net they hid entangle them,
may they fall into the pit, to their ruin.
[9] Then my soul will rejoice in the LORD
and delight in his salvation.
[10] My whole being will exclaim,
"Who is like you, LORD?
You rescue the poor from those too strong for them,
the poor and needy from those who rob them."
[11] Ruthless witnesses come forward;
they question me on things I know nothing about.
[12] They repay me evil for good
and leave me like one bereaved.
[13] Yet when they were ill, I put on sackcloth
and humbled myself with fasting.
When my prayers returned to me unanswered,
[14] I went about mourning
as though for my friend or brother.
I bowed my head in grief
as though weeping for my mother.
[15] But when I stumbled, they gathered in glee;
assailants gathered against me without my knowledge.
They slandered me without ceasing.
[16] Like the ungodly they maliciously mocked;[a]
they gnashed their teeth at me.

[17] How long, Lord, will you look on?
Rescue me from their ravages,
my precious life from these lions.
[18] I will give you thanks in the great assembly;
among the throngs I will praise you.
[19] Do not let those gloat over me
who are my enemies without cause;
do not let those who hate me without reason
maliciously wink the eye.
[20] They do not speak peaceably,
but devise false accusations
against those who live quietly in the land.
[21] They sneer at me and say, "Aha! Aha!
With our own eyes we have seen it."

[22] LORD, you have seen this; do not be silent.
Do not be far from me, Lord.
[23] Awake, and rise to my defense!
Contend for me, my God and Lord.
[24] Vindicate me in your righteousness, LORD my God;
do not let them gloat over me.
[25] Do not let them think, "Aha, just what we wanted!"
or say, "We have swallowed him up."

[26] May all who gloat over my distress
be put to shame and confusion;
may all who exalt themselves over me
be clothed with shame and disgrace.

---

[a] *16* Septuagint; Hebrew may mean *Like an ungodly circle of mockers,*

PSALM 35:1 – 28

A PRAYER FOR VINDICATION

When difficulty comes in the form of personal attacks, it is easy to feel alone and forgotten, and as if enemies have the upper hand. Such was David's attitude when he opened Psalm 35 with an earnest plea for God to come to his aid and vindicate him (vv. 1 – 3). Blindsided by the hatred of his adversaries, Israel's king proclaimed his innocence, insisting he had done nothing to incur their wrath. Despite David's sincere prayers for their well-being, his foes continued to slander and attack him at every turn (vv. 11 – 16).

While it is often difficult to understand the motives behind the actions of those who deliberately plot the demise of God-fearing people, some insight comes by understanding that residing in the hearts of unbelievers is a fundamental opposition to the supremacy of God. Those who do not acknowledge Jesus as Lord not only reject their Creator, but in prideful arrogance set themselves up as ultimate arbiters of what is good and right (Pr 16:25; 21:2). This often subconscious (and always futile) struggle with the Lord for control makes them hostile to anything that suggests that they are not "god" in their own lives.

Against this backdrop, it becomes understandable how the Pharisees would oppose Jesus despite his many miracles and obvious good works. All the deeds of the Son of God pointed to a higher authority: his Father in heaven (Jn 5:19; 12:49). But because the Pharisees had rejected God's authority in favor of their own, Jesus' activities became a threat to their political and religious power and personal control of their own lives. Even though they outwardly appeared to follow God through legalistic adherence to the law, their attitudes betrayed their fundamental rejection of him as their head. Jesus' presence and uncompromising devotion to the truth reminded them that they were then and would always be subject to the Lord's authority.

Encounters with those who resist and reject God's message are not uncommon. Jesus reminded his followers that they should expect to receive the same kind of treatment that he himself received (Mt 10:24 – 25). More specifically, he warned that in this world, his followers would have trouble (Jn 16:33). Because Christ's presence and teachings are reflected in the lives of believers (Lk 6:43 – 49; Jn 16:13), their actions will always remind the unbelieving world that there is a God above all gods to whom everyone is accountable regardless of race, nationality, religion or worldview (Ro 14:11 – 12; Php 2:10; Heb 14:13).

[27] May those who delight in my vindication
shout for joy and gladness;
may they always say, "The LORD be exalted,
who delights in the well-being of his servant."

[28] My tongue will proclaim your righteousness,
your praises all day long.

Psalm 36[a]

For the director of music. Of David the servant of the LORD.

[1] I have a message from God in my heart
concerning the sinfulness of the wicked:[b]
There is no fear of God
before their eyes.

[2] In their own eyes they flatter themselves
too much to detect or hate their sin.
[3] The words of their mouths are wicked and deceitful;
they fail to act wisely or do good.
[4] Even on their beds they plot evil;
they commit themselves to a sinful course
and do not reject what is wrong.

[5] Your love, LORD, reaches to the heavens,
your faithfulness to the skies.
[6] Your righteousness is like the highest mountains,
your justice like the great deep.
You, LORD, preserve both people and animals.
[7] How priceless is your unfailing love, O God!
People take refuge in the shadow of your wings.
[8] They feast on the abundance of your house;
you give them drink from your river of delights.
[9] For with you is the fountain of life;
in your light we see light.

[10] Continue your love to those who know you,
your righteousness to the upright in heart.
[11] May the foot of the proud not come against me,
nor the hand of the wicked drive me away.
[12] See how the evildoers lie fallen—
thrown down, not able to rise!

Psalm 37[c]

Of David.

[1] Do not fret because of those who are evil
or be envious of those who do wrong;
[2] for like the grass they will soon wither,
like green plants they will soon die away.

[3] Trust in the LORD and do good;
dwell in the land and enjoy safe pasture.
[4] Take delight in the LORD,
and he will give you the desires of your heart.

[a] In Hebrew texts 36:1-12 is numbered 36:2-13. [b] 1 Or *A message from God: The transgression of the wicked / resides in their hearts.* [c] This psalm is an acrostic poem, the stanzas of which begin with the successive letters of the Hebrew alphabet.

PSALM 36:1–12

LOVE DEMONSTRATED

In the midst of decrying Judah's sin, the prophet Jeremiah made this observation: "The heart is deceitful above all things and beyond cure" (Jer 17:9). The opening section of Psalm 36 helps readers further understand this universal condition with a blunt description of the wickedness that resides in the hearts of unbelievers and the subsequent sin that results from rejecting their Creator. Left to themselves, people gravitate away from the Lord and toward an arrogant and destructive sense of ambivalence toward spiritual truth, which leads to self-deceit, evil and, ultimately, the willful rejection of all that is good (vv. 1–4).

Contrast this desperate state with the righteousness, purity and faithfulness of God. Struggling to describe divine justice and mercy adequately, the psalmist pointed to the vastness of the heavens, the height of the mountains and the depths of the sea as mere hints of the overwhelming goodness and love of the Almighty (vv. 5–7). In light of his grasp of God's holiness and its vast difference from humanity's fallen condition, the psalmist made an impassioned plea to the Lord to "continue your love to those who know you" (v. 10). Jesus, who is the very image of God (2Co 4:4; Col 1:15), definitively answered the psalmist's request on behalf of all people by giving his life as a "ransom for many" (Mt 20:28) so that all who believe "might live through him" (1Jn 4:9).

PSALM 37:4

DESIRES OF THE HEART

Hopes, aspirations and desires often push people to excel and be their best. But when longings remain unfulfilled, people tend to become frustrated, bewildered and disappointed. Christians grappling with deep and unsatisfied yearnings are comforted often by the promise recorded in Psalm 37:4: "Take delight in the LORD, and he will give you the desires of your heart." Unfortunately, when the reader's attention is solely focused on how to receive things from the Lord, the important context of this verse is missed. While Scripture does identify God as the source of all that is good (Jas 1:17), his primary intent is not to dole out a limitless supply of gifts or to fulfill self-centered and worldly dreams. Prayers that are focused on the object of desire fail to include the fundamental key to fulfillment of this promise: delighting oneself in the Lord. When a person shifts his or her affection away from objects and to God (and knowing him through Christ), he or she finds that the Almighty supplants that which is less worthy of pursuit and becomes the only true goal and source of satisfaction. Then the Lord is pleased to bestow upon his children their heart's deepest longing—which turns out to be God himself!

5 Commit your way to the LORD;
trust in him and he will do this:
6 He will make your righteous reward shine like the dawn,
your vindication like the noonday sun.

7 Be still before the LORD
and wait patiently for him;
do not fret when people succeed in their ways,
when they carry out their wicked schemes.

8 Refrain from anger and turn from wrath;
do not fret—it leads only to evil.
9 For those who are evil will be destroyed,
but those who hope in the LORD will inherit the land.

10 A little while, and the wicked will be no more;
though you look for them, they will not be found.
11 But the meek will inherit the land
and enjoy peace and prosperity.

12 The wicked plot against the righteous
and gnash their teeth at them;
13 but the Lord laughs at the wicked,
for he knows their day is coming.

14 The wicked draw the sword
and bend the bow
to bring down the poor and needy,
to slay those whose ways are upright.
15 But their swords will pierce their own hearts,
and their bows will be broken.

16 Better the little that the righteous have
than the wealth of many wicked;
17 for the power of the wicked will be broken,
but the LORD upholds the righteous.

18 The blameless spend their days under the LORD's care,
and their inheritance will endure forever.
19 In times of disaster they will not wither;
in days of famine they will enjoy plenty.

20 But the wicked will perish:
Though the LORD's enemies are like the flowers of the field,
they will be consumed, they will go up in smoke.

21 The wicked borrow and do not repay,
but the righteous give generously;
22 those the LORD blesses will inherit the land,
but those he curses will be destroyed.

23 The LORD makes firm the steps
of the one who delights in him;
24 though he may stumble, he will not fall,
for the LORD upholds him with his hand.

25 I was young and now I am old,
yet I have never seen the righteous forsaken
or their children begging bread.
26 They are always generous and lend freely;
their children will be a blessing.[a]

[a] *26* Or *freely; / the names of their children will be used in blessings* (see Gen. 48:20); or *freely; / others will see that their children are blessed*

27 Turn from evil and do good;
then you will dwell in the land forever.
28 For the LORD loves the just
and will not forsake his faithful ones.

Wrongdoers will be completely destroyed[a];
the offspring of the wicked will perish.
29 The righteous will inherit the land
and dwell in it forever.

30 The mouths of the righteous utter wisdom,
and their tongues speak what is just.
31 The law of their God is in their hearts;
their feet do not slip.
32 The wicked lie in wait for the righteous,
intent on putting them to death;
33 but the LORD will not leave them in the power of the wicked
or let them be condemned when brought to trial.
34 Hope in the LORD
and keep his way.
He will exalt you to inherit the land;
when the wicked are destroyed, you will see it.
35 I have seen a wicked and ruthless man
flourishing like a luxuriant native tree,
36 but he soon passed away and was no more;
though I looked for him, he could not be found.

37 Consider the blameless, observe the upright;
a future awaits those who seek peace.[b]
38 But all sinners will be destroyed;
there will be no future[c] for the wicked.

39 The salvation of the righteous comes from the LORD;
he is their stronghold in time of trouble.
40 The LORD helps them and delivers them;
he delivers them from the wicked and saves them,
because they take refuge in him.

Psalm 38[d]

A psalm of David. A petition.

1 LORD, do not rebuke me in your anger
or discipline me in your wrath.
2 Your arrows have pierced me,
and your hand has come down on me.
3 Because of your wrath there is no health in my body;
there is no soundness in my bones because of my sin.
4 My guilt has overwhelmed me
like a burden too heavy to bear.

5 My wounds fester and are loathsome
because of my sinful folly.
6 I am bowed down and brought very low;
all day long I go about mourning.
7 My back is filled with searing pain;
there is no health in my body.

PSALM 38:1 – 22

THE IMPACT OF SIN

Psalm 38 begins with David's jarring words penned as he confessed the overwhelming guilt he experienced as a result of sin (vv. 1 – 4). It is difficult to reconcile the confident assertion of his familiar pastoral psalm that "the LORD is my shepherd" (Ps 23:1) with this lament over wrongdoing that caused wounds that "fester and are loathsome" (38:5) and left him "feeble and utterly crushed" (v. 8). Such language causes some to suggest the psalm was inspired by a life-threatening illness. However, verse 18 clearly reveals this passage to be a depiction of the destruction sin inflicts upon a person's body, mind, soul and spirit. Realizing his guilt, David's only recourse was to acknowledge his helpless condition and cry out, "Come quickly to help me, my Lord and my Savior" (v. 22).

The New Testament declares this repentant attitude to be critical for receiving the only remedy for humanity's sinful condition: salvation through Jesus Christ. While all parts of salvation, including repentance, faith, belief and desire, find their source in God (Jn 6:44), one cannot express faith without first realizing personal need and acknowledging Christ as the only One capable of delivering humanity from sin's grip (Ac 16:31; Ro 10:9 – 10). Then, believers can be confident they have bypassed God's wrath and entered into his grace (Ro 8:1 – 2). Though consequences of sin may remain, the Lord even uses those to his children's benefit and for his glory (Ro 8:28; Heb 12:4 – 10).

[a] 28 See Septuagint; Hebrew *They will be protected forever* [b] 37 Or *upright; / those who seek peace will have posterity* [c] 38 Or *posterity* [d] In Hebrew texts 38:1-22 is numbered 38:2-23.

PROMISES TO THE MEEK

History is filled with stories where it appears that those who do evil prosper while righteous and God-loving people suffer without cause. In Psalm 37, troubled people find the encouraging reminder that wrongdoers will not endure forever, and that "the meek will inherit the land and enjoy peace and prosperity" (v. 11). Hundreds of years later, Jesus made a similar statement in the Sermon on the Mount, reassuring his disciples that regardless of their present situation, the meek "will inherit the earth" (Mt 5:5). Often, the meaning of both verses is unclear to present-day readers because of an incomplete understanding of the word "meek." Modern dictionaries often add to its generally negative connotation by equating it with words like "timid," "tame," "submissive" and "docile." But since Jesus used the same Greek term to describe himself (Mt 11:28 – 29; translated "gentle"), the better definition of meekness is a more accurate characterization of the biblical meaning.

Scripture declares Christ to be unequaled in power and authority (Mt 26:53; 28:18; Jn 1:1 – 4; Col 1:16; Heb 1:3). Yet despite his rightful position as the Son of God, he willingly submitted himself to his Father (Jn 8:28; 12:49 – 50; 14:10; Php 2:6 – 8). In his interactions with people on earth, he was confident, firm and spoke fearlessly to those who opposed or misrepresented God (Mt 23:13 – 39); at the same time, to those in need he was approachable, compassionate and gentle (Mt 9:36; 14:14; 20:34; Mk 6:34; Lk 7:13; Jn 11:34 – 38).

Jesus used the agricultural analogy of two oxen joined by a yoke to invite his followers to embrace an attitude of meekness as they enter into relationship with him (Mt 11:28 – 29). A yoke is a wooden crosspiece fastened over the neck of two or more animals to unite them in pulling a plow or cart. As believers voluntarily yield their rights and submit to Christ, he promises to replace their futile efforts to make themselves right with God (Ro 3:20) with divine "rest for your souls" (Mt 11:29). In a world where so many things leave people depleted and empty, Jesus promises restoration, nurture and rekindled strength to the spiritually meek. He grants them the power to face whatever life brings with a confident assurance that God is "their stronghold in time of trouble" (Ps 37:39) and that "the righteous will inherit the land and dwell in it forever" (v. 29).

8 I am feeble and utterly crushed;
I groan in anguish of heart.

9 All my longings lie open before you, Lord;
my sighing is not hidden from you.
10 My heart pounds, my strength fails me;
even the light has gone from my eyes.
11 My friends and companions avoid me because of my wounds;
my neighbors stay far away.
12 Those who want to kill me set their traps,
those who would harm me talk of my ruin;
all day long they scheme and lie.

13 I am like the deaf, who cannot hear,
like the mute, who cannot speak;
14 I have become like one who does not hear,
whose mouth can offer no reply.
15 LORD, I wait for you;
you will answer, Lord my God.
16 For I said, "Do not let them gloat
or exalt themselves over me when my feet slip."

17 For I am about to fall,
and my pain is ever with me.
18 I confess my iniquity;
I am troubled by my sin.
19 Many have become my enemies without cause[a];
those who hate me without reason are numerous.
20 Those who repay my good with evil
lodge accusations against me,
though I seek only to do what is good.

21 LORD, do not forsake me;
do not be far from me, my God.
22 Come quickly to help me,
my Lord and my Savior.

Psalm 39[b]

For the director of music. For Jeduthun.
A psalm of David.

1 I said, "I will watch my ways
and keep my tongue from sin;
I will put a muzzle on my mouth
while in the presence of the wicked."
2 So I remained utterly silent,
not even saying anything good.
But my anguish increased;
3 my heart grew hot within me.
While I meditated, the fire burned;
then I spoke with my tongue:

4 "Show me, LORD, my life's end
and the number of my days;
let me know how fleeting my life is.
5 You have made my days a mere handbreadth;
the span of my years is as nothing before you.

[a] 19 One Dead Sea Scrolls manuscript; Masoretic Text *my vigorous enemies* [b] In Hebrew texts 39:1-13 is numbered 39:2-14.

PSALM 39:4–7

BREVITY

It often feels as though the older one gets, the shorter life seems. David seemed to grasp this irony when he wrote of the fleeting nature of life (vv. 4–5). Pointing to the vanity of worldly pursuits that promise fulfillment through fading things such as wealth, power and prestige, he illustrated how such things are meaningless against the backdrop of the brevity of life on earth (vv. 6,11). Understanding this ultimate futility led him to cry out to the Lord as his only hope (vv. 7,12).

Jesus also derided the senselessness of worrying over temporary things such as food, clothing and length of life (Mt 6:25–27). He exhorted his followers to make an essential shift to storing up treasure in heaven. Since wealth and possessions can be threatened by theft, destruction and decay and will ultimately pass away (Lk 21:33), the only true security can be found by investing in things that last for eternity (Mt 6:19–21).

Like worldly possessions, the physical bodies of people are also subject to destruction and decay. However, the New Testament reminds those who believe in Jesus that they have experienced a fundamental change in their lives (2Co 5:17; Col 2:13), and though their bodies waste away, inwardly they are continually renewed (2Co 4:16). Since being born of eternal seed which never perishes through faith in Christ (1Pe 1:23), they can trust God to continue his good work in them until the day of Jesus Christ (Php 1:6).

Everyone is but a breath,
even those who seem secure.[a]

6 "Surely everyone goes around like a mere phantom;
in vain they rush about, heaping up wealth
without knowing whose it will finally be.

7 "But now, Lord, what do I look for?
My hope is in you.
8 Save me from all my transgressions;
do not make me the scorn of fools.
9 I was silent; I would not open my mouth,
for you are the one who has done this.
10 Remove your scourge from me;
I am overcome by the blow of your hand.
11 When you rebuke and discipline anyone for their sin,
you consume their wealth like a moth —
surely everyone is but a breath.

12 "Hear my prayer, LORD,
listen to my cry for help;
do not be deaf to my weeping.
I dwell with you as a foreigner,
a stranger, as all my ancestors were.
13 Look away from me, that I may enjoy life again
before I depart and am no more."

Psalm 40[b]

For the director of music. Of David. A psalm.

1 I waited patiently for the LORD;
he turned to me and heard my cry.
2 He lifted me out of the slimy pit,
out of the mud and mire;
he set my feet on a rock
and gave me a firm place to stand.
3 He put a new song in my mouth,
a hymn of praise to our God.
Many will see and fear the LORD
and put their trust in him.

4 Blessed is the one
who trusts in the LORD,
who does not look to the proud,
to those who turn aside to false gods.[c]
5 Many, LORD my God,
are the wonders you have done,
the things you planned for us.
None can compare with you;
were I to speak and tell of your deeds,
they would be too many to declare.

6 Sacrifice and offering you did not desire —
but my ears you have opened[d] —
burnt offerings and sin offerings[e] you did not
require.

---

[a] 5 The Hebrew has *Selah* (a word of uncertain meaning) here and at the end of verse 11.
[b] In Hebrew texts 40:1-17 is numbered 40:2-18. [c] 4 Or *to lies* [d] 6 Hebrew; some Septuagint manuscripts *but a body you have prepared for me* [e] 6 Or *purification offerings*

DESIRING TO DO GOD'S WILL

In Psalm 40, David showed a remarkable example of obedience through troubled and difficult times. These troubles brought him to continual dependence on the Lord, trusting the Lord's plan and strength over his own. In verses 6 – 8, perhaps David had brought a sacrifice and offering. But his focus was on presenting his life to the Lord. He stated, "Here I am, I have come — it is written about me in the scroll. I desire to do your will, my God; your law is within my heart." According to Hebrews 10:5 – 7, Christ spoke these same words to express his obedient submission to the Father in coming to earth. Both Christ and David showed delight in doing God's will over their own.

Although important, the sacrifices themselves were not pleasing to God. He desired obedience. In David's time, sacrifices were a ritual delivering temporary atonement for sin. "Day after day every priest stands and performs his religious duties; again and again he offers the same sacrifices, which can never take away sins" (Heb 10:11). But through Jesus' obedience to his Father's plan, God provided a sacrifice made perfect forever (Php 2:8). "And by that will, we have been made holy through the sacrifice of the body of Jesus Christ once for all" (Heb 10:10).

In the same way that Jesus offered himself in obedience to God's will, his followers are called to do the same. "Offer yourselves to God as those who have been brought from death to life; and offer every part of yourself to him as an instrument of righteousness" (Ro 6:13). God's Word presents the human body as a sacred place, the place the Holy Spirit dwells. God paid a high price, the sacrifice of Jesus' body, and in doing so asks his people to honor him through total obedience to God's will. "You are not your own; you were bought at a price. Therefore honor God with your bodies" (1Co 6:19 – 20).

Doing God's will is a practical act of discipleship, a reflection of a heart obedient to God. God asks for the sacrifice of an obedient life, and he sends the Spirit to live in the hearts of his followers in order to empower them to accomplish his purposes. This requires daily surrendering one's own will, allowing the body to die to self and conform to God's will (Ro 12:1 – 2). Throughout his life on earth, Jesus was the ultimate model of this way of life.

7 Then I said, "Here I am, I have come—
it is written about me in the scroll.[a]
8 I desire to do your will, my God;
your law is within my heart."

9 I proclaim your saving acts in the great assembly;
I do not seal my lips, LORD,
as you know.
10 I do not hide your righteousness in my heart;
I speak of your faithfulness and your saving help.
I do not conceal your love and your faithfulness
from the great assembly.

11 Do not withhold your mercy from me, LORD;
may your love and faithfulness always protect me.
12 For troubles without number surround me;
my sins have overtaken me, and I cannot see.
They are more than the hairs of my head,
and my heart fails within me.
13 Be pleased to save me, LORD;
come quickly, LORD, to help me.

14 May all who want to take my life
be put to shame and confusion;
may all who desire my ruin
be turned back in disgrace.
15 May those who say to me, "Aha! Aha!"
be appalled at their own shame.
16 But may all who seek you
rejoice and be glad in you;
may those who long for your saving help always say,
"The LORD is great!"

17 But as for me, I am poor and needy;
may the Lord think of me.
You are my help and my deliverer;
you are my God, do not delay.

Psalm 41[b]

For the director of music. A psalm of David.

1 Blessed are those who have regard for the weak;
the LORD delivers them in times of trouble.
2 The LORD protects and preserves them—
they are counted among the blessed in the land—
he does not give them over to the desire of their foes.
3 The LORD sustains them on their sickbed
and restores them from their bed of illness.

4 I said, "Have mercy on me, LORD;
heal me, for I have sinned against you."
5 My enemies say of me in malice,
"When will he die and his name perish?"
6 When one of them comes to see me,
he speaks falsely, while his heart gathers slander;
then he goes out and spreads it around.

7 All my enemies whisper together against me;
they imagine the worst for me, saying,

[a] 7 Or *come / with the scroll written for me* [b] In Hebrew texts 41:1-13 is numbered 41:2-14.

[8] "A vile disease has afflicted him;
he will never get up from the place where he lies."
[9] Even my close friend,
someone I trusted,
one who shared my bread,
has turned[a] against me.

[10] But may you have mercy on me, LORD;
raise me up, that I may repay them.
[11] I know that you are pleased with me,
for my enemy does not triumph over me.
[12] Because of my integrity you uphold me
and set me in your presence forever.

[13] Praise be to the LORD, the God of Israel,
from everlasting to everlasting.
Amen and Amen.

BOOK II

Psalms 42–72

Psalm 42[b,c]

For the director of music. A maskil[d] *of the Sons of Korah.*

[1] As the deer pants for streams of water,
so my soul pants for you, my God.
[2] My soul thirsts for God, for the living God.
When can I go and meet with God?
[3] My tears have been my food
day and night,
while people say to me all day long,
"Where is your God?"
[4] These things I remember
as I pour out my soul:
how I used to go to the house of God
under the protection of the Mighty One[e]
with shouts of joy and praise
among the festive throng.

[5] Why, my soul, are you downcast?
Why so disturbed within me?
Put your hope in God,
for I will yet praise him,
my Savior and my God.

[6] My soul is downcast within me;
therefore I will remember you
from the land of the Jordan,
the heights of Hermon—from Mount Mizar.
[7] Deep calls to deep
in the roar of your waterfalls;
all your waves and breakers
have swept over me.

[a] 9 Hebrew *has lifted up his heel* [b] In many Hebrew manuscripts Psalms 42 and 43 constitute one psalm. [c] In Hebrew texts 42:1-11 is numbered 42:2-12. [d] Title: Probably a literary or musical term [e] 4 See Septuagint and Syriac; the meaning of the Hebrew for this line is uncertain.

PSALM 41:9

DOUBLE-CROSSED

Wounds from a friend cut deep. David and Jesus have both felt this pain. In the midst of the Last Supper with his beloved disciples, shortly after Jesus washed their feet, he quoted David's words: "He who shared my bread has turned against me" (Jn 13:18). Jesus knew Judas would soon betray him. As the perfect Son of God, Jesus intimately knows all people—including their sin and shame—yet he loves them anyway. Jesus' followers are commanded to love like this. Love is a choice, and in times of hurt and betrayal, it will not be easy. Yet through this act of love for others, Jesus says that the watching world will recognize his followers (Jn 13:35). People know that even their closest friends might abandon them if they knew the truth about their sin. But not Jesus. Jesus loves with a perfect, unconditional love. He never gives up on his people. And through this great love, his followers are redeemed (Eph 1:7).

PSALM 42:5–11

THE DOWNCAST SOUL

Feelings of sadness and discouragement are inevitable. This life has times of dancing and praising, but also times of deep anguish and despair. The psalmist cried out to God, declaring his downcast soul. Jesus understands. In Luke 22, preceding his impending crucifixion, Jesus cried out to his Father, "'Take this cup from me' … And being in anguish, he prayed more earnestly, and his sweat was like drops of blood falling to the ground" (Lk 22:42,44). This passage shows Jesus' very real and

(continued on page 837)

PSALM 41:1 – 13

NO MORE HATRED

This psalm was written by David at a time when he found himself betrayed by someone he once trusted (v. 9). It is a prayer asking God, the source of all blessings, to deliver, protect, sustain and restore him from his undeserved suffering (vv. 1 – 3). His enemies spread lies about him, wanted the worst for him and tarnished his reputation by spreading gossip (vv. 6 – 8), all the while preferring him dead and forgotten (v. 5).

In the midst of this trial, instead of hating his enemies, David turned to God. He prayerfully pleaded for mercy, knowing God would raise him up and repay his enemies in due time (v. 10). David claimed victory over his enemies and looked to God for his affirmation and praise (v. 11). Through intense pain and hardship, David kept his integrity, knowing that God would uphold him (v. 12). And he called for praise of the one true God, "from everlasting to everlasting" (v. 13).

Jesus Christ, the very Son of God, became flesh and knew the pain of betrayal and hatred. One of his closest associates, enticed by a monetary reward, turned him over to the authorities. Judas approached Jesus in the garden and kissed him on the cheek, signaling to Jesus' enemies that he was the one for whom they were looking (Lk 22:48). Jesus did not allow hate in his heart, but he showed only compassion and gentleness to his friend who betrayed him and to those who arrested him (Lk 22:49 – 51).

The wisdom of Proverbs teaches the consequences of love versus hate — "hatred stirs up conflict, but love covers over all wrongs" (Pr 10:12). Jesus' life modeled perfect love, and the church is called to love "because he first loved us" (1Jn 4:19). For "whoever claims to love God yet hates a brother or sister is a liar" (1Jn 4:20). Followers of Christ who do not love those they do life with, those they can see, are told they cannot love God, whom they have not seen (1Jn 4:20). Jesus commands believers to love even their enemies and those that persecute them (Mt 5:44).

8 By day the LORD directs his love,
at night his song is with me —
a prayer to the God of my life.

9 I say to God my Rock,
"Why have you forgotten me?
Why must I go about mourning,
oppressed by the enemy?"
10 My bones suffer mortal agony
as my foes taunt me,
saying to me all day long,
"Where is your God?"

11 Why, my soul, are you downcast?
Why so disturbed within me?
Put your hope in God,
for I will yet praise him,
my Savior and my God.

Psalm 43[a]

1 Vindicate me, my God,
and plead my cause
against an unfaithful nation.
Rescue me from those who are
deceitful and wicked.
2 You are God my stronghold.
Why have you rejected me?
Why must I go about mourning,
oppressed by the enemy?
3 Send me your light and your faithful care,
let them lead me;
let them bring me to your holy mountain,
to the place where you dwell.
4 Then I will go to the altar of God,
to God, my joy and my delight.
I will praise you with the lyre,
O God, my God.

5 Why, my soul, are you downcast?
Why so disturbed within me?
Put your hope in God,
for I will yet praise him,
my Savior and my God.

Psalm 44[b]

For the director of music. Of the Sons of Korah. A maskil.[c]

1 We have heard it with our ears, O God;
our ancestors have told us
what you did in their days,
in days long ago.
2 With your hand you drove out the nations
and planted our ancestors;
you crushed the peoples
and made our ancestors flourish.

[a] In many Hebrew manuscripts Psalms 42 and 43 constitute one psalm. [b] In Hebrew texts 44:1-26 is numbered 44:2-27. [c] Title: Probably a literary or musical term

(The Downcast Soul, continued)

deep despair. However, in the midst of crying out to God, he declared his longing for the Father's will to be accomplished, not his own. In the same way, God hears and answers prayer, even when it may seem he has forgotten his people. And because God the Son left his throne in heaven to walk the earth in human flesh, he knows and understands the human experience on every level — physical, spiritual and emotional. Therefore, God's people can confidently praise him and put their hope in him (Ps 42:11), knowing that one day, through Jesus' costly sacrifice, they will experience anew the presence of God and his goodness.

PSALM 43:5

HOPE IN GOD

Psalm 43 is a prayer to God in a time of trouble. Through doubt and stress, the psalmist urged his inner being, by the power of God, to keep believing. "Why, my soul, are you downcast?" he questioned himself (Ps 43:5). Yet he stood firm, keeping his hope in God and praising him through his distress. Hope in God, through Jesus, is one of the central messages of the New Testament. Without Christ, people have no hope. However, the shed blood of Christ brings believers back to their Creator and gives them the hope they once lacked (Eph 2:12–13). He then prayed that God would give spiritual understanding to his people, opening the eyes of their hearts, allowing them to know the hope to which he has called them — "the riches of his glorious inheritance in his holy people" (Eph 1:18). People may hope in many things, but there is one hope that all

(continued on next page)

(Hope in God, continued)

Christians have in common, the Lord Jesus Christ. It is in him alone that believers find true hope and eternal riches.

PSALM 44:24

THE FACE OF CHRIST

Why does God look the other way? The psalmist asked this, thinking God had forgotten the people of Israel in their misery and oppression. The Israelites were conquered by their enemies, scattered and dishonored, yet they had not fallen away from God. They had remained faithful and obedient to his covenant (Ps 44:17). Yet, God chose to allow afflictions on his people, as if he were hiding his face from them (v. 24). They sought God in their darkness, asking him to reveal himself and his glory.

The New Testament affirms that Jesus came to reveal God to all people, displaying the glory of God in the face of Jesus. "For God, who said, 'Let light shine out of darkness,' made his light shine in our hearts to give us the light of the knowledge of God's glory displayed in the face of Christ" (2Co 4:6). No one has seen the Father (Ex 33:20; Jn 6:46), yet through the face of Christ, God's people see his glory revealed. And keeping hearts focused on eternity, Jesus' followers long for Christ's return — when "they will see his face, and his name will be on their foreheads ... They will not need the light of a lamp or the light of the sun, for the Lord God will give them light" (Rev 22:4–5).

3 It was not by their sword that they won the land,
nor did their arm bring them victory;
it was your right hand, your arm,
and the light of your face, for you loved them.

4 You are my King and my God,
who decrees[a] victories for Jacob.
5 Through you we push back our enemies;
through your name we trample our foes.
6 I put no trust in my bow,
my sword does not bring me victory;
7 but you give us victory over our enemies,
you put our adversaries to shame.
8 In God we make our boast all day long,
and we will praise your name forever.[b]

9 But now you have rejected and humbled us;
you no longer go out with our armies.
10 You made us retreat before the enemy,
and our adversaries have plundered us.
11 You gave us up to be devoured like sheep
and have scattered us among the nations.
12 You sold your people for a pittance,
gaining nothing from their sale.

13 You have made us a reproach to our neighbors,
the scorn and derision of those around us.
14 You have made us a byword among the nations;
the peoples shake their heads at us.
15 I live in disgrace all day long,
and my face is covered with shame
16 at the taunts of those who reproach and revile me,
because of the enemy, who is bent on revenge.

17 All this came upon us,
though we had not forgotten you;
we had not been false to your covenant.
18 Our hearts had not turned back;
our feet had not strayed from your path.
19 But you crushed us and made us a haunt for jackals;
you covered us over with deep darkness.

20 If we had forgotten the name of our God
or spread out our hands to a foreign god,
21 would not God have discovered it,
since he knows the secrets of the heart?
22 Yet for your sake we face death all day long;
we are considered as sheep to be slaughtered.

23 Awake, Lord! Why do you sleep?
Rouse yourself! Do not reject us forever.
24 Why do you hide your face
and forget our misery and oppression?

25 We are brought down to the dust;
our bodies cling to the ground.
26 Rise up and help us;
rescue us because of your unfailing love.

[a] *4* Septuagint, Aquila and Syriac; Hebrew *King, O God; / command* [b] *8* The Hebrew has *Selah* (a word of uncertain meaning) here.

Psalm 45[a]

For the director of music. To the tune of "Lilies." Of the Sons of Korah. A maskil.[b] *A wedding song.*

[1] My heart is stirred by a noble theme
as I recite my verses for the king;
my tongue is the pen of a skillful writer.

[2] You are the most excellent of men
and your lips have been anointed with grace,
since God has blessed you forever.

[3] Gird your sword on your side, you mighty one;
clothe yourself with splendor and majesty.
[4] In your majesty ride forth victoriously
in the cause of truth, humility and justice;
let your right hand achieve awesome deeds.
[5] Let your sharp arrows pierce the hearts of the king's enemies;
let the nations fall beneath your feet.
[6] Your throne, O God,[c] will last for ever and ever;
a scepter of justice will be the scepter of your kingdom.
[7] You love righteousness and hate wickedness;
therefore God, your God, has set you above your companions
by anointing you with the oil of joy.
[8] All your robes are fragrant with myrrh and aloes and cassia;
from palaces adorned with ivory
the music of the strings makes you glad.
[9] Daughters of kings are among your honored women;
at your right hand is the royal bride in gold of Ophir.

[10] Listen, daughter, and pay careful attention:
Forget your people and your father's house.
[11] Let the king be enthralled by your beauty;
honor him, for he is your lord.
[12] The city of Tyre will come with a gift,[d]
people of wealth will seek your favor.
[13] All glorious is the princess within her chamber;
her gown is interwoven with gold.
[14] In embroidered garments she is led to the king;
her virgin companions follow her —
those brought to be with her.
[15] Led in with joy and gladness,
they enter the palace of the king.

[16] Your sons will take the place of your fathers;
you will make them princes throughout the land.

[17] I will perpetuate your memory through all generations;
therefore the nations will praise you for ever and ever.

Psalm 46[e]

For the director of music. Of the Sons of Korah. According to alamoth.[f] *A song.*

[1] God is our refuge and strength,
an ever-present help in trouble.

---

[a] In Hebrew texts 45:1-17 is numbered 45:2-18. [b] Title: Probably a literary or musical term
[c] *6* Here the king is addressed as God's representative. [d] *12* Or *A Tyrian robe is among the gifts* [e] In Hebrew texts 46:1-11 is numbered 46:2-12. [f] Title: Probably a musical term

THE KING AND HIS BRIDE

The Israelite king described in this psalm is a king above many kings. He is well respected by the people and by God. He is described as the "most excellent of men" (v. 2) — one who makes his cause "truth, humility and justice" (v. 4), who always defeats his enemies (v. 5), and who establishes a throne that lasts forever (v. 6). All these qualities point directly to Jesus. He is the King of all kings, "exalted … to the highest place" by God (Php 2:7 – 9). Jesus is truth (Jn 14:6), the humblest man to walk the earth (Php 2:8), and his ministry and life constantly challenged people to live for God and pursue righteousness (Mt 5:6). God gives his people "victory through our Lord Jesus Christ" (1Co 15:57). Jesus sits at the right hand of God and his throne "will last for ever and ever" (Heb 1:8).

Psalm 45 is a song of love — a royal wedding song that celebrates marriage in a grand manner — a wedding between a king and his beloved. The king is completely in love with his bride, and she is asked to honor and adore him (v. 11). This psalm prophetically portrays the glorious reign of Jesus — God's promised Messiah and the final and ultimate King (vv. 6 – 7) — and how his church is his holy bride.

In his great and unfailing love, Jesus, the King over all, invites his church to become his holy bride, asking them to be ready for his return (Rev 19:7). The anticipation of a bride awaiting her groom as the wedding approaches is immeasurable. Months and months of preparation are spent on this one day. The bride is at her very best, with the best of intentions and expectations. Her heart overflows with joy, longing for her groom. This is an exact representation of how the church should be longing, preparing and eagerly anticipating the coming of King Jesus — singing and praying, "Come, Lord Jesus" (Rev 22:20).

[2] Therefore we will not fear, though the earth give way
and the mountains fall into the heart of the sea,
[3] though its waters roar and foam
and the mountains quake with their surging.[a]

[4] There is a river whose streams make glad the city of God,
the holy place where the Most High dwells.
[5] God is within her, she will not fall;
God will help her at break of day.
[6] Nations are in uproar, kingdoms fall;
he lifts his voice, the earth melts.
[7] The LORD Almighty is with us;
the God of Jacob is our fortress.

[8] Come and see what the LORD has done,
the desolations he has brought on the earth.
[9] He makes wars cease
to the ends of the earth.
He breaks the bow and shatters the spear;
he burns the shields[b] with fire.
[10] He says, "Be still, and know that I am God;
I will be exalted among the nations,
I will be exalted in the earth."

[11] The LORD Almighty is with us;
the God of Jacob is our fortress.

Psalm 47[c]

For the director of music. Of the Sons of Korah. A psalm.

[1] Clap your hands, all you nations;
shout to God with cries of joy.

[2] For the LORD Most High is awesome,
the great King over all the earth.
[3] He subdued nations under us,
peoples under our feet.
[4] He chose our inheritance for us,
the pride of Jacob, whom he loved.[d]

[5] God has ascended amid shouts of joy,
the LORD amid the sounding of trumpets.
[6] Sing praises to God, sing praises;
sing praises to our King, sing praises.
[7] For God is the King of all the earth;
sing to him a psalm of praise.

[8] God reigns over the nations;
God is seated on his holy throne.
[9] The nobles of the nations assemble
as the people of the God of Abraham,
for the kings[e] of the earth belong to God;
he is greatly exalted.

[a] 3 The Hebrew has *Selah* (a word of uncertain meaning) here and at the end of verses 7 and 11. [b] 9 Or *chariots* [c] In Hebrew texts 47:1-9 is numbered 47:2-10. [d] 4 The Hebrew has *Selah* (a word of uncertain meaning) here. [e] 9 Or *shields*

PSALM 47:1–9

KING OVER ALL

All kings have derived authority; only one King, the great God of heaven, is absolute in power and righteousness. This psalm not only exalts and worships God as King, but foreshadows Jesus as the coming King. Jesus is "the blessed and only Ruler, the King of kings and Lord of lords" (1Ti 6:15) who reigns over the people (Lk 1:33), chooses an inheritance for them (Eph 1:11), was exalted by God (Php 2:9) and ascended into heaven, where he is seated once again on his holy throne (Ac 2:33).

Through King Jesus, victory is promised for God's people, determined long ago by God when "he subdued nations under us, peoples under our feet" (Ps 47:3). The church longs for the day when Jesus will return — a day when he will display all his glory. He will sit on his throne in all heavenly glory with all the nations gathered before him. And he will say to his people, "Come, you who are blessed by my Father; take your inheritance, the kingdom prepared for you since the creation of the world" (Mt 25:34).

OUR GOD REIGNS

God reigns — over his city, over the earth and over all the nations (vv. 4 – 5,10). Jerusalem is God's chosen city. And God is the strength and refuge of his city (v. 1). He is within her — not just watching over or in control of, but present and in the midst of the people (v. 7). And he promises that, as long as the people stay faithful to him, the city will not fall (vv. 5,7). Surrounding nations are in turmoil, but the city of God is not to fear, for he is in control; just the sound of his voice can destroy the earth (v. 6). God's people must fix their eyes on what he can do (v. 8), to be still and wait on him — allowing him to be exalted on high among the nations (v. 10).

The people of Israel had God as their king, but that didn't satisfy them. They wanted a king they could see. A military king — one who would come and rescue them from their surrounding enemies. God promised his people a king, although the plan was nothing like what they expected or wanted. Jesus, God's Son, came to earth to lead the people and be their Savior — not from their enemies, but from their sins (Mt 1:21). He reigned in a new way — set apart from all other kings. He reigned in humility, not from an earthly throne (Php 2:7). His message was "the good news of peace" (Ac 10:36). He came to serve, not to be served (Mt 20:28). And paradoxically, the glory of Jesus' reign is the result of his humble service, gentleness, and self-sacrifice. Jesus did not seek his own glory. Instead, he sought the glory of his Father alone — which resulted in the Father glorifying him (Jn 8:54; Php 2:9 – 11).

Jesus, the King of the Jews, conquered death and now lives within the heart of every believer (Gal 2:20). He is with his believers at all times, never changing (Ps 46:7; Heb 13:8). "Therefore [they] will not fear" (Ps 46:2) because he is "an ever-present help in trouble" (Ps 46:1). Thus those who accept Jesus as Savior and believe in him will experience firsthand the comfort of his strength, his power, his protection and his counsel. He is the One true King, the Savior of all humankind, who is seated at the right hand of God, reigning over the whole earth in all majesty and glory. He is Immanuel — God with us.

Psalm 48[a]

A song. A psalm of the Sons of Korah.

1 Great is the LORD, and most worthy of praise,
in the city of our God, his holy mountain.

2 Beautiful in its loftiness,
the joy of the whole earth,
like the heights of Zaphon[b] is Mount Zion,
the city of the Great King.
3 God is in her citadels;
he has shown himself to be her fortress.

4 When the kings joined forces,
when they advanced together,
5 they saw her and were astounded;
they fled in terror.
6 Trembling seized them there,
pain like that of a woman in labor.
7 You destroyed them like ships of Tarshish
shattered by an east wind.

8 As we have heard,
so we have seen
in the city of the LORD Almighty,
in the city of our God:
God makes her secure
forever.[c]

9 Within your temple, O God,
we meditate on your unfailing love.
10 Like your name, O God,
your praise reaches to the ends of the earth;
your right hand is filled with righteousness.
11 Mount Zion rejoices,
the villages of Judah are glad
because of your judgments.

12 Walk about Zion, go around her,
count her towers,
13 consider well her ramparts,
view her citadels,
that you may tell of them
to the next generation.

14 For this God is our God for ever and ever;
he will be our guide even to the end.

Psalm 49[d]

For the director of music. Of the Sons of Korah. A psalm.

1 Hear this, all you peoples;
listen, all who live in this world,
2 both low and high,
rich and poor alike:
3 My mouth will speak words of wisdom;
the meditation of my heart will give you understanding.

[a] In Hebrew texts 48:1-14 is numbered 48:2-15. [b] *2 Zaphon* was the most sacred mountain of the Canaanites. [c] *8* The Hebrew has *Selah* (a word of uncertain meaning) here. [d] In Hebrew texts 49:1-20 is numbered 49:2-21.

PSALM 49:15

REDEEMED

God is a perfect God. His creation was perfect and humankind was created in his perfect image. Yet God's people fell away. They chose sin. They chose their own way, a way that led to death. But God promised to redeem his people, knowing the only way to life was by purchasing their freedom. "You were bought at a price" (1Co 6:20). Christ went ahead of God's people, preparing a place for them and making a way for them, ultimately giving "his life as a ransom for many" (Mt 20:28). Through the blood of his Son, God redeemed humankind. They were once dead in their transgressions, but now are promised to be alive with Christ once again. The psalmist foreshadowed this, stating, "He will surely take me to himself" (Ps 49:15). Although risen from the dead and reunited with God (Mk 16:6), Christ showed himself to his disciples and those who loved him. After Christ's resurrection, the disciples were told, "He is going ahead of you into Galilee. There you will see him, just as he told you" (Mk 16:7). In the same way as for his first disciples, Christ has gone ahead of all believers, redeeming them to their Father and giving them hope of eternal life, which was "promised before the beginning of time" (Titus 1:2).

4 I will turn my ear to a proverb;
with the harp I will expound my riddle:

5 Why should I fear when evil days come,
when wicked deceivers surround me—
6 those who trust in their wealth
and boast of their great riches?
7 No one can redeem the life of another
or give to God a ransom for them—
8 the ransom for a life is costly,
no payment is ever enough—
9 so that they should live on forever
and not see decay.
10 For all can see that the wise die,
that the foolish and the senseless also perish,
leaving their wealth to others.
11 Their tombs will remain their houses[a] forever,
their dwellings for endless generations,
though they had[b] named lands after themselves.

12 People, despite their wealth, do not endure;
they are like the beasts that perish.

13 This is the fate of those who trust in themselves,
and of their followers, who approve their sayings.[c]
14 They are like sheep and are destined to die;
death will be their shepherd
(but the upright will prevail over them in the morning).
Their forms will decay in the grave,
far from their princely mansions.
15 But God will redeem me from the realm of the dead;
he will surely take me to himself.
16 Do not be overawed when others grow rich,
when the splendor of their houses increases;
17 for they will take nothing with them when they die,
their splendor will not descend with them.
18 Though while they live they count themselves blessed—
and people praise you when you prosper—
19 they will join those who have gone before them,
who will never again see the light of life.

20 People who have wealth but lack understanding
are like the beasts that perish.

Psalm 50

A psalm of Asaph.

1 The Mighty One, God, the LORD,
speaks and summons the earth
from the rising of the sun to where it sets.
2 From Zion, perfect in beauty,
God shines forth.
3 Our God comes
and will not be silent;
a fire devours before him,
and around him a tempest rages.

---

[a] 11 Septuagint and Syriac; Hebrew *In their thoughts their houses will remain*
[b] 11 Or *generations, / for they have* [c] 13 The Hebrew has *Selah* (a word of uncertain meaning) here and at the end of verse 15.

[4] He summons the heavens above,
and the earth, that he may judge his people:
[5] "Gather to me this consecrated people,
who made a covenant with me by sacrifice."
[6] And the heavens proclaim his righteousness,
for he is a God of justice.[a,b]

[7] "Listen, my people, and I will speak;
I will testify against you, Israel:
I am God, your God.
[8] I bring no charges against you concerning your sacrifices
or concerning your burnt offerings, which are ever before me.
[9] I have no need of a bull from your stall
or of goats from your pens,
[10] for every animal of the forest is mine,
and the cattle on a thousand hills.
[11] I know every bird in the mountains,
and the insects in the fields are mine.
[12] If I were hungry I would not tell you,
for the world is mine, and all that is in it.
[13] Do I eat the flesh of bulls
or drink the blood of goats?

[14] "Sacrifice thank offerings to God,
fulfill your vows to the Most High,
[15] and call on me in the day of trouble;
I will deliver you, and you will honor me."

[16] But to the wicked person, God says:

"What right have you to recite my laws
or take my covenant on your lips?
[17] You hate my instruction
and cast my words behind you.
[18] When you see a thief, you join with him;
you throw in your lot with adulterers.
[19] You use your mouth for evil
and harness your tongue to deceit.
[20] You sit and testify against your brother
and slander your own mother's son.
[21] When you did these things and I kept silent,
you thought I was exactly[c] like you.
But I now arraign you
and set my accusations before you.

[22] "Consider this, you who forget God,
or I will tear you to pieces, with no one to rescue you:
[23] Those who sacrifice thank offerings honor me,
and to the blameless[d] I will show my salvation."

Psalm 51[e]

For the director of music. A psalm of David. When the prophet Nathan came to him after David had committed adultery with Bathsheba.

[1] Have mercy on me, O God,
according to your unfailing love;

---

[a] *6* With a different word division of the Hebrew; Masoretic Text *for God himself is judge*
[b] *6* The Hebrew has *Selah* (a word of uncertain meaning) here. [c] *21* Or *thought the 'I AM' was* [d] *23* Probable reading of the original Hebrew text; the meaning of the Masoretic Text for this phrase is uncertain. [e] In Hebrew texts 51:1-19 is numbered 51:3-21.

according to your great compassion
blot out my transgressions.
2 Wash away all my iniquity
and cleanse me from my sin.

3 For I know my transgressions,
and my sin is always before me.
4 Against you, you only, have I sinned
and done what is evil in your sight;
so you are right in your verdict
and justified when you judge.
5 Surely I was sinful at birth,
sinful from the time my mother conceived me.
6 Yet you desired faithfulness even in the womb;
you taught me wisdom in that secret place.

7 Cleanse me with hyssop, and I will be clean;
wash me, and I will be whiter than snow.
8 Let me hear joy and gladness;
let the bones you have crushed rejoice.
9 Hide your face from my sins
and blot out all my iniquity.

10 Create in me a pure heart, O God,
and renew a steadfast spirit within me.
11 Do not cast me from your presence
or take your Holy Spirit from me.
12 Restore to me the joy of your salvation
and grant me a willing spirit, to sustain me.

13 Then I will teach transgressors your ways,
so that sinners will turn back to you.
14 Deliver me from the guilt of bloodshed, O God,
you who are God my Savior,
and my tongue will sing of your righteousness.
15 Open my lips, Lord,
and my mouth will declare your praise.
16 You do not delight in sacrifice, or I would bring it;
you do not take pleasure in burnt offerings.
17 My sacrifice, O God, is[a] a broken spirit;
a broken and contrite heart
you, God, will not despise.

18 May it please you to prosper Zion,
to build up the walls of Jerusalem.
19 Then you will delight in the sacrifices of the righteous,
in burnt offerings offered whole;
then bulls will be offered on your altar.

Psalm 52[b]

For the director of music. A maskil[c] *of David. When Doeg the Edomite had gone to Saul and told him: "David has gone to the house of Ahimelek."*

1 Why do you boast of evil, you mighty hero?
Why do you boast all day long,
you who are a disgrace in the eyes of God?

[a] 17 Or *The sacrifices of God are* [b] In Hebrew texts 52:1-9 is numbered 52:3-11. [c] Title: Probably a literary or musical term

PSALM 51:1 – 19

SECOND CHANCES

David sinned against God and his own people. Because of his great sin, people's lives were forever impacted (2Sa 11). When confronted with his failure, David cried out to God with a repentant heart and asked for a second chance. He asked for a chance to choose God's way over his sinful ways. He asked for mercy (Ps 51:1), a pure heart and steadfast spirit (v. 10), a restored relationship with God (v. 12) and deliverance from his guilt (v. 14). David knew he deserved punishment and judgment for his wrongdoings, recognizing that his sin was against God and God alone (v. 4), yet he also knew that God is a God of forgiveness, mercy and compassion (v. 1).

Even though David, a man after God's own heart, fell into sin, God didn't give up on him. God took David's sin and used it to display his goodness and his glory. Solomon, son of David and Bathsheba, grew up to be the wisest man on earth (1Ki 4:30 – 31). And about a thousand years later, Jesus would come from that same lineage. The Savior of the world was born into a lineage tainted by sin.

God is a God of second chances. He is in every detail and is sovereign over all. Although sin is never a part of his plan, he makes "light shine out of darkness" (2Co 4:6) and "in all things God works for the good of those who love him" (Ro 8:28). This was Jesus' ultimate mission during his time on earth — to restore God's people, giving them the gift of life instead of death (Jn 10:10). His blood covered over all the sins of humankind, washing them whiter than snow (Ps 51:7; Rev 7:14) — not because they deserved such a gift, but because of God's great love for them (Jn 3:16; Eph 2:4). God promises "that neither death nor life, neither angels nor demons, neither the present nor the future, nor any powers, neither height nor depth, nor anything else in all creation, will be able to separate us from the love of God that is in Christ Jesus our Lord" (Ro 8:38 – 39).

[2]You who practice deceit,
your tongue plots destruction;
it is like a sharpened razor.
[3]You love evil rather than good,
falsehood rather than speaking the truth.[a]
[4]You love every harmful word,
you deceitful tongue!

[5]Surely God will bring you down to everlasting ruin:
He will snatch you up and pluck you from your tent;
he will uproot you from the land of the living.
[6]The righteous will see and fear;
they will laugh at you, saying,
[7]"Here now is the man
who did not make God his stronghold
but trusted in his great wealth
and grew strong by destroying others!"
[8]But I am like an olive tree
flourishing in the house of God;
I trust in God's unfailing love
for ever and ever.
[9]For what you have done I will always praise you
in the presence of your faithful people.
And I will hope in your name,
for your name is good.

PSALM 53:1–3

NO GOOD

Everyone—that means all people, believers and unbelievers alike—has sinned. Sin is universal and inescapable. If this concept is not understood, one misses a foundational aspect of the gospel message. No one can live up to what God created humans to be. "For all have sinned and fall short of the glory of God" (Ro 3:23). Knowing people couldn't save themselves, God made a way through his Son. God's people are "justified freely by his grace through the redemption that came by Christ Jesus" (Ro 3:24). Jesus, the only perfect human to walk the earth, was presented as a sacrifice of atonement for the sins of his people. "He was pierced for our transgressions, he was crushed for our iniquities; the punishment that brought us peace was on him, and by his wounds we are healed" (Isa 53:5). And because "there is no one who does good" (Ps 53:3; quoted in Ro 3:12), Jesus paid the ultimate sacrifice, suffering in the place of sinners. It is the people's sin that Jesus bore on the cross. And through this act of immeasurable love, he gives hope and life to all who believe.

Psalm 53[b]

For the director of music. According to mahalath.[c]
A maskil[d] *of David.*

[1]The fool says in his heart,
"There is no God."
They are corrupt, and their ways are vile;
there is no one who does good.

[2]God looks down from heaven
on all mankind
to see if there are any who understand,
any who seek God.
[3]Everyone has turned away, all have become corrupt;
there is no one who does good,
not even one.

[4]Do all these evildoers know nothing?

They devour my people as though eating bread;
they never call on God.
[5]But there they are, overwhelmed with dread,
where there was nothing to dread.
God scattered the bones of those who attacked you;
you put them to shame, for God despised them.

[6]Oh, that salvation for Israel would come out of Zion!
When God restores his people,
let Jacob rejoice and Israel be glad!

[a] *3* The Hebrew has *Selah* (a word of uncertain meaning) here and at the end of verse 5.
[b] In Hebrew texts 53:1-6 is numbered 53:2-7. [c] Title: Probably a musical term [d] Title: Probably a literary or musical term

Psalm 54[a]

For the director of music. With stringed instruments. A maskil[b] *of David. When the Ziphites had gone to Saul and said, "Is not David hiding among us?"*

1 Save me, O God, by your name;
vindicate me by your might.
2 Hear my prayer, O God;
listen to the words of my mouth.

3 Arrogant foes are attacking me;
ruthless people are trying to kill me—
people without regard for God.[c]

4 Surely God is my help;
the Lord is the one who sustains me.

5 Let evil recoil on those who slander me;
in your faithfulness destroy them.

6 I will sacrifice a freewill offering to you;
I will praise your name, LORD, for it is good.
7 You have delivered me from all my troubles,
and my eyes have looked in triumph on my foes.

Psalm 55[d]

For the director of music. With stringed instruments. A maskil[b] *of David.*

1 Listen to my prayer, O God,
do not ignore my plea;
2 hear me and answer me.
My thoughts trouble me and I am distraught
3 because of what my enemy is saying,
because of the threats of the wicked;
for they bring down suffering on me
and assail me in their anger.

4 My heart is in anguish within me;
the terrors of death have fallen on me.
5 Fear and trembling have beset me;
horror has overwhelmed me.
6 I said, "Oh, that I had the wings of a dove!
I would fly away and be at rest.
7 I would flee far away
and stay in the desert;[e]
8 I would hurry to my place of shelter,
far from the tempest and storm."

9 Lord, confuse the wicked, confound their words,
for I see violence and strife in the city.
10 Day and night they prowl about on its walls;
malice and abuse are within it.
11 Destructive forces are at work in the city;
threats and lies never leave its streets.

12 If an enemy were insulting me,
I could endure it;

---

[a] In Hebrew texts 54:1-7 is numbered 54:3-9. [b] Title: Probably a literary or musical term
[c] 3 The Hebrew has *Selah* (a word of uncertain meaning) here. [d] In Hebrew texts 55:1-23 is numbered 55:2-24. [e] 7 The Hebrew has *Selah* (a word of uncertain meaning) here and in the middle of verse 19.

if a foe were rising against me,
  I could hide.
13 But it is you, a man like myself,
  my companion, my close friend,
14 with whom I once enjoyed sweet fellowship
  at the house of God,
as we walked about
  among the worshipers.

15 Let death take my enemies by surprise;
  let them go down alive to the realm of the dead,
  for evil finds lodging among them.

16 As for me, I call to God,
  and the LORD saves me.
17 Evening, morning and noon
  I cry out in distress,
  and he hears my voice.
18 He rescues me unharmed
  from the battle waged against me,
  even though many oppose me.
19 God, who is enthroned from of old,
  who does not change —
he will hear them and humble them,
  because they have no fear of God.

20 My companion attacks his friends;
  he violates his covenant.
21 His talk is smooth as butter,
  yet war is in his heart;
his words are more soothing than oil,
  yet they are drawn swords.

22 Cast your cares on the LORD
  and he will sustain you;
he will never let
  the righteous be shaken.
23 But you, God, will bring down the wicked
  into the pit of decay;
the bloodthirsty and deceitful
  will not live out half their days.

But as for me, I trust in you.

Psalm 56[a]

For the director of music. To the tune of "A Dove on Distant Oaks." Of David. A miktam.[b] *When the Philistines had seized him in Gath.*

1 Be merciful to me, my God,
  for my enemies are in hot pursuit;
  all day long they press their attack.
2 My adversaries pursue me all day long;
  in their pride many are attacking me.

3 When I am afraid, I put my trust in you.
4   In God, whose word I praise —
in God I trust and am not afraid.
  What can mere mortals do to me?

[a] In Hebrew texts 56:1-13 is numbered 56:2-14. [b] Title: Probably a literary or musical term

[5] All day long they twist my words;
all their schemes are for my ruin.
[6] They conspire, they lurk,
they watch my steps,
hoping to take my life.
[7] Because of their wickedness do not[a] let them escape;
in your anger, God, bring the nations down.

[8] Record my misery;
list my tears on your scroll[b] —
are they not in your record?
[9] Then my enemies will turn back
when I call for help.
By this I will know that God is for me.

[10] In God, whose word I praise,
in the LORD, whose word I praise —
[11] in God I trust and am not afraid.
What can man do to me?

[12] I am under vows to you, my God;
I will present my thank offerings to you.
[13] For you have delivered me from death
and my feet from stumbling,
that I may walk before God
in the light of life.

Psalm 57[c]

For the director of music. To the tune of "Do Not Destroy." Of David.
A miktam.[d] *When he had fled from Saul into the cave.*

[1] Have mercy on me, my God, have mercy on me,
for in you I take refuge.
I will take refuge in the shadow of your wings
until the disaster has passed.

[2] I cry out to God Most High,
to God, who vindicates me.
[3] He sends from heaven and saves me,
rebuking those who hotly pursue me —[e]
God sends forth his love and his faithfulness.

[4] I am in the midst of lions;
I am forced to dwell among ravenous beasts —
men whose teeth are spears and arrows,
whose tongues are sharp swords.

[5] Be exalted, O God, above the heavens;
let your glory be over all the earth.

[6] They spread a net for my feet —
I was bowed down in distress.
They dug a pit in my path —
but they have fallen into it themselves.

[7] My heart, O God, is steadfast,
my heart is steadfast;
I will sing and make music.

---

[a] *7* Probable reading of the original Hebrew text; Masoretic Text does not have *do not*.
[b] *8* Or *misery; / put my tears in your wineskin* [c] In Hebrew texts 57:1-11 is numbered 57:2-12.
[d] Title: Probably a literary or musical term [e] *3* The Hebrew has *Selah* (a word of uncertain meaning) here and at the end of verse 6.

[8] Awake, my soul!
Awake, harp and lyre!
I will awaken the dawn.

[9] I will praise you, Lord, among the nations;
I will sing of you among the peoples.
[10] For great is your love, reaching to the heavens;
your faithfulness reaches to the skies.

[11] Be exalted, O God, above the heavens;
let your glory be over all the earth.

PSALM 58:1 – 11

JUSTICE

The psalmist knew that the God he served is a God of justice. He is a "God who judges the earth" (v. 11). The judges on earth were ruling unjustly. They were merely humans but acting as if they had divine power (vv. 1 – 2). Yet, the psalmist prayed to God, asking him to provide justice for his people and for sudden judgment to come upon the unrighteous (vv. 9 – 11). The psalmist was confident in God and his mighty power to bring divine justice upon these evil judges. Jesus echoed the admonition to rule with justice when he spoke to the Pharisees. He scolded them because they had "neglected the more important matters of the law — justice, mercy and faithfulness" (Mt 23:23). In the end, Jesus Christ will judge the living and the dead (2Ti 4:1). God's justice will be final and established forever. And the righteous, confident in their future reward (Ps 58:11), wait with great joy, recognizing that their Savior King has already won the victory (Rev 19:11 – 21).

Psalm 58[a]

For the director of music. To the tune of "Do Not Destroy." Of David. A miktam.[b]

[1] Do you rulers indeed speak justly?
Do you judge people with equity?
[2] No, in your heart you devise injustice,
and your hands mete out violence on the earth.

[3] Even from birth the wicked go astray;
from the womb they are wayward, spreading lies.
[4] Their venom is like the venom of a snake,
like that of a cobra that has stopped its ears,
[5] that will not heed the tune of the charmer,
however skillful the enchanter may be.

[6] Break the teeth in their mouths, O God;
LORD, tear out the fangs of those lions!
[7] Let them vanish like water that flows away;
when they draw the bow, let their arrows fall short.
[8] May they be like a slug that melts away as it moves along,
like a stillborn child that never sees the sun.

[9] Before your pots can feel the heat of the thorns —
whether they be green or dry — the wicked will be swept away.[c]
[10] The righteous will be glad when they are avenged,
when they dip their feet in the blood of the wicked.
[11] Then people will say,
"Surely the righteous still are rewarded;
surely there is a God who judges the earth."

Psalm 59[d]

For the director of music. To the tune of "Do Not Destroy." Of David. A miktam.[b] *When Saul had sent men to watch David's house in order to kill him.*

[1] Deliver me from my enemies, O God;
be my fortress against those who are attacking me.
[2] Deliver me from evildoers
and save me from those who are after my blood.

[3] See how they lie in wait for me!
Fierce men conspire against me
for no offense or sin of mine, LORD.
[4] I have done no wrong, yet they are ready to attack me.
Arise to help me; look on my plight!

[a] In Hebrew texts 58:1-11 is numbered 58:2-12. [b] Title: Probably a literary or musical term
[c] 9 The meaning of the Hebrew for this verse is uncertain. [d] In Hebrew texts 59:1-17 is numbered 59:2-18.

PSALM 57:1 – 11

SOVEREIGN OVER ALL

This psalm was David's response to a desperate situation. David was fleeing for his life from King Saul, and he had hidden in a cave. In this moment of distress and uncertainty, David put his dependence and trust in God. He cried out to God, certain that God would send down his mercy and rescue him (Ps 57:1 – 3). He found "refuge in the shadow of [God's] wings," knowing God was with him in the midst of this disaster (v. 1). Although all the circumstances of his life seemed to indicate that God had forgotten him, David knew that God was still sovereign over all. And in the midst of "men whose teeth are spears and arrows, whose tongues are sharp swords" (v. 4), his primary desire was for God to be exalted over all (vv. 5,11).

How difficult it is, in the middle of a storm, through all the deep emotions and uncertainty, to have a steadfast heart, singing and praising God (v. 7). Yet this was exactly David's response. He sang, "I will praise you, Lord, among the nations; I will sing of you among the peoples. For great is your love, reaching to the heavens; your faithfulness reaches to the skies" (vv. 9 – 10). Without knowing the outcome — whether he would live or die — David chose God's glory.

Jesus showed that same steadfast heart. On the hardest day of his life, knowing he was about to walk a difficult road of suffering and death, he chose to trust God's sovereignty. Praying to God, he knelt down and asked, "Father, if you are willing, take this cup from me; yet not my will, but yours be done" (Lk 22:42). God's will required Jesus to lay down his life. However, God knew every detail, orchestrating all things, bringing forth a much bigger plan. God had a plan that defeated death, not only for Jesus, but for every believer — "for a time is coming when all who are in their graves will hear his voice and come out — those who have done what is good will rise to live" (Jn 5:28 – 29). So in difficult times, through the fog of uncertainty, God's people can confidently trust him. They can fix their eyes on Jesus and hold on tight knowing victory is coming!

[5] You, LORD God Almighty,
you who are the God of Israel,
rouse yourself to punish all the nations;
show no mercy to wicked traitors.[a]

[6] They return at evening,
snarling like dogs,
and prowl about the city.
[7] See what they spew from their mouths —
the words from their lips are sharp as swords,
and they think, "Who can hear us?"
[8] But you laugh at them, LORD;
you scoff at all those nations.

[9] You are my strength, I watch for you;
you, God, are my fortress,
10 my God on whom I can rely.

God will go before me
and will let me gloat over those who slander me.
[11] But do not kill them, Lord our shield,[b]
or my people will forget.
In your might uproot them
and bring them down.
[12] For the sins of their mouths,
for the words of their lips,
let them be caught in their pride.
For the curses and lies they utter,
13 consume them in your wrath,
consume them till they are no more.
Then it will be known to the ends of the earth
that God rules over Jacob.

[14] They return at evening,
snarling like dogs,
and prowl about the city.
[15] They wander about for food
and howl if not satisfied.
[16] But I will sing of your strength,
in the morning I will sing of your love;
for you are my fortress,
my refuge in times of trouble.

[17] You are my strength, I sing praise to you;
you, God, are my fortress,
my God on whom I can rely.

Psalm 60[c]

For the director of music. To the tune of "The Lily of the Covenant." A miktam[d] of David. For teaching. When he fought Aram Naharaim[e] and Aram Zobah,[f] and when Joab returned and struck down twelve thousand Edomites in the Valley of Salt.

[1] You have rejected us, God, and burst upon us;
you have been angry — now restore us!
[2] You have shaken the land and torn it open;
mend its fractures, for it is quaking.

---

[a] 5 The Hebrew has *Selah* (a word of uncertain meaning) here and at the end of verse 13.
[b] 11 Or *sovereign* [c] In Hebrew texts 60:1-12 is numbered 60:3-14. [d] Title: Probably a literary or musical term [e] Title: That is, Arameans of Northwest Mesopotamia [f] Title: That is, Arameans of central Syria

[3] You have shown your people desperate times;
you have given us wine that makes us stagger.
[4] But for those who fear you, you have raised a banner
to be unfurled against the bow.[a]

[5] Save us and help us with your right hand,
that those you love may be delivered.
[6] God has spoken from his sanctuary:
"In triumph I will parcel out Shechem
and measure off the Valley of Sukkoth.
[7] Gilead is mine, and Manasseh is mine;
Ephraim is my helmet,
Judah is my scepter.
[8] Moab is my washbasin,
on Edom I toss my sandal;
over Philistia I shout in triumph."

[9] Who will bring me to the fortified city?
Who will lead me to Edom?
[10] Is it not you, God, you who have now rejected us
and no longer go out with our armies?
[11] Give us aid against the enemy,
for human help is worthless.
[12] With God we will gain the victory,
and he will trample down our enemies.

Psalm 61[b]

For the director of music. With stringed instruments. Of David.

[1] Hear my cry, O God;
listen to my prayer.

[2] From the ends of the earth I call to you,
I call as my heart grows faint;
lead me to the rock that is higher than I.
[3] For you have been my refuge,
a strong tower against the foe.

[4] I long to dwell in your tent forever
and take refuge in the shelter of your wings.[a]
[5] For you, God, have heard my vows;
you have given me the heritage of those who fear your name.

[6] Increase the days of the king's life,
his years for many generations.
[7] May he be enthroned in God's presence forever;
appoint your love and faithfulness to protect him.

[8] Then I will ever sing in praise of your name
and fulfill my vows day after day.

Psalm 62[c]

For the director of music. For Jeduthun. A psalm of David.

[1] Truly my soul finds rest in God;
my salvation comes from him.
[2] Truly he is my rock and my salvation;
he is my fortress, I will never be shaken.

[a] *4,4* The Hebrew has *Selah* (a word of uncertain meaning) here. [b] In Hebrew texts 61:1-8 is numbered 61:2-9. [c] In Hebrew texts 62:1-12 is numbered 62:2-13.

PSALM 61:2

THE ROCK HIGHER THAN I

Aware of his own fragility, the psalmist longed for the stability and security he could find in God — his rock of strength. God is unshakable. He is unalterable in his purposes — not at all fazed by opposition or resistance. Nothing can challenge his strength. The psalmist was wise to recognize his own vulnerability, turning to lean on someone whose position is forever fixed — trusting in his immovable God.

The New Testament compares Jesus to a spiritual rock — identifying him as the source that once sustained Moses and the Israelites liberated from Egypt (1Co 10:4). From this rock, they enjoyed a miraculous supply of desperately needed water (Nu 20:6–11). Jesus provides life for people without hope. All who call on him and believe in his name will be saved (Ro 10:13). Jesus is also referred to as a rock that makes people stumble (1Pe 2:8). Even today his uncompromising call to repentance causes some people to reject him because they love sin and the stuff of earth. Jesus' clear message of salvation through his name alone is too much for many people to accept — they refuse to put faith in him as the long-awaited Messiah.

PSALM 63:1–8

PERSONAL WORSHIP

The psalmist's affection for God and his great need of God's help combined to become a beautiful example of personal worship. The psalmist approached God, savoring his goodness and power as the answers to his heart's hunger and thirst (Ps 63:5). All through the night, the psalmist privately contemplated and remembered God as his help, protector, advocate and provider (vv. 6–8).

In a similar way, Jesus had a habit of private prayer. He regularly withdrew from others to commune with God (Mk 1:35). In the theological mystery of the Trinity, God the Son desired behind-the-scenes time with God the Father. He got up very early in the morning to secure intimate moments of worshipful gratitude and submission to the Father's will. In this way, Jesus modeled the importance of approaching God as an individual—above and beyond corporate gatherings of worship. Private prayer, intimate thanksgiving and nonpublic praise are essential disciplines of the Christian life.

3 How long will you assault me?
Would all of you throw me down—
this leaning wall, this tottering fence?
4 Surely they intend to topple me
from my lofty place;
they take delight in lies.
With their mouths they bless,
but in their hearts they curse.[a]

5 Yes, my soul, find rest in God;
my hope comes from him.
6 Truly he is my rock and my salvation;
he is my fortress, I will not be shaken.
7 My salvation and my honor depend on God[b];
he is my mighty rock, my refuge.
8 Trust in him at all times, you people;
pour out your hearts to him,
for God is our refuge.

9 Surely the lowborn are but a breath,
the highborn are but a lie.
If weighed on a balance, they are nothing;
together they are only a breath.
10 Do not trust in extortion
or put vain hope in stolen goods;
though your riches increase,
do not set your heart on them.

11 One thing God has spoken,
two things I have heard:
"Power belongs to you, God,
12 and with you, Lord, is unfailing love";
and, "You reward everyone
according to what they have done."

Psalm 63[c]

A psalm of David. When he was in the Desert of Judah.

1 You, God, are my God,
earnestly I seek you;
I thirst for you,
my whole being longs for you,
in a dry and parched land
where there is no water.
2 I have seen you in the sanctuary
and beheld your power and your glory.
3 Because your love is better than life,
my lips will glorify you.
4 I will praise you as long as I live,
and in your name I will lift up my hands.
5 I will be fully satisfied as with the richest of foods;
with singing lips my mouth will praise you.
6 On my bed I remember you;
I think of you through the watches of the night.

[a] 4 The Hebrew has *Selah* (a word of uncertain meaning) here and at the end of verse 8.
[b] 7 Or */ God Most High is my salvation and my honor* [c] In Hebrew texts 63:1-11 is numbered 63:2-12.

[7] Because you are my help,
I sing in the shadow of your wings.
[8] I cling to you;
your right hand upholds me.

[9] Those who want to kill me will be destroyed;
they will go down to the depths of the earth.
[10] They will be given over to the sword
and become food for jackals.

[11] But the king will rejoice in God;
all who swear by God will glory in him,
while the mouths of liars will be silenced.

Psalm 64[a]

For the director of music. A psalm of David.

[1] Hear me, my God, as I voice my complaint;
protect my life from the threat of the enemy.
[2] Hide me from the conspiracy of the wicked,
from the plots of evildoers.
[3] They sharpen their tongues like swords
and aim cruel words like deadly arrows.
[4] They shoot from ambush at the innocent;
they shoot suddenly, without fear.

[5] They encourage each other in evil plans,
they talk about hiding their snares;
they say, "Who will see it[b]?"
[6] They plot injustice and say,
"We have devised a perfect plan!"
Surely the human mind and heart are cunning.

[7] But God will shoot them with his arrows;
they will suddenly be struck down.
[8] He will turn their own tongues against them
and bring them to ruin;
all who see them will shake their heads in scorn.
[9] All people will fear;
they will proclaim the works of God
and ponder what he has done.

[10] The righteous will rejoice in the LORD
and take refuge in him;
all the upright in heart will glory in him!

Psalm 65[c]

For the director of music. A psalm of David. A song.

[1] Praise awaits[d] you, our God, in Zion;
to you our vows will be fulfilled.
[2] You who answer prayer,
to you all people will come.
[3] When we were overwhelmed by sins,
you forgave[e] our transgressions.

[a] In Hebrew texts 64:1-10 is numbered 64:2-11. [b] 5 Or *us* [c] In Hebrew texts 65:1-13 is numbered 65:2-14. [d] 1 Or *befits*; the meaning of the Hebrew for this word is uncertain.
[e] 3 Or *made atonement for*

PSALM 64:1 – 10

PLOTTING EVIL

David was familiar with the reality of having enemies who plotted to end his life. He cried out for God to show his strength in these moments in order that God would ultimately receive glory and recognition as the one who holds all power.

In reading this psalm, believers can detect a foreshadowing of Jesus and his dealings with the religious Jewish leaders who plotted to end his life because of who he claimed to be — the Son of God (Mt 26:3 – 4). Though the religious leaders, like David's enemies, had devised a plan, God showed his power and ultimately received glory. Yet, God's glory came in a way that no one at that time expected. In Psalm 64, God was glorified through the prolonged life of David whom he protected and spared. In the New Testament, God was glorified through the death of his Son sent as a sacrifice for humankind's sin. The attempted destruction of Jesus — his arrest, trial and crucifixion — actually accomplished the defeat of sin for all who put faith in Jesus for salvation.

PSALM 65:1 – 13

SALVATION AND GOD'S PROVIDENCE

The psalmist considered a debt of praise still owed to God, remembering the dramatic ways God showed his might through the creation of the world (vv. 6 – 7). The psalmist also thanked God for the forgiveness of sins — mindful that in the time before God intervened, the people had

(continued on next page)

(Salvation and God's Providence, continued)

been overwhelmed (v. 3). In addition, Psalm 65 celebrates God's providence over all of the blessings people enjoy (vv. 9 – 13). All good things that happen on the earth are the result of God's intentional works of love, faithfulness and care.

When Jesus entered the world, people were still helpless under the guilt of sin. Yet Christ died and rose again for the ungodly as a demonstration of God's love for sinners (Ro 5:6 – 8). Jesus' sacrifice enabled everyone who will trust Jesus to have a relationship with God through faith. This relationship provides access to the providential benefits of God's power. Those who believe in Jesus enjoy the blessings that accompany God's favor. He is a good Father to his adopted sons and daughters.

4 Blessed are those you choose
and bring near to live in your courts!
We are filled with the good things of your house,
of your holy temple.

5 You answer us with awesome and righteous deeds,
God our Savior,
the hope of all the ends of the earth
and of the farthest seas,
6 who formed the mountains by your power,
having armed yourself with strength,
7 who stilled the roaring of the seas,
the roaring of their waves,
and the turmoil of the nations.
8 The whole earth is filled with awe at your wonders;
where morning dawns, where evening fades,
you call forth songs of joy.

9 You care for the land and water it;
you enrich it abundantly.
The streams of God are filled with water
to provide the people with grain,
for so you have ordained it.[a]
10 You drench its furrows and level its ridges;
you soften it with showers and bless its crops.
11 You crown the year with your bounty,
and your carts overflow with abundance.
12 The grasslands of the wilderness overflow;
the hills are clothed with gladness.
13 The meadows are covered with flocks
and the valleys are mantled with grain;
they shout for joy and sing.

Psalm 66

For the director of music. A song. A psalm.

1 Shout for joy to God, all the earth!
2 Sing the glory of his name;
make his praise glorious.
3 Say to God, "How awesome are your deeds!
So great is your power
that your enemies cringe before you.
4 All the earth bows down to you;
they sing praise to you,
they sing the praises of your name."[b]

5 Come and see what God has done,
his awesome deeds for mankind!
6 He turned the sea into dry land,
they passed through the waters on foot—
come, let us rejoice in him.
7 He rules forever by his power,
his eyes watch the nations—
let not the rebellious rise up against him.

8 Praise our God, all peoples,
let the sound of his praise be heard;

[a] 9 Or *for that is how you prepare the land* [b] 4 The Hebrew has *Selah* (a word of uncertain meaning) here and at the end of verses 7 and 15.

[9] he has preserved our lives
and kept our feet from slipping.
[10] For you, God, tested us;
you refined us like silver.
[11] You brought us into prison
and laid burdens on our backs.
[12] You let people ride over our heads;
we went through fire and water,
but you brought us to a place of abundance.

[13] I will come to your temple with burnt offerings
and fulfill my vows to you—
[14] vows my lips promised and my mouth spoke
when I was in trouble.
[15] I will sacrifice fat animals to you
and an offering of rams;
I will offer bulls and goats.

[16] Come and hear, all you who fear God;
let me tell you what he has done for me.
[17] I cried out to him with my mouth;
his praise was on my tongue.
[18] If I had cherished sin in my heart,
the Lord would not have listened;
[19] but God has surely listened
and has heard my prayer.
[20] Praise be to God,
who has not rejected my prayer
or withheld his love from me!

Psalm 67[a]

For the director of music. With stringed instruments. A psalm. A song.

[1] May God be gracious to us and bless us
and make his face shine on us—[b]
[2] so that your ways may be known on earth,
your salvation among all nations.

[3] May the peoples praise you, God;
may all the peoples praise you.
[4] May the nations be glad and sing for joy,
for you rule the peoples with equity
and guide the nations of the earth.
[5] May the peoples praise you, God;
may all the peoples praise you.

[6] The land yields its harvest;
God, our God, blesses us.
[7] May God bless us still,
so that all the ends of the earth will fear him.

Psalm 68[c]

For the director of music. Of David. A psalm. A song.

[1] May God arise, may his enemies be scattered;
may his foes flee before him.

[a] In Hebrew texts 67:1-7 is numbered 67:2-8. [b] *1* The Hebrew has *Selah* (a word of uncertain meaning) here and at the end of verse 4. [c] In Hebrew texts 68:1-35 is numbered 68:2-36.

PSALM 66:16–20

CHERISHING SIN HINDERS PRAYER

The psalmist invited all to hear about the opportunity for securing God's favor (v. 16). He was full of joy because the Lord had heard his prayers. He knew this was only possible because of his genuine humility and distaste for the sins present in his life. "If I had cherished sin in my heart, the Lord would not have listened" (v. 18). Jesus taught that if someone is holding a grudge against someone, they must forgive them in order to receive forgiveness themselves from the Lord (Mk 11:25). This is not a contradiction to grace—adding some formula of work before one can receive pardon. Jesus wants people to go to God with integrity, refusing to make requests while harboring things God hates. It puts people into a position of humility—yielded to God's authority and aligned with his Word.

PSALM 67:1–7

LET ALL PEOPLES PRAISE YOU

The psalmist desired the blessings of God so that he could bring fame to God among the nations. The hope was that all people would see the benefits of following the Lord. From the beginning, God's plan was expansive, involving all the peoples of the earth (Ge 12:3). The evangelistic perspective of this psalm points toward the New Testament focus on sharing the gospel.

Before ascending to heaven, Jesus gave a clear mission to the disciples.

(continued on next page)

(Let All Peoples Praise You, continued)

They were to make new disciples of people from all nations — teaching and baptizing in his name (Mt 28:18 – 20). The primary way of making disciples is speaking the good news of the gospel — spelling out God's grace, Christ's sacrifice, the defeat of sin and the hope of eternal life.

When people experience life change through Jesus, he transforms them so that they bring light to the world. Satisfaction in Jesus turns into a living announcement about the sufficiency of Jesus. Christians shine their joyous light in the world — all for the glory of God (Mt 5:14 – 16).

2 May you blow them away like smoke —
as wax melts before the fire,
may the wicked perish before God.
3 But may the righteous be glad
and rejoice before God;
may they be happy and joyful.

4 Sing to God, sing in praise of his name,
extol him who rides on the clouds[a];
rejoice before him — his name is the LORD.
5 A father to the fatherless, a defender of widows,
is God in his holy dwelling.
6 God sets the lonely in families,[b]
he leads out the prisoners with singing;
but the rebellious live in a sun-scorched land.

7 When you, God, went out before your people,
when you marched through the wilderness,[c]
8 the earth shook, the heavens poured down rain,
before God, the One of Sinai,
before God, the God of Israel.
9 You gave abundant showers, O God;
you refreshed your weary inheritance.
10 Your people settled in it,
and from your bounty, God, you provided for the poor.

11 The Lord announces the word,
and the women who proclaim it are a mighty throng:
12 "Kings and armies flee in haste;
the women at home divide the plunder.
13 Even while you sleep among the sheep pens,[d]
the wings of my dove are sheathed with silver,
its feathers with shining gold."
14 When the Almighty[e] scattered the kings in the land,
it was like snow fallen on Mount Zalmon.

15 Mount Bashan, majestic mountain,
Mount Bashan, rugged mountain,
16 why gaze in envy, you rugged mountain,
at the mountain where God chooses to reign,
where the LORD himself will dwell forever?
17 The chariots of God are tens of thousands
and thousands of thousands;
the Lord has come from Sinai into his sanctuary.[f]
18 When you ascended on high,
you took many captives;
you received gifts from people,
even from[g] the rebellious —
that you,[h] LORD God, might dwell there.

19 Praise be to the Lord, to God our Savior,
who daily bears our burdens.
20 Our God is a God who saves;
from the Sovereign LORD comes escape from death.

[a] 4 Or *name, / prepare the way for him who rides through the deserts* [b] 6 Or *the desolate in a homeland* [c] 7 The Hebrew has *Selah* (a word of uncertain meaning) here and at the end of verses 19 and 32. [d] 13 Or *the campfires;* or *the saddlebags* [e] 14 Hebrew *Shaddai* [f] 17 Probable reading of the original Hebrew text; Masoretic Text *Lord is among them at Sinai in holiness* [g] 18 Or *gifts for people, / even* [h] 18 Or *they*

21 Surely God will crush the heads of his enemies,
the hairy crowns of those who go on in their sins.
22 The Lord says, "I will bring them from Bashan;
I will bring them from the depths of the sea,
23 that your feet may wade in the blood of your foes,
while the tongues of your dogs have their share."

24 Your procession, God, has come into view,
the procession of my God and King into the sanctuary.
25 In front are the singers, after them the musicians;
with them are the young women playing the timbrels.
26 Praise God in the great congregation;
praise the LORD in the assembly of Israel.
27 There is the little tribe of Benjamin, leading them,
there the great throng of Judah's princes,
and there the princes of Zebulun and of Naphtali.

28 Summon your power, God[a];
show us your strength, our God, as you have done before.
29 Because of your temple at Jerusalem
kings will bring you gifts.
30 Rebuke the beast among the reeds,
the herd of bulls among the calves of the nations.
Humbled, may the beast bring bars of silver.
Scatter the nations who delight in war.
31 Envoys will come from Egypt;
Cush[b] will submit herself to God.

32 Sing to God, you kingdoms of the earth,
sing praise to the Lord,
33 to him who rides across the highest heavens, the ancient heavens,
who thunders with mighty voice.
34 Proclaim the power of God,
whose majesty is over Israel,
whose power is in the heavens.
35 You, God, are awesome in your sanctuary;
the God of Israel gives power and strength to his people.

Praise be to God!

Psalm 69[c]

For the director of music. To the tune of "Lilies." Of David.

1 Save me, O God,
for the waters have come up to my neck.
2 I sink in the miry depths,
where there is no foothold.
I have come into the deep waters;
the floods engulf me.
3 I am worn out calling for help;
my throat is parched.
My eyes fail,
looking for my God.
4 Those who hate me without reason
outnumber the hairs of my head;

---

[a] *28* Many Hebrew manuscripts, Septuagint and Syriac; most Hebrew manuscripts *Your God has summoned power for you* [b] *31* That is, the upper Nile region [c] In Hebrew texts 69:1-36 is numbered 69:2-37.

many are my enemies without cause,
those who seek to destroy me.
I am forced to restore
what I did not steal.

5 You, God, know my folly;
my guilt is not hidden from you.

6 Lord, the LORD Almighty,
may those who hope in you
not be disgraced because of me;
God of Israel,
may those who seek you
not be put to shame because of me.
7 For I endure scorn for your sake,
and shame covers my face.
8 I am a foreigner to my own family,
a stranger to my own mother's children;
9 for zeal for your house consumes me,
and the insults of those who insult you fall on me.
10 When I weep and fast,
I must endure scorn;
11 when I put on sackcloth,
people make sport of me.
12 Those who sit at the gate mock me,
and I am the song of the drunkards.

13 But I pray to you, LORD,
in the time of your favor;
in your great love, O God,
answer me with your sure salvation.
14 Rescue me from the mire,
do not let me sink;
deliver me from those who hate me,
from the deep waters.
15 Do not let the floodwaters engulf me
or the depths swallow me up
or the pit close its mouth over me.

16 Answer me, LORD, out of the goodness of your love;
in your great mercy turn to me.
17 Do not hide your face from your servant;
answer me quickly, for I am in trouble.
18 Come near and rescue me;
deliver me because of my foes.

19 You know how I am scorned, disgraced and shamed;
all my enemies are before you.
20 Scorn has broken my heart
and has left me helpless;
I looked for sympathy, but there was none,
for comforters, but I found none.
21 They put gall in my food
and gave me vinegar for my thirst.

22 May the table set before them become a snare;
may it become retribution and[a] a trap.
23 May their eyes be darkened so they cannot see,
and their backs be bent forever.

[a] 22 Or *snare / and their fellowship become*

24 Pour out your wrath on them;
  let your fierce anger overtake them.
25 May their place be deserted;
  let there be no one to dwell in their tents.
26 For they persecute those you wound
  and talk about the pain of those you hurt.
27 Charge them with crime upon crime;
  do not let them share in your salvation.
28 May they be blotted out of the book of life
  and not be listed with the righteous.

29 But as for me, afflicted and in pain—
  may your salvation, God, protect me.

30 I will praise God's name in song
  and glorify him with thanksgiving.
31 This will please the LORD more than an ox,
  more than a bull with its horns and hooves.
32 The poor will see and be glad—
  you who seek God, may your hearts live!
33 The LORD hears the needy
  and does not despise his captive people.

34 Let heaven and earth praise him,
  the seas and all that move in them,
35 for God will save Zion
  and rebuild the cities of Judah.
 Then people will settle there and possess it;
36 the children of his servants will inherit it,
  and those who love his name will dwell there.

Psalm 70[a]

For the director of music. Of David. A petition.

1 Hasten, O God, to save me;
  come quickly, LORD, to help me.

2 May those who want to take my life
  be put to shame and confusion;
 may all who desire my ruin
  be turned back in disgrace.
3 May those who say to me, "Aha! Aha!"
  turn back because of their shame.
4 But may all who seek you
  rejoice and be glad in you;
 may those who long for your saving help always say,
  "The LORD is great!"

5 But as for me, I am poor and needy;
  come quickly to me, O God.
 You are my help and my deliverer;
  LORD, do not delay.

Psalm 71

1 In you, LORD, I have taken refuge;
  let me never be put to shame.
2 In your righteousness, rescue me and deliver me;
  turn your ear to me and save me.

[a] In Hebrew texts 70:1-5 is numbered 70:2-6.

PSALM 70:1 – 5

SAVE ME: YES OR NO?

In Psalm 70, David asked God to deliver him from the oppression and suffering brought about by his enemies. He sought refuge in God, expecting the result to include great glory for the Lord (v. 4).

Jesus voiced a prayer in the Gospel of John that includes some similarity to David's prayer (Jn 12:27 – 28). Laboring under the weight of the task before him, Jesus considered the depth of what he was about to suffer on the cross. He contemplated a request for God to deliver him, but quickly changed direction—affirming that what he was about to endure was the very reason why he came to earth.

In David's words, God is glorified by delivering him from the hands of his enemies. In Jesus' words, God the Father is glorified not by sparing the Son but through the Son's death. If Jesus had avoided the cross, there would be no way for people to have access to God. Through the willing sacrifice of Jesus, God makes possible the deliverance of all people who place their faith in Jesus for salvation.

[3] Be my rock of refuge,
to which I can always go;
give the command to save me,
for you are my rock and my fortress.
[4] Deliver me, my God, from the hand of the wicked,
from the grasp of those who are evil and cruel.

[5] For you have been my hope, Sovereign LORD,
my confidence since my youth.
[6] From birth I have relied on you;
you brought me forth from my mother's womb.
I will ever praise you.
[7] I have become a sign to many;
you are my strong refuge.
[8] My mouth is filled with your praise,
declaring your splendor all day long.

[9] Do not cast me away when I am old;
do not forsake me when my strength is gone.
[10] For my enemies speak against me;
those who wait to kill me conspire together.
[11] They say, "God has forsaken him;
pursue him and seize him,
for no one will rescue him."
[12] Do not be far from me, my God;
come quickly, God, to help me.
[13] May my accusers perish in shame;
may those who want to harm me
be covered with scorn and disgrace.

[14] As for me, I will always have hope;
I will praise you more and more.
[15] My mouth will tell of your righteous deeds,
of your saving acts all day long—
though I know not how to relate them all.
[16] I will come and proclaim your mighty acts, Sovereign LORD;
I will proclaim your righteous deeds, yours alone.
[17] Since my youth, God, you have taught me,
and to this day I declare your marvelous deeds.
[18] Even when I am old and gray,
do not forsake me, my God,
till I declare your power to the next generation,
your mighty acts to all who are to come.

[19] Your righteousness, God, reaches to the heavens,
you who have done great things.
Who is like you, God?
[20] Though you have made me see troubles,
many and bitter,
you will restore my life again;
from the depths of the earth
you will again bring me up.
[21] You will increase my honor
and comfort me once more.

[22] I will praise you with the harp
for your faithfulness, my God;
I will sing praise to you with the lyre,
Holy One of Israel.

PSALM 71:14–18

DECLARING GOD'S GREATNESS AT EVERY AGE

There are many reasons people want to live long lives. Some want to enjoy the fruits of careers—savoring the rewards of retirement. Others want to witness the successes of children and grandchildren. This psalmist had a God-centered reason for wanting to continue to live, and thrive, in his old age. He desired more time to declare the greatness of God's power—to tell the stories of God's faithfulness to the younger people around him.

Jesus encouraged Peter that, though he had sinned, his life would testify to the greatness of God—and he would continue to be used by God in powerful ways (Jn 21:18–19). Even at the end of his life, Peter would faithfully serve Christ. His very death would glorify God. Christians do not reach an age of discharge from the mission—a threshold of years beyond which they can rest from kingdom labors. Believers have the privilege and responsibility to tell the succeeding generations about the goodness and greatness of God. Stories of God's faithfulness inspire the young to trust God—to live boldly, refusing to waste any days of life.

23 My lips will shout for joy
when I sing praise to you —
I whom you have delivered.
24 My tongue will tell of your righteous acts
all day long,
for those who wanted to harm me
have been put to shame and confusion.

Psalm 72

Of Solomon.

1 Endow the king with your justice, O God,
the royal son with your righteousness.
2 May he judge your people in righteousness,
your afflicted ones with justice.

3 May the mountains bring prosperity to the people,
the hills the fruit of righteousness.
4 May he defend the afflicted among the people
and save the children of the needy;
may he crush the oppressor.
5 May he endure[a] as long as the sun,
as long as the moon, through all generations.
6 May he be like rain falling on a mown field,
like showers watering the earth.
7 In his days may the righteous flourish
and prosperity abound till the moon is no more.

8 May he rule from sea to sea
and from the River[b] to the ends of the earth.
9 May the desert tribes bow before him
and his enemies lick the dust.
10 May the kings of Tarshish and of distant shores
bring tribute to him.
May the kings of Sheba and Seba
present him gifts.
11 May all kings bow down to him
and all nations serve him.

12 For he will deliver the needy who cry out,
the afflicted who have no one to help.
13 He will take pity on the weak and the needy
and save the needy from death.
14 He will rescue them from oppression and violence,
for precious is their blood in his sight.

15 Long may he live!
May gold from Sheba be given him.
May people ever pray for him
and bless him all day long.
16 May grain abound throughout the land;
on the tops of the hills may it sway.
May the crops flourish like Lebanon
and thrive[c] like the grass of the field.
17 May his name endure forever;
may it continue as long as the sun.

[a] 5 Septuagint; Hebrew *You will be feared* [b] 8 That is, the Euphrates [c] 16 Probable reading of the original Hebrew text; Masoretic Text *Lebanon, / from the city*

Then all nations will be blessed through him,[a]
and they will call him blessed.

18 Praise be to the LORD God, the God of Israel,
who alone does marvelous deeds.
19 Praise be to his glorious name forever;
may the whole earth be filled with his glory.
Amen and Amen.

20 This concludes the prayers of David son of Jesse.

BOOK III

Psalms 73–89

Psalm 73

A psalm of Asaph.

1 Surely God is good to Israel,
to those who are pure in heart.

2 But as for me, my feet had almost slipped;
I had nearly lost my foothold.
3 For I envied the arrogant
when I saw the prosperity of the wicked.

4 They have no struggles;
their bodies are healthy and strong.[b]
5 They are free from common human burdens;
they are not plagued by human ills.
6 Therefore pride is their necklace;
they clothe themselves with violence.
7 From their callous hearts comes iniquity[c];
their evil imaginations have no limits.
8 They scoff, and speak with malice;
with arrogance they threaten oppression.
9 Their mouths lay claim to heaven,
and their tongues take possession of the earth.
10 Therefore their people turn to them
and drink up waters in abundance.[d]
11 They say, "How would God know?
Does the Most High know anything?"

12 This is what the wicked are like—
always free of care, they go on amassing wealth.

13 Surely in vain I have kept my heart pure
and have washed my hands in innocence.
14 All day long I have been afflicted,
and every morning brings new punishments.

15 If I had spoken out like that,
I would have betrayed your children.
16 When I tried to understand all this,
it troubled me deeply

---

[a] 17 Or *will use his name in blessings* (see Gen. 48:20) [b] 4 With a different word division of the Hebrew; Masoretic Text *struggles at their death; / their bodies are healthy* [c] 7 Syriac (see also Septuagint); Hebrew *Their eyes bulge with fat* [d] 10 The meaning of the Hebrew for this verse is uncertain.

17 till I entered the sanctuary of God;
then I understood their final destiny.

18 Surely you place them on slippery ground;
you cast them down to ruin.
19 How suddenly are they destroyed,
completely swept away by terrors!
20 They are like a dream when one awakes;
when you arise, Lord,
you will despise them as fantasies.

21 When my heart was grieved
and my spirit embittered,
22 I was senseless and ignorant;
I was a brute beast before you.

23 Yet I am always with you;
you hold me by my right hand.
24 You guide me with your counsel,
and afterward you will take me into glory.
25 Whom have I in heaven but you?
And earth has nothing I desire besides you.
26 My flesh and my heart may fail,
but God is the strength of my heart
and my portion forever.

27 Those who are far from you will perish;
you destroy all who are unfaithful to you.
28 But as for me, it is good to be near God.
I have made the Sovereign LORD my refuge;
I will tell of all your deeds.

Psalm 74

A maskil[a] of Asaph.

1 O God, why have you rejected us forever?
Why does your anger smolder against the sheep of your pasture?
2 Remember the nation you purchased long ago,
the people of your inheritance, whom you redeemed—
Mount Zion, where you dwelt.
3 Turn your steps toward these everlasting ruins,
all this destruction the enemy has brought on the sanctuary.

4 Your foes roared in the place where you met with us;
they set up their standards as signs.
5 They behaved like men wielding axes
to cut through a thicket of trees.
6 They smashed all the carved paneling
with their axes and hatchets.
7 They burned your sanctuary to the ground;
they defiled the dwelling place of your Name.
8 They said in their hearts, "We will crush them completely!"
They burned every place where God was worshiped in the land.

9 We are given no signs from God;
no prophets are left,
and none of us knows how long this will be.
10 How long will the enemy mock you, God?
Will the foe revile your name forever?

[a] Title: Probably a literary or musical term

PSALM 73:25–26

TREASURE IN HEAVEN

The writer of this psalm likely encountered many beautiful and impressive things while serving in the temple. Yet the confession of his heart was that God in heaven was his greatest treasure. Nothing on earth could compete with the glories of God. Nothing stirred his affections like the Sovereign Lord.

Jesus taught people to pull back from pursuing the treasures of earth—to stop storing them away for status and security. Money and possessions are temporary bits of wealth, and all of it can be stolen or ruined (Mt 6:19). As the psalmist's greatest prize was in heaven, so Jesus encouraged his listeners to invest in things that would last forever (Mt 6:20). On another occasion, Jesus used a parable to compare the kingdom of heaven to a treasure hidden in a field. "When a man found it, he ... sold all he had and bought that field" (Mt 13:44). Life on earth features many luxuries and objects of worth. Jesus teaches people to resist the temptation to chase after things that will not last. Rather, those who believe in Jesus should spend their years investing in their relationship with God and the people he loves—dispensing grace, making disciples and loving unconditionally. These treasures of heaven will endure forever and bring much glory to God.

PSALM 74:1–12

PAIN

Pain in life is a universal experience—it falls on the righteous and

(continued on next page)

(Pain, continued)

the unrighteous. People often search for a reason behind trials and tragedies, but answers are elusive since humans cannot fully know the purposes of God. The Bible suggests that in some instances, pain might be punishment for specific sins, a test of faith, fatherly discipline or a means to drive people to repentance. Usually clear meaning is absent, especially in situations of ongoing suffering. From the pit of pain, the psalmist reached for confidence in God — the one who had been his faithful King for a long time (v. 12). He knew of God's capabilities, yet wondered when relief would come.

Jesus frequently stepped into people's lives during a point of great pain. He performed a miracle for a grieving mother at a funeral (Lk 7:13 – 15). He touched and healed a man with leprosy (Mt 8:2 – 3). He changed the lives of a bleeding woman and a worried father over the course of just a few minutes (Mk 5:22 – 42). Jesus is full of compassion for the pain caused by this world. He is eager for people to know that he cares deeply about their trouble. Jesus is a dependable source of comfort in the face of suffering (2Co 1:3 – 6).

11 Why do you hold back your hand, your right hand?
Take it from the folds of your garment and destroy them!

12 But God is my King from long ago;
he brings salvation on the earth.

13 It was you who split open the sea by your power;
you broke the heads of the monster in the waters.
14 It was you who crushed the heads of Leviathan
and gave it as food to the creatures of the desert.
15 It was you who opened up springs and streams;
you dried up the ever-flowing rivers.
16 The day is yours, and yours also the night;
you established the sun and moon.
17 It was you who set all the boundaries of the earth;
you made both summer and winter.

18 Remember how the enemy has mocked you, LORD,
how foolish people have reviled your name.
19 Do not hand over the life of your dove to wild beasts;
do not forget the lives of your afflicted people forever.
20 Have regard for your covenant,
because haunts of violence fill the dark places of the land.
21 Do not let the oppressed retreat in disgrace;
may the poor and needy praise your name.
22 Rise up, O God, and defend your cause;
remember how fools mock you all day long.
23 Do not ignore the clamor of your adversaries,
the uproar of your enemies, which rises continually.

Psalm 75[a]

For the director of music. To the tune of "Do Not Destroy."
A psalm of Asaph. A song.

1 We praise you, God,
we praise you, for your Name is near;
people tell of your wonderful deeds.

2 You say, "I choose the appointed time;
it is I who judge with equity.
3 When the earth and all its people quake,
it is I who hold its pillars firm.[b]
4 To the arrogant I say, 'Boast no more,'
and to the wicked, 'Do not lift up your horns.[c]
5 Do not lift your horns against heaven;
do not speak so defiantly.' "

6 No one from the east or the west
or from the desert can exalt themselves.
7 It is God who judges:
He brings one down, he exalts another.
8 In the hand of the LORD is a cup
full of foaming wine mixed with spices;
he pours it out, and all the wicked of the earth
drink it down to its very dregs.

9 As for me, I will declare this forever;
I will sing praise to the God of Jacob,

[a] In Hebrew texts 75:1-10 is numbered 75:2-11. [b] *3* The Hebrew has *Selah* (a word of uncertain meaning) here. [c] *4* *Horns* here symbolize strength; also in verses 5 and 10.

[10]who says, "I will cut off the horns of all the wicked,
but the horns of the righteous will be lifted up."

Psalm 76[a]

For the director of music. With stringed instruments. A psalm of Asaph. A song.

[1]God is renowned in Judah;
in Israel his name is great.
[2]His tent is in Salem,
his dwelling place in Zion.
[3]There he broke the flashing arrows,
the shields and the swords, the weapons of war.[b]

[4]You are radiant with light,
more majestic than mountains rich with game.
[5]The valiant lie plundered,
they sleep their last sleep;
not one of the warriors
can lift his hands.
[6]At your rebuke, God of Jacob,
both horse and chariot lie still.

[7]It is you alone who are to be feared.
Who can stand before you when you are angry?
[8]From heaven you pronounced judgment,
and the land feared and was quiet—
[9]when you, God, rose up to judge,
to save all the afflicted of the land.
[10]Surely your wrath against mankind brings you praise,
and the survivors of your wrath are restrained.[c]

[11]Make vows to the LORD your God and fulfill them;
let all the neighboring lands
bring gifts to the One to be feared.
[12]He breaks the spirit of rulers;
he is feared by the kings of the earth.

Psalm 77[d]

For the director of music. For Jeduthun. Of Asaph. A psalm.

[1]I cried out to God for help;
I cried out to God to hear me.
[2]When I was in distress, I sought the Lord;
at night I stretched out untiring hands,
and I would not be comforted.

[3]I remembered you, God, and I groaned;
I meditated, and my spirit grew faint.[e]
[4]You kept my eyes from closing;
I was too troubled to speak.
[5]I thought about the former days,
the years of long ago;
[6]I remembered my songs in the night.
My heart meditated and my spirit asked:

[a] In Hebrew texts 76:1-12 is numbered 76:2-13. [b] *3* The Hebrew has *Selah* (a word of uncertain meaning) here and at the end of verse 9. [c] *10* Or *Surely the wrath of mankind brings you praise, / and with the remainder of wrath you arm yourself* [d] In Hebrew texts 77:1-20 is numbered 77:2-21. [e] *3* The Hebrew has *Selah* (a word of uncertain meaning) here and at the end of verses 9 and 15.

PSALM 77:1 – 20

OUR HELP IN AGES PAST

This is one psalm, but it reads like two distinct chapters. In the first nine verses, the author bared his soul. He cried out for help, but remained uncomforted (v. 2). The difficulties he faced kept his eyes open at night and his mouth shut during the day (v. 4). In the midst of trouble, he asked the honest questions many in this broken world ask: Does God still love me? Are God's promises still true? (vv. 7 – 8). That is the first "chapter" of this psalm.

Then the psalmist remembered something else, namely, the character of the God he cried out to. In this second "chapter," he meditated upon the deeds of his God (vv. 10 – 12), the character of his God (v. 13) and the power of his God (vv. 14 – 20). Long before the psalmist's sufferings, the people of God were in bondage in Egypt. God heard their cry, redeeming them with a mighty arm (vv. 15 – 19). In the midst of trouble, the psalmist's only hope was the character of his God.

Jesus instructed his disciples along the same lines in John 14. Though he never promised them a life of ease, he encouraged them to believe *in the midst* of trouble (Jn 14:1). Their only hope, too, was the character of the God who spoke to them. This Jesus — God incarnate — heard their cries and put his power on display by redeeming them.

[7] "Will the Lord reject forever?
Will he never show his favor again?
[8] Has his unfailing love vanished forever?
Has his promise failed for all time?
[9] Has God forgotten to be merciful?
Has he in anger withheld his compassion?"

[10] Then I thought, "To this I will appeal:
the years when the Most High stretched out his
right hand.
[11] I will remember the deeds of the LORD;
yes, I will remember your miracles of long ago.
[12] I will consider all your works
and meditate on all your mighty deeds."

[13] Your ways, God, are holy.
What god is as great as our God?
[14] You are the God who performs miracles;
you display your power among the peoples.
[15] With your mighty arm you redeemed your people,
the descendants of Jacob and Joseph.

[16] The waters saw you, God,
the waters saw you and writhed;
the very depths were convulsed.
[17] The clouds poured down water,
the heavens resounded with thunder;
your arrows flashed back and forth.
[18] Your thunder was heard in the whirlwind,
your lightning lit up the world;
the earth trembled and quaked.
[19] Your path led through the sea,
your way through the mighty waters,
though your footprints were not seen.

[20] You led your people like a flock
by the hand of Moses and Aaron.

Psalm 78

A maskil[a] *of Asaph.*

[1] My people, hear my teaching;
listen to the words of my mouth.
[2] I will open my mouth with a parable;
I will utter hidden things, things from of old—
[3] things we have heard and known,
things our ancestors have told us.
[4] We will not hide them from their descendants;
we will tell the next generation
the praiseworthy deeds of the LORD,
his power, and the wonders he has done.
[5] He decreed statutes for Jacob
and established the law in Israel,
which he commanded our ancestors
to teach their children,
[6] so the next generation would know them,
even the children yet to be born,
and they in turn would tell their children.

[a] Title: Probably a literary or musical term

7 Then they would put their trust in God
and would not forget his deeds
but would keep his commands.
8 They would not be like their ancestors —
a stubborn and rebellious generation,
whose hearts were not loyal to God,
whose spirits were not faithful to him.

9 The men of Ephraim, though armed with bows,
turned back on the day of battle;
10 they did not keep God's covenant
and refused to live by his law.
11 They forgot what he had done,
the wonders he had shown them.
12 He did miracles in the sight of their ancestors
in the land of Egypt, in the region of Zoan.
13 He divided the sea and led them through;
he made the water stand up like a wall.
14 He guided them with the cloud by day
and with light from the fire all night.
15 He split the rocks in the wilderness
and gave them water as abundant as the seas;
16 he brought streams out of a rocky crag
and made water flow down like rivers.

17 But they continued to sin against him,
rebelling in the wilderness against the Most High.
18 They willfully put God to the test
by demanding the food they craved.
19 They spoke against God;
they said, "Can God really
spread a table in the wilderness?
20 True, he struck the rock,
and water gushed out,
streams flowed abundantly,
but can he also give us bread?
Can he supply meat for his people?"
21 When the LORD heard them, he was furious;
his fire broke out against Jacob,
and his wrath rose against Israel,
22 for they did not believe in God
or trust in his deliverance.
23 Yet he gave a command to the skies above
and opened the doors of the heavens;
24 he rained down manna for the people to eat,
he gave them the grain of heaven.
25 Human beings ate the bread of angels;
he sent them all the food they could eat.
26 He let loose the east wind from the heavens
and by his power made the south wind blow.
27 He rained meat down on them like dust,
birds like sand on the seashore.
28 He made them come down inside their camp,
all around their tents.
29 They ate till they were gorged —
he had given them what they craved.
30 But before they turned from what they craved,
even while the food was still in their mouths,

TEACHING IN PARABLES

In Matthew 13, Jesus used parables to explain the kingdom of God. In fact, he chose not to say much of anything to the gathered crowds in that passage *without* using parables. Though the purposes behind Jesus' teaching style are more than can be enumerated here, it certainly fulfilled the psalmist's words in Psalm 78:2: "I will open my mouth with a parable; I will utter hidden things, things from of old" (quoted in Mt 13:35).

The parables Jesus taught — the Good Samaritan, the Lost Son, etc. — rank as some of the best-known passages in all of Scripture. Rather than giving complicated teachings wrapped in theologically dense language, Jesus usually used simple, everyday realities to teach the intended truth. For example, he used a lost coin in Luke 15 and differing kinds of soil in Matthew 13.

A few times Jesus applied the parable to his audience by asking the crowd a question, as in the parable of the Good Samaritan: "Which of these three do you think was a neighbor to the man who fell into the hands of robbers?" (Lk 10:36). Other times he interpreted the parable himself (Mt 13:18–23). There were also times when the parable was told only to confirm unbelievers in their rejection of him (Mk 4:11–12). In such cases, the simplicity of the parable only highlighted their blindness.

While there might be a few characters in a parable that need to be interpreted, parables are not necessarily strict allegories where every detail demands an attached spiritual symbolism. In the parable of the Lost Son, for example, spiritual significance might wrongly be attached to details of the ring the father gives. Even so, parables do not need to be limited to only one application point. For example, the father in that parable represents God, but it is also clear that the older brother represents the self-righteous Pharisees to whom Jesus spoke.

Jesus' teaching style shared many of the same aims of Psalm 78. Like the psalmist's words long before, Jesus' parables taught "the next generation the praiseworthy deeds of the LORD, his power, and the wonders he has done" (Ps 78:4).

31 God's anger rose against them;
he put to death the sturdiest among them,
cutting down the young men of Israel.

32 In spite of all this, they kept on sinning;
in spite of his wonders, they did not believe.
33 So he ended their days in futility
and their years in terror.
34 Whenever God slew them, they would seek him;
they eagerly turned to him again.
35 They remembered that God was their Rock,
that God Most High was their Redeemer.
36 But then they would flatter him with their mouths,
lying to him with their tongues;
37 their hearts were not loyal to him,
they were not faithful to his covenant.
38 Yet he was merciful;
he forgave their iniquities
and did not destroy them.
Time after time he restrained his anger
and did not stir up his full wrath.
39 He remembered that they were but flesh,
a passing breeze that does not return.

40 How often they rebelled against him in the wilderness
and grieved him in the wasteland!
41 Again and again they put God to the test;
they vexed the Holy One of Israel.
42 They did not remember his power —
the day he redeemed them from the oppressor,
43 the day he displayed his signs in Egypt,
his wonders in the region of Zoan.
44 He turned their river into blood;
they could not drink from their streams.
45 He sent swarms of flies that devoured them,
and frogs that devastated them.
46 He gave their crops to the grasshopper,
their produce to the locust.
47 He destroyed their vines with hail
and their sycamore-figs with sleet.
48 He gave over their cattle to the hail,
their livestock to bolts of lightning.
49 He unleashed against them his hot anger,
his wrath, indignation and hostility —
a band of destroying angels.
50 He prepared a path for his anger;
he did not spare them from death
but gave them over to the plague.
51 He struck down all the firstborn of Egypt,
the firstfruits of manhood in the tents of Ham.
52 But he brought his people out like a flock;
he led them like sheep through the wilderness.
53 He guided them safely, so they were unafraid;
but the sea engulfed their enemies.
54 And so he brought them to the border of his holy land,
to the hill country his right hand had taken.
55 He drove out nations before them
and allotted their lands to them as an inheritance;
he settled the tribes of Israel in their homes.

56 But they put God to the test
and rebelled against the Most High;
they did not keep his statutes.
57 Like their ancestors they were disloyal and faithless,
as unreliable as a faulty bow.
58 They angered him with their high places;
they aroused his jealousy with their idols.
59 When God heard them, he was furious;
he rejected Israel completely.
60 He abandoned the tabernacle of Shiloh,
the tent he had set up among humans.
61 He sent the ark of his might into captivity,
his splendor into the hands of the enemy.
62 He gave his people over to the sword;
he was furious with his inheritance.
63 Fire consumed their young men,
and their young women had no wedding songs;
64 their priests were put to the sword,
and their widows could not weep.

65 Then the Lord awoke as from sleep,
as a warrior wakes from the stupor of wine.
66 He beat back his enemies;
he put them to everlasting shame.
67 Then he rejected the tents of Joseph,
he did not choose the tribe of Ephraim;
68 but he chose the tribe of Judah,
Mount Zion, which he loved.
69 He built his sanctuary like the heights,
like the earth that he established forever.
70 He chose David his servant
and took him from the sheep pens;
71 from tending the sheep he brought him
to be the shepherd of his people Jacob,
of Israel his inheritance.
72 And David shepherded them with integrity of heart;
with skillful hands he led them.

Psalm 79

A psalm of Asaph.

1 O God, the nations have invaded your inheritance;
they have defiled your holy temple,
they have reduced Jerusalem to rubble.
2 They have left the dead bodies of your servants
as food for the birds of the sky,
the flesh of your own people for the animals of the wild.
3 They have poured out blood like water
all around Jerusalem,
and there is no one to bury the dead.
4 We are objects of contempt to our neighbors,
of scorn and derision to those around us.

5 How long, LORD? Will you be angry forever?
How long will your jealousy burn like fire?
6 Pour out your wrath on the nations
that do not acknowledge you,
on the kingdoms
that do not call on your name;

[7] for they have devoured Jacob
and devastated his homeland.

[8] Do not hold against us the sins of past generations;
may your mercy come quickly to meet us,
for we are in desperate need.
[9] Help us, God our Savior,
for the glory of your name;
deliver us and forgive our sins
for your name's sake.
[10] Why should the nations say,
"Where is their God?"

Before our eyes, make known among the nations
that you avenge the outpoured blood of your servants.
[11] May the groans of the prisoners come before you;
with your strong arm preserve those condemned to die.
[12] Pay back into the laps of our neighbors seven times
the contempt they have hurled at you, Lord.
[13] Then we your people, the sheep of your pasture,
will praise you forever;
from generation to generation
we will proclaim your praise.

Psalm 80[a]

For the director of music. To the tune of "The Lilies of the Covenant." Of Asaph. A psalm.

[1] Hear us, Shepherd of Israel,
you who lead Joseph like a flock.
You who sit enthroned between the cherubim,
shine forth [2] before Ephraim, Benjamin and Manasseh.
Awaken your might;
come and save us.

[3] Restore us, O God;
make your face shine on us,
that we may be saved.

[4] How long, LORD God Almighty,
will your anger smolder
against the prayers of your people?
[5] You have fed them with the bread of tears;
you have made them drink tears by the bowlful.
[6] You have made us an object of derision[b] to our neighbors,
and our enemies mock us.

[7] Restore us, God Almighty;
make your face shine on us,
that we may be saved.

[8] You transplanted a vine from Egypt;
you drove out the nations and planted it.
[9] You cleared the ground for it,
and it took root and filled the land.
[10] The mountains were covered with its shade,
the mighty cedars with its branches.

[a] In Hebrew texts 80:1-19 is numbered 80:2-20. [b] *6* Probable reading of the original Hebrew text; Masoretic Text *contention*

PSALM 79:8–10

JUDAH'S REPENTANCE

In this psalm, the reader gets a glimpse into the horror that followed Nebuchadnezzar's invasion of Judah. The birds and wild animals feasted upon bodies left unburied. The temple of God—the locus of the Lord's worship—was defiled. Furthermore, the pagan nations mocked the people of God.

In their recent history, the people of God had stiffened their necks a thousand too many times. They were stubbornly disobedient. But in this psalm, after seeing and experiencing the judgment of God, the psalmist was brought low. He asked the Lord to be compassionate and to remember their sins no longer.

But this was not for Judah's sake alone. Instead, the pleas for help centered upon God's reputation (vv. 9–10). The psalmist lamented the pagan nations' taunt: "Where is their God?" (v. 10). True repentance not only turns away from sin, but turns toward God's honor.

[11] Its branches reached as far as the Sea,[a]
its shoots as far as the River.[b]

[12] Why have you broken down its walls
so that all who pass by pick its grapes?
[13] Boars from the forest ravage it,
and insects from the fields feed on it.
[14] Return to us, God Almighty!
Look down from heaven and see!
Watch over this vine,
[15] the root your right hand has planted,
the son[c] you have raised up for yourself.

[16] Your vine is cut down, it is burned with fire;
at your rebuke your people perish.
[17] Let your hand rest on the man at your right hand,
the son of man you have raised up for yourself.
[18] Then we will not turn away from you;
revive us, and we will call on your name.

[19] Restore us, LORD God Almighty;
make your face shine on us,
that we may be saved.

Psalm 81[d]

For the director of music. According to gittith.[e] *Of Asaph.*

[1] Sing for joy to God our strength;
shout aloud to the God of Jacob!
[2] Begin the music, strike the timbrel,
play the melodious harp and lyre.

[3] Sound the ram's horn at the New Moon,
and when the moon is full, on the day of our festival;
[4] this is a decree for Israel,
an ordinance of the God of Jacob.
[5] When God went out against Egypt,
he established it as a statute for Joseph.

I heard an unknown voice say:

[6] "I removed the burden from their shoulders;
their hands were set free from the basket.
[7] In your distress you called and I rescued you,
I answered you out of a thundercloud;
I tested you at the waters of Meribah.[f]
[8] Hear me, my people, and I will warn you —
if you would only listen to me, Israel!
[9] You shall have no foreign god among you;
you shall not worship any god other than me.
[10] I am the LORD your God,
who brought you up out of Egypt.
Open wide your mouth and I will fill it.

[11] "But my people would not listen to me;
Israel would not submit to me.
[12] So I gave them over to their stubborn hearts
to follow their own devices.

[a] *11* Probably the Mediterranean [b] *11* That is, the Euphrates [c] *15* Or *branch* [d] In Hebrew texts 81:1-16 is numbered 81:2-17. [e] Title: Probably a musical term [f] *7* The Hebrew has *Selah* (a word of uncertain meaning) here.

PLACE OF HONOR

While the "man at your right hand" (Ps 80:17) originally referred to Israel, Jesus — the "Son of Man" — ultimately fulfills Israel's calling as the Scriptures unfold. Jesus now sits in the place of honor described in this psalm.

Having been raised from the dead, Jesus ascended to the right hand of the Father. Paul spoke of God's power, which "he exerted when he raised Christ from the dead and seated him at his right hand in the heavenly realms" (Eph 1:20). At Pentecost, Peter proclaimed that Jesus had been "exalted to the right hand of God" (Ac 2:33). Though the ascension is sometimes treated as something of an afterthought to the life, death and resurrection of Jesus, the Scriptures reveal its importance. The ascension marks a decisive moment when God the Father placed honor squarely on his Son.

What is Jesus doing, seated in the place of honor? He reigns as King. The ascension and the kingdom of God are connected. Jesus ascended to be coronated; he ascended to rule. Peter wrote that Jesus "has gone into heaven and is at God's right hand — with angels, authorities and powers in submission to him" (1Pe 3:22). There is a present kingdom because there is a present, living King. Sitting in the place of honor, ruling as King, Jesus intercedes for his people (Ro 8:34).

In the Scriptures, being seated signifies a completed work. For Old Testament believers, a "seated priest" would likely have seemed like a contradiction in terms. Priests never sat in the tabernacle, reflecting the fact that their priestly work was never complete or final. Every sacrifice and offering was provisional and would need to be repeated. But all this changed with the coming of a true and better priest: "But when this priest had offered for all time one sacrifice for sins, he sat down at the right hand of God" (Heb 10:12). Those who trust in the man at God's right hand will never be put to shame (1Pe 2:6).

13 "If my people would only listen to me,
if Israel would only follow my ways,
14 how quickly I would subdue their enemies
and turn my hand against their foes!
15 Those who hate the LORD would cringe before him,
and their punishment would last forever.
16 But you would be fed with the finest of wheat;
with honey from the rock I would satisfy you."

Psalm 82

A psalm of Asaph.

1 God presides in the great assembly;
he renders judgment among the "gods":

2 "How long will you[a] defend the unjust
and show partiality to the wicked?[b]
3 Defend the weak and the fatherless;
uphold the cause of the poor and the oppressed.
4 Rescue the weak and the needy;
deliver them from the hand of the wicked.

5 "The 'gods' know nothing, they understand nothing.
They walk about in darkness;
all the foundations of the earth are shaken.

6 "I said, 'You are "gods";
you are all sons of the Most High.'
7 But you will die like mere mortals;
you will fall like every other ruler."

8 Rise up, O God, judge the earth,
for all the nations are your inheritance.

Psalm 83[c]

A song. A psalm of Asaph.

1 O God, do not remain silent;
do not turn a deaf ear,
do not stand aloof, O God.
2 See how your enemies growl,
how your foes rear their heads.
3 With cunning they conspire against your people;
they plot against those you cherish.
4 "Come," they say, "let us destroy them as a nation,
so that Israel's name is remembered no more."

5 With one mind they plot together;
they form an alliance against you—
6 the tents of Edom and the Ishmaelites,
of Moab and the Hagrites,
7 Byblos, Ammon and Amalek,
Philistia, with the people of Tyre.
8 Even Assyria has joined them
to reinforce Lot's descendants.[b]

9 Do to them as you did to Midian,
as you did to Sisera and Jabin at the river Kishon,

---

[a] *2* The Hebrew is plural. [b] *2,8* The Hebrew has *Selah* (a word of uncertain meaning) here.
[c] In Hebrew texts 83:1-18 is numbered 83:2-19.

SON OF THE MOST HIGH

In the Gospel of John, men holding stones told Jesus that they intended to kill him for blasphemy. This was because he, merely a man in their minds, claimed to be God (Jn 10:33).

In response, Jesus reasoned with them, quoting from Psalm 82:6: "Is it not written in your Law, 'I have said you are "gods" '?" (Jn 10:34). Jesus used the word *Law* in more general terms, referring to the entire Old Testament. Jesus offered the following argument to his would-be murderers: If Scripture can apply the word *gods* to mere humans, how much more should it be applied to the One whom the Father sent into the world (Jn 10:35–36). Jesus appealed to the Word of God to address the charge of blasphemy.

A few verses prior in the Gospel of John, Jesus made clear that he and the Father are one (Jn 10:30). Though some had argued that Jesus never claimed to be God, here was his golden opportunity to assert something different. To keep these men from stoning him, all he needed to do was deny this oneness. But Jesus would not.

While children often bear a resemblance to their father, the Son of the Most High shows the world *exactly* what God is like. The author of Hebrews made this point explicit, telling readers that Jesus is "the exact representation of [God's] being" (Heb 1:3). Paul expressed the same point in different language: "The Son is the image of the invisible God" (Col 1:15).

Jesus did not cease to be God when he became human. In John's Gospel, these men's Creator and Sustainer stood in the flesh before them. Such was their blindness that they had no idea who he was. If only they could have seen that Jesus was their ultimate source of salvation. He wanted to connect them to God, yet they wanted to stone him.

10 who perished at Endor
and became like dung on the ground.
11 Make their nobles like Oreb and Zeeb,
all their princes like Zebah and Zalmunna,
12 who said, "Let us take possession
of the pasturelands of God."
13 Make them like tumbleweed, my God,
like chaff before the wind.
14 As fire consumes the forest
or a flame sets the mountains ablaze,
15 so pursue them with your tempest
and terrify them with your storm.
16 Cover their faces with shame, LORD,
so that they will seek your name.

17 May they ever be ashamed and dismayed;
may they perish in disgrace.
18 Let them know that you, whose name is the LORD—
that you alone are the Most High over all the earth.

Psalm 84[a]

For the director of music. According to gittith.[b]
Of the Sons of Korah. A psalm.

1 How lovely is your dwelling place,
LORD Almighty!
2 My soul yearns, even faints,
for the courts of the LORD;
my heart and my flesh cry out
for the living God.
3 Even the sparrow has found a home,
and the swallow a nest for herself,
where she may have her young—
a place near your altar,
LORD Almighty, my King and my God.
4 Blessed are those who dwell in your house;
they are ever praising you.[c]

5 Blessed are those whose strength is in you,
whose hearts are set on pilgrimage.
6 As they pass through the Valley of Baka,
they make it a place of springs;
the autumn rains also cover it with pools.[d]
7 They go from strength to strength,
till each appears before God in Zion.

8 Hear my prayer, LORD God Almighty;
listen to me, God of Jacob.
9 Look on our shield,[e] O God;
look with favor on your anointed one.

10 Better is one day in your courts
than a thousand elsewhere;
I would rather be a doorkeeper in the house of my God
than dwell in the tents of the wicked.

PSALM 84:1–12

SPARROWS AND SWALLOWS

The psalmist desired nothing more than to be with God. This psalm seems to indicate that—at that moment—the psalmist, likely a Levite who normally served in the temple, did not have the physical access his soul desired. In the first stanza, he gave the readers an illustration. While the psalmist found himself away from the temple, nothing hindered the birds from staying as long as they desired (v. 3). The psalmist would go on to pen that one day in the temple courts was better than a thousand elsewhere (v. 10). He would sing that the blessed dwell in that temple (v. 4). These sparrows and swallows enjoyed the highest of privileges: never having to leave God's house.

Since the fall, humanity suffers from this separation. The Gospel of John says that Jesus came and made his dwelling among humans (Jn 1:14). He bridged the gulf caused by human sin and made a way for mankind to be made right with God once more. God's people, like the birds in this psalm, enjoy unfettered access to God through this Christ.

[a] In Hebrew texts 84:1-12 is numbered 84:2-13. [b] Title: Probably a musical term [c] *4* The Hebrew has *Selah* (a word of uncertain meaning) here and at the end of verse 8. [d] *6* Or *blessings* [e] *9* Or *sovereign*

[11] For the LORD God is a sun and shield;
the LORD bestows favor and honor;
no good thing does he withhold
from those whose walk is blameless.

[12] LORD Almighty,
blessed is the one who trusts in you.

Psalm 85[a]

For the director of music. Of the Sons of Korah. A psalm.

[1] You, LORD, showed favor to your land;
you restored the fortunes of Jacob.
[2] You forgave the iniquity of your people
and covered all their sins.[b]
[3] You set aside all your wrath
and turned from your fierce anger.

[4] Restore us again, God our Savior,
and put away your displeasure toward us.
[5] Will you be angry with us forever?
Will you prolong your anger through all generations?
[6] Will you not revive us again,
that your people may rejoice in you?
[7] Show us your unfailing love, LORD,
and grant us your salvation.

[8] I will listen to what God the LORD says;
he promises peace to his people, his faithful servants—
but let them not turn to folly.
[9] Surely his salvation is near those who fear him,
that his glory may dwell in our land.

[10] Love and faithfulness meet together;
righteousness and peace kiss each other.
[11] Faithfulness springs forth from the earth,
and righteousness looks down from heaven.
[12] The LORD will indeed give what is good,
and our land will yield its harvest.
[13] Righteousness goes before him
and prepares the way for his steps.

Psalm 86

A prayer of David.

[1] Hear me, LORD, and answer me,
for I am poor and needy.
[2] Guard my life, for I am faithful to you;
save your servant who trusts in you.
You are my God; [3] have mercy on me, Lord,
for I call to you all day long.
[4] Bring joy to your servant, Lord,
for I put my trust in you.

[5] You, Lord, are forgiving and good,
abounding in love to all who call to you.
[6] Hear my prayer, LORD;
listen to my cry for mercy.

[a] In Hebrew texts 85:1-13 is numbered 85:2-14. [b] 2 The Hebrew has *Selah* (a word of uncertain meaning) here.

PSALM 85:10–11

RIGHTEOUSNESS AND PEACE

Righteousness and peace demonstrate God's favor toward his people. The things the prophet longed for—peace, justice and hope—are found in the Lord. Only God can be both just in his judgment of sin and bring about peace through the forgiveness of sin. The blessing the psalmist seeks here will be given to those who fear God and submit to him. The apostle Paul put this coming together on display most explicitly in the letter to the Romans. He wrote that a righteousness that comes from God has been made known through faith in Jesus Christ (Ro 3:21–22). This righteousness embraces peace: "Therefore, since we have been justified through faith, we have peace with God through our Lord Jesus Christ" (Ro 5:1). God has judged sin in Jesus' death and, through that death, granted peace to his children. Mercy and truth meet in Jesus, and in the end, true peace is found in that convergence.

PSALM 86:1–17

HEART CONDITION

This psalm holds the distinction of being one of the few psalms labeled "A Prayer of David." Without question, David lifted his heart to the Lord in these verses. The introduction makes clear his poverty of spirit (v. 1). His cries for mercy continued throughout the day (v. 3). As men sought his life (v. 14), David sought the Lord. In the middle of this prayer—comparing his God to the gods of the world—he erupted in praise: "There is none

(continued on next page)

(Heart Condition, continued)

like you, Lord; no deeds can compare with yours" (v. 8). However, he still confessed to having a *divided* heart, a heart not solely focused upon God. David believed it would take nothing less than a work of God to change him. So he prayed: "Give me an *undivided* heart, that I may fear your name. I will praise you, Lord my God, with *all* my heart; I will glorify your name forever" (vv. 11–12, emphasis added).

7 When I am in distress, I call to you,
because you answer me.

8 Among the gods there is none like you, Lord;
no deeds can compare with yours.
9 All the nations you have made
will come and worship before you, Lord;
they will bring glory to your name.
10 For you are great and do marvelous deeds;
you alone are God.

11 Teach me your way, LORD,
that I may rely on your faithfulness;
give me an undivided heart,
that I may fear your name.
12 I will praise you, Lord my God, with all my heart;
I will glorify your name forever.
13 For great is your love toward me;
you have delivered me from the depths,
from the realm of the dead.

14 Arrogant foes are attacking me, O God;
ruthless people are trying to kill me—
they have no regard for you.
15 But you, Lord, are a compassionate and gracious God,
slow to anger, abounding in love and faithfulness.
16 Turn to me and have mercy on me;
show your strength in behalf of your servant;
save me, because I serve you
just as my mother did.
17 Give me a sign of your goodness,
that my enemies may see it and be put to shame,
for you, LORD, have helped me and comforted me.

Psalm 87

Of the Sons of Korah. A psalm. A song.

1 He has founded his city on the holy mountain.
2 The LORD loves the gates of Zion
more than all the other dwellings of Jacob.

3 Glorious things are said of you,
city of God:[a]
4 "I will record Rahab[b] and Babylon
among those who acknowledge me—
Philistia too, and Tyre, along with Cush[c]—
and will say, 'This one was born in Zion.' "[d]
5 Indeed, of Zion it will be said,
"This one and that one were born in her,
and the Most High himself will establish her."
6 The LORD will write in the register of the peoples:
"This one was born in Zion."

7 As they make music they will sing,
"All my fountains are in you."

[a] 3 The Hebrew has *Selah* (a word of uncertain meaning) here and at the end of verse 6.
[b] 4 A poetic name for Egypt [c] 4 That is, the upper Nile region [d] 4 Or *"I will record concerning those who acknowledge me: / 'This one was born in Zion.' / Hear this, Rahab and Babylon, / and you too, Philistia, Tyre and Cush."*

Psalm 88[a]

A song. A psalm of the Sons of Korah. For the director of music. According to mahalath leannoth.[b] *A* maskil[c] *of Heman the Ezrahite.*

1 LORD, you are the God who saves me;
day and night I cry out to you.
2 May my prayer come before you;
turn your ear to my cry.

3 I am overwhelmed with troubles
and my life draws near to death.
4 I am counted among those who go down to the pit;
I am like one without strength.
5 I am set apart with the dead,
like the slain who lie in the grave,
whom you remember no more,
who are cut off from your care.

6 You have put me in the lowest pit,
in the darkest depths.
7 Your wrath lies heavily on me;
you have overwhelmed me with all your waves.[d]
8 You have taken from me my closest friends
and have made me repulsive to them.
I am confined and cannot escape;
9 my eyes are dim with grief.

I call to you, LORD, every day;
I spread out my hands to you.
10 Do you show your wonders to the dead?
Do their spirits rise up and praise you?
11 Is your love declared in the grave,
your faithfulness in Destruction[e]?
12 Are your wonders known in the place of darkness,
or your righteous deeds in the land of oblivion?

13 But I cry to you for help, LORD;
in the morning my prayer comes before you.
14 Why, LORD, do you reject me
and hide your face from me?

15 From my youth I have suffered and been close to death;
I have borne your terrors and am in despair.
16 Your wrath has swept over me;
your terrors have destroyed me.
17 All day long they surround me like a flood;
they have completely engulfed me.
18 You have taken from me friend and neighbor—
darkness is my closest friend.

Psalm 89[f]

A maskil[c] *of Ethan the Ezrahite.*

1 I will sing of the LORD's great love forever;
with my mouth I will make your faithfulness known
through all generations.

[a] In Hebrew texts 88:1-18 is numbered 88:2-19. [b] Title: Possibly a tune, "The Suffering of Affliction" [c] Title: Probably a literary or musical term [d] *7* The Hebrew has *Selah* (a word of uncertain meaning) here and at the end of verse 10. [e] *11* Hebrew *Abaddon* [f] In Hebrew texts 89:1-52 is numbered 89:2-53.

PSALM 88:1 – 18

THE AGONY OF SEPARATION

No one would accuse this songwriter of holding back how he really felt. He described his life as if he were in the grave. Some of the psalmist's phrasing recalls Job's story: "You have taken from me my closest friends and have made me repulsive to them. I am confined and cannot escape" (v. 8). The psalmist was experiencing separation from the blessing and favor of God. "You have put me in the lowest pit, in the darkest depths," he complains to the Lord (v. 6). However, while most of this psalm speaks to the writer's isolation, he still addressed God as the one who saves him (v. 1).

The silence of God must not be mistaken for the absence of God. Jesus felt abandoned by God at his crucifixion. This abandoned One would cry out, in darkness, on a wooden cross: "My God, my God, why have you forsaken me?" (Mt 27:46). Because of this, nothing in all of creation can separate God's people from his love (Ro 8:39). Jesus experienced separation from God so that his people would never have to.

[2] I will declare that your love stands firm forever,
that you have established your faithfulness in heaven itself.
[3] You said, "I have made a covenant with my chosen one,
I have sworn to David my servant,
[4] 'I will establish your line forever
and make your throne firm through all generations.'"[a]

[5] The heavens praise your wonders, LORD,
your faithfulness too, in the assembly of the holy ones.
[6] For who in the skies above can compare with the LORD?
Who is like the LORD among the heavenly beings?
[7] In the council of the holy ones God is greatly feared;
he is more awesome than all who surround him.
[8] Who is like you, LORD God Almighty?
You, LORD, are mighty, and your faithfulness surrounds you.

[9] You rule over the surging sea;
when its waves mount up, you still them.
[10] You crushed Rahab like one of the slain;
with your strong arm you scattered your enemies.
[11] The heavens are yours, and yours also the earth;
you founded the world and all that is in it.
[12] You created the north and the south;
Tabor and Hermon sing for joy at your name.
[13] Your arm is endowed with power;
your hand is strong, your right hand exalted.

[14] Righteousness and justice are the foundation of your throne;
love and faithfulness go before you.
[15] Blessed are those who have learned to acclaim you,
who walk in the light of your presence, LORD.
[16] They rejoice in your name all day long;
they celebrate your righteousness.
[17] For you are their glory and strength,
and by your favor you exalt our horn.[b]
[18] Indeed, our shield[c] belongs to the LORD,
our king to the Holy One of Israel.

[19] Once you spoke in a vision,
to your faithful people you said:
"I have bestowed strength on a warrior;
I have raised up a young man from among the people.
[20] I have found David my servant;
with my sacred oil I have anointed him.
[21] My hand will sustain him;
surely my arm will strengthen him.
[22] The enemy will not get the better of him;
the wicked will not oppress him.
[23] I will crush his foes before him
and strike down his adversaries.
[24] My faithful love will be with him,
and through my name his horn[d] will be exalted.
[25] I will set his hand over the sea,
his right hand over the rivers.
[26] He will call out to me, 'You are my Father,
my God, the Rock my Savior.'

[a] *4* The Hebrew has *Selah* (a word of uncertain meaning) here and at the end of verses 37, 45 and 48. [b] *17 Horn* here symbolizes strong one. [c] *18* Or *sovereign* [d] *24 Horn* here symbolizes strength.

[27] And I will appoint him to be my firstborn,
the most exalted of the kings of the earth.
[28] I will maintain my love to him forever,
and my covenant with him will never fail.
[29] I will establish his line forever,
his throne as long as the heavens endure.

[30] "If his sons forsake my law
and do not follow my statutes,
[31] if they violate my decrees
and fail to keep my commands,
[32] I will punish their sin with the rod,
their iniquity with flogging;
[33] but I will not take my love from him,
nor will I ever betray my faithfulness.
[34] I will not violate my covenant
or alter what my lips have uttered.
[35] Once for all, I have sworn by my holiness—
and I will not lie to David—
[36] that his line will continue forever
and his throne endure before me like the sun;
[37] it will be established forever like the moon,
the faithful witness in the sky."

[38] But you have rejected, you have spurned,
you have been very angry with your anointed one.
[39] You have renounced the covenant with your servant
and have defiled his crown in the dust.
[40] You have broken through all his walls
and reduced his strongholds to ruins.
[41] All who pass by have plundered him;
he has become the scorn of his neighbors.
[42] You have exalted the right hand of his foes;
you have made all his enemies rejoice.
[43] Indeed, you have turned back the edge of his sword
and have not supported him in battle.
[44] You have put an end to his splendor
and cast his throne to the ground.
[45] You have cut short the days of his youth;
you have covered him with a mantle of shame.

[46] How long, LORD? Will you hide yourself forever?
How long will your wrath burn like fire?
[47] Remember how fleeting is my life.
For what futility you have created all humanity!
[48] Who can live and not see death,
or who can escape the power of the grave?
[49] Lord, where is your former great love,
which in your faithfulness you swore to David?
[50] Remember, Lord, how your servant has[a] been mocked,
how I bear in my heart the taunts of all the nations,
[51] the taunts with which your enemies, LORD, have mocked,
with which they have mocked every step of your
anointed one.

[52] Praise be to the LORD forever!
Amen and Amen.

[a] 50 Or *your servants have*

PSALM 89:46

WAITING PATIENTLY

"How long, LORD?" The psalmist — having likely just seen the destruction of Jerusalem — asked the God of heaven this honest question.

In the first verse, the psalmist declared that his song concerning God's love would never end. His mouth would forever declare the faithfulness of God. However, though he kept singing, the song changed key. God's people no longer enjoyed the Lord's favor, it seemed. Though God had promised to David a throne throughout all generations (v. 4), the splendor of Israel's king was no longer on display (v. 44). The throne having been cast to the ground, the psalmist wondered where God's love had hidden (v. 49).

No matter what God had said, to the psalmist the promises *felt* as if they were false. This is not uncommon, because God spoke regularly to the saints waiting on the deliverance of the Lord. To the Israelites exiled in Babylon, God promised to bring them out of captivity (Jer 29:14). To the New Testament exiles undergoing persecution in 1 Peter, God promised an inheritance that neither spoils nor fades. But that inheritance is not yet fully revealed — it is being kept in heaven "until the coming of the salvation that is ready to be revealed in the last time" (1Pe 1:5).

Hebrews 11 sings a waiting song. After mentioning Abel's, Enoch's, Noah's, Abraham's and Sarah's lives of faith, the author wrote, "All these people were still living by faith when they died. They did not receive the things promised; they only saw them and welcomed them from a distance" (Heb 11:13). They were certain of what they hoped for, but it remained unseen. They waited, believing.

The psalmist did the same. He waited patiently, remembering the promises of God. In fact, after baring his soul in questioning the Lord's purposes, he still ended the psalm in praise.

The promises never seemed as false as when the promised One took a spear in the side on a Roman cross. Yet three days later when Jesus rose from the dead, the promises were never truer.

BOOK IV

Psalms 90–106

Psalm 90

A prayer of Moses the man of God.

1 Lord, you have been our dwelling place
throughout all generations.
2 Before the mountains were born
or you brought forth the whole world,
from everlasting to everlasting you are God.

3 You turn people back to dust,
saying, "Return to dust, you mortals."
4 A thousand years in your sight
are like a day that has just gone by,
or like a watch in the night.
5 Yet you sweep people away in the sleep of death—
they are like the new grass of the morning:
6 In the morning it springs up new,
but by evening it is dry and withered.

7 We are consumed by your anger
and terrified by your indignation.
8 You have set our iniquities before you,
our secret sins in the light of your presence.
9 All our days pass away under your wrath;
we finish our years with a moan.
10 Our days may come to seventy years,
or eighty, if our strength endures;
yet the best of them are but trouble and sorrow,
for they quickly pass, and we fly away.
11 If only we knew the power of your anger!
Your wrath is as great as the fear that is your due.
12 Teach us to number our days,
that we may gain a heart of wisdom.

13 Relent, LORD! How long will it be?
Have compassion on your servants.
14 Satisfy us in the morning with your unfailing love,
that we may sing for joy and be glad all our days.
15 Make us glad for as many days as you have afflicted us,
for as many years as we have seen trouble.
16 May your deeds be shown to your servants,
your splendor to their children.

17 May the favor[a] of the Lord our God rest on us;
establish the work of our hands for us—
yes, establish the work of our hands.

Psalm 91

1 Whoever dwells in the shelter of the Most High
will rest in the shadow of the Almighty.[b]
2 I will say of the LORD, "He is my refuge and my fortress,
my God, in whom I trust."

PSALM 90:1–12

THE ETERNAL GOD

Before Genesis 1:1, God was. The eternal God knows no beginning, nor will he know an end. A thousand years are as a day to him (v. 4). While the mountain peaks were born one day, God was not (v. 2). In fact, creation exists because of this eternal God.

Psalm 90 includes multiple reminders that humankind is not by nature eternal. The psalmist, identified as Moses in the superscription, noted that it generally takes 70 or 80 years for humans to turn back to dust (vv. 3,10). In light of this, he prayed that God would help his people to number their days (v. 12).

God is eternal. Humans are not, due to their fallen nature. A merciful Jesus interrupts the ordinary nature of things, declaring, "Now this is eternal life: that they know you, the only true God, and Jesus Christ, whom you have sent" (Jn 17:3). Only an eternal God could give eternal life. Only an eternal and merciful God would.

[a] *17* Or *beauty* [b] *1* Hebrew *Shaddai*

3 Surely he will save you
from the fowler's snare
and from the deadly pestilence.
4 He will cover you with his feathers,
and under his wings you will find refuge;
his faithfulness will be your shield and rampart.
5 You will not fear the terror of night,
nor the arrow that flies by day,
6 nor the pestilence that stalks in the darkness,
nor the plague that destroys at midday.
7 A thousand may fall at your side,
ten thousand at your right hand,
but it will not come near you.
8 You will only observe with your eyes
and see the punishment of the wicked.

9 If you say, "The LORD is my refuge,"
and you make the Most High your dwelling,
10 no harm will overtake you,
no disaster will come near your tent.
11 For he will command his angels concerning you
to guard you in all your ways;
12 they will lift you up in their hands,
so that you will not strike your foot against a stone.
13 You will tread on the lion and the cobra;
you will trample the great lion and the serpent.

14 "Because he[a] loves me," says the LORD, "I will rescue him;
I will protect him, for he acknowledges my name.
15 He will call on me, and I will answer him;
I will be with him in trouble,
I will deliver him and honor him.
16 With long life I will satisfy him
and show him my salvation."

Psalm 92[b]

A psalm. A song. For the Sabbath day.

1 It is good to praise the LORD
and make music to your name, O Most High,
2 proclaiming your love in the morning
and your faithfulness at night,
3 to the music of the ten-stringed lyre
and the melody of the harp.

4 For you make me glad by your deeds, LORD;
I sing for joy at what your hands have done.
5 How great are your works, LORD,
how profound your thoughts!
6 Senseless people do not know,
fools do not understand,
7 that though the wicked spring up like grass
and all evildoers flourish,
they will be destroyed forever.

8 But you, LORD, are forever exalted.

---

[a] *14* That is, probably the king [b] In Hebrew texts 92:1-15 is numbered 92:2-16.

ANGELS

Scripture seems to indicate that there are tens of thousands of angels. Though angels do not have physical bodies, God created them with both moral discernment and high intelligence. In fact, Hebrews suggests that angels are pervasive enough that believers occasionally show hospitality to angels without knowing it (Heb 13:2).

The psalmist notes here that God "will command his angels concerning you to guard you in all your ways; they will lift you up in their hands, so that you will not strike your foot against a stone" (Ps 91:11 – 12). Satan would use this text while speaking with Jesus, imploring him to put God to the test (Mt 4:6). Jesus refused to misapply this text, interpreting Psalm 91 in light of the rest of God's Word.

Angels function as examples for believers, as they obey and worship the Lord without ceasing (Isa 6:3). Paul referred to angelic beings as powers, rulers, dominions and authorities (Eph 1:21; Col 1:16). Though a post-Enlightenment world pushes the nonphysical to the margins, the Bible's descriptions of angels remind the believer that the spiritual world is real.

However, some angels fell from grace and became demonic forces in our world. Unlike humans, who are made in the image of God, God did not show these angels mercy. Peter wrote, "God did not spare angels when they sinned, but sent them to hell, putting them in chains of darkness to be held for judgment" (2Pe 2:4). This reminds the believer of the grace God showed in sending Jesus for the salvation of sinners. In no way was God obligated to save.

The author of Hebrews began his letter by making clear the supremacy of Jesus over the angels. Alluding to Psalm 2, the author noted that God never called any of the angels his Son (Heb 1:5). Quoting from the Old Testament, the author further pointed out that God calls upon all the angels to worship Jesus (Heb 1:6). Finally, the author asked, "To which of the angels did God ever say, 'Sit at my right hand until I make your enemies a footstool for your feet'?" (Heb 1:13). Jesus is supremely better than anything. He alone is the source of a life of joy and contentment.

9 For surely your enemies, LORD,
surely your enemies will perish;
all evildoers will be scattered.
10 You have exalted my horn[a] like that of a wild ox;
fine oils have been poured on me.
11 My eyes have seen the defeat of my adversaries;
my ears have heard the rout of my wicked foes.

12 The righteous will flourish like a palm tree,
they will grow like a cedar of Lebanon;
13 planted in the house of the LORD,
they will flourish in the courts of our God.
14 They will still bear fruit in old age,
they will stay fresh and green,
15 proclaiming, "The LORD is upright;
he is my Rock, and there is no wickedness in him."

Psalm 93

1 The LORD reigns, he is robed in majesty;
the LORD is robed in majesty and armed with strength;
indeed, the world is established, firm and secure.
2 Your throne was established long ago;
you are from all eternity.
3 The seas have lifted up, LORD,
the seas have lifted up their voice;
the seas have lifted up their pounding waves.
4 Mightier than the thunder of the great waters,
mightier than the breakers of the sea—
the LORD on high is mighty.

5 Your statutes, LORD, stand firm;
holiness adorns your house
for endless days.

Psalm 94

1 The LORD is a God who avenges.
O God who avenges, shine forth.
2 Rise up, Judge of the earth;
pay back to the proud what they deserve.
3 How long, LORD, will the wicked,
how long will the wicked be jubilant?

4 They pour out arrogant words;
all the evildoers are full of boasting.
5 They crush your people, LORD;
they oppress your inheritance.
6 They slay the widow and the foreigner;
they murder the fatherless.
7 They say, "The LORD does not see;
the God of Jacob takes no notice."

8 Take notice, you senseless ones among the people;
you fools, when will you become wise?
9 Does he who fashioned the ear not hear?
Does he who formed the eye not see?
10 Does he who disciplines nations not punish?
Does he who teaches mankind lack knowledge?

[a] 10 *Horn* here symbolizes strength.

[11] The LORD knows all human plans;
he knows that they are futile.

[12] Blessed is the one you discipline, LORD,
the one you teach from your law;
[13] you grant them relief from days of trouble,
till a pit is dug for the wicked.
[14] For the LORD will not reject his people;
he will never forsake his inheritance.
[15] Judgment will again be founded on righteousness,
and all the upright in heart will follow it.

[16] Who will rise up for me against the wicked?
Who will take a stand for me against evildoers?
[17] Unless the LORD had given me help,
I would soon have dwelt in the silence of death.
[18] When I said, "My foot is slipping,"
your unfailing love, LORD, supported me.
[19] When anxiety was great within me,
your consolation brought me joy.

[20] Can a corrupt throne be allied with you—
a throne that brings on misery by its decrees?
[21] The wicked band together against the righteous
and condemn the innocent to death.
[22] But the LORD has become my fortress,
and my God the rock in whom I take refuge.
[23] He will repay them for their sins
and destroy them for their wickedness;
the LORD our God will destroy them.

Psalm 95

[1] Come, let us sing for joy to the LORD;
let us shout aloud to the Rock of our salvation.
[2] Let us come before him with thanksgiving
and extol him with music and song.

[3] For the LORD is the great God,
the great King above all gods.
[4] In his hand are the depths of the earth,
and the mountain peaks belong to him.
[5] The sea is his, for he made it,
and his hands formed the dry land.

[6] Come, let us bow down in worship,
let us kneel before the LORD our Maker;
[7] for he is our God
and we are the people of his pasture,
the flock under his care.

Today, if only you would hear his voice,
[8] "Do not harden your hearts as you did at Meribah,[a]
as you did that day at Massah[b] in the wilderness,
[9] where your ancestors tested me;
they tried me, though they had seen what I did.
[10] For forty years I was angry with that generation;
I said, 'They are a people whose hearts go astray,
and they have not known my ways.'

[a] 8 *Meribah* means *quarreling.* [b] 8 *Massah* means *testing.*

PSALM 95:1–11

A PLACE OF REST

God speaks in verses 8 through 11 of this psalm, taking a few verses to remind the readers of the disobedience of the generation of the exodus. Though the ancestors of the original readers had seen the wonders God performed in their deliverance from slavery, they still hardened their hearts and tested the Lord. In fact, the name "Massah" means "testing" (v. 8). Because of this, God declared that they would never enter his rest (v. 11). The Israelite narrative teaches that seeing God's works does not necessarily lead to knowing his ways (v. 10).

Hebrews 3 and 4 make clear that the "rest" referred to in this psalm points beyond Canaan. "Now we who have believed enter that rest" (Heb 4:3). While the exodus generation failed to obey, the author of Hebrews holds out the promise that his readers might enter God's rest "today" (Heb 4:7). Therefore, they were to make every effort to enter (Heb 4:11).

[11] So I declared on oath in my anger,
'They shall never enter my rest.' "

Psalm 96

[1] Sing to the LORD a new song;
sing to the LORD, all the earth.
[2] Sing to the LORD, praise his name;
proclaim his salvation day after day.
[3] Declare his glory among the nations,
his marvelous deeds among all peoples.

[4] For great is the LORD and most worthy of praise;
he is to be feared above all gods.
[5] For all the gods of the nations are idols,
but the LORD made the heavens.
[6] Splendor and majesty are before him;
strength and glory are in his sanctuary.

[7] Ascribe to the LORD, all you families of nations,
ascribe to the LORD glory and strength.
[8] Ascribe to the LORD the glory due his name;
bring an offering and come into his courts.
[9] Worship the LORD in the splendor of his[a] holiness;
tremble before him, all the earth.
[10] Say among the nations, "The LORD reigns."
The world is firmly established, it cannot be moved;
he will judge the peoples with equity.

[11] Let the heavens rejoice, let the earth be glad;
let the sea resound, and all that is in it.
[12] Let the fields be jubilant, and everything in them;
let all the trees of the forest sing for joy.
[13] Let all creation rejoice before the LORD, for he comes,
he comes to judge the earth.
He will judge the world in righteousness
and the peoples in his faithfulness.

Psalm 97

[1] The LORD reigns, let the earth be glad;
let the distant shores rejoice.
[2] Clouds and thick darkness surround him;
righteousness and justice are the foundation of his throne.
[3] Fire goes before him
and consumes his foes on every side.
[4] His lightning lights up the world;
the earth sees and trembles.
[5] The mountains melt like wax before the LORD,
before the Lord of all the earth.
[6] The heavens proclaim his righteousness,
and all peoples see his glory.

[7] All who worship images are put to shame,
those who boast in idols —
worship him, all you gods!

[8] Zion hears and rejoices
and the villages of Judah are glad
because of your judgments, LORD.

[a] 9 Or *LORD with the splendor of*

PSALM 96:1 – 13

THE MISSION OF GOD

Everyone worships. The question is not *whether* humans worship, but *whom or what* they worship. In this psalm, the reader finds the Old Testament rationale for joining in God's mission to make himself known. Although the pagan nations were worshiping idols they made, God made the entire world, including these pagans and the materials they used to carve idols (v. 5). Nevertheless, the first verse of this psalm calls upon *all* the earth to sing to God — including idolaters who have turned away from him. Since the creation of the world, God intended to fill the earth with true worshipers. Seeking that which God desires, the people of God declare his glory among pagan nations (v. 3). The apostle John's vision in the book of Revelation gave the reader a peek into God's eternal purposes. John wrote, "And they sang a new song, saying: 'You are worthy to take the scroll and to open its seals, because you were slain, and with your blood you purchased for God persons from every tribe and language and people and nation'" (Rev 5:9). False gods make false promises. However, the true God, in sending his Son, brought glory to himself by redeeming worshipers from every nation on earth. Let the earth be glad (Ps 96:11).

9 For you, LORD, are the Most High over all the earth;
you are exalted far above all gods.
10 Let those who love the LORD hate evil,
for he guards the lives of his faithful ones
and delivers them from the hand of the wicked.
11 Light shines[a] on the righteous
and joy on the upright in heart.
12 Rejoice in the LORD, you who are righteous,
and praise his holy name.

Psalm 98

A psalm.

1 Sing to the LORD a new song,
for he has done marvelous things;
his right hand and his holy arm
have worked salvation for him.
2 The LORD has made his salvation known
and revealed his righteousness to the nations.
3 He has remembered his love
and his faithfulness to Israel;
all the ends of the earth have seen
the salvation of our God.

4 Shout for joy to the LORD, all the earth,
burst into jubilant song with music;
5 make music to the LORD with the harp,
with the harp and the sound of singing,
6 with trumpets and the blast of the ram's horn —
shout for joy before the LORD, the King.

7 Let the sea resound, and everything in it,
the world, and all who live in it.
8 Let the rivers clap their hands,
let the mountains sing together for joy;
9 let them sing before the LORD,
for he comes to judge the earth.
He will judge the world in righteousness
and the peoples with equity.

Psalm 99

1 The LORD reigns,
let the nations tremble;
he sits enthroned between the cherubim,
let the earth shake.
2 Great is the LORD in Zion;
he is exalted over all the nations.
3 Let them praise your great and awesome name —
he is holy.

4 The King is mighty, he loves justice —
you have established equity;
in Jacob you have done
what is just and right.
5 Exalt the LORD our God
and worship at his footstool;
he is holy.

[a] *11* One Hebrew manuscript and ancient versions (see also 112:4); most Hebrew manuscripts *Light is sown*

PSALM 99:1 – 9

HOLY, HOLY, HOLY

The first verse says that the nations tremble at the One who reigns, enthroned between the cherubim. Many understand that this alludes to the cherubim placed at either end of the atonement cover on top of the ark with their outstretched wings forming a throne. The psalmist called upon the reader to visualize God sitting enthroned upon this stunning structure. The earth rightly shakes.

The psalmist went on to describe the One who reigns as holy. Since they could not underline or bold something in the Hebrew Scriptures, the author would repeat whatever he intended to emphasize. So, three different times in this psalm, this King is described as holy (vv. 3,5,9). It seems as if the readers of this psalm might never approach such a holy, justice-loving King (v. 4). But Israel's history told a different story. Moses, Aaron and Samuel all cried out to this King (v. 6). Mercifully, he answered and forgave (vv. 7 – 8). For the reader, the question arises: How can this holy God who loves justice also forgive the guilty?

God upheld his righteous character by sending his blameless Son to take the punishment his holy justice demanded. The holy life his Son lived is now credited to those who believe. When the innocent One stands in their place, the guilty can be called holy (Eph 1:3 – 4).

SALVATION IS HERE!

God is a God of salvation! By his holy arm, God worked salvation, making it known to his people (Ps 98:1 – 2). Therefore, accompanied by a host of instruments, the people of God were to sing and shout to the Lord (vv. 4 – 6). This psalm makes clear that God did great things for Israel, reminding the people of all his promises to them. But his blessing did not terminate at the nation's borders, nor was it intended to. This salvation that God made known was seen by all the ends of the earth (v. 3).

The salvation that God has brought to his people is to be shouted about with joy, and the people are to burst into jubilant song (v. 4). It cannot be celebrated in somber tones but must be celebrated in exuberant chorus. The sea and all who live in the earth will "resound" in this chorus (v. 7).

The psalmist wrote that the Lord has revealed his righteousness to the nations (v. 2). Certainly God did this in part through the law, but in Jesus righteousness was revealed apart from the law (Ro 3:21). In the New Testament, Paul wrote, "In the gospel the righteousness of God is revealed — a righteousness that is by faith" (Ro 1:17). In Jesus, God sent his righteous Savior. The people that he came to save did not earn salvation on their own merit, but it was given by the grace and righteousness of God. This fact gives all people something to celebrate and shout about!

[6] Moses and Aaron were among his priests,
Samuel was among those who called on his name;
they called on the LORD
and he answered them.
[7] He spoke to them from the pillar of cloud;
they kept his statutes and the decrees he gave them.

[8] LORD our God,
you answered them;
you were to Israel a forgiving God,
though you punished their misdeeds.[a]
[9] Exalt the LORD our God
and worship at his holy mountain,
for the LORD our God is holy.

Psalm 100

A psalm. For giving grateful praise.

[1] Shout for joy to the LORD, all the earth.
[2] Worship the LORD with gladness;
come before him with joyful songs.
[3] Know that the LORD is God.
It is he who made us, and we are his[b];
we are his people, the sheep of his pasture.

[4] Enter his gates with thanksgiving
and his courts with praise;
give thanks to him and praise his name.
[5] For the LORD is good and his love endures forever;
his faithfulness continues through all generations.

Psalm 101

Of David. A psalm.

[1] I will sing of your love and justice;
to you, LORD, I will sing praise.
[2] I will be careful to lead a blameless life—
when will you come to me?

I will conduct the affairs of my house
with a blameless heart.
[3] I will not look with approval
on anything that is vile.

I hate what faithless people do;
I will have no part in it.
[4] The perverse of heart shall be far from me;
I will have nothing to do with what is evil.
[5] Whoever slanders their neighbor in secret,
I will put to silence;
whoever has haughty eyes and a proud heart,
I will not tolerate.

[6] My eyes will be on the faithful in the land,
that they may dwell with me;
the one whose walk is blameless
will minister to me.

[a] 8 Or *God, / an avenger of the wrongs done to them* [b] 3 Or *and not we ourselves*

PSALM 100:1–5

GIVE THANKS

The structure of this psalm is fairly simple. The songwriter encouraged the people of God to sing and shout to the Lord and subsequently reminded them why they should. The psalmist then instructed the people of God to give thanks to the Lord. Then, in similar fashion, readers are given a solid, lasting rationale for why their thanksgiving should be unceasing. This psalm prompts worship with the truths of God's person and deeds.

So, why should they give thanks? The God to whom these readers gave thanks is the unchanging standard for goodness. Furthermore, this good God never ceased to love his people. In the book of Psalms, the Hebrew word *hesed*, translated "love" in Psalm 100:5, appears as a characteristic of God over 120 times. The book makes its point. Not only is God both good and loving, but no generation has known God to be unfaithful (v. 5). The New Testament equivalent to Old Testament love and faithfulness is grace and truth, seen most clearly in Jesus Christ (Jn 1:17).

7 No one who practices deceit
will dwell in my house;
no one who speaks falsely
will stand in my presence.

8 Every morning I will put to silence
all the wicked in the land;
I will cut off every evildoer
from the city of the LORD.

Psalm 102[a]

A prayer of an afflicted person who has grown weak and pours out a lament before the LORD.

1 Hear my prayer, LORD;
let my cry for help come to you.
2 Do not hide your face from me
when I am in distress.
Turn your ear to me;
when I call, answer me quickly.

3 For my days vanish like smoke;
my bones burn like glowing embers.
4 My heart is blighted and withered like grass;
I forget to eat my food.
5 In my distress I groan aloud
and am reduced to skin and bones.
6 I am like a desert owl,
like an owl among the ruins.
7 I lie awake; I have become
like a bird alone on a roof.
8 All day long my enemies taunt me;
those who rail against me use my name as a curse.
9 For I eat ashes as my food
and mingle my drink with tears
10 because of your great wrath,
for you have taken me up and thrown me aside.
11 My days are like the evening shadow;
I wither away like grass.

12 But you, LORD, sit enthroned forever;
your renown endures through all generations.
13 You will arise and have compassion on Zion,
for it is time to show favor to her;
the appointed time has come.
14 For her stones are dear to your servants;
her very dust moves them to pity.
15 The nations will fear the name of the LORD,
all the kings of the earth will revere your glory.
16 For the LORD will rebuild Zion
and appear in his glory.
17 He will respond to the prayer of the destitute;
he will not despise their plea.

18 Let this be written for a future generation,
that a people not yet created may praise the LORD:
19 "The LORD looked down from his sanctuary on high,
from heaven he viewed the earth,

[a] In Hebrew texts 102:1-28 is numbered 102:2-29.

[20] to hear the groans of the prisoners
and release those condemned to death."
[21] So the name of the LORD will be declared in Zion
and his praise in Jerusalem
[22] when the peoples and the kingdoms
assemble to worship the LORD.

[23] In the course of my life[a] he broke my strength;
he cut short my days.
[24] So I said:
"Do not take me away, my God, in the midst of my days;
your years go on through all generations.
[25] In the beginning you laid the foundations of the earth,
and the heavens are the work of your hands.
[26] They will perish, but you remain;
they will all wear out like a garment.
Like clothing you will change them
and they will be discarded.
[27] But you remain the same,
and your years will never end.
[28] The children of your servants will live in your presence;
their descendants will be established before you."

Psalm 103

Of David.

[1] Praise the LORD, my soul;
all my inmost being, praise his holy name.
[2] Praise the LORD, my soul,
and forget not all his benefits—
[3] who forgives all your sins
and heals all your diseases,
[4] who redeems your life from the pit
and crowns you with love and compassion,
[5] who satisfies your desires with good things
so that your youth is renewed like the eagle's.

[6] The LORD works righteousness
and justice for all the oppressed.

[7] He made known his ways to Moses,
his deeds to the people of Israel:
[8] The LORD is compassionate and gracious,
slow to anger, abounding in love.
[9] He will not always accuse,
nor will he harbor his anger forever;
[10] he does not treat us as our sins deserve
or repay us according to our iniquities.
[11] For as high as the heavens are above the earth,
so great is his love for those who fear him;
[12] as far as the east is from the west,
so far has he removed our transgressions from us.

[13] As a father has compassion on his children,
so the LORD has compassion on those who fear him;
[14] for he knows how we are formed,
he remembers that we are dust.

[a] 23 Or *By his power*

PSALM 102:25–27

GOD NEVER CHANGES

The psalmist contrasted, in these few verses, that which perishes with that which is imperishable. In the beginning, God made the heavens and the earth. The rationale follows that if the uncreated God preceded and made the heavens, then clearly he need not perish or change as they do.

All the promises of God depend upon the truth that God is unchanging. The apostle Peter used language similar to the psalmist to assure believers of the finality of God's Word. Quoting the prophet Isaiah, he wrote, "The grass withers and the flowers fall, but the word of the Lord endures forever" (1Pe 1:24–25).

Each autumn, yards are covered with the evidence of the world's perishable nature. Yet, in the midst of this earthly fading, God does not change. The author of Hebrews quoted Ps 102:25–27 and applied it specifically to the Son of God (Heb 1:10–12), going on to argue that Jesus remains the same yesterday, today and forever (Heb 13:8). Because of this—an unchanging God making unchanging promises—an imperishable inheritance awaits God's people (1Pe 1:4).

PSALM 103:3

HEALING

The psalmist, in this single verse, spoke of both healing and forgiveness of sins. During one instance in Jesus' ministry, he used a single miracle to prove his authority to accomplish both physical healing and spiritual forgiveness. In the Gospel

(continued on page 899)

GUILT IS GONE

Psalm 103 focuses on how God dealt with his people with compassion and grace (v. 8), not treating them as their sins deserved (v. 10). He will not harbor his anger forever (v. 9).

Sin is not only defined by commission, but also by omission. James makes clear that anyone who "knows the good they ought to do and doesn't do it, it is sin for them" (Jas 4:17). With the greatest commandment demanding the devotion of the entirety of our hearts, minds and strength to loving God (Mk 12:29 – 30), the biblical case for humanity's guilt is clear. Furthermore, James told his readers that one violation of God's law makes a person guilty of breaking the entirety of it (Jas 2:10).

The apostle Paul made plain humanity's guilt in his letter to the Romans. Regarding the Gentile without God's law, he wrote, "All who sin apart from the law will also perish apart from the law" (Ro 2:12). Regarding the Jew devoted to God's law, Paul added, "All who sin under the law will be judged by the law" (Ro 2:12). To summarize Paul's argument in the first three chapters of Romans: all mouths are stopped; no one is righteous (Ro 3:10). Humankind stands guilty before a holy God.

But psalms like this one reveal to the people of God that the Lord is "compassionate and gracious, slow to anger, abounding in love" (Ps 103:8). This psalm reveals that God's love is immeasurable in human terms. Using terms like "as high as the heavens are above the earth" (v. 11) and "as far as the east is from the west" (v. 12), the author describes the love of God.

The righteous Lord must also be a compassionate Lord (v. 13). This psalm reveals him, pointing the reader to the God-man who would one day look at people with compassion (Mt 9:36). Jesus, the embodiment of grace and love, came to set people free and offer a new way to have a relationship with God the Father.

[15]The life of mortals is like grass,
they flourish like a flower of the field;
[16]the wind blows over it and it is gone,
and its place remembers it no more.
[17]But from everlasting to everlasting
the LORD's love is with those who fear him,
and his righteousness with their children's children—
[18]with those who keep his covenant
and remember to obey his precepts.

[19]The LORD has established his throne in heaven,
and his kingdom rules over all.

[20]Praise the LORD, you his angels,
you mighty ones who do his bidding,
who obey his word.
[21]Praise the LORD, all his heavenly hosts,
you his servants who do his will.
[22]Praise the LORD, all his works
everywhere in his dominion.

Praise the LORD, my soul.

Psalm 104

[1]Praise the LORD, my soul.

LORD my God, you are very great;
you are clothed with splendor and majesty.

[2]The LORD wraps himself in light as with a garment;
he stretches out the heavens like a tent
[3]and lays the beams of his upper chambers on their waters.
He makes the clouds his chariot
and rides on the wings of the wind.
[4]He makes winds his messengers,[a]
flames of fire his servants.

[5]He set the earth on its foundations;
it can never be moved.
[6]You covered it with the watery depths as with a garment;
the waters stood above the mountains.
[7]But at your rebuke the waters fled,
at the sound of your thunder they took to flight;
[8]they flowed over the mountains,
they went down into the valleys,
to the place you assigned for them.
[9]You set a boundary they cannot cross;
never again will they cover the earth.

[10]He makes springs pour water into the ravines;
it flows between the mountains.
[11]They give water to all the beasts of the field;
the wild donkeys quench their thirst.
[12]The birds of the sky nest by the waters;
they sing among the branches.
[13]He waters the mountains from his upper chambers;
the land is satisfied by the fruit of his work.
[14]He makes grass grow for the cattle,
and plants for people to cultivate—
bringing forth food from the earth:

[a] 4 Or *angels*

(Healing, continued)

of Mark, while Jesus was teaching, a crowd pressed in on him. Unable to reach Jesus through the crowd, a group of people lowered their paralyzed friend through the roof of the house to be healed by Jesus. This man's need was obvious—he needed physical healing. Jesus, seemingly insensitive, said, "Son, your sins are forgiven" (Mk 2:5). The teachers of the law nearby thought Jesus blasphemed by claiming to do something only God could do. So Jesus, knowing their innermost thoughts, asked which would be easier: to heal someone or to *say* he forgave his sins? The idea was that it would be easier to *say* his sins were forgiven, since no one could verify that kind of spiritual transformation.

Jesus chose the harder thing to prove his authority. He said, "But I want you to know that the Son of Man has authority on earth to forgive sins . . . I tell you, get up, take your mat and go home" (Mk 2:10–11). The man stood up, proving what Psalm 103:3 says: Jesus can both heal and forgive.

PSALM 104:10–28

GOD'S CARE

Psalm 104 spells out the details of God's care for the world. The beasts of the field get their water from a spring, but ultimately that water comes from the hand of God (vv. 10–11). God planted the trees that the birds nest in (vv. 16–17). The teeming creatures of the sea look to the Lord for provision (vv. 25–27).

The psalmist made clear God's care for his creation. Jesus would much later take this truth and apply it to his hearers, saying, "Look at the

(continued on next page)

(God's Care, continued)

birds of the air; they do not sow or reap or store away in barns, and yet your heavenly Father feeds them. Are you not much more valuable than they?" (Mt 6:26). Peter, who surely heard these words, would later write, "Cast all your anxiety on him because he cares for you" (1Pe 5:7).

15 wine that gladdens human hearts,
oil to make their faces shine,
and bread that sustains their hearts.
16 The trees of the LORD are well watered,
the cedars of Lebanon that he planted.
17 There the birds make their nests;
the stork has its home in the junipers.
18 The high mountains belong to the wild goats;
the crags are a refuge for the hyrax.

19 He made the moon to mark the seasons,
and the sun knows when to go down.
20 You bring darkness, it becomes night,
and all the beasts of the forest prowl.
21 The lions roar for their prey
and seek their food from God.
22 The sun rises, and they steal away;
they return and lie down in their dens.
23 Then people go out to their work,
to their labor until evening.

24 How many are your works, LORD!
In wisdom you made them all;
the earth is full of your creatures.
25 There is the sea, vast and spacious,
teeming with creatures beyond number—
living things both large and small.
26 There the ships go to and fro,
and Leviathan, which you formed to frolic there.

27 All creatures look to you
to give them their food at the proper time.
28 When you give it to them,
they gather it up;
when you open your hand,
they are satisfied with good things.
29 When you hide your face,
they are terrified;
when you take away their breath,
they die and return to the dust.
30 When you send your Spirit,
they are created,
and you renew the face of the ground.

31 May the glory of the LORD endure forever;
may the LORD rejoice in his works—
32 he who looks at the earth, and it trembles,
who touches the mountains, and they smoke.

33 I will sing to the LORD all my life;
I will sing praise to my God as long as I live.
34 May my meditation be pleasing to him,
as I rejoice in the LORD.
35 But may sinners vanish from the earth
and the wicked be no more.

Praise the LORD, my soul.

Praise the LORD.[a]

[a] *35* Hebrew *Hallelu Yah;* in the Septuagint this line stands at the beginning of Psalm 105.

Psalm 105

[1] Give praise to the LORD, proclaim his name;
make known among the nations what he has done.
[2] Sing to him, sing praise to him;
tell of all his wonderful acts.
[3] Glory in his holy name;
let the hearts of those who seek the LORD rejoice.
[4] Look to the LORD and his strength;
seek his face always.

[5] Remember the wonders he has done,
his miracles, and the judgments he pronounced,
[6] you his servants, the descendants of Abraham,
his chosen ones, the children of Jacob.
[7] He is the LORD our God;
his judgments are in all the earth.

[8] He remembers his covenant forever,
the promise he made, for a thousand generations,
[9] the covenant he made with Abraham,
the oath he swore to Isaac.
[10] He confirmed it to Jacob as a decree,
to Israel as an everlasting covenant:
[11] "To you I will give the land of Canaan
as the portion you will inherit."

[12] When they were but few in number,
few indeed, and strangers in it,
[13] they wandered from nation to nation,
from one kingdom to another.
[14] He allowed no one to oppress them;
for their sake he rebuked kings:
[15] "Do not touch my anointed ones;
do my prophets no harm."

[16] He called down famine on the land
and destroyed all their supplies of food;
[17] and he sent a man before them—
Joseph, sold as a slave.
[18] They bruised his feet with shackles,
his neck was put in irons,
[19] till what he foretold came to pass,
till the word of the LORD proved him true.
[20] The king sent and released him,
the ruler of peoples set him free.
[21] He made him master of his household,
ruler over all he possessed,
[22] to instruct his princes as he pleased
and teach his elders wisdom.

[23] Then Israel entered Egypt;
Jacob resided as a foreigner in the land of Ham.
[24] The LORD made his people very fruitful;
he made them too numerous for their foes,
[25] whose hearts he turned to hate his people,
to conspire against his servants.
[26] He sent Moses his servant,
and Aaron, whom he had chosen.
[27] They performed his signs among them,
his wonders in the land of Ham.

PSALM 105:1–45

A HISTORY OF FAITHFULNESS

The audience for this psalm is clear: "the descendants of Abraham, his chosen ones, the children of Jacob" (v. 6). The people of God were to hear and heed these words.

The people of Israel seemed to have suffered from spiritual amnesia. So, beginning with Abraham, the psalmist recounted the faithfulness of God over the span of 40 verses. The God of Israel allowed no one to oppress them (vv. 14–15). The word of the Lord was fulfilled in the rise of Joseph (vv. 17–22). The Lord made his people fruitful, more numerous than their foes (v. 24). When they were enslaved, God sent Moses (v. 26).

While the psalm lists various names, God proves to be the main character. It was God who powerfully delivered them from Pharaoh (vv. 27–38). Though this psalm includes only highlights from Israel's history, the point is clear: nothing God purposed has failed.

The psalmist began with Abraham. Yet, Jesus would assert plainly in the Gospel of John, "Before Abraham was born, I am" (Jn 8:58). The epicenter of God's faithfulness not only preceded the father of Israel, all God's promises eventually find their "Yes" in him (2Co 1:20). God remembers his covenant; God's people remember his wonders (Ps 105:5–11).

28 He sent darkness and made the land dark—
for had they not rebelled against his words?
29 He turned their waters into blood,
causing their fish to die.
30 Their land teemed with frogs,
which went up into the bedrooms of their rulers.
31 He spoke, and there came swarms of flies,
and gnats throughout their country.
32 He turned their rain into hail,
with lightning throughout their land;
33 he struck down their vines and fig trees
and shattered the trees of their country.
34 He spoke, and the locusts came,
grasshoppers without number;
35 they ate up every green thing in their land,
ate up the produce of their soil.
36 Then he struck down all the firstborn in their land,
the firstfruits of all their manhood.
37 He brought out Israel, laden with silver and gold,
and from among their tribes no one faltered.
38 Egypt was glad when they left,
because dread of Israel had fallen on them.

39 He spread out a cloud as a covering,
and a fire to give light at night.
40 They asked, and he brought them quail;
he fed them well with the bread of heaven.
41 He opened the rock, and water gushed out;
it flowed like a river in the desert.

42 For he remembered his holy promise
given to his servant Abraham.
43 He brought out his people with rejoicing,
his chosen ones with shouts of joy;
44 he gave them the lands of the nations,
and they fell heir to what others had toiled for—
45 that they might keep his precepts
and observe his laws.

Praise the LORD.[a]

Psalm 106

1 Praise the LORD.[b]

Give thanks to the LORD, for he is good;
his love endures forever.

2 Who can proclaim the mighty acts of the LORD
or fully declare his praise?
3 Blessed are those who act justly,
who always do what is right.

4 Remember me, LORD, when you show favor to your people,
come to my aid when you save them,
5 that I may enjoy the prosperity of your chosen ones,
that I may share in the joy of your nation
and join your inheritance in giving praise.

[a] *45* Hebrew *Hallelu Yah* [b] *1* Hebrew *Hallelu Yah*; also in verse 48

6 We have sinned, even as our ancestors did;
we have done wrong and acted wickedly.
7 When our ancestors were in Egypt,
they gave no thought to your miracles;
they did not remember your many kindnesses,
and they rebelled by the sea, the Red Sea.[a]
8 Yet he saved them for his name's sake,
to make his mighty power known.
9 He rebuked the Red Sea, and it dried up;
he led them through the depths as through a desert.
10 He saved them from the hand of the foe;
from the hand of the enemy he redeemed them.
11 The waters covered their adversaries;
not one of them survived.
12 Then they believed his promises
and sang his praise.

13 But they soon forgot what he had done
and did not wait for his plan to unfold.
14 In the desert they gave in to their craving;
in the wilderness they put God to the test.
15 So he gave them what they asked for,
but sent a wasting disease among them.

16 In the camp they grew envious of Moses
and of Aaron, who was consecrated to the LORD.
17 The earth opened up and swallowed Dathan;
it buried the company of Abiram.
18 Fire blazed among their followers;
a flame consumed the wicked.
19 At Horeb they made a calf
and worshiped an idol cast from metal.
20 They exchanged their glorious God
for an image of a bull, which eats grass.
21 They forgot the God who saved them,
who had done great things in Egypt,
22 miracles in the land of Ham
and awesome deeds by the Red Sea.
23 So he said he would destroy them —
had not Moses, his chosen one,
stood in the breach before him
to keep his wrath from destroying them.

24 Then they despised the pleasant land;
they did not believe his promise.
25 They grumbled in their tents
and did not obey the LORD.
26 So he swore to them with uplifted hand
that he would make them fall in the wilderness,
27 make their descendants fall among the nations
and scatter them throughout the lands.

28 They yoked themselves to the Baal of Peor
and ate sacrifices offered to lifeless gods;
29 they aroused the LORD's anger by their wicked deeds,
and a plague broke out among them.
30 But Phinehas stood up and intervened,
and the plague was checked.

[a] 7 Or *the Sea of Reeds*; also in verses 9 and 22

PSALM 107:1–32

MERCY ENDURES

The fifth and final book of Psalms begins with a call for the redeemed to give thanks to the Lord, in light of his enduring love (vv. 1–3). Then, using four particular narratives, it illustrates this enduring love of God.

The first narrative tells of a group that suffered from hunger out in the desert, their lives fading away. Then (with the first appearance of a common denominator in all four stories), they cried out to the Lord (vv. 6,13,19,28). The Lord answered, leading them from the desert to a city where their hunger might be satisfied (vv. 6–7). The second group suffered from the punishment of slavery to foreign oppressors. They cried to the Lord and he delivered them (vv. 13–14). The third group suffered from the punishment of wasting disease; however, when they cried to the Lord he showed nothing but mercy (vv. 19–20). The fourth group suffered from fear of the sea's power, their lives being threatened. They too cried to the Lord and the storm was stilled (vv. 28–29).

Not only does each scene show someone crying to the Lord and subsequently being delivered by the Lord's mercy, each one includes the response that should follow: "Let them give thanks to the LORD for his unfailing love and his wonderful deeds for mankind" (vv. 8,15,21,31). The height of the demonstration of this mercy was in the sending of Jesus, who would die a substitutionary death on behalf of his people. The only response to an enduring love like this is a thankfulness that knows no end.

31 This was credited to him as righteousness
for endless generations to come.
32 By the waters of Meribah they angered the LORD,
and trouble came to Moses because of them;
33 for they rebelled against the Spirit of God,
and rash words came from Moses' lips.[a]

34 They did not destroy the peoples
as the LORD had commanded them,
35 but they mingled with the nations
and adopted their customs.
36 They worshiped their idols,
which became a snare to them.
37 They sacrificed their sons
and their daughters to false gods.
38 They shed innocent blood,
the blood of their sons and daughters,
whom they sacrificed to the idols of Canaan,
and the land was desecrated by their blood.
39 They defiled themselves by what they did;
by their deeds they prostituted themselves.

40 Therefore the LORD was angry with his people
and abhorred his inheritance.
41 He gave them into the hands of the nations,
and their foes ruled over them.
42 Their enemies oppressed them
and subjected them to their power.
43 Many times he delivered them,
but they were bent on rebellion
and they wasted away in their sin.
44 Yet he took note of their distress
when he heard their cry;
45 for their sake he remembered his covenant
and out of his great love he relented.
46 He caused all who held them captive
to show them mercy.

47 Save us, LORD our God,
and gather us from the nations,
that we may give thanks to your holy name
and glory in your praise.

48 Praise be to the LORD, the God of Israel,
from everlasting to everlasting.

Let all the people say, "Amen!"

Praise the LORD.

BOOK V

Psalms 107–150

Psalm 107

1 Give thanks to the LORD, for he is good;
his love endures forever.

[a] 33 Or *against his spirit, / and rash words came from his lips*

PSALM 106:1 – 48

DELIVERED BUT ENSLAVED

This psalm details the Israelites' harrowing deliverance from captivity in Egypt. As just one example, the Red Sea transformed into dry land long enough for the people of God to pass. Then, in a matter of moments, that dry land became a watery graveyard for Israel's adversaries. God saved his people, not for their sake primarily, but to make his power known (v. 8).

Although the people were delivered miraculously from their physical slavery, the rest of the psalm speaks to their continuing slavery to sin. Though they sang of God's promises on the shores of the sea, they soon forgot that melody (v. 13). They no longer trusted the leaders God gave them (v. 16). At the height of their rebellion, they crafted and worshiped idols (vv. 19 – 20). Rather than standing in contrast to the pagan nations as God commanded them, they assimilated, even to the point of sacrificing their own children to false gods (vv. 34 – 38). This is not what God delivered them for.

The people of God forgot more than the song of God's deliverance; they forgot their God (v. 21). Therefore, God allowed the pagan nations to overrun them (vv. 40 – 42). Their enslavement to sin led once again to physical enslavement.

Throughout this psalm, two themes emerge. The people of God forget. God remembers. In fact, these two themes fill the pages of Scripture. The unfaithfulness of God's people does not rub off on their God; he continues to deliver. As Paul would later say, "If we are faithless, he remains faithful, for he cannot disown himself" (2Ti 2:13).

In his letter to the church at Rome, Paul described an act of God more miraculous than the parting of the Red Sea: "You have been set free from sin and have become slaves to righteousness" (Ro 6:18). The chains of the pagan nations could not enslave believers' hearts. Through the work of the resurrection, God destroyed the shackles of sin, making Jesus the new master of all who put their faith in him.

[2] Let the redeemed of the LORD tell their story—
those he redeemed from the hand of the foe,
[3] those he gathered from the lands,
from east and west, from north and south.[a]

[4] Some wandered in desert wastelands,
finding no way to a city where they could settle.
[5] They were hungry and thirsty,
and their lives ebbed away.
[6] Then they cried out to the LORD in their trouble,
and he delivered them from their distress.
[7] He led them by a straight way
to a city where they could settle.
[8] Let them give thanks to the LORD for his unfailing love
and his wonderful deeds for mankind,
[9] for he satisfies the thirsty
and fills the hungry with good things.

[10] Some sat in darkness, in utter darkness,
prisoners suffering in iron chains,
[11] because they rebelled against God's commands
and despised the plans of the Most High.
[12] So he subjected them to bitter labor;
they stumbled, and there was no one to help.
[13] Then they cried to the LORD in their trouble,
and he saved them from their distress.
[14] He brought them out of darkness, the utter darkness,
and broke away their chains.
[15] Let them give thanks to the LORD for his unfailing love
and his wonderful deeds for mankind,
[16] for he breaks down gates of bronze
and cuts through bars of iron.

[17] Some became fools through their rebellious ways
and suffered affliction because of their iniquities.
[18] They loathed all food
and drew near the gates of death.
[19] Then they cried to the LORD in their trouble,
and he saved them from their distress.
[20] He sent out his word and healed them;
he rescued them from the grave.
[21] Let them give thanks to the LORD for his unfailing love
and his wonderful deeds for mankind.
[22] Let them sacrifice thank offerings
and tell of his works with songs of joy.

[23] Some went out on the sea in ships;
they were merchants on the mighty waters.
[24] They saw the works of the LORD,
his wonderful deeds in the deep.
[25] For he spoke and stirred up a tempest
that lifted high the waves.
[26] They mounted up to the heavens and went down to the depths;
in their peril their courage melted away.
[27] They reeled and staggered like drunkards;
they were at their wits' end.
[28] Then they cried out to the LORD in their trouble,
and he brought them out of their distress.

---

[a] *3* Hebrew *north and the sea*

[29]He stilled the storm to a whisper;
the waves of the sea[a] were hushed.
[30]They were glad when it grew calm,
and he guided them to their desired haven.
[31]Let them give thanks to the LORD for his unfailing love
and his wonderful deeds for mankind.
[32]Let them exalt him in the assembly of the people
and praise him in the council of the elders.

[33]He turned rivers into a desert,
flowing springs into thirsty ground,
[34]and fruitful land into a salt waste,
because of the wickedness of those who lived there.
[35]He turned the desert into pools of water
and the parched ground into flowing springs;
[36]there he brought the hungry to live,
and they founded a city where they could settle.
[37]They sowed fields and planted vineyards
that yielded a fruitful harvest;
[38]he blessed them, and their numbers greatly increased,
and he did not let their herds diminish.

[39]Then their numbers decreased, and they were humbled
by oppression, calamity and sorrow;
[40]he who pours contempt on nobles
made them wander in a trackless waste.
[41]But he lifted the needy out of their affliction
and increased their families like flocks.
[42]The upright see and rejoice,
but all the wicked shut their mouths.

[43]Let the one who is wise heed these things
and ponder the loving deeds of the LORD.

Psalm 108[b]

A song. A psalm of David.

[1]My heart, O God, is steadfast;
I will sing and make music with all my soul.
[2]Awake, harp and lyre!
I will awaken the dawn.
[3]I will praise you, LORD, among the nations;
I will sing of you among the peoples.
[4]For great is your love, higher than the heavens;
your faithfulness reaches to the skies.
[5]Be exalted, O God, above the heavens;
let your glory be over all the earth.

[6]Save us and help us with your right hand,
that those you love may be delivered.
[7]God has spoken from his sanctuary:
"In triumph I will parcel out Shechem
and measure off the Valley of Sukkoth.
[8]Gilead is mine, Manasseh is mine;
Ephraim is my helmet,
Judah is my scepter.

[a] 29 Dead Sea Scrolls; Masoretic Text / *their waves* [b] In Hebrew texts 108:1-13 is numbered 108:2-14.

[9] Moab is my washbasin,
on Edom I toss my sandal;
over Philistia I shout in triumph."
[10] Who will bring me to the fortified city?
Who will lead me to Edom?
[11] Is it not you, God, you who have rejected us
and no longer go out with our armies?
[12] Give us aid against the enemy,
for human help is worthless.
[13] With God we will gain the victory,
and he will trample down our enemies.

Psalm 109

For the director of music. Of David. A psalm.

[1] My God, whom I praise,
do not remain silent,
[2] for people who are wicked and deceitful
have opened their mouths against me;
they have spoken against me with lying tongues.
[3] With words of hatred they surround me;
they attack me without cause.
[4] In return for my friendship they accuse me,
but I am a man of prayer.
[5] They repay me evil for good,
and hatred for my friendship.

[6] Appoint someone evil to oppose my enemy;
let an accuser stand at his right hand.
[7] When he is tried, let him be found guilty,
and may his prayers condemn him.
[8] May his days be few;
may another take his place of leadership.
[9] May his children be fatherless
and his wife a widow.
[10] May his children be wandering beggars;
may they be driven[a] from their ruined homes.
[11] May a creditor seize all he has;
may strangers plunder the fruits of his labor.
[12] May no one extend kindness to him
or take pity on his fatherless children.
[13] May his descendants be cut off,
their names blotted out from the next generation.
[14] May the iniquity of his fathers be remembered before
the LORD;
may the sin of his mother never be blotted out.
[15] May their sins always remain before the LORD,
that he may blot out their name from the earth.

[16] For he never thought of doing a kindness,
but hounded to death the poor
and the needy and the brokenhearted.
[17] He loved to pronounce a curse—
may it come back on him.
He found no pleasure in blessing—
may it be far from him.

[a] *10* Septuagint; Hebrew *sought*

PSALM 109:1–5

PERSECUTED UNJUSTLY

"'A servant is not greater than his master.' If they persecuted me, they will persecute you also," Jesus told his disciples (Jn 15:20). Immediately preceding a section of prayers for delivery, here David detailed the persecution he faced. Wicked men spoke dishonestly against him (Ps 109:2). Without cause they spoke words of hate (v. 3). He showed them friendship; they attacked him (v. 4). He did good toward them; they returned evil (v. 5).

Jesus would tell his kingdom citizens to receive this kind of treatment as a blessing: "Blessed are you when people insult you, persecute you and falsely say all kinds of evil against you because of me" (Mt 5:11). The world's ire often means the Father's blessing. Anyone who desires to live a godly life should expect persecution (2Ti 3:12). Jesus epitomized this type of reality. Though he never sinned, he was consistently harassed by people. If they persecuted him, certainly they will persecute his followers. A servant is not greater than his master.

[18] He wore cursing as his garment;
it entered into his body like water,
into his bones like oil.
[19] May it be like a cloak wrapped about him,
like a belt tied forever around him.
[20] May this be the LORD's payment to my accusers,
to those who speak evil of me.

[21] But you, Sovereign LORD,
help me for your name's sake;
out of the goodness of your love, deliver me.
[22] For I am poor and needy,
and my heart is wounded within me.
[23] I fade away like an evening shadow;
I am shaken off like a locust.
[24] My knees give way from fasting;
my body is thin and gaunt.
[25] I am an object of scorn to my accusers;
when they see me, they shake their heads.

[26] Help me, LORD my God;
save me according to your unfailing love.
[27] Let them know that it is your hand,
that you, LORD, have done it.
[28] While they curse, may you bless;
may those who attack me be put to shame,
but may your servant rejoice.
[29] May my accusers be clothed with disgrace
and wrapped in shame as in a cloak.

[30] With my mouth I will greatly extol the LORD;
in the great throng of worshipers I will praise him.
[31] For he stands at the right hand of the needy,
to save their lives from those who would condemn them.

Psalm 110

Of David. A psalm.

[1] The LORD says to my lord:[a]

"Sit at my right hand
until I make your enemies
a footstool for your feet."

[2] The LORD will extend your mighty scepter from Zion, saying,
"Rule in the midst of your enemies!"
[3] Your troops will be willing
on your day of battle.
Arrayed in holy splendor,
your young men will come to you
like dew from the morning's womb.[b]

[4] The LORD has sworn
and will not change his mind:
"You are a priest forever,
in the order of Melchizedek."

[5] The Lord is at your right hand[c];
he will crush kings on the day of his wrath.

[a] *1* Or *Lord* [b] *3* The meaning of the Hebrew for this sentence is uncertain. [c] *5* Or *My lord is at your right hand, LORD*

PSALM 110:1

WHOSE SON IS HE?

No psalm is quoted more frequently in the New Testament than this one. While the same English word (*lord*) is used twice in verse 1, the Hebrew uses two different words. The question for the interpreter centers on the identity of this second "lord."

Jesus posed a form of this question to the Pharisees in Matthew's Gospel. Speaking of the long-expected Messiah, he asked, "Whose son is he?" (Mt 22:42). When the Pharisees responded "The son of David," Jesus quoted Psalm 110:1. In essence, Jesus asked them how, if David wrote this psalm, he can call his son "Lord" (Mt 22:45). Jesus asserted that this Messiah must be more than just the son of David.

Surely Peter was in the audience that day. Not long afterward, at Pentecost, he also quoted Psalm 110:1. Peter made plain to that crowd that David did not ascend to the heavens, though he wrote that this "Lord" would sit at God's right hand (Ac 2:29 – 35). Though Jesus made the case that this "Lord" could not be *just* the son of David, Peter stated clearly his identity: "Let all Israel be assured of this: God has made this Jesus, whom you crucified, both Lord and Messiah" (Ac 2:36). Jesus was not just the son of David; he is the Son of God. He is both David's descendant and his Lord.

[6] He will judge the nations, heaping up the dead
and crushing the rulers of the whole earth.
[7] He will drink from a brook along the way,[a]
and so he will lift his head high.

Psalm 111[b]

[1] Praise the LORD.[c]

I will extol the LORD with all my heart
in the council of the upright and in the assembly.

[2] Great are the works of the LORD;
they are pondered by all who delight in them.
[3] Glorious and majestic are his deeds,
and his righteousness endures forever.
[4] He has caused his wonders to be remembered;
the LORD is gracious and compassionate.
[5] He provides food for those who fear him;
he remembers his covenant forever.

[6] He has shown his people the power of his works,
giving them the lands of other nations.
[7] The works of his hands are faithful and just;
all his precepts are trustworthy.
[8] They are established for ever and ever,
enacted in faithfulness and uprightness.
[9] He provided redemption for his people;
he ordained his covenant forever—
holy and awesome is his name.

[10] The fear of the LORD is the beginning of wisdom;
all who follow his precepts have good understanding.
To him belongs eternal praise.

Psalm 112[b]

[1] Praise the LORD.[c]

Blessed are those who fear the LORD,
who find great delight in his commands.

[2] Their children will be mighty in the land;
the generation of the upright will be blessed.
[3] Wealth and riches are in their houses,
and their righteousness endures forever.
[4] Even in darkness light dawns for the upright,
for those who are gracious and compassionate and
righteous.
[5] Good will come to those who are generous and lend freely,
who conduct their affairs with justice.

[6] Surely the righteous will never be shaken;
they will be remembered forever.
[7] They will have no fear of bad news;
their hearts are steadfast, trusting in the LORD.
[8] Their hearts are secure, they will have no fear;
in the end they will look in triumph on their foes.

[a] *7* The meaning of the Hebrew for this clause is uncertain. [b] This psalm is an acrostic poem, the lines of which begin with the successive letters of the Hebrew alphabet.
[c] *1,1* Hebrew *Hallelu Yah*

JESUS, THE PRIEST-KING

In Genesis 14, Moses wrote about a mysterious priest named Melchizedek. He served as priest in Salem, the place later known as Jerusalem. His symbolically rich name means "king of righteousness." Interestingly, Melchizedek not only served as priest of Salem, he ruled as king.

The New Testament makes clear that Melchizedek was a representation of the Messiah who was to come. Psalm 110 speaks of the One whom the New Testament makes clear is Jesus Christ (Ac 2:22 – 36). God exalted him, seating him at his right hand to rule and reign (Ps 110:1; Eph 1:20).

During the Old Testament era, in every case other than in the person of Melchizedek, the kingly and priestly offices remained separate. One person could not fulfill both roles. The king represented God to humanity; the priest represented humanity to God. However, the role of the Old Testament priest was not the full realization of the plans of God.

In the Old Testament priests had limited authority and ultimately died. Jesus, on the other hand, has ultimate authority and ever lives to make intercession for his people (Heb 7:23 – 25). Melchizedek did not reign forever, but the Old Testament timeline gives no end to his reign or priesthood. It seemed to continue on, pointing readers to a priest-king who would reign forever: Jesus, in the order of Melchizedek (Ps 110:4).

Not only did Jesus' priesthood surpass the Levitical priesthood, but his sacrifice surpassed the priestly sacrifice. With no need to make atonement for his own sin, Jesus sacrificed himself as a pure and spotless lamb (1Pe 1:19). Not only did he *make* the perfect offering, he *was* that offering.

In Jesus, that which Melchizedek pointed to is perfectly fulfilled. Both offices come together in one person. Only one who was both God and human could represent both God and humanity. Jesus rules as King until all his enemies become his footstool, while interceding as priest for those being reconciled to God.

[9] They have freely scattered their gifts to the poor,
their righteousness endures forever;
their horn[a] will be lifted high in honor.

[10] The wicked will see and be vexed,
they will gnash their teeth and waste away;
the longings of the wicked will come to nothing.

Psalm 113

[1] Praise the LORD.[b]

Praise the LORD, you his servants;
praise the name of the LORD.
[2] Let the name of the LORD be praised,
both now and forevermore.
[3] From the rising of the sun to the place where it sets,
the name of the LORD is to be praised.

[4] The LORD is exalted over all the nations,
his glory above the heavens.
[5] Who is like the LORD our God,
the One who sits enthroned on high,
[6] who stoops down to look
on the heavens and the earth?

[7] He raises the poor from the dust
and lifts the needy from the ash heap;
[8] he seats them with princes,
with the princes of his people.
[9] He settles the childless woman in her home
as a happy mother of children.

Praise the LORD.

Psalm 114

[1] When Israel came out of Egypt,
Jacob from a people of foreign tongue,
[2] Judah became God's sanctuary,
Israel his dominion.

[3] The sea looked and fled,
the Jordan turned back;
[4] the mountains leaped like rams,
the hills like lambs.

[5] Why was it, sea, that you fled?
Why, Jordan, did you turn back?
[6] Why, mountains, did you leap like rams,
you hills, like lambs?

[7] Tremble, earth, at the presence of the Lord,
at the presence of the God of Jacob,
[8] who turned the rock into a pool,
the hard rock into springs of water.

Psalm 115

[1] Not to us, LORD, not to us
but to your name be the glory,
because of your love and faithfulness.

PSALMS 113–118

LAST MEAL

Psalms 113–118, called the Egyptian Hallel, came to be sung at the yearly Passover. Hallel means "praise." Generally, the first two psalms were sung prior to the meal, with the final four being sung after the meal.

While only one of them clearly references the exodus (Ps 114), other appropriate themes emerge. Psalm 113 speaks of the Lord raising the poor and needy from the dust, not unlike the Hebrew slaves. The same themes of the Old Testament Passover meal would eventually be seen in the New Testament Lord's Supper—a meal of remembrance and thanks. Psalm 116 addresses thanksgiving based on God's gracious action. Since these psalms usually accompanied the Passover, it is likely that these were the final songs Jesus sang before going to Gethsemane (Mt 26:30). Though he knew a terrible fate awaited, he was able to give thanks to God for his ongoing faithfulness to his redemptive work.

---

[a] *9 Horn* here symbolizes dignity. [b] *1* Hebrew *Hallelu Yah*; also in verse 9

2 Why do the nations say,
"Where is their God?"
3 Our God is in heaven;
he does whatever pleases him.
4 But their idols are silver and gold,
made by human hands.
5 They have mouths, but cannot speak,
eyes, but cannot see.
6 They have ears, but cannot hear,
noses, but cannot smell.
7 They have hands, but cannot feel,
feet, but cannot walk,
nor can they utter a sound with their throats.
8 Those who make them will be like them,
and so will all who trust in them.

9 All you Israelites, trust in the LORD—
he is their help and shield.
10 House of Aaron, trust in the LORD—
he is their help and shield.
11 You who fear him, trust in the LORD—
he is their help and shield.

12 The LORD remembers us and will bless us:
He will bless his people Israel,
he will bless the house of Aaron,
13 he will bless those who fear the LORD—
small and great alike.

14 May the LORD cause you to flourish,
both you and your children.
15 May you be blessed by the LORD,
the Maker of heaven and earth.

16 The highest heavens belong to the LORD,
but the earth he has given to mankind.
17 It is not the dead who praise the LORD,
those who go down to the place of silence;
18 it is we who extol the LORD,
both now and forevermore.

Praise the LORD.[a]

Psalm 116

1 I love the LORD, for he heard my voice;
he heard my cry for mercy.
2 Because he turned his ear to me,
I will call on him as long as I live.

3 The cords of death entangled me,
the anguish of the grave came over me;
I was overcome by distress and sorrow.
4 Then I called on the name of the LORD:
"LORD, save me!"

5 The LORD is gracious and righteous;
our God is full of compassion.
6 The LORD protects the unwary;
when I was brought low, he saved me.

[a] 18 Hebrew *Hallelu Yah*

[7] Return to your rest, my soul,
for the LORD has been good to you.

[8] For you, LORD, have delivered me from death,
my eyes from tears,
my feet from stumbling,
[9] that I may walk before the LORD
in the land of the living.

[10] I trusted in the LORD when I said,
"I am greatly afflicted";
[11] in my alarm I said,
"Everyone is a liar."

[12] What shall I return to the LORD
for all his goodness to me?

[13] I will lift up the cup of salvation
and call on the name of the LORD.
[14] I will fulfill my vows to the LORD
in the presence of all his people.

[15] Precious in the sight of the LORD
is the death of his faithful servants.
[16] Truly I am your servant, LORD;
I serve you just as my mother did;
you have freed me from my chains.

[17] I will sacrifice a thank offering to you
and call on the name of the LORD.
[18] I will fulfill my vows to the LORD
in the presence of all his people,
[19] in the courts of the house of the LORD—
in your midst, Jerusalem.

Praise the LORD.[a]

Psalm 117

[1] Praise the LORD, all you nations;
extol him, all you peoples.
[2] For great is his love toward us,
and the faithfulness of the LORD endures forever.

Praise the LORD.[a]

Psalm 118

[1] Give thanks to the LORD, for he is good;
his love endures forever.

[2] Let Israel say:
"His love endures forever."
[3] Let the house of Aaron say:
"His love endures forever."
[4] Let those who fear the LORD say:
"His love endures forever."

[5] When hard pressed, I cried to the LORD;
he brought me into a spacious place.
[6] The LORD is with me; I will not be afraid.
What can mere mortals do to me?

[a] *19,2* Hebrew *Hallelu Yah*

PSALM 116:15

DEATH

The psalmist mentioned here an enemy of humankind: death (Ps 116:3), though he referred to it here as "precious"—an overwhelmingly positive term. According to Paul, death came to humanity because of sin: in Adam all die (Ro 5:12). While the scientific advances of the last century—even the last ten years—preserve and extend life in amazing ways, no one evades death forever.

Psalm 110 speaks of Jesus reigning until all his enemies become a footstool for his feet (v. 1). Building upon that truth, Paul wrote, "The last enemy to be destroyed is death" (1Co 15:26). Paul went on to argue in that letter that the resurrection of Jesus makes possible the resurrection of his followers: "Since death came through a man, the resurrection of the dead comes also through a man. For as in Adam all die, so in Christ all will be made alive" (1Co 15:21–22). Only through the work of Christ can his followers taunt death: "Where, O death, is your sting?" (1Co 15:55). Though no one evades death, it need not have the final word.

THE NATIONS PRAISE THE LORD

This is the shortest psalm. However, its brevity should not be confused for insignificance. The psalmist calls upon all the earth — each and every nation — to praise the Lord of the nations (v. 1).

Though many of the psalms speak of God's work among the Israelites, God called Israel to himself for the sake of the world. Genesis 1 – 11 portrays the sinful descent of humanity culminating in the scattering of the people at Babel, but Genesis 12 indicates a brand new start for humanity through God's covenant with Abraham: "All peoples on earth will be blessed through you" (Ge 12:3). God promised that *all the nations* would be blessed through Abraham. In fact, God blessed Abraham *so that* he might be a blessing.

Then at the exodus, God orchestrated events to assert his unrivaled authority over all the nations, including the enemies of Israel. Even after being conquered by their enemies and forced into exile hundreds of years later, the Israelites continued to claim that their God rules sovereignly over all (Eze 36:16 – 38). God chose Israel to make himself known to all the world.

The Gospel of Luke — by going back beyond Abraham to Adam in its genealogy — hints at the global scope of the gospel's intent (Lk 3:37). At the end of Luke's Gospel, Jesus' commission states that repentance for the forgiveness of sins should be proclaimed *to all nations* (Lk 24:47). In Acts 1:8, Luke picks up on this movement of God from Jerusalem to the ends of the earth, corroborated by the conversion of Gentiles, beginning with Cornelius and others in Acts 10. Erasing any doubt about the global reach of the gospel, Jesus commanded his disciples to make disciples *of every nation* (Mt 28:16 – 20).

In the context of calling believers to welcome one another as Christ welcomed them, Paul quoted from Psalm 117, making clear that the Gentiles were to glorify God for his mercy (Ro 15:11). God's plan has always been that all the nations praise him. The book of Revelation confirms that he will certainly bring this to pass (Rev 7:9 – 10). This is a global God, deserving and desiring global praise.

HIS LOVE ENDURES FOREVER

God is love (1Jn 4:16). Some might avoid this seeming sentimentality because believers often exalt this attribute of God while at the same time minimizing his holiness, sovereignty or justice. Additionally, people can misuse the phrase *God is love* and impose a culturally shaped human-centered definition of love, thereby redefining the very character of God. However, it must be said that if the other attributes of God are true, that is, if this God is inflexibly just and infallibly righteous, humanity's only hope is that he also is love.

The psalmists make sure to repeat the truth of God's love throughout the book, and this psalm is especially focused on repetition. Israel, the house of Aaron, and all who feared the Lord were to join in the chorus: "His love endures forever" (Ps 118:2 – 4). In the Old Testament context, this psalm would have been sung as a deliverance song after victory in battle. The phrase "His love endures forever" finds constant refrain throughout Scripture as the people's way of expressing their gratitude and hope.

Each Gospel actually uses this psalm during the triumphal entry. Jesus' "passion week" began with this kind of fanfare. Though he would be crucified soon, the crowds took palm branches (Jn 12:13) and shouted praises as he rode by on a donkey, quoting from Psalm 118: "LORD, save us!... Blessed is he who comes in the name of the LORD" (vv. 25 – 26). However, the expression they used for "save us" was actually "Hosanna." Hosanna is both a call to save and an expression of praise. With this word, the people praised the one who came to save them.

Little did this crowd know the appropriateness of their chosen psalm. Though Jesus rode on a donkey, they were indeed welcoming a King. And nowhere would the enduring love of God be more apparent than in the days to come. God is love. The apostle John would explain: "This is how God showed his love among us: He sent his one and only Son into the world that we might live through him" (1Jn 4:9).

[7] The LORD is with me; he is my helper.
I look in triumph on my enemies.

[8] It is better to take refuge in the LORD
than to trust in humans.
[9] It is better to take refuge in the LORD
than to trust in princes.
[10] All the nations surrounded me,
but in the name of the LORD I cut them down.
[11] They surrounded me on every side,
but in the name of the LORD I cut them down.
[12] They swarmed around me like bees,
but they were consumed as quickly as burning thorns;
in the name of the LORD I cut them down.
[13] I was pushed back and about to fall,
but the LORD helped me.
[14] The LORD is my strength and my defense[a];
he has become my salvation.

[15] Shouts of joy and victory
resound in the tents of the righteous:
"The LORD's right hand has done mighty things!
[16] The LORD's right hand is lifted high;
the LORD's right hand has done mighty things!"
[17] I will not die but live,
and will proclaim what the LORD has done.
[18] The LORD has chastened me severely,
but he has not given me over to death.
[19] Open for me the gates of the righteous;
I will enter and give thanks to the LORD.
[20] This is the gate of the LORD
through which the righteous may enter.
[21] I will give you thanks, for you answered me;
you have become my salvation.

[22] The stone the builders rejected
has become the cornerstone;
[23] the LORD has done this,
and it is marvelous in our eyes.
[24] The LORD has done it this very day;
let us rejoice today and be glad.

[25] LORD, save us!
LORD, grant us success!

[26] Blessed is he who comes in the name of the LORD.
From the house of the LORD we bless you.[b]
[27] The LORD is God,
and he has made his light shine on us.
With boughs in hand, join in the festal procession
up[c] to the horns of the altar.

[28] You are my God, and I will praise you;
you are my God, and I will exalt you.

[29] Give thanks to the LORD, for he is good;
his love endures forever.

[a] *14* Or *song* [b] *26* The Hebrew is plural. [c] *27* Or *Bind the festal sacrifice with ropes / and take it*

PSALM 118:22–23

CORNERSTONE

The writers of Scripture often used building imagery to make their point. This included references to the large stone set at the corner of the building's foundation — integral to the rest of construction — which they called the cornerstone. This psalm, quoted often in the New Testament, makes clear that during one of humanity's building projects, "the stone the builders rejected has become the cornerstone" (v. 22).

Here the psalmist celebrates the victory of a reigning king who had once been looked upon with disdain by the rival kingdoms. The builders of worldly empires once viewed him as a failure by kings who invaded his kingdom, yet, in time, it was shown that this king was in fact to be celebrated in his victory. God will also use his people, the nation of Israel, to establish his new world order on this earth — though they may appear weak, frail and defeated.

Peter calls believers in the New Testament living stones, being built together into a spiritual house. Then he quotes from the prophet Isaiah: "See, I lay a stone in Zion, a chosen and precious cornerstone, and the one who trusts in him will never be put to shame" (1Pe 2:6). His point was this: just like the pagan nations who rejected David to their eventual demise, a tragic end awaits those who trip over the cornerstone God laid, Jesus Christ. In God's sight, this stone is precious (1Pe 2:4). Those who trust Jesus by faith will be built into a victorious people — even though it may not always appear so in this life.

PSALM 119:1–176

THE WORD

The structure of Psalm 119, the longest psalm (and the longest chapter) in Scripture, is fascinating. The 22 stanzas follow in order the 22 letters of the Hebrew alphabet. Within each eight-verse stanza, the first letter of each line corresponds to the same Hebrew letter. So, in English, this would be eight verses beginning with "A" followed by eight verses beginning with "B," eight verses beginning with "C," and so on.

But the focus of this psalm is not Hebrew letters. The focus of Psalm 119 is the Word. As the most extended treatment of this topic in Scripture, Psalm 119 uses various terms (precepts, law, decrees, statutes, commands) to speak about the Word of God. God's Word is eternal (v. 89). His commands are wise (v. 98). Those who walk in God's commands, God considers blessed (vv. 1–2). If one wants to be pure, the Word of God needs to be his or her guide (v. 9).

The psalm is arranged in an acrostic fashion to help facilitate memorization, likely among children. Memorization of the Word leads to meditation upon the Word, producing the strength the psalmist described: "Cause me to understand the way of your precepts, that I may meditate on your wonderful deeds ... strengthen me according to your word" (vv. 27–28). As the Word made flesh, Jesus would exemplify God's ways and guide God's people.

Psalm 119[a]

א Aleph

1 Blessed are those whose ways are blameless,
who walk according to the law of the LORD.
2 Blessed are those who keep his statutes
and seek him with all their heart—
3 they do no wrong
but follow his ways.
4 You have laid down precepts
that are to be fully obeyed.
5 Oh, that my ways were steadfast
in obeying your decrees!
6 Then I would not be put to shame
when I consider all your commands.
7 I will praise you with an upright heart
as I learn your righteous laws.
8 I will obey your decrees;
do not utterly forsake me.

ב Beth

9 How can a young person stay on the path of purity?
By living according to your word.
10 I seek you with all my heart;
do not let me stray from your commands.
11 I have hidden your word in my heart
that I might not sin against you.
12 Praise be to you, LORD;
teach me your decrees.
13 With my lips I recount
all the laws that come from your mouth.
14 I rejoice in following your statutes
as one rejoices in great riches.
15 I meditate on your precepts
and consider your ways.
16 I delight in your decrees;
I will not neglect your word.

ג Gimel

17 Be good to your servant while I live,
that I may obey your word.
18 Open my eyes that I may see
wonderful things in your law.
19 I am a stranger on earth;
do not hide your commands from me.
20 My soul is consumed with longing
for your laws at all times.
21 You rebuke the arrogant, who are accursed,
those who stray from your commands.
22 Remove from me their scorn and contempt,
for I keep your statutes.
23 Though rulers sit together and slander me,
your servant will meditate on your decrees.

[a] This psalm is an acrostic poem, the stanzas of which begin with successive letters of the Hebrew alphabet; moreover, the verses of each stanza begin with the same letter of the Hebrew alphabet.

24 Your statutes are my delight;
they are my counselors.

ד Daleth

25 I am laid low in the dust;
preserve my life according to your word.
26 I gave an account of my ways and you answered me;
teach me your decrees.
27 Cause me to understand the way of your precepts,
that I may meditate on your wonderful deeds.
28 My soul is weary with sorrow;
strengthen me according to your word.
29 Keep me from deceitful ways;
be gracious to me and teach me your law.
30 I have chosen the way of faithfulness;
I have set my heart on your laws.
31 I hold fast to your statutes, LORD;
do not let me be put to shame.
32 I run in the path of your commands,
for you have broadened my understanding.

ה He

33 Teach me, LORD, the way of your decrees,
that I may follow it to the end.[a]
34 Give me understanding, so that I may keep your law
and obey it with all my heart.
35 Direct me in the path of your commands,
for there I find delight.
36 Turn my heart toward your statutes
and not toward selfish gain.
37 Turn my eyes away from worthless things;
preserve my life according to your word.[b]
38 Fulfill your promise to your servant,
so that you may be feared.
39 Take away the disgrace I dread,
for your laws are good.
40 How I long for your precepts!
In your righteousness preserve my life.

ו Waw

41 May your unfailing love come to me, LORD,
your salvation, according to your promise;
42 then I can answer anyone who taunts me,
for I trust in your word.
43 Never take your word of truth from my mouth,
for I have put my hope in your laws.
44 I will always obey your law,
for ever and ever.
45 I will walk about in freedom,
for I have sought out your precepts.
46 I will speak of your statutes before kings
and will not be put to shame,
47 for I delight in your commands
because I love them.

---

[a] 33 Or *follow it for its reward* [b] 37 Two manuscripts of the Masoretic Text and Dead Sea Scrolls; most manuscripts of the Masoretic Text *life in your way*

48 I reach out for your commands, which I love,
that I may meditate on your decrees.

ז Zayin

49 Remember your word to your servant,
for you have given me hope.
50 My comfort in my suffering is this:
Your promise preserves my life.
51 The arrogant mock me unmercifully,
but I do not turn from your law.
52 I remember, LORD, your ancient laws,
and I find comfort in them.
53 Indignation grips me because of the wicked,
who have forsaken your law.
54 Your decrees are the theme of my song
wherever I lodge.
55 In the night, LORD, I remember your name,
that I may keep your law.
56 This has been my practice:
I obey your precepts.

ח Heth

57 You are my portion, LORD;
I have promised to obey your words.
58 I have sought your face with all my heart;
be gracious to me according to your promise.
59 I have considered my ways
and have turned my steps to your statutes.
60 I will hasten and not delay
to obey your commands.
61 Though the wicked bind me with ropes,
I will not forget your law.
62 At midnight I rise to give you thanks
for your righteous laws.
63 I am a friend to all who fear you,
to all who follow your precepts.
64 The earth is filled with your love, LORD;
teach me your decrees.

ט Teth

65 Do good to your servant
according to your word, LORD.
66 Teach me knowledge and good judgment,
for I trust your commands.
67 Before I was afflicted I went astray,
but now I obey your word.
68 You are good, and what you do is good;
teach me your decrees.
69 Though the arrogant have smeared me with lies,
I keep your precepts with all my heart.
70 Their hearts are callous and unfeeling,
but I delight in your law.
71 It was good for me to be afflicted
so that I might learn your decrees.
72 The law from your mouth is more precious to me
than thousands of pieces of silver and gold.

י Yodh

73 Your hands made me and formed me;
give me understanding to learn your commands.
74 May those who fear you rejoice when they see me,
for I have put my hope in your word.
75 I know, LORD, that your laws are righteous,
and that in faithfulness you have afflicted me.
76 May your unfailing love be my comfort,
according to your promise to your servant.
77 Let your compassion come to me that I may live,
for your law is my delight.
78 May the arrogant be put to shame for wronging me without cause;
but I will meditate on your precepts.
79 May those who fear you turn to me,
those who understand your statutes.
80 May I wholeheartedly follow your decrees,
that I may not be put to shame.

כ Kaph

81 My soul faints with longing for your salvation,
but I have put my hope in your word.
82 My eyes fail, looking for your promise;
I say, "When will you comfort me?"
83 Though I am like a wineskin in the smoke,
I do not forget your decrees.
84 How long must your servant wait?
When will you punish my persecutors?
85 The arrogant dig pits to trap me,
contrary to your law.
86 All your commands are trustworthy;
help me, for I am being persecuted without cause.
87 They almost wiped me from the earth,
but I have not forsaken your precepts.
88 In your unfailing love preserve my life,
that I may obey the statutes of your mouth.

ל Lamedh

89 Your word, LORD, is eternal;
it stands firm in the heavens.
90 Your faithfulness continues through all generations;
you established the earth, and it endures.
91 Your laws endure to this day,
for all things serve you.
92 If your law had not been my delight,
I would have perished in my affliction.
93 I will never forget your precepts,
for by them you have preserved my life.
94 Save me, for I am yours;
I have sought out your precepts.
95 The wicked are waiting to destroy me,
but I will ponder your statutes.
96 To all perfection I see a limit,
but your commands are boundless.

מ Mem

97 Oh, how I love your law!
I meditate on it all day long.

98 Your commands are always with me
and make me wiser than my enemies.
99 I have more insight than all my teachers,
for I meditate on your statutes.
100 I have more understanding than the elders,
for I obey your precepts.
101 I have kept my feet from every evil path
so that I might obey your word.
102 I have not departed from your laws,
for you yourself have taught me.
103 How sweet are your words to my taste,
sweeter than honey to my mouth!
104 I gain understanding from your precepts;
therefore I hate every wrong path.

נ Nun

105 Your word is a lamp for my feet,
a light on my path.
106 I have taken an oath and confirmed it,
that I will follow your righteous laws.
107 I have suffered much;
preserve my life, LORD, according to your word.
108 Accept, LORD, the willing praise of my mouth,
and teach me your laws.
109 Though I constantly take my life in my hands,
I will not forget your law.
110 The wicked have set a snare for me,
but I have not strayed from your precepts.
111 Your statutes are my heritage forever;
they are the joy of my heart.
112 My heart is set on keeping your decrees
to the very end.[a]

ס Samekh

113 I hate double-minded people,
but I love your law.
114 You are my refuge and my shield;
I have put my hope in your word.
115 Away from me, you evildoers,
that I may keep the commands of my God!
116 Sustain me, my God, according to your promise,
and I will live;
do not let my hopes be dashed.
117 Uphold me, and I will be delivered;
I will always have regard for your decrees.
118 You reject all who stray from your decrees,
for their delusions come to nothing.
119 All the wicked of the earth you discard like dross;
therefore I love your statutes.
120 My flesh trembles in fear of you;
I stand in awe of your laws.

ע Ayin

121 I have done what is righteous and just;
do not leave me to my oppressors.

---

[a] *112* Or *decrees / for their enduring reward*

[122] Ensure your servant's well-being;
do not let the arrogant oppress me.
[123] My eyes fail, looking for your salvation,
looking for your righteous promise.
[124] Deal with your servant according to your love
and teach me your decrees.
[125] I am your servant; give me discernment
that I may understand your statutes.
[126] It is time for you to act, LORD;
your law is being broken.
[127] Because I love your commands
more than gold, more than pure gold,
[128] and because I consider all your precepts right,
I hate every wrong path.

פ Pe

[129] Your statutes are wonderful;
therefore I obey them.
[130] The unfolding of your words gives light;
it gives understanding to the simple.
[131] I open my mouth and pant,
longing for your commands.
[132] Turn to me and have mercy on me,
as you always do to those who love your name.
[133] Direct my footsteps according to your word;
let no sin rule over me.
[134] Redeem me from human oppression,
that I may obey your precepts.
[135] Make your face shine on your servant
and teach me your decrees.
[136] Streams of tears flow from my eyes,
for your law is not obeyed.

צ Tsadhe

[137] You are righteous, LORD,
and your laws are right.
[138] The statutes you have laid down are righteous;
they are fully trustworthy.
[139] My zeal wears me out,
for my enemies ignore your words.
[140] Your promises have been thoroughly tested,
and your servant loves them.
[141] Though I am lowly and despised,
I do not forget your precepts.
[142] Your righteousness is everlasting
and your law is true.
[143] Trouble and distress have come upon me,
but your commands give me delight.
[144] Your statutes are always righteous;
give me understanding that I may live.

ק Qoph

[145] I call with all my heart; answer me, LORD,
and I will obey your decrees.
[146] I call out to you; save me
and I will keep your statutes.

147 I rise before dawn and cry for help;
I have put my hope in your word.
148 My eyes stay open through the watches of the night,
that I may meditate on your promises.
149 Hear my voice in accordance with your love;
preserve my life, LORD, according to your laws.
150 Those who devise wicked schemes are near,
but they are far from your law.
151 Yet you are near, LORD,
and all your commands are true.
152 Long ago I learned from your statutes
that you established them to last forever.

ר Resh

153 Look on my suffering and deliver me,
for I have not forgotten your law.
154 Defend my cause and redeem me;
preserve my life according to your promise.
155 Salvation is far from the wicked,
for they do not seek out your decrees.
156 Your compassion, LORD, is great;
preserve my life according to your laws.
157 Many are the foes who persecute me,
but I have not turned from your statutes.
158 I look on the faithless with loathing,
for they do not obey your word.
159 See how I love your precepts;
preserve my life, LORD, in accordance with
your love.
160 All your words are true;
all your righteous laws are eternal.

ש Sin and Shin

161 Rulers persecute me without cause,
but my heart trembles at your word.
162 I rejoice in your promise
like one who finds great spoil.
163 I hate and detest falsehood
but I love your law.
164 Seven times a day I praise you
for your righteous laws.
165 Great peace have those who love your law,
and nothing can make them stumble.
166 I wait for your salvation, LORD,
and I follow your commands.
167 I obey your statutes,
for I love them greatly.
168 I obey your precepts and your statutes,
for all my ways are known to you.

ת Taw

169 May my cry come before you, LORD;
give me understanding according to your
word.
170 May my supplication come before you;
deliver me according to your promise.

[171] May my lips overflow with praise,
for you teach me your decrees.
[172] May my tongue sing of your word,
for all your commands are righteous.
[173] May your hand be ready to help me,
for I have chosen your precepts.
[174] I long for your salvation, LORD,
and your law gives me delight.
[175] Let me live that I may praise you,
and may your laws sustain me.
[176] I have strayed like a lost sheep.
Seek your servant,
for I have not forgotten your commands.

Psalm 120

A song of ascents.

[1] I call on the LORD in my distress,
and he answers me.
[2] Save me, LORD,
from lying lips
and from deceitful tongues.
[3] What will he do to you,
and what more besides,
you deceitful tongue?
[4] He will punish you with a warrior's sharp arrows,
with burning coals of the broom bush.
[5] Woe to me that I dwell in Meshek,
that I live among the tents of Kedar!
[6] Too long have I lived
among those who hate peace.
[7] I am for peace;
but when I speak, they are for war.

Psalm 121

A song of ascents.

[1] I lift up my eyes to the mountains —
where does my help come from?
[2] My help comes from the LORD,
the Maker of heaven and earth.

[3] He will not let your foot slip —
he who watches over you will not slumber;
[4] indeed, he who watches over Israel
will neither slumber nor sleep.
[5] The LORD watches over you —
the LORD is your shade at your right hand;
[6] the sun will not harm you by day,
nor the moon by night.

[7] The LORD will keep you from all harm —
he will watch over your life;
[8] the LORD will watch over your coming and going
both now and forevermore.

HELP

While looking at the mountains, the psalmist asked a question. Because the psalmist immediately answered his own question, the reader knows this question was rhetorical. There was no doubt in the psalmist's mind: the one who made the mountains is also the one who helps.

The psalmist placed his confidence in the Creator God. The "songs of ascents" (beginning at Ps 120) were likely sung as Israelite pilgrims traveled toward Jerusalem. It seems that this psalm narrates the experience of the journey itself, as the pilgrims looked toward the mountains that surrounded their destination. Rather than wasting this moment, the psalmist chose to use the sight as an object lesson. The mountains were impressive. So was their Creator. And, most significant for the people making their way to Jerusalem, that Creator was the traveling pilgrim's helper.

The rest of the psalm speaks of the specifics of God's help. As the people journeyed, the Maker of heaven and earth would keep their feet from slipping. To a crowd likely traveling in rough terrain, this would be a comfort. Furthermore, to a crowd sleeping seemingly in dangerous conditions, the psalmist said, "Indeed, he who watches over Israel will neither slumber nor sleep" (v. 4). As they rested, maybe restlessly, God watched over them. The word "watch" indicates that he guarded and protected them. Filling these pilgrims with peace was this truth: the Maker of heaven and earth was their guardian.

The psalm ends with an overview of the aspects of life the Lord watches over. "Your coming and going" points to everything in the pilgrim's life, even hinting at the beginning and ending of one's days (v. 8). Nothing is outside the purview of God's watch and keep. The duration of this promise makes this apparent: The Lord watches over his people now and forevermore.

When the psalmist wrote that they would be kept from all harm, he did not contradict those passages that refer to the persecution that follows those who follow the Lord (Jn 15:20). Instead, the Lord protects his people in the midst of difficulty. Jesus prayed along these lines in his high priestly prayer: "Holy Father, protect them by the power of your name" (Jn 17:11). Followers of Christ will not be kept from difficulty, but they will be kept.

Psalm 122

A song of ascents. Of David.

[1]I rejoiced with those who said to me,
"Let us go to the house of the LORD."
[2]Our feet are standing
in your gates, Jerusalem.

[3]Jerusalem is built like a city
that is closely compacted together.
[4]That is where the tribes go up —
the tribes of the LORD —
to praise the name of the LORD
according to the statute given to Israel.
[5]There stand the thrones for judgment,
the thrones of the house of David.

[6]Pray for the peace of Jerusalem:
"May those who love you be secure.
[7]May there be peace within your walls
and security within your citadels."
[8]For the sake of my family and friends,
I will say, "Peace be within you."
[9]For the sake of the house of the LORD our God,
I will seek your prosperity.

Psalm 123

A song of ascents.

[1]I lift up my eyes to you,
to you who sit enthroned in heaven.
[2]As the eyes of slaves look to the hand of their master,
as the eyes of a female slave look to the hand of her
mistress,
so our eyes look to the LORD our God,
till he shows us his mercy.

[3]Have mercy on us, LORD, have mercy on us,
for we have endured no end of contempt.
[4]We have endured no end
of ridicule from the arrogant,
of contempt from the proud.

Psalm 124

A song of ascents. Of David.

[1]If the LORD had not been on our side —
let Israel say —
[2]if the LORD had not been on our side
when people attacked us,
[3]they would have swallowed us alive
when their anger flared against us;
[4]the flood would have engulfed us,
the torrent would have swept over us,
[5]the raging waters
would have swept us away.

[6]Praise be to the LORD,
who has not let us be torn by their teeth.

PSALM 122:1 – 9

PRAYING FOR PEACE

The Israelites sang this "song of ascents" as they journeyed toward Jerusalem. This long, difficult pilgrimage was not simply a matter of duty. After a few details about the city, the psalm points out the reason for this trip: the Israelites went to Jerusalem for the purpose of praise (v. 4). At the very mention of worshiping the Lord in the Lord's city — at the Lord's house — the psalmist rejoiced (v. 1).

However, if Jerusalem were to become dangerous — or if war were to break out — it would make it more difficult for families to venture out. So, the psalmist prayed for peace. The peace he desired certainly brought him benefit, but the psalmist prayed for his fellow pilgrims as well (v. 8). For the sake of the temple of God, he asked for strife to cease (v. 9). War would hinder worship; peace would facilitate praise. Ultimately this peace was only possible through the finished work of Jesus Christ, who came to bring peace between fallen humans and God and peace between his created people (Ro 5:1).

PSALM 123:1 – 4

PLEADING FOR MERCY

The people of God sang songs and prayers in the hopes that God would vindicate them and foil the contempt of the proud. These songs bolstered their hope through years of oppression and pain — when it looked as if God had forgotten them and the

(continued on next page)

(Pleading for Mercy, continued)

arrogant were winning. Later, these songs would become the anthems sung by the people as they journeyed to Jerusalem.

The psalmist pled for mercy, but not for him alone (v. 3). He sang for his fellow people. While the proud and those at ease heaped insults, he asked that God might show favor to his people.

The psalmist pled patiently. Rather than attempting to strong-arm the hand of God, the people of God submit. A picture gives readers insight into how they should plead with the Lord. Slaves live under the authority of their master, watching the hand of the master until an order comes. So how long will these people continue to look and ask for mercy? The end of verse 2 says, "till he shows us his mercy."

In this same city, years later, the people of Jerusalem were hostile to God and his appointed One. The very radiance of God walked among them, endured the scorn of those at ease and received the contempt of the proud. In the end, they nailed him to a cross. In stark irony, however, this great act of violence proved the beauty of the mercy of God.

PSALM 124:1–8

IF GOD IS FOR HIS PEOPLE

The Old Testament narrative gives example after example of the Lord's protection of his people. Though the details of each story differ and feature a variety of people used by God—Moses, Joshua, David and others—the main character remains

(continued on page 930)

7 We have escaped like a bird
from the fowler's snare;
the snare has been broken,
and we have escaped.
8 Our help is in the name of the LORD,
the Maker of heaven and earth.

Psalm 125

A song of ascents.

1 Those who trust in the LORD are like Mount Zion,
which cannot be shaken but endures forever.
2 As the mountains surround Jerusalem,
so the LORD surrounds his people
both now and forevermore.

3 The scepter of the wicked will not remain
over the land allotted to the righteous,
for then the righteous might use
their hands to do evil.

4 LORD, do good to those who are good,
to those who are upright in heart.
5 But those who turn to crooked ways
the LORD will banish with the evildoers.

Peace be on Israel.

Psalm 126

A song of ascents.

1 When the LORD restored the fortunes of[a] Zion,
we were like those who dreamed.[b]
2 Our mouths were filled with laughter,
our tongues with songs of joy.
Then it was said among the nations,
"The LORD has done great things for them."
3 The LORD has done great things for us,
and we are filled with joy.

4 Restore our fortunes,[c] LORD,
like streams in the Negev.
5 Those who sow with tears
will reap with songs of joy.
6 Those who go out weeping,
carrying seed to sow,
will return with songs of joy,
carrying sheaves with them.

Psalm 127

A song of ascents. Of Solomon.

1 Unless the LORD builds the house,
the builders labor in vain.
Unless the LORD watches over the city,
the guards stand watch in vain.

[a] *1* Or *LORD brought back the captives to our captives* [b] *1* Or *those restored to health* [c] *4* Or *Bring back*

PSALM 126:1 – 6

PAST, PRESENT AND FUTURE GRACE

The first half of this psalm (vv. 1 – 3) looks back at an event in Israel's past when the Lord displayed his greatness, restoring the fortunes of the people of God. The writer indicated that the people of God were not calloused and dull to the fortunes of God's grace. They responded appropriately, with laughter and songs of joy. In fact, the Lord's greatness on their behalf increased their gladness (v. 3). Furthermore, this was a publicized joy. Even the pagan nations observed, looking on as bystanders and marveling at the Lord's goodness (v. 2).

The second half of this song (vv. 4 – 6) finds the people of God further from fortune. What the psalmist remembered the Lord doing, he prayed for, appealing to God's grace in the past for grace in the present. For the arid Negev, he prayed for flourishing streams. For those sowing with tears, he prayed for restoration. It seems that the Israelites' grief was so unending that it accompanied them in the mundane acts of their day, even the sowing of seeds (v. 6). As they cast seed, they shed their tears.

For God's people, present difficulties need not dissuade them from trusting in future grace. The psalmist wrote, "Those who sow with tears will reap with songs of joy" (v. 5). God's grace remains inevitable, though full restoration might be paused. In the end, suffering will not triumph. Paul considered present sufferings unworthy to be compared to future glory (Ro 8:18). Elsewhere he wrote that "light and momentary troubles" achieve for God's people a surpassing future glory (2Co 4:17).

However, God's certain deliverance does not negate the reality of present suffering. Jesus, with more certainty than anyone, knew Lazarus would rise. Yet, he wept (Jn 11:35). Additionally, the inevitability of God's future grace does not negate the obligation of God's people to pray. Jesus prayed to the Father upon Lazarus's death (Jn 11:41). God's goodness in the past (remembered by the people of God) and promises for the future (trusted by the people of God) compel prayer in the present.

(If God Is for His People, continued)

the same: God himself. Apart from the Lord's intervention, the people of God would have long ago been swept away by the flood's raging waters (v. 5).

Though it seems obvious, the psalmist endeavored to point out the side the Lord chose in the ongoing conflict between God's people and their enemies. This psalm looks back—reviewing the battles—to clarify beyond any doubt that the people of God overcame only by the power of the Lord.

The apostle Paul made this same point in his letter to the Romans, though he did not only look at past deliverances. Believers root their assurance in the work of Christ. In Christ, condemnation no longer has any teeth (Ro 8:1). God will conform those he calls to the image of his Son (Ro 8:29). Furthermore, those whom he justified freely, he will most certainly glorify in the future (Ro 8:30). Paul looked *back* to the work of Christ while also looking *forward* to a future hope. In light of these truths he wrote, "If God is for us, who can be against us?" (Ro 8:31). Though people have tried, no one has yet come up with a worthy opponent.

PSALM 125:2

SURROUNDED

The issue for the believer is not the intensity of their faith, but the object of it. The enemies of God sought to conquer the city of Jerusalem. To overrun Jerusalem, however, would mean traversing the mountains that surrounded it. So the mountains protected the city, making it more difficult to attack.

(continued on next page)

[2] In vain you rise early
and stay up late,
toiling for food to eat—
for he grants sleep to[a] those he loves.

[3] Children are a heritage from the LORD,
offspring a reward from him.
[4] Like arrows in the hands of a warrior
are children born in one's youth.
[5] Blessed is the man
whose quiver is full of them.
They will not be put to shame
when they contend with their opponents in court.

Psalm 128

A song of ascents.

[1] Blessed are all who fear the LORD,
who walk in obedience to him.
[2] You will eat the fruit of your labor;
blessings and prosperity will be yours.
[3] Your wife will be like a fruitful vine
within your house;
your children will be like olive shoots
around your table.
[4] Yes, this will be the blessing
for the man who fears the LORD.
[5] May the LORD bless you from Zion;
may you see the prosperity of Jerusalem
all the days of your life.
[6] May you live to see your children's children—
peace be on Israel.

Psalm 129

A song of ascents.

[1] "They have greatly oppressed me from my youth,"
let Israel say;
[2] "they have greatly oppressed me from my youth,
but they have not gained the victory over me.
[3] Plowmen have plowed my back
and made their furrows long.
[4] But the LORD is righteous;
he has cut me free from the cords of the wicked."

[5] May all who hate Zion
be turned back in shame.
[6] May they be like grass on the roof,
which withers before it can grow;
[7] a reaper cannot fill his hands with it,
nor one who gathers fill his arms.
[8] May those who pass by not say to them,
"The blessing of the LORD be on you;
we bless you in the name of the LORD."

[a] 2 Or *eat— / for while they sleep he provides for*

Psalm 130

A song of ascents.

[1]Out of the depths I cry to you, LORD;
[2] Lord, hear my voice.
Let your ears be attentive
to my cry for mercy.

[3]If you, LORD, kept a record of sins,
Lord, who could stand?
[4]But with you there is forgiveness,
so that we can, with reverence, serve you.

[5]I wait for the LORD, my whole being waits,
and in his word I put my hope.
[6]I wait for the Lord
more than watchmen wait for the morning,
more than watchmen wait for the morning.

[7]Israel, put your hope in the LORD,
for with the LORD is unfailing love
and with him is full redemption.
[8]He himself will redeem Israel
from all their sins.

Psalm 131

A song of ascents. Of David.

[1]My heart is not proud, LORD,
my eyes are not haughty;
I do not concern myself with great matters
or things too wonderful for me.
[2]But I have calmed and quieted myself,
I am like a weaned child with its mother;
like a weaned child I am content.

[3]Israel, put your hope in the LORD
both now and forevermore.

Psalm 132

A song of ascents.

[1]LORD, remember David
and all his self-denial.

[2]He swore an oath to the LORD,
he made a vow to the Mighty One of Jacob:
[3]"I will not enter my house
or go to my bed,
[4]I will allow no sleep to my eyes
or slumber to my eyelids,
[5]till I find a place for the LORD,
a dwelling for the Mighty One of Jacob."

[6]We heard it in Ephrathah,
we came upon it in the fields of Jaar:[a]
[7]"Let us go to his dwelling place,
let us worship at his footstool, saying,

[a] 6 Or *heard of it in Ephrathah, / we found it in the fields of Jearim.* (See 1 Chron. 13:5,6) (And no quotation marks around verses 7-9)

(Surrounded, continued)

When these songs were sung by traveling pilgrims after their ascent, the people would see the mountains which surrounded them every day. The psalmist takes that reality and points them to the Lord's protection. As the mountains surround Jerusalem, so the Lord surrounds his people. The Lord, in much more significant but unseen ways, protects his people from attack.

Peter described the Lord's protection via salvation by stating that God's people are "through faith ... shielded by God's power" (1Pe 1:5). The word "shield" indicates protection — probably from sin, suffering or Satan. Peter makes the point, however, that God also protects the inheritance awaiting the people of God. God purchased it by the death of his Son; he guards it by his power, as surely as the mountains surround Jerusalem.

PSALM 127:1 – 5

DEPENDING ON GOD

Many accomplished people have come face to face with their weaknesses and sin while raising children. Though a parent might be able to control countless dynamics at work, at the gym, in school or elsewhere, a screaming newborn is a different matter. This psalm, which includes some of the most cherished verses on children in Scripture, points the reader to dependence upon the Lord.

Using a series of metaphors, the psalmist (identified as Solomon in the superscription) asserted that the builders of a house profit nothing if they do not recognize who the builder is; the guards might as well

(continued on page 934)

THE MISSING RECORD OF OUR SIN

If God kept a record of every human's past sins, then no one would be able to stand before him when their turn came to give an account for their life. But Psalm 130:3 explains that the Lord does not keep a record of all the times each believer sins. He will not have everyone come before him so that he can scold them for every single sin they committed since they were born. Hebrews 10:17 says, "Their sins and lawless acts I will remember no more."

God is not looking to discover the faults of man, but instead he is gracious. His memory is short when it comes to humanity's wrongdoing. God's grace is evident. He does not keep score in the midst of mankind's propensity toward waywardness.

This forgiveness, grace and mercy that God is so eager to give his followers comes through the sinless life, death and resurrection of Jesus. He is the only way in which humans can receive God's forgiveness (Mt 26:28; Eph 1:7; 1Jn 1:9; 2:12). First John 4:10 explains that Jesus is the "atoning sacrifice" for all sins, which means he is the sacrifice that can repair every person's relationship with God, bringing about perfect reconciliation between God and sinners. God no longer has to keep track of everyone's sins because he placed all sin on Jesus when he was on the cross (2Co 5:21). With the sacrifice of Jesus, God provided a remedy for the guilt and shame of all humankind, offering them a clean slate. With the resurrection of Jesus, sin and death have been defeated, and God is now solely focused on bringing everyone to himself through the forgiveness, grace and mercy that can be found through belief in Jesus and what he did on the cross (Jn 3:16).

JESUS GIVES REST FOR OUR SOUL

Psalm 131 is one of the shortest psalms in the Bible. It provides a simple and easy-to-understand message, which is that God provides rest for the soul that follows him. In the first verse, the psalmist showed that he was aware that there are heavenly things that are outside his knowledge and unattainable for his own understanding. Instead of choosing to try to understand everything that God was doing, he decided not to occupy himself with "great matters or things too wonderful for me." Instead, the psalmist compared himself to a weaned child that is at ultimate peace with its mother. Young children are not worried about getting a job, making money, providing for a family or any other stresses that may come with being a parent. A child trusts that its mother is going to care for him or her. The psalmist was saying that his relationship with God was similar. There may be a lot of events going on in the world that God is involved in, but all the psalmist concerned himself with was his personal relationship with God.

A right relationship with God is intended to be a high priority for the believer. Once someone is able to grasp an understanding of that concept, the natural result is a calm and quiet soul. The psalmist understood that if everything was fine between him and God, he did not need to concern himself with whatever was going on outside of that.

Believers can be confident in knowing that a healthy relationship with Jesus produces peace that "transcends all understanding" (Php 4:7). Practicing the disciplines of the spiritual life will ultimately bring an unshakable confidence. When one regularly prays and meditates on Scripture, they build a foundation for their life that will stand strong when the torrents hit. A believer will be at peace knowing that their life is anchored in an unmovable Savior, Jesus Christ.

(Depending on God, continued)

drop their swords if they think they ultimately protect. In the same way, believers toil in vain if they fail to depend upon their God (vv. 1–2).

Jesus said something similar to the disciples. Without equivocation, he stated: "Apart from me, you can do nothing" (Jn 15:5). As branches separated from the vine cannot bear fruit, so humans separated from Christ invariably discover that even their best efforts yield zero results. But if the Lord builds something, nothing can tear it down. Furthermore, if the Lord protects something, nothing can harm it.

PSALM 128:1–6

THE BLESSED LIFE

Psalm 128 focuses on the man who receives blessings. Humanity generally thinks of "blessing" in terms of material abundance or a certain degree of health. If one is healthy or enjoys some measure of familial/financial prosperity, he or she is blessed.

In the introduction of his Sermon on the Mount, Jesus used blessing language to describe citizens of his kingdom. Each beatitude begins with this phrase: "Blessed are ..." (Mt 5:3–11). In a counterintuitive reversal, Jesus taught that those who are poor in spirit, meek and persecuted all fit this description. Jesus used the term "blessed" to describe not material abundance, mere happiness or some other trite application. Instead, he used it to describe someone approved or favored by God. The circumstances might not smile upon them, but the God of the circumstances did. How can God

(continued on page 936)

8 'Arise, LORD, and come to your resting place,
you and the ark of your might.
9 May your priests be clothed with your
righteousness;
may your faithful people sing for joy.'"
10 For the sake of your servant David,
do not reject your anointed one.

11 The LORD swore an oath to David,
a sure oath he will not revoke:
"One of your own descendants
I will place on your throne.
12 If your sons keep my covenant
and the statutes I teach them,
then their sons will sit
on your throne for ever and ever."

13 For the LORD has chosen Zion,
he has desired it for his dwelling, saying,
14 "This is my resting place for ever and ever;
here I will sit enthroned, for I have desired it.
15 I will bless her with abundant provisions;
her poor I will satisfy with food.
16 I will clothe her priests with salvation,
and her faithful people will ever sing for joy.

17 "Here I will make a horn[a] grow for David
and set up a lamp for my anointed one.
18 I will clothe his enemies with shame,
but his head will be adorned with a radiant
crown."

Psalm 133

A song of ascents. Of David.

1 How good and pleasant it is
when God's people live together in unity!

2 It is like precious oil poured on the head,
running down on the beard,
running down on Aaron's beard,
down on the collar of his robe.
3 It is as if the dew of Hermon
were falling on Mount Zion.
For there the LORD bestows his blessing,
even life forevermore.

Psalm 134

A song of ascents.

1 Praise the LORD, all you servants of the LORD
who minister by night in the house of the LORD.
2 Lift up your hands in the sanctuary
and praise the LORD.

3 May the LORD bless you from Zion,
he who is the Maker of heaven and earth.

[a] *17 Horn* here symbolizes strong one, that is, king.

FULFILLING A ROYAL PSALM

Covenant-grounded worship centers on the promise of the covenant keeper. The psalmist asks God to remember all that David endured in bringing the ark to Jerusalem. Prior to arriving in Jerusalem, the ark had lain in obscurity in Kiriath Jearim for many years.

As the king, David could afford to live at ease. Yet at a significant cost to himself, David desired God to be honored by his people. David made a vow to find a dwelling place for the Mighty One of Jacob (vv. 1 – 5). In 2 Samuel 6, David fulfilled that promise. After a difficult journey that included the sudden death of Uzzah, the ark arrived in Jerusalem. When the ark arrived, great celebration ensued. This psalm asks the Lord to remember this in David's favor.

The psalmist (perhaps Solomon) asked: "For the sake of your servant David, do not reject your anointed one" (Ps 132:10). This is covenantal language. David's promise to God fills the first half of this psalm. The second half of the text reveals God's promise to David.

True to character, God gave much more than even the psalmist asked for. When the Lord makes an oath, he always stands by it. God promised that he would place one of David's descendants on his throne (v. 11). And if David's sons kept God's covenant and statutes, their sons would reign forever and ever (v. 12).

However, a man from the lineage of David is not sitting on a literal throne in literal Israel today. So what of this promise from God? Have any of David's sons kept the covenant without fail?

Yes, one Son of David kept the covenant and is worthy to sit on the throne for all eternity. And right now, at this moment, he rules and reigns. God kept his promise in the person of Jesus. Jesus today sits at the right hand of God the Father, interceding on behalf of his children.

(The Blessed Life, continued)

smile upon, and approve of, a people so broken? Jesus took upon himself a curse — the antithesis of blessing — so that broken people might enjoy the blessing of reconciliation with God (Gal 3:13 – 14).

PSALM 133:1

UNITY

Psalm 133 exclaims the wonderful experience of God's people living and worshiping together as one. If David was the author, he may have written the psalm to commemorate when all Israel joined together at Hebron to make him king (2Sa 5:1 – 3). Jesus shared the psalmist's sentiment and gave an exhortation in John 13:34 when he said, "As I have loved you, so you must love one another." He went on to say that everyone should know who God's people are by the way they love each other, and that believers should be identified by the way they live and treat each other. Paul expanded even further upon the idea of unity among believers in Ephesians 4:3: "Make every effort to keep the unity of the Spirit through the bond of peace." The importance of unity among believers is clearly important since the psalmist, Jesus and Paul all thought it to be something worth writing about. Here in Psalms, the psalmist rejoiced about "how good and pleasant it is," and it is clear that he was currently experiencing unity with God's people. By the time Jesus and Paul taught the importance of unity in the New Testament, it came in the form of a command. If God's people listen to the exhortations of Paul and Jesus and live in love and unity, then they too will be able to experience the joy that the psalmist experienced and wrote about in Psalm 133.

Psalm 135

1 Praise the LORD.[a]

Praise the name of the LORD;
praise him, you servants of the LORD,
2 you who minister in the house of the LORD,
in the courts of the house of our God.

3 Praise the LORD, for the LORD is good;
sing praise to his name, for that is pleasant.
4 For the LORD has chosen Jacob to be his own,
Israel to be his treasured possession.

5 I know that the LORD is great,
that our Lord is greater than all gods.
6 The LORD does whatever pleases him,
in the heavens and on the earth,
in the seas and all their depths.
7 He makes clouds rise from the ends of the earth;
he sends lightning with the rain
and brings out the wind from his storehouses.

8 He struck down the firstborn of Egypt,
the firstborn of people and animals.
9 He sent his signs and wonders into your midst,
Egypt,
against Pharaoh and all his servants.
10 He struck down many nations
and killed mighty kings —
11 Sihon king of the Amorites,
Og king of Bashan,
and all the kings of Canaan —
12 and he gave their land as an inheritance,
an inheritance to his people Israel.

13 Your name, LORD, endures forever,
your renown, LORD, through all generations.
14 For the LORD will vindicate his people
and have compassion on his servants.

15 The idols of the nations are silver and gold,
made by human hands.
16 They have mouths, but cannot speak,
eyes, but cannot see.
17 They have ears, but cannot hear,
nor is there breath in their mouths.
18 Those who make them will be like them,
and so will all who trust in them.

19 All you Israelites, praise the LORD;
house of Aaron, praise the LORD;
20 house of Levi, praise the LORD;
you who fear him, praise the LORD.
21 Praise be to the LORD from Zion,
to him who dwells in Jerusalem.

Praise the LORD.

[a] *1* Hebrew *Hallelu Yah*; also in verses 3 and 21

Psalm 136

1 Give thanks to the LORD, for he is good.
His love endures forever.
2 Give thanks to the God of gods.
His love endures forever.
3 Give thanks to the Lord of lords:
His love endures forever.
4 to him who alone does great wonders,
His love endures forever.
5 who by his understanding made the heavens,
His love endures forever.
6 who spread out the earth upon the waters,
His love endures forever.
7 who made the great lights—
His love endures forever.
8 the sun to govern the day,
His love endures forever.
9 the moon and stars to govern the night;
His love endures forever.
10 to him who struck down the firstborn of Egypt
His love endures forever.
11 and brought Israel out from among them
His love endures forever.
12 with a mighty hand and outstretched arm;
His love endures forever.
13 to him who divided the Red Sea[a] asunder
His love endures forever.
14 and brought Israel through the midst of it,
His love endures forever.
15 but swept Pharaoh and his army into the Red Sea;
His love endures forever.
16 to him who led his people through the wilderness;
His love endures forever.
17 to him who struck down great kings,
His love endures forever.
18 and killed mighty kings—
His love endures forever.
19 Sihon king of the Amorites
His love endures forever.
20 and Og king of Bashan—
His love endures forever.
21 and gave their land as an inheritance,
His love endures forever.
22 an inheritance to his servant Israel.
His love endures forever.
23 He remembered us in our low estate
His love endures forever.
24 and freed us from our enemies.
His love endures forever.

[a] *13* Or *the Sea of Reeds*; also in verse 15

PSALM 135:13

YOUR NAME, YOUR FAME

In Psalm 135, the psalmist urged the people of God to praise the Lord because of all the things he had done for them. The psalm lists several historical events that have brought God glory and show how he is worthy of praise. In verse 13, the author changes from focusing on what God has done in the past to deserve praise, and says that the name and renown of the Lord will endure forever and last "through all generations." The glory of God is not limited to past historical experiences, but it is something that will continue to increase as time moves on. In Acts, the words of Psalm 135:13 came true as the name of Jesus grew and spread throughout all the nations. Throughout the beginning of Acts, the church was growing, the disciples were doing everything to spread the name of Jesus, and those who accepted him were "walking and jumping, and praising God" (Ac 3:8). God's renown did not stop when he rescued the Israelites from Egypt or when he struck down the enemies of the Israelites, as is written in Psalm 135:8–12. Instead, those events were merely the beginning of his glory and his renown. Jesus came and God's glory became apparent to all who saw him and heard of him. Today his name continues to endure.

25 He gives food to every creature.
His love endures forever.
26 Give thanks to the God of heaven.
His love endures forever.

Psalm 137

1 By the rivers of Babylon we sat and wept
when we remembered Zion.
2 There on the poplars
we hung our harps,
3 for there our captors asked us for songs,
our tormentors demanded songs of joy;
they said, "Sing us one of the songs of Zion!"

4 How can we sing the songs of the LORD
while in a foreign land?
5 If I forget you, Jerusalem,
may my right hand forget its skill.
6 May my tongue cling to the roof of my mouth
if I do not remember you,
if I do not consider Jerusalem
my highest joy.

7 Remember, LORD, what the Edomites did
on the day Jerusalem fell.
"Tear it down," they cried,
"tear it down to its foundations!"
8 Daughter Babylon, doomed to destruction,
happy is the one who repays you
according to what you have done to us.
9 Happy is the one who seizes your infants
and dashes them against the rocks.

Psalm 138

Of David.

1 I will praise you, LORD, with all my heart;
before the "gods" I will sing your praise.
2 I will bow down toward your holy temple
and will praise your name
for your unfailing love and your faithfulness,
for you have so exalted your solemn decree
that it surpasses your fame.
3 When I called, you answered me;
you greatly emboldened me.

4 May all the kings of the earth praise you, LORD,
when they hear what you have decreed.
5 May they sing of the ways of the LORD,
for the glory of the LORD is great.

6 Though the LORD is exalted, he looks kindly on the
lowly;
though lofty, he sees them from afar.
7 Though I walk in the midst of trouble,
you preserve my life.
You stretch out your hand against the anger of my foes;
with your right hand you save me.

A SONG OF PRAISE IN DIFFICULT TIMES

Psalm 137 was written about the difficulties of praising God in hard circumstances. Though the author had recently returned home from captivity in Babylon, he describes how nothing could remove the pain and sorrow that he and his fellow Israelites experienced while living in exile. Despite their captors asking them to "sing us one of the songs of Zion," the Israelites were unable to do so in a foreign land. All the blessings of the Lord had been taken from them, and they did not see how they could offer praise to God at a time of great sadness.

Jesus promised his disciples that they would one day face persecution and hard times (Mt 5:10 – 11; Lk 21:12; Jn 15:20). In Acts, there are descriptions of the violence that the early church initially faced. Perhaps like the Israelite captives in Babylon, the early Christians did not feel like singing songs of praise.

However, the story of Paul shows how it is possible for the people of God to sing songs in a strange land. In Acts 8:1 – 3, he was one of the people bent on destroying the church. But in Acts 9 he had an encounter with Jesus that completely changed his life. Paul became one of the greatest missionaries ever to live, and he did amazing things to spread the name of Jesus. As a leader of the church, Paul was constantly in and out of prison and facing hard persecution, yet he never ceased to praise God. Acts 16:25 tells the story of Paul and Silas in prison singing hymns to God. The reason they were in prison in the first place was because of their ministry on behalf of Jesus, but rather than sulking silently in their cell, they sang praises to God.

While the Israelites in exile had a difficult time singing songs of praise, God shows that he desires his people to praise him constantly, regardless of their circumstances. In Philippians 4, Paul charged the believers to "rejoice in the Lord always" (v. 4), and he made it clear that he had learned to be "content whatever the circumstances" (v. 11). Paul did not base his ability to praise God on his current situation, but rather he showed that circumstances do not change the fact that it is important to praise God always.

[8]The LORD will vindicate me;
your love, LORD, endures forever—
do not abandon the works of your hands.

Psalm 139

For the director of music. Of David. A psalm.

[1]You have searched me, LORD,
and you know me.
[2]You know when I sit and when I rise;
you perceive my thoughts from afar.
[3]You discern my going out and my lying down;
you are familiar with all my ways.
[4]Before a word is on my tongue
you, LORD, know it completely.
[5]You hem me in behind and before,
and you lay your hand upon me.
[6]Such knowledge is too wonderful for me,
too lofty for me to attain.

[7]Where can I go from your Spirit?
Where can I flee from your presence?
[8]If I go up to the heavens, you are there;
if I make my bed in the depths, you are there.
[9]If I rise on the wings of the dawn,
if I settle on the far side of the sea,
[10]even there your hand will guide me,
your right hand will hold me fast.
[11]If I say, "Surely the darkness will hide me
and the light become night around me,"
[12]even the darkness will not be dark to you;
the night will shine like the day,
for darkness is as light to you.

[13]For you created my inmost being;
you knit me together in my mother's womb.
[14]I praise you because I am fearfully and wonderfully made;
your works are wonderful,
I know that full well.
[15]My frame was not hidden from you
when I was made in the secret place,
when I was woven together in the depths of the earth.
[16]Your eyes saw my unformed body;
all the days ordained for me were written in your book
before one of them came to be.
[17]How precious to me are your thoughts,[a] God!
How vast is the sum of them!
[18]Were I to count them,
they would outnumber the grains of sand—
when I awake, I am still with you.

[19]If only you, God, would slay the wicked!
Away from me, you who are bloodthirsty!
[20]They speak of you with evil intent;
your adversaries misuse your name.
[21]Do I not hate those who hate you, LORD,
and abhor those who are in rebellion against you?

[a] 17 Or *How amazing are your thoughts concerning me*

PSALM 139:13–14

THE UNBORN

Psalm 139 is a beautiful picture of how God is involved in every single aspect of every person's life. The first 12 verses discuss how, no matter where David went, God was always with him. God knew his thoughts (v. 2), God knew his ways (v. 3) and God knew his words (v. 4). Furthermore, God knew David when he was in his mother's womb, long before he had thoughts, ways or words (vv. 13–14). The same holds true for every person in the world. God is involved in every aspect of a human's life. While some think a person's life, as well as God's involvement in it, starts the day they are born, it is clear that God is involved well before the day of birth: "You created my inmost being; you knit me together in my mother's womb" (v. 13). In Luke 1:26–38, the angel Gabriel explained to Mary that she would give birth to the Son of God. She was understandably confused because she was a virgin. However, the angel explained that the Holy Spirit would conceive a child in her. Just as Psalm 139 describes, that child would be formed and knit by the hand of God. While Jesus is the only human ever to have been conceived by the Holy Spirit, all children are formed by the Creator.

[22] I have nothing but hatred for them;
I count them my enemies.
[23] Search me, God, and know my heart;
test me and know my anxious thoughts.
[24] See if there is any offensive way in me,
and lead me in the way everlasting.

Psalm 140[a]

For the director of music. A psalm of David.

[1] Rescue me, LORD, from evildoers;
protect me from the violent,
[2] who devise evil plans in their hearts
and stir up war every day.
[3] They make their tongues as sharp as a serpent's;
the poison of vipers is on their lips.[b]

[4] Keep me safe, LORD, from the hands of the wicked;
protect me from the violent,
who devise ways to trip my feet.
[5] The arrogant have hidden a snare for me;
they have spread out the cords of their net
and have set traps for me along my path.

[6] I say to the LORD, "You are my God."
Hear, LORD, my cry for mercy.
[7] Sovereign LORD, my strong deliverer,
you shield my head in the day of battle.
[8] Do not grant the wicked their desires, LORD;
do not let their plans succeed.

[9] Those who surround me proudly rear their heads;
may the mischief of their lips engulf them.
[10] May burning coals fall on them;
may they be thrown into the fire,
into miry pits, never to rise.
[11] May slanderers not be established in the land;
may disaster hunt down the violent.

[12] I know that the LORD secures justice for the poor
and upholds the cause of the needy.
[13] Surely the righteous will praise your name,
and the upright will live in your presence.

Psalm 141

A psalm of David.

[1] I call to you, LORD, come quickly to me;
hear me when I call to you.
[2] May my prayer be set before you like incense;
may the lifting up of my hands be like the evening sacrifice.

[3] Set a guard over my mouth, LORD;
keep watch over the door of my lips.
[4] Do not let my heart be drawn to what is evil
so that I take part in wicked deeds
along with those who are evildoers;
do not let me eat their delicacies.

[a] In Hebrew texts 140:1-13 is numbered 140:2-14. [b] *3* The Hebrew has *Selah* (a word of uncertain meaning) here and at the end of verses 5 and 8.

PSALM 140:12

JUSTICE FOR THE POOR

Jesus is the justice for the poor that the psalmist, possibly David, wrote about here. Throughout Jesus' teachings there is constant mention of the poor and Jesus' intention of saving them. Luke 4:18 says, "He has anointed me to proclaim good news to the poor." Jesus told the rich young man that if he wanted to inherit eternal life, he had to "go, sell everything you have and give to the poor" (Mk 10:21). And in the parable of the Good Samaritan, Jesus showed how in order to be obedient to God and a good neighbor, one must help those in need (Lk 10:25–37). Indeed, what the psalmist wrote in Psalm 140 was confirmed through Jesus and is continuing to come true today. Jesus used his ministry to show how important the poor are to God, and he encouraged believers to treat the poor as he treated them—with love and care.

PSALM 141:1–2

PRAYER AS INCENSE

In Psalm 141, the psalmist asked God to hear his voice and to accept his prayer "like incense," which is to say a sweet-smelling fragrance. Today, believers can pray with confidence, knowing that God hears their prayers. Hebrews 7:25 says that Jesus "always lives to intercede for them." Jesus serves as the intermediary between believers and God, and he takes the requests of believers and presents them before God. First John 2:1 adds, "We have an advocate with the

(continued on next page)

(Prayer as Incense, continued)

Father — Jesus Christ, the Righteous One." While the psalmist begged God to hear and accept his prayers, believers today can pray confidently knowing that Jesus will take their prayers to God on their behalf. There is no uncertainty about whether or not God hears the prayers of those who follow him. Jesus made it possible for believers to present their requests to God "in every situation, by prayer and petition" (Php 4:6). The prayers of believers are like incense to God who hears them.

5 Let a righteous man strike me — that is a kindness;
let him rebuke me — that is oil on my head.
My head will not refuse it,
for my prayer will still be against the deeds of evildoers.
6 Their rulers will be thrown down from the cliffs,
and the wicked will learn that my words were well spoken.
7 They will say, "As one plows and breaks up the earth,
so our bones have been scattered at the mouth of the grave."
8 But my eyes are fixed on you, Sovereign LORD;
in you I take refuge — do not give me over to death.
9 Keep me safe from the traps set by evildoers,
from the snares they have laid for me.
10 Let the wicked fall into their own nets,
while I pass by in safety.

Psalm 142[a]

A maskil[b] *of David. When he was in the cave. A prayer.*

1 I cry aloud to the LORD;
I lift up my voice to the LORD for mercy.
2 I pour out before him my complaint;
before him I tell my trouble.

3 When my spirit grows faint within me,
it is you who watch over my way.
In the path where I walk
people have hidden a snare for me.
4 Look and see, there is no one at my right hand;
no one is concerned for me.
I have no refuge;
no one cares for my life.

5 I cry to you, LORD;
I say, "You are my refuge,
my portion in the land of the living."

6 Listen to my cry,
for I am in desperate need;
rescue me from those who pursue me,
for they are too strong for me.
7 Set me free from my prison,
that I may praise your name.
Then the righteous will gather about me
because of your goodness to me.

Psalm 143

A psalm of David.

1 LORD, hear my prayer,
listen to my cry for mercy;
in your faithfulness and righteousness
come to my relief.
2 Do not bring your servant into judgment,
for no one living is righteous before you.
3 The enemy pursues me,
he crushes me to the ground;

[a] In Hebrew texts 142:1-7 is numbered 142:2-8. [b] Title: Probably a literary or musical term

OUR REFUGE

According to the superscription attached to Psalm 142, David wrote this psalm when he was hiding in a cave — no doubt because Saul was trying to kill him. In his dire circumstances, he sought refuge in the Lord. David had been anointed to be Israel's next king, and that was why Saul was jealous of him. Yet even though David knew Saul was wrong for trying to kill him, he stayed faithful and refused to act violently toward the king appointed by God. However, it is clear in Psalm 142 that it was not easy for David to sit quietly in a cave and wait for redemption. He cried out to God and offered his complaints, but amidst all of his words, he never gave up faith and he continually recognized that the Lord was his "refuge" and his "portion" (v. 5).

Jesus prayed a similar prayer in John 17:1 – 5. In the hours before his arrest and crucifixion, Jesus cried out to God and prayed for God to be glorified in what he was about to do. Jesus showed incredible resolve and selflessness as he spent only five verses praying for himself, but fourteen verses praying for his disciples and another seven for all future believers. Jesus was about to begin the hardest trial of his life, and his reaction was to seek refuge in his Father and to pray for others.

In praying for future believers, Jesus provided encouragement for believers today to seek refuge in God as he himself did. David and Jesus both knew how important it was to seek refuge and safety in the Father through prayer, and believers are able to do the same amidst their own hardships. Even in the hardest situation of his life, Jesus remembered his followers. While it would have been easy for him to pray solely for himself, he took the time to pray for those around him and for those he knew would one day need his prayers. The examples of David and Jesus are worth emulating, and they each show exactly what prayer should look like in times of crisis and need.

he makes me dwell in the darkness
like those long dead.
4 So my spirit grows faint within me;
my heart within me is dismayed.
5 I remember the days of long ago;
I meditate on all your works
and consider what your hands have done.
6 I spread out my hands to you;
I thirst for you like a parched land.[a]

7 Answer me quickly, LORD;
my spirit fails.
Do not hide your face from me
or I will be like those who go down to the pit.
8 Let the morning bring me word of your unfailing love,
for I have put my trust in you.
Show me the way I should go,
for to you I entrust my life.
9 Rescue me from my enemies, LORD,
for I hide myself in you.
10 Teach me to do your will,
for you are my God;
may your good Spirit
lead me on level ground.

11 For your name's sake, LORD, preserve my life;
in your righteousness, bring me out of trouble.
12 In your unfailing love, silence my enemies;
destroy all my foes,
for I am your servant.

Psalm 144

Of David.

1 Praise be to the LORD my Rock,
who trains my hands for war,
my fingers for battle.
2 He is my loving God and my fortress,
my stronghold and my deliverer,
my shield, in whom I take refuge,
who subdues peoples[b] under me.

3 LORD, what are human beings that you care for them,
mere mortals that you think of them?
4 They are like a breath;
their days are like a fleeting shadow.

5 Part your heavens, LORD, and come down;
touch the mountains, so that they smoke.
6 Send forth lightning and scatter the enemy;
shoot your arrows and rout them.
7 Reach down your hand from on high;
deliver me and rescue me
from the mighty waters,
from the hands of foreigners

---

[a] 6 The Hebrew has *Selah* (a word of uncertain meaning) here. [b] 2 Many manuscripts of the Masoretic Text, Dead Sea Scrolls, Aquila, Jerome and Syriac; most manuscripts of the Masoretic Text *subdues my people*

GOD'S AMAZING LOVE FOR US

Psalm 144:3 shows David's deep appreciation and amazement at God's ability to care for humanity. Despite everything that God has control over, David wondered at the fact that God takes time to think of humans. This verse is one of those moments for David when he thought over the vastness of creation and realized how small he was in comparison to all that God has made. And it is at that moment that he was struck by how deeply profound God's love for him was. God has created everything on the earth and in the rest of the universe, yet he is able to care deeply for the beating heart of an individual person. David compared human life to a breath and a fleeting shadow (v. 4), both things that are present one moment and gone the next. In the vastness of eternity, the life of one person is incredibly small, yet God cares for each and every life.

John 3:16 explains how much God loved the world and how he was willing to sacrifice his only Son for the sake of mortal humans. David wrote of his amazement at God's ability to give thought to human beings, yet God does infinitely more than simply give thought. He gives life. To a God who lives forever, a human life is fleeting. However, God not only pays attention to each and every human life, he also gave an ultimate sacrifice in his Son Jesus, so that every human life can have value and purpose. God created a way for fleeting human lives one day to join him in the vastness of eternity through Jesus. He promises humans that "whoever believes in him shall not perish but have eternal life" (Jn 3:16).

David was right to be amazed at God's ability to regard humans, yet believers today know that God does so much more than simply regard them. A response of shock and amazement is entirely appropriate when one realizes how extraordinary the sacrifice of Jesus was for the life of each individual human. God did not stop at merely giving thought to humanity. He saved humanity.

8 whose mouths are full of lies,
whose right hands are deceitful.
9 I will sing a new song to you, my God;
on the ten-stringed lyre I will make music to you,
10 to the One who gives victory to kings,
who delivers his servant David.

From the deadly sword 11 deliver me;
rescue me from the hands of foreigners
whose mouths are full of lies,
whose right hands are deceitful.
12 Then our sons in their youth
will be like well-nurtured plants,
and our daughters will be like pillars
carved to adorn a palace.
13 Our barns will be filled
with every kind of provision.
Our sheep will increase by thousands,
by tens of thousands in our fields;
14 our oxen will draw heavy loads.[a]
There will be no breaching of walls,
no going into captivity,
no cry of distress in our streets.
15 Blessed is the people of whom this is true;
blessed is the people whose God is the LORD.

Psalm 145[b]

A psalm of praise. Of David.

1 I will exalt you, my God the King;
I will praise your name for ever and ever.
2 Every day I will praise you
and extol your name for ever and ever.
3 Great is the LORD and most worthy of praise;
his greatness no one can fathom.
4 One generation commends your works to another;
they tell of your mighty acts.
5 They speak of the glorious splendor of your majesty—
and I will meditate on your wonderful works.[c]
6 They tell of the power of your awesome works—
and I will proclaim your great deeds.
7 They celebrate your abundant goodness
and joyfully sing of your righteousness.

8 The LORD is gracious and compassionate,
slow to anger and rich in love.

9 The LORD is good to all;
he has compassion on all he has made.
10 All your works praise you, LORD;
your faithful people extol you.
11 They tell of the glory of your kingdom
and speak of your might,

PSALM 145:1–7

THE GLORY OF GOD

The superscription added to Psalm 145 credits David with authorship of this psalm. Traditionally referred to as "the sweet psalmist of Israel," David was intimately aware of "the glorious splendor of [God's] majesty" (v. 5). He wrote countless verses praising and glorifying God. Psalm 145 shows how God-followers like David come to understand God so well: "Every day I will praise you . . . I will meditate on your wonderful works" (vv. 2,5). The idea of spending time with God daily is also mentioned in Psalm 1:2, which describes a blessed person as one who "meditates on [God's] law day and night." David consistently spent quality time with the Lord, and it was because he spent so much time conversing with God that he was able to praise him so readily for his goodness and glory.

In the Gospels there are many instances where Jesus went away to pray and be alone with God (Mt 14:23; Mk 1:35; Lk 6:12; 22:41), so it is clear that Jesus highly valued time spent with his Father. To better understand the glory of God, it is crucial to spend time talking with God and meditating on his Word.

[a] 14 Or *our chieftains will be firmly established* [b] This psalm is an acrostic poem, the verses of which (including verse 13b) begin with the successive letters of the Hebrew alphabet.
[c] 5 Dead Sea Scrolls and Syriac (see also Septuagint); Masoretic Text *On the glorious splendor of your majesty / and on your wonderful works I will meditate*

[12] so that all people may know of your mighty acts
and the glorious splendor of your kingdom.
[13] Your kingdom is an everlasting kingdom,
and your dominion endures through all
generations.

The LORD is trustworthy in all he promises
and faithful in all he does.[a]
[14] The LORD upholds all who fall
and lifts up all who are bowed down.
[15] The eyes of all look to you,
and you give them their food at the proper time.
[16] You open your hand
and satisfy the desires of every living thing.

[17] The LORD is righteous in all his ways
and faithful in all he does.
[18] The LORD is near to all who call on him,
to all who call on him in truth.
[19] He fulfills the desires of those who fear him;
he hears their cry and saves them.
[20] The LORD watches over all who love him,
but all the wicked he will destroy.

[21] My mouth will speak in praise of the LORD.
Let every creature praise his holy name
for ever and ever.

Psalm 146

[1] Praise the LORD.[b]

Praise the LORD, my soul.

[2] I will praise the LORD all my life;
I will sing praise to my God as long as I live.
[3] Do not put your trust in princes,
in human beings, who cannot save.
[4] When their spirit departs, they return to the
ground;
on that very day their plans come to nothing.
[5] Blessed are those whose help is the God of Jacob,
whose hope is in the LORD their God.

[6] He is the Maker of heaven and earth,
the sea, and everything in them—
he remains faithful forever.
[7] He upholds the cause of the oppressed
and gives food to the hungry.
The LORD sets prisoners free,
[8] the LORD gives sight to the blind,
the LORD lifts up those who are bowed down,
the LORD loves the righteous.
[9] The LORD watches over the foreigner
and sustains the fatherless and the widow,
but he frustrates the ways of the wicked.

[a] *13* One manuscript of the Masoretic Text, Dead Sea Scrolls and Syriac (see also Septuagint); most manuscripts of the Masoretic Text do not have the last two lines of verse 13.
[b] *1* Hebrew *Hallelu Yah*; also in verse 10

PSALM 146:1–10

REIGN FOREVER

The first nine verses of Psalm 146 offer praise to God for all that he does and is doing. The psalm ends with a declaration that "the LORD reigns forever." First Corinthians 15:24–26 echoes the idea that God will reign forever, and Revelation 11:15 says, "The kingdom of the world has become the kingdom of our Lord and of his Messiah, and he will reign for ever and ever." In biblical times, kings struggled to hold their reign over their kingdom for as long as they could, and they placed a high priority on having sons to continue the lineage of their rule after their death. Unlike these kings, God does not have to fight to maintain his rule. In Psalms, 1 Corinthians and Revelation, it is written that God's reign will never come to an end. And he only needed one Son to confirm his reign here on earth. Jesus reminded people that his Father is the one true Ruler. It is the responsibility of Jesus' followers to continue to follow their King and to bring others along to do the same.

[10] The LORD reigns forever,
your God, O Zion, for all generations.

Praise the LORD.

Psalm 147

[1] Praise the LORD.[a]

How good it is to sing praises to our God,
how pleasant and fitting to praise him!

[2] The LORD builds up Jerusalem;
he gathers the exiles of Israel.
[3] He heals the brokenhearted
and binds up their wounds.
[4] He determines the number of the stars
and calls them each by name.
[5] Great is our Lord and mighty in power;
his understanding has no limit.
[6] The LORD sustains the humble
but casts the wicked to the ground.

[7] Sing to the LORD with grateful praise;
make music to our God on the harp.

[8] He covers the sky with clouds;
he supplies the earth with rain
and makes grass grow on the hills.
[9] He provides food for the cattle
and for the young ravens when they call.

[10] His pleasure is not in the strength of the horse,
nor his delight in the legs of the warrior;
[11] the LORD delights in those who fear him,
who put their hope in his unfailing love.

[12] Extol the LORD, Jerusalem;
praise your God, Zion.

[13] He strengthens the bars of your gates
and blesses your people within you.
[14] He grants peace to your borders
and satisfies you with the finest of wheat.

[15] He sends his command to the earth;
his word runs swiftly.
[16] He spreads the snow like wool
and scatters the frost like ashes.
[17] He hurls down his hail like pebbles.
Who can withstand his icy blast?
[18] He sends his word and melts them;
he stirs up his breezes, and the waters flow.

[19] He has revealed his word to Jacob,
his laws and decrees to Israel.
[20] He has done this for no other nation;
they do not know his laws.[b]

Praise the LORD.

[a] *1* Hebrew *Hallelu Yah*; also in verse 20 [b] *20* Masoretic Text; Dead Sea Scrolls and Septuagint *nation; / he has not made his laws known to them*

PSALM 147:1–20

SEE WHAT GOD HAS DONE

Throughout the psalms, the psalmists constantly praised God for all of the works that he had done. These works proved God's faithfulness to his people. In Psalm 147, the psalmist listed promises that God had upheld and would continue to uphold, all of which are a testament to his faithfulness. The psalmist praised God for his wondrous deeds to the nation of Israel, likely at a time when they rebuilt the walls around the city of Jerusalem (Ne 2:17–20; 4:1–23). These mighty acts of the Lord demonstrate that he had not forgotten his exilic people and would, once again, give them reason for great praise. Believers will never run out of things to be amazed by as they see all that God has done for them. Like Israel, God always provides for his people. His provision culminated in sending his Son Jesus to provide believers with ultimate salvation, which is in itself everything they could ever need.

Psalm 148

[1] Praise the LORD.[a]

Praise the LORD from the heavens;
praise him in the heights above.
[2] Praise him, all his angels;
praise him, all his heavenly hosts.
[3] Praise him, sun and moon;
praise him, all you shining stars.
[4] Praise him, you highest heavens
and you waters above the skies.

[5] Let them praise the name of the LORD,
for at his command they were created,
[6] and he established them for ever and ever—
he issued a decree that will never pass away.

[7] Praise the LORD from the earth,
you great sea creatures and all ocean depths,
[8] lightning and hail, snow and clouds,
stormy winds that do his bidding,
[9] you mountains and all hills,
fruit trees and all cedars,
[10] wild animals and all cattle,
small creatures and flying birds,
[11] kings of the earth and all nations,
you princes and all rulers on earth,
[12] young men and women,
old men and children.

[13] Let them praise the name of the LORD,
for his name alone is exalted;
his splendor is above the earth and the heavens.
[14] And he has raised up for his people a horn,[b]
the praise of all his faithful servants,
of Israel, the people close to his heart.

Praise the LORD.

Psalm 149

[1] Praise the LORD.[c]

Sing to the LORD a new song,
his praise in the assembly of his faithful people.
[2] Let Israel rejoice in their Maker;
let the people of Zion be glad in their King.
[3] Let them praise his name with dancing
and make music to him with timbrel and harp.
[4] For the LORD takes delight in his people;
he crowns the humble with victory.
[5] Let his faithful people rejoice in this honor
and sing for joy on their beds.

[6] May the praise of God be in their mouths
and a double-edged sword in their hands,
[7] to inflict vengeance on the nations
and punishment on the peoples,

[a] *1* Hebrew *Hallelu Yah*; also in verse 14 [b] *14* *Horn* here symbolizes strength.
[c] *1* Hebrew *Hallelu Yah*; also in verse 9

PSALM 148:1–14

PRAISE: OUR SPONTANEOUS RESPONSE

Psalm 148 provides an appropriate response to everything that was written in Psalm 147. The word *praise* is used 13 times in 14 verses, which shows just how important it is to praise God for who he is and what he has done. Praising God is mentioned many times in the New Testament, including in the greetings of many of Paul's letters (2Co 1:3; Eph 1:3; Php 1:11). Clearly, it was a priority to Paul to start his letters by offering praise to God. In Hebrews 13:15, believers are encouraged to praise God: "Let us continually offer to God a sacrifice of praise." First Peter 1:7 talks about how everything that believers experience is intended to "result in praise, glory and honor" to God. And in 1 Peter 4:11 the apostle Peter wrote that believers should use their spiritual gifts "so that in all things God may be praised through Jesus Christ." Today, God has given countless blessings to his people, including the blessing of Jesus. The natural response of everyone who knows of these blessings and who knows Jesus should be thanksgiving and praise.

GIVING OUR BEST PRAISE

Psalm 149 gives a great summary of every psalm that comes before it, and it also provides a charge to believers going forward. Throughout the book of Psalms, there are a multitude of different praises given to God, and Psalm 149 reminds the people who are singing the praises to continue to do so because of the great pleasure it brings God (v. 4). There is no greater purpose for a human than to praise the Creator, and that is exactly what the book of Psalms is intended for. The psalms provide reasons for praising God, as well as examples of how to praise God. In Psalm 149, the psalmist pauses to make sure everyone is aware of why they sing praises to God. The people of God sing because "the LORD takes delight in his people" (v. 4). It is important to remember that believers are not only supposed to sing praises because God deserves them, but also because God enjoys them.

Also, Psalm 149 serves as a challenge to God's people to give God their best effort when praising him. Believers are not called to recite praises mundanely to God with little to no care about the actual words they are saying, but rather they are to enter into praise with great joy and with heartfelt emotion. The psalmist encourages people to sing "a new song," to "praise [God's] name with dancing," and to "sing for joy on their beds" (vv. 1,3,5). There is a reason that Psalms has the most chapters of any book in the Bible; there are so many ways to sing to God and to bring him praise!

When believers realize all that God has done for them through his Son Jesus, it is natural to respond with joy and praise. It is also important for that praise to be the best possible praise that each person can muster. It is the heart behind the praise that matters more than the words themselves, and that is what the psalmist was trying to say here. Continue to worship God in the ways that he has always been worshiped, but also sing new songs and dance new dances. God is deserving of nothing less than the best praise.

[8]to bind their kings with fetters,
their nobles with shackles of iron,
[9]to carry out the sentence written against them—
this is the glory of all his faithful people.

Praise the LORD.

Psalm 150

[1]Praise the LORD.[a]

Praise God in his sanctuary;
praise him in his mighty heavens.
[2]Praise him for his acts of power;
praise him for his surpassing greatness.
[3]Praise him with the sounding of the trumpet,
praise him with the harp and lyre,
[4]praise him with timbrel and dancing,
praise him with the strings and pipe,
[5]praise him with the clash of cymbals,
praise him with resounding cymbals.

[6]Let everything that has breath praise the LORD.

Praise the LORD.

[a] *1* Hebrew *Hallelu Yah*; also in verse 6

PSALM 150:6

LET EVERYTHING THAT HAS BREATH PRAISE HIM

Psalm 150 provides a summation of the entire book of Psalms in its final verse: "Let everything that has breath praise the LORD." Everyone who reads Psalms is exhorted to praise God in all that they do, and Paul encourages believers to do the same (1Th 5:18). While there have been many blessings from God to his people, Jesus and the salvation and grace that come with knowing him are the ultimate blessing from God. Jesus is enough reason to give God praise, and someday all those who are in Christ will give God praise because of Christ and his work. One day "every knee will bow before me; every tongue will acknowledge God" (Ro 14:11)—those who have failed to trust in Christ will acknowledge this in shame and remorse, while Christians will do so in overwhelming praise. Jesus echoed the fact that everything will eventually give praise to God in Luke 19:40 when he said, "I tell you ... if [the people] keep quiet, the stones will cry out." It is the responsibility of believers to begin and encourage the praise of God. They are at the forefront of a movement toward a day when every believer and everything will fully embrace the God who created them and give him the praise that only he is worthy of.

JESUS: OUR DIVINE WISDOM

PROVERBS

PROVERBS

BIRTH OF SOLOMON, TO WHOM MOST PROVERBS ARE ASCRIBED *c. 991 BC*	DEATH OF SOLOMON *c. 930 BC*	REIGN OF HEZEKIAH, DURING WHICH SOME OR ALL OF PROVERBS WAS COMPILED *c. 715 – 686 BC*

The writers of the book of Proverbs distill God's divine wisdom to provide insight for obedient worship in a world wrecked by sin. As a collection of practical wisdom sayings inspired by God, this book provides specific insight into the wisdom that God graciously offers throughout history. Solomon, Lemuel, Agur, and others communicated their wealth of God-given insight to the nation of Israel and to all subsequent readers of Proverbs.

The range of topics throughout the book demonstrates the complexity of human existence. From money to marriage, power to possessions, Proverbs presents practical wisdom for those seeking to follow God faithfully. These subjects are addressed throughout Proverbs in repeated and memorable sayings that were meant to be shared by God's people.

The main contrast in the book is between wisdom and foolishness (1:1 – 7). Foolishness is presented as humanity's natural propensity and, without God's intervention, a dangerous and destructive path for life, ultimately culminating in death and destruction in this life and the next (3:35).

Wisdom, on the other hand, is a gift from God and is the path to the life he intends (2:6). Because all people are born dead in sin and enslaved to foolishness, only God can deliver people from their impending doom. God graciously gives wisdom to those who, through faith, fear him and seek after him with all of their heart. Wisdom fosters a love for God, fulfillment in life and intimacy with God — in this life and the next (2:1 – 6).

Sin renders all humankind incapable of following the path of wisdom described in the book of Proverbs. Jesus, however, could and did follow that perfect path. He is the embodiment of the divine wisdom spoken of throughout the book. In his life and sacrificial death, he perfectly obeyed God's commands at great cost to himself. By looking at the life of Jesus, all people can see the One who perfectly followed the path wisdom affords. Jesus, who is the wisdom of God, lived the life humankind was meant to live but could not due to sin. By faith, believers can receive the gift of Jesus' righteous life and perfect standing before God. God gives his children the gift of his Spirit, which empowers them to follow his perfect path of wisdom.

THE FEAR OF THE LORD IS THE BEGINNING OF WISDOM, AND KNOWLEDGE OF THE HOLY ONE IS UNDERSTANDING.

Proverbs 9:10

PROVERBS

PROVERBS 1:8–19

AMONG THE CRIMINALS

In this passage Solomon warned his son against the temptation to use illicit means of gaining wealth. Through the voice of a gang that kills and robs people, Solomon presented the enticing prospect of filling one's house with plunder taken from the unsuspecting and innocent. His warning focused on the destructive effects such a lifestyle has — not only on the victims but on the perpetrators of the crimes. Solomon knew where the path of violence and theft leads — to death. The wisdom principle is clear both here and throughout Proverbs: those who gain money the wrong way bring about their own destruction (Pr 10:2; 15:27).

But what about apparent exceptions to this principle? After all, many people enrich themselves in the wrong ways and seem to get away with it. Consider how this story points to the life of Jesus, the One who will someday rectify all injustice. Judas joined forces with a "gang" to set a trap for an innocent man. The gang set the trap, the innocent man was executed among criminals and Judas became richer by thirty pieces of silver. At first blush, this story seems to disprove the proverb. The innocent man died the death that criminals deserved to die, and the guilty man lined his pockets. But on Sunday morning, Judas was in the grave and Jesus walked out of his, proving that "ill-gotten treasures have no lasting value, but righteousness delivers from death" (Pr 10:2).

Purpose and Theme

1 The proverbs of Solomon son of David, king of Israel:

2 for gaining wisdom and instruction;
for understanding words of insight;
3 for receiving instruction in prudent behavior,
doing what is right and just and fair;
4 for giving prudence to those who are simple,[a]
knowledge and discretion to the young—
5 let the wise listen and add to their learning,
and let the discerning get guidance—
6 for understanding proverbs and parables,
the sayings and riddles of the wise.[b]

7 The fear of the LORD is the beginning of knowledge,
but fools[c] despise wisdom and instruction.

Prologue: Exhortations to Embrace Wisdom

Warning Against the Invitation of Sinful Men

8 Listen, my son, to your father's instruction
and do not forsake your mother's teaching.
9 They are a garland to grace your head
and a chain to adorn your neck.

10 My son, if sinful men entice you,
do not give in to them.
11 If they say, "Come along with us;
let's lie in wait for innocent blood,
let's ambush some harmless soul;
12 let's swallow them alive, like the grave,
and whole, like those who go down to the pit;
13 we will get all sorts of valuable things
and fill our houses with plunder;
14 cast lots with us;
we will all share the loot"—
15 my son, do not go along with them,
do not set foot on their paths;
16 for their feet rush into evil,
they are swift to shed blood.
17 How useless to spread a net
where every bird can see it!
18 These men lie in wait for their own blood;
they ambush only themselves!
19 Such are the paths of all who go after ill-gotten
gain;
it takes away the life of those who get it.

[a] *4* The Hebrew word rendered *simple* in Proverbs denotes a person who is gullible, without moral direction and inclined to evil. [b] *6* Or *understanding a proverb, namely, a parable, / and the sayings of the wise, their riddles* [c] *7* The Hebrew words rendered *fool* in Proverbs, and often elsewhere in the Old Testament, denote a person who is morally deficient.

PROVERBS 1:1 – 7

THE WISE KING

King Solomon was the wisest man in ancient Israel, and he sought to impart that wisdom to the nation by speaking and writing proverbs (1Ki 4:32). Proverbs opens with an introduction that describes the purpose of the book. The wise king, desiring to produce wisdom in the people of Israel, asserted that wisdom begins with the fear of the Lord (Pr 1:7). Thus, wisdom is more than intellect — it is a spiritual attitude.

The problem for the Israelites was that not only were they not wise, but their kings were fools, too. Solomon repeatedly warned his sons not to fall for immoral women, but Solomon fell for foreign women (1Ki 11:1 – 13). Solomon attempted to train his son in wisdom, but his son foolishly split the nation in two by listening to his peers rather than the wise counsel of the elders (1Ki 12:1 – 20). Israel's kings' failures led to the development of a hope for a future king who would be truly wise.

Eventually, Isaiah described the Messiah as one who would embody the kind of wisdom described in the introduction of Proverbs. Drawing upon the language of Proverbs 1:1 – 7, Isaiah wrote, "A shoot will come up from the stump of Jesse; from his roots a Branch will bear fruit. The Spirit of the LORD will rest on him — the Spirit of wisdom and of understanding, the Spirit of counsel and of might, the Spirit of the knowledge and fear of the LORD — and he will delight in the fear of the LORD" (Isa 11:1 – 3).

The fulfillment of this promise can be found in Jesus Christ. He was given the throne of David (Lk 1:32). He was anointed with the Holy Spirit at his baptism (Mt 3:16). And, Jesus himself said, "The Queen of the South will rise at the judgment with this generation and condemn it; for she came from the ends of the earth to listen to Solomon's wisdom, and now something greater than Solomon is here" (Mt 12:42). Jesus is the Spirit-anointed King who is wiser than Solomon. Not only does he teach wisdom, he actually lives it out and enables his followers to do so as well.

Wisdom's Rebuke

[20] Out in the open wisdom calls aloud,
she raises her voice in the public square;
[21] on top of the wall[a] she cries out,
at the city gate she makes her speech:

[22] "How long will you who are simple love your simple ways?
How long will mockers delight in mockery
and fools hate knowledge?
[23] Repent at my rebuke!
Then I will pour out my thoughts to you,
I will make known to you my teachings.
[24] But since you refuse to listen when I call
and no one pays attention when I stretch out my hand,
[25] since you disregard all my advice
and do not accept my rebuke,
[26] I in turn will laugh when disaster strikes you;
I will mock when calamity overtakes you—
[27] when calamity overtakes you like a storm,
when disaster sweeps over you like a whirlwind,
when distress and trouble overwhelm you.

[28] "Then they will call to me but I will not answer;
they will look for me but will not find me,
[29] since they hated knowledge
and did not choose to fear the LORD.
[30] Since they would not accept my advice
and spurned my rebuke,
[31] they will eat the fruit of their ways
and be filled with the fruit of their schemes.
[32] For the waywardness of the simple will kill them,
and the complacency of fools will destroy them;
[33] but whoever listens to me will live in safety
and be at ease, without fear of harm."

Moral Benefits of Wisdom

2 My son, if you accept my words
and store up my commands within you,
[2] turning your ear to wisdom
and applying your heart to understanding—
[3] indeed, if you call out for insight
and cry aloud for understanding,
[4] and if you look for it as for silver
and search for it as for hidden treasure,
[5] then you will understand the fear of the LORD
and find the knowledge of God.
[6] For the LORD gives wisdom;
from his mouth come knowledge and understanding.
[7] He holds success in store for the upright,
he is a shield to those whose walk is blameless,
[8] for he guards the course of the just
and protects the way of his faithful ones.

[9] Then you will understand what is right and just
and fair—every good path.
[10] For wisdom will enter your heart,
and knowledge will be pleasant to your soul.

---

[a] *21* Septuagint; Hebrew / *at noisy street corners*

11 Discretion will protect you,
and understanding will guard you.

12 Wisdom will save you from the ways of wicked men,
from men whose words are perverse,
13 who have left the straight paths
to walk in dark ways,
14 who delight in doing wrong
and rejoice in the perverseness of evil,
15 whose paths are crooked
and who are devious in their ways.

16 Wisdom will save you also from the adulterous woman,
from the wayward woman with her seductive words,
17 who has left the partner of her youth
and ignored the covenant she made before God.[a]
18 Surely her house leads down to death
and her paths to the spirits of the dead.
19 None who go to her return
or attain the paths of life.

20 Thus you will walk in the ways of the good
and keep to the paths of the righteous.
21 For the upright will live in the land,
and the blameless will remain in it;
22 but the wicked will be cut off from the land,
and the unfaithful will be torn from it.

Wisdom Bestows Well-Being

3 My son, do not forget my teaching,
but keep my commands in your heart,
2 for they will prolong your life many years
and bring you peace and prosperity.

3 Let love and faithfulness never leave you;
bind them around your neck,
write them on the tablet of your heart.
4 Then you will win favor and a good name
in the sight of God and man.

5 Trust in the LORD with all your heart
and lean not on your own understanding;
6 in all your ways submit to him,
and he will make your paths straight.[b]

7 Do not be wise in your own eyes;
fear the LORD and shun evil.
8 This will bring health to your body
and nourishment to your bones.

9 Honor the LORD with your wealth,
with the firstfruits of all your crops;
10 then your barns will be filled to overflowing,
and your vats will brim over with new wine.

11 My son, do not despise the LORD's discipline,
and do not resent his rebuke,
12 because the LORD disciplines those he loves,
as a father the son he delights in.[c]

PROVERBS 2:20–22

INHERITING THE EARTH

Solomon urged his son to listen to his wisdom: avoid sexual sin with the adulterous woman. And he clearly outlined the judgment for those who fall for the temptation and the reward for those who avoid it—the upright will dwell in the land, and the wicked will be exiled. To ancient Israel, these promises and warnings were part of the fabric of the nation. If they were unfaithful to God, then they would be exiled from the land, but if they remained faithful to God, then they would remain in the land. To those of us on the other side of the New Testament, these words take on a different meaning. The New Testament expanded the land promise to include the entire earth. As Jesus said, "Blessed are the meek, for they will inherit the earth" (Mt 5:5). There is only one who was perfectly faithful to God and entirely meek—Jesus of Nazareth. He inherits the whole world, and those who believe in him are his co-heirs who inherit a new creation with him (Ro 8:17). But those who reject Christ will be exiled from the Lord's presence forever.

[a] 17 Or *covenant of her God* [b] 6 Or *will direct your paths* [c] 12 Hebrew; Septuagint *loves, / and he chastens everyone he accepts as his child*

FAVOR WITH GOD AND MAN

This passage is about being in a faithful covenant relationship with God where each partner has obligations to uphold. The odd verses here seem to be about the obligation of the human partner in the covenant, and the even verses are about the obligations of the divine partner. Verses 1, 3, 5, 7, 9 and 11 describe expectations on readers to keep God the Father's commands, to bind steadfast love around their necks, to trust in the Lord with all their hearts, not to be wise in their own eyes, to give generously and to welcome the Lord's discipline. Verses 2, 4, 6, 8, 10 and 12 tell readers what the Lord will do in return, such as granting longer life, favor with God and man, guidance, health, provision and loving discipline. Those who meet the obligations of being faithful to the Lord and walking in wisdom will experience the Lord meeting his obligations to bless and grow them.

The question that must be asked is, "Who has ever kept the covenant and received these rewards?" The answer is clearly Jesus Christ. Luke 2:52 alludes directly to Proverbs 3:4 to show its fulfillment in Jesus: "And Jesus grew in wisdom and stature, and in favor with God and man." Now, the good news is that he represents his people before the Father in this covenant relationship. He lived up to humanity's obligations on their behalf, and then he took the curses of humanity's covenant-breaking in their place. He experienced sickness, sorrows, enemies and a premature death. Because of who Jesus is and all he has done, he is able to offer full pardon to every covenant-breaker who believes in him. His righteous record of keeping the covenant is credited to the account of all who are united to him by faith, and as a result, they will experience the blessings of covenant faithfulness by his merits, not their own. For all those who are in Christ, God will do the work by the power of the Spirit to conform them into the image of his covenant-keeping Son — sometimes through discipline (Pr 3:11 – 12; Heb 12:5 – 6).

13 Blessed are those who find wisdom,
those who gain understanding,
14 for she is more profitable than silver
and yields better returns than gold.
15 She is more precious than rubies;
nothing you desire can compare with her.
16 Long life is in her right hand;
in her left hand are riches and honor.
17 Her ways are pleasant ways,
and all her paths are peace.
18 She is a tree of life to those who take hold of her;
those who hold her fast will be blessed.

19 By wisdom the LORD laid the earth's foundations,
by understanding he set the heavens in place;
20 by his knowledge the watery depths were divided,
and the clouds let drop the dew.

21 My son, do not let wisdom and understanding out of
your sight,
preserve sound judgment and discretion;
22 they will be life for you,
an ornament to grace your neck.
23 Then you will go on your way in safety,
and your foot will not stumble.
24 When you lie down, you will not be afraid;
when you lie down, your sleep will be sweet.
25 Have no fear of sudden disaster
or of the ruin that overtakes the wicked,
26 for the LORD will be at your side
and will keep your foot from being snared.

27 Do not withhold good from those to whom it is due,
when it is in your power to act.
28 Do not say to your neighbor,
"Come back tomorrow and I'll give it to you" —
when you already have it with you.
29 Do not plot harm against your neighbor,
who lives trustfully near you.
30 Do not accuse anyone for no reason —
when they have done you no harm.

31 Do not envy the violent
or choose any of their ways.

32 For the LORD detests the perverse
but takes the upright into his confidence.
33 The LORD's curse is on the house of the wicked,
but he blesses the home of the righteous.
34 He mocks proud mockers
but shows favor to the humble and oppressed.
35 The wise inherit honor,
but fools get only shame.

Get Wisdom at Any Cost

4 Listen, my sons, to a father's instruction;
pay attention and gain understanding.
2 I give you sound learning,
so do not forsake my teaching.

PROVERBS 3:13 – 18

THE PEARL OF GREAT VALUE

In this poem about the supreme value of wisdom, Solomon personified wisdom as a woman, telling his readers to seek her above everything else. In the fullness of time, the New Testament revealed that this personification pointed to a real person — Jesus of Nazareth — who should be pursued and treasured above all else (1Co 1:24,30). Wisdom's profits are better than silver, gold or jewels, so people should seek Jesus at any cost. No other object of desire compares with him. Jesus — like the kingdom of God, the pearl of great value, the treasure hidden in a field (Mt 13:44 – 46) — is worth selling everything in order to acquire. When people seek Jesus — the wisdom of God — above all else, other things will be added (Pr 3:16 – 18; Mt 6:33). Solomon knew the value of wisdom from God. In 1 Kings 3, God told Solomon he would grant whatever Solomon asked for. Solomon could have asked for riches, long life, victory over his enemies or the most glorious empire any king has ever ruled, but instead he asked for wisdom above all else. So God gave him supreme wisdom, and God added to it long life, wealth and great honor. Jesus is worth more than anything anyone could ever desire, and to those who seek him first he adds many additional blessings.

PROVERBS 3:18

TREE OF LIFE

The term "tree of life" is only found in three books of Scripture: Genesis, Proverbs and Revelation. In the

(continued on next page)

(Tree of Life, continued)

Garden of Eden, eating from the tree of life granted immortality (Ge 3:22). Proverbs says that wisdom is a tree of life, and the New Testament reveals not only that Jesus is the wisdom of God (1Co 1:24) but also that he grants access to the tree of life (Rev 2:7). Proverbs 3:18, along with the rest of Proverbs, calls humanity back to paradise. Indeed, in the garden, humankind reached for knowledge apart from God and his Word. Humans sought to determine right and wrong for themselves. As a result, humans became unwise and inherited death—cut off from access to the tree of life. Proverbs reveals the path back to life—wisdom. But only in Christ, who is the wisdom of God, does that path become a reality for finite humans. If they will humble themselves and take hold of Jesus in faith, they will receive back what was lost in Eden.

3 For I too was a son to my father,
still tender, and cherished by my mother.
4 Then he taught me, and he said to me,
"Take hold of my words with all your heart;
keep my commands, and you will live.
5 Get wisdom, get understanding;
do not forget my words or turn away from them.
6 Do not forsake wisdom, and she will protect you;
love her, and she will watch over you.
7 The beginning of wisdom is this: Get[a] wisdom.
Though it cost all you have,[b] get understanding.
8 Cherish her, and she will exalt you;
embrace her, and she will honor you.
9 She will give you a garland to grace your head
and present you with a glorious crown."

10 Listen, my son, accept what I say,
and the years of your life will be many.
11 I instruct you in the way of wisdom
and lead you along straight paths.
12 When you walk, your steps will not be hampered;
when you run, you will not stumble.
13 Hold on to instruction, do not let it go;
guard it well, for it is your life.
14 Do not set foot on the path of the wicked
or walk in the way of evildoers.
15 Avoid it, do not travel on it;
turn from it and go on your way.
16 For they cannot rest until they do evil;
they are robbed of sleep till they make someone
stumble.
17 They eat the bread of wickedness
and drink the wine of violence.

18 The path of the righteous is like the morning sun,
shining ever brighter till the full light of day.
19 But the way of the wicked is like deep darkness;
they do not know what makes them stumble.

20 My son, pay attention to what I say;
turn your ear to my words.
21 Do not let them out of your sight,
keep them within your heart;
22 for they are life to those who find them
and health to one's whole body.
23 Above all else, guard your heart,
for everything you do flows from it.
24 Keep your mouth free of perversity;
keep corrupt talk far from your lips.
25 Let your eyes look straight ahead;
fix your gaze directly before you.
26 Give careful thought to the[c] paths for your
feet
and be steadfast in all your ways.
27 Do not turn to the right or the left;
keep your foot from evil.

---

[a] 7 Or *Wisdom is supreme; therefore get* [b] 7 Or *wisdom. / Whatever else you get*
[c] 26 Or *Make level*

THE HEART

This verse is one of the keys to understanding Proverbs. The human heart is the source of each person's actions, words and thoughts. People have a problem though; their hearts are broken and sinful. Proverbs makes this clear when it says, "Who can say, 'I have kept my heart pure; I am clean and without sin'?" (Pr 20:9; cf. 22:15). The reason why people behave badly is because of their hearts. Jesus observed this reality when he said that evil words proceed from an evil heart (Mt 12:33 – 37), and that deceit, sexual immorality, murder, theft and other sins flow from the heart (Mk 7:20 – 23).

Since humans have heart issues, they need new hearts for real and lasting change. Deuteronomy said that people fail to obey the law when their hearts are not turned toward God (cf. Dt 5:29; 30:1 – 20). It promised that one day the Lord would perform an inner transformation of the heart that would enable obedience (Dt 30:6). This promise was repeated in Ezekiel when the Lord said he would someday give his followers a new heart (Eze 36:26) and in Jeremiah when the Lord said of the new covenant, "I will put my law in their minds and write it on their hearts" (Jer 31:33).

Proverbs refers to the same hope — the hope for a heart that has God's wisdom and ways written on it (Pr 3:3; 7:3). Foolishness is described in the Hebrew of Proverbs as literally "lacking a heart," which is translated with some form of the English phrase "having no sense" in the NIV (Pr 6:32; 7:7; 9:4; 10:13; 11:12; 12:11; 17:18; 24:30; cf. Dt 5:29). The adulterer "lacks a heart" (Pr 6:32; 7:7). Both wisdom and folly seek the affection of the one who "lacks a heart" (9:4,16). The one who "lacks a heart" will die (10:21). And the lazy fool is one who "lacks a heart" (24:30). But, the wise person who listens to wisdom "gains" a heart (15:32; cf. Eze 36:26).

People need to be born again with a new heart through faith in Jesus Christ, who inaugurated the new covenant with his blood. Jesus said, "This is my blood of the covenant, which is poured out for many for the forgiveness of sins" (Mt 26:28). Only through renewal in Christ can people walk in wisdom.

Warning Against Adultery

5 My son, pay attention to my wisdom,
turn your ear to my words of insight,
2 that you may maintain discretion
and your lips may preserve knowledge.
3 For the lips of the adulterous woman drip honey,
and her speech is smoother than oil;
4 but in the end she is bitter as gall,
sharp as a double-edged sword.
5 Her feet go down to death;
her steps lead straight to the grave.
6 She gives no thought to the way of life;
her paths wander aimlessly, but she does not know it.

7 Now then, my sons, listen to me;
do not turn aside from what I say.
8 Keep to a path far from her,
do not go near the door of her house,
9 lest you lose your honor to others
and your dignity[a] to one who is cruel,
10 lest strangers feast on your wealth
and your toil enrich the house of another.
11 At the end of your life you will groan,
when your flesh and body are spent.
12 You will say, "How I hated discipline!
How my heart spurned correction!
13 I would not obey my teachers
or turn my ear to my instructors.
14 And I was soon in serious trouble
in the assembly of God's people."

15 Drink water from your own cistern,
running water from your own well.
16 Should your springs overflow in the streets,
your streams of water in the public squares?
17 Let them be yours alone,
never to be shared with strangers.
18 May your fountain be blessed,
and may you rejoice in the wife of your youth.
19 A loving doe, a graceful deer—
may her breasts satisfy you always,
may you ever be intoxicated with her love.
20 Why, my son, be intoxicated with another man's wife?
Why embrace the bosom of a wayward woman?

21 For your ways are in full view of the LORD,
and he examines all your paths.
22 The evil deeds of the wicked ensnare them;
the cords of their sins hold them fast.
23 For lack of discipline they will die,
led astray by their own great folly.

Warnings Against Folly

6 My son, if you have put up security for your neighbor,
if you have shaken hands in pledge for a stranger,
2 you have been trapped by what you said,
ensnared by the words of your mouth.

[a] 9 Or *years*

PROVERBS 5:3–6

THE ADULTEROUS WOMAN

Not only did Solomon personify wisdom, he also personified foolishness (Pr 9:13–18). Foolishness is a predator hunting people down and trying to kill them, often through sexual temptation. Just like Satan is tracking people down and attempting to ensnare them in sexual sin (1Co 7:5), so foolishness wants to trap and kill (Pr 7:22–23; 23:26–28). Solomon illustrates the lure of foolishness with the smooth words of the adulterous woman (Pr 5:3), which mirror and rival the father's words to the son (Pr 5:1–2). There is both a vertical means of rescue from this predator and a horizontal means. Vertically, a person can be rescued by having a personal relationship with wisdom—who is Jesus Christ (Pr 2:1–22; 7:4–5; 1Co 1:24,30). Horizontally, a person can be rescued by having an intimate relationship with a spouse (Pr 5:15–20). Paul employed this same strategy in 1 Corinthians. He warned his readers to flee sexual immorality (1Co 6:12–18), and encouraged them by reminding them of redemption in Christ (1Co 6:19–20) and calling them to preserve intimacy with their spouses (1Co 7:1–5).

3 So do this, my son, to free yourself,
since you have fallen into your neighbor's hands:
Go — to the point of exhaustion — [a]
and give your neighbor no rest!
4 Allow no sleep to your eyes,
no slumber to your eyelids.
5 Free yourself, like a gazelle from the hand of the hunter,
like a bird from the snare of the fowler.

6 Go to the ant, you sluggard;
consider its ways and be wise!
7 It has no commander,
no overseer or ruler,
8 yet it stores its provisions in summer
and gathers its food at harvest.

9 How long will you lie there, you sluggard?
When will you get up from your sleep?
10 A little sleep, a little slumber,
a little folding of the hands to rest —
11 and poverty will come on you like a thief
and scarcity like an armed man.

12 A troublemaker and a villain,
who goes about with a corrupt mouth,
13 who winks maliciously with his eye,
signals with his feet
and motions with his fingers,
14 who plots evil with deceit in his heart —
he always stirs up conflict.
15 Therefore disaster will overtake him in an instant;
he will suddenly be destroyed — without remedy.

16 There are six things the LORD hates,
seven that are detestable to him:
17 haughty eyes,
a lying tongue,
hands that shed innocent blood,
18 a heart that devises wicked schemes,
feet that are quick to rush into evil,
19 a false witness who pours out lies
and a person who stirs up conflict in the community.

Warning Against Adultery

20 My son, keep your father's command
and do not forsake your mother's teaching.
21 Bind them always on your heart;
fasten them around your neck.
22 When you walk, they will guide you;
when you sleep, they will watch over you;
when you awake, they will speak to you.
23 For this command is a lamp,
this teaching is a light,
and correction and instruction
are the way to life,
24 keeping you from your neighbor's wife,
from the smooth talk of a wayward woman.

---

[a] 3 Or *Go and humble yourself,*

25 Do not lust in your heart after her beauty
or let her captivate you with her eyes.

26 For a prostitute can be had for a loaf of bread,
but another man's wife preys on your very life.
27 Can a man scoop fire into his lap
without his clothes being burned?
28 Can a man walk on hot coals
without his feet being scorched?
29 So is he who sleeps with another man's wife;
no one who touches her will go unpunished.

30 People do not despise a thief if he steals
to satisfy his hunger when he is starving.
31 Yet if he is caught, he must pay sevenfold,
though it costs him all the wealth of his house.
32 But a man who commits adultery has no sense;
whoever does so destroys himself.
33 Blows and disgrace are his lot,
and his shame will never be wiped away.
34 For jealousy arouses a husband's fury,
and he will show no mercy when he takes revenge.
35 He will not accept any compensation;
he will refuse a bribe, however great it is.

Warning Against the Adulterous Woman

7 My son, keep my words
and store up my commands within you.
2 Keep my commands and you will live;
guard my teachings as the apple of your eye.
3 Bind them on your fingers;
write them on the tablet of your heart.
4 Say to wisdom, "You are my sister,"
and to insight, "You are my relative."
5 They will keep you from the adulterous woman,
from the wayward woman with her seductive words.

6 At the window of my house
I looked down through the lattice.
7 I saw among the simple,
I noticed among the young men,
a youth who had no sense.
8 He was going down the street near her corner,
walking along in the direction of her house
9 at twilight, as the day was fading,
as the dark of night set in.

10 Then out came a woman to meet him,
dressed like a prostitute and with crafty intent.
11 (She is unruly and defiant,
her feet never stay at home;
12 now in the street, now in the squares,
at every corner she lurks.)
13 She took hold of him and kissed him
and with a brazen face she said:

14 "Today I fulfilled my vows,
and I have food from my fellowship offering at home.
15 So I came out to meet you;
I looked for you and have found you!

16 I have covered my bed
with colored linens from Egypt.
17 I have perfumed my bed
with myrrh, aloes and cinnamon.
18 Come, let's drink deeply of love till morning;
let's enjoy ourselves with love!
19 My husband is not at home;
he has gone on a long journey.
20 He took his purse filled with money
and will not be home till full moon."

21 With persuasive words she led him astray;
she seduced him with her smooth talk.
22 All at once he followed her
like an ox going to the slaughter,
like a deer[a] stepping into a noose[b]
23 till an arrow pierces his liver,
like a bird darting into a snare,
little knowing it will cost him his life.

24 Now then, my sons, listen to me;
pay attention to what I say.
25 Do not let your heart turn to her ways
or stray into her paths.
26 Many are the victims she has brought down;
her slain are a mighty throng.
27 Her house is a highway to the grave,
leading down to the chambers of death.

Wisdom's Call

8 Does not wisdom call out?
Does not understanding raise her voice?
2 At the highest point along the way,
where the paths meet, she takes her stand;
3 beside the gate leading into the city,
at the entrance, she cries aloud:
4 "To you, O people, I call out;
I raise my voice to all mankind.
5 You who are simple, gain prudence;
you who are foolish, set your hearts on it.[c]
6 Listen, for I have trustworthy things to say;
I open my lips to speak what is right.
7 My mouth speaks what is true,
for my lips detest wickedness.
8 All the words of my mouth are just;
none of them is crooked or perverse.
9 To the discerning all of them are right;
they are upright to those who have found
knowledge.
10 Choose my instruction instead of silver,
knowledge rather than choice gold,
11 for wisdom is more precious than rubies,
and nothing you desire can compare with her.

12 "I, wisdom, dwell together with prudence;
I possess knowledge and discretion.

---

[a] *22* Syriac (see also Septuagint); Hebrew *fool* [b] *22* The meaning of the Hebrew for this line is uncertain. [c] *5* Septuagint; Hebrew *foolish, instruct your minds*

13 To fear the LORD is to hate evil;
I hate pride and arrogance,
evil behavior and perverse speech.
14 Counsel and sound judgment are mine;
I have insight, I have power.
15 By me kings reign
and rulers issue decrees that are just;
16 by me princes govern,
and nobles — all who rule on earth.[a]
17 I love those who love me,
and those who seek me find me.
18 With me are riches and honor,
enduring wealth and prosperity.
19 My fruit is better than fine gold;
what I yield surpasses choice silver.
20 I walk in the way of righteousness,
along the paths of justice,
21 bestowing a rich inheritance on those who love me
and making their treasuries full.

22 "The LORD brought me forth as the first of his works,[b,c]
before his deeds of old;
23 I was formed long ages ago,
at the very beginning, when the world came to be.
24 When there were no watery depths, I was given birth,
when there were no springs overflowing with water;
25 before the mountains were settled in place,
before the hills, I was given birth,
26 before he made the world or its fields
or any of the dust of the earth.
27 I was there when he set the heavens in place,
when he marked out the horizon on the face of the deep,
28 when he established the clouds above
and fixed securely the fountains of the deep,
29 when he gave the sea its boundary
so the waters would not overstep his command,
and when he marked out the foundations of the earth.
30 Then I was constantly[d] at his side.
I was filled with delight day after day,
rejoicing always in his presence,
31 rejoicing in his whole world
and delighting in mankind.

32 "Now then, my children, listen to me;
blessed are those who keep my ways.
33 Listen to my instruction and be wise;
do not disregard it.
34 Blessed are those who listen to me,
watching daily at my doors,
waiting at my doorway.
35 For those who find me find life
and receive favor from the LORD.
36 But those who fail to find me harm themselves;
all who hate me love death."

[a] *16* Some Hebrew manuscripts and Septuagint; other Hebrew manuscripts *all righteous rulers* [b] *22* Or *way*; or *dominion* [c] *22* Or *The LORD possessed me at the beginning of his work*; or *The LORD brought me forth at the beginning of his work* [d] *30* Or *was the artisan*; or *was a little child*

THE WISDOM OF GOD

Throughout the first nine chapters of Proverbs, Solomon personified wisdom as a woman. Personification gives human characteristics to an abstract idea. For example, the phrase "Lady Justice is blind" personifies justice as someone who does not look at appearances, thus highlighting the ideal of objectivity in the justice system. Solomon presented wisdom as a woman for at least two reasons. First, wisdom is a feminine noun in Hebrew, and so the personification takes on the gender of the word. Second, Solomon appealed to his son to embrace the wisdom of Proverbs, and what would be more appealing to a young man than an alluring woman?

However, there are several indications that Solomon's personification of wisdom was more than merely a literary device. In Proverbs 8:22 – 31, Solomon heightened wisdom's status beyond his own knowledge or understanding. All true wisdom, he taught, is God's wisdom. Wisdom comes from God and accompanies him in all his works. The New Testament further reveals that Jesus is the wisdom of God (1Co 1:24,30). Consider the following facts:

First, Solomon describes wisdom as the first thing brought forth from God (Pr 8:22). Revelation 3:14 alludes to this exact phrasing in Proverbs 8:22 and applies it to Jesus. This statement does not mean that Jesus was created, but rather that he is supreme over the creation (Jn 1:1 – 3; Col 1:15). After all, he is God's one and only Son (Jn 3:16). He is the wisdom of God.

Second, wisdom existed prior to the creation of the world (Pr 8:23 – 26). The New Testament discloses the same thing about Jesus. The night of his betrayal, Jesus prayed, "And now, Father, glorify me in your presence with the glory I had with you before the world began" (Jn 17:5). Jesus existed before the creation — he is the wisdom of God.

Finally, Proverbs 8 says that not only did wisdom exist prior to the creation, but wisdom seems to have assisted in creating the world (vv. 27 – 31). The New Testament said the same thing about Jesus. Colossians 1:15 – 16 says, "The Son is the image of the invisible God, the firstborn over all creation. For in him all things were created." Like a firstborn son in the biblical world, Jesus had certain rights over creation since Jesus is the wisdom of God who assisted him in creating the world.

PROVERBS 9:10

THE FEAR OF THE LORD

According to Solomon, wisdom is based on the fear of the Lord. Proverbs opens with a similar refrain (1:7), demonstrating that the ability to obey all of the practical guidance found throughout Solomon's writings derives from the same source — the fear of the Lord. Often attempts are made to soften or minimize the nature of this fear, leading some to conclude that Solomon was merely referring to awe or reverence for God. Yet, the biblical notion of fearing God is far more holistic (Ecc 12:13 – 14). The power and judgment of God should cause frail and fallen humans to have a profound sense of fear and submission to the rightful ruler of all things because it is a fearful thing to fall into the hands of the living God (Heb 10:31). Christians should live in fear of God (Mt 10:28), and this fear is manifest in a life of obedience to God's commands (2Co 7:1). People like Joseph, who are marked by such wisdom, are often referred to as God-fearing individuals (Ge 42:18). Ultimately, however, it is only Jesus whose entire life was lived in the fear of God. Even as he faced death, Jesus willingly laid down his life in obedience to the Father's plan, demonstrating that his desire to obey God was greater than the fear of a brutal death (Lk 22:42). Empowered by the Spirit, Christians are transformed to fear God, and in so doing, find true wisdom.

Invitations of Wisdom and Folly

9 Wisdom has built her house;
she has set up[a] its seven pillars.
2 She has prepared her meat and mixed her wine;
she has also set her table.
3 She has sent out her servants, and she calls
from the highest point of the city,
4 "Let all who are simple come to my house!"
To those who have no sense she says,
5 "Come, eat my food
and drink the wine I have mixed.
6 Leave your simple ways and you will live;
walk in the way of insight."

7 Whoever corrects a mocker invites insults;
whoever rebukes the wicked incurs abuse.
8 Do not rebuke mockers or they will hate you;
rebuke the wise and they will love you.
9 Instruct the wise and they will be wiser still;
teach the righteous and they will add to their learning.

10 The fear of the LORD is the beginning of wisdom,
and knowledge of the Holy One is understanding.
11 For through wisdom[b] your days will be many,
and years will be added to your life.
12 If you are wise, your wisdom will reward you;
if you are a mocker, you alone will suffer.

13 Folly is an unruly woman;
she is simple and knows nothing.
14 She sits at the door of her house,
on a seat at the highest point of the city,
15 calling out to those who pass by,
who go straight on their way,
16 "Let all who are simple come to my house!"
To those who have no sense she says,
17 "Stolen water is sweet;
food eaten in secret is delicious!"
18 But little do they know that the dead are there,
that her guests are deep in the realm of the dead.

Proverbs of Solomon

10 The proverbs of Solomon:

A wise son brings joy to his father,
but a foolish son brings grief to his mother.

2 Ill-gotten treasures have no lasting value,
but righteousness delivers from death.

3 The LORD does not let the righteous go hungry,
but he thwarts the craving of the wicked.

4 Lazy hands make for poverty,
but diligent hands bring wealth.

5 He who gathers crops in summer is a prudent son,
but he who sleeps during harvest is a disgraceful son.

---

[a] *1* Septuagint, Syriac and Targum; Hebrew *has hewn out* [b] *11* Septuagint, Syriac and Targum; Hebrew *me*

6 Blessings crown the head of the righteous,
but violence overwhelms the mouth of the wicked.[a]

7 The name of the righteous is used in blessings,[b]
but the name of the wicked will rot.

8 The wise in heart accept commands,
but a chattering fool comes to ruin.

9 Whoever walks in integrity walks securely,
but whoever takes crooked paths will be found out.

10 Whoever winks maliciously causes grief,
and a chattering fool comes to ruin.

11 The mouth of the righteous is a fountain of life,
but the mouth of the wicked conceals violence.

12 Hatred stirs up conflict,
but love covers over all wrongs.

13 Wisdom is found on the lips of the discerning,
but a rod is for the back of one who has no sense.

14 The wise store up knowledge,
but the mouth of a fool invites ruin.

15 The wealth of the rich is their fortified city,
but poverty is the ruin of the poor.

16 The wages of the righteous is life,
but the earnings of the wicked are sin and death.

17 Whoever heeds discipline shows the way to life,
but whoever ignores correction leads others astray.

18 Whoever conceals hatred with lying lips
and spreads slander is a fool.

19 Sin is not ended by multiplying words,
but the prudent hold their tongues.

20 The tongue of the righteous is choice silver,
but the heart of the wicked is of little value.

21 The lips of the righteous nourish many,
but fools die for lack of sense.

22 The blessing of the LORD brings wealth,
without painful toil for it.

23 A fool finds pleasure in wicked schemes,
but a person of understanding delights in wisdom.

24 What the wicked dread will overtake them;
what the righteous desire will be granted.

25 When the storm has swept by, the wicked are gone,
but the righteous stand firm forever.

26 As vinegar to the teeth and smoke to the eyes,
so are sluggards to those who send them.

27 The fear of the LORD adds length to life,
but the years of the wicked are cut short.

28 The prospect of the righteous is joy,
but the hopes of the wicked come to nothing.

---

[a] 6 Or *righteous, / but the mouth of the wicked conceals violence* [b] 7 See Gen. 48:20.

LIVING GOD'S WAY

Solomon described the human life as a walk. All people move though life like a walk, yet not all people walk through life in the same way. Some do so in crooked and perverse ways, while others walk uprightly. The way in which they walk is influenced, not by their aptitude or ability, but by their companion along life's journey. Those who walk with God follow him into paths of righteousness; those who do not walk with him follow "the ways of this world and of the ruler of the kingdom of the air, the spirit who is now at work in those who are disobedient" (Eph 2:2).

Godly men and women of faith are singled out as those who walk with God. For example, the enigmatic figure Enoch "walked faithfully with God" and was taken by God directly to his presence at the end of his life (Ge 5:22 – 24; Heb 11:5). Noah, who was spared the destruction brought about by the flood, "was a righteous man, blameless among the people of his time, and he walked faithfully with God" (Ge 6:9; Heb 11:7). Likewise, Abraham trusted God and walked with him, though he did not know where he was going (Ge 12:1 – 3; Heb 11:8). In Jesus' day, his disciples literally walked with him as they followed him to fish for people (Mt 4:19). As the Good Shepherd, God knows how best to lead his people to green pastures and still waters (Ps 23:1 – 2). His children know his voice and follow his leadership because they know that he guides them in the path of life (Jn 10:1 – 6).

It is impossible to walk with God apart from Jesus. All people, by virtue of their inborn sin nature, live counter to God's wisdom and are unwilling to follow his leadership. Jesus was the only man who ever followed God's path perfectly. He walked with God — each day and each moment of each day. He earned a righteous standing before the Father, more than sinners could ever produce on their own. By grace, he gives his righteous standing to his followers, who are seen by God as having lived the upright life God demands (2Co 5:17 – 21). This gift of righteousness then motivates and mobilizes God's people to walk in a manner worthy of their calling, with God as their constant companion through life's journey (Eph 4:1).

[29] The way of the LORD is a refuge for the blameless,
but it is the ruin of those who do evil.

[30] The righteous will never be uprooted,
but the wicked will not remain in the land.

[31] From the mouth of the righteous comes the fruit of wisdom,
but a perverse tongue will be silenced.

[32] The lips of the righteous know what finds favor,
but the mouth of the wicked only what is perverse.

11 The LORD detests dishonest scales,
but accurate weights find favor with him.

[2] When pride comes, then comes disgrace,
but with humility comes wisdom.

[3] The integrity of the upright guides them,
but the unfaithful are destroyed by their duplicity.

[4] Wealth is worthless in the day of wrath,
but righteousness delivers from death.

[5] The righteousness of the blameless makes their paths straight,
but the wicked are brought down by their own wickedness.

[6] The righteousness of the upright delivers them,
but the unfaithful are trapped by evil desires.

[7] Hopes placed in mortals die with them;
all the promise of[a] their power comes to nothing.

[8] The righteous person is rescued from trouble,
and it falls on the wicked instead.

[9] With their mouths the godless destroy their neighbors,
but through knowledge the righteous escape.

[10] When the righteous prosper, the city rejoices;
when the wicked perish, there are shouts of joy.

[11] Through the blessing of the upright a city is exalted,
but by the mouth of the wicked it is destroyed.

[12] Whoever derides their neighbor has no sense,
but the one who has understanding holds their tongue.

[13] A gossip betrays a confidence,
but a trustworthy person keeps a secret.

[14] For lack of guidance a nation falls,
but victory is won through many advisers.

[15] Whoever puts up security for a stranger will surely suffer,
but whoever refuses to shake hands in pledge is safe.

[16] A kindhearted woman gains honor,
but ruthless men gain only wealth.

[17] Those who are kind benefit themselves,
but the cruel bring ruin on themselves.

[18] A wicked person earns deceptive wages,
but the one who sows righteousness reaps a sure reward.

[a] 7 Two Hebrew manuscripts; most Hebrew manuscripts, Vulgate, Syriac and Targum *When the wicked die, their hope perishes; / all they expected from*

PROVERBS 11:2

ATTITUDE

Pride and humility are defining traits of the human heart. No one can see either characteristic, but the manifestations of both pride and humility are seen in the actions of all humans. Throughout the proverbs, Solomon connected pride with foolishness and ultimate destruction (Pr 16:18). In contrast, he linked humility with wisdom and the fear of the Lord, leading to life and blessing (Pr 22:4; 29:23). Pride vaunts the person to the supreme arbitrator of life and demonstrates a lack of submission to God as the One who knows how best life should be lived. Discounting God's wisdom through human pride invariably leads to destruction in this life and the next. Humility, in contrast, affirms God is sovereign, omnipotent and omniscient. He knows how life should be lived far better than humans, whose vision is always limited in this life (1Co 13:12). God stands in opposition to the proud, but promises his faithfulness and grace to the humble in heart (Jas 4:6).

19 Truly the righteous attain life,
but whoever pursues evil finds death.

20 The LORD detests those whose hearts are perverse,
but he delights in those whose ways are blameless.

21 Be sure of this: The wicked will not go unpunished,
but those who are righteous will go free.

22 Like a gold ring in a pig's snout
is a beautiful woman who shows no discretion.

23 The desire of the righteous ends only in good,
but the hope of the wicked only in wrath.

24 One person gives freely, yet gains even more;
another withholds unduly, but comes to poverty.

25 A generous person will prosper;
whoever refreshes others will be refreshed.

26 People curse the one who hoards grain,
but they pray God's blessing on the one who is willing
to sell.

27 Whoever seeks good finds favor,
but evil comes to one who searches for it.

28 Those who trust in their riches will fall,
but the righteous will thrive like a green leaf.

29 Whoever brings ruin on their family will inherit only wind,
and the fool will be servant to the wise.

30 The fruit of the righteous is a tree of life,
and the one who is wise saves lives.

31 If the righteous receive their due on earth,
how much more the ungodly and the sinner!

12 Whoever loves discipline loves knowledge,
but whoever hates correction is stupid.

2 Good people obtain favor from the LORD,
but he condemns those who devise wicked schemes.

3 No one can be established through wickedness,
but the righteous cannot be uprooted.

4 A wife of noble character is her husband's crown,
but a disgraceful wife is like decay in his bones.

5 The plans of the righteous are just,
but the advice of the wicked is deceitful.

6 The words of the wicked lie in wait for blood,
but the speech of the upright rescues them.

7 The wicked are overthrown and are no more,
but the house of the righteous stands firm.

8 A person is praised according to their prudence,
and one with a warped mind is despised.

9 Better to be a nobody and yet have a servant
than pretend to be somebody and have no food.

10 The righteous care for the needs of their animals,
but the kindest acts of the wicked are cruel.

11 Those who work their land will have abundant food,
but those who chase fantasies have no sense.

12 The wicked desire the stronghold of evildoers,
but the root of the righteous endures.

13 Evildoers are trapped by their sinful talk,
and so the innocent escape trouble.

14 From the fruit of their lips people are filled with good things,
and the work of their hands brings them reward.

15 The way of fools seems right to them,
but the wise listen to advice.

16 Fools show their annoyance at once,
but the prudent overlook an insult.

17 An honest witness tells the truth,
but a false witness tells lies.

18 The words of the reckless pierce like swords,
but the tongue of the wise brings healing.

19 Truthful lips endure forever,
but a lying tongue lasts only a moment.

20 Deceit is in the hearts of those who plot evil,
but those who promote peace have joy.

21 No harm overtakes the righteous,
but the wicked have their fill of trouble.

22 The LORD detests lying lips,
but he delights in people who are trustworthy.

23 The prudent keep their knowledge to themselves,
but a fool's heart blurts out folly.

24 Diligent hands will rule,
but laziness ends in forced labor.

25 Anxiety weighs down the heart,
but a kind word cheers it up.

26 The righteous choose their friends carefully,
but the way of the wicked leads them astray.

27 The lazy do not roast[a] any game,
but the diligent feed on the riches of the hunt.

28 In the way of righteousness there is life;
along that path is immortality.

13 A wise son heeds his father's instruction,
but a mocker does not respond to rebukes.

2 From the fruit of their lips people enjoy good things,
but the unfaithful have an appetite for violence.

3 Those who guard their lips preserve their lives,
but those who speak rashly will come to ruin.

4 A sluggard's appetite is never filled,
but the desires of the diligent are fully satisfied.

[a] 27 The meaning of the Hebrew for this word is uncertain.

PROVERBS 12:28

ETERNAL LIFE

When read apart from the context of the whole Scripture, this verse may lead readers to believe a false gospel. It seems to say that if anyone lives a righteous life, then that person will inherit eternal life. And this hints that a person's good works can secure a place in heaven after death. The problem is that absolutely no one is righteous (Ro 3:10). Taken within the full context of Scripture, Proverbs 12:28 is actually bad news for sinful humanity. The only righteous one in history is Jesus of Nazareth. Second Corinthians 5:21 describes the good news: "God made him who had no sin to be sin for us, so that in him we might become the righteousness of God." Christ has brought "life and immortality to light through the gospel" (2Ti 1:10). So, for those who believe in Christ, Proverbs 12:28 is the best news in the entire world because believers are counted as righteous in Christ and will receive eternal life.

5 The righteous hate what is false,
but the wicked make themselves a stench
and bring shame on themselves.

6 Righteousness guards the person of integrity,
but wickedness overthrows the sinner.

7 One person pretends to be rich, yet has nothing;
another pretends to be poor, yet has great wealth.

8 A person's riches may ransom their life,
but the poor cannot respond to threatening rebukes.

9 The light of the righteous shines brightly,
but the lamp of the wicked is snuffed out.

10 Where there is strife, there is pride,
but wisdom is found in those who take advice.

11 Dishonest money dwindles away,
but whoever gathers money little by little makes it grow.

12 Hope deferred makes the heart sick,
but a longing fulfilled is a tree of life.

13 Whoever scorns instruction will pay for it,
but whoever respects a command is rewarded.

14 The teaching of the wise is a fountain of life,
turning a person from the snares of death.

15 Good judgment wins favor,
but the way of the unfaithful leads to their destruction.[a]

16 All who are prudent act with[b] knowledge,
but fools expose their folly.

17 A wicked messenger falls into trouble,
but a trustworthy envoy brings healing.

18 Whoever disregards discipline comes to poverty and shame,
but whoever heeds correction is honored.

19 A longing fulfilled is sweet to the soul,
but fools detest turning from evil.

20 Walk with the wise and become wise,
for a companion of fools suffers harm.

21 Trouble pursues the sinner,
but the righteous are rewarded with good things.

22 A good person leaves an inheritance for their children's
children,
but a sinner's wealth is stored up for the righteous.

23 An unplowed field produces food for the poor,
but injustice sweeps it away.

24 Whoever spares the rod hates their children,
but the one who loves their children is careful to discipline
them.

25 The righteous eat to their hearts' content,
but the stomach of the wicked goes hungry.

---

[a] 15 Septuagint and Syriac; the meaning of the Hebrew for this phrase is uncertain.
[b] 16 Or *prudent protect themselves through*

14 The wise woman builds her house,
but with her own hands the foolish one tears hers down.

2 Whoever fears the LORD walks uprightly,
but those who despise him are devious in their ways.

3 A fool's mouth lashes out with pride,
but the lips of the wise protect them.

4 Where there are no oxen, the manger is empty,
but from the strength of an ox come abundant harvests.

5 An honest witness does not deceive,
but a false witness pours out lies.

6 The mocker seeks wisdom and finds none,
but knowledge comes easily to the discerning.

7 Stay away from a fool,
for you will not find knowledge on their lips.

8 The wisdom of the prudent is to give thought to their ways,
but the folly of fools is deception.

9 Fools mock at making amends for sin,
but goodwill is found among the upright.

10 Each heart knows its own bitterness,
and no one else can share its joy.

11 The house of the wicked will be destroyed,
but the tent of the upright will flourish.

12 There is a way that appears to be right,
but in the end it leads to death.

13 Even in laughter the heart may ache,
and rejoicing may end in grief.

14 The faithless will be fully repaid for their ways,
and the good rewarded for theirs.

15 The simple believe anything,
but the prudent give thought to their steps.

16 The wise fear the LORD and shun evil,
but a fool is hotheaded and yet feels secure.

17 A quick-tempered person does foolish things,
and the one who devises evil schemes is hated.

18 The simple inherit folly,
but the prudent are crowned with knowledge.

19 Evildoers will bow down in the presence of the good,
and the wicked at the gates of the righteous.

20 The poor are shunned even by their neighbors,
but the rich have many friends.

21 It is a sin to despise one's neighbor,
but blessed is the one who is kind to the needy.

22 Do not those who plot evil go astray?
But those who plan what is good find[a] love and faithfulness.

23 All hard work brings a profit,
but mere talk leads only to poverty.

---

[a] 22 Or *show*

24 The wealth of the wise is their crown,
but the folly of fools yields folly.

25 A truthful witness saves lives,
but a false witness is deceitful.

26 Whoever fears the LORD has a secure fortress,
and for their children it will be a refuge.

27 The fear of the LORD is a fountain of life,
turning a person from the snares of death.

28 A large population is a king's glory,
but without subjects a prince is ruined.

29 Whoever is patient has great understanding,
but one who is quick-tempered displays folly.

30 A heart at peace gives life to the body,
but envy rots the bones.

31 Whoever oppresses the poor shows contempt for their Maker,
but whoever is kind to the needy honors God.

32 When calamity comes, the wicked are brought down,
but even in death the righteous seek refuge in God.

33 Wisdom reposes in the heart of the discerning
and even among fools she lets herself be known.[a]

34 Righteousness exalts a nation,
but sin condemns any people.

35 A king delights in a wise servant,
but a shameful servant arouses his fury.

15 A gentle answer turns away wrath,
but a harsh word stirs up anger.

2 The tongue of the wise adorns knowledge,
but the mouth of the fool gushes folly.

3 The eyes of the LORD are everywhere,
keeping watch on the wicked and the good.

4 The soothing tongue is a tree of life,
but a perverse tongue crushes the spirit.

5 A fool spurns a parent's discipline,
but whoever heeds correction shows prudence.

6 The house of the righteous contains great treasure,
but the income of the wicked brings ruin.

7 The lips of the wise spread knowledge,
but the hearts of fools are not upright.

8 The LORD detests the sacrifice of the wicked,
but the prayer of the upright pleases him.

9 The LORD detests the way of the wicked,
but he loves those who pursue righteousness.

10 Stern discipline awaits anyone who leaves the path;
the one who hates correction will die.

---

[a] *33* Hebrew; Septuagint and Syriac *discerning / but in the heart of fools she is not known*

[11] Death and Destruction[a] lie open before the LORD —
how much more do human hearts!

[12] Mockers resent correction,
so they avoid the wise.

[13] A happy heart makes the face cheerful,
but heartache crushes the spirit.

[14] The discerning heart seeks knowledge,
but the mouth of a fool feeds on folly.

[15] All the days of the oppressed are wretched,
but the cheerful heart has a continual feast.

[16] Better a little with the fear of the LORD
than great wealth with turmoil.

[17] Better a small serving of vegetables with love
than a fattened calf with hatred.

[18] A hot-tempered person stirs up conflict,
but the one who is patient calms a quarrel.

[19] The way of the sluggard is blocked with thorns,
but the path of the upright is a highway.

[20] A wise son brings joy to his father,
but a foolish man despises his mother.

[21] Folly brings joy to one who has no sense,
but whoever has understanding keeps a straight course.

[22] Plans fail for lack of counsel,
but with many advisers they succeed.

[23] A person finds joy in giving an apt reply —
and how good is a timely word!

[24] The path of life leads upward for the prudent
to keep them from going down to the realm of the dead.

[25] The LORD tears down the house of the proud,
but he sets the widow's boundary stones in place.

[26] The LORD detests the thoughts of the wicked,
but gracious words are pure in his sight.

[27] The greedy bring ruin to their households,
but the one who hates bribes will live.

[28] The heart of the righteous weighs its answers,
but the mouth of the wicked gushes evil.

[29] The LORD is far from the wicked,
but he hears the prayer of the righteous.

[30] Light in a messenger's eyes brings joy to the heart,
and good news gives health to the bones.

[31] Whoever heeds life-giving correction
will be at home among the wise.

[32] Those who disregard discipline despise themselves,
but the one who heeds correction gains understanding.

[33] Wisdom's instruction is to fear the LORD,
and humility comes before honor.

[a] 11 Hebrew *Abaddon*

PROVERBS 15:29

PRAYER

While God is aware of every prayer, this verse says that in a certain sense, he does not "hear" every prayer. The righteous can pray to God and be heard, but God is far from the wicked. That does not mean that God does not have any awareness of the prayers of the wicked, but rather that he does not respond to them. Isaiah 59:2 says something very similar: "But your iniquities have separated you from your God; your sins have hidden his face from you, so that he will not hear." Most people do not think they are wicked, but Proverbs says that the prayers of those who ignore God's law are detestable to him (28:9). All people have sinned and broken God's law. So can anyone hope to be heard by God? Jesus Christ — the righteous one — died for people so that they could be accounted righteous before God, and then he entered into the heavenly sanctuary as their mediator before God (2Co 5:21; 1Ti 2:5; Heb 7:25; 9:24). That's why people pray in Jesus' name: it is only through Jesus that the prayers of sinful humans can be heard and answered!

PROVERBS 16:4 – 6

THROUGH LOVE AND FAITHFULNESS

Solomon affirmed that God is ultimately in control and his good purposes will prevail, even in spite of human sin. Even the wicked, who seem to avoid destruction in this life, will surely face the judgment of God. The prideful person will not escape the coming day of disaster, and the folly of pride will be exposed on that day. In contrast, those whose lives are marked by humility — who understand the fear of the Lord — they will experience the love and faithfulness of God and in turn love God and walk faithfully with him. This is the glorious truth about the character of God. Though he is holy and pure, he is not quick to anger, nor is he vindictive or capricious in his wrath. He is "the LORD, the LORD, the compassionate and gracious God, slow to anger, abounding in love and faithfulness" (Ex 34:6). God extends mercy in allowing prideful rebels time to confess their sins and humble themselves before the mighty hand of God. As Peter says, "He is patient with you, not wanting anyone to perish, but everyone to come to repentance" (2Pe 3:9). Each day God gives is evidence of his love, and those who hear his voice should turn to him in faith as long as today is called today (Heb 3:12 – 15).

16 To humans belong the plans of the heart,
but from the LORD comes the proper answer of the tongue.

2 All a person's ways seem pure to them,
but motives are weighed by the LORD.

3 Commit to the LORD whatever you do,
and he will establish your plans.

4 The LORD works out everything to its proper end —
even the wicked for a day of disaster.

5 The LORD detests all the proud of heart.
Be sure of this: They will not go unpunished.

6 Through love and faithfulness sin is atoned for;
through the fear of the LORD evil is avoided.

7 When the LORD takes pleasure in anyone's way,
he causes their enemies to make peace with them.

8 Better a little with righteousness
than much gain with injustice.

9 In their hearts humans plan their course,
but the LORD establishes their steps.

10 The lips of a king speak as an oracle,
and his mouth does not betray justice.

11 Honest scales and balances belong to the LORD;
all the weights in the bag are of his making.

12 Kings detest wrongdoing,
for a throne is established through righteousness.

13 Kings take pleasure in honest lips;
they value the one who speaks what is right.

14 A king's wrath is a messenger of death,
but the wise will appease it.

15 When a king's face brightens, it means life;
his favor is like a rain cloud in spring.

16 How much better to get wisdom than gold,
to get insight rather than silver!

17 The highway of the upright avoids evil;
those who guard their ways preserve their lives.

18 Pride goes before destruction,
a haughty spirit before a fall.

19 Better to be lowly in spirit along with the oppressed
than to share plunder with the proud.

20 Whoever gives heed to instruction prospers,[a]
and blessed is the one who trusts in the LORD.

21 The wise in heart are called discerning,
and gracious words promote instruction.[b]

22 Prudence is a fountain of life to the prudent,
but folly brings punishment to fools.

[a] 20 Or *whoever speaks prudently finds what is good* [b] 21 Or *words make a person persuasive*

[23] The hearts of the wise make their mouths prudent,
and their lips promote instruction.[a]

[24] Gracious words are a honeycomb,
sweet to the soul and healing to the bones.

[25] There is a way that appears to be right,
but in the end it leads to death.

[26] The appetite of laborers works for them;
their hunger drives them on.

[27] A scoundrel plots evil,
and on their lips it is like a scorching fire.

[28] A perverse person stirs up conflict,
and a gossip separates close friends.

[29] A violent person entices their neighbor
and leads them down a path that is not good.

[30] Whoever winks with their eye is plotting perversity;
whoever purses their lips is bent on evil.

[31] Gray hair is a crown of splendor;
it is attained in the way of righteousness.

[32] Better a patient person than a warrior,
one with self-control than one who takes a city.

[33] The lot is cast into the lap,
but its every decision is from the LORD.

17 Better a dry crust with peace and quiet
than a house full of feasting, with strife.

[2] A prudent servant will rule over a disgraceful son
and will share the inheritance as one of the family.

[3] The crucible for silver and the furnace for gold,
but the LORD tests the heart.

[4] A wicked person listens to deceitful lips;
a liar pays attention to a destructive tongue.

[5] Whoever mocks the poor shows contempt for their Maker;
whoever gloats over disaster will not go unpunished.

[6] Children's children are a crown to the aged,
and parents are the pride of their children.

[7] Eloquent lips are unsuited to a godless fool—
how much worse lying lips to a ruler!

[8] A bribe is seen as a charm by the one who gives it;
they think success will come at every turn.

[9] Whoever would foster love covers over an offense,
but whoever repeats the matter separates close friends.

[10] A rebuke impresses a discerning person
more than a hundred lashes a fool.

[11] Evildoers foster rebellion against God;
the messenger of death will be sent against them.

[12] Better to meet a bear robbed of her cubs
than a fool bent on folly.

---

[a] 23 Or *prudent / and make their lips persuasive*

PROVERBS 16:25

NO ALTERNATE ROUTE

The wisdom of man is folly in the eyes of God. Solomon proclaimed a reality that fallen sinners know all too well. The pseudo-wisdom that guides life, more often than not, leads to destruction and disaster. Sinners who presume to know the best way to life often leave a wake of shattered dreams, broken promises and failure when they pursue their own plans.

What is true with minor decisions is also true on a grand scale. The path that many choose to follow leads to eternal destruction. There is a broad way that seems right to humans, but it ends in eternal separation from God. Jesus warns that many take this way of death (Mt 7:13). Few are those who walk the narrow path — the path to life — and find the joy and salvation that God offers (Mt 7:14). In fact, Jesus is the only one who perfectly walked the narrow way, faithfully obeying God at every turn. By walking this narrow path, Jesus did more than call sinners to follow his example. He gives those who trust him in faith the gift of eternal life. This is why Jesus is the only means of salvation. No one else walked the narrow path in the place of sinners. No one else earned a perfect standing before the Father. And no one else offered his perfect righteousness to sinners as a gift. For this reason Peter proclaimed, "Salvation is found in no one else, for there is no other name under heaven given to mankind by which we must be saved" (Ac 4:12).

The path of faith and repentance seems counterintuitive to many. Why not simply try harder to obey God, live a good life in comparison to the world's standards and seek to avoid major sins? Many try to follow this path that "seems right" only to find that it leads to disaster because, despite the best efforts of sinners, no one can obey God perfectly. Those who choose this path may hear the startling words from the Father on the last day: "I never knew you. Away from me" (Mt 7:23). God will only grant salvation to those who know they cannot walk the narrow way, but cling to the One who has, knowing that "in Christ Jesus" they, too, can avoid the way that leads to death and find the way that leads to life (Ro 8:1; Gal 3:26 – 28).

13 Evil will never leave the house
of one who pays back evil for good.

14 Starting a quarrel is like breaching a dam;
so drop the matter before a dispute breaks out.

15 Acquitting the guilty and condemning the innocent—
the LORD detests them both.

16 Why should fools have money in hand to buy wisdom,
when they are not able to understand it?

17 A friend loves at all times,
and a brother is born for a time of adversity.

18 One who has no sense shakes hands in pledge
and puts up security for a neighbor.

19 Whoever loves a quarrel loves sin;
whoever builds a high gate invites destruction.

20 One whose heart is corrupt does not prosper;
one whose tongue is perverse falls into trouble.

21 To have a fool for a child brings grief;
there is no joy for the parent of a godless fool.

22 A cheerful heart is good medicine,
but a crushed spirit dries up the bones.

23 The wicked accept bribes in secret
to pervert the course of justice.

24 A discerning person keeps wisdom in view,
but a fool's eyes wander to the ends of the earth.

25 A foolish son brings grief to his father
and bitterness to the mother who bore him.

26 If imposing a fine on the innocent is not good,
surely to flog honest officials is not right.

27 The one who has knowledge uses words with
restraint,
and whoever has understanding is even-tempered.

28 Even fools are thought wise if they keep silent,
and discerning if they hold their tongues.

18 An unfriendly person pursues selfish ends
and against all sound judgment starts quarrels.

2 Fools find no pleasure in understanding
but delight in airing their own opinions.

3 When wickedness comes, so does contempt,
and with shame comes reproach.

4 The words of the mouth are deep waters,
but the fountain of wisdom is a rushing stream.

5 It is not good to be partial to the wicked
and so deprive the innocent of justice.

6 The lips of fools bring them strife,
and their mouths invite a beating.

7 The mouths of fools are their undoing,
and their lips are a snare to their very lives.

[8] The words of a gossip are like choice morsels;
they go down to the inmost parts.

[9] One who is slack in his work
is brother to one who destroys.

[10] The name of the LORD is a fortified tower;
the righteous run to it and are safe.

[11] The wealth of the rich is their fortified city;
they imagine it a wall too high to scale.

[12] Before a downfall the heart is haughty,
but humility comes before honor.

[13] To answer before listening—
that is folly and shame.

[14] The human spirit can endure in sickness,
but a crushed spirit who can bear?

[15] The heart of the discerning acquires knowledge,
for the ears of the wise seek it out.

[16] A gift opens the way
and ushers the giver into the presence of the great.

[17] In a lawsuit the first to speak seems right,
until someone comes forward and cross-examines.

[18] Casting the lot settles disputes
and keeps strong opponents apart.

[19] A brother wronged is more unyielding than a fortified city;
disputes are like the barred gates of a citadel.

[20] From the fruit of their mouth a person's stomach is filled;
with the harvest of their lips they are satisfied.

[21] The tongue has the power of life and death,
and those who love it will eat its fruit.

[22] He who finds a wife finds what is good
and receives favor from the LORD.

[23] The poor plead for mercy,
but the rich answer harshly.

[24] One who has unreliable friends soon comes to ruin,
but there is a friend who sticks closer than a brother.

19 Better the poor whose walk is blameless
than a fool whose lips are perverse.

[2] Desire without knowledge is not good—
how much more will hasty feet miss the way!

[3] A person's own folly leads to their ruin,
yet their heart rages against the LORD.

[4] Wealth attracts many friends,
but even the closest friend of the poor person deserts
them.

[5] A false witness will not go unpunished,
and whoever pours out lies will not go free.

[6] Many curry favor with a ruler,
and everyone is the friend of one who gives gifts.

PROVERBS 18:24

FRIENDSHIP

Everyone has experienced to some extent the force of the first line in this verse: "One who has unreliable friends soon comes to ruin." Unfortunately, no one is exempt from being let down and letting others down. This proverb is a reminder that everyone needs a friend who is more than just a casual association—and each person needs to be that kind of friend to others. People need true friends who will be closer and more loyal than even blood relatives. This proverb clearly points to Jesus Christ, who is a friend that is better than family. Jesus described what true friendship is: "Greater love has no one than this: to lay down one's life for one's friends" (Jn 15:13). Jesus displayed the greatest love and friendship to us through his death on the cross. In Christ, we have the friend we need (Jn 15:15), and we can become the kind of friend that others need.

[7] The poor are shunned by all their relatives—
how much more do their friends avoid them!
Though the poor pursue them with pleading,
they are nowhere to be found.[a]

[8] The one who gets wisdom loves life;
the one who cherishes understanding will soon prosper.

[9] A false witness will not go unpunished,
and whoever pours out lies will perish.

[10] It is not fitting for a fool to live in luxury—
how much worse for a slave to rule over princes!

[11] A person's wisdom yields patience;
it is to one's glory to overlook an offense.

[12] A king's rage is like the roar of a lion,
but his favor is like dew on the grass.

[13] A foolish child is a father's ruin,
and a quarrelsome wife is like
the constant dripping of a leaky roof.

[14] Houses and wealth are inherited from parents,
but a prudent wife is from the LORD.

[15] Laziness brings on deep sleep,
and the shiftless go hungry.

[16] Whoever keeps commandments keeps their life,
but whoever shows contempt for their ways will die.

[17] Whoever is kind to the poor lends to the LORD,
and he will reward them for what they have done.

[18] Discipline your children, for in that there is hope;
do not be a willing party to their death.

[19] A hot-tempered person must pay the penalty;
rescue them, and you will have to do it again.

[20] Listen to advice and accept discipline,
and at the end you will be counted among the wise.

[21] Many are the plans in a person's heart,
but it is the LORD's purpose that prevails.

[22] What a person desires is unfailing love[b];
better to be poor than a liar.

[23] The fear of the LORD leads to life;
then one rests content, untouched by trouble.

[24] A sluggard buries his hand in the dish;
he will not even bring it back to his mouth!

[25] Flog a mocker, and the simple will learn prudence;
rebuke the discerning, and they will gain knowledge.

[26] Whoever robs their father and drives out their mother
is a child who brings shame and disgrace.

[27] Stop listening to instruction, my son,
and you will stray from the words of knowledge.

[a] 7 The meaning of the Hebrew for this sentence is uncertain. [b] 22 Or *Greed is a person's shame*

KINDNESS TO THE POOR

Compassion for the poor is an unmistakable mark of God's people. Throughout the Old Testament, the nation of Israel was consistently reminded of their responsibility to care for the poor, the outcast and the sojourner in their midst. This care was to begin with their own people, as they were to see to it that there were no poor among them (Dt 15:7 – 8). Yet, it was also to extend beyond the ranks of the Israelites, to all those to whom they came in contact (Lev 19:34).

The pattern continues in the New Testament. In Luke 10 an expert in religious law asked Jesus what he must do in order to inherit eternal life. The scholar, attempting to justify himself, tried to prove that he had, in fact, loved God and his neighbor. But he asked Jesus to identify his neighbor. Jesus answered by telling a parable of a man who was robbed, beaten and left for dead. Two men, who should have known their responsibility to meet this man's needs, passed by on the other side of the road. But the third man, a hated Samaritan, modeled neighbor-love by caring for the beaten man and seeing to it that his needs were met. The last one, the most unlikely of all characters in the story, was the one followers of Jesus should emulate. Such compassion and love is only possible as God's people come to understand that they are, ultimately, the man left for dead on the side of the road. God, like the Samaritan, came to their aid and saved them when they could do nothing to save themselves. Paul reminded the church in Corinth that their love and generosity should be motivated by a deep reflection on this gospel truth: "For you know the grace of our Lord Jesus Christ, that though he was rich, yet for your sake he became poor, so that you through his poverty might become rich" (2Co 8:9).

The New Testament church is marked by this type of gospel understanding through their care for one another. Luke documents the nature of the early church, pointing out that they "sold property and possessions to give to anyone who had need" (Ac 2:45). In so doing they proved to know and follow God. As John writes, "If anyone has material possessions and sees a brother or sister in need but has no pity on them, how can the love of God be in that person? Dear children, let us not love with words or speech but with actions and in truth" (1Jn 3:17 – 18).

[28] A corrupt witness mocks at justice,
and the mouth of the wicked gulps down evil.

[29] Penalties are prepared for mockers,
and beatings for the backs of fools.

20 Wine is a mocker and beer a brawler;
whoever is led astray by them is not wise.

[2] A king's wrath strikes terror like the roar of a lion;
those who anger him forfeit their lives.

[3] It is to one's honor to avoid strife,
but every fool is quick to quarrel.

[4] Sluggards do not plow in season;
so at harvest time they look but find nothing.

[5] The purposes of a person's heart are deep waters,
but one who has insight draws them out.

[6] Many claim to have unfailing love,
but a faithful person who can find?

[7] The righteous lead blameless lives;
blessed are their children after them.

[8] When a king sits on his throne to judge,
he winnows out all evil with his eyes.

[9] Who can say, "I have kept my heart pure;
I am clean and without sin"?

[10] Differing weights and differing measures—
the LORD detests them both.

[11] Even small children are known by their actions,
so is their conduct really pure and upright?

[12] Ears that hear and eyes that see—
the LORD has made them both.

[13] Do not love sleep or you will grow poor;
stay awake and you will have food to spare.

[14] "It's no good, it's no good!" says the buyer—
then goes off and boasts about the purchase.

[15] Gold there is, and rubies in abundance,
but lips that speak knowledge are a rare jewel.

[16] Take the garment of one who puts up security for a
stranger;
hold it in pledge if it is done for an outsider.

[17] Food gained by fraud tastes sweet,
but one ends up with a mouth full of gravel.

[18] Plans are established by seeking advice;
so if you wage war, obtain guidance.

[19] A gossip betrays a confidence;
so avoid anyone who talks too much.

[20] If someone curses their father or mother,
their lamp will be snuffed out in pitch darkness.

[21] An inheritance claimed too soon
will not be blessed at the end.

PROVERBS 20:1

ALCOHOL

Drunkenness is condemned throughout the Bible. Here, Solomon noted the outcome of drunkenness—it produces sin in one's actions and speech. These sinful actions stem from the control alcohol exercises over the one who overindulges. Because this person is controlled by alcohol, he or she acts in foolish and sinful ways. In contrast, God's people are to be controlled by his Spirit, who dwells within them (Eph 5:18). Those who are filled with the Spirit and led according to his wishes are guided into all truth and protected from the type of sin that results from drunkenness (Jn 16:13). What makes alcohol so destructive is that it controls a person, whereas God's Spirit desires to have complete control. Those controlled by the Spirit are empowered to produce godly characteristics such as love, joy, peace, kindness, gentleness, and self-control (Gal 5:22–23). These godly fruits are only produced in the heart of one who is controlled by God's Spirit.

[22] Do not say, "I'll pay you back for this wrong!"
Wait for the LORD, and he will avenge you.

[23] The LORD detests differing weights,
and dishonest scales do not please him.

[24] A person's steps are directed by the LORD.
How then can anyone understand their own way?

[25] It is a trap to dedicate something rashly
and only later to consider one's vows.

[26] A wise king winnows out the wicked;
he drives the threshing wheel over them.

[27] The human spirit is[a] the lamp of the LORD
that sheds light on one's inmost being.

[28] Love and faithfulness keep a king safe;
through love his throne is made secure.

[29] The glory of young men is their strength,
gray hair the splendor of the old.

[30] Blows and wounds scrub away evil,
and beatings purge the inmost being.

21 In the LORD's hand the king's heart is a stream of water
that he channels toward all who please him.

[2] A person may think their own ways are right,
but the LORD weighs the heart.

[3] To do what is right and just
is more acceptable to the LORD than sacrifice.

[4] Haughty eyes and a proud heart—
the unplowed field of the wicked—produce sin.

[5] The plans of the diligent lead to profit
as surely as haste leads to poverty.

[6] A fortune made by a lying tongue
is a fleeting vapor and a deadly snare.[b]

[7] The violence of the wicked will drag them away,
for they refuse to do what is right.

[8] The way of the guilty is devious,
but the conduct of the innocent is upright.

[9] Better to live on a corner of the roof
than share a house with a quarrelsome wife.

[10] The wicked crave evil;
their neighbors get no mercy from them.

[11] When a mocker is punished, the simple gain wisdom;
by paying attention to the wise they get knowledge.

[12] The Righteous One[c] takes note of the house of the
wicked
and brings the wicked to ruin.

[13] Whoever shuts their ears to the cry of the poor
will also cry out and not be answered.

[a] 27 Or *A person's words are* [b] 6 Some Hebrew manuscripts, Septuagint and Vulgate; most Hebrew manuscripts *vapor for those who seek death* [c] 12 Or *The righteous person*

PROVERBS 21:12

THE RIGHTEOUS ONE

Though Solomon was the wisest man who ever lived (until Jesus came), there is a Righteous One who is beyond compare. Solomon portrayed this one as sovereign over all human history and watching the actions of all those whom he made. This same Righteous One looks over the earth seeking "to strengthen those whose hearts are fully committed to him" (2Ch 16:9). Here, the same One notices the rebellion of the wicked and promises to bring them to ruin. The psalmist lamented the reality that, in this life, it may often seem that the wicked prosper and suffer no harm for their sin (Ps 73:3). But God is not blind to their sin. He sees. He knows. And he will judge. Should they fail to repent, God will cast them away from his presence forever (Mt 25:30). The Righteous One will not allow sin to go unpunished. Thankfully, God provided a way to maintain his righteousness and yet punish sin by pouring out his wrath on his Son (Ro 3:21–26). Faith in Jesus' finished work is the only hope all sinners have for escaping sure ruin from the hand of the Righteous One.

[14] A gift given in secret soothes anger,
and a bribe concealed in the cloak pacifies great wrath.

[15] When justice is done, it brings joy to the righteous
but terror to evildoers.

[16] Whoever strays from the path of prudence
comes to rest in the company of the dead.

[17] Whoever loves pleasure will become poor;
whoever loves wine and olive oil will never be rich.

[18] The wicked become a ransom for the righteous,
and the unfaithful for the upright.

[19] Better to live in a desert
than with a quarrelsome and nagging wife.

[20] The wise store up choice food and olive oil,
but fools gulp theirs down.

[21] Whoever pursues righteousness and love
finds life, prosperity[a] and honor.

[22] One who is wise can go up against the city of the mighty
and pull down the stronghold in which they trust.

[23] Those who guard their mouths and their tongues
keep themselves from calamity.

[24] The proud and arrogant person — "Mocker" is his name —
behaves with insolent fury.

[25] The craving of a sluggard will be the death of him,
because his hands refuse to work.
[26] All day long he craves for more,
but the righteous give without sparing.

[27] The sacrifice of the wicked is detestable —
how much more so when brought with evil intent!

[28] A false witness will perish,
but a careful listener will testify successfully.

[29] The wicked put up a bold front,
but the upright give thought to their ways.

[30] There is no wisdom, no insight, no plan
that can succeed against the LORD.

[31] The horse is made ready for the day of battle,
but victory rests with the LORD.

22 A good name is more desirable than great riches;
to be esteemed is better than silver or gold.

[2] Rich and poor have this in common:
The LORD is the Maker of them all.

[3] The prudent see danger and take refuge,
but the simple keep going and pay the penalty.

[4] Humility is the fear of the LORD;
its wages are riches and honor and life.

[5] In the paths of the wicked are snares and pitfalls,
but those who would preserve their life stay far from them.

---

[a] 21 Or *righteousness*

PROVERBS 22:6

TRAIN A CHILD

Many Christian parents feel guilty when their children do not "turn out right," and some of that guilt finds its root in this verse (traditionally rendered "Train up a child in the way he should go; and when he is old, he will not depart from it"). The logic seems straightforward: If a parent has children who rebel, then that parent must not have raised them right. Yet, a proverb is not a prophecy or a promise. It is a general principle that God will use the discipline and instruction of the parents to start their children off in the way they should go, and the child will continue on that path, or return to it, when they are old. As such, it is a message of hope, even if the child seems to be rebelling from God at any given time. Children will, as a general rule, take what they've learned and integrate it into their personal walk with God as they age. Fallen sinners can find confidence that, though their parenting may seem inadequate and flawed, God will often use this instruction to point children to the way of life everlasting. Also, parents can find hope that God can convict the rebellious and bring them to repentance in his time.

6 Start children off on the way they should go,
and even when they are old they will not turn from it.

7 The rich rule over the poor,
and the borrower is slave to the lender.

8 Whoever sows injustice reaps calamity,
and the rod they wield in fury will be broken.

9 The generous will themselves be blessed,
for they share their food with the poor.

10 Drive out the mocker, and out goes strife;
quarrels and insults are ended.

11 One who loves a pure heart and who speaks with grace
will have the king for a friend.

12 The eyes of the LORD keep watch over knowledge,
but he frustrates the words of the unfaithful.

13 The sluggard says, "There's a lion outside!
I'll be killed in the public square!"

14 The mouth of an adulterous woman is a deep pit;
a man who is under the LORD's wrath falls into it.

15 Folly is bound up in the heart of a child,
but the rod of discipline will drive it far away.

16 One who oppresses the poor to increase his wealth
and one who gives gifts to the rich — both come to poverty.

Thirty Sayings of the Wise

Saying 1

17 Pay attention and turn your ear to the sayings of the wise;
apply your heart to what I teach,
18 for it is pleasing when you keep them in your heart
and have all of them ready on your lips.
19 So that your trust may be in the LORD,
I teach you today, even you.
20 Have I not written thirty sayings for you,
sayings of counsel and knowledge,
21 teaching you to be honest and to speak the truth,
so that you bring back truthful reports
to those you serve?

Saying 2

22 Do not exploit the poor because they are poor
and do not crush the needy in court,
23 for the LORD will take up their case
and will exact life for life.

Saying 3

24 Do not make friends with a hot-tempered person,
do not associate with one easily angered,
25 or you may learn their ways
and get yourself ensnared.

Saying 4

26 Do not be one who shakes hands in pledge
or puts up security for debts;

[27] if you lack the means to pay,
your very bed will be snatched from under you.

Saying 5

[28] Do not move an ancient boundary stone
set up by your ancestors.

Saying 6

[29] Do you see someone skilled in their work?
They will serve before kings;
they will not serve before officials of low rank.

Saying 7

23 When you sit to dine with a ruler,
note well what[a] is before you,
[2] and put a knife to your throat
if you are given to gluttony.
[3] Do not crave his delicacies,
for that food is deceptive.

Saying 8

[4] Do not wear yourself out to get rich;
do not trust your own cleverness.
[5] Cast but a glance at riches, and they are gone,
for they will surely sprout wings
and fly off to the sky like an eagle.

Saying 9

[6] Do not eat the food of a begrudging host,
do not crave his delicacies;
[7] for he is the kind of person
who is always thinking about the cost.[b]
"Eat and drink," he says to you,
but his heart is not with you.
[8] You will vomit up the little you have eaten
and will have wasted your compliments.

Saying 10

[9] Do not speak to fools,
for they will scorn your prudent words.

Saying 11

[10] Do not move an ancient boundary stone
or encroach on the fields of the fatherless,
[11] for their Defender is strong;
he will take up their case against you.

Saying 12

[12] Apply your heart to instruction
and your ears to words of knowledge.

Saying 13

[13] Do not withhold discipline from a child;
if you punish them with the rod, they will not die.

[a] *1* Or *who he is* [b] *7* Or *for as he thinks within himself, / so he is*; or *for as he puts on a feast, / so*

PROVERBS 23:4–5

CONTENTMENT

This passage joins a chorus of verses in Proverbs that urge a balance of diligence and contentment in life with what one has — rather than laziness or a workaholic craving for things that will not last. Jesus told a parable about a rich fool who focused entirely on acquiring and preserving his possessions, only to lose everything he had worked so hard for when he died (Lk 12:15–21). Hebrews gives a good perspective on the kind of contentment Proverbs urges: "Keep your lives free from the love of money and be content with what you have, because God has said, 'Never will I leave you; never will I forsake you.' So we say with confidence, 'The Lord is my helper; I will not be afraid. What can mere mortals do to me?'" (Heb 13:5–6). Believers do not ultimately look to money for help but to God. Trust Jesus and be content with what he has provided.

[14] Punish them with the rod
and save them from death.

Saying 14

[15] My son, if your heart is wise,
then my heart will be glad indeed;
[16] my inmost being will rejoice
when your lips speak what is right.

Saying 15

[17] Do not let your heart envy sinners,
but always be zealous for the fear of the LORD.
[18] There is surely a future hope for you,
and your hope will not be cut off.

Saying 16

[19] Listen, my son, and be wise,
and set your heart on the right path:
[20] Do not join those who drink too much wine
or gorge themselves on meat,
[21] for drunkards and gluttons become poor,
and drowsiness clothes them in rags.

Saying 17

[22] Listen to your father, who gave you life,
and do not despise your mother when she is old.
[23] Buy the truth and do not sell it—
wisdom, instruction and insight as well.
[24] The father of a righteous child has great joy;
a man who fathers a wise son rejoices in him.
[25] May your father and mother rejoice;
may she who gave you birth be joyful!

Saying 18

[26] My son, give me your heart
and let your eyes delight in my ways,
[27] for an adulterous woman is a deep pit,
and a wayward wife is a narrow well.
[28] Like a bandit she lies in wait
and multiplies the unfaithful among men.

Saying 19

[29] Who has woe? Who has sorrow?
Who has strife? Who has complaints?
Who has needless bruises? Who has bloodshot eyes?
[30] Those who linger over wine,
who go to sample bowls of mixed wine.
[31] Do not gaze at wine when it is red,
when it sparkles in the cup,
when it goes down smoothly!
[32] In the end it bites like a snake
and poisons like a viper.
[33] Your eyes will see strange sights,
and your mind will imagine confusing things.
[34] You will be like one sleeping on the high seas,
lying on top of the rigging.

PROVERBS 23:19–21

GLUTTONS AND DRUNKARDS

Overindulgence in food and drink, a sin which runs rampant today, brings terrible consequences. These verses recall the law commanding that rebellious sons who were gluttons and drunkards were to be executed outside the city gates (Dt 21:18–21). Interestingly, Jesus' opponents accused him of violating this principle because he spent time with a disreputable crowd. Jesus said, "The Son of Man came eating and drinking, and you say, 'Here is a glutton and a drunkard, a friend of tax collectors and sinners'" (Lk 7:34). Jesus not only associated with gluttons and drunkards, but he died the death that they should suffer for sin. Jesus was executed outside the city gates (Heb 13:12)—condemned by the elders and hung on a pole, or tree, under the curse of God (Gal 3:13). His death provides forgiveness for all who lack self-control, and he gives his Spirit to produce fruit (including self-control) in the lives of his followers (Gal 5:22–23).

35 "They hit me," you will say, "but I'm not hurt!
They beat me, but I don't feel it!
When will I wake up
so I can find another drink?"

Saying 20

24 Do not envy the wicked,
do not desire their company;
2 for their hearts plot violence,
and their lips talk about making trouble.

Saying 21

3 By wisdom a house is built,
and through understanding it is established;
4 through knowledge its rooms are filled
with rare and beautiful treasures.

Saying 22

5 The wise prevail through great power,
and those who have knowledge muster their strength.
6 Surely you need guidance to wage war,
and victory is won through many advisers.

Saying 23

7 Wisdom is too high for fools;
in the assembly at the gate they must not open their
mouths.

Saying 24

8 Whoever plots evil
will be known as a schemer.
9 The schemes of folly are sin,
and people detest a mocker.

Saying 25

10 If you falter in a time of trouble,
how small is your strength!
11 Rescue those being led away to death;
hold back those staggering toward slaughter.
12 If you say, "But we knew nothing about this,"
does not he who weighs the heart perceive it?
Does not he who guards your life know it?
Will he not repay everyone according to what they have
done?

Saying 26

13 Eat honey, my son, for it is good;
honey from the comb is sweet to your taste.
14 Know also that wisdom is like honey for you:
If you find it, there is a future hope for you,
and your hope will not be cut off.

Saying 27

15 Do not lurk like a thief near the house of the righteous,
do not plunder their dwelling place;
16 for though the righteous fall seven times, they rise again,
but the wicked stumble when calamity strikes.

Saying 28

[17] Do not gloat when your enemy falls;
when they stumble, do not let your heart rejoice,
[18] or the LORD will see and disapprove
and turn his wrath away from them.

Saying 29

[19] Do not fret because of evildoers
or be envious of the wicked,
[20] for the evildoer has no future hope,
and the lamp of the wicked will be snuffed out.

Saying 30

[21] Fear the LORD and the king, my son,
and do not join with rebellious officials,
[22] for those two will send sudden destruction on them,
and who knows what calamities they can bring?

Further Sayings of the Wise

[23] These also are sayings of the wise:

To show partiality in judging is not good:
[24] Whoever says to the guilty, "You are innocent,"
will be cursed by peoples and denounced by nations.
[25] But it will go well with those who convict the guilty,
and rich blessing will come on them.

[26] An honest answer
is like a kiss on the lips.

[27] Put your outdoor work in order
and get your fields ready;
after that, build your house.

[28] Do not testify against your neighbor without cause—
would you use your lips to mislead?
[29] Do not say, "I'll do to them as they have done to me;
I'll pay them back for what they did."

[30] I went past the field of a sluggard,
past the vineyard of someone who has no sense;
[31] thorns had come up everywhere,
the ground was covered with weeds,
and the stone wall was in ruins.
[32] I applied my heart to what I observed
and learned a lesson from what I saw:
[33] A little sleep, a little slumber,
a little folding of the hands to rest—
[34] and poverty will come on you like a thief
and scarcity like an armed man.

More Proverbs of Solomon

25 These are more proverbs of Solomon, compiled by the men of Hezekiah
king of Judah:

[2] It is the glory of God to conceal a matter;
to search out a matter is the glory of kings.
[3] As the heavens are high and the earth is deep,
so the hearts of kings are unsearchable.

PROVERBS 24:30–34

LAZINESS AND SIN'S CURSE

Proverbs clearly says that laziness will lead to poverty, but laziness is not just a character defect that makes life a little more difficult. Laziness is a sin according to Proverbs. The lazy man has his field overgrown with thorns, which is a result of the curse on the ground because of Adam and Eve's sin (Ge 3:18). Paul also connected laziness with sin in 1 Timothy 5:8: "Anyone who does not provide for their relatives, and especially for their own household, has denied the faith and is worse than an unbeliever." The lack of a work ethic may be evidence of an insincere faith.

The good news is that Proverbs points to Jesus—the wisdom of God. During his time on earth, Jesus was a hard worker. Not only was he a carpenter, but he was supremely concerned with finishing the work the Father sent him to do. " 'My food,' said Jesus, 'is to do the will of him who sent me and to finish his work' " (Jn 4:34). As Jesus was praying to his Father he said, "I have brought you glory on earth by finishing the work you gave me to do" (Jn 17:4). Also, Hebrews 1:3 states that Jesus is at work right now sustaining the world. In addition to being an example of a wise man who works hard, Jesus also transforms those who believe in him into his image—which includes overcoming the sin of laziness and becoming diligent in doing good (Gal 6:9).

4 Remove the dross from the silver,
and a silversmith can produce a vessel;
5 remove wicked officials from the king's presence,
and his throne will be established through righteousness.

6 Do not exalt yourself in the king's presence,
and do not claim a place among his great men;
7 it is better for him to say to you, "Come up here,"
than for him to humiliate you before his nobles.

What you have seen with your eyes
8 do not bring[a] hastily to court,
for what will you do in the end
if your neighbor puts you to shame?

9 If you take your neighbor to court,
do not betray another's confidence,
10 or the one who hears it may shame you
and the charge against you will stand.

11 Like apples[b] of gold in settings of silver
is a ruling rightly given.
12 Like an earring of gold or an ornament of fine gold
is the rebuke of a wise judge to a listening ear.

13 Like a snow-cooled drink at harvest time
is a trustworthy messenger to the one who sends him;
he refreshes the spirit of his master.
14 Like clouds and wind without rain
is one who boasts of gifts never given.

15 Through patience a ruler can be persuaded,
and a gentle tongue can break a bone.

16 If you find honey, eat just enough—
too much of it, and you will vomit.
17 Seldom set foot in your neighbor's house—
too much of you, and they will hate you.

18 Like a club or a sword or a sharp arrow
is one who gives false testimony against a neighbor.
19 Like a broken tooth or a lame foot
is reliance on the unfaithful in a time of trouble.
20 Like one who takes away a garment on a cold day,
or like vinegar poured on a wound,
is one who sings songs to a heavy heart.

21 If your enemy is hungry, give him food to eat;
if he is thirsty, give him water to drink.
22 In doing this, you will heap burning coals on his head,
and the LORD will reward you.

23 Like a north wind that brings unexpected rain
is a sly tongue—which provokes a horrified look.

24 Better to live on a corner of the roof
than share a house with a quarrelsome wife.

25 Like cold water to a weary soul
is good news from a distant land.
26 Like a muddied spring or a polluted well
are the righteous who give way to the wicked.

[a] *7,8* Or *nobles / on whom you had set your eyes. / [8]Do not go* [b] *11* Or possibly *apricots*

PROVERBS 25:21–22

DO GOOD TO ENEMIES

Paul quotes these verses in the context of teaching that the key to doing good to one's enemies is trusting God's justice (Ro 12:17–21). Often the biggest obstacle to releasing a grudge is the fear that it will unjustly discount how bad or hurtful certain actions were. Proverbs and Paul say that the way to let grudges go is by trusting that God will take care of it. Burning coals represent the pricking of the conscience of the wrongdoer, rather than responding in violence. Failing to forgive enemies indicates a lack of trust in the gospel. In effect, holding a grudge says, "The cross of Jesus Christ is enough to forgive the sins I commit against God, but it is not enough to forgive the sins committed against me."

God's people can experience freedom from grudges and do good toward their enemies for two reasons. First, there is a possibility that responding with goodness will open an enemy's heart to the gospel and bring about reconciliation. Second, believers can afford to suffer injustices temporarily knowing that God will someday judge the unrepentant. Trusting in the justice of God enabled Jesus to endure his suffering. The apostle Peter told believers, "To this you were called, because Christ suffered for you, leaving you an example, that you should follow in his steps ... When they hurled their insults at him, he did not retaliate; when he suffered, he made no threats. Instead, he entrusted himself to him who judges justly" (1Pe 2:21,23).

PROVERBS 26:4 – 5

ANSWERING A FOOL

These verses do not contradict one another. They should be read together. The point is to teach discernment. In some cases, fools are not worth correcting if answering them requires stooping to their level. In other cases, fools should be corrected, particularly if there is a possibility that answering them will clarify for them the difference between wisdom and their folly. Wisdom is the discernment to know when to answer and when not to answer.

Jesus amazed people with this ability. He knew when a reply would do no good, and in those situations chose to stay silent. And he knew when to offer correction. He knew exactly how to respond or not respond. Jesus answered the Pharisees' challenge about the disciples not washing their hands (Mt 15:1 – 9), and he rebuked Peter's assertion that the notion of Jesus suffering and dying was inconceivable and wrong (Mt 16:23). But he also refused to play the chief priests' game about where Jesus' authority came from (Mt 21:23 – 27), and he remained silent at his trial (Mk 15:5). Jesus grew in wisdom (Lk 2:52), which involved developing the ability to read people and situations. And the Spirit produces this Christ-like wisdom in Jesus' followers.

27 It is not good to eat too much honey,
nor is it honorable to search out matters that are
too deep.

28 Like a city whose walls are broken through
is a person who lacks self-control.

26 Like snow in summer or rain in harvest,
honor is not fitting for a fool.
2 Like a fluttering sparrow or a darting swallow,
an undeserved curse does not come to rest.
3 A whip for the horse, a bridle for the donkey,
and a rod for the backs of fools!
4 Do not answer a fool according to his folly,
or you yourself will be just like him.
5 Answer a fool according to his folly,
or he will be wise in his own eyes.
6 Sending a message by the hands of a fool
is like cutting off one's feet or drinking poison.
7 Like the useless legs of one who is lame
is a proverb in the mouth of a fool.
8 Like tying a stone in a sling
is the giving of honor to a fool.
9 Like a thornbush in a drunkard's hand
is a proverb in the mouth of a fool.
10 Like an archer who wounds at random
is one who hires a fool or any passer-by.
11 As a dog returns to its vomit,
so fools repeat their folly.
12 Do you see a person wise in their own eyes?
There is more hope for a fool than for them.

13 A sluggard says, "There's a lion in the road,
a fierce lion roaming the streets!"
14 As a door turns on its hinges,
so a sluggard turns on his bed.
15 A sluggard buries his hand in the dish;
he is too lazy to bring it back to his mouth.
16 A sluggard is wiser in his own eyes
than seven people who answer discreetly.

17 Like one who grabs a stray dog by the ears
is someone who rushes into a quarrel not their own.

18 Like a maniac shooting
flaming arrows of death
19 is one who deceives their neighbor
and says, "I was only joking!"

20 Without wood a fire goes out;
without a gossip a quarrel dies down.
21 As charcoal to embers and as wood to fire,
so is a quarrelsome person for kindling strife.
22 The words of a gossip are like choice morsels;
they go down to the inmost parts.

23 Like a coating of silver dross on earthenware
are fervent[a] lips with an evil heart.
24 Enemies disguise themselves with their lips,
but in their hearts they harbor deceit.

[a] 23 Hebrew; Septuagint *smooth*

[25] Though their speech is charming, do not believe them,
for seven abominations fill their hearts.
[26] Their malice may be concealed by deception,
but their wickedness will be exposed in the assembly.
[27] Whoever digs a pit will fall into it;
if someone rolls a stone, it will roll back on them.
[28] A lying tongue hates those it hurts,
and a flattering mouth works ruin.

27 Do not boast about tomorrow,
for you do not know what a day may bring.
[2] Let someone else praise you, and not your own mouth;
an outsider, and not your own lips.
[3] Stone is heavy and sand a burden,
but a fool's provocation is heavier than both.
[4] Anger is cruel and fury overwhelming,
but who can stand before jealousy?
[5] Better is open rebuke
than hidden love.
[6] Wounds from a friend can be trusted,
but an enemy multiplies kisses.
[7] One who is full loathes honey from the comb,
but to the hungry even what is bitter tastes sweet.
[8] Like a bird that flees its nest
is anyone who flees from home.
[9] Perfume and incense bring joy to the heart,
and the pleasantness of a friend
springs from their heartfelt advice.
[10] Do not forsake your friend or a friend of your family,
and do not go to your relative's house when disaster strikes you—
better a neighbor nearby than a relative far away.
[11] Be wise, my son, and bring joy to my heart;
then I can answer anyone who treats me with contempt.
[12] The prudent see danger and take refuge,
but the simple keep going and pay the penalty.
[13] Take the garment of one who puts up security for a stranger;
hold it in pledge if it is done for an outsider.
[14] If anyone loudly blesses their neighbor early in the morning,
it will be taken as a curse.
[15] A quarrelsome wife is like the dripping
of a leaky roof in a rainstorm;
[16] restraining her is like restraining the wind
or grasping oil with the hand.
[17] As iron sharpens iron,
so one person sharpens another.
[18] The one who guards a fig tree will eat its fruit,
and whoever protects their master will be honored.
[19] As water reflects the face,
so one's life reflects the heart.[a]

[a] 19 Or *so others reflect your heart back to you*

PROVERBS 27:5–6

OPEN REBUKE

Pushing against the grain of modern culture's "can't we all just get along" mentality, these verses say that having a friend who will tell the truth is valuable—even when that truth is difficult or unwelcome. In fact, people who only tell their acquaintances what they want to hear are not friends but enemies. These verses point to the gospel of Jesus Christ, not only because Jesus was kissed by an enemy masquerading as a friend (Mt 26:49), but also because the cross of Christ is meant to transform the daily lives of believers. If God's people really believe what Scripture says about the cross, then they can both give and receive a rebuke without getting angry. The cross reveals that all people are sinners, so believers should be able to accept a friend's correction. Believers in the cross find comfort not in delusional self-righteousness but in the knowledge that Christ paid the penalty for their sins!

[20] Death and Destruction[a] are never satisfied,
and neither are human eyes.

[21] The crucible for silver and the furnace for gold,
but people are tested by their praise.

[22] Though you grind a fool in a mortar,
grinding them like grain with a pestle,
you will not remove their folly from them.

[23] Be sure you know the condition of your flocks,
give careful attention to your herds;
[24] for riches do not endure forever,
and a crown is not secure for all generations.
[25] When the hay is removed and new growth appears
and the grass from the hills is gathered in,
[26] the lambs will provide you with clothing,
and the goats with the price of a field.
[27] You will have plenty of goats' milk to feed your family
and to nourish your female servants.

28

The wicked flee though no one pursues,
but the righteous are as bold as a lion.

[2] When a country is rebellious, it has many rulers,
but a ruler with discernment and knowledge maintains order.

[3] A ruler[b] who oppresses the poor
is like a driving rain that leaves no crops.

[4] Those who forsake instruction praise the wicked,
but those who heed it resist them.

[5] Evildoers do not understand what is right,
but those who seek the LORD understand it fully.

[6] Better the poor whose walk is blameless
than the rich whose ways are perverse.

[7] A discerning son heeds instruction,
but a companion of gluttons disgraces his father.

[8] Whoever increases wealth by taking interest or profit from the poor
amasses it for another, who will be kind to the poor.

[9] If anyone turns a deaf ear to my instruction,
even their prayers are detestable.

[10] Whoever leads the upright along an evil path
will fall into their own trap,
but the blameless will receive a good inheritance.

[11] The rich are wise in their own eyes;
one who is poor and discerning sees how deluded they are.

[12] When the righteous triumph, there is great elation;
but when the wicked rise to power, people go into hiding.

[13] Whoever conceals their sins does not prosper,
but the one who confesses and renounces them finds mercy.

[14] Blessed is the one who always trembles before God,
but whoever hardens their heart falls into trouble.

---

[a] 20 Hebrew *Abaddon* [b] 3 Or *A poor person*

[15] Like a roaring lion or a charging bear
is a wicked ruler over a helpless people.

[16] A tyrannical ruler practices extortion,
but one who hates ill-gotten gain will enjoy a long reign.

[17] Anyone tormented by the guilt of murder
will seek refuge in the grave;
let no one hold them back.

[18] The one whose walk is blameless is kept safe,
but the one whose ways are perverse will fall into the pit.[a]

[19] Those who work their land will have abundant food,
but those who chase fantasies will have their fill of poverty.

[20] A faithful person will be richly blessed,
but one eager to get rich will not go unpunished.

[21] To show partiality is not good—
yet a person will do wrong for a piece of bread.

[22] The stingy are eager to get rich
and are unaware that poverty awaits them.

[23] Whoever rebukes a person will in the end gain favor
rather than one who has a flattering tongue.

[24] Whoever robs their father or mother
and says, "It's not wrong,"
is partner to one who destroys.

[25] The greedy stir up conflict,
but those who trust in the LORD will prosper.

[26] Those who trust in themselves are fools,
but those who walk in wisdom are kept safe.

[27] Those who give to the poor will lack nothing,
but those who close their eyes to them receive many curses.

[28] When the wicked rise to power, people go into hiding;
but when the wicked perish, the righteous thrive.

29 Whoever remains stiff-necked after many rebukes
will suddenly be destroyed—without remedy.

[2] When the righteous thrive, the people rejoice;
when the wicked rule, the people groan.

[3] A man who loves wisdom brings joy to his father,
but a companion of prostitutes squanders his wealth.

[4] By justice a king gives a country stability,
but those who are greedy for[b] bribes tear it down.

[5] Those who flatter their neighbors
are spreading nets for their feet.

[6] Evildoers are snared by their own sin,
but the righteous shout for joy and are glad.

[7] The righteous care about justice for the poor,
but the wicked have no such concern.

[8] Mockers stir up a city,
but the wise turn away anger.

[a] 18 Syriac (see Septuagint); Hebrew *into one* [b] 4 Or *who give*

PROVERBS 28:27

GENEROSITY TO THE POOR

Generosity to the poor is a central concern of the book of Proverbs. Strikingly, this verse asserts that giving money away leads not to poverty but rather ensures that the giver "will lack nothing." The wisdom of God goes against the grain of human wisdom, which often promotes hoarding as the only way to guarantee sufficient resources. The Lord will bless a lifestyle of generosity, but he will curse those who ignore the poor.

The wisdom of Proverbs finds its fulfillment in Jesus of Nazareth, who at the outset of his ministry said, "The Spirit of the Lord is on me, because he has anointed me to proclaim good news to the poor" (Lk 4:18). Jesus modeled for believers a generous lifestyle and also grants them the ability to be generous in sharing the gospel, which is true spiritual wealth. Paul wrote, "For you know the grace of our Lord Jesus Christ, that though he was rich, yet for your sake he became poor, so that you through his poverty might become rich" (2Co 8:9). When people believe the good news that Christ gave up everything for them so that they could be co-heirs and receive everything with him, they are enabled to hold loosely to their possessions and give them away to others.

PROVERBS 29:14

ETERNAL KINGDOM

The proverbs of Solomon referred to a faithful king who would establish an eternal kingdom. A key characteristic of this ideal king was fair treatment of the poor. This principle connects up with God's promise to David that one of his descendants would establish a kingdom that lasts forever (2Sa 7:12 – 16). The problem was that Solomon and the rest of David's descendants leading up to the time of Christ failed. Not one of them was the ideal king. Yet these disappointments only increased the expectation that someday a son of David would be the ideal king and establish an eternal kingdom. Isaiah 11:1 – 5 described that future king as the embodiment of Proverbs who is anointed with the Spirit of wisdom. The New Testament presents Jesus of Nazareth as that King. He is the Son of David who came ministering to the poor, and he was given the kingdom of David (Lk 1:32).

9 If a wise person goes to court with a fool,
the fool rages and scoffs, and there is no peace.

10 The bloodthirsty hate a person of integrity
and seek to kill the upright.

11 Fools give full vent to their rage,
but the wise bring calm in the end.

12 If a ruler listens to lies,
all his officials become wicked.

13 The poor and the oppressor have this in common:
The LORD gives sight to the eyes of both.

14 If a king judges the poor with fairness,
his throne will be established forever.

15 A rod and a reprimand impart wisdom,
but a child left undisciplined disgraces its mother.

16 When the wicked thrive, so does sin,
but the righteous will see their downfall.

17 Discipline your children, and they will give you peace;
they will bring you the delights you desire.

18 Where there is no revelation, people cast off restraint;
but blessed is the one who heeds wisdom's instruction.

19 Servants cannot be corrected by mere words;
though they understand, they will not respond.

20 Do you see someone who speaks in haste?
There is more hope for a fool than for them.

21 A servant pampered from youth
will turn out to be insolent.

22 An angry person stirs up conflict,
and a hot-tempered person commits many sins.

23 Pride brings a person low,
but the lowly in spirit gain honor.

24 The accomplices of thieves are their own enemies;
they are put under oath and dare not testify.

25 Fear of man will prove to be a snare,
but whoever trusts in the LORD is kept safe.

26 Many seek an audience with a ruler,
but it is from the LORD that one gets justice.

27 The righteous detest the dishonest;
the wicked detest the upright.

Sayings of Agur

30 The sayings of Agur son of Jakeh — an inspired utterance.

This man's utterance to Ithiel:

"I am weary, God,
but I can prevail.[a]

[a] *1* With a different word division of the Hebrew; Masoretic Text *utterance to Ithiel, / to Ithiel and Ukal:*

2 Surely I am only a brute, not a man;
I do not have human understanding.
3 I have not learned wisdom,
nor have I attained to the knowledge of the
Holy One.
4 Who has gone up to heaven and come down?
Whose hands have gathered up the wind?
Who has wrapped up the waters in a cloak?
Who has established all the ends of the earth?
What is his name, and what is the name of his son?
Surely you know!

5 "Every word of God is flawless;
he is a shield to those who take refuge in him.
6 Do not add to his words,
or he will rebuke you and prove you a liar.

7 "Two things I ask of you, LORD;
do not refuse me before I die:
8 Keep falsehood and lies far from me;
give me neither poverty nor riches,
but give me only my daily bread.
9 Otherwise, I may have too much and disown you
and say, 'Who is the LORD?'
Or I may become poor and steal,
and so dishonor the name of my God.

10 "Do not slander a servant to their master,
or they will curse you, and you will pay for it.

11 "There are those who curse their fathers
and do not bless their mothers;
12 those who are pure in their own eyes
and yet are not cleansed of their filth;
13 those whose eyes are ever so haughty,
whose glances are so disdainful;
14 those whose teeth are swords
and whose jaws are set with knives
to devour the poor from the earth
and the needy from among mankind.

15 "The leech has two daughters.
'Give! Give!' they cry.

"There are three things that are never satisfied,
four that never say, 'Enough!':
16 the grave, the barren womb,
land, which is never satisfied with water,
and fire, which never says, 'Enough!'

17 "The eye that mocks a father,
that scorns an aged mother,
will be pecked out by the ravens of the valley,
will be eaten by the vultures.

18 "There are three things that are too amazing for me,
four that I do not understand:
19 the way of an eagle in the sky,
the way of a snake on a rock,
the way of a ship on the high seas,
and the way of a man with a young woman.

THE WISE SON OF GOD

The author of this passage was Agur, the son of Jakeh. This man's exact identity remains unknown because this is the only place he is mentioned in the Bible, but clearly he was a follower of God. He started the passage by claiming to be ignorant and unwise (vv. 2 – 3). He confessed that he was limited in terms of his wisdom. Wisdom begins with God, and Agur's problem was that he did not have access to God in heaven. Humanity is limited because they cannot go up to heaven and come down. No human has the wisdom to create the world or hold the wind, so they have no access to true wisdom. Agur asked a series of rhetorical questions to indicate that humanity's wisdom is limited; Agur implies that true wisdom belongs to the Almighty Creator — and *his son* (v. 4).

No human has gone up to heaven and come back down. No human can gather the wind in his fist. No human created the world. However, we read this passage from a different vantage point than Agur. Agur asked the name of the son, but he did not know what it was. We know it — Jesus Christ. We know that Jesus is the God-Man who came down from heaven as wisdom for us. In a roundabout way, Jesus answered Agur's question in his conversation with Nicodemus. He said, "No one has ever gone into heaven except the one who came from heaven — the Son of Man" (Jn 3:13). So, God's Son has access to God's wisdom, and in the goodness of God, he sent his Son to earth to make people wise!

Where should people look for that wisdom? Agur answered that question in the next two verses. They should look to the Word of God and refrain from adding to it or taking away from it because "every word of God is flawless" (Pr 30:5). Jesus is not just the Son of God; Jesus is the Word of God made flesh (Jn 1:1 – 14). Look to Jesus and his Word for the wisdom of God.

20 "This is the way of an adulterous woman:
She eats and wipes her mouth
and says, 'I've done nothing wrong.'

21 "Under three things the earth trembles,
under four it cannot bear up:
22 a servant who becomes king,
a godless fool who gets plenty to eat,
23 a contemptible woman who gets married,
and a servant who displaces her mistress.

24 "Four things on earth are small,
yet they are extremely wise:
25 Ants are creatures of little strength,
yet they store up their food in the summer;
26 hyraxes are creatures of little power,
yet they make their home in the crags;
27 locusts have no king,
yet they advance together in ranks;
28 a lizard can be caught with the hand,
yet it is found in kings' palaces.

29 "There are three things that are stately in their stride,
four that move with stately bearing:
30 a lion, mighty among beasts,
who retreats before nothing;
31 a strutting rooster, a he-goat,
and a king secure against revolt.[a]

32 "If you play the fool and exalt yourself,
or if you plan evil,
clap your hand over your mouth!
33 For as churning cream produces butter,
and as twisting the nose produces blood,
so stirring up anger produces strife."

Sayings of King Lemuel

31 The sayings of King Lemuel—an inspired utterance his mother taught him.

2 Listen, my son! Listen, son of my womb!
Listen, my son, the answer to my prayers!
3 Do not spend your strength[b] on women,
your vigor on those who ruin kings.

4 It is not for kings, Lemuel—
it is not for kings to drink wine,
not for rulers to crave beer,
5 lest they drink and forget what has been decreed,
and deprive all the oppressed of their rights.
6 Let beer be for those who are perishing,
wine for those who are in anguish!
7 Let them drink and forget their poverty
and remember their misery no more.

8 Speak up for those who cannot speak for themselves,
for the rights of all who are destitute.
9 Speak up and judge fairly;
defend the rights of the poor and needy.

[a] *31* The meaning of the Hebrew for this phrase is uncertain. [b] *3* Or *wealth*

Epilogue: The Wife of Noble Character

10 [a]A wife of noble character who can find?
She is worth far more than rubies.
11 Her husband has full confidence in her
and lacks nothing of value.
12 She brings him good, not harm,
all the days of her life.
13 She selects wool and flax
and works with eager hands.
14 She is like the merchant ships,
bringing her food from afar.
15 She gets up while it is still night;
she provides food for her family
and portions for her female servants.
16 She considers a field and buys it;
out of her earnings she plants a vineyard.
17 She sets about her work vigorously;
her arms are strong for her tasks.
18 She sees that her trading is profitable,
and her lamp does not go out at night.
19 In her hand she holds the distaff
and grasps the spindle with her fingers.
20 She opens her arms to the poor
and extends her hands to the needy.
21 When it snows, she has no fear for her household;
for all of them are clothed in scarlet.
22 She makes coverings for her bed;
she is clothed in fine linen and purple.
23 Her husband is respected at the city gate,
where he takes his seat among the elders of the land.
24 She makes linen garments and sells them,
and supplies the merchants with sashes.
25 She is clothed with strength and dignity;
she can laugh at the days to come.
26 She speaks with wisdom,
and faithful instruction is on her tongue.
27 She watches over the affairs of her household
and does not eat the bread of idleness.
28 Her children arise and call her blessed;
her husband also, and he praises her:
29 "Many women do noble things,
but you surpass them all."
30 Charm is deceptive, and beauty is fleeting;
but a woman who fears the LORD is to be praised.
31 Honor her for all that her hands have done,
and let her works bring her praise at the city gate.

[a] *10* Verses 10-31 are an acrostic poem, the verses of which begin with the successive letters of the Hebrew alphabet.

JESUS: OUR TRUE HOPE

ECCLESIASTES

ECCLESIASTES

REIGN OF DAVID	REIGN OF SOLOMON	FALL OF JUDAH
c. 1010 – 970 BC	*c. 970 – 930 BC*	*c. 586 BC*

Meaningless. This is the conclusion of Solomon, traditionally assumed to be the author of Ecclesiastes, regarding life in this world. Everything is meaningless.

Solomon could make this claim because he *had* everything. First, Solomon considered the outcome of pursuing wisdom (1:12 – 18). Having received wisdom as a gift from God, Solomon was uniquely able to assess the result of searching for knowledge apart from God. He described it as madness and folly, "a chasing after the wind" (1:17). His assessment was that no matter how much wisdom humankind possesses, it is ultimately futile compared to God's wisdom and his plans.

Up next was the pursuit of pleasure (2:1 – 11). Though Solomon could have had anything his heart desired, and pursued these pleasures with perfect wisdom, nothing that he found satisfied his heart for the long term. Pleasures, too, were meaningless. Solomon also assessed the work of his hands (2:17 – 26). This toil, although a good and meaningful aspect of human existence, led to frustration and failure, grief and pain. Even his youthful aspirations for advancement were meaningless for Solomon (4:13 – 16). A man renowned throughout the world for his wealth, Solomon determined that riches were futile as well (5:8 – 20).

The meaninglessness and brevity of life forced Solomon to conclude that life under the sun, no matter how well lived, is not enough. The best humankind can do is eat, drink and find joy in life with those they love (2:24 – 25). Throughout the book, Solomon shares proverbial wisdom for how to honor God and obey him in this life. These exhortations, no matter how true, can sound hollow for modern readers in light of the overall depressive tone of the book.

Solomon's conclusion forces readers of Ecclesiastes to look beyond this life for the ultimate hope for human existence. No human experience — not wealth, power, success, wisdom or relationships — will ever satisfy the longing of the human heart. Only Jesus can provide what nothing on this earth can deliver. Those saved by Jesus' work are then sent back into the world with newfound vitality. Life remains toilsome, frustrating and fraught with failure, but Jesus gives meaning and mission to those who will believe and trust in him for their salvation. These people can have hope in the midst of a broken world, knowing they are loved by God and secure for all eternity. They do not have to follow the path of this world and seek fulfillment in things that will always leave them empty. Instead, God's children can find meaning in worshiping God and in giving their lives away to his mission in the world.

THERE IS A TIME FOR EVERYTHING,
AND A SEASON FOR EVERY ACTIVITY
UNDER THE HEAVENS.

Ecclesiastes 3:1

ECCLESIASTES

Everything Is Meaningless

1 The words of the Teacher,[a] son of David, king in Jerusalem:

2 "Meaningless! Meaningless!"
says the Teacher.
"Utterly meaningless!
Everything is meaningless."
3 What do people gain from all their labors
at which they toil under the sun?
4 Generations come and generations go,
but the earth remains forever.
5 The sun rises and the sun sets,
and hurries back to where it rises.
6 The wind blows to the south
and turns to the north;
round and round it goes,
ever returning on its course.
7 All streams flow into the sea,
yet the sea is never full.
To the place the streams come from,
there they return again.
8 All things are wearisome,
more than one can say.
The eye never has enough of seeing,
nor the ear its fill of hearing.
9 What has been will be again,
what has been done will be done again;
there is nothing new under the sun.
10 Is there anything of which one can say,
"Look! This is something new"?
It was here already, long ago;
it was here before our time.
11 No one remembers the former generations,
and even those yet to come
will not be remembered
by those who follow them.

Wisdom Is Meaningless

12 I, the Teacher, was king over Israel in Jerusalem. 13 I applied my mind to
study and to explore by wisdom all that is done under the heavens. What a heavy
burden God has laid on mankind! 14 I have seen all the things that are done under
the sun; all of them are meaningless, a chasing after the wind.

15 What is crooked cannot be straightened;
what is lacking cannot be counted.

16 I said to myself, "Look, I have increased in wisdom more than anyone who
has ruled over Jerusalem before me; I have experienced much of wisdom and
knowledge." 17 Then I applied myself to the understanding of wisdom, and also
of madness and folly, but I learned that this, too, is a chasing after the wind.

---

[a] *1* Or *the leader of the assembly;* also in verses 2 and 12

ECCLESIASTES 1:2

THE SEARCH FOR MEANING

In Hebrew, repeating the same word makes that word a superlative — it indicates incomparability. For example, doubling the word "holy" to describe the inner chamber of the tabernacle or temple emphasizes that this room was the "Most Holy Place" (Ex 26:33). In the same way, when Solomon, traditionally assumed to be the author of Ecclesiastes, wrote that everything is "Meaningless! Meaningless!" he was claiming that life is utterly futile, without purpose or worth. Why would he make such a terrible claim?

The Hebrew word *hebel,* translated as "meaningless" in this passage, literally means "vapor" or "breath." It resonates with other Scripture passages that emphasize the inherent worthlessness of things that do not last, from the temporary lives of mortals, to idols and false worship practices (1Ki 16:13; Job 7:16; Ps 35:5; Isa 57:13). As James 4:14 says, "You are a mist that appears for a little while and then vanishes." Sin transformed human life into suffering and death. And it was in the course of wrestling with this reality that Solomon cried out, "Everything is meaningless"!

Yet, Scripture does not teach that human lives are without meaning. Despite its dark tone, this book presses toward hope by asking readers to ponder where meaning could come from. If death is the final destination for every human regardless of how they have lived, does any of it really matter (Ecc 9:2 – 6)? What can bring true, lasting value to a human's short, vapor-like existence?

Thankfully, Jesus came and gave everyone the opportunity to seek fulfillment beyond his or her own life. While life here on earth would be meaningless in and of itself, Jesus says that humans are made for more than this sinful world (Jn 15:19). Jesus calls everyone to seek eternal life, as opposed to the meaninglessness of an earthly life disconnected from God. First John 2:25 says, "And this is what he promised us — eternal life." The meaninglessness that Solomon referred to is life under the burdensome limits of sin and death. But those who follow Jesus will receive the resurrection of the body and eternal life. This new life in Christ brings genuine meaning — and every Christian's hope of eternity infuses temporal life with renewed purpose.

No one has to look for fulfillment in this broken, fleeting world. Jesus reaches out to mortal humans — whose lives are like vapor — and offers them eternal life with him. Believers today can be encouraged by the knowledge that an eternity with Jesus is anything but meaningless.

[18] For with much wisdom comes much sorrow;
the more knowledge, the more grief.

Pleasures Are Meaningless

2 I said to myself, "Come now, I will test you with pleasure to find out what is
good." But that also proved to be meaningless. [2]"Laughter," I said, "is madness. And what does pleasure accomplish?" [3]I tried cheering myself with wine,
and embracing folly — my mind still guiding me with wisdom. I wanted to see
what was good for people to do under the heavens during the few days of their
lives.

[4]I undertook great projects: I built houses for myself and planted vineyards. [5]I
made gardens and parks and planted all kinds of fruit trees in them. [6]I made reservoirs to water groves of flourishing trees. [7]I bought male and female slaves and
had other slaves who were born in my house. I also owned more herds and flocks
than anyone in Jerusalem before me. [8]I amassed silver and gold for myself, and
the treasure of kings and provinces. I acquired male and female singers, and a
harem[a] as well — the delights of a man's heart. [9]I became greater by far than anyone in Jerusalem before me. In all this my wisdom stayed with me.

[10] I denied myself nothing my eyes desired;
I refused my heart no pleasure.
My heart took delight in all my labor,
and this was the reward for all my toil.
[11] Yet when I surveyed all that my hands had done
and what I had toiled to achieve,
everything was meaningless, a chasing after the wind;
nothing was gained under the sun.

Wisdom and Folly Are Meaningless

[12] Then I turned my thoughts to consider wisdom,
and also madness and folly.
What more can the king's successor do
than what has already been done?
[13] I saw that wisdom is better than folly,
just as light is better than darkness.
[14] The wise have eyes in their heads,
while the fool walks in the darkness;
but I came to realize
that the same fate overtakes them both.

[15]Then I said to myself,

"The fate of the fool will overtake me also.
What then do I gain by being wise?"
I said to myself,
"This too is meaningless."
[16] For the wise, like the fool, will not be long remembered;
the days have already come when both have been forgotten.
Like the fool, the wise too must die!

Toil Is Meaningless

[17]So I hated life, because the work that is done under the sun was grievous
to me. All of it is meaningless, a chasing after the wind. [18]I hated all the things
I had toiled for under the sun, because I must leave them to the one who comes
after me. [19]And who knows whether that person will be wise or foolish? Yet they
will have control over all the fruit of my toil into which I have poured my effort
and skill under the sun. This too is meaningless. [20]So my heart began to despair

[a] *8* The meaning of the Hebrew for this phrase is uncertain.

ECCLESIASTES 1:18

WITH MUCH WISDOM COMES MUCH SORROW

In verse 18, Solomon lamented the fact that his great wisdom and knowledge had brought him great sorrow and grief. He was not alone in this feeling. In Matthew 26:38, Jesus talked about his soul being deeply grieved. That sorrow was rooted in the knowledge that God had given him. Jesus knew what it was going to take to save humankind. He knew the price of sin would be his own life, and this knowledge weighed heavily on his heart. Yet, Jesus did not let sorrow overtake him. He stayed the course, remaining obedient to the point of death on the cross (Php 2:8). Even though his knowledge and wisdom brought him grief — about the world's sin and the price he would pay on the cross to overcome sin — he gave his life so that believers could experience the joy of a relationship with him. Though wisdom may bring sorrow, knowing Jesus brings ultimate joy.

over all my toilsome labor under the sun. 21For a person may labor with wisdom,
knowledge and skill, and then they must leave all they own to another who has
not toiled for it. This too is meaningless and a great misfortune. 22What do people get for all the toil and anxious striving with which they labor under the sun?
23All their days their work is grief and pain; even at night their minds do not rest.
This too is meaningless.

24A person can do nothing better than to eat and drink and find satisfaction
in their own toil. This too, I see, is from the hand of God, 25for without him, who
can eat or find enjoyment? 26To the person who pleases him, God gives wisdom,
knowledge and happiness, but to the sinner he gives the task of gathering and
storing up wealth to hand it over to the one who pleases God. This too is meaningless, a chasing after the wind.

A Time for Everything

3 There is a time for everything,
and a season for every activity under the heavens:

2 a time to be born and a time to die,
a time to plant and a time to uproot,
3 a time to kill and a time to heal,
a time to tear down and a time to build,
4 a time to weep and a time to laugh,
a time to mourn and a time to dance,
5 a time to scatter stones and a time to gather them,
a time to embrace and a time to refrain from embracing,
6 a time to search and a time to give up,
a time to keep and a time to throw away,
7 a time to tear and a time to mend,
a time to be silent and a time to speak,
8 a time to love and a time to hate,
a time for war and a time for peace.

9What do workers gain from their toil? 10I have seen the burden God has laid
on the human race. 11He has made everything beautiful in its time. He has also
set eternity in the human heart; yet[a] no one can fathom what God has done from
beginning to end. 12I know that there is nothing better for people than to be happy and to do good while they live. 13That each of them may eat and drink, and
find satisfaction in all their toil—this is the gift of God. 14I know that everything
God does will endure forever; nothing can be added to it and nothing taken from
it. God does it so that people will fear him.

15Whatever is has already been,
and what will be has been before;
and God will call the past to account.[b]

16And I saw something else under the sun:

In the place of judgment—wickedness was there,
in the place of justice—wickedness was there.

17I said to myself,

"God will bring into judgment
both the righteous and the wicked,
for there will be a time for every activity,
a time to judge every deed."

18I also said to myself, "As for humans, God tests them so that they may see
that they are like the animals. 19Surely the fate of human beings is like that of
the animals; the same fate awaits them both: As one dies, so dies the other. All

ECCLESIASTES 3:11

ETERNAL LIFE

Ecclesiastes tells us that God has "set eternity in the human heart." Humans are created in the image of God (Ge 1:27), and God lives in eternity (Rev 1:8). Solomon poses the idea that humans have an innate desire in their hearts for something beyond their earthly lives. Humans were not made to live, die and cease existing. Something about how God designed humans makes them stretch toward the eternal God. Scripture eventually reveals that humans were made to live eternally with God. It is natural for our hearts to feel as if there has to be something more—because there *is* something more. John 3:16 and 1 John 2:25 both confirm that God promises eternal life to those who believe. The reason eternity is so appealing to humans is because that is exactly what God created humans for in the first place—to live in relationship with eternal God himself.

[a] *11* Or *also placed ignorance in the human heart, so that* [b] *15* Or *God calls back the past*

TIME

Ecclesiastes 3 starts with the reassurance that there is a time for everything. If there was anything that Solomon was sure of, it was that God is the sovereign ruler over everything. Birth and death, love and hate, war and peace all have their own time under God's control. Amidst chapters that seem to question the meaningfulness of the universe itself, Solomon assured his readers that God remains completely sovereign over everything that happens under the sun.

Jesus was also aware of the truth that there is a time for everything. Early in Jesus' ministry, he attended a wedding in Cana. As the celebration progressed, the host ran out of wine. Jesus' mother asked him to help, but he responded by saying, "My hour has not yet come" (Jn 2:4). Jesus ended up turning water into wine, his first miracle recorded in Scripture. But it is interesting to note that he was not eager to perform a miracle and draw attention to himself. The wedding in Cana is not the only instance where Jesus tried to maintain a low profile. On multiple occasions Jesus performed a miracle and then instructed people not to spread the word about him (Mt 8:2 – 4; 9:29 – 30; Mk 1:40 – 45; 5:21 – 43; Lk 5:13 – 16). Jesus understood that after he performed miracles for people they would want to tell everyone about him — but he also knew that there was a specific time for his name to spread and he was keen to wait until that time.

Jesus was not trying to hide. Rather, he wanted to reveal his glory in the right place and at the right time. He knew his works and words would lead to the cross, in keeping with God's plan to bring salvation to sinful humanity. But Jesus also wanted to spend sufficient time teaching his disciples in order to prepare them for the task of building the church after his resurrection and ascension. Believers today know that Jesus' time came on the cross, and his name has been spread far and wide since the miracle of his resurrection. God is sovereign over everything that happens under the sun, and God's people can be sure that now is the time to share the Good News about Jesus with all who will listen.

have the same breath[a]; humans have no advantage over animals. Everything
is meaningless. 20All go to the same place; all come from dust, and to dust all
return. 21Who knows if the human spirit rises upward and if the spirit of the animal goes down into the earth?"

22So I saw that there is nothing better for a person than to enjoy their work, because that is their lot. For who can bring them to see what will happen after them?

Oppression, Toil, Friendlessness

4 Again I looked and saw all the oppression that was taking place under the
sun:

I saw the tears of the oppressed—
  and they have no comforter;
power was on the side of their oppressors—
  and they have no comforter.
2And I declared that the dead,
  who had already died,
are happier than the living,
  who are still alive.
3But better than both
  is the one who has never been born,
who has not seen the evil
  that is done under the sun.

4And I saw that all toil and all achievement spring from one person's envy of
another. This too is meaningless, a chasing after the wind.

5Fools fold their hands
  and ruin themselves.
6Better one handful with tranquillity
  than two handfuls with toil
  and chasing after the wind.

7Again I saw something meaningless under the sun:

8There was a man all alone;
  he had neither son nor brother.
There was no end to his toil,
  yet his eyes were not content with his wealth.
"For whom am I toiling," he asked,
  "and why am I depriving myself of enjoyment?"
This too is meaningless—
  a miserable business!

9Two are better than one,
  because they have a good return for their labor:
10If either of them falls down,
  one can help the other up.
But pity anyone who falls
  and has no one to help them up.
11Also, if two lie down together, they will keep warm.
  But how can one keep warm alone?
12Though one may be overpowered,
  two can defend themselves.
A cord of three strands is not quickly broken.

Advancement Is Meaningless

13Better a poor but wise youth than an old but foolish king who no longer
knows how to heed a warning. 14The youth may have come from prison to the

[a] 19 Or *spirit*

kingship, or he may have been born in poverty within his kingdom. [15]I saw that
all who lived and walked under the sun followed the youth, the king's successor.
[16]There was no end to all the people who were before them. But those who came
later were not pleased with the successor. This too is meaningless, a chasing
after the wind.

Fulfill Your Vow to God

5[a] Guard your steps when you go to the house of God. Go near to listen rather than to offer the sacrifice of fools, who do not know that they do wrong.

[2] Do not be quick with your mouth,
do not be hasty in your heart
to utter anything before God.
God is in heaven
and you are on earth,
so let your words be few.
[3] A dream comes when there are many cares,
and many words mark the speech of a fool.

[4]When you make a vow to God, do not delay to fulfill it. He has no pleasure in
fools; fulfill your vow. [5]It is better not to make a vow than to make one and not
fulfill it. [6]Do not let your mouth lead you into sin. And do not protest to the temple messenger, "My vow was a mistake." Why should God be angry at what you
say and destroy the work of your hands? [7]Much dreaming and many words are
meaningless. Therefore fear God.

Riches Are Meaningless

[8]If you see the poor oppressed in a district, and justice and rights denied, do
not be surprised at such things; for one official is eyed by a higher one, and over
them both are others higher still. [9]The increase from the land is taken by all; the
king himself profits from the fields.

[10] Whoever loves money never has enough;
whoever loves wealth is never satisfied with their
income.
This too is meaningless.

[11] As goods increase,
so do those who consume them.
And what benefit are they to the owners
except to feast their eyes on them?

[12] The sleep of a laborer is sweet,
whether they eat little or much,
but as for the rich, their abundance
permits them no sleep.

[13]I have seen a grievous evil under the sun:

wealth hoarded to the harm of its owners,
14 or wealth lost through some misfortune,
so that when they have children
there is nothing left for them to inherit.
[15] Everyone comes naked from their mother's womb,
and as everyone comes, so they depart.
They take nothing from their toil
that they can carry in their hands.

[16]This too is a grievous evil:

ECCLESIASTES 5:10

LOVE OF MONEY

In addition to being the wisest man ever to live (until Jesus), Solomon was arguably one of the richest men in history (1Ki 10:14–25). So when he wrote about wealth, he did so from his own experience. Despite all that Solomon was able to accumulate through his lifetime, he came to the ultimate conclusion that money is ultimately futile and fails to satisfy. Jesus taught about money in Matthew 19:16–24 in his encounter with the rich young ruler, and he concluded by saying, "It is easier for a camel to go through the eye of a needle than for someone who is rich to enter the kingdom of God." While money is important for survival, love of money is a detriment to one's spiritual health. Combining Solomon's and Jesus' teachings about money, it becomes clear that money fails to satisfy while on earth, and it can be a stumbling block that keeps people from finding ultimate satisfaction in Jesus. However, when people give away their money and possessions to the poor in the name of Jesus, they store up for themselves treasure in heaven (Mt 19:21). Such lasting, heavenly treasure is much more valuable and beneficial than any possession gained on earth (Mt 6:19–21).

---

[a] In Hebrew texts 5:1 is numbered 4:17, and 5:2-20 is numbered 5:1-19.

As everyone comes, so they depart,
  and what do they gain,
  since they toil for the wind?
17 All their days they eat in darkness,
  with great frustration, affliction and anger.

18 This is what I have observed to be good: that it is appropriate for a person to
eat, to drink and to find satisfaction in their toilsome labor under the sun during
the few days of life God has given them—for this is their lot. 19 Moreover, when
God gives someone wealth and possessions, and the ability to enjoy them, to accept their lot and be happy in their toil—this is a gift of God. 20 They seldom reflect
on the days of their life, because God keeps them occupied with gladness of heart.

6 I have seen another evil under the sun, and it weighs heavily on mankind:
2 God gives some people wealth, possessions and honor, so that they lack
nothing their hearts desire, but God does not grant them the ability to enjoy
them, and strangers enjoy them instead. This is meaningless, a grievous evil.
3 A man may have a hundred children and live many years; yet no matter how
long he lives, if he cannot enjoy his prosperity and does not receive proper burial, I say that a stillborn child is better off than he. 4 It comes without meaning,
it departs in darkness, and in darkness its name is shrouded. 5 Though it never
saw the sun or knew anything, it has more rest than does that man— 6 even if
he lives a thousand years twice over but fails to enjoy his prosperity. Do not all
go to the same place?

7 Everyone's toil is for their mouth,
  yet their appetite is never satisfied.
8 What advantage have the wise over fools?
What do the poor gain
  by knowing how to conduct themselves before others?
9 Better what the eye sees
  than the roving of the appetite.
This too is meaningless,
  a chasing after the wind.

10 Whatever exists has already been named,
  and what humanity is has been known;
no one can contend
  with someone who is stronger.
11 The more the words,
  the less the meaning,
  and how does that profit anyone?

12 For who knows what is good for a person in life, during the few and meaningless days they pass through like a shadow? Who can tell them what will happen under the sun after they are gone?

Wisdom

7 A good name is better than fine perfume,
  and the day of death better than the day of birth.
2 It is better to go to a house of mourning
  than to go to a house of feasting,
for death is the destiny of everyone;
  the living should take this to heart.
3 Frustration is better than laughter,
  because a sad face is good for the heart.
4 The heart of the wise is in the house of mourning,
  but the heart of fools is in the house of pleasure.
5 It is better to heed the rebuke of a wise person
  than to listen to the song of fools.

[6] Like the crackling of thorns under the pot,
so is the laughter of fools.
This too is meaningless.

[7] Extortion turns a wise person into a fool,
and a bribe corrupts the heart.

[8] The end of a matter is better than its beginning,
and patience is better than pride.
[9] Do not be quickly provoked in your spirit,
for anger resides in the lap of fools.
[10] Do not say, "Why were the old days better than these?"
For it is not wise to ask such questions.

[11] Wisdom, like an inheritance, is a good thing
and benefits those who see the sun.
[12] Wisdom is a shelter
as money is a shelter,
but the advantage of knowledge is this:
Wisdom preserves those who have it.

[13] Consider what God has done:

Who can straighten
what he has made crooked?
[14] When times are good, be happy;
but when times are bad, consider this:
God has made the one
as well as the other.
Therefore, no one can discover
anything about their future.

[15] In this meaningless life of mine I have seen both of these:

the righteous perishing in their righteousness,
and the wicked living long in their wickedness.
[16] Do not be overrighteous,
neither be overwise—
why destroy yourself?
[17] Do not be overwicked,
and do not be a fool—
why die before your time?
[18] It is good to grasp the one
and not let go of the other.
Whoever fears God will avoid all extremes.[a]

[19] Wisdom makes one wise person more powerful
than ten rulers in a city.

[20] Indeed, there is no one on earth who is righteous,
no one who does what is right and never sins.

[21] Do not pay attention to every word people say,
or you may hear your servant cursing you—
[22] for you know in your heart
that many times you yourself have cursed others.

[23] All this I tested by wisdom and I said,

"I am determined to be wise"—
but this was beyond me.

[a] *18* Or *will follow them both*

ECCLESIASTES 7:16–18

AVOID EXTREMES

Ecclesiastes 7:18 balances the statements in the preceding two verses. It is important to be neither a wicked fool, nor an over-righteous zealot. Solomon advised finding a balance between wearing oneself out in the pursuit of perfection and abandoning oneself to sinful excess. That place of moderation and balance is found in the knowledge and fear of God. In Matthew 23, Jesus harshly criticized the Pharisees for being exactly like the people Solomon mentioned in verse 16. He said that the Pharisees were hypocrites. They thought they were living the right way, but they were actually worshiping religion itself and not God, upon whom the religion was founded. Jesus must be the focus of Christianity. Believers are responsible for avoiding extremes and living a balanced life in pursuit of him and him alone. Perfection is unattainable, and sin is unavoidable this side of heaven. In light of this, Jesus simply asks his people to be faithful and follow him.

24 Whatever exists is far off and most profound—
who can discover it?
25 So I turned my mind to understand,
to investigate and to search out wisdom and the scheme of things
and to understand the stupidity of wickedness
and the madness of folly.

26 I find more bitter than death
the woman who is a snare,
whose heart is a trap
and whose hands are chains.
The man who pleases God will escape her,
but the sinner she will ensnare.

27 "Look," says the Teacher,[a] "this is what I have discovered:

"Adding one thing to another to discover the scheme of things—
28 while I was still searching
but not finding—
I found one upright man among a thousand,
but not one upright woman among them all.
29 This only have I found:
God created mankind upright,
but they have gone in search of many schemes."

8 Who is like the wise?
Who knows the explanation of things?
A person's wisdom brightens their face
and changes its hard appearance.

Obey the King

2 Obey the king's command, I say, because you took an oath before God. 3 Do
not be in a hurry to leave the king's presence. Do not stand up for a bad cause,
for he will do whatever he pleases. 4 Since a king's word is supreme, who can say
to him, "What are you doing?"

5 Whoever obeys his command will come to no harm,
and the wise heart will know the proper time and procedure.
6 For there is a proper time and procedure for every matter,
though a person may be weighed down by misery.

7 Since no one knows the future,
who can tell someone else what is to come?
8 As no one has power over the wind to contain it,
so[b] no one has power over the time of their death.
As no one is discharged in time of war,
so wickedness will not release those who practice it.

9 All this I saw, as I applied my mind to everything done under the sun. There
is a time when a man lords it over others to his own[c] hurt. 10 Then too, I saw the
wicked buried—those who used to come and go from the holy place and receive
praise[d] in the city where they did this. This too is meaningless.
11 When the sentence for a crime is not quickly carried out, people's hearts
are filled with schemes to do wrong. 12 Although a wicked person who commits
a hundred crimes may live a long time, I know that it will go better with those
who fear God, who are reverent before him. 13 Yet because the wicked do not fear
God, it will not go well with them, and their days will not lengthen like a shadow.

---

[a] 27 Or *the leader of the assembly* [b] 8 Or *over the human spirit to retain it, / and so*
[c] 9 Or *to their* [d] 10 Some Hebrew manuscripts and Septuagint (Aquila); most Hebrew
manuscripts *and are forgotten*

14There is something else meaningless that occurs on earth: the righteous
who get what the wicked deserve, and the wicked who get what the righteous
deserve. This too, I say, is meaningless. 15So I commend the enjoyment of life,
because there is nothing better for a person under the sun than to eat and drink
and be glad. Then joy will accompany them in their toil all the days of the life
God has given them under the sun.
16When I applied my mind to know wisdom and to observe the labor that is
done on earth — people getting no sleep day or night — 17then I saw all that God
has done. No one can comprehend what goes on under the sun. Despite all their
efforts to search it out, no one can discover its meaning. Even if the wise claim
they know, they cannot really comprehend it.

A Common Destiny for All

9 So I reflected on all this and concluded that the righteous and the wise and
what they do are in God's hands, but no one knows whether love or hate
awaits them. 2All share a common destiny — the righteous and the wicked, the
good and the bad,[a] the clean and the unclean, those who offer sacrifices and
those who do not.

As it is with the good,
so with the sinful;
as it is with those who take oaths,
so with those who are afraid to take them.

3This is the evil in everything that happens under the sun: The same destiny
overtakes all. The hearts of people, moreover, are full of evil and there is madness in their hearts while they live, and afterward they join the dead. 4Anyone
who is among the living has hope[b] — even a live dog is better off than a dead lion!

5For the living know that they will die,
but the dead know nothing;
they have no further reward,
and even their name is forgotten.
6Their love, their hate
and their jealousy have long since vanished;
never again will they have a part
in anything that happens under the sun.

7Go, eat your food with gladness, and drink your wine with a joyful heart, for
God has already approved what you do. 8Always be clothed in white, and always
anoint your head with oil. 9Enjoy life with your wife, whom you love, all the days
of this meaningless life that God has given you under the sun — all your meaningless days. For this is your lot in life and in your toilsome labor under the sun.
10Whatever your hand finds to do, do it with all your might, for in the realm of
the dead, where you are going, there is neither working nor planning nor knowledge nor wisdom.
11I have seen something else under the sun:

The race is not to the swift
or the battle to the strong,
nor does food come to the wise
or wealth to the brilliant
or favor to the learned;
but time and chance happen to them all.

12Moreover, no one knows when their hour will come:

---

[a] 2 Septuagint (Aquila), Vulgate and Syriac; Hebrew does not have *and the bad.*
[b] 4 Or *What then is to be chosen? With all who live, there is hope*

As fish are caught in a cruel net,
or birds are taken in a snare,
so people are trapped by evil times
that fall unexpectedly upon them.

Wisdom Better Than Folly

13I also saw under the sun this example of wisdom that greatly impressed
me: 14There was once a small city with only a few people in it. And a powerful
king came against it, surrounded it and built huge siege works against it. 15Now
there lived in that city a man poor but wise, and he saved the city by his wisdom. But nobody remembered that poor man. 16So I said, "Wisdom is better than
strength." But the poor man's wisdom is despised, and his words are no longer
heeded.

17 The quiet words of the wise are more to be heeded
than the shouts of a ruler of fools.
18 Wisdom is better than weapons of war,
but one sinner destroys much good.

10 As dead flies give perfume a bad smell,
so a little folly outweighs wisdom and honor.
2 The heart of the wise inclines to the right,
but the heart of the fool to the left.
3 Even as fools walk along the road,
they lack sense
and show everyone how stupid they are.
4 If a ruler's anger rises against you,
do not leave your post;
calmness can lay great offenses to rest.

5 There is an evil I have seen under the sun,
the sort of error that arises from a ruler:
6 Fools are put in many high positions,
while the rich occupy the low ones.
7 I have seen slaves on horseback,
while princes go on foot like slaves.

8 Whoever digs a pit may fall into it;
whoever breaks through a wall may be bitten by
a snake.
9 Whoever quarries stones may be injured by them;
whoever splits logs may be endangered by them.
10 If the ax is dull
and its edge unsharpened,
more strength is needed,
but skill will bring success.

11 If a snake bites before it is charmed,
the charmer receives no fee.

12 Words from the mouth of the wise are gracious,
but fools are consumed by their own lips.
13 At the beginning their words are folly;
at the end they are wicked madness—
14 and fools multiply words.

No one knows what is coming—
who can tell someone else what will happen after them?

15 The toil of fools wearies them;
they do not know the way to town.

ECCLESIASTES 10:2

JESUS AT GOD'S RIGHT HAND

Solomon's statement about the wise inclining toward the right while the foolish turn toward the left reflects a tendency common in several ancient cultures to associate "the right" or "the right hand" with strength, wisdom or favor. For example, various Scripture passages refer to God's right hand as a source of deliverance and safety (Ps 17:7; Isa 62:8). Similarly, those who have God at their right hand or side are favored by God and receive his help (Ps 109:31; Isa 63:12). In Ecclesiastes, Solomon extended the "right" motif to describe how wise people set themselves apart by choosing paths that lead to life. The notion that "right" signifies wisdom and power is reflected again in the New Testament. After Jesus had reappeared to the disciples following his death and resurrection, he was taken up into heaven, where he is seated at the right hand of God (Lk 22:69; 24:51). Paul tells believers that this crucified and risen Christ, sitting in authority at God's right hand, is the very power and wisdom of God (1Co 1:22–24; Eph 1:20; Col 3:1). For believers today, inclining their hearts toward the right means turning toward the One who sits at the right hand of God—for Jesus is God's power and wisdom, and the only path to life (Jn 14:6).

ECCLESIASTES 9:11 – 12

LIFE IS UNFAIR

Ecclesiastes wrestles with the fact that life is unfair. The fastest person does not always win the race; the best warrior does not always win the battle; wisdom, intelligence and knowledge do not always result in wealth, prestige or favor. Solomon understood that sometimes life simply does not work out the way people want it to. People are like fish or birds that get caught in nets and traps — despite their best efforts, people's lives are surrounded by things that remain outside their control. Sometimes young people die. Sometimes evil people experience temporary success. Life is not fair.

However, while the unfairness of life may seem like something to be upset about, consider this: If life were fair, then everyone would receive the just reward for his or her actions. Everyone has sinned, and the just consequence for every sinful action is immediate, eternal separation from God. Thankfully, Jesus came to earth, lived a perfect life, died on the cross for humanity's sins, rose from the grave and made life completely unfair. Now, everyone who has ever sinned has the opportunity to go to heaven through belief in Jesus. In a fair life, no such opportunity for grace would exist. Everyone would have to receive punishment for their actions. Instead God gives out grace and mercy unconditionally.

Sin made life on earth unfair — but God, in his grace, allows this sinful, unfair world to continue, creating time for sinners to accept his gracious offer of reconciliation through Christ. It is still hard to understand why bad things happen to good people or why good things happen to bad people. Even so, readers of Scripture know that those kinds of injustices are the result of sin, and Solomon does not avoid pointing out the negative consequences of living in a world marked by sin. But when faced with the world's injustices, believers today can celebrate the fact that Jesus' offer of eternal life is an altogether unfair and undeserved gift. All the sinful unfairness of this broken world pales in comparison to the gracious unfairness of salvation, which God lovingly makes available through Christ's death and resurrection.

[16] Woe to the land whose king was a servant[a]
and whose princes feast in the morning.
[17] Blessed is the land whose king is of noble birth
and whose princes eat at a proper time —
for strength and not for drunkenness.

[18] Through laziness, the rafters sag;
because of idle hands, the house leaks.

[19] A feast is made for laughter,
wine makes life merry,
and money is the answer for everything.

[20] Do not revile the king even in your thoughts,
or curse the rich in your bedroom,
because a bird in the sky may carry your words,
and a bird on the wing may report what you say.

Invest in Many Ventures

11 Ship your grain across the sea;
after many days you may receive a return.
[2] Invest in seven ventures, yes, in eight;
you do not know what disaster may come upon the land.

[3] If clouds are full of water,
they pour rain on the earth.
Whether a tree falls to the south or to the north,
in the place where it falls, there it will lie.
[4] Whoever watches the wind will not plant;
whoever looks at the clouds will not reap.

[5] As you do not know the path of the wind,
or how the body is formed[b] in a mother's womb,
so you cannot understand the work of God,
the Maker of all things.

[6] Sow your seed in the morning,
and at evening let your hands not be idle,
for you do not know which will succeed,
whether this or that,
or whether both will do equally well.

Remember Your Creator While Young

[7] Light is sweet,
and it pleases the eyes to see the sun.
[8] However many years anyone may live,
let them enjoy them all.
But let them remember the days of darkness,
for there will be many.
Everything to come is meaningless.

[9] You who are young, be happy while you are young,
and let your heart give you joy in the days of your youth.
Follow the ways of your heart
and whatever your eyes see,
but know that for all these things
God will bring you into judgment.
[10] So then, banish anxiety from your heart
and cast off the troubles of your body,
for youth and vigor are meaningless.

[a] 16 Or *king is a child* [b] 5 Or *know how life* (or *the spirit*) / *enters the body being formed*

ECCLESIASTES 11:9 – 10

ANXIETY AND HAPPINESS

Solomon almost certainly experienced anxiety and worry as he built for himself an incredible kingdom on earth. But by the time Solomon wrote Ecclesiastes, he had realized the futility of worrying. Drawing from his own experience that worry never brings anything positive in life, he advised his readers to be happy and enjoy the life that God had given them. Solomon's teaching on anxiety is similar to Paul's teaching in Philippians 4:6, where he exhorted believers to combat anxiety with prayer in order to experience the fullness of the peace of God. This emphasis on contentment rooted in Christ reflects Jesus' own teachings about the folly of anxiety (Lk 12:22 – 31). Worrying indicates a lack of faith in the God who provides for his creatures. As Jesus pointed out, the birds neither sow nor reap, yet they are fed; the wild flowers do not toil to make clothes, yet "not even Solomon in all his splendor was dressed like one of these" (Lk 12:27). Through faith, believers can experience freedom from anxiety and true happiness with the life God has given them. They can cast their anxiety on the God who offers "eternal glory in Christ" (1Pe 5:7,10; cf. Ps 55:22).

JESUS AND LIFE BEYOND DEATH

Solomon closes Ecclesiastes the same way he began: " 'Meaningless! Meaningless!' says the Teacher. 'Everything is meaningless!' " However, Solomon adds an important observation at the end of the book: he differentiates the mere human body, which returns to dust, and the human spirit, which returns to God. Solomon's claim that the body will return to the ground echoes the affirmation in Genesis that creatures are mortal; unlike the eternal, living God, humanity's life is a gift, granted and sustained by the breath of God (Ge 2:7). Every human life ends with the burial of a body, and that body returns to the dust from which it was made.

Life is meaningless if a decomposing body in the grave marks the end of the story. But Solomon asserted that in some sense God keeps and preserves human life beyond the grave. While the body of every human turns back into dust after death, "the spirit returns to God who gave it" (Ecc 12:7). There is more to the human body than flesh, blood and bones.

In Genesis, God made the first human out of dust, but this human did not become a living being until God breathed "into his nostrils the breath of life" (Ge 2:7). The breath of God is in each and every human being. That is what Solomon was referring to when he said that the spirit will return to God. He understood that God's gift of life somehow extended beyond bodily death.

The New Testament affirms and expands the insight that death is not the end. Jesus warned his disciples not to fear those who can only kill the body, but to fear the one who can kill both the body and the soul. God is the only one who has power over the human soul, and his final judgment will answer all the temporary injustices of this sinful world (Mt 10:28; Rev 21:1 – 8). Each soul is of infinite value (Mt 16:26), and believers should devote their souls fully to God (Mt 22:37). Ultimately, the hope found in Christ provides the decisive answer to the troubling questions Solomon raised in Ecclesiastes. Solomon found some solace in the knowledge that the spirit would return to God. But God's people today know that everything is transformed by the hope of heaven: "For you died, and your life is now hidden with Christ in God. When Christ, who is your life, appears, then you also will appear with him in glory" (Col 3:3 – 4).

12 Remember your Creator
in the days of your youth,
before the days of trouble come
and the years approach when you will say,
"I find no pleasure in them" —
2 before the sun and the light
and the moon and the stars grow dark,
and the clouds return after the rain;
3 when the keepers of the house tremble,
and the strong men stoop,
when the grinders cease because they are few,
and those looking through the windows grow dim;
4 when the doors to the street are closed
and the sound of grinding fades;
when people rise up at the sound of birds,
but all their songs grow faint;
5 when people are afraid of heights
and of dangers in the streets;
when the almond tree blossoms
and the grasshopper drags itself along
and desire no longer is stirred.
Then people go to their eternal home
and mourners go about the streets.

6 Remember him — before the silver cord is severed,
and the golden bowl is broken;
before the pitcher is shattered at the spring,
and the wheel broken at the well,
7 and the dust returns to the ground it came from,
and the spirit returns to God who gave it.

8 "Meaningless! Meaningless!" says the Teacher.[a]
"Everything is meaningless!"

The Conclusion of the Matter

9 Not only was the Teacher wise, but he also imparted knowledge to the people. He pondered and searched out and set in order many proverbs. 10 The Teacher searched to find just the right words, and what he wrote was upright and true.
11 The words of the wise are like goads, their collected sayings like firmly em-
bedded nails — given by one shepherd.[b] 12 Be warned, my son, of anything in addition to them.

Of making many books there is no end, and much study wearies the body.

13 Now all has been heard;
here is the conclusion of the matter:
Fear God and keep his commandments,
for this is the duty of all mankind.
14 For God will bring every deed into judgment,
including every hidden thing,
whether it is good or evil.

ECCLESIASTES 12:13

FEAR GOD AND KEEP HIS COMMANDMENTS

After all of his teaching and exhortation, Solomon closed the book of Ecclesiastes with a simple command: "Fear God and keep his commandments." Solomon wrote from an incredibly unique perspective. He had experienced the best that life has to offer in terms of fortune, fame and pleasure, yet he boiled all of life down into this one simple phrase. Jesus was asked to define the single most important commandment in all the law. He responded with a simple, twofold command: love God and love your neighbor (Mt 22:37 – 39). The final counsel of Solomon's great wisdom combines with Christ's clarification of the law to reveal an amazing connection between wisdom, obedience and love. The pinnacle of wisdom is respecting and obeying God — and the heart of obedience to God's law consists of loving God and other people. Amidst all the wisdom and counsel within the book of Ecclesiastes, this insight is something that anyone should be able to apply to their life. Solomon's words of wisdom connect directly to Christ's way of obedience and love.

[a] *8* Or *the leader of the assembly*; also in verses 9 and 10 [b] *11* Or *Shepherd*

JESUS: OUR DEEPEST COMPANION

SONG OF SONGS

SONG OF SONGS

REIGN OF DAVID	REIGN OF SOLOMON	ISRAEL DIVIDED
c. 1010 – 970 BC	*c. 970 – 930 BC*	*c. 930 BC*

The Song of Songs, traditionally assumed to be written by Solomon, provides lyrical insight into the depth of human love and desire. Like the other areas of wisdom discussed in the books of Proverbs, Ecclesiastes, Job and Psalms, Song of Songs is meant to describe practical aspects of God's intentions for his people. In this book, the emphasis is on the marriage relationship between a man and a woman: the beauty of the marriage union seen in the passionate pursuit of the lover and his beloved. While human relationships are described in other places in the wisdom literature, the Song of Songs stands alone in its portrayal of human love and sexuality.

Allegorical interpretations of the book seek to compare God's love for his people, epitomized in the work of Jesus Christ, to the bridegroom in Song of Songs and the church to the bride. The pursuit, love and faithfulness seen in the book are certainly emblematic of the way God loves his people; however, the main focus of the book centers on the God-ordained priority of marriage and sexual intimacy.

As part of his "very good" creation, God gave away the first bride, Eve, to her husband, Adam. Since that time, God has used marriage to provide love and companionship to his image-bearers and to allow them, together, to accomplish his good purposes on this earth. Together, a married couple models the love God has for his church.

Song of Songs provides wisdom for lovers on how to pursue one another and love each other well. Using poetic imagery, the book models how couples can speak words of affirmation, seek the fulfillment of their spouse and find delight in sexual intimacy. This book reveals the practical nature of the Scripture and shows that God cares about all aspects of human existence.

However, as with all other aspects of life in the fallen world, marriage is not intended to be the ultimate pursuit of God's children. While these relationships are a source of great joy and fulfillment, they are a mere shadow of the love found in Christ. Ultimately, marriage is a temporary relationship that embodies the love of Christ through sacrificial service and selfless love. In heaven there will no longer be marriage (Mt 22:30); there God's followers will revel in their beloved Savior, Jesus Christ. Until then, God's people see in the beauty of God-honoring human relationships a picture of the divine companion, Jesus Christ, who will always love us with a never-ending, ever-pursuing love.

MY BELOVED IS MINE AND I AM HIS.

Song of Songs 2:16

SONG OF SONGS

1 Solomon's Song of Songs.

She[a]

[2] Let him kiss me with the kisses of his mouth—
for your love is more delightful than wine.
[3] Pleasing is the fragrance of your perfumes;
your name is like perfume poured out.
No wonder the young women love you!
[4] Take me away with you—let us hurry!
Let the king bring me into his chambers.

Friends

We rejoice and delight in you[b];
we will praise your love more than wine.

She

How right they are to adore you!

[5] Dark am I, yet lovely,
daughters of Jerusalem,
dark like the tents of Kedar,
like the tent curtains of Solomon.[c]
[6] Do not stare at me because I am dark,
because I am darkened by the sun.
My mother's sons were angry with me
and made me take care of the vineyards;
my own vineyard I had to neglect.
[7] Tell me, you whom I love,
where you graze your flock
and where you rest your sheep at midday.
Why should I be like a veiled woman
beside the flocks of your friends?

Friends

[8] If you do not know, most beautiful of women,
follow the tracks of the sheep
and graze your young goats
by the tents of the shepherds.

He

[9] I liken you, my darling, to a mare
among Pharaoh's chariot horses.
[10] Your cheeks are beautiful with earrings,
your neck with strings of jewels.
[11] We will make you earrings of gold,
studded with silver.

SONG OF SONGS 1:7

LOVE SONG

The Song of Songs portrays the height of human love. Here, the woman asks Solomon where he leads his flocks so that she can arrange to be near him. Her heart is captivated by innocent desire for this man. She does not waste time with emotional innuendo, merely hinting at her affections. She is unashamed and unafraid, freely expressing her interest in the king.

Between a husband and a wife, fear of rejection often veils actual affection. This exists because sin has corrupted human relationships. Jesus—who conquered sin—liberates men and women to live freely in love with a spouse, secure in their marriage commitment. Those who believe in him have right standing with God by faith—trusting grace to cover all aspects of life, including love relationships. The two lovers in this passage illustrate God's delight in joyful marriage marked by unfiltered desire. Perfect love, ultimately realized in the person of Jesus, drives out all fear (1Jn 4:18).

---

[a] The main male and female speakers (identified primarily on the basis of the gender of the relevant Hebrew forms) are indicated by the captions *He* and *She* respectively. The words of others are marked *Friends*. In some instances the divisions and their captions are debatable.
[b] 4 The Hebrew is masculine singular. [c] 5 Or *Salma*

She

[12] While the king was at his table,
my perfume spread its fragrance.
[13] My beloved is to me a sachet of myrrh
resting between my breasts.
[14] My beloved is to me a cluster of henna blossoms
from the vineyards of En Gedi.

He

[15] How beautiful you are, my darling!
Oh, how beautiful!
Your eyes are doves.

She

[16] How handsome you are, my beloved!
Oh, how charming!
And our bed is verdant.

He

[17] The beams of our house are cedars;
our rafters are firs.

She[a]

2 I am a rose[b] of Sharon,
a lily of the valleys.

He

[2] Like a lily among thorns
is my darling among the young women.

She

[3] Like an apple[c] tree among the trees of the forest
is my beloved among the young men.
I delight to sit in his shade,
and his fruit is sweet to my taste.
[4] Let him lead me to the banquet hall,
and let his banner over me be love.
[5] Strengthen me with raisins,
refresh me with apples,
for I am faint with love.
[6] His left arm is under my head,
and his right arm embraces me.
[7] Daughters of Jerusalem, I charge you
by the gazelles and by the does of the field:
Do not arouse or awaken love
until it so desires.

[8] Listen! My beloved!
Look! Here he comes,
leaping across the mountains,
bounding over the hills.
[9] My beloved is like a gazelle or a young stag.
Look! There he stands behind our wall,
gazing through the windows,
peering through the lattice.

[a] Or *He* [b] *1* Probably a member of the crocus family [c] *3* Or possibly *apricot*; here and elsewhere in Song of Songs

SONG OF SONGS 2:4

JESUS IS OUR ETERNAL BANNER OF LOVE

King Solomon's banquet hall was a place of splendor, utilized for occasions of great joy. It was furnished with the finest things so that celebrations were extravagant and luxurious. The woman looked forward to joining the king there, aware that the privilege of being in such a place happened only because she was with him. His *banner* over her is a symbol of the permanence of his commitment to his beloved. More than just association, she was chosen—claimed not by force but with love.

When Jesus completed his mission on earth, he ascended to the Father to prepare a place for his bride, the church (Jn 14:2–3). Men and women in Christ are chosen and claimed by love. They are saved by grace—a priceless gift from God (Eph 2:8–9). Their future in the extravagance of heaven is established and guaranteed because they belong to the King. At life's end, those who believe in Jesus will enjoy an everlasting banquet. They will delight in the pleasures of heaven—the greatest of these is the presence of the One who *is* love (1Jn 4:8).

[10] My beloved spoke and said to me,
"Arise, my darling,
my beautiful one, come with me.
[11] See! The winter is past;
the rains are over and gone.
[12] Flowers appear on the earth;
the season of singing has come,
the cooing of doves
is heard in our land.
[13] The fig tree forms its early fruit;
the blossoming vines spread their fragrance.
Arise, come, my darling;
my beautiful one, come with me."

He

[14] My dove in the clefts of the rock,
in the hiding places on the mountainside,
show me your face,
let me hear your voice;
for your voice is sweet,
and your face is lovely.
[15] Catch for us the foxes,
the little foxes
that ruin the vineyards,
our vineyards that are in bloom.

She

[16] My beloved is mine and I am his;
he browses among the lilies.
[17] Until the day breaks
and the shadows flee,
turn, my beloved,
and be like a gazelle
or like a young stag
on the rugged hills.[a]

3 All night long on my bed
I looked for the one my heart loves;
I looked for him but did not find him.
[2] I will get up now and go about the city,
through its streets and squares;
I will search for the one my heart loves.
So I looked for him but did not find him.
[3] The watchmen found me
as they made their rounds in the city.
"Have you seen the one my heart loves?"
[4] Scarcely had I passed them
when I found the one my heart loves.
I held him and would not let him go
till I had brought him to my mother's house,
to the room of the one who conceived me.
[5] Daughters of Jerusalem, I charge you
by the gazelles and by the does of the field:
Do not arouse or awaken love
until it so desires.

[a] 17 Or *the hills of Bether*

[6] Who is this coming up from the wilderness
 like a column of smoke,
perfumed with myrrh and incense
 made from all the spices of the merchant?
[7] Look! It is Solomon's carriage,
 escorted by sixty warriors,
 the noblest of Israel,
[8] all of them wearing the sword,
 all experienced in battle,
each with his sword at his side,
 prepared for the terrors of the night.
[9] King Solomon made for himself the carriage;
 he made it of wood from Lebanon.
[10] Its posts he made of silver,
 its base of gold.
Its seat was upholstered with purple,
 its interior inlaid with love.
Daughters of Jerusalem, [11] come out,
 and look, you daughters of Zion.
Look[a] on King Solomon wearing a crown,
 the crown with which his mother crowned him
on the day of his wedding,
 the day his heart rejoiced.

He

4 How beautiful you are, my darling!
 Oh, how beautiful!
 Your eyes behind your veil are doves.
Your hair is like a flock of goats
 descending from the hills of Gilead.
[2] Your teeth are like a flock of sheep just shorn,
 coming up from the washing.
Each has its twin;
 not one of them is alone.
[3] Your lips are like a scarlet ribbon;
 your mouth is lovely.
Your temples behind your veil
 are like the halves of a pomegranate.
[4] Your neck is like the tower of David,
 built with courses of stone[b];
on it hang a thousand shields,
 all of them shields of warriors.
[5] Your breasts are like two fawns,
 like twin fawns of a gazelle
 that browse among the lilies.
[6] Until the day breaks
 and the shadows flee,
I will go to the mountain of myrrh
 and to the hill of incense.
[7] You are altogether beautiful, my darling;
 there is no flaw in you.

[8] Come with me from Lebanon, my bride,
 come with me from Lebanon.

---

[a] 10,11 Or *interior lovingly inlaid / by the daughters of Jerusalem. / [11] Come out, you daughters of Zion, / and look* [b] 4 The meaning of the Hebrew for this phrase is uncertain.

THE WEDDING

Chapter 3 of Song of Songs depicts the wedding between the two lovers. Verse 6 starts with Solomon's entrance to the wedding ceremony. The king and his escorts arrive to meet the woman, creating a dramatic spectacle. The procession is extravagant. Solomon has spared no expense in presenting himself to his bride. In verses 9 through 11, the text describes two objects connected with the king's arrival: a carriage and a crown.

The carriage was made of wood from Lebanon, some of the most prized material in the world. Its posts were crafted from silver, its base fashioned with gold and the seat upholstered with purple cloth. Solomon's carriage was unmistakably royal — luxurious and impressive. The other object of note is a crown placed on his head by his mother. This was likely a special wedding wreath, distinguishing him as the day's honored hero and celebrated victor.

The New Testament describes two major entrances by Jesus the Son of God. The first is his birth in a Bethlehem manger (Lk 2:7). This quiet arrival is marked by chosen humility. He could have arrived with fanfare befitting the King of the universe. Yet Jesus chose to take on the nature of a servant (Php 2:7) in order to call his eventual followers to faith. Jesus is worthy of all honor and glory, but his earthly ministry began in near obscurity, celebrated by only a few observers. His other entrance — his future coming from heaven to gather his own and to end sin's reign — will be exponentially more dramatic (1Th 4:14 – 17). The entire population of earth will stop to give stunned attention. Those who believe will rejoice and celebrate. Those who reject salvation in Christ's name will tremble and weep. Jesus will come as a conqueror and King (Titus 2:13).

Solomon's kingship, though significant, is miniscule in comparison to the power and authority of the Son of God. Jesus is not simply king over one nation or region; he is the eternal King above all things in existence. When Jesus comes for his own, creation's King will wear a victor's crown and will also dispense unfading crowns to all those who have believed (1Pe 5:4).

Descend from the crest of Amana,
from the top of Senir, the summit of Hermon,
from the lions' dens
and the mountain haunts of leopards.
9 You have stolen my heart, my sister, my bride;
you have stolen my heart
with one glance of your eyes,
with one jewel of your necklace.
10 How delightful is your love, my sister, my bride!
How much more pleasing is your love than wine,
and the fragrance of your perfume
more than any spice!
11 Your lips drop sweetness as the honeycomb, my bride;
milk and honey are under your tongue.
The fragrance of your garments
is like the fragrance of Lebanon.
12 You are a garden locked up, my sister, my bride;
you are a spring enclosed, a sealed fountain.
13 Your plants are an orchard of pomegranates
with choice fruits,
with henna and nard,
14 nard and saffron,
calamus and cinnamon,
with every kind of incense tree,
with myrrh and aloes
and all the finest spices.
15 You are[a] a garden fountain,
a well of flowing water
streaming down from Lebanon.

She

16 Awake, north wind,
and come, south wind!
Blow on my garden,
that its fragrance may spread everywhere.
Let my beloved come into his garden
and taste its choice fruits.

He

5 I have come into my garden, my sister, my bride;
I have gathered my myrrh with my spice.
I have eaten my honeycomb and my honey;
I have drunk my wine and my milk.

Friends

Eat, friends, and drink;
drink your fill of love.

She

2 I slept but my heart was awake.
Listen! My beloved is knocking:
"Open to me, my sister, my darling,
my dove, my flawless one.
My head is drenched with dew,
my hair with the dampness of the night."

[a] 15 Or *I am* (spoken by *She*)

3 I have taken off my robe —
must I put it on again?
I have washed my feet —
must I soil them again?
4 My beloved thrust his hand through the latch-opening;
my heart began to pound for him.
5 I arose to open for my beloved,
and my hands dripped with myrrh,
my fingers with flowing myrrh,
on the handles of the bolt.
6 I opened for my beloved,
but my beloved had left; he was gone.
My heart sank at his departure.[a]
I looked for him but did not find him.
I called him but he did not answer.
7 The watchmen found me
as they made their rounds in the city.
They beat me, they bruised me;
they took away my cloak,
those watchmen of the walls!
8 Daughters of Jerusalem, I charge you —
if you find my beloved,
what will you tell him?
Tell him I am faint with love.

Friends

9 How is your beloved better than others,
most beautiful of women?
How is your beloved better than others,
that you so charge us?

She

10 My beloved is radiant and ruddy,
outstanding among ten thousand.
11 His head is purest gold;
his hair is wavy
and black as a raven.
12 His eyes are like doves
by the water streams,
washed in milk,
mounted like jewels.
13 His cheeks are like beds of spice
yielding perfume.
His lips are like lilies
dripping with myrrh.
14 His arms are rods of gold
set with topaz.
His body is like polished ivory
decorated with lapis lazuli.
15 His legs are pillars of marble
set on bases of pure gold.
His appearance is like Lebanon,
choice as its cedars.
16 His mouth is sweetness itself;
he is altogether lovely.

---

[a] 6 Or *heart had gone out to him when he spoke*

EMOTIONS

Every relationship experiences highs and lows, and the two lovers in Song of Songs are no exception. In chapter 5, Solomon withdrew from the woman, and she quickly realized a gap started to form between them. She cried for his return but heard no answer. The emotions of the two lovers are clear throughout the entire book, but most often they are emotions of great joy. Chapter 5 shows a severe emotional swing toward separation and sadness, as the woman's heart sank after being away from her lover.

The young bride is not unique in her experience of heavy emotions. Jesus showed he was capable of great emotional depth. He illustrated the joy a shepherd experiences when a lost sheep is found, pointing to his own happiness (Lk 15:5 – 6). Additionally, there were times when Jesus was filled with tremendous sorrow (Jn 11:35). One of Jesus' most emotional moments is recorded in Mark 14 while praying in the Garden of Gethsemane before his imminent arrest. Verse 34 says, "My soul is overwhelmed with sorrow to the point of death." He knew that he was on his way to the cross to die for the sins of humankind, and similar to the woman in Song of Songs, his heart sank. Jesus' last words recorded in Matthew's Gospel are " '*Eli, Eli, lema sabachthani?*' (which means 'My God, my God, why have you forsaken me?')" (Mt 27:46). Every past, present and future sin was heaped upon Jesus at the moment when he cried out, and it was in that moment that Jesus experienced separation from God for the first time in all eternity.

It is important to know that Jesus' separation from God on the cross was only momentary. He died on the cross, atoning for sin, and he rose to life in victory over death (1Co 15:55 – 56). In Song of Songs, the separation of the lovers was only temporary as well.

This is my beloved, this is my friend,
daughters of Jerusalem.

Friends

6 Where has your beloved gone,
most beautiful of women?
Which way did your beloved turn,
that we may look for him with you?

She

2 My beloved has gone down to his garden,
to the beds of spices,
to browse in the gardens
and to gather lilies.
3 I am my beloved's and my beloved is mine;
he browses among the lilies.

He

4 You are as beautiful as Tirzah, my darling,
as lovely as Jerusalem,
as majestic as troops with banners.
5 Turn your eyes from me;
they overwhelm me.
Your hair is like a flock of goats
descending from Gilead.
6 Your teeth are like a flock of sheep
coming up from the washing.
Each has its twin,
not one of them is missing.
7 Your temples behind your veil
are like the halves of a pomegranate.
8 Sixty queens there may be,
and eighty concubines,
and virgins beyond number;
9 but my dove, my perfect one, is unique,
the only daughter of her mother,
the favorite of the one who bore her.
The young women saw her and called her blessed;
the queens and concubines praised her.

Friends

10 Who is this that appears like the dawn,
fair as the moon, bright as the sun,
majestic as the stars in procession?

He

11 I went down to the grove of nut trees
to look at the new growth in the valley,
to see if the vines had budded
or the pomegranates were in bloom.
12 Before I realized it,
my desire set me among the royal chariots of my people.[a]

Friends

13 Come back, come back, O Shulammite;
come back, come back, that we may gaze on you!

---

[a] 12 Or *among the chariots of Amminadab*; or *among the chariots of the people of the prince*

He

Why would you gaze on the Shulammite
as on the dance of Mahanaim?[a]

7

[b] How beautiful your sandaled feet,
O prince's daughter!
Your graceful legs are like jewels,
the work of an artist's hands.
2 Your navel is a rounded goblet
that never lacks blended wine.
Your waist is a mound of wheat
encircled by lilies.
3 Your breasts are like two fawns,
like twin fawns of a gazelle.
4 Your neck is like an ivory tower.
Your eyes are the pools of Heshbon
by the gate of Bath Rabbim.
Your nose is like the tower of Lebanon
looking toward Damascus.
5 Your head crowns you like Mount Carmel.
Your hair is like royal tapestry;
the king is held captive by its tresses.
6 How beautiful you are and how pleasing,
my love, with your delights!
7 Your stature is like that of the palm,
and your breasts like clusters of fruit.
8 I said, "I will climb the palm tree;
I will take hold of its fruit."
May your breasts be like clusters of grapes on the vine,
the fragrance of your breath like apples,
9 and your mouth like the best wine.

She

May the wine go straight to my beloved,
flowing gently over lips and teeth.[c]
10 I belong to my beloved,
and his desire is for me.
11 Come, my beloved, let us go to the countryside,
let us spend the night in the villages.[d]
12 Let us go early to the vineyards
to see if the vines have budded,
if their blossoms have opened,
and if the pomegranates are in bloom—
there I will give you my love.
13 The mandrakes send out their fragrance,
and at our door is every delicacy,
both new and old,
that I have stored up for you, my beloved.

8

If only you were to me like a brother,
who was nursed at my mother's breasts!
Then, if I found you outside,
I would kiss you,
and no one would despise me.

---

[a] *13* In Hebrew texts this verse (6:13) is numbered 7:1. [b] In Hebrew texts 7:1-13 is numbered 7:2-14. [c] *9* Septuagint, Aquila, Vulgate and Syriac; Hebrew *lips of sleepers* [d] *11* Or *the henna bushes*

[2] I would lead you
and bring you to my mother's house —
she who has taught me.
I would give you spiced wine to drink,
the nectar of my pomegranates.
[3] His left arm is under my head
and his right arm embraces me.
[4] Daughters of Jerusalem, I charge you:
Do not arouse or awaken love
until it so desires.

Friends

[5] Who is this coming up from the wilderness
leaning on her beloved?

She

Under the apple tree I roused you;
there your mother conceived you,
there she who was in labor gave you birth.
[6] Place me like a seal over your heart,
like a seal on your arm;
for love is as strong as death,
its jealousy[a] unyielding as the grave.
It burns like blazing fire,
like a mighty flame.[b]
[7] Many waters cannot quench love;
rivers cannot sweep it away.
If one were to give
all the wealth of one's house for love,
it[c] would be utterly scorned.

Friends

[8] We have a little sister,
and her breasts are not yet grown.
What shall we do for our sister
on the day she is spoken for?
[9] If she is a wall,
we will build towers of silver on her.
If she is a door,
we will enclose her with panels of cedar.

She

[10] I am a wall,
and my breasts are like towers.
Thus I have become in his eyes
like one bringing contentment.
[11] Solomon had a vineyard in Baal Hamon;
he let out his vineyard to tenants.
Each was to bring for its fruit
a thousand shekels[d] of silver.
[12] But my own vineyard is mine to give;
the thousand shekels are for you, Solomon,
and two hundred[e] are for those who tend its fruit.

---

[a] *6* Or *ardor* [b] *6* Or *fire, / like the very flame of the LORD* [c] *7* Or *he* [d] *11* That is, about 25 pounds or about 12 kilograms; also in verse 12 [e] *12* That is, about 5 pounds or about 2.3 kilograms

LOVE AS STRONG AS DEATH

Song of Songs describes the relationship between two people who are in love. But the book offers more than specific descriptions of a particular relationship. As the book concludes, the author shares a powerful reflection on the nature and essence of the love between husbands and wives. Love is not superficial in nature, but it is a strong bond that ties two individuals together.

"Love is as strong as death." Nothing personifies love more than Jesus and his outrageous act of grace. He loves people so much that he was willing to die an undeserving death. Solomon's bride knew the depths of earthly love as an overwhelming force and unbreakable bond. Jesus defined the strength of love by dying for undeserving people (Ro 5:6 – 8).

The phrase "until death do us part" — a common wedding vow today — is another way of saying "our love is as strong as death." This phrase is a vow to a lifelong commitment to one's spouse, and it is not something to be said lightly. Jesus said that there was no greater love than the kind that makes one willing to lay down one's life for a friend, and he followed through (Jn 15:13).

In the same way that marriage begins with a profound and permanent commitment, beginning a relationship with God means committing to live one's entire life fully devoted to Jesus. Nothing can separate a Christian from God's strong love (Ro 8:37 – 39). Those who believe in Jesus cling to the promise that love endures beyond physical death because of the hope of eternal life.

He

13 You who dwell in the gardens
with friends in attendance,
let me hear your voice!

She

14 Come away, my beloved,
and be like a gazelle
or like a young stag
on the spice-laden mountains.

SONG OF SONGS 8:14

JESUS' REUNION WITH HIS BRIDE

Secure and free in each other's love, the woman calls her beloved to her—longing for Solomon to overtake her in delight. She beckons him to rush to her, satisfying a long-anticipated togetherness.

Scripture here describes righteous desire—passion between a married man and woman. Their commitment to each other and their past experiences together fuel longing for new moments of intimacy. The calling and invitation in this text reflect the longing in the heart of the Christian to see Jesus face to face (Rev 19:7). One day, the anticipation of every believer will be satisfied. Until then, there is a calling back and forth between heaven and earth. "The Spirit and the bride say, 'Come!' And let the one who hears say, 'Come!' Let the one who is thirsty come; and let the one who wishes take the free gift of the water of life" (Rev 22:17). Jesus answers, "Yes, I am coming soon" (Rev 22:20). Hallelujah!

JESUS: OUR SOVEREIGN SAVIOR

ISAIAH

ISAIAH

REIGN OF UZZIAH BEGINS *c. 792 BC*	PROPHETIC MINISTRY OF ISAIAH BEGINS *c. 740 BC*	FALL OF ISRAEL *c. 722 BC*

Isaiah's vision of God's glory (6:1 – 5) propelled his message and mission. The words he proclaimed were filled with warning, confrontation and rebuke for God's people due to their spiritual unfaithfulness. As a result, Isaiah was opposed by his contemporaries, those who needed his message most.

Isaiah, Jeremiah and Ezekiel are known as the "Major Prophets." This title does not denote the importance of these books compared to the "Minor Prophets," but rather refers to the length and the scope of their writings. All of the prophets were God-ordained spokespersons who God called, appointed and used to declare his word to his people.

Isaiah, like many of the prophets, warned a spiritually adulterous and morally corrupt people of the coming consequences for their waywardness. As God had promised, the disobedient nation of Israel would not be immune to God's wrath. As he had done to the nations before them, God would drive his people from the land if they did not turn to him in repentance and faith. The first portion of the book, chapters 1 – 39, describes the coming judgment at the hands of the Assyrians in the second half of the eighth century BC. The final portion of the book, chapters 40 – 66, looks forward more than a century to encourage the people of Judah who would be taken into exile in Babylon. In spite of the nation's rebellion, however, Isaiah pictured a coming day when God would demonstrate the majesty of his mercy and grace. Central to Isaiah's prophetic writings are the vivid images of the promised Messiah who would suffer and die for the sins of God's people (52:13 — 53:12). The images portray the coming One as a humble servant, a willing substitute and a sacrificial lamb who would give his life for the transgressions of his people.

To scattered exiles languishing under the consequences of their sin, the lasting legacy of Isaiah's message was hope and assurance in God's enduring faithfulness. God's people could be assured of God's provision, in spite of their continual proclivity toward sin. The long-awaited Messiah, Jesus Christ, would finally and fully fulfill the glorious reality to which Isaiah pointed. Jesus' work secured peace with God, forgiveness for sin and hope for all those who trust in him.

BUT HE WAS PIERCED FOR OUR TRANSGRESSIONS,
HE WAS CRUSHED FOR OUR INIQUITIES;
THE PUNISHMENT THAT BROUGHT US PEACE
WAS ON HIM, AND BY HIS WOUNDS WE ARE HEALED.

Isaiah 53:5

ISAIAH

1 The vision concerning Judah and Jerusalem that Isaiah son of Amoz saw during the reigns of Uzziah, Jotham, Ahaz and Hezekiah, kings of Judah.

A Rebellious Nation

[2] Hear me, you heavens! Listen, earth!
For the LORD has spoken:
"I reared children and brought them up,
but they have rebelled against me.
[3] The ox knows its master,
the donkey its owner's manger,
but Israel does not know,
my people do not understand."
[4] Woe to the sinful nation,
a people whose guilt is great,
a brood of evildoers,
children given to corruption!
They have forsaken the LORD;
they have spurned the Holy One of Israel
and turned their backs on him.

[5] Why should you be beaten anymore?
Why do you persist in rebellion?
Your whole head is injured,
your whole heart afflicted.
[6] From the sole of your foot to the top of your head
there is no soundness—
only wounds and welts
and open sores,
not cleansed or bandaged
or soothed with olive oil.

[7] Your country is desolate,
your cities burned with fire;
your fields are being stripped by foreigners
right before you,
laid waste as when overthrown by strangers.
[8] Daughter Zion is left
like a shelter in a vineyard,
like a hut in a cucumber field,
like a city under siege.
[9] Unless the LORD Almighty
had left us some survivors,
we would have become like Sodom,
we would have been like Gomorrah.

[10] Hear the word of the LORD,
you rulers of Sodom;
listen to the instruction of our God,
you people of Gomorrah!
[11] "The multitude of your sacrifices—
what are they to me?" says the LORD.

"I have more than enough of burnt offerings,
of rams and the fat of fattened animals;
I have no pleasure
in the blood of bulls and lambs and goats.
12 When you come to appear before me,
who has asked this of you,
this trampling of my courts?
13 Stop bringing meaningless offerings!
Your incense is detestable to me.
New Moons, Sabbaths and convocations —
I cannot bear your worthless assemblies.
14 Your New Moon feasts and your appointed festivals
I hate with all my being.
They have become a burden to me;
I am weary of bearing them.
15 When you spread out your hands in prayer,
I hide my eyes from you;
even when you offer many prayers,
I am not listening.

Your hands are full of blood!

16 Wash and make yourselves clean.
Take your evil deeds out of my sight;
stop doing wrong.
17 Learn to do right; seek justice.
Defend the oppressed.[a]
Take up the cause of the fatherless;
plead the case of the widow.

18 "Come now, let us settle the matter,"
says the LORD.
"Though your sins are like scarlet,
they shall be as white as snow;
though they are red as crimson,
they shall be like wool.
19 If you are willing and obedient,
you will eat the good things of the land;
20 but if you resist and rebel,
you will be devoured by the sword."
For the mouth of the LORD has spoken.

21 See how the faithful city
has become a prostitute!
She once was full of justice;
righteousness used to dwell in her —
but now murderers!
22 Your silver has become dross,
your choice wine is diluted with water.
23 Your rulers are rebels,
partners with thieves;
they all love bribes
and chase after gifts.
They do not defend the cause of the fatherless;
the widow's case does not come before them.

24 Therefore the Lord, the LORD Almighty,
the Mighty One of Israel, declares:

[a] 17 Or *justice. / Correct the oppressor*

ISAIAH 1:14

GOD-HONORING WORSHIP

The first chapter of Isaiah records the prophet's lament that God's people had abandoned true worship and instead chose to rebel against their God. While the people continued to go through the motions and maintained their rituals and religious practices, God was burdened by the weight of their empty worship. God does not want his people to monotonously obey his rules out of blind obligation; rather, he desires that praise for him would come from the deepest longing of the heart.

As always, God's priority is the heart of his people and not their outward actions or appearance. God chose David to be king by looking at his heart and not his outward appearance (1Sa 16:7). Jesus similarly taught that God knows people's hearts and has little regard for the things that humans value, such as money (Lk 16:15). God's concern is that a person worship him rightly, from the heart. Wise Solomon wrote, "Above all else, guard your heart, for everything you do flows from it" (Pr 4:23). Acts of true worship that are pleasing to God flow from hearts that are faithful to him.

ISAIAH 2:3–5

NO MORE WAR

Isaiah chapter 2, in direct contrast to chapter 1, pictures a coming day when God's people would worship him rightly — with pure hearts. This is an inclusive look into God's righteous reign, a day when "many peoples" will look to God for wisdom (v. 3). On this great and future day, war will cease because God's peace will reign in the world once more (v. 4). The people, however, failed to heed the warnings that Isaiah told them about, so God judged them with the sword of invading foreign armies.

The coming of Jesus, likewise, brings a "sword" that purifies a people for himself and exposes mere religious observance that is not driven from a heart in love with God (Mt 10:34). And a spear found the side of Jesus himself (Jn 19:34), who, though he knew no sin, became sin for his people so that they would not have to experience the wrath of God that their sin deserved.

"Ah! I will vent my wrath on my foes
and avenge myself on my enemies.
25 I will turn my hand against you;[a]
I will thoroughly purge away your dross
and remove all your impurities.
26 I will restore your leaders as in days of old,
your rulers as at the beginning.
Afterward you will be called
the City of Righteousness,
the Faithful City."

27 Zion will be delivered with justice,
her penitent ones with righteousness.
28 But rebels and sinners will both be broken,
and those who forsake the LORD will perish.

29 "You will be ashamed because of the sacred oaks
in which you have delighted;
you will be disgraced because of the gardens
that you have chosen.
30 You will be like an oak with fading leaves,
like a garden without water.
31 The mighty man will become tinder
and his work a spark;
both will burn together,
with no one to quench the fire."

The Mountain of the LORD

2 This is what Isaiah son of Amoz saw concerning Judah and Jerusalem:

2 In the last days

the mountain of the LORD's temple will be established
as the highest of the mountains;
it will be exalted above the hills,
and all nations will stream to it.

3 Many peoples will come and say,

"Come, let us go up to the mountain of the LORD,
to the temple of the God of Jacob.
He will teach us his ways,
so that we may walk in his paths."
The law will go out from Zion,
the word of the LORD from Jerusalem.
4 He will judge between the nations
and will settle disputes for many peoples.
They will beat their swords into plowshares
and their spears into pruning hooks.
Nation will not take up sword against nation,
nor will they train for war anymore.

5 Come, descendants of Jacob,
let us walk in the light of the LORD.

The Day of the LORD

6 You, LORD, have abandoned your people,
the descendants of Jacob.

[a] 25 That is, against Jerusalem

They are full of superstitions from the East;
they practice divination like the Philistines
and embrace pagan customs.
7 Their land is full of silver and gold;
there is no end to their treasures.
Their land is full of horses;
there is no end to their chariots.
8 Their land is full of idols;
they bow down to the work of their hands,
to what their fingers have made.
9 So people will be brought low
and everyone humbled—
do not forgive them.[a]

10 Go into the rocks, hide in the ground
from the fearful presence of the LORD
and the splendor of his majesty!
11 The eyes of the arrogant will be humbled
and human pride brought low;
the LORD alone will be exalted in that day.

12 The LORD Almighty has a day in store
for all the proud and lofty,
for all that is exalted
(and they will be humbled),
13 for all the cedars of Lebanon, tall and lofty,
and all the oaks of Bashan,
14 for all the towering mountains
and all the high hills,
15 for every lofty tower
and every fortified wall,
16 for every trading ship[b]
and every stately vessel.
17 The arrogance of man will be brought low
and human pride humbled;
the LORD alone will be exalted in that day,
18 and the idols will totally disappear.

19 People will flee to caves in the rocks
and to holes in the ground
from the fearful presence of the LORD
and the splendor of his majesty,
when he rises to shake the earth.
20 In that day people will throw away
to the moles and bats
their idols of silver and idols of gold,
which they made to worship.
21 They will flee to caverns in the rocks
and to the overhanging crags
from the fearful presence of the LORD
and the splendor of his majesty,
when he rises to shake the earth.

22 Stop trusting in mere humans,
who have but a breath in their nostrils.
Why hold them in esteem?

---

[a] 9 Or *not raise them up* [b] 16 Hebrew *every ship of Tarshish*

Judgment on Jerusalem and Judah

3 See now, the Lord,
the LORD Almighty,
is about to take from Jerusalem and Judah
both supply and support:
all supplies of food and all supplies of water,
2 the hero and the warrior,
the judge and the prophet,
the diviner and the elder,
3 the captain of fifty and the man of rank,
the counselor, skilled craftsman and clever enchanter.

4 "I will make mere youths their officials;
children will rule over them."

5 People will oppress each other—
man against man, neighbor against neighbor.
The young will rise up against the old,
the nobody against the honored.

6 A man will seize one of his brothers
in his father's house, and say,
"You have a cloak, you be our leader;
take charge of this heap of ruins!"
7 But in that day he will cry out,
"I have no remedy.
I have no food or clothing in my house;
do not make me the leader of the people."

8 Jerusalem staggers,
Judah is falling;
their words and deeds are against the LORD,
defying his glorious presence.
9 The look on their faces testifies against them;
they parade their sin like Sodom;
they do not hide it.
Woe to them!
They have brought disaster upon themselves.

10 Tell the righteous it will be well with them,
for they will enjoy the fruit of their deeds.
11 Woe to the wicked!
Disaster is upon them!
They will be paid back
for what their hands have done.

12 Youths oppress my people,
women rule over them.
My people, your guides lead you astray;
they turn you from the path.

13 The LORD takes his place in court;
he rises to judge the people.
14 The LORD enters into judgment
against the elders and leaders of his people:
"It is you who have ruined my vineyard;
the plunder from the poor is in your houses.
15 What do you mean by crushing my people
and grinding the faces of the poor?"
declares the Lord, the LORD Almighty.

16 The LORD says,
"The women of Zion are haughty,
walking along with outstretched necks,
flirting with their eyes,
strutting along with swaying hips,
with ornaments jingling on their ankles.
17 Therefore the Lord will bring sores on the heads of the women of Zion;
the LORD will make their scalps bald."

18 In that day the Lord will snatch away their finery: the bangles and head-
bands and crescent necklaces, 19 the earrings and bracelets and veils, 20 the head-
dresses and anklets and sashes, the perfume bottles and charms, 21 the signet
rings and nose rings, 22 the fine robes and the capes and cloaks, the purses 23 and
mirrors, and the linen garments and tiaras and shawls.

24 Instead of fragrance there will be a stench;
instead of a sash, a rope;
instead of well-dressed hair, baldness;
instead of fine clothing, sackcloth;
instead of beauty, branding.
25 Your men will fall by the sword,
your warriors in battle.
26 The gates of Zion will lament and mourn;
destitute, she will sit on the ground.

4 1 In that day seven women
will take hold of one man
and say, "We will eat our own food
and provide our own clothes;
only let us be called by your name.
Take away our disgrace!"

The Branch of the LORD

2 In that day the Branch of the LORD will be beautiful and glorious, and the
fruit of the land will be the pride and glory of the survivors in Israel. 3 Those
who are left in Zion, who remain in Jerusalem, will be called holy, all who are
recorded among the living in Jerusalem. 4 The Lord will wash away the filth of
the women of Zion; he will cleanse the bloodstains from Jerusalem by a spirit[a]
of judgment and a spirit[a] of fire. 5 Then the LORD will create over all of Mount
Zion and over those who assemble there a cloud of smoke by day and a glow of
flaming fire by night; over everything the glory[b] will be a canopy. 6 It will be a
shelter and shade from the heat of the day, and a refuge and hiding place from
the storm and rain.

The Song of the Vineyard

5 I will sing for the one I love
a song about his vineyard:
My loved one had a vineyard
on a fertile hillside.
2 He dug it up and cleared it of stones
and planted it with the choicest vines.
He built a watchtower in it
and cut out a winepress as well.
Then he looked for a crop of good grapes,
but it yielded only bad fruit.

3 "Now you dwellers in Jerusalem and people of Judah,
judge between me and my vineyard.

[a] 4 Or *the Spirit* [b] 5 Or *over all the glory there*

ISAIAH 4:2

THE BRANCH

The image of the branch in this passage is used to represent both Judah and the coming Messiah. The word *branch* is derived from the Hebrew verb meaning "to sprout up" or "to come from death to life." In a literal sense, Isaiah is describing the prosperity and blessing that the people of Judah will one day experience following God's judgment for their unfaithfulness as described in Isaiah 3:1 — 4:1. However, the other important aspect of this section is the Messianic references that it contains. This is the first reference to the Messiah as the "Branch" of the Lord, yet there are several other mentions throughout Scripture (Isa 11:1; Jer 23:5; 33:15; Zec 3:8). The branch is an image for life and prosperity, and these verses point to the blessing that Jesus would one day bring to God's people. His blessing would allow fallen sinners to once again have fellowship and peace with God. This prophecy gives hope to the Israelites that the coming Messiah will bring life to the otherwise dying religion and law under which they were living. Jesus is not only the giver of life; he is life itself.

ISAIAH 5:1 – 7

THE SONG OF THE VINEYARD

In this song, Israel is a vineyard that has been planted by God. From this vineyard, he expects to receive fruit (v. 2). God established his people and positioned them in the promised land so that his glory might be seen

(continued on next page)

(The Song of the Vineyard, continued)

throughout the world. The Law that he gave (and the sacrificial system he instituted) was God's appointed way for his people to worship a God who was altogether different than the false gods of the surrounding nations. The fruit of the nation that God desired to see was worshipful obedience, but they failed in this task and would be judged as a result.

Jesus taught that God is the gardener who has established his people to bear fruit as well. As the gardener, Jesus said, God will prune branches that do not bear fruit (Jn 15:1–2). But he also taught that those who abide in him will bear fruit as a result of that connection: "I am the vine; you are the branches. If you remain in me and I in you, you will bear much fruit; apart from me you can do nothing" (Jn 15:5).

[4] What more could have been done for my vineyard
than I have done for it?
When I looked for good grapes,
why did it yield only bad?
[5] Now I will tell you
what I am going to do to my vineyard:
I will take away its hedge,
and it will be destroyed;
I will break down its wall,
and it will be trampled.
[6] I will make it a wasteland,
neither pruned nor cultivated,
and briers and thorns will grow there.
I will command the clouds
not to rain on it."

[7] The vineyard of the LORD Almighty
is the nation of Israel,
and the people of Judah
are the vines he delighted in.
And he looked for justice, but saw bloodshed;
for righteousness, but heard cries of distress.

Woes and Judgments

[8] Woe to you who add house to house
and join field to field
till no space is left
and you live alone in the land.

[9] The LORD Almighty has declared in my hearing:

"Surely the great houses will become desolate,
the fine mansions left without occupants.
[10] A ten-acre vineyard will produce only a bath[a] of wine;
a homer[b] of seed will yield only an ephah[c] of grain."
[11] Woe to those who rise early in the morning
to run after their drinks,
who stay up late at night
till they are inflamed with wine.
[12] They have harps and lyres at their banquets,
pipes and timbrels and wine,
but they have no regard for the deeds of the LORD,
no respect for the work of his hands.
[13] Therefore my people will go into exile
for lack of understanding;
those of high rank will die of hunger
and the common people will be parched with thirst.
[14] Therefore Death expands its jaws,
opening wide its mouth;
into it will descend their nobles and masses
with all their brawlers and revelers.
[15] So people will be brought low
and everyone humbled,
the eyes of the arrogant humbled.
[16] But the LORD Almighty will be exalted by his justice,
and the holy God will be proved holy by his righteous acts.

[a] *10* That is, about 6 gallons or about 22 liters [b] *10* That is, probably about 360 pounds or about 160 kilograms [c] *10* That is, probably about 36 pounds or about 16 kilograms

17 Then sheep will graze as in their own pasture;
lambs will feed[a] among the ruins of the rich.

18 Woe to those who draw sin along with cords of deceit,
and wickedness as with cart ropes,
19 to those who say, "Let God hurry;
let him hasten his work
so we may see it.
The plan of the Holy One of Israel—
let it approach, let it come into view,
so we may know it."

20 Woe to those who call evil good
and good evil,
who put darkness for light
and light for darkness,
who put bitter for sweet
and sweet for bitter.

21 Woe to those who are wise in their own eyes
and clever in their own sight.

22 Woe to those who are heroes at drinking wine
and champions at mixing drinks,
23 who acquit the guilty for a bribe,
but deny justice to the innocent.
24 Therefore, as tongues of fire lick up straw
and as dry grass sinks down in the flames,
so their roots will decay
and their flowers blow away like dust;
for they have rejected the law of the LORD Almighty
and spurned the word of the Holy One of Israel.
25 Therefore the LORD's anger burns against his people;
his hand is raised and he strikes them down.
The mountains shake,
and the dead bodies are like refuse in the streets.

Yet for all this, his anger is not turned away,
his hand is still upraised.

26 He lifts up a banner for the distant nations,
he whistles for those at the ends of the earth.
Here they come,
swiftly and speedily!
27 Not one of them grows tired or stumbles,
not one slumbers or sleeps;
not a belt is loosened at the waist,
not a sandal strap is broken.
28 Their arrows are sharp,
all their bows are strung;
their horses' hooves seem like flint,
their chariot wheels like a whirlwind.
29 Their roar is like that of the lion,
they roar like young lions;
they growl as they seize their prey
and carry it off with no one to rescue.
30 In that day they will roar over it
like the roaring of the sea.

[a] 17 Septuagint; Hebrew / *strangers will eat*

And if one looks at the land,
there is only darkness and distress;
even the sun will be darkened by clouds.

Isaiah's Commission

6 In the year that King Uzziah died, I saw the Lord, high and exalted, seated
on a throne; and the train of his robe filled the temple. 2Above him were seraphim, each with six wings: With two wings they covered their faces, with two
they covered their feet, and with two they were flying. 3And they were calling
to one another:

"Holy, holy, holy is the LORD Almighty;
the whole earth is full of his glory."

4At the sound of their voices the doorposts and thresholds shook and the temple
was filled with smoke.
5"Woe to me!" I cried. "I am ruined! For I am a man of unclean lips, and I live
among a people of unclean lips, and my eyes have seen the King, the LORD Almighty."
6Then one of the seraphim flew to me with a live coal in his hand, which he
had taken with tongs from the altar. 7With it he touched my mouth and said,
"See, this has touched your lips; your guilt is taken away and your sin atoned for."
8Then I heard the voice of the Lord saying, "Whom shall I send? And who will
go for us?"

And I said, "Here am I. Send me!"
9He said, "Go and tell this people:
" 'Be ever hearing, but never understanding;
be ever seeing, but never perceiving.'
10 Make the heart of this people calloused;
make their ears dull
and close their eyes.[a]
Otherwise they might see with their eyes,
hear with their ears,
understand with their hearts,
and turn and be healed."
11Then I said, "For how long, Lord?"
And he answered:

"Until the cities lie ruined
and without inhabitant,
until the houses are left deserted
and the fields ruined and ravaged,
12 until the LORD has sent everyone far away
and the land is utterly forsaken.
13 And though a tenth remains in the land,
it will again be laid waste.
But as the terebinth and oak
leave stumps when they are cut down,
so the holy seed will be the stump in the land."

The Sign of Immanuel

7 When Ahaz son of Jotham, the son of Uzziah, was king of Judah, King Rezin of Aram and Pekah son of Remaliah king of Israel marched up to fight
against Jerusalem, but they could not overpower it.
2Now the house of David was told, "Aram has allied itself with[b] Ephraim";

[a] 9,10 Hebrew; Septuagint *'You will be ever hearing, but never understanding; / you will be ever seeing, but never perceiving.' / 10This people's heart has become calloused; / they hardly hear with their ears, / and they have closed their eyes* [b] 2 Or *has set up camp in*

ISAIAH 6:2–3

HOLY, HOLY, HOLY

The description of the seraphim provides an image that shows how one is supposed to act in the presence of God. God is holy—altogether pure and without blemish or sin. He is spotless and perfect, and as such is set apart from everything that is not as holy as he is. The seraphim cover their faces because even though they are supernatural beings, they are evidently unworthy to look on God. The fact that they humbly cover their feet implies that they are created beings. When one realizes the immensity of God's holiness, the only appropriate response is exactly what is described in this passage. (Read Isaiah's response in v. 5.)

Believers who read this passage can get a glimpse of how intense and pure God's holiness is. Likewise, God calls believers to be holy (1Pe 1:15–16). Once a person believes in God and who he says he is, they can begin to live a life empowered by the Holy Spirit, in accordance with his Word, and can join a community of imperfect people who have been set apart by God (1Pe 2:9). Although the struggle is real, believers can claim victory over sin through Christ's death and resurrection. And, by setting themselves apart from this world and the sin that entangles it, believers take steps to one day be united with God in holiness (Heb 12:1–3).

PROPHECIES FULFILLED

God used Isaiah to speak his word, but God also told Isaiah that many people would not repent as they would be hardened in their unbelief. Moses faced a similar situation when he went before Pharaoh to demand the release of the Israelites. Before Moses even spoke to Pharaoh, God told him that he would harden Pharaoh's heart (Ex 7:3). In that instance, God used Pharaoh to show his sovereign power by freeing his people despite their oppressor's intentions. In both instances, the people on the receiving end had the opportunity to hear God's warnings and turn, but neither Pharaoh nor the Israelites chose to believe what they heard. As they chose to ignore God's prophets, their hearts only grew harder and more opposed to God.

God chose to use their hardened hearts for his glory. When Pharaoh's heart was hardened, God freed his people through many signs and acts of his greatness. When the Israelites refused to listen to Isaiah, they went into exile. Later, God sent his Son to the earth to fulfill many of Isaiah's prophecies and bring fruition to Isaiah's words. Even in justifying Isaiah, God brought mercy and a second chance for the people to hear what he had to say. However, just as before, their hearts remained hardened (Mt 13:14 – 15; Mk 4:12; Lk 8:10; Jn 12:37 – 41).

Jesus came and fulfilled many of the prophecies of Isaiah, and these verses are an example of how even the people around Jesus fulfilled Isaiah's prophecies (Ac 28:25 – 27). God knew that there would be people who heard Jesus' good news, yet failed to repent and adhere to what he said. God used those hardened hearts to orchestrate Jesus' crucifixion, and through his death on the cross he paid for the sins of the world.

so the hearts of Ahaz and his people were shaken, as the trees of the forest are shaken by the wind.

3 Then the LORD said to Isaiah, "Go out, you and your son Shear-Jashub,[a] to meet Ahaz at the end of the aqueduct of the Upper Pool, on the road to the Launderer's Field. 4 Say to him, 'Be careful, keep calm and don't be afraid. Do not lose heart because of these two smoldering stubs of firewood — because of the fierce anger of Rezin and Aram and of the son of Remaliah. 5 Aram, Ephraim and Remaliah's son have plotted your ruin, saying, 6 "Let us invade Judah; let us tear it apart and divide it among ourselves, and make the son of Tabeel king over it." 7 Yet this is what the Sovereign LORD says:

" 'It will not take place,
  it will not happen,
8 for the head of Aram is Damascus,
  and the head of Damascus is only Rezin.
Within sixty-five years
  Ephraim will be too shattered to be a people.
9 The head of Ephraim is Samaria,
  and the head of Samaria is only Remaliah's son.
If you do not stand firm in your faith,
  you will not stand at all.' "

10 Again the LORD spoke to Ahaz, 11 "Ask the LORD your God for a sign, whether in the deepest depths or in the highest heights."

12 But Ahaz said, "I will not ask; I will not put the LORD to the test."

13 Then Isaiah said, "Hear now, you house of David! Is it not enough to try the patience of humans? Will you try the patience of my God also? 14 Therefore the Lord himself will give you[b] a sign: The virgin[c] will conceive and give birth to a son, and[d] will call him Immanuel.[e] 15 He will be eating curds and honey when he knows enough to reject the wrong and choose the right, 16 for before the boy knows enough to reject the wrong and choose the right, the land of the two kings you dread will be laid waste. 17 The LORD will bring on you and on your people and on the house of your father a time unlike any since Ephraim broke away from Judah — he will bring the king of Assyria."

Assyria, the LORD's Instrument

18 In that day the LORD will whistle for flies from the Nile delta in Egypt and for bees from the land of Assyria. 19 They will all come and settle in the steep ravines and in the crevices in the rocks, on all the thornbushes and at all the water holes. 20 In that day the Lord will use a razor hired from beyond the Euphrates River — the king of Assyria — to shave your head and private parts, and to cut off your beard also. 21 In that day, a person will keep alive a young cow and two goats. 22 And because of the abundance of the milk they give, there will be curds to eat. All who remain in the land will eat curds and honey. 23 In that day, in every place where there were a thousand vines worth a thousand silver shekels,[f] there will be only briers and thorns. 24 Hunters will go there with bow and arrow, for the land will be covered with briers and thorns. 25 As for all the hills once cultivated by the hoe, you will no longer go there for fear of the briers and thorns; they will become places where cattle are turned loose and where sheep run.

Isaiah and His Children as Signs

8 The LORD said to me, "Take a large scroll and write on it with an ordinary pen: Maher-Shalal-Hash-Baz."[g] 2 So I called in Uriah the priest and Zechariah son of Jeberekiah as reliable witnesses for me. 3 Then I made love to the

[a] 3 *Shear-Jashub* means *a remnant will return.* [b] 14 The Hebrew is plural. [c] 14 Or *young woman* [d] 14 Masoretic Text; Dead Sea Scrolls *son, and he* or *son, and they* [e] 14 *Immanuel* means *God with us.* [f] 23 That is, about 25 pounds or about 12 kilograms [g] 1 *Maher-Shalal-Hash-Baz* means *quick to the plunder, swift to the spoil*; also in verse 3.

ISAIAH 7:14

IMMANUEL

Immanuel is a Hebrew word meaning "God with us," and it is a fitting name for the promised son in Isaiah's day and for Jesus, the One prophesied about in Isaiah. Because of the sin of mankind, a debt had to be paid in order to free humanity from living and dying in eternal separation from God. In order to pay this debt, God sent his Son Jesus to the earth to be born in desperately poor conditions, live a perfect life, die an undeserving death and rise again so that humans may one day be united with God in heaven.

When Isaiah wrote about a child named Immanuel, he was referring to Jesus, who was "God with us" to the people he encountered while he was on earth. God the Son willingly laid aside his position in heaven and descended to the earth, taking on human form in order to save his sinful image-bearers (Php 2:5 – 11). God continues to be Immanuel, "God with us," through the indwelling presence of his Holy Spirit who fills believers, comforts them in a fallen world and empowers them to live holy lives.

IMMANUEL IS COMING

As is true for many prophecies, here Isaiah portrays two coming events. First, during Ahaz's day, a child would be born who would witness the destruction of Judah's two prominent enemies — Israel and Aram. The word translated in English Bibles as *virgin* (*'almah*) is used to refer to an unmarried woman who is young (Ge 24:43; Pr 30:19). Some believe this is a prophecy that a child will be born to a young woman from the house of Ahaz who will marry and give birth to this promised son. Other writers feel that Isaiah's prophecy concerns a young woman who would become Isaiah's wife following the death of his first wife after she gave birth to Shear-Jashub (Isa 7:3). In that case, the initial fulfillment of this prophecy is found in Isaiah 8:3. Regardless of the exact nature of this promised son, he would grow up during a time when God would crush the surrounding nations and fulfill his good promises to his people.

The second application of this prophecy was fulfilled by the coming of Jesus Christ, whose name *Immanuel,* means "God with us." Born to a young virgin, Jesus was the promised Messiah of which all Old Testament deliverers ultimately foreshadow. What Ahaz lacked in vision and purpose, Jesus had — and more. He was the incarnate Son of God, miraculously born of a virgin and with a mission to fulfill God's plan to save his people. Jesus would be the perfect King who would rule from a position of humility and grace, not tyranny and self-aggrandizement. Through God's miraculous provision, the coming Messiah would take on human flesh while retaining his full divinity. This promised Son would do far more than the son would accomplish or represent in Isaiah's day. Jesus would crush Satan, sin and death through his sacrificial death and miraculous resurrection.

prophetess, and she conceived and gave birth to a son. And the LORD said to me,
"Name him Maher-Shalal-Hash-Baz. 4 For before the boy knows how to say 'My
father' or 'My mother,' the wealth of Damascus and the plunder of Samaria will
be carried off by the king of Assyria."

5 The LORD spoke to me again:

6 "Because this people has rejected
the gently flowing waters of Shiloah
and rejoices over Rezin
and the son of Remaliah,
7 therefore the Lord is about to bring against them
the mighty floodwaters of the Euphrates—
the king of Assyria with all his pomp.
It will overflow all its channels,
run over all its banks
8 and sweep on into Judah, swirling over it,
passing through it and reaching up to the neck.
Its outspread wings will cover the breadth of your land,
Immanuel[a]!"
9 Raise the war cry,[b] you nations, and be shattered!
Listen, all you distant lands.
Prepare for battle, and be shattered!
Prepare for battle, and be shattered!
10 Devise your strategy, but it will be thwarted;
propose your plan, but it will not stand,
for God is with us.[c]

11 This is what the LORD says to me with his strong hand upon me, warning me
not to follow the way of this people:

12 "Do not call conspiracy
everything this people calls a conspiracy;
do not fear what they fear,
and do not dread it.
13 The LORD Almighty is the one you are to regard
as holy,
he is the one you are to fear,
he is the one you are to dread.
14 He will be a holy place;
for both Israel and Judah he will be
a stone that causes people to stumble
and a rock that makes them fall.
And for the people of Jerusalem he will be
a trap and a snare.
15 Many of them will stumble;
they will fall and be broken,
they will be snared and captured."

16 Bind up this testimony of warning
and seal up God's instruction among my disciples.
17 I will wait for the LORD,
who is hiding his face from the descendants
of Jacob.
I will put my trust in him.

18 Here am I, and the children the LORD has given me. We are signs and symbols in Israel from the LORD Almighty, who dwells on Mount Zion.

[a] 8 *Immanuel* means *God with us.* [b] 9 Or *Do your worst* [c] 10 Hebrew *Immanuel*

ISAIAH 8:14

HOLY PLACE OR STUMBLING BLOCK?

Isaiah describes God as a holy place, which is a sanctuary for peace and refuge. But Isaiah also uses this image to portray God's holy place as a stumbling block leading to destruction for his people because his holy place would also expose the sin of those who entered.

Those who enter God's holy place, who earnestly seek after God, encounter God who is perfect. But because of their own imperfections and their inability to obey his commandments and follow him humbly, this same holy place that was meant for their good can also be the cause of stumbling. Paul wrote that pursuing God by works as opposed to faith is a similar stumbling block today (Ro 9:32–33). Faith is what brings believers into the holy place, and obedience to God's Word keeps believers from stumbling over the very thing that is meant to save them (1Pe 2:7–8).

The Darkness Turns to Light

19When someone tells you to consult mediums and spiritists, who whisper
and mutter, should not a people inquire of their God? Why consult the dead on
behalf of the living? 20Consult God's instruction and the testimony of warning. If
anyone does not speak according to this word, they have no light of dawn. 21Dis-
tressed and hungry, they will roam through the land; when they are famished,
they will become enraged and, looking upward, will curse their king and their
God. 22Then they will look toward the earth and see only distress and darkness
and fearful gloom, and they will be thrust into utter darkness.

9[a] Nevertheless, there will be no more gloom for those who were in distress.
In the past he humbled the land of Zebulun and the land of Naphtali, but
in the future he will honor Galilee of the nations, by the Way of the Sea, beyond
the Jordan—

2The people walking in darkness
have seen a great light;
on those living in the land of deep darkness
a light has dawned.
3You have enlarged the nation
and increased their joy;
they rejoice before you
as people rejoice at the harvest,
as warriors rejoice
when dividing the plunder.
4For as in the day of Midian's defeat,
you have shattered
the yoke that burdens them,
the bar across their shoulders,
the rod of their oppressor.
5Every warrior's boot used in battle
and every garment rolled in blood
will be destined for burning,
will be fuel for the fire.
6For to us a child is born,
to us a son is given,
and the government will be on his shoulders.
And he will be called
Wonderful Counselor, Mighty God,
Everlasting Father, Prince of Peace.
7Of the greatness of his government and peace
there will be no end.
He will reign on David's throne
and over his kingdom,
establishing and upholding it
with justice and righteousness
from that time on and forever.
The zeal of the LORD Almighty
will accomplish this.

The LORD's Anger Against Israel

8The Lord has sent a message against Jacob;
it will fall on Israel.
9All the people will know it—
Ephraim and the inhabitants of Samaria—
who say with pride
and arrogance of heart,

[a] In Hebrew texts 9:1 is numbered 8:23, and 9:2-21 is numbered 9:1-20.

ISAIAH 9:1–2

A LIGHT HAS DAWNED

The light Isaiah describes in this passage is Jesus, the One who would bring salvation to the people of the world when he came to earth. Isaiah even specifically identified the region of Galilee as the place where the light would come, which was the place Jesus spent a majority of his time teaching and ministering (Mt 4:13–16). In verse 2, Isaiah shifts into the past tense, demonstrating the certainty of his prophecy, indicating that what was to happen in the future was as sure to happen as if it had already occurred. God would bring light to a people in darkness, and they would see that light dawning and bringing joy to their lives. Jesus fulfilled Isaiah's prophecy; he is the light of the world (Jn 8:12), and no one who trusts Jesus for salvation has to walk in the darkness of unforgiven sin ever again.

ISAIAH 9:2 – 7

HOPE FOR PEACE

Isaiah portrays the eternal hope of God's people in this passage. Again, this prophecy refers directly to Jesus, the One who was to fulfill Isaiah's words (Lk 1:32 – 33). The coming of Jesus represented a new rule and a new King who would reign forever, and ultimately he will establish God's rule and reign forever (Rev 21:5 – 7). "Of the greatness of his government and peace there will be no end" (Isa 9:7). Earthly kingdoms advance through greed, war and oppression. God's kingdom advances through righteousness and peace (Jn 14:27) — peace that will prevail forever in God's new heaven and new earth.

The people of God longed for this type of peace. Though the promised land was meant to be marked by God's provision and freedom from war, this had not been the case. Israel's persistent rebellion and idolatry prevented the kind of peaceful situation that God had promised, had they been obedient (Dt 6:3).

Isaiah encouraged the people to maintain hope that God's peace would prevail, but it would come in a future day inaugurated by the appearance of the Messiah. Believers today can have this hope as well. Though the world has been broken with strife and sin, Isaiah pictured a day when peace will cover the earth and all pain will cease (Isa 9:7; Rev 21:4). Jesus encouraged believers to have hope, for he overcame this world and is bringing about a new and better one (Jn 16:33). It is this hope that believers cling to, and it is their faith that makes hope possible. Jesus came to earth to seek and save those who were lost and wandering from him (Lk 19:10). He came to establish a way for people to enter into his kingdom and find the peace he offers. Believers find peace with God, knowing that their sins are forgiven and they can rely on the presence of a holy God, both now and forever. And they experience peace knowing that they will, one day, inhabit a world ruled by God himself that is free from violence, where peace reigns supreme.

10 “The bricks have fallen down,
but we will rebuild with dressed stone;
the fig trees have been felled,
but we will replace them with cedars.”
11 But the LORD has strengthened Rezin’s foes against them
and has spurred their enemies on.
12 Arameans from the east and Philistines from the west
have devoured Israel with open mouth.

Yet for all this, his anger is not turned away,
his hand is still upraised.

13 But the people have not returned to him who struck them,
nor have they sought the LORD Almighty.
14 So the LORD will cut off from Israel both head and tail,
both palm branch and reed in a single day;
15 the elders and dignitaries are the head,
the prophets who teach lies are the tail.
16 Those who guide this people mislead them,
and those who are guided are led astray.
17 Therefore the Lord will take no pleasure in the young men,
nor will he pity the fatherless and widows,
for everyone is ungodly and wicked,
every mouth speaks folly.

Yet for all this, his anger is not turned away,
his hand is still upraised.

18 Surely wickedness burns like a fire;
it consumes briers and thorns,
it sets the forest thickets ablaze,
so that it rolls upward in a column of smoke.
19 By the wrath of the LORD Almighty
the land will be scorched
and the people will be fuel for the fire;
they will not spare one another.
20 On the right they will devour,
but still be hungry;
on the left they will eat,
but not be satisfied.
Each will feed on the flesh of their own offspring[a]:
21 Manasseh will feed on Ephraim, and Ephraim on
Manasseh;
together they will turn against Judah.
Yet for all this, his anger is not turned away,
his hand is still upraised.

10 Woe to those who make unjust laws,
to those who issue oppressive decrees,
2 to deprive the poor of their rights
and withhold justice from the oppressed of my people,
making widows their prey
and robbing the fatherless.
3 What will you do on the day of reckoning,
when disaster comes from afar?
To whom will you run for help?
Where will you leave your riches?

[a] 20 Or *arm*

[4] Nothing will remain but to cringe among the captives
or fall among the slain.

Yet for all this, his anger is not turned away,
his hand is still upraised.

God's Judgment on Assyria

[5] "Woe to the Assyrian, the rod of my anger,
in whose hand is the club of my wrath!
[6] I send him against a godless nation,
I dispatch him against a people who anger me,
to seize loot and snatch plunder,
and to trample them down like mud in the streets.
[7] But this is not what he intends,
this is not what he has in mind;
his purpose is to destroy,
to put an end to many nations.
[8] 'Are not my commanders all kings?' he says.
[9] 'Has not Kalno fared like Carchemish?
Is not Hamath like Arpad,
and Samaria like Damascus?
[10] As my hand seized the kingdoms of the idols,
kingdoms whose images excelled those of Jerusalem and
Samaria—
[11] shall I not deal with Jerusalem and her images
as I dealt with Samaria and her idols?' "

[12] When the Lord has finished all his work against Mount Zion and Jerusalem,
he will say, "I will punish the king of Assyria for the willful pride of his heart and
the haughty look in his eyes. [13] For he says:

" 'By the strength of my hand I have done this,
and by my wisdom, because I have understanding.
I removed the boundaries of nations,
I plundered their treasures;
like a mighty one I subdued[a] their kings.
[14] As one reaches into a nest,
so my hand reached for the wealth of the nations;
as people gather abandoned eggs,
so I gathered all the countries;
not one flapped a wing,
or opened its mouth to chirp.' "

[15] Does the ax raise itself above the person who swings it,
or the saw boast against the one who uses it?
As if a rod were to wield the person who lifts it up,
or a club brandish the one who is not wood!
[16] Therefore, the Lord, the LORD Almighty,
will send a wasting disease upon his sturdy warriors;
under his pomp a fire will be kindled
like a blazing flame.
[17] The Light of Israel will become a fire,
their Holy One a flame;
in a single day it will burn and consume
his thorns and his briers.
[18] The splendor of his forests and fertile fields
it will completely destroy,
as when a sick person wastes away.

---

[a] *13* Or *treasures; / I subdued the mighty,*

19 And the remaining trees of his forests will be so few
that a child could write them down.

The Remnant of Israel

20 In that day the remnant of Israel,
the survivors of Jacob,
will no longer rely on him
who struck them down
but will truly rely on the LORD,
the Holy One of Israel.
21 A remnant will return,[a] a remnant of Jacob
will return to the Mighty God.
22 Though your people be like the sand by the sea, Israel,
only a remnant will return.
Destruction has been decreed,
overwhelming and righteous.
23 The Lord, the LORD Almighty, will carry out
the destruction decreed upon the whole land.

24 Therefore this is what the Lord, the LORD Almighty, says:

"My people who live in Zion,
do not be afraid of the Assyrians,
who beat you with a rod
and lift up a club against you, as Egypt did.
25 Very soon my anger against you will end
and my wrath will be directed to their destruction."
26 The LORD Almighty will lash them with a whip,
as when he struck down Midian at the rock of Oreb;
and he will raise his staff over the waters,
as he did in Egypt.
27 In that day their burden will be lifted from your
shoulders,
their yoke from your neck;
the yoke will be broken
because you have grown so fat.[b]

28 They enter Aiath;
they pass through Migron;
they store supplies at Mikmash.
29 They go over the pass, and say,
"We will camp overnight at Geba."
Ramah trembles;
Gibeah of Saul flees.
30 Cry out, Daughter Gallim!
Listen, Laishah!
Poor Anathoth!
31 Madmenah is in flight;
the people of Gebim take cover.
32 This day they will halt at Nob;
they will shake their fist
at the mount of Daughter Zion,
at the hill of Jerusalem.

33 See, the Lord, the LORD Almighty,
will lop off the boughs with great power.

[a] 21 Hebrew *shear-jashub* (see 7:3 and note); also in verse 22 [b] 27 Hebrew; Septuagint *broken / from your shoulders*

ISAIAH 10:20–21

REMNANT

This passage is written in a tone of hope for the future. Though the Assyrian army had nearly conquered Judah in 701 BC, it was through that same invasion that God drew his people to himself. Later, a remnant would return to Judah after the destruction of Jerusalem by the Babylonians in 586 BC.

This passage demonstrates the fact that God always has a plan to bring people to the saving knowledge of himself. The Israelites would learn through God's judgment and his mercy that they should not trust in any earthly leader but rather trust in God alone. Despite the turmoil that surrounded Judah, Isaiah focused on the point of hope for the remnant, and he encouraged them to trust and believe that God was in control.

Believers should adhere to this same focus and encouragement today. God is ultimately in control; he sent Jesus as salvation for the lost, and he will one day return and redeem all of his people.

The lofty trees will be felled,
 the tall ones will be brought low.
34 He will cut down the forest thickets with an ax;
 Lebanon will fall before the Mighty One.

The Branch From Jesse

11 A shoot will come up from the stump of Jesse;
 from his roots a Branch will bear fruit.
2 The Spirit of the LORD will rest on him—
 the Spirit of wisdom and of understanding,
 the Spirit of counsel and of might,
 the Spirit of the knowledge and fear of the LORD—
3 and he will delight in the fear of the LORD.

He will not judge by what he sees with his eyes,
 or decide by what he hears with his ears;
4 but with righteousness he will judge the needy,
 with justice he will give decisions for the poor of the earth.
He will strike the earth with the rod of his mouth;
 with the breath of his lips he will slay the wicked.
5 Righteousness will be his belt
 and faithfulness the sash around his waist.

6 The wolf will live with the lamb,
 the leopard will lie down with the goat,
the calf and the lion and the yearling[a] together;
 and a little child will lead them.
7 The cow will feed with the bear,
 their young will lie down together,
 and the lion will eat straw like the ox.
8 The infant will play near the cobra's den,
 and the young child will put its hand into the viper's nest.
9 They will neither harm nor destroy
 on all my holy mountain,
for the earth will be filled with the knowledge of the LORD
 as the waters cover the sea.

10 In that day the Root of Jesse will stand as a banner for the peoples; the nations will rally to him, and his resting place will be glorious. 11 In that day the
Lord will reach out his hand a second time to reclaim the surviving remnant
of his people from Assyria, from Lower Egypt, from Upper Egypt, from Cush,[b]
from Elam, from Babylonia,[c] from Hamath and from the islands of the Mediterranean.

12 He will raise a banner for the nations
 and gather the exiles of Israel;
he will assemble the scattered people of Judah
 from the four quarters of the earth.
13 Ephraim's jealousy will vanish,
 and Judah's enemies[d] will be destroyed;
Ephraim will not be jealous of Judah,
 nor Judah hostile toward Ephraim.
14 They will swoop down on the slopes of Philistia to the west;
 together they will plunder the people to the east.
They will subdue Edom and Moab,
 and the Ammonites will be subject to them.

---

[a] 6 Hebrew; Septuagint *lion will feed* [b] 11 That is, the upper Nile region [c] 11 Hebrew *Shinar* [d] 13 Or *hostility*

ISAIAH 11:1 – 3,10

A BRANCH FROM JESSE

Isaiah again points Judah forward to the coming of the Messiah — this time emphasizing that he would come from the line of Jesse. Because the Jews during the time that Jesus lived studied Israel's prophets of old, they knew what they were looking for when it came to the Messiah. Matthew knew this truth, so he began his gospel witness by confirming that Jesus was from the line of Abraham, Isaac, Jacob and David, as well as from David's father Jesse (Mt 1:1 – 6). Paul continued to confirm this truth in his letter to the Romans by pointing to the fact that Jesus was the one of whom Isaiah prophesied (Ro 15:12).

Isaiah used the images of a branch and a root to once again show that this coming One would be a source of life and blessing, removing the curse of disobedience and setting things right in concern for justice. These images, combined with the prophecies found throughout Isaiah, provide a robust picture of the nature of God's chosen One and serve to confirm the truthfulness of God's Word from cover to cover.

The second verse of Isaiah 11 says that "the Spirit of the LORD will rest on him." In multiple Gospels, God's Spirit is described as resting on Jesus following his baptism (Mt 3:16; Mk 1:10; Lk 3:21 – 22). In each account, God's Spirit descends in the form of a dove and God the Father confirms Jesus' identity as his beloved Son. Furthermore, Isaiah wrote that the coming Messiah would be given "the Spirit of wisdom and of understanding, the Spirit of counsel and of might, the Spirit of the knowledge and fear of the LORD" (Isa 11:2). In this Spirit, he would speak the wisdom of God and live in perfect conformity to it (Lk 2:52; 24:44; Heb 4:15). This branch from Jesse would embody the vibrant life of God's Spirit and demonstrate the life that could come to those who place their faith in his finished work. They could be born anew by the power of God's Spirit and live in the power of that same Spirit.

[15]The LORD will dry up
the gulf of the Egyptian sea;
with a scorching wind he will sweep his hand
over the Euphrates River.
He will break it up into seven streams
so that anyone can cross over in sandals.
[16]There will be a highway for the remnant of his people
that is left from Assyria,
as there was for Israel
when they came up from Egypt.

Songs of Praise

12 In that day you will say:

"I will praise you, LORD.
Although you were angry with me,
your anger has turned away
and you have comforted me.
[2]Surely God is my salvation;
I will trust and not be afraid.
The LORD, the LORD himself, is my strength and my
defense[a];
he has become my salvation."
[3]With joy you will draw water
from the wells of salvation.

[4]In that day you will say:

"Give praise to the LORD, proclaim his name;
make known among the nations what he has done,
and proclaim that his name is exalted.
[5]Sing to the LORD, for he has done glorious things;
let this be known to all the world.
[6]Shout aloud and sing for joy, people of Zion,
for great is the Holy One of Israel among you."

A Prophecy Against Babylon

13 A prophecy against Babylon that Isaiah son of Amoz saw:

[2]Raise a banner on a bare hilltop,
shout to them;
beckon to them
to enter the gates of the nobles.
[3]I have commanded those I prepared for battle;
I have summoned my warriors to carry out my wrath —
those who rejoice in my triumph.

[4]Listen, a noise on the mountains,
like that of a great multitude!
Listen, an uproar among the kingdoms,
like nations massing together!
The LORD Almighty is mustering
an army for war.
[5]They come from faraway lands,
from the ends of the heavens —
the LORD and the weapons of his wrath —
to destroy the whole country.

[a] 2 Or *song*

JOY

Great joy and happiness comes with knowing the Lord. One who is overjoyed and excited sings these two songs, and the verses describe someone who is completely and utterly amazed at what God has done for them. The fact that the Israelites could look forward to singing these songs is a testimony to the grace of God. Nothing about their current situation would occasion such rejoicing. Their moral and spiritual failure resulted in God's judgment, yet the future promise of hope remained.

Isaiah proclaimed a coming day when God's faithfulness would be seen clearly in the coming Messiah. On this day, God's people would shout for joy at the undeserved grace they had been shown. These songs of praise are for the remnant who will be gathered from the ends of the earth (11:12), and they can also be sung by believers today in celebration of the salvation that comes from Jesus. Joy-filled worship is indicative of intimate fellowship with God. To know God and be known by him is a source of great joy — in Isaiah's time and over the centuries to today.

Isaiah also describes the joy that comes from drawing water from "the wells of salvation" (12:3). While the task of drawing water from a well would have been arduous, water is a source of life. God's saving love would be like water — it would satisfy the thirst of his people forever. Those who drank from the water he provided would find life, delight and joy. This joy described by Isaiah was symbolized at the Festival of Tabernacles, in which all of Israel would come together and remember God's promise to deliver them out of slavery and into the promised land (Lev 23:39 – 43). One of the rituals on each of the seven days involved the priests taking water from the Pool of Siloam. There, they would draw the clear, cool water into their beautiful ceremonial golden vases. All the while, the trumpets blared and the people celebrated in remembrance of what God had done for them in the exodus.

When Jesus was at a well talking with a Samaritan woman, she was eager to learn how Jesus would offer her water that would allow her to never be thirsty again (Jn 4:10 – 11). Jesus provides his followers with much more than physical water from a normal well. Instead, what he offers is eternal life. Believers today can sing with the same joy and hope that the Israelites celebrated in their Festival of Tabernacles because Jesus is the wellspring of salvation (Jn 7:37 – 38). The songs of praise in Isaiah 12 are intended to encourage believers to recognize this gift and to draw others to trust God for their salvation.

6 Wail, for the day of the LORD is near;
it will come like destruction from the Almighty.[a]
7 Because of this, all hands will go limp,
every heart will melt with fear.
8 Terror will seize them,
pain and anguish will grip them;
they will writhe like a woman in labor.
They will look aghast at each other,
their faces aflame.

9 See, the day of the LORD is coming
—a cruel day, with wrath and fierce anger—
to make the land desolate
and destroy the sinners within it.
10 The stars of heaven and their constellations
will not show their light.
The rising sun will be darkened
and the moon will not give its light.
11 I will punish the world for its evil,
the wicked for their sins.
I will put an end to the arrogance of the haughty
and will humble the pride of the ruthless.
12 I will make people scarcer than pure gold,
more rare than the gold of Ophir.
13 Therefore I will make the heavens tremble;
and the earth will shake from its place
at the wrath of the LORD Almighty,
in the day of his burning anger.

14 Like a hunted gazelle,
like sheep without a shepherd,
they will all return to their own people,
they will flee to their native land.
15 Whoever is captured will be thrust through;
all who are caught will fall by the sword.
16 Their infants will be dashed to pieces before their eyes;
their houses will be looted and their wives violated.
17 See, I will stir up against them the Medes,
who do not care for silver
and have no delight in gold.
18 Their bows will strike down the young men;
they will have no mercy on infants,
nor will they look with compassion on children.
19 Babylon, the jewel of kingdoms,
the pride and glory of the Babylonians,[b]
will be overthrown by God
like Sodom and Gomorrah.
20 She will never be inhabited
or lived in through all generations;
there no nomads will pitch their tents,
there no shepherds will rest their flocks.
21 But desert creatures will lie there,
jackals will fill her houses;
there the owls will dwell,
and there the wild goats will leap about.

[a] 6 Hebrew *Shaddai* [b] 19 Or *Chaldeans*

22 Hyenas will inhabit her strongholds,
jackals her luxurious palaces.
Her time is at hand,
and her days will not be prolonged.

14 The LORD will have compassion on Jacob;
once again he will choose Israel
and will settle them in their own land.
Foreigners will join them
and unite with the descendants of Jacob.
2 Nations will take them
and bring them to their own place.
And Israel will take possession of the nations
and make them male and female servants in the LORD's land.
They will make captives of their captors
and rule over their oppressors.

3 On the day the LORD gives you relief from your suffering and turmoil and
from the harsh labor forced on you, 4 you will take up this taunt against the king
of Babylon:

How the oppressor has come to an end!
How his fury[a] has ended!
5 The LORD has broken the rod of the wicked,
the scepter of the rulers,
6 which in anger struck down peoples
with unceasing blows,
and in fury subdued nations
with relentless aggression.
7 All the lands are at rest and at peace;
they break into singing.
8 Even the junipers and the cedars of Lebanon
gloat over you and say,
"Now that you have been laid low,
no one comes to cut us down."

9 The realm of the dead below is all astir
to meet you at your coming;
it rouses the spirits of the departed to greet you—
all those who were leaders in the world;
it makes them rise from their thrones—
all those who were kings over the nations.
10 They will all respond,
they will say to you,
"You also have become weak, as we are;
you have become like us."
11 All your pomp has been brought down to the grave,
along with the noise of your harps;
maggots are spread out beneath you
and worms cover you.

12 How you have fallen from heaven,
morning star, son of the dawn!
You have been cast down to the earth,
you who once laid low the nations!
13 You said in your heart,
"I will ascend to the heavens;

[a] 4 Dead Sea Scrolls, Septuagint and Syriac; the meaning of the word in the Masoretic Text is uncertain.

ISAIAH 14:12–15

THE FALL OF THE PRIDEFUL

Isaiah wrote this passage promising that Israelites would one day use these words to taunt the king of Babylon who had brought destruction on them. Isaiah prophesies that arrogant Babylon, once powerful and mighty, will be thrown down.

How ironic that the thing that sets something or someone most in opposition to God is the desire to be God's equal. Some scholars suggest that although this text is directed at the ruler of Babylon, it also depicts the fall of Satan. Regardless of its target, the text makes clear that a desire to be on equal footing with God is a pride-generated desire that will result in destruction. God has no equal, and his greatness is beyond attainable. For believers, it is crucial to recognize the fact that the character of God is not something to be attained; rather it is something to be worshiped. True to the old adage, pride always comes before a fall, so it is best for believers to approach the unattainable greatness of God with sincere humility and respect.

I will raise my throne
above the stars of God;
I will sit enthroned on the mount of assembly,
on the utmost heights of Mount Zaphon.[a]
14 I will ascend above the tops of the clouds;
I will make myself like the Most High."
15 But you are brought down to the realm of the dead,
to the depths of the pit.

16 Those who see you stare at you,
they ponder your fate:
"Is this the man who shook the earth
and made kingdoms tremble,
17 the man who made the world a wilderness,
who overthrew its cities
and would not let his captives go home?"

18 All the kings of the nations lie in state,
each in his own tomb.
19 But you are cast out of your tomb
like a rejected branch;
you are covered with the slain,
with those pierced by the sword,
those who descend to the stones of the pit.
Like a corpse trampled underfoot,
20 you will not join them in burial,
for you have destroyed your land
and killed your people.

Let the offspring of the wicked
never be mentioned again.
21 Prepare a place to slaughter his children
for the sins of their ancestors;
they are not to rise to inherit the land
and cover the earth with their cities.

22 "I will rise up against them,"
declares the LORD Almighty.
"I will wipe out Babylon's name and survivors,
her offspring and descendants,"
declares the LORD.
23 "I will turn her into a place for owls
and into swampland;
I will sweep her with the broom of destruction,"
declares the LORD Almighty.

24 The LORD Almighty has sworn,

"Surely, as I have planned, so it will be,
and as I have purposed, so it will happen.
25 I will crush the Assyrian in my land;
on my mountains I will trample him down.
His yoke will be taken from my people,
and his burden removed from their shoulders."

26 This is the plan determined for the whole world;
this is the hand stretched out over all nations.
27 For the LORD Almighty has purposed, and who can thwart him?
His hand is stretched out, and who can turn it back?

[a] 13 Or *of the north*; Zaphon was the most sacred mountain of the Canaanites.

A Prophecy Against the Philistines

28 This prophecy came in the year King Ahaz died:

29 Do not rejoice, all you Philistines,
that the rod that struck you is broken;
from the root of that snake will spring up a viper,
its fruit will be a darting, venomous serpent.
30 The poorest of the poor will find pasture,
and the needy will lie down in safety.
But your root I will destroy by famine;
it will slay your survivors.

31 Wail, you gate! Howl, you city!
Melt away, all you Philistines!
A cloud of smoke comes from the north,
and there is not a straggler in its ranks.
32 What answer shall be given
to the envoys of that nation?
"The LORD has established Zion,
and in her his afflicted people will find refuge."

A Prophecy Against Moab

15 A prophecy against Moab:

Ar in Moab is ruined,
destroyed in a night!
Kir in Moab is ruined,
destroyed in a night!
2 Dibon goes up to its temple,
to its high places to weep;
Moab wails over Nebo and Medeba.
Every head is shaved
and every beard cut off.
3 In the streets they wear sackcloth;
on the roofs and in the public squares
they all wail,
prostrate with weeping.
4 Heshbon and Elealeh cry out,
their voices are heard all the way to Jahaz.
Therefore the armed men of Moab cry out,
and their hearts are faint.

5 My heart cries out over Moab;
her fugitives flee as far as Zoar,
as far as Eglath Shelishiyah.
They go up the hill to Luhith,
weeping as they go;
on the road to Horonaim
they lament their destruction.
6 The waters of Nimrim are dried up
and the grass is withered;
the vegetation is gone
and nothing green is left.
7 So the wealth they have acquired and stored up
they carry away over the Ravine of the Poplars.
8 Their outcry echoes along the border of Moab;
their wailing reaches as far as Eglaim,
their lamentation as far as Beer Elim.

9 The waters of Dimon[a] are full of blood,
but I will bring still more upon Dimon[a] —
a lion upon the fugitives of Moab
and upon those who remain in the land.

16 Send lambs as tribute
to the ruler of the land,
from Sela, across the desert,
to the mount of Daughter Zion.
2 Like fluttering birds
pushed from the nest,
so are the women of Moab
at the fords of the Arnon.

3 "Make up your mind," Moab says.
"Render a decision.
Make your shadow like night —
at high noon.
Hide the fugitives,
do not betray the refugees.
4 Let the Moabite fugitives stay with you;
be their shelter from the destroyer."

The oppressor will come to an end,
and destruction will cease;
the aggressor will vanish from the land.
5 In love a throne will be established;
in faithfulness a man will sit on it —
one from the house[b] of David —
one who in judging seeks justice
and speeds the cause of righteousness.

6 We have heard of Moab's pride —
how great is her arrogance! —
of her conceit, her pride and her insolence;
but her boasts are empty.
7 Therefore the Moabites wail,
they wail together for Moab.
Lament and grieve
for the raisin cakes of Kir Hareseth.
8 The fields of Heshbon wither,
the vines of Sibmah also.
The rulers of the nations
have trampled down the choicest vines,
which once reached Jazer
and spread toward the desert.
Their shoots spread out
and went as far as the sea.[c]
9 So I weep, as Jazer weeps,
for the vines of Sibmah.
Heshbon and Elealeh,
I drench you with tears!
The shouts of joy over your ripened fruit
and over your harvests have been stilled.
10 Joy and gladness are taken away from the orchards;
no one sings or shouts in the vineyards;

[a] 9 *Dimon*, a wordplay on *Dibon* (see verse 2), sounds like the Hebrew for *blood*.
[b] 5 Hebrew *tent* [c] 8 Probably the Dead Sea

no one treads out wine at the presses,
for I have put an end to the shouting.
11 My heart laments for Moab like a harp,
my inmost being for Kir Hareseth.
12 When Moab appears at her high place,
she only wears herself out;
when she goes to her shrine to pray,
it is to no avail.

13 This is the word the LORD has already spoken concerning Moab. 14 But now
the LORD says: "Within three years, as a servant bound by contract would count
them, Moab's splendor and all her many people will be despised, and her survivors will be very few and feeble."

A Prophecy Against Damascus

17 A prophecy against Damascus:

"See, Damascus will no longer be a city
but will become a heap of ruins.
2 The cities of Aroer will be deserted
and left to flocks, which will lie down,
with no one to make them afraid.
3 The fortified city will disappear from Ephraim,
and royal power from Damascus;
the remnant of Aram will be
like the glory of the Israelites,"
declares the LORD Almighty.

4 "In that day the glory of Jacob will fade;
the fat of his body will waste away.
5 It will be as when reapers harvest the standing grain,
gathering the grain in their arms—
as when someone gleans heads of grain
in the Valley of Rephaim.
6 Yet some gleanings will remain,
as when an olive tree is beaten,
leaving two or three olives on the topmost branches,
four or five on the fruitful boughs,"
declares the LORD, the God of Israel.

7 In that day people will look to their Maker
and turn their eyes to the Holy One of Israel.
8 They will not look to the altars,
the work of their hands,
and they will have no regard for the Asherah poles[a]
and the incense altars their fingers have made.

9 In that day their strong cities, which they left because of the Israelites, will be
like places abandoned to thickets and undergrowth. And all will be desolation.

10 You have forgotten God your Savior;
you have not remembered the Rock, your fortress.
Therefore, though you set out the finest plants
and plant imported vines,
11 though on the day you set them out, you make them grow,
and on the morning when you plant them, you bring them to bud,
yet the harvest will be as nothing
in the day of disease and incurable pain.

---

[a] 8 That is, wooden symbols of the goddess Asherah

ISAIAH 18:7

ZION

The question of worship is not a question of "if" but a question of "when." Eventually the Lord will consummate his victory over his enemies—the victory that was secured once and for all through the crucifixion and resurrection of Jesus. Though secured, that victory has not yet been fully realized throughout every corner of the universe; even though God's ultimate victory is certain, the fight still goes on. But someday, Jesus will not only be the declared king, but the acknowledged One. Once all the enemies of God have been defeated, people from every tribe and nation will bow in worship at Jesus' feet, bringing gifts to God in Zion as a sign of their loyalty and desire to honor God for destroying their enemy. People upon people and nation upon nation will unite despite their previous differences and will stream to Zion under the banner of the victory of Jesus Christ.

12 Woe to the many nations that rage—
they rage like the raging sea!
Woe to the peoples who roar—
they roar like the roaring of great waters!
13 Although the peoples roar like the roar of surging waters,
when he rebukes them they flee far away,
driven before the wind like chaff on the hills,
like tumbleweed before a gale.
14 In the evening, sudden terror!
Before the morning, they are gone!
This is the portion of those who loot us,
the lot of those who plunder us.

A Prophecy Against Cush

18 Woe to the land of whirring wings[a]
along the rivers of Cush,[b]
2 which sends envoys by sea
in papyrus boats over the water.

Go, swift messengers,
to a people tall and smooth-skinned,
to a people feared far and wide,
an aggressive nation of strange speech,
whose land is divided by rivers.

3 All you people of the world,
you who live on the earth,
when a banner is raised on the mountains,
you will see it,
and when a trumpet sounds,
you will hear it.
4 This is what the LORD says to me:
"I will remain quiet and will look on from my dwelling place,
like shimmering heat in the sunshine,
like a cloud of dew in the heat of harvest."
5 For, before the harvest, when the blossom is gone
and the flower becomes a ripening grape,
he will cut off the shoots with pruning knives,
and cut down and take away the spreading branches.
6 They will all be left to the mountain birds of prey
and to the wild animals;
the birds will feed on them all summer,
the wild animals all winter.

7 At that time gifts will be brought to the LORD Almighty

from a people tall and smooth-skinned,
from a people feared far and wide,
an aggressive nation of strange speech,
whose land is divided by rivers—

the gifts will be brought to Mount Zion, the place of the Name of the LORD Almighty.

A Prophecy Against Egypt

19 A prophecy against Egypt:

See, the LORD rides on a swift cloud
and is coming to Egypt.

[a] 1 Or *of locusts* [b] 1 That is, the upper Nile region

The idols of Egypt tremble before him,
  and the hearts of the Egyptians melt with fear.

[2] "I will stir up Egyptian against Egyptian —
  brother will fight against brother,
  neighbor against neighbor,
  city against city,
  kingdom against kingdom.
[3] The Egyptians will lose heart,
  and I will bring their plans to nothing;
they will consult the idols and the spirits of the dead,
  the mediums and the spiritists.
[4] I will hand the Egyptians over
  to the power of a cruel master,
and a fierce king will rule over them,"
  declares the Lord, the LORD Almighty.

[5] The waters of the river will dry up,
  and the riverbed will be parched and dry.
[6] The canals will stink;
  the streams of Egypt will dwindle and dry up.
The reeds and rushes will wither,
[7]   also the plants along the Nile,
  at the mouth of the river.
Every sown field along the Nile
  will become parched, will blow away and be no more.
[8] The fishermen will groan and lament,
  all who cast hooks into the Nile;
those who throw nets on the water
  will pine away.
[9] Those who work with combed flax will despair,
  the weavers of fine linen will lose hope.
[10] The workers in cloth will be dejected,
  and all the wage earners will be sick at heart.

[11] The officials of Zoan are nothing but fools;
  the wise counselors of Pharaoh give senseless advice.
How can you say to Pharaoh,
  "I am one of the wise men,
  a disciple of the ancient kings"?

[12] Where are your wise men now?
  Let them show you and make known
what the LORD Almighty
  has planned against Egypt.
[13] The officials of Zoan have become fools,
  the leaders of Memphis are deceived;
the cornerstones of her peoples
  have led Egypt astray.
[14] The LORD has poured into them
  a spirit of dizziness;
they make Egypt stagger in all that she does,
  as a drunkard staggers around in his vomit.
[15] There is nothing Egypt can do —
  head or tail, palm branch or reed.

[16]In that day the Egyptians will become weaklings. They will shudder with
fear at the uplifted hand that the LORD Almighty raises against them. [17]And
the land of Judah will bring terror to the Egyptians; everyone to whom Judah

is mentioned will be terrified, because of what the LORD Almighty is planning
against them.

18 In that day five cities in Egypt will speak the language of Canaan and swear
allegiance to the LORD Almighty. One of them will be called the City of the Sun.[a]

19 In that day there will be an altar to the LORD in the heart of Egypt, and a
monument to the LORD at its border. 20 It will be a sign and witness to the LORD
Almighty in the land of Egypt. When they cry out to the LORD because of their
oppressors, he will send them a savior and defender, and he will rescue them.
21 So the LORD will make himself known to the Egyptians, and in that day they
will acknowledge the LORD. They will worship with sacrifices and grain offerings; they will make vows to the LORD and keep them. 22 The LORD will strike
Egypt with a plague; he will strike them and heal them. They will turn to the
LORD, and he will respond to their pleas and heal them.

23 In that day there will be a highway from Egypt to Assyria. The Assyrians will
go to Egypt and the Egyptians to Assyria. The Egyptians and Assyrians will worship together. 24 In that day Israel will be the third, along with Egypt and Assyria,
a blessing[b] on the earth. 25 The LORD Almighty will bless them, saying, "Blessed
be Egypt my people, Assyria my handiwork, and Israel my inheritance."

A Prophecy Against Egypt and Cush

20 In the year that the supreme commander, sent by Sargon king of Assyria,
came to Ashdod and attacked and captured it— 2 at that time the LORD
spoke through Isaiah son of Amoz. He said to him, "Take off the sackcloth from
your body and the sandals from your feet." And he did so, going around stripped
and barefoot.

3 Then the LORD said, "Just as my servant Isaiah has gone stripped and barefoot for three years, as a sign and portent against Egypt and Cush,[c] 4 so the king
of Assyria will lead away stripped and barefoot the Egyptian captives and Cushite exiles, young and old, with buttocks bared—to Egypt's shame. 5 Those who
trusted in Cush and boasted in Egypt will be dismayed and put to shame. 6 In
that day the people who live on this coast will say, 'See what has happened to
those we relied on, those we fled to for help and deliverance from the king of
Assyria! How then can we escape?'"

A Prophecy Against Babylon

21 A prophecy against the Desert by the Sea:

Like whirlwinds sweeping through the southland,
  an invader comes from the desert,
  from a land of terror.

2 A dire vision has been shown to me:
  The traitor betrays, the looter takes loot.
Elam, attack! Media, lay siege!
  I will bring to an end all the groaning she caused.

3 At this my body is racked with pain,
  pangs seize me, like those of a woman in labor;
I am staggered by what I hear,
  I am bewildered by what I see.
4 My heart falters,
  fear makes me tremble;
the twilight I longed for
  has become a horror to me.

---

[a] *18* Some manuscripts of the Masoretic Text, Dead Sea Scrolls, Symmachus and Vulgate; most manuscripts of the Masoretic Text *City of Destruction* [b] *24* Or *Assyria, whose names will be used in blessings* (see Gen. 48:20); or *Assyria, who will be seen by others as blessed* [c] *3* That is, the upper Nile region; also in verse 5

[5]They set the tables,
they spread the rugs,
they eat, they drink!
Get up, you officers,
oil the shields!

[6]This is what the Lord says to me:

"Go, post a lookout
and have him report what he sees.
[7]When he sees chariots
with teams of horses,
riders on donkeys
or riders on camels,
let him be alert,
fully alert."

[8]And the lookout[a] shouted,

"Day after day, my lord, I stand on the watchtower;
every night I stay at my post.
[9]Look, here comes a man in a chariot
with a team of horses.
And he gives back the answer:
'Babylon has fallen, has fallen!
All the images of its gods
lie shattered on the ground!' "

[10]My people who are crushed on the threshing floor,
I tell you what I have heard
from the LORD Almighty,
from the God of Israel.

A Prophecy Against Edom

[11]A prophecy against Dumah[b]:

Someone calls to me from Seir,
"Watchman, what is left of the night?
Watchman, what is left of the night?"
[12]The watchman replies,
"Morning is coming, but also the night.
If you would ask, then ask;
and come back yet again."

A Prophecy Against Arabia

[13]A prophecy against Arabia:

You caravans of Dedanites,
who camp in the thickets of Arabia,
14 bring water for the thirsty;
you who live in Tema,
bring food for the fugitives.
[15]They flee from the sword,
from the drawn sword,
from the bent bow
and from the heat of battle.

[16]This is what the Lord says to me: "Within one year, as a servant bound by
contract would count it, all the splendor of Kedar will come to an end. [17]The

[a] 8 Dead Sea Scrolls and Syriac; Masoretic Text *A lion* [b] 11 *Dumah*, a wordplay on *Edom*, means *silence* or *stillness.*

survivors of the archers, the warriors of Kedar, will be few." The LORD, the God
of Israel, has spoken.

A Prophecy About Jerusalem

22 A prophecy against the Valley of Vision:

What troubles you now,
 that you have all gone up on the roofs,
2 you town so full of commotion,
 you city of tumult and revelry?
Your slain were not killed by the sword,
 nor did they die in battle.
3 All your leaders have fled together;
 they have been captured without using the bow.
All you who were caught were taken prisoner together,
 having fled while the enemy was still far away.
4 Therefore I said, "Turn away from me;
 let me weep bitterly.
Do not try to console me
 over the destruction of my people."

5 The Lord, the LORD Almighty, has a day
 of tumult and trampling and terror
 in the Valley of Vision,
a day of battering down walls
 and of crying out to the mountains.
6 Elam takes up the quiver,
 with her charioteers and horses;
 Kir uncovers the shield.
7 Your choicest valleys are full of chariots,
 and horsemen are posted at the city gates.

8 The Lord stripped away the defenses of Judah,
 and you looked in that day
 to the weapons in the Palace of the Forest.
9 You saw that the walls of the City of David
 were broken through in many places;
you stored up water
 in the Lower Pool.
10 You counted the buildings in Jerusalem
 and tore down houses to strengthen the wall.
11 You built a reservoir between the two walls
 for the water of the Old Pool,
but you did not look to the One who made it,
 or have regard for the One who planned it long ago.

12 The Lord, the LORD Almighty,
 called you on that day
to weep and to wail,
 to tear out your hair and put on sackcloth.
13 But see, there is joy and revelry,
 slaughtering of cattle and killing of sheep,
 eating of meat and drinking of wine!
"Let us eat and drink," you say,
 "for tomorrow we die!"

14 The LORD Almighty has revealed this in my hearing: "Till your dying day
this sin will not be atoned for," says the Lord, the LORD Almighty.

15 This is what the Lord, the LORD Almighty, says:

"Go, say to this steward,
to Shebna the palace administrator:
16 What are you doing here and who gave you permission
to cut out a grave for yourself here,
hewing your grave on the height
and chiseling your resting place in the rock?

17 "Beware, the LORD is about to take firm hold of you
and hurl you away, you mighty man.
18 He will roll you up tightly like a ball
and throw you into a large country.
There you will die
and there the chariots you were so proud of
will become a disgrace to your master's house.
19 I will depose you from your office,
and you will be ousted from your position.

20 "In that day I will summon my servant, Eliakim son of Hilkiah. 21 I will clothe
him with your robe and fasten your sash around him and hand your authority
over to him. He will be a father to those who live in Jerusalem and to the people of
Judah. 22 I will place on his shoulder the key to the house of David; what he opens
no one can shut, and what he shuts no one can open. 23 I will drive him like a peg
into a firm place; he will become a seat[a] of honor for the house of his father. 24 All
the glory of his family will hang on him: its offspring and offshoots—all its lesser
vessels, from the bowls to all the jars.

25 "In that day," declares the LORD Almighty, "the peg driven into the firm
place will give way; it will be sheared off and will fall, and the load hanging on it
will be cut down." The LORD has spoken.

A Prophecy Against Tyre

23 A prophecy against Tyre:

Wail, you ships of Tarshish!
For Tyre is destroyed
and left without house or harbor.
From the land of Cyprus
word has come to them.

2 Be silent, you people of the island
and you merchants of Sidon,
whom the seafarers have enriched.
3 On the great waters
came the grain of the Shihor;
the harvest of the Nile[b] was the revenue of Tyre,
and she became the marketplace of the nations.

4 Be ashamed, Sidon, and you fortress of the sea,
for the sea has spoken:
"I have neither been in labor nor given birth;
I have neither reared sons nor brought up daughters."
5 When word comes to Egypt,
they will be in anguish at the report from Tyre.

6 Cross over to Tarshish;
wail, you people of the island.
7 Is this your city of revelry,
the old, old city,

---

[a] 23 Or *throne* [b] 2,3 Masoretic Text; Dead Sea Scrolls *Sidon, / who cross over the sea; / your envoys* [3] *are on the great waters. / The grain of the Shihor, / the harvest of the Nile,*

THE OPEN DOOR

A steward is chiefly concerned with the affairs of his master. But here we find Shebna, identified as a steward in charge of the king's palace (a position second only to the king), more concerned with providing for himself than serving the king. While he should have been preparing the way for the siege that would come to the city, he was busy instead preparing a tomb for himself that was fit for a king. In this, Shebna represented Judah: he was more concerned with meeting his needs and pursuing the desires of his heart than he was in honoring God.

In contrast to the selfish intent of Shebna, Isaiah predicted that a new steward would rise up in his place. He would inherit the royal clothes and the authoritative seal. Unlike his self-serving predecessor, he would care for the people like a father, and he would put his own desires to the side for their good. He would inherit the keys to the kingdom and control who gets into the palace to see the king and who does not. Isaiah identifies this new steward as Eliakim, and yet we know that this compassionate and welcoming steward is just a shadow of the even greater One to come.

Jesus didn't only put aside his ambition for the sake of God's people; he gave up his life for their eternal benefit. Jesus holds not only the keys to an earthly palace, but also the keys to the kingdom of God. His servanthood stands in direct contrast to Shebna, in that Jesus took on the form of a servant, considered others as being more important than himself, and submitted himself to death on behalf of those whom he loved. He doesn't merely open the door for a one-time audience with a king; rather, through his own sacrifice he has provided complete access to the King of the universe for all who will believe. Through Jesus, the greatest door is freely opened to whoever will walk through it and accept his free gift of salvation. Those who believe in Jesus find him not only ready to open the door, but to actually *be* the door (Lk 13:22 – 29; Jn 10:9; 14:6), and through him to find unending and open access to God's throne room. It is through him, and only through him, that the door to God and the life he offers is open (Rev 3:7).

whose feet have taken her
to settle in far-off lands?
8 Who planned this against Tyre,
the bestower of crowns,
whose merchants are princes,
whose traders are renowned in the earth?
9 The LORD Almighty planned it,
to bring down her pride in all her splendor
and to humble all who are renowned on the earth.

10 Till[a] your land as they do along the Nile,
Daughter Tarshish,
for you no longer have a harbor.
11 The LORD has stretched out his hand over the sea
and made its kingdoms tremble.
He has given an order concerning Phoenicia
that her fortresses be destroyed.
12 He said, "No more of your reveling,
Virgin Daughter Sidon, now crushed!

"Up, cross over to Cyprus;
even there you will find no rest."
13 Look at the land of the Babylonians,[b]
this people that is now of no account!
The Assyrians have made it
a place for desert creatures;
they raised up their siege towers,
they stripped its fortresses bare
and turned it into a ruin.

14 Wail, you ships of Tarshish;
your fortress is destroyed!

15 At that time Tyre will be forgotten for seventy years, the span of a king's life.
But at the end of these seventy years, it will happen to Tyre as in the song of the
prostitute:

16 "Take up a harp, walk through the city,
you forgotten prostitute;
play the harp well, sing many a song,
so that you will be remembered."

17 At the end of seventy years, the LORD will deal with Tyre. She will return to
her lucrative prostitution and will ply her trade with all the kingdoms on the face
of the earth. 18 Yet her profit and her earnings will be set apart for the LORD; they
will not be stored up or hoarded. Her profits will go to those who live before the
LORD, for abundant food and fine clothes.

The LORD's Devastation of the Earth

24 See, the LORD is going to lay waste the earth
and devastate it;
he will ruin its face
and scatter its inhabitants—
2 it will be the same
for priest as for people,
for the master as for his servant,
for the mistress as for her servant,

[a] *10* Dead Sea Scrolls and some Septuagint manuscripts; Masoretic Text *Go through*
[b] *13* Or *Chaldeans*

for seller as for buyer,
for borrower as for lender,
for debtor as for creditor.
3 The earth will be completely laid waste
and totally plundered.
The LORD has spoken this word.

4 The earth dries up and withers,
the world languishes and withers,
the heavens languish with the earth.
5 The earth is defiled by its people;
they have disobeyed the laws,
violated the statutes
and broken the everlasting covenant.
6 Therefore a curse consumes the earth;
its people must bear their guilt.
Therefore earth's inhabitants are burned up,
and very few are left.
7 The new wine dries up and the vine withers;
all the merrymakers groan.
8 The joyful timbrels are stilled,
the noise of the revelers has stopped,
the joyful harp is silent.
9 No longer do they drink wine with a song;
the beer is bitter to its drinkers.
10 The ruined city lies desolate;
the entrance to every house is barred.
11 In the streets they cry out for wine;
all joy turns to gloom,
all joyful sounds are banished from the earth.
12 The city is left in ruins,
its gate is battered to pieces.
13 So will it be on the earth
and among the nations,
as when an olive tree is beaten,
or as when gleanings are left after the grape
harvest.

14 They raise their voices, they shout for joy;
from the west they acclaim the LORD's majesty.
15 Therefore in the east give glory to the LORD;
exalt the name of the LORD, the God of Israel,
in the islands of the sea.
16 From the ends of the earth we hear singing:
"Glory to the Righteous One."

But I said, "I waste away, I waste away!
Woe to me!
The treacherous betray!
With treachery the treacherous betray!"
17 Terror and pit and snare await you,
people of the earth.
18 Whoever flees at the sound of terror
will fall into a pit;
whoever climbs out of the pit
will be caught in a snare.

The floodgates of the heavens are opened,
the foundations of the earth shake.

[19] The earth is broken up,
the earth is split asunder,
the earth is violently shaken.
[20] The earth reels like a drunkard,
it sways like a hut in the wind;
so heavy upon it is the guilt of its rebellion
that it falls — never to rise again.

[21] In that day the LORD will punish
the powers in the heavens above
and the kings on the earth below.
[22] They will be herded together
like prisoners bound in a dungeon;
they will be shut up in prison
and be punished[a] after many days.
[23] The moon will be dismayed,
the sun ashamed;
for the LORD Almighty will reign
on Mount Zion and in Jerusalem,
and before its elders — with great glory.

Praise to the LORD

25 LORD, you are my God;
I will exalt you and praise your name,
for in perfect faithfulness
you have done wonderful things,
things planned long ago.
[2] You have made the city a heap of rubble,
the fortified town a ruin,
the foreigners' stronghold a city no more;
it will never be rebuilt.
[3] Therefore strong peoples will honor you;
cities of ruthless nations will revere you.
[4] You have been a refuge for the poor,
a refuge for the needy in their distress,
a shelter from the storm
and a shade from the heat.
For the breath of the ruthless
is like a storm driving against a wall
[5] and like the heat of the desert.
You silence the uproar of foreigners;
as heat is reduced by the shadow of a cloud,
so the song of the ruthless is stilled.

[6] On this mountain the LORD Almighty will prepare
a feast of rich food for all peoples,
a banquet of aged wine —
the best of meats and the finest of wines.
[7] On this mountain he will destroy
the shroud that enfolds all peoples,
the sheet that covers all nations;
[8] he will swallow up death forever.
The Sovereign LORD will wipe away the tears
from all faces;
he will remove his people's disgrace
from all the earth.

The LORD has spoken.

---

[a] 22 Or *released*

PROMISES

"It's better." That phrase can be applied to what waits for the people of God when they are fully with him someday — in comparison to almost anything in this life now. Every relationship, every emotion, every sense, every celebration — every aspect of what's good and right and joyful that believers experience in this life — is only a foretaste of what's coming.

Isaiah looks forward to a great banquet, a joyous celebration of God's rule by people from around the world. The kinds of things available at this banquet remind believers of God's extravagant generosity toward his people. At this banquet, the food will not be just good food; it will be the choicest of food. The wine will not be just good wine; it will be the choicest of wine. This is the unending and lavish celebration, the absolute fullness of joy, that waits for God's people in his presence (Ps 16:11). At this feast, all of God's people — those from every tribe, tongue and nation, will gather together to celebrate the bountiful provision of God (Lk 13:29; 14:15).

Not only do believers see God's generosity on display in this passage, but they also see that the great shroud that hangs over humanity right now — that shadow that clouds over even the best of earthly celebrations — will one day be wiped out forever. Humans know that eventually birthdays will become memorials; that holidays will eventually be tinged with the sense of loss; that every celebration will eventually pass away as our loved ones do. Death is that cloud, that shroud, which hangs constantly in the background of the earthly experience reminding us that even the best of times on this earth have limitations and will eventually come to an end.

But one day that shroud will be no more. God will swallow up death forever, for the risen Christ has defeated it once and for all. Through him, death has died and been swallowed up in victory (Isa 25:8; 1Co 15:54). The punishment for sin has been paid and all who trust in Jesus will live and celebrate forever.

This is the unshakable, unalterable, eternal Word of God. God will provide a feast for his people, even though they may find hunger and pain in this life. These promises are as sure as the eternal character of God. And God keeps his promises (Jos 23:14).

[9]In that day they will say,
"Surely this is our God;
we trusted in him, and he saved us.
This is the LORD, we trusted in him;
let us rejoice and be glad in his salvation."
[10]The hand of the LORD will rest on this mountain;
but Moab will be trampled in their land
as straw is trampled down in the manure.
[11]They will stretch out their hands in it,
as swimmers stretch out their hands to swim.
God will bring down their pride
despite the cleverness[a] of their hands.
[12]He will bring down your high fortified walls
and lay them low;
he will bring them down to the ground,
to the very dust.

A Song of Praise

26 In that day this song will be sung in the land of Judah:

We have a strong city;
God makes salvation
its walls and ramparts.
[2]Open the gates
that the righteous nation may enter,
the nation that keeps faith.
[3]You will keep in perfect peace
those whose minds are steadfast,
because they trust in you.
[4]Trust in the LORD forever,
for the LORD, the LORD himself, is the Rock eternal.
[5]He humbles those who dwell on high,
he lays the lofty city low;
he levels it to the ground
and casts it down to the dust.
[6]Feet trample it down—
the feet of the oppressed,
the footsteps of the poor.
[7]The path of the righteous is level;
you, the Upright One, make the way of the righteous smooth.
[8]Yes, LORD, walking in the way of your laws,[b]
we wait for you;
your name and renown
are the desire of our hearts.
[9]My soul yearns for you in the night;
in the morning my spirit longs for you.
When your judgments come upon the earth,
the people of the world learn righteousness.
[10]But when grace is shown to the wicked,
they do not learn righteousness;
even in a land of uprightness they go on doing evil
and do not regard the majesty of the LORD.
[11]LORD, your hand is lifted high,
but they do not see it.

[a] *11* The meaning of the Hebrew for this word is uncertain. [b] *8* Or *judgments*

ISAIAH 26:4

THE ETERNAL ROCK

This verse contains the simple imperative: "Trust." Though simple in word, trust is difficult to maintain in life. Most people have had negative life experiences that have taught them that trust is a commodity not to trade in easily, for anyone and everyone we fully trust will eventually fail. Many times failure is unintentional, but failure is inevitable. Humans, it seems, were not built to fully carry that kind of weight for each other.

But the Lord is the Rock. Unmovable. Unshakable. Unchangeable. His character stands more firmly than stone. Though any human will eventually crack under the pressure of the weight of carrying another's trust, the Lord is more than capable of carrying the trust of all who have faith in him. We know this is true because he has proven himself to be trustworthy time and time again—most of all through the life, death and resurrection of Jesus. Jesus validates all of the trust that believers place in God; his saving work on our behalf proves that God, the Eternal Rock, can bear that weight.

ISAIAH 26:8

WAITING

Isaiah describes those who waited and remained faithful to the Lord. As God's judgment on Judah unfolded around them, many waited patiently while remaining steadfast in their love for and devotion to the Lord. Waiting reflects a relinquishing of power, a trust in someone else for the future, and that is exactly how

(continued on next page)

(Waiting, continued)

the people of Judah are pictured here. They know that God is ultimately the one in control, and they are content to wait for the ultimate blessing that God had promised them. To those who wait, God's names and his renown were the desire of their hearts. This kind of faith serves as an excellent example for how believers should continually carry themselves today. The people of God are waiting for Jesus to return and to bring justice to the earth. It is important to realize that there is nothing they can do to speed up his return. Instead, believers should ensure that God's name and his renown are the desire of their hearts, and in their waiting, remain patient in their praise and faithful to tell others about him.

Let them see your zeal for your people and be put to shame;
  let the fire reserved for your enemies consume them.

12 LORD, you establish peace for us;
  all that we have accomplished you have done for us.
13 LORD our God, other lords besides you have ruled over us,
  but your name alone do we honor.
14 They are now dead, they live no more;
  their spirits do not rise.
You punished them and brought them to ruin;
  you wiped out all memory of them.
15 You have enlarged the nation, LORD;
  you have enlarged the nation.
You have gained glory for yourself;
  you have extended all the borders of the land.

16 LORD, they came to you in their distress;
  when you disciplined them,
  they could barely whisper a prayer.[a]
17 As a pregnant woman about to give birth
  writhes and cries out in her pain,
  so were we in your presence, LORD.
18 We were with child, we writhed in labor,
  but we gave birth to wind.
We have not brought salvation to the earth,
  and the people of the world have not come to life.

19 But your dead will live, LORD;
  their bodies will rise—
let those who dwell in the dust
  wake up and shout for joy—
your dew is like the dew of the morning;
  the earth will give birth to her dead.

20 Go, my people, enter your rooms
  and shut the doors behind you;
hide yourselves for a little while
  until his wrath has passed by.
21 See, the LORD is coming out of his dwelling
  to punish the people of the earth for their sins.
The earth will disclose the blood shed on it;
  the earth will conceal its slain no longer.

Deliverance of Israel

27 In that day,

the LORD will punish with his sword—
  his fierce, great and powerful sword—
Leviathan the gliding serpent,
  Leviathan the coiling serpent;
he will slay the monster of the sea.

2 In that day—

"Sing about a fruitful vineyard:
3 I, the LORD, watch over it;
  I water it continually.
I guard it day and night
  so that no one may harm it.

[a] 16 The meaning of the Hebrew for this clause is uncertain.

4 I am not angry.
If only there were briers and thorns confronting me!
I would march against them in battle;
I would set them all on fire.
5 Or else let them come to me for refuge;
let them make peace with me,
yes, let them make peace with me."

6 In days to come Jacob will take root,
Israel will bud and blossom
and fill all the world with fruit.

7 Has the LORD struck her
as he struck down those who struck her?
Has she been killed
as those were killed who killed her?
8 By warfare[a] and exile you contend with her—
with his fierce blast he drives her out,
as on a day the east wind blows.
9 By this, then, will Jacob's guilt be atoned for,
and this will be the full fruit of the removal of his sin:
When he makes all the altar stones
to be like limestone crushed to pieces,
no Asherah poles[b] or incense altars
will be left standing.
10 The fortified city stands desolate,
an abandoned settlement, forsaken like the wilderness;
there the calves graze,
there they lie down;
they strip its branches bare.
11 When its twigs are dry, they are broken off
and women come and make fires with them.
For this is a people without understanding;
so their Maker has no compassion on them,
and their Creator shows them no favor.

12 In that day the LORD will thresh from the flowing Euphrates to the Wadi of
Egypt, and you, Israel, will be gathered up one by one. 13 And in that day a great
trumpet will sound. Those who were perishing in Assyria and those who were
exiled in Egypt will come and worship the LORD on the holy mountain in Jerusalem.

Woe to the Leaders of Ephraim and Judah

28 Woe to that wreath, the pride of Ephraim's drunkards,
to the fading flower, his glorious beauty,
set on the head of a fertile valley—
to that city, the pride of those laid low by wine!
2 See, the Lord has one who is powerful and strong.
Like a hailstorm and a destructive wind,
like a driving rain and a flooding downpour,
he will throw it forcefully to the ground.
3 That wreath, the pride of Ephraim's drunkards,
will be trampled underfoot.
4 That fading flower, his glorious beauty,
set on the head of a fertile valley,

[a] 8 See Septuagint; the meaning of the Hebrew for this word is uncertain. [b] 9 That is, wooden symbols of the goddess Asherah

ISAIAH 28:14 – 16

A PRECIOUS CORNERSTONE

Because of their quickly changing political situation, the people of Isaiah's day were habitually looking for something sure and steadfast in which to find security and safety. Time and time again, their alliances and efforts to find such security and stability were thwarted. They foolishly made covenants that had deadly consequences and tried to secure themselves on less than firm footing. They should have turned to God to receive that sure foundation for which the people were searching.

The cornerstone was the first stone laid in building a structure; this single stone gave shape, security and integrity to the rest of the structure; it was the stone off of which everything else about the structure was aligned. When it comes to the Christian faith, Jesus Christ is that precious cornerstone. When believers build their lives on Jesus and on him alone, they can know that on him, there is eternal integrity and security (1Pe 2:6). What is the basis for all hope? What stands at the cornerstone of life? What gives shape to every relationship, decision and priority humans hold dear? If it's something other than Jesus, then people who are building their lives on that something else are building on sinking sand (Mt 7:26).

will be like figs ripe before harvest—
as soon as people see them and take them in hand,
they swallow them.

5 In that day the LORD Almighty
will be a glorious crown,
a beautiful wreath
for the remnant of his people.
6 He will be a spirit of justice
to the one who sits in judgment,
a source of strength
to those who turn back the battle at the gate.

7 And these also stagger from wine
and reel from beer:
Priests and prophets stagger from beer
and are befuddled with wine;
they reel from beer,
they stagger when seeing visions,
they stumble when rendering decisions.
8 All the tables are covered with vomit
and there is not a spot without filth.

9 "Who is it he is trying to teach?
To whom is he explaining his message?
To children weaned from their milk,
to those just taken from the breast?
10 For it is:
Do this, do that,
a rule for this, a rule for that[a];
a little here, a little there."

11 Very well then, with foreign lips and strange tongues
God will speak to this people,
12 to whom he said,
"This is the resting place, let the weary rest";
and, "This is the place of repose"—
but they would not listen.
13 So then, the word of the LORD to them will become:
Do this, do that,
a rule for this, a rule for that;
a little here, a little there—
so that as they go they will fall backward;
they will be injured and snared and captured.

14 Therefore hear the word of the LORD, you scoffers
who rule this people in Jerusalem.
15 You boast, "We have entered into a covenant with death,
with the realm of the dead we have made an agreement.
When an overwhelming scourge sweeps by,
it cannot touch us,
for we have made a lie our refuge
and falsehood[b] our hiding place."

16 So this is what the Sovereign LORD says:

"See, I lay a stone in Zion, a tested stone,
a precious cornerstone for a sure foundation;

[a] *10* Hebrew / *sav lasav sav lasav / kav lakav kav lakav* (probably meaningless sounds mimicking the prophet's words); also in verse 13 [b] *15* Or *false gods*

the one who relies on it
will never be stricken with panic.
17 I will make justice the measuring line
and righteousness the plumb line;
hail will sweep away your refuge, the lie,
and water will overflow your hiding place.
18 Your covenant with death will be annulled;
your agreement with the realm of the dead will not stand.
When the overwhelming scourge sweeps by,
you will be beaten down by it.
19 As often as it comes it will carry you away;
morning after morning, by day and by night,
it will sweep through."

The understanding of this message
will bring sheer terror.
20 The bed is too short to stretch out on,
the blanket too narrow to wrap around you.
21 The LORD will rise up as he did at Mount Perazim,
he will rouse himself as in the Valley of Gibeon —
to do his work, his strange work,
and perform his task, his alien task.
22 Now stop your mocking,
or your chains will become heavier;
the Lord, the LORD Almighty, has told me
of the destruction decreed against the whole land.

23 Listen and hear my voice;
pay attention and hear what I say.
24 When a farmer plows for planting, does he plow continually?
Does he keep on breaking up and working the soil?
25 When he has leveled the surface,
does he not sow caraway and scatter cumin?
Does he not plant wheat in its place,[a]
barley in its plot,[a]
and spelt in its field?
26 His God instructs him
and teaches him the right way.
27 Caraway is not threshed with a sledge,
nor is the wheel of a cart rolled over cumin;
caraway is beaten out with a rod,
and cumin with a stick.
28 Grain must be ground to make bread;
so one does not go on threshing it forever.
The wheels of a threshing cart may be rolled over it,
but one does not use horses to grind grain.
29 All this also comes from the LORD Almighty,
whose plan is wonderful,
whose wisdom is magnificent.

Woe to David's City

29 Woe to you, Ariel, Ariel,
the city where David settled!
Add year to year
and let your cycle of festivals go on.

---

[a] 25 The meaning of the Hebrew for this word is uncertain.

ISAIAH 29:9 – 13

RELIGIOUSNESS

Idolatry takes many forms and is as insidious as it is destructive. While some might think of an idol as a form of something made of stone or wood, the human heart has a remarkable capacity to take even that which is good and twist it into something idolatrous. Because this is our tendency, believers must recognize that something as seemingly good and right as devotion to God can be twisted into a form to which they bow. Such was the case for the people in Isaiah's day.

Though they might not have worshiped a physical idol, the people of Judah were intoxicated with their own religiousness. They were devoted to their own devotion; committed to their own commitment. And in so doing, they were trusting and loving their own religious efforts to the point that they were blind and deaf to the true Word of God. Jesus fought the same tendency toward misdirected devotion in the Pharisees of his own day who loved the law not for the sake of God, but because it filled them with pride at their own accomplishments (Mt 15:8 – 9). Jesus, both then and now, desires the heart of a person, not merely their religious actions. He requires their genuine love, not a self-serving and ultimately empty form of devotion.

[2] Yet I will besiege Ariel;
she will mourn and lament,
she will be to me like an altar hearth.[a]
[3] I will encamp against you on all sides;
I will encircle you with towers
and set up my siege works against you.
[4] Brought low, you will speak from the ground;
your speech will mumble out of the dust.
Your voice will come ghostlike from the earth;
out of the dust your speech will whisper.

[5] But your many enemies will become like fine dust,
the ruthless hordes like blown chaff.
Suddenly, in an instant,
[6] the LORD Almighty will come
with thunder and earthquake and great noise,
with windstorm and tempest and flames of a devouring fire.
[7] Then the hordes of all the nations that fight against Ariel,
that attack her and her fortress and besiege her,
will be as it is with a dream,
with a vision in the night—
[8] as when a hungry person dreams of eating,
but awakens hungry still;
as when a thirsty person dreams of drinking,
but awakens faint and thirsty still.
So will it be with the hordes of all the nations
that fight against Mount Zion.

[9] Be stunned and amazed,
blind yourselves and be sightless;
be drunk, but not from wine,
stagger, but not from beer.
[10] The LORD has brought over you a deep sleep:
He has sealed your eyes (the prophets);
he has covered your heads (the seers).

[11] For you this whole vision is nothing but words sealed in a scroll. And if you
give the scroll to someone who can read, and say, "Read this, please," they will
answer, "I can't; it is sealed." [12] Or if you give the scroll to someone who cannot
read, and say, "Read this, please," they will answer, "I don't know how to read."

[13] The Lord says:

"These people come near to me with their mouth
and honor me with their lips,
but their hearts are far from me.
Their worship of me
is based on merely human rules they have been taught.[b]
[14] Therefore once more I will astound these people
with wonder upon wonder;
the wisdom of the wise will perish,
the intelligence of the intelligent will vanish."
[15] Woe to those who go to great depths
to hide their plans from the LORD,
who do their work in darkness and think,
"Who sees us? Who will know?"

[a] 2 The Hebrew for *altar hearth* sounds like the Hebrew for *Ariel*. [b] 13 Hebrew; Septuagint *They worship me in vain; / their teachings are merely human rules*

16 You turn things upside down,
as if the potter were thought to be like the clay!
Shall what is formed say to the one who formed it,
"You did not make me"?
Can the pot say to the potter,
"You know nothing"?

17 In a very short time, will not Lebanon be turned into a fertile field
and the fertile field seem like a forest?
18 In that day the deaf will hear the words of the scroll,
and out of gloom and darkness
the eyes of the blind will see.
19 Once more the humble will rejoice in the LORD;
the needy will rejoice in the Holy One of Israel.
20 The ruthless will vanish,
the mockers will disappear,
and all who have an eye for evil will be cut down —
21 those who with a word make someone out to be guilty,
who ensnare the defender in court
and with false testimony deprive the innocent of justice.

22 Therefore this is what the LORD, who redeemed Abraham, says to the descendants of Jacob:

"No longer will Jacob be ashamed;
no longer will their faces grow pale.
23 When they see among them their children,
the work of my hands,
they will keep my name holy;
they will acknowledge the holiness of the Holy One of Jacob,
and will stand in awe of the God of Israel.
24 Those who are wayward in spirit will gain understanding;
those who complain will accept instruction."

Woe to the Obstinate Nation

30 "Woe to the obstinate children,"
declares the LORD,
"to those who carry out plans that are not mine,
forming an alliance, but not by my Spirit,
heaping sin upon sin;
2 who go down to Egypt
without consulting me;
who look for help to Pharaoh's protection,
to Egypt's shade for refuge.
3 But Pharaoh's protection will be to your shame,
Egypt's shade will bring you disgrace.
4 Though they have officials in Zoan
and their envoys have arrived in Hanes,
5 everyone will be put to shame
because of a people useless to them,
who bring neither help nor advantage,
but only shame and disgrace."

6 A prophecy concerning the animals of the Negev:

Through a land of hardship and distress,
of lions and lionesses,
of adders and darting snakes,
the envoys carry their riches on donkeys' backs,
their treasures on the humps of camels,

to that unprofitable nation,
7 to Egypt, whose help is utterly useless.
Therefore I call her
Rahab the Do-Nothing.

8 Go now, write it on a tablet for them,
inscribe it on a scroll,
that for the days to come
it may be an everlasting witness.
9 For these are rebellious people, deceitful children,
children unwilling to listen to the LORD's instruction.
10 They say to the seers,
"See no more visions!"
and to the prophets,
"Give us no more visions of what is right!
Tell us pleasant things,
prophesy illusions.
11 Leave this way,
get off this path,
and stop confronting us
with the Holy One of Israel!"

12 Therefore this is what the Holy One of Israel says:

"Because you have rejected this message,
relied on oppression
and depended on deceit,
13 this sin will become for you
like a high wall, cracked and bulging,
that collapses suddenly, in an instant.
14 It will break in pieces like pottery,
shattered so mercilessly
that among its pieces not a fragment will be found
for taking coals from a hearth
or scooping water out of a cistern."

15 This is what the Sovereign LORD, the Holy One of Israel, says:

"In repentance and rest is your salvation,
in quietness and trust is your strength,
but you would have none of it.
16 You said, 'No, we will flee on horses.'
Therefore you will flee!
You said, 'We will ride off on swift horses.'
Therefore your pursuers will be swift!
17 A thousand will flee
at the threat of one;
at the threat of five
you will all flee away,
till you are left
like a flagstaff on a mountaintop,
like a banner on a hill."

18 Yet the LORD longs to be gracious to you;
therefore he will rise up to show you compassion.
For the LORD is a God of justice.
Blessed are all who wait for him!

19 People of Zion, who live in Jerusalem, you will weep no more. How gracious
he will be when you cry for help! As soon as he hears, he will answer you. 20 Although the Lord gives you the bread of adversity and the water of affliction, your

ISAIAH 30:15

REST AND TRUST

There is something inside the heart of people that requires a human response to adversity. We demand action both from others and from ourselves when difficulties come. So the response God desires, as pictured in this verse, is counterintuitive. Quietness? Trust? Most people, whether now or in Isaiah's day, would say that these are not common ways to react in times of crisis. It's far easier to trust in horses and chariots than to rest and find strength in the Lord (v. 16; Ps 20:7). Nevertheless, when people know, understand and believe in the character of the Holy One of Israel, they can fully and completely rest in him.

For the people of Isaiah's day, this trust was too much and they felt as though they must take matters into their own hands. People who believe in and follow the gospel must fight the urge to do the same, taking up arms as a replacement for faith in God's ability to save completely. Walking in the way of Jesus means fully resting in him and his ability alone to fight on our behalf and win the battles his people experience (Jn 14:5–6).

teachers will be hidden no more; with your own eyes you will see them. [21]Wheth-
er you turn to the right or to the left, your ears will hear a voice behind you, saying, "This is the way; walk in it." [22]Then you will desecrate your idols overlaid
with silver and your images covered with gold; you will throw them away like a
menstrual cloth and say to them, "Away with you!"

[23]He will also send you rain for the seed you sow in the ground, and the food
that comes from the land will be rich and plentiful. In that day your cattle will
graze in broad meadows. [24]The oxen and donkeys that work the soil will eat fodder and mash, spread out with fork and shovel. [25]In the day of great slaughter,
when the towers fall, streams of water will flow on every high mountain and
every lofty hill. [26]The moon will shine like the sun, and the sunlight will be sev-
en times brighter, like the light of seven full days, when the LORD binds up the
bruises of his people and heals the wounds he inflicted.

[27]See, the Name of the LORD comes from afar,
with burning anger and dense clouds of smoke;
his lips are full of wrath,
and his tongue is a consuming fire.
[28]His breath is like a rushing torrent,
rising up to the neck.
He shakes the nations in the sieve of destruction;
he places in the jaws of the peoples
a bit that leads them astray.
[29]And you will sing
as on the night you celebrate a holy festival;
your hearts will rejoice
as when people playing pipes go up
to the mountain of the LORD,
to the Rock of Israel.
[30]The LORD will cause people to hear his majestic voice
and will make them see his arm coming down
with raging anger and consuming fire,
with cloudburst, thunderstorm and hail.
[31]The voice of the LORD will shatter Assyria;
with his rod he will strike them down.
[32]Every stroke the LORD lays on them
with his punishing club
will be to the music of timbrels and harps,
as he fights them in battle with the blows of his arm.
[33]Topheth has long been prepared;
it has been made ready for the king.
Its fire pit has been made deep and wide,
with an abundance of fire and wood;
the breath of the LORD,
like a stream of burning sulfur,
sets it ablaze.

Woe to Those Who Rely on Egypt

31 Woe to those who go down to Egypt for help,
who rely on horses,
who trust in the multitude of their chariots
and in the great strength of their horsemen,
but do not look to the Holy One of Israel,
or seek help from the LORD.
[2]Yet he too is wise and can bring disaster;
he does not take back his words.
He will rise up against that wicked nation,
against those who help evildoers.

ISAIAH 32:1–8

THE KINGDOM OF RIGHTEOUSNESS

The kingdom of God is an upside-down kingdom; it stands in direct opposition to the kingdom of the world into which we all have been born. For that reason, coming into the kingdom of God can have a whiplash kind of effect—it's a process of unlearning and relearning what is truly good and righteous and valuable in God's eyes.

Jesus told us about this dramatic reversal in his Sermon on the Mount (Mt 5–7). In this kingdom, the hungry are filled. The mourners rejoice. The poor are rich. God reverses the principles that lie at the foundation of the way we observe the world as we enter into his kingdom of righteousness. Here, God's prophet predicts this reversal in the coming kingdom when what is high will be brought low and what has been humiliated will be exalted. In this kingdom of righteousness, God's people will no longer know the hard work of seeking righteousness on their own merit but will instead know the quietness, assurance and peace that can only come from a righteousness given through the sacrifice of Jesus.

3 But the Egyptians are mere mortals and not God;
their horses are flesh and not spirit.
When the LORD stretches out his hand,
those who help will stumble,
those who are helped will fall;
all will perish together.

4 This is what the LORD says to me:

"As a lion growls,
a great lion over its prey—
and though a whole band of shepherds
is called together against it,
it is not frightened by their shouts
or disturbed by their clamor—
so the LORD Almighty will come down
to do battle on Mount Zion and on its heights.
5 Like birds hovering overhead,
the LORD Almighty will shield Jerusalem;
he will shield it and deliver it,
he will 'pass over' it and will rescue it."

6 Return, you Israelites, to the One you have so greatly revolted against. 7 For
in that day every one of you will reject the idols of silver and gold your sinful
hands have made.

8 "Assyria will fall by no human sword;
a sword, not of mortals, will devour them.
They will flee before the sword
and their young men will be put to forced labor.
9 Their stronghold will fall because of terror;
at the sight of the battle standard their commanders will panic,"
declares the LORD,
whose fire is in Zion,
whose furnace is in Jerusalem.

The Kingdom of Righteousness

32 See, a king will reign in righteousness
and rulers will rule with justice.
2 Each one will be like a shelter from the wind
and a refuge from the storm,
like streams of water in the desert
and the shadow of a great rock in a thirsty land.

3 Then the eyes of those who see will no longer be closed,
and the ears of those who hear will listen.
4 The fearful heart will know and understand,
and the stammering tongue will be fluent and clear.
5 No longer will the fool be called noble
nor the scoundrel be highly respected.
6 For fools speak folly,
their hearts are bent on evil:
They practice ungodliness
and spread error concerning the LORD;
the hungry they leave empty
and from the thirsty they withhold water.
7 Scoundrels use wicked methods,
they make up evil schemes
to destroy the poor with lies,
even when the plea of the needy is just.

[8] But the noble make noble plans,
and by noble deeds they stand.

The Women of Jerusalem

[9] You women who are so complacent,
rise up and listen to me;
you daughters who feel secure,
hear what I have to say!
[10] In little more than a year
you who feel secure will tremble;
the grape harvest will fail,
and the harvest of fruit will not come.
[11] Tremble, you complacent women;
shudder, you daughters who feel secure!
Strip off your fine clothes
and wrap yourselves in rags.
[12] Beat your breasts for the pleasant fields,
for the fruitful vines
[13] and for the land of my people,
a land overgrown with thorns and briers —
yes, mourn for all houses of merriment
and for this city of revelry.
[14] The fortress will be abandoned,
the noisy city deserted;
citadel and watchtower will become a wasteland forever,
the delight of donkeys, a pasture for flocks,
[15] till the Spirit is poured on us from on high,
and the desert becomes a fertile field,
and the fertile field seems like a forest.
[16] The LORD's justice will dwell in the desert,
his righteousness live in the fertile field.
[17] The fruit of that righteousness will be peace;
its effect will be quietness and confidence forever.
[18] My people will live in peaceful dwelling places,
in secure homes,
in undisturbed places of rest.
[19] Though hail flattens the forest
and the city is leveled completely,
[20] how blessed you will be,
sowing your seed by every stream,
and letting your cattle and donkeys range free.

Distress and Help

33 Woe to you, destroyer,
you who have not been destroyed!
Woe to you, betrayer,
you who have not been betrayed!
When you stop destroying,
you will be destroyed;
when you stop betraying,
you will be betrayed.

[2] LORD, be gracious to us;
we long for you.
Be our strength every morning,
our salvation in time of distress.
[3] At the uproar of your army, the peoples flee;
when you rise up, the nations scatter.

[4] Your plunder, O nations, is harvested as by young
locusts;
like a swarm of locusts people pounce on it.

[5] The LORD is exalted, for he dwells on high;
he will fill Zion with his justice and righteousness.
[6] He will be the sure foundation for your times,
a rich store of salvation and wisdom and knowledge;
the fear of the LORD is the key to this treasure.[a]

[7] Look, their brave men cry aloud in the streets;
the envoys of peace weep bitterly.
[8] The highways are deserted,
no travelers are on the roads.
The treaty is broken,
its witnesses[b] are despised,
no one is respected.
[9] The land dries up and wastes away,
Lebanon is ashamed and withers;
Sharon is like the Arabah,
and Bashan and Carmel drop their leaves.

[10] "Now will I arise," says the LORD.
"Now will I be exalted;
now will I be lifted up.
[11] You conceive chaff,
you give birth to straw;
your breath is a fire that consumes you.
[12] The peoples will be burned to ashes;
like cut thornbushes they will be set ablaze."

[13] You who are far away, hear what I have done;
you who are near, acknowledge my power!
[14] The sinners in Zion are terrified;
trembling grips the godless:
"Who of us can dwell with the consuming fire?
Who of us can dwell with everlasting burning?"
[15] Those who walk righteously
and speak what is right,
who reject gain from extortion
and keep their hands from accepting bribes,
who stop their ears against plots of murder
and shut their eyes against contemplating evil—
[16] they are the ones who will dwell on the heights,
whose refuge will be the mountain fortress.
Their bread will be supplied,
and water will not fail them.

[17] Your eyes will see the king in his beauty
and view a land that stretches afar.
[18] In your thoughts you will ponder the former terror:
"Where is that chief officer?
Where is the one who took the revenue?
Where is the officer in charge of the towers?"
[19] You will see those arrogant people no more,
people whose speech is obscure,
whose language is strange and incomprehensible.

ISAIAH 33:13–17

THE BEAUTY OF THE KING

Judgment is a fearsome thing, and it is coming. God is a consuming fire (v. 14), and because he is, the prophet asked a somewhat rhetorical question in verse 14. Who indeed can live with God's consuming fire? Who can remain upright when the holiness of God burns away the hypocritical acts of righteousness along with the rebellious sin of humanity? Shockingly, after this we see in verse 17 a picture not of the fire of judgment from just a few verses earlier, but instead of the beauty of the King.

Such is the difference between the perspective of those who have, in humility, thrown themselves on the mercy of the King and those who, in arrogance, have presumed upon his patience. The fact that every human will bend their knee and give honor to Jesus is not a question of "if"; it's a question of "when." *Every* knee will bow. *Every* tongue will acknowledge. And it will be done to the glory of God the Father (Php 2:10–11). Some will bow in great joy at the beauty of the King; others will bow in terror at his judgment. But make no mistake—every person will bend their knee to Jesus.

[a] 6 Or *is a treasure from him* [b] 8 Dead Sea Scrolls; Masoretic Text / *the cities*

[20] Look on Zion, the city of our festivals;
your eyes will see Jerusalem,
a peaceful abode, a tent that will not be moved;
its stakes will never be pulled up,
nor any of its ropes broken.
[21] There the LORD will be our Mighty One.
It will be like a place of broad rivers and streams.
No galley with oars will ride them,
no mighty ship will sail them.
[22] For the LORD is our judge,
the LORD is our lawgiver,
the LORD is our king;
it is he who will save us.

[23] Your rigging hangs loose:
The mast is not held secure,
the sail is not spread.
Then an abundance of spoils will be divided
and even the lame will carry off plunder.
[24] No one living in Zion will say, "I am ill";
and the sins of those who dwell there will be forgiven.

Judgment Against the Nations

34 Come near, you nations, and listen;
pay attention, you peoples!
Let the earth hear, and all that is in it,
the world, and all that comes out of it!
[2] The LORD is angry with all nations;
his wrath is on all their armies.
He will totally destroy[a] them,
he will give them over to slaughter.
[3] Their slain will be thrown out,
their dead bodies will stink;
the mountains will be soaked with their blood.
[4] All the stars in the sky will be dissolved
and the heavens rolled up like a scroll;
all the starry host will fall
like withered leaves from the vine,
like shriveled figs from the fig tree.

[5] My sword has drunk its fill in the heavens;
see, it descends in judgment on Edom,
the people I have totally destroyed.
[6] The sword of the LORD is bathed in blood,
it is covered with fat—
the blood of lambs and goats,
fat from the kidneys of rams.
For the LORD has a sacrifice in Bozrah
and a great slaughter in the land of Edom.
[7] And the wild oxen will fall with them,
the bull calves and the great bulls.
Their land will be drenched with blood,
and the dust will be soaked with fat.

[8] For the LORD has a day of vengeance,
a year of retribution, to uphold Zion's cause.

---

[a] *2* The Hebrew term refers to the irrevocable giving over of things or persons to the LORD, often by totally destroying them; also in verse 5.

[9] Edom's streams will be turned into pitch,
her dust into burning sulfur;
her land will become blazing pitch!
[10] It will not be quenched night or day;
its smoke will rise forever.
From generation to generation it will lie desolate;
no one will ever pass through it again.
[11] The desert owl[a] and screech owl[a] will possess it;
the great owl[a] and the raven will nest there.
God will stretch out over Edom
the measuring line of chaos
and the plumb line of desolation.
[12] Her nobles will have nothing there to be called a kingdom,
all her princes will vanish away.
[13] Thorns will overrun her citadels,
nettles and brambles her strongholds.
She will become a haunt for jackals,
a home for owls.
[14] Desert creatures will meet with hyenas,
and wild goats will bleat to each other;
there the night creatures will also lie down
and find for themselves places of rest.
[15] The owl will nest there and lay eggs,
she will hatch them, and care for her young
under the shadow of her wings;
there also the falcons will gather,
each with its mate.

[16] Look in the scroll of the LORD and read:

None of these will be missing,
not one will lack her mate.
For it is his mouth that has given the order,
and his Spirit will gather them together.
[17] He allots their portions;
his hand distributes them by measure.
They will possess it forever
and dwell there from generation to generation.

Joy of the Redeemed

35 The desert and the parched land will be glad;
the wilderness will rejoice and blossom.
Like the crocus, [2] it will burst into bloom;
it will rejoice greatly and shout for joy.
The glory of Lebanon will be given to it,
the splendor of Carmel and Sharon;
they will see the glory of the LORD,
the splendor of our God.

[3] Strengthen the feeble hands,
steady the knees that give way;
[4] say to those with fearful hearts,
"Be strong, do not fear;
your God will come,
he will come with vengeance;
with divine retribution
he will come to save you."

---

[a] *11* The precise identification of these birds is uncertain.

POWER TO HEAL

God's plan, since the fall of the first humans in Genesis 3, has been to return all of creation to a restored and redeemed state. His ongoing work, exercised through the ministry of Jesus Christ, is to return all things to what they were. And this redemptive work goes beyond the scope of humanity. True, God's redemptive work will include the salvation of his people, who will be freed from the tyranny of sin forever. But God's plan also includes the salvation of a fallen world, which will be purged from the curse of sin and purified so that it radiates the very glory of God.

Isaiah 35 stands in contrast to the promise of divine judgment in Isaiah 34. This later chapter describes God's promises — his willingness, ability and intent to bring healing to his creation. This healing will be all-encompassing as God transforms nature (vv. 1 – 2), broken humanity (vv. 3 – 6) and then eventually returns God's transformed creation and people to himself (vv. 6 – 10). Though the Israelites would certainly find hope in these verses as they looked forward to returning from their exile in foreign territory, we know that the greatest fulfillment of these verses, and of God's glory, will come when Jesus returns to the earth.

We might look on these promises about God's power to heal with cynicism when we see them in light of life as it stands today. Here, now, we see much evidence to the contrary as wars, violence, pain, disease and famine define our current reality, and even believers find it difficult to envision that they are on the road to a fully and completely healed creation. In the New Testament, John the Baptist felt the same tension when he was imprisoned. In response to John's own questions about whether Jesus was the One to bring about this kind of holistic redemption, Jesus pointed his cousin back to this very passage (Mt 11:2 – 6).

By faith, we believe that Jesus can do what he promised. By faith, we trust that everything old and broken will be restored and made new again. By faith, we believe that not only our souls, but also our bodies and the rest of creation around us will be redeemed (Ro 8:18 – 23). Though today's surrounding circumstances might tell us otherwise, we trust not in what we visibly see but in the promises of the God who heals, restores and makes everything new (Rev 21:5).

5 Then will the eyes of the blind be opened
  and the ears of the deaf unstopped.
6 Then will the lame leap like a deer,
  and the mute tongue shout for joy.
Water will gush forth in the wilderness
  and streams in the desert.
7 The burning sand will become a pool,
  the thirsty ground bubbling springs.
In the haunts where jackals once lay,
  grass and reeds and papyrus will grow.

8 And a highway will be there;
  it will be called the Way of Holiness;
  it will be for those who walk on that Way.
The unclean will not journey on it;
  wicked fools will not go about on it.
9 No lion will be there,
  nor any ravenous beast;
  they will not be found there.
But only the redeemed will walk there,
10 and those the LORD has rescued will return.
They will enter Zion with singing;
  everlasting joy will crown their heads.
Gladness and joy will overtake them,
  and sorrow and sighing will flee away.

Sennacherib Threatens Jerusalem

36 In the fourteenth year of King Hezekiah's reign, Sennacherib king of Assyria attacked all the fortified cities of Judah and captured them. 2 Then the king of Assyria sent his field commander with a large army from Lachish to King Hezekiah at Jerusalem. When the commander stopped at the aqueduct of the Upper Pool, on the road to the Launderer's Field, 3 Eliakim son of Hilkiah the palace administrator, Shebna the secretary, and Joah son of Asaph the recorder went out to him.

4 The field commander said to them, "Tell Hezekiah:

"'This is what the great king, the king of Assyria, says: On what are you basing this confidence of yours? 5 You say you have counsel and might for war — but you speak only empty words. On whom are you depending, that you rebel against me? 6 Look, I know you are depending on Egypt, that splintered reed of a staff, which pierces the hand of anyone who leans on it! Such is Pharaoh king of Egypt to all who depend on him. 7 But if you say to me, "We are depending on the LORD our God" — isn't he the one whose high places and altars Hezekiah removed, saying to Judah and Jerusalem, "You must worship before this altar"?

8 "'Come now, make a bargain with my master, the king of Assyria: I will give you two thousand horses — if you can put riders on them! 9 How then can you repulse one officer of the least of my master's officials, even though you are depending on Egypt for chariots and horsemen[a]? 10 Furthermore, have I come to attack and destroy this land without the LORD? The LORD himself told me to march against this country and destroy it.'"

11 Then Eliakim, Shebna and Joah said to the field commander, "Please speak to your servants in Aramaic, since we understand it. Don't speak to us in Hebrew in the hearing of the people on the wall."

12 But the commander replied, "Was it only to your master and you that my master sent me to say these things, and not to the people sitting on the wall — who, like you, will have to eat their own excrement and drink their own urine?"

---

[a] 9 Or *charioteers*

13Then the commander stood and called out in Hebrew, "Hear the words of the great king, the king of Assyria! 14This is what the king says: Do not let Hezekiah deceive you. He cannot deliver you! 15Do not let Hezekiah persuade you to trust in the LORD when he says, 'The LORD will surely deliver us; this city will not be given into the hand of the king of Assyria.'

16"Do not listen to Hezekiah. This is what the king of Assyria says: Make peace with me and come out to me. Then each of you will eat fruit from your own vine and fig tree and drink water from your own cistern, 17until I come and take you to a land like your own — a land of grain and new wine, a land of bread and vineyards.

18"Do not let Hezekiah mislead you when he says, 'The LORD will deliver us.' Have the gods of any nations ever delivered their lands from the hand of the king of Assyria? 19Where are the gods of Hamath and Arpad? Where are the gods of Sepharvaim? Have they rescued Samaria from my hand? 20Who of all the gods of these countries have been able to save their lands from me? How then can the LORD deliver Jerusalem from my hand?"

21But the people remained silent and said nothing in reply, because the king had commanded, "Do not answer him."

22Then Eliakim son of Hilkiah the palace administrator, Shebna the secretary and Joah son of Asaph the recorder went to Hezekiah, with their clothes torn, and told him what the field commander had said.

Jerusalem's Deliverance Foretold

37 When King Hezekiah heard this, he tore his clothes and put on sackcloth and went into the temple of the LORD. 2He sent Eliakim the palace administrator, Shebna the secretary, and the leading priests, all wearing sackcloth, to the prophet Isaiah son of Amoz. 3They told him, "This is what Hezekiah says: This day is a day of distress and rebuke and disgrace, as when children come to the moment of birth and there is no strength to deliver them. 4It may be that the LORD your God will hear the words of the field commander, whom his master, the king of Assyria, has sent to ridicule the living God, and that he will rebuke him for the words the LORD your God has heard. Therefore pray for the remnant that still survives."

5When King Hezekiah's officials came to Isaiah, 6Isaiah said to them, "Tell your master, 'This is what the LORD says: Do not be afraid of what you have heard — those words with which the underlings of the king of Assyria have blasphemed me. 7Listen! When he hears a certain report, I will make him want to return to his own country, and there I will have him cut down with the sword.' "

8When the field commander heard that the king of Assyria had left Lachish, he withdrew and found the king fighting against Libnah.

9Now Sennacherib received a report that Tirhakah, the king of Cush,[a] was marching out to fight against him. When he heard it, he sent messengers to Hezekiah with this word: 10"Say to Hezekiah king of Judah: Do not let the god you depend on deceive you when he says, 'Jerusalem will not be given into the hands of the king of Assyria.' 11Surely you have heard what the kings of Assyria have done to all the countries, destroying them completely. And will you be delivered? 12Did the gods of the nations that were destroyed by my predecessors deliver them — the gods of Gozan, Harran, Rezeph and the people of Eden who were in Tel Assar? 13Where is the king of Hamath or the king of Arpad? Where are the kings of Lair, Sepharvaim, Hena and Ivvah?"

Hezekiah's Prayer

14Hezekiah received the letter from the messengers and read it. Then he went up to the temple of the LORD and spread it out before the LORD. 15And Hezekiah prayed to the LORD: 16"LORD Almighty, the God of Israel, enthroned between the

[a] 9 That is, the upper Nile region

THE DANGER OF MOCKING GOD

Hezekiah and his people were facing an extreme threat. But up to this point, Hezekiah had failed to do the very thing he should have done at first. Instead of turning directly to the God who can save, he attempted to make an alliance with Egypt (Isa 30:1 – 2; 36:4 – 6) and probably with Babylon. Only when those alliances failed did he turn in desperation to the God who held Judah's future in his hands all along.

Hezekiah's appeal to the Lord was based not only in God's character, but also in the fact that Sennacherib had mocked God (37:9 – 13). He had called into question the reality and power of the Almighty. In their arrogance, the Assyrians had ruthlessly and mercilessly conquered all the nations before them, and in so doing had triumphed over their gods. Their victories had set the nation up to believe they were the captains of their destiny, the navigators of their own course, and that no one — neither God nor man — could stand in their way.

Hezekiah, though, knew better. Despite his attempts to form earthly alliances in the past, he was at this point aware that the true battle belonged to the Lord alone. God answered through his prophet to let Hezekiah know that he would defend his city from the Assyrians for his own sake and for the sake of his servant David (37:33 – 37). Here is another reminder that God delivers on his promises; that even in this desperate time, with a ruthless army standing in opposition to his people, against all reasonable human odds, he would continue to act on the promises he had previously made — to the honor of his own glory.

Like Hezekiah, we find ourselves in desperate situations. Like Hezekiah, we face a seemingly unbeatable foe in the prince of darkness. This is the fight behind the fight and the enemy behind all the other enemies. Whether we recognize it or not, we are all caught up in this broad, cosmic struggle that will not end until Jesus returns and brings final judgment. Like Hezekiah, we have the tendency to trust in our earthly alliances and weapons, but Paul would later write that in this fight we don't wage war like the world does. We do not use the weapons of the world, but instead we fight in the spiritual realm with spiritual weapons, and as we do, we demolish strongholds in that arena (2Co 10:3 – 5). For the Christian, the war is already won, though the battles rage on. For the Christian, in the end we will see Jesus demonstrate his power against those who mock God just as God demonstrated his power on behalf of Hezekiah.

cherubim, you alone are God over all the kingdoms of the earth. You have made heaven and earth. [17]Give ear, LORD, and hear; open your eyes, LORD, and see; listen to all the words Sennacherib has sent to ridicule the living God.

[18]"It is true, LORD, that the Assyrian kings have laid waste all these peoples and their lands. [19]They have thrown their gods into the fire and destroyed them, for they were not gods but only wood and stone, fashioned by human hands. [20]Now, LORD our God, deliver us from his hand, so that all the kingdoms of the earth may know that you, LORD, are the only God.[a]"

Sennacherib's Fall

[21]Then Isaiah son of Amoz sent a message to Hezekiah: "This is what the LORD, the God of Israel, says: Because you have prayed to me concerning Sennacherib king of Assyria, [22]this is the word the LORD has spoken against him:

"Virgin Daughter Zion
despises and mocks you.
Daughter Jerusalem
tosses her head as you flee.
[23]Who is it you have ridiculed and blasphemed?
Against whom have you raised your voice
and lifted your eyes in pride?
Against the Holy One of Israel!
[24]By your messengers
you have ridiculed the Lord.
And you have said,
'With my many chariots
I have ascended the heights of the mountains,
the utmost heights of Lebanon.
I have cut down its tallest cedars,
the choicest of its junipers.
I have reached its remotest heights,
the finest of its forests.
[25]I have dug wells in foreign lands[b]
and drunk the water there.
With the soles of my feet
I have dried up all the streams of Egypt.'

[26]"Have you not heard?
Long ago I ordained it.
In days of old I planned it;
now I have brought it to pass,
that you have turned fortified cities
into piles of stone.
[27]Their people, drained of power,
are dismayed and put to shame.
They are like plants in the field,
like tender green shoots,
like grass sprouting on the roof,
scorched[c] before it grows up.

[28]"But I know where you are
and when you come and go
and how you rage against me.

---

[a] *20* Dead Sea Scrolls (see also 2 Kings 19:19); Masoretic Text *you alone are the LORD*
[b] *25* Dead Sea Scrolls (see also 2 Kings 19:24); Masoretic Text does not have *in foreign lands.*
[c] *27* Some manuscripts of the Masoretic Text, Dead Sea Scrolls and some Septuagint manuscripts (see also 2 Kings 19:26); most manuscripts of the Masoretic Text *roof / and terraced fields*

29 Because you rage against me
and because your insolence has reached my ears,
I will put my hook in your nose
and my bit in your mouth,
and I will make you return
by the way you came.

30 "This will be the sign for you, Hezekiah:

"This year you will eat what grows by itself,
and the second year what springs from that.
But in the third year sow and reap,
plant vineyards and eat their fruit.
31 Once more a remnant of the kingdom of Judah
will take root below and bear fruit above.
32 For out of Jerusalem will come a remnant,
and out of Mount Zion a band of survivors.
The zeal of the LORD Almighty
will accomplish this.

33 "Therefore this is what the LORD says concerning the king of Assyria:

"He will not enter this city
or shoot an arrow here.
He will not come before it with shield
or build a siege ramp against it.
34 By the way that he came he will return;
he will not enter this city,"
declares the LORD.
35 "I will defend this city and save it,
for my sake and for the sake of David my servant!"

36 Then the angel of the LORD went out and put to death a hundred and
eighty-five thousand in the Assyrian camp. When the people got up the next
morning — there were all the dead bodies! 37 So Sennacherib king of Assyria
broke camp and withdrew. He returned to Nineveh and stayed there.
38 One day, while he was worshiping in the temple of his god Nisrok, his sons
Adrammelek and Sharezer killed him with the sword, and they escaped to the
land of Ararat. And Esarhaddon his son succeeded him as king.

Hezekiah's Illness

38 In those days Hezekiah became ill and was at the point of death. The
prophet Isaiah son of Amoz went to him and said, "This is what the LORD
says: Put your house in order, because you are going to die; you will not recover."
2 Hezekiah turned his face to the wall and prayed to the LORD, 3 "Remember,
LORD, how I have walked before you faithfully and with wholehearted devotion
and have done what is good in your eyes." And Hezekiah wept bitterly.
4 Then the word of the LORD came to Isaiah: 5 "Go and tell Hezekiah, 'This is
what the LORD, the God of your father David, says: I have heard your prayer and
seen your tears; I will add fifteen years to your life. 6 And I will deliver you and
this city from the hand of the king of Assyria. I will defend this city.
7 " 'This is the LORD's sign to you that the LORD will do what he has promised:
8 I will make the shadow cast by the sun go back the ten steps it has gone down
on the stairway of Ahaz.' " So the sunlight went back the ten steps it had gone
down.

9 A writing of Hezekiah king of Judah after his illness and recovery:
10 I said, "In the prime of my life
must I go through the gates of death
and be robbed of the rest of my years?"

[11]I said, "I will not again see the LORD himself
in the land of the living;
no longer will I look on my fellow man,
or be with those who now dwell in this world.
[12]Like a shepherd's tent my house
has been pulled down and taken from me.
Like a weaver I have rolled up my life,
and he has cut me off from the loom;
day and night you made an end of me.
[13]I waited patiently till dawn,
but like a lion he broke all my bones;
day and night you made an end of me.
[14]I cried like a swift or thrush,
I moaned like a mourning dove.
My eyes grew weak as I looked to the heavens.
I am being threatened; Lord, come to my aid!"

[15]But what can I say?
He has spoken to me, and he himself has done this.
I will walk humbly all my years
because of this anguish of my soul.
[16]Lord, by such things people live;
and my spirit finds life in them too.
You restored me to health
and let me live.
[17]Surely it was for my benefit
that I suffered such anguish.
In your love you kept me
from the pit of destruction;
you have put all my sins
behind your back.
[18]For the grave cannot praise you,
death cannot sing your praise;
those who go down to the pit
cannot hope for your faithfulness.
[19]The living, the living—they praise you,
as I am doing today;
parents tell their children
about your faithfulness.

[20]The LORD will save me,
and we will sing with stringed instruments
all the days of our lives
in the temple of the LORD.

[21]Isaiah had said, "Prepare a poultice of figs and apply it to the boil, and he will recover."

[22]Hezekiah had asked, "What will be the sign that I will go up to the temple of the LORD?"

Envoys From Babylon

39 At that time Marduk-Baladan son of Baladan king of Babylon sent Hezekiah letters and a gift, because he had heard of his illness and recovery.
[2]Hezekiah received the envoys gladly and showed them what was in his storehouses—the silver, the gold, the spices, the fine olive oil—his entire armory and
everything found among his treasures. There was nothing in his palace or in all
his kingdom that Hezekiah did not show them.
[3]Then Isaiah the prophet went to King Hezekiah and asked, "What did those
men say, and where did they come from?"

ISAIAH 40:1 – 8

COMFORT FOR GOD'S PEOPLE

Comfort is a powerful thing, especially when a person's situation is dire. That's precisely the kind of situation in which the Babylonian exiles found themselves. Because of their unfaithfulness to the Lord, they had been stripped of their land, their temple and their very identity, and yet the prophet spoke to them this message of comfort. Though they were far away from their homeland, though they were in exile, though they might have been filled with fear and apprehension about the future, God had not forgotten them. Neither had his plan for redemption been put aside.

The comfort offered here is better than a physical return to their homeland and greater than a restoration of their temple; the comfort God offers is that he will someday meet them in the form of the Suffering Servant — the One who would become their great King. Though some of the people would indeed return to their homeland, this was just a foretaste of the greater homecoming that awaited them — and that awaits all of God's people — when they will dwell with him for all eternity.

Just as Isaiah announced this comfort to the people of Judah, so came John the Baptist later heralding the way of Jesus Christ. John's cry was that a ruler was coming from the desert, from a distant land, and that the people should prepare the way for the glory of the Lord to be revealed in Jesus Christ (Mt 3:3).

"From a distant land," Hezekiah replied. "They came to me from Babylon."
4 The prophet asked, "What did they see in your palace?"
"They saw everything in my palace," Hezekiah said. "There is nothing among
my treasures that I did not show them."
5 Then Isaiah said to Hezekiah, "Hear the word of the LORD Almighty: 6 The
time will surely come when everything in your palace, and all that your predecessors have stored up until this day, will be carried off to Babylon. Nothing will
be left, says the LORD. 7 And some of your descendants, your own flesh and blood
who will be born to you, will be taken away, and they will become eunuchs in the
palace of the king of Babylon."
8 "The word of the LORD you have spoken is good," Hezekiah replied. For he
thought, "There will be peace and security in my lifetime."

Comfort for God's People

40 Comfort, comfort my people,
says your God.
2 Speak tenderly to Jerusalem,
and proclaim to her
that her hard service has been completed,
that her sin has been paid for,
that she has received from the LORD's hand
double for all her sins.

3 A voice of one calling:
"In the wilderness prepare
the way for the LORD[a];
make straight in the desert
a highway for our God.[b]
4 Every valley shall be raised up,
every mountain and hill made low;
the rough ground shall become level,
the rugged places a plain.
5 And the glory of the LORD will be revealed,
and all people will see it together.
For the mouth of the LORD has spoken."

6 A voice says, "Cry out."
And I said, "What shall I cry?"

"All people are like grass,
and all their faithfulness is like the flowers of the field.
7 The grass withers and the flowers fall,
because the breath of the LORD blows on them.
Surely the people are grass.
8 The grass withers and the flowers fall,
but the word of our God endures forever."

9 You who bring good news to Zion,
go up on a high mountain.
You who bring good news to Jerusalem,[c]
lift up your voice with a shout,
lift it up, do not be afraid;
say to the towns of Judah,
"Here is your God!"
10 See, the Sovereign LORD comes with power,
and he rules with a mighty arm.

[a] 3 Or *A voice of one calling in the wilderness: / "Prepare the way for the LORD* [b] 3 Hebrew; Septuagint *make straight the paths of our God* [c] 9 Or *Zion, bringer of good news, / go up on a high mountain. / Jerusalem, bringer of good news*

THE FOLLY OF A WORLDLY FOCUS

Hezekiah suffered from the shortsightedness that is one of the great weaknesses of humanity. After his illness and recovery, envoys from Babylon came to the kingdom, and Hezekiah welcomed them warmly. He was happy not only to receive them, but to show them everything in his kingdom without exception. He went so far as to show them the deepest parts of his palace, including everything he had in his treasury.

"Why not?" he might have reasoned. After all, they were from a country that was far away; what harm could it do? This was the answer, in short, that Hezekiah gave to Isaiah when Isaiah confronted him about his actions. Hezekiah was both worldly and unwise, for Isaiah gave him the bad news: his foolish actions would one day pay bitter dividends. Even though Babylon was indeed far away, there would come a day when the armies of that nation would come and carry off the people and plunder of Judah in victory. All the treasures Hezekiah had accumulated and then boastfully and carelessly revealed to the Babylonians would eventually be theirs.

Hezekiah's shortsightedness went well beyond the fact that he showed off before the foreign dignitaries. His response when Isaiah told him that his palace and country would be plundered revealed his acceptance of the Lord's coming judgment (v. 8). He was also surely thankful for the time of peace that the people would experience before this judgment would come.

God has "set eternity in the human heart" (Ecc 3:11), but we seem to go to remarkable lengths to deny its existence. Jesus talked about the great folly of this worldly focus when he told the parable of the successful farmer who built bigger and bigger barns, storing up more and more for himself without ever considering that today could be his last day. While he was eating, drinking and being merry in the present moment, God demanded his life from him (Lk 12:13 – 21). The reality of human mortality and God's immortality requires that we maintain more than a temporary and worldly focus. We must think about the impact our words and actions have for eternity, not only for the sake of our own souls but also for the sake of those around us.

See, his reward is with him,
and his recompense accompanies him.
11 He tends his flock like a shepherd:
He gathers the lambs in his arms
and carries them close to his heart;
he gently leads those that have young.

12 Who has measured the waters in the hollow of his hand,
or with the breadth of his hand marked off the heavens?
Who has held the dust of the earth in a basket,
or weighed the mountains on the scales
and the hills in a balance?
13 Who can fathom the Spirit[a] of the LORD,
or instruct the LORD as his counselor?
14 Whom did the LORD consult to enlighten him,
and who taught him the right way?
Who was it that taught him knowledge,
or showed him the path of understanding?

15 Surely the nations are like a drop in a bucket;
they are regarded as dust on the scales;
he weighs the islands as though they were fine dust.
16 Lebanon is not sufficient for altar fires,
nor its animals enough for burnt offerings.
17 Before him all the nations are as nothing;
they are regarded by him as worthless
and less than nothing.

18 With whom, then, will you compare God?
To what image will you liken him?
19 As for an idol, a metalworker casts it,
and a goldsmith overlays it with gold
and fashions silver chains for it.
20 A person too poor to present such an offering
selects wood that will not rot;
they look for a skilled worker
to set up an idol that will not topple.

21 Do you not know?
Have you not heard?
Has it not been told you from the beginning?
Have you not understood since the earth was founded?
22 He sits enthroned above the circle of the earth,
and its people are like grasshoppers.
He stretches out the heavens like a canopy,
and spreads them out like a tent to live in.
23 He brings princes to naught
and reduces the rulers of this world to nothing.
24 No sooner are they planted,
no sooner are they sown,
no sooner do they take root in the ground,
than he blows on them and they wither,
and a whirlwind sweeps them away like chaff.

25 "To whom will you compare me?
Or who is my equal?" says the Holy One.
26 Lift up your eyes and look to the heavens:
Who created all these?

---

[a] *13* Or *mind*

He who brings out the starry host one by one
and calls forth each of them by name.
Because of his great power and mighty strength,
not one of them is missing.

27 Why do you complain, Jacob?
Why do you say, Israel,
"My way is hidden from the LORD;
my cause is disregarded by my God"?
28 Do you not know?
Have you not heard?
The LORD is the everlasting God,
the Creator of the ends of the earth.
He will not grow tired or weary,
and his understanding no one can fathom.
29 He gives strength to the weary
and increases the power of the weak.
30 Even youths grow tired and weary,
and young men stumble and fall;
31 but those who hope in the LORD
will renew their strength.
They will soar on wings like eagles;
they will run and not grow weary,
they will walk and not be faint.

The Helper of Israel

41 "Be silent before me, you islands!
Let the nations renew their strength!
Let them come forward and speak;
let us meet together at the place of judgment.

2 "Who has stirred up one from the east,
calling him in righteousness to his service[a]?
He hands nations over to him
and subdues kings before him.
He turns them to dust with his sword,
to windblown chaff with his bow.
3 He pursues them and moves on unscathed,
by a path his feet have not traveled before.
4 Who has done this and carried it through,
calling forth the generations from the beginning?
I, the LORD—with the first of them
and with the last—I am he."

5 The islands have seen it and fear;
the ends of the earth tremble.
They approach and come forward;
6 they help each other
and say to their companions, "Be strong!"
7 The metalworker encourages the goldsmith,
and the one who smooths with the hammer
spurs on the one who strikes the anvil.
One says of the welding, "It is good."
The other nails down the idol so it will not topple.

8 "But you, Israel, my servant,
Jacob, whom I have chosen,
you descendants of Abraham my friend,

[a] 2 Or *east, / whom victory meets at every step*

ISAIAH 41:8–14

GOD'S CHOOSING

True security can only be found in the grace and mercy of God. This was the case for the Israelites. Though time and time again they had rebelled against their God, testing his patience with their consistent return to idolatry, he just as consistently reminded them that they were, and are, his chosen people.

The people of Israel did not earn this right; they did not pursue it on their own. Rather, God's choice of Israel was based on his good pleasure and will. For that reason, his choice of a people to be his favored nation is also to his great glory alone. Because God's choice of his people is based on himself, and for himself, security comes not in making a claim to personal righteousness, but rather in knowing and trusting that God keeps his promises to his people.

Like the Israelites then, we too can be free from fear. We can trust in his strength. We can know that ultimately God will be victorious, and that we will share in that victory. This is not because we can merit any such claim, but only because we have been chosen to be the recipients of God's grace in the sacrifice and resurrection of Jesus Christ.

9 I took you from the ends of the earth,
from its farthest corners I called you.
I said, 'You are my servant';
I have chosen you and have not rejected you.
10 So do not fear, for I am with you;
do not be dismayed, for I am your God.
I will strengthen you and help you;
I will uphold you with my righteous right hand.

11 "All who rage against you
will surely be ashamed and disgraced;
those who oppose you
will be as nothing and perish.
12 Though you search for your enemies,
you will not find them.
Those who wage war against you
will be as nothing at all.
13 For I am the LORD your God
who takes hold of your right hand
and says to you, Do not fear;
I will help you.
14 Do not be afraid, you worm Jacob,
little Israel, do not fear,
for I myself will help you," declares the LORD,
your Redeemer, the Holy One of Israel.
15 "See, I will make you into a threshing sledge,
new and sharp, with many teeth.
You will thresh the mountains and crush them,
and reduce the hills to chaff.
16 You will winnow them, the wind will pick them up,
and a gale will blow them away.
But you will rejoice in the LORD
and glory in the Holy One of Israel.

17 "The poor and needy search for water,
but there is none;
their tongues are parched with thirst.
But I the LORD will answer them;
I, the God of Israel, will not forsake them.
18 I will make rivers flow on barren heights,
and springs within the valleys.
I will turn the desert into pools of water,
and the parched ground into springs.
19 I will put in the desert
the cedar and the acacia, the myrtle and the olive.
I will set junipers in the wasteland,
the fir and the cypress together,
20 so that people may see and know,
may consider and understand,
that the hand of the LORD has done this,
that the Holy One of Israel has created it.

21 "Present your case," says the LORD.
"Set forth your arguments," says Jacob's King.
22 "Tell us, you idols,
what is going to happen.
Tell us what the former things were,
so that we may consider them
and know their final outcome.

Or declare to us the things to come,
23 tell us what the future holds,
so we may know that you are gods.
Do something, whether good or bad,
so that we will be dismayed and filled with fear.
24 But you are less than nothing
and your works are utterly worthless;
whoever chooses you is detestable.

25 "I have stirred up one from the north, and he comes —
one from the rising sun who calls on my name.
He treads on rulers as if they were mortar,
as if he were a potter treading the clay.
26 Who told of this from the beginning, so we could know,
or beforehand, so we could say, 'He was right'?
No one told of this,
no one foretold it,
no one heard any words from you.
27 I was the first to tell Zion, 'Look, here they are!'
I gave to Jerusalem a messenger of good news.
28 I look but there is no one —
no one among the gods to give counsel,
no one to give answer when I ask them.
29 See, they are all false!
Their deeds amount to nothing;
their images are but wind and confusion.

The Servant of the Lord

42 "Here is my servant, whom I uphold,
my chosen one in whom I delight;
I will put my Spirit on him,
and he will bring justice to the nations.
2 He will not shout or cry out,
or raise his voice in the streets.
3 A bruised reed he will not break,
and a smoldering wick he will not snuff out.
In faithfulness he will bring forth justice;
4 he will not falter or be discouraged
till he establishes justice on earth.
In his teaching the islands will put their hope."

5 This is what God the Lord says —
the Creator of the heavens, who stretches them out,
who spreads out the earth with all that springs from it,
who gives breath to its people,
and life to those who walk on it:
6 "I, the Lord, have called you in righteousness;
I will take hold of your hand.
I will keep you and will make you
to be a covenant for the people
and a light for the Gentiles,
7 to open eyes that are blind,
to free captives from prison
and to release from the dungeon those who sit in darkness.

8 "I am the Lord; that is my name!
I will not yield my glory to another
or my praise to idols.

ISAIAH 42:1 – 4

HEALING THE BROKEN

Truth and justice can be wielded like a jackhammer; they can come with such force that even those who are eventual beneficiaries of these realities feel destroyed in their path. But this description of the servant of the Lord makes it clear that, though God's Anointed One will indeed bring in these kingdom realities, he will not do so at the expense of the broken.

It is as true today as it was in Isaiah's day that in the world there are many people who are hanging on by a thread: it might be a thread of faith, a thread of fragile health or a thread of hope. These people are bruised reeds, beaten down by their circumstances and their attempts at remaining faithful to God in their own broken world. God's chosen One is *for* these people: for those who know what it means to mourn, to hunger, to thirst and to wait with patience. Consequently Jesus, this "chosen one" of whom Isaiah prophesied, did not withhold his power or compassion from those who were broken in body and spirit. Instead, he healed them. He brought — and still brings — justice to those who are overlooked and despised by the kingdom of this world.

HUMBLE AND FAITHFUL SERVICE

Isaiah's prophecies would have filled God's people with encouragement and hope as they looked to God alone for strength and deliverance. God alone held their destiny in their hands, and he would not reject them as his people. But in Isaiah 42, we see the true greatness of the message: that God's special servant would be the very embodiment of God's help, deliverance, justice and truth.

Though the original audience was no doubt primarily concerned about their nation and their destiny in particular, God wanted to expand the vision of his people to the entire world. The justice God was to establish would not only apply to Judah but to all the nations of the earth; the coming kingdom would not just be made up of one nation but would rather spread throughout the world. This kingdom would be the fulfillment of all God's promises and the true hope of everyone who is defeated and hopeless. All of this is found in the person and work of Jesus Christ (Lk 2:25 – 32).

In addition to announcing this One who was to come, these verses also help pave the way for a different kind of ruler, a different kind of king. In his coming, he will not be marked by fanfare or military conquest, and his ministry will not be characterized by vanquishing his foes in earthly battle. Instead, this chosen one will lift up the low and make smooth all the ways that had been rough (Isa 42:16). Eventually, all the ends of the earth will sing a song of praise to him (v. 10), for he will welcome all who are willing to follow him into this kingdom. He will not simply be the king of a particular nation; he will be the rightful king of the entire world who will gather together his subjects from all of the peoples of the earth.

Make no mistake — Isaiah's Spirit-inspired description of God's servant tells us that he will go out like a mighty warrior and destroy all his enemies (v. 13), but he will do so in a way that is unexpected. In fact, time would demonstrate that many in Israel would be so convinced of their own ideas about God's chosen One that they would actually miss the true Messiah who would come to serve in humbleness and faithfulness.

[9] See, the former things have taken place,
and new things I declare;
before they spring into being
I announce them to you."

Song of Praise to the LORD

[10] Sing to the LORD a new song,
his praise from the ends of the earth,
you who go down to the sea, and all that is in it,
you islands, and all who live in them.
[11] Let the wilderness and its towns raise their voices;
let the settlements where Kedar lives rejoice.
Let the people of Sela sing for joy;
let them shout from the mountaintops.
[12] Let them give glory to the LORD
and proclaim his praise in the islands.
[13] The LORD will march out like a champion,
like a warrior he will stir up his zeal;
with a shout he will raise the battle cry
and will triumph over his enemies.

[14] "For a long time I have kept silent,
I have been quiet and held myself back.
But now, like a woman in childbirth,
I cry out, I gasp and pant.
[15] I will lay waste the mountains and hills
and dry up all their vegetation;
I will turn rivers into islands
and dry up the pools.
[16] I will lead the blind by ways they have not known,
along unfamiliar paths I will guide them;
I will turn the darkness into light before them
and make the rough places smooth.
These are the things I will do;
I will not forsake them.
[17] But those who trust in idols,
who say to images, 'You are our gods,'
will be turned back in utter shame.

Israel Blind and Deaf

[18] "Hear, you deaf;
look, you blind, and see!
[19] Who is blind but my servant,
and deaf like the messenger I send?
Who is blind like the one in covenant with me,
blind like the servant of the LORD?
[20] You have seen many things, but you pay no attention;
your ears are open, but you do not listen."
[21] It pleased the LORD
for the sake of his righteousness
to make his law great and glorious.
[22] But this is a people plundered and looted,
all of them trapped in pits
or hidden away in prisons.
They have become plunder,
with no one to rescue them;
they have been made loot,
with no one to say, "Send them back."

ISAIAH 43:1

REDEMPTION

To "redeem" means literally "to buy back." Redemption is one of the key accomplishments of God's Son, Jesus. As this passage states, God's people were created and formed by God's own divine activity, and God himself through Jesus' sacrificial ministry would buy them back.

But the word "redeemed" itself begs the question: From what are God's people being bought back? The answer is that we all have willingly sold ourselves in slavery to sin; death is the cost of our disobedience. We are, both by nature and by our consistently sinful choices, rebels against God's kingdom. The consequence for that rebellion against the righteousness and holiness of God is death, and this price must be paid.

But God, in his mercy, has paid that price himself. He truly has redeemed those who trust in him, having paid the price for our sinful pride and rebellion. God has now the right not only as our Creator, but also as our Redeemer, to say that believers are his and to expect them to live lives that reflect gratitude for his gracious redemption.

23 Which of you will listen to this
or pay close attention in time to come?
24 Who handed Jacob over to become loot,
and Israel to the plunderers?
Was it not the LORD,
against whom we have sinned?
For they would not follow his ways;
they did not obey his law.
25 So he poured out on them his burning anger,
the violence of war.
It enveloped them in flames, yet they did not understand;
it consumed them, but they did not take it to heart.

Israel's Only Savior

43 But now, this is what the LORD says—
he who created you, Jacob,
he who formed you, Israel:
"Do not fear, for I have redeemed you;
I have summoned you by name; you are mine.
2 When you pass through the waters,
I will be with you;
and when you pass through the rivers,
they will not sweep over you.
When you walk through the fire,
you will not be burned;
the flames will not set you ablaze.
3 For I am the LORD your God,
the Holy One of Israel, your Savior;
I give Egypt for your ransom,
Cush[a] and Seba in your stead.
4 Since you are precious and honored in my sight,
and because I love you,
I will give people in exchange for you,
nations in exchange for your life.
5 Do not be afraid, for I am with you;
I will bring your children from the east
and gather you from the west.
6 I will say to the north, 'Give them up!'
and to the south, 'Do not hold them back.'
Bring my sons from afar
and my daughters from the ends of the earth—
7 everyone who is called by my name,
whom I created for my glory,
whom I formed and made."

8 Lead out those who have eyes but are blind,
who have ears but are deaf.
9 All the nations gather together
and the peoples assemble.
Which of their gods foretold this
and proclaimed to us the former things?
Let them bring in their witnesses to prove they were right,
so that others may hear and say, "It is true."
10 "You are my witnesses," declares the LORD,
"and my servant whom I have chosen,

[a] 3 That is, the upper Nile region

so that you may know and believe me
and understand that I am he.
Before me no god was formed,
nor will there be one after me.
11 I, even I, am the LORD,
and apart from me there is no savior.
12 I have revealed and saved and proclaimed —
I, and not some foreign god among you.
You are my witnesses," declares the LORD, "that I am God.
13 Yes, and from ancient days I am he.
No one can deliver out of my hand.
When I act, who can reverse it?"

God's Mercy and Israel's Unfaithfulness

14 This is what the LORD says —
your Redeemer, the Holy One of Israel:
"For your sake I will send to Babylon
and bring down as fugitives all the Babylonians,[a]
in the ships in which they took pride.
15 I am the LORD, your Holy One,
Israel's Creator, your King."

16 This is what the LORD says —
he who made a way through the sea,
a path through the mighty waters,
17 who drew out the chariots and horses,
the army and reinforcements together,
and they lay there, never to rise again,
extinguished, snuffed out like a wick:
18 "Forget the former things;
do not dwell on the past.
19 See, I am doing a new thing!
Now it springs up; do you not perceive it?
I am making a way in the wilderness
and streams in the wasteland.
20 The wild animals honor me,
the jackals and the owls,
because I provide water in the wilderness
and streams in the wasteland,
to give drink to my people, my chosen,
21 the people I formed for myself
that they may proclaim my praise.

22 "Yet you have not called on me, Jacob,
you have not wearied yourselves for[b] me, Israel.
23 You have not brought me sheep for burnt offerings,
nor honored me with your sacrifices.
I have not burdened you with grain offerings
nor wearied you with demands for incense.
24 You have not bought any fragrant calamus for me,
or lavished on me the fat of your sacrifices.
But you have burdened me with your sins
and wearied me with your offenses.

25 "I, even I, am he who blots out
your transgressions, for my own sake,
and remembers your sins no more.

---

[a] 14 Or *Chaldeans* [b] 22 Or *Jacob; / surely you have grown weary of*

[26] Review the past for me,
let us argue the matter together;
state the case for your innocence.
[27] Your first father sinned;
those I sent to teach you rebelled against me.
[28] So I disgraced the dignitaries of your temple;
I consigned Jacob to destruction[a]
and Israel to scorn.

Israel the Chosen

44 "But now listen, Jacob, my servant,
Israel, whom I have chosen.
[2] This is what the LORD says—
he who made you, who formed you in the womb,
and who will help you:
Do not be afraid, Jacob, my servant,
Jeshurun,[b] whom I have chosen.
[3] For I will pour water on the thirsty land,
and streams on the dry ground;
I will pour out my Spirit on your offspring,
and my blessing on your descendants.
[4] They will spring up like grass in a meadow,
like poplar trees by flowing streams.
[5] Some will say, 'I belong to the LORD';
others will call themselves by the name of Jacob;
still others will write on their hand, 'The LORD's,'
and will take the name Israel.

The LORD, Not Idols

[6] "This is what the LORD says—
Israel's King and Redeemer, the LORD Almighty:
I am the first and I am the last;
apart from me there is no God.
[7] Who then is like me? Let him proclaim it.
Let him declare and lay out before me
what has happened since I established my ancient people,
and what is yet to come—
yes, let them foretell what will come.
[8] Do not tremble, do not be afraid.
Did I not proclaim this and foretell it long ago?
You are my witnesses. Is there any God besides me?
No, there is no other Rock; I know not one."

[9] All who make idols are nothing,
and the things they treasure are worthless.
Those who would speak up for them are blind;
they are ignorant, to their own shame.
[10] Who shapes a god and casts an idol,
which can profit nothing?
[11] People who do that will be put to shame;
such craftsmen are only human beings.
Let them all come together and take their stand;
they will be brought down to terror and shame.

[12] The blacksmith takes a tool
and works with it in the coals;

ISAIAH 44:6

KING AND REDEEMER

Depending on the context, the word *king* conjures up different images. Throughout biblical history, there were as many kings and rulers marked by their greed, vengeance and cruelty as by their compassion and mercy. Power is incredibly seductive, and few individuals can wield it well. But here we see not only the power of God as our King, but also the compassion of God as our Redeemer.

The implications of both words, when taken together, are staggering. This King has every power, luxury, honor and glory at his disposal. However, instead of pronouncing ultimate judgment on human rebellion, God willingly paid that price to redeem his people. Amazingly, the God to whom humans owed their very lives as payment for sin took it upon himself to pay that debt on our behalf.

Though the Israelites had many earthly kings, God's intent for his people has always been for them not to follow an earthly ruler but instead to view and follow him and him alone as their true King. By becoming the Redeemer we needed, God has bought us and brought us back from the far country of disobedience. By his own gracious actions and for his glory, he has reestablished us in his kingdom.

[a] *28* The Hebrew term refers to the irrevocable giving over of things or persons to the LORD, often by totally destroying them. [b] *2* *Jeshurun* means *the upright one,* that is, Israel.

he shapes an idol with hammers,
he forges it with the might of his arm.
He gets hungry and loses his strength;
he drinks no water and grows faint.
13 The carpenter measures with a line
and makes an outline with a marker;
he roughs it out with chisels
and marks it with compasses.
He shapes it in human form,
human form in all its glory,
that it may dwell in a shrine.
14 He cut down cedars,
or perhaps took a cypress or oak.
He let it grow among the trees of the forest,
or planted a pine, and the rain made it grow.
15 It is used as fuel for burning;
some of it he takes and warms himself,
he kindles a fire and bakes bread.
But he also fashions a god and worships it;
he makes an idol and bows down to it.
16 Half of the wood he burns in the fire;
over it he prepares his meal,
he roasts his meat and eats his fill.
He also warms himself and says,
"Ah! I am warm; I see the fire."
17 From the rest he makes a god, his idol;
he bows down to it and worships.
He prays to it and says,
"Save me! You are my god!"
18 They know nothing, they understand nothing;
their eyes are plastered over so they cannot see,
and their minds closed so they cannot understand.
19 No one stops to think,
no one has the knowledge or understanding to say,
"Half of it I used for fuel;
I even baked bread over its coals,
I roasted meat and I ate.
Shall I make a detestable thing from what is left?
Shall I bow down to a block of wood?"
20 Such a person feeds on ashes; a deluded heart misleads him;
he cannot save himself, or say,
"Is not this thing in my right hand a lie?"

21 "Remember these things, Jacob,
for you, Israel, are my servant.
I have made you, you are my servant;
Israel, I will not forget you.
22 I have swept away your offenses like a cloud,
your sins like the morning mist.
Return to me,
for I have redeemed you."

23 Sing for joy, you heavens, for the LORD has done this;
shout aloud, you earth beneath.
Burst into song, you mountains,
you forests and all your trees,
for the LORD has redeemed Jacob,
he displays his glory in Israel.

Jerusalem to Be Inhabited

24 "This is what the LORD says—
your Redeemer, who formed you in the womb:

I am the LORD,
the Maker of all things,
who stretches out the heavens,
who spreads out the earth by myself,
25 who foils the signs of false prophets
and makes fools of diviners,
who overthrows the learning of the wise
and turns it into nonsense,
26 who carries out the words of his servants
and fulfills the predictions of his messengers,

who says of Jerusalem, 'It shall be inhabited,'
of the towns of Judah, 'They shall be rebuilt,'
and of their ruins, 'I will restore them,'
27 who says to the watery deep, 'Be dry,
and I will dry up your streams,'
28 who says of Cyrus, 'He is my shepherd
and will accomplish all that I please;
he will say of Jerusalem, "Let it be rebuilt,"
and of the temple, "Let its foundations be laid."'

45 "This is what the LORD says to his anointed,
to Cyrus, whose right hand I take hold of
to subdue nations before him
and to strip kings of their armor,
to open doors before him
so that gates will not be shut:
2 I will go before you
and will level the mountains[a];
I will break down gates of bronze
and cut through bars of iron.
3 I will give you hidden treasures,
riches stored in secret places,
so that you may know that I am the LORD,
the God of Israel, who summons you by name.
4 For the sake of Jacob my servant,
of Israel my chosen,
I summon you by name
and bestow on you a title of honor,
though you do not acknowledge me.
5 I am the LORD, and there is no other;
apart from me there is no God.
I will strengthen you,
though you have not acknowledged me,
6 so that from the rising of the sun
to the place of its setting
people may know there is none besides me.
I am the LORD, and there is no other.
7 I form the light and create darkness,
I bring prosperity and create disaster;
I, the LORD, do all these things.

---

[a] 2 Dead Sea Scrolls and Septuagint; the meaning of the word in the Masoretic Text is uncertain.

[8] "You heavens above, rain down my righteousness;
let the clouds shower it down.
Let the earth open wide,
let salvation spring up,
let righteousness flourish with it;
I, the LORD, have created it.

[9] "Woe to those who quarrel with their Maker,
those who are nothing but potsherds
among the potsherds on the ground.
Does the clay say to the potter,
'What are you making?'
Does your work say,
'The potter has no hands'?
[10] Woe to the one who says to a father,
'What have you begotten?'
or to a mother,
'What have you brought to birth?'

[11] "This is what the LORD says —
the Holy One of Israel, and its Maker:
Concerning things to come,
do you question me about my children,
or give me orders about the work of my hands?
[12] It is I who made the earth
and created mankind on it.
My own hands stretched out the heavens;
I marshaled their starry hosts.
[13] I will raise up Cyrus[a] in my righteousness:
I will make all his ways straight.
He will rebuild my city
and set my exiles free,
but not for a price or reward,
says the LORD Almighty."

[14] This is what the LORD says:

"The products of Egypt and the merchandise
of Cush,[b]
and those tall Sabeans —
they will come over to you
and will be yours;
they will trudge behind you,
coming over to you in chains.
They will bow down before you
and plead with you, saying,
'Surely God is with you, and there is no other;
there is no other god.' "

[15] Truly you are a God who has been hiding himself,
the God and Savior of Israel.
[16] All the makers of idols will be put to shame and
disgraced;
they will go off into disgrace together.
[17] But Israel will be saved by the LORD
with an everlasting salvation;
you will never be put to shame or disgraced,
to ages everlasting.

---

[a] *13* Hebrew *him* [b] *14* That is, the upper Nile region

ISAIAH 45:22–23

SWORN BY HIMSELF

Why would God swear by himself? The writer of Hebrews answers the question for us in the context of the promise God made to Abraham: God swore by himself because he could swear by no one greater (Heb 6:13). When God swears by himself, he is declaring once and for all that his word is good and unshakeable. Here we see God putting his stamp of absolute certitude on the fact that his word will accomplish its purposes, and that when it does, every tongue will confess its truth. This is an oath that God makes by himself, to himself and for himself.

The oath will be fulfilled when every knee bows and every tongue confesses that Jesus Christ is Lord, all to the glory of God the Father (Php 2:10–11). This is not mere aspiration; it's not a pie-in-the-sky hope for God. Rather, it is so sure and certain that God has sealed the promise by himself. The question of Jesus' acknowledged reign in the universe is not in doubt; it's only a question of when it will be fully realized and acknowledged by all creation.

18 For this is what the LORD says—
he who created the heavens,
he is God;
he who fashioned and made the earth,
he founded it;
he did not create it to be empty,
but formed it to be inhabited—
he says:
"I am the LORD,
and there is no other.
19 I have not spoken in secret,
from somewhere in a land of darkness;
I have not said to Jacob's descendants,
'Seek me in vain.'
I, the LORD, speak the truth;
I declare what is right.

20 "Gather together and come;
assemble, you fugitives from the nations.
Ignorant are those who carry about idols of wood,
who pray to gods that cannot save.
21 Declare what is to be, present it—
let them take counsel together.
Who foretold this long ago,
who declared it from the distant past?
Was it not I, the LORD?
And there is no God apart from me,
a righteous God and a Savior;
there is none but me.

22 "Turn to me and be saved,
all you ends of the earth;
for I am God, and there is no other.
23 By myself I have sworn,
my mouth has uttered in all integrity
a word that will not be revoked:
Before me every knee will bow;
by me every tongue will swear.
24 They will say of me, 'In the LORD alone
are deliverance and strength.'"
All who have raged against him
will come to him and be put to shame.
25 But all the descendants of Israel
will find deliverance in the LORD
and will make their boast in him.

Gods of Babylon

46 Bel bows down, Nebo stoops low;
their idols are borne by beasts of burden.[a]
The images that are carried about are burdensome,
a burden for the weary.
2 They stoop and bow down together;
unable to rescue the burden,
they themselves go off into captivity.

3 "Listen to me, you descendants of Jacob,
all the remnant of the people of Israel,

[a] *1* Or *are but beasts and cattle*

you whom I have upheld since your birth,
and have carried since you were born.
4 Even to your old age and gray hairs
I am he, I am he who will sustain you.
I have made you and I will carry you;
I will sustain you and I will rescue you.

5 "With whom will you compare me or count me equal?
To whom will you liken me that we may be compared?
6 Some pour out gold from their bags
and weigh out silver on the scales;
they hire a goldsmith to make it into a god,
and they bow down and worship it.
7 They lift it to their shoulders and carry it;
they set it up in its place, and there it stands.
From that spot it cannot move.
Even though someone cries out to it, it cannot answer;
it cannot save them from their troubles.

8 "Remember this, keep it in mind,
take it to heart, you rebels.
9 Remember the former things, those of long ago;
I am God, and there is no other;
I am God, and there is none like me.
10 I make known the end from the beginning,
from ancient times, what is still to come.
I say, 'My purpose will stand,
and I will do all that I please.'
11 From the east I summon a bird of prey;
from a far-off land, a man to fulfill my purpose.
What I have said, that I will bring about;
what I have planned, that I will do.
12 Listen to me, you stubborn-hearted,
you who are now far from my righteousness.
13 I am bringing my righteousness near,
it is not far away;
and my salvation will not be delayed.
I will grant salvation to Zion,
my splendor to Israel.

The Fall of Babylon

47 "Go down, sit in the dust,
Virgin Daughter Babylon;
sit on the ground without a throne,
queen city of the Babylonians.[a]
No more will you be called
tender or delicate.
2 Take millstones and grind flour;
take off your veil.
Lift up your skirts, bare your legs,
and wade through the streams.
3 Your nakedness will be exposed
and your shame uncovered.
I will take vengeance;
I will spare no one."

[a] *1* Or *Chaldeans*; also in verse 5

ISAIAH 46:9 – 11

DECLARING THE END FROM THE BEGINNING

As the sovereign ruler of the cosmos, God can do anything he pleases. His word is not merely advice or a prediction; it is a declaration, even if humans do not yet see the visible evidence of that declaration in the world. He who knew the very end before the very beginning can be trusted to not only know what will transpire but to bring it about in the way and time in which he sees fit.

As a prophet, Jesus too had the ability to declare what would and would not occur. Consider his declarations that he would rebuild the temple in three days, that Jerusalem would be destroyed and even his straightforward declaration of his own suffering, death and resurrection to come (Mt 16:21). Just as God declared his word through the prophet Isaiah, so also Jesus makes declarations as a prophet: words not born of his own opinion or logical deduction, but instead from the knowledge of God from the very beginning. As we trust the declarations of God the Father, so also can we trust in the declarations of Jesus, God's Son.

ISAIAH 47:12–15

WARNINGS ABOUT MAGIC

The Old Testament warned the people of Israel against practicing magic and sorcery (Lev 19:26,31; Dt 18:9–14). The breaking point for Saul, the first king of Israel, was his association with the medium at Endor who conjured up the spirit of Samuel to solicit his counsel for the king. After that, the Lord removed Saul as king and gave the crown to David (1Sa 28:3–19). As with Saul's pursuit of a word from beyond, modern pursuit of magic and superstition represents misplaced human faith and confidence. When we choose to engage in and trust in processes like these, we show that we will not accept the Word of God and trust in him alone to guide us into his will.

In this passage, the prophet taunts the Babylonian effort to try to avert God's judgment through magic. He dares them to stand fast by their sorcery, knowing the foolishness of doing so. God alone holds true power, and anything else that people look to for guidance is a mere fabrication, a pathetic and blurry copy of what God provides. Believers in Christ have seen the power and glory of God displayed in the life, death and resurrection of Jesus. Because of this, we no longer hold to meaningless superstitions and magic incantations. All our faith is in him.

4 Our Redeemer — the LORD Almighty is his name —
is the Holy One of Israel.

5 "Sit in silence, go into darkness,
queen city of the Babylonians;
no more will you be called
queen of kingdoms.
6 I was angry with my people
and desecrated my inheritance;
I gave them into your hand,
and you showed them no mercy.
Even on the aged
you laid a very heavy yoke.
7 You said, 'I am forever —
the eternal queen!'
But you did not consider these things
or reflect on what might happen.

8 "Now then, listen, you lover of pleasure,
lounging in your security
and saying to yourself,
'I am, and there is none besides me.
I will never be a widow
or suffer the loss of children.'
9 Both of these will overtake you
in a moment, on a single day:
loss of children and widowhood.
They will come upon you in full measure,
in spite of your many sorceries
and all your potent spells.
10 You have trusted in your wickedness
and have said, 'No one sees me.'
Your wisdom and knowledge mislead you
when you say to yourself,
'I am, and there is none besides me.'
11 Disaster will come upon you,
and you will not know how to conjure it away.
A calamity will fall upon you
that you cannot ward off with a ransom;
a catastrophe you cannot foresee
will suddenly come upon you.

12 "Keep on, then, with your magic spells
and with your many sorceries,
which you have labored at since childhood.
Perhaps you will succeed,
perhaps you will cause terror.
13 All the counsel you have received has only worn
you out!
Let your astrologers come forward,
those stargazers who make predictions month by
month,
let them save you from what is coming upon you.
14 Surely they are like stubble;
the fire will burn them up.
They cannot even save themselves
from the power of the flame.
These are not coals for warmth;
this is not a fire to sit by.

15 That is all they are to you—
these you have dealt with
and labored with since childhood.
All of them go on in their error;
there is not one that can save you.

Stubborn Israel

48 "Listen to this, you descendants of Jacob,
you who are called by the name of Israel
and come from the line of Judah,
you who take oaths in the name of the LORD
and invoke the God of Israel—
but not in truth or righteousness—
2 you who call yourselves citizens of the holy city
and claim to rely on the God of Israel—
the LORD Almighty is his name:
3 I foretold the former things long ago,
my mouth announced them and I made them known;
then suddenly I acted, and they came to pass.
4 For I knew how stubborn you were;
your neck muscles were iron,
your forehead was bronze.
5 Therefore I told you these things long ago;
before they happened I announced them to you
so that you could not say,
'My images brought them about;
my wooden image and metal god ordained them.'
6 You have heard these things; look at them all.
Will you not admit them?

"From now on I will tell you of new things,
of hidden things unknown to you.
7 They are created now, and not long ago;
you have not heard of them before today.
So you cannot say,
'Yes, I knew of them.'
8 You have neither heard nor understood;
from of old your ears have not been open.
Well do I know how treacherous you are;
you were called a rebel from birth.
9 For my own name's sake I delay my wrath;
for the sake of my praise I hold it back from you,
so as not to destroy you completely.
10 See, I have refined you, though not as silver;
I have tested you in the furnace of affliction.
11 For my own sake, for my own sake, I do this.
How can I let myself be defamed?
I will not yield my glory to another.

Israel Freed

12 "Listen to me, Jacob,
Israel, whom I have called:
I am he;
I am the first and I am the last.
13 My own hand laid the foundations of the earth,
and my right hand spread out the heavens;
when I summon them,
they all stand up together.

ISAIAH 48:12–15

THE FIRST AND THE LAST

Time is the great equalizer. Whether people are rich or poor, educated or not, prominent or lowly, time does not speed up or slow down for anyone. Each day offers the same amount of time for each of us, and not one of us knows when the present day could be our last. In contrast to our human limitations, God stands apart from time. He is the first and the last; he is the beginning and the ending.

Being both the first and the last is a unique claim that only God can make; in so doing, he separates himself from the supposed gods of the nations. Unlike these gods, who are fashioned from wood or stone, God has no beginning or ending. He has and will control every event from the beginning until the end of time. He laid the foundations of the earth, named the stars one by one and will eventually redeem all of creation for his glory. In making this pronouncement, God reminded this Israelite audience that they would do well to listen to what he has to say, because the idols of the other nations are mute on any and every subject (v. 14).

Similarly, the risen Christ addressed the New Testament churches in Revelation, calling them to heed his words through the same pronouncement of his eternal nature. He is "the First and the Last" (Rev 1:17; 2:8), and his Word is sure.

14 "Come together, all of you, and listen:
Which of the idols has foretold these things?
The LORD's chosen ally
will carry out his purpose against Babylon;
his arm will be against the Babylonians.[a]
15 I, even I, have spoken;
yes, I have called him.
I will bring him,
and he will succeed in his mission.

16 "Come near me and listen to this:

"From the first announcement I have not spoken in secret;
at the time it happens, I am there."

And now the Sovereign LORD has sent me,
endowed with his Spirit.

17 This is what the LORD says —
your Redeemer, the Holy One of Israel:
"I am the LORD your God,
who teaches you what is best for you,
who directs you in the way you should go.
18 If only you had paid attention to my commands,
your peace would have been like a river,
your well-being like the waves of the sea.
19 Your descendants would have been like the sand,
your children like its numberless grains;
their name would never be blotted out
nor destroyed from before me."

20 Leave Babylon,
flee from the Babylonians!
Announce this with shouts of joy
and proclaim it.
Send it out to the ends of the earth;
say, "The LORD has redeemed his servant Jacob."
21 They did not thirst when he led them through the deserts;
he made water flow for them from the rock;
he split the rock
and water gushed out.

22 "There is no peace," says the LORD, "for the wicked."

The Servant of the LORD

49 Listen to me, you islands;
hear this, you distant nations:
Before I was born the LORD called me;
from my mother's womb he has spoken my name.
2 He made my mouth like a sharpened sword,
in the shadow of his hand he hid me;
he made me into a polished arrow
and concealed me in his quiver.
3 He said to me, "You are my servant,
Israel, in whom I will display my splendor."
4 But I said, "I have labored in vain;
I have spent my strength for nothing at all.
Yet what is due me is in the LORD's hand,
and my reward is with my God."

[a] *14* Or *Chaldeans*; also in verse 20

5 And now the LORD says—
he who formed me in the womb to be his servant
to bring Jacob back to him
and gather Israel to himself,
for I am[a] honored in the eyes of the LORD
and my God has been my strength—
6 he says:
"It is too small a thing for you to be my servant
to restore the tribes of Jacob
and bring back those of Israel I have kept.
I will also make you a light for the Gentiles,
that my salvation may reach to the ends of the earth."

7 This is what the LORD says—
the Redeemer and Holy One of Israel—
to him who was despised and abhorred by the nation,
to the servant of rulers:
"Kings will see you and stand up,
princes will see and bow down,
because of the LORD, who is faithful,
the Holy One of Israel, who has chosen you."

Restoration of Israel

8 This is what the LORD says:

"In the time of my favor I will answer you,
and in the day of salvation I will help you;
I will keep you and will make you
to be a covenant for the people,
to restore the land
and to reassign its desolate inheritances,
9 to say to the captives, 'Come out,'
and to those in darkness, 'Be free!'

"They will feed beside the roads
and find pasture on every barren hill.
10 They will neither hunger nor thirst,
nor will the desert heat or the sun beat down on them.
He who has compassion on them will guide them
and lead them beside springs of water.
11 I will turn all my mountains into roads,
and my highways will be raised up.
12 See, they will come from afar—
some from the north, some from the west,
some from the region of Aswan.[b]"

13 Shout for joy, you heavens;
rejoice, you earth;
burst into song, you mountains!
For the LORD comforts his people
and will have compassion on his afflicted ones.

14 But Zion said, "The LORD has forsaken me,
the Lord has forgotten me."

15 "Can a mother forget the baby at her breast
and have no compassion on the child she has borne?

[a] 5 Or *him, / but Israel would not be gathered; / yet I will be* [b] 12 Dead Sea Scrolls; Masoretic Text *Sinim*

ISAIAH 49:6

A LIGHT FOR THE GENTILES

The greatness and glory of Jesus is meant to spread to every corner of the globe. This is what God promised through the prophet in this verse: that his coming servant would not be confined to the worship of a single nation.

Importantly, this intent has existed in the heart of God from the beginning of time; throughout redemptive history, he has been raising up a people for himself from every tribe, tongue and nation. The expansion of the gospel was not initiated in the Great Commission of Jesus; in fact, it extends even further back in time than when the prophet Isaiah lived. When God chose Abraham as the father of his people, he did so not to the exclusion of all the other peoples of the earth, but for their sake. God intended (and still intends) that his people will be a blessing to all the nations of the earth (Ge 12:2–3). This was fulfilled through the ministry of Jesus who then commissioned his followers to move past the traditional boundary lines of culture and bring the message of salvation to the furthest corners of the globe (Mt 28:18–20).

Though she may forget,
I will not forget you!
16 See, I have engraved you on the palms of my
hands;
your walls are ever before me.
17 Your children hasten back,
and those who laid you waste depart from you.
18 Lift up your eyes and look around;
all your children gather and come to you.
As surely as I live," declares the LORD,
"you will wear them all as ornaments;
you will put them on, like a bride.

19 "Though you were ruined and made desolate
and your land laid waste,
now you will be too small for your people,
and those who devoured you will be far away.
20 The children born during your bereavement
will yet say in your hearing,
'This place is too small for us;
give us more space to live in.'
21 Then you will say in your heart,
'Who bore me these?
I was bereaved and barren;
I was exiled and rejected.
Who brought these up?
I was left all alone,
but these — where have they come from?' "

22 This is what the Sovereign LORD says:

"See, I will beckon to the nations,
I will lift up my banner to the peoples;
they will bring your sons in their arms
and carry your daughters on their hips.
23 Kings will be your foster fathers,
and their queens your nursing mothers.
They will bow down before you with their faces to
the ground;
they will lick the dust at your feet.
Then you will know that I am the LORD;
those who hope in me will not be disappointed."

24 Can plunder be taken from warriors,
or captives be rescued from the fierce[a]?

25 But this is what the LORD says:

"Yes, captives will be taken from warriors,
and plunder retrieved from the fierce;
I will contend with those who contend with you,
and your children I will save.
26 I will make your oppressors eat their own flesh;
they will be drunk on their own blood, as with wine.
Then all mankind will know
that I, the LORD, am your Savior,
your Redeemer, the Mighty One of Jacob."

---

[a] *24* Dead Sea Scrolls, Vulgate and Syriac (see also Septuagint and verse 25); Masoretic Text *righteous*

Israel's Sin and the Servant's Obedience

50 This is what the LORD says:

"Where is your mother's certificate of divorce
with which I sent her away?
Or to which of my creditors
did I sell you?
Because of your sins you were sold;
because of your transgressions your mother was
sent away.
2 When I came, why was there no one?
When I called, why was there no one to answer?
Was my arm too short to deliver you?
Do I lack the strength to rescue you?
By a mere rebuke I dry up the sea,
I turn rivers into a desert;
their fish rot for lack of water
and die of thirst.
3 I clothe the heavens with darkness
and make sackcloth its covering."
4 The Sovereign LORD has given me a well-instructed tongue,
to know the word that sustains the weary.
He wakens me morning by morning,
wakens my ear to listen like one being instructed.
5 The Sovereign LORD has opened my ears;
I have not been rebellious,
I have not turned away.
6 I offered my back to those who beat me,
my cheeks to those who pulled out my beard;
I did not hide my face
from mocking and spitting.
7 Because the Sovereign LORD helps me,
I will not be disgraced.
Therefore have I set my face like flint,
and I know I will not be put to shame.
8 He who vindicates me is near.
Who then will bring charges against me?
Let us face each other!
Who is my accuser?
Let him confront me!
9 It is the Sovereign LORD who helps me.
Who will condemn me?
They will all wear out like a garment;
the moths will eat them up.

10 Who among you fears the LORD
and obeys the word of his servant?
Let the one who walks in the dark,
who has no light,
trust in the name of the LORD
and rely on their God.
11 But now, all you who light fires
and provide yourselves with flaming torches,
go, walk in the light of your fires
and of the torches you have set ablaze.
This is what you shall receive from my hand:
You will lie down in torment.

ISAIAH 50:6

VOLUNTARY SUFFERING

What would mark the coming of God's chosen one? The prophet foretold of songs of joy, glory, renown and praise for his coming. But here we find another more surprising aspect of the Messiah's coming — that of suffering. The idea that the coming King would meet this kind of humiliation and hatred seems counterintuitive, but that's exactly what Isaiah's prophecy describes. While many Israelites expected the servant of God to be heralded as a king, conquering his enemies in triumph and riding into the city on a war horse, they would instead witness the rise of an inauspicious son of a tradesman — one who associated with the lowest and the least — riding into Jerusalem on the back of a donkey. Jesus Christ would be the King that no one expected, and he would receive brutal treatment that he did not deserve.

In ancient culture, people sometimes struck the back of a fool (Pr 19:29), and pulling someone's beard was a sign of contempt and disrespect (2Sa 10:4 – 5). Even today there is no greater insult than spitting in one's face, and yet Jesus willingly endured the mocking of his enemies (Mt 26:67 – 68; 27:26 – 31).

Note, however, the posture of the servant described in this verse: "I *offered* my back to those who beat me" (emphasis added). Isaiah testified that these terrible things would not just be done to God's chosen one; they would be done with his permission. He would give them his back to strike; he would give them his cheeks, and they would mock him to his face. He would not turn away from the spit in his face.

We see in Matthew's crucifixion account that Jesus allowed all these things to happen. This is the great irony of the cross. The King of the universe who could, in a moment, defeat his enemies and free himself from their abuse, willingly submitted to the cross in order to satisfy the Father's wrath upon human sin. The King of kings became the suffering servant out of love for his chosen people.

Jesus, God's chosen servant, willingly took all these sufferings on himself even to the point of death. He did so not because his own life merited such suffering and humiliation, but because ours does. Jesus took that which we deserved so that we might accept what we do not deserve. Because of his willing suffering, we can be the recipients of his unmerited grace and favor.

Everlasting Salvation for Zion

51 "Listen to me, you who pursue righteousness
and who seek the LORD:
Look to the rock from which you were cut
and to the quarry from which you were hewn;
2 look to Abraham, your father,
and to Sarah, who gave you birth.
When I called him he was only one man,
and I blessed him and made him many.
3 The LORD will surely comfort Zion
and will look with compassion on all her ruins;
he will make her deserts like Eden,
her wastelands like the garden of the LORD.
Joy and gladness will be found in her,
thanksgiving and the sound of singing.

4 "Listen to me, my people;
hear me, my nation:
Instruction will go out from me;
my justice will become a light to the nations.
5 My righteousness draws near speedily,
my salvation is on the way,
and my arm will bring justice to the nations.
The islands will look to me
and wait in hope for my arm.
6 Lift up your eyes to the heavens,
look at the earth beneath;
the heavens will vanish like smoke,
the earth will wear out like a garment
and its inhabitants die like flies.
But my salvation will last forever,
my righteousness will never fail.

7 "Hear me, you who know what is right,
you people who have taken my instruction to heart:
Do not fear the reproach of mere mortals
or be terrified by their insults.
8 For the moth will eat them up like a garment;
the worm will devour them like wool.
But my righteousness will last forever,
my salvation through all generations."

9 Awake, awake, arm of the LORD,
clothe yourself with strength!
Awake, as in days gone by,
as in generations of old.
Was it not you who cut Rahab to pieces,
who pierced that monster through?
10 Was it not you who dried up the sea,
the waters of the great deep,
who made a road in the depths of the sea
so that the redeemed might cross over?
11 Those the LORD has rescued will return.
They will enter Zion with singing;
everlasting joy will crown their heads.
Gladness and joy will overtake them,
and sorrow and sighing will flee away.

ISAIAH 51:4–6

SALVATION FOREVER

The prophet Isaiah spoke of the nearness of the righteousness and salvation of God. His arm, or his power, will go forth in judgment, but that same power will be used to deliver and save those who trust in him. Though the prophecy about God's righteousness drawing near "speedily" (v. 5) refers to the Jews returning from exile in Babylon, the rest of this stanza (vv. 4–6) clearly looks beyond that event.

Just as judgment lies with God alone—he alone sets the standards of justice, righteousness and holiness in the universe according to his good character—so too does salvation lie with him. God alone has the power to truly save, for he saves his people from the very judgment that he will execute in the world.

This text reminds readers that the entire cosmos is in a state of downward entropy; things are getting worse and worse and will continue to do so. Just as humans have been, so God's creation has also been mired and corrupted by sin. While the earth will pass away, God's salvation will stand forever. This salvation is accomplished through Jesus and Jesus alone; indeed, salvation was and is his mission on earth. God shows his eternal commitment to save those who trust in him through the life, death and resurrection of Christ. Salvation, then, can only be had through Christ. This is why the New Testament echoes the fact that "salvation belongs to our God" (Rev 7:10).

12 "I, even I, am he who comforts you.
Who are you that you fear mere mortals,
human beings who are but grass,
13 that you forget the LORD your Maker,
who stretches out the heavens
and who lays the foundations of the earth,
that you live in constant terror every day
because of the wrath of the oppressor,
who is bent on destruction?
For where is the wrath of the oppressor?
14 The cowering prisoners will soon be set free;
they will not die in their dungeon,
nor will they lack bread.
15 For I am the LORD your God,
who stirs up the sea so that its waves roar—
the LORD Almighty is his name.
16 I have put my words in your mouth
and covered you with the shadow of my hand—
I who set the heavens in place,
who laid the foundations of the earth,
and who say to Zion, 'You are my people.'"

The Cup of the LORD's Wrath

17 Awake, awake!
Rise up, Jerusalem,
you who have drunk from the hand of the LORD
the cup of his wrath,
you who have drained to its dregs
the goblet that makes people stagger.
18 Among all the children she bore
there was none to guide her;
among all the children she reared
there was none to take her by the hand.
19 These double calamities have come upon you—
who can comfort you?—
ruin and destruction, famine and sword—
who can[a] console you?
20 Your children have fainted;
they lie at every street corner,
like antelope caught in a net.
They are filled with the wrath of the LORD,
with the rebuke of your God.

21 Therefore hear this, you afflicted one,
made drunk, but not with wine.
22 This is what your Sovereign LORD says,
your God, who defends his people:
"See, I have taken out of your hand
the cup that made you stagger;
from that cup, the goblet of my wrath,
you will never drink again.
23 I will put it into the hands of your tormentors,
who said to you,
'Fall prostrate that we may walk on you.'
And you made your back like the ground,
like a street to be walked on."

[a] *19* Dead Sea Scrolls, Septuagint, Vulgate and Syriac; Masoretic Text / *how can I*

52 Awake, awake, Zion,
clothe yourself with strength!
Put on your garments of splendor,
Jerusalem, the holy city.
The uncircumcised and defiled
will not enter you again.
2 Shake off your dust;
rise up, sit enthroned, Jerusalem.
Free yourself from the chains on your neck,
Daughter Zion, now a captive.

3 For this is what the LORD says:

"You were sold for nothing,
and without money you will be redeemed."

4 For this is what the Sovereign LORD says:

"At first my people went down to Egypt to live;
lately, Assyria has oppressed them.

5 "And now what do I have here?" declares the LORD.

"For my people have been taken away for nothing,
and those who rule them mock,[a]"
declares the LORD.
"And all day long
my name is constantly blasphemed.
6 Therefore my people will know my name;
therefore in that day they will know
that it is I who foretold it.
Yes, it is I."
7 How beautiful on the mountains
are the feet of those who bring good news,
who proclaim peace,
who bring good tidings,
who proclaim salvation,
who say to Zion,
"Your God reigns!"
8 Listen! Your watchmen lift up their voices;
together they shout for joy.
When the LORD returns to Zion,
they will see it with their own eyes.
9 Burst into songs of joy together,
you ruins of Jerusalem,
for the LORD has comforted his people,
he has redeemed Jerusalem.
10 The LORD will lay bare his holy arm
in the sight of all the nations,
and all the ends of the earth will see
the salvation of our God.
11 Depart, depart, go out from there!
Touch no unclean thing!
Come out from it and be pure,
you who carry the articles of the LORD's house.
12 But you will not leave in haste
or go in flight;
for the LORD will go before you,
the God of Israel will be your rear guard.

ISAIAH 52:7

BEAUTIFUL FEET

In the days of Isaiah, news of the outcome of a battle would be carried on foot by a messenger from the battle, bringing either good or bad news to the waiting population. In this case, the glorious message of this runner involved the announcement of the return from exile.

In the New Testament, the apostle Paul refers to this imagery for the sake of the gospel. He quotes this verse in Romans 10:15 to bolster his point about the importance of the proclamation of the good news. There is no greater victory than that which God has won in Christ; this is the ultimate victory over the last and final enemy. Through Christ, the victory over sin and death has been fully accomplished, but the news of that victory must still be shared.

For those who follow Jesus, the task remains to herald that victory far and wide. It's the calling of every follower of Jesus to make this declaration until all have heard the good news that people can, at long last, have peace with God because of the sacrifice of Jesus Christ.

[a] 5 Dead Sea Scrolls and Vulgate; Masoretic Text *wail*

EXALTED SERVANT

Through his prophet Isaiah, the Lord promised that his servant would be exalted because of his obedience to his mission from God. We see in Jesus' exaltation a number of things about God's redemptive purposes in Christ.

Initially, we are reminded that the cross and resurrection of Jesus happened not by accident, but according to God's specific plan. People throughout history have sometimes considered the crucifixion of Jesus to be a tragic accident, a case of misappropriated justice and anger by the judicial system of the time. But this was no accident. Indeed, God was pleased by Jesus' sacrifice and even specifically sent him to offer himself up as that sacrifice (Gal 4:4 – 5; Eph 1:7 – 10). God orchestrated Jesus' life, death and resurrection to happen in his predetermined time and according to his sovereign plan.

Because this was no accident, we must also conclude that this was not a secondary option to God. Others in history have seen the cross in this light, that God's initial plan was thwarted in the garden, and the crucifixion and resurrection of Jesus was God's last-ditch effort to save at least some of his creation. But God, who knows the beginning and the end, always knew that his one and only Son would be the required sacrifice to atone for humanity's sin.

Because of Christ's work, we also understand that it's only a matter of time before God's plan is completed and creation is redeemed. While God has exalted Jesus to the highest place (Ps 89:27; Php 2:9 – 10), eventually the rest of creation will follow suit. The recognition that God gave to Jesus after his resurrection will eventually be given by all of creation. Jesus will be recognized by Christian and non-Christian alike as the rightful King, and the honor that is due him because of his willing and obedient sacrifice will be paid. Every knee will bow and every tongue will acknowledge that Jesus is Lord, to the glory of God the Father (Php 2:10 – 11). Now, though the world is broken, Jesus the King sits on the throne, ruling and reigning at the right hand of the Father. He is worthy of all worship — in this life and the next (Rev 5:12).

The Suffering and Glory of the Servant

13 See, my servant will act wisely[a];
he will be raised and lifted up and highly exalted.
14 Just as there were many who were appalled at him[b]—
his appearance was so disfigured beyond that of any
human being
and his form marred beyond human likeness—
15 so he will sprinkle many nations,[c]
and kings will shut their mouths because of him.
For what they were not told, they will see,
and what they have not heard, they will understand.

53 Who has believed our message
and to whom has the arm of the LORD been revealed?
2 He grew up before him like a tender shoot,
and like a root out of dry ground.
He had no beauty or majesty to attract us to him,
nothing in his appearance that we should desire him.
3 He was despised and rejected by mankind,
a man of suffering, and familiar with pain.
Like one from whom people hide their faces
he was despised, and we held him in low esteem.

4 Surely he took up our pain
and bore our suffering,
yet we considered him punished by God,
stricken by him, and afflicted.
5 But he was pierced for our transgressions,
he was crushed for our iniquities;
the punishment that brought us peace was on him,
and by his wounds we are healed.
6 We all, like sheep, have gone astray,
each of us has turned to our own way;
and the LORD has laid on him
the iniquity of us all.

7 He was oppressed and afflicted,
yet he did not open his mouth;
he was led like a lamb to the slaughter,
and as a sheep before its shearers is silent,
so he did not open his mouth.
8 By oppression[d] and judgment he was taken away.
Yet who of his generation protested?
For he was cut off from the land of the living;
for the transgression of my people he was punished.[e]
9 He was assigned a grave with the wicked,
and with the rich in his death,
though he had done no violence,
nor was any deceit in his mouth.

10 Yet it was the LORD's will to crush him and cause him to
suffer,
and though the LORD makes[f] his life an offering for sin,
he will see his offspring and prolong his days,
and the will of the LORD will prosper in his hand.

---

[a] 13 Or *will prosper* [b] 14 Hebrew *you* [c] 15 Or *so will many nations be amazed at him* (see also Septuagint) [d] 8 Or *From arrest* [e] 8 Or *generation considered / that he was cut off from the land of the living, / that he was punished for the transgression of my people?* [f] 10 Hebrew *though you make*

ISAIAH 53:1 – 12

MAN OF SORROWS

There is perhaps no passage in the Old Testament that so clearly predicts and describes the character, life and mission of Jesus Christ. We see from this chapter as a whole that God's servant would be humiliated and disfigured by suffering (v. 3; Mk 15:17,19); he would be widely rejected (v. 3; Jn 12:37 – 38); he would bear our sins and suffering (vv. 4 – 6; Ro 4:25; 1Pe 2:24); he would make a blood atonement (vv. 7 – 8; Ro 3:25); he would become our substitute (v. 7; 2Co 5:21); he would voluntarily accept our guilt and punishment (v. 7; Jn 10:11); he would remain silent in the face of his enemies (v. 8); he would justify many from their sin (vv. 8,11; Ro 5:15 – 19); he would die with transgressors (vv. 9,12; Mk 15:27); and he would be buried in a rich man's tomb (v. 9; Jn 19:38 – 42). And there are many more connections to be made in this chapter to the life of Jesus.

Isaiah 53 paints a stark picture of God's chosen One, but it does so in surprising ways. What we see here is the vivid picture of One who would be characterized by trial and suffering. No wonder Jesus is called the man of suffering (v. 3; some translations use "man of sorrows").

This title doesn't mean that Jesus lived a sad life or that he was incapable of humor. It does mean, though, that Jesus would be even more acquainted with sorrow than any of the rest of humanity would ever be. This is a startling statement given that so much suffering is possible for a single person. The world is — and, since the fall, always has been — riddled with disease, famine, injustice and more; yet all of these things are the result of the condition of sin.

When sin entered the world, it not only corrupted the relationship between humankind and God; it flipped all of creation on its head. Sin is the condition of the universe, and as a result of that condition, there are not only acts of sin, but also natural disasters, disease and all manner of negative and painful realities in the universe. While all of us are acquainted with sin because we all live in this sinful world, not one of us has had the experience with sin that Jesus has. He has felt it more deeply, suffered under its burden more completely and ultimately triumphed over it fully.

The man of sorrows has experienced the worst the world has to offer and come out victorious on the other side. And for that, believers have reason to thank and praise him for all eternity.

11 After he has suffered,
he will see the light of life[a] and be satisfied[b];
by his knowledge[c] my righteous servant will justify many,
and he will bear their iniquities.
12 Therefore I will give him a portion among the great,[d]
and he will divide the spoils with the strong,[e]
because he poured out his life unto death,
and was numbered with the transgressors.
For he bore the sin of many,
and made intercession for the transgressors.

The Future Glory of Zion

54 "Sing, barren woman,
you who never bore a child;
burst into song, shout for joy,
you who were never in labor;
because more are the children of the desolate woman
than of her who has a husband,"
says the LORD.

2 "Enlarge the place of your tent,
stretch your tent curtains wide,
do not hold back;
lengthen your cords,
strengthen your stakes.
3 For you will spread out to the right and to the left;
your descendants will dispossess nations
and settle in their desolate cities.

4 "Do not be afraid; you will not be put to shame.
Do not fear disgrace; you will not be humiliated.
You will forget the shame of your youth
and remember no more the reproach of your widowhood.
5 For your Maker is your husband—
the LORD Almighty is his name—
the Holy One of Israel is your Redeemer;
he is called the God of all the earth.
6 The LORD will call you back
as if you were a wife deserted and distressed in spirit—
a wife who married young,
only to be rejected," says your God.
7 "For a brief moment I abandoned you,
but with deep compassion I will bring you back.
8 In a surge of anger
I hid my face from you for a moment,
but with everlasting kindness
I will have compassion on you,"
says the LORD your Redeemer.

9 "To me this is like the days of Noah,
when I swore that the waters of Noah would never again cover the
earth.
So now I have sworn not to be angry with you,
never to rebuke you again.
10 Though the mountains be shaken
and the hills be removed,

---

[a] 11 Dead Sea Scrolls (see also Septuagint); Masoretic Text does not have *the light of life.*
[b] 11 Or (with Masoretic Text) [11]*He will see the fruit of his suffering / and will be satisfied*
[c] 11 Or *by knowledge of him* [d] 12 Or *many* [e] 12 Or *numerous*

YOUR MAKER, YOUR HUSBAND

One of the most beautiful images representative of the relationship between God and his people is that of marriage. Here God is seen as the husband with Israel as his bride. This image reminds us of the great love and compassion God has for his people. In the Bible, sin is often compared to adultery. Yet God demonstrates the profound nature of his love by pursuing his wayward, adulterous people, keeping his promises and loving them anyway. It further reminds us of the commitment God has to his people.

Like Gomer's unfaithfulness to Hosea (Hos 1:2; 3:1), Israel's past was riddled with infidelity to their covenant with God. But like Hosea's faithfulness to Gomer, the Lord steadfastly remained faithful to his people and even in their exile would not reject them (Isa 54:6 – 8). He is the husband who remained true, for his covenant was based on his own character.

In the same way that wedding vows include the commitment "for better, for worse," so God has joined himself to his people. This verse is meant to comfort the people in understanding that, no matter where they might find themselves in exile, God has not rejected them. Like a faithful spouse, he promised to continually pursue them in his love, call them with his kindness and seek to restore them to right relationship with himself.

Along with the title of husband in this verse, we also see the title of "LORD Almighty." If the husband imagery reminds us of God's love and commitment, this second title speaks of his power. He is the Lord of hosts, commander of the armies of heaven, so there is nothing in all the universe that will prevent him from carrying out his will and protecting his own people. In the New Testament, Jesus is the husband of the church (Rev 19:7), who has the power to bring his people to himself. He is called "Faithful and True" (Rev 19:11), and we, as his bride, are secure in him. Despite our unfaithfulness, believers can rest assured that our keeping in God is based not on our own righteousness but instead on the strength of Jesus that God graciously credits to us.

yet my unfailing love for you will not be shaken
nor my covenant of peace be removed,"
says the LORD, who has compassion on you.

11 "Afflicted city, lashed by storms and not comforted,
I will rebuild you with stones of turquoise,[a]
your foundations with lapis lazuli.
12 I will make your battlements of rubies,
your gates of sparkling jewels,
and all your walls of precious stones.
13 All your children will be taught by the LORD,
and great will be their peace.
14 In righteousness you will be established:
Tyranny will be far from you;
you will have nothing to fear.
Terror will be far removed;
it will not come near you.
15 If anyone does attack you, it will not be my doing;
whoever attacks you will surrender to you.

16 "See, it is I who created the blacksmith
who fans the coals into flame
and forges a weapon fit for its work.
And it is I who have created the destroyer to wreak havoc;
17 no weapon forged against you will prevail,
and you will refute every tongue that accuses you.
This is the heritage of the servants of the LORD,
and this is their vindication from me,"
declares the LORD.

Invitation to the Thirsty

55 "Come, all you who are thirsty,
come to the waters;
and you who have no money,
come, buy and eat!
Come, buy wine and milk
without money and without cost.
2 Why spend money on what is not bread,
and your labor on what does not satisfy?
Listen, listen to me, and eat what is good,
and you will delight in the richest of fare.
3 Give ear and come to me;
listen, that you may live.
I will make an everlasting covenant with you,
my faithful love promised to David.
4 See, I have made him a witness to the peoples,
a ruler and commander of the peoples.
5 Surely you will summon nations you know not,
and nations you do not know will come running to you,
because of the LORD your God,
the Holy One of Israel,
for he has endowed you with splendor."

6 Seek the LORD while he may be found;
call on him while he is near.
7 Let the wicked forsake their ways
and the unrighteous their thoughts.

[a] *11* The meaning of the Hebrew for this word is uncertain.

ISAIAH 54:11–12

THE FUTURE GLORY OF ZION

These verses begin with the misery and affliction of the people of Jerusalem. The residents had been terrorized by an attack on the city, and God had not yet intervened to stop the invaders. But God, through Isaiah, detailed the bold plans he had to personally step into the city and gloriously transform it. This passage stunningly pictures everything from the foundation of the city to its ornamentation. The imagery described in terms of the jewels and precious stones is meant to help people visualize something beyond their wildest imagination.

Though Jerusalem has been destroyed and rebuilt many times throughout history, nothing has been erected by human hands that comes anywhere close to the glittering vision God presented in this passage. That's because the true fulfillment of the future glory of Zion is yet to come. The new Jerusalem is God's future city; it will be inhabited by his people from every tribe, tongue and nation. United once and for all in his city, God's people will worship him in the splendor of his beauty and holiness. And Jesus, the Lamb of God, will be its centerpiece (Rev 21:18–23).

ISAIAH 55:3–5

AN INVITATION

It's staggering to consider that God, though wronged and rejected time and time again, actually extends an invitation of salvation to his sinful people. He did and does just that,

(continued on page 1137)

INVITATION TO THE THIRSTY

God holds out his invitation in this passage to all who are willing to come, including Israel and the Gentile nations. God's invitation is not merely for the basic stuff of life; rather, he invites us to come to him to find that which is truly satisfying and fulfilling.

What do we find in God's presence? What can he alone give? These verses show us the futility we experience when we try to find satisfaction and joy apart from God. While we might spend a lifetime working hard to purchase things that will ultimately leave us frustrated and empty, God alone holds satisfaction in himself. In him, we can finally and ultimately be delighted (Ps 37:4), for God created us with a unique capacity to know and enjoy him for all eternity.

Remarkably, this great satisfaction is free to us. God made sure through his prophet Isaiah to emphasize that what is found in him cannot be purchased with money. There are no wells to be dug; there is no seed to be planted; there are no animals to tend. Instead, God's overwhelming bounty comes to us by grace alone, free to all who are willing to come. Though all the goodness of God is free, it is not without cost. Jesus himself paid that price on behalf of those who believe. Because of the death and resurrection of Jesus, God holds his arms open and says, "Come." The proper response to God's invitation is for all who hear it to "seek the LORD while he may be found" (Isa 55:6). Because he is the foundation of life, the fountain who won't run dry, the source of all human satisfaction, all people should willingly seek after and come to him.

When we "seek the LORD while he may be found," it means we agree with God's assessments of ourselves and the world around us. We no longer rebel against his calling us sinners but instead wholeheartedly accept his word to us. It's that word of God that issues his invitation, and it's through accepting the word that we actually find him. Jesus, as God's living Word (Jn 1:1), went out from him and accomplished the purposes God had for him. And it's through accepting the free gift of this living Word that we can ultimately return to God.

Let them turn to the LORD, and he will have mercy
on them,
and to our God, for he will freely pardon.
8 "For my thoughts are not your thoughts,
neither are your ways my ways,"
declares the LORD.
9 "As the heavens are higher than the earth,
so are my ways higher than your ways
and my thoughts than your thoughts.
10 As the rain and the snow
come down from heaven,
and do not return to it
without watering the earth
and making it bud and flourish,
so that it yields seed for the sower and bread for
the eater,
11 so is my word that goes out from my mouth:
It will not return to me empty,
but will accomplish what I desire
and achieve the purpose for which I sent it.
12 You will go out in joy
and be led forth in peace;
the mountains and hills
will burst into song before you,
and all the trees of the field
will clap their hands.
13 Instead of the thornbush will grow the juniper,
and instead of briers the myrtle will grow.
This will be for the LORD's renown,
for an everlasting sign,
that will endure forever."

Salvation for Others

56 This is what the LORD says:

"Maintain justice
and do what is right,
for my salvation is close at hand
and my righteousness will soon be revealed.
2 Blessed is the one who does this—
the person who holds it fast,
who keeps the Sabbath without desecrating it,
and keeps their hands from doing any evil."

3 Let no foreigner who is bound to the LORD say,
"The LORD will surely exclude me from his people."
And let no eunuch complain,
"I am only a dry tree."

4 For this is what the LORD says:

"To the eunuchs who keep my Sabbaths,
who choose what pleases me
and hold fast to my covenant—
5 to them I will give within my temple and its walls
a memorial and a name
better than sons and daughters;
I will give them an everlasting name
that will endure forever.

(An Invitation, continued)

inviting all people to consider the promises he made to David in his covenant. This invitation comes through God's Word to us; if we listen to it, we will find ourselves drawn to him over and over again. This is what the Word of God does; it engenders faith in sinners as they hear God's Word (Ro 10:17).

Years before Isaiah prophesied these words, God made David a promise that David would have a descendant who would reign on Israel's throne forever. This, of course, is Jesus Christ (Ac 13:32–39), through whom God continues to make his great invitation to sinners of every sort and origin. Through Jesus, the door is open to all who are willing to admit their need of cleansing and salvation in light of the holy standard of God, submitting themselves to that standard as revealed in God's Word and coming to him to accept this free gift.

ISAIAH 56:6–7

HOUSE OF PRAYER

The Gentiles, God promised, would one day be welcomed at his holy temple, and he would receive their sacrifices and prayers. Indeed, the temple, to which many Israelites of Isaiah's day had a nationalistic and prideful attachment, would become known as a house of prayer for *all* nations, not just the singular nation of Israel.

During the days of Jesus, Gentiles were indeed coming to the temple. But what he encountered in Jerusalem was far from the joyful celebration about which Isaiah prophesied. Instead, those from other parts of the world were being swindled out of their money as they had to exchange their currency for that of the temple. The Jews who traveled to the temple from a great distance could buy sacrificial animals in the outer court and it was here that they were being exploited by the merchants. As he approached the temple, Jesus discovered a system designed to exploit foreigners rather than welcome them. This exploitation, in contrast to the prophecy of Isaiah, incensed Jesus to take action (Mt 21:12–16).

6 And foreigners who bind themselves to the LORD
to minister to him,
to love the name of the LORD,
and to be his servants,
all who keep the Sabbath without desecrating it
and who hold fast to my covenant—
7 these I will bring to my holy mountain
and give them joy in my house of prayer.
Their burnt offerings and sacrifices
will be accepted on my altar;
for my house will be called
a house of prayer for all nations."
8 The Sovereign LORD declares—
he who gathers the exiles of Israel:
"I will gather still others to them
besides those already gathered."

God's Accusation Against the Wicked

9 Come, all you beasts of the field,
come and devour, all you beasts of the forest!
10 Israel's watchmen are blind,
they all lack knowledge;
they are all mute dogs,
they cannot bark;
they lie around and dream,
they love to sleep.
11 They are dogs with mighty appetites;
they never have enough.
They are shepherds who lack understanding;
they all turn to their own way,
they seek their own gain.
12 "Come," each one cries, "let me get wine!
Let us drink our fill of beer!
And tomorrow will be like today,
or even far better."

57 The righteous perish,
and no one takes it to heart;
the devout are taken away,
and no one understands
that the righteous are taken away
to be spared from evil.
2 Those who walk uprightly
enter into peace;
they find rest as they lie in death.

3 "But you—come here, you children of a sorceress,
you offspring of adulterers and prostitutes!
4 Who are you mocking?
At whom do you sneer
and stick out your tongue?
Are you not a brood of rebels,
the offspring of liars?
5 You burn with lust among the oaks
and under every spreading tree;
you sacrifice your children in the ravines
and under the overhanging crags.

[6]The idols among the smooth stones of the ravines are
your portion;
indeed, they are your lot.
Yes, to them you have poured out drink offerings
and offered grain offerings.
In view of all this, should I relent?
[7]You have made your bed on a high and lofty hill;
there you went up to offer your sacrifices.
[8]Behind your doors and your doorposts
you have put your pagan symbols.
Forsaking me, you uncovered your bed,
you climbed into it and opened it wide;
you made a pact with those whose beds you love,
and you looked with lust on their naked bodies.
[9]You went to Molek[a] with olive oil
and increased your perfumes.
You sent your ambassadors[b] far away;
you descended to the very realm of the dead!
[10]You wearied yourself by such going about,
but you would not say, 'It is hopeless.'
You found renewal of your strength,
and so you did not faint.

[11]"Whom have you so dreaded and feared
that you have not been true to me,
and have neither remembered me
nor taken this to heart?
Is it not because I have long been silent
that you do not fear me?
[12]I will expose your righteousness and your works,
and they will not benefit you.
[13]When you cry out for help,
let your collection of idols save you!
The wind will carry all of them off,
a mere breath will blow them away.
But whoever takes refuge in me
will inherit the land
and possess my holy mountain."

Comfort for the Contrite

[14]And it will be said:

"Build up, build up, prepare the road!
Remove the obstacles out of the way of my people."
[15]For this is what the high and exalted One says—
he who lives forever, whose name is holy:
"I live in a high and holy place,
but also with the one who is contrite and lowly in spirit,
to revive the spirit of the lowly
and to revive the heart of the contrite.
[16]I will not accuse them forever,
nor will I always be angry,
for then they would faint away because of me—
the very people I have created.
[17]I was enraged by their sinful greed;
I punished them, and hid my face in anger,
yet they kept on in their willful ways.

[a] 9 Or *to the king* [b] 9 Or *idols*

ISAIAH 57:14–19

THE WAY OF HUMILITY

Humans have no room for pride in God's presence, and pride is the root of the same idolatry that heightened the Lord's anger toward Isaiah's people. Idolatry is the prideful attempt to supplant the rule and reign of God over an individual's destiny; and in this case, over an entire nation. But God promised that his anger would not last forever. Though he is holy and as such has no room for any impurity or sin in his presence, he will still receive those who come to him in a contrite and humble way.

The hope of salvation is in Jesus alone, and yet the only way to truly come to Jesus is through humility. In coming to Jesus, we must first admit and confess our great sin of self-worship and self-lordship, accepting and owning the fact that we have rebelled against our true and right Master. The one who persists in pride, convinced of their own righteousness and goodness, will find no comfort and no forgiveness. But those who come to the cross with confession on their lips will find the grace and mercy they need from him (Jn 1:14,17).

ISAIAH 58:3 – 9

FASTING THAT GOD ACCEPTS

Fasting is the intentional choice to deprive oneself of something, most often food, for a period of time. But fasting is also a spiritual discipline that can easily become corrupted and self-serving. The Israelites had fasted in times of national calamity and as a regular part of their liturgical calendar. While true fasting is done to heighten one's awareness of the things of God and move one toward holiness, the fasting Isaiah wrote about was largely hypocritical. It was focused on self-righteousness and not on the kind of justice for others that God desired. Ironically, the self-righteous were busy depriving themselves of food while others in their community and their nation went hungry because of their poverty. This, said the prophet, was not the fast that God desired.

Similarly, Jesus condemned the fasting he witnessed in his day. Fasting had become a way to publicly demonstrate one's righteousness, but Jesus pointed people back to the heart of the matter. This discipline was meant to be a private matter between the individual and God (Mt 6:16 – 18), with the goal of fostering greater commitment to God and a greater commitment to helping those in need.

18 I have seen their ways, but I will heal them;
I will guide them and restore comfort to Israel's mourners,
19 creating praise on their lips.
Peace, peace, to those far and near,"
says the LORD. "And I will heal them."
20 But the wicked are like the tossing sea,
which cannot rest,
whose waves cast up mire and mud.
21 "There is no peace," says my God, "for the wicked."

True Fasting

58 "Shout it aloud, do not hold back.
Raise your voice like a trumpet.
Declare to my people their rebellion
and to the descendants of Jacob their sins.
2 For day after day they seek me out;
they seem eager to know my ways,
as if they were a nation that does what is right
and has not forsaken the commands of its God.
They ask me for just decisions
and seem eager for God to come near them.
3 'Why have we fasted,' they say,
'and you have not seen it?
Why have we humbled ourselves,
and you have not noticed?'

"Yet on the day of your fasting, you do as you please
and exploit all your workers.
4 Your fasting ends in quarreling and strife,
and in striking each other with wicked fists.
You cannot fast as you do today
and expect your voice to be heard on high.
5 Is this the kind of fast I have chosen,
only a day for people to humble themselves?
Is it only for bowing one's head like a reed
and for lying in sackcloth and ashes?
Is that what you call a fast,
a day acceptable to the LORD?

6 "Is not this the kind of fasting I have chosen:
to loose the chains of injustice
and untie the cords of the yoke,
to set the oppressed free
and break every yoke?
7 Is it not to share your food with the hungry
and to provide the poor wanderer with shelter —
when you see the naked, to clothe them,
and not to turn away from your own flesh and blood?
8 Then your light will break forth like the dawn,
and your healing will quickly appear;
then your righteousness[a] will go before you,
and the glory of the LORD will be your rear guard.
9 Then you will call, and the LORD will answer;
you will cry for help, and he will say: Here am I.

[a] 8 Or *your righteous One*

"If you do away with the yoke of oppression,
with the pointing finger and malicious talk,
10 and if you spend yourselves in behalf of the hungry
and satisfy the needs of the oppressed,
then your light will rise in the darkness,
and your night will become like the noonday.
11 The LORD will guide you always;
he will satisfy your needs in a sun-scorched land
and will strengthen your frame.
You will be like a well-watered garden,
like a spring whose waters never fail.
12 Your people will rebuild the ancient ruins
and will raise up the age-old foundations;
you will be called Repairer of Broken Walls,
Restorer of Streets with Dwellings.

13 "If you keep your feet from breaking the Sabbath
and from doing as you please on my holy day,
if you call the Sabbath a delight
and the LORD's holy day honorable,
and if you honor it by not going your own way
and not doing as you please or speaking idle words,
14 then you will find your joy in the LORD,
and I will cause you to ride in triumph on the heights of the land
and to feast on the inheritance of your father Jacob."
For the mouth of the LORD has spoken.

Sin, Confession and Redemption

59 Surely the arm of the LORD is not too short to save,
nor his ear too dull to hear.
2 But your iniquities have separated
you from your God;
your sins have hidden his face from you,
so that he will not hear.
3 For your hands are stained with blood,
your fingers with guilt.
Your lips have spoken falsely,
and your tongue mutters wicked things.
4 No one calls for justice;
no one pleads a case with integrity.
They rely on empty arguments, they utter lies;
they conceive trouble and give birth to evil.
5 They hatch the eggs of vipers
and spin a spider's web.
Whoever eats their eggs will die,
and when one is broken, an adder is hatched.
6 Their cobwebs are useless for clothing;
they cannot cover themselves with what they make.
Their deeds are evil deeds,
and acts of violence are in their hands.
7 Their feet rush into sin;
they are swift to shed innocent blood.
They pursue evil schemes;
acts of violence mark their ways.
8 The way of peace they do not know;
there is no justice in their paths.
They have turned them into crooked roads;
no one who walks along them will know peace.

9 So justice is far from us,
and righteousness does not reach us.
We look for light, but all is darkness;
for brightness, but we walk in deep shadows.
10 Like the blind we grope along the wall,
feeling our way like people without eyes.
At midday we stumble as if it were twilight;
among the strong, we are like the dead.
11 We all growl like bears;
we moan mournfully like doves.
We look for justice, but find none;
for deliverance, but it is far away.

12 For our offenses are many in your sight,
and our sins testify against us.
Our offenses are ever with us,
and we acknowledge our iniquities:
13 rebellion and treachery against the LORD,
turning our backs on our God,
inciting revolt and oppression,
uttering lies our hearts have conceived.
14 So justice is driven back,
and righteousness stands at a distance;
truth has stumbled in the streets,
honesty cannot enter.
15 Truth is nowhere to be found,
and whoever shuns evil becomes a prey.

The LORD looked and was displeased
that there was no justice.
16 He saw that there was no one,
he was appalled that there was no one to intervene;
so his own arm achieved salvation for him,
and his own righteousness sustained him.
17 He put on righteousness as his breastplate,
and the helmet of salvation on his head;
he put on the garments of vengeance
and wrapped himself in zeal as in a cloak.
18 According to what they have done,
so will he repay
wrath to his enemies
and retribution to his foes;
he will repay the islands their due.
19 From the west, people will fear the name of the LORD,
and from the rising of the sun, they will revere
his glory.
For he will come like a pent-up flood
that the breath of the LORD drives along.[a]

20 "The Redeemer will come to Zion,
to those in Jacob who repent of their sins,"
declares the LORD.

21 "As for me, this is my covenant with them," says the LORD. "My Spirit, who
is on you, will not depart from you, and my words that I have put in your mouth
will always be on your lips, on the lips of your children and on the lips of their
descendants — from this time on and forever," says the LORD.

[a] *19* Or *When enemies come in like a flood, / the Spirit of the LORD will put them to flight*

UNCONFESSED SIN

The land was filled with injustice during Isaiah's day. Though the people appeared to be very religious, their actions showed a shocking disregard for the needy around them. Instead of mercy and compassion, the land was filled with exploitation and hypocrisy. To this point, the people were unwilling to confess their sin to God, repent and turn toward obedience.

This unconfessed sin might have seemed like a trivial matter; after all, the people might have argued, it was a private matter between themselves and God. Even worse, they might have been living in a web of self-deception, refusing to see the truth of their sin even when Isaiah confronted them. But unconfessed sin festers inside a person; it destroys one from the inside out.

Similarly, when believers are confronted by the Word of God which calls their sin exactly what it is, they have the choice about whether to agree with God or to continue in their obstinate pride. When they agree with God, they are acknowledging that God knows them better than they know themselves; indeed, that God will tell them the truth even when they are intentionally or unintentionally blind to it themselves. In this light, confession of sin is really simply agreeing with God, who is — lest believers fool themselves into thinking they're hiding anything — well aware of all sin.

Ultimately, the people's refusal to agree with God when he told them the truth resulted in his judgment. He raised up the Babylonians to destroy Judah and Jerusalem as a lasting reminder that God is right in his pronouncements. God's judgment on his people stands as a reminder today that in the future, every nation will be judged by the same God who raised up the Babylonians. Knowing this judgment is coming, the proper response is to agree with God and his Word.

Believers agree with God when they confess their sin; they agree with him when they repent of that sin; they agree with God when they look to the cross of Christ alone as the atoning sacrifice for their sin. Christians follow this pattern of agreement, repentance and forgiveness time and time again as they look forward to the day when sin will be a thing of the past.

The Glory of Zion

60 "Arise, shine, for your light has come,
and the glory of the LORD rises upon you.
2 See, darkness covers the earth
and thick darkness is over the peoples,
but the LORD rises upon you
and his glory appears over you.
3 Nations will come to your light,
and kings to the brightness of your dawn.

4 "Lift up your eyes and look about you:
All assemble and come to you;
your sons come from afar,
and your daughters are carried on the hip.
5 Then you will look and be radiant,
your heart will throb and swell with joy;
the wealth on the seas will be brought to you,
to you the riches of the nations will come.
6 Herds of camels will cover your land,
young camels of Midian and Ephah.
And all from Sheba will come,
bearing gold and incense
and proclaiming the praise of the LORD.
7 All Kedar's flocks will be gathered to you,
the rams of Nebaioth will serve you;
they will be accepted as offerings on my altar,
and I will adorn my glorious temple.

8 "Who are these that fly along like clouds,
like doves to their nests?
9 Surely the islands look to me;
in the lead are the ships of Tarshish,[a]
bringing your children from afar,
with their silver and gold,
to the honor of the LORD your God,
the Holy One of Israel,
for he has endowed you with splendor.

10 "Foreigners will rebuild your walls,
and their kings will serve you.
Though in anger I struck you,
in favor I will show you compassion.
11 Your gates will always stand open,
they will never be shut, day or night,
so that people may bring you the wealth of the nations —
their kings led in triumphal procession.
12 For the nation or kingdom that will not serve you will perish;
it will be utterly ruined.

13 "The glory of Lebanon will come to you,
the juniper, the fir and the cypress together,
to adorn my sanctuary;
and I will glorify the place for my feet.
14 The children of your oppressors will come bowing before you;
all who despise you will bow down at your feet
and will call you the City of the LORD,
Zion of the Holy One of Israel.

[a] 9 Or *the trading ships*

ISAIAH 60:1–3

LIGHT IN THE DARKNESS

In darkness there is wandering, apprehension, confusion and fear. Conversely, light brings clarity, truth, understanding and comfort. Isaiah spoke of the darkness that covered the whole earth. This description goes beyond the darkness that would come as the people were exiled to Babylon; this is the spiritual darkness that pervades a lost and broken world. It's the darkness into which all humanity has been born, blinded to the truth. But Jesus Christ is the light of the world (Jn 8:12). In him, we can know truth, life and comfort, for Jesus alone shows us the true way to God.

In this context, it's beautiful to remember that on the night of Jesus' birth, a literal light from above pierced the darkness. The angel of the Lord, shining with "the glory of the Lord," surprised and frightened the shepherds. But the angel's message figuratively and literally pointed the way to the true Light of the world, the One who would eliminate all darkness in the future (Lk 2:8–12). Because of Jesus, there is no longer any need to languish in spiritual darkness, for he himself is the light.

15 "Although you have been forsaken and hated,
with no one traveling through,
I will make you the everlasting pride
and the joy of all generations.
16 You will drink the milk of nations
and be nursed at royal breasts.
Then you will know that I, the LORD, am your Savior,
your Redeemer, the Mighty One of Jacob.
17 Instead of bronze I will bring you gold,
and silver in place of iron.
Instead of wood I will bring you bronze,
and iron in place of stones.
I will make peace your governor
and well-being your ruler.
18 No longer will violence be heard in your land,
nor ruin or destruction within your borders,
but you will call your walls Salvation
and your gates Praise.
19 The sun will no more be your light by day,
nor will the brightness of the moon shine on you,
for the LORD will be your everlasting light,
and your God will be your glory.
20 Your sun will never set again,
and your moon will wane no more;
the LORD will be your everlasting light,
and your days of sorrow will end.
21 Then all your people will be righteous
and they will possess the land forever.
They are the shoot I have planted,
the work of my hands,
for the display of my splendor.
22 The least of you will become a thousand,
the smallest a mighty nation.
I am the LORD;
in its time I will do this swiftly."

The Year of the LORD's Favor

61 The Spirit of the Sovereign LORD is on me,
because the LORD has anointed me
to proclaim good news to the poor.
He has sent me to bind up the brokenhearted,
to proclaim freedom for the captives
and release from darkness for the prisoners,[a]
2 to proclaim the year of the LORD's favor
and the day of vengeance of our God,
to comfort all who mourn,
3 and provide for those who grieve in Zion—
to bestow on them a crown of beauty
instead of ashes,
the oil of joy
instead of mourning,
and a garment of praise
instead of a spirit of despair.
They will be called oaks of righteousness,
a planting of the LORD
for the display of his splendor.

[a] *1* Hebrew; Septuagint *the blind*

ISAIAH 61:1–2

YEAR OF JUBILEE

These verses describe the Year of Jubilee (Lev 25:8–55). According to the Levitical law, every seven years God's people were to observe not just a day of Sabbath, but a sabbatical year in which they allowed the land to lie unplowed. After seven sabbaticals, or forty-nine years, they were to celebrate the Year of Jubilee. During that year, the people were commanded to cancel all debts, return all land to the original owners and free their fellow Israelites who had sold themselves as indentured servants. This Year of Jubilee signified a fresh start for God's people.

As Jesus was beginning his public ministry, he made a stop in his hometown of Nazareth. Upon visiting the synagogue, he stood up to read and chose this passage from Isaiah. When he concluded his reading, he boldly proclaimed that these verses had been fulfilled that day in the presence of the people (Lk 4:16–21).

Jesus is the one who will usher in the true Year of Jubilee. Through faith in him, the One who gives us his righteousness, we can be released from our debt to sin and truly start again.

[4] They will rebuild the ancient ruins
and restore the places long devastated;
they will renew the ruined cities
that have been devastated for generations.
[5] Strangers will shepherd your flocks;
foreigners will work your fields and vineyards.
[6] And you will be called priests of the LORD,
you will be named ministers of our God.
You will feed on the wealth of nations,
and in their riches you will boast.

[7] Instead of your shame
you will receive a double portion,
and instead of disgrace
you will rejoice in your inheritance.
And so you will inherit a double portion in your land,
and everlasting joy will be yours.

[8] "For I, the LORD, love justice;
I hate robbery and wrongdoing.
In my faithfulness I will reward my people
and make an everlasting covenant with them.
[9] Their descendants will be known among the nations
and their offspring among the peoples.
All who see them will acknowledge
that they are a people the LORD has blessed."

[10] I delight greatly in the LORD;
my soul rejoices in my God.
For he has clothed me with garments of salvation
and arrayed me in a robe of his righteousness,
as a bridegroom adorns his head like a priest,
and as a bride adorns herself with her jewels.
[11] For as the soil makes the sprout come up
and a garden causes seeds to grow,
so the Sovereign LORD will make righteousness
and praise spring up before all nations.

Zion's New Name

62 For Zion's sake I will not keep silent,
for Jerusalem's sake I will not remain quiet,
till her vindication shines out like the dawn,
her salvation like a blazing torch.
[2] The nations will see your vindication,
and all kings your glory;
you will be called by a new name
that the mouth of the LORD will bestow.
[3] You will be a crown of splendor in the LORD's hand,
a royal diadem in the hand of your God.
[4] No longer will they call you Deserted,
or name your land Desolate.
But you will be called Hephzibah,[a]
and your land Beulah[b];
for the LORD will take delight in you,
and your land will be married.
[5] As a young man marries a young woman,
so will your Builder marry you;

[a] 4 *Hephzibah* means *my delight is in her.* [b] 4 *Beulah* means *married.*

ISAIAH 62:1–4

HEPHZIBAH AND BEULAH

In the biblical context, one's name carried great significance. Far from being a mere moniker, a person's name was the description of their character and identity, the summation of the very core of who they were. In these verses, we see that Jerusalem, or Zion, will go through a time when it will be called Deserted and Desolate, but that time will not last forever. Though there would be years of exile and a great season of wandering and doubt, the Lord would one day, at the appropriate time, reconcile with his people, represented by the special city.

In that reconciliation, God would give the city a new name. Hephzibah means "my delight is in her." The old name Desolate would be replaced by Beulah, which means "married." Here stands another promise of God that he has not, and will not, abandon his people. His relationship with them and reconciliation with them is bound by his own character.

Similarly, through Christ alone we are given a new name. No matter who we were prior to our reconciliation with God through Christ, God has given us a new name as his own adopted sons and daughters (1Jn 3:1–2; Rev 2:17), and he will not revoke this name.

as a bridegroom rejoices over his bride,
so will your God rejoice over you.

6 I have posted watchmen on your walls, Jerusalem;
they will never be silent day or night.
You who call on the LORD,
give yourselves no rest,
7 and give him no rest till he establishes Jerusalem
and makes her the praise of the earth.

8 The LORD has sworn by his right hand
and by his mighty arm:
"Never again will I give your grain
as food for your enemies,
and never again will foreigners drink the new wine
for which you have toiled;
9 but those who harvest it will eat it
and praise the LORD,
and those who gather the grapes will drink it
in the courts of my sanctuary."

10 Pass through, pass through the gates!
Prepare the way for the people.
Build up, build up the highway!
Remove the stones.
Raise a banner for the nations.

11 The LORD has made proclamation
to the ends of the earth:
"Say to Daughter Zion,
'See, your Savior comes!
See, his reward is with him,
and his recompense accompanies him.' "
12 They will be called the Holy People,
the Redeemed of the LORD;
and you will be called Sought After,
the City No Longer Deserted.

God's Day of Vengeance and Redemption

63 Who is this coming from Edom,
from Bozrah, with his garments stained crimson?
Who is this, robed in splendor,
striding forward in the greatness of his strength?

"It is I, proclaiming victory,
mighty to save."

2 Why are your garments red,
like those of one treading the winepress?

3 "I have trodden the winepress alone;
from the nations no one was with me.
I trampled them in my anger
and trod them down in my wrath;
their blood spattered my garments,
and I stained all my clothing.
4 It was for me the day of vengeance;
the year for me to redeem had come.
5 I looked, but there was no one to help,
I was appalled that no one gave support;

ISAIAH 63:1–6

GOD'S DAY OF VENGEANCE

Jesus came into the world the first time in an inauspicious way. Born in a stable in a backwater town, he inaugurated the year of true Jubilee, inviting all who are willing to repent and return to God to find true and lasting peace. When he comes the second time, it will not be with the message of peace but of vengeance and judgment. This second coming is described in Isaiah 63: God's day of vengeance.

The imagery in this chapter is vivid; among the most powerful images is that of the winepress. In those days, grapes were put into a large, hollowed rock for the people to tread on them. The juice of the grapes would run out of a hole in the rock to be caught, and as the grapes were crushed, some of the juice would stain the garments of the people. In this passage, the Lord's garments drip with the blood of his enemies as a result of his great victory.

Still, Isaiah concludes the chapter with a plea for God to demonstrate his power to his people before this great and terrible day. He asks the Lord for mercy so that people might trust in him before it is too late (63:15–19).

so my own arm achieved salvation for me,
and my own wrath sustained me.
6 I trampled the nations in my anger;
in my wrath I made them drunk
and poured their blood on the ground."

Praise and Prayer

7 I will tell of the kindnesses of the LORD,
the deeds for which he is to be praised,
according to all the LORD has done for us —
yes, the many good things
he has done for Israel,
according to his compassion and many kindnesses.
8 He said, "Surely they are my people,
children who will be true to me";
and so he became their Savior.
9 In all their distress he too was distressed,
and the angel of his presence saved them.[a]
In his love and mercy he redeemed them;
he lifted them up and carried them
all the days of old.
10 Yet they rebelled
and grieved his Holy Spirit.
So he turned and became their enemy
and he himself fought against them.

11 Then his people recalled[b] the days of old,
the days of Moses and his people —
where is he who brought them through the sea,
with the shepherd of his flock?
Where is he who set
his Holy Spirit among them,
12 who sent his glorious arm of power
to be at Moses' right hand,
who divided the waters before them,
to gain for himself everlasting renown,
13 who led them through the depths?
Like a horse in open country,
they did not stumble;
14 like cattle that go down to the plain,
they were given rest by the Spirit of the LORD.
This is how you guided your people
to make for yourself a glorious name.

15 Look down from heaven and see,
from your lofty throne, holy and glorious.
Where are your zeal and your might?
Your tenderness and compassion are withheld from us.
16 But you are our Father,
though Abraham does not know us
or Israel acknowledge us;
you, LORD, are our Father,
our Redeemer from of old is your name.
17 Why, LORD, do you make us wander from your ways
and harden our hearts so we do not revere you?

---

[a] 9 Or *Savior* [9]*in their distress. / It was no envoy or angel / but his own presence that saved them*
[b] 11 Or *But may he recall*

Return for the sake of your servants,
the tribes that are your inheritance.
18 For a little while your people possessed your holy place,
but now our enemies have trampled down your sanctuary.
19 We are yours from of old;
but you have not ruled over them,
they have not been called[a] by your name.

64 [b] Oh, that you would rend the heavens and come down,
that the mountains would tremble before you!
2 As when fire sets twigs ablaze
and causes water to boil,
come down to make your name known to your enemies
and cause the nations to quake before you!
3 For when you did awesome things that we did not expect,
you came down, and the mountains trembled before you.
4 Since ancient times no one has heard,
no ear has perceived,
no eye has seen any God besides you,
who acts on behalf of those who wait for him.
5 You come to the help of those who gladly do right,
who remember your ways.
But when we continued to sin against them,
you were angry.
How then can we be saved?
6 All of us have become like one who is unclean,
and all our righteous acts are like filthy rags;
we all shrivel up like a leaf,
and like the wind our sins sweep us away.
7 No one calls on your name
or strives to lay hold of you;
for you have hidden your face from us
and have given us over to[c] our sins.

8 Yet you, LORD, are our Father.
We are the clay, you are the potter;
we are all the work of your hand.
9 Do not be angry beyond measure, LORD;
do not remember our sins forever.
Oh, look on us, we pray,
for we are all your people.
10 Your sacred cities have become a wasteland;
even Zion is a wasteland, Jerusalem a desolation.
11 Our holy and glorious temple, where our ancestors praised you,
has been burned with fire,
and all that we treasured lies in ruins.
12 After all this, LORD, will you hold yourself back?
Will you keep silent and punish us beyond measure?

Judgment and Salvation

65 "I revealed myself to those who did not ask for me;
I was found by those who did not seek me.
To a nation that did not call on my name,
I said, 'Here am I, here am I.'

[a] 19 Or *We are like those you have never ruled, / like those never called* [b] In Hebrew texts 64:1 is numbered 63:19b, and 64:2-12 is numbered 64:1-11. [c] 7 Septuagint, Syriac and Targum; Hebrew *have made us melt because of*

ISAIAH 64:6–12

PUNISHMENT LEADING TO REPENTANCE

God's judgment on the world is a future reality. It's not a question of if it will come; rather, it's a question of when. But God is also patient; he desires that all people come to repentance (2Pe 3:9). Judgment is long in coming not because God is negligent, but because he is kind and generous.

These verses depict not only the reality of God's judgment, but also the apathy of the people. As it was in Isaiah's day, among unbelievers the judgment of God seems to be at best a distant reality, at worst a myth. We would do well to realize ourselves, and to help others see, the reality of what's to come. These promises are to us a warning so that we will not delay in our repentance. Because we have no righteousness to merit God's favor, our only choice is to throw ourselves at his feet asking for mercy and forgiveness. The time we have until God's great judgment and punishment for sin gives us and others an opportunity to repent and return to him (Ro 2:4). We must not neglect this chance, for we do not know when God's longsuffering patience will run out.

[2] All day long I have held out my hands
to an obstinate people,
who walk in ways not good,
pursuing their own imaginations —
[3] a people who continually provoke me
to my very face,
offering sacrifices in gardens
and burning incense on altars of brick;
[4] who sit among the graves
and spend their nights keeping secret vigil;
who eat the flesh of pigs,
and whose pots hold broth of impure meat;
[5] who say, 'Keep away; don't come near me,
for I am too sacred for you!'
Such people are smoke in my nostrils,
a fire that keeps burning all day.

[6] "See, it stands written before me:
I will not keep silent but will pay back in full;
I will pay it back into their laps —
[7] both your sins and the sins of your ancestors,"
says the LORD.
"Because they burned sacrifices on the mountains
and defied me on the hills,
I will measure into their laps
the full payment for their former deeds."

[8] This is what the LORD says:

"As when juice is still found in a cluster of grapes
and people say, 'Don't destroy it,
there is still a blessing in it,'
so will I do in behalf of my servants;
I will not destroy them all.
[9] I will bring forth descendants from Jacob,
and from Judah those who will possess my mountains;
my chosen people will inherit them,
and there will my servants live.
[10] Sharon will become a pasture for flocks,
and the Valley of Achor a resting place for herds,
for my people who seek me.

[11] "But as for you who forsake the LORD
and forget my holy mountain,
who spread a table for Fortune
and fill bowls of mixed wine for Destiny,
[12] I will destine you for the sword,
and all of you will fall in the slaughter;
for I called but you did not answer,
I spoke but you did not listen.
You did evil in my sight
and chose what displeases me."

[13] Therefore this is what the Sovereign LORD says:

"My servants will eat,
but you will go hungry;
my servants will drink,
but you will go thirsty;

JUDGMENT AND SALVATION

God is waiting. As these verses tell us, God's desire is to receive those who come to him. Throughout history, he has implored all who hear his voice to respond and come to him. God has revealed his righteous character through nature (Ro 1:20), through the Law of Moses (Ro 2:12 – 13) and even through the human conscience that testifies to God's own righteousness and holiness (Ro 2:14 – 15). His hands are outstretched and his invitation is open even though time and time again people have chosen to walk in the way that seems best to them.

Though God is and has been ready to receive all who come, people obstinately persist in their self-governance. They continue to go their own way so much so that Paul the apostle would echo the sentiment of Isaiah the prophet: "There is no one righteous, not even one; there is no one who understands; there is no one who seeks God. All have turned away, they have together become worthless; there is no one who does good, not even one" (Ro 3:10 – 12). But God's love is strong and his desire to dwell with his people is lasting. He will save his people from judgment though they might not even be seeking after him (Isa 65:1). He is powerful to break the shackles of sin and open blind eyes to see the beauty of his love. All those who come to him are empowered to do so by the work of his Spirit, who convicts men and women of their sin, of the righteousness of Christ and of their need for him.

This is the true peril of sin. Humanity is so blinded and so deeply corrupted by sin that all people must be awakened by the Spirit of God to even know that they are lost. Through the power of the Holy Spirit, God does this work, breaking through the blindness of sin to reveal the light of the gospel of Jesus Christ. Though we do not seek him, he has sought us. Though we have not called out to him, he has found us and brought us home. When God's judgment does come, then, there is no other option for those who have been saved but to revel completely in the grace alone that has saved them. Jesus alone will receive the honor of salvation even as he receives the honor that comes through judgment.

my servants will rejoice,
but you will be put to shame.
14 My servants will sing
out of the joy of their hearts,
but you will cry out
from anguish of heart
and wail in brokenness of spirit.
15 You will leave your name
for my chosen ones to use in their curses;
the Sovereign LORD will put you to death,
but to his servants he will give another name.
16 Whoever invokes a blessing in the land
will do so by the one true God;
whoever takes an oath in the land
will swear by the one true God.
For the past troubles will be forgotten
and hidden from my eyes.

New Heavens and a New Earth

17 "See, I will create
new heavens and a new earth.
The former things will not be remembered,
nor will they come to mind.
18 But be glad and rejoice forever
in what I will create,
for I will create Jerusalem to be a delight
and its people a joy.
19 I will rejoice over Jerusalem
and take delight in my people;
the sound of weeping and of crying
will be heard in it no more.

20 "Never again will there be in it
an infant who lives but a few days,
or an old man who does not live out his years;
the one who dies at a hundred
will be thought a mere child;
the one who fails to reach[a] a hundred
will be considered accursed.
21 They will build houses and dwell in them;
they will plant vineyards and eat their fruit.
22 No longer will they build houses and others live in them,
or plant and others eat.
For as the days of a tree,
so will be the days of my people;
my chosen ones will long enjoy
the work of their hands.
23 They will not labor in vain,
nor will they bear children doomed to misfortune;
for they will be a people blessed by the LORD,
they and their descendants with them.
24 Before they call I will answer;
while they are still speaking I will hear.
25 The wolf and the lamb will feed together,
and the lion will eat straw like the ox,
and dust will be the serpent's food.

---

[a] *20* Or *the sinner who reaches*

They will neither harm nor destroy
 on all my holy mountain,"
 says the LORD.

Judgment and Hope

66 This is what the LORD says:

"Heaven is my throne,
 and the earth is my footstool.
Where is the house you will build for me?
 Where will my resting place be?
2 Has not my hand made all these things,
 and so they came into being?"
 declares the LORD.

"These are the ones I look on with favor:
 those who are humble and contrite in spirit,
 and who tremble at my word.
3 But whoever sacrifices a bull
 is like one who kills a person,
and whoever offers a lamb
 is like one who breaks a dog's neck;
whoever makes a grain offering
 is like one who presents pig's blood,
and whoever burns memorial incense
 is like one who worships an idol.
They have chosen their own ways,
 and they delight in their abominations;
4 so I also will choose harsh treatment for them
 and will bring on them what they dread.
For when I called, no one answered,
 when I spoke, no one listened.
They did evil in my sight
 and chose what displeases me."
5 Hear the word of the LORD,
 you who tremble at his word:
"Your own people who hate you,
 and exclude you because of my name, have said,
'Let the LORD be glorified,
 that we may see your joy!'
 Yet they will be put to shame.
6 Hear that uproar from the city,
 hear that noise from the temple!
It is the sound of the LORD
 repaying his enemies all they deserve.

7 "Before she goes into labor,
 she gives birth;
before the pains come upon her,
 she delivers a son.
8 Who has ever heard of such things?
 Who has ever seen things like this?
Can a country be born in a day
 or a nation be brought forth in a moment?
Yet no sooner is Zion in labor
 than she gives birth to her children.
9 Do I bring to the moment of birth
 and not give delivery?" says the LORD.

ISAIAH 66:18–24

FINAL WARNINGS

Isaiah's prophecy closes with the promise that God's Word will go out to the ends of the earth (v. 19). As a result, the kingdom of God will be filled with both the people of Israel and with those from the Gentile nations. Though in the past these idolatrous nations have attacked God and his people, they will one day come to worship and glorify their true King.

But there will also be those who do not come, those who do not receive God's Word in repentance and faith. Isaiah's prophecy closes with a vision of judgment, looking upon a scene filled with the corpses of rebels (v. 24). Jesus quoted this verse in picturing a grisly image of hell (Mk 9:48). These two descriptions define two alternatives for those who hear the message. They can either trust in the Lord and claim the salvation that comes through his servant Jesus and live, or they can continue in rebellion and die. The stark reality of these two alternatives shows people not only the greatness of the salvation that can only come through Jesus, but also the urgency with which believers must join Isaiah in proclaiming the message of God.

"Do I close up the womb
when I bring to delivery?" says your God.
10 "Rejoice with Jerusalem and be glad for her,
all you who love her;
rejoice greatly with her,
all you who mourn over her.
11 For you will nurse and be satisfied
at her comforting breasts;
you will drink deeply
and delight in her overflowing abundance."

12 For this is what the LORD says:

"I will extend peace to her like a river,
and the wealth of nations like a flooding stream;
you will nurse and be carried on her arm
and dandled on her knees.
13 As a mother comforts her child,
so will I comfort you;
and you will be comforted over Jerusalem."

14 When you see this, your heart will rejoice
and you will flourish like grass;
the hand of the LORD will be made known to his servants,
but his fury will be shown to his foes.
15 See, the LORD is coming with fire,
and his chariots are like a whirlwind;
he will bring down his anger with fury,
and his rebuke with flames of fire.
16 For with fire and with his sword
the LORD will execute judgment on all people,
and many will be those slain by the LORD.

17 "Those who consecrate and purify themselves to go into the gardens, following one who is among those who eat the flesh of pigs, rats and other unclean things—they will meet their end together with the one they follow," declares the LORD.

18 "And I, because of what they have planned and done, am about to come[a] and gather the people of all nations and languages, and they will come and see my glory.

19 "I will set a sign among them, and I will send some of those who survive to the nations—to Tarshish, to the Libyans[b] and Lydians (famous as archers), to Tubal and Greece, and to the distant islands that have not heard of my fame or seen my glory. They will proclaim my glory among the nations.
20 And they will bring all your people, from all the nations, to my holy mountain in Jerusalem as an offering to the LORD—on horses, in chariots and wagons, and on mules and camels," says the LORD. "They will bring them, as the Israelites bring their grain offerings, to the temple of the LORD in ceremonially clean vessels.
21 And I will select some of them also to be priests and Levites," says the LORD.

22 "As the new heavens and the new earth that I make will endure before me," declares the LORD, "so will your name and descendants endure.
23 From one New Moon to another and from one Sabbath to another, all mankind will come and bow down before me," says the LORD.
24 "And they will go out and look on the dead bodies of those who rebelled against me; the worms that eat them will not die, the fire that burns them will not be quenched, and they will be loathsome to all mankind."

[a] *18* The meaning of the Hebrew for this clause is uncertain. [b] *19* Some Septuagint manuscripts *Put* (Libyans); Hebrew *Pul*

JESUS: OUR NEW COVENANT

JEREMIAH

JEREMIAH

PROPHETIC MINISTRY OF JEREMIAH BEGINS *c. 626 BC*	FALL OF JUDAH *c. 586 BC*	SOME JEWS FLEE TO EGYPT, TAKING JEREMIAH *c. 586 BC*

Jeremiah symbolized the overwhelming burden that God's spokespersons faced during the continual decline of the people of Israel. Called and appointed by God, Jeremiah undertook the daunting task of proclaiming a message of judgment against the Israelites and their removal from the land they had once received as a gift from God's hand. While overwhelming, Jeremiah's prophetic warnings came from God alone, and the prophet had no recourse but to share them with the people (Jer 20:9).

Jeremiah's words drip with anguish and grief over the spiritual state of Judah. In spite of their chosen status in God's eyes, the people had continually given themselves to idolatry and proven themselves incapable of keeping their covenant commitment to God. God had willingly bound himself to these people in covenant love, and the people were expected to respond with worshipful obedience. But they did not. As a result, God's coming judgment would be sure, swift and severe.

At the time of Jeremiah's warnings, the nation of Judah was in its last days. Jeremiah warned that God would raise up the nation of Babylon to defeat God's people and haul them off into captivity. The fall of Jerusalem in 586 BC fulfilled the long-standing warnings of the prophets regarding the results of Judah's sinful rebellion.

Jeremiah's writings are not without a glimmer of hope. The prophet knew that God's character was unchanging and his mission was sure. God would secure a remnant of worshipers from among the exiled nation. Because of his faithful love for his people, God would bring the people back from captivity and into right relationship with himself

(Jer 30:18 — 31:6; Eze 11:19). As a result, the people would once again sing for joy at the glory of God's salvation.

Through Jesus, the prophet's words still ring true today. These new covenant promises (Jer 31:31 – 34) are fulfilled in the person and work of Jesus Christ, who secured salvation through his righteous life, substitutionary death and victorious resurrection. Through faith, God's people can be born again to a living hope that pulsates with life. Though sin is grotesque and the consequences painful, Jesus' work is altogether complete and provides the sure hope that God will fulfill his promises to his people.

" 'FOR I KNOW THE PLANS I HAVE FOR YOU,' DECLARES THE LORD, 'PLANS TO PROSPER YOU AND NOT TO HARM YOU, PLANS TO GIVE YOU HOPE AND A FUTURE.' "

Jeremiah 29:11

JEREMIAH

1 The words of Jeremiah son of Hilkiah, one of the priests at Anathoth in the
territory of Benjamin. 2The word of the LORD came to him in the thirteenth
year of the reign of Josiah son of Amon king of Judah, 3and through the reign of
Jehoiakim son of Josiah king of Judah, down to the fifth month of the eleventh
year of Zedekiah son of Josiah king of Judah, when the people of Jerusalem went
into exile.

The Call of Jeremiah

4The word of the LORD came to me, saying,

5"Before I formed you in the womb I knew[a] you,
before you were born I set you apart;
I appointed you as a prophet to the nations."

6"Alas, Sovereign LORD," I said, "I do not know how to speak; I am too young."
7But the LORD said to me, "Do not say, 'I am too young.' You must go to everyone I send you to and say whatever I command you. 8Do not be afraid of them,
for I am with you and will rescue you," declares the LORD.
9Then the LORD reached out his hand and touched my mouth and said to me, "I
have put my words in your mouth. 10See, today I appoint you over nations and kingdoms to uproot and tear down, to destroy and overthrow, to build and to plant."
11The word of the LORD came to me: "What do you see, Jeremiah?"
"I see the branch of an almond tree," I replied.
12The LORD said to me, "You have seen correctly, for I am watching[b] to see that
my word is fulfilled."
13The word of the LORD came to me again: "What do you see?"
"I see a pot that is boiling," I answered. "It is tilting toward us from the north."
14The LORD said to me, "From the north disaster will be poured out on all who
live in the land. 15I am about to summon all the peoples of the northern kingdoms," declares the LORD.

"Their kings will come and set up their thrones
in the entrance of the gates of Jerusalem;
they will come against all her surrounding walls
and against all the towns of Judah.
16I will pronounce my judgments on my people
because of their wickedness in forsaking me,
in burning incense to other gods
and in worshiping what their hands have made.

17"Get yourself ready! Stand up and say to them whatever I command you. Do
not be terrified by them, or I will terrify you before them. 18Today I have made
you a fortified city, an iron pillar and a bronze wall to stand against the whole
land — against the kings of Judah, its officials, its priests and the people of the
land. 19They will fight against you but will not overcome you, for I am with you
and will rescue you," declares the LORD.

Israel Forsakes God

2 The word of the LORD came to me: 2"Go and proclaim in the hearing of Jerusalem:

"This is what the LORD says:

[a] 5 Or *chose* [b] 12 The Hebrew for *watching* sounds like the Hebrew for *almond tree.*

JEREMIAH 1:5

BEFORE BIRTH

When God calls a person to fulfill a mission, that mission can seem overwhelming. Thoughts flood one's mind: "I'm not qualified," "I'm not good enough," "I'm not ready" or "What could I possibly have to offer?" Yet, for every assignment, God is faithful to provide an outpouring of grace, courage and strength.

Jeremiah spent over 40 years as God's prophet to Judah. Even though he experienced many hardships, Jeremiah also experienced his ever-faithful God giving him the words and perseverance necessary to accomplish the work.

Like Jeremiah, Jesus was set apart for a divine mission. Jeremiah lived as a prophet sent to call the people back to God; Jesus, the fulfillment of over 300 prophesies, came as the living and literal *Way* back to God. Jeremiah revealed the grip of sin on the nation of Judah; Jesus came to deliver the people from their sin. As God called Jeremiah before he was born, the Father also knew how, when and where the Messiah would be born and how he would redeem mankind.

" 'I remember the devotion of your youth,
how as a bride you loved me
and followed me through the wilderness,
through a land not sown.
3 Israel was holy to the LORD,
the firstfruits of his harvest;
all who devoured her were held guilty,
and disaster overtook them,' "

declares the LORD.

4 Hear the word of the LORD, you descendants of Jacob,
all you clans of Israel.

5 This is what the LORD says:

"What fault did your ancestors find in me,
that they strayed so far from me?
They followed worthless idols
and became worthless themselves.
6 They did not ask, 'Where is the LORD,
who brought us up out of Egypt
and led us through the barren wilderness,
through a land of deserts and ravines,
a land of drought and utter darkness,
a land where no one travels and no one lives?'
7 I brought you into a fertile land
to eat its fruit and rich produce.
But you came and defiled my land
and made my inheritance detestable.
8 The priests did not ask,
'Where is the LORD?'
Those who deal with the law did not know me;
the leaders rebelled against me.
The prophets prophesied by Baal,
following worthless idols.

9 "Therefore I bring charges against you again,"

declares the LORD.

"And I will bring charges against your children's
children.
10 Cross over to the coasts of Cyprus and look,
send to Kedar[a] and observe closely;
see if there has ever been anything like this:
11 Has a nation ever changed its gods?
(Yet they are not gods at all.)
But my people have exchanged their glorious God
for worthless idols.
12 Be appalled at this, you heavens,
and shudder with great horror,"

declares the LORD.

13 "My people have committed two sins:
They have forsaken me,
the spring of living water,
and have dug their own cisterns,
broken cisterns that cannot hold water.
14 Is Israel a servant, a slave by birth?
Why then has he become plunder?

---

[a] *10* In the Syro-Arabian desert

SPRING OF LIVING WATER

God's pronouncement of judgment through Jeremiah likely carried a tone of raw emotion. God was livid — the enraged epitome of one betrayed. The Lord was not shocked at Judah's adultery as if he had suddenly become aware of it. Rather, he was stunned by what the people were willing to trade: "My people have exchanged their glorious God for worthless idols" (Jer 2:11).

The root sins of the people in Jeremiah 2:13 were forsaking him, "the spring of living water," and digging their own cisterns. The first charge against the people is that they abandoned God. They forgot his faithfulness and discarded their covenant obligations. The issue that's larger than the fact that they walked away is *who* they walked away *from* and *for what*. The key word in this part of verse 13 is "me," and the exchange is utterly irrational. God is incredulous — how could they reject the One who is always attentive, faithful and sufficient? The very spring from which life-giving water originates?

The second charge against the people is they put faith in gods of their own design, trading God's living water for dead, dry, useless idols. Cisterns were receptacles for storing rain water to use during the dry season. Ancient peoples also used large pottery containers or, when possible, dug massive holding tanks into the rock face of a mountain or hill. It was a contingency of control, of supplying for one's own needs. God uses this metaphor to describe Judah's adoption of false gods. God describes himself as *the spring of living water* — always flowing, perpetually satisfying. His love and mercy are unfathomable, his power inexhaustible. His knowledge and wisdom are perfect and unrivaled. The Israelites' trade of their life-giving God for worthless idols was more than rebellion; it was utter foolishness. With the Lord, they had all that they would ever need. Their cisterns — the idols of wood and stone — would never answer a prayer, and they could never hold the people's hope.

During a conversation with a Samaritan woman, Jesus declared that he was, and is still today, the source of "a spring of water welling up to eternal life" (Jn 4:14). Men and women look to many things of human design for joy and satisfaction. None of them offers lasting hope. But if anyone believes in Christ, their soul's thirst is permanently quenched. Jesus is all that believers will ever need. He is the spring of living water — the constant source of abundant life, both now and throughout eternity.

15 Lions have roared;
they have growled at him.
They have laid waste his land;
his towns are burned and deserted.
16 Also, the men of Memphis and Tahpanhes
have cracked your skull.
17 Have you not brought this on yourselves
by forsaking the LORD your God
when he led you in the way?
18 Now why go to Egypt
to drink water from the Nile[a]?
And why go to Assyria
to drink water from the Euphrates?
19 Your wickedness will punish you;
your backsliding will rebuke you.
Consider then and realize
how evil and bitter it is for you
when you forsake the LORD your God
and have no awe of me,"
declares the Lord, the LORD Almighty.

20 "Long ago you broke off your yoke
and tore off your bonds;
you said, 'I will not serve you!'
Indeed, on every high hill
and under every spreading tree
you lay down as a prostitute.
21 I had planted you like a choice vine
of sound and reliable stock.
How then did you turn against me
into a corrupt, wild vine?
22 Although you wash yourself with soap
and use an abundance of cleansing powder,
the stain of your guilt is still before me,"
declares the Sovereign LORD.
23 "How can you say, 'I am not defiled;
I have not run after the Baals'?
See how you behaved in the valley;
consider what you have done.
You are a swift she-camel
running here and there,
24 a wild donkey accustomed to the desert,
sniffing the wind in her craving —
in her heat who can restrain her?
Any males that pursue her need not tire themselves;
at mating time they will find her.
25 Do not run until your feet are bare
and your throat is dry.
But you said, 'It's no use!
I love foreign gods,
and I must go after them.'

26 "As a thief is disgraced when he is caught,
so the people of Israel are disgraced —
they, their kings and their officials,
their priests and their prophets.

---

[a] *18* Hebrew *Shihor*; that is, a branch of the Nile

27 They say to wood, 'You are my father,'
and to stone, 'You gave me birth.'
They have turned their backs to me
and not their faces;
yet when they are in trouble, they say,
'Come and save us!'
28 Where then are the gods you made for yourselves?
Let them come if they can save you
when you are in trouble!
For you, Judah, have as many gods
as you have towns.

29 "Why do you bring charges against me?
You have all rebelled against me,"
declares the LORD.
30 "In vain I punished your people;
they did not respond to correction.
Your sword has devoured your prophets
like a ravenous lion.

31 "You of this generation, consider the word of the LORD:

"Have I been a desert to Israel
or a land of great darkness?
Why do my people say, 'We are free to roam;
we will come to you no more'?
32 Does a young woman forget her jewelry,
a bride her wedding ornaments?
Yet my people have forgotten me,
days without number.
33 How skilled you are at pursuing love!
Even the worst of women can learn from your ways.
34 On your clothes is found
the lifeblood of the innocent poor,
though you did not catch them breaking in.
Yet in spite of all this
35 you say, 'I am innocent;
he is not angry with me.'
But I will pass judgment on you
because you say, 'I have not sinned.'
36 Why do you go about so much,
changing your ways?
You will be disappointed by Egypt
as you were by Assyria.
37 You will also leave that place
with your hands on your head,
for the LORD has rejected those you trust;
you will not be helped by them.

3 "If a man divorces his wife
and she leaves him and marries another man,
should he return to her again?
Would not the land be completely defiled?
But you have lived as a prostitute with many lovers —
would you now return to me?"
declares the LORD.

2 "Look up to the barren heights and see.
Is there any place where you have not been ravished?

By the roadside you sat waiting for lovers,
sat like a nomad in the desert.
You have defiled the land
with your prostitution and wickedness.
3 Therefore the showers have been withheld,
and no spring rains have fallen.
Yet you have the brazen look of a prostitute;
you refuse to blush with shame.
4 Have you not just called to me:
'My Father, my friend from my youth,
5 will you always be angry?
Will your wrath continue forever?'
This is how you talk,
but you do all the evil you can."

Unfaithful Israel

6 During the reign of King Josiah, the LORD said to me, "Have you seen what
faithless Israel has done? She has gone up on every high hill and under every
spreading tree and has committed adultery there. 7 I thought that after she had
done all this she would return to me but she did not, and her unfaithful sister
Judah saw it. 8 I gave faithless Israel her certificate of divorce and sent her away
because of all her adulteries. Yet I saw that her unfaithful sister Judah had no
fear; she also went out and committed adultery. 9 Because Israel's immorality
mattered so little to her, she defiled the land and committed adultery with stone
and wood. 10 In spite of all this, her unfaithful sister Judah did not return to me
with all her heart, but only in pretense," declares the LORD.
11 The LORD said to me, "Faithless Israel is more righteous than unfaithful Judah. 12 Go, proclaim this message toward the north:

" 'Return, faithless Israel,' declares the LORD,
'I will frown on you no longer,
for I am faithful,' declares the LORD,
'I will not be angry forever.
13 Only acknowledge your guilt—
you have rebelled against the LORD your God,
you have scattered your favors to foreign gods
under every spreading tree,
and have not obeyed me,' "
declares the LORD.

14 "Return, faithless people," declares the LORD, "for I am your husband. I will
choose you—one from a town and two from a clan—and bring you to Zion.
15 Then I will give you shepherds after my own heart, who will lead you with
knowledge and understanding. 16 In those days, when your numbers have increased greatly in the land," declares the LORD, "people will no longer say, 'The
ark of the covenant of the LORD.' It will never enter their minds or be remembered; it will not be missed, nor will another one be made. 17 At that time they will
call Jerusalem The Throne of the LORD, and all nations will gather in Jerusalem
to honor the name of the LORD. No longer will they follow the stubbornness of
their evil hearts. 18 In those days the people of Judah will join the people of Israel,
and together they will come from a northern land to the land I gave your ancestors as an inheritance.
19 "I myself said,

" 'How gladly would I treat you like my children
and give you a pleasant land,
the most beautiful inheritance of any nation.'
I thought you would call me 'Father'
and not turn away from following me.

JEREMIAH 3:14

UNFAITHFUL MARRIAGE

Here God uses the human institution of marriage as a picture of his love relationship with Israel. He considers the unfaithfulness of Judah, along with her faithless "sister" Israel, as being equal to adultery (vv. 6–9). The people have betrayed their beloved—giving themselves over to idol worship. They have abandoned God, their provider and protector, spurning the One who chose them as the object of his affection and care. But God issues an astonishing call, an open-armed offer for the Israelites to return to him. He promises to take them back and live as their husband if they will simply return to him (v. 14).

This invitation to grace reflects God's desire to save sinners through faith in Jesus. Even while humankind wandered in sin, Christ died for the ungodly (Ro 5:8). God's call to salvation is an offer to receive the opposite of what humanity deserves. Although he was betrayed, God paid the debt of human rebellion so he could be reconciled with the ones he loves.

FORGIVENESS OF SIN

God occasionally uses the metaphor of marriage in Scripture to portray his relationship with his people. He builds on this illustration in the book of Jeremiah by defining the worship of false gods as spiritual adultery and prostitution (Jer 3:1). Adultery — sharing intimate physical affection with someone outside of marriage — cuts deep personal wounds. And God felt those same wounds: The Israelites had rebelled against God, disobeying his commands and giving their intimate spiritual selves to idols.

Even though this breach of trust dishonored God and moved him to anger, he was willing to forgive their sin. He invited the people to return to him — to experience the end of his anger (v. 12). God implored the Israelites to return to him; he was eager to treat them like his children (v. 19). Though their sins were many, God's love never wavered. Above and beyond restoring the relationship, God even offered to do rehabilitating work on their souls — to cure their backsliding (v. 22).

All people have sinned against God, violating his commands or worshiping other people and things in his place (Ro 3:23). Even so, God sent Jesus into the world — not to condemn it, but to make a way for sin to be forgiven (Jn 3:17). God did not forgive sin by decree, but he arranged for it to be paid for through the death of his own Son. Jesus sacrificed himself on a cross to pay the debt for every single sin against God. Believing in Christ's death and resurrection enables men and women to have all of their sins forgiven (Ac 13:38 – 39). Through faith, Christ's atoning sacrifice is applied to their lives; their guilt is exchanged for Christ's perfect righteousness (Php 3:9).

These spiritual realities support the relationship realities between people and God. Sins against him are betrayals, as ugly and as terrible as the adultery of the Israelites. Yet God, who is rich in mercy, is eager to forgive those who turn to him through repentance and faith in Jesus. Like God's offer to the Israelites, those who believe in Christ enter a process of sanctification, of becoming holy — a blessing and benefit on top of forgiveness. Because of Jesus' sacrifice on the cross, human sin is paid for. Because of his victorious resurrection, he still helps believers today, through the Holy Spirit, to transform his followers more and more into his own character.

20 But like a woman unfaithful to her husband,
so you, Israel, have been unfaithful to me,"
declares the LORD.

21 A cry is heard on the barren heights,
the weeping and pleading of the people of Israel,
because they have perverted their ways
and have forgotten the LORD their God.

22 "Return, faithless people;
I will cure you of backsliding."

"Yes, we will come to you,
for you are the LORD our God.
23 Surely the idolatrous commotion on the hills
and mountains is a deception;
surely in the LORD our God
is the salvation of Israel.
24 From our youth shameful gods have consumed
the fruits of our ancestors' labor—
their flocks and herds,
their sons and daughters.
25 Let us lie down in our shame,
and let our disgrace cover us.
We have sinned against the LORD our God,
both we and our ancestors;
from our youth till this day
we have not obeyed the LORD our God."

4 "If you, Israel, will return,
then return to me,"
declares the LORD.

"If you put your detestable idols out of my sight
and no longer go astray,
2 and if in a truthful, just and righteous way
you swear, 'As surely as the LORD lives,'
then the nations will invoke blessings by him
and in him they will boast."

3 This is what the LORD says to the people of Judah and to Jerusalem:

"Break up your unplowed ground
and do not sow among thorns.
4 Circumcise yourselves to the LORD,
circumcise your hearts,
you people of Judah and inhabitants of Jerusalem,
or my wrath will flare up and burn like fire
because of the evil you have done—
burn with no one to quench it.

Disaster From the North

5 "Announce in Judah and proclaim in Jerusalem and say:
'Sound the trumpet throughout the land!'
Cry aloud and say:
'Gather together!
Let us flee to the fortified cities!'
6 Raise the signal to go to Zion!
Flee for safety without delay!
For I am bringing disaster from the north,
even terrible destruction."

JEREMIAH 4:4

CIRCUMCISION OF THE HEART

God sent Jeremiah to remind the people of Judah of their covenant with God. God had promised to lead and care for the Israelites, and they had pledged faithful obedience. Circumcision—removing a small part of the physical flesh—was a sign of this covenant, permanently marking a person's relationship with God as an outward sign of an inward reality. However, over time, most observances of the symbol became disconnected from the expression of an internal commitment. Jeremiah called the people to circumcise their hearts as an internal symbol of their honor and affection, declaring their allegiance, love and commitment to obey God.

Jesus continued this emphasis on mankind's internal condition when he challenged the religious leaders of his day. He confronted the Pharisees about living lives that looked good on the outside while their hearts remained unclean (Mt 23:27–28). Salvation through Jesus results in a new kind of circumcision of the heart—a believer's "whole self ruled by the flesh" is permanently "put off" (Col 2:11). And while Christians still continue to struggle with sin, they can also claim victory over it (1Co 15:56–57).

7 A lion has come out of his lair;
a destroyer of nations has set out.
He has left his place
to lay waste your land.
Your towns will lie in ruins
without inhabitant.
8 So put on sackcloth,
lament and wail,
for the fierce anger of the LORD
has not turned away from us.

9 "In that day," declares the LORD,
"the king and the officials will lose heart,
the priests will be horrified,
and the prophets will be appalled."

10 Then I said, "Alas, Sovereign LORD! How completely you have deceived this people and Jerusalem by saying, 'You will have peace,' when the sword is at our throats!"
11 At that time this people and Jerusalem will be told, "A scorching wind from
the barren heights in the desert blows toward my people, but not to winnow or
cleanse; 12 a wind too strong for that comes from me. Now I pronounce my judgments against them."

13 Look! He advances like the clouds,
his chariots come like a whirlwind,
his horses are swifter than eagles.
Woe to us! We are ruined!
14 Jerusalem, wash the evil from your heart and be saved.
How long will you harbor wicked thoughts?
15 A voice is announcing from Dan,
proclaiming disaster from the hills of Ephraim.
16 "Tell this to the nations,
proclaim concerning Jerusalem:
'A besieging army is coming from a distant land,
raising a war cry against the cities of Judah.
17 They surround her like men guarding a field,
because she has rebelled against me,' "

declares the LORD.

18 "Your own conduct and actions
have brought this on you.
This is your punishment.
How bitter it is!
How it pierces to the heart!"

19 Oh, my anguish, my anguish!
I writhe in pain.
Oh, the agony of my heart!
My heart pounds within me,
I cannot keep silent.
For I have heard the sound of the trumpet;
I have heard the battle cry.
20 Disaster follows disaster;
the whole land lies in ruins.
In an instant my tents are destroyed,
my shelter in a moment.
21 How long must I see the battle standard
and hear the sound of the trumpet?

22 "My people are fools;
they do not know me.

They are senseless children;
they have no understanding.
They are skilled in doing evil;
they know not how to do good."

23 I looked at the earth,
and it was formless and empty;
and at the heavens,
and their light was gone.
24 I looked at the mountains,
and they were quaking;
all the hills were swaying.
25 I looked, and there were no people;
every bird in the sky had flown away.
26 I looked, and the fruitful land was a desert;
all its towns lay in ruins
before the LORD, before his fierce anger.

27 This is what the LORD says:

"The whole land will be ruined,
though I will not destroy it completely.
28 Therefore the earth will mourn
and the heavens above grow dark,
because I have spoken and will not relent,
I have decided and will not turn back."

29 At the sound of horsemen and archers
every town takes to flight.
Some go into the thickets;
some climb up among the rocks.
All the towns are deserted;
no one lives in them.

30 What are you doing, you devastated one?
Why dress yourself in scarlet
and put on jewels of gold?
Why highlight your eyes with makeup?
You adorn yourself in vain.
Your lovers despise you;
they want to kill you.

31 I hear a cry as of a woman in labor,
a groan as of one bearing her first child—
the cry of Daughter Zion gasping for breath,
stretching out her hands and saying,
"Alas! I am fainting;
my life is given over to murderers."

Not One Is Upright

5 "Go up and down the streets of Jerusalem,
look around and consider,
search through her squares.
If you can find but one person
who deals honestly and seeks the truth,
I will forgive this city.
2 Although they say, 'As surely as the LORD lives,'
still they are swearing falsely."

3 LORD, do not your eyes look for truth?
You struck them, but they felt no pain;
you crushed them, but they refused correction.

They made their faces harder than stone
and refused to repent.
4 I thought, "These are only the poor;
they are foolish,
for they do not know the way of the LORD,
the requirements of their God.
5 So I will go to the leaders
and speak to them;
surely they know the way of the LORD,
the requirements of their God."
But with one accord they too had broken off the
yoke
and torn off the bonds.
6 Therefore a lion from the forest will attack them,
a wolf from the desert will ravage them,
a leopard will lie in wait near their towns
to tear to pieces any who venture out,
for their rebellion is great
and their backslidings many.

7 "Why should I forgive you?
Your children have forsaken me
and sworn by gods that are not gods.
I supplied all their needs,
yet they committed adultery
and thronged to the houses of prostitutes.
8 They are well-fed, lusty stallions,
each neighing for another man's wife.
9 Should I not punish them for this?"
declares the LORD.
"Should I not avenge myself
on such a nation as this?

10 "Go through her vineyards and ravage them,
but do not destroy them completely.
Strip off her branches,
for these people do not belong to the LORD.
11 The people of Israel and the people of Judah
have been utterly unfaithful to me,"
declares the LORD.

12 They have lied about the LORD;
they said, "He will do nothing!
No harm will come to us;
we will never see sword or famine.
13 The prophets are but wind
and the word is not in them;
so let what they say be done to them."

14 Therefore this is what the LORD God Almighty says:

"Because the people have spoken these words,
I will make my words in your mouth a fire
and these people the wood it consumes.
15 People of Israel," declares the LORD,
"I am bringing a distant nation against you—
an ancient and enduring nation,
a people whose language you do not know,
whose speech you do not understand.
16 Their quivers are like an open grave;
all of them are mighty warriors.

17 They will devour your harvests and food,
devour your sons and daughters;
they will devour your flocks and herds,
devour your vines and fig trees.
With the sword they will destroy
the fortified cities in which you trust.

18 "Yet even in those days," declares the LORD, "I will not destroy you completely. 19 And when the people ask, 'Why has the LORD our God done all this to
us?' you will tell them, 'As you have forsaken me and served foreign gods in your
own land, so now you will serve foreigners in a land not your own.'

20 "Announce this to the descendants of Jacob
and proclaim it in Judah:
21 Hear this, you foolish and senseless people,
who have eyes but do not see,
who have ears but do not hear:
22 Should you not fear me?" declares the LORD.
"Should you not tremble in my presence?
I made the sand a boundary for the sea,
an everlasting barrier it cannot cross.
The waves may roll, but they cannot prevail;
they may roar, but they cannot cross it.
23 But these people have stubborn and rebellious hearts;
they have turned aside and gone away.
24 They do not say to themselves,
'Let us fear the LORD our God,
who gives autumn and spring rains in season,
who assures us of the regular weeks of harvest.'
25 Your wrongdoings have kept these away;
your sins have deprived you of good.

26 "Among my people are the wicked
who lie in wait like men who snare birds
and like those who set traps to catch people.
27 Like cages full of birds,
their houses are full of deceit;
they have become rich and powerful
28 and have grown fat and sleek.
Their evil deeds have no limit;
they do not seek justice.
They do not promote the case of the fatherless;
they do not defend the just cause of the poor.
29 Should I not punish them for this?"
declares the LORD.
"Should I not avenge myself
on such a nation as this?

30 "A horrible and shocking thing
has happened in the land:
31 The prophets prophesy lies,
the priests rule by their own authority,
and my people love it this way.
But what will you do in the end?

Jerusalem Under Siege

6 "Flee for safety, people of Benjamin!
Flee from Jerusalem!
Sound the trumpet in Tekoa!
Raise the signal over Beth Hakkerem!

A HORRIBLE AND SHOCKING THING

Jeremiah's was not the only voice in Jerusalem speaking about what God was about to do in response to the people's disobedience. The anointed priests and acknowledged prophets addressed the people — but they contradicted Jeremiah's warnings. Both priests and prophets had succumbed to the temptation of abusing their power, rejecting their responsibilities as messengers and servants of God. These official religious leaders provoked God by overtly lying, denying the truth of the imminent judgment. While Jeremiah sounded the alarm in an attempt to bring the Israelites to their senses, Jerusalem's spiritual leaders urged calm and confidence.

These false teachers asserted that God would not exert his discipline — that God would never initiate something so devastating to his chosen ones. The people were soothed by these words; they relaxed from their fear of war or famine (Jer 5:12). The priests and prophets did not rouse the people toward repentance. Instead, they offered words with neither substance nor weight, their speeches becoming like the sound of an empty wind. The *word* was not in them (v. 13). Perhaps the most shocking aspect of this predicament is seen in the people's contentment with compromised leaders. God observed, "My people love it this way" (v. 31).

Centuries later, Jesus confronted the spiritual leaders of Jerusalem for their refusal to embrace the truth about what God was doing among them. Apparently they had abandoned all efforts to discern God's work in the world, spending their energies on preserving the institution of temple life. Jesus issued harsh rebukes against the teachers of the law and the religious leaders whose role should have included support for works performed to the glory of God. They failed to recognize Jesus as the promised Messiah (Lk 5:20 – 24), scoffing at his claims of authority and dismissing his pronouncements about the kingdom of God. Eventually, they would resist Jesus to the point of arresting him, putting him on trial and calling for his execution.

Clearly, these scholars had not learned the lessons of the exile, even though they should have known Jeremiah's prophecies. Despite their intentions, Jesus went to the cross as a willing sacrifice and not as a victim. Through his death and resurrection, Jesus accomplished the purpose and mission of his life (Mk 10:45).

For disaster looms out of the north,
even terrible destruction.
2 I will destroy Daughter Zion,
so beautiful and delicate.
3 Shepherds with their flocks will come against her;
they will pitch their tents around her,
each tending his own portion."

4 "Prepare for battle against her!
Arise, let us attack at noon!
But, alas, the daylight is fading,
and the shadows of evening grow long.
5 So arise, let us attack at night
and destroy her fortresses!"

6 This is what the LORD Almighty says:

"Cut down the trees
and build siege ramps against Jerusalem.
This city must be punished;
it is filled with oppression.
7 As a well pours out its water,
so she pours out her wickedness.
Violence and destruction resound in her;
her sickness and wounds are ever before me.
8 Take warning, Jerusalem,
or I will turn away from you
and make your land desolate
so no one can live in it."

9 This is what the LORD Almighty says:

"Let them glean the remnant of Israel
as thoroughly as a vine;
pass your hand over the branches again,
like one gathering grapes."

10 To whom can I speak and give warning?
Who will listen to me?
Their ears are closed[a]
so they cannot hear.
The word of the LORD is offensive to them;
they find no pleasure in it.
11 But I am full of the wrath of the LORD,
and I cannot hold it in.

"Pour it out on the children in the street
and on the young men gathered together;
both husband and wife will be caught in it,
and the old, those weighed down with years.
12 Their houses will be turned over to others,
together with their fields and their wives,
when I stretch out my hand
against those who live in the land,"
declares the LORD.

13 "From the least to the greatest,
all are greedy for gain;
prophets and priests alike,
all practice deceit.

[a] 10 Hebrew *uncircumcised*

JEREMIAH 6:19

JUDGMENT IS COMING

God invited the nations of the world to witness what was about to happen to his people. The impending disaster would result not from ambition in the hearts of foreign kings; rather, God himself would orchestrate the disaster. The Israelites earned God's judgment by disregarding his call to repentance and his clear warning of consequences for disobedience. Judah's rebellion altered their history. Jerusalem suffered ruin and God allowed Judah's people to be killed or captured because they chose to act as if God's decrees did not matter— as if God would not actually hold them accountable.

On a day of God's choosing, Jesus will return to earth and administer judgment over all mankind (Heb 10:30–31). Those who have faith in Jesus will be saved, and those who do not believe will endure everlasting punishment. Similar to Jeremiah's announcements, the world needs to know that God is real and that a coming day of judgment is certain. But Jesus promised that those who believe would not be judged (Jn 5:24).

14 They dress the wound of my people
as though it were not serious.
'Peace, peace,' they say,
when there is no peace.
15 Are they ashamed of their detestable conduct?
No, they have no shame at all;
they do not even know how to blush.
So they will fall among the fallen;
they will be brought down when I punish them,"
says the LORD.

16 This is what the LORD says:

"Stand at the crossroads and look;
ask for the ancient paths,
ask where the good way is, and walk in it,
and you will find rest for your souls.
But you said, 'We will not walk in it.'
17 I appointed watchmen over you and said,
'Listen to the sound of the trumpet!'
But you said, 'We will not listen.'
18 Therefore hear, you nations;
you who are witnesses,
observe what will happen to them.
19 Hear, you earth:
I am bringing disaster on this people,
the fruit of their schemes,
because they have not listened to my words
and have rejected my law.
20 What do I care about incense from Sheba
or sweet calamus from a distant land?
Your burnt offerings are not acceptable;
your sacrifices do not please me."

21 Therefore this is what the LORD says:

"I will put obstacles before this people.
Parents and children alike will stumble over them;
neighbors and friends will perish."

22 This is what the LORD says:

"Look, an army is coming
from the land of the north;
a great nation is being stirred up
from the ends of the earth.
23 They are armed with bow and spear;
they are cruel and show no mercy.
They sound like the roaring sea
as they ride on their horses;
they come like men in battle formation
to attack you, Daughter Zion."

24 We have heard reports about them,
and our hands hang limp.
Anguish has gripped us,
pain like that of a woman in labor.
25 Do not go out to the fields
or walk on the roads,
for the enemy has a sword,
and there is terror on every side.

[26] Put on sackcloth, my people,
and roll in ashes;
mourn with bitter wailing
as for an only son,
for suddenly the destroyer
will come upon us.

[27] "I have made you a tester of metals
and my people the ore,
that you may observe
and test their ways.
[28] They are all hardened rebels,
going about to slander.
They are bronze and iron;
they all act corruptly.
[29] The bellows blow fiercely
to burn away the lead with fire,
but the refining goes on in vain;
the wicked are not purged out.
[30] They are called rejected silver,
because the LORD has rejected them."

False Religion Worthless

7 This is the word that came to Jeremiah from the LORD: [2] "Stand at the gate of
the LORD's house and there proclaim this message:
" 'Hear the word of the LORD, all you people of Judah who come through these
gates to worship the LORD. [3] This is what the LORD Almighty, the God of Israel,
says: Reform your ways and your actions, and I will let you live in this place. [4] Do
not trust in deceptive words and say, "This is the temple of the LORD, the temple
of the LORD, the temple of the LORD!" [5] If you really change your ways and your
actions and deal with each other justly, [6] if you do not oppress the foreigner, the
fatherless or the widow and do not shed innocent blood in this place, and if you
do not follow other gods to your own harm, [7] then I will let you live in this place,
in the land I gave your ancestors for ever and ever. [8] But look, you are trusting in
deceptive words that are worthless.
[9] " 'Will you steal and murder, commit adultery and perjury,[a] burn incense to
Baal and follow other gods you have not known, [10] and then come and stand before me in this house, which bears my Name, and say, "We are safe" — safe to do
all these detestable things? [11] Has this house, which bears my Name, become a
den of robbers to you? But I have been watching! declares the LORD.
[12] " 'Go now to the place in Shiloh where I first made a dwelling for my Name,
and see what I did to it because of the wickedness of my people Israel. [13] While
you were doing all these things, declares the LORD, I spoke to you again and
again, but you did not listen; I called you, but you did not answer. [14] Therefore,
what I did to Shiloh I will now do to the house that bears my Name, the temple
you trust in, the place I gave to you and your ancestors. [15] I will thrust you from
my presence, just as I did all your fellow Israelites, the people of Ephraim.'
[16] "So do not pray for this people nor offer any plea or petition for them; do not
plead with me, for I will not listen to you. [17] Do you not see what they are doing in
the towns of Judah and in the streets of Jerusalem? [18] The children gather wood,
the fathers light the fire, and the women knead the dough and make cakes to offer to the Queen of Heaven. They pour out drink offerings to other gods to arouse
my anger. [19] But am I the one they are provoking? declares the LORD. Are they not
rather harming themselves, to their own shame?
[20] " 'Therefore this is what the Sovereign LORD says: My anger and my wrath

[a] 9 Or *and swear by false gods*

JEREMIAH 7:9 – 11

REAL SECURITY

Long before the Law, the tabernacle and the temple, God desired that his people love and follow him — joyfully reflecting his worth to the world. Disappointingly, the Israelites lost sight of the relationship's purpose and the very reason for their existence as a nation. They rejected an exclusive relationship with God yet continued to enter the temple gates to worship — going through the motions, treating the physical temple as a kind of good-luck charm. They missed the love story into which God invited them.

As they spiraled into following the same immoral and demonic practices of their ungodly neighbors, the community no longer resembled the one that God initially chose. Jeremiah used the blunt word picture of thieves hiding in a cave to confront Judah's broken moral compass and their false sense of security. Judah's association with the temple could not protect them. Even so God, in his covenant faithfulness, resolved to rescue them from themselves. He allowed Jerusalem and the temple to be utterly destroyed, arranging Babylon's invasion as a radical form of intervention for the sinful people he continued to love.

Jesus quoted part of this passage when he forcibly removed the buyers and sellers from the temple (Mt 21:13). He resented the manmade obstacles in the temple that prevented worshipers from drawing near to the Father. God will not ignore anything that hinders his people from following him wholeheartedly.

will be poured out on this place — on man and beast, on the trees of the field and
on the crops of your land — and it will burn and not be quenched.
21“ ‘This is what the LORD Almighty, the God of Israel, says: Go ahead, add
your burnt offerings to your other sacrifices and eat the meat yourselves! 22For
when I brought your ancestors out of Egypt and spoke to them, I did not just
give them commands about burnt offerings and sacrifices, 23but I gave them this
command: Obey me, and I will be your God and you will be my people. Walk
in obedience to all I command you, that it may go well with you. 24But they did
not listen or pay attention; instead, they followed the stubborn inclinations of
their evil hearts. They went backward and not forward. 25From the time your
ancestors left Egypt until now, day after day, again and again I sent you my servants the prophets. 26But they did not listen to me or pay attention. They were
stiff-necked and did more evil than their ancestors.’

27“When you tell them all this, they will not listen to you; when you call to
them, they will not answer. 28Therefore say to them, ‘This is the nation that has
not obeyed the LORD its God or responded to correction. Truth has perished; it
has vanished from their lips.

29“ ‘Cut off your hair and throw it away; take up a lament on the barren heights,
for the LORD has rejected and abandoned this generation that is under his wrath.

The Valley of Slaughter

30“ ‘The people of Judah have done evil in my eyes, declares the LORD. They
have set up their detestable idols in the house that bears my Name and have
defiled it. 31They have built the high places of Topheth in the Valley of Ben Hinnom to burn their sons and daughters in the fire — something I did not command, nor did it enter my mind. 32So beware, the days are coming, declares the
LORD, when people will no longer call it Topheth or the Valley of Ben Hinnom,
but the Valley of Slaughter, for they will bury the dead in Topheth until there
is no more room. 33Then the carcasses of this people will become food for the
birds and the wild animals, and there will be no one to frighten them away. 34I
will bring an end to the sounds of joy and gladness and to the voices of bride
and bridegroom in the towns of Judah and the streets of Jerusalem, for the land
will become desolate.

8 “ ‘At that time, declares the LORD, the bones of the kings and officials of Judah, the bones of the priests and prophets, and the bones of the people of
Jerusalem will be removed from their graves. 2They will be exposed to the sun
and the moon and all the stars of the heavens, which they have loved and served
and which they have followed and consulted and worshiped. They will not be
gathered up or buried, but will be like dung lying on the ground. 3Wherever I
banish them, all the survivors of this evil nation will prefer death to life, declares
the LORD Almighty.’

Sin and Punishment

4“Say to them, ‘This is what the LORD says:

“ ‘When people fall down, do they not get up?
    When someone turns away, do they not return?
5Why then have these people turned away?
    Why does Jerusalem always turn away?
They cling to deceit;
    they refuse to return.
6I have listened attentively,
    but they do not say what is right.
None of them repent of their wickedness,
    saying, “What have I done?”
Each pursues their own course
    like a horse charging into battle.

[7] Even the stork in the sky
knows her appointed seasons,
and the dove, the swift and the thrush
observe the time of their migration.
But my people do not know
the requirements of the LORD.

[8] " 'How can you say, "We are wise,
for we have the law of the LORD,"
when actually the lying pen of the scribes
has handled it falsely?
[9] The wise will be put to shame;
they will be dismayed and trapped.
Since they have rejected the word of the
LORD,
what kind of wisdom do they have?
[10] Therefore I will give their wives to other men
and their fields to new owners.
From the least to the greatest,
all are greedy for gain;
prophets and priests alike,
all practice deceit.
[11] They dress the wound of my people
as though it were not serious.
"Peace, peace," they say,
when there is no peace.
[12] Are they ashamed of their detestable conduct?
No, they have no shame at all;
they do not even know how to blush.
So they will fall among the fallen;
they will be brought down when they are
punished,
says the LORD.

[13] " 'I will take away their harvest,
declares the LORD.

There will be no grapes on the vine.
There will be no figs on the tree,
and their leaves will wither.
What I have given them
will be taken from them.[a] ' "
[14] Why are we sitting here?
Gather together!
Let us flee to the fortified cities
and perish there!
For the LORD our God has doomed us to perish
and given us poisoned water to drink,
because we have sinned against him.
[15] We hoped for peace
but no good has come,
for a time of healing
but there is only terror.
[16] The snorting of the enemy's horses
is heard from Dan;
at the neighing of their stallions
the whole land trembles.

[a] *13* The meaning of the Hebrew for this sentence is uncertain.

SUPERFICIAL HEALING

Jerusalem's religious officials failed to lead the people to take God seriously regarding their sin and God's judgment, but God was not issuing an idle threat in response to the Israelites' compromise and idolatry. God likens this placating behavior to medical malpractice: "They dress the wound of my people as though it were not serious" (Jer 8:11).

There was a cruelty in the religious leaders' choice to be dishonest — to withhold truth because it would have been uncomfortable and unpopular in the ears of the people. The prognosis for Jerusalem should have included warnings that their condition was terminal. Given the clarity of Jeremiah's charges against the sinful nation, the priests and prophets grossly understated the situation. God had pronounced destruction for Jerusalem, and the leaders responded with the medical equivalent of a Band-Aid® on a severed limb. The people were living in the final days of God's judgment that would result in their exile to Babylon. The false hope proclaimed by the priests and prophets offered them no genuine peace.

During the years of Jesus' earthly ministry, the people of Jerusalem were similarly unaware of the coming destruction at the hands of the Romans in 70 AD. Jesus, as God, knew all things and alluded to the trouble that lay ahead (Lk 19:41 – 44). He taught the people with an aim toward giving them peace for all eternity — not just for the next few decades. As crowds listened to Jesus teach and watched his works of compassion, they marveled at the genuine concern he had for the poor, for children, for women, for the downtrodden — for people who truly needed lasting peace. They saw in his own life that the peace Jesus desired to give was of a superior quality to anything the world could offer. And Jesus himself promised as much (Jn 14:27).

Jesus never held back on the reality of the life-and-death crisis brought about by sin. He was clear about the need for personal repentance, and just as clear about his place as the exclusive path to the Father (Jn 14:6). Sent by God, Jesus proclaimed a message of good news (Ac 10:36). Christ's words and his actions did more than comfort; they are powerful enough to heal the condition of the sinful heart.

They have come to devour
the land and everything in it,
the city and all who live there.

17 "See, I will send venomous snakes among you,
vipers that cannot be charmed,
and they will bite you,"
declares the LORD.

18 You who are my Comforter[a] in sorrow,
my heart is faint within me.
19 Listen to the cry of my people
from a land far away:
"Is the LORD not in Zion?
Is her King no longer there?"
"Why have they aroused my anger with their images,
with their worthless foreign idols?"

20 "The harvest is past,
the summer has ended,
and we are not saved."

21 Since my people are crushed, I am crushed;
I mourn, and horror grips me.
22 Is there no balm in Gilead?
Is there no physician there?
Why then is there no healing
for the wound of my people?

9[b] 1 Oh, that my head were a spring of water
and my eyes a fountain of tears!
I would weep day and night
for the slain of my people.
2 Oh, that I had in the desert
a lodging place for travelers,
so that I might leave my people
and go away from them;
for they are all adulterers,
a crowd of unfaithful people.

3 "They make ready their tongue
like a bow, to shoot lies;
it is not by truth
that they triumph[c] in the land.
They go from one sin to another;
they do not acknowledge me,"
declares the LORD.

4 "Beware of your friends;
do not trust anyone in your clan.
For every one of them is a deceiver,[d]
and every friend a slanderer.
5 Friend deceives friend,
and no one speaks the truth.
They have taught their tongues to lie;
they weary themselves with sinning.

[a] *18* The meaning of the Hebrew for this word is uncertain. [b] In Hebrew texts 9:1 is numbered 8:23, and 9:2-26 is numbered 9:1-25. [c] *3* Or *lies; / they are not valiant for truth*
[d] *4* Or *a deceiving Jacob*

JEREMIAH 9:1

A BROKEN HEART

Jeremiah was undone, overwhelmed by the state of the relationship between God and his people. God had pronounced judgment and set in motion the wheels of destruction and captivity. The prophet's grief over his people went beyond mere dread of Babylonian invasion and the subsequent slaughter. He ached over the hard hearts that prevented repentance and reconciliation with the living God, knowing that the coming judgment could have been avoided. He lamented that God's hand was forced — the people must be disciplined. "Since my people are crushed, I am crushed; I mourn, and horror grips me" (Jer 8:21). The weeping prophet lived in a storm of emotions ranging from anger to sadness to shame.

Sin grips men and women in ways that make them forget who God is and what he has done. Lack of immediate retribution leads people to doubt that God will ever act in response to their rebellion. The world teems with young and old sinners, oblivious to their future judgment. Others remain so fixated on living everyday life on earth that death and eternity seem too far off to matter. Sin is so dark that it can lead people to reject the one true God for idols made of wood, stone, silver or gold.

Jeremiah's tears mark the tragedy of a relationship wasted, of an invitation to repentance unaccepted. Jerusalem's people threw away the blessings of being chosen. They rejected the God who is infinite in glory and boundless in his desire to show love. God is worthy of unwavering faithfulness. Therefore, sin is an act of dishonor. For the people, for the Lord, for the loss and death that are to come — for all of these things, Jeremiah wept.

Jesus expressed sorrowful emotions over the way the teachers of the law misled and blinded the people to the truth. "Jerusalem, Jerusalem, you who kill the prophets and stone those sent to you, how often I have longed to gather your children together, as a hen gathers her chicks under her wings, and you were not willing" (Mt 23:37).

Heartbreak over sin is both appropriate and necessary if men and women are to find forgiveness in Jesus (Jas 4:9). Repentance — turning away from sinful ways — is the response that comes from a holy grief when a person realizes the magnitude of their offenses against God. When people confess their sin, God replaces the conviction of disobedience with forgiveness and a clean heart.

6 You[a] live in the midst of deception;
in their deceit they refuse to acknowledge me,"
declares the LORD.

7 Therefore this is what the LORD Almighty says:

"See, I will refine and test them,
for what else can I do
because of the sin of my people?
8 Their tongue is a deadly arrow;
it speaks deceitfully.
With their mouths they all speak cordially to their neighbors,
but in their hearts they set traps for them.
9 Should I not punish them for this?"
declares the LORD.
"Should I not avenge myself
on such a nation as this?"

10 I will weep and wail for the mountains
and take up a lament concerning the wilderness grasslands.
They are desolate and untraveled,
and the lowing of cattle is not heard.
The birds have all fled
and the animals are gone.

11 "I will make Jerusalem a heap of ruins,
a haunt of jackals;
and I will lay waste the towns of Judah
so no one can live there."

12 Who is wise enough to understand this? Who has been instructed by the
LORD and can explain it? Why has the land been ruined and laid waste like a
desert that no one can cross?
13 The LORD said, "It is because they have forsaken my law, which I set before
them; they have not obeyed me or followed my law. 14 Instead, they have followed the stubbornness of their hearts; they have followed the Baals, as their
ancestors taught them." 15 Therefore this is what the LORD Almighty, the God
of Israel, says: "See, I will make this people eat bitter food and drink poisoned
water. 16 I will scatter them among nations that neither they nor their ancestors
have known, and I will pursue them with the sword until I have made an end
of them."

17 This is what the LORD Almighty says:

"Consider now! Call for the wailing women to come;
send for the most skillful of them.
18 Let them come quickly
and wail over us
till our eyes overflow with tears
and water streams from our eyelids.
19 The sound of wailing is heard from Zion:
'How ruined we are!
How great is our shame!
We must leave our land
because our houses are in ruins.' "

20 Now, you women, hear the word of the LORD;
open your ears to the words of his mouth.

---

[a] 6 That is, Jeremiah (the Hebrew is singular)

Teach your daughters how to wail;
  teach one another a lament.
21 Death has climbed in through our windows
  and has entered our fortresses;
it has removed the children from the streets
  and the young men from the public squares.

22 Say, "This is what the LORD declares:

" 'Dead bodies will lie
  like dung on the open field,
like cut grain behind the reaper,
  with no one to gather them.' "

23 This is what the LORD says:

"Let not the wise boast of their wisdom
  or the strong boast of their strength
  or the rich boast of their riches,
24 but let the one who boasts boast about this:
  that they have the understanding to know me,
that I am the LORD, who exercises kindness,
  justice and righteousness on earth,
  for in these I delight,"
declares the LORD.

25 "The days are coming," declares the LORD, "when I will punish all who are
circumcised only in the flesh— 26 Egypt, Judah, Edom, Ammon, Moab and all
who live in the wilderness in distant places.[a] For all these nations are really uncircumcised, and even the whole house of Israel is uncircumcised in heart."

God and Idols

10 Hear what the LORD says to you, people of Israel. 2 This is what the LORD says:

"Do not learn the ways of the nations
  or be terrified by signs in the heavens,
  though the nations are terrified by them.
3 For the practices of the peoples are worthless;
  they cut a tree out of the forest,
  and a craftsman shapes it with his chisel.
4 They adorn it with silver and gold;
  they fasten it with hammer and nails
  so it will not totter.
5 Like a scarecrow in a cucumber field,
  their idols cannot speak;
they must be carried
  because they cannot walk.
Do not fear them;
  they can do no harm
  nor can they do any good."

6 No one is like you, LORD;
  you are great,
  and your name is mighty in power.
7 Who should not fear you,
  King of the nations?
  This is your due.

[a] 26 Or *wilderness and who clip the hair by their foreheads*

JEREMIAH 9:23–24

BOASTING

Human wisdom, strength and wealth are not the highest reasons to boast. These three blessings, though significant, are fleeting and temporary. Their value is virtually nothing when compared with the undeserved honor of knowing the God of all.

The Lord led Jeremiah to encourage boasting as long as it glorifies God as the greatest of treasures. After all, God is the One whose very nature includes grace, even though he never compromises on justice. God is the only One whose every act is right and good. Knowing God, who delights in being God, is the greatest privilege and the only reason to boast.

Knowing certain facts about God is insufficient; truly knowing him requires having a relationship with him. This is only possible now through faith in Jesus and what he accomplished by his death and resurrection (Jn 14:6). The person made new in salvation should boast out of sheer gratitude (1Co 1:31), fully aware that nothing, compared to knowing Christ Jesus as Lord, amounts to anything (Php 3:7–8).

Among all the wise leaders of the nations
 and in all their kingdoms,
 there is no one like you.

8 They are all senseless and foolish;
 they are taught by worthless wooden idols.
9 Hammered silver is brought from Tarshish
 and gold from Uphaz.
What the craftsman and goldsmith have made
 is then dressed in blue and purple —
 all made by skilled workers.
10 But the LORD is the true God;
 he is the living God, the eternal King.
When he is angry, the earth trembles;
 the nations cannot endure his wrath.

11 "Tell them this: 'These gods, who did not make the heavens and the earth, will perish from the earth and from under the heavens.' "[a]

12 But God made the earth by his power;
 he founded the world by his wisdom
 and stretched out the heavens by his understanding.
13 When he thunders, the waters in the heavens roar;
 he makes clouds rise from the ends of the earth.
He sends lightning with the rain
 and brings out the wind from his storehouses.
14 Everyone is senseless and without knowledge;
 every goldsmith is shamed by his idols.
The images he makes are a fraud;
 they have no breath in them.
15 They are worthless, the objects of mockery;
 when their judgment comes, they will perish.
16 He who is the Portion of Jacob is not like these,
 for he is the Maker of all things,
including Israel, the people of his inheritance —
 the LORD Almighty is his name.

Coming Destruction

17 Gather up your belongings to leave the land,
 you who live under siege.
18 For this is what the LORD says:
 "At this time I will hurl out
 those who live in this land;
I will bring distress on them
 so that they may be captured."

19 Woe to me because of my injury!
 My wound is incurable!
Yet I said to myself,
 "This is my sickness, and I must endure it."
20 My tent is destroyed;
 all its ropes are snapped.
My children are gone from me and are no more;
 no one is left now to pitch my tent
 or to set up my shelter.
21 The shepherds are senseless
 and do not inquire of the LORD;

[a] *11* The text of this verse is in Aramaic.

JEREMIAH 10:10

GOD IS IN CONTROL

The preceding verses point to the absurdity of worshiping idols of wood, silver or gold. *Yahweh* — Judah's God, is the *true* God. He is real and full of power. He is alive and always has been — eternally existing, neither conceived nor crafted by anyone. He is the Creator of all things seen and unseen. As the eternal King, he is supreme with no rival and no place in existence where his authority is overridden. The idols are worse than powerless — they are false, not at all alive, completely devoid of any authority.

It is right and good to hope in and pray to the living God, the eternal King. God is in control of everything that happens, and he is absolutely worthy of trust. Jesus — who is the very image of God — is "the firstborn over all creation" (Col 1:15). In him, all things — including the lives of every man and woman — hold together (Col 1:17).

so they do not prosper
and all their flock is scattered.
22 Listen! The report is coming—
a great commotion from the land of the north!
It will make the towns of Judah desolate,
a haunt of jackals.

Jeremiah's Prayer

23 LORD, I know that people's lives are not their own;
it is not for them to direct their steps.
24 Discipline me, LORD, but only in due measure—
not in your anger,
or you will reduce me to nothing.
25 Pour out your wrath on the nations
that do not acknowledge you,
on the peoples who do not call on your name.
For they have devoured Jacob;
they have devoured him completely
and destroyed his homeland.

The Covenant Is Broken

11 This is the word that came to Jeremiah from the LORD: 2"Listen to the
terms of this covenant and tell them to the people of Judah and to those
who live in Jerusalem. 3Tell them that this is what the LORD, the God of Israel,
says: 'Cursed is the one who does not obey the terms of this covenant— 4the
terms I commanded your ancestors when I brought them out of Egypt, out of
the iron-smelting furnace.' I said, 'Obey me and do everything I command you,
and you will be my people, and I will be your God. 5Then I will fulfill the oath I
swore to your ancestors, to give them a land flowing with milk and honey'—the
land you possess today."

I answered, "Amen, LORD."

6The LORD said to me, "Proclaim all these words in the towns of Judah and in
the streets of Jerusalem: 'Listen to the terms of this covenant and follow them.
7From the time I brought your ancestors up from Egypt until today, I warned
them again and again, saying, "Obey me." 8But they did not listen or pay attention; instead, they followed the stubbornness of their evil hearts. So I brought
on them all the curses of the covenant I had commanded them to follow but that
they did not keep.'"

9Then the LORD said to me, "There is a conspiracy among the people of Judah
and those who live in Jerusalem. 10They have returned to the sins of their ancestors, who refused to listen to my words. They have followed other gods to serve
them. Both Israel and Judah have broken the covenant I made with their ancestors. 11Therefore this is what the LORD says: 'I will bring on them a disaster they
cannot escape. Although they cry out to me, I will not listen to them. 12The towns
of Judah and the people of Jerusalem will go and cry out to the gods to whom
they burn incense, but they will not help them at all when disaster strikes. 13You,
Judah, have as many gods as you have towns; and the altars you have set up to
burn incense to that shameful god Baal are as many as the streets of Jerusalem.'

14"Do not pray for this people or offer any plea or petition for them, because I
will not listen when they call to me in the time of their distress.

15 "What is my beloved doing in my temple
as she, with many others, works out her evil schemes?
Can consecrated meat avert your punishment?
When you engage in your wickedness,
then you rejoice.[a]"

[a] 15 Or *Could consecrated meat avert your punishment? / Then you would rejoice*

JEREMIAH 11:1–17

COVENANT TERMS

Even though the entire earth belonged to him, God chose the nation of Israel to be in a relationship with him so he could put his goodness and greatness on display (Ex 19:4–6). He promised to be with them and to give them a land of their own. God's pledge to the people would endure even through the nation's most horrific betrayal. This covenant relationship was both unconditional and conditional: God maintained expectations for how the people would live, and the threshold for honoring the covenant was complete obedience. The benefit to Israel was astonishing—"And you will be my people, and I will be your God" (Jer 11:4). When the Israelites obeyed the Lord, they enjoyed abundant blessings. When they resisted his leadership or defied his commands, consequences always followed. Jeremiah reminds the people about the clear terms of the covenant in chapter 11.

Jesus ushered in a new covenant relationship for men and women when he suffered death and arose again (Mt 26:28). Inspired by God, Jeremiah actually predicted this new covenant (Jer 31:31). Grace enables sinful people to receive adoption as God's chosen children (Eph 1:4–5). This new covenant relationship, like the old one, includes great blessings and expectations for believers to respond to Jesus' amazing love—with acts of love for others out of gratitude to him.

16 The LORD called you a thriving olive tree
with fruit beautiful in form.
But with the roar of a mighty storm
he will set it on fire,
and its branches will be broken.

17 The LORD Almighty, who planted you, has decreed disaster for you, because
the people of both Israel and Judah have done evil and aroused my anger by
burning incense to Baal.

Plot Against Jeremiah

18 Because the LORD revealed their plot to me, I knew it, for at that time he
showed me what they were doing. 19 I had been like a gentle lamb led to the
slaughter; I did not realize that they had plotted against me, saying,

"Let us destroy the tree and its fruit;
let us cut him off from the land of the living,
that his name be remembered no more."
20 But you, LORD Almighty, who judge righteously
and test the heart and mind,
let me see your vengeance on them,
for to you I have committed my cause.

21 Therefore this is what the LORD says about the people of Anathoth who are
threatening to kill you, saying, "Do not prophesy in the name of the LORD or you
will die by our hands" — 22 therefore this is what the LORD Almighty says: "I will
punish them. Their young men will die by the sword, their sons and daughters
by famine. 23 Not even a remnant will be left to them, because I will bring disaster
on the people of Anathoth in the year of their punishment."

Jeremiah's Complaint

12 You are always righteous, LORD,
when I bring a case before you.
Yet I would speak with you about your justice:
Why does the way of the wicked prosper?
Why do all the faithless live at ease?
2 You have planted them, and they have taken root;
they grow and bear fruit.
You are always on their lips
but far from their hearts.
3 Yet you know me, LORD;
you see me and test my thoughts about you.
Drag them off like sheep to be butchered!
Set them apart for the day of slaughter!
4 How long will the land lie parched
and the grass in every field be withered?
Because those who live in it are wicked,
the animals and birds have perished.
Moreover, the people are saying,
"He will not see what happens to us."

God's Answer

5 "If you have raced with men on foot
and they have worn you out,
how can you compete with horses?
If you stumble[a] in safe country,
how will you manage in the thickets by[b] the Jordan?

[a] 5 Or *you feel secure only* [b] 5 Or *the flooding of*

JEREMIAH 12:14–16

HOPE FOR THE GENTILES

God's promise to Abraham included a future when all peoples and nations would partake in the covenant blessings (Ge 12:2–3). God desired to show all nations what life could be like when led by the one true God; through his relationship with the Israelites, he demonstrated faithful provision, constant protection and dependable intervention. Even the judgment announced and carried out in the book of Jeremiah points to the value that God placed on his relationship with Israel. The Lord would use the Babylonians to uproot both Judah and the nation's wicked neighbors. But he promised to bring exiles from each country back to their lands and to give the foreigners an opportunity to establish themselves among the Israelites (Jer 12:16).

Jesus came as Israel's Messiah, but he would also become the Savior for whoever chooses to turn to him in trust (Jn 3:16). This included the Gentiles—that is, anyone not born of Jewish descent (Lk 2:30–32). Through the Good News of salvation in Jesus Christ, men and women of every nation, tribe and tongue can have a relationship with God.

6 Your relatives, members of your own family—
even they have betrayed you;
they have raised a loud cry against you.
Do not trust them,
though they speak well of you.

7 "I will forsake my house,
abandon my inheritance;
I will give the one I love
into the hands of her enemies.
8 My inheritance has become to me
like a lion in the forest.
She roars at me;
therefore I hate her.
9 Has not my inheritance become to me
like a speckled bird of prey
that other birds of prey surround and attack?
Go and gather all the wild beasts;
bring them to devour.
10 Many shepherds will ruin my vineyard
and trample down my field;
they will turn my pleasant field
into a desolate wasteland.
11 It will be made a wasteland,
parched and desolate before me;
the whole land will be laid waste
because there is no one who cares.
12 Over all the barren heights in the desert
destroyers will swarm,
for the sword of the LORD will devour
from one end of the land to the other;
no one will be safe.
13 They will sow wheat but reap thorns;
they will wear themselves out but gain nothing.
They will bear the shame of their harvest
because of the LORD's fierce anger."

14 This is what the LORD says: "As for all my wicked neighbors who seize the
inheritance I gave my people Israel, I will uproot them from their lands and I
will uproot the people of Judah from among them. 15 But after I uproot them, I
will again have compassion and will bring each of them back to their own inheritance and their own country. 16 And if they learn well the ways of my people
and swear by my name, saying, 'As surely as the LORD lives'—even as they once
taught my people to swear by Baal—then they will be established among my
people. 17 But if any nation does not listen, I will completely uproot and destroy
it," declares the LORD.

A Linen Belt

13 This is what the LORD said to me: "Go and buy a linen belt and put it
around your waist, but do not let it touch water." 2 So I bought a belt, as the
LORD directed, and put it around my waist.
3 Then the word of the LORD came to me a second time: 4 "Take the belt you
bought and are wearing around your waist, and go now to Perath[a] and hide
it there in a crevice in the rocks." 5 So I went and hid it at Perath, as the LORD
told me.
6 Many days later the LORD said to me, "Go now to Perath and get the belt I

[a] 4 Or possibly *to the Euphrates*; similarly in verses 5-7

told you to hide there." [7]So I went to Perath and dug up the belt and took it from
the place where I had hidden it, but now it was ruined and completely useless.
[8]Then the word of the LORD came to me: [9]"This is what the LORD says: 'In the
same way I will ruin the pride of Judah and the great pride of Jerusalem. [10]These
wicked people, who refuse to listen to my words, who follow the stubbornness
of their hearts and go after other gods to serve and worship them, will be like
this belt — completely useless! [11]For as a belt is bound around the waist, so I
bound all the people of Israel and all the people of Judah to me,' declares the
LORD, 'to be my people for my renown and praise and honor. But they have not
listened.'

Wineskins

[12]"Say to them: 'This is what the LORD, the God of Israel, says: Every wineskin
should be filled with wine.' And if they say to you, 'Don't we know that every
wineskin should be filled with wine?' [13]then tell them, 'This is what the LORD
says: I am going to fill with drunkenness all who live in this land, including the
kings who sit on David's throne, the priests, the prophets and all those living in
Jerusalem. [14]I will smash them one against the other, parents and children alike,
declares the LORD. I will allow no pity or mercy or compassion to keep me from
destroying them.'"

Threat of Captivity

[15]Hear and pay attention,
  do not be arrogant,
  for the LORD has spoken.
[16]Give glory to the LORD your God
  before he brings the darkness,
before your feet stumble
  on the darkening hills.
You hope for light,
  but he will turn it to utter darkness
  and change it to deep gloom.
[17]If you do not listen,
  I will weep in secret
  because of your pride;
my eyes will weep bitterly,
  overflowing with tears,
  because the LORD's flock will be taken captive.

[18]Say to the king and to the queen mother,
  "Come down from your thrones,
for your glorious crowns
  will fall from your heads."
[19]The cities in the Negev will be shut up,
  and there will be no one to open them.
All Judah will be carried into exile,
  carried completely away.

[20]Look up and see
  those who are coming from the north.
Where is the flock that was entrusted to you,
  the sheep of which you boasted?
[21]What will you say when the LORD sets over you
  those you cultivated as your special allies?
Will not pain grip you
  like that of a woman in labor?
[22]And if you ask yourself,
  "Why has this happened to me?" —

JEREMIAH 14:8

THE HOPE AND SAVIOR OF ISRAEL

Judah experienced a terrible drought that greatly affected both people and animals. Wells dried up and the land, parched and cracked, would not produce food. Jeremiah asked God to mercifully intervene even though the people had sinned (Jer 14:7). God's silence in their situation felt like God's absence from their lives. Jeremiah prayed with informed faith, acknowledging that God was "the hope of Israel" and "its Savior in times of distress" (v. 8). Many times before, God had proven his power by rescuing the people from trouble. Jeremiah asked him to do so again.

Between the days of the Old Testament and the era of the New Testament, some 400 years went by without a word from God. The people longed for the spiritual drought to end—they were desperate for God to speak or move (Lk 2:25). Jesus came into these dark and dry times to bring light and life (Jn 1:4). He was and is the answer to the hope of all nations; a Savior who brings the possibility of grace and eternal life to all people (2Ti 1:9–10).

it is because of your many sins
that your skirts have been torn off
and your body mistreated.
23 Can an Ethiopian[a] change his skin
or a leopard its spots?
Neither can you do good
who are accustomed to doing evil.

24 "I will scatter you like chaff
driven by the desert wind.
25 This is your lot,
the portion I have decreed for you,"
declares the LORD,
"because you have forgotten me
and trusted in false gods.
26 I will pull up your skirts over your face
that your shame may be seen—
27 your adulteries and lustful neighings,
your shameless prostitution!
I have seen your detestable acts
on the hills and in the fields.
Woe to you, Jerusalem!
How long will you be unclean?"

Drought, Famine, Sword

14 This is the word of the LORD that came to Jeremiah concerning the drought:

2 "Judah mourns,
her cities languish;
they wail for the land,
and a cry goes up from Jerusalem.
3 The nobles send their servants for water;
they go to the cisterns
but find no water.
They return with their jars unfilled;
dismayed and despairing,
they cover their heads.
4 The ground is cracked
because there is no rain in the land;
the farmers are dismayed
and cover their heads.
5 Even the doe in the field
deserts her newborn fawn
because there is no grass.
6 Wild donkeys stand on the barren heights
and pant like jackals;
their eyes fail
for lack of food."

7 Although our sins testify against us,
do something, LORD, for the sake of your name.
For we have often rebelled;
we have sinned against you.
8 You who are the hope of Israel,
its Savior in times of distress,

[a] 23 Hebrew *Cushite* (probably a person from the upper Nile region)

why are you like a stranger in the land,
like a traveler who stays only a night?
9 Why are you like a man taken by surprise,
like a warrior powerless to save?
You are among us, LORD,
and we bear your name;
do not forsake us!

10 This is what the LORD says about this people:

"They greatly love to wander;
they do not restrain their feet.
So the LORD does not accept them;
he will now remember their wickedness
and punish them for their sins."

11 Then the LORD said to me, "Do not pray for the well-being of this people.
12 Although they fast, I will not listen to their cry; though they offer burnt offerings and grain offerings, I will not accept them. Instead, I will destroy them with
the sword, famine and plague."
13 But I said, "Alas, Sovereign LORD! The prophets keep telling them, 'You will
not see the sword or suffer famine. Indeed, I will give you lasting peace in this
place.' "
14 Then the LORD said to me, "The prophets are prophesying lies in my name.
I have not sent them or appointed them or spoken to them. They are prophesying to you false visions, divinations, idolatries[a] and the delusions of their own
minds. 15 Therefore this is what the LORD says about the prophets who are prophesying in my name: I did not send them, yet they are saying, 'No sword or famine will touch this land.' Those same prophets will perish by sword and famine.
16 And the people they are prophesying to will be thrown out into the streets of
Jerusalem because of the famine and sword. There will be no one to bury them,
their wives, their sons and their daughters. I will pour out on them the calamity
they deserve.

17 "Speak this word to them:

" 'Let my eyes overflow with tears
night and day without ceasing;
for the Virgin Daughter, my people,
has suffered a grievous wound,
a crushing blow.
18 If I go into the country,
I see those slain by the sword;
if I go into the city,
I see the ravages of famine.
Both prophet and priest
have gone to a land they know not.' "
19 Have you rejected Judah completely?
Do you despise Zion?
Why have you afflicted us
so that we cannot be healed?
We hoped for peace
but no good has come,
for a time of healing
but there is only terror.
20 We acknowledge our wickedness, LORD,
and the guilt of our ancestors;
we have indeed sinned against you.

[a] 14 Or *visions, worthless divinations*

[21] For the sake of your name do not despise us;
do not dishonor your glorious throne.
Remember your covenant with us
and do not break it.
[22] Do any of the worthless idols of the nations bring rain?
Do the skies themselves send down showers?
No, it is you, LORD our God.
Therefore our hope is in you,
for you are the one who does all this.

15 Then the LORD said to me: "Even if Moses and Samuel were to stand before me, my heart would not go out to this people. Send them away from
my presence! Let them go! [2]And if they ask you, 'Where shall we go?' tell them,
'This is what the LORD says:

" 'Those destined for death, to death;
those for the sword, to the sword;
those for starvation, to starvation;
those for captivity, to captivity.'

[3]"I will send four kinds of destroyers against them," declares the LORD, "the
sword to kill and the dogs to drag away and the birds and the wild animals to
devour and destroy. [4]I will make them abhorrent to all the kingdoms of the earth
because of what Manasseh son of Hezekiah king of Judah did in Jerusalem.

[5] "Who will have pity on you, Jerusalem?
Who will mourn for you?
Who will stop to ask how you are?
[6] You have rejected me," declares the LORD.
"You keep on backsliding.
So I will reach out and destroy you;
I am tired of holding back.
[7] I will winnow them with a winnowing fork
at the city gates of the land.
I will bring bereavement and destruction on my people,
for they have not changed their ways.
[8] I will make their widows more numerous
than the sand of the sea.
At midday I will bring a destroyer
against the mothers of their young men;
suddenly I will bring down on them
anguish and terror.
[9] The mother of seven will grow faint
and breathe her last.
Her sun will set while it is still day;
she will be disgraced and humiliated.
I will put the survivors to the sword
before their enemies,"
declares the LORD.

[10] Alas, my mother, that you gave me birth,
a man with whom the whole land strives and contends!
I have neither lent nor borrowed,
yet everyone curses me.

[11] The LORD said,

"Surely I will deliver you for a good purpose;
surely I will make your enemies plead with you
in times of disaster and times of distress.

12 "Can a man break iron —
iron from the north — or bronze?
13 "Your wealth and your treasures
I will give as plunder, without charge,
because of all your sins
throughout your country.
14 I will enslave you to your enemies
in[a] a land you do not know,
for my anger will kindle a fire
that will burn against you."

15 LORD, you understand;
remember me and care for me.
Avenge me on my persecutors.
You are long-suffering — do not take me away;
think of how I suffer reproach for your sake.
16 When your words came, I ate them;
they were my joy and my heart's delight,
for I bear your name,
LORD God Almighty.
17 I never sat in the company of revelers,
never made merry with them;
I sat alone because your hand was on me
and you had filled me with indignation.
18 Why is my pain unending
and my wound grievous and incurable?
You are to me like a deceptive brook,
like a spring that fails.

19 Therefore this is what the LORD says:

"If you repent, I will restore you
that you may serve me;
if you utter worthy, not worthless, words,
you will be my spokesman.
Let this people turn to you,
but you must not turn to them.
20 I will make you a wall to this people,
a fortified wall of bronze;
they will fight against you
but will not overcome you,
for I am with you
to rescue and save you,"

declares the LORD.

21 "I will save you from the hands of the wicked
and deliver you from the grasp of the cruel."

Day of Disaster

16 Then the word of the LORD came to me: 2 "You must not marry and have
sons or daughters in this place." 3 For this is what the LORD says about the
sons and daughters born in this land and about the women who are their mothers and the men who are their fathers: 4 "They will die of deadly diseases. They
will not be mourned or buried but will be like dung lying on the ground. They
will perish by sword and famine, and their dead bodies will become food for the
birds and the wild animals."

[a] *14* Some Hebrew manuscripts, Septuagint and Syriac (see also 17:4); most Hebrew manuscripts *I will cause your enemies to bring you / into*

JEREMIAH 15:18

STREAMS OF LIVING WATER?

God called Jeremiah to announce the coming judgment, and God protected his life. Yet the prophet was grieved by the message he had to proclaim, and he suffered under the hardship and rejection he experienced from the people (Jer 15:10). Jeremiah continually pleaded with God to relent from punishing his people — to forgive and to spare them. But God held his ground, intent on dispensing justice to those who had abandoned him to worship idols. Jeremiah's pain was a mixture of grief and frustration. He was sickened by the situation — he saw the inevitable disaster and knew that Judah deserved it, yet he still pleaded with God on behalf of the people. Jeremiah was disappointed that God would not change his mind; he compared God to a spring that fails to produce water.

In a conversation with a woman at a well, Jesus compared himself to a spring producing living water (Jn 4:10). While life as a disciple of Jesus includes a flow of many blessings, there are no guarantees that life will be free of hardship or suffering. Grace covers sin, and salvation through Jesus provides eternal life. But grace does not preclude dark and difficult days (Jn 16:33). Following Jesus requires faith in God's sovereign plan; this faith provides perspective on every event in life. Jesus offers an antidote to the frustration and disappointment believers might experience when some prayers go unanswered. He has promised to be with us wherever we go (Mt 28:20).

[5]For this is what the LORD says: "Do not enter a house where there is a funeral meal; do not go to mourn or show sympathy, because I have withdrawn my
blessing, my love and my pity from this people," declares the LORD. [6]"Both high
and low will die in this land. They will not be buried or mourned, and no one
will cut themselves or shave their head for the dead. [7]No one will offer food to
comfort those who mourn for the dead — not even for a father or a mother — nor
will anyone give them a drink to console them.

[8]"And do not enter a house where there is feasting and sit down to eat and
drink. [9]For this is what the LORD Almighty, the God of Israel, says: Before your
eyes and in your days I will bring an end to the sounds of joy and gladness and to
the voices of bride and bridegroom in this place.

[10]"When you tell these people all this and they ask you, 'Why has the LORD
decreed such a great disaster against us? What wrong have we done? What sin
have we committed against the LORD our God?' [11]then say to them, 'It is because your ancestors forsook me,' declares the LORD, 'and followed other gods
and served and worshiped them. They forsook me and did not keep my law.
[12]But you have behaved more wickedly than your ancestors. See how all of you
are following the stubbornness of your evil hearts instead of obeying me. [13]So
I will throw you out of this land into a land neither you nor your ancestors have
known, and there you will serve other gods day and night, for I will show you
no favor.'

[14]"However, the days are coming," declares the LORD, "when it will no longer
be said, 'As surely as the LORD lives, who brought the Israelites up out of Egypt,'
[15]but it will be said, 'As surely as the LORD lives, who brought the Israelites up out
of the land of the north and out of all the countries where he had banished them.'
For I will restore them to the land I gave their ancestors.

[16]"But now I will send for many fishermen," declares the LORD, "and they will
catch them. After that I will send for many hunters, and they will hunt them
down on every mountain and hill and from the crevices of the rocks. [17]My eyes
are on all their ways; they are not hidden from me, nor is their sin concealed from
my eyes. [18]I will repay them double for their wickedness and their sin, because
they have defiled my land with the lifeless forms of their vile images and have
filled my inheritance with their detestable idols."

[19]LORD, my strength and my fortress,
my refuge in time of distress,
to you the nations will come
from the ends of the earth and say,
"Our ancestors possessed nothing but false gods,
worthless idols that did them no good.
[20]Do people make their own gods?
Yes, but they are not gods!"

[21]"Therefore I will teach them —
this time I will teach them
my power and might.
Then they will know
that my name is the LORD.

17 "Judah's sin is engraved with an iron tool,
inscribed with a flint point,
on the tablets of their hearts
and on the horns of their altars.
[2]Even their children remember
their altars and Asherah poles[a]
beside the spreading trees
and on the high hills.

[a] 2 That is, wooden symbols of the goddess Asherah

JEREMIAH 16:14 – 15

GATHERING THE SCATTERED

Just after God declared that he would exile Judah, he promised a future restoration. The Babylonian exile was a terrible and traumatic season — the people of Judah were scattered to foreign territory, enslaved and separated from worship. But God, through Jeremiah, assured the people that one day they would return and be restored to their land.

Those who know and follow Jesus cling to the promise that Christ will one day return to gather his people from this sin-corrupted earth (Mt 24:31). Jesus pledged that no matter how much his church suffered and regardless of how far they became scattered, he would one day call them to be with him. In the same way that God called his people out of exile to return to their land, Jesus will call his church out of exile in the world to enjoy him forever in heaven (1Th 4:16 – 17).

3 My mountain in the land
and your[a] wealth and all your treasures
I will give away as plunder,
together with your high places,
because of sin throughout your country.
4 Through your own fault you will lose
the inheritance I gave you.
I will enslave you to your enemies
in a land you do not know,
for you have kindled my anger,
and it will burn forever."

5 This is what the LORD says:

"Cursed is the one who trusts in man,
who draws strength from mere flesh
and whose heart turns away from the LORD.
6 That person will be like a bush in the wastelands;
they will not see prosperity when it comes.
They will dwell in the parched places of the desert,
in a salt land where no one lives.

7 "But blessed is the one who trusts in the LORD,
whose confidence is in him.
8 They will be like a tree planted by the water
that sends out its roots by the stream.
It does not fear when heat comes;
its leaves are always green.
It has no worries in a year of drought
and never fails to bear fruit."

9 The heart is deceitful above all things
and beyond cure.
Who can understand it?

10 "I the LORD search the heart
and examine the mind,
to reward each person according to their conduct,
according to what their deeds deserve."

11 Like a partridge that hatches eggs it did not lay
are those who gain riches by unjust means.
When their lives are half gone, their riches will desert them,
and in the end they will prove to be fools.

12 A glorious throne, exalted from the beginning,
is the place of our sanctuary.
13 LORD, you are the hope of Israel;
all who forsake you will be put to shame.
Those who turn away from you will be written in the dust
because they have forsaken the LORD,
the spring of living water.

14 Heal me, LORD, and I will be healed;
save me and I will be saved,
for you are the one I praise.
15 They keep saying to me,
"Where is the word of the LORD?
Let it now be fulfilled!"

---

[a] 2,3 Or *hills* / [3]*and the mountains of the land.* / *Your*

JEREMIAH 17:9

DECEITFUL HEARTS

Men and women were created in perfection with a pure heart to enjoy God. When Adam and Eve chose to defy God and to embrace sin, all that was perfect, including the human heart, became corrupted. This defiance of God separated people from their Creator, and the sin of Adam passed down to the whole human race. The root of this original sin is present at conception and leads to actual sin in the life of every man, woman and child. All people have sinned against God, turning away from his laws and expectations (Ro 3:10).

God has been absolutely clear about what he requires. He has proclaimed warnings about disobedience. He has anointed prophets to remind people of what a life lived in obedience looks like as opposed to death through sin. Yet the human heart's default inclination is toward defiance and self-service.

The solution to a person's corrupted heart is not an attempt to try harder, to work toward a change of behavior. There is no hope for forced or natural improvement (Jer 17:9). Beyond simple selfishness or unkindness, sinful nature carries people to dark and wicked places far from God's life-giving paths (Mt 15:19). Men and women need a new nature — a new heart. The prophet Ezekiel announced that one day God would provide the cure for the sickness of sin: "I will give you a new heart and put a new spirit in you; I will remove from you your heart of stone and give you a heart of flesh" (Eze 36:26).

Jesus came into the world and lived a sinless life. He gave himself as a perfect sacrifice to pay in full the debt of humankind's sin. He rose from the dead to defeat the power of death for all time. Believing in him and trusting in his saving work secures forgiveness for any person. On top of this, faith in Jesus gives men and women what they desperately need — a new heart. Everyone who believes in him is made new (2Co 5:17). Through the power of the Holy Spirit, Christians can put off the old, corrupted self and put on the new self that is created through faith in Jesus.

16I have not run away from being your shepherd;
  you know I have not desired the day of despair.
  What passes my lips is open before you.
17Do not be a terror to me;
  you are my refuge in the day of disaster.
18Let my persecutors be put to shame,
  but keep me from shame;
let them be terrified,
  but keep me from terror.
Bring on them the day of disaster;
  destroy them with double destruction.

Keeping the Sabbath Day Holy

19This is what the LORD said to me: "Go and stand at the Gate of the People,[a]
through which the kings of Judah go in and out; stand also at all the other gates
of Jerusalem. 20Say to them, 'Hear the word of the LORD, you kings of Judah and
all people of Judah and everyone living in Jerusalem who come through these
gates. 21This is what the LORD says: Be careful not to carry a load on the Sabbath day or bring it through the gates of Jerusalem. 22Do not bring a load out of
your houses or do any work on the Sabbath, but keep the Sabbath day holy, as
I commanded your ancestors. 23Yet they did not listen or pay attention; they
were stiff-necked and would not listen or respond to discipline. 24But if you are
careful to obey me, declares the LORD, and bring no load through the gates of
this city on the Sabbath, but keep the Sabbath day holy by not doing any work
on it, 25then kings who sit on David's throne will come through the gates of this
city with their officials. They and their officials will come riding in chariots and
on horses, accompanied by the men of Judah and those living in Jerusalem,
and this city will be inhabited forever. 26People will come from the towns of Judah and the villages around Jerusalem, from the territory of Benjamin and the
western foothills, from the hill country and the Negev, bringing burnt offerings
and sacrifices, grain offerings and incense, and bringing thank offerings to the
house of the LORD. 27But if you do not obey me to keep the Sabbath day holy by
not carrying any load as you come through the gates of Jerusalem on the Sabbath day, then I will kindle an unquenchable fire in the gates of Jerusalem that
will consume her fortresses.' "

At the Potter's House

18 This is the word that came to Jeremiah from the LORD: 2"Go down to the
potter's house, and there I will give you my message." 3So I went down to
the potter's house, and I saw him working at the wheel. 4But the pot he was shaping from the clay was marred in his hands; so the potter formed it into another
pot, shaping it as seemed best to him.

5Then the word of the LORD came to me. 6He said, "Can I not do with you, Israel, as this potter does?" declares the LORD. "Like clay in the hand of the potter, so
are you in my hand, Israel. 7If at any time I announce that a nation or kingdom is
to be uprooted, torn down and destroyed, 8and if that nation I warned repents of
its evil, then I will relent and not inflict on it the disaster I had planned. 9And if at
another time I announce that a nation or kingdom is to be built up and planted,
10and if it does evil in my sight and does not obey me, then I will reconsider the
good I had intended to do for it.

11"Now therefore say to the people of Judah and those living in Jerusalem,
'This is what the LORD says: Look! I am preparing a disaster for you and devising
a plan against you. So turn from your evil ways, each one of you, and reform your
ways and your actions.' 12But they will reply, 'It's no use. We will continue with
our own plans; we will all follow the stubbornness of our evil hearts.' "

---

[a] *19* Or *Army*

GOD IS THE POTTER

God proposed the analogy of potter and clay as a picture of his power and sovereignty and to illustrate the futility of his people's stubbornness. At the Lord's instruction, Jeremiah observed the potter engaging the soft clay — determining its final form according to his pleasure and will (Jer 18:4). The same lump of clay could end up as an oil lamp, a bowl, a vessel for water or any other creation. The purpose in the mind of the artist determined the pull and pressure on the clay, combining with the speed of the wheel to spin out a desired shape. The potter was the sole determiner of the clay's destiny.

In the same way, the Lord alone controlled the Israelites' destiny. At any point, God could position Judah as a most-favored nation — thriving and advancing beyond all other peoples. At any point, the process of building could be halted and the form collapsed to begin something different (Jer 18:7 – 10). The Israelites attempted to resist God, but they did not succeed. They rejected the design he wanted for his people, pressing their own desires for going their own way. Over time, they abandoned their covenant with God to worship false gods. Faithful to his word, God arranged to discipline his children when they refused to repent.

The judgment of Judah through being conquered and exiled was a reminder that the clay was never free to determine its own form. Following a siege and the people's capture, the ruins of Jerusalem would become a monument to foolishness — of the people's attempt to defy the living God (Jer 18:16 – 17).

In his letter to the Romans, Paul asserted the same principle the Lord showed to Jeremiah: In the end, the fate of the clay is always dependent on the will of the potter (Ro 9:19 – 21). The rebel's resolve is irrelevant. God will not be mocked. People who sin never actually *get away* with defying him. At the cross of Christ, God demonstrated his justice to eventually punish previously unaddressed sin (Ro 3:25).

God invites all people to enjoy a relationship with him, to participate in abundant life through happy obedience to his ways. Jesus modeled the ideal of cooperating with God, demonstrating perfect obedience to the Father. On the night of his betrayal, completely aware of the horrors ahead, Jesus yielded to his Father's ultimate will (Mt 26:39).

[13]Therefore this is what the LORD says:

"Inquire among the nations:
Who has ever heard anything like this?
A most horrible thing has been done
by Virgin Israel.
[14]Does the snow of Lebanon
ever vanish from its rocky slopes?
Do its cool waters from distant sources
ever stop flowing?[a]
[15]Yet my people have forgotten me;
they burn incense to worthless idols,
which made them stumble in their ways,
in the ancient paths.
They made them walk in byways,
on roads not built up.
[16]Their land will be an object of horror
and of lasting scorn;
all who pass by will be appalled
and will shake their heads.
[17]Like a wind from the east,
I will scatter them before their enemies;
I will show them my back and not my face
in the day of their disaster."

[18]They said, "Come, let's make plans against Jeremiah; for the teaching of the
law by the priest will not cease, nor will counsel from the wise, nor the word from
the prophets. So come, let's attack him with our tongues and pay no attention to
anything he says."

[19]Listen to me, LORD;
hear what my accusers are saying!
[20]Should good be repaid with evil?
Yet they have dug a pit for me.
Remember that I stood before you
and spoke in their behalf
to turn your wrath away from them.
[21]So give their children over to famine;
hand them over to the power of the sword.
Let their wives be made childless and widows;
let their men be put to death,
their young men slain by the sword in battle.
[22]Let a cry be heard from their houses
when you suddenly bring invaders against them,
for they have dug a pit to capture me
and have hidden snares for my feet.
[23]But you, LORD, know
all their plots to kill me.
Do not forgive their crimes
or blot out their sins from your sight.
Let them be overthrown before you;
deal with them in the time of your anger.

19 This is what the LORD says: "Go and buy a clay jar from a potter. Take along
some of the elders of the people and of the priests [2]and go out to the Valley of Ben Hinnom, near the entrance of the Potsherd Gate. There proclaim the
words I tell you, [3]and say, 'Hear the word of the LORD, you kings of Judah and

[a] *14* The meaning of the Hebrew for this sentence is uncertain.

people of Jerusalem. This is what the LORD Almighty, the God of Israel, says: Listen! I am going to bring a disaster on this place that will make the ears of everyone who hears of it tingle. 4For they have forsaken me and made this a place of foreign gods; they have burned incense in it to gods that neither they nor their ancestors nor the kings of Judah ever knew, and they have filled this place with the blood of the innocent. 5They have built the high places of Baal to burn their children in the fire as offerings to Baal — something I did not command or mention, nor did it enter my mind. 6So beware, the days are coming, declares the LORD, when people will no longer call this place Topheth or the Valley of Ben Hinnom, but the Valley of Slaughter.

7" 'In this place I will ruin[a] the plans of Judah and Jerusalem. I will make them fall by the sword before their enemies, at the hands of those who want to kill them, and I will give their carcasses as food to the birds and the wild animals. 8I will devastate this city and make it an object of horror and scorn; all who pass by will be appalled and will scoff because of all its wounds. 9I will make them eat the flesh of their sons and daughters, and they will eat one another's flesh because their enemies will press the siege so hard against them to destroy them.'

10"Then break the jar while those who go with you are watching, 11and say to them, 'This is what the LORD Almighty says: I will smash this nation and this city just as this potter's jar is smashed and cannot be repaired. They will bury the dead in Topheth until there is no more room. 12This is what I will do to this place and to those who live here, declares the LORD. I will make this city like Topheth. 13The houses in Jerusalem and those of the kings of Judah will be defiled like this place, Topheth — all the houses where they burned incense on the roofs to all the starry hosts and poured out drink offerings to other gods.' "

14Jeremiah then returned from Topheth, where the LORD had sent him to prophesy, and stood in the court of the LORD's temple and said to all the people, 15"This is what the LORD Almighty, the God of Israel, says: 'Listen! I am going to bring on this city and all the villages around it every disaster I pronounced against them, because they were stiff-necked and would not listen to my words.' "

Jeremiah and Pashhur

20 When the priest Pashhur son of Immer, the official in charge of the temple of the LORD, heard Jeremiah prophesying these things, 2he had Jeremiah the prophet beaten and put in the stocks at the Upper Gate of Benjamin at the LORD's temple. 3The next day, when Pashhur released him from the stocks, Jeremiah said to him, "The LORD's name for you is not Pashhur, but Terror on Every Side. 4For this is what the LORD says: 'I will make you a terror to yourself and to all your friends; with your own eyes you will see them fall by the sword of their enemies. I will give all Judah into the hands of the king of Babylon, who will carry them away to Babylon or put them to the sword. 5I will deliver all the wealth of this city into the hands of their enemies — all its products, all its valuables and all the treasures of the kings of Judah. They will take it away as plunder and carry it off to Babylon. 6And you, Pashhur, and all who live in your house will go into exile to Babylon. There you will die and be buried, you and all your friends to whom you have prophesied lies.' "

Jeremiah's Complaint

7You deceived[b] me, LORD, and I was deceived[b];
you overpowered me and prevailed.
I am ridiculed all day long;
everyone mocks me.
8Whenever I speak, I cry out
proclaiming violence and destruction.

[a] 7 The Hebrew for *ruin* sounds like the Hebrew for *jar* (see verses 1 and 10).
[b] 7 Or *persuaded*

JEREMIAH 20:7 – 9

FIRED UP TO SHARE THE WORD

Jeremiah lamented that serving as the Lord's messenger of warning had brought him unending insult and rejection (Jer 20:7 – 8). Yet he could not physically withhold the news of God's impending judgment; the words were like a raging fire within him (v. 9). He could not remain silent about Judah's need to repent and return to the Lord, and the people needed to connect the coming tragedy to God's punishment for their disobedience and betrayal. Regardless of the resulting mistreatment, Jeremiah had no choice but to speak the words God put in his heart.

When John the Baptist saw Jesus approaching, he, like Jeremiah, found himself unable to remain silent. With joy John blurted out, "Look, the Lamb of God, who takes away the sin of the world!" (Jn 1:29). Similarly, the apostle Paul's life was so radically changed by Christ that he could not keep the gospel to himself (Ac 26:19 – 20). Throughout history, Christ's true followers have experienced the same compelling desire: to tell others that God is real and that a relationship with him is possible through Jesus. Communicating a person's need for the Savior includes highlighting the reality of sin. This message can result in mistreatment when prideful people resist the notion of their sinfulness. Yet, the bad news about sin and the good news about grace through Jesus are too important for Christians to keep to themselves.

So the word of the LORD has brought me
  insult and reproach all day long.
[9] But if I say, "I will not mention his word
  or speak anymore in his name,"
his word is in my heart like a fire,
  a fire shut up in my bones.
I am weary of holding it in;
  indeed, I cannot.
[10] I hear many whispering,
  "Terror on every side!
  Denounce him! Let's denounce him!"
All my friends
  are waiting for me to slip, saying,
"Perhaps he will be deceived;
  then we will prevail over him
  and take our revenge on him."

[11] But the LORD is with me like a mighty warrior;
  so my persecutors will stumble and not prevail.
They will fail and be thoroughly disgraced;
  their dishonor will never be forgotten.
[12] LORD Almighty, you who examine the righteous
  and probe the heart and mind,
let me see your vengeance on them,
  for to you I have committed my cause.

[13] Sing to the LORD!
  Give praise to the LORD!
He rescues the life of the needy
  from the hands of the wicked.

[14] Cursed be the day I was born!
  May the day my mother bore me not be blessed!
[15] Cursed be the man who brought my father the news,
  who made him very glad, saying,
  "A child is born to you — a son!"
[16] May that man be like the towns
  the LORD overthrew without pity.
May he hear wailing in the morning,
  a battle cry at noon.
[17] For he did not kill me in the womb,
  with my mother as my grave,
  her womb enlarged forever.
[18] Why did I ever come out of the womb
  to see trouble and sorrow
  and to end my days in shame?

God Rejects Zedekiah's Request

21 The word came to Jeremiah from the LORD when King Zedekiah sent to
him Pashhur son of Malkijah and the priest Zephaniah son of Maaseiah.
They said: [2] "Inquire now of the LORD for us because Nebuchadnezzar[a] king of
Babylon is attacking us. Perhaps the LORD will perform wonders for us as in
times past so that he will withdraw from us."
[3] But Jeremiah answered them, "Tell Zedekiah, [4] 'This is what the LORD, the
God of Israel, says: I am about to turn against you the weapons of war that
are in your hands, which you are using to fight the king of Babylon and the

[a] 2 Hebrew *Nebuchadrezzar,* of which *Nebuchadnezzar* is a variant; here and often in Jeremiah and Ezekiel

Babylonians[a] who are outside the wall besieging you. And I will gather them
inside this city. 5I myself will fight against you with an outstretched hand and a
mighty arm in furious anger and in great wrath. 6I will strike down those who
live in this city—both man and beast—and they will die of a terrible plague.
7After that, declares the LORD, I will give Zedekiah king of Judah, his officials
and the people in this city who survive the plague, sword and famine, into the
hands of Nebuchadnezzar king of Babylon and to their enemies who want to
kill them. He will put them to the sword; he will show them no mercy or pity or
compassion.'

8"Furthermore, tell the people, 'This is what the LORD says: See, I am setting
before you the way of life and the way of death. 9Whoever stays in this city will
die by the sword, famine or plague. But whoever goes out and surrenders to the
Babylonians who are besieging you will live; they will escape with their lives.
10I have determined to do this city harm and not good, declares the LORD. It will
be given into the hands of the king of Babylon, and he will destroy it with fire.'

11"Moreover, say to the royal house of Judah, 'Hear the word of the LORD.
12This is what the LORD says to you, house of David:

"'Administer justice every morning;
  rescue from the hand of the oppressor
  the one who has been robbed,
or my wrath will break out and burn like fire
  because of the evil you have done—
  burn with no one to quench it.
13I am against you, Jerusalem,
  you who live above this valley
  on the rocky plateau, declares the LORD—
you who say, "Who can come against us?
  Who can enter our refuge?"
14I will punish you as your deeds deserve,
  declares the LORD.
I will kindle a fire in your forests
  that will consume everything around you.'"

Judgment Against Wicked Kings

22 This is what the LORD says: "Go down to the palace of the king of Judah
and proclaim this message there: 2'Hear the word of the LORD to you, king
of Judah, you who sit on David's throne—you, your officials and your people
who come through these gates. 3This is what the LORD says: Do what is just and
right. Rescue from the hand of the oppressor the one who has been robbed. Do
no wrong or violence to the foreigner, the fatherless or the widow, and do not
shed innocent blood in this place. 4For if you are careful to carry out these commands, then kings who sit on David's throne will come through the gates of this
palace, riding in chariots and on horses, accompanied by their officials and their
people. 5But if you do not obey these commands, declares the LORD, I swear by
myself that this palace will become a ruin.'"

6For this is what the LORD says about the palace of the king of Judah:

"Though you are like Gilead to me,
  like the summit of Lebanon,
I will surely make you like a wasteland,
  like towns not inhabited.
7I will send destroyers against you,
  each man with his weapons,
and they will cut up your fine cedar beams
  and throw them into the fire.

[a] 4 Or *Chaldeans*; also in verse 9

THE LEAST OF THESE

Jeremiah delivered a word from the Lord to the king's court. In light of the Israelites' behavior, the Lord had a lot to say regarding their potential destruction. However, Jeremiah did not start out his prophetic word with destruction. Instead, he started with a command: "Do what is just and right" (v. 3). The verse continues on to command that those listening to Jeremiah rescue those who have been robbed; that they not violate the foreigner, the fatherless or the widow, and that they avoid shedding innocent blood. Despite how far away the people drifted from the Lord, God gave them a few simple commands that gave them the opportunity to bring back the blessings they so strongly desired.

Jesus taught that whatever anyone does for "the least of these" they do for him (Mt 25:45). His teaching echoes the same commandments that God gave the people in Jeremiah 22:3. God deeply desires that his people care for those who need to be cared for the most; so much so that he considers it directly serving him when they serve someone in need. James 1:27 also says that pure and faultless religion is "to look after orphans and widows in their distress," and at the time when James wrote his letter, the idea of caring for those who were less fortunate was not a novel concept. God had been telling his people to care for and rescue those in need since the Law of Moses; Jesus told his followers the same thing, and James wrote to remind everyone of the same truth once more. God's pattern of urging his people to care for "the least of these" is crystal clear in Scripture.

The first five verses of Jeremiah 22 describe God's desires for King Zedekiah and his people: how they can obey him, and what will happen if they do. However, the next four verses give a tragic description of what was about to happen because they did not listen. For believers today, God has given his own word, Jesus' word and James's word. Zedekiah and his court failed to listen to Jeremiah and they suffered for it, but the same does not have to be true of God's people today. God's desire is straightforward, and his commandment is clear: Love the least of these.

[8]"People from many nations will pass by this city and will ask one another,
'Why has the LORD done such a thing to this great city?' [9]And the answer will
be: 'Because they have forsaken the covenant of the LORD their God and have
worshiped and served other gods.' "

[10]Do not weep for the dead king or mourn his loss;
rather, weep bitterly for him who is exiled,
because he will never return
nor see his native land again.

[11]For this is what the LORD says about Shallum[a] son of Josiah, who succeeded
his father as king of Judah but has gone from this place: "He will never return.
[12]He will die in the place where they have led him captive; he will not see this
land again."

[13]"Woe to him who builds his palace by unrighteousness,
his upper rooms by injustice,
making his own people work for nothing,
not paying them for their labor.
[14]He says, 'I will build myself a great palace
with spacious upper rooms.'
So he makes large windows in it,
panels it with cedar
and decorates it in red.

[15]"Does it make you a king
to have more and more cedar?
Did not your father have food and drink?
He did what was right and just,
so all went well with him.
[16]He defended the cause of the poor and needy,
and so all went well.
Is that not what it means to know me?"
declares the LORD.
[17]"But your eyes and your heart
are set only on dishonest gain,
on shedding innocent blood
and on oppression and extortion."

[18]Therefore this is what the LORD says about Jehoiakim son of Josiah king of Judah:

"They will not mourn for him:
'Alas, my brother! Alas, my sister!'
They will not mourn for him:
'Alas, my master! Alas, his splendor!'
[19]He will have the burial of a donkey—
dragged away and thrown
outside the gates of Jerusalem."

[20]"Go up to Lebanon and cry out,
let your voice be heard in Bashan,
cry out from Abarim,
for all your allies are crushed.
[21]I warned you when you felt secure,
but you said, 'I will not listen!'
This has been your way from your youth;
you have not obeyed me.

---

[a] *11* Also called *Jehoahaz*

22 The wind will drive all your shepherds away,
and your allies will go into exile.
Then you will be ashamed and disgraced
because of all your wickedness.
23 You who live in 'Lebanon,[a]'
who are nestled in cedar buildings,
how you will groan when pangs come upon you,
pain like that of a woman in labor!

24 "As surely as I live," declares the LORD, "even if you, Jehoiachin[b] son of
Jehoiakim king of Judah, were a signet ring on my right hand, I would still pull
you off. 25 I will deliver you into the hands of those who want to kill you, those
you fear — Nebuchadnezzar king of Babylon and the Babylonians.[c] 26 I will
hurl you and the mother who gave you birth into another country, where neither
of you was born, and there you both will die. 27 You will never come back to the
land you long to return to."

28 Is this man Jehoiachin a despised, broken pot,
an object no one wants?
Why will he and his children be hurled out,
cast into a land they do not know?
29 O land, land, land,
hear the word of the LORD!
30 This is what the LORD says:
"Record this man as if childless,
a man who will not prosper in his lifetime,
for none of his offspring will prosper,
none will sit on the throne of David
or rule anymore in Judah."

The Righteous Branch

23 "Woe to the shepherds who are destroying and scattering the sheep of my
pasture!" declares the LORD. 2 Therefore this is what the LORD, the God
of Israel, says to the shepherds who tend my people: "Because you have scattered my flock and driven them away and have not bestowed care on them, I
will bestow punishment on you for the evil you have done," declares the LORD.
3 "I myself will gather the remnant of my flock out of all the countries where I
have driven them and will bring them back to their pasture, where they will be
fruitful and increase in number. 4 I will place shepherds over them who will tend
them, and they will no longer be afraid or terrified, nor will any be missing,"
declares the LORD.

5 "The days are coming," declares the LORD,
"when I will raise up for David[d] a righteous Branch,
a King who will reign wisely
and do what is just and right in the land.
6 In his days Judah will be saved
and Israel will live in safety.
This is the name by which he will be called:
The LORD Our Righteous Savior.

7 "So then, the days are coming," declares the LORD, "when people will no longer
say, 'As surely as the LORD lives, who brought the Israelites up out of Egypt,' 8 but
they will say, 'As surely as the LORD lives, who brought the descendants of Israel
up out of the land of the north and out of all the countries where he had banished
them.' Then they will live in their own land."

---

[a] *23* That is, the palace in Jerusalem (see 1 Kings 7:2) [b] *24* Hebrew *Koniah,* a variant of *Jehoiachin;* also in verse 28 [c] *25* Or *Chaldeans* [d] *5* Or *up from David's line*

OUR RIGHTEOUS SAVIOR

The first two verses of Jeremiah 23 describe the Lord's lament at how poorly the kings took care of his people. He blamed the kings leading up to and including Zedekiah for leading the people away from God and into exile, for which he promised punishment. However, God's justice comes hand in hand with his mercy: while verse 3 promises punishment in exile, it also promises a united future back in the land. Not only did God promise to bring his people back to him, but he also said that they would one day no longer have to fear or worry because he himself would "place shepherds over them" to rule and protect them (v. 4).

Then Jeremiah described the ultimate ruler that God planned to raise up: a king from the line of David who would rule with wisdom, justice and righteousness. The ruler is described as "a righteous Branch" of this family that God had blessed, a shepherd for his people who would be the ultimate ruler in every way: the Messiah, whom we know is Jesus. The people of Jeremiah's time were left to wonder about who God was promising through this passage, but believers today know the end of this particular story, having a different picture of the righteous and risen Savior.

Given the tumult of Jeremiah's time, the idea of a wise, just and righteous ruler was undoubtedly appealing. Today, Jesus is the Savior of all who believe, but he is also the ruler over God's people as well. He is the shepherd who is responsible for bringing God's people back from the nations where they were scattered, and he wears the crown under which all believers are able to unite. God's people have a ruler under which they can live safely and securely, and his name is Jesus.

Lying Prophets

[9]Concerning the prophets:

My heart is broken within me;
 all my bones tremble.
I am like a drunken man,
 like a strong man overcome by wine,
because of the LORD
 and his holy words.
[10]The land is full of adulterers;
 because of the curse[a] the land lies parched
 and the pastures in the wilderness are withered.
The prophets follow an evil course
 and use their power unjustly.

[11]"Both prophet and priest are godless;
 even in my temple I find their wickedness,"
 declares the LORD.
[12]"Therefore their path will become slippery;
 they will be banished to darkness
 and there they will fall.
I will bring disaster on them
 in the year they are punished,"
 declares the LORD.

[13]"Among the prophets of Samaria
 I saw this repulsive thing:
They prophesied by Baal
 and led my people Israel astray.
[14]And among the prophets of Jerusalem
 I have seen something horrible:
 They commit adultery and live a lie.
They strengthen the hands of evildoers,
 so that not one of them turns from their wickedness.
They are all like Sodom to me;
 the people of Jerusalem are like Gomorrah."

[15]Therefore this is what the LORD Almighty says concerning the prophets:

"I will make them eat bitter food
 and drink poisoned water,
because from the prophets of Jerusalem
 ungodliness has spread throughout the land."

[16]This is what the LORD Almighty says:

"Do not listen to what the prophets are prophesying to you;
 they fill you with false hopes.
They speak visions from their own minds,
 not from the mouth of the LORD.
[17]They keep saying to those who despise me,
 'The LORD says: You will have peace.'
And to all who follow the stubbornness of their hearts
 they say, 'No harm will come to you.'
[18]But which of them has stood in the council of the LORD
 to see or to hear his word?
 Who has listened and heard his word?
[19]See, the storm of the LORD
 will burst out in wrath,

[a] 10 Or *because of these things*

a whirlwind swirling down
on the heads of the wicked.
20 The anger of the LORD will not turn back
until he fully accomplishes
the purposes of his heart.
In days to come
you will understand it clearly.
21 I did not send these prophets,
yet they have run with their message;
I did not speak to them,
yet they have prophesied.
22 But if they had stood in my council,
they would have proclaimed my words to my people
and would have turned them from their evil ways
and from their evil deeds.

23 "Am I only a God nearby,"
declares the LORD,
"and not a God far away?
24 Who can hide in secret places
so that I cannot see them?"
declares the LORD.
"Do not I fill heaven and earth?"
declares the LORD.

25 "I have heard what the prophets say who prophesy lies in my name. They
say, 'I had a dream! I had a dream!' 26 How long will this continue in the hearts
of these lying prophets, who prophesy the delusions of their own minds? 27 They
think the dreams they tell one another will make my people forget my name,
just as their ancestors forgot my name through Baal worship. 28 Let the prophet
who has a dream recount the dream, but let the one who has my word speak
it faithfully. For what has straw to do with grain?" declares the LORD. 29 "Is not
my word like fire," declares the LORD, "and like a hammer that breaks a rock
in pieces?

30 "Therefore," declares the LORD, "I am against the prophets who steal from
one another words supposedly from me. 31 Yes," declares the LORD, "I am against
the prophets who wag their own tongues and yet declare, 'The LORD declares.'
32 Indeed, I am against those who prophesy false dreams," declares the LORD.
"They tell them and lead my people astray with their reckless lies, yet I did not
send or appoint them. They do not benefit these people in the least," declares
the LORD.

False Prophecy

33 "When these people, or a prophet or a priest, ask you, 'What is the message
from the LORD?' say to them, 'What message? I will forsake you, declares the
LORD.' 34 If a prophet or a priest or anyone else claims, 'This is a message from
the LORD,' I will punish them and their household. 35 This is what each of you
keeps saying to your friends and other Israelites: 'What is the LORD's answer?'
or 'What has the LORD spoken?' 36 But you must not mention 'a message from the
LORD' again, because each one's word becomes their own message. So you distort the words of the living God, the LORD Almighty, our God. 37 This is what you
keep saying to a prophet: 'What is the LORD's answer to you?' or 'What has the
LORD spoken?' 38 Although you claim, 'This is a message from the LORD,' this is
what the LORD says: You used the words, 'This is a message from the LORD,' even
though I told you that you must not claim, 'This is a message from the LORD.'
39 Therefore, I will surely forget you and cast you out of my presence along with
the city I gave to you and your ancestors. 40 I will bring on you everlasting disgrace — everlasting shame that will not be forgotten."

JEREMIAH 23:25

TRUTH TELLERS

The Lord was aware that prophets were falsely claiming that they had dreams inspired by him. The people were misled and confused as to what God was actually saying. God has great disdain for those who teach falsely in his name and lead people astray.

In Matthew 7:15, Jesus warned his followers to beware of false prophets, comparing them to wolves disguised as sheep. How can believers tell the difference? Jesus answered that question: "By their fruit you will recognize them" (Mt 7:16). Look closely for the end results of their teachings. Are they bringing division rather than unity? Are they following the teachings of the Bible? And do these teachers personally exhibit the fruit of the Spirit (Gal 5:22–23)? False teachers will one day be brought to justice for leading God's people astray (2Pe 2), but until that day, it is the responsibility of believers to ensure that the teachers they follow are truly leading them closer to Jesus.

Two Baskets of Figs

24 After Jehoiachin[a] son of Jehoiakim king of Judah and the officials, the
skilled workers and the artisans of Judah were carried into exile from Jerusalem to Babylon by Nebuchadnezzar king of Babylon, the LORD showed me
two baskets of figs placed in front of the temple of the LORD. 2One basket had very
good figs, like those that ripen early; the other basket had very bad figs, so bad
they could not be eaten.
3Then the LORD asked me, "What do you see, Jeremiah?"
"Figs," I answered. "The good ones are very good, but the bad ones are so bad
they cannot be eaten."
4Then the word of the LORD came to me: 5"This is what the LORD, the God of
Israel, says: 'Like these good figs, I regard as good the exiles from Judah, whom
I sent away from this place to the land of the Babylonians.[b] 6My eyes will watch
over them for their good, and I will bring them back to this land. I will build them
up and not tear them down; I will plant them and not uproot them. 7I will give
them a heart to know me, that I am the LORD. They will be my people, and I will
be their God, for they will return to me with all their heart.
8"'But like the bad figs, which are so bad they cannot be eaten,' says the LORD,
'so will I deal with Zedekiah king of Judah, his officials and the survivors from
Jerusalem, whether they remain in this land or live in Egypt. 9I will make them
abhorrent and an offense to all the kingdoms of the earth, a reproach and a byword, a curse[c] and an object of ridicule, wherever I banish them. 10I will send the
sword, famine and plague against them until they are destroyed from the land I
gave to them and their ancestors.'"

Seventy Years of Captivity

25 The word came to Jeremiah concerning all the people of Judah in the
fourth year of Jehoiakim son of Josiah king of Judah, which was the first
year of Nebuchadnezzar king of Babylon. 2So Jeremiah the prophet said to all the
people of Judah and to all those living in Jerusalem: 3For twenty-three years—
from the thirteenth year of Josiah son of Amon king of Judah until this very
day—the word of the LORD has come to me and I have spoken to you again and
again, but you have not listened.
4And though the LORD has sent all his servants the prophets to you again and
again, you have not listened or paid any attention. 5They said, "Turn now, each
of you, from your evil ways and your evil practices, and you can stay in the land
the LORD gave to you and your ancestors for ever and ever. 6Do not follow other
gods to serve and worship them; do not arouse my anger with what your hands
have made. Then I will not harm you."
7"But you did not listen to me," declares the LORD, "and you have aroused my
anger with what your hands have made, and you have brought harm to yourselves."
8Therefore the LORD Almighty says this: "Because you have not listened to
my words, 9I will summon all the peoples of the north and my servant Nebuchadnezzar king of Babylon," declares the LORD, "and I will bring them against
this land and its inhabitants and against all the surrounding nations. I will
completely destroy[d] them and make them an object of horror and scorn, and
an everlasting ruin. 10I will banish from them the sounds of joy and gladness,
the voices of bride and bridegroom, the sound of millstones and the light of the
lamp. 11This whole country will become a desolate wasteland, and these nations
will serve the king of Babylon seventy years.
12"But when the seventy years are fulfilled, I will punish the king of Babylon and

[a] *1* Hebrew *Jeconiah,* a variant of *Jehoiachin* [b] *5* Or *Chaldeans* [c] *9* That is, their names will be used in cursing (see 29:22); or, others will see that they are cursed. [d] *9* The Hebrew term refers to the irrevocable giving over of things or persons to the LORD, often by totally destroying them.

JEREMIAH 24:1–10

WORKING TOGETHER FOR GOD

This description of the good and bad figs is used to show that God had a purpose for sending some of his people away from their land. In allowing some of his people to be exiled, God was actually separating them from the influences of those who remained defiantly in Jerusalem with hardened hearts toward God. As Romans 8:28 says, "In all things God works for the good of those who love him." Although exile may have seemed like a punishment, God was actually preparing and refining his people for when they would return.

God's good plan for his people is consistent throughout the Old Testament, and it continues to hold true for believers today. In John 10:28, Jesus said of his followers, "No one will snatch them out of my hand." Those who belong to Jesus cannot be removed from his hand, and God will always work toward the good of those who love him. These verses affirm Jeremiah's word to the people of his day that God would be with them. They also affirm Jesus' promise of care and concern for his followers today.

JEREMIAH 25:11–12

GOD'S TIMING

These verses describe God's timeline for allowing Jerusalem to fall under the rule of Babylon for 70 years. Despite the fact that the people had turned away from following him and felt the consequences of that disobedience, God promised deliverance

(continued on next page)

(God's Timing, continued)

and retribution for the oppression the people experienced under Babylonian rule. God maintained a steadfast timeline for what would happen to them next, determined how long they would be punished, and promised that they would eventually be redeemed. Seventy years may seem like a long time, but there is no doubt that God had a very specific purpose for his timing.

In Mark 13:32, Jesus discussed the time and day of his return, and he made it clear that no one knows the day except for the Father. Neither the angels nor even Jesus himself knows the day and hour when he is to return, so Jesus warned his followers that it could be any day. Seventy years was God's timeline during the time of Jeremiah, but for believers today the only certainty regarding God's timing is that it is completely up to him. Therefore, remember these words of Jesus: "Be on guard! Be alert! You do not know when that time will come" (Mk 13:33).

his nation, the land of the Babylonians,[a] for their guilt," declares the LORD, "and
will make it desolate forever. 13 I will bring on that land all the things I have spoken
against it, all that are written in this book and prophesied by Jeremiah against all
the nations. 14 They themselves will be enslaved by many nations and great kings;
I will repay them according to their deeds and the work of their hands."

The Cup of God's Wrath

15 This is what the LORD, the God of Israel, said to me: "Take from my hand this
cup filled with the wine of my wrath and make all the nations to whom I send
you drink it. 16 When they drink it, they will stagger and go mad because of the
sword I will send among them."

17 So I took the cup from the LORD's hand and made all the nations to whom
he sent me drink it: 18 Jerusalem and the towns of Judah, its kings and officials,
to make them a ruin and an object of horror and scorn, a curse[b]—as they are
today; 19 Pharaoh king of Egypt, his attendants, his officials and all his people,
20 and all the foreign people there; all the kings of Uz; all the kings of the Philistines (those of Ashkelon, Gaza, Ekron, and the people left at Ashdod); 21 Edom,
Moab and Ammon; 22 all the kings of Tyre and Sidon; the kings of the coastlands
across the sea; 23 Dedan, Tema, Buz and all who are in distant places[c]; 24 all the
kings of Arabia and all the kings of the foreign people who live in the wilderness;
25 all the kings of Zimri, Elam and Media; 26 and all the kings of the north, near
and far, one after the other—all the kingdoms on the face of the earth. And after
all of them, the king of Sheshak[d] will drink it too.

27 "Then tell them, 'This is what the LORD Almighty, the God of Israel, says:
Drink, get drunk and vomit, and fall to rise no more because of the sword I will
send among you.' 28 But if they refuse to take the cup from your hand and drink,
tell them, 'This is what the LORD Almighty says: You must drink it! 29 See, I am
beginning to bring disaster on the city that bears my Name, and will you indeed
go unpunished? You will not go unpunished, for I am calling down a sword on
all who live on the earth, declares the LORD Almighty.'

30 "Now prophesy all these words against them and say to them:

" 'The LORD will roar from on high;
  he will thunder from his holy dwelling
  and roar mightily against his land.
He will shout like those who tread the grapes,
  shout against all who live on the earth.
31 The tumult will resound to the ends of the earth,
  for the LORD will bring charges against the nations;
he will bring judgment on all mankind
  and put the wicked to the sword,' "

declares the LORD.

32 This is what the LORD Almighty says:

"Look! Disaster is spreading
  from nation to nation;
a mighty storm is rising
  from the ends of the earth."

33 At that time those slain by the LORD will be everywhere—from one end of the
earth to the other. They will not be mourned or gathered up or buried, but will
be like dung lying on the ground.

34 Weep and wail, you shepherds;
  roll in the dust, you leaders of the flock.

[a] 12 Or *Chaldeans* [b] 18 That is, their names to be used in cursing (see 29:22); or, to be seen by others as cursed [c] 23 Or *who clip the hair by their foreheads* [d] 26 *Sheshak* is a cryptogram for Babylon.

For your time to be slaughtered has come;
you will fall like the best of the rams.[a]
35 The shepherds will have nowhere to flee,
the leaders of the flock no place to escape.
36 Hear the cry of the shepherds,
the wailing of the leaders of the flock,
for the LORD is destroying their pasture.
37 The peaceful meadows will be laid waste
because of the fierce anger of the LORD.
38 Like a lion he will leave his lair,
and their land will become desolate
because of the sword[b] of the oppressor
and because of the LORD's fierce anger.

Jeremiah Threatened With Death

26 Early in the reign of Jehoiakim son of Josiah king of Judah, this word came
from the LORD: 2 "This is what the LORD says: Stand in the courtyard of the
LORD's house and speak to all the people of the towns of Judah who come to worship in the house of the LORD. Tell them everything I command you; do not omit
a word. 3 Perhaps they will listen and each will turn from their evil ways. Then I
will relent and not inflict on them the disaster I was planning because of the evil
they have done. 4 Say to them, 'This is what the LORD says: If you do not listen to
me and follow my law, which I have set before you, 5 and if you do not listen to
the words of my servants the prophets, whom I have sent to you again and again
(though you have not listened), 6 then I will make this house like Shiloh and this
city a curse[c] among all the nations of the earth.' "
7 The priests, the prophets and all the people heard Jeremiah speak these
words in the house of the LORD. 8 But as soon as Jeremiah finished telling all
the people everything the LORD had commanded him to say, the priests, the
prophets and all the people seized him and said, "You must die! 9 Why do you
prophesy in the LORD's name that this house will be like Shiloh and this city will
be desolate and deserted?" And all the people crowded around Jeremiah in the
house of the LORD.
10 When the officials of Judah heard about these things, they went up from the
royal palace to the house of the LORD and took their places at the entrance of
the New Gate of the LORD's house. 11 Then the priests and the prophets said to the
officials and all the people, "This man should be sentenced to death because
he has prophesied against this city. You have heard it with your own ears!"
12 Then Jeremiah said to all the officials and all the people: "The LORD sent
me to prophesy against this house and this city all the things you have heard.
13 Now reform your ways and your actions and obey the LORD your God. Then
the LORD will relent and not bring the disaster he has pronounced against you.
14 As for me, I am in your hands; do with me whatever you think is good and
right. 15 Be assured, however, that if you put me to death, you will bring the
guilt of innocent blood on yourselves and on this city and on those who live
in it, for in truth the LORD has sent me to you to speak all these words in your
hearing."
16 Then the officials and all the people said to the priests and the prophets,
"This man should not be sentenced to death! He has spoken to us in the name
of the LORD our God."
17 Some of the elders of the land stepped forward and said to the entire assembly of people, 18 "Micah of Moresheth prophesied in the days of Hezekiah king
of Judah. He told all the people of Judah, 'This is what the LORD Almighty says:

---

[a] *34* Septuagint; Hebrew *fall and be shattered like fine pottery* [b] *38* Some Hebrew manuscripts and Septuagint (see also 46:16 and 50:16); most Hebrew manuscripts *anger*
[c] *6* That is, its name will be used in cursing (see 29:22); or, others will see that it is cursed.

JEREMIAH 26:1 – 9

PERSECUTED FOR SPEAKING THE TRUTH

God was very clear with Jeremiah that he did not want him to edit anything out of the message God had for his people. And in return for speaking God's truth just as he was asked to, Jeremiah faced death threats from the very people he was trying to help.

In the same way, Jesus experienced persecution for the truth that he spoke. On multiple occasions people tried to kill Jesus because of something he said, but he never backed down from the truth that he proclaimed (Lk 4:29; Jn 8:59; 10:22 – 39). Jeremiah's treatment for speaking God's message foreshadowed the treatment Jesus would receive. Jesus warned that his followers were sure to face some level of persecution, but he taught that suffering should be regarded as a blessing (Mt 5:10 – 12) — a sign that God's countercultural message to a sinful world is having an impact.

“ ‘Zion will be plowed like a field,
Jerusalem will become a heap of rubble,
the temple hill a mound overgrown with thickets.’[a]

19“Did Hezekiah king of Judah or anyone else in Judah put him to death? Did not
Hezekiah fear the LORD and seek his favor? And did not the LORD relent, so that
he did not bring the disaster he pronounced against them? We are about to bring
a terrible disaster on ourselves!”

20(Now Uriah son of Shemaiah from Kiriath Jearim was another man who
prophesied in the name of the LORD; he prophesied the same things against this
city and this land as Jeremiah did. 21When King Jehoiakim and all his officers
and officials heard his words, the king was determined to put him to death. But
Uriah heard of it and fled in fear to Egypt. 22King Jehoiakim, however, sent Elnathan son of Akbor to Egypt, along with some other men. 23They brought Uriah
out of Egypt and took him to King Jehoiakim, who had him struck down with a
sword and his body thrown into the burial place of the common people.)
24Furthermore, Ahikam son of Shaphan supported Jeremiah, and so he was
not handed over to the people to be put to death.

Judah to Serve Nebuchadnezzar

27 Early in the reign of Zedekiah[b] son of Josiah king of Judah, this word came
to Jeremiah from the LORD: 2This is what the LORD said to me: “Make a
yoke out of straps and crossbars and put it on your neck. 3Then send word to
the kings of Edom, Moab, Ammon, Tyre and Sidon through the envoys who
have come to Jerusalem to Zedekiah king of Judah. 4Give them a message for
their masters and say, ‘This is what the LORD Almighty, the God of Israel, says:
“Tell this to your masters: 5With my great power and outstretched arm I made
the earth and its people and the animals that are on it, and I give it to anyone I
please. 6Now I will give all your countries into the hands of my servant Nebuchadnezzar king of Babylon; I will make even the wild animals subject to him.
7All nations will serve him and his son and his grandson until the time for his
land comes; then many nations and great kings will subjugate him.
8“ ‘ “If, however, any nation or kingdom will not serve Nebuchadnezzar king
of Babylon or bow its neck under his yoke, I will punish that nation with the
sword, famine and plague, declares the LORD, until I destroy it by his hand. 9So
do not listen to your prophets, your diviners, your interpreters of dreams, your
mediums or your sorcerers who tell you, ‘You will not serve the king of Babylon.’
10They prophesy lies to you that will only serve to remove you far from your
lands; I will banish you and you will perish. 11But if any nation will bow its neck
under the yoke of the king of Babylon and serve him, I will let that nation remain
in its own land to till it and to live there, declares the LORD.” ’ ”
12I gave the same message to Zedekiah king of Judah. I said, “Bow your neck
under the yoke of the king of Babylon; serve him and his people, and you will
live. 13Why will you and your people die by the sword, famine and plague with
which the LORD has threatened any nation that will not serve the king of Babylon? 14Do not listen to the words of the prophets who say to you, ‘You will not
serve the king of Babylon,’ for they are prophesying lies to you. 15‘I have not sent
them,’ declares the LORD. ‘They are prophesying lies in my name. Therefore, I
will banish you and you will perish, both you and the prophets who prophesy
to you.’ ”

16Then I said to the priests and all these people, “This is what the LORD says:
Do not listen to the prophets who say, ‘Very soon now the articles from the
LORD’s house will be brought back from Babylon.’ They are prophesying lies to
you. 17Do not listen to them. Serve the king of Babylon, and you will live. Why
should this city become a ruin? 18If they are prophets and have the word of the

[a] *18* Micah 3:12 [b] *1* A few Hebrew manuscripts and Syriac (see also 27:3,12 and 28:1); most Hebrew manuscripts *Jehoiakim* (Most Septuagint manuscripts do not have this verse.)

LORD, let them plead with the LORD Almighty that the articles remaining in the
house of the LORD and in the palace of the king of Judah and in Jerusalem not
be taken to Babylon. 19For this is what the LORD Almighty says about the pillars,
the bronze Sea, the movable stands and the other articles that are left in this city,
20which Nebuchadnezzar king of Babylon did not take away when he carried Jehoiachin[a] son of Jehoiakim king of Judah into exile from Jerusalem to Babylon,
along with all the nobles of Judah and Jerusalem— 21yes, this is what the LORD
Almighty, the God of Israel, says about the things that are left in the house of
the LORD and in the palace of the king of Judah and in Jerusalem: 22'They will
be taken to Babylon and there they will remain until the day I come for them,'
declares the LORD. 'Then I will bring them back and restore them to this place.' "

The False Prophet Hananiah

28 In the fifth month of that same year, the fourth year, early in the reign
of Zedekiah king of Judah, the prophet Hananiah son of Azzur, who was
from Gibeon, said to me in the house of the LORD in the presence of the priests
and all the people: 2"This is what the LORD Almighty, the God of Israel, says: 'I
will break the yoke of the king of Babylon. 3Within two years I will bring back
to this place all the articles of the LORD's house that Nebuchadnezzar king of
Babylon removed from here and took to Babylon. 4I will also bring back to this
place Jehoiachin[a] son of Jehoiakim king of Judah and all the other exiles from
Judah who went to Babylon,' declares the LORD, 'for I will break the yoke of the
king of Babylon.' "

5Then the prophet Jeremiah replied to the prophet Hananiah before the
priests and all the people who were standing in the house of the LORD. 6He said,
"Amen! May the LORD do so! May the LORD fulfill the words you have prophesied
by bringing the articles of the LORD's house and all the exiles back to this place
from Babylon. 7Nevertheless, listen to what I have to say in your hearing and in
the hearing of all the people: 8From early times the prophets who preceded you
and me have prophesied war, disaster and plague against many countries and
great kingdoms. 9But the prophet who prophesies peace will be recognized as
one truly sent by the LORD only if his prediction comes true."

10Then the prophet Hananiah took the yoke off the neck of the prophet Jeremiah and broke it, 11and he said before all the people, "This is what the LORD
says: 'In the same way I will break the yoke of Nebuchadnezzar king of Babylon
off the neck of all the nations within two years.' " At this, the prophet Jeremiah
went on his way.

12After the prophet Hananiah had broken the yoke off the neck of the prophet Jeremiah, the word of the LORD came to Jeremiah: 13"Go and tell Hananiah,
'This is what the LORD says: You have broken a wooden yoke, but in its place you
will get a yoke of iron. 14This is what the LORD Almighty, the God of Israel, says: I
will put an iron yoke on the necks of all these nations to make them serve Nebuchadnezzar king of Babylon, and they will serve him. I will even give him control
over the wild animals.' "

15Then the prophet Jeremiah said to Hananiah the prophet, "Listen, Hananiah! The LORD has not sent you, yet you have persuaded this nation to trust in
lies. 16Therefore this is what the LORD says: 'I am about to remove you from the
face of the earth. This very year you are going to die, because you have preached
rebellion against the LORD.' "

17In the seventh month of that same year, Hananiah the prophet died.

A Letter to the Exiles

29 This is the text of the letter that the prophet Jeremiah sent from Jerusalem
to the surviving elders among the exiles and to the priests, the prophets
and all the other people Nebuchadnezzar had carried into exile from Jerusalem

[a] *20,4* Hebrew *Jeconiah,* a variant of *Jehoiachin*

JEREMIAH 27:21–22

PUNISHMENT AND REDEMPTION

These verses refer to valuable treasures and articles that decorated the house of the Lord and the palace of the king. No doubt these would be some of the first things that the Babylonians would take as they gained control of the city. However, even though God said he was going to allow Jerusalem to be overrun and the temple treasures removed, he also promised that these treasures would one day be returned.

This prophecy is similar to the parable of the lost coin in Luke 15:8–10. Although God allowed the valuable treasures of the temple to be taken, he assured the people that he would bring them back. God used the Babylonians to exact the justice that his people had brought upon themselves, but God also showed the greatness of his mercy by promising to one day bring the people, his true temple treasures, back to himself and to their land. No matter how far away a thing or person may seem to be away from God, he is always capable of rescuing and redeeming that which belongs to him.

JEREMIAH 28:1–17

CONFRONTING FALSE PROPHETS

Here Jeremiah was forced to stand up to one of the false prophets that God had been warning his people against for so long. He was told by God to wear a yoke around his neck—demonstrating that he would

(continued on next page)

(Confronting False Prophets, continued)

soon put the nations under the yoke of Nebuchadnezzar, king of Babylon (Jer 27:2). Hananiah had been prophesying directly against everything that Jeremiah was saying, telling the people what they wanted to hear as opposed to the actual truth of God (Jer 28:1–11). Finally God told Jeremiah to go to Hananiah and condemn him for the lies that he had been spreading (vv. 12–14). Jeremiah did so, also prophesying that Hananiah would die within that same year (vv. 15–16).

In a similar way, Jesus constantly battled the Pharisees and other religious leaders who claimed to speak for God and undermined the message of Jesus (Jn 8:42–58). After his resurrection, Jesus was vindicated and the religious leaders were exposed as frauds. Similarly, after Hananiah's death that same year (Jer 28:17) and the fulfillment of the rest of Jeremiah's prophecies, Jeremiah too was vindicated and his word was proven as truth.

to Babylon. 2(This was after King Jehoiachin[a] and the queen mother, the court
officials and the leaders of Judah and Jerusalem, the skilled workers and the artisans had gone into exile from Jerusalem.) 3He entrusted the letter to Elasah son
of Shaphan and to Gemariah son of Hilkiah, whom Zedekiah king of Judah sent
to King Nebuchadnezzar in Babylon. It said:

4This is what the LORD Almighty, the God of Israel, says to all those I
carried into exile from Jerusalem to Babylon: 5"Build houses and settle
down; plant gardens and eat what they produce. 6Marry and have sons and
daughters; find wives for your sons and give your daughters in marriage,
so that they too may have sons and daughters. Increase in number there;
do not decrease. 7Also, seek the peace and prosperity of the city to which
I have carried you into exile. Pray to the LORD for it, because if it prospers,
you too will prosper." 8Yes, this is what the LORD Almighty, the God of Israel, says: "Do not let the prophets and diviners among you deceive you. Do
not listen to the dreams you encourage them to have. 9They are prophesying lies to you in my name. I have not sent them," declares the LORD.

10This is what the LORD says: "When seventy years are completed for
Babylon, I will come to you and fulfill my good promise to bring you back to
this place. 11For I know the plans I have for you," declares the LORD, "plans
to prosper you and not to harm you, plans to give you hope and a future.
12Then you will call on me and come and pray to me, and I will listen to
you. 13You will seek me and find me when you seek me with all your heart.
14I will be found by you," declares the LORD, "and will bring you back from
captivity.[b] I will gather you from all the nations and places where I have
banished you," declares the LORD, "and will bring you back to the place
from which I carried you into exile."

15You may say, "The LORD has raised up prophets for us in Babylon,"
16but this is what the LORD says about the king who sits on David's throne
and all the people who remain in this city, your fellow citizens who did
not go with you into exile — 17yes, this is what the LORD Almighty says: "I
will send the sword, famine and plague against them and I will make them
like figs that are so bad they cannot be eaten. 18I will pursue them with the
sword, famine and plague and will make them abhorrent to all the kingdoms of the earth, a curse[c] and an object of horror, of scorn and reproach,
among all the nations where I drive them. 19For they have not listened to
my words," declares the LORD, "words that I sent to them again and again
by my servants the prophets. And you exiles have not listened either," declares the LORD.

20Therefore, hear the word of the LORD, all you exiles whom I have sent
away from Jerusalem to Babylon. 21This is what the LORD Almighty, the
God of Israel, says about Ahab son of Kolaiah and Zedekiah son of Maaseiah, who are prophesying lies to you in my name: "I will deliver them
into the hands of Nebuchadnezzar king of Babylon, and he will put them
to death before your very eyes. 22Because of them, all the exiles from Judah
who are in Babylon will use this curse: 'May the LORD treat you like Zedekiah and Ahab, whom the king of Babylon burned in the fire.' 23For they have
done outrageous things in Israel; they have committed adultery with their
neighbors' wives, and in my name they have uttered lies — which I did not
authorize. I know it and am a witness to it," declares the LORD.

Message to Shemaiah

24Tell Shemaiah the Nehelamite, 25"This is what the LORD Almighty, the God
of Israel, says: You sent letters in your own name to all the people in Jerusalem,
to the priest Zephaniah son of Maaseiah, and to all the other priests. You said

[a] *2* Hebrew *Jeconiah,* a variant of *Jehoiachin* [b] *14* Or *will restore your fortunes* [c] *18* That is, their names will be used in cursing (see verse 22); or, others will see that they are cursed.

HOPE FOR THE FUTURE

Chapter 29 is Jeremiah's letter to those exiled in 597 BC, and it was written sometime between that deportation in 597 and the destruction of Jerusalem — and final exile — in 586. God told Jeremiah that he had allowed some of his people to be taken to Babylon and that he would one day bring them back to the city of Jerusalem. The idea of exile could hardly be seen as a blessing for Jeremiah's audience, a fact made even more difficult because not everyone had been taken away. Of the people who were still in Jerusalem, many remained defiant to God and lived with hardened hearts. Therefore, Jeremiah wrote this letter to the people who had been sent into exile to assure them that God had a plan for them and that everything was going to work out for their good. Verse 11 would have greatly encouraged these Israelites who were captives in foreign territory.

Taken in a broader context, this verse can also be seen as God's promise to all his people. The term "you" is plural, not singular, and we can expand it to point toward God's plan for anyone and everyone who follows him. Although believers may want to take this verse and apply it to their own life as an assurance of God's individual plan for them, it is much bigger than the everyday decisions modern-day believers often apply it to: Deciding which college to attend, which job to take and which city to move to are all trivial matters when compared to the future hope that God promises to all of his people.

Does God have plans for individuals? Absolutely, but this verse is so much more than a promise of personal benefit. This promise of redemption and salvation is brought about through the generous sovereignty of God. Jeremiah 29:11 was a future hope for the scattered people, and believers today can also see it as a future hope of eternal redemption and life with God — strong encouragement for those who endure serious hardship and trial. Then as now, God is the only reason for our hope for the future.

to Zephaniah, [26]'The LORD has appointed you priest in place of Jehoiada to be
in charge of the house of the LORD; you should put any maniac who acts like
a prophet into the stocks and neck-irons. [27]So why have you not reprimanded
Jeremiah from Anathoth, who poses as a prophet among you? [28]He has sent this
message to us in Babylon: It will be a long time. Therefore build houses and settle
down; plant gardens and eat what they produce.' "

[29]Zephaniah the priest, however, read the letter to Jeremiah the prophet.
[30]Then the word of the LORD came to Jeremiah: [31]"Send this message to all the
exiles: 'This is what the LORD says about Shemaiah the Nehelamite: Because
Shemaiah has prophesied to you, even though I did not send him, and has persuaded you to trust in lies, [32]this is what the LORD says: I will surely punish Shemaiah the Nehelamite and his descendants. He will have no one left among this
people, nor will he see the good things I will do for my people, declares the LORD,
because he has preached rebellion against me.' "

Restoration of Israel

30 This is the word that came to Jeremiah from the LORD: [2]"This is what the
LORD, the God of Israel, says: 'Write in a book all the words I have spoken
to you. [3]The days are coming,' declares the LORD, 'when I will bring my people
Israel and Judah back from captivity[a] and restore them to the land I gave their
ancestors to possess,' says the LORD."

[4]These are the words the LORD spoke concerning Israel and Judah: [5]"This is
what the LORD says:

" 'Cries of fear are heard—
terror, not peace.
[6]Ask and see:
Can a man bear children?
Then why do I see every strong man
with his hands on his stomach like a woman in labor,
every face turned deathly pale?
[7]How awful that day will be!
No other will be like it.
It will be a time of trouble for Jacob,
but he will be saved out of it.

[8]" 'In that day,' declares the LORD Almighty,
'I will break the yoke off their necks
and will tear off their bonds;
no longer will foreigners enslave them.
[9]Instead, they will serve the LORD their God
and David their king,
whom I will raise up for them.

[10]" 'So do not be afraid, Jacob my servant;
do not be dismayed, Israel,'
declares the LORD.

'I will surely save you out of a distant place,
your descendants from the land of their exile.
Jacob will again have peace and security,
and no one will make him afraid.
[11]I am with you and will save you,'
declares the LORD.
'Though I completely destroy all the nations
among which I scatter you,
I will not completely destroy you.

[a] 3 Or *will restore the fortunes of my people Israel and Judah*

I will discipline you but only in due measure;
I will not let you go entirely unpunished.'

12 "This is what the LORD says:

" 'Your wound is incurable,
your injury beyond healing.
13 There is no one to plead your cause,
no remedy for your sore,
no healing for you.
14 All your allies have forgotten you;
they care nothing for you.
I have struck you as an enemy would
and punished you as would the cruel,
because your guilt is so great
and your sins so many.
15 Why do you cry out over your wound,
your pain that has no cure?
Because of your great guilt and many sins
I have done these things to you.

16 " 'But all who devour you will be devoured;
all your enemies will go into exile.
Those who plunder you will be plundered;
all who make spoil of you I will despoil.
17 But I will restore you to health
and heal your wounds,'
declares the LORD,

'because you are called an outcast,
Zion for whom no one cares.'

18 "This is what the LORD says:

" 'I will restore the fortunes of Jacob's tents
and have compassion on his dwellings;
the city will be rebuilt on her ruins,
and the palace will stand in its proper place.
19 From them will come songs of thanksgiving
and the sound of rejoicing.
I will add to their numbers,
and they will not be decreased;
I will bring them honor,
and they will not be disdained.
20 Their children will be as in days of old,
and their community will be established
before me;
I will punish all who oppress them.
21 Their leader will be one of their own;
their ruler will arise from among them.
I will bring him near and he will come close to me—
for who is he who will devote himself
to be close to me?'
declares the LORD.

22 " 'So you will be my people,
and I will be your God.' "

23 See, the storm of the LORD
will burst out in wrath,
a driving wind swirling down
on the heads of the wicked.

[24] The fierce anger of the LORD will not turn back
until he fully accomplishes
the purposes of his heart.
In days to come
you will understand this.

31 "At that time," declares the LORD, "I will be the God of all the families of
Israel, and they will be my people."
[2] This is what the LORD says:

"The people who survive the sword
will find favor in the wilderness;
I will come to give rest to Israel."

[3] The LORD appeared to us in the past,[a] saying:

"I have loved you with an everlasting love;
I have drawn you with unfailing kindness.
[4] I will build you up again,
and you, Virgin Israel, will be rebuilt.
Again you will take up your timbrels
and go out to dance with the joyful.
[5] Again you will plant vineyards
on the hills of Samaria;
the farmers will plant them
and enjoy their fruit.
[6] There will be a day when watchmen cry out
on the hills of Ephraim,
'Come, let us go up to Zion,
to the LORD our God.'"

[7] This is what the LORD says:

"Sing with joy for Jacob;
shout for the foremost of the nations.
Make your praises heard, and say,
'LORD, save your people,
the remnant of Israel.'
[8] See, I will bring them from the land of the north
and gather them from the ends of the earth.
Among them will be the blind and the lame,
expectant mothers and women in labor;
a great throng will return.
[9] They will come with weeping;
they will pray as I bring them back.
I will lead them beside streams of water
on a level path where they will not stumble,
because I am Israel's father,
and Ephraim is my firstborn son.

[10] "Hear the word of the LORD, you nations;
proclaim it in distant coastlands:
'He who scattered Israel will gather them
and will watch over his flock like a shepherd.'
[11] For the LORD will deliver Jacob
and redeem them from the hand of those stronger than they.

[a] 3 Or *LORD has appeared to us from afar*

12 They will come and shout for joy on the heights of Zion;
they will rejoice in the bounty of the LORD —
the grain, the new wine and the olive oil,
the young of the flocks and herds.
They will be like a well-watered garden,
and they will sorrow no more.
13 Then young women will dance and be glad,
young men and old as well.
I will turn their mourning into gladness;
I will give them comfort and joy instead of sorrow.
14 I will satisfy the priests with abundance,
and my people will be filled with my bounty,"
declares the LORD.

15 This is what the LORD says:

"A voice is heard in Ramah,
mourning and great weeping,
Rachel weeping for her children
and refusing to be comforted,
because they are no more."

16 This is what the LORD says:

"Restrain your voice from weeping
and your eyes from tears,
for your work will be rewarded,"
declares the LORD.

"They will return from the land of the enemy.
17 So there is hope for your descendants,"
declares the LORD.

"Your children will return to their own land.
18 "I have surely heard Ephraim's moaning:
'You disciplined me like an unruly calf,
and I have been disciplined.
Restore me, and I will return,
because you are the LORD my God.
19 After I strayed,
I repented;
after I came to understand,
I beat my breast.
I was ashamed and humiliated
because I bore the disgrace of my youth.'
20 Is not Ephraim my dear son,
the child in whom I delight?
Though I often speak against him,
I still remember him.
Therefore my heart yearns for him;
I have great compassion for him,"
declares the LORD.

21 "Set up road signs;
put up guideposts.
Take note of the highway,
the road that you take.
Return, Virgin Israel,
return to your towns.
22 How long will you wander,
unfaithful Daughter Israel?

JEREMIAH 31:15

WEEPING FOR HER CHILDREN

In chapter 31, Jeremiah prophesies the future restoration of the people of God. From glowing predictions of grace and mercy, Jeremiah once again confronts the tragic conditions of his day. He speaks of Rachel at Ramah weeping over the loss of her children (v. 15). An ancestress of the people of God, Rachel was also weeping over the exile of God's people. The Lord invites Rachel to stop mourning because God would be faithful to restore his wayward people once again (vv. 16–17).

Matthew quotes Jeremiah 31:15 in Matthew 2:18 when Herod, in an attempt to kill the newborn Jesus, killed all of the infant boys born in Bethlehem. It is impossible to come to terms with the deaths of the infant boys in Matthew 2. But Jesus and his parents escaped this attempt on his life and went to Egypt for a time after having been warned in a dream. In the book of Jeremiah, God took his people through exile, but he eventually brought them back to their home country to live and worship him. Similarly, God brought his Son Jesus through attempted murder, both in Bethlehem and on the cross, to save and redeem the world so that they may live and worship him. In great darkness, there is great hope.

The LORD will create a new thing on earth —
  the woman will return to[a] the man."

23This is what the LORD Almighty, the God of Israel, says: "When I bring them
back from captivity,[b] the people in the land of Judah and in its towns will once
again use these words: 'The LORD bless you, you prosperous city, you sacred
mountain.' 24People will live together in Judah and all its towns — farmers and
those who move about with their flocks. 25I will refresh the weary and satisfy
the faint."

26At this I awoke and looked around. My sleep had been pleasant to me.

27"The days are coming," declares the LORD, "when I will plant the kingdoms of Israel and Judah with the offspring of people and of animals. 28Just as I
watched over them to uproot and tear down, and to overthrow, destroy and bring
disaster, so I will watch over them to build and to plant," declares the LORD. 29"In
those days people will no longer say,

'The parents have eaten sour grapes,
  and the children's teeth are set on edge.'

30Instead, everyone will die for their own sin; whoever eats sour grapes — their
own teeth will be set on edge.

31"The days are coming," declares the LORD,
  "when I will make a new covenant
with the people of Israel
  and with the people of Judah.
32It will not be like the covenant
  I made with their ancestors
when I took them by the hand
  to lead them out of Egypt,
because they broke my covenant,
  though I was a husband to[c] them,[d]"
declares the LORD.

33"This is the covenant I will make with the people of Israel
  after that time," declares the LORD.
"I will put my law in their minds
  and write it on their hearts.
I will be their God,
  and they will be my people.
34No longer will they teach their neighbor,
  or say to one another, 'Know the LORD,'
because they will all know me,
  from the least of them to the greatest,"
declares the LORD.

"For I will forgive their wickedness
  and will remember their sins no more."

35This is what the LORD says,

he who appoints the sun
  to shine by day,
who decrees the moon and stars
  to shine by night,
who stirs up the sea
  so that its waves roar —
  the LORD Almighty is his name:
36"Only if these decrees vanish from my sight,"
  declares the LORD,

[a] 22 Or *will protect* [b] 23 Or *I restore their fortunes* [c] 32 Hebrew; Septuagint and Syriac / *and I turned away from* [d] 32 Or *was their master*

NEW COVENANT

In this passage, Jeremiah wrote of the new covenant that was to be later fulfilled by the Messiah. In Luke 22:20, when Jesus said, "This cup is the new covenant in my blood," his reference to a new covenant echoed this passage from Jeremiah.

Writing during a time of great national turmoil, Jeremiah described what the people's relationship with their God would one day look like, and believers today can say that they now live in the time to which Jeremiah was referring. Jesus fulfilled this Scripture, and the lives of believers are today defined by the terms of this new covenant.

Hebrews 8 explains that God wrote this new covenant for his people, and in doing so, he made the old covenant "obsolete and outdated" (Heb 8:13). When Jesus came and sealed the new covenant between God and his people, he eliminated the covenant he had made with Israel at Sinai. This is why Christians are no longer required to live in accordance with much of the Old Testament law. Under the old covenant, the Israelites had a plethora of tangible requirements to perform to show their obedience to God. For example, they had to sacrifice animals to atone for their sins. However, under the new covenant, believers who recognize their need for a Savior joyfully accept Jesus as the Son of God and the perfect sacrifice for their sins, and they show their obedience by telling others about this great news. There is no longer a need to sacrifice animals because Jesus is the final and eternal sacrifice for sins.

Jeremiah's words showed why he had great reason to hope in what was yet to come. When he said "the days are coming," he pointed toward a time when the antiquated religion of the past was to be replaced with a greater one that better reflected God's close and personal relationship with his people. He looked forward to a time when everyone will know the Lord, "from the least of them to the greatest" (Jer 31:34). Jesus came to earth to offer salvation to everyone, both "the least … and the greatest," and in doing so he fulfilled the new covenant between mankind and God that allows believers to know God and to have his law written on their hearts (vv. 33 – 34).

"will Israel ever cease
being a nation before me."

37This is what the LORD says:

"Only if the heavens above can be measured
and the foundations of the earth below be searched out
will I reject all the descendants of Israel
because of all they have done,"

declares the LORD.

38"The days are coming," declares the LORD, "when this city will be rebuilt
for me from the Tower of Hananel to the Corner Gate. 39The measuring line will
stretch from there straight to the hill of Gareb and then turn to Goah. 40The
whole valley where dead bodies and ashes are thrown, and all the terraces out
to the Kidron Valley on the east as far as the corner of the Horse Gate, will be holy
to the LORD. The city will never again be uprooted or demolished."

Jeremiah Buys a Field

32 This is the word that came to Jeremiah from the LORD in the tenth year of
Zedekiah king of Judah, which was the eighteenth year of Nebuchadnezzar.
2The army of the king of Babylon was then besieging Jerusalem, and Jeremiah the
prophet was confined in the courtyard of the guard in the royal palace of Judah.
3Now Zedekiah king of Judah had imprisoned him there, saying, "Why do
you prophesy as you do? You say, 'This is what the LORD says: I am about to give
this city into the hands of the king of Babylon, and he will capture it. 4Zedekiah
king of Judah will not escape the Babylonians[a] but will certainly be given into
the hands of the king of Babylon, and will speak with him face to face and see
him with his own eyes. 5He will take Zedekiah to Babylon, where he will remain
until I deal with him, declares the LORD. If you fight against the Babylonians,
you will not succeed.' "

6Jeremiah said, "The word of the LORD came to me: 7Hanamel son of Shallum
your uncle is going to come to you and say, 'Buy my field at Anathoth, because as
nearest relative it is your right and duty to buy it.'

8"Then, just as the LORD had said, my cousin Hanamel came to me in the
courtyard of the guard and said, 'Buy my field at Anathoth in the territory of
Benjamin. Since it is your right to redeem it and possess it, buy it for yourself.'

"I knew that this was the word of the LORD; 9so I bought the field at Anathoth
from my cousin Hanamel and weighed out for him seventeen shekels[b] of silver.
10I signed and sealed the deed, had it witnessed, and weighed out the silver on
the scales. 11I took the deed of purchase — the sealed copy containing the terms
and conditions, as well as the unsealed copy — 12and I gave this deed to Baruch
son of Neriah, the son of Mahseiah, in the presence of my cousin Hanamel and
of the witnesses who had signed the deed and of all the Jews sitting in the courtyard of the guard.

13"In their presence I gave Baruch these instructions: 14'This is what the LORD
Almighty, the God of Israel, says: Take these documents, both the sealed and unsealed copies of the deed of purchase, and put them in a clay jar so they will last
a long time. 15For this is what the LORD Almighty, the God of Israel, says: Houses,
fields and vineyards will again be bought in this land.'

16"After I had given the deed of purchase to Baruch son of Neriah, I prayed
to the LORD:

17"Ah, Sovereign LORD, you have made the heavens and the earth by your
great power and outstretched arm. Nothing is too hard for you. 18You show
love to thousands but bring the punishment for the parents' sins into the
laps of their children after them. Great and mighty God, whose name is the

JEREMIAH 32:8–9

JUST WAIT

Jeremiah's opportunity to purchase land in this chapter tested whether or not he truly believed that the Lord would bring a remnant of Judah back home after the imminent exile. Jeremiah was imprisoned for his message when his cousin Hanamel gave him the opportunity to buy a piece of land from him. At this point, the Babylonians had already laid siege to Jerusalem, and the field at Anathoth that Hanamel wanted to sell him was already in enemy hands. Furthermore, once the Babylonians were in control of all of Judah, it was highly unlikely that they would recognize Jeremiah as the rightful owner of this property.

Despite all of the conventional wisdom that went against this purchase, Jeremiah obeyed God and bought the land from his cousin. He made a point to pay for the land, fill out the proper paperwork and do everything publicly for others to see that he fully believed everything he had been preaching. In doing so, Jeremiah showed he was confident that God would be true to his promise and restore the land back to his people. Jeremiah had a literal investment in the fulfillment of God's word, and he showed he was willing to persevere (Jas 1:3) through anything and everything to stay true to what God had told him.

[a] *4* Or *Chaldeans*; also in verses 5, 24, 25, 28, 29 and 43 [b] *9* That is, about 7 ounces or about 200 grams

LORD Almighty, 19great are your purposes and mighty are your deeds. Your
eyes are open to the ways of all mankind; you reward each person according to their conduct and as their deeds deserve. 20You performed signs and
wonders in Egypt and have continued them to this day, in Israel and among
all mankind, and have gained the renown that is still yours. 21You brought
your people Israel out of Egypt with signs and wonders, by a mighty hand
and an outstretched arm and with great terror. 22You gave them this land
you had sworn to give their ancestors, a land flowing with milk and honey.
23They came in and took possession of it, but they did not obey you or follow
your law; they did not do what you commanded them to do. So you brought
all this disaster on them.

24"See how the siege ramps are built up to take the city. Because of the
sword, famine and plague, the city will be given into the hands of the Babylonians who are attacking it. What you said has happened, as you now see.
25And though the city will be given into the hands of the Babylonians, you,
Sovereign LORD, say to me, 'Buy the field with silver and have the transaction witnessed.' "

26Then the word of the LORD came to Jeremiah: 27"I am the LORD, the God of
all mankind. Is anything too hard for me? 28Therefore this is what the LORD says:
I am about to give this city into the hands of the Babylonians and to Nebuchadnezzar king of Babylon, who will capture it. 29The Babylonians who are attacking
this city will come in and set it on fire; they will burn it down, along with the
houses where the people aroused my anger by burning incense on the roofs to
Baal and by pouring out drink offerings to other gods.

30"The people of Israel and Judah have done nothing but evil in my sight from
their youth; indeed, the people of Israel have done nothing but arouse my anger
with what their hands have made, declares the LORD. 31From the day it was built
until now, this city has so aroused my anger and wrath that I must remove it from
my sight. 32The people of Israel and Judah have provoked me by all the evil they
have done—they, their kings and officials, their priests and prophets, the people
of Judah and those living in Jerusalem. 33They turned their backs to me and not
their faces; though I taught them again and again, they would not listen or respond
to discipline. 34They set up their vile images in the house that bears my Name and
defiled it. 35They built high places for Baal in the Valley of Ben Hinnom to sacrifice
their sons and daughters to Molek, though I never commanded—nor did it enter
my mind—that they should do such a detestable thing and so make Judah sin.

36"You are saying about this city, 'By the sword, famine and plague it will be
given into the hands of the king of Babylon'; but this is what the LORD, the God
of Israel, says: 37I will surely gather them from all the lands where I banish them
in my furious anger and great wrath; I will bring them back to this place and
let them live in safety. 38They will be my people, and I will be their God. 39I will
give them singleness of heart and action, so that they will always fear me and
that all will then go well for them and for their children after them. 40I will make
an everlasting covenant with them: I will never stop doing good to them, and I
will inspire them to fear me, so that they will never turn away from me. 41I will
rejoice in doing them good and will assuredly plant them in this land with all
my heart and soul.

42"This is what the LORD says: As I have brought all this great calamity on this
people, so I will give them all the prosperity I have promised them. 43Once more
fields will be bought in this land of which you say, 'It is a desolate waste, without people or animals, for it has been given into the hands of the Babylonians.'
44Fields will be bought for silver, and deeds will be signed, sealed and witnessed
in the territory of Benjamin, in the villages around Jerusalem, in the towns of
Judah and in the towns of the hill country, of the western foothills and of the
Negev, because I will restore their fortunes,[a] declares the LORD."

---

[a] 44 Or *will bring them back from captivity*

Promise of Restoration

33 While Jeremiah was still confined in the courtyard of the guard, the word
of the LORD came to him a second time: 2"This is what the LORD says, he
who made the earth, the LORD who formed it and established it—the LORD is
his name: 3'Call to me and I will answer you and tell you great and unsearchable
things you do not know.' 4For this is what the LORD, the God of Israel, says about
the houses in this city and the royal palaces of Judah that have been torn down
to be used against the siege ramps and the sword 5in the fight with the Babylonians[a]: 'They will be filled with the dead bodies of the people I will slay in my
anger and wrath. I will hide my face from this city because of all its wickedness.
6" 'Nevertheless, I will bring health and healing to it; I will heal my people and
will let them enjoy abundant peace and security. 7I will bring Judah and Israel
back from captivity[b] and will rebuild them as they were before. 8I will cleanse
them from all the sin they have committed against me and will forgive all their
sins of rebellion against me. 9Then this city will bring me renown, joy, praise
and honor before all nations on earth that hear of all the good things I do for it;
and they will be in awe and will tremble at the abundant prosperity and peace
I provide for it.'
10"This is what the LORD says: 'You say about this place, "It is a desolate waste,
without people or animals." Yet in the towns of Judah and the streets of Jerusalem that are deserted, inhabited by neither people nor animals, there will be
heard once more 11the sounds of joy and gladness, the voices of bride and bridegroom, and the voices of those who bring thank offerings to the house of the
LORD, saying,

"Give thanks to the LORD Almighty,
for the LORD is good;
his love endures forever."

For I will restore the fortunes of the land as they were before,' says the LORD.
12"This is what the LORD Almighty says: 'In this place, desolate and without
people or animals—in all its towns there will again be pastures for shepherds to
rest their flocks. 13In the towns of the hill country, of the western foothills and of
the Negev, in the territory of Benjamin, in the villages around Jerusalem and in
the towns of Judah, flocks will again pass under the hand of the one who counts
them,' says the LORD.
14" 'The days are coming,' declares the LORD, 'when I will fulfill the good
promise I made to the people of Israel and Judah.

15" 'In those days and at that time
I will make a righteous Branch sprout from David's line;
he will do what is just and right in the land.
16In those days Judah will be saved
and Jerusalem will live in safety.
This is the name by which it[c] will be called:
The LORD Our Righteous Savior.'

17For this is what the LORD says: 'David will never fail to have a man to sit on the
throne of Israel, 18nor will the Levitical priests ever fail to have a man to stand
before me continually to offer burnt offerings, to burn grain offerings and to
present sacrifices.' "
19The word of the LORD came to Jeremiah: 20"This is what the LORD says: 'If
you can break my covenant with the day and my covenant with the night, so that
day and night no longer come at their appointed time, 21then my covenant with
David my servant—and my covenant with the Levites who are priests ministering before me—can be broken and David will no longer have a descendant to
reign on his throne. 22I will make the descendants of David my servant and the

---

[a] 5 Or *Chaldeans* [b] 7 Or *will restore the fortunes of Judah and Israel* [c] 16 Or *he*

JEREMIAH 33:3

CALL TO ME

Throughout the book of Jeremiah, it is clear that the people had forsaken God and had completely wandered away from him. However, in spite of their sin, God promised to stay with them. All he desired was that they call to him and ask him for help. God sent the people into exile, but he also clearly promised that they would one day return to the land.

Chapter 33 includes a beautiful listing of the blessings God would shower on his people to show that he still wanted them back, despite their unfaithfulness. God only asked that they pray to him and simply ask for wisdom and direction. In Matthew 7:7, Jesus said, "Ask and it will be given to you; seek and you will find; knock and the door will be opened to you." Many people have misinterpreted this verse to mean that God will give believers whatever they ask for, but this is simply not true. Anyone who has prayed for a new car and found the same old car sitting in the driveway the next morning knows that God is not some sort of heavenly vending machine. He does not simply say yes to every prayer. However, for those who ask in faith and seek him, God will give them whatever it is he wants for them. Thankfully, the gifts and direction that God gives to his people are invariably better than what they ask for.

In times of hardship and turmoil, God wants his people to turn to him so that he can help them. Jeremiah 33:3 says that if God's people call to him, he will tell them "great and unsearchable things" that they do not know. The same is true for believers today who find themselves confused and in need. Through his Word, through his Son and through his Spirit, God offers answers for his people's deepest life questions, no matter their circumstances.

Levites who minister before me as countless as the stars in the sky and as measureless as the sand on the seashore.' "

[23]The word of the LORD came to Jeremiah: [24]"Have you not noticed that these people are saying, 'The LORD has rejected the two kingdoms[a] he chose'? So they despise my people and no longer regard them as a nation. [25]This is what the LORD says: 'If I have not made my covenant with day and night and established the laws of heaven and earth, [26]then I will reject the descendants of Jacob and David my servant and will not choose one of his sons to rule over the descendants of Abraham, Isaac and Jacob. For I will restore their fortunes[b] and have compassion on them.' "

Warning to Zedekiah

34 While Nebuchadnezzar king of Babylon and all his army and all the kingdoms and peoples in the empire he ruled were fighting against Jerusalem and all its surrounding towns, this word came to Jeremiah from the LORD: [2]"This is what the LORD, the God of Israel, says: Go to Zedekiah king of Judah and tell him, 'This is what the LORD says: I am about to give this city into the hands of the king of Babylon, and he will burn it down. [3]You will not escape from his grasp but will surely be captured and given into his hands. You will see the king of Babylon with your own eyes, and he will speak with you face to face. And you will go to Babylon.

[4]" 'Yet hear the LORD's promise to you, Zedekiah king of Judah. This is what the LORD says concerning you: You will not die by the sword; [5]you will die peacefully. As people made a funeral fire in honor of your predecessors, the kings who ruled before you, so they will make a fire in your honor and lament, "Alas, master!" I myself make this promise, declares the LORD.' "

[6]Then Jeremiah the prophet told all this to Zedekiah king of Judah, in Jerusalem, [7]while the army of the king of Babylon was fighting against Jerusalem and the other cities of Judah that were still holding out — Lachish and Azekah. These were the only fortified cities left in Judah.

Freedom for Slaves

[8]The word came to Jeremiah from the LORD after King Zedekiah had made a covenant with all the people in Jerusalem to proclaim freedom for the slaves. [9]Everyone was to free their Hebrew slaves, both male and female; no one was to hold a fellow Hebrew in bondage. [10]So all the officials and people who entered into this covenant agreed that they would free their male and female slaves and no longer hold them in bondage. They agreed, and set them free. [11]But afterward they changed their minds and took back the slaves they had freed and enslaved them again.

[12]Then the word of the LORD came to Jeremiah: [13]"This is what the LORD, the God of Israel, says: I made a covenant with your ancestors when I brought them out of Egypt, out of the land of slavery. I said, [14]'Every seventh year each of you must free any fellow Hebrews who have sold themselves to you. After they have served you six years, you must let them go free.'[c] Your ancestors, however, did not listen to me or pay attention to me. [15]Recently you repented and did what is right in my sight: Each of you proclaimed freedom to your own people. You even made a covenant before me in the house that bears my Name. [16]But now you have turned around and profaned my name; each of you has taken back the male and female slaves you had set free to go where they wished. You have forced them to become your slaves again.

[17]"Therefore this is what the LORD says: You have not obeyed me; you have not proclaimed freedom to your own people. So I now proclaim 'freedom' for you, declares the LORD — 'freedom' to fall by the sword, plague and famine. I will make you abhorrent to all the kingdoms of the earth. [18]Those who have violated

[a] *24* Or *families* [b] *26* Or *will bring them back from captivity* [c] *14* Deut. 15:12

my covenant and have not fulfilled the terms of the covenant they made before
me, I will treat like the calf they cut in two and then walked between its pieces.
19The leaders of Judah and Jerusalem, the court officials, the priests and all the
people of the land who walked between the pieces of the calf, 20I will deliver into
the hands of their enemies who want to kill them. Their dead bodies will become
food for the birds and the wild animals.

21"I will deliver Zedekiah king of Judah and his officials into the hands of their
enemies who want to kill them, to the army of the king of Babylon, which has
withdrawn from you. 22I am going to give the order, declares the LORD, and I will
bring them back to this city. They will fight against it, take it and burn it down.
And I will lay waste the towns of Judah so no one can live there."

The Rekabites

35 This is the word that came to Jeremiah from the LORD during the reign
of Jehoiakim son of Josiah king of Judah: 2"Go to the Rekabite family and
invite them to come to one of the side rooms of the house of the LORD and give
them wine to drink."

3So I went to get Jaazaniah son of Jeremiah, the son of Habazziniah, and his
brothers and all his sons — the whole family of the Rekabites. 4I brought them
into the house of the LORD, into the room of the sons of Hanan son of Igdaliah
the man of God. It was next to the room of the officials, which was over that of
Maaseiah son of Shallum the doorkeeper. 5Then I set bowls full of wine and some
cups before the Rekabites and said to them, "Drink some wine."

6But they replied, "We do not drink wine, because our forefather Jehonadab[a]
son of Rekab gave us this command: 'Neither you nor your descendants must
ever drink wine. 7Also you must never build houses, sow seed or plant vineyards;
you must never have any of these things, but must always live in tents. Then
you will live a long time in the land where you are nomads.' 8We have obeyed
everything our forefather Jehonadab son of Rekab commanded us. Neither we
nor our wives nor our sons and daughters have ever drunk wine 9or built houses to live in or had vineyards, fields or crops. 10We have lived in tents and have
fully obeyed everything our forefather Jehonadab commanded us. 11But when
Nebuchadnezzar king of Babylon invaded this land, we said, 'Come, we must
go to Jerusalem to escape the Babylonian[b] and Aramean armies.' So we have
remained in Jerusalem."

12Then the word of the LORD came to Jeremiah, saying: 13"This is what the
LORD Almighty, the God of Israel, says: Go and tell the people of Judah and those
living in Jerusalem, 'Will you not learn a lesson and obey my words?' declares
the LORD. 14'Jehonadab son of Rekab ordered his descendants not to drink wine
and this command has been kept. To this day they do not drink wine, because
they obey their forefather's command. But I have spoken to you again and again,
yet you have not obeyed me. 15Again and again I sent all my servants the prophets to you. They said, "Each of you must turn from your wicked ways and reform
your actions; do not follow other gods to serve them. Then you will live in the
land I have given to you and your ancestors." But you have not paid attention or
listened to me. 16The descendants of Jehonadab son of Rekab have carried out
the command their forefather gave them, but these people have not obeyed me.'

17"Therefore this is what the LORD God Almighty, the God of Israel, says: 'Listen! I am going to bring on Judah and on everyone living in Jerusalem every
disaster I pronounced against them. I spoke to them, but they did not listen; I
called to them, but they did not answer.' "

18Then Jeremiah said to the family of the Rekabites, "This is what the LORD
Almighty, the God of Israel, says: 'You have obeyed the command of your forefather Jehonadab and have followed all his instructions and have done everything

[a] 6 Hebrew *Jonadab*, a variant of *Jehonadab*; here and often in this chapter
[b] *11* Or *Chaldean*

he ordered.' [19]Therefore this is what the LORD Almighty, the God of Israel, says: 'Jehonadab son of Rekab will never fail to have a descendant to serve me.' "

Jehoiakim Burns Jeremiah's Scroll

36 In the fourth year of Jehoiakim son of Josiah king of Judah, this word came to Jeremiah from the LORD: [2]"Take a scroll and write on it all the words I have spoken to you concerning Israel, Judah and all the other nations from the time I began speaking to you in the reign of Josiah till now. [3]Perhaps when the people of Judah hear about every disaster I plan to inflict on them, they will each turn from their wicked ways; then I will forgive their wickedness and their sin."

[4]So Jeremiah called Baruch son of Neriah, and while Jeremiah dictated all the words the LORD had spoken to him, Baruch wrote them on the scroll. [5]Then Jeremiah told Baruch, "I am restricted; I am not allowed to go to the LORD's temple. [6]So you go to the house of the LORD on a day of fasting and read to the people from the scroll the words of the LORD that you wrote as I dictated. Read them to all the people of Judah who come in from their towns. [7]Perhaps they will bring their petition before the LORD and will each turn from their wicked ways, for the anger and wrath pronounced against this people by the LORD are great."

[8]Baruch son of Neriah did everything Jeremiah the prophet told him to do; at the LORD's temple he read the words of the LORD from the scroll. [9]In the ninth month of the fifth year of Jehoiakim son of Josiah king of Judah, a time of fasting before the LORD was proclaimed for all the people in Jerusalem and those who had come from the towns of Judah. [10]From the room of Gemariah son of Shaphan the secretary, which was in the upper courtyard at the entrance of the New Gate of the temple, Baruch read to all the people at the LORD's temple the words of Jeremiah from the scroll.

[11]When Micaiah son of Gemariah, the son of Shaphan, heard all the words of the LORD from the scroll, [12]he went down to the secretary's room in the royal palace, where all the officials were sitting: Elishama the secretary, Delaiah son of Shemaiah, Elnathan son of Akbor, Gemariah son of Shaphan, Zedekiah son of Hananiah, and all the other officials. [13]After Micaiah told them everything he had heard Baruch read to the people from the scroll, [14]all the officials sent Jehudi son of Nethaniah, the son of Shelemiah, the son of Cushi, to say to Baruch, "Bring the scroll from which you have read to the people and come." So Baruch son of Neriah went to them with the scroll in his hand. [15]They said to him, "Sit down, please, and read it to us."

So Baruch read it to them. [16]When they heard all these words, they looked at each other in fear and said to Baruch, "We must report all these words to the king." [17]Then they asked Baruch, "Tell us, how did you come to write all this? Did Jeremiah dictate it?"

[18]"Yes," Baruch replied, "he dictated all these words to me, and I wrote them in ink on the scroll."

[19]Then the officials said to Baruch, "You and Jeremiah, go and hide. Don't let anyone know where you are."

[20]After they put the scroll in the room of Elishama the secretary, they went to the king in the courtyard and reported everything to him. [21]The king sent Jehudi to get the scroll, and Jehudi brought it from the room of Elishama the secretary and read it to the king and all the officials standing beside him. [22]It was the ninth month and the king was sitting in the winter apartment, with a fire burning in the firepot in front of him. [23]Whenever Jehudi had read three or four columns of the scroll, the king cut them off with a scribe's knife and threw them into the firepot, until the entire scroll was burned in the fire. [24]The king and all his attendants who heard all these words showed no fear, nor did they tear their clothes. [25]Even though Elnathan, Delaiah and Gemariah urged the king not to burn the scroll, he would not listen to them. [26]Instead, the king commanded Jerahmeel, a son of the king, Seraiah son of Azriel and Shelemiah son of Abdeel to arrest Baruch the scribe and Jeremiah the prophet. But the LORD had hidden them.

JEREMIAH 36:1–32

JEHOIAKIM AND REPENTANCE

Upon hearing a description of the wickedness of the people of Judah and God's declarations of judgment, there were two ways King Jehoiakim could have responded. He could have either expressed great sorrow at what was written and led the nation in repenting of their actions, or he could have ignored the call to repent and continued living in sin. Jehoiakim went further than simply ignoring the scroll—he actually cut it up and burned it in the firepot, as if that action would make God's message go away.

Jeremiah saw the people sinning. He rebuked them, but they failed to repent. In Acts 3:19, Peter says that if people repent and turn to God, their sins will be wiped out. Jehoiakim had a chance to repent, but he ignored the rebuke of God through Jeremiah, and he now represents a perfect example of how people are not supposed to respond when they're called to account for their sins.

27 After the king burned the scroll containing the words that Baruch had written at Jeremiah's dictation, the word of the LORD came to Jeremiah: 28 "Take
another scroll and write on it all the words that were on the first scroll, which
Jehoiakim king of Judah burned up. 29 Also tell Jehoiakim king of Judah, 'This
is what the LORD says: You burned that scroll and said, "Why did you write on it
that the king of Babylon would certainly come and destroy this land and wipe
from it both man and beast?" 30 Therefore this is what the LORD says about Jehoiakim king of Judah: He will have no one to sit on the throne of David; his body
will be thrown out and exposed to the heat by day and the frost by night. 31 I will
punish him and his children and his attendants for their wickedness; I will bring
on them and those living in Jerusalem and the people of Judah every disaster I
pronounced against them, because they have not listened.' "
32 So Jeremiah took another scroll and gave it to the scribe Baruch son of Neriah, and as Jeremiah dictated, Baruch wrote on it all the words of the scroll that
Jehoiakim king of Judah had burned in the fire. And many similar words were
added to them.

Jeremiah in Prison

37 Zedekiah son of Josiah was made king of Judah by Nebuchadnezzar king
of Babylon; he reigned in place of Jehoiachin[a] son of Jehoiakim. 2 Neither
he nor his attendants nor the people of the land paid any attention to the words
the LORD had spoken through Jeremiah the prophet.
3 King Zedekiah, however, sent Jehukal son of Shelemiah with the priest Zephaniah son of Maaseiah to Jeremiah the prophet with this message: "Please pray
to the LORD our God for us."
4 Now Jeremiah was free to come and go among the people, for he had not yet
been put in prison. 5 Pharaoh's army had marched out of Egypt, and when the
Babylonians[b] who were besieging Jerusalem heard the report about them, they
withdrew from Jerusalem.
6 Then the word of the LORD came to Jeremiah the prophet: 7 "This is what the
LORD, the God of Israel, says: Tell the king of Judah, who sent you to inquire of
me, 'Pharaoh's army, which has marched out to support you, will go back to its
own land, to Egypt. 8 Then the Babylonians will return and attack this city; they
will capture it and burn it down.'
9 "This is what the LORD says: Do not deceive yourselves, thinking, 'The Babylonians will surely leave us.' They will not! 10 Even if you were to defeat the entire
Babylonian[c] army that is attacking you and only wounded men were left in their
tents, they would come out and burn this city down."
11 After the Babylonian army had withdrawn from Jerusalem because of Pharaoh's army, 12 Jeremiah started to leave the city to go to the territory of Benjamin
to get his share of the property among the people there. 13 But when he reached
the Benjamin Gate, the captain of the guard, whose name was Irijah son of Shelemiah, the son of Hananiah, arrested him and said, "You are deserting to the
Babylonians!"
14 "That's not true!" Jeremiah said. "I am not deserting to the Babylonians."
But Irijah would not listen to him; instead, he arrested Jeremiah and brought
him to the officials. 15 They were angry with Jeremiah and had him beaten and
imprisoned in the house of Jonathan the secretary, which they had made into
a prison.
16 Jeremiah was put into a vaulted cell in a dungeon, where he remained a long
time. 17 Then King Zedekiah sent for him and had him brought to the palace,
where he asked him privately, "Is there any word from the LORD?"
"Yes," Jeremiah replied, "you will be delivered into the hands of the king of
Babylon."
18 Then Jeremiah said to King Zedekiah, "What crime have I committed

JEREMIAH 37:16–21

SECRETLY SEEKING A WORD FROM GOD

Despite the fact that Jeremiah was imprisoned for his prophecies against Judah, Zedekiah still sought him out to hear if he had any word from the Lord. King Zedekiah clearly desired to hear the truth, but he risked serious retribution from his officials for consulting with this hated prophet. That led him to keep his conversations with Jeremiah secret (Jer 37:17; 38:14–27).

Nicodemus had a similar struggle in John 3. As a member of the Jewish ruling council, he took a great risk in meeting Jesus at night to discuss religious issues. What his actions showed is that he sought to discover who Jesus was. In the same way that Jeremiah spoke the truth from the Lord to Zedekiah, so Jesus spoke truth to Nicodemus about spiritual matters. While Jesus did not hesitate to speak strongly to religious hypocrites, he was always willing to answer anyone who was seeking truth.

[a] *1* Hebrew *Koniah,* a variant of *Jehoiachin* [b] *5* Or *Chaldeans*; also in verses 8, 9, 13 and 14
[c] *10* Or *Chaldean*; also in verse 11

against you or your attendants or this people, that you have put me in prison? [19]Where are your prophets who prophesied to you, 'The king of Babylon will not attack you or this land'? [20]But now, my lord the king, please listen. Let me bring my petition before you: Do not send me back to the house of Jonathan the secretary, or I will die there."

[21]King Zedekiah then gave orders for Jeremiah to be placed in the courtyard of the guard and given a loaf of bread from the street of the bakers each day until all the bread in the city was gone. So Jeremiah remained in the courtyard of the guard.

Jeremiah Thrown Into a Cistern

38 Shephatiah son of Mattan, Gedaliah son of Pashhur, Jehukal[a] son of Shelemiah, and Pashhur son of Malkijah heard what Jeremiah was telling all the people when he said, [2]"This is what the LORD says: 'Whoever stays in this city will die by the sword, famine or plague, but whoever goes over to the Babylonians[b] will live. They will escape with their lives; they will live.' [3]And this is what the LORD says: 'This city will certainly be given into the hands of the army of the king of Babylon, who will capture it.'"

[4]Then the officials said to the king, "This man should be put to death. He is discouraging the soldiers who are left in this city, as well as all the people, by the things he is saying to them. This man is not seeking the good of these people but their ruin."

[5]"He is in your hands," King Zedekiah answered. "The king can do nothing to oppose you."

[6]So they took Jeremiah and put him into the cistern of Malkijah, the king's son, which was in the courtyard of the guard. They lowered Jeremiah by ropes into the cistern; it had no water in it, only mud, and Jeremiah sank down into the mud.

[7]But Ebed-Melek, a Cushite,[c] an official[d] in the royal palace, heard that they had put Jeremiah into the cistern. While the king was sitting in the Benjamin Gate, [8]Ebed-Melek went out of the palace and said to him, [9]"My lord the king, these men have acted wickedly in all they have done to Jeremiah the prophet. They have thrown him into a cistern, where he will starve to death when there is no longer any bread in the city."

[10]Then the king commanded Ebed-Melek the Cushite, "Take thirty men from here with you and lift Jeremiah the prophet out of the cistern before he dies."

[11]So Ebed-Melek took the men with him and went to a room under the treasury in the palace. He took some old rags and worn-out clothes from there and let them down with ropes to Jeremiah in the cistern. [12]Ebed-Melek the Cushite said to Jeremiah, "Put these old rags and worn-out clothes under your arms to pad the ropes." Jeremiah did so, [13]and they pulled him up with the ropes and lifted him out of the cistern. And Jeremiah remained in the courtyard of the guard.

Zedekiah Questions Jeremiah Again

[14]Then King Zedekiah sent for Jeremiah the prophet and had him brought to the third entrance to the temple of the LORD. "I am going to ask you something," the king said to Jeremiah. "Do not hide anything from me."

[15]Jeremiah said to Zedekiah, "If I give you an answer, will you not kill me? Even if I did give you counsel, you would not listen to me."

[16]But King Zedekiah swore this oath secretly to Jeremiah: "As surely as the LORD lives, who has given us breath, I will neither kill you nor hand you over to those who want to kill you."

[17]Then Jeremiah said to Zedekiah, "This is what the LORD God Almighty, the God of Israel, says: 'If you surrender to the officers of the king of Babylon, your

---

JEREMIAH 38:14–18

PATIENCE AND PERSEVERANCE

Jeremiah had a very difficult time getting the people of Jerusalem to listen to him. He was imprisoned multiple times for his message and even thrown into a water cistern and left to die. However, King Zedekiah still asked this prophet of God to tell him the word of the Lord. In response, Jeremiah exclaimed his frustration and fear that Zedekiah would either put him to death or ignore him no matter what truth from God he shared.

Jesus had a similar moment to Jeremiah in Luke 9:41 in which he expressed frustration at the weak faith of the people around him. However, both Jesus and Jeremiah persevered through their frustration. Jeremiah told Zedekiah God's truth, and Jesus healed the boy that had been put in front of him. Both Jeremiah and Jesus showed great patience and shared God's truth, continuing the work they were called to do.

---

[a] *1* Hebrew *Jukal,* a variant of *Jehukal* [b] *2* Or *Chaldeans*; also in verses 18, 19 and 23
[c] *7* Probably from the upper Nile region [d] *7* Or *a eunuch*

life will be spared and this city will not be burned down; you and your family will
live. [18]But if you will not surrender to the officers of the king of Babylon, this city
will be given into the hands of the Babylonians and they will burn it down; you
yourself will not escape from them.' "

[19]King Zedekiah said to Jeremiah, "I am afraid of the Jews who have gone over
to the Babylonians, for the Babylonians may hand me over to them and they will
mistreat me."

[20]"They will not hand you over," Jeremiah replied. "Obey the LORD by doing
what I tell you. Then it will go well with you, and your life will be spared. [21]But if
you refuse to surrender, this is what the LORD has revealed to me: [22]All the wom-
en left in the palace of the king of Judah will be brought out to the officials of the
king of Babylon. Those women will say to you:

" 'They misled you and overcame you—
those trusted friends of yours.
Your feet are sunk in the mud;
your friends have deserted you.'

[23]"All your wives and children will be brought out to the Babylonians. You
yourself will not escape from their hands but will be captured by the king of
Babylon; and this city will[a] be burned down."

[24]Then Zedekiah said to Jeremiah, "Do not let anyone know about this conversation, or you may die. [25]If the officials hear that I talked with you, and they
come to you and say, 'Tell us what you said to the king and what the king said to
you; do not hide it from us or we will kill you,' [26]then tell them, 'I was pleading
with the king not to send me back to Jonathan's house to die there.' "

[27]All the officials did come to Jeremiah and question him, and he told them
everything the king had ordered him to say. So they said no more to him, for no
one had heard his conversation with the king.

[28]And Jeremiah remained in the courtyard of the guard until the day Jerusalem was captured.

The Fall of Jerusalem

39 This is how Jerusalem was taken: [1]In the ninth year of Zedekiah king of
Judah, in the tenth month, Nebuchadnezzar king of Babylon marched
against Jerusalem with his whole army and laid siege to it. [2]And on the ninth
day of the fourth month of Zedekiah's eleventh year, the city wall was broken
through. [3]Then all the officials of the king of Babylon came and took seats in the
Middle Gate: Nergal-Sharezer of Samgar, Nebo-Sarsekim a chief officer, Nergal-
Sharezer a high official and all the other officials of the king of Babylon. [4]When
Zedekiah king of Judah and all the soldiers saw them, they fled; they left the city
at night by way of the king's garden, through the gate between the two walls, and
headed toward the Arabah.[b]

[5]But the Babylonian[c] army pursued them and overtook Zedekiah in the plains
of Jericho. They captured him and took him to Nebuchadnezzar king of Babylon
at Riblah in the land of Hamath, where he pronounced sentence on him. [6]There
at Riblah the king of Babylon slaughtered the sons of Zedekiah before his eyes
and also killed all the nobles of Judah. [7]Then he put out Zedekiah's eyes and
bound him with bronze shackles to take him to Babylon.

[8]The Babylonians[d] set fire to the royal palace and the houses of the people
and broke down the walls of Jerusalem. [9]Nebuzaradan commander of the imperial guard carried into exile to Babylon the people who remained in the city,
along with those who had gone over to him, and the rest of the people. [10]But Nebuzaradan the commander of the guard left behind in the land of Judah some of
the poor people, who owned nothing; and at that time he gave them vineyards
and fields.

---

[a] 23 Or *and you will cause this city to* [b] 4 Or *the Jordan Valley* [c] 5 Or *Chaldean*
[d] 8 Or *Chaldeans*

JEREMIAH 39:1 – 18

CONSEQUENCES

Despite all of Jeremiah's attempts to warn the people, chapter 39 depicts the fall of Jerusalem just as God's prophet had predicted it throughout this book. Through Jeremiah, God warned his people that their actions would have consequences, and their failure to ask for forgiveness and to repent from their wrongdoing sealed their fate. The Israelites sowed ignorance of God's truth, and they reaped destruction and exile (Gal 6:7). Verses 1 through 10 depict the horror of the punishment meted out against the people of the city for their disobedience.

True to Zedekiah's character, he tried to sneak out by night, but he was ultimately caught and taken as a prisoner to Babylon, where he was imprisoned until he died (Jer 52:11). God does not make empty promises in the Bible; he was not bluffing when he spoke words of judgment through Jeremiah.

For believers today, it is important to understand that everything God says in the Bible is his word, and his word has weight to it. Therefore, when Jesus said, "Whoever acknowledges me before others, I will also acknowledge before my Father in heaven. But whoever disowns me before others, I will disown before my Father in heaven" (Mt 10:32 – 33), he is not bluffing either. These very words will come true on judgment day.

The people of Jerusalem chose to disown God, and they lived with the consequences of their disobedience. Yes, God brought some of the exiles back to their land, but that did not happen until 70 years after the first deportation in 605 BC. Most individuals died before the people were able to return to Jerusalem and experience God's mercy. Believers need to recognize who God is now and what he desires for them as citizens of his kingdom so that they may experience his grace when the time comes for him to return and give it to those who have been waiting.

11 Now Nebuchadnezzar king of Babylon had given these orders about Jeremiah through Nebuzaradan commander of the imperial guard: 12 "Take him and look after him; don't harm him but do for him whatever he asks." 13 So Nebuzaradan the commander of the guard, Nebushazban a chief officer, Nergal-Sharezer a high official and all the other officers of the king of Babylon 14 sent and had Jeremiah taken out of the courtyard of the guard. They turned him over to Gedaliah son of Ahikam, the son of Shaphan, to take him back to his home. So he remained among his own people.

15 While Jeremiah had been confined in the courtyard of the guard, the word of the LORD came to him: 16 "Go and tell Ebed-Melek the Cushite, 'This is what the LORD Almighty, the God of Israel, says: I am about to fulfill my words against this city—words concerning disaster, not prosperity. At that time they will be fulfilled before your eyes. 17 But I will rescue you on that day, declares the LORD; you will not be given into the hands of those you fear. 18 I will save you; you will not fall by the sword but will escape with your life, because you trust in me, declares the LORD.'"

Jeremiah Freed

40 The word came to Jeremiah from the LORD after Nebuzaradan commander of the imperial guard had released him at Ramah. He had found Jeremiah bound in chains among all the captives from Jerusalem and Judah who were being carried into exile to Babylon. 2 When the commander of the guard found Jeremiah, he said to him, "The LORD your God decreed this disaster for this place. 3 And now the LORD has brought it about; he has done just as he said he would. All this happened because you people sinned against the LORD and did not obey him. 4 But today I am freeing you from the chains on your wrists. Come with me to Babylon, if you like, and I will look after you; but if you do not want to, then don't come. Look, the whole country lies before you; go wherever you please." 5 However, before Jeremiah turned to go,[a] Nebuzaradan added, "Go back to Gedaliah son of Ahikam, the son of Shaphan, whom the king of Babylon has appointed over the towns of Judah, and live with him among the people, or go anywhere else you please."

Then the commander gave him provisions and a present and let him go. 6 So Jeremiah went to Gedaliah son of Ahikam at Mizpah and stayed with him among the people who were left behind in the land.

Gedaliah Assassinated

7 When all the army officers and their men who were still in the open country heard that the king of Babylon had appointed Gedaliah son of Ahikam as governor over the land and had put him in charge of the men, women and children who were the poorest in the land and who had not been carried into exile to Babylon, 8 they came to Gedaliah at Mizpah—Ishmael son of Nethaniah, Johanan and Jonathan the sons of Kareah, Seraiah son of Tanhumeth, the sons of Ephai the Netophathite, and Jaazaniah[b] the son of the Maakathite, and their men. 9 Gedaliah son of Ahikam, the son of Shaphan, took an oath to reassure them and their men. "Do not be afraid to serve the Babylonians,[c]" he said. "Settle down in the land and serve the king of Babylon, and it will go well with you. 10 I myself will stay at Mizpah to represent you before the Babylonians who come to us, but you are to harvest the wine, summer fruit and olive oil, and put them in your storage jars, and live in the towns you have taken over."

11 When all the Jews in Moab, Ammon, Edom and all the other countries heard that the king of Babylon had left a remnant in Judah and had appointed Gedaliah son of Ahikam, the son of Shaphan, as governor over them, 12 they all came back to the land of Judah, to Gedaliah at Mizpah, from all the countries where

[a] 5 Or *Jeremiah answered* [b] 8 Hebrew *Jezaniah,* a variant of *Jaazaniah*
[c] 9 Or *Chaldeans*; also in verse 10

JEREMIAH 40:1–4

SPIRITUAL TRUTH FROM AN UNBELIEVER

Despite the fact that the people of Judah ignored Jeremiah's prophecies, the Babylonians listened and believed what he had said. In chapter 40, the commander of the imperial guard spoke Jeremiah's words back to him and essentially confirmed what Jeremiah had been saying all along: that the Lord had brought about the destruction of Jerusalem because of the people's rebellion against the Lord. This instance was not the last time truth was to come from the mouth of an unbeliever.

When Jesus died on the cross, the Roman centurion who had supervised his crucifixion exclaimed, "Surely this man was the Son of God" (Mk 15:39). The centurion's realization and the Babylonian commander's knowledge of Jeremiah's prophecies show how the truth of God is for anyone and everyone—believers and nonbelievers alike. Jesus came to save the lost (Lk 19:10), so no matter what unconventional manner the message may take, anyone can hear God's truth.

they had been scattered. And they harvested an abundance of wine and summer fruit.
13 Johanan son of Kareah and all the army officers still in the open country
came to Gedaliah at Mizpah 14 and said to him, "Don't you know that Baalis king
of the Ammonites has sent Ishmael son of Nethaniah to take your life?" But Gedaliah son of Ahikam did not believe them.
15 Then Johanan son of Kareah said privately to Gedaliah in Mizpah, "Let me
go and kill Ishmael son of Nethaniah, and no one will know it. Why should he
take your life and cause all the Jews who are gathered around you to be scattered
and the remnant of Judah to perish?"
16 But Gedaliah son of Ahikam said to Johanan son of Kareah, "Don't do such
a thing! What you are saying about Ishmael is not true."

41 In the seventh month Ishmael son of Nethaniah, the son of Elishama,
who was of royal blood and had been one of the king's officers, came with
ten men to Gedaliah son of Ahikam at Mizpah. While they were eating together
there, 2 Ishmael son of Nethaniah and the ten men who were with him got up and
struck down Gedaliah son of Ahikam, the son of Shaphan, with the sword, killing the one whom the king of Babylon had appointed as governor over the land.
3 Ishmael also killed all the men of Judah who were with Gedaliah at Mizpah, as
well as the Babylonian[a] soldiers who were there.
4 The day after Gedaliah's assassination, before anyone knew about it, 5 eighty
men who had shaved off their beards, torn their clothes and cut themselves came
from Shechem, Shiloh and Samaria, bringing grain offerings and incense with
them to the house of the LORD. 6 Ishmael son of Nethaniah went out from Mizpah
to meet them, weeping as he went. When he met them, he said, "Come to Gedaliah son of Ahikam." 7 When they went into the city, Ishmael son of Nethaniah
and the men who were with him slaughtered them and threw them into a cistern.
8 But ten of them said to Ishmael, "Don't kill us! We have wheat and barley, olive oil
and honey, hidden in a field." So he let them alone and did not kill them with the
others. 9 Now the cistern where he threw all the bodies of the men he had killed
along with Gedaliah was the one King Asa had made as part of his defense against
Baasha king of Israel. Ishmael son of Nethaniah filled it with the dead.
10 Ishmael made captives of all the rest of the people who were in Mizpah—
the king's daughters along with all the others who were left there, over whom
Nebuzaradan commander of the imperial guard had appointed Gedaliah son of
Ahikam. Ishmael son of Nethaniah took them captive and set out to cross over
to the Ammonites.
11 When Johanan son of Kareah and all the army officers who were with him
heard about all the crimes Ishmael son of Nethaniah had committed, 12 they took
all their men and went to fight Ishmael son of Nethaniah. They caught up with
him near the great pool in Gibeon. 13 When all the people Ishmael had with him
saw Johanan son of Kareah and the army officers who were with him, they were
glad. 14 All the people Ishmael had taken captive at Mizpah turned and went over
to Johanan son of Kareah. 15 But Ishmael son of Nethaniah and eight of his men
escaped from Johanan and fled to the Ammonites.

Flight to Egypt

16 Then Johanan son of Kareah and all the army officers who were with him led
away all the people of Mizpah who had survived, whom Johanan had recovered
from Ishmael son of Nethaniah after Ishmael had assassinated Gedaliah son of
Ahikam—the soldiers, women, children and court officials he had recovered
from Gibeon. 17 And they went on, stopping at Geruth Kimham near Bethlehem
on their way to Egypt 18 to escape the Babylonians.[b] They were afraid of them because Ishmael son of Nethaniah had killed Gedaliah son of Ahikam, whom the
king of Babylon had appointed as governor over the land.

---

[a] *3* Or *Chaldean* [b] *18* Or *Chaldeans*

42 Then all the army officers, including Johanan son of Kareah and Jezaniah[a] son of Hoshaiah, and all the people from the least to the greatest approached [2]Jeremiah the prophet and said to him, "Please hear our petition and
pray to the LORD your God for this entire remnant. For as you now see, though
we were once many, now only a few are left. [3]Pray that the LORD your God will
tell us where we should go and what we should do."
[4]"I have heard you," replied Jeremiah the prophet. "I will certainly pray to the
LORD your God as you have requested; I will tell you everything the LORD says
and will keep nothing back from you."
[5]Then they said to Jeremiah, "May the LORD be a true and faithful witness
against us if we do not act in accordance with everything the LORD your God
sends you to tell us. [6]Whether it is favorable or unfavorable, we will obey the
LORD our God, to whom we are sending you, so that it will go well with us, for we
will obey the LORD our God."
[7]Ten days later the word of the LORD came to Jeremiah. [8]So he called together
Johanan son of Kareah and all the army officers who were with him and all the
people from the least to the greatest. [9]He said to them, "This is what the LORD,
the God of Israel, to whom you sent me to present your petition, says: [10]'If you
stay in this land, I will build you up and not tear you down; I will plant you and
not uproot you, for I have relented concerning the disaster I have inflicted on
you. [11]Do not be afraid of the king of Babylon, whom you now fear. Do not be
afraid of him, declares the LORD, for I am with you and will save you and deliver
you from his hands. [12]I will show you compassion so that he will have compassion on you and restore you to your land.'
[13]"However, if you say, 'We will not stay in this land,' and so disobey the LORD
your God, [14]and if you say, 'No, we will go and live in Egypt, where we will not
see war or hear the trumpet or be hungry for bread,' [15]then hear the word of the
LORD, you remnant of Judah. This is what the LORD Almighty, the God of Israel,
says: 'If you are determined to go to Egypt and you do go to settle there, [16]then
the sword you fear will overtake you there, and the famine you dread will follow
you into Egypt, and there you will die. [17]Indeed, all who are determined to go to
Egypt to settle there will die by the sword, famine and plague; not one of them
will survive or escape the disaster I will bring on them.' [18]This is what the LORD
Almighty, the God of Israel, says: 'As my anger and wrath have been poured out
on those who lived in Jerusalem, so will my wrath be poured out on you when
you go to Egypt. You will be a curse[b] and an object of horror, a curse[b] and an object of reproach; you will never see this place again.'
[19]"Remnant of Judah, the LORD has told you, 'Do not go to Egypt.' Be sure of
this: I warn you today [20]that you made a fatal mistake when you sent me to the
LORD your God and said, 'Pray to the LORD our God for us; tell us everything he
says and we will do it.' [21]I have told you today, but you still have not obeyed the
LORD your God in all he sent me to tell you. [22]So now, be sure of this: You will die
by the sword, famine and plague in the place where you want to go to settle."

43 When Jeremiah had finished telling the people all the words of the LORD
their God — everything the LORD had sent him to tell them — [2]Azariah
son of Hoshaiah and Johanan son of Kareah and all the arrogant men said to
Jeremiah, "You are lying! The LORD our God has not sent you to say, 'You must
not go to Egypt to settle there.' [3]But Baruch son of Neriah is inciting you against
us to hand us over to the Babylonians,[c] so they may kill us or carry us into exile
to Babylon."
[4]So Johanan son of Kareah and all the army officers and all the people disobeyed the LORD's command to stay in the land of Judah. [5]Instead, Johanan son
of Kareah and all the army officers led away all the remnant of Judah who had
come back to live in the land of Judah from all the nations where they had been

[a] *1* Hebrew; Septuagint (see also 43:2) *Azariah* [b] *18* That is, your name will be used in cursing (see 29:22); or, others will see that you are cursed. [c] *3* Or *Chaldeans*

JEREMIAH 42:1 – 22

WHEN WILL THEY LEARN?

After Jeremiah correctly prophesied the fall of Jerusalem, one would think that the people would have been more prone to listen to him and heed his message. Here a remnant that escaped death and exile ask Jeremiah to pray to the Lord and ask him what they should do. Jeremiah does so, telling them to stay where they are and not go to Egypt. The word of the Lord seems pretty straightforward, but what did the people do? They called Jeremiah a liar and went directly to Egypt in direct defiance of God's word (Jer 43:1 – 5).

Sometimes God's truth is obvious and explicit. For the Israelites, Jeremiah spelled out exactly what they should not do. For believers today, the truth revealed in Jesus Christ is written in Scripture. Everything that is necessary for life is found in Jesus. He can be trusted because his ways are perfect. Jesus says that he is "the way and the truth and the life" (Jn 14:6).

scattered. 6They also led away all those whom Nebuzaradan commander of the imperial guard had left with Gedaliah son of Ahikam, the son of Shaphan — the men, the women, the children and the king's daughters. And they took Jeremiah the prophet and Baruch son of Neriah along with them. 7So they entered Egypt in disobedience to the LORD and went as far as Tahpanhes.

8In Tahpanhes the word of the LORD came to Jeremiah: 9"While the Jews are watching, take some large stones with you and bury them in clay in the brick pavement at the entrance to Pharaoh's palace in Tahpanhes. 10Then say to them, 'This is what the LORD Almighty, the God of Israel, says: I will send for my servant Nebuchadnezzar king of Babylon, and I will set his throne over these stones I have buried here; he will spread his royal canopy above them. 11He will come and attack Egypt, bringing death to those destined for death, captivity to those destined for captivity, and the sword to those destined for the sword. 12He will set fire to the temples of the gods of Egypt; he will burn their temples and take their gods captive. As a shepherd picks his garment clean of lice, so he will pick Egypt clean and depart. 13There in the temple of the sun[a] in Egypt he will demolish the sacred pillars and will burn down the temples of the gods of Egypt.' "

Disaster Because of Idolatry

44 This word came to Jeremiah concerning all the Jews living in Lower Egypt — in Migdol, Tahpanhes and Memphis — and in Upper Egypt: 2"This is what the LORD Almighty, the God of Israel, says: You saw the great disaster I brought on Jerusalem and on all the towns of Judah. Today they lie deserted and in ruins 3because of the evil they have done. They aroused my anger by burning incense to and worshiping other gods that neither they nor you nor your ancestors ever knew. 4Again and again I sent my servants the prophets, who said, 'Do not do this detestable thing that I hate!' 5But they did not listen or pay attention; they did not turn from their wickedness or stop burning incense to other gods. 6Therefore, my fierce anger was poured out; it raged against the towns of Judah and the streets of Jerusalem and made them the desolate ruins they are today.

7"Now this is what the LORD God Almighty, the God of Israel, says: Why bring such great disaster on yourselves by cutting off from Judah the men and women, the children and infants, and so leave yourselves without a remnant? 8Why arouse my anger with what your hands have made, burning incense to other gods in Egypt, where you have come to live? You will destroy yourselves and make yourselves a curse[b] and an object of reproach among all the nations on earth. 9Have you forgotten the wickedness committed by your ancestors and by the kings and queens of Judah and the wickedness committed by you and your wives in the land of Judah and the streets of Jerusalem? 10To this day they have not humbled themselves or shown reverence, nor have they followed my law and the decrees I set before you and your ancestors.

11"Therefore this is what the LORD Almighty, the God of Israel, says: I am determined to bring disaster on you and to destroy all Judah. 12I will take away the remnant of Judah who were determined to go to Egypt to settle there. They will all perish in Egypt; they will fall by the sword or die from famine. From the least to the greatest, they will die by sword or famine. They will become a curse and an object of horror, a curse and an object of reproach. 13I will punish those who live in Egypt with the sword, famine and plague, as I punished Jerusalem. 14None of the remnant of Judah who have gone to live in Egypt will escape or survive to return to the land of Judah, to which they long to return and live; none will return except a few fugitives."

15Then all the men who knew that their wives were burning incense to other gods, along with all the women who were present — a large assembly — and all

[a] *13* Or *in Heliopolis* [b] *8* That is, your name will be used in cursing (see 29:22); or, others will see that you are cursed; also in verse 12; similarly in verse 22.

JEREMIAH 43:8

PERSECUTED FOR RIGHTEOUSNESS' SAKE

Despite Jeremiah's warning to those left behind in Jerusalem to not go to Egypt, the people completely ignored him. They left for Egypt, and even forced Jeremiah to go along with them (Jer 43:6). Jeremiah simply did what he did best and continued to preach the truth of God. In verse 8, Jeremiah heard the word of the Lord, and again he proclaimed it to the people. He did not hold back because of how poorly they had treated him in the past; rather, he remained obedient to his calling and passed along the truth that God gave him to share.

Jesus taught about being persecuted for the sake of righteousness (Mt 5:10 – 11), and few people experienced persecution like Jeremiah did. Almost every time he did what was right and shared God's truth, he received some sort of negative backlash. The story of Jeremiah can be encouraging to believers who experience persecution as a result of standing strong in the faith.

JEREMIAH 44:14 – 18

RULER OF HEAVEN

God consistently warned his people throughout the Old Testament not to worship other gods. Yet many Israelites intermarried with people who practiced other religions, which often led the Israelites away from worshiping God. Unfortunately, the people did not understand that God was the true Ruler of heaven. Had they

(continued on next page)

the people living in Lower and Upper Egypt, said to Jeremiah, 16"We will not listen to the message you have spoken to us in the name of the LORD! 17We will certainly do everything we said we would: We will burn incense to the Queen of Heaven and will pour out drink offerings to her just as we and our ancestors, our kings and our officials did in the towns of Judah and in the streets of Jerusalem. At that time we had plenty of food and were well off and suffered no harm. 18But ever since we stopped burning incense to the Queen of Heaven and pouring out drink offerings to her, we have had nothing and have been perishing by sword and famine."

19The women added, "When we burned incense to the Queen of Heaven and poured out drink offerings to her, did not our husbands know that we were making cakes impressed with her image and pouring out drink offerings to her?"

20Then Jeremiah said to all the people, both men and women, who were answering him, 21"Did not the LORD remember and call to mind the incense burned in the towns of Judah and the streets of Jerusalem by you and your ancestors, your kings and your officials and the people of the land? 22When the LORD could no longer endure your wicked actions and the detestable things you did, your land became a curse and a desolate waste without inhabitants, as it is today. 23Because you have burned incense and have sinned against the LORD and have not obeyed him or followed his law or his decrees or his stipulations, this disaster has come upon you, as you now see."

24Then Jeremiah said to all the people, including the women, "Hear the word of the LORD, all you people of Judah in Egypt. 25This is what the LORD Almighty, the God of Israel, says: You and your wives have done what you said you would do when you promised, 'We will certainly carry out the vows we made to burn incense and pour out drink offerings to the Queen of Heaven.'

"Go ahead then, do what you promised! Keep your vows! 26But hear the word of the LORD, all you Jews living in Egypt: 'I swear by my great name,' says the LORD, 'that no one from Judah living anywhere in Egypt will ever again invoke my name or swear, "As surely as the Sovereign LORD lives." 27For I am watching over them for harm, not for good; the Jews in Egypt will perish by sword and famine until they are all destroyed. 28Those who escape the sword and return to the land of Judah from Egypt will be very few. Then the whole remnant of Judah who came to live in Egypt will know whose word will stand — mine or theirs.

29" 'This will be the sign to you that I will punish you in this place,' declares the LORD, 'so that you will know that my threats of harm against you will surely stand.' 30This is what the LORD says: 'I am going to deliver Pharaoh Hophra king of Egypt into the hands of his enemies who want to kill him, just as I gave Zedekiah king of Judah into the hands of Nebuchadnezzar king of Babylon, the enemy who wanted to kill him.' "

A Message to Baruch

45 When Baruch son of Neriah wrote on a scroll the words Jeremiah the prophet dictated in the fourth year of Jehoiakim son of Josiah king of Judah, Jeremiah said this to Baruch: 2"This is what the LORD, the God of Israel, says to you, Baruch: 3You said, 'Woe to me! The LORD has added sorrow to my pain; I am worn out with groaning and find no rest.' 4But the LORD has told me to say to you, 'This is what the LORD says: I will overthrow what I have built and uproot what I have planted, throughout the earth. 5Should you then seek great things for yourself? Do not seek them. For I will bring disaster on all people, declares the LORD, but wherever you go I will let you escape with your life.' "

A Message About Egypt

46 This is the word of the LORD that came to Jeremiah the prophet concerning the nations:

2Concerning Egypt:

(Ruler of Heaven, continued)

stopped worshiping false gods and instead listened to Jeremiah and followed the one true God, their circumstances could have been drastically different.

Jesus echoed Jeremiah's message when he was tempted by Satan in the wilderness: "Worship the Lord your God, and serve him only" (Mt 4:10). Even today believers worship false gods of money, pride, power and other entities that promise rewards but don't deliver. While modern believers no longer offer sacrifices to the "Queen of Heaven," it is important for believers to be consistently aware of anything that may be distracting them from worshiping and obeying God.

This is the message against the army of Pharaoh Necho king of Egypt, which was defeated at Carchemish on the Euphrates River by Nebuchadnezzar king of Babylon in the fourth year of Jehoiakim son of Josiah king of Judah:

3 "Prepare your shields, both large and small,
and march out for battle!
4 Harness the horses,
mount the steeds!
Take your positions
with helmets on!
Polish your spears,
put on your armor!
5 What do I see?
They are terrified,
they are retreating,
their warriors are defeated.
They flee in haste
without looking back,
and there is terror on every side,"
declares the LORD.
6 "The swift cannot flee
nor the strong escape.
In the north by the River Euphrates
they stumble and fall.
7 "Who is this that rises like the Nile,
like rivers of surging waters?
8 Egypt rises like the Nile,
like rivers of surging waters.
She says, 'I will rise and cover the earth;
I will destroy cities and their people.'
9 Charge, you horses!
Drive furiously, you charioteers!
March on, you warriors — men of Cush[a] and Put who carry shields,
men of Lydia who draw the bow.
10 But that day belongs to the Lord, the LORD Almighty —
a day of vengeance, for vengeance on his foes.
The sword will devour till it is satisfied,
till it has quenched its thirst with blood.
For the Lord, the LORD Almighty, will offer sacrifice
in the land of the north by the River Euphrates.

11 "Go up to Gilead and get balm,
Virgin Daughter Egypt.
But you try many medicines in vain;
there is no healing for you.
12 The nations will hear of your shame;
your cries will fill the earth.
One warrior will stumble over another;
both will fall down together."

13 This is the message the LORD spoke to Jeremiah the prophet about the coming of Nebuchadnezzar king of Babylon to attack Egypt:

14 "Announce this in Egypt, and proclaim it in Migdol;
proclaim it also in Memphis and Tahpanhes:
'Take your positions and get ready,
for the sword devours those around you.'

[a] 9 That is, the upper Nile region

15 Why will your warriors be laid low?
They cannot stand, for the LORD will push them down.
16 They will stumble repeatedly;
they will fall over each other.
They will say, 'Get up, let us go back
to our own people and our native lands,
away from the sword of the oppressor.'
17 There they will exclaim,
'Pharaoh king of Egypt is only a loud noise;
he has missed his opportunity.'

18 "As surely as I live," declares the King,
whose name is the LORD Almighty,
"one will come who is like Tabor among the mountains,
like Carmel by the sea.
19 Pack your belongings for exile,
you who live in Egypt,
for Memphis will be laid waste
and lie in ruins without inhabitant.

20 "Egypt is a beautiful heifer,
but a gadfly is coming
against her from the north.
21 The mercenaries in her ranks
are like fattened calves.
They too will turn and flee together,
they will not stand their ground,
for the day of disaster is coming upon them,
the time for them to be punished.
22 Egypt will hiss like a fleeing serpent
as the enemy advances in force;
they will come against her with axes,
like men who cut down trees.
23 They will chop down her forest,"
declares the LORD,
"dense though it be.
They are more numerous than locusts,
they cannot be counted.
24 Daughter Egypt will be put to shame,
given into the hands of the people of the north."

25 The LORD Almighty, the God of Israel, says: "I am about to bring punishment on Amon god of Thebes, on Pharaoh, on Egypt and her gods and her kings,
and on those who rely on Pharaoh. 26 I will give them into the hands of those
who want to kill them — Nebuchadnezzar king of Babylon and his officers. Later,
however, Egypt will be inhabited as in times past," declares the LORD.

27 "Do not be afraid, Jacob my servant;
do not be dismayed, Israel.
I will surely save you out of a distant place,
your descendants from the land of their exile.
Jacob will again have peace and security,
and no one will make him afraid.
28 Do not be afraid, Jacob my servant,
for I am with you," declares the LORD.
"Though I completely destroy all the nations
among which I scatter you,
I will not completely destroy you.
I will discipline you but only in due measure;
I will not let you go entirely unpunished."

A Message About the Philistines

47 This is the word of the LORD that came to Jeremiah the prophet concerning the Philistines before Pharaoh attacked Gaza:

2 This is what the LORD says:

"See how the waters are rising in the north;
they will become an overflowing torrent.
They will overflow the land and everything in it,
the towns and those who live in them.
The people will cry out;
all who dwell in the land will wail
3 at the sound of the hooves of galloping steeds,
at the noise of enemy chariots
and the rumble of their wheels.
Parents will not turn to help their children;
their hands will hang limp.
4 For the day has come
to destroy all the Philistines
and to remove all survivors
who could help Tyre and Sidon.
The LORD is about to destroy the Philistines,
the remnant from the coasts of Caphtor.[a]
5 Gaza will shave her head in mourning;
Ashkelon will be silenced.
You remnant on the plain,
how long will you cut yourselves?

6 " 'Alas, sword of the LORD,
how long till you rest?
Return to your sheath;
cease and be still.'
7 But how can it rest
when the LORD has commanded it,
when he has ordered it
to attack Ashkelon and the coast?"

A Message About Moab

48 Concerning Moab:

This is what the LORD Almighty, the God of Israel, says:
"Woe to Nebo, for it will be ruined.
Kiriathaim will be disgraced and captured;
the stronghold[b] will be disgraced and shattered.
2 Moab will be praised no more;
in Heshbon[c] people will plot her downfall:
'Come, let us put an end to that nation.'
You, the people of Madmen,[d] will also be silenced;
the sword will pursue you.
3 Cries of anguish arise from Horonaim,
cries of great havoc and destruction.
4 Moab will be broken;
her little ones will cry out.[e]
5 They go up the hill to Luhith,
weeping bitterly as they go;

---

[a] 4 That is, Crete [b] 1 Or *captured; / Misgab* [c] 2 The Hebrew for *Heshbon* sounds like the Hebrew for *plot.* [d] 2 The name of the Moabite town Madmen sounds like the Hebrew for *be silenced.* [e] 4 Hebrew; Septuagint / *proclaim it to Zoar*

on the road down to Horonaim
anguished cries over the destruction are heard.
6 Flee! Run for your lives;
become like a bush[a] in the desert.
7 Since you trust in your deeds and riches,
you too will be taken captive,
and Chemosh will go into exile,
together with his priests and officials.
8 The destroyer will come against every town,
and not a town will escape.
The valley will be ruined
and the plateau destroyed,
because the LORD has spoken.
9 Put salt on Moab,
for she will be laid waste[b];
her towns will become desolate,
with no one to live in them.

10 "A curse on anyone who is lax in doing the LORD's work!
A curse on anyone who keeps their sword from bloodshed!

11 "Moab has been at rest from youth,
like wine left on its dregs,
not poured from one jar to another—
she has not gone into exile.
So she tastes as she did,
and her aroma is unchanged.
12 But days are coming,"
declares the LORD,
"when I will send men who pour from pitchers,
and they will pour her out;
they will empty her pitchers
and smash her jars.
13 Then Moab will be ashamed of Chemosh,
as Israel was ashamed
when they trusted in Bethel.

14 "How can you say, 'We are warriors,
men valiant in battle'?
15 Moab will be destroyed and her towns invaded;
her finest young men will go down in the slaughter,"
declares the King, whose name is the LORD Almighty.
16 "The fall of Moab is at hand;
her calamity will come quickly.
17 Mourn for her, all who live around her,
all who know her fame;
say, 'How broken is the mighty scepter,
how broken the glorious staff!'

18 "Come down from your glory
and sit on the parched ground,
you inhabitants of Daughter Dibon,
for the one who destroys Moab
will come up against you
and ruin your fortified cities.
19 Stand by the road and watch,
you who live in Aroer.

[a] 6 Or *like Aroer* [b] 9 Or *Give wings to Moab, / for she will fly away*

JEREMIAH 48:9

SALT

In the Old Testament, the image of salt is used to describe judgment and destruction. Look, for example, at Lot's wife (Ge 19:26), or at Abimelek's action after conquering Shechem (Jdg 9:45). Jeremiah 48:9 is reminiscent of Abimelek's story in that God wanted Moab to be completely destroyed and perpetually barren.

However, the image of salt is completely transformed in the New Testament. There Jesus used salt as an image of preservation and life enrichment (Mt 5:13). Salt is a savoring element meant to make food taste better; therefore, Christians are called to be the salt of the earth in order to bring out the fullness of life, which is only realized when living in accordance with Jesus.

Ask the man fleeing and the woman escaping,
ask them, 'What has happened?'
20 Moab is disgraced, for she is shattered.
Wail and cry out!
Announce by the Arnon
that Moab is destroyed.
21 Judgment has come to the plateau —
to Holon, Jahzah and Mephaath,
22 to Dibon, Nebo and Beth Diblathaim,
23 to Kiriathaim, Beth Gamul and Beth Meon,
24 to Kerioth and Bozrah —
to all the towns of Moab, far and near.
25 Moab's horn[a] is cut off;
her arm is broken,"
declares the LORD.

26 "Make her drunk,
for she has defied the LORD.
Let Moab wallow in her vomit;
let her be an object of ridicule.
27 Was not Israel the object of your ridicule?
Was she caught among thieves,
that you shake your head in scorn
whenever you speak of her?
28 Abandon your towns and dwell among the rocks,
you who live in Moab.
Be like a dove that makes its nest
at the mouth of a cave.

29 "We have heard of Moab's pride —
how great is her arrogance! —
of her insolence, her pride, her conceit
and the haughtiness of her heart.
30 I know her insolence but it is futile,"
declares the LORD,
"and her boasts accomplish nothing.
31 Therefore I wail over Moab,
for all Moab I cry out,
I moan for the people of Kir Hareseth.
32 I weep for you, as Jazer weeps,
you vines of Sibmah.
Your branches spread as far as the sea[b];
they reached as far as[c] Jazer.
The destroyer has fallen
on your ripened fruit and grapes.
33 Joy and gladness are gone
from the orchards and fields of Moab.
I have stopped the flow of wine from the presses;
no one treads them with shouts of joy.
Although there are shouts,
they are not shouts of joy.

34 "The sound of their cry rises
from Heshbon to Elealeh and Jahaz,
from Zoar as far as Horonaim and Eglath Shelishiyah,
for even the waters of Nimrim are dried up.

[a] 25 *Horn* here symbolizes strength. [b] 32 Probably the Dead Sea [c] 32 Two Hebrew manuscripts and Septuagint; most Hebrew manuscripts *as far as the Sea of*

35 In Moab I will put an end
to those who make offerings on the high places
and burn incense to their gods,"
declares the LORD.
36 "So my heart laments for Moab like the music of a pipe;
it laments like a pipe for the people of Kir Hareseth.
The wealth they acquired is gone.
37 Every head is shaved
and every beard cut off;
every hand is slashed
and every waist is covered with sackcloth.
38 On all the roofs in Moab
and in the public squares
there is nothing but mourning,
for I have broken Moab
like a jar that no one wants,"
declares the LORD.

39 "How shattered she is! How they wail!
How Moab turns her back in shame!
Moab has become an object of ridicule,
an object of horror to all those around her."

40 This is what the LORD says:

"Look! An eagle is swooping down,
spreading its wings over Moab.
41 Kerioth[a] will be captured
and the strongholds taken.
In that day the hearts of Moab's warriors
will be like the heart of a woman in labor.
42 Moab will be destroyed as a nation
because she defied the LORD.
43 Terror and pit and snare await you,
you people of Moab,"
declares the LORD.
44 "Whoever flees from the terror
will fall into a pit,
whoever climbs out of the pit
will be caught in a snare;
for I will bring on Moab
the year of her punishment,"
declares the LORD.

45 "In the shadow of Heshbon
the fugitives stand helpless,
for a fire has gone out from Heshbon,
a blaze from the midst of Sihon;
it burns the foreheads of Moab,
the skulls of the noisy boasters.
46 Woe to you, Moab!
The people of Chemosh are destroyed;
your sons are taken into exile
and your daughters into captivity.

47 "Yet I will restore the fortunes of Moab
in days to come,"
declares the LORD.

Here ends the judgment on Moab.

[a] 41 Or *The cities*

A Message About Ammon

49 Concerning the Ammonites:

This is what the LORD says:

"Has Israel no sons?
Has Israel no heir?
Why then has Molek[a] taken possession of Gad?
Why do his people live in its towns?
2 But the days are coming,"
declares the LORD,
"when I will sound the battle cry
against Rabbah of the Ammonites;
it will become a mound of ruins,
and its surrounding villages will be set on fire.
Then Israel will drive out
those who drove her out,"

says the LORD.

3 "Wail, Heshbon, for Ai is destroyed!
Cry out, you inhabitants of Rabbah!
Put on sackcloth and mourn;
rush here and there inside the walls,
for Molek will go into exile,
together with his priests and officials.
4 Why do you boast of your valleys,
boast of your valleys so fruitful?
Unfaithful Daughter Ammon,
you trust in your riches and say,
'Who will attack me?'
5 I will bring terror on you
from all those around you,"

declares the Lord, the LORD Almighty.

"Every one of you will be driven away,
and no one will gather the fugitives.

6 "Yet afterward, I will restore the fortunes of the Ammonites,"

declares the LORD.

A Message About Edom

7 Concerning Edom:

This is what the LORD Almighty says:

"Is there no longer wisdom in Teman?
Has counsel perished from the prudent?
Has their wisdom decayed?
8 Turn and flee, hide in deep caves,
you who live in Dedan,
for I will bring disaster on Esau
at the time when I punish him.
9 If grape pickers came to you,
would they not leave a few grapes?
If thieves came during the night,
would they not steal only as much as they wanted?
10 But I will strip Esau bare;
I will uncover his hiding places,
so that he cannot conceal himself.

---

[a] *1* Or *their king*; also in verse 3

His armed men are destroyed,
also his allies and neighbors,
so there is no one to say,
11 'Leave your fatherless children; I will keep them alive.
Your widows too can depend on me.' "

12 This is what the LORD says: "If those who do not deserve to drink the cup
must drink it, why should you go unpunished? You will not go unpunished, but
must drink it. 13 I swear by myself," declares the LORD, "that Bozrah will become
a ruin and a curse,[a] an object of horror and reproach; and all its towns will be
in ruins forever."

14 I have heard a message from the LORD;
an envoy was sent to the nations to say,
"Assemble yourselves to attack it!
Rise up for battle!"

15 "Now I will make you small among the nations,
despised by mankind.
16 The terror you inspire
and the pride of your heart have deceived you,
you who live in the clefts of the rocks,
who occupy the heights of the hill.
Though you build your nest as high as the eagle's,
from there I will bring you down,"
declares the LORD.

17 "Edom will become an object of horror;
all who pass by will be appalled and will scoff
because of all its wounds.
18 As Sodom and Gomorrah were overthrown,
along with their neighboring towns,"
says the LORD,

"so no one will live there;
no people will dwell in it.

19 "Like a lion coming up from Jordan's thickets
to a rich pastureland,
I will chase Edom from its land in an instant.
Who is the chosen one I will appoint for this?
Who is like me and who can challenge me?
And what shepherd can stand against me?"

20 Therefore, hear what the LORD has planned against Edom,
what he has purposed against those who live in Teman:
The young of the flock will be dragged away;
their pasture will be appalled at their fate.
21 At the sound of their fall the earth will tremble;
their cry will resound to the Red Sea.[b]
22 Look! An eagle will soar and swoop down,
spreading its wings over Bozrah.
In that day the hearts of Edom's warriors
will be like the heart of a woman in labor.

A Message About Damascus

23 Concerning Damascus:

"Hamath and Arpad are dismayed,
for they have heard bad news.

---

[a] *13* That is, its name will be used in cursing (see 29:22); or, others will see that it is cursed.
[b] *21* Or *the Sea of Reeds*

They are disheartened,
troubled like[a] the restless sea.
24 Damascus has become feeble,
she has turned to flee
and panic has gripped her;
anguish and pain have seized her,
pain like that of a woman in labor.
25 Why has the city of renown not been abandoned,
the town in which I delight?
26 Surely, her young men will fall in the streets;
all her soldiers will be silenced in that day,"
declares the LORD Almighty.

27 "I will set fire to the walls of Damascus;
it will consume the fortresses of Ben-Hadad."

A Message About Kedar and Hazor

28 Concerning Kedar and the kingdoms of Hazor, which Nebuchadnezzar king
of Babylon attacked:

This is what the LORD says:

"Arise, and attack Kedar
and destroy the people of the East.
29 Their tents and their flocks will be taken;
their shelters will be carried off
with all their goods and camels.
People will shout to them,
'Terror on every side!'

30 "Flee quickly away!
Stay in deep caves, you who live in Hazor,"
declares the LORD.

"Nebuchadnezzar king of Babylon has plotted against you;
he has devised a plan against you.

31 "Arise and attack a nation at ease,
which lives in confidence,"
declares the LORD,

"a nation that has neither gates nor bars;
its people live far from danger.
32 Their camels will become plunder,
and their large herds will be spoils of war.
I will scatter to the winds those who are in distant places[b]
and will bring disaster on them from every side,"
declares the LORD.

33 "Hazor will become a haunt of jackals,
a desolate place forever.
No one will live there;
no people will dwell in it."

A Message About Elam

34 This is the word of the LORD that came to Jeremiah the prophet concerning
Elam, early in the reign of Zedekiah king of Judah:

35 This is what the LORD Almighty says:

"See, I will break the bow of Elam,
the mainstay of their might.

[a] 23 Hebrew *on* or *by* [b] 32 Or *who clip the hair by their foreheads*

36 I will bring against Elam the four winds
from the four quarters of heaven;
I will scatter them to the four winds,
and there will not be a nation
where Elam's exiles do not go.
37 I will shatter Elam before their foes,
before those who want to kill them;
I will bring disaster on them,
even my fierce anger,"
declares the LORD.

"I will pursue them with the sword
until I have made an end of them.
38 I will set my throne in Elam
and destroy her king and officials,"
declares the LORD.

39 "Yet I will restore the fortunes of Elam
in days to come,"
declares the LORD.

A Message About Babylon

50 This is the word the LORD spoke through Jeremiah the prophet concerning Babylon and the land of the Babylonians[a]:

2 "Announce and proclaim among the nations,
lift up a banner and proclaim it;
keep nothing back, but say,
'Babylon will be captured;
Bel will be put to shame,
Marduk filled with terror.
Her images will be put to shame
and her idols filled with terror.'
3 A nation from the north will attack her
and lay waste her land.
No one will live in it;
both people and animals will flee away.

4 "In those days, at that time,"
declares the LORD,
"the people of Israel and the people of Judah together
will go in tears to seek the LORD their God.
5 They will ask the way to Zion
and turn their faces toward it.
They will come and bind themselves to the LORD
in an everlasting covenant
that will not be forgotten.
6 "My people have been lost sheep;
their shepherds have led them astray
and caused them to roam on the mountains.
They wandered over mountain and hill
and forgot their own resting place.
7 Whoever found them devoured them;
their enemies said, 'We are not guilty,
for they sinned against the LORD, their verdant
pasture,
the LORD, the hope of their ancestors.'

[a] *1* Or *Chaldeans*; also in verses 8, 25, 35 and 45

SCATTERED SHEEP

The Lord allowed Babylon to overtake Judah as punishment for the people's constant and consistent disobedience. However, God never intended for the nation of Babylon to remain in power over his people. This chapter describes the Lord's judgment on Babylon that would eventually come. Verses 4 – 5 speak of when the people of Israel and Judah together would seek the Lord and "come and bind themselves to the LORD in an everlasting covenant." Though this could refer to a remnant from both nations returning to the land of Judah after the Babylonian captivity, the ultimate fulfillment will be found in the Messianic age when God's divided people will be brought together and live in righteousness, peace and unity.

In verse 6, Jeremiah compares his people to a flock of sheep that had wandered and been led astray. The false prophets and false gods acted as irresponsible and evil shepherds to the flock of Israel, and they caused the people to wander away from God and to forget from where they had come. The sheep of Israel needed to return to the one true Shepherd (Jn 10:11; Heb 13:20). In Luke 15:1 – 7, Jesus told the parable of the lost sheep and explained how a good shepherd will do everything within his power to keep his flock together. Even if 99 sheep are accounted for and one is missing, a good shepherd will go after the missing one and bring it back to the flock. Jeremiah pointed out that God, the Shepherd of the Israelites, was working to bring his flock back to him again.

These verses in Jeremiah provide great encouragement for believers today, for no matter how far someone may have wandered away from God, they are never fully out of his reach. The Israelites had wandered very far away from him, yet God continued to mercifully call for them to return to him. Psalm 51:17 says, "A broken and contrite heart you, God, will not despise." God has a strong desire for his followers to stay near him, but even if they wander away, a broken heart of true repentance can always bring them back.

8 "Flee out of Babylon;
leave the land of the Babylonians,
and be like the goats that lead the flock.
9 For I will stir up and bring against Babylon
an alliance of great nations from the land of the north.
They will take up their positions against her,
and from the north she will be captured.
Their arrows will be like skilled warriors
who do not return empty-handed.
10 So Babylonia[a] will be plundered;
all who plunder her will have their fill,"
declares the LORD.

11 "Because you rejoice and are glad,
you who pillage my inheritance,
because you frolic like a heifer threshing grain
and neigh like stallions,
12 your mother will be greatly ashamed;
she who gave you birth will be disgraced.
She will be the least of the nations —
a wilderness, a dry land, a desert.
13 Because of the LORD's anger she will not be inhabited
but will be completely desolate.
All who pass Babylon will be appalled;
they will scoff because of all her wounds.

14 "Take up your positions around Babylon,
all you who draw the bow.
Shoot at her! Spare no arrows,
for she has sinned against the LORD.
15 Shout against her on every side!
She surrenders, her towers fall,
her walls are torn down.
Since this is the vengeance of the LORD,
take vengeance on her;
do to her as she has done to others.
16 Cut off from Babylon the sower,
and the reaper with his sickle at harvest.
Because of the sword of the oppressor
let everyone return to their own people,
let everyone flee to their own land.

17 "Israel is a scattered flock
that lions have chased away.
The first to devour them
was the king of Assyria;
the last to crush their bones
was Nebuchadnezzar king of Babylon."

18 Therefore this is what the LORD Almighty, the God of Israel, says:

"I will punish the king of Babylon and his land
as I punished the king of Assyria.
19 But I will bring Israel back to their own pasture,
and they will graze on Carmel and Bashan;
their appetite will be satisfied
on the hills of Ephraim and Gilead.

[a] 10 Or *Chaldea*

20 In those days, at that time,"
declares the LORD,
"search will be made for Israel's guilt,
but there will be none,
and for the sins of Judah,
but none will be found,
for I will forgive the remnant I spare.

21 "Attack the land of Merathaim
and those who live in Pekod.
Pursue, kill and completely destroy[a] them,"
declares the LORD.

"Do everything I have commanded you.
22 The noise of battle is in the land,
the noise of great destruction!
23 How broken and shattered
is the hammer of the whole earth!
How desolate is Babylon
among the nations!
24 I set a trap for you, Babylon,
and you were caught before you knew it;
you were found and captured
because you opposed the LORD.
25 The LORD has opened his arsenal
and brought out the weapons of his wrath,
for the Sovereign LORD Almighty has work to do
in the land of the Babylonians.
26 Come against her from afar.
Break open her granaries;
pile her up like heaps of grain.
Completely destroy her
and leave her no remnant.
27 Kill all her young bulls;
let them go down to the slaughter!
Woe to them! For their day has come,
the time for them to be punished.
28 Listen to the fugitives and refugees from Babylon
declaring in Zion
how the LORD our God has taken vengeance,
vengeance for his temple.

29 "Summon archers against Babylon,
all those who draw the bow.
Encamp all around her;
let no one escape.
Repay her for her deeds;
do to her as she has done.
For she has defied the LORD,
the Holy One of Israel.
30 Therefore, her young men will fall in the streets;
all her soldiers will be silenced in that day,"
declares the LORD.
31 "See, I am against you, you arrogant one,"
declares the Lord, the LORD Almighty,
"for your day has come,
the time for you to be punished.

[a] *21* The Hebrew term refers to the irrevocable giving over of things or persons to the LORD, often by totally destroying them; also in verse 26.

32 The arrogant one will stumble and fall
and no one will help her up;
I will kindle a fire in her towns
that will consume all who are around her."

33 This is what the LORD Almighty says:

"The people of Israel are oppressed,
and the people of Judah as well.
All their captors hold them fast,
refusing to let them go.
34 Yet their Redeemer is strong;
the LORD Almighty is his name.
He will vigorously defend their cause
so that he may bring rest to their land,
but unrest to those who live in Babylon.

35 "A sword against the Babylonians!"
declares the LORD —
"against those who live in Babylon
and against her officials and wise men!
36 A sword against her false prophets!
They will become fools.
A sword against her warriors!
They will be filled with terror.
37 A sword against her horses and chariots
and all the foreigners in her ranks!
They will become weaklings.
A sword against her treasures!
They will be plundered.
38 A drought on[a] her waters!
They will dry up.
For it is a land of idols,
idols that will go mad with terror.

39 "So desert creatures and hyenas will live there,
and there the owl will dwell.
It will never again be inhabited
or lived in from generation to generation.
40 As I overthrew Sodom and Gomorrah
along with their neighboring towns,"
declares the LORD,
"so no one will live there;
no people will dwell in it.

41 "Look! An army is coming from the north;
a great nation and many kings
are being stirred up from the ends of the earth.
42 They are armed with bows and spears;
they are cruel and without mercy.
They sound like the roaring sea
as they ride on their horses;
they come like men in battle formation
to attack you, Daughter Babylon.
43 The king of Babylon has heard reports about them,
and his hands hang limp.
Anguish has gripped him,
pain like that of a woman in labor.

---

[a] 38 Or *A sword against*

44 Like a lion coming up from Jordan's thickets
to a rich pastureland,
I will chase Babylon from its land in an instant.
Who is the chosen one I will appoint for this?
Who is like me and who can challenge me?
And what shepherd can stand against me?"

45 Therefore, hear what the LORD has planned against Babylon,
what he has purposed against the land of the Babylonians:
The young of the flock will be dragged away;
their pasture will be appalled at their fate.
46 At the sound of Babylon's capture the earth will tremble;
its cry will resound among the nations.

51 This is what the LORD says:

"See, I will stir up the spirit of a destroyer
against Babylon and the people of Leb Kamai.[a]
2 I will send foreigners to Babylon
to winnow her and to devastate her land;
they will oppose her on every side
in the day of her disaster.
3 Let not the archer string his bow,
nor let him put on his armor.
Do not spare her young men;
completely destroy[b] her army.
4 They will fall down slain in Babylon,[c]
fatally wounded in her streets.
5 For Israel and Judah have not been forsaken
by their God, the LORD Almighty,
though their land[d] is full of guilt
before the Holy One of Israel.

6 "Flee from Babylon!
Run for your lives!
Do not be destroyed because of her sins.
It is time for the LORD's vengeance;
he will repay her what she deserves.
7 Babylon was a gold cup in the LORD's hand;
she made the whole earth drunk.
The nations drank her wine;
therefore they have now gone mad.
8 Babylon will suddenly fall and be broken.
Wail over her!
Get balm for her pain;
perhaps she can be healed.
9 " 'We would have healed Babylon,
but she cannot be healed;
let us leave her and each go to our own land,
for her judgment reaches to the skies,
it rises as high as the heavens.'

10 " 'The LORD has vindicated us;
come, let us tell in Zion
what the LORD our God has done.'

---

[a] 1 *Leb Kamai* is a cryptogram for Chaldea, that is, Babylonia. [b] 3 The Hebrew term refers to the irrevocable giving over of things or persons to the LORD, often by totally destroying them. [c] 4 Or *Chaldea* [d] 5 Or *Almighty, / and the land of the Babylonians*

[11] "Sharpen the arrows,
take up the shields!
The LORD has stirred up the kings of the Medes,
because his purpose is to destroy Babylon.
The LORD will take vengeance,
vengeance for his temple.
[12] Lift up a banner against the walls of Babylon!
Reinforce the guard,
station the watchmen,
prepare an ambush!
The LORD will carry out his purpose,
his decree against the people of Babylon.
[13] You who live by many waters
and are rich in treasures,
your end has come,
the time for you to be destroyed.
[14] The LORD Almighty has sworn by himself:
I will surely fill you with troops, as with a swarm of locusts,
and they will shout in triumph over you.

[15] "He made the earth by his power;
he founded the world by his wisdom
and stretched out the heavens by his understanding.
[16] When he thunders, the waters in the heavens roar;
he makes clouds rise from the ends of the earth.
He sends lightning with the rain
and brings out the wind from his storehouses.

[17] "Everyone is senseless and without knowledge;
every goldsmith is shamed by his idols.
The images he makes are a fraud;
they have no breath in them.
[18] They are worthless, the objects of mockery;
when their judgment comes, they will perish.
[19] He who is the Portion of Jacob is not like these,
for he is the Maker of all things,
including the people of his inheritance —
the LORD Almighty is his name.

[20] "You are my war club,
my weapon for battle —
with you I shatter nations,
with you I destroy kingdoms,
[21] with you I shatter horse and rider,
with you I shatter chariot and driver,
[22] with you I shatter man and woman,
with you I shatter old man and youth,
with you I shatter young man and young woman,
[23] with you I shatter shepherd and flock,
with you I shatter farmer and oxen,
with you I shatter governors and officials.

[24] "Before your eyes I will repay Babylon and all who live in Babylonia[a] for all
the wrong they have done in Zion," declares the LORD.

[25] "I am against you, you destroying mountain,
you who destroy the whole earth,"
declares the LORD.

[a] 24 Or *Chaldea*; also in verse 35

"I will stretch out my hand against you,
roll you off the cliffs,
and make you a burned-out mountain.
26 No rock will be taken from you for a cornerstone,
nor any stone for a foundation,
for you will be desolate forever,"
declares the LORD.

27 "Lift up a banner in the land!
Blow the trumpet among the nations!
Prepare the nations for battle against her;
summon against her these kingdoms:
Ararat, Minni and Ashkenaz.
Appoint a commander against her;
send up horses like a swarm of locusts.
28 Prepare the nations for battle against her —
the kings of the Medes,
their governors and all their officials,
and all the countries they rule.
29 The land trembles and writhes,
for the LORD's purposes against Babylon stand —
to lay waste the land of Babylon
so that no one will live there.
30 Babylon's warriors have stopped fighting;
they remain in their strongholds.
Their strength is exhausted;
they have become weaklings.
Her dwellings are set on fire;
the bars of her gates are broken.
31 One courier follows another
and messenger follows messenger
to announce to the king of Babylon
that his entire city is captured,
32 the river crossings seized,
the marshes set on fire,
and the soldiers terrified."

33 This is what the LORD Almighty, the God of Israel, says:

"Daughter Babylon is like a threshing floor
at the time it is trampled;
the time to harvest her will soon come."

34 "Nebuchadnezzar king of Babylon has devoured us,
he has thrown us into confusion,
he has made us an empty jar.
Like a serpent he has swallowed us
and filled his stomach with our delicacies,
and then has spewed us out.
35 May the violence done to our flesh[a] be on Babylon,"
say the inhabitants of Zion.
"May our blood be on those who live in Babylonia,"
says Jerusalem.

36 Therefore this is what the LORD says:

"See, I will defend your cause
and avenge you;

[a] 35 Or *done to us and to our children*

I will dry up her sea
and make her springs dry.
37 Babylon will be a heap of ruins,
a haunt of jackals,
an object of horror and scorn,
a place where no one lives.
38 Her people all roar like young lions,
they growl like lion cubs.
39 But while they are aroused,
I will set out a feast for them
and make them drunk,
so that they shout with laughter —
then sleep forever and not awake,"
declares the LORD.

40 "I will bring them down
like lambs to the slaughter,
like rams and goats.

41 "How Sheshak[a] will be captured,
the boast of the whole earth seized!
How desolate Babylon will be
among the nations!
42 The sea will rise over Babylon;
its roaring waves will cover her.
43 Her towns will be desolate,
a dry and desert land,
a land where no one lives,
through which no one travels.
44 I will punish Bel in Babylon
and make him spew out what he has swallowed.
The nations will no longer stream to him.
And the wall of Babylon will fall.

45 "Come out of her, my people!
Run for your lives!
Run from the fierce anger of the LORD.
46 Do not lose heart or be afraid
when rumors are heard in the land;
one rumor comes this year, another the next,
rumors of violence in the land
and of ruler against ruler.
47 For the time will surely come
when I will punish the idols of Babylon;
her whole land will be disgraced
and her slain will all lie fallen within her.
48 Then heaven and earth and all that is in them
will shout for joy over Babylon,
for out of the north
destroyers will attack her,"
declares the LORD.

49 "Babylon must fall because of Israel's slain,
just as the slain in all the earth
have fallen because of Babylon.
50 You who have escaped the sword,
leave and do not linger!

[a] 41 *Sheshak* is a cryptogram for Babylon.

Remember the LORD in a distant land,
and call to mind Jerusalem."

51 "We are disgraced,
for we have been insulted
and shame covers our faces,
because foreigners have entered
the holy places of the LORD's house."

52 "But days are coming," declares the LORD,
"when I will punish her idols,
and throughout her land
the wounded will groan.
53 Even if Babylon ascends to the heavens
and fortifies her lofty stronghold,
I will send destroyers against her,"
declares the LORD.

54 "The sound of a cry comes from Babylon,
the sound of great destruction
from the land of the Babylonians.[a]
55 The LORD will destroy Babylon;
he will silence her noisy din.
Waves of enemies will rage like great waters;
the roar of their voices will resound.
56 A destroyer will come against Babylon;
her warriors will be captured,
and their bows will be broken.
For the LORD is a God of retribution;
he will repay in full.
57 I will make her officials and wise men drunk,
her governors, officers and warriors as well;
they will sleep forever and not awake,"
declares the King, whose name is the LORD Almighty.

58 This is what the LORD Almighty says:

"Babylon's thick wall will be leveled
and her high gates set on fire;
the peoples exhaust themselves for nothing,
the nations' labor is only fuel for the flames."

59 This is the message Jeremiah the prophet gave to the staff officer Seraiah
son of Neriah, the son of Mahseiah, when he went to Babylon with Zedekiah king
of Judah in the fourth year of his reign. 60 Jeremiah had written on a scroll about
all the disasters that would come upon Babylon — all that had been recorded
concerning Babylon. 61 He said to Seraiah, "When you get to Babylon, see that
you read all these words aloud. 62 Then say, 'LORD, you have said you will destroy
this place, so that neither people nor animals will live in it; it will be desolate
forever.' 63 When you finish reading this scroll, tie a stone to it and throw it into
the Euphrates. 64 Then say, 'So will Babylon sink to rise no more because of the
disaster I will bring on her. And her people will fall.' "

The words of Jeremiah end here.

JEREMIAH 52:1 – 34

ASSURANCE OF TRUTH

The text of Jeremiah ends with the fulfillment of the prophecy that Jeremiah had been preaching throughout the entire book. It details the fall of Jerusalem in 586 BC and reports how many people were sent into exile — all just as Jeremiah had said. Finally, it ends with the release of Jehoiachin, an earlier king of Judah, from prison.

Jehoiachin had been taken as one of the captives under Nebuchadnezzar in the deportation of 597 BC, but once Awel-Marduk became king in 561, he released Jehoiachin from prison and gave him a regular allotment of provisions. The story of Jehoiachin's release ends the book of Jeremiah on a note of hope, and it also represents the story of the Israelites, which then points toward our ultimate hope for the future. Because everything that the Lord said through Jeremiah came true, believers today have an assurance that God will also deliver on his promise of eternal life for those who believe in Jesus Christ. God's Word held true in the past, it is true in the present and it will remain true in the future.

The Fall of Jerusalem

52 Zedekiah was twenty-one years old when he became king, and he reigned
in Jerusalem eleven years. His mother's name was Hamutal daughter
of Jeremiah; she was from Libnah. 2 He did evil in the eyes of the LORD, just as

[a] 54 Or *Chaldeans*

Jehoiakim had done. 3It was because of the LORD's anger that all this happened to Jerusalem and Judah, and in the end he thrust them from his presence.

Now Zedekiah rebelled against the king of Babylon.

4So in the ninth year of Zedekiah's reign, on the tenth day of the tenth month, Nebuchadnezzar king of Babylon marched against Jerusalem with his whole army. They encamped outside the city and built siege works all around it. 5The city was kept under siege until the eleventh year of King Zedekiah.

6By the ninth day of the fourth month the famine in the city had become so severe that there was no food for the people to eat. 7Then the city wall was broken through, and the whole army fled. They left the city at night through the gate between the two walls near the king's garden, though the Babylonians[a] were surrounding the city. They fled toward the Arabah,[b] 8but the Babylonian[c] army pursued King Zedekiah and overtook him in the plains of Jericho. All his soldiers were separated from him and scattered, 9and he was captured.

He was taken to the king of Babylon at Riblah in the land of Hamath, where he pronounced sentence on him. 10There at Riblah the king of Babylon killed the sons of Zedekiah before his eyes; he also killed all the officials of Judah. 11Then he put out Zedekiah's eyes, bound him with bronze shackles and took him to Babylon, where he put him in prison till the day of his death.

12On the tenth day of the fifth month, in the nineteenth year of Nebuchadnezzar king of Babylon, Nebuzaradan commander of the imperial guard, who served the king of Babylon, came to Jerusalem. 13He set fire to the temple of the LORD, the royal palace and all the houses of Jerusalem. Every important building he burned down. 14The whole Babylonian army, under the commander of the imperial guard, broke down all the walls around Jerusalem. 15Nebuzaradan the commander of the guard carried into exile some of the poorest people and those who remained in the city, along with the rest of the craftsmen[d] and those who had deserted to the king of Babylon. 16But Nebuzaradan left behind the rest of the poorest people of the land to work the vineyards and fields.

17The Babylonians broke up the bronze pillars, the movable stands and the bronze Sea that were at the temple of the LORD and they carried all the bronze to Babylon. 18They also took away the pots, shovels, wick trimmers, sprinkling bowls, dishes and all the bronze articles used in the temple service. 19The commander of the imperial guard took away the basins, censers, sprinkling bowls, pots, lampstands, dishes and bowls used for drink offerings — all that were made of pure gold or silver.

20The bronze from the two pillars, the Sea and the twelve bronze bulls under it, and the movable stands, which King Solomon had made for the temple of the LORD, was more than could be weighed. 21Each pillar was eighteen cubits high and twelve cubits in circumference[e]; each was four fingers thick, and hollow. 22The bronze capital on top of one pillar was five cubits[f] high and was decorated with a network and pomegranates of bronze all around. The other pillar, with its pomegranates, was similar. 23There were ninety-six pomegranates on the sides; the total number of pomegranates above the surrounding network was a hundred.

24The commander of the guard took as prisoners Seraiah the chief priest, Zephaniah the priest next in rank and the three doorkeepers. 25Of those still in the city, he took the officer in charge of the fighting men, and seven royal advisers. He also took the secretary who was chief officer in charge of conscripting the people of the land, sixty of whom were found in the city. 26Nebuzaradan the commander took them all and brought them to the king of Babylon at Riblah. 27There at Riblah, in the land of Hamath, the king had them executed.

---

[a] *7* Or *Chaldeans*; also in verse 17 [b] *7* Or *the Jordan Valley* [c] *8* Or *Chaldean*; also in verse 14 [d] *15* Or *the populace* [e] *21* That is, about 27 feet high and 18 feet in circumference or about 8.1 meters high and 5.4 meters in circumference [f] *22* That is, about 7 1/2 feet or about 2.3 meters

So Judah went into captivity, away from her land. [28]This is the number of the
people Nebuchadnezzar carried into exile:

in the seventh year, 3,023 Jews;
[29]in Nebuchadnezzar's eighteenth year,
832 people from Jerusalem;
[30]in his twenty-third year,
745 Jews taken into exile by Nebuzaradan the commander of the imperial guard.
There were 4,600 people in all.

Jehoiachin Released

[31]In the thirty-seventh year of the exile of Jehoiachin king of Judah, in the year
Awel-Marduk became king of Babylon, on the twenty-fifth day of the twelfth
month, he released Jehoiachin king of Judah and freed him from prison. [32]He
spoke kindly to him and gave him a seat of honor higher than those of the other
kings who were with him in Babylon. [33]So Jehoiachin put aside his prison clothes
and for the rest of his life ate regularly at the king's table. [34]Day by day the king
of Babylon gave Jehoiachin a regular allowance as long as he lived, till the day
of his death.

JESUS: OUR FAITHFUL LORD

LAMENTATIONS

LAMENTATIONS

PROPHETIC MINISTRY OF JEREMIAH BEGINS	FALL OF JUDAH	WRITING OF BOOK OF LAMENTATIONS
c. 626 BC	*c. 586 BC*	*Not long after 586 BC*

The aptly named book of Lamentations portrays the broken heart of its author, traditionally assumed to be the prophet Jeremiah, after the fall of Jerusalem to the Babylonians. This national tragedy was an unprecedented act of God's judgment for the people's unfaithfulness. Almost inconceivably, God had allowed the very center of worship for his people to be ransacked and demolished by a pagan nation.

Jeremiah's lament derived from his personal sorrow at the fate of those whom he dearly loved. Even more, he agonized over the people's unwillingness to turn from their sin when confronted by the prophet's clear and consistent warnings.

This short book is composed of five poems; specifically, laments. Chapters 1 and 5 summarize the siege and fall of Jerusalem at the hands of the Babylonians. The great city of Jerusalem was defeated, and with that the hopes of God's people faltered. Jeremiah begged God to remember his people and turn back to them in love once more. Chapters 2 and 4 focus on the destruction and devastation that resulted from God's judgment. The consequences of sin ravaged all segments of society, leaving no one untouched.

The third chapter functions as the climax and focal point of Jeremiah's writing. Jeremiah proclaimed the greatness of God's faithfulness in the face of his judgment (3:23). Though Judah was in shambles, God had not abandoned his people forever. His intention was to use Jerusalem's destruction to remind his people of the heinousness of their sin and draw them back to himself through his relentless grace. The circumstances of God's people may have obscured their view of God's faithfulness, but Jeremiah reminded the people that their sin had not irrevocably destroyed God's promises, and that God would certainly remain faithful. While the nation's rebellion was great, God's faithfulness was greater: "his compassions never fail" (3:22).

These never-ending mercies are seen most clearly in the life, death and resurrection of Jesus Christ, who came to earth as the perfect embodiment of God's faithfulness. All those who have been defeated and destroyed by sin need to look no further than Jesus to see God's great faithfulness on display. They can turn to Christ and find the hope that all people so desperately need.

BECAUSE OF THE LORD'S GREAT LOVE
WE ARE NOT CONSUMED, FOR HIS
COMPASSIONS NEVER FAIL.

Lamentations 3:22

LAMENTATIONS

LAMENTATIONS 1:1 – 10

THE TEMPLE

The first half of the first chapter of Lamentations describes the destruction of Jerusalem from the point of view of someone directly observing what had happened. The prophet Jeremiah shows, with extensive poetic language, how Jerusalem's sins have caused it to be completely desolated. Verse 10 shifts from the view of objective observer and makes the destruction of the city more personal for readers. By referring to "your assembly," Jeremiah pointed out that the pagan enemy has not just entered into any building. The assembly, or the temple, was a house of worship and a very important building for the people of Jerusalem to communicate with God. The author was saying it is not simply *a* building, it is *your* building, and furthermore it is a representation of one's relationship with God.

However, once Jesus arrived, the whole meaning and imagery of the temple changed. In John 2:19, Jesus said that he was going to destroy the temple and rebuild it in three days. What Jesus was saying is that he is now the temple, and with his crucifixion, the temple (his body) would be destroyed only to rise again (or be rebuilt) in three days. While the temple was the way God's people used to communicate with God, Jesus is the way Christians communicate with God today.

1 [a] How deserted lies the city,
once so full of people!
How like a widow is she,
who once was great among the nations!
She who was queen among the provinces
has now become a slave.

2 Bitterly she weeps at night,
tears are on her cheeks.
Among all her lovers
there is no one to comfort her.
All her friends have betrayed her;
they have become her enemies.

3 After affliction and harsh labor,
Judah has gone into exile.
She dwells among the nations;
she finds no resting place.
All who pursue her have overtaken her
in the midst of her distress.

4 The roads to Zion mourn,
for no one comes to her appointed festivals.
All her gateways are desolate,
her priests groan,
her young women grieve,
and she is in bitter anguish.

5 Her foes have become her masters;
her enemies are at ease.
The LORD has brought her grief
because of her many sins.
Her children have gone into exile,
captive before the foe.

6 All the splendor has departed
from Daughter Zion.
Her princes are like deer
that find no pasture;
in weakness they have fled
before the pursuer.

7 In the days of her affliction and wandering
Jerusalem remembers all the treasures
that were hers in days of old.
When her people fell into enemy hands,
there was no one to help her.
Her enemies looked at her
and laughed at her destruction.

8 Jerusalem has sinned greatly
and so has become unclean.

[a] This chapter is an acrostic poem, the verses of which begin with the successive letters of the Hebrew alphabet.

All who honored her despise her,
for they have all seen her naked;
she herself groans
and turns away.

9 Her filthiness clung to her skirts;
she did not consider her future.
Her fall was astounding;
there was none to comfort her.
"Look, LORD, on my affliction,
for the enemy has triumphed."

10 The enemy laid hands
on all her treasures;
she saw pagan nations
enter her sanctuary—
those you had forbidden
to enter your assembly.

11 All her people groan
as they search for bread;
they barter their treasures for food
to keep themselves alive.
"Look, LORD, and consider,
for I am despised."

12 "Is it nothing to you, all you who pass by?
Look around and see.
Is any suffering like my suffering
that was inflicted on me,
that the LORD brought on me
in the day of his fierce anger?

13 "From on high he sent fire,
sent it down into my bones.
He spread a net for my feet
and turned me back.
He made me desolate,
faint all the day long.

14 "My sins have been bound into a yoke[a];
by his hands they were woven together.
They have been hung on my neck,
and the Lord has sapped my strength.
He has given me into the hands
of those I cannot withstand.

15 "The Lord has rejected
all the warriors in my midst;
he has summoned an army against me
to[b] crush my young men.
In his winepress the Lord has trampled
Virgin Daughter Judah.

16 "This is why I weep
and my eyes overflow with tears.
No one is near to comfort me,
no one to restore my spirit.

---

[a] *14* Most Hebrew manuscripts; many Hebrew manuscripts and Septuagint *He kept watch over my sins* [b] *15* Or *has set a time for me / when he will*

My children are destitute
because the enemy has prevailed."

17 Zion stretches out her hands,
but there is no one to comfort her.
The LORD has decreed for Jacob
that his neighbors become his foes;
Jerusalem has become
an unclean thing among them.

18 "The LORD is righteous,
yet I rebelled against his command.
Listen, all you peoples;
look on my suffering.
My young men and young women
have gone into exile.

19 "I called to my allies
but they betrayed me.
My priests and my elders
perished in the city
while they searched for food
to keep themselves alive.

20 "See, LORD, how distressed I am!
I am in torment within,
and in my heart I am disturbed,
for I have been most rebellious.
Outside, the sword bereaves;
inside, there is only death.

21 "People have heard my groaning,
but there is no one to comfort me.
All my enemies have heard of my distress;
they rejoice at what you have done.
May you bring the day you have announced
so they may become like me.

22 "Let all their wickedness come before you;
deal with them
as you have dealt with me
because of all my sins.
My groans are many
and my heart is faint."

2[a] How the Lord has covered Daughter Zion
with the cloud of his anger[b]!
He has hurled down the splendor of Israel
from heaven to earth;
he has not remembered his footstool
in the day of his anger.

2 Without pity the Lord has swallowed up
all the dwellings of Jacob;
in his wrath he has torn down
the strongholds of Daughter Judah.
He has brought her kingdom and its princes
down to the ground in dishonor.

---

[a] This chapter is an acrostic poem, the verses of which begin with the successive letters of the Hebrew alphabet. [b] 1 Or *How the Lord in his anger / has treated Daughter Zion with contempt*

3 In fierce anger he has cut off
every horn[a,b] of Israel.
He has withdrawn his right hand
at the approach of the enemy.
He has burned in Jacob like a flaming fire
that consumes everything around it.

4 Like an enemy he has strung his bow;
his right hand is ready.
Like a foe he has slain
all who were pleasing to the eye;
he has poured out his wrath like fire
on the tent of Daughter Zion.

5 The Lord is like an enemy;
he has swallowed up Israel.
He has swallowed up all her palaces
and destroyed her strongholds.
He has multiplied mourning and lamentation
for Daughter Judah.

6 He has laid waste his dwelling like a garden;
he has destroyed his place of meeting.
The LORD has made Zion forget
her appointed festivals and her Sabbaths;
in his fierce anger he has spurned
both king and priest.

7 The Lord has rejected his altar
and abandoned his sanctuary.
He has given the walls of her palaces
into the hands of the enemy;
they have raised a shout in the house of the LORD
as on the day of an appointed festival.

8 The LORD determined to tear down
the wall around Daughter Zion.
He stretched out a measuring line
and did not withhold his hand from destroying.
He made ramparts and walls lament;
together they wasted away.

9 Her gates have sunk into the ground;
their bars he has broken and destroyed.
Her king and her princes are exiled among the nations,
the law is no more,
and her prophets no longer find
visions from the LORD.

10 The elders of Daughter Zion
sit on the ground in silence;
they have sprinkled dust on their heads
and put on sackcloth.
The young women of Jerusalem
have bowed their heads to the ground.

11 My eyes fail from weeping,
I am in torment within;
my heart is poured out on the ground
because my people are destroyed,

---

[a] 3 Or *off / all the strength*; or *every king* [b] 3 *Horn* here symbolizes strength.

because children and infants faint
 in the streets of the city.

12 They say to their mothers,
 "Where is bread and wine?"
as they faint like the wounded
 in the streets of the city,
as their lives ebb away
 in their mothers' arms.

13 What can I say for you?
 With what can I compare you,
 Daughter Jerusalem?
To what can I liken you,
 that I may comfort you,
 Virgin Daughter Zion?
Your wound is as deep as the sea.
 Who can heal you?

14 The visions of your prophets
 were false and worthless;
they did not expose your sin
 to ward off your captivity.
The prophecies they gave you
 were false and misleading.

15 All who pass your way
 clap their hands at you;
they scoff and shake their heads
 at Daughter Jerusalem:
"Is this the city that was called
 the perfection of beauty,
 the joy of the whole earth?"

16 All your enemies open their mouths
 wide against you;
they scoff and gnash their teeth
 and say, "We have swallowed her up.
This is the day we have waited for;
 we have lived to see it."

17 The LORD has done what he planned;
 he has fulfilled his word,
 which he decreed long ago.
He has overthrown you without pity,
 he has let the enemy gloat over you,
 he has exalted the horn[a] of your foes.

18 The hearts of the people
 cry out to the Lord.
You walls of Daughter Zion,
 let your tears flow like a river
 day and night;
give yourself no relief,
 your eyes no rest.

19 Arise, cry out in the night,
 as the watches of the night begin;
pour out your heart like water
 in the presence of the Lord.

[a] 17 *Horn* here symbolizes strength.

Lift up your hands to him
for the lives of your children,
who faint from hunger
at every street corner.

20 "Look, LORD, and consider:
Whom have you ever treated like this?
Should women eat their offspring,
the children they have cared for?
Should priest and prophet be killed
in the sanctuary of the Lord?

21 "Young and old lie together
in the dust of the streets;
my young men and young women
have fallen by the sword.
You have slain them in the day of your anger;
you have slaughtered them without pity.

22 "As you summon to a feast day,
so you summoned against me terrors on every side.
In the day of the LORD's anger
no one escaped or survived;
those I cared for and reared
my enemy has destroyed."

3[a] I am the man who has seen affliction
by the rod of the LORD's wrath.
2 He has driven me away and made me walk
in darkness rather than light;
3 indeed, he has turned his hand against me
again and again, all day long.

4 He has made my skin and my flesh grow old
and has broken my bones.
5 He has besieged me and surrounded me
with bitterness and hardship.
6 He has made me dwell in darkness
like those long dead.

7 He has walled me in so I cannot escape;
he has weighed me down with chains.
8 Even when I call out or cry for help,
he shuts out my prayer.
9 He has barred my way with blocks of stone;
he has made my paths crooked.

10 Like a bear lying in wait,
like a lion in hiding,
11 he dragged me from the path and mangled me
and left me without help.
12 He drew his bow
and made me the target for his arrows.

13 He pierced my heart
with arrows from his quiver.
14 I became the laughingstock of all my people;
they mock me in song all day long.

[a] This chapter is an acrostic poem; the verses of each stanza begin with the successive letters of the Hebrew alphabet, and the verses within each stanza begin with the same letter.

LAMENTATIONS 3:64

THE LORD'S REVENGE

The third chapter of Lamentations displays a wide range of emotions. The entire chapter is written from the personal experience of the author, Jeremiah. In verses 1–20, Jeremiah describes his sorrows and despair, verses 21–39 provide reminders of God's faithfulness and the purpose of affliction, verses 40–47 are an encouragement to the Israelites to repent and return to God, and verses 48–66 represent the Israelites' prayer. The last section of chapter three specifically depicts the people's feelings toward their enemies who have attacked Jerusalem, and their injustices are provided in great detail. The prayer in verse 64 expresses the wish that God would "pay them back what they deserve." While this prayer may seem somewhat malicious, Jeremiah was simply asking God to follow through on what he had already promised to those who broke their covenant with him.

In Exodus 23:22, God said, "If you . . . do all that I say, I will be an enemy to your enemies and will oppose those who oppose you." In Lamentations, Jeremiah asked God to be an enemy to his enemies and to provide justice. Christians know now that God promises more than just justice on this earth, but that he offers eternal justice for the ultimate enemy. Revelation 20:10 says that "the devil, who deceived them, was thrown into the lake of burning sulfur" where he will be "tormented day and night for ever and ever." Jesus' death on the cross and his resurrection were the first of many victories yet to come to achieve God's ultimate justice.

15 He has filled me with bitter herbs
and given me gall to drink.

16 He has broken my teeth with gravel;
he has trampled me in the dust.
17 I have been deprived of peace;
I have forgotten what prosperity is.
18 So I say, "My splendor is gone
and all that I had hoped from the LORD."

19 I remember my affliction and my wandering,
the bitterness and the gall.
20 I well remember them,
and my soul is downcast within me.
21 Yet this I call to mind
and therefore I have hope:

22 Because of the LORD's great love we are not consumed,
for his compassions never fail.
23 They are new every morning;
great is your faithfulness.
24 I say to myself, "The LORD is my portion;
therefore I will wait for him."

25 The LORD is good to those whose hope is in him,
to the one who seeks him;
26 it is good to wait quietly
for the salvation of the LORD.
27 It is good for a man to bear the yoke
while he is young.

28 Let him sit alone in silence,
for the LORD has laid it on him.
29 Let him bury his face in the dust—
there may yet be hope.
30 Let him offer his cheek to one who would strike him,
and let him be filled with disgrace.

31 For no one is cast off
by the Lord forever.
32 Though he brings grief, he will show compassion,
so great is his unfailing love.
33 For he does not willingly bring affliction
or grief to anyone.

34 To crush underfoot
all prisoners in the land,
35 to deny people their rights
before the Most High,
36 to deprive them of justice—
would not the Lord see such things?

37 Who can speak and have it happen
if the Lord has not decreed it?
38 Is it not from the mouth of the Most High
that both calamities and good things come?
39 Why should the living complain
when punished for their sins?

40 Let us examine our ways and test them,
and let us return to the LORD.

LAMENTATIONS 3:21 – 23

GREAT IS HIS FAITHFULNESS

A complete shift in the prophet Jeremiah's tone and focus occurs in 3:21. While every verse up until this point has discussed the hardships of God's wrath, suddenly the prophet's hope is renewed and he proclaims God's love, compassion and faithfulness. Despite all that has happened to Jerusalem and her people, verse 23 declares that God's compassions are "new every morning." It may not seem as though Jeremiah had much reason to declare praise for God, but he chose to remember that God had been faithful to his people all along.

God responds compassionately to his people's needs. One instance of such a response is in Exodus 16, when the Israelites were traveling through the desert and complaining of hunger. God heard their complaints and responded by raining manna (bread) from heaven every morning for the people to gather and eat. There was never a shortage of manna for the people, and they were able to live off of what God gave them.

In Matthew 6:11, Jesus referred to the manna that God gave the Israelites in his instructions regarding prayer. He told his followers to pray and ask God to "give us today our daily bread." God met the daily needs of the Israelites, and he promises to do the same for his people today. Now, this does not mean that God will rain down from heaven whatever his people ask for, but it does show that he has compassion for his people's needs and responds to their cries.

Lamentations appeals to God's compassion and faithfulness. Even though those who survived the destruction of Jerusalem were facing incredible pain and hardship, Jeremiah reminded them that God had been faithful to his people in the past and he would continue to be faithful to them in the future. While Lamentations is about difficulty and hardship, the central verses focus on the Lord's great love. Not only did Jeremiah remind readers of the goodness of God, but he also challenged his audience to remember God's love and live in it daily.

41 Let us lift up our hearts and our hands
to God in heaven, and say:
42 "We have sinned and rebelled
and you have not forgiven.

43 "You have covered yourself with anger and
pursued us;
you have slain without pity.
44 You have covered yourself with a cloud
so that no prayer can get through.
45 You have made us scum and refuse
among the nations.

46 "All our enemies have opened their mouths
wide against us.
47 We have suffered terror and pitfalls,
ruin and destruction."
48 Streams of tears flow from my eyes
because my people are destroyed.

49 My eyes will flow unceasingly,
without relief,
50 until the LORD looks down
from heaven and sees.
51 What I see brings grief to my soul
because of all the women of my city.

52 Those who were my enemies without cause
hunted me like a bird.
53 They tried to end my life in a pit
and threw stones at me;
54 the waters closed over my head,
and I thought I was about to perish.

55 I called on your name, LORD,
from the depths of the pit.
56 You heard my plea: "Do not close your ears
to my cry for relief."
57 You came near when I called you,
and you said, "Do not fear."

58 You, Lord, took up my case;
you redeemed my life.
59 LORD, you have seen the wrong done to me.
Uphold my cause!
60 You have seen the depth of their vengeance,
all their plots against me.

61 LORD, you have heard their insults,
all their plots against me —
62 what my enemies whisper and mutter
against me all day long.
63 Look at them! Sitting or standing,
they mock me in their songs.

64 Pay them back what they deserve, LORD,
for what their hands have done.
65 Put a veil over their hearts,
and may your curse be on them!
66 Pursue them in anger and destroy them
from under the heavens of the LORD.

4 [a] How the gold has lost its luster,
the fine gold become dull!
The sacred gems are scattered
at every street corner.

2 How the precious children of Zion,
once worth their weight in gold,
are now considered as pots of clay,
the work of a potter's hands!

3 Even jackals offer their breasts
to nurse their young,
but my people have become heartless
like ostriches in the desert.

4 Because of thirst the infant's tongue
sticks to the roof of its mouth;
the children beg for bread,
but no one gives it to them.

5 Those who once ate delicacies
are destitute in the streets.
Those brought up in royal purple
now lie on ash heaps.

6 The punishment of my people
is greater than that of Sodom,
which was overthrown in a moment
without a hand turned to help her.

7 Their princes were brighter than snow
and whiter than milk,
their bodies more ruddy than rubies,
their appearance like lapis lazuli.

8 But now they are blacker than soot;
they are not recognized in the streets.
Their skin has shriveled on their bones;
it has become as dry as a stick.

9 Those killed by the sword are better off
than those who die of famine;
racked with hunger, they waste away
for lack of food from the field.

10 With their own hands compassionate women
have cooked their own children,
who became their food
when my people were destroyed.

11 The LORD has given full vent to his wrath;
he has poured out his fierce anger.
He kindled a fire in Zion
that consumed her foundations.

12 The kings of the earth did not believe,
nor did any of the peoples of the world,
that enemies and foes could enter
the gates of Jerusalem.

---

[a] This chapter is an acrostic poem, the verses of which begin with the successive letters of the Hebrew alphabet.

[13] But it happened because of the sins of her prophets
and the iniquities of her priests,
who shed within her
the blood of the righteous.

[14] Now they grope through the streets
as if they were blind.
They are so defiled with blood
that no one dares to touch their garments.

[15] "Go away! You are unclean!" people cry to them.
"Away! Away! Don't touch us!"
When they flee and wander about,
people among the nations say,
"They can stay here no longer."

[16] The LORD himself has scattered them;
he no longer watches over them.
The priests are shown no honor,
the elders no favor.

[17] Moreover, our eyes failed,
looking in vain for help;
from our towers we watched
for a nation that could not save us.

[18] People stalked us at every step,
so we could not walk in our streets.
Our end was near, our days were numbered,
for our end had come.

[19] Our pursuers were swifter
than eagles in the sky;
they chased us over the mountains
and lay in wait for us in the desert.

[20] The LORD's anointed, our very life breath,
was caught in their traps.
We thought that under his shadow
we would live among the nations.

[21] Rejoice and be glad, Daughter Edom,
you who live in the land of Uz.
But to you also the cup will be passed;
you will be drunk and stripped naked.

[22] Your punishment will end, Daughter Zion;
he will not prolong your exile.
But he will punish your sin, Daughter Edom,
and expose your wickedness.

5 Remember, LORD, what has happened to us;
look, and see our disgrace.
[2] Our inheritance has been turned over to strangers,
our homes to foreigners.
[3] We have become fatherless,
our mothers are widows.
[4] We must buy the water we drink;
our wood can be had only at a price.
[5] Those who pursue us are at our heels;
we are weary and find no rest.

LAMENTATIONS 4:13

A JUST GOD

Lamentations may seem like a book that is full of strong sorrow and bitterness, and through most of the book, it is. The prophet Jeremiah continually complained about the plight of the city, and he was distraught at how the Lord had brought judgment upon his people. However, it is important to note that these complaints are never against God. Jeremiah was certainly upset about the situation, but there was no suggestion that God's judgment was somehow unjust. Lamentations 4:13 says, "But it happened because of the sins of her prophets and the iniquities of her priests." The blame for the destruction of Jerusalem lay squarely on the shoulders of the prophets, priests and people of the city. Never did the author lament about why God chose to destroy the city, nor did he ever wonder about why Jerusalem was facing such judgment. The people of the city had rebelled against God, and they were receiving their just reward.

Romans 6:23 says, "The wages of sin is death," which means someone had to die for sin. The wages had to be paid, and God did not simply remove the debt that was owed. Instead, he paid for the wages of sin himself with his perfect Son (Jn 3:16). Jesus fulfilled God's justice, so that believers may receive his mercy.

IS THERE HOPE?

Lamentations concludes with Jeremiah's desperate, tenacious hope against the backdrop of the recent destruction of Jerusalem. He summarized the hardships that he had described in great detail in the previous chapters. However, instead of Lamentations ending with mourning, it ends with a plea.

Just because God is faithful does not mean that everything is going to go perfectly. Chapters 4 and 5 vividly describe the suffering of the people of Jerusalem. Sovereignty does not eliminate calamity, and Jeremiah is fully aware of that. The writer realizes that the people deserve the judgment they are facing (4:13), but he also knows that God is in control over everything both good and bad (3:37).

Therefore, the book ends with a humble plea as the writer recognized the sovereign rule of God and begged that he not ignore the cries of his people. The final two verses ask that God restore his people unless he is angered beyond measure. Does this mean that it is possible for God to be angered to the point where he remains separated from his people? In Romans 8:35 – 39, Paul wrote that nothing "will be able to separate us from the love of God that is in Christ Jesus our Lord." Before Moses died, he promised Joshua, "The LORD himself goes before you and will be with you; he will never leave you nor forsake you" (Dt 31:8). And in Matthew, Jesus' last words are, "Surely I am with you always, to the very end of the age" (Mt 28:20).

Lamentations reminds us that there is always hope for God's people. Through the Old Testament, despite all of the calamities that the Israelites brought upon themselves, God stayed with them. In the New Testament, Jesus saved the world and sent the Holy Spirit to be with and lead those who believe. Nothing — whether the foolish acts of the Israelites, or ignorance of modern-day believers, or death or life — can ever separate God's people from his love.

6 We submitted to Egypt and Assyria
to get enough bread.
7 Our ancestors sinned and are no more,
and we bear their punishment.
8 Slaves rule over us,
and there is no one to free us from their hands.
9 We get our bread at the risk of our lives
because of the sword in the desert.
10 Our skin is hot as an oven,
feverish from hunger.
11 Women have been violated in Zion,
and virgins in the towns of Judah.
12 Princes have been hung up by their hands;
elders are shown no respect.
13 Young men toil at the millstones;
boys stagger under loads of wood.
14 The elders are gone from the city gate;
the young men have stopped their music.
15 Joy is gone from our hearts;
our dancing has turned to mourning.
16 The crown has fallen from our head.
Woe to us, for we have sinned!
17 Because of this our hearts are faint,
because of these things our eyes grow dim
18 for Mount Zion, which lies desolate,
with jackals prowling over it.

19 You, LORD, reign forever;
your throne endures from generation to generation.
20 Why do you always forget us?
Why do you forsake us so long?
21 Restore us to yourself, LORD, that we may return;
renew our days as of old
22 unless you have utterly rejected us
and are angry with us beyond measure.

JESUS: OUR TRUE TEMPLE

EZEKIEL

EZEKIEL

EZEKIEL EXILED TO BABYLON	EZEKIEL'S VISIONS	FALL OF JUDAH/ TEMPLE DESTROYED
c. 597 BC	*c. 593 – 573 BC*	*c. 586 BC*

God used Ezekiel to speak to God's people after their exile to Babylon. While Jeremiah warned the people in Jerusalem of the coming destruction, Ezekiel spoke to those who had already been taken captive. The messages of Jeremiah and Ezekiel are quite similar, though they spoke to people hundreds of miles away from one another who were facing differing stages of God's judgment.

Ezekiel knew the fate that awaited God's people. He knew of the similar deportation of the northern kingdom (Israel) at the hands of the Assyrians in 722 BC. The southern kingdom (Judah) remained faithful to God for about a century longer, but eventually they too became engrossed in the idolatry of the surrounding nations. God used the nation of Babylon to enact judgment on the southern kingdom of Judah, and Ezekiel was a part of that deportation to pagan Babylon.

In exile, Ezekiel experienced and shared with the people a number of visions. These were meant to remind God's people of their responsibility before God even though they were far away from the promised land. Ezekiel, a priest and a prophet, was well acquainted with God's Law and its covenant-keeping implications for God's people. Through Ezekiel, God called the people to return to follow him in worshipful obedience.

God, through Ezekiel, also reminded the exiles that God's judgment was purposeful and not vindictive. As God had used the years of wandering in the wilderness, so he was also using their exile to foster humility, remind them of their dependence and bring about genuine repentance. Ultimately, God's purpose was that the people would know that he alone is

Lord and deserving of their worship. This refrain echoes throughout the book, reminding the people of the glorious privilege of knowing God and their need for spiritual renewal.

Like other prophets, Ezekiel sounded a message of hope to accompany his warnings of judgment (Eze 33–48). He concluded his prophecy with the news of a coming day when God would restore proper worship in a new temple in a new, and better, city. There a renewed nation would one day worship their glorious King.

I WILL GIVE THEM AN UNDIVIDED HEART AND PUT A NEW SPIRIT IN THEM; I WILL REMOVE FROM THEM THEIR HEART OF STONE AND GIVE THEM A HEART OF FLESH.

Ezekiel 11:19

EZEKIEL

EZEKIEL 1:4–28

GOD'S GLORY

This book of prophecy opens with an incredible display of God's glory. This is important to recognize at the outset of a book that is full of prophecy from God, through God's prophet Ezekiel, to God's people Israel.

Through his prophet, God was delivering a firm word to his people. His people had lived in sin despite the fact that God had shown them so much grace. Sin has consequences, and God was preparing to tell them what their sin would cost. But before delivering that message, God showed his glory (v. 28); God's glory is the basis for everything that follows.

God is holy—completely pure and good. Humanity is not. As an expression of God's holiness, God disciplines his disobedient children. Reading the book of Ezekiel should lead people who are far from God to see his glory, hear of his grace and draw near in repentance. This book should lead followers of Jesus to remember the perfect character of God—how he has already accomplished the gracious salvation this book looks forward to—and to depend on the Spirit of God to help them live for God in every area of life.

Ezekiel's Inaugural Vision

1 In my thirtieth year, in the fourth month on the fifth day, while I was among the exiles by the Kebar River, the heavens were opened and I saw visions of God.

2 On the fifth of the month—it was the fifth year of the exile of King Jehoiachin— 3 the word of the LORD came to Ezekiel the priest, the son of Buzi, by the Kebar River in the land of the Babylonians.[a] There the hand of the LORD was on him.

4 I looked, and I saw a windstorm coming out of the north—an immense cloud with flashing lightning and surrounded by brilliant light. The center of the fire looked like glowing metal, 5 and in the fire was what looked like four living creatures. In appearance their form was human, 6 but each of them had four faces and four wings. 7 Their legs were straight; their feet were like those of a calf and gleamed like burnished bronze. 8 Under their wings on their four sides they had human hands. All four of them had faces and wings, 9 and the wings of one touched the wings of another. Each one went straight ahead; they did not turn as they moved.

10 Their faces looked like this: Each of the four had the face of a human being, and on the right side each had the face of a lion, and on the left the face of an ox; each also had the face of an eagle. 11 Such were their faces. They each had two wings spreading out upward, each wing touching that of the creature on either side; and each had two other wings covering its body. 12 Each one went straight ahead. Wherever the spirit would go, they would go, without turning as they went. 13 The appearance of the living creatures was like burning coals of fire or like torches. Fire moved back and forth among the creatures; it was bright, and lightning flashed out of it. 14 The creatures sped back and forth like flashes of lightning.

15 As I looked at the living creatures, I saw a wheel on the ground beside each creature with its four faces. 16 This was the appearance and structure of the wheels: They sparkled like topaz, and all four looked alike. Each appeared to be made like a wheel intersecting a wheel. 17 As they moved, they would go in any one of the four directions the creatures faced; the wheels did not change direction as the creatures went. 18 Their rims were high and awesome, and all four rims were full of eyes all around.

19 When the living creatures moved, the wheels beside them moved; and when the living creatures rose from the ground, the wheels also rose. 20 Wherever the spirit would go, they would go, and the wheels would rise along with them, because the spirit of the living creatures was in the wheels. 21 When the creatures moved, they also moved; when the creatures stood still, they also stood still; and when the creatures rose from the ground, the wheels rose along with them, because the spirit of the living creatures was in the wheels.

22 Spread out above the heads of the living creatures was what looked something like a vault, sparkling like crystal, and awesome. 23 Under the vault their wings were stretched out one toward the other, and each had two wings covering its body. 24 When the creatures moved, I heard the sound of their wings, like the roar of rushing waters, like the voice of the Almighty,[b] like the tumult of an army. When they stood still, they lowered their wings.

25 Then there came a voice from above the vault over their heads as they stood with lowered wings. 26 Above the vault over their heads was what looked like a

[a] 3 Or *Chaldeans* [b] 24 Hebrew *Shaddai*

throne of lapis lazuli, and high above on the throne was a figure like that of a man. [27]I saw that from what appeared to be his waist up he looked like glowing metal, as if full of fire, and that from there down he looked like fire; and brilliant light surrounded him. [28]Like the appearance of a rainbow in the clouds on a rainy day, so was the radiance around him.

This was the appearance of the likeness of the glory of the LORD. When I saw it, I fell facedown, and I heard the voice of one speaking.

Ezekiel's Call to Be a Prophet

2 He said to me, "Son of man,[a] stand up on your feet and I will speak to you." [2]As he spoke, the Spirit came into me and raised me to my feet, and I heard him speaking to me.

[3]He said: "Son of man, I am sending you to the Israelites, to a rebellious nation that has rebelled against me; they and their ancestors have been in revolt against me to this very day. [4]The people to whom I am sending you are obstinate and stubborn. Say to them, 'This is what the Sovereign LORD says.' [5]And whether they listen or fail to listen — for they are a rebellious people — they will know that a prophet has been among them. [6]And you, son of man, do not be afraid of them or their words. Do not be afraid, though briers and thorns are all around you and you live among scorpions. Do not be afraid of what they say or be terrified by them, though they are a rebellious people. [7]You must speak my words to them, whether they listen or fail to listen, for they are rebellious. [8]But you, son of man, listen to what I say to you. Do not rebel like that rebellious people; open your mouth and eat what I give you."

[9]Then I looked, and I saw a hand stretched out to me. In it was a scroll, [10]which he unrolled before me. On both sides of it were written words of lament and mourning and woe.

3 And he said to me, "Son of man, eat what is before you, eat this scroll; then go and speak to the people of Israel." [2]So I opened my mouth, and he gave me the scroll to eat.

[3]Then he said to me, "Son of man, eat this scroll I am giving you and fill your stomach with it." So I ate it, and it tasted as sweet as honey in my mouth.

[4]He then said to me: "Son of man, go now to the people of Israel and speak my words to them. [5]You are not being sent to a people of obscure speech and strange language, but to the people of Israel — [6]not to many peoples of obscure speech and strange language, whose words you cannot understand. Surely if I had sent you to them, they would have listened to you. [7]But the people of Israel are not willing to listen to you because they are not willing to listen to me, for all the Israelites are hardened and obstinate. [8]But I will make you as unyielding and hardened as they are. [9]I will make your forehead like the hardest stone, harder than flint. Do not be afraid of them or terrified by them, though they are a rebellious people."

[10]And he said to me, "Son of man, listen carefully and take to heart all the words I speak to you. [11]Go now to your people in exile and speak to them. Say to them, 'This is what the Sovereign LORD says,' whether they listen or fail to listen."

[12]Then the Spirit lifted me up, and I heard behind me a loud rumbling sound as the glory of the LORD rose from the place where it was standing.[b] [13]It was the sound of the wings of the living creatures brushing against each other and the sound of the wheels beside them, a loud rumbling sound. [14]The Spirit then lifted me up and took me away, and I went in bitterness and in the anger of my spirit, with the strong hand of the LORD on me. [15]I came to the exiles who lived at Tel Aviv near the Kebar River. And there, where they were living, I sat among them for seven days — deeply distressed.

---

[a] *1* The Hebrew phrase *ben adam* means *human being*. The phrase *son of man* is retained as a form of address here and throughout Ezekiel because of its possible association with "Son of Man" in the New Testament. [b] *12* Probable reading of the original Hebrew text; Masoretic Text *sound — may the glory of the LORD be praised from his place*

EZEKIEL 3:1 – 3

EAT A SCROLL?

Life as a prophet was often bittersweet, and painful experiences regularly outweighed the pleasant. The symbolic act of eating the scroll demonstrated that Ezekiel internalized God's message in preparation for speaking to the people. Eating a physical scroll does not seem appetizing, but in this case it tasted sweet like honey. At the same time, the message the scroll contained was full of lament and woe (Eze 2:9 – 10).

This was not the only time God told one of his people to eat a scroll. In the New Testament, the apostle John prophesied about what God was going to do during the end times. God told John to eat that scroll as well — it was sweet to taste, but it made his stomach sour (Rev 10:9 – 11). It is a sweet thing to be empowered to speak God's truth, but at the same time it can be bitter when it contains a condemnation against sin.

God the Son spoke the same message as God the Father. Jesus came and preached the "sweet" news of God's love for all people and his offer to forgive their sins, but this message included the "bitter" news that people are sick and need to be healed (Mk 2:17), lost and in need of being found (Lk 15:1 – 32), in infinitely deep debt to God, and in desperate need of deliverance (Mt 18:21 – 35). God saves people who taste the bitterness of sin and cling to the sweet hope that only Jesus can save.

SON OF MAN

The phrase "son of man" is used as a title for Ezekiel the prophet 93 times throughout the book of Ezekiel. The name highlights the mortality of the prophet and places him at a distance from God. It is clear that Ezekiel is far from God and cannot compare to God. When Ezekiel stood in the presence of God, he noted that it was only possible with the help of God's Spirit (vv. 1 – 2).

Jesus used the title "Son of Man" to refer to himself more than any other name — more than 75 times through the Gospels. Whereas the phrase was used to refer to Ezekiel's distance from God, Jesus used it to refer to his nearness to us. Jesus is a "son of man" in the sense of being human in every way. Because Jesus is a member of the Trinity, the one true and holy God, he is not separated from God like the other prophets who had gone before him — Jesus is God.

There are many things that Jesus came to reveal to humanity. Although he is the eternal Word, he was made flesh to reveal God to the world (Jn 1:14). Jesus came to show the world God's love (Jn 3:16). Although he is God, Jesus relinquished the privileges of heaven so that he could seek and save the lost (Lk 19:10; Php 2:5 – 8). Jesus Christ lived the greatest life that anyone has ever lived. He was humble in character and mighty in word and deed. He came to fulfill God's Law and show himself to be Lord over it. He perfectly fulfilled the major offices of the Old Testament as he lived as the one true prophet, priest and king. He died to atone for the sins of the world and rose from the dead, proving that he is God and that sin has been defeated. He will return as reigning royalty (Da 7:13 – 14), and all the nations will mourn their judgment. Until that day comes, he is with his church, guiding and nurturing them in every way.

Jesus is the only perfect person who ever lived. He was completely human and completely identified with the full range of human emotions, and yet he remained sinless. Hebrews 4:15 reads, "For we do not have a high priest who is unable to empathize with our weaknesses, but we have one who has been tempted in every way, just as we are — yet he did not sin." Jesus invites people to follow him. This involves casting off sin and the former sense of self and finding new identity in him. God is high above humanity in holiness and yet has drawn near to all people in Jesus.

Ezekiel's Task as Watchman

[16]At the end of seven days the word of the LORD came to me: [17]"Son of man, I have made you a watchman for the people of Israel; so hear the word I speak and give them warning from me. [18]When I say to a wicked person, 'You will surely die,' and you do not warn them or speak out to dissuade them from their evil ways in order to save their life, that wicked person will die for[a] their sin, and I will hold you accountable for their blood. [19]But if you do warn the wicked person and they do not turn from their wickedness or from their evil ways, they will die for their sin; but you will have saved yourself.

[20]"Again, when a righteous person turns from their righteousness and does evil, and I put a stumbling block before them, they will die. Since you did not warn them, they will die for their sin. The righteous things that person did will not be remembered, and I will hold you accountable for their blood. [21]But if you do warn the righteous person not to sin and they do not sin, they will surely live because they took warning, and you will have saved yourself."

[22]The hand of the LORD was on me there, and he said to me, "Get up and go out to the plain, and there I will speak to you." [23]So I got up and went out to the plain. And the glory of the LORD was standing there, like the glory I had seen by the Kebar River, and I fell facedown.

[24]Then the Spirit came into me and raised me to my feet. He spoke to me and said: "Go, shut yourself inside your house. [25]And you, son of man, they will tie with ropes; you will be bound so that you cannot go out among the people. [26]I will make your tongue stick to the roof of your mouth so that you will be silent and unable to rebuke them, for they are a rebellious people. [27]But when I speak to you, I will open your mouth and you shall say to them, 'This is what the Sovereign LORD says.' Whoever will listen let them listen, and whoever will refuse let them refuse; for they are a rebellious people.

Siege of Jerusalem Symbolized

4 "Now, son of man, take a block of clay, put it in front of you and draw the city of Jerusalem on it. [2]Then lay siege to it: Erect siege works against it, build a ramp up to it, set up camps against it and put battering rams around it. [3]Then take an iron pan, place it as an iron wall between you and the city and turn your face toward it. It will be under siege, and you shall besiege it. This will be a sign to the people of Israel.

[4]"Then lie on your left side and put the sin of the people of Israel upon yourself.[b] You are to bear their sin for the number of days you lie on your side. [5]I have assigned you the same number of days as the years of their sin. So for 390 days you will bear the sin of the people of Israel.

[6]"After you have finished this, lie down again, this time on your right side, and bear the sin of the people of Judah. I have assigned you 40 days, a day for each year. [7]Turn your face toward the siege of Jerusalem and with bared arm prophesy against her. [8]I will tie you up with ropes so that you cannot turn from one side to the other until you have finished the days of your siege.

[9]"Take wheat and barley, beans and lentils, millet and spelt; put them in a storage jar and use them to make bread for yourself. You are to eat it during the 390 days you lie on your side. [10]Weigh out twenty shekels[c] of food to eat each day and eat it at set times. [11]Also measure out a sixth of a hin[d] of water and drink it at set times. [12]Eat the food as you would a loaf of barley bread; bake it in the sight of the people, using human excrement for fuel." [13]The LORD said, "In this way the people of Israel will eat defiled food among the nations where I will drive them."

[14]Then I said, "Not so, Sovereign LORD! I have never defiled myself. From my youth until now I have never eaten anything found dead or torn by wild animals. No impure meat has ever entered my mouth."

---

[a] *18* Or *in*; also in verses 19 and 20 [b] *4* Or *upon your side* [c] *10* That is, about 8 ounces or about 230 grams [d] *11* That is, about 2/3 quart or about 0.6 liter

15"Very well," he said, "I will let you bake your bread over cow dung instead
of human excrement."
16He then said to me: "Son of man, I am about to cut off the food supply in Jerusalem. The people will eat rationed food in anxiety and drink rationed water
in despair, 17for food and water will be scarce. They will be appalled at the sight
of each other and will waste away because of[a] their sin.

God's Razor of Judgment

5 "Now, son of man, take a sharp sword and use it as a barber's razor to shave
your head and your beard. Then take a set of scales and divide up the hair.
2When the days of your siege come to an end, burn a third of the hair inside the
city. Take a third and strike it with the sword all around the city. And scatter a
third to the wind. For I will pursue them with drawn sword. 3But take a few hairs
and tuck them away in the folds of your garment. 4Again, take a few of these and
throw them into the fire and burn them up. A fire will spread from there to all
Israel.
5"This is what the Sovereign LORD says: This is Jerusalem, which I have set in
the center of the nations, with countries all around her. 6Yet in her wickedness
she has rebelled against my laws and decrees more than the nations and countries around her. She has rejected my laws and has not followed my decrees.
7"Therefore this is what the Sovereign LORD says: You have been more unruly
than the nations around you and have not followed my decrees or kept my laws.
You have not even[b] conformed to the standards of the nations around you.
8"Therefore this is what the Sovereign LORD says: I myself am against you,
Jerusalem, and I will inflict punishment on you in the sight of the nations. 9Be-
cause of all your detestable idols, I will do to you what I have never done before
and will never do again. 10Therefore in your midst parents will eat their children,
and children will eat their parents. I will inflict punishment on you and will
scatter all your survivors to the winds. 11Therefore as surely as I live, declares
the Sovereign LORD, because you have defiled my sanctuary with all your vile
images and detestable practices, I myself will shave you; I will not look on you
with pity or spare you. 12A third of your people will die of the plague or perish by
famine inside you; a third will fall by the sword outside your walls; and a third I
will scatter to the winds and pursue with drawn sword.
13"Then my anger will cease and my wrath against them will subside, and I
will be avenged. And when I have spent my wrath on them, they will know that I
the LORD have spoken in my zeal.
14"I will make you a ruin and a reproach among the nations around you, in the
sight of all who pass by. 15You will be a reproach and a taunt, a warning and an
object of horror to the nations around you when I inflict punishment on you in
anger and in wrath and with stinging rebuke. I the LORD have spoken. 16When
I shoot at you with my deadly and destructive arrows of famine, I will shoot to
destroy you. I will bring more and more famine upon you and cut off your supply
of food. 17I will send famine and wild beasts against you, and they will leave you
childless. Plague and bloodshed will sweep through you, and I will bring the
sword against you. I the LORD have spoken."

Doom for the Mountains of Israel

6 The word of the LORD came to me: 2"Son of man, set your face against the
mountains of Israel; prophesy against them 3and say: 'You mountains of
Israel, hear the word of the Sovereign LORD. This is what the Sovereign LORD
says to the mountains and hills, to the ravines and valleys: I am about to bring
a sword against you, and I will destroy your high places. 4Your altars will be demolished and your incense altars will be smashed; and I will slay your people
in front of your idols. 5I will lay the dead bodies of the Israelites in front of their

---

EZEKIEL 5:5–11

MORE ACCOUNTABLE

The entire Bible, from cover to cover, is the story of God's plan to create a people, choose a people, transform that people and then work through his transformed people to change the world. God's people are supposed to be like a light that shines into the dark world, but this passage reveals that the Israelites literally outdid the world in sinning. While the other nations worshiped idols, Israel left the One true living God to turn to idols—a choice that brought dire consequences. God judged them, and his judgment was harsh because his mercy to them had been unfathomable. Of all the people in the world, God chose to love these people in a special way. For them to forsake that love was unthinkable.

The judgments of God are always relative based on the level of light people have received. All people will suffer if they never hear of God; this is why God's people are supposed to run to people with good news to share! At the same time, those who receive more are more accountable. Ezekiel 5:5–7 teaches about this enduring scriptural truth that Jesus repeated in his teaching: "From everyone who has been given much, much will be demanded" (Lk 12:48). If that was true for Israel, who spent their lives looking forward to Jesus' arrival, how much more true is it of believers today who have the Holy Spirit?

---

[a] *17* Or *away in* [b] *7* Most Hebrew manuscripts; some Hebrew manuscripts and Syriac *You have*

idols, and I will scatter your bones around your altars. [6]Wherever you live, the
towns will be laid waste and the high places demolished, so that your altars will
be laid waste and devastated, your idols smashed and ruined, your incense altars broken down, and what you have made wiped out. [7]Your people will fall
slain among you, and you will know that I am the LORD.
[8]" 'But I will spare some, for some of you will escape the sword when you are
scattered among the lands and nations. [9]Then in the nations where they have
been carried captive, those who escape will remember me — how I have been
grieved by their adulterous hearts, which have turned away from me, and by
their eyes, which have lusted after their idols. They will loathe themselves for the
evil they have done and for all their detestable practices. [10]And they will know
that I am the LORD; I did not threaten in vain to bring this calamity on them.
[11]" 'This is what the Sovereign LORD says: Strike your hands together and
stamp your feet and cry out "Alas!" because of all the wicked and detestable
practices of the people of Israel, for they will fall by the sword, famine and
plague. [12]One who is far away will die of the plague, and one who is near will fall
by the sword, and anyone who survives and is spared will die of famine. So will I
pour out my wrath on them. [13]And they will know that I am the LORD, when their
people lie slain among their idols around their altars, on every high hill and on
all the mountaintops, under every spreading tree and every leafy oak — places
where they offered fragrant incense to all their idols. [14]And I will stretch out my
hand against them and make the land a desolate waste from the desert to Dib-
lah[a] — wherever they live. Then they will know that I am the LORD.' "

The End Has Come

7 The word of the LORD came to me: [2]"Son of man, this is what the Sovereign
LORD says to the land of Israel:

" 'The end! The end has come
upon the four corners of the land!
[3]The end is now upon you,
and I will unleash my anger against you.
I will judge you according to your conduct
and repay you for all your detestable practices.
[4]I will not look on you with pity;
I will not spare you.
I will surely repay you for your conduct
and for the detestable practices among you.

" 'Then you will know that I am the LORD.'

[5]"This is what the Sovereign LORD says:

" 'Disaster! Unheard-of[b] disaster!
See, it comes!
[6]The end has come!
The end has come!
It has roused itself against you.
See, it comes!
[7]Doom has come upon you,
upon you who dwell in the land.
The time has come! The day is near!
There is panic, not joy, on the mountains.
[8]I am about to pour out my wrath on you
and spend my anger against you.
I will judge you according to your conduct
and repay you for all your detestable practices.

[a] *14* Most Hebrew manuscripts; a few Hebrew manuscripts *Riblah* [b] *5* Most Hebrew manuscripts; some Hebrew manuscripts and Syriac *Disaster after*

EZEKIEL 7:6

THE END HAS COME!

Predictions about the end of the world tend to get people's attention, as they have a natural tendency to wonder when the end will come. In the book of Ezekiel, God delivered a clear word to Judah not that the end of the world was coming, but that the end of this season of God's favor had come. Ezekiel told them they would experience punishment as their nation was conquered and they were sent away to live as exiles.

A few hundred years later, in the New Testament, Jesus' followers asked him how they could tell when the end would come. Jesus responded, "You will hear of wars and rumors of wars, but see to it that you are not alarmed. Such things must happen, but the end is still to come. Nation will rise against nation, and kingdom against kingdom. There will be famines and earthquakes in various places" (Mt 24:6 – 7). And then, Jesus went on to declare, "This gospel of the kingdom will be preached in the whole world as a testimony to all nations, and then the end will come" (Mt 24:14).

God doesn't expect his people to know the exact time when his kingdom will come in fullness. He does, however, expect his church to be faithful and obedient in preparing for it.

EZEKIEL 6:7

YOU WILL KNOW

One of the recurring themes of Ezekiel revolves around the phrase, "and you will know that I am the LORD" (v. 7). The best way to experience God is through an encounter with his mercy. At the same time, it is possible to experience God through an encounter with his judgment. At this point, God's people had sinned so much that they were about to experience the judgment of God in an encounter they would never forget.

The recurring theme of "and you will know" testifies to the God-centeredness of this book. God's sovereignty, glory and love for his people converge in a powerful way. This combination of ideas is also found in Jeremiah's prophecy. It certainly seems that Ezekiel drew upon Jeremiah to develop these ideas further by focusing on the Babylonians' destruction of Jerusalem.

Ezekiel 6 is full of references to the theme of God's power and might for his people (vv. 7,10, 13 – 14). In this case, God was dealing with a stiff-necked and rebellious people, who would discover that he was the Lord through judgment. The emphasis is not necessarily on the fact that God judges, though that is certainly true. The real goal is that people would know and experience the character of God. The emphasis is on getting to know God and experience God. Judgment is never for judgment's sake; its goal is for people to experience more truth about who God is.

Judgment is a critical way for people to experience the character of God. The most wonderful part of the idea of judgment is that God substituted Jesus for undeserving sinners. It was not until Jesus was "lifted up" via crucifixion that people could really get to know him and understand him in the fullest sense: "So Jesus said, 'When you have lifted up the Son of Man, then you will know that I am he and that I do nothing on my own but speak just what the Father has taught me' " (Jn 8:28).

It is only through seeing that God substituted Jesus for the sins of the world that people are able to see the truth that sets them free (Jn 8:32).

9 I will not look on you with pity;
I will not spare you.
I will repay you for your conduct
and for the detestable practices among you.

" 'Then you will know that it is I the LORD who strikes you.

10 " 'See, the day!
See, it comes!
Doom has burst forth,
the rod has budded,
arrogance has blossomed!
11 Violence has arisen,[a]
a rod to punish the wicked.
None of the people will be left,
none of that crowd—
none of their wealth,
nothing of value.
12 The time has come!
The day has arrived!
Let not the buyer rejoice
nor the seller grieve,
for my wrath is on the whole crowd.
13 The seller will not recover
the property that was sold—
as long as both buyer and seller live.
For the vision concerning the whole crowd
will not be reversed.
Because of their sins, not one of them
will preserve their life.

14 " 'They have blown the trumpet,
they have made all things ready,
but no one will go into battle,
for my wrath is on the whole crowd.
15 Outside is the sword;
inside are plague and famine.
Those in the country
will die by the sword;
those in the city
will be devoured by famine and plague.
16 The fugitives who escape
will flee to the mountains.
Like doves of the valleys,
they will all moan,
each for their own sins.
17 Every hand will go limp;
every leg will be wet with urine.
18 They will put on sackcloth
and be clothed with terror.
Every face will be covered with shame,
and every head will be shaved.

19 " 'They will throw their silver into the streets,
and their gold will be treated as a thing unclean.
Their silver and gold
will not be able to deliver them
in the day of the LORD's wrath.

---

[a] 11 Or *The violent one has become*

It will not satisfy their hunger
or fill their stomachs,
for it has caused them to stumble into sin.
20 They took pride in their beautiful jewelry
and used it to make their detestable idols.
They made it into vile images;
therefore I will make it a thing unclean for them.
21 I will give their wealth as plunder to foreigners
and as loot to the wicked of the earth,
who will defile it.
22 I will turn my face away from the people,
and robbers will desecrate the place I treasure.
They will enter it
and will defile it.

23 " 'Prepare chains!
For the land is full of bloodshed,
and the city is full of violence.
24 I will bring the most wicked of nations
to take possession of their houses.
I will put an end to the pride of the mighty,
and their sanctuaries will be desecrated.
25 When terror comes,
they will seek peace in vain.
26 Calamity upon calamity will come,
and rumor upon rumor.
They will go searching for a vision from the prophet,
priestly instruction in the law will cease,
the counsel of the elders will come to an end.
27 The king will mourn,
the prince will be clothed with despair,
and the hands of the people of the land will tremble.
I will deal with them according to their conduct,
and by their own standards I will judge them.

" 'Then they will know that I am the LORD.' "

Idolatry in the Temple

8 In the sixth year, in the sixth month on the fifth day, while I was sitting in my
house and the elders of Judah were sitting before me, the hand of the Sovereign LORD came on me there. 2 I looked, and I saw a figure like that of a man.[a]
From what appeared to be his waist down he was like fire, and from there up his
appearance was as bright as glowing metal. 3 He stretched out what looked like a
hand and took me by the hair of my head. The Spirit lifted me up between earth
and heaven and in visions of God he took me to Jerusalem, to the entrance of
the north gate of the inner court, where the idol that provokes to jealousy stood.
4 And there before me was the glory of the God of Israel, as in the vision I had
seen in the plain.

5 Then he said to me, "Son of man, look toward the north." So I looked, and in
the entrance north of the gate of the altar I saw this idol of jealousy.

6 And he said to me, "Son of man, do you see what they are doing—the utterly
detestable things the Israelites are doing here, things that will drive me far from
my sanctuary? But you will see things that are even more detestable."

7 Then he brought me to the entrance to the court. I looked, and I saw a hole
in the wall. 8 He said to me, "Son of man, now dig into the wall." So I dug into the
wall and saw a doorway there.

9 And he said to me, "Go in and see the wicked and detestable things they are

[a] 2 Or *saw a fiery figure*

EZEKIEL 8:9–12

SIN OF THE PEOPLE

God's judgment was coming upon the Israelites because of their sin. This sin was not contained to a few lunatics on the fringes of their community; instead, the leaders of the community were committing it. In the temple, the very place where God's presence was meant to dwell with his people, they were committing wicked acts against God.

Like so many of the prophets, Ezekiel analyzed and spoke against the sins of the people. He focused especially on the sin of idolatry—the worship of other gods or other things in place of God. God's people were hiding in the dark and doing dark things. In his ministry, Jesus taught that what happens in the dark will eventually be brought into the light: "For there is nothing hidden that will not be disclosed, and nothing concealed that will not be known or brought out into the open. Therefore consider carefully how you listen. Whoever has will be given more; whoever does not have, even what they think they have will be taken from them" (Lk 8:17–18).

In Ezekiel, God's people were judged because they had so much favor from God and did so little with it. God gives great things to his people and then expects great things from his people. Sin keeps God's people from experiencing God's best for them.

doing here." 10So I went in and looked, and I saw portrayed all over the walls all
kinds of crawling things and unclean animals and all the idols of Israel. 11In
front of them stood seventy elders of Israel, and Jaazaniah son of Shaphan was
standing among them. Each had a censer in his hand, and a fragrant cloud of
incense was rising.
12He said to me, "Son of man, have you seen what the elders of Israel are doing
in the darkness, each at the shrine of his own idol? They say, 'The LORD does not
see us; the LORD has forsaken the land.' " 13Again, he said, "You will see them
doing things that are even more detestable."
14Then he brought me to the entrance of the north gate of the house of the
LORD, and I saw women sitting there, mourning the god Tammuz. 15He said to
me, "Do you see this, son of man? You will see things that are even more detestable than this."
16He then brought me into the inner court of the house of the LORD, and there
at the entrance to the temple, between the portico and the altar, were about
twenty-five men. With their backs toward the temple of the LORD and their faces
toward the east, they were bowing down to the sun in the east.
17He said to me, "Have you seen this, son of man? Is it a trivial matter for the
people of Judah to do the detestable things they are doing here? Must they also
fill the land with violence and continually arouse my anger? Look at them putting the branch to their nose! 18Therefore I will deal with them in anger; I will
not look on them with pity or spare them. Although they shout in my ears, I will
not listen to them."

Judgment on the Idolaters

9 Then I heard him call out in a loud voice, "Bring near those who are appointed to execute judgment on the city, each with a weapon in his hand." 2And
I saw six men coming from the direction of the upper gate, which faces north,
each with a deadly weapon in his hand. With them was a man clothed in linen
who had a writing kit at his side. They came in and stood beside the bronze altar.
3Now the glory of the God of Israel went up from above the cherubim, where
it had been, and moved to the threshold of the temple. Then the LORD called to
the man clothed in linen who had the writing kit at his side 4and said to him, "Go
throughout the city of Jerusalem and put a mark on the foreheads of those who
grieve and lament over all the detestable things that are done in it."
5As I listened, he said to the others, "Follow him through the city and kill,
without showing pity or compassion. 6Slaughter the old men, the young men
and women, the mothers and children, but do not touch anyone who has the
mark. Begin at my sanctuary." So they began with the old men who were in front
of the temple.
7Then he said to them, "Defile the temple and fill the courts with the slain.
Go!" So they went out and began killing throughout the city. 8While they were
killing and I was left alone, I fell facedown, crying out, "Alas, Sovereign LORD!
Are you going to destroy the entire remnant of Israel in this outpouring of your
wrath on Jerusalem?"
9He answered me, "The sin of the people of Israel and Judah is exceedingly
great; the land is full of bloodshed and the city is full of injustice. They say, 'The
LORD has forsaken the land; the LORD does not see.' 10So I will not look on them
with pity or spare them, but I will bring down on their own heads what they
have done."
11Then the man in linen with the writing kit at his side brought back word,
saying, "I have done as you commanded."

God's Glory Departs From the Temple

10 I looked, and I saw the likeness of a throne of lapis lazuli above the vault
that was over the heads of the cherubim. 2The LORD said to the man
clothed in linen, "Go in among the wheels beneath the cherubim. Fill your

hands with burning coals from among the cherubim and scatter them over the
city." And as I watched, he went in.
3Now the cherubim were standing on the south side of the temple when the
man went in, and a cloud filled the inner court. 4Then the glory of the LORD rose
from above the cherubim and moved to the threshold of the temple. The cloud
filled the temple, and the court was full of the radiance of the glory of the LORD.
5The sound of the wings of the cherubim could be heard as far away as the outer
court, like the voice of God Almighty[a] when he speaks.
6When the LORD commanded the man in linen, "Take fire from among the
wheels, from among the cherubim," the man went in and stood beside a wheel.
7Then one of the cherubim reached out his hand to the fire that was among them.
He took up some of it and put it into the hands of the man in linen, who took it
and went out. 8(Under the wings of the cherubim could be seen what looked like
human hands.)
9I looked, and I saw beside the cherubim four wheels, one beside each of the
cherubim; the wheels sparkled like topaz. 10As for their appearance, the four of
them looked alike; each was like a wheel intersecting a wheel. 11As they moved,
they would go in any one of the four directions the cherubim faced; the wheels
did not turn about[b] as the cherubim went. The cherubim went in whatever direction the head faced, without turning as they went. 12Their entire bodies, including their backs, their hands and their wings, were completely full of eyes, as were
their four wheels. 13I heard the wheels being called "the whirling wheels." 14Each
of the cherubim had four faces: One face was that of a cherub, the second the face
of a human being, the third the face of a lion, and the fourth the face of an eagle.
15Then the cherubim rose upward. These were the living creatures I had
seen by the Kebar River. 16When the cherubim moved, the wheels beside them
moved; and when the cherubim spread their wings to rise from the ground, the
wheels did not leave their side. 17When the cherubim stood still, they also stood
still; and when the cherubim rose, they rose with them, because the spirit of the
living creatures was in them.
18Then the glory of the LORD departed from over the threshold of the temple
and stopped above the cherubim. 19While I watched, the cherubim spread their
wings and rose from the ground, and as they went, the wheels went with them.
They stopped at the entrance of the east gate of the LORD's house, and the glory
of the God of Israel was above them.
20These were the living creatures I had seen beneath the God of Israel by the
Kebar River, and I realized that they were cherubim. 21Each had four faces and
four wings, and under their wings was what looked like human hands. 22Their
faces had the same appearance as those I had seen by the Kebar River. Each one
went straight ahead.

God's Sure Judgment on Jerusalem

11 Then the Spirit lifted me up and brought me to the gate of the house of the
LORD that faces east. There at the entrance of the gate were twenty-five
men, and I saw among them Jaazaniah son of Azzur and Pelatiah son of Benaiah, leaders of the people. 2The LORD said to me, "Son of man, these are the men
who are plotting evil and giving wicked advice in this city. 3They say, 'Haven't
our houses been recently rebuilt? This city is a pot, and we are the meat in it.'
4Therefore prophesy against them; prophesy, son of man."
5Then the Spirit of the LORD came on me, and he told me to say: "This is what
the LORD says: That is what you are saying, you leaders in Israel, but I know what
is going through your mind. 6You have killed many people in this city and filled
its streets with the dead.
7"Therefore this is what the Sovereign LORD says: The bodies you have thrown
there are the meat and this city is the pot, but I will drive you out of it. 8You fear

[a] 5 Hebrew *El-Shaddai* [b] 11 Or *aside*

EZEKIEL 10:18 – 19

GLORY DEPARTING, GLORY COMING

God's glory in the temple was a manifestation of his presence, but since sin was happening in the temple, God removed his presence. Beginning with Ezekiel 9:3, the prophet recounts the steady withdrawal of God's presence from the temple. The removal of God's glory was a shocking reminder that God was not going to tolerate the Israelites' sin.

Thankfully, Jesus made a way for God's glory to remain with his people in a permanent way. Jesus was God's glory living on earth (Jn 17:24), but people did not see it. In time, Jesus' disciples realized that in Jesus' incarnation, death and resurrection, they had witnessed the coming glory of God (Jn 1:14). Jesus came to live a perfect life and die as the perfect sacrifice for human sin.

When God took the sins of the entire world and heaped them on Jesus, sin was accounted for and punished. As a result, believers can experience God's glory and live because their sin is no longer an obstacle to them. Ezekiel taught about the removal of God's glory, and Jesus taught about the coming of God's glory (Mt 24:30; 25:31). Christians joyfully remember how gracious God is to save them and then dedicate their lives to loving and serving him wholeheartedly.

the sword, and the sword is what I will bring against you, declares the Sovereign LORD. [9]I will drive you out of the city and deliver you into the hands of foreigners and inflict punishment on you. [10]You will fall by the sword, and I will execute judgment on you at the borders of Israel. Then you will know that I am the LORD. [11]This city will not be a pot for you, nor will you be the meat in it; I will execute judgment on you at the borders of Israel. [12]And you will know that I am the LORD, for you have not followed my decrees or kept my laws but have conformed to the standards of the nations around you."

[13]Now as I was prophesying, Pelatiah son of Benaiah died. Then I fell facedown and cried out in a loud voice, "Alas, Sovereign LORD! Will you completely destroy the remnant of Israel?"

The Promise of Israel's Return

[14]The word of the LORD came to me: [15]"Son of man, the people of Jerusalem have said of your fellow exiles and all the other Israelites, 'They are far away from the LORD; this land was given to us as our possession.'

[16]"Therefore say: 'This is what the Sovereign LORD says: Although I sent them far away among the nations and scattered them among the countries, yet for a little while I have been a sanctuary for them in the countries where they have gone.'

[17]"Therefore say: 'This is what the Sovereign LORD says: I will gather you from the nations and bring you back from the countries where you have been scattered, and I will give you back the land of Israel again.'

[18]"They will return to it and remove all its vile images and detestable idols. [19]I will give them an undivided heart and put a new spirit in them; I will remove from them their heart of stone and give them a heart of flesh. [20]Then they will follow my decrees and be careful to keep my laws. They will be my people, and I will be their God. [21]But as for those whose hearts are devoted to their vile images and detestable idols, I will bring down on their own heads what they have done, declares the Sovereign LORD."

[22]Then the cherubim, with the wheels beside them, spread their wings, and the glory of the God of Israel was above them. [23]The glory of the LORD went up from within the city and stopped above the mountain east of it. [24]The Spirit lifted me up and brought me to the exiles in Babylonia[a] in the vision given by the Spirit of God.

Then the vision I had seen went up from me, [25]and I told the exiles everything the LORD had shown me.

The Exile Symbolized

12 The word of the LORD came to me: [2]"Son of man, you are living among a rebellious people. They have eyes to see but do not see and ears to hear but do not hear, for they are a rebellious people.

[3]"Therefore, son of man, pack your belongings for exile and in the daytime, as they watch, set out and go from where you are to another place. Perhaps they will understand, though they are a rebellious people. [4]During the daytime, while they watch, bring out your belongings packed for exile. Then in the evening, while they are watching, go out like those who go into exile. [5]While they watch, dig through the wall and take your belongings out through it. [6]Put them on your shoulder as they are watching and carry them out at dusk. Cover your face so that you cannot see the land, for I have made you a sign to the Israelites."

[7]So I did as I was commanded. During the day I brought out my things packed for exile. Then in the evening I dug through the wall with my hands. I took my belongings out at dusk, carrying them on my shoulders while they watched.

[8]In the morning the word of the LORD came to me: [9]"Son of man, did not the Israelites, that rebellious people, ask you, 'What are you doing?'

---

[a] 24 Or *Chaldea*

WHERE GOD'S GLORY RESIDES

The word *glory* here literally means "weight" or "significance" and refers to the wonder and majesty of the living God. At times in the Old Testament, God's glory was displayed to his people to show that he was with them. When Moses set up the tabernacle, God's glory filled the tent and Moses was not able to enter it (Ex 40:34 – 35). Later, when Solomon built the temple, the cloud of God's glory appeared again (1Ki 8:10 – 12; 2Ch 7:1 – 2). But during Ezekiel's ministry, the prophet saw a vision of God's glory leaving the temple in Jerusalem.

God's glory left the presence of God's people because God's people were involved in unrelenting sin. Their idol worship permeated everything to the point that they went to the temple to pay homage to other idols instead of the one true and living God (Eze 8:3,14 – 16). They even painted images of idols and unclean animals on the walls of the temple (Eze 8:9 – 11). God's message to his people about their sin was clear: it was wrong. He told them to stop sinning. He warned them about its consequences. And he warned them that he would not tolerate it forever.

God took the most precious thing that he could have from his people: his presence. Regardless of what God's people valued, God's glory was the best reality they had ever experienced. It is interesting to note how God slowly removed his glory from his people. God's glory moved from above the cherubim in the Most Holy Place to the threshold of the temple (Eze 9:3), then moved to the east gate of the temple (Eze 10:19), and then made one final stop above the Mount of Olives (Eze 11:23). God slowly and reluctantly removed himself from his people with a display that left no doubt as to what was happening. Not long after God removed his glory from Solomon's temple, the temple was destroyed, and God's glory never returned to that temple.

But God's glory did return to the world, and it returned in a way that was unlike anything the world had ever seen. John explains, "The Word became flesh and made his dwelling among us. We have seen his glory, the glory of the one and only Son, who came from the Father, full of grace and truth" (Jn 1:14). Jesus fully embodied the glory of God. To see God, one only needs to look to Jesus (Heb 1:3). Following his short life, Jesus offered himself up as the perfect sacrifice for sin to end all other sacrifices. He gave parting words to his followers and departed to heaven from the Mount of Olives (Ac 1:7 – 12). His glory is with his people today because all who trust in Jesus possess his Spirit and live their lives reflecting God's glory in an ever-increasing way (2Co 3:18).

THE REBELLION

God's prophet had to speak to God's "rebellious people": a phrase the Lord used twice in this verse to describe the community of exiles in Babylon among whom Ezekiel ministered. They refused to listen to the prophet's words or heed his dramatizations of their coming judgments.

All people struggle with a rebellious heart toward God. The word "rebellious" is used all throughout Scripture to explain the condition of people's hearts as a result of sin. It depicts someone opposing an authority figure out of stubborn pride (Dt 21:18). Ezekiel described the Israelites as a rebellious people a dozen times, meaning they were willfully disobedient and persistent in their refusal to listen to God's message through Ezekiel (Eze 2:3 – 8). These people wanted nothing to do with God's authority in their lives.

Jesus was accused of being a rebel throughout his life. Religious leaders accused him of leading a rebellion (Lk 23:1 – 2,13 – 14). They had created an established system of religion to manage their relationship with God. Their man-made solution to their sin problem with God had no need of Jesus. When Jesus came preaching the gospel of repentance, the leaders hated it because it meant that their whole system was inadequate. Jesus was arrested, put on trial and sentenced to death. As Jesus hung on the cross, he was crucified between two rebels (Mt 27:38,44).

The great irony is that Jesus was the ultimate example of someone who was not a rebel! Jesus obediently died as the substitute for sinners. He was not a sinner, but he willfully gave his life to die for everyone who has ever had a rebellious thought, season or life. All people need to do is trust in him to claim the life that is truly life (1Ti 6:19). Jesus' life was perfectly aligned with God the Father in every way. In John 5:9, he stated that he would do only what he saw the Father doing. When teaching his followers to pray, he told them to say to the Father, "Your kingdom come, your will be done, on earth as it is in heaven" (Mt 6:10).

God sent both Ezekiel and Jesus to speak to a rebellious people. Jesus was a perfect man who lived a life of perfect obedience to God for undeserving people. Despite their rebellion, God launched a counter-rebellion against the defiance of his people. He has waged a war of love on the misplaced desires of human hearts.

10“Say to them, ‘This is what the Sovereign LORD says: This prophecy concerns
the prince in Jerusalem and all the Israelites who are there.’ 11Say to them, ‘I am
a sign to you.’

“As I have done, so it will be done to them. They will go into exile as captives.
12“The prince among them will put his things on his shoulder at dusk and
leave, and a hole will be dug in the wall for him to go through. He will cover his
face so that he cannot see the land. 13I will spread my net for him, and he will
be caught in my snare; I will bring him to Babylonia, the land of the Chaldeans,
but he will not see it, and there he will die. 14I will scatter to the winds all those
around him — his staff and all his troops — and I will pursue them with drawn
sword.

15“They will know that I am the LORD, when I disperse them among the nations and scatter them through the countries. 16But I will spare a few of them
from the sword, famine and plague, so that in the nations where they go they
may acknowledge all their detestable practices. Then they will know that I am
the LORD.”

17The word of the LORD came to me: 18“Son of man, tremble as you eat your
food, and shudder in fear as you drink your water. 19Say to the people of the land:
‘This is what the Sovereign LORD says about those living in Jerusalem and in the
land of Israel: They will eat their food in anxiety and drink their water in despair, for their land will be stripped of everything in it because of the violence of
all who live there. 20The inhabited towns will be laid waste and the land will be
desolate. Then you will know that I am the LORD.’ ”

There Will Be No Delay

21The word of the LORD came to me: 22“Son of man, what is this proverb you
have in the land of Israel: ‘The days go by and every vision comes to nothing’?
23Say to them, ‘This is what the Sovereign LORD says: I am going to put an end to
this proverb, and they will no longer quote it in Israel.’ Say to them, ‘The days are
near when every vision will be fulfilled. 24For there will be no more false visions
or flattering divinations among the people of Israel. 25But I the LORD will speak
what I will, and it shall be fulfilled without delay. For in your days, you rebellious
people, I will fulfill whatever I say, declares the Sovereign LORD.’ ”

26The word of the LORD came to me: 27“Son of man, the Israelites are saying,
‘The vision he sees is for many years from now, and he prophesies about the
distant future.’

28“Therefore say to them, ‘This is what the Sovereign LORD says: None of my
words will be delayed any longer; whatever I say will be fulfilled, declares the
Sovereign LORD.’ ”

False Prophets Condemned

13 The word of the LORD came to me: 2“Son of man, prophesy against the
prophets of Israel who are now prophesying. Say to those who prophesy out of their own imagination: ‘Hear the word of the LORD! 3This is what the
Sovereign LORD says: Woe to the foolish[a] prophets who follow their own spirit
and have seen nothing! 4Your prophets, Israel, are like jackals among ruins. 5You
have not gone up to the breaches in the wall to repair it for the people of Israel so
that it will stand firm in the battle on the day of the LORD. 6Their visions are false
and their divinations a lie. Even though the LORD has not sent them, they say,
“The LORD declares,” and expect him to fulfill their words. 7Have you not seen
false visions and uttered lying divinations when you say, “The LORD declares,”
though I have not spoken?

8“ ‘Therefore this is what the Sovereign LORD says: Because of your false words
and lying visions, I am against you, declares the Sovereign LORD. 9My hand will
be against the prophets who see false visions and utter lying divinations. They

[a] 3 Or *wicked*

will not belong to the council of my people or be listed in the records of Israel, nor will they enter the land of Israel. Then you will know that I am the Sovereign LORD.

10" 'Because they lead my people astray, saying, "Peace," when there is no peace, and because, when a flimsy wall is built, they cover it with whitewash, 11therefore tell those who cover it with whitewash that it is going to fall. Rain will come in torrents, and I will send hailstones hurtling down, and violent winds will burst forth. 12When the wall collapses, will people not ask you, "Where is the whitewash you covered it with?"

13" 'Therefore this is what the Sovereign LORD says: In my wrath I will unleash a violent wind, and in my anger hailstones and torrents of rain will fall with destructive fury. 14I will tear down the wall you have covered with whitewash and will level it to the ground so that its foundation will be laid bare. When it[a] falls, you will be destroyed in it; and you will know that I am the LORD. 15So I will pour out my wrath against the wall and against those who covered it with whitewash. I will say to you, "The wall is gone and so are those who whitewashed it, 16those prophets of Israel who prophesied to Jerusalem and saw visions of peace for her when there was no peace, declares the Sovereign LORD." '

17"Now, son of man, set your face against the daughters of your people who prophesy out of their own imagination. Prophesy against them 18and say, 'This is what the Sovereign LORD says: Woe to the women who sew magic charms on all their wrists and make veils of various lengths for their heads in order to ensnare people. Will you ensnare the lives of my people but preserve your own? 19You have profaned me among my people for a few handfuls of barley and scraps of bread. By lying to my people, who listen to lies, you have killed those who should not have died and have spared those who should not live.

20" 'Therefore this is what the Sovereign LORD says: I am against your magic charms with which you ensnare people like birds and I will tear them from your arms; I will set free the people that you ensnare like birds. 21I will tear off your veils and save my people from your hands, and they will no longer fall prey to your power. Then you will know that I am the LORD. 22Because you disheartened the righteous with your lies, when I had brought them no grief, and because you encouraged the wicked not to turn from their evil ways and so save their lives, 23therefore you will no longer see false visions or practice divination. I will save my people from your hands. And then you will know that I am the LORD.' "

Idolaters Condemned

14 Some of the elders of Israel came to me and sat down in front of me. 2Then the word of the LORD came to me: 3"Son of man, these men have set up idols in their hearts and put wicked stumbling blocks before their faces. Should I let them inquire of me at all? 4Therefore speak to them and tell them, 'This is what the Sovereign LORD says: When any of the Israelites set up idols in their hearts and put a wicked stumbling block before their faces and then go to a prophet, I the LORD will answer them myself in keeping with their great idolatry. 5I will do this to recapture the hearts of the people of Israel, who have all deserted me for their idols.'

6"Therefore say to the people of Israel, 'This is what the Sovereign LORD says: Repent! Turn from your idols and renounce all your detestable practices!

7" 'When any of the Israelites or any foreigner residing in Israel separate themselves from me and set up idols in their hearts and put a wicked stumbling block before their faces and then go to a prophet to inquire of me, I the LORD will answer them myself. 8I will set my face against them and make them an example and a byword. I will remove them from my people. Then you will know that I am the LORD.

9" 'And if the prophet is enticed to utter a prophecy, I the LORD have enticed

[a] 14 Or *the city*

EZEKIEL 13:10 – 16

COVERING UP THE REAL PROBLEM

God's rage burned against Jerusalem's false prophets, and his message was clear: Their city was going to be destroyed because of the sins of its inhabitants. Still these deceitful prophets gave God's people a false sense of hope. They reassured the people that their society's problems were not that bad, and they minimized the consequences of their sins. God spoke through Ezekiel to tell these prophets that they had "whitewashed" the sin problem in their city, covering over what was a deadly serious problem with whitewash paint. Because they covered up the problem of the people's sin but never really dealt with it, God would crush these false prophets under that same whitewashed stone wall when the city was destroyed.

Jesus warned the religious leaders during his day in a similar way, saying they were like "whitewashed tombs" (Mt 23:27 – 28). From the outside, their religious exterior looked good and presentable, but their empty religious practices were like rotting decay and dry bones on the inside. Sinful people will never be made whole until their problems are addressed all the way down to the core. Covering up the problem of sin never makes that sin go away. Only Jesus can heal the brokenness and restore relationships between people, and between believers and God (Ro 6:1 – 14).

IDOLS IN THE HEART

Loyalty is an important word; it has to do with what or whom a person relies on when a need arises, and it carries a sense of being dedicated and faithful to an idea or to a person. The elders here were double-minded men (1Ki 18:21). Outwardly, they came to the prophet Ezekiel in order to hear from God, but in their hearts their loyalty to God was divided. God told Ezekiel that he would not give revelatory guidance to these men who were not fully committed to worshiping him above all other gods. Loyalty to God means worshiping him alone. The religious leaders were not loyal to God because they had a heart problem.

Idolatry may sound primitive. Many people think of figures made from wood or stone to which people pray and offer sacrifices. When people engage in idolatrous practices they "put a wicked stumbling block before their faces" (Eze 14:4). Idols are not only carved objects that sit in pagan temples; idols are the godless cravings and sinful commitments that rule people's hearts.

God's people during Ezekiel's day struggled with the same things that people struggle with today: "idols in their hearts" (vv. 3,4). Everyone struggled with this; it was not just a problem for a select few. Even the religious leaders were committed to godless purposes. Their hearts' divided loyalties manifested in mixing the worship of idols with the worship of the one true and living God. Their idols would fail when God's judgment came (vv. 4 – 5).

God announced his restorative purpose through loving rebuke and discipline of those he loves (Rev 3:19). Jesus came to rid the world of idols, and he accomplished this by focusing on the hearts of humanity. Jesus confronted people who struggled with idolatry in order to save them from their idolatry. He knew that idolatry was not a simple behavior problem but a deep and abiding heart problem.

God's work of salvation is "heart work." Humanity's idolatry is not a little issue that needs to be fixed but a path that will lead to judgment (Ro 2:5). God promised to give his people new hearts so they could worship him fully (Eze 11:19 – 20; 36:26). The resurrection of Jesus means that believers can have new life. As a promise of his love, God puts his Spirit in the hearts of his children; he has "set his seal of ownership on us, and put his Spirit in our hearts as a deposit, guaranteeing what is to come" (2Co 1:22).

that prophet, and I will stretch out my hand against him and destroy him from among my people Israel. [10]They will bear their guilt — the prophet will be as guilty as the one who consults him. [11]Then the people of Israel will no longer stray from me, nor will they defile themselves anymore with all their sins. They will be my people, and I will be their God, declares the Sovereign LORD.' "

Jerusalem's Judgment Inescapable

[12]The word of the LORD came to me: [13]"Son of man, if a country sins against me by being unfaithful and I stretch out my hand against it to cut off its food supply and send famine upon it and kill its people and their animals, [14]even if these three men — Noah, Daniel[a] and Job — were in it, they could save only themselves by their righteousness, declares the Sovereign LORD.

[15]"Or if I send wild beasts through that country and they leave it childless and it becomes desolate so that no one can pass through it because of the beasts, [16]as surely as I live, declares the Sovereign LORD, even if these three men were in it, they could not save their own sons or daughters. They alone would be saved, but the land would be desolate.

[17]"Or if I bring a sword against that country and say, 'Let the sword pass throughout the land,' and I kill its people and their animals, [18]as surely as I live, declares the Sovereign LORD, even if these three men were in it, they could not save their own sons or daughters. They alone would be saved.

[19]"Or if I send a plague into that land and pour out my wrath on it through bloodshed, killing its people and their animals, [20]as surely as I live, declares the Sovereign LORD, even if Noah, Daniel and Job were in it, they could save neither son nor daughter. They would save only themselves by their righteousness.

[21]"For this is what the Sovereign LORD says: How much worse will it be when I send against Jerusalem my four dreadful judgments — sword and famine and wild beasts and plague — to kill its men and their animals! [22]Yet there will be some survivors — sons and daughters who will be brought out of it. They will come to you, and when you see their conduct and their actions, you will be consoled regarding the disaster I have brought on Jerusalem — every disaster I have brought on it. [23]You will be consoled when you see their conduct and their actions, for you will know that I have done nothing in it without cause, declares the Sovereign LORD."

Jerusalem as a Useless Vine

15 The word of the LORD came to me: [2]"Son of man, how is the wood of a vine different from that of a branch from any of the trees in the forest? [3]Is wood ever taken from it to make anything useful? Do they make pegs from it to hang things on? [4]And after it is thrown on the fire as fuel and the fire burns both ends and chars the middle, is it then useful for anything? [5]If it was not useful for anything when it was whole, how much less can it be made into something useful when the fire has burned it and it is charred?

[6]"Therefore this is what the Sovereign LORD says: As I have given the wood of the vine among the trees of the forest as fuel for the fire, so will I treat the people living in Jerusalem. [7]I will set my face against them. Although they have come out of the fire, the fire will yet consume them. And when I set my face against them, you will know that I am the LORD. [8]I will make the land desolate because they have been unfaithful, declares the Sovereign LORD."

Jerusalem as an Adulterous Wife

16 The word of the LORD came to me: [2]"Son of man, confront Jerusalem with her detestable practices [3]and say, 'This is what the Sovereign LORD says to Jerusalem: Your ancestry and birth were in the land of the Canaanites; your father was an Amorite and your mother a Hittite. [4]On the day you were born

[a] *14* Or *Danel,* a man of renown in ancient literature; also in verse 20

EZEKIEL 15:1 – 5

FRUITFUL VINE OR FIREWOOD?

The symbol of a grapevine is frequently used in the Bible to refer to God's people, Israel (Ge 49:22; Ps 80:8). God intended for his people to be a "vine" that would produce "fruit," revealing to the surrounding nations who God is and how to be in relationship with him. In the book of Ezekiel, God described his people as a grapevine that was bearing no grapes — a fruitless vine that was useless except as firewood. In the New Testament, Jesus appears to compare the religious leaders of Jerusalem to a fig tree that failed to produce fruit. Desiring to eat the fruit from the tree and having none to eat, Jesus cursed the tree, and the tree withered (Mk 11:12 – 14,20 – 21).

Jesus encourages believers, saying that he is the true vine to whom we must be attached in order to be fruitful: "I am the true vine, and my Father is the gardener. He cuts off every branch in me that bears no fruit, while every branch that does bear fruit he prunes so that it will be even more fruitful" (Jn 15:1 – 2). In Ezekiel, God's people failed to depend on God, and they withered away. Today the evidence of real Christian growth is found in the fruit that God's people bear (Gal 5:22 – 23; Eph 5:9) so that others will see the hope that we have in Jesus and believe (1Pe 3:15 – 16).

EZEKIEL 16:1–6

FORGETTING WHERE YOU COME FROM

God's people forgot all that God had done for them. They became proud and arrogant, and God loved them too much to let them remain in that pitiful condition. Sometimes hard words are required to break a hard heart, and that is exactly what God provided here.

God's people, living in Jerusalem, had forgotten where they came from. God reminded them of their hopeless past and all that he did for them to bring them to where they were: he had rescued them like an abandoned newborn child, unwashed and left exposed to the elements to die. A baby like that is utterly dependent upon the mercy of another to intervene and save, and God reminded them that he alone had rescued his people and given them life and blessing.

Centuries later Jesus spoke harsh words to the self-assured people living in Jerusalem. He warned them against the dangers of taking their right standing with God for granted. Jesus even went as far as to tell the religious leaders that they did not align themselves with God, but Satan (Jn 8:44)—harsh words for hard hearts. Because of their sin, the religious leaders in Jesus' day had once again become like a helpless infant, abandoned and at the mercy of the elements.

Believers today also do well to remember God's mercy to them in Jesus' work on the cross. Remembering where they came from and understanding where they are in Christ leads believers to humility and gratitude.

your cord was not cut, nor were you washed with water to make you clean, nor
were you rubbed with salt or wrapped in cloths. 5No one looked on you with
pity or had compassion enough to do any of these things for you. Rather, you
were thrown out into the open field, for on the day you were born you were
despised.

6" 'Then I passed by and saw you kicking about in your blood, and as you lay
there in your blood I said to you, "Live!"[a] 7I made you grow like a plant of the
field. You grew and developed and entered puberty. Your breasts had formed
and your hair had grown, yet you were stark naked.

8" 'Later I passed by, and when I looked at you and saw that you were old
enough for love, I spread the corner of my garment over you and covered your
naked body. I gave you my solemn oath and entered into a covenant with you,
declares the Sovereign LORD, and you became mine.

9" 'I bathed you with water and washed the blood from you and put ointments
on you. 10I clothed you with an embroidered dress and put sandals of fine leather on you. I dressed you in fine linen and covered you with costly garments. 11I
adorned you with jewelry: I put bracelets on your arms and a necklace around
your neck, 12and I put a ring on your nose, earrings on your ears and a beautiful
crown on your head. 13So you were adorned with gold and silver; your clothes
were of fine linen and costly fabric and embroidered cloth. Your food was honey,
olive oil and the finest flour. You became very beautiful and rose to be a queen.
14And your fame spread among the nations on account of your beauty, because
the splendor I had given you made your beauty perfect, declares the Sovereign
LORD.

15" 'But you trusted in your beauty and used your fame to become a prostitute.
You lavished your favors on anyone who passed by and your beauty became his.
16You took some of your garments to make gaudy high places, where you carried
on your prostitution. You went to him, and he possessed your beauty.[b] 17You also
took the fine jewelry I gave you, the jewelry made of my gold and silver, and you
made for yourself male idols and engaged in prostitution with them. 18And you
took your embroidered clothes to put on them, and you offered my oil and incense before them. 19Also the food I provided for you—the flour, olive oil and
honey I gave you to eat—you offered as fragrant incense before them. That is
what happened, declares the Sovereign LORD.

20" 'And you took your sons and daughters whom you bore to me and sacrificed
them as food to the idols. Was your prostitution not enough? 21You slaughtered
my children and sacrificed them to the idols. 22In all your detestable practices
and your prostitution you did not remember the days of your youth, when you
were naked and bare, kicking about in your blood.

23" 'Woe! Woe to you, declares the Sovereign LORD. In addition to all your other wickedness, 24you built a mound for yourself and made a lofty shrine in every
public square. 25At every street corner you built your lofty shrines and degraded
your beauty, spreading your legs with increasing promiscuity to anyone who
passed by. 26You engaged in prostitution with the Egyptians, your neighbors
with large genitals, and aroused my anger with your increasing promiscuity.
27So I stretched out my hand against you and reduced your territory; I gave you
over to the greed of your enemies, the daughters of the Philistines, who were
shocked by your lewd conduct. 28You engaged in prostitution with the Assyrians too, because you were insatiable; and even after that, you still were not satisfied. 29Then you increased your promiscuity to include Babylonia,[c] a land of
merchants, but even with this you were not satisfied.

30" 'I am filled with fury against you,[d] declares the Sovereign LORD, when
you do all these things, acting like a brazen prostitute! 31When you built your

[a] 6 A few Hebrew manuscripts, Septuagint and Syriac; most Hebrew manuscripts repeat *and as you lay there in your blood I said to you, "Live!"* [b] 16 The meaning of the Hebrew for this sentence is uncertain. [c] 29 Or *Chaldea* [d] 30 Or *How feverish is your heart,*

mounds at every street corner and made your lofty shrines in every public
square, you were unlike a prostitute, because you scorned payment.
32“ ‘You adulterous wife! You prefer strangers to your own husband! 33All prostitutes receive gifts, but you give gifts to all your lovers, bribing them to come to
you from everywhere for your illicit favors. 34So in your prostitution you are the
opposite of others; no one runs after you for your favors. You are the very opposite, for you give payment and none is given to you.
35“ ‘Therefore, you prostitute, hear the word of the LORD! 36This is what the Sovereign LORD says: Because you poured out your lust and exposed your naked body
in your promiscuity with your lovers, and because of all your detestable idols, and
because you gave them your children’s blood, 37therefore I am going to gather all
your lovers, with whom you found pleasure, those you loved as well as those you
hated. I will gather them against you from all around and will strip you in front of
them, and they will see you stark naked. 38I will sentence you to the punishment
of women who commit adultery and who shed blood; I will bring on you the blood
vengeance of my wrath and jealous anger. 39Then I will deliver you into the hands
of your lovers, and they will tear down your mounds and destroy your lofty shrines.
They will strip you of your clothes and take your fine jewelry and leave you stark
naked. 40They will bring a mob against you, who will stone you and hack you to
pieces with their swords. 41They will burn down your houses and inflict punishment on you in the sight of many women. I will put a stop to your prostitution, and
you will no longer pay your lovers. 42Then my wrath against you will subside and
my jealous anger will turn away from you; I will be calm and no longer angry.
43“ ‘Because you did not remember the days of your youth but enraged me
with all these things, I will surely bring down on your head what you have done,
declares the Sovereign LORD. Did you not add lewdness to all your other detestable practices?
44“ ‘Everyone who quotes proverbs will quote this proverb about you: “Like
mother, like daughter.” 45You are a true daughter of your mother, who despised
her husband and her children; and you are a true sister of your sisters, who despised their husbands and their children. Your mother was a Hittite and your
father an Amorite. 46Your older sister was Samaria, who lived to the north of you
with her daughters; and your younger sister, who lived to the south of you with
her daughters, was Sodom. 47You not only followed their ways and copied their
detestable practices, but in all your ways you soon became more depraved than
they. 48As surely as I live, declares the Sovereign LORD, your sister Sodom and her
daughters never did what you and your daughters have done.
49“ ‘Now this was the sin of your sister Sodom: She and her daughters were arrogant, overfed and unconcerned; they did not help the poor and needy. 50They
were haughty and did detestable things before me. Therefore I did away with
them as you have seen. 51Samaria did not commit half the sins you did. You have
done more detestable things than they, and have made your sisters seem righteous by all these things you have done. 52Bear your disgrace, for you have furnished some justification for your sisters. Because your sins were more vile than
theirs, they appear more righteous than you. So then, be ashamed and bear your
disgrace, for you have made your sisters appear righteous.
53“ ‘However, I will restore the fortunes of Sodom and her daughters and of Samaria and her daughters, and your fortunes along with them, 54so that you may
bear your disgrace and be ashamed of all you have done in giving them comfort.
55And your sisters, Sodom with her daughters and Samaria with her daughters,
will return to what they were before; and you and your daughters will return to
what you were before. 56You would not even mention your sister Sodom in the
day of your pride, 57before your wickedness was uncovered. Even so, you are now
scorned by the daughters of Edom[a] and all her neighbors and the daughters of

[a] 57 Many Hebrew manuscripts and Syriac; most Hebrew manuscripts, Septuagint and Vulgate *Aram*

EZEKIEL 16:63

MAKING ATONEMENT

God made great promises to his people long before he spoke to them through Ezekiel. Centuries before, God made a covenant with Abraham; that covenant was God's promise to make his name great by blessing Abraham and Abraham's descendants (Ge 15:1 – 6). The covenant was based on God's character; God had made the promises and God would keep them.

In the midst of judging Israel for their sin, God never forgot that he had promises to keep. In the course of keeping the covenant, God's people would inevitably compare their unfaithfulness with God's unending faithfulness and feel shame. Yet God promised his people, through Ezekiel, that he would appropriately punish the sin of his people so that he could reestablish a relationship with them.

As the story of God's faithfulness to his people unfolded, it eventually became clear that Jesus' death would be the sacrifice that would restore sinners to God (Ro 5:18 – 19). All of God's promises are kept in Jesus, the living Savior of all who will believe in him.

EZEKIEL 17:22 – 23

A BRANCH OF DAVID

God intended for his people to be a tree that would provide saving fruit by which the nations would be nourished. But God's tree didn't grow as big and as strong as God desired because it was infected by the disease of sin. Quite simply, God had a good plan and his people messed it up. God's people were unfaithful sinners,

(continued on next page)

the Philistines — all those around you who despise you. 58You will bear the consequences of your lewdness and your detestable practices, declares the LORD.
59" 'This is what the Sovereign LORD says: I will deal with you as you deserve,
because you have despised my oath by breaking the covenant. 60Yet I will remember the covenant I made with you in the days of your youth, and I will establish an everlasting covenant with you. 61Then you will remember your ways and
be ashamed when you receive your sisters, both those who are older than you
and those who are younger. I will give them to you as daughters, but not on the
basis of my covenant with you. 62So I will establish my covenant with you, and
you will know that I am the LORD. 63Then, when I make atonement for you for all
you have done, you will remember and be ashamed and never again open your
mouth because of your humiliation, declares the Sovereign LORD.' "

Two Eagles and a Vine

17 The word of the LORD came to me: 2"Son of man, set forth an allegory and
tell it to the Israelites as a parable. 3Say to them, 'This is what the Sovereign
LORD says: A great eagle with powerful wings, long feathers and full plumage of
varied colors came to Lebanon. Taking hold of the top of a cedar, 4he broke off
its topmost shoot and carried it away to a land of merchants, where he planted
it in a city of traders.
5" 'He took one of the seedlings of the land and put it in fertile soil. He planted
it like a willow by abundant water, 6and it sprouted and became a low, spreading
vine. Its branches turned toward him, but its roots remained under it. So it became a vine and produced branches and put out leafy boughs.
7" 'But there was another great eagle with powerful wings and full plumage.
The vine now sent out its roots toward him from the plot where it was planted
and stretched out its branches to him for water. 8It had been planted in good soil
by abundant water so that it would produce branches, bear fruit and become a
splendid vine.'
9"Say to them, 'This is what the Sovereign LORD says: Will it thrive? Will it not
be uprooted and stripped of its fruit so that it withers? All its new growth will
wither. It will not take a strong arm or many people to pull it up by the roots. 10It
has been planted, but will it thrive? Will it not wither completely when the east
wind strikes it — wither away in the plot where it grew?' "
11Then the word of the LORD came to me: 12"Say to this rebellious people, 'Do
you not know what these things mean?' Say to them: 'The king of Babylon went to
Jerusalem and carried off her king and her nobles, bringing them back with him
to Babylon. 13Then he took a member of the royal family and made a treaty with
him, putting him under oath. He also carried away the leading men of the land,
14so that the kingdom would be brought low, unable to rise again, surviving only
by keeping his treaty. 15But the king rebelled against him by sending his envoys
to Egypt to get horses and a large army. Will he succeed? Will he who does such
things escape? Will he break the treaty and yet escape?
16" 'As surely as I live, declares the Sovereign LORD, he shall die in Babylon,
in the land of the king who put him on the throne, whose oath he despised and
whose treaty he broke. 17Pharaoh with his mighty army and great horde will be
of no help to him in war, when ramps are built and siege works erected to destroy
many lives. 18He despised the oath by breaking the covenant. Because he had
given his hand in pledge and yet did all these things, he shall not escape.
19" 'Therefore this is what the Sovereign LORD says: As surely as I live, I will
repay him for despising my oath and breaking my covenant. 20I will spread my
net for him, and he will be caught in my snare. I will bring him to Babylon and
execute judgment on him there because he was unfaithful to me. 21All his choice
troops will fall by the sword, and the survivors will be scattered to the winds.
Then you will know that I the LORD have spoken.
22" 'This is what the Sovereign LORD says: I myself will take a shoot from the
very top of a cedar and plant it; I will break off a tender sprig from its topmost

shoots and plant it on a high and lofty mountain. 23On the mountain heights of
Israel I will plant it; it will produce branches and bear fruit and become a splendid cedar. Birds of every kind will nest in it; they will find shelter in the shade of
its branches. 24All the trees of the forest will know that I the LORD bring down
the tall tree and make the low tree grow tall. I dry up the green tree and make
the dry tree flourish.

"'I the LORD have spoken, and I will do it.'"

The One Who Sins Will Die

18 The word of the LORD came to me: 2"What do you people mean by quoting
this proverb about the land of Israel:

"'The parents eat sour grapes,
and the children's teeth are set on edge'?

3"As surely as I live, declares the Sovereign LORD, you will no longer quote this
proverb in Israel. 4For everyone belongs to me, the parent as well as the child—
both alike belong to me. The one who sins is the one who will die.

5"Suppose there is a righteous man
who does what is just and right.
6He does not eat at the mountain shrines
or look to the idols of Israel.
He does not defile his neighbor's wife
or have sexual relations with a woman during her period.
7He does not oppress anyone,
but returns what he took in pledge for a loan.
He does not commit robbery
but gives his food to the hungry
and provides clothing for the naked.
8He does not lend to them at interest
or take a profit from them.
He withholds his hand from doing wrong
and judges fairly between two parties.
9He follows my decrees
and faithfully keeps my laws.
That man is righteous;
he will surely live,
declares the Sovereign LORD.

10"Suppose he has a violent son, who sheds blood or does any of these other
things[a] 11(though the father has done none of them):

"He eats at the mountain shrines.
He defiles his neighbor's wife.
12He oppresses the poor and needy.
He commits robbery.
He does not return what he took in pledge.
He looks to the idols.
He does detestable things.
13He lends at interest and takes a profit.

Will such a man live? He will not! Because he has done all these detestable
things, he is to be put to death; his blood will be on his own head.

14"But suppose this son has a son who sees all the sins his father commits, and
though he sees them, he does not do such things:

15"He does not eat at the mountain shrines
or look to the idols of Israel.

[a] 10 Or *things to a brother*

(A Branch of David, continued)

yet God assured them that he was going to be a great Savior.

God used incredibly personal words to communicate this message by saying, "I myself will take ... " (v. 22). God does not leave human sin to chance. He takes it upon himself and deals with it personally. God himself declared his plan to set apart a special part of the tree to be the saving work the world desperately needs, pointing to his sending Jesus, the "Branch" of Isaiah 11:1, to earth. Jesus' ministry would reveal God's greater plan to redeem fallen humanity, and his sacrifice on the cross would bring about the kind of blessing that "will produce branches and bear fruit" (Eze 17:23) for the salvation of millions who trust in him for their salvation.

BLAME SHIFTING

No one likes to accept blame. That is one of the hallmarks of the fallen nature of humanity. Sin makes people self-serving and self-protective. By nature, people are defensive against anyone or anything that threatens their wellbeing and reputation. People do not like blame because blame infers guilt and guilt means imperfection. And people want to be seen as perfect — or at the very least, not the biggest part of the problem.

Ezekiel was careful to stress the themes of sin, judgment and restoration not only for the nation as a whole, but especially for the individual. As Ezekiel spoke against the sins of the people, the people naturally tried to shift the blame to their ancestors who made mistakes that they were forced to live with. Ezekiel denounced this popular proverb conveying that children pay the penalty for their parents' actions. They wanted to shift the blame of their own sin to their parents so that they could not be held responsible for the coming judgment. To counter this, Ezekiel stressed individual sin and judgment, and individual righteousness and salvation. In Ezekiel 14:14 and 14:20, the prophet noted that even Noah, Daniel and Job were able to save only themselves. A day was coming when Jesus would be the ultimate Deliverer, but even after his coming, people would be held individually accountable for the way they respond to him.

God's people were suffering from generations of sin and rebellion against God. They found it easier to blame their ancestors for the tough place their actions had put them in, rather than to accept responsibility for the sins they had committed that contributed to the situation. God reminded his people that experiencing hardship as a consequence of the sins of ancestors was not the same as being judged for one's own sins. Though it is unfortunate to suffer because of the sins that someone else has committed, God does not excuse willfully sinful behavior that occurs within that context.

God invites all people to accept responsibility, repent of sin and have a full life. The prophet John the Baptist sounded a lot like the prophet Ezekiel: "Repent, for the kingdom of heaven has come near" (Mt 3:2; compare with Eze 18:30). God meets repentance with the gift of a new heart and a new spirit (Eze 18:31). Ezekiel invited people to turn to God and live (v. 32). Jesus came so that people may have life and have it to the full (Jn 10:10).

He does not defile his neighbor's wife.
[16]He does not oppress anyone
or require a pledge for a loan.
He does not commit robbery
but gives his food to the hungry
and provides clothing for the naked.
[17]He withholds his hand from mistreating the poor
and takes no interest or profit from them.
He keeps my laws and follows my decrees.

He will not die for his father's sin; he will surely live. [18]But his father will die for
his own sin, because he practiced extortion, robbed his brother and did what
was wrong among his people.

[19]"Yet you ask, 'Why does the son not share the guilt of his father?' Since the
son has done what is just and right and has been careful to keep all my decrees,
he will surely live. [20]The one who sins is the one who will die. The child will not
share the guilt of the parent, nor will the parent share the guilt of the child. The
righteousness of the righteous will be credited to them, and the wickedness of
the wicked will be charged against them.

[21]"But if a wicked person turns away from all the sins they have committed
and keeps all my decrees and does what is just and right, that person will surely live; they will not die. [22]None of the offenses they have committed will be
remembered against them. Because of the righteous things they have done,
they will live. [23]Do I take any pleasure in the death of the wicked? declares
the Sovereign LORD. Rather, am I not pleased when they turn from their ways
and live?

[24]"But if a righteous person turns from their righteousness and commits sin
and does the same detestable things the wicked person does, will they live?
None of the righteous things that person has done will be remembered. Because
of the unfaithfulness they are guilty of and because of the sins they have committed, they will die.

[25]"Yet you say, 'The way of the Lord is not just.' Hear, you Israelites: Is my way
unjust? Is it not your ways that are unjust? [26]If a righteous person turns from
their righteousness and commits sin, they will die for it; because of the sin they
have committed they will die. [27]But if a wicked person turns away from the wickedness they have committed and does what is just and right, they will save their
life. [28]Because they consider all the offenses they have committed and turn away
from them, that person will surely live; they will not die. [29]Yet the Israelites say,
'The way of the Lord is not just.' Are my ways unjust, people of Israel? Is it not
your ways that are unjust?

[30]"Therefore, you Israelites, I will judge each of you according to your own
ways, declares the Sovereign LORD. Repent! Turn away from all your offenses;
then sin will not be your downfall. [31]Rid yourselves of all the offenses you have
committed, and get a new heart and a new spirit. Why will you die, people of
Israel? [32]For I take no pleasure in the death of anyone, declares the Sovereign
LORD. Repent and live!

A Lament Over Israel's Princes

19 "Take up a lament concerning the princes of Israel [2]and say:

"'What a lioness was your mother
among the lions!
She lay down among them
and reared her cubs.
[3]She brought up one of her cubs,
and he became a strong lion.
He learned to tear the prey
and he became a man-eater.

EZEKIEL 18:30

MAKING A U-TURN

Repentance involves conscious sorrow and regret over the former way of life and a change of course to a new direction. In short, it's like making a U-turn, a 180-degree about-face away from the path one has been following. Mere remorse over sin is not enough, and simply acknowledging sin without turning from it only leads to death. God requires this change in people because sin, without God's intervening grace, forcefully and destructively controls people's lives.

The first step of change is simply acknowledging the sin and fostering the desire to change—that is where repentance starts. God calls people to repentance, and the Bible contains some gripping examples of people who repented in prayer (Ezr 9–10; Ps 51). God's desire is that all people will repent of their sin and live a life in relationship with him. He issued this call to repentance through prophets such as Ezekiel, John the Baptist, Jesus and Jesus' disciples. To those who confess their sin and turn to Jesus, God promises forgiveness and eternal life. The call to repentance is still given today, and those who heed it find God's grace and peace in this life.

EZEKIEL 19:1–9

BEHAVING LIKE A LION

The lion was a symbol of the tribe of Judah (Ge 49:9). Lions are known for their great strength, agility and goose-bump-raising roars. The lioness in Ezekiel's lament represents

(continued on next page)

(Behaving Like a Lion, continued)

the nation or tribe of Judah, whose emblem was a lion (Ge 49:9). The first cub (Eze 19:3 – 4) stands for King Jehoahaz, whom Pharaoh Necho took in chains to Egypt. The second cub (Eze 19:5 – 9) symbolizes either King Jehoiachin or King Zedekiah, both of whom were carried off to Babylon. As the kings from David's tribe were expelled, the roar from the lion of Judah was silenced. God created his people to be a beautiful and a bold force in the world. Sin tames, tricks and neutralizes the good things that God created his people to be about. Jesus was the sacrificial lamb who died for the sins of the world and will return as the conquering lion-king. Revelation 5:5 promises, "Then one of the elders said to me, 'Do not weep! See, the Lion of the tribe of Judah, the Root of David, has triumphed. He is able to open the scroll and its seven seals.'" With the death and resurrection of Jesus, God's mighty lion sprang to life and its roar shakes the silence.

4 The nations heard about him,
and he was trapped in their pit.
They led him with hooks
to the land of Egypt.

5 " 'When she saw her hope unfulfilled,
her expectation gone,
she took another of her cubs
and made him a strong lion.
6 He prowled among the lions,
for he was now a strong lion.
He learned to tear the prey
and he became a man-eater.
7 He broke down[a] their strongholds
and devastated their towns.
The land and all who were in it
were terrified by his roaring.
8 Then the nations came against him,
those from regions round about.
They spread their net for him,
and he was trapped in their pit.
9 With hooks they pulled him into a cage
and brought him to the king of Babylon.
They put him in prison,
so his roar was heard no longer
on the mountains of Israel.

10 " 'Your mother was like a vine in your vineyard[b]
planted by the water;
it was fruitful and full of branches
because of abundant water.
11 Its branches were strong,
fit for a ruler's scepter.
It towered high
above the thick foliage,
conspicuous for its height
and for its many branches.
12 But it was uprooted in fury
and thrown to the ground.
The east wind made it shrivel,
it was stripped of its fruit;
its strong branches withered
and fire consumed them.
13 Now it is planted in the desert,
in a dry and thirsty land.
14 Fire spread from one of its main[c] branches
and consumed its fruit.
No strong branch is left on it
fit for a ruler's scepter.'

"This is a lament and is to be used as a lament."

Rebellious Israel Purged

20 In the seventh year, in the fifth month on the tenth day, some of the elders
of Israel came to inquire of the LORD, and they sat down in front of me.
2 Then the word of the LORD came to me: 3 "Son of man, speak to the elders of

---

[a] 7 Targum (see Septuagint); Hebrew *He knew* [b] 10 Two Hebrew manuscripts; most Hebrew manuscripts *your blood* [c] 14 Or *from under its*

Israel and say to them, 'This is what the Sovereign LORD says: Have you come to inquire of me? As surely as I live, I will not let you inquire of me, declares the Sovereign LORD.'
4"Will you judge them? Will you judge them, son of man? Then confront them with the detestable practices of their ancestors
5and say to them: 'This is what the Sovereign LORD says: On the day I chose Israel, I swore with uplifted hand to the descendants of Jacob and revealed myself to them in Egypt. With uplifted hand I said to them, "I am the LORD your God."
6On that day I swore to them that I would bring them out of Egypt into a land I had searched out for them, a land flowing with milk and honey, the most beautiful of all lands.
7And I said to them, "Each of you, get rid of the vile images you have set your eyes on, and do not defile yourselves with the idols of Egypt. I am the LORD your God."
8" 'But they rebelled against me and would not listen to me; they did not get rid of the vile images they had set their eyes on, nor did they forsake the idols of Egypt. So I said I would pour out my wrath on them and spend my anger against them in Egypt.
9But for the sake of my name, I brought them out of Egypt. I did it to keep my name from being profaned in the eyes of the nations among whom they lived and in whose sight I had revealed myself to the Israelites.
10Therefore I led them out of Egypt and brought them into the wilderness.
11I gave them my decrees and made known to them my laws, by which the person who obeys them will live.
12Also I gave them my Sabbaths as a sign between us, so they would know that I the LORD made them holy.
13" 'Yet the people of Israel rebelled against me in the wilderness. They did not follow my decrees but rejected my laws — by which the person who obeys them will live — and they utterly desecrated my Sabbaths. So I said I would pour out my wrath on them and destroy them in the wilderness.
14But for the sake of my name I did what would keep it from being profaned in the eyes of the nations in whose sight I had brought them out.
15Also with uplifted hand I swore to them in the wilderness that I would not bring them into the land I had given them — a land flowing with milk and honey, the most beautiful of all lands —
16because they rejected my laws and did not follow my decrees and desecrated my Sabbaths. For their hearts were devoted to their idols.
17Yet I looked on them with pity and did not destroy them or put an end to them in the wilderness.
18I said to their children in the wilderness, "Do not follow the statutes of your parents or keep their laws or defile yourselves with their idols.
19I am the LORD your God; follow my decrees and be careful to keep my laws.
20Keep my Sabbaths holy, that they may be a sign between us. Then you will know that I am the LORD your God."
21" 'But the children rebelled against me: They did not follow my decrees, they were not careful to keep my laws, of which I said, "The person who obeys them will live by them," and they desecrated my Sabbaths. So I said I would pour out my wrath on them and spend my anger against them in the wilderness.
22But I withheld my hand, and for the sake of my name I did what would keep it from being profaned in the eyes of the nations in whose sight I had brought them out.
23Also with uplifted hand I swore to them in the wilderness that I would disperse them among the nations and scatter them through the countries,
24because they had not obeyed my laws but had rejected my decrees and desecrated my Sabbaths, and their eyes lusted after their parents' idols.
25So I gave them other statutes that were not good and laws through which they could not live;
26I defiled them through their gifts — the sacrifice of every firstborn — that I might fill them with horror so they would know that I am the LORD.'
27"Therefore, son of man, speak to the people of Israel and say to them, 'This is what the Sovereign LORD says: In this also your ancestors blasphemed me by being unfaithful to me:
28When I brought them into the land I had sworn to give them and they saw any high hill or any leafy tree, there they offered their sacrifices, made offerings that aroused my anger, presented their fragrant incense

EZEKIEL 20:4–29

A SIN HABIT

Old habits die hard. God spoke words of judgment through Ezekiel to his people. These words of judgment were not the first time God had spoken to his people in this way. Long before this time, God's people had habitually committed the same sins over and over again. Ezekiel had spoken to the people figuratively and in allegory, and now he spoke to the people plainly by simply retelling their story.

As Ezekiel rehearsed their history to them, he was careful to point out how their present sins were actually part of a long sin pattern that their ancestors struggled with as well. They forgot where they came from, they forgot God's exclusive claim on their lives through his covenant and they became proud. In their pride, they thought they were good enough in God's eyes; they were surprised when God moved toward them in judgment.

God sent Jesus to deliver people from their sins (Mt 1:21). The way out of a sin pattern is to simply look to Jesus (Heb 12:1 – 2). God saves people from their sins to make them his special people, to purify them in every way and to enable them to develop the new habit of doing good works (Titus 2:11 – 14).

and poured out their drink offerings. [29]Then I said to them: What is this high place you go to?'" (It is called Bamah[a] to this day.)

Rebellious Israel Renewed

[30]"Therefore say to the Israelites: 'This is what the Sovereign LORD says: Will you defile yourselves the way your ancestors did and lust after their vile images? [31]When you offer your gifts — the sacrifice of your children in the fire — you continue to defile yourselves with all your idols to this day. Am I to let you inquire of me, you Israelites? As surely as I live, declares the Sovereign LORD, I will not let you inquire of me.

[32]" 'You say, "We want to be like the nations, like the peoples of the world, who serve wood and stone." But what you have in mind will never happen. [33]As surely as I live, declares the Sovereign LORD, I will reign over you with a mighty hand and an outstretched arm and with outpoured wrath. [34]I will bring you from the nations and gather you from the countries where you have been scattered — with a mighty hand and an outstretched arm and with outpoured wrath. [35]I will bring you into the wilderness of the nations and there, face to face, I will execute judgment upon you. [36]As I judged your ancestors in the wilderness of the land of Egypt, so I will judge you, declares the Sovereign LORD. [37]I will take note of you as you pass under my rod, and I will bring you into the bond of the covenant. [38]I will purge you of those who revolt and rebel against me. Although I will bring them out of the land where they are living, yet they will not enter the land of Israel. Then you will know that I am the LORD.

[39]" 'As for you, people of Israel, this is what the Sovereign LORD says: Go and serve your idols, every one of you! But afterward you will surely listen to me and no longer profane my holy name with your gifts and idols. [40]For on my holy mountain, the high mountain of Israel, declares the Sovereign LORD, there in the land all the people of Israel will serve me, and there I will accept them. There I will require your offerings and your choice gifts,[b] along with all your holy sacrifices. [41]I will accept you as fragrant incense when I bring you out from the nations and gather you from the countries where you have been scattered, and I will be proved holy through you in the sight of the nations. [42]Then you will know that I am the LORD, when I bring you into the land of Israel, the land I had sworn with uplifted hand to give to your ancestors. [43]There you will remember your conduct and all the actions by which you have defiled yourselves, and you will loathe yourselves for all the evil you have done. [44]You will know that I am the LORD, when I deal with you for my name's sake and not according to your evil ways and your corrupt practices, you people of Israel, declares the Sovereign LORD.'"

Prophecy Against the South

[45]The word of the LORD came to me: [46]"Son of man, set your face toward the south; preach against the south and prophesy against the forest of the southland. [47]Say to the southern forest: 'Hear the word of the LORD. This is what the Sovereign LORD says: I am about to set fire to you, and it will consume all your trees, both green and dry. The blazing flame will not be quenched, and every face from south to north will be scorched by it. [48]Everyone will see that I the LORD have kindled it; it will not be quenched.'"

[49]Then I said, "Sovereign LORD, they are saying of me, 'Isn't he just telling parables?'"[c]

Babylon as God's Sword of Judgment

21 [d] The word of the LORD came to me: [2]"Son of man, set your face against Jerusalem and preach against the sanctuary. Prophesy against the land of Israel [3]and say to her: 'This is what the LORD says: I am against you. I will draw

[a] 29 *Bamah* means *high place.* [b] 40 Or *and the gifts of your firstfruits* [c] 49 In Hebrew texts 20:45-49 is numbered 21:1-5. [d] In Hebrew texts 21:1-32 is numbered 21:6-37.

EZEKIEL 21:1 – 5

PREACH AGAINST THE SANCTUARY

Every religion has a place where one goes or a thing that one does to meet with God. For Israel, the place they went to was the temple, and the thing they did was to make sacrifices. People went to the temple to worship because that is the place where God's glory — his majesty and presence — lived. Ezekiel had terrible news to deliver to the people: Earlier he had communicated that they were so sinful that God had withdrawn his presence from the temple. And here the Lord stirred his prophet to "preach against the sanctuary" (Eze 21:2). The most holy place was dark and empty instead of bright and the source of life. The sins of the people had pushed the glory of God out of their lives, and their punishment would be destruction and grief.

Centuries later, Jesus would preach against the empty practices of the Pharisees and religious leaders (Mt 23); he also predicted the destruction of that temple as well (Mt 24:1 – 2). Ezekiel and Jesus never spoke against the temple itself. Instead, they spoke against the way that God's people made little of the presence of God. Jesus rose from the grave so that people can experience the presence of God wherever they are. People were never meant to encounter God in a mere building. Instead, God is building a great temple called his church, person by person (1Pe 2:5). God doesn't live in a temple made with human hands (Ac 17:24 – 25) but chooses to live in his people through his Holy Spirit.

my sword from its sheath and cut off from you both the righteous and the wicked. [4]Because I am going to cut off the righteous and the wicked, my sword will
be unsheathed against everyone from south to north. [5]Then all people will know
that I the LORD have drawn my sword from its sheath; it will not return again.'

[6]"Therefore groan, son of man! Groan before them with broken heart and bitter grief. [7]And when they ask you, 'Why are you groaning?' you shall say, 'Because of the news that is coming. Every heart will melt with fear and every hand
go limp; every spirit will become faint and every leg will be wet with urine.' It is
coming! It will surely take place, declares the Sovereign LORD."

[8]The word of the LORD came to me: [9]"Son of man, prophesy and say, 'This is
what the Lord says:

" 'A sword, a sword,
  sharpened and polished—
[10] sharpened for the slaughter,
  polished to flash like lightning!

" 'Shall we rejoice in the scepter of my royal son? The sword despises every
such stick.

[11] " 'The sword is appointed to be polished,
  to be grasped with the hand;
it is sharpened and polished,
  made ready for the hand of the slayer.
[12] Cry out and wail, son of man,
  for it is against my people;
  it is against all the princes of Israel.
They are thrown to the sword
  along with my people.
Therefore beat your breast.

[13]" 'Testing will surely come. And what if even the scepter, which the sword
despises, does not continue? declares the Sovereign LORD.'

[14] "So then, son of man, prophesy
  and strike your hands together.
Let the sword strike twice,
  even three times.
It is a sword for slaughter—
  a sword for great slaughter,
  closing in on them from every side.
[15] So that hearts may melt with fear
  and the fallen be many,
I have stationed the sword for slaughter[a]
  at all their gates.
Look! It is forged to strike like lightning,
  it is grasped for slaughter.
[16] Slash to the right, you sword,
  then to the left,
  wherever your blade is turned.
[17] I too will strike my hands together,
  and my wrath will subside.
I the LORD have spoken."

[18]The word of the LORD came to me: [19]"Son of man, mark out two roads for
the sword of the king of Babylon to take, both starting from the same country.
Make a signpost where the road branches off to the city. [20]Mark out one road
for the sword to come against Rabbah of the Ammonites and another against
Judah and fortified Jerusalem. [21]For the king of Babylon will stop at the fork in

[a] 15 Septuagint; the meaning of the Hebrew for this word is uncertain.

the road, at the junction of the two roads, to seek an omen: He will cast lots with
arrows, he will consult his idols, he will examine the liver. 22Into his right hand
will come the lot for Jerusalem, where he is to set up battering rams, to give the
command to slaughter, to sound the battle cry, to set battering rams against the
gates, to build a ramp and to erect siege works. 23It will seem like a false omen to
those who have sworn allegiance to him, but he will remind them of their guilt
and take them captive.

24"Therefore this is what the Sovereign LORD says: 'Because you people have
brought to mind your guilt by your open rebellion, revealing your sins in all that
you do — because you have done this, you will be taken captive.

25" 'You profane and wicked prince of Israel, whose day has come, whose time
of punishment has reached its climax, 26this is what the Sovereign LORD says:
Take off the turban, remove the crown. It will not be as it was: The lowly will be
exalted and the exalted will be brought low. 27A ruin! A ruin! I will make it a ruin!
The crown will not be restored until he to whom it rightfully belongs shall come;
to him I will give it.'

28"And you, son of man, prophesy and say, 'This is what the Sovereign LORD
says about the Ammonites and their insults:

" 'A sword, a sword,
drawn for the slaughter,
polished to consume
and to flash like lightning!
29 Despite false visions concerning you
and lying divinations about you,
it will be laid on the necks
of the wicked who are to be slain,
whose day has come,
whose time of punishment has reached its climax.
30 " 'Let the sword return to its sheath.
In the place where you were created,
in the land of your ancestry,
I will judge you.
31 I will pour out my wrath on you
and breathe out my fiery anger against you;
I will deliver you into the hands of brutal men,
men skilled in destruction.
32 You will be fuel for the fire,
your blood will be shed in your land,
you will be remembered no more;
for I the LORD have spoken.' "

Judgment on Jerusalem's Sins

22 The word of the LORD came to me:

2"Son of man, will you judge her? Will you judge this city of bloodshed? Then
confront her with all her detestable practices 3and say: 'This is what the Sovereign LORD says: You city that brings on herself doom by shedding blood in her
midst and defiles herself by making idols, 4you have become guilty because of
the blood you have shed and have become defiled by the idols you have made.
You have brought your days to a close, and the end of your years has come.
Therefore I will make you an object of scorn to the nations and a laughingstock
to all the countries. 5Those who are near and those who are far away will mock
you, you infamous city, full of turmoil.

6" 'See how each of the princes of Israel who are in you uses his power to shed
blood. 7In you they have treated father and mother with contempt; in you they
have oppressed the foreigner and mistreated the fatherless and the widow. 8You

EZEKIEL 21:25–27

THE CROWN

Ezekiel spoke of the turban and the crown as a way of referencing the coming king who would rule over God's people. God's campaign against sin is severe, and nothing will remain after God's work is done. The current system would be wrecked and ruined. Israel never had a perfect king, though it seemed that several leaders would assume this role. They longed for a king. Yet, no mere human could ever perform the kingly role for which the people longed. They needed a kingly Messiah who would perfectly do what others had failed to accomplish.

The crown does not belong to any person but Jesus (Ge 49:10). Jesus is the ultimate King who sits on the throne (Lk 1:32–33). Jesus is worthy not only of the crown from God, but also of every measure of worth from the lives of his people. One day everyone who trusts in Jesus will be able to cast their glory and accomplishments at his feet and recognize him as the One who is worthy of all honor, because he and he alone has won salvation for those who believe in him.

have despised my holy things and desecrated my Sabbaths. 9In you are slanderers who are bent on shedding blood; in you are those who eat at the mountain
shrines and commit lewd acts. 10In you are those who dishonor their father's
bed; in you are those who violate women during their period, when they are
ceremonially unclean. 11In you one man commits a detestable offense with his
neighbor's wife, another shamefully defiles his daughter-in-law, and another violates his sister, his own father's daughter. 12In you are people who accept bribes
to shed blood; you take interest and make a profit from the poor. You extort unjust gain from your neighbors. And you have forgotten me, declares the Sovereign LORD.

13" 'I will surely strike my hands together at the unjust gain you have made
and at the blood you have shed in your midst. 14Will your courage endure or your
hands be strong in the day I deal with you? I the LORD have spoken, and I will do
it. 15I will disperse you among the nations and scatter you through the countries;
and I will put an end to your uncleanness. 16When you have been defiled[a] in the
eyes of the nations, you will know that I am the LORD.' "

17Then the word of the LORD came to me: 18"Son of man, the people of Israel
have become dross to me; all of them are the copper, tin, iron and lead left inside
a furnace. They are but the dross of silver. 19Therefore this is what the Sovereign
LORD says: 'Because you have all become dross, I will gather you into Jerusalem.
20As silver, copper, iron, lead and tin are gathered into a furnace to be melted
with a fiery blast, so will I gather you in my anger and my wrath and put you
inside the city and melt you. 21I will gather you and I will blow on you with my
fiery wrath, and you will be melted inside her. 22As silver is melted in a furnace,
so you will be melted inside her, and you will know that I the LORD have poured
out my wrath on you.' "

23Again the word of the LORD came to me: 24"Son of man, say to the land, 'You
are a land that has not been cleansed or rained on in the day of wrath.' 25There
is a conspiracy of her princes[b] within her like a roaring lion tearing its prey;
they devour people, take treasures and precious things and make many widows
within her. 26Her priests do violence to my law and profane my holy things; they
do not distinguish between the holy and the common; they teach that there is
no difference between the unclean and the clean; and they shut their eyes to the
keeping of my Sabbaths, so that I am profaned among them. 27Her officials within her are like wolves tearing their prey; they shed blood and kill people to make
unjust gain. 28Her prophets whitewash these deeds for them by false visions and
lying divinations. They say, 'This is what the Sovereign LORD says'—when the
LORD has not spoken. 29The people of the land practice extortion and commit
robbery; they oppress the poor and needy and mistreat the foreigner, denying
them justice.

30"I looked for someone among them who would build up the wall and stand
before me in the gap on behalf of the land so I would not have to destroy it, but
I found no one. 31So I will pour out my wrath on them and consume them with
my fiery anger, bringing down on their own heads all they have done, declares
the Sovereign LORD."

Two Adulterous Sisters

23 The word of the LORD came to me: 2"Son of man, there were two women,
daughters of the same mother. 3They became prostitutes in Egypt, engaging in prostitution from their youth. In that land their breasts were fondled
and their virgin bosoms caressed. 4The older was named Oholah, and her sister
was Oholibah. They were mine and gave birth to sons and daughters. Oholah is
Samaria, and Oholibah is Jerusalem.

5"Oholah engaged in prostitution while she was still mine; and she lusted after her lovers, the Assyrians—warriors 6clothed in blue, governors and

[a] 16 Or *When I have allotted you your inheritance* [b] 25 Septuagint; Hebrew *prophets*

EZEKIEL 22:30

SOMEONE TO STAND IN THE GAP

God always follows through with both his warnings and his promises to his people. For generations, God had warned his people that he would destroy the nation of Judah because of their sin. They had had plenty of warnings and plenty of opportunities to turn to God before he acted in judgment. Before his judgment came, however, God gave Judah one final opportunity: If he could find one prophet to intercede to him on behalf of the nation, God would relent. Not a single person could be found in all the nation to fulfill this role, and consequently God's judgment fell upon the people.

Ezekiel 22:30 teaches that God desires to make things right with the world through a mediator, and thankfully, Jesus is that mediator (Ro 8:34; 1Ti 2:5–6). In his death he stood before the Father on behalf of his people and received punishment for their sins so that they could receive his righteousness (Heb 9:15; 1Jn 2:1). Because Jesus was and still is the means of grace for his church, his church is able to intercede on behalf of the nations for God to exercise mercy. Beyond this, his church is able to go to the nations to share the news of God's unrelenting love for them through Jesus.

EZEKIEL 23:1–49

A TALE OF TWO CITIES

God's kingdom was torn in two because of sin: Israel, the northern kingdom, and Judah, the southern

(continued on next page)

(A Tale of Two Cities, continued)

kingdom. In this chapter Ezekiel graphically depicts Israel and Judah, represented by their capital cities of Samaria and Jerusalem, as sisters who were guilty of political and spiritual prostitution — they had turned away from worshiping him and looked to other nations for security, and also adopted the idolatrous practices of their allies.

As the ultimate suitor to both Israel and Judah, God was furious at their betrayal. The imagery of prostitution represents the deep spiritual treason that God's people had committed against him. Jesus used similar language to talk about his contemporaries in calling them "a wicked and adulterous generation" (Mt 12:39). God was outraged because the culture-shapers in Israel and Judah had led the people of these nations away from him. But Jesus died for the idolatrous rebellion of all of humanity. His atoning death provided forgiveness for the sins of his people who, like the cities of Samaria and Jerusalem, rebelled against God.

commanders, all of them handsome young men, and mounted horsemen. 7She
gave herself as a prostitute to all the elite of the Assyrians and defiled herself
with all the idols of everyone she lusted after. 8She did not give up the prostitution she began in Egypt, when during her youth men slept with her, caressed her
virgin bosom and poured out their lust on her.
9"Therefore I delivered her into the hands of her lovers, the Assyrians, for
whom she lusted. 10They stripped her naked, took away her sons and daughters
and killed her with the sword. She became a byword among women, and punishment was inflicted on her.
11"Her sister Oholibah saw this, yet in her lust and prostitution she was more
depraved than her sister. 12She too lusted after the Assyrians — governors and
commanders, warriors in full dress, mounted horsemen, all handsome young
men. 13I saw that she too defiled herself; both of them went the same way.
14"But she carried her prostitution still further. She saw men portrayed on a
wall, figures of Chaldeans[a] portrayed in red, 15with belts around their waists
and flowing turbans on their heads; all of them looked like Babylonian chariot officers, natives of Chaldea.[b] 16As soon as she saw them, she lusted after
them and sent messengers to them in Chaldea. 17Then the Babylonians came
to her, to the bed of love, and in their lust they defiled her. After she had been
defiled by them, she turned away from them in disgust. 18When she carried on
her prostitution openly and exposed her naked body, I turned away from her
in disgust, just as I had turned away from her sister. 19Yet she became more
and more promiscuous as she recalled the days of her youth, when she was a
prostitute in Egypt. 20There she lusted after her lovers, whose genitals were like
those of donkeys and whose emission was like that of horses. 21So you longed for
the lewdness of your youth, when in Egypt your bosom was caressed and your
young breasts fondled.[c]
22"Therefore, Oholibah, this is what the Sovereign LORD says: I will stir up
your lovers against you, those you turned away from in disgust, and I will bring
them against you from every side — 23the Babylonians and all the Chaldeans,
the men of Pekod and Shoa and Koa, and all the Assyrians with them, handsome
young men, all of them governors and commanders, chariot officers and men of
high rank, all mounted on horses. 24They will come against you with weapons,[d]
chariots and wagons and with a throng of people; they will take up positions
against you on every side with large and small shields and with helmets. I will
turn you over to them for punishment, and they will punish you according to
their standards. 25I will direct my jealous anger against you, and they will deal
with you in fury. They will cut off your noses and your ears, and those of you who
are left will fall by the sword. They will take away your sons and daughters, and
those of you who are left will be consumed by fire. 26They will also strip you of
your clothes and take your fine jewelry. 27So I will put a stop to the lewdness and
prostitution you began in Egypt. You will not look on these things with longing
or remember Egypt anymore.
28"For this is what the Sovereign LORD says: I am about to deliver you into the
hands of those you hate, to those you turned away from in disgust. 29They will
deal with you in hatred and take away everything you have worked for. They will
leave you stark naked, and the shame of your prostitution will be exposed. Your
lewdness and promiscuity 30have brought this on you, because you lusted after
the nations and defiled yourself with their idols. 31You have gone the way of your
sister; so I will put her cup into your hand.
32"This is what the Sovereign LORD says:

"You will drink your sister's cup,
  a cup large and deep;

[a] 14 Or *Babylonians* [b] 15 Or *Babylonia*; also in verse 16 [c] 21 Syriac (see also verse 3); Hebrew *caressed because of your young breasts* [d] 24 The meaning of the Hebrew for this word is uncertain.

it will bring scorn and derision,
for it holds so much.
33 You will be filled with drunkenness and sorrow,
the cup of ruin and desolation,
the cup of your sister Samaria.
34 You will drink it and drain it dry
and chew on its pieces—
and you will tear your breasts.

I have spoken, declares the Sovereign LORD.

35 "Therefore this is what the Sovereign LORD says: Since you have forgotten
me and turned your back on me, you must bear the consequences of your lewdness and prostitution."
36 The LORD said to me: "Son of man, will you judge Oholah and Oholibah?
Then confront them with their detestable practices, 37 for they have committed
adultery and blood is on their hands. They committed adultery with their idols;
they even sacrificed their children, whom they bore to me, as food for them.
38 They have also done this to me: At that same time they defiled my sanctuary
and desecrated my Sabbaths. 39 On the very day they sacrificed their children to
their idols, they entered my sanctuary and desecrated it. That is what they did
in my house.
40 "They even sent messengers for men who came from far away, and when
they arrived you bathed yourself for them, applied eye makeup and put on your
jewelry. 41 You sat on an elegant couch, with a table spread before it on which you
had placed the incense and olive oil that belonged to me.
42 "The noise of a carefree crowd was around her; drunkards were brought
from the desert along with men from the rabble, and they put bracelets on the
wrists of the woman and her sister and beautiful crowns on their heads. 43 Then
I said about the one worn out by adultery, 'Now let them use her as a prostitute,
for that is all she is.' 44 And they slept with her. As men sleep with a prostitute, so
they slept with those lewd women, Oholah and Oholibah. 45 But righteous judges
will sentence them to the punishment of women who commit adultery and shed
blood, because they are adulterous and blood is on their hands.
46 "This is what the Sovereign LORD says: Bring a mob against them and give
them over to terror and plunder. 47 The mob will stone them and cut them down
with their swords; they will kill their sons and daughters and burn down their
houses.
48 "So I will put an end to lewdness in the land, that all women may take warning and not imitate you. 49 You will suffer the penalty for your lewdness and bear
the consequences of your sins of idolatry. Then you will know that I am the Sovereign LORD."

Jerusalem as a Cooking Pot

24 In the ninth year, in the tenth month on the tenth day, the word of the
LORD came to me: 2 "Son of man, record this date, this very date, because
the king of Babylon has laid siege to Jerusalem this very day. 3 Tell this rebellious
people a parable and say to them: 'This is what the Sovereign LORD says:

" 'Put on the cooking pot; put it on
and pour water into it.
4 Put into it the pieces of meat,
all the choice pieces—the leg and the shoulder.
Fill it with the best of these bones;
5 take the pick of the flock.
Pile wood beneath it for the bones;
bring it to a boil
and cook the bones in it.

EZEKIEL 24:21

JUDGMENT

Sin always leads to judgment. God's people had opposed God for some time, despite God's multiple warnings and opportunities to repent. Their hearts were stubborn, and they did not want to change, so God moved in to judge them because what God says he will do, he will do.

God told the people that Jerusalem would fall, that the temple of God would be desecrated and that the people would be either destroyed or carried off into exile. Ezekiel reserved the harshest words of judgment for the leaders of God's people. All of this might sound severe, but it was just. God's chosen people had disobeyed their infinitely holy God in the face of his persistent pleas for them to stop.

This was a judgment day of sorts; God's judgment was coming down upon his people because of their disobedience. At the cross, another judgment day occurred: God sacrificed Jesus because of the sins of his people. The city of Jerusalem railed against him. His body was beaten and bloodied; he died, and was exiled to the grave. Then he arose from the grave in victory so that all who look to him for salvation can escape judgment.

[6]" 'For this is what the Sovereign LORD says:

" 'Woe to the city of bloodshed,
to the pot now encrusted,
whose deposit will not go away!
Take the meat out piece by piece
in whatever order it comes.

[7]" 'For the blood she shed is in her midst:
She poured it on the bare rock;
she did not pour it on the ground,
where the dust would cover it.
[8]To stir up wrath and take revenge
I put her blood on the bare rock,
so that it would not be covered.

[9]" 'Therefore this is what the Sovereign LORD says:

" 'Woe to the city of bloodshed!
I, too, will pile the wood high.
[10]So heap on the wood
and kindle the fire.
Cook the meat well,
mixing in the spices;
and let the bones be charred.
[11]Then set the empty pot on the coals
till it becomes hot and its copper glows,
so that its impurities may be melted
and its deposit burned away.
[12]It has frustrated all efforts;
its heavy deposit has not been removed,
not even by fire.

[13]" 'Now your impurity is lewdness. Because I tried to cleanse you but you
would not be cleansed from your impurity, you will not be clean again until my
wrath against you has subsided.

[14]" 'I the LORD have spoken. The time has come for me to act. I will not hold
back; I will not have pity, nor will I relent. You will be judged according to your
conduct and your actions, declares the Sovereign LORD.' "

Ezekiel's Wife Dies

[15]The word of the LORD came to me: [16]"Son of man, with one blow I am about
to take away from you the delight of your eyes. Yet do not lament or weep or shed
any tears. [17]Groan quietly; do not mourn for the dead. Keep your turban fastened
and your sandals on your feet; do not cover your mustache and beard or eat the
customary food of mourners."

[18]So I spoke to the people in the morning, and in the evening my wife died.
The next morning I did as I had been commanded.

[19]Then the people asked me, "Won't you tell us what these things have to do
with us? Why are you acting like this?"

[20]So I said to them, "The word of the LORD came to me: [21]Say to the people of
Israel, 'This is what the Sovereign LORD says: I am about to desecrate my sanctuary — the stronghold in which you take pride, the delight of your eyes, the object
of your affection. The sons and daughters you left behind will fall by the sword.
[22]And you will do as I have done. You will not cover your mustache and beard or
eat the customary food of mourners. [23]You will keep your turbans on your heads
and your sandals on your feet. You will not mourn or weep but will waste away
because of[a] your sins and groan among yourselves. [24]Ezekiel will be a sign to

---

[a] 23 Or *away in*

UNABLE TO GRIEVE

God wanted to show his people how much their sin hurt his heart. To do this, God told Ezekiel that he was going to take his wife, "the delight of your eyes," in order to illustrate for the people how great a loss God felt over the loss of Jerusalem. Though the nation of Israel had been warned, their grief over the fall of Jerusalem would be unimaginable. The conventional means of expressing grief would be insufficient for the great pain the exiles would feel.

People express sorrow in different ways. A long period of mourning was a normal response to the death of a loved one in the ancient Near East (Mic 1:8). There were certain things that mourners would do to illustrate their sorrow: weep, take off their turbans and put dust on their heads, and fast or eat the "food of mourners" (Eze 24:17) — Ezekiel was to do none of those things. Ezekiel's apparent indifference to the death of his beloved wife was a powerful object lesson to God's people about how they would feel in the future when they learned about the fall of Israel (Eze 33:21).

Ezekiel reveals that God was about to administer a far greater calamity than the death of a wife. Jerusalem was going to fall, and the temple — the delight of the people's eyes — was going to fall as well. After this the people who weren't killed were going to be taken to Babylon, joining Ezekiel and the other Israelites already in exile. What made this worse was that many of the sons and daughters of those Ezekiel spoke to were going to be murdered in the process.

The death of Ezekiel's wife points the reader to the death of the only truly innocent person who ever lived — Jesus Christ. People may be tempted to look to the death of Ezekiel's wife and call it unfair. Yet, if anything in the Bible is unfair, it is that Jesus died for people who did not deserve it. Paul explained what God intended through the death of his Son: "God demonstrates his own love for us in this: While we were still sinners, Christ died for us" (Ro 5:8). Jesus' death was a necessary death; no one can be saved without it. God the Father allowed his Son to die to show us the depth of the love he has for his children. God is not heartless toward human pain. People may not always understand his ways (Isa 55:9), but his children can trust that he is working things for good for those who love him (Ro 8:28).

you; you will do just as he has done. When this happens, you will know that I am
the Sovereign LORD.'

25“And you, son of man, on the day I take away their stronghold, their joy and
glory, the delight of their eyes, their heart's desire, and their sons and daughters
as well — 26on that day a fugitive will come to tell you the news. 27At that time
your mouth will be opened; you will speak with him and will no longer be silent.
So you will be a sign to them, and they will know that I am the LORD.”

A Prophecy Against Ammon

25 The word of the LORD came to me: 2“Son of man, set your face against
the Ammonites and prophesy against them. 3Say to them, ‘Hear the word
of the Sovereign LORD. This is what the Sovereign LORD says: Because you said
“Aha!” over my sanctuary when it was desecrated and over the land of Israel
when it was laid waste and over the people of Judah when they went into exile, 4therefore I am going to give you to the people of the East as a possession.
They will set up their camps and pitch their tents among you; they will eat your
fruit and drink your milk. 5I will turn Rabbah into a pasture for camels and Ammon into a resting place for sheep. Then you will know that I am the LORD. 6For
this is what the Sovereign LORD says: Because you have clapped your hands and
stamped your feet, rejoicing with all the malice of your heart against the land of
Israel, 7therefore I will stretch out my hand against you and give you as plunder
to the nations. I will wipe you out from among the nations and exterminate you
from the countries. I will destroy you, and you will know that I am the LORD.’ ”

A Prophecy Against Moab

8“This is what the Sovereign LORD says: ‘Because Moab and Seir said, “Look,
Judah has become like all the other nations,” 9therefore I will expose the flank
of Moab, beginning at its frontier towns — Beth Jeshimoth, Baal Meon and Kiriathaim — the glory of that land. 10I will give Moab along with the Ammonites to
the people of the East as a possession, so that the Ammonites will not be remembered among the nations; 11and I will inflict punishment on Moab. Then they
will know that I am the LORD.’ ”

A Prophecy Against Edom

12“This is what the Sovereign LORD says: ‘Because Edom took revenge on Judah and became very guilty by doing so, 13therefore this is what the Sovereign
LORD says: I will stretch out my hand against Edom and kill both man and beast.
I will lay it waste, and from Teman to Dedan they will fall by the sword. 14I will
take vengeance on Edom by the hand of my people Israel, and they will deal
with Edom in accordance with my anger and my wrath; they will know my vengeance, declares the Sovereign LORD.’ ”

A Prophecy Against Philistia

15“This is what the Sovereign LORD says: ‘Because the Philistines acted in
vengeance and took revenge with malice in their hearts, and with ancient hostility sought to destroy Judah, 16therefore this is what the Sovereign LORD says: I
am about to stretch out my hand against the Philistines, and I will wipe out the
Kerethites and destroy those remaining along the coast. 17I will carry out great
vengeance on them and punish them in my wrath. Then they will know that I am
the LORD, when I take vengeance on them.’ ”

A Prophecy Against Tyre

26 In the eleventh month of the twelfth[a] year, on the first day of the month,
the word of the LORD came to me: 2“Son of man, because Tyre has said of
Jerusalem, ‘Aha! The gate to the nations is broken, and its doors have swung open
to me; now that she lies in ruins I will prosper,’ 3therefore this is what the Sovereign

[a] *1* Probable reading of the original Hebrew text; Masoretic Text does not have *month of the twelfth.*

EZEKIEL 26:1 – 21

PREYING ON GOD'S PEOPLE

Tyre was a Phoenician city off the coast of Lebanon, north of Israel. The city was known for shipping and commerce as it exercised great influence throughout the ancient Mediterranean world. The king of Tyre was once a friend to David and Solomon and assisted them in the construction of God's temple.

During the days of Ezekiel, Tyre was a pagan commercial city that had completely forgotten about God. God judged this city in the midst of judging his own people because Tyre was opposed to God's purposes. The people of Tyre didn't lead God's people deeper into God's purposes for them, but further away. Furthermore, the greedy and materialistic people of Tyre saw a vulnerable Jerusalem as their opportunity to serve themselves (v. 2).

God's judgment against Tyre teaches that God is fiercely committed to his purposes. All who do not stand with God are against God and will face his judgment. Interestingly, God in his grace was not done with Tyre forever. Jesus ministered in “the vicinity of Tyre,” one of the few places outside of Israel he traveled, and there he healed the demon-possessed daughter of a woman from Syrian Phoenicia (Mk 7:24 – 30).

TRAGICALLY MISSING THE POINT

God's actions may sometimes be mysterious to his children. But God's enemies face a very different difficulty when confronted by God's actions: they fail to see him working at all. This was true for the nations of Moab and Edom, which were enemies of God's people Israel. As they watched God's judgment play out from a distance, they did not recognize it as such. When they saw the people of Judah being captured and their city and temple being destroyed, they concluded that the God of Israel was powerless in this situation. These nations taunted the Israelite people because they thought their God had failed them. In so doing, they taunted God.

But God was certainly present and active and was carrying out his great plan to punish, purify and prepare his people for their coming Deliverer. God was at work; the fact that the Moabites and the Edomites could not see God's activity did not change the reality.

The Jewish religious leaders taunted Jesus in a way that echoed the Moabites and Edomites. The situation was more complex than even the one referred to in Ezekiel. Jesus came preaching the gospel of the kingdom of God. He was gathering a following, challenging the status quo and talking about how different the future was going to be. Then the unthinkable happened: he was crucified. In ignorance, people taunted him by jeering, "You who are going to destroy the temple and build it in three days, save yourself! Come down from the cross, if you are the Son of God!" (Mt 27:40). They could not see the bigger picture. " 'He saved others,' they said, 'but he can't save himself! He's the king of Israel! Let him come down now from the cross, and we will believe in him' " (Mt 27:42).

Tragically, they missed the point. The fact that Jesus did not come down from the cross demonstrated the magnitude of his power. In his sacrifice, Jesus displayed his power over sin, over death, over Satan and hell. In that moment, as people taunted him, they assumed he lacked power. In reality, they were witnessing the greatest power the world has ever seen. They simply did not have the spiritual "eyes" to see it.

LORD says: I am against you, Tyre, and I will bring many nations against you, like the sea casting up its waves. [4]They will destroy the walls of Tyre and pull down her towers; I will scrape away her rubble and make her a bare rock. [5]Out in the sea she will become a place to spread fishnets, for I have spoken, declares the Sovereign LORD. She will become plunder for the nations, [6]and her settlements on the mainland will be ravaged by the sword. Then they will know that I am the LORD.

[7]"For this is what the Sovereign LORD says: From the north I am going to bring against Tyre Nebuchadnezzar[a] king of Babylon, king of kings, with horses and chariots, with horsemen and a great army. [8]He will ravage your settlements on the mainland with the sword; he will set up siege works against you, build a ramp up to your walls and raise his shields against you. [9]He will direct the blows of his battering rams against your walls and demolish your towers with his weapons. [10]His horses will be so many that they will cover you with dust. Your walls will tremble at the noise of the warhorses, wagons and chariots when he enters your gates as men enter a city whose walls have been broken through. [11]The hooves of his horses will trample all your streets; he will kill your people with the sword, and your strong pillars will fall to the ground. [12]They will plunder your wealth and loot your merchandise; they will break down your walls and demolish your fine houses and throw your stones, timber and rubble into the sea. [13]I will put an end to your noisy songs, and the music of your harps will be heard no more. [14]I will make you a bare rock, and you will become a place to spread fishnets. You will never be rebuilt, for I the LORD have spoken, declares the Sovereign LORD.

[15]"This is what the Sovereign LORD says to Tyre: Will not the coastlands tremble at the sound of your fall, when the wounded groan and the slaughter takes place in you? [16]Then all the princes of the coast will step down from their thrones and lay aside their robes and take off their embroidered garments. Clothed with terror, they will sit on the ground, trembling every moment, appalled at you. [17]Then they will take up a lament concerning you and say to you:

" 'How you are destroyed, city of renown,
  peopled by men of the sea!
You were a power on the seas,
  you and your citizens;
you put your terror
  on all who lived there.
[18]Now the coastlands tremble
  on the day of your fall;
the islands in the sea
  are terrified at your collapse.'

[19]"This is what the Sovereign LORD says: When I make you a desolate city, like cities no longer inhabited, and when I bring the ocean depths over you and its vast waters cover you, [20]then I will bring you down with those who go down to the pit, to the people of long ago. I will make you dwell in the earth below, as in ancient ruins, with those who go down to the pit, and you will not return or take your place[b] in the land of the living. [21]I will bring you to a horrible end and you will be no more. You will be sought, but you will never again be found, declares the Sovereign LORD."

A Lament Over Tyre

27 The word of the LORD came to me: [2]"Son of man, take up a lament concerning Tyre. [3]Say to Tyre, situated at the gateway to the sea, merchant of peoples on many coasts, 'This is what the Sovereign LORD says:

" 'You say, Tyre,
  "I am perfect in beauty."

---

[a] *7* Hebrew *Nebuchadrezzar,* of which *Nebuchadnezzar* is a variant; here and often in Ezekiel and Jeremiah [b] *20* Septuagint; Hebrew *return, and I will give glory*

4 Your domain was on the high seas;
your builders brought your beauty to perfection.
5 They made all your timbers
of juniper from Senir[a];
they took a cedar from Lebanon
to make a mast for you.
6 Of oaks from Bashan
they made your oars;
of cypress wood[b] from the coasts of Cyprus
they made your deck, adorned with ivory.
7 Fine embroidered linen from Egypt was your sail
and served as your banner;
your awnings were of blue and purple
from the coasts of Elishah.
8 Men of Sidon and Arvad were your oarsmen;
your skilled men, Tyre, were aboard as your sailors.
9 Veteran craftsmen of Byblos were on board
as shipwrights to caulk your seams.
All the ships of the sea and their sailors
came alongside to trade for your wares.

10 " 'Men of Persia, Lydia and Put
served as soldiers in your army.
They hung their shields and helmets on your walls,
bringing you splendor.
11 Men of Arvad and Helek
guarded your walls on every side;
men of Gammad
were in your towers.
They hung their shields around your walls;
they brought your beauty to perfection.

12 " 'Tarshish did business with you because of your great wealth of goods; they
exchanged silver, iron, tin and lead for your merchandise.
13 " 'Greece, Tubal and Meshek did business with you; they traded human beings and articles of bronze for your wares.
14 " 'Men of Beth Togarmah exchanged chariot horses, cavalry horses and
mules for your merchandise.
15 " 'The men of Rhodes[c] traded with you, and many coastlands were your customers; they paid you with ivory tusks and ebony.
16 " 'Aram[d] did business with you because of your many products; they exchanged turquoise, purple fabric, embroidered work, fine linen, coral and rubies for your merchandise.
17 " 'Judah and Israel traded with you; they exchanged wheat from Minnith
and confections,[e] honey, olive oil and balm for your wares.
18 " 'Damascus did business with you because of your many products and great
wealth of goods. They offered wine from Helbon, wool from Zahar 19 and casks
of wine from Izal in exchange for your wares: wrought iron, cassia and calamus.
20 " 'Dedan traded in saddle blankets with you.
21 " 'Arabia and all the princes of Kedar were your customers; they did business
with you in lambs, rams and goats.
22 " 'The merchants of Sheba and Raamah traded with you; for your merchandise they exchanged the finest of all kinds of spices and precious stones, and
gold.

[a] *5* That is, Mount Hermon [b] *6* Targum; the Masoretic Text has a different division of the consonants. [c] *15* Septuagint; Hebrew *Dedan* [d] *16* Most Hebrew manuscripts; some Hebrew manuscripts and Syriac *Edom* [e] *17* The meaning of the Hebrew for this word is uncertain.

[23]" 'Harran, Kanneh and Eden and merchants of Sheba, Ashur and Kilmad
traded with you. [24]In your marketplace they traded with you beautiful garments,
blue fabric, embroidered work and multicolored rugs with cords twisted and
tightly knotted.

[25]" 'The ships of Tarshish serve
as carriers for your wares.
You are filled with heavy cargo
as you sail the sea.
[26]Your oarsmen take you
out to the high seas.
But the east wind will break you to pieces
far out at sea.
[27]Your wealth, merchandise and wares,
your mariners, sailors and shipwrights,
your merchants and all your soldiers,
and everyone else on board
will sink into the heart of the sea
on the day of your shipwreck.
[28]The shorelands will quake
when your sailors cry out.
[29]All who handle the oars
will abandon their ships;
the mariners and all the sailors
will stand on the shore.
[30]They will raise their voice
and cry bitterly over you;
they will sprinkle dust on their heads
and roll in ashes.
[31]They will shave their heads because of you
and will put on sackcloth.
They will weep over you with anguish of soul
and with bitter mourning.
[32]As they wail and mourn over you,
they will take up a lament concerning you:
"Who was ever silenced like Tyre,
surrounded by the sea?"
[33]When your merchandise went out on the seas,
you satisfied many nations;
with your great wealth and your wares
you enriched the kings of the earth.
[34]Now you are shattered by the sea
in the depths of the waters;
your wares and all your company
have gone down with you.
[35]All who live in the coastlands
are appalled at you;
their kings shudder with horror
and their faces are distorted with fear.
[36]The merchants among the nations scoff at you;
you have come to a horrible end
and will be no more.' "

A Prophecy Against the King of Tyre

28 The word of the LORD came to me: [2]"Son of man, say to the ruler of Tyre,
'This is what the Sovereign LORD says:

" 'In the pride of your heart
you say, "I am a god;

I sit on the throne of a god
in the heart of the seas."
But you are a mere mortal and not a god,
though you think you are as wise as a god.
3 Are you wiser than Daniel[a]?
Is no secret hidden from you?
4 By your wisdom and understanding
you have gained wealth for yourself
and amassed gold and silver
in your treasuries.
5 By your great skill in trading
you have increased your wealth,
and because of your wealth
your heart has grown proud.

6 " 'Therefore this is what the Sovereign LORD says:

" 'Because you think you are wise,
as wise as a god,
7 I am going to bring foreigners against you,
the most ruthless of nations;
they will draw their swords against your beauty
and wisdom
and pierce your shining splendor.
8 They will bring you down to the pit,
and you will die a violent death
in the heart of the seas.
9 Will you then say, "I am a god,"
in the presence of those who kill you?
You will be but a mortal, not a god,
in the hands of those who slay you.
10 You will die the death of the uncircumcised
at the hands of foreigners.

I have spoken, declares the Sovereign LORD.' "

11 The word of the LORD came to me: 12 "Son of man, take up a lament concerning the king of Tyre and say to him: 'This is what the Sovereign LORD says:

" 'You were the seal of perfection,
full of wisdom and perfect in beauty.
13 You were in Eden,
the garden of God;
every precious stone adorned you:
carnelian, chrysolite and emerald,
topaz, onyx and jasper,
lapis lazuli, turquoise and beryl.[b]
Your settings and mountings[c] were made of gold;
on the day you were created they were prepared.
14 You were anointed as a guardian cherub,
for so I ordained you.
You were on the holy mount of God;
you walked among the fiery stones.
15 You were blameless in your ways
from the day you were created
till wickedness was found in you.

[a] 3 Or *Danel*, a man of renown in ancient literature [b] 13 The precise identification of some of these precious stones is uncertain. [c] 13 The meaning of the Hebrew for this phrase is uncertain.

EZEKIEL 28:25–26

SCATTERED AND THEN GATHERED

God is the gathering and scattering God. He gathers his people together to give them a new purpose and then scatters them out in order to live for that purpose. His ultimate purpose is to bring his people to a place where they will dwell with him forever and he will be their God. All of God's gathering and scattering finds its unity in that one great purpose of eventually having God's people live in perfect communion with each other and with God.

In this particular instance, God had scattered his people because they did not trust him in faith. But God also promised his people that he would one day gather them from their dispersion among the nations and return them to live with him in their own land.

This promise reflects God's previous promise to their forefathers Abraham and Isaac (Ge 26:3). While not a direct reference, this "gathering" provides another illustration of Jesus' promise to prepare places for his followers and then bring believers one day to be with him (Jn 14:2–3).

16 Through your widespread trade
you were filled with violence,
and you sinned.
So I drove you in disgrace from the mount of God,
and I expelled you, guardian cherub,
from among the fiery stones.
17 Your heart became proud
on account of your beauty,
and you corrupted your wisdom
because of your splendor.
So I threw you to the earth;
I made a spectacle of you before kings.
18 By your many sins and dishonest trade
you have desecrated your sanctuaries.
So I made a fire come out from you,
and it consumed you,
and I reduced you to ashes on the ground
in the sight of all who were watching.
19 All the nations who knew you
are appalled at you;
you have come to a horrible end
and will be no more.' "

A Prophecy Against Sidon

20 The word of the LORD came to me: 21 "Son of man, set your face against Sidon;
prophesy against her 22 and say: 'This is what the Sovereign LORD says:

" 'I am against you, Sidon,
and among you I will display my glory.
You will know that I am the LORD,
when I inflict punishment on you
and within you am proved to be holy.
23 I will send a plague upon you
and make blood flow in your streets.
The slain will fall within you,
with the sword against you on every side.
Then you will know that I am the LORD.

24 " 'No longer will the people of Israel have malicious neighbors who are painful briers and sharp thorns. Then they will know that I am the Sovereign LORD.
25 " 'This is what the Sovereign LORD says: When I gather the people of Israel
from the nations where they have been scattered, I will be proved holy through
them in the sight of the nations. Then they will live in their own land, which I
gave to my servant Jacob. 26 They will live there in safety and will build houses
and plant vineyards; they will live in safety when I inflict punishment on all
their neighbors who maligned them. Then they will know that I am the LORD
their God.' "

A Prophecy Against Egypt

Judgment on Pharaoh

29 In the tenth year, in the tenth month on the twelfth day, the word of the
LORD came to me: 2 "Son of man, set your face against Pharaoh king of
Egypt and prophesy against him and against all Egypt. 3 Speak to him and say:
'This is what the Sovereign LORD says:

" 'I am against you, Pharaoh king of Egypt,
you great monster lying among your streams.
You say, "The Nile belongs to me;
I made it for myself."

4 But I will put hooks in your jaws
and make the fish of your streams stick to your scales.
I will pull you out from among your streams,
with all the fish sticking to your scales.
5 I will leave you in the desert,
you and all the fish of your streams.
You will fall on the open field
and not be gathered or picked up.
I will give you as food
to the beasts of the earth and the birds of the sky.

6 Then all who live in Egypt will know that I am the LORD.

" 'You have been a staff of reed for the people of Israel. 7 When they grasped
you with their hands, you splintered and you tore open their shoulders; when
they leaned on you, you broke and their backs were wrenched.[a]
8 " 'Therefore this is what the Sovereign LORD says: I will bring a sword against
you and kill both man and beast. 9 Egypt will become a desolate wasteland. Then
they will know that I am the LORD.
" 'Because you said, "The Nile is mine; I made it," 10 therefore I am against you
and against your streams, and I will make the land of Egypt a ruin and a desolate waste from Migdol to Aswan, as far as the border of Cush.[b] 11 The foot of neither man nor beast will pass through it; no one will live there for forty years. 12 I
will make the land of Egypt desolate among devastated lands, and her cities will
lie desolate forty years among ruined cities. And I will disperse the Egyptians
among the nations and scatter them through the countries.
13 " 'Yet this is what the Sovereign LORD says: At the end of forty years I will
gather the Egyptians from the nations where they were scattered. 14 I will bring
them back from captivity and return them to Upper Egypt, the land of their ancestry. There they will be a lowly kingdom. 15 It will be the lowliest of kingdoms
and will never again exalt itself above the other nations. I will make it so weak
that it will never again rule over the nations. 16 Egypt will no longer be a source of
confidence for the people of Israel but will be a reminder of their sin in turning to
her for help. Then they will know that I am the Sovereign LORD.' "

Nebuchadnezzar's Reward

17 In the twenty-seventh year, in the first month on the first day, the word of
the LORD came to me: 18 "Son of man, Nebuchadnezzar king of Babylon drove his
army in a hard campaign against Tyre; every head was rubbed bare and every
shoulder made raw. Yet he and his army got no reward from the campaign he
led against Tyre. 19 Therefore this is what the Sovereign LORD says: I am going to
give Egypt to Nebuchadnezzar king of Babylon, and he will carry off its wealth.
He will loot and plunder the land as pay for his army. 20 I have given him Egypt
as a reward for his efforts because he and his army did it for me, declares the
Sovereign LORD.
21 "On that day I will make a horn[c] grow for the Israelites, and I will open your
mouth among them. Then they will know that I am the LORD."

A Lament Over Egypt

30 The word of the LORD came to me: 2 "Son of man, prophesy and say: 'This
is what the Sovereign LORD says:

" 'Wail and say,
"Alas for that day!"
3 For the day is near,
the day of the LORD is near—

[a] 7 Syriac (see also Septuagint and Vulgate); Hebrew *and you caused their backs to stand*
[b] 10 That is, the upper Nile region [c] 21 *Horn* here symbolizes strength.

EZEKIEL 29:16

MISPLACED HOPE

People are created to have hope. Be it a person, a place, a thing, a status or a destination—everyone hopes in something or someone. God's people, the Israelites, were supposed to hope in God, but they frequently struggled to do so and instead placed their security in alliances with foreign nations.

God promised to bring down the neighboring nation of Egypt, and then Judah would no longer look to them as a source of hope and help. God took seriously his people's tendency to misplace their trust and hope. Jesus rebuked those who trusted in anything other than God—those who trusted in riches (Mt 6:19–21), in religious heritage (Mt 3:9) or in their religious activities (Mk 13:1–2). Confidence in anyone or anything other than God is an issue of misplaced hope. Like the Israelites before, all of God's people must learn to trust him today.

EZEKIEL 30:1–3

THE DAY OF THE LORD

Throughout the prophetic books of the Old Testament and parts of the New Testament, "the day of the LORD" is a common expression for God's judgment, especially his future judgment. This is a comforting concept for those who follow God and are weary of the injustice of the world, those who long for God to set things right as he has promised to do in Scripture. God will come near to a sin-soaked world and make all things right. But those who

(continued on next page)

(The Day of the Lord, continued)

oppose God will have to deal with Jesus on that day. Jesus taught that he would ultimately act as the final judge for all humanity (Mt 25:31 – 46; Jn 5:22). He came to provide people with a chance to escape the future judgment that is surely coming to all people. Jesus already paid the debt of sin, and all people are encouraged to cry out to him for mercy in order to escape the coming judgment on their sin.

a day of clouds,
a time of doom for the nations.
4 A sword will come against Egypt,
and anguish will come upon Cush.[a]
When the slain fall in Egypt,
her wealth will be carried away
and her foundations torn down.

5 Cush and Libya, Lydia and all Arabia, Kub and the people of the covenant land
will fall by the sword along with Egypt.

6 " 'This is what the LORD says:

" 'The allies of Egypt will fall
and her proud strength will fail.
From Migdol to Aswan
they will fall by the sword within her,
declares the Sovereign LORD.
7 " 'They will be desolate
among desolate lands,
and their cities will lie
among ruined cities.
8 Then they will know that I am the LORD,
when I set fire to Egypt
and all her helpers are crushed.

9 " 'On that day messengers will go out from me in ships to frighten Cush out
of her complacency. Anguish will take hold of them on the day of Egypt's doom,
for it is sure to come.

10 " 'This is what the Sovereign LORD says:

" 'I will put an end to the hordes of Egypt
by the hand of Nebuchadnezzar king of Babylon.
11 He and his army — the most ruthless of nations —
will be brought in to destroy the land.
They will draw their swords against Egypt
and fill the land with the slain.
12 I will dry up the waters of the Nile
and sell the land to an evil nation;
by the hand of foreigners
I will lay waste the land and everything in it.

I the LORD have spoken.

13 " 'This is what the Sovereign LORD says:

" 'I will destroy the idols
and put an end to the images in Memphis.
No longer will there be a prince in Egypt,
and I will spread fear throughout the land.
14 I will lay waste Upper Egypt,
set fire to Zoan
and inflict punishment on Thebes.
15 I will pour out my wrath on Pelusium,
the stronghold of Egypt,
and wipe out the hordes of Thebes.
16 I will set fire to Egypt;
Pelusium will writhe in agony.
Thebes will be taken by storm;
Memphis will be in constant distress.

[a] 4 That is, the upper Nile region; also in verses 5 and 9

[17] The young men of Heliopolis and Bubastis
will fall by the sword,
and the cities themselves will go into captivity.
[18] Dark will be the day at Tahpanhes
when I break the yoke of Egypt;
there her proud strength will come to an end.
She will be covered with clouds,
and her villages will go into captivity.
[19] So I will inflict punishment on Egypt,
and they will know that I am the LORD.' "

Pharaoh's Arms Are Broken

[20] In the eleventh year, in the first month on the seventh day, the word of the
LORD came to me: [21] "Son of man, I have broken the arm of Pharaoh king of Egypt.
It has not been bound up to be healed or put in a splint so that it may become
strong enough to hold a sword. [22] Therefore this is what the Sovereign LORD says:
I am against Pharaoh king of Egypt. I will break both his arms, the good arm as
well as the broken one, and make the sword fall from his hand. [23] I will disperse
the Egyptians among the nations and scatter them through the countries. [24] I
will strengthen the arms of the king of Babylon and put my sword in his hand,
but I will break the arms of Pharaoh, and he will groan before him like a mortally
wounded man. [25] I will strengthen the arms of the king of Babylon, but the arms
of Pharaoh will fall limp. Then they will know that I am the LORD, when I put my
sword into the hand of the king of Babylon and he brandishes it against Egypt.
[26] I will disperse the Egyptians among the nations and scatter them through the
countries. Then they will know that I am the LORD."

Pharaoh as a Felled Cedar of Lebanon

31 In the eleventh year, in the third month on the first day, the word of the
LORD came to me: [2] "Son of man, say to Pharaoh king of Egypt and to his
hordes:

" 'Who can be compared with you in majesty?
[3] Consider Assyria, once a cedar in Lebanon,
with beautiful branches overshadowing the forest;
it towered on high,
its top above the thick foliage.
[4] The waters nourished it,
deep springs made it grow tall;
their streams flowed
all around its base
and sent their channels
to all the trees of the field.
[5] So it towered higher
than all the trees of the field;
its boughs increased
and its branches grew long,
spreading because of abundant waters.
[6] All the birds of the sky
nested in its boughs,
all the animals of the wild
gave birth under its branches;
all the great nations
lived in its shade.
[7] It was majestic in beauty,
with its spreading boughs,
for its roots went down
to abundant waters.

EZEKIEL 31:3–17

PRIDE GOES BEFORE A FALL

The bigger they are, the harder they fall. The powerful nations in the Bible can seem as if they are untouchable or immoveable. Ezekiel compared Assyria to a massive tree. This tree had its roots deep in the earth and the top branches in the clouds and was higher and mightier than all the trees of the earth (vv. 3–7). It was the greatest and overlord of the nations, but the great tree of Assyria fell because it became proud (Pr 16:18).

Assyria never recognized that her lofty status came from God. The Lord had elevated her to such a great status, but she considered her attainments something of which to be proud (Eze 31:10). As great as Assyria was, the Lord easily cast her down.

Jesus came to save people from the terrible sin of pride. Jesus was full of humility, and he showed this by giving his life for others (Php 2:5–11). Jesus taught that the humble would be exalted (Mt 23:12). And so, Jesus turns the values of the world on their head: the way to earn glory in God's kingdom is to be humble.

[8] The cedars in the garden of God
could not rival it,
nor could the junipers
equal its boughs,
nor could the plane trees
compare with its branches—
no tree in the garden of God
could match its beauty.
[9] I made it beautiful
with abundant branches,
the envy of all the trees of Eden
in the garden of God.

[10] " 'Therefore this is what the Sovereign LORD says: Because the great cedar
towered over the thick foliage, and because it was proud of its height, [11] I gave
it into the hands of the ruler of the nations, for him to deal with according to its
wickedness. I cast it aside, [12] and the most ruthless of foreign nations cut it down
and left it. Its boughs fell on the mountains and in all the valleys; its branches lay
broken in all the ravines of the land. All the nations of the earth came out from
under its shade and left it. [13] All the birds settled on the fallen tree, and all the wild
animals lived among its branches. [14] Therefore no other trees by the waters are
ever to tower proudly on high, lifting their tops above the thick foliage. No other trees so well-watered are ever to reach such a height; they are all destined for
death, for the earth below, among mortals who go down to the realm of the dead.
[15] " 'This is what the Sovereign LORD says: On the day it was brought down
to the realm of the dead I covered the deep springs with mourning for it; I held
back its streams, and its abundant waters were restrained. Because of it I clothed
Lebanon with gloom, and all the trees of the field withered away. [16] I made the
nations tremble at the sound of its fall when I brought it down to the realm of
the dead to be with those who go down to the pit. Then all the trees of Eden, the
choicest and best of Lebanon, the well-watered trees, were consoled in the earth
below. [17] They too, like the great cedar, had gone down to the realm of the dead,
to those killed by the sword, along with the armed men who lived in its shade
among the nations.
[18] " 'Which of the trees of Eden can be compared with you in splendor and
majesty? Yet you, too, will be brought down with the trees of Eden to the earth
below; you will lie among the uncircumcised, with those killed by the sword.
" 'This is Pharaoh and all his hordes, declares the Sovereign LORD.' "

A Lament Over Pharaoh

32 In the twelfth year, in the twelfth month on the first day, the word of the
LORD came to me: [2] "Son of man, take up a lament concerning Pharaoh
king of Egypt and say to him:

" 'You are like a lion among the nations;
you are like a monster in the seas
thrashing about in your streams,
churning the water with your feet
and muddying the streams.

[3] " 'This is what the Sovereign LORD says:

" 'With a great throng of people
I will cast my net over you,
and they will haul you up in my net.
[4] I will throw you on the land
and hurl you on the open field.
I will let all the birds of the sky settle on you
and all the animals of the wild gorge themselves on you.

[5] I will spread your flesh on the mountains
and fill the valleys with your remains.
[6] I will drench the land with your flowing blood
all the way to the mountains,
and the ravines will be filled with your flesh.
[7] When I snuff you out, I will cover the heavens
and darken their stars;
I will cover the sun with a cloud,
and the moon will not give its light.
[8] All the shining lights in the heavens
I will darken over you;
I will bring darkness over your land,
declares the Sovereign LORD.
[9] I will trouble the hearts of many peoples
when I bring about your destruction among the nations,
among[a] lands you have not known.
[10] I will cause many peoples to be appalled at you,
and their kings will shudder with horror because of you
when I brandish my sword before them.
On the day of your downfall
each of them will tremble
every moment for his life.

[11] " 'For this is what the Sovereign LORD says:

" 'The sword of the king of Babylon
will come against you.
[12] I will cause your hordes to fall
by the swords of mighty men —
the most ruthless of all nations.
They will shatter the pride of Egypt,
and all her hordes will be overthrown.
[13] I will destroy all her cattle
from beside abundant waters
no longer to be stirred by the foot of man
or muddied by the hooves of cattle.
[14] Then I will let her waters settle
and make her streams flow like oil,
declares the Sovereign LORD.
[15] When I make Egypt desolate
and strip the land of everything in it,
when I strike down all who live there,
then they will know that I am the LORD.'

[16] "This is the lament they will chant for her. The daughters of the nations will
chant it; for Egypt and all her hordes they will chant it, declares the Sovereign
LORD."

Egypt's Descent Into the Realm of the Dead

[17] In the twelfth year, on the fifteenth day of the month, the word of the LORD
came to me: [18] "Son of man, wail for the hordes of Egypt and consign to the earth
below both her and the daughters of mighty nations, along with those who go
down to the pit. [19] Say to them, 'Are you more favored than others? Go down and be
laid among the uncircumcised.' [20] They will fall among those killed by the sword.
The sword is drawn; let her be dragged off with all her hordes. [21] From within the
realm of the dead the mighty leaders will say of Egypt and her allies, 'They have
come down and they lie with the uncircumcised, with those killed by the sword.'

[a] 9 Hebrew; Septuagint *bring you into captivity among the nations, / to*

22“Assyria is there with her whole army; she is surrounded by the graves of all her slain, all who have fallen by the sword. 23Their graves are in the depths of the pit and her army lies around her grave. All who had spread terror in the land of the living are slain, fallen by the sword.

24“Elam is there, with all her hordes around her grave. All of them are slain, fallen by the sword. All who had spread terror in the land of the living went down uncircumcised to the earth below. They bear their shame with those who go down to the pit. 25A bed is made for her among the slain, with all her hordes around her grave. All of them are uncircumcised, killed by the sword. Because their terror had spread in the land of the living, they bear their shame with those who go down to the pit; they are laid among the slain.

26“Meshek and Tubal are there, with all their hordes around their graves. All of them are uncircumcised, killed by the sword because they spread their terror in the land of the living. 27But they do not lie with the fallen warriors of old,[a] who went down to the realm of the dead with their weapons of war—their swords placed under their heads and their shields[b] resting on their bones—though these warriors also had terrorized the land of the living.

28“You too, Pharaoh, will be broken and will lie among the uncircumcised, with those killed by the sword.

29“Edom is there, her kings and all her princes; despite their power, they are laid with those killed by the sword. They lie with the uncircumcised, with those who go down to the pit.

30“All the princes of the north and all the Sidonians are there; they went down with the slain in disgrace despite the terror caused by their power. They lie uncircumcised with those killed by the sword and bear their shame with those who go down to the pit.

31“Pharaoh—he and all his army—will see them and he will be consoled for all his hordes that were killed by the sword, declares the Sovereign LORD. 32Although I had him spread terror in the land of the living, Pharaoh and all his hordes will be laid among the uncircumcised, with those killed by the sword, declares the Sovereign LORD.”

Renewal of Ezekiel’s Call as Watchman

33 The word of the LORD came to me: 2“Son of man, speak to your people and say to them: ‘When I bring the sword against a land, and the people of the land choose one of their men and make him their watchman, 3and he sees the sword coming against the land and blows the trumpet to warn the people, 4then if anyone hears the trumpet but does not heed the warning and the sword comes and takes their life, their blood will be on their own head. 5Since they heard the sound of the trumpet but did not heed the warning, their blood will be on their own head. If they had heeded the warning, they would have saved themselves. 6But if the watchman sees the sword coming and does not blow the trumpet to warn the people and the sword comes and takes someone’s life, that person’s life will be taken because of their sin, but I will hold the watchman accountable for their blood.’

7“Son of man, I have made you a watchman for the people of Israel; so hear the word I speak and give them warning from me. 8When I say to the wicked, ‘You wicked person, you will surely die,’ and you do not speak out to dissuade them from their ways, that wicked person will die for[c] their sin, and I will hold you accountable for their blood. 9But if you do warn the wicked person to turn from their ways and they do not do so, they will die for their sin, though you yourself will be saved.

10“Son of man, say to the Israelites, ‘This is what you are saying: “Our offenses and sins weigh us down, and we are wasting away because of[d] them. How

---

[a] *27* Septuagint; Hebrew *warriors who were uncircumcised* [b] *27* Probable reading of the original Hebrew text; Masoretic Text *punishment* [c] *8* Or *in*; also in verse 9 [d] *10* Or *away in*

WATCH AND WARN

In the ancient world, a watchman was an official military title. The person was to watch in anticipation and be on the lookout for opposition and attacks. Watchmen were positioned on the city wall and were responsible for spotting approaching armies and sounding the alarm to alert the city to their approach (1Sa 14:16; 2Sa 18:24).

God used the title watchman here to assign Ezekiel the role of reporting to the people the things that God showed him. This was not the only time God assigned the role of watchman to a prophet (Hos 9:8; Hab 2:1). Like a military watchman, Ezekiel's task was to alert God's people at the sight of alarm so that they could respond in repentance. The watchman was an important role to fulfill, and failure to report to the people meant punishment by death (Eze 33:8).

Jesus taught his disciples to be watchful as well so that they could be ready for his return (Mt 24:42 – 43). His disciples were to look to Jesus as the great model and to be ready to respond when they saw God at work.

God is gracious to provide elders to "watch" and oversee his church today. Their role is similar to the prophets and disciples who came before them. The apostle Paul reminded the Ephesian elders of how he served as a watchman when he said, "So be on your guard! Remember that for three years I never stopped warning each of you night and day with tears" (Ac 20:31). The author of Hebrews later encouraged God's people to "have confidence in your leaders and submit to their authority, because they keep watch over you as those who must give an account. Do this so that their work will be a joy, not a burden, for that would be of no benefit to you" (Heb 13:17).

God's best for his people is to lead them and guide them through the lives of other people. Only Jesus is able to give people the humility to submit to others in authority, and to grant those in authority the compassion to lead well (1Pe 5:1 – 4).

then can we live?" ' [11]Say to them, 'As surely as I live, declares the Sovereign LORD, I take no pleasure in the death of the wicked, but rather that they turn from their ways and live. Turn! Turn from your evil ways! Why will you die, people of Israel?'

[12]"Therefore, son of man, say to your people, 'If someone who is righteous disobeys, that person's former righteousness will count for nothing. And if someone who is wicked repents, that person's former wickedness will not bring condemnation. The righteous person who sins will not be allowed to live even though they were formerly righteous.' [13]If I tell a righteous person that they will surely live, but then they trust in their righteousness and do evil, none of the righteous things that person has done will be remembered; they will die for the evil they have done. [14]And if I say to a wicked person, 'You will surely die,' but they then turn away from their sin and do what is just and right — [15]if they give back what they took in pledge for a loan, return what they have stolen, follow the decrees that give life, and do no evil — that person will surely live; they will not die. [16]None of the sins that person has committed will be remembered against them. They have done what is just and right; they will surely live.

[17]"Yet your people say, 'The way of the Lord is not just.' But it is their way that is not just. [18]If a righteous person turns from their righteousness and does evil, they will die for it. [19]And if a wicked person turns away from their wickedness and does what is just and right, they will live by doing so. [20]Yet you Israelites say, 'The way of the Lord is not just.' But I will judge each of you according to your own ways."

Jerusalem's Fall Explained

[21]In the twelfth year of our exile, in the tenth month on the fifth day, a man who had escaped from Jerusalem came to me and said, "The city has fallen!" [22]Now the evening before the man arrived, the hand of the LORD was on me, and he opened my mouth before the man came to me in the morning. So my mouth was opened and I was no longer silent.

[23]Then the word of the LORD came to me: [24]"Son of man, the people living in those ruins in the land of Israel are saying, 'Abraham was only one man, yet he possessed the land. But we are many; surely the land has been given to us as our possession.' [25]Therefore say to them, 'This is what the Sovereign LORD says: Since you eat meat with the blood still in it and look to your idols and shed blood, should you then possess the land? [26]You rely on your sword, you do detestable things, and each of you defiles his neighbor's wife. Should you then possess the land?'

[27]"Say this to them: 'This is what the Sovereign LORD says: As surely as I live, those who are left in the ruins will fall by the sword, those out in the country I will give to the wild animals to be devoured, and those in strongholds and caves will die of a plague. [28]I will make the land a desolate waste, and her proud strength will come to an end, and the mountains of Israel will become desolate so that no one will cross them. [29]Then they will know that I am the LORD, when I have made the land a desolate waste because of all the detestable things they have done.'

[30]"As for you, son of man, your people are talking together about you by the walls and at the doors of the houses, saying to each other, 'Come and hear the message that has come from the LORD.' [31]My people come to you, as they usually do, and sit before you to hear your words, but they do not put them into practice. Their mouths speak of love, but their hearts are greedy for unjust gain. [32]Indeed, to them you are nothing more than one who sings love songs with a beautiful voice and plays an instrument well, for they hear your words but do not put them into practice.

[33]"When all this comes true — and it surely will — then they will know that a prophet has been among them."

The LORD Will Be Israel's Shepherd

34 The word of the LORD came to me: 2“Son of man, prophesy against the
shepherds of Israel; prophesy and say to them: ‘This is what the Sovereign LORD says: Woe to you shepherds of Israel who only take care of yourselves!
Should not shepherds take care of the flock? 3You eat the curds, clothe yourselves with the wool and slaughter the choice animals, but you do not take care
of the flock. 4You have not strengthened the weak or healed the sick or bound up
the injured. You have not brought back the strays or searched for the lost. You
have ruled them harshly and brutally. 5So they were scattered because there was
no shepherd, and when they were scattered they became food for all the wild animals. 6My sheep wandered over all the mountains and on every high hill. They
were scattered over the whole earth, and no one searched or looked for them.

7“ ‘Therefore, you shepherds, hear the word of the LORD: 8As surely as I live,
declares the Sovereign LORD, because my flock lacks a shepherd and so has been
plundered and has become food for all the wild animals, and because my shepherds did not search for my flock but cared for themselves rather than for my
flock, 9therefore, you shepherds, hear the word of the LORD: 10This is what the
Sovereign LORD says: I am against the shepherds and will hold them accountable for my flock. I will remove them from tending the flock so that the shepherds can no longer feed themselves. I will rescue my flock from their mouths,
and it will no longer be food for them.

11“ ‘For this is what the Sovereign LORD says: I myself will search for my sheep
and look after them. 12As a shepherd looks after his scattered flock when he is
with them, so will I look after my sheep. I will rescue them from all the places
where they were scattered on a day of clouds and darkness. 13I will bring them
out from the nations and gather them from the countries, and I will bring them
into their own land. I will pasture them on the mountains of Israel, in the ravines and in all the settlements in the land. 14I will tend them in a good pasture,
and the mountain heights of Israel will be their grazing land. There they will
lie down in good grazing land, and there they will feed in a rich pasture on the
mountains of Israel. 15I myself will tend my sheep and have them lie down, declares the Sovereign LORD. 16I will search for the lost and bring back the strays. I
will bind up the injured and strengthen the weak, but the sleek and the strong I
will destroy. I will shepherd the flock with justice.

17“ ‘As for you, my flock, this is what the Sovereign LORD says: I will judge between one sheep and another, and between rams and goats. 18Is it not enough for
you to feed on the good pasture? Must you also trample the rest of your pasture
with your feet? Is it not enough for you to drink clear water? Must you also mud-
dy the rest with your feet? 19Must my flock feed on what you have trampled and
drink what you have muddied with your feet?

20“ ‘Therefore this is what the Sovereign LORD says to them: See, I myself will
judge between the fat sheep and the lean sheep. 21Because you shove with flank
and shoulder, butting all the weak sheep with your horns until you have driven
them away, 22I will save my flock, and they will no longer be plundered. I will
judge between one sheep and another. 23I will place over them one shepherd, my
servant David, and he will tend them; he will tend them and be their shepherd.
24I the LORD will be their God, and my servant David will be prince among them.
I the LORD have spoken.

25“ ‘I will make a covenant of peace with them and rid the land of savage
beasts so that they may live in the wilderness and sleep in the forests in safety.
26I will make them and the places surrounding my hill a blessing.[a] I will send
down showers in season; there will be showers of blessing. 27The trees will yield
their fruit and the ground will yield its crops; the people will be secure in their
land. They will know that I am the LORD, when I break the bars of their yoke and

---

[a] 26 Or *I will cause them and the places surrounding my hill to be named in blessings* (see Gen. 48:20); or *I will cause them and the places surrounding my hill to be seen as blessed*

THE GREAT SHEPHERD

Shepherds are important. Sheep lack common-sense intelligence. Therefore, they are constantly getting into trouble, eating things that are bad for them and unknowingly endangering their own lives. Sheep need a shepherd, someone who would give his very life to care for the sheep and find those that wander.

God acknowledges that his people are like sheep: careless, helpless, easily led astray, and yet so precious to the shepherd. God called his people to care for others as a way of reflecting his goodness; that was his desire for his people Israel. But God's leaders ended up caring for themselves a lot more than they cared for others. As a result, God got involved. God became the personal shepherd of his people and tended to their needs himself.

God makes many promises to his sheep: he will search for and rescue them in times of trouble (vv. 11 – 12); he will lead them to good grass that will allow for flourishing (vv. 13 – 14); he will tend to their needs and give them strength when they are hurting and weak (vv. 15 – 16).

Jesus is the Good Shepherd (Jn 10:11). He personally leads his sheep (Jn 10:3 – 4) and delivers them from danger when they stray (Jn 10:11 – 13). Many good shepherds care for their sheep, but Jesus uniquely gave his life to save his sheep. Jesus' sacrificial death entitles him to be called the Great Shepherd (Heb 13:20).

Jesus' example allows "under-shepherds" to lead God's people well. Paul did not mince words in describing how pastors are supposed to shepherd God's flock: "Keep watch over yourselves and all the flock of which the Holy Spirit has made you overseers. Be shepherds of the church of God, which he bought with his own blood. I know that after I leave, savage wolves will come in among you and will not spare the flock" (Ac 20:28 – 29).

While it is good to hold God's under-shepherds in great respect as they lead God's church, there is a sense in which all of God's people are under-shepherds; they reflect the caring character of God in how they love and look after one another.

rescue them from the hands of those who enslaved them. 28They will no longer be plundered by the nations, nor will wild animals devour them. They will live in safety, and no one will make them afraid. 29I will provide for them a land renowned for its crops, and they will no longer be victims of famine in the land or bear the scorn of the nations. 30Then they will know that I, the LORD their God, am with them and that they, the Israelites, are my people, declares the Sovereign LORD. 31You are my sheep, the sheep of my pasture, and I am your God, declares the Sovereign LORD.' "

A Prophecy Against Edom

35 The word of the LORD came to me: 2"Son of man, set your face against Mount Seir; prophesy against it 3and say: 'This is what the Sovereign LORD says: I am against you, Mount Seir, and I will stretch out my hand against you and make you a desolate waste. 4I will turn your towns into ruins and you will be desolate. Then you will know that I am the LORD.

5" 'Because you harbored an ancient hostility and delivered the Israelites over to the sword at the time of their calamity, the time their punishment reached its climax, 6therefore as surely as I live, declares the Sovereign LORD, I will give you over to bloodshed and it will pursue you. Since you did not hate bloodshed, bloodshed will pursue you. 7I will make Mount Seir a desolate waste and cut off from it all who come and go. 8I will fill your mountains with the slain; those killed by the sword will fall on your hills and in your valleys and in all your ravines. 9I will make you desolate forever; your towns will not be inhabited. Then you will know that I am the LORD.

10" 'Because you have said, "These two nations and countries will be ours and we will take possession of them," even though I the LORD was there, 11therefore as surely as I live, declares the Sovereign LORD, I will treat you in accordance with the anger and jealousy you showed in your hatred of them and I will make myself known among them when I judge you. 12Then you will know that I the LORD have heard all the contemptible things you have said against the mountains of Israel. You said, "They have been laid waste and have been given over to us to devour." 13You boasted against me and spoke against me without restraint, and I heard it. 14This is what the Sovereign LORD says: While the whole earth rejoices, I will make you desolate. 15Because you rejoiced when the inheritance of Israel became desolate, that is how I will treat you. You will be desolate, Mount Seir, you and all of Edom. Then they will know that I am the LORD.' "

Hope for the Mountains of Israel

36 "Son of man, prophesy to the mountains of Israel and say, 'Mountains of Israel, hear the word of the LORD. 2This is what the Sovereign LORD says: The enemy said of you, "Aha! The ancient heights have become our possession." ' 3Therefore prophesy and say, 'This is what the Sovereign LORD says: Because they ravaged and crushed you from every side so that you became the possession of the rest of the nations and the object of people's malicious talk and slander, 4therefore, mountains of Israel, hear the word of the Sovereign LORD: This is what the Sovereign LORD says to the mountains and hills, to the ravines and valleys, to the desolate ruins and the deserted towns that have been plundered and ridiculed by the rest of the nations around you— 5this is what the Sovereign LORD says: In my burning zeal I have spoken against the rest of the nations, and against all Edom, for with glee and with malice in their hearts they made my land their own possession so that they might plunder its pastureland.' 6Therefore prophesy concerning the land of Israel and say to the mountains and hills, to the ravines and valleys: 'This is what the Sovereign LORD says: I speak in my jealous wrath because you have suffered the scorn of the nations. 7Therefore this is what the Sovereign LORD says: I swear with uplifted hand that the nations around you will also suffer scorn.

8" 'But you, mountains of Israel, will produce branches and fruit for my people

EZEKIEL 35:1–4

EDOM

The people of Israel and the people of Edom (referred to as Mount Seir here) were longtime enemies. Edom had a heritage of not only wanting bad things for the Israelites but also celebrating when things went badly for them (Eze 35:12–15). When Judah lost their city of Jerusalem, the Edomites swarmed to loot the city, and they also handed over those who fled to their attackers (Ob 12–14). Their attitude went beyond contempt for the people of Judah; they spurned the work of God and God's decision to choose and love the people of Judah.

Their problem was not merely with another group of people; their problem was with the God who loved these people and acted on their behalf. Because of their continued hatred of the Israelites, God gave them over to devastation and spiritual barrenness. So it will be with everyone who denies God's lordship and the work of Jesus toward salvation.

Israel, for they will soon come home. 9I am concerned for you and will look on you with favor; you will be plowed and sown, 10and I will cause many people to live on you—yes, all of Israel. The towns will be inhabited and the ruins rebuilt. 11I will increase the number of people and animals living on you, and they will be fruitful and become numerous. I will settle people on you as in the past and will make you prosper more than before. Then you will know that I am the LORD. 12I will cause people, my people Israel, to live on you. They will possess you, and you will be their inheritance; you will never again deprive them of their children.

13" 'This is what the Sovereign LORD says: Because some say to you, "You devour people and deprive your nation of its children," 14therefore you will no longer devour people or make your nation childless, declares the Sovereign LORD. 15No longer will I make you hear the taunts of the nations, and no longer will you suffer the scorn of the peoples or cause your nation to fall, declares the Sovereign LORD.' "

Israel's Restoration Assured

16Again the word of the LORD came to me: 17"Son of man, when the people of Israel were living in their own land, they defiled it by their conduct and their actions. Their conduct was like a woman's monthly uncleanness in my sight. 18So I poured out my wrath on them because they had shed blood in the land and because they had defiled it with their idols. 19I dispersed them among the nations, and they were scattered through the countries; I judged them according to their conduct and their actions. 20And wherever they went among the nations they profaned my holy name, for it was said of them, 'These are the LORD's people, and yet they had to leave his land.' 21I had concern for my holy name, which the people of Israel profaned among the nations where they had gone.

22"Therefore say to the Israelites, 'This is what the Sovereign LORD says: It is not for your sake, people of Israel, that I am going to do these things, but for the sake of my holy name, which you have profaned among the nations where you have gone. 23I will show the holiness of my great name, which has been profaned among the nations, the name you have profaned among them. Then the nations will know that I am the LORD, declares the Sovereign LORD, when I am proved holy through you before their eyes.

24" 'For I will take you out of the nations; I will gather you from all the countries and bring you back into your own land. 25I will sprinkle clean water on you, and you will be clean; I will cleanse you from all your impurities and from all your idols. 26I will give you a new heart and put a new spirit in you; I will remove from you your heart of stone and give you a heart of flesh. 27And I will put my Spirit in you and move you to follow my decrees and be careful to keep my laws. 28Then you will live in the land I gave your ancestors; you will be my people, and I will be your God. 29I will save you from all your uncleanness. I will call for the grain and make it plentiful and will not bring famine upon you. 30I will increase the fruit of the trees and the crops of the field, so that you will no longer suffer disgrace among the nations because of famine. 31Then you will remember your evil ways and wicked deeds, and you will loathe yourselves for your sins and detestable practices. 32I want you to know that I am not doing this for your sake, declares the Sovereign LORD. Be ashamed and disgraced for your conduct, people of Israel!

33" 'This is what the Sovereign LORD says: On the day I cleanse you from all your sins, I will resettle your towns, and the ruins will be rebuilt. 34The desolate land will be cultivated instead of lying desolate in the sight of all who pass through it. 35They will say, "This land that was laid waste has become like the garden of Eden; the cities that were lying in ruins, desolate and destroyed, are now fortified and inhabited." 36Then the nations around you that remain will know that I the LORD have rebuilt what was destroyed and have replanted what was desolate. I the LORD have spoken, and I will do it.'

37"This is what the Sovereign LORD says: Once again I will yield to Israel's plea

HEART TRANSPLANT

God loves to send his message of hope into situations of despair. God was clear that his people's sin broke his heart. As a result of their sin they were sent into exile, many of their children were murdered, their city was overtaken and their temple was destroyed. In the midst of this hopelessness, God sent a message of hope: he would give his people a new heart, a new start and most importantly a new spirit (v. 26).

God's people had a fundamental problem: they could not change themselves because they had hearts that were full of sin (Jer 17:9). To change their problem, God was going to have to change their hearts.

God is a heart surgeon of incomparable skill. He does not simply fix a small problem in the hearts of his people; he gives them brand-new spiritual hearts. The problem with the sinful heart is that it is hard and unresponsive to correction and warning. For those who trust in him, God removes that old heart and replaces it with a new one that is soft, tender and responsive to God's leading and guiding (Eze 36:26). The new heart won't resist in the same way the old one did. The old one was dead, and this new one is alive.

To accompany the new heart, God promises to fill his people with the very Spirit of God (v. 27). In the Old Testament, the Spirit of God would come upon people from time to time, but in the New Testament, because of what Jesus accomplished, the Spirit comes to live in people. The change in how the Spirit would be given under this new covenant would make all the difference. Jesus made this same promise to his people: that his Spirit would live in them and guide them into all truth (Jn 16:12 – 15).

Jesus made it clear that people speak from the overflow of their hearts (Mt 12:34). God gave his people the Law in order to expose the sinful tendencies of their hearts so that they would cry out to God for help. Jesus gives his people a new heart so that they may finally love him fully and completely. To tell if God's love is reigning in the hearts of his children, one needs only to look at the lives his people are living.

and do this for them: I will make their people as numerous as sheep, 38as numerous as the flocks for offerings at Jerusalem during her appointed festivals. So will the ruined cities be filled with flocks of people. Then they will know that I am the LORD."

The Valley of Dry Bones

37 The hand of the LORD was on me, and he brought me out by the Spirit of the LORD and set me in the middle of a valley; it was full of bones. 2He led me back and forth among them, and I saw a great many bones on the floor of the valley, bones that were very dry. 3He asked me, "Son of man, can these bones live?"

I said, "Sovereign LORD, you alone know."

4Then he said to me, "Prophesy to these bones and say to them, 'Dry bones, hear the word of the LORD! 5This is what the Sovereign LORD says to these bones: I will make breath[a] enter you, and you will come to life. 6I will attach tendons to you and make flesh come upon you and cover you with skin; I will put breath in you, and you will come to life. Then you will know that I am the LORD.' "

7So I prophesied as I was commanded. And as I was prophesying, there was a noise, a rattling sound, and the bones came together, bone to bone. 8I looked, and tendons and flesh appeared on them and skin covered them, but there was no breath in them.

9Then he said to me, "Prophesy to the breath; prophesy, son of man, and say to it, 'This is what the Sovereign LORD says: Come, breath, from the four winds and breathe into these slain, that they may live.' " 10So I prophesied as he commanded me, and breath entered them; they came to life and stood up on their feet—a vast army.

11Then he said to me: "Son of man, these bones are the people of Israel. They say, 'Our bones are dried up and our hope is gone; we are cut off.' 12Therefore prophesy and say to them: 'This is what the Sovereign LORD says: My people, I am going to open your graves and bring you up from them; I will bring you back to the land of Israel. 13Then you, my people, will know that I am the LORD, when I open your graves and bring you up from them. 14I will put my Spirit in you and you will live, and I will settle you in your own land. Then you will know that I the LORD have spoken, and I have done it, declares the LORD.' "

One Nation Under One King

15The word of the LORD came to me: 16"Son of man, take a stick of wood and write on it, 'Belonging to Judah and the Israelites associated with him.' Then take another stick of wood, and write on it, 'Belonging to Joseph (that is, to Ephraim) and all the Israelites associated with him.' 17Join them together into one stick so that they will become one in your hand.

18"When your people ask you, 'Won't you tell us what you mean by this?' 19say to them, 'This is what the Sovereign LORD says: I am going to take the stick of Joseph—which is in Ephraim's hand—and of the Israelite tribes associated with him, and join it to Judah's stick. I will make them into a single stick of wood, and they will become one in my hand.' 20Hold before their eyes the sticks you have written on 21and say to them, 'This is what the Sovereign LORD says: I will take the Israelites out of the nations where they have gone. I will gather them from all around and bring them back into their own land. 22I will make them one nation in the land, on the mountains of Israel. There will be one king over all of them and they will never again be two nations or be divided into two kingdoms. 23They will no longer defile themselves with their idols and vile images or with any of their offenses, for I will save them from all their sinful backsliding,[b] and I will cleanse them. They will be my people, and I will be their God.

[a] 5 The Hebrew for this word can also mean *wind* or *spirit* (see verses 6-14). [b] 23 Many Hebrew manuscripts (see also Septuagint); most Hebrew manuscripts *all their dwelling places where they sinned*

EZEKIEL 37:1 – 14

THE VALLEY OF DRY BONES

God can put the pieces back together. God can reassemble what was once beautiful in people's lives, relationships and circumstances. More importantly, God can put his people's hearts back together. To prove this, God took Ezekiel on an amazing journey around a valley full of dry bones.

God asked Ezekiel a simple question: "Son of man, can these bones live?" (37:3). When asked to reply, Ezekiel really had to think about it: to deny that the bones could live would mean that Ezekiel doubted God's power; to agree that the bones could live would mean that Ezekiel was embracing a human impossibility. The prophet responded with the safest answer: "Sovereign LORD, you alone know" (v. 3).

Then God gave Ezekiel an unthinkable directive. God told him to prophesy to the bones so that the bones would come to life. It is one thing for God to bring the dead to life; it is quite another thing for God to involve mere mortals in the process. Ezekiel began to speak to the bones, and God worked through Ezekiel's words: the bones started to come back together. Tendons and skin appeared, and Ezekiel marveled as a resurrection took place. At the end of the process, an entire army stood before Ezekiel awaiting God's command. God did this miracle to remind Ezekiel that his word is powerful and effective. God is the Lord, and his promises are powerful and true (vv. 13 – 14).

God's Word has incredible effects; it brings the dead to life. As God's Word is proclaimed, the Spirit of God uses the Word of God to revitalize the people of God. Jesus told his followers that their only hope was to depend on him in every way (Jn 15:5). God's Word always does what he intends: "So is my word that goes out from my mouth: It will not return to me empty, but will accomplish what I desire and achieve the purpose for which I sent it" (Isa 55:11). God's Word can bring light into darkness and life into dead places. People are encouraged to read and listen to the Word of God to live.

God is building an army to tell the world who he is and what he has done. His army is totally dependent on the Word of God to accomplish the mission of God. When believing in God's ability is hard, Ezekiel 37:1 – 14 is a wonderful reminder of the great things God has done and is capable of doing.

[24]" 'My servant David will be king over them, and they will all have one shepherd. They will follow my laws and be careful to keep my decrees. [25]They will live in the land I gave to my servant Jacob, the land where your ancestors lived. They and their children and their children's children will live there forever, and David my servant will be their prince forever. [26]I will make a covenant of peace with them; it will be an everlasting covenant. I will establish them and increase their numbers, and I will put my sanctuary among them forever. [27]My dwelling place will be with them; I will be their God, and they will be my people. [28]Then the nations will know that I the LORD make Israel holy, when my sanctuary is among them forever.' "

The LORD's Great Victory Over the Nations

38 The word of the LORD came to me: [2]"Son of man, set your face against Gog, of the land of Magog, the chief prince of[a] Meshek and Tubal; prophesy against him [3]and say: 'This is what the Sovereign LORD says: I am against you, Gog, chief prince of[b] Meshek and Tubal. [4]I will turn you around, put hooks in your jaws and bring you out with your whole army — your horses, your horsemen fully armed, and a great horde with large and small shields, all of them brandishing their swords. [5]Persia, Cush[c] and Put will be with them, all with shields and helmets, [6]also Gomer with all its troops, and Beth Togarmah from the far north with all its troops — the many nations with you.

[7]" 'Get ready; be prepared, you and all the hordes gathered about you, and take command of them. [8]After many days you will be called to arms. In future years you will invade a land that has recovered from war, whose people were gathered from many nations to the mountains of Israel, which had long been desolate. They had been brought out from the nations, and now all of them live in safety. [9]You and all your troops and the many nations with you will go up, advancing like a storm; you will be like a cloud covering the land.

[10]" 'This is what the Sovereign LORD says: On that day thoughts will come into your mind and you will devise an evil scheme. [11]You will say, "I will invade a land of unwalled villages; I will attack a peaceful and unsuspecting people — all of them living without walls and without gates and bars. [12]I will plunder and loot and turn my hand against the resettled ruins and the people gathered from the nations, rich in livestock and goods, living at the center of the land.[d]" [13]Sheba and Dedan and the merchants of Tarshish and all her villages[e] will say to you, "Have you come to plunder? Have you gathered your hordes to loot, to carry off silver and gold, to take away livestock and goods and to seize much plunder?" '

[14]"Therefore, son of man, prophesy and say to Gog: 'This is what the Sovereign LORD says: In that day, when my people Israel are living in safety, will you not take notice of it? [15]You will come from your place in the far north, you and many nations with you, all of them riding on horses, a great horde, a mighty army. [16]You will advance against my people Israel like a cloud that covers the land. In days to come, Gog, I will bring you against my land, so that the nations may know me when I am proved holy through you before their eyes.

[17]" 'This is what the Sovereign LORD says: You are the one I spoke of in former days by my servants the prophets of Israel. At that time they prophesied for years that I would bring you against them. [18]This is what will happen in that day: When Gog attacks the land of Israel, my hot anger will be aroused, declares the Sovereign LORD. [19]In my zeal and fiery wrath I declare that at that time there shall be a great earthquake in the land of Israel. [20]The fish in the sea, the birds in the sky, the beasts of the field, every creature that moves along the ground, and all the people on the face of the earth will tremble at my presence. The mountains will be overturned, the cliffs will crumble and every wall will fall to the ground. [21]I will summon a sword against Gog on all my mountains, declares the Sovereign

[a] 2 Or *the prince of Rosh,* [b] 3 Or *Gog, prince of Rosh,* [c] 5 That is, the upper Nile region
[d] 12 The Hebrew for this phrase means *the navel of the earth.* [e] 13 Or *her strong lions*

LORD. Every man's sword will be against his brother. 22I will execute judgment on him with plague and bloodshed; I will pour down torrents of rain, hailstones and burning sulfur on him and on his troops and on the many nations with him. 23And so I will show my greatness and my holiness, and I will make myself known in the sight of many nations. Then they will know that I am the LORD.'

39 "Son of man, prophesy against Gog and say: 'This is what the Sovereign LORD says: I am against you, Gog, chief prince of[a] Meshek and Tubal. 2I will turn you around and drag you along. I will bring you from the far north and send you against the mountains of Israel. 3Then I will strike your bow from your left hand and make your arrows drop from your right hand. 4On the mountains of Israel you will fall, you and all your troops and the nations with you. I will give you as food to all kinds of carrion birds and to the wild animals. 5You will fall in the open field, for I have spoken, declares the Sovereign LORD. 6I will send fire on Magog and on those who live in safety in the coastlands, and they will know that I am the LORD.

7" 'I will make known my holy name among my people Israel. I will no longer let my holy name be profaned, and the nations will know that I the LORD am the Holy One in Israel. 8It is coming! It will surely take place, declares the Sovereign LORD. This is the day I have spoken of.

9" 'Then those who live in the towns of Israel will go out and use the weapons for fuel and burn them up — the small and large shields, the bows and arrows, the war clubs and spears. For seven years they will use them for fuel. 10They will not need to gather wood from the fields or cut it from the forests, because they will use the weapons for fuel. And they will plunder those who plundered them and loot those who looted them, declares the Sovereign LORD.

11" 'On that day I will give Gog a burial place in Israel, in the valley of those who travel east of the Sea. It will block the way of travelers, because Gog and all his hordes will be buried there. So it will be called the Valley of Hamon Gog.[b]

12" 'For seven months the Israelites will be burying them in order to cleanse the land. 13All the people of the land will bury them, and the day I display my glory will be a memorable day for them, declares the Sovereign LORD. 14People will be continually employed in cleansing the land. They will spread out across the land and, along with others, they will bury any bodies that are lying on the ground.

" 'After the seven months they will carry out a more detailed search. 15As they go through the land, anyone who sees a human bone will leave a marker beside it until the gravediggers bury it in the Valley of Hamon Gog, 16near a town called Hamonah.[c] And so they will cleanse the land.'

17"Son of man, this is what the Sovereign LORD says: Call out to every kind of bird and all the wild animals: 'Assemble and come together from all around to the sacrifice I am preparing for you, the great sacrifice on the mountains of Israel. There you will eat flesh and drink blood. 18You will eat the flesh of mighty men and drink the blood of the princes of the earth as if they were rams and lambs, goats and bulls — all of them fattened animals from Bashan. 19At the sacrifice I am preparing for you, you will eat fat till you are glutted and drink blood till you are drunk. 20At my table you will eat your fill of horses and riders, mighty men and soldiers of every kind,' declares the Sovereign LORD.

21"I will display my glory among the nations, and all the nations will see the punishment I inflict and the hand I lay on them. 22From that day forward the people of Israel will know that I am the LORD their God. 23And the nations will know that the people of Israel went into exile for their sin, because they were unfaithful to me. So I hid my face from them and handed them over to their enemies, and they all fell by the sword. 24I dealt with them according to their uncleanness and their offenses, and I hid my face from them.

---

[a] *1* Or *Gog, prince of Rosh,* [b] *11 Hamon Gog* means *hordes of Gog.* [c] *16 Hamonah* means *horde.*

GLORY AMONG THE NATIONS

God's ultimate purpose is to make his glory known in all parts of the earth. God made this promise to Abraham (Ge 12:2 – 3) and has been working for its fulfillment ever since. Here Ezekiel joins the sweeping prophetic voice of Scripture that God is working to make his glory known among all peoples in general and among the people of Israel in particular.

All of this is good news for a book that is filled with so much prophecy about judgment. The Israelites had disobeyed God, and God made it absolutely clear that they would suffer for their disobedience. Yet in the midst of his prophecies of God's judgment against the nations, Ezekiel focused on the wonderful, unexpected outcome: that one day when his glory is revealed to the nations, Israel would know that God is the Lord.

God's desire is for all people to know him and love him. When this does not happen, God's heart breaks. Jesus longed for the people of Jerusalem to know him as well, though he lamented that they were not willing to do so. He said, "Jerusalem, Jerusalem, you who kill the prophets and stone those sent to you, how often I have longed to gather your children together, as a hen gathers her chicks under her wings, and you were not willing" (Mt 23:37). God's desire is for all people, including all of Israel, to repent and believe the gospel (Ro 11:25 – 27), though some will refuse to believe.

While we don't know all that God will do in the last days, we know this truth: People are saved when they confess that Jesus is Lord and believe in their hearts that God raised him from the dead (Ro 10:9 – 10). So, in his grace, God plans to do something in the end times that will turn Israel toward Jesus as Lord. And one day people from all nations will surround the throne of God in worship (Rev 15:4; 21:26).

God's church ought to see God's plan for the world, which is clearly revealed in his Word, and join God in his redemptive purposes. The fact that God's throne will be surrounded with representatives from all nations (Rev 5) should propel believers to approach all people with the confidence that they may repent and believe after hearing the good news of the gospel.

[25]"Therefore this is what the Sovereign LORD says: I will now restore the fortunes of Jacob[a] and will have compassion on all the people of Israel, and I will be zealous for my holy name. [26]They will forget their shame and all the unfaithfulness they showed toward me when they lived in safety in their land with no one to make them afraid. [27]When I have brought them back from the nations and have gathered them from the countries of their enemies, I will be proved holy through them in the sight of many nations. [28]Then they will know that I am the LORD their God, for though I sent them into exile among the nations, I will gather them to their own land, not leaving any behind. [29]I will no longer hide my face from them, for I will pour out my Spirit on the people of Israel, declares the Sovereign LORD."

The Temple Area Restored

40 In the twenty-fifth year of our exile, at the beginning of the year, on the tenth of the month, in the fourteenth year after the fall of the city — on that very day the hand of the LORD was on me and he took me there. [2]In visions of God he took me to the land of Israel and set me on a very high mountain, on whose south side were some buildings that looked like a city. [3]He took me there, and I saw a man whose appearance was like bronze; he was standing in the gateway with a linen cord and a measuring rod in his hand. [4]The man said to me, "Son of man, look carefully and listen closely and pay attention to everything I am going to show you, for that is why you have been brought here. Tell the people of Israel everything you see."

The East Gate to the Outer Court

[5]I saw a wall completely surrounding the temple area. The length of the measuring rod in the man's hand was six long cubits,[b] each of which was a cubit and a handbreadth. He measured the wall; it was one measuring rod thick and one rod high.

[6]Then he went to the east gate. He climbed its steps and measured the threshold of the gate; it was one rod deep. [7]The alcoves for the guards were one rod long and one rod wide, and the projecting walls between the alcoves were five cubits[c] thick. And the threshold of the gate next to the portico facing the temple was one rod deep.

[8]Then he measured the portico of the gateway; [9]it[d] was eight cubits[e] deep and its jambs were two cubits[f] thick. The portico of the gateway faced the temple.

[10]Inside the east gate were three alcoves on each side; the three had the same measurements, and the faces of the projecting walls on each side had the same measurements. [11]Then he measured the width of the entrance of the gateway; it was ten cubits and its length was thirteen cubits.[g] [12]In front of each alcove was a wall one cubit high, and the alcoves were six cubits square. [13]Then he measured the gateway from the top of the rear wall of one alcove to the top of the opposite one; the distance was twenty-five cubits[h] from one parapet opening to the opposite one. [14]He measured along the faces of the projecting walls all around the inside of the gateway — sixty cubits.[i] The measurement was up to the portico[j] facing the courtyard.[k] [15]The distance from the entrance of the gateway to the far end of its portico was fifty cubits.[l] [16]The alcoves and the projecting walls inside

[a] *25* Or *now bring Jacob back from captivity* [b] *5* That is, about 11 feet or about 3.2 meters; also in verse 12. The long cubit of about 21 inches or about 53 centimeters is the basic unit of measurement of length throughout chapters 40 – 48. [c] *7* That is, about 8 3/4 feet or about 2.7 meters; also in verse 48 [d] *8,9* Many Hebrew manuscripts, Septuagint, Vulgate and Syriac; most Hebrew manuscripts *gateway facing the temple; it was one rod deep.* [9]*Then he measured the portico of the gateway; it* [e] *9* That is, about 14 feet or about 4.2 meters [f] *9* That is, about 3 1/2 feet or about 1 meter [g] *11* That is, about 18 feet wide and 23 feet long or about 5.3 meters wide and 6.9 meters long [h] *13* That is, about 44 feet or about 13 meters; also in verses 21, 25, 29, 30, 33 and 36 [i] *14* That is, about 105 feet or about 32 meters [j] *14* Septuagint; Hebrew *projecting wall* [k] *14* The meaning of the Hebrew for this verse is uncertain. [l] *15* That is, about 88 feet or about 27 meters; also in verses 21, 25, 29, 33 and 36

the gateway were surmounted by narrow parapet openings all around, as was the portico; the openings all around faced inward. The faces of the projecting walls were decorated with palm trees.

The Outer Court

[17]Then he brought me into the outer court. There I saw some rooms and a pavement that had been constructed all around the court; there were thirty rooms along the pavement. [18]It abutted the sides of the gateways and was as wide as they were long; this was the lower pavement. [19]Then he measured the distance from the inside of the lower gateway to the outside of the inner court; it was a hundred cubits[a] on the east side as well as on the north.

The North Gate

[20]Then he measured the length and width of the north gate, leading into the outer court. [21]Its alcoves — three on each side — its projecting walls and its portico had the same measurements as those of the first gateway. It was fifty cubits long and twenty-five cubits wide. [22]Its openings, its portico and its palm tree decorations had the same measurements as those of the gate facing east. Seven steps led up to it, with its portico opposite them. [23]There was a gate to the inner court facing the north gate, just as there was on the east. He measured from one gate to the opposite one; it was a hundred cubits.

The South Gate

[24]Then he led me to the south side and I saw the south gate. He measured its jambs and its portico, and they had the same measurements as the others. [25]The gateway and its portico had narrow openings all around, like the openings of the others. It was fifty cubits long and twenty-five cubits wide. [26]Seven steps led up to it, with its portico opposite them; it had palm tree decorations on the faces of the projecting walls on each side. [27]The inner court also had a gate facing south, and he measured from this gate to the outer gate on the south side; it was a hundred cubits.

The Gates to the Inner Court

[28]Then he brought me into the inner court through the south gate, and he measured the south gate; it had the same measurements as the others. [29]Its alcoves, its projecting walls and its portico had the same measurements as the others. The gateway and its portico had openings all around. It was fifty cubits long and twenty-five cubits wide. [30](The porticoes of the gateways around the inner court were twenty-five cubits wide and five cubits deep.) [31]Its portico faced the outer court; palm trees decorated its jambs, and eight steps led up to it.

[32]Then he brought me to the inner court on the east side, and he measured the gateway; it had the same measurements as the others. [33]Its alcoves, its projecting walls and its portico had the same measurements as the others. The gateway and its portico had openings all around. It was fifty cubits long and twenty-five cubits wide. [34]Its portico faced the outer court; palm trees decorated the jambs on either side, and eight steps led up to it.

[35]Then he brought me to the north gate and measured it. It had the same measurements as the others, [36]as did its alcoves, its projecting walls and its portico, and it had openings all around. It was fifty cubits long and twenty-five cubits wide. [37]Its portico[b] faced the outer court; palm trees decorated the jambs on either side, and eight steps led up to it.

The Rooms for Preparing Sacrifices

[38]A room with a doorway was by the portico in each of the inner gateways, where the burnt offerings were washed. [39]In the portico of the gateway were

---

EZEKIEL 40:38–43

ONCE AND FOR ALL

No sacrifice before or after Jesus can accomplish salvation. They only point to him, the one true Lamb who takes away sin. Jesus is the one-time sacrifice to make things right forever: "But when this priest had offered for all time one sacrifice for sins, he sat down at the right hand of God, and since that time he waits for his enemies to be made his footstool. For by one sacrifice he has made perfect forever those who are being made holy" (Heb 10:12–14). Throughout all time, Jesus is the Lamb of God who takes away the sin of the world (Jn 1:29). Only through Jesus are all the wrong things made right.

---

[a] *19* That is, about 175 feet or about 53 meters; also in verses 23, 27 and 47 [b] *37* Septuagint (see also verses 31 and 34); Hebrew *jambs*

two tables on each side, on which the burnt offerings, sin offerings[a] and guilt offerings were slaughtered. 40By the outside wall of the portico of the gateway, near the steps at the entrance of the north gateway were two tables, and on the other side of the steps were two tables. 41So there were four tables on one side of the gateway and four on the other — eight tables in all — on which the sacrifices were slaughtered. 42There were also four tables of dressed stone for the burnt offerings, each a cubit and a half long, a cubit and a half wide and a cubit high.[b] On them were placed the utensils for slaughtering the burnt offerings and the other sacrifices. 43And double-pronged hooks, each a handbreadth[c] long, were attached to the wall all around. The tables were for the flesh of the offerings.

The Rooms for the Priests

44Outside the inner gate, within the inner court, were two rooms, one[d] at the side of the north gate and facing south, and another at the side of the south[e] gate and facing north. 45He said to me, "The room facing south is for the priests who guard the temple, 46and the room facing north is for the priests who guard the altar. These are the sons of Zadok, who are the only Levites who may draw near to the LORD to minister before him."

47Then he measured the court: It was square — a hundred cubits long and a hundred cubits wide. And the altar was in front of the temple.

The New Temple

48He brought me to the portico of the temple and measured the jambs of the portico; they were five cubits wide on either side. The width of the entrance was fourteen cubits[f] and its projecting walls were[g] three cubits[h] wide on either side. 49The portico was twenty cubits[i] wide, and twelve[j] cubits[k] from front to back. It was reached by a flight of stairs,[l] and there were pillars on each side of the jambs.

41 Then the man brought me to the main hall and measured the jambs; the width of the jambs was six cubits[m] on each side.[n] 2The entrance was ten cubits[o] wide, and the projecting walls on each side of it were five cubits[p] wide. He also measured the main hall; it was forty cubits long and twenty cubits wide.[q]

3Then he went into the inner sanctuary and measured the jambs of the entrance; each was two cubits[r] wide. The entrance was six cubits wide, and the projecting walls on each side of it were seven cubits[s] wide. 4And he measured the length of the inner sanctuary; it was twenty cubits, and its width was twenty cubits across the end of the main hall. He said to me, "This is the Most Holy Place."

5Then he measured the wall of the temple; it was six cubits thick, and each side room around the temple was four cubits[t] wide. 6The side rooms were on three levels, one above another, thirty on each level. There were ledges all around the wall of the temple to serve as supports for the side rooms, so that the supports were not inserted into the wall of the temple. 7The side rooms all around the temple were wider at each successive level. The structure surrounding the temple was built in ascending stages, so that the rooms widened as one went upward. A stairway went up from the lowest floor to the top floor through the middle floor.

---

[a] *39* Or *purification offerings* [b] *42* That is, about 2 2/3 feet long and wide and 21 inches high or about 80 centimeters long and wide and 53 centimeters high [c] *43* That is, about 3 1/2 inches or about 9 centimeters [d] *44* Septuagint; Hebrew *were rooms for singers, which were* [e] *44* Septuagint; Hebrew *east* [f] *48* That is, about 25 feet or about 7.4 meters [g] *48* Septuagint; Hebrew *entrance was* [h] *48* That is, about 5 1/4 feet or about 1.6 meters [i] *49* That is, about 35 feet or about 11 meters [j] *49* Septuagint; Hebrew *eleven* [k] *49* That is, about 21 feet or about 6.4 meters [l] *49* Hebrew; Septuagint *Ten steps led up to it* [m] *1* That is, about 11 feet or about 3.2 meters; also in verses 3, 5 and 8 [n] *1* One Hebrew manuscript and Septuagint; most Hebrew manuscripts *side, the width of the tent* [o] *2* That is, about 18 feet or about 5.3 meters [p] *2* That is, about 8 3/4 feet or about 2.7 meters; also in verses 9, 11 and 12 [q] *2* That is, about 70 feet long and 35 feet wide or about 21 meters long and 11 meters wide [r] *3* That is, about 3 1/2 feet or about 1.1 meters; also in verse 22 [s] *3* That is, about 12 feet or about 3.7 meters [t] *5* That is, about 7 feet or about 2.1 meters

[8]I saw that the temple had a raised base all around it, forming the foundation of the side rooms. It was the length of the rod, six long cubits. [9]The outer wall of the side rooms was five cubits thick. The open area between the side rooms of the temple [10]and the priests' rooms was twenty cubits wide all around the temple. [11]There were entrances to the side rooms from the open area, one on the north and another on the south; and the base adjoining the open area was five cubits wide all around.

[12]The building facing the temple courtyard on the west side was seventy cubits[a] wide. The wall of the building was five cubits thick all around, and its length was ninety cubits.[b]

[13]Then he measured the temple; it was a hundred cubits[c] long, and the temple courtyard and the building with its walls were also a hundred cubits long. [14]The width of the temple courtyard on the east, including the front of the temple, was a hundred cubits.

[15]Then he measured the length of the building facing the courtyard at the rear of the temple, including its galleries on each side; it was a hundred cubits.

The main hall, the inner sanctuary and the portico facing the court, [16]as well as the thresholds and the narrow windows and galleries around the three of them — everything beyond and including the threshold was covered with wood. The floor, the wall up to the windows, and the windows were covered. [17]In the space above the outside of the entrance to the inner sanctuary and on the walls at regular intervals all around the inner and outer sanctuary [18]were carved cherubim and palm trees. Palm trees alternated with cherubim. Each cherub had two faces: [19]the face of a human being toward the palm tree on one side and the face of a lion toward the palm tree on the other. They were carved all around the whole temple. [20]From the floor to the area above the entrance, cherubim and palm trees were carved on the wall of the main hall.

[21]The main hall had a rectangular doorframe, and the one at the front of the Most Holy Place was similar. [22]There was a wooden altar three cubits[d] high and two cubits square[e]; its corners, its base[f] and its sides were of wood. The man said to me, "This is the table that is before the LORD." [23]Both the main hall and the Most Holy Place had double doors. [24]Each door had two leaves — two hinged leaves for each door. [25]And on the doors of the main hall were carved cherubim and palm trees like those carved on the walls, and there was a wooden overhang on the front of the portico. [26]On the sidewalls of the portico were narrow windows with palm trees carved on each side. The side rooms of the temple also had overhangs.

The Rooms for the Priests

42 Then the man led me northward into the outer court and brought me to the rooms opposite the temple courtyard and opposite the outer wall on the north side. [2]The building whose door faced north was a hundred cubits long and fifty cubits wide.[g] [3]Both in the section twenty cubits[h] from the inner court and in the section opposite the pavement of the outer court, gallery faced gallery at the three levels. [4]In front of the rooms was an inner passageway ten cubits wide and a hundred cubits[i] long.[j] Their doors were on the north. [5]Now the upper rooms were narrower, for the galleries took more space from them than from the rooms on the lower and middle floors of the building. [6]The rooms on the top floor had no pillars, as the courts had; so they were smaller in floor space than those on the lower and middle floors. [7]There was an outer wall parallel to

[a] *12* That is, about 123 feet or about 37 meters [b] *12* That is, about 158 feet or about 48 meters [c] *13* That is, about 175 feet or about 53 meters; also in verses 14 and 15
[d] *22* That is, about 5 1/4 feet or about 1.5 meters [e] *22* Septuagint; Hebrew *long*
[f] *22* Septuagint; Hebrew *length* [g] *2* That is, about 175 feet long and 88 feet wide or about 53 meters long and 27 meters wide [h] *3* That is, about 35 feet or about 11 meters
[i] *4* Septuagint and Syriac; Hebrew *and one cubit* [j] *4* That is, about 18 feet wide and 175 feet long or about 5.3 meters wide and 53 meters long

the rooms and the outer court; it extended in front of the rooms for fifty cubits. 8While the row of rooms on the side next to the outer court was fifty cubits long, the row on the side nearest the sanctuary was a hundred cubits long. 9The lower rooms had an entrance on the east side as one enters them from the outer court.

10On the south side[a] along the length of the wall of the outer court, adjoining the temple courtyard and opposite the outer wall, were rooms 11with a passageway in front of them. These were like the rooms on the north; they had the same length and width, with similar exits and dimensions. Similar to the doorways on the north 12were the doorways of the rooms on the south. There was a doorway at the beginning of the passageway that was parallel to the corresponding wall extending eastward, by which one enters the rooms.

13Then he said to me, "The north and south rooms facing the temple courtyard are the priests' rooms, where the priests who approach the LORD will eat the most holy offerings. There they will put the most holy offerings — the grain offerings, the sin offerings[b] and the guilt offerings — for the place is holy. 14Once the priests enter the holy precincts, they are not to go into the outer court until they leave behind the garments in which they minister, for these are holy. They are to put on other clothes before they go near the places that are for the people."

15When he had finished measuring what was inside the temple area, he led me out by the east gate and measured the area all around: 16He measured the east side with the measuring rod; it was five hundred cubits.[c,d] 17He measured the north side; it was five hundred cubits[e] by the measuring rod. 18He measured the south side; it was five hundred cubits by the measuring rod. 19Then he turned to the west side and measured; it was five hundred cubits by the measuring rod. 20So he measured the area on all four sides. It had a wall around it, five hundred cubits long and five hundred cubits wide, to separate the holy from the common.

God's Glory Returns to the Temple

43 Then the man brought me to the gate facing east, 2and I saw the glory of the God of Israel coming from the east. His voice was like the roar of rushing waters, and the land was radiant with his glory. 3The vision I saw was like the vision I had seen when he[f] came to destroy the city and like the visions I had seen by the Kebar River, and I fell facedown. 4The glory of the LORD entered the temple through the gate facing east. 5Then the Spirit lifted me up and brought me into the inner court, and the glory of the LORD filled the temple.

6While the man was standing beside me, I heard someone speaking to me from inside the temple. 7He said: "Son of man, this is the place of my throne and the place for the soles of my feet. This is where I will live among the Israelites forever. The people of Israel will never again defile my holy name — neither they nor their kings — by their prostitution and the funeral offerings[g] for their kings at their death.[h] 8When they placed their threshold next to my threshold and their doorposts beside my doorposts, with only a wall between me and them, they defiled my holy name by their detestable practices. So I destroyed them in my anger. 9Now let them put away from me their prostitution and the funeral offerings for their kings, and I will live among them forever.

10"Son of man, describe the temple to the people of Israel, that they may be ashamed of their sins. Let them consider its perfection, 11and if they are ashamed of all they have done, make known to them the design of the temple — its arrangement, its exits and entrances — its whole design and all its regulations[i] and laws. Write these down before them so that they may be faithful to its design and follow all its regulations.

[a] *10* Septuagint; Hebrew *Eastward* [b] *13* Or *purification offerings* [c] *16* See Septuagint of verse 17; Hebrew *rods*; also in verses 18 and 19. [d] *16* Five hundred cubits equal about 875 feet or about 265 meters; also in verses 17, 18 and 19. [e] *17* Septuagint; Hebrew *rods* [f] *3* Some Hebrew manuscripts and Vulgate; most Hebrew manuscripts *I* [g] *7* Or *the memorial monuments*; also in verse 9 [h] *7* Or *their high places* [i] *11* Some Hebrew manuscripts and Septuagint; most Hebrew manuscripts *regulations and its whole design*

EZEKIEL 43:1–12

THE GLORY RETURNS TO THE TEMPLE

The vision of the return of God's glory to the temple is one of the high points of the book of Ezekiel. On its return, the glory of God not only fills the temple, it even causes the land itself to shine (v. 2). Without the presence of God at the heart of a community, there can be no life at all; there will simply be a collection of dry bones.

Ezekiel's vision of the return of God's glory is a picture of what must happen before people can be restored. God's presence must arrive for healing to take place. This vision gives readers a picture of the future city of God, when his glory will be revealed and there will be no need for the sun (Rev 22:5); it also points toward the time when God himself would live inside his people and reside in the temples that he has made them to be. In both the present and future, God dwells with his people. By dwelling with them, God will make all things new. He lives within his believers today through his Spirit; he will gather all people who love him to himself one day in the future.

12 “This is the law of the temple: All the surrounding area on top of the mountain will be most holy. Such is the law of the temple.

The Great Altar Restored

13 “These are the measurements of the altar in long cubits,[a] that cubit being a cubit and a handbreadth: Its gutter is a cubit deep and a cubit wide, with a rim of one span[b] around the edge. And this is the height of the altar: 14 From the gutter on the ground up to the lower ledge that goes around the altar it is two cubits high, and the ledge is a cubit wide.[c] From this lower ledge to the upper ledge that goes around the altar it is four cubits high, and that ledge is also a cubit wide.[d] 15 Above that, the altar hearth is four cubits high, and four horns project upward from the hearth. 16 The altar hearth is square, twelve cubits[e] long and twelve cubits wide. 17 The upper ledge also is square, fourteen cubits[f] long and fourteen cubits wide. All around the altar is a gutter of one cubit with a rim of half a cubit.[b] The steps of the altar face east.”

18 Then he said to me, “Son of man, this is what the Sovereign LORD says: These will be the regulations for sacrificing burnt offerings and splashing blood against the altar when it is built: 19 You are to give a young bull as a sin offering[g] to the Levitical priests of the family of Zadok, who come near to minister before me, declares the Sovereign LORD. 20 You are to take some of its blood and put it on the four horns of the altar and on the four corners of the upper ledge and all around the rim, and so purify the altar and make atonement for it. 21 You are to take the bull for the sin offering and burn it in the designated part of the temple area outside the sanctuary.

22 “On the second day you are to offer a male goat without defect for a sin offering, and the altar is to be purified as it was purified with the bull. 23 When you have finished purifying it, you are to offer a young bull and a ram from the flock, both without defect. 24 You are to offer them before the LORD, and the priests are to sprinkle salt on them and sacrifice them as a burnt offering to the LORD.

25 “For seven days you are to provide a male goat daily for a sin offering; you are also to provide a young bull and a ram from the flock, both without defect. 26 For seven days they are to make atonement for the altar and cleanse it; thus they will dedicate it. 27 At the end of these days, from the eighth day on, the priests are to present your burnt offerings and fellowship offerings on the altar. Then I will accept you, declares the Sovereign LORD.”

The Priesthood Restored

44 Then the man brought me back to the outer gate of the sanctuary, the one facing east, and it was shut. 2 The LORD said to me, “This gate is to remain shut. It must not be opened; no one may enter through it. It is to remain shut because the LORD, the God of Israel, has entered through it. 3 The prince himself is the only one who may sit inside the gateway to eat in the presence of the LORD. He is to enter by way of the portico of the gateway and go out the same way.”

4 Then the man brought me by way of the north gate to the front of the temple. I looked and saw the glory of the LORD filling the temple of the LORD, and I fell facedown.

5 The LORD said to me, “Son of man, look carefully, listen closely and give attention to everything I tell you concerning all the regulations and instructions regarding the temple of the LORD. Give attention to the entrance to the temple and all the exits of the sanctuary. 6 Say to rebellious Israel, ‘This is what the

---

[a] *13* That is, about 21 inches or about 53 centimeters; also in verses 14 and 17. The long cubit is the basic unit for linear measurement throughout Ezekiel 40 – 48. [b] *13,17* That is, about 11 inches or about 27 centimeters [c] *14* That is, about 3 1/2 feet high and 1 3/4 feet wide or about 105 centimeters high and 53 centimeters wide [d] *14* That is, about 7 feet high and 1 3/4 feet wide or about 2.1 meters high and 53 centimeters wide [e] *16* That is, about 21 feet or about 6.4 meters [f] *17* That is, about 25 feet or about 7.4 meters [g] *19* Or *purification offering*; also in verses 21, 22 and 25

Sovereign LORD says: Enough of your detestable practices, people of Israel! 7In addition to all your other detestable practices, you brought foreigners uncircumcised in heart and flesh into my sanctuary, desecrating my temple while you offered me food, fat and blood, and you broke my covenant. 8Instead of carrying out your duty in regard to my holy things, you put others in charge of my sanctuary. 9This is what the Sovereign LORD says: No foreigner uncircumcised in heart and flesh is to enter my sanctuary, not even the foreigners who live among the Israelites.

10" 'The Levites who went far from me when Israel went astray and who wandered from me after their idols must bear the consequences of their sin. 11They may serve in my sanctuary, having charge of the gates of the temple and serving in it; they may slaughter the burnt offerings and sacrifices for the people and stand before the people and serve them. 12But because they served them in the presence of their idols and made the people of Israel fall into sin, therefore I have sworn with uplifted hand that they must bear the consequences of their sin, declares the Sovereign LORD. 13They are not to come near to serve me as priests or come near any of my holy things or my most holy offerings; they must bear the shame of their detestable practices. 14And I will appoint them to guard the temple for all the work that is to be done in it.

15" 'But the Levitical priests, who are descendants of Zadok and who guarded my sanctuary when the Israelites went astray from me, are to come near to minister before me; they are to stand before me to offer sacrifices of fat and blood, declares the Sovereign LORD. 16They alone are to enter my sanctuary; they alone are to come near my table to minister before me and serve me as guards.

17" 'When they enter the gates of the inner court, they are to wear linen clothes; they must not wear any woolen garment while ministering at the gates of the inner court or inside the temple. 18They are to wear linen turbans on their heads and linen undergarments around their waists. They must not wear anything that makes them perspire. 19When they go out into the outer court where the people are, they are to take off the clothes they have been ministering in and are to leave them in the sacred rooms, and put on other clothes, so that the people are not consecrated through contact with their garments.

20" 'They must not shave their heads or let their hair grow long, but they are to keep the hair of their heads trimmed. 21No priest is to drink wine when he enters the inner court. 22They must not marry widows or divorced women; they may marry only virgins of Israelite descent or widows of priests. 23They are to teach my people the difference between the holy and the common and show them how to distinguish between the unclean and the clean.

24" 'In any dispute, the priests are to serve as judges and decide it according to my ordinances. They are to keep my laws and my decrees for all my appointed festivals, and they are to keep my Sabbaths holy.

25" 'A priest must not defile himself by going near a dead person; however, if the dead person was his father or mother, son or daughter, brother or unmarried sister, then he may defile himself. 26After he is cleansed, he must wait seven days. 27On the day he goes into the inner court of the sanctuary to minister in the sanctuary, he is to offer a sin offering[a] for himself, declares the Sovereign LORD.

28" 'I am to be the only inheritance the priests have. You are to give them no possession in Israel; I will be their possession. 29They will eat the grain offerings, the sin offerings and the guilt offerings; and everything in Israel devoted[b] to the LORD will belong to them. 30The best of all the firstfruits and of all your special gifts will belong to the priests. You are to give them the first portion of your ground meal so that a blessing may rest on your household. 31The priests must not eat anything, whether bird or animal, found dead or torn by wild animals.

[a] *27* Or *purification offering*; also in verse 29 [b] *29* The Hebrew term refers to the irrevocable giving over of things or persons to the LORD.

Israel Fully Restored

45 "'When you allot the land as an inheritance, you are to present to the LORD a portion of the land as a sacred district, 25,000 cubits[a] long and 20,000[b] cubits[c] wide; the entire area will be holy. 2Of this, a section 500 cubits[d] square is to be for the sanctuary, with 50 cubits[e] around it for open land. 3In the sacred district, measure off a section 25,000 cubits long and 10,000 cubits[f] wide. In it will be the sanctuary, the Most Holy Place. 4It will be the sacred portion of the land for the priests, who minister in the sanctuary and who draw near to minister before the LORD. It will be a place for their houses as well as a holy place for the sanctuary. 5An area 25,000 cubits long and 10,000 cubits wide will belong to the Levites, who serve in the temple, as their possession for towns to live in.[g]

6"'You are to give the city as its property an area 5,000 cubits[h] wide and 25,000 cubits long, adjoining the sacred portion; it will belong to all Israel.

7"'The prince will have the land bordering each side of the area formed by the sacred district and the property of the city. It will extend westward from the west side and eastward from the east side, running lengthwise from the western to the eastern border parallel to one of the tribal portions. 8This land will be his possession in Israel. And my princes will no longer oppress my people but will allow the people of Israel to possess the land according to their tribes.

9"'This is what the Sovereign LORD says: You have gone far enough, princes of Israel! Give up your violence and oppression and do what is just and right. Stop dispossessing my people, declares the Sovereign LORD. 10You are to use accurate scales, an accurate ephah[i] and an accurate bath.[j] 11The ephah and the bath are to be the same size, the bath containing a tenth of a homer and the ephah a tenth of a homer; the homer is to be the standard measure for both. 12The shekel[k] is to consist of twenty gerahs. Twenty shekels plus twenty-five shekels plus fifteen shekels equal one mina.[l]

13"'This is the special gift you are to offer: a sixth of an ephah[m] from each homer of wheat and a sixth of an ephah[n] from each homer of barley. 14The prescribed portion of olive oil, measured by the bath, is a tenth of a bath[o] from each cor (which consists of ten baths or one homer, for ten baths are equivalent to a homer). 15Also one sheep is to be taken from every flock of two hundred from the well-watered pastures of Israel. These will be used for the grain offerings, burnt offerings and fellowship offerings to make atonement for the people, declares the Sovereign LORD. 16All the people of the land will be required to give this special offering to the prince in Israel. 17It will be the duty of the prince to provide the burnt offerings, grain offerings and drink offerings at the festivals, the New Moons and the Sabbaths—at all the appointed festivals of Israel. He will provide the sin offerings,[p] grain offerings, burnt offerings and fellowship offerings to make atonement for the Israelites.

18"'This is what the Sovereign LORD says: In the first month on the first day you are to take a young bull without defect and purify the sanctuary. 19The priest is to take some of the blood of the sin offering and put it on the doorposts of the

---

[a] *1* That is, about 8 miles or about 13 kilometers; also in verses 3, 5 and 6 [b] *1* Septuagint (see also verses 3 and 5 and 48:9); Hebrew *10,000* [c] *1* That is, about 6 1/2 miles or about 11 kilometers [d] *2* That is, about 875 feet or about 265 meters [e] *2* That is, about 88 feet or about 27 meters [f] *3* That is, about 3 1/3 miles or about 5.3 kilometers; also in verse 5 [g] *5* Septuagint; Hebrew *temple; they will have as their possession 20 rooms* [h] *6* That is, about 1 2/3 miles or about 2.7 kilometers [i] *10* An ephah was a dry measure having the capacity of about 3/5 bushel or about 22 liters. [j] *10* A bath was a liquid measure equaling about 6 gallons or about 22 liters. [k] *12* A shekel weighed about 2/5 ounce or about 12 grams. [l] *12* That is, 60 shekels; the common mina was 50 shekels. Sixty shekels were about 1 1/2 pounds or about 690 grams. [m] *13* That is, probably about 6 pounds or about 2.7 kilograms [n] *13* That is, probably about 5 pounds or about 2.3 kilograms [o] *14* That is, about 2 1/2 quarts or about 2.2 liters [p] *17* Or *purification offerings*; also in verses 19, 22, 23 and 25

temple, on the four corners of the upper ledge of the altar and on the gateposts of the inner court. 20You are to do the same on the seventh day of the month for anyone who sins unintentionally or through ignorance; so you are to make atonement for the temple.

21" 'In the first month on the fourteenth day you are to observe the Passover, a festival lasting seven days, during which you shall eat bread made without yeast. 22On that day the prince is to provide a bull as a sin offering for himself and for all the people of the land. 23Every day during the seven days of the festival he is to provide seven bulls and seven rams without defect as a burnt offering to the LORD, and a male goat for a sin offering. 24He is to provide as a grain offering an ephah for each bull and an ephah for each ram, along with a hin[a] of olive oil for each ephah.

25" 'During the seven days of the festival, which begins in the seventh month on the fifteenth day, he is to make the same provision for sin offerings, burnt offerings, grain offerings and oil.

46 " 'This is what the Sovereign LORD says: The gate of the inner court facing east is to be shut on the six working days, but on the Sabbath day and on the day of the New Moon it is to be opened. 2The prince is to enter from the outside through the portico of the gateway and stand by the gatepost. The priests are to sacrifice his burnt offering and his fellowship offerings. He is to bow down in worship at the threshold of the gateway and then go out, but the gate will not be shut until evening. 3On the Sabbaths and New Moons the people of the land are to worship in the presence of the LORD at the entrance of that gateway. 4The burnt offering the prince brings to the LORD on the Sabbath day is to be six male lambs and a ram, all without defect. 5The grain offering given with the ram is to be an ephah,[b] and the grain offering with the lambs is to be as much as he pleases, along with a hin[c] of olive oil for each ephah. 6On the day of the New Moon he is to offer a young bull, six lambs and a ram, all without defect. 7He is to provide as a grain offering one ephah with the bull, one ephah with the ram, and with the lambs as much as he wants to give, along with a hin of oil for each ephah. 8When the prince enters, he is to go in through the portico of the gateway, and he is to come out the same way.

9" 'When the people of the land come before the LORD at the appointed festivals, whoever enters by the north gate to worship is to go out the south gate; and whoever enters by the south gate is to go out the north gate. No one is to return through the gate by which they entered, but each is to go out the opposite gate. 10The prince is to be among them, going in when they go in and going out when they go out. 11At the feasts and the appointed festivals, the grain offering is to be an ephah with a bull, an ephah with a ram, and with the lambs as much as he pleases, along with a hin of oil for each ephah.

12" 'When the prince provides a freewill offering to the LORD—whether a burnt offering or fellowship offerings—the gate facing east is to be opened for him. He shall offer his burnt offering or his fellowship offerings as he does on the Sabbath day. Then he shall go out, and after he has gone out, the gate will be shut.

13" 'Every day you are to provide a year-old lamb without defect for a burnt offering to the LORD; morning by morning you shall provide it. 14You are also to provide with it morning by morning a grain offering, consisting of a sixth of an ephah[d] with a third of a hin[e] of oil to moisten the flour. The presenting of this grain offering to the LORD is a lasting ordinance. 15So the lamb and the grain offering and the oil shall be provided morning by morning for a regular burnt offering.

16" 'This is what the Sovereign LORD says: If the prince makes a gift from his

[a] *24* That is, about 1 gallon or about 3.8 liters [b] *5* That is, probably about 35 pounds or about 16 kilograms; also in verses 7 and 11 [c] *5* That is, about 1 gallon or about 3.8 liters; also in verses 7 and 11 [d] *14* That is, probably about 6 pounds or about 2.7 kilograms [e] *14* That is, about 1 1/2 quarts or about 1.3 liters

ALL OF LIFE IS HOLY

Holy places are incredibly important for the world's major religions. For many people, the concept of holy places brings to mind cities, cathedrals and temples. It would be easy to think of holiness as simply something that happens in such a place, especially when there are so many references to these kinds of "holy places" in the Old Testament.

The description of holy places continues with Ezekiel's vision of the new temple. But despite the fact that holiness has often been attached to certain places, holiness is less about places and more about how God's people ought to live. Jesus' work and teaching redefines everything. Instead of inhabiting a holy temple as the exclusive place of worship, Jesus makes his home in the life of every believer and promises to be with them whenever they get together (Mt 18:20). Instead of people trying to work hard to do good and earn Jesus' acceptance, Jesus' own righteous life is applied to sinners, who only need to look to him in order to be made right with God (2Co 5:17).

Jesus redefines what it means to be holy. All of life is to be holy, no matter where one is. Ezekiel pinpoints some very practical and even mundane aspects of holiness that are all made possible because of Jesus: God's people are supposed to stop the use of violence and oppression (Eze 45:9); they are to conduct their business and entrepreneurial ventures with integrity and trust (45:10 – 12); they are also to live with a sense of purposeful balance, working six days and taking one day to be refreshed and rejuvenated (46:1 – 15).

All of life is meant to be holy. There is nothing wrong with being more reverent in certain places and on certain occasions, but worshiping in particular holy places or undertaking certain rituals to symbolize holiness is no longer necessary for one to be made right with God. Jesus Christ has already provided his people access to the most holy place possible, and he did that by giving his life as a sacrifice for sin (Heb 9:11 – 15). As people who already have unprecedented access to him, God's people are now free to live for God in all of life: "Let us hold unswervingly to the hope we profess, for he who promised is faithful. And let us consider how we may spur one another on toward love and good deeds, not giving up meeting together, as some are in the habit of doing, but encouraging one another — and all the more as you see the Day approaching" (Heb 10:23 – 25).

inheritance to one of his sons, it will also belong to his descendants; it is to be their property by inheritance. [17]If, however, he makes a gift from his inheritance to one of his servants, the servant may keep it until the year of freedom; then it will revert to the prince. His inheritance belongs to his sons only; it is theirs. [18]The prince must not take any of the inheritance of the people, driving them off their property. He is to give his sons their inheritance out of his own property, so that not one of my people will be separated from their property.' "

[19]Then the man brought me through the entrance at the side of the gate to the sacred rooms facing north, which belonged to the priests, and showed me a place at the western end. [20]He said to me, "This is the place where the priests are to cook the guilt offering and the sin offering[a] and bake the grain offering, to avoid bringing them into the outer court and consecrating the people."

[21]He then brought me to the outer court and led me around to its four corners, and I saw in each corner another court. [22]In the four corners of the outer court were enclosed[b] courts, forty cubits long and thirty cubits wide;[c] each of the courts in the four corners was the same size. [23]Around the inside of each of the four courts was a ledge of stone, with places for fire built all around under the ledge. [24]He said to me, "These are the kitchens where those who minister at the temple are to cook the sacrifices of the people."

The River From the Temple

47 The man brought me back to the entrance to the temple, and I saw water coming out from under the threshold of the temple toward the east (for the temple faced east). The water was coming down from under the south side of the temple, south of the altar. [2]He then brought me out through the north gate and led me around the outside to the outer gate facing east, and the water was trickling from the south side.

[3]As the man went eastward with a measuring line in his hand, he measured off a thousand cubits[d] and then led me through water that was ankle-deep. [4]He measured off another thousand cubits and led me through water that was knee-deep. He measured off another thousand and led me through water that was up to the waist. [5]He measured off another thousand, but now it was a river that I could not cross, because the water had risen and was deep enough to swim in — a river that no one could cross. [6]He asked me, "Son of man, do you see this?"

Then he led me back to the bank of the river. [7]When I arrived there, I saw a great number of trees on each side of the river. [8]He said to me, "This water flows toward the eastern region and goes down into the Arabah,[e] where it enters the Dead Sea. When it empties into the sea, the salty water there becomes fresh. [9]Swarms of living creatures will live wherever the river flows. There will be large numbers of fish, because this water flows there and makes the salt water fresh; so where the river flows everything will live. [10]Fishermen will stand along the shore; from En Gedi to En Eglaim there will be places for spreading nets. The fish will be of many kinds — like the fish of the Mediterranean Sea. [11]But the swamps and marshes will not become fresh; they will be left for salt. [12]Fruit trees of all kinds will grow on both banks of the river. Their leaves will not wither, nor will their fruit fail. Every month they will bear fruit, because the water from the sanctuary flows to them. Their fruit will serve for food and their leaves for healing."

The Boundaries of the Land

[13]This is what the Sovereign LORD says: "These are the boundaries of the land that you will divide among the twelve tribes of Israel as their inheritance, with

[a] 20 Or *purification offering* [b] 22 The meaning of the Hebrew for this word is uncertain.
[c] 22 That is, about 70 feet long and 53 feet wide or about 21 meters long and 16 meters wide
[d] 3 That is, about 1,700 feet or about 530 meters [e] 8 Or *the Jordan Valley*

EZEKIEL 47:1 – 12

THE RIVER OF LIFE

The Dead Sea is the saltiest body of water on the planet. It is presently unable to support life of any kind. Ezekiel 47 tells of a wonderful moment that is coming in the future when the Dead Sea will one day teem with all kinds of life. This will happen when God's restoring salvation starts to make its way through every sphere of life.

Ezekiel foretells a time when God's restoring presence will flow out from the temple and into every part of life. The progress of his presence will leave nothing but restoration and new life in its wake. This is pictured as a river flowing from the temple and to the Dead Sea. Much later, the apostle John saw a similar vision. He saw a river flowing from the throne of God. On the banks of this river was the tree of life whose leaves were for the "healing of the nations" (Rev 22:2). Both visions peer into the future in which God's presence and provision for his people are unmistakably central. Jesus likened himself to the river of life when he said, "Everyone who drinks this water will be thirsty again, but whoever drinks the water I give them will never thirst. Indeed, the water I give them will become in them a spring of water welling up to eternal life" (Jn 4:13 – 14).

two portions for Joseph. 14 You are to divide it equally among them. Because I
swore with uplifted hand to give it to your ancestors, this land will become your
inheritance.

15 “This is to be the boundary of the land:

“On the north side it will run from the Mediterranean Sea by the Hethlon road
past Lebo Hamath to Zedad, 16 Berothah[a] and Sibraim (which lies on the
border between Damascus and Hamath), as far as Hazer Hattikon, which
is on the border of Hauran. 17 The boundary will extend from the sea to
Hazar Enan,[b] along the northern border of Damascus, with the border of
Hamath to the north. This will be the northern boundary.

18 “On the east side the boundary will run between Hauran and Damascus,
along the Jordan between Gilead and the land of Israel, to the Dead Sea
and as far as Tamar.[c] This will be the eastern boundary.

19 “On the south side it will run from Tamar as far as the waters of Meribah Kadesh, then along the Wadi of Egypt to the Mediterranean Sea. This will be
the southern boundary.

20 “On the west side, the Mediterranean Sea will be the boundary to a point opposite Lebo Hamath. This will be the western boundary.

21 “You are to distribute this land among yourselves according to the tribes of
Israel. 22 You are to allot it as an inheritance for yourselves and for the foreigners
residing among you and who have children. You are to consider them as native-
born Israelites; along with you they are to be allotted an inheritance among the
tribes of Israel. 23 In whatever tribe a foreigner resides, there you are to give them
their inheritance,” declares the Sovereign LORD.

The Division of the Land

48 “These are the tribes, listed by name: At the northern frontier, Dan will
have one portion; it will follow the Hethlon road to Lebo Hamath; Hazar
Enan and the northern border of Damascus next to Hamath will be part of its
border from the east side to the west side.

2 “Asher will have one portion; it will border the territory of Dan from east to
west.

3 “Naphtali will have one portion; it will border the territory of Asher from east
to west.

4 “Manasseh will have one portion; it will border the territory of Naphtali from
east to west.

5 “Ephraim will have one portion; it will border the territory of Manasseh from
east to west.

6 “Reuben will have one portion; it will border the territory of Ephraim from
east to west.

7 “Judah will have one portion; it will border the territory of Reuben from east
to west.

8 “Bordering the territory of Judah from east to west will be the portion you
are to present as a special gift. It will be 25,000 cubits[d] wide, and its length from
east to west will equal one of the tribal portions; the sanctuary will be in the
center of it.

9 “The special portion you are to offer to the LORD will be 25,000 cubits long
and 10,000 cubits[e] wide. 10 This will be the sacred portion for the priests. It will be
25,000 cubits long on the north side, 10,000 cubits wide on the west side, 10,000
cubits wide on the east side and 25,000 cubits long on the south side. In the
center of it will be the sanctuary of the LORD. 11 This will be for the consecrated

[a] *15,16* See Septuagint and 48:1; Hebrew *road to go into Zedad, 16 Hamath, Berothah.*
[b] *17* Hebrew *Enon,* a variant of *Enan* [c] *18* See Syriac; Hebrew *Israel. You will measure to the Dead Sea.* [d] *8* That is, about 8 miles or about 13 kilometers; also in verses 9, 10, 13, 15, 20 and 21 [e] *9* That is, about 3 1/3 miles or about 5.3 kilometers; also in verses 10, 13 and 18

priests, the Zadokites, who were faithful in serving me and did not go astray as the Levites did when the Israelites went astray. 12It will be a special gift to them from the sacred portion of the land, a most holy portion, bordering the territory of the Levites.

13"Alongside the territory of the priests, the Levites will have an allotment 25,000 cubits long and 10,000 cubits wide. Its total length will be 25,000 cubits and its width 10,000 cubits. 14They must not sell or exchange any of it. This is the best of the land and must not pass into other hands, because it is holy to the LORD.

15"The remaining area, 5,000 cubits[a] wide and 25,000 cubits long, will be for the common use of the city, for houses and for pastureland. The city will be in the center of it 16and will have these measurements: the north side 4,500 cubits,[b] the south side 4,500 cubits, the east side 4,500 cubits, and the west side 4,500 cubits. 17The pastureland for the city will be 250 cubits[c] on the north, 250 cubits on the south, 250 cubits on the east, and 250 cubits on the west. 18What remains of the area, bordering on the sacred portion and running the length of it, will be 10,000 cubits on the east side and 10,000 cubits on the west side. Its produce will supply food for the workers of the city. 19The workers from the city who farm it will come from all the tribes of Israel. 20The entire portion will be a square, 25,000 cubits on each side. As a special gift you will set aside the sacred portion, along with the property of the city.

21"What remains on both sides of the area formed by the sacred portion and the property of the city will belong to the prince. It will extend eastward from the 25,000 cubits of the sacred portion to the eastern border, and westward from the 25,000 cubits to the western border. Both these areas running the length of the tribal portions will belong to the prince, and the sacred portion with the temple sanctuary will be in the center of them. 22So the property of the Levites and the property of the city will lie in the center of the area that belongs to the prince. The area belonging to the prince will lie between the border of Judah and the border of Benjamin.

23"As for the rest of the tribes: Benjamin will have one portion; it will extend from the east side to the west side.

24"Simeon will have one portion; it will border the territory of Benjamin from east to west.

25"Issachar will have one portion; it will border the territory of Simeon from east to west.

26"Zebulun will have one portion; it will border the territory of Issachar from east to west.

27"Gad will have one portion; it will border the territory of Zebulun from east to west.

28"The southern boundary of Gad will run south from Tamar to the waters of Meribah Kadesh, then along the Wadi of Egypt to the Mediterranean Sea.

29"This is the land you are to allot as an inheritance to the tribes of Israel, and these will be their portions," declares the Sovereign LORD.

The Gates of the New City

30"These will be the exits of the city: Beginning on the north side, which is 4,500 cubits long, 31the gates of the city will be named after the tribes of Israel. The three gates on the north side will be the gate of Reuben, the gate of Judah and the gate of Levi.

32"On the east side, which is 4,500 cubits long, will be three gates: the gate of Joseph, the gate of Benjamin and the gate of Dan.

33"On the south side, which measures 4,500 cubits, will be three gates: the gate of Simeon, the gate of Issachar and the gate of Zebulun.

EZEKIEL 48:30–35

THE GATES OF THE CITY

From the very beginning, God's plan has been to have a pure and permanent relationship with his people. Ezekiel's final vision is one of the city in which this will happen, and the name of the city is literally "THE LORD IS THERE." The prophet saw 12 gates surrounding the city, representing the 12 tribes of Israel. The apostle John later saw similar gates in his vision of the new Jerusalem (Rev 21:12–14). Both visions foreshadow the physical presence of the Lord in the future, perfect city where God and his people will live in eternal harmony.

Revelation 21:3 summarizes this theme wonderfully, "And I heard a loud voice from the throne saying, 'Look! God's dwelling place is now among the people, and he will dwell with them. They will be his people, and God himself will be with them and be their God.'" God has always desired a permanent relationship with his people, and God will have it. Jesus Christ made that relationship with God possible by dying on the cross to remove the sin barrier that separated people from God (Eph 2:13–14). Jesus then secured the presence of God for his people by rising from the dead to bring his people to God (1Pe 3:18).

[a] *15* That is, about 1 2/3 miles or about 2.7 kilometers [b] *16* That is, about 1 1/2 miles or about 2.4 kilometers; also in verses 30, 32, 33 and 34 [c] *17* That is, about 440 feet or about 135 meters

[34]"On the west side, which is 4,500 cubits long, will be three gates: the gate of
Gad, the gate of Asher and the gate of Naphtali.
[35]"The distance all around will be 18,000 cubits.[a]
"And the name of the city from that time on will be:

THE LORD IS THERE."

[a] 35 That is, about 6 miles or about 9.5 kilometers

JESUS: OUR GREAT KING

DANIEL

DANIEL

DANIEL EXILED TO BABYLON *c. 605 BC*	BABYLONIANS DESTROY JERUSALEM *c. 586 BC*	DECREE OF CYRUS ALLOWING JEWS TO RETURN *c. 538 BC*

The book of Daniel is a unique combination of two types of literature: first, it presents a historical narrative about the people of God in exile in Babylon; second, it details prophetic visions of the coming rule and reign of God. Daniel, a Jewish exile in Babylon, provided an insider's perspective on the plight of God's people during this critical stage in God's mission. As a well-educated Jew and advisor to the Babylonian king Nebuchadnezzar, God used Daniel to model faithfulness in a pagan culture and to testify to God's faithfulness in a time of judgment.

Later, through his influential relationship with the Persian king Cyrus, Daniel was in another unique position. Cyrus had defeated the Babylonians and enacted a number of new policies — one of which was to allow exiled peoples to return to their homelands. Under Cyrus, the Jews returned to their homeland as well to rebuild their capital city and their temple. Perhaps God used Daniel to influence the king so that God's people could return to the promised land and seek to rebuild their life under leaders such as Zerubbabel, Haggai and Zechariah initially, and later Nehemiah and Ezra.

In his writings, Daniel reminded God's people of two main themes. First, God is in control of all things — even mighty pagan nations are pawns in God's hand. God had used these nations to judge his people, and whenever and however he wanted to, God could restore the fortunes of his people. In due time, God would destroy the other nations; Daniel pictured a coming day when the Babylonian and Persian Empires, as well as others in the distant future, would come to an end. History would continue to see empires rise and fall, all according to God's will and under his control.

Second, Daniel reminded the people that God was faithful and would not forget them. Though they would suffer under these empires for a lengthy period, their time under punishment would one day come to a close. God would preserve his people despite the exile, and reestablish them at the time of his choosing.

With Daniel's encouragement, the hope of God's people rested on the fact that God is a great king and is far more powerful than any kingdom of this earth. In Jesus, God will usher in his divine kingdom on earth and invite anyone who will trust in him into the realm of his benevolent rule and reign. In his eternal kingdom, peace will reign forever.

IN THE TIME OF THOSE KINGS, THE GOD OF HEAVEN WILL SET UP A KINGDOM THAT WILL NEVER BE DESTROYED, NOR WILL IT BE LEFT TO ANOTHER PEOPLE. IT WILL CRUSH ALL THOSE KINGDOMS AND BRING THEM TO AN END, BUT IT WILL ITSELF ENDURE FOREVER.

Daniel 2:44

DANIEL

Daniel's Training in Babylon

1 In the third year of the reign of Jehoiakim king of Judah, Nebuchadnezzar king of Babylon came to Jerusalem and besieged it. 2And the Lord delivered Jehoiakim king of Judah into his hand, along with some of the articles from the temple of God. These he carried off to the temple of his god in Babylonia[a] and put in the treasure house of his god.

3Then the king ordered Ashpenaz, chief of his court officials, to bring into the king's service some of the Israelites from the royal family and the nobility—4young men without any physical defect, handsome, showing aptitude for every kind of learning, well informed, quick to understand, and qualified to serve in the king's palace. He was to teach them the language and literature of the Babylonians.[b] 5The king assigned them a daily amount of food and wine from the king's table. They were to be trained for three years, and after that they were to enter the king's service.

6Among those who were chosen were some from Judah: Daniel, Hananiah, Mishael and Azariah. 7The chief official gave them new names: to Daniel, the name Belteshazzar; to Hananiah, Shadrach; to Mishael, Meshach; and to Azariah, Abednego.

8But Daniel resolved not to defile himself with the royal food and wine, and he asked the chief official for permission not to defile himself this way. 9Now God had caused the official to show favor and compassion to Daniel, 10but the official told Daniel, "I am afraid of my lord the king, who has assigned your[c] food and drink. Why should he see you looking worse than the other young men your age? The king would then have my head because of you."

11Daniel then said to the guard whom the chief official had appointed over Daniel, Hananiah, Mishael and Azariah, 12"Please test your servants for ten days: Give us nothing but vegetables to eat and water to drink. 13Then compare our appearance with that of the young men who eat the royal food, and treat your servants in accordance with what you see." 14So he agreed to this and tested them for ten days.

15At the end of the ten days they looked healthier and better nourished than any of the young men who ate the royal food. 16So the guard took away their choice food and the wine they were to drink and gave them vegetables instead.

17To these four young men God gave knowledge and understanding of all kinds of literature and learning. And Daniel could understand visions and dreams of all kinds.

18At the end of the time set by the king to bring them into his service, the chief official presented them to Nebuchadnezzar. 19The king talked with them, and he found none equal to Daniel, Hananiah, Mishael and Azariah; so they entered the king's service. 20In every matter of wisdom and understanding about which the king questioned them, he found them ten times better than all the magicians and enchanters in his whole kingdom.

21And Daniel remained there until the first year of King Cyrus.

Nebuchadnezzar's Dream

2 In the second year of his reign, Nebuchadnezzar had dreams; his mind was troubled and he could not sleep. 2So the king summoned the magicians, enchanters, sorcerers and astrologers[d] to tell him what he had dreamed. When

---

[a] *2* Hebrew *Shinar* [b] *4* Or *Chaldeans* [c] *10* The Hebrew for *your* and *you* in this verse is plural. [d] *2* Or *Chaldeans*; also in verses 4, 5 and 10

they came in and stood before the king, 3he said to them, "I have had a dream
that troubles me and I want to know what it means.[a]"
4Then the astrologers answered the king,[b] "May the king live forever! Tell your
servants the dream, and we will interpret it."
5The king replied to the astrologers, "This is what I have firmly decided: If you
do not tell me what my dream was and interpret it, I will have you cut into pieces
and your houses turned into piles of rubble. 6But if you tell me the dream and
explain it, you will receive from me gifts and rewards and great honor. So tell me
the dream and interpret it for me."
7Once more they replied, "Let the king tell his servants the dream, and we
will interpret it."
8Then the king answered, "I am certain that you are trying to gain time, because you realize that this is what I have firmly decided: 9If you do not tell me
the dream, there is only one penalty for you. You have conspired to tell me misleading and wicked things, hoping the situation will change. So then, tell me the
dream, and I will know that you can interpret it for me."
10The astrologers answered the king, "There is no one on earth who can do what
the king asks! No king, however great and mighty, has ever asked such a thing of
any magician or enchanter or astrologer. 11What the king asks is too difficult. No
one can reveal it to the king except the gods, and they do not live among humans."
12This made the king so angry and furious that he ordered the execution of
all the wise men of Babylon. 13So the decree was issued to put the wise men to
death, and men were sent to look for Daniel and his friends to put them to death.
14When Arioch, the commander of the king's guard, had gone out to put to
death the wise men of Babylon, Daniel spoke to him with wisdom and tact. 15He
asked the king's officer, "Why did the king issue such a harsh decree?" Arioch
then explained the matter to Daniel. 16At this, Daniel went in to the king and
asked for time, so that he might interpret the dream for him.
17Then Daniel returned to his house and explained the matter to his friends
Hananiah, Mishael and Azariah. 18He urged them to plead for mercy from the God
of heaven concerning this mystery, so that he and his friends might not be executed with the rest of the wise men of Babylon. 19During the night the mystery was
revealed to Daniel in a vision. Then Daniel praised the God of heaven 20and said:

"Praise be to the name of God for ever and ever;
wisdom and power are his.
21 He changes times and seasons;
he deposes kings and raises up others.
He gives wisdom to the wise
and knowledge to the discerning.
22 He reveals deep and hidden things;
he knows what lies in darkness,
and light dwells with him.
23 I thank and praise you, God of my ancestors:
You have given me wisdom and power,
you have made known to me what we asked of you,
you have made known to us the dream of the king."

Daniel Interprets the Dream

24Then Daniel went to Arioch, whom the king had appointed to execute the
wise men of Babylon, and said to him, "Do not execute the wise men of Babylon.
Take me to the king, and I will interpret his dream for him."
25Arioch took Daniel to the king at once and said, "I have found a man among
the exiles from Judah who can tell the king what his dream means."
26The king asked Daniel (also called Belteshazzar), "Are you able to tell me
what I saw in my dream and interpret it?"

---

[a] 3 Or *was* [b] 4 At this point the Hebrew text has *in Aramaic*, indicating that the text from
here through the end of chapter 7 is in Aramaic.

[27]Daniel replied, "No wise man, enchanter, magician or diviner can explain to the king the mystery he has asked about, [28]but there is a God in heaven who reveals mysteries. He has shown King Nebuchadnezzar what will happen in days to come. Your dream and the visions that passed through your mind as you were lying in bed are these:

[29]"As Your Majesty was lying there, your mind turned to things to come, and the revealer of mysteries showed you what is going to happen. [30]As for me, this mystery has been revealed to me, not because I have greater wisdom than anyone else alive, but so that Your Majesty may know the interpretation and that you may understand what went through your mind.

[31]"Your Majesty looked, and there before you stood a large statue — an enormous, dazzling statue, awesome in appearance. [32]The head of the statue was made of pure gold, its chest and arms of silver, its belly and thighs of bronze, [33]its legs of iron, its feet partly of iron and partly of baked clay. [34]While you were watching, a rock was cut out, but not by human hands. It struck the statue on its feet of iron and clay and smashed them. [35]Then the iron, the clay, the bronze, the silver and the gold were all broken to pieces and became like chaff on a threshing floor in the summer. The wind swept them away without leaving a trace. But the rock that struck the statue became a huge mountain and filled the whole earth.

[36]"This was the dream, and now we will interpret it to the king. [37]Your Majesty, you are the king of kings. The God of heaven has given you dominion and power and might and glory; [38]in your hands he has placed all mankind and the beasts of the field and the birds in the sky. Wherever they live, he has made you ruler over them all. You are that head of gold.

[39]"After you, another kingdom will arise, inferior to yours. Next, a third kingdom, one of bronze, will rule over the whole earth. [40]Finally, there will be a fourth kingdom, strong as iron — for iron breaks and smashes everything — and as iron breaks things to pieces, so it will crush and break all the others. [41]Just as you saw that the feet and toes were partly of baked clay and partly of iron, so this will be a divided kingdom; yet it will have some of the strength of iron in it, even as you saw iron mixed with clay. [42]As the toes were partly iron and partly clay, so this kingdom will be partly strong and partly brittle. [43]And just as you saw the iron mixed with baked clay, so the people will be a mixture and will not remain united, any more than iron mixes with clay.

[44]"In the time of those kings, the God of heaven will set up a kingdom that will never be destroyed, nor will it be left to another people. It will crush all those kingdoms and bring them to an end, but it will itself endure forever. [45]This is the meaning of the vision of the rock cut out of a mountain, but not by human hands — a rock that broke the iron, the bronze, the clay, the silver and the gold to pieces.

"The great God has shown the king what will take place in the future. The dream is true and its interpretation is trustworthy."

[46]Then King Nebuchadnezzar fell prostrate before Daniel and paid him honor and ordered that an offering and incense be presented to him. [47]The king said to Daniel, "Surely your God is the God of gods and the Lord of kings and a revealer of mysteries, for you were able to reveal this mystery."

[48]Then the king placed Daniel in a high position and lavished many gifts on him. He made him ruler over the entire province of Babylon and placed him in charge of all its wise men. [49]Moreover, at Daniel's request the king appointed Shadrach, Meshach and Abednego administrators over the province of Babylon, while Daniel himself remained at the royal court.

DANIEL 2:44–45

THE STONE

Daniel interpreted King Nebuchadnezzar's dream about the giant statue (Da 2:31–32). The dream showed what would take place in the future, and Daniel explained that the statue stood for four kingdoms which would succeed one another. Daniel 7 describes another vision that parallels this one. Daniel explains the main point of Nebuchadnezzar's dream: the kingdoms of the world would fall, and the kingdom of God would topple them as God would establish his eternal kingdom.

This vision would have been unthinkable in Daniel's day. The kingdoms of this earth were vast. Surely these kingdoms would stand forever. Yet, God promised that these kingdoms would come to an end. The image of a stone is later used by the apostle Paul to describe the person and work of Jesus (Eph 2:20). He is the cornerstone the builders rejected but is the means by which God will establish his kingdom forever. He has been given the throne of David (Lk 1:32). Jesus taught about the kingdom of God — how the kingdom would start small and seemingly insignificant but grow like the rock of Daniel 2:34–35 (Mt 13:31–32). And Revelation 11:15 promises that the kingdom of the world will "become the kingdom of our Lord and of his Messiah, and he will reign for ever and ever."

The Image of Gold and the Blazing Furnace

3 King Nebuchadnezzar made an image of gold, sixty cubits high and six cubits wide,[a] and set it up on the plain of Dura in the province of Babylon. [2]He then summoned the satraps, prefects, governors, advisers, treasurers, judges,

[a] *1* That is, about 90 feet high and 9 feet wide or about 27 meters high and 2.7 meters wide

magistrates and all the other provincial officials to come to the dedication of
the image he had set up. 3So the satraps, prefects, governors, advisers, treasurers, judges, magistrates and all the other provincial officials assembled for the
dedication of the image that King Nebuchadnezzar had set up, and they stood
before it.
4Then the herald loudly proclaimed, "Nations and peoples of every language,
this is what you are commanded to do: 5As soon as you hear the sound of the
horn, flute, zither, lyre, harp, pipe and all kinds of music, you must fall down and
worship the image of gold that King Nebuchadnezzar has set up. 6Whoever does
not fall down and worship will immediately be thrown into a blazing furnace."
7Therefore, as soon as they heard the sound of the horn, flute, zither, lyre,
harp and all kinds of music, all the nations and peoples of every language fell
down and worshiped the image of gold that King Nebuchadnezzar had set up.
8At this time some astrologers[a] came forward and denounced the Jews. 9They
said to King Nebuchadnezzar, "May the king live forever! 10Your Majesty has issued a decree that everyone who hears the sound of the horn, flute, zither, lyre,
harp, pipe and all kinds of music must fall down and worship the image of gold,
11and that whoever does not fall down and worship will be thrown into a blazing furnace. 12But there are some Jews whom you have set over the affairs of the
province of Babylon — Shadrach, Meshach and Abednego — who pay no attention to you, Your Majesty. They neither serve your gods nor worship the image
of gold you have set up."
13Furious with rage, Nebuchadnezzar summoned Shadrach, Meshach and
Abednego. So these men were brought before the king, 14and Nebuchadnezzar
said to them, "Is it true, Shadrach, Meshach and Abednego, that you do not serve
my gods or worship the image of gold I have set up? 15Now when you hear the
sound of the horn, flute, zither, lyre, harp, pipe and all kinds of music, if you are
ready to fall down and worship the image I made, very good. But if you do not
worship it, you will be thrown immediately into a blazing furnace. Then what
god will be able to rescue you from my hand?"
16Shadrach, Meshach and Abednego replied to him, "King Nebuchadnezzar,
we do not need to defend ourselves before you in this matter. 17If we are thrown
into the blazing furnace, the God we serve is able to deliver us from it, and he
will deliver us[b] from Your Majesty's hand. 18But even if he does not, we want you
to know, Your Majesty, that we will not serve your gods or worship the image of
gold you have set up."
19Then Nebuchadnezzar was furious with Shadrach, Meshach and Abednego, and his attitude toward them changed. He ordered the furnace heated sev-
en times hotter than usual 20and commanded some of the strongest soldiers in
his army to tie up Shadrach, Meshach and Abednego and throw them into the
blazing furnace. 21So these men, wearing their robes, trousers, turbans and other clothes, were bound and thrown into the blazing furnace. 22The king's command was so urgent and the furnace so hot that the flames of the fire killed the
soldiers who took up Shadrach, Meshach and Abednego, 23and these three men,
firmly tied, fell into the blazing furnace.
24Then King Nebuchadnezzar leaped to his feet in amazement and asked his
advisers, "Weren't there three men that we tied up and threw into the fire?"
They replied, "Certainly, Your Majesty."
25He said, "Look! I see four men walking around in the fire, unbound and unharmed, and the fourth looks like a son of the gods."
26Nebuchadnezzar then approached the opening of the blazing furnace and
shouted, "Shadrach, Meshach and Abednego, servants of the Most High God,
come out! Come here!"
So Shadrach, Meshach and Abednego came out of the fire, 27and the satraps,

---

[a] 8 Or *Chaldeans* [b] 17 Or *If the God we serve is able to deliver us, then he will deliver us from the blazing furnace and*

THE NEW EXODUS AND GREAT COMMISSION

Shadrach, Meshach and Abednego trusted in the Lord and refused to bow down to the statue King Nebuchadnezzar made. As a result, the king had them thrown into a blazing furnace. It is important to remember the context for this event. The Babylonian exile was not the first time that God's people had been captives in a foreign country. They had been slaves in Egypt, and God miraculously brought them out. Deuteronomy 4:20 describes the exodus in this way: "But as for you, the LORD took you and brought you out of the iron-smelting furnace, out of Egypt, to be the people of his inheritance, as you now are." God had rescued his people from a powerful empire and a fiery furnace before, and in Daniel 3 he did it again, which is exactly what these three Hebrews trusted God could do. Amazingly, when the men were thrown into the furnace, the king saw four men instead of three, and the additional man looked like "a son of the gods." Some believe this fourth figure was an angel, while others believe it was a pre-incarnate appearance of Jesus, the second person of the Trinity. Regardless of the exact nature of this person, the words of the prophet Isaiah ring true: "When you pass through the waters, I will be with you ... When you walk through the fire, you will not be burned; the flames will not set you ablaze" (Isa 43:2).

After seeing the men walk out of the furnace unharmed, King Nebuchadnezzar exclaimed that no other god is able to save like this, and that was a true statement. There is no other god who walks through the fire *with* his people. God, through Jesus Christ, took on the suffering and death of his people at the cross to rescue them, ultimately, from suffering and death. Like these three Hebrews, Jesus was held captive under a pagan world empire, Rome. He was handed over to die, and then he emerged from death three days later.

When Jesus emerged from his death, he commissioned his disciples to take the gospel to the ends of the earth because his blood was spilled to redeem people for God from every tribe, language, people and nation (Rev 5:9; 7:9). In Daniel 3, the pagan king praised the Hebrews' God and prohibited the people of any nation or language from speaking against him. God's deliverance and his message of salvation are always meant to be declared among all nations.

prefects, governors and royal advisers crowded around them. They saw that the fire had not harmed their bodies, nor was a hair of their heads singed; their robes were not scorched, and there was no smell of fire on them.

28 Then Nebuchadnezzar said, "Praise be to the God of Shadrach, Meshach and Abednego, who has sent his angel and rescued his servants! They trusted in him and defied the king's command and were willing to give up their lives rather than serve or worship any god except their own God. 29 Therefore I decree that the people of any nation or language who say anything against the God of Shadrach, Meshach and Abednego be cut into pieces and their houses be turned into piles of rubble, for no other god can save in this way."

30 Then the king promoted Shadrach, Meshach and Abednego in the province of Babylon.

Nebuchadnezzar's Dream of a Tree

4 [a] King Nebuchadnezzar,

To the nations and peoples of every language, who live in all the earth:

May you prosper greatly!

2 It is my pleasure to tell you about the miraculous signs and wonders that the Most High God has performed for me.

3 How great are his signs,
how mighty his wonders!
His kingdom is an eternal kingdom;
his dominion endures from generation to generation.

4 I, Nebuchadnezzar, was at home in my palace, contented and prosperous. 5 I had a dream that made me afraid. As I was lying in bed, the images and visions that passed through my mind terrified me. 6 So I commanded that all the wise men of Babylon be brought before me to interpret the dream for me. 7 When the magicians, enchanters, astrologers[b] and diviners came, I told them the dream, but they could not interpret it for me. 8 Finally, Daniel came into my presence and I told him the dream. (He is called Belteshazzar, after the name of my god, and the spirit of the holy gods is in him.)

9 I said, "Belteshazzar, chief of the magicians, I know that the spirit of the holy gods is in you, and no mystery is too difficult for you. Here is my dream; interpret it for me. 10 These are the visions I saw while lying in bed: I looked, and there before me stood a tree in the middle of the land. Its height was enormous. 11 The tree grew large and strong and its top touched the sky; it was visible to the ends of the earth. 12 Its leaves were beautiful, its fruit abundant, and on it was food for all. Under it the wild animals found shelter, and the birds lived in its branches; from it every creature was fed.

13 "In the visions I saw while lying in bed, I looked, and there before me was a holy one, a messenger,[c] coming down from heaven. 14 He called in a loud voice: 'Cut down the tree and trim off its branches; strip off its leaves and scatter its fruit. Let the animals flee from under it and the birds from its branches. 15 But let the stump and its roots, bound with iron and bronze, remain in the ground, in the grass of the field.

" 'Let him be drenched with the dew of heaven, and let him live with the animals among the plants of the earth. 16 Let his mind be changed from that of a man and let him be given the mind of an animal, till seven times[d] pass by for him.

17 " 'The decision is announced by messengers, the holy ones declare the

[a] In Aramaic texts 4:1-3 is numbered 3:31-33, and 4:4-37 is numbered 4:1-34. [b] *7* Or *Chaldeans* [c] *13* Or *watchman*; also in verses 17 and 23 [d] *16* Or *years*; also in verses 23, 25 and 32

DANIEL 4:17

GOD IS SOVEREIGN

King Nebuchadnezzar had a dream about a tree that grew and provided food and protection for the whole earth. It was cut down, but the roots were preserved for the future. Inspired by God, Daniel interpreted the dream as being about the king himself. In essence, Daniel says that because of King Nebuchadnezzar's pride in his kingdom and his accomplishments, God would humble him to show that God alone gives power and takes it away. In this act God would show that his kingdom reigns supreme over all. The dream came true when the most powerful man on earth began to crawl on the ground and eat grass like an ox.

Ultimately God determines who is or isn't in positions of authority and influence. The vision of Daniel 7 continued the point that God made here in Daniel 4. The powerful empires of the world (represented by four beasts) would eventually fall, and "one like a son of man" (referring to the Messiah, Jesus) would be given an eternal kingdom (Da 7:13–14). Who is this "one like a son of man"? He is the One who humbled himself and then was exalted (Php 2:8–9). He is the One who receives and transforms the kingdom of the world (Rev 11:15). Daniel 4 encouraged God's people that eventually he would flip the tables on the world's kingdom and establish his kingdom. This promise was spoken after the fall (Ge 3:15) and began through the choice of Israel as God's people; it blossomed in the person and work of Jesus Christ and will ultimately be fulfilled in the future — in God's perfect timing (1Th 5:2).

verdict, so that the living may know that the Most High is sovereign over
all kingdoms on earth and gives them to anyone he wishes and sets over
them the lowliest of people.'

18"This is the dream that I, King Nebuchadnezzar, had. Now, Belteshazzar, tell me what it means, for none of the wise men in my kingdom can
interpret it for me. But you can, because the spirit of the holy gods is in you."

Daniel Interprets the Dream

19Then Daniel (also called Belteshazzar) was greatly perplexed for a
time, and his thoughts terrified him. So the king said, "Belteshazzar, do
not let the dream or its meaning alarm you."

Belteshazzar answered, "My lord, if only the dream applied to your enemies and its meaning to your adversaries! 20The tree you saw, which grew
large and strong, with its top touching the sky, visible to the whole earth,
21with beautiful leaves and abundant fruit, providing food for all, giving
shelter to the wild animals, and having nesting places in its branches for
the birds — 22Your Majesty, you are that tree! You have become great and
strong; your greatness has grown until it reaches the sky, and your dominion extends to distant parts of the earth.

23"Your Majesty saw a holy one, a messenger, coming down from heaven
and saying, 'Cut down the tree and destroy it, but leave the stump, bound
with iron and bronze, in the grass of the field, while its roots remain in the
ground. Let him be drenched with the dew of heaven; let him live with the
wild animals, until seven times pass by for him.'

24"This is the interpretation, Your Majesty, and this is the decree the
Most High has issued against my lord the king: 25You will be driven away
from people and will live with the wild animals; you will eat grass like the
ox and be drenched with the dew of heaven. Seven times will pass by for
you until you acknowledge that the Most High is sovereign over all kingdoms on earth and gives them to anyone he wishes. 26The command to
leave the stump of the tree with its roots means that your kingdom will
be restored to you when you acknowledge that Heaven rules. 27Therefore,
Your Majesty, be pleased to accept my advice: Renounce your sins by doing
what is right, and your wickedness by being kind to the oppressed. It may
be that then your prosperity will continue."

The Dream Is Fulfilled

28All this happened to King Nebuchadnezzar. 29Twelve months later,
as the king was walking on the roof of the royal palace of Babylon, 30he
said, "Is not this the great Babylon I have built as the royal residence, by my
mighty power and for the glory of my majesty?"

31Even as the words were on his lips, a voice came from heaven, "This is
what is decreed for you, King Nebuchadnezzar: Your royal authority has
been taken from you. 32You will be driven away from people and will live
with the wild animals; you will eat grass like the ox. Seven times will pass
by for you until you acknowledge that the Most High is sovereign over all
kingdoms on earth and gives them to anyone he wishes."

33Immediately what had been said about Nebuchadnezzar was fulfilled.
He was driven away from people and ate grass like the ox. His body was
drenched with the dew of heaven until his hair grew like the feathers of an
eagle and his nails like the claws of a bird.

34At the end of that time, I, Nebuchadnezzar, raised my eyes toward
heaven, and my sanity was restored. Then I praised the Most High; I honored and glorified him who lives forever.

His dominion is an eternal dominion;
his kingdom endures from generation to generation.

[35]All the peoples of the earth
are regarded as nothing.
He does as he pleases
with the powers of heaven
and the peoples of the earth.
No one can hold back his hand
or say to him: "What have you done?"

[36]At the same time that my sanity was restored, my honor and splendor were returned to me for the glory of my kingdom. My advisers and nobles sought me out, and I was restored to my throne and became even greater than before. [37]Now I, Nebuchadnezzar, praise and exalt and glorify the King of heaven, because everything he does is right and all his ways are just. And those who walk in pride he is able to humble.

The Writing on the Wall

5 King Belshazzar gave a great banquet for a thousand of his nobles and drank wine with them. [2]While Belshazzar was drinking his wine, he gave orders to bring in the gold and silver goblets that Nebuchadnezzar his father[a] had taken from the temple in Jerusalem, so that the king and his nobles, his wives and his concubines might drink from them. [3]So they brought in the gold goblets that had been taken from the temple of God in Jerusalem, and the king and his nobles, his wives and his concubines drank from them. [4]As they drank the wine, they praised the gods of gold and silver, of bronze, iron, wood and stone.

[5]Suddenly the fingers of a human hand appeared and wrote on the plaster of the wall, near the lampstand in the royal palace. The king watched the hand as it wrote. [6]His face turned pale and he was so frightened that his legs became weak and his knees were knocking.

[7]The king summoned the enchanters, astrologers[b] and diviners. Then he said to these wise men of Babylon, "Whoever reads this writing and tells me what it means will be clothed in purple and have a gold chain placed around his neck, and he will be made the third highest ruler in the kingdom."

[8]Then all the king's wise men came in, but they could not read the writing or tell the king what it meant. [9]So King Belshazzar became even more terrified and his face grew more pale. His nobles were baffled.

[10]The queen,[c] hearing the voices of the king and his nobles, came into the banquet hall. "May the king live forever!" she said. "Don't be alarmed! Don't look so pale! [11]There is a man in your kingdom who has the spirit of the holy gods in him. In the time of your father he was found to have insight and intelligence and wisdom like that of the gods. Your father, King Nebuchadnezzar, appointed him chief of the magicians, enchanters, astrologers and diviners. [12]He did this because Daniel, whom the king called Belteshazzar, was found to have a keen mind and knowledge and understanding, and also the ability to interpret dreams, explain riddles and solve difficult problems. Call for Daniel, and he will tell you what the writing means."

[13]So Daniel was brought before the king, and the king said to him, "Are you Daniel, one of the exiles my father the king brought from Judah? [14]I have heard that the spirit of the gods is in you and that you have insight, intelligence and outstanding wisdom. [15]The wise men and enchanters were brought before me to read this writing and tell me what it means, but they could not explain it. [16]Now I have heard that you are able to give interpretations and to solve difficult problems. If you can read this writing and tell me what it means, you will be clothed in purple and have a gold chain placed around your neck, and you will be made the third highest ruler in the kingdom."

[17]Then Daniel answered the king, "You may keep your gifts for yourself and

---

[a] *2* Or *ancestor*; or *predecessor*; also in verses 11, 13 and 18 [b] *7* Or *Chaldeans*; also in verse 11 [c] *10* Or *queen mother*

give your rewards to someone else. Nevertheless, I will read the writing for the
king and tell him what it means.
[18]"Your Majesty, the Most High God gave your father Nebuchadnezzar sovereignty and greatness and glory and splendor. [19]Because of the high position
he gave him, all the nations and peoples of every language dreaded and feared
him. Those the king wanted to put to death, he put to death; those he wanted to
spare, he spared; those he wanted to promote, he promoted; and those he wanted to humble, he humbled. [20]But when his heart became arrogant and hardened
with pride, he was deposed from his royal throne and stripped of his glory. [21]He
was driven away from people and given the mind of an animal; he lived with the
wild donkeys and ate grass like the ox; and his body was drenched with the dew
of heaven, until he acknowledged that the Most High God is sovereign over all
kingdoms on earth and sets over them anyone he wishes.
[22]"But you, Belshazzar, his son,[a] have not humbled yourself, though you knew
all this. [23]Instead, you have set yourself up against the Lord of heaven. You had
the goblets from his temple brought to you, and you and your nobles, your wives
and your concubines drank wine from them. You praised the gods of silver and
gold, of bronze, iron, wood and stone, which cannot see or hear or understand.
But you did not honor the God who holds in his hand your life and all your ways.
[24]Therefore he sent the hand that wrote the inscription.
[25]"This is the inscription that was written:

MENE, MENE, TEKEL, PARSIN

[26]"Here is what these words mean:

Mene[b]: God has numbered the days of your reign and brought it to an end.

[27] *Tekel*[c]: You have been weighed on the scales and found wanting.

[28] *Peres*[d]: Your kingdom is divided and given to the Medes and Persians."

[29]Then at Belshazzar's command, Daniel was clothed in purple, a gold chain
was placed around his neck, and he was proclaimed the third highest ruler in
the kingdom.
[30]That very night Belshazzar, king of the Babylonians,[e] was slain, [31]and Darius the Mede took over the kingdom, at the age of sixty-two.[f]

Daniel in the Den of Lions

6[g] It pleased Darius to appoint 120 satraps to rule throughout the kingdom,
[2]with three administrators over them, one of whom was Daniel. The satraps
were made accountable to them so that the king might not suffer loss. [3]Now Daniel so distinguished himself among the administrators and the satraps by his
exceptional qualities that the king planned to set him over the whole kingdom.
[4]At this, the administrators and the satraps tried to find grounds for charges
against Daniel in his conduct of government affairs, but they were unable to
do so. They could find no corruption in him, because he was trustworthy and
neither corrupt nor negligent. [5]Finally these men said, "We will never find any
basis for charges against this man Daniel unless it has something to do with the
law of his God."
[6]So these administrators and satraps went as a group to the king and said:
"May King Darius live forever! [7]The royal administrators, prefects, satraps, advisers and governors have all agreed that the king should issue an edict and enforce the decree that anyone who prays to any god or human being during the
next thirty days, except to you, Your Majesty, shall be thrown into the lions' den.

---

[a] 22 Or *descendant*; or *successor* [b] 26 *Mene* can mean *numbered* or *mina* (a unit of money). [c] 27 *Tekel* can mean *weighed* or *shekel*. [d] 28 *Peres* (the singular of *Parsin*) can mean *divided* or *Persia* or *a half mina* or *a half shekel*. [e] 30 Or *Chaldeans* [f] 31 In Aramaic texts this verse (5:31) is numbered 6:1. [g] In Aramaic texts 6:1-28 is numbered 6:2-29.

8Now, Your Majesty, issue the decree and put it in writing so that it cannot be altered—in accordance with the law of the Medes and Persians, which cannot be
repealed." 9So King Darius put the decree in writing.

10Now when Daniel learned that the decree had been published, he went
home to his upstairs room where the windows opened toward Jerusalem. Three
times a day he got down on his knees and prayed, giving thanks to his God, just
as he had done before. 11Then these men went as a group and found Daniel praying and asking God for help. 12So they went to the king and spoke to him about
his royal decree: "Did you not publish a decree that during the next thirty days
anyone who prays to any god or human being except to you, Your Majesty, would
be thrown into the lions' den?"

The king answered, "The decree stands—in accordance with the law of the Medes and Persians, which cannot be repealed."

13Then they said to the king, "Daniel, who is one of the exiles from Judah, pays
no attention to you, Your Majesty, or to the decree you put in writing. He still
prays three times a day." 14When the king heard this, he was greatly distressed;
he was determined to rescue Daniel and made every effort until sundown to
save him.

15Then the men went as a group to King Darius and said to him, "Remember,
Your Majesty, that according to the law of the Medes and Persians no decree or
edict that the king issues can be changed."

16So the king gave the order, and they brought Daniel and threw him into the
lions' den. The king said to Daniel, "May your God, whom you serve continually,
rescue you!"

17A stone was brought and placed over the mouth of the den, and the king
sealed it with his own signet ring and with the rings of his nobles, so that Daniel's situation might not be changed. 18Then the king returned to his palace and
spent the night without eating and without any entertainment being brought to
him. And he could not sleep.

19At the first light of dawn, the king got up and hurried to the lions' den.
20When he came near the den, he called to Daniel in an anguished voice, "Daniel, servant of the living God, has your God, whom you serve continually, been
able to rescue you from the lions?"

21Daniel answered, "May the king live forever! 22My God sent his angel, and
he shut the mouths of the lions. They have not hurt me, because I was found innocent in his sight. Nor have I ever done any wrong before you, Your Majesty."

23The king was overjoyed and gave orders to lift Daniel out of the den. And
when Daniel was lifted from the den, no wound was found on him, because he
had trusted in his God.

24At the king's command, the men who had falsely accused Daniel were
brought in and thrown into the lions' den, along with their wives and children.
And before they reached the floor of the den, the lions overpowered them and
crushed all their bones.

25Then King Darius wrote to all the nations and peoples of every language in
all the earth:

"May you prosper greatly!

26"I issue a decree that in every part of my kingdom people must fear and
reverence the God of Daniel.

"For he is the living God
and he endures forever;
his kingdom will not be destroyed,
his dominion will never end.
27He rescues and he saves;
he performs signs and wonders
in the heavens and on the earth.

DANIEL 6:17–23

THE STONE AND THE PIT

When the Medo-Persian Empire toppled the Babylonian Empire and King Darius reigned, Daniel—who had served under Babylon's defeated King Nebuchadnezzar—rose in the government ranks, which made other officials jealous. Their devious plot to bolster the king's self-image and entrap Daniel is well known—as is their fate when God intervened to save Daniel from the lions.

This episode points to Jesus. Like Daniel, Jesus was unjustly condemned by his enemies. The pagan ruler, Pontius Pilate, though he knew Jesus was innocent, agreed to send him to his death. He was placed in a pit—a tomb—and had a sealed stone rolled over it. Both rose victoriously from the pit; however, Daniel didn't experience death, and Jesus did. Daniel didn't defeat death in his own power, but Jesus did. Daniel and Jesus were both faithful to God, but Jesus conquered death so that all believers can have victory over sin and death through him.

He has rescued Daniel
from the power of the lions."

[28]So Daniel prospered during the reign of Darius and the reign of Cyrus[a] the Persian.

Daniel's Dream of Four Beasts

7 In the first year of Belshazzar king of Babylon, Daniel had a dream, and visions passed through his mind as he was lying in bed. He wrote down the substance of his dream.

[2]Daniel said: "In my vision at night I looked, and there before me were the four
winds of heaven churning up the great sea. [3]Four great beasts, each different
from the others, came up out of the sea.

[4]"The first was like a lion, and it had the wings of an eagle. I watched until its wings were torn off and it was lifted from the ground so that it stood on two feet like a human being, and the mind of a human was given to it.

[5]"And there before me was a second beast, which looked like a bear. It was raised up on one of its sides, and it had three ribs in its mouth between its teeth. It was told, 'Get up and eat your fill of flesh!'

[6]"After that, I looked, and there before me was another beast, one that looked like a leopard. And on its back it had four wings like those of a bird. This beast had four heads, and it was given authority to rule.

[7]"After that, in my vision at night I looked, and there before me was a fourth beast—terrifying and frightening and very powerful. It had large iron teeth; it crushed and devoured its victims and trampled underfoot whatever was left. It was different from all the former beasts, and it had ten horns.

[8]"While I was thinking about the horns, there before me was another horn, a little one, which came up among them; and three of the first horns were uprooted before it. This horn had eyes like the eyes of a human being and a mouth that spoke boastfully.

[9]"As I looked,

"thrones were set in place,
and the Ancient of Days took his seat.
His clothing was as white as snow;
the hair of his head was white like wool.
His throne was flaming with fire,
and its wheels were all ablaze.
[10]A river of fire was flowing,
coming out from before him.
Thousands upon thousands attended him;
ten thousand times ten thousand stood before him.
The court was seated,
and the books were opened.

[11]"Then I continued to watch because of the boastful words the horn was speaking. I kept looking until the beast was slain and its body destroyed and thrown into the blazing fire. [12](The other beasts had been stripped of their authority, but were allowed to live for a period of time.)

[13]"In my vision at night I looked, and there before me was one like a son of man,[b] coming with the clouds of heaven. He approached the Ancient of Days and was led into his presence. [14]He was given authority, glory and sovereign power; all nations and peoples of every language worshiped him. His dominion is an everlasting dominion that will not pass away, and his kingdom is one that will never be destroyed.

DANIEL 7:13–14

SON OF MAN

The promise of Daniel 7 is that "one like a son of man" will come with the clouds of heaven and be given authority. People speaking every language on the planet will worship him, and his kingdom will last forever.

While Jesus walked the earth, he repeatedly called himself "Son of Man" (Mk 2:27–28; 9:11–13; 10:45; Lk 9:58), a title used at least 29 times in the Gospel of Matthew alone. At his trial, Jesus alluded to Daniel 7:13 to identify himself as the Son of Man: "You will see the Son of Man sitting at the right hand of the Mighty One and coming on the clouds of heaven" (Mk 14:62). Stephen saw this at his martyrdom and proclaimed, "Look . . . I see heaven open and the Son of Man standing at the right hand of God" (Ac 7:56). And this promise will be fulfilled when Jesus returns at the end of the age to establish his eternal kingdom, which will be made up of people from every nation and language on the earth (Rev 7:9).

---

[a] 28 Or *Darius, that is, the reign of Cyrus* [b] 13 The Aramaic phrase *bar enash* means *human being.* The phrase *son of man* is retained here because of its use in the New Testament as a title of Jesus, probably based largely on this verse.

BEASTS FROM THE SEA

Daniel's prophetic vision of four beasts coming out of the sea stand symbolically for pagan kings or kingdoms. Who were they? Since the visions and dreams of Daniel 2, 7 and 8 are parallel, three of the four beasts were actually named in Daniel.

The first beast was Babylon, as named by Daniel when he said to Nebuchadnezzar, "You are that head of gold" (2:38). The second beast was the Medo-Persian Empire, which was made clear in Daniel 8:20: "The two-horned ram that you saw represents the kings of Media and Persia." The third beast was the Greek Empire, which was named in Daniel 8:21: "The shaggy goat is the king of Greece." The reader can surmise that the shaggy goat is parallel to the third beast in the vision of Daniel 7:6, which was a leopard with four heads, because the shaggy goat has "four horns that replaced the one that was broken off" (Da 8:22). When Alexander the Great — the king who spread Greek culture across the known world in the fourth century BC — died, his kingdom broke into four kingdoms. The fourth beast was not named in the book, but it appears to symbolize every evil empire that would succeed these others, beginning with the Roman Empire and continuing until the antichrist's final empire. In the end, the good news of the gospel is that Jesus will defeat evil and rule over an eternal kingdom (Rev 19:19 – 21).

Daniel demonstrates that the greatest kingdoms on earth are no match for the sovereign King of the universe. All earthly kingdoms will crumble. History has already testified to this reality as numerous mighty kingdoms have collapsed already. The same will ultimately be true for all earthly kingdoms. Only one kingdom will last in the end — the great and glorious kingdom of our God and Savior, Jesus Christ.

The Interpretation of the Dream

[15]"I, Daniel, was troubled in spirit, and the visions that passed through my mind disturbed me. [16]I approached one of those standing there and asked him the meaning of all this.

"So he told me and gave me the interpretation of these things: [17]'The four great beasts are four kings that will rise from the earth. [18]But the holy people of the Most High will receive the kingdom and will possess it forever—yes, for ever and ever.'

[19]"Then I wanted to know the meaning of the fourth beast, which was different from all the others and most terrifying, with its iron teeth and bronze claws—the beast that crushed and devoured its victims and trampled underfoot whatever was left. [20]I also wanted to know about the ten horns on its head and about the other horn that came up, before which three of them fell—the horn that looked more imposing than the others and that had eyes and a mouth that spoke boastfully. [21]As I watched, this horn was waging war against the holy people and defeating them, [22]until the Ancient of Days came and pronounced judgment in favor of the holy people of the Most High, and the time came when they possessed the kingdom.

[23]"He gave me this explanation: 'The fourth beast is a fourth kingdom that will appear on earth. It will be different from all the other kingdoms and will devour the whole earth, trampling it down and crushing it. [24]The ten horns are ten kings who will come from this kingdom. After them another king will arise, different from the earlier ones; he will subdue three kings. [25]He will speak against the Most High and oppress his holy people and try to change the set times and the laws. The holy people will be delivered into his hands for a time, times and half a time.[a]

[26]" 'But the court will sit, and his power will be taken away and completely destroyed forever. [27]Then the sovereignty, power and greatness of all the kingdoms under heaven will be handed over to the holy people of the Most High. His kingdom will be an everlasting kingdom, and all rulers will worship and obey him.'

[28]"This is the end of the matter. I, Daniel, was deeply troubled by my thoughts, and my face turned pale, but I kept the matter to myself."

Daniel's Vision of a Ram and a Goat

8 In the third year of King Belshazzar's reign, I, Daniel, had a vision, after the one that had already appeared to me. [2]In my vision I saw myself in the citadel of Susa in the province of Elam; in the vision I was beside the Ulai Canal. [3]I looked up, and there before me was a ram with two horns, standing beside the canal, and the horns were long. One of the horns was longer than the other but grew up later. [4]I watched the ram as it charged toward the west and the north and the south. No animal could stand against it, and none could rescue from its power. It did as it pleased and became great.

[5]As I was thinking about this, suddenly a goat with a prominent horn between its eyes came from the west, crossing the whole earth without touching the ground. [6]It came toward the two-horned ram I had seen standing beside the canal and charged at it in great rage. [7]I saw it attack the ram furiously, striking the ram and shattering its two horns. The ram was powerless to stand against it; the goat knocked it to the ground and trampled on it, and none could rescue the ram from its power. [8]The goat became very great, but at the height of its power the large horn was broken off, and in its place four prominent horns grew up toward the four winds of heaven.

[9]Out of one of them came another horn, which started small but grew in power to the south and to the east and toward the Beautiful Land. [10]It grew until it reached the host of the heavens, and it threw some of the starry host down to the earth and trampled on them. [11]It set itself up to be as great as the commander of the army of the LORD; it took away the daily sacrifice from the LORD, and his

---

[a] 25 Or *for a year, two years and half a year*

sanctuary was thrown down. 12Because of rebellion, the LORD's people[a] and the daily sacrifice were given over to it. It prospered in everything it did, and truth was thrown to the ground.

13Then I heard a holy one speaking, and another holy one said to him, "How long will it take for the vision to be fulfilled — the vision concerning the daily sacrifice, the rebellion that causes desolation, the surrender of the sanctuary and the trampling underfoot of the LORD's people?"

14He said to me, "It will take 2,300 evenings and mornings; then the sanctuary will be reconsecrated."

The Interpretation of the Vision

15While I, Daniel, was watching the vision and trying to understand it, there before me stood one who looked like a man. 16And I heard a man's voice from the Ulai calling, "Gabriel, tell this man the meaning of the vision."

17As he came near the place where I was standing, I was terrified and fell prostrate. "Son of man,"[b] he said to me, "understand that the vision concerns the time of the end."

18While he was speaking to me, I was in a deep sleep, with my face to the ground. Then he touched me and raised me to my feet.

19He said: "I am going to tell you what will happen later in the time of wrath, because the vision concerns the appointed time of the end.[c] 20The two-horned ram that you saw represents the kings of Media and Persia. 21The shaggy goat is the king of Greece, and the large horn between its eyes is the first king. 22The four horns that replaced the one that was broken off represent four kingdoms that will emerge from his nation but will not have the same power.

23"In the latter part of their reign, when rebels have become completely wicked, a fierce-looking king, a master of intrigue, will arise. 24He will become very strong, but not by his own power. He will cause astounding devastation and will succeed in whatever he does. He will destroy those who are mighty, the holy people. 25He will cause deceit to prosper, and he will consider himself superior. When they feel secure, he will destroy many and take his stand against the Prince of princes. Yet he will be destroyed, but not by human power.

26"The vision of the evenings and mornings that has been given you is true, but seal up the vision, for it concerns the distant future."

27I, Daniel, was worn out. I lay exhausted for several days. Then I got up and went about the king's business. I was appalled by the vision; it was beyond understanding.

Daniel's Prayer

9 In the first year of Darius son of Xerxes[d] (a Mede by descent), who was made ruler over the Babylonian[e] kingdom — 2in the first year of his reign, I, Daniel, understood from the Scriptures, according to the word of the LORD given to Jeremiah the prophet, that the desolation of Jerusalem would last seventy years. 3So I turned to the Lord God and pleaded with him in prayer and petition, in fasting, and in sackcloth and ashes.

4I prayed to the LORD my God and confessed:

> "Lord, the great and awesome God, who keeps his covenant of love with those who love him and keep his commandments, 5we have sinned and done wrong. We have been wicked and have rebelled; we have turned away from your commands and laws. 6We have not listened to your servants the prophets, who spoke in your name to our kings, our princes and our ancestors, and to all the people of the land.

---

[a] 12 Or *rebellion, the armies*   [b] 17 The Hebrew phrase *ben adam* means *human being.* The phrase *son of man* is retained as a form of address here because of its possible association with "Son of Man" in the New Testament.   [c] 19 Or *because the end will be at the appointed time*   [d] 1 Hebrew *Ahasuerus*   [e] 1 Or *Chaldean*

7“Lord, you are righteous, but this day we are covered with shame — the people of Judah and the inhabitants of Jerusalem and all Israel, both near and far, in all the countries where you have scattered us because of our unfaithfulness to you. 8We and our kings, our princes and our ancestors are covered with shame, LORD, because we have sinned against you. 9The Lord our God is merciful and forgiving, even though we have rebelled against him; 10we have not obeyed the LORD our God or kept the laws he gave us through his servants the prophets. 11All Israel has transgressed your law and turned away, refusing to obey you.

“Therefore the curses and sworn judgments written in the Law of Moses, the servant of God, have been poured out on us, because we have sinned against you. 12You have fulfilled the words spoken against us and against our rulers by bringing on us great disaster. Under the whole heaven nothing has ever been done like what has been done to Jerusalem. 13Just as it is written in the Law of Moses, all this disaster has come on us, yet we have not sought the favor of the LORD our God by turning from our sins and giving attention to your truth. 14The LORD did not hesitate to bring the disaster on us, for the LORD our God is righteous in everything he does; yet we have not obeyed him.

15“Now, Lord our God, who brought your people out of Egypt with a mighty hand and who made for yourself a name that endures to this day, we have sinned, we have done wrong. 16Lord, in keeping with all your righteous acts, turn away your anger and your wrath from Jerusalem, your city, your holy hill. Our sins and the iniquities of our ancestors have made Jerusalem and your people an object of scorn to all those around us.

17“Now, our God, hear the prayers and petitions of your servant. For your sake, Lord, look with favor on your desolate sanctuary. 18Give ear, our God, and hear; open your eyes and see the desolation of the city that bears your Name. We do not make requests of you because we are righteous, but because of your great mercy. 19Lord, listen! Lord, forgive! Lord, hear and act! For your sake, my God, do not delay, because your city and your people bear your Name.”

The Seventy “Sevens”

20While I was speaking and praying, confessing my sin and the sin of my people Israel and making my request to the LORD my God for his holy hill — 21while I was still in prayer, Gabriel, the man I had seen in the earlier vision, came to me in swift flight about the time of the evening sacrifice. 22He instructed me and said to me, “Daniel, I have now come to give you insight and understanding. 23As soon as you began to pray, a word went out, which I have come to tell you, for you are highly esteemed. Therefore, consider the word and understand the vision:

24“Seventy ‘sevens’[a] are decreed for your people and your holy city to finish[b] transgression, to put an end to sin, to atone for wickedness, to bring in everlasting righteousness, to seal up vision and prophecy and to anoint the Most Holy Place.[c]

25“Know and understand this: From the time the word goes out to restore and rebuild Jerusalem until the Anointed One,[d] the ruler, comes, there will be seven ‘sevens,’ and sixty-two ‘sevens.’ It will be rebuilt with streets and a trench, but in times of trouble. 26After the sixty-two ‘sevens,’ the Anointed One will be put to death and will have nothing.[e] The people of the ruler who will come will destroy the city and the sanctuary. The end will come like a flood: War will continue until the end, and desolations have been decreed. 27He will confirm a covenant with many for one ‘seven.’[f] In the middle of the ‘seven’[f] he will put an end to

[a] 24 Or *‘weeks’*; also in verses 25 and 26 [b] 24 Or *restrain* [c] 24 Or *the most holy One* [d] 25 Or *an anointed one*; also in verse 26 [e] 26 Or *death and will have no one*; or *death, but not for himself* [f] 27 Or *‘week’*

DANIEL 9:23 – 27

SEVENTY “SEVENS”

When Daniel was reading Jeremiah’s writings — specifically 25:11 – 12 and 29:10 — he realized the exile would only last seventy years (Da 9:2). That realization sparked a prayer of repentance to prepare the Israelites to reenter the promised land. Daniel’s prayer prompted God to send Gabriel with a vision to explain more about the exile to Daniel. Gabriel said, “Seventy ‘sevens’ are decreed for your people.” This prophecy is complex, but many scholars agree that the word “sevens” refers to seven-year periods.

While many point to this timeline as predicting the arrival of the Messiah (the “Anointed One”), the dates themselves are debatable. What is important to note is that Daniel affirmed that this One will be cut off from his people and have nothing (v. 26). Though he will be the promised provision of God, he would be rejected. Years later, Jesus’ death fulfilled this promise as the Anointed One was cut off from his people in order to accomplish a far greater exile for sinful humans — making it possible for them to return to God himself.

sacrifice and offering. And at the temple[a] he will set up an abomination that causes desolation, until the end that is decreed is poured out on him.[b][c]

Daniel's Vision of a Man

10 In the third year of Cyrus king of Persia, a revelation was given to Daniel (who was called Belteshazzar). Its message was true and it concerned a great war.[d] The understanding of the message came to him in a vision.

2 At that time I, Daniel, mourned for three weeks. 3 I ate no choice food; no meat or wine touched my lips; and I used no lotions at all until the three weeks were over.

4 On the twenty-fourth day of the first month, as I was standing on the bank of the great river, the Tigris, 5 I looked up and there before me was a man dressed in linen, with a belt of fine gold from Uphaz around his waist. 6 His body was like topaz, his face like lightning, his eyes like flaming torches, his arms and legs like the gleam of burnished bronze, and his voice like the sound of a multitude.

7 I, Daniel, was the only one who saw the vision; those who were with me did not see it, but such terror overwhelmed them that they fled and hid themselves. 8 So I was left alone, gazing at this great vision; I had no strength left, my face turned deathly pale and I was helpless. 9 Then I heard him speaking, and as I listened to him, I fell into a deep sleep, my face to the ground.

10 A hand touched me and set me trembling on my hands and knees. 11 He said, "Daniel, you who are highly esteemed, consider carefully the words I am about to speak to you, and stand up, for I have now been sent to you." And when he said this to me, I stood up trembling.

12 Then he continued, "Do not be afraid, Daniel. Since the first day that you set your mind to gain understanding and to humble yourself before your God, your words were heard, and I have come in response to them. 13 But the prince of the Persian kingdom resisted me twenty-one days. Then Michael, one of the chief princes, came to help me, because I was detained there with the king of Persia. 14 Now I have come to explain to you what will happen to your people in the future, for the vision concerns a time yet to come."

15 While he was saying this to me, I bowed with my face toward the ground and was speechless. 16 Then one who looked like a man[e] touched my lips, and I opened my mouth and began to speak. I said to the one standing before me, "I am overcome with anguish because of the vision, my lord, and I feel very weak. 17 How can I, your servant, talk with you, my lord? My strength is gone and I can hardly breathe."

18 Again the one who looked like a man touched me and gave me strength. 19 "Do not be afraid, you who are highly esteemed," he said. "Peace! Be strong now; be strong."

When he spoke to me, I was strengthened and said, "Speak, my lord, since you have given me strength."

20 So he said, "Do you know why I have come to you? Soon I will return to fight against the prince of Persia, and when I go, the prince of Greece will come; 21 but first I will tell you what is written in the Book of Truth. (No one supports me against them except Michael, your prince.

11 1 And in the first year of Darius the Mede, I took my stand to support and protect him.)

The Kings of the South and the North

2 "Now then, I tell you the truth: Three more kings will arise in Persia, and then a fourth, who will be far richer than all the others. When he has gained power by his wealth, he will stir up everyone against the kingdom of Greece. 3 Then a

[a] 27 Septuagint and Theodotion; Hebrew *wing* [b] 27 Or *it* [c] 27 Or *And one who causes desolation will come upon the wing of the abominable temple, until the end that is decreed is poured out on the desolated city* [d] 1 Or *true and burdensome* [e] 16 Most manuscripts of the Masoretic Text; one manuscript of the Masoretic Text, Dead Sea Scrolls and Septuagint *Then something that looked like a human hand*

mighty king will arise, who will rule with great power and do as he pleases. [4]Af-
ter he has arisen, his empire will be broken up and parceled out toward the four
winds of heaven. It will not go to his descendants, nor will it have the power he
exercised, because his empire will be uprooted and given to others.

[5]"The king of the South will become strong, but one of his commanders will
become even stronger than he and will rule his own kingdom with great power.
[6]After some years, they will become allies. The daughter of the king of the South
will go to the king of the North to make an alliance, but she will not retain her
power, and he and his power[a] will not last. In those days she will be betrayed,
together with her royal escort and her father[b] and the one who supported her.

[7]"One from her family line will arise to take her place. He will attack the forces
of the king of the North and enter his fortress; he will fight against them and be
victorious. [8]He will also seize their gods, their metal images and their valuable
articles of silver and gold and carry them off to Egypt. For some years he will
leave the king of the North alone. [9]Then the king of the North will invade the
realm of the king of the South but will retreat to his own country. [10]His sons will
prepare for war and assemble a great army, which will sweep on like an irresist-
ible flood and carry the battle as far as his fortress.

[11]"Then the king of the South will march out in a rage and fight against the
king of the North, who will raise a large army, but it will be defeated. [12]When
the army is carried off, the king of the South will be filled with pride and will
slaughter many thousands, yet he will not remain triumphant. [13]For the king of
the North will muster another army, larger than the first; and after several years,
he will advance with a huge army fully equipped.

[14]"In those times many will rise against the king of the South. Those who are
violent among your own people will rebel in fulfillment of the vision, but without
success. [15]Then the king of the North will come and build up siege ramps and
will capture a fortified city. The forces of the South will be powerless to resist;
even their best troops will not have the strength to stand. [16]The invader will do
as he pleases; no one will be able to stand against him. He will establish himself
in the Beautiful Land and will have the power to destroy it. [17]He will determine
to come with the might of his entire kingdom and will make an alliance with
the king of the South. And he will give him a daughter in marriage in order to
overthrow the kingdom, but his plans[c] will not succeed or help him. [18]Then he
will turn his attention to the coastlands and will take many of them, but a commander will put an end to his insolence and will turn his insolence back on him.
[19]After this, he will turn back toward the fortresses of his own country but will
stumble and fall, to be seen no more.

[20]"His successor will send out a tax collector to maintain the royal splendor.
In a few years, however, he will be destroyed, yet not in anger or in battle.

[21]"He will be succeeded by a contemptible person who has not been given the
honor of royalty. He will invade the kingdom when its people feel secure, and
he will seize it through intrigue. [22]Then an overwhelming army will be swept
away before him; both it and a prince of the covenant will be destroyed. [23]After
coming to an agreement with him, he will act deceitfully, and with only a few
people he will rise to power. [24]When the richest provinces feel secure, he will
invade them and will achieve what neither his fathers nor his forefathers did.
He will distribute plunder, loot and wealth among his followers. He will plot the
overthrow of fortresses — but only for a time.

[25]"With a large army he will stir up his strength and courage against the king
of the South. The king of the South will wage war with a large and very powerful army, but he will not be able to stand because of the plots devised against
him. [26]Those who eat from the king's provisions will try to destroy him; his
army will be swept away, and many will fall in battle. [27]The two kings, with their
hearts bent on evil, will sit at the same table and lie to each other, but to no avail,

---

[a] 6 Or *offspring* [b] 6 Or *child* (see Vulgate and Syriac) [c] 17 Or *but she*

because an end will still come at the appointed time. 28The king of the North will
return to his own country with great wealth, but his heart will be set against the
holy covenant. He will take action against it and then return to his own country.
29"At the appointed time he will invade the South again, but this time the outcome will be different from what it was before. 30Ships of the western coastlands
will oppose him, and he will lose heart. Then he will turn back and vent his fury
against the holy covenant. He will return and show favor to those who forsake
the holy covenant.
31"His armed forces will rise up to desecrate the temple fortress and will abolish the daily sacrifice. Then they will set up the abomination that causes desolation. 32With flattery he will corrupt those who have violated the covenant, but
the people who know their God will firmly resist him.
33"Those who are wise will instruct many, though for a time they will fall by
the sword or be burned or captured or plundered. 34When they fall, they will
receive a little help, and many who are not sincere will join them. 35Some of the
wise will stumble, so that they may be refined, purified and made spotless until
the time of the end, for it will still come at the appointed time.

The King Who Exalts Himself

36"The king will do as he pleases. He will exalt and magnify himself above
every god and will say unheard-of things against the God of gods. He will be
successful until the time of wrath is completed, for what has been determined
must take place. 37He will show no regard for the gods of his ancestors or for the
one desired by women, nor will he regard any god, but will exalt himself above
them all. 38Instead of them, he will honor a god of fortresses; a god unknown to
his ancestors he will honor with gold and silver, with precious stones and costly
gifts. 39He will attack the mightiest fortresses with the help of a foreign god and
will greatly honor those who acknowledge him. He will make them rulers over
many people and will distribute the land at a price.[a]
40"At the time of the end the king of the South will engage him in battle, and
the king of the North will storm out against him with chariots and cavalry and a
great fleet of ships. He will invade many countries and sweep through them like
a flood. 41He will also invade the Beautiful Land. Many countries will fall, but
Edom, Moab and the leaders of Ammon will be delivered from his hand. 42He
will extend his power over many countries; Egypt will not escape. 43He will gain
control of the treasures of gold and silver and all the riches of Egypt, with the Libyans and Cushites[b] in submission. 44But reports from the east and the north will
alarm him, and he will set out in a great rage to destroy and annihilate many.
45He will pitch his royal tents between the seas at[c] the beautiful holy mountain.
Yet he will come to his end, and no one will help him.

The End Times

12 "At that time Michael, the great prince who protects your people, will
arise. There will be a time of distress such as has not happened from the
beginning of nations until then. But at that time your people — everyone whose
name is found written in the book — will be delivered. 2Multitudes who sleep in
the dust of the earth will awake: some to everlasting life, others to shame and
everlasting contempt. 3Those who are wise[d] will shine like the brightness of the
heavens, and those who lead many to righteousness, like the stars for ever and
ever. 4But you, Daniel, roll up and seal the words of the scroll until the time of the
end. Many will go here and there to increase knowledge."

5Then I, Daniel, looked, and there before me stood two others, one on this
bank of the river and one on the opposite bank. 6One of them said to the man

[a] 39 Or *land for a reward* [b] 43 That is, people from the upper Nile region [c] 45 Or *the sea and* [d] 3 Or *who impart wisdom*

DANIEL 12:1 – 3

THE RESURRECTION

Daniel 12 looks to the end of the world. The great distress caused by the beastly empires would end as God would judge evil and vindicate the righteous. Some would be raised from the dead to everlasting life and others to everlasting shame.

In the New Testament, God did pour out his final judgment on sin when Jesus submitted by giving his life on the cross so that sinners could be made right with God. And God vindicated Jesus — the only righteous human to ever walk the earth — in his resurrection from the dead.

Paul made this truth clear in 1 Corinthians 15:20 – 23 when he wrote, "But Christ has indeed been raised from the dead, the firstfruits of those who have fallen asleep. For since death came through a man, the resurrection of the dead comes also through a man. For as in Adam all die, so in Christ all will be made alive. But each in turn: Christ, the firstfruits; then, when he comes, those who belong to him."

When Jesus returns to judge the nations, those who are in Christ will be raised to everlasting life. Those who reject Jesus' gracious offer of salvation will be raised to everlasting shame. God's judgment on sin and death has already happened; how each person responds to Jesus' work makes an eternal difference on how each will be regarded by him at the end of this age.

clothed in linen, who was above the waters of the river, "How long will it be before these astonishing things are fulfilled?"

[7]The man clothed in linen, who was above the waters of the river, lifted his right hand and his left hand toward heaven, and I heard him swear by him who lives forever, saying, "It will be for a time, times and half a time.[a] When the power of the holy people has been finally broken, all these things will be completed."

[8]I heard, but I did not understand. So I asked, "My lord, what will the outcome of all this be?"

[9]He replied, "Go your way, Daniel, because the words are rolled up and sealed until the time of the end. [10]Many will be purified, made spotless and refined, but the wicked will continue to be wicked. None of the wicked will understand, but those who are wise will understand.

[11]"From the time that the daily sacrifice is abolished and the abomination that causes desolation is set up, there will be 1,290 days. [12]Blessed is the one who waits for and reaches the end of the 1,335 days.

[13]"As for you, go your way till the end. You will rest, and then at the end of the days you will rise to receive your allotted inheritance."

[a] 7 Or *a year, two years and half a year*

JESUS: OUR PURSUING SPOUSE

HOSEA

HOSEA

REIGN OF JEROBOAM II *c. 793 – 753 BC*	PROPHETIC MINISTRY OF HOSEA *c. 753 – 715 BC*	FALL OF ISRAEL *c. 722 BC*

Hosea was the only writing prophet to come from the northern kingdom of Israel, and his messages were primarily directed to that kingdom. Like others before him, Hosea experienced firsthand the challenges that come from being a prophet. God often used the prophets to do more than proclaim the word of God; at times they were also asked to provide living object lessons for the people to see and experience the ramifications of their sin.

Hosea was asked to do just that. At the outset of his ministry, God told Hosea to marry a woman whose adultery God would use to illustrate Israel's spiritual adultery. Hosea obeyed God and took Gomer as his wife. Together they had three children, who each received a name that symbolized the sin of the people. The first child, a son named Jezreel, was a reminder of the calamity that occurred in that city and a foreshadowing of ensuing judgment. The second, a daughter whose name meant "not loved," forced the people to consider the consequences of God temporarily removing his love from them. The final child, "not my people," foreshadowed the consequences of Israel's sin on their relationship with God.

Throughout the Bible, marriage serves as a tangible picture of God's love for his beloved people. The intimacy, fidelity and love seen between a husband and wife in a committed marriage are meant to vividly portray God's deep passion for his people. For this reason, adultery paints an equally profound picture of disobedience to God. The unfaithfulness, treachery and rejection demonstrated through an adulterous and promiscuous relationship highlights the detestable nature of sin.

Hosea's life and ministry were meant to shock the Israelites and awaken them from spiritual adultery before it was too late. Their sin was put on display as they heard from Hosea about his wife's adultery. Israel proved, time and again, to be unfaithful to their covenant commitments to God. As a jealous spouse, God longed for the singular love of his people.

More importantly, however, God demonstrated his faithful love for Israel in Hosea's ongoing pursuit of his wayward bride. Though Israel suffered under God's judgment, God remained loyal to his people. Like a faithful spouse, God continued to demonstrate a faithfulness to his covenant promise regardless of the ongoing adultery of his people. God's love for his people was — and is — not based on their faithfulness, but on his faithfulness to his word. He would never give up on his people, even though his love would come at the cost of his Son. Jesus perfectly and finally pursued, and now claims, his wayward bride.

FOR I DESIRE MERCY, NOT SACRIFICE,
AND ACKNOWLEDGMENT OF GOD RATHER
THAN BURNT OFFERINGS.

Hosea 6:6

HOSEA

HOSEA 1:2

AN UNFAITHFUL SPOUSE

The opening chapter of Hosea unveils a clear problem between God and his people: they had been unfaithful. God commanded Hosea to take a wife who would be unfaithful to him. Hosea and Gomer's ensuing relationship symbolized the way the people of Israel had departed from God to pursue the Canaanites' false gods. Hosea was instructed to love Gomer despite her promiscuous actions and knowing she would continue to be unfaithful.

Unfaithfulness is not just a character flaw reserved for the Israelites of the Old Testament; it is a problem for all of humanity. Sin by definition is forsaking God's way and going one's own way, resulting in a broken relationship between humans and God. This is the very foundation of why Jesus came. Isaiah 53:6 beautifully says it this way: "We all, like sheep, have gone astray, each of us has turned to our own way; and the LORD has laid on him the iniquity of us all." With the heart of humanity bent on pursuing false gods, or going "our own way," all people would have been utterly lost and separated from God forever if not for the pursuit of God sending his Son to bring humanity back to himself (1Pe 3:18). Those who believe and follow Christ are invited into the perfect love Christ has for the church, his bride, for whom he gave his life (Eph 5:25–27).

1 The word of the LORD that came to Hosea son of Beeri during the reigns of
Uzziah, Jotham, Ahaz and Hezekiah, kings of Judah, and during the reign of
Jeroboam son of Jehoash[a] king of Israel:

Hosea's Wife and Children

2 When the LORD began to speak through Hosea, the LORD said to him, "Go,
marry a promiscuous woman and have children with her, for like an adulterous
wife this land is guilty of unfaithfulness to the LORD." 3 So he married Gomer
daughter of Diblaim, and she conceived and bore him a son.
4 Then the LORD said to Hosea, "Call him Jezreel, because I will soon punish
the house of Jehu for the massacre at Jezreel, and I will put an end to the kingdom
of Israel. 5 In that day I will break Israel's bow in the Valley of Jezreel."
6 Gomer conceived again and gave birth to a daughter. Then the LORD said
to Hosea, "Call her Lo-Ruhamah (which means "not loved"), for I will no longer
show love to Israel, that I should at all forgive them. 7 Yet I will show love to Judah;
and I will save them — not by bow, sword or battle, or by horses and horsemen,
but I, the LORD their God, will save them."
8 After she had weaned Lo-Ruhamah, Gomer had another son. 9 Then the
LORD said, "Call him Lo-Ammi (which means "not my people"), for you are not
my people, and I am not your God.[b]
10 "Yet the Israelites will be like the sand on the seashore, which cannot be
measured or counted. In the place where it was said to them, 'You are not my
people,' they will be called 'children of the living God.' 11 The people of Judah
and the people of Israel will come together; they will appoint one leader and will
come up out of the land, for great will be the day of Jezreel.[c]

2 [d] "Say of your brothers, 'My people,' and of your sisters, 'My loved one.'

Israel Punished and Restored

2 "Rebuke your mother, rebuke her,
for she is not my wife,
and I am not her husband.
Let her remove the adulterous look from her face
and the unfaithfulness from between her breasts.
3 Otherwise I will strip her naked
and make her as bare as on the day she was born;
I will make her like a desert,
turn her into a parched land,
and slay her with thirst.
4 I will not show my love to her children,
because they are the children of adultery.
5 Their mother has been unfaithful
and has conceived them in disgrace.
She said, 'I will go after my lovers,
who give me my food and my water,
my wool and my linen, my olive oil and my drink.'
6 Therefore I will block her path with thornbushes;
I will wall her in so that she cannot find her way.
7 She will chase after her lovers but not catch them;
she will look for them but not find them.

[a] *1* Hebrew *Joash,* a variant of *Jehoash* [b] *9* Or *your I AM* [c] *11* In Hebrew texts 1:10,11 is numbered 2:1,2. [d] In Hebrew texts 2:1-23 is numbered 2:3-25.

AN OBEDIENT SON

In the Old Testament, God carefully outlined the blessings of obedience and the punishments that would follow in the wake of disobedience (Hos 4:1–6). Hosea 1:9 presents a living picture of this principle when God told Hosea to name one of his children Lo-Ammi, meaning "not my people." Though Israel was always in covenant relationship with God, their rebellion kept them from experiencing their rights and privileges as dearly loved children. Yet even in their disobedience, God promised restoration (v. 10). Throughout all of Hosea, God is pictured as Israel's steadfast pursuer despite the nation's continued unfaithfulness and rebellion.

The fullness of this illustration was not realized until the coming of Jesus, God's perfect Son, the One who refused to rebel against his Father. Through his perfect obedience and sinless death, he would absorb the wrath rightfully incurred by God's disobedient son, Israel, as well as the whole world. Jesus came from God, and as John 1:1–2 notes, he "was God" and "was with God in the beginning." Matthew 2:15 helps us to see Jesus' early exile in Egypt as an infant as the fulfillment of the prophecy from Hosea 11:1: "When Israel was a child, I loved him, and out of Egypt I called my son." Matthew applies to Christ what Hosea spoke about the Israelites in Moses' time.

Through his death and resurrection, Jesus made a way for the deliverance and restoration of the original children of God, the Jews, and of all those outside the nation of Israel as well. This salvation occurs for both groups by believing and trusting Jesus as Savior. Through faith, the promise of Hosea 1:10 applies to believers today: "In the place where it was said to them, 'You are not my people,' they will be called 'children of the living God.'" By trusting and believing in the Son, all people can become children of the living God.

Then she will say,
'I will go back to my husband as at first,
for then I was better off than now.'
8 She has not acknowledged that I was the one
who gave her the grain, the new wine and oil,
who lavished on her the silver and gold —
which they used for Baal.

9 "Therefore I will take away my grain when it ripens,
and my new wine when it is ready.
I will take back my wool and my linen,
intended to cover her naked body.
10 So now I will expose her lewdness
before the eyes of her lovers;
no one will take her out of my hands.
11 I will stop all her celebrations:
her yearly festivals, her New Moons,
her Sabbath days — all her appointed festivals.
12 I will ruin her vines and her fig trees,
which she said were her pay from her lovers;
I will make them a thicket,
and wild animals will devour them.
13 I will punish her for the days
she burned incense to the Baals;
she decked herself with rings and jewelry,
and went after her lovers,
but me she forgot,"
declares the LORD.

14 "Therefore I am now going to allure her;
I will lead her into the wilderness
and speak tenderly to her.
15 There I will give her back her vineyards,
and will make the Valley of Achor[a] a door of hope.
There she will respond[b] as in the days of her youth,
as in the day she came up out of Egypt.

16 "In that day," declares the LORD,
"you will call me 'my husband';
you will no longer call me 'my master.[c]'
17 I will remove the names of the Baals from her lips;
no longer will their names be invoked.
18 In that day I will make a covenant for them
with the beasts of the field, the birds in the sky
and the creatures that move along the ground.
Bow and sword and battle
I will abolish from the land,
so that all may lie down in safety.
19 I will betroth you to me forever;
I will betroth you in[d] righteousness and justice,
in[d] love and compassion.
20 I will betroth you in[d] faithfulness,
and you will acknowledge the LORD.

21 "In that day I will respond,"
declares the LORD —
"I will respond to the skies,
and they will respond to the earth;

[a] *15 Achor* means *trouble.* [b] *15* Or *sing* [c] *16* Hebrew *baal* [d] *19,20* Or *with*

HOSEA 2:19 – 23

A DIVINE LOVE

Since names in the Old Testament often held great meaning and purpose, the people of Hosea's day would have recognized the special significance God intended when he instructed the prophet to name his children Jezreel ("God scatters"), Lo-Ruhamah ("not loved") and Lo-Ammi ("not my people") (1:4,6,9). In Hosea's culture, unrepentant idolatry infected the land, and as symbolized by these names, Israel was poised to reap the consequences of their disobedience and waywardness. Yet, even as they experienced God's discipline, he indicated that his divine love and mercy would ultimately triumph over judgment (2:19 – 23; Jas 2:13). In fact, in Hosea 2:22, Jezreel is used in the reversed sense: "God plants" rather than "God scatters."

By pursuing and restoring Gomer to her rightful place as his wife (Hos 3:1 – 3), Hosea paralleled (though imperfectly) God's unrelenting desire for fellowship with his people and the high price he was willing to pay to purchase his people back from their slavery to sin. Hosea highlighted not only God's original covenant with his people, but also his unending commitment that continued despite Israel's superficial claims to faithfulness. Carrying forward the theme of restoration, he reminded them that it is he alone who could provide comfort, companionship, fruitfulness and the hope that they would eventually be called his people once again (2:14 – 16).

Just as Hosea pursued an unfaithful wife, God pursues an unfaithful people, based solely in his own unchanging love, faithfulness and glory. With the redemption plan of Jesus in play before the beginning of the world (Eph 1:4), God declared his intention even before people became aware of their need. Humanity was chosen as the unlikely recipient of unmerited favor, an extravagant grace.

While God's heart has always desired relationship with his people, the coming of Christ revealed the fullness of the promise. All people were once cut off from mercy and could not attain it through personal effort, but now all can possess it through faith in Jesus and stand in his righteousness, being fully redeemed by his blood (Eph 2:11 – 13). Fulfilling the prophecy of Hosea, Jesus alone makes it possible for all believers to be the mercy-lavished children of God. Peter wrote triumphantly: "Once you were not a people, but now you are the people of God; once you had not received mercy, but now you have received mercy" (1Pe 2:10). The people of God are loved by a divine love pictured most perfectly in Jesus, who would pursue all of humanity through his life, death and resurrection. "Greater love has no one than this: to lay down one's life for one's friends" (Jn 15:13).

22 and the earth will respond to the grain,
the new wine and the olive oil,
and they will respond to Jezreel.[a]
23 I will plant her for myself in the land;
I will show my love to the one I called 'Not my loved one.[b]'
I will say to those called 'Not my people,[c]' 'You are my people';
and they will say, 'You are my God.' "

Hosea's Reconciliation With His Wife

3 The LORD said to me, "Go, show your love to your wife again, though she is
loved by another man and is an adulteress. Love her as the LORD loves the
Israelites, though they turn to other gods and love the sacred raisin cakes."
2 So I bought her for fifteen shekels[d] of silver and about a homer and a lethek[e] of
barley. 3 Then I told her, "You are to live with me many days; you must not be a prostitute or be intimate with any man, and I will behave the same way toward you."
4 For the Israelites will live many days without king or prince, without sacrifice
or sacred stones, without ephod or household gods. 5 Afterward the Israelites will
return and seek the LORD their God and David their king. They will come trembling to the LORD and to his blessings in the last days.

The Charge Against Israel

4 Hear the word of the LORD, you Israelites,
because the LORD has a charge to bring
against you who live in the land:
"There is no faithfulness, no love,
no acknowledgment of God in the land.
2 There is only cursing,[f] lying and murder,
stealing and adultery;
they break all bounds,
and bloodshed follows bloodshed.
3 Because of this the land dries up,
and all who live in it waste away;
the beasts of the field, the birds in the sky
and the fish in the sea are swept away.

4 "But let no one bring a charge,
let no one accuse another,
for your people are like those
who bring charges against a priest.
5 You stumble day and night,
and the prophets stumble with you.
So I will destroy your mother—
6 my people are destroyed from lack of knowledge.
"Because you have rejected knowledge,
I also reject you as my priests;
because you have ignored the law of your God,
I also will ignore your children.
7 The more priests there were,
the more they sinned against me;
they exchanged their glorious God[g] for something disgraceful.
8 They feed on the sins of my people
and relish their wickedness.

---

[a] 22 *Jezreel* means *God plants.* [b] 23 Hebrew *Lo-Ruhamah* (see 1:6) [c] 23 Hebrew *Lo-Ammi* (see 1:9) [d] 2 That is, about 6 ounces or about 170 grams [e] 2 A homer and a lethek possibly weighed about 430 pounds or about 195 kilograms. [f] 2 That is, to pronounce a curse on [g] 7 Syriac (see also an ancient Hebrew scribal tradition); Masoretic Text *me; / I will exchange their glory*

HOSEA 3:1 – 3

REDEEMED

Redemption is a primary theme in Hosea, as evidenced by the way the prophet's personal story mirrors the love and redemption of God Almighty. In Hosea 3:1, God said to him, "Go, show your love to your wife again, though she is loved by another man and is an adulteress. Love her as the LORD loves the Israelites, though they turn to other gods." Through her illicit lifestyle, Hosea's wife, Gomer, became enslaved to her passions and eventually found herself in a state of literal slavery. Despite the heartbreak he must have felt, Hosea honored God's command to pursue and rescue her from her own folly.

Hosea's experience mirrored the devastating betrayal God felt from his own people. Despite his people's rebellious wandering, God's deep affection for them manifested itself in a constant quest to show them his unconditional love. Hosea took Gomer back to live with him, paralleling the way God's heart is bent toward his people with an everlasting devotion.

Just as Hosea was steadfast in his desire to restore his relationship with his wife despite her unfaithfulness, so also God persists in pursuing his people and graciously bringing them back to their proper (though undeserved) place with him.

The account of Hosea's rescue of his unfaithful wife beautifully prefigures the way God went to the utmost lengths to pursue an adulterous people and win them back by sending his own Son Jesus to pay their ransom. Hosea's story is but a shadow image of God's perfect love for the people of Israel and also for all people through Jesus Christ. Now, believers in Christ can express a genuine love relationship with God since, as 1 John 4:19 reminds Christians, "We love because he first loved us."

God fully expressed his love to his people by purchasing them with the precious blood of Christ (1Pe 1:18 – 19). As a result of this redemption, those who were called "not my people" now are embraced fully as "God's chosen people, holy and dearly loved" (Col 3:12). Quoting Hosea twice, Paul declares that all people, whether Jew or Gentile, have the opportunity to become children of God (Ro 9:22 – 26). By looking at Hosea in light of what Jesus has done, it is clear that despite sinful choices or deliberate rebellion, God is always at work redeeming his people with the end goal of full recovery and restoration for those who will claim that redemption in Jesus.

[9] And it will be: Like people, like priests.
I will punish both of them for their ways
and repay them for their deeds.

[10] "They will eat but not have enough;
they will engage in prostitution but not
flourish,
because they have deserted the LORD
to give themselves [11] to prostitution;
old wine and new wine
take away their understanding.
[12] My people consult a wooden idol,
and a diviner's rod speaks to them.
A spirit of prostitution leads them astray;
they are unfaithful to their God.
[13] They sacrifice on the mountaintops
and burn offerings on the hills,
under oak, poplar and terebinth,
where the shade is pleasant.
Therefore your daughters turn to prostitution
and your daughters-in-law to adultery.

[14] "I will not punish your daughters
when they turn to prostitution,
nor your daughters-in-law
when they commit adultery,
because the men themselves consort with harlots
and sacrifice with shrine prostitutes —
a people without understanding will come
to ruin!

[15] "Though you, Israel, commit adultery,
do not let Judah become guilty.

"Do not go to Gilgal;
do not go up to Beth Aven.[a]
And do not swear, 'As surely as the LORD lives!'
[16] The Israelites are stubborn,
like a stubborn heifer.
How then can the LORD pasture them
like lambs in a meadow?
[17] Ephraim is joined to idols;
leave him alone!
[18] Even when their drinks are gone,
they continue their prostitution;
their rulers dearly love shameful ways.
[19] A whirlwind will sweep them away,
and their sacrifices will bring them shame.

HOSEA 4:12 – 13

ADULTERY

The religious practices associated with Baal worship included worshiping wooden idols made by human hands and engaging in sexual fertility rituals. The Israelites got tangled up in both of these activities, as many were corrupted by the surrounding pagan religious practices and led astray from the one true God. Instead of worshiping the Lord and trusting in him alone for their provision, they were offering their bodies to prostitutes as a way of appealing to other gods (Hos 4:14).

This provides a sobering picture of the heart of humanity and what happens when people stray from God — whether literally committing adultery or being unfaithful in heart or word. It also describes the condition of a heart before being redeemed by God through Jesus' work on the cross — a heart divided and eyes that prize created things over the Creator. Pondering the saving work of Jesus at the cross through the filter of personal unfaithfulness to God highlights the incredible lengths God went to for the sake of winning back each one of his adulterous people.

Judgment Against Israel

5 "Hear this, you priests!
Pay attention, you Israelites!
Listen, royal house!
This judgment is against you:
You have been a snare at Mizpah,
a net spread out on Tabor.

[a] 15 *Beth Aven* means *house of wickedness* (a derogatory name for Bethel, which means *house of God*).

TIME OF JUDGMENT

By the time Hosea prophesied in the land, these religious and civic leaders had abandoned their prime responsibilities of inspiring faithfulness and leading the people to worship only God. Instead, they often encouraged and supported blatant idolatry and led the people to worship false gods. Chapter 5 opens with a strong word of impending judgment against three groups of people: the priests, the nation of Israel and the royal family. The ongoing rebellion of each of these groups was such that God should, and surely would, judge them for their sin.

Chapter 6 breathes some hope into this desperate situation, reminding Israel that divine justice is always delivered against a backdrop of divine love and the promise of coming redemption (Hos 6:1 – 3). Whether the consequences are imminent (as Israel was soon to experience at the hands of a conquering nation) or delayed (as all can expect at the end of time), judgment from a perfect and holy God on human unfaithfulness and rampant wickedness is sure and certain. Because even the best effort and most consistent faithfulness still fail to live up to God's righteous standards, the rightful and impending consequence that awaits humanity is separation, wrath and ultimately death.

But that is not the end of the story. Even though it's definitely true that "the wages of sin is death," God stepped in to provide the only payment that could satisfy his righteous standards and offer to all his free alternative: "eternal life in Christ Jesus" (Ro 6:23). Jesus didn't come to make bad people good, but rather to give spiritually dead people life "to the full" when they place their trust in him (Jn 10:10).

The prophecies in Hosea represented judgments that would happen for Israel's idolatrous rebellion and also future judgment for all people. The ultimate Judge, the Son of God, Jesus Christ himself, will one day determine rewards for service by faithful followers or just punishment for rebellion and unbelief. He himself will "reward each person according to what they have done" (Mt 16:27). Since Christ satisfied the sentence of death by offering his life on the cross, when the day of the Lord comes, those who have trusted him will find their sins covered and not counted against them (Ro 4:7 – 8).

2 The rebels are knee-deep in slaughter.
    I will discipline all of them.
3 I know all about Ephraim;
    Israel is not hidden from me.
Ephraim, you have now turned to prostitution;
    Israel is corrupt.

4 "Their deeds do not permit them
    to return to their God.
A spirit of prostitution is in their heart;
    they do not acknowledge the LORD.
5 Israel's arrogance testifies against them;
    the Israelites, even Ephraim, stumble in their sin;
    Judah also stumbles with them.
6 When they go with their flocks and herds
    to seek the LORD,
they will not find him;
    he has withdrawn himself from them.
7 They are unfaithful to the LORD;
    they give birth to illegitimate children.
When they celebrate their New Moon feasts,
    he will devour[a] their fields.

8 "Sound the trumpet in Gibeah,
    the horn in Ramah.
Raise the battle cry in Beth Aven[b];
    lead on, Benjamin.
9 Ephraim will be laid waste
    on the day of reckoning.
Among the tribes of Israel
    I proclaim what is certain.
10 Judah's leaders are like those
    who move boundary stones.
I will pour out my wrath on them
    like a flood of water.
11 Ephraim is oppressed,
    trampled in judgment,
    intent on pursuing idols.[c]
12 I am like a moth to Ephraim,
    like rot to the people of Judah.

13 "When Ephraim saw his sickness,
    and Judah his sores,
then Ephraim turned to Assyria,
    and sent to the great king for help.
But he is not able to cure you,
    not able to heal your sores.
14 For I will be like a lion to Ephraim,
    like a great lion to Judah.
I will tear them to pieces and go away;
    I will carry them off, with no one to rescue
        them.
15 Then I will return to my lair
    until they have borne their guilt
    and seek my face—

[a] 7 Or *Now their New Moon feasts / will devour them and* [b] 8 *Beth Aven* means *house of wickedness* (a derogatory name for Bethel, which means *house of God*). [c] 11 The meaning of the Hebrew for this word is uncertain.

in their misery
they will earnestly seek me."

Israel Unrepentant

6 "Come, let us return to the LORD.
He has torn us to pieces
but he will heal us;
he has injured us
but he will bind up our wounds.
2 After two days he will revive us;
on the third day he will restore us,
that we may live in his presence.
3 Let us acknowledge the LORD;
let us press on to acknowledge him.
As surely as the sun rises,
he will appear;
he will come to us like the winter rains,
like the spring rains that water the earth."

4 "What can I do with you, Ephraim?
What can I do with you, Judah?
Your love is like the morning mist,
like the early dew that disappears.
5 Therefore I cut you in pieces with my prophets,
I killed you with the words of my mouth—
then my judgments go forth like the sun.[a]
6 For I desire mercy, not sacrifice,
and acknowledgment of God rather than burnt
offerings.
7 As at Adam,[b] they have broken the covenant;
they were unfaithful to me there.
8 Gilead is a city of evildoers,
stained with footprints of blood.
9 As marauders lie in ambush for a victim,
so do bands of priests;
they murder on the road to Shechem,
carrying out their wicked schemes.
10 I have seen a horrible thing in Israel:
There Ephraim is given to prostitution,
Israel is defiled.

11 "Also for you, Judah,
a harvest is appointed.

"Whenever I would restore the fortunes of my people,
7 1 whenever I would heal Israel,
the sins of Ephraim are exposed
and the crimes of Samaria revealed.
They practice deceit,
thieves break into houses,
bandits rob in the streets;
2 but they do not realize
that I remember all their evil deeds.
Their sins engulf them;
they are always before me.

[a] 5 The meaning of the Hebrew for this line is uncertain. [b] 7 Or *Like Adam*; or *Like human beings*

HOSEA 6:6

THE HEART OF THE LAW

The heart of the Law was concerned with just that: the heart. God's rules were always for the benefit of his people, intended to draw their hearts toward himself so that they would be transformed and so they would lean on him completely (Pr 3:5). It is clear in Hosea 6:6 that God desires "mercy," or loyal hearts that are wholly devoted to him and compassionate toward others, over lives filled with lip service and empty sacrifices. God desires people actually to know him, not just know about him while ignoring what God considers important. Living a life of obedience and love is the hallmark of a worshiping heart, which stands in stark contrast to a life of going through the motions: outwardly sacrificing and saying the right things, yet inwardly remaining far from God.

Jesus gave himself as the final sacrifice to satisfy God, to be both the mercy *and* the sacrifice. As Jesus emphatically asserted, "Do not think that I have come to abolish the Law or the Prophets; I have not come to abolish them but to fulfill them" (Mt 5:17). Worship is made possible through a relationship with Jesus, and it happens as one increasingly devotes one's entire life to God (Ro 12:1). When believers joyfully surrender every day to Jesus, with loyal hearts and expectant obedience and with compassion toward others, they are actually living, breathing representations of proper worship toward God.

3 "They delight the king with their wickedness,
the princes with their lies.
4 They are all adulterers,
burning like an oven
whose fire the baker need not stir
from the kneading of the dough till it rises.
5 On the day of the festival of our king
the princes become inflamed with wine,
and he joins hands with the mockers.
6 Their hearts are like an oven;
they approach him with intrigue.
Their passion smolders all night;
in the morning it blazes like a flaming fire.
7 All of them are hot as an oven;
they devour their rulers.
All their kings fall,
and none of them calls on me.

8 "Ephraim mixes with the nations;
Ephraim is a flat loaf not turned over.
9 Foreigners sap his strength,
but he does not realize it.
His hair is sprinkled with gray,
but he does not notice.
10 Israel's arrogance testifies against him,
but despite all this
he does not return to the LORD his God
or search for him.

11 "Ephraim is like a dove,
easily deceived and senseless —
now calling to Egypt,
now turning to Assyria.
12 When they go, I will throw my net over them;
I will pull them down like the birds in the sky.
When I hear them flocking together,
I will catch them.
13 Woe to them,
because they have strayed from me!
Destruction to them,
because they have rebelled against me!
I long to redeem them
but they speak about me falsely.
14 They do not cry out to me from their hearts
but wail on their beds.
They slash themselves,[a] appealing to their gods
for grain and new wine,
but they turn away from me.
15 I trained them and strengthened their arms,
but they plot evil against me.
16 They do not turn to the Most High;
they are like a faulty bow.
Their leaders will fall by the sword
because of their insolent words.
For this they will be ridiculed
in the land of Egypt.

---

[a] *14* Some Hebrew manuscripts and Septuagint; most Hebrew manuscripts *They gather together*

Israel to Reap the Whirlwind

8 "Put the trumpet to your lips!
An eagle is over the house of the LORD
because the people have broken my covenant
and rebelled against my law.
2 Israel cries out to me,
'Our God, we acknowledge you!'
3 But Israel has rejected what is good;
an enemy will pursue him.
4 They set up kings without my consent;
they choose princes without my approval.
With their silver and gold
they make idols for themselves
to their own destruction.
5 Samaria, throw out your calf-idol!
My anger burns against them.
How long will they be incapable of purity?
6 They are from Israel!
This calf—a metalworker has made it;
it is not God.
It will be broken in pieces,
that calf of Samaria.

7 "They sow the wind
and reap the whirlwind.
The stalk has no head;
it will produce no flour.
Were it to yield grain,
foreigners would swallow it up.
8 Israel is swallowed up;
now she is among the nations
like something no one wants.
9 For they have gone up to Assyria
like a wild donkey wandering alone.
Ephraim has sold herself to lovers.
10 Although they have sold themselves among the
nations,
I will now gather them together.
They will begin to waste away
under the oppression of the mighty king.

11 "Though Ephraim built many altars for sin
offerings,
these have become altars for sinning.
12 I wrote for them the many things of my law,
but they regarded them as something foreign.
13 Though they offer sacrifices as gifts to me,
and though they eat the meat,
the LORD is not pleased with them.
Now he will remember their wickedness
and punish their sins:
They will return to Egypt.
14 Israel has forgotten their Maker
and built palaces;
Judah has fortified many towns.
But I will send fire on their cities
that will consume their fortresses."

HOSEA 8:7

SOWING THE WIND

Hosea 8 references sowing and reaping. It is used as an image of judgment: the people have rebelled ("sow the wind") and will therefore experience judgment ("reap the whirlwind"). Under the law, Israel was to repent and follow God's every command in order to receive his blessing. But the never-ending cycle of failure and repentance persisted, for who could perfectly live up to the law? What is done in selfishness and sin will always reap death and ruin.

But Christ's work on the cross enables all people to choose to live, or "sow," Spirit-filled lives. Galatians 6:7–8 outlines this principle: "A man reaps what he sows. Whoever sows to please their flesh, from the flesh will reap destruction; whoever sows to please the Spirit, from the Spirit will reap eternal life." When followers of Jesus walk with the Holy Spirit and live intentional lives for God, the natural overflow will be lives that yield a righteous and blessed harvest and impact God's kingdom for all eternity.

Punishment for Israel

9 Do not rejoice, Israel;
do not be jubilant like the other nations.
For you have been unfaithful to your God;
you love the wages of a prostitute
at every threshing floor.
2 Threshing floors and winepresses will not feed the people;
the new wine will fail them.
3 They will not remain in the LORD's land;
Ephraim will return to Egypt
and eat unclean food in Assyria.
4 They will not pour out wine offerings to the LORD,
nor will their sacrifices please him.
Such sacrifices will be to them like the bread of mourners;
all who eat them will be unclean.
This food will be for themselves;
it will not come into the temple of the LORD.

5 What will you do on the day of your appointed festivals,
on the feast days of the LORD?
6 Even if they escape from destruction,
Egypt will gather them,
and Memphis will bury them.
Their treasures of silver will be taken over by briers,
and thorns will overrun their tents.
7 The days of punishment are coming,
the days of reckoning are at hand.
Let Israel know this.
Because your sins are so many
and your hostility so great,
the prophet is considered a fool,
the inspired person a maniac.
8 The prophet, along with my God,
is the watchman over Ephraim,[a]
yet snares await him on all his paths,
and hostility in the house of his God.
9 They have sunk deep into corruption,
as in the days of Gibeah.
God will remember their wickedness
and punish them for their sins.

10 "When I found Israel,
it was like finding grapes in the desert;
when I saw your ancestors,
it was like seeing the early fruit on the fig tree.
But when they came to Baal Peor,
they consecrated themselves to that shameful idol
and became as vile as the thing they loved.
11 Ephraim's glory will fly away like a bird —
no birth, no pregnancy, no conception.
12 Even if they rear children,
I will bereave them of every one.
Woe to them
when I turn away from them!
13 I have seen Ephraim, like Tyre,
planted in a pleasant place.

[a] 8 Or *The prophet is the watchman over Ephraim, / the people of my God*

But Ephraim will bring out
their children to the slayer."

14 Give them, LORD—
what will you give them?
Give them wombs that miscarry
and breasts that are dry.

15 "Because of all their wickedness in Gilgal,
I hated them there.
Because of their sinful deeds,
I will drive them out of my house.
I will no longer love them;
all their leaders are rebellious.
16 Ephraim is blighted,
their root is withered,
they yield no fruit.
Even if they bear children,
I will slay their cherished offspring."

17 My God will reject them
because they have not obeyed him;
they will be wanderers among the nations.

10 Israel was a spreading vine;
he brought forth fruit for himself.
As his fruit increased,
he built more altars;
as his land prospered,
he adorned his sacred stones.
2 Their heart is deceitful,
and now they must bear their guilt.
The LORD will demolish their altars
and destroy their sacred stones.

3 Then they will say, "We have no king
because we did not revere the LORD.
But even if we had a king,
what could he do for us?"
4 They make many promises,
take false oaths
and make agreements;
therefore lawsuits spring up
like poisonous weeds in a plowed field.
5 The people who live in Samaria fear
for the calf-idol of Beth Aven.[a]
Its people will mourn over it,
and so will its idolatrous priests,
those who had rejoiced over its splendor,
because it is taken from them into exile.
6 It will be carried to Assyria
as tribute for the great king.
Ephraim will be disgraced;
Israel will be ashamed of its foreign alliances.
7 Samaria's king will be destroyed,
swept away like a twig on the surface of the
waters.

[a] 5 *Beth Aven* means *house of wickedness* (a derogatory name for Bethel, which means *house of God*).

HOSEA 10:5

IN THE SPIRIT AND IN TRUTH

In Hosea 10:5, "Beth Aven" means "house of wickedness," a derogatory name for "Bethel," which means "house of God." Years earlier, the schism following Solomon's reign had resulted in two kingdoms. Jeroboam I, the first king of the northern kingdom (Israel), moved worship from Jerusalem by establishing golden calves in the towns of Bethel and Dan (1Ki 12:28–30). Under this king and nearly all of his successors, the people of Israel went further and further astray. They intermingled worship of the one true God with worship of foreign gods. Eventually the city of Samaria became the capital of the northern kingdom, and "Samaria" became another name for the entire nation.

By the time of Jesus, a bitter hostility existed between the Jews and Samaritans. When Jesus passed through Samaria and spoke with a woman at a well, she was living with the difficult history between Jews and Samaritans every single day. This outcast among outcasts challenged Jesus with a question about worship in John 4:20: "Our ancestors worshiped on this mountain, but you Jews claim that the place where we must worship is in Jerusalem." Jesus explained that ultimately it was not going to be about the location of where a person worships, but, because of the Messiah, a time was coming—and indeed, "has now come"—when God's people would worship "in the Spirit and in truth" (Jn 4:23). He revealed that he was, in fact, the Messiah. Jesus made returning to God a reality with his life,

(continued on next page)

(In the Spirit and in Truth, continued)

death and resurrection. Now, through faith in Jesus, people can worship God in the Spirit and in truth.

HOSEA 11:1

EXODUS FROM EGYPT

In Hosea 11:1, God spoke through Hosea of his great love for his people, a promised love that was deep and parental. God regarded Israel as a child, and the Israelites were often referred to as God's children. When God said he called his people out of Egypt, he was referring to how he redeemed his people from slavery and bondage in Egypt during the exodus. This great act was *the* act of redemption the Israelites associated with God as Redeemer of his people. This was the event that exemplified true redemption for the people of Israel in Old Testament times.

Now, living in the shadow of the cross, followers of Jesus can see how God is always redeeming, and just like he brought his people out of Egypt and out of slavery, he has now brought all people out of slavery to sin through the life, death and resurrection of Jesus Christ, giving them the title "children of God." In Romans 8:14–15, the promise is clear: "Those who are led by the Spirit of God are the children of God. The Spirit you received does not make you slaves, so that you live in fear again; rather, the Spirit you received brought about your adoption to sonship." As the Israelites walked out of slavery, so also people today can make their exodus from fear and death into the freedom and life found in Christ.

8 The high places of wickedness[a] will be destroyed —
it is the sin of Israel.
Thorns and thistles will grow up
and cover their altars.
Then they will say to the mountains, "Cover us!"
and to the hills, "Fall on us!"

9 "Since the days of Gibeah, you have sinned, Israel,
and there you have remained.[b]
Will not war again overtake
the evildoers in Gibeah?
10 When I please, I will punish them;
nations will be gathered against them
to put them in bonds for their double sin.
11 Ephraim is a trained heifer
that loves to thresh;
so I will put a yoke
on her fair neck.
I will drive Ephraim,
Judah must plow,
and Jacob must break up the ground.
12 Sow righteousness for yourselves,
reap the fruit of unfailing love,
and break up your unplowed ground;
for it is time to seek the LORD,
until he comes
and showers his righteousness on you.
13 But you have planted wickedness,
you have reaped evil,
you have eaten the fruit of deception.
Because you have depended on your own strength
and on your many warriors,
14 the roar of battle will rise against your people,
so that all your fortresses will be devastated —
as Shalman devastated Beth Arbel on the day of battle,
when mothers were dashed to the ground with their children.
15 So will it happen to you, Bethel,
because your wickedness is great.
When that day dawns,
the king of Israel will be completely destroyed.

God's Love for Israel

11 "When Israel was a child, I loved him,
and out of Egypt I called my son.
2 But the more they were called,
the more they went away from me.[c]
They sacrificed to the Baals
and they burned incense to images.
3 It was I who taught Ephraim to walk,
taking them by the arms;
but they did not realize
it was I who healed them.
4 I led them with cords of human kindness,
with ties of love.

[a] 8 Hebrew *aven,* a reference to Beth Aven (a derogatory name for Bethel); see verse 5.
[b] 9 Or *there a stand was taken* [c] 2 Septuagint; Hebrew *them*

To them I was like one who lifts
a little child to the cheek,
and I bent down to feed them.

5 "Will they not return to Egypt
and will not Assyria rule over them
because they refuse to repent?
6 A sword will flash in their cities;
it will devour their false prophets
and put an end to their plans.
7 My people are determined to turn from me.
Even though they call me God Most High,
I will by no means exalt them.
8 "How can I give you up, Ephraim?
How can I hand you over, Israel?
How can I treat you like Admah?
How can I make you like Zeboyim?
My heart is changed within me;
all my compassion is aroused.
9 I will not carry out my fierce anger,
nor will I devastate Ephraim again.
For I am God, and not a man—
the Holy One among you.
I will not come against their cities.
10 They will follow the LORD;
he will roar like a lion.
When he roars,
his children will come trembling from the west.
11 They will come from Egypt,
trembling like sparrows,
from Assyria, fluttering like doves.
I will settle them in their homes,"
declares the LORD.

Israel's Sin

12 Ephraim has surrounded me with lies,
Israel with deceit.
And Judah is unruly against God,
even against the faithful Holy One.[a]

12 [b] 1 Ephraim feeds on the wind;
he pursues the east wind all day
and multiplies lies and violence.
He makes a treaty with Assyria
and sends olive oil to Egypt.
2 The LORD has a charge to bring against Judah;
he will punish Jacob[c] according to his ways
and repay him according to his deeds.
3 In the womb he grasped his brother's heel;
as a man he struggled with God.
4 He struggled with the angel and overcame him;
he wept and begged for his favor.
He found him at Bethel
and talked with him there—

[a] *12* In Hebrew texts this verse (11:12) is numbered 12:1. [b] In Hebrew texts 12:1-14 is numbered 12:2-15. [c] *2* *Jacob* means *he grasps the heel*, a Hebrew idiom for *he takes advantage of* or *he deceives*.

A REBELLIOUS SON

Scripture records the unique relationship that God established between himself and Israel. Referred to as God's child or son (Hos 11:1), God deeply loved the people of Israel and gifted them with special rights, privileges, promises and an inheritance corresponding to that which is reserved for children by their fathers. Grasping this foundational bond helps the reader to understand the great heartbreak God felt when the Israelites rejected his affection and chose to go their own way. It also points to the steadfast character of God as a loving Father to his people.

Jesus told a parable about a lost son in Luke 15:11 – 32 in which a son decided to go his own way and leave his father's house in rebellion. Jesus described the son's downward spiral as he tried to find fulfillment in worldly things. When the son came to the end of himself and realized his terrible error in judgment, he decided to return home. Before he could even get the full apology out of his mouth, the father had run to embrace him in his repentance with open arms and a joyful celebration. The father also had an older son who never left his side, yet this son held both his father and brother in contempt when the father accepted his brother so easily. Despite the actions of and the conflict between the sons, the true heart of the story is the extravagant grace of the father toward both of the sons.

Israel and the sons in Jesus' parable had in common their disobedience and their quest to find satisfaction apart from God, either in outright rebellion or through moral performance. A person can be near the things of God without recognizing the grace of God — saying and doing the right things without actually knowing God (Hos 6:6). Rebellion separates people from God, but both Hosea and the parable of the lost son reveal that God's heart is full of abundant grace and a kindness that leads to repentance (Ro 2:4). When Jesus came, he came as the true and perfect Son, a ransom for Israel and the Savior for all people who will trust in him. And he displayed the heart of God as the perfect Father who welcomes all those who call upon Christ into his family.

5 the LORD God Almighty,
the LORD is his name!
6 But you must return to your God;
maintain love and justice,
and wait for your God always.

7 The merchant uses dishonest scales
and loves to defraud.
8 Ephraim boasts,
"I am very rich; I have become wealthy.
With all my wealth they will not find in me
any iniquity or sin."

9 "I have been the LORD your God
ever since you came out of Egypt;
I will make you live in tents again,
as in the days of your appointed festivals.
10 I spoke to the prophets,
gave them many visions
and told parables through them."

11 Is Gilead wicked?
Its people are worthless!
Do they sacrifice bulls in Gilgal?
Their altars will be like piles of stones
on a plowed field.
12 Jacob fled to the country of Aram[a];
Israel served to get a wife,
and to pay for her he tended sheep.
13 The LORD used a prophet to bring Israel up from Egypt,
by a prophet he cared for him.
14 But Ephraim has aroused his bitter anger;
his Lord will leave on him the guilt of his
bloodshed
and will repay him for his contempt.

The LORD's Anger Against Israel

13 When Ephraim spoke, people trembled;
he was exalted in Israel.
But he became guilty of Baal worship and died.
2 Now they sin more and more;
they make idols for themselves from their silver,
cleverly fashioned images,
all of them the work of craftsmen.
It is said of these people,
"They offer human sacrifices!
They kiss[b] calf-idols!"
3 Therefore they will be like the morning mist,
like the early dew that disappears,
like chaff swirling from a threshing floor,
like smoke escaping through a window.

4 "But I have been the LORD your God
ever since you came out of Egypt.
You shall acknowledge no God but me,
no Savior except me.
5 I cared for you in the wilderness,
in the land of burning heat.

[a] 12 That is, Northwest Mesopotamia [b] 2 Or *"Men who sacrifice / kiss*

HOSEA 13:14

RANSOM AND REDEMPTION

Relentless judgment seems to be rampant throughout the pages of Hosea. But God's love is revealed to be even more unstoppable than divine judgment when readers view this Scripture through the lens of love personified — that is, through Jesus Christ. The extensive judgment in this text is followed by rhetorical questions that point toward redemption and ransom: God seems to be asking himself, "Will I ransom my people?" and, "Will I redeem them from death?" The unfaithfulness of the people has incited extreme judgment and wrath, yet God still holds out a promise of hope (Hos 14:4 – 8).

Despite their sin, God was faithful and loving to save his people. There is no more beautiful expression of this love than when Jesus arrived on the scene hundreds of years later, leaving heaven to walk on earth with the primary purpose of ransoming his people and defeating death once and for all. Hosea 13:14 is quoted in 1 Corinthians 15:55 – 57, in what is perhaps one of the most triumphant and victorious exclamations of the finished work of Jesus: "Where, O death, is your victory? Where, O death, is your sting? The sting of death is sin, and the power of sin is the law. But thanks be to God! He gives us the victory through our Lord Jesus Christ." God's people are redeemed from punishment into glorious life both now and forever.

6 When I fed them, they were satisfied;
when they were satisfied, they became proud;
then they forgot me.
7 So I will be like a lion to them,
like a leopard I will lurk by the path.
8 Like a bear robbed of her cubs,
I will attack them and rip them open;
like a lion I will devour them —
a wild animal will tear them apart.

9 "You are destroyed, Israel,
because you are against me, against your helper.
10 Where is your king, that he may save you?
Where are your rulers in all your towns,
of whom you said,
'Give me a king and princes'?
11 So in my anger I gave you a king,
and in my wrath I took him away.
12 The guilt of Ephraim is stored up,
his sins are kept on record.
13 Pains as of a woman in childbirth come to him,
but he is a child without wisdom;
when the time arrives,
he doesn't have the sense to come out of the
womb.

14 "I will deliver this people from the power of the grave;
I will redeem them from death.
Where, O death, are your plagues?
Where, O grave, is your destruction?

"I will have no compassion,
15 even though he thrives among his brothers.
An east wind from the LORD will come,
blowing in from the desert;
his spring will fail
and his well dry up.
His storehouse will be plundered
of all its treasures.
16 The people of Samaria must bear their guilt,
because they have rebelled against their God.
They will fall by the sword;
their little ones will be dashed to the ground,
their pregnant women ripped open."[a]

Repentance to Bring Blessing

14 [b] Return, Israel, to the LORD your God.
Your sins have been your downfall!
2 Take words with you
and return to the LORD.
Say to him:
"Forgive all our sins
and receive us graciously,
that we may offer the fruit of our lips.[c]
3 Assyria cannot save us;
we will not mount warhorses.

[a] *16* In Hebrew texts this verse (13:16) is numbered 14:1. [b] In Hebrew texts 14:1-9 is numbered 14:2-10. [c] *2* Or *offer our lips as sacrifices of bulls*

We will never again say 'Our gods'
to what our own hands have made,
for in you the fatherless find compassion."

4 "I will heal their waywardness
and love them freely,
for my anger has turned away from them.
5 I will be like the dew to Israel;
he will blossom like a lily.
Like a cedar of Lebanon
he will send down his roots;
6 his young shoots will grow.
His splendor will be like an olive tree,
his fragrance like a cedar of Lebanon.
7 People will dwell again in his shade;
they will flourish like the grain,
they will blossom like the vine—
Israel's fame will be like the wine of Lebanon.
8 Ephraim, what more have I[a] to do with idols?
I will answer him and care for him.
I am like a flourishing juniper;
your fruitfulness comes from me."

9 Who is wise? Let them realize these things.
Who is discerning? Let them understand.
The ways of the LORD are right;
the righteous walk in them,
but the rebellious stumble in them.

[a] 8 Or Hebrew; Septuagint *What more has Ephraim*

HOSEA 14:4–8

HOPE FOR A FUTURE

In the stunning conclusion to the book of Hosea, God puts the exclamation mark on his intention for his people, the chosen ones of God: he has chosen to redeem them despite their blatant rebellion. When Israel returns to God, he will not turn away from them as they deserve, but will rather provide healing and a home for them with himself, allowing them to once again belong to him; they will put their roots down in him and be fruitful because of his care and compassion to them. Instead of cutting them off forever, God will give them a beautiful future with him as his people.

There is perhaps no better parallel than one that comes from the prophet Jeremiah, although it came over a century later. It also reveals God's heart and purpose for his people in the midst of their struggle, and reminds them of the hope only he can provide: " 'For I know the plans I have for you,' declares the LORD, 'plans to prosper you and not to harm you, plans to give you hope and a future' " (Jer 29:11). God reminded his people continually of his love throughout their trials, assuring them that when they repented and sought him, he would bring them back to himself. This is shown in the most ultimate way through Jesus—who is "the way and the truth and the life" (Jn 14:6). Jesus gives those who will trust in him the best hope: everlasting life with him.

JESUS: OUR BLESSED HOPE

JOEL

JOEL

ELISHA SUCCEEDS ELIJAH *c. 848 BC*	ESTIMATED DATE FOR THE PROPHETIC MINISTRY OF JOEL *c. 830 BC*	FALL OF ISRAEL *c. 722 BC*

Joel used the image of a natural disaster to picture God's forthcoming judgment. Floods, earthquakes, famine and other calamities provoke fear and dread among all people. They are usually unexpected and often unexplained — leaving a wake of destruction, despair and confusion in their path.

This time, however, the disaster would have a clear cause. Joel began with a terrifying image — a plague of ravenous locusts that would wreak havoc on the people, their land and their crops. Nothing would escape the locusts' devastating work. This plague, like those God used to release the Israelites from slavery in Egypt, was meant to demonstrate the all-surpassing power of the one true God and provoke repentance from all those who witnessed the stunning devastation. Joel called the people of Judah to return to God based on their experience of his judgment in the locust plague (2:12 – 14). He warned that, should they continue in their rebellion, a greater and more devastating judgment would soon come. The intervening time between the plague of locusts and the forthcoming judgment of God would allow space for the people to return humbly to God.

Joel knew that the people's propensity to sin would unleash the coming acts of judgment as well. God's patience would be tested again, as there seemed to be no end to the people's rebellion and recklessness against God. Would he finally give up on his people forever? Had they finally crossed the line and gone too far for the love of God?

The answer, once again, is a resounding, no! A day would come when God would pour out his Spirit on his people (2:28 – 32). This coming day, known only by God, would restore the fortunes of God's people and demonstrate God's faithfulness. God would restore the prosperity of the land, destroy the pagan nations and once again dwell in Zion.

Following the sending of the Spirit at Pentecost, Peter proclaimed that the prophet Joel's words had been fulfilled in their day (Ac 2:16 – 21). The Spirit would serve as an ever-present reminder of the faithfulness of God to fulfill his promises to restore his people and "repay you for the years the locusts have eaten" (Joel 2:25).

RETURN TO THE LORD YOUR GOD, FOR HE IS GRACIOUS AND COMPASSIONATE, SLOW TO ANGER AND ABOUNDING IN LOVE, AND HE RELENTS FROM SENDING CALAMITY.

Joel 2:13

JOEL

1 The word of the LORD that came to Joel son of Pethuel.

An Invasion of Locusts

[2] Hear this, you elders;
listen, all who live in the land.
Has anything like this ever happened in your days
or in the days of your ancestors?
[3] Tell it to your children,
and let your children tell it to their children,
and their children to the next generation.
[4] What the locust swarm has left
the great locusts have eaten;
what the great locusts have left
the young locusts have eaten;
what the young locusts have left
other locusts[a] have eaten.

[5] Wake up, you drunkards, and weep!
Wail, all you drinkers of wine;
wail because of the new wine,
for it has been snatched from your lips.
[6] A nation has invaded my land,
a mighty army without number;
it has the teeth of a lion,
the fangs of a lioness.
[7] It has laid waste my vines
and ruined my fig trees.
It has stripped off their bark
and thrown it away,
leaving their branches white.

[8] Mourn like a virgin in sackcloth
grieving for the betrothed of her youth.
[9] Grain offerings and drink offerings
are cut off from the house of the LORD.
The priests are in mourning,
those who minister before the LORD.
[10] The fields are ruined,
the ground is dried up;
the grain is destroyed,
the new wine is dried up,
the olive oil fails.

[11] Despair, you farmers,
wail, you vine growers;
grieve for the wheat and the barley,
because the harvest of the field is destroyed.
[12] The vine is dried up
and the fig tree is withered;

---

[a] *4* The precise meaning of the four Hebrew words used here for locusts is uncertain.

the pomegranate, the palm and the apple[a] tree —
all the trees of the field — are dried up.
Surely the people's joy
is withered away.

A Call to Lamentation

13 Put on sackcloth, you priests, and mourn;
wail, you who minister before the altar.
Come, spend the night in sackcloth,
you who minister before my God;
for the grain offerings and drink offerings
are withheld from the house of your God.
14 Declare a holy fast;
call a sacred assembly.
Summon the elders
and all who live in the land
to the house of the LORD your God,
and cry out to the LORD.

15 Alas for that day!
For the day of the LORD is near;
it will come like destruction from the Almighty.[b]

16 Has not the food been cut off
before our very eyes —
joy and gladness
from the house of our God?
17 The seeds are shriveled
beneath the clods.[c]
The storehouses are in ruins,
the granaries have been broken down,
for the grain has dried up.
18 How the cattle moan!
The herds mill about
because they have no pasture;
even the flocks of sheep are suffering.

19 To you, LORD, I call,
for fire has devoured the pastures in the wilderness
and flames have burned up all the trees of the field.
20 Even the wild animals pant for you;
the streams of water have dried up
and fire has devoured the pastures in the wilderness.

An Army of Locusts

2 Blow the trumpet in Zion;
sound the alarm on my holy hill.
Let all who live in the land tremble,
for the day of the LORD is coming.
It is close at hand —
2 a day of darkness and gloom,
a day of clouds and blackness.
Like dawn spreading across the mountains
a large and mighty army comes,
such as never was in ancient times
nor ever will be in ages to come.

[a] *12* Or possibly *apricot* [b] *15* Hebrew *Shaddai* [c] *17* The meaning of the Hebrew for this word is uncertain.

3 Before them fire devours,
behind them a flame blazes.
Before them the land is like the garden of Eden,
behind them, a desert waste —
nothing escapes them.
4 They have the appearance of horses;
they gallop along like cavalry.
5 With a noise like that of chariots
they leap over the mountaintops,
like a crackling fire consuming stubble,
like a mighty army drawn up for battle.

6 At the sight of them, nations are in anguish;
every face turns pale.
7 They charge like warriors;
they scale walls like soldiers.
They all march in line,
not swerving from their course.
8 They do not jostle each other;
each marches straight ahead.
They plunge through defenses
without breaking ranks.
9 They rush upon the city;
they run along the wall.
They climb into the houses;
like thieves they enter through the windows.

10 Before them the earth shakes,
the heavens tremble,
the sun and moon are darkened,
and the stars no longer shine.
11 The LORD thunders
at the head of his army;
his forces are beyond number,
and mighty is the army that obeys his command.
The day of the LORD is great;
it is dreadful.
Who can endure it?

Rend Your Heart

12 "Even now," declares the LORD,
"return to me with all your heart,
with fasting and weeping and mourning."

13 Rend your heart
and not your garments.
Return to the LORD your God,
for he is gracious and compassionate,
slow to anger and abounding in love,
and he relents from sending calamity.
14 Who knows? He may turn and relent
and leave behind a blessing —
grain offerings and drink offerings
for the LORD your God.

15 Blow the trumpet in Zion,
declare a holy fast,
call a sacred assembly.
16 Gather the people,
consecrate the assembly;

bring together the elders,
gather the children,
those nursing at the breast.
Let the bridegroom leave his room
and the bride her chamber.
17 Let the priests, who minister before the LORD,
weep between the portico and the altar.
Let them say, "Spare your people, LORD.
Do not make your inheritance an object of scorn,
a byword among the nations.
Why should they say among the peoples,
'Where is their God?' "

The LORD's Answer

18 Then the LORD was jealous for his land
and took pity on his people.

19 The LORD replied[a] to them:

"I am sending you grain, new wine and olive oil,
enough to satisfy you fully;
never again will I make you
an object of scorn to the nations.

20 "I will drive the northern horde far from you,
pushing it into a parched and barren land;
its eastern ranks will drown in the Dead Sea
and its western ranks in the Mediterranean Sea.
And its stench will go up;
its smell will rise."

Surely he has done great things!
21 Do not be afraid, land of Judah;
be glad and rejoice.
Surely the LORD has done great things!
22 Do not be afraid, you wild animals,
for the pastures in the wilderness are becoming green.
The trees are bearing their fruit;
the fig tree and the vine yield their riches.
23 Be glad, people of Zion,
rejoice in the LORD your God,
for he has given you the autumn rains
because he is faithful.
He sends you abundant showers,
both autumn and spring rains, as before.
24 The threshing floors will be filled with grain;
the vats will overflow with new wine and oil.

25 "I will repay you for the years the locusts have eaten —
the great locust and the young locust,
the other locusts and the locust swarm[b] —
my great army that I sent among you.
26 You will have plenty to eat, until you are full,
and you will praise the name of the LORD your God,
who has worked wonders for you;
never again will my people be shamed.

---

[a] *18,19* Or *LORD will be jealous . . . / and take pity . . . / 19The LORD will reply* [b] *25* The precise meaning of the four Hebrew words used here for locusts is uncertain.

[27] Then you will know that I am in Israel,
 that I am the LORD your God,
 and that there is no other;
never again will my people be shamed.

The Day of the LORD

[28] "And afterward,
 I will pour out my Spirit on all people.
Your sons and daughters will prophesy,
 your old men will dream dreams,
 your young men will see visions.
[29] Even on my servants, both men and women,
 I will pour out my Spirit in those days.
[30] I will show wonders in the heavens
 and on the earth,
 blood and fire and billows of smoke.
[31] The sun will be turned to darkness
 and the moon to blood
 before the coming of the great and dreadful day
 of the LORD.
[32] And everyone who calls
 on the name of the LORD will be saved;
for on Mount Zion and in Jerusalem
 there will be deliverance,
 as the LORD has said,
even among the survivors
 whom the LORD calls.[a]

The Nations Judged

3 [b] "In those days and at that time,
 when I restore the fortunes of Judah and Jerusalem,
[2] I will gather all nations
 and bring them down to the Valley of Jehoshaphat.[c]
There I will put them on trial
 for what they did to my inheritance, my people Israel,
because they scattered my people among the nations
 and divided up my land.
[3] They cast lots for my people
 and traded boys for prostitutes;
 they sold girls for wine to drink.

[4] "Now what have you against me, Tyre and Sidon and all you regions of Philistia? Are you repaying me for something I have done? If you are paying me back, I
will swiftly and speedily return on your own heads what you have done. [5] For you
took my silver and my gold and carried off my finest treasures to your temples.[d]
[6] You sold the people of Judah and Jerusalem to the Greeks, that you might send
them far from their homeland.

[7] "See, I am going to rouse them out of the places to which you sold them, and
I will return on your own heads what you have done. [8] I will sell your sons and
daughters to the people of Judah, and they will sell them to the Sabeans, a nation
far away." The LORD has spoken.

[9] Proclaim this among the nations:
 Prepare for war!
Rouse the warriors!
 Let all the fighting men draw near and attack.

JOEL 2:28–32

CALLING ON JESUS' NAME

Joel began his prophecy by declaring God's judgment on the people of Judah for their sins. He urged his listeners to repent and to return to God. This was Joel's core message: Repentance brings about salvation. He promised that as the people repented and sought after God (Joel 1:13–14; 2:12–13), God would answer them and come to their rescue (2:25–27).

Joel 2:28–32 details that God not only wanted to rescue his people, he also wanted to bring his people to a place of complete and future restoration. The Lord promised that he would place his Spirit on all people. He desired to make a way for his presence to dwell within humankind. He also promised that anyone who would call on the name of the Lord would be saved. Later, in Acts 2:14–41, Peter preached the same message as Joel. He called the people to repent from their sins and call on the name of Jesus to be forgiven and to receive the gift of the Holy Spirit of God. Since that day, the Holy Spirit has been fueling and building the church.

---

[a] *32* In Hebrew texts 2:28-32 is numbered 3:1-5. [b] In Hebrew texts 3:1-21 is numbered 4:1-21.
[c] *2* *Jehoshaphat* means *the LORD judges*; also in verse 12. [d] *5* Or *palaces*

THE SIGNIFICANCE OF PENTECOST

The outpouring of the Holy Spirit was an extraordinary event that happened on the day of Pentecost. After the crucifixion, Jesus' disciples had seen him alive and risen from the dead. Before Jesus ascended to heaven, he told them to remain in Jerusalem and wait for the gift of the Holy Spirit. They were all gathered in one room when "suddenly a sound like the blowing of a violent wind came from heaven and filled the whole house where they were sitting" (Ac 2:2). Then "they saw what seemed to be tongues of fire that separated and came to rest on each of them" (v. 3). They were all "filled with the Holy Spirit and began to speak in other tongues" (v. 4), "declaring the wonders of God" in different languages (v. 11).

Because of the festival of Pentecost (the ancient Jewish Festival of Harvest; Ex 23:16), people from many nations were gathered in Jerusalem. As a crowd gathered around the disciples, many were bewildered to hear Galileans speaking in their native language. Peter stood up and preached to the crowd, proclaiming that the prophecy in Joel 2:28–32 had been fulfilled (Ac 2:14–21): The Holy Spirit had come to be with God's people. The disciples were filled with and empowered to speak in other languages by the Holy Spirit of God. Peter declared that Jesus was the way to salvation and anyone who put their faith in him could have eternal life. As Joel prophesied, "Everyone who calls on the name of the LORD will be saved" (Joel 2:32). On that day of Pentecost, three thousand people were added to the church (Ac 2:41).

Jesus was the one who made possible the indwelling of the Holy Spirit. Because sin separated humans from God, God's presence could not live inside of his people. Jesus' atoning sacrifice made a way for the Holy Spirit to come and make his home in the hearts and lives of believers (Ro 8:1–4).

The Holy Spirit is one member of the Trinity, along with the Son and the Father. His role is to reveal and magnify Jesus (Jn 14:26; 15:26; 16:13–14; Ac 1:8), to restore and refine his people into the image of Christ (Ro 8:5–13) and unite and lead the church (1Co 12:12–31).

The day of Pentecost ushered in a new era of history. The church was born, and God's Spirit became accessible for everybody. Today, the Holy Spirit is still at work in the lives of those who trust in Jesus alone for salvation and surrender to the Spirit's leading.

JOEL 3:17–21

A FUTURE HOPE

Joel prophesied that God would judge other nations for how they treated his people. On the day of the Lord, this future judgment would come; however, on that terrible day, the Lord promised to be a refuge for his people. In this passage, God promised to be the God of his people and live among them in Jerusalem. As a result of God's presence among the people, the land would be blessed, fruitful and safe from foreign invasion.

This blessing points believers to the day referenced in Revelation 22:1–2, where in the new heaven and the new earth, the river of life will flow from the throne of God and bring life to all the city—including the tree of life, which will continually bear fruit. The people of God can take part in this beautiful blessing because of the work of Jesus on the cross. When Jesus died on the cross, he took on the guilt of all who will trust in him for salvation, and he became the one way that God would pardon human sin.

Jesus, then, is the ultimate refuge for the people of God. He not only protects them from their enemies, but he has also absorbed the wrath of God on their behalf. This is what makes it possible for God to dwell within his people. Now, the people of God, with the indwelling of the Holy Spirit, live each day of their lives with the hope of a great future and wait for this promise of eternal blessing to be realized.

10 Beat your plowshares into swords
and your pruning hooks into spears.
Let the weakling say,
"I am strong!"
11 Come quickly, all you nations from every side,
and assemble there.

Bring down your warriors, LORD!

12 "Let the nations be roused;
let them advance into the Valley of Jehoshaphat,
for there I will sit
to judge all the nations on every side.
13 Swing the sickle,
for the harvest is ripe.
Come, trample the grapes,
for the winepress is full
and the vats overflow—
so great is their wickedness!"

14 Multitudes, multitudes
in the valley of decision!
For the day of the LORD is near
in the valley of decision.
15 The sun and moon will be darkened,
and the stars no longer shine.
16 The LORD will roar from Zion
and thunder from Jerusalem;
the earth and the heavens will tremble.
But the LORD will be a refuge for his people,
a stronghold for the people of Israel.

Blessings for God's People

17 "Then you will know that I, the LORD your God,
dwell in Zion, my holy hill.
Jerusalem will be holy;
never again will foreigners invade her.

18 "In that day the mountains will drip new wine,
and the hills will flow with milk;
all the ravines of Judah will run with water.
A fountain will flow out of the LORD's house
and will water the valley of acacias.[a]
19 But Egypt will be desolate,
Edom a desert waste,
because of violence done to the people of Judah,
in whose land they shed innocent blood.
20 Judah will be inhabited forever
and Jerusalem through all generations.
21 Shall I leave their innocent blood unavenged?
No, I will not."

The LORD dwells in Zion!

[a] 18 Or *Valley of Shittim*

JESUS: OUR JUSTICE BEARER

AMOS

AMOS

REIGN OF UZZIAH OF JUDAH	REIGN OF JEROBOAM II OF ISRAEL	PROPHETIC MINISTRY OF AMOS
c. 792 – 740 BC	*c. 793 – 753 BC*	*c. 760 – 750 BC*

The striking metaphors and dynamic themes of the book of Amos make it one of the most familiar of all of the Minor Prophets. Amos, a shepherd, prophesied during the reigns of Uzziah king of Judah and Jeroboam II king of Israel. Though his home was in Judah, Amos was sent to announce God's judgment on the northern kingdom of Israel. His familiarity with the needs of the people of Israel prompted the remarkable clarity of his prophetic call.

Amos's words contain a different tone than many of the other prophets. His main concern was justice among God's people. Their spiritual failures resulted in ongoing injustice within the nation of Israel itself.

Justice is meant to be tangible. Injustice fosters hostility, hatred, jealousy and rage. Justice, on the other hand, fosters loving-kindness, care and service. God's people are to be marked by justice because God acts justly toward his people.

God's bountiful provision to the nation of Israel produced a spirit of superiority between the wealthy and those whom they were called to love. The upper class, bolstered by the prosperity brought about under the rule of Jeroboam II, neglected their social responsibility to care for their own countrymen. As in many societies in our world today, people of means marginalized and exploited people who were poor in order to advance their selfish pursuits.

God, through Amos, warns that such divisiveness is unfit for his people. God's law demanded that his people care for the downtrodden and marginalized and supply their needs — even if they were outsiders and sojourners living among the nation of Israel. If there was ever a place where social inequity and injustice should not have been found, it should have been among the people of Israel.

Yet injustice was pervasive in the hearts of the Israelites. Amos warned Israel's leaders to repent, to lead the people to right the inequality and to restore justice in the land. He longed for Israel to "let justice roll on like a river, righteousness like a never-failing stream!" (5:24). These days would fully come only when God ushered in his kingdom through the work of his Son, Jesus Christ, who would come to seek and save all those who were lost — poor and rich, weak and strong, marginalized and powerful. Today all who come to him, regardless of their social status, can become children of God and be part of his family, the church, where all people can find love, acceptance and care.

BUT LET JUSTICE ROLL ON LIKE A RIVER, RIGHTEOUSNESS LIKE A NEVER-FAILING STREAM!

Amos 5:24

AMOS

1 The words of Amos, one of the shepherds of Tekoa — the vision he saw concerning Israel two years before the earthquake, when Uzziah was king of Judah and Jeroboam son of Jehoash[a] was king of Israel.
2 He said:

"The LORD roars from Zion
    and thunders from Jerusalem;
the pastures of the shepherds dry up,
    and the top of Carmel withers."

Judgment on Israel's Neighbors

3 This is what the LORD says:

"For three sins of Damascus,
    even for four, I will not relent.
Because she threshed Gilead
    with sledges having iron teeth,
4 I will send fire on the house of Hazael
    that will consume the fortresses of Ben-Hadad.
5 I will break down the gate of Damascus;
    I will destroy the king who is in[b] the Valley of Aven[c]
and the one who holds the scepter in Beth Eden.
    The people of Aram will go into exile to Kir,"

says the LORD.

6 This is what the LORD says:

"For three sins of Gaza,
    even for four, I will not relent.
Because she took captive whole communities
    and sold them to Edom,
7 I will send fire on the walls of Gaza
    that will consume her fortresses.
8 I will destroy the king[d] of Ashdod
    and the one who holds the scepter in Ashkelon.
I will turn my hand against Ekron,
    till the last of the Philistines are dead,"

says the Sovereign LORD.

9 This is what the LORD says:

"For three sins of Tyre,
    even for four, I will not relent.
Because she sold whole communities of captives to Edom,
    disregarding a treaty of brotherhood,
10 I will send fire on the walls of Tyre
    that will consume her fortresses."

11 This is what the LORD says:

"For three sins of Edom,
    even for four, I will not relent.
Because he pursued his brother with a sword
    and slaughtered the women of the land,

---

[a] *1* Hebrew *Joash,* a variant of *Jehoash* [b] *5* Or *the inhabitants of* [c] *5* *Aven* means *wickedness.* [d] *8* Or *inhabitants*

because his anger raged continually
and his fury flamed unchecked,
12 I will send fire on Teman
that will consume the fortresses of Bozrah."

13 This is what the LORD says:

"For three sins of Ammon,
even for four, I will not relent.
Because he ripped open the pregnant women of Gilead
in order to extend his borders,
14 I will set fire to the walls of Rabbah
that will consume her fortresses
amid war cries on the day of battle,
amid violent winds on a stormy day.
15 Her king[a] will go into exile,
he and his officials together,"
says the LORD.

2 This is what the LORD says:

"For three sins of Moab,
even for four, I will not relent.
Because he burned to ashes
the bones of Edom's king,
2 I will send fire on Moab
that will consume the fortresses of Kerioth.[b]
Moab will go down in great tumult
amid war cries and the blast of the trumpet.
3 I will destroy her ruler
and kill all her officials with him,"
says the LORD.

4 This is what the LORD says:

"For three sins of Judah,
even for four, I will not relent.
Because they have rejected the law of the LORD
and have not kept his decrees,
because they have been led astray by false gods,[c]
the gods[d] their ancestors followed,
5 I will send fire on Judah
that will consume the fortresses of Jerusalem."

Judgment on Israel

6 This is what the LORD says:

"For three sins of Israel,
even for four, I will not relent.
They sell the innocent for silver,
and the needy for a pair of sandals.
7 They trample on the heads of the poor
as on the dust of the ground
and deny justice to the oppressed.
Father and son use the same girl
and so profane my holy name.
8 They lie down beside every altar
on garments taken in pledge.

AMOS 2:6–16

JUDGMENT COMES

From the time he established the Mosaic covenant at Mount Sinai (Ex 19:1–8), God had clearly laid out his expectation that his people would treat others fairly. In this portion of Amos, God told the people of Israel that they would be judged severely for continually oppressing others—including selling people, mistreating the poor and the persistent practice of sexual immorality.

Similarly, Jesus told the people of his day that judgment would soon come because they also had continued to oppress others. When confronted by a temple system that valued the pocketbooks of merchants more than providing an opportunity for non-Jews to worship the true God, he literally turned the tables on the money changers (Mk 11:15–17).

Jesus refused to tolerate the mistreatment of others. In Matthew 23:13–39, Jesus made it clear that God would soon judge Israel's religious leaders who spiritually oppressed others, saying they had "neglected the more important matters of the law—justice, mercy and faithfulness" (v. 23).

[a] 15 Or / *Molek* [b] 2 Or *of her cities* [c] 4 Or *by lies* [d] 4 Or *lies*

HAPPY TO JUDGE OTHERS

God's call on our lives is rarely easy, and Amos's call was no exception. The Lord told this shepherd of Tekoa (a town about six miles south of Bethlehem) to leave his home in the southern kingdom of Judah to preach divine judgment to the people of the northern kingdom of Israel. Yet Amos's unflinching prophetic message didn't begin with Israel, but instead with her neighbors.

Imagine the smiles on the faces of the Israelites as Amos systematically proclaimed God's judgment on Aram and its capital city Damascus (1:3 – 5), Philistia and its major cities (1:6 – 8), Phoenicia and its principal city Tyre (1:9 – 10), Edom (1:11 – 12), Ammon (1:13 – 15), Moab (2:1 – 3) and even Judah (2:4 – 5). These countries (with the exception of Phoenicia) had been Israel's enemies for generations.

However, God reserved most of Amos's prophetic message for Israel. The people of Israel may have been cheering the beginning of Amos's message, but they likely didn't appreciate the rest of his message.

Jesus had strong words for religious leaders in his day who were quick to pile judgment upon others without looking at themselves first. Jesus said, "Do not judge, or you too will be judged. For in the same way you judge others, you will be judged, and with the measure you use, it will be measured to you" (Mt 7:1 – 2). Jesus went on to make his famous analogy urging his listeners not to look at the speck of sawdust in their brother's eye and ignore the plank in their own (Mt 7:3 – 5).

Jesus never celebrated the sin of others, nor did he celebrate the impending judgment of that sin. Instead, he mourned the coming judgment of God. In Matthew 23, Jesus lamented the impending devastation of Jerusalem that he knew was coming; its residents had killed the prophets and stoned those whom God had sent to warn the city (vv. 37 – 39), and so they were marked for judgment. Jesus modeled a truly broken heart when confronted with God's impending judgment on sin-stained humanity.

Jesus wasn't suggesting that the sins of others be ignored — far from it. Jesus always took sin seriously. Rather he instructed his followers to deal first with their own rebellious hearts before they concerned themselves with the challenges that others faced. Amos's message to the people of Israel was similar, as he called them to face their own sin rather than judging the sins of the surrounding nations.

In the house of their god
they drink wine taken as fines.

9 "Yet I destroyed the Amorites before them,
though they were tall as the cedars
and strong as the oaks.
I destroyed their fruit above
and their roots below.
10 I brought you up out of Egypt
and led you forty years in the wilderness
to give you the land of the Amorites.

11 "I also raised up prophets from among your children
and Nazirites from among your youths.
Is this not true, people of Israel?"
declares the LORD.

12 "But you made the Nazirites drink wine
and commanded the prophets not to prophesy.

13 "Now then, I will crush you
as a cart crushes when loaded with grain.
14 The swift will not escape,
the strong will not muster their strength,
and the warrior will not save his life.
15 The archer will not stand his ground,
the fleet-footed soldier will not get away,
and the horseman will not save his life.
16 Even the bravest warriors
will flee naked on that day,"
declares the LORD.

Witnesses Summoned Against Israel

3 Hear this word, people of Israel, the word the LORD has spoken against you—
against the whole family I brought up out of Egypt:

2 "You only have I chosen
of all the families of the earth;
therefore I will punish you
for all your sins."

3 Do two walk together
unless they have agreed to do so?
4 Does a lion roar in the thicket
when it has no prey?
Does it growl in its den
when it has caught nothing?
5 Does a bird swoop down to a trap on the ground
when no bait is there?
Does a trap spring up from the ground
if it has not caught anything?
6 When a trumpet sounds in a city,
do not the people tremble?
When disaster comes to a city,
has not the LORD caused it?

7 Surely the Sovereign LORD does nothing
without revealing his plan
to his servants the prophets.

8 The lion has roared—
who will not fear?

The Sovereign LORD has spoken —
who can but prophesy?

9 Proclaim to the fortresses of Ashdod
and to the fortresses of Egypt:
"Assemble yourselves on the mountains of Samaria;
see the great unrest within her
and the oppression among her people."

10 "They do not know how to do right," declares the LORD,
"who store up in their fortresses
what they have plundered and looted."

11 Therefore this is what the Sovereign LORD says:

"An enemy will overrun your land,
pull down your strongholds
and plunder your fortresses."

12 This is what the LORD says:

"As a shepherd rescues from the lion's mouth
only two leg bones or a piece of an ear,
so will the Israelites living in Samaria be rescued,
with only the head of a bed
and a piece of fabric[a] from a couch.[b]"

13 "Hear this and testify against the descendants of Jacob," declares the Lord, the LORD God Almighty.

14 "On the day I punish Israel for her sins,
I will destroy the altars of Bethel;
the horns of the altar will be cut off
and fall to the ground.
15 I will tear down the winter house
along with the summer house;
the houses adorned with ivory will be destroyed
and the mansions will be demolished,"
declares the LORD.

Israel Has Not Returned to God

4 Hear this word, you cows of Bashan on Mount Samaria,
you women who oppress the poor and crush the needy
and say to your husbands, "Bring us some drinks!"
2 The Sovereign LORD has sworn by his holiness:
"The time will surely come
when you will be taken away with hooks,
the last of you with fishhooks.[c]
3 You will each go straight out
through breaches in the wall,
and you will be cast out toward Harmon,[d]"
declares the LORD.

4 "Go to Bethel and sin;
go to Gilgal and sin yet more.
Bring your sacrifices every morning,
your tithes every three years.[e]

[a] 12 The meaning of the Hebrew for this phrase is uncertain. [b] 12 Or *Israelites be rescued, / those who sit in Samaria / on the edge of their beds / and in Damascus on their couches.* [c] 2 Or *away in baskets, / the last of you in fish baskets* [d] 3 Masoretic Text; with a different word division of the Hebrew (see Septuagint) *out, you mountain of oppression* [e] 4 Or *days*

DEMOLISHING STRONGHOLDS

Concerned that citizens of the northern kingdom might return their allegiance to the house of David, Jeroboam had, after his revolt against Judah (1Ki 12:1 – 24), built sanctuaries in Bethel and Dan where his people could go and worship. These "convenient" places of worship quickly drifted into outright false worship: Like his pagan neighbors, Jeroboam established high places for worship; he then enrolled people into the priesthood who were not a part of Levitical families, and he altered the Hebrew religious calendar. Jeroboam even had two golden calves built (1Ki 12:25 – 30), which were a key part of Canaanite Baal worship — and eerily similar to the idols the people built at the base of Mount Sinai when Moses was on the mountain receiving the Ten Commandments (Ex 32:1,4).

Amos's message was clear: God would judge the nation for their apostasy by destroying the altars of Bethel. Jeroboam and the people of the northern kingdom had practiced their religion within these structures of false worship without considering the inevitable judgment that God would bring.

Throughout the Bible, God consistently judges spiritual strongholds that keep people in bondage to false religions. The good news is that the Bible gives us the battle plan we need as we set about to demolish the spiritual strongholds that seek to dethrone King Jesus in our world. Paul said that we must "take captive every thought to make it obedient to Christ" (2Co 10:5), following Christ's example of complete devotion to his Father.

Jeroboam tried to "protect" Israel by setting up an intricate yet false system of religion that kept the people from drifting back to the house of David. Yet he didn't realize that he had become a pawn in a cosmic battle — one in which Jesus had already been declared the winner.

AMOS 4:12

PREPARE TO MEET YOUR GOD

Amos told the Israelites that they would need to "prepare to meet [their] God," as the nation would soon be held accountable for its ongoing mistreatment of others and its broken religious system. This language recalls God's encounter with Israel at Mount Sinai (Ex 19:10 – 19), but instead of founding a new covenant, this meeting would be to institute firm discipline for Israel's failure to follow the covenant. Since Israel would soon meet their all-powerful Creator, they had to prepare themselves.

Jesus frequently told his followers to prepare to meet him when he returned. He told a parable about ten virgins who took lamps to go out and meet the bridegroom (Mt 25:1 – 13). Five of the virgins were unwise and left the house unprepared with not enough oil to keep the lamps going. When their lamps went out, these unwise young women had to leave to find more. While they were gone, the groom came.

Jesus urged the people of his day not to be unprepared for his return. Instead, as Amos warned the people of Israel and as Jesus warned his followers — including believers today — we are always to be prepared to meet our God.

5 Burn leavened bread as a thank offering
and brag about your freewill offerings —
boast about them, you Israelites,
for this is what you love to do,"
declares the Sovereign LORD.

6 "I gave you empty stomachs in every city
and lack of bread in every town,
yet you have not returned to me,"
declares the LORD.

7 "I also withheld rain from you
when the harvest was still three months away.
I sent rain on one town,
but withheld it from another.
One field had rain;
another had none and dried up.
8 People staggered from town to town for water
but did not get enough to drink,
yet you have not returned to me,"
declares the LORD.
9 "Many times I struck your gardens and vineyards,
destroying them with blight and mildew.
Locusts devoured your fig and olive trees,
yet you have not returned to me,"
declares the LORD.
10 "I sent plagues among you
as I did to Egypt.
I killed your young men with the sword,
along with your captured horses.
I filled your nostrils with the stench of your camps,
yet you have not returned to me,"
declares the LORD.
11 "I overthrew some of you
as I overthrew Sodom and Gomorrah.
You were like a burning stick snatched from the fire,
yet you have not returned to me,"
declares the LORD.

12 "Therefore this is what I will do to you, Israel,
and because I will do this to you, Israel,
prepare to meet your God."

13 He who forms the mountains,
who creates the wind,
and who reveals his thoughts to mankind,
who turns dawn to darkness,
and treads on the heights of the earth —
the LORD God Almighty is his name.

A Lament and Call to Repentance

5 Hear this word, Israel, this lament I take up concerning you:

2 "Fallen is Virgin Israel,
never to rise again,
deserted in her own land,
with no one to lift her up."

3This is what the Sovereign LORD says to Israel:

"Your city that marches out a thousand strong
will have only a hundred left;
your town that marches out a hundred strong
will have only ten left."

4This is what the LORD says to Israel:

"Seek me and live;
5 do not seek Bethel,
do not go to Gilgal,
do not journey to Beersheba.
For Gilgal will surely go into exile,
and Bethel will be reduced to nothing.[a]"
6 Seek the LORD and live,
or he will sweep through the tribes of Joseph like a fire;
it will devour them,
and Bethel will have no one to quench it.

7 There are those who turn justice into bitterness
and cast righteousness to the ground.

8 He who made the Pleiades and Orion,
who turns midnight into dawn
and darkens day into night,
who calls for the waters of the sea
and pours them out over the face of the land—
the LORD is his name.
9 With a blinding flash he destroys the stronghold
and brings the fortified city to ruin.

10 There are those who hate the one who upholds justice in court
and detest the one who tells the truth.

11 You levy a straw tax on the poor
and impose a tax on their grain.
Therefore, though you have built stone mansions,
you will not live in them;
though you have planted lush vineyards,
you will not drink their wine.
12 For I know how many are your offenses
and how great your sins.

There are those who oppress the innocent and take bribes
and deprive the poor of justice in the courts.
13 Therefore the prudent keep quiet in such times,
for the times are evil.

14 Seek good, not evil,
that you may live.
Then the LORD God Almighty will be with you,
just as you say he is.
15 Hate evil, love good;
maintain justice in the courts.
Perhaps the LORD God Almighty will have mercy
on the remnant of Joseph.

16Therefore this is what the Lord, the LORD God Almighty, says:

"There will be wailing in all the streets
and cries of anguish in every public square.

[a] 5 Hebrew *aven,* a reference to Beth Aven (a derogatory name for Bethel); see Hosea 4:15.

The farmers will be summoned to weep
and the mourners to wail.
[17] There will be wailing in all the vineyards,
for I will pass through your midst,"
says the LORD.

The Day of the LORD

[18] Woe to you who long
for the day of the LORD!
Why do you long for the day of the LORD?
That day will be darkness, not light.
[19] It will be as though a man fled from a lion
only to meet a bear,
as though he entered his house
and rested his hand on the wall
only to have a snake bite him.
[20] Will not the day of the LORD be darkness, not light—
pitch-dark, without a ray of brightness?

[21] "I hate, I despise your religious festivals;
your assemblies are a stench to me.
[22] Even though you bring me burnt offerings and grain offerings,
I will not accept them.
Though you bring choice fellowship offerings,
I will have no regard for them.
[23] Away with the noise of your songs!
I will not listen to the music of your harps.
[24] But let justice roll on like a river,
righteousness like a never-failing stream!

[25] "Did you bring me sacrifices and offerings
forty years in the wilderness, people of Israel?
[26] You have lifted up the shrine of your king,
the pedestal of your idols,
the star of your god[a]—
which you made for yourselves.
[27] Therefore I will send you into exile beyond Damascus,"
says the LORD, whose name is God Almighty.

Woe to the Complacent

6 Woe to you who are complacent in Zion,
and to you who feel secure on Mount Samaria,
you notable men of the foremost nation,
to whom the people of Israel come!
[2] Go to Kalneh and look at it;
go from there to great Hamath,
and then go down to Gath in Philistia.
Are they better off than your two kingdoms?
Is their land larger than yours?
[3] You put off the day of disaster
and bring near a reign of terror.
[4] You lie on beds adorned with ivory
and lounge on your couches.
You dine on choice lambs
and fattened calves.

[a] 26 Or *lifted up Sakkuth your king / and Kaiwan your idols, / your star-gods;* Septuagint *lifted up the shrine of Molek / and the star of your god Rephan, / their idols*

AMOS 5:18–20

THE DAY OF THE LORD

Apparently a popular theory in Amos's day was that the coming day of the Lord would be a positive development for Israel as God would restore her military, political and economic status. But God through Amos warned the people that their expectations were severely misdirected, as that day would be one of "darkness, not light." Instead of restoring Israel's greatness, God's judgment would fall on the nation for its generational disobedience.

Jesus, too, told the people of his day that many people would be surprised at his return. In fact, some would say that they had done many wonderful things in Jesus' name, yet he would declare that he did not know them (Mt 7:21–23). True conversion is necessitated for one to know God and await his coming. Those who are truly saved will await the coming of Jesus like a bride waits for her groom (Mt 25:1–13). The love of God's people for their Savior prompts expectant hearts that long for his coming, knowing they will be spared his judgment and granted the joy of living forever in his presence.

FALSE CONFIDENCE

Though Amos's primary calling was to proclaim God's judgment upon the northern kingdom of Israel, represented here by its fortress capital city of "Mount Samaria," he also pronounced woe upon Judah, represented here by "Zion" (Jerusalem). Both Israel and Judah had great confidence in their own military strength and their ability to overcome the challenge of outside invaders. But at God's direction, foreign powers eventually conquered both nations, and their people were taken into exile.

When Jesus began his earthly ministry hundreds of years later, he did so with the descendants of those two nations, and it's clear they hadn't yet learned their lesson. Even under Roman occupation, the people of Jesus' day felt secure in their situation and proud of their temple and ever-expanding system of worship. They thought they had no reason to expect that their way of life would soon come to an end. God would judge their misplaced priorities and hard hearts with swift and decisive action. Still, the people did not listen — and God's judgment came.

God's decisive judgment on people and nations never comes without consistent warnings, yet there's no doubt that Scripture presents that judgment as something people do not expect. Jesus compared the people of his day to those in Noah's day, who "were eating and drinking, marrying and giving in marriage, up to the day Noah entered the ark; and they knew nothing about what would happen until the flood came and took them all away" (Mt 24:38 – 39). Yet judgment, Jesus said again, was coming quickly, as "the Son of Man will come at an hour when you do not expect him" (Mt 24:44).

Spiritual complacency and false confidence are themes of at least two of Jesus' letters to the seven churches in Revelation chapters 2 and 3. He told the church in Ephesus that although he appreciated their hard work and perseverance, those works did not replace a relationship with him. Jesus said they had "forsaken the love you had at first" (Rev 2:4). The church in Laodicea also seemed to have an overconfidence that drew them away from Jesus, yet theirs was based upon an abundance of material possessions. Though they had much wealth and prosperity, Jesus said they had also grown "lukewarm" (Rev 3:16). As believers anticipate the day of Jesus' return, they can expect to be surprised. But they are also called to keep watch in anticipation of that day that is sure to come (Mt 25:13).

[5]You strum away on your harps like David
and improvise on musical instruments.
[6]You drink wine by the bowlful
and use the finest lotions,
but you do not grieve over the ruin of Joseph.
[7]Therefore you will be among the first to go into exile;
your feasting and lounging will end.

The LORD Abhors the Pride of Israel

[8]The Sovereign LORD has sworn by himself—the LORD God Almighty declares:

"I abhor the pride of Jacob
and detest his fortresses;
I will deliver up the city
and everything in it."

[9]If ten people are left in one house, they too will die. [10]And if the relative who
comes to carry the bodies out of the house to burn them[a] asks anyone who might
be hiding there, "Is anyone else with you?" and he says, "No," then he will go on
to say, "Hush! We must not mention the name of the LORD."

[11]For the LORD has given the command,
and he will smash the great house into pieces
and the small house into bits.

[12]Do horses run on the rocky crags?
Does one plow the sea[b] with oxen?
But you have turned justice into poison
and the fruit of righteousness into bitterness—
[13]you who rejoice in the conquest of Lo Debar[c]
and say, "Did we not take Karnaim[d] by our own strength?"

[14]For the LORD God Almighty declares,
"I will stir up a nation against you, Israel,
that will oppress you all the way
from Lebo Hamath to the valley of the Arabah."

Locusts, Fire and a Plumb Line

7 This is what the Sovereign LORD showed me: He was preparing swarms of
locusts after the king's share had been harvested and just as the late crops
were coming up. [2]When they had stripped the land clean, I cried out, "Sovereign
LORD, forgive! How can Jacob survive? He is so small!"
[3]So the LORD relented.
"This will not happen," the LORD said.
[4]This is what the Sovereign LORD showed me: The Sovereign LORD was calling for judgment by fire; it dried up the great deep and devoured the land. [5]Then
I cried out, "Sovereign LORD, I beg you, stop! How can Jacob survive? He is so
small!"
[6]So the LORD relented.
"This will not happen either," the Sovereign LORD said.
[7]This is what he showed me: The Lord was standing by a wall that had been
built true to plumb,[e] with a plumb line[f] in his hand. [8]And the LORD asked me,
"What do you see, Amos?"
"A plumb line," I replied.

[a] 10 Or *to make a funeral fire in honor of the dead* [b] 12 With a different word division of the Hebrew; Masoretic Text *plow there* [c] 13 *Lo Debar* means *nothing.* [d] 13 *Karnaim* means *horns; horn* here symbolizes strength. [e] 7 The meaning of the Hebrew for this phrase is uncertain. [f] 7 The meaning of the Hebrew for this phrase is uncertain; also in verse 8.

AMOS 7:7–9

THE PLUMB LINE

To help illustrate the message of God's judgment upon Israel, Amos described a vision that he had of a plumb line. A plumb line is a string with a weight attached to the end. As the string is held against a wall, the weight is allowed to hang freely. Using this device it soon becomes clear whether the wall is precisely vertical ("plumb") or not. God, through Amos, was telling the people of Israel that their lives simply didn't line up with God's standards.

Jesus clarified this plumb line concept in his conversation with a rich young man (Mt 19:16–24). This man saw himself as blameless when compared to the law, yet Jesus told him there was more to God's standards than merely outward behavior. God cares more about the heart and motivation of a person than he does about their outward appearances or actions. Jesus presented this wealthy young man with an opportunity to see his life in terms of God's plumb line and to repent. Unfortunately the young man—like so many others in Jesus' day and in our modern day as well—thought he was already aligned with God's standards. He went away confused and disheartened. May this never be the case for seekers who ask Jesus' followers about the hope that they have in him (1Pe 3:15).

Then the Lord said, "Look, I am setting a plumb line among my people Israel;
I will spare them no longer.

9 "The high places of Isaac will be destroyed
and the sanctuaries of Israel will be ruined;
with my sword I will rise against the house of Jeroboam."

Amos and Amaziah

10 Then Amaziah the priest of Bethel sent a message to Jeroboam king of Israel: "Amos is raising a conspiracy against you in the very heart of Israel. The land
cannot bear all his words. 11 For this is what Amos is saying:

" 'Jeroboam will die by the sword,
and Israel will surely go into exile,
away from their native land.' "

12 Then Amaziah said to Amos, "Get out, you seer! Go back to the land of Judah. Earn your bread there and do your prophesying there. 13 Don't prophesy
anymore at Bethel, because this is the king's sanctuary and the temple of the
kingdom."

14 Amos answered Amaziah, "I was neither a prophet nor the son of a prophet,
but I was a shepherd, and I also took care of sycamore-fig trees. 15 But the LORD
took me from tending the flock and said to me, 'Go, prophesy to my people Israel.' 16 Now then, hear the word of the LORD. You say,

" 'Do not prophesy against Israel,
and stop preaching against the descendants of Isaac.'

17 "Therefore this is what the LORD says:

" 'Your wife will become a prostitute in the city,
and your sons and daughters will fall by the sword.
Your land will be measured and divided up,
and you yourself will die in a pagan[a] country.
And Israel will surely go into exile,
away from their native land.' "

A Basket of Ripe Fruit

8 This is what the Sovereign LORD showed me: a basket of ripe fruit. 2 "What do
you see, Amos?" he asked.

"A basket of ripe fruit," I answered.

Then the LORD said to me, "The time is ripe for my people Israel; I will spare
them no longer.

3 "In that day," declares the Sovereign LORD, "the songs in the temple will turn
to wailing.[b] Many, many bodies — flung everywhere! Silence!"

4 Hear this, you who trample the needy
and do away with the poor of the land,

5 saying,

"When will the New Moon be over
that we may sell grain,
and the Sabbath be ended
that we may market wheat?" —
skimping on the measure,
boosting the price
and cheating with dishonest scales,
6 buying the poor with silver
and the needy for a pair of sandals,
selling even the sweepings with the wheat.

---

[a] 17 Hebrew *an unclean* [b] 3 Or *"the temple singers will wail*

[7]The LORD has sworn by himself, the Pride of Jacob: "I will never forget anything they have done.

[8] "Will not the land tremble for this,
and all who live in it mourn?
The whole land will rise like the Nile;
it will be stirred up and then sink
like the river of Egypt.

[9]"In that day," declares the Sovereign LORD,

"I will make the sun go down at noon
and darken the earth in broad daylight.
[10] I will turn your religious festivals into mourning
and all your singing into weeping.
I will make all of you wear sackcloth
and shave your heads.
I will make that time like mourning for an only son
and the end of it like a bitter day.

[11] "The days are coming," declares the Sovereign LORD,
"when I will send a famine through the land —
not a famine of food or a thirst for water,
but a famine of hearing the words of the LORD.
[12] People will stagger from sea to sea
and wander from north to east,
searching for the word of the LORD,
but they will not find it.

[13]"In that day

"the lovely young women and strong young men
will faint because of thirst.
[14] Those who swear by the sin of Samaria —
who say, 'As surely as your god lives, Dan,'
or, 'As surely as the god[a] of Beersheba lives' —
they will fall, never to rise again."

Israel to Be Destroyed

9 I saw the Lord standing by the altar, and he said:

"Strike the tops of the pillars
so that the thresholds shake.
Bring them down on the heads of all the people;
those who are left I will kill with the sword.
Not one will get away,
none will escape.
[2] Though they dig down to the depths below,
from there my hand will take them.
Though they climb up to the heavens above,
from there I will bring them down.
[3] Though they hide themselves on the top of Carmel,
there I will hunt them down and seize them.
Though they hide from my eyes at the bottom of
the sea,
there I will command the serpent to bite them.
[4] Though they are driven into exile by their enemies,
there I will command the sword to slay them.

[a] 14 Hebrew *the way*

AMOS 8:11–13

A FAMINE OF GOD'S WORD

The people of Amos's day desperately feared famine, disease, and plagues. These were among the most devastating disasters in the known world at the time. Yet Israel's history pointed to a more desperate situation — a dearth of hearing a word from God. They saw this in the downfall of their first king, Saul (1Sa 14:37; 28:6).

Micah expressed the possibility of the loss of the word of the Lord in the bleakest terms: "Therefore night will come over you, without visions, and darkness, without divination. The sun will set for the prophets, and the day will go dark for them. The seers will be ashamed and the diviners disgraced. They will all cover their faces because there is no answer from God" (Mic 3:6 – 7).

Jesus, too, knew that it was better to lack food than be deprived of the word of God. He reminded Satan of this when he was tempted in the wilderness (Mt 4:4). Praise God that he sent Jesus to be the living Word and living bread for those who will believe in him (Jn 6:51). When people trust in Jesus alone for their salvation, he tells them that they will live forever.

"I will keep my eye on them
for harm and not for good."

5 The Lord, the LORD Almighty—
he touches the earth and it melts,
and all who live in it mourn;
the whole land rises like the Nile,
then sinks like the river of Egypt;
6 he builds his lofty palace[a] in the heavens
and sets its foundation[b] on the earth;
he calls for the waters of the sea
and pours them out over the face of the land—
the LORD is his name.

7 "Are not you Israelites
the same to me as the Cushites[c]?"
declares the LORD.

"Did I not bring Israel up from Egypt,
the Philistines from Caphtor[d]
and the Arameans from Kir?

8 "Surely the eyes of the Sovereign LORD
are on the sinful kingdom.
I will destroy it
from the face of the earth.
Yet I will not totally destroy
the descendants of Jacob,"
declares the LORD.

9 "For I will give the command,
and I will shake the people of Israel
among all the nations
as grain is shaken in a sieve,
and not a pebble will reach the ground.
10 All the sinners among my people
will die by the sword,
all those who say,
'Disaster will not overtake or meet us.'

Israel's Restoration

11 "In that day

"I will restore David's fallen shelter—
I will repair its broken walls
and restore its ruins—
and will rebuild it as it used to be,
12 so that they may possess the remnant of Edom
and all the nations that bear my name,[e]"
declares the LORD, who will do these things.

13 "The days are coming," declares the LORD,

"when the reaper will be overtaken by the plowman
and the planter by the one treading grapes.
New wine will drip from the mountains
and flow from all the hills,
14 and I will bring my people Israel back from exile.[f]

[a] *6* The meaning of the Hebrew for this phrase is uncertain. [b] *6* The meaning of the Hebrew for this word is uncertain. [c] *7* That is, people from the upper Nile region
[d] *7* That is, Crete [e] *12* Hebrew; Septuagint *so that the remnant of people / and all the nations that bear my name may seek me* [f] *14* Or *will restore the fortunes of my people Israel*

AMOS 9:11–15

SALVATION FOR THE GENTILES

At the Council of Jerusalem, James quoted the first two verses of this passage from the Septuagint (a Greek translation of the Old Testament completed between 250 and 150 BC). The early church leader quoted the following words from the Greek translation of Amos to make a case for Gentile inclusion in the church: "After this I will return and rebuild David's fallen tent. Its ruins I will rebuild, and I will restore it, that the rest of mankind may seek the Lord, even all the Gentiles who bear my name" (Ac 15:16–17).

James' quote was spoken at a pivotal moment in likely the most significant event in the history of the post-Pentecost church. The letter that resulted from the council clarified that Gentiles would no longer be required to follow traditional Jewish customs either before or after becoming Christians. Jesus himself predicted this unconditional enfolding of the Gentiles into the church in John 10:16 when he said, "I have other sheep that are not of this sheep pen"—sheep that he would bring into a united movement of his followers. Praise God that his vision for salvation expands to all people of the world, Jews and Gentiles alike.

"They will rebuild the ruined cities and live in them.
They will plant vineyards and drink their wine;
they will make gardens and eat their fruit.
15 I will plant Israel in their own land,
never again to be uprooted
from the land I have given them,"

says the LORD your God.

JESUS: OUR RIGHTEOUS JUDGE

OBADIAH

OBADIAH

BABYLONIAN INVASIONS OF JUDAH	FALL OF JERUSALEM	WRITING OF BOOK OF OBADIAH
c. 605, 597 and 586 BC	*c. 586 BC*	*Shortly after 586 BC*

Obadiah announced God's judgment on the nation of Edom. His prophetic ministry is unusual in the Old Testament because it was not addressed primarily to either Israel or Judah. Rather, Obadiah wrote to the descendants of Esau, the nation of Edom, in light of the ongoing feud between them and the descendants of Esau's brother Jacob, the people of Israel.

Though some scholars believe the historical setting of this book takes place around 850 BC, it is more likely that the context is the fall of Judah in 586 BC. When King Nebuchadnezzar's army demolished Jerusalem and deported the survivors to Babylon, the people of Edom watched with delight. Because the Edomites were related to the Israelites, they should have rallied in support of the people of Judah and offered them refuge in their land. Instead, the Edomites handed God's people over to the Babylonians, killing some of the refugees in the process. And they went into Jerusalem and looted the Israelites' possessions.

The Edomites' prideful self-sufficiency led to their demise, as God allowed them to fall prey to their Arab neighbors. Eventually the Edomites disappeared from history.

The nation about whom Obadiah wrote his prophecy likely never heard or read his words. The prophecy was primarily meant to encourage the people of Judah: even though it appeared that the pagan nations were going unpunished and often emerging victorious over God's people, their fate was sealed. They would not go unpunished. God would care for his people in spite of the rejection they faced at the hands of the Edomites and ultimately bring them back as a remnant to the land he had promised.

This little-known prophet declares a message of resounding familiarity throughout the history of God's people: God is in control of all things, even pagan nations, and will use them to accomplish his sovereign purposes and judge them in due time. Nothing escapes the reach of an all-powerful God, and nothing is hidden from his eyes. Through Christ, God rules and reigns as a righteous judge. Those who turn to him in faith and repentance will escape his just wrath. Those who do not, like the nation of Edom, will face the consequences of their rejection.

THE DAY OF THE LORD IS NEAR FOR ALL NATIONS.
AS YOU HAVE DONE, IT WILL BE DONE TO YOU;
YOUR DEEDS WILL RETURN UPON YOUR OWN HEAD.

Obadiah 15

OBADIAH

Obadiah's Vision

1 The vision of Obadiah.

This is what the Sovereign LORD says about Edom—

We have heard a message from the LORD:
An envoy was sent to the nations to say,
"Rise, let us go against her for battle"—

2 "See, I will make you small among the nations;
you will be utterly despised.
3 The pride of your heart has deceived you,
you who live in the clefts of the rocks[a]
and make your home on the heights,
you who say to yourself,
'Who can bring me down to the ground?'
4 Though you soar like the eagle
and make your nest among the stars,
from there I will bring you down,"
declares the LORD.
5 "If thieves came to you,
if robbers in the night—
oh, what a disaster awaits you!—
would they not steal only as much as they wanted?
If grape pickers came to you,
would they not leave a few grapes?
6 But how Esau will be ransacked,
his hidden treasures pillaged!
7 All your allies will force you to the border;
your friends will deceive and overpower you;
those who eat your bread will set a trap for you,[b]
but you will not detect it.

8 "In that day," declares the LORD,
"will I not destroy the wise men of Edom,
those of understanding in the mountains of Esau?
9 Your warriors, Teman, will be terrified,
and everyone in Esau's mountains
will be cut down in the slaughter.
10 Because of the violence against your brother Jacob,
you will be covered with shame;
you will be destroyed forever.
11 On the day you stood aloof
while strangers carried off his wealth
and foreigners entered his gates
and cast lots for Jerusalem,
you were like one of them.
12 You should not gloat over your brother
in the day of his misfortune,
nor rejoice over the people of Judah
in the day of their destruction,

[a] 3 Or *of Sela* [b] 7 The meaning of the Hebrew for this clause is uncertain.

JUDGMENT DAY

God used Obadiah to stand up for Judah and speak a stern warning against its brotherly enemy, Edom. The two nations had a contentious past that started with the twin brothers Jacob and Esau (Ge 25:21 – 34; 27:1 – 41), continued after the exodus of Israel (Nu 20:14 – 21) and persisted until Israel's exile. In fact, in 586 BC, when Nebuchadnezzar's army devastated Jerusalem, the Edomites handed fleeing refugees over to the Babylonians instead of coming to their aid. In God's message through the prophet Obadiah, he makes it clear that Edom will pay for its history of mistreating the people of Israel.

In verse 10 Obadiah says, "Because of the violence against your brother Jacob, you will be covered with shame; you will be destroyed forever." Although at times it may seem as if God ignores the pain and suffering of his people, the Bible is crystal clear that the sovereign God of Scripture will not overlook evil forever.

Scripture says one day God will decisively judge evil and make right all that is wrong in the world. Obadiah speaks of this day throughout his prophecy but addresses it specifically in verse 15 when he declares that "the day of the LORD is near for all nations," not just Edom. On this day Edom will finally pay a price for its treachery against Judah.

Called by multiple names (such as "the day of the LORD/Lord," "the day of wrath" and "the day of the Lord Jesus"), the foreshadowing of the last judgment permeates much of the story of Scripture. Jesus, too, speaks of a day when all people on the planet will be judged. Even careless words will be judged on this day of days (Mt 12:36 – 37). The activities of our lives — and the lives of all who have ever walked the earth — will be judged then (2Co 5:10).

Scripture says that Jesus himself is the Judge who will preside over that monumental day (Ac 10:42). Not only was Jesus present and active in creation (Col 1:16) and made the payment for believers' sin (Jn 1:29), but he is also the satisfaction of God's judgment (Ro 3:25). The Bible teaches that Jesus' death on the cross satisfies the wrath and judgment of God for any and all who believe in him.

nor boast so much
in the day of their trouble.
13 You should not march through the gates of my people
in the day of their disaster,
nor gloat over them in their calamity
in the day of their disaster,
nor seize their wealth
in the day of their disaster.
14 You should not wait at the crossroads
to cut down their fugitives,
nor hand over their survivors
in the day of their trouble.

15 "The day of the LORD is near
for all nations.
As you have done, it will be done to you;
your deeds will return upon your own head.
16 Just as you drank on my holy hill,
so all the nations will drink continually;
they will drink and drink
and be as if they had never been.
17 But on Mount Zion will be deliverance;
it will be holy,
and Jacob will possess his inheritance.
18 Jacob will be a fire
and Joseph a flame;
Esau will be stubble,
and they will set him on fire and destroy him.
There will be no survivors
from Esau."

The LORD has spoken.

19 People from the Negev will occupy
the mountains of Esau,
and people from the foothills will possess
the land of the Philistines.
They will occupy the fields of Ephraim and Samaria,
and Benjamin will possess Gilead.
20 This company of Israelite exiles who are in Canaan
will possess the land as far as Zarephath;
the exiles from Jerusalem who are in Sepharad
will possess the towns of the Negev.
21 Deliverers will go up on[a] Mount Zion
to govern the mountains of Esau.
And the kingdom will be the LORD's.

[a] 21 Or *from*

JESUS: OUR MISSIONARY GOD

JONAH

REIGN OF JEROBOAM II	PROPHETIC MINISTRY OF JONAH	FALL OF NINEVEH
c. 793 – 753 BC	*c. 800 – 750 BC*	*c. 612 BC*

God called Jonah to a difficult and intimidating mission. He commissioned Jonah to go to "the great city of Nineveh" in Assyria and preach against it (1:2), warning this militarily brutal and spiritually pagan nation of God's coming judgment, should the inhabitants fail to repent.

Instead, Jonah boarded a ship heading in the opposite direction. What follows is a very well-known story: God raised a powerful storm, enlightened an insightful crew and delivered a great fish to thwart Jonah's rebellion. Jonah cried out to God for deliverance, proclaiming his faith in God and his belief that "salvation comes from the LORD" (2:9). God heard Jonah's prayer and once again called him to go to Nineveh and proclaim God's warning. This time Jonah obeyed and warned the people of God's coming judgment and the city's impending destruction.

Much to Jonah's chagrin, the king of Nineveh and the city's inhabitants responded to his message by believing God and repenting of their sin (3:7 – 10). Their response revealed Jonah's initial motive for disobeying God: Assyria was Israel's hated enemy, and Jonah firmly believed that God's judgment and punishment on this nation was richly deserved. He further erroneously believed that God's saving work should be limited to the chosen people of Israel. Their superiority, in Jonah's mind, came from God's unique call on the nation and his promises to Abraham, Isaac and Jacob. While God continued to demonstrate patience and persistent love toward Israel, Jonah failed to appreciate the fact that God may do the same for other nations.

Yet God's mission includes all the nations of the world. He is the rightful King who can do with the nations as he sees fit — even choosing to bless those who turn to him for salvation. God is free to show mercy to any person and any nation at any time that he wills. Jonah's sorrow over Nineveh's repentance shows his narrow view of God's kindness.

While the book of Jonah contains no specific prophecies, its narrative structure demonstrates God's passion to bring salvation to the nations. All those who turn to him, even residents of a pagan city at the heart of an evil empire, can find God's mercy (Jer 29:13).

Jesus' stated mission makes this point clear. His mission focused on the Jews first, but extended to graft in Gentile believers who turned to him (Mt 15:21 – 28). Following his resurrection, the church was commissioned, like Jonah, to take the message of the gospel to Gentiles everywhere and invite them to trust in the One who holds salvation in his hands.

WHEN MY LIFE WAS EBBING AWAY, I REMEMBERED YOU, LORD, AND MY PRAYER ROSE TO YOU, TO YOUR HOLY TEMPLE.

Jonah 2:7

JONAH

JONAH 1:12

WATER AS JUDGMENT

When Jonah fled from the Lord's call and booked passage on a ship headed toward Tarshish, God sent a mighty storm that threatened the lives of everyone in the boat. Jonah knew the wind and the waves were God's judgment on his decision, and that the only solution to this problem was to throw him into the waters.

Throughout the Old Testament, water is a sign of God's judgment. Jesus also uses water imagery to characterize his crucifixion (Lk 12:50). All of humanity has sinned, and the wages of that sin is death (Ro 6:23), but the good news is that Jesus drowned under God's overwhelming wrath against sin at the cross and walked away alive three days later so that all who believe on him could be forgiven.

In fact, we picture this gospel story in the sacrament of baptism. The baptismal waters symbolize judgment and salvation, death and resurrection. In baptism, the church announces to the individual in the water, "You have already died, been buried and walked away from death to new life in Christ." Baptism replays Noah's flood, the Red Sea crossing and Jonah's rescue from the fish. It tells the story over and over again of a God who rescues his people through the water of judgment.

Jonah Flees From the Lord

1 The word of the Lord came to Jonah son of Amittai: 2 "Go to the great city
of Nineveh and preach against it, because its wickedness has come up before me."

3 But Jonah ran away from the Lord and headed for Tarshish. He went down to
Joppa, where he found a ship bound for that port. After paying the fare, he went
aboard and sailed for Tarshish to flee from the Lord.

4 Then the Lord sent a great wind on the sea, and such a violent storm arose
that the ship threatened to break up. 5 All the sailors were afraid and each cried
out to his own god. And they threw the cargo into the sea to lighten the ship.

But Jonah had gone below deck, where he lay down and fell into a deep sleep.
6 The captain went to him and said, "How can you sleep? Get up and call on your
god! Maybe he will take notice of us so that we will not perish."

7 Then the sailors said to each other, "Come, let us cast lots to find out who is
responsible for this calamity." They cast lots and the lot fell on Jonah. 8 So they
asked him, "Tell us, who is responsible for making all this trouble for us? What
kind of work do you do? Where do you come from? What is your country? From
what people are you?"

9 He answered, "I am a Hebrew and I worship the Lord, the God of heaven,
who made the sea and the dry land."

10 This terrified them and they asked, "What have you done?" (They knew he
was running away from the Lord, because he had already told them so.)

11 The sea was getting rougher and rougher. So they asked him, "What should
we do to you to make the sea calm down for us?"

12 "Pick me up and throw me into the sea," he replied, "and it will become
calm. I know that it is my fault that this great storm has come upon you."

13 Instead, the men did their best to row back to land. But they could not, for
the sea grew even wilder than before. 14 Then they cried out to the Lord, "Please,
Lord, do not let us die for taking this man's life. Do not hold us accountable for
killing an innocent man, for you, Lord, have done as you pleased." 15 Then they
took Jonah and threw him overboard, and the raging sea grew calm. 16 At this
the men greatly feared the Lord, and they offered a sacrifice to the Lord and
made vows to him.

Jonah's Prayer

17 Now the Lord provided a huge fish to swallow Jonah, and Jonah was in the
2[a] belly of the fish three days and three nights. 1 From inside the fish Jonah
prayed to the Lord his God. 2 He said:

"In my distress I called to the Lord,
  and he answered me.
From deep in the realm of the dead I called for help,
  and you listened to my cry.
3 You hurled me into the depths,
  into the very heart of the seas,
  and the currents swirled about me;
all your waves and breakers
  swept over me.
4 I said, 'I have been banished
  from your sight;

[a] In Hebrew texts 2:1 is numbered 1:17, and 2:1-10 is numbered 2:2-11.

COMPARING JESUS AND JONAH

Jesus clearly linked his life with the prophet Jonah. When some of the Pharisees challenged Jesus to give them a sign that he was the Messiah, Jesus rebuked them and said that they would only receive the sign of Jonah (Mt 12:38 – 39). He went on to make this comparison: "For as Jonah was three days and three nights in the belly of a huge fish, so the Son of Man will be three days and three nights in the heart of the earth" (12:40).

Though there are similarities in Jesus' and Jonah's stories, Jesus is much greater! Jonah was a disobedient prophet who ran from his mission to proclaim judgment on the lost people of Nineveh; Jesus was the true, obedient prophet who came to seek and save the lost people of the entire world. When faced with a storm that raged and threatened the lives of the crew, both Jonah and Jesus slept deeply in the boat they were in and had to be awakened. However, while Jonah's crew threw him into the sea to calm the wind and the waves, Jesus told the wind and the waves to be still, and they obeyed his voice (Mk 4:35 – 41)!

Ultimately Jonah experienced punishment for his own sin, and by his punishment the sailors were saved. Jesus lived a life that was without sin, but at his death he experienced judgment for the sins of the world in order to save others.

In Matthew 12, Jesus essentially told the Pharisees, "I'll give you a sign, but it's not the kind of sign you want. It's a sign of judgment for your resistance toward God." Whether it's the flood of Noah's day, or the Red Sea crashing in on the Egyptian army, or a reluctant prophet thrown overboard into the sea, water consistently represents judgment in the Old Testament. That is why Jesus refers to his cross as a "baptism" (Lk 12:50). That is the sign of Jonah. Jonah almost drown under the wrath of God, spent three days in the belly of the fish and then he was brought out alive on the other side to carry out his commission to go to Nineveh. But Jesus, the true and better Jonah, was engulfed under God's complete wrath at Calvary's cross, spent three days in the belly of the earth, then came out alive on the other side to carry out his commission to the nations through his followers (Mt 28:18 – 20).

Jesus gives the Jewish leaders the sign of Jonah to reveal his identity and mission. They longed for a sign they could see, and Jesus pointed them to the faithfulness of God in history.

JONAH 2:4–6

ALL WHO CALL ON THE NAME OF THE LORD

As he was sinking into the depths of the Mediterranean, Jonah cried out to God. After he was swallowed into the belly of the huge fish, he lifted up a prayer of thanksgiving for God's deliverance. He proclaimed his faith in God and his belief that "salvation comes from the LORD" (2:9). Jonah spent three days and three nights in the belly of that fish before being vomited onto the shore. According to Jonah, those who look to the God's dwelling will be saved.

The New Testament reveals to us that the temple is no longer a building made with stone and mortar; the new temple is a person—Jesus Christ himself (Jn 2:21; Rev 21:22). All who look to him in trust and repentance and call on his name will be delivered (Ro 10:13).

JONAH 4:1–3

JONAH AND THE OLDER BROTHER

Instead of celebrating God's salvation of the people of Nineveh, Jonah became very angry that God would show mercy to the Ninevites. The story of Jonah is similar to a parable that Jesus told about a lost son (Lk 15:11–32). The younger of two sons, violating every cultural norm, demanded his inheritance from his father and wasted it all in wild living in a foreign country. When the younger son runs out of resources and returns home, the father shows

(continued on page 1434)

yet I will look again
 toward your holy temple.'
5 The engulfing waters threatened me,[a]
 the deep surrounded me;
 seaweed was wrapped around my head.
6 To the roots of the mountains I sank down;
 the earth beneath barred me in forever.
But you, LORD my God,
 brought my life up from the pit.

7 "When my life was ebbing away,
 I remembered you, LORD,
and my prayer rose to you,
 to your holy temple.

8 "Those who cling to worthless idols
 turn away from God's love for them.
9 But I, with shouts of grateful praise,
 will sacrifice to you.
What I have vowed I will make good.
 I will say, 'Salvation comes from the LORD.'"

10 And the LORD commanded the fish, and it vomited Jonah onto dry land.

Jonah Goes to Nineveh

3 Then the word of the LORD came to Jonah a second time: 2 "Go to the great
city of Nineveh and proclaim to it the message I give you."
3 Jonah obeyed the word of the LORD and went to Nineveh. Now Nineveh was
a very large city; it took three days to go through it. 4 Jonah began by going a day's
journey into the city, proclaiming, "Forty more days and Nineveh will be overthrown." 5 The Ninevites believed God. A fast was proclaimed, and all of them,
from the greatest to the least, put on sackcloth.
6 When Jonah's warning reached the king of Nineveh, he rose from his throne,
took off his royal robes, covered himself with sackcloth and sat down in the dust.
7 This is the proclamation he issued in Nineveh:

"By the decree of the king and his nobles:

Do not let people or animals, herds or flocks, taste anything; do not let
them eat or drink. 8 But let people and animals be covered with sackcloth.
Let everyone call urgently on God. Let them give up their evil ways and
their violence. 9 Who knows? God may yet relent and with compassion turn
from his fierce anger so that we will not perish."

10 When God saw what they did and how they turned from their evil ways, he
relented and did not bring on them the destruction he had threatened.

Jonah's Anger at the LORD's Compassion

4 But to Jonah this seemed very wrong, and he became angry. 2 He prayed to
the LORD, "Isn't this what I said, LORD, when I was still at home? That is what
I tried to forestall by fleeing to Tarshish. I knew that you are a gracious and compassionate God, slow to anger and abounding in love, a God who relents from
sending calamity. 3 Now, LORD, take away my life, for it is better for me to die
than to live."
4 But the LORD replied, "Is it right for you to be angry?"
5 Jonah had gone out and sat down at a place east of the city. There he made
himself a shelter, sat in its shade and waited to see what would happen to the city.
6 Then the LORD God provided a leafy plant[b] and made it grow up over Jonah to

[a] 5 Or *waters were at my throat* [b] 6 The precise identification of this plant is uncertain; also in verses 7, 9 and 10.

GOD'S HEART FOR THE NATIONS

Jonah resisted God's call to bring his word to the Ninevites because he hated the people of Nineveh and did not want them to be saved. In some ways, his disposition was understandable. After all, Nineveh was known as the Assyrian Empire's "great city" (Jnh 1:2). Because they were a militarily ruthless people, the Assyrians were the most feared threat in that era.

Jonah ran from his mission not because he was scared of what the Ninevites might do to him; rather, he was afraid of what God would do for the Ninevites. He knew that God's mercy is an intimate part of God's revealed character (Jnh 4:2), and he wanted judgment for Nineveh, not forgiveness. True to form, throughout the book of Jonah God repeatedly shows mercy: not only to the Ninevites, but also to the sailors and especially to his rebellious prophet Jonah.

Jonah does not share God's heart for the nations. But from the beginning of Israel's history, the divinely chosen people of Israel were meant to be a light to the nations. When God chose Abraham, God said that he would bless all the peoples of the earth through this family (Ge 12:3). The book of Jonah is not just an indictment on God's runaway prophet; it's also a condemnation of the people of Israel, who failed to be a light to the nations.

And yet, God loves Nineveh so much that he will not allow Jonah to fail. Through the fish, he transports Jonah to shore, giving him a second chance to preach the message so that the people of Nineveh can repent. Jonah walks away from death, then walks many miles to the gates of the city to fulfill his commission. Upon hearing God's pronouncement, the king and the people of Nineveh repent and the city is saved.

Believers must be reminded that Paul says that Jesus is the seed of Abraham who will bring salvation to the world (Gal 3:16). Jesus also walked away from death to give the Great Commission to the church. Corporately, we as the church are commanded to go to all nations — regardless of our cultural, political or ideological differences with those nations — to make disciples. Why? Because the God who loves the entire world has saved us. God has a heart for and plan to save all people who will come to him in faith and trust; in his goodness, he allows us to be part of that plan: "The Lord is not slow in keeping his promise, as some understand slowness. Instead he is patient with you, not wanting anyone to perish, but everyone to come to repentance" (2Pe 3:9).

(Jonah and the Older Brother, continued)

mercy to him, embracing him and throwing a party. But instead of celebrating, the father's older son — like Jonah — gets angry and protests the unfairness of the father's decision.

These stories are similar in that they end with Jonah and the older brother being corrected for their anger. The stories are also open-ended, because God hopes the reader will get the point that those who struggle to show mercy to the lost need to repent. After all, God is a "gracious and compassionate God, slow to anger and abounding in love, a God who relents from sending calamity" (Jnh 4:2). Isn't it right that a gracious God would seek out the lost and show mercy to them?

The book of Jonah is in the Old Testament to teach us that lesson; the parable of the lost son is in the New Testament to teach us that seeking out and saving the lost is perfectly in line with Jesus' character and his plan of salvation for all who will believe in him.

give shade for his head to ease his discomfort, and Jonah was very happy about
the plant. 7But at dawn the next day God provided a worm, which chewed the
plant so that it withered. 8When the sun rose, God provided a scorching east
wind, and the sun blazed on Jonah's head so that he grew faint. He wanted to die,
and said, "It would be better for me to die than to live."

9But God said to Jonah, "Is it right for you to be angry about the plant?"
"It is," he said. "And I'm so angry I wish I were dead."

10But the LORD said, "You have been concerned about this plant, though you
did not tend it or make it grow. It sprang up overnight and died overnight. 11And
should I not have concern for the great city of Nineveh, in which there are more
than a hundred and twenty thousand people who cannot tell their right hand
from their left — and also many animals?"

JESUS: OUR COMPASSIONATE KING

MICAH

MICAH

PROPHETIC MINISTRY OF MICAH *c. 735 – 700 BC*	FALL OF ISRAEL *c. 722 BC*	FALL OF JUDAH *c. 586 BC*

Micah, who was from a town in southern Judah, prophesied mostly to the southern kingdom of Judah, though he also spoke to the northern kingdom of Israel. Micah's hope-filled message was meant to encourage God's people in the face of God's judgment. This message did not minimize the impending destruction; in fact, Micah went to great lengths to demonstrate the severity of the punishment God would unleash on the people for their sin.

Micah countered their self-assurance that they would be protected because of their unique covenant relationship with God. Ignoring the warnings of the prophets, many within Judah felt that Jerusalem was impenetrable because it was the site of God's temple — his dwelling place among his people. Surely God would not allow the destruction of the holy city, regardless of how wicked the nation became. Micah sternly warned Judah against such prideful thinking and flawed logic. God would protect his name among the nations. He would not allow the Israelites to defame his glory or tarnish his reputation through their bold-faced idol worship in the very heart of the promised land. Micah assured them that God would purge the people from the land if they did not quickly repent. In kindness, God spared Jerusalem from destruction for over a hundred years after Micah's prophecies. But because of the people's ongoing sin, he finally acted in judgment in 586 BC when the Babylonians captured Jerusalem, destroyed the temple and led the people into exile.

But Micah weaved threads of hope into his dire warnings for the people of God. Micah pointed back to God's covenant promises as the basis for his ongoing faithfulness to those whom he loves, assuring them that, because God is intent on keeping his promises to Abraham, he will always act to sustain a remnant of his people. Micah also pointed to a future day when a true King would rule over God's people (4:2 – 3). This King would reign in peace and would bring justice to the earth once more. Hundreds of years before Jesus' birth, Micah prophesied that this King would be born in Bethlehem and would one day rule over all Israel (5:2).

The twin themes of judgment and mercy that characterize the prophetic writings derive from God's perfect nature and character. He is a God of holy judgment for sin who, at the same time, shows merciful compassion to his people. God put these characteristics on display time and again for the people of Israel. Micah's writings, and the glorious and specific promises of God's compassionate Messiah, Jesus Christ, provide hope that God will indeed show compassion to his chosen ones once more.

HE HAS SHOWN YOU, O MORTAL, WHAT IS GOOD.
AND WHAT DOES THE LORD REQUIRE OF YOU?
TO ACT JUSTLY AND TO LOVE MERCY AND
TO WALK HUMBLY WITH YOUR GOD.

Micah 6:8

MICAH

1 The word of the LORD that came to Micah of Moresheth during the reigns of
Jotham, Ahaz and Hezekiah, kings of Judah — the vision he saw concerning
Samaria and Jerusalem.

2 Hear, you peoples, all of you,
listen, earth and all who live in it,
that the Sovereign LORD may bear witness against you,
the Lord from his holy temple.

Judgment Against Samaria and Jerusalem

3 Look! The LORD is coming from his dwelling place;
he comes down and treads on the heights of the earth.
4 The mountains melt beneath him
and the valleys split apart,
like wax before the fire,
like water rushing down a slope.
5 All this is because of Jacob's transgression,
because of the sins of the people of Israel.
What is Jacob's transgression?
Is it not Samaria?
What is Judah's high place?
Is it not Jerusalem?

6 "Therefore I will make Samaria a heap of rubble,
a place for planting vineyards.
I will pour her stones into the valley
and lay bare her foundations.
7 All her idols will be broken to pieces;
all her temple gifts will be burned with fire;
I will destroy all her images.
Since she gathered her gifts from the wages of prostitutes,
as the wages of prostitutes they will again be used."

Weeping and Mourning

8 Because of this I will weep and wail;
I will go about barefoot and naked.
I will howl like a jackal
and moan like an owl.
9 For Samaria's plague is incurable;
it has spread to Judah.
It has reached the very gate of my people,
even to Jerusalem itself.
10 Tell it not in Gath[a];
weep not at all.
In Beth Ophrah[b]
roll in the dust.
11 Pass by naked and in shame,
you who live in Shaphir.[c]
Those who live in Zaanan[d]
will not come out.

---

[a] 10 *Gath* sounds like the Hebrew for *tell*. [b] 10 *Beth Ophrah* means *house of dust*.
[c] 11 *Shaphir* means *pleasant*. [d] 11 *Zaanan* sounds like the Hebrew for *come out*.

Beth Ezel is in mourning;
it no longer protects you.
12 Those who live in Maroth[a] writhe in pain,
waiting for relief,
because disaster has come from the LORD,
even to the gate of Jerusalem.
13 You who live in Lachish,
harness fast horses to the chariot.
You are where the sin of Daughter Zion began,
for the transgressions of Israel were found in you.
14 Therefore you will give parting gifts
to Moresheth Gath.
The town of Akzib[b] will prove deceptive
to the kings of Israel.
15 I will bring a conqueror against you
who live in Mareshah.[c]
The nobles of Israel
will flee to Adullam.
16 Shave your head in mourning
for the children in whom you delight;
make yourself as bald as the vulture,
for they will go from you into exile.

Human Plans and God's Plans

2 Woe to those who plan iniquity,
to those who plot evil on their beds!
At morning's light they carry it out
because it is in their power to do it.
2 They covet fields and seize them,
and houses, and take them.
They defraud people of their homes,
they rob them of their inheritance.

3 Therefore, the LORD says:

"I am planning disaster against this people,
from which you cannot save yourselves.
You will no longer walk proudly,
for it will be a time of calamity.
4 In that day people will ridicule you;
they will taunt you with this mournful song:
'We are utterly ruined;
my people's possession is divided up.
He takes it from me!
He assigns our fields to traitors.'"

5 Therefore you will have no one in the assembly of the LORD
to divide the land by lot.

False Prophets

6 "Do not prophesy," their prophets say.
"Do not prophesy about these things;
disgrace will not overtake us."
7 You descendants of Jacob, should it be said,
"Does the LORD become[d] impatient?
Does he do such things?"

---

[a] 12 *Maroth* sounds like the Hebrew for *bitter*. [b] 14 *Akzib* means *deception*.
[c] 15 *Mareshah* sounds like the Hebrew for *conqueror*. [d] 7 Or *Is the Spirit of the LORD*

"Do not my words do good
to the one whose ways are upright?
8 Lately my people have risen up
like an enemy.
You strip off the rich robe
from those who pass by without a care,
like men returning from battle.
9 You drive the women of my people
from their pleasant homes.
You take away my blessing
from their children forever.
10 Get up, go away!
For this is not your resting place,
because it is defiled,
it is ruined, beyond all remedy.
11 If a liar and deceiver comes and says,
'I will prophesy for you plenty of wine and beer,'
that would be just the prophet for this people!

Deliverance Promised

12 "I will surely gather all of you, Jacob;
I will surely bring together the remnant of Israel.
I will bring them together like sheep in a pen,
like a flock in its pasture;
the place will throng with people.
13 The One who breaks open the way will go up before
them;
they will break through the gate and go out.
Their King will pass through before them,
the LORD at their head."

MICAH 2:12

THE GOOD SHEPHERD

God, through the prophet Micah, emphatically demonstrates his fierce determination to gather his people from wherever they are scattered, to bring them back to himself and to shepherd them to the place where they belong (Mic 2:12). Like a good shepherd, God promised to lead and protect his sheep at all costs; Jesus, God's Son, spoke of himself as the good shepherd who would lay down his very life for his sheep (Jn 10:11).

The people of Israel in Micah's day walked the path of all sinners: As sheep without a shepherd, they were lost, helpless and doomed to wander aimlessly. God's promise to draw his wayward sheep back was accomplished in Jesus, who through his work on the cross leads believers beside quiet waters and restores their souls (Ps 23:1 – 3).

Leaders and Prophets Rebuked

3 Then I said,

"Listen, you leaders of Jacob,
you rulers of Israel.
Should you not embrace justice,
2 you who hate good and love evil;
who tear the skin from my people
and the flesh from their bones;
3 who eat my people's flesh,
strip off their skin
and break their bones in pieces;
who chop them up like meat for the pan,
like flesh for the pot?"
4 Then they will cry out to the LORD,
but he will not answer them.
At that time he will hide his face from them
because of the evil they have done.

5 This is what the LORD says:

"As for the prophets
who lead my people astray,
they proclaim 'peace'
if they have something to eat,
but prepare to wage war against anyone
who refuses to feed them.

6 Therefore night will come over you, without visions,
and darkness, without divination.
The sun will set for the prophets,
and the day will go dark for them.
7 The seers will be ashamed
and the diviners disgraced.
They will all cover their faces
because there is no answer from God."
8 But as for me, I am filled with power,
with the Spirit of the LORD,
and with justice and might,
to declare to Jacob his transgression,
to Israel his sin.

9 Hear this, you leaders of Jacob,
you rulers of Israel,
who despise justice
and distort all that is right;
10 who build Zion with bloodshed,
and Jerusalem with wickedness.
11 Her leaders judge for a bribe,
her priests teach for a price,
and her prophets tell fortunes for money.
Yet they look for the LORD's support and say,
"Is not the LORD among us?
No disaster will come upon us."
12 Therefore because of you,
Zion will be plowed like a field,
Jerusalem will become a heap of rubble,
the temple hill a mound overgrown with thickets.

The Mountain of the LORD

4 In the last days

the mountain of the LORD's temple will be established
as the highest of the mountains;
it will be exalted above the hills,
and peoples will stream to it.

2 Many nations will come and say,

"Come, let us go up to the mountain of the LORD,
to the temple of the God of Jacob.
He will teach us his ways,
so that we may walk in his paths."
The law will go out from Zion,
the word of the LORD from Jerusalem.
3 He will judge between many peoples
and will settle disputes for strong nations far and wide.
They will beat their swords into plowshares
and their spears into pruning hooks.
Nation will not take up sword against nation,
nor will they train for war anymore.
4 Everyone will sit under their own vine
and under their own fig tree,
and no one will make them afraid,
for the LORD Almighty has spoken.
5 All the nations may walk
in the name of their gods,

MICAH 4:1 – 5

IN THE LAST DAYS

Micah and Isaiah were contemporaries, and Micah 4:1 – 3 is a nearly identical echo of Isaiah 2:2 – 4. Both prophets knew that there would be a time in the last days when a Savior King would rule the nations. Although the people of God would experience hardship in the days before, they would, in this day, live under the protection of the Lord their God, and no one would be able to make them afraid (Mic 4:4 – 5).

Believers in Christ hold this to be true as well today. Jesus tells his followers, "In this world you will have trouble. But take heart! I have overcome the world" (Jn 16:33). When Jesus comes again, he will come to judge the people (Jn 5:22), and God will wipe away every tear from every eye of every believer (Rev 21:4). Those who follow Jesus will never be put to shame (Ro 10:11), for they have received by the Spirit a hope that does not disappoint (Ro 5:5). A person who abides in Christ through the Holy Spirit can live a God-glorifying life, since Jesus provides life and peace and salvation both now and forever. And for that, believers will eternally praise "God our Savior" (Jude 24 – 25).

but we will walk in the name of the LORD
our God for ever and ever.

The LORD's Plan

6 "In that day," declares the LORD,

"I will gather the lame;
I will assemble the exiles
and those I have brought to grief.
7 I will make the lame my remnant,
those driven away a strong nation.
The LORD will rule over them in Mount Zion
from that day and forever.
8 As for you, watchtower of the flock,
stronghold[a] of Daughter Zion,
the former dominion will be restored to you;
kingship will come to Daughter Jerusalem."

9 Why do you now cry aloud —
have you no king[b]?
Has your ruler[c] perished,
that pain seizes you like that of a woman in labor?
10 Writhe in agony, Daughter Zion,
like a woman in labor,
for now you must leave the city
to camp in the open field.
You will go to Babylon;
there you will be rescued.
There the LORD will redeem you
out of the hand of your enemies.

11 But now many nations
are gathered against you.
They say, "Let her be defiled,
let our eyes gloat over Zion!"
12 But they do not know
the thoughts of the LORD;
they do not understand his plan,
that he has gathered them like sheaves to the
threshing floor.
13 "Rise and thresh, Daughter Zion,
for I will give you horns of iron;
I will give you hooves of bronze,
and you will break to pieces many nations."
You will devote their ill-gotten gains to the LORD,
their wealth to the Lord of all the earth.

A Promised Ruler From Bethlehem

5 [d] Marshal your troops now, city of troops,
for a siege is laid against us.
They will strike Israel's ruler
on the cheek with a rod.

2 "But you, Bethlehem Ephrathah,
though you are small among the clans[e] of Judah,
out of you will come for me
one who will be ruler over Israel,

[a] 8 Or *hill* [b] 9 Or *King* [c] 9 Or *Ruler* [d] In Hebrew texts 5:1 is numbered 4:14, and 5:2-15 is numbered 5:1-14. [e] 2 Or *rulers*

whose origins are from of old,
from ancient times."

3 Therefore Israel will be abandoned
until the time when she who is in labor bears
a son,
and the rest of his brothers return
to join the Israelites.

4 He will stand and shepherd his flock
in the strength of the LORD,
in the majesty of the name of the LORD his God.
And they will live securely, for then his greatness
will reach to the ends of the earth.

5 And he will be our peace
when the Assyrians invade our land
and march through our fortresses.
We will raise against them seven shepherds,
even eight commanders,
6 who will rule[a] the land of Assyria with the sword,
the land of Nimrod with drawn sword.[b]
He will deliver us from the Assyrians
when they invade our land
and march across our borders.

7 The remnant of Jacob will be
in the midst of many peoples
like dew from the LORD,
like showers on the grass,
which do not wait for anyone
or depend on man.
8 The remnant of Jacob will be among the nations,
in the midst of many peoples,
like a lion among the beasts of the forest,
like a young lion among flocks of sheep,
which mauls and mangles as it goes,
and no one can rescue.
9 Your hand will be lifted up in triumph over your
enemies,
and all your foes will be destroyed.

10 "In that day," declares the LORD,

"I will destroy your horses from among you
and demolish your chariots.
11 I will destroy the cities of your land
and tear down all your strongholds.
12 I will destroy your witchcraft
and you will no longer cast spells.
13 I will destroy your idols
and your sacred stones from among you;
you will no longer bow down
to the work of your hands.
14 I will uproot from among you your Asherah poles[c]
when I demolish your cities.
15 I will take vengeance in anger and wrath
on the nations that have not obeyed me."

[a] 6 Or *crush* [b] 6 Or *Nimrod in its gates* [c] *14* That is, wooden symbols of the goddess Asherah

A PROMISED RULER FROM BETHLEHEM

God prophesied through the prophet Micah that the Savior of the world — the Davidic king who would rule forever — would come from a small, obscure town called Bethlehem (Mic 5:2). He would shepherd God's people and be their peace (vv. 4 – 5). Bethlehem had its fair share of lows, such as times of moral decay during the judges (Jdg 19). However, the chief priests and teachers of the law confirmed Bethlehem as the birthplace of the Messiah when Herod questioned them, citing Micah as their source of information (Mt 2:1 – 6).

Bethlehem means "house of bread." Bread was critical in ancient times as it signified economic stability and sustained physical life. In a spiritual sense, it also represented provision from God, who had provided manna, which was actual "bread from heaven" (Ex 16:4), in the desert, demonstrating his willingness and power to supply his people with all that they needed.

At one point in his ministry, Jesus reminded the Jewish crowd listening to him that although God provided for their forefathers by giving them manna in the wilderness, there was now a new picture of provision: Jesus himself (Jn 6:31 – 35). The true bread from heaven was standing in front of them as the One who came down from heaven to give life to the world (Jn 6:33). Jesus is the true "bread of life," and anyone who comes to him will never go hungry (Jn 6:35).

Micah also described this Messianic shepherd as one whose greatness "will reach to the ends of the earth" (Mic 5:4) and defines him as one who "will be our peace" (5:5). Paul encourages Christians in the church at Ephesus that Jesus "himself is our peace" (Eph 2:14). Bethlehem is significant — both as a sweet promise for the people of Israel in Micah's time and also for all who follow Jesus. Believers can point back to this city as the birthplace of their Savior, their peace, the fulfillment of God's prophecy through Micah, which is perfectly and completely satisfied in Christ.

The LORD's Case Against Israel

6 Listen to what the LORD says:

"Stand up, plead my case before the mountains;
let the hills hear what you have to say.

2 "Hear, you mountains, the LORD's accusation;
listen, you everlasting foundations of the earth.
For the LORD has a case against his people;
he is lodging a charge against Israel.

3 "My people, what have I done to you?
How have I burdened you? Answer me.
4 I brought you up out of Egypt
and redeemed you from the land of slavery.
I sent Moses to lead you,
also Aaron and Miriam.
5 My people, remember
what Balak king of Moab plotted
and what Balaam son of Beor answered.
Remember your journey from Shittim to Gilgal,
that you may know the righteous acts of the LORD."

6 With what shall I come before the LORD
and bow down before the exalted God?
Shall I come before him with burnt offerings,
with calves a year old?
7 Will the LORD be pleased with thousands of rams,
with ten thousand rivers of olive oil?
Shall I offer my firstborn for my transgression,
the fruit of my body for the sin of my soul?
8 He has shown you, O mortal, what is good.
And what does the LORD require of you?
To act justly and to love mercy
and to walk humbly[a] with your God.

Israel's Guilt and Punishment

9 Listen! The LORD is calling to the city—
and to fear your name is wisdom—
"Heed the rod and the One who appointed it.[b]
10 Am I still to forget your ill-gotten treasures, you wicked house,
and the short ephah,[c] which is accursed?
11 Shall I acquit someone with dishonest scales,
with a bag of false weights?
12 Your rich people are violent;
your inhabitants are liars
and their tongues speak deceitfully.
13 Therefore, I have begun to destroy you,
to ruin[d] you because of your sins.
14 You will eat but not be satisfied;
your stomach will still be empty.[e]
You will store up but save nothing,
because what you save[f] I will give to the sword.

[a] *8* Or *prudently* [b] *9* The meaning of the Hebrew for this line is uncertain. [c] *10* An ephah was a dry measure. [d] *13* Or *Therefore, I will make you ill and destroy you; / I will ruin* [e] *14* The meaning of the Hebrew for this word is uncertain. [f] *14* Or *You will press toward birth but not give birth, / and what you bring to birth*

MICAH 6:8

WHAT DOES GOD REQUIRE OF US?

These beautiful, famous words of the prophet Micah outline God's simple expectations of his people: "To act justly and to love mercy and to walk humbly with your God" (Mic 6:8). These qualities of the heart that lead to a God-pleasing life have stood the test of time because they reflect the heart of God himself. Throughout the history of his interaction with his people, God has longed for them to remember his goodness and generosity to his people and to live in response to all they know about the Lord.

Jesus confronted the religious leaders of his day, the teachers of the law and Pharisees, for turning worship into drudgery and for outwardly doing all the right things but inwardly neglecting to show justice and mercy. He harshly criticized them, calling them "hypocrites" and "blind guides" (Mt 23:23–24). God desires that his people walk humbly with him, for as they walk with him, they become more like him. Jesus is the way (Jn 14:6). He is the One who came to serve, not to be served (Mk 10:45). When a crowd asked him what kind of works God requires, he simply answered, "The work of God is this: to believe in the one he has sent" (Jn 6:28–29). When Jesus' people follow him with their whole hearts, they develop hearts like his—hearts that are compassionate and swift to do justice.

15 You will plant but not harvest;
you will press olives but not use the oil,
you will crush grapes but not drink the wine.
16 You have observed the statutes of Omri
and all the practices of Ahab's house;
you have followed their traditions.
Therefore I will give you over to ruin
and your people to derision;
you will bear the scorn of the nations.[a]

Israel's Misery

7 What misery is mine!
I am like one who gathers summer fruit
at the gleaning of the vineyard;
there is no cluster of grapes to eat,
none of the early figs that I crave.
2 The faithful have been swept from the land;
not one upright person remains.
Everyone lies in wait to shed blood;
they hunt each other with nets.
3 Both hands are skilled in doing evil;
the ruler demands gifts,
the judge accepts bribes,
the powerful dictate what they desire—
they all conspire together.
4 The best of them is like a brier,
the most upright worse than a thorn hedge.
The day God visits you has come,
the day your watchmen sound the alarm.
Now is the time of your confusion.
5 Do not trust a neighbor;
put no confidence in a friend.
Even with the woman who lies in your embrace
guard the words of your lips.
6 For a son dishonors his father,
a daughter rises up against her mother,
a daughter-in-law against her mother-in-law—
a man's enemies are the members of his own household.

7 But as for me, I watch in hope for the LORD,
I wait for God my Savior;
my God will hear me.

Israel Will Rise

8 Do not gloat over me, my enemy!
Though I have fallen, I will rise.
Though I sit in darkness,
the LORD will be my light.
9 Because I have sinned against him,
I will bear the LORD's wrath,
until he pleads my case
and upholds my cause.
He will bring me out into the light;
I will see his righteousness.
10 Then my enemy will see it
and will be covered with shame,

[a] 16 Septuagint; Hebrew *scorn due my people*

MICAH 7:18–19

FORGIVENESS

Forgiveness and compassion is at the very heart of who God is: a God who hurls "all our iniquities into the depths of the sea" (Mic 7:19). What a beautiful exclamation point with which to finish out the book of Micah. As his prophecy comes to a close, Micah ends with this vivid picture of the forgiveness God offers. This promise recalls a similar promise made to the people of Israel through Moses at Mount Sinai (Ex 34:6–9).

God's promise unfolds as his people confess their sin earlier in the chapter (Mic 7:9). Micah likens it to sitting in darkness, yet holding onto the hope that through God's grace the people will be brought into the light (7:8). The prophet goes on to explain that the people will experience God's wrath as a consequence of their sin, until there is someone to plead their case (7:9). Incredibly, Jesus came to do just that.

The divine verdict against human sin is "guilty," and its consequence is death (Ro 6:23). But God delights to show mercy (Mic 7:18), and his own arm works salvation (Isa 59:16). Before Jesus, no one else could satisfy God's wrath against sin. No one in history was righteous — not even one person (Ro 3:10)! Yet God's promise of forgiveness remained. That's why "God made him who had no sin to be sin for us, so that in him we might become the righteousness of God" (2Co 5:21). Because Jesus is the Righteous One, followers of Christ now have an Advocate who will stand at their side before the Father — that Advocate is the Son, Jesus Christ (1Jn 2:1).

There is now a responsibility on the forgiven to extend forgiveness to the world around them. Jesus clearly calls his followers to a higher standard by telling them to forgive others just as their heavenly Father has forgiven them. He warns them that if forgiveness is withheld, God will withhold it from them as well (Mt 6:14–15). Paul exhorts the church at Ephesus in the same way, encouraging them to be kind and compassionate, "forgiving each other, just as in Christ God forgave you" (Eph 4:32). This type of forgiveness should mark God's church throughout all generations as well.

she who said to me,
"Where is the LORD your God?"
My eyes will see her downfall;
even now she will be trampled underfoot
like mire in the streets.

11 The day for building your walls will come,
the day for extending your boundaries.
12 In that day people will come to you
from Assyria and the cities of Egypt,
even from Egypt to the Euphrates
and from sea to sea
and from mountain to mountain.
13 The earth will become desolate because of its inhabitants,
as the result of their deeds.

Prayer and Praise

14 Shepherd your people with your staff,
the flock of your inheritance,
which lives by itself in a forest,
in fertile pasturelands.[a]
Let them feed in Bashan and Gilead
as in days long ago.

15 "As in the days when you came out of Egypt,
I will show them my wonders."

16 Nations will see and be ashamed,
deprived of all their power.
They will put their hands over their mouths
and their ears will become deaf.
17 They will lick dust like a snake,
like creatures that crawl on the ground.
They will come trembling out of their dens;
they will turn in fear to the LORD our God
and will be afraid of you.
18 Who is a God like you,
who pardons sin and forgives the transgression
of the remnant of his inheritance?
You do not stay angry forever
but delight to show mercy.
19 You will again have compassion on us;
you will tread our sins underfoot
and hurl all our iniquities into the depths of the sea.
20 You will be faithful to Jacob,
and show love to Abraham,
as you pledged on oath to our ancestors
in days long ago.

[a] *14* Or *in the middle of Carmel*

JESUS: OUR WRATH BEARER

NAHUM

NAHUM

ASSYRIA CONQUERS ISRAEL	WRITING OF BOOK OF NAHUM	FALL OF NINEVEH
c. 722 BC	*Probably shortly before 612 BC*	*c. 612 BC*

Nahum, like Jonah, addressed the city of Nineveh. During the century or more in between these two prophets, King Sennacherib made Nineveh the capital of Assyria. In Jonah's day, the Ninevites heeded the prophet's warning and appeared to repent of their sin. Not long after that, however, Nineveh returned to its extremely wicked, cruel and prideful ways. Rather than extending another warning to Nineveh, God called Nahum to announce a message of doom. Though most of his prophecies are addressed to Nineveh — representing the entire nation of Assyria — Nahum wrote this book to comfort and encourage the people of Judah.

God had used the Assyrians to execute judgment against his own people. By 722 BC, Assyria had routed Samaria and deported many Israelites into exile. Diabolical and cruel, the Assyrian regime enacted swift and severe punishment upon their enemies. Nineveh earned a reputation for bloodthirsty and deplorable acts of terror and war. These atrocities, wrote Nahum, had not escaped God's notice (Na 1:3).

Even though God used the Assyrians to accomplish his purposes, they were not excused from their own guilt before God. God could, at the same time, use them and judge them. God would surely do to them what they had done to the Israelites. However, God's judgment (unlike Assyria's) would be righteous and pure. He would not dole out punishment in a capricious manner; rather, he would rightly judge these rebellious people.

Nineveh's judgment serves as a prototype of the wrath of God that comes to all those who scorn his mercy and rebelliously pursue their wicked ways. Because he is omniscient,

God sees and knows everything that humanity does. Because he is sovereign, he can act at any time to crush any form of evil. And because he is just, he will perfectly judge evildoers in due time.

The people of Judah, and subsequent believers, can find hope in the fact that while this life is filled with evil and pain, God will ultimately right all wrongs. Because of Jesus, believers can take joy in the fact that the wrath of God that was due them as a result of their sin has been poured out on Christ. They will not suffer in the coming day of God's wrath; until God ushers in his new heaven and new earth, believers must cry out to the nations to turn from their sin and turn to Christ for salvation. Jesus' followers must tell their friends, family members, coworkers and the nations about the salvation that's freely available before they, like Nineveh, face the judgment of a holy and just Judge.

THE LORD IS SLOW TO ANGER BUT GREAT IN POWER;
THE LORD WILL NOT LEAVE THE GUILTY UNPUNISHED.
HIS WAY IS IN THE WHIRLWIND AND THE STORM,
AND CLOUDS ARE THE DUST OF HIS FEET.

Nahum 1:3

NAHUM

1 A prophecy concerning Nineveh. The book of the vision of Nahum the Elkoshite.

The Lord's Anger Against Nineveh

2 The Lord is a jealous and avenging God;
the Lord takes vengeance and is filled with wrath.
The Lord takes vengeance on his foes
and vents his wrath against his enemies.
3 The Lord is slow to anger but great in power;
the Lord will not leave the guilty unpunished.
His way is in the whirlwind and the storm,
and clouds are the dust of his feet.
4 He rebukes the sea and dries it up;
he makes all the rivers run dry.
Bashan and Carmel wither
and the blossoms of Lebanon fade.
5 The mountains quake before him
and the hills melt away.
The earth trembles at his presence,
the world and all who live in it.
6 Who can withstand his indignation?
Who can endure his fierce anger?
His wrath is poured out like fire;
the rocks are shattered before him.

7 The Lord is good,
a refuge in times of trouble.
He cares for those who trust in him,
8 but with an overwhelming flood
he will make an end of Nineveh;
he will pursue his foes into the realm of darkness.

9 Whatever they plot against the Lord
he will bring[a] to an end;
trouble will not come a second time.
10 They will be entangled among thorns
and drunk from their wine;
they will be consumed like dry stubble.[b]
11 From you, Nineveh, has one come forth
who plots evil against the Lord
and devises wicked plans.

12 This is what the Lord says:

"Although they have allies and are numerous,
they will be destroyed and pass away.
Although I have afflicted you, Judah,
I will afflict you no more.
13 Now I will break their yoke from your neck
and tear your shackles away."

---

[a] 9 Or *What do you foes plot against the Lord? / He will bring it* [b] *10* The meaning of the Hebrew for this verse is uncertain.

A GOSPEL CASE STUDY

The people of Israel and Judah had suffered because of the evil actions of the people of Nineveh. Yet as Nahum waited in hope, he affirmed that God is good all the time, providing a refuge in times of trouble. Rather than faltering in faith, Nahum declared that God cares for those who trust in him.

Years earlier, God had commanded the prophet Jonah to travel to Nineveh and warn the people of God's coming wrath if they did not repent (Jnh 1:1 – 2; 3:1 – 2). In spite of Jonah's efforts and hopes to the contrary, the people of Nineveh repented and God withheld his judgment (Jnh 3:10). Unfortunately, as the years passed their commitment faded, and the people of Nineveh returned to their evil ways. Knowing the impact of Nineveh's short-lived repentance, Nahum prophesied God's coming judgment. In a message filled with gospel truth, Nahum extolled God's patience and mercy, but also God's judgment.

The people of Nineveh became an Old Testament case study of the gospel story. They lived in the destructive power of sin, yet Nineveh experienced God's inexplicable mercy through the reluctant prophet Jonah, who brought them the minimum possible warning to repent (Jnh 3:4). Nineveh's reprieve from judgment proclaimed for all times the extent of God's love. Yet Nineveh's return to sin and its turning away from the one true God clarifies to all who read the book of Nahum that sin brings profound consequences. The wages of sin is death (Ro 6:23), so the people of Nineveh died rejecting his mercy.

Ultimately, Jesus exemplified the truth that Nahum's experience foreshadowed. Jesus came preaching a gospel of repentance, declaring that people need to turn from sin and toward God (Mt 4:17). Jesus led people who took sin seriously to realize that sin pervaded their lives to a degree they had never imagined (Mt 5:27 – 28). To those trapped in sin and assumed to be lost by the religious elite, Jesus extended the hope of forgiveness through the full extent of God's love. In the end, Jesus quantified the high price of sin when he, the only perfect One, died for all who would never be truly good, much less perfect. Then, through his resurrection and resounding defeat of death itself, Jesus punctuated all that he had previously promised.

Nahum had declared that God is good, a refuge in times of trouble. Jesus embodied the goodness of God; the good news about Jesus offers refuge to all who will respond in faith.

14 The LORD has given a command concerning you,
Nineveh:
"You will have no descendants to bear your name.
I will destroy the images and idols
that are in the temple of your gods.
I will prepare your grave,
for you are vile."

15 Look, there on the mountains,
the feet of one who brings good news,
who proclaims peace!
Celebrate your festivals, Judah,
and fulfill your vows.
No more will the wicked invade you;
they will be completely destroyed.[a]

Nineveh to Fall

2[b] An attacker advances against you, Nineveh.
Guard the fortress,
watch the road,
brace yourselves,
marshal all your strength!

2 The LORD will restore the splendor of Jacob
like the splendor of Israel,
though destroyers have laid them waste
and have ruined their vines.

3 The shields of the soldiers are red;
the warriors are clad in scarlet.
The metal on the chariots flashes
on the day they are made ready;
the spears of juniper are brandished.[c]
4 The chariots storm through the streets,
rushing back and forth through the squares.
They look like flaming torches;
they dart about like lightning.

5 Nineveh summons her picked troops,
yet they stumble on their way.
They dash to the city wall;
the protective shield is put in place.
6 The river gates are thrown open
and the palace collapses.
7 It is decreed[d] that Nineveh
be exiled and carried away.
Her female slaves moan like doves
and beat on their breasts.
8 Nineveh is like a pool
whose water is draining away.
"Stop! Stop!" they cry,
but no one turns back.
9 Plunder the silver!
Plunder the gold!
The supply is endless,
the wealth from all its treasures!

[a] *15* In Hebrew texts this verse (1:15) is numbered 2:1. [b] In Hebrew texts 2:1-13 is numbered 2:2-14. [c] *3* Hebrew; Septuagint and Syriac *ready; / the horsemen rush to and fro.*
[d] *7* The meaning of the Hebrew for this word is uncertain.

NAHUM 2:2

RESTORING WHAT WAS LOST

For years, the people of Israel had suffered under the onslaught of the nation of Assyria and its flagship city, Nineveh. Earlier, the Assyrians had crushed the northern kingdom of Israel, and now the southern kingdom of Judah was subject to Assyria. Having fallen from their days of glory under David and Solomon, the Israelites heard the offer of restoration and a return to splendor through the prophet Nahum: Everything that sin had destroyed could be rebuilt through God's strength. Years earlier Moses had affirmed a similar promise, telling the people that even if they were exiled among the nations God would reclaim and restore them to himself (Dt 30:1 – 3). Later Isaiah expanded this promise to include the gospel purpose for which Israel existed: to become a light to the Gentiles so that all nations could experience his salvation (Isa 49:6).

Ultimately, Jesus offered the promise of restoration. Lives devastated by sin's brutal attack could be made new. The people in Nahum's day likely struggled to believe such good news could be true. Yet the tide changed; Nineveh faltered and failed. The Israelites experienced temporary relief, but Jesus now offers complete restoration from sin's domination. Through faith, Jesus transforms lives so thoroughly that those impacted can best be described as new creations (2Co 5:17).

[10] She is pillaged, plundered, stripped!
Hearts melt, knees give way,
bodies tremble, every face grows pale.

[11] Where now is the lions' den,
the place where they fed their young,
where the lion and lioness went,
and the cubs, with nothing to fear?
[12] The lion killed enough for his cubs
and strangled the prey for his mate,
filling his lairs with the kill
and his dens with the prey.

[13] "I am against you,"
declares the LORD Almighty.
"I will burn up your chariots in smoke,
and the sword will devour your young lions.
I will leave you no prey on the earth.
The voices of your messengers
will no longer be heard."

Woe to Nineveh

3 Woe to the city of blood,
full of lies,
full of plunder,
never without victims!
[2] The crack of whips,
the clatter of wheels,
galloping horses
and jolting chariots!
[3] Charging cavalry,
flashing swords
and glittering spears!
Many casualties,
piles of dead,
bodies without number,
people stumbling over the corpses —
[4] all because of the wanton lust of a prostitute,
alluring, the mistress of sorceries,
who enslaved nations by her prostitution
and peoples by her witchcraft.

[5] "I am against you," declares the LORD Almighty.
"I will lift your skirts over your face.
I will show the nations your nakedness
and the kingdoms your shame.
[6] I will pelt you with filth,
I will treat you with contempt
and make you a spectacle.
[7] All who see you will flee from you and say,
'Nineveh is in ruins — who will mourn
for her?'
Where can I find anyone to comfort you?"

[8] Are you better than Thebes,
situated on the Nile,
with water around her?
The river was her defense,
the waters her wall.

NAHUM 3:5

WHEN GOD IS AGAINST YOU

Once the people of Nineveh rejected God's mercy and returned to their pattern of sin, they experienced God's wrath through judgment. For a short season, Assyria and its "great city of Nineveh" had glimpsed the grace that flowed when God was acting mercifully on their behalf (Jnh 3:10; 4:10 – 11). Yet as their pride swelled and they flexed their military might once again, Nineveh encountered the practical implications of rejecting God. Nahum's declaration against Nineveh lays out in graphic detail the ramifications of their choices. As they stood for themselves, God stood against them. God's perfect holiness requires that he stand against sin. As a result God stands against all people, since all people sin and fall short of the glory of God (Ro 3:23). The gospel offers an elegant escape from inevitable judgment: Jesus took on the death penalty for the sin of all who would believe in him.

With sin's debt paid in full, those who place their faith in Jesus enter a new reality, an eternally altered standing with God. This right standing with God is so complete that it doesn't matter if anyone or anything else stands against the believer (Ro 8:31 – 32). In the end, only two options exist: God standing against or God standing for. Jesus makes the second option possible through the good news of the gospel, and that option changes eternity for those who trust in him for salvation.

[9] Cush[a] and Egypt were her boundless strength;
Put and Libya were among her allies.
[10] Yet she was taken captive
and went into exile.
Her infants were dashed to pieces
at every street corner.
Lots were cast for her nobles,
and all her great men were put in chains.
[11] You too will become drunk;
you will go into hiding
and seek refuge from the enemy.

[12] All your fortresses are like fig trees
with their first ripe fruit;
when they are shaken,
the figs fall into the mouth of the eater.
[13] Look at your troops —
they are all weaklings.
The gates of your land
are wide open to your enemies;
fire has consumed the bars of your gates.

[14] Draw water for the siege,
strengthen your defenses!
Work the clay,
tread the mortar,
repair the brickwork!
[15] There the fire will consume you;
the sword will cut you down —
they will devour you like a swarm of locusts.
Multiply like grasshoppers,
multiply like locusts!
[16] You have increased the number of your merchants
till they are more numerous than the stars in the sky,
but like locusts they strip the land
and then fly away.
[17] Your guards are like locusts,
your officials like swarms of locusts
that settle in the walls on a cold day —
but when the sun appears they fly away,
and no one knows where.

[18] King of Assyria, your shepherds[b] slumber;
your nobles lie down to rest.
Your people are scattered on the mountains
with no one to gather them.
[19] Nothing can heal you;
your wound is fatal.
All who hear the news about you
clap their hands at your fall,
for who has not felt
your endless cruelty?

[a] *9* That is, the upper Nile region [b] *18* That is, rulers

JESUS: OUR JOYFUL SALVATION

HABAKKUK

HABAKKUK

BABYLONIANS ATTACK JUDAH	WRITING OF BOOK OF HABAKKUK	BABYLONIANS CONQUER JUDAH
c. 605 and 597 BC	*c. 605 BC*	*c. 586 BC*

The prophet Habakkuk was filled with questions for God. Unlike many other God-appointed spokesmen, Habakkuk publicly expressed his inner frustration at evil and at God's perceived lack of response to it. The prophet pleaded, "How long, LORD, must I call for help, but you do not listen?" (1:2). Habakkuk's longing for answers and his cries for deliverance match the fervor of many of the psalms that David wrote during a similarly treacherous time in his own life.

The tone of Habakkuk's questions reveal two central frustrations. First, he did not understand why evil ran unchecked among the people of God; it seemed as if God left the sins of Judah unpunished. Second, Habakkuk watched as the pagan Babylonians prospered and were even used as God's instrument to conquer his own people. How could God bless a nation that so obviously stood in opposition to God's commands?

God graciously responded to Habakkuk's laments, and he pronounced five woes on the Babylonians because of their evil deeds (2:6 – 19). While it may seem that the Babylonians prospered while the people of God perished, God would see to it that all would be made right in the end: God would judge — and judge perfectly.

Habakkuk concluded this brief book with a prayer of praise to God (3:17 – 19). In it, he beautifully captured the deep-rooted faith that is sustained by a high view of God's control in the world. Though outwardly it may seem that evil is winning and the righteous are perishing, God will judge justly and set things right. Habakkuk called Judah to not lose hope, even if external signs of blessing from God's hand were scarce. With the prophet, God's people “will be joyful in God my Savior” (3:18), knowing that he is good and his perfect purposes will prevail.

Ultimately, such joyful hope is only possible because of the work of Jesus Christ. He is God’s perfect answer to the evil that pervades our fallen world. God took the greatest act of evil in human history — the murder of his innocent Son — and used it to open the way of salvation for all who will trust in Jesus’ saving work. And God, through Christ, will one day purge the world of evil, sin and death forever and prove once again to be the God who saves.

YET I WILL REJOICE IN THE LORD, I WILL BE JOYFUL IN GOD MY SAVIOR. THE SOVEREIGN LORD IS MY STRENGTH; HE MAKES MY FEET LIKE THE FEET OF A DEER, HE ENABLES ME TO TREAD ON THE HEIGHTS.

Habakkuk 3:18 – 19

HABAKKUK

1 The prophecy that Habakkuk the prophet received.

Habakkuk's Complaint

2 How long, LORD, must I call for help,
but you do not listen?
Or cry out to you, "Violence!"
but you do not save?
3 Why do you make me look at injustice?
Why do you tolerate wrongdoing?
Destruction and violence are before me;
there is strife, and conflict abounds.
4 Therefore the law is paralyzed,
and justice never prevails.
The wicked hem in the righteous,
so that justice is perverted.

The LORD's Answer

5 "Look at the nations and watch —
and be utterly amazed.
For I am going to do something in your days
that you would not believe,
even if you were told.
6 I am raising up the Babylonians,[a]
that ruthless and impetuous people,
who sweep across the whole earth
to seize dwellings not their own.
7 They are a feared and dreaded people;
they are a law to themselves
and promote their own honor.
8 Their horses are swifter than leopards,
fiercer than wolves at dusk.
Their cavalry gallops headlong;
their horsemen come from afar.
They fly like an eagle swooping to devour;
9 they all come intent on violence.
Their hordes[b] advance like a desert wind
and gather prisoners like sand.
10 They mock kings
and scoff at rulers.
They laugh at all fortified cities;
by building earthen ramps they capture them.
11 Then they sweep past like the wind and go on —
guilty people, whose own strength is their god."

Habakkuk's Second Complaint

12 LORD, are you not from everlasting?
My God, my Holy One, you[c] will never die.
You, LORD, have appointed them to execute judgment;
you, my Rock, have ordained them to punish.

[a] *6* Or *Chaldeans* [b] *9* The meaning of the Hebrew for this word is uncertain.
[c] *12* An ancient Hebrew scribal tradition; Masoretic Text *we*

HABAKKUK 1:5 – 6

DON'T BE FOOLISH

Habakkuk questioned how a loving God could surrender his chosen people to defeat by the cruel and pagan Babylonians. While Judah had sinned, most of its people continued to assume that they were automatically entitled to God's blessing, yet God had consistently communicated that their physical and emotional comfort were not his top priority. In fact, he promised through the prophet Habakkuk that he would do things in their day that they would not believe, even if they were told what was coming. While some could have interpreted this as good news, it was not. God would call the wicked nation of Babylon to bring judgment to his people.

Years later, the apostle Paul quoted Habakkuk 1:5 while speaking to a congregation in a Jewish synagogue. He encouraged his hearers not to allow religious tradition to prevent them from accepting Jesus as God's Messiah (Ac 13:38 – 41). God had instructed Habakkuk and his people that he would punish evil and establish righteousness, and in the end redeem his people in an amazing way. Paul pointed his hearers to the fulfillment of this prophecy: the work of Jesus Christ on their behalf. He exhorted them that they would be foolish not to see God at work through this amazing Messiah, Jesus, to whose saving work the prophet Habakkuk and others had pointed.

[13]Your eyes are too pure to look on evil;
you cannot tolerate wrongdoing.
Why then do you tolerate the treacherous?
Why are you silent while the wicked
swallow up those more righteous than themselves?
[14]You have made people like the fish in the sea,
like the sea creatures that have no ruler.
[15]The wicked foe pulls all of them up with hooks,
he catches them in his net,
he gathers them up in his dragnet;
and so he rejoices and is glad.
[16]Therefore he sacrifices to his net
and burns incense to his dragnet,
for by his net he lives in luxury
and enjoys the choicest food.
[17]Is he to keep on emptying his net,
destroying nations without mercy?

2 I will stand at my watch
and station myself on the ramparts;
I will look to see what he will say to me,
and what answer I am to give to this complaint.[a]

The LORD's Answer

[2]Then the LORD replied:

"Write down the revelation
and make it plain on tablets
so that a herald[b] may run with it.
[3]For the revelation awaits an appointed time;
it speaks of the end
and will not prove false.
Though it linger, wait for it;
it[c] will certainly come
and will not delay.

[4]"See, the enemy is puffed up;
his desires are not upright—
but the righteous person will live by his
faithfulness[d]—
[5]indeed, wine betrays him;
he is arrogant and never at rest.
Because he is as greedy as the grave
and like death is never satisfied,
he gathers to himself all the nations
and takes captive all the peoples.

[6]"Will not all of them taunt him with ridicule and scorn, saying,

"'Woe to him who piles up stolen goods
and makes himself wealthy by extortion!
How long must this go on?'
[7]Will not your creditors suddenly arise?
Will they not wake up and make you tremble?
Then you will become their prey.
[8]Because you have plundered many nations,
the peoples who are left will plunder you.

[a] 1 Or *and what to answer when I am rebuked* [b] 2 Or *so that whoever reads it*
[c] 3 Or *Though he linger, wait for him; / he* [d] 4 Or *faith*

HABAKKUK 2:1–3

MAKE IT CLEAR

God instructed Habakkuk to write down the revelation and make it plain on tablets so that a herald could run with it (Hab 2:2). He wanted the people to understand, without any room for misinterpretation or doubt, what he was saying, and he wanted to make certain that everyone had the opportunity to respond. The message was about what would happen in the future—initially in God's judgment of the Babylonians and ultimately in the earth being filled with the knowledge of God's glory (2:14).

In the New Testament, God gave the apostle John a more complete vision, which compelled John to refer to the message as "the revelation from Jesus Christ" (Rev 1:1). Through time, God has communicated in different ways (Heb 1:1) but has spoken with ultimate clarity through Jesus (Jn 1:17; Heb 1:2). God's Word, and all that God has revealed, works like a surgeon's knife in human hearts—penetrating and dividing as it exposes the truth (Heb 4:12). In Habakkuk's day, God communicated because he expected people to respond. Because of his crystal-clear communication in Jesus, God desires that those who hear his Word today choose life's most important response—turning to Jesus for the forgiveness of their sin and accepting God's free gift of new life as his adopted children.

HABAKKUK 3:1–2

IN WRATH REMEMBER MERCY

In the midst of his confusion about God's revealed ways and plans, Habakkuk expressed his faith through prayer. He affirmed that he had heard of God's fame and stood in awe of God's deeds, and he pleaded with God to renew his work in the past so it would be known in the present. Yet, since God had clearly communicated his plans to judge Judah, Habakkuk asked God to remember mercy even as he poured out his wrath.

What Habakkuk could not understand at the time was that God's mercy was woven through all that was to come. Without having mercy, God would have completely destroyed the people of Judah. Without God's mercy, the nation would never return from exile to rebuild Jerusalem and the temple. Without his mercy, God would not send Jesus into the world to die. Without his mercy, God would not offer Jesus' perfect payment for sin to a hopelessly sinful world so that people who deserved only judgment could experience only grace.

Even as Habakkuk prayed, God continued the work he had started. This work encompassed all that would happen to Judah through Babylon, but it continued purposefully through the death, resurrection and ascension of Jesus. Jesus now reigns forever in heaven, surrounded by all those who did not get what they deserved but rather received what they could never have hoped to earn: complete forgiveness, utter peace and eternal life with God.

For you have shed human blood;
you have destroyed lands and cities and everyone in them.

9 "Woe to him who builds his house by unjust gain,
setting his nest on high
to escape the clutches of ruin!
10 You have plotted the ruin of many peoples,
shaming your own house and forfeiting your life.
11 The stones of the wall will cry out,
and the beams of the woodwork will echo it.

12 "Woe to him who builds a city with bloodshed
and establishes a town by injustice!
13 Has not the LORD Almighty determined
that the people's labor is only fuel for the fire,
that the nations exhaust themselves for nothing?
14 For the earth will be filled with the knowledge of the glory of the LORD
as the waters cover the sea.

15 "Woe to him who gives drink to his neighbors,
pouring it from the wineskin till they are drunk,
so that he can gaze on their naked bodies!
16 You will be filled with shame instead of glory.
Now it is your turn! Drink and let your nakedness be
exposed[a]!
The cup from the LORD's right hand is coming around
to you,
and disgrace will cover your glory.
17 The violence you have done to Lebanon will overwhelm you,
and your destruction of animals will terrify you.
For you have shed human blood;
you have destroyed lands and cities and everyone in them.

18 "Of what value is an idol carved by a craftsman?
Or an image that teaches lies?
For the one who makes it trusts in his own creation;
he makes idols that cannot speak.
19 Woe to him who says to wood, 'Come to life!'
Or to lifeless stone, 'Wake up!'
Can it give guidance?
It is covered with gold and silver;
there is no breath in it."

20 The LORD is in his holy temple;
let all the earth be silent before him.

Habakkuk's Prayer

3 A prayer of Habakkuk the prophet. On *shigionoth*.[b]

2 LORD, I have heard of your fame;
I stand in awe of your deeds, LORD.
Repeat them in our day,
in our time make them known;
in wrath remember mercy.

3 God came from Teman,
the Holy One from Mount Paran.[c]

[a] 16 Masoretic Text; Dead Sea Scrolls, Aquila, Vulgate and Syriac (see also Septuagint) *and stagger* [b] 1 Probably a literary or musical term [c] 3 The Hebrew has *Selah* (a word of uncertain meaning) here and at the middle of verse 9 and at the end of verse 13.

His glory covered the heavens
and his praise filled the earth.
4 His splendor was like the sunrise;
rays flashed from his hand,
where his power was hidden.
5 Plague went before him;
pestilence followed his steps.
6 He stood, and shook the earth;
he looked, and made the nations tremble.
The ancient mountains crumbled
and the age-old hills collapsed —
but he marches on forever.
7 I saw the tents of Cushan in distress,
the dwellings of Midian in anguish.
8 Were you angry with the rivers, LORD?
Was your wrath against the streams?
Did you rage against the sea
when you rode your horses
and your chariots to victory?
9 You uncovered your bow,
you called for many arrows.
You split the earth with rivers;
10 the mountains saw you and writhed.
Torrents of water swept by;
the deep roared
and lifted its waves on high.

11 Sun and moon stood still in the heavens
at the glint of your flying arrows,
at the lightning of your flashing spear.
12 In wrath you strode through the earth
and in anger you threshed the nations.
13 You came out to deliver your people,
to save your anointed one.
You crushed the leader of the land of wickedness,
you stripped him from head to foot.
14 With his own spear you pierced his head
when his warriors stormed out to scatter us,
gloating as though about to devour
the wretched who were in hiding.
15 You trampled the sea with your horses,
churning the great waters.

16 I heard and my heart pounded,
my lips quivered at the sound;
decay crept into my bones,
and my legs trembled.
Yet I will wait patiently for the day of calamity
to come on the nation invading us.
17 Though the fig tree does not bud
and there are no grapes on the vines,
though the olive crop fails
and the fields produce no food,
though there are no sheep in the pen
and no cattle in the stalls,
18 yet I will rejoice in the LORD,
I will be joyful in God my Savior.

YET I WILL REJOICE

Habakkuk saw the sin of his day, its impact on the people of Judah and the collective corrosion of the nation. Seeking to frame what he saw with a lens of faith, he waited on God, calling out for divine help. But Habakkuk struggled when God told him his plan to punish evilness with more evilness. Would God actually use the wicked nation of Babylon to punish the (relatively less wicked) nation of Judah (Hab 1:6)?

Habakkuk waited for God to answer his questions (1:2 – 3; 2:1). He listened as God explained that the righteous would live by faith (2:4) and marveled as God promised that, in time, the earth would be filled with the knowledge of the glory of the Lord as the waters cover the sea (2:3,14).

As Habakkuk reflected on all that was happening in Judah and the devastation to come, he turned to God in prayer. He poured out his praise, his questions, his longing and confusion. He recalled Israel's past, the era when God's glory covered the heavens and his praise filled the earth (3:3). He reveled in the memory of how God had chastened Israel's enemies and delivered Israel from those who sought to devour them (3:13 – 15).

Habakkuk acted in faith during this dark and difficult time. He thought about the future and imagined fig trees no longer budding, vines without grapes, olive crops failing, fields with no food, pens with no sheep and stalls with no cattle (3:17).

Centuries later, as Jesus walked into Jerusalem, he knew he would soon be crucified. Like Habakkuk, he knew the Father's will and acknowledged that horrific events were coming that he would have to endure. Unlike Habakkuk, Jesus could have altered the course of his life on earth and traveled the easier path. Yet no other path would make Jesus the way, the truth and the life through which every person would be able to gain access to the Father (Jn 14:6).

On earth, Jesus was a real person, experiencing life as we all do, yet without sin. In his humanity, like the prophet Habakkuk, he experienced a troubled heart. He knew he could ask to be saved from that dark hour to come. But he also fully knew that the brutal path of crucifixion was the reason he had come to the world (Jn 12:27). So in this intense hour he prayed, "Father, glorify your name!" (Jn 12:28). In that moment Jesus, the Son of God, lived by faith and perfectly modeled for us complete reliance on God.

19 The Sovereign LORD is my strength;
he makes my feet like the feet of a deer,
he enables me to tread on the heights.

For the director of music. On my stringed instruments.

JESUS: OUR MIGHTY ONE

ZEPHANIAH

ZEPHANIAH

REIGN OF JOSIAH	WRITING OF BOOK OF ZEPHANIAH	FALL OF JUDAH
c. 640 – 609 BC	*Probably between 640 and 627 BC*	*c. 586 BC*

Zephaniah wrote to warn God's people of the coming day of the Lord. Certainly, he was not the only prophet to use this theme, though the looming judgment of this day featured more prominently in Zephaniah's ministry than in some of the other prophets' writings.

He began with a stern word of warning to his fellow Israelites in Judah. Instead of following God's commands, they had modeled the pagan ways of the surrounding nations. They disregarded God's law, engaged in idolatrous worship and lived without remorse. Zephaniah begged the people to repent and turn back to God before it was too late.

History records that they did heed Zephaniah's warning, at least for a time. The southern kingdom, Judah, had watched as Assyria destroyed the northern kingdom, Israel. It had seemed that the same fate was imminent for Judah as well. Under the evil reign of Manasseh, the people had engaged in deplorable acts of wickedness. But God used godly King Josiah to foster a revival in the nation. Under Josiah's leadership, the people heard the Book of the Law and were broken by their sin. Their repentance led to a number of reforms, which promoted worship and obedience among the people once again (2Ki 22:1 — 23:25). Zephaniah ministered during Josiah's reign (Zep 1:1), and this prophecy was likely delivered early in Josiah's reign — helping to spur Josiah on in his reforms. This spiritual transformation, though short-lived, prevented an Assyrian invasion and the destruction of Jerusalem for a time.

God's judgment on his appointed day — through the Babylonians — would certainly come. Zephaniah knew that the people's obedience was a faulty basis for confidence; they were sinful through and through. Yet, Zephaniah's conclusion expressed hope based not on the moral uprightness of the people but on the power of God. He is "the Mighty Warrior" who would save a remnant of his people from the coming judgment (3:17). Zephaniah encouraged the people that God "will take great delight in you; in his love he will no longer rebuke you, but will rejoice over you with singing" (3:17). These poetic refrains depict an astonishing act of God's grace. In the person and work of Jesus, God's mighty power and tender affections meet. Jesus proves that God is mighty to save his people through the sacrifice of his Son.

THE LORD WITHIN HER IS RIGHTEOUS;
HE DOES NO WRONG. MORNING BY MORNING
HE DISPENSES HIS JUSTICE, AND EVERY
NEW DAY HE DOES NOT FAIL, YET THE
UNRIGHTEOUS KNOW NO SHAME.

Zephaniah 3:5

ZEPHANIAH

1 The word of the LORD that came to Zephaniah son of Cushi, the son of Gedaliah, the son of Amariah, the son of Hezekiah, during the reign of Josiah son of Amon king of Judah:

Judgment on the Whole Earth in the Day of the LORD

2 "I will sweep away everything
from the face of the earth,"
declares the LORD.
3 "I will sweep away both man and beast;
I will sweep away the birds in the sky
and the fish in the sea—
and the idols that cause the wicked to stumble."[a]

"When I destroy all mankind
on the face of the earth,"
declares the LORD,
4 "I will stretch out my hand against Judah
and against all who live in Jerusalem.
I will destroy every remnant of Baal worship in this place,
the very names of the idolatrous priests—
5 those who bow down on the roofs
to worship the starry host,
those who bow down and swear by the LORD
and who also swear by Molek,[b]
6 those who turn back from following the LORD
and neither seek the LORD nor inquire of him."
7 Be silent before the Sovereign LORD,
for the day of the LORD is near.
The LORD has prepared a sacrifice;
he has consecrated those he has invited.

8 "On the day of the LORD's sacrifice
I will punish the officials
and the king's sons
and all those clad
in foreign clothes.
9 On that day I will punish
all who avoid stepping on the threshold,[c]
who fill the temple of their gods
with violence and deceit.

10 "On that day,"
declares the LORD,
"a cry will go up from the Fish Gate,
wailing from the New Quarter,
and a loud crash from the hills.
11 Wail, you who live in the market district[d];
all your merchants will be wiped out,
all who trade with[e] silver will be destroyed.

[a] *3* The meaning of the Hebrew for this line is uncertain. [b] *5* Hebrew *Malkam*
[c] *9* See 1 Samuel 5:5. [d] *11* Or *the Mortar* [e] *11* Or *in*

12 At that time I will search Jerusalem with lamps
and punish those who are complacent,
who are like wine left on its dregs,
who think, 'The LORD will do nothing,
either good or bad.'
13 Their wealth will be plundered,
their houses demolished.
Though they build houses,
they will not live in them;
though they plant vineyards,
they will not drink the wine."

14 The great day of the LORD is near —
near and coming quickly.
The cry on the day of the LORD is bitter;
the Mighty Warrior shouts his battle cry.
15 That day will be a day of wrath —
a day of distress and anguish,
a day of trouble and ruin,
a day of darkness and gloom,
a day of clouds and blackness —
16 a day of trumpet and battle cry
against the fortified cities
and against the corner towers.

17 "I will bring such distress on all people
that they will grope about like those who are blind,
because they have sinned against the LORD.
Their blood will be poured out like dust
and their entrails like dung.
18 Neither their silver nor their gold
will be able to save them
on the day of the LORD's wrath."

In the fire of his jealousy
the whole earth will be consumed,
for he will make a sudden end
of all who live on the earth.

Judah and Jerusalem Judged Along With the Nations

Judah Summoned to Repent

2 Gather together, gather yourselves together,
you shameful nation,
2 before the decree takes effect
and that day passes like windblown chaff,
before the LORD's fierce anger
comes upon you,
before the day of the LORD's wrath
comes upon you.
3 Seek the LORD, all you humble of the land,
you who do what he commands.
Seek righteousness, seek humility;
perhaps you will be sheltered
on the day of the LORD's anger.

Philistia

4 Gaza will be abandoned
and Ashkelon left in ruins.

ZEPHANIAH 2:3

SEEK HUMILITY

Zephaniah — the prophet to Judah — devoted the early part of his manuscript to warning Judah and Jerusalem of the coming day of the Lord (1:4 – 7). For those who continued to sin against the Lord, this day's approach only meant the increasing proximity of God's judgment. Though the northern kingdom of Israel experienced destruction nearly 100 years earlier — something these readers knew well — the southern kingdom of Judah continued to stiffen its neck against the Lord's warnings.

In mercy, God sent Zephaniah to call them to repentance once again. He commanded them to seek the Lord, particularly in a spirit of humility. It is evident that pride had contributed to their rebellion in some sense, as the author referred to humility twice in 2:3.

Paul wrote about the day of the Lord in a letter to the Thessalonian church, describing it as coming "like a thief in the night" (1Th 5:2). Paul describes two categories of people in that text as well. Those who are in the *darkness* will not escape the coming destruction (1Th 5:4). However, Christ died so that children of the *light* might be sheltered from the coming wrath of God (1Th 5:5,9). While God opposes pride, his grace and favor await the humble (1Pe 5:5).

At midday Ashdod will be emptied
and Ekron uprooted.
5 Woe to you who live by the sea,
you Kerethite people;
the word of the LORD is against you,
Canaan, land of the Philistines.
He says, "I will destroy you,
and none will be left."
6 The land by the sea will become pastures
having wells for shepherds
and pens for flocks.
7 That land will belong
to the remnant of the people of Judah;
there they will find pasture.
In the evening they will lie down
in the houses of Ashkelon.
The LORD their God will care for them;
he will restore their fortunes.[a]

Moab and Ammon

8 "I have heard the insults of Moab
and the taunts of the Ammonites,
who insulted my people
and made threats against their land.
9 Therefore, as surely as I live,"
declares the LORD Almighty,
the God of Israel,
"surely Moab will become like Sodom,
the Ammonites like Gomorrah —
a place of weeds and salt pits,
a wasteland forever.
The remnant of my people will plunder them;
the survivors of my nation will inherit their land."
10 This is what they will get in return for their pride,
for insulting and mocking
the people of the LORD Almighty.
11 The LORD will be awesome to them
when he destroys all the gods of the earth.
Distant nations will bow down to him,
all of them in their own lands.

Cush

12 "You Cushites,[b] too,
will be slain by my sword."

Assyria

13 He will stretch out his hand against the north
and destroy Assyria,
leaving Nineveh utterly desolate
and dry as the desert.
14 Flocks and herds will lie down there,
creatures of every kind.
The desert owl and the screech owl
will roost on her columns.

[a] 7 Or *will bring back their captives* [b] 12 That is, people from the upper Nile region

Their hooting will echo through the windows,
rubble will fill the doorways,
the beams of cedar will be exposed.
15 This is the city of revelry
that lived in safety.
She said to herself,
"I am the one! And there is none besides me."
What a ruin she has become,
a lair for wild beasts!
All who pass by her scoff
and shake their fists.

Jerusalem

3 Woe to the city of oppressors,
rebellious and defiled!
2 She obeys no one,
she accepts no correction.
She does not trust in the LORD,
she does not draw near to her God.
3 Her officials within her
are roaring lions;
her rulers are evening wolves,
who leave nothing for the morning.
4 Her prophets are unprincipled;
they are treacherous people.
Her priests profane the sanctuary
and do violence to the law.
5 The LORD within her is righteous;
he does no wrong.
Morning by morning he dispenses his justice,
and every new day he does not fail,
yet the unrighteous know no shame.

Jerusalem Remains Unrepentant

6 "I have destroyed nations;
their strongholds are demolished.
I have left their streets deserted,
with no one passing through.
Their cities are laid waste;
they are deserted and empty.
7 Of Jerusalem I thought,
'Surely you will fear me
and accept correction!'
Then her place of refuge[a] would not be destroyed,
nor all my punishments come upon[b] her.
But they were still eager
to act corruptly in all they did.
8 Therefore wait for me,"
declares the LORD,
"for the day I will stand up to testify.[c]
I have decided to assemble the nations,
to gather the kingdoms
and to pour out my wrath on them —
all my fierce anger.

[a] 7 Or *her sanctuary will rise up to plunder* [b] 7 Or *all those I appointed over* [c] 8 Septuagint and Syriac; Hebrew

ZEPHANIAH 3:5

JUSTICE

Zephaniah began this chapter describing the city of Jerusalem. God's image bearers — living inside the walls of God's city — continued to reject God's word. An oppressing and rebellious metropolis, the corruption within this city knew no bounds. Zephaniah described the officials and rulers as bloodthirsty animals; the prophets and priests he labeled treacherous and perverse (vv. 3 – 4).

However, the Lord of the city remained righteous, having never done wrong. He had no trouble meeting the standard of justice he maintained. In fact, the prophet portrayed each dawn as fresh evidence of the Lord's faithfulness (v. 5).

As the pages of the Gospels reveal, Jesus puts this perfect justice on display, even declaring, "I always do what pleases [the Father]" (Jn 8:29). Jesus always did what was right. Therefore, he proved to be the only one who could rightly judge the world. God's ways are perfect, and in his grace he provides a way, through Jesus, for people to come to him.

The whole world will be consumed
by the fire of my jealous anger.

Restoration of Israel's Remnant

9 "Then I will purify the lips of the peoples,
that all of them may call on the name of the LORD
and serve him shoulder to shoulder.
10 From beyond the rivers of Cush[a]
my worshipers, my scattered people,
will bring me offerings.
11 On that day you, Jerusalem, will not be put to shame
for all the wrongs you have done to me,
because I will remove from you
your arrogant boasters.
Never again will you be haughty
on my holy hill.
12 But I will leave within you
the meek and humble.
The remnant of Israel
will trust in the name of the LORD.
13 They will do no wrong;
they will tell no lies.
A deceitful tongue
will not be found in their mouths.
They will eat and lie down
and no one will make them afraid."

14 Sing, Daughter Zion;
shout aloud, Israel!
Be glad and rejoice with all your heart,
Daughter Jerusalem!
15 The LORD has taken away your punishment,
he has turned back your enemy.
The LORD, the King of Israel, is with you;
never again will you fear any harm.
16 On that day
they will say to Jerusalem,
"Do not fear, Zion;
do not let your hands hang limp.
17 The LORD your God is with you,
the Mighty Warrior who saves.
He will take great delight in you;
in his love he will no longer rebuke you,
but will rejoice over you with singing."

18 "I will remove from you
all who mourn over the loss of your appointed festivals,
which is a burden and reproach for you.
19 At that time I will deal
with all who oppressed you.
I will rescue the lame;
I will gather the exiles.
I will give them praise and honor
in every land where they have suffered shame.
20 At that time I will gather you;
at that time I will bring you home.

[a] *10* That is, the upper Nile region

HE WILL REJOICE OVER US WITH SINGING

Zephaniah closed his book by pointing his audience to the coming day of the Lord. The impending judgment will be extensive, as the jealous anger of the Lord removes all prideful people from his city, Jerusalem (3:7 – 8,11). On that day, God's wrath will leave no rebel untouched.

However, within his city, God will leave people who are humble — his remnant (vv. 12 – 13). As a foreshadowing of later teaching (Mt 5:5), the meek will inherit Jerusalem. In an appropriate response to the swift and decisive judgment on their enemies, Zephaniah called upon believers to rejoice (Zep 3:14 – 15). Their God — the "Mighty Warrior" — was with them (vv. 16 – 17).

Their rejoicing is reflective of another's rejoicing. Zephaniah goes on to detail the Lord's affections toward his people. Zephaniah does not portray God as indifferent to his people. Rather, God delights in those whom he delivers. In fact, the one who created music — soaring melodies and resonant harmonies — actually sings over his people (v. 17).

Though God sees his people this way, God's people often fail to see God this way — as one who enthusiastically rejoices over them. The apostle Paul, knowing the calloused human heart, prayed that believers' eyes would be enlightened to see God's joy in the redeemed. His prayer for the Ephesian church included a request that they might see the "riches of his glorious inheritance in his holy people" (Eph 1:18). The inheritance Paul described does not appear to be one awaiting God's people; rather, the inheritance is one that awaits God. God sees a diverse body of believers, united in and clothed with Christ's righteousness. The meek inherit the earth; God inherits the meek.

Zephaniah described a mighty-to-save God who would be with his people (3:17). In the Gospel of Matthew, an angel appeared to Joseph to tell him to name his soon-to-arrive son "Jesus, because he will save his people from their sins" (Mt 1:21). Matthew goes on to interpret this as a fulfillment of another name, Immanuel, meaning "God with us" (Mt 1:22 – 23). This saving God dwells with — and *delights in* — his people. God rejoices over those who choose to trust him, expressing his delight in song.

I will give you honor and praise
among all the peoples of the earth
when I restore your fortunes[a]
before your very eyes,"

says the LORD.

[a] 20 Or *I bring back your captives*

JESUS: OUR MAIN PRIORITY

HAGGAI

HAGGAI

FALL OF JUDAH/ TEMPLE DESTROYED *c. 586 BC*	HAGGAI PROPHESIES/ WORK ON TEMPLE RENEWED *c. 520 BC*	TEMPLE COMPLETED *c. 516 BC*

Haggai proclaimed the word of God to the Jews who had returned from exile in Babylon and were attempting to rebuild their lives in the promised land. After conquering the Babylonians, in 538 BC King Cyrus of Persia allowed the Jews to go back to their homeland. Led by Zerubbabel, about 50,000 Jews made the long journey and began working to restore God-centered worship among their people by rebuilding Jerusalem and the temple.

But the zeal that should have marked the people of God for this work was lacking. The extent of the work combined with criticism from hostile neighbors produced a defeated spirit among the remnant who returned. More than that, they focused on their own selfish desires and abandoned God's work in favor of their own individual pursuits. Claiming that it was not yet the right time to begin work on God's house, they were passionately building their own houses (1:2 – 4).

Haggai directed the people's attention to the problems of their day — namely, the challenging economic times and the infertility of the land. These factors were not the result of poor planning or strategy on the part of the people, but were rather the direct result of their spiritual lethargy. God himself withheld rain and brought about economic turmoil to demonstrate the folly of the people's priorities. They had willingly chosen to prioritize their own desires over the explicit commands of God (1:5 – 11).

As a result, the temple remained in ruins. The place where God chose to dwell among his people was still in shambles, and to make matters worse, the people seemingly didn't care. The ruined temple site served as a tangible symbol of the ruined spiritual state of God's people.

Thankfully, the people heeded Haggai's message and promptly began work on the temple. Haggai followed with another simple yet profound message of hope. He assured them that God was with them in their work and would continue to dwell in their midst. "'Be strong, all you people of the land,' declares the LORD, 'and work. For I am with you'" (2:4). Though the people would continue to falter, God's full and final dwelling among his people would find its fulfillment in "God with us," Immanuel (Mt 1:23) — Jesus the Christ, who would rightly receive his people's worship forever.

NOW THIS IS WHAT THE LORD ALMIGHTY SAYS: "GIVE CAREFUL THOUGHT TO YOUR WAYS."

Haggai 1:5

HAGGAI

HAGGAI 1:5–6

THE DISCIPLINE OF A SMALL HARVEST

For agrarian societies like those of the ancient world, harvest was a cultural event that was central to the lives of most of the people. Israel celebrated feast days three times a year (Firstfruits, Weeks and Tabernacles), with each one tied to a harvest. As God's people celebrated the feast days, plentiful harvests assured them that God was with them and cared for them.

Unfortunately, those who returned to Judah from exile prioritized building their own houses over rebuilding God's temple (Hag 1:2–4). In response, God disciplined his people with a drought (v. 11). Though they "planted much," they "harvested little" (v. 6). After receiving the discipline of a small harvest and hearing Haggai's message, God's people began to rebuild the temple.

Christians today experience God's discipline as a form of protection, a reminder that they belong to a loving Father (Heb 12:5–10). Such discipline "produces a harvest of righteousness and peace" in believers' lives (Heb 12:11). Jesus used the imagery of harvest to teach spiritual truths about his mission. He described people who needed to hear the gospel as a field ripe for harvest, and he exhorted his disciples to pray for more laborers to be sent to gather the harvest (Mt 9:35–38). In Haggai's day, God was ready to bless his

(continued on page 1482)

A Call to Build the House of the Lord

1 In the second year of King Darius, on the first day of the sixth month, the
word of the Lord came through the prophet Haggai to Zerubbabel son of
Shealtiel, governor of Judah, and to Joshua son of Jozadak,[a] the high priest:
[2]This is what the Lord Almighty says: "These people say, 'The time has not yet
come to rebuild the Lord's house.' "
[3]Then the word of the Lord came through the prophet Haggai: [4]"Is it a time
for you yourselves to be living in your paneled houses, while this house remains
a ruin?"
[5]Now this is what the Lord Almighty says: "Give careful thought to your ways.
[6]You have planted much, but harvested little. You eat, but never have enough.
You drink, but never have your fill. You put on clothes, but are not warm. You
earn wages, only to put them in a purse with holes in it."
[7]This is what the Lord Almighty says: "Give careful thought to your ways.
[8]Go up into the mountains and bring down timber and build my house, so that
I may take pleasure in it and be honored," says the Lord. [9]"You expected much,
but see, it turned out to be little. What you brought home, I blew away. Why?"
declares the Lord Almighty. "Because of my house, which remains a ruin, while
each of you is busy with your own house. [10]Therefore, because of you the heavens
have withheld their dew and the earth its crops. [11]I called for a drought on the
fields and the mountains, on the grain, the new wine, the olive oil and everything else the ground produces, on people and livestock, and on all the labor of
your hands."

[12]Then Zerubbabel son of Shealtiel, Joshua son of Jozadak, the high priest,
and the whole remnant of the people obeyed the voice of the Lord their God and
the message of the prophet Haggai, because the Lord their God had sent him.
And the people feared the Lord.
[13]Then Haggai, the Lord's messenger, gave this message of the Lord to the
people: "I am with you," declares the Lord. [14]So the Lord stirred up the spirit
of Zerubbabel son of Shealtiel, governor of Judah, and the spirit of Joshua son of
Jozadak, the high priest, and the spirit of the whole remnant of the people. They
came and began to work on the house of the Lord Almighty, their God, [15]on the
twenty-fourth day of the sixth month.

The Promised Glory of the New House

2 In the second year of King Darius, [1]on the twenty-first day of the seventh
month, the word of the Lord came through the prophet Haggai: [2]"Speak to
Zerubbabel son of Shealtiel, governor of Judah, to Joshua son of Jozadak,[b] the
high priest, and to the remnant of the people. Ask them, [3]'Who of you is left who
saw this house in its former glory? How does it look to you now? Does it not seem
to you like nothing? [4]But now be strong, Zerubbabel,' declares the Lord. 'Be
strong, Joshua son of Jozadak, the high priest. Be strong, all you people of the
land,' declares the Lord, 'and work. For I am with you,' declares the Lord Almighty. [5]'This is what I covenanted with you when you came out of Egypt. And
my Spirit remains among you. Do not fear.'
[6]"This is what the Lord Almighty says: 'In a little while I will once more shake
the heavens and the earth, the sea and the dry land. [7]I will shake all nations, and

[a] *1* Hebrew *Jehozadak,* a variant of *Jozadak*; also in verses 12 and 14 [b] *2* Hebrew *Jehozadak,* a variant of *Jozadak*; also in verse 4

PRESENT AND FUTURE HOPE IN CHRIST

In different seasons of life, the people of God face the possibility of discouragement. Discouragement can hold believers back from fulfilling God's plans for their lives. This is exactly where those who had returned from exile were when God, through Haggai, brought them a message of hope.

Through Haggai's ministry, this remnant renewed their passion for God and began to rebuild the temple, the place where God's people gathered for worship. When the temple was in shambles, the Israelites' relationship with God suffered. God had disciplined his people through drought (1:11); when they listened to Haggai's message, they were ready to get to work on rebuilding the temple (1:14 – 15). However, discouragement quickly began to creep in as they remembered the glory of the former temple. How could they ever restore the temple to its former beauty and majesty? Yet, this was exactly what God promised.

God spoke directly to the people's discouragement with hope. He told them to be strong; he told them he was with them (2:4). He reminded them of his covenant with them, he assured them that his Spirit was with them, and he admonished them not to fear (2:5).

These are the same words of hope that God gives Christians today. He exhorts believers to be strong (1Co 16:13). God has promised never to leave his people (Heb 13:5); Jesus has told his followers not to fear (Jn 14:27).

The temple was completed in Haggai's day, yet without the ark of the covenant, it lacked the former glory. Still, hope remained. The Messiah was still to come to his temple (Mal 3:1). Haggai pointed to the appearance of that which is "desired by all nations" (Hag 2:7); both of these prophecies likely found their fulfillment in Jesus Christ. Jesus would fill the temple with the greatest glory it had ever known when he came to Jerusalem and taught in it (Hag 2:9). Jesus personified the rebuilding of the temple with a greater glory through his death, burial and resurrection (Jn 2:19 – 22). Even now, Jesus is drawing all nations to himself, and God's people wait with great hope for the final fulfillment of Haggai 2:7, when those from "every nation, tribe, people and language" will gather around the throne to worship Jesus Christ (Rev 7:9 – 10).

(The Discipline of a Small Harvest, continued)

people with a plentiful harvest when they prioritized the building of the temple.

In Jesus' death, the need for the temple as a conduit for salvation was eliminated (Mk 15:38). Today, believers participate in the building of the church as they share the good news of Jesus with the people around them. The church that Jesus is building (unlike the temple in Haggai's time) will be indestructible and serves as a living sign of the kingdom of God until Christ's return (Mt 16:18).

what is desired by all nations will come, and I will fill this house with glory,' says
the LORD Almighty. [8]'The silver is mine and the gold is mine,' declares the LORD
Almighty. [9]'The glory of this present house will be greater than the glory of the
former house,' says the LORD Almighty. 'And in this place I will grant peace,' declares the LORD Almighty."

Blessings for a Defiled People

[10]On the twenty-fourth day of the ninth month, in the second year of Darius,
the word of the LORD came to the prophet Haggai: [11]"This is what the LORD Almighty says: 'Ask the priests what the law says: [12]If someone carries consecrated
meat in the fold of their garment, and that fold touches some bread or stew, some
wine, olive oil or other food, does it become consecrated?' "

The priests answered, "No."

[13]Then Haggai said, "If a person defiled by contact with a dead body touches
one of these things, does it become defiled?"

"Yes," the priests replied, "it becomes defiled."

[14]Then Haggai said, " 'So it is with this people and this nation in my sight,'
declares the LORD. 'Whatever they do and whatever they offer there is defiled.

[15]" 'Now give careful thought to this from this day on[a]—consider how things
were before one stone was laid on another in the LORD's temple. [16]When anyone
came to a heap of twenty measures, there were only ten. When anyone went to a
wine vat to draw fifty measures, there were only twenty. [17]I struck all the work of
your hands with blight, mildew and hail, yet you did not return to me,' declares
the LORD. [18]'From this day on, from this twenty-fourth day of the ninth month,
give careful thought to the day when the foundation of the LORD's temple was
laid. Give careful thought: [19]Is there yet any seed left in the barn? Until now, the
vine and the fig tree, the pomegranate and the olive tree have not borne fruit.

" 'From this day on I will bless you.' "

Zerubbabel the LORD's Signet Ring

[20]The word of the LORD came to Haggai a second time on the twenty-fourth
day of the month: [21]"Tell Zerubbabel governor of Judah that I am going to shake
the heavens and the earth. [22]I will overturn royal thrones and shatter the power
of the foreign kingdoms. I will overthrow chariots and their drivers; horses and
their riders will fall, each by the sword of his brother.

[23]" 'On that day,' declares the LORD Almighty, 'I will take you, my servant Zerubbabel son of Shealtiel,' declares the LORD, 'and I will make you like my signet
ring, for I have chosen you,' declares the LORD Almighty."

[a] 15 Or *to the days past*

JESUS: OUR HUMBLE KING

ZECHARIAH

ZECHARIAH

DECREE OF CYRUS ALLOWING JEWS TO RETURN	ZECHARIAH'S PROPHECIES	WORK ON TEMPLE RENEWED AND COMPLETED
c. 538 BC	*c. 520 – 480 BC*	*c. 520 – 516 BC*

Zechariah, whose name means "The LORD remembers," testified about God's faithfulness to the remnant of Jews who returned to rebuild Jerusalem. Along with Haggai, Zechariah served to enliven the faith and confidence of God's people as they rebuilt the temple.

Of primary importance for Zechariah was encouraging the people's loyalty to God and faithfulness to his word throughout their labors. Encouraging them to avoid the sins of their predecessors, Zechariah reminded the people to stay true to God, forsake all idolatry and maintain their covenant promises to God (1:2 – 6). Zechariah also encouraged the people by assuring them of God's faithfulness to bless their work and restore their fortunes.

These promises were based on a coming Anointed One who would rule and reign as God's Messiah from Zion, ushering in a desperately longed-for era of peace. Zechariah employed a number of images to refer to this Messiah: God's servant (3:8), the Branch (3:8), a stone (3:9) and God's shepherd (13:7). He would serve both as a king, ruling over God's people with righteousness; and a priest, caring for the people with loving-kindness.

Zechariah's clear message also revealed a number of fascinating details about this coming One: he would enter Jerusalem on a donkey colt (9:9), he would be betrayed for 30 pieces of silver (11:12 – 13) and his body would be pierced (12:10). Most importantly, Zechariah spoke of the forgiveness of sins that would come through the Messiah's death (13:1). The prophet's writings provide striking parallels with the writings of the New Testament authors. Zechariah also looked forward to the second coming of Christ, when he would ultimately save his people (12:10 — 13:1), vanquish their enemies (14:3,12 – 15), and reign in the new Jerusalem (14:9,16).

Zechariah detailed God's clear plan for salvation: they need only to repent, turn to him and trust in the provision he offers. These decisions make it possible for fallen, sinful humans to have a restored relationship with God and live a life of worshipful obedience. Because Jesus, as God's Anointed One, fulfilled the prophecies of Zechariah and other Old Testament prophets, he alone provides the purification and righteousness all people so desperately need.

THEREFORE TELL THE PEOPLE: THIS IS WHAT THE LORD ALMIGHTY SAYS: "RETURN TO ME," DECLARES THE LORD ALMIGHTY, "AND I WILL RETURN TO YOU," SAYS THE LORD ALMIGHTY.

Zechariah 1:3

ZECHARIAH

A Call to Return to the Lord

1 In the eighth month of the second year of Darius, the word of the LORD came
to the prophet Zechariah son of Berekiah, the son of Iddo:
2“The LORD was very angry with your ancestors. 3Therefore tell the people:
This is what the LORD Almighty says: ‘Return to me,’ declares the LORD Almighty, ‘and I will return to you,’ says the LORD Almighty. 4Do not be like your
ancestors, to whom the earlier prophets proclaimed: This is what the LORD Almighty says: ‘Turn from your evil ways and your evil practices.’ But they would
not listen or pay attention to me, declares the LORD. 5Where are your ancestors
now? And the prophets, do they live forever? 6But did not my words and my decrees, which I commanded my servants the prophets, overtake your ancestors?
“Then they repented and said, ‘The LORD Almighty has done to us what our
ways and practices deserve, just as he determined to do.’ ”

The Man Among the Myrtle Trees

7On the twenty-fourth day of the eleventh month, the month of Shebat, in the
second year of Darius, the word of the LORD came to the prophet Zechariah son
of Berekiah, the son of Iddo.
8During the night I had a vision, and there before me was a man mounted on a
red horse. He was standing among the myrtle trees in a ravine. Behind him were
red, brown and white horses.
9I asked, “What are these, my lord?”
The angel who was talking with me answered, “I will show you what they are.”
10Then the man standing among the myrtle trees explained, “They are the
ones the LORD has sent to go throughout the earth.”
11And they reported to the angel of the LORD who was standing among the
myrtle trees, “We have gone throughout the earth and found the whole world
at rest and in peace.”
12Then the angel of the LORD said, “LORD Almighty, how long will you withhold mercy from Jerusalem and from the towns of Judah, which you have been
angry with these seventy years?” 13So the LORD spoke kind and comforting
words to the angel who talked with me.
14Then the angel who was speaking to me said, “Proclaim this word: This is
what the LORD Almighty says: ‘I am very jealous for Jerusalem and Zion, 15and I
am very angry with the nations that feel secure. I was only a little angry, but they
went too far with the punishment.’
16“Therefore this is what the LORD says: ‘I will return to Jerusalem with mercy,
and there my house will be rebuilt. And the measuring line will be stretched out
over Jerusalem,’ declares the LORD Almighty.
17“Proclaim further: This is what the LORD Almighty says: ‘My towns will
again overflow with prosperity, and the LORD will again comfort Zion and
choose Jerusalem.’ ”

Four Horns and Four Craftsmen

18Then I looked up, and there before me were four horns. 19I asked the angel
who was speaking to me, “What are these?”
He answered me, “These are the horns that scattered Judah, Israel and Jerusalem.”
20Then the LORD showed me four craftsmen. 21I asked, “What are these coming to do?”
He answered, “These are the horns that scattered Judah so that no one could

ZECHARIAH 1:8–17

THE MAN AMONG THE MYRTLE TREES

The book of Zechariah finds the Israelites back in the promised land after exile, though the temple remained in ruins. The Lord used the prophet Haggai to begin spurring the people of God to take on this construction project. A couple of months later, Zechariah joined with Haggai in calling Judah to return to their God and rebuild the temple.

The book of Zechariah contains eight visions; this is the first. During this vision, the conversation between the man on a horse and the angel of the Lord came to this conclusion: the world seemed to be at peace (v. 11).

However, the Lord’s anger was kindled against the nations who had added atrocity to the punishment that God allowed his people to experience in exile (vv. 12–15). As a result, God would turn again with favor toward his people and celebrate his renewed presence in Jerusalem and the surrounding towns (vv. 16–17). This beautiful picture of God’s blessing and care points believers today toward the city that will be fully established when Jesus comes again (Rev 21:2–10).

raise their head, but the craftsmen have come to terrify them and throw down these horns of the nations who lifted up their horns against the land of Judah to scatter its people."[a]

A Man With a Measuring Line

2 [b] Then I looked up, and there before me was a man with a measuring line in his hand. 2 I asked, "Where are you going?"

He answered me, "To measure Jerusalem, to find out how wide and how long it is."

3 While the angel who was speaking to me was leaving, another angel came to meet him 4 and said to him: "Run, tell that young man, 'Jerusalem will be a city without walls because of the great number of people and animals in it. 5 And I myself will be a wall of fire around it,' declares the LORD, 'and I will be its glory within.'

6 "Come! Come! Flee from the land of the north," declares the LORD, "for I have scattered you to the four winds of heaven," declares the LORD.

7 "Come, Zion! Escape, you who live in Daughter Babylon!" 8 For this is what the LORD Almighty says: "After the Glorious One has sent me against the nations that have plundered you — for whoever touches you touches the apple of his eye — 9 I will surely raise my hand against them so that their slaves will plunder them.[c] Then you will know that the LORD Almighty has sent me.

10 "Shout and be glad, Daughter Zion. For I am coming, and I will live among you," declares the LORD. 11 "Many nations will be joined with the LORD in that day and will become my people. I will live among you and you will know that the LORD Almighty has sent me to you. 12 The LORD will inherit Judah as his portion in the holy land and will again choose Jerusalem. 13 Be still before the LORD, all mankind, because he has roused himself from his holy dwelling."

Clean Garments for the High Priest

3 Then he showed me Joshua the high priest standing before the angel of the LORD, and Satan[d] standing at his right side to accuse him. 2 The LORD said to Satan, "The LORD rebuke you, Satan! The LORD, who has chosen Jerusalem, rebuke you! Is not this man a burning stick snatched from the fire?"

3 Now Joshua was dressed in filthy clothes as he stood before the angel. 4 The angel said to those who were standing before him, "Take off his filthy clothes."

Then he said to Joshua, "See, I have taken away your sin, and I will put fine garments on you."

5 Then I said, "Put a clean turban on his head." So they put a clean turban on his head and clothed him, while the angel of the LORD stood by.

6 The angel of the LORD gave this charge to Joshua: 7 "This is what the LORD Almighty says: 'If you will walk in obedience to me and keep my requirements, then you will govern my house and have charge of my courts, and I will give you a place among these standing here.

8 "'Listen, High Priest Joshua, you and your associates seated before you, who are men symbolic of things to come: I am going to bring my servant, the Branch. 9 See, the stone I have set in front of Joshua! There are seven eyes[e] on that one stone, and I will engrave an inscription on it,' says the LORD Almighty, 'and I will remove the sin of this land in a single day.

10 "'In that day each of you will invite your neighbor to sit under your vine and fig tree,' declares the LORD Almighty."

The Gold Lampstand and the Two Olive Trees

4 Then the angel who talked with me returned and woke me up, like someone awakened from sleep. 2 He asked me, "What do you see?"

I answered, "I see a solid gold lampstand with a bowl at the top and seven

---

[a] *21* In Hebrew texts 1:18-21 is numbered 2:1-4. [b] In Hebrew texts 2:1-13 is numbered 2:5-17. [c] *8,9* Or *says after . . . eye:* [9] *"I . . . plunder them."* [d] *1* Hebrew *satan* means *adversary.* [e] *9* Or *facets*

ZECHARIAH 3:1 – 2

OUR DEFENDER

This text details the fourth of eight visions, and this vision appears to be located in a courtroom in the heavens. Verse 1 sets the scene. The angel of the Lord sat as judge. The high priest Joshua, here representing the sinful nation, stood in the room as the defendant. The fallen angel, Satan, opposed and accused Joshua.

Scripture records other such scenes where an accuser points a finger at God's people. Job 1:1 – 12 records the classic scene where Satan accuses Job of only giving lip service to God because he's been blessed and protected by God. Revelation 12:7 – 12 details a vision of Satan, "the accuser of our brothers and sisters" (v. 10), losing a future battle. In each of these scenes, the accuser loses his argument under the defense of One who advocates for fallen humans.

In a precursor to later revelation, the Lord defended his people before Satan (Zec 3:2). And believers today have One who still stands as our advocate before the Father (1Jn 2:1). The book of Revelation reveals the Lord's power over the accuser. Out of the fire, God snatched Joshua; through the person and work of the living Savior, Jesus Christ, he still does the same today.

ZECHARIAH 3:3 – 5

CLEAN CLOTHES

As the courtroom scene of verses 1 and 2 continued, Zechariah revealed that Joshua wore filthy clothes, indicating Satan's case was not entirely

(continued on next page)

(Clean Clothes, continued)

without merit. Tragically, the high priest—an intermediary for the defiled—was himself defiled. The angel ordered Joshua's filthy clothes to be removed, interpreting that action as sin being taken away (v. 4). While this certainly served as evidence of God's grace, clearing humanity's debt only keeps the believer from sin's punishment. A neutral position does not give the believer access to a righteous and holy God.

The book of Zechariah pictured the other aspect of salvation. Not only did the angel have the filthy garments removed, but Joshua also received fine, clean garments in their place. To be reconciled to a holy God, believers must claim the righteousness of Christ as their own. Paul puts in clear terms what Zechariah pictured: "God made him who had no sin to be sin for us, so that in him we might become the righteousness of God" (2Co 5:21). In Revelation 3:5, the risen Christ similarly talks about believers being dressed in new garments in heaven, using courtroom language as well: "The one who is victorious will, like them, be dressed in white. I will never blot out the name of that person from the book of life, but will acknowledge that name before my Father and his angels."

ZECHARIAH 4:1–14

SEEKING ANSWERS

Zechariah asked the Lord three times what the meaning of the two olive trees and branches was (vv. 4,11,14). At first, the Lord does not answer him directly. He is wanting Zechariah to trust him and seek him in a deeper way.

(continued on page 1490)

lamps on it, with seven channels to the lamps. 3Also there are two olive trees by
it, one on the right of the bowl and the other on its left."
4I asked the angel who talked with me, "What are these, my lord?"
5He answered, "Do you not know what these are?"
"No, my lord," I replied.
6So he said to me, "This is the word of the LORD to Zerubbabel: 'Not by might
nor by power, but by my Spirit,' says the LORD Almighty.
7"What are you, mighty mountain? Before Zerubbabel you will become level ground. Then he will bring out the capstone to shouts of 'God bless it! God
bless it!' "
8Then the word of the LORD came to me: 9"The hands of Zerubbabel have
laid the foundation of this temple; his hands will also complete it. Then you will
know that the LORD Almighty has sent me to you.
10"Who dares despise the day of small things, since the seven eyes of the LORD
that range throughout the earth will rejoice when they see the chosen capstone[a]
in the hand of Zerubbabel?"
11Then I asked the angel, "What are these two olive trees on the right and the
left of the lampstand?"
12Again I asked him, "What are these two olive branches beside the two gold
pipes that pour out golden oil?"
13He replied, "Do you not know what these are?"
"No, my lord," I said.
14So he said, "These are the two who are anointed to[b] serve the Lord of all
the earth."

The Flying Scroll

5 I looked again, and there before me was a flying scroll.
2He asked me, "What do you see?"
I answered, "I see a flying scroll, twenty cubits long and ten cubits wide.[c]"
3And he said to me, "This is the curse that is going out over the whole land;
for according to what it says on one side, every thief will be banished, and according to what it says on the other, everyone who swears falsely will be banished. 4The LORD Almighty declares, 'I will send it out, and it will enter the
house of the thief and the house of anyone who swears falsely by my name. It
will remain in that house and destroy it completely, both its timbers and its
stones.' "

The Woman in a Basket

5Then the angel who was speaking to me came forward and said to me, "Look
up and see what is appearing."
6I asked, "What is it?"
He replied, "It is a basket." And he added, "This is the iniquity[d] of the people
throughout the land."
7Then the cover of lead was raised, and there in the basket sat a woman! 8He
said, "This is wickedness," and he pushed her back into the basket and pushed
its lead cover down on it.
9Then I looked up—and there before me were two women, with the wind in
their wings! They had wings like those of a stork, and they lifted up the basket
between heaven and earth.
10"Where are they taking the basket?" I asked the angel who was speaking
to me.
11He replied, "To the country of Babylonia[e] to build a house for it. When the
house is ready, the basket will be set there in its place."

[a] 10 Or *the plumb line* [b] 14 Or *two who bring oil and* [c] 2 That is, about 30 feet long and 15 feet wide or about 9 meters long and 4.5 meters wide [d] 6 Or *appearance* [e] 11 Hebrew *Shinar*

ZECHARIAH 4:6 – 10

GOD LAYS THE FOUNDATION

Haggai charged Judah's high priest Joshua and governor Zerubbabel to rebuild the temple. In the face of construction obstacles, the Lord's angel gave Zechariah a message to encourage Zerubbabel in the work. Though it might have seemed natural to the Israelites to depend upon their own strength or ingenuity for this project, God said the temple would only be built by depending upon his Spirit (v. 6).

With the Spirit's aid, Zechariah revealed that the obstacles the people faced were not as insurmountable as they seemed. Using metaphoric language, the prophet asserted that mighty mountains would become like level ground (v. 7). Though opposition slowed the process, Zerubbabel would indeed complete the construction (v. 9). Then, as the capstone was set, the people would shout in praise (v. 7). These promises proved to be true in the days that followed.

The New Testament calls the church the temple of God (Eph 2:21). Christ himself serves as the chosen and precious cornerstone (1Pe 2:6). Like the prophetic vision in Zechariah 4 says of the building of the temple, the building of this New Testament temple depends entirely upon the Spirit (1Co 12:13). Similarly, apparent obstacles — even the gates of Hades — will not prevail against it (Mt 16:18). The construction will be completed (1Pe 2:5). Nothing thwarts God's purposes in building his church.

The purposes of the New Testament church reflect the temple's purposes as well. God dwelled with his people at the temple. By his Spirit, God dwells with his people in the church (Eph 2:22). The praises of God filled the temple; God builds his church so they might declare his praises (1Pe 2:9).

Viable buildings depend upon viable foundations. However, God's people always face the temptation of attempting to build the church without the Spirit. God's people might endeavor to create pseudo-community, devoid of essential unity in Christ. God's people might attempt to live on mission, while missing God entirely. Paul wrote, "No one can lay any foundation other than the one already laid, which is Jesus Christ" (1Co 3:11). Therefore, each one should be careful how they build. One day, all will be brought to light (1Co 3:10,12 – 13).

(Seeking Answers, continued)

God will often times speak indirectly with his children. This is not because he does not care for them or that he does not want to answer them, but he is wanting them to seek in a deeper way and to trust that his actions are perfect.

Zechariah was persistent in his questioning about the identity of the two olive trees. Finally, the Lord through an angel responded, indicating that the two olive trees represented two anointed men. The vision, according to many interpreters, referred to Zerubbabel and Joshua. Joshua served the Lord as high priest; Zerubbabel, a descendant of King David, served the Lord as the governor. The Lord anointed these men for his purposes.

These anointed offices point the reader toward one who is to come. In fact, the terms "Messiah" and "Christ" come from Hebrew and Greek words that mean "anointed one."

God anointed Zerubbabel and Joshua to serve Israel. The Anointed One—Jesus Christ—"did not come to be served, but to serve, and to give his life as a ransom for many" (Mt 20:28).

ZECHARIAH 6:9–15

KING AND PRIEST

In mercy, the Lord continued to reveal his purposes and plans. The word of the Lord came to Zechariah, instructing him to get silver and gold from a few of the exiles for the purpose of making a crown.

Typically, a crown was reserved for a king. However, the Lord told Zechariah in this text to place it upon the

(continued on next page)

Four Chariots

6 I looked up again, and there before me were four chariots coming out from between two mountains—mountains of bronze. 2The first chariot had red horses, the second black, 3the third white, and the fourth dappled—all of them powerful. 4I asked the angel who was speaking to me, "What are these, my lord?"

5The angel answered me, "These are the four spirits[a] of heaven, going out from standing in the presence of the Lord of the whole world. 6The one with the black horses is going toward the north country, the one with the white horses toward the west,[b] and the one with the dappled horses toward the south."

7When the powerful horses went out, they were straining to go throughout the earth. And he said, "Go throughout the earth!" So they went throughout the earth.

8Then he called to me, "Look, those going toward the north country have given my Spirit[c] rest in the land of the north."

A Crown for Joshua

9The word of the LORD came to me: 10"Take silver and gold from the exiles Heldai, Tobijah and Jedaiah, who have arrived from Babylon. Go the same day to the house of Josiah son of Zephaniah. 11Take the silver and gold and make a crown, and set it on the head of the high priest, Joshua son of Jozadak.[d] 12Tell him this is what the LORD Almighty says: 'Here is the man whose name is the Branch, and he will branch out from his place and build the temple of the LORD. 13It is he who will build the temple of the LORD, and he will be clothed with majesty and will sit and rule on his throne. And he[e] will be a priest on his throne. And there will be harmony between the two.' 14The crown will be given to Heldai,[f] Tobijah, Jedaiah and Hen[g] son of Zephaniah as a memorial in the temple of the LORD. 15Those who are far away will come and help to build the temple of the LORD, and you will know that the LORD Almighty has sent me to you. This will happen if you diligently obey the LORD your God."

Justice and Mercy, Not Fasting

7 In the fourth year of King Darius, the word of the LORD came to Zechariah on the fourth day of the ninth month, the month of Kislev. 2The people of Bethel had sent Sharezer and Regem-Melek, together with their men, to entreat the LORD 3by asking the priests of the house of the LORD Almighty and the prophets, "Should I mourn and fast in the fifth month, as I have done for so many years?"

4Then the word of the LORD Almighty came to me: 5"Ask all the people of the land and the priests, 'When you fasted and mourned in the fifth and seventh months for the past seventy years, was it really for me that you fasted? 6And when you were eating and drinking, were you not just feasting for yourselves? 7Are these not the words the LORD proclaimed through the earlier prophets when Jerusalem and its surrounding towns were at rest and prosperous, and the Negev and the western foothills were settled?' "

8And the word of the LORD came again to Zechariah: 9"This is what the LORD Almighty said: 'Administer true justice; show mercy and compassion to one another. 10Do not oppress the widow or the fatherless, the foreigner or the poor. Do not plot evil against each other.'

11"But they refused to pay attention; stubbornly they turned their backs and covered their ears. 12They made their hearts as hard as flint and would not listen to the law or to the words that the LORD Almighty had sent by his Spirit through the earlier prophets. So the LORD Almighty was very angry.

13" 'When I called, they did not listen; so when they called, I would not listen,'

---

[a] 5 Or *winds* [b] 6 Or *horses after them* [c] 8 Or *spirit* [d] 11 Hebrew *Jehozadak,* a variant of *Jozadak* [e] 13 Or *there* [f] 14 Syriac; Hebrew *Helem* [g] 14 Or *and the gracious one, the*

says the LORD Almighty. 14'I scattered them with a whirlwind among all the nations, where they were strangers. The land they left behind them was so desolate that no one traveled through it. This is how they made the pleasant land
desolate.' "

The LORD Promises to Bless Jerusalem

8 The word of the LORD Almighty came to me.
2This is what the LORD Almighty says: "I am very jealous for Zion; I am burning with jealousy for her."
3This is what the LORD says: "I will return to Zion and dwell in Jerusalem.
Then Jerusalem will be called the Faithful City, and the mountain of the LORD
Almighty will be called the Holy Mountain."
4This is what the LORD Almighty says: "Once again men and women of ripe old
age will sit in the streets of Jerusalem, each of them with cane in hand because
of their age. 5The city streets will be filled with boys and girls playing there."
6This is what the LORD Almighty says: "It may seem marvelous to the remnant of this people at that time, but will it seem marvelous to me?" declares the
LORD Almighty.
7This is what the LORD Almighty says: "I will save my people from the countries of the east and the west. 8I will bring them back to live in Jerusalem; they
will be my people, and I will be faithful and righteous to them as their God."
9This is what the LORD Almighty says: "Now hear these words, 'Let your
hands be strong so that the temple may be built.' This is also what the prophets said who were present when the foundation was laid for the house of the
LORD Almighty. 10Before that time there were no wages for people or hire for
animals. No one could go about their business safely because of their enemies,
since I had turned everyone against their neighbor. 11But now I will not deal
with the remnant of this people as I did in the past," declares the LORD Almighty.
12"The seed will grow well, the vine will yield its fruit, the ground will produce
its crops, and the heavens will drop their dew. I will give all these things as an
inheritance to the remnant of this people. 13Just as you, Judah and Israel, have
been a curse[a] among the nations, so I will save you, and you will be a blessing.[b]
Do not be afraid, but let your hands be strong."
14This is what the LORD Almighty says: "Just as I had determined to bring disaster on you and showed no pity when your ancestors angered me," says the
LORD Almighty, 15"so now I have determined to do good again to Jerusalem and
Judah. Do not be afraid. 16These are the things you are to do: Speak the truth to
each other, and render true and sound judgment in your courts; 17do not plot
evil against each other, and do not love to swear falsely. I hate all this," declares
the LORD.
18The word of the LORD Almighty came to me.
19This is what the LORD Almighty says: "The fasts of the fourth, fifth, seventh
and tenth months will become joyful and glad occasions and happy festivals for
Judah. Therefore love truth and peace."
20This is what the LORD Almighty says: "Many peoples and the inhabitants of
many cities will yet come, 21and the inhabitants of one city will go to another and
say, 'Let us go at once to entreat the LORD and seek the LORD Almighty. I myself
am going.' 22And many peoples and powerful nations will come to Jerusalem to
seek the LORD Almighty and to entreat him."
23This is what the LORD Almighty says: "In those days ten people from all languages and nations will take firm hold of one Jew by the hem of his robe and say,
'Let us go with you, because we have heard that God is with you.' "

[a] *13* That is, your name has been used in cursing (see Jer. 29:22); or, you have been regarded as under a curse. [b] *13* Or *and your name will be used in blessings* (see Gen. 48:20); or *and you will be seen as blessed*

(King and Priest, continued)

high priest's head. Joshua took on some kingly symbolism in this vision, showing his significant role in the rebuilding of the temple (v. 12). As the passage continues, it details a certain harmony between these two offices (v. 13). The people needed governance to build the temple; yet the temple needed priests to offer sacrifices.

The degree of unity between these offices depicted in Zechariah foreshadowed a perfect harmony to come. While Zerubbabel and Joshua served individually, Jesus—the Branch of Jesse (Isa 11:1)—would come to unite the offices; he would rule as King and intercede as Priest. He now sits at the right hand of God and governs perfectly while also interceding for the imperfect.

God instructed the people to store this crown as a reminder that God acted on their behalf (v. 14). The people of God must not forget his gracious actions toward them.

ZECHARIAH 8:20–23

ONE JEW, MANY NATIONS

The Old Testament focused upon God's choice of Israel. However, God saved Israel not for their sake alone, but for the good of the nations. This passage defines the mission of God as one that will compel the nations to come to Jerusalem to seek the Lord (v. 22). The inhabitants of many cities will flock to the city of God (v. 20). In fact, residents of each city will share the good news with another (v. 21).

Verse 23 pointed to a future day when a diverse group of people—

(continued on next page)

(One Jew, Many Nations, continued)

ten people from all languages and nations — will take hold of one Jew. Grabbing him by the hem of his robe indicates that they desire his company and presence.

In Genesis 11, the nations of the world were scattered among the world. However, as we start to see in Zechariah, God ultimately desires for the nations of the world to be united. This unity will come in the person of Jesus. In Acts 2:9–11, one of the first acts of the Holy Spirit is to begin unifying the nations of the world so that they are able to understand the "wonders of God" in a common language. Paul asserted that Jesus' death and resurrection transformed two divided groups — Jew and Gentile — into one new humanity (Eph 2:14–16).

All people from every nation who grasp at Jesus' robe, who desire a relationship with him, will certainly find God.

Judgment on Israel's Enemies

9 A prophecy:

The word of the LORD is against the land of Hadrak
and will come to rest on Damascus —
for the eyes of all people and all the tribes of Israel
are on the LORD —[a]
2 and on Hamath too, which borders on it,
and on Tyre and Sidon, though they are very skillful.
3 Tyre has built herself a stronghold;
she has heaped up silver like dust,
and gold like the dirt of the streets.
4 But the Lord will take away her possessions
and destroy her power on the sea,
and she will be consumed by fire.
5 Ashkelon will see it and fear;
Gaza will writhe in agony,
and Ekron too, for her hope will wither.
Gaza will lose her king
and Ashkelon will be deserted.
6 A mongrel people will occupy Ashdod,
and I will put an end to the pride of the Philistines.
7 I will take the blood from their mouths,
the forbidden food from between their teeth.
Those who are left will belong to our God
and become a clan in Judah,
and Ekron will be like the Jebusites.
8 But I will encamp at my temple
to guard it against marauding forces.
Never again will an oppressor overrun my people,
for now I am keeping watch.

The Coming of Zion's King

9 Rejoice greatly, Daughter Zion!
Shout, Daughter Jerusalem!
See, your king comes to you,
righteous and victorious,
lowly and riding on a donkey,
on a colt, the foal of a donkey.
10 I will take away the chariots from Ephraim
and the warhorses from Jerusalem,
and the battle bow will be broken.
He will proclaim peace to the nations.
His rule will extend from sea to sea
and from the River[b] to the ends of the earth.
11 As for you, because of the blood of my covenant with you,
I will free your prisoners from the waterless pit.
12 Return to your fortress, you prisoners of hope;
even now I announce that I will restore twice as much to you.
13 I will bend Judah as I bend my bow
and fill it with Ephraim.
I will rouse your sons, Zion,
against your sons, Greece,
and make you like a warrior's sword.

[a] *1* Or *Damascus. / For the eye of the LORD is on all people, / as well as on the tribes of Israel,*
[b] *10* That is, the Euphrates

LOWLY AND RIDING ON A DONKEY

Zechariah points toward a coming king. While the first part of this chapter concerns God's judgment on Judah's enemies, it goes on to declare that true peace ultimately comes through this coming King, the Messiah.

Zechariah announced his imminent arrival, admonishing Zion, or Jerusalem, to rejoice and shout. According to verse 9, this king proves to be righteous. Furthermore, his arrival brings salvation.

In a typical ancient Near Eastern context, a king's arrival to a city would be marked by conspicuous pomp and pageantry. In this honor- and shame-based culture, anything less would be an affront to the king's rule. Royalty traveled with an entourage. Here Zechariah's royal prophecy pointed to the well-known ancient practice of kings who came in peace, riding into town on a donkey rather than a war horse.

Entering the final week of Jesus' earthly ministry, he asked his disciples to run an errand. If anyone asked the disciples what they sought, they were to respond that the Lord required it (Mt 21:2 – 3).

More than anyone else, Jesus knew who he was. He knew — in fact he inspired — the prophecy in Zechariah. So, in what many now call the Triumphal Entry, Jesus rode into Jerusalem on the back of a humble colt, the foal of a donkey; the symbol of a king arriving in peace. The whole city, Matthew records, wondered about the identity of this man (Mt 21:10). However, Jesus was not confused. As he rode in on the donkey, he claimed — in visible terms — to be the Messiah that this prophecy foretold.

Though Zechariah told them this was to come, the Jews failed to connect the prophetic dots. In tragic ways, they misunderstood Jesus. They celebrated him as a king on Sunday; they crucified him as a criminal the next Friday.

While the palm branches and shouting were appropriate, so was the donkey. This King ruled perfectly, including the attitudes with which he ruled. Deserving of all honor, he humbled himself, even to the point of death on a cross (Php 2:8). No one had ever seen a King like this. The next Sunday proved it.

ZECHARIAH 10:4

THE CORNERSTONE

While the Lord's anger burned against Judah's shepherds, he promised to care for the flock. In this verse, he used metaphoric language to describe how he planned to tend to those who were ultimately *his* people.

He assured them, initially, that a cornerstone would soon come. As any builder knows, the cornerstone determines the position of the rest of the foundation; furthermore, the foundation is vital to the structural integrity of the building. From the Lord would come the tent peg as well, referring to a certain capability to carry weight (Isa 22:20–23) and the battle bow, an image representing military power.

Though each of these images could be elaborated upon, Jesus employed the cornerstone image most frequently in his teaching. In the parable of the wicked tenants, he called himself the stone the builders rejected that has become the cornerstone (Mt 21:42). In Zechariah's day, the Jewish leaders hindered the people's relationship with their God. In Jesus' day, the Jewish leaders rejected the cornerstone, God in the flesh. In fact, they sought his arrest (Mt 21:46), plotted to kill him (Mt 26:4) and eventually influenced Pilate to crucify him.

God replaced the leaders of Old Testament Israel, providing faithfully for his people. For New Testament believers, the stone that the leaders rejected became the cornerstone. Once again, God took care of his people, as he still does today.

The LORD Will Appear

14 Then the LORD will appear over them;
his arrow will flash like lightning.
The Sovereign LORD will sound the trumpet;
he will march in the storms of the south,
15 and the LORD Almighty will shield them.
They will destroy
and overcome with slingstones.
They will drink and roar as with wine;
they will be full like a bowl
used for sprinkling[a] the corners of the altar.
16 The LORD their God will save his people on that day
as a shepherd saves his flock.
They will sparkle in his land
like jewels in a crown.
17 How attractive and beautiful they will be!
Grain will make the young men thrive,
and new wine the young women.

The LORD Will Care for Judah

10 Ask the LORD for rain in the springtime;
it is the LORD who sends the thunderstorms.
He gives showers of rain to all people,
and plants of the field to everyone.
2 The idols speak deceitfully,
diviners see visions that lie;
they tell dreams that are false,
they give comfort in vain.
Therefore the people wander like sheep
oppressed for lack of a shepherd.

3 "My anger burns against the shepherds,
and I will punish the leaders;
for the LORD Almighty will care
for his flock, the people of Judah,
and make them like a proud horse in battle.
4 From Judah will come the cornerstone,
from him the tent peg,
from him the battle bow,
from him every ruler.
5 Together they[b] will be like warriors in battle
trampling their enemy into the mud of the streets.
They will fight because the LORD is with them,
and they will put the enemy horsemen to shame.

6 "I will strengthen Judah
and save the tribes of Joseph.
I will restore them
because I have compassion on them.
They will be as though
I had not rejected them,
for I am the LORD their God
and I will answer them.
7 The Ephraimites will become like warriors,
and their hearts will be glad as with wine.
Their children will see it and be joyful;
their hearts will rejoice in the LORD.

---

[a] 15 Or *bowl, / like* [b] 4,5 Or *ruler, all of them together. / [5]They*

[8]I will signal for them
and gather them in.
Surely I will redeem them;
they will be as numerous as before.
[9]Though I scatter them among the peoples,
yet in distant lands they will remember me.
They and their children will survive,
and they will return.
[10]I will bring them back from Egypt
and gather them from Assyria.
I will bring them to Gilead and Lebanon,
and there will not be room enough for them.
[11]They will pass through the sea of trouble;
the surging sea will be subdued
and all the depths of the Nile will dry up.
Assyria's pride will be brought down
and Egypt's scepter will pass away.
[12]I will strengthen them in the LORD
and in his name they will live securely,"
declares the LORD.

11 Open your doors, Lebanon,
so that fire may devour your cedars!
[2]Wail, you juniper, for the cedar has fallen;
the stately trees are ruined!
Wail, oaks of Bashan;
the dense forest has been cut down!
[3]Listen to the wail of the shepherds;
their rich pastures are destroyed!
Listen to the roar of the lions;
the lush thicket of the Jordan is ruined!

Two Shepherds

[4]This is what the LORD my God says: "Shepherd the flock marked for slaughter. [5]Their buyers slaughter them and go unpunished. Those who sell them say,
'Praise the LORD, I am rich!' Their own shepherds do not spare them. [6]For I will
no longer have pity on the people of the land," declares the LORD. "I will give everyone into the hands of their neighbors and their king. They will devastate the
land, and I will not rescue anyone from their hands."
[7]So I shepherded the flock marked for slaughter, particularly the oppressed of
the flock. Then I took two staffs and called one Favor and the other Union, and I
shepherded the flock. [8]In one month I got rid of the three shepherds.
The flock detested me, and I grew weary of them [9]and said, "I will not be your
shepherd. Let the dying die, and the perishing perish. Let those who are left eat
one another's flesh."
[10]Then I took my staff called Favor and broke it, revoking the covenant I had
made with all the nations. [11]It was revoked on that day, and so the oppressed of
the flock who were watching me knew it was the word of the LORD.
[12]I told them, "If you think it best, give me my pay; but if not, keep it." So they
paid me thirty pieces of silver.
[13]And the LORD said to me, "Throw it to the potter"—the handsome price at
which they valued me! So I took the thirty pieces of silver and threw them to the
potter at the house of the LORD.
[14]Then I broke my second staff called Union, breaking the family bond between Judah and Israel.
[15]Then the LORD said to me, "Take again the equipment of a foolish shepherd.
[16]For I am going to raise up a shepherd over the land who will not care for the lost,

ZECHARIAH 11:12–13

THIRTY PIECES OF SILVER

In these latter chapters, Judah's situation escalated quickly. Zechariah got rid of three prominent shepherds, assuming their leadership role. However, he quickly tired of the people; they, in turn, detested him (v. 8). He, presumably to leave them to their sinful ways, promptly resigned from leadership (v. 9).

Zechariah's severance package had not been made clear, so Zechariah gave them the option to pay him or not (v. 12). In a most inadequate middle ground, they sent him off for the price of a slave—thirty pieces of silver. He rejected this devaluation, hurling the coins to the potter at the house of the Lord as the Lord directed him (v. 13).

The flock underestimated the worth of Zechariah's leadership, assigning him a value the Lord found insufficient. However, this pales in comparison to the narrative in Matthew's Gospel, which reports history's worst appraisal of worth. God incarnate came to dwell with humanity. Humanity promptly sold him for thirty pieces of silver (Mt 27:1–10).

or seek the young, or heal the injured, or feed the healthy, but will eat the meat
of the choice sheep, tearing off their hooves.

17 "Woe to the worthless shepherd,
 who deserts the flock!
May the sword strike his arm and his right eye!
 May his arm be completely withered,
 his right eye totally blinded!"

Jerusalem's Enemies to Be Destroyed

12 A prophecy: The word of the LORD concerning Israel.

The LORD, who stretches out the heavens, who lays the foundation of the
earth, and who forms the human spirit within a person, declares: 2"I am going
to make Jerusalem a cup that sends all the surrounding peoples reeling. Judah
will be besieged as well as Jerusalem. 3On that day, when all the nations of the
earth are gathered against her, I will make Jerusalem an immovable rock for
all the nations. All who try to move it will injure themselves. 4On that day I will
strike every horse with panic and its rider with madness," declares the LORD. "I
will keep a watchful eye over Judah, but I will blind all the horses of the nations.
5Then the clans of Judah will say in their hearts, 'The people of Jerusalem are
strong, because the LORD Almighty is their God.'

6"On that day I will make the clans of Judah like a firepot in a woodpile, like a
flaming torch among sheaves. They will consume all the surrounding peoples
right and left, but Jerusalem will remain intact in her place.

7"The LORD will save the dwellings of Judah first, so that the honor of the
house of David and of Jerusalem's inhabitants may not be greater than that of
Judah. 8On that day the LORD will shield those who live in Jerusalem, so that the
feeblest among them will be like David, and the house of David will be like God,
like the angel of the LORD going before them. 9On that day I will set out to destroy
all the nations that attack Jerusalem.

Mourning for the One They Pierced

10"And I will pour out on the house of David and the inhabitants of Jerusalem a spirit[a] of grace and supplication. They will look on[b] me, the one they
have pierced, and they will mourn for him as one mourns for an only child,
and grieve bitterly for him as one grieves for a firstborn son. 11On that day the
weeping in Jerusalem will be as great as the weeping of Hadad Rimmon in
the plain of Megiddo. 12The land will mourn, each clan by itself, with their
wives by themselves: the clan of the house of David and their wives, the clan of
the house of Nathan and their wives, 13the clan of the house of Levi and their
wives, the clan of Shimei and their wives, 14and all the rest of the clans and
their wives.

Cleansing From Sin

13 "On that day a fountain will be opened to the house of David and the inhabitants of Jerusalem, to cleanse them from sin and impurity.

2"On that day, I will banish the names of the idols from the land, and they will
be remembered no more," declares the LORD Almighty. "I will remove both the
prophets and the spirit of impurity from the land. 3And if anyone still prophesies, their father and mother, to whom they were born, will say to them, 'You
must die, because you have told lies in the LORD's name.' Then their own parents
will stab the one who prophesies.

4"On that day every prophet will be ashamed of their prophetic vision. They
will not put on a prophet's garment of hair in order to deceive. 5Each will say,
'I am not a prophet. I am a farmer; the land has been my livelihood since my

ZECHARIAH 11:12–13

THIRTY PIECES OF SILVER

In these latter chapters, Judah's situation escalated quickly. Zechariah got rid of three prominent shepherds, assuming their leadership role. However, he quickly tired of the people. They, in turn, detested him (v. 8). He, presumably to leave them to their sinful ways, promptly resigned from leadership (v. 9).

Zechariah's severance package had not been made clear, so Zechariah gave them the option to pay him or not (v. 12). In a most inadequate middle ground, they sent him off for the price of a slave — thirty pieces of silver. He rejected this devaluation, hurling the coins to the potter at the house of the Lord as the Lord directed him (v. 13).

The flock underestimated the worth of Zechariah's leadership, assigning him a value the Lord found insufficient. However, this pales in comparison to the narrative in Matthew's Gospel, which reports history's worst appraisal of worth. God incarnate came to dwell with humanity. Humanity promptly sold him for thirty pieces of silver (Mt 27:3 – 10).

[a] 10 Or *the Spirit* [b] 10 Or *to*

SEEING THE ONE WHOM THEY HAVE PIERCED

A number of centuries before Christ, the Word of God alluded to crucifixion as a form of execution — specifically, what would happen to the Messiah in his death. Immediately after sharing God's promise to pour out a "spirit of grace" on his people, Zechariah mentioned the people looking upon "the one they have pierced" (Zec 12:10). Hundreds of years after the time Zechariah wrote, the Romans utilized crucifixion as a way to discourage subversive activity. In a crucifixion, authorities nailed the criminal to a cross where they often hung in agony for days until they died of multiple traumas (Ps 22:16).

The cross signified the deepest shame — the convicted criminal died, naked and suffering, in front of a public audience whose jeering or sheer horror at the sight only made it worse. Incredibly, almost impossibly, the One who spoke creation into existence submitted to this horrible form of death. On the cross, he sacrificed himself for the sins of all humanity; he hung on a cross between two criminals to forge a new pathway for people to find their way to God.

On the day of Jesus' execution, the Jewish leaders asked that his legs be broken so death would occur more quickly; they wanted the bodies down before the Sabbath. Pilate agreed. But after the soldiers broke the legs of the two rebels, they found Jesus already dead. Rather than breaking Jesus' legs, one of the soldiers pierced Jesus' side with a spear (Jn 19:33 – 34). John, knowing well the book of Zechariah, saw these events with his own eyes (Jn 19:35). In his Gospel, he made clear that nothing about Jesus' crucifixion happened by chance. When he watched the spear pierce Jesus' side, he remembered Zechariah's prophecy. God continued to fulfill his Word, even in the death of God's Son (Jn 19:37).

Of course, Jesus did not remain dead. John went on to tell God's people much more about the Jesus who lived *after* the cross. When John described the return of this risen Christ, he used these words: "'Look, he is coming with the clouds,' and 'every eye will see him, even those who *pierced* him'" (Rev 1:7, emphasis added). The pierced, crucified and risen Christ will return to rule over his people forever.

ZECHARIAH 13:7

SHEPHERD STRUCK, SHEEP SCATTERED

Sheep are not the smartest creatures on the planet. In fact, their survival largely depends upon the care of their shepherd. In the final sections of Zechariah's book, God described the leaders of Israel as cruel shepherds and the people as oppressed sheep.

Nevertheless, when a good shepherd finally began to care for the people of God, the sheep rejected him as well. Zechariah quoted these words: "Strike the shepherd, and the sheep will be scattered" (v. 7). God's good shepherd would die, the flock would scatter and many would perish (v. 8). However, the Lord indicated that through that testing he would refine his remaining people (v. 9).

Jesus quoted this prophecy on the evening of Judas' betrayal. With the disciples gathered, he told them they would *all* scatter that night (Mt 26:31). And, just as Jesus foretold, the Gospels reveal that all the disciples soon fled (Mt 26:56).

Soon after, the Good Shepherd laid down his life for his wandering sheep (Jn 10:14–15). Though the shepherd would be struck, Jesus assured his disciples this would not be the end. He comforted them, saying, "After I have risen, I will go ahead of you into Galilee" (Mt 26:32). The rest of Matthew's Gospel relates the fulfillment of this promise.

The balance of the New Testament details the full restoration of all of God's people. Ultimately, Jesus' death did not scatter his sheep. When the Good Shepherd was struck, God gathered them together (Jn 10:27).

youth.[a]' 6If someone asks, 'What are these wounds on your body[b]?' they will answer, 'The wounds I was given at the house of my friends.'

The Shepherd Struck, the Sheep Scattered

7 "Awake, sword, against my shepherd,
against the man who is close to me!"
declares the LORD Almighty.
"Strike the shepherd,
and the sheep will be scattered,
and I will turn my hand against the little ones.
8 In the whole land," declares the LORD,
"two-thirds will be struck down and perish;
yet one-third will be left in it.
9 This third I will put into the fire;
I will refine them like silver
and test them like gold.
They will call on my name
and I will answer them;
I will say, 'They are my people,'
and they will say, 'The LORD is our God.'"

The LORD Comes and Reigns

14 A day of the LORD is coming, Jerusalem, when your possessions will be
plundered and divided up within your very walls.
2I will gather all the nations to Jerusalem to fight against it; the city will be
captured, the houses ransacked, and the women raped. Half of the city will go
into exile, but the rest of the people will not be taken from the city. 3Then the
LORD will go out and fight against those nations, as he fights on a day of battle.
4On that day his feet will stand on the Mount of Olives, east of Jerusalem, and
the Mount of Olives will be split in two from east to west, forming a great valley,
with half of the mountain moving north and half moving south. 5You will flee
by my mountain valley, for it will extend to Azel. You will flee as you fled from
the earthquake[c] in the days of Uzziah king of Judah. Then the LORD my God will
come, and all the holy ones with him.
6On that day there will be neither sunlight nor cold, frosty darkness. 7It will
be a unique day—a day known only to the LORD—with no distinction between
day and night. When evening comes, there will be light.
8On that day living water will flow out from Jerusalem, half of it east to the
Dead Sea and half of it west to the Mediterranean Sea, in summer and in winter.
9The LORD will be king over the whole earth. On that day there will be one
LORD, and his name the only name.
10The whole land, from Geba to Rimmon, south of Jerusalem, will become like
the Arabah. But Jerusalem will be raised up high from the Benjamin Gate to the
site of the First Gate, to the Corner Gate, and from the Tower of Hananel to the
royal winepresses, and will remain in its place. 11It will be inhabited; never again
will it be destroyed. Jerusalem will be secure.
12This is the plague with which the LORD will strike all the nations that fought
against Jerusalem: Their flesh will rot while they are still standing on their feet,
their eyes will rot in their sockets, and their tongues will rot in their mouths.
13On that day people will be stricken by the LORD with great panic. They will
seize each other by the hand and attack one another. 14Judah too will fight at
Jerusalem. The wealth of all the surrounding nations will be collected—great
quantities of gold and silver and clothing. 15A similar plague will strike the horses and mules, the camels and donkeys, and all the animals in those camps.

[a] 5 Or *farmer; a man sold me in my youth* [b] 6 Or *wounds between your hands* [c] 5 Or *5My mountain valley will be blocked and will extend to Azel. It will be blocked as it was blocked because of the earthquake*

SET APART AS HOLY

Scripture describes the God of creation as holy (Isa 6:3). Holiness, a much-used term that is seldom carefully defined, necessitates the idea of separation. In fact, to the degree that God is holy, he expects his people to be holy (Lev 19:2). God called the people of Israel, and he calls his church today, to be set apart from the world: visibly and demonstrably different as a reflection of his holiness.

After the Lord delivered the Israelites from slavery, he labeled this newly formed people a *holy* nation (Ex 19:5 – 6). Much of the Old Testament outlined in specific terms how the Israelites were to relate to one another as well as to God. This careful instruction was intended to distinguish Israel from other pagan nations, just as God was distinguished from their false gods. Israel's conduct before the world was intended to show God's intent for all human life.

The purity of God's people serves as a recurring theme in the final chapters of Zechariah's prophecy. In this passage, Zechariah looked forward to a time when normal cooking pots would be considered holy — like the bowls used before the altar (Zec 14:20 – 21). Even the bells of horses were to include the inscription "HOLY TO THE LORD," a phrase usually reserved for the high priest's turban (Ex 28:36 – 38). The extensiveness of these descriptions indicated that nothing lay outside God's purview. Israel's relationship to God was to infuse every aspect of their lives.

Through his chosen people, God intended to put on display his holy character before the world. He chose and set apart Israel not only for privilege but also for missionary responsibility.

As any cursory reading of the Scripture reveals, the Old Testament people of God failed to embody God's holy standard. But rather than judging all of humanity irrevocably, God sent his Son to be that which he intended for Israel. In every detail of his life, Jesus perfectly embodied holiness.

Jesus' holy life makes possible a holy people today. The New Testament uses the term "holy people" (Ro 1:7) to describe the people of God for this reason. The Holy Spirit applies Christ's holy work to each believer's heart.

To truly understand holiness, today's people of God look to Jesus as their standard. In seeing the impossibility of perfectly imitating Christ's perfect life, they continue looking to him as their present and future hope.

16 Then the survivors from all the nations that have attacked Jerusalem will
go up year after year to worship the King, the LORD Almighty, and to celebrate
the Festival of Tabernacles. 17 If any of the peoples of the earth do not go up to Jerusalem to worship the King, the LORD Almighty, they will have no rain. 18 If the
Egyptian people do not go up and take part, they will have no rain. The LORD[a]
will bring on them the plague he inflicts on the nations that do not go up to celebrate the Festival of Tabernacles. 19 This will be the punishment of Egypt and
the punishment of all the nations that do not go up to celebrate the Festival of
Tabernacles.

20 On that day HOLY TO THE LORD will be inscribed on the bells of the horses,
and the cooking pots in the LORD's house will be like the sacred bowls in front of
the altar. 21 Every pot in Jerusalem and Judah will be holy to the LORD Almighty,
and all who come to sacrifice will take some of the pots and cook in them. And on
that day there will no longer be a Canaanite[b] in the house of the LORD Almighty.

---

[a] 18 Or *part, then the LORD* [b] 21 Or *merchant*

JESUS: OUR COMING MESSIAH

MALACHI

MALACHI

COMPLETION OF REBUILT TEMPLE	RECONSTRUCTION OF JERUSALEM'S WALL	WRITING OF BOOK OF MALACHI
c. 516 BC	*c. 444 BC*	*c. 430 BC*

The final prophecy of the Old Testament challenges Israel to remember the glorious nature of God's love.

The theme of forgetfulness was prominent throughout the Old Testament. When the nation prepared to cross the Jordan River and possess the land, Moses warned them of the danger of forgetting God (Dt 8:10 – 20). Their years in the wilderness had taught the people to depend on God, quite literally, for their daily bread. Once they entered the land, however, they found ample provision, just as God had promised. But rather than prompting the people to worship, this surplus often caused them to forget God and trust in their own resources.

In a similar fashion, the Jews who lived in Judah in Malachi's day, about a century after the Babylonian exile, were prone to forget God. They were blessed by the fact that they were established in the land, enjoying a rebuilt temple and wall around Jerusalem and thus given the chance to restore united worship among God's people. But their hopes for the glory that the prophets had promised flagged in the face of their low political status and the lack of a visible symbol of God's presence in the temple. Their worship became listless and rote rather than being inspiring.

Malachi reminded the people that rightly remembering God comes about by proper worship; but the priests, who offered blemished animals and were otherwise negligent about worship, offered a poor example that resulted in lackluster worship practices among God's people. The spillover effect of this faulty worship was broken social relationships; especially the relationships between husbands and wives (Mal 2:10 – 16). Rather than modeling God's covenant love, marriages among the people of God were broken by divorce. Also, Malachi chided the nation for robbing God by withholding tithes and offerings meant for the needy and to fund worship.

At the end of his prophecy, Malachi pointed forward to a coming messenger who would both speak the word of God and model conformity to his message (4:5). This messenger would minister "in the spirit and power of Elijah" (Lk 1:17) and point the way to the Messiah, who would worship God perfectly and give his very life on behalf of his people. Malachi's prophecy culminated the ministry of the prophets before God's Word came in the flesh, centuries later, as Jesus Christ, God's promised Messiah.

"ON THE DAY WHEN I ACT," SAYS THE LORD ALMIGHTY, "THEY WILL BE MY TREASURED POSSESSION. I WILL SPARE THEM, JUST AS A FATHER HAS COMPASSION AND SPARES HIS SON WHO SERVES HIM."

Malachi 3:17

MALACHI

1 A prophecy: The word of the LORD to Israel through Malachi.[a]

Israel Doubts God's Love

2"I have loved you," says the LORD.
"But you ask, 'How have you loved us?'
"Was not Esau Jacob's brother?" declares the LORD. "Yet I have loved Jacob,
3but Esau I have hated, and I have turned his hill country into a wasteland and
left his inheritance to the desert jackals."
4Edom may say, "Though we have been crushed, we will rebuild the ruins."
But this is what the LORD Almighty says: "They may build, but I will demolish. They will be called the Wicked Land, a people always under the wrath of
the LORD. 5You will see it with your own eyes and say, 'Great is the LORD—even
beyond the borders of Israel!'

Breaking Covenant Through Blemished Sacrifices

6"A son honors his father, and a slave his master. If I am a father, where is the
honor due me? If I am a master, where is the respect due me?" says the LORD
Almighty.
"It is you priests who show contempt for my name.
"But you ask, 'How have we shown contempt for your name?'
7"By offering defiled food on my altar.
"But you ask, 'How have we defiled you?'
"By saying that the LORD's table is contemptible. 8When you offer blind animals for sacrifice, is that not wrong? When you sacrifice lame or diseased animals, is that not wrong? Try offering them to your governor! Would he be pleased
with you? Would he accept you?" says the LORD Almighty.
9"Now plead with God to be gracious to us. With such offerings from your
hands, will he accept you?"—says the LORD Almighty.
10"Oh, that one of you would shut the temple doors, so that you would not light
useless fires on my altar! I am not pleased with you," says the LORD Almighty,
"and I will accept no offering from your hands. 11My name will be great among
the nations, from where the sun rises to where it sets. In every place incense and
pure offerings will be brought to me, because my name will be great among the
nations," says the LORD Almighty.
12"But you profane it by saying, 'The Lord's table is defiled,' and, 'Its food is
contemptible.' 13And you say, 'What a burden!' and you sniff at it contemptuous-
ly," says the LORD Almighty.
"When you bring injured, lame or diseased animals and offer them as sacrifices, should I accept them from your hands?" says the LORD. 14"Cursed is the
cheat who has an acceptable male in his flock and vows to give it, but then sacrifices a blemished animal to the Lord. For I am a great king," says the LORD
Almighty, "and my name is to be feared among the nations.

Additional Warning to the Priests

2 "And now, you priests, this warning is for you. 2If you do not listen, and if
you do not resolve to honor my name," says the LORD Almighty, "I will send
a curse on you, and I will curse your blessings. Yes, I have already cursed them,
because you have not resolved to honor me.
3"Because of you I will rebuke your descendants[b]; I will smear on your faces

---

[a] 1 *Malachi* means *my messenger.* [b] 3 Or *will blight your grain*

the dung from your festival sacrifices, and you will be carried off with it. 4And
you will know that I have sent you this warning so that my covenant with Levi
may continue," says the LORD Almighty. 5"My covenant was with him, a covenant of life and peace, and I gave them to him; this called for reverence and he
revered me and stood in awe of my name. 6True instruction was in his mouth
and nothing false was found on his lips. He walked with me in peace and uprightness, and turned many from sin.
7"For the lips of a priest ought to preserve knowledge, because he is the
messenger of the LORD Almighty and people seek instruction from his mouth.
8But you have turned from the way and by your teaching have caused many to
stumble; you have violated the covenant with Levi," says the LORD Almighty.
9"So I have caused you to be despised and humiliated before all the people,
because you have not followed my ways but have shown partiality in matters
of the law."

Breaking Covenant Through Divorce

10Do we not all have one Father[a]? Did not one God create us? Why do we profane the covenant of our ancestors by being unfaithful to one another?
11Judah has been unfaithful. A detestable thing has been committed in Israel
and in Jerusalem: Judah has desecrated the sanctuary the LORD loves by marrying women who worship a foreign god. 12As for the man who does this, whoever
he may be, may the LORD remove him from the tents of Jacob[b] — even though he
brings an offering to the LORD Almighty.
13Another thing you do: You flood the LORD's altar with tears. You weep and
wail because he no longer looks with favor on your offerings or accepts them
with pleasure from your hands. 14You ask, "Why?" It is because the LORD is the
witness between you and the wife of your youth. You have been unfaithful to her,
though she is your partner, the wife of your marriage covenant.
15Has not the one God made you? You belong to him in body and spirit. And
what does the one God seek? Godly offspring.[c] So be on your guard, and do not
be unfaithful to the wife of your youth.
16"The man who hates and divorces his wife," says the LORD, the God of Israel,
"does violence to the one he should protect,"[d] says the LORD Almighty.
So be on your guard, and do not be unfaithful.

Breaking Covenant Through Injustice

17You have wearied the LORD with your words.
"How have we wearied him?" you ask.
By saying, "All who do evil are good in the eyes of the LORD, and he is pleased
with them" or "Where is the God of justice?"
3 "I will send my messenger, who will prepare the way before me. Then suddenly the Lord you are seeking will come to his temple; the messenger of the
covenant, whom you desire, will come," says the LORD Almighty.
2But who can endure the day of his coming? Who can stand when he appears?
For he will be like a refiner's fire or a launderer's soap. 3He will sit as a refiner and
purifier of silver; he will purify the Levites and refine them like gold and silver.
Then the LORD will have men who will bring offerings in righteousness, 4and the
offerings of Judah and Jerusalem will be acceptable to the LORD, as in days gone
by, as in former years.
5"So I will come to put you on trial. I will be quick to testify against sorcerers,
adulterers and perjurers, against those who defraud laborers of their wages, who
oppress the widows and the fatherless, and deprive the foreigners among you of
justice, but do not fear me," says the LORD Almighty.

[a] *10* Or *father* [b] *12* Or *12May the LORD remove from the tents of Jacob anyone who gives testimony in behalf of the man who does this* [c] *15* The meaning of the Hebrew for the first part of this verse is uncertain. [d] *16* Or *"I hate divorce," says the LORD, the God of Israel, "because the man who divorces his wife covers his garment with violence,"*

MALACHI 2:16

DIVORCE MATTERS

God's verdict concerning divorce was severe, noting that the one who pursues divorce acts violently and shows hatred for their spouse.

The fact that Malachi singled out marriage in his prophecy shows the significance God places on marriage. The nation's spiritual regression was demonstrated in their inability to keep their marriage commitments and in their open embrace of pagan immorality. Therefore, God said, his people should "be on your guard, and do not be unfaithful."

These commands are rooted in the nature and character of God, who is always faithful to his covenant promises. The fact that God always keeps his word to his people is seen throughout the Old Testament. Time and time again, God sought out his wayward people and loved them in spite of their sin (Hos 3:1). Since marriage is a picture of God's relationship with his church, his people should keep their promises to one another — especially the covenant promises of marriage vows (Eph 5:32).

MALACHI 3:1

PREPARE THE WAY

Malachi prophesied of a coming messenger who would prepare the way for the Messiah (called "the Lord" in this passage). Matthew and Luke's Gospels identify this messenger as John the Baptist, the forerunner of Jesus Christ (Mt 11:10; Mk 1:2 – 3). John's ministry did not look like what one might expect for one chosen to

(continued on page 1507)

THE DAY OF THE LORD

The book of Malachi concludes the Old Testament in a somewhat cryptic way. After encouraging his audience to turn from their spiritual apathy and return to God, Malachi pointed to a righteous remnant of people who would hold fast to God and fear his name. To these faithful ones, God promised to send healing; they would find joy and gladness and "frolic like well-fed calves" (v. 2). To the unfaithful, he promised his coming judgment (vv. 1,3).

Before this day comes, Malachi said, the prophet Elijah would return. Elijah's story appears in 1 Kings 17 through 2 Kings 2. During a dreadful time in Israel's history, Elijah was faithful to the Lord and called people to repent and return to God. But Malachi said that he would come again. There are three commonly identified possibilities in which this prophecy has been or will be fulfilled.

First, the Gospel writers identify John the Baptist with Elijah (Mt 11:14; 17:10 – 12; Mk 9:11 – 13; Lk 1:17). Elijah and John share much in common, including their message of the need for repentance, their ascetic lifestyle and the rejection they faced at the hands of the people of their respective cultures.

Second, two leading Old Testament figures appeared with Jesus at his transfiguration — Moses and Elijah (Mt 17:1 – 8). Clearly, those in Jesus' day were looking for Elijah to come as a precursor to the establishment of the kingdom of God. The transfiguration radically demonstrated that Jesus was the Son of God who had come to do the very things Malachi described in this text.

Finally, some believe that an Elijah-like figure will come before Jesus' second coming. This person may, like Elijah, call down fire from heaven and bring the judgment of God upon those who reject the gospel message (Rev 11:3 – 6).

Malachi's concluding statement portrays the twin themes of the character of God that have been seen throughout the Old Testament: On the one hand, he is a God of judgment. He will curse those who live and die in their sin and who never turn to him in repentance and faith. But he is also a God who gives grace. Because of Jesus' work on the cross, all people have the opportunity to seek and find the Lord before it is too late.

Breaking Covenant by Withholding Tithes

[6]"I the LORD do not change. So you, the descendants of Jacob, are not destroyed. [7]Ever since the time of your ancestors you have turned away from my
decrees and have not kept them. Return to me, and I will return to you," says the
LORD Almighty.

"But you ask, 'How are we to return?'

[8]"Will a mere mortal rob God? Yet you rob me.

"But you ask, 'How are we robbing you?'

"In tithes and offerings. [9]You are under a curse — your whole nation — because you are robbing me. [10]Bring the whole tithe into the storehouse, that there
may be food in my house. Test me in this," says the LORD Almighty, "and see if I
will not throw open the floodgates of heaven and pour out so much blessing that
there will not be room enough to store it. [11]I will prevent pests from devouring
your crops, and the vines in your fields will not drop their fruit before it is ripe,"
says the LORD Almighty. [12]"Then all the nations will call you blessed, for yours
will be a delightful land," says the LORD Almighty.

Israel Speaks Arrogantly Against God

[13]"You have spoken arrogantly against me," says the LORD.

"Yet you ask, 'What have we said against you?'

[14]"You have said, 'It is futile to serve God. What do we gain by carrying out his
requirements and going about like mourners before the LORD Almighty? [15]But
now we call the arrogant blessed. Certainly evildoers prosper, and even when
they put God to the test, they get away with it.'"

The Faithful Remnant

[16]Then those who feared the LORD talked with each other, and the LORD listened and heard. A scroll of remembrance was written in his presence concerning those who feared the LORD and honored his name.

[17]"On the day when I act," says the LORD Almighty, "they will be my treasured
possession. I will spare them, just as a father has compassion and spares his son
who serves him. [18]And you will again see the distinction between the righteous
and the wicked, between those who serve God and those who do not.

Judgment and Covenant Renewal

4 [a] "Surely the day is coming; it will burn like a furnace. All the arrogant and
every evildoer will be stubble, and the day that is coming will set them on
fire," says the LORD Almighty. "Not a root or a branch will be left to them. [2]But
for you who revere my name, the sun of righteousness will rise with healing in its
rays. And you will go out and frolic like well-fed calves. [3]Then you will trample
on the wicked; they will be ashes under the soles of your feet on the day when I
act," says the LORD Almighty.

[4]"Remember the law of my servant Moses, the decrees and laws I gave him at
Horeb for all Israel.

[5]"See, I will send the prophet Elijah to you before that great and dreadful day
of the LORD comes. [6]He will turn the hearts of the parents to their children, and
the hearts of the children to their parents; or else I will come and strike the land
with total destruction."

(Prepare the Way, continued)

prepare the way for the King of the universe. John's unique lifestyle and prophetic message countered the culture of his day (Mk 1:4 – 8).

Like John, those who declare the message of Jesus today will often be shunned. The "pleasing aroma of Christ" will be compelling to some and lead them to repentance and faith, but to others it will be "an aroma that brings death" and they will reject the gospel message (2Co 2:15 – 16). God's people should find confidence in knowing that God has commissioned them to proclaim his message until Jesus returns.

[a] In Hebrew texts 4:1-6 is numbered 3:19-24.

INTERTESTAMENTAL PERIOD

Approximately 400 years lie between the time of Malachi, the final prophetic book of the Old Testament, and the birth of Jesus Christ. During this time, God was "silent" — the Bible records no revelation from God to his people during this period. The absence of God's written word through his prophets was surely a fearful reality for his people. Had God finally given up on them? Had their sin caused him to reject them forever?

God's four-hundred-year silence stands in stark contrast to his previous interaction with humanity. He had a close relationship with Adam and Eve and was quick to call out to Adam when he hid from God's presence in the garden (Ge 3:9). When corruption filled the earth and God regretted even making humans because of the darkness of their hearts, he still called to Noah and protected him and his family from the coming destruction (Ge 6:13). After the debacle at Babel, God called Abram and chose him to be the father of his people (Ge 12:1 – 3). And God led his people, powerfully and visibly, out of Egypt and through their wilderness wanderings (Dt 1:1 — 2:3). From the beginning of time, God had been a speaking God, always calling out to his people, inviting them to repentance and faith and assuring them of his love.

For years he spoke through his prophets. Some — such as Hosea, Amos and Micah — warned the nation of Israel of God's coming judgment prior to the exile. They called the people to spiritual reform and renewal, warning them of the consequences of disobedience. God's people did not listen, but God continued to speak. During the exile, prophets such as Ezekiel and Daniel reminded the people of the reason for their punishment and continued to encourage them to return to God and live faithful lives, even though they were now scattered throughout the pagan world. Finally, the prophets Haggai, Zechariah and Malachi spoke God's word to his people as they began to return to the land to rebuild the city of Jerusalem and the temple of God. Through it all, God spoke clearly and often.

But then he did stop — for over 400 years. The people were left to hope that the prophets' words of restoration and redemption would come true one day. They longed for God to send his promised One, his Messiah, to save his people and usher in his rule and reign forever. However, with each passing year it must have been more and more difficult for the people to maintain their hope that the promised One would ever come.

Those who held out hope had all sorts of notions as to what the Messiah would be like. Some likely expected a military ruler who would rid the world of those who oppressed God's people and would bring God's kingdom to preeminence through military might. Others likely expected a political king who would enact justice in the land and lead God's people into the peace and stability foreshadowed by King David's rule. The people's perspectives, hopes and dreams about the coming Messiah differed widely during this period, which we now know as the intertestamental period. (Some also refer to this time as the "Second Temple" period, due to the fact that a remnant of Jews was allowed to rebuild the temple that was destroyed during the exile.)

Throughout the world, various nations such as the Greeks and the Romans rose to power through this time. These nations continued to influence the people of God and shape the spiritual vitality (or lack thereof) of God's people. Roman rule and Greek influence also greatly impacted the cultural milieu into which Jesus was born.

Throughout Israel and Judah, various factions also developed between the time when the Old and New Testaments were written. The Pharisees, Sadducees, Essenes and Zealots each maintained differing understandings of God's Law and the promises related to the coming of his Messiah. These groups also had varying ideas regarding how God's people should live obedient lives in light of the wickedness of the surrounding society. By the time of Jesus, these different entities exerted influence over the religious practices of God's people and shaped the way in which the people understood Jesus' life and ministry.

God's apparent silence, compounded by the pagan culture, ongoing moral depravity, and internal factionalism, created a dark world indeed for the chosen people of God. Those who still held out hope of the coming of the Messiah longed for a word from God. But "when the set time had fully come" (Gal 4:4), when God chose to reveal more of himself and his plan to redeem his people, Israel did not merely get *a* word from God, they got *the* Word from God.

The New Testament opens with the announcement that God's word took on flesh and made his dwelling among a sin-darkened world (Jn 1:14). The birth of Jesus, his redeeming work and ministry, and his sacrifice and resurrection confirm for his people — both believers in the distant past, now and in the future — that though God may at times seem silent, he will never forget his people.

BEGINNINGS	REVOLT	PEOPLE	INTERTESTAMENTAL PERIOD	SAVIOR	CHURCH	FOREVER
GENESIS 1–2 (pg. 8)	GENESIS 3–11 (pg. 24)	GENESIS 12 to MALACHI (pg. 266)	(pg. 1508)	GOSPELS to ACTS 1 (pg. 1560)	ACTS 2 to REVELATION 20 (pg. 1736)	REVELATION 21–22 (pg. 1996)

NEW TESTAMENT

JESUS: OUR PROMISED KING

MATTHEW

MATTHEW

BIRTH OF JESUS *c. 5 BC*	HEROD ANTIPAS RULES GALILEE AND PEREA *4 BC – AD 39*	JESUS' MINISTRY, DEATH, RESURRECTION *c. AD 27 – 30*

Kings came and went throughout the Old Testament. With each successive king, the hope of the people of God continued to fade. Israel longed for the promised king who would usher in God's peace and deliverance. With their own eyes, they witnessed the failure of even the best kings, the demise of the nation and the exile of God's people. Though the prophets spoke of a coming day when God would prove faithful, the lengthy silence after Malachi's writing left the fate of God's people seemingly in question.

Matthew's Gospel proclaims Jesus to be the long awaited King of kings — the one to whom the entire Old Testament points. Matthew, a Jewish believer, began his summary of Jesus' life and ministry with a lengthy genealogy that served to connect the Lord's coming to the promises God made to David so long ago. He was a king like David, but one who would succeed where David failed and accomplish what David had been incapable of doing in his life. At the conclusion of the book, the sign that hung above Jesus' head on the cross ironically makes the same claim: "THIS IS JESUS, THE KING OF THE JEWS" (27:37). Between these two bookends, Matthew makes a clear and compelling argument for the divine origin of Jesus and his kingly role among his people.

Though many Jews in Jesus' day were blind to his identity, Matthew anchors Jesus' life and mission in the Old Testament promises of God. Using more than 70 quotations or allusions from the Old Testament, Matthew demonstrates that Jesus is the promised king who came to fulfill the hope of his people. Matthew invites his readers to embrace the rightful king through faith and repentance and submit to life in "the kingdom of heaven" or "the kingdom of God."

Those who come under the rule and reign of the King find this king to be a righteous and loving ruler who humbly serves his beloved kingdom citizens. This king invites his people to participate in his mission to the world and the establishment of his kingdom on earth as it is in heaven (28:18 – 20). In his kingdom, Jews and Gentiles alike find forgiveness of sin, peace with God and hope for this life and the next.

SEEK FIRST HIS KINGDOM AND HIS RIGHTEOUSNESS, AND ALL THESE THINGS WILL BE GIVEN TO YOU AS WELL.

Matthew 6:33

MATTHEW

MATTHEW 1:1 – 17

THE GENEALOGY OF JESUS

Part of Matthew's goal in writing his Gospel was to show Jesus as the true Messiah for whom the Jews had been waiting. Because the Messiah had to come from the line of David, it was important for Matthew to show Jesus' legitimacy by connecting him not only to David, but all the way back to Abraham (v. 2; Ge 12:3). Another interesting point in Matthew's genealogy is the mention of five women, specifically Tamar (Mt 1:3), Rahab (v. 5) and Bathsheba (simply called "Uriah's wife" in v. 6). Tamar had deceitfully posed as a prostitute to bear her children (Ge 38), Rahab was a prostitute in the city of Jericho (Jos 2), and Bathsheba was the woman with whom David committed adultery (2Sa 11). Not only was it unusual for women to be mentioned in genealogies, but it was even stranger that Matthew decided to list three women of relatively low moral standing. The inclusion of Tamar, Rahab and Bathsheba shows that God is able to use anyone to accomplish his plan. God could have handpicked anyone to be in the genealogy of Jesus, but he included these and many other imperfect people to comprise the line that would eventually bring his Son into the world. These women are an incredible image of God's sovereign desire to take what is broken and make it new. Matthew begins his Gospel by showing the legitimacy of Jesus and the redemptive power of God.

The Genealogy of Jesus the Messiah

1 This is the genealogy[a] of Jesus the Messiah[b] the son of David, the son of Abraham:

2 Abraham was the father of Isaac,
Isaac the father of Jacob,
Jacob the father of Judah and his brothers,
3 Judah the father of Perez and Zerah, whose mother was Tamar,
Perez the father of Hezron,
Hezron the father of Ram,
4 Ram the father of Amminadab,
Amminadab the father of Nahshon,
Nahshon the father of Salmon,
5 Salmon the father of Boaz, whose mother was Rahab,
Boaz the father of Obed, whose mother was Ruth,
Obed the father of Jesse,
6 and Jesse the father of King David.

David was the father of Solomon, whose mother had been Uriah's wife,
7 Solomon the father of Rehoboam,
Rehoboam the father of Abijah,
Abijah the father of Asa,
8 Asa the father of Jehoshaphat,
Jehoshaphat the father of Jehoram,
Jehoram the father of Uzziah,
9 Uzziah the father of Jotham,
Jotham the father of Ahaz,
Ahaz the father of Hezekiah,
10 Hezekiah the father of Manasseh,
Manasseh the father of Amon,
Amon the father of Josiah,
11 and Josiah the father of Jeconiah[c] and his brothers at the time of the exile
to Babylon.

12 After the exile to Babylon:
Jeconiah was the father of Shealtiel,
Shealtiel the father of Zerubbabel,
13 Zerubbabel the father of Abihud,
Abihud the father of Eliakim,
Eliakim the father of Azor,
14 Azor the father of Zadok,
Zadok the father of Akim,
Akim the father of Elihud,
15 Elihud the father of Eleazar,
Eleazar the father of Matthan,
Matthan the father of Jacob,
16 and Jacob the father of Joseph, the husband of Mary, and Mary was the
mother of Jesus who is called the Messiah.

17 Thus there were fourteen generations in all from Abraham to David, fourteen
from David to the exile to Babylon, and fourteen from the exile to the Messiah.

---

[a] *1* Or *is an account of the origin* [b] *1* Or *Jesus Christ. Messiah* (Hebrew) and *Christ* (Greek) both mean *Anointed One*; also in verse 18. [c] *11* That is, Jehoiachin; also in verse 12

Joseph Accepts Jesus as His Son

18This is how the birth of Jesus the Messiah came about[a]: His mother Mary
was pledged to be married to Joseph, but before they came together, she was
found to be pregnant through the Holy Spirit. 19Because Joseph her husband was
faithful to the law, and yet[b] did not want to expose her to public disgrace, he had
in mind to divorce her quietly.

20But after he had considered this, an angel of the Lord appeared to him in
a dream and said, "Joseph son of David, do not be afraid to take Mary home as
your wife, because what is conceived in her is from the Holy Spirit. 21She will give
birth to a son, and you are to give him the name Jesus,[c] because he will save his
people from their sins."

22All this took place to fulfill what the Lord had said through the prophet:
23"The virgin will conceive and give birth to a son, and they will call him Immanuel"[d] (which means "God with us").

24When Joseph woke up, he did what the angel of the Lord had commanded
him and took Mary home as his wife. 25But he did not consummate their marriage until she gave birth to a son. And he gave him the name Jesus.

The Magi Visit the Messiah

2 After Jesus was born in Bethlehem in Judea, during the time of King Herod,
Magi[e] from the east came to Jerusalem 2and asked, "Where is the one who
has been born king of the Jews? We saw his star when it rose and have come to
worship him."

3When King Herod heard this he was disturbed, and all Jerusalem with him.
4When he had called together all the people's chief priests and teachers of the
law, he asked them where the Messiah was to be born. 5"In Bethlehem in Judea,"
they replied, "for this is what the prophet has written:

6"'But you, Bethlehem, in the land of Judah,
  are by no means least among the rulers of Judah;
for out of you will come a ruler
  who will shepherd my people Israel.'[f]"

7Then Herod called the Magi secretly and found out from them the exact time
the star had appeared. 8He sent them to Bethlehem and said, "Go and search
carefully for the child. As soon as you find him, report to me, so that I too may
go and worship him."

9After they had heard the king, they went on their way, and the star they had
seen when it rose went ahead of them until it stopped over the place where the
child was. 10When they saw the star, they were overjoyed. 11On coming to the
house, they saw the child with his mother Mary, and they bowed down and worshiped him. Then they opened their treasures and presented him with gifts of
gold, frankincense and myrrh. 12And having been warned in a dream not to go
back to Herod, they returned to their country by another route.

The Escape to Egypt

13When they had gone, an angel of the Lord appeared to Joseph in a dream.
"Get up," he said, "take the child and his mother and escape to Egypt. Stay there
until I tell you, for Herod is going to search for the child to kill him."

14So he got up, took the child and his mother during the night and left for
Egypt, 15where he stayed until the death of Herod. And so was fulfilled what the
Lord had said through the prophet: "Out of Egypt I called my son."[g]

16When Herod realized that he had been outwitted by the Magi, he was furious, and he gave orders to kill all the boys in Bethlehem and its vicinity who were

---

[a] *18* Or *The origin of Jesus the Messiah was like this* [b] *19* Or *was a righteous man and*
[c] *21* *Jesus* is the Greek form of *Joshua,* which means *the LORD saves.* [d] *23* Isaiah 7:14
[e] *1* Traditionally *wise men* [f] *6* Micah 5:2,4 [g] *15* Hosea 11:1

two years old and under, in accordance with the time he had learned from the Magi. [17]Then what was said through the prophet Jeremiah was fulfilled:

> [18]"A voice is heard in Ramah,
> weeping and great mourning,
> Rachel weeping for her children
> and refusing to be comforted,
> because they are no more."[a]

The Return to Nazareth

[19]After Herod died, an angel of the Lord appeared in a dream to Joseph in Egypt [20]and said, "Get up, take the child and his mother and go to the land of Israel, for those who were trying to take the child's life are dead."

[21]So he got up, took the child and his mother and went to the land of Israel. [22]But when he heard that Archelaus was reigning in Judea in place of his father Herod, he was afraid to go there. Having been warned in a dream, he withdrew to the district of Galilee, [23]and he went and lived in a town called Nazareth. So was fulfilled what was said through the prophets, that he would be called a Nazarene.

John the Baptist Prepares the Way

3 In those days John the Baptist came, preaching in the wilderness of Judea [2]and saying, "Repent, for the kingdom of heaven has come near." [3]This is he who was spoken of through the prophet Isaiah:

> "A voice of one calling in the wilderness,
> 'Prepare the way for the Lord,
> make straight paths for him.'"[b]

[4]John's clothes were made of camel's hair, and he had a leather belt around his waist. His food was locusts and wild honey. [5]People went out to him from Jerusalem and all Judea and the whole region of the Jordan. [6]Confessing their sins, they were baptized by him in the Jordan River.

[7]But when he saw many of the Pharisees and Sadducees coming to where he was baptizing, he said to them: "You brood of vipers! Who warned you to flee from the coming wrath? [8]Produce fruit in keeping with repentance. [9]And do not think you can say to yourselves, 'We have Abraham as our father.' I tell you that out of these stones God can raise up children for Abraham. [10]The ax is already at the root of the trees, and every tree that does not produce good fruit will be cut down and thrown into the fire.

[11]"I baptize you with[c] water for repentance. But after me comes one who is more powerful than I, whose sandals I am not worthy to carry. He will baptize you with[c] the Holy Spirit and fire. [12]His winnowing fork is in his hand, and he will clear his threshing floor, gathering his wheat into the barn and burning up the chaff with unquenchable fire."

The Baptism of Jesus

[13]Then Jesus came from Galilee to the Jordan to be baptized by John. [14]But John tried to deter him, saying, "I need to be baptized by you, and do you come to me?"

[15]Jesus replied, "Let it be so now; it is proper for us to do this to fulfill all righteousness." Then John consented.

[16]As soon as Jesus was baptized, he went up out of the water. At that moment heaven was opened, and he saw the Spirit of God descending like a dove and alighting on him. [17]And a voice from heaven said, "This is my Son, whom I love; with him I am well pleased."

MATTHEW 3:1–2

JOHN'S BAPTISM OF REPENTANCE

John the Baptist was the son of Zechariah and Elizabeth and was a cousin of Jesus (Lk 1). His birth was a signal of the coming of the Messiah, and Jesus himself said that there was none "greater than John the Baptist" (Mt 11:11). John called his followers to repent from their wrongdoing because of the nearness of the kingdom of heaven. In order for people to repent, they had to recognize and acknowledge the fact that they were not living lives that glorified God. In Matthew 4:17, Jesus echoes John's call as he preaches the same message of repentance. Believers are expected to live lives that honor and glorify God. Throughout Jesus' ministry, he explained what it means to live according to the standard that God has set — in a way that mirrors the Father's heart — and he also lived a life that believers are meant to imitate. Obviously it is impossible to be completely like Jesus; after all, he was perfect. But the first step for anyone to begin to live according to Scripture is to repent and turn away from that which is wrong or sinful.

---

[a] *18* Jer. 31:15 [b] *3* Isaiah 40:3 [c] *11* Or *in*

MATTHEW 3:13 – 17

MY BELOVED SON

The Father confirmed the identity of the Son at his baptism. Though Jesus had no sin, he willingly submitted to John's baptism. This action further identified him with those he came to save. As the author of Hebrews writes, "Since the children have flesh and blood, he too shared in their humanity" (Heb 2:14). His association with frail humans allowed him to understand their pain, sympathize with their weakness and enter into their suffering.

It is fitting that God spoke from the heavens upon this significant event. Jesus knew his identity as the preexistent Son of God, who was the central agent of God's created handiwork at the dawn of creation (Col 1:15 – 20). Yet, God the Father publically proclaimed that Jesus was his beloved Son before he fully inaugurated his earthly mission. This statement was certainly a source of encouragement to Jesus, but it was also a public testimony to all those who heard that Jesus was, in fact, God's Messiah — the One who was promised so long ago (Ge 3:15).

The same motive lies at the heart of the Gospel writers, who sought to demonstrate that Jesus was the Son of God. Matthew, writing to a Jewish audience, established that Jesus was the fulfillment of both the Abrahamic and Davidic covenants (Mt 1:17). Mark used Jesus' miracles and message to show that he was "the Son of God" (Mk 1:1). Luke complied an orderly account of the life and ministry of Jesus — focused on his death, burial and resurrection — in order to prove the validity of the message concerning Jesus the Christ (Lk 1:1 – 4). John focuses on Christ as the *logos*. Jesus reveals the Father to God's people in a way that is reminiscent of, but much clearer than, the Word of God that had revealed him throughout the Old Testament (Jn 1:1 – 14). Though the contextual realities differed, each Gospel story sought to affirm Jesus' identity and convince the original hearers, and all subsequent humanity, "that Jesus is the Messiah, the Son of God, and that by believing you may have life in his name" (Jn 20:31). The Father's pronouncement at Jesus' baptism is affirmed whenever a person repents of their sins and trusts in Christ.

Jesus Is Tested in the Wilderness

4 Then Jesus was led by the Spirit into the wilderness to be tempted[a] by the devil. [2]After fasting forty days and forty nights, he was hungry. [3]The tempter came to him and said, "If you are the Son of God, tell these stones to become bread."

[4]Jesus answered, "It is written: 'Man shall not live on bread alone, but on every word that comes from the mouth of God.'[b]"

[5]Then the devil took him to the holy city and had him stand on the highest point of the temple. [6]"If you are the Son of God," he said, "throw yourself down. For it is written:

"'He will command his angels concerning you,
and they will lift you up in their hands,
so that you will not strike your foot against a stone.'[c]"

[7]Jesus answered him, "It is also written: 'Do not put the Lord your God to the test.'[d]"

[8]Again, the devil took him to a very high mountain and showed him all the kingdoms of the world and their splendor. [9]"All this I will give you," he said, "if you will bow down and worship me."

[10]Jesus said to him, "Away from me, Satan! For it is written: 'Worship the Lord your God, and serve him only.'[e]"

[11]Then the devil left him, and angels came and attended him.

Jesus Begins to Preach

[12]When Jesus heard that John had been put in prison, he withdrew to Galilee. [13]Leaving Nazareth, he went and lived in Capernaum, which was by the lake in the area of Zebulun and Naphtali— [14]to fulfill what was said through the prophet Isaiah:

[15]"Land of Zebulun and land of Naphtali,
the Way of the Sea, beyond the Jordan,
Galilee of the Gentiles—
[16]the people living in darkness
have seen a great light;
on those living in the land of the shadow of death
a light has dawned."[f]

[17]From that time on Jesus began to preach, "Repent, for the kingdom of heaven has come near."

Jesus Calls His First Disciples

[18]As Jesus was walking beside the Sea of Galilee, he saw two brothers, Simon called Peter and his brother Andrew. They were casting a net into the lake, for they were fishermen. [19]"Come, follow me," Jesus said, "and I will send you out to fish for people." [20]At once they left their nets and followed him.

[21]Going on from there, he saw two other brothers, James son of Zebedee and his brother John. They were in a boat with their father Zebedee, preparing their nets. Jesus called them, [22]and immediately they left the boat and their father and followed him.

Jesus Heals the Sick

[23]Jesus went throughout Galilee, teaching in their synagogues, proclaiming the good news of the kingdom, and healing every disease and sickness among the people. [24]News about him spread all over Syria, and people brought to him all who were ill with various diseases, those suffering severe pain, the demon-possessed, those having seizures, and the paralyzed; and he healed them.

[a] *1* The Greek for *tempted* can also mean *tested.* [b] *4* Deut. 8:3 [c] *6* Psalm 91:11,12
[d] *7* Deut. 6:16 [e] *10* Deut. 6:13 [f] *16* Isaiah 9:1,2

MATTHEW 4:1–11

THE TEMPTATION OF THE SON OF GOD

As a human, Jesus experienced everything that any other human has experienced, including temptation. Matthew 4 describes Jesus' experience of being tempted by the devil for 40 days and 40 nights. Jesus was tempted by the opportunity to use his power to meet his own needs rather than relying on God (v. 3), to put God to the test in order to win a large following (v. 5) and to compromise with Satan to win the kingdoms of the world, thereby avoiding the cross (v. 9). Jesus' experience was no less real than any sort of temptation that other people experience. However, the difference is that Jesus did not give in to the temptation he faced (Heb 4:15). Jesus boldly and convincingly refuted with Scripture each of the temptations he faced. Jesus defeated Satan by using a weapon that every believer has at their disposal: "the sword of the Spirit, which is the word of God" (Eph 6:17).

[25]Large crowds from Galilee, the Decapolis,[a] Jerusalem, Judea and the region
across the Jordan followed him.

Introduction to the Sermon on the Mount

5 Now when Jesus saw the crowds, he went up on a mountainside and sat
down. His disciples came to him, [2]and he began to teach them.

The Beatitudes

He said:

[3]"Blessed are the poor in spirit,
for theirs is the kingdom of heaven.
[4]Blessed are those who mourn,
for they will be comforted.
[5]Blessed are the meek,
for they will inherit the earth.
[6]Blessed are those who hunger and thirst for righteousness,
for they will be filled.
[7]Blessed are the merciful,
for they will be shown mercy.
[8]Blessed are the pure in heart,
for they will see God.
[9]Blessed are the peacemakers,
for they will be called children of God.
[10]Blessed are those who are persecuted because of righteousness,
for theirs is the kingdom of heaven.

[11]"Blessed are you when people insult you, persecute you and falsely say all
kinds of evil against you because of me. [12]Rejoice and be glad, because great is
your reward in heaven, for in the same way they persecuted the prophets who
were before you.

Salt and Light

[13]"You are the salt of the earth. But if the salt loses its saltiness, how can it be
made salty again? It is no longer good for anything, except to be thrown out and
trampled underfoot.

[14]"You are the light of the world. A town built on a hill cannot be hidden. [15]Nei-
ther do people light a lamp and put it under a bowl. Instead they put it on its
stand, and it gives light to everyone in the house. [16]In the same way, let your
light shine before others, that they may see your good deeds and glorify your
Father in heaven.

The Fulfillment of the Law

[17]"Do not think that I have come to abolish the Law or the Prophets; I have not
come to abolish them but to fulfill them. [18]For truly I tell you, until heaven and
earth disappear, not the smallest letter, not the least stroke of a pen, will by any
means disappear from the Law until everything is accomplished. [19]Therefore
anyone who sets aside one of the least of these commands and teaches others
accordingly will be called least in the kingdom of heaven, but whoever practices and teaches these commands will be called great in the kingdom of heaven.
[20]For I tell you that unless your righteousness surpasses that of the Pharisees
and the teachers of the law, you will certainly not enter the kingdom of heaven.

Murder

[21]"You have heard that it was said to the people long ago, 'You shall not murder,[b] and anyone who murders will be subject to judgment.' [22]But I tell you that

[a] 25 That is, the Ten Cities [b] 21 Exodus 20:13

MATTHEW 5:2

JESUS AND THE LAW

The Sermon on the Mount includes Jesus' explanation of how he is the fulfillment of the law. This discourse was not meant to replace Old Testament law, but rather it points to the ultimate fulfillment of the spiritual intention of the law. Jesus explained the true meaning and purpose of the Old Testament law. The law was designed not to confine people to their own futile efforts but rather to show complete dependence on God.

Here in the book of Matthew, Jesus created a standard that no human can fully achieve. He did not preach such a high standard of law in order to discourage his followers from obeying it, but rather he taught it in such a way as to show how necessary is human dependence on the Spirit of God. Jesus expects his followers to give their fullest effort to obey his commandments, yet he knows they will fall short. He gives them his Spirit to empower them whenever they ask.

anyone who is angry with a brother or sister[a,b] will be subject to judgment. Again, anyone who says to a brother or sister, 'Raca,'[c] is answerable to the court. And anyone who says, 'You fool!' will be in danger of the fire of hell.

23 "Therefore, if you are offering your gift at the altar and there remember that your brother or sister has something against you, 24 leave your gift there in front of the altar. First go and be reconciled to them; then come and offer your gift.

25 "Settle matters quickly with your adversary who is taking you to court. Do it while you are still together on the way, or your adversary may hand you over to the judge, and the judge may hand you over to the officer, and you may be thrown into prison. 26 Truly I tell you, you will not get out until you have paid the last penny.

Adultery

27 "You have heard that it was said, 'You shall not commit adultery.'[d] 28 But I tell you that anyone who looks at a woman lustfully has already committed adultery with her in his heart. 29 If your right eye causes you to stumble, gouge it out and throw it away. It is better for you to lose one part of your body than for your whole body to be thrown into hell. 30 And if your right hand causes you to stumble, cut it off and throw it away. It is better for you to lose one part of your body than for your whole body to go into hell.

Divorce

31 "It has been said, 'Anyone who divorces his wife must give her a certificate of divorce.'[e] 32 But I tell you that anyone who divorces his wife, except for sexual immorality, makes her the victim of adultery, and anyone who marries a divorced woman commits adultery.

Oaths

33 "Again, you have heard that it was said to the people long ago, 'Do not break your oath, but fulfill to the Lord the vows you have made.' 34 But I tell you, do not swear an oath at all: either by heaven, for it is God's throne; 35 or by the earth, for it is his footstool; or by Jerusalem, for it is the city of the Great King. 36 And do not swear by your head, for you cannot make even one hair white or black. 37 All you need to say is simply 'Yes' or 'No'; anything beyond this comes from the evil one.[f]

Eye for Eye

38 "You have heard that it was said, 'Eye for eye, and tooth for tooth.'[g] 39 But I tell you, do not resist an evil person. If anyone slaps you on the right cheek, turn to them the other cheek also. 40 And if anyone wants to sue you and take your shirt, hand over your coat as well. 41 If anyone forces you to go one mile, go with them two miles. 42 Give to the one who asks you, and do not turn away from the one who wants to borrow from you.

Love for Enemies

43 "You have heard that it was said, 'Love your neighbor[h] and hate your enemy.' 44 But I tell you, love your enemies and pray for those who persecute you, 45 that you may be children of your Father in heaven. He causes his sun to rise on the evil and the good, and sends rain on the righteous and the unrighteous. 46 If you love those who love you, what reward will you get? Are not even the tax collectors doing that? 47 And if you greet only your own people, what are you doing more than others? Do not even pagans do that? 48 Be perfect, therefore, as your heavenly Father is perfect.

---

[a] 22 The Greek word for *brother or sister* (*adelphos*) refers here to a fellow disciple, whether man or woman; also in verse 23. [b] 22 Some manuscripts *brother or sister without cause* [c] 22 An Aramaic term of contempt [d] 27 Exodus 20:14 [e] 31 Deut. 24:1 [f] 37 Or *from evil* [g] 38 Exodus 21:24; Lev. 24:20; Deut. 19:21 [h] 43 Lev. 19:18

Giving to the Needy

6 “Be careful not to practice your righteousness in front of others to be seen by
them. If you do, you will have no reward from your Father in heaven.
2“So when you give to the needy, do not announce it with trumpets, as the
hypocrites do in the synagogues and on the streets, to be honored by others.
Truly I tell you, they have received their reward in full. 3But when you give to
the needy, do not let your left hand know what your right hand is doing, 4so that
your giving may be in secret. Then your Father, who sees what is done in secret,
will reward you.

Prayer

5“And when you pray, do not be like the hypocrites, for they love to pray standing in the synagogues and on the street corners to be seen by others. Truly I tell
you, they have received their reward in full. 6But when you pray, go into your
room, close the door and pray to your Father, who is unseen. Then your Father,
who sees what is done in secret, will reward you. 7And when you pray, do not
keep on babbling like pagans, for they think they will be heard because of their
many words. 8Do not be like them, for your Father knows what you need before
you ask him.
9“This, then, is how you should pray:

“ ‘Our Father in heaven,
hallowed be your name,
10 your kingdom come,
your will be done,
on earth as it is in heaven.
11 Give us today our daily bread.
12 And forgive us our debts,
as we also have forgiven our debtors.
13 And lead us not into temptation,[a]
but deliver us from the evil one.[b]’

14For if you forgive other people when they sin against you, your heavenly Father
will also forgive you. 15But if you do not forgive others their sins, your Father will
not forgive your sins.

Fasting

16“When you fast, do not look somber as the hypocrites do, for they disfigure
their faces to show others they are fasting. Truly I tell you, they have received
their reward in full. 17But when you fast, put oil on your head and wash your
face, 18so that it will not be obvious to others that you are fasting, but only to
your Father, who is unseen; and your Father, who sees what is done in secret,
will reward you.

Treasures in Heaven

19“Do not store up for yourselves treasures on earth, where moths and vermin
destroy, and where thieves break in and steal. 20But store up for yourselves treasures in heaven, where moths and vermin do not destroy, and where thieves do
not break in and steal. 21For where your treasure is, there your heart will be also.
22“The eye is the lamp of the body. If your eyes are healthy,[c] your whole body
will be full of light. 23But if your eyes are unhealthy,[d] your whole body will be full
of darkness. If then the light within you is darkness, how great is that darkness!
24“No one can serve two masters. Either you will hate the one and love the

---

[a] *13* The Greek for *temptation* can also mean *testing*. [b] *13* Or *from evil*; some late manuscripts *one, / for yours is the kingdom and the power and the glory forever. Amen.*
[c] *22* The Greek for *healthy* here implies *generous*. [d] *23* The Greek for *unhealthy* here implies *stingy*.

other, or you will be devoted to the one and despise the other. You cannot serve both God and money.

Do Not Worry

25“Therefore I tell you, do not worry about your life, what you will eat or drink; or about your body, what you will wear. Is not life more than food, and the body more than clothes? 26Look at the birds of the air; they do not sow or reap or store away in barns, and yet your heavenly Father feeds them. Are you not much more valuable than they? 27Can any one of you by worrying add a single hour to your life[a]?

28“And why do you worry about clothes? See how the flowers of the field grow. They do not labor or spin. 29Yet I tell you that not even Solomon in all his splendor was dressed like one of these. 30If that is how God clothes the grass of the field, which is here today and tomorrow is thrown into the fire, will he not much more clothe you — you of little faith? 31So do not worry, saying, ‘What shall we eat?’ or ‘What shall we drink?’ or ‘What shall we wear?’ 32For the pagans run after all these things, and your heavenly Father knows that you need them. 33But seek first his kingdom and his righteousness, and all these things will be given to you as well. 34Therefore do not worry about tomorrow, for tomorrow will worry about itself. Each day has enough trouble of its own.

Judging Others

7 “Do not judge, or you too will be judged. 2For in the same way you judge others, you will be judged, and with the measure you use, it will be measured to you.

3“Why do you look at the speck of sawdust in your brother’s eye and pay no attention to the plank in your own eye? 4How can you say to your brother, ‘Let me take the speck out of your eye,’ when all the time there is a plank in your own eye? 5You hypocrite, first take the plank out of your own eye, and then you will see clearly to remove the speck from your brother’s eye.

6“Do not give dogs what is sacred; do not throw your pearls to pigs. If you do, they may trample them under their feet, and turn and tear you to pieces.

Ask, Seek, Knock

7“Ask and it will be given to you; seek and you will find; knock and the door will be opened to you. 8For everyone who asks receives; the one who seeks finds; and to the one who knocks, the door will be opened.

9“Which of you, if your son asks for bread, will give him a stone? 10Or if he asks for a fish, will give him a snake? 11If you, then, though you are evil, know how to give good gifts to your children, how much more will your Father in heaven give good gifts to those who ask him! 12So in everything, do to others what you would have them do to you, for this sums up the Law and the Prophets.

The Narrow and Wide Gates

13“Enter through the narrow gate. For wide is the gate and broad is the road that leads to destruction, and many enter through it. 14But small is the gate and narrow the road that leads to life, and only a few find it.

True and False Prophets

15“Watch out for false prophets. They come to you in sheep’s clothing, but inwardly they are ferocious wolves. 16By their fruit you will recognize them. Do people pick grapes from thornbushes, or figs from thistles? 17Likewise, every good tree bears good fruit, but a bad tree bears bad fruit. 18A good tree cannot bear bad fruit, and a bad tree cannot bear good fruit. 19Every tree that does not bear good fruit is cut down and thrown into the fire. 20Thus, by their fruit you will recognize them.

[a] 27 Or *single cubit to your height*

MATTHEW 7:13 – 14

THE WIDE AND THE NARROW GATES

Jesus explained that the roads to life and destruction are roads guarded by narrow and wide gates, respectively. In doing so, he taught that many people walk down the road that leads to destruction, while few people choose to walk down the road that leads to life. The road that leads to destruction is easy to find (Pr 14:12). Anyone who chases after the cares of the world without the mind of the Spirit (Php 2:1 – 11) walks along the broad road that leads to destruction, and they do so with many other people. In contrast, the narrow road is smaller, and fewer people travel upon it. In John 14:6, Jesus said, “I am the way and the truth and the life. No one comes to the Father except through me.” Jesus is the narrow gate, and by following him and living in his power, believers are able to walk upon the path of life.

True and False Disciples

21“Not everyone who says to me, ‘Lord, Lord,’ will enter the kingdom of heav-
en, but only the one who does the will of my Father who is in heaven. 22Many will
say to me on that day, ‘Lord, Lord, did we not prophesy in your name and in your
name drive out demons and in your name perform many miracles?’ 23Then I will
tell them plainly, ‘I never knew you. Away from me, you evildoers!’

The Wise and Foolish Builders

24“Therefore everyone who hears these words of mine and puts them into
practice is like a wise man who built his house on the rock. 25The rain came
down, the streams rose, and the winds blew and beat against that house; yet it
did not fall, because it had its foundation on the rock. 26But everyone who hears
these words of mine and does not put them into practice is like a foolish man
who built his house on sand. 27The rain came down, the streams rose, and the
winds blew and beat against that house, and it fell with a great crash.”

28When Jesus had finished saying these things, the crowds were amazed at
his teaching, 29because he taught as one who had authority, and not as their
teachers of the law.

Jesus Heals a Man With Leprosy

8 When Jesus came down from the mountainside, large crowds followed him.
2A man with leprosy[a] came and knelt before him and said, “Lord, if you are
willing, you can make me clean.”

3Jesus reached out his hand and touched the man. “I am willing,” he said. “Be
clean!” Immediately he was cleansed of his leprosy. 4Then Jesus said to him, “See
that you don’t tell anyone. But go, show yourself to the priest and offer the gift
Moses commanded, as a testimony to them.”

The Faith of the Centurion

5When Jesus had entered Capernaum, a centurion came to him, asking for
help. 6“Lord,” he said, “my servant lies at home paralyzed, suffering terribly.”

7Jesus said to him, “Shall I come and heal him?”

8The centurion replied, “Lord, I do not deserve to have you come under my
roof. But just say the word, and my servant will be healed. 9For I myself am a
man under authority, with soldiers under me. I tell this one, ‘Go,’ and he goes;
and that one, ‘Come,’ and he comes. I say to my servant, ‘Do this,’ and he does it.”

10When Jesus heard this, he was amazed and said to those following him,
“Truly I tell you, I have not found anyone in Israel with such great faith. 11I say to
you that many will come from the east and the west, and will take their places
at the feast with Abraham, Isaac and Jacob in the kingdom of heaven. 12But the
subjects of the kingdom will be thrown outside, into the darkness, where there
will be weeping and gnashing of teeth.”

13Then Jesus said to the centurion, “Go! Let it be done just as you believed it
would.” And his servant was healed at that moment.

Jesus Heals Many

14When Jesus came into Peter’s house, he saw Peter’s mother-in-law lying in
bed with a fever. 15He touched her hand and the fever left her, and she got up and
began to wait on him.

16When evening came, many who were demon-possessed were brought to
him, and he drove out the spirits with a word and healed all the sick. 17This was
to fulfill what was spoken through the prophet Isaiah:

“He took up our infirmities
and bore our diseases.”[b]

---

[a] *2* The Greek word traditionally translated *leprosy* was used for various diseases affecting the skin. [b] *17* Isaiah 53:4 (see Septuagint)

MATTHEW 8:1–17

JESUS' POWER OVER DISEASE

Matthew 8 begins with three stories of Jesus' healing miracles. Throughout the Gospels, Jesus healed many people; in doing so, he fulfilled the Old Testament prophecy of Isaiah 53:4: "He took up our pain and bore our suffering." Not only did Jesus heal physical infirmities while he was on earth, but he also healed all infirmities, physical and spiritual, through his death on the cross. The stories of Jesus' healing miracles are precursors to his ultimate healing miracle on the cross.

The key phrase worth noting in the story of the man with leprosy is "Lord, if you are willing" (Mt 8:2). As a leper, this man was a social outcast because leprosy was thought to be highly contagious. This man was incredibly bold even to approach Jesus in light of his disease, yet he did so confidently. He knew that having faith was no guarantee that Jesus *would* heal him, but he knew Jesus *could* heal him (Da 3:17–18).

The next story shows, for the first time in the Gospels, Jesus interacting with someone who was not Jewish. As a Gentile, the centurion had little reason to interact with, let alone believe in, Jesus. However, he showed faith similar to that of the leper in asking Jesus to heal his servant. The centurion, a man in charge of roughly 80 to 100 soldiers, rebuffed Jesus' offer to come into his home. He knew that if Jesus would only say the word, his servant would be healed, which even further showed his confidence in Jesus' power. Jesus was astonished at the faith of the centurion: "Truly I tell you, I have not found anyone in Israel with such great faith" (Mt 8:10).

These two stories are remarkable in Scripture specifically because they tell stories of two individuals' great faith despite the supposed odds against Jesus acting on their behalf. The social outcast and the Gentile showed more faith in Jesus than he had seen before, and they reaped the rewards of their faith and trust.

The Cost of Following Jesus

[18]When Jesus saw the crowd around him, he gave orders to cross to the other side of the lake. [19]Then a teacher of the law came to him and said, "Teacher, I will follow you wherever you go."

[20]Jesus replied, "Foxes have dens and birds have nests, but the Son of Man has no place to lay his head."

[21]Another disciple said to him, "Lord, first let me go and bury my father."

[22]But Jesus told him, "Follow me, and let the dead bury their own dead."

Jesus Calms the Storm

[23]Then he got into the boat and his disciples followed him. [24]Suddenly a furious storm came up on the lake, so that the waves swept over the boat. But Jesus was sleeping. [25]The disciples went and woke him, saying, "Lord, save us! We're going to drown!"

[26]He replied, "You of little faith, why are you so afraid?" Then he got up and rebuked the winds and the waves, and it was completely calm.

[27]The men were amazed and asked, "What kind of man is this? Even the winds and the waves obey him!"

Jesus Restores Two Demon-Possessed Men

[28]When he arrived at the other side in the region of the Gadarenes,[a] two demon-possessed men coming from the tombs met him. They were so violent that no one could pass that way. [29]"What do you want with us, Son of God?" they shouted. "Have you come here to torture us before the appointed time?"

[30]Some distance from them a large herd of pigs was feeding. [31]The demons begged Jesus, "If you drive us out, send us into the herd of pigs."

[32]He said to them, "Go!" So they came out and went into the pigs, and the whole herd rushed down the steep bank into the lake and died in the water. [33]Those tending the pigs ran off, went into the town and reported all this, including what had happened to the demon-possessed men. [34]Then the whole town went out to meet Jesus. And when they saw him, they pleaded with him to leave their region.

Jesus Forgives and Heals a Paralyzed Man

9 Jesus stepped into a boat, crossed over and came to his own town. [2]Some men brought to him a paralyzed man, lying on a mat. When Jesus saw their faith, he said to the man, "Take heart, son; your sins are forgiven."

[3]At this, some of the teachers of the law said to themselves, "This fellow is blaspheming!"

[4]Knowing their thoughts, Jesus said, "Why do you entertain evil thoughts in your hearts? [5]Which is easier: to say, 'Your sins are forgiven,' or to say, 'Get up and walk'? [6]But I want you to know that the Son of Man has authority on earth to forgive sins." So he said to the paralyzed man, "Get up, take your mat and go home." [7]Then the man got up and went home. [8]When the crowd saw this, they were filled with awe; and they praised God, who had given such authority to man.

The Calling of Matthew

[9]As Jesus went on from there, he saw a man named Matthew sitting at the tax collector's booth. "Follow me," he told him, and Matthew got up and followed him.

[10]While Jesus was having dinner at Matthew's house, many tax collectors and sinners came and ate with him and his disciples. [11]When the Pharisees saw this, they asked his disciples, "Why does your teacher eat with tax collectors and sinners?"

---

[a] 28 Some manuscripts *Gergesenes*; other manuscripts *Gerasenes*

MATTHEW 9:1 – 8

THE SON OF MAN HAS AUTHORITY TO FORGIVE SINS

This story has been a favorite of children and adults over the centuries. The image of these concerned and loving friends breaking through every obstacle to get their friend to the Lord is endearing — a very physical, material story of faith and persistence. Yet in the midst of this story, Jesus redirects those who read this story as he redirected the men who believed that their friend would be healed. What must they have been thinking as they heard this great healer, who had performed many healing and other miracles in the region, declare that their friend's sins were forgiven?

Imagine their puzzlement. This is not what they were expecting. Yet Jesus decided to use this very public forum to demonstrate his power to forgive sins as well as his power to heal this man's body.

Jesus had performed other miracles before this one, yet this is the first instance in which he claimed to forgive someone's sins. Jesus wanted to prove that his ministry did not only involve healing people of their illnesses; his ministry was so much more than that, and in this instance he gave further notice of what he truly came to earth to accomplish. How easy would it have been to merely *say* that the man who was paralyzed was forgiven of his sins, yet Jesus showed that he was able to back up everything he claimed: that not only could he provide physical healing, but that he could provide spiritual healing as well. His words and this miracle point to the ultimate purpose of Jesus' ministry on earth: "But he was pierced for our transgressions, he was crushed for our iniquities; the punishment that brought us peace was on him, and by his wounds we are healed" (Isa 53:5). Through Jesus' ministry in his life, death and resurrection, we are completely, and gloriously, healed.

12 On hearing this, Jesus said, "It is not the healthy who need a doctor, but the sick. 13 But go and learn what this means: 'I desire mercy, not sacrifice.'[a] For I have not come to call the righteous, but sinners."

Jesus Questioned About Fasting

14 Then John's disciples came and asked him, "How is it that we and the Pharisees fast often, but your disciples do not fast?"

15 Jesus answered, "How can the guests of the bridegroom mourn while he is with them? The time will come when the bridegroom will be taken from them; then they will fast.

16 "No one sews a patch of unshrunk cloth on an old garment, for the patch will pull away from the garment, making the tear worse. 17 Neither do people pour new wine into old wineskins. If they do, the skins will burst; the wine will run out and the wineskins will be ruined. No, they pour new wine into new wineskins, and both are preserved."

Jesus Raises a Dead Girl and Heals a Sick Woman

18 While he was saying this, a synagogue leader came and knelt before him and said, "My daughter has just died. But come and put your hand on her, and she will live." 19 Jesus got up and went with him, and so did his disciples.

20 Just then a woman who had been subject to bleeding for twelve years came up behind him and touched the edge of his cloak. 21 She said to herself, "If I only touch his cloak, I will be healed."

22 Jesus turned and saw her. "Take heart, daughter," he said, "your faith has healed you." And the woman was healed at that moment.

23 When Jesus entered the synagogue leader's house and saw the noisy crowd and people playing pipes, 24 he said, "Go away. The girl is not dead but asleep." But they laughed at him. 25 After the crowd had been put outside, he went in and took the girl by the hand, and she got up. 26 News of this spread through all that region.

Jesus Heals the Blind and the Mute

27 As Jesus went on from there, two blind men followed him, calling out, "Have mercy on us, Son of David!"

28 When he had gone indoors, the blind men came to him, and he asked them, "Do you believe that I am able to do this?"

"Yes, Lord," they replied.

29 Then he touched their eyes and said, "According to your faith let it be done to you"; 30 and their sight was restored. Jesus warned them sternly, "See that no one knows about this." 31 But they went out and spread the news about him all over that region.

32 While they were going out, a man who was demon-possessed and could not talk was brought to Jesus. 33 And when the demon was driven out, the man who had been mute spoke. The crowd was amazed and said, "Nothing like this has ever been seen in Israel."

34 But the Pharisees said, "It is by the prince of demons that he drives out demons."

The Workers Are Few

35 Jesus went through all the towns and villages, teaching in their synagogues, proclaiming the good news of the kingdom and healing every disease and sickness. 36 When he saw the crowds, he had compassion on them, because they were harassed and helpless, like sheep without a shepherd. 37 Then he said to his disciples, "The harvest is plentiful but the workers are few. 38 Ask the Lord of the harvest, therefore, to send out workers into his harvest field."

---

[a] *13* Hosea 6:6

Jesus Sends Out the Twelve

10 Jesus called his twelve disciples to him and gave them authority to drive out impure spirits and to heal every disease and sickness.

2These are the names of the twelve apostles: first, Simon (who is called Peter) and his brother Andrew; James son of Zebedee, and his brother John; 3Philip and Bartholomew; Thomas and Matthew the tax collector; James son of Alphaeus, and Thaddaeus; 4Simon the Zealot and Judas Iscariot, who betrayed him.

5These twelve Jesus sent out with the following instructions: "Do not go among the Gentiles or enter any town of the Samaritans. 6Go rather to the lost sheep of Israel. 7As you go, proclaim this message: 'The kingdom of heaven has come near.' 8Heal the sick, raise the dead, cleanse those who have leprosy,[a] drive out demons. Freely you have received; freely give.

9"Do not get any gold or silver or copper to take with you in your belts — 10no bag for the journey or extra shirt or sandals or a staff, for the worker is worth his keep. 11Whatever town or village you enter, search there for some worthy person and stay at their house until you leave. 12As you enter the home, give it your greeting. 13If the home is deserving, let your peace rest on it; if it is not, let your peace return to you. 14If anyone will not welcome you or listen to your words, leave that home or town and shake the dust off your feet. 15Truly I tell you, it will be more bearable for Sodom and Gomorrah on the day of judgment than for that town.

16"I am sending you out like sheep among wolves. Therefore be as shrewd as snakes and as innocent as doves. 17Be on your guard; you will be handed over to the local councils and be flogged in the synagogues. 18On my account you will be brought before governors and kings as witnesses to them and to the Gentiles. 19But when they arrest you, do not worry about what to say or how to say it. At that time you will be given what to say, 20for it will not be you speaking, but the Spirit of your Father speaking through you.

21"Brother will betray brother to death, and a father his child; children will rebel against their parents and have them put to death. 22You will be hated by everyone because of me, but the one who stands firm to the end will be saved. 23When you are persecuted in one place, flee to another. Truly I tell you, you will not finish going through the towns of Israel before the Son of Man comes.

24"The student is not above the teacher, nor a servant above his master. 25It is enough for students to be like their teachers, and servants like their masters. If the head of the house has been called Beelzebul, how much more the members of his household!

26"So do not be afraid of them, for there is nothing concealed that will not be disclosed, or hidden that will not be made known. 27What I tell you in the dark, speak in the daylight; what is whispered in your ear, proclaim from the roofs. 28Do not be afraid of those who kill the body but cannot kill the soul. Rather, be afraid of the One who can destroy both soul and body in hell. 29Are not two sparrows sold for a penny? Yet not one of them will fall to the ground outside your Father's care.[b] 30And even the very hairs of your head are all numbered. 31So don't be afraid; you are worth more than many sparrows.

32"Whoever acknowledges me before others, I will also acknowledge before my Father in heaven. 33But whoever disowns me before others, I will disown before my Father in heaven.

34"Do not suppose that I have come to bring peace to the earth. I did not come to bring peace, but a sword. 35For I have come to turn

"'a man against his father,
a daughter against her mother,
a daughter-in-law against her mother-in-law —
36 a man's enemies will be the members of his own household.'[c]

[a] 8 The Greek word traditionally translated *leprosy* was used for various diseases affecting the skin. [b] 29 Or *will*; or *knowledge* [c] 36 Micah 7:6

37“Anyone who loves their father or mother more than me is not worthy of me; anyone who loves their son or daughter more than me is not worthy of me. 38Whoever does not take up their cross and follow me is not worthy of me. 39Whoever finds their life will lose it, and whoever loses their life for my sake will find it.

40“Anyone who welcomes you welcomes me, and anyone who welcomes me welcomes the one who sent me. 41Whoever welcomes a prophet as a prophet will receive a prophet’s reward, and whoever welcomes a righteous person as a righteous person will receive a righteous person’s reward. 42And if anyone gives even a cup of cold water to one of these little ones who is my disciple, truly I tell you, that person will certainly not lose their reward.”

Jesus and John the Baptist

11 After Jesus had finished instructing his twelve disciples, he went on from there to teach and preach in the towns of Galilee.[a]

2When John, who was in prison, heard about the deeds of the Messiah, he sent his disciples 3to ask him, “Are you the one who is to come, or should we expect someone else?”

4Jesus replied, “Go back and report to John what you hear and see: 5The blind receive sight, the lame walk, those who have leprosy[b] are cleansed, the deaf hear, the dead are raised, and the good news is proclaimed to the poor. 6Blessed is anyone who does not stumble on account of me.”

7As John’s disciples were leaving, Jesus began to speak to the crowd about John: “What did you go out into the wilderness to see? A reed swayed by the wind? 8If not, what did you go out to see? A man dressed in fine clothes? No, those who wear fine clothes are in kings’ palaces. 9Then what did you go out to see? A prophet? Yes, I tell you, and more than a prophet. 10This is the one about whom it is written:

“ ‘I will send my messenger ahead of you,
who will prepare your way before you.’[c]

11Truly I tell you, among those born of women there has not risen anyone greater than John the Baptist; yet whoever is least in the kingdom of heaven is greater than he. 12From the days of John the Baptist until now, the kingdom of heaven has been subjected to violence,[d] and violent people have been raiding it. 13For all the Prophets and the Law prophesied until John. 14And if you are willing to accept it, he is the Elijah who was to come. 15Whoever has ears, let them hear.

16“To what can I compare this generation? They are like children sitting in the marketplaces and calling out to others:

17“ ‘We played the pipe for you,
and you did not dance;
we sang a dirge,
and you did not mourn.’

18For John came neither eating nor drinking, and they say, ‘He has a demon.’ 19The Son of Man came eating and drinking, and they say, ‘Here is a glutton and a drunkard, a friend of tax collectors and sinners.’ But wisdom is proved right by her deeds.”

Woe on Unrepentant Towns

20Then Jesus began to denounce the towns in which most of his miracles had been performed, because they did not repent. 21“Woe to you, Chorazin! Woe to you, Bethsaida! For if the miracles that were performed in you had been performed in Tyre and Sidon, they would have repented long ago in sackcloth and ashes. 22But I tell you, it will be more bearable for Tyre and Sidon on the

[a] *1* Greek *in their towns* [b] *5* The Greek word traditionally translated *leprosy* was used for various diseases affecting the skin. [c] *10* Mal. 3:1 [d] *12* Or *been forcefully advancing*

MATTHEW 11:2–3

THE CHRIST

Today, the title “Christ” naturally follows the name of Jesus. However, during the time that the Gospels were written, people sparingly and carefully used the word “Christ,” the Greek form of the Hebrew word “Messiah,” which literally means “Anointed One.” In the Old Testament, the three types of people who were anointed were prophets (1Ki 19:16), priests (Ex 28:41) and kings (1Sa 16:13). In the New Testament, Jesus is God’s preeminent Anointed One who was anointed by God to be the ultimate prophet, priest and king (Mt 27:11; Heb 6:20; cf. Isa 61:1). The Pharisees and religious leaders during that time viewed such a claim as blasphemous and punishable by death. However, the word “Christ” is used to refer to Jesus 470 times throughout the New Testament. When the word “Christ” was used anywhere in the New Testament, the author was very aware of the implications of his use of that word—what it meant for him as an author, and what it said about his Savior.

JESUS SENDS OUT THE TWELVE

Matthew 10 is the first place where Jesus referred to the twelve disciples as "apostles." The word "apostle" is derivative of the Greek word *apostello*, which means "to send." Here Jesus gave the apostles the authority to drive out evil spirits and heal the sick, which up until this point only Jesus had been able to do. He then sent them to go into other towns and preach the message that "the kingdom of heaven has come near" (v. 7).

It is one thing that Jesus was able to heal and cast out demons himself, but the fact that he was able to give the same authority to his disciples only further shows the strength of his divine nature and power. To represent the fact that these apostles did not act in their own strength, but fully relied on God's provision, Jesus told them not to take provisions for themselves (vv. 9 – 10). Jesus instructed them to rely solely on God. His power was enough to sustain their entire journey.

Jesus also warned them that they would face opposition. Verses 16 through 23 of this chapter have been both a warning and a comfort to believers in Jesus around the world for centuries. As the apostles found out, some will not accept the message that believers in Jesus have to bring to a broken and fallen world. Millions have faced the opposition that Jesus was describing in these verses and have faithfully withstood persecution of many types, even to the point of death, relying on the Holy Spirit to give them the words to say in the face of persecution. Jesus told the apostles not to worry when they were arrested, and notice he said "when" and not "if" (v. 19). Later each of the disciples, with the exception of Judas, experienced the opposition that Jesus described. They were called to a gritty, physical, desperate, minute-by-minute faith and reliance on the person and work of Jesus to be manifested in their lives.

The authority that Jesus gave to each disciple was enough to get them through any hardship that they might have faced upon their journey, and the same is true for believers today.

day of judgment than for you. [23]And you, Capernaum, will you be lifted to the
heavens? No, you will go down to Hades.[a] For if the miracles that were performed in you had been performed in Sodom, it would have remained to this
day. [24]But I tell you that it will be more bearable for Sodom on the day of judgment than for you."

The Father Revealed in the Son

[25]At that time Jesus said, "I praise you, Father, Lord of heaven and earth, because you have hidden these things from the wise and learned, and revealed
them to little children. [26]Yes, Father, for this is what you were pleased to do.
[27]"All things have been committed to me by my Father. No one knows the
Son except the Father, and no one knows the Father except the Son and those to
whom the Son chooses to reveal him.
[28]"Come to me, all you who are weary and burdened, and I will give you rest.
[29]Take my yoke upon you and learn from me, for I am gentle and humble in heart,
and you will find rest for your souls. [30]For my yoke is easy and my burden is
light."

Jesus Is Lord of the Sabbath

12 At that time Jesus went through the grainfields on the Sabbath. His disciples were hungry and began to pick some heads of grain and eat them.
[2]When the Pharisees saw this, they said to him, "Look! Your disciples are doing
what is unlawful on the Sabbath."
[3]He answered, "Haven't you read what David did when he and his companions were hungry? [4]He entered the house of God, and he and his companions
ate the consecrated bread — which was not lawful for them to do, but only for the
priests. [5]Or haven't you read in the Law that the priests on Sabbath duty in the
temple desecrate the Sabbath and yet are innocent? [6]I tell you that something
greater than the temple is here. [7]If you had known what these words mean, 'I
desire mercy, not sacrifice,'[b] you would not have condemned the innocent. [8]For
the Son of Man is Lord of the Sabbath."
[9]Going on from that place, he went into their synagogue, [10]and a man with a
shriveled hand was there. Looking for a reason to bring charges against Jesus,
they asked him, "Is it lawful to heal on the Sabbath?"
[11]He said to them, "If any of you has a sheep and it falls into a pit on the Sabbath, will you not take hold of it and lift it out? [12]How much more valuable is a
person than a sheep! Therefore it is lawful to do good on the Sabbath."
[13]Then he said to the man, "Stretch out your hand." So he stretched it out and
it was completely restored, just as sound as the other. [14]But the Pharisees went
out and plotted how they might kill Jesus.

God's Chosen Servant

[15]Aware of this, Jesus withdrew from that place. A large crowd followed him,
and he healed all who were ill. [16]He warned them not to tell others about him.
[17]This was to fulfill what was spoken through the prophet Isaiah:

[18] "Here is my servant whom I have chosen,
the one I love, in whom I delight;
I will put my Spirit on him,
and he will proclaim justice to the nations.
[19] He will not quarrel or cry out;
no one will hear his voice in the streets.
[20] A bruised reed he will not break,
and a smoldering wick he will not snuff out,
till he has brought justice through to victory.
[21] In his name the nations will put their hope."[c]

[a] *23* That is, the realm of the dead [b] *7* Hosea 6:6 [c] *21* Isaiah 42:1-4

Jesus and Beelzebul

[22]Then they brought him a demon-possessed man who was blind and mute, and Jesus healed him, so that he could both talk and see. [23]All the people were astonished and said, "Could this be the Son of David?"

[24]But when the Pharisees heard this, they said, "It is only by Beelzebul, the prince of demons, that this fellow drives out demons."

[25]Jesus knew their thoughts and said to them, "Every kingdom divided against itself will be ruined, and every city or household divided against itself will not stand. [26]If Satan drives out Satan, he is divided against himself. How then can his kingdom stand? [27]And if I drive out demons by Beelzebul, by whom do your people drive them out? So then, they will be your judges. [28]But if it is by the Spirit of God that I drive out demons, then the kingdom of God has come upon you.

[29]"Or again, how can anyone enter a strong man's house and carry off his possessions unless he first ties up the strong man? Then he can plunder his house.

[30]"Whoever is not with me is against me, and whoever does not gather with me scatters. [31]And so I tell you, every kind of sin and slander can be forgiven, but blasphemy against the Spirit will not be forgiven. [32]Anyone who speaks a word against the Son of Man will be forgiven, but anyone who speaks against the Holy Spirit will not be forgiven, either in this age or in the age to come.

[33]"Make a tree good and its fruit will be good, or make a tree bad and its fruit will be bad, for a tree is recognized by its fruit. [34]You brood of vipers, how can you who are evil say anything good? For the mouth speaks what the heart is full of. [35]A good man brings good things out of the good stored up in him, and an evil man brings evil things out of the evil stored up in him. [36]But I tell you that everyone will have to give account on the day of judgment for every empty word they have spoken. [37]For by your words you will be acquitted, and by your words you will be condemned."

The Sign of Jonah

[38]Then some of the Pharisees and teachers of the law said to him, "Teacher, we want to see a sign from you."

[39]He answered, "A wicked and adulterous generation asks for a sign! But none will be given it except the sign of the prophet Jonah. [40]For as Jonah was three days and three nights in the belly of a huge fish, so the Son of Man will be three days and three nights in the heart of the earth. [41]The men of Nineveh will stand up at the judgment with this generation and condemn it; for they repented at the preaching of Jonah, and now something greater than Jonah is here. [42]The Queen of the South will rise at the judgment with this generation and condemn it; for she came from the ends of the earth to listen to Solomon's wisdom, and now something greater than Solomon is here.

[43]"When an impure spirit comes out of a person, it goes through arid places seeking rest and does not find it. [44]Then it says, 'I will return to the house I left.' When it arrives, it finds the house unoccupied, swept clean and put in order. [45]Then it goes and takes with it seven other spirits more wicked than itself, and they go in and live there. And the final condition of that person is worse than the first. That is how it will be with this wicked generation."

Jesus' Mother and Brothers

[46]While Jesus was still talking to the crowd, his mother and brothers stood outside, wanting to speak to him. [47]Someone told him, "Your mother and brothers are standing outside, wanting to speak to you."

[48]He replied to him, "Who is my mother, and who are my brothers?" [49]Pointing to his disciples, he said, "Here are my mother and my brothers. [50]For whoever does the will of my Father in heaven is my brother and sister and mother."

MATTHEW 12:38–42

JONAH AND THE RESURRECTION

Jesus referred to those who asked for a sign as proof of Jesus' identity as a "wicked and adulterous generation" (Mt 12:39), saying that the only sign they would receive was the sign of Jonah. But what did this mean? Jonah had spent three days and three nights in the belly of a fish; in the same way, Jesus said he would spend three days and three nights in "the heart of the earth" (v. 40). Jesus was clearly foreshadowing his death, burial and resurrection; yet it is doubtful that the Pharisees understood what he was saying. In John 20:29, Jesus said, "Blessed are those who have not seen and yet have believed"; Jesus' frustration with the Pharisees stemmed from the fact that they saw and heard him and yet still did not believe. They were the opposite of the "blessed" he referred to in John 20:29. His purpose in referring to Jonah, however, was twofold: to give a picture of his death and resurrection and to call those who heard these words to repentance, in imitation of the people of Nineveh now that One greater than Jonah had come.

The Parable of the Sower

13 That same day Jesus went out of the house and sat by the lake. 2Such large
crowds gathered around him that he got into a boat and sat in it, while
all the people stood on the shore. 3Then he told them many things in parables,
saying: “A farmer went out to sow his seed. 4As he was scattering the seed, some
fell along the path, and the birds came and ate it up. 5Some fell on rocky places, where it did not have much soil. It sprang up quickly, because the soil was
shallow. 6But when the sun came up, the plants were scorched, and they withered because they had no root. 7Other seed fell among thorns, which grew up
and choked the plants. 8Still other seed fell on good soil, where it produced a
crop — a hundred, sixty or thirty times what was sown. 9Whoever has ears, let
them hear.”

10The disciples came to him and asked, “Why do you speak to the people in
parables?”

11He replied, “Because the knowledge of the secrets of the kingdom of heaven
has been given to you, but not to them. 12Whoever has will be given more, and
they will have an abundance. Whoever does not have, even what they have will
be taken from them. 13This is why I speak to them in parables:

“Though seeing, they do not see;
 though hearing, they do not hear or understand.

14In them is fulfilled the prophecy of Isaiah:

“ ‘You will be ever hearing but never understanding;
 you will be ever seeing but never perceiving.
15For this people’s heart has become calloused;
 they hardly hear with their ears,
 and they have closed their eyes.
Otherwise they might see with their eyes,
 hear with their ears,
 understand with their hearts
and turn, and I would heal them.’[a]

16But blessed are your eyes because they see, and your ears because they hear.
17For truly I tell you, many prophets and righteous people longed to see what you
see but did not see it, and to hear what you hear but did not hear it.

18“Listen then to what the parable of the sower means: 19When anyone hears
the message about the kingdom and does not understand it, the evil one comes
and snatches away what was sown in their heart. This is the seed sown along the
path. 20The seed falling on rocky ground refers to someone who hears the word
and at once receives it with joy. 21But since they have no root, they last only a
short time. When trouble or persecution comes because of the word, they quickly fall away. 22The seed falling among the thorns refers to someone who hears the
word, but the worries of this life and the deceitfulness of wealth choke the word,
making it unfruitful. 23But the seed falling on good soil refers to someone who
hears the word and understands it. This is the one who produces a crop, yielding
a hundred, sixty or thirty times what was sown.”

The Parable of the Weeds

24Jesus told them another parable: “The kingdom of heaven is like a man who
sowed good seed in his field. 25But while everyone was sleeping, his enemy came
and sowed weeds among the wheat, and went away. 26When the wheat sprouted
and formed heads, then the weeds also appeared.

27“The owner’s servants came to him and said, ‘Sir, didn’t you sow good seed
in your field? Where then did the weeds come from?’

28“ ‘An enemy did this,’ he replied.

---

[a] *15* Isaiah 6:9,10 (see Septuagint)

"The servants asked him, 'Do you want us to go and pull them up?'
[29]"'No,' he answered, 'because while you are pulling the weeds, you may uproot the wheat with them. [30]Let both grow together until the harvest. At that time
I will tell the harvesters: First collect the weeds and tie them in bundles to be
burned; then gather the wheat and bring it into my barn.'"

The Parables of the Mustard Seed and the Yeast

[31]He told them another parable: "The kingdom of heaven is like a mustard
seed, which a man took and planted in his field. [32]Though it is the smallest of all
seeds, yet when it grows, it is the largest of garden plants and becomes a tree, so
that the birds come and perch in its branches."
[33]He told them still another parable: "The kingdom of heaven is like yeast that
a woman took and mixed into about sixty pounds[a] of flour until it worked all
through the dough."
[34]Jesus spoke all these things to the crowd in parables; he did not say anything
to them without using a parable. [35]So was fulfilled what was spoken through
the prophet:

"I will open my mouth in parables,
I will utter things hidden since the creation of the world."[b]

The Parable of the Weeds Explained

[36]Then he left the crowd and went into the house. His disciples came to him
and said, "Explain to us the parable of the weeds in the field."
[37]He answered, "The one who sowed the good seed is the Son of Man. [38]The
field is the world, and the good seed stands for the people of the kingdom. The
weeds are the people of the evil one, [39]and the enemy who sows them is the devil.
The harvest is the end of the age, and the harvesters are angels.
[40]"As the weeds are pulled up and burned in the fire, so it will be at the end of
the age. [41]The Son of Man will send out his angels, and they will weed out of his
kingdom everything that causes sin and all who do evil. [42]They will throw them
into the blazing furnace, where there will be weeping and gnashing of teeth.
[43]Then the righteous will shine like the sun in the kingdom of their Father. Whoever has ears, let them hear.

The Parables of the Hidden Treasure and the Pearl

[44]"The kingdom of heaven is like treasure hidden in a field. When a man
found it, he hid it again, and then in his joy went and sold all he had and bought
that field.
[45]"Again, the kingdom of heaven is like a merchant looking for fine pearls.
[46]When he found one of great value, he went away and sold everything he had
and bought it.

The Parable of the Net

[47]"Once again, the kingdom of heaven is like a net that was let down into the
lake and caught all kinds of fish. [48]When it was full, the fishermen pulled it up on
the shore. Then they sat down and collected the good fish in baskets, but threw
the bad away. [49]This is how it will be at the end of the age. The angels will come
and separate the wicked from the righteous [50]and throw them into the blazing
furnace, where there will be weeping and gnashing of teeth.
[51]"Have you understood all these things?" Jesus asked.
"Yes," they replied.
[52]He said to them, "Therefore every teacher of the law who has become a disciple in the kingdom of heaven is like the owner of a house who brings out of his
storeroom new treasures as well as old."

---

[a] *33* Or about 27 kilograms [b] *35* Psalm 78:2

MATTHEW 13:1 – 50

JESUS AND HIS PARABLES

Jesus commonly taught the crowds and his followers through parables, which are stories that illustrate a moral or spiritual truth. In Matthew 13, Jesus told parables relating to soil, weeds, a mustard seed, yeast, hidden treasure, a pearl and a fishing net. Jesus' parables cover a spectrum of topics and truths, and they also represent the confirmation of a Messianic prophecy from Isaiah 6:9 – 10: "Go and tell this people: 'Be ever hearing, but never understanding; be ever seeing, but never perceiving.' Make the heart of this people calloused; make their ears dull and close their eyes. Otherwise they might see with their eyes, hear with their ears, understand with their hearts, and turn and be healed."

Jesus told parables to teach God's truth to those who were ready and willing to hear it, but he also knew there were people in his audience who would not understand his words because their hearts were calloused. At times, parables were Jesus' tools to reveal truth to the faithful and to conceal it from those who would object to it and seek to stop his ministry and mission.

Jesus used six of the seven parables in this chapter to describe the nature of the kingdom of heaven. The people who rejected Jesus' teaching because of their inability to understand it, including the Jewish religious leaders, only further blinded themselves to the spiritual nature of the kingdom of God. On the other hand, those who had ears to hear — including believers who read these stories today — receive a great blessing in knowing and understanding Jesus' truth.

As to the parables themselves, notice that even Jesus' disciples, the men who had left their jobs, businesses and families for the sake of this amazing teacher, misunderstood some of Jesus' parables (Mt 13:36). Jesus carefully and patiently explained to the disciples who sought to learn more. They asked for wisdom, and Jesus provided it (Jas 1:5) along with meaningful word pictures of the coming kingdom loaded with meaning and nuance. For believers today, these parables and teachings provide a rich picture of the kingdom as it exists and also as it is to come.

A Prophet Without Honor

[53]When Jesus had finished these parables, he moved on from there. [54]Coming to his hometown, he began teaching the people in their synagogue, and they were amazed. "Where did this man get this wisdom and these miraculous powers?" they asked. [55]"Isn't this the carpenter's son? Isn't his mother's name Mary, and aren't his brothers James, Joseph, Simon and Judas? [56]Aren't all his sisters with us? Where then did this man get all these things?" [57]And they took offense at him.

But Jesus said to them, "A prophet is not without honor except in his own town and in his own home."

[58]And he did not do many miracles there because of their lack of faith.

John the Baptist Beheaded

14 At that time Herod the tetrarch heard the reports about Jesus, [2]and he said to his attendants, "This is John the Baptist; he has risen from the dead! That is why miraculous powers are at work in him."

[3]Now Herod had arrested John and bound him and put him in prison because of Herodias, his brother Philip's wife, [4]for John had been saying to him: "It is not lawful for you to have her." [5]Herod wanted to kill John, but he was afraid of the people, because they considered John a prophet.

[6]On Herod's birthday the daughter of Herodias danced for the guests and pleased Herod so much [7]that he promised with an oath to give her whatever she asked. [8]Prompted by her mother, she said, "Give me here on a platter the head of John the Baptist." [9]The king was distressed, but because of his oaths and his dinner guests, he ordered that her request be granted [10]and had John beheaded in the prison. [11]His head was brought in on a platter and given to the girl, who carried it to her mother. [12]John's disciples came and took his body and buried it. Then they went and told Jesus.

Jesus Feeds the Five Thousand

[13]When Jesus heard what had happened, he withdrew by boat privately to a solitary place. Hearing of this, the crowds followed him on foot from the towns. [14]When Jesus landed and saw a large crowd, he had compassion on them and healed their sick.

[15]As evening approached, the disciples came to him and said, "This is a remote place, and it's already getting late. Send the crowds away, so they can go to the villages and buy themselves some food."

[16]Jesus replied, "They do not need to go away. You give them something to eat."

[17]"We have here only five loaves of bread and two fish," they answered.

[18]"Bring them here to me," he said. [19]And he directed the people to sit down on the grass. Taking the five loaves and the two fish and looking up to heaven, he gave thanks and broke the loaves. Then he gave them to the disciples, and the disciples gave them to the people. [20]They all ate and were satisfied, and the disciples picked up twelve basketfuls of broken pieces that were left over. [21]The number of those who ate was about five thousand men, besides women and children.

Jesus Walks on the Water

[22]Immediately Jesus made the disciples get into the boat and go on ahead of him to the other side, while he dismissed the crowd. [23]After he had dismissed them, he went up on a mountainside by himself to pray. Later that night, he was there alone, [24]and the boat was already a considerable distance from land, buffeted by the waves because the wind was against it.

[25]Shortly before dawn Jesus went out to them, walking on the lake. [26]When the disciples saw him walking on the lake, they were terrified. "It's a ghost," they said, and cried out in fear.

[27]But Jesus immediately said to them: "Take courage! It is I. Don't be afraid."

MATTHEW 14:13–21

FEEDING THE FIVE THOUSAND

Jesus' feeding of the five thousand is the only pre-crucifixion miracle recorded in all four Gospels, and it is significant for a multitude of reasons. Through this miracle, Jesus fulfilled the expectation of those looking forward to a new prophet after Moses (Jn 1:21; Ac 3:22; 7:37). While Moses was their prophet-leader, the Israelites received manna from heaven. Jesus' provision of bread parallels the miracle that the Israelites experienced under Moses and thus fulfills Deuteronomy 18:15 (quoted twice in Acts, referred to above). Also, Jesus showed that he could supply both the physical and the spiritual "daily bread" requested in the prayer in Matthew 6:11. Finally, Jesus showed that he is the Messiah who will provide the coming Messianic banquet (Ps 132:15; Isa 25:6; Mt 22:1–14; 26:29). Not only does the feeding of the five thousand preview that kingdom banquet, but it also provides a wholesome contrast to the degenerate banquet held by Herod in Matthew 14:1–12. In giving the people physical bread, Jesus showed that he was the compassionate provider that his people needed.

28“Lord, if it’s you,” Peter replied, “tell me to come to you on the water.”

29“Come,” he said.

Then Peter got down out of the boat, walked on the water and came toward Jesus. 30But when he saw the wind, he was afraid and, beginning to sink, cried out, “Lord, save me!”

31Immediately Jesus reached out his hand and caught him. “You of little faith,” he said, “why did you doubt?”

32And when they climbed into the boat, the wind died down. 33Then those who were in the boat worshiped him, saying, “Truly you are the Son of God.”

34When they had crossed over, they landed at Gennesaret. 35And when the men of that place recognized Jesus, they sent word to all the surrounding country. People brought all their sick to him 36and begged him to let the sick just touch the edge of his cloak, and all who touched it were healed.

That Which Defiles

15 Then some Pharisees and teachers of the law came to Jesus from Jerusalem and asked, 2“Why do your disciples break the tradition of the elders? They don’t wash their hands before they eat!”

3Jesus replied, “And why do you break the command of God for the sake of your tradition? 4For God said, ‘Honor your father and mother’[a] and ‘Anyone who curses their father or mother is to be put to death.’[b] 5But you say that if anyone declares that what might have been used to help their father or mother is ‘devoted to God,’ 6they are not to ‘honor their father or mother’ with it. Thus you nullify the word of God for the sake of your tradition. 7You hypocrites! Isaiah was right when he prophesied about you:

8“ ‘These people honor me with their lips,
but their hearts are far from me.
9They worship me in vain;
their teachings are merely human rules.’[c]”

10Jesus called the crowd to him and said, “Listen and understand. 11What goes into someone’s mouth does not defile them, but what comes out of their mouth, that is what defiles them.”

12Then the disciples came to him and asked, “Do you know that the Pharisees were offended when they heard this?”

13He replied, “Every plant that my heavenly Father has not planted will be pulled up by the roots. 14Leave them; they are blind guides.[d] If the blind lead the blind, both will fall into a pit.”

15Peter said, “Explain the parable to us.”

16“Are you still so dull?” Jesus asked them. 17“Don’t you see that whatever enters the mouth goes into the stomach and then out of the body? 18But the things that come out of a person’s mouth come from the heart, and these defile them. 19For out of the heart come evil thoughts — murder, adultery, sexual immorality, theft, false testimony, slander. 20These are what defile a person; but eating with unwashed hands does not defile them.”

The Faith of a Canaanite Woman

21Leaving that place, Jesus withdrew to the region of Tyre and Sidon. 22A Canaanite woman from that vicinity came to him, crying out, “Lord, Son of David, have mercy on me! My daughter is demon-possessed and suffering terribly.”

23Jesus did not answer a word. So his disciples came to him and urged him, “Send her away, for she keeps crying out after us.”

24He answered, “I was sent only to the lost sheep of Israel.”

25The woman came and knelt before him. “Lord, help me!” she said.

26He replied, “It is not right to take the children’s bread and toss it to the dogs.”

[a] *4* Exodus 20:12; Deut. 5:16 [b] *4* Exodus 21:17; Lev. 20:9 [c] *9* Isaiah 29:13 [d] *14* Some manuscripts *blind guides of the blind*

MATTHEW 15:1 – 9

TRADITIONS OF THE ELDERS

The tradition of the elders referred to in verse two was not the Law of Moses. It was the oral tradition that had had been built up over the centuries and was based on human interpretations of the law. But these rules were not of God; rather they were simply traditions invented by humans. Jesus used this opportunity to expose these men in the hypocritical way in which they lived their lives. They cared more about the ceremonial washing of hands than they did about faithfully obeying God’s commands. God cares more about the hearts of his followers than any human tradition (1Sa 16:7).

27“Yes it is, Lord,” she said. “Even the dogs eat the crumbs that fall from their master’s table.”

28Then Jesus said to her, “Woman, you have great faith! Your request is granted.” And her daughter was healed at that moment.

Jesus Feeds the Four Thousand

29Jesus left there and went along the Sea of Galilee. Then he went up on a mountainside and sat down. 30Great crowds came to him, bringing the lame, the blind, the crippled, the mute and many others, and laid them at his feet; and he healed them. 31The people were amazed when they saw the mute speaking, the crippled made well, the lame walking and the blind seeing. And they praised the God of Israel.

32Jesus called his disciples to him and said, “I have compassion for these people; they have already been with me three days and have nothing to eat. I do not want to send them away hungry, or they may collapse on the way.”

33His disciples answered, “Where could we get enough bread in this remote place to feed such a crowd?”

34“How many loaves do you have?” Jesus asked.

“Seven,” they replied, “and a few small fish.”

35He told the crowd to sit down on the ground. 36Then he took the seven loaves and the fish, and when he had given thanks, he broke them and gave them to the disciples, and they in turn to the people. 37They all ate and were satisfied. Afterward the disciples picked up seven basketfuls of broken pieces that were left over. 38The number of those who ate was four thousand men, besides women and children. 39After Jesus had sent the crowd away, he got into the boat and went to the vicinity of Magadan.

The Demand for a Sign

16 The Pharisees and Sadducees came to Jesus and tested him by asking him to show them a sign from heaven.

2He replied, “When evening comes, you say, ‘It will be fair weather, for the sky is red,’ 3and in the morning, ‘Today it will be stormy, for the sky is red and overcast.’ You know how to interpret the appearance of the sky, but you cannot interpret the signs of the times.[a] 4A wicked and adulterous generation looks for a sign, but none will be given it except the sign of Jonah.” Jesus then left them and went away.

The Yeast of the Pharisees and Sadducees

5When they went across the lake, the disciples forgot to take bread. 6“Be careful,” Jesus said to them. “Be on your guard against the yeast of the Pharisees and Sadducees.”

7They discussed this among themselves and said, “It is because we didn’t bring any bread.”

8Aware of their discussion, Jesus asked, “You of little faith, why are you talking among yourselves about having no bread? 9Do you still not understand? Don’t you remember the five loaves for the five thousand, and how many basketfuls you gathered? 10Or the seven loaves for the four thousand, and how many basketfuls you gathered? 11How is it you don’t understand that I was not talking to you about bread? But be on your guard against the yeast of the Pharisees and Sadducees.” 12Then they understood that he was not telling them to guard against the yeast used in bread, but against the teaching of the Pharisees and Sadducees.

Peter Declares That Jesus Is the Messiah

13When Jesus came to the region of Caesarea Philippi, he asked his disciples, “Who do people say the Son of Man is?”

---

[a] 2,3 Some early manuscripts do not have *When evening comes . . . of the times.*

14They replied, "Some say John the Baptist; others say Elijah; and still others, Jeremiah or one of the prophets."

15"But what about you?" he asked. "Who do you say I am?"

16Simon Peter answered, "You are the Messiah, the Son of the living God."

17Jesus replied, "Blessed are you, Simon son of Jonah, for this was not revealed to you by flesh and blood, but by my Father in heaven. 18And I tell you that you are Peter,[a] and on this rock I will build my church, and the gates of Hades[b] will not overcome it. 19I will give you the keys of the kingdom of heaven; whatever you bind on earth will be[c] bound in heaven, and whatever you loose on earth will be[c] loosed in heaven." 20Then he ordered his disciples not to tell anyone that he was the Messiah.

Jesus Predicts His Death

21From that time on Jesus began to explain to his disciples that he must go to Jerusalem and suffer many things at the hands of the elders, the chief priests and the teachers of the law, and that he must be killed and on the third day be raised to life.

22Peter took him aside and began to rebuke him. "Never, Lord!" he said. "This shall never happen to you!"

23Jesus turned and said to Peter, "Get behind me, Satan! You are a stumbling block to me; you do not have in mind the concerns of God, but merely human concerns."

24Then Jesus said to his disciples, "Whoever wants to be my disciple must deny themselves and take up their cross and follow me. 25For whoever wants to save their life[d] will lose it, but whoever loses their life for me will find it. 26What good will it be for someone to gain the whole world, yet forfeit their soul? Or what can anyone give in exchange for their soul? 27For the Son of Man is going to come in his Father's glory with his angels, and then he will reward each person according to what they have done.

28"Truly I tell you, some who are standing here will not taste death before they see the Son of Man coming in his kingdom."

The Transfiguration

17 After six days Jesus took with him Peter, James and John the brother of James, and led them up a high mountain by themselves. 2There he was transfigured before them. His face shone like the sun, and his clothes became as white as the light. 3Just then there appeared before them Moses and Elijah, talking with Jesus.

4Peter said to Jesus, "Lord, it is good for us to be here. If you wish, I will put up three shelters — one for you, one for Moses and one for Elijah."

5While he was still speaking, a bright cloud covered them, and a voice from the cloud said, "This is my Son, whom I love; with him I am well pleased. Listen to him!"

6When the disciples heard this, they fell facedown to the ground, terrified. 7But Jesus came and touched them. "Get up," he said. "Don't be afraid." 8When they looked up, they saw no one except Jesus.

9As they were coming down the mountain, Jesus instructed them, "Don't tell anyone what you have seen, until the Son of Man has been raised from the dead."

10The disciples asked him, "Why then do the teachers of the law say that Elijah must come first?"

11Jesus replied, "To be sure, Elijah comes and will restore all things. 12But I tell you, Elijah has already come, and they did not recognize him, but have done to him everything they wished. In the same way the Son of Man is going to suffer at their hands." 13Then the disciples understood that he was talking to them about John the Baptist.

---

[a] *18* The Greek word for *Peter* means *rock*. [b] *18* That is, the realm of the dead
[c] *19* Or *will have been* [d] *25* The Greek word means either *life* or *soul*; also in verse 26.

MATTHEW 16:13 – 17

WHO DO YOU SAY I AM?

A critically important question Jesus asks his followers is: "Who do you say I am?" (Mt 16:15). Jesus knew that a proper understanding of who he is would lead to a right relationship with God. He first asked the disciples to tell him who other people thought he was, then who they thought he was. Peter answered by professing what millions have come to acknowledge throughout the centuries: "You are the Messiah, the Son of the living God" (v. 16). This answer could not be a more accurate description of who Jesus is. And Peter was only beginning to find out what his statement of belief would mean not only to his life, but to the life of the church that Jesus would establish on the basis of his testimony (v. 18).

The faith of any believer today can be determined by their answer to this question. True believers are those who say that Jesus is the Christ and the Son of God, and anyone who says otherwise does not fully understand the character and nature of Jesus. Some say that Jesus was simply a great moral teacher or a prophet, but Jesus never claimed to be anything other than the Son of God. When theories abounded about who he might be, he acknowledged that Peter alone had a correct understanding of who he was.

For believers today, it is crucial that they understand the power and truth of Peter's proclamation of Jesus as the Son of God. To say that Jesus was, and is, the Son of God is to say that he is the truth and the one way to enter into a right relationship with God. Through Jesus, believers are able to experience everything that comes with knowing God and having a relationship with his Son — grace, peace, mercy in this life, and eternity with him in the next.

Jesus Heals a Demon-Possessed Boy

[14]When they came to the crowd, a man approached Jesus and knelt before
him. [15]"Lord, have mercy on my son," he said. "He has seizures and is suffering
greatly. He often falls into the fire or into the water. [16]I brought him to your disciples, but they could not heal him."

[17]"You unbelieving and perverse generation," Jesus replied, "how long shall
I stay with you? How long shall I put up with you? Bring the boy here to me."
[18]Jesus rebuked the demon, and it came out of the boy, and he was healed at
that moment.

[19]Then the disciples came to Jesus in private and asked, "Why couldn't we
drive it out?"

[20]He replied, "Because you have so little faith. Truly I tell you, if you have faith
as small as a mustard seed, you can say to this mountain, 'Move from here to
there,' and it will move. Nothing will be impossible for you." [21][a]

Jesus Predicts His Death a Second Time

[22]When they came together in Galilee, he said to them, "The Son of Man is going to be delivered into the hands of men. [23]They will kill him, and on the third
day he will be raised to life." And the disciples were filled with grief.

The Temple Tax

[24]After Jesus and his disciples arrived in Capernaum, the collectors of the
two-drachma temple tax came to Peter and asked, "Doesn't your teacher pay
the temple tax?"

[25]"Yes, he does," he replied.

When Peter came into the house, Jesus was the first to speak. "What do you
think, Simon?" he asked. "From whom do the kings of the earth collect duty and
taxes — from their own children or from others?"

[26]"From others," Peter answered.

"Then the children are exempt," Jesus said to him. [27]"But so that we may not
cause offense, go to the lake and throw out your line. Take the first fish you catch;
open its mouth and you will find a four-drachma coin. Take it and give it to them
for my tax and yours."

The Greatest in the Kingdom of Heaven

18 At that time the disciples came to Jesus and asked, "Who, then, is the
greatest in the kingdom of heaven?"

[2]He called a little child to him, and placed the child among them. [3]And he
said: "Truly I tell you, unless you change and become like little children, you will
never enter the kingdom of heaven. [4]Therefore, whoever takes the lowly position
of this child is the greatest in the kingdom of heaven. [5]And whoever welcomes
one such child in my name welcomes me.

Causing to Stumble

[6]"If anyone causes one of these little ones — those who believe in me — to
stumble, it would be better for them to have a large millstone hung around their
neck and to be drowned in the depths of the sea. [7]Woe to the world because of
the things that cause people to stumble! Such things must come, but woe to
the person through whom they come! [8]If your hand or your foot causes you to
stumble, cut it off and throw it away. It is better for you to enter life maimed or
crippled than to have two hands or two feet and be thrown into eternal fire.
[9]And if your eye causes you to stumble, gouge it out and throw it away. It is better for you to enter life with one eye than to have two eyes and be thrown into
the fire of hell.

[a] *21* Some manuscripts include here words similar to Mark 9:29.

MATTHEW 17:24–27

PAYING THE TEMPLE TAX

The temple tax was paid annually by every adult Jewish male over 20 years old to fund maintenance of the temple. This tax was based on Exodus 30:13 and amounted to two days' wages for a common laborer. Evidently, Jesus had not yet paid the tax, and the temple tax collector was following up. However, instead of speaking to Jesus, the tax collector spoke to Peter regarding his teacher's payment. Through the resulting conversation, Jesus showed that he (and his followers) are a part of a different kingdom, a heavenly kingdom. He does not live by the rules set by mankind but by the will of God the Father. However, not wanting to "cause offense," Jesus paid the temple tax, but he delivered it in a way that showed that he was the Son of God.

The Parable of the Wandering Sheep

10"See that you do not despise one of these little ones. For I tell you that their angels in heaven always see the face of my Father in heaven. [11][a]

12"What do you think? If a man owns a hundred sheep, and one of them wanders away, will he not leave the ninety-nine on the hills and go to look for the one that wandered off? 13And if he finds it, truly I tell you, he is happier about that one sheep than about the ninety-nine that did not wander off. 14In the same way your Father in heaven is not willing that any of these little ones should perish.

Dealing With Sin in the Church

15"If your brother or sister[b] sins,[c] go and point out their fault, just between the two of you. If they listen to you, you have won them over. 16But if they will not listen, take one or two others along, so that 'every matter may be established by the testimony of two or three witnesses.'[d] 17If they still refuse to listen, tell it to the church; and if they refuse to listen even to the church, treat them as you would a pagan or a tax collector.

18"Truly I tell you, whatever you bind on earth will be[e] bound in heaven, and whatever you loose on earth will be[e] loosed in heaven.

19"Again, truly I tell you that if two of you on earth agree about anything they ask for, it will be done for them by my Father in heaven. 20For where two or three gather in my name, there am I with them."

The Parable of the Unmerciful Servant

21Then Peter came to Jesus and asked, "Lord, how many times shall I forgive my brother or sister who sins against me? Up to seven times?"

22Jesus answered, "I tell you, not seven times, but seventy-seven times.[f]

23"Therefore, the kingdom of heaven is like a king who wanted to settle accounts with his servants. 24As he began the settlement, a man who owed him ten thousand bags of gold[g] was brought to him. 25Since he was not able to pay, the master ordered that he and his wife and his children and all that he had be sold to repay the debt.

26"At this the servant fell on his knees before him. 'Be patient with me,' he begged, 'and I will pay back everything.' 27The servant's master took pity on him, canceled the debt and let him go.

28"But when that servant went out, he found one of his fellow servants who owed him a hundred silver coins.[h] He grabbed him and began to choke him. 'Pay back what you owe me!' he demanded.

29"His fellow servant fell to his knees and begged him, 'Be patient with me, and I will pay it back.'

30"But he refused. Instead, he went off and had the man thrown into prison until he could pay the debt. 31When the other servants saw what had happened, they were outraged and went and told their master everything that had happened.

32"Then the master called the servant in. 'You wicked servant,' he said, 'I canceled all that debt of yours because you begged me to. 33Shouldn't you have had mercy on your fellow servant just as I had on you?' 34In anger his master handed him over to the jailers to be tortured, until he should pay back all he owed.

35"This is how my heavenly Father will treat each of you unless you forgive your brother or sister from your heart."

---

[a] *11* Some manuscripts include here the words of Luke 19:10. [b] *15* The Greek word for *brother or sister* (*adelphos*) refers here to a fellow disciple, whether man or woman; also in verses 21 and 35. [c] *15* Some manuscripts *sins against you* [d] *16* Deut. 19:15 [e] *18* Or *will have been* [f] *22* Or *seventy times seven* [g] *24* Greek *ten thousand talents*; a talent was worth about 20 years of a day laborer's wages. [h] *28* Greek *a hundred denarii*; a denarius was the usual daily wage of a day laborer (see 20:2).

Divorce

19 When Jesus had finished saying these things, he left Galilee and went into
the region of Judea to the other side of the Jordan. 2Large crowds followed
him, and he healed them there.
3Some Pharisees came to him to test him. They asked, "Is it lawful for a man
to divorce his wife for any and every reason?"
4"Haven't you read," he replied, "that at the beginning the Creator 'made them
male and female,'[a] 5and said, 'For this reason a man will leave his father and
mother and be united to his wife, and the two will become one flesh'[b]? 6So they
are no longer two, but one flesh. Therefore what God has joined together, let no
one separate."
7"Why then," they asked, "did Moses command that a man give his wife a certificate of divorce and send her away?"
8Jesus replied, "Moses permitted you to divorce your wives because your
hearts were hard. But it was not this way from the beginning. 9I tell you that anyone who divorces his wife, except for sexual immorality, and marries another
woman commits adultery."
10The disciples said to him, "If this is the situation between a husband and
wife, it is better not to marry."
11Jesus replied, "Not everyone can accept this word, but only those to whom
it has been given. 12For there are eunuchs who were born that way, and there
are eunuchs who have been made eunuchs by others—and there are those who
choose to live like eunuchs for the sake of the kingdom of heaven. The one who
can accept this should accept it."

The Little Children and Jesus

13Then people brought little children to Jesus for him to place his hands on
them and pray for them. But the disciples rebuked them.
14Jesus said, "Let the little children come to me, and do not hinder them, for
the kingdom of heaven belongs to such as these." 15When he had placed his
hands on them, he went on from there.

The Rich and the Kingdom of God

16Just then a man came up to Jesus and asked, "Teacher, what good thing must
I do to get eternal life?"
17"Why do you ask me about what is good?" Jesus replied. "There is only One
who is good. If you want to enter life, keep the commandments."
18"Which ones?" he inquired.
Jesus replied, "'You shall not murder, you shall not commit adultery, you shall
not steal, you shall not give false testimony, 19honor your father and mother,'[c]
and 'love your neighbor as yourself.'[d]"
20"All these I have kept," the young man said. "What do I still lack?"
21Jesus answered, "If you want to be perfect, go, sell your possessions and give
to the poor, and you will have treasure in heaven. Then come, follow me."
22When the young man heard this, he went away sad, because he had great
wealth.
23Then Jesus said to his disciples, "Truly I tell you, it is hard for someone who
is rich to enter the kingdom of heaven. 24Again I tell you, it is easier for a camel
to go through the eye of a needle than for someone who is rich to enter the kingdom of God."
25When the disciples heard this, they were greatly astonished and asked,
"Who then can be saved?"
26Jesus looked at them and said, "With man this is impossible, but with God
all things are possible."
27Peter answered him, "We have left everything to follow you! What then will
there be for us?"

[a] *4* Gen. 1:27 [b] *5* Gen. 2:24 [c] *19* Exodus 20:12-16; Deut. 5:16-20 [d] *19* Lev. 19:18

MATTHEW 19:16–26

WEALTH AND THE KINGDOM OF GOD

This story's application is not to imply that believers need to give away all of their possessions in order to get into heaven. Rather, it is intended to show that Jesus cared about the hearts of those who were following him. Knowing all things, he knew that this rich young man's heart was preoccupied with his wealth. So when he asked about eternal life, Jesus showed him that right standing with God flows from a pure heart. It is not enough merely to follow external standards. That sort of life tends to foster a spirit of self-righteousness. Followers of Jesus are expected to rely on Jesus alone as the one and only way to heaven, and to have a heart for God and his kingdom before all else (Mt 6:33).

[28]Jesus said to them, "Truly I tell you, at the renewal of all things, when the
Son of Man sits on his glorious throne, you who have followed me will also sit on
twelve thrones, judging the twelve tribes of Israel. [29]And everyone who has left
houses or brothers or sisters or father or mother or wife[a] or children or fields for
my sake will receive a hundred times as much and will inherit eternal life. [30]But
many who are first will be last, and many who are last will be first.

The Parable of the Workers in the Vineyard

20 "For the kingdom of heaven is like a landowner who went out early in the
morning to hire workers for his vineyard. [2]He agreed to pay them a denarius[b] for the day and sent them into his vineyard.
[3]"About nine in the morning he went out and saw others standing in the marketplace doing nothing. [4]He told them, 'You also go and work in my vineyard,
and I will pay you whatever is right.' [5]So they went.
"He went out again about noon and about three in the afternoon and did
the same thing. [6]About five in the afternoon he went out and found still others
standing around. He asked them, 'Why have you been standing here all day long
doing nothing?'
[7]" 'Because no one has hired us,' they answered.
"He said to them, 'You also go and work in my vineyard.'
[8]"When evening came, the owner of the vineyard said to his foreman, 'Call
the workers and pay them their wages, beginning with the last ones hired and
going on to the first.'
[9]"The workers who were hired about five in the afternoon came and each received a denarius. [10]So when those came who were hired first, they expected to
receive more. But each one of them also received a denarius. [11]When they received it, they began to grumble against the landowner. [12]'These who were hired
last worked only one hour,' they said, 'and you have made them equal to us who
have borne the burden of the work and the heat of the day.'
[13]"But he answered one of them, 'I am not being unfair to you, friend. Didn't
you agree to work for a denarius? [14]Take your pay and go. I want to give the one
who was hired last the same as I gave you. [15]Don't I have the right to do what I
want with my own money? Or are you envious because I am generous?'
[16]"So the last will be first, and the first will be last."

Jesus Predicts His Death a Third Time

[17]Now Jesus was going up to Jerusalem. On the way, he took the Twelve aside
and said to them, [18]"We are going up to Jerusalem, and the Son of Man will be
delivered over to the chief priests and the teachers of the law. They will condemn
him to death [19]and will hand him over to the Gentiles to be mocked and flogged
and crucified. On the third day he will be raised to life!"

A Mother's Request

[20]Then the mother of Zebedee's sons came to Jesus with her sons and, kneeling down, asked a favor of him.
[21]"What is it you want?" he asked.
She said, "Grant that one of these two sons of mine may sit at your right and
the other at your left in your kingdom."
[22]"You don't know what you are asking," Jesus said to them. "Can you drink
the cup I am going to drink?"
"We can," they answered.
[23]Jesus said to them, "You will indeed drink from my cup, but to sit at my right
or left is not for me to grant. These places belong to those for whom they have
been prepared by my Father."
[24]When the ten heard about this, they were indignant with the two brothers.

MATTHEW 20:20–28

SERVANTHOOD

This exchange provides an interesting view on Jesus' perception of what it takes to be able to sit in the seat of power. Here, two disciples were seeking to advance their own status. James and John were the ones asking, but the other ten were indignant as well, so all of the disciples' attitudes are on display in this story. Each of the twelve wanted to occupy seats of authority and power in heaven. However, they did not understand that those seats required partnership in suffering (v. 22). Jesus' "cup" was not only that he, as God, allowed himself to become human, but also that he was to be crucified on the cross as the perfect, sinless sacrifice for the sins of humankind (Php 2:6–9). The "cup" for James and John would be one of suffering for the kingdom. As Jesus often did, he was emphasizing that one must be willing to sacrifice their own comfort and livelihood in order to follow him.

[a] 29 Some manuscripts do not have *or wife*. [b] 2 A denarius was the usual daily wage of a day laborer.

25 Jesus called them together and said, "You know that the rulers of the Gentiles
lord it over them, and their high officials exercise authority over them. 26 Not so
with you. Instead, whoever wants to become great among you must be your servant, 27 and whoever wants to be first must be your slave— 28 just as the Son of Man
did not come to be served, but to serve, and to give his life as a ransom for many."

Two Blind Men Receive Sight

29 As Jesus and his disciples were leaving Jericho, a large crowd followed him.
30 Two blind men were sitting by the roadside, and when they heard that Jesus
was going by, they shouted, "Lord, Son of David, have mercy on us!"

31 The crowd rebuked them and told them to be quiet, but they shouted all the
louder, "Lord, Son of David, have mercy on us!"

32 Jesus stopped and called them. "What do you want me to do for you?" he
asked.

33 "Lord," they answered, "we want our sight."

34 Jesus had compassion on them and touched their eyes. Immediately they
received their sight and followed him.

Jesus Comes to Jerusalem as King

21 As they approached Jerusalem and came to Bethphage on the Mount of
Olives, Jesus sent two disciples, 2 saying to them, "Go to the village ahead
of you, and at once you will find a donkey tied there, with her colt by her. Untie
them and bring them to me. 3 If anyone says anything to you, say that the Lord
needs them, and he will send them right away."

4 This took place to fulfill what was spoken through the prophet:

5 "Say to Daughter Zion,
'See, your king comes to you,
gentle and riding on a donkey,
and on a colt, the foal of a donkey.'"[a]

6 The disciples went and did as Jesus had instructed them. 7 They brought the
donkey and the colt and placed their cloaks on them for Jesus to sit on. 8 A very
large crowd spread their cloaks on the road, while others cut branches from the
trees and spread them on the road. 9 The crowds that went ahead of him and
those that followed shouted,

"Hosanna[b] to the Son of David!"

"Blessed is he who comes in the name of the Lord!"[c]

"Hosanna[b] in the highest heaven!"

10 When Jesus entered Jerusalem, the whole city was stirred and asked, "Who
is this?"

11 The crowds answered, "This is Jesus, the prophet from Nazareth in Galilee."

Jesus at the Temple

12 Jesus entered the temple courts and drove out all who were buying and selling there. He overturned the tables of the money changers and the benches of
those selling doves. 13 "It is written," he said to them, "'My house will be called a
house of prayer,'[d] but you are making it 'a den of robbers.'[e]"

14 The blind and the lame came to him at the temple, and he healed them.
15 But when the chief priests and the teachers of the law saw the wonderful things
he did and the children shouting in the temple courts, "Hosanna to the Son of
David," they were indignant.

16 "Do you hear what these children are saying?" they asked him.

"Yes," replied Jesus, "have you never read,

---

[a] 5 Zech. 9:9 [b] 9 A Hebrew expression meaning "Save!" which became an exclamation of praise; also in verse 15 [c] 9 Psalm 118:25,26 [d] 13 Isaiah 56:7 [e] 13 Jer. 7:11

JESUS COMES TO JERUSALEM AS KING

Jesus' coming to Jerusalem riding on a donkey, to the accolades and praise of the gathered crowd, fulfilled the Old Testament prophecies of Jesus as King. Isaiah 62:11 calls for "Daughter Zion" to watch for this King, and Zechariah 9:9 depicts the King "lowly and riding on a donkey, on a colt, the foal of a donkey." While most royal processions feature incredible extravagance, Jesus humbly entered town on a simple donkey. While horses were ridden during times of war, rulers rode donkeys during times of peace as a sign of humility toward the people (1Ki 1:38 – 40). Here, Jesus exemplified the peaceful return of a king to Jerusalem. By riding on a donkey, he showed that he came to bring grace and not judgment. Also, it is significant that Jesus rode a colt, which is a young and untrained donkey. Normally, it would be incredibly difficult for someone to ride an unbroken animal through a crowded and chaotic scene with an unfamiliar burden on its back. But this was Jesus, Creator of the world!

This scene was nothing less than a royal procession (2Ki 9:13), yet up until this point, Jesus had consistently avoided such displays (Mt 8:4; 9:30; 12:16). However, he was now ready to present himself publicly as the Messiah and King. This was Jesus' last trip to Jerusalem, and he chose to enter in such a way as to leave no doubt that he was the promised Messiah who had come to save the nation. No one in the city could possibly miss the procession or the prophecy-fulfilling reference Jesus' entry conveyed.

" 'From the lips of children and infants
you, Lord, have called forth your praise'[a]?"

17 And he left them and went out of the city to Bethany, where he spent the
night.

Jesus Curses a Fig Tree

18 Early in the morning, as Jesus was on his way back to the city, he was hungry. 19 Seeing a fig tree by the road, he went up to it but found nothing on it except
leaves. Then he said to it, "May you never bear fruit again!" Immediately the
tree withered.

20 When the disciples saw this, they were amazed. "How did the fig tree wither
so quickly?" they asked.

21 Jesus replied, "Truly I tell you, if you have faith and do not doubt, not only
can you do what was done to the fig tree, but also you can say to this mountain,
'Go, throw yourself into the sea,' and it will be done. 22 If you believe, you will receive whatever you ask for in prayer."

The Authority of Jesus Questioned

23 Jesus entered the temple courts, and, while he was teaching, the chief
priests and the elders of the people came to him. "By what authority are you doing these things?" they asked. "And who gave you this authority?"

24 Jesus replied, "I will also ask you one question. If you answer me, I will tell
you by what authority I am doing these things. 25 John's baptism — where did it
come from? Was it from heaven, or of human origin?"

They discussed it among themselves and said, "If we say, 'From heaven,' he
will ask, 'Then why didn't you believe him?' 26 But if we say, 'Of human origin' —
we are afraid of the people, for they all hold that John was a prophet."

27 So they answered Jesus, "We don't know."

Then he said, "Neither will I tell you by what authority I am doing these things.

The Parable of the Two Sons

28 "What do you think? There was a man who had two sons. He went to the first
and said, 'Son, go and work today in the vineyard.'

29 " 'I will not,' he answered, but later he changed his mind and went.

30 "Then the father went to the other son and said the same thing. He answered, 'I will, sir,' but he did not go.

31 "Which of the two did what his father wanted?"

"The first," they answered.

Jesus said to them, "Truly I tell you, the tax collectors and the prostitutes are
entering the kingdom of God ahead of you. 32 For John came to you to show you
the way of righteousness, and you did not believe him, but the tax collectors and
the prostitutes did. And even after you saw this, you did not repent and believe
him.

The Parable of the Tenants

33 "Listen to another parable: There was a landowner who planted a vineyard. He put a wall around it, dug a winepress in it and built a watchtower.
Then he rented the vineyard to some farmers and moved to another place.
34 When the harvest time approached, he sent his servants to the tenants to
collect his fruit.

35 "The tenants seized his servants; they beat one, killed another, and stoned
a third. 36 Then he sent other servants to them, more than the first time, and the
tenants treated them the same way. 37 Last of all, he sent his son to them. 'They
will respect my son,' he said.

38 "But when the tenants saw the son, they said to each other, 'This is the heir.

---

[a] *16* Psalm 8:2 (see Septuagint)

Come, let's kill him and take his inheritance.' 39So they took him and threw him out of the vineyard and killed him.

40"Therefore, when the owner of the vineyard comes, what will he do to those tenants?"

41"He will bring those wretches to a wretched end," they replied, "and he will rent the vineyard to other tenants, who will give him his share of the crop at harvest time."

42Jesus said to them, "Have you never read in the Scriptures:

"'The stone the builders rejected
has become the cornerstone;
the Lord has done this,
and it is marvelous in our eyes'[a]?

43"Therefore I tell you that the kingdom of God will be taken away from you and given to a people who will produce its fruit. 44Anyone who falls on this stone will be broken to pieces; anyone on whom it falls will be crushed."[b]

45When the chief priests and the Pharisees heard Jesus' parables, they knew he was talking about them. 46They looked for a way to arrest him, but they were afraid of the crowd because the people held that he was a prophet.

The Parable of the Wedding Banquet

22 Jesus spoke to them again in parables, saying: 2"The kingdom of heaven is like a king who prepared a wedding banquet for his son. 3He sent his servants to those who had been invited to the banquet to tell them to come, but they refused to come.

4"Then he sent some more servants and said, 'Tell those who have been invited that I have prepared my dinner: My oxen and fattened cattle have been butchered, and everything is ready. Come to the wedding banquet.'

5"But they paid no attention and went off—one to his field, another to his business. 6The rest seized his servants, mistreated them and killed them. 7The king was enraged. He sent his army and destroyed those murderers and burned their city.

8"Then he said to his servants, 'The wedding banquet is ready, but those I invited did not deserve to come. 9So go to the street corners and invite to the banquet anyone you find.' 10So the servants went out into the streets and gathered all the people they could find, the bad as well as the good, and the wedding hall was filled with guests.

11"But when the king came in to see the guests, he noticed a man there who was not wearing wedding clothes. 12He asked, 'How did you get in here without wedding clothes, friend?' The man was speechless.

13"Then the king told the attendants, 'Tie him hand and foot, and throw him outside, into the darkness, where there will be weeping and gnashing of teeth.'

14"For many are invited, but few are chosen."

Paying the Imperial Tax to Caesar

15Then the Pharisees went out and laid plans to trap him in his words. 16They sent their disciples to him along with the Herodians. "Teacher," they said, "we know that you are a man of integrity and that you teach the way of God in accordance with the truth. You aren't swayed by others, because you pay no attention to who they are. 17Tell us then, what is your opinion? Is it right to pay the imperial tax[c] to Caesar or not?"

18But Jesus, knowing their evil intent, said, "You hypocrites, why are you trying to trap me? 19Show me the coin used for paying the tax." They brought him a denarius, 20and he asked them, "Whose image is this? And whose inscription?"

[a] *42* Psalm 118:22,23 [b] *44* Some manuscripts do not have verse 44. [c] *17* A special tax levied on subject peoples, not on Roman citizens

MATTHEW 22:1–14

THE WEDDING FEAST

When families planned Jewish weddings, they sent out two invitations (similar to our "save-the-date" mailings that sometimes come before the actual invitation). In this instance, the first invitation portrays the ministry of John the Baptist. He told people to repent and prepare, for the kingdom of God was coming (Mt 3:2). The indifferent response describes Israel—specifically, the religious authorities—at the time of Jesus' earthly ministry. They ignored John's call to repent, and they opposed the arrival of the second invitation as well in the ministry of Jesus. But God is in the business of drawing people to himself, so the king in the story still instructs his servants to invite others to attend his wedding. Those who accept these gracious invitations and are truly prepared to engage in this banquet as citizens of the kingdom (which the religious leaders were not, 22:11–13) are welcomed in. The point of this parable is to portray how God shows grace in extending invitations to his kingdom while at the same time mandating requirements for entrance.

21“Caesar’s,” they replied.

Then he said to them, “So give back to Caesar what is Caesar’s, and to God what is God’s.”

22When they heard this, they were amazed. So they left him and went away.

Marriage at the Resurrection

23That same day the Sadducees, who say there is no resurrection, came to him with a question. 24“Teacher,” they said, “Moses told us that if a man dies without having children, his brother must marry the widow and raise up offspring for him. 25Now there were seven brothers among us. The first one married and died, and since he had no children, he left his wife to his brother. 26The same thing happened to the second and third brother, right on down to the seventh. 27Finally, the woman died. 28Now then, at the resurrection, whose wife will she be of the seven, since all of them were married to her?”

29Jesus replied, “You are in error because you do not know the Scriptures or the power of God. 30At the resurrection people will neither marry nor be given in marriage; they will be like the angels in heaven. 31But about the resurrection of the dead — have you not read what God said to you, 32‘I am the God of Abraham, the God of Isaac, and the God of Jacob’[a]? He is not the God of the dead but of the living.”

33When the crowds heard this, they were astonished at his teaching.

The Greatest Commandment

34Hearing that Jesus had silenced the Sadducees, the Pharisees got together. 35One of them, an expert in the law, tested him with this question: 36“Teacher, which is the greatest commandment in the Law?”

37Jesus replied: “ ‘Love the Lord your God with all your heart and with all your soul and with all your mind.’[b] 38This is the first and greatest commandment. 39And the second is like it: ‘Love your neighbor as yourself.’[c] 40All the Law and the Prophets hang on these two commandments.”

Whose Son Is the Messiah?

41While the Pharisees were gathered together, Jesus asked them, 42“What do you think about the Messiah? Whose son is he?”

“The son of David,” they replied.

43He said to them, “How is it then that David, speaking by the Spirit, calls him ‘Lord’? For he says,

44“ ‘The Lord said to my Lord:
“Sit at my right hand
until I put your enemies
under your feet.” ’[d]

45If then David calls him ‘Lord,’ how can he be his son?” 46No one could say a word in reply, and from that day on no one dared to ask him any more questions.

A Warning Against Hypocrisy

23 Then Jesus said to the crowds and to his disciples: 2“The teachers of the law and the Pharisees sit in Moses’ seat. 3So you must be careful to do everything they tell you. But do not do what they do, for they do not practice what they preach. 4They tie up heavy, cumbersome loads and put them on other people’s shoulders, but they themselves are not willing to lift a finger to move them.

5“Everything they do is done for people to see: They make their phylacteries[e] wide and the tassels on their garments long; 6they love the place of honor at banquets and the most important seats in the synagogues; 7they love to be greeted with respect in the marketplaces and to be called ‘Rabbi’ by others.

[a] 32 Exodus 3:6 [b] 37 Deut. 6:5 [c] 39 Lev. 19:18 [d] 44 Psalm 110:1 [e] 5 That is, boxes containing Scripture verses, worn on forehead and arm

MATTHEW 23:1 – 39

HYPOCRISY

Throughout his ministry, Jesus consistently confronted hypocrisy, especially in the Jewish religious leaders of his day. Chapter 23 includes Jesus’ angry condemnation of those who were much more concerned about securing their power base than they were about bringing their followers closer to God. The rules that they forced on others were manmade responses to their study of the law, and while they required strict adherence to those rules, they themselves did not practice what they preached (v. 4). Notice the language with which the perfect, sinless Son of God addressed them: lazy (v. 4), prideful (v. 6), hypocrites (vv. 25,27,29), blind (v. 26), “full of hypocrisy and wickedness” (v. 28), deluded (v. 30), self-incriminating (v. 31), hell-bound vipers (v. 33), murderers (v. 34), and condemned because of their blood-guilt (v. 35). Jesus’ righteous indignation burned against these self-important men who were leading others astray. Their devotion was not to God but to a set of rules they held over the people beneath them, and Jesus was not shy to point out the contradiction that manifested itself in their daily lives. In contrast, Jesus lived without any misalignment between his heart and his actions. He lived with perfect integrity in service to God, and believers are called to desire to be like him and share his mindset (1Co 2:16).

[8]“But you are not to be called ‘Rabbi,’ for you have one Teacher, and you are all brothers. [9]And do not call anyone on earth ‘father,’ for you have one Father, and he is in heaven. [10]Nor are you to be called instructors, for you have one Instructor, the Messiah. [11]The greatest among you will be your servant. [12]For those who exalt themselves will be humbled, and those who humble themselves will be exalted.

Seven Woes on the Teachers of the Law and the Pharisees

[13]“Woe to you, teachers of the law and Pharisees, you hypocrites! You shut the door of the kingdom of heaven in people’s faces. You yourselves do not enter, nor will you let those enter who are trying to. [14][a]

[15]“Woe to you, teachers of the law and Pharisees, you hypocrites! You travel over land and sea to win a single convert, and when you have succeeded, you make them twice as much a child of hell as you are.

[16]“Woe to you, blind guides! You say, ‘If anyone swears by the temple, it means nothing; but anyone who swears by the gold of the temple is bound by that oath.’ [17]You blind fools! Which is greater: the gold, or the temple that makes the gold sacred? [18]You also say, ‘If anyone swears by the altar, it means nothing; but anyone who swears by the gift on the altar is bound by that oath.’ [19]You blind men! Which is greater: the gift, or the altar that makes the gift sacred? [20]Therefore, anyone who swears by the altar swears by it and by everything on it. [21]And anyone who swears by the temple swears by it and by the one who dwells in it. [22]And anyone who swears by heaven swears by God’s throne and by the one who sits on it.

[23]“Woe to you, teachers of the law and Pharisees, you hypocrites! You give a tenth of your spices — mint, dill and cumin. But you have neglected the more important matters of the law — justice, mercy and faithfulness. You should have practiced the latter, without neglecting the former. [24]You blind guides! You strain out a gnat but swallow a camel.

[25]“Woe to you, teachers of the law and Pharisees, you hypocrites! You clean the outside of the cup and dish, but inside they are full of greed and self-indulgence. [26]Blind Pharisee! First clean the inside of the cup and dish, and then the outside also will be clean.

[27]“Woe to you, teachers of the law and Pharisees, you hypocrites! You are like whitewashed tombs, which look beautiful on the outside but on the inside are full of the bones of the dead and everything unclean. [28]In the same way, on the outside you appear to people as righteous but on the inside you are full of hypocrisy and wickedness.

[29]“Woe to you, teachers of the law and Pharisees, you hypocrites! You build tombs for the prophets and decorate the graves of the righteous. [30]And you say, ‘If we had lived in the days of our ancestors, we would not have taken part with them in shedding the blood of the prophets.’ [31]So you testify against yourselves that you are the descendants of those who murdered the prophets. [32]Go ahead, then, and complete what your ancestors started!

[33]“You snakes! You brood of vipers! How will you escape being condemned to hell? [34]Therefore I am sending you prophets and sages and teachers. Some of them you will kill and crucify; others you will flog in your synagogues and pursue from town to town. [35]And so upon you will come all the righteous blood that has been shed on earth, from the blood of righteous Abel to the blood of Zechariah son of Berekiah, whom you murdered between the temple and the altar. [36]Truly I tell you, all this will come on this generation.

[37]“Jerusalem, Jerusalem, you who kill the prophets and stone those sent to you, how often I have longed to gather your children together, as a hen gathers her chicks under her wings, and you were not willing. [38]Look, your house is left to you desolate. [39]For I tell you, you will not see me again until you say, ‘Blessed is he who comes in the name of the Lord.’[b]”

---

[a] *14* Some manuscripts include here words similar to Mark 12:40 and Luke 20:47.
[b] *39* Psalm 118:26

The Destruction of the Temple and Signs of the End Times

24 Jesus left the temple and was walking away when his disciples came up to him to call his attention to its buildings. 2"Do you see all these things?" he asked. "Truly I tell you, not one stone here will be left on another; every one will be thrown down."

3As Jesus was sitting on the Mount of Olives, the disciples came to him privately. "Tell us," they said, "when will this happen, and what will be the sign of your coming and of the end of the age?"

4Jesus answered: "Watch out that no one deceives you. 5For many will come in my name, claiming, 'I am the Messiah,' and will deceive many. 6You will hear of wars and rumors of wars, but see to it that you are not alarmed. Such things must happen, but the end is still to come. 7Nation will rise against nation, and kingdom against kingdom. There will be famines and earthquakes in various places. 8All these are the beginning of birth pains.

9"Then you will be handed over to be persecuted and put to death, and you will be hated by all nations because of me. 10At that time many will turn away from the faith and will betray and hate each other, 11and many false prophets will appear and deceive many people. 12Because of the increase of wickedness, the love of most will grow cold, 13but the one who stands firm to the end will be saved. 14And this gospel of the kingdom will be preached in the whole world as a testimony to all nations, and then the end will come.

15"So when you see standing in the holy place 'the abomination that causes desolation,'[a] spoken of through the prophet Daniel—let the reader understand— 16then let those who are in Judea flee to the mountains. 17Let no one on the housetop go down to take anything out of the house. 18Let no one in the field go back to get their cloak. 19How dreadful it will be in those days for pregnant women and nursing mothers! 20Pray that your flight will not take place in winter or on the Sabbath. 21For then there will be great distress, unequaled from the beginning of the world until now—and never to be equaled again.

22"If those days had not been cut short, no one would survive, but for the sake of the elect those days will be shortened. 23At that time if anyone says to you, 'Look, here is the Messiah!' or, 'There he is!' do not believe it. 24For false messiahs and false prophets will appear and perform great signs and wonders to deceive, if possible, even the elect. 25See, I have told you ahead of time.

26"So if anyone tells you, 'There he is, out in the wilderness,' do not go out; or, 'Here he is, in the inner rooms,' do not believe it. 27For as lightning that comes from the east is visible even in the west, so will be the coming of the Son of Man. 28Wherever there is a carcass, there the vultures will gather.

29"Immediately after the distress of those days

"'the sun will be darkened,
    and the moon will not give its light;
the stars will fall from the sky,
    and the heavenly bodies will be shaken.'[b]

30"Then will appear the sign of the Son of Man in heaven. And then all the peoples of the earth[c] will mourn when they see the Son of Man coming on the clouds of heaven, with power and great glory.[d] 31And he will send his angels with a loud trumpet call, and they will gather his elect from the four winds, from one end of the heavens to the other.

32"Now learn this lesson from the fig tree: As soon as its twigs get tender and its leaves come out, you know that summer is near. 33Even so, when you see all these things, you know that it[e] is near, right at the door. 34Truly I tell you, this generation will certainly not pass away until all these things have happened. 35Heaven and earth will pass away, but my words will never pass away.

---

[a] *15* Daniel 9:27; 11:31; 12:11 [b] *29* Isaiah 13:10; 34:4 [c] *30* Or *the tribes of the land*
[d] *30* See Daniel 7:13-14. [e] *33* Or *he*

MATTHEW 24:1–14,36–42

THE SECOND COMING (PART 1)

Here Jesus described the second coming by using symbolic language. While these words and various proposed timelines have been interpreted differently by committed Christians over the centuries, we do know that Jesus' second coming will be preceded by persecution and opposition (vv. 9–10), marked by false prophets claiming to be the Messiah (v. 5), and will include a time of testing for believers whose persistence and commitment will be rewarded (v. 14). Above all, the second coming of Christ will be sudden (v. 36). Altogether, Jesus made it clear that there will be no mistaking the second coming when it happens, and it is important for his followers to be prepared, each and every day, for that day.

The Day and Hour Unknown

[36]"But about that day or hour no one knows, not even the angels in heaven, nor
the Son,[a] but only the Father. [37]As it was in the days of Noah, so it will be at the
coming of the Son of Man. [38]For in the days before the flood, people were eating
and drinking, marrying and giving in marriage, up to the day Noah entered the
ark; [39]and they knew nothing about what would happen until the flood came
and took them all away. That is how it will be at the coming of the Son of Man.
[40]Two men will be in the field; one will be taken and the other left. [41]Two women
will be grinding with a hand mill; one will be taken and the other left.

[42]"Therefore keep watch, because you do not know on what day your Lord will
come. [43]But understand this: If the owner of the house had known at what time
of night the thief was coming, he would have kept watch and would not have let
his house be broken into. [44]So you also must be ready, because the Son of Man
will come at an hour when you do not expect him.

[45]"Who then is the faithful and wise servant, whom the master has put in
charge of the servants in his household to give them their food at the proper time?
[46]It will be good for that servant whose master finds him doing so when he returns.
[47]Truly I tell you, he will put him in charge of all his possessions. [48]But suppose
that servant is wicked and says to himself, 'My master is staying away a long time,'
[49]and he then begins to beat his fellow servants and to eat and drink with drunkards. [50]The master of that servant will come on a day when he does not expect him
and at an hour he is not aware of. [51]He will cut him to pieces and assign him a place
with the hypocrites, where there will be weeping and gnashing of teeth.

MATTHEW 25:1–46

THE SECOND COMING (PART 2)

The final section of this discourse involves judgment, which is not a new theme in the Gospel of Matthew (3:12; 6:2; 13:30; 18:23–35; 21:33–43; 22:1–14). Because Matthew spent a significant portion of his Gospel focusing on the coming of the kingdom, he also needed to discuss the judgment that comes with it. In the first two parables in this chapter, Jesus spoke about the judgment that will come upon those who are not prepared for his return, and in the last parable he focuses on all of the nations of the earth. To fully understand Jesus, it is important to see not only his love but also the reality that his coming will be accompanied by judgment. With the opportunity for people to accept his sacrifice and the grace and forgiveness that come with it, there also is an opportunity for people to reject that same sacrifice. Jesus came so that those who love God may devote their lives to following him, but his offer has another side: judgment on those who willfully choose to turn their backs on God.

The Parable of the Ten Virgins

25 "At that time the kingdom of heaven will be like ten virgins who took their
lamps and went out to meet the bridegroom. [2]Five of them were foolish
and five were wise. [3]The foolish ones took their lamps but did not take any oil with
them. [4]The wise ones, however, took oil in jars along with their lamps. [5]The bridegroom was a long time in coming, and they all became drowsy and fell asleep.

[6]"At midnight the cry rang out: 'Here's the bridegroom! Come out to meet
him!'

[7]"Then all the virgins woke up and trimmed their lamps. [8]The foolish ones
said to the wise, 'Give us some of your oil; our lamps are going out.'

[9]"'No,' they replied, 'there may not be enough for both us and you. Instead, go
to those who sell oil and buy some for yourselves.'

[10]"But while they were on their way to buy the oil, the bridegroom arrived.
The virgins who were ready went in with him to the wedding banquet. And the
door was shut.

[11]"Later the others also came. 'Lord, Lord,' they said, 'open the door for us!'

[12]"But he replied, 'Truly I tell you, I don't know you.'

[13]"Therefore keep watch, because you do not know the day or the hour.

The Parable of the Bags of Gold

[14]"Again, it will be like a man going on a journey, who called his servants and
entrusted his wealth to them. [15]To one he gave five bags of gold, to another two
bags, and to another one bag,[b] each according to his ability. Then he went on his
journey. [16]The man who had received five bags of gold went at once and put his
money to work and gained five bags more. [17]So also, the one with two bags of gold
gained two more. [18]But the man who had received one bag went off, dug a hole in
the ground and hid his master's money.

[19]"After a long time the master of those servants returned and settled accounts with them. [20]The man who had received five bags of gold brought the

[a] *36* Some manuscripts do not have *nor the Son.* [b] *15* Greek *five talents . . . two talents . . . one talent*; also throughout this parable; a talent was worth about 20 years of a day laborer's wage.

other five. 'Master,' he said, 'you entrusted me with five bags of gold. See, I have
gained five more.'
[21]"His master replied, 'Well done, good and faithful servant! You have been
faithful with a few things; I will put you in charge of many things. Come and
share your master's happiness!'
[22]"The man with two bags of gold also came. 'Master,' he said, 'you entrusted
me with two bags of gold; see, I have gained two more.'
[23]"His master replied, 'Well done, good and faithful servant! You have been
faithful with a few things; I will put you in charge of many things. Come and
share your master's happiness!'
[24]"Then the man who had received one bag of gold came. 'Master,' he said, 'I
knew that you are a hard man, harvesting where you have not sown and gathering where you have not scattered seed. [25]So I was afraid and went out and hid
your gold in the ground. See, here is what belongs to you.'
[26]"His master replied, 'You wicked, lazy servant! So you knew that I harvest
where I have not sown and gather where I have not scattered seed? [27]Well then,
you should have put my money on deposit with the bankers, so that when I returned I would have received it back with interest.
[28]" 'So take the bag of gold from him and give it to the one who has ten bags.
[29]For whoever has will be given more, and they will have an abundance. Whoever does not have, even what they have will be taken from them. [30]And throw
that worthless servant outside, into the darkness, where there will be weeping
and gnashing of teeth.'

The Sheep and the Goats

[31]"When the Son of Man comes in his glory, and all the angels with him, he
will sit on his glorious throne. [32]All the nations will be gathered before him, and
he will separate the people one from another as a shepherd separates the sheep
from the goats. [33]He will put the sheep on his right and the goats on his left.
[34]"Then the King will say to those on his right, 'Come, you who are blessed by
my Father; take your inheritance, the kingdom prepared for you since the creation of the world. [35]For I was hungry and you gave me something to eat, I was
thirsty and you gave me something to drink, I was a stranger and you invited me
in, [36]I needed clothes and you clothed me, I was sick and you looked after me, I
was in prison and you came to visit me.'
[37]"Then the righteous will answer him, 'Lord, when did we see you hungry
and feed you, or thirsty and give you something to drink? [38]When did we see you
a stranger and invite you in, or needing clothes and clothe you? [39]When did we
see you sick or in prison and go to visit you?'
[40]"The King will reply, 'Truly I tell you, whatever you did for one of the least of
these brothers and sisters of mine, you did for me.'
[41]"Then he will say to those on his left, 'Depart from me, you who are cursed,
into the eternal fire prepared for the devil and his angels. [42]For I was hungry
and you gave me nothing to eat, I was thirsty and you gave me nothing to drink,
[43]I was a stranger and you did not invite me in, I needed clothes and you did not
clothe me, I was sick and in prison and you did not look after me.'
[44]"They also will answer, 'Lord, when did we see you hungry or thirsty or a
stranger or needing clothes or sick or in prison, and did not help you?'
[45]"He will reply, 'Truly I tell you, whatever you did not do for one of the least of
these, you did not do for me.'
[46]"Then they will go away to eternal punishment, but the righteous to eternal life."

The Plot Against Jesus

26 When Jesus had finished saying all these things, he said to his disciples,
[2]"As you know, the Passover is two days away — and the Son of Man will
be handed over to be crucified."

[3]Then the chief priests and the elders of the people assembled in the palace of the high priest, whose name was Caiaphas, [4]and they schemed to arrest Jesus secretly and kill him. [5]"But not during the festival," they said, "or there may be a riot among the people."

Jesus Anointed at Bethany

[6]While Jesus was in Bethany in the home of Simon the Leper, [7]a woman came to him with an alabaster jar of very expensive perfume, which she poured on his head as he was reclining at the table.

[8]When the disciples saw this, they were indignant. "Why this waste?" they asked. [9]"This perfume could have been sold at a high price and the money given to the poor."

[10]Aware of this, Jesus said to them, "Why are you bothering this woman? She has done a beautiful thing to me. [11]The poor you will always have with you,[a] but you will not always have me. [12]When she poured this perfume on my body, she did it to prepare me for burial. [13]Truly I tell you, wherever this gospel is preached throughout the world, what she has done will also be told, in memory of her."

Judas Agrees to Betray Jesus

[14]Then one of the Twelve — the one called Judas Iscariot — went to the chief priests [15]and asked, "What are you willing to give me if I deliver him over to you?" So they counted out for him thirty pieces of silver. [16]From then on Judas watched for an opportunity to hand him over.

The Last Supper

[17]On the first day of the Festival of Unleavened Bread, the disciples came to Jesus and asked, "Where do you want us to make preparations for you to eat the Passover?"

[18]He replied, "Go into the city to a certain man and tell him, 'The Teacher says: My appointed time is near. I am going to celebrate the Passover with my disciples at your house.' " [19]So the disciples did as Jesus had directed them and prepared the Passover.

[20]When evening came, Jesus was reclining at the table with the Twelve. [21]And while they were eating, he said, "Truly I tell you, one of you will betray me."

[22]They were very sad and began to say to him one after the other, "Surely you don't mean me, Lord?"

[23]Jesus replied, "The one who has dipped his hand into the bowl with me will betray me. [24]The Son of Man will go just as it is written about him. But woe to that man who betrays the Son of Man! It would be better for him if he had not been born."

[25]Then Judas, the one who would betray him, said, "Surely you don't mean me, Rabbi?"

Jesus answered, "You have said so."

[26]While they were eating, Jesus took bread, and when he had given thanks, he broke it and gave it to his disciples, saying, "Take and eat; this is my body."

[27]Then he took a cup, and when he had given thanks, he gave it to them, saying, "Drink from it, all of you. [28]This is my blood of the[b] covenant, which is poured out for many for the forgiveness of sins. [29]I tell you, I will not drink from this fruit of the vine from now on until that day when I drink it new with you in my Father's kingdom."

[30]When they had sung a hymn, they went out to the Mount of Olives.

Jesus Predicts Peter's Denial

[31]Then Jesus told them, "This very night you will all fall away on account of me, for it is written:

---

[a] *11* See Deut. 15:11. [b] *28* Some manuscripts *the new*

"'I will strike the shepherd,
and the sheep of the flock will be scattered.'[a]
[32]But after I have risen, I will go ahead of you into Galilee."
[33]Peter replied, "Even if all fall away on account of you, I never will."
[34]"Truly I tell you," Jesus answered, "this very night, before the rooster crows,
you will disown me three times."
[35]But Peter declared, "Even if I have to die with you, I will never disown you."
And all the other disciples said the same.

Gethsemane

[36]Then Jesus went with his disciples to a place called Gethsemane, and he
said to them, "Sit here while I go over there and pray." [37]He took Peter and the
two sons of Zebedee along with him, and he began to be sorrowful and troubled.
[38]Then he said to them, "My soul is overwhelmed with sorrow to the point of
death. Stay here and keep watch with me."
[39]Going a little farther, he fell with his face to the ground and prayed, "My
Father, if it is possible, may this cup be taken from me. Yet not as I will, but as
you will."
[40]Then he returned to his disciples and found them sleeping. "Couldn't you
men keep watch with me for one hour?" he asked Peter. [41]"Watch and pray so
that you will not fall into temptation. The spirit is willing, but the flesh is weak."
[42]He went away a second time and prayed, "My Father, if it is not possible for
this cup to be taken away unless I drink it, may your will be done."
[43]When he came back, he again found them sleeping, because their eyes were
heavy. [44]So he left them and went away once more and prayed the third time,
saying the same thing.
[45]Then he returned to the disciples and said to them, "Are you still sleeping
and resting? Look, the hour has come, and the Son of Man is delivered into the
hands of sinners. [46]Rise! Let us go! Here comes my betrayer!"

Jesus Arrested

[47]While he was still speaking, Judas, one of the Twelve, arrived. With him was
a large crowd armed with swords and clubs, sent from the chief priests and the
elders of the people. [48]Now the betrayer had arranged a signal with them: "The
one I kiss is the man; arrest him." [49]Going at once to Jesus, Judas said, "Greetings,
Rabbi!" and kissed him.
[50]Jesus replied, "Do what you came for, friend."[b]
Then the men stepped forward, seized Jesus and arrested him. [51]With that,
one of Jesus' companions reached for his sword, drew it out and struck the servant of the high priest, cutting off his ear.
[52]"Put your sword back in its place," Jesus said to him, "for all who draw the
sword will die by the sword. [53]Do you think I cannot call on my Father, and he
will at once put at my disposal more than twelve legions of angels? [54]But how
then would the Scriptures be fulfilled that say it must happen in this way?"
[55]In that hour Jesus said to the crowd, "Am I leading a rebellion, that you have
come out with swords and clubs to capture me? Every day I sat in the temple
courts teaching, and you did not arrest me. [56]But this has all taken place that
the writings of the prophets might be fulfilled." Then all the disciples deserted
him and fled.

Jesus Before the Sanhedrin

[57]Those who had arrested Jesus took him to Caiaphas the high priest, where
the teachers of the law and the elders had assembled. [58]But Peter followed him at
a distance, right up to the courtyard of the high priest. He entered and sat down
with the guards to see the outcome.

---

[a] *31* Zech. 13:7 [b] *50* Or *"Why have you come, friend?"*

OLD TESTAMENT FULFILLMENTS

The events that led up to the crucifixion of Jesus directly parallel what was prophesied about the Messiah as the Suffering Servant in the Old Testament. But not only did Jesus fulfill Old Testament prophecy; others around Jesus did as well.

Judas betrayed Jesus for 30 pieces of silver (v. 14), which was the equivalent to the price of a slave (Ex 21:32). Zechariah wrote about this exact price in his Messianic foreshadowing (Zec 11:12 – 13). Thirty pieces of silver was not a very large sum of money in that era, and in Matthew, Judas' story provides a stark contrast to the verses preceding his betrayal (Mt 26:6 – 13). While Mary went to great expense to anoint Jesus with precious oil, giving to Jesus what was probably her entire dowry (and therefore her entire future), Judas turned against Jesus for a relatively small price. Great is the cost of devotion, but cheap is the price of betrayal.

After the description of Judas' betrayal, Matthew transitioned to the preparations of the Passover meal. The Passover was celebrated in remembrance of God freeing his people from Egypt (Nu 9:2). However, for believers, Jesus completely transformed the way the meal was celebrated. It is now in remembrance of God freeing his people from sin and death through Jesus. In honoring old traditions, Jesus also created new traditions for believers to follow today. During this Passover celebration, Jesus represented the very fulfillment of the Passover's promise of deliverance from sin, ushering in a new covenant to replace the old covenant. This new covenant had been promised in the Old Testament multiple times (Jer 31:31 – 34; Eze 34:25 – 31; 37:26 – 28), and Jesus finally fulfilled it.

In addition to Judas and Jesus, Peter and the rest of the disciples also fulfilled Old Testament prophecies. While Peter's denial was a blatant betrayal against Jesus, it is important to remember that Peter was not the only disciple to avoid being associated with Jesus after his arrest. None of the other disciples had the courage to follow Jesus on that night; they all hid, which Jesus referred to by quoting Zechariah 13:7 (Mt 26:31). After Jesus' resurrection, ever the Good Shepherd, Jesus brought his flock back together (28:16 – 20), as he will again in the last days (Ac 2:17 – 21).

59The chief priests and the whole Sanhedrin were looking for false evidence
against Jesus so that they could put him to death. 60But they did not find any,
though many false witnesses came forward.
Finally two came forward 61and declared, "This fellow said, 'I am able to destroy the temple of God and rebuild it in three days.'"
62Then the high priest stood up and said to Jesus, "Are you not going to answer? What is this testimony that these men are bringing against you?" 63But
Jesus remained silent.
The high priest said to him, "I charge you under oath by the living God: Tell us
if you are the Messiah, the Son of God."
64"You have said so," Jesus replied. "But I say to all of you: From now on you
will see the Son of Man sitting at the right hand of the Mighty One and coming
on the clouds of heaven."[a]
65Then the high priest tore his clothes and said, "He has spoken blasphemy!
Why do we need any more witnesses? Look, now you have heard the blasphemy.
66What do you think?"
"He is worthy of death," they answered.
67Then they spit in his face and struck him with their fists. Others slapped him
68and said, "Prophesy to us, Messiah. Who hit you?"

Peter Disowns Jesus

69Now Peter was sitting out in the courtyard, and a servant girl came to him.
"You also were with Jesus of Galilee," she said.
70But he denied it before them all. "I don't know what you're talking about,"
he said.
71Then he went out to the gateway, where another servant girl saw him and
said to the people there, "This fellow was with Jesus of Nazareth."
72He denied it again, with an oath: "I don't know the man!"
73After a little while, those standing there went up to Peter and said, "Surely
you are one of them; your accent gives you away."
74Then he began to call down curses, and he swore to them, "I don't know
the man!"
Immediately a rooster crowed. 75Then Peter remembered the word Jesus had
spoken: "Before the rooster crows, you will disown me three times." And he went
outside and wept bitterly.

Judas Hangs Himself

27 Early in the morning, all the chief priests and the elders of the people
made their plans how to have Jesus executed. 2So they bound him, led
him away and handed him over to Pilate the governor.
3When Judas, who had betrayed him, saw that Jesus was condemned, he was
seized with remorse and returned the thirty pieces of silver to the chief priests
and the elders. 4"I have sinned," he said, "for I have betrayed innocent blood."
"What is that to us?" they replied. "That's your responsibility."
5So Judas threw the money into the temple and left. Then he went away and
hanged himself.
6The chief priests picked up the coins and said, "It is against the law to put this
into the treasury, since it is blood money." 7So they decided to use the money to
buy the potter's field as a burial place for foreigners. 8That is why it has been called
the Field of Blood to this day. 9Then what was spoken by Jeremiah the prophet was
fulfilled: "They took the thirty pieces of silver, the price set on him by the people of
Israel, 10and they used them to buy the potter's field, as the Lord commanded me."[b]

Jesus Before Pilate

11Meanwhile Jesus stood before the governor, and the governor asked him,
"Are you the king of the Jews?"

---

[a] *64* See Psalm 110:1; Daniel 7:13. [b] *10* See Zech. 11:12,13; Jer. 19:1-13; 32:6-9.

SAVIOR

THE UNIQUENESS OF JESUS

— *RAVI ZACHARIAS*

GOSPELS TO ACTS 1

A common phrase heard in the West for years was "Jesus is the answer." Tired of that glib statement, some replied cynically, "But what is the question?" Under this taunting response actually lies a gem of truth, for we cannot understand the depth of our own questions until we first understand ourselves as questioners. Indeed, one of the most thought-provoking scenes in Scripture is the exchange between Jesus and Pilate, the Roman governor. The question Pilate asked is one of the most important questions of life: "What is truth?" (Jn 18:38). How tragic that he asked it of the One who embodied the answer, but never waited to hear that answer. He proved that *intent is prior to content:* before the mind receives any content, the intent of the heart is already influencing perception (Mt 13:13).

Is it not often the same with us? I remember many times in my youth how I dreaded the truth in incriminating situations. Like the poet Francis Thompson wrote in the *Hound of Heaven,* "I fled him, down the nights and down the days; I fled him, down the arches of the years." We may ask Jesus why he is the truth, yet we never take the time to examine why he made such a claim. The answer has ramifications for us that often we don't want to hear.

Yet the fact remains that we will never understand who we are until we understand who Jesus is. He made the incredible statement to Pilate, "Everyone on the side of truth listens to me" (Jn 18:37).

John, who knew Jesus personally and closely, declares in the first chapter of his Gospel the definitive way in which Jesus is not merely unique but is the consummate embodiment of truth: "In the beginning was the Word, and the Word was with God, and the Word was God. He was with God in the beginning. Through him all things were made; without him nothing was made that has been made. In him was life, and that life was the light of all mankind" (Jn 1:1 – 4). Truth is primarily a property of propositions. Truthfulness is the embodiment of truth. Jesus was the Word and the Word made flesh. In him, Word and incarnation combined in truth.

John tells us that Jesus not only proclaims the words of God but is the Word, who *is* God. "Through him all things were made; without him nothing was made." Reflect upon that stupendous phrase! In Jesus we see the blending of all reality lived out in truth. Scottish theologian James Stewart wrote that in Jesus we find a "startling coalescence of contrarieties." This is how he worded it:

He was the meekest and lowliest of all the sons of men: yet He said that He would come on the clouds of heaven in the glory of God. He was so austere that evil spirits and demons cried out at terror of His coming: yet He was so genial and winsome and approachable that the children loved to play with him, and the little ones nestled in His arms; and His company in the innocent gaiety of a village wedding was like the sunshine. No one was ever half so kind or compassionate to sinners: yet no one ever spoke such red-hot, scorching words about sin. He would not break the bruised reed, and His whole life was love: yet on one occasion He demanded of the Pharisees how they expected to escape the damnation of hell. He was a dreamer of dreams and a seer of visions: yet for sheer stark naked realism He has all our self-styled "realists" beaten. He was the servant of all, washing the disciples' feet: yet masterfully He strode into the Temple, and the hucksters and traders fell over one another in their mad rush to get away from the fire they saw blazing in His eyes. He saved others: yet at the last, Himself He would not save. There is nothing in history like the union of contrasts that confronts you in the Gospels. The mystery of Jesus is the mystery of divine personality.*

A *contradiction,* according to *Webster's Dictionary,* is a statement or proposition that denies another statement or itself and is logically incongruous. A *contrariety,* however, holds two aspects of an issue in balance and in tension without violating the logical congruency of either. For example, the two poles of meekness and authority are not contradictory. They both have their excellences, and when blended in perfection, they embody truth. In the contrarieties within Jesus we see how he represents to us the answer for all the tensions we feel within ourselves. His being and incarnation are unique.

How is Jesus unique so as to claim our hearts? There are many reasons, but consider four distinctives:

1. Jesus' description of the human condition: "Out of the heart come evil thoughts — murder, adultery, sexual immorality, theft, false testimony, slander" (Mt 15:19).

Malcolm Muggeridge wisely remarked, "The depravity of man is at once the most empirically verifiable reality but at the same time the most intellectually resisted fact." That is well put. And ironically, the more we argue against it, the more we end up proving the point.

*James Stewart, *The Strong Name* (Baker Book House: Grand Rapids, Michigan, 1972), 72 – 73.

SAVIOR

(CONTINUED)

I was at the 2014 World Cup of football in Brazil. There were fans from all over the world, ranging from those closest to the field of play to those proverbially described as in the "nosebleed section." But no one was as close as about one hundred able-bodied men surrounding the playing field at the perimeter. Ironically, they did not witness the game. They had their backs to the game, and their sole purpose was to watch the fans and keep them from disruptive or violent behavior. They were there to protect the players. Other security personnel were in the stands to protect the spectators from each other! On the field were the uniformed referees to keep the players from violating the rules — and even to keep them from taking a bite off an opposing player's shoulder! (Yes, that did happen, and the culprit was a player considered by many to be the best all-round player in the world.) Later we found out that the very officials leading the organization were corrupt. Nobody was watching *them*. The insidiousness of human sin is quite amazing.

The systemic human bent toward autonomy and pride spares no one. G.K. Chesterton once responded to the question, "What's wrong with the world?" with "I am. Yours truly, G.K Chesterton." Evil is within us before it is "out there." Take a look at our world today as it skids out of control. None of our efforts to tame the heart, from laws to education, have changed the horrific things we do to ourselves and each other. The heart is at rebellion with God and therefore at rebellion with ourselves and our fellow human beings (Mt 9:3 – 5; 12:33 – 35; Mk 7:21; Jn 12:40).

2. Jesus' provision for our malady.

The provision he gives for you and me is absolutely one of a kind, and it is not cheap. It is the cross. The graciousness of God's forgiveness is singularly true. In every other religion, whether pantheistic or monotheistic, the devotee has to earn salvation. One pays either through karma or by being weighed in the balances at death's door. Jesus alone tells us our forgiveness is a gift. The grace of God provides it for us. If we chose to receive the gift, the heart changes. When Jesus paid with his own sacrifice, justice and mercy blended in remarkable splendor. Yes, there is only one place in the world where law and love, justice and forgiveness are embodied in one person. That is on the cross of Calvary. Jesus Christ claimed to be the way, the truth, and the life because he is what the absolute truth really is. Our greatest malady is sin. Our greatest need is a Savior. In his life he was perfect. In his death he died for imperfect humanity. The truth is awe-inspiring.

In May of 2014, NBA basketball superstar Kevin Durant made a memorable speech when he received the MVP award. He said, "There's only one who deserves this, and that is my mother, the true MVP." The media said it was the greatest speech at an award ceremony. Apply that to the cross. Jesus traded the award for the recognition he wanted to make. Jesus was the ultimate being of purity and worth. He transferred his purity to us. He proved our worth by his sacrifice.

3. The purity of Jesus' own life.

Pontius Pilate could find no fault in Jesus (Lk 23:4). The thief on the cross said, "We are punished justly, for we are getting what our deeds deserve. But this man has done nothing wrong" (Lk 23:41). "A lamb without blemish or defect" is the description given to him (1Pe 1:19). Jesus is unique. We can be covered by his perfect life. No one who has claimed to be divine or prophetic has claimed or demonstrated purity. Jesus alone is spotless.

4. Jesus' resurrection from the dead.

This event is deemed the most relevant and critical aspect in demonstrating Jesus' divinity. The Danish philosopher Søren Kierkegaard said, "Life can only be understood backwards; but it must be lived forwards." The "end" or "purpose" of life must define the journey to get there. The destiny and destination determine the path taken. Without the resurrection, two realities become inescapable: the finality of all earthly relationships — a loss of hope, and the impossibility of ultimate justice — the weakness of law. In the Christian faith, the resurrection of Jesus promises both hope and justice. This alone ought to make us aware of how important his grace is when we come to him for forgiveness.

We are meant to live for eternity in a relationship that will never be broken. Love has its eternal expression. Law's demands were met and death was conquered. Justice was kissed by grace. That is why Jesus sent the message of hope specifically to Peter, who had denied him.

The resurrection is so definitively important that if the early skeptics had wanted to debunk Jesus' divinity, all they had to do was produce the body. The very claim that he would bodily rise again was an enormously tangible promise. Two of the most inquiring minds, Saul of Tarsus and Thomas, submitted to the lordship of the resurrected Jesus. Thomas said he wouldn't believe until he touched and felt Jesus' wounds. Saul of Tarsus had persecuted the church. He stood by as Stephen was murdered by a hostile crowd of Jewish leaders. Saul's transformed life following his encounter with the risen Jesus changed history. One headed west and the other headed east. Both were willing to pay with their lives because

SAVIOR

(CONTINUED)

GOSPELS TO ACTS 1

they defined life on the basis of that resurrection hope. Today there are churches in both extremities of the world because of these men's contact with the resurrected Son of God.

The Christian message can be summarized this way: The greatest ethic is love. Where love is a reality, freedom has to be given. Where there is freedom, there will always be the possibility of sin. Where there is sin, there is the need of a Savior. Where there is a Savior, there is the hope of redemption. Only in the Judeo-Christian worldview does this sequence find its total expression and answer. That in a nutshell is the entire gospel story, and that is uniquely true of the message of Jesus Christ.

We know behind every question is a questioner. In God's Word we find that behind the ultimate answer is also a person — the very Word of God who is "the way and the truth and the life" (Jn 14:6). He is the answer to the cry of every human heart for a Savior, a Champion and a personal Redeemer. Jesus is the ultimate hope for our destiny. No one else comes even close to meeting our greatest need and our greatest longing. He invites you to know him and find ultimate freedom.

"You have said so," Jesus replied.

12When he was accused by the chief priests and the elders, he gave no answer. 13Then Pilate asked him, "Don't you hear the testimony they are bringing against you?" 14But Jesus made no reply, not even to a single charge — to the great amazement of the governor.

15Now it was the governor's custom at the festival to release a prisoner chosen by the crowd. 16At that time they had a well-known prisoner whose name was Jesus[a] Barabbas. 17So when the crowd had gathered, Pilate asked them, "Which one do you want me to release to you: Jesus Barabbas, or Jesus who is called the Messiah?" 18For he knew it was out of self-interest that they had handed Jesus over to him.

19While Pilate was sitting on the judge's seat, his wife sent him this message: "Don't have anything to do with that innocent man, for I have suffered a great deal today in a dream because of him."

20But the chief priests and the elders persuaded the crowd to ask for Barabbas and to have Jesus executed.

21"Which of the two do you want me to release to you?" asked the governor.

"Barabbas," they answered.

22"What shall I do, then, with Jesus who is called the Messiah?" Pilate asked.

They all answered, "Crucify him!"

23"Why? What crime has he committed?" asked Pilate.

But they shouted all the louder, "Crucify him!"

24When Pilate saw that he was getting nowhere, but that instead an uproar was starting, he took water and washed his hands in front of the crowd. "I am innocent of this man's blood," he said. "It is your responsibility!"

25All the people answered, "His blood is on us and on our children!"

26Then he released Barabbas to them. But he had Jesus flogged, and handed him over to be crucified.

The Soldiers Mock Jesus

27Then the governor's soldiers took Jesus into the Praetorium and gathered the whole company of soldiers around him. 28They stripped him and put a scarlet robe on him, 29and then twisted together a crown of thorns and set it on his head. They put a staff in his right hand. Then they knelt in front of him and mocked him. "Hail, king of the Jews!" they said. 30They spit on him, and took the staff and struck him on the head again and again. 31After they had mocked him, they took off the robe and put his own clothes on him. Then they led him away to crucify him.

The Crucifixion of Jesus

32As they were going out, they met a man from Cyrene, named Simon, and they forced him to carry the cross. 33They came to a place called Golgotha (which means "the place of the skull"). 34There they offered Jesus wine to drink, mixed with gall; but after tasting it, he refused to drink it. 35When they had crucified him, they divided up his clothes by casting lots. 36And sitting down, they kept watch over him there. 37Above his head they placed the written charge against him: THIS IS JESUS, THE KING OF THE JEWS.

38Two rebels were crucified with him, one on his right and one on his left. 39Those who passed by hurled insults at him, shaking their heads 40and saying, "You who are going to destroy the temple and build it in three days, save yourself! Come down from the cross, if you are the Son of God!" 41In the same way the chief priests, the teachers of the law and the elders mocked him. 42"He saved others," they said, "but he can't save himself! He's the king of Israel! Let him come down now from the cross, and we will believe in him. 43He trusts in God. Let God rescue him now if he wants him, for he said, 'I am the Son of

---

[a] *16* Many manuscripts do not have *Jesus*; also in verse 17.

MATTHEW 27:62–66

WORRIED ABOUT A RESURRECTION

Matthew made sure to emphasize the fact that the tomb was sealed in order to show that there was no possible way for the disciples to steal the body. The Jewish leaders and the guard were instructed to "make the tomb as secure as you know how" (v. 65), and they did so by placing a seal on the stone that was rolled in front of the tomb and also by placing a guard there. After the grave was reported empty and the disciples began telling others about the resurrection, those who opposed Jesus attempted to spread the rumor that the disciples had stolen the body (Mt 28:11–15). However, Matthew made it clear in his Gospel that the religious leaders had sealed the tomb specifically for the purpose of preventing anyone from stealing the body and faking a resurrection, which directly contradicts the false narrative they attempted to spread. There is no way the disciples could have stolen the body of Christ, and Matthew did well to show that despite the chief priests and Pharisees' attempts to guard the tomb, there was nothing they could do to prevent Jesus' actual, physical resurrection from the dead.

God.' " 44In the same way the rebels who were crucified with him also heaped
insults on him.

The Death of Jesus

45From noon until three in the afternoon darkness came over all the land.
46About three in the afternoon Jesus cried out in a loud voice, *"Eli, Eli,*[a] *lema
sabachthani?"* (which means "My God, my God, why have you forsaken me?").[b]
47When some of those standing there heard this, they said, "He's calling Elijah."
48Immediately one of them ran and got a sponge. He filled it with wine vinegar, put it on a staff, and offered it to Jesus to drink. 49The rest said, "Now leave
him alone. Let's see if Elijah comes to save him."
50And when Jesus had cried out again in a loud voice, he gave up his spirit.
51At that moment the curtain of the temple was torn in two from top to bottom.
The earth shook, the rocks split 52and the tombs broke open. The bodies of many
holy people who had died were raised to life. 53They came out of the tombs after
Jesus' resurrection and[c] went into the holy city and appeared to many people.
54When the centurion and those with him who were guarding Jesus saw the
earthquake and all that had happened, they were terrified, and exclaimed,
"Surely he was the Son of God!"
55Many women were there, watching from a distance. They had followed
Jesus from Galilee to care for his needs. 56Among them were Mary Magdalene,
Mary the mother of James and Joseph,[d] and the mother of Zebedee's sons.

The Burial of Jesus

57As evening approached, there came a rich man from Arimathea, named Joseph, who had himself become a disciple of Jesus. 58Going to Pilate, he asked for
Jesus' body, and Pilate ordered that it be given to him. 59Joseph took the body,
wrapped it in a clean linen cloth, 60and placed it in his own new tomb that he
had cut out of the rock. He rolled a big stone in front of the entrance to the tomb
and went away. 61Mary Magdalene and the other Mary were sitting there opposite the tomb.

The Guard at the Tomb

62The next day, the one after Preparation Day, the chief priests and the Pharisees went to Pilate. 63"Sir," they said, "we remember that while he was still alive
that deceiver said, 'After three days I will rise again.' 64So give the order for the
tomb to be made secure until the third day. Otherwise, his disciples may come
and steal the body and tell the people that he has been raised from the dead. This
last deception will be worse than the first."
65"Take a guard," Pilate answered. "Go, make the tomb as secure as you know
how." 66So they went and made the tomb secure by putting a seal on the stone
and posting the guard.

Jesus Has Risen

28 After the Sabbath, at dawn on the first day of the week, Mary Magdalene
and the other Mary went to look at the tomb.
2There was a violent earthquake, for an angel of the Lord came down from
heaven and, going to the tomb, rolled back the stone and sat on it. 3His appearance was like lightning, and his clothes were white as snow. 4The guards were so
afraid of him that they shook and became like dead men.
5The angel said to the women, "Do not be afraid, for I know that you are looking for Jesus, who was crucified. 6He is not here; he has risen, just as he said.
Come and see the place where he lay. 7Then go quickly and tell his disciples: 'He

[a] 46 Some manuscripts *Eli, Eloi* [b] 46 Psalm 22:1 [c] 53 Or *tombs, and after Jesus' resurrection they* [d] 56 Greek *Joses,* a variant of *Joseph*

JESUS' ASSIGNMENT TO HIS DISCIPLES

The Great Commission (vv. 19 – 20) is a command that rests on the authority of Christ described in the preceding verse. The phrase "Go and make disciples" is commonly spoken among believers, but it is important to note the word "therefore" that comes before. Followers of Jesus are expected to *go and make disciples* solely because of who Jesus is and with the power and authority that he has been given (v. 18). Jesus has all authority on heaven and earth, and he doesn't give this command without empowering his followers to go and tell others about who he is.

The Great Commission is not the first call for world evangelism in the Bible. In fact, Genesis 12:1 – 3 describes God's promise that Abraham and his descendants would be a blessing to all nations. Jesus was simply building on what God had already told his people long before. Believers are expected to share the true and life-giving story of Jesus to every nation far and wide; this command has always been true for people who follow Jesus.

Jesus' command involves a simple three-step process; go, baptize and teach. Within this phrase, Jesus clarified exactly what he expects of his followers. They are to first go and tell others about him so that others can know and understand his story. Then they are to baptize those who have heard the story so that they can publicly declare their belief in who he is. Finally, believers need to teach and encourage one another (Col 3:16). Believers will never stop teaching each other and learning about the nature of God. The command to go, baptize and teach was Jesus' last command in the book of Matthew, and it is of the utmost importance for followers of Christ.

However, Jesus did not ask his disciples to do so alone. He promised that although he was leaving them physically he would always be with them through his Spirit. As long as believers hold fast to Jesus and rely on the Holy Spirit, the pathway is open for his followers to do what they have been called to do (Php 4:13).

has risen from the dead and is going ahead of you into Galilee. There you will see
him.' Now I have told you."
[8]So the women hurried away from the tomb, afraid yet filled with joy, and ran
to tell his disciples. [9]Suddenly Jesus met them. "Greetings," he said. They came
to him, clasped his feet and worshiped him. [10]Then Jesus said to them, "Do not
be afraid. Go and tell my brothers to go to Galilee; there they will see me."

The Guards' Report

[11]While the women were on their way, some of the guards went into the city
and reported to the chief priests everything that had happened. [12]When the
chief priests had met with the elders and devised a plan, they gave the soldiers
a large sum of money, [13]telling them, "You are to say, 'His disciples came during
the night and stole him away while we were asleep.' [14]If this report gets to the
governor, we will satisfy him and keep you out of trouble." [15]So the soldiers took
the money and did as they were instructed. And this story has been widely cir-
culated among the Jews to this very day.

The Great Commission

[16]Then the eleven disciples went to Galilee, to the mountain where Jesus had
told them to go. [17]When they saw him, they worshiped him; but some doubted.
[18]Then Jesus came to them and said, "All authority in heaven and on earth has
been given to me. [19]Therefore go and make disciples of all nations, baptizing
them in the name of the Father and of the Son and of the Holy Spirit, [20]and teaching them to obey everything I have commanded you. And surely I am with you
always, to the very end of the age."

JESUS: OUR TRUE GOD

MARK

MARK

BIRTH OF JESUS *c. 5 BC*	PONTIUS PILATE GOVERNS JUDEA *c. AD 26 – 36*	JESUS' MINISTRY, DEATH, RESURRECTION *c. AD 27 – 30*

Jesus is the Son of God. This is the message of Mark's Gospel, which contains an action-packed summary of the life and accomplishments of God's Son, Jesus Christ. Mark provides his readers with vivid, compelling and emotional descriptions of many of Jesus' greatest works. Informed by eyewitness accounts, especially by the disciple Peter, Mark wrote with the clarity and precision of one who knew the life-transforming implications of Jesus' life, death and resurrection.

The shortest of the Gospels, Mark's Gospel is written to Gentile believers, especially Romans, in an effort to show that Jesus' might and miracles prove that he is God in the flesh. Jesus' birth and baptism are covered in the span of only 13 verses, with Mark's main focus being the ministry of the second person of the Trinity.

Mark selected critical episodes and interactions from Jesus' ministry and often arranged them in thematic order to show that Jesus is "the Son of God" (1:1). The status is validated through Jesus' breathtaking power over all of his creation. He is powerful over the wind and the waves, the demonic kingdom and even sickness and death. For Mark, there was no denying the fact that these miracles prove Jesus is who he says he is and that all people owe him their supreme allegiance.

Mark invites his readers to hear and respond to the invitation offered by the Son of God. Since Jesus is God, his words are the word of God. This message is good news for those who have ears to hear the gracious call of God through Jesus. The kingdom of God has come on earth in the person of Jesus. The throne of David is occupied by the true anointed one, the King of kings, who rules and reigns with perfect justice and righteousness. Of his kingdom, there will be no end.

Kingdom citizens are sent to declare and demonstrate this gospel message to the world. Disciples are sent in the power of God to do the work of God. Their passionate zeal spreads the message of the availability of the kingdom and plants the seeds for the development of the church. Mark himself gave his life to this mission by serving as a travel companion to Paul and Barnabas as they established the church throughout the book of Acts. These churches would continue to proclaim the message: Jesus is the Son of God.

A VOICE CAME FROM HEAVEN:
"YOU ARE MY SON, WHOM I LOVE;
WITH YOU I AM WELL PLEASED."

Mark 1:11

MARK

John the Baptist Prepares the Way

1 The beginning of the good news about Jesus the Messiah,[a] the Son of God,[b]
2as it is written in Isaiah the prophet:

"I will send my messenger ahead of you,
who will prepare your way"[c] —
3"a voice of one calling in the wilderness,
'Prepare the way for the Lord,
make straight paths for him.' "[d]

4And so John the Baptist appeared in the wilderness, preaching a baptism of
repentance for the forgiveness of sins. 5The whole Judean countryside and all
the people of Jerusalem went out to him. Confessing their sins, they were baptized by him in the Jordan River. 6John wore clothing made of camel's hair, with
a leather belt around his waist, and he ate locusts and wild honey. 7And this was
his message: "After me comes the one more powerful than I, the straps of whose
sandals I am not worthy to stoop down and untie. 8I baptize you with[e] water, but
he will baptize you with[e] the Holy Spirit."

The Baptism and Testing of Jesus

9At that time Jesus came from Nazareth in Galilee and was baptized by John
in the Jordan. 10Just as Jesus was coming up out of the water, he saw heaven being
torn open and the Spirit descending on him like a dove. 11And a voice came from
heaven: "You are my Son, whom I love; with you I am well pleased."

12At once the Spirit sent him out into the wilderness, 13and he was in the wilderness forty days, being tempted[f] by Satan. He was with the wild animals, and
angels attended him.

Jesus Announces the Good News

14After John was put in prison, Jesus went into Galilee, proclaiming the good
news of God. 15"The time has come," he said. "The kingdom of God has come
near. Repent and believe the good news!"

Jesus Calls His First Disciples

16As Jesus walked beside the Sea of Galilee, he saw Simon and his brother Andrew casting a net into the lake, for they were fishermen. 17"Come, follow me,"
Jesus said, "and I will send you out to fish for people." 18At once they left their
nets and followed him.

19When he had gone a little farther, he saw James son of Zebedee and his
brother John in a boat, preparing their nets. 20Without delay he called them, and
they left their father Zebedee in the boat with the hired men and followed him.

Jesus Drives Out an Impure Spirit

21They went to Capernaum, and when the Sabbath came, Jesus went into the
synagogue and began to teach. 22The people were amazed at his teaching, because he taught them as one who had authority, not as the teachers of the law.
23Just then a man in their synagogue who was possessed by an impure spirit
cried out, 24"What do you want with us, Jesus of Nazareth? Have you come to
destroy us? I know who you are — the Holy One of God!"

[a] *1* Or *Jesus Christ. Messiah* (Hebrew) and *Christ* (Greek) both mean *Anointed One.*
[b] *1* Some manuscripts do not have *the Son of God.* [c] *2* Mal. 3:1 [d] *3* Isaiah 40:3
[e] *8* Or *in* [f] *13* The Greek for *tempted* can also mean *tested.*

MARK 1:14

THE GOOD NEWS

The world is full of bad news, and all of the bad news the world has ever known can be traced back to the Garden of Eden when Adam and Eve disobeyed God (Ge 3:1 – 24). Disobeying God's Word always leads to pain and suffering. Thankfully, God doesn't leave people in their pain. As soon as Adam and Eve brought chaos into God's good world, God promised to one day make everything right again (Ge 3:15). Humanity's fall corrupted God's perfect world and brought all of this bad news. But God comes to people with the gospel, the "Good News" that God has covered believers' sins through the work of Jesus and will one day make all things right through him. The gospel is not the news of what people must do in order to get to God; rather, the gospel is the news of what God has done to make a bridge to people. With Jesus, the reign and presence of God came into the world in a special way. Jesus came to fix the wrongs by going to the cross and by being broken for the sin of the world. God is in the business of "making everything new" (Rev 21:5). This is the Good News that Jesus came to share, and this is the news his people can tell their friends, family and others throughout the world as well.

25"Be quiet!" said Jesus sternly. "Come out of him!" 26The impure spirit shook the man violently and came out of him with a shriek.

27The people were all so amazed that they asked each other, "What is this? A new teaching — and with authority! He even gives orders to impure spirits and they obey him." 28News about him spread quickly over the whole region of Galilee.

Jesus Heals Many

29As soon as they left the synagogue, they went with James and John to the home of Simon and Andrew. 30Simon's mother-in-law was in bed with a fever, and they immediately told Jesus about her. 31So he went to her, took her hand and helped her up. The fever left her and she began to wait on them.

32That evening after sunset the people brought to Jesus all the sick and demon-possessed. 33The whole town gathered at the door, 34and Jesus healed many who had various diseases. He also drove out many demons, but he would not let the demons speak because they knew who he was.

Jesus Prays in a Solitary Place

35Very early in the morning, while it was still dark, Jesus got up, left the house and went off to a solitary place, where he prayed. 36Simon and his companions went to look for him, 37and when they found him, they exclaimed: "Everyone is looking for you!"

38Jesus replied, "Let us go somewhere else — to the nearby villages — so I can preach there also. That is why I have come." 39So he traveled throughout Galilee, preaching in their synagogues and driving out demons.

Jesus Heals a Man With Leprosy

40A man with leprosy[a] came to him and begged him on his knees, "If you are willing, you can make me clean."

41Jesus was indignant.[b] He reached out his hand and touched the man. "I am willing," he said. "Be clean!" 42Immediately the leprosy left him and he was cleansed.

43Jesus sent him away at once with a strong warning: 44"See that you don't tell this to anyone. But go, show yourself to the priest and offer the sacrifices that Moses commanded for your cleansing, as a testimony to them." 45Instead he went out and began to talk freely, spreading the news. As a result, Jesus could no longer enter a town openly but stayed outside in lonely places. Yet the people still came to him from everywhere.

Jesus Forgives and Heals a Paralyzed Man

2 A few days later, when Jesus again entered Capernaum, the people heard that he had come home. 2They gathered in such large numbers that there was no room left, not even outside the door, and he preached the word to them. 3Some men came, bringing to him a paralyzed man, carried by four of them. 4Since they could not get him to Jesus because of the crowd, they made an opening in the roof above Jesus by digging through it and then lowered the mat the man was lying on. 5When Jesus saw their faith, he said to the paralyzed man, "Son, your sins are forgiven."

6Now some teachers of the law were sitting there, thinking to themselves, 7"Why does this fellow talk like that? He's blaspheming! Who can forgive sins but God alone?"

8Immediately Jesus knew in his spirit that this was what they were thinking in their hearts, and he said to them, "Why are you thinking these things? 9Which is easier: to say to this paralyzed man, 'Your sins are forgiven,' or to say, 'Get up, take your mat and walk'? 10But I want you to know that the Son of Man has

---

[a] *40* The Greek word traditionally translated *leprosy* was used for various diseases affecting the skin. [b] *41* Many manuscripts *Jesus was filled with compassion*

authority on earth to forgive sins." So he said to the man, 11"I tell you, get up, take your mat and go home." 12He got up, took his mat and walked out in full view of them all. This amazed everyone and they praised God, saying, "We have never seen anything like this!"

Jesus Calls Levi and Eats With Sinners

13Once again Jesus went out beside the lake. A large crowd came to him, and he began to teach them. 14As he walked along, he saw Levi son of Alphaeus sitting at the tax collector's booth. "Follow me," Jesus told him, and Levi got up and followed him.

15While Jesus was having dinner at Levi's house, many tax collectors and sinners were eating with him and his disciples, for there were many who followed him. 16When the teachers of the law who were Pharisees saw him eating with the sinners and tax collectors, they asked his disciples: "Why does he eat with tax collectors and sinners?"

17On hearing this, Jesus said to them, "It is not the healthy who need a doctor, but the sick. I have not come to call the righteous, but sinners."

Jesus Questioned About Fasting

18Now John's disciples and the Pharisees were fasting. Some people came and asked Jesus, "How is it that John's disciples and the disciples of the Pharisees are fasting, but yours are not?"

19Jesus answered, "How can the guests of the bridegroom fast while he is with them? They cannot, so long as they have him with them. 20But the time will come when the bridegroom will be taken from them, and on that day they will fast.

21"No one sews a patch of unshrunk cloth on an old garment. Otherwise, the new piece will pull away from the old, making the tear worse. 22And no one pours new wine into old wineskins. Otherwise, the wine will burst the skins, and both the wine and the wineskins will be ruined. No, they pour new wine into new wineskins."

Jesus Is Lord of the Sabbath

23One Sabbath Jesus was going through the grainfields, and as his disciples walked along, they began to pick some heads of grain. 24The Pharisees said to him, "Look, why are they doing what is unlawful on the Sabbath?"

25He answered, "Have you never read what David did when he and his companions were hungry and in need? 26In the days of Abiathar the high priest, he entered the house of God and ate the consecrated bread, which is lawful only for priests to eat. And he also gave some to his companions."

27Then he said to them, "The Sabbath was made for man, not man for the Sabbath. 28So the Son of Man is Lord even of the Sabbath."

Jesus Heals on the Sabbath

3 Another time Jesus went into the synagogue, and a man with a shriveled hand was there. 2Some of them were looking for a reason to accuse Jesus, so they watched him closely to see if he would heal him on the Sabbath. 3Jesus said to the man with the shriveled hand, "Stand up in front of everyone."

4Then Jesus asked them, "Which is lawful on the Sabbath: to do good or to do evil, to save life or to kill?" But they remained silent.

5He looked around at them in anger and, deeply distressed at their stubborn hearts, said to the man, "Stretch out your hand." He stretched it out, and his hand was completely restored. 6Then the Pharisees went out and began to plot with the Herodians how they might kill Jesus.

Crowds Follow Jesus

7Jesus withdrew with his disciples to the lake, and a large crowd from Galilee followed. 8When they heard about all he was doing, many people came

MARK 2:13–17

TAX COLLECTORS AND SINNERS

Religion that leaves Jesus out of the equation teaches that people can do enough good to earn God's love and acceptance. This kind of religion manipulates the system by putting God in your debt. Religious people have difficulty with Jesus because he challenges their understanding of God and salvation. Too often people believe they can earn their way to heaven, but Jesus came to save people who will never be good enough to save themselves. For people who think too highly of themselves, the free gift of salvation that Jesus offers is offensive. Tragically, people who think they are good enough don't see any need for a Savior. During Jesus' ministry, the people who knew they had problems flocked to him: tax collectors, women of questionable character and others who saw their own desperate need. The religious leaders of his day didn't understand how or why a good, moral religious teacher like Jesus could spend time with such bad people. But Jesus knew that all people, without exception, need saving. As a Good Shepherd, Jesus came to seek and to save the lost (Lk 19:10).

to him from Judea, Jerusalem, Idumea, and the regions across the Jordan and
around Tyre and Sidon. [9]Because of the crowd he told his disciples to have a
small boat ready for him, to keep the people from crowding him. [10]For he had
healed many, so that those with diseases were pushing forward to touch him.
[11]Whenever the impure spirits saw him, they fell down before him and cried
out, "You are the Son of God." [12]But he gave them strict orders not to tell others
about him.

Jesus Appoints the Twelve

[13]Jesus went up on a mountainside and called to him those he wanted, and
they came to him. [14]He appointed twelve[a] that they might be with him and that
he might send them out to preach [15]and to have authority to drive out demons.
[16]These are the twelve he appointed: Simon (to whom he gave the name Peter),
[17]James son of Zebedee and his brother John (to them he gave the name Boaner-
ges, which means "sons of thunder"), [18]Andrew, Philip, Bartholomew, Matthew,
Thomas, James son of Alphaeus, Thaddaeus, Simon the Zealot [19]and Judas Iscariot, who betrayed him.

Jesus Accused by His Family and by Teachers of the Law

[20]Then Jesus entered a house, and again a crowd gathered, so that he and his
disciples were not even able to eat. [21]When his family[b] heard about this, they
went to take charge of him, for they said, "He is out of his mind."
[22]And the teachers of the law who came down from Jerusalem said, "He is possessed by Beelzebul! By the prince of demons he is driving out demons."
[23]So Jesus called them over to him and began to speak to them in parables:
"How can Satan drive out Satan? [24]If a kingdom is divided against itself, that
kingdom cannot stand. [25]If a house is divided against itself, that house cannot
stand. [26]And if Satan opposes himself and is divided, he cannot stand; his end
has come. [27]In fact, no one can enter a strong man's house without first tying him
up. Then he can plunder the strong man's house. [28]Truly I tell you, people can
be forgiven all their sins and every slander they utter, [29]but whoever blasphemes
against the Holy Spirit will never be forgiven; they are guilty of an eternal sin."
[30]He said this because they were saying, "He has an impure spirit."
[31]Then Jesus' mother and brothers arrived. Standing outside, they sent someone in to call him. [32]A crowd was sitting around him, and they told him, "Your
mother and brothers are outside looking for you."
[33]"Who are my mother and my brothers?" he asked.
[34]Then he looked at those seated in a circle around him and said, "Here are
my mother and my brothers! [35]Whoever does God's will is my brother and sister
and mother."

The Parable of the Sower

4 Again Jesus began to teach by the lake. The crowd that gathered around him
was so large that he got into a boat and sat in it out on the lake, while all the
people were along the shore at the water's edge. [2]He taught them many things by
parables, and in his teaching said: [3]"Listen! A farmer went out to sow his seed.
[4]As he was scattering the seed, some fell along the path, and the birds came and
ate it up. [5]Some fell on rocky places, where it did not have much soil. It sprang
up quickly, because the soil was shallow. [6]But when the sun came up, the plants
were scorched, and they withered because they had no root. [7]Other seed fell
among thorns, which grew up and choked the plants, so that they did not bear
grain. [8]Still other seed fell on good soil. It came up, grew and produced a crop,
some multiplying thirty, some sixty, some a hundred times."
[9]Then Jesus said, "Whoever has ears to hear, let them hear."
[10]When he was alone, the Twelve and the others around him asked him about

---

[a] 14 Some manuscripts *twelve—designating them apostles—* [b] 21 Or *his associates*

THE TWELVE APOSTLES

Jesus' strategy to influence the world was to invest in people and then unleash them to be his ambassadors.

Note several characteristics of the men he chose as his disciples. First, he chose ordinary people. One might think a global strategy would include people of global influence; however, Jesus chose the ordinary. He picked fishermen and tax collectors and others of humble routine, those we would consider "blue-collar" status. They were no-names. Nobodies.

Second, Jesus' disciples were invited. Discipleship for these men began with an invitation. He invited them to eat with him, talk with him, travel with him and learn from him. He cared for them personally. He instilled in them everything that they would need to preach and cast out demons (vv. 14 – 15). His instruction over their lives came not through lecture but through life. These men observed Jesus in the good moments and the bad, and in so doing learned how to emulate his life.

Third, some of the disciples received new names. Jesus gave James and John the moniker "sons of thunder." We know he also gave Simon the name Peter, meaning "rock." Through the Bible we see instances of God changing the names of people when something significant happened in their life. God changed the name of Abram ("high father") to Abraham ("father of a multitude") (Ge 17:3 – 5), and Jacob ("deceiver") became Israel ("he struggles with God") (Ge 32:28). Individuals in the Bible receive new names as a sign of the new purpose that God intends: Their lives were once headed in a particular direction, and now, under divine authority, they are headed in a completely new trajectory.

Jesus' leadership model and strategy to influence the world is one that his followers today can use. Paul implemented this model himself by personally investing his life into Timothy. To Timothy he wrote, "And the things you have heard me say in the presence of many witnesses entrust to reliable people who will also be qualified to teach others" (2Ti 2:2). Likewise, followers of Jesus should spend their lives inviting a few people into an intentional and life-giving relationship, just like Jesus did.

the parables. [11]He told them, "The secret of the kingdom of God has been given
to you. But to those on the outside everything is said in parables [12]so that,

"'they may be ever seeing but never perceiving,
and ever hearing but never understanding;
otherwise they might turn and be forgiven!'[a]"

[13]Then Jesus said to them, "Don't you understand this parable? How then will
you understand any parable? [14]The farmer sows the word. [15]Some people are
like seed along the path, where the word is sown. As soon as they hear it, Satan
comes and takes away the word that was sown in them. [16]Others, like seed sown
on rocky places, hear the word and at once receive it with joy. [17]But since they
have no root, they last only a short time. When trouble or persecution comes
because of the word, they quickly fall away. [18]Still others, like seed sown among
thorns, hear the word; [19]but the worries of this life, the deceitfulness of wealth
and the desires for other things come in and choke the word, making it unfruitful. [20]Others, like seed sown on good soil, hear the word, accept it, and produce a
crop — some thirty, some sixty, some a hundred times what was sown."

A Lamp on a Stand

[21]He said to them, "Do you bring in a lamp to put it under a bowl or a bed?
Instead, don't you put it on its stand? [22]For whatever is hidden is meant to be disclosed, and whatever is concealed is meant to be brought out into the open. [23]If
anyone has ears to hear, let them hear."
[24]"Consider carefully what you hear," he continued. "With the measure you
use, it will be measured to you — and even more. [25]Whoever has will be given
more; whoever does not have, even what they have will be taken from them."

The Parable of the Growing Seed

[26]He also said, "This is what the kingdom of God is like. A man scatters seed
on the ground. [27]Night and day, whether he sleeps or gets up, the seed sprouts
and grows, though he does not know how. [28]All by itself the soil produces grain —
first the stalk, then the head, then the full kernel in the head. [29]As soon as the
grain is ripe, he puts the sickle to it, because the harvest has come."

The Parable of the Mustard Seed

[30]Again he said, "What shall we say the kingdom of God is like, or what parable shall we use to describe it? [31]It is like a mustard seed, which is the smallest
of all seeds on earth. [32]Yet when planted, it grows and becomes the largest of
all garden plants, with such big branches that the birds can perch in its shade."
[33]With many similar parables Jesus spoke the word to them, as much as they
could understand. [34]He did not say anything to them without using a parable.
But when he was alone with his own disciples, he explained everything.

Jesus Calms the Storm

[35]That day when evening came, he said to his disciples, "Let us go over to the
other side." [36]Leaving the crowd behind, they took him along, just as he was, in
the boat. There were also other boats with him. [37]A furious squall came up, and
the waves broke over the boat, so that it was nearly swamped. [38]Jesus was in the
stern, sleeping on a cushion. The disciples woke him and said to him, "Teacher,
don't you care if we drown?"
[39]He got up, rebuked the wind and said to the waves, "Quiet! Be still!" Then the
wind died down and it was completely calm.
[40]He said to his disciples, "Why are you so afraid? Do you still have no faith?"
[41]They were terrified and asked each other, "Who is this? Even the wind and
the waves obey him!"

[a] *12* Isaiah 6:9,10

MARK 4:11

THE SECRET OF THE KINGDOM

Jesus' parables were like wrapped gifts given for people to enjoy. Jesus taught people about the kingdom by using these short stories that contained deeper meanings. Like all packages, the wrapping can either distract or captivate, and unless the package is opened, the gift remains unseen and not yet enjoyed. In the same way, Jesus' parables have to be unwrapped in order to uncover the application and understand the intent. Jesus said that even those who had physical sight and hearing might not understand what was presented to them (4:12, quoting Isa 6:9). Isaiah's words point to the fact that people's "hardness of heart" is created by sin. Those who seek the wisdom of God need to humble themselves, soften their hearts and honestly seek truth in order to find it. The religious leaders in this account were unwilling to give up their pride, humble themselves and learn from Jesus.

God is the One who fills us with understanding and gives wisdom (Col 1:9). All of this happens through Jesus, of whom John wrote, "We know also that the Son of God has come and has given us understanding, so that we may know him who is true. And we are in him who is true by being in his Son Jesus Christ. He is the true God and eternal life" (1Jn 5:20).

MARK 5:24–34

FAITH AND UNBELIEF

Faith is different from feelings. Feelings are based on circumstances, and they change like the weather. Faith involves acting, trusting and believing that God is real, at work and working for believers' good—regardless of what one may happen to feel at the moment. In fact, sometimes faith leads believers in the opposite direction of feelings.

The woman in this passage had been suffering for a long time. As her disorder involved blood, she was perpetually "unclean" (according to Jewish law), and as a result had likely been ostracized by her community. When she heard about the healing power of Jesus, she boldly braved the large crowd and reached out to him in faith. His response: "Daughter, your faith has healed you" (Mk 5:34).

God invites people to faithfully trust him for all of life (Pr 3:5–6). The way of Jesus is the way of trust. All throughout his life on earth, Jesus demonstrated absolute faith in his Father and challenged his followers to exercise the same kind of faith.

For many reasons, people are prone to doubt. Modern western culture is fraught with skepticism. The contemporary search for truth says, "Understand in order to believe." And against this thinking, Jesus has always maintained, "Believe in order to understand." In the struggle with doubt and unbelief, Jesus encourages people, "Don't be afraid; just believe" (Mk 5:36). The way of Jesus is the way of trusting God every day, for this life and the next.

Jesus Restores a Demon-Possessed Man

5 They went across the lake to the region of the Gerasenes.[a] 2When Jesus got out of the boat, a man with an impure spirit came from the tombs to meet him. 3This man lived in the tombs, and no one could bind him anymore, not even with a chain. 4For he had often been chained hand and foot, but he tore the chains apart and broke the irons on his feet. No one was strong enough to subdue him. 5Night and day among the tombs and in the hills he would cry out and cut himself with stones.

6When he saw Jesus from a distance, he ran and fell on his knees in front of him. 7He shouted at the top of his voice, "What do you want with me, Jesus, Son of the Most High God? In God's name don't torture me!" 8For Jesus had said to him, "Come out of this man, you impure spirit!"

9Then Jesus asked him, "What is your name?"

"My name is Legion," he replied, "for we are many." 10And he begged Jesus again and again not to send them out of the area.

11A large herd of pigs was feeding on the nearby hillside. 12The demons begged Jesus, "Send us among the pigs; allow us to go into them." 13He gave them permission, and the impure spirits came out and went into the pigs. The herd, about two thousand in number, rushed down the steep bank into the lake and were drowned.

14Those tending the pigs ran off and reported this in the town and countryside, and the people went out to see what had happened. 15When they came to Jesus, they saw the man who had been possessed by the legion of demons, sitting there, dressed and in his right mind; and they were afraid. 16Those who had seen it told the people what had happened to the demon-possessed man—and told about the pigs as well. 17Then the people began to plead with Jesus to leave their region.

18As Jesus was getting into the boat, the man who had been demon-possessed begged to go with him. 19Jesus did not let him, but said, "Go home to your own people and tell them how much the Lord has done for you, and how he has had mercy on you." 20So the man went away and began to tell in the Decapolis[b] how much Jesus had done for him. And all the people were amazed.

Jesus Raises a Dead Girl and Heals a Sick Woman

21When Jesus had again crossed over by boat to the other side of the lake, a large crowd gathered around him while he was by the lake. 22Then one of the synagogue leaders, named Jairus, came, and when he saw Jesus, he fell at his feet. 23He pleaded earnestly with him, "My little daughter is dying. Please come and put your hands on her so that she will be healed and live." 24So Jesus went with him.

A large crowd followed and pressed around him. 25And a woman was there who had been subject to bleeding for twelve years. 26She had suffered a great deal under the care of many doctors and had spent all she had, yet instead of getting better she grew worse. 27When she heard about Jesus, she came up behind him in the crowd and touched his cloak, 28because she thought, "If I just touch his clothes, I will be healed." 29Immediately her bleeding stopped and she felt in her body that she was freed from her suffering.

30At once Jesus realized that power had gone out from him. He turned around in the crowd and asked, "Who touched my clothes?"

31"You see the people crowding against you," his disciples answered, "and yet you can ask, 'Who touched me?' "

32But Jesus kept looking around to see who had done it. 33Then the woman, knowing what had happened to her, came and fell at his feet and, trembling with fear, told him the whole truth. 34He said to her, "Daughter, your faith has healed you. Go in peace and be freed from your suffering."

---

[a] *1* Some manuscripts *Gadarenes;* other manuscripts *Gergesenes* [b] *20* That is, the Ten Cities

[35]While Jesus was still speaking, some people came from the house of Jairus, the synagogue leader. "Your daughter is dead," they said. "Why bother the
teacher anymore?"
[36]Overhearing[a] what they said, Jesus told him, "Don't be afraid; just believe."
[37]He did not let anyone follow him except Peter, James and John the brother of James. [38]When they came to the home of the synagogue leader, Jesus saw
a commotion, with people crying and wailing loudly. [39]He went in and said to
them, "Why all this commotion and wailing? The child is not dead but asleep."
[40]But they laughed at him.
After he put them all out, he took the child's father and mother and the disciples who were with him, and went in where the child was. [41]He took her by the
hand and said to her, *"Talitha koum!"* (which means "Little girl, I say to you, get
up!"). [42]Immediately the girl stood up and began to walk around (she was twelve
years old). At this they were completely astonished. [43]He gave strict orders not to
let anyone know about this, and told them to give her something to eat.

A Prophet Without Honor

6 Jesus left there and went to his hometown, accompanied by his disciples.
[2]When the Sabbath came, he began to teach in the synagogue, and many
who heard him were amazed.
"Where did this man get these things?" they asked. "What's this wisdom that
has been given him? What are these remarkable miracles he is performing?
[3]Isn't this the carpenter? Isn't this Mary's son and the brother of James, Joseph,[b]
Judas and Simon? Aren't his sisters here with us?" And they took offense at him.
[4]Jesus said to them, "A prophet is not without honor except in his own town,
among his relatives and in his own home." [5]He could not do any miracles there,
except lay his hands on a few sick people and heal them. [6]He was amazed at
their lack of faith.

Jesus Sends Out the Twelve

Then Jesus went around teaching from village to village. [7]Calling the Twelve
to him, he began to send them out two by two and gave them authority over impure spirits.
[8]These were his instructions: "Take nothing for the journey except a staff—
no bread, no bag, no money in your belts. [9]Wear sandals but not an extra shirt.
[10]Whenever you enter a house, stay there until you leave that town. [11]And if any
place will not welcome you or listen to you, leave that place and shake the dust
off your feet as a testimony against them."
[12]They went out and preached that people should repent. [13]They drove out
many demons and anointed many sick people with oil and healed them.

John the Baptist Beheaded

[14]King Herod heard about this, for Jesus' name had become well known. Some
were saying,[c] "John the Baptist has been raised from the dead, and that is why
miraculous powers are at work in him."
[15]Others said, "He is Elijah."
And still others claimed, "He is a prophet, like one of the prophets of long ago."
[16]But when Herod heard this, he said, "John, whom I beheaded, has been
raised from the dead!"
[17]For Herod himself had given orders to have John arrested, and he had him
bound and put in prison. He did this because of Herodias, his brother Philip's
wife, whom he had married. [18]For John had been saying to Herod, "It is not lawful for you to have your brother's wife." [19]So Herodias nursed a grudge against
John and wanted to kill him. But she was not able to, [20]because Herod feared

---

[a] *36* Or *Ignoring* [b] *3* Greek *Joses*, a variant of *Joseph* [c] *14* Some early manuscripts *He was saying*

MIRACLES: A FORESHADOWING OF THE RESTORED CREATION

In his model prayer, Jesus prayed that the kingdom of God would come "on earth as it is in heaven" (Mt 6:10). In praying for this, he recognized the effects that sin has on the earth, pointing to God's much greater kingdom plans. When we pray this prayer, we look forward to the kingdom of God, where creation will be made new and the effects of sin completely removed. What a day that will be!

Mark 5 shows three people who had been deeply impacted by the imperfection of this physical world and the terrors of the spiritual world. The first was a man "with an impure spirit." This spirit caused him to do many destructive things to others and to himself. He was a social outcast, banished to live in the tombs because no one in his community could manage his demon possession. Scripture says that he tried to deal with his pain by crying out and cutting himself with stones (5:5). These behaviors are a far cry from the peace and flourishing life that God desires for people, so Jesus stepped into the man's reality and saved him. He restored the possessed man to "his right mind" (5:15). In bringing the man back to his right mind, Jesus pointed to the way things will be in the kingdom of God, when all things will someday be made right.

The next encounters were with a woman who was sick and a girl who had died. In both instances, Jesus stepped into their reality and restored their lives. Death and sickness are not a part of the kingdom of God; therefore as a sign of that coming kingdom, Jesus healed both of these people.

The accounts of Jesus' miracles give believers a look in three directions. First, miracles cause believers to look back to God's original intention for creation to see how things were meant to be. Second, miracles cause believers to look inward to consider the pervasive effects of sin in the world and to cry out to God for deliverance. Finally, miracles are also a glimpse ahead to the kingdom of God in its fullness, where we eagerly anticipate the complete restoration of creation.

John and protected him, knowing him to be a righteous and holy man. When Herod heard John, he was greatly puzzled[a]; yet he liked to listen to him.

[21]Finally the opportune time came. On his birthday Herod gave a banquet for his high officials and military commanders and the leading men of Galilee. [22]When the daughter of[b] Herodias came in and danced, she pleased Herod and his dinner guests.

The king said to the girl, "Ask me for anything you want, and I'll give it to you." [23]And he promised her with an oath, "Whatever you ask I will give you, up to half my kingdom."

[24]She went out and said to her mother, "What shall I ask for?"

"The head of John the Baptist," she answered.

[25]At once the girl hurried in to the king with the request: "I want you to give me right now the head of John the Baptist on a platter."

[26]The king was greatly distressed, but because of his oaths and his dinner guests, he did not want to refuse her. [27]So he immediately sent an executioner with orders to bring John's head. The man went, beheaded John in the prison, [28]and brought back his head on a platter. He presented it to the girl, and she gave it to her mother. [29]On hearing of this, John's disciples came and took his body and laid it in a tomb.

Jesus Feeds the Five Thousand

[30]The apostles gathered around Jesus and reported to him all they had done and taught. [31]Then, because so many people were coming and going that they did not even have a chance to eat, he said to them, "Come with me by yourselves to a quiet place and get some rest."

[32]So they went away by themselves in a boat to a solitary place. [33]But many who saw them leaving recognized them and ran on foot from all the towns and got there ahead of them. [34]When Jesus landed and saw a large crowd, he had compassion on them, because they were like sheep without a shepherd. So he began teaching them many things.

[35]By this time it was late in the day, so his disciples came to him. "This is a remote place," they said, "and it's already very late. [36]Send the people away so that they can go to the surrounding countryside and villages and buy themselves something to eat."

[37]But he answered, "You give them something to eat."

They said to him, "That would take more than half a year's wages[c]! Are we to go and spend that much on bread and give it to them to eat?"

[38]"How many loaves do you have?" he asked. "Go and see."

When they found out, they said, "Five — and two fish."

[39]Then Jesus directed them to have all the people sit down in groups on the green grass. [40]So they sat down in groups of hundreds and fifties. [41]Taking the five loaves and the two fish and looking up to heaven, he gave thanks and broke the loaves. Then he gave them to his disciples to distribute to the people. He also divided the two fish among them all. [42]They all ate and were satisfied, [43]and the disciples picked up twelve basketfuls of broken pieces of bread and fish. [44]The number of the men who had eaten was five thousand.

Jesus Walks on the Water

[45]Immediately Jesus made his disciples get into the boat and go on ahead of him to Bethsaida, while he dismissed the crowd. [46]After leaving them, he went up on a mountainside to pray.

[47]Later that night, the boat was in the middle of the lake, and he was alone on land. [48]He saw the disciples straining at the oars, because the wind was against them. Shortly before dawn he went out to them, walking on the lake. He

---

[a] 20 Some early manuscripts *he did many things* [b] 22 Some early manuscripts *When his daughter* [c] 37 Greek *take two hundred denarii*

was about to pass by them, [49]but when they saw him walking on the lake, they thought he was a ghost. They cried out, [50]because they all saw him and were terrified.

Immediately he spoke to them and said, "Take courage! It is I. Don't be afraid." [51]Then he climbed into the boat with them, and the wind died down. They were completely amazed, [52]for they had not understood about the loaves; their hearts were hardened.

[53]When they had crossed over, they landed at Gennesaret and anchored there. [54]As soon as they got out of the boat, people recognized Jesus. [55]They ran throughout that whole region and carried the sick on mats to wherever they heard he was. [56]And wherever he went — into villages, towns or countryside — they placed the sick in the marketplaces. They begged him to let them touch even the edge of his cloak, and all who touched it were healed.

That Which Defiles

7 The Pharisees and some of the teachers of the law who had come from Jerusalem gathered around Jesus [2]and saw some of his disciples eating food with hands that were defiled, that is, unwashed. [3](The Pharisees and all the Jews do not eat unless they give their hands a ceremonial washing, holding to the tradition of the elders. [4]When they come from the marketplace they do not eat unless they wash. And they observe many other traditions, such as the washing of cups, pitchers and kettles.[a])

[5]So the Pharisees and teachers of the law asked Jesus, "Why don't your disciples live according to the tradition of the elders instead of eating their food with defiled hands?"

[6]He replied, "Isaiah was right when he prophesied about you hypocrites; as it is written:

" 'These people honor me with their lips,
  but their hearts are far from me.
[7]They worship me in vain;
  their teachings are merely human rules.'[b]

[8]You have let go of the commands of God and are holding on to human traditions."

[9]And he continued, "You have a fine way of setting aside the commands of God in order to observe[c] your own traditions! [10]For Moses said, 'Honor your father and mother,'[d] and, 'Anyone who curses their father or mother is to be put to death.'[e] [11]But you say that if anyone declares that what might have been used to help their father or mother is Corban (that is, devoted to God) — [12]then you no longer let them do anything for their father or mother. [13]Thus you nullify the word of God by your tradition that you have handed down. And you do many things like that."

[14]Again Jesus called the crowd to him and said, "Listen to me, everyone, and understand this. [15]Nothing outside a person can defile them by going into them. Rather, it is what comes out of a person that defiles them." [16][f]

[17]After he had left the crowd and entered the house, his disciples asked him about this parable. [18]"Are you so dull?" he asked. "Don't you see that nothing that enters a person from the outside can defile them? [19]For it doesn't go into their heart but into their stomach, and then out of the body." (In saying this, Jesus declared all foods clean.)

[20]He went on: "What comes out of a person is what defiles them. [21]For it is from within, out of a person's heart, that evil thoughts come — sexual immorality, theft, murder, [22]adultery, greed, malice, deceit, lewdness, envy, slander, arrogance and folly. [23]All these evils come from inside and defile a person."

---

[a] *4* Some early manuscripts *pitchers, kettles and dining couches* [b] *6,7* Isaiah 29:13
[c] *9* Some manuscripts *set up* [d] *10* Exodus 20:12; Deut. 5:16 [e] *10* Exodus 21:17; Lev. 20:9
[f] *16* Some manuscripts include here the words of 4:23.

Jesus Honors a Syrophoenician Woman's Faith

[24]Jesus left that place and went to the vicinity of Tyre.[a] He entered a house and did not want anyone to know it; yet he could not keep his presence secret. [25]In fact, as soon as she heard about him, a woman whose little daughter was possessed by an impure spirit came and fell at his feet. [26]The woman was a Greek, born in Syrian Phoenicia. She begged Jesus to drive the demon out of her daughter.

[27]"First let the children eat all they want," he told her, "for it is not right to take the children's bread and toss it to the dogs."

[28]"Lord," she replied, "even the dogs under the table eat the children's crumbs."

[29]Then he told her, "For such a reply, you may go; the demon has left your daughter."

[30]She went home and found her child lying on the bed, and the demon gone.

Jesus Heals a Deaf and Mute Man

[31]Then Jesus left the vicinity of Tyre and went through Sidon, down to the Sea of Galilee and into the region of the Decapolis.[b] [32]There some people brought to him a man who was deaf and could hardly talk, and they begged Jesus to place his hand on him.

[33]After he took him aside, away from the crowd, Jesus put his fingers into the man's ears. Then he spit and touched the man's tongue. [34]He looked up to heaven and with a deep sigh said to him, *"Ephphatha!"* (which means "Be opened!"). [35]At this, the man's ears were opened, his tongue was loosened and he began to speak plainly.

[36]Jesus commanded them not to tell anyone. But the more he did so, the more they kept talking about it. [37]People were overwhelmed with amazement. "He has done everything well," they said. "He even makes the deaf hear and the mute speak."

Jesus Feeds the Four Thousand

8 During those days another large crowd gathered. Since they had nothing to eat, Jesus called his disciples to him and said, [2]"I have compassion for these people; they have already been with me three days and have nothing to eat. [3]If I send them home hungry, they will collapse on the way, because some of them have come a long distance."

[4]His disciples answered, "But where in this remote place can anyone get enough bread to feed them?"

[5]"How many loaves do you have?" Jesus asked.

"Seven," they replied.

[6]He told the crowd to sit down on the ground. When he had taken the seven loaves and given thanks, he broke them and gave them to his disciples to distribute to the people, and they did so. [7]They had a few small fish as well; he gave thanks for them also and told the disciples to distribute them. [8]The people ate and were satisfied. Afterward the disciples picked up seven basketfuls of broken pieces that were left over. [9]About four thousand were present. After he had sent them away, [10]he got into the boat with his disciples and went to the region of Dalmanutha.

[11]The Pharisees came and began to question Jesus. To test him, they asked him for a sign from heaven. [12]He sighed deeply and said, "Why does this generation ask for a sign? Truly I tell you, no sign will be given to it." [13]Then he left them, got back into the boat and crossed to the other side.

The Yeast of the Pharisees and Herod

[14]The disciples had forgotten to bring bread, except for one loaf they had with them in the boat. [15]"Be careful," Jesus warned them. "Watch out for the yeast of the Pharisees and that of Herod."

[16]They discussed this with one another and said, "It is because we have no bread."

[a] *24* Many early manuscripts *Tyre and Sidon* [b] *31* That is, the Ten Cities

MARK 7:24–30

"MEAN" JESUS?

During dinner, a local woman sought Jesus' attention and care. Jesus responded in a way that could be misinterpreted as mean or rude (v. 27). But Jesus was not attempting to insult the woman with this metaphor. In fact, he was testing her faith. He wanted the woman to consider what she felt about him: whether she thought he was merely another religious guru or he was the only way her daughter could be healed.

Matthew, one of the other Gospel writers, records Jesus' response to this hopeful mother in this way: "Then Jesus said to her, 'Woman, you have great faith! Your request is granted.' And her daughter was healed at that moment" (Mt 15:28). This wise woman understood the test and persisted in seeking Jesus' help. Believers today can learn a valuable lesson from the faith and practice of this mother who cared enough to push the envelope, in faith.

17 Aware of their discussion, Jesus asked them: "Why are you talking about
having no bread? Do you still not see or understand? Are your hearts hardened?
18 Do you have eyes but fail to see, and ears but fail to hear? And don't you remember? 19 When I broke the five loaves for the five thousand, how many basketfuls
of pieces did you pick up?"

"Twelve," they replied.

20 "And when I broke the seven loaves for the four thousand, how many basketfuls of pieces did you pick up?"

They answered, "Seven."

21 He said to them, "Do you still not understand?"

Jesus Heals a Blind Man at Bethsaida

22 They came to Bethsaida, and some people brought a blind man and begged
Jesus to touch him. 23 He took the blind man by the hand and led him outside
the village. When he had spit on the man's eyes and put his hands on him, Jesus
asked, "Do you see anything?"

24 He looked up and said, "I see people; they look like trees walking around."

25 Once more Jesus put his hands on the man's eyes. Then his eyes were
opened, his sight was restored, and he saw everything clearly. 26 Jesus sent him
home, saying, "Don't even go into[a] the village."

Peter Declares That Jesus Is the Messiah

27 Jesus and his disciples went on to the villages around Caesarea Philippi. On
the way he asked them, "Who do people say I am?"

28 They replied, "Some say John the Baptist; others say Elijah; and still others,
one of the prophets."

29 "But what about you?" he asked. "Who do you say I am?"

Peter answered, "You are the Messiah."

30 Jesus warned them not to tell anyone about him.

Jesus Predicts His Death

31 He then began to teach them that the Son of Man must suffer many things
and be rejected by the elders, the chief priests and the teachers of the law, and
that he must be killed and after three days rise again. 32 He spoke plainly about
this, and Peter took him aside and began to rebuke him.

33 But when Jesus turned and looked at his disciples, he rebuked Peter. "Get
behind me, Satan!" he said. "You do not have in mind the concerns of God, but
merely human concerns."

The Way of the Cross

34 Then he called the crowd to him along with his disciples and said: "Whoever
wants to be my disciple must deny themselves and take up their cross and follow
me. 35 For whoever wants to save their life[b] will lose it, but whoever loses their
life for me and for the gospel will save it. 36 What good is it for someone to gain
the whole world, yet forfeit their soul? 37 Or what can anyone give in exchange for
their soul? 38 If anyone is ashamed of me and my words in this adulterous and
sinful generation, the Son of Man will be ashamed of them when he comes in his
Father's glory with the holy angels."

9 And he said to them, "Truly I tell you, some who are standing here will not
taste death before they see that the kingdom of God has come with power."

The Transfiguration

2 After six days Jesus took Peter, James and John with him and led them up
a high mountain, where they were all alone. There he was transfigured before
them. 3 His clothes became dazzling white, whiter than anyone in the world

---

[a] 26 Some manuscripts *go and tell anyone in*

[b] 35 The Greek word means either *life* or *soul*; also in verses 36 and 37.

could bleach them. [4]And there appeared before them Elijah and Moses, who
were talking with Jesus.
[5]Peter said to Jesus, "Rabbi, it is good for us to be here. Let us put up three
shelters — one for you, one for Moses and one for Elijah." [6](He did not know what
to say, they were so frightened.)
[7]Then a cloud appeared and covered them, and a voice came from the cloud:
"This is my Son, whom I love. Listen to him!"
[8]Suddenly, when they looked around, they no longer saw anyone with them
except Jesus.
[9]As they were coming down the mountain, Jesus gave them orders not to tell
anyone what they had seen until the Son of Man had risen from the dead. [10]They
kept the matter to themselves, discussing what "rising from the dead" meant.
[11]And they asked him, "Why do the teachers of the law say that Elijah must
come first?"
[12]Jesus replied, "To be sure, Elijah does come first, and restores all things.
Why then is it written that the Son of Man must suffer much and be rejected?
[13]But I tell you, Elijah has come, and they have done to him everything they
wished, just as it is written about him."

Jesus Heals a Boy Possessed by an Impure Spirit

[14]When they came to the other disciples, they saw a large crowd around them
and the teachers of the law arguing with them. [15]As soon as all the people saw
Jesus, they were overwhelmed with wonder and ran to greet him.
[16]"What are you arguing with them about?" he asked.
[17]A man in the crowd answered, "Teacher, I brought you my son, who is possessed by a spirit that has robbed him of speech. [18]Whenever it seizes him, it
throws him to the ground. He foams at the mouth, gnashes his teeth and becomes rigid. I asked your disciples to drive out the spirit, but they could not."
[19]"You unbelieving generation," Jesus replied, "how long shall I stay with you?
How long shall I put up with you? Bring the boy to me."
[20]So they brought him. When the spirit saw Jesus, it immediately threw the boy
into a convulsion. He fell to the ground and rolled around, foaming at the mouth.
[21]Jesus asked the boy's father, "How long has he been like this?"
"From childhood," he answered. [22]"It has often thrown him into fire or water
to kill him. But if you can do anything, take pity on us and help us."
[23]" 'If you can'?" said Jesus. "Everything is possible for one who believes."
[24]Immediately the boy's father exclaimed, "I do believe; help me overcome
my unbelief!"
[25]When Jesus saw that a crowd was running to the scene, he rebuked the impure spirit. "You deaf and mute spirit," he said, "I command you, come out of
him and never enter him again."
[26]The spirit shrieked, convulsed him violently and came out. The boy looked
so much like a corpse that many said, "He's dead." [27]But Jesus took him by the
hand and lifted him to his feet, and he stood up.
[28]After Jesus had gone indoors, his disciples asked him privately, "Why
couldn't we drive it out?"
[29]He replied, "This kind can come out only by prayer.[a]"

Jesus Predicts His Death a Second Time

[30]They left that place and passed through Galilee. Jesus did not want anyone
to know where they were, [31]because he was teaching his disciples. He said to
them, "The Son of Man is going to be delivered into the hands of men. They will
kill him, and after three days he will rise." [32]But they did not understand what he
meant and were afraid to ask him about it.
[33]They came to Capernaum. When he was in the house, he asked them, "What

[a] 29 Some manuscripts *prayer and fasting*

MARK 9:7

SON OF GOD

In the Old Testament, Moses asked God to show him his glory to confirm his calling on Moses' life (Ex 33:18 – 23). God could not fully reveal his glory to a mere man, so God showed Moses only a shielded portion of his glory. It was so intense that Moses reflected that glory on his face for a couple of days (Ge 34:29 – 32)!

In the episode of the transfiguration, God the Father showed his glory in a special way to Jesus in front of a few of his disciples. God revealed his glory in his Son to prove that Jesus is the Son of God, a title that is used often through the Gospel of Mark (here; 3:11; 5:7; 13:32).

Both the sun and the moon give light so that people can see, but the moon only reflects the sun's light and shines just a fraction of it into the world. In a similar way, Moses was like the moon, but Jesus, the Son of God and the full revelation of God himself, reflects God's brilliant and blazing presence: "The Son is the radiance of God's glory and the exact representation of his being" (Heb 1:3).

were you arguing about on the road?" 34But they kept quiet because on the way
they had argued about who was the greatest.
35Sitting down, Jesus called the Twelve and said, "Anyone who wants to be
first must be the very last, and the servant of all."
36He took a little child whom he placed among them. Taking the child in his
arms, he said to them, 37"Whoever welcomes one of these little children in my
name welcomes me; and whoever welcomes me does not welcome me but the
one who sent me."

Whoever Is Not Against Us Is for Us

38"Teacher," said John, "we saw someone driving out demons in your name
and we told him to stop, because he was not one of us."
39"Do not stop him," Jesus said. "For no one who does a miracle in my name
can in the next moment say anything bad about me, 40for whoever is not against
us is for us. 41Truly I tell you, anyone who gives you a cup of water in my name
because you belong to the Messiah will certainly not lose their reward.

Causing to Stumble

42"If anyone causes one of these little ones — those who believe in me — to stumble, it would be better for them if a large millstone were hung around their neck and
they were thrown into the sea. 43If your hand causes you to stumble, cut it off. It is
better for you to enter life maimed than with two hands to go into hell, where the
fire never goes out. [44][a] 45And if your foot causes you to stumble, cut it off. It is better
for you to enter life crippled than to have two feet and be thrown into hell. [46][a] 47And
if your eye causes you to stumble, pluck it out. It is better for you to enter the kingdom of God with one eye than to have two eyes and be thrown into hell, 48where

> " 'the worms that eat them do not die,
> and the fire is not quenched.'[b]

49Everyone will be salted with fire.
50"Salt is good, but if it loses its saltiness, how can you make it salty again?
Have salt among yourselves, and be at peace with each other."

Divorce

10 Jesus then left that place and went into the region of Judea and across the
Jordan. Again crowds of people came to him, and as was his custom, he
taught them.
2Some Pharisees came and tested him by asking, "Is it lawful for a man to
divorce his wife?"
3"What did Moses command you?" he replied.
4They said, "Moses permitted a man to write a certificate of divorce and send
her away."
5"It was because your hearts were hard that Moses wrote you this law," Jesus
replied. 6"But at the beginning of creation God 'made them male and female.'[c]
7'For this reason a man will leave his father and mother and be united to his
wife,[d] 8and the two will become one flesh.'[e] So they are no longer two, but one
flesh. 9Therefore what God has joined together, let no one separate."
10When they were in the house again, the disciples asked Jesus about this.
11He answered, "Anyone who divorces his wife and marries another woman
commits adultery against her. 12And if she divorces her husband and marries
another man, she commits adultery."

The Little Children and Jesus

13People were bringing little children to Jesus for him to place his hands on
them, but the disciples rebuked them. 14When Jesus saw this, he was indignant.

[a] 44,46 Some manuscripts include here the words of verse 48. [b] 48 Isaiah 66:24 [c] 6 Gen.
1:27 [d] 7 Some early manuscripts do not have *and be united to his wife.* [e] 8 Gen. 2:24

He said to them, "Let the little children come to me, and do not hinder them,
for the kingdom of God belongs to such as these. 15Truly I tell you, anyone who
will not receive the kingdom of God like a little child will never enter it." 16And
he took the children in his arms, placed his hands on them and blessed them.

The Rich and the Kingdom of God

17As Jesus started on his way, a man ran up to him and fell on his knees before
him. "Good teacher," he asked, "what must I do to inherit eternal life?"

18"Why do you call me good?" Jesus answered. "No one is good — except God
alone. 19You know the commandments: 'You shall not murder, you shall not
commit adultery, you shall not steal, you shall not give false testimony, you shall
not defraud, honor your father and mother.'[a]"

20"Teacher," he declared, "all these I have kept since I was a boy."

21Jesus looked at him and loved him. "One thing you lack," he said. "Go, sell
everything you have and give to the poor, and you will have treasure in heaven.
Then come, follow me."

22At this the man's face fell. He went away sad, because he had great wealth.

23Jesus looked around and said to his disciples, "How hard it is for the rich to
enter the kingdom of God!"

24The disciples were amazed at his words. But Jesus said again, "Children,
how hard it is[b] to enter the kingdom of God! 25It is easier for a camel to go through
the eye of a needle than for someone who is rich to enter the kingdom of God."

26The disciples were even more amazed, and said to each other, "Who then
can be saved?"

27Jesus looked at them and said, "With man this is impossible, but not with
God; all things are possible with God."

28Then Peter spoke up, "We have left everything to follow you!"

29"Truly I tell you," Jesus replied, "no one who has left home or brothers or
sisters or mother or father or children or fields for me and the gospel 30will fail
to receive a hundred times as much in this present age: homes, brothers, sisters,
mothers, children and fields — along with persecutions — and in the age to come
eternal life. 31But many who are first will be last, and the last first."

Jesus Predicts His Death a Third Time

32They were on their way up to Jerusalem, with Jesus leading the way, and the
disciples were astonished, while those who followed were afraid. Again he took
the Twelve aside and told them what was going to happen to him. 33"We are going up to Jerusalem," he said, "and the Son of Man will be delivered over to the
chief priests and the teachers of the law. They will condemn him to death and
will hand him over to the Gentiles, 34who will mock him and spit on him, flog
him and kill him. Three days later he will rise."

The Request of James and John

35Then James and John, the sons of Zebedee, came to him. "Teacher," they
said, "we want you to do for us whatever we ask."

36"What do you want me to do for you?" he asked.

37They replied, "Let one of us sit at your right and the other at your left in your
glory."

38"You don't know what you are asking," Jesus said. "Can you drink the cup I
drink or be baptized with the baptism I am baptized with?"

39"We can," they answered.

Jesus said to them, "You will drink the cup I drink and be baptized with the
baptism I am baptized with, 40but to sit at my right or left is not for me to grant.
These places belong to those for whom they have been prepared."

41When the ten heard about this, they became indignant with James and

---

[a] *19* Exodus 20:12-16; Deut. 5:16-20 [b] *24* Some manuscripts *is for those who trust in riches*

John. 42Jesus called them together and said, "You know that those who are regarded as rulers of the Gentiles lord it over them, and their high officials exercise
authority over them. 43Not so with you. Instead, whoever wants to become great
among you must be your servant, 44and whoever wants to be first must be slave
of all. 45For even the Son of Man did not come to be served, but to serve, and to
give his life as a ransom for many."

Blind Bartimaeus Receives His Sight

46Then they came to Jericho. As Jesus and his disciples, together with a large
crowd, were leaving the city, a blind man, Bartimaeus (which means "son of Ti-
maeus"), was sitting by the roadside begging. 47When he heard that it was Jesus
of Nazareth, he began to shout, "Jesus, Son of David, have mercy on me!"

48Many rebuked him and told him to be quiet, but he shouted all the more,
"Son of David, have mercy on me!"

49Jesus stopped and said, "Call him."

So they called to the blind man, "Cheer up! On your feet! He's calling you."
50Throwing his cloak aside, he jumped to his feet and came to Jesus.

51"What do you want me to do for you?" Jesus asked him.

The blind man said, "Rabbi, I want to see."

52"Go," said Jesus, "your faith has healed you." Immediately he received his
sight and followed Jesus along the road.

Jesus Comes to Jerusalem as King

11 As they approached Jerusalem and came to Bethphage and Bethany at the
Mount of Olives, Jesus sent two of his disciples, 2saying to them, "Go to the
village ahead of you, and just as you enter it, you will find a colt tied there, which
no one has ever ridden. Untie it and bring it here. 3If anyone asks you, 'Why are
you doing this?' say, 'The Lord needs it and will send it back here shortly.' "

4They went and found a colt outside in the street, tied at a doorway. As they
untied it, 5some people standing there asked, "What are you doing, untying that
colt?" 6They answered as Jesus had told them to, and the people let them go.
7When they brought the colt to Jesus and threw their cloaks over it, he sat on it.
8Many people spread their cloaks on the road, while others spread branches they
had cut in the fields. 9Those who went ahead and those who followed shouted,

"Hosanna![a]"

"Blessed is he who comes in the name of the Lord!"[b]

10"Blessed is the coming kingdom of our father David!"

"Hosanna in the highest heaven!"

11Jesus entered Jerusalem and went into the temple courts. He looked around
at everything, but since it was already late, he went out to Bethany with the
Twelve.

Jesus Curses a Fig Tree and Clears the Temple Courts

12The next day as they were leaving Bethany, Jesus was hungry. 13Seeing in the
distance a fig tree in leaf, he went to find out if it had any fruit. When he reached
it, he found nothing but leaves, because it was not the season for figs. 14Then he
said to the tree, "May no one ever eat fruit from you again." And his disciples
heard him say it.

15On reaching Jerusalem, Jesus entered the temple courts and began driving out those who were buying and selling there. He overturned the tables of
the money changers and the benches of those selling doves, 16and would not allow anyone to carry merchandise through the temple courts. 17And as he taught

---

[a] 9 A Hebrew expression meaning "Save!" which became an exclamation of praise; also in verse 10 [b] 9 Psalm 118:25,26

them, he said, "Is it not written: 'My house will be called a house of prayer for all nations'[a]? But you have made it 'a den of robbers.'[b]"
[18]The chief priests and the teachers of the law heard this and began looking for a way to kill him, for they feared him, because the whole crowd was amazed at his teaching.
[19]When evening came, Jesus and his disciples[c] went out of the city.
[20]In the morning, as they went along, they saw the fig tree withered from the
roots. [21]Peter remembered and said to Jesus, "Rabbi, look! The fig tree you cursed has withered!"
[22]"Have faith in God," Jesus answered. [23]"Truly[d] I tell you, if anyone says to this mountain, 'Go, throw yourself into the sea,' and does not doubt in their heart
but believes that what they say will happen, it will be done for them. [24]Therefore I tell you, whatever you ask for in prayer, believe that you have received it, and it
will be yours. [25]And when you stand praying, if you hold anything against anyone, forgive them, so that your Father in heaven may forgive you your sins." [26][e]

The Authority of Jesus Questioned

[27]They arrived again in Jerusalem, and while Jesus was walking in the temple courts, the chief priests, the teachers of the law and the elders came to him.
[28]"By what authority are you doing these things?" they asked. "And who gave you authority to do this?"
[29]Jesus replied, "I will ask you one question. Answer me, and I will tell you by
what authority I am doing these things. [30]John's baptism—was it from heaven, or of human origin? Tell me!"
[31]They discussed it among themselves and said, "If we say, 'From heaven,' he
will ask, 'Then why didn't you believe him?' [32]But if we say, 'Of human origin' . . ." (They feared the people, for everyone held that John really was a prophet.)
[33]So they answered Jesus, "We don't know."
Jesus said, "Neither will I tell you by what authority I am doing these things."

The Parable of the Tenants

12 Jesus then began to speak to them in parables: "A man planted a vineyard. He put a wall around it, dug a pit for the winepress and built a watchtower.
Then he rented the vineyard to some farmers and moved to another place. [2]At
harvest time he sent a servant to the tenants to collect from them some of the
fruit of the vineyard. [3]But they seized him, beat him and sent him away empty-handed. [4]Then he sent another servant to them; they struck this man on the
head and treated him shamefully. [5]He sent still another, and that one they killed. He sent many others; some of them they beat, others they killed.
[6]"He had one left to send, a son, whom he loved. He sent him last of all, saying, 'They will respect my son.'
[7]"But the tenants said to one another, 'This is the heir. Come, let's kill him,
and the inheritance will be ours.' [8]So they took him and killed him, and threw him out of the vineyard.
[9]"What then will the owner of the vineyard do? He will come and kill those tenants and give the vineyard to others. [10]Haven't you read this passage of Scripture:

" 'The stone the builders rejected
has become the cornerstone;
[11]the Lord has done this,
and it is marvelous in our eyes'[f]?"

[12]Then the chief priests, the teachers of the law and the elders looked for a way to arrest him because they knew he had spoken the parable against them. But they were afraid of the crowd; so they left him and went away.

[a] *17* Isaiah 56:7 [b] *17* Jer. 7:11 [c] *19* Some early manuscripts *came, Jesus* [d] *22,23* Some early manuscripts *"If you have faith in God," Jesus answered,* [23]*"truly* [e] *26* Some manuscripts include here words similar to Matt. 6:15. [f] *11* Psalm 118:22,23

MARK 12:9–11

THE CORNERSTONE

Jesus, as a trained carpenter and possibly also a stonemason, knew that building requires precision. In biblical times, buildings were often made of cut stones that were squared together, side by side. To keep the entire building "plumb," the builders would establish a "cornerstone" and work off that. The cornerstone would help align the two intersecting walls of the building and would serve to show if another stone was out of line. Appropriately, at various points in the New Testament, Jesus is referred to as the "cornerstone" (Ac 4:10,11; Eph 2:20). He is the stone that the builders rejected (Ps 118:22). Some people, in their pride, trip and stumble over Jesus' teaching. Thus, Jesus is a stumbling block for some and the source of life for others.

Jesus is the chief cornerstone of the church because "salvation is found in no one else, for there is no other name under heaven given to mankind by which we must be saved" (Ac 4:12). God continues to build his church—a throng of people who will exist as his temple in the world and will help others encounter God. The church is all about Jesus, because "In him the whole building is joined together and rises to become a holy temple in the Lord" (Eph 2:21).

Paying the Imperial Tax to Caesar

[13]Later they sent some of the Pharisees and Herodians to Jesus to catch him in his words. [14]They came to him and said, "Teacher, we know that you are a man of integrity. You aren't swayed by others, because you pay no attention to who they are; but you teach the way of God in accordance with the truth. Is it right to pay the imperial tax[a] to Caesar or not? [15]Should we pay or shouldn't we?"

But Jesus knew their hypocrisy. "Why are you trying to trap me?" he asked. "Bring me a denarius and let me look at it." [16]They brought the coin, and he asked them, "Whose image is this? And whose inscription?"

"Caesar's," they replied.

[17]Then Jesus said to them, "Give back to Caesar what is Caesar's and to God what is God's."

And they were amazed at him.

Marriage at the Resurrection

[18]Then the Sadducees, who say there is no resurrection, came to him with a question. [19]"Teacher," they said, "Moses wrote for us that if a man's brother dies and leaves a wife but no children, the man must marry the widow and raise up offspring for his brother. [20]Now there were seven brothers. The first one married and died without leaving any children. [21]The second one married the widow, but he also died, leaving no child. It was the same with the third. [22]In fact, none of the seven left any children. Last of all, the woman died too. [23]At the resurrection[b] whose wife will she be, since the seven were married to her?"

[24]Jesus replied, "Are you not in error because you do not know the Scriptures or the power of God? [25]When the dead rise, they will neither marry nor be given in marriage; they will be like the angels in heaven. [26]Now about the dead rising—have you not read in the Book of Moses, in the account of the burning bush, how God said to him, 'I am the God of Abraham, the God of Isaac, and the God of Jacob'[c]? [27]He is not the God of the dead, but of the living. You are badly mistaken!"

The Greatest Commandment

[28]One of the teachers of the law came and heard them debating. Noticing that Jesus had given them a good answer, he asked him, "Of all the commandments, which is the most important?"

[29]"The most important one," answered Jesus, "is this: 'Hear, O Israel: The Lord our God, the Lord is one.[d] [30]Love the Lord your God with all your heart and with all your soul and with all your mind and with all your strength.'[e] [31]The second is this: 'Love your neighbor as yourself.'[f] There is no commandment greater than these."

[32]"Well said, teacher," the man replied. "You are right in saying that God is one and there is no other but him. [33]To love him with all your heart, with all your understanding and with all your strength, and to love your neighbor as yourself is more important than all burnt offerings and sacrifices."

[34]When Jesus saw that he had answered wisely, he said to him, "You are not far from the kingdom of God." And from then on no one dared ask him any more questions.

Whose Son Is the Messiah?

[35]While Jesus was teaching in the temple courts, he asked, "Why do the teachers of the law say that the Messiah is the son of David? [36]David himself, speaking by the Holy Spirit, declared:

" 'The Lord said to my Lord:
"Sit at my right hand

---

[a] *14* A special tax levied on subject peoples, not on Roman citizens [b] *23* Some manuscripts *resurrection, when people rise from the dead,* [c] *26* Exodus 3:6 [d] *29* Or *The Lord our God is one Lord* [e] *30* Deut. 6:4,5 [f] *31* Lev. 19:18

until I put your enemies
under your feet."'[a]

[37]David himself calls him 'Lord.' How then can he be his son?"
The large crowd listened to him with delight.

Warning Against the Teachers of the Law

[38]As he taught, Jesus said, "Watch out for the teachers of the law. They like to
walk around in flowing robes and be greeted with respect in the marketplaces,
[39]and have the most important seats in the synagogues and the places of honor at
banquets. [40]They devour widows' houses and for a show make lengthy prayers.
These men will be punished most severely."

The Widow's Offering

[41]Jesus sat down opposite the place where the offerings were put and watched
the crowd putting their money into the temple treasury. Many rich people threw
in large amounts. [42]But a poor widow came and put in two very small copper
coins, worth only a few cents.

[43]Calling his disciples to him, Jesus said, "Truly I tell you, this poor widow has
put more into the treasury than all the others. [44]They all gave out of their wealth;
but she, out of her poverty, put in everything—all she had to live on."

The Destruction of the Temple and Signs of the End Times

13 As Jesus was leaving the temple, one of his disciples said to him, "Look,
Teacher! What massive stones! What magnificent buildings!"

[2]"Do you see all these great buildings?" replied Jesus. "Not one stone here will
be left on another; every one will be thrown down."

[3]As Jesus was sitting on the Mount of Olives opposite the temple, Peter, James,
John and Andrew asked him privately, [4]"Tell us, when will these things happen?
And what will be the sign that they are all about to be fulfilled?"

[5]Jesus said to them: "Watch out that no one deceives you. [6]Many will come in
my name, claiming, 'I am he,' and will deceive many. [7]When you hear of wars
and rumors of wars, do not be alarmed. Such things must happen, but the end
is still to come. [8]Nation will rise against nation, and kingdom against kingdom.
There will be earthquakes in various places, and famines. These are the beginning of birth pains.

[9]"You must be on your guard. You will be handed over to the local councils
and flogged in the synagogues. On account of me you will stand before governors and kings as witnesses to them. [10]And the gospel must first be preached to
all nations. [11]Whenever you are arrested and brought to trial, do not worry beforehand about what to say. Just say whatever is given you at the time, for it is not
you speaking, but the Holy Spirit.

[12]"Brother will betray brother to death, and a father his child. Children will
rebel against their parents and have them put to death. [13]Everyone will hate you
because of me, but the one who stands firm to the end will be saved.

[14]"When you see 'the abomination that causes desolation'[b] standing where
it[c] does not belong—let the reader understand—then let those who are in Judea flee to the mountains. [15]Let no one on the housetop go down or enter the
house to take anything out. [16]Let no one in the field go back to get their cloak.
[17]How dreadful it will be in those days for pregnant women and nursing mothers! [18]Pray that this will not take place in winter, [19]because those will be days
of distress unequaled from the beginning, when God created the world, until
now—and never to be equaled again.

[20]"If the Lord had not cut short those days, no one would survive. But for the
sake of the elect, whom he has chosen, he has shortened them. [21]At that time
if anyone says to you, 'Look, here is the Messiah!' or, 'Look, there he is!' do not

---

[a] *36* Psalm 110:1 [b] *14* Daniel 9:27; 11:31; 12:11 [c] *14* Or *he*

believe it. 22For false messiahs and false prophets will appear and perform signs and wonders to deceive, if possible, even the elect. 23So be on your guard; I have told you everything ahead of time.

24"But in those days, following that distress,

"'the sun will be darkened,
and the moon will not give its light;
25the stars will fall from the sky,
and the heavenly bodies will be shaken.'[a]

26"At that time people will see the Son of Man coming in clouds with great power and glory. 27And he will send his angels and gather his elect from the four winds, from the ends of the earth to the ends of the heavens.

28"Now learn this lesson from the fig tree: As soon as its twigs get tender and its leaves come out, you know that summer is near. 29Even so, when you see these things happening, you know that it[b] is near, right at the door. 30Truly I tell you, this generation will certainly not pass away until all these things have happened. 31Heaven and earth will pass away, but my words will never pass away.

The Day and Hour Unknown

32"But about that day or hour no one knows, not even the angels in heaven, nor the Son, but only the Father. 33Be on guard! Be alert[c]! You do not know when that time will come. 34It's like a man going away: He leaves his house and puts his servants in charge, each with their assigned task, and tells the one at the door to keep watch.

35"Therefore keep watch because you do not know when the owner of the house will come back—whether in the evening, or at midnight, or when the rooster crows, or at dawn. 36If he comes suddenly, do not let him find you sleeping. 37What I say to you, I say to everyone: 'Watch!'"

Jesus Anointed at Bethany

14 Now the Passover and the Festival of Unleavened Bread were only two days away, and the chief priests and the teachers of the law were scheming to arrest Jesus secretly and kill him. 2"But not during the festival," they said, "or the people may riot."

3While he was in Bethany, reclining at the table in the home of Simon the Leper, a woman came with an alabaster jar of very expensive perfume, made of pure nard. She broke the jar and poured the perfume on his head.

4Some of those present were saying indignantly to one another, "Why this waste of perfume? 5It could have been sold for more than a year's wages[d] and the money given to the poor." And they rebuked her harshly.

6"Leave her alone," said Jesus. "Why are you bothering her? She has done a beautiful thing to me. 7The poor you will always have with you,[e] and you can help them any time you want. But you will not always have me. 8She did what she could. She poured perfume on my body beforehand to prepare for my burial. 9Truly I tell you, wherever the gospel is preached throughout the world, what she has done will also be told, in memory of her."

10Then Judas Iscariot, one of the Twelve, went to the chief priests to betray Jesus to them. 11They were delighted to hear this and promised to give him money. So he watched for an opportunity to hand him over.

The Last Supper

12On the first day of the Festival of Unleavened Bread, when it was customary to sacrifice the Passover lamb, Jesus' disciples asked him, "Where do you want us to go and make preparations for you to eat the Passover?"

[a] 25 Isaiah 13:10; 34:4 [b] 29 Or *he* [c] 33 Some manuscripts *alert and pray* [d] 5 Greek *than three hundred denarii* [e] 7 See Deut. 15:11.

MARK 13:32–36

JESUS: GOD INCARNATE

Jesus is unlike any man who ever lived. He was at the same time both fully God and fully human, and he is able to identify with us as humans in every way. When Jesus came to earth, he never stopped being anything less than God. Yet he set aside his divine power in order to live as a human being (Php 2:7). Jesus' ability to heal, knowledge of the unknowable, and command over demonic spirits and nature alike came from his anointing by the Holy Spirit at his baptism.

This mystery illustrates the wonder of the incarnation: "For God so loved the world that he gave his one and only Son, that whoever believes in him shall not perish but have eternal life" (Jn 3:16). Jesus' life represented the love of God. He testified to the fact that he is the only way that people can come to God (Jn 14:6). He knew that he must give his life for others to have life, and Jesus willingly gave his earthly life so that others could live eternally (Mk 10:45).

13So he sent two of his disciples, telling them, "Go into the city, and a man
carrying a jar of water will meet you. Follow him. 14Say to the owner of the house
he enters, 'The Teacher asks: Where is my guest room, where I may eat the Passover with my disciples?' 15He will show you a large room upstairs, furnished and
ready. Make preparations for us there."

16The disciples left, went into the city and found things just as Jesus had told
them. So they prepared the Passover.

17When evening came, Jesus arrived with the Twelve. 18While they were reclining at the table eating, he said, "Truly I tell you, one of you will betray me —
one who is eating with me."

19They were saddened, and one by one they said to him, "Surely you don't
mean me?"

20"It is one of the Twelve," he replied, "one who dips bread into the bowl with
me. 21The Son of Man will go just as it is written about him. But woe to that man
who betrays the Son of Man! It would be better for him if he had not been born."

22While they were eating, Jesus took bread, and when he had given thanks, he
broke it and gave it to his disciples, saying, "Take it; this is my body."

23Then he took a cup, and when he had given thanks, he gave it to them, and
they all drank from it.

24"This is my blood of the[a] covenant, which is poured out for many," he said
to them. 25"Truly I tell you, I will not drink again from the fruit of the vine until
that day when I drink it new in the kingdom of God."

26When they had sung a hymn, they went out to the Mount of Olives.

Jesus Predicts Peter's Denial

27"You will all fall away," Jesus told them, "for it is written:

" 'I will strike the shepherd,
and the sheep will be scattered.'[b]

28But after I have risen, I will go ahead of you into Galilee."

29Peter declared, "Even if all fall away, I will not."

30"Truly I tell you," Jesus answered, "today — yes, tonight — before the rooster
crows twice[c] you yourself will disown me three times."

31But Peter insisted emphatically, "Even if I have to die with you, I will never
disown you." And all the others said the same.

Gethsemane

32They went to a place called Gethsemane, and Jesus said to his disciples, "Sit
here while I pray." 33He took Peter, James and John along with him, and he began
to be deeply distressed and troubled. 34"My soul is overwhelmed with sorrow to
the point of death," he said to them. "Stay here and keep watch."

35Going a little farther, he fell to the ground and prayed that if possible the
hour might pass from him. 36"*Abba*,[d] Father," he said, "everything is possible for
you. Take this cup from me. Yet not what I will, but what you will."

37Then he returned to his disciples and found them sleeping. "Simon," he said
to Peter, "are you asleep? Couldn't you keep watch for one hour? 38Watch and
pray so that you will not fall into temptation. The spirit is willing, but the flesh
is weak."

39Once more he went away and prayed the same thing. 40When he came back,
he again found them sleeping, because their eyes were heavy. They did not know
what to say to him.

41Returning the third time, he said to them, "Are you still sleeping and resting? Enough! The hour has come. Look, the Son of Man is delivered into the
hands of sinners. 42Rise! Let us go! Here comes my betrayer!"

[a] 24 Some manuscripts *the new* [b] 27 Zech. 13:7 [c] 30 Some early manuscripts do not have *twice.* [d] 36 Aramaic for *father*

MARK 14:35 – 36

ABBA, FATHER

Jesus was a Son. Understanding Jesus' relationship to his Father is essential to understanding who Jesus is. When Jesus prayed in this passage, he used the word "*Abba*," which is the Aramaic word for "dad." When Jesus uttered his Father's name in both terms, it revealed a love both in his heart language and in the common language of the day, and it represents Jesus talking to God in the most personal of terms. Jesus talked to his Father as a loving son would talk to his dad.

The circumstances of this conversation were dire. Jesus was talking about "the hour" and "the cup" he was to drink, which foreshadowed his impending death (Mk 10:38). Figuratively, the cup held God's judgment for the sin of the world. Jesus knew that he had to drink it in order to fulfill the Father's plan for his life, for the redemption of his people.

In Jesus' suffering, we discover a wonderful truth about God's love. Our heavenly Father works everything together for the greatest good in the long run, even if that good requires difficult seasons for his children in the short run. The presence of pain and suffering does not negate the goodness of God as a Father to his children. Instead, God's presence is what helps carry his people through pain and suffering. Believers can look to God and call him "dad" as well: "The Spirit you received does not make you slaves, so that you live in fear again; rather, the Spirit you received brought about your adoption to sonship. And by him we cry, '*Abba*, Father' " (Ro 8:15).

Jesus Arrested

43Just as he was speaking, Judas, one of the Twelve, appeared. With him was
a crowd armed with swords and clubs, sent from the chief priests, the teachers
of the law, and the elders.

44Now the betrayer had arranged a signal with them: "The one I kiss is the
man; arrest him and lead him away under guard." 45Going at once to Jesus, Judas
said, "Rabbi!" and kissed him. 46The men seized Jesus and arrested him. 47Then
one of those standing near drew his sword and struck the servant of the high
priest, cutting off his ear.

48"Am I leading a rebellion," said Jesus, "that you have come out with swords
and clubs to capture me? 49Every day I was with you, teaching in the temple
courts, and you did not arrest me. But the Scriptures must be fulfilled." 50Then
everyone deserted him and fled.

51A young man, wearing nothing but a linen garment, was following Jesus.
When they seized him, 52he fled naked, leaving his garment behind.

Jesus Before the Sanhedrin

53They took Jesus to the high priest, and all the chief priests, the elders and
the teachers of the law came together. 54Peter followed him at a distance, right
into the courtyard of the high priest. There he sat with the guards and warmed
himself at the fire.

55The chief priests and the whole Sanhedrin were looking for evidence against
Jesus so that they could put him to death, but they did not find any. 56Many testified falsely against him, but their statements did not agree.

57Then some stood up and gave this false testimony against him: 58"We heard
him say, 'I will destroy this temple made with human hands and in three days
will build another, not made with hands.'" 59Yet even then their testimony did
not agree.

60Then the high priest stood up before them and asked Jesus, "Are you not going to answer? What is this testimony that these men are bringing against you?"
61But Jesus remained silent and gave no answer.

Again the high priest asked him, "Are you the Messiah, the Son of the Blessed
One?"

62"I am," said Jesus. "And you will see the Son of Man sitting at the right hand
of the Mighty One and coming on the clouds of heaven."

63The high priest tore his clothes. "Why do we need any more witnesses?" he
asked. 64"You have heard the blasphemy. What do you think?"

They all condemned him as worthy of death. 65Then some began to spit at
him; they blindfolded him, struck him with their fists, and said, "Prophesy!" And
the guards took him and beat him.

Peter Disowns Jesus

66While Peter was below in the courtyard, one of the servant girls of the high
priest came by. 67When she saw Peter warming himself, she looked closely at him.

"You also were with that Nazarene, Jesus," she said.

68But he denied it. "I don't know or understand what you're talking about," he
said, and went out into the entryway.[a]

69When the servant girl saw him there, she said again to those standing
around, "This fellow is one of them." 70Again he denied it.

After a little while, those standing near said to Peter, "Surely you are one of
them, for you are a Galilean."

71He began to call down curses, and he swore to them, "I don't know this man
you're talking about."

72Immediately the rooster crowed the second time.[b] Then Peter remembered

[a] 68 Some early manuscripts *entryway and the rooster crowed* [b] 72 Some early
manuscripts do not have *the second time.*

the word Jesus had spoken to him: "Before the rooster crows twice[a] you will disown me three times." And he broke down and wept.

Jesus Before Pilate

15 Very early in the morning, the chief priests, with the elders, the teachers of the law and the whole Sanhedrin, made their plans. So they bound Jesus, led him away and handed him over to Pilate.

2"Are you the king of the Jews?" asked Pilate.

"You have said so," Jesus replied.

3The chief priests accused him of many things. 4So again Pilate asked him, "Aren't you going to answer? See how many things they are accusing you of."

5But Jesus still made no reply, and Pilate was amazed.

6Now it was the custom at the festival to release a prisoner whom the people requested.
7A man called Barabbas was in prison with the insurrectionists who had committed murder in the uprising.
8The crowd came up and asked Pilate to do for them what he usually did.

9"Do you want me to release to you the king of the Jews?" asked Pilate,
10knowing it was out of self-interest that the chief priests had handed Jesus over to him.
11But the chief priests stirred up the crowd to have Pilate release Barabbas instead.

12"What shall I do, then, with the one you call the king of the Jews?" Pilate asked them.

13"Crucify him!" they shouted.

14"Why? What crime has he committed?" asked Pilate.

But they shouted all the louder, "Crucify him!"

15Wanting to satisfy the crowd, Pilate released Barabbas to them. He had Jesus flogged, and handed him over to be crucified.

The Soldiers Mock Jesus

16The soldiers led Jesus away into the palace (that is, the Praetorium) and
called together the whole company of soldiers. 17They put a purple robe on him,
then twisted together a crown of thorns and set it on him. 18And they began to
call out to him, "Hail, king of the Jews!" 19Again and again they struck him on
the head with a staff and spit on him. Falling on their knees, they paid homage
to him. 20And when they had mocked him, they took off the purple robe and put
his own clothes on him. Then they led him out to crucify him.

The Crucifixion of Jesus

21A certain man from Cyrene, Simon, the father of Alexander and Rufus, was passing by on his way in from the country, and they forced him to carry the cross.
22They brought Jesus to the place called Golgotha (which means "the place of
the skull"). 23Then they offered him wine mixed with myrrh, but he did not take
it. 24And they crucified him. Dividing up his clothes, they cast lots to see what each would get.

25It was nine in the morning when they crucified him. 26The written notice of the charge against him read: THE KING OF THE JEWS.

27They crucified two rebels with him, one on his right and one on his left. [28][b]
29Those who passed by hurled insults at him, shaking their heads and saying,
"So! You who are going to destroy the temple and build it in three days, 30come
down from the cross and save yourself!" 31In the same way the chief priests and
the teachers of the law mocked him among themselves. "He saved others," they
said, "but he can't save himself! 32Let this Messiah, this king of Israel, come
down now from the cross, that we may see and believe." Those crucified with him also heaped insults on him.

---

[a] 72 Some early manuscripts do not have *twice*. [b] 28 Some manuscripts include here words similar to Luke 22:37.

The Death of Jesus

[33]At noon, darkness came over the whole land until three in the afternoon. [34]And at three in the afternoon Jesus cried out in a loud voice, *"Eloi, Eloi, lema sabachthani?"* (which means "My God, my God, why have you forsaken me?").[a]

[35]When some of those standing near heard this, they said, "Listen, he's calling Elijah."

[36]Someone ran, filled a sponge with wine vinegar, put it on a staff, and offered it to Jesus to drink. "Now leave him alone. Let's see if Elijah comes to take him down," he said.

[37]With a loud cry, Jesus breathed his last.

[38]The curtain of the temple was torn in two from top to bottom. [39]And when the centurion, who stood there in front of Jesus, saw how he died,[b] he said, "Surely this man was the Son of God!"

[40]Some women were watching from a distance. Among them were Mary Magdalene, Mary the mother of James the younger and of Joseph,[c] and Salome. [41]In Galilee these women had followed him and cared for his needs. Many other women who had come up with him to Jerusalem were also there.

The Burial of Jesus

[42]It was Preparation Day (that is, the day before the Sabbath). So as evening approached, [43]Joseph of Arimathea, a prominent member of the Council, who was himself waiting for the kingdom of God, went boldly to Pilate and asked for Jesus' body. [44]Pilate was surprised to hear that he was already dead. Summoning the centurion, he asked him if Jesus had already died. [45]When he learned from the centurion that it was so, he gave the body to Joseph. [46]So Joseph bought some linen cloth, took down the body, wrapped it in the linen, and placed it in a tomb cut out of rock. Then he rolled a stone against the entrance of the tomb. [47]Mary Magdalene and Mary the mother of Joseph saw where he was laid.

Jesus Has Risen

16 When the Sabbath was over, Mary Magdalene, Mary the mother of James, and Salome bought spices so that they might go to anoint Jesus' body. [2]Very early on the first day of the week, just after sunrise, they were on their way to the tomb [3]and they asked each other, "Who will roll the stone away from the entrance of the tomb?"

[4]But when they looked up, they saw that the stone, which was very large, had been rolled away. [5]As they entered the tomb, they saw a young man dressed in a white robe sitting on the right side, and they were alarmed.

[6]"Don't be alarmed," he said. "You are looking for Jesus the Nazarene, who was crucified. He has risen! He is not here. See the place where they laid him. [7]But go, tell his disciples and Peter, 'He is going ahead of you into Galilee. There you will see him, just as he told you.'"

[8]Trembling and bewildered, the women went out and fled from the tomb. They said nothing to anyone, because they were afraid.[d]

[The earliest manuscripts and some other ancient witnesses do not have verses 9 – 20.]

[9]When Jesus rose early on the first day of the week, he appeared first to Mary Magdalene, out of whom he had driven seven demons. [10]She went and told those who had been with him

---

[a] *34* Psalm 22:1 [b] *39* Some manuscripts *saw that he died with such a cry* [c] *40* Greek *Joses,* a variant of *Joseph*; also in verse 47 [d] *8* Some manuscripts have the following ending between verses 8 and 9, and one manuscript has it after verse 8 (omitting verses 9-20): *Then they quickly reported all these instructions to those around Peter. After this, Jesus himself also sent out through them from east to west the sacred and imperishable proclamation of eternal salvation. Amen.*

UNDEFEATED

Living in this broken world, people know defeat all too well. Everyone has experienced a relationship where someone let them down, or a situation that didn't work out the way they hoped. These moments of disappointment or frustration reveal the tragic fact that this world is deeply flawed. Even though believers live in the hope of the resurrection and the victorious life that Jesus promises through his Spirit, he still calls us to live in this world, where we experience death, brokenness, mourning and pain (in contrast to the coming kingdom: Rev 21:4).

Jesus' resurrection reveals to believers the true way to life. Those who think that the abundant life consists of finding one's way around suffering and hardship have a misguided perception of what Jesus promised. Jesus' life and example teach that the way to a full life consists of service, hardship, opposition, pain and suffering. Believers look at Jesus' life and see that God's best plan for his Son was to stay close to him through the most unimaginable of circumstances. The New Testament shows many times over that God was with his Son until the end, when Jesus took our sin upon himself and suffered on the cross.

But the good news is God didn't leave his Son in the grave! Because Jesus submitted to the point of death, and then defeated death, he paved the way for all people to find eternal life. By submitting himself to death, Jesus found life. "For whoever wants to save their life will lose it, but whoever loses their life for me and for the gospel will save it" (Mk 8:35). It's only in surrendering to his will and his way that believers actually find the fullness of life as God intended it. Giving is the key to gaining.

In all of this, Jesus is victorious. He was, is, and will always be undefeated by sin, by death and by the grave. His victory is found in the fact that he was, and is, a selfless servant. In graciously giving his life, he also created a pathway to the life that is truly life eternal.

and who were mourning and weeping. [11] *When they heard that Jesus was alive and that she had seen him, they did not believe it.*

[12] *Afterward Jesus appeared in a different form to two of them while they were walking in the country.* [13] *These returned and reported it to the rest; but they did not believe them either.*

[14] *Later Jesus appeared to the Eleven as they were eating; he rebuked them for their lack of faith and their stubborn refusal to believe those who had seen him after he had risen.*

[15] *He said to them, "Go into all the world and preach the gospel to all creation.* [16] *Whoever believes and is baptized will be saved, but whoever does not believe will be condemned.* [17] *And these signs will accompany those who believe: In my name they will drive out demons; they will speak in new tongues;* [18] *they will pick up snakes with their hands; and when they drink deadly poison, it will not hurt them at all; they will place their hands on sick people, and they will get well."*

[19] *After the Lord Jesus had spoken to them, he was taken up into heaven and he sat at the right hand of God.* [20] *Then the disciples went out and preached everywhere, and the Lord worked with them and confirmed his word by the signs that accompanied it.*

JESUS: OUR GRACIOUS SAVIOR

LUKE

LUKE

TIBERIUS CAESAR IS ROMAN EMPEROR *c. AD 14 – 37*	JOHN THE BAPTIST'S MINISTRY *c. AD 25 – 27*	JESUS' MINISTRY, DEATH, RESURRECTION *c. AD 27 – 30*

Jesus was sent by God to save sinners. Luke was one such sinner saved by the perfect life and substitutionary death of Jesus, the Messiah. Though Luke never met Jesus personally, it is clear that his life was radically transformed by the message he received from those who had.

Luke, a physician by trade, compiled information concerning the Christ from eyewitnesses to his life, death and resurrection. The letter is addressed to Theophilus, presumably a Gentile convert who served among the Christian community established through Jesus' work. This neophyte church was facing persecution, and Luke sought to reassure Theophilus of God's faithfulness throughout history, seen most clearly in the sending of Jesus Christ. God would surely not abandon his people in the face of persecution when he had already gone to such great lengths to secure their salvation through Christ.

Luke's Gospel is the only one with a sequel — the book of Acts. There Luke continues to describe the ongoing acts of God through the power of the Holy Spirit as the church spread throughout the known world of the first century. Through the church's proclamation of Jesus, God continues to seek and save sinners.

This mission is vividly portrayed in the life of Christ seen throughout Luke's Gospel. Jesus was sent by God to fulfill his pledge to save his people from their sins. Though many would fail to trust him, Jesus relentlessly pursued them in his love. This passionate, gracious love is portrayed in the three stories found in Luke 15 — a lost sheep, a lost coin and two lost sons. There Jesus is pictured as a loving Savior who will go to any length to find what belongs to him.

The message of salvation is available to all through Christ's work. But, as Luke shows, few will accept this gracious offer. Even his own people, the Jews, turn their backs on him and reject Jesus and his disciples. The brutal execution of the Son of God shows the widening gulf between followers of Jesus and those hardened in rebellion. Yet, the grace of God would overcome the height of human folly. In God's wisdom, the death of Jesus was God's perfect plan to defeat Satan, sin and death once and for all. Through this sacrifice, the lost could be saved. Not only the Jews, but also Gentiles could receive the priceless gift of salvation. God's people could then give their lives for the sake of God's mission, the world — a mission that continues through the founding of the church in the book of Acts.

THE SPIRIT OF THE LORD IS ON ME,
BECAUSE HE HAS ANOINTED ME TO PROCLAIM
GOOD NEWS TO THE POOR. HE HAS SENT ME
TO PROCLAIM FREEDOM FOR THE PRISONERS
AND RECOVERY OF SIGHT FOR THE BLIND,
TO SET THE OPPRESSED FREE.

Luke 4:18

LUKE

Introduction

1 Many have undertaken to draw up an account of the things that have been fulfilled[a] among us, 2just as they were handed down to us by those who from the first were eyewitnesses and servants of the word. 3With this in mind, since I myself have carefully investigated everything from the beginning, I too decided to write an orderly account for you, most excellent Theophilus, 4so that you may know the certainty of the things you have been taught.

The Birth of John the Baptist Foretold

5In the time of Herod king of Judea there was a priest named Zechariah, who belonged to the priestly division of Abijah; his wife Elizabeth was also a descendant of Aaron. 6Both of them were righteous in the sight of God, observing all the Lord's commands and decrees blamelessly. 7But they were childless because Elizabeth was not able to conceive, and they were both very old.

8Once when Zechariah's division was on duty and he was serving as priest before God, 9he was chosen by lot, according to the custom of the priesthood, to go into the temple of the Lord and burn incense. 10And when the time for the burning of incense came, all the assembled worshipers were praying outside.

11Then an angel of the Lord appeared to him, standing at the right side of the altar of incense. 12When Zechariah saw him, he was startled and was gripped with fear. 13But the angel said to him: "Do not be afraid, Zechariah; your prayer has been heard. Your wife Elizabeth will bear you a son, and you are to call him John. 14He will be a joy and delight to you, and many will rejoice because of his birth, 15for he will be great in the sight of the Lord. He is never to take wine or other fermented drink, and he will be filled with the Holy Spirit even before he is born. 16He will bring back many of the people of Israel to the Lord their God. 17And he will go on before the Lord, in the spirit and power of Elijah, to turn the hearts of the parents to their children and the disobedient to the wisdom of the righteous — to make ready a people prepared for the Lord."

18Zechariah asked the angel, "How can I be sure of this? I am an old man and my wife is well along in years."

19The angel said to him, "I am Gabriel. I stand in the presence of God, and I have been sent to speak to you and to tell you this good news. 20And now you will be silent and not able to speak until the day this happens, because you did not believe my words, which will come true at their appointed time."

21Meanwhile, the people were waiting for Zechariah and wondering why he stayed so long in the temple. 22When he came out, he could not speak to them. They realized he had seen a vision in the temple, for he kept making signs to them but remained unable to speak.

23When his time of service was completed, he returned home. 24After this his wife Elizabeth became pregnant and for five months remained in seclusion. 25"The Lord has done this for me," she said. "In these days he has shown his favor and taken away my disgrace among the people."

The Birth of Jesus Foretold

26In the sixth month of Elizabeth's pregnancy, God sent the angel Gabriel to Nazareth, a town in Galilee, 27to a virgin pledged to be married to a man named Joseph, a descendant of David. The virgin's name was Mary. 28The angel went to her and said, "Greetings, you who are highly favored! The Lord is with you."

[a] *1* Or *been surely believed*

29 Mary was greatly troubled at his words and wondered what kind of greeting this might be. 30 But the angel said to her, "Do not be afraid, Mary; you have
found favor with God. 31 You will conceive and give birth to a son, and you are to
call him Jesus. 32 He will be great and will be called the Son of the Most High. The
Lord God will give him the throne of his father David, 33 and he will reign over
Jacob's descendants forever; his kingdom will never end."
34 "How will this be," Mary asked the angel, "since I am a virgin?"
35 The angel answered, "The Holy Spirit will come on you, and the power of
the Most High will overshadow you. So the holy one to be born will be called[a]
the Son of God. 36 Even Elizabeth your relative is going to have a child in her old
age, and she who was said to be unable to conceive is in her sixth month. 37 For
no word from God will ever fail."
38 "I am the Lord's servant," Mary answered. "May your word to me be fulfilled." Then the angel left her.

Mary Visits Elizabeth

39 At that time Mary got ready and hurried to a town in the hill country of
Judea, 40 where she entered Zechariah's home and greeted Elizabeth. 41 When
Elizabeth heard Mary's greeting, the baby leaped in her womb, and Elizabeth
was filled with the Holy Spirit. 42 In a loud voice she exclaimed: "Blessed are you
among women, and blessed is the child you will bear! 43 But why am I so favored,
that the mother of my Lord should come to me? 44 As soon as the sound of your
greeting reached my ears, the baby in my womb leaped for joy. 45 Blessed is she
who has believed that the Lord would fulfill his promises to her!"

Mary's Song

46 And Mary said:

"My soul glorifies the Lord
47 and my spirit rejoices in God my Savior,
48 for he has been mindful
of the humble state of his servant.
From now on all generations will call me blessed,
49 for the Mighty One has done great things for me—
holy is his name.
50 His mercy extends to those who fear him,
from generation to generation.
51 He has performed mighty deeds with his arm;
he has scattered those who are proud in their inmost thoughts.
52 He has brought down rulers from their thrones
but has lifted up the humble.
53 He has filled the hungry with good things
but has sent the rich away empty.
54 He has helped his servant Israel,
remembering to be merciful
55 to Abraham and his descendants forever,
just as he promised our ancestors."

56 Mary stayed with Elizabeth for about three months and then returned
home.

The Birth of John the Baptist

57 When it was time for Elizabeth to have her baby, she gave birth to a son.
58 Her neighbors and relatives heard that the Lord had shown her great mercy,
and they shared her joy.
59 On the eighth day they came to circumcise the child, and they were going to

---

[a] 35 Or *So the child to be born will be called holy,*

SON OF THE MOST HIGH

When Gabriel announced to Mary that she would have a son, the angel invoked a promise that had echoed throughout the Old Testament. Her son would be called the Son of the Most High and would reign on the throne of his father, David. Those familiar with the Law and the Prophets, including Mary herself, would have quickly begun to connect the prophetic dots.

God had picked David, a young shepherd boy, from among an entire family of brothers and made him the ruler over Israel. God promised to make David's name great. In addition, God promised that after David died, God would raise up one of his offspring to establish the throne of his kingdom forever (2Sa 7:8 – 16).

During his life, as David faced enemies and conspiracy, he sang songs of praise to God for protecting him as God's anointed (Ps 2:1 – 12) and for establishing his line for as long as the heavens endure (Ps 89:19 – 29). David intoned a psalm of praise that contained a phrase that Jesus later quoted to confound his critics: "The LORD says to my lord …" (Ps 110:1; Mt 22:44). Another psalm affirmed that God, in his promise to David about the duration of his throne, had sworn an oath that could not be revoked (Ps 132:11 – 12).

The prophet Isaiah continued to prophesy the fulfillment of God's promise to David. He wrote that to his people a child would be born, a son would be given and the government would be on his shoulders (Isa 9:6 – 7). Isaiah also affirmed that a shoot would come up from the stump of Jesse, David's father, and from its roots a Branch (referring to Jesus) would bear fruit (Isa 11:1 – 15).

In time, God's plan became clear: he would fulfill this promise through his Son, Jesus. When the angel appeared to Mary, God provided the ultimate update on God's plan to keep his promise. The baby in Mary's womb, conceived by the Holy Spirit though Mary was a virgin, is God's Son who would reign eternally (Lk 1:31 – 33). As a capstone to the astounding declaration, the angel reminded Mary that no word from God would ever fail (v. 37).

The intricate history of God's initial promise realized so fully at Jesus' first coming increases confidence that the rest of God's promises will be fulfilled at Jesus' second coming and after that, into eternity.

name him after his father Zechariah, 60 but his mother spoke up and said, "No!
He is to be called John."
61 They said to her, "There is no one among your relatives who has that name."
62 Then they made signs to his father, to find out what he would like to name
the child. 63 He asked for a writing tablet, and to everyone's astonishment he
wrote, "His name is John." 64 Immediately his mouth was opened and his tongue
set free, and he began to speak, praising God. 65 All the neighbors were filled
with awe, and throughout the hill country of Judea people were talking about all
these things. 66 Everyone who heard this wondered about it, asking, "What then
is this child going to be?" For the Lord's hand was with him.

Zechariah's Song

67 His father Zechariah was filled with the Holy Spirit and prophesied:

68 "Praise be to the Lord, the God of Israel,
because he has come to his people and redeemed them.
69 He has raised up a horn[a] of salvation for us
in the house of his servant David
70 (as he said through his holy prophets of long ago),
71 salvation from our enemies
and from the hand of all who hate us —
72 to show mercy to our ancestors
and to remember his holy covenant,
73 the oath he swore to our father Abraham:
74 to rescue us from the hand of our enemies,
and to enable us to serve him without fear
75 in holiness and righteousness before him all our days.

76 And you, my child, will be called a prophet of the Most High;
for you will go on before the Lord to prepare the way for him,
77 to give his people the knowledge of salvation
through the forgiveness of their sins,
78 because of the tender mercy of our God,
by which the rising sun will come to us from heaven
79 to shine on those living in darkness
and in the shadow of death,
to guide our feet into the path of peace."

80 And the child grew and became strong in spirit[b]; and he lived in the wilderness until he appeared publicly to Israel.

The Birth of Jesus

2 In those days Caesar Augustus issued a decree that a census should be tak-
en of the entire Roman world. 2 (This was the first census that took place
while[c] Quirinius was governor of Syria.) 3 And everyone went to their own town
to register.
4 So Joseph also went up from the town of Nazareth in Galilee to Judea, to Bethlehem the town of David, because he belonged to the house and line of David.
5 He went there to register with Mary, who was pledged to be married to him and
was expecting a child. 6 While they were there, the time came for the baby to be
born, 7 and she gave birth to her firstborn, a son. She wrapped him in cloths and
placed him in a manger, because there was no guest room available for them.
8 And there were shepherds living out in the fields nearby, keeping watch over
their flocks at night. 9 An angel of the Lord appeared to them, and the glory of
the Lord shone around them, and they were terrified. 10 But the angel said to
them, "Do not be afraid. I bring you good news that will cause great joy for all

[a] 69 *Horn* here symbolizes a strong king. [b] 80 Or *in the Spirit* [c] 2 Or *This census took place before*

the people. [11]Today in the town of David a Savior has been born to you; he is the
Messiah, the Lord. [12]This will be a sign to you: You will find a baby wrapped in
cloths and lying in a manger."
[13]Suddenly a great company of the heavenly host appeared with the angel,
praising God and saying,

[14]"Glory to God in the highest heaven,
and on earth peace to those on whom his favor rests."

[15]When the angels had left them and gone into heaven, the shepherds said to
one another, "Let's go to Bethlehem and see this thing that has happened, which
the Lord has told us about."
[16]So they hurried off and found Mary and Joseph, and the baby, who was lying in the manger. [17]When they had seen him, they spread the word concerning
what had been told them about this child, [18]and all who heard it were amazed at
what the shepherds said to them. [19]But Mary treasured up all these things and
pondered them in her heart. [20]The shepherds returned, glorifying and praising God for all the things they had heard and seen, which were just as they had
been told.
[21]On the eighth day, when it was time to circumcise the child, he was named
Jesus, the name the angel had given him before he was conceived.

Jesus Presented in the Temple

[22]When the time came for the purification rites required by the Law of Moses, Joseph and Mary took him to Jerusalem to present him to the Lord [23](as it is
written in the Law of the Lord, "Every firstborn male is to be consecrated to the
Lord"[a]), [24]and to offer a sacrifice in keeping with what is said in the Law of the
Lord: "a pair of doves or two young pigeons."[b]
[25]Now there was a man in Jerusalem called Simeon, who was righteous and
devout. He was waiting for the consolation of Israel, and the Holy Spirit was on
him. [26]It had been revealed to him by the Holy Spirit that he would not die before
he had seen the Lord's Messiah. [27]Moved by the Spirit, he went into the temple
courts. When the parents brought in the child Jesus to do for him what the custom of the Law required, [28]Simeon took him in his arms and praised God, saying:

[29]"Sovereign Lord, as you have promised,
you may now dismiss[c] your servant in peace.
[30]For my eyes have seen your salvation,
[31]which you have prepared in the sight of all nations:
[32]a light for revelation to the Gentiles,
and the glory of your people Israel."

[33]The child's father and mother marveled at what was said about him. [34]Then
Simeon blessed them and said to Mary, his mother: "This child is destined to
cause the falling and rising of many in Israel, and to be a sign that will be spoken
against, [35]so that the thoughts of many hearts will be revealed. And a sword will
pierce your own soul too."
[36]There was also a prophet, Anna, the daughter of Penuel, of the tribe of Asher.
She was very old; she had lived with her husband seven years after her marriage,
[37]and then was a widow until she was eighty-four.[d] She never left the temple but
worshiped night and day, fasting and praying. [38]Coming up to them at that very
moment, she gave thanks to God and spoke about the child to all who were looking forward to the redemption of Jerusalem.
[39]When Joseph and Mary had done everything required by the Law of the
Lord, they returned to Galilee to their own town of Nazareth. [40]And the child
grew and became strong; he was filled with wisdom, and the grace of God was
on him.

[a] *23* Exodus 13:2,12 [b] *24* Lev. 12:8 [c] *29* Or *promised, / now dismiss* [d] *37* Or *then had been a widow for eighty-four years.*

LUKE 2:11

SAVIOR, MESSIAH, LORD

The three titles "Savior," "Messiah" and "Lord" summarize the work of Christ to save. What God was called in 1:47 ("Savior"), Jesus is called here. This description includes the related meanings of deliverer, protector or preserver. The word "Messiah" means "anointed one," referring to Jesus' royal position, the One who was promised and long expected. The word "Lord" is the title of a ruler. The use of "Lord" throughout the New Testament is also significant because, out of reverence for God's covenant name, the Greek word for "Lord" stood in place of *Yahweh* in the Greek translation of the Old Testament.

Peter elaborated on the meaning of these words in Acts 2:30–36 where Jesus is pictured as sitting on a throne and distributing the gift of salvation from God's side, ruling with the Father. In this way, Peter connected Jesus with God's promises to give David an everlasting kingdom. To refer to Jesus as a good man or a good teacher falls immeasurably short of reality. Jesus came to save people from their sin, as promised. He came to minister, to suffer and die, to rise again, and rule and reign forever as Lord. This was the outworking of God's grand plan, what the writer of Hebrews would call "so great a salvation" (Heb 2:3).

The Boy Jesus at the Temple

41Every year Jesus' parents went to Jerusalem for the Festival of the Passover.
42When he was twelve years old, they went up to the festival, according to the
custom. 43After the festival was over, while his parents were returning home, the
boy Jesus stayed behind in Jerusalem, but they were unaware of it. 44Thinking
he was in their company, they traveled on for a day. Then they began looking
for him among their relatives and friends. 45When they did not find him, they
went back to Jerusalem to look for him. 46After three days they found him in the
temple courts, sitting among the teachers, listening to them and asking them
questions. 47Everyone who heard him was amazed at his understanding and his
answers. 48When his parents saw him, they were astonished. His mother said to
him, "Son, why have you treated us like this? Your father and I have been anxiously searching for you."

49"Why were you searching for me?" he asked. "Didn't you know I had to be in
my Father's house?"[a] 50But they did not understand what he was saying to them.

51Then he went down to Nazareth with them and was obedient to them. But
his mother treasured all these things in her heart. 52And Jesus grew in wisdom
and stature, and in favor with God and man.

John the Baptist Prepares the Way

3 In the fifteenth year of the reign of Tiberius Caesar—when Pontius Pilate
was governor of Judea, Herod tetrarch of Galilee, his brother Philip tetrarch
of Iturea and Traconitis, and Lysanias tetrarch of Abilene— 2during the high-
priesthood of Annas and Caiaphas, the word of God came to John son of Zechariah in the wilderness. 3He went into all the country around the Jordan, preaching
a baptism of repentance for the forgiveness of sins. 4As it is written in the book of
the words of Isaiah the prophet:

"A voice of one calling in the wilderness,
'Prepare the way for the Lord,
make straight paths for him.
5Every valley shall be filled in,
every mountain and hill made low.
The crooked roads shall become straight,
the rough ways smooth.
6And all people will see God's salvation.' "[b]

7John said to the crowds coming out to be baptized by him, "You brood of vipers! Who warned you to flee from the coming wrath? 8Produce fruit in keeping
with repentance. And do not begin to say to yourselves, 'We have Abraham as
our father.' For I tell you that out of these stones God can raise up children for
Abraham. 9The ax is already at the root of the trees, and every tree that does not
produce good fruit will be cut down and thrown into the fire."

10"What should we do then?" the crowd asked.

11John answered, "Anyone who has two shirts should share with the one who
has none, and anyone who has food should do the same."

12Even tax collectors came to be baptized. "Teacher," they asked, "what
should we do?"

13"Don't collect any more than you are required to," he told them.

14Then some soldiers asked him, "And what should we do?"

He replied, "Don't extort money and don't accuse people falsely—be content with your pay."

15The people were waiting expectantly and were all wondering in their hearts
if John might possibly be the Messiah. 16John answered them all, "I baptize you
with[c] water. But one who is more powerful than I will come, the straps of whose
sandals I am not worthy to untie. He will baptize you with[c] the Holy Spirit and

[a] 49 Or *be about my Father's business* [b] 6 Isaiah 40:3-5 [c] 16 Or *in*

LUKE 2:49

MY FATHER'S BUSINESS

The Bible provides limited information about Jesus' life as a child. We know his parents took him to the temple when he was eight days old to present him to the Lord, to circumcise him, and to offer a sacrifice as prescribed by the law (Lk 2:21–24). Then when Jesus was age 12, he and his family returned to the temple. There Jesus demonstrated an understanding of the work God had commissioned him to accomplish. This evocative statement in the Greek text is an elliptical clause that leaves out a key word. It reads, "I must be in the . . . of my Father," without specifying a place or activity. So what young Jesus proclaimed here is that either he must be in the house of God discussing God's truth as the translation suggests, or he must be busy with the Father's work in another context. In the end, the two possibilities are not very different. Over time, it became clear that Jesus understood fully the work he had to do—preaching the good news while traveling to Jerusalem to be killed and to rise on the third day (Lk 9:22). In anticipation of the day he would begin his earthly ministry, he "grew in wisdom and stature, and in favor with God and man" (Lk 2:52).

fire. 17 His winnowing fork is in his hand to clear his threshing floor and to gather
the wheat into his barn, but he will burn up the chaff with unquenchable fire."
18 And with many other words John exhorted the people and proclaimed the
good news to them.

19 But when John rebuked Herod the tetrarch because of his marriage to Herodias, his brother's wife, and all the other evil things he had done, 20 Herod added
this to them all: He locked John up in prison.

The Baptism and Genealogy of Jesus

21 When all the people were being baptized, Jesus was baptized too. And as
he was praying, heaven was opened 22 and the Holy Spirit descended on him in
bodily form like a dove. And a voice came from heaven: "You are my Son, whom
I love; with you I am well pleased."

23 Now Jesus himself was about thirty years old when he began his ministry.
He was the son, so it was thought, of Joseph,

the son of Heli, 24 the son of Matthat,
the son of Levi, the son of Melki,
the son of Jannai, the son of Joseph,
25 the son of Mattathias, the son of Amos,
the son of Nahum, the son of Esli,
the son of Naggai, 26 the son of Maath,
the son of Mattathias, the son of Semein,
the son of Josek, the son of Joda,
27 the son of Joanan, the son of Rhesa,
the son of Zerubbabel, the son of Shealtiel,
the son of Neri, 28 the son of Melki,
the son of Addi, the son of Cosam,
the son of Elmadam, the son of Er,
29 the son of Joshua, the son of Eliezer,
the son of Jorim, the son of Matthat,
the son of Levi, 30 the son of Simeon,
the son of Judah, the son of Joseph,
the son of Jonam, the son of Eliakim,
31 the son of Melea, the son of Menna,
the son of Mattatha, the son of Nathan,
the son of David, 32 the son of Jesse,
the son of Obed, the son of Boaz,
the son of Salmon,[a] the son of Nahshon,
33 the son of Amminadab, the son of Ram,[b]
the son of Hezron, the son of Perez,
the son of Judah, 34 the son of Jacob,
the son of Isaac, the son of Abraham,
the son of Terah, the son of Nahor,
35 the son of Serug, the son of Reu,
the son of Peleg, the son of Eber,
the son of Shelah, 36 the son of Cainan,
the son of Arphaxad, the son of Shem,
the son of Noah, the son of Lamech,
37 the son of Methuselah, the son of Enoch,
the son of Jared, the son of Mahalalel,
the son of Kenan, 38 the son of Enosh,
the son of Seth, the son of Adam,
the son of God.

---

[a] *32* Some early manuscripts *Sala* [b] *33* Some manuscripts *Amminadab, the son of Admin, the son of Arni*; other manuscripts vary widely.

ONE MORE POWERFUL

When John began to preach in the wilderness, crowds flocked to see him. He baptized those who confessed their sins but rebuked the pious religious leaders for their self-reliance (Mt 3:7 – 10). After 400 years without a prophet, people rushed to John, wondering if he might be the Christ, the one for whom they as a people had been waiting for centuries. John pointed them to one more powerful than himself who was to come — Jesus. While John baptized with water as a sign of repentance, Jesus would baptize with the Holy Spirit and fire (Mt 3:11).

The power Jesus demonstrated in his baptism differed from John's to an infinite degree. To observers, their physical actions looked similar. While both used water, Jesus' baptism pointed to an imminent change, the time when God would take up residence in the lives of believers through the person of the Holy Spirit. Each of the Gospel writers reference this distinctive element of Jesus' work (Mt 3:11; Mk 1:8; Jn 1:33), foreshadowing the nature of the Trinity: one God in three persons — Father, Son and Holy Spirit.

During Jesus' earthly ministry, his disciples experienced power for immediate tasks in Jesus' name (Lk 10:17 – 20). While the disciples relished these experiences, Jesus knew they would soon experience a substantively different reality — something that could only happen when he returned to his Father (Jn 16:7). Before he ascended into heaven after his resurrection, Jesus commanded his disciples not to leave Jerusalem but to wait for the gift his Father had promised, the Holy Spirit (Ac 1:4 – 5). Once the Spirit came in fullness, the Holy Spirit's filling became the confirmation that God had accepted people by grace through faith in Jesus. This grace extended even to Gentiles who had not kept the Law of Moses (Ac 11:15 – 17).

Throughout his ministry, John stated firmly that Jesus must become greater while he became less (Jn 3:30). John understood that he was responsible for preparing the way for Jesus, calling people to repentance. Jesus affirmed this role, stating that John was a great man (Mt 11:10 – 11) who had faithfully fulfilled his purpose. During his life, John never confused his role or ministry with that of Jesus. He knew Jesus was the Lamb of God who would take away the sin of the world — one who was more powerful than himself and greater in all possible ways (Jn 1:36).

Jesus Is Tested in the Wilderness

4 Jesus, full of the Holy Spirit, left the Jordan and was led by the Spirit into the wilderness, [2]where for forty days he was tempted[a] by the devil. He ate nothing during those days, and at the end of them he was hungry.

[3]The devil said to him, "If you are the Son of God, tell this stone to become bread."

[4]Jesus answered, "It is written: 'Man shall not live on bread alone.'[b]"

[5]The devil led him up to a high place and showed him in an instant all the kingdoms of the world. [6]And he said to him, "I will give you all their authority and splendor; it has been given to me, and I can give it to anyone I want to. [7]If you worship me, it will all be yours."

[8]Jesus answered, "It is written: 'Worship the Lord your God and serve him only.'[c]"

[9]The devil led him to Jerusalem and had him stand on the highest point of the temple. "If you are the Son of God," he said, "throw yourself down from here. [10]For it is written:

"'He will command his angels concerning you
to guard you carefully;
[11] they will lift you up in their hands,
so that you will not strike your foot against a stone.'[d]"

[12]Jesus answered, "It is said: 'Do not put the Lord your God to the test.'[e]"

[13]When the devil had finished all this tempting, he left him until an opportune time.

Jesus Rejected at Nazareth

[14]Jesus returned to Galilee in the power of the Spirit, and news about him spread through the whole countryside. [15]He was teaching in their synagogues, and everyone praised him.

[16]He went to Nazareth, where he had been brought up, and on the Sabbath day he went into the synagogue, as was his custom. He stood up to read, [17]and the scroll of the prophet Isaiah was handed to him. Unrolling it, he found the place where it is written:

[18] "The Spirit of the Lord is on me,
because he has anointed me
to proclaim good news to the poor.
He has sent me to proclaim freedom for the prisoners
and recovery of sight for the blind,
to set the oppressed free,
19 to proclaim the year of the Lord's favor."[f]

[20]Then he rolled up the scroll, gave it back to the attendant and sat down. The eyes of everyone in the synagogue were fastened on him. [21]He began by saying to them, "Today this scripture is fulfilled in your hearing."

[22]All spoke well of him and were amazed at the gracious words that came from his lips. "Isn't this Joseph's son?" they asked.

[23]Jesus said to them, "Surely you will quote this proverb to me: 'Physician, heal yourself!' And you will tell me, 'Do here in your hometown what we have heard that you did in Capernaum.'"

[24]"Truly I tell you," he continued, "no prophet is accepted in his hometown. [25]I assure you that there were many widows in Israel in Elijah's time, when the sky was shut for three and a half years and there was a severe famine throughout the land. [26]Yet Elijah was not sent to any of them, but to a widow in Zarephath in the region of Sidon. [27]And there were many in Israel with leprosy[g] in

LUKE 4:1 – 13

TEMPTATION AND SCRIPTURE

In his humanity, Jesus experienced every temptation that humans do, yet he was without sin (Heb 4:15). When Satan tempted Jesus in the wilderness, Jesus demonstrated his ability to resist the devil and declared his allegiance to God. What Adam failed to do in the garden, Jesus did in the wilderness. When Satan challenged Jesus' identity and authority, Jesus responded by quoting Scripture (Dt 8:3), a succinct way to demonstrate his refusal to live independently from his Father. Next, when Satan enticed Jesus to avoid the cross and gain power in an easier way, Jesus confronted Satan's exaggerated claims about power and authority with another scriptural quote (Dt 6:13). Finally, Satan suggested that Jesus jump from the highest point on the temple, fighting fire with fire and bolstering this temptation with a Scripture passage (Ps 91:11 – 12). Refusing to put God to a test, Jesus withstood this last temptation by quoting Scripture once again (Dt 6:16). Satan retreated, defeated for the moment by Jesus, who resisted his advances by submitting humbly to God (Jas 4:7). Using the sword of the Spirit, which is the Word of God, Jesus demonstrated how to defeat the devil's schemes and extinguish the flaming arrows directed at God's children (Eph 6:10 – 17).

[a] *2* The Greek for *tempted* can also mean *tested.* [b] *4* Deut. 8:3 [c] *8* Deut. 6:13
[d] *11* Psalm 91:11,12 [e] *12* Deut. 6:16 [f] *19* Isaiah 61:1,2 (see Septuagint); Isaiah 58:6
[g] *27* The Greek word traditionally translated *leprosy* was used for various diseases affecting the skin.

the time of Elisha the prophet, yet not one of them was cleansed — only Naaman the Syrian."
[28]All the people in the synagogue were furious when they heard this. [29]They
got up, drove him out of the town, and took him to the brow of the hill on which
the town was built, in order to throw him off the cliff. [30]But he walked right
through the crowd and went on his way.

Jesus Drives Out an Impure Spirit

[31]Then he went down to Capernaum, a town in Galilee, and on the Sabbath
he taught the people. [32]They were amazed at his teaching, because his words
had authority.
[33]In the synagogue there was a man possessed by a demon, an impure spirit.
He cried out at the top of his voice, [34]"Go away! What do you want with us, Jesus
of Nazareth? Have you come to destroy us? I know who you are — the Holy One
of God!"
[35]"Be quiet!" Jesus said sternly. "Come out of him!" Then the demon threw the
man down before them all and came out without injuring him.
[36]All the people were amazed and said to each other, "What words these are!
With authority and power he gives orders to impure spirits and they come out!"
[37]And the news about him spread throughout the surrounding area.

Jesus Heals Many

[38]Jesus left the synagogue and went to the home of Simon. Now Simon's mother-in-law was suffering from a high fever, and they asked Jesus to help her. [39]So
he bent over her and rebuked the fever, and it left her. She got up at once and
began to wait on them.
[40]At sunset, the people brought to Jesus all who had various kinds of sickness,
and laying his hands on each one, he healed them. [41]Moreover, demons came
out of many people, shouting, "You are the Son of God!" But he rebuked them
and would not allow them to speak, because they knew he was the Messiah.
[42]At daybreak, Jesus went out to a solitary place. The people were looking for
him and when they came to where he was, they tried to keep him from leaving
them. [43]But he said, "I must proclaim the good news of the kingdom of God to
the other towns also, because that is why I was sent." [44]And he kept on preaching
in the synagogues of Judea.

Jesus Calls His First Disciples

5 One day as Jesus was standing by the Lake of Gennesaret,[a] the people were
crowding around him and listening to the word of God. [2]He saw at the water's edge two boats, left there by the fishermen, who were washing their nets.
[3]He got into one of the boats, the one belonging to Simon, and asked him to put
out a little from shore. Then he sat down and taught the people from the boat.
[4]When he had finished speaking, he said to Simon, "Put out into deep water,
and let down the nets for a catch."
[5]Simon answered, "Master, we've worked hard all night and haven't caught
anything. But because you say so, I will let down the nets."
[6]When they had done so, they caught such a large number of fish that their nets
began to break. [7]So they signaled their partners in the other boat to come and
help them, and they came and filled both boats so full that they began to sink.
[8]When Simon Peter saw this, he fell at Jesus' knees and said, "Go away from
me, Lord; I am a sinful man!" [9]For he and all his companions were astonished at
the catch of fish they had taken, [10]and so were James and John, the sons of Zebedee, Simon's partners.
Then Jesus said to Simon, "Don't be afraid; from now on you will fish for people." [11]So they pulled their boats up on shore, left everything and followed him.

---

[a] *1* That is, the Sea of Galilee

Jesus Heals a Man With Leprosy

12 While Jesus was in one of the towns, a man came along who was covered
with leprosy.[a] When he saw Jesus, he fell with his face to the ground and begged
him, "Lord, if you are willing, you can make me clean."

13 Jesus reached out his hand and touched the man. "I am willing," he said. "Be
clean!" And immediately the leprosy left him.

14 Then Jesus ordered him, "Don't tell anyone, but go, show yourself to the
priest and offer the sacrifices that Moses commanded for your cleansing, as a
testimony to them."

15 Yet the news about him spread all the more, so that crowds of people came
to hear him and to be healed of their sicknesses. 16 But Jesus often withdrew to
lonely places and prayed.

Jesus Forgives and Heals a Paralyzed Man

17 One day Jesus was teaching, and Pharisees and teachers of the law were sitting there. They had come from every village of Galilee and from Judea and Jerusalem. And the power of the Lord was with Jesus to heal the sick. 18 Some men
came carrying a paralyzed man on a mat and tried to take him into the house to
lay him before Jesus. 19 When they could not find a way to do this because of the
crowd, they went up on the roof and lowered him on his mat through the tiles
into the middle of the crowd, right in front of Jesus.

20 When Jesus saw their faith, he said, "Friend, your sins are forgiven."

21 The Pharisees and the teachers of the law began thinking to themselves,
"Who is this fellow who speaks blasphemy? Who can forgive sins but God alone?"

22 Jesus knew what they were thinking and asked, "Why are you thinking
these things in your hearts? 23 Which is easier: to say, 'Your sins are forgiven,'
or to say, 'Get up and walk'? 24 But I want you to know that the Son of Man has
authority on earth to forgive sins." So he said to the paralyzed man, "I tell you,
get up, take your mat and go home." 25 Immediately he stood up in front of them,
took what he had been lying on and went home praising God. 26 Everyone was
amazed and gave praise to God. They were filled with awe and said, "We have
seen remarkable things today."

Jesus Calls Levi and Eats With Sinners

27 After this, Jesus went out and saw a tax collector by the name of Levi sitting
at his tax booth. "Follow me," Jesus said to him, 28 and Levi got up, left everything
and followed him.

29 Then Levi held a great banquet for Jesus at his house, and a large crowd of
tax collectors and others were eating with them. 30 But the Pharisees and the
teachers of the law who belonged to their sect complained to his disciples, "Why
do you eat and drink with tax collectors and sinners?"

31 Jesus answered them, "It is not the healthy who need a doctor, but the sick.
32 I have not come to call the righteous, but sinners to repentance."

Jesus Questioned About Fasting

33 They said to him, "John's disciples often fast and pray, and so do the disciples of the Pharisees, but yours go on eating and drinking."

34 Jesus answered, "Can you make the friends of the bridegroom fast while he
is with them? 35 But the time will come when the bridegroom will be taken from
them; in those days they will fast."

36 He told them this parable: "No one tears a piece out of a new garment to patch
an old one. Otherwise, they will have torn the new garment, and the patch from the
new will not match the old. 37 And no one pours new wine into old wineskins. Otherwise, the new wine will burst the skins; the wine will run out and the wineskins

[a] *12* The Greek word traditionally translated *leprosy* was used for various diseases affecting the skin.

LUKE 5:24

SON OF MAN

The religious leaders watched to see if Jesus would heal on the Sabbath. Jesus increased the stakes by stating that he, as the Son of Man, had the power and authority to forgive sin. The phrase "Son of Man" was an Aramaic idiom that referred to a human being, meaning "someone" or "I." But in this situation, Jesus referenced a title from Daniel 7:13, something he did regularly during his ministry, especially when he wanted to emphasize the nature of his relationship to the Father (Lk 21:27; 22:69). Daniel used the title "son of man" to describe one who shared authority with the Ancient of Days, a powerful reference to the one true God. By invoking this image, Jesus tapped into the supernatural impression of this figure, for only God rides the clouds (Ex 14:20; Ps 104:3).

The question Jesus posed to the religious leaders was whether he had the authority to forgive sin. By referring to himself as the Son of Man in that context, Jesus claimed the authority to forgive sins with the full understanding that such authority was limited only to God.

will be ruined. [38]No, new wine must be poured into new wineskins. [39]And no one
after drinking old wine wants the new, for they say, 'The old is better.' "

Jesus Is Lord of the Sabbath

6 One Sabbath Jesus was going through the grainfields, and his disciples began
to pick some heads of grain, rub them in their hands and eat the kernels. [2]Some
of the Pharisees asked, "Why are you doing what is unlawful on the Sabbath?"
[3]Jesus answered them, "Have you never read what David did when he and his
companions were hungry? [4]He entered the house of God, and taking the consecrated bread, he ate what is lawful only for priests to eat. And he also gave some to his
companions." [5]Then Jesus said to them, "The Son of Man is Lord of the Sabbath."
[6]On another Sabbath he went into the synagogue and was teaching, and a
man was there whose right hand was shriveled. [7]The Pharisees and the teachers
of the law were looking for a reason to accuse Jesus, so they watched him closely
to see if he would heal on the Sabbath. [8]But Jesus knew what they were thinking
and said to the man with the shriveled hand, "Get up and stand in front of everyone." So he got up and stood there.
[9]Then Jesus said to them, "I ask you, which is lawful on the Sabbath: to do
good or to do evil, to save life or to destroy it?"
[10]He looked around at them all, and then said to the man, "Stretch out your
hand." He did so, and his hand was completely restored. [11]But the Pharisees and
the teachers of the law were furious and began to discuss with one another what
they might do to Jesus.

The Twelve Apostles

[12]One of those days Jesus went out to a mountainside to pray, and spent the
night praying to God. [13]When morning came, he called his disciples to him and
chose twelve of them, whom he also designated apostles: [14]Simon (whom he
named Peter), his brother Andrew, James, John, Philip, Bartholomew, [15]Mat-
thew, Thomas, James son of Alphaeus, Simon who was called the Zealot, [16]Judas
son of James, and Judas Iscariot, who became a traitor.

Blessings and Woes

[17]He went down with them and stood on a level place. A large crowd of his
disciples was there and a great number of people from all over Judea, from Jerusalem, and from the coastal region around Tyre and Sidon, [18]who had come
to hear him and to be healed of their diseases. Those troubled by impure spirits
were cured, [19]and the people all tried to touch him, because power was coming
from him and healing them all.
[20]Looking at his disciples, he said:

"Blessed are you who are poor,
for yours is the kingdom of God.
[21]Blessed are you who hunger now,
for you will be satisfied.
Blessed are you who weep now,
for you will laugh.
[22]Blessed are you when people hate you,
when they exclude you and insult you
and reject your name as evil,
because of the Son of Man.

[23]"Rejoice in that day and leap for joy, because great is your reward in heaven.
For that is how their ancestors treated the prophets.

[24]"But woe to you who are rich,
for you have already received your comfort.
[25]Woe to you who are well fed now,
for you will go hungry.

JESUS AND THE POOR

Many, if not most, of the people who listened to Jesus' words that day were poor. The difficulties and hardships of their lives drove them to listen to this prophet, Jesus. As those who lacked material wealth, they may have hoped Jesus would tell them more about the kingdom of God — the day when the righteous Messiah and not the cruel Romans would govern them.

From his initial statement, Jesus launched into a series of statements that turned the crowd's perceptions upside down. Jesus' speech contrasted possessions and values with those that flow from a heavenly perspective. In a few sentences, Jesus affirmed that things in this world are not always what they seem and certainly are not what they will one day be.

At face value, it seemed as though Jesus was making a blanket promise of salvation and blessing to everyone who was poor materially. Based on this interpretation, some have viewed the poor as God's chosen people — those who suffer in this world but can expect immeasurable blessings in the next. Those holding this view often advocate that God's people, the church, should prioritize ministry to the poor and in this way advance the kingdom of God.

Others view Jesus' statement as an insight into spiritual poverty, referencing a similar sermon in which Jesus talked about the "poor in spirit" (Mt 5:3). In their view, Jesus was offering great blessing to those who recognize their spiritual poverty before God. Because they acknowledge that nothing they do can enhance their spiritual standing, these people, the poor in spirit, receive God's unmerited favor. So, in this second view, Jesus is not affirming the value of being poor materially but warning against the profound danger of being self-sufficient spiritually.

Since Jesus referenced both the "poor" and the "poor in spirit," the implications of his words can be intertwined. Throughout his ministry on earth, Jesus met the practical needs of the poor — feeding, healing and honoring them. In spite of this emphasis, Jesus refused to place a higher priority on meeting physical needs than on meeting spiritual needs. Through his words and his actions, Jesus demonstrated the divine balance — pay attention to those with physical needs but never forget the priority of spiritual needs.

Woe to you who laugh now,
for you will mourn and weep.
[26]Woe to you when everyone speaks well of you,
for that is how their ancestors treated the false prophets.

Love for Enemies

[27]"But to you who are listening I say: Love your enemies, do good to those who
hate you, [28]bless those who curse you, pray for those who mistreat you. [29]If someone slaps you on one cheek, turn to them the other also. If someone takes your
coat, do not withhold your shirt from them. [30]Give to everyone who asks you, and
if anyone takes what belongs to you, do not demand it back. [31]Do to others as you
would have them do to you.

[32]"If you love those who love you, what credit is that to you? Even sinners love
those who love them. [33]And if you do good to those who are good to you, what
credit is that to you? Even sinners do that. [34]And if you lend to those from whom
you expect repayment, what credit is that to you? Even sinners lend to sinners,
expecting to be repaid in full. [35]But love your enemies, do good to them, and lend
to them without expecting to get anything back. Then your reward will be great,
and you will be children of the Most High, because he is kind to the ungrateful
and wicked. [36]Be merciful, just as your Father is merciful.

Judging Others

[37]"Do not judge, and you will not be judged. Do not condemn, and you will not
be condemned. Forgive, and you will be forgiven. [38]Give, and it will be given to
you. A good measure, pressed down, shaken together and running over, will be
poured into your lap. For with the measure you use, it will be measured to you."

[39]He also told them this parable: "Can the blind lead the blind? Will they not
both fall into a pit? [40]The student is not above the teacher, but everyone who is
fully trained will be like their teacher.

[41]"Why do you look at the speck of sawdust in your brother's eye and pay no attention to the plank in your own eye? [42]How can you say to your brother, 'Brother, let me take the speck out of your eye,' when you yourself fail to see the plank
in your own eye? You hypocrite, first take the plank out of your eye, and then you
will see clearly to remove the speck from your brother's eye.

A Tree and Its Fruit

[43]"No good tree bears bad fruit, nor does a bad tree bear good fruit. [44]Each
tree is recognized by its own fruit. People do not pick figs from thornbushes, or
grapes from briers. [45]A good man brings good things out of the good stored up in
his heart, and an evil man brings evil things out of the evil stored up in his heart.
For the mouth speaks what the heart is full of.

The Wise and Foolish Builders

[46]"Why do you call me, 'Lord, Lord,' and do not do what I say? [47]As for everyone who comes to me and hears my words and puts them into practice, I will
show you what they are like. [48]They are like a man building a house, who dug
down deep and laid the foundation on rock. When a flood came, the torrent
struck that house but could not shake it, because it was well built. [49]But the one
who hears my words and does not put them into practice is like a man who built
a house on the ground without a foundation. The moment the torrent struck that
house, it collapsed and its destruction was complete."

The Faith of the Centurion

7 When Jesus had finished saying all this to the people who were listening, he
entered Capernaum. [2]There a centurion's servant, whom his master valued
highly, was sick and about to die. [3]The centurion heard of Jesus and sent some
elders of the Jews to him, asking him to come and heal his servant. [4]When they

LUKE 7:1 – 10

AUTHORITY

A Roman soldier who was a centurion demonstrated insight into Jesus' authority. After asking Jesus to heal his servant, the soldier exhorted Jesus not to travel to him; Jesus needed only to issue the command for the request to be granted. The centurion reasoned that since he exercised authority over the soldiers he led, Jesus could exercise far greater authority. Upon hearing what the centurion said, Jesus affirmed his great faith (Lk 7:9 – 10).

This Roman discerned what the spiritual leaders of the day missed as they questioned Jesus repeatedly about his authority (Mt 21:23 – 27; Lk 20:2). The centurion and the common people recognized Jesus' authority, contrasting his powerful teaching with that of the teachers of the law (Mt 7:29). Before his ascension into heaven, Jesus explained to his disciples that all authority in heaven and on earth had been given to him (Mt 28:18). Years later, the apostle Paul would proclaim that God the Father had placed everything in the present age and the age to come under Jesus' feet (Eph 1:19 – 21). As a result, acknowledging or denying Jesus' absolute authority changes people's eternal destinities, as well as their lives now.

came to Jesus, they pleaded earnestly with him, “This man deserves to have you
do this, 5because he loves our nation and has built our synagogue.” 6So Jesus
went with them.

He was not far from the house when the centurion sent friends to say to him:
“Lord, don’t trouble yourself, for I do not deserve to have you come under my
roof. 7That is why I did not even consider myself worthy to come to you. But say
the word, and my servant will be healed. 8For I myself am a man under authority,
with soldiers under me. I tell this one, ‘Go,’ and he goes; and that one, ‘Come,’
and he comes. I say to my servant, ‘Do this,’ and he does it.”

9When Jesus heard this, he was amazed at him, and turning to the crowd following him, he said, “I tell you, I have not found such great faith even in Israel.”
10Then the men who had been sent returned to the house and found the servant
well.

Jesus Raises a Widow’s Son

11Soon afterward, Jesus went to a town called Nain, and his disciples and a
large crowd went along with him. 12As he approached the town gate, a dead person was being carried out — the only son of his mother, and she was a widow.
And a large crowd from the town was with her. 13When the Lord saw her, his
heart went out to her and he said, “Don’t cry.”

14Then he went up and touched the bier they were carrying him on, and the
bearers stood still. He said, “Young man, I say to you, get up!” 15The dead man sat
up and began to talk, and Jesus gave him back to his mother.

16They were all filled with awe and praised God. “A great prophet has appeared among us,” they said. “God has come to help his people.” 17This news
about Jesus spread throughout Judea and the surrounding country.

Jesus and John the Baptist

18John’s disciples told him about all these things. Calling two of them, 19he
sent them to the Lord to ask, “Are you the one who is to come, or should we expect someone else?”

20When the men came to Jesus, they said, “John the Baptist sent us to you to
ask, ‘Are you the one who is to come, or should we expect someone else?’ ”

21At that very time Jesus cured many who had diseases, sicknesses and evil
spirits, and gave sight to many who were blind. 22So he replied to the messengers, “Go back and report to John what you have seen and heard: The blind receive sight, the lame walk, those who have leprosy[a] are cleansed, the deaf hear,
the dead are raised, and the good news is proclaimed to the poor. 23Blessed is
anyone who does not stumble on account of me.”

24After John’s messengers left, Jesus began to speak to the crowd about John:
“What did you go out into the wilderness to see? A reed swayed by the wind? 25If
not, what did you go out to see? A man dressed in fine clothes? No, those who
wear expensive clothes and indulge in luxury are in palaces. 26But what did you
go out to see? A prophet? Yes, I tell you, and more than a prophet. 27This is the
one about whom it is written:

“ ‘I will send my messenger ahead of you,
who will prepare your way before you.’[b]

28I tell you, among those born of women there is no one greater than John; yet the
one who is least in the kingdom of God is greater than he.”

29(All the people, even the tax collectors, when they heard Jesus’ words, acknowledged that God’s way was right, because they had been baptized by John.
30But the Pharisees and the experts in the law rejected God’s purpose for themselves, because they had not been baptized by John.)

31Jesus went on to say, “To what, then, can I compare the people of this

---

[a] 22 The Greek word traditionally translated *leprosy* was used for various diseases affecting the skin. [b] 27 Mal. 3:1

generation? What are they like? 32They are like children sitting in the marketplace and calling out to each other:

"'We played the pipe for you,
    and you did not dance;
we sang a dirge,
    and you did not cry.'

33For John the Baptist came neither eating bread nor drinking wine, and you say, 'He has a demon.' 34The Son of Man came eating and drinking, and you say, 'Here is a glutton and a drunkard, a friend of tax collectors and sinners.' 35But wisdom is proved right by all her children."

Jesus Anointed by a Sinful Woman

36When one of the Pharisees invited Jesus to have dinner with him, he went to the Pharisee's house and reclined at the table. 37A woman in that town who lived a sinful life learned that Jesus was eating at the Pharisee's house, so she came there with an alabaster jar of perfume. 38As she stood behind him at his feet weeping, she began to wet his feet with her tears. Then she wiped them with her hair, kissed them and poured perfume on them.

39When the Pharisee who had invited him saw this, he said to himself, "If this man were a prophet, he would know who is touching him and what kind of woman she is — that she is a sinner."

40Jesus answered him, "Simon, I have something to tell you."

"Tell me, teacher," he said.

41"Two people owed money to a certain moneylender. One owed him five hundred denarii,[a] and the other fifty. 42Neither of them had the money to pay him back, so he forgave the debts of both. Now which of them will love him more?"

43Simon replied, "I suppose the one who had the bigger debt forgiven."

"You have judged correctly," Jesus said.

44Then he turned toward the woman and said to Simon, "Do you see this woman? I came into your house. You did not give me any water for my feet, but she wet my feet with her tears and wiped them with her hair. 45You did not give me a kiss, but this woman, from the time I entered, has not stopped kissing my feet. 46You did not put oil on my head, but she has poured perfume on my feet. 47Therefore, I tell you, her many sins have been forgiven — as her great love has shown. But whoever has been forgiven little loves little."

48Then Jesus said to her, "Your sins are forgiven."

49The other guests began to say among themselves, "Who is this who even forgives sins?"

50Jesus said to the woman, "Your faith has saved you; go in peace."

The Parable of the Sower

8 After this, Jesus traveled about from one town and village to another, proclaiming the good news of the kingdom of God. The Twelve were with him, 2and also some women who had been cured of evil spirits and diseases: Mary (called Magdalene) from whom seven demons had come out; 3Joanna the wife of Chuza, the manager of Herod's household; Susanna; and many others. These women were helping to support them out of their own means.

4While a large crowd was gathering and people were coming to Jesus from town after town, he told this parable: 5"A farmer went out to sow his seed. As he was scattering the seed, some fell along the path; it was trampled on, and the birds ate it up. 6Some fell on rocky ground, and when it came up, the plants withered because they had no moisture. 7Other seed fell among thorns, which grew up with it and choked the plants. 8Still other seed fell on good soil. It came up and yielded a crop, a hundred times more than was sown."

---

[a] *41* A denarius was the usual daily wage of a day laborer (see Matt. 20:2).

When he said this, he called out, "Whoever has ears to hear, let them hear."
[9]His disciples asked him what this parable meant. [10]He said, "The knowledge of the secrets of the kingdom of God has been given to you, but to others I speak in parables, so that,

" 'though seeing, they may not see;
though hearing, they may not understand.'[a]

[11]"This is the meaning of the parable: The seed is the word of God. [12]Those along the path are the ones who hear, and then the devil comes and takes away the word from their hearts, so that they may not believe and be saved. [13]Those on the rocky ground are the ones who receive the word with joy when they hear it, but they have no root. They believe for a while, but in the time of testing they fall away. [14]The seed that fell among thorns stands for those who hear, but as they go on their way they are choked by life's worries, riches and pleasures, and they do not mature. [15]But the seed on good soil stands for those with a noble and good heart, who hear the word, retain it, and by persevering produce a crop.

A Lamp on a Stand

[16]"No one lights a lamp and hides it in a clay jar or puts it under a bed. Instead, they put it on a stand, so that those who come in can see the light. [17]For there is nothing hidden that will not be disclosed, and nothing concealed that will not be known or brought out into the open. [18]Therefore consider carefully how you listen. Whoever has will be given more; whoever does not have, even what they think they have will be taken from them."

Jesus' Mother and Brothers

[19]Now Jesus' mother and brothers came to see him, but they were not able to get near him because of the crowd. [20]Someone told him, "Your mother and brothers are standing outside, wanting to see you."
[21]He replied, "My mother and brothers are those who hear God's word and put it into practice."

Jesus Calms the Storm

[22]One day Jesus said to his disciples, "Let us go over to the other side of the lake." So they got into a boat and set out. [23]As they sailed, he fell asleep. A squall came down on the lake, so that the boat was being swamped, and they were in great danger.
[24]The disciples went and woke him, saying, "Master, Master, we're going to drown!"
He got up and rebuked the wind and the raging waters; the storm subsided, and all was calm. [25]"Where is your faith?" he asked his disciples.
In fear and amazement they asked one another, "Who is this? He commands even the winds and the water, and they obey him."

Jesus Restores a Demon-Possessed Man

[26]They sailed to the region of the Gerasenes,[b] which is across the lake from Galilee. [27]When Jesus stepped ashore, he was met by a demon-possessed man from the town. For a long time this man had not worn clothes or lived in a house, but had lived in the tombs. [28]When he saw Jesus, he cried out and fell at his feet, shouting at the top of his voice, "What do you want with me, Jesus, Son of the Most High God? I beg you, don't torture me!" [29]For Jesus had commanded the impure spirit to come out of the man. Many times it had seized him, and though he was chained hand and foot and kept under guard, he had broken his chains and had been driven by the demon into solitary places.

[a] *10* Isaiah 6:9 [b] *26* Some manuscripts *Gadarenes;* other manuscripts *Gergesenes;* also in verse 37

LUKE 8:19–21

JESUS' FAMILY

One of the mysteries of the incarnation (Jesus' coming to earth as a human being without ceasing to be God), is the fact that Jesus had a flesh-and-blood family — a mother, father and siblings (Mt 13:55–56). While many if not all of his family members ultimately became his disciples, the Gospels demonstrate that they did not follow him initially. On one occasion they traveled "to take charge of him" because they believed he was out of his mind (Mk 3:21). Another time, his brothers taunted that he should travel to Jerusalem so his disciples could see his works there. "No one who wants to become a public figure acts in secret. Since you are doing these things, show yourself to the world" (Jn 7:2–4).

Through his life and teachings, Jesus framed the context of family in terms of the kingdom of God. He expanded the concept of family to include all who did the will of his Father in heaven (Mt 12:50). While he rebuked religious leaders who failed to honor their parents for the sake of their traditions, he called his disciples to love him more than all else, including their families (Mt 10:37). Yet from the cross, Jesus assigned his disciple John to care for Mary, his mother, demonstrating his love and concern for her (Jn 19:26–27). For Jesus, family remained important but not ultimate, aligning with his mandate to seek God's kingdom first so that all other realities in life could align correctly (Mt 6:33).

[30]Jesus asked him, "What is your name?"

"Legion," he replied, because many demons had gone into him. [31]And they begged Jesus repeatedly not to order them to go into the Abyss.

[32]A large herd of pigs was feeding there on the hillside. The demons begged Jesus to let them go into the pigs, and he gave them permission. [33]When the demons came out of the man, they went into the pigs, and the herd rushed down the steep bank into the lake and was drowned.

[34]When those tending the pigs saw what had happened, they ran off and reported this in the town and countryside, [35]and the people went out to see what had happened. When they came to Jesus, they found the man from whom the demons had gone out, sitting at Jesus' feet, dressed and in his right mind; and they were afraid. [36]Those who had seen it told the people how the demon-possessed man had been cured. [37]Then all the people of the region of the Gerasenes asked Jesus to leave them, because they were overcome with fear. So he got into the boat and left.

[38]The man from whom the demons had gone out begged to go with him, but Jesus sent him away, saying, [39]"Return home and tell how much God has done for you." So the man went away and told all over town how much Jesus had done for him.

Jesus Raises a Dead Girl and Heals a Sick Woman

[40]Now when Jesus returned, a crowd welcomed him, for they were all expecting him. [41]Then a man named Jairus, a synagogue leader, came and fell at Jesus' feet, pleading with him to come to his house [42]because his only daughter, a girl of about twelve, was dying.

As Jesus was on his way, the crowds almost crushed him. [43]And a woman was there who had been subject to bleeding for twelve years,[a] but no one could heal her. [44]She came up behind him and touched the edge of his cloak, and immediately her bleeding stopped.

[45]"Who touched me?" Jesus asked.

When they all denied it, Peter said, "Master, the people are crowding and pressing against you."

[46]But Jesus said, "Someone touched me; I know that power has gone out from me."

[47]Then the woman, seeing that she could not go unnoticed, came trembling and fell at his feet. In the presence of all the people, she told why she had touched him and how she had been instantly healed. [48]Then he said to her, "Daughter, your faith has healed you. Go in peace."

[49]While Jesus was still speaking, someone came from the house of Jairus, the synagogue leader. "Your daughter is dead," he said. "Don't bother the teacher anymore."

[50]Hearing this, Jesus said to Jairus, "Don't be afraid; just believe, and she will be healed."

[51]When he arrived at the house of Jairus, he did not let anyone go in with him except Peter, John and James, and the child's father and mother. [52]Meanwhile, all the people were wailing and mourning for her. "Stop wailing," Jesus said. "She is not dead but asleep."

[53]They laughed at him, knowing that she was dead. [54]But he took her by the hand and said, "My child, get up!" [55]Her spirit returned, and at once she stood up. Then Jesus told them to give her something to eat. [56]Her parents were astonished, but he ordered them not to tell anyone what had happened.

Jesus Sends Out the Twelve

9 When Jesus had called the Twelve together, he gave them power and authority to drive out all demons and to cure diseases, [2]and he sent them out to proclaim the kingdom of God and to heal the sick. [3]He told them: "Take nothing

[a] 43 Many manuscripts *years, and she had spent all she had on doctors*

for the journey — no staff, no bag, no bread, no money, no extra shirt. 4Whatever house you enter, stay there until you leave that town. 5If people do not welcome you, leave their town and shake the dust off your feet as a testimony against them." 6So they set out and went from village to village, proclaiming the good news and healing people everywhere.

7Now Herod the tetrarch heard about all that was going on. And he was perplexed because some were saying that John had been raised from the dead, 8others that Elijah had appeared, and still others that one of the prophets of long ago had come back to life. 9But Herod said, "I beheaded John. Who, then, is this I hear such things about?" And he tried to see him.

Jesus Feeds the Five Thousand

10When the apostles returned, they reported to Jesus what they had done. Then he took them with him and they withdrew by themselves to a town called Bethsaida, 11but the crowds learned about it and followed him. He welcomed them and spoke to them about the kingdom of God, and healed those who needed healing.

12Late in the afternoon the Twelve came to him and said, "Send the crowd away so they can go to the surrounding villages and countryside and find food and lodging, because we are in a remote place here."

13He replied, "You give them something to eat."

They answered, "We have only five loaves of bread and two fish — unless we go and buy food for all this crowd." 14(About five thousand men were there.)

But he said to his disciples, "Have them sit down in groups of about fifty each." 15The disciples did so, and everyone sat down. 16Taking the five loaves and the two fish and looking up to heaven, he gave thanks and broke them. Then he gave them to the disciples to distribute to the people. 17They all ate and were satisfied, and the disciples picked up twelve basketfuls of broken pieces that were left over.

Peter Declares That Jesus Is the Messiah

18Once when Jesus was praying in private and his disciples were with him, he asked them, "Who do the crowds say I am?"

19They replied, "Some say John the Baptist; others say Elijah; and still others, that one of the prophets of long ago has come back to life."

20"But what about you?" he asked. "Who do you say I am?"

Peter answered, "God's Messiah."

Jesus Predicts His Death

21Jesus strictly warned them not to tell this to anyone. 22And he said, "The Son of Man must suffer many things and be rejected by the elders, the chief priests and the teachers of the law, and he must be killed and on the third day be raised to life."

23Then he said to them all: "Whoever wants to be my disciple must deny themselves and take up their cross daily and follow me. 24For whoever wants to save their life will lose it, but whoever loses their life for me will save it. 25What good is it for someone to gain the whole world, and yet lose or forfeit their very self? 26Whoever is ashamed of me and my words, the Son of Man will be ashamed of them when he comes in his glory and in the glory of the Father and of the holy angels.

27"Truly I tell you, some who are standing here will not taste death before they see the kingdom of God."

The Transfiguration

28About eight days after Jesus said this, he took Peter, John and James with him and went up onto a mountain to pray. 29As he was praying, the appearance of his face changed, and his clothes became as bright as a flash of lightning. 30Two men, Moses and Elijah, appeared in glorious splendor, talking with Jesus.

LUKE 9:21

JESUS' SECRET

After Simon Peter affirmed that Jesus was God's Messiah, Jesus "strictly warned" his disciples not to tell anyone. This was not the first time Jesus cautioned against sharing his identity. After healing a man from leprosy, he said, "See that you don't tell anyone" (Mt 8:4). When Jesus came down from the mountain after Peter, James and John had seen him transfigured, Jesus told them, "Don't tell anyone what you have seen, until the Son of Man has been raised from the dead" (Mt 17:9).

Scholars have pondered this "Messianic secret," seeking to understand why Jesus commanded his disciples not to share what they knew. The problem was not that the disciples knew too much; it was that they knew too little. For example, on the way to Jerusalem where Jesus would be crucified, James and John became indignant by the way a village of Samaritans treated them. "Lord, do you want us to call fire down from heaven to destroy them?" they asked (Lk 9:54). At that moment, they were prepared to kill those for whom Jesus came to die. Clearly, they needed to know more, to experience more: Jesus' trial, torture, crucifixion, death, resurrection and ascension to heaven. After that, Jesus commanded them to go to the whole world and make disciples, teaching them to obey everything he had commanded them (Mt 28:19 – 20). Only then, after their understanding had increased, would the disciples be ready and free to share the Good News.

31They spoke about his departure,[a] which he was about to bring to fulfillment at Jerusalem. 32Peter and his companions were very sleepy, but when they became fully awake, they saw his glory and the two men standing with him. 33As the men were leaving Jesus, Peter said to him, "Master, it is good for us to be here. Let us put up three shelters — one for you, one for Moses and one for Elijah." (He did not know what he was saying.)

34While he was speaking, a cloud appeared and covered them, and they were afraid as they entered the cloud. 35A voice came from the cloud, saying, "This is my Son, whom I have chosen; listen to him." 36When the voice had spoken, they found that Jesus was alone. The disciples kept this to themselves and did not tell anyone at that time what they had seen.

Jesus Heals a Demon-Possessed Boy

37The next day, when they came down from the mountain, a large crowd met him. 38A man in the crowd called out, "Teacher, I beg you to look at my son, for he is my only child. 39A spirit seizes him and he suddenly screams; it throws him into convulsions so that he foams at the mouth. It scarcely ever leaves him and is destroying him. 40I begged your disciples to drive it out, but they could not."

41"You unbelieving and perverse generation," Jesus replied, "how long shall I stay with you and put up with you? Bring your son here."

42Even while the boy was coming, the demon threw him to the ground in a convulsion. But Jesus rebuked the impure spirit, healed the boy and gave him back to his father. 43And they were all amazed at the greatness of God.

Jesus Predicts His Death a Second Time

While everyone was marveling at all that Jesus did, he said to his disciples, 44"Listen carefully to what I am about to tell you: The Son of Man is going to be delivered into the hands of men." 45But they did not understand what this meant. It was hidden from them, so that they did not grasp it, and they were afraid to ask him about it.

46An argument started among the disciples as to which of them would be the greatest. 47Jesus, knowing their thoughts, took a little child and had him stand beside him. 48Then he said to them, "Whoever welcomes this little child in my name welcomes me; and whoever welcomes me welcomes the one who sent me. For it is the one who is least among you all who is the greatest."

49"Master," said John, "we saw someone driving out demons in your name and we tried to stop him, because he is not one of us."

50"Do not stop him," Jesus said, "for whoever is not against you is for you."

Samaritan Opposition

51As the time approached for him to be taken up to heaven, Jesus resolutely set out for Jerusalem. 52And he sent messengers on ahead, who went into a Samaritan village to get things ready for him; 53but the people there did not welcome him, because he was heading for Jerusalem. 54When the disciples James and John saw this, they asked, "Lord, do you want us to call fire down from heaven to destroy them[b]?" 55But Jesus turned and rebuked them. 56Then he and his disciples went to another village.

The Cost of Following Jesus

57As they were walking along the road, a man said to him, "I will follow you wherever you go."

58Jesus replied, "Foxes have dens and birds have nests, but the Son of Man has no place to lay his head."

59He said to another man, "Follow me."

But he replied, "Lord, first let me go and bury my father."

---

[a] *31* Greek *exodos* [b] *54* Some manuscripts *them, just as Elijah did*

[60]Jesus said to him, "Let the dead bury their own dead, but you go and proclaim the kingdom of God."

[61]Still another said, "I will follow you, Lord; but first let me go back and say goodbye to my family."

[62]Jesus replied, "No one who puts a hand to the plow and looks back is fit for service in the kingdom of God."

Jesus Sends Out the Seventy-Two

10 After this the Lord appointed seventy-two[a] others and sent them two by two ahead of him to every town and place where he was about to go. [2]He told them, "The harvest is plentiful, but the workers are few. Ask the Lord of the harvest, therefore, to send out workers into his harvest field. [3]Go! I am sending you out like lambs among wolves. [4]Do not take a purse or bag or sandals; and do not greet anyone on the road.

[5]"When you enter a house, first say, 'Peace to this house.' [6]If someone who promotes peace is there, your peace will rest on them; if not, it will return to you. [7]Stay there, eating and drinking whatever they give you, for the worker deserves his wages. Do not move around from house to house.

[8]"When you enter a town and are welcomed, eat what is offered to you. [9]Heal the sick who are there and tell them, 'The kingdom of God has come near to you.' [10]But when you enter a town and are not welcomed, go into its streets and say, [11]'Even the dust of your town we wipe from our feet as a warning to you. Yet be sure of this: The kingdom of God has come near.' [12]I tell you, it will be more bearable on that day for Sodom than for that town.

[13]"Woe to you, Chorazin! Woe to you, Bethsaida! For if the miracles that were performed in you had been performed in Tyre and Sidon, they would have repented long ago, sitting in sackcloth and ashes. [14]But it will be more bearable for Tyre and Sidon at the judgment than for you. [15]And you, Capernaum, will you be lifted to the heavens? No, you will go down to Hades.[b]

[16]"Whoever listens to you listens to me; whoever rejects you rejects me; but whoever rejects me rejects him who sent me."

[17]The seventy-two returned with joy and said, "Lord, even the demons submit to us in your name."

[18]He replied, "I saw Satan fall like lightning from heaven. [19]I have given you authority to trample on snakes and scorpions and to overcome all the power of the enemy; nothing will harm you. [20]However, do not rejoice that the spirits submit to you, but rejoice that your names are written in heaven."

[21]At that time Jesus, full of joy through the Holy Spirit, said, "I praise you, Father, Lord of heaven and earth, because you have hidden these things from the wise and learned, and revealed them to little children. Yes, Father, for this is what you were pleased to do.

[22]"All things have been committed to me by my Father. No one knows who the Son is except the Father, and no one knows who the Father is except the Son and those to whom the Son chooses to reveal him."

[23]Then he turned to his disciples and said privately, "Blessed are the eyes that see what you see. [24]For I tell you that many prophets and kings wanted to see what you see but did not see it, and to hear what you hear but did not hear it."

The Parable of the Good Samaritan

[25]On one occasion an expert in the law stood up to test Jesus. "Teacher," he asked, "what must I do to inherit eternal life?"

[26]"What is written in the Law?" he replied. "How do you read it?"

[27]He answered, " 'Love the Lord your God with all your heart and with all your soul and with all your strength and with all your mind'[c]; and, 'Love your neighbor as yourself.'[d]"

---

[a] *1* Some manuscripts *seventy;* also in verse 17 [b] *15* That is, the realm of the dead
[c] *27* Deut. 6:5 [d] *27* Lev. 19:18

28"You have answered correctly," Jesus replied. "Do this and you will live."
29But he wanted to justify himself, so he asked Jesus, "And who is my neighbor?"
30In reply Jesus said: "A man was going down from Jerusalem to Jericho, when
he was attacked by robbers. They stripped him of his clothes, beat him and went
away, leaving him half dead. 31A priest happened to be going down the same
road, and when he saw the man, he passed by on the other side. 32So too, a Levite, when he came to the place and saw him, passed by on the other side. 33But
a Samaritan, as he traveled, came where the man was; and when he saw him,
he took pity on him. 34He went to him and bandaged his wounds, pouring on oil
and wine. Then he put the man on his own donkey, brought him to an inn and
took care of him. 35The next day he took out two denarii[a] and gave them to the
innkeeper. 'Look after him,' he said, 'and when I return, I will reimburse you for
any extra expense you may have.'
36"Which of these three do you think was a neighbor to the man who fell into
the hands of robbers?"
37The expert in the law replied, "The one who had mercy on him."
Jesus told him, "Go and do likewise."

At the Home of Martha and Mary

38As Jesus and his disciples were on their way, he came to a village where a
woman named Martha opened her home to him. 39She had a sister called Mary,
who sat at the Lord's feet listening to what he said. 40But Martha was distracted by
all the preparations that had to be made. She came to him and asked, "Lord, don't
you care that my sister has left me to do the work by myself? Tell her to help me!"
41"Martha, Martha," the Lord answered, "you are worried and upset about
many things, 42but few things are needed — or indeed only one.[b] Mary has chosen what is better, and it will not be taken away from her."

Jesus' Teaching on Prayer

11 One day Jesus was praying in a certain place. When he finished, one of
his disciples said to him, "Lord, teach us to pray, just as John taught his
disciples."
2He said to them, "When you pray, say:

"'Father,[c]
hallowed be your name,
your kingdom come.[d]
3Give us each day our daily bread.
4Forgive us our sins,
for we also forgive everyone who sins against us.[e]
And lead us not into temptation.[f]'"

5Then Jesus said to them, "Suppose you have a friend, and you go to him at
midnight and say, 'Friend, lend me three loaves of bread; 6a friend of mine on a
journey has come to me, and I have no food to offer him.' 7And suppose the one
inside answers, 'Don't bother me. The door is already locked, and my children
and I are in bed. I can't get up and give you anything.' 8I tell you, even though
he will not get up and give you the bread because of friendship, yet because of
your shameless audacity[g] he will surely get up and give you as much as you need.
9"So I say to you: Ask and it will be given to you; seek and you will find; knock
and the door will be opened to you. 10For everyone who asks receives; the one
who seeks finds; and to the one who knocks, the door will be opened.

---

[a] 35 A denarius was the usual daily wage of a day laborer (see Matt. 20:2). [b] 42 Some manuscripts *but only one thing is needed* [c] 2 Some manuscripts *Our Father in heaven* [d] 2 Some manuscripts *come. May your will be done on earth as it is in heaven.* [e] 4 Greek *everyone who is indebted to us* [f] 4 Some manuscripts *temptation, but deliver us from the evil one* [g] 8 Or *yet to preserve his good name*

11“Which of you fathers, if your son asks for[a] a fish, will give him a snake instead? 12Or if he asks for an egg, will give him a scorpion? 13If you then, though you are evil, know how to give good gifts to your children, how much more will your Father in heaven give the Holy Spirit to those who ask him!”

Jesus and Beelzebul

14Jesus was driving out a demon that was mute. When the demon left, the man who had been mute spoke, and the crowd was amazed. 15But some of them said, “By Beelzebul, the prince of demons, he is driving out demons.” 16Others tested him by asking for a sign from heaven.

17Jesus knew their thoughts and said to them: “Any kingdom divided against itself will be ruined, and a house divided against itself will fall. 18If Satan is divided against himself, how can his kingdom stand? I say this because you claim that I drive out demons by Beelzebul. 19Now if I drive out demons by Beelzebul, by whom do your followers drive them out? So then, they will be your judges. 20But if I drive out demons by the finger of God, then the kingdom of God has come upon you.

21“When a strong man, fully armed, guards his own house, his possessions are safe. 22But when someone stronger attacks and overpowers him, he takes away the armor in which the man trusted and divides up his plunder.

23“Whoever is not with me is against me, and whoever does not gather with me scatters.

24“When an impure spirit comes out of a person, it goes through arid places seeking rest and does not find it. Then it says, ‘I will return to the house I left.’ 25When it arrives, it finds the house swept clean and put in order. 26Then it goes and takes seven other spirits more wicked than itself, and they go in and live there. And the final condition of that person is worse than the first.”

27As Jesus was saying these things, a woman in the crowd called out, “Blessed is the mother who gave you birth and nursed you.”

28He replied, “Blessed rather are those who hear the word of God and obey it.”

The Sign of Jonah

29As the crowds increased, Jesus said, “This is a wicked generation. It asks for a sign, but none will be given it except the sign of Jonah. 30For as Jonah was a sign to the Ninevites, so also will the Son of Man be to this generation. 31The Queen of the South will rise at the judgment with the people of this generation and condemn them, for she came from the ends of the earth to listen to Solomon’s wisdom; and now something greater than Solomon is here. 32The men of Nineveh will stand up at the judgment with this generation and condemn it, for they repented at the preaching of Jonah; and now something greater than Jonah is here.

The Lamp of the Body

33“No one lights a lamp and puts it in a place where it will be hidden, or under a bowl. Instead they put it on its stand, so that those who come in may see the light. 34Your eye is the lamp of your body. When your eyes are healthy,[b] your whole body also is full of light. But when they are unhealthy,[c] your body also is full of darkness. 35See to it, then, that the light within you is not darkness. 36Therefore, if your whole body is full of light, and no part of it dark, it will be just as full of light as when a lamp shines its light on you.”

Woes on the Pharisees and the Experts in the Law

37When Jesus had finished speaking, a Pharisee invited him to eat with him; so he went in and reclined at the table. 38But the Pharisee was surprised when he noticed that Jesus did not first wash before the meal.

[a] *11* Some manuscripts *for bread, will give him a stone? Or if he asks for* [b] *34* The Greek for *healthy* here implies *generous.* [c] *34* The Greek for *unhealthy* here implies *stingy.*

LUKE 11:20

THE KINGDOM OF GOD

Jesus proclaimed and explained the kingdom of God — God’s rule over all things. In the Old Testament, God established his kingdom politically under David. When the Babylonians destroyed Jerusalem, the prophets continued to speak of the reestablishment of the kingdom of God under the coming Messiah (Isa 9:6 – 7). When Jesus came to earth, he preached that the kingdom of God had arrived (Mt 4:17; 5:3; Lk 11:20). With Jesus’ coming, God’s redemptive rule has freed men and women from Satan’s power. When Jesus cast out demons, he demonstrated the reality of the kingdom. And through his parables, Jesus described what the kingdom was like (Mt 25).

What we know from Jesus’ own accounts of the kingdom is that, from an earthly perspective, it turns worldly values and priorities upside down. In God’s kingdom, the poor are rich, those who mourn will be comforted, the meek are powerful, and seekers, mercy-givers, peacemakers, and those who are persecuted are the ones who will inherit the kingdom (Mt 5:3 – 12). Jesus’ ministry on earth ushered in the kingdom; the coming of the Spirit (Ac 2:1 – 13) brought it into a new phase; and someday, when the dead in Christ are raised and Jesus comes again to establish his earthly kingdom, it will be fully realized in all of its splendor, justice and perfection (Rev 22:1 – 5).

JESUS AND THE HOLY SPIRIT

One of the cautions in studying exclusively about Jesus is the implication that Jesus was and is separate from the Father and the Holy Spirit. While the truth remains mysterious, the Bible clearly teaches that God exists in three persons, the Trinity. The Bible does not use that term, but it is impossible to understand the Bible's teaching without embracing this reality. Luke, in his writings (Luke and Acts), focused on the Holy Spirit to provide insight into Jesus and the Holy Spirit. Here's an overview:

The Holy Spirit filled John the Baptist in his mother's womb (Lk 1:15 – 17).

The Holy Spirit was the agent of divine conception with Mary, the mother of Jesus (Lk 1:35).

The Holy Spirit filled Mary's relative, Elizabeth, the mother of John the Baptist, and empowered her to encourage Mary (Lk 1:41 – 45).

The Holy Spirit filled Zacharias, John's father, so he could prophesy about the Messiah (Lk 1:67 – 75).

At Jesus' baptism, the Holy Spirit descended in bodily form like a dove as God the Father spoke (Lk 3:22).

The Holy Spirit led Jesus into the wilderness to be tempted by the devil (Lk 4:1 – 13).

The Holy Spirit empowered Jesus as he began his earthly ministry (Lk 4:14 – 21).

Jesus spoke of the Father giving the Holy Spirit as he taught his disciples about prayer (Lk 11:1 – 4,13).

The Holy Spirit filled Jesus' disciples at Pentecost and empowered them to preach the Good News (Ac 2:1 – 21).

Before his crucifixion, Jesus encouraged his disciples with deep spiritual realities about the Father and the Holy Spirit. He said, "If you love me, keep my commands. And I will ask the Father, and he will give you another advocate to help you and be with you forever — the Spirit of truth" (Jn 14:15 – 17). Then, as the disciples struggled to understand, Jesus said, "I will not leave you as orphans; I will come to you. Before long, the world will not see me anymore, but you will see me. Because I live, you also will live. On that day you will realize that I am in my Father, and you are in me, and I am in you" (Jn 14:18 – 20).

[39]Then the Lord said to him, "Now then, you Pharisees clean the outside of the cup and dish, but inside you are full of greed and wickedness. [40]You foolish people! Did not the one who made the outside make the inside also? [41]But now as for what is inside you — be generous to the poor, and everything will be clean for you.

[42]"Woe to you Pharisees, because you give God a tenth of your mint, rue and all other kinds of garden herbs, but you neglect justice and the love of God. You should have practiced the latter without leaving the former undone.

[43]"Woe to you Pharisees, because you love the most important seats in the synagogues and respectful greetings in the marketplaces.

[44]"Woe to you, because you are like unmarked graves, which people walk over without knowing it."

[45]One of the experts in the law answered him, "Teacher, when you say these things, you insult us also."

[46]Jesus replied, "And you experts in the law, woe to you, because you load people down with burdens they can hardly carry, and you yourselves will not lift one finger to help them.

[47]"Woe to you, because you build tombs for the prophets, and it was your ancestors who killed them. [48]So you testify that you approve of what your ancestors did; they killed the prophets, and you build their tombs. [49]Because of this, God in his wisdom said, 'I will send them prophets and apostles, some of whom they will kill and others they will persecute.' [50]Therefore this generation will be held responsible for the blood of all the prophets that has been shed since the beginning of the world, [51]from the blood of Abel to the blood of Zechariah, who was killed between the altar and the sanctuary. Yes, I tell you, this generation will be held responsible for it all.

[52]"Woe to you experts in the law, because you have taken away the key to knowledge. You yourselves have not entered, and you have hindered those who were entering."

[53]When Jesus went outside, the Pharisees and the teachers of the law began to oppose him fiercely and to besiege him with questions, [54]waiting to catch him in something he might say.

Warnings and Encouragements

12 Meanwhile, when a crowd of many thousands had gathered, so that they were trampling on one another, Jesus began to speak first to his disciples, saying: "Be[a] on your guard against the yeast of the Pharisees, which is hypocrisy. [2]There is nothing concealed that will not be disclosed, or hidden that will not be made known. [3]What you have said in the dark will be heard in the daylight, and what you have whispered in the ear in the inner rooms will be proclaimed from the roofs.

[4]"I tell you, my friends, do not be afraid of those who kill the body and after that can do no more. [5]But I will show you whom you should fear: Fear him who, after your body has been killed, has authority to throw you into hell. Yes, I tell you, fear him. [6]Are not five sparrows sold for two pennies? Yet not one of them is forgotten by God. [7]Indeed, the very hairs of your head are all numbered. Don't be afraid; you are worth more than many sparrows.

[8]"I tell you, whoever publicly acknowledges me before others, the Son of Man will also acknowledge before the angels of God. [9]But whoever disowns me before others will be disowned before the angels of God. [10]And everyone who speaks a word against the Son of Man will be forgiven, but anyone who blasphemes against the Holy Spirit will not be forgiven.

[11]"When you are brought before synagogues, rulers and authorities, do not worry about how you will defend yourselves or what you will say, [12]for the Holy Spirit will teach you at that time what you should say."

[a] *1* Or *speak to his disciples, saying: "First of all, be*

LUKE 12:10

BLASPHEMY

Jesus' critics accused him of blasphemy, the act of showing contempt or lack of reverence for God. In the Old Testament, blaspheming God was a crime punishable by death (Lev 24:15 – 16). Blasphemy violated the third of the Ten Commandments, which required people to uphold the name and reputation of the Lord (Ex 20:7). The unbelieving Jewish leaders of Jesus' day charged Jesus with blasphemy since, in their view, he was a man who falsely claimed to be God's Son (Mt 9:3).

Actually, the Jewish leaders' own lawlessness and hypocrisy caused God's name to be blasphemed among the Gentiles (Ro 2:24). Also, their bitter opposition to Jesus and his gospel blasphemed God (Ac 18:6), and Jesus confronted their blasphemy as they attributed the work of the Holy Spirit to Satan (Mt 12:31 – 32). In the Scripture, Christians are commanded to avoid words or actions that blaspheme the Lord's name and teaching (1Ti 6:1). Rejecting Jesus' gracious gift of salvation remains the ultimate form of blasphemy, one with eternal repercussions.

The Parable of the Rich Fool

13 Someone in the crowd said to him, "Teacher, tell my brother to divide the
inheritance with me."
14 Jesus replied, "Man, who appointed me a judge or an arbiter between you?"
15 Then he said to them, "Watch out! Be on your guard against all kinds of greed;
life does not consist in an abundance of possessions."
16 And he told them this parable: "The ground of a certain rich man yielded
an abundant harvest. 17 He thought to himself, 'What shall I do? I have no place
to store my crops.'
18 "Then he said, 'This is what I'll do. I will tear down my barns and build bigger ones, and there I will store my surplus grain. 19 And I'll say to myself, "You
have plenty of grain laid up for many years. Take life easy; eat, drink and be
merry." '
20 "But God said to him, 'You fool! This very night your life will be demanded
from you. Then who will get what you have prepared for yourself?'
21 "This is how it will be with whoever stores up things for themselves but is
not rich toward God."

Do Not Worry

22 Then Jesus said to his disciples: "Therefore I tell you, do not worry about
your life, what you will eat; or about your body, what you will wear. 23 For life is
more than food, and the body more than clothes. 24 Consider the ravens: They
do not sow or reap, they have no storeroom or barn; yet God feeds them. And
how much more valuable you are than birds! 25 Who of you by worrying can add
a single hour to your life[a]? 26 Since you cannot do this very little thing, why do
you worry about the rest?
27 "Consider how the wild flowers grow. They do not labor or spin. Yet I tell you,
not even Solomon in all his splendor was dressed like one of these. 28 If that is how
God clothes the grass of the field, which is here today, and tomorrow is thrown
into the fire, how much more will he clothe you—you of little faith! 29 And do not
set your heart on what you will eat or drink; do not worry about it. 30 For the pagan world runs after all such things, and your Father knows that you need them.
31 But seek his kingdom, and these things will be given to you as well.
32 "Do not be afraid, little flock, for your Father has been pleased to give you
the kingdom. 33 Sell your possessions and give to the poor. Provide purses for
yourselves that will not wear out, a treasure in heaven that will never fail, where
no thief comes near and no moth destroys. 34 For where your treasure is, there
your heart will be also.

Watchfulness

35 "Be dressed ready for service and keep your lamps burning, 36 like servants
waiting for their master to return from a wedding banquet, so that when he
comes and knocks they can immediately open the door for him. 37 It will be good
for those servants whose master finds them watching when he comes. Truly I
tell you, he will dress himself to serve, will have them recline at the table and
will come and wait on them. 38 It will be good for those servants whose master
finds them ready, even if he comes in the middle of the night or toward daybreak. 39 But understand this: If the owner of the house had known at what hour
the thief was coming, he would not have let his house be broken into. 40 You also
must be ready, because the Son of Man will come at an hour when you do not
expect him."
41 Peter asked, "Lord, are you telling this parable to us, or to everyone?"
42 The Lord answered, "Who then is the faithful and wise manager, whom the
master puts in charge of his servants to give them their food allowance at the
proper time? 43 It will be good for that servant whom the master finds doing so

---

[a] 25 Or *single cubit to your height*

when he returns. [44]Truly I tell you, he will put him in charge of all his possessions. [45]But suppose the servant says to himself, 'My master is taking a long time in coming,' and he then begins to beat the other servants, both men and women, and to eat and drink and get drunk. [46]The master of that servant will come on a day when he does not expect him and at an hour he is not aware of. He will cut him to pieces and assign him a place with the unbelievers.

[47]"The servant who knows the master's will and does not get ready or does not do what the master wants will be beaten with many blows. [48]But the one who does not know and does things deserving punishment will be beaten with few blows. From everyone who has been given much, much will be demanded; and from the one who has been entrusted with much, much more will be asked.

Not Peace but Division

[49]"I have come to bring fire on the earth, and how I wish it were already kindled! [50]But I have a baptism to undergo, and what constraint I am under until it is completed! [51]Do you think I came to bring peace on earth? No, I tell you, but division. [52]From now on there will be five in one family divided against each other, three against two and two against three. [53]They will be divided, father against son and son against father, mother against daughter and daughter against mother, mother-in-law against daughter-in-law and daughter-in-law against mother-in-law."

Interpreting the Times

[54]He said to the crowd: "When you see a cloud rising in the west, immediately you say, 'It's going to rain,' and it does. [55]And when the south wind blows, you say, 'It's going to be hot,' and it is. [56]Hypocrites! You know how to interpret the appearance of the earth and the sky. How is it that you don't know how to interpret this present time?

[57]"Why don't you judge for yourselves what is right? [58]As you are going with your adversary to the magistrate, try hard to be reconciled on the way, or your adversary may drag you off to the judge, and the judge turn you over to the officer, and the officer throw you into prison. [59]I tell you, you will not get out until you have paid the last penny."

Repent or Perish

13 Now there were some present at that time who told Jesus about the Galileans whose blood Pilate had mixed with their sacrifices. [2]Jesus answered, "Do you think that these Galileans were worse sinners than all the other Galileans because they suffered this way? [3]I tell you, no! But unless you repent, you too will all perish. [4]Or those eighteen who died when the tower in Siloam fell on them — do you think they were more guilty than all the others living in Jerusalem? [5]I tell you, no! But unless you repent, you too will all perish."

[6]Then he told this parable: "A man had a fig tree growing in his vineyard, and he went to look for fruit on it but did not find any. [7]So he said to the man who took care of the vineyard, 'For three years now I've been coming to look for fruit on this fig tree and haven't found any. Cut it down! Why should it use up the soil?'

[8]" 'Sir,' the man replied, 'leave it alone for one more year, and I'll dig around it and fertilize it. [9]If it bears fruit next year, fine! If not, then cut it down.' "

Jesus Heals a Crippled Woman on the Sabbath

[10]On a Sabbath Jesus was teaching in one of the synagogues, [11]and a woman was there who had been crippled by a spirit for eighteen years. She was bent over and could not straighten up at all. [12]When Jesus saw her, he called her forward and said to her, "Woman, you are set free from your infirmity." [13]Then he put his hands on her, and immediately she straightened up and praised God.

[14]Indignant because Jesus had healed on the Sabbath, the synagogue leader said to the people, "There are six days for work. So come and be healed on those days, not on the Sabbath."

15The Lord answered him, "You hypocrites! Doesn't each of you on the Sabbath untie your ox or donkey from the stall and lead it out to give it water? 16Then
should not this woman, a daughter of Abraham, whom Satan has kept bound
for eighteen long years, be set free on the Sabbath day from what bound her?"
17When he said this, all his opponents were humiliated, but the people were
delighted with all the wonderful things he was doing.

The Parables of the Mustard Seed and the Yeast

18Then Jesus asked, "What is the kingdom of God like? What shall I compare
it to? 19It is like a mustard seed, which a man took and planted in his garden. It
grew and became a tree, and the birds perched in its branches."
20Again he asked, "What shall I compare the kingdom of God to? 21It is like
yeast that a woman took and mixed into about sixty pounds[a] of flour until it
worked all through the dough."

The Narrow Door

22Then Jesus went through the towns and villages, teaching as he made his
way to Jerusalem. 23Someone asked him, "Lord, are only a few people going to
be saved?"
He said to them, 24"Make every effort to enter through the narrow door, because many, I tell you, will try to enter and will not be able to. 25Once the owner
of the house gets up and closes the door, you will stand outside knocking and
pleading, 'Sir, open the door for us.'
"But he will answer, 'I don't know you or where you come from.'
26"Then you will say, 'We ate and drank with you, and you taught in our streets.'
27"But he will reply, 'I don't know you or where you come from. Away from me,
all you evildoers!'
28"There will be weeping there, and gnashing of teeth, when you see Abraham, Isaac and Jacob and all the prophets in the kingdom of God, but you yourselves thrown out. 29People will come from east and west and north and south,
and will take their places at the feast in the kingdom of God. 30Indeed there are
those who are last who will be first, and first who will be last."

Jesus' Sorrow for Jerusalem

31At that time some Pharisees came to Jesus and said to him, "Leave this place
and go somewhere else. Herod wants to kill you."
32He replied, "Go tell that fox, 'I will keep on driving out demons and healing people today and tomorrow, and on the third day I will reach my goal.' 33In
any case, I must press on today and tomorrow and the next day—for surely no
prophet can die outside Jerusalem!
34"Jerusalem, Jerusalem, you who kill the prophets and stone those sent to
you, how often I have longed to gather your children together, as a hen gathers
her chicks under her wings, and you were not willing. 35Look, your house is left
to you desolate. I tell you, you will not see me again until you say, 'Blessed is he
who comes in the name of the Lord.'[b]"

Jesus at a Pharisee's House

14 One Sabbath, when Jesus went to eat in the house of a prominent Pharisee,
he was being carefully watched. 2There in front of him was a man suffering
from abnormal swelling of his body. 3Jesus asked the Pharisees and experts in
the law, "Is it lawful to heal on the Sabbath or not?" 4But they remained silent. So
taking hold of the man, he healed him and sent him on his way.
5Then he asked them, "If one of you has a child[c] or an ox that falls into a well
on the Sabbath day, will you not immediately pull it out?" 6And they had nothing to say.

[a] *21* Or about 27 kilograms [b] *35* Psalm 118:26 [c] *5* Some manuscripts *donkey*

LUKE 13:31–35

PROPHETS DYING IN JERUSALEM

Near the end of Jesus' earthly ministry, he moved purposefully toward Jerusalem knowing that he would be mocked, flogged and crucified in that city (Mt 20:18–20). Jesus followed a long line of prophets who were executed in the nation's capital (1Ki 18:4; 2Ch 24:21). During the last week before his death, Jesus looked out over the city and cried, "Jerusalem, Jerusalem" (v. 34). Repeating the name twice was a sign of intense sorrow, like one mourning the loss of a child (2Sa 18:33). Jesus' emotion expressed his love for the people despite the bitter experience that he knew was coming by way of their hands. In the end, like the prophets of old, Jesus issued a declaration of judgment on the city, calling it a house that would be desolated (v. 35). Unlike the prophets of old who died as martyrs, Jesus' death and resurrection brought everlasting life—life that would explode in resurrection power (Php 3:10).

JESUS AND THE SABBATH

Jesus clashed with the religious leaders of his day over many issues: religious traditions, associating with sinners, spiritual authority and more. On one issue in particular — the Sabbath — these leaders monitored Jesus' actions scrupulously. The Ten Commandments prohibited work on the Sabbath since it was a holy day set apart (Ex 20:8 – 11). Just as the Israelites were commanded to tithe part of their earnings to God, they were to give him their time as well. Breaking the Sabbath was a grave matter, for God's law demanded death for those who ignored it (Ex 31:14 – 15).

The question, though, was what activities constituted "work." In the years after the temple was rebuilt following the exile (515 BC – AD 70), scribes and rabbis studied the words of Scripture, interpreting every detail. What kinds of work could be allowed on the Sabbath within the Law? For example, according to the Law, no work was to be done on the Sabbath, so that meant burdens were not to be carried on that day. So scholars debated what constituted a "burden." On the surface, the scribes had good reasons for interpreting the Law carefully since they did not want anyone to break it inadvertently. But their interpretations increasingly emphasized external adherence to the Law rather than cultivating an attitude of submission before God. Obeying their own interpretations became a source of pride instead of an expression of love for God. By Jesus' day, the rabbis and scribes had become so strict that they accused Jesus' disciples of breaking the Sabbath because they picked some grain and ate it as they walked through a field on the Sabbath (Lk 6:1 – 2).

Jesus' healings on the Sabbath enraged the religious teachers who classified healing as "work" and therefore prohibited it (Dt 5:15). He revealed the rabbis' hypocrisy with his response.

God had given the Law to encourage the Israelites to love him and to love others (Mk 12:30 – 31). He had never prohibited doing good on the Sabbath. The Pharisees acted as if God had created people so that he would have someone to keep the Sabbath, but Jesus clarified that God had given the Sabbath as a gift to the people he had created (Mk 2:27). For the Pharisees, the Ten Commandments provided great restrictions punishable by death. For Jesus, the Law outlined great freedoms that led to real life (Mt 5:17).

7When he noticed how the guests picked the places of honor at the table, he
told them this parable: 8"When someone invites you to a wedding feast, do not
take the place of honor, for a person more distinguished than you may have
been invited. 9If so, the host who invited both of you will come and say to you,
'Give this person your seat.' Then, humiliated, you will have to take the least
important place. 10But when you are invited, take the lowest place, so that when
your host comes, he will say to you, 'Friend, move up to a better place.' Then
you will be honored in the presence of all the other guests. 11For all those who
exalt themselves will be humbled, and those who humble themselves will be
exalted."

12Then Jesus said to his host, "When you give a luncheon or dinner, do not invite your friends, your brothers or sisters, your relatives, or your rich neighbors;
if you do, they may invite you back and so you will be repaid. 13But when you give
a banquet, invite the poor, the crippled, the lame, the blind, 14and you will be
blessed. Although they cannot repay you, you will be repaid at the resurrection
of the righteous."

The Parable of the Great Banquet

15When one of those at the table with him heard this, he said to Jesus, "Blessed
is the one who will eat at the feast in the kingdom of God."

16Jesus replied: "A certain man was preparing a great banquet and invited
many guests. 17At the time of the banquet he sent his servant to tell those who
had been invited, 'Come, for everything is now ready.'

18"But they all alike began to make excuses. The first said, 'I have just bought
a field, and I must go and see it. Please excuse me.'

19"Another said, 'I have just bought five yoke of oxen, and I'm on my way to try
them out. Please excuse me.'

20"Still another said, 'I just got married, so I can't come.'

21"The servant came back and reported this to his master. Then the owner
of the house became angry and ordered his servant, 'Go out quickly into the
streets and alleys of the town and bring in the poor, the crippled, the blind and
the lame.'

22" 'Sir,' the servant said, 'what you ordered has been done, but there is still
room.'

23"Then the master told his servant, 'Go out to the roads and country lanes
and compel them to come in, so that my house will be full. 24I tell you, not one of
those who were invited will get a taste of my banquet.' "

The Cost of Being a Disciple

25Large crowds were traveling with Jesus, and turning to them he said: 26"If
anyone comes to me and does not hate father and mother, wife and children,
brothers and sisters — yes, even their own life — such a person cannot be my
disciple. 27And whoever does not carry their cross and follow me cannot be my
disciple.

28"Suppose one of you wants to build a tower. Won't you first sit down and esti-
mate the cost to see if you have enough money to complete it? 29For if you lay the
foundation and are not able to finish it, everyone who sees it will ridicule you,
30saying, 'This person began to build and wasn't able to finish.'

31"Or suppose a king is about to go to war against another king. Won't he first
sit down and consider whether he is able with ten thousand men to oppose the
one coming against him with twenty thousand? 32If he is not able, he will send a
delegation while the other is still a long way off and will ask for terms of peace.
33In the same way, those of you who do not give up everything you have cannot
be my disciples.

34"Salt is good, but if it loses its saltiness, how can it be made salty again? 35It
is fit neither for the soil nor for the manure pile; it is thrown out.

"Whoever has ears to hear, let them hear."

LUKE 14:25–34

THE COST OF DISCIPLESHIP

Jesus paid an incalculable price for the salvation of sinners. As the Romans executed him on trumped up charges (Lk 23:22), the Father substituted the death of his innocent Son for the lives of all believers, who are justly charged with the capital offense of sinning against a holy God. This substitution made it possible for a just God to forgive guilty sinners. This divine pardon cannot be bought or earned but only received by grace through faith (Eph 2:8). The miracle of the gospel is that God would accept sinners because of what Jesus did through his life, death and resurrection.

The high cost Jesus paid for salvation demands a high price for discipleship. Jesus clarified this truth when he said that whoever wanted to be his disciples must take up their cross and follow him (Lk 9:23). Jesus' disciples were to surrender completely to God and his will, just as Jesus submitted completely to his Father's will (Jn 5:19). Then, as now, the ones who desire to follow Jesus must obey him (Jn 14:15).

Robust discipleship reflects a realistic understanding of salvation: the price paid, the pain borne and the great gift delivered. Those who seek to follow Jesus casually have failed to think deeply about his death on the cross. While God gives sinners salvation freely, living a life of discipleship costs everything, as what is required is daily and complete surrender to God and his will.

The Parable of the Lost Sheep

15 Now the tax collectors and sinners were all gathering around to hear Jesus. 2But the Pharisees and the teachers of the law muttered, "This man welcomes sinners and eats with them."

3Then Jesus told them this parable: 4"Suppose one of you has a hundred sheep and loses one of them. Doesn't he leave the ninety-nine in the open country and go after the lost sheep until he finds it? 5And when he finds it, he joyfully puts it on his shoulders 6and goes home. Then he calls his friends and neighbors together and says, 'Rejoice with me; I have found my lost sheep.' 7I tell you that in the same way there will be more rejoicing in heaven over one sinner who repents than over ninety-nine righteous persons who do not need to repent.

The Parable of the Lost Coin

8"Or suppose a woman has ten silver coins[a] and loses one. Doesn't she light a lamp, sweep the house and search carefully until she finds it? 9And when she finds it, she calls her friends and neighbors together and says, 'Rejoice with me; I have found my lost coin.' 10In the same way, I tell you, there is rejoicing in the presence of the angels of God over one sinner who repents."

The Parable of the Lost Son

11Jesus continued: "There was a man who had two sons. 12The younger one said to his father, 'Father, give me my share of the estate.' So he divided his property between them.

13"Not long after that, the younger son got together all he had, set off for a distant country and there squandered his wealth in wild living. 14After he had spent everything, there was a severe famine in that whole country, and he began to be in need. 15So he went and hired himself out to a citizen of that country, who sent him to his fields to feed pigs. 16He longed to fill his stomach with the pods that the pigs were eating, but no one gave him anything.

17"When he came to his senses, he said, 'How many of my father's hired servants have food to spare, and here I am starving to death! 18I will set out and go back to my father and say to him: Father, I have sinned against heaven and against you. 19I am no longer worthy to be called your son; make me like one of your hired servants.' 20So he got up and went to his father.

"But while he was still a long way off, his father saw him and was filled with compassion for him; he ran to his son, threw his arms around him and kissed him.

21"The son said to him, 'Father, I have sinned against heaven and against you. I am no longer worthy to be called your son.'

22"But the father said to his servants, 'Quick! Bring the best robe and put it on him. Put a ring on his finger and sandals on his feet. 23Bring the fattened calf and kill it. Let's have a feast and celebrate. 24For this son of mine was dead and is alive again; he was lost and is found.' So they began to celebrate.

25"Meanwhile, the older son was in the field. When he came near the house, he heard music and dancing. 26So he called one of the servants and asked him what was going on. 27'Your brother has come,' he replied, 'and your father has killed the fattened calf because he has him back safe and sound.'

28"The older brother became angry and refused to go in. So his father went out and pleaded with him. 29But he answered his father, 'Look! All these years I've been slaving for you and never disobeyed your orders. Yet you never gave me even a young goat so I could celebrate with my friends. 30But when this son of yours who has squandered your property with prostitutes comes home, you kill the fattened calf for him!'

31"'My son,' the father said, 'you are always with me, and everything I have is yours. 32But we had to celebrate and be glad, because this brother of yours was dead and is alive again; he was lost and is found.'"

---

[a] 8 Greek *ten drachmas,* each worth about a day's wages

CELEBRATING WHEN THE LOST ARE FOUND

Throughout his earthly ministry, Jesus' association with sinners chafed his religious critics, but Jesus consistently explained that he had come to seek and save the lost (Lk 19:10). To reinforce this truth, Jesus told three stories about a search for lost things.

With each story, Jesus confronted the religious leaders with the truth they kept missing — God is in the business of restoration and celebration (Lk 15:7). These leaders failed to listen with discernment as Jesus confronted them with the fact that they were like the older brother in the third story who had stayed home, served his father grudgingly, judged his brother unfairly, then distanced himself from his father without leaving home (Lk 15:25 – 30).

Jesus came to earth to launch a search-and-rescue mission, seeking and saving those who were spiritually lost. The sinners of his day loved to invite Jesus to their gatherings (Lk 5:29). The Pharisees stood by, scowled and judged. They complained to Jesus' disciples about his eating and drinking with tax collectors and sinners. Jesus responded that it was not the healthy who needed a doctor but rather those who were sick (Mt 9:12).

The Pharisees and other religious leaders loved the trappings of their offices — respectful greetings, sitting in the most important seats and having the opportunity to load others with religious burdens they personally had no intention of carrying (Lk 11:4 – 6). In contrast, Jesus did not come to be served but to serve and give his life as a ransom for many (Mt 20:28). The Pharisees thanked God that they were not needy like the sinners around them. Jesus rebuked them with a story about a tax collector who cried out to God in his spiritual poverty and found salvation (Lk 18:9 – 14).

Earthly concerns clouded the judgment of the religious leaders and caused them to disregard the spiritual truths Jesus taught. Confident that they knew God's will and that God was pleased with them, they resisted Jesus. As Jesus submitted to the grand plan of the gospel, the religious leaders manipulated the political system to ensure Jesus' death. Unwittingly, their actions set in motion all that was required for the lost to be found and for celebration to erupt in heaven.

The Parable of the Shrewd Manager

16 Jesus told his disciples: "There was a rich man whose manager was accused of wasting his possessions. [2]So he called him in and asked him,
'What is this I hear about you? Give an account of your management, because
you cannot be manager any longer.'
[3]"The manager said to himself, 'What shall I do now? My master is taking
away my job. I'm not strong enough to dig, and I'm ashamed to beg— [4]I know
what I'll do so that, when I lose my job here, people will welcome me into their
houses.'
[5]"So he called in each one of his master's debtors. He asked the first, 'How
much do you owe my master?'
[6]" 'Nine hundred gallons[a] of olive oil,' he replied.
"The manager told him, 'Take your bill, sit down quickly, and make it four
hundred and fifty.'
[7]"Then he asked the second, 'And how much do you owe?'
" 'A thousand bushels[b] of wheat,' he replied.
"He told him, 'Take your bill and make it eight hundred.'
[8]"The master commended the dishonest manager because he had acted
shrewdly. For the people of this world are more shrewd in dealing with their
own kind than are the people of the light. [9]I tell you, use worldly wealth to gain
friends for yourselves, so that when it is gone, you will be welcomed into eternal
dwellings.
[10]"Whoever can be trusted with very little can also be trusted with much, and
whoever is dishonest with very little will also be dishonest with much. [11]So if you
have not been trustworthy in handling worldly wealth, who will trust you with
true riches? [12]And if you have not been trustworthy with someone else's property, who will give you property of your own?
[13]"No one can serve two masters. Either you will hate the one and love the
other, or you will be devoted to the one and despise the other. You cannot serve
both God and money."
[14]The Pharisees, who loved money, heard all this and were sneering at Jesus.
[15]He said to them, "You are the ones who justify yourselves in the eyes of others, but God knows your hearts. What people value highly is detestable in God's
sight.

Additional Teachings

[16]"The Law and the Prophets were proclaimed until John. Since that time,
the good news of the kingdom of God is being preached, and everyone is forcing
their way into it. [17]It is easier for heaven and earth to disappear than for the least
stroke of a pen to drop out of the Law.
[18]"Anyone who divorces his wife and marries another woman commits adultery, and the man who marries a divorced woman commits adultery.

The Rich Man and Lazarus

[19]"There was a rich man who was dressed in purple and fine linen and lived
in luxury every day. [20]At his gate was laid a beggar named Lazarus, covered with
sores [21]and longing to eat what fell from the rich man's table. Even the dogs came
and licked his sores.
[22]"The time came when the beggar died and the angels carried him to Abraham's side. The rich man also died and was buried. [23]In Hades, where he was in
torment, he looked up and saw Abraham far away, with Lazarus by his side. [24]So
he called to him, 'Father Abraham, have pity on me and send Lazarus to dip the
tip of his finger in water and cool my tongue, because I am in agony in this fire.'
[25]"But Abraham replied, 'Son, remember that in your lifetime you received
your good things, while Lazarus received bad things, but now he is comforted

[a] 6 Or about 3,000 liters [b] 7 Or about 30 tons

here and you are in agony. [26]And besides all this, between us and you a great chasm has been set in place, so that those who want to go from here to you cannot, nor can anyone cross over from there to us.'

[27]"He answered, 'Then I beg you, father, send Lazarus to my family, [28]for I have five brothers. Let him warn them, so that they will not also come to this place of torment.'

[29]"Abraham replied, 'They have Moses and the Prophets; let them listen to them.'

[30]" 'No, father Abraham,' he said, 'but if someone from the dead goes to them, they will repent.'

[31]"He said to him, 'If they do not listen to Moses and the Prophets, they will not be convinced even if someone rises from the dead.' "

Sin, Faith, Duty

17 Jesus said to his disciples: "Things that cause people to stumble are bound to come, but woe to anyone through whom they come. [2]It would be better for them to be thrown into the sea with a millstone tied around their neck than to cause one of these little ones to stumble. [3]So watch yourselves.

"If your brother or sister[a] sins against you, rebuke them; and if they repent, forgive them. [4]Even if they sin against you seven times in a day and seven times come back to you saying 'I repent,' you must forgive them."

[5]The apostles said to the Lord, "Increase our faith!"

[6]He replied, "If you have faith as small as a mustard seed, you can say to this mulberry tree, 'Be uprooted and planted in the sea,' and it will obey you.

[7]"Suppose one of you has a servant plowing or looking after the sheep. Will he say to the servant when he comes in from the field, 'Come along now and sit down to eat'? [8]Won't he rather say, 'Prepare my supper, get yourself ready and wait on me while I eat and drink; after that you may eat and drink'? [9]Will he thank the servant because he did what he was told to do? [10]So you also, when you have done everything you were told to do, should say, 'We are unworthy servants; we have only done our duty.' "

Jesus Heals Ten Men With Leprosy

[11]Now on his way to Jerusalem, Jesus traveled along the border between Samaria and Galilee. [12]As he was going into a village, ten men who had leprosy[b] met him. They stood at a distance [13]and called out in a loud voice, "Jesus, Master, have pity on us!"

[14]When he saw them, he said, "Go, show yourselves to the priests." And as they went, they were cleansed.

[15]One of them, when he saw he was healed, came back, praising God in a loud voice. [16]He threw himself at Jesus' feet and thanked him — and he was a Samaritan.

[17]Jesus asked, "Were not all ten cleansed? Where are the other nine? [18]Has no one returned to give praise to God except this foreigner?" [19]Then he said to him, "Rise and go; your faith has made you well."

The Coming of the Kingdom of God

[20]Once, on being asked by the Pharisees when the kingdom of God would come, Jesus replied, "The coming of the kingdom of God is not something that can be observed, [21]nor will people say, 'Here it is,' or 'There it is,' because the kingdom of God is in your midst."[c]

[22]Then he said to his disciples, "The time is coming when you will long to see one of the days of the Son of Man, but you will not see it. [23]People will tell you, 'There he is!' or 'Here he is!' Do not go running off after them. [24]For the Son of

LUKE 17:20–21

THE KINGDOM OF GOD IN YOUR MIDST

In Jesus' day, people wanted to know about the kingdom of God, and they asked Jesus about it. Jesus confounded their assumptions by asserting that the kingdom of God was already in their midst. Clearly, an aspect of the kingdom promise was fulfilled in Jesus' first coming. The kingdom of God operates among earthly kingdoms today, but one day, God's kingdom will swallow up all rival kingdoms (Rev 11:15).

The kingdom of God is not the same as the church, though the church is part of the kingdom. The kingdom now is the presence of God alongside earthly kingdoms. The power of God is shown now in the distribution and work of the Holy Spirit (Heb 2:4). One day, however, Jesus will rule over all, and he will share that rule with his people (Rev 5:9–10). Until then, believers wait in anticipation for God's kingdom rule to be complete.

[a] *3* The Greek word for *brother or sister* (*adelphos*) refers here to a fellow disciple, whether man or woman. [b] *12* The Greek word traditionally translated *leprosy* was used for various diseases affecting the skin. [c] *21* Or *is within you*

JESUS AND HELL

Jesus taught more about hell than he taught about heaven. Through the parable of the rich man and a poor man named Lazarus, Jesus provided unforgettable insights into life now and the life to come.

While they lived on earth, a great economic chasm separated the rich man from Lazarus. While the rich man feasted, Lazarus starved. While the rich man lived in pleasure, Lazarus lived in pain. If Jesus had asked his disciples which of these men God favored, they would not have faltered: their answer would have been "the rich man." That's why the disciples were so surprised when Jesus explained that it was easier for a camel to go through the eye of a needle than for a rich man to go to heaven. They exclaimed, "Who then can be saved?" Jesus responded, "With man this is impossible, but with God all things are possible" (Mt 19:25 – 26).

In the parable, after the rich man and Lazarus died, a great spiritual chasm separated them. While Lazarus enjoyed comfort, the rich man writhed in torment. For these two men, eternity brought about a great reversal. Jesus' story teaches that there is an unbridgeable divide between heaven and hell; no one can travel from one to the other. The good news is that eternity in hell is not inevitable. Choices made in this life impact what happens after death.

The Pharisees and other religious leaders listened that day but clearly missed the point. Later, Jesus raised another man, Lazarus, from the dead. Only God could perform such a miracle. Some placed their faith in Jesus, but others, especially the religious leaders, left and began plotting how and when to kill Jesus (Jn 11:38 – 53). Jesus had enough power to raise Lazarus from the dead, yet the religious elite pooled their political power to trap, accuse, bring to trial and then crucify Jesus. Jesus confronted them with the truth that they were in league with their father, the devil, and working to carry out his murderous desires (Jn 8:44).

Jesus graciously explained the reality of hell so that people would understand the consequences of their choices. Because of the gospel, everyone can call on the name of the Lord before they die and be saved (Ac 2:21).

Man in his day[a] will be like the lightning, which flashes and lights up the sky
from one end to the other. [25]But first he must suffer many things and be rejected
by this generation.

[26]"Just as it was in the days of Noah, so also will it be in the days of the Son of
Man. [27]People were eating, drinking, marrying and being given in marriage up
to the day Noah entered the ark. Then the flood came and destroyed them all.

[28]"It was the same in the days of Lot. People were eating and drinking, buying
and selling, planting and building. [29]But the day Lot left Sodom, fire and sulfur
rained down from heaven and destroyed them all.

[30]"It will be just like this on the day the Son of Man is revealed. [31]On that day
no one who is on the housetop, with possessions inside, should go down to get
them. Likewise, no one in the field should go back for anything. [32]Remember
Lot's wife! [33]Whoever tries to keep their life will lose it, and whoever loses their
life will preserve it. [34]I tell you, on that night two people will be in one bed; one
will be taken and the other left. [35]Two women will be grinding grain together;
one will be taken and the other left." [36][b]

[37]"Where, Lord?" they asked.

He replied, "Where there is a dead body, there the vultures will gather."

The Parable of the Persistent Widow

18 Then Jesus told his disciples a parable to show them that they should always pray and not give up. [2]He said: "In a certain town there was a judge
who neither feared God nor cared what people thought. [3]And there was a widow
in that town who kept coming to him with the plea, 'Grant me justice against
my adversary.'

[4]"For some time he refused. But finally he said to himself, 'Even though I don't
fear God or care what people think, [5]yet because this widow keeps bothering me,
I will see that she gets justice, so that she won't eventually come and attack me!' "

[6]And the Lord said, "Listen to what the unjust judge says. [7]And will not God
bring about justice for his chosen ones, who cry out to him day and night? Will
he keep putting them off? [8]I tell you, he will see that they get justice, and quickly.
However, when the Son of Man comes, will he find faith on the earth?"

The Parable of the Pharisee and the Tax Collector

[9]To some who were confident of their own righteousness and looked down on
everyone else, Jesus told this parable: [10]"Two men went up to the temple to pray, one
a Pharisee and the other a tax collector. [11]The Pharisee stood by himself and prayed:
'God, I thank you that I am not like other people—robbers, evildoers, adulterers—
or even like this tax collector. [12]I fast twice a week and give a tenth of all I get.'

[13]"But the tax collector stood at a distance. He would not even look up to heav-
en, but beat his breast and said, 'God, have mercy on me, a sinner.'

[14]"I tell you that this man, rather than the other, went home justified before
God. For all those who exalt themselves will be humbled, and those who humble
themselves will be exalted."

The Little Children and Jesus

[15]People were also bringing babies to Jesus for him to place his hands on
them. When the disciples saw this, they rebuked them. [16]But Jesus called the
children to him and said, "Let the little children come to me, and do not hinder
them, for the kingdom of God belongs to such as these. [17]Truly I tell you, anyone
who will not receive the kingdom of God like a little child will never enter it."

The Rich and the Kingdom of God

[18]A certain ruler asked him, "Good teacher, what must I do to inherit eternal
life?"

---

[a] *24* Some manuscripts do not have *in his day.* [b] *36* Some manuscripts include here words similar to Matt. 24:40.

LUKE 18:9–14

JESUS AND MERCY

The Greek word translated "have mercy" can also mean "to be favorably inclined." This word is used only one other time in the New Testament, and there it describes how Christ made reconciliation possible between God and humanity by his sacrifice on the cross (Heb 2:17). The noun form appears in 1 John 2:2 and 4:10; in both places, Jesus is called the atoning sacrifice for our sins. Jesus, as our sacrifice, paid the price our sins required, thereby making it possible for God to turn aside his righteous wrath.

The tax collector in Jesus' story understood his sinful condition and asked God for mercy. Thankfully, God does not save people because of their righteous acts but solely through his rich mercy (Eph 2:4–5; Titus 3:5). Later, the apostle Peter would write that in God's great mercy, he has given believers new birth into a living hope through the resurrection of Jesus Christ from the dead (1Pe 1:3). When people cry out to God for mercy, God's merciful response is Jesus.

19“Why do you call me good?” Jesus answered. “No one is good—except God
alone. 20You know the commandments: ‘You shall not commit adultery, you
shall not murder, you shall not steal, you shall not give false testimony, honor
your father and mother.’[a]”
21“All these I have kept since I was a boy,” he said.
22When Jesus heard this, he said to him, “You still lack one thing. Sell everything you have and give to the poor, and you will have treasure in heaven. Then
come, follow me.”
23When he heard this, he became very sad, because he was very wealthy.
24Jesus looked at him and said, “How hard it is for the rich to enter the kingdom
of God! 25Indeed, it is easier for a camel to go through the eye of a needle than for
someone who is rich to enter the kingdom of God.”
26Those who heard this asked, “Who then can be saved?”
27Jesus replied, “What is impossible with man is possible with God.”
28Peter said to him, “We have left all we had to follow you!”
29“Truly I tell you,” Jesus said to them, “no one who has left home or wife or
brothers or sisters or parents or children for the sake of the kingdom of God 30will
fail to receive many times as much in this age, and in the age to come eternal life.”

Jesus Predicts His Death a Third Time

31Jesus took the Twelve aside and told them, “We are going up to Jerusalem,
and everything that is written by the prophets about the Son of Man will be fulfilled. 32He will be delivered over to the Gentiles. They will mock him, insult
him and spit on him; 33they will flog him and kill him. On the third day he will
rise again.”
34The disciples did not understand any of this. Its meaning was hidden from
them, and they did not know what he was talking about.

A Blind Beggar Receives His Sight

35As Jesus approached Jericho, a blind man was sitting by the roadside begging. 36When he heard the crowd going by, he asked what was happening. 37They
told him, “Jesus of Nazareth is passing by.”
38He called out, “Jesus, Son of David, have mercy on me!”
39Those who led the way rebuked him and told him to be quiet, but he shouted
all the more, “Son of David, have mercy on me!”
40Jesus stopped and ordered the man to be brought to him. When he came
near, Jesus asked him, 41“What do you want me to do for you?”
“Lord, I want to see,” he replied.
42Jesus said to him, “Receive your sight; your faith has healed you.” 43Immedi-
ately he received his sight and followed Jesus, praising God. When all the people
saw it, they also praised God.

Zacchaeus the Tax Collector

19 Jesus entered Jericho and was passing through. 2A man was there by the
name of Zacchaeus; he was a chief tax collector and was wealthy. 3He
wanted to see who Jesus was, but because he was short he could not see over the
crowd. 4So he ran ahead and climbed a sycamore-fig tree to see him, since Jesus
was coming that way.
5When Jesus reached the spot, he looked up and said to him, “Zacchaeus,
come down immediately. I must stay at your house today.” 6So he came down at
once and welcomed him gladly.
7All the people saw this and began to mutter, “He has gone to be the guest of
a sinner.”
8But Zacchaeus stood up and said to the Lord, “Look, Lord! Here and now
I give half of my possessions to the poor, and if I have cheated anybody out of
anything, I will pay back four times the amount.”

---

[a] *20* Exodus 20:12-16; Deut. 5:16-20

[9]Jesus said to him, "Today salvation has come to this house, because this man, too, is a son of Abraham. [10]For the Son of Man came to seek and to save the lost."

The Parable of the Ten Minas

[11]While they were listening to this, he went on to tell them a parable, because he was near Jerusalem and the people thought that the kingdom of God was going to appear at once. [12]He said: "A man of noble birth went to a distant country to have himself appointed king and then to return. [13]So he called ten of his servants and gave them ten minas.[a] 'Put this money to work,' he said, 'until I come back.'

[14]"But his subjects hated him and sent a delegation after him to say, 'We don't want this man to be our king.'

[15]"He was made king, however, and returned home. Then he sent for the servants to whom he had given the money, in order to find out what they had gained with it.

[16]"The first one came and said, 'Sir, your mina has earned ten more.'

[17]" 'Well done, my good servant!' his master replied. 'Because you have been trustworthy in a very small matter, take charge of ten cities.'

[18]"The second came and said, 'Sir, your mina has earned five more.'

[19]"His master answered, 'You take charge of five cities.'

[20]"Then another servant came and said, 'Sir, here is your mina; I have kept it laid away in a piece of cloth. [21]I was afraid of you, because you are a hard man. You take out what you did not put in and reap what you did not sow.'

[22]"His master replied, 'I will judge you by your own words, you wicked servant! You knew, did you, that I am a hard man, taking out what I did not put in, and reaping what I did not sow? [23]Why then didn't you put my money on deposit, so that when I came back, I could have collected it with interest?'

[24]"Then he said to those standing by, 'Take his mina away from him and give it to the one who has ten minas.'

[25]" 'Sir,' they said, 'he already has ten!'

[26]"He replied, 'I tell you that to everyone who has, more will be given, but as for the one who has nothing, even what they have will be taken away. [27]But those enemies of mine who did not want me to be king over them — bring them here and kill them in front of me.' "

Jesus Comes to Jerusalem as King

[28]After Jesus had said this, he went on ahead, going up to Jerusalem. [29]As he approached Bethphage and Bethany at the hill called the Mount of Olives, he sent two of his disciples, saying to them, [30]"Go to the village ahead of you, and as you enter it, you will find a colt tied there, which no one has ever ridden. Untie it and bring it here. [31]If anyone asks you, 'Why are you untying it?' say, 'The Lord needs it.' "

[32]Those who were sent ahead went and found it just as he had told them. [33]As they were untying the colt, its owners asked them, "Why are you untying the colt?"

[34]They replied, "The Lord needs it."

[35]They brought it to Jesus, threw their cloaks on the colt and put Jesus on it. [36]As he went along, people spread their cloaks on the road.

[37]When he came near the place where the road goes down the Mount of Olives, the whole crowd of disciples began joyfully to praise God in loud voices for all the miracles they had seen:

[38]"Blessed is the king who comes in the name of the Lord!"[b]

"Peace in heaven and glory in the highest!"

[39]Some of the Pharisees in the crowd said to Jesus, "Teacher, rebuke your disciples!"

---

[a] *13* A mina was about three months' wages. [b] *38* Psalm 118:26

LUKE 19:28 – 44

THE TRIUMPHAL ENTRY

Jesus' entry into Jerusalem bears the unmistakable marks of a royal procession — the arrival of a king greeted by his people with celebration and joy. In the space of a few verses, Luke deftly weaves together historical allusions and nods to prophecy to emphasize that Jesus was indeed Israel's promised king. The ride on the colt strongly resembles Solomon's journey to Gihon where he was to be proclaimed king (1Ki 1:33 – 35). The description of people eagerly spreading their outer garments to create a pathway for Jesus (roughly equivalent to "rolling out the red carpet" today) recalls the scene of Jehu's coronation (2Ki 9:13). Luke's account of Christ's triumphal entry culminates with a citation from Psalm 118:26, adding the title of "king" so as to leave no doubt: Jesus was the long-awaited King who would bring peace between people and God.

40“I tell you,” he replied, “if they keep quiet, the stones will cry out.”

41As he approached Jerusalem and saw the city, he wept over it 42and said, “If you, even you, had only known on this day what would bring you peace — but now it is hidden from your eyes. 43The days will come upon you when your enemies will build an embankment against you and encircle you and hem you in on every side. 44They will dash you to the ground, you and the children within your walls. They will not leave one stone on another, because you did not recognize the time of God’s coming to you.”

Jesus at the Temple

45When Jesus entered the temple courts, he began to drive out those who were selling. 46“It is written,” he said to them, “ ‘My house will be a house of prayer’[a]; but you have made it ‘a den of robbers.’[b]”

47Every day he was teaching at the temple. But the chief priests, the teachers of the law and the leaders among the people were trying to kill him. 48Yet they could not find any way to do it, because all the people hung on his words.

The Authority of Jesus Questioned

20 One day as Jesus was teaching the people in the temple courts and proclaiming the good news, the chief priests and the teachers of the law, together with the elders, came up to him. 2“Tell us by what authority you are doing these things,” they said. “Who gave you this authority?”

3He replied, “I will also ask you a question. Tell me: 4John’s baptism — was it from heaven, or of human origin?”

5They discussed it among themselves and said, “If we say, ‘From heaven,’ he will ask, ‘Why didn’t you believe him?’ 6But if we say, ‘Of human origin,’ all the people will stone us, because they are persuaded that John was a prophet.”

7So they answered, “We don’t know where it was from.”

8Jesus said, “Neither will I tell you by what authority I am doing these things.”

The Parable of the Tenants

9He went on to tell the people this parable: “A man planted a vineyard, rented it to some farmers and went away for a long time. 10At harvest time he sent a servant to the tenants so they would give him some of the fruit of the vineyard. But the tenants beat him and sent him away empty-handed. 11He sent another servant, but that one also they beat and treated shamefully and sent away empty-handed. 12He sent still a third, and they wounded him and threw him out.

13“Then the owner of the vineyard said, ‘What shall I do? I will send my son, whom I love; perhaps they will respect him.’

14“But when the tenants saw him, they talked the matter over. ‘This is the heir,’ they said. ‘Let’s kill him, and the inheritance will be ours.’ 15So they threw him out of the vineyard and killed him.

“What then will the owner of the vineyard do to them? 16He will come and kill those tenants and give the vineyard to others.”

When the people heard this, they said, “God forbid!”

17Jesus looked directly at them and asked, “Then what is the meaning of that which is written:

“ ‘The stone the builders rejected
has become the cornerstone’[c]?

18Everyone who falls on that stone will be broken to pieces; anyone on whom it falls will be crushed.”

19The teachers of the law and the chief priests looked for a way to arrest him immediately, because they knew he had spoken this parable against them. But they were afraid of the people.

[a] 46 Isaiah 56:7 [b] 46 Jer. 7:11 [c] 17 Psalm 118:22

LUKE 20:19 – 26

“WHOSE IMAGE?”

Jesus and his teachings posed a direct challenge to Jewish religious leaders. Yet, because of Jesus’ popularity, the chief priests and scribes remained wary of taking direct action against either Jesus or his teachings. Instead, they watched and waited, hoping Jesus’ words would be his own downfall. In this passage, the religious leaders set a subtle trap for Jesus by asking a question for which there was no easy answer: Should Jews pay a citizenship tax to Caesar? If Jesus said yes, this would indicate his acceptance of foreign rule and undermine his standing with the people. If Jesus said no, he would sound like a political revolutionary.

But Jesus knew their hearts and risked neither losing the support of the people or being handed over to the Roman governor for sedition. Jesus sidestepped the trap — and set a trap of his own. When Jesus asked for a coin, the Pharisees produced a Roman denarius, proving that they already recognized Roman sovereignty. Jesus pointed out that since this coin bore the image of Caesar, it belonged to Caesar. Caesar had the right to require taxes, and the Jews were not exempt. But Jesus went a step further, taking the opportunity to turn a political debate into a spiritual lesson. Alluding to the fact that human beings are “stamped” with the image of God (Ge 1:26 – 27), Jesus reminded the religious leaders of the vital importance of giving to God what is due to him. God’s people, as bearers of God’s image, belong to him alone.

Paying Taxes to Caesar

[20]Keeping a close watch on him, they sent spies, who pretended to be sincere.
They hoped to catch Jesus in something he said, so that they might hand him
over to the power and authority of the governor. [21]So the spies questioned him:
"Teacher, we know that you speak and teach what is right, and that you do not
show partiality but teach the way of God in accordance with the truth. [22]Is it right
for us to pay taxes to Caesar or not?"

[23]He saw through their duplicity and said to them, [24]"Show me a denarius.
Whose image and inscription are on it?"

"Caesar's," they replied.

[25]He said to them, "Then give back to Caesar what is Caesar's, and to God
what is God's."

[26]They were unable to trap him in what he had said there in public. And astonished by his answer, they became silent.

The Resurrection and Marriage

[27]Some of the Sadducees, who say there is no resurrection, came to Jesus with
a question. [28]"Teacher," they said, "Moses wrote for us that if a man's brother dies
and leaves a wife but no children, the man must marry the widow and raise up
offspring for his brother. [29]Now there were seven brothers. The first one married
a woman and died childless. [30]The second [31]and then the third married her, and
in the same way the seven died, leaving no children. [32]Finally, the woman died
too. [33]Now then, at the resurrection whose wife will she be, since the seven were
married to her?"

[34]Jesus replied, "The people of this age marry and are given in marriage. [35]But
those who are considered worthy of taking part in the age to come and in the resurrection from the dead will neither marry nor be given in marriage, [36]and they
can no longer die; for they are like the angels. They are God's children, since they
are children of the resurrection. [37]But in the account of the burning bush, even
Moses showed that the dead rise, for he calls the Lord 'the God of Abraham, and
the God of Isaac, and the God of Jacob.'[a] [38]He is not the God of the dead, but of
the living, for to him all are alive."

[39]Some of the teachers of the law responded, "Well said, teacher!" [40]And no
one dared to ask him any more questions.

Whose Son Is the Messiah?

[41]Then Jesus said to them, "Why is it said that the Messiah is the son of David?
[42]David himself declares in the Book of Psalms:

"'The Lord said to my Lord:
"Sit at my right hand
[43]until I make your enemies
a footstool for your feet."'[b]

[44]David calls him 'Lord.' How then can he be his son?"

Warning Against the Teachers of the Law

[45]While all the people were listening, Jesus said to his disciples, [46]"Beware of
the teachers of the law. They like to walk around in flowing robes and love to be
greeted with respect in the marketplaces and have the most important seats in the
synagogues and the places of honor at banquets. [47]They devour widows' houses
and for a show make lengthy prayers. These men will be punished most severely."

The Widow's Offering

21 As Jesus looked up, he saw the rich putting their gifts into the temple treasury. [2]He also saw a poor widow put in two very small copper coins. [3]"Truly I tell you," he said, "this poor widow has put in more than all the others. [4]All

[a] 37 Exodus 3:6 [b] 43 Psalm 110:1

these people gave their gifts out of their wealth; but she out of her poverty put in all she had to live on."

The Destruction of the Temple and Signs of the End Times

5Some of his disciples were remarking about how the temple was adorned with beautiful stones and with gifts dedicated to God. But Jesus said, 6"As for what you see here, the time will come when not one stone will be left on another; every one of them will be thrown down."

7"Teacher," they asked, "when will these things happen? And what will be the sign that they are about to take place?"

8He replied: "Watch out that you are not deceived. For many will come in my name, claiming, 'I am he,' and, 'The time is near.' Do not follow them. 9When you hear of wars and uprisings, do not be frightened. These things must happen first, but the end will not come right away."

10Then he said to them: "Nation will rise against nation, and kingdom against kingdom. 11There will be great earthquakes, famines and pestilences in various places, and fearful events and great signs from heaven.

12"But before all this, they will seize you and persecute you. They will hand you over to synagogues and put you in prison, and you will be brought before kings and governors, and all on account of my name. 13And so you will bear testimony to me. 14But make up your mind not to worry beforehand how you will defend yourselves. 15For I will give you words and wisdom that none of your adversaries will be able to resist or contradict. 16You will be betrayed even by parents, brothers and sisters, relatives and friends, and they will put some of you to death. 17Everyone will hate you because of me. 18But not a hair of your head will perish. 19Stand firm, and you will win life.

20"When you see Jerusalem being surrounded by armies, you will know that its desolation is near. 21Then let those who are in Judea flee to the mountains, let those in the city get out, and let those in the country not enter the city. 22For this is the time of punishment in fulfillment of all that has been written. 23How dreadful it will be in those days for pregnant women and nursing mothers! There will be great distress in the land and wrath against this people. 24They will fall by the sword and will be taken as prisoners to all the nations. Jerusalem will be trampled on by the Gentiles until the times of the Gentiles are fulfilled.

25"There will be signs in the sun, moon and stars. On the earth, nations will be in anguish and perplexity at the roaring and tossing of the sea. 26People will faint from terror, apprehensive of what is coming on the world, for the heavenly bodies will be shaken. 27At that time they will see the Son of Man coming in a cloud with power and great glory. 28When these things begin to take place, stand up and lift up your heads, because your redemption is drawing near."

29He told them this parable: "Look at the fig tree and all the trees. 30When they sprout leaves, you can see for yourselves and know that summer is near. 31Even so, when you see these things happening, you know that the kingdom of God is near.

32"Truly I tell you, this generation will certainly not pass away until all these things have happened. 33Heaven and earth will pass away, but my words will never pass away.

34"Be careful, or your hearts will be weighed down with carousing, drunkenness and the anxieties of life, and that day will close on you suddenly like a trap. 35For it will come on all those who live on the face of the whole earth. 36Be always on the watch, and pray that you may be able to escape all that is about to happen, and that you may be able to stand before the Son of Man."

37Each day Jesus was teaching at the temple, and each evening he went out to spend the night on the hill called the Mount of Olives, 38and all the people came early in the morning to hear him at the temple.

LUKE 21:5–6

FULFILLED PROPHECY

When Jesus prophesied the destruction of the temple, he was standing on the grounds of that magnificently adorned place of worship. The temple was at the heart of Israel's religious life, and Herod the Great had initiated an extravagant refurbishing process: residents and tourists saw gold- and silver-plated gates, golden grapevine clusters that decorated the courtyard, and ornate Babylonian linen tapestries that hung from the temple veil. Even a Roman historian, Tacitus, was impressed, declaring it to be an "immensely opulent temple."

Jesus' prediction must have seemed unlikely, even unthinkable, to the people listening. Not only was the temple itself impressive, but Jesus lived during a time when Judaism was experiencing great Messianic fervor, with high expectations of national deliverance from Roman rule. How could it be that this building that stood at the center of Jewish life and hope would be reduced to a heap of rubble? But just a few short decades later, in AD 70, Roman forces attacked the city of Jerusalem and ransacked, demolished and burned the temple.

Despite the tragic nature of this episode in history, it highlights a great truth: Jesus' words are reliable. As God's people now live in the hope of Jesus' return, the final resurrection and all the other promises of Jesus that have yet to come to pass, they can find reassurance in knowing that Jesus' prophecies have proven reliable time and time again. Christian hope is well founded on the One who does not change (Mal 3:6; Jas 1:17).

Judas Agrees to Betray Jesus

22 Now the Festival of Unleavened Bread, called the Passover, was approaching, [2]and the chief priests and the teachers of the law were looking for some way to get rid of Jesus, for they were afraid of the people. [3]Then Satan entered Judas, called Iscariot, one of the Twelve. [4]And Judas went to the chief priests and the officers of the temple guard and discussed with them how he might betray Jesus. [5]They were delighted and agreed to give him money. [6]He consented, and watched for an opportunity to hand Jesus over to them when no crowd was present.

The Last Supper

[7]Then came the day of Unleavened Bread on which the Passover lamb had to be sacrificed. [8]Jesus sent Peter and John, saying, "Go and make preparations for us to eat the Passover."

[9]"Where do you want us to prepare for it?" they asked.

[10]He replied, "As you enter the city, a man carrying a jar of water will meet you. Follow him to the house that he enters, [11]and say to the owner of the house, 'The Teacher asks: Where is the guest room, where I may eat the Passover with my disciples?' [12]He will show you a large room upstairs, all furnished. Make preparations there."

[13]They left and found things just as Jesus had told them. So they prepared the Passover.

[14]When the hour came, Jesus and his apostles reclined at the table. [15]And he said to them, "I have eagerly desired to eat this Passover with you before I suffer. [16]For I tell you, I will not eat it again until it finds fulfillment in the kingdom of God."

[17]After taking the cup, he gave thanks and said, "Take this and divide it among you. [18]For I tell you I will not drink again from the fruit of the vine until the kingdom of God comes."

[19]And he took bread, gave thanks and broke it, and gave it to them, saying, "This is my body given for you; do this in remembrance of me."

[20]In the same way, after the supper he took the cup, saying, "This cup is the new covenant in my blood, which is poured out for you.[a] [21]But the hand of him who is going to betray me is with mine on the table. [22]The Son of Man will go as it has been decreed. But woe to that man who betrays him!" [23]They began to question among themselves which of them it might be who would do this.

[24]A dispute also arose among them as to which of them was considered to be greatest. [25]Jesus said to them, "The kings of the Gentiles lord it over them; and those who exercise authority over them call themselves Benefactors. [26]But you are not to be like that. Instead, the greatest among you should be like the youngest, and the one who rules like the one who serves. [27]For who is greater, the one who is at the table or the one who serves? Is it not the one who is at the table? But I am among you as one who serves. [28]You are those who have stood by me in my trials. [29]And I confer on you a kingdom, just as my Father conferred one on me, [30]so that you may eat and drink at my table in my kingdom and sit on thrones, judging the twelve tribes of Israel.

[31]"Simon, Simon, Satan has asked to sift all of you as wheat. [32]But I have prayed for you, Simon, that your faith may not fail. And when you have turned back, strengthen your brothers."

[33]But he replied, "Lord, I am ready to go with you to prison and to death."

[34]Jesus answered, "I tell you, Peter, before the rooster crows today, you will deny three times that you know me."

[35]Then Jesus asked them, "When I sent you without purse, bag or sandals, did you lack anything?"

"Nothing," they answered.

[36]He said to them, "But now if you have a purse, take it, and also a bag; and if you don't have a sword, sell your cloak and buy one. [37]It is written: 'And he was

---

[a] *19,20* Some manuscripts do not have *given for you . . . poured out for you.*

numbered with the transgressors'[a]; and I tell you that this must be fulfilled in
me. Yes, what is written about me is reaching its fulfillment."
38The disciples said, "See, Lord, here are two swords."
"That's enough!" he replied.

Jesus Prays on the Mount of Olives

39Jesus went out as usual to the Mount of Olives, and his disciples followed
him. 40On reaching the place, he said to them, "Pray that you will not fall into
temptation." 41He withdrew about a stone's throw beyond them, knelt down and
prayed, 42"Father, if you are willing, take this cup from me; yet not my will, but
yours be done." 43An angel from heaven appeared to him and strengthened him.
44And being in anguish, he prayed more earnestly, and his sweat was like drops
of blood falling to the ground.[b]
45When he rose from prayer and went back to the disciples, he found them
asleep, exhausted from sorrow. 46"Why are you sleeping?" he asked them. "Get
up and pray so that you will not fall into temptation."

Jesus Arrested

47While he was still speaking a crowd came up, and the man who was called
Judas, one of the Twelve, was leading them. He approached Jesus to kiss him,
48but Jesus asked him, "Judas, are you betraying the Son of Man with a kiss?"
49When Jesus' followers saw what was going to happen, they said, "Lord,
should we strike with our swords?" 50And one of them struck the servant of the
high priest, cutting off his right ear.
51But Jesus answered, "No more of this!" And he touched the man's ear and
healed him.
52Then Jesus said to the chief priests, the officers of the temple guard, and the
elders, who had come for him, "Am I leading a rebellion, that you have come with
swords and clubs? 53Every day I was with you in the temple courts, and you did
not lay a hand on me. But this is your hour — when darkness reigns."

Peter Disowns Jesus

54Then seizing him, they led him away and took him into the house of the high
priest. Peter followed at a distance. 55And when some there had kindled a fire
in the middle of the courtyard and had sat down together, Peter sat down with
them. 56A servant girl saw him seated there in the firelight. She looked closely at
him and said, "This man was with him."
57But he denied it. "Woman, I don't know him," he said.
58A little later someone else saw him and said, "You also are one of them."
"Man, I am not!" Peter replied.
59About an hour later another asserted, "Certainly this fellow was with him,
for he is a Galilean."
60Peter replied, "Man, I don't know what you're talking about!" Just as he was
speaking, the rooster crowed. 61The Lord turned and looked straight at Peter. Then
Peter remembered the word the Lord had spoken to him: "Before the rooster crows
today, you will disown me three times." 62And he went outside and wept bitterly.

The Guards Mock Jesus

63The men who were guarding Jesus began mocking and beating him. 64They
blindfolded him and demanded, "Prophesy! Who hit you?" 65And they said
many other insulting things to him.

Jesus Before Pilate and Herod

66At daybreak the council of the elders of the people, both the chief priests and
the teachers of the law, met together, and Jesus was led before them. 67"If you are
the Messiah," they said, "tell us."

---

[a] *37* Isaiah 53:12 [b] *43,44* Many early manuscripts do not have verses 43 and 44.

Jesus answered, "If I tell you, you will not believe me, [68]and if I asked you, you would not answer. [69]But from now on, the Son of Man will be seated at the right hand of the mighty God."

[70]They all asked, "Are you then the Son of God?"

He replied, "You say that I am."

[71]Then they said, "Why do we need any more testimony? We have heard it from his own lips."

23 Then the whole assembly rose and led him off to Pilate. [2]And they began to accuse him, saying, "We have found this man subverting our nation. He opposes payment of taxes to Caesar and claims to be Messiah, a king."

[3]So Pilate asked Jesus, "Are you the king of the Jews?"

"You have said so," Jesus replied.

[4]Then Pilate announced to the chief priests and the crowd, "I find no basis for a charge against this man."

[5]But they insisted, "He stirs up the people all over Judea by his teaching. He started in Galilee and has come all the way here."

[6]On hearing this, Pilate asked if the man was a Galilean. [7]When he learned that Jesus was under Herod's jurisdiction, he sent him to Herod, who was also in Jerusalem at that time.

[8]When Herod saw Jesus, he was greatly pleased, because for a long time he had been wanting to see him. From what he had heard about him, he hoped to see him perform a sign of some sort. [9]He plied him with many questions, but Jesus gave him no answer. [10]The chief priests and the teachers of the law were standing there, vehemently accusing him. [11]Then Herod and his soldiers ridiculed and mocked him. Dressing him in an elegant robe, they sent him back to Pilate. [12]That day Herod and Pilate became friends — before this they had been enemies.

[13]Pilate called together the chief priests, the rulers and the people, [14]and said to them, "You brought me this man as one who was inciting the people to rebellion. I have examined him in your presence and have found no basis for your charges against him. [15]Neither has Herod, for he sent him back to us; as you can see, he has done nothing to deserve death. [16]Therefore, I will punish him and then release him." [17] [a]

[18]But the whole crowd shouted, "Away with this man! Release Barabbas to us!" [19](Barabbas had been thrown into prison for an insurrection in the city, and for murder.)

[20]Wanting to release Jesus, Pilate appealed to them again. [21]But they kept shouting, "Crucify him! Crucify him!"

[22]For the third time he spoke to them: "Why? What crime has this man committed? I have found in him no grounds for the death penalty. Therefore I will have him punished and then release him."

[23]But with loud shouts they insistently demanded that he be crucified, and their shouts prevailed. [24]So Pilate decided to grant their demand. [25]He released the man who had been thrown into prison for insurrection and murder, the one they asked for, and surrendered Jesus to their will.

The Crucifixion of Jesus

[26]As the soldiers led him away, they seized Simon from Cyrene, who was on his way in from the country, and put the cross on him and made him carry it behind Jesus. [27]A large number of people followed him, including women who mourned and wailed for him. [28]Jesus turned and said to them, "Daughters of Jerusalem, do not weep for me; weep for yourselves and for your children. [29]For the time will come when you will say, 'Blessed are the childless women, the wombs that never bore and the breasts that never nursed!' [30]Then

> "'they will say to the mountains, "Fall on us!"
> and to the hills, "Cover us!"' [b]

---

[a] *17* Some manuscripts include here words similar to Matt. 27:15 and Mark 15:6.
[b] *30* Hosea 10:8

LUKE 23:1 – 25

JESUS' TRIAL

Jesus' multistage trial — from the Jewish religious council, to the initial hearing before the Roman governor Pilate, to Herod's court, and finally back to Pilate for sentencing — marked the culmination of a lengthy plot by certain religious leaders to trap and condemn Jesus. After various unsuccessful attempts to undermine Jesus' popularity or frame him for sedition, the elders, chief priests and scribes finally had Jesus in their clutches. They were not about to waste the opportunity. Outraged at Jesus' claim to be the Son of God (Lk 22:70 – 71), these religious leaders brought Jesus before Pilate and leveled three accusations (23:2), each designed to frame Jesus as a threat to Roman authority. The first charge, "subverting our nation," was a general complaint implying that Jesus was disturbing the peace and stirring up civil unrest. The second and third charges were more directly related to Roman rule: Jesus, they claimed, forbade paying taxes to Caesar (a blatant fabrication; see Lk 20:25) and had declared himself to be the king over Israel. The final charge had an element of truth, but the religious leaders deliberately twisted Jesus' claim into one that usurped Caesar's earthly reign. Pilate himself saw through the unjust accusations, but his repeated attempts to set Jesus free were to no avail. The farcical nature of the trial is just one more indication that Jesus' suffering and death were those of an innocent and righteous man (Lk 23:47).

31 For if people do these things when the tree is green, what will happen when it is dry?"

32 Two other men, both criminals, were also led out with him to be executed. 33 When they came to the place called the Skull, they crucified him there, along with the criminals — one on his right, the other on his left. 34 Jesus said, "Father, forgive them, for they do not know what they are doing."[a] And they divided up his clothes by casting lots.

35 The people stood watching, and the rulers even sneered at him. They said, "He saved others; let him save himself if he is God's Messiah, the Chosen One."

36 The soldiers also came up and mocked him. They offered him wine vinegar 37 and said, "If you are the king of the Jews, save yourself."

38 There was a written notice above him, which read: THIS IS THE KING OF THE JEWS.

39 One of the criminals who hung there hurled insults at him: "Aren't you the Messiah? Save yourself and us!"

40 But the other criminal rebuked him. "Don't you fear God," he said, "since you are under the same sentence? 41 We are punished justly, for we are getting what our deeds deserve. But this man has done nothing wrong."

42 Then he said, "Jesus, remember me when you come into your kingdom.[b]"

43 Jesus answered him, "Truly I tell you, today you will be with me in paradise."

The Death of Jesus

44 It was now about noon, and darkness came over the whole land until three in the afternoon, 45 for the sun stopped shining. And the curtain of the temple was torn in two. 46 Jesus called out with a loud voice, "Father, into your hands I commit my spirit."[c] When he had said this, he breathed his last.

47 The centurion, seeing what had happened, praised God and said, "Surely this was a righteous man." 48 When all the people who had gathered to witness this sight saw what took place, they beat their breasts and went away. 49 But all those who knew him, including the women who had followed him from Galilee, stood at a distance, watching these things.

The Burial of Jesus

50 Now there was a man named Joseph, a member of the Council, a good and upright man, 51 who had not consented to their decision and action. He came from the Judean town of Arimathea, and he himself was waiting for the kingdom of God. 52 Going to Pilate, he asked for Jesus' body. 53 Then he took it down, wrapped it in linen cloth and placed it in a tomb cut in the rock, one in which no one had yet been laid. 54 It was Preparation Day, and the Sabbath was about to begin.

55 The women who had come with Jesus from Galilee followed Joseph and saw the tomb and how his body was laid in it. 56 Then they went home and prepared spices and perfumes. But they rested on the Sabbath in obedience to the commandment.

Jesus Has Risen

24 On the first day of the week, very early in the morning, the women took the spices they had prepared and went to the tomb. 2 They found the stone rolled away from the tomb, 3 but when they entered, they did not find the body of the Lord Jesus. 4 While they were wondering about this, suddenly two men in clothes that gleamed like lightning stood beside them. 5 In their fright the women bowed down with their faces to the ground, but the men said to them, "Why do you look for the living among the dead? 6 He is not here; he has risen! Remember how he told you, while he was still with you in Galilee: 7 'The Son of Man must

[a] *34* Some early manuscripts do not have this sentence. [b] *42* Some manuscripts *come with your kingly power* [c] *46* Psalm 31:5

LUKE 23:33

CRUCIFIXION

At the time of Jesus' death, crucifixion was the Roman Empire's most brutal and degrading form of capital punishment — a death so horrible it was reserved for slaves and the vilest of criminals. No Roman citizen could be subjected to crucifixion. Indeed, church tradition indicates that while the Jewish apostle Peter eventually was crucified for following Christ, the apostle Paul, who was a Roman citizen, suffered the relatively humane fate of being beheaded.

Crucifixion seems to have taken various forms throughout the Roman Empire, but biblical and historical sources reveal a pattern. First, the condemned person usually was scourged with a flagellum, a whip constructed of leather thongs interwoven with bits of metal or bone. Greatly weakened by the scourging, the victim then carried the crossbeam through a crowd of people to the place of execution, enduring their taunts and jeers along the way. Sometimes a sign specifying the crime was hung around the criminal's neck. At the place of execution, the condemned was forced to lie on the ground with the crossbeam under his shoulders. Adding degradation to suffering, the executioners stripped the victim naked before nailing or binding him with ropes to the crossbeam.

After the condemned had been nailed or tied to the crossbeam, executioners lifted the crossbeam and secured it to a post, with the person's feet hanging above the ground. Archaeological evidence indicates that sometimes a pin or wooden block was placed halfway up the post to provide a seat for the body — allowing the prisoner to rest periodically, further prolonging the agony — and preventing the nails from tearing open the wounds and allowing the body to fall. The feet were also nailed or tied to the post. Finally, as in the case of the two criminals crucified with Jesus, executioners would sometimes break the legs of the crucified. This last brutal tactic sped up death for those lingering on the cross by causing massive shock, loss of circulation and heart failure.

Jesus, completely innocent of all sin and wrongdoing, suffered the ancient world's most horrific and disgraceful punishment. But this was no ordinary case of wrongful condemnation. This perfect man was also the Son of God, and what appeared to be his defeat gave way to the most glorious victory the world has ever known. After suffering and dying for the sins of the world, Jesus Christ rose from the dead three days later. Jesus' glorious resurrection broke the power of sin and death and empowered his disciples to preach the Good News: through his suffering on the cross and his resurrection, Jesus offers salvation to all who believe in him.

be delivered over to the hands of sinners, be crucified and on the third day be raised again.' " [8]Then they remembered his words.

[9]When they came back from the tomb, they told all these things to the Eleven and to all the others. [10]It was Mary Magdalene, Joanna, Mary the mother of James, and the others with them who told this to the apostles. [11]But they did not believe the women, because their words seemed to them like nonsense. [12]Peter, however, got up and ran to the tomb. Bending over, he saw the strips of linen lying by themselves, and he went away, wondering to himself what had happened.

On the Road to Emmaus

[13]Now that same day two of them were going to a village called Emmaus, about seven miles[a] from Jerusalem. [14]They were talking with each other about everything that had happened. [15]As they talked and discussed these things with each other, Jesus himself came up and walked along with them; [16]but they were kept from recognizing him.

[17]He asked them, "What are you discussing together as you walk along?"

They stood still, their faces downcast. [18]One of them, named Cleopas, asked him, "Are you the only one visiting Jerusalem who does not know the things that have happened there in these days?"

[19]"What things?" he asked.

"About Jesus of Nazareth," they replied. "He was a prophet, powerful in word and deed before God and all the people. [20]The chief priests and our rulers handed him over to be sentenced to death, and they crucified him; [21]but we had hoped that he was the one who was going to redeem Israel. And what is more, it is the third day since all this took place. [22]In addition, some of our women amazed us. They went to the tomb early this morning [23]but didn't find his body. They came and told us that they had seen a vision of angels, who said he was alive. [24]Then some of our companions went to the tomb and found it just as the women had said, but they did not see Jesus."

[25]He said to them, "How foolish you are, and how slow to believe all that the prophets have spoken! [26]Did not the Messiah have to suffer these things and then enter his glory?" [27]And beginning with Moses and all the Prophets, he explained to them what was said in all the Scriptures concerning himself.

[28]As they approached the village to which they were going, Jesus continued on as if he were going farther. [29]But they urged him strongly, "Stay with us, for it is nearly evening; the day is almost over." So he went in to stay with them.

[30]When he was at the table with them, he took bread, gave thanks, broke it and began to give it to them. [31]Then their eyes were opened and they recognized him, and he disappeared from their sight. [32]They asked each other, "Were not our hearts burning within us while he talked with us on the road and opened the Scriptures to us?"

[33]They got up and returned at once to Jerusalem. There they found the Eleven and those with them, assembled together [34]and saying, "It is true! The Lord has risen and has appeared to Simon." [35]Then the two told what had happened on the way, and how Jesus was recognized by them when he broke the bread.

Jesus Appears to the Disciples

[36]While they were still talking about this, Jesus himself stood among them and said to them, "Peace be with you."

[37]They were startled and frightened, thinking they saw a ghost. [38]He said to them, "Why are you troubled, and why do doubts rise in your minds? [39]Look at my hands and my feet. It is I myself! Touch me and see; a ghost does not have flesh and bones, as you see I have."

[40]When he had said this, he showed them his hands and feet. [41]And while they still did not believe it because of joy and amazement, he asked them, "Do

---

[a] *13* Or about 11 kilometers

you have anything here to eat?" [42]They gave him a piece of broiled fish, [43]and he
took it and ate it in their presence.
[44]He said to them, "This is what I told you while I was still with you: Everything must be fulfilled that is written about me in the Law of Moses, the Prophets
and the Psalms."
[45]Then he opened their minds so they could understand the Scriptures.
[46]He told them, "This is what is written: The Messiah will suffer and rise from
the dead on the third day, [47]and repentance for the forgiveness of sins will be
preached in his name to all nations, beginning at Jerusalem. [48]You are witnesses
of these things. [49]I am going to send you what my Father has promised; but stay
in the city until you have been clothed with power from on high."

The Ascension of Jesus

[50]When he had led them out to the vicinity of Bethany, he lifted up his hands
and blessed them. [51]While he was blessing them, he left them and was taken up
into heaven. [52]Then they worshiped him and returned to Jerusalem with great
joy. [53]And they stayed continually at the temple, praising God.

LUKE 24:46–47

REMISSION OF SINS

Jesus' power over sin had been called into question early in his ministry. Witnessing the faith of a group of people who made an extraordinary effort to bring their paralyzed friend to him for healing, Jesus said, "Friend, your sins are forgiven" (Lk 5:20). The Pharisees and teachers of the law recognized that only God could forgive sins — and not believing that Jesus was indeed God, they accused him of blasphemy. After Jesus' resurrection, there was no longer room for questioning or doubt. In defeating death, Jesus proved he was neither a pretender nor a blasphemer but the very Son of God. This victory over death signaled his divine authority to forgive sin.

Luke connects the preaching of the life-changing, sin-defeating gospel with Christ's resurrection. The good news of repentance and remission of sins, which the disciples began preaching following Jesus' ascension and the coming of the Holy Spirit in power, is rooted in this fundamental truth: In fulfillment of God's promises in Scripture, Christ suffered and died and was raised to life on the third day. Death is defeated; sin's power is broken. The remission of sins is now available to all who believe in the powerful name of Jesus.

JESUS: OUR GREAT I AM

JOHN

JOHN

BIRTH OF JESUS *c. 5 BC*	JESUS' MINISTRY, DEATH, RESURRECTION *c. AD 27 – 30*	JOHN'S GOSPEL WRITTEN *c. AD 90*

John writes with one clear purpose: to show that Jesus is the path to eternal life (20:31). There is no other way to peace with God, in this life or the next, apart from having a saving faith in Jesus. For salvation to happen, a person who is dead in sin must be born again by the power of God's Spirit (3:1 – 21). John invites his readers to do just that — to be born again — to a living hope made possible by Jesus' work.

John did not write as a detached observer to these truths; rather he was one who trusted and followed after Jesus personally. The beloved disciple, John, knew firsthand the joy found in a loving relationship with God's Son. He longed to see others respond in faith and repentance to the good news that had transformed his life.

This good news is based on God's plans and promises throughout history. In John's Gospel, Jesus is described as the Word made flesh, the dwelling of God among men, the true light of the world. These images serve to connect readers with powerful ideas found throughout the Old Testament — ideas related to the coming of God's promised Savior. These images also remind readers of the all-encompassing scope of Jesus' mission.

The most prominent feature of John's Gospel is his repeated use of Jesus' "I am" statements, which communicate his identity to his hearers. Jesus is the bread of life (6:35,48), the light of the world (8:12), the door (10:7,9), the good shepherd (10:11,14), the resurrection and the life (11:25), the way, the truth and the life (14:6) and the true vine (15:1). Jesus uses these images to communicate his offer of salvation, but more importantly to communicate that he is the same God who told Moses "I am" so long ago (Ex 3:14). Jesus boldly proclaims:

"Before Abraham was born, I am" (Jn 8:58). His eternal status as the God who was, who is and who will always be is seen in the perfect fulfillment of his plans in the coming of Jesus. God perfectly executed his plan to send his Son, at just the right time, to secure the salvation of his people. Throughout all generations, those who look to him in faith will be saved because he is the only One powerful enough to save.

JESUS ANSWERED, "I AM THE WAY AND THE TRUTH AND THE LIFE. NO ONE COMES TO THE FATHER EXCEPT THROUGH ME."

John 14:6

JOHN

The Word Became Flesh

1 In the beginning was the Word, and the Word was with God, and the Word was God. [2]He was with God in the beginning. [3]Through him all things were made; without him nothing was made that has been made. [4]In him was life, and that life was the light of all mankind. [5]The light shines in the darkness, and the darkness has not overcome[a] it.

[6]There was a man sent from God whose name was John. [7]He came as a witness to testify concerning that light, so that through him all might believe. [8]He himself was not the light; he came only as a witness to the light.

[9]The true light that gives light to everyone was coming into the world. [10]He was in the world, and though the world was made through him, the world did not recognize him. [11]He came to that which was his own, but his own did not receive him. [12]Yet to all who did receive him, to those who believed in his name, he gave the right to become children of God — [13]children born not of natural descent, nor of human decision or a husband's will, but born of God.

[14]The Word became flesh and made his dwelling among us. We have seen his glory, the glory of the one and only Son, who came from the Father, full of grace and truth.

[15](John testified concerning him. He cried out, saying, "This is the one I spoke about when I said, 'He who comes after me has surpassed me because he was before me.' ") [16]Out of his fullness we have all received grace in place of grace already given. [17]For the law was given through Moses; grace and truth came through Jesus Christ. [18]No one has ever seen God, but the one and only Son, who is himself God and[b] is in closest relationship with the Father, has made him known.

John the Baptist Denies Being the Messiah

[19]Now this was John's testimony when the Jewish leaders[c] in Jerusalem sent priests and Levites to ask him who he was. [20]He did not fail to confess, but confessed freely, "I am not the Messiah."

[21]They asked him, "Then who are you? Are you Elijah?"

He said, "I am not."

"Are you the Prophet?"

He answered, "No."

[22]Finally they said, "Who are you? Give us an answer to take back to those who sent us. What do you say about yourself?"

[23]John replied in the words of Isaiah the prophet, "I am the voice of one calling in the wilderness, 'Make straight the way for the Lord.' "[d]

[24]Now the Pharisees who had been sent [25]questioned him, "Why then do you baptize if you are not the Messiah, nor Elijah, nor the Prophet?"

[26]"I baptize with[e] water," John replied, "but among you stands one you do not know. [27]He is the one who comes after me, the straps of whose sandals I am not worthy to untie."

[28]This all happened at Bethany on the other side of the Jordan, where John was baptizing.

---

[a] *5* Or *understood* [b] *18* Some manuscripts *but the only Son, who* [c] *19* The Greek term traditionally translated *the Jews* (*hoi Ioudaioi*) refers here and elsewhere in John's Gospel to those Jewish leaders who opposed Jesus; also in 5:10, 15, 16; 7:1, 11, 13; 9:22; 18:14, 28, 36; 19:7, 12, 31, 38; 20:19. [d] *23* Isaiah 40:3 [e] *26* Or *in*; also in verses 31 and 33 (twice)

THE WORD OF GOD

From the very beginning of creation, God has been making himself known to people by his revealed word. In Genesis 1 we read the account of God speaking the world into existence, then speaking relationally to Adam (Ge 1:27 – 30). In Exodus 3, God spoke to Moses from a burning bush, calling him to be his agent to liberate Israel from slavery in Egypt. Throughout the Torah (the first five books of the Bible), God gave instructions to his chosen people so that they would know the glories of his righteousness and wonders of his love.

God taught his people how to worship through the words of the psalmists, and he reminded them of their coming hope through the words of the prophets. But God gave his greatest revelation when Jesus, the Son and the very "Word" of God, came to earth. The author of Hebrews explains this well (Heb 1:1 – 3).

From the beginning, Jesus, the Word, was with God and was God (Jn 1:1). In this verse, John is making a very important Trinitarian statement: Jesus is not just *like* God; rather, Jesus actually *is* God. But Jesus is also *with* God, meaning that Jesus is separate from God. This mystery is explained through the Christian doctrine of the Trinity. This biblical doctrine explains that God exists in three persons, being of one substance, power and eternity. This doctrine is clear in Scripture, and without it, the message of the gospel falls apart. For example, in delivering the Great Commission, Jesus commands his church to baptize his disciples "in the name of the Father and of the Son and of the Holy Spirit" (Mt 28:19), the three members of the Trinity. This doctrine has been affirmed throughout church history.

Jesus is the eternal "Word of the Father." Therefore we understand his powerful role in creation, for "through him all things were made" (Jn 1:3). But the great mystery of the gospel is that Jesus came to live with us; he left his position as creator and ruler of the universe to become human and endure all of the miseries of this life. He came to earth to completely identify with us in order that we might in turn identify with him and receive him as our Savior and Lord. And to those who receive him, he gives the amazing promise that they will be the very children of God (v. 12), not simply permitted into the presence of God as servants or guests. Rather, they are eternally welcomed into the house of God as his own sons and daughters, heirs of all of God's promised blessings (Gal 4:4 – 7).

JOHN 2:1–12

THE HOUR OF CHRIST

At first glance, Jesus' response to his mother at the wedding in Cana can be confusing or even troubling: "Woman, why do you involve me? My hour has not yet come." But then he proceeds to perform his first miracle, producing somewhere between 120 and 180 gallons of wine.

When considering Jesus' evident change of heart, it is important to remember the setting of this miracle: a wedding. Whenever people attend a wedding, they inevitably entertain thoughts about their own wedding. This is true for married people, but many single people as well long for their wedding day, when it will be their "hour"—when they will be the bride or groom, finally joined to the one they love.

So in this moment, as Jesus looked on at the bride and groom in Cana, perhaps he too was longing for his "hour," when he would be joined with his bride, his church. Perhaps he looked forward to the wedding banquet that is to come, when men and women from every tribe and language will be joined with him at the marriage supper of the Lamb in the new heavens and new earth (Rev 19:6–9). How utterly appropriate that Jesus' first sign pointed toward the ultimate celebration and the ultimate wedding: his own with his church.

John Testifies About Jesus

[29]The next day John saw Jesus coming toward him and said, "Look, the Lamb of God, who takes away the sin of the world! [30]This is the one I meant when I said, 'A man who comes after me has surpassed me because he was before me.' [31]I myself did not know him, but the reason I came baptizing with water was that he might be revealed to Israel."

[32]Then John gave this testimony: "I saw the Spirit come down from heaven as a dove and remain on him. [33]And I myself did not know him, but the one who sent me to baptize with water told me, 'The man on whom you see the Spirit come down and remain is the one who will baptize with the Holy Spirit.' [34]I have seen and I testify that this is God's Chosen One."[a]

John's Disciples Follow Jesus

[35]The next day John was there again with two of his disciples. [36]When he saw Jesus passing by, he said, "Look, the Lamb of God!"

[37]When the two disciples heard him say this, they followed Jesus. [38]Turning around, Jesus saw them following and asked, "What do you want?"

They said, "Rabbi" (which means "Teacher"), "where are you staying?"

[39]"Come," he replied, "and you will see."

So they went and saw where he was staying, and they spent that day with him. It was about four in the afternoon.

[40]Andrew, Simon Peter's brother, was one of the two who heard what John had said and who had followed Jesus. [41]The first thing Andrew did was to find his brother Simon and tell him, "We have found the Messiah" (that is, the Christ). [42]And he brought him to Jesus.

Jesus looked at him and said, "You are Simon son of John. You will be called Cephas" (which, when translated, is Peter[b]).

Jesus Calls Philip and Nathanael

[43]The next day Jesus decided to leave for Galilee. Finding Philip, he said to him, "Follow me."

[44]Philip, like Andrew and Peter, was from the town of Bethsaida. [45]Philip found Nathanael and told him, "We have found the one Moses wrote about in the Law, and about whom the prophets also wrote—Jesus of Nazareth, the son of Joseph."

[46]"Nazareth! Can anything good come from there?" Nathanael asked.

"Come and see," said Philip.

[47]When Jesus saw Nathanael approaching, he said of him, "Here truly is an Israelite in whom there is no deceit."

[48]"How do you know me?" Nathanael asked.

Jesus answered, "I saw you while you were still under the fig tree before Philip called you."

[49]Then Nathanael declared, "Rabbi, you are the Son of God; you are the king of Israel."

[50]Jesus said, "You believe[c] because I told you I saw you under the fig tree. You will see greater things than that." [51]He then added, "Very truly I tell you,[d] you[d] will see 'heaven open, and the angels of God ascending and descending on'[e] the Son of Man."

Jesus Changes Water Into Wine

2 On the third day a wedding took place at Cana in Galilee. Jesus' mother was there, [2]and Jesus and his disciples had also been invited to the wedding. [3]When the wine was gone, Jesus' mother said to him, "They have no more wine."

[a] *34* See Isaiah 42:1; many manuscripts *is the Son of God.* [b] *42* *Cephas* (Aramaic) and *Peter* (Greek) both mean *rock.* [c] *50* Or *Do you believe . . . ?* [d] *51* The Greek is plural. [e] *51* Gen. 28:12

4"Woman,[a] why do you involve me?" Jesus replied. "My hour has not yet
come."
5His mother said to the servants, "Do whatever he tells you."
6Nearby stood six stone water jars, the kind used by the Jews for ceremonial
washing, each holding from twenty to thirty gallons.[b]
7Jesus said to the servants, "Fill the jars with water"; so they filled them to
the brim.
8Then he told them, "Now draw some out and take it to the master of the banquet."
They did so, 9and the master of the banquet tasted the water that had been
turned into wine. He did not realize where it had come from, though the servants
who had drawn the water knew. Then he called the bridegroom aside 10and said,
"Everyone brings out the choice wine first and then the cheaper wine after the
guests have had too much to drink; but you have saved the best till now."
11What Jesus did here in Cana of Galilee was the first of the signs through
which he revealed his glory; and his disciples believed in him.
12After this he went down to Capernaum with his mother and brothers and his
disciples. There they stayed for a few days.

Jesus Clears the Temple Courts

13When it was almost time for the Jewish Passover, Jesus went up to Jerusalem. 14In the temple courts he found people selling cattle, sheep and doves, and
others sitting at tables exchanging money. 15So he made a whip out of cords, and
drove all from the temple courts, both sheep and cattle; he scattered the coins
of the money changers and overturned their tables. 16To those who sold doves he
said, "Get these out of here! Stop turning my Father's house into a market!" 17His
disciples remembered that it is written: "Zeal for your house will consume me."[c]
18The Jews then responded to him, "What sign can you show us to prove your
authority to do all this?"
19Jesus answered them, "Destroy this temple, and I will raise it again in three
days."
20They replied, "It has taken forty-six years to build this temple, and you are
going to raise it in three days?" 21But the temple he had spoken of was his body.
22After he was raised from the dead, his disciples recalled what he had said. Then
they believed the scripture and the words that Jesus had spoken.
23Now while he was in Jerusalem at the Passover Festival, many people saw
the signs he was performing and believed in his name.[d] 24But Jesus would not
entrust himself to them, for he knew all people. 25He did not need any testimony
about mankind, for he knew what was in each person.

Jesus Teaches Nicodemus

3 Now there was a Pharisee, a man named Nicodemus who was a member of
the Jewish ruling council. 2He came to Jesus at night and said, "Rabbi, we
know that you are a teacher who has come from God. For no one could perform
the signs you are doing if God were not with him."
3Jesus replied, "Very truly I tell you, no one can see the kingdom of God unless
they are born again.[e]"
4"How can someone be born when they are old?" Nicodemus asked. "Surely
they cannot enter a second time into their mother's womb to be born!"
5Jesus answered, "Very truly I tell you, no one can enter the kingdom of God
unless they are born of water and the Spirit. 6Flesh gives birth to flesh, but the
Spirit[f] gives birth to spirit. 7You should not be surprised at my saying, 'You[g] must
be born again.' 8The wind blows wherever it pleases. You hear its sound, but you

---

[a] 4 The Greek for *Woman* does not denote any disrespect. [b] 6 Or from about 75 to about 115 liters [c] 17 Psalm 69:9 [d] 23 Or *in him* [e] 3 The Greek for *again* also means *from above*; also in verse 7. [f] 6 Or *but spirit* [g] 7 The Greek is plural.

JOHN 4:1–26

THE FIRST REVELATION

Throughout his ministry, Jesus revealed himself to the most unlikely people in the most unlikely places; his encounter with the Samaritan woman is no exception. Centuries of bitterness and disagreement divided the Jewish people and the Samaritans. Though they lived near one another and had a common heritage, the Samaritans were of mixed race — Hebrew people whose ancestors had intermarried with the Assyrians, a pagan enemy nation. They had developed a different culture and a different place of worship, at Mount Gerizim (4:20). No respectable Jewish man would have lowered himself to interact with a Samaritan, much less a Samaritan *woman*, as Jewish culture dictated strict social division between men and women who were not married or close relatives.

But there's even more to Jesus' surprising choice: this woman was an outcast even among her own people. She had been married five times and was living with a man who was not her husband; in a very conservative and traditional culture, Jesus' conversation with her is doubly puzzling. Still, Jesus, a Jewish rabbi, engages in conversation with this woman. He speaks to her with love and offers her salvation (4:14). More than that, she is the first person to whom Jesus reveals his identity as the Messiah (4:25–26). By revealing his identity first to this woman, Jesus emphasized his interest in outcasts. Jesus seeks out those who are broken and poor in spirit (Mt 5:3), and he offers himself as living water to all who thirst for him.

cannot tell where it comes from or where it is going. So it is with everyone born of the Spirit."[a]

9"How can this be?" Nicodemus asked.

10"You are Israel's teacher," said Jesus, "and do you not understand these things? 11Very truly I tell you, we speak of what we know, and we testify to what we have seen, but still you people do not accept our testimony. 12I have spoken to you of earthly things and you do not believe; how then will you believe if I speak of heavenly things? 13No one has ever gone into heaven except the one who came from heaven — the Son of Man.[b] 14Just as Moses lifted up the snake in the wilderness, so the Son of Man must be lifted up,[c] 15that everyone who believes may have eternal life in him."[d]

16For God so loved the world that he gave his one and only Son, that whoever believes in him shall not perish but have eternal life. 17For God did not send his Son into the world to condemn the world, but to save the world through him. 18Whoever believes in him is not condemned, but whoever does not believe stands condemned already because they have not believed in the name of God's one and only Son. 19This is the verdict: Light has come into the world, but people loved darkness instead of light because their deeds were evil. 20Everyone who does evil hates the light, and will not come into the light for fear that their deeds will be exposed. 21But whoever lives by the truth comes into the light, so that it may be seen plainly that what they have done has been done in the sight of God.

John Testifies Again About Jesus

22After this, Jesus and his disciples went out into the Judean countryside, where he spent some time with them, and baptized. 23Now John also was baptizing at Aenon near Salim, because there was plenty of water, and people were coming and being baptized. 24(This was before John was put in prison.) 25An argument developed between some of John's disciples and a certain Jew over the matter of ceremonial washing. 26They came to John and said to him, "Rabbi, that man who was with you on the other side of the Jordan — the one you testified about — look, he is baptizing, and everyone is going to him."

27To this John replied, "A person can receive only what is given them from heaven. 28You yourselves can testify that I said, 'I am not the Messiah but am sent ahead of him.' 29The bride belongs to the bridegroom. The friend who attends the bridegroom waits and listens for him, and is full of joy when he hears the bridegroom's voice. That joy is mine, and it is now complete. 30He must become greater; I must become less."[e]

31The one who comes from above is above all; the one who is from the earth belongs to the earth, and speaks as one from the earth. The one who comes from heaven is above all. 32He testifies to what he has seen and heard, but no one accepts his testimony. 33Whoever has accepted it has certified that God is truthful. 34For the one whom God has sent speaks the words of God, for God[f] gives the Spirit without limit. 35The Father loves the Son and has placed everything in his hands. 36Whoever believes in the Son has eternal life, but whoever rejects the Son will not see life, for God's wrath remains on them.

Jesus Talks With a Samaritan Woman

4 Now Jesus learned that the Pharisees had heard that he was gaining and baptizing more disciples than John — 2although in fact it was not Jesus who baptized, but his disciples. 3So he left Judea and went back once more to Galilee.

4Now he had to go through Samaria. 5So he came to a town in Samaria called Sychar, near the plot of ground Jacob had given to his son Joseph. 6Jacob's well

[a] *8* The Greek for *Spirit* is the same as that for *wind*. [b] *13* Some manuscripts *Man, who is in heaven* [c] *14* The Greek for *lifted up* also means *exalted*. [d] *15* Some interpreters end the quotation with verse 21. [e] *30* Some interpreters end the quotation with verse 36. [f] *34* Greek *he*

THE NEW BIRTH

Throughout his ministry, Jesus taught about God's kingdom. He preached about the kingdom to crowds, to small groups and to individuals like Nicodemus. Nicodemus was a teacher of the Hebrew Scriptures and must have been taken aback when Jesus said, "No one can see the kingdom of God unless they are born again" (v. 3).

Nicodemus, like most teachers of the Hebrew law, would have expected the Jewish Messiah to come and establish his kingdom in a very forceful and very visible way. As Alexander the Great and Julius Caesar had come and ushered in their kingdoms by force, the Jewish people expected a messiah to come with authoritative power to reestablish the Jewish kingdom. But when Jesus, the true Messiah, came, he did not rule with an iron fist or crush his enemies; rather, he came in humility to serve and to lay down his life for other people (Mk 10:45). In his first coming, Jesus did establish his authority over men and women — not externally, but internally in their hearts (Mt 9:8; Mk 1:27; Lk 4:36).

That authority is absolute. So the allegiance of a Christian is not ultimately with Caesar, or with Rome, or with any king or country (Mk 12:17); the allegiance of a Christian is rather with Jesus, and a believer's citizenship is in his eternal kingdom (Php 3:20). Therefore, followers of Christ are born again — not as citizens of any earthly country, but as Christians born with Christ and born into his kingdom.

How does this new birth occur? How does Jesus establish his authority in our hearts? Again, unlike the kingdoms of this world, Jesus does not establish his present rule with an army or by force; rather, he establishes his rule with love. His kingdom is not of this world (Jn 18:36). "For God so loved the world that he gave his one and only Son, that whoever believes in him shall not perish but have eternal life. For God did not send his Son into the world to condemn the world, but to save the world through him" (3:16 – 17). When, with the help of the Holy Spirit, individuals see their own sin and need for a Savior, and when they see Jesus for all that he is and realize how deep his sacrifice was and how deep his love is, then the believer is "captured" by the love and beauty of Christ. When his followers see how deeply God has loved his people in Christ, then they are inspired, by their own desire for him, to surrender to his lordship. Such an experience is salvation, the new birth.

was there, and Jesus, tired as he was from the journey, sat down by the well. It was about noon.

[7]When a Samaritan woman came to draw water, Jesus said to her, "Will you give me a drink?" [8](His disciples had gone into the town to buy food.)

[9]The Samaritan woman said to him, "You are a Jew and I am a Samaritan woman. How can you ask me for a drink?" (For Jews do not associate with Samaritans.[a])

[10]Jesus answered her, "If you knew the gift of God and who it is that asks you for a drink, you would have asked him and he would have given you living water."

[11]"Sir," the woman said, "you have nothing to draw with and the well is deep. Where can you get this living water? [12]Are you greater than our father Jacob, who gave us the well and drank from it himself, as did also his sons and his livestock?"

[13]Jesus answered, "Everyone who drinks this water will be thirsty again, [14]but whoever drinks the water I give them will never thirst. Indeed, the water I give them will become in them a spring of water welling up to eternal life."

[15]The woman said to him, "Sir, give me this water so that I won't get thirsty and have to keep coming here to draw water."

[16]He told her, "Go, call your husband and come back."

[17]"I have no husband," she replied.

Jesus said to her, "You are right when you say you have no husband. [18]The fact is, you have had five husbands, and the man you now have is not your husband. What you have just said is quite true."

[19]"Sir," the woman said, "I can see that you are a prophet. [20]Our ancestors worshiped on this mountain, but you Jews claim that the place where we must worship is in Jerusalem."

[21]"Woman," Jesus replied, "believe me, a time is coming when you will worship the Father neither on this mountain nor in Jerusalem. [22]You Samaritans worship what you do not know; we worship what we do know, for salvation is from the Jews. [23]Yet a time is coming and has now come when the true worshipers will worship the Father in the Spirit and in truth, for they are the kind of worshipers the Father seeks. [24]God is spirit, and his worshipers must worship in the Spirit and in truth."

[25]The woman said, "I know that Messiah" (called Christ) "is coming. When he comes, he will explain everything to us."

[26]Then Jesus declared, "I, the one speaking to you — I am he."

The Disciples Rejoin Jesus

[27]Just then his disciples returned and were surprised to find him talking with a woman. But no one asked, "What do you want?" or "Why are you talking with her?"

[28]Then, leaving her water jar, the woman went back to the town and said to the people, [29]"Come, see a man who told me everything I ever did. Could this be the Messiah?" [30]They came out of the town and made their way toward him.

[31]Meanwhile his disciples urged him, "Rabbi, eat something."

[32]But he said to them, "I have food to eat that you know nothing about."

[33]Then his disciples said to each other, "Could someone have brought him food?"

[34]"My food," said Jesus, "is to do the will of him who sent me and to finish his work. [35]Don't you have a saying, 'It's still four months until harvest'? I tell you, open your eyes and look at the fields! They are ripe for harvest. [36]Even now the one who reaps draws a wage and harvests a crop for eternal life, so that the sower and the reaper may be glad together. [37]Thus the saying 'One sows and another reaps' is true. [38]I sent you to reap what you have not worked for. Others have done the hard work, and you have reaped the benefits of their labor."

[a] 9 Or *do not use dishes Samaritans have used*

Many Samaritans Believe

[39]Many of the Samaritans from that town believed in him because of the woman's testimony, "He told me everything I ever did." [40]So when the Samaritans came to him, they urged him to stay with them, and he stayed two days. [41]And because of his words many more became believers.

[42]They said to the woman, "We no longer believe just because of what you said; now we have heard for ourselves, and we know that this man really is the Savior of the world."

Jesus Heals an Official's Son

[43]After the two days he left for Galilee. [44](Now Jesus himself had pointed out that a prophet has no honor in his own country.) [45]When he arrived in Galilee, the Galileans welcomed him. They had seen all that he had done in Jerusalem at the Passover Festival, for they also had been there.

[46]Once more he visited Cana in Galilee, where he had turned the water into wine. And there was a certain royal official whose son lay sick at Capernaum. [47]When this man heard that Jesus had arrived in Galilee from Judea, he went to him and begged him to come and heal his son, who was close to death.

[48]"Unless you people see signs and wonders," Jesus told him, "you will never believe."

[49]The royal official said, "Sir, come down before my child dies."

[50]"Go," Jesus replied, "your son will live."

The man took Jesus at his word and departed. [51]While he was still on the way, his servants met him with the news that his boy was living. [52]When he inquired as to the time when his son got better, they said to him, "Yesterday, at one in the afternoon, the fever left him."

[53]Then the father realized that this was the exact time at which Jesus had said to him, "Your son will live." So he and his whole household believed.

[54]This was the second sign Jesus performed after coming from Judea to Galilee.

The Healing at the Pool

5 Some time later, Jesus went up to Jerusalem for one of the Jewish festivals. [2]Now there is in Jerusalem near the Sheep Gate a pool, which in Aramaic is called Bethesda[a] and which is surrounded by five covered colonnades. [3]Here a great number of disabled people used to lie—the blind, the lame, the paralyzed. [4][b] [5]One who was there had been an invalid for thirty-eight years. [6]When Jesus saw him lying there and learned that he had been in this condition for a long time, he asked him, "Do you want to get well?"

[7]"Sir," the invalid replied, "I have no one to help me into the pool when the water is stirred. While I am trying to get in, someone else goes down ahead of me."

[8]Then Jesus said to him, "Get up! Pick up your mat and walk." [9]At once the man was cured; he picked up his mat and walked.

The day on which this took place was a Sabbath, [10]and so the Jewish leaders said to the man who had been healed, "It is the Sabbath; the law forbids you to carry your mat."

[11]But he replied, "The man who made me well said to me, 'Pick up your mat and walk.'"

[12]So they asked him, "Who is this fellow who told you to pick it up and walk?"

[13]The man who was healed had no idea who it was, for Jesus had slipped away into the crowd that was there.

[14]Later Jesus found him at the temple and said to him, "See, you are well again. Stop sinning or something worse may happen to you." [15]The man went away and told the Jewish leaders that it was Jesus who had made him well.

---

[a] 2 Some manuscripts *Bethzatha*; other manuscripts *Bethsaida* [b] 3,4 Some manuscripts include here, wholly or in part, *paralyzed—and they waited for the moving of the waters. [4]From time to time an angel of the Lord would come down and stir up the waters. The first one into the pool after each such disturbance would be cured of whatever disease they had.*

JOHN 5:1–15

SALVATION THROUGH JESUS

Before and while Jesus walked the earth, the people of Israel had been given to systems and superstitions in trying to know and experience God. The meticulous laws of the Sabbath, as shown in this story, were a prime example of such a Hebrew system; the pool of Bethesda is a prime example of a Hebrew superstition.

Evidently the pool would stir or bubble periodically, and allegedly this bubbling brought healing to the first person to jump in the pool after it began. Jesus came across a man who, in 38 years, had not been able to get into the pool first. Coincidentally, 38 years is the same amount of time that the people of Israel wandered in the wilderness from Kadesh Barnea to the Zered Valley (Dt 2:14); and he, the man who at 38 years was an invalid, was just as depressed and helpless as they were. But Jesus looked beyond the man's excuses and superstition. He looked beyond this man's depression and his poor theology. Jesus looked beyond all this, and he showed him grace and brought him healing.

Such is the salvation of Jesus; it cannot be earned by obedience to a system, good theological knowledge, a good attitude or familial connections. Salvation is a gift of God; it is only by his grace that we are saved (Eph 2:8–9). It is appropriate that Jesus asked this man if he *wanted* to be healed; it's the same question he asks of those who would believe in him today.

The Authority of the Son

[16]So, because Jesus was doing these things on the Sabbath, the Jewish leaders began to persecute him. [17]In his defense Jesus said to them, "My Father is always at his work to this very day, and I too am working." [18]For this reason they tried all the more to kill him; not only was he breaking the Sabbath, but he was even calling God his own Father, making himself equal with God.

[19]Jesus gave them this answer: "Very truly I tell you, the Son can do nothing by himself; he can do only what he sees his Father doing, because whatever the Father does the Son also does. [20]For the Father loves the Son and shows him all he does. Yes, and he will show him even greater works than these, so that you will be amazed. [21]For just as the Father raises the dead and gives them life, even so the Son gives life to whom he is pleased to give it. [22]Moreover, the Father judges no one, but has entrusted all judgment to the Son, [23]that all may honor the Son just as they honor the Father. Whoever does not honor the Son does not honor the Father, who sent him.

[24]"Very truly I tell you, whoever hears my word and believes him who sent me has eternal life and will not be judged but has crossed over from death to life. [25]Very truly I tell you, a time is coming and has now come when the dead will hear the voice of the Son of God and those who hear will live. [26]For as the Father has life in himself, so he has granted the Son also to have life in himself. [27]And he has given him authority to judge because he is the Son of Man.

[28]"Do not be amazed at this, for a time is coming when all who are in their graves will hear his voice [29]and come out — those who have done what is good will rise to live, and those who have done what is evil will rise to be condemned. [30]By myself I can do nothing; I judge only as I hear, and my judgment is just, for I seek not to please myself but him who sent me.

Testimonies About Jesus

[31]"If I testify about myself, my testimony is not true. [32]There is another who testifies in my favor, and I know that his testimony about me is true.

[33]"You have sent to John and he has testified to the truth. [34]Not that I accept human testimony; but I mention it that you may be saved. [35]John was a lamp that burned and gave light, and you chose for a time to enjoy his light.

[36]"I have testimony weightier than that of John. For the works that the Father has given me to finish — the very works that I am doing — testify that the Father has sent me. [37]And the Father who sent me has himself testified concerning me. You have never heard his voice nor seen his form, [38]nor does his word dwell in you, for you do not believe the one he sent. [39]You study[a] the Scriptures diligently because you think that in them you have eternal life. These are the very Scriptures that testify about me, [40]yet you refuse to come to me to have life.

[41]"I do not accept glory from human beings, [42]but I know you. I know that you do not have the love of God in your hearts. [43]I have come in my Father's name, and you do not accept me; but if someone else comes in his own name, you will accept him. [44]How can you believe since you accept glory from one another but do not seek the glory that comes from the only God[b]?

[45]"But do not think I will accuse you before the Father. Your accuser is Moses, on whom your hopes are set. [46]If you believed Moses, you would believe me, for he wrote about me. [47]But since you do not believe what he wrote, how are you going to believe what I say?"

Jesus Feeds the Five Thousand

6 Some time after this, Jesus crossed to the far shore of the Sea of Galilee (that is, the Sea of Tiberias), [2]and a great crowd of people followed him because they saw the signs he had performed by healing the sick. [3]Then Jesus went up on

[a] *39* Or [39]*Study* [b] *44* Some early manuscripts *the Only One*

JOHN 6:1–15

KING FOR A DAY

On this enormously notable day in the life of Jesus, the people tried to make him king. Yet, rather than accepting their praise and love, he escaped the crowd in order to go experience the praise and love of his Father. After Jesus miraculously multiplied the fish and loaves, many people believed that he was the promised Messiah and wanted him to establish his earthly rule. Jesus had his sights set on a different throne and a different kingdom.

God the Father had sent Jesus to earth not to be exalted but to be humbled. Throughout Jesus' ministry, even when he was standing atop a hill in Galilee, he had his sights set on another hill — one just outside of Jerusalem, where he would give his life as a ransom payment for many (Mk 10:45). In this instance, as always, Jesus did not consider his power and eternal equality with God something to be used for his own advantage. He could have taken the glory for this miracle, but he refused. Instead, he took "the very nature of a servant" and "humbled himself by becoming obedient to death — even death on a cross" (Php 2:6–9). Because of his complete obedience, God the Father raised him from the dead and exalted him to the highest place in heaven, giving him the name that is above every name.

Jesus understood that earthly accolades are empty and fickle. He remained obedient to God's plan. The throne where Jesus now sits is infinitely higher than any earthly throne.

a mountainside and sat down with his disciples. [4]The Jewish Passover Festival
was near.
[5]When Jesus looked up and saw a great crowd coming toward him, he said to
Philip, "Where shall we buy bread for these people to eat?" [6]He asked this only
to test him, for he already had in mind what he was going to do.
[7]Philip answered him, "It would take more than half a year's wages[a] to buy
enough bread for each one to have a bite!"
[8]Another of his disciples, Andrew, Simon Peter's brother, spoke up, [9]"Here is
a boy with five small barley loaves and two small fish, but how far will they go
among so many?"
[10]Jesus said, "Have the people sit down." There was plenty of grass in that
place, and they sat down (about five thousand men were there). [11]Jesus then took
the loaves, gave thanks, and distributed to those who were seated as much as
they wanted. He did the same with the fish.
[12]When they had all had enough to eat, he said to his disciples, "Gather the
pieces that are left over. Let nothing be wasted." [13]So they gathered them and
filled twelve baskets with the pieces of the five barley loaves left over by those
who had eaten.
[14]After the people saw the sign Jesus performed, they began to say, "Surely
this is the Prophet who is to come into the world." [15]Jesus, knowing that they
intended to come and make him king by force, withdrew again to a mountain
by himself.

Jesus Walks on the Water

[16]When evening came, his disciples went down to the lake, [17]where they got
into a boat and set off across the lake for Capernaum. By now it was dark, and
Jesus had not yet joined them. [18]A strong wind was blowing and the waters grew
rough. [19]When they had rowed about three or four miles,[b] they saw Jesus approaching the boat, walking on the water; and they were frightened. [20]But he
said to them, "It is I; don't be afraid." [21]Then they were willing to take him into
the boat, and immediately the boat reached the shore where they were heading.
[22]The next day the crowd that had stayed on the opposite shore of the lake realized that only one boat had been there, and that Jesus had not entered it with
his disciples, but that they had gone away alone. [23]Then some boats from Tiberias landed near the place where the people had eaten the bread after the Lord
had given thanks. [24]Once the crowd realized that neither Jesus nor his disciples
were there, they got into the boats and went to Capernaum in search of Jesus.

Jesus the Bread of Life

[25]When they found him on the other side of the lake, they asked him, "Rabbi,
when did you get here?"
[26]Jesus answered, "Very truly I tell you, you are looking for me, not because
you saw the signs I performed but because you ate the loaves and had your fill.
[27]Do not work for food that spoils, but for food that endures to eternal life, which
the Son of Man will give you. For on him God the Father has placed his seal of
approval."
[28]Then they asked him, "What must we do to do the works God requires?"
[29]Jesus answered, "The work of God is this: to believe in the one he has sent."
[30]So they asked him, "What sign then will you give that we may see it and believe you? What will you do? [31]Our ancestors ate the manna in the wilderness; as
it is written: 'He gave them bread from heaven to eat.'[c]"
[32]Jesus said to them, "Very truly I tell you, it is not Moses who has given you
the bread from heaven, but it is my Father who gives you the true bread from
heaven. [33]For the bread of God is the bread that comes down from heaven and
gives life to the world."

---

[a] *7* Greek *take two hundred denarii* [b] *19* Or about 5 or 6 kilometers [c] *31* Exodus 16:4; Neh. 9:15; Psalm 78:24,25

34“Sir,” they said, “always give us this bread.”

35Then Jesus declared, “I am the bread of life. Whoever comes to me will never go hungry, and whoever believes in me will never be thirsty. 36But as I told you, you have seen me and still you do not believe. 37All those the Father gives me will come to me, and whoever comes to me I will never drive away. 38For I have come down from heaven not to do my will but to do the will of him who sent me. 39And this is the will of him who sent me, that I shall lose none of all those he has given me, but raise them up at the last day. 40For my Father’s will is that everyone who looks to the Son and believes in him shall have eternal life, and I will raise them up at the last day.”

41At this the Jews there began to grumble about him because he said, “I am the bread that came down from heaven.” 42They said, “Is this not Jesus, the son of Joseph, whose father and mother we know? How can he now say, ‘I came down from heaven’?”

43“Stop grumbling among yourselves,” Jesus answered. 44“No one can come to me unless the Father who sent me draws them, and I will raise them up at the last day. 45It is written in the Prophets: ‘They will all be taught by God.’[a] Everyone who has heard the Father and learned from him comes to me. 46No one has seen the Father except the one who is from God; only he has seen the Father. 47Very truly I tell you, the one who believes has eternal life. 48I am the bread of life. 49Your ancestors ate the manna in the wilderness, yet they died. 50But here is the bread that comes down from heaven, which anyone may eat and not die. 51I am the living bread that came down from heaven. Whoever eats this bread will live forever. This bread is my flesh, which I will give for the life of the world.”

52Then the Jews began to argue sharply among themselves, “How can this man give us his flesh to eat?”

53Jesus said to them, “Very truly I tell you, unless you eat the flesh of the Son of Man and drink his blood, you have no life in you. 54Whoever eats my flesh and drinks my blood has eternal life, and I will raise them up at the last day. 55For my flesh is real food and my blood is real drink. 56Whoever eats my flesh and drinks my blood remains in me, and I in them. 57Just as the living Father sent me and I live because of the Father, so the one who feeds on me will live because of me. 58This is the bread that came down from heaven. Your ancestors ate manna and died, but whoever feeds on this bread will live forever.” 59He said this while teaching in the synagogue in Capernaum.

Many Disciples Desert Jesus

60On hearing it, many of his disciples said, “This is a hard teaching. Who can accept it?”

61Aware that his disciples were grumbling about this, Jesus said to them, “Does this offend you? 62Then what if you see the Son of Man ascend to where he was before! 63The Spirit gives life; the flesh counts for nothing. The words I have spoken to you — they are full of the Spirit[b] and life. 64Yet there are some of you who do not believe.” For Jesus had known from the beginning which of them did not believe and who would betray him. 65He went on to say, “This is why I told you that no one can come to me unless the Father has enabled them.”

66From this time many of his disciples turned back and no longer followed him.

67“You do not want to leave too, do you?” Jesus asked the Twelve.

68Simon Peter answered him, “Lord, to whom shall we go? You have the words of eternal life. 69We have come to believe and to know that you are the Holy One of God.”

70Then Jesus replied, “Have I not chosen you, the Twelve? Yet one of you is a devil!” 71(He meant Judas, the son of Simon Iscariot, who, though one of the Twelve, was later to betray him.)

---

[a] *45* Isaiah 54:13 [b] *63* Or *are Spirit*; or *are spirit*

Jesus Goes to the Festival of Tabernacles

7 After this, Jesus went around in Galilee. He did not want[a] to go about in Judea because the Jewish leaders there were looking for a way to kill him. 2But when the Jewish Festival of Tabernacles was near, 3Jesus' brothers said to him, "Leave Galilee and go to Judea, so that your disciples there may see the works you do. 4No one who wants to become a public figure acts in secret. Since you are doing these things, show yourself to the world." 5For even his own brothers did not believe in him.

6Therefore Jesus told them, "My time is not yet here; for you any time will do. 7The world cannot hate you, but it hates me because I testify that its works are evil. 8You go to the festival. I am not[b] going up to this festival, because my time has not yet fully come." 9After he had said this, he stayed in Galilee.

10However, after his brothers had left for the festival, he went also, not publicly, but in secret. 11Now at the festival the Jewish leaders were watching for Jesus and asking, "Where is he?"

12Among the crowds there was widespread whispering about him. Some said, "He is a good man."

Others replied, "No, he deceives the people." 13But no one would say anything publicly about him for fear of the leaders.

Jesus Teaches at the Festival

14Not until halfway through the festival did Jesus go up to the temple courts and begin to teach. 15The Jews there were amazed and asked, "How did this man get such learning without having been taught?"

16Jesus answered, "My teaching is not my own. It comes from the one who sent me. 17Anyone who chooses to do the will of God will find out whether my teaching comes from God or whether I speak on my own. 18Whoever speaks on their own does so to gain personal glory, but he who seeks the glory of the one who sent him is a man of truth; there is nothing false about him. 19Has not Moses given you the law? Yet not one of you keeps the law. Why are you trying to kill me?"

20"You are demon-possessed," the crowd answered. "Who is trying to kill you?"

21Jesus said to them, "I did one miracle, and you are all amazed. 22Yet, because Moses gave you circumcision (though actually it did not come from Moses, but from the patriarchs), you circumcise a boy on the Sabbath. 23Now if a boy can be circumcised on the Sabbath so that the law of Moses may not be broken, why are you angry with me for healing a man's whole body on the Sabbath? 24Stop judging by mere appearances, but instead judge correctly."

Division Over Who Jesus Is

25At that point some of the people of Jerusalem began to ask, "Isn't this the man they are trying to kill? 26Here he is, speaking publicly, and they are not saying a word to him. Have the authorities really concluded that he is the Messiah? 27But we know where this man is from; when the Messiah comes, no one will know where he is from."

28Then Jesus, still teaching in the temple courts, cried out, "Yes, you know me, and you know where I am from. I am not here on my own authority, but he who sent me is true. You do not know him, 29but I know him because I am from him and he sent me."

30At this they tried to seize him, but no one laid a hand on him, because his hour had not yet come. 31Still, many in the crowd believed in him. They said, "When the Messiah comes, will he perform more signs than this man?"

32The Pharisees heard the crowd whispering such things about him. Then the chief priests and the Pharisees sent temple guards to arrest him.

33Jesus said, "I am with you for only a short time, and then I am going to the one who sent me. 34You will look for me, but you will not find me; and where I am, you cannot come."

---

[a] *1* Some manuscripts *not have authority* [b] *8* Some manuscripts *not yet*

35The Jews said to one another, "Where does this man intend to go that we cannot find him? Will he go where our people live scattered among the Greeks, and teach the Greeks? 36What did he mean when he said, 'You will look for me, but you will not find me,' and 'Where I am, you cannot come'?"

37On the last and greatest day of the festival, Jesus stood and said in a loud voice, "Let anyone who is thirsty come to me and drink. 38Whoever believes in me, as Scripture has said, rivers of living water will flow from within them."[a] 39By this he meant the Spirit, whom those who believed in him were later to receive. Up to that time the Spirit had not been given, since Jesus had not yet been glorified.

40On hearing his words, some of the people said, "Surely this man is the Prophet."

41Others said, "He is the Messiah."

Still others asked, "How can the Messiah come from Galilee? 42Does not Scripture say that the Messiah will come from David's descendants and from Bethlehem, the town where David lived?" 43Thus the people were divided because of Jesus. 44Some wanted to seize him, but no one laid a hand on him.

Unbelief of the Jewish Leaders

45Finally the temple guards went back to the chief priests and the Pharisees, who asked them, "Why didn't you bring him in?"

46"No one ever spoke the way this man does," the guards replied.

47"You mean he has deceived you also?" the Pharisees retorted. 48"Have any of the rulers or of the Pharisees believed in him? 49No! But this mob that knows nothing of the law — there is a curse on them."

50Nicodemus, who had gone to Jesus earlier and who was one of their own number, asked, 51"Does our law condemn a man without first hearing him to find out what he has been doing?"

52They replied, "Are you from Galilee, too? Look into it, and you will find that a prophet does not come out of Galilee."

[The earliest manuscripts and many other ancient witnesses do not have John 7:53 — 8:11. A few manuscripts include these verses, wholly or in part, after John 7:36, John 21:25, Luke 21:38 or Luke 24:53.]

8 *53Then they all went home, 1but Jesus went to the Mount of Olives.*

2At dawn he appeared again in the temple courts, where all the people gathered around him, and he sat down to teach them. 3The teachers of the law and the Pharisees brought in a woman caught in adultery. They made her stand before the group 4and said to Jesus, "Teacher, this woman was caught in the act of adultery. 5In the Law Moses commanded us to stone such women. Now what do you say?" 6They were using this question as a trap, in order to have a basis for accusing him.

But Jesus bent down and started to write on the ground with his finger. 7When they kept on questioning him, he straightened up and said to them, "Let any one of you who is without sin be the first to throw a stone at her." 8Again he stooped down and wrote on the ground.

9At this, those who heard began to go away one at a time, the older ones first, until only Jesus was left, with the woman still standing there. 10Jesus straightened up and asked her, "Woman, where are they? Has no one condemned you?"

11"No one, sir," she said.

"Then neither do I condemn you," Jesus declared. "Go now and leave your life of sin."

Dispute Over Jesus' Testimony

12When Jesus spoke again to the people, he said, "I am the light of the world. Whoever follows me will never walk in darkness, but will have the light of life."

---

[a] 37,38 Or *me. And let anyone drink 38who believes in me." As Scripture has said, "Out of him* (or *them*) *will flow rivers of living water."*

THE "I AM" STATEMENTS OF CHRIST

A defining mark of the Gospel of John is Jesus' seven "I Am" statements. The statements are all revelations from Jesus that he is the promised Messiah, the Anointed One for which Israel had been waiting for centuries.

I am the bread of life — Jn 6:35,48. In identifying himself as such, Jesus references the bread from heaven that the people of Israel ate in the wilderness; yet, eventually, they still died. Jesus says believers will have endless life if they "eat him" (6:51), meaning, believe in and follow him.

I am the light of the world — Jn 8:12. Again Jesus references the people of ancient Israel and the pillar of fire that they followed through the wilderness (Ex 13:21). It is fitting that Jesus makes this statement in the temple courts during the Festival of Tabernacles, which commemorates Israel's sojourn in the desert with a display of bright lights. Jesus is a better and eternal light; whoever follows him will never walk in darkness, but will have the light of life (Jn 8:12).

I am the gate for the sheep — Jn 10:7,9 and I am the good shepherd — v. 11. In these statements Jesus is likely referencing Jerusalem's Sheep Gate (Ne 3:1,32) and the shepherd of Psalm 23. The sacrificial sheep and lambs were brought through the Sheep Gate to the temple for sacrifice, providing a way for the sins of the people of Israel to be covered. But Jesus is a better gate and a better shepherd; he is the gateway to eternal forgiveness and salvation for all people, and he is the ultimate Good Shepherd who restores the souls of everyone who believes in him.

I am the resurrection and the life — Jn 11:25. Jesus' words follow Martha's reference to the final resurrection of the body that Daniel prophesied (Da 12:2). Jesus explains that the resurrection and life is found in more than just an event; it is found in a person — more specifically, in him.

I am the way and the truth and the life — Jn 14:6. As the only sinless human ever to walk the earth, only Jesus was able to keep all of the decrees, commands and laws of God and thus walk in the way and truth of God that leads to life (Dt 26:17).

I am the true vine — Jn 15:1,5. Jesus drew on the many Old Testament references to Israel as a vine (Ps 80:8 – 16; Isa 5:1 – 7; Jer 2:21; Eze 15:1 – 8; 17:5 – 10; 19:10 – 14; Hos 10:1). Though Israel was the vine God transplanted from Egypt and planted on a hillside, it became a vine that was cut down (Ps 80:16), corrupt (Jer 2:21) and ultimately destroyed (Isa 5:5). Jesus, however, is the true vine. He fulfills Israel's promise to obey the commands of God and bear fruit on her behalf. Whoever is connected to him will have life and bear much fruit (Jn 15:5).

[13]The Pharisees challenged him, "Here you are, appearing as your own witness; your testimony is not valid."

[14]Jesus answered, "Even if I testify on my own behalf, my testimony is valid, for I know where I came from and where I am going. But you have no idea where I come from or where I am going. [15]You judge by human standards; I pass judgment on no one. [16]But if I do judge, my decisions are true, because I am not alone. I stand with the Father, who sent me. [17]In your own Law it is written that the testimony of two witnesses is true. [18]I am one who testifies for myself; my other witness is the Father, who sent me."

[19]Then they asked him, "Where is your father?"

"You do not know me or my Father," Jesus replied. "If you knew me, you would know my Father also." [20]He spoke these words while teaching in the temple courts near the place where the offerings were put. Yet no one seized him, because his hour had not yet come.

Dispute Over Who Jesus Is

[21]Once more Jesus said to them, "I am going away, and you will look for me, and you will die in your sin. Where I go, you cannot come."

[22]This made the Jews ask, "Will he kill himself? Is that why he says, 'Where I go, you cannot come'?"

[23]But he continued, "You are from below; I am from above. You are of this world; I am not of this world. [24]I told you that you would die in your sins; if you do not believe that I am he, you will indeed die in your sins."

[25]"Who are you?" they asked.

"Just what I have been telling you from the beginning," Jesus replied. [26]"I have much to say in judgment of you. But he who sent me is trustworthy, and what I have heard from him I tell the world."

[27]They did not understand that he was telling them about his Father. [28]So Jesus said, "When you have lifted up[a] the Son of Man, then you will know that I am he and that I do nothing on my own but speak just what the Father has taught me. [29]The one who sent me is with me; he has not left me alone, for I always do what pleases him." [30]Even as he spoke, many believed in him.

Dispute Over Whose Children Jesus' Opponents Are

[31]To the Jews who had believed him, Jesus said, "If you hold to my teaching, you are really my disciples. [32]Then you will know the truth, and the truth will set you free."

[33]They answered him, "We are Abraham's descendants and have never been slaves of anyone. How can you say that we shall be set free?"

[34]Jesus replied, "Very truly I tell you, everyone who sins is a slave to sin. [35]Now a slave has no permanent place in the family, but a son belongs to it forever. [36]So if the Son sets you free, you will be free indeed. [37]I know that you are Abraham's descendants. Yet you are looking for a way to kill me, because you have no room for my word. [38]I am telling you what I have seen in the Father's presence, and you are doing what you have heard from your father.[b]"

[39]"Abraham is our father," they answered.

"If you were Abraham's children," said Jesus, "then you would[c] do what Abraham did. [40]As it is, you are looking for a way to kill me, a man who has told you the truth that I heard from God. Abraham did not do such things. [41]You are doing the works of your own father."

"We are not illegitimate children," they protested. "The only Father we have is God himself."

[42]Jesus said to them, "If God were your Father, you would love me, for I have come here from God. I have not come on my own; God sent me. [43]Why is my

---

[a] 28 The Greek for *lifted up* also means *exalted.* [b] 38 Or *presence. Therefore do what you have heard from the Father.* [c] 39 Some early manuscripts *"If you are Abraham's children," said Jesus, "then*

language not clear to you? Because you are unable to hear what I say. 44You belong to your father, the devil, and you want to carry out your father's desires.
He was a murderer from the beginning, not holding to the truth, for there is no
truth in him. When he lies, he speaks his native language, for he is a liar and the
father of lies. 45Yet because I tell the truth, you do not believe me! 46Can any of
you prove me guilty of sin? If I am telling the truth, why don't you believe me?
47Whoever belongs to God hears what God says. The reason you do not hear is
that you do not belong to God."

Jesus' Claims About Himself

48The Jews answered him, "Aren't we right in saying that you are a Samaritan
and demon-possessed?"

49"I am not possessed by a demon," said Jesus, "but I honor my Father and
you dishonor me. 50I am not seeking glory for myself; but there is one who seeks
it, and he is the judge. 51Very truly I tell you, whoever obeys my word will never
see death."

52At this they exclaimed, "Now we know that you are demon-possessed! Abraham died and so did the prophets, yet you say that whoever obeys your word will
never taste death. 53Are you greater than our father Abraham? He died, and so
did the prophets. Who do you think you are?"

54Jesus replied, "If I glorify myself, my glory means nothing. My Father, whom
you claim as your God, is the one who glorifies me. 55Though you do not know
him, I know him. If I said I did not, I would be a liar like you, but I do know him
and obey his word. 56Your father Abraham rejoiced at the thought of seeing my
day; he saw it and was glad."

57"You are not yet fifty years old," they said to him, "and you have seen Abraham!"

58"Very truly I tell you," Jesus answered, "before Abraham was born, I am!"
59At this, they picked up stones to stone him, but Jesus hid himself, slipping away
from the temple grounds.

Jesus Heals a Man Born Blind

9 As he went along, he saw a man blind from birth. 2His disciples asked him,
"Rabbi, who sinned, this man or his parents, that he was born blind?"

3"Neither this man nor his parents sinned," said Jesus, "but this happened so
that the works of God might be displayed in him. 4As long as it is day, we must do
the works of him who sent me. Night is coming, when no one can work. 5While I
am in the world, I am the light of the world."

6After saying this, he spit on the ground, made some mud with the saliva,
and put it on the man's eyes. 7"Go," he told him, "wash in the Pool of Siloam"
(this word means "Sent"). So the man went and washed, and came home seeing.

8His neighbors and those who had formerly seen him begging asked, "Isn't
this the same man who used to sit and beg?" 9Some claimed that he was.

Others said, "No, he only looks like him."

But he himself insisted, "I am the man."

10"How then were your eyes opened?" they asked.

11He replied, "The man they call Jesus made some mud and put it on my eyes.
He told me to go to Siloam and wash. So I went and washed, and then I could
see."

12"Where is this man?" they asked him.

"I don't know," he said.

The Pharisees Investigate the Healing

13They brought to the Pharisees the man who had been blind. 14Now the day
on which Jesus had made the mud and opened the man's eyes was a Sabbath.
15Therefore the Pharisees also asked him how he had received his sight. "He put
mud on my eyes," the man replied, "and I washed, and now I see."

JOHN 9:1 – 12

NOW I SEE

Christians will be plumbing the depths of God's truth for all of eternity. We will learn all about the nature and the work of God and how he is meticulously working all things together for his glory. The more we learn about him, the more we will be amazed at his power, character and love.

But becoming a Christian does not require deep knowledge of God. It simply requires recognition of our brokenness and an experience with Jesus that causes us to follow him. The man in this story did not know who Jesus was, where he came from or what he was like. All he knew was that he had been born blind, and that Jesus had caused him to see (9:25). That was all he needed to know to begin following Jesus.

In the same way, when we really encounter Jesus, he heals us of our spiritual blindness. When we understand his work, we are able to see our sin and our need for him, which draws us to his free gift of salvation. When we are drawn to him, we begin to follow him. This man who had been born blind first saw the light because of Jesus' gracious work on his behalf. So also for believers who seek him — in Jesus' light, everything else begins to make sense.

16Some of the Pharisees said, "This man is not from God, for he does not keep the Sabbath."

But others asked, "How can a sinner perform such signs?" So they were divided.

17Then they turned again to the blind man, "What have you to say about him? It was your eyes he opened."

The man replied, "He is a prophet."

18They still did not believe that he had been blind and had received his sight until they sent for the man's parents. 19"Is this your son?" they asked. "Is this the one you say was born blind? How is it that now he can see?"

20"We know he is our son," the parents answered, "and we know he was born blind. 21But how he can see now, or who opened his eyes, we don't know. Ask him. He is of age; he will speak for himself." 22His parents said this because they were afraid of the Jewish leaders, who already had decided that anyone who acknowledged that Jesus was the Messiah would be put out of the synagogue. 23That was why his parents said, "He is of age; ask him."

24A second time they summoned the man who had been blind. "Give glory to God by telling the truth," they said. "We know this man is a sinner."

25He replied, "Whether he is a sinner or not, I don't know. One thing I do know. I was blind but now I see!"

26Then they asked him, "What did he do to you? How did he open your eyes?"

27He answered, "I have told you already and you did not listen. Why do you want to hear it again? Do you want to become his disciples too?"

28Then they hurled insults at him and said, "You are this fellow's disciple! We are disciples of Moses! 29We know that God spoke to Moses, but as for this fellow, we don't even know where he comes from."

30The man answered, "Now that is remarkable! You don't know where he comes from, yet he opened my eyes. 31We know that God does not listen to sinners. He listens to the godly person who does his will. 32Nobody has ever heard of opening the eyes of a man born blind. 33If this man were not from God, he could do nothing."

34To this they replied, "You were steeped in sin at birth; how dare you lecture us!" And they threw him out.

Spiritual Blindness

35Jesus heard that they had thrown him out, and when he found him, he said, "Do you believe in the Son of Man?"

36"Who is he, sir?" the man asked. "Tell me so that I may believe in him."

37Jesus said, "You have now seen him; in fact, he is the one speaking with you."

38Then the man said, "Lord, I believe," and he worshiped him.

39Jesus said,[a] "For judgment I have come into this world, so that the blind will see and those who see will become blind."

40Some Pharisees who were with him heard him say this and asked, "What? Are we blind too?"

41Jesus said, "If you were blind, you would not be guilty of sin; but now that you claim you can see, your guilt remains.

The Good Shepherd and His Sheep

10 "Very truly I tell you Pharisees, anyone who does not enter the sheep pen by the gate, but climbs in by some other way, is a thief and a robber. 2The one who enters by the gate is the shepherd of the sheep. 3The gatekeeper opens the gate for him, and the sheep listen to his voice. He calls his own sheep by name and leads them out. 4When he has brought out all his own, he goes on ahead of them, and his sheep follow him because they know his voice. 5But they will never follow a stranger; in fact, they will run away from him because they

[a] 38,39 Some early manuscripts do not have *Then the man said . . . 39Jesus said.*

do not recognize a stranger's voice." [6]Jesus used this figure of speech, but the
Pharisees did not understand what he was telling them.
[7]Therefore Jesus said again, "Very truly I tell you, I am the gate for the
sheep. [8]All who have come before me are thieves and robbers, but the sheep
have not listened to them. [9]I am the gate; whoever enters through me will be
saved.[a] They will come in and go out, and find pasture. [10]The thief comes only
to steal and kill and destroy; I have come that they may have life, and have it
to the full.
[11]"I am the good shepherd. The good shepherd lays down his life for the sheep.
[12]The hired hand is not the shepherd and does not own the sheep. So when he
sees the wolf coming, he abandons the sheep and runs away. Then the wolf attacks the flock and scatters it. [13]The man runs away because he is a hired hand
and cares nothing for the sheep.
[14]"I am the good shepherd; I know my sheep and my sheep know me— [15]just
as the Father knows me and I know the Father—and I lay down my life for the
sheep. [16]I have other sheep that are not of this sheep pen. I must bring them also.
They too will listen to my voice, and there shall be one flock and one shepherd.
[17]The reason my Father loves me is that I lay down my life—only to take it up
again. [18]No one takes it from me, but I lay it down of my own accord. I have authority to lay it down and authority to take it up again. This command I received
from my Father."
[19]The Jews who heard these words were again divided. [20]Many of them said,
"He is demon-possessed and raving mad. Why listen to him?"
[21]But others said, "These are not the sayings of a man possessed by a demon.
Can a demon open the eyes of the blind?"

Further Conflict Over Jesus' Claims

[22]Then came the Festival of Dedication[b] at Jerusalem. It was winter, [23]and
Jesus was in the temple courts walking in Solomon's Colonnade. [24]The Jews who
were there gathered around him, saying, "How long will you keep us in suspense? If you are the Messiah, tell us plainly."
[25]Jesus answered, "I did tell you, but you do not believe. The works I do in my
Father's name testify about me, [26]but you do not believe because you are not my
sheep. [27]My sheep listen to my voice; I know them, and they follow me. [28]I give
them eternal life, and they shall never perish; no one will snatch them out of my
hand. [29]My Father, who has given them to me, is greater than all[c]; no one can
snatch them out of my Father's hand. [30]I and the Father are one."
[31]Again his Jewish opponents picked up stones to stone him, [32]but Jesus said
to them, "I have shown you many good works from the Father. For which of these
do you stone me?"
[33]"We are not stoning you for any good work," they replied, "but for blasphemy, because you, a mere man, claim to be God."
[34]Jesus answered them, "Is it not written in your Law, 'I have said you are
"gods"'[d]? [35]If he called them 'gods,' to whom the word of God came—and Scripture cannot be set aside— [36]what about the one whom the Father set apart as
his very own and sent into the world? Why then do you accuse me of blasphemy
because I said, 'I am God's Son'? [37]Do not believe me unless I do the works of my
Father. [38]But if I do them, even though you do not believe me, believe the works,
that you may know and understand that the Father is in me, and I in the Father."
[39]Again they tried to seize him, but he escaped their grasp.
[40]Then Jesus went back across the Jordan to the place where John had been
baptizing in the early days. There he stayed, [41]and many people came to him.
They said, "Though John never performed a sign, all that John said about this
man was true." [42]And in that place many believed in Jesus.

[a] 9 Or *kept safe* [b] 22 That is, Hanukkah [c] 29 Many early manuscripts *What my Father has given me is greater than all* [d] 34 Psalm 82:6

JOHN 10:22–30

I AND THE FATHER ARE ONE

Throughout his ministry, Jesus regularly made bold claims that the Jewish leaders either didn't like or didn't understand. His claim to be one with the Father (Jn 10:30) might have been the boldest, most disliked and most misunderstood of all his claims. The Jewish leaders and the crowd charged him with blasphemy and tried to stone him.

For a man to claim to be one with God was unthinkable. This is the great miracle of Christ, the miracle of the incarnation: that Jesus is fully God and as such is utterly holy, yet also fully man and completely human. Christians believe that the divinity of Christ is fully present in the person of Jesus but is veiled in flesh (Jn 1:14). Because of his miraculous incarnation, people can identify with Christ. He is a man, but he simultaneously has the power to save since he is also fully God.

The amazing truth of the gospel is that Jesus left the power, peace and love of his Father to endure the miseries of this life and to willingly take the guilt of human sin upon himself, bearing the brunt of God's wrath on the cross. Now, in exchange for our sin, he offers us his righteousness. This righteousness is so complete that when we are clothed in it, we become united with Christ and one with God the Father (Jn 17:11,21).

The Death of Lazarus

11 Now a man named Lazarus was sick. He was from Bethany, the village
of Mary and her sister Martha. 2(This Mary, whose brother Lazarus now
lay sick, was the same one who poured perfume on the Lord and wiped his feet
with her hair.) 3So the sisters sent word to Jesus, "Lord, the one you love is sick."
4When he heard this, Jesus said, "This sickness will not end in death. No, it is
for God's glory so that God's Son may be glorified through it." 5Now Jesus loved
Martha and her sister and Lazarus. 6So when he heard that Lazarus was sick, he
stayed where he was two more days, 7and then he said to his disciples, "Let us
go back to Judea."
8"But Rabbi," they said, "a short while ago the Jews there tried to stone you,
and yet you are going back?"
9Jesus answered, "Are there not twelve hours of daylight? Anyone who walks
in the daytime will not stumble, for they see by this world's light. 10It is when a
person walks at night that they stumble, for they have no light."
11After he had said this, he went on to tell them, "Our friend Lazarus has fallen
asleep; but I am going there to wake him up."
12His disciples replied, "Lord, if he sleeps, he will get better." 13Jesus had been
speaking of his death, but his disciples thought he meant natural sleep.
14So then he told them plainly, "Lazarus is dead, 15and for your sake I am glad
I was not there, so that you may believe. But let us go to him."
16Then Thomas (also known as Didymus[a]) said to the rest of the disciples,
"Let us also go, that we may die with him."

Jesus Comforts the Sisters of Lazarus

17On his arrival, Jesus found that Lazarus had already been in the tomb for
four days. 18Now Bethany was less than two miles[b] from Jerusalem, 19and many
Jews had come to Martha and Mary to comfort them in the loss of their brother. 20When Martha heard that Jesus was coming, she went out to meet him, but
Mary stayed at home.
21"Lord," Martha said to Jesus, "if you had been here, my brother would not
have died. 22But I know that even now God will give you whatever you ask."
23Jesus said to her, "Your brother will rise again."
24Martha answered, "I know he will rise again in the resurrection at the last
day."
25Jesus said to her, "I am the resurrection and the life. The one who believes
in me will live, even though they die; 26and whoever lives by believing in me will
never die. Do you believe this?"
27"Yes, Lord," she replied, "I believe that you are the Messiah, the Son of God,
who is to come into the world."
28After she had said this, she went back and called her sister Mary aside. "The
Teacher is here," she said, "and is asking for you." 29When Mary heard this, she
got up quickly and went to him. 30Now Jesus had not yet entered the village,
but was still at the place where Martha had met him. 31When the Jews who had
been with Mary in the house, comforting her, noticed how quickly she got up
and went out, they followed her, supposing she was going to the tomb to mourn
there.
32When Mary reached the place where Jesus was and saw him, she fell at his
feet and said, "Lord, if you had been here, my brother would not have died."
33When Jesus saw her weeping, and the Jews who had come along with her
also weeping, he was deeply moved in spirit and troubled. 34"Where have you
laid him?" he asked.
"Come and see, Lord," they replied.
35Jesus wept.
36Then the Jews said, "See how he loved him!"

[a] *16 Thomas* (Aramaic) and *Didymus* (Greek) both mean *twin.* [b] *18* Or about 3 kilometers

[37]But some of them said, "Could not he who opened the eyes of the blind man have kept this man from dying?"

Jesus Raises Lazarus From the Dead

[38]Jesus, once more deeply moved, came to the tomb. It was a cave with a stone laid across the entrance. [39]"Take away the stone," he said.

"But, Lord," said Martha, the sister of the dead man, "by this time there is a bad odor, for he has been there four days."

[40]Then Jesus said, "Did I not tell you that if you believe, you will see the glory of God?"

[41]So they took away the stone. Then Jesus looked up and said, "Father, I thank you that you have heard me. [42]I knew that you always hear me, but I said this for the benefit of the people standing here, that they may believe that you sent me."

[43]When he had said this, Jesus called in a loud voice, "Lazarus, come out!" [44]The dead man came out, his hands and feet wrapped with strips of linen, and a cloth around his face.

Jesus said to them, "Take off the grave clothes and let him go."

The Plot to Kill Jesus

[45]Therefore many of the Jews who had come to visit Mary, and had seen what Jesus did, believed in him. [46]But some of them went to the Pharisees and told them what Jesus had done. [47]Then the chief priests and the Pharisees called a meeting of the Sanhedrin.

"What are we accomplishing?" they asked. "Here is this man performing many signs. [48]If we let him go on like this, everyone will believe in him, and then the Romans will come and take away both our temple and our nation."

[49]Then one of them, named Caiaphas, who was high priest that year, spoke up, "You know nothing at all! [50]You do not realize that it is better for you that one man die for the people than that the whole nation perish."

[51]He did not say this on his own, but as high priest that year he prophesied that Jesus would die for the Jewish nation, [52]and not only for that nation but also for the scattered children of God, to bring them together and make them one. [53]So from that day on they plotted to take his life.

[54]Therefore Jesus no longer moved about publicly among the people of Judea. Instead he withdrew to a region near the wilderness, to a village called Ephraim, where he stayed with his disciples.

[55]When it was almost time for the Jewish Passover, many went up from the country to Jerusalem for their ceremonial cleansing before the Passover. [56]They kept looking for Jesus, and as they stood in the temple courts they asked one another, "What do you think? Isn't he coming to the festival at all?" [57]But the chief priests and the Pharisees had given orders that anyone who found out where Jesus was should report it so that they might arrest him.

Jesus Anointed at Bethany

12 Six days before the Passover, Jesus came to Bethany, where Lazarus lived, whom Jesus had raised from the dead. [2]Here a dinner was given in Jesus' honor. Martha served, while Lazarus was among those reclining at the table with him. [3]Then Mary took about a pint[a] of pure nard, an expensive perfume; she poured it on Jesus' feet and wiped his feet with her hair. And the house was filled with the fragrance of the perfume.

[4]But one of his disciples, Judas Iscariot, who was later to betray him, objected, [5]"Why wasn't this perfume sold and the money given to the poor? It was worth a year's wages.[b]" [6]He did not say this because he cared about the poor but because he was a thief; as keeper of the money bag, he used to help himself to what was put into it.

---

[a] 3 Or about 0.5 liter [b] 5 Greek *three hundred denarii*

THE HOPE OF LIFE

Of the many miracles in the Gospel of John, one of the most dramatic is Jesus' raising of Lazarus. Not only is this sign one of the most vivid, it also tells us the most about the ministry and purpose of Jesus. From the very beginning of time God could have certainly kept sin, pain and even death out of the world that he created. However, God allowed sin to enter into his good creation through the serpent's temptation and the man and woman's disobedience, so that through the power of redemption, God's glory might be displayed. Similarly, Jesus allowed Lazarus to die "for God's glory so that God's Son might be glorified through it" (Jn 11:4).

God sent that redemption through his own Son, Jesus, who came to earth to sympathize with us in every way. We see that sympathy in this story as he goes to comfort Mary and Martha, Lazarus's sisters and his dear friends (11:35). We understand from Scripture that Jesus can sympathize with us in our weaknesses and in our temptations (Heb 4:15). Jesus even identified with us to the point of becoming our sin and dying the death that we should have died because of our rebellion against God (2Co 5:21; Php 2:8). But Jesus is the resurrection and the life (Jn 11:25), and by the power of God he overcame death, was raised to eternal life, and now reigns forever in his eternal kingdom.

As Lazarus was undeniably physically dead, so we are spiritually dead and separated from God in our own sins. Like Lazarus, any hope of life is gone, and the stench of our spiritual decomposition is pungent. As Paul explained, we "were dead in [our] transgressions and sins … we were by nature deserving of wrath" (Eph 2:1 – 3). But just as Jesus raised Lazarus from his physical death, if we believe that Jesus is the resurrection and the life, he promises to raise us from our spiritual death and gives us the promise of a physical resurrection on the last day.

Understand that last statement: Just as Jesus physically raised Lazarus from the dead, so he will one day do that with each of us who believe in and trust him alone for our salvation. In fact, we will do one better: our bodies will be reinvigorated, but not to their old, imperfect state; instead, in that day we will be like him (1Jn 3:2).

7“Leave her alone,” Jesus replied. “It was intended that she should save this
perfume for the day of my burial. 8You will always have the poor among you,[a] but
you will not always have me.”
9Meanwhile a large crowd of Jews found out that Jesus was there and came,
not only because of him but also to see Lazarus, whom he had raised from the
dead. 10So the chief priests made plans to kill Lazarus as well, 11for on account of
him many of the Jews were going over to Jesus and believing in him.

Jesus Comes to Jerusalem as King

12The next day the great crowd that had come for the festival heard that Jesus
was on his way to Jerusalem. 13They took palm branches and went out to meet
him, shouting,

“Hosanna![b]”

“Blessed is he who comes in the name of the Lord!”[c]

“Blessed is the king of Israel!”

14Jesus found a young donkey and sat on it, as it is written:

15“Do not be afraid, Daughter Zion;
see, your king is coming,
seated on a donkey’s colt.”[d]

16At first his disciples did not understand all this. Only after Jesus was glorified did they realize that these things had been written about him and that these
things had been done to him.
17Now the crowd that was with him when he called Lazarus from the tomb
and raised him from the dead continued to spread the word. 18Many people,
because they had heard that he had performed this sign, went out to meet him.
19So the Pharisees said to one another, “See, this is getting us nowhere. Look how
the whole world has gone after him!”

Jesus Predicts His Death

20Now there were some Greeks among those who went up to worship at the
festival. 21They came to Philip, who was from Bethsaida in Galilee, with a request. “Sir,” they said, “we would like to see Jesus.” 22Philip went to tell Andrew;
Andrew and Philip in turn told Jesus.
23Jesus replied, “The hour has come for the Son of Man to be glorified. 24Very
truly I tell you, unless a kernel of wheat falls to the ground and dies, it remains
only a single seed. But if it dies, it produces many seeds. 25Anyone who loves
their life will lose it, while anyone who hates their life in this world will keep it
for eternal life. 26Whoever serves me must follow me; and where I am, my servant
also will be. My Father will honor the one who serves me.
27“Now my soul is troubled, and what shall I say? ‘Father, save me from this hour’?
No, it was for this very reason I came to this hour. 28Father, glorify your name!”
Then a voice came from heaven, “I have glorified it, and will glorify it again.”
29The crowd that was there and heard it said it had thundered; others said an
angel had spoken to him.
30Jesus said, “This voice was for your benefit, not mine. 31Now is the time for
judgment on this world; now the prince of this world will be driven out. 32And
I, when I am lifted up[e] from the earth, will draw all people to myself.” 33He said
this to show the kind of death he was going to die.
34The crowd spoke up, “We have heard from the Law that the Messiah will
remain forever, so how can you say, ‘The Son of Man must be lifted up’? Who is
this ‘Son of Man’?”

---

[a] *8* See Deut. 15:11. [b] *13* A Hebrew expression meaning “Save!” which became an exclamation of praise [c] *13* Psalm 118:25,26 [d] *15* Zech. 9:9 [e] *32* The Greek for *lifted up* also means *exalted*.

JOHN 12:37–43

THE PRAISE OF GOD

One of the most haunting stories in the Bible is this story of the Jews who were fearful of following Jesus. Jesus, the Messiah, the one whom the people of Israel had been expecting for generations, was standing right in front of them. Jesus had spoken the truth about God's kingdom, had given them many miraculous signs and had just raised Lazarus from the dead. Many believed that Jesus was the Messiah, but they were too afraid to acknowledge him and follow him because "they loved human praise more than praise from God" (Jn 12:43).

This is a great warning to all. Following Jesus is not always convenient or popular. Often, the call to follow Christ is a call to forsake comfort, wealth, status and the approval of others; in some contexts, following Jesus is quite literally a call to die. Those who follow Jesus may forsake "human praise," but in return they gain "praise from God."

Christ promises that believers will one day see the incredible riches of God's grace (Eph 2:7) and sit with Jesus on his eternal throne (Rev 3:21). These fearful Jewish people traded the eternal throne of Christ for the temporal praise of humans. Believers today reject this bad trade, choosing rather by God's grace to forsake the small things of this world for the eternal things of God.

JOHN 13:1–17,34–35

A NEW COMMAND

During the Passover meal, Jesus, the master and teacher of the twelve

(continued on next page)

[35]Then Jesus told them, "You are going to have the light just a little while longer. Walk while you have the light, before darkness overtakes you. Whoever
walks in the dark does not know where they are going. [36]Believe in the light while
you have the light, so that you may become children of light." When he had finished speaking, Jesus left and hid himself from them.

Belief and Unbelief Among the Jews

[37]Even after Jesus had performed so many signs in their presence, they still
would not believe in him. [38]This was to fulfill the word of Isaiah the prophet:

"Lord, who has believed our message
and to whom has the arm of the Lord been revealed?"[a]

[39]For this reason they could not believe, because, as Isaiah says elsewhere:

[40]"He has blinded their eyes
and hardened their hearts,
so they can neither see with their eyes,
nor understand with their hearts,
nor turn—and I would heal them."[b]

[41]Isaiah said this because he saw Jesus' glory and spoke about him.
[42]Yet at the same time many even among the leaders believed in him. But because of the Pharisees they would not openly acknowledge their faith for fear
they would be put out of the synagogue; [43]for they loved human praise more
than praise from God.
[44]Then Jesus cried out, "Whoever believes in me does not believe in me only,
but in the one who sent me. [45]The one who looks at me is seeing the one who
sent me. [46]I have come into the world as a light, so that no one who believes in
me should stay in darkness.
[47]"If anyone hears my words but does not keep them, I do not judge that person. For I did not come to judge the world, but to save the world. [48]There is a judge
for the one who rejects me and does not accept my words; the very words I have
spoken will condemn them at the last day. [49]For I did not speak on my own, but
the Father who sent me commanded me to say all that I have spoken. [50]I know
that his command leads to eternal life. So whatever I say is just what the Father
has told me to say."

Jesus Washes His Disciples' Feet

13 It was just before the Passover Festival. Jesus knew that the hour had come
for him to leave this world and go to the Father. Having loved his own who
were in the world, he loved them to the end.
[2]The evening meal was in progress, and the devil had already prompted Judas, the son of Simon Iscariot, to betray Jesus. [3]Jesus knew that the Father had
put all things under his power, and that he had come from God and was returning to God; [4]so he got up from the meal, took off his outer clothing, and wrapped
a towel around his waist. [5]After that, he poured water into a basin and began to
wash his disciples' feet, drying them with the towel that was wrapped around
him.
[6]He came to Simon Peter, who said to him, "Lord, are you going to wash my
feet?"
[7]Jesus replied, "You do not realize now what I am doing, but later you will
understand."
[8]"No," said Peter, "you shall never wash my feet."
Jesus answered, "Unless I wash you, you have no part with me."
[9]"Then, Lord," Simon Peter replied, "not just my feet but my hands and my
head as well!"
[10]Jesus answered, "Those who have had a bath need only to wash their feet;

[a] *38* Isaiah 53:1 [b] *40* Isaiah 6:10

their whole body is clean. And you are clean, though not every one of you." 11For
he knew who was going to betray him, and that was why he said not every one
was clean.
12When he had finished washing their feet, he put on his clothes and returned
to his place. "Do you understand what I have done for you?" he asked them.
13"You call me 'Teacher' and 'Lord,' and rightly so, for that is what I am. 14Now
that I, your Lord and Teacher, have washed your feet, you also should wash one
another's feet. 15I have set you an example that you should do as I have done for
you. 16Very truly I tell you, no servant is greater than his master, nor is a messenger greater than the one who sent him. 17Now that you know these things, you
will be blessed if you do them.

Jesus Predicts His Betrayal

18"I am not referring to all of you; I know those I have chosen. But this is to fulfill this passage of Scripture: 'He who shared my bread has turned[a] against me.'[b]
19"I am telling you now before it happens, so that when it does happen you will
believe that I am who I am. 20Very truly I tell you, whoever accepts anyone I send
accepts me; and whoever accepts me accepts the one who sent me."
21After he had said this, Jesus was troubled in spirit and testified, "Very truly
I tell you, one of you is going to betray me."
22His disciples stared at one another, at a loss to know which of them he
meant. 23One of them, the disciple whom Jesus loved, was reclining next to him.
24Simon Peter motioned to this disciple and said, "Ask him which one he means."
25Leaning back against Jesus, he asked him, "Lord, who is it?"
26Jesus answered, "It is the one to whom I will give this piece of bread when
I have dipped it in the dish." Then, dipping the piece of bread, he gave it to Judas, the son of Simon Iscariot. 27As soon as Judas took the bread, Satan entered
into him.

So Jesus told him, "What you are about to do, do quickly." 28But no one at
the meal understood why Jesus said this to him. 29Since Judas had charge of the
money, some thought Jesus was telling him to buy what was needed for the festival, or to give something to the poor. 30As soon as Judas had taken the bread, he
went out. And it was night.

Jesus Predicts Peter's Denial

31When he was gone, Jesus said, "Now the Son of Man is glorified and God is
glorified in him. 32If God is glorified in him,[c] God will glorify the Son in himself,
and will glorify him at once.
33"My children, I will be with you only a little longer. You will look for me,
and just as I told the Jews, so I tell you now: Where I am going, you cannot come.
34"A new command I give you: Love one another. As I have loved you, so you
must love one another. 35By this everyone will know that you are my disciples,
if you love one another."
36Simon Peter asked him, "Lord, where are you going?"

Jesus replied, "Where I am going, you cannot follow now, but you will follow
later."
37Peter asked, "Lord, why can't I follow you now? I will lay down my life for you."
38Then Jesus answered, "Will you really lay down your life for me? Very truly I
tell you, before the rooster crows, you will disown me three times!

Jesus Comforts His Disciples

14 "Do not let your hearts be troubled. You believe in God[d]; believe also in
me. 2My Father's house has many rooms; if that were not so, would I have
told you that I am going there to prepare a place for you? 3And if I go and prepare

[a] 18 Greek *has lifted up his heel* [b] 18 Psalm 41:9 [c] 32 Many early manuscripts do not have *If God is glorified in him.* [d] 1 Or *Believe in God*

(A New Command, continued)

disciples, got up, wrapped a towel around his waist and began to wash the disciples' feet. This was a dirty job normally reserved for a lowly servant. But Jesus, the obvious leader of this group, decided to wash feet to serve his disciples and make a profound point. While it's true that the disciples had dirty feet, Jesus' motive was far beyond the circumstances. The disciples knew this was an important night, yet none of them had bothered to wash their own, much less one another's, feet. Jesus realized this was the perfect opportunity to show them that the way of his kingdom is very different from the way of earthly kingdoms.

Jesus came to serve and love, and so he gave his disciples a new command: "Love one another"; he then went on to say, "By this everyone will know that you are my disciples, if you love one another" (13:34–35). It's this kind of aspiration that Jesus wanted his disciples to pursue; its countercultural nature is just as radical today. God's love in believers' lives is to be evident as they show his love to a lost and broken world today, pointing toward a kingdom that is not of this world (Jn 18:36).

a place for you, I will come back and take you to be with me that you also may be where I am. 4You know the way to the place where I am going."

Jesus the Way to the Father

5Thomas said to him, "Lord, we don't know where you are going, so how can we know the way?"

6Jesus answered, "I am the way and the truth and the life. No one comes to the Father except through me. 7If you really know me, you will know[a] my Father as well. From now on, you do know him and have seen him."

8Philip said, "Lord, show us the Father and that will be enough for us."

9Jesus answered: "Don't you know me, Philip, even after I have been among you such a long time? Anyone who has seen me has seen the Father. How can you say, 'Show us the Father'? 10Don't you believe that I am in the Father, and that the Father is in me? The words I say to you I do not speak on my own authority. Rather, it is the Father, living in me, who is doing his work. 11Believe me when I say that I am in the Father and the Father is in me; or at least believe on the evidence of the works themselves. 12Very truly I tell you, whoever believes in me will do the works I have been doing, and they will do even greater things than these, because I am going to the Father. 13And I will do whatever you ask in my name, so that the Father may be glorified in the Son. 14You may ask me for anything in my name, and I will do it.

Jesus Promises the Holy Spirit

15"If you love me, keep my commands. 16And I will ask the Father, and he will give you another advocate to help you and be with you forever — 17the Spirit of truth. The world cannot accept him, because it neither sees him nor knows him. But you know him, for he lives with you and will be[b] in you. 18I will not leave you as orphans; I will come to you. 19Before long, the world will not see me anymore, but you will see me. Because I live, you also will live. 20On that day you will realize that I am in my Father, and you are in me, and I am in you. 21Whoever has my commands and keeps them is the one who loves me. The one who loves me will be loved by my Father, and I too will love them and show myself to them."

22Then Judas (not Judas Iscariot) said, "But, Lord, why do you intend to show yourself to us and not to the world?"

23Jesus replied, "Anyone who loves me will obey my teaching. My Father will love them, and we will come to them and make our home with them. 24Anyone who does not love me will not obey my teaching. These words you hear are not my own; they belong to the Father who sent me.

25"All this I have spoken while still with you. 26But the Advocate, the Holy Spirit, whom the Father will send in my name, will teach you all things and will remind you of everything I have said to you. 27Peace I leave with you; my peace I give you. I do not give to you as the world gives. Do not let your hearts be troubled and do not be afraid.

28"You heard me say, 'I am going away and I am coming back to you.' If you loved me, you would be glad that I am going to the Father, for the Father is greater than I. 29I have told you now before it happens, so that when it does happen you will believe. 30I will not say much more to you, for the prince of this world is coming. He has no hold over me, 31but he comes so that the world may learn that I love the Father and do exactly what my Father has commanded me.

"Come now; let us leave.

The Vine and the Branches

15 "I am the true vine, and my Father is the gardener. 2He cuts off every branch in me that bears no fruit, while every branch that does bear fruit he prunes[c] so that it will be even more fruitful. 3You are already clean because

[a] 7 Some manuscripts *If you really knew me, you would know* [b] 17 Some early manuscripts *and is* [c] 2 The Greek for *he prunes* also means *he cleans.*

JOHN 15:1–8

THE VINE AND THE BRANCHES

Jesus here draws on Old Testament "vine" language (Isa 5:1) in his final "I am" statement to declare that all of the prophecies and laws of Israel are fulfilled in him (Mt 5:17). By this statement, believers discover that the secret of staying connected to God is to stay connected to Christ.

When his followers are connected to Jesus, they will "bear much fruit" (Jn 15:8), but apart from him they can do "nothing" (v. 5). Practically then, to remain in the "vine of Christ," believers must be faithful to pursue God on a regular basis. Regular worship, prayer and Bible study are essential in the life of a believer. The more disciplined they are in pursuing God through these disciplines, the more fruit they will bear.

of the word I have spoken to you. 4Remain in me, as I also remain in you. No branch can bear fruit by itself; it must remain in the vine. Neither can you bear fruit unless you remain in me.

5"I am the vine; you are the branches. If you remain in me and I in you, you will bear much fruit; apart from me you can do nothing. 6If you do not remain in me, you are like a branch that is thrown away and withers; such branches are picked up, thrown into the fire and burned. 7If you remain in me and my words remain in you, ask whatever you wish, and it will be done for you. 8This is to my Father's glory, that you bear much fruit, showing yourselves to be my disciples.

9"As the Father has loved me, so have I loved you. Now remain in my love. 10If you keep my commands, you will remain in my love, just as I have kept my Father's commands and remain in his love. 11I have told you this so that my joy may be in you and that your joy may be complete. 12My command is this: Love each other as I have loved you. 13Greater love has no one than this: to lay down one's life for one's friends. 14You are my friends if you do what I command. 15I no longer call you servants, because a servant does not know his master's business. Instead, I have called you friends, for everything that I learned from my Father I have made known to you. 16You did not choose me, but I chose you and appointed you so that you might go and bear fruit — fruit that will last — and so that whatever you ask in my name the Father will give you. 17This is my command: Love each other.

The World Hates the Disciples

18"If the world hates you, keep in mind that it hated me first. 19If you belonged to the world, it would love you as its own. As it is, you do not belong to the world, but I have chosen you out of the world. That is why the world hates you. 20Remember what I told you: 'A servant is not greater than his master.'[a] If they persecuted me, they will persecute you also. If they obeyed my teaching, they will obey yours also. 21They will treat you this way because of my name, for they do not know the one who sent me. 22If I had not come and spoken to them, they would not be guilty of sin; but now they have no excuse for their sin. 23Whoever hates me hates my Father as well. 24If I had not done among them the works no one else did, they would not be guilty of sin. As it is, they have seen, and yet they have hated both me and my Father. 25But this is to fulfill what is written in their Law: 'They hated me without reason.'[b]

The Work of the Holy Spirit

26"When the Advocate comes, whom I will send to you from the Father — the Spirit of truth who goes out from the Father — he will testify about me. 27And you also must testify, for you have been with me from the beginning.

16 "All this I have told you so that you will not fall away. 2They will put you out of the synagogue; in fact, the time is coming when anyone who kills you will think they are offering a service to God. 3They will do such things because they have not known the Father or me. 4I have told you this, so that when their time comes you will remember that I warned you about them. I did not tell you this from the beginning because I was with you, 5but now I am going to him who sent me. None of you asks me, 'Where are you going?' 6Rather, you are filled with grief because I have said these things. 7But very truly I tell you, it is for your good that I am going away. Unless I go away, the Advocate will not come to you; but if I go, I will send him to you. 8When he comes, he will prove the world to be in the wrong about sin and righteousness and judgment: 9about sin, because people do not believe in me; 10about righteousness, because I am going to the Father, where you can see me no longer; 11and about judgment, because the prince of this world now stands condemned.

12"I have much more to say to you, more than you can now bear. 13But when

---

[a] *20* John 13:16 [b] *25* Psalms 35:19; 69:4

he, the Spirit of truth, comes, he will guide you into all the truth. He will not speak on his own; he will speak only what he hears, and he will tell you what is yet to come. [14]He will glorify me because it is from me that he will receive what he will make known to you. [15]All that belongs to the Father is mine. That is why I said the Spirit will receive from me what he will make known to you."

The Disciples' Grief Will Turn to Joy

[16]Jesus went on to say, "In a little while you will see me no more, and then after a little while you will see me."

[17]At this, some of his disciples said to one another, "What does he mean by saying, 'In a little while you will see me no more, and then after a little while you will see me,' and 'Because I am going to the Father'?" [18]They kept asking, "What does he mean by 'a little while'? We don't understand what he is saying."

[19]Jesus saw that they wanted to ask him about this, so he said to them, "Are you asking one another what I meant when I said, 'In a little while you will see me no more, and then after a little while you will see me'? [20]Very truly I tell you, you will weep and mourn while the world rejoices. You will grieve, but your grief will turn to joy. [21]A woman giving birth to a child has pain because her time has come; but when her baby is born she forgets the anguish because of her joy that a child is born into the world. [22]So with you: Now is your time of grief, but I will see you again and you will rejoice, and no one will take away your joy. [23]In that day you will no longer ask me anything. Very truly I tell you, my Father will give you whatever you ask in my name. [24]Until now you have not asked for anything in my name. Ask and you will receive, and your joy will be complete.

[25]"Though I have been speaking figuratively, a time is coming when I will no longer use this kind of language but will tell you plainly about my Father. [26]In that day you will ask in my name. I am not saying that I will ask the Father on your behalf. [27]No, the Father himself loves you because you have loved me and have believed that I came from God. [28]I came from the Father and entered the world; now I am leaving the world and going back to the Father."

[29]Then Jesus' disciples said, "Now you are speaking clearly and without figures of speech. [30]Now we can see that you know all things and that you do not even need to have anyone ask you questions. This makes us believe that you came from God."

[31]"Do you now believe?" Jesus replied. [32]"A time is coming and in fact has come when you will be scattered, each to your own home. You will leave me all alone. Yet I am not alone, for my Father is with me.

[33]"I have told you these things, so that in me you may have peace. In this world you will have trouble. But take heart! I have overcome the world."

Jesus Prays to Be Glorified

17 After Jesus said this, he looked toward heaven and prayed:

"Father, the hour has come. Glorify your Son, that your Son may glorify you. [2]For you granted him authority over all people that he might give eternal life to all those you have given him. [3]Now this is eternal life: that they know you, the only true God, and Jesus Christ, whom you have sent. [4]I have brought you glory on earth by finishing the work you gave me to do. [5]And now, Father, glorify me in your presence with the glory I had with you before the world began.

Jesus Prays for His Disciples

[6]"I have revealed you[a] to those whom you gave me out of the world. They were yours; you gave them to me and they have obeyed your word. [7]Now they know that everything you have given me comes from you. [8]For I gave

---

JOHN 17:1–26

THE PRAYER OF CHRIST

One of the great blessings of being a follower of Jesus is to know that right now he is interceding for his people before the Father (Ro 8:34; Heb 7:25). While we do not know exactly what Jesus says to the Father, we do have an example of Jesus' prayer here in John 17.

First, Jesus prays that the Father would protect his church. He not only prays for physical protection, but even more he prays for spiritual protection—that the church's faith would stay strong after Jesus left them to return to his Father (17:11).

Second, Jesus prays for his church to be sanctified, that they would be made holy; that they would know the truth of God and reflect the glory of God on earth (17:17,19).

Third, Jesus prays for those who will believe through the message of the disciples (17:20). Jesus prays that his church will grow and that many people in all the earth will come to know him through the faithful ministry of all his disciples.

What an amazing gift to believers today to be able to read this prayer and know that Jesus was, and still is, going to God—directly and personally—on their behalf.

---

[a] 6 Greek *your name*

JOHN 16:1 – 15

THE ADVOCATE

While the Gospel of John covers most of the significant events in Jesus' ministry, nearly a third of the book covers the events of just one night. This night was, of course, one of the most important nights of his life: his last night with his disciples before he was betrayed and arrested. On this night he comforted his disciples by promising them the greatest gift they could ever receive: the indwelling power of the Holy Spirit of God.

The Holy Spirit is the third person of the holy Trinity; he is fully God, and his will is always in line with God the Father and God the Son. The Holy Spirit was present at creation (Ge 1:2) and was with the people of Israel in the tabernacle (Ex 40:34 – 35) and the temple (1Ki 8:6 – 13). This same Spirit had led Jesus throughout his earthly ministry (Mt 3:16), but on this final night of Jesus' life, he promised his disciples that the Holy Spirit would be present with each one of them: "I will ask the Father, and he will give you another advocate to help you and be with you forever — the Spirit of truth" (Jn 14:16 – 17).

The disciples, like many believers throughout history, did not understand what Jesus was promising; they undoubtedly would have preferred for Jesus to stay with them. But Jesus emphasized the benefits of the Spirit's indwelling when he said, "It is for your good [for your advantage] that I am going away. Unless I go away, the Advocate will not come to you; but if I go, I will send him to you" (Jn 16:7). After the Spirit came at Pentecost (Ac 2:1 – 18), the disciples must have remembered Jesus' teaching about the ministry of the Holy Spirit: "When he comes, he will prove the world to be in the wrong about sin and righteousness and judgment" (Jn 16:8). "He will guide you into all the truth" (16:13).

The Holy Spirit teaches Christians that sin is wrong, and when believers surrender to him, he begins to take away their desire for sin. The Spirit reminds Christians of Christ's righteousness. Jesus has gone to the Father to advocate for those who believe (16:10). Since we no longer have Jesus to show us righteousness through his earthly life, believers now have the Holy Spirit to lead us into what is good, right and true. Finally, the Holy Spirit reminds believers of the coming judgment (16:11): that one day Jesus will return to condemn all evil and reward all good. He will settle all accounts, bring justice to the world and will renew his creation (Isa 43:18 – 19; Rev 21:5).

them the words you gave me and they accepted them. They knew with certainty that I came from you, and they believed that you sent me. [9]I pray for
them. I am not praying for the world, but for those you have given me, for
they are yours. [10]All I have is yours, and all you have is mine. And glory has
come to me through them. [11]I will remain in the world no longer, but they
are still in the world, and I am coming to you. Holy Father, protect them by
the power of[a] your name, the name you gave me, so that they may be one as
we are one. [12]While I was with them, I protected them and kept them safe
by[b] that name you gave me. None has been lost except the one doomed to
destruction so that Scripture would be fulfilled.

[13]"I am coming to you now, but I say these things while I am still in the
world, so that they may have the full measure of my joy within them. [14]I
have given them your word and the world has hated them, for they are not
of the world any more than I am of the world. [15]My prayer is not that you
take them out of the world but that you protect them from the evil one.
[16]They are not of the world, even as I am not of it. [17]Sanctify them by[c] the
truth; your word is truth. [18]As you sent me into the world, I have sent them
into the world. [19]For them I sanctify myself, that they too may be truly
sanctified.

Jesus Prays for All Believers

[20]"My prayer is not for them alone. I pray also for those who will believe
in me through their message, [21]that all of them may be one, Father, just as
you are in me and I am in you. May they also be in us so that the world may
believe that you have sent me. [22]I have given them the glory that you gave
me, that they may be one as we are one — [23]I in them and you in me — so
that they may be brought to complete unity. Then the world will know that
you sent me and have loved them even as you have loved me.

[24]"Father, I want those you have given me to be with me where I am, and
to see my glory, the glory you have given me because you loved me before
the creation of the world.

[25]"Righteous Father, though the world does not know you, I know you,
and they know that you have sent me. [26]I have made you[d] known to them,
and will continue to make you known in order that the love you have for me
may be in them and that I myself may be in them."

Jesus Arrested

18 When he had finished praying, Jesus left with his disciples and crossed
the Kidron Valley. On the other side there was a garden, and he and his
disciples went into it.

[2]Now Judas, who betrayed him, knew the place, because Jesus had often met
there with his disciples. [3]So Judas came to the garden, guiding a detachment of
soldiers and some officials from the chief priests and the Pharisees. They were
carrying torches, lanterns and weapons.

[4]Jesus, knowing all that was going to happen to him, went out and asked
them, "Who is it you want?"

[5]"Jesus of Nazareth," they replied.

"I am he," Jesus said. (And Judas the traitor was standing there with them.)
[6]When Jesus said, "I am he," they drew back and fell to the ground.

[7]Again he asked them, "Who is it you want?"

"Jesus of Nazareth," they said.

[8]Jesus answered, "I told you that I am he. If you are looking for me, then let
these men go." [9]This happened so that the words he had spoken would be fulfilled: "I have not lost one of those you gave me."[e]

---

[a] *11* Or *Father, keep them faithful to* [b] *12* Or *kept them faithful to* [c] *17* Or *them to live in accordance with* [d] *26* Greek *your name* [e] *9* John 6:39

[10]Then Simon Peter, who had a sword, drew it and struck the high priest's servant, cutting off his right ear. (The servant's name was Malchus.)

[11]Jesus commanded Peter, "Put your sword away! Shall I not drink the cup the Father has given me?"

[12]Then the detachment of soldiers with its commander and the Jewish officials arrested Jesus. They bound him [13]and brought him first to Annas, who was the father-in-law of Caiaphas, the high priest that year. [14]Caiaphas was the one who had advised the Jewish leaders that it would be good if one man died for the people.

Peter's First Denial

[15]Simon Peter and another disciple were following Jesus. Because this disciple was known to the high priest, he went with Jesus into the high priest's courtyard, [16]but Peter had to wait outside at the door. The other disciple, who was known to the high priest, came back, spoke to the servant girl on duty there and brought Peter in.

[17]"You aren't one of this man's disciples too, are you?" she asked Peter.

He replied, "I am not."

[18]It was cold, and the servants and officials stood around a fire they had made to keep warm. Peter also was standing with them, warming himself.

The High Priest Questions Jesus

[19]Meanwhile, the high priest questioned Jesus about his disciples and his teaching.

[20]"I have spoken openly to the world," Jesus replied. "I always taught in synagogues or at the temple, where all the Jews come together. I said nothing in secret. [21]Why question me? Ask those who heard me. Surely they know what I said."

[22]When Jesus said this, one of the officials nearby slapped him in the face. "Is this the way you answer the high priest?" he demanded.

[23]"If I said something wrong," Jesus replied, "testify as to what is wrong. But if I spoke the truth, why did you strike me?" [24]Then Annas sent him bound to Caiaphas the high priest.

Peter's Second and Third Denials

[25]Meanwhile, Simon Peter was still standing there warming himself. So they asked him, "You aren't one of his disciples too, are you?"

He denied it, saying, "I am not."

[26]One of the high priest's servants, a relative of the man whose ear Peter had cut off, challenged him, "Didn't I see you with him in the garden?" [27]Again Peter denied it, and at that moment a rooster began to crow.

Jesus Before Pilate

[28]Then the Jewish leaders took Jesus from Caiaphas to the palace of the Roman governor. By now it was early morning, and to avoid ceremonial uncleanness they did not enter the palace, because they wanted to be able to eat the Passover. [29]So Pilate came out to them and asked, "What charges are you bringing against this man?"

[30]"If he were not a criminal," they replied, "we would not have handed him over to you."

[31]Pilate said, "Take him yourselves and judge him by your own law."

"But we have no right to execute anyone," they objected. [32]This took place to fulfill what Jesus had said about the kind of death he was going to die.

[33]Pilate then went back inside the palace, summoned Jesus and asked him, "Are you the king of the Jews?"

[34]"Is that your own idea," Jesus asked, "or did others talk to you about me?"

[35]"Am I a Jew?" Pilate replied. "Your own people and chief priests handed you over to me. What is it you have done?"

36 Jesus said, "My kingdom is not of this world. If it were, my servants would fight to prevent my arrest by the Jewish leaders. But now my kingdom is from another place."

37 "You are a king, then!" said Pilate.

Jesus answered, "You say that I am a king. In fact, the reason I was born and came into the world is to testify to the truth. Everyone on the side of truth listens to me."

38 "What is truth?" retorted Pilate. With this he went out again to the Jews gathered there and said, "I find no basis for a charge against him. 39 But it is your custom for me to release to you one prisoner at the time of the Passover. Do you want me to release 'the king of the Jews'?"

40 They shouted back, "No, not him! Give us Barabbas!" Now Barabbas had taken part in an uprising.

Jesus Sentenced to Be Crucified

19 Then Pilate took Jesus and had him flogged. 2 The soldiers twisted together a crown of thorns and put it on his head. They clothed him in a purple robe 3 and went up to him again and again, saying, "Hail, king of the Jews!" And they slapped him in the face.

4 Once more Pilate came out and said to the Jews gathered there, "Look, I am bringing him out to you to let you know that I find no basis for a charge against him." 5 When Jesus came out wearing the crown of thorns and the purple robe, Pilate said to them, "Here is the man!"

6 As soon as the chief priests and their officials saw him, they shouted, "Crucify! Crucify!"

But Pilate answered, "You take him and crucify him. As for me, I find no basis for a charge against him."

7 The Jewish leaders insisted, "We have a law, and according to that law he must die, because he claimed to be the Son of God."

8 When Pilate heard this, he was even more afraid, 9 and he went back inside the palace. "Where do you come from?" he asked Jesus, but Jesus gave him no answer. 10 "Do you refuse to speak to me?" Pilate said. "Don't you realize I have power either to free you or to crucify you?"

11 Jesus answered, "You would have no power over me if it were not given to you from above. Therefore the one who handed me over to you is guilty of a greater sin."

12 From then on, Pilate tried to set Jesus free, but the Jewish leaders kept shouting, "If you let this man go, you are no friend of Caesar. Anyone who claims to be a king opposes Caesar."

13 When Pilate heard this, he brought Jesus out and sat down on the judge's seat at a place known as the Stone Pavement (which in Aramaic is Gabbatha). 14 It was the day of Preparation of the Passover; it was about noon.

"Here is your king," Pilate said to the Jews.

15 But they shouted, "Take him away! Take him away! Crucify him!"

"Shall I crucify your king?" Pilate asked.

"We have no king but Caesar," the chief priests answered.

16 Finally Pilate handed him over to them to be crucified.

The Crucifixion of Jesus

So the soldiers took charge of Jesus. 17 Carrying his own cross, he went out to the place of the Skull (which in Aramaic is called Golgotha). 18 There they crucified him, and with him two others — one on each side and Jesus in the middle.

19 Pilate had a notice prepared and fastened to the cross. It read: JESUS OF NAZARETH, THE KING OF THE JEWS. 20 Many of the Jews read this sign, for the place where Jesus was crucified was near the city, and the sign was written in Aramaic, Latin and Greek. 21 The chief priests of the Jews protested to Pilate, "Do not write 'The King of the Jews,' but that this man claimed to be king of the Jews."

22Pilate answered, "What I have written, I have written."

23When the soldiers crucified Jesus, they took his clothes, dividing them into four shares, one for each of them, with the undergarment remaining. This garment was seamless, woven in one piece from top to bottom.

24"Let's not tear it," they said to one another. "Let's decide by lot who will get it."

This happened that the scripture might be fulfilled that said,

"They divided my clothes among them
and cast lots for my garment."[a]

So this is what the soldiers did.

25Near the cross of Jesus stood his mother, his mother's sister, Mary the wife of Clopas, and Mary Magdalene. 26When Jesus saw his mother there, and the disciple whom he loved standing nearby, he said to her, "Woman,[b] here is your son," 27and to the disciple, "Here is your mother." From that time on, this disciple took her into his home.

The Death of Jesus

28Later, knowing that everything had now been finished, and so that Scripture would be fulfilled, Jesus said, "I am thirsty." 29A jar of wine vinegar was there, so they soaked a sponge in it, put the sponge on a stalk of the hyssop plant, and lifted it to Jesus' lips. 30When he had received the drink, Jesus said, "It is finished." With that, he bowed his head and gave up his spirit.

31Now it was the day of Preparation, and the next day was to be a special Sabbath. Because the Jewish leaders did not want the bodies left on the crosses during the Sabbath, they asked Pilate to have the legs broken and the bodies taken down. 32The soldiers therefore came and broke the legs of the first man who had been crucified with Jesus, and then those of the other. 33But when they came to Jesus and found that he was already dead, they did not break his legs. 34Instead, one of the soldiers pierced Jesus' side with a spear, bringing a sudden flow of blood and water. 35The man who saw it has given testimony, and his testimony is true. He knows that he tells the truth, and he testifies so that you also may believe. 36These things happened so that the scripture would be fulfilled: "Not one of his bones will be broken,"[c] 37and, as another scripture says, "They will look on the one they have pierced."[d]

The Burial of Jesus

38Later, Joseph of Arimathea asked Pilate for the body of Jesus. Now Joseph was a disciple of Jesus, but secretly because he feared the Jewish leaders. With Pilate's permission, he came and took the body away. 39He was accompanied by Nicodemus, the man who earlier had visited Jesus at night. Nicodemus brought a mixture of myrrh and aloes, about seventy-five pounds.[e] 40Taking Jesus' body, the two of them wrapped it, with the spices, in strips of linen. This was in accordance with Jewish burial customs. 41At the place where Jesus was crucified, there was a garden, and in the garden a new tomb, in which no one had ever been laid. 42Because it was the Jewish day of Preparation and since the tomb was nearby, they laid Jesus there.

The Empty Tomb

20 Early on the first day of the week, while it was still dark, Mary Magdalene went to the tomb and saw that the stone had been removed from the entrance. 2So she came running to Simon Peter and the other disciple, the one Jesus loved, and said, "They have taken the Lord out of the tomb, and we don't know where they have put him!"

[a] *24* Psalm 22:18 [b] *26* The Greek for *Woman* does not denote any disrespect.
[c] *36* Exodus 12:46; Num. 9:12; Psalm 34:20 [d] *37* Zech. 12:10 [e] *39* Or about 34 kilograms

JOHN 19:30

IT IS FINISHED

"It is finished"—a simple sentence, made of only three simple words, but the significance of this sentence has eternal consequences for billions of people. When Jesus declared, "It is finished," he indicated that his work of salvation was finished; that he had paid the full price for our sins. The cross is about so much more than a man enduring pain and suffering; it is about so much more than a man being abandoned by his friends and family. The cross is about Jesus, the eternal Son of God, being forsaken by his Father. Jesus, who had forever been one with the Father, was willing to come to earth and identify with sinners like us. He was even willing to become our sin (2Co 5:21), so that on the cross he could die in our place. On the cross, the hellish punishment that we deserved was placed on him; he willingly endured God's wrath in order to set us free.

The prophet Isaiah says of him, "You who have drunk from the hand of the LORD the cup of his wrath, you who have drained to its dregs the goblet that makes people stagger" (Isa 51:17)—this is what Jesus did on the cross for everyone who believes in him. Our sins have been paid for, and the work of redemption is, gloriously, "finished"!

3So Peter and the other disciple started for the tomb. 4Both were running, but the other disciple outran Peter and reached the tomb first. 5He bent over and looked in at the strips of linen lying there but did not go in. 6Then Simon Peter came along behind him and went straight into the tomb. He saw the strips of linen lying there, 7as well as the cloth that had been wrapped around Jesus' head. The cloth was still lying in its place, separate from the linen. 8Finally the other disciple, who had reached the tomb first, also went inside. He saw and believed. 9(They still did not understand from Scripture that Jesus had to rise from the dead.) 10Then the disciples went back to where they were staying.

Jesus Appears to Mary Magdalene

11Now Mary stood outside the tomb crying. As she wept, she bent over to look into the tomb 12and saw two angels in white, seated where Jesus' body had been, one at the head and the other at the foot.

13They asked her, "Woman, why are you crying?"

"They have taken my Lord away," she said, "and I don't know where they have put him." 14At this, she turned around and saw Jesus standing there, but she did not realize that it was Jesus.

15He asked her, "Woman, why are you crying? Who is it you are looking for?"

Thinking he was the gardener, she said, "Sir, if you have carried him away, tell me where you have put him, and I will get him."

16Jesus said to her, "Mary."

She turned toward him and cried out in Aramaic, "Rabboni!" (which means "Teacher").

17Jesus said, "Do not hold on to me, for I have not yet ascended to the Father. Go instead to my brothers and tell them, 'I am ascending to my Father and your Father, to my God and your God.'"

18Mary Magdalene went to the disciples with the news: "I have seen the Lord!" And she told them that he had said these things to her.

Jesus Appears to His Disciples

19On the evening of that first day of the week, when the disciples were together, with the doors locked for fear of the Jewish leaders, Jesus came and stood among them and said, "Peace be with you!" 20After he said this, he showed them his hands and side. The disciples were overjoyed when they saw the Lord.

21Again Jesus said, "Peace be with you! As the Father has sent me, I am sending you." 22And with that he breathed on them and said, "Receive the Holy Spirit. 23If you forgive anyone's sins, their sins are forgiven; if you do not forgive them, they are not forgiven."

Jesus Appears to Thomas

24Now Thomas (also known as Didymus[a]), one of the Twelve, was not with the disciples when Jesus came. 25So the other disciples told him, "We have seen the Lord!"

But he said to them, "Unless I see the nail marks in his hands and put my finger where the nails were, and put my hand into his side, I will not believe."

26A week later his disciples were in the house again, and Thomas was with them. Though the doors were locked, Jesus came and stood among them and said, "Peace be with you!" 27Then he said to Thomas, "Put your finger here; see my hands. Reach out your hand and put it into my side. Stop doubting and believe."

28Thomas said to him, "My Lord and my God!"

29Then Jesus told him, "Because you have seen me, you have believed; blessed are those who have not seen and yet have believed."

---

[a] 24 *Thomas* (Aramaic) and *Didymus* (Greek) both mean *twin.*

THE POWER OF THE RESURRECTION

In many of the accounts of Jesus' resurrection, people who saw him had a difficult time recognizing him. Before he spoke her name (v. 16), Mary thought Jesus was the gardener (vv. 14 – 15); the disciples had difficulty recognizing Jesus on the shore (Jn 21:4); and the men on the road to Emmaus did not realize they were talking to Jesus (Lk 24:15 – 16). In these resurrection accounts, all of the people ultimately do recognize Jesus. Yet there is something different about him, some new quality that makes his appearance different than it was before his arrest and crucifixion. This is helpful for us as we seek to understand our own resurrection in Christ.

The ultimate hope of the believer is not heaven, but the new heavens and new earth, of which Jesus emphatically says, "I am making everything new!" (Rev 21:5). The essence of the word "new" in that phrase is not "different," or "new" in terms of time, but rather "new" in terms of quality. One day Jesus will make all things that do exist new or better, fuller, more complete; this is certainly resurrection language.

In other words, the ultimate hope of the believer is the resurrection — when God will do for us and for all creation what he did for Jesus on Easter. The resurrected Jesus was still the same Jesus who had lived for more than thirty-three years and worked among the disciples for more than three years, but he was changed; he was "new," he was more, he was resurrected.

Paul gives us an exciting glimpse of this coming reality (1Co 15:42 – 44;49 – 54). God's plans for his people in Christ are so good. The sure hope that believers have is that, one day, the whole creation will be made new, and all will be made right. God himself will dwell among his people, and he will wipe every tear from their eyes. More than that, there will be no more death or mourning or crying or pain (Rev 21:4).

In the new heavens and new earth, Jesus will reign fully and forever, and everything will be as it should be. There will be no sin and no possibility of sin, and believers will finally live the lives God had designed them to live from the beginning of time. So as believers think back to the glorious resurrection of Christ, it also becomes a reminder of the future resurrection in Christ.

The Purpose of John's Gospel

[30]Jesus performed many other signs in the presence of his disciples, which are not recorded in this book. [31]But these are written that you may believe[a] that Jesus is the Messiah, the Son of God, and that by believing you may have life in his name.

Jesus and the Miraculous Catch of Fish

21 Afterward Jesus appeared again to his disciples, by the Sea of Galilee.[b] It happened this way: [2]Simon Peter, Thomas (also known as Didymus[c]), Nathanael from Cana in Galilee, the sons of Zebedee, and two other disciples were together. [3]"I'm going out to fish," Simon Peter told them, and they said, "We'll go with you." So they went out and got into the boat, but that night they caught nothing.

[4]Early in the morning, Jesus stood on the shore, but the disciples did not realize that it was Jesus.

[5]He called out to them, "Friends, haven't you any fish?"

"No," they answered.

[6]He said, "Throw your net on the right side of the boat and you will find some." When they did, they were unable to haul the net in because of the large number of fish.

[7]Then the disciple whom Jesus loved said to Peter, "It is the Lord!" As soon as Simon Peter heard him say, "It is the Lord," he wrapped his outer garment around him (for he had taken it off) and jumped into the water. [8]The other disciples followed in the boat, towing the net full of fish, for they were not far from shore, about a hundred yards.[d] [9]When they landed, they saw a fire of burning coals there with fish on it, and some bread.

[10]Jesus said to them, "Bring some of the fish you have just caught." [11]So Simon Peter climbed back into the boat and dragged the net ashore. It was full of large fish, 153, but even with so many the net was not torn. [12]Jesus said to them, "Come and have breakfast." None of the disciples dared ask him, "Who are you?" They knew it was the Lord. [13]Jesus came, took the bread and gave it to them, and did the same with the fish. [14]This was now the third time Jesus appeared to his disciples after he was raised from the dead.

Jesus Reinstates Peter

[15]When they had finished eating, Jesus said to Simon Peter, "Simon son of John, do you love me more than these?"

"Yes, Lord," he said, "you know that I love you."

Jesus said, "Feed my lambs."

[16]Again Jesus said, "Simon son of John, do you love me?"

He answered, "Yes, Lord, you know that I love you."

Jesus said, "Take care of my sheep."

[17]The third time he said to him, "Simon son of John, do you love me?"

Peter was hurt because Jesus asked him the third time, "Do you love me?" He said, "Lord, you know all things; you know that I love you."

Jesus said, "Feed my sheep. [18]Very truly I tell you, when you were younger you dressed yourself and went where you wanted; but when you are old you will stretch out your hands, and someone else will dress you and lead you where you do not want to go." [19]Jesus said this to indicate the kind of death by which Peter would glorify God. Then he said to him, "Follow me!"

[20]Peter turned and saw that the disciple whom Jesus loved was following them. (This was the one who had leaned back against Jesus at the supper and had said, "Lord, who is going to betray you?") [21]When Peter saw him, he asked, "Lord, what about him?"

JOHN 21:15–19

TRUE LOVE

Even though the disciples had seen the resurrected Jesus, they did not really know what they were supposed to do next. For three years they had been following Jesus and carrying out his ministry, but now Jesus was not with them on a regular basis. That being the case, it only made sense for the disciples to return to what they knew: fishing.

Peter, in particular, had not seen Jesus for more than a few moments since he had denied knowing him three times in Jesus' hour of greatest need (Mt 26:69–75; Lk 22:54–62; Jn 18:15–27). Usually when a person knows that they have hurt someone, or done something to wrong someone, they are not eager to see that person. Yet Peter was so confident in Jesus' love and forgiveness that as soon as he realized it was Jesus standing on the shore, he jumped from the boat and swam to shore so that he could be face to face with his Lord. There Jesus lovingly and gently reinstated his bold disciple and went on to use him greatly for the sake of his kingdom. This story reminds all believers that those who repent of the pain they have caused Jesus and others in the past can have full confidence that his arms of grace are open to all who are willing to run into them.

[a] *31* Or *may continue to believe* [b] *1* Greek *Tiberias* [c] *2* *Thomas* (Aramaic) and *Didymus* (Greek) both mean *twin.* [d] *8* Or about 90 meters

[22]Jesus answered, "If I want him to remain alive until I return, what is that to
you? You must follow me." [23]Because of this, the rumor spread among the believers that this disciple would not die. But Jesus did not say that he would not die;
he only said, "If I want him to remain alive until I return, what is that to you?"

[24]This is the disciple who testifies to these things and who wrote them down.
We know that his testimony is true.

[25]Jesus did many other things as well. If every one of them were written down,
I suppose that even the whole world would not have room for the books that
would be written.

JESUS: OUR CONTINUED MISSION

ACTS

ACTS

PENTECOST *c. AD 30 – 35*	PAUL'S MISSIONARY JOURNEYS *c. AD 47 – 57*	PAUL IMPRISONED IN ROME *c. AD 60 – 62*

The news of Jesus cannot be stopped. Beginning with a fledgling band of disciples, the transforming message of hope offered by Jesus would spread from Jerusalem to Rome in less than 35 years. The leaders of Jesus' day assumed his death would forever stamp out his claims. In God-sized irony, Jesus' death only fueled the spread of this message because he did not remain dead but defeated death through his glorious resurrection.

The resurrected Christ forever changed those who witnessed these events. They trusted that he would send them his Spirit to empower them for the mission that lay ahead (2:1 – 4). At Pentecost, the Spirit came in might and power and established the church that will prevail over the gates of Hades for all time (Mt 16:18). Peter's sermon following the sending of the Spirit made it clear that this miracle was the fulfillment of God's promises and further validated the claims of Jesus to be God's Messiah and the Savior of the world.

Luke provides Theophilus and all subsequent readers with a glimpse into the culture of this young church. Those who trusted Jesus gathered together in teaching, singing, prayer, fellowship and shared meals. By the power of God, many placed their faith in Christ and were added to the church (Ac 2:42 – 47).

The church would never permanently escape the fires of persecution, but through this opposition the church would continue to spread. The stoning of Stephen in Acts 8 scattered believers throughout the known world, and with them went God's Spirit and the message of the gospel. These displaced believers established churches and invited the inhabitants of new cities to place their faith in Christ.

A primary catalyst for the spread of the gospel was the conversion of Saul, a vehement persecutor of the church (9:1 – 22). God revealed himself in a blinding flash of light and altered Saul's fate forever. Saul began to be called Paul (Ac 13:9). Paul's subsequent mission work focused on the Gentiles and is central to the later portion of Luke's writing in the book of Acts. Luke describes Paul's three chief missionary journeys, his labor among the churches and the countless obstacles he faced in his mission. Through it all, however, God continued to show himself faithful to his promise to build his church and use his people in that grand mission.

BUT YOU WILL RECEIVE POWER WHEN
THE HOLY SPIRIT COMES ON YOU;
AND YOU WILL BE MY WITNESSES IN JERUSALEM,
AND IN ALL JUDEA AND SAMARIA,
AND TO THE ENDS OF THE EARTH.

Acts 1:8

ACTS

ACTS 1:5–8

EMPOWERED BY THE SPIRIT

Central to the book of Acts is the role the Holy Spirit plays in advancing the church. Prior to beginning their earthly mission, Jesus instructed his followers to wait until he sent his Spirit, who would supply the power behind the task that lay ahead. This mission would necessitate such power. It was massive — this small group of disciples were instructed to take the good news of Jesus to the very ends of the earth. One wonders what thoughts played in the minds of these first followers of Jesus. Were they afraid? Certainly. Did they understand all that was ahead? Certainly not. Yet they trusted God. Verse 8 serves as an outline of the book of Acts, as Luke describes the faith-filled mission of this group to spread the gospel in Jerusalem, then Judea and Samaria, and then to the ends of the known world of that day. The very same Spirit that empowered the disciples for this great mission is the Spirit who indwells all followers of Jesus (Lk 11:13; Gal 3:14; Eph 1:13 – 14). He propels ordinary disciples to do extraordinary things through the power only God can supply.

Jesus Taken Up Into Heaven

1 In my former book, Theophilus, I wrote about all that Jesus began to do and to teach 2until the day he was taken up to heaven, after giving instructions through the Holy Spirit to the apostles he had chosen. 3After his suffering, he presented himself to them and gave many convincing proofs that he was alive. He appeared to them over a period of forty days and spoke about the kingdom of God. 4On one occasion, while he was eating with them, he gave them this command: "Do not leave Jerusalem, but wait for the gift my Father promised, which you have heard me speak about. 5For John baptized with[a] water, but in a few days you will be baptized with[a] the Holy Spirit."

6Then they gathered around him and asked him, "Lord, are you at this time going to restore the kingdom to Israel?"

7He said to them: "It is not for you to know the times or dates the Father has set by his own authority. 8But you will receive power when the Holy Spirit comes on you; and you will be my witnesses in Jerusalem, and in all Judea and Samaria, and to the ends of the earth."

9After he said this, he was taken up before their very eyes, and a cloud hid him from their sight.

10They were looking intently up into the sky as he was going, when suddenly two men dressed in white stood beside them. 11"Men of Galilee," they said, "why do you stand here looking into the sky? This same Jesus, who has been taken from you into heaven, will come back in the same way you have seen him go into heaven."

Matthias Chosen to Replace Judas

12Then the apostles returned to Jerusalem from the hill called the Mount of Olives, a Sabbath day's walk[b] from the city. 13When they arrived, they went upstairs to the room where they were staying. Those present were Peter, John, James and Andrew; Philip and Thomas, Bartholomew and Matthew; James son of Alphaeus and Simon the Zealot, and Judas son of James. 14They all joined together constantly in prayer, along with the women and Mary the mother of Jesus, and with his brothers.

15In those days Peter stood up among the believers (a group numbering about a hundred and twenty) 16and said, "Brothers and sisters,[c] the Scripture had to be fulfilled in which the Holy Spirit spoke long ago through David concerning Judas, who served as guide for those who arrested Jesus. 17He was one of our number and shared in our ministry."

18(With the payment he received for his wickedness, Judas bought a field; there he fell headlong, his body burst open and all his intestines spilled out. 19Everyone in Jerusalem heard about this, so they called that field in their language Akeldama, that is, Field of Blood.)

20"For," said Peter, "it is written in the Book of Psalms:

"'May his place be deserted;
let there be no one to dwell in it,'[d]

and,

"'May another take his place of leadership.'[e]

---

[a] *5* Or *in* [b] *12* That is, about 5/8 mile or about 1 kilometer [c] *16* The Greek word for *brothers and sisters* (*adelphoi*) refers here to believers, both men and women, as part of God's family; also in 6:3; 11:29; 12:17; 16:40; 18:18, 27; 21:7, 17; 28:14, 15. [d] *20* Psalm 69:25 [e] *20* Psalm 109:8

[21]Therefore it is necessary to choose one of the men who have been with us the
whole time the Lord Jesus was living among us, [22]beginning from John's baptism
to the time when Jesus was taken up from us. For one of these must become a
witness with us of his resurrection."

[23]So they nominated two men: Joseph called Barsabbas (also known as Justus) and Matthias. [24]Then they prayed, "Lord, you know everyone's heart. Show
us which of these two you have chosen [25]to take over this apostolic ministry,
which Judas left to go where he belongs." [26]Then they cast lots, and the lot fell to
Matthias; so he was added to the eleven apostles.

The Holy Spirit Comes at Pentecost

2 When the day of Pentecost came, they were all together in one place. [2]Sud-
denly a sound like the blowing of a violent wind came from heaven and filled
the whole house where they were sitting. [3]They saw what seemed to be tongues
of fire that separated and came to rest on each of them. [4]All of them were filled
with the Holy Spirit and began to speak in other tongues[a] as the Spirit enabled
them.

[5]Now there were staying in Jerusalem God-fearing Jews from every nation
under heaven. [6]When they heard this sound, a crowd came together in bewil-
derment, because each one heard their own language being spoken. [7]Utterly
amazed, they asked: "Aren't all these who are speaking Galileans? [8]Then how
is it that each of us hears them in our native language? [9]Parthians, Medes and
Elamites; residents of Mesopotamia, Judea and Cappadocia, Pontus and Asia,[b]
[10]Phrygia and Pamphylia, Egypt and the parts of Libya near Cyrene; visitors
from Rome [11](both Jews and converts to Judaism); Cretans and Arabs—we hear
them declaring the wonders of God in our own tongues!" [12]Amazed and perplexed, they asked one another, "What does this mean?"

[13]Some, however, made fun of them and said, "They have had too much wine."

Peter Addresses the Crowd

[14]Then Peter stood up with the Eleven, raised his voice and addressed the
crowd: "Fellow Jews and all of you who live in Jerusalem, let me explain this to
you; listen carefully to what I say. [15]These people are not drunk, as you suppose.
It's only nine in the morning! [16]No, this is what was spoken by the prophet Joel:

[17]" 'In the last days, God says,
I will pour out my Spirit on all people.
Your sons and daughters will prophesy,
your young men will see visions,
your old men will dream dreams.
[18]Even on my servants, both men and women,
I will pour out my Spirit in those days,
and they will prophesy.
[19]I will show wonders in the heavens above
and signs on the earth below,
blood and fire and billows of smoke.
[20]The sun will be turned to darkness
and the moon to blood
before the coming of the great and glorious day of the Lord.
[21]And everyone who calls
on the name of the Lord will be saved.'[c]

[22]"Fellow Israelites, listen to this: Jesus of Nazareth was a man accredited by
God to you by miracles, wonders and signs, which God did among you through
him, as you yourselves know. [23]This man was handed over to you by God's deliberate plan and foreknowledge; and you, with the help of wicked men,[d] put him

[a] *4* Or *languages*; also in verse 11 [b] *9* That is, the Roman province by that name
[c] *21* Joel 2:28-32 [d] *23* Or *of those not having the law* (that is, Gentiles)

ACTS 2:14–21

THE SPIRIT AND THE OLD TESTAMENT

Peter quoted the prophet Joel to explain the supernatural phenomenon of Pentecost. Joel predicted that an outpouring of God's Spirit would come on the young and the old, on men and women alike, as a sign of God's commitment to deliver those "who [call] on the name of the LORD" (Joel 2:32). Joel explained that those who oppressed God's people and those who refused to repent would be judged, yet the opportunity to be saved was—and still is—clearly offered. Given the context of Joel's proclamation then, it seems that the author (Luke) also uses this passage to underscore the assuring message of salvation for those who believe. In sum, Peter's speech makes clear the idea that Jesus is the long-awaited Messiah who fulfills the prophecies of old, who issues the anticipated outpouring of God's Spirit on his people and who offers salvation from judgment to any and all who will repent and follow Christ.

to death by nailing him to the cross. [24]But God raised him from the dead, freeing
him from the agony of death, because it was impossible for death to keep its hold
on him. [25]David said about him:

"'I saw the Lord always before me.
Because he is at my right hand,
I will not be shaken.
[26]Therefore my heart is glad and my tongue rejoices;
my body also will rest in hope,
[27]because you will not abandon me to the realm of the dead,
you will not let your holy one see decay.
[28]You have made known to me the paths of life;
you will fill me with joy in your presence.'[a]

[29]"Fellow Israelites, I can tell you confidently that the patriarch David died
and was buried, and his tomb is here to this day. [30]But he was a prophet and knew
that God had promised him on oath that he would place one of his descendants
on his throne. [31]Seeing what was to come, he spoke of the resurrection of the
Messiah, that he was not abandoned to the realm of the dead, nor did his body
see decay. [32]God has raised this Jesus to life, and we are all witnesses of it. [33]Ex-
alted to the right hand of God, he has received from the Father the promised
Holy Spirit and has poured out what you now see and hear. [34]For David did not
ascend to heaven, and yet he said,

"'The Lord said to my Lord:
"Sit at my right hand
[35]until I make your enemies
a footstool for your feet."'[b]

[36]"Therefore let all Israel be assured of this: God has made this Jesus, whom
you crucified, both Lord and Messiah."

[37]When the people heard this, they were cut to the heart and said to Peter and
the other apostles, "Brothers, what shall we do?"

[38]Peter replied, "Repent and be baptized, every one of you, in the name of
Jesus Christ for the forgiveness of your sins. And you will receive the gift of the
Holy Spirit. [39]The promise is for you and your children and for all who are far
off—for all whom the Lord our God will call."

[40]With many other words he warned them; and he pleaded with them, "Save
yourselves from this corrupt generation." [41]Those who accepted his message
were baptized, and about three thousand were added to their number that day.

The Fellowship of the Believers

[42]They devoted themselves to the apostles' teaching and to fellowship, to
the breaking of bread and to prayer. [43]Everyone was filled with awe at the many
wonders and signs performed by the apostles. [44]All the believers were together
and had everything in common. [45]They sold property and possessions to give to
anyone who had need. [46]Every day they continued to meet together in the temple
courts. They broke bread in their homes and ate together with glad and sincere
hearts, [47]praising God and enjoying the favor of all the people. And the Lord
added to their number daily those who were being saved.

Peter Heals a Lame Beggar

3 One day Peter and John were going up to the temple at the time of prayer—at
three in the afternoon. [2]Now a man who was lame from birth was being carried to the temple gate called Beautiful, where he was put every day to beg from
those going into the temple courts. [3]When he saw Peter and John about to enter,
he asked them for money. [4]Peter looked straight at him, as did John. Then Peter

[a] *28* Psalm 16:8-11 (see Septuagint) [b] *35* Psalm 110:1

ACTS 3:1–26

BEARING WITNESS TO JESUS

In Acts 3, Luke focuses on the importance of Jesus' name by documenting the disciples' empowerment to heal people "in the name of Jesus Christ of Nazareth" (3:6). This theme is seen throughout the book as the disciples continue to perform miracles and baptize in Jesus' name, as well as witnessing to and suffering "disgrace for the Name" (e.g., 5:41; 9:16; 10:48; 21:13). Not only is their power to do these things directly sourced from Jesus himself, but also their *purpose* is, unquestionably, to proclaim Jesus' name. The core of discipleship is always centered on the person of Christ, nothing else. The mission is always to know Jesus and to make him known. Jesus' disciples give, serve, heal, witness, are empowered, and live for Jesus—not for their own glory, but to bring glory and honor to his name above all others (Ac 4:12; Php 2:9–11; Rev 15:4).

said, "Look at us!" 5So the man gave them his attention, expecting to get something from them.
6Then Peter said, "Silver or gold I do not have, but what I do have I give you.
In the name of Jesus Christ of Nazareth, walk." 7Taking him by the right hand,
he helped him up, and instantly the man's feet and ankles became strong. 8He
jumped to his feet and began to walk. Then he went with them into the temple
courts, walking and jumping, and praising God. 9When all the people saw him
walking and praising God, 10they recognized him as the same man who used to
sit begging at the temple gate called Beautiful, and they were filled with wonder
and amazement at what had happened to him.

Peter Speaks to the Onlookers

11While the man held on to Peter and John, all the people were astonished and
came running to them in the place called Solomon's Colonnade. 12When Peter
saw this, he said to them: "Fellow Israelites, why does this surprise you? Why do
you stare at us as if by our own power or godliness we had made this man walk?
13The God of Abraham, Isaac and Jacob, the God of our fathers, has glorified his
servant Jesus. You handed him over to be killed, and you disowned him before
Pilate, though he had decided to let him go. 14You disowned the Holy and Righteous One and asked that a murderer be released to you. 15You killed the author
of life, but God raised him from the dead. We are witnesses of this. 16By faith in
the name of Jesus, this man whom you see and know was made strong. It is Jesus'
name and the faith that comes through him that has completely healed him, as
you can all see.

17"Now, fellow Israelites, I know that you acted in ignorance, as did your leaders. 18But this is how God fulfilled what he had foretold through all the prophets,
saying that his Messiah would suffer. 19Repent, then, and turn to God, so that
your sins may be wiped out, that times of refreshing may come from the Lord,
20and that he may send the Messiah, who has been appointed for you — even
Jesus. 21Heaven must receive him until the time comes for God to restore everything, as he promised long ago through his holy prophets. 22For Moses said,
'The Lord your God will raise up for you a prophet like me from among your own
people; you must listen to everything he tells you. 23Anyone who does not listen
to him will be completely cut off from their people.'[a]

24"Indeed, beginning with Samuel, all the prophets who have spoken have
foretold these days. 25And you are heirs of the prophets and of the covenant God
made with your fathers. He said to Abraham, 'Through your offspring all peoples
on earth will be blessed.'[b] 26When God raised up his servant, he sent him first to
you to bless you by turning each of you from your wicked ways."

Peter and John Before the Sanhedrin

4 The priests and the captain of the temple guard and the Sadducees came up
to Peter and John while they were speaking to the people. 2They were greatly
disturbed because the apostles were teaching the people, proclaiming in Jesus
the resurrection of the dead. 3They seized Peter and John and, because it was
evening, they put them in jail until the next day. 4But many who heard the message believed; so the number of men who believed grew to about five thousand.
5The next day the rulers, the elders and the teachers of the law met in Jerusalem. 6Annas the high priest was there, and so were Caiaphas, John, Alexander
and others of the high priest's family. 7They had Peter and John brought before
them and began to question them: "By what power or what name did you do
this?"
8Then Peter, filled with the Holy Spirit, said to them: "Rulers and elders of the
people! 9If we are being called to account today for an act of kindness shown to
a man who was lame and are being asked how he was healed, 10then know this,

[a] *23* Deut. 18:15,18,19 [b] *25* Gen. 22:18; 26:4

you and all the people of Israel: It is by the name of Jesus Christ of Nazareth,
whom you crucified but whom God raised from the dead, that this man stands
before you healed. 11Jesus is

> " 'the stone you builders rejected,
> which has become the cornerstone.'[a]

12Salvation is found in no one else, for there is no other name under heaven given
to mankind by which we must be saved."
13When they saw the courage of Peter and John and realized that they were
unschooled, ordinary men, they were astonished and they took note that these
men had been with Jesus. 14But since they could see the man who had been
healed standing there with them, there was nothing they could say. 15So they
ordered them to withdraw from the Sanhedrin and then conferred together.
16"What are we going to do with these men?" they asked. "Everyone living in Jerusalem knows they have performed a notable sign, and we cannot deny it. 17But
to stop this thing from spreading any further among the people, we must warn
them to speak no longer to anyone in this name."
18Then they called them in again and commanded them not to speak or teach
at all in the name of Jesus. 19But Peter and John replied, "Which is right in God's
eyes: to listen to you, or to him? You be the judges! 20As for us, we cannot help
speaking about what we have seen and heard."
21After further threats they let them go. They could not decide how to punish
them, because all the people were praising God for what had happened. 22For
the man who was miraculously healed was over forty years old.

The Believers Pray

23On their release, Peter and John went back to their own people and reported
all that the chief priests and the elders had said to them. 24When they heard this,
they raised their voices together in prayer to God. "Sovereign Lord," they said,
"you made the heavens and the earth and the sea, and everything in them. 25You
spoke by the Holy Spirit through the mouth of your servant, our father David:

> " 'Why do the nations rage
> and the peoples plot in vain?
> 26The kings of the earth rise up
> and the rulers band together
> against the Lord
> and against his anointed one.'[b,c]

27Indeed Herod and Pontius Pilate met together with the Gentiles and the people of Israel in this city to conspire against your holy servant Jesus, whom you
anointed. 28They did what your power and will had decided beforehand should
happen. 29Now, Lord, consider their threats and enable your servants to speak
your word with great boldness. 30Stretch out your hand to heal and perform signs
and wonders through the name of your holy servant Jesus."
31After they prayed, the place where they were meeting was shaken. And they
were all filled with the Holy Spirit and spoke the word of God boldly.

The Believers Share Their Possessions

32All the believers were one in heart and mind. No one claimed that any of
their possessions was their own, but they shared everything they had. 33With
great power the apostles continued to testify to the resurrection of the Lord
Jesus. And God's grace was so powerfully at work in them all 34that there were
no needy persons among them. For from time to time those who owned land or
houses sold them, brought the money from the sales 35and put it at the apostles'
feet, and it was distributed to anyone who had need.

ACTS 4:32

UNITY

It is difficult to overstate the importance of unity among believers. Unity was one of the most obvious characteristics of the early church (Ac 2:42), and at least in part led to the remarkably effective spread of the gospel. And, as this verse indicates, unity played an important role in providing holistic provision for all the believers' needs. Jesus himself emphasized the importance of unity when he said, "By this everyone will know that you are my disciples, if you love one another" (Jn 13:35).

Still today believers must consistently and intentionally prioritize unity. It is the most obvious means to meet each other's needs (spiritually, economically and socially), to demonstrate God's love to an unbelieving world and to facilitate harmony and peace. Psalm 133:1 says it best: "How good and pleasant it is when God's people live together in unity!"

---

[a] *11* Psalm 118:22 [b] *26* That is, Messiah or Christ [c] *26* Psalm 2:1,2

SALVATION IN NO ONE ELSE

God created the world to display his glory to all creation. The Garden of Eden was the first temple of God, where God showed his glory and lived with his people. The first humans, Adam and Eve, rebelled against God, even after he gave them directives about what would harm them. They chose to doubt God's goodness, failed to trust him and acted against God in disobedience, but God showed his glory by being patient with them. He provided consequences for their sin, but he promised deliverance as well. Immediately after their punishment was enacted, God promised to send a Savior to fix the relationship between himself and his people (Ge 3:15). He would have been justified in letting his creation degrade in its sin and collapse into confusion. And yet, he showed his glory in being patient with his people.

As part of his eternal, perfect nature, God makes and keeps his promises. Time and time again throughout the Old Testament, God made promises to his people and delivered on those promises (Jos 21:45). Whenever God's people fell into trouble, God's heart was to bring them out, restore them and commission them to live as his people once again.

The great saving event of the Old Testament was the exodus. God's people were bound in physical slavery in Egypt, and God sent a deliverer named Moses to bring them out. Once they were set free, God himself, not some ill-defined deity that operated in obscurity, renewed the covenant promises he had made with Israel's ancestors Abram (Ge 15:1 – 20), Isaac (Ge 26:2 – 5) and Jacob (Ge 28:13 – 15) and gave them his law and taught them how to live.

God wants to show his glory in this world by saving sinners. The entire Bible, from cover to cover, tells the one story of God's desire to save sinners from their sin. God kept all of his promises by sending Jesus to die for sinners and then rise again from the dead. Jesus was the true and better Moses, the ultimate liberator who broke people out of the ultimate form of bondage — slavery to sin and death.

[36]Joseph, a Levite from Cyprus, whom the apostles called Barnabas (which means "son of encouragement"), [37]sold a field he owned and brought the money and put it at the apostles' feet.

Ananias and Sapphira

5 Now a man named Ananias, together with his wife Sapphira, also sold a piece of property. [2]With his wife's full knowledge he kept back part of the money for himself, but brought the rest and put it at the apostles' feet.

[3]Then Peter said, "Ananias, how is it that Satan has so filled your heart that you have lied to the Holy Spirit and have kept for yourself some of the money you received for the land? [4]Didn't it belong to you before it was sold? And after it was sold, wasn't the money at your disposal? What made you think of doing such a thing? You have not lied just to human beings but to God."

[5]When Ananias heard this, he fell down and died. And great fear seized all who heard what had happened. [6]Then some young men came forward, wrapped up his body, and carried him out and buried him.

[7]About three hours later his wife came in, not knowing what had happened. [8]Peter asked her, "Tell me, is this the price you and Ananias got for the land?"

"Yes," she said, "that is the price."

[9]Peter said to her, "How could you conspire to test the Spirit of the Lord? Listen! The feet of the men who buried your husband are at the door, and they will carry you out also."

[10]At that moment she fell down at his feet and died. Then the young men came in and, finding her dead, carried her out and buried her beside her husband. [11]Great fear seized the whole church and all who heard about these events.

The Apostles Heal Many

[12]The apostles performed many signs and wonders among the people. And all the believers used to meet together in Solomon's Colonnade. [13]No one else dared join them, even though they were highly regarded by the people. [14]Nevertheless, more and more men and women believed in the Lord and were added to their number. [15]As a result, people brought the sick into the streets and laid them on beds and mats so that at least Peter's shadow might fall on some of them as he passed by. [16]Crowds gathered also from the towns around Jerusalem, bringing their sick and those tormented by impure spirits, and all of them were healed.

The Apostles Persecuted

[17]Then the high priest and all his associates, who were members of the party of the Sadducees, were filled with jealousy. [18]They arrested the apostles and put them in the public jail. [19]But during the night an angel of the Lord opened the doors of the jail and brought them out. [20]"Go, stand in the temple courts," he said, "and tell the people all about this new life."

[21]At daybreak they entered the temple courts, as they had been told, and began to teach the people.

When the high priest and his associates arrived, they called together the Sanhedrin — the full assembly of the elders of Israel — and sent to the jail for the apostles. [22]But on arriving at the jail, the officers did not find them there. So they went back and reported, [23]"We found the jail securely locked, with the guards standing at the doors; but when we opened them, we found no one inside." [24]On hearing this report, the captain of the temple guard and the chief priests were at a loss, wondering what this might lead to.

[25]Then someone came and said, "Look! The men you put in jail are standing in the temple courts teaching the people." [26]At that, the captain went with his officers and brought the apostles. They did not use force, because they feared that the people would stone them.

[27]The apostles were brought in and made to appear before the Sanhedrin to be questioned by the high priest. [28]"We gave you strict orders not to teach in this

ACTS 5:1 – 11

GIVING OUR ALL TO JESUS

The sudden deaths of Ananias and Sapphira are jarring at first glance. After all, the couple voluntarily gave up part of their profits to the church, so what could possibly warrant their deaths? The problem was that they lied about their gift and withheld money for themselves, desiring the status of the large donation and the appearance of radical generosity in the eyes of the apostles and the other members of the church. Furthermore, Peter says that they allowed Satan to fill their hearts (5:3). They lied to the Holy Spirit (5:4), who had filled their community of believers. In the midst of the church's miraculous growth, remarkable unity and amazing gospel message, Ananias and Sapphira's deceitful plan stood as the antithesis of the church's faith-filled generosity and brotherly love.

The Good Shepherd refuses to tolerate wolves roaming freely among his sheep. In contrast, the preceding story of Barnabas (4:36 – 37) reveals the greater truth that authentic allegiance to Jesus is characterized by the kind of cheerful generosity that both honors God and cares for his people. May those who follow Jesus be so struck by his worth, so confident of his care and so committed to his ways that they likewise "seek first his kingdom and his righteousness" (Mt 6:33).

name," he said. "Yet you have filled Jerusalem with your teaching and are determined to make us guilty of this man's blood."
29Peter and the other apostles replied: "We must obey God rather than human
beings! 30The God of our ancestors raised Jesus from the dead — whom you killed
by hanging him on a cross. 31God exalted him to his own right hand as Prince
and Savior that he might bring Israel to repentance and forgive their sins. 32We
are witnesses of these things, and so is the Holy Spirit, whom God has given to
those who obey him."
33When they heard this, they were furious and wanted to put them to death.
34But a Pharisee named Gamaliel, a teacher of the law, who was honored by all
the people, stood up in the Sanhedrin and ordered that the men be put outside for
a little while. 35Then he addressed the Sanhedrin: "Men of Israel, consider carefully what you intend to do to these men. 36Some time ago Theudas appeared,
claiming to be somebody, and about four hundred men rallied to him. He was
killed, all his followers were dispersed, and it all came to nothing. 37After him,
Judas the Galilean appeared in the days of the census and led a band of people
in revolt. He too was killed, and all his followers were scattered. 38Therefore, in
the present case I advise you: Leave these men alone! Let them go! For if their
purpose or activity is of human origin, it will fail. 39But if it is from God, you will
not be able to stop these men; you will only find yourselves fighting against God."
40His speech persuaded them. They called the apostles in and had them
flogged. Then they ordered them not to speak in the name of Jesus, and let
them go.
41The apostles left the Sanhedrin, rejoicing because they had been counted
worthy of suffering disgrace for the Name. 42Day after day, in the temple courts
and from house to house, they never stopped teaching and proclaiming the good
news that Jesus is the Messiah.

The Choosing of the Seven

6 In those days when the number of disciples was increasing, the Hellenistic
Jews[a] among them complained against the Hebraic Jews because their widows were being overlooked in the daily distribution of food. 2So the Twelve gathered all the disciples together and said, "It would not be right for us to neglect
the ministry of the word of God in order to wait on tables. 3Brothers and sisters,
choose seven men from among you who are known to be full of the Spirit and
wisdom. We will turn this responsibility over to them 4and will give our attention to prayer and the ministry of the word."
5This proposal pleased the whole group. They chose Stephen, a man full of
faith and of the Holy Spirit; also Philip, Procorus, Nicanor, Timon, Parmenas,
and Nicolas from Antioch, a convert to Judaism. 6They presented these men to
the apostles, who prayed and laid their hands on them.
7So the word of God spread. The number of disciples in Jerusalem increased
rapidly, and a large number of priests became obedient to the faith.

Stephen Seized

8Now Stephen, a man full of God's grace and power, performed great wonders
and signs among the people. 9Opposition arose, however, from members of the
Synagogue of the Freedmen (as it was called) — Jews of Cyrene and Alexandria
as well as the provinces of Cilicia and Asia — who began to argue with Stephen.
10But they could not stand up against the wisdom the Spirit gave him as he spoke.
11Then they secretly persuaded some men to say, "We have heard Stephen
speak blasphemous words against Moses and against God."
12So they stirred up the people and the elders and the teachers of the law.
They seized Stephen and brought him before the Sanhedrin. 13They produced
false witnesses, who testified, "This fellow never stops speaking against this holy

[a] 1 That is, Jews who had adopted the Greek language and culture

place and against the law. [14]For we have heard him say that this Jesus of Nazareth will destroy this place and change the customs Moses handed down to us."

[15]All who were sitting in the Sanhedrin looked intently at Stephen, and they saw that his face was like the face of an angel.

Stephen's Speech to the Sanhedrin

7 Then the high priest asked Stephen, "Are these charges true?"

[2]To this he replied: "Brothers and fathers, listen to me! The God of glory appeared to our father Abraham while he was still in Mesopotamia, before he lived in Harran. [3]'Leave your country and your people,' God said, 'and go to the land I will show you.'[a]

[4]"So he left the land of the Chaldeans and settled in Harran. After the death of his father, God sent him to this land where you are now living. [5]He gave him no inheritance here, not even enough ground to set his foot on. But God promised him that he and his descendants after him would possess the land, even though at that time Abraham had no child. [6]God spoke to him in this way: 'For four hundred years your descendants will be strangers in a country not their own, and they will be enslaved and mistreated. [7]But I will punish the nation they serve as slaves,' God said, 'and afterward they will come out of that country and worship me in this place.'[b] [8]Then he gave Abraham the covenant of circumcision. And Abraham became the father of Isaac and circumcised him eight days after his birth. Later Isaac became the father of Jacob, and Jacob became the father of the twelve patriarchs.

[9]"Because the patriarchs were jealous of Joseph, they sold him as a slave into Egypt. But God was with him [10]and rescued him from all his troubles. He gave Joseph wisdom and enabled him to gain the goodwill of Pharaoh king of Egypt. So Pharaoh made him ruler over Egypt and all his palace.

[11]"Then a famine struck all Egypt and Canaan, bringing great suffering, and our ancestors could not find food. [12]When Jacob heard that there was grain in Egypt, he sent our forefathers on their first visit. [13]On their second visit, Joseph told his brothers who he was, and Pharaoh learned about Joseph's family. [14]After this, Joseph sent for his father Jacob and his whole family, seventy-five in all. [15]Then Jacob went down to Egypt, where he and our ancestors died. [16]Their bodies were brought back to Shechem and placed in the tomb that Abraham had bought from the sons of Hamor at Shechem for a certain sum of money.

[17]"As the time drew near for God to fulfill his promise to Abraham, the number of our people in Egypt had greatly increased. [18]Then 'a new king, to whom Joseph meant nothing, came to power in Egypt.'[c] [19]He dealt treacherously with our people and oppressed our ancestors by forcing them to throw out their newborn babies so that they would die.

[20]"At that time Moses was born, and he was no ordinary child.[d] For three months he was cared for by his family. [21]When he was placed outside, Pharaoh's daughter took him and brought him up as her own son. [22]Moses was educated in all the wisdom of the Egyptians and was powerful in speech and action.

[23]"When Moses was forty years old, he decided to visit his own people, the Israelites. [24]He saw one of them being mistreated by an Egyptian, so he went to his defense and avenged him by killing the Egyptian. [25]Moses thought that his own people would realize that God was using him to rescue them, but they did not. [26]The next day Moses came upon two Israelites who were fighting. He tried to reconcile them by saying, 'Men, you are brothers; why do you want to hurt each other?'

[27]"But the man who was mistreating the other pushed Moses aside and said, 'Who made you ruler and judge over us? [28]Are you thinking of killing me as you killed the Egyptian yesterday?'[e] [29]When Moses heard this, he fled to Midian, where he settled as a foreigner and had two sons.

[a] *3* Gen. 12:1 [b] *7* Gen. 15:13,14 [c] *18* Exodus 1:8 [d] *20* Or *was fair in the sight of God*
[e] *28* Exodus 2:14

ACTS 7:1–53

STEPHEN'S SPEECH

Having been falsely accused of blasphemy, Stephen replied to his accusers by speaking to them about that which they "knew"—the prophecies and teachings of the Old Testament. The crowd was filled with experts on Jewish history and law, yet they failed to understand the significance of the *whole* story. Stephen deftly highlighted what they had long since overlooked: Israel's long history of rejecting God and his prophets, despite God's repeated provision of clear, specific messages through his spokespeople.

Here is a classic example of history forgotten becoming history repeated. What the Jewish leaders had done in the past, they had done again by rejecting Jesus, the ultimate deliverer. This tendency to forget how God has been faithful is all too common among his people. Christians today remember God's goodness by faithfully reading the Scriptures and gathering with other believers. Stephen faithfully bore witness to Jesus as the first Christian martyr because he had this awareness of redemptive history, the embracing presence of Christ and a personal commitment to remain sensitive to the Holy Spirit.

30“After forty years had passed, an angel appeared to Moses in the flames
of a burning bush in the desert near Mount Sinai. 31When he saw this, he was
amazed at the sight. As he went over to get a closer look, he heard the Lord say:
32‘I am the God of your fathers, the God of Abraham, Isaac and Jacob.’[a] Moses
trembled with fear and did not dare to look.
33“Then the Lord said to him, ‘Take off your sandals, for the place where you
are standing is holy ground. 34I have indeed seen the oppression of my people in
Egypt. I have heard their groaning and have come down to set them free. Now
come, I will send you back to Egypt.’[b]
35“This is the same Moses they had rejected with the words, ‘Who made you
ruler and judge?’ He was sent to be their ruler and deliverer by God himself,
through the angel who appeared to him in the bush. 36He led them out of Egypt
and performed wonders and signs in Egypt, at the Red Sea and for forty years in
the wilderness.
37“This is the Moses who told the Israelites, ‘God will raise up for you a prophet like me from your own people.’[c] 38He was in the assembly in the wilderness,
with the angel who spoke to him on Mount Sinai, and with our ancestors; and he
received living words to pass on to us.
39“But our ancestors refused to obey him. Instead, they rejected him and in
their hearts turned back to Egypt. 40They told Aaron, ‘Make us gods who will go
before us. As for this fellow Moses who led us out of Egypt — we don’t know what
has happened to him!’[d] 41That was the time they made an idol in the form of a
calf. They brought sacrifices to it and reveled in what their own hands had made.
42But God turned away from them and gave them over to the worship of the sun,
moon and stars. This agrees with what is written in the book of the prophets:

“ ‘Did you bring me sacrifices and offerings
    forty years in the wilderness, people of Israel?
43You have taken up the tabernacle of Molek
    and the star of your god Rephan,
    the idols you made to worship.
Therefore I will send you into exile’[e] beyond Babylon.

44“Our ancestors had the tabernacle of the covenant law with them in the wilderness. It had been made as God directed Moses, according to the pattern he
had seen. 45After receiving the tabernacle, our ancestors under Joshua brought it
with them when they took the land from the nations God drove out before them.
It remained in the land until the time of David, 46who enjoyed God’s favor and
asked that he might provide a dwelling place for the God of Jacob.[f] 47But it was
Solomon who built a house for him.
48“However, the Most High does not live in houses made by human hands. As
the prophet says:

49“ ‘Heaven is my throne,
    and the earth is my footstool.
What kind of house will you build for me?
                                                says the Lord.
    Or where will my resting place be?
50Has not my hand made all these things?’[g]

51“You stiff-necked people! Your hearts and ears are still uncircumcised. You
are just like your ancestors: You always resist the Holy Spirit! 52Was there ever a
prophet your ancestors did not persecute? They even killed those who predicted
the coming of the Righteous One. And now you have betrayed and murdered
him — 53you who have received the law that was given through angels but have
not obeyed it.”

---

[a] *32* Exodus 3:6 [b] *34* Exodus 3:5,7,8,10 [c] *37* Deut. 18:15 [d] *40* Exodus 32:1
[e] *43* Amos 5:25-27 (see Septuagint) [f] *46* Some early manuscripts *the house of Jacob*
[g] *50* Isaiah 66:1,2

The Stoning of Stephen

[54]When the members of the Sanhedrin heard this, they were furious and gnashed their teeth at him. [55]But Stephen, full of the Holy Spirit, looked up to heaven and saw the glory of God, and Jesus standing at the right hand of God. [56]"Look," he said, "I see heaven open and the Son of Man standing at the right hand of God."

[57]At this they covered their ears and, yelling at the top of their voices, they all rushed at him, [58]dragged him out of the city and began to stone him. Meanwhile, the witnesses laid their coats at the feet of a young man named Saul.

[59]While they were stoning him, Stephen prayed, "Lord Jesus, receive my spirit." [60]Then he fell on his knees and cried out, "Lord, do not hold this sin against them." When he had said this, he fell asleep.

8 And Saul approved of their killing him.

The Church Persecuted and Scattered

On that day a great persecution broke out against the church in Jerusalem, and all except the apostles were scattered throughout Judea and Samaria. [2]Godly men buried Stephen and mourned deeply for him. [3]But Saul began to destroy the church. Going from house to house, he dragged off both men and women and put them in prison.

Philip in Samaria

[4]Those who had been scattered preached the word wherever they went. [5]Philip went down to a city in Samaria and proclaimed the Messiah there. [6]When the crowds heard Philip and saw the signs he performed, they all paid close attention to what he said. [7]For with shrieks, impure spirits came out of many, and many who were paralyzed or lame were healed. [8]So there was great joy in that city.

Simon the Sorcerer

[9]Now for some time a man named Simon had practiced sorcery in the city and amazed all the people of Samaria. He boasted that he was someone great, [10]and all the people, both high and low, gave him their attention and exclaimed, "This man is rightly called the Great Power of God." [11]They followed him because he had amazed them for a long time with his sorcery. [12]But when they believed Philip as he proclaimed the good news of the kingdom of God and the name of Jesus Christ, they were baptized, both men and women. [13]Simon himself believed and was baptized. And he followed Philip everywhere, astonished by the great signs and miracles he saw.

[14]When the apostles in Jerusalem heard that Samaria had accepted the word of God, they sent Peter and John to Samaria. [15]When they arrived, they prayed for the new believers there that they might receive the Holy Spirit, [16]because the Holy Spirit had not yet come on any of them; they had simply been baptized in the name of the Lord Jesus. [17]Then Peter and John placed their hands on them, and they received the Holy Spirit.

[18]When Simon saw that the Spirit was given at the laying on of the apostles' hands, he offered them money [19]and said, "Give me also this ability so that everyone on whom I lay my hands may receive the Holy Spirit."

[20]Peter answered: "May your money perish with you, because you thought you could buy the gift of God with money! [21]You have no part or share in this ministry, because your heart is not right before God. [22]Repent of this wickedness and pray to the Lord in the hope that he may forgive you for having such a thought in your heart. [23]For I see that you are full of bitterness and captive to sin."

[24]Then Simon answered, "Pray to the Lord for me so that nothing you have said may happen to me."

[25]After they had further proclaimed the word of the Lord and testified about

---

ACTS 8:4

PROCLAIMING THE MESSAGE

The early church is well known for caring for one another (i.e., "They sold property and possessions to give to anyone who had need" [2:45]; "There were no needy persons among them" [4:34]), but it is also known for its commitment to boldly preaching the Good News.

Both deeds *and* words defined the early church. But what was the main message? Looking at three of the sermons in Acts (2:14–36; 4:8–22; 13:16–41), the primary points can be summarized as: (1) Through Jesus, the Scriptures are fulfilled. (2) Jesus is the long-awaited Messiah, Savior and Lord who lived, died and rose again to new life. (3) Jesus is able to forgive sin and will return again as judge. (4) Repent, believe and be baptized.

The responsibility for all Christians remains the same: to live in a Christ-like manner, which includes the call to preach the Good News of Jesus to the world (Mt 28:19–20; Mk 16:15; Ac 1:8; 2Co 5:20).

Jesus, Peter and John returned to Jerusalem, preaching the gospel in many Samaritan villages.

Philip and the Ethiopian

[26]Now an angel of the Lord said to Philip, "Go south to the road — the desert
road — that goes down from Jerusalem to Gaza." [27]So he started out, and on his
way he met an Ethiopian[a] eunuch, an important official in charge of all the treasury of the Kandake (which means "queen of the Ethiopians"). This man had
gone to Jerusalem to worship, [28]and on his way home was sitting in his chariot
reading the Book of Isaiah the prophet. [29]The Spirit told Philip, "Go to that chariot and stay near it."
[30]Then Philip ran up to the chariot and heard the man reading Isaiah the
prophet. "Do you understand what you are reading?" Philip asked.
[31]"How can I," he said, "unless someone explains it to me?" So he invited Philip to come up and sit with him.
[32]This is the passage of Scripture the eunuch was reading:

"He was led like a sheep to the slaughter,
and as a lamb before its shearer is silent,
so he did not open his mouth.
[33]In his humiliation he was deprived of justice.
Who can speak of his descendants?
For his life was taken from the earth."[b]

[34]The eunuch asked Philip, "Tell me, please, who is the prophet talking about,
himself or someone else?" [35]Then Philip began with that very passage of Scripture and told him the good news about Jesus.
[36]As they traveled along the road, they came to some water and the eunuch
said, "Look, here is water. What can stand in the way of my being baptized?" [37][c]
[38]And he gave orders to stop the chariot. Then both Philip and the eunuch went
down into the water and Philip baptized him. [39]When they came up out of the
water, the Spirit of the Lord suddenly took Philip away, and the eunuch did not
see him again, but went on his way rejoicing. [40]Philip, however, appeared at Azo-
tus and traveled about, preaching the gospel in all the towns until he reached
Caesarea.

Saul's Conversion

9 Meanwhile, Saul was still breathing out murderous threats against the
Lord's disciples. He went to the high priest [2]and asked him for letters to the
synagogues in Damascus, so that if he found any there who belonged to the Way,
whether men or women, he might take them as prisoners to Jerusalem. [3]As he
neared Damascus on his journey, suddenly a light from heaven flashed around
him. [4]He fell to the ground and heard a voice say to him, "Saul, Saul, why do you
persecute me?"
[5]"Who are you, Lord?" Saul asked.
"I am Jesus, whom you are persecuting," he replied. [6]"Now get up and go into
the city, and you will be told what you must do."
[7]The men traveling with Saul stood there speechless; they heard the sound
but did not see anyone. [8]Saul got up from the ground, but when he opened his
eyes he could see nothing. So they led him by the hand into Damascus. [9]For
three days he was blind, and did not eat or drink anything.
[10]In Damascus there was a disciple named Ananias. The Lord called to him
in a vision, "Ananias!"
"Yes, Lord," he answered.
[11]The Lord told him, "Go to the house of Judas on Straight Street and ask for a

[a] 27 That is, from the southern Nile region [b] 33 Isaiah 53:7,8 (see Septuagint)
[c] 37 Some manuscripts include here *Philip said, "If you believe with all your heart, you may."*
The eunuch answered, "I believe that Jesus Christ is the Son of God."

ACTS 8:26 – 40

USING THE OLD TESTAMENT TO REVEAL JESUS

Because God is unchanging, his plan of salvation has been steadfast since the beginning. The Old Testament is thus the firm foundation for all of redemptive history; it provides the framework for understanding Jesus, which is why the New Testament authors took such great pains to quote, allude to, echo and interpret the Old Testament in their writings. These authors recognized that Jesus' birth and ministry confirmed his identity as the Davidic Messiah in fulfillment of Old Testament prophecy. Furthermore, since many of the early Christians had a strong Jewish background, the New Testament writers were careful to honor their audience as they addressed Jesus' fulfillment of the law and readily drew typological connections between Jesus and Old Testament characters.

Through this rigorous method of harkening back to the ancient Scriptures, the writers highlighted the good news that God has always been faithful to his people, and Jesus has always been the pinnacle of his plan.

SAUL'S CONVERSION

Saul's conversion teaches many truths about how people come to God and what it means to live for God.

As a member of the religious leadership, Saul was actively and vehemently opposed to the work of Jesus and his disciples. He was a staunch follower of the traditions of the Pharisees, which had been developed over time to supplement God's direct revelations to Israel's ancestors. Although many of the rules taught by the Pharisees were intended to help God's people honor God, they very often had the opposite effect: alienating the lowest of society and fostering religious pride. This religious spirit could not accept a crucified Messiah, so Saul refused to believe that Jesus was who he had claimed to be. Therefore, Saul "persecuted the church" violently (Gal 1:13 – 15) and opposed Christianity with all he had. But even Saul was not beyond God's reach.

Up until the day that God saved him, Saul believed he was advancing God's cause and doing work that would please the Lord. He wasn't scared, and he didn't feel guilty. On the surface, it appeared that he had it all together. He had the right education from the right teachers and was part of the right family (Php 3:1 – 9). He was on his way, ascending the ranks of the Jewish hierarchy — and then, suddenly, God broke through to him.

God saved Saul by grace, through faith, in Christ. Jesus, who was completely sovereign over Saul's conversion, confronted Saul in his sin. He showed up in a blinding light (Ac 9:3 – 4), then simply told this suddenly former persecutor what city to go to and what to do (9:5 – 6).

Saul's conversion teaches that the gospel message isn't only for "the right kind of person." Saul was deeply opposed to Jesus and deeply committed to his own path, but none of that stopped God's plan. God works through all kinds of people and situations to bring people to himself.

Saul's conversion teaches that coming to Christ is personal and absolutely possible even in the most unlikely situations. Saul was personally changed; he saw his past differently, and he understood his present situation with new eyes. After Jesus' revelation, Saul looked at the future with a changed perspective. For many throughout the centuries and still today, conversion means a radical U-turn, and Jesus Christ himself is the turning point.

man from Tarsus named Saul, for he is praying. [12]In a vision he has seen a man
named Ananias come and place his hands on him to restore his sight."
[13]"Lord," Ananias answered, "I have heard many reports about this man and
all the harm he has done to your holy people in Jerusalem. [14]And he has come
here with authority from the chief priests to arrest all who call on your name."
[15]But the Lord said to Ananias, "Go! This man is my chosen instrument to
proclaim my name to the Gentiles and their kings and to the people of Israel. [16]I
will show him how much he must suffer for my name."
[17]Then Ananias went to the house and entered it. Placing his hands on Saul,
he said, "Brother Saul, the Lord — Jesus, who appeared to you on the road as you
were coming here — has sent me so that you may see again and be filled with the
Holy Spirit." [18]Immediately, something like scales fell from Saul's eyes, and he
could see again. He got up and was baptized, [19]and after taking some food, he
regained his strength.

Saul in Damascus and Jerusalem

Saul spent several days with the disciples in Damascus. [20]At once he began
to preach in the synagogues that Jesus is the Son of God. [21]All those who heard
him were astonished and asked, "Isn't he the man who raised havoc in Jerusalem among those who call on this name? And hasn't he come here to take them
as prisoners to the chief priests?" [22]Yet Saul grew more and more powerful and
baffled the Jews living in Damascus by proving that Jesus is the Messiah.
[23]After many days had gone by, there was a conspiracy among the Jews to kill
him, [24]but Saul learned of their plan. Day and night they kept close watch on the
city gates in order to kill him. [25]But his followers took him by night and lowered
him in a basket through an opening in the wall.
[26]When he came to Jerusalem, he tried to join the disciples, but they were all
afraid of him, not believing that he really was a disciple. [27]But Barnabas took
him and brought him to the apostles. He told them how Saul on his journey had
seen the Lord and that the Lord had spoken to him, and how in Damascus he
had preached fearlessly in the name of Jesus. [28]So Saul stayed with them and
moved about freely in Jerusalem, speaking boldly in the name of the Lord. [29]He
talked and debated with the Hellenistic Jews,[a] but they tried to kill him. [30]When
the believers learned of this, they took him down to Caesarea and sent him off
to Tarsus.
[31]Then the church throughout Judea, Galilee and Samaria enjoyed a time of
peace and was strengthened. Living in the fear of the Lord and encouraged by
the Holy Spirit, it increased in numbers.

Aeneas and Dorcas

[32]As Peter traveled about the country, he went to visit the Lord's people who
lived in Lydda. [33]There he found a man named Aeneas, who was paralyzed and
had been bedridden for eight years. [34]"Aeneas," Peter said to him, "Jesus Christ
heals you. Get up and roll up your mat." Immediately Aeneas got up. [35]All those
who lived in Lydda and Sharon saw him and turned to the Lord.
[36]In Joppa there was a disciple named Tabitha (in Greek her name is Dorcas);
she was always doing good and helping the poor. [37]About that time she became
sick and died, and her body was washed and placed in an upstairs room. [38]Lydda
was near Joppa; so when the disciples heard that Peter was in Lydda, they sent
two men to him and urged him, "Please come at once!"
[39]Peter went with them, and when he arrived he was taken upstairs to the
room. All the widows stood around him, crying and showing him the robes and
other clothing that Dorcas had made while she was still with them.
[40]Peter sent them all out of the room; then he got down on his knees and
prayed. Turning toward the dead woman, he said, "Tabitha, get up." She opened

[a] *29* That is, Jews who had adopted the Greek language and culture

her eyes, and seeing Peter she sat up. [41]He took her by the hand and helped her to her feet. Then he called for the believers, especially the widows, and presented her to them alive. [42]This became known all over Joppa, and many people believed in the Lord. [43]Peter stayed in Joppa for some time with a tanner named Simon.

Cornelius Calls for Peter

10 At Caesarea there was a man named Cornelius, a centurion in what was known as the Italian Regiment. [2]He and all his family were devout and God-fearing; he gave generously to those in need and prayed to God regularly. [3]One day at about three in the afternoon he had a vision. He distinctly saw an angel of God, who came to him and said, "Cornelius!"

[4]Cornelius stared at him in fear. "What is it, Lord?" he asked.

The angel answered, "Your prayers and gifts to the poor have come up as a memorial offering before God. [5]Now send men to Joppa to bring back a man named Simon who is called Peter. [6]He is staying with Simon the tanner, whose house is by the sea."

[7]When the angel who spoke to him had gone, Cornelius called two of his servants and a devout soldier who was one of his attendants. [8]He told them everything that had happened and sent them to Joppa.

Peter's Vision

[9]About noon the following day as they were on their journey and approaching the city, Peter went up on the roof to pray. [10]He became hungry and wanted something to eat, and while the meal was being prepared, he fell into a trance. [11]He saw heaven opened and something like a large sheet being let down to earth by its four corners. [12]It contained all kinds of four-footed animals, as well as reptiles and birds. [13]Then a voice told him, "Get up, Peter. Kill and eat."

[14]"Surely not, Lord!" Peter replied. "I have never eaten anything impure or unclean."

[15]The voice spoke to him a second time, "Do not call anything impure that God has made clean."

[16]This happened three times, and immediately the sheet was taken back to heaven.

[17]While Peter was wondering about the meaning of the vision, the men sent by Cornelius found out where Simon's house was and stopped at the gate. [18]They called out, asking if Simon who was known as Peter was staying there.

[19]While Peter was still thinking about the vision, the Spirit said to him, "Simon, three[a] men are looking for you. [20]So get up and go downstairs. Do not hesitate to go with them, for I have sent them."

[21]Peter went down and said to the men, "I'm the one you're looking for. Why have you come?"

[22]The men replied, "We have come from Cornelius the centurion. He is a righteous and God-fearing man, who is respected by all the Jewish people. A holy angel told him to ask you to come to his house so that he could hear what you have to say." [23]Then Peter invited the men into the house to be his guests.

Peter at Cornelius's House

The next day Peter started out with them, and some of the believers from Joppa went along. [24]The following day he arrived in Caesarea. Cornelius was expecting them and had called together his relatives and close friends. [25]As Peter entered the house, Cornelius met him and fell at his feet in reverence. [26]But Peter made him get up. "Stand up," he said, "I am only a man myself."

[27]While talking with him, Peter went inside and found a large gathering of people. [28]He said to them: "You are well aware that it is against our law for a Jew

[a] *19* One early manuscript *two*; other manuscripts do not have the number.

ACTS 10:1–23

BREAKING BARRIERS

Ethnic divides were deeply ingrained in the culture of first-century Israel. Even Jewish Christians such as Peter thought of themselves as being among God's favorites. This is why a thorough reading of the New Testament, especially noting the literary structure of many of the books, reveals a careful progression in thought to lead the audience out of their biases and into the truth that Jesus came for *all* people. For example, the author (Luke) hints at God's work in non-Jewish nations when he records Stephen's references to God showing up in Mesopotamia (7:2), Harran (7:4), Egypt (7:9) and Sinai (7:38). And it's why the first half of the book of Acts is focused on Peter's ministry to the Jews before widening the lens to incorporate Paul's ministry to the Gentiles.

Quite tactfully, Luke aims to help the eyes of his audience to adjust as he slowly turns one light on at a time, ultimately illuminating the good news that Jesus brought the Gentiles into the kingdom. Luke's choice to repeat the episode of Peter's dream in both chapters 10 and 11, as well as to explain the interaction between Peter and Cornelius, serves to cement the truths that God shows no partiality and that God desires that people from all nations be welcomed into his kingdom (Mt 28:19; Ro 2:11; Gal 3:8; 1Ti 2:4; Rev 15:4).

to associate with or visit a Gentile. But God has shown me that I should not call
anyone impure or unclean. 29So when I was sent for, I came without raising any
objection. May I ask why you sent for me?"
30Cornelius answered: "Three days ago I was in my house praying at this hour,
at three in the afternoon. Suddenly a man in shining clothes stood before me
31and said, 'Cornelius, God has heard your prayer and remembered your gifts to
the poor. 32Send to Joppa for Simon who is called Peter. He is a guest in the home
of Simon the tanner, who lives by the sea.' 33So I sent for you immediately, and it
was good of you to come. Now we are all here in the presence of God to listen to
everything the Lord has commanded you to tell us."
34Then Peter began to speak: "I now realize how true it is that God does not
show favoritism 35but accepts from every nation the one who fears him and does
what is right. 36You know the message God sent to the people of Israel, announcing the good news of peace through Jesus Christ, who is Lord of all. 37You know
what has happened throughout the province of Judea, beginning in Galilee after
the baptism that John preached — 38how God anointed Jesus of Nazareth with
the Holy Spirit and power, and how he went around doing good and healing all
who were under the power of the devil, because God was with him.
39"We are witnesses of everything he did in the country of the Jews and in Jerusalem. They killed him by hanging him on a cross, 40but God raised him from
the dead on the third day and caused him to be seen. 41He was not seen by all
the people, but by witnesses whom God had already chosen — by us who ate and
drank with him after he rose from the dead. 42He commanded us to preach to the
people and to testify that he is the one whom God appointed as judge of the living
and the dead. 43All the prophets testify about him that everyone who believes in
him receives forgiveness of sins through his name."
44While Peter was still speaking these words, the Holy Spirit came on all who
heard the message. 45The circumcised believers who had come with Peter were
astonished that the gift of the Holy Spirit had been poured out even on Gentiles.
46For they heard them speaking in tongues[a] and praising God.
Then Peter said, 47"Surely no one can stand in the way of their being baptized
with water. They have received the Holy Spirit just as we have." 48So he ordered
that they be baptized in the name of Jesus Christ. Then they asked Peter to stay
with them for a few days.

Peter Explains His Actions

11 The apostles and the believers throughout Judea heard that the Gentiles
also had received the word of God. 2So when Peter went up to Jerusalem,
the circumcised believers criticized him 3and said, "You went into the house of
uncircumcised men and ate with them."
4Starting from the beginning, Peter told them the whole story: 5"I was in the
city of Joppa praying, and in a trance I saw a vision. I saw something like a large
sheet being let down from heaven by its four corners, and it came down to where
I was. 6I looked into it and saw four-footed animals of the earth, wild beasts,
reptiles and birds. 7Then I heard a voice telling me, 'Get up, Peter. Kill and eat.'
8"I replied, 'Surely not, Lord! Nothing impure or unclean has ever entered my
mouth.'
9"The voice spoke from heaven a second time, 'Do not call anything impure
that God has made clean.' 10This happened three times, and then it was all
pulled up to heaven again.
11"Right then three men who had been sent to me from Caesarea stopped at
the house where I was staying. 12The Spirit told me to have no hesitation about
going with them. These six brothers also went with me, and we entered the man's
house. 13He told us how he had seen an angel appear in his house and say, 'Send
to Joppa for Simon who is called Peter. 14He will bring you a message through
which you and all your household will be saved.'

---

[a] *46* Or *other languages*

[15]"As I began to speak, the Holy Spirit came on them as he had come on us
at the beginning. [16]Then I remembered what the Lord had said: 'John baptized
with[a] water, but you will be baptized with[a] the Holy Spirit.' [17]So if God gave them
the same gift he gave us who believed in the Lord Jesus Christ, who was I to think
that I could stand in God's way?"

[18]When they heard this, they had no further objections and praised God, saying, "So then, even to Gentiles God has granted repentance that leads to life."

The Church in Antioch

[19]Now those who had been scattered by the persecution that broke out when
Stephen was killed traveled as far as Phoenicia, Cyprus and Antioch, spreading
the word only among Jews. [20]Some of them, however, men from Cyprus and Cyrene, went to Antioch and began to speak to Greeks also, telling them the good
news about the Lord Jesus. [21]The Lord's hand was with them, and a great number
of people believed and turned to the Lord.

[22]News of this reached the church in Jerusalem, and they sent Barnabas to
Antioch. [23]When he arrived and saw what the grace of God had done, he was glad
and encouraged them all to remain true to the Lord with all their hearts. [24]He
was a good man, full of the Holy Spirit and faith, and a great number of people
were brought to the Lord.

[25]Then Barnabas went to Tarsus to look for Saul, [26]and when he found him,
he brought him to Antioch. So for a whole year Barnabas and Saul met with the
church and taught great numbers of people. The disciples were called Christians
first at Antioch.

[27]During this time some prophets came down from Jerusalem to Antioch.
[28]One of them, named Agabus, stood up and through the Spirit predicted that
a severe famine would spread over the entire Roman world. (This happened
during the reign of Claudius.) [29]The disciples, as each one was able, decided to
provide help for the brothers and sisters living in Judea. [30]This they did, sending
their gift to the elders by Barnabas and Saul.

Peter's Miraculous Escape From Prison

12 It was about this time that King Herod arrested some who belonged to the
church, intending to persecute them. [2]He had James, the brother of John,
put to death with the sword. [3]When he saw that this met with approval among
the Jews, he proceeded to seize Peter also. This happened during the Festival of
Unleavened Bread. [4]After arresting him, he put him in prison, handing him over
to be guarded by four squads of four soldiers each. Herod intended to bring him
out for public trial after the Passover.

[5]So Peter was kept in prison, but the church was earnestly praying to God
for him.

[6]The night before Herod was to bring him to trial, Peter was sleeping between
two soldiers, bound with two chains, and sentries stood guard at the entrance.
[7]Suddenly an angel of the Lord appeared and a light shone in the cell. He struck
Peter on the side and woke him up. "Quick, get up!" he said, and the chains fell
off Peter's wrists.

[8]Then the angel said to him, "Put on your clothes and sandals." And Peter
did so. "Wrap your cloak around you and follow me," the angel told him. [9]Peter
followed him out of the prison, but he had no idea that what the angel was doing
was really happening; he thought he was seeing a vision. [10]They passed the first
and second guards and came to the iron gate leading to the city. It opened for
them by itself, and they went through it. When they had walked the length of one
street, suddenly the angel left him.

[11]Then Peter came to himself and said, "Now I know without a doubt that the
Lord has sent his angel and rescued me from Herod's clutches and from everything the Jewish people were hoping would happen."

[a] *16* Or *in*

ACTS 11:26

CHRISTIANS

Given the marked diversity in religious backgrounds, social status, economic power, age and ethnicity among the early Christians, it's a miracle that the young church ever gained its footing. What was it that unified and identified believers despite all these differences? In short, Christians were known by what they said and did. They preached about Jesus and they acted like Jesus. Originally called "followers of the Way," the term "Christians" was eventually coined, likely by nonbelievers, to mean "ones who are like Christ." Paul says that Christians are "captives in Christ's triumphal procession [used by God] to spread the aroma of the knowledge of him everywhere. For we are to God the pleasing aroma of Christ among those who are being saved and those who are perishing" (2Co 2:14–15). The descriptions of the church in Acts are distinctive and profound, painting Christians as compassionate, prophetic, selfless, committed and loving followers of Christ. True Christians have always been committed to more than a set of ideas and beliefs; they are active, giving people who reach out to others in service, joyfully telling them about their relationship with Jesus. In short, they are "ones who are like Christ," devoted to their King who makes a way for all who will repent and be saved (2Pe 3:9).

UNJUST PERSECUTION

The early church experienced intense persecution. Herod saw some political advantage in persecuting the fledgling church, yet those who are in opposition to God's ways and his plan to redeem the world through Jesus Christ cite many other reasons for persecuting the church. The Jewish leadership during the time of the early church perpetuated this persecution. Their historical lineage included being God's chosen people, Israel. But they presumed upon God's kindness and didn't really trust God in their hearts. They were proud: They believed that their outward actions as defined by their ancestors earned God's favor, and this showed in how they lived their lives. Many Jews persecuted the church with incredible vigor. They saw Jesus as a blasphemer and a rebel, and they actively tried to stop what the early church was doing in and around Jerusalem.

Jesus was persecuted, and he promised that his followers would also endure persecution (Jn 16:33). In their own pride, the Jewish leaders believed they were doing what was required to please God and earn his favor, but Jesus represented a radically different perspective. Jesus came to fulfill the law that they so closely followed (Mt 5:17), but they could not see that the entire Old Testament had pointed to him all along (Lk 24:27).

Jesus taught his followers that persecution was real and was coming. "If the world hates you, keep in mind that it hated me first. If you belonged to the world, it would love you as its own. As it is, you do not belong to the world, but I have chosen you out of the world. That is why the world hates you. Remember what I told you: 'A servant is not greater than his master.' If they persecuted me, they will persecute you also. If they obeyed my teaching, they will obey yours also. They will treat you this way because of my name, for they do not know the one who sent me" (Jn 15:18 – 21).

Jesus' promise still stands today as the worldwide church experiences opposition and persecution. The persecuted can "take heart" that Jesus voluntarily endured brutal persecution and died on the cross so that, regardless of the "trouble" they experience, Jesus has indeed "overcome the world" (Jn 16:33). Inspired by Jesus' example under persecution, the church continues to bring the message of God's unending love to a lost world.

[12]When this had dawned on him, he went to the house of Mary the mother
of John, also called Mark, where many people had gathered and were praying.
[13]Peter knocked at the outer entrance, and a servant named Rhoda came to answer the door. [14]When she recognized Peter's voice, she was so overjoyed she ran
back without opening it and exclaimed, "Peter is at the door!"
[15]"You're out of your mind," they told her. When she kept insisting that it was
so, they said, "It must be his angel."
[16]But Peter kept on knocking, and when they opened the door and saw him,
they were astonished. [17]Peter motioned with his hand for them to be quiet and
described how the Lord had brought him out of prison. "Tell James and the other brothers and sisters about this," he said, and then he left for another place.
[18]In the morning, there was no small commotion among the soldiers as to
what had become of Peter. [19]After Herod had a thorough search made for him
and did not find him, he cross-examined the guards and ordered that they be
executed.

Herod's Death

Then Herod went from Judea to Caesarea and stayed there. [20]He had been
quarreling with the people of Tyre and Sidon; they now joined together and
sought an audience with him. After securing the support of Blastus, a trusted
personal servant of the king, they asked for peace, because they depended on
the king's country for their food supply.
[21]On the appointed day Herod, wearing his royal robes, sat on his throne and
delivered a public address to the people. [22]They shouted, "This is the voice of a
god, not of a man." [23]Immediately, because Herod did not give praise to God, an
angel of the Lord struck him down, and he was eaten by worms and died.
[24]But the word of God continued to spread and flourish.

Barnabas and Saul Sent Off

[25]When Barnabas and Saul had finished their mission, they returned from[a]
13 Jerusalem, taking with them John, also called Mark. [1]Now in the church
at Antioch there were prophets and teachers: Barnabas, Simeon called
Niger, Lucius of Cyrene, Manaen (who had been brought up with Herod the tetrarch) and Saul. [2]While they were worshiping the Lord and fasting, the Holy
Spirit said, "Set apart for me Barnabas and Saul for the work to which I have
called them." [3]So after they had fasted and prayed, they placed their hands on
them and sent them off.

On Cyprus

[4]The two of them, sent on their way by the Holy Spirit, went down to Seleucia
and sailed from there to Cyprus. [5]When they arrived at Salamis, they proclaimed
the word of God in the Jewish synagogues. John was with them as their helper.
[6]They traveled through the whole island until they came to Paphos. There
they met a Jewish sorcerer and false prophet named Bar-Jesus, [7]who was an attendant of the proconsul, Sergius Paulus. The proconsul, an intelligent man,
sent for Barnabas and Saul because he wanted to hear the word of God. [8]But
Elymas the sorcerer (for that is what his name means) opposed them and tried
to turn the proconsul from the faith. [9]Then Saul, who was also called Paul, filled
with the Holy Spirit, looked straight at Elymas and said, [10]"You are a child of the
devil and an enemy of everything that is right! You are full of all kinds of deceit
and trickery. Will you never stop perverting the right ways of the Lord? [11]Now
the hand of the Lord is against you. You are going to be blind for a time, not even
able to see the light of the sun."
Immediately mist and darkness came over him, and he groped about, seeking
someone to lead him by the hand. [12]When the proconsul saw what had happened, he believed, for he was amazed at the teaching about the Lord.

---

[a] *25* Some manuscripts *to*

THE ACTS OF THE HOLY SPIRIT

The Holy Spirit is the power that God has provided to move his kingdom mission forward. God's mission has always been to work through his people to show his glory to the world: first through the nation of Israel, and now through his Christian church. But God doesn't leave his people without help: Thankfully, God sent the Holy Spirit to be our helper and Advocate (Jn 14:15 – 17,25 – 27).

The book of Acts tells about many functions of the Holy Spirit: giving boldness and power to preach the gospel (Ac 6:10), inspiring people to prophesy (Ac 2:18) and directing ministry activity (Ac 13:2). Ultimately, the Spirit leads the church through the proper exercise of her different ministry offices and gifts.

God creates a unique unity in believers through the Holy Spirit. This unity is unlike anything that can be found anywhere else in the world. An example of this is found in Acts 13:1 – 3. The church in Antioch sent missionaries to other locations at an incredible rate. Interestingly, the church at Antioch was birthed by ordinary believers who had traveled to the city to escape persecution (Ac 11:19 – 21). The greatest local congregation in the world at the time was started by everyday people living for God in their everyday lives.

From what we know of it, the church in Antioch was also diverse, which gives us another picture of the Spirit's unifying work. Barnabas was a bicultural Hellenistic Jew, and he was one of the leaders of the church. Simeon, who was called Niger, was a leader in the church — no one knows his background. Another leader was Lucius the Cyrene from North Africa. Manaen used to keep terrible company; he was a lifelong friend of the man who had John the Baptist beheaded. And finally there was Paul, the Jewish Pharisee and persecutor-turned-evangelist. This was the group of people who came together to advance the message of Jesus as the Messiah. They were empowered by the Holy Spirit of God leading and guiding them.

The Spirit of Jesus created unity in the past through unthinkable combinations of diverse people coming together to advance one cause in the world: the kingdom of God. And the same Spirit still works in and through believers to do the same today.

In Pisidian Antioch

[13]From Paphos, Paul and his companions sailed to Perga in Pamphylia, where
John left them to return to Jerusalem. [14]From Perga they went on to Pisidian
Antioch. On the Sabbath they entered the synagogue and sat down. [15]After the
reading from the Law and the Prophets, the leaders of the synagogue sent word
to them, saying, "Brothers, if you have a word of exhortation for the people,
please speak."

[16]Standing up, Paul motioned with his hand and said: "Fellow Israelites and
you Gentiles who worship God, listen to me! [17]The God of the people of Israel chose our ancestors; he made the people prosper during their stay in Egypt;
with mighty power he led them out of that country; [18]for about forty years he
endured their conduct[a] in the wilderness; [19]and he overthrew seven nations in
Canaan, giving their land to his people as their inheritance. [20]All this took about
450 years.

"After this, God gave them judges until the time of Samuel the prophet. [21]Then
the people asked for a king, and he gave them Saul son of Kish, of the tribe of Benjamin, who ruled forty years. [22]After removing Saul, he made David their king.
God testified concerning him: 'I have found David son of Jesse, a man after my
own heart; he will do everything I want him to do.'

[23]"From this man's descendants God has brought to Israel the Savior Jesus,
as he promised. [24]Before the coming of Jesus, John preached repentance and
baptism to all the people of Israel. [25]As John was completing his work, he said:
'Who do you suppose I am? I am not the one you are looking for. But there is one
coming after me whose sandals I am not worthy to untie.'

[26]"Fellow children of Abraham and you God-fearing Gentiles, it is to us that
this message of salvation has been sent. [27]The people of Jerusalem and their rulers did not recognize Jesus, yet in condemning him they fulfilled the words of
the prophets that are read every Sabbath. [28]Though they found no proper ground
for a death sentence, they asked Pilate to have him executed. [29]When they had
carried out all that was written about him, they took him down from the cross
and laid him in a tomb. [30]But God raised him from the dead, [31]and for many days
he was seen by those who had traveled with him from Galilee to Jerusalem. They
are now his witnesses to our people.

[32]"We tell you the good news: What God promised our ancestors [33]he has fulfilled for us, their children, by raising up Jesus. As it is written in the second
Psalm:

> " 'You are my son;
> today I have become your father.'[b]

[34]God raised him from the dead so that he will never be subject to decay. As God
has said,

> " 'I will give you the holy and sure blessings promised to David.'[c]

[35]So it is also stated elsewhere:

> " 'You will not let your holy one see decay.'[d]

[36]"Now when David had served God's purpose in his own generation, he fell
asleep; he was buried with his ancestors and his body decayed. [37]But the one
whom God raised from the dead did not see decay.

[38]"Therefore, my friends, I want you to know that through Jesus the forgiveness of sins is proclaimed to you. [39]Through him everyone who believes is set
free from every sin, a justification you were not able to obtain under the law of
Moses. [40]Take care that what the prophets have said does not happen to you:

> [41]" 'Look, you scoffers,
> wonder and perish,

---

[a] *18* Some manuscripts *he cared for them* [b] *33* Psalm 2:7 [c] *34* Isaiah 55:3
[d] *35* Psalm 16:10 (see Septuagint)

for I am going to do something in your days
that you would never believe,
even if someone told you.'[a]"

42As Paul and Barnabas were leaving the synagogue, the people invited them
to speak further about these things on the next Sabbath. 43When the congregation was dismissed, many of the Jews and devout converts to Judaism followed
Paul and Barnabas, who talked with them and urged them to continue in the
grace of God.
44On the next Sabbath almost the whole city gathered to hear the word of the
Lord. 45When the Jews saw the crowds, they were filled with jealousy. They began to contradict what Paul was saying and heaped abuse on him.
46Then Paul and Barnabas answered them boldly: "We had to speak the word
of God to you first. Since you reject it and do not consider yourselves worthy of
eternal life, we now turn to the Gentiles. 47For this is what the Lord has commanded us:

"'I have made you[b] a light for the Gentiles,
that you[b] may bring salvation to the ends of the earth.'[c]"

48When the Gentiles heard this, they were glad and honored the word of the
Lord; and all who were appointed for eternal life believed.
49The word of the Lord spread through the whole region. 50But the Jewish
leaders incited the God-fearing women of high standing and the leading men of
the city. They stirred up persecution against Paul and Barnabas, and expelled
them from their region. 51So they shook the dust off their feet as a warning to
them and went to Iconium. 52And the disciples were filled with joy and with the
Holy Spirit.

In Iconium

14 At Iconium Paul and Barnabas went as usual into the Jewish synagogue.
There they spoke so effectively that a great number of Jews and Greeks
believed. 2But the Jews who refused to believe stirred up the other Gentiles and
poisoned their minds against the brothers. 3So Paul and Barnabas spent considerable time there, speaking boldly for the Lord, who confirmed the message of
his grace by enabling them to perform signs and wonders. 4The people of the city
were divided; some sided with the Jews, others with the apostles. 5There was a
plot afoot among both Gentiles and Jews, together with their leaders, to mistreat
them and stone them. 6But they found out about it and fled to the Lycaonian cities of Lystra and Derbe and to the surrounding country, 7where they continued
to preach the gospel.

In Lystra and Derbe

8In Lystra there sat a man who was lame. He had been that way from birth and
had never walked. 9He listened to Paul as he was speaking. Paul looked directly
at him, saw that he had faith to be healed 10and called out, "Stand up on your
feet!" At that, the man jumped up and began to walk.
11When the crowd saw what Paul had done, they shouted in the Lycaonian
language, "The gods have come down to us in human form!" 12Barnabas they
called Zeus, and Paul they called Hermes because he was the chief speaker.
13The priest of Zeus, whose temple was just outside the city, brought bulls and
wreaths to the city gates because he and the crowd wanted to offer sacrifices to
them.
14But when the apostles Barnabas and Paul heard of this, they tore their
clothes and rushed out into the crowd, shouting: 15"Friends, why are you doing
this? We too are only human, like you. We are bringing you good news, telling
you to turn from these worthless things to the living God, who made the heavens

[a] *41* Hab. 1:5 [b] *47* The Greek is singular. [c] *47* Isaiah 49:6

and the earth and the sea and everything in them. 16In the past, he let all nations go their own way. 17Yet he has not left himself without testimony: He has shown kindness by giving you rain from heaven and crops in their seasons; he provides you with plenty of food and fills your hearts with joy." 18Even with these words, they had difficulty keeping the crowd from sacrificing to them.

19Then some Jews came from Antioch and Iconium and won the crowd over. They stoned Paul and dragged him outside the city, thinking he was dead. 20But after the disciples had gathered around him, he got up and went back into the city. The next day he and Barnabas left for Derbe.

The Return to Antioch in Syria

21They preached the gospel in that city and won a large number of disciples. Then they returned to Lystra, Iconium and Antioch, 22strengthening the disciples and encouraging them to remain true to the faith. "We must go through many hardships to enter the kingdom of God," they said. 23Paul and Barnabas appointed elders[a] for them in each church and, with prayer and fasting, committed them to the Lord, in whom they had put their trust. 24After going through Pisidia, they came into Pamphylia, 25and when they had preached the word in Perga, they went down to Attalia.

26From Attalia they sailed back to Antioch, where they had been committed to the grace of God for the work they had now completed. 27On arriving there, they gathered the church together and reported all that God had done through them and how he had opened a door of faith to the Gentiles. 28And they stayed there a long time with the disciples.

The Council at Jerusalem

15 Certain people came down from Judea to Antioch and were teaching the believers: "Unless you are circumcised, according to the custom taught by Moses, you cannot be saved." 2This brought Paul and Barnabas into sharp dispute and debate with them. So Paul and Barnabas were appointed, along with some other believers, to go up to Jerusalem to see the apostles and elders about this question. 3The church sent them on their way, and as they traveled through Phoenicia and Samaria, they told how the Gentiles had been converted. This news made all the believers very glad. 4When they came to Jerusalem, they were welcomed by the church and the apostles and elders, to whom they reported everything God had done through them.

5Then some of the believers who belonged to the party of the Pharisees stood up and said, "The Gentiles must be circumcised and required to keep the law of Moses."

6The apostles and elders met to consider this question. 7After much discussion, Peter got up and addressed them: "Brothers, you know that some time ago God made a choice among you that the Gentiles might hear from my lips the message of the gospel and believe. 8God, who knows the heart, showed that he accepted them by giving the Holy Spirit to them, just as he did to us. 9He did not discriminate between us and them, for he purified their hearts by faith. 10Now then, why do you try to test God by putting on the necks of Gentiles a yoke that neither we nor our ancestors have been able to bear? 11No! We believe it is through the grace of our Lord Jesus that we are saved, just as they are."

12The whole assembly became silent as they listened to Barnabas and Paul telling about the signs and wonders God had done among the Gentiles through them. 13When they finished, James spoke up. "Brothers," he said, "listen to me. 14Simon[b] has described to us how God first intervened to choose a people for his name from the Gentiles. 15The words of the prophets are in agreement with this, as it is written:

[a] 23 Or *Barnabas ordained elders*; or *Barnabas had elders elected* [b] 14 Greek *Simeon*, a variant of *Simon*; that is, Peter

ACTS 14:19–20

SUFFERING FOR JESUS

Paul was well acquainted with suffering. He was imprisoned, stoned, beaten, flogged, shipwrecked, starved, exhausted and endangered throughout his life as a follower of Christ (2Co 11:16–33). Because of his experiences, throughout his letters Paul was intent on reminding Christians that hardship is to be *expected*. He said it quite clearly in Philippians: "For it has been granted to you on behalf of Christ not only to believe in him, but also to suffer for him" (Php 1:29).

Though the typical human response is to avoid pain at all costs, Paul calls Christians to accept their trials in light of the fact that God suffers with us and because God causes good things to come from our difficulties (Ps 34:18; Ro 8:28). He says, "We also glory in our sufferings, because we know that suffering produces perseverance; perseverance, character; and character, hope" (Ro 5:3–4). Furthermore, suffering is part of being united with Jesus (Php 3:10–11) and, thankfully, it is temporary: "Therefore we do not lose heart. Though outwardly we are wasting away, yet inwardly we are being renewed day by day. For our light and momentary troubles are achieving for us an eternal glory that far outweighs them all" (2Co 4:16–17).

[16]“ ‘After this I will return
and rebuild David’s fallen tent.
Its ruins I will rebuild,
and I will restore it,
[17]that the rest of mankind may seek the Lord,
even all the Gentiles who bear my name,
says the Lord, who does these things’[a]—
[18] things known from long ago.[b]

[19]“It is my judgment, therefore, that we should not make it difficult for the
Gentiles who are turning to God. [20]Instead we should write to them, telling them
to abstain from food polluted by idols, from sexual immorality, from the meat of
strangled animals and from blood. [21]For the law of Moses has been preached in
every city from the earliest times and is read in the synagogues on every Sabbath.”

The Council’s Letter to Gentile Believers

[22]Then the apostles and elders, with the whole church, decided to choose
some of their own men and send them to Antioch with Paul and Barnabas. They
chose Judas (called Barsabbas) and Silas, men who were leaders among the believers. [23]With them they sent the following letter:

The apostles and elders, your brothers,

To the Gentile believers in Antioch, Syria and Cilicia:

Greetings.

[24]We have heard that some went out from us without our authorization
and disturbed you, troubling your minds by what they said. [25]So we all
agreed to choose some men and send them to you with our dear friends
Barnabas and Paul— [26]men who have risked their lives for the name of our
Lord Jesus Christ. [27]Therefore we are sending Judas and Silas to confirm
by word of mouth what we are writing. [28]It seemed good to the Holy Spirit
and to us not to burden you with anything beyond the following requirements: [29]You are to abstain from food sacrificed to idols, from blood, from
the meat of strangled animals and from sexual immorality. You will do well
to avoid these things.

Farewell.

[30]So the men were sent off and went down to Antioch, where they gathered the
church together and delivered the letter. [31]The people read it and were glad for
its encouraging message. [32]Judas and Silas, who themselves were prophets, said
much to encourage and strengthen the believers. [33]After spending some time
there, they were sent off by the believers with the blessing of peace to return to
those who had sent them. [34][c] [35]But Paul and Barnabas remained in Antioch,
where they and many others taught and preached the word of the Lord.

Disagreement Between Paul and Barnabas

[36]Some time later Paul said to Barnabas, “Let us go back and visit the believers
in all the towns where we preached the word of the Lord and see how they are doing.” [37]Barnabas wanted to take John, also called Mark, with them, [38]but Paul did
not think it wise to take him, because he had deserted them in Pamphylia and
had not continued with them in the work. [39]They had such a sharp disagreement
that they parted company. Barnabas took Mark and sailed for Cyprus, [40]but Paul

[a] *17* Amos 9:11,12 (see Septuagint) [b] *17,18* Some manuscripts *things’— / [18]the Lord’s work is known to him from long ago* [c] *34* Some manuscripts include here *But Silas decided to remain there.*

ACTS 15:24–29

JESUS IS EVERYTHING

At the heart of what it means to be fallen human beings, people are proud and want to do things for themselves. Even Christians, after God saves them, struggle with trying to earn their way to God. Yet people who have surrendered their life to Christ grow with God the same way they were saved by God: by grace, through faith, in Christ.

Some of the first converts to Christianity struggled with this same issue of wanting to contribute in some way to their salvation. A group of Jewish Christians believed that to be Christians, Gentile converts must follow the Old Testament laws and traditions. In contrast to this, Peter and others argued that Christians did not need to follow the law in the same way—because Jesus had already fulfilled the law for everyone (Mt 5:17).

Even today there is a danger that well-meaning Christians will burden themselves and others with “add-ons” to the core of the gospel message, which is simply that Jesus is enough. As people try to add good works and other requirements to that message, the message of salvation by grace is lost: “For it is by grace you have been saved, through faith—and this is not from yourselves, it is the gift of God—not by works, so that no one can boast. For we are God’s handiwork, created in Christ Jesus to do good works, which God prepared in advance for us to do” (Eph 2:8–10).

ACTS 16:24–34

"WHAT MUST I DO TO BE SAVED?"

Faith is about trusting in Jesus regardless of daily circumstances. Paul and Silas had been beaten, stripped and thrown in jail for following Jesus (16:22–23), but the real test of their faith came in how they responded to their imprisonment. They didn't seek legal action or resort to grumbling; they didn't question God's plan. Instead, they decided to pray and sing to God (16:25). This activity and their attitude must have seemed strange to the other prisoners—and to the jailer!

To show his glory through Paul and Silas's circumstances, God sent an earthquake to shake things up. The jailer thought the prisoners had escaped; desperate, he prepared to take his own life: he knew he would be sentenced to death if the prisoners escaped under his watch. Instead of seeking their own welfare, Paul and Silas stayed in the prison and ministered to the jailer. It had to be mind-boggling to see two prisoners respond to his cruelty in such a tender way.

He asked the question that is "The Question" for people who have seen God and his people at work: "What must I do to be saved?" (16:30). The answer is simple because the message is clear: "Believe in the Lord Jesus, and you will be saved" (16:31). Paul was a brilliant theologian, but he also knew that the message of Jesus was beautifully simple, and he was ready to share it clearly in a moment of openness and opportunity.

chose Silas and left, commended by the believers to the grace of the Lord. [41]He went through Syria and Cilicia, strengthening the churches.

Timothy Joins Paul and Silas

16 Paul came to Derbe and then to Lystra, where a disciple named Timothy lived, whose mother was Jewish and a believer but whose father was a Greek. [2]The believers at Lystra and Iconium spoke well of him. [3]Paul wanted to take him along on the journey, so he circumcised him because of the Jews who lived in that area, for they all knew that his father was a Greek. [4]As they traveled from town to town, they delivered the decisions reached by the apostles and elders in Jerusalem for the people to obey. [5]So the churches were strengthened in the faith and grew daily in numbers.

Paul's Vision of the Man of Macedonia

[6]Paul and his companions traveled throughout the region of Phrygia and Galatia, having been kept by the Holy Spirit from preaching the word in the province of Asia. [7]When they came to the border of Mysia, they tried to enter Bithynia, but the Spirit of Jesus would not allow them to. [8]So they passed by Mysia and went down to Troas. [9]During the night Paul had a vision of a man of Macedonia standing and begging him, "Come over to Macedonia and help us." [10]After Paul had seen the vision, we got ready at once to leave for Macedonia, concluding that God had called us to preach the gospel to them.

Lydia's Conversion in Philippi

[11]From Troas we put out to sea and sailed straight for Samothrace, and the next day we went on to Neapolis. [12]From there we traveled to Philippi, a Roman colony and the leading city of that district[a] of Macedonia. And we stayed there several days.

[13]On the Sabbath we went outside the city gate to the river, where we expected to find a place of prayer. We sat down and began to speak to the women who had gathered there. [14]One of those listening was a woman from the city of Thyatira named Lydia, a dealer in purple cloth. She was a worshiper of God. The Lord opened her heart to respond to Paul's message. [15]When she and the members of her household were baptized, she invited us to her home. "If you consider me a believer in the Lord," she said, "come and stay at my house." And she persuaded us.

Paul and Silas in Prison

[16]Once when we were going to the place of prayer, we were met by a female slave who had a spirit by which she predicted the future. She earned a great deal of money for her owners by fortune-telling. [17]She followed Paul and the rest of us, shouting, "These men are servants of the Most High God, who are telling you the way to be saved." [18]She kept this up for many days. Finally Paul became so annoyed that he turned around and said to the spirit, "In the name of Jesus Christ I command you to come out of her!" At that moment the spirit left her.

[19]When her owners realized that their hope of making money was gone, they seized Paul and Silas and dragged them into the marketplace to face the authorities. [20]They brought them before the magistrates and said, "These men are Jews, and are throwing our city into an uproar [21]by advocating customs unlawful for us Romans to accept or practice."

[22]The crowd joined in the attack against Paul and Silas, and the magistrates ordered them to be stripped and beaten with rods. [23]After they had been severely flogged, they were thrown into prison, and the jailer was commanded to guard them carefully. [24]When he received these orders, he put them in the inner cell and fastened their feet in the stocks.

---

[a] 12 The text and meaning of the Greek for *the leading city of that district* are uncertain.

25About midnight Paul and Silas were praying and singing hymns to God, and the other prisoners were listening to them. 26Suddenly there was such a violent earthquake that the foundations of the prison were shaken. At once all the prison doors flew open, and everyone's chains came loose. 27The jailer woke up, and when he saw the prison doors open, he drew his sword and was about to kill himself because he thought the prisoners had escaped. 28But Paul shouted, "Don't harm yourself! We are all here!"

29The jailer called for lights, rushed in and fell trembling before Paul and Silas. 30He then brought them out and asked, "Sirs, what must I do to be saved?"

31They replied, "Believe in the Lord Jesus, and you will be saved — you and your household." 32Then they spoke the word of the Lord to him and to all the others in his house. 33At that hour of the night the jailer took them and washed their wounds; then immediately he and all his household were baptized. 34The jailer brought them into his house and set a meal before them; he was filled with joy because he had come to believe in God — he and his whole household.

35When it was daylight, the magistrates sent their officers to the jailer with the order: "Release those men." 36The jailer told Paul, "The magistrates have ordered that you and Silas be released. Now you can leave. Go in peace."

37But Paul said to the officers: "They beat us publicly without a trial, even though we are Roman citizens, and threw us into prison. And now do they want to get rid of us quietly? No! Let them come themselves and escort us out."

38The officers reported this to the magistrates, and when they heard that Paul and Silas were Roman citizens, they were alarmed. 39They came to appease them and escorted them from the prison, requesting them to leave the city. 40After Paul and Silas came out of the prison, they went to Lydia's house, where they met with the brothers and sisters and encouraged them. Then they left.

In Thessalonica

17 When Paul and his companions had passed through Amphipolis and Apollonia, they came to Thessalonica, where there was a Jewish synagogue. 2As was his custom, Paul went into the synagogue, and on three Sabbath days he reasoned with them from the Scriptures, 3explaining and proving that the Messiah had to suffer and rise from the dead. "This Jesus I am proclaiming to you is the Messiah," he said. 4Some of the Jews were persuaded and joined Paul and Silas, as did a large number of God-fearing Greeks and quite a few prominent women.

5But other Jews were jealous; so they rounded up some bad characters from the marketplace, formed a mob and started a riot in the city. They rushed to Jason's house in search of Paul and Silas in order to bring them out to the crowd.[a] 6But when they did not find them, they dragged Jason and some other believers before the city officials, shouting: "These men who have caused trouble all over the world have now come here, 7and Jason has welcomed them into his house. They are all defying Caesar's decrees, saying that there is another king, one called Jesus." 8When they heard this, the crowd and the city officials were thrown into turmoil. 9Then they made Jason and the others post bond and let them go.

In Berea

10As soon as it was night, the believers sent Paul and Silas away to Berea. On arriving there, they went to the Jewish synagogue. 11Now the Berean Jews were of more noble character than those in Thessalonica, for they received the message with great eagerness and examined the Scriptures every day to see if what Paul said was true. 12As a result, many of them believed, as did also a number of prominent Greek women and many Greek men.

13But when the Jews in Thessalonica learned that Paul was preaching the

[a] 5 Or *the assembly of the people*

word of God at Berea, some of them went there too, agitating the crowds and stirring them up. 14The believers immediately sent Paul to the coast, but Silas and
Timothy stayed at Berea. 15Those who escorted Paul brought him to Athens and
then left with instructions for Silas and Timothy to join him as soon as possible.

In Athens

16While Paul was waiting for them in Athens, he was greatly distressed to see
that the city was full of idols. 17So he reasoned in the synagogue with both Jews
and God-fearing Greeks, as well as in the marketplace day by day with those who
happened to be there. 18A group of Epicurean and Stoic philosophers began to
debate with him. Some of them asked, "What is this babbler trying to say?" Others remarked, "He seems to be advocating foreign gods." They said this because
Paul was preaching the good news about Jesus and the resurrection. 19Then they
took him and brought him to a meeting of the Areopagus, where they said to
him, "May we know what this new teaching is that you are presenting? 20You are
bringing some strange ideas to our ears, and we would like to know what they
mean." 21(All the Athenians and the foreigners who lived there spent their time
doing nothing but talking about and listening to the latest ideas.)

22Paul then stood up in the meeting of the Areopagus and said: "People of
Athens! I see that in every way you are very religious. 23For as I walked around
and looked carefully at your objects of worship, I even found an altar with this
inscription: TO AN UNKNOWN GOD. So you are ignorant of the very thing you worship — and this is what I am going to proclaim to you.

24"The God who made the world and everything in it is the Lord of heaven and
earth and does not live in temples built by human hands. 25And he is not served
by human hands, as if he needed anything. Rather, he himself gives everyone
life and breath and everything else. 26From one man he made all the nations,
that they should inhabit the whole earth; and he marked out their appointed
times in history and the boundaries of their lands. 27God did this so that they
would seek him and perhaps reach out for him and find him, though he is not far
from any one of us. 28'For in him we live and move and have our being.'[a] As some
of your own poets have said, 'We are his offspring.'[b]

29"Therefore since we are God's offspring, we should not think that the divine
being is like gold or silver or stone — an image made by human design and skill.
30In the past God overlooked such ignorance, but now he commands all people
everywhere to repent. 31For he has set a day when he will judge the world with
justice by the man he has appointed. He has given proof of this to everyone by
raising him from the dead."

32When they heard about the resurrection of the dead, some of them sneered,
but others said, "We want to hear you again on this subject." 33At that, Paul
left the Council. 34Some of the people became followers of Paul and believed.
Among them was Dionysius, a member of the Areopagus, also a woman named
Damaris, and a number of others.

In Corinth

18 After this, Paul left Athens and went to Corinth. 2There he met a Jew
named Aquila, a native of Pontus, who had recently come from Italy with
his wife Priscilla, because Claudius had ordered all Jews to leave Rome. Paul
went to see them, 3and because he was a tentmaker as they were, he stayed and
worked with them. 4Every Sabbath he reasoned in the synagogue, trying to persuade Jews and Greeks.

5When Silas and Timothy came from Macedonia, Paul devoted himself exclusively to preaching, testifying to the Jews that Jesus was the Messiah. 6But when
they opposed Paul and became abusive, he shook out his clothes in protest and

ACTS 17:23

AN UNKNOWN GOD

Sharing the story of Jesus begins with understanding the story people are living. Paul traveled the then-known world planting churches and sharing the story of Jesus. As he did, he shared the story in different ways, depending on people's life experiences. He looked for a simple way to connect with the people he met in order to talk about Jesus, "the way and the truth and the life" (Jn 14:6). As Paul looked around Athens to uncover the residents' story, he saw many idols to artificial gods that the people worshiped. Just in case they missed a god, they also had an altar set up with the inscription, "TO AN UNKNOWN GOD" (Ac 17:23). Paul knew this was his opportunity.

Paul did not ridicule the Athenians for their struggle with sin, nor did he blindly approve of it. Instead, Paul engaged their idolatry as an essential part of their story and turned their attention to Jesus. Since Mars Hill was directly opposite the Acropolis with its temples, it was clear to everyone that the people were very religious. Paul points out this reality and directs their attention to the true and living God.

Christians need to have a similar posture with the great cities of the world today. The church is a group of people who look for brokenness, connect with others on that basis and then bring the story of Jesus into the conversation.

[a] *28* From the Cretan philosopher Epimenides [b] *28* From the Cilician Stoic philosopher Aratus

said to them, "Your blood be on your own heads! I am innocent of it. From now
on I will go to the Gentiles."

[7]Then Paul left the synagogue and went next door to the house of Titius Justus, a worshiper of God. [8]Crispus, the synagogue leader, and his entire household believed in the Lord; and many of the Corinthians who heard Paul believed
and were baptized.

[9]One night the Lord spoke to Paul in a vision: "Do not be afraid; keep on
speaking, do not be silent. [10]For I am with you, and no one is going to attack and
harm you, because I have many people in this city." [11]So Paul stayed in Corinth
for a year and a half, teaching them the word of God.

[12]While Gallio was proconsul of Achaia, the Jews of Corinth made a united
attack on Paul and brought him to the place of judgment. [13]"This man," they
charged, "is persuading the people to worship God in ways contrary to the law."

[14]Just as Paul was about to speak, Gallio said to them, "If you Jews were making a complaint about some misdemeanor or serious crime, it would be reasonable for me to listen to you. [15]But since it involves questions about words and
names and your own law — settle the matter yourselves. I will not be a judge
of such things." [16]So he drove them off. [17]Then the crowd there turned on Sosthenes the synagogue leader and beat him in front of the proconsul; and Gallio
showed no concern whatever.

Priscilla, Aquila and Apollos

[18]Paul stayed on in Corinth for some time. Then he left the brothers and sisters and sailed for Syria, accompanied by Priscilla and Aquila. Before he sailed,
he had his hair cut off at Cenchreae because of a vow he had taken. [19]They arrived at Ephesus, where Paul left Priscilla and Aquila. He himself went into the
synagogue and reasoned with the Jews. [20]When they asked him to spend more
time with them, he declined. [21]But as he left, he promised, "I will come back if it
is God's will." Then he set sail from Ephesus. [22]When he landed at Caesarea, he
went up to Jerusalem and greeted the church and then went down to Antioch.

[23]After spending some time in Antioch, Paul set out from there and traveled
from place to place throughout the region of Galatia and Phrygia, strengthening
all the disciples.

[24]Meanwhile a Jew named Apollos, a native of Alexandria, came to Ephesus. He was a learned man, with a thorough knowledge of the Scriptures. [25]He
had been instructed in the way of the Lord, and he spoke with great fervor[a] and
taught about Jesus accurately, though he knew only the baptism of John. [26]He began to speak boldly in the synagogue. When Priscilla and Aquila heard him, they
invited him to their home and explained to him the way of God more adequately.

[27]When Apollos wanted to go to Achaia, the brothers and sisters encouraged
him and wrote to the disciples there to welcome him. When he arrived, he was
a great help to those who by grace had believed. [28]For he vigorously refuted his
Jewish opponents in public debate, proving from the Scriptures that Jesus was
the Messiah.

Paul in Ephesus

19 While Apollos was at Corinth, Paul took the road through the interior and
arrived at Ephesus. There he found some disciples [2]and asked them, "Did
you receive the Holy Spirit when[b] you believed?"

They answered, "No, we have not even heard that there is a Holy Spirit."

[3]So Paul asked, "Then what baptism did you receive?"

"John's baptism," they replied.

[4]Paul said, "John's baptism was a baptism of repentance. He told the people
to believe in the one coming after him, that is, in Jesus." [5]On hearing this, they
were baptized in the name of the Lord Jesus. [6]When Paul placed his hands on

[a] 25 Or *with fervor in the Spirit* [b] 2 Or *after*

them, the Holy Spirit came on them, and they spoke in tongues[a] and prophesied.
7There were about twelve men in all.

8Paul entered the synagogue and spoke boldly there for three months, arguing persuasively about the kingdom of God. 9But some of them became obstinate; they refused to believe and publicly maligned the Way. So Paul left them.
He took the disciples with him and had discussions daily in the lecture hall of
Tyrannus. 10This went on for two years, so that all the Jews and Greeks who lived
in the province of Asia heard the word of the Lord.

11God did extraordinary miracles through Paul, 12so that even handkerchiefs
and aprons that had touched him were taken to the sick, and their illnesses were
cured and the evil spirits left them.

13Some Jews who went around driving out evil spirits tried to invoke the name
of the Lord Jesus over those who were demon-possessed. They would say, "In the
name of the Jesus whom Paul preaches, I command you to come out." 14Seven
sons of Sceva, a Jewish chief priest, were doing this. 15One day the evil spirit answered them, "Jesus I know, and Paul I know about, but who are you?" 16Then the
man who had the evil spirit jumped on them and overpowered them all. He gave
them such a beating that they ran out of the house naked and bleeding.

17When this became known to the Jews and Greeks living in Ephesus, they
were all seized with fear, and the name of the Lord Jesus was held in high honor.
18Many of those who believed now came and openly confessed what they had
done. 19A number who had practiced sorcery brought their scrolls together and
burned them publicly. When they calculated the value of the scrolls, the total
came to fifty thousand drachmas.[b] 20In this way the word of the Lord spread
widely and grew in power.

21After all this had happened, Paul decided[c] to go to Jerusalem, passing
through Macedonia and Achaia. "After I have been there," he said, "I must visit
Rome also." 22He sent two of his helpers, Timothy and Erastus, to Macedonia,
while he stayed in the province of Asia a little longer.

The Riot in Ephesus

23About that time there arose a great disturbance about the Way. 24A silversmith named Demetrius, who made silver shrines of Artemis, brought in a lot
of business for the craftsmen there. 25He called them together, along with the
workers in related trades, and said: "You know, my friends, that we receive a
good income from this business. 26And you see and hear how this fellow Paul has
convinced and led astray large numbers of people here in Ephesus and in practically the whole province of Asia. He says that gods made by human hands are
no gods at all. 27There is danger not only that our trade will lose its good name,
but also that the temple of the great goddess Artemis will be discredited; and
the goddess herself, who is worshiped throughout the province of Asia and the
world, will be robbed of her divine majesty."

28When they heard this, they were furious and began shouting: "Great is Artemis of the Ephesians!" 29Soon the whole city was in an uproar. The people seized
Gaius and Aristarchus, Paul's traveling companions from Macedonia, and all
of them rushed into the theater together. 30Paul wanted to appear before the
crowd, but the disciples would not let him. 31Even some of the officials of the
province, friends of Paul, sent him a message begging him not to venture into
the theater.

32The assembly was in confusion: Some were shouting one thing, some another. Most of the people did not even know why they were there. 33The Jews in
the crowd pushed Alexander to the front, and they shouted instructions to him.
He motioned for silence in order to make a defense before the people. 34But when
they realized he was a Jew, they all shouted in unison for about two hours: "Great
is Artemis of the Ephesians!"

ACTS 19:13–17

"JESUS I KNOW . . . BUT WHO ARE YOU?"

Throughout history, religious practitioners and those who are involved in the occult have attempted to co-opt the name of Jesus, and the results are never good.

The Ephesian participants in these dark arts were aware of the apostle Paul and the incredible miracles that he was doing in the name of Jesus. Recognizing the power that came when the Name was used, they attempted to use it as well. The demon's verbal response is chilling, and these men paid the physical price for their misuse of Jesus' name (Ac 19:15–16).

The Bible tells us that demons have a great respect for Jesus. James says, "You believe that there is one God. Good! Even the demons believe that—and shudder" (Jas 2:19). Even though they do not love God, they know about and tremble at the thought of him. The would-be exorcists had a weak theology compared to the demons. They tried to use Jesus' name without really identifying with him or following him in their own lives.

The name of Jesus is never to be used to enhance one's status. Instead, it is a gift that should be upheld with reverence and used to honor God. Jesus has rescued his people from the dominion of darkness so that they can live as his agents of light (Col 1:13–15).

[a] 6 Or *other languages* [b] 19 A drachma was a silver coin worth about a day's wages.
[c] 21 Or *decided in the Spirit*

PAUL'S THIRD MISSIONARY JOURNEY

We see from Paul's life that God's people are sometimes called to be mobile. Paul took three major missionary journeys. Each of these trips had a different strategy, but all of them had the same goal: spreading God's glory by planting and strengthening churches among the unreached parts of the Greco-Roman world.

Paul fostered many close relationships during his journeys, spending three full years in Ephesus that were especially formative periods in his ministry. He maintained contact with the church in Corinth, a church that actually sent people to Paul to update him on what was happening in the life of their congregation (1Co 1:11; 16:17). Paul wrote at least two letters to those believers in Corinth while in Ephesus, and he visited Corinth on his missionary journeys.

During Paul's missionary journeys, the Holy Spirit created extraordinary gospel unity. We see this in the networking that Paul did with other churches during his journeys. As Paul was passing through Macedonia, he received a substantial financial gift to take to the poorer Christians living in Jerusalem. He also asked the believers in Corinth to contribute, and they did as well. These were largely Gentile believers raising support for their Jewish brothers and sisters.

Finally, Paul found opportunity to write letters during his journeys. During the three months that Paul was in Corinth, before he left for Jerusalem, Paul wrote his letter to the church in Rome. God worked through Paul to lay out a masterful exposition of theology in order to foster understanding in the church and to motivate believers in Rome to support his missionary efforts.

As believers read about Paul's example, they see him taking God's Word to the ends of what was the known world at the time. They can take that as inspiration to follow Jesus' call, as Paul did, to teach, baptize and tell others about Jesus — whether that be in the family, in the neighborhood, or on the other side of the world.

35The city clerk quieted the crowd and said: "Fellow Ephesians, doesn't all the world know that the city of Ephesus is the guardian of the temple of the great Artemis and of her image, which fell from heaven? 36Therefore, since these facts are undeniable, you ought to calm down and not do anything rash. 37You have brought these men here, though they have neither robbed temples nor blasphemed our goddess. 38If, then, Demetrius and his fellow craftsmen have a grievance against anybody, the courts are open and there are proconsuls. They can press charges. 39If there is anything further you want to bring up, it must be settled in a legal assembly. 40As it is, we are in danger of being charged with rioting because of what happened today. In that case we would not be able to account for this commotion, since there is no reason for it." 41After he had said this, he dismissed the assembly.

Through Macedonia and Greece

20 When the uproar had ended, Paul sent for the disciples and, after encouraging them, said goodbye and set out for Macedonia. 2He traveled through that area, speaking many words of encouragement to the people, and finally arrived in Greece, 3where he stayed three months. Because some Jews had plotted against him just as he was about to sail for Syria, he decided to go back through Macedonia. 4He was accompanied by Sopater son of Pyrrhus from Berea, Aristarchus and Secundus from Thessalonica, Gaius from Derbe, Timothy also, and Tychicus and Trophimus from the province of Asia. 5These men went on ahead and waited for us at Troas. 6But we sailed from Philippi after the Festival of Unleavened Bread, and five days later joined the others at Troas, where we stayed seven days.

Eutychus Raised From the Dead at Troas

7On the first day of the week we came together to break bread. Paul spoke to the people and, because he intended to leave the next day, kept on talking until midnight. 8There were many lamps in the upstairs room where we were meeting. 9Seated in a window was a young man named Eutychus, who was sinking into a deep sleep as Paul talked on and on. When he was sound asleep, he fell to the ground from the third story and was picked up dead. 10Paul went down, threw himself on the young man and put his arms around him. "Don't be alarmed," he said. "He's alive!" 11Then he went upstairs again and broke bread and ate. After talking until daylight, he left. 12The people took the young man home alive and were greatly comforted.

Paul's Farewell to the Ephesian Elders

13We went on ahead to the ship and sailed for Assos, where we were going to take Paul aboard. He had made this arrangement because he was going there on foot. 14When he met us at Assos, we took him aboard and went on to Mitylene. 15The next day we set sail from there and arrived off Chios. The day after that we crossed over to Samos, and on the following day arrived at Miletus. 16Paul had decided to sail past Ephesus to avoid spending time in the province of Asia, for he was in a hurry to reach Jerusalem, if possible, by the day of Pentecost.

17From Miletus, Paul sent to Ephesus for the elders of the church. 18When they arrived, he said to them: "You know how I lived the whole time I was with you, from the first day I came into the province of Asia. 19I served the Lord with great humility and with tears and in the midst of severe testing by the plots of my Jewish opponents. 20You know that I have not hesitated to preach anything that would be helpful to you but have taught you publicly and from house to house. 21I have declared to both Jews and Greeks that they must turn to God in repentance and have faith in our Lord Jesus.

22"And now, compelled by the Spirit, I am going to Jerusalem, not knowing what will happen to me there. 23I only know that in every city the Holy Spirit warns me that prison and hardships are facing me. 24However, I consider my life

ACTS 20:24

THE GOOD NEWS OF GOD'S GRACE

Telling people about Jesus is a joy for those who realize what God has saved them from and what God has saved them to do. Paul laid out the single ambition of his life: to testify to the good news of God's grace. Grace refers to the love God shows to us through Jesus. We don't deserve it, and we could never earn it. Every person who ever lived is responsible for the death of Jesus (Ro 4:25; 5:8). Our sin made the cross necessary. Each of us is guilty and deserving of punishment forever. But God pursues people in his love (Lk 19:10) and freely forgives people when they turn to Jesus in repentance (Heb 9:14).

Paul invited the church to join him in sharing about the grace of God: "Join with me in suffering for the gospel, by the power of God. He has saved us and called us to a holy life—not because of anything we have done but because of his own purpose and grace. This grace was given us in Christ Jesus before the beginning of time" (2Ti 1:8–9). God has saved his people from eternal punishment by his generous and merciful grace. For those who remember that they are saved to new life in Jesus by his grace alone, sharing about this Good News is an incredible joy!

worth nothing to me; my only aim is to finish the race and complete the task the
Lord Jesus has given me — the task of testifying to the good news of God's grace.
25“Now I know that none of you among whom I have gone about preaching
the kingdom will ever see me again. 26Therefore, I declare to you today that I am
innocent of the blood of any of you. 27For I have not hesitated to proclaim to you
the whole will of God. 28Keep watch over yourselves and all the flock of which the
Holy Spirit has made you overseers. Be shepherds of the church of God,[a] which
he bought with his own blood.[b] 29I know that after I leave, savage wolves will
come in among you and will not spare the flock. 30Even from your own number
men will arise and distort the truth in order to draw away disciples after them.
31So be on your guard! Remember that for three years I never stopped warning
each of you night and day with tears.
32“Now I commit you to God and to the word of his grace, which can build
you up and give you an inheritance among all those who are sanctified. 33I have
not coveted anyone's silver or gold or clothing. 34You yourselves know that these
hands of mine have supplied my own needs and the needs of my companions.
35In everything I did, I showed you that by this kind of hard work we must help
the weak, remembering the words the Lord Jesus himself said: ‘It is more blessed
to give than to receive.’ ”
36When Paul had finished speaking, he knelt down with all of them and
prayed. 37They all wept as they embraced him and kissed him. 38What grieved
them most was his statement that they would never see his face again. Then they
accompanied him to the ship.

On to Jerusalem

21 After we had torn ourselves away from them, we put out to sea and sailed
straight to Kos. The next day we went to Rhodes and from there to Patara.
2We found a ship crossing over to Phoenicia, went on board and set sail. 3After
sighting Cyprus and passing to the south of it, we sailed on to Syria. We landed at
Tyre, where our ship was to unload its cargo. 4We sought out the disciples there
and stayed with them seven days. Through the Spirit they urged Paul not to go
on to Jerusalem. 5When it was time to leave, we left and continued on our way.
All of them, including wives and children, accompanied us out of the city, and
there on the beach we knelt to pray. 6After saying goodbye to each other, we went
aboard the ship, and they returned home.
7We continued our voyage from Tyre and landed at Ptolemais, where we
greeted the brothers and sisters and stayed with them for a day. 8Leaving the
next day, we reached Caesarea and stayed at the house of Philip the evangelist,
one of the Seven. 9He had four unmarried daughters who prophesied.
10After we had been there a number of days, a prophet named Agabus came
down from Judea. 11Coming over to us, he took Paul's belt, tied his own hands and
feet with it and said, “The Holy Spirit says, ‘In this way the Jewish leaders in Jerusalem will bind the owner of this belt and will hand him over to the Gentiles.’ ”
12When we heard this, we and the people there pleaded with Paul not to go
up to Jerusalem. 13Then Paul answered, “Why are you weeping and breaking my
heart? I am ready not only to be bound, but also to die in Jerusalem for the name
of the Lord Jesus.” 14When he would not be dissuaded, we gave up and said, “The
Lord's will be done.”
15After this, we started on our way up to Jerusalem. 16Some of the disciples
from Caesarea accompanied us and brought us to the home of Mnason, where
we were to stay. He was a man from Cyprus and one of the early disciples.

Paul's Arrival at Jerusalem

17When we arrived at Jerusalem, the brothers and sisters received us warmly.
18The next day Paul and the rest of us went to see James, and all the elders were

[a] *28* Many manuscripts *of the Lord* [b] *28* Or *with the blood of his own Son.*

PETER AND PAUL

The Bible tells the story of God's mission to heal the world through Jesus. Through the book of Acts, the focus of God's advancing of this mission narrows to the lives of two people in the early church: Peter and Paul. In these two men we find many similarities, but also some deep contrasts.

Peter was one of Jesus' original disciples. He followed Jesus through his entire ministry and experienced Jesus' miracles and teachings firsthand. Yet Peter also struggled with his belief in and loyalty to Jesus. As such, Peter is a comforting character for many Christians today. One might expect Peter to have had a clear picture of Jesus as the Messiah, as he professed (Mt 16:16). And yet, like the other disciples, he struggled with Jesus' teachings (Jn 16:17 – 18); Jesus even had to rebuke him several times during their ministry together (Mt 26:31 – 35; Mk 8:32 – 33; 14:37). Peter is an example of someone who took a long time to "get it." Nevertheless, Jesus was faithful to Peter even when Peter struggled to be faithful to him.

Paul was an opponent of the church and an enemy of God — by all human accounts, he was the last kind of person one would expect to become a Christian. Paul was caught up in his own way of life, in his own way of practicing religion. But Jesus broke through to Paul, rocked his world to its foundations and saved him. Paul's life changed dramatically. He went from being a great opponent of Jesus to a great leader in the church within a few years. Unlike Peter, Paul's understanding of Jesus' identity and mission seemed instantaneous.

The author of Acts records many parallel events involving Peter and Paul to show that they were both effective servants of God. They both had direct encounters with Jesus (Peter, Mt 14:22 – 34; Paul, Ac 9:1 – 19), and they repented of their sins and trusted in him. Each man pronounced judgment against a sorcerer (Peter, Ac 8:20 – 23; Paul, Ac 13:9 – 11), healed men who had been disabled from birth (Peter, Ac 3:6; Paul, Ac 14:8 – 10) and exhibited amazing Spirit-empowered healing (Peter, Ac 5:15; Paul, Ac 19:12).

Peter and Paul represent different extremes of the same process. Peter's path to ministry was one of following Jesus up close for a season and then becoming a builder of the church after Jesus' ascension. Paul, on the other hand, took a different path. But both men's lives were transformed by Jesus, and their ministries were Spirit empowered. No matter what one's spiritual heritage is, Jesus can transform any life, and the Spirit is available to empower a life of ministry.

present. [19]Paul greeted them and reported in detail what God had done among the Gentiles through his ministry.

[20]When they heard this, they praised God. Then they said to Paul: "You see, brother, how many thousands of Jews have believed, and all of them are zealous for the law. [21]They have been informed that you teach all the Jews who live among the Gentiles to turn away from Moses, telling them not to circumcise their children or live according to our customs. [22]What shall we do? They will certainly hear that you have come, [23]so do what we tell you. There are four men with us who have made a vow. [24]Take these men, join in their purification rites and pay their expenses, so that they can have their heads shaved. Then everyone will know there is no truth in these reports about you, but that you yourself are living in obedience to the law. [25]As for the Gentile believers, we have written to them our decision that they should abstain from food sacrificed to idols, from blood, from the meat of strangled animals and from sexual immorality."

[26]The next day Paul took the men and purified himself along with them. Then he went to the temple to give notice of the date when the days of purification would end and the offering would be made for each of them.

Paul Arrested

[27]When the seven days were nearly over, some Jews from the province of Asia saw Paul at the temple. They stirred up the whole crowd and seized him, [28]shouting, "Fellow Israelites, help us! This is the man who teaches everyone everywhere against our people and our law and this place. And besides, he has brought Greeks into the temple and defiled this holy place." [29](They had previously seen Trophimus the Ephesian in the city with Paul and assumed that Paul had brought him into the temple.)

[30]The whole city was aroused, and the people came running from all directions. Seizing Paul, they dragged him from the temple, and immediately the gates were shut. [31]While they were trying to kill him, news reached the commander of the Roman troops that the whole city of Jerusalem was in an uproar. [32]He at once took some officers and soldiers and ran down to the crowd. When the rioters saw the commander and his soldiers, they stopped beating Paul.

[33]The commander came up and arrested him and ordered him to be bound with two chains. Then he asked who he was and what he had done. [34]Some in the crowd shouted one thing and some another, and since the commander could not get at the truth because of the uproar, he ordered that Paul be taken into the barracks. [35]When Paul reached the steps, the violence of the mob was so great he had to be carried by the soldiers. [36]The crowd that followed kept shouting, "Get rid of him!"

Paul Speaks to the Crowd

[37]As the soldiers were about to take Paul into the barracks, he asked the commander, "May I say something to you?"

"Do you speak Greek?" he replied. [38]"Aren't you the Egyptian who started a revolt and led four thousand terrorists out into the wilderness some time ago?"

[39]Paul answered, "I am a Jew, from Tarsus in Cilicia, a citizen of no ordinary city. Please let me speak to the people."

[40]After receiving the commander's permission, Paul stood on the steps and motioned to the crowd. When they were all silent, he said to them in

22 Aramaic[a]: [1]"Brothers and fathers, listen now to my defense."

[2]When they heard him speak to them in Aramaic, they became very quiet.

Then Paul said: [3]"I am a Jew, born in Tarsus of Cilicia, but brought up in this city. I studied under Gamaliel and was thoroughly trained in the law of our ancestors. I was just as zealous for God as any of you are today. [4]I persecuted the followers of this Way to their death, arresting both men and women and throwing

[a] *40* Or possibly *Hebrew*; also in 22:2

them into prison, [5]as the high priest and all the Council can themselves testify. I even obtained letters from them to their associates in Damascus, and went there to bring these people as prisoners to Jerusalem to be punished.

[6]"About noon as I came near Damascus, suddenly a bright light from heaven flashed around me. [7]I fell to the ground and heard a voice say to me, 'Saul! Saul! Why do you persecute me?'

[8]" 'Who are you, Lord?' I asked.

" 'I am Jesus of Nazareth, whom you are persecuting,' he replied. [9]My companions saw the light, but they did not understand the voice of him who was speaking to me.

[10]" 'What shall I do, Lord?' I asked.

" 'Get up,' the Lord said, 'and go into Damascus. There you will be told all that you have been assigned to do.' [11]My companions led me by the hand into Damascus, because the brilliance of the light had blinded me.

[12]"A man named Ananias came to see me. He was a devout observer of the law and highly respected by all the Jews living there. [13]He stood beside me and said, 'Brother Saul, receive your sight!' And at that very moment I was able to see him.

[14]"Then he said: 'The God of our ancestors has chosen you to know his will and to see the Righteous One and to hear words from his mouth. [15]You will be his witness to all people of what you have seen and heard. [16]And now what are you waiting for? Get up, be baptized and wash your sins away, calling on his name.'

[17]"When I returned to Jerusalem and was praying at the temple, I fell into a trance [18]and saw the Lord speaking to me. 'Quick!' he said. 'Leave Jerusalem immediately, because the people here will not accept your testimony about me.'

[19]" 'Lord,' I replied, 'these people know that I went from one synagogue to another to imprison and beat those who believe in you. [20]And when the blood of your martyr[a] Stephen was shed, I stood there giving my approval and guarding the clothes of those who were killing him.'

[21]"Then the Lord said to me, 'Go; I will send you far away to the Gentiles.' "

Paul the Roman Citizen

[22]The crowd listened to Paul until he said this. Then they raised their voices and shouted, "Rid the earth of him! He's not fit to live!"

[23]As they were shouting and throwing off their cloaks and flinging dust into the air, [24]the commander ordered that Paul be taken into the barracks. He directed that he be flogged and interrogated in order to find out why the people were shouting at him like this. [25]As they stretched him out to flog him, Paul said to the centurion standing there, "Is it legal for you to flog a Roman citizen who hasn't even been found guilty?"

[26]When the centurion heard this, he went to the commander and reported it. "What are you going to do?" he asked. "This man is a Roman citizen."

[27]The commander went to Paul and asked, "Tell me, are you a Roman citizen?"

"Yes, I am," he answered.

[28]Then the commander said, "I had to pay a lot of money for my citizenship."

"But I was born a citizen," Paul replied.

[29]Those who were about to interrogate him withdrew immediately. The commander himself was alarmed when he realized that he had put Paul, a Roman citizen, in chains.

Paul Before the Sanhedrin

[30]The commander wanted to find out exactly why Paul was being accused by the Jews. So the next day he released him and ordered the chief priests and all the members of the Sanhedrin to assemble. Then he brought Paul and had him stand before them.

[a] 20 Or *witness*

ACTS 22:6–10

THE PERSONAL GOSPEL

Many kinds of people, living all around the world and down through the centuries, have believed the truth of Christianity. Though the scope of Christianity is universal, Christianity is a very personal religion for those who trust in God. Before Paul was a follower of Jesus, he was an enemy of Jesus and his cause. He spent his early years trying to stop God's redemptive work in the world through his Messiah. When Jesus confronted Saul, he said, "Saul! Saul! Why do you persecute me?" (Ac 22:7). Jesus took Saul's persecution of the church personally.

In addition to this, the implications of Christianity are personal as well. Jesus is not simply an idea to be thought about; rather, he is a person who invites us into relationship with him. When Paul became a follower of Jesus, he learned that his Savior had a specific assignment for him (Ac 22:10). Jesus took Saul's opposition personally. And after he confronted Paul, this former enemy took the implications of that call just as personally. Every single believer in the church has a joyful responsibility to do the same—to take Jesus' call to heart and to play their own unique role in God's mission to show his glory to the world.

23 Paul looked straight at the Sanhedrin and said, "My brothers, I have fulfilled my duty to God in all good conscience to this day." 2At this the high priest Ananias ordered those standing near Paul to strike him on the mouth. 3Then Paul said to him, "God will strike you, you whitewashed wall! You sit there to judge me according to the law, yet you yourself violate the law by commanding that I be struck!"

4Those who were standing near Paul said, "How dare you insult God's high priest!"

5Paul replied, "Brothers, I did not realize that he was the high priest; for it is written: 'Do not speak evil about the ruler of your people.'[a]"

6Then Paul, knowing that some of them were Sadducees and the others Pharisees, called out in the Sanhedrin, "My brothers, I am a Pharisee, descended from Pharisees. I stand on trial because of the hope of the resurrection of the dead." 7When he said this, a dispute broke out between the Pharisees and the Sadducees, and the assembly was divided. 8(The Sadducees say that there is no resurrection, and that there are neither angels nor spirits, but the Pharisees believe all these things.)

9There was a great uproar, and some of the teachers of the law who were Pharisees stood up and argued vigorously. "We find nothing wrong with this man," they said. "What if a spirit or an angel has spoken to him?" 10The dispute became so violent that the commander was afraid Paul would be torn to pieces by them. He ordered the troops to go down and take him away from them by force and bring him into the barracks.

11The following night the Lord stood near Paul and said, "Take courage! As you have testified about me in Jerusalem, so you must also testify in Rome."

The Plot to Kill Paul

12The next morning some Jews formed a conspiracy and bound themselves with an oath not to eat or drink until they had killed Paul. 13More than forty men were involved in this plot. 14They went to the chief priests and the elders and said, "We have taken a solemn oath not to eat anything until we have killed Paul. 15Now then, you and the Sanhedrin petition the commander to bring him before you on the pretext of wanting more accurate information about his case. We are ready to kill him before he gets here."

16But when the son of Paul's sister heard of this plot, he went into the barracks and told Paul.

17Then Paul called one of the centurions and said, "Take this young man to the commander; he has something to tell him." 18So he took him to the commander.

The centurion said, "Paul, the prisoner, sent for me and asked me to bring this young man to you because he has something to tell you."

19The commander took the young man by the hand, drew him aside and asked, "What is it you want to tell me?"

20He said: "Some Jews have agreed to ask you to bring Paul before the Sanhedrin tomorrow on the pretext of wanting more accurate information about him. 21Don't give in to them, because more than forty of them are waiting in ambush for him. They have taken an oath not to eat or drink until they have killed him. They are ready now, waiting for your consent to their request."

22The commander dismissed the young man with this warning: "Don't tell anyone that you have reported this to me."

Paul Transferred to Caesarea

23Then he called two of his centurions and ordered them, "Get ready a detachment of two hundred soldiers, seventy horsemen and two hundred spearmen[b] to go to Caesarea at nine tonight. 24Provide horses for Paul so that he may be taken safely to Governor Felix."

ACTS 23:11

PERSONAL SAVIOR

Jesus is a personal Savior. He came to save the world, and he does that by saving people individually as they trust in him. Jesus is not a distant cosmic deity, unaware of what is happening in his world. Instead, Jesus is intensely and personally aware of and concerned about every detail of our lives.

Paul was on trial in front of the Jewish religious leadership of his day. A near-riot broke out, and Paul suffered because of it. These leaders wanted to kill Paul because of the message he shared. In the midst of this hardship, Jesus showed up personally to care for his apostle. Our living Savior physically appeared to Paul and gave him his next assignment.

As he wrote in his letter to the Romans (Ro 8:38 – 39), nothing could keep Paul from Jesus. Paul was in a difficult circumstance, but Jesus was aware of it and chose to interact with him personally. While such interactions are not common, they are real. Jesus' awareness and concern for individuals continues today. He is the great God of the universe who has come near to love people individually.

[a] *5* Exodus 22:28 [b] *23* The meaning of the Greek for this word is uncertain.

ACTS 24:14 – 16

THE WAY

The entire Bible is the story of how people gain access to God. In the first part of the Bible, God established the Law as a way for people to atone for their sins. In the second part, God called prophets to mediate the relationship between God and his people. Finally, God sent Jesus to be the fulfillment of the Law and the Prophets and to personally give people eternal access to God.

Jesus is the only way to God; he said, "I am the way and the truth and the life. No one comes to the Father except through me" (Jn 14:6). Human sin has created an impassable canyon between God and his people. Paul testified that Jesus is "the Way" back to God and believed that Jesus' claims were consistent with the Law and the Prophets.

The Old Testament provides a rich and detailed backdrop for Jesus' life and helps people see Jesus more clearly. In a sense, viewing Jesus against the backdrop of the Old Testament is like seeing a movie in 3D. Three-dimensional movies accomplish depth by adding different visual dimensions on the screen. In a similar way, our relationship with Jesus becomes more vivid when we understand him within the story of the Bible as the fulfillment of the Law. Jesus taught his followers to read the whole Bible in reference to him: "Beginning with Moses and all the Prophets, he explained to them what was said in all the Scriptures concerning himself" (Lk 24:27).

25He wrote a letter as follows:

26Claudius Lysias,
To His Excellency, Governor Felix:
Greetings.

27This man was seized by the Jews and they were about to kill him, but I
came with my troops and rescued him, for I had learned that he is a Roman
citizen. 28I wanted to know why they were accusing him, so I brought him
to their Sanhedrin. 29I found that the accusation had to do with questions
about their law, but there was no charge against him that deserved death
or imprisonment. 30When I was informed of a plot to be carried out against
the man, I sent him to you at once. I also ordered his accusers to present to
you their case against him.

31So the soldiers, carrying out their orders, took Paul with them during the
night and brought him as far as Antipatris. 32The next day they let the cavalry go
on with him, while they returned to the barracks. 33When the cavalry arrived in
Caesarea, they delivered the letter to the governor and handed Paul over to him.
34The governor read the letter and asked what province he was from. Learning
that he was from Cilicia, 35he said, "I will hear your case when your accusers get
here." Then he ordered that Paul be kept under guard in Herod's palace.

Paul's Trial Before Felix

24 Five days later the high priest Ananias went down to Caesarea with some
of the elders and a lawyer named Tertullus, and they brought their charges against Paul before the governor. 2When Paul was called in, Tertullus presented his case before Felix: "We have enjoyed a long period of peace under you,
and your foresight has brought about reforms in this nation. 3Everywhere and in
every way, most excellent Felix, we acknowledge this with profound gratitude.
4But in order not to weary you further, I would request that you be kind enough
to hear us briefly.
5"We have found this man to be a troublemaker, stirring up riots among the
Jews all over the world. He is a ringleader of the Nazarene sect 6and even tried to
desecrate the temple; so we seized him. [7][a] 8By examining him yourself you will
be able to learn the truth about all these charges we are bringing against him."
9The other Jews joined in the accusation, asserting that these things were
true.
10When the governor motioned for him to speak, Paul replied: "I know that
for a number of years you have been a judge over this nation; so I gladly make
my defense. 11You can easily verify that no more than twelve days ago I went up
to Jerusalem to worship. 12My accusers did not find me arguing with anyone
at the temple, or stirring up a crowd in the synagogues or anywhere else in the
city. 13And they cannot prove to you the charges they are now making against
me. 14However, I admit that I worship the God of our ancestors as a follower of
the Way, which they call a sect. I believe everything that is in accordance with
the Law and that is written in the Prophets, 15and I have the same hope in God
as these men themselves have, that there will be a resurrection of both the righteous and the wicked. 16So I strive always to keep my conscience clear before
God and man.
17"After an absence of several years, I came to Jerusalem to bring my people
gifts for the poor and to present offerings. 18I was ceremonially clean when they
found me in the temple courts doing this. There was no crowd with me, nor was

[a] 6-8 Some manuscripts include here *him, and we would have judged him in accordance with our law. 7But the commander Lysias came and took him from us with much violence, 8ordering his accusers to come before you.*

I involved in any disturbance. [19]But there are some Jews from the province of
Asia, who ought to be here before you and bring charges if they have anything
against me. [20]Or these who are here should state what crime they found in me
when I stood before the Sanhedrin— [21]unless it was this one thing I shouted as
I stood in their presence: 'It is concerning the resurrection of the dead that I am
on trial before you today.' "

[22]Then Felix, who was well acquainted with the Way, adjourned the proceed-
ings. "When Lysias the commander comes," he said, "I will decide your case."
[23]He ordered the centurion to keep Paul under guard but to give him some freedom and permit his friends to take care of his needs.

[24]Several days later Felix came with his wife Drusilla, who was Jewish. He
sent for Paul and listened to him as he spoke about faith in Christ Jesus. [25]As
Paul talked about righteousness, self-control and the judgment to come, Felix
was afraid and said, "That's enough for now! You may leave. When I find it convenient, I will send for you." [26]At the same time he was hoping that Paul would
offer him a bribe, so he sent for him frequently and talked with him.

[27]When two years had passed, Felix was succeeded by Porcius Festus, but because Felix wanted to grant a favor to the Jews, he left Paul in prison.

Paul's Trial Before Festus

25 Three days after arriving in the province, Festus went up from Caesarea to
Jerusalem, [2]where the chief priests and the Jewish leaders appeared before
him and presented the charges against Paul. [3]They requested Festus, as a favor to
them, to have Paul transferred to Jerusalem, for they were preparing an ambush
to kill him along the way. [4]Festus answered, "Paul is being held at Caesarea, and
I myself am going there soon. [5]Let some of your leaders come with me, and if the
man has done anything wrong, they can press charges against him there."

[6]After spending eight or ten days with them, Festus went down to Caesarea.
The next day he convened the court and ordered that Paul be brought before
him. [7]When Paul came in, the Jews who had come down from Jerusalem stood
around him. They brought many serious charges against him, but they could
not prove them.

[8]Then Paul made his defense: "I have done nothing wrong against the Jewish
law or against the temple or against Caesar."

[9]Festus, wishing to do the Jews a favor, said to Paul, "Are you willing to go up
to Jerusalem and stand trial before me there on these charges?"

[10]Paul answered: "I am now standing before Caesar's court, where I ought to
be tried. I have not done any wrong to the Jews, as you yourself know very well.
[11]If, however, I am guilty of doing anything deserving death, I do not refuse to
die. But if the charges brought against me by these Jews are not true, no one has
the right to hand me over to them. I appeal to Caesar!"

[12]After Festus had conferred with his council, he declared: "You have appealed to Caesar. To Caesar you will go!"

Festus Consults King Agrippa

[13]A few days later King Agrippa and Bernice arrived at Caesarea to pay their
respects to Festus. [14]Since they were spending many days there, Festus discussed Paul's case with the king. He said: "There is a man here whom Felix left
as a prisoner. [15]When I went to Jerusalem, the chief priests and the elders of the
Jews brought charges against him and asked that he be condemned.

[16]"I told them that it is not the Roman custom to hand over anyone before they
have faced their accusers and have had an opportunity to defend themselves
against the charges. [17]When they came here with me, I did not delay the case, but
convened the court the next day and ordered the man to be brought in. [18]When
his accusers got up to speak, they did not charge him with any of the crimes I
had expected. [19]Instead, they had some points of dispute with him about their
own religion and about a dead man named Jesus who Paul claimed was alive.

[20]I was at a loss how to investigate such matters; so I asked if he would be willing to go to Jerusalem and stand trial there on these charges. [21]But when Paul made his appeal to be held over for the Emperor's decision, I ordered him held until I could send him to Caesar."

[22]Then Agrippa said to Festus, "I would like to hear this man myself."

He replied, "Tomorrow you will hear him."

Paul Before Agrippa

[23]The next day Agrippa and Bernice came with great pomp and entered the audience room with the high-ranking military officers and the prominent men of the city. At the command of Festus, Paul was brought in. [24]Festus said: "King Agrippa, and all who are present with us, you see this man! The whole Jewish community has petitioned me about him in Jerusalem and here in Caesarea, shouting that he ought not to live any longer. [25]I found he had done nothing deserving of death, but because he made his appeal to the Emperor I decided to send him to Rome. [26]But I have nothing definite to write to His Majesty about him. Therefore I have brought him before all of you, and especially before you, King Agrippa, so that as a result of this investigation I may have something to write. [27]For I think it is unreasonable to send a prisoner on to Rome without specifying the charges against him."

26 Then Agrippa said to Paul, "You have permission to speak for yourself." So Paul motioned with his hand and began his defense: [2]"King Agrippa, I consider myself fortunate to stand before you today as I make my defense against all the accusations of the Jews, [3]and especially so because you are well acquainted with all the Jewish customs and controversies. Therefore, I beg you to listen to me patiently.

[4]"The Jewish people all know the way I have lived ever since I was a child, from the beginning of my life in my own country, and also in Jerusalem. [5]They have known me for a long time and can testify, if they are willing, that I conformed to the strictest sect of our religion, living as a Pharisee. [6]And now it is because of my hope in what God has promised our ancestors that I am on trial today. [7]This is the promise our twelve tribes are hoping to see fulfilled as they earnestly serve God day and night. King Agrippa, it is because of this hope that these Jews are accusing me. [8]Why should any of you consider it incredible that God raises the dead?

[9]"I too was convinced that I ought to do all that was possible to oppose the name of Jesus of Nazareth. [10]And that is just what I did in Jerusalem. On the authority of the chief priests I put many of the Lord's people in prison, and when they were put to death, I cast my vote against them. [11]Many a time I went from one synagogue to another to have them punished, and I tried to force them to blaspheme. I was so obsessed with persecuting them that I even hunted them down in foreign cities.

[12]"On one of these journeys I was going to Damascus with the authority and commission of the chief priests. [13]About noon, King Agrippa, as I was on the road, I saw a light from heaven, brighter than the sun, blazing around me and my companions. [14]We all fell to the ground, and I heard a voice saying to me in Aramaic,[a] 'Saul, Saul, why do you persecute me? It is hard for you to kick against the goads.'

[15]"Then I asked, 'Who are you, Lord?'

"'I am Jesus, whom you are persecuting,' the Lord replied. [16]'Now get up and stand on your feet. I have appeared to you to appoint you as a servant and as a witness of what you have seen and will see of me. [17]I will rescue you from your own people and from the Gentiles. I am sending you to them [18]to open their eyes and turn them from darkness to light, and from the power of Satan to God, so that they may receive forgiveness of sins and a place among those who are sanctified by faith in me.'

---

[a] *14* Or *Hebrew*

TURNING THE WORLD UPSIDE DOWN

In the book of Acts, God's people caused great trouble for the government and religious establishments of their day. That's what living according to the values of the coming kingdom does — it's countercultural; it's disruptive; it challenges the status quo.

The kingdom of God operates according to values that are antithetical to the world. The world values self-advancement by stepping on or over other people; in God's kingdom, true reward is found in humility and in service to others. The world sees hard work and status as the key identifiers of success; in God's kingdom, the only way to find your life is to lose it for the sake of the gospel, surrendering yourself in the interest of advancing the cause of Jesus in the world. When God's people live according to the values of the kingdom, it causes trouble because God is in the business of turning the ways of the world upside down.

Acts 25 details Paul's confrontations with the authorities of his day; Jesus caused trouble for the Roman authorities as well (Mk 15:1 – 15). Also following Jesus' lead (Mk 14:53 – 65), Paul caused trouble and was opposed by Jewish religious leaders for his beliefs.

In the eyes of the prevailing religious and political authorities, Paul was a troublemaker. He was completely devoted to Jesus, and Jesus was turning the world upside down through him. The authorities couldn't stop him. If they put Paul on trial, then he simply shared the gospel. If they put Paul in prison, then he would befriend and disciple everyone there. Paul was causing trouble because he refused to settle for anything less than advancing the values of Christ's kingdom. Paul knew that the way of Jesus would mean suffering at times (Ac 9:15 – 16). Therefore, he was not alarmed when he found himself in prison. God continued to use him wherever he found himself. And God does the same for believers today. Around the dinner table, in the workplace, or in a remote corner of the world, they can represent kingdom values, no matter where they find themselves.

Jesus came to bring God's kingdom — a kingdom set on turning the values of the world upside down through the mission of the church. Then as now, any attempts to stop the church only propel it forward. God's work will not be stopped. He is using his followers, his own children, to bring about an entirely new world and way of life.

19“So then, King Agrippa, I was not disobedient to the vision from heaven.
20First to those in Damascus, then to those in Jerusalem and in all Judea, and
then to the Gentiles, I preached that they should repent and turn to God and
demonstrate their repentance by their deeds. 21That is why some Jews seized
me in the temple courts and tried to kill me. 22But God has helped me to this
very day; so I stand here and testify to small and great alike. I am saying nothing
beyond what the prophets and Moses said would happen — 23that the Messiah
would suffer and, as the first to rise from the dead, would bring the message of
light to his own people and to the Gentiles.”

24At this point Festus interrupted Paul's defense. “You are out of your mind,
Paul!” he shouted. “Your great learning is driving you insane.”

25“I am not insane, most excellent Festus,” Paul replied. “What I am saying is
true and reasonable. 26The king is familiar with these things, and I can speak freely to him. I am convinced that none of this has escaped his notice, because it was
not done in a corner. 27King Agrippa, do you believe the prophets? I know you do.”

28Then Agrippa said to Paul, “Do you think that in such a short time you can
persuade me to be a Christian?”

29Paul replied, “Short time or long — I pray to God that not only you but all
who are listening to me today may become what I am, except for these chains.”

30The king rose, and with him the governor and Bernice and those sitting with
them. 31After they left the room, they began saying to one another, “This man is
not doing anything that deserves death or imprisonment.”

32Agrippa said to Festus, “This man could have been set free if he had not
appealed to Caesar.”

Paul Sails for Rome

27 When it was decided that we would sail for Italy, Paul and some other
prisoners were handed over to a centurion named Julius, who belonged to
the Imperial Regiment. 2We boarded a ship from Adramyttium about to sail for
ports along the coast of the province of Asia, and we put out to sea. Aristarchus,
a Macedonian from Thessalonica, was with us.

3The next day we landed at Sidon; and Julius, in kindness to Paul, allowed him
to go to his friends so they might provide for his needs. 4From there we put out
to sea again and passed to the lee of Cyprus because the winds were against us.
5When we had sailed across the open sea off the coast of Cilicia and Pamphylia,
we landed at Myra in Lycia. 6There the centurion found an Alexandrian ship
sailing for Italy and put us on board. 7We made slow headway for many days
and had difficulty arriving off Cnidus. When the wind did not allow us to hold
our course, we sailed to the lee of Crete, opposite Salmone. 8We moved along
the coast with difficulty and came to a place called Fair Havens, near the town
of Lasea.

9Much time had been lost, and sailing had already become dangerous because by now it was after the Day of Atonement.[a] So Paul warned them, 10“Men,
I can see that our voyage is going to be disastrous and bring great loss to ship and
cargo, and to our own lives also.” 11But the centurion, instead of listening to what
Paul said, followed the advice of the pilot and of the owner of the ship. 12Since
the harbor was unsuitable to winter in, the majority decided that we should sail
on, hoping to reach Phoenix and winter there. This was a harbor in Crete, facing
both southwest and northwest.

The Storm

13When a gentle south wind began to blow, they saw their opportunity; so they
weighed anchor and sailed along the shore of Crete. 14Before very long, a wind of
hurricane force, called the Northeaster, swept down from the island. 15The ship
was caught by the storm and could not head into the wind; so we gave way to it
and were driven along. 16As we passed to the lee of a small island called Cauda,

[a] 9 That is, Yom Kippur

ACTS 26:24 – 29

SHARING OUR STORY

Paul was once a highly educated religious leader in the Jewish faith. He found his identity in that expertise; because of his deep knowledge, after Jesus confronted him, Paul could make all of the connections between Jesus and the prophets. He was so convinced and his life changed so dramatically that Paul couldn't help but tell people the gospel story no matter where he was.

As Jesus promised (Ac 23:11), Paul found himself before the most influential rulers of the day. Even in that situation, Paul wasn't concerned about self-preservation. Instead of defending himself, Paul shared about his background, his encounter with Jesus and his subsequent change of heart. Quite simply, Paul shared his story because it was all about Jesus. The rulers responded with shock and ridicule, but they listened and considered what he said against the charges that were levied against him (Ac 26:31 – 32). This encounter between Paul and the secular leaders of his day teaches that the message of Jesus always runs counter to the culture. Paul taught with his teaching and modeled with his life how to share the story of Jesus with others (2Ti 2:2). The church's story of God's radical grace in the face of consistent human sin should draw a similar reaction from the surrounding culture. Believers need only to plant the seed and let the Spirit do the rest (1Co 3:6).

we were hardly able to make the lifeboat secure, 17so the men hoisted it aboard.
Then they passed ropes under the ship itself to hold it together. Because they
were afraid they would run aground on the sandbars of Syrtis, they lowered the
sea anchor[a] and let the ship be driven along. 18We took such a violent battering from the storm that the next day they began to throw the cargo overboard.
19On the third day, they threw the ship's tackle overboard with their own hands.
20When neither sun nor stars appeared for many days and the storm continued
raging, we finally gave up all hope of being saved.
21After they had gone a long time without food, Paul stood up before them
and said: "Men, you should have taken my advice not to sail from Crete; then
you would have spared yourselves this damage and loss. 22But now I urge you to
keep up your courage, because not one of you will be lost; only the ship will be
destroyed. 23Last night an angel of the God to whom I belong and whom I serve
stood beside me 24and said, 'Do not be afraid, Paul. You must stand trial before
Caesar; and God has graciously given you the lives of all who sail with you.' 25So
keep up your courage, men, for I have faith in God that it will happen just as he
told me. 26Nevertheless, we must run aground on some island."

The Shipwreck

27On the fourteenth night we were still being driven across the Adriatic[b] Sea,
when about midnight the sailors sensed they were approaching land. 28They
took soundings and found that the water was a hundred and twenty feet[c] deep.
A short time later they took soundings again and found it was ninety feet[d] deep.
29Fearing that we would be dashed against the rocks, they dropped four anchors
from the stern and prayed for daylight. 30In an attempt to escape from the ship,
the sailors let the lifeboat down into the sea, pretending they were going to lower
some anchors from the bow. 31Then Paul said to the centurion and the soldiers,
"Unless these men stay with the ship, you cannot be saved." 32So the soldiers cut
the ropes that held the lifeboat and let it drift away.
33Just before dawn Paul urged them all to eat. "For the last fourteen days," he
said, "you have been in constant suspense and have gone without food — you
haven't eaten anything. 34Now I urge you to take some food. You need it to survive. Not one of you will lose a single hair from his head." 35After he said this,
he took some bread and gave thanks to God in front of them all. Then he broke
it and began to eat. 36They were all encouraged and ate some food themselves.
37Altogether there were 276 of us on board. 38When they had eaten as much as
they wanted, they lightened the ship by throwing the grain into the sea.
39When daylight came, they did not recognize the land, but they saw a bay
with a sandy beach, where they decided to run the ship aground if they could.
40Cutting loose the anchors, they left them in the sea and at the same time untied the ropes that held the rudders. Then they hoisted the foresail to the wind
and made for the beach. 41But the ship struck a sandbar and ran aground. The
bow stuck fast and would not move, and the stern was broken to pieces by the
pounding of the surf.
42The soldiers planned to kill the prisoners to prevent any of them from swim-
ming away and escaping. 43But the centurion wanted to spare Paul's life and kept
them from carrying out their plan. He ordered those who could swim to jump
overboard first and get to land. 44The rest were to get there on planks or on other
pieces of the ship. In this way everyone reached land safely.

Paul Ashore on Malta

28 Once safely on shore, we found out that the island was called Malta.
2The islanders showed us unusual kindness. They built a fire and
welcomed us all because it was raining and cold. 3Paul gathered a pile of

---

[a] 17 Or *the sails* [b] 27 In ancient times the name referred to an area extending well south of Italy. [c] 28 Or about 37 meters [d] 28 Or about 27 meters

CHURCH

JESUS ON DISPLAY TO THE WORLD

—MAX LUCADO

ACTS 2 TO REVELATION 20

A short time after his resurrection, Jesus appeared to his followers and proclaimed, "You will receive power when the Holy Spirit comes on you; and you will be my witnesses in Jerusalem, and in all Judea and Samaria, and to the ends of the earth" (Ac 1:8).

A powerful witness. This is what Jesus intends the church to be.

This powerful witness shows the world what transformed lives look like. Not perfect lives, mind you, but lives testifying to what is possible when Jesus is at the center of our lives.

What was the mightiest miracle of the New Testament church? As you think about the early days of the church, what stands out as the most powerful moment? Mentally thumb through the book of Acts and consider the greatest events:

- The falling of the Holy Spirit on the apostles in the upper room.
- The baptism of three thousand people on the day of Pentecost.
- The healing of the lame man at the temple gate.
- The conversion of Saul. The deliverance of Peter. The vision of Stephen.

These are all amazing and miraculous events. If you were to list any one of them as the greatest of the New Testament church, I wouldn't blame you. But I wouldn't agree with you. As stunning as these are, I feel there is one even greater. One that is often overlooked, easily neglected, yet absolutely amazing. What was this mighty event? Unity. This church loved each other, and this is what set it apart as an amazing display of God's grace to the world.

"All the believers were together and had everything in common. They sold property and possessions to give to anyone who had need. Every day they continued to meet together in the temple courts. They broke bread in their homes and ate together with glad and sincere hearts, praising God and enjoying the favor of all the people. And the Lord added to their number daily those who were being saved" (Ac 2:44–47).

The charter members of Jesus Christ's church were Jews who had come to Jerusalem to celebrate the Passover. "Those who accepted his message were baptized, and about three thousand were added to their number that day" (Ac 2:41).

The church exploded. Membership went from zero to three thousand overnight! "The Lord added to their number daily those who were being saved" (Ac 2:47). Every meeting had more faces. Every service had new members. The Jerusalem 101 class was bursting at the seams. This was a dynamic church.

And this was a diverse church! They were from different places: Parthia, Media, Elam, Mesopotamia, Judea, Cappadocia, Pontus, Asia, Phrygia, Pamphylia, Egypt, the areas of Libya near Cyrene, Rome (both Jews and those who had become Jews), Crete, and Arabia (Ac 2:8 – 11).

Fifteen different regions were represented! The Parthinians came from the east. The Egyptians came from the south. The Romans were from the north. They had different cultures and spoke different languages; they ate different types of food. They came to be a part of the Passover. They stayed to be a part of the church.

Within a short time, the church grew to as many as 20,000 men, women and children (Ac 4:4).* What was the church's strategy? They had no buildings. They were not affiliated with any denomination. No mention is made of a budget or program. What enabled them to increase in number and deepen in faith? It was simple: "They devoted themselves to the apostles' teaching and to fellowship, to the breaking of bread and to prayer" (Ac 2:42).

The verb "devoted" means *steadfast determination*. They were steadfastly determined to grow in four areas: teaching, fellowship, the breaking of bread, (likely communion) and prayer. Three of the four activities are done with others. We may pray alone, but teaching, the breaking of bread, and fellowship require community. The church was devoted to develop this community.

Could the world use such community today?

Conflicts rage on every continent. Loneliness stalks our streets. Neighbors live next door to each other without sharing a word. Our world is hungry for community.

The church is God's way of giving it. The church is a community of saved sinners. No economic level required. No education level expected. If you call God your Father and Jesus your Savior then I call you brother or sister. Period.

We:

"Form one body, and each member belongs to all the others" (Ro 12:5).

*The reference of 5,000 men implies that, with women and children, the church could have numbered 20,000 people.

CHURCH

(CONTINUED)

ACTS 2 TO REVELATION 20

We are told to:

"Accept one another" (Ro 15:7).

"Instruct one another" (Ro 15:14).

"Greet one another" (Ro 16:16).

"Serve one another" (Gal 5:13).

"Carry each other's burdens" (Gal 6:2).

"Be patient, bearing with one another in love" (Eph 4:2).

"Submit to one another" (Eph 5:21)

"Encourage one another and build each other up" (1Th 5:11)

What would happen if we took these verses seriously? What if we truly devoted ourselves to one another?

I spoke at each Good Friday service of a nearby Episcopal church for many years. On one occasion, I shared the responsibility with the bishop of the diocese of West Texas. He wore a robe and a large gold cross around his neck. My church background didn't make me too keen on preachers wearing religious jewelry. So, I was less than impressed. And, I confess, even a bit judgmental.

But as he shared the story behind his gold cross, my attitude began to change. In order to assume his role as bishop, he had to leave behind St. Mark's Episcopal, a church where he was loved dearly. The people tried to talk him into staying, but he felt it was God's will to leave. The members, then, expressed their gratitude by making him this cross. Two hundred and forty-two households contributed gold pieces which were melted down and forged together. Some of the gold provided was from the wedding bands of widow and widowers. Three couples who had divorced and then reconciled each gave a set of wedding rings to the cross. One friend of the bishop was a bachelor who was rejected by "the love of his life" just days before the ceremony contributed her ring to the cross as a symbolic surrendering of the pain of his lost love. The cross includes a college ring as well as the bridge from a fellow bishop's mouth. One mom donated some gold beads. When her son was four, he found them on a dresser, thought they were toys and damaged them. He died soon thereafter in an accident. She donated them on the day before what would have been his seventh birthday.

Two hundred and forty-two stories. Stories of celebration, stories of sorrow. Stories of peace, stories of pain. But when forged together they form the cross of Christ.

What happened literally with the bishop's cross happens spiritually in every church that devotes itself to fellowship. When your story intermingles with mine, and our stories interweave with others, the cross is formed. When one hand holds another in a hospital, the cross is lifted up. When a conservative loves a liberal; when an Anglo seeks to understand a Hispanic; when the redneck and the tree-hugger stand side by side at the communion table, the cross is lifted up.

When Jesus is at the center of the church:

People with a diversity of backgrounds serve and love each other.

Prejudices and biases are replaced with love and grace.

Peace, not conflict, is the goal of all of our relationships.

This is what was on display in the first church. Those early believers were a powerful testimony of what is possible in Jesus. This same possibility is available for us today. May we, through the example of Jesus and the power of the Holy Spirit, strive to pattern our lives after theirs.

BEGINNINGS	REVOLT	PEOPLE	INTERTESTAMENTAL PERIOD	SAVIOR	CHURCH	FOREVER
GENESIS 1–2 (pg. 8)	GENESIS 3–11 (pg. 24)	GENESIS 12 to MALACHI (pg. 266)	(pg. 1508)	GOSPELS to ACTS 1 (pg. 1560)	ACTS 2 to REVELATION 20 (pg. 1736)	REVELATION 21–22 (pg. 1996)

brushwood and, as he put it on the fire, a viper, driven out by the heat, fastened
itself on his hand. [4]When the islanders saw the snake hanging from his hand,
they said to each other, "This man must be a murderer; for though he escaped
from the sea, the goddess Justice has not allowed him to live." [5]But Paul shook
the snake off into the fire and suffered no ill effects. [6]The people expected him
to swell up or suddenly fall dead; but after waiting a long time and seeing
nothing unusual happen to him, they changed their minds and said he was a
god.

[7]There was an estate nearby that belonged to Publius, the chief official of
the island. He welcomed us to his home and showed us generous hospitality
for three days. [8]His father was sick in bed, suffering from fever and dysentery.
Paul went in to see him and, after prayer, placed his hands on him and healed
him. [9]When this had happened, the rest of the sick on the island came and were
cured. [10]They honored us in many ways; and when we were ready to sail, they
furnished us with the supplies we needed.

Paul's Arrival at Rome

[11]After three months we put out to sea in a ship that had wintered in the island—it was an Alexandrian ship with the figurehead of the twin gods Castor
and Pollux. [12]We put in at Syracuse and stayed there three days. [13]From there we
set sail and arrived at Rhegium. The next day the south wind came up, and on
the following day we reached Puteoli. [14]There we found some brothers and sisters who invited us to spend a week with them. And so we came to Rome. [15]The
brothers and sisters there had heard that we were coming, and they traveled as
far as the Forum of Appius and the Three Taverns to meet us. At the sight of these
people Paul thanked God and was encouraged. [16]When we got to Rome, Paul was
allowed to live by himself, with a soldier to guard him.

Paul Preaches at Rome Under Guard

[17]Three days later he called together the local Jewish leaders. When they
had assembled, Paul said to them: "My brothers, although I have done nothing
against our people or against the customs of our ancestors, I was arrested in Jerusalem and handed over to the Romans. [18]They examined me and wanted to
release me, because I was not guilty of any crime deserving death. [19]The Jews
objected, so I was compelled to make an appeal to Caesar. I certainly did not intend to bring any charge against my own people. [20]For this reason I have asked
to see you and talk with you. It is because of the hope of Israel that I am bound
with this chain."

[21]They replied, "We have not received any letters from Judea concerning you,
and none of our people who have come from there has reported or said anything
bad about you. [22]But we want to hear what your views are, for we know that people everywhere are talking against this sect."

[23]They arranged to meet Paul on a certain day, and came in even larger numbers to the place where he was staying. He witnessed to them from morning
till evening, explaining about the kingdom of God, and from the Law of Moses
and from the Prophets he tried to persuade them about Jesus. [24]Some were convinced by what he said, but others would not believe. [25]They disagreed among
themselves and began to leave after Paul had made this final statement: "The
Holy Spirit spoke the truth to your ancestors when he said through Isaiah the
prophet:

[26]" 'Go to this people and say,
  "You will be ever hearing but never understanding;
    you will be ever seeing but never perceiving."
[27]For this people's heart has become calloused;
    they hardly hear with their ears,
    and they have closed their eyes.

Otherwise they might see with their eyes,
hear with their ears,
understand with their hearts
and turn, and I would heal them.'[a]

28"Therefore I want you to know that God's salvation has been sent to the Gentiles, and they will listen!" [29][b]
30For two whole years Paul stayed there in his own rented house and welcomed all who came to see him. 31He proclaimed the kingdom of God and taught
about the Lord Jesus Christ—with all boldness and without hindrance!

[a] 27 Isaiah 6:9,10 (see Septuagint) [b] 29 Some manuscripts include here *After he said this, the Jews left, arguing vigorously among themselves.*

JESUS: OUR ETERNAL SALVATION

ROMANS

ROMANS

THE JERUSALEM COUNCIL *c. AD 50*	PAUL WRITES ROMANS *c. AD 57*	PAUL MARTYRED IN ROME *c. AD 67 – 68*

The letter to the church at Rome is one of Paul's most magisterial books. At the time of writing, Paul had never visited the vibrant church at Rome, though he clearly held the church in high regard and longed to visit it soon (1:8 – 15). He wrote this theological treatise in order to summarize the message of the gospel for a church at such a critical cultural nexus in the world of that day.

Paul began with a formal introduction of himself and his calling as a slave or servant of Jesus (1:1 – 7). Paul then described the plight of sinners living in a fallen world, who willingly chose to worship created things rather than the Creator (1:25). All human sin is explained by this foolish exchange.

God must judge human sin. His holiness cannot dwell in the presence of sin, and his justice necessitates a proper punishment for all wickedness. Death is the only just wage for sin (6:23) and all people — Jew and Gentile alike — should receive their just condemnation (3:23).

But God graciously made a way for salvation through Jesus. God poured out his punishment for human sin on Christ, who served as God's appointed wrath-bearing substitute (5:6 – 11). Those who place their faith in Christ are forgiven because of Jesus' work on the cross. Jesus pays for their sin. In addition, God's people are given the righteousness that Christ earned through his perfect life. They can now know peace and fellowship with God (5:12 – 20). This is true for Jews, though most will scorn Jesus' offer of salvation, and for Gentiles, who can now be grafted into God's family tree (chs. 9 – 11). Nothing in all of creation can take God's love away from those he has saved because salvation is of God, from God and for God.

Those whom God saves offer up their lives as "living sacrifice[s]" to God, which is their act of proper worship (12:1). Paul ends his letter by demonstrating the scope of the transformation that the gospel should produce. Christians should worship God through their gifts in service to the church, by loving what is good, by rejoicing in all things, by serving one another in love, by submitting to governmental leaders, by making wise decisions and by bearing one another's burdens. These actions, and a host of others like them, demonstrate God's work of salvation in a person's life and produce in them a hope, joy and peace that can never be taken away.

FOR THE WAGES OF SIN IS DEATH,
BUT THE GIFT OF GOD IS ETERNAL LIFE
IN CHRIST JESUS OUR LORD.

Romans 6:23

ROMANS

1 Paul, a servant of Christ Jesus, called to be an apostle and set apart for the gospel of God— [2]the gospel he promised beforehand through his prophets in the Holy Scriptures [3]regarding his Son, who as to his earthly life[a] was a descendant of David, [4]and who through the Spirit of holiness was appointed the Son of God in power[b] by his resurrection from the dead: Jesus Christ our Lord. [5]Through him we received grace and apostleship to call all the Gentiles to the obedience that comes from[c] faith for his name's sake. [6]And you also are among those Gentiles who are called to belong to Jesus Christ.

[7]To all in Rome who are loved by God and called to be his holy people:

Grace and peace to you from God our Father and from the Lord Jesus Christ.

Paul's Longing to Visit Rome

[8]First, I thank my God through Jesus Christ for all of you, because your faith is being reported all over the world. [9]God, whom I serve in my spirit in preaching the gospel of his Son, is my witness how constantly I remember you [10]in my prayers at all times; and I pray that now at last by God's will the way may be opened for me to come to you.

[11]I long to see you so that I may impart to you some spiritual gift to make you strong— [12]that is, that you and I may be mutually encouraged by each other's faith. [13]I do not want you to be unaware, brothers and sisters,[d] that I planned many times to come to you (but have been prevented from doing so until now) in order that I might have a harvest among you, just as I have had among the other Gentiles.

[14]I am obligated both to Greeks and non-Greeks, both to the wise and the foolish. [15]That is why I am so eager to preach the gospel also to you who are in Rome.

[16]For I am not ashamed of the gospel, because it is the power of God that brings salvation to everyone who believes: first to the Jew, then to the Gentile. [17]For in the gospel the righteousness of God is revealed—a righteousness that is by faith from first to last,[e] just as it is written: "The righteous will live by faith."[f]

God's Wrath Against Sinful Humanity

[18]The wrath of God is being revealed from heaven against all the godlessness and wickedness of people, who suppress the truth by their wickedness, [19]since what may be known about God is plain to them, because God has made it plain to them. [20]For since the creation of the world God's invisible qualities—his eternal power and divine nature—have been clearly seen, being understood from what has been made, so that people are without excuse.

[21]For although they knew God, they neither glorified him as God nor gave thanks to him, but their thinking became futile and their foolish hearts were darkened. [22]Although they claimed to be wise, they became fools [23]and exchanged the glory of the immortal God for images made to look like a mortal human being and birds and animals and reptiles.

[24]Therefore God gave them over in the sinful desires of their hearts to sexual impurity for the degrading of their bodies with one another. [25]They exchanged the truth about God for a lie, and worshiped and served created things rather than the Creator—who is forever praised. Amen.

---

[a] *3* Or *who according to the flesh* [b] *4* Or *was declared with power to be the Son of God* [c] *5* Or *that is* [d] *13* The Greek word for *brothers and sisters* (*adelphoi*) refers here to believers, both men and women, as part of God's family; also in 7:1, 4; 8:12, 29; 10:1; 11:25; 12:1; 15:14, 30; 16:14, 17. [e] *17* Or *is from faith to faith* [f] *17* Hab. 2:4

SALVATION

The letter to the church in Rome contains a comprehensive, clear and detailed explanation of the gospel message. Paul's thesis statement — not only of this letter, but also, in many ways, of his entire ministry — can be summed up in Romans 1:16 – 17: "For I am not ashamed of the gospel, because it is the power of God that brings salvation to everyone who believes: first to the Jew, then to the Gentile. For in the gospel the righteousness of God is revealed — a righteousness that is by faith from first to last, just as it is written: 'The righteous will live by faith.'"

Paul and the other New Testament writers portray Jesus Christ as the author and provider of salvation on the basis of his sacrificial death on the cross in the place of sinners. This salvation is by grace alone and through faith in Jesus alone. Through faith, the righteousness of Christ is credited to sinners, who are declared righteous on the basis of that faith.

The word *salvation* itself implies rescue. Paul makes it clear in Romans chapters 1 – 3 that all humanity is desperately lost in sin. The just punishment from a holy God for that sin is death. Salvation, then, is not only rescue from our sin, but it is also rescue from the justified punishment of God. God is perfect in his justice, and because of that, is justified in his wrath toward those who don't trust him. However, the rescue that comes through faith in Jesus completely erases the eternal separation between a holy God and imperfect humanity.

What is the result of this great salvation that comes by grace and through faith? The answer is a reconciled relationship with God (Ro 5:1). The fact that stands at the heart of the gospel is that God desires to be in relationship with his people. Rebellious people are reconciled with their holy God through the cross. Ultimately, all who come to Jesus in faith and trust are saved to the great glory of God. Because salvation is by grace alone, apart from good works, God alone receives the credit for this complete and astonishing deliverance.

[26]Because of this, God gave them over to shameful lusts. Even their women exchanged natural sexual relations for unnatural ones. [27]In the same way the men also abandoned natural relations with women and were inflamed with lust for one another. Men committed shameful acts with other men, and received in themselves the due penalty for their error.

[28]Furthermore, just as they did not think it worthwhile to retain the knowledge of God, so God gave them over to a depraved mind, so that they do what ought not to be done. [29]They have become filled with every kind of wickedness, evil, greed and depravity. They are full of envy, murder, strife, deceit and malice. They are gossips, [30]slanderers, God-haters, insolent, arrogant and boastful; they invent ways of doing evil; they disobey their parents; [31]they have no understanding, no fidelity, no love, no mercy. [32]Although they know God's righteous decree that those who do such things deserve death, they not only continue to do these very things but also approve of those who practice them.

God's Righteous Judgment

2 You, therefore, have no excuse, you who pass judgment on someone else, for at whatever point you judge another, you are condemning yourself, because you who pass judgment do the same things. [2]Now we know that God's judgment against those who do such things is based on truth. [3]So when you, a mere human being, pass judgment on them and yet do the same things, do you think you will escape God's judgment? [4]Or do you show contempt for the riches of his kindness, forbearance and patience, not realizing that God's kindness is intended to lead you to repentance?

[5]But because of your stubbornness and your unrepentant heart, you are storing up wrath against yourself for the day of God's wrath, when his righteous judgment will be revealed. [6]God "will repay each person according to what they have done."[a] [7]To those who by persistence in doing good seek glory, honor and immortality, he will give eternal life. [8]But for those who are self-seeking and who reject the truth and follow evil, there will be wrath and anger. [9]There will be trouble and distress for every human being who does evil: first for the Jew, then for the Gentile; [10]but glory, honor and peace for everyone who does good: first for the Jew, then for the Gentile. [11]For God does not show favoritism.

[12]All who sin apart from the law will also perish apart from the law, and all who sin under the law will be judged by the law. [13]For it is not those who hear the law who are righteous in God's sight, but it is those who obey the law who will be declared righteous. [14](Indeed, when Gentiles, who do not have the law, do by nature things required by the law, they are a law for themselves, even though they do not have the law. [15]They show that the requirements of the law are written on their hearts, their consciences also bearing witness, and their thoughts sometimes accusing them and at other times even defending them.) [16]This will take place on the day when God judges people's secrets through Jesus Christ, as my gospel declares.

The Jews and the Law

[17]Now you, if you call yourself a Jew; if you rely on the law and boast in God; [18]if you know his will and approve of what is superior because you are instructed by the law; [19]if you are convinced that you are a guide for the blind, a light for those who are in the dark, [20]an instructor of the foolish, a teacher of little children, because you have in the law the embodiment of knowledge and truth— [21]you, then, who teach others, do you not teach yourself? You who preach against stealing, do you steal? [22]You who say that people should not commit adultery, do you commit adultery? You who abhor idols, do you rob temples? [23]You who boast in the law, do you dishonor God by breaking the law? [24]As it is written: "God's name is blasphemed among the Gentiles because of you."[b]

[a] *6* Psalm 62:12; Prov. 24:12 [b] *24* Isaiah 52:5 (see Septuagint); Ezek. 36:20,22

ROMANS 2:1–4

WITHOUT EXCUSE

Paul's description of sin throughout the book of Romans is cosmic in scope. Not only is the whole of creation itself broken by sin, but also all people—Jew and Gentile alike—are dead in sin. Though Paul seems to focus his attention on the Gentiles at the outset of the book of Romans, he turns his attention to the Jews starting in chapter 2. These people had every opportunity to live by faith. Instead of taking full advantage of being the recipients of the revelation and blessing of being God's chosen people, the Jews had become self-righteous, focusing on outward symbols related to God's standards while neglecting the heart behind those standards. In the process, they underestimated their own sinfulness.

One can almost imagine the self-righteous audience of Jewish Christians in Rome, full of their own religiosity, at first reading with a smug smile on their faces about the sinfulness of the Gentiles, only to read a bit further and find their own guilt exposed. In the end, whether someone has a religious pedigree, hears the gospel early in life, or has access to clear explanations of the gospel only late in life, they still stand guilty before a holy God. Both the religious and the nonreligious alike stand condemned before him, so the ground is completely level when it comes to our own sinfulness. Each person must decide whether or not they will turn to Jesus Christ and trust him alone for their salvation.

25Circumcision has value if you observe the law, but if you break the law, you
have become as though you had not been circumcised. 26So then, if those who
are not circumcised keep the law's requirements, will they not be regarded as
though they were circumcised? 27The one who is not circumcised physically and
yet obeys the law will condemn you who, even though you have the[a] written
code and circumcision, are a lawbreaker.

28A person is not a Jew who is one only outwardly, nor is circumcision merely
outward and physical. 29No, a person is a Jew who is one inwardly; and circumcision is circumcision of the heart, by the Spirit, not by the written code. Such a
person's praise is not from other people, but from God.

God's Faithfulness

3 What advantage, then, is there in being a Jew, or what value is there in circumcision? 2Much in every way! First of all, the Jews have been entrusted
with the very words of God.

3What if some were unfaithful? Will their unfaithfulness nullify God's faithfulness? 4Not at all! Let God be true, and every human being a liar. As it is written:

"So that you may be proved right when you speak
and prevail when you judge."[b]

5But if our unrighteousness brings out God's righteousness more clearly, what
shall we say? That God is unjust in bringing his wrath on us? (I am using a human argument.) 6Certainly not! If that were so, how could God judge the world?
7Someone might argue, "If my falsehood enhances God's truthfulness and so
increases his glory, why am I still condemned as a sinner?" 8Why not say — as
some slanderously claim that we say — "Let us do evil that good may result"?
Their condemnation is just!

No One Is Righteous

9What shall we conclude then? Do we have any advantage? Not at all! For we
have already made the charge that Jews and Gentiles alike are all under the power of sin. 10As it is written:

"There is no one righteous, not even one;
11 there is no one who understands;
there is no one who seeks God.
12 All have turned away,
they have together become worthless;
there is no one who does good,
not even one."[c]
13 "Their throats are open graves;
their tongues practice deceit."[d]
"The poison of vipers is on their lips."[e]
14 "Their mouths are full of cursing and bitterness."[f]
15 "Their feet are swift to shed blood;
16 ruin and misery mark their ways,
17 and the way of peace they do not know."[g]
18 "There is no fear of God before their eyes."[h]

19Now we know that whatever the law says, it says to those who are under the
law, so that every mouth may be silenced and the whole world held accountable
to God. 20Therefore no one will be declared righteous in God's sight by the works
of the law; rather, through the law we become conscious of our sin.

---

[a] *27* Or *who, by means of a* [b] *4* Psalm 51:4 [c] *12* Psalms 14:1-3; 53:1-3; Eccles. 7:20
[d] *13* Psalm 5:9 [e] *13* Psalm 140:3 [f] *14* Psalm 10:7 (see Septuagint) [g] *17* Isaiah 59:7,8
[h] *18* Psalm 36:1

ROMANS 4:3

ABRAHAM: SAVED THROUGH FAITH

The gospel is not only the central message of the New Testament, it's also the storyline of the entire Bible. For Paul in Romans 4, Abraham is the case study of salvation by faith. By the time Paul wrote this letter, Jewish belief was that Abraham was justified because of his circumcision and his willingness to sacrifice Isaac. If that were the case, Abraham would have earned righteousness with his works. As he builds his argument for salvation by faith in Jesus alone, Paul's concern is that his audience understand that there is only one way a person is made righteous before God — through faith.

In verses 9 – 16, Paul confronts the issue of Abraham's righteousness with the simple issue of chronology. God declared Abraham righteous prior to his obedience and hundreds of years before God gave the Law to Moses. Therefore Abraham's faith saved him, just as today God's people are only saved through the same kind of faith.

Righteousness Through Faith

21 But now apart from the law the righteousness of God has been made known,
to which the Law and the Prophets testify. 22 This righteousness is given through
faith in[a] Jesus Christ to all who believe. There is no difference between Jew and
Gentile, 23 for all have sinned and fall short of the glory of God, 24 and all are justified freely by his grace through the redemption that came by Christ Jesus.
25 God presented Christ as a sacrifice of atonement,[b] through the shedding of his
blood — to be received by faith. He did this to demonstrate his righteousness,
because in his forbearance he had left the sins committed beforehand unpunished — 26 he did it to demonstrate his righteousness at the present time, so as to
be just and the one who justifies those who have faith in Jesus.
27 Where, then, is boasting? It is excluded. Because of what law? The law that
requires works? No, because of the law that requires faith. 28 For we maintain
that a person is justified by faith apart from the works of the law. 29 Or is God the
God of Jews only? Is he not the God of Gentiles too? Yes, of Gentiles too, 30 since
there is only one God, who will justify the circumcised by faith and the uncircumcised through that same faith. 31 Do we, then, nullify the law by this faith?
Not at all! Rather, we uphold the law.

Abraham Justified by Faith

4 What then shall we say that Abraham, our forefather according to the flesh,
discovered in this matter? 2 If, in fact, Abraham was justified by works, he
had something to boast about — but not before God. 3 What does Scripture say?
"Abraham believed God, and it was credited to him as righteousness."[c]
4 Now to the one who works, wages are not credited as a gift but as an obligation. 5 However, to the one who does not work but trusts God who justifies
the ungodly, their faith is credited as righteousness. 6 David says the same thing
when he speaks of the blessedness of the one to whom God credits righteousness
apart from works:

7 "Blessed are those
whose transgressions are forgiven,
whose sins are covered.
8 Blessed is the one
whose sin the Lord will never count against them."[d]

9 Is this blessedness only for the circumcised, or also for the uncircumcised?
We have been saying that Abraham's faith was credited to him as righteousness.
10 Under what circumstances was it credited? Was it after he was circumcised, or
before? It was not after, but before! 11 And he received circumcision as a sign, a
seal of the righteousness that he had by faith while he was still uncircumcised.
So then, he is the father of all who believe but have not been circumcised, in
order that righteousness might be credited to them. 12 And he is then also the father of the circumcised who not only are circumcised but who also follow in the
footsteps of the faith that our father Abraham had before he was circumcised.
13 It was not through the law that Abraham and his offspring received the
promise that he would be heir of the world, but through the righteousness that
comes by faith. 14 For if those who depend on the law are heirs, faith means nothing and the promise is worthless, 15 because the law brings wrath. And where
there is no law there is no transgression.
16 Therefore, the promise comes by faith, so that it may be by grace and may
be guaranteed to all Abraham's offspring — not only to those who are of the law
but also to those who have the faith of Abraham. He is the father of us all. 17 As
it is written: "I have made you a father of many nations."[e] He is our father in the

[a] *22* Or *through the faithfulness of* [b] *25* The Greek for *sacrifice of atonement* refers to the atonement cover on the ark of the covenant (see Lev. 16:15,16). [c] *3* Gen. 15:6; also in verse 22 [d] *8* Psalm 32:1,2 [e] *17* Gen. 17:5

THE RIGHTEOUSNESS OF GOD

Righteousness is a core component of the gospel message. The holy and eternal God expects that people who are in relationship with him to be without sin. This is, as we all know, a requirement that is utterly impossible for any of us to meet on our own! However, in the gospel, God delivers his righteousness to unrighteous people without sacrificing his own righteousness in the process.

Paul spends the opening chapters of this book making his case that all people are guilty of sin, regardless of their supposed morality or their association with the things of God. There is no wiggle room in this argument (3:23) — all people have sinned; all have fallen short of God's righteous standard. The only hope for humanity, then, is the gift of righteousness that comes not by works of the law but instead through faith alone.

This righteousness by faith is not a departure from God's work in the Old Testament; then as now, no one can live up to God's righteous standard. The only way men and women have ever come into righteousness is through faith. But before Jesus came to earth, there was in the air a lingering question of cosmic importance: How could a righteous God, perfect in every way, freely forgive and justify sinful and guilty human beings? Because God is perfectly holy and perfectly righteous, there must be punishment for sin. Otherwise, God's perfect character would be compromised.

This pivotal moment in universal history, the day when Jesus took away the sin of the world, was not only about the souls of men and women; it was about the very character of God. The cross is the answer to the question above; the crucifixion is the apex of God's love and mercy but also of his justice and righteousness. At the cross, God not only provided the ultimate answer for how a person can be made righteous by faith, but he also dispensed his justice. At the cross, God poured out his wrath on his own Son so that sinful human beings might be forgiven and granted the righteousness of Jesus' life. At the cross, the God of righteousness both demonstrates and grants righteousness, for he is both just and the One who justifies.

ROMANS 5:1

JUSTIFIED

The word *justify* is a legal term. Behind that word is a courtroom setting, and in this case, God is the judge who has on the docket before him the guilt or innocence of every person ever born. Paul has already in chapters 1–3 made it clear that the guilt of all humanity is not in question. But here is an amazing declaration: despite our clear guilt, God the Judge declares his people righteous. This happens not only because of God's great love, but because God has demonstrated his justice through the death of Jesus. When someone believes in Jesus, God gives that person the righteousness of Christ and in so doing declares them to be right before God. In other words, God declaring our innocence is not an exception to justice because justice was fully dispensed on Jesus instead of on the sinner who repents. This is truly amazing grace. Because God's people have been justified by faith, they have eternal life and peace with God. Of course, if someone can only have peace with God through faith, then the opposite is also true. Outside of a personal faith commitment, all people stand in eternal conflict with God.

ROMANS 5:10

RECONCILIATION

Could there be anything more terrifying than to be considered an enemy of God? But apart from Christ, that's the status of all people. This is not a relationship of neutrality, but instead of hostility, for all people are born under God's just judgment for sin. However, through Jesus and the gospel

(continued on page 1754)

sight of God, in whom he believed — the God who gives life to the dead and calls into being things that were not.

18Against all hope, Abraham in hope believed and so became the father of many nations, just as it had been said to him, "So shall your offspring be."[a] 19Without weakening in his faith, he faced the fact that his body was as good as dead — since he was about a hundred years old — and that Sarah's womb was also dead. 20Yet he did not waver through unbelief regarding the promise of God, but was strengthened in his faith and gave glory to God, 21being fully persuaded that God had power to do what he had promised. 22This is why "it was credited to him as righteousness." 23The words "it was credited to him" were written not for him alone, 24but also for us, to whom God will credit righteousness — for us who believe in him who raised Jesus our Lord from the dead. 25He was delivered over to death for our sins and was raised to life for our justification.

Peace and Hope

5 Therefore, since we have been justified through faith, we[b] have peace with God through our Lord Jesus Christ, 2through whom we have gained access by faith into this grace in which we now stand. And we[c] boast in the hope of the glory of God. 3Not only so, but we[c] also glory in our sufferings, because we know that suffering produces perseverance; 4perseverance, character; and character, hope. 5And hope does not put us to shame, because God's love has been poured out into our hearts through the Holy Spirit, who has been given to us.

6You see, at just the right time, when we were still powerless, Christ died for the ungodly. 7Very rarely will anyone die for a righteous person, though for a good person someone might possibly dare to die. 8But God demonstrates his own love for us in this: While we were still sinners, Christ died for us.

9Since we have now been justified by his blood, how much more shall we be saved from God's wrath through him! 10For if, while we were God's enemies, we were reconciled to him through the death of his Son, how much more, having been reconciled, shall we be saved through his life! 11Not only is this so, but we also boast in God through our Lord Jesus Christ, through whom we have now received reconciliation.

Death Through Adam, Life Through Christ

12Therefore, just as sin entered the world through one man, and death through sin, and in this way death came to all people, because all sinned —

13To be sure, sin was in the world before the law was given, but sin is not charged against anyone's account where there is no law. 14Nevertheless, death reigned from the time of Adam to the time of Moses, even over those who did not sin by breaking a command, as did Adam, who is a pattern of the one to come.

15But the gift is not like the trespass. For if the many died by the trespass of the one man, how much more did God's grace and the gift that came by the grace of the one man, Jesus Christ, overflow to the many! 16Nor can the gift of God be compared with the result of one man's sin: The judgment followed one sin and brought condemnation, but the gift followed many trespasses and brought justification. 17For if, by the trespass of the one man, death reigned through that one man, how much more will those who receive God's abundant provision of grace and of the gift of righteousness reign in life through the one man, Jesus Christ!

18Consequently, just as one trespass resulted in condemnation for all people, so also one righteous act resulted in justification and life for all people. 19For just as through the disobedience of the one man the many were made sinners, so also through the obedience of the one man the many will be made righteous.

20The law was brought in so that the trespass might increase. But where sin increased, grace increased all the more, 21so that, just as sin reigned in death, so

[a] *18* Gen. 15:5 [b] *1* Many manuscripts *let us* [c] *2,3* Or *let us*

ROMANS 5:12 – 21

JESUS AS THE LAST ADAM

It has been said that those who fail to learn the lessons of history are doomed to repeat them. To reinterpret this quote in light of redemptive history, one might say that believers who fail to understand where they have come from will also fail to understand where humanity has been, where they themselves, as followers of Christ, are now and where they are going.

Paul helps his readers see the overwhelming consequence of Adam's sin. When the "one man" of verse 12 disobeyed God's direct command, sin and death entered the world. Adam represented all future humanity. He was, in many ways, the first and best hope of humanity: there was and never would be a more idyllic situation in which to have perfect and unbroken fellowship with God, and yet he fell. With Adam's choice to sin came the inherited implications to every person born into Adam's race: namely, that all people have a sinful nature at their core. All people are born into sin; all are under the curse of disobedience that came from the Garden of Eden. Any parent can testify to the truth that they never taught their toddlers how to be selfish; they came by that inclination naturally.

But Jesus Christ is the new and last Adam. Adam faced temptation in the garden under the best of circumstances; Jesus Christ faced temptation in another garden under the worst of circumstances. Adam bent to his selfish pride and desire to be like God. Jesus withstood temptation and submitted himself to the will of God. "Consequently, just as one trespass resulted in condemnation for all people, so also one righteous act resulted in justification and life for all people" (Ro 5:18). But there's even more.

As Paul wrote, although the disobedience that brought about condemnation and alienation was purely evil, the work of Jesus did more good. Through the cross, Jesus overcame sin and death and is now able to bring sons and daughters of God into glory. Where Adam failed, Jesus won.

also grace might reign through righteousness to bring eternal life through Jesus Christ our Lord.

Dead to Sin, Alive in Christ

6 What shall we say, then? Shall we go on sinning so that grace may increase? [2]By no means! We are those who have died to sin; how can we live in it any longer? [3]Or don't you know that all of us who were baptized into Christ Jesus were baptized into his death? [4]We were therefore buried with him through baptism into death in order that, just as Christ was raised from the dead through the glory of the Father, we too may live a new life.

[5]For if we have been united with him in a death like his, we will certainly also be united with him in a resurrection like his. [6]For we know that our old self was crucified with him so that the body ruled by sin might be done away with,[a] that we should no longer be slaves to sin — [7]because anyone who has died has been set free from sin.

[8]Now if we died with Christ, we believe that we will also live with him. [9]For we know that since Christ was raised from the dead, he cannot die again; death no longer has mastery over him. [10]The death he died, he died to sin once for all; but the life he lives, he lives to God.

[11]In the same way, count yourselves dead to sin but alive to God in Christ Jesus. [12]Therefore do not let sin reign in your mortal body so that you obey its evil desires. [13]Do not offer any part of yourself to sin as an instrument of wickedness, but rather offer yourselves to God as those who have been brought from death to life; and offer every part of yourself to him as an instrument of righteousness. [14]For sin shall no longer be your master, because you are not under the law, but under grace.

Slaves to Righteousness

[15]What then? Shall we sin because we are not under the law but under grace? By no means! [16]Don't you know that when you offer yourselves to someone as obedient slaves, you are slaves of the one you obey — whether you are slaves to sin, which leads to death, or to obedience, which leads to righteousness? [17]But thanks be to God that, though you used to be slaves to sin, you have come to obey from your heart the pattern of teaching that has now claimed your allegiance. [18]You have been set free from sin and have become slaves to righteousness.

[19]I am using an example from everyday life because of your human limitations. Just as you used to offer yourselves as slaves to impurity and to ever-increasing wickedness, so now offer yourselves as slaves to righteousness leading to holiness. [20]When you were slaves to sin, you were free from the control of righteousness. [21]What benefit did you reap at that time from the things you are now ashamed of? Those things result in death! [22]But now that you have been set free from sin and have become slaves of God, the benefit you reap leads to holiness, and the result is eternal life. [23]For the wages of sin is death, but the gift of God is eternal life in[b] Christ Jesus our Lord.

Released From the Law, Bound to Christ

7 Do you not know, brothers and sisters — for I am speaking to those who know the law — that the law has authority over someone only as long as that person lives? [2]For example, by law a married woman is bound to her husband as long as he is alive, but if her husband dies, she is released from the law that binds her to him. [3]So then, if she has sexual relations with another man while her husband is still alive, she is called an adulteress. But if her husband dies, she is released from that law and is not an adulteress if she marries another man.

[4]So, my brothers and sisters, you also died to the law through the body of Christ, that you might belong to another, to him who was raised from the dead,

[a] 6 Or *be rendered powerless* [b] 23 Or *through*

(Reconciliation, continued)

the unthinkable happens: God grants reconciliation to those who turn to Jesus in repentance and trust. The word *reconciliation* means "change" or "exchange," but it's important to remember that true reconciliation involves a change in the attitudes of both parties who had been previously estranged or at odds. Through Christ, sinners are not left as beggars on the doorstep of heaven, hoping God will somehow open the door. Instead, his attitude toward those who believe has been wholly changed because of Jesus Christ's sacrifice. His wrath and justice have been satisfied, and his people are made right with him based on the righteousness of Christ. God sees his people not as former enemies, but as dearly beloved and adopted children. Like the father in the story of the lost son, God's people are welcomed home — not as slaves, but with celebration as returning sons and daughters (Lk 15:11 – 32).

ROMANS 6:22 – 23

GIFT OF ETERNAL LIFE

Workers are paid for the work they do, and while at times that wage is merited on the quality of the work performed, quite often it is static based on economic realities — especially in entry-level jobs. Similarly, Paul notes that all sin, no matter how seemingly innocuous, has earned every person who has ever lived a single and eternal wage from the hand of a just God: death. The gift of God's grace, however, stands in stark contrast to the wages of sin. God gives eternal life not because sinners merit it, but because his Son earned it. Eternal life

(continued on page 1756)

FIGHTING SIN

Paul the apostle was a realist. He knew that though conversion and justification might happen in a moment, the process of sanctification, or becoming more and more like Christ, is a progression that happens over time for the Christian. In fact, as believers come closer and closer in relationship with Christ they will find not that they are more confident of their own holiness, but less so; in coming closer to Christ, they find more and more corners of their dark hearts exposed in his light. For the Christian, then, fighting sin is a part of life — it's a battle in which they must fully engage to take up the work God has done and is doing in their lives.

The key difference in this battle for the Christian is that in Christ, a person is no longer fighting *for* victory; he or she is fighting *from* victory. Because one's position in respect to salvation has changed and God has initiated an irrevocable change in the heart, this person is no longer under the dominion of sin. Take a moment to let this thought sink in: *Sin is no longer in control.* That person now has access to the power of the Holy Spirit, who aids in the ongoing, everyday fight for holiness. This is why Paul can speak in such definite terms here — that Christians have died and been raised to life in Christ. This death and resurrection is a reference to one's eternal position of salvation in Jesus.

In light of that position, believers are to "count," or "reckon," themselves dead to sin (vv. 10 – 11). This counting and reckoning involves reminding oneself of what has been done for us and in us through Christ, and then bringing the truth of our position in him to bear on any given situation. When Christians count themselves dead to sin, they remind themselves that they are the blood-bought children of God. Then they allow that truth to impact their daily choices as they "remain" in Jesus throughout the course of their everyday life (Jn 15:5 – 8).

The process of sanctification requires that Christians continually rely on Jesus' teachings and the Holy Spirit, time and time again, as they "take captive every thought to make it obedient to Christ" (2Co 10:5). As they do, believers are offering daily actions, thoughts and attitudes as worship to God because of his glory. Christians no longer give themselves over to the old desires they had before their new life in Christ, but instead they align more and more with the work of the Holy Spirit to become more like Jesus to their families, friends and coworkers.

(Gift of Eternal Life, continued)

is a gracious gift from a loving God to his people who repent and trust in his salvation.

This gift of eternal life is not static; it's not something that will only be actualized upon physical death. Rather, eternal life is a dynamic relationship that believers enter into through faith in Jesus Christ and experience right here and now. Jesus promised his followers that they could have life to the full while living on this earth (Jn 10:10). This joyful, victorious life is possible through a deep and abiding relationship with God (Jn 15:4–6). Eternal life in heaven and on the new earth is, then, the glorious and unimaginably awe-inspiring extension of the believer's dynamic and growing relationship with God on earth.

ROMANS 7:25

THANKS BE TO GOD, WHO DELIVERS ME

Romans 7 is nothing if not a verbal picture of struggle. In this chapter, readers get a firsthand glimpse into the inner thoughts of the apostle, which can either be uplifting and encouraging or crushing and discouraging depending on one's perspective.

It might be discouraging to know that even Paul — who had experienced Jesus in a personal way and had seen the explosive growth of the early church — still struggled so violently with his own heart. But this chapter can also be encouraging for the same reason. When the weight of sin is particularly oppressive, Christians can take heart, knowing that all people struggle; even the

(continued on next page)

in order that we might bear fruit for God. 5For when we were in the realm of the
flesh,[a] the sinful passions aroused by the law were at work in us, so that we bore
fruit for death. 6But now, by dying to what once bound us, we have been released
from the law so that we serve in the new way of the Spirit, and not in the old way
of the written code.

The Law and Sin

7What shall we say, then? Is the law sinful? Certainly not! Nevertheless, I
would not have known what sin was had it not been for the law. For I would
not have known what coveting really was if the law had not said, "You shall not
covet."[b] 8But sin, seizing the opportunity afforded by the commandment, produced in me every kind of coveting. For apart from the law, sin was dead. 9Once
I was alive apart from the law; but when the commandment came, sin sprang
to life and I died. 10I found that the very commandment that was intended to
bring life actually brought death. 11For sin, seizing the opportunity afforded
by the commandment, deceived me, and through the commandment put me
to death. 12So then, the law is holy, and the commandment is holy, righteous
and good.

13Did that which is good, then, become death to me? By no means! Nevertheless, in order that sin might be recognized as sin, it used what is good to bring
about my death, so that through the commandment sin might become utterly
sinful.

14We know that the law is spiritual; but I am unspiritual, sold as a slave to sin.
15I do not understand what I do. For what I want to do I do not do, but what I hate
I do. 16And if I do what I do not want to do, I agree that the law is good. 17As it is,
it is no longer I myself who do it, but it is sin living in me. 18For I know that good
itself does not dwell in me, that is, in my sinful nature.[c] For I have the desire to
do what is good, but I cannot carry it out. 19For I do not do the good I want to do,
but the evil I do not want to do — this I keep on doing. 20Now if I do what I do not
want to do, it is no longer I who do it, but it is sin living in me that does it.

21So I find this law at work: Although I want to do good, evil is right there with
me. 22For in my inner being I delight in God's law; 23but I see another law at work
in me, waging war against the law of my mind and making me a prisoner of the
law of sin at work within me. 24What a wretched man I am! Who will rescue me
from this body that is subject to death? 25Thanks be to God, who delivers me
through Jesus Christ our Lord!

So then, I myself in my mind am a slave to God's law, but in my sinful nature[d]
a slave to the law of sin.

Life Through the Spirit

8 Therefore, there is now no condemnation for those who are in Christ Jesus,
2because through Christ Jesus the law of the Spirit who gives life has set you[e]
free from the law of sin and death. 3For what the law was powerless to do because
it was weakened by the flesh,[f] God did by sending his own Son in the likeness of
sinful flesh to be a sin offering.[g] And so he condemned sin in the flesh, 4in order
that the righteous requirement of the law might be fully met in us, who do not
live according to the flesh but according to the Spirit.

5Those who live according to the flesh have their minds set on what the flesh
desires; but those who live in accordance with the Spirit have their minds set
on what the Spirit desires. 6The mind governed by the flesh is death, but the
mind governed by the Spirit is life and peace. 7The mind governed by the flesh is

[a] 5 In contexts like this, the Greek word for *flesh* (*sarx*) refers to the sinful state of human beings, often presented as a power in opposition to the Spirit. [b] 7 Exodus 20:17; Deut. 5:21
[c] 18 Or *my flesh* [d] 25 Or *in the flesh* [e] 2 The Greek is singular; some manuscripts *me*
[f] 3 In contexts like this, the Greek word for *flesh* (*sarx*) refers to the sinful state of human beings, often presented as a power in opposition to the Spirit; also in verses 4-13.
[g] 3 Or *flesh, for sin*

hostile to God; it does not submit to God's law, nor can it do so. 8Those who are in the realm of the flesh cannot please God.

9You, however, are not in the realm of the flesh but are in the realm of the Spirit, if indeed the Spirit of God lives in you. And if anyone does not have the Spirit of Christ, they do not belong to Christ. 10But if Christ is in you, then even though your body is subject to death because of sin, the Spirit gives life[a] because of righteousness. 11And if the Spirit of him who raised Jesus from the dead is living in you, he who raised Christ from the dead will also give life to your mortal bodies because of[b] his Spirit who lives in you.

12Therefore, brothers and sisters, we have an obligation — but it is not to the flesh, to live according to it. 13For if you live according to the flesh, you will die; but if by the Spirit you put to death the misdeeds of the body, you will live.

14For those who are led by the Spirit of God are the children of God. 15The Spirit you received does not make you slaves, so that you live in fear again; rather, the Spirit you received brought about your adoption to sonship.[c] And by him we cry, *"Abba,*[d] Father." 16The Spirit himself testifies with our spirit that we are God's children. 17Now if we are children, then we are heirs — heirs of God and co-heirs with Christ, if indeed we share in his sufferings in order that we may also share in his glory.

Present Suffering and Future Glory

18I consider that our present sufferings are not worth comparing with the glory that will be revealed in us. 19For the creation waits in eager expectation for the children of God to be revealed. 20For the creation was subjected to frustration, not by its own choice, but by the will of the one who subjected it, in hope 21that[e] the creation itself will be liberated from its bondage to decay and brought into the freedom and glory of the children of God.

22We know that the whole creation has been groaning as in the pains of childbirth right up to the present time. 23Not only so, but we ourselves, who have the firstfruits of the Spirit, groan inwardly as we wait eagerly for our adoption to sonship, the redemption of our bodies. 24For in this hope we were saved. But hope that is seen is no hope at all. Who hopes for what they already have? 25But if we hope for what we do not yet have, we wait for it patiently.

26In the same way, the Spirit helps us in our weakness. We do not know what we ought to pray for, but the Spirit himself intercedes for us through wordless groans. 27And he who searches our hearts knows the mind of the Spirit, because the Spirit intercedes for God's people in accordance with the will of God.

28And we know that in all things God works for the good of those who love him, who[f] have been called according to his purpose. 29For those God foreknew he also predestined to be conformed to the image of his Son, that he might be the firstborn among many brothers and sisters. 30And those he predestined, he also called; those he called, he also justified; those he justified, he also glorified.

More Than Conquerors

31What, then, shall we say in response to these things? If God is for us, who can be against us? 32He who did not spare his own Son, but gave him up for us all — how will he not also, along with him, graciously give us all things? 33Who will bring any charge against those whom God has chosen? It is God who justifies. 34Who then is the one who condemns? No one. Christ Jesus who died — more than that, who was raised to life — is at the right hand of God and is also interceding for us. 35Who shall separate us from the love of Christ? Shall trouble

[a] *10* Or *you, your body is dead because of sin, yet your spirit is alive* [b] *11* Some manuscripts *bodies through* [c] *15* The Greek word for *adoption to sonship* is a term referring to the full legal standing of an adopted male heir in Roman culture; also in verse 23. [d] *15* Aramaic for *father* [e] *20,21* Or *subjected it in hope.* [21]*For* [f] *28* Or *that all things work together for good to those who love God, who*; or *that in all things God works together with those who love him to bring about what is good — with those who*

(Thanks Be to God, Who Delivers Me, continued)

apostle Paul battled mightily with sin. The New Testament never characterizes Christians as those who do not struggle with sin; rather they are those who stay in the fight.

When Christians feel the weight of sin's burden; when they're torn between righteousness and unrighteousness, between the desires of the Spirit and the desires of the flesh, then the only solution is Jesus. He is the only One who can deliver those who are dead in sin and, through the Holy Spirit, help his followers to resist sin. The Christian needs the gospel as much as the non-Christian does, for it is by the gospel God's people were saved from their slavery to sin. It is the same gospel that reminds the believer that they are "more than conquerors through him who loved us" (Ro 8:37).

ROMANS 8:1–2

NO CONDEMNATION

God did not give the law to his people as the means of their salvation, for he knew that no sinful person could ever perfectly keep the law. Instead, the law both exposes the sinfulness of the human heart and displays the perfect holiness of God's character. In both cases, the law reminds all people that apart from Christ, there is only condemnation.

But in Christ, there is no condemnation. None. In Christ, believers have been given the gift of his hard-won righteousness. This gift comes by faith in Jesus, who fulfilled the law on their behalf. Along with the imputed righteousness of Christ comes the gift of the Holy Spirit, who gives

(continued on page 1759)

ELECTION

Throughout the ages, theologians have debated the doctrine of election that Paul brings into consideration in these verses. This doctrine is more than a matter of theological debate; in this context, it is one of the reasons for the great assurance Christians have of God's love that is available in Christ.

There are two main opinions that have arisen over the ages in regard to this doctrine. The first opinion is that God's foreknowledge involves his future knowledge of the people who will respond to him by faith and those who will not. Those who accept Christ and the gospel are the elect, for they were predestined according to the choice God knew they would make. Those who take this position find that it reconciles well with the fact that God desires that all people come to a saving knowledge of him (1Ti 2:3 – 4; 2Pe 3:9) and that salvation is universally available to all who will claim this free gift. It is a "whosoever will come" kind of call, in which people have the real choice to either accept or reject God's offer of salvation.

The other viewpoint understands God's foreknowledge as an unconditional choice. Anyone who is saved, according to this view, is saved only because God chose some that they would believe; indeed, apart from God's active choosing of individuals, all people are so lost in sin that not one would actively choose Christ if left to themself to decide. Supporting this position is the doctrine of absolute human depravity (Eph 2:1 – 10), which holds that sinners are dead in their trespasses and incapable of responding to God apart from his divine intervention. God changes the human heart, removes the scales from the eyes of some, and gives them the gift of faith that allows them to believe the gospel message.

Where these two views come together is that every person, apart from God's intervening grace in sending Jesus, is hopelessly lost, and the only way to salvation is through his grace and mercy. Furthermore, each understanding of the doctrine, when rightly applied, results in the glory of God alone rather than human pride. Regardless of where we land on the particulars of the doctrine of election, in the end it inspires our worship because we are directed back to the gospel of Jesus Christ, our only hope.

or hardship or persecution or famine or nakedness or danger or sword? [36]As it is written:

"For your sake we face death all day long;
we are considered as sheep to be slaughtered."[a]

[37]No, in all these things we are more than conquerors through him who loved us. [38]For I am convinced that neither death nor life, neither angels nor demons,[b] neither the present nor the future, nor any powers, [39]neither height nor depth, nor anything else in all creation, will be able to separate us from the love of God that is in Christ Jesus our Lord.

Paul's Anguish Over Israel

9 I speak the truth in Christ—I am not lying, my conscience confirms it through the Holy Spirit— [2]I have great sorrow and unceasing anguish in my heart. [3]For I could wish that I myself were cursed and cut off from Christ for the sake of my people, those of my own race, [4]the people of Israel. Theirs is the adoption to sonship; theirs the divine glory, the covenants, the receiving of the law, the temple worship and the promises. [5]Theirs are the patriarchs, and from them is traced the human ancestry of the Messiah, who is God over all, forever praised![c] Amen.

God's Sovereign Choice

[6]It is not as though God's word had failed. For not all who are descended from Israel are Israel. [7]Nor because they are his descendants are they all Abraham's children. On the contrary, "It is through Isaac that your offspring will be reckoned."[d] [8]In other words, it is not the children by physical descent who are God's children, but it is the children of the promise who are regarded as Abraham's offspring. [9]For this was how the promise was stated: "At the appointed time I will return, and Sarah will have a son."[e]

[10]Not only that, but Rebekah's children were conceived at the same time by our father Isaac. [11]Yet, before the twins were born or had done anything good or bad—in order that God's purpose in election might stand: [12]not by works but by him who calls—she was told, "The older will serve the younger."[f] [13]Just as it is written: "Jacob I loved, but Esau I hated."[g]

[14]What then shall we say? Is God unjust? Not at all! [15]For he says to Moses,

"I will have mercy on whom I have mercy,
and I will have compassion on whom I have compassion."[h]

[16]It does not, therefore, depend on human desire or effort, but on God's mercy. [17]For Scripture says to Pharaoh: "I raised you up for this very purpose, that I might display my power in you and that my name might be proclaimed in all the earth."[i] [18]Therefore God has mercy on whom he wants to have mercy, and he hardens whom he wants to harden.

[19]One of you will say to me: "Then why does God still blame us? For who is able to resist his will?" [20]But who are you, a human being, to talk back to God? "Shall what is formed say to the one who formed it, 'Why did you make me like this?'"[j] [21]Does not the potter have the right to make out of the same lump of clay some pottery for special purposes and some for common use?

[22]What if God, although choosing to show his wrath and make his power known, bore with great patience the objects of his wrath—prepared for destruction? [23]What if he did this to make the riches of his glory known to the objects of his mercy, whom he prepared in advance for glory— [24]even us, whom he also called, not only from the Jews but also from the Gentiles? [25]As he says in Hosea:

(No Condemnation, continued)

Christians the power to live for Jesus every day. Rather than having a law written on tablets of stone, the Holy Spirit writes the law on the hearts of God's people. It's only through the Spirit, and his power, that his people can bring glory to God and help to build his kingdom.

---

[a] *36* Psalm 44:22 [b] *38* Or *nor heavenly rulers* [c] *5* Or *Messiah, who is over all. God be forever praised!* Or *Messiah. God who is over all be forever praised!* [d] *7* Gen. 21:12
[e] *9* Gen. 18:10,14 [f] *12* Gen. 25:23 [g] *13* Mal. 1:2,3 [h] *15* Exodus 33:19
[i] *17* Exodus 9:16 [j] *20* Isaiah 29:16; 45:9

"I will call them 'my people' who are not my people;
and I will call her 'my loved one' who is not my loved one,"[a]

26 and,

"In the very place where it was said to them,
'You are not my people,'
there they will be called 'children of the living God.'"[b]

27 Isaiah cries out concerning Israel:

"Though the number of the Israelites be like the sand by the sea,
only the remnant will be saved.
28 For the Lord will carry out
his sentence on earth with speed and finality."[c]

29 It is just as Isaiah said previously:

"Unless the Lord Almighty
had left us descendants,
we would have become like Sodom,
we would have been like Gomorrah."[d]

Israel's Unbelief

30 What then shall we say? That the Gentiles, who did not pursue righteousness, have obtained it, a righteousness that is by faith; 31 but the people of Israel, who pursued the law as the way of righteousness, have not attained their goal. 32 Why not? Because they pursued it not by faith but as if it were by works. They stumbled over the stumbling stone. 33 As it is written:

"See, I lay in Zion a stone that causes people to stumble
and a rock that makes them fall,
and the one who believes in him will never be put to shame."[e]

10 Brothers and sisters, my heart's desire and prayer to God for the Israelites is that they may be saved. 2 For I can testify about them that they are zealous for God, but their zeal is not based on knowledge. 3 Since they did not know the righteousness of God and sought to establish their own, they did not submit to God's righteousness. 4 Christ is the culmination of the law so that there may be righteousness for everyone who believes.

5 Moses writes this about the righteousness that is by the law: "The person who does these things will live by them."[f] 6 But the righteousness that is by faith says: "Do not say in your heart, 'Who will ascend into heaven?'"[g] (that is, to bring Christ down) 7 "or 'Who will descend into the deep?'"[h] (that is, to bring Christ up from the dead). 8 But what does it say? "The word is near you; it is in your mouth and in your heart,"[i] that is, the message concerning faith that we proclaim: 9 If you declare with your mouth, "Jesus is Lord," and believe in your heart that God raised him from the dead, you will be saved. 10 For it is with your heart that you believe and are justified, and it is with your mouth that you profess your faith and are saved. 11 As Scripture says, "Anyone who believes in him will never be put to shame."[j] 12 For there is no difference between Jew and Gentile—the same Lord is Lord of all and richly blesses all who call on him, 13 for, "Everyone who calls on the name of the Lord will be saved."[k]

14 How, then, can they call on the one they have not believed in? And how can they believe in the one of whom they have not heard? And how can they hear without someone preaching to them? 15 And how can anyone preach unless they are sent? As it is written: "How beautiful are the feet of those who bring good news!"[l]

16 But not all the Israelites accepted the good news. For Isaiah says, "Lord, who

[a] 25 Hosea 2:23 [b] 26 Hosea 1:10 [c] 28 Isaiah 10:22,23 (see Septuagint) [d] 29 Isaiah 1:9 [e] 33 Isaiah 8:14; 28:16 [f] 5 Lev. 18:5 [g] 6 Deut. 30:12 [h] 7 Deut. 30:13 [i] 8 Deut. 30:14 [j] 11 Isaiah 28:16 (see Septuagint) [k] 13 Joel 2:32 [l] 15 Isaiah 52:7

ROMANS 9:33

STUMBLING

Expectation is a powerful thing. When it comes to God, people can easily convince themselves of what God *should* do in a given situation and end up missing what God is actually doing. Such were the tragic ironies of many Jews in Paul's day: Though they had for centuries looked with longing toward a day when God would send a deliverer, a Messiah, they were so committed to their expectations of what that Messiah should do and be that many missed the reality of God's work in Jesus Christ.

The prophet Isaiah said it would be so—he said that Israel would reject their own Messiah (Isa 8:14; 28:16) in prophecies echoed here by the apostle Paul. Many Jews were busy looking for a political leader like King David of old; they were focused on deliverance from the Roman oppression and so they neglected the greater King who was sent and the greater deliverance he offered. Jesus, the cornerstone for all Christian faith and righteousness, was—and still is—a stumbling block for many.

ROMANS 10:4

RIGHTEOUSNESS

One of the predominant themes in both the Old and New Testaments is that of righteousness. Paul's understanding of this word is not that it is an extensive list of rules to keep, but rather something that Jesus earned through his perfectly obedient life and credits to believers by faith. For Paul, righteousness is not so much a *description* of conduct as it is a *condition* of a proper relationship between God and a person.

In the Old Testament, righteousness is established fundamentally as a characteristic of God. He alone is truly righteous. Because this is true, God always kept his promises even when his people, Israel, were not faithful to theirs. Time and time again, the people abandoned God through their pursuit of idols and their unfaithfulness to the covenant God had made with them, but time and time again, God remained faithful and restored his people. However, eventually God took drastic measures to discipline his people, raising up the pagan nations of Assyria and Babylon to conquer Israel and Judah and bring them into exile in foreign lands. When Judah returned, the people returned with the understanding that their unrighteousness and idolatry had led to God's judgment.

Because they realized this, their leaders encouraged the people of Judah to foster a new zeal for the law; they were determined never to let what happened in the exile happen again. Unfortunately, though, the people confused this external and rule-based adherence to the law with true righteousness. True righteousness goes well beyond external compliance to a set of rules; true righteousness comes from a heart that is bent toward loving God and participating in joyful worship.

This is why true righteousness can only come about through faith and through the gospel. Jesus alone is fully righteous, inside and out; the only way in which a person can become righteous is by faith in him. When a person believes in Jesus, that person's sin is laid upon Jesus and is paid for by his sacrifice. Meanwhile, the believer in exchange receives the perfect righteousness of Christ. By faith, a person can at long last not only act in a righteous way, but can actually become more and more righteous as their heart is changed by the continual influence of the Holy Spirit.

has believed our message?"[a] 17Consequently, faith comes from hearing the message, and the message is heard through the word about Christ. 18But I ask: Did they not hear? Of course they did:

"Their voice has gone out into all the earth,
their words to the ends of the world."[b]

19Again I ask: Did Israel not understand? First, Moses says,

"I will make you envious by those who are not a nation;
I will make you angry by a nation that has no understanding."[c]

20And Isaiah boldly says,

"I was found by those who did not seek me;
I revealed myself to those who did not ask for me."[d]

21But concerning Israel he says,

"All day long I have held out my hands
to a disobedient and obstinate people."[e]

The Remnant of Israel

11 I ask then: Did God reject his people? By no means! I am an Israelite myself, a descendant of Abraham, from the tribe of Benjamin. 2God did not reject his people, whom he foreknew. Don't you know what Scripture says in the passage about Elijah — how he appealed to God against Israel: 3"Lord, they have killed your prophets and torn down your altars; I am the only one left, and they are trying to kill me"[f]? 4And what was God's answer to him? "I have reserved for myself seven thousand who have not bowed the knee to Baal."[g] 5So too, at the present time there is a remnant chosen by grace. 6And if by grace, then it cannot be based on works; if it were, grace would no longer be grace.

7What then? What the people of Israel sought so earnestly they did not obtain. The elect among them did, but the others were hardened, 8as it is written:

"God gave them a spirit of stupor,
eyes that could not see
and ears that could not hear,
to this very day."[h]

9And David says:

"May their table become a snare and a trap,
a stumbling block and a retribution for them.
10May their eyes be darkened so they cannot see,
and their backs be bent forever."[i]

Ingrafted Branches

11Again I ask: Did they stumble so as to fall beyond recovery? Not at all! Rather, because of their transgression, salvation has come to the Gentiles to make Israel envious. 12But if their transgression means riches for the world, and their loss means riches for the Gentiles, how much greater riches will their full inclusion bring!

13I am talking to you Gentiles. Inasmuch as I am the apostle to the Gentiles, I take pride in my ministry 14in the hope that I may somehow arouse my own people to envy and save some of them. 15For if their rejection brought reconciliation to the world, what will their acceptance be but life from the dead? 16If the part of the dough offered as firstfruits is holy, then the whole batch is holy; if the root is holy, so are the branches.

17If some of the branches have been broken off, and you, though a wild olive

---

[a] *16* Isaiah 53:1 [b] *18* Psalm 19:4 [c] *19* Deut. 32:21 [d] *20* Isaiah 65:1 [e] *21* Isaiah 65:2
[f] *3* 1 Kings 19:10,14 [g] *4* 1 Kings 19:18 [h] *8* Deut. 29:4; Isaiah 29:10 [i] *10* Psalm 69:22,23

shoot, have been grafted in among the others and now share in the nourishing
sap from the olive root, [18]do not consider yourself to be superior to those other
branches. If you do, consider this: You do not support the root, but the root supports you. [19]You will say then, "Branches were broken off so that I could be grafted in." [20]Granted. But they were broken off because of unbelief, and you stand
by faith. Do not be arrogant, but tremble. [21]For if God did not spare the natural
branches, he will not spare you either.

[22]Consider therefore the kindness and sternness of God: sternness to those
who fell, but kindness to you, provided that you continue in his kindness. Otherwise, you also will be cut off. [23]And if they do not persist in unbelief, they will
be grafted in, for God is able to graft them in again. [24]After all, if you were cut out
of an olive tree that is wild by nature, and contrary to nature were grafted into
a cultivated olive tree, how much more readily will these, the natural branches,
be grafted into their own olive tree!

All Israel Will Be Saved

[25]I do not want you to be ignorant of this mystery, brothers and sisters, so
that you may not be conceited: Israel has experienced a hardening in part until
the full number of the Gentiles has come in, [26]and in this way[a] all Israel will be
saved. As it is written:

"The deliverer will come from Zion;
he will turn godlessness away from Jacob.
[27]And this is[b] my covenant with them
when I take away their sins."[c]

[28]As far as the gospel is concerned, they are enemies for your sake; but as far
as election is concerned, they are loved on account of the patriarchs, [29]for God's
gifts and his call are irrevocable. [30]Just as you who were at one time disobedient
to God have now received mercy as a result of their disobedience, [31]so they too
have now become disobedient in order that they too may now[d] receive mercy as
a result of God's mercy to you. [32]For God has bound everyone over to disobedience so that he may have mercy on them all.

Doxology

[33]Oh, the depth of the riches of the wisdom and[e] knowledge of God!
How unsearchable his judgments,
and his paths beyond tracing out!
[34]"Who has known the mind of the Lord?
Or who has been his counselor?"[f]
[35]"Who has ever given to God,
that God should repay them?"[g]
[36]For from him and through him and for him are all things.
To him be the glory forever! Amen.

A Living Sacrifice

12 Therefore, I urge you, brothers and sisters, in view of God's mercy, to offer
your bodies as a living sacrifice, holy and pleasing to God—this is your
true and proper worship. [2]Do not conform to the pattern of this world, but be
transformed by the renewing of your mind. Then you will be able to test and approve what God's will is—his good, pleasing and perfect will.

Humble Service in the Body of Christ

[3]For by the grace given me I say to every one of you: Do not think of yourself
more highly than you ought, but rather think of yourself with sober judgment,

[a] *26* Or *and so* [b] *27* Or *will be* [c] *27* Isaiah 59:20,21; 27:9 (see Septuagint); Jer. 31:33,34
[d] *31* Some manuscripts do not have *now.* [e] *33* Or *riches and the wisdom and the*
[f] *34* Isaiah 40:13 [g] *35* Job 41:11

ROMANS 11:33–36

DOXOLOGY

Paul's pattern of writing letters was broadly the same—he built his convincing arguments by explaining doctrine, but then brought it to a more practical level by discussing behavior. This holds true in the book of Romans. Having spent 11 chapters extrapolating the gravity of sin, the necessity of faith and the profound grace of the gospel, Paul is ready to turn the corner into the practical implications of behavior in Romans 12. As he closes the first section of his letter, he erupts in praise for who God is and for what he has done.

In this passage, Paul acknowledges the mysterious and incomparable nature of God and his plan. The gospel, which Paul has explained in detail in the previous pages, was not something any human could have devised. Rather, it took God's great and unsearchable wisdom to provide the solution for the terrible and universal problem of sin. He acted in history in such a way that men and women could be made righteous.

Because the foundation of the gospel is not humanity but God, God alone can and should receive the glory and honor he is due. The gospel, as with all things, begins and ends with God, for he is the center of all things.

ROMANS 12:3–8

MEMBERS OF ONE BODY

Christian unity is one of the imperatives of the gospel. When someone is born again, he or she is born into a

(continued on next page)

(Members of One Body, continued)

family of faith for all eternity. This family, God's people, is the church. Unlike any other earthly entity, the church is not divided according to physical boundary, race, culture, education or any other reality. Instead, the church is unified because of its members' common experience with the grace of Jesus Christ.

Unity, however, does not mean uniformity or a lack of diversity. Indeed, the great diversity of the church's members is one of its unique aspects. Though each member is gifted differently, every member comes together to form the whole church. Furthermore, because of the variety of gifts possessed, every member is integral to the church's healthy functioning. There is, then, no member greater than another, just as there is no part of the body that would boast over its position. The proper response of the Christian is to love and value the other members of the church because of their essential contributions to the health and well-being of the church worldwide.

in accordance with the faith God has distributed to each of you. [4]For just as each
of us has one body with many members, and these members do not all have the
same function, [5]so in Christ we, though many, form one body, and each member
belongs to all the others. [6]We have different gifts, according to the grace given to
each of us. If your gift is prophesying, then prophesy in accordance with your[a]
faith; [7]if it is serving, then serve; if it is teaching, then teach; [8]if it is to encourage,
then give encouragement; if it is giving, then give generously; if it is to lead,[b] do
it diligently; if it is to show mercy, do it cheerfully.

Love in Action

[9]Love must be sincere. Hate what is evil; cling to what is good. [10]Be devoted to
one another in love. Honor one another above yourselves. [11]Never be lacking in
zeal, but keep your spiritual fervor, serving the Lord. [12]Be joyful in hope, patient
in affliction, faithful in prayer. [13]Share with the Lord's people who are in need.
Practice hospitality.

[14]Bless those who persecute you; bless and do not curse. [15]Rejoice with those
who rejoice; mourn with those who mourn. [16]Live in harmony with one another.
Do not be proud, but be willing to associate with people of low position.[c] Do
not be conceited.

[17]Do not repay anyone evil for evil. Be careful to do what is right in the eyes of
everyone. [18]If it is possible, as far as it depends on you, live at peace with everyone.
[19]Do not take revenge, my dear friends, but leave room for God's wrath, for
it is written: "It is mine to avenge; I will repay,"[d] says the Lord. [20]On the contrary:

"If your enemy is hungry, feed him;
if he is thirsty, give him something to drink.
In doing this, you will heap burning coals on his head."[e]

[21]Do not be overcome by evil, but overcome evil with good.

Submission to Governing Authorities

13 Let everyone be subject to the governing authorities, for there is no authority
except that which God has established. The authorities that exist
have been established by God. [2]Consequently, whoever rebels against the authority
is rebelling against what God has instituted, and those who do so will
bring judgment on themselves. [3]For rulers hold no terror for those who do right,
but for those who do wrong. Do you want to be free from fear of the one in authority?
Then do what is right and you will be commended. [4]For the one in authority
is God's servant for your good. But if you do wrong, be afraid, for rulers
do not bear the sword for no reason. They are God's servants, agents of wrath
to bring punishment on the wrongdoer. [5]Therefore, it is necessary to submit to
the authorities, not only because of possible punishment but also as a matter of
conscience.

[6]This is also why you pay taxes, for the authorities are God's servants, who
give their full time to governing. [7]Give to everyone what you owe them: If you
owe taxes, pay taxes; if revenue, then revenue; if respect, then respect; if honor,
then honor.

Love Fulfills the Law

[8]Let no debt remain outstanding, except the continuing debt to love one another,
for whoever loves others has fulfilled the law. [9]The commandments, "You
shall not commit adultery," "You shall not murder," "You shall not steal," "You
shall not covet,"[f] and whatever other command there may be, are summed up in
this one command: "Love your neighbor as yourself."[g] [10]Love does no harm to a
neighbor. Therefore love is the fulfillment of the law.

---

[a] 6 Or *the* [b] 8 Or *to provide for others* [c] 16 Or *willing to do menial work*
[d] 19 Deut. 32:35 [e] 20 Prov. 25:21,22 [f] 9 Exodus 20:13-15,17; Deut. 5:17-19,21
[g] 9 Lev. 19:18

ROMANS 13:8–10

KEY TERMS OF SALVATION

The more one understands the key terms Paul chose to explain the gospel, the deeper one's experience will be with the gospel.

Atonement (3:25): "The satisfaction of God's holy wrath against sin." The consequence of our sin is the righteous judgment that God will exercise on sinners. By dying in our place and taking our sins on himself, Jesus makes "atonement" for our sin: he satisfies God's righteous anger against all who believe.

Faith (1:17): Meaning "belief" or "trust," faith is the means by which sinful people come into right standing with God. It is a complete and active trust in Jesus alone for salvation.

Gospel (1:16): Literally means "good news" and is the word Paul uses to refer to the message of forgiveness, eternal life and the lordship of Christ.

Grace (6:14): "The unmerited favor of God." This refers to God's inexplicable and unwarranted giving of good things (especially salvation) to those who could never earn it. There is power for holy living in the grace of God.

Justification (5:18): A legal term that means "the act of being declared righteous." This exchange happens at salvation when God the Judge declares righteous those who trust in Christ and his work at the cross. Christ took on the punishment for the sins of those who believe.

Law (13:8): "The commandments given by God." The law is good, yet sinful people are incapable of fully keeping it. The law then serves to fully expose our sin. That's why Paul emphasizes the law in comparison with God's grace (5:20; 6:14–15).

Redemption (3:23–24): What we experience when we are saved. This is "the act of freeing someone by paying a price," an economic term Paul employed to show how God buys us back with the blood of his own Son.

Righteousness (1:17): As God buys us back, he gifts us with righteousness, "God's standard of purity" or "God's own truthfulness and faithfulness." Amazingly, in the gospel we are not only forgiven, but we are also granted perfect purity in Christ.

Salvation (1:16): Means "deliverance" or "healing" and is the word Paul most often uses to denote deliverance from sin and its deadly consequences.

Sin (3:20): Means "missing the mark" or "disobedience to God's law." Sin is more than an action; it's a condition that leads to disobedient action. Broadly defined, it's the tendency of humans to rebel against God, which leads to any action or attitude that opposes God's character and will.

Paul uses these terms throughout the book of Romans to describe the free gift of salvation and eternal transformation that is available to all who will believe and trust in Jesus for the forgiveness of their sin.

The Day Is Near

11 And do this, understanding the present time: The hour has already come for you to wake up from your slumber, because our salvation is nearer now than when we first believed. 12 The night is nearly over; the day is almost here. So let us put aside the deeds of darkness and put on the armor of light. 13 Let us behave decently, as in the daytime, not in carousing and drunkenness, not in sexual immorality and debauchery, not in dissension and jealousy. 14 Rather, clothe yourselves with the Lord Jesus Christ, and do not think about how to gratify the desires of the flesh.[a]

The Weak and the Strong

14 Accept the one whose faith is weak, without quarreling over disputable matters. 2 One person's faith allows them to eat anything, but another, whose faith is weak, eats only vegetables. 3 The one who eats everything must not treat with contempt the one who does not, and the one who does not eat everything must not judge the one who does, for God has accepted them. 4 Who are you to judge someone else's servant? To their own master, servants stand or fall. And they will stand, for the Lord is able to make them stand.

5 One person considers one day more sacred than another; another considers every day alike. Each of them should be fully convinced in their own mind. 6 Whoever regards one day as special does so to the Lord. Whoever eats meat does so to the Lord, for they give thanks to God; and whoever abstains does so to the Lord and gives thanks to God. 7 For none of us lives for ourselves alone, and none of us dies for ourselves alone. 8 If we live, we live for the Lord; and if we die, we die for the Lord. So, whether we live or die, we belong to the Lord. 9 For this very reason, Christ died and returned to life so that he might be the Lord of both the dead and the living.

10 You, then, why do you judge your brother or sister[b]? Or why do you treat them with contempt? For we will all stand before God's judgment seat. 11 It is written:

> "'As surely as I live,' says the Lord,
> 'every knee will bow before me;
> every tongue will acknowledge God.'"[c]

12 So then, each of us will give an account of ourselves to God.

13 Therefore let us stop passing judgment on one another. Instead, make up your mind not to put any stumbling block or obstacle in the way of a brother or sister. 14 I am convinced, being fully persuaded in the Lord Jesus, that nothing is unclean in itself. But if anyone regards something as unclean, then for that person it is unclean. 15 If your brother or sister is distressed because of what you eat, you are no longer acting in love. Do not by your eating destroy someone for whom Christ died. 16 Therefore do not let what you know is good be spoken of as evil. 17 For the kingdom of God is not a matter of eating and drinking, but of righteousness, peace and joy in the Holy Spirit, 18 because anyone who serves Christ in this way is pleasing to God and receives human approval.

19 Let us therefore make every effort to do what leads to peace and to mutual edification. 20 Do not destroy the work of God for the sake of food. All food is clean, but it is wrong for a person to eat anything that causes someone else to stumble. 21 It is better not to eat meat or drink wine or to do anything else that will cause your brother or sister to fall.

22 So whatever you believe about these things keep between yourself and God. Blessed is the one who does not condemn himself by what he approves. 23 But

---

[a] *14* In contexts like this, the Greek word for *flesh* (*sarx*) refers to the sinful state of human beings, often presented as a power in opposition to the Spirit. [b] *10* The Greek word for *brother or sister* (*adelphos*) refers here to a believer, whether man or woman, as part of God's family; also in verses 13, 15 and 21. [c] *11* Isaiah 45:23

whoever has doubts is condemned if they eat, because their eating is not from
faith; and everything that does not come from faith is sin.[a]

15 We who are strong ought to bear with the failings of the weak and not to
please ourselves. [2]Each of us should please our neighbors for their good, to
build them up. [3]For even Christ did not please himself but, as it is written: "The
insults of those who insult you have fallen on me."[b] [4]For everything that was
written in the past was written to teach us, so that through the endurance taught
in the Scriptures and the encouragement they provide we might have hope.
[5]May the God who gives endurance and encouragement give you the same
attitude of mind toward each other that Christ Jesus had, [6]so that with one mind
and one voice you may glorify the God and Father of our Lord Jesus Christ.
[7]Accept one another, then, just as Christ accepted you, in order to bring praise
to God. [8]For I tell you that Christ has become a servant of the Jews[c] on behalf of
God's truth, so that the promises made to the patriarchs might be confirmed
[9]and, moreover, that the Gentiles might glorify God for his mercy. As it is written:

"Therefore I will praise you among the Gentiles;
I will sing the praises of your name."[d]

[10]Again, it says,

"Rejoice, you Gentiles, with his people."[e]

[11]And again,

"Praise the Lord, all you Gentiles;
let all the peoples extol him."[f]

[12]And again, Isaiah says,

"The Root of Jesse will spring up,
one who will arise to rule over the nations;
in him the Gentiles will hope."[g]

[13]May the God of hope fill you with all joy and peace as you trust in him, so
that you may overflow with hope by the power of the Holy Spirit.

Paul the Minister to the Gentiles

[14]I myself am convinced, my brothers and sisters, that you yourselves are full
of goodness, filled with knowledge and competent to instruct one another. [15]Yet
I have written you quite boldly on some points to remind you of them again, because of the grace God gave me [16]to be a minister of Christ Jesus to the Gentiles.
He gave me the priestly duty of proclaiming the gospel of God, so that the Gentiles might become an offering acceptable to God, sanctified by the Holy Spirit.
[17]Therefore I glory in Christ Jesus in my service to God. [18]I will not venture to
speak of anything except what Christ has accomplished through me in leading
the Gentiles to obey God by what I have said and done— [19]by the power of signs
and wonders, through the power of the Spirit of God. So from Jerusalem all the
way around to Illyricum, I have fully proclaimed the gospel of Christ. [20]It has always been my ambition to preach the gospel where Christ was not known, so that
I would not be building on someone else's foundation. [21]Rather, as it is written:

"Those who were not told about him will see,
and those who have not heard will understand."[h]

[22]This is why I have often been hindered from coming to you.

Paul's Plan to Visit Rome

[23]But now that there is no more place for me to work in these regions, and
since I have been longing for many years to visit you, [24]I plan to do so when I go to

---

[a] *23* Some manuscripts place 16:25-27 here; others after 15:33. [b] *3* Psalm 69:9 [c] *8* Greek *circumcision* [d] *9* 2 Samuel 22:50; Psalm 18:49 [e] *10* Deut. 32:43 [f] *11* Psalm 117:1 [g] *12* Isaiah 11:10 (see Septuagint) [h] *21* Isaiah 52:15 (see Septuagint)

ROMANS 15:1–4

AN UNSELFISH ATTITUDE

The Bible does not speak clearly about every specific issue people encounter in this life. Paul recognized this and penned for his readers a key principle to follow in those matters not specifically addressed. In Romans 14, Paul laid out the law of liberty in which the Christian chooses not to exercise all the freedom at their disposal, but instead processes decisions about debatable matters based on what's best for their brothers and sisters. The first four verses of chapter 15 summarize and close out that section of the book and provide the true fuel for such an attitude.

When a Christian faces a questionable matter, one in which they are not constrained by their conscience or guided by a clear biblical mandate, they should be willing to forgo their personal freedom for the sake of a brother or sister. This is what Jesus modeled for us. He did not live to benefit himself, but instead willingly and unselfishly gave himself over to insult and injury for the sake of others (1Pe 2:23). For those who follow Jesus, the same attitude is expected—being willing to give up our freedom for the edification of another.

Spain. I hope to see you while passing through and to have you assist me on my journey there, after I have enjoyed your company for a while. 25Now, however, I am on my way to Jerusalem in the service of the Lord's people there. 26For Macedonia and Achaia were pleased to make a contribution for the poor among the Lord's people in Jerusalem. 27They were pleased to do it, and indeed they owe it to them. For if the Gentiles have shared in the Jews' spiritual blessings, they owe it to the Jews to share with them their material blessings. 28So after I have completed this task and have made sure that they have received this contribution, I will go to Spain and visit you on the way. 29I know that when I come to you, I will come in the full measure of the blessing of Christ.

30I urge you, brothers and sisters, by our Lord Jesus Christ and by the love of the Spirit, to join me in my struggle by praying to God for me. 31Pray that I may be kept safe from the unbelievers in Judea and that the contribution I take to Jerusalem may be favorably received by the Lord's people there, 32so that I may come to you with joy, by God's will, and in your company be refreshed. 33The God of peace be with you all. Amen.

Personal Greetings

16 I commend to you our sister Phoebe, a deacon[a,b] of the church in Cenchreae. 2I ask you to receive her in the Lord in a way worthy of his people and to give her any help she may need from you, for she has been the benefactor of many people, including me.

3Greet Priscilla[c] and Aquila, my co-workers in Christ Jesus. 4They risked their lives for me. Not only I but all the churches of the Gentiles are grateful to them.

5Greet also the church that meets at their house.

Greet my dear friend Epenetus, who was the first convert to Christ in the province of Asia.

6Greet Mary, who worked very hard for you.

7Greet Andronicus and Junia, my fellow Jews who have been in prison with me. They are outstanding among[d] the apostles, and they were in Christ before I was.

8Greet Ampliatus, my dear friend in the Lord.

9Greet Urbanus, our co-worker in Christ, and my dear friend Stachys.

10Greet Apelles, whose fidelity to Christ has stood the test.

Greet those who belong to the household of Aristobulus.

11Greet Herodion, my fellow Jew.

Greet those in the household of Narcissus who are in the Lord.

12Greet Tryphena and Tryphosa, those women who work hard in the Lord.

Greet my dear friend Persis, another woman who has worked very hard in the Lord.

13Greet Rufus, chosen in the Lord, and his mother, who has been a mother to me, too.

14Greet Asyncritus, Phlegon, Hermes, Patrobas, Hermas and the other brothers and sisters with them.

15Greet Philologus, Julia, Nereus and his sister, and Olympas and all the Lord's people who are with them.

16Greet one another with a holy kiss.

All the churches of Christ send greetings.

17I urge you, brothers and sisters, to watch out for those who cause divisions and put obstacles in your way that are contrary to the teaching you have learned. Keep away from them. 18For such people are not serving our Lord Christ, but their own appetites. By smooth talk and flattery they deceive the minds of naive

---

[a] *1* Or *servant* [b] *1* The word *deacon* refers here to a Christian designated to serve with the overseers/elders of the church in a variety of ways; similarly in Phil. 1:1 and 1 Tim. 3:8,12.
[c] *3* Greek *Prisca*, a variant of *Priscilla* [d] *7* Or *are esteemed by*

people. [19]Everyone has heard about your obedience, so I rejoice because of you;
but I want you to be wise about what is good, and innocent about what is evil.
[20]The God of peace will soon crush Satan under your feet.
The grace of our Lord Jesus be with you.
[21]Timothy, my co-worker, sends his greetings to you, as do Lucius, Jason and
Sosipater, my fellow Jews.
[22]I, Tertius, who wrote down this letter, greet you in the Lord.
[23]Gaius, whose hospitality I and the whole church here enjoy, sends you his
greetings.
Erastus, who is the city's director of public works, and our brother Quartus
send you their greetings. [24] [a]

[25]Now to him who is able to establish you in accordance with my gospel, the
message I proclaim about Jesus Christ, in keeping with the revelation of the mystery hidden for long ages past, [26]but now revealed and made known through the
prophetic writings by the command of the eternal God, so that all the Gentiles
might come to the obedience that comes from[b] faith— [27]to the only wise God be
glory forever through Jesus Christ! Amen.

ROMANS 16:25–27

BENEDICTION

How does one conclude the greatest theological treatise ever written? For Paul, the answer was to refer back to what he had already said. Indeed, this is what Paul's ministry was, as he was committed to preaching only Christ and Christ crucified time and time again (1Co 2:2). This good-news message is the only lasting hope for humanity.

In his final benediction to the letter of Romans, Paul again reminds readers of the great and mysterious gospel of Jesus Christ, which is immensely available to all who believe, whether Jew or Gentile. This is the central storyline of all Scripture, and now through the work of Jesus, God's plans are fulfilled. Appropriately, this letter ends in the same way that all of history will end: on bended knee, eyes on Christ alone, with Paul—and by extension, us as well—giving glory to God for what he has done and what he will surely do in the future.

[a] *24* Some manuscripts include here *May the grace of our Lord Jesus Christ be with all of you. Amen.* [b] *26* Or *that is*

JESUS: OUR HOPE FOR CHANGE

1 CORINTHIANS

1 CORINTHIANS

PAUL'S MISSIONARY JOURNEYS	PAUL PLANTS CHURCH AT CORINTH	PAUL WRITES 1 CORINTHIANS
c. AD 47 – 57	*c. AD 51*	*c. AD 54*

The New Testament church was far from perfect. The idyllic pictures of the church found in small sections of the book of Acts might lead one to believe that all the churches of the first century were permeated by purity and holiness. The church in Corinth dispels that faulty belief due to its gross immorality and wickedness.

In Acts 18:1 – 18, Luke records the founding of the church in Corinth. Paul was well acquainted with this church, having visited it on his second mission journey. Paul served the church for a year and a half, seeking to establish the predominately Gentile believers in the ways of the Lord. This work was vital since Corinth was an important, cosmopolitan city in ancient Greece. Believers in that region were faced with constant temptation to succumb to the idolatry of the pagans living throughout the region.

The Corinthian letters differ in style from Paul's other writings. Rather than his typical pattern of first describing the good news of Jesus, followed by a summary of the ethical implications of this message, Paul uses the Corinthian letters to respond to particular issues facing the young church after his departure. Paul received troubling reports about the church and their ongoing proclivity toward waywardness, and he wrote to address the issues that continued to plague the church, such as divisions, abuse of liberty, sexual immorality, drunkenness and the influence of false teaching.

As he wrote, Paul demonstrated the holistic and communal effects of the gospel. Every facet of life is shaped by Jesus' work, and all decisions can and should be informed by what was accomplished in his death and resurrection. Also, the gospel is pervasive among the people of God as the church gathers in worship and scatters in mission. The hope of the gospel is not merely a means of personal salvation, but it transforms the corporate life of God's people.

While the overall tone of this book is forceful and passionate, Paul ends with a reminder of the great hope that the gospel brings. Satan, sin and death are defeated, and as a result, God's people can experience victory over Satan, sin and death themselves. At the appointed time, God will vindicate himself before the watching world and prove, once and for all, that he has accomplished his plan of redeeming the world (15:50 – 58).

YET FOR US THERE IS BUT ONE GOD, THE FATHER, FROM WHOM ALL THINGS CAME AND FOR WHOM WE LIVE; AND THERE IS BUT ONE LORD, JESUS CHRIST, THROUGH WHOM ALL THINGS CAME AND THROUGH WHOM WE LIVE.

---

1 Corinthians 8:6

1 CORINTHIANS

1 Paul, called to be an apostle of Christ Jesus by the will of God, and our brother Sosthenes,

[2]To the church of God in Corinth, to those sanctified in Christ Jesus and called to be his holy people, together with all those everywhere who call on the name of our Lord Jesus Christ— their Lord and ours:

[3]Grace and peace to you from God our Father and the Lord Jesus Christ.

Thanksgiving

[4]I always thank my God for you because of his grace given you in Christ Jesus. [5]For in him you have been enriched in every way—with all kinds of speech and with all knowledge— [6]God thus confirming our testimony about Christ among you. [7]Therefore you do not lack any spiritual gift as you eagerly wait for our Lord Jesus Christ to be revealed. [8]He will also keep you firm to the end, so that you will be blameless on the day of our Lord Jesus Christ. [9]God is faithful, who has called you into fellowship with his Son, Jesus Christ our Lord.

A Church Divided Over Leaders

[10]I appeal to you, brothers and sisters,[a] in the name of our Lord Jesus Christ, that all of you agree with one another in what you say and that there be no divisions among you, but that you be perfectly united in mind and thought. [11]My brothers and sisters, some from Chloe's household have informed me that there are quarrels among you. [12]What I mean is this: One of you says, "I follow Paul"; another, "I follow Apollos"; another, "I follow Cephas[b]"; still another, "I follow Christ."

[13]Is Christ divided? Was Paul crucified for you? Were you baptized in the name of Paul? [14]I thank God that I did not baptize any of you except Crispus and Gaius, [15]so no one can say that you were baptized in my name. [16](Yes, I also baptized the household of Stephanas; beyond that, I don't remember if I baptized anyone else.) [17]For Christ did not send me to baptize, but to preach the gospel— not with wisdom and eloquence, lest the cross of Christ be emptied of its power.

Christ Crucified Is God's Power and Wisdom

[18]For the message of the cross is foolishness to those who are perishing, but to us who are being saved it is the power of God. [19]For it is written:

"I will destroy the wisdom of the wise;
  the intelligence of the intelligent I will frustrate."[c]

[20]Where is the wise person? Where is the teacher of the law? Where is the philosopher of this age? Has not God made foolish the wisdom of the world? [21]For since in the wisdom of God the world through its wisdom did not know him, God was pleased through the foolishness of what was preached to save those who believe. [22]Jews demand signs and Greeks look for wisdom, [23]but we preach Christ crucified: a stumbling block to Jews and foolishness to Gentiles, [24]but to those whom God has called, both Jews and Greeks, Christ the power of God and the wisdom of God. [25]For the foolishness of God is wiser than human wisdom, and the weakness of God is stronger than human strength.

[26]Brothers and sisters, think of what you were when you were called. Not

---

[a] *10* The Greek word for *brothers and sisters* (*adelphoi*) refers here to believers, both men and women, as part of God's family; also in verses 11 and 26; and in 2:1; 3:1; 4:6; 6:8; 7:24, 29; 10:1; 11:33; 12:1; 14:6, 20, 26, 39; 15:1, 6, 50, 58; 16:15, 20. [b] *12* That is, Peter [c] *19* Isaiah 29:14

UNITY IN CHRIST

Paul challenged this newly formed Corinthian church based on a troubling report he received (v. 11). Because of pervasive pride, these new believers were cultivating a disruptive spirit: some championed Paul, others Apollos, and some Cephas (v. 12). Teaching preference divided the church.

In response to this division, Paul exhorted the church to unite around the person and work of Jesus Christ, not those who are used by him to lead the church. Paul asked, "Is Christ divided?" (v. 13). The implied and obvious answer is a clear "no." A unified Christ works to unify believers one with another. Therefore, Paul appealed to them, asking "that all of you agree with one another in what you say and that there be no divisions among you, but that you be perfectly united in mind and thought" (v. 10). One Christ necessitates one united church.

Few divisions marked this New Testament era as much as the chasm between Jews and Greeks (Gentiles). However, this chapter makes it clear that for those God called from among both Jews and Gentiles, Christ is both the power and the wisdom of God (v. 24). In the gospel, these two groups become one (Eph 2:15). That which sin divides, Christ gathers together.

Therefore, any division that remains among God's people repudiates the gospel. Elsewhere, Paul admonishes the church to maintain the unity created by Christ (Eph 4:3). Jesus prayed that this unity might further God's mission (Jn 17:20–26). Inasmuch as the church becomes a single community, it portrays to the world the unifying work of the gospel (Jn 17:21). So Christians should be marked by unity, regardless of what earthly barriers threaten to divide them, be they racial, socioeconomic or cultural.

Christ unites a divided people, purchasing unity rather than uniformity. In the beginning, God created a united humanity of worshipers. In the end, God will restore a united humanity of diverse worshipers under the banner of his crucified and risen Son (Rev 5:9). In fact, this diversity on display will only magnify the glory of the unifier. Christ unites Christians in his church, for this life and for all eternity.

1 CORINTHIANS 2:2

JESUS CHRIST AND HIM CRUCIFIED

Paul told the Corinthians that he decided to know *nothing* but "Jesus Christ and him crucified." This immediately raises the question: Did Paul mean he intended cognitively to forget all other knowledge, such as the alphabet, the direction to Corinth or how to make a tent? Of course not. The thrust of the language pointed instead to a surpassing knowledge; the other information in his brain paled in comparison to the message about Jesus and his work. Furthermore, the balance of the New Testament makes plain that the crucified Jesus informs and directs all other knowledge.

Believers never graduate from the cross. Though some teach that the crucifixion and resurrection of Jesus only informs initial conversion, the New Testament describes the entirety of a Christian's life as a working out of salvation (Php 2:12). A well-educated man like Paul — never to be confused with an intellectual slouch — spoke of the cross as if he was always moving into a deeper understanding of it, continually seeing new facets of this inexhaustible gospel. He did not intend to move on to lesser pursuits. Neither should the church.

1 CORINTHIANS 3:1–9

INFANTS IN CHRIST

No adult likes to be called a baby. However, Paul refused to sugarcoat his words to the toddling Corinthian church. While it is acceptable to be a baby for a season — in fact, unavoidable — a 30-year-old depending

(continued on next page)

many of you were wise by human standards; not many were influential; not
many were of noble birth. 27But God chose the foolish things of the world to
shame the wise; God chose the weak things of the world to shame the strong.
28God chose the lowly things of this world and the despised things — and the
things that are not — to nullify the things that are, 29so that no one may boast
before him. 30It is because of him that you are in Christ Jesus, who has become
for us wisdom from God — that is, our righteousness, holiness and redemption.
31Therefore, as it is written: "Let the one who boasts boast in the Lord."[a]

2 And so it was with me, brothers and sisters. When I came to you, I did not
come with eloquence or human wisdom as I proclaimed to you the testimony about God.[b] 2For I resolved to know nothing while I was with you except
Jesus Christ and him crucified. 3I came to you in weakness with great fear and
trembling. 4My message and my preaching were not with wise and persuasive
words, but with a demonstration of the Spirit's power, 5so that your faith might
not rest on human wisdom, but on God's power.

God's Wisdom Revealed by the Spirit

6We do, however, speak a message of wisdom among the mature, but not the
wisdom of this age or of the rulers of this age, who are coming to nothing. 7No,
we declare God's wisdom, a mystery that has been hidden and that God destined for our glory before time began. 8None of the rulers of this age understood
it, for if they had, they would not have crucified the Lord of glory. 9However, as
it is written:

"What no eye has seen,
what no ear has heard,
and what no human mind has conceived"[c] —
the things God has prepared for those who love him —

10these are the things God has revealed to us by his Spirit.
The Spirit searches all things, even the deep things of God. 11For who knows
a person's thoughts except their own spirit within them? In the same way no one
knows the thoughts of God except the Spirit of God. 12What we have received is
not the spirit of the world, but the Spirit who is from God, so that we may understand what God has freely given us. 13This is what we speak, not in words taught
us by human wisdom but in words taught by the Spirit, explaining spiritual realities with Spirit-taught words.[d] 14The person without the Spirit does not accept
the things that come from the Spirit of God but considers them foolishness, and
cannot understand them because they are discerned only through the Spirit.
15The person with the Spirit makes judgments about all things, but such a person
is not subject to merely human judgments, 16for,

"Who has known the mind of the Lord
so as to instruct him?"[e]

But we have the mind of Christ.

The Church and Its Leaders

3 Brothers and sisters, I could not address you as people who live by the Spirit
but as people who are still worldly — mere infants in Christ. 2I gave you milk,
not solid food, for you were not yet ready for it. Indeed, you are still not ready.
3You are still worldly. For since there is jealousy and quarreling among you, are
you not worldly? Are you not acting like mere humans? 4For when one says, "I
follow Paul," and another, "I follow Apollos," are you not mere human beings?
5What, after all, is Apollos? And what is Paul? Only servants, through whom
you came to believe — as the Lord has assigned to each his task. 6I planted the
seed, Apollos watered it, but God has been making it grow. 7So neither the one

[a] *31* Jer. 9:24 [b] *1* Some manuscripts *proclaimed to you God's mystery* [c] *9* Isaiah 64:4
[d] *13* Or *Spirit, interpreting spiritual truths to those who are spiritual* [e] *16* Isaiah 40:13

who plants nor the one who waters is anything, but only God, who makes things grow. 8The one who plants and the one who waters have one purpose, and they will each be rewarded according to their own labor. 9For we are co-workers in God's service; you are God's field, God's building.

10By the grace God has given me, I laid a foundation as a wise builder, and someone else is building on it. But each one should build with care. 11For no one can lay any foundation other than the one already laid, which is Jesus Christ. 12If anyone builds on this foundation using gold, silver, costly stones, wood, hay or straw, 13their work will be shown for what it is, because the Day will bring it to light. It will be revealed with fire, and the fire will test the quality of each person's work. 14If what has been built survives, the builder will receive a reward. 15If it is burned up, the builder will suffer loss but yet will be saved — even though only as one escaping through the flames.

16Don't you know that you yourselves are God's temple and that God's Spirit dwells in your midst? 17If anyone destroys God's temple, God will destroy that person; for God's temple is sacred, and you together are that temple.

18Do not deceive yourselves. If any of you think you are wise by the standards of this age, you should become "fools" so that you may become wise. 19For the wisdom of this world is foolishness in God's sight. As it is written: "He catches the wise in their craftiness"[a]; 20and again, "The Lord knows that the thoughts of the wise are futile."[b] 21So then, no more boasting about human leaders! All things are yours, 22whether Paul or Apollos or Cephas[c] or the world or life or death or the present or the future — all are yours, 23and you are of Christ, and Christ is of God.

The Nature of True Apostleship

4 This, then, is how you ought to regard us: as servants of Christ and as those entrusted with the mysteries God has revealed. 2Now it is required that those who have been given a trust must prove faithful. 3I care very little if I am judged by you or by any human court; indeed, I do not even judge myself. 4My conscience is clear, but that does not make me innocent. It is the Lord who judges me. 5Therefore judge nothing before the appointed time; wait until the Lord comes. He will bring to light what is hidden in darkness and will expose the motives of the heart. At that time each will receive their praise from God.

6Now, brothers and sisters, I have applied these things to myself and Apollos for your benefit, so that you may learn from us the meaning of the saying, "Do not go beyond what is written." Then you will not be puffed up in being a follower of one of us over against the other. 7For who makes you different from anyone else? What do you have that you did not receive? And if you did receive it, why do you boast as though you did not?

8Already you have all you want! Already you have become rich! You have begun to reign — and that without us! How I wish that you really had begun to reign so that we also might reign with you! 9For it seems to me that God has put us apostles on display at the end of the procession, like those condemned to die in the arena. We have been made a spectacle to the whole universe, to angels as well as to human beings. 10We are fools for Christ, but you are so wise in Christ! We are weak, but you are strong! You are honored, we are dishonored! 11To this very hour we go hungry and thirsty, we are in rags, we are brutally treated, we are homeless. 12We work hard with our own hands. When we are cursed, we bless; when we are persecuted, we endure it; 13when we are slandered, we answer kindly. We have become the scum of the earth, the garbage of the world — right up to this moment.

Paul's Appeal and Warning

14I am writing this not to shame you but to warn you as my dear children. 15Even if you had ten thousand guardians in Christ, you do not have many

[a] *19* Job 5:13 [b] *20* Psalm 94:11 [c] *22* That is, Peter

(Infants in Christ, continued)

entirely upon his mother needs to be admonished. Such is the nature of Paul's rebuke in this text.

To continue the imagery Paul employed, no one teaches a baby the intricacies of selfishness. Infants only pursue what makes them happy at all times. The Corinthians' sinful pride seems to have perpetuated this selfishness into full adulthood. They continued to be jealous of and quarrel with one another, demonstrating attitudes and actions that were at odds with mature Christian living.

Not only did Paul call these believers infants, but he also went on to rebuke them for modeling the pagan ways of nonbelievers. In the Corinthian context — alluding back to chapter 1 — a spirit of favoritism led individuals to place an undue emphasis upon their preferred teacher. This kind of behavior resembled the prevailing worldly patterns more than it resembled Christ. So Paul quickly reminded these believers of the role he and Apollos played. Human teachers merely plant and water; God gives the growth. Contrary to some teaching, Paul did not indicate that there were two acceptable kinds of Christians in this text. Rather, he called upon the immature to grow up and to trust that God will be faithful to do his part.

1 CORINTHIANS 4:1

SERVANTS OF CHRIST

The Corinthian church admired celebrities. Prizing lofty rhetoric, they focused upon the teacher more than the teaching. And once they elevated their teacher of choice — branding and marketing him — they chose a tribe to which they would belong. In

(continued on next page)

(Servants of Christ, continued)

response to the Corinthian climate, Paul wrote plainly: "No more boasting about human leaders!" (1Co 3:21).

Paul penned an image he wanted the believers to keep in mind as they considered their teachers. Rather than viewing their teachers as rhetoricians waxing eloquent upon their pedestals, the Corinthians should envision teachers as *servants*, Paul said. The word used in this passage refers often to the rower on a ship, listening to and obeying the orders of a supervisor. As long as the rowers listened and obeyed, the ship moved smoothly toward its destination. With that humble language, Paul made clear that he, Apollos and Cephas were merely servants of the true teacher: Jesus Christ.

These teachers — actually servants — stewarded the mysteries of God. When Paul used the term *mystery*, he did not mean to imply something that cannot be figured out. *Mystery* refers instead to truths that God knew before time and has now revealed to his people. In this case, Paul used mystery language to describe the gospel of Jesus Christ. God entrusted his servants with the faithful stewardship of this mystery as they taught the glorious gospel of Jesus.

fathers, for in Christ Jesus I became your father through the gospel. 16Therefore I urge you to imitate me. 17For this reason I have sent to you Timothy, my son whom I love, who is faithful in the Lord. He will remind you of my way of life in Christ Jesus, which agrees with what I teach everywhere in every church.

18Some of you have become arrogant, as if I were not coming to you. 19But I will come to you very soon, if the Lord is willing, and then I will find out not only how these arrogant people are talking, but what power they have. 20For the kingdom of God is not a matter of talk but of power. 21What do you prefer? Shall I come to you with a rod of discipline, or shall I come in love and with a gentle spirit?

Dealing With a Case of Incest

5 It is actually reported that there is sexual immorality among you, and of a kind that even pagans do not tolerate: A man is sleeping with his father's wife. 2And you are proud! Shouldn't you rather have gone into mourning and have put out of your fellowship the man who has been doing this? 3For my part, even though I am not physically present, I am with you in spirit. As one who is present with you in this way, I have already passed judgment in the name of our Lord Jesus on the one who has been doing this. 4So when you are assembled and I am with you in spirit, and the power of our Lord Jesus is present, 5hand this man over to Satan for the destruction of the flesh,[a,b] so that his spirit may be saved on the day of the Lord.

6Your boasting is not good. Don't you know that a little yeast leavens the whole batch of dough? 7Get rid of the old yeast, so that you may be a new unleavened batch — as you really are. For Christ, our Passover lamb, has been sacrificed. 8Therefore let us keep the Festival, not with the old bread leavened with malice and wickedness, but with the unleavened bread of sincerity and truth.

9I wrote to you in my letter not to associate with sexually immoral people — 10not at all meaning the people of this world who are immoral, or the greedy and swindlers, or idolaters. In that case you would have to leave this world. 11But now I am writing to you that you must not associate with anyone who claims to be a brother or sister[c] but is sexually immoral or greedy, an idolater or slanderer, a drunkard or swindler. Do not even eat with such people.

12What business is it of mine to judge those outside the church? Are you not to judge those inside? 13God will judge those outside. "Expel the wicked person from among you."[d]

Lawsuits Among Believers

6 If any of you has a dispute with another, do you dare to take it before the ungodly for judgment instead of before the Lord's people? 2Or do you not know that the Lord's people will judge the world? And if you are to judge the world, are you not competent to judge trivial cases? 3Do you not know that we will judge angels? How much more the things of this life! 4Therefore, if you have disputes about such matters, do you ask for a ruling from those whose way of life is scorned in the church? 5I say this to shame you. Is it possible that there is nobody among you wise enough to judge a dispute between believers? 6But instead, one brother takes another to court — and this in front of unbelievers!

7The very fact that you have lawsuits among you means you have been completely defeated already. Why not rather be wronged? Why not rather be cheated? 8Instead, you yourselves cheat and do wrong, and you do this to your

---

[a] *5* In contexts like this, the Greek word for *flesh* (*sarx*) refers to the sinful state of human beings, often presented as a power in opposition to the Spirit. [b] *5* Or *of his body*
[c] *11* The Greek word for *brother or sister* (*adelphos*) refers here to a believer, whether man or woman, as part of God's family; also in 8:11, 13. [d] *13* Deut. 13:5; 17:7; 19:19; 21:21; 22:21,24; 24:7

CHRIST, THE PASSOVER LAMB

The Corinthian believers seemed to misunderstand what Paul meant when he described the church as those who were "called to be his holy people" (1Co 1:2). Preceding this letter, Paul received word that a man living in open immorality continued to fellowship with the rest of the Corinthian church. Responding in this passage, Paul addressed not only this man's culpability, but the corporate body's as well.

It seemed that rather than the church being sorrowful over the sin in their midst, they boasted. Rather than rebuking this man corporately, they continued to worship and fellowship as if nothing was amiss. The absence of corporate grief grieved Paul.

Paul consistently connected the church's conduct with the gospel, calling believers to live in a way that reflects their new life in Christ (Ro 12:1 – 2; Gal 2:14; 5:1 – 26; Eph 4 – 6; Col 3). As an implication of the gospel's power, God expects his people to live in a manner distinct from the mindsets and practices of the world.

Paul recognized that an unbeliever might do exactly what the immoral man did, though God does not call believers to judge those outside the church. But when this sort of behavior occurs within the body of Christ, the church must act (1Co 5:12). Though some might consider this instruction harsh, Paul admonished the Corinthians to put the man living in sin out of their fellowship (v. 13).

The apostle connected the Corinthians' conduct with the Israelites' preparation for the Passover. Before Passover, the Jewish family would make sure no yeast remained in their home, as even a little yeast leavened the whole lump (v. 6). The analogy Paul used here implies that this individual's sin affected the corporate body, though their approval was only implicit.

Paul goes on to reason that if the Israelites showed this amount of care in preparation for Passover, how much more should the church deal with sin in light of the cross? At Passover, the Israelites sacrificed an unknowing lamb so others might live (Ex 12:1 – 30). However, the Corinthians' Passover Lamb was not an ignorant sheep. Nor did he die unwillingly. The precious Lamb of God died in the Corinthians' place so they might live a life of obedience out of gratitude to him.

brothers and sisters. 9Or do you not know that wrongdoers will not inherit the kingdom of God? Do not be deceived: Neither the sexually immoral nor idolaters nor adulterers nor men who have sex with men[a] 10nor thieves nor the greedy nor drunkards nor slanderers nor swindlers will inherit the kingdom of God. 11And that is what some of you were. But you were washed, you were sanctified, you were justified in the name of the Lord Jesus Christ and by the Spirit of our God.

Sexual Immorality

12"I have the right to do anything," you say—but not everything is beneficial. "I have the right to do anything"—but I will not be mastered by anything. 13You say, "Food for the stomach and the stomach for food, and God will destroy them both." The body, however, is not meant for sexual immorality but for the Lord, and the Lord for the body. 14By his power God raised the Lord from the dead, and he will raise us also. 15Do you not know that your bodies are members of Christ himself? Shall I then take the members of Christ and unite them with a prostitute? Never! 16Do you not know that he who unites himself with a prostitute is one with her in body? For it is said, "The two will become one flesh."[b] 17But whoever is united with the Lord is one with him in spirit.[c]

18Flee from sexual immorality. All other sins a person commits are outside the body, but whoever sins sexually, sins against their own body. 19Do you not know that your bodies are temples of the Holy Spirit, who is in you, whom you have received from God? You are not your own; 20you were bought at a price. Therefore honor God with your bodies.

Concerning Married Life

7 Now for the matters you wrote about: "It is good for a man not to have sexual relations with a woman." 2But since sexual immorality is occurring, each man should have sexual relations with his own wife, and each woman with her own husband. 3The husband should fulfill his marital duty to his wife, and likewise the wife to her husband. 4The wife does not have authority over her own body but yields it to her husband. In the same way, the husband does not have authority over his own body but yields it to his wife. 5Do not deprive each other except perhaps by mutual consent and for a time, so that you may devote yourselves to prayer. Then come together again so that Satan will not tempt you because of your lack of self-control. 6I say this as a concession, not as a command. 7I wish that all of you were as I am. But each of you has your own gift from God; one has this gift, another has that.

8Now to the unmarried[d] and the widows I say: It is good for them to stay unmarried, as I do. 9But if they cannot control themselves, they should marry, for it is better to marry than to burn with passion.

10To the married I give this command (not I, but the Lord): A wife must not separate from her husband. 11But if she does, she must remain unmarried or else be reconciled to her husband. And a husband must not divorce his wife.

12To the rest I say this (I, not the Lord): If any brother has a wife who is not a believer and she is willing to live with him, he must not divorce her. 13And if a woman has a husband who is not a believer and he is willing to live with her, she must not divorce him. 14For the unbelieving husband has been sanctified through his wife, and the unbelieving wife has been sanctified through her believing husband. Otherwise your children would be unclean, but as it is, they are holy.

15But if the unbeliever leaves, let it be so. The brother or the sister is not bound in such circumstances; God has called us to live in peace. 16How do you know,

[a] 9 The words *men who have sex with men* translate two Greek words that refer to the passive and active participants in homosexual acts. [b] *16* Gen. 2:24 [c] *17* Or *in the Spirit*
[d] *8* Or *widowers*

1 CORINTHIANS 6:19–20

MEMBERS OF CHRIST

Though some draw a sharp distinction between the spiritual and the physical, God made humanity neither a soulless body nor a body-less soul. Instead, God made humans as spiritual and physical creatures, integrating both in a complex whole that cannot be divided. Therefore, that which a human being does physically directly affects their spirituality, and vice versa.

While the fall of humanity in Genesis 3 perverted every aspect of creation, the created order should never be described as evil in its essence. If the Bible considered creation evil, Jesus could not have become human in the incarnation. Jesus did not come as a mirage, but instead he took on human flesh (Jn 1:14). Coming as a man, Jesus reconciled all things—the spiritual and the physical—to himself on the cross (Col 1:20). Because of this, the physical aspects of creation—including our bodies—can be directed toward good or evil (Ro 6:5–7).

This passage indicates that salvation created unity to such a degree that believers actually become members of Christ himself (1Co 6:15). Paul described the corporate body of Christ as a temple of the Holy Spirit. God did not purchase the believer's body at a discount store for a small price; he purchased each person on the cross at the cost of his Son's life. Therefore, the Christian is to honor God spiritually with their physical body (v. 20).

wife, whether you will save your husband? Or, how do you know, husband, whether you will save your wife?

Concerning Change of Status

17Nevertheless, each person should live as a believer in whatever situation the Lord has assigned to them, just as God has called them. This is the rule I lay down in all the churches. 18Was a man already circumcised when he was called? He should not become uncircumcised. Was a man uncircumcised when he was called? He should not be circumcised. 19Circumcision is nothing and uncircumcision is nothing. Keeping God's commands is what counts. 20Each person should remain in the situation they were in when God called them.

21Were you a slave when you were called? Don't let it trouble you—although if you can gain your freedom, do so. 22For the one who was a slave when called to faith in the Lord is the Lord's freed person; similarly, the one who was free when called is Christ's slave. 23You were bought at a price; do not become slaves of human beings. 24Brothers and sisters, each person, as responsible to God, should remain in the situation they were in when God called them.

Concerning the Unmarried

25Now about virgins: I have no command from the Lord, but I give a judgment as one who by the Lord's mercy is trustworthy. 26Because of the present crisis, I think that it is good for a man to remain as he is. 27Are you pledged to a woman? Do not seek to be released. Are you free from such a commitment? Do not look for a wife. 28But if you do marry, you have not sinned; and if a virgin marries, she has not sinned. But those who marry will face many troubles in this life, and I want to spare you this.

29What I mean, brothers and sisters, is that the time is short. From now on those who have wives should live as if they do not; 30those who mourn, as if they did not; those who are happy, as if they were not; those who buy something, as if it were not theirs to keep; 31those who use the things of the world, as if not engrossed in them. For this world in its present form is passing away.

32I would like you to be free from concern. An unmarried man is concerned about the Lord's affairs—how he can please the Lord. 33But a married man is concerned about the affairs of this world—how he can please his wife— 34and his interests are divided. An unmarried woman or virgin is concerned about the Lord's affairs: Her aim is to be devoted to the Lord in both body and spirit. But a married woman is concerned about the affairs of this world—how she can please her husband. 35I am saying this for your own good, not to restrict you, but that you may live in a right way in undivided devotion to the Lord.

36If anyone is worried that he might not be acting honorably toward the virgin he is engaged to, and if his passions are too strong[a] and he feels he ought to marry, he should do as he wants. He is not sinning. They should get married. 37But the man who has settled the matter in his own mind, who is under no compulsion but has control over his own will, and who has made up his mind not to marry the virgin—this man also does the right thing. 38So then, he who marries the virgin does right, but he who does not marry her does better.[b]

39A woman is bound to her husband as long as he lives. But if her husband dies, she is free to marry anyone she wishes, but he must belong to the Lord. 40In my judgment, she is happier if she stays as she is—and I think that I too have the Spirit of God.

[a] 36 Or *if she is getting beyond the usual age for marriage* [b] 36-38 Or *36If anyone thinks he is not treating his daughter properly, and if she is getting along in years* (or *if her passions are too strong*), *and he feels she ought to marry, he should do as he wants. He is not sinning. He should let her get married. 37But the man who has settled the matter in his own mind, who is under no compulsion but has control over his own will, and who has made up his mind to keep the virgin unmarried—this man also does the right thing. 38So then, he who gives his virgin in marriage does right, but he who does not give her in marriage does better.*

1 CORINTHIANS 7:19

OBEDIENCE

Though many see obedience as being opposed to their personal freedom, individuals find true freedom in embracing the right restrictions. Any relationship based on absolute freedom quickly erodes: one need only ask the abandoned spouse. Paul—in the middle of a complex section on marriage—argues for the necessity of obedience.

Disobedience to God's Word often stems from a misunderstanding of God's character. Deceived by their own deceptive hearts, believers often wonder whether God intends to do them harm. However, as God's commands reflect his flawless character, believers can assuredly trust in God's directives. The one who created all things knows perfectly how believers should live. In fact, in obedience the believer finds true joy (Jn 15:10–11).

In this context, some Corinthian believers wanted to blame their circumstances for their lack of Christian growth. It seemed that a few of them even wanted to be circumcised for some perceived spiritual benefit. However, Paul pointedly rebuked that desire: "Circumcision is nothing and uncircumcision is nothing" (1Co 7:19). Paul made clear that the believer must continue to faithfully follow the Lord whatever their circumstances (vv. 17,20). God not only carefully wrote his Word and gave us a perfect example of faithfulness in the life of Jesus Christ, he also carefully orchestrates the circumstances in which the believer lives and in which God's Word is to be obeyed.

Concerning Food Sacrificed to Idols

8 Now about food sacrificed to idols: We know that "We all possess knowledge." But knowledge puffs up while love builds up. 2Those who think they know something do not yet know as they ought to know. 3But whoever loves God is known by God.[a]

4So then, about eating food sacrificed to idols: We know that "An idol is nothing at all in the world" and that "There is no God but one." 5For even if there are so-called gods, whether in heaven or on earth (as indeed there are many "gods" and many "lords"), 6yet for us there is but one God, the Father, from whom all things came and for whom we live; and there is but one Lord, Jesus Christ, through whom all things came and through whom we live.

7But not everyone possesses this knowledge. Some people are still so accustomed to idols that when they eat sacrificial food they think of it as having been sacrificed to a god, and since their conscience is weak, it is defiled. 8But food does not bring us near to God; we are no worse if we do not eat, and no better if we do.

9Be careful, however, that the exercise of your rights does not become a stumbling block to the weak. 10For if someone with a weak conscience sees you, with all your knowledge, eating in an idol's temple, won't that person be emboldened to eat what is sacrificed to idols? 11So this weak brother or sister, for whom Christ died, is destroyed by your knowledge. 12When you sin against them in this way and wound their weak conscience, you sin against Christ. 13Therefore, if what I eat causes my brother or sister to fall into sin, I will never eat meat again, so that I will not cause them to fall.

Paul's Rights as an Apostle

9 Am I not free? Am I not an apostle? Have I not seen Jesus our Lord? Are you not the result of my work in the Lord? 2Even though I may not be an apostle to others, surely I am to you! For you are the seal of my apostleship in the Lord.

3This is my defense to those who sit in judgment on me. 4Don't we have the right to food and drink? 5Don't we have the right to take a believing wife along with us, as do the other apostles and the Lord's brothers and Cephas[b]? 6Or is it only I and Barnabas who lack the right to not work for a living?

7Who serves as a soldier at his own expense? Who plants a vineyard and does not eat its grapes? Who tends a flock and does not drink the milk? 8Do I say this merely on human authority? Doesn't the Law say the same thing? 9For it is written in the Law of Moses: "Do not muzzle an ox while it is treading out the grain."[c] Is it about oxen that God is concerned? 10Surely he says this for us, doesn't he? Yes, this was written for us, because whoever plows and threshes should be able to do so in the hope of sharing in the harvest. 11If we have sown spiritual seed among you, is it too much if we reap a material harvest from you? 12If others have this right of support from you, shouldn't we have it all the more?

But we did not use this right. On the contrary, we put up with anything rather than hinder the gospel of Christ.

13Don't you know that those who serve in the temple get their food from the temple, and that those who serve at the altar share in what is offered on the altar? 14In the same way, the Lord has commanded that those who preach the gospel should receive their living from the gospel.

15But I have not used any of these rights. And I am not writing this in the hope that you will do such things for me, for I would rather die than allow anyone to deprive me of this boast. 16For when I preach the gospel, I cannot boast, since I am compelled to preach. Woe to me if I do not preach the gospel! 17If I preach voluntarily, I have a reward; if not voluntarily, I am simply discharging the trust

---

1 CORINTHIANS 9:12

EXERCISING RIGHTS

To illustrate the emphasis in chapter 8 on love's priority over liberty, in this text the apostle Paul described one of his own rights he personally curtailed. As Paul served the Corinthians with the gospel, it may have been appropriate to receive some form of financial compensation (v. 11); however, Paul chose not to demand this right (v. 12).

Paul intended his refusal of this personal liberty as a means to further the gospel. The Corinthians likely encountered traveling charlatans—preachers who proclaimed a message for the express purpose of receiving compensation. With that context in mind, Paul refused to exercise his right so that no one would accuse him of the same. Rather than hinder the gospel's message, he worked while he was among them so to provide for his own financial needs.

Paul considered the integrity of the message to be bound up in the integrity of the messenger. If false accusations about Paul gained traction, the gospel's credibility would be undermined. Though the gospel might offend, Paul endeavored to make sure his actions would not. Paul taught a love that trumped liberty (1Co 8; 13). He also modeled it.

---

[a] 2,3 An early manuscript and another ancient witness *think they have knowledge do not yet know as they ought to know. 3But whoever loves truly knows.* [b] 5 That is, Peter
[c] 9 Deut. 25:4

SINNING AGAINST JESUS

The Bible often outlines broad principles that guide behavior, rather than telling the believer explicitly what he or she can or cannot do. In other words, the Bible does not detail a particular style of music one must enjoy, as if eighteenth-century harpsichord sonatas please the Lord's ears more than modern worship led with an acoustic guitar. Instead, the Bible tells the believer what kinds of things to think about and meditate upon (Php 4:8). This principle helps guide the believer's choices.

If the Scriptures do not condemn a particular activity, and the believer's conscience is not convicted by the Spirit's application of a biblical principle, then God gives the believer liberty to engage in it. Legalism goes beyond what the Scriptures teach, requiring more in the way of rules and regulations than Jesus did. Libertinism, conversely, believes the Bible requires almost nothing of the believer. Scripture, however, opposes both views and the lifestyles that proceed from them.

Nevertheless, believers regularly abuse their liberty in Christ. Just as we do today, the Corinthians found this balance to be elusive. It seems that some in the Corinthian church prioritized their personal liberty over love for their neighbor. In this text, the details involved some Corinthians eating meat that had been sacrificed to idols, an issue a mature follower might have long ago settled in their hearts. However, someone with a weaker conscience — for example, one recently converted out of paganism — may have continued to struggle with this complicated issue.

Paul pointed out that if the mature believer ate this meat in front of the newer or weaker believer, the new believer might stumble spiritually (v. 10). In essence, Paul confronted the individualistic liberty so often prized in Corinth. Contrary to today's more popular notions, one's personal liberties do not trump everyone else's. Paul emphasized love over liberty. The controlling factor in the believer's decision to do something or act in a certain way is not whether they have the liberty, but whether love motivates their action.

Furthermore, when the stronger believer refuses to consider the weaker, he sins against Christ (v. 12). Paul knew this truth well. As a former persecutor of believers in Christ, Paul (known as Saul at the time) met the God of those martyrs. On the road to Damascus, Jesus did not ask Paul why he persecuted God's people. Instead, he asked Paul why he persecuted him personally (Ac 9:4). To sin against the body of Christ is to sin against Christ.

committed to me. [18]What then is my reward? Just this: that in preaching the gospel I may offer it free of charge, and so not make full use of my rights as a preacher
of the gospel.

Paul's Use of His Freedom

[19]Though I am free and belong to no one, I have made myself a slave to everyone, to win as many as possible. [20]To the Jews I became like a Jew, to win the
Jews. To those under the law I became like one under the law (though I myself
am not under the law), so as to win those under the law. [21]To those not having the
law I became like one not having the law (though I am not free from God's law
but am under Christ's law), so as to win those not having the law. [22]To the weak
I became weak, to win the weak. I have become all things to all people so that
by all possible means I might save some. [23]I do all this for the sake of the gospel,
that I may share in its blessings.

The Need for Self-Discipline

[24]Do you not know that in a race all the runners run, but only one gets the
prize? Run in such a way as to get the prize. [25]Everyone who competes in the
games goes into strict training. They do it to get a crown that will not last, but we
do it to get a crown that will last forever. [26]Therefore I do not run like someone
running aimlessly; I do not fight like a boxer beating the air. [27]No, I strike a blow
to my body and make it my slave so that after I have preached to others, I myself
will not be disqualified for the prize.

Warnings From Israel's History

10 For I do not want you to be ignorant of the fact, brothers and sisters, that
our ancestors were all under the cloud and that they all passed through
the sea. [2]They were all baptized into Moses in the cloud and in the sea. [3]They all
ate the same spiritual food [4]and drank the same spiritual drink; for they drank
from the spiritual rock that accompanied them, and that rock was Christ. [5]Nev-
ertheless, God was not pleased with most of them; their bodies were scattered
in the wilderness.

[6]Now these things occurred as examples to keep us from setting our hearts on
evil things as they did. [7]Do not be idolaters, as some of them were; as it is written: "The people sat down to eat and drink and got up to indulge in revelry."[a]
[8]We should not commit sexual immorality, as some of them did — and in one
day twenty-three thousand of them died. [9]We should not test Christ,[b] as some
of them did — and were killed by snakes. [10]And do not grumble, as some of them
did — and were killed by the destroying angel.

[11]These things happened to them as examples and were written down as
warnings for us, on whom the culmination of the ages has come. [12]So, if you
think you are standing firm, be careful that you don't fall! [13]No temptation[c] has
overtaken you except what is common to mankind. And God is faithful; he will
not let you be tempted[c] beyond what you can bear. But when you are tempted,[c]
he will also provide a way out so that you can endure it.

Idol Feasts and the Lord's Supper

[14]Therefore, my dear friends, flee from idolatry. [15]I speak to sensible people;
judge for yourselves what I say. [16]Is not the cup of thanksgiving for which we give
thanks a participation in the blood of Christ? And is not the bread that we break
a participation in the body of Christ? [17]Because there is one loaf, we, who are
many, are one body, for we all share the one loaf.

[18]Consider the people of Israel: Do not those who eat the sacrifices participate
in the altar? [19]Do I mean then that food sacrificed to an idol is anything, or that

[a] *7* Exodus 32:6 [b] *9* Some manuscripts *test the Lord* [c] *13* The Greek for *temptation* and *tempted* can also mean *testing* and *tested.*

1 CORINTHIANS 10:4

JESUS: THE ROCK

God's provision does not always mean life will be easy. Citing Israel's experience in the wilderness, Paul warned the Corinthians of this reality. Though God delivered these Israelites from bondage in Egypt, turned the Red Sea into dry land and led them by a cloud through the wilderness, miraculous intervention did not necessarily indicate God's approval (v. 5). Out of the thousands of first-generation Israelites who left Egypt, only Joshua and Caleb made it to the promised land. In the wilderness, funerals were a very common activity.

However, neither does humankind's faithlessness demonstrate God's distance. Paul said that despite the Israelites' rebellion, God stayed near to them. When their throats were parched, the Israelites drank from a rock (Ex 17). Though God judged them temporarily, he did not leave them.

Using this well-known Exodus narrative — as a clear display of God's nearness — Paul points to an unseen character. Along with a literal rock, a spiritual rock accompanied the Israelites throughout the wilderness (1Co 10:4). In plain language, Paul identifies this spiritual rock. Though he remained invisible in Moses' narrative, Jesus Christ provided the miracle and made water pour from the rock. As they wandered, Christ remained their compass and their provision.

This episode in Israel's history serves as a warning to idolaters (v. 6). Without qualification, God's image-bearers benefit from God's provision. In gratitude, the proper response is to flee from idolatry, preferring instead the pleasure of God (v. 14).

an idol is anything? [20]No, but the sacrifices of pagans are offered to demons, not to God, and I do not want you to be participants with demons. [21]You cannot drink the cup of the Lord and the cup of demons too; you cannot have a part in both the Lord's table and the table of demons. [22]Are we trying to arouse the Lord's jealousy? Are we stronger than he?

The Believer's Freedom

[23]"I have the right to do anything," you say — but not everything is beneficial. "I have the right to do anything" — but not everything is constructive. [24]No one should seek their own good, but the good of others.

[25]Eat anything sold in the meat market without raising questions of conscience, [26]for, "The earth is the Lord's, and everything in it."[a]

[27]If an unbeliever invites you to a meal and you want to go, eat whatever is put before you without raising questions of conscience. [28]But if someone says to you, "This has been offered in sacrifice," then do not eat it, both for the sake of the one who told you and for the sake of conscience. [29]I am referring to the other person's conscience, not yours. For why is my freedom being judged by another's conscience? [30]If I take part in the meal with thankfulness, why am I denounced because of something I thank God for?

[31]So whether you eat or drink or whatever you do, do it all for the glory of God. [32]Do not cause anyone to stumble, whether Jews, Greeks or the church of God — [33]even as I try to please everyone in every way. For I am not seeking my own good

11 but the good of many, so that they may be saved. [1]Follow my example, as I follow the example of Christ.

On Covering the Head in Worship

[2]I praise you for remembering me in everything and for holding to the traditions just as I passed them on to you. [3]But I want you to realize that the head of every man is Christ, and the head of the woman is man,[b] and the head of Christ is God. [4]Every man who prays or prophesies with his head covered dishonors his head. [5]But every woman who prays or prophesies with her head uncovered dishonors her head — it is the same as having her head shaved. [6]For if a woman does not cover her head, she might as well have her hair cut off; but if it is a disgrace for a woman to have her hair cut off or her head shaved, then she should cover her head.

[7]A man ought not to cover his head,[c] since he is the image and glory of God; but woman is the glory of man. [8]For man did not come from woman, but woman from man; [9]neither was man created for woman, but woman for man. [10]It is for this reason that a woman ought to have authority over her own[d] head, because of the angels. [11]Nevertheless, in the Lord woman is not independent of man, nor is man independent of woman. [12]For as woman came from man, so also man is born of woman. But everything comes from God.

[13]Judge for yourselves: Is it proper for a woman to pray to God with her head uncovered? [14]Does not the very nature of things teach you that if a man has long hair, it is a disgrace to him, [15]but that if a woman has long hair, it is her glory? For long hair is given to her as a covering. [16]If anyone wants to be contentious about this, we have no other practice — nor do the churches of God.

Correcting an Abuse of the Lord's Supper

[17]In the following directives I have no praise for you, for your meetings do more harm than good. [18]In the first place, I hear that when you come together

[a] *26* Psalm 24:1 [b] *3* Or *of the wife is her husband* [c] *4-7* Or [4]*Every man who prays or prophesies with long hair dishonors his head.* [5]*But every woman who prays or prophesies with no covering of hair dishonors her head — she is just like one of the "shorn women."* [6]*If a woman has no covering, let her be for now with short hair; but since it is a disgrace for a woman to have her hair shorn or shaved, she should grow it again.* [7]*A man ought not to have long hair*
[d] *10* Or *have a sign of authority on her*

1 CORINTHIANS 11:17 – 34

THE LORD'S SUPPER

This passage outlines some of the clearest instruction concerning the church's worship gatherings. While diverse understandings of the Lord's Supper often separate churches from one another, the Lord's Supper is intended to be a visible display of the unity of the church. In Paul's instruction, the church as a whole is to proclaim Christ's death (v. 26).

Although the exact role and function the Lord's Supper is to play in a believers' life remains a matter of debate among Christians, Paul makes it very clear that the Lord's Supper can be taken incorrectly (v. 27). Paul wrote that those who celebrate the meal should examine their lives prior to partaking of the bread and the cup (v. 28). This examination includes both personal and corporate elements. The recognition of "the body of Christ" in this passage (v. 29) included both Jesus' body *and* the church, outlined in the chapter that follows (1Co 12:12 – 27). Therefore, at the Supper believers are to examine their lives concerning sin toward Christ and any offense toward one another.

At the communion table, believers celebrate with other believers their unity in Christ, renewing their commitment to God, his people and his mission.

1 CORINTHIANS 12:12–30

THE BODY OF CHRIST

Many of the three-year-olds in Corinth could probably have comprehended Paul's main point in this passage. He essentially wrote: "The body is one. And the body has many parts." Even most toddlers understand that a person who has two ears and two eyes is still one body and, thus, one person.

Paul used the human body as an analogy to describe the church as the body of Christ. While elsewhere this image points to the headship of Jesus Christ, in this passage Paul emphasizes unity within diversity. At salvation, God baptizes by his Spirit both Jews and Gentiles into one body (v. 13).

Paul laid out two aspects of the diversity. For those troubled with a sense of inferiority, he reminded them that the foot is no less part of the body than the hand (v. 15). For those convinced of their superiority, Paul reminded them that the rest of the body would be limited without feet (v. 21). God composed the body just as he saw fit (v. 18). God created this unity to such a degree that whatever happens to one, happens to all, whether joy or pain (v. 26).

Paul taught simple truths in this text, though the church's application continues to be far from simple. People tend to surround themselves with people just like them — those who share the same hobbies, possess the same ethnicity or have similar jobs. But the body of Christ crosses every racial, cultural and social barrier, uniting people under one umbrella alone: the Christ of the gospel.

as a church, there are divisions among you, and to some extent I believe it. [19]No
doubt there have to be differences among you to show which of you have God's
approval. [20]So then, when you come together, it is not the Lord's Supper you eat,
[21]for when you are eating, some of you go ahead with your own private suppers.
As a result, one person remains hungry and another gets drunk. [22]Don't you
have homes to eat and drink in? Or do you despise the church of God by humiliating those who have nothing? What shall I say to you? Shall I praise you?
Certainly not in this matter!

[23]For I received from the Lord what I also passed on to you: The Lord Jesus,
on the night he was betrayed, took bread, [24]and when he had given thanks, he
broke it and said, "This is my body, which is for you; do this in remembrance of
me." [25]In the same way, after supper he took the cup, saying, "This cup is the new
covenant in my blood; do this, whenever you drink it, in remembrance of me."
[26]For whenever you eat this bread and drink this cup, you proclaim the Lord's
death until he comes.

[27]So then, whoever eats the bread or drinks the cup of the Lord in an unworthy manner will be guilty of sinning against the body and blood of the Lord. [28]Everyone ought to examine themselves before they eat of the bread and drink from
the cup. [29]For those who eat and drink without discerning the body of Christ eat
and drink judgment on themselves. [30]That is why many among you are weak and
sick, and a number of you have fallen asleep. [31]But if we were more discerning
with regard to ourselves, we would not come under such judgment. [32]Nevertheless, when we are judged in this way by the Lord, we are being disciplined so that
we will not be finally condemned with the world.

[33]So then, my brothers and sisters, when you gather to eat, you should all eat
together. [34]Anyone who is hungry should eat something at home, so that when
you meet together it may not result in judgment.

And when I come I will give further directions.

Concerning Spiritual Gifts

12 Now about the gifts of the Spirit, brothers and sisters, I do not want you to
be uninformed. [2]You know that when you were pagans, somehow or other
you were influenced and led astray to mute idols. [3]Therefore I want you to know
that no one who is speaking by the Spirit of God says, "Jesus be cursed," and no
one can say, "Jesus is Lord," except by the Holy Spirit.

[4]There are different kinds of gifts, but the same Spirit distributes them. [5]There
are different kinds of service, but the same Lord. [6]There are different kinds of
working, but in all of them and in everyone it is the same God at work.

[7]Now to each one the manifestation of the Spirit is given for the common
good. [8]To one there is given through the Spirit a message of wisdom, to another a
message of knowledge by means of the same Spirit, [9]to another faith by the same
Spirit, to another gifts of healing by that one Spirit, [10]to another miraculous powers, to another prophecy, to another distinguishing between spirits, to another
speaking in different kinds of tongues,[a] and to still another the interpretation of
tongues.[a] [11]All these are the work of one and the same Spirit, and he distributes
them to each one, just as he determines.

Unity and Diversity in the Body

[12]Just as a body, though one, has many parts, but all its many parts form one
body, so it is with Christ. [13]For we were all baptized by[b] one Spirit so as to form
one body — whether Jews or Gentiles, slave or free — and we were all given the
one Spirit to drink. [14]Even so the body is not made up of one part but of many.

[15]Now if the foot should say, "Because I am not a hand, I do not belong to the
body," it would not for that reason stop being part of the body. [16]And if the ear
should say, "Because I am not an eye, I do not belong to the body," it would not

[a] *10* Or *languages*; also in verse 28 [b] *13* Or *with*; or *in*

for that reason stop being part of the body. 17 If the whole body were an eye, where would the sense of hearing be? If the whole body were an ear, where would the sense of smell be? 18 But in fact God has placed the parts in the body, every one of them, just as he wanted them to be. 19 If they were all one part, where would the body be? 20 As it is, there are many parts, but one body.

21 The eye cannot say to the hand, "I don't need you!" And the head cannot say to the feet, "I don't need you!" 22 On the contrary, those parts of the body that seem to be weaker are indispensable, 23 and the parts that we think are less honorable we treat with special honor. And the parts that are unpresentable are treated with special modesty, 24 while our presentable parts need no special treatment. But God has put the body together, giving greater honor to the parts that lacked it, 25 so that there should be no division in the body, but that its parts should have equal concern for each other. 26 If one part suffers, every part suffers with it; if one part is honored, every part rejoices with it.

27 Now you are the body of Christ, and each one of you is a part of it. 28 And God has placed in the church first of all apostles, second prophets, third teachers, then miracles, then gifts of healing, of helping, of guidance, and of different kinds of tongues. 29 Are all apostles? Are all prophets? Are all teachers? Do all work miracles? 30 Do all have gifts of healing? Do all speak in tongues[a]? Do all interpret? 31 Now eagerly desire the greater gifts.

Love Is Indispensable

And yet I will show you the most excellent way.

13 If I speak in the tongues[b] of men or of angels, but do not have love, I am only a resounding gong or a clanging cymbal. 2 If I have the gift of prophecy and can fathom all mysteries and all knowledge, and if I have a faith that can move mountains, but do not have love, I am nothing. 3 If I give all I possess to the poor and give over my body to hardship that I may boast,[c] but do not have love, I gain nothing.

4 Love is patient, love is kind. It does not envy, it does not boast, it is not proud. 5 It does not dishonor others, it is not self-seeking, it is not easily angered, it keeps no record of wrongs. 6 Love does not delight in evil but rejoices with the truth. 7 It always protects, always trusts, always hopes, always perseveres.

8 Love never fails. But where there are prophecies, they will cease; where there are tongues, they will be stilled; where there is knowledge, it will pass away. 9 For we know in part and we prophesy in part, 10 but when completeness comes, what is in part disappears. 11 When I was a child, I talked like a child, I thought like a child, I reasoned like a child. When I became a man, I put the ways of childhood behind me. 12 For now we see only a reflection as in a mirror; then we shall see face to face. Now I know in part; then I shall know fully, even as I am fully known.

13 And now these three remain: faith, hope and love. But the greatest of these is love.

Intelligibility in Worship

14 Follow the way of love and eagerly desire gifts of the Spirit, especially prophecy. 2 For anyone who speaks in a tongue[d] does not speak to people but to God. Indeed, no one understands them; they utter mysteries by the Spirit. 3 But the one who prophesies speaks to people for their strengthening, encouraging and comfort. 4 Anyone who speaks in a tongue edifies themselves, but the one who prophesies edifies the church. 5 I would like every one of you to speak in tongues,[e] but I would rather have you prophesy. The one who prophesies is greater than the one who speaks in tongues,[e] unless someone interprets, so that the church may be edified.

---

[a] *30* Or *other languages* [b] *1* Or *languages* [c] *3* Some manuscripts *body to the flames*
[d] *2* Or *in another language*; also in verses 4, 13, 14, 19, 26 and 27 [e] *5* Or *in other languages*; also in verses 6, 18, 22, 23 and 39

LOVE

In recent history, few Christian women have worn a wedding dress and not heard this passage. While it certainly can be applied to the marriage relationship, Paul originally wrote it to describe a love that was to characterize the Corinthians' relationships with one another. However, Paul did not command the church to do anything the Lord Jesus had not already done perfectly. While this chapter is famous for its description of love, the Gospels provide further insight about the characteristics of genuine love by holding up the example of Christ's own life. For instance, Jesus embodied patience (v. 4). Consider the passage in the Gospel of Mark in which James and John asked Jesus to do whatever they asked of him. They boldly asked — maybe even with a hint of demand — to sit on either side of him in glory. However, rather than chiding them for such brashness, Jesus spoke to them patiently (Mk 10:35 – 40).

Jesus' patience was matched by his kindness. While his disciples thought he would not have the time or the inclination to visit with children, Jesus welcomed little children to come to him, laying his hands on them graciously (Mt 19:14). In the upper room, he took on the role of a servant, washing his disciples' feet (Jn 13:5). Love is not proud (1Co 13:4).

Jesus was not easily angered, either. The careful reader might immediately think of the Lord driving out the moneychangers in the temple. Clearly, these people angered the Lord. However, Jesus' anger was not an easily triggered rage over something insignificant. Instead, love for his Father's house consumed him (Jn 2:17). Rather than delighting in evil, Jesus rejoiced in the truth. In fact, before Pilate he declared, "The reason I was born and came into the world is to testify to the truth" (Jn 18:37). Jesus would not back down nor compromise truth, though it would ultimately lead to his crucifixion. He chose not to protect himself so that others might be protected. That's what perfect love does (1Co 13:7).

Jesus died believing the Father would raise him from the dead. Love always perseveres (v. 7). Scorning the shame, he endured the cross for his people (Heb 12:2). This patient, kind, truth-rejoicing, protecting, trusting and persevering love kept no record of wrongs (1Co 13:5). Because of Jesus' death, the amassed wrongs committed by the people of God were forgiven. The love demonstrated on the cross will forever remain unmatched (1Jn 4:10). First Corinthians 13 certainly applies to marriage, but it's more about a loving Groom who died for his bride, the church (Eph 5:25).

6 Now, brothers and sisters, if I come to you and speak in tongues, what good will I be to you, unless I bring you some revelation or knowledge or prophecy or word of instruction? 7 Even in the case of lifeless things that make sounds, such as the pipe or harp, how will anyone know what tune is being played unless there is a distinction in the notes? 8 Again, if the trumpet does not sound a clear call, who will get ready for battle? 9 So it is with you. Unless you speak intelligible words with your tongue, how will anyone know what you are saying? You will just be speaking into the air. 10 Undoubtedly there are all sorts of languages in the world, yet none of them is without meaning. 11 If then I do not grasp the meaning of what someone is saying, I am a foreigner to the speaker, and the speaker is a foreigner to me. 12 So it is with you. Since you are eager for gifts of the Spirit, try to excel in those that build up the church.

13 For this reason the one who speaks in a tongue should pray that they may interpret what they say. 14 For if I pray in a tongue, my spirit prays, but my mind is unfruitful. 15 So what shall I do? I will pray with my spirit, but I will also pray with my understanding; I will sing with my spirit, but I will also sing with my understanding. 16 Otherwise when you are praising God in the Spirit, how can someone else, who is now put in the position of an inquirer,[a] say "Amen" to your thanksgiving, since they do not know what you are saying? 17 You are giving thanks well enough, but no one else is edified.

18 I thank God that I speak in tongues more than all of you. 19 But in the church I would rather speak five intelligible words to instruct others than ten thousand words in a tongue.

20 Brothers and sisters, stop thinking like children. In regard to evil be infants, but in your thinking be adults. 21 In the Law it is written:

"With other tongues
    and through the lips of foreigners
I will speak to this people,
    but even then they will not listen to me,
        says the Lord."[b]

22 Tongues, then, are a sign, not for believers but for unbelievers; prophecy, however, is not for unbelievers but for believers. 23 So if the whole church comes together and everyone speaks in tongues, and inquirers or unbelievers come in, will they not say that you are out of your mind? 24 But if an unbeliever or an inquirer comes in while everyone is prophesying, they are convicted of sin and are brought under judgment by all, 25 as the secrets of their hearts are laid bare. So they will fall down and worship God, exclaiming, "God is really among you!"

Good Order in Worship

26 What then shall we say, brothers and sisters? When you come together, each of you has a hymn, or a word of instruction, a revelation, a tongue or an interpretation. Everything must be done so that the church may be built up. 27 If anyone speaks in a tongue, two — or at the most three — should speak, one at a time, and someone must interpret. 28 If there is no interpreter, the speaker should keep quiet in the church and speak to himself and to God.

29 Two or three prophets should speak, and the others should weigh carefully what is said. 30 And if a revelation comes to someone who is sitting down, the first speaker should stop. 31 For you can all prophesy in turn so that everyone may be instructed and encouraged. 32 The spirits of prophets are subject to the control of prophets. 33 For God is not a God of disorder but of peace — as in all the congregations of the Lord's people.

34 Women[c] should remain silent in the churches. They are not allowed to speak, but must be in submission, as the law says. 35 If they want to inquire about

---

[a] *16* The Greek word for *inquirer* is a technical term for someone not fully initiated into a religion; also in verses 23 and 24. [b] *21* Isaiah 28:11,12 [c] *33,34* Or *peace. As in all the congregations of the Lord's people, 34 women*

something, they should ask their own husbands at home; for it is disgraceful for a woman to speak in the church.[a]

36 Or did the word of God originate with you? Or are you the only people it has reached? 37 If anyone thinks they are a prophet or otherwise gifted by the Spirit, let them acknowledge that what I am writing to you is the Lord's command. 38 But if anyone ignores this, they will themselves be ignored.[b]

39 Therefore, my brothers and sisters, be eager to prophesy, and do not forbid speaking in tongues. 40 But everything should be done in a fitting and orderly way.

The Resurrection of Christ

15 Now, brothers and sisters, I want to remind you of the gospel I preached to you, which you received and on which you have taken your stand. 2 By this gospel you are saved, if you hold firmly to the word I preached to you. Otherwise, you have believed in vain.

3 For what I received I passed on to you as of first importance[c]: that Christ died for our sins according to the Scriptures, 4 that he was buried, that he was raised on the third day according to the Scriptures, 5 and that he appeared to Cephas,[d] and then to the Twelve. 6 After that, he appeared to more than five hundred of the brothers and sisters at the same time, most of whom are still living, though some have fallen asleep. 7 Then he appeared to James, then to all the apostles, 8 and last of all he appeared to me also, as to one abnormally born.

9 For I am the least of the apostles and do not even deserve to be called an apostle, because I persecuted the church of God. 10 But by the grace of God I am what I am, and his grace to me was not without effect. No, I worked harder than all of them — yet not I, but the grace of God that was with me. 11 Whether, then, it is I or they, this is what we preach, and this is what you believed.

The Resurrection of the Dead

12 But if it is preached that Christ has been raised from the dead, how can some of you say that there is no resurrection of the dead? 13 If there is no resurrection of the dead, then not even Christ has been raised. 14 And if Christ has not been raised, our preaching is useless and so is your faith. 15 More than that, we are then found to be false witnesses about God, for we have testified about God that he raised Christ from the dead. But he did not raise him if in fact the dead are not raised. 16 For if the dead are not raised, then Christ has not been raised either. 17 And if Christ has not been raised, your faith is futile; you are still in your sins. 18 Then those also who have fallen asleep in Christ are lost. 19 If only for this life we have hope in Christ, we are of all people most to be pitied.

20 But Christ has indeed been raised from the dead, the firstfruits of those who have fallen asleep. 21 For since death came through a man, the resurrection of the dead comes also through a man. 22 For as in Adam all die, so in Christ all will be made alive. 23 But each in turn: Christ, the firstfruits; then, when he comes, those who belong to him. 24 Then the end will come, when he hands over the kingdom to God the Father after he has destroyed all dominion, authority and power. 25 For he must reign until he has put all his enemies under his feet. 26 The last enemy to be destroyed is death. 27 For he "has put everything under his feet."[e] Now when it says that "everything" has been put under him, it is clear that this does not include God himself, who put everything under Christ. 28 When he has done this, then the Son himself will be made subject to him who put everything under him, so that God may be all in all.

29 Now if there is no resurrection, what will those do who are baptized for the dead? If the dead are not raised at all, why are people baptized for them? 30 And as for us, why do we endanger ourselves every hour? 31 I face death every day —

[a] *34,35* In a few manuscripts these verses come after verse 40. [b] *38* Some manuscripts *But anyone who is ignorant of this will be ignorant* [c] *3* Or *you at the first* [d] *5* That is, Peter [e] *27* Psalm 8:6

1 CORINTHIANS 15:1 – 58

RESURRECTION FACTS

To be a Christian, one must affirm the resurrection of Jesus Christ from the dead. Paul argues in this key chapter that any alternative to the resurrection of Jesus results in a dismantling of every other aspect of the faith. In other words, Christianity hinges on whether or not Jesus rose from the dead. If he did not, Christianity is irrelevant. If he did, then faith in Christ is all that matters. The following points outline Paul's explanation of the significance of Jesus' resurrection:

1 Corinthians 15:4: There are Old Testament prophesies about Christ's resurrection (Ps 16:10). Peter made this claim in his sermon at Pentecost (Ac 2:25 – 31).

1 Corinthians 15:5 – 8: The resurrected Jesus appeared to more than 500 witnesses. The Gospels describe some of those who saw him (Mt 28:1 – 10,16 – 17). Paul mentioned the reality of witnesses in part to challenge those who doubted the resurrection to ask one of the witnesses themselves. Most of the witnesses were still alive at the time of Paul's writing.

1 Corinthians 15:14 – 15: If Jesus did not rise, the believer's faith is empty and void, and the believer proves to be nothing more than a liar.

1 Corinthians 15:17 – 19: Jesus' resurrection assures believers that God accepted Jesus' sacrifice for sins. Paul mentioned the alternative in this verse; namely, that if Jesus has not been raised, there would have been no assurance that God accepted his sacrifice. If that were true, then individuals would remain under sin's punishment, and those who died would have truly perished without hope.

1 Corinthians 15:20 – 26: However, Jesus did rise. His resurrection foreshadows the resurrection of all those who would trust in him. Paul described Jesus as the "firstfruits." If he lives, so will those who believe in him (v. 22). Adam's sin infected the entire human race, resulting in spiritual death. Christ represented all those who would believe in him, and his resurrected life becomes theirs.

1 Corinthians 15:50: Bodies marked by corruption cannot inherit the kingdom of God.

1 Corinthians 15:52: At the resurrection, perishable bodies will become imperishable. For those who believe in Christ, what is now mortal will put on immortality.

1 Corinthians 15:55 – 58: Jesus' resurrection conquered death, the final enemy. In light of that truth, believers can and should give thanks to God, who gives them victory. Furthermore, the resurrection gives the believer confidence that their labor is not void of purpose, and it strengthens their resolve to give themselves fully to God's work.

yes, just as surely as I boast about you in Christ Jesus our Lord. [32]If I fought wild beasts in Ephesus with no more than human hopes, what have I gained? If the dead are not raised,

"Let us eat and drink,
for tomorrow we die."[a]

[33]Do not be misled: "Bad company corrupts good character."[b] [34]Come back to your senses as you ought, and stop sinning; for there are some who are ignorant of God—I say this to your shame.

The Resurrection Body

[35]But someone will ask, "How are the dead raised? With what kind of body will they come?" [36]How foolish! What you sow does not come to life unless it dies. [37]When you sow, you do not plant the body that will be, but just a seed, perhaps of wheat or of something else. [38]But God gives it a body as he has determined, and to each kind of seed he gives its own body. [39]Not all flesh is the same: People have one kind of flesh, animals have another, birds another and fish another. [40]There are also heavenly bodies and there are earthly bodies; but the splendor of the heavenly bodies is one kind, and the splendor of the earthly bodies is another. [41]The sun has one kind of splendor, the moon another and the stars another; and star differs from star in splendor.

[42]So will it be with the resurrection of the dead. The body that is sown is perishable, it is raised imperishable; [43]it is sown in dishonor, it is raised in glory; it is sown in weakness, it is raised in power; [44]it is sown a natural body, it is raised a spiritual body.

If there is a natural body, there is also a spiritual body. [45]So it is written: "The first man Adam became a living being"[c]; the last Adam, a life-giving spirit. [46]The spiritual did not come first, but the natural, and after that the spiritual. [47]The first man was of the dust of the earth; the second man is of heaven. [48]As was the earthly man, so are those who are of the earth; and as is the heavenly man, so also are those who are of heaven. [49]And just as we have borne the image of the earthly man, so shall we[d] bear the image of the heavenly man.

[50]I declare to you, brothers and sisters, that flesh and blood cannot inherit the kingdom of God, nor does the perishable inherit the imperishable. [51]Listen, I tell you a mystery: We will not all sleep, but we will all be changed— [52]in a flash, in the twinkling of an eye, at the last trumpet. For the trumpet will sound, the dead will be raised imperishable, and we will be changed. [53]For the perishable must clothe itself with the imperishable, and the mortal with immortality. [54]When the perishable has been clothed with the imperishable, and the mortal with immortality, then the saying that is written will come true: "Death has been swallowed up in victory."[e]

[55]"Where, O death, is your victory?
Where, O death, is your sting?"[f]

[56]The sting of death is sin, and the power of sin is the law. [57]But thanks be to God! He gives us the victory through our Lord Jesus Christ.

[58]Therefore, my dear brothers and sisters, stand firm. Let nothing move you. Always give yourselves fully to the work of the Lord, because you know that your labor in the Lord is not in vain.

The Collection for the Lord's People

16 Now about the collection for the Lord's people: Do what I told the Galatian churches to do. [2]On the first day of every week, each one of you should set aside a sum of money in keeping with your income, saving it up, so that when I come no collections will have to be made. [3]Then, when I arrive, I will give letters

[a] *32* Isaiah 22:13 [b] *33* From the Greek poet Menander [c] *45* Gen. 2:7 [d] *49* Some early manuscripts *so let us* [e] *54* Isaiah 25:8 [f] *55* Hosea 13:14

of introduction to the men you approve and send them with your gift to Jerusalem. 4If it seems advisable for me to go also, they will accompany me.

Personal Requests

5After I go through Macedonia, I will come to you — for I will be going through
Macedonia. 6Perhaps I will stay with you for a while, or even spend the winter,
so that you can help me on my journey, wherever I go. 7For I do not want to see
you now and make only a passing visit; I hope to spend some time with you, if
the Lord permits. 8But I will stay on at Ephesus until Pentecost, 9because a great
door for effective work has opened to me, and there are many who oppose me.

10When Timothy comes, see to it that he has nothing to fear while he is with
you, for he is carrying on the work of the Lord, just as I am. 11No one, then, should
treat him with contempt. Send him on his way in peace so that he may return to
me. I am expecting him along with the brothers.

12Now about our brother Apollos: I strongly urged him to go to you with the
brothers. He was quite unwilling to go now, but he will go when he has the opportunity.

13Be on your guard; stand firm in the faith; be courageous; be strong. 14Do
everything in love.

15You know that the household of Stephanas were the first converts in Achaia, and they have devoted themselves to the service of the Lord's people. I urge
you, brothers and sisters, 16to submit to such people and to everyone who joins
in the work and labors at it. 17I was glad when Stephanas, Fortunatus and Acha-
icus arrived, because they have supplied what was lacking from you. 18For they
refreshed my spirit and yours also. Such men deserve recognition.

Final Greetings

19The churches in the province of Asia send you greetings. Aquila and Priscilla[a] greet you warmly in the Lord, and so does the church that meets at their
house. 20All the brothers and sisters here send you greetings. Greet one another
with a holy kiss.

21I, Paul, write this greeting in my own hand.

22If anyone does not love the Lord, let that person be cursed! Come, Lord[b]!

23The grace of the Lord Jesus be with you.

24My love to all of you in Christ Jesus. Amen.[c]

---

[a] *19* Greek *Prisca*, a variant of *Priscilla* [b] *22* The Greek for *Come, Lord* reproduces an Aramaic expression (*Marana tha*) used by early Christians. [c] *24* Some manuscripts do not have *Amen*.

JESUS: OUR INVITATION TO REPENTANCE

2 CORINTHIANS

2 CORINTHIANS

PAUL'S MISSIONARY JOURNEYS *c. AD 47 – 57*	PAUL PLANTS CHURCH AT CORINTH *c. AD 51*	PAUL WRITES 2 CORINTHIANS *c. AD 54*

God loves his church and desires that its worshipful obedience proclaims his glory to the watching world. The rampant sin in the Corinthian church harmed not only those engaged in such sin, but also sabotaged the church's witness. Paul's passionate challenge in the first letter to the Corinthian church was designed to awaken them from their sin-induced spiritual stupor and remind them of the necessity of obedience motivated by God's grace.

Some disregarded Paul's appeal and continued to scorn the grace of God. False teachers led many in the church to question Paul's authority as an apostle and thus to ignore his message. As a result, 2 Corinthians reads like an autobiography in which Paul defends his life's mission and the truthfulness of his message. These personal reflections reveal the trials, problems and suffering Paul faced as a traveling minister in the first century. Through his letter, Paul models the hope that only comes to those who find their comfort in Christ alone (1:5). All Christians should embrace suffering, like Paul, as a way of following after the suffering servant, who gave his life as a ransom for many.

Paul's ongoing interaction with the church fostered a personal tone throughout the correspondence in which Paul was both forceful yet gracious, stern yet hopeful, realistic yet joyful. He was also able to speak with specificity to the problems within the church — many of which he already addressed in his first letter to the church. He also cautions all people, particularly false teachers, that they will stand before the judgment seat of God and be called to account for their actions.

The church, according to Paul, faces the continual onslaught of Satan's opposition and the disastrous effects of sin. Believers must fight Satan and sin with the power afforded to them by virtue of Christ's resurrection and his indwelling Spirit. Should they genuinely repent, they will find a merciful and gracious God who will grant forgiveness and empower them to live holy lives that are pleasing to God. Paul longs for the church in Corinth to turn from their sin and joyfully submit to God's good purposes for their individual lives and the corporate life of the church.

WE ARE THEREFORE CHRIST'S AMBASSADORS, AS THOUGH GOD WERE MAKING HIS APPEAL THROUGH US. WE IMPLORE YOU ON CHRIST'S BEHALF: BE RECONCILED TO GOD.

---

2 Corinthians 5:20

2 CORINTHIANS

1 Paul, an apostle of Christ Jesus by the will of God, and Timothy our brother,

To the church of God in Corinth, together with all his holy people throughout Achaia:

2 Grace and peace to you from God our Father and the Lord Jesus Christ.

Praise to the God of All Comfort

3 Praise be to the God and Father of our Lord Jesus Christ, the Father of compassion and the God of all comfort, 4 who comforts us in all our troubles, so that we can comfort those in any trouble with the comfort we ourselves receive from God. 5 For just as we share abundantly in the sufferings of Christ, so also our comfort abounds through Christ. 6 If we are distressed, it is for your comfort and salvation; if we are comforted, it is for your comfort, which produces in you patient endurance of the same sufferings we suffer. 7 And our hope for you is firm, because we know that just as you share in our sufferings, so also you share in our comfort.

8 We do not want you to be uninformed, brothers and sisters,[a] about the troubles we experienced in the province of Asia. We were under great pressure, far beyond our ability to endure, so that we despaired of life itself. 9 Indeed, we felt we had received the sentence of death. But this happened that we might not rely on ourselves but on God, who raises the dead. 10 He has delivered us from such a deadly peril, and he will deliver us again. On him we have set our hope that he will continue to deliver us, 11 as you help us by your prayers. Then many will give thanks on our behalf for the gracious favor granted us in answer to the prayers of many.

Paul's Change of Plans

12 Now this is our boast: Our conscience testifies that we have conducted ourselves in the world, and especially in our relations with you, with integrity[b] and godly sincerity. We have done so, relying not on worldly wisdom but on God's grace. 13 For we do not write you anything you cannot read or understand. And I hope that, 14 as you have understood us in part, you will come to understand fully that you can boast of us just as we will boast of you in the day of the Lord Jesus.

15 Because I was confident of this, I wanted to visit you first so that you might benefit twice. 16 I wanted to visit you on my way to Macedonia and to come back to you from Macedonia, and then to have you send me on my way to Judea. 17 Was I fickle when I intended to do this? Or do I make my plans in a worldly manner so that in the same breath I say both "Yes, yes" and "No, no"?

18 But as surely as God is faithful, our message to you is not "Yes" and "No." 19 For the Son of God, Jesus Christ, who was preached among you by us — by me and Silas[c] and Timothy — was not "Yes" and "No," but in him it has always been "Yes." 20 For no matter how many promises God has made, they are "Yes" in Christ. And so through him the "Amen" is spoken by us to the glory of God. 21 Now it is God who makes both us and you stand firm in Christ. He anointed us, 22 set his seal of ownership on us, and put his Spirit in our hearts as a deposit, guaranteeing what is to come.

---

[a] *8* The Greek word for *brothers and sisters* (*adelphoi*) refers here to believers, both men and women, as part of God's family; also in 8:1; 13:11. [b] *12* Many manuscripts *holiness*
[c] *19* Greek *Silvanus,* a variant of *Silas*

---

2 CORINTHIANS 1:3 – 11

SUFFERING WITH PURPOSE

Paul understood the reality of suffering as well as anyone. His troubles extended to the point that he "despaired of life itself" (v. 8). But Paul recognized that just as believers share in the sufferings of Christ, "comfort abounds through Christ" (v. 5). Knowing this, Paul found joy in his own sufferings and encouraged the believers in Corinth to do the same. Further, Paul recognized that Christ comforts believers in their sufferings so that they, in turn, can bring comfort to others. Paul used his own times of suffering as opportunities to bless those around him. Even when all seemed lost, Paul knew that his suffering occurred so that he would learn to rely less on himself and more fully on God. Having seen Christ work in his own trials in the past, Paul had even greater confidence that God would continue to deliver him so that he might, in turn, continue to minister to the young church.

Just as Paul did, believers today can view struggles and suffering as opportunities to bless those around them. Just as he did not abandon Paul, Jesus will be faithful to his people in all circumstances.

[23]I call God as my witness — and I stake my life on it — that it was in order to
spare you that I did not return to Corinth. [24]Not that we lord it over your faith, but
2 we work with you for your joy, because it is by faith you stand firm. [1]So I made
up my mind that I would not make another painful visit to you. [2]For if I grieve
you, who is left to make me glad but you whom I have grieved? [3]I wrote as I did,
so that when I came I would not be distressed by those who should have made
me rejoice. I had confidence in all of you, that you would all share my joy. [4]For I
wrote you out of great distress and anguish of heart and with many tears, not to
grieve you but to let you know the depth of my love for you.

Forgiveness for the Offender

[5]If anyone has caused grief, he has not so much grieved me as he has grieved
all of you to some extent — not to put it too severely. [6]The punishment inflicted
on him by the majority is sufficient. [7]Now instead, you ought to forgive and comfort him, so that he will not be overwhelmed by excessive sorrow. [8]I urge you,
therefore, to reaffirm your love for him. [9]Another reason I wrote you was to see if
you would stand the test and be obedient in everything. [10]Anyone you forgive, I
also forgive. And what I have forgiven — if there was anything to forgive — I have
forgiven in the sight of Christ for your sake, [11]in order that Satan might not outwit
us. For we are not unaware of his schemes.

Ministers of the New Covenant

[12]Now when I went to Troas to preach the gospel of Christ and found that the
Lord had opened a door for me, [13]I still had no peace of mind, because I did not
find my brother Titus there. So I said goodbye to them and went on to Macedonia.

[14]But thanks be to God, who always leads us as captives in Christ's triumphal procession and uses us to spread the aroma of the knowledge of him everywhere. [15]For we are to God the pleasing aroma of Christ among those who
are being saved and those who are perishing. [16]To the one we are an aroma that
brings death; to the other, an aroma that brings life. And who is equal to such
a task? [17]Unlike so many, we do not peddle the word of God for profit. On the
contrary, in Christ we speak before God with sincerity, as those sent from God.
3 Are we beginning to commend ourselves again? Or do we need, like some
people, letters of recommendation to you or from you? [2]You yourselves are
our letter, written on our hearts, known and read by everyone. [3]You show that
you are a letter from Christ, the result of our ministry, written not with ink but
with the Spirit of the living God, not on tablets of stone but on tablets of human
hearts.

[4]Such confidence we have through Christ before God. [5]Not that we are competent in ourselves to claim anything for ourselves, but our competence comes
from God. [6]He has made us competent as ministers of a new covenant — not of
the letter but of the Spirit; for the letter kills, but the Spirit gives life.

The Greater Glory of the New Covenant

[7]Now if the ministry that brought death, which was engraved in letters on
stone, came with glory, so that the Israelites could not look steadily at the face
of Moses because of its glory, transitory though it was, [8]will not the ministry of
the Spirit be even more glorious? [9]If the ministry that brought condemnation
was glorious, how much more glorious is the ministry that brings righteousness!
[10]For what was glorious has no glory now in comparison with the surpassing glory. [11]And if what was transitory came with glory, how much greater is the glory
of that which lasts!

[12]Therefore, since we have such a hope, we are very bold. [13]We are not like
Moses, who would put a veil over his face to prevent the Israelites from seeing the
end of what was passing away. [14]But their minds were made dull, for to this day
the same veil remains when the old covenant is read. It has not been removed,

---

2 CORINTHIANS 3:13 – 18

FREEDOM

Moses' face physically glowed when he spent time in the presence of God (Ex 34:29 – 30). The Israelites were so disturbed by his otherworldly appearance that Moses actually had to wear a veil for their benefit (Ex 34:33 – 35). The veil shielded the people from the remaining reflection of the glory of God on Moses' face, for which their hearts and minds were not prepared.

Paul compared the physical veil worn by Moses with the spiritual veil covering the hearts and minds of the Israelites who did not believe in Jesus. He explained that the spiritual veil could be removed only through faith in Christ.

As long as the veil remains, it is impossible to completely understand the old covenant. "But whenever anyone turns to the Lord, the veil is taken away" (2Co 3:16). Through faith in Christ, believers are able not only to understand the law itself, but also to revel in the freedom that comes through Christ's fulfillment of the law. Indeed, when the veil is removed from the hearts of those who come to faith in Christ, their lives are freed to reflect God's glory. Just as the glory of the Lord was evident on Moses' face, Jesus' glory should be unmistakably evident in the lives of his followers when they experience freedom in Christ.

THE VICTORY PARADE

After great victories, triumphant armies often conduct massive parades to revel in the glory of the victory won. This has been true throughout history. In ancient times, soldiers from victorious armies would march in parade to receive the adulation of the masses. In addition, the surviving soldiers from the defeated armies were often forced to participate in the parade as humiliated captives to demonstrate the power and the glory of the conquering heroes.

Ever aware of his own prior violent hostility toward the gospel, Paul now envisioned himself and the host of believers as those captives. Those who were formerly adversarial to the cause of Christ were now joyfully able to participate in Christ's victory parade. Rather than being humiliated by being Christ's captive, Paul found great honor in that position.

As part of these victory parades, conquering generals would often have their attendants carry censers of incense, the fragrance of which became, quite literally, the "smell of victory." Paul declared that Christ similarly uses his people to "spread the aroma of the knowledge of him everywhere" (v. 14). Christ's followers are to carry the gospel to the nations so that the knowledge of Christ and his great victory over sin and death can be spread far and wide.

But Paul recognized that the scent of Jesus' victory would not be pleasing to all. There are unbelievers to whom the smell of Christ in believers' lives serves as a reminder of the darkness in which they live. It may be jealousy of the freedom believers have found in Jesus' victory or merely the fundamental repulsion between light and darkness, life and death. Sadly, the light of Christ in his followers will be violently rejected by some.

Regardless of the reception, followers of Christ have the amazing opportunity to participate in his victory procession throughout the world. While all people, like Paul, once rebelled against the gospel, Christians now revel in the incredible privilege and honor of raising his banner and spreading his glory with their lives and their words.

THE SOURCE OF PAUL'S CONFIDENCE

Paul here responded directly to his opponents in Corinth. He outlined two questions in verse 1, presumably rhetorical, to frame the apparent objections to the authority of his ministry. First he asked if he was bragging about himself and his credentials, and second if he needed some sort of recommendation to the believers at Corinth from a higher authority.

The answer to both questions was a resounding "No!" Paul's ministry stood in contrast to the itinerant preachers and philosophers referenced in chapter 2 who peddled "the word of God for profit" (v. 17). Paul wanted to be very clear with the Corinthian believers that he was not like this crowd, but that his only interest was their continued maturity in Christ.

In the early church, it was not uncommon for a visiting preacher or believer to take to the believers in a new locale a letter of recommendation or introduction from a leader known to them (Ac 18:27). The letter served as a voucher of the sincerity and credibility of the visiting preacher and acknowledged his status in the church. Paul wasn't opposed to the use of such letters. Paul's letter to Philemon is, to some extent, just such a letter and Paul references such letters in his other writings (1Co 16:3).

However, Paul in this passage argues that the only letter of recommendation that he needs at this point is the Corinthian believers themselves. Their new lives in Christ were testimony enough of the validity of Paul's ministry. Significantly, just as traditional letters of recommendation were written in ink, the old covenant was written on stone tablets. In stark contrast, the new covenant was written "not on tablets of stone but on tablets of human hearts" (v. 3). Remarkably, this covenant was etched on the lives of the first-century believers.

Speaking in the confidence of the new covenant, Paul recognized and proclaimed that his authority was validated not by adherence to the old covenant but by the glory directed to God as a result of the power of Jesus Christ manifested in the lives of the Corinthian believers. The power and authority of this new covenant continues today in the lives of believers everywhere.

because only in Christ is it taken away. 15Even to this day when Moses is read, a veil covers their hearts. 16But whenever anyone turns to the Lord, the veil is taken away. 17Now the Lord is the Spirit, and where the Spirit of the Lord is, there is freedom. 18And we all, who with unveiled faces contemplate[a] the Lord's glory, are being transformed into his image with ever-increasing glory, which comes from the Lord, who is the Spirit.

Present Weakness and Resurrection Life

4 Therefore, since through God's mercy we have this ministry, we do not lose heart. 2Rather, we have renounced secret and shameful ways; we do not use deception, nor do we distort the word of God. On the contrary, by setting forth the truth plainly we commend ourselves to everyone's conscience in the sight of God. 3And even if our gospel is veiled, it is veiled to those who are perishing. 4The god of this age has blinded the minds of unbelievers, so that they cannot see the light of the gospel that displays the glory of Christ, who is the image of God. 5For what we preach is not ourselves, but Jesus Christ as Lord, and ourselves as your servants for Jesus' sake. 6For God, who said, "Let light shine out of darkness,"[b] made his light shine in our hearts to give us the light of the knowledge of God's glory displayed in the face of Christ.

7But we have this treasure in jars of clay to show that this all-surpassing power is from God and not from us. 8We are hard pressed on every side, but not crushed; perplexed, but not in despair; 9persecuted, but not abandoned; struck down, but not destroyed. 10We always carry around in our body the death of Jesus, so that the life of Jesus may also be revealed in our body. 11For we who are alive are always being given over to death for Jesus' sake, so that his life may also be revealed in our mortal body. 12So then, death is at work in us, but life is at work in you.

13It is written: "I believed; therefore I have spoken."[c] Since we have that same spirit of[d] faith, we also believe and therefore speak, 14because we know that the one who raised the Lord Jesus from the dead will also raise us with Jesus and present us with you to himself. 15All this is for your benefit, so that the grace that is reaching more and more people may cause thanksgiving to overflow to the glory of God.

16Therefore we do not lose heart. Though outwardly we are wasting away, yet inwardly we are being renewed day by day. 17For our light and momentary troubles are achieving for us an eternal glory that far outweighs them all. 18So we fix our eyes not on what is seen, but on what is unseen, since what is seen is temporary, but what is unseen is eternal.

Awaiting the New Body

5 For we know that if the earthly tent we live in is destroyed, we have a building from God, an eternal house in heaven, not built by human hands. 2Meanwhile we groan, longing to be clothed instead with our heavenly dwelling, 3because when we are clothed, we will not be found naked. 4For while we are in this tent, we groan and are burdened, because we do not wish to be unclothed but to be clothed instead with our heavenly dwelling, so that what is mortal may be swallowed up by life. 5Now the one who has fashioned us for this very purpose is God, who has given us the Spirit as a deposit, guaranteeing what is to come.

6Therefore we are always confident and know that as long as we are at home in the body we are away from the Lord. 7For we live by faith, not by sight. 8We are confident, I say, and would prefer to be away from the body and at home with the Lord. 9So we make it our goal to please him, whether we are at home in the body or away from it. 10For we must all appear before the judgment seat of Christ, so that each of us may receive what is due us for the things done while in the body, whether good or bad.

---

[a] *18* Or *reflect* [b] *6* Gen. 1:3 [c] *13* Psalm 116:10 (see Septuagint) [d] *13* Or *Spirit-given*

MINISTRY THROUGH JARS OF CLAY

Paul described his ministry fully in this letter to the Corinthian church. In this passage, he explained that he had this ministry because of God's mercy and because he was being transformed into God's likeness.

Paul explained that the message of his ministry was focused on the glory of God as revealed through Jesus Christ and mediated through the Spirit. This focus on God's glory required Paul's singular focus and devotion, just as it requires the same of believers today.

The joy of carrying this message was not without challenges for Paul. Few before or since have faced the kind of suffering Paul experienced on a regular basis in his ministry. And yet, despite the incredible suffering he endured for the sake of the gospel, Paul rejoiced because his own weakness revealed the incredible power of God. Indeed, he continued by explaining that the glory of the gospel is carried by believers in "jars of clay" (v. 7). Believers themselves are those fragile jars — ordinary and common creatures. Despite this, or even because of this, God has chosen believers to take the unsurpassed glory of his name to the world, to proclaim reconciliation and freedom to the broken and lost so that they might find new life in Jesus.

Paul acknowledged the persecution that would come to believers as they spread the good news of Jesus Christ. But in every circumstance, he explained, there is victory. Jesus' followers may be "hard pressed on every side, but not crushed; perplexed, but not in despair; persecuted, but not abandoned; struck down, but not destroyed" (vv. 8 – 9). No matter one's circumstances, it is never too late and no one is ever too far gone for Christ to bring victory into their lives. Paul knew that Jesus Christ had overcome the grave, and as a result he can overcome any and every situation and circumstance that threatens to defeat his followers.

Even today, believers around the world experience all kinds of suffering and persecution because they carry the gospel message of reconciliation to others. Just like Paul, believers today can find joy in knowing that their weakness and suffering reveal the awe-inspiring power of God on display in the gospel of Jesus Christ.

THE JUDGMENT SEAT

At the judgment seat, Jesus will evaluate the faithfulness and work of each believer as Paul explained in 1 Corinthians 3:13 – 15. One must be careful to recognize that the works evaluated at the judgment seat do not determine an individual's eternal salvation. That issue is resolved solely by the redeeming work of Jesus Christ at the moment the believer places their faith in Christ, and it is validated at the great white throne as believers' names are found written in the book of life (Rev 20:15). In contrast, the judgment seat provides opportunity for Christ to evaluate the faithfulness of each believer. Those who invested in the kingdom of God will receive rewards from Christ, while believers who wasted their opportunities will "suffer loss" (1Co 3:15).

While Scripture is not specific about the timing of the judgment seat, it does indicate that believers will be judged and rewarded at the time of Christ's second coming and the resurrection of the dead (Lk 14:14; 1Co 4:5).

The nature of the rewards distributed at the judgment seat is not clear. Several New Testament passages refer to "crowns" as rewards (1Co 9:25; 1Pe 5:4). Revelation 4:10 explains that these crowns will ultimately be laid at the feet of Jesus. The parable of the minas in Luke 19:11 – 27 suggests that the rewards could also include the opportunity to serve and to govern in eternity. In any event, the Bible indicates that eternal benefit will be bestowed at the judgment seat.

In light of the knowledge that believers will one day stand before the judgment seat of Christ and be rewarded for their faithfulness in life, it is important for all of those who call Jesus Lord to be diligent to their calling to bring him glory in all things, including their efforts to invest in the kingdom of God on earth. It is a privilege not to be ignored.

The Ministry of Reconciliation

[11]Since, then, we know what it is to fear the Lord, we try to persuade others.
What we are is plain to God, and I hope it is also plain to your conscience. [12]We
are not trying to commend ourselves to you again, but are giving you an opportunity to take pride in us, so that you can answer those who take pride in what is
seen rather than in what is in the heart. [13]If we are "out of our mind," as some say,
it is for God; if we are in our right mind, it is for you. [14]For Christ's love compels
us, because we are convinced that one died for all, and therefore all died. [15]And
he died for all, that those who live should no longer live for themselves but for him who died for them and was raised again.

[16]So from now on we regard no one from a worldly point of view. Though we
once regarded Christ in this way, we do so no longer. [17]Therefore, if anyone is in
Christ, the new creation has come:[a] The old has gone, the new is here! [18]All this is
from God, who reconciled us to himself through Christ and gave us the ministry
of reconciliation: [19]that God was reconciling the world to himself in Christ, not counting people's sins against them. And he has committed to us the message
of reconciliation. [20]We are therefore Christ's ambassadors, as though God were making his appeal through us. We implore you on Christ's behalf: Be reconciled
to God. [21]God made him who had no sin to be sin[b] for us, so that in him we might become the righteousness of God.

6 As God's co-workers we urge you not to receive God's grace in vain. [2]For he
says,

"In the time of my favor I heard you,
and in the day of salvation I helped you."[c]

I tell you, now is the time of God's favor, now is the day of salvation.

Paul's Hardships

[3]We put no stumbling block in anyone's path, so that our ministry will not be
discredited. [4]Rather, as servants of God we commend ourselves in every way:
in great endurance; in troubles, hardships and distresses; [5]in beatings, imprisonments and riots; in hard work, sleepless nights and hunger; [6]in purity, understanding, patience and kindness; in the Holy Spirit and in sincere love; [7]in
truthful speech and in the power of God; with weapons of righteousness in the
right hand and in the left; [8]through glory and dishonor, bad report and good
report; genuine, yet regarded as impostors; [9]known, yet regarded as unknown;
dying, and yet we live on; beaten, and yet not killed; [10]sorrowful, yet always
rejoicing; poor, yet making many rich; having nothing, and yet possessing everything.

[11]We have spoken freely to you, Corinthians, and opened wide our hearts to
you. [12]We are not withholding our affection from you, but you are withholding
yours from us. [13]As a fair exchange — I speak as to my children — open wide your hearts also.

Warning Against Idolatry

[14]Do not be yoked together with unbelievers. For what do righteousness and wickedness have in common? Or what fellowship can light have with darkness?
[15]What harmony is there between Christ and Belial[d]? Or what does a believer
have in common with an unbeliever? [16]What agreement is there between the
temple of God and idols? For we are the temple of the living God. As God has said:

"I will live with them
and walk among them,
and I will be their God,
and they will be my people."[e]

---

[a] *17* Or *Christ, that person is a new creation.* [b] *21* Or *be a sin offering* [c] *2* Isaiah 49:8
[d] *15* Greek *Beliar,* a variant of *Belial* [e] *16* Lev. 26:12; Jer. 32:38; Ezek. 37:27

---

2 CORINTHIANS 5:18–20

RECONCILIATION

Reconciliation happens when two parties at odds with one another are brought back together. It occurs when one party reaches out to the other and seeks to establish peace in the conflict.

Sin brought war between God and humanity. As created beings, men and women were powerless to reconcile with their Creator. Recognizing this, God sent his Son, Jesus Christ, as the ultimate peace offering, laying down his life so that those who would accept his forgiveness of sin could be reconciled to himself.

In turn, God has "committed to [his followers] the message of reconciliation" (v. 19). This offer of reconciliation is for the whole world. Because God has reached out to believers, they are instructed to take this message of reconciliation to the world. Christ's followers must share the good news of Jesus everywhere they go.

2 CORINTHIANS 7:8–13

GODLY SORROW

How often do people in today's culture express sorrow for their actions once they are confronted and the consequences of their actions are manifested? The expressed "sorrow" is really disappointment that they were caught in their misdeeds, not true regret over the underlying actions. Sadly, this is often true for believers and nonbelievers alike.

In the case of the Corinthian church, Paul had sent an earlier letter calling out the inappropriate behavior in the church. This letter, now lost, was written between the letters now canonized as 1 and 2 Corinthians. This intermediate letter may have caused the Corinthians sorrow, but this sorrow led to true repentance.

Paul contrasts "godly sorrow," which leads to repentance, with "worldly sorrow," which leads to death (v. 10). Being confronted with one's sin can be painful. However, it can be a powerful and productive exercise when it leads to repentance and spiritual growth — a genuine turning from the sinful behavior. Christ's followers must be receptive to godly confrontation and must be ready and willing to alter their own behavior in order to grow in their relationship with Christ. In their repentance, the Corinthian believers set an example that can still be followed today.

17Therefore,

"Come out from them
and be separate,
says the Lord.
Touch no unclean thing,
and I will receive you."[a]
18And,
"I will be a Father to you,
and you will be my sons and daughters,
says the Lord Almighty."[b]

7 Therefore, since we have these promises, dear friends, let us purify ourselves
from everything that contaminates body and spirit, perfecting holiness out
of reverence for God.

Paul's Joy Over the Church's Repentance

2Make room for us in your hearts. We have wronged no one, we have corrupted no one, we have exploited no one. 3I do not say this to condemn you; I have
said before that you have such a place in our hearts that we would live or die with
you. 4I have spoken to you with great frankness; I take great pride in you. I am
greatly encouraged; in all our troubles my joy knows no bounds.
5For when we came into Macedonia, we had no rest, but we were harassed
at every turn — conflicts on the outside, fears within. 6But God, who comforts
the downcast, comforted us by the coming of Titus, 7and not only by his coming
but also by the comfort you had given him. He told us about your longing for
me, your deep sorrow, your ardent concern for me, so that my joy was greater
than ever.
8Even if I caused you sorrow by my letter, I do not regret it. Though I did regret
it — I see that my letter hurt you, but only for a little while — 9yet now I am happy,
not because you were made sorry, but because your sorrow led you to repentance.
For you became sorrowful as God intended and so were not harmed in any way
by us. 10Godly sorrow brings repentance that leads to salvation and leaves no regret, but worldly sorrow brings death. 11See what this godly sorrow has produced
in you: what earnestness, what eagerness to clear yourselves, what indignation,
what alarm, what longing, what concern, what readiness to see justice done. At
every point you have proved yourselves to be innocent in this matter. 12So even
though I wrote to you, it was neither on account of the one who did the wrong nor
on account of the injured party, but rather that before God you could see for yourselves how devoted to us you are. 13By all this we are encouraged.
In addition to our own encouragement, we were especially delighted to see
how happy Titus was, because his spirit has been refreshed by all of you. 14I had
boasted to him about you, and you have not embarrassed me. But just as everything we said to you was true, so our boasting about you to Titus has proved to
be true as well. 15And his affection for you is all the greater when he remembers
that you were all obedient, receiving him with fear and trembling. 16I am glad I
can have complete confidence in you.

The Collection for the Lord's People

8 And now, brothers and sisters, we want you to know about the grace that God
has given the Macedonian churches. 2In the midst of a very severe trial, their
overflowing joy and their extreme poverty welled up in rich generosity. 3For I
testify that they gave as much as they were able, and even beyond their ability.
Entirely on their own, 4they urgently pleaded with us for the privilege of sharing
in this service to the Lord's people. 5And they exceeded our expectations: They

[a] *17* Isaiah 52:11; Ezek. 20:34,41 [b] *18* 2 Samuel 7:14; 7:8

2 CORINTHIANS 6:17 – 18

BE SEPARATE

A prosperous metropolitan center, Corinth was a seaport and hub of art and industry in the Roman world. It was also a center for immorality and materialism, which was the context in which the church in Corinth was planted. And it was in this environment that the Corinthian church struggled with understanding how to relate to the surrounding culture.

This is the background for Paul's admonition in verse 17 to "come out from them and be separate." Paul phrased this as a directive from God that quoted Old Testament prophecy. This command also closely mirrors John's prophecy in Revelation 18:4. With this instruction, Paul called out the church in Corinth to stop imitating the immoral practices of their pagan neighbors.

Paul's charge to "be separate" has been interpreted in many ways throughout the centuries. Some believers segregate themselves from the world (in whole or in part), and refuse to participate as members of the larger society outside of their circle of belief and practice. Some groups shun modern conveniences as basic as electricity and live in cloistered seclusion from the world. Other groups refuse to build relationships of any significance with nonbelievers for fear of becoming entangled with the world.

But rather than requiring believers to live in isolation from the world, Paul called the Corinthian believers — and by extension, all believers throughout history — to be set apart in their lifestyles. Instead of participating in the base and immoral activities of the people around them, the Corinthian believers were to come out of that pagan lifestyle and pursue holiness. In so doing, they would draw attention to Jesus.

Paul's admonition follows closely with Jesus' call to be salt and light in Matthew 5:13 – 16. Just as salt loses its value if it loses its saltiness, so too if a believer has patterns and behaviors that mimic the sinfulness of the world, the believer's spiritual value in reaching others is lost. Instead, like a light on a lamp stand, believers are to live in such a way as to shine in the darkness. This can only occur when the believer chooses a life of holiness and purity, standing in contrast to the sinful behavior of the surrounding culture.

2 CORINTHIANS 8:9

TRADING PLACES

Christ's grace to us was manifested when he became poor, according to Paul. While his earthly life was certainly austere, there is no evidence to suggest that Jesus was any poorer than most first-century Galileans. However, when viewed through an eternal lens, it is clear that Christ laid down riches beyond measure in order to enter time and history on behalf of those who would follow him. Even though he possessed all the wealth of heaven, Jesus chose to set aside his own glory and become a man so that his followers could ultimately share in his glory.

The believer's relationship with God is based on this incredible juxtaposition. Jesus gave up his wealth of glory so that his followers, in their own spiritual poverty, could share in his relationship with God the Father—a relationship of more value than anything earthly. Because Jesus was willing to become poor, his followers are able to become rich beyond measure if they merely accept the grace he offers.

2 CORINTHIANS 9:6–8

GIVING

Christ's followers have received the most incredible gift imaginable in the love, grace and mercy of God. It costs them nothing, but it cost Jesus everything. Not only has Christ given his followers life and breath, but by his death and resurrection, he has defeated sin and death.

Because of this, when it comes to giving, strict percentages are a thing

(continued on next page)

gave themselves first of all to the Lord, and then by the will of God also to us. 6So
we urged Titus, just as he had earlier made a beginning, to bring also to completion this act of grace on your part. 7But since you excel in everything—in faith, in
speech, in knowledge, in complete earnestness and in the love we have kindled
in you[a]—see that you also excel in this grace of giving.

8I am not commanding you, but I want to test the sincerity of your love by
comparing it with the earnestness of others. 9For you know the grace of our Lord
Jesus Christ, that though he was rich, yet for your sake he became poor, so that
you through his poverty might become rich.

10And here is my judgment about what is best for you in this matter. Last year
you were the first not only to give but also to have the desire to do so. 11Now finish
the work, so that your eager willingness to do it may be matched by your completion of it, according to your means. 12For if the willingness is there, the gift is
acceptable according to what one has, not according to what one does not have.

13Our desire is not that others might be relieved while you are hard pressed,
but that there might be equality. 14At the present time your plenty will supply
what they need, so that in turn their plenty will supply what you need. The goal
is equality, 15as it is written: "The one who gathered much did not have too much,
and the one who gathered little did not have too little."[b]

Titus Sent to Receive the Collection

16Thanks be to God, who put into the heart of Titus the same concern I have
for you. 17For Titus not only welcomed our appeal, but he is coming to you with
much enthusiasm and on his own initiative. 18And we are sending along with
him the brother who is praised by all the churches for his service to the gospel.
19What is more, he was chosen by the churches to accompany us as we carry the
offering, which we administer in order to honor the Lord himself and to show
our eagerness to help. 20We want to avoid any criticism of the way we administer
this liberal gift. 21For we are taking pains to do what is right, not only in the eyes
of the Lord but also in the eyes of man.

22In addition, we are sending with them our brother who has often proved to
us in many ways that he is zealous, and now even more so because of his great
confidence in you. 23As for Titus, he is my partner and co-worker among you; as
for our brothers, they are representatives of the churches and an honor to Christ.
24Therefore show these men the proof of your love and the reason for our pride in
you, so that the churches can see it.

9 There is no need for me to write to you about this service to the Lord's people.
2For I know your eagerness to help, and I have been boasting about it to the
Macedonians, telling them that since last year you in Achaia were ready to give;
and your enthusiasm has stirred most of them to action. 3But I am sending the
brothers in order that our boasting about you in this matter should not prove
hollow, but that you may be ready, as I said you would be. 4For if any Macedonians come with me and find you unprepared, we—not to say anything about
you—would be ashamed of having been so confident. 5So I thought it necessary
to urge the brothers to visit you in advance and finish the arrangements for the
generous gift you had promised. Then it will be ready as a generous gift, not as
one grudgingly given.

Generosity Encouraged

6Remember this: Whoever sows sparingly will also reap sparingly, and whoever sows generously will also reap generously. 7Each of you should give what
you have decided in your heart to give, not reluctantly or under compulsion, for
God loves a cheerful giver. 8And God is able to bless you abundantly, so that in
all things at all times, having all that you need, you will abound in every good
work. 9As it is written:

[a] 7 Some manuscripts *and in your love for us*   [b] 15 Exodus 16:18

"They have freely scattered their gifts to the poor;
their righteousness endures forever."[a]

10Now he who supplies seed to the sower and bread for food will also supply and
increase your store of seed and will enlarge the harvest of your righteousness.
11You will be enriched in every way so that you can be generous on every occasion, and through us your generosity will result in thanksgiving to God.
12This service that you perform is not only supplying the needs of the Lord's
people but is also overflowing in many expressions of thanks to God. 13Because
of the service by which you have proved yourselves, others will praise God for
the obedience that accompanies your confession of the gospel of Christ, and
for your generosity in sharing with them and with everyone else. 14And in their
prayers for you their hearts will go out to you, because of the surpassing grace
God has given you. 15Thanks be to God for his indescribable gift!

Paul's Defense of His Ministry

10 By the humility and gentleness of Christ, I appeal to you — I, Paul, who am
"timid" when face to face with you, but "bold" toward you when away! 2I
beg you that when I come I may not have to be as bold as I expect to be toward
some people who think that we live by the standards of this world. 3For though
we live in the world, we do not wage war as the world does. 4The weapons we
fight with are not the weapons of the world. On the contrary, they have divine
power to demolish strongholds. 5We demolish arguments and every preten-
sion that sets itself up against the knowledge of God, and we take captive every
thought to make it obedient to Christ. 6And we will be ready to punish every act
of disobedience, once your obedience is complete.
7You are judging by appearances.[b] If anyone is confident that they belong
to Christ, they should consider again that we belong to Christ just as much as
they do. 8So even if I boast somewhat freely about the authority the Lord gave
us for building you up rather than tearing you down, I will not be ashamed
of it. 9I do not want to seem to be trying to frighten you with my letters. 10For
some say, "His letters are weighty and forceful, but in person he is unimpres-
sive and his speaking amounts to nothing." 11Such people should realize that
what we are in our letters when we are absent, we will be in our actions when
we are present.
12We do not dare to classify or compare ourselves with some who commend
themselves. When they measure themselves by themselves and compare themselves with themselves, they are not wise. 13We, however, will not boast beyond
proper limits, but will confine our boasting to the sphere of service God himself
has assigned to us, a sphere that also includes you. 14We are not going too far in
our boasting, as would be the case if we had not come to you, for we did get as far
as you with the gospel of Christ. 15Neither do we go beyond our limits by boasting of work done by others. Our hope is that, as your faith continues to grow,
our sphere of activity among you will greatly expand, 16so that we can preach
the gospel in the regions beyond you. For we do not want to boast about work
already done in someone else's territory. 17But, "Let the one who boasts boast in
the Lord."[c] 18For it is not the one who commends himself who is approved, but
the one whom the Lord commends.

Paul and the False Apostles

11 I hope you will put up with me in a little foolishness. Yes, please put up
with me! 2I am jealous for you with a godly jealousy. I promised you to one
husband, to Christ, so that I might present you as a pure virgin to him. 3But I am
afraid that just as Eve was deceived by the serpent's cunning, your minds may
somehow be led astray from your sincere and pure devotion to Christ. 4For if
someone comes to you and preaches a Jesus other than the Jesus we preached, or

[a] 9 Psalm 112:9 [b] 7 Or *Look at the obvious facts* [c] 17 Jer. 9:24

(Giving, continued)

of the past and Christians do not live under the weight of obligation. Instead, Paul makes it clear that believers are to give generously and may enjoy a generous return. What is more, the attitude of the giver is more important than the size of their gift.

Giving is intended to be an act of worship — the believer's opportunity to respond to the extravagant grace and glory of God. God generously meets the needs of his people, both physical and spiritual. Giving is an opportunity for his people to use those gifts to return honor and glory to him. Just as he was extravagant in his giving, so too Christ's followers have the opportunity to be extravagant in their gifts back to him.

2 CORINTHIANS 10:17

BOASTING

Paul circled back in this passage to the same issue he addressed at the end of chapter 2 and the beginning of chapter 3. Specifically, he again argued the legitimacy of his own authority in the gospel. In doing so, he started by summarizing the prophet's admonition in Jeremiah 9:23 – 24.

Given his education in the law of the Old Testament through his training as a Pharisee, Paul was well versed in the idea that one should not boast about himself. And yet, in this single letter he felt compelled to defend himself and his ministry repeatedly.

Paul's motive is of utmost importance in this matter. His purposes in establishing his authority were not to bring honor to himself. Instead, his intent was to distinguish the authority of his ministry from the deceptive

(continued on next page)

(Boasting, continued)

influence of the false leaders who wanted to build themselves up at the expense of the Corinthian church.

In any event, Paul concluded his own defense by pointing out that the approval of humans should not be the goal of believers, but instead they should seek the approval of God. He who created everything knows the hearts and motives of those who follow him. It is his glory and his approval that his followers should seek.

2 CORINTHIANS 11:21–29

SUFFERING

Jesus' followers are not promised a life of comfort and wealth. Indeed, Jesus himself warned his followers of the suffering they should expect (Mt 10:16–39). Paul's own experience certainly confirms that the earthly life of a believer will not be easy.

In this passage, Paul recounted for the church at Corinth his own struggles. He experienced prison, beatings and was near death with remarkable regularity. Danger seemed to have become a lifestyle for him. Hunger, thirst, exposure to the elements and sleeplessness all became a part of Paul's experience when he began using his life to lift up the name of Jesus.

Suffering this extreme may seem foreign to believers who have found lives of relative comfort in many parts of the world in the twenty-first century. However, the reality of suffering for the cause of Christ continues today. Whether in cultures where the worship of Jesus is outlawed or in nations where Christianity is embraced, the

(continued on next page)

if you receive a different spirit from the Spirit you received, or a different gospel
from the one you accepted, you put up with it easily enough.
5 I do not think I am in the least inferior to those "super-apostles."[a] 6 I may
indeed be untrained as a speaker, but I do have knowledge. We have made this
perfectly clear to you in every way. 7 Was it a sin for me to lower myself in order to
elevate you by preaching the gospel of God to you free of charge? 8 I robbed other
churches by receiving support from them so as to serve you. 9 And when I was
with you and needed something, I was not a burden to anyone, for the brothers
who came from Macedonia supplied what I needed. I have kept myself from being a burden to you in any way, and will continue to do so. 10 As surely as the truth
of Christ is in me, nobody in the regions of Achaia will stop this boasting of mine.
11 Why? Because I do not love you? God knows I do!
12 And I will keep on doing what I am doing in order to cut the ground from under those who want an opportunity to be considered equal with us in the things
they boast about. 13 For such people are false apostles, deceitful workers, masquerading as apostles of Christ. 14 And no wonder, for Satan himself masquerades as an angel of light. 15 It is not surprising, then, if his servants also masquer-
ade as servants of righteousness. Their end will be what their actions deserve.

Paul Boasts About His Sufferings

16 I repeat: Let no one take me for a fool. But if you do, then tolerate me just as
you would a fool, so that I may do a little boasting. 17 In this self-confident boasting I am not talking as the Lord would, but as a fool. 18 Since many are boasting
in the way the world does, I too will boast. 19 You gladly put up with fools since
you are so wise! 20 In fact, you even put up with anyone who enslaves you or exploits you or takes advantage of you or puts on airs or slaps you in the face. 21 To
my shame I admit that we were too weak for that!
Whatever anyone else dares to boast about — I am speaking as a fool — I also
dare to boast about. 22 Are they Hebrews? So am I. Are they Israelites? So am
I. Are they Abraham's descendants? So am I. 23 Are they servants of Christ? (I
am out of my mind to talk like this.) I am more. I have worked much harder,
been in prison more frequently, been flogged more severely, and been exposed
to death again and again. 24 Five times I received from the Jews the forty lashes
minus one. 25 Three times I was beaten with rods, once I was pelted with stones,
three times I was shipwrecked, I spent a night and a day in the open sea, 26 I
have been constantly on the move. I have been in danger from rivers, in danger
from bandits, in danger from my fellow Jews, in danger from Gentiles; in danger
in the city, in danger in the country, in danger at sea; and in danger from false
believers. 27 I have labored and toiled and have often gone without sleep; I have
known hunger and thirst and have often gone without food; I have been cold and
naked. 28 Besides everything else, I face daily the pressure of my concern for all
the churches. 29 Who is weak, and I do not feel weak? Who is led into sin, and I
do not inwardly burn?
30 If I must boast, I will boast of the things that show my weakness. 31 The God
and Father of the Lord Jesus, who is to be praised forever, knows that I am not
lying. 32 In Damascus the governor under King Aretas had the city of the Dam-
ascenes guarded in order to arrest me. 33 But I was lowered in a basket from a
window in the wall and slipped through his hands.

Paul's Vision and His Thorn

12 I must go on boasting. Although there is nothing to be gained, I will go
on to visions and revelations from the Lord. 2 I know a man in Christ who
fourteen years ago was caught up to the third heaven. Whether it was in the body
or out of the body I do not know — God knows. 3 And I know that this man —
whether in the body or apart from the body I do not know, but God knows — 4 was

[a] 5 Or *to the most eminent apostles*

caught up to paradise and heard inexpressible things, things that no one is permitted to tell. 5I will boast about a man like that, but I will not boast about myself, except about my weaknesses. 6Even if I should choose to boast, I would not be a fool, because I would be speaking the truth. But I refrain, so no one will think more of me than is warranted by what I do or say, 7or because of these surpassingly great revelations. Therefore, in order to keep me from becoming conceited, I was given a thorn in my flesh, a messenger of Satan, to torment me. 8Three times I pleaded with the Lord to take it away from me. 9But he said to me, "My grace is sufficient for you, for my power is made perfect in weakness." Therefore I will boast all the more gladly about my weaknesses, so that Christ's power may rest on me. 10That is why, for Christ's sake, I delight in weaknesses, in insults, in hardships, in persecutions, in difficulties. For when I am weak, then I am strong.

Paul's Concern for the Corinthians

11I have made a fool of myself, but you drove me to it. I ought to have been commended by you, for I am not in the least inferior to the "super-apostles,"[a] even though I am nothing. 12I persevered in demonstrating among you the marks of a true apostle, including signs, wonders and miracles. 13How were you inferior to the other churches, except that I was never a burden to you? Forgive me this wrong!

14Now I am ready to visit you for the third time, and I will not be a burden to you, because what I want is not your possessions but you. After all, children should not have to save up for their parents, but parents for their children. 15So I will very gladly spend for you everything I have and expend myself as well. If I love you more, will you love me less? 16Be that as it may, I have not been a burden to you. Yet, crafty fellow that I am, I caught you by trickery! 17Did I exploit you through any of the men I sent to you? 18I urged Titus to go to you and I sent our brother with him. Titus did not exploit you, did he? Did we not walk in the same footsteps by the same Spirit?

19Have you been thinking all along that we have been defending ourselves to you? We have been speaking in the sight of God as those in Christ; and everything we do, dear friends, is for your strengthening. 20For I am afraid that when I come I may not find you as I want you to be, and you may not find me as you want me to be. I fear that there may be discord, jealousy, fits of rage, selfish ambition, slander, gossip, arrogance and disorder. 21I am afraid that when I come again my God will humble me before you, and I will be grieved over many who have sinned earlier and have not repented of the impurity, sexual sin and debauchery in which they have indulged.

Final Warnings

13 This will be my third visit to you. "Every matter must be established by the testimony of two or three witnesses."[b] 2I already gave you a warning when I was with you the second time. I now repeat it while absent: On my return I will not spare those who sinned earlier or any of the others, 3since you are demanding proof that Christ is speaking through me. He is not weak in dealing with you, but is powerful among you. 4For to be sure, he was crucified in weakness, yet he lives by God's power. Likewise, we are weak in him, yet by God's power we will live with him in our dealing with you.

5Examine yourselves to see whether you are in the faith; test yourselves. Do you not realize that Christ Jesus is in you — unless, of course, you fail the test? 6And I trust that you will discover that we have not failed the test. 7Now we pray to God that you will not do anything wrong — not so that people will see that we have stood the test but so that you will do what is right even though we may seem to have failed. 8For we cannot do anything against the truth, but only for the truth. 9We are glad whenever we are weak but you are strong; and our prayer

[a] *11* Or *the most eminent apostles* [b] *1* Deut. 19:15

(Suffering, continued)

possibility of suffering for one's faith remains. Believers should not be surprised when they face suffering of any kind but should recognize that their suffering places them in good company.

---

2 CORINTHIANS 12:7 – 10

THORN IN THE FLESH

Paul recognized his inclination to become conceited because of his own apostolic authority and impressive spiritual credentials. To keep Paul humble and maximize the glory given to God through Paul's ministry, God gave Paul a "thorn in [his] flesh" (v. 7).

Paul referred to this thorn as "a messenger of Satan" (v. 7), and therefore it may have been that God allowed the devil to attack Paul in some limited way in order to serve the Lord's own good purposes (Job 2:1). Beyond this, however, Scripture is not clear as to the precise nature of Paul's struggle. Some have speculated that it was an issue related to his eyesight based on his comments in Galatians 4:13 – 15. In any event, it is clear that the issue was chronic and debilitating and was a hindrance to his work and ministry.

Regardless of the nature of Paul's thorn, two things are clear. First, God's grace was sufficient to sustain Paul through his struggle. And second, because of the disability in Paul's life, God received even more glory through Paul's ministry. It is for this reason that Paul was able to rejoice in his own suffering and delight in his own weakness.

The same principles apply to believers today. While God uses the

(continued on next page)

(Thorn in the Flesh, continued)

strengths and skills of his people, even more glory can be attributed to God when his people rely on him, serve him and make themselves available despite their weaknesses and struggles.

is that you may be fully restored. [10]This is why I write these things when I am
absent, that when I come I may not have to be harsh in my use of authority — the
authority the Lord gave me for building you up, not for tearing you down.

Final Greetings

[11]Finally, brothers and sisters, rejoice! Strive for full restoration, encourage
one another, be of one mind, live in peace. And the God of love and peace will
be with you.

[12]Greet one another with a holy kiss. [13]All God's people here send their greetings.

[14]May the grace of the Lord Jesus Christ, and the love of God, and the fellowship of the Holy Spirit be with you all.

JESUS: OUR JUSTIFICATION BY FAITH

GALATIANS

GALATIANS

PAUL'S MISSIONARY JOURNEYS	PAUL VISITS, WRITES TO GALATIANS	PAUL MARTYRED IN ROME
c. AD 47 – 57	*c. AD 48*	*c. AD 67 – 68*

How can sinful people be made right with a holy God? This question is central to understanding Paul's letter to the churches of Galatia, and also the entirety of the Bible.

The churches in this region were established by Paul on either his first or second missionary journey. Since his departure, false teachers had perverted the gospel he proclaimed. These teachers led many to conclude erroneously that keeping the law, especially practicing circumcision, was essential for salvation.

Paul did not mince words in countering this heresy, which Paul argued had fundamentally altered the message of the gospel. Salvation is found through faith in Jesus Christ alone (2:16; 3:11 – 12). The law was used by God to reveal the extent of human sin and point forward to the coming of Christ. It was, as it had always been, a response to the grace of God. Those who try to earn salvation by keeping the law will find themselves cursed by God because they cannot obey it perfectly (3:10).

With fatherly affection, Paul writes to his "dear children" (4:19) in the faith and hope that they would not abandon the gospel he proclaimed. Works-based salvation is not good news. It is crushing, burdensome and condemning. The good news is that God pursued his people in love, knowing full well the extent of their sinfulness. Jesus lived a life of perfect conformity to the law and gives his righteous standing before God as a gift to his people. On the cross, Jesus became a curse on behalf of believers so they would never face the condemnation sin deserves (3:13). These gifts — right standing before God and freedom from the wrath of God — are given apart from the works of the law. They are a gift of grace.

God then indwells believers by means of his Holy Spirit, who empowers them to live the lives for which God created them. The Spirit produces in them what the law never could (5:22 – 23). Those who are saved by faith will find this faith working in them to produce lives marked by love of God and of one another (5:5 – 6). Jesus alone is the basis for the church's hope — both for their salvation and their ongoing sanctification.

I HAVE BEEN CRUCIFIED WITH CHRIST AND I NO LONGER LIVE, BUT CHRIST LIVES IN ME. THE LIFE I NOW LIVE IN THE BODY, I LIVE BY FAITH IN THE SON OF GOD, WHO LOVED ME AND GAVE HIMSELF FOR ME.

Galatians 2:20

GALATIANS

1 Paul, an apostle — sent not from men nor by a man, but by Jesus Christ and
God the Father, who raised him from the dead — [2]and all the brothers and
sisters[a] with me,

To the churches in Galatia:

[3]Grace and peace to you from God our Father and the Lord Jesus Christ, [4]who
gave himself for our sins to rescue us from the present evil age, according to the
will of our God and Father, [5]to whom be glory for ever and ever. Amen.

No Other Gospel

[6]I am astonished that you are so quickly deserting the one who called you to
live in the grace of Christ and are turning to a different gospel — [7]which is really
no gospel at all. Evidently some people are throwing you into confusion and are
trying to pervert the gospel of Christ. [8]But even if we or an angel from heaven
should preach a gospel other than the one we preached to you, let them be under
God's curse! [9]As we have already said, so now I say again: If anybody is preaching
to you a gospel other than what you accepted, let them be under God's curse!
[10]Am I now trying to win the approval of human beings, or of God? Or am I
trying to please people? If I were still trying to please people, I would not be a
servant of Christ.

Paul Called by God

[11]I want you to know, brothers and sisters, that the gospel I preached is not of
human origin. [12]I did not receive it from any man, nor was I taught it; rather, I
received it by revelation from Jesus Christ.
[13]For you have heard of my previous way of life in Judaism, how intensely I
persecuted the church of God and tried to destroy it. [14]I was advancing in Judaism beyond many of my own age among my people and was extremely zealous for the traditions of my fathers. [15]But when God, who set me apart from my
mother's womb and called me by his grace, was pleased [16]to reveal his Son in
me so that I might preach him among the Gentiles, my immediate response was
not to consult any human being. [17]I did not go up to Jerusalem to see those who
were apostles before I was, but I went into Arabia. Later I returned to Damascus.
[18]Then after three years, I went up to Jerusalem to get acquainted with Cephas[b] and stayed with him fifteen days. [19]I saw none of the other apostles — only
James, the Lord's brother. [20]I assure you before God that what I am writing you
is no lie.
[21]Then I went to Syria and Cilicia. [22]I was personally unknown to the churches of Judea that are in Christ. [23]They only heard the report: "The man who formerly persecuted us is now preaching the faith he once tried to destroy." [24]And
they praised God because of me.

Paul Accepted by the Apostles

2 Then after fourteen years, I went up again to Jerusalem, this time with Barnabas. I took Titus along also. [2]I went in response to a revelation and, meeting privately with those esteemed as leaders, I presented to them the gospel that
I preach among the Gentiles. I wanted to be sure I was not running and had
not been running my race in vain. [3]Yet not even Titus, who was with me, was

GALATIANS 1:6–7

AMAZING GRACE

Often believers find it difficult to rest in the undeserved, amazing grace of Jesus. With gratitude and good intentions, believers look to prove themselves worthy of their unearned position. In this letter, Paul confronts the church of Galatia on this point. They had become confused and were trying to work out their salvation by suggesting they should add the rules and legalism of Jewish laws to the saving grace God the Father offered through Jesus' death and resurrection. Paul reasoned that if believers were required to keep the law in order to be saved, a savior wasn't necessary — "which is really no gospel at all" (v. 7).

[a] *2* The Greek word for *brothers and sisters* (*adelphoi*) refers here to believers, both men and women, as part of God's family; also in verse 11; and in 3:15; 4:12, 28, 31; 5:11, 13; 6:1, 18.
[b] *18* That is, Peter

compelled to be circumcised, even though he was a Greek. 4This matter arose because some false believers had infiltrated our ranks to spy on the freedom we have in Christ Jesus and to make us slaves. 5We did not give in to them for a moment, so that the truth of the gospel might be preserved for you.

6As for those who were held in high esteem — whatever they were makes no difference to me; God does not show favoritism — they added nothing to my message. 7On the contrary, they recognized that I had been entrusted with the task of preaching the gospel to the uncircumcised,[a] just as Peter had been to the circumcised.[b] 8For God, who was at work in Peter as an apostle to the circumcised, was also at work in me as an apostle to the Gentiles. 9James, Cephas[c] and John, those esteemed as pillars, gave me and Barnabas the right hand of fellowship when they recognized the grace given to me. They agreed that we should go to the Gentiles, and they to the circumcised. 10All they asked was that we should continue to remember the poor, the very thing I had been eager to do all along.

Paul Opposes Cephas

11When Cephas came to Antioch, I opposed him to his face, because he stood condemned. 12For before certain men came from James, he used to eat with the Gentiles. But when they arrived, he began to draw back and separate himself from the Gentiles because he was afraid of those who belonged to the circumcision group. 13The other Jews joined him in his hypocrisy, so that by their hypocrisy even Barnabas was led astray.

14When I saw that they were not acting in line with the truth of the gospel, I said to Cephas in front of them all, "You are a Jew, yet you live like a Gentile and not like a Jew. How is it, then, that you force Gentiles to follow Jewish customs?

15"We who are Jews by birth and not sinful Gentiles 16know that a person is not justified by the works of the law, but by faith in Jesus Christ. So we, too, have put our faith in Christ Jesus that we may be justified by faith in[d] Christ and not by the works of the law, because by the works of the law no one will be justified.

17"But if, in seeking to be justified in Christ, we Jews find ourselves also among the sinners, doesn't that mean that Christ promotes sin? Absolutely not! 18If I rebuild what I destroyed, then I really would be a lawbreaker.

19"For through the law I died to the law so that I might live for God. 20I have been crucified with Christ and I no longer live, but Christ lives in me. The life I now live in the body, I live by faith in the Son of God, who loved me and gave himself for me. 21I do not set aside the grace of God, for if righteousness could be gained through the law, Christ died for nothing!"[e]

Faith or Works of the Law

3 You foolish Galatians! Who has bewitched you? Before your very eyes Jesus Christ was clearly portrayed as crucified. 2I would like to learn just one thing from you: Did you receive the Spirit by the works of the law, or by believing what you heard? 3Are you so foolish? After beginning by means of the Spirit, are you now trying to finish by means of the flesh?[f] 4Have you experienced[g] so much in vain — if it really was in vain? 5So again I ask, does God give you his Spirit and work miracles among you by the works of the law, or by your believing what you heard? 6So also Abraham "believed God, and it was credited to him as righteousness."[h]

7Understand, then, that those who have faith are children of Abraham. 8Scripture foresaw that God would justify the Gentiles by faith, and announced the gospel in advance to Abraham: "All nations will be blessed through you."[i] 9So those who rely on faith are blessed along with Abraham, the man of faith.

---

[a] *7* That is, Gentiles [b] *7* That is, Jews; also in verses 8 and 9 [c] *9* That is, Peter; also in verses 11 and 14 [d] *16* Or *but through the faithfulness of . . . justified on the basis of the faithfulness of* [e] *21* Some interpreters end the quotation after verse 14. [f] *3* In contexts like this, the Greek word for *flesh* (*sarx*) refers to the sinful state of human beings, often presented as a power in opposition to the Spirit. [g] *4* Or *suffered* [h] *6* Gen. 15:6 [i] *8* Gen. 12:3; 18:18; 22:18

CRUCIFIED WITH CHRIST

To truly appreciate the claim Paul makes in Galatians 2:20, "I have been crucified with Christ," first consider the symbol of the cross in Jesus' day. An excruciating, shameful death by crucifixion was reserved for society's worst criminal offenders. So why would Paul choose to align himself with the cross? The gospel flips everything on its head. Not until his conversion did Paul really see what the cross stood for. Only God could turn a horrible death on a cross into something beautiful. On the cross, Jesus exchanged the punishment we deserved for his grace — a gift so profound and so complete that nothing could be added to it.

So Paul couldn't understand why the church leaders would want to make symbols of righteousness through Jewish law requirements for salvation. He stood firm in his belief: Either salvation was through faith alone or it wasn't (2:15)! For the believer, works are not a *prerequisite* for salvation; rather, they are a *response* to salvation. Paul's identity with Christ's crucifixion symbolized the reality that Jesus removed the stain of his sin once and for all and brought life, grace and freedom to this former persecutor of the church. His letter to the Galatians reinforces the completeness of this transformation to convince them that nothing needed to be added to their faith to assure their salvation.

In their first meeting together after Paul's conversion (2:1 – 10), Paul and Peter confirmed the unity and oneness they shared in the gospel and affirmed each other's unique call. However, when the two met again in Antioch, Paul called Peter out for acting one way around Gentiles and another way around those who still practiced the Jewish law. Paul was concerned that Peter's behavior could be perceived by the Gentiles that there must be something more that believers have to do to continue in God's grace after salvation. Paul fiercely protected the freedom that grace offers (2:21).

With Jesus, the entire concept of "the cross" was changed to the point that Paul would "boast ... in the cross of ... Christ" (6:14). He would never belittle the cross by adding elements of the Jewish law to it — elements that fell short of true righteousness before God. Christianity centers on complete change — a change in our status before God, in our view of the present world, and even in the way we think about the cross. Paul emphasized that Christ's one sacrifice covers all of our sin completely; we need not add even one more thing to that sacrifice to somehow earn more favor with God.

[10]For all who rely on the works of the law are under a curse, as it is written: "Cursed is everyone who does not continue to do everything written in the Book of the Law."[a] [11]Clearly no one who relies on the law is justified before God, because "the righteous will live by faith."[b] [12]The law is not based on faith; on the contrary, it says, "The person who does these things will live by them."[c] [13]Christ redeemed us from the curse of the law by becoming a curse for us, for it is written: "Cursed is everyone who is hung on a pole."[d] [14]He redeemed us in order that the blessing given to Abraham might come to the Gentiles through Christ Jesus, so that by faith we might receive the promise of the Spirit.

The Law and the Promise

[15]Brothers and sisters, let me take an example from everyday life. Just as no one can set aside or add to a human covenant that has been duly established, so it is in this case. [16]The promises were spoken to Abraham and to his seed. Scripture does not say "and to seeds," meaning many people, but "and to your seed,"[e] meaning one person, who is Christ. [17]What I mean is this: The law, introduced 430 years later, does not set aside the covenant previously established by God and thus do away with the promise. [18]For if the inheritance depends on the law, then it no longer depends on the promise; but God in his grace gave it to Abraham through a promise.

[19]Why, then, was the law given at all? It was added because of transgressions until the Seed to whom the promise referred had come. The law was given through angels and entrusted to a mediator. [20]A mediator, however, implies more than one party; but God is one.

[21]Is the law, therefore, opposed to the promises of God? Absolutely not! For if a law had been given that could impart life, then righteousness would certainly have come by the law. [22]But Scripture has locked up everything under the control of sin, so that what was promised, being given through faith in Jesus Christ, might be given to those who believe.

Children of God

[23]Before the coming of this faith,[f] we were held in custody under the law, locked up until the faith that was to come would be revealed. [24]So the law was our guardian until Christ came that we might be justified by faith. [25]Now that this faith has come, we are no longer under a guardian.

[26]So in Christ Jesus you are all children of God through faith, [27]for all of you who were baptized into Christ have clothed yourselves with Christ. [28]There is neither Jew nor Gentile, neither slave nor free, nor is there male and female, for you are all one in Christ Jesus. [29]If you belong to Christ, then you are Abraham's seed, and heirs according to the promise.

4 What I am saying is that as long as an heir is underage, he is no different from a slave, although he owns the whole estate. [2]The heir is subject to guardians and trustees until the time set by his father. [3]So also, when we were underage, we were in slavery under the elemental spiritual forces[g] of the world. [4]But when the set time had fully come, God sent his Son, born of a woman, born under the law, [5]to redeem those under the law, that we might receive adoption to sonship.[h] [6]Because you are his sons, God sent the Spirit of his Son into our hearts, the Spirit who calls out, *"Abba,*[i] Father." [7]So you are no longer a slave, but God's child; and since you are his child, God has made you also an heir.

Paul's Concern for the Galatians

[8]Formerly, when you did not know God, you were slaves to those who by nature are not gods. [9]But now that you know God — or rather are known by God —

[a] *10* Deut. 27:26 [b] *11* Hab. 2:4 [c] *12* Lev. 18:5 [d] *13* Deut. 21:23 [e] *16* Gen. 12:7; 13:15; 24:7 [f] *22,23* Or *through the faithfulness of Jesus . . .* [23]*Before faith came* [g] *3* Or *under the basic principles* [h] *5* The Greek word for *adoption to sonship* is a legal term referring to the full legal standing of an adopted male heir in Roman culture. [i] *6* Aramaic for *Father*

GALATIANS 4:4–5

CHILDREN OF GOD'S PROMISE

The law was given as a guardian, a steward of the relationship between God and his people until the promise of the coming Messiah was fulfilled. It was established by God to uphold a standard of holiness and make a way for people to temporarily atone for their sins. God determined the time between the giving of the law and the fulfillment of the promise for our benefit. Not a moment of what went on before Jesus came was wasted.

The Israelites of the Old Testament lived with expectation, waiting for God to fulfill his promises. Like underage heirs, they were subject to their guardian, the law — and that arrangement made them no better off than slaves. But Jesus came "to redeem those under the law, that [they] might receive adoption to sonship" (v. 5). He was the fulfilled promise that made adoption into God's eternal family possible.

Believers are children of God. And they share in the mind-blowingly abundant inheritance of the Lord himself! There is no more uncertainty: God calls believers his beloved and they walk in the close, deeply affectionate, committed love of their heavenly Father.

GALATIANS 3:23–29

GRACE VERSUS THE LAW

Paul didn't waste words. He saw that his Galatian brothers and sisters were headed down a dangerous path. They may or may not have been ready for a heavyweight theological match, but Paul was ready to throw down. While the Galatians were led astray by those who wanted to add such Jewish traditions as circumcision to the requirements for salvation, Paul stood firm on the issue of righteousness gained through faith alone. Paul considered this a hill worth dying on; Jesus did too. Salvation by grace alone centers on the cross of Christ, and any human law, Jewish or otherwise, centers on submitting to human requirements. Paul is clear: The enemy wants Christ-followers to believe that faith in Jesus alone is not sufficient for salvation.

Faith is a matter of trust, not a pursuit of perfection. These believers were mistakenly trying to achieve perfection through their own efforts. Sound familiar? Paul emphasized that the law is based on works and depends on human effort, whereas grace is based on faith and depends on the power of the Holy Spirit. Paul challenged his audience, "After beginning by means of the Spirit, are you now trying to finish by means of the flesh?" (3:3). Does the Spirit come to believers because they perfectly keep all the rules? Of course not. "But God demonstrates his own love for us in this: While we were still sinners, Christ died for us" (Ro 5:8).

The Holy Spirit frees us from the rule of law and empowers us, changing our desires so that we want to live holy, godly lives. This reality moves believers away from being "sanctified scorekeepers" to people who live joyfully for Jesus: "But you are a chosen people, a royal priesthood, a holy nation, God's special possession, *that you may* declare the praises of him who called you out of darkness into his wonderful light" (1Pe 2:9, emphasis added). This "that we may" attitude involves a complete mind shift: Believers don't *have* to ... they *get* to respond to Jesus' love by showing love to others in return.

Children of God don't live to keep all the rules and then concern themselves with how they rank as compared to others. Life under the law is motivated by pride. Life under grace is motivated by love. To support his argument, Paul points out that it can't go both ways. Even if some believed they could keep parts of the law, they were essentially condemning themselves to keep the whole law. James taught similarly (Jas 2:10). Paul wrote to convince the Galatians — and us as well — that living under the law, or even part of the law, brings bondage. But grace brings liberty.

how is it that you are turning back to those weak and miserable forces[a]? Do you
wish to be enslaved by them all over again? [10]You are observing special days and
months and seasons and years! [11]I fear for you, that somehow I have wasted my
efforts on you.

[12]I plead with you, brothers and sisters, become like me, for I became like
you. You did me no wrong. [13]As you know, it was because of an illness that I first
preached the gospel to you, [14]and even though my illness was a trial to you, you
did not treat me with contempt or scorn. Instead, you welcomed me as if I were
an angel of God, as if I were Christ Jesus himself. [15]Where, then, is your blessing
of me now? I can testify that, if you could have done so, you would have torn out
your eyes and given them to me. [16]Have I now become your enemy by telling
you the truth?

[17]Those people are zealous to win you over, but for no good. What they want
is to alienate you from us, so that you may have zeal for them. [18]It is fine to be
zealous, provided the purpose is good, and to be so always, not just when I am
with you. [19]My dear children, for whom I am again in the pains of childbirth until Christ is formed in you, [20]how I wish I could be with you now and change my
tone, because I am perplexed about you!

Hagar and Sarah

[21]Tell me, you who want to be under the law, are you not aware of what the
law says? [22]For it is written that Abraham had two sons, one by the slave woman and the other by the free woman. [23]His son by the slave woman was born
according to the flesh, but his son by the free woman was born as the result of a
divine promise.

[24]These things are being taken figuratively: The women represent two covenants. One covenant is from Mount Sinai and bears children who are to be slaves:
This is Hagar. [25]Now Hagar stands for Mount Sinai in Arabia and corresponds to
the present city of Jerusalem, because she is in slavery with her children. [26]But the
Jerusalem that is above is free, and she is our mother. [27]For it is written:

> "Be glad, barren woman,
>   you who never bore a child;
> shout for joy and cry aloud,
>   you who were never in labor;
> because more are the children of the desolate woman
>   than of her who has a husband."[b]

[28]Now you, brothers and sisters, like Isaac, are children of promise. [29]At that
time the son born according to the flesh persecuted the son born by the power
of the Spirit. It is the same now. [30]But what does Scripture say? "Get rid of the
slave woman and her son, for the slave woman's son will never share in the inheritance with the free woman's son."[c] [31]Therefore, brothers and sisters, we are
not children of the slave woman, but of the free woman.

Freedom in Christ

5 It is for freedom that Christ has set us free. Stand firm, then, and do not let
yourselves be burdened again by a yoke of slavery.

[2]Mark my words! I, Paul, tell you that if you let yourselves be circumcised,
Christ will be of no value to you at all. [3]Again I declare to every man who lets
himself be circumcised that he is obligated to obey the whole law. [4]You who are
trying to be justified by the law have been alienated from Christ; you have fall-
en away from grace. [5]For through the Spirit we eagerly await by faith the righteousness for which we hope. [6]For in Christ Jesus neither circumcision nor uncircumcision has any value. The only thing that counts is faith expressing itself
through love.

---

[a] 9 Or *principles* [b] *27* Isaiah 54:1 [c] *30* Gen. 21:10

7You were running a good race. Who cut in on you to keep you from obeying the truth? 8That kind of persuasion does not come from the one who calls you. 9"A little yeast works through the whole batch of dough." 10I am confident in the Lord that you will take no other view. The one who is throwing you into confusion, whoever that may be, will have to pay the penalty. 11Brothers and sisters, if I am still preaching circumcision, why am I still being persecuted? In that case the offense of the cross has been abolished. 12As for those agitators, I wish they would go the whole way and emasculate themselves!

Life by the Spirit

13You, my brothers and sisters, were called to be free. But do not use your freedom to indulge the flesh[a]; rather, serve one another humbly in love. 14For the entire law is fulfilled in keeping this one command: "Love your neighbor as yourself."[b] 15If you bite and devour each other, watch out or you will be destroyed by each other.

16So I say, walk by the Spirit, and you will not gratify the desires of the flesh. 17For the flesh desires what is contrary to the Spirit, and the Spirit what is contrary to the flesh. They are in conflict with each other, so that you are not to do whatever[c] you want. 18But if you are led by the Spirit, you are not under the law.

19The acts of the flesh are obvious: sexual immorality, impurity and debauchery; 20idolatry and witchcraft; hatred, discord, jealousy, fits of rage, selfish ambition, dissensions, factions 21and envy; drunkenness, orgies, and the like. I warn you, as I did before, that those who live like this will not inherit the kingdom of God.

22But the fruit of the Spirit is love, joy, peace, forbearance, kindness, goodness, faithfulness, 23gentleness and self-control. Against such things there is no law. 24Those who belong to Christ Jesus have crucified the flesh with its passions and desires. 25Since we live by the Spirit, let us keep in step with the Spirit. 26Let us not become conceited, provoking and envying each other.

Doing Good to All

6 Brothers and sisters, if someone is caught in a sin, you who live by the Spirit should restore that person gently. But watch yourselves, or you also may be tempted. 2Carry each other's burdens, and in this way you will fulfill the law of Christ. 3If anyone thinks they are something when they are not, they deceive themselves. 4Each one should test their own actions. Then they can take pride in themselves alone, without comparing themselves to someone else, 5for each one should carry their own load. 6Nevertheless, the one who receives instruction in the word should share all good things with their instructor.

7Do not be deceived: God cannot be mocked. A man reaps what he sows. 8Whoever sows to please their flesh, from the flesh will reap destruction; whoever sows to please the Spirit, from the Spirit will reap eternal life. 9Let us not become weary in doing good, for at the proper time we will reap a harvest if we do not give up. 10Therefore, as we have opportunity, let us do good to all people, especially to those who belong to the family of believers.

Not Circumcision but the New Creation

11See what large letters I use as I write to you with my own hand!

12Those who want to impress people by means of the flesh are trying to compel you to be circumcised. The only reason they do this is to avoid being persecuted for the cross of Christ. 13Not even those who are circumcised keep the law, yet they want you to be circumcised that they may boast about your circumcision in the flesh. 14May I never boast except in the cross of our Lord Jesus Christ,

GALATIANS 5:22–23

FRUIT OF THE SPIRIT

As Christians begin to live lives that are transformed more and more into the image of Christ, certain character traits begin to show up: love, joy, peace, kindness and the like. Paul tells his audience that as a person's heart changes, their outward disposition, demeanor and actions will also change. This "fruit" comes as the Holy Spirit works and changes the way believers live. This passage tells us that the words, actions, character and values of a believer will increasingly align with the behavior Jesus modeled during his earthly ministry. Paul's preview to the fruit describes how the process works: "So I say, walk by the Spirit, and you will not gratify the desires of the flesh" (v. 16).

All believers have days when love or joy is less evident. But overall, the transformational nature of salvation—when a believer's eternal status is converted once and for all time—can't help but begin to change their daily attitudes and actions.

[a] *13* In contexts like this, the Greek word for *flesh* (*sarx*) refers to the sinful state of human beings, often presented as a power in opposition to the Spirit; also in verses 16, 17, 19 and 24; and in 6:8. [b] *14* Lev. 19:18 [c] *17* Or *you do not do what*

through which[a] the world has been crucified to me, and I to the world. [15]Neither
circumcision nor uncircumcision means anything; what counts is the new creation. [16]Peace and mercy to all who follow this rule — to[b] the Israel of God.
[17]From now on, let no one cause me trouble, for I bear on my body the marks
of Jesus.
[18]The grace of our Lord Jesus Christ be with your spirit, brothers and sisters.
Amen.

[a] *14* Or *whom* [b] *16* Or *rule and to*

JESUS: OUR PEACE WITH GOD

EPHESIANS

EPHESIANS

PAUL PLANTS EPHESIAN CHURCH	PAUL'S EXTENDED STAY IN EPHESUS	PAUL IMPRISONED, WRITES EPHESIANS
c. AD 53	*c. AD 54 – 56*	*c. AD 60 – 62*

The depth of the gospel's message is unfathomable. Since the beginning of the church, pastors and scholars have written countless books attempting to address the nature and implications of Jesus' work. There is perhaps no greater and more succinct summary of the gospel message, however, than the book of Ephesians.

Ephesus was the capital of the Roman province of Asia and was a major thoroughfare in the Roman Empire. Its location made it a multicultural, cosmopolitan city, bustling with activity and influence.

Paul visited Ephesus on his second missionary journey and witnessed the birth of the church in that region. He then returned on his third missionary journey and spent three years working to establish the church (Ac 18:18 – 21; 19:1 – 41). God used the inhabitants' spiritual fervor and the strategic location of the city to make the church a center for evangelism and mission to the surrounding region (Ac 19:18 – 20). Upon leaving, Paul warned the church that fierce wolves would attack the church from inside and outside (Ac 20:17 – 38).

Years later, Paul wrote from a Roman prison to his beloved friends in Ephesus. He wanted to remind them of the gospel he proclaimed, spur them on to perseverance in the face of suffering and encourage them with the blessed hope the gospel brings. There is evidence to suggest that Ephesians may also have been a circular letter that was used to instruct and encourage believers in the broader world. The first three chapters explore many of the central doctrines of the Christian faith to show that Jesus' work brings peace with God and peace with others. The grace of God lies at the heart of Paul's letter

(Eph 2:8 – 9). This grace saves God's people apart from their works so that, through salvation, God gets all the glory.

In light of Jesus' work, then, Paul discusses the "good works" that naturally flow from a high view of God's grace and a proper understanding of the peace he brings (2:10). The peace God provides transforms every aspect of life — especially the relationships Christians have with one another. As the head of his church, Jesus shapes human relationships to model and display the love, grace and mercy he demonstrated through his death and resurrection. Dynamic, countercultural love for God and one another was to distinguish the church, in Ephesus and throughout all history, as God's people.

BUT BECAUSE OF HIS GREAT LOVE FOR US, GOD, WHO IS RICH IN MERCY, MADE US ALIVE WITH CHRIST EVEN WHEN WE WERE DEAD IN TRANSGRESSIONS — IT IS BY GRACE YOU HAVE BEEN SAVED.

Ephesians 2:4 – 5

EPHESIANS

EPHESIANS 2:1 – 10

DEATH TO LIFE

There is a stark contrast between death and life. Ephesians 2:1 – 3 explores the terrible reality for unbelievers. Using such words as “transgressions,” “disobedient,” “cravings of our flesh” and “wrath,” these verses communicate that there is something dreadfully wrong with the identity and life experience of people who are not followers of Christ. What an appalling description! There is no worse condition than spiritual death.

But hope emerges from the ashes of death (vv. 4 – 5). Those who are in Christ are “God’s handiwork” (v. 10), meaning he has crafted something beautiful. But how could beauty come from desperation, ugliness and complete destruction? It seems unfathomable that life could come from death and despair. The apostle Paul communicated this stark contrast to teach believers where ultimate praise and glory belong. Christians have nothing to offer for their salvation — it comes about only by God’s rich mercy (v. 4), kindness (v. 7), grace (v. 8) and gift (v. 8).

A Christian has no grounds for boasting about their status as a child of God (v. 9): not their wisdom, effort to obey, morality ... nothing! Every ounce of the believer’s being must therefore give absolute adoration to the Lord God, thus fulfilling the first great commandment (Mt 22:37). Closely flowing from this praise is the second great commandment (Mt 22:39). God’s handiwork of

(continued on page 1830)

1 Paul, an apostle of Christ Jesus by the will of God,

To God’s holy people in Ephesus,[a] the faithful in Christ Jesus:
[2]Grace and peace to you from God our Father and the Lord Jesus Christ.

Praise for Spiritual Blessings in Christ

[3]Praise be to the God and Father of our Lord Jesus Christ, who has blessed us
in the heavenly realms with every spiritual blessing in Christ. [4]For he chose us
in him before the creation of the world to be holy and blameless in his sight. In
love [5]he[b] predestined us for adoption to sonship[c] through Jesus Christ, in accordance with his pleasure and will — [6]to the praise of his glorious grace, which
he has freely given us in the One he loves. [7]In him we have redemption through
his blood, the forgiveness of sins, in accordance with the riches of God’s grace
[8]that he lavished on us. With all wisdom and understanding, [9]he[d] made known
to us the mystery of his will according to his good pleasure, which he purposed
in Christ, [10]to be put into effect when the times reach their fulfillment — to bring
unity to all things in heaven and on earth under Christ.
[11]In him we were also chosen,[e] having been predestined according to the plan
of him who works out everything in conformity with the purpose of his will, [12]in
order that we, who were the first to put our hope in Christ, might be for the praise
of his glory. [13]And you also were included in Christ when you heard the message
of truth, the gospel of your salvation. When you believed, you were marked in
him with a seal, the promised Holy Spirit, [14]who is a deposit guaranteeing our
inheritance until the redemption of those who are God’s possession — to the
praise of his glory.

Thanksgiving and Prayer

[15]For this reason, ever since I heard about your faith in the Lord Jesus and
your love for all God’s people, [16]I have not stopped giving thanks for you, remembering you in my prayers. [17]I keep asking that the God of our Lord Jesus Christ,
the glorious Father, may give you the Spirit[f] of wisdom and revelation, so that
you may know him better. [18]I pray that the eyes of your heart may be enlightened
in order that you may know the hope to which he has called you, the riches of
his glorious inheritance in his holy people, [19]and his incomparably great power
for us who believe. That power is the same as the mighty strength [20]he exerted
when he raised Christ from the dead and seated him at his right hand in the
heavenly realms, [21]far above all rule and authority, power and dominion, and
every name that is invoked, not only in the present age but also in the one to
come. [22]And God placed all things under his feet and appointed him to be head
over everything for the church, [23]which is his body, the fullness of him who fills
everything in every way.

Made Alive in Christ

2 As for you, you were dead in your transgressions and sins, [2]in which you used
to live when you followed the ways of this world and of the ruler of the kingdom of the air, the spirit who is now at work in those who are disobedient. [3]All of

---

[a] *1* Some early manuscripts do not have *in Ephesus.* [b] *4,5* Or *sight in love.* [5]*He* [c] *5* The Greek word for *adoption to sonship* is a legal term referring to the full legal standing of an adopted male heir in Roman culture. [d] *8,9* Or *us with all wisdom and understanding.* [9]*And he* [e] *11* Or *were made heirs* [f] *17* Or *a spirit*

A DOXOLOGY OF PRAISE

This text relates the ultimate purpose for which all creation exists and to which all human activity should lead: the praise and glory of God. As seen throughout these verses, God acts according to his good pleasure (v. 5) and glorious grace (v. 6). The richness of God's grace toward his children is not an obligation. It is, instead, a free act of God that dumbfounds all rational explanation — it is completely awe-inspiring. What reason could God possibly have to redeem sinful humanity? For Adam and his descendants, nothing but condemnation should be expected (Ro 5:12 – 19). There is nothing good in humankind that warrants redemption. In fact, all people have turned aside, choosing to revolt against God's way (Ro 3:9 – 20). In light of humanity's complete rebellion, the idea that God would offer a gift as magnificent as redemption is truly astonishing. And yet, shortly after Adam and Eve first sinned, God promised that he would bring about that redemption (Ge 3:15). He reaffirmed this promise to his servant David (2Sa 7:12 – 17) and at many other times throughout Old Testament history.

The Lord's promises are never empty words. Our triune God has carried out his plan of redemption through specific acts. Knowing that humanity would sin and ruin his creation and bring about the need for redemption, God the Father crafted a plan before the creation of the world (Eph 1:4). He would not leave his precious creation without hope, so he provided a way out of the mess produced by humanity's father, Adam. God the Father's plan required the "God-man" to pay the ultimate penalty for human rebellion. It was a penalty that was too much for humans to pay; only God could do it. Yet, a human had to pay it because it was the failure of Adam that brought about the curses of Genesis 3. Thus, only someone who was fully God and fully human could satisfy the justice due to all of fallen creation.

Jesus, being completely God and also fully human, was the one whose sacrifice provided the necessary redemption. This plan, laid out by the Father and secured by the Son, is now guaranteed by the indwelling of the Spirit (v. 13). The Holy Spirit is the seal, or guarantee, of these promises to Christians for all eternity. The word "guarantee" in this text conveys the same idea as that of a wedding ring — a mark of belonging, which reflects God's unbreakable relationship with his people. Thus, the God of glory initiated, secured and guaranteed a promise that forms a doxology of praise due to the Father, Son and Holy Spirit.

(Death to Life, continued)

recreating Christians from death to life, according to Ephesians 2:10, is meant to result in good works toward one's neighbors out of sheer gratitude to God.

us also lived among them at one time, gratifying the cravings of our flesh[a] and following its desires and thoughts. Like the rest, we were by nature deserving of wrath. [4]But because of his great love for us, God, who is rich in mercy, [5]made us alive with Christ even when we were dead in transgressions — it is by grace you have been saved. [6]And God raised us up with Christ and seated us with him in the heavenly realms in Christ Jesus, [7]in order that in the coming ages he might show the incomparable riches of his grace, expressed in his kindness to us in Christ Jesus. [8]For it is by grace you have been saved, through faith — and this is not from yourselves, it is the gift of God — [9]not by works, so that no one can boast. [10]For we are God's handiwork, created in Christ Jesus to do good works, which God prepared in advance for us to do.

Jew and Gentile Reconciled Through Christ

[11]Therefore, remember that formerly you who are Gentiles by birth and called "uncircumcised" by those who call themselves "the circumcision" (which is done in the body by human hands) — [12]remember that at that time you were separate from Christ, excluded from citizenship in Israel and foreigners to the covenants of the promise, without hope and without God in the world. [13]But now in Christ Jesus you who once were far away have been brought near by the blood of Christ.

[14]For he himself is our peace, who has made the two groups one and has destroyed the barrier, the dividing wall of hostility, [15]by setting aside in his flesh the law with its commands and regulations. His purpose was to create in himself one new humanity out of the two, thus making peace, [16]and in one body to reconcile both of them to God through the cross, by which he put to death their hostility. [17]He came and preached peace to you who were far away and peace to those who were near. [18]For through him we both have access to the Father by one Spirit.

[19]Consequently, you are no longer foreigners and strangers, but fellow citizens with God's people and also members of his household, [20]built on the foundation of the apostles and prophets, with Christ Jesus himself as the chief cornerstone. [21]In him the whole building is joined together and rises to become a holy temple in the Lord. [22]And in him you too are being built together to become a dwelling in which God lives by his Spirit.

God's Marvelous Plan for the Gentiles

3 For this reason I, Paul, the prisoner of Christ Jesus for the sake of you Gentiles —

[2]Surely you have heard about the administration of God's grace that was given to me for you, [3]that is, the mystery made known to me by revelation, as I have already written briefly. [4]In reading this, then, you will be able to understand my insight into the mystery of Christ, [5]which was not made known to people in other generations as it has now been revealed by the Spirit to God's holy apostles and prophets. [6]This mystery is that through the gospel the Gentiles are heirs together with Israel, members together of one body, and sharers together in the promise in Christ Jesus.

[7]I became a servant of this gospel by the gift of God's grace given me through the working of his power. [8]Although I am less than the least of all the Lord's people, this grace was given me: to preach to the Gentiles the boundless riches of Christ, [9]and to make plain to everyone the administration of this mystery, which for ages past was kept hidden in God, who created all things. [10]His intent was that now, through the church, the manifold wisdom of God should be made known to the rulers and authorities in the heavenly realms, [11]according to his eternal purpose that he accomplished in Christ Jesus our Lord. [12]In him

---

[a] *3* In contexts like this, the Greek word for *flesh* (*sarx*) refers to the sinful state of human beings, often presented as a power in opposition to the Spirit.

and through faith in him we may approach God with freedom and confidence.
[13]I ask you, therefore, not to be discouraged because of my sufferings for you, which are your glory.

A Prayer for the Ephesians

[14]For this reason I kneel before the Father, [15]from whom every family[a] in heaven and on earth derives its name. [16]I pray that out of his glorious riches he may strengthen you with power through his Spirit in your inner being, [17]so that Christ may dwell in your hearts through faith. And I pray that you, being rooted and established in love, [18]may have power, together with all the Lord's holy people, to grasp how wide and long and high and deep is the love of Christ, [19]and to know this love that surpasses knowledge — that you may be filled to the measure of all the fullness of God.

[20]Now to him who is able to do immeasurably more than all we ask or imagine, according to his power that is at work within us, [21]to him be glory in the church and in Christ Jesus throughout all generations, for ever and ever! Amen.

Unity and Maturity in the Body of Christ

4 As a prisoner for the Lord, then, I urge you to live a life worthy of the calling you have received. [2]Be completely humble and gentle; be patient, bearing with one another in love. [3]Make every effort to keep the unity of the Spirit through the bond of peace. [4]There is one body and one Spirit, just as you were called to one hope when you were called; [5]one Lord, one faith, one baptism; [6]one God and Father of all, who is over all and through all and in all.

[7]But to each one of us grace has been given as Christ apportioned it. [8]This is why it[b] says:

"When he ascended on high,
he took many captives
and gave gifts to his people."[c]

[9](What does "he ascended" mean except that he also descended to the lower, earthly regions[d]? [10]He who descended is the very one who ascended higher than all the heavens, in order to fill the whole universe.) [11]So Christ himself gave the apostles, the prophets, the evangelists, the pastors and teachers, [12]to equip his people for works of service, so that the body of Christ may be built up [13]until we all reach unity in the faith and in the knowledge of the Son of God and become mature, attaining to the whole measure of the fullness of Christ.

[14]Then we will no longer be infants, tossed back and forth by the waves, and blown here and there by every wind of teaching and by the cunning and craftiness of people in their deceitful scheming. [15]Instead, speaking the truth in love, we will grow to become in every respect the mature body of him who is the head, that is, Christ. [16]From him the whole body, joined and held together by every supporting ligament, grows and builds itself up in love, as each part does its work.

Instructions for Christian Living

[17]So I tell you this, and insist on it in the Lord, that you must no longer live as the Gentiles do, in the futility of their thinking. [18]They are darkened in their understanding and separated from the life of God because of the ignorance that is in them due to the hardening of their hearts. [19]Having lost all sensitivity, they have given themselves over to sensuality so as to indulge in every kind of impurity, and they are full of greed.

[20]That, however, is not the way of life you learned [21]when you heard about Christ and were taught in him in accordance with the truth that is in Jesus. [22]You

[a] *15* The Greek for *family* (*patria*) is derived from the Greek for *father* (*pater*). [b] *8* Or *God*
[c] *8* Psalm 68:18 [d] *9* Or *the depths of the earth*

EPHESIANS 3:14 – 19

THE FULLNESS OF GOD

Paul prayed for God to grant something to his Ephesian readers, something that all Christians should desire with the very essence of their beings: the "fullness of God" (v. 19). As opposed to the emptiness offered by the fleeting — and often unattainable — pleasures of this world, experiencing the fullness of God is much preferred.

Simply surveying the descriptive words Paul used to describe God's fullness is impressive: "glorious riches," Jesus' "dwell[ing]" presence, "rooted and established in love," "wide and long and high and deep," "knowledge" and "fullness." Rather than scarcity, Christ's love offers us great riches. In contrast to humiliating embarrassment, Jesus is glorious. Whereas some promises and hopes go unfulfilled or abandoned, Christ's everlasting love and presence are rooted and dwell in the believer. Rather than having limits or strict parameters, God's fullness is boundless. In Christ, believers can know a love beyond any other relationship or possession, something that is unimaginably satisfying. In fact, the reality Paul conveyed so shatters human categories that he said it "surpasses knowledge." Jesus' essence is defined not by emptiness but by completeness. Nothing and no one can separate a believer from the full height and depth of God's love in Christ (Ro 8:38 – 39).

BLESSINGS AND RESPONSIBILITIES OF BELIEVERS

These verses speak of a stark contrast between believers and unbelievers as Paul encouraged the Ephesian church to live according to their status as God's children. Christians have been enlightened, awakened from the darkness and the ignorant pursuits that consume non-Christians. According to the apostle Paul, nonbelievers walk in futility (v. 17), have darkened understanding (v. 18), are "separated from the life of God" (v. 18), are ignorant (v. 18), are impure (v. 19) and are "full of greed" (v. 19). Not so with a child of God. These descriptions apply to the believer's "old self" and have nothing to do with Christ (vv. 21 – 22).

The believer's status has completely shifted — from old to new, from death and blindness to life and light. Yet this beautiful gift of the believer's new identity is not simply meant to benefit the individual. This new standing before God also entails obligations as stated in verse 28: Paul commanded the believing thief to steal no longer but rather work with their own hands in order to have means to bless others. In short, the former thief received the blessing of redemption and was therefore obligated to become a blessing to others.

The following list shows the blessing of new life along with certain responsibilities associated with the believer's new status as a child of God.

Blessings Christians Enjoy

- Chosen by God; election (1:4)
- Adoption into God's family (1:5; 2:19)
- Acceptance before God (1:6)
- Forgiveness of sins (1:7)
- Insight into God's will (1:9)
- An eternal inheritance (1:11)
- The seal of the Spirit (1:13; 2:18)
- God's mercy and love (2:4; 3:17 – 19)
- Wisdom and knowledge (1:17)
- Divine power (1:19 – 20; 3:16,20)
- Spiritual life (2:1,5)
- The promise of eternal kindness (2:7)
- The knowledge that God's plan for believers is good (2:10)
- Unity and peace with all believers (2:11 – 18; 3:6)
- Heavenly citizenship (2:19)
- Access to God through Christ (3:12)

Responsibilities of Believers

- To keep the unity of the Spirit (4:3 – 6)
- To use one's gifts for the church's benefit (4:7 – 13)
- To keep growing and maturing (4:14 – 15)
- To put away old, sinful ways (4:17 – 24; 5:2 – 14)
- To speak honestly and purely (4:25,29)
- To do what the Spirit leads us to do (4:30)
- To imitate God (5:1)
- To walk in love (5:2)
- To know what is acceptable to the Lord (5:10)
- To make the most of our time (5:16)
- To be filled with the Spirit (5:18)
- To submit to one another (5:21)
- To have marriages that honor God (5:22 – 33)
- To honor God in family contexts (6:1 – 4)
- To demonstrate integrity before those who have authority over us, including in the workplace (6:5 – 9)
- To stand strong against the forces of evil (6:10 – 18)

were taught, with regard to your former way of life, to put off your old self, which
is being corrupted by its deceitful desires; 23to be made new in the attitude of
your minds; 24and to put on the new self, created to be like God in true righteousness and holiness.

25Therefore each of you must put off falsehood and speak truthfully to your
neighbor, for we are all members of one body. 26"In your anger do not sin"[a]: Do
not let the sun go down while you are still angry, 27and do not give the devil a
foothold. 28Anyone who has been stealing must steal no longer, but must work,
doing something useful with their own hands, that they may have something to
share with those in need.

29Do not let any unwholesome talk come out of your mouths, but only what
is helpful for building others up according to their needs, that it may benefit
those who listen. 30And do not grieve the Holy Spirit of God, with whom you
were sealed for the day of redemption. 31Get rid of all bitterness, rage and anger,
brawling and slander, along with every form of malice. 32Be kind and compassionate to one another, forgiving each other, just as in Christ God forgave you.

5 1Follow God's example, therefore, as dearly loved children 2and walk in the
way of love, just as Christ loved us and gave himself up for us as a fragrant
offering and sacrifice to God.

3But among you there must not be even a hint of sexual immorality, or of any
kind of impurity, or of greed, because these are improper for God's holy people.
4Nor should there be obscenity, foolish talk or coarse joking, which are out of
place, but rather thanksgiving. 5For of this you can be sure: No immoral, impure or greedy person — such a person is an idolater — has any inheritance in
the kingdom of Christ and of God.[b] 6Let no one deceive you with empty words,
for because of such things God's wrath comes on those who are disobedient.
7Therefore do not be partners with them.

8For you were once darkness, but now you are light in the Lord. Live as children of light 9(for the fruit of the light consists in all goodness, righteousness
and truth) 10and find out what pleases the Lord. 11Have nothing to do with the
fruitless deeds of darkness, but rather expose them. 12It is shameful even to mention what the disobedient do in secret. 13But everything exposed by the light
becomes visible — and everything that is illuminated becomes a light. 14This is
why it is said:

"Wake up, sleeper,
  rise from the dead,
  and Christ will shine on you."

15Be very careful, then, how you live — not as unwise but as wise, 16making the
most of every opportunity, because the days are evil. 17Therefore do not be foolish, but understand what the Lord's will is. 18Do not get drunk on wine, which
leads to debauchery. Instead, be filled with the Spirit, 19speaking to one another
with psalms, hymns, and songs from the Spirit. Sing and make music from your
heart to the Lord, 20always giving thanks to God the Father for everything, in the
name of our Lord Jesus Christ.

Instructions for Christian Households

21Submit to one another out of reverence for Christ.

22Wives, submit yourselves to your own husbands as you do to the Lord. 23For
the husband is the head of the wife as Christ is the head of the church, his body,
of which he is the Savior. 24Now as the church submits to Christ, so also wives
should submit to their husbands in everything.

25Husbands, love your wives, just as Christ loved the church and gave himself
up for her 26to make her holy, cleansing[c] her by the washing with water through
the word, 27and to present her to himself as a radiant church, without stain or

[a] *26* Psalm 4:4 (see Septuagint) [b] *5* Or *kingdom of the Messiah and God* [c] *26* Or *having cleansed*

CHRISTIAN BAPTISM

In the Jewish tradition, ceremonial washing and baptism are key elements of faith. Gentiles receive baptism when they embrace the religion of the Jews, and some Jewish sects regularly practice baptism as a symbol of purification. Serving as an early example of this practice, John the Baptist emphasized baptism as a foundational part of his ministry, calling his listeners to repent and receive baptism as an expression of their sincere faith. At least for part of his ministry, Jesus offered baptism to his followers, though it seems his disciples performed the baptisms rather than Jesus himself (Jn 4:1 – 2). We also know that he received baptism personally (Mk 1:9 – 11). And Paul stated that Jesus' disciples baptized people "into Christ" (Gal 3:27).

A clear shift from Jewish baptism to a distinctively Christian understanding of baptism is recorded in texts such as Acts 18:26 – 27 when Priscilla and Aquila redirected Apollos' understanding of the act. The early church understood baptism in various ways — as a symbol of a person's death to sin (Ro 6:4), of the cleansing from sin (Ac 22:16; Eph 5:26) and of the new life in Christ (Ac 2:41; Ro 6:3).

Throughout church history, the Christian understanding of the command to baptize has been linked to evangelism and making disciples. For instance, Matthew 28:19 has a clear mandate to make disciples, which is the command of this passage that ties together the other three commands — to go, evangelize and baptize. These three words describe how to make disciples. Specific traditions within the Christian faith have understood the relationship of these three words to making disciples in different ways. When someone is baptized, they join the fellowship of Jesus' disciples, so it makes sense that the Great Commission links evangelism with baptism. Evangelism invites lost people into the community of saints; baptism is a sign of their membership within that community.

Despite the different interpretations of these questions in the Christian faith, one issue is clear: the New Testament modification of Jewish baptism was distinct. For Christians, baptism is linked directly to redemption and being a disciple. In baptism, believers carry out this rite as an act of obedience to genuine faith, signifying a change in the person by burying the Christian's "old Adam" and being raised to life in Christ (Ro 5:12 – 18; 1Co 15:20 – 22; Col 2:11 – 12).

wrinkle or any other blemish, but holy and blameless. [28]In this same way, husbands ought to love their wives as their own bodies. He who loves his wife loves
himself. [29]After all, no one ever hated their own body, but they feed and care for
their body, just as Christ does the church— [30]for we are members of his body.
[31]"For this reason a man will leave his father and mother and be united to his
wife, and the two will become one flesh."[a] [32]This is a profound mystery—but I
am talking about Christ and the church. [33]However, each one of you also must
love his wife as he loves himself, and the wife must respect her husband.

6 Children, obey your parents in the Lord, for this is right. [2]"Honor your father
and mother"—which is the first commandment with a promise— [3]"so that
it may go well with you and that you may enjoy long life on the earth."[b]

[4]Fathers,[c] do not exasperate your children; instead, bring them up in the
training and instruction of the Lord.

[5]Slaves, obey your earthly masters with respect and fear, and with sincerity
of heart, just as you would obey Christ. [6]Obey them not only to win their favor
when their eye is on you, but as slaves of Christ, doing the will of God from your
heart. [7]Serve wholeheartedly, as if you were serving the Lord, not people, [8]be-
cause you know that the Lord will reward each one for whatever good they do,
whether they are slave or free.

[9]And masters, treat your slaves in the same way. Do not threaten them, since
you know that he who is both their Master and yours is in heaven, and there is
no favoritism with him.

The Armor of God

[10]Finally, be strong in the Lord and in his mighty power. [11]Put on the full armor of God, so that you can take your stand against the devil's schemes. [12]For
our struggle is not against flesh and blood, but against the rulers, against the
authorities, against the powers of this dark world and against the spiritual forces
of evil in the heavenly realms. [13]Therefore put on the full armor of God, so that
when the day of evil comes, you may be able to stand your ground, and after you
have done everything, to stand. [14]Stand firm then, with the belt of truth buckled
around your waist, with the breastplate of righteousness in place, [15]and with
your feet fitted with the readiness that comes from the gospel of peace. [16]In addition to all this, take up the shield of faith, with which you can extinguish all
the flaming arrows of the evil one. [17]Take the helmet of salvation and the sword
of the Spirit, which is the word of God.

[18]And pray in the Spirit on all occasions with all kinds of prayers and requests.
With this in mind, be alert and always keep on praying for all the Lord's people.
[19]Pray also for me, that whenever I speak, words may be given me so that I will
fearlessly make known the mystery of the gospel, [20]for which I am an ambassa-
dor in chains. Pray that I may declare it fearlessly, as I should.

Final Greetings

[21]Tychicus, the dear brother and faithful servant in the Lord, will tell you everything, so that you also may know how I am and what I am doing. [22]I am sending him to you for this very purpose, that you may know how we are, and that he
may encourage you.

[23]Peace to the brothers and sisters,[d] and love with faith from God the Father
and the Lord Jesus Christ. [24]Grace to all who love our Lord Jesus Christ with an
undying love.[e]

[a] *31* Gen. 2:24 [b] *3* Deut. 5:16 [c] *4* Or *Parents* [d] *23* The Greek word for *brothers and sisters* (*adelphoi*) refers here to believers, both men and women, as part of God's family.
[e] *24* Or *Grace and immortality to all who love our Lord Jesus Christ.*

EPHESIANS 6:12

SPIRITUAL WARFARE

Ephesians offers a window into the spiritual realities that underlie the struggles and difficulties of life many people face. Sins that people commit against God, themselves and others spring from a deeper well than simple bad choices or mere circumstances. Believers are engaged in spiritual warfare.

Second Corinthians 10:1–6 (particularly vv. 4–5) offers a helpful addition to Paul's teachings here concerning spiritual warfare. These passages combined offer a picture of the spiritual battle taking place behind the scenes of many human experiences. Arguments against the gospel, failures of biblical morality and lines of unbiblical thinking are not merely the skewed actions and beliefs of humans. According to Paul's teachings, these issues come from the intentional activity of an enemy who influences people each and every day. When a Christian faces overwhelming trials and oppressive circumstances, the evil one may be intimately involved.

Yet, believers must not despair. The Christian has every reason to be confident as he takes up the approach to spiritual warfare prescribed by God. The means of success are the spiritual disciplines commanded by God in Ephesians 6. Using the familiar image of Roman armor, this passage reveals how to do battle against spiritual enemies and outlines the rules of engagement for this specific fight. The end goal of spiritual warfare is to make every thought captive to Christ (2Co 10:5).

JESUS: OUR JOY IN SUFFERING

PHILIPPIANS

PHILIPPIANS

PAUL PLANTS PHILIPPIAN CHURCH	PAUL REVISITS PHILIPPI	PAUL IMPRISONED, WRITES PHILIPPIANS
c. AD 50	*c. AD 56*	*c. AD 60 – 62*

Christians can have joy in all circumstances, even in the face of immense suffering. Paul's life testified to the truthfulness of this claim, and he wrote the letter of Philippians to remind the church in Philippi that they, too, could find joy in suffering.

The church in Philippi was established during Paul's second missionary journey, in response to a vision from God instructing Paul to travel to Macedonia and proclaim the gospel. As the first church in Europe, the Philippian church represented a mixture of races, classes and cultures. Paul wrote to remind the church of the hope they have by virtue of Christ's work.

Throughout the letter, Paul spends considerable time thanking the church for their partnership in the gospel. Clearly, the church has been an encouragement to Paul — through their prayers and financial support. In their generosity, the believers in Philippi became partakers in the missionary advance of the church.

The continued spread of the gospel, however, faced considerable opposition — both in Paul's ministry and in the ongoing work of the church at Philippi. Therefore, Paul reminded the church that suffering should not be seen as evidence of God's lack of care and concern for his church. In fact, suffering is a God-ordained means of spreading the message of salvation. As Christians suffer with joy and find contentment in all things, they have the privilege of modeling a hope that this world cannot provide. This type of joy is only possible if the church has a deep understanding of the gospel and continues to grow in knowledge and discernment of God's will and ways.

The Philippian church needed to look no further than Paul for their example. By the time Paul wrote Philippians, he had suffered greatly for his faith in Jesus and his work to spread the message of the gospel. Writing from a Roman prison, Paul reminds the church that he can find joy in all things. His hope and confidence is not based on his circumstances but is firmly rooted in the inalterable truth of Jesus' work. All people, including believers today, can look to this letter to find encouragement to face life with pervasive joy, even in a fallen world.

I KNOW WHAT IT IS TO BE IN NEED, AND I KNOW WHAT IT IS TO HAVE PLENTY. I HAVE LEARNED THE SECRET OF BEING CONTENT IN ANY AND EVERY SITUATION, WHETHER WELL FED OR HUNGRY, WHETHER LIVING IN PLENTY OR IN WANT. I CAN DO ALL THIS THROUGH HIM WHO GIVES ME STRENGTH.

Philippians 4:12 – 13

PHILIPPIANS

1 Paul and Timothy, servants of Christ Jesus,

To all God's holy people in Christ Jesus at Philippi, together with the overseers
and deacons[a]:

[2]Grace and peace to you from God our Father and the Lord Jesus Christ.

Thanksgiving and Prayer

[3]I thank my God every time I remember you. [4]In all my prayers for all of you,
I always pray with joy [5]because of your partnership in the gospel from the first
day until now, [6]being confident of this, that he who began a good work in you will
carry it on to completion until the day of Christ Jesus.

[7]It is right for me to feel this way about all of you, since I have you in my heart
and, whether I am in chains or defending and confirming the gospel, all of you
share in God's grace with me. [8]God can testify how I long for all of you with the
affection of Christ Jesus.

[9]And this is my prayer: that your love may abound more and more in knowledge and depth of insight, [10]so that you may be able to discern what is best and
may be pure and blameless for the day of Christ, [11]filled with the fruit of righteousness that comes through Jesus Christ — to the glory and praise of God.

Paul's Chains Advance the Gospel

[12]Now I want you to know, brothers and sisters,[b] that what has happened to
me has actually served to advance the gospel. [13]As a result, it has become clear
throughout the whole palace guard[c] and to everyone else that I am in chains for
Christ. [14]And because of my chains, most of the brothers and sisters have become confident in the Lord and dare all the more to proclaim the gospel without
fear.

[15]It is true that some preach Christ out of envy and rivalry, but others out of
goodwill. [16]The latter do so out of love, knowing that I am put here for the defense
of the gospel. [17]The former preach Christ out of selfish ambition, not sincerely,
supposing that they can stir up trouble for me while I am in chains. [18]But what
does it matter? The important thing is that in every way, whether from false motives or true, Christ is preached. And because of this I rejoice.

Yes, and I will continue to rejoice, [19]for I know that through your prayers
and God's provision of the Spirit of Jesus Christ what has happened to me will
turn out for my deliverance.[d] [20]I eagerly expect and hope that I will in no way be
ashamed, but will have sufficient courage so that now as always Christ will be
exalted in my body, whether by life or by death. [21]For to me, to live is Christ and
to die is gain. [22]If I am to go on living in the body, this will mean fruitful labor for
me. Yet what shall I choose? I do not know! [23]I am torn between the two: I desire
to depart and be with Christ, which is better by far; [24]but it is more necessary
for you that I remain in the body. [25]Convinced of this, I know that I will remain,
and I will continue with all of you for your progress and joy in the faith, [26]so that
through my being with you again your boasting in Christ Jesus will abound on
account of me.

---

[a] *1* The word *deacons* refers here to Christians designated to serve with the overseers/elders of the church in a variety of ways; similarly in Romans 16:1 and 1 Tim. 3:8,12. [b] *12* The Greek word for *brothers and sisters* (*adelphoi*) refers here to believers, both men and women, as part of God's family; also in verse 14; and in 3:1, 13, 17; 4:1, 8, 21. [c] *13* Or *whole palace* [d] *19* Or *vindication*; or *salvation*

Life Worthy of the Gospel

27Whatever happens, conduct yourselves in a manner worthy of the gospel of
Christ. Then, whether I come and see you or only hear about you in my absence,
I will know that you stand firm in the one Spirit,[a] striving together as one for
the faith of the gospel 28without being frightened in any way by those who oppose you. This is a sign to them that they will be destroyed, but that you will be
saved — and that by God. 29For it has been granted to you on behalf of Christ not
only to believe in him, but also to suffer for him, 30since you are going through
the same struggle you saw I had, and now hear that I still have.

Imitating Christ's Humility

2 Therefore if you have any encouragement from being united with Christ, if
any comfort from his love, if any common sharing in the Spirit, if any tenderness and compassion, 2then make my joy complete by being like-minded,
having the same love, being one in spirit and of one mind. 3Do nothing out of
selfish ambition or vain conceit. Rather, in humility value others above yourselves, 4not looking to your own interests but each of you to the interests of the
others.

5In your relationships with one another, have the same mindset as Christ
Jesus:

6Who, being in very nature[b] God,
did not consider equality with God something to be used to his own advantage;
7rather, he made himself nothing
by taking the very nature[c] of a servant,
being made in human likeness.
8And being found in appearance as a man,
he humbled himself
by becoming obedient to death —
even death on a cross!

9Therefore God exalted him to the highest place
and gave him the name that is above every name,
10that at the name of Jesus every knee should bow,
in heaven and on earth and under the earth,
11and every tongue acknowledge that Jesus Christ is Lord,
to the glory of God the Father.

Do Everything Without Grumbling

12Therefore, my dear friends, as you have always obeyed — not only in my
presence, but now much more in my absence — continue to work out your salvation with fear and trembling, 13for it is God who works in you to will and to act in
order to fulfill his good purpose.

14Do everything without grumbling or arguing, 15so that you may become
blameless and pure, "children of God without fault in a warped and crooked
generation."[d] Then you will shine among them like stars in the sky 16as you hold
firmly to the word of life. And then I will be able to boast on the day of Christ that
I did not run or labor in vain. 17But even if I am being poured out like a drink offering on the sacrifice and service coming from your faith, I am glad and rejoice
with all of you. 18So you too should be glad and rejoice with me.

Timothy and Epaphroditus

19I hope in the Lord Jesus to send Timothy to you soon, that I also may be
cheered when I receive news about you. 20I have no one else like him, who will
show genuine concern for your welfare. 21For everyone looks out for their own

---

[a] 27 Or *in one spirit* [b] 6 Or *in the form of* [c] 7 Or *the form* [d] 15 Deut. 32:5

PHILIPPIANS 2:6–11

TRUE HUMILITY

The words of this beloved passage may have existed as a hymn for the early church. Paul's description of Jesus is quite lyrical — a crescendo of praise for the matchless Son of God. Jesus is celebrated as the One worthy to receive the highest place because he chose to become a servant. He is the epitome of true humility.

Jesus did not stop being God, but he willfully released the glorious entitlements of his position and power. He laid aside his deserved privilege as God's Son in order to accomplish the will of his Father. Believers begin to appreciate the magnitude of Jesus' choice to empty himself when they contrast it to the immeasurable honor due his name. The One worthy of the finest throne began life on earth by being placed in a manger. The Word became flesh and lived among humans (Jn 1:14). The eternal King became a servant.

Jesus served humankind by yielding to God's plan for atonement on the gruesome cross of Calvary. Christ sacrificed himself to redeem humanity from the debt of sin. Though Jesus never sinned, he took the place of the guilty, absorbing punishment that he did not deserve (2Co 5:21). Mocked and exposed, Jesus experienced the shame and humiliation of public execution. Death by crucifixion was agonizing, yet Jesus endured it with a vision of greater purposes. He willingly endured the cross because of the "joy set before him" (Heb 12:2).

Jesus served the Father by making a way for people to be reconciled with their Creator (2Co 5:18). God gave Jesus to the world because he loved people and desired a relationship with them. Jesus bridged the separation between God and humankind. At the same time, the cross provided a public declaration of God's unwavering commitment to his Word — finally dealing with sin long passed over (Ro 3:25). Christ's sacrifice and victorious resurrection also won worshipers for God — those who believe and find new life and joy in him.

In recognition of Jesus' obedience through restraint and suffering, the Father gave him the highest place, establishing his name above every other name. And a day is coming when every person in all of history will bow to the Son who served. All will humble themselves to exalt and praise Christ the Lord (Php 2:10–11).

interests, not those of Jesus Christ. 22But you know that Timothy has proved himself, because as a son with his father he has served with me in the work of the gospel. 23I hope, therefore, to send him as soon as I see how things go with me. 24And I am confident in the Lord that I myself will come soon.

25But I think it is necessary to send back to you Epaphroditus, my brother, co-worker and fellow soldier, who is also your messenger, whom you sent to take care of my needs. 26For he longs for all of you and is distressed because you heard he was ill. 27Indeed he was ill, and almost died. But God had mercy on him, and not on him only but also on me, to spare me sorrow upon sorrow. 28Therefore I am all the more eager to send him, so that when you see him again you may be glad and I may have less anxiety. 29So then, welcome him in the Lord with great joy, and honor people like him, 30because he almost died for the work of Christ. He risked his life to make up for the help you yourselves could not give me.

No Confidence in the Flesh

3 Further, my brothers and sisters, rejoice in the Lord! It is no trouble for me to write the same things to you again, and it is a safeguard for you. 2Watch out for those dogs, those evildoers, those mutilators of the flesh. 3For it is we who are the circumcision, we who serve God by his Spirit, who boast in Christ Jesus, and who put no confidence in the flesh— 4though I myself have reasons for such confidence.

If someone else thinks they have reasons to put confidence in the flesh, I have more: 5circumcised on the eighth day, of the people of Israel, of the tribe of Benjamin, a Hebrew of Hebrews; in regard to the law, a Pharisee; 6as for zeal, persecuting the church; as for righteousness based on the law, faultless.

7But whatever were gains to me I now consider loss for the sake of Christ. 8What is more, I consider everything a loss because of the surpassing worth of knowing Christ Jesus my Lord, for whose sake I have lost all things. I consider them garbage, that I may gain Christ 9and be found in him, not having a righteousness of my own that comes from the law, but that which is through faith in[a] Christ—the righteousness that comes from God on the basis of faith. 10I want to know Christ—yes, to know the power of his resurrection and participation in his sufferings, becoming like him in his death, 11and so, somehow, attaining to the resurrection from the dead.

12Not that I have already obtained all this, or have already arrived at my goal, but I press on to take hold of that for which Christ Jesus took hold of me. 13Brothers and sisters, I do not consider myself yet to have taken hold of it. But one thing I do: Forgetting what is behind and straining toward what is ahead, 14I press on toward the goal to win the prize for which God has called me heavenward in Christ Jesus.

Following Paul's Example

15All of us, then, who are mature should take such a view of things. And if on some point you think differently, that too God will make clear to you. 16Only let us live up to what we have already attained.

17Join together in following my example, brothers and sisters, and just as you have us as a model, keep your eyes on those who live as we do. 18For, as I have often told you before and now tell you again even with tears, many live as enemies of the cross of Christ. 19Their destiny is destruction, their god is their stomach, and their glory is in their shame. Their mind is set on earthly things. 20But our citizenship is in heaven. And we eagerly await a Savior from there, the Lord Jesus Christ, 21who, by the power that enables him to bring everything under his control, will transform our lowly bodies so that they will be like his glorious body.

[a] 9 Or *through the faithfulness of*

PHILIPPIANS 3:8–9

KNOWING CHRIST

The apostle Paul's standard summary of a Christian is one who is "in Christ." All of salvation takes place in Christ. Before the creation, believers were chosen in him (Eph 1:4). Through faith, Christians are justified in him (Ro 5:1) and sealed in him (Eph 1:13). Throughout life, believers are sanctified in him (2Co 3:18).

Chapter 3 of Philippians highlights Paul's intense desire to be found in Christ when his life comes to an end (Php 3:8–9). To be "in Christ" is to trust in his work on the cross as the basis for salvation. Noah survived judgment in the ark that God provided (Ge 6:17–18). In a similar way, sinful people can pass through the coming judgment by believing in Christ, the one and only Savior. For Christians, their present experience of life is in Christ. When death comes, they will die in Christ. When God initiates the return of Christ, those who believe will be made alive in him and reign with him (2Ti 2:12).

PHILIPPIANS 4:19

ALL WE NEED

Humans are fundamentally needy creatures — newborns instinctively gasp for oxygen, kids hunger for afternoon snacks, high schoolers seek friends and popularity, young adults chase careers, and so on. People are needy by design — physically, socially, emotionally and most importantly, spiritually. God is intimately acquainted with the needs of his people. As all-knowing God, he anticipates his people's needs; as a loving Father, he tenderly provides (Mt 7:7 – 11).

Having a laugh with friends or grabbing a bite to eat cannot result in lasting satisfaction. The deepest needs are of the soul, not the body. Thankfully, this passage proclaims that these needs can be satisfied through Jesus, who is rich in glory. The more we grow in our faith in Christ, the more our needs are satisfied by the riches he offers. Paul confirmed that the God of the universe is able: the One who created humans will also be their continuing resource. God can be trusted to take care of those who believe in Christ and who follow him with their lives. His supply of mercy is endless — flowing from the glory that is in Christ Jesus, who left heaven to show love and mercy to rebels. The God whom believers trust for provision is the same God with the power to conquer sin and death. He can meet any need.

Closing Appeal for Steadfastness and Unity

4 Therefore, my brothers and sisters, you whom I love and long for, my joy and
crown, stand firm in the Lord in this way, dear friends!
[2]I plead with Euodia and I plead with Syntyche to be of the same mind in the
Lord. [3]Yes, and I ask you, my true companion, help these women since they have
contended at my side in the cause of the gospel, along with Clement and the rest
of my co-workers, whose names are in the book of life.

Final Exhortations

[4]Rejoice in the Lord always. I will say it again: Rejoice! [5]Let your gentleness be
evident to all. The Lord is near. [6]Do not be anxious about anything, but in every
situation, by prayer and petition, with thanksgiving, present your requests to
God. [7]And the peace of God, which transcends all understanding, will guard
your hearts and your minds in Christ Jesus.
[8]Finally, brothers and sisters, whatever is true, whatever is noble, whatever is
right, whatever is pure, whatever is lovely, whatever is admirable — if anything
is excellent or praiseworthy — think about such things. [9]Whatever you have
learned or received or heard from me, or seen in me — put it into practice. And
the God of peace will be with you.

Thanks for Their Gifts

[10]I rejoiced greatly in the Lord that at last you renewed your concern for me.
Indeed, you were concerned, but you had no opportunity to show it. [11]I am not
saying this because I am in need, for I have learned to be content whatever the
circumstances. [12]I know what it is to be in need, and I know what it is to have
plenty. I have learned the secret of being content in any and every situation,
whether well fed or hungry, whether living in plenty or in want. [13]I can do all
this through him who gives me strength.
[14]Yet it was good of you to share in my troubles. [15]Moreover, as you Philippians know, in the early days of your acquaintance with the gospel, when I set out
from Macedonia, not one church shared with me in the matter of giving and receiving, except you only; [16]for even when I was in Thessalonica, you sent me aid
more than once when I was in need. [17]Not that I desire your gifts; what I desire is
that more be credited to your account. [18]I have received full payment and have
more than enough. I am amply supplied, now that I have received from Epaphroditus the gifts you sent. They are a fragrant offering, an acceptable sacrifice,
pleasing to God. [19]And my God will meet all your needs according to the riches
of his glory in Christ Jesus.
[20]To our God and Father be glory for ever and ever. Amen.

Final Greetings

[21]Greet all God's people in Christ Jesus. The brothers and sisters who are with
me send greetings. [22]All God's people here send you greetings, especially those
who belong to Caesar's household.
[23]The grace of the Lord Jesus Christ be with your spirit. Amen.[a]

[a] 23 Some manuscripts do not have *Amen*.

JESUS: OUR HEAD OF ALL THINGS

COLOSSIANS

COLOSSIANS

PAUL EVANGELIZES COLOSSAE	PAUL IMPRISONED, WRITES COLOSSIANS	PAUL MARTYRED IN ROME
c. AD 54 – 56	*c. AD 60 – 62*	*c. AD 67 – 68*

Jesus is the supreme head of all things (2:10). As the image of the invisible God, Jesus shows the world what God is like. He also demonstrates the scope of the rule and reign of God. God is not some ill-defined deity, unseen and unknowable. In his grace, God has made himself known in the person of Christ.

These truths lie at the heart of Paul's letter to the church at Colossae. This church, located about a hundred miles east of Ephesus, was likely evangelized during Paul's three-year stay in that region. Like many of the churches Paul established, false teachers wreaked havoc on the church after his departure. Some apparently taught that the works of the law were vital for salvation. Others seemingly promoted a form of mysticism that affirmed Jesus as a higher being but not God.

While in prison in Rome, Paul wrote this letter to confront these two errors. This letter mirrors a similar one Paul sent to the church at Ephesus, leading many to presume that they were written around the same time. Both follow the classic outline common to many of Paul's writings. They begin with an introduction and word of encouragement, followed by a summary of the gospel and concluding with the way these truths should shape all of life.

Colossians is unique in its emphasis on the cosmic rule of Christ. Jesus is the head of his people, the church. He leads them as a benevolent king, who rules over his beloved people with sacrificial love. But his reign does not stop with the church. He is the head over all of creation — with authority over the natural world and also over the principalities and authorities of the unseen world. He is the head of all and the one to whom all allegiance is due (2:10).

Since Jesus is the head of all things, the church at Colossae can depend on him alone for salvation. Works of the flesh do not save — only the singular work of Christ in the flesh can save. Paul reminds the church to seek the things that are above and worship God alone because he is their life and only hope (3:1 – 4). This worship should permeate every aspect of the life of the church. As Paul does elsewhere, he called the church's attention to the various implications of the gospel message. This includes that Jesus, as the head of all things, deserves all worship and praise (3:1 — 4:6).

FOR IN HIM ALL THINGS WERE CREATED: THINGS IN HEAVEN AND ON EARTH, VISIBLE AND INVISIBLE, WHETHER THRONES OR POWERS OR RULERS OR AUTHORITIES; ALL THINGS HAVE BEEN CREATED THROUGH HIM AND FOR HIM.

Colossians 1:16

COLOSSIANS

1 Paul, an apostle of Christ Jesus by the will of God, and Timothy our brother,

[2]To God's holy people in Colossae, the faithful brothers and sisters[a] in Christ:

Grace and peace to you from God our Father.[b]

Thanksgiving and Prayer

[3]We always thank God, the Father of our Lord Jesus Christ, when we pray for you, [4]because we have heard of your faith in Christ Jesus and of the love you have for all God's people— [5]the faith and love that spring from the hope stored up for you in heaven and about which you have already heard in the true message of the gospel [6]that has come to you. In the same way, the gospel is bearing fruit and growing throughout the whole world—just as it has been doing among you since the day you heard it and truly understood God's grace. [7]You learned it from Epaphras, our dear fellow servant,[c] who is a faithful minister of Christ on our[d] behalf, [8]and who also told us of your love in the Spirit.

[9]For this reason, since the day we heard about you, we have not stopped praying for you. We continually ask God to fill you with the knowledge of his will through all the wisdom and understanding that the Spirit gives,[e] [10]so that you may live a life worthy of the Lord and please him in every way: bearing fruit in every good work, growing in the knowledge of God, [11]being strengthened with all power according to his glorious might so that you may have great endurance and patience, [12]and giving joyful thanks to the Father, who has qualified you[f] to share in the inheritance of his holy people in the kingdom of light. [13]For he has rescued us from the dominion of darkness and brought us into the kingdom of the Son he loves, [14]in whom we have redemption, the forgiveness of sins.

The Supremacy of the Son of God

[15]The Son is the image of the invisible God, the firstborn over all creation. [16]For in him all things were created: things in heaven and on earth, visible and invisible, whether thrones or powers or rulers or authorities; all things have been created through him and for him. [17]He is before all things, and in him all things hold together. [18]And he is the head of the body, the church; he is the beginning and the firstborn from among the dead, so that in everything he might have the supremacy. [19]For God was pleased to have all his fullness dwell in him, [20]and through him to reconcile to himself all things, whether things on earth or things in heaven, by making peace through his blood, shed on the cross.

[21]Once you were alienated from God and were enemies in your minds because of[g] your evil behavior. [22]But now he has reconciled you by Christ's physical body through death to present you holy in his sight, without blemish and free from accusation— [23]if you continue in your faith, established and firm, and do not move from the hope held out in the gospel. This is the gospel that you heard and that has been proclaimed to every creature under heaven, and of which I, Paul, have become a servant.

Paul's Labor for the Church

[24]Now I rejoice in what I am suffering for you, and I fill up in my flesh what is still lacking in regard to Christ's afflictions, for the sake of his body, which is the

---

[a] 2 The Greek word for *brothers and sisters* (*adelphoi*) refers here to believers, both men and women, as part of God's family; also in 4:15. [b] 2 Some manuscripts *Father and the Lord Jesus Christ* [c] 7 Or *slave* [d] 7 Some manuscripts *your* [e] 9 Or *all spiritual wisdom and understanding* [f] 12 Some manuscripts *us* [g] 21 Or *minds, as shown by*

THE PREEMINENCE OF CHRIST

Everyone worships someone or something. All people give someone or something first place in their life. The apostle Paul was determined that the church at Colossae give Jesus Christ preeminence in everything. Paul used what is most likely an early Christian hymn to explain how Jesus is preeminent in the entire universe and worthy of the church's allegiance and affection.

The beginning of the hymn explains that when people see Jesus, they see God. Remarkably, even in his human form, Jesus is God. Jesus himself affirmed when he said, "I and the Father are one" (Jn 10:30). Jesus' deity displays his preeminence. Paul then used a phrase that has often been misunderstood. He said Jesus is the "firstborn over all creation" (Col 1:15). At times, people have mistakenly taken this to mean that God the Father created the Son. The immediate context reveals otherwise, describing Jesus as the creator of all things, who existed "before all things" (vv. 16 – 17). Additionally, John affirmed that Jesus was in existence with the Father at the very beginning: "In the beginning was the Word, and the Word was with God, and the Word was God. He was with God in the beginning" (Jn 1:1 – 2). The description of Jesus as "firstborn" points to his exalted position. In the Jewish context, "firstborn" implied the highest rank and value.

Paul then pointed to the fact that Jesus created the universe. He hoped to stretch his readers' minds by leading them to think about invisible things that Jesus created, including the unseen angelic realm. When Christians ponder all of creation, galaxies upon galaxies, unexplored oceans and the complexity of the human body, they only begin to understand the majesty and power of Jesus. All of creation exists to bring glory to God.

Jesus is preeminent in his church. Jesus creates, sustains and leads his church as its head. Every church has its challenges and problems; however, because the church belongs to Jesus, Christians should have a heart to build up the church rather than tear it down. Jesus' preeminence shines brightly through his work of reconciling all things through his death on the cross. Jesus' death and resurrection are among the ultimate displays of his preeminence. Jesus is greater than humanity's sin. Jesus is greater than death. Jesus is greater than the devil. Indeed, in a world that often feels out of control, Christians can rejoice and take hope that Jesus Christ is reconciling all things to the Father and will bring peace to the cosmos.

COLOSSIANS 2:11 – 14

SALVATION IS A MIRACULOUS ACT

Salvation is a miracle. Scripture paints a bleak picture of humanity's spiritual condition. The problem is not just that people are bad. The problem is that people are spiritually dead. Every person needs a spiritual resurrection to be able to know God and live for him. The good news is that Jesus Christ provides spiritual resurrection.

In the Bible, circumcision usually refers to the practice of cutting away the foreskin of males on the eighth day after birth, signifying the child's entrance into the Old Testament community of faith. Paul picked up on this well-known imagery when he wrote, "you were also circumcised with a circumcision not performed by human hands" to describe the miraculous act of being made alive spiritually in Christ (v. 11). This echoes the promise made by God in Ezekiel 36:26: "I will give you a new heart and put a new spirit in you; I will remove from you your heart of stone and give you a heart of flesh." It is only because Jesus died and rose again that people can experience life today, and the resurrection of their bodies in the future. Anyone can experience spiritual resurrection by placing their faith in Jesus Christ. Jesus does not just help people become better people; he raises people from spiritual death to new life. Salvation is at the hands of God alone. Mankind cannot do any level of work that would bring approval in the sight of God. No ritual, whether ancient or modern, can replace the gracious work of God in the salvation of humanity.

church. [25]I have become its servant by the commission God gave me to present
to you the word of God in its fullness — [26]the mystery that has been kept hidden
for ages and generations, but is now disclosed to the Lord's people. [27]To them
God has chosen to make known among the Gentiles the glorious riches of this
mystery, which is Christ in you, the hope of glory.

[28]He is the one we proclaim, admonishing and teaching everyone with all
wisdom, so that we may present everyone fully mature in Christ. [29]To this end I
strenuously contend with all the energy Christ so powerfully works in me.

2 I want you to know how hard I am contending for you and for those at Laodicea, and for all who have not met me personally. [2]My goal is that they may
be encouraged in heart and united in love, so that they may have the full riches
of complete understanding, in order that they may know the mystery of God,
namely, Christ, [3]in whom are hidden all the treasures of wisdom and knowledge.
[4]I tell you this so that no one may deceive you by fine-sounding arguments. [5]For
though I am absent from you in body, I am present with you in spirit and delight
to see how disciplined you are and how firm your faith in Christ is.

Spiritual Fullness in Christ

[6]So then, just as you received Christ Jesus as Lord, continue to live your lives
in him, [7]rooted and built up in him, strengthened in the faith as you were taught,
and overflowing with thankfulness.

[8]See to it that no one takes you captive through hollow and deceptive philos-
ophy, which depends on human tradition and the elemental spiritual forces[a] of
this world rather than on Christ.

[9]For in Christ all the fullness of the Deity lives in bodily form, [10]and in Christ
you have been brought to fullness. He is the head over every power and authority. [11]In him you were also circumcised with a circumcision not performed by
human hands. Your whole self ruled by the flesh[b] was put off when you were
circumcised by[c] Christ, [12]having been buried with him in baptism, in which you
were also raised with him through your faith in the working of God, who raised
him from the dead.

[13]When you were dead in your sins and in the uncircumcision of your flesh,
God made you[d] alive with Christ. He forgave us all our sins, [14]having canceled the
charge of our legal indebtedness, which stood against us and condemned us; he
has taken it away, nailing it to the cross. [15]And having disarmed the powers and authorities, he made a public spectacle of them, triumphing over them by the cross.[e]

Freedom From Human Rules

[16]Therefore do not let anyone judge you by what you eat or drink, or with regard to a religious festival, a New Moon celebration or a Sabbath day. [17]These are
a shadow of the things that were to come; the reality, however, is found in Christ.
[18]Do not let anyone who delights in false humility and the worship of angels dis-
qualify you. Such a person also goes into great detail about what they have seen;
they are puffed up with idle notions by their unspiritual mind. [19]They have lost
connection with the head, from whom the whole body, supported and held together by its ligaments and sinews, grows as God causes it to grow.

[20]Since you died with Christ to the elemental spiritual forces of this world,
why, as though you still belonged to the world, do you submit to its rules: [21]"Do
not handle! Do not taste! Do not touch!"? [22]These rules, which have to do with
things that are all destined to perish with use, are based on merely human
commands and teachings. [23]Such regulations indeed have an appearance of
wisdom, with their self-imposed worship, their false humility and their harsh
treatment of the body, but they lack any value in restraining sensual indulgence.

[a] *8* Or *the basic principles*; also in verse 20 [b] *11* In contexts like this, the Greek word for *flesh* (*sarx*) refers to the sinful state of human beings, often presented as a power in opposition to the Spirit; also in verse 13. [c] *11* Or *put off in the circumcision of* [d] *13* Some manuscripts *us* [e] *15* Or *them in him*

Living as Those Made Alive in Christ

3 Since, then, you have been raised with Christ, set your hearts on things above, where Christ is, seated at the right hand of God. 2Set your minds on things above, not on earthly things. 3For you died, and your life is now hidden with Christ in God. 4When Christ, who is your[a] life, appears, then you also will appear with him in glory.

5Put to death, therefore, whatever belongs to your earthly nature: sexual immorality, impurity, lust, evil desires and greed, which is idolatry. 6Because of these, the wrath of God is coming.[b] 7You used to walk in these ways, in the life you once lived. 8But now you must also rid yourselves of all such things as these: anger, rage, malice, slander, and filthy language from your lips. 9Do not lie to each other, since you have taken off your old self with its practices 10and have put on the new self, which is being renewed in knowledge in the image of its Creator. 11Here there is no Gentile or Jew, circumcised or uncircumcised, barbarian, Scythian, slave or free, but Christ is all, and is in all.

12Therefore, as God's chosen people, holy and dearly loved, clothe yourselves with compassion, kindness, humility, gentleness and patience. 13Bear with each other and forgive one another if any of you has a grievance against someone. Forgive as the Lord forgave you. 14And over all these virtues put on love, which binds them all together in perfect unity.

15Let the peace of Christ rule in your hearts, since as members of one body you were called to peace. And be thankful. 16Let the message of Christ dwell among you richly as you teach and admonish one another with all wisdom through psalms, hymns, and songs from the Spirit, singing to God with gratitude in your hearts. 17And whatever you do, whether in word or deed, do it all in the name of the Lord Jesus, giving thanks to God the Father through him.

Instructions for Christian Households

18Wives, submit yourselves to your husbands, as is fitting in the Lord.

19Husbands, love your wives and do not be harsh with them.

20Children, obey your parents in everything, for this pleases the Lord.

21Fathers,[c] do not embitter your children, or they will become discouraged.

22Slaves, obey your earthly masters in everything; and do it, not only when their eye is on you and to curry their favor, but with sincerity of heart and reverence for the Lord. 23Whatever you do, work at it with all your heart, as working for the Lord, not for human masters, 24since you know that you will receive an inheritance from the Lord as a reward. It is the Lord Christ you are serving. 25Anyone who does wrong will be repaid for their wrongs, and there is no favoritism.

4 Masters, provide your slaves with what is right and fair, because you know that you also have a Master in heaven.

Further Instructions

2Devote yourselves to prayer, being watchful and thankful. 3And pray for us, too, that God may open a door for our message, so that we may proclaim the mystery of Christ, for which I am in chains. 4Pray that I may proclaim it clearly, as I should. 5Be wise in the way you act toward outsiders; make the most of every opportunity. 6Let your conversation be always full of grace, seasoned with salt, so that you may know how to answer everyone.

Final Greetings

7Tychicus will tell you all the news about me. He is a dear brother, a faithful minister and fellow servant[d] in the Lord. 8I am sending him to you for the express purpose that you may know about our[e] circumstances and that he may

[a] 4 Some manuscripts *our* [b] 6 Some early manuscripts *coming on those who are disobedient* [c] 21 Or *Parents* [d] 7 Or *slave*; also in verse 12 [e] 8 Some manuscripts *that he may know about your*

COLOSSIANS 4:2–6

DEVOTED TO PRAYER

Almost every Christian knows that prayer is important. Even many unbelievers think prayer is a good thing. Devoting oneself to prayer, however, is a challenge for many people. Nevertheless, this is exactly what Paul instructed the church at Colossae to do as he concluded his letter. Paul gave an immediate explanation of what he meant by "devote yourselves to prayer," when he followed up with "being watchful and thankful" (v. 2). Remaining watchful for the "flaming arrows of the evil one" (Eph 6:16) keeps believers in a posture of prayerful dependence upon God.

Paul then directed the church to pray for his proclamation of Jesus. Specifically, he needed opportunities (open doors) and God's help in making sure he proclaimed the mystery of Jesus with clarity.

Jesus is the very One who makes prayer possible. Jesus paved the way for prayer to be possible by removing the sin barrier between God and humanity through his death, burial and resurrection. The author of Hebrews said it this way: "Since we have a great priest over the house of God, let us draw near to God with a sincere heart and with the full assurance that faith brings, having our hearts sprinkled to cleanse us from a guilty conscience and having our bodies washed with pure water" (Heb 10:21–22). Jesus makes prayer possible, allowing Christians to draw near to God with the confidence that God will hear and act according to his will.

RENEWAL IN THE IMAGE OF GOD

Humanity has been blessed with the unique privilege of being created in the image of God. People alone enjoy the special blessing of reflecting the image of God like a mirror. Unfortunately, sin has changed the reflection of God in humanity, twisting and distorting his reflection like a funhouse mirror. His image is still there, yet it is not in focus. Indeed, sin has darkened the hearts and minds of all of humanity. Out of these darkened hearts flow all kinds of sins: "sexual immorality, impurity, lust, evil desires and greed, which is idolatry ... anger, rage, malice, slander, and filthy language" (vv. 5,8). Paul warned that the wrath of God is coming because of sins like these. But Jesus changes everything.

Jesus offers forgiveness of sin and the removal of God's wrath. In his grace, God sent Jesus to rescue people from their sin. When people become believers by repenting of their sin and trusting in Jesus Christ, God's Spirit comes to dwell inside them. The Holy Spirit then begins to transform believers from the inside out, helping them to repent of further sin and to walk in holiness. Paul described these radical changes as "putting to death" the old self and "putting on" the new self. The old self consists of the attitudes and lifestyles that are governed by sin. The new self consists of the new attitude and lifestyle that are governed by Jesus and empowered by the indwelling of the Holy Spirit. The result of putting off the old self and putting on the new self is a renewed reflection of the image of God. As believers are increasingly renewed in the image of God, the beauty, love and holiness of God shines through and becomes visible to other people.

Essentially, Paul's challenge to Christians is to become who they are. Paul wrote, "Therefore, if anyone is in Christ, the new creation has come: The old has gone, the new is here!" (2Co 5:17). For the Christian, recognizing that Jesus has already made him or her new is foundational to the daily process of putting on the new self.

encourage your hearts. [9]He is coming with Onesimus, our faithful and dear
brother, who is one of you. They will tell you everything that is happening here.

[10]My fellow prisoner Aristarchus sends you his greetings, as does Mark, the
cousin of Barnabas. (You have received instructions about him; if he comes to
you, welcome him.) [11]Jesus, who is called Justus, also sends greetings. These
are the only Jews[a] among my co-workers for the kingdom of God, and they have
proved a comfort to me. [12]Epaphras, who is one of you and a servant of Christ
Jesus, sends greetings. He is always wrestling in prayer for you, that you may
stand firm in all the will of God, mature and fully assured. [13]I vouch for him that
he is working hard for you and for those at Laodicea and Hierapolis. [14]Our dear
friend Luke, the doctor, and Demas send greetings. [15]Give my greetings to the
brothers and sisters at Laodicea, and to Nympha and the church in her house.

[16]After this letter has been read to you, see that it is also read in the church of
the Laodiceans and that you in turn read the letter from Laodicea.

[17]Tell Archippus: "See to it that you complete the ministry you have received
in the Lord."

[18]I, Paul, write this greeting in my own hand. Remember my chains. Grace
be with you.

---

[a] *11* Greek *only ones of the circumcision group*

JESUS: OUR SOURCE OF COMFORT

1 THESSALONIANS

1 THESSALONIANS

THESSALONIAN CHURCH IS STARTED	PAUL WRITES 1 THESSALONIANS	PAUL MARTYRED IN ROME
c. AD 51	*c. AD 51*	*c. AD 67 – 68*

Lives were changed everywhere the gospel message was proclaimed. Paul and Silas saw many converted to faith in Jesus Christ in Thessalonica, a wealthy trade center on the continent of Europe. The church that developed from these converts was filled with young believers who needed grounding in their newly formed faith. After leaving Thessalonica, Paul sent his protégé Timothy back to the church to assess their health and spiritual vitality. Timothy rejoined Paul in Corinth and brought with him an encouraging report about the faithfulness of the church, even in the face of continued persecution. As with all new converts, however, they were filled with questions concerning the nature of the gospel and particularly the second coming of Jesus. Paul wrote his first letter to the church to answer these questions and to encourage the church to continue to grow, mature and persevere as they await the coming of Christ.

The hope in Christ's return intensified due to the death of a number of believers in the church. Some may have believed that Jesus would return during their lifetimes and usher in his full and total reign on earth. This had not yet happened, and some in the church had begun to doubt that it would.

Paul wrote to encourage the church that they should not be dismayed by the delay in Christ's second coming. He will return, as he had promised; he will give his people renewed, resurrected bodies, and they will reign with him forever (4:13 – 18). This promise was meant to comfort the church in their mourning and motivate them to keep watch for his return (5:1 – 11).

Paul exhorts the church to live godly lives in the meantime, as they anticipate this coming. They should not lose heart in light of the persecution they were facing or doubt the truthfulness of Paul's message because of the influence of false teachers. The church must persevere, knowing that nothing they face in this world can take away the hope they have in Christ. The One who made these promises is faithful, as he has been throughout history, and he will surely accomplish all that he sets out to do (5:24).

GIVE THANKS IN ALL CIRCUMSTANCES; FOR THIS IS GOD'S WILL FOR YOU IN CHRIST JESUS.

---

1 Thessalonians 5:18

1 THESSALONIANS

1 Paul, Silas[a] and Timothy,

To the church of the Thessalonians in God the Father and the Lord Jesus Christ:

Grace and peace to you.

Thanksgiving for the Thessalonians' Faith

2We always thank God for all of you and continually mention you in our prayers. 3We remember before our God and Father your work produced by faith, your labor prompted by love, and your endurance inspired by hope in our Lord Jesus Christ.

4For we know, brothers and sisters[b] loved by God, that he has chosen you, 5because our gospel came to you not simply with words but also with power, with the Holy Spirit and deep conviction. You know how we lived among you for your sake. 6You became imitators of us and of the Lord, for you welcomed the message in the midst of severe suffering with the joy given by the Holy Spirit. 7And so you became a model to all the believers in Macedonia and Achaia. 8The Lord's message rang out from you not only in Macedonia and Achaia — your faith in God has become known everywhere. Therefore we do not need to say anything about it, 9for they themselves report what kind of reception you gave us. They tell how you turned to God from idols to serve the living and true God, 10and to wait for his Son from heaven, whom he raised from the dead — Jesus, who rescues us from the coming wrath.

Paul's Ministry in Thessalonica

2 You know, brothers and sisters, that our visit to you was not without results. 2We had previously suffered and been treated outrageously in Philippi, as you know, but with the help of our God we dared to tell you his gospel in the face of strong opposition. 3For the appeal we make does not spring from error or impure motives, nor are we trying to trick you. 4On the contrary, we speak as those approved by God to be entrusted with the gospel. We are not trying to please people but God, who tests our hearts. 5You know we never used flattery, nor did we put on a mask to cover up greed — God is our witness. 6We were not looking for praise from people, not from you or anyone else, even though as apostles of Christ we could have asserted our authority. 7Instead, we were like young children[c] among you.

Just as a nursing mother cares for her children, 8so we cared for you. Because we loved you so much, we were delighted to share with you not only the gospel of God but our lives as well. 9Surely you remember, brothers and sisters, our toil and hardship; we worked night and day in order not to be a burden to anyone while we preached the gospel of God to you. 10You are witnesses, and so is God, of how holy, righteous and blameless we were among you who believed. 11For you know that we dealt with each of you as a father deals with his own children, 12encouraging, comforting and urging you to live lives worthy of God, who calls you into his kingdom and glory.

13And we also thank God continually because, when you received the word of God, which you heard from us, you accepted it not as a human word, but as it

---

1 THESSALONIANS 1:10

HOPE

The people to whom Paul wrote as part of the church in Thessalonica were new followers of Jesus. They had many questions and challenges in the midst of severe opposition from the Jews. Therefore it seems natural that Paul would inject hope into every chapter of 1 Thessalonians. In much of the book, Jesus is pictured as the hope of salvation — both for this life and when he returns to earth. This message was especially vital to this audience since the gospel originally came to them amidst great suffering and affliction (1Th 1:6).

Paul encouraged the Thessalonians to hope, or "wait for" Jesus, who would rescue them from the coming wrath (v. 10). This phrase "wait for" implies looking forward, eagerly and expectantly, to the return of the Lord. This hope is a confident waiting and not a wishful thinking. Those who believe in and follow Christ can face life confidently despite their surrounding circumstances, and they can most assuredly wait in joyful expectation for his second coming.

---

[a] *1* Greek *Silvanus,* a variant of *Silas* [b] *4* The Greek word for *brothers and sisters* (*adelphoi*) refers here to believers, both men and women, as part of God's family; also in 2:1, 9, 14, 17; 3:7; 4:1, 10, 13; 5:1, 4, 12, 14, 25, 27. [c] *7* Some manuscripts *were gentle*

SUFFERING

Paul was no stranger to trouble and suffering. He experienced escape after harrowing escape (2Co 11:23). He was beaten, imprisoned, shipwrecked, stoned and left for dead (Ac 14:19; 2Co 11:24 – 27). In addition to the physical suffering he faced, he carried the emotional strain and stress of caring for the churches he planted (2Co 11:28). Similarly, he and Timothy faced turbulent opposition from the Jews when they began to preach the gospel message to the Thessalonians. This came on the heels of the mistreatment that they had endured at Philippi. Yet Paul said their work with this church was not in vain (1Th 2:1). Paul's life exemplifies following God in hard times and in "the face of strong opposition" (v. 2).

Jesus himself said, "In this world you will have trouble. But take heart! I have overcome the world" (Jn 16:33). Jesus taught that any who would be his disciples would have to "deny themselves and take up their cross daily and follow me" (Lk 9:23). It should be no surprise to the disciple of Christ when he or she experiences resistance, pressure, trials or suffering as he or she spiritually matures. But the glorious, and seemingly paradoxical, result of this suffering is "pure joy" (Jas 1:2). The Thessalonians experienced this firsthand as they had received the gospel with great joy amidst "severe suffering" (1Th 1:6). Their joyful faith was contagious. Their steadfast faith in the midst of suffering made them an example to all the believers and had "become known everywhere" (1:8).

The Christ-follower is called to this "pure joy" faith. It is in looking to Jesus, "the pioneer and perfecter of faith," that the Christian can rest in times of trouble and hardship, because "for the joy set before [Jesus], he endured the cross" (Heb 12:2). In the same way, because we have eternal life in Christ, we can endure our "light and momentary troubles," trusting that they are achieving "an eternal glory that far outweighs them all" (2Co 4:17). Jesus is a beacon of hope and a light in the midst of trial and suffering; Christ is alive and has defeated death through his own suffering, bringing peace both now and forever and eternal victory to those who follow him.

actually is, the word of God, which is indeed at work in you who believe. 14For you,
brothers and sisters, became imitators of God's churches in Judea, which are in
Christ Jesus: You suffered from your own people the same things those churches
suffered from the Jews 15who killed the Lord Jesus and the prophets and also drove
us out. They displease God and are hostile to everyone 16in their effort to keep us
from speaking to the Gentiles so that they may be saved. In this way they always
heap up their sins to the limit. The wrath of God has come upon them at last.[a]

Paul's Longing to See the Thessalonians

17But, brothers and sisters, when we were orphaned by being separated from
you for a short time (in person, not in thought), out of our intense longing we
made every effort to see you. 18For we wanted to come to you — certainly I, Paul,
did, again and again — but Satan blocked our way. 19For what is our hope, our
joy, or the crown in which we will glory in the presence of our Lord Jesus when
he comes? Is it not you? 20Indeed, you are our glory and joy.

3 So when we could stand it no longer, we thought it best to be left by ourselves
in Athens. 2We sent Timothy, who is our brother and co-worker in God's service in spreading the gospel of Christ, to strengthen and encourage you in your
faith, 3so that no one would be unsettled by these trials. For you know quite well
that we are destined for them. 4In fact, when we were with you, we kept telling
you that we would be persecuted. And it turned out that way, as you well know.
5For this reason, when I could stand it no longer, I sent to find out about your
faith. I was afraid that in some way the tempter had tempted you and that our
labors might have been in vain.

Timothy's Encouraging Report

6But Timothy has just now come to us from you and has brought good news
about your faith and love. He has told us that you always have pleasant memories
of us and that you long to see us, just as we also long to see you. 7Therefore, brothers and sisters, in all our distress and persecution we were encouraged about you
because of your faith. 8For now we really live, since you are standing firm in the
Lord. 9How can we thank God enough for you in return for all the joy we have in
the presence of our God because of you? 10Night and day we pray most earnestly
that we may see you again and supply what is lacking in your faith.

11Now may our God and Father himself and our Lord Jesus clear the way for
us to come to you. 12May the Lord make your love increase and overflow for each
other and for everyone else, just as ours does for you. 13May he strengthen your
hearts so that you will be blameless and holy in the presence of our God and Father when our Lord Jesus comes with all his holy ones.

Living to Please God

4 As for other matters, brothers and sisters, we instructed you how to live in
order to please God, as in fact you are living. Now we ask you and urge you
in the Lord Jesus to do this more and more. 2For you know what instructions we
gave you by the authority of the Lord Jesus.

3It is God's will that you should be sanctified: that you should avoid sexual immorality; 4that each of you should learn to control your own body[b] in a way that
is holy and honorable, 5not in passionate lust like the pagans, who do not know
God; 6and that in this matter no one should wrong or take advantage of a brother
or sister.[c] The Lord will punish all those who commit such sins, as we told you
and warned you before. 7For God did not call us to be impure, but to live a holy
life. 8Therefore, anyone who rejects this instruction does not reject a human being but God, the very God who gives you his Holy Spirit.

[a] 16 Or *them fully* [b] 4 Or *learn to live with your own wife*; or *learn to acquire a wife*
[c] 6 The Greek word for *brother or sister* (*adelphos*) refers here to a believer, whether man or woman, as part of God's family.

1 THESSALONIANS 4:3 – 8

SANCTIFICATION

Sanctification is simply the process of becoming more like God. Believers become more like him in holiness out of gratitude to God for what he's done in their lives. The Greek word "sanctify" means "to set apart" for God's special plans. Paul urged the new believers in Thessalonica to live this kind of life, outlining that it was God's will for them to walk with Jesus, thus pleasing God with their lives (1Th 4:1,3). He expressed that holy living is very practical and that rejecting the instruction of God brings consequences (v. 8). God has called his people to make daily choices through a different lens: the lens of gospel truth.

When someone puts their faith in Christ, he or she has been sanctified, or "made holy" through the sacrifice of Jesus Christ once and for all (Heb 10:10). Sin is completely wiped away, death is defeated and eternal life is at hand. This is the good news! At the same time, the believer enters into a lifelong process of being purified and becoming more like God through the power of the Holy Spirit (1Th 4:8). Paul echoes this reality, declaring that God would sanctify the Thessalonians "through and through," and keep them "blameless at the coming of our Lord Jesus Christ" (1Th 5:23).

Followers of Jesus today can hold on to that promise, for "the one who calls you is faithful, and he will do it" (1Th 5:24).

9Now about your love for one another we do not need to write to you, for you
yourselves have been taught by God to love each other. 10And in fact, you do love
all of God's family throughout Macedonia. Yet we urge you, brothers and sisters,
to do so more and more, 11and to make it your ambition to lead a quiet life: You
should mind your own business and work with your hands, just as we told you,
12so that your daily life may win the respect of outsiders and so that you will not
be dependent on anybody.

Believers Who Have Died

13Brothers and sisters, we do not want you to be uninformed about those who
sleep in death, so that you do not grieve like the rest of mankind, who have no
hope. 14For we believe that Jesus died and rose again, and so we believe that God
will bring with Jesus those who have fallen asleep in him. 15According to the
Lord's word, we tell you that we who are still alive, who are left until the coming
of the Lord, will certainly not precede those who have fallen asleep. 16For the
Lord himself will come down from heaven, with a loud command, with the voice
of the archangel and with the trumpet call of God, and the dead in Christ will
rise first. 17After that, we who are still alive and are left will be caught up together
with them in the clouds to meet the Lord in the air. And so we will be with the
Lord forever. 18Therefore encourage one another with these words.

The Day of the Lord

5 Now, brothers and sisters, about times and dates we do not need to write to
you, 2for you know very well that the day of the Lord will come like a thief in
the night. 3While people are saying, "Peace and safety," destruction will come on
them suddenly, as labor pains on a pregnant woman, and they will not escape.
4But you, brothers and sisters, are not in darkness so that this day should surprise you like a thief. 5You are all children of the light and children of the day.
We do not belong to the night or to the darkness. 6So then, let us not be like others, who are asleep, but let us be awake and sober. 7For those who sleep, sleep at
night, and those who get drunk, get drunk at night. 8But since we belong to the
day, let us be sober, putting on faith and love as a breastplate, and the hope of
salvation as a helmet. 9For God did not appoint us to suffer wrath but to receive
salvation through our Lord Jesus Christ. 10He died for us so that, whether we are
awake or asleep, we may live together with him. 11Therefore encourage one another and build each other up, just as in fact you are doing.

Final Instructions

12Now we ask you, brothers and sisters, to acknowledge those who work hard
among you, who care for you in the Lord and who admonish you. 13Hold them in
the highest regard in love because of their work. Live in peace with each other.
14And we urge you, brothers and sisters, warn those who are idle and disruptive,
encourage the disheartened, help the weak, be patient with everyone. 15Make
sure that nobody pays back wrong for wrong, but always strive to do what is good
for each other and for everyone else.
16Rejoice always, 17pray continually, 18give thanks in all circumstances; for
this is God's will for you in Christ Jesus.
19Do not quench the Spirit. 20Do not treat prophecies with contempt 21but test
them all; hold on to what is good, 22reject every kind of evil.
23May God himself, the God of peace, sanctify you through and through. May
your whole spirit, soul and body be kept blameless at the coming of our Lord
Jesus Christ. 24The one who calls you is faithful, and he will do it.

25Brothers and sisters, pray for us. 26Greet all God's people with a holy kiss. 27I
charge you before the Lord to have this letter read to all the brothers and sisters.
28The grace of our Lord Jesus Christ be with you.

1 THESSALONIANS 5:1–8

THIEF IN THE NIGHT

In the Old Testament, the prophets spoke repeatedly of a "day of the LORD" which was to be a day of much judgment, yet also a day of blessing and restoration for the people of God (Joel 2:28; 3:14,18). Paul refers to this "day of the Lord" as the day Jesus returns and describes it as one that will come "like a thief in the night" (1Th 5:2). Jesus himself made clear that no one knows the time or date, "not even the angels in heaven, nor the Son, but only the Father" (Mt 24:36).

It is not for believers to know the hour or day that Jesus will come again, but rather for them to be awake and ready at any time (1Th 5:6). Paul describes Christ-followers as those who "belong to the day" as a stark contrast to the night, where people do sinful things and are unaware of Christ and his pending return (vv. 5,8). The Jesus-follower, therefore, should be living with eyes wide open to the things of God, full of faith, love and the hope of salvation — not caught off guard when Jesus returns.

JESUS: OUR COMING KING

2 THESSALONIANS

2 THESSALONIANS

THESSALONIAN CHURCH IS STARTED	PAUL WRITES 1 THESSALONIANS	PAUL WRITES 2 THESSALONIANS
c. AD 51	*c. AD 51*	*c. AD 51 – 52*

The day of the Lord's return will come suddenly (1Th 5:2). This reality was meant to encourage the church to persevere in the face of suffering and not lose heart when members of the church died prior to Christ's return.

Apparently, some in the church twisted Paul's words and distorted the truthfulness of his message. False teachers had deceived the church into believing that the day of the Lord was already at hand. As a result, some in the church had stopped working altogether and were waiting passively for Christ's return.

Paul wrote his second letter to counter this theology and compel the church to active obedience as they wait for the day of the Lord. While Christ will return, his second coming will be preceded by a number of signs that had not yet taken place (2Th 2:1 – 12). Therefore, the church should continue to anticipate Christ's coming, though there would be an intervening period of time before the end would come.

The faithfulness of God would guard his people during this time of lawlessness that would proceed Christ's second coming. God had done the work to save his people, and he would continue to demonstrate his faithfulness by protecting them from the evil one. Thus, the church could live with confidence, knowing that while suffering and pain awaited, God's purposes would ultimately prevail.

This confidence should embolden the church to steward their gifts and the time allotted to them to bring God glory. Rather than squandering the days in idleness, God's people should redeem the time in prayerfulness, worship and meaningful service to one another.

They should not grow weary in these good works because they know that God has called them by his grace, transformed them by his Spirit and entrusted them with a mission to declare his glory to all mankind. Paul challenged the church to follow his model of missionary zeal, passionate proclamation and fervent prayer in the time between the first and second coming of Christ. In so doing, they would be found faithful on that glorious day when Christ fulfills his promise to come again and, with his people, rule and reign over a new heaven and new earth where righteousness dwells forever.

ON THE DAY HE COMES TO BE GLORIFIED IN HIS HOLY PEOPLE AND TO BE MARVELED AT AMONG ALL THOSE WHO HAVE BELIEVED. THIS INCLUDES YOU, BECAUSE YOU BELIEVED OUR TESTIMONY TO YOU.

---

2 Thessalonians 1:10

2 THESSALONIANS

2 THESSALONIANS 1:4–12

THE NAME OF JESUS GLORIFIED IN YOU

Steeped in suffering and opposition, the Thessalonians were steadfast in their faith as they persevered through the trials they encountered (vv. 4–5). It is against this backdrop that Paul wrote his second letter to the believers in Thessalonica. Paul reminded the church that God is triumphant over evil, and that their faith in him and obedience to Jesus is more than enough for them to hold on to, even and especially in times of trouble (vv. 6–10). In the midst of great trial, their enduring trust in Jesus demonstrated the hope they had in Christ.

The same holds true for Christians today. The watching world should see in Christians a joyful and compelling hope, even in the midst of trials. God's power in each believer is at work in both good and bad circumstances, as "in all things God works for the good of those who love him" (Ro 8:28). God has called, justified and glorified every Christian through Christ (Ro 8:30). Thus, in every season, circumstance and relationship, Christ-followers are enabled to love and serve those around them. Through the Holy Spirit's power, the believer can live a life "worthy of his calling": a life that makes a difference for the kingdom and magnifies Jesus' name (2Th 1:11).

1 Paul, Silas[a] and Timothy,

To the church of the Thessalonians in God our Father and the Lord Jesus Christ:

2 Grace and peace to you from God the Father and the Lord Jesus Christ.

Thanksgiving and Prayer

3 We ought always to thank God for you, brothers and sisters,[b] and rightly so, because your faith is growing more and more, and the love all of you have for one another is increasing. 4 Therefore, among God's churches we boast about your perseverance and faith in all the persecutions and trials you are enduring.

5 All this is evidence that God's judgment is right, and as a result you will be counted worthy of the kingdom of God, for which you are suffering. 6 God is just: He will pay back trouble to those who trouble you 7 and give relief to you who are troubled, and to us as well. This will happen when the Lord Jesus is revealed from heaven in blazing fire with his powerful angels. 8 He will punish those who do not know God and do not obey the gospel of our Lord Jesus. 9 They will be punished with everlasting destruction and shut out from the presence of the Lord and from the glory of his might 10 on the day he comes to be glorified in his holy people and to be marveled at among all those who have believed. This includes you, because you believed our testimony to you.

11 With this in mind, we constantly pray for you, that our God may make you worthy of his calling, and that by his power he may bring to fruition your every desire for goodness and your every deed prompted by faith. 12 We pray this so that the name of our Lord Jesus may be glorified in you, and you in him, according to the grace of our God and the Lord Jesus Christ.[c]

The Man of Lawlessness

2 Concerning the coming of our Lord Jesus Christ and our being gathered to him, we ask you, brothers and sisters, 2 not to become easily unsettled or alarmed by the teaching allegedly from us—whether by a prophecy or by word of mouth or by letter—asserting that the day of the Lord has already come. 3 Don't let anyone deceive you in any way, for that day will not come until the rebellion occurs and the man of lawlessness[d] is revealed, the man doomed to destruction. 4 He will oppose and will exalt himself over everything that is called God or is worshiped, so that he sets himself up in God's temple, proclaiming himself to be God.

5 Don't you remember that when I was with you I used to tell you these things? 6 And now you know what is holding him back, so that he may be revealed at the proper time. 7 For the secret power of lawlessness is already at work; but the one who now holds it back will continue to do so till he is taken out of the way. 8 And then the lawless one will be revealed, whom the Lord Jesus will overthrow with the breath of his mouth and destroy by the splendor of his coming. 9 The coming of the lawless one will be in accordance with how Satan works. He will use all sorts of displays of power through signs and wonders that serve the lie, 10 and all the ways that wickedness deceives those who are perishing. They perish because they refused to love the truth and so be saved. 11 For this reason God sends

[a] *1* Greek *Silvanus,* a variant of *Silas* [b] *3* The Greek word for *brothers and sisters* (*adelphoi*) refers here to believers, both men and women, as part of God's family; also in 2:1, 13, 15; 3:1, 6, 13. [c] *12* Or *God and Lord, Jesus Christ* [d] *3* Some manuscripts *sin*

BUSY WAITING

How is the Christian to live until Jesus returns? This question has confronted every generation of Jesus' followers. Throughout history some people have lived as they please, as though Christ will not return. Others have tried to figure out the date and time of Jesus' coming, even though Scripture says that day will come "like a thief in the night" (1Th 5:2), and no one will "know the day or the hour" (Mt 25:13). Believers in Christ are to live expecting that he will return at any time, never tiring of doing good works, continually abiding in Christ and in God's purpose for their lives (Gal 6:9).

In the second letter to the believers at Thessalonica, Paul addressed his young church and encouraged them to stand firm by living a life "worthy of his calling" that they had received (2Th 1:11). Some of the believers had become lazy "busybodies" (3:11), and he strongly warned the church against this kind of idle and disruptive behavior (3:6,11,14). Paul reminded them that they weren't called to simply wait around for Jesus' return or to take advantage of their fellow Christians in the meantime. Paul knew that such people could easily hide under a guise of spirituality or a misguided logic that assumed if Christ was coming back at any moment, working hard was not necessary. Paul exhorted them, rather, to "settle down," "earn the food they eat" and "never tire of doing what is good" (3:12 – 13).

Jesus taught a parable about ten virgins who were to put oil in their lamps and wait for the return of the bridegroom (Mt 25:1 – 13). Five of them were wise, keeping enough oil on hand to light their lamps at any time; five were foolish, not possessing enough oil to keep their lamps lit when the bridegroom arrived (Mt 25:2,7 – 9). Jesus commanded those listening to keep watch since they didn't know the day or hour of his return (Mt 25:13).

Followers of Jesus are to have their "oil" with them at all times; in other words, they are to be ready, keeping busy with the works prepared in advance for them (Eph 2:10). They are to work hard and ardently pursue the things of God, building his kingdom and bringing heaven to earth (Mt 6:10). Although Christians are still awaiting the return of Christ, they are to be "busy waiting," not tiring in doing good works and holding fast to the hope of Christ's return.

them a powerful delusion so that they will believe the lie [12]and so that all will be condemned who have not believed the truth but have delighted in wickedness.

Stand Firm

[13]But we ought always to thank God for you, brothers and sisters loved by the Lord, because God chose you as firstfruits[a] to be saved through the sanctifying work of the Spirit and through belief in the truth. [14]He called you to this through our gospel, that you might share in the glory of our Lord Jesus Christ.

[15]So then, brothers and sisters, stand firm and hold fast to the teachings[b] we passed on to you, whether by word of mouth or by letter.

[16]May our Lord Jesus Christ himself and God our Father, who loved us and by his grace gave us eternal encouragement and good hope, [17]encourage your hearts and strengthen you in every good deed and word.

Request for Prayer

3 As for other matters, brothers and sisters, pray for us that the message of the Lord may spread rapidly and be honored, just as it was with you. [2]And pray that we may be delivered from wicked and evil people, for not everyone has faith. [3]But the Lord is faithful, and he will strengthen you and protect you from the evil one. [4]We have confidence in the Lord that you are doing and will continue to do the things we command. [5]May the Lord direct your hearts into God's love and Christ's perseverance.

Warning Against Idleness

[6]In the name of the Lord Jesus Christ, we command you, brothers and sisters, to keep away from every believer who is idle and disruptive and does not live according to the teaching[c] you received from us. [7]For you yourselves know how you ought to follow our example. We were not idle when we were with you, [8]nor did we eat anyone's food without paying for it. On the contrary, we worked night and day, laboring and toiling so that we would not be a burden to any of you. [9]We did this, not because we do not have the right to such help, but in order to offer ourselves as a model for you to imitate. [10]For even when we were with you, we gave you this rule: "The one who is unwilling to work shall not eat."

[11]We hear that some among you are idle and disruptive. They are not busy; they are busybodies. [12]Such people we command and urge in the Lord Jesus Christ to settle down and earn the food they eat. [13]And as for you, brothers and sisters, never tire of doing what is good.

[14]Take special note of anyone who does not obey our instruction in this letter. Do not associate with them, in order that they may feel ashamed. [15]Yet do not regard them as an enemy, but warn them as you would a fellow believer.

Final Greetings

[16]Now may the Lord of peace himself give you peace at all times and in every way. The Lord be with all of you.

[17]I, Paul, write this greeting in my own hand, which is the distinguishing mark in all my letters. This is how I write.

[18]The grace of our Lord Jesus Christ be with you all.

---

[a] *13* Some manuscripts *because from the beginning God chose you* [b] *15* Or *traditions*
[c] *6* Or *tradition*

JESUS: OUR ONE MEDIATOR

1 TIMOTHY

1 TIMOTHY

TIMOTHY JOINS PAUL'S SECOND JOURNEY	TIMOTHY JOINS PAUL'S THIRD JOURNEY	PAUL IN ROME, WRITES 1 TIMOTHY
c. AD 50	*c. AD 54*	*c. AD 62*

Paul lived the message he proclaimed. God radically saved Paul and called him to spread God's message to those who had not yet heard it. Along the way, Paul saw many come to saving faith in Jesus and was a vital catalyst for the planting of churches throughout Asia Minor. Timothy was one such convert who came to faith during Paul's first missionary journey. The strong paternal language Paul uses to speak of Timothy leads many to surmise that Timothy was converted directly under Paul's teaching.

Whatever the case, Timothy's newfound faith was evident to those in his hometown, and when Paul returned to the region, Timothy was a clear choice to take along for his ongoing missionary labors. For many years, Timothy accompanied Paul in his travels — often venturing out on his own to work among the churches that Paul could not visit himself. Paul's trust in Timothy allowed him to send him to difficult churches in the hopes that Timothy could root the believers there in gospel fidelity and faithful worship.

The church in Ephesus was one such church. The church faced numerous threats in the forms of satanic attack, false teaching, impoverished leadership and internal divisiveness. Timothy was sent by Paul to lead the church during a critical season in the life of the newly formed congregation.

Paul wrote 1 Timothy to his young protégé from Macedonia in an effort to encourage him in this daunting work. He reminded Timothy of his great love for him and the clear call God had placed on Timothy's life. Now, in Ephesus, Timothy should apply theological acumen and the leadership savvy he had observed from Paul through the years. Paul gave instructions for the appointment of godly leaders (3:1 – 13) and conduct in Christian worship (3:15). Timothy would also have to consider how to provide care for church members, such as widows who would need special consideration by the leaders of the church (5:1 – 16).

While Timothy was a young pastor and the leadership of the church was complex, Paul reminded Timothy that his confidence was not in his wisdom or ability but in the Lord. He must not let others look down on him because of his age, but set an example to others for godly living and maturity (4:12). He could do this because of Jesus, who served as his mediator and advocate with the Father (2:5). What Timothy lacked in age and experience, he could find in dependence on the wisdom that comes from God above.

FOR THERE IS ONE GOD AND ONE MEDIATOR BETWEEN GOD AND MANKIND, THE MAN CHRIST JESUS.

---

1 Timothy 2:5

1 TIMOTHY

1 TIMOTHY 1:12–17

THE WORST SINNER

Although he was one of the most devout and influential Christians to ever live, Paul described himself as "the worst" of sinners. While this statement might at first appear hyperbolic, Paul believed it to be an accurate self-assessment because he knew his own heart. Paul knew not only every sinful action he had committed, but also his sinful thoughts and motivations that were hidden from everyone else. When he examined himself, he saw the depths of his personal battle with sin (Ro 7:13–25).

Likewise, if we are honest with ourselves, we will assess our lives the same way: we are the worst of sinners. While we might make a futile guess at the sinful thoughts and motivations in others, we know the depths of our own sinful heart. Jesus referenced this reality when he told his hearers to mind the plank in their own eye before removing the speck of sawdust in another's (Mt 7:3).

Yet, the recognition of this truth should not lead to depression but worship. Jesus came to seek and save the lost; Paul knew this meant that Jesus came to save *him*. This fueled his passionate desire to spend his life spreading the gospel. In the same way, our honest recognition of the depths of our own sinfulness should lead us to praise Jesus for the mercy he has shown us. And as a gesture of gratitude for our salvation, we are to share this message of grace with all who will listen, just as Paul did.

1 Paul, an apostle of Christ Jesus by the command of God our Savior and of
Christ Jesus our hope,

[2]To Timothy my true son in the faith:

Grace, mercy and peace from God the Father and Christ Jesus our Lord.

Timothy Charged to Oppose False Teachers

[3]As I urged you when I went into Macedonia, stay there in Ephesus so that you
may command certain people not to teach false doctrines any longer [4]or to devote themselves to myths and endless genealogies. Such things promote contro-
versial speculations rather than advancing God's work—which is by faith. [5]The
goal of this command is love, which comes from a pure heart and a good conscience and a sincere faith. [6]Some have departed from these and have turned
to meaningless talk. [7]They want to be teachers of the law, but they do not know
what they are talking about or what they so confidently affirm.

[8]We know that the law is good if one uses it properly. [9]We also know that the
law is made not for the righteous but for lawbreakers and rebels, the ungodly and
sinful, the unholy and irreligious, for those who kill their fathers or mothers, for
murderers, [10]for the sexually immoral, for those practicing homosexuality, for
slave traders and liars and perjurers—and for whatever else is contrary to the
sound doctrine [11]that conforms to the gospel concerning the glory of the blessed
God, which he entrusted to me.

The Lord's Grace to Paul

[12]I thank Christ Jesus our Lord, who has given me strength, that he considered me trustworthy, appointing me to his service. [13]Even though I was once a
blasphemer and a persecutor and a violent man, I was shown mercy because I
acted in ignorance and unbelief. [14]The grace of our Lord was poured out on me
abundantly, along with the faith and love that are in Christ Jesus.

[15]Here is a trustworthy saying that deserves full acceptance: Christ Jesus
came into the world to save sinners—of whom I am the worst. [16]But for that very
reason I was shown mercy so that in me, the worst of sinners, Christ Jesus might
display his immense patience as an example for those who would believe in him
and receive eternal life. [17]Now to the King eternal, immortal, invisible, the only
God, be honor and glory for ever and ever. Amen.

The Charge to Timothy Renewed

[18]Timothy, my son, I am giving you this command in keeping with the prophecies once made about you, so that by recalling them you may fight the battle
well, [19]holding on to faith and a good conscience, which some have rejected
and so have suffered shipwreck with regard to the faith. [20]Among them are Hymenaeus and Alexander, whom I have handed over to Satan to be taught not to
blaspheme.

Instructions on Worship

2 I urge, then, first of all, that petitions, prayers, intercession and thanksgiving be made for all people— [2]for kings and all those in authority, that we
may live peaceful and quiet lives in all godliness and holiness. [3]This is good,
and pleases God our Savior, [4]who wants all people to be saved and to come
to a knowledge of the truth. [5]For there is one God and one mediator between
God and mankind, the man Christ Jesus, [6]who gave himself as a ransom for all

APPOINTED TO HIS SERVICE

After coming to know Christ, Paul was consumed by a desire to share the good news of Christ's work with as many people as possible. Not only that, but Paul felt especially burdened to preach the gospel where it had never been shared (Ro 15:20). We know from Acts 13:1 — 21:16 that Paul went on three missionary journeys, planting churches in Asia Minor and Macedonia before his arrest in Jerusalem (Ac 21:27 – 36) and eventual transportation to Rome to stand trial (Ac 27:1 — 28:31).

These travels brought immense suffering into Paul's life. He was the constant target of hostility from those around him (Ac 13:45; 14:5; 18:12; 26:24; 27:9 – 11). He was repeatedly arrested (Ac 16:23; 21:33; 22:24; 23:35) and beaten (Ac 16:22; 21:30 – 31; 23:2). He was once even stoned and left for dead (Ac 14:19).

Despite these trials, Paul remained steadfast in his commitment to preach Christ where there were not yet any churches. The beauty of the gospel captivated him to the point that he willingly sacrificed his own safety that others might hear.

In addition to these three journeys, it is possible Paul made a fourth journey after his release from the Roman imprisonment recorded in Acts 28:16. The conclusion that such a journey did indeed take place is based on Paul's declared intention to go to Spain (Ro 15:24,28) and statements in early Christian literature that indicate that Paul took the gospel as far as Spain.

Whether or not Paul was able to make an additional journey, believers today should seek to emulate his passion for the spread of the gospel. After his resurrection, Jesus charged his followers to take the gospel to the ends of the globe (Mt 28:19 – 20). This Great Commission, as it is known, motivated Paul and should motivate us to make sacrifices so others might hear the message of Jesus. Just as the spread of the gospel was Paul's primary concern until the end of his life (2Ti 2:1 – 13), so believers today should also seek to discover how their lives can be leveraged to spread the good news of Jesus Christ to the nations.

people. This has now been witnessed to at the proper time. [7]And for this purpose I was appointed a herald and an apostle—I am telling the truth, I am not lying—and a true and faithful teacher of the Gentiles.

[8]Therefore I want the men everywhere to pray, lifting up holy hands without anger or disputing. [9]I also want the women to dress modestly, with decency and propriety, adorning themselves, not with elaborate hairstyles or gold or pearls or expensive clothes, [10]but with good deeds, appropriate for women who profess to worship God.

[11]A woman[a] should learn in quietness and full submission. [12]I do not permit a woman to teach or to assume authority over a man;[b] she must be quiet. [13]For Adam was formed first, then Eve. [14]And Adam was not the one deceived; it was the woman who was deceived and became a sinner. [15]But women[c] will be saved through childbearing—if they continue in faith, love and holiness with propriety.

Qualifications for Overseers and Deacons

3 Here is a trustworthy saying: Whoever aspires to be an overseer desires a noble task. [2]Now the overseer is to be above reproach, faithful to his wife, temperate, self-controlled, respectable, hospitable, able to teach, [3]not given to drunkenness, not violent but gentle, not quarrelsome, not a lover of money. [4]He must manage his own family well and see that his children obey him, and he must do so in a manner worthy of full[d] respect. [5](If anyone does not know how to manage his own family, how can he take care of God's church?) [6]He must not be a recent convert, or he may become conceited and fall under the same judgment as the devil. [7]He must also have a good reputation with outsiders, so that he will not fall into disgrace and into the devil's trap.

[8]In the same way, deacons[e] are to be worthy of respect, sincere, not indulging in much wine, and not pursuing dishonest gain. [9]They must keep hold of the deep truths of the faith with a clear conscience. [10]They must first be tested; and then if there is nothing against them, let them serve as deacons.

[11]In the same way, the women[f] are to be worthy of respect, not malicious talkers but temperate and trustworthy in everything.

[12]A deacon must be faithful to his wife and must manage his children and his household well. [13]Those who have served well gain an excellent standing and great assurance in their faith in Christ Jesus.

Reasons for Paul's Instructions

[14]Although I hope to come to you soon, I am writing you these instructions so that, [15]if I am delayed, you will know how people ought to conduct themselves in God's household, which is the church of the living God, the pillar and foundation of the truth. [16]Beyond all question, the mystery from which true godliness springs is great:

He appeared in the flesh,
    was vindicated by the Spirit,[g]
was seen by angels,
    was preached among the nations,
was believed on in the world,
    was taken up in glory.

4 The Spirit clearly says that in later times some will abandon the faith and follow deceiving spirits and things taught by demons. [2]Such teachings come through hypocritical liars, whose consciences have been seared as with a hot iron. [3]They forbid people to marry and order them to abstain from certain

[a] *11* Or *wife*; also in verse 12 [b] *12* Or *over her husband* [c] *15* Greek *she* [d] *4* Or *him with proper* [e] *8* The word *deacons* refers here to Christians designated to serve with the overseers/elders of the church in a variety of ways; similarly in verse 12; and in Romans 16:1 and Phil. 1:1. [f] *11* Possibly deacons' wives or women who are deacons
[g] *16* Or *vindicated in spirit*

---

1 TIMOTHY 2:5

MEDIATOR

If you asked someone to list the titles of Jesus in the Bible, it would likely be a while before they said "mediator." Yet this often-overlooked title is of critical importance for believers. A mediator enters into a dispute between two parties and brings about a resolution. According to the Bible, sin has placed every human being in conflict with the perfectly righteous God of the universe (Ro 3:10). There is nothing a person can do to bridge this chasm that sin creates between himself or herself and God.

Despite this problem originating because of human sin, God took it upon himself to resolve the conflict. Instead of letting people experience the just result of their rebellion against him, God sent Jesus, his own Son, to act as a mediator of his new covenant of grace (Heb 9:15). For those who place their faith in him, the Bible says Jesus bore their sin so that they could become the righteousness of God (2Co 5:21). Now Jesus sits at the right hand of the Father, interceding on their behalf (Ro 8:34).

If we are in Christ, he paid the penalty for our sin, and his perfect obedience is credited to us. Because of Jesus' work, we are no longer in conflict with God and we have been adopted as children and co-heirs with Christ (Ro 8:17). With Jesus as our mediator, we partake in God's amazing grace!

foods, which God created to be received with thanksgiving by those who believe and who know the truth. [4]For everything God created is good, and nothing is to be rejected if it is received with thanksgiving, [5]because it is consecrated by the word of God and prayer.

[6]If you point these things out to the brothers and sisters,[a] you will be a good minister of Christ Jesus, nourished on the truths of the faith and of the good teaching that you have followed. [7]Have nothing to do with godless myths and old wives' tales; rather, train yourself to be godly. [8]For physical training is of some value, but godliness has value for all things, holding promise for both the present life and the life to come. [9]This is a trustworthy saying that deserves full acceptance. [10]That is why we labor and strive, because we have put our hope in the living God, who is the Savior of all people, and especially of those who believe.

[11]Command and teach these things. [12]Don't let anyone look down on you because you are young, but set an example for the believers in speech, in conduct, in love, in faith and in purity. [13]Until I come, devote yourself to the public reading of Scripture, to preaching and to teaching. [14]Do not neglect your gift, which was given you through prophecy when the body of elders laid their hands on you.

[15]Be diligent in these matters; give yourself wholly to them, so that everyone may see your progress. [16]Watch your life and doctrine closely. Persevere in them, because if you do, you will save both yourself and your hearers.

Widows, Elders and Slaves

5 Do not rebuke an older man harshly, but exhort him as if he were your father. Treat younger men as brothers, [2]older women as mothers, and younger women as sisters, with absolute purity.

[3]Give proper recognition to those widows who are really in need. [4]But if a widow has children or grandchildren, these should learn first of all to put their religion into practice by caring for their own family and so repaying their parents and grandparents, for this is pleasing to God. [5]The widow who is really in need and left all alone puts her hope in God and continues night and day to pray and to ask God for help. [6]But the widow who lives for pleasure is dead even while she lives. [7]Give the people these instructions, so that no one may be open to blame. [8]Anyone who does not provide for their relatives, and especially for their own household, has denied the faith and is worse than an unbeliever.

[9]No widow may be put on the list of widows unless she is over sixty, has been faithful to her husband, [10]and is well known for her good deeds, such as bringing up children, showing hospitality, washing the feet of the Lord's people, helping those in trouble and devoting herself to all kinds of good deeds.

[11]As for younger widows, do not put them on such a list. For when their sensual desires overcome their dedication to Christ, they want to marry. [12]Thus they bring judgment on themselves, because they have broken their first pledge. [13]Besides, they get into the habit of being idle and going about from house to house. And not only do they become idlers, but also busybodies who talk nonsense, saying things they ought not to. [14]So I counsel younger widows to marry, to have children, to manage their homes and to give the enemy no opportunity for slander. [15]Some have in fact already turned away to follow Satan.

[16]If any woman who is a believer has widows in her care, she should continue to help them and not let the church be burdened with them, so that the church can help those widows who are really in need.

[17]The elders who direct the affairs of the church well are worthy of double honor, especially those whose work is preaching and teaching. [18]For Scripture says, "Do not muzzle an ox while it is treading out the grain,"[b] and "The worker deserves his wages."[c] [19]Do not entertain an accusation against an elder unless it is brought by two or three witnesses. [20]But those elders who are sinning you are

[a] *6* The Greek word for *brothers and sisters* (*adelphoi*) refers here to believers, both men and women, as part of God's family. [b] *18* Deut. 25:4 [c] *18* Luke 10:7

1 TIMOTHY 4:1 – 2

DO NOT ABANDON THE FAITH

Paul warned Timothy to guard against false teachers who lead people astray. For Paul, false teachers represented a serious danger to the church, prompting him to frequently warn those under his care about them. He wrote to other churches about false teachers (2Th 2:3 – 12), warning the elders several years earlier at the church in Ephesus, where Timothy ministered (Ac 20:29 – 30). He focused on this subject extensively in his final letter to Timothy.

Paul was not alone in his concern. Peter wrote about false teachers (2Pe 2:1 – 3), as did John (1Jn 2:18 – 19; 4:3; 2Jn 7 – 11) and Jude (Jude 18). The author of Hebrews repeatedly warned about falling away from the faith (Heb 3:12; 5:11 — 6:8; 10:26 – 31). Throughout the New Testament epistles, one finds frequent warnings that in the last days — from the time of the life of Jesus until his return (Eph 5:6; Col 2:4; 2Th 2:3,10) — deceivers would pose a threat to the church.

How did these authors come to share this concern? From Jesus himself. He told his disciples to beware of false teachers "in sheep's clothing, but inwardly they are ferocious wolves" (Mt 7:15) who would come and attempt to deceive people with their message (Mt 24:4 – 12). It is clear the apostles of Jesus took these words to heart as they sought to remind the early church, and us today, of the dangers that accepting the ideas of false teachers can have on our faith.

1 TIMOTHY 6:13 – 16

LIGHT

The Bible often speaks of God in connection with light. Here Paul uses this imagery to communicate an important truth: God is concealed from us. This is not because God is hiding in the shadows, but rather because our human eyes are too weak to perceive him due to the brightness of the light in which he dwells. This metaphoric picture reveals the spiritual reality of sinful humanity. Instead of walking with God in close relationship (Ge 2:4 – 25), sin has rendered humanity utterly unable to approach God (Ex 33:20).

Thankfully, the story does not end there. At Jesus' incarnation, the light of God came into the world so that we might be given the ability to see God (Jn 12:46; 14:9). Because of what Jesus accomplished on our behalf, we have the ability to see some of God's light (Ps 36:9). However, even after we come to know God through Christ, we cannot know him fully in this life (1Co 13:9 – 12). Christians look forward to a time when this will not still be the case. The Bible teaches that there will come a time when God will make all things new and once again dwell face-to-face with his people. When describing that day, the Bible again speaks of the light of God, as it will illuminate the New Jerusalem like the sun (Rev 21:23), and believers will live in the glory of that light for eternity.

to reprove before everyone, so that the others may take warning. [21]I charge you,
in the sight of God and Christ Jesus and the elect angels, to keep these instructions without partiality, and to do nothing out of favoritism.
[22]Do not be hasty in the laying on of hands, and do not share in the sins of
others. Keep yourself pure.
[23]Stop drinking only water, and use a little wine because of your stomach and
your frequent illnesses.
[24]The sins of some are obvious, reaching the place of judgment ahead of them;
the sins of others trail behind them. [25]In the same way, good deeds are obvious,
and even those that are not obvious cannot remain hidden forever.

6 All who are under the yoke of slavery should consider their masters worthy
of full respect, so that God's name and our teaching may not be slandered.
[2]Those who have believing masters should not show them disrespect just because they are fellow believers. Instead, they should serve them even better because their masters are dear to them as fellow believers and are devoted to the
welfare[a] of their slaves.

False Teachers and the Love of Money

These are the things you are to teach and insist on. [3]If anyone teaches otherwise and does not agree to the sound instruction of our Lord Jesus Christ and
to godly teaching, [4]they are conceited and understand nothing. They have an
unhealthy interest in controversies and quarrels about words that result in envy,
strife, malicious talk, evil suspicions [5]and constant friction between people of
corrupt mind, who have been robbed of the truth and who think that godliness
is a means to financial gain.
[6]But godliness with contentment is great gain. [7]For we brought nothing into
the world, and we can take nothing out of it. [8]But if we have food and clothing,
we will be content with that. [9]Those who want to get rich fall into temptation
and a trap and into many foolish and harmful desires that plunge people into
ruin and destruction. [10]For the love of money is a root of all kinds of evil. Some
people, eager for money, have wandered from the faith and pierced themselves
with many griefs.

Final Charge to Timothy

[11]But you, man of God, flee from all this, and pursue righteousness, godliness,
faith, love, endurance and gentleness. [12]Fight the good fight of the faith. Take
hold of the eternal life to which you were called when you made your good confession in the presence of many witnesses. [13]In the sight of God, who gives life to
everything, and of Christ Jesus, who while testifying before Pontius Pilate made
the good confession, I charge you [14]to keep this command without spot or blame
until the appearing of our Lord Jesus Christ, [15]which God will bring about in his
own time — God, the blessed and only Ruler, the King of kings and Lord of lords,
[16]who alone is immortal and who lives in unapproachable light, whom no one
has seen or can see. To him be honor and might forever. Amen.

[17]Command those who are rich in this present world not to be arrogant nor to
put their hope in wealth, which is so uncertain, but to put their hope in God, who
richly provides us with everything for our enjoyment. [18]Command them to do
good, to be rich in good deeds, and to be generous and willing to share. [19]In this
way they will lay up treasure for themselves as a firm foundation for the coming
age, so that they may take hold of the life that is truly life.
[20]Timothy, guard what has been entrusted to your care. Turn away from godless chatter and the opposing ideas of what is falsely called knowledge, [21]which
some have professed and in so doing have departed from the faith.

Grace be with you all.

---

[a] 2 Or *and benefit from the service*

JESUS: OUR SOURCE OF STRENGTH

2 TIMOTHY

2 TIMOTHY

PAUL IN ROME, WRITES 1 TIMOTHY	PAUL IMPRISONED, WRITES 2 TIMOTHY	PAUL MARTYRED IN ROME
c. AD 62	*c. AD 64 – 67*	*c. AD 67 – 68*

The faithful transmission of the gospel message from one generation to the next is at the heart of the mission of God's people. Paul, the foremost missionary of the Christian faith, spent his life investing in others in the hopes that the message he proclaimed would continue to resound throughout the world long after his death.

Paul knew that his death was imminent as he wrote his second letter to pastor Timothy in Ephesus. Imprisoned in a hole in the ground in Rome, Paul penned a passionate letter to his son in the faith. By this time, it was clear that Paul's life would soon end and, though he longed to see Timothy again, he knew that might never be possible.

Second Timothy drips with emotion as the aging Paul begged his beloved Timothy to stay true to the faith in an age of apostasy. Paul knew that the life of a pastor is fraught with dangers and challenges and that Timothy would face overwhelming burdens in the days ahead. He compared the Christian life, and ministry in particular, to the work of a soldier, an athlete and a farmer — since each job requires diligent perseverance in the face of obstacles in order to accomplish their objectives (2:1 – 13). As a pastor, Timothy would need to tirelessly labor and not give up in order to properly care for God's people.

Central to his pastoral duties is the preaching of the Word of God (2:12 – 26; 4:1 – 5). He needed to handle this responsibility with all seriousness — guarding the proper content of the gospel message and protecting the church from aberrant teaching and heretical doctrine. Paul's life and mission served as an example to Timothy of the type of persecution that would await those who continue to boldly proclaim the Word of God. Yet Paul reminded

Timothy of the great reward that awaits those who keep their focus fixed on Christ and persevere to the end (4:8). Timothy must not lose heart, though the world is broken and marred by sin and his mentor would soon be gone. Jesus was a sufficient source of strength to faithfully fulfill the ministry with which Timothy was entrusted. Just as Timothy did, all of God's people will find in 2 Timothy a reminder of the glorious privilege of representing God to others and the need to continue in this work, even in the face of opposition.

FOR THE SPIRIT GOD GAVE US DOES NOT MAKE US TIMID, BUT GIVES US POWER, LOVE AND SELF-DISCIPLINE.

---

2 Timothy 1:7

2 TIMOTHY

1 Paul, an apostle of Christ Jesus by the will of God, in keeping with the promise of life that is in Christ Jesus,

2To Timothy, my dear son:
Grace, mercy and peace from God the Father and Christ Jesus our Lord.

Thanksgiving

3I thank God, whom I serve, as my ancestors did, with a clear conscience, as
night and day I constantly remember you in my prayers. 4Recalling your tears,
I long to see you, so that I may be filled with joy. 5I am reminded of your sincere
faith, which first lived in your grandmother Lois and in your mother Eunice and,
I am persuaded, now lives in you also.

Appeal for Loyalty to Paul and the Gospel

6For this reason I remind you to fan into flame the gift of God, which is in you
through the laying on of my hands. 7For the Spirit God gave us does not make us
timid, but gives us power, love and self-discipline. 8So do not be ashamed of the
testimony about our Lord or of me his prisoner. Rather, join with me in suffering for the gospel, by the power of God. 9He has saved us and called us to a holy
life — not because of anything we have done but because of his own purpose and
grace. This grace was given us in Christ Jesus before the beginning of time, 10but
it has now been revealed through the appearing of our Savior, Christ Jesus, who
has destroyed death and has brought life and immortality to light through the
gospel. 11And of this gospel I was appointed a herald and an apostle and a teacher. 12That is why I am suffering as I am. Yet this is no cause for shame, because
I know whom I have believed, and am convinced that he is able to guard what I
have entrusted to him until that day.

13What you heard from me, keep as the pattern of sound teaching, with faith
and love in Christ Jesus. 14Guard the good deposit that was entrusted to you —
guard it with the help of the Holy Spirit who lives in us.

Examples of Disloyalty and Loyalty

15You know that everyone in the province of Asia has deserted me, including
Phygelus and Hermogenes.

16May the Lord show mercy to the household of Onesiphorus, because he often refreshed me and was not ashamed of my chains. 17On the contrary, when he
was in Rome, he searched hard for me until he found me. 18May the Lord grant
that he will find mercy from the Lord on that day! You know very well in how
many ways he helped me in Ephesus.

The Appeal Renewed

2 You then, my son, be strong in the grace that is in Christ Jesus. 2And the
things you have heard me say in the presence of many witnesses entrust to
reliable people who will also be qualified to teach others. 3Join with me in suffering, like a good soldier of Christ Jesus. 4No one serving as a soldier gets entangled
in civilian affairs, but rather tries to please his commanding officer. 5Similarly,
anyone who competes as an athlete does not receive the victor's crown except by
competing according to the rules. 6The hardworking farmer should be the first
to receive a share of the crops. 7Reflect on what I am saying, for the Lord will give
you insight into all this.

8Remember Jesus Christ, raised from the dead, descended from David. This

2 TIMOTHY 2:1 – 26

HANDBOOK FOR THE CHRISTIAN LIFE

In this his final letter to Timothy, his "son" in the faith, Paul summarizes the essential elements of faithful Christian ministry based on the good news of Jesus. All believers, not just pastors like Timothy, can have an eternal impact on the world if they follow Paul's timeless advice.

First, Paul tells Timothy to find his strength in the grace of God (v. 1). A Christian's relationship with God begins with grace, not works. God freely gives salvation, forgiveness and the indwelling of the Holy Spirit to everyone who believes the good news about Jesus (1:5 – 6,9 – 10; 3:15). These are gifts; they are not something earned. Therefore, Timothy would find the strength he needed to weather life's storms by clinging in faith to the gifts he had already received from God.

Second, faithful ministry is built upon the inspired Word of God. The Bible is no mere book; it contains God's very words recorded without error, capable of equipping Christians for every good deed (3:16 – 17). Therefore, Timothy needed to hold fast to the essential truths revealed in Scripture (1:13 – 14; 2:2 – 8; 3:14 – 15). Any drifting away from these truths would have jeopardized both his public ministry and personal walk with the Lord. So Paul challenged Timothy to continue studying and teaching God's Word (4:1 – 5). Only then would he be able to stand before God as a "worker who does not need to be ashamed" (2:15). Furthermore, as Timothy entrusted the truths he learned from the Word of God to other believers who would, in turn, entrust those truths to others, he would ensure that his ministry would last long after his life ended (2:2). The secret to building a ministry that honors God for decades to come is keeping God's Word at the center.

Third, character matters in ministry. It is not enough to simply know and teach the Word of God. One must live it. In particular, all those who wish to follow Timothy's example must flee from youthful lusts and pointless arguments and instead pursue righteousness, faith, love and peace (2:22 – 24).

Finally, faithful ministry requires endurance in the midst of suffering. Anyone who desires to serve the Lord faithfully will face persecution in this life (3:12). Timothy needed to accept suffering as an unavoidable part of a faithful life. He had to learn to look beyond the pain and see the reward that God has in store for those who endure persecution because of their allegiance to Jesus (1:8,12; 2:3 – 6,12; 3:1; 4:5 – 8).

is my gospel, [9]for which I am suffering even to the point of being chained like a criminal. But God's word is not chained. [10]Therefore I endure everything for the sake of the elect, that they too may obtain the salvation that is in Christ Jesus, with eternal glory.

[11]Here is a trustworthy saying:

If we died with him,
we will also live with him;
[12]if we endure,
we will also reign with him.
If we disown him,
he will also disown us;
[13]if we are faithless,
he remains faithful,
for he cannot disown himself.

Dealing With False Teachers

[14]Keep reminding God's people of these things. Warn them before God against quarreling about words; it is of no value, and only ruins those who listen. [15]Do your best to present yourself to God as one approved, a worker who does not need to be ashamed and who correctly handles the word of truth. [16]Avoid godless chatter, because those who indulge in it will become more and more ungodly. [17]Their teaching will spread like gangrene. Among them are Hymenaeus and Philetus, [18]who have departed from the truth. They say that the resurrection has already taken place, and they destroy the faith of some. [19]Nevertheless, God's solid foundation stands firm, sealed with this inscription: "The Lord knows those who are his," and, "Everyone who confesses the name of the Lord must turn away from wickedness."

[20]In a large house there are articles not only of gold and silver, but also of wood and clay; some are for special purposes and some for common use. [21]Those who cleanse themselves from the latter will be instruments for special purposes, made holy, useful to the Master and prepared to do any good work.

[22]Flee the evil desires of youth and pursue righteousness, faith, love and peace, along with those who call on the Lord out of a pure heart. [23]Don't have anything to do with foolish and stupid arguments, because you know they produce quarrels. [24]And the Lord's servant must not be quarrelsome but must be kind to everyone, able to teach, not resentful. [25]Opponents must be gently instructed, in the hope that God will grant them repentance leading them to a knowledge of the truth, [26]and that they will come to their senses and escape from the trap of the devil, who has taken them captive to do his will.

3 But mark this: There will be terrible times in the last days. [2]People will be lovers of themselves, lovers of money, boastful, proud, abusive, disobedient to their parents, ungrateful, unholy, [3]without love, unforgiving, slanderous, without self-control, brutal, not lovers of the good, [4]treacherous, rash, conceited, lovers of pleasure rather than lovers of God— [5]having a form of godliness but denying its power. Have nothing to do with such people.

[6]They are the kind who worm their way into homes and gain control over gullible women, who are loaded down with sins and are swayed by all kinds of evil desires, [7]always learning but never able to come to a knowledge of the truth. [8]Just as Jannes and Jambres opposed Moses, so also these teachers oppose the truth. They are men of depraved minds, who, as far as the faith is concerned, are rejected. [9]But they will not get very far because, as in the case of those men, their folly will be clear to everyone.

A Final Charge to Timothy

[10]You, however, know all about my teaching, my way of life, my purpose, faith, patience, love, endurance, [11]persecutions, sufferings—what kinds of things happened to me in Antioch, Iconium and Lystra, the persecutions I endured.

2 TIMOTHY 3:15–17

A GOD-BREATHED BOOK

In 2 Timothy 3:16, Paul declares that Scripture is "God-breathed," a word that combines the Greek words *theos* meaning "God" with *pneo* meaning "to breathe." Paul's point is that the Bible is not a man-made book. All sixty-six of the Bible's books were "breathed out" by God through the unique writing styles and vocabulary of each biblical author. Since God is always truthful (Nu 23:19; Titus 1:2; Heb 6:18) and since the Bible is his own word, then the Bible must therefore be completely true. Theologians call it "inerrant," meaning "without error." So while our understanding of Scripture may be fallible, the Bible itself is as true as God himself is true.

Furthermore, because the Bible comes from God, it carries his own authority. The authoritative Word, the One who spoke all things into existence and brought the dead to life during his ministry on earth—Jesus himself—continues to exert the same power over God's people today through the Scripture, God's revelation to his people. Scripture defines our values, directs our lives and commands our obedience. It is, therefore, useful for "teaching, rebuking, correcting and training in righteousness" (2Ti 3:16). It can lead a person to salvation (v. 15) and equip a believer to face every opportunity and challenge in life (v. 17).

DESCRIPTIONS OF THE CHRISTIAN LIFE

In describing how Christians should live, Paul and other New Testament writers often used analogies or metaphors. These word pictures help believers to understand more clearly God's expectations for his people. This article lists some of the metaphors of the Christian life found in the New Testament.

Soldiers (2Ti 2:3–4). Like good soldiers, we should accept hardships and keep our lives focused on the mission that our commander, Jesus, has given us.

Athletes (2Ti 4:6–8). Just as athletes follow strict rules and train hard to win their races, so we must follow the Lord's commands (2:1–3) to receive our reward from him.

Farmers (2Ti 2:6). Like farmers who work ceaselessly to reap a fruitful harvest, so we must also work hard in ministry to receive our reward from Jesus.

Workers (2Ti 2:15). As a craftsman is honored for his skillful construction, so the Lord honors believers for their skillful use of his Word.

Articles/Dishes (2Ti 2:20–21). Like a dish kept clean and ready for use, so we must keep our lives pure and righteous to be useful to the Lord.

Fishers of people (Mt 4:19). We are called to "catch" people for God's kingdom with God's good news, the gospel.

Salt (Mt 5:13). Like salt, we can act as a godly preservative in an evil society if we remain righteous.

Light (Mt 5:14–16). If we obey God's Word we will shine brightly in the midst of a dark world and attract others to know and follow God.

Branches (Jn 15:5). As branches, we bear godly fruit so long as we abide in the vine, Jesus, by obeying and surrendering to him.

Servants (1Co 4:1–2). Like household servants entrusted with resources and responsibilities, we will be evaluated by our Master based on our faithfulness to his commands.

Ambassadors (2Co 5:20). We are representatives of God's kingdom to the lost citizens of this world.

Living stones (1Pe 2:5). In the Old Testament, God presence dwelled in a physical temple. Now he dwells within his people, the church.

Priests (1Pe 2:9). Like priests, we have the privilege of drawing near to God and the responsibility of helping others find reconciliation with God.

Foreigners and Exiles (1Pe 2:11). As children of God, we do not belong to this world. It is not our home; we await our true home, which is being in the presence of God for eternity.

Yet the Lord rescued me from all of them. [12]In fact, everyone who wants to live a godly life in Christ Jesus will be persecuted, [13]while evildoers and impostors will go from bad to worse, deceiving and being deceived. [14]But as for you, continue in what you have learned and have become convinced of, because you know those from whom you learned it, [15]and how from infancy you have known the Holy Scriptures, which are able to make you wise for salvation through faith in Christ Jesus. [16]All Scripture is God-breathed and is useful for teaching, rebuking, correcting and training in righteousness, [17]so that the servant of God[a] may be thoroughly equipped for every good work.

4 In the presence of God and of Christ Jesus, who will judge the living and the dead, and in view of his appearing and his kingdom, I give you this charge: [2]Preach the word; be prepared in season and out of season; correct, rebuke and encourage — with great patience and careful instruction. [3]For the time will come when people will not put up with sound doctrine. Instead, to suit their own desires, they will gather around them a great number of teachers to say what their itching ears want to hear. [4]They will turn their ears away from the truth and turn aside to myths. [5]But you, keep your head in all situations, endure hardship, do the work of an evangelist, discharge all the duties of your ministry.

[6]For I am already being poured out like a drink offering, and the time for my departure is near. [7]I have fought the good fight, I have finished the race, I have kept the faith. [8]Now there is in store for me the crown of righteousness, which the Lord, the righteous Judge, will award to me on that day — and not only to me, but also to all who have longed for his appearing.

Personal Remarks

[9]Do your best to come to me quickly, [10]for Demas, because he loved this world, has deserted me and has gone to Thessalonica. Crescens has gone to Galatia, and Titus to Dalmatia. [11]Only Luke is with me. Get Mark and bring him with you, because he is helpful to me in my ministry. [12]I sent Tychicus to Ephesus. [13]When you come, bring the cloak that I left with Carpus at Troas, and my scrolls, especially the parchments.

[14]Alexander the metalworker did me a great deal of harm. The Lord will repay him for what he has done. [15]You too should be on your guard against him, because he strongly opposed our message.

[16]At my first defense, no one came to my support, but everyone deserted me. May it not be held against them. [17]But the Lord stood at my side and gave me strength, so that through me the message might be fully proclaimed and all the Gentiles might hear it. And I was delivered from the lion's mouth. [18]The Lord will rescue me from every evil attack and will bring me safely to his heavenly kingdom. To him be glory for ever and ever. Amen.

Final Greetings

[19]Greet Priscilla[b] and Aquila and the household of Onesiphorus. [20]Erastus stayed in Corinth, and I left Trophimus sick in Miletus. [21]Do your best to get here before winter. Eubulus greets you, and so do Pudens, Linus, Claudia and all the brothers and sisters.[c]

[22]The Lord be with your spirit. Grace be with you all.

---

[a] *17* Or *that you, a man of God,* [b] *19* Greek *Prisca,* a variant of *Priscilla* [c] *21* The Greek word for *brothers and sisters* (*adelphoi*) refers here to believers, both men and women, as part of God's family.

JESUS: OUR GREAT GOD AND SAVIOR

TITUS

TITUS

TITUS MINISTERS WITH PAUL *c. AD 53 – 57*	PAUL WRITES TITUS *c. AD 63*	PAUL MARTYRED IN ROME *c. AD 67 – 68*

The work of the church is central to God's plan. Paul invested his life in the establishment of the church and wrote a number of letters to these churches in order to encourage their ongoing faithfulness and gospel fidelity. Two pastors, Timothy and Titus, received personal letters instructing them in how to lead their respective churches — Timothy in Ephesus and Titus on the island of Crete. Together these letters form what are commonly known as the Pastoral Epistles, due to the recipient's task in each letter and the instructions they contain regarding leadership in the church. The church at Crete, a large island near Greece, was a newly formed congregation located among a radically pagan culture. Paul left Titus to lead the church and bring order to the young church (1:5). This challenge was made all the more difficult due to the fact that Crete had a reputation for wickedness that was known throughout the region (1:12).

Titus was an appropriate choice for this challenging role since he had been discipled personally under the apostle Paul. Like Timothy, Titus traveled with Paul on numerous missionary journeys, received personal training in doctrine and theology under his care and was sent by Paul to minister among the churches they established.

The organization of the church was central to Paul's instructions in this short letter. He instructed Titus on the role and qualifications of elders and deacons, which contrasted sharply with the false teachers that were pervasive in that day (1:5 – 16). As in the letters to Timothy, Paul exhorted Titus to proclaim the Word of God with boldness and confidence because it was the God-ordained means of bringing transformation to God's people (2:1).

Paul concluded his letter with the motive for such challenging work. The grace of God compels leaders to invest their lives in God's church. Because of Jesus, all people should live godly, honorable lives as they await his second coming (2:11). They can shun immorality and idolatry, knowing that the worship of Jesus far surpasses anything this world has to offer. And they can run the race God has given them, knowing that they are heirs to the abundant riches of God through our great God and Savior, Jesus Christ (2:13).

HE SAVED US, NOT BECAUSE OF RIGHTEOUS THINGS WE HAD DONE, BUT BECAUSE OF HIS MERCY. HE SAVED US THROUGH THE WASHING OF REBIRTH AND RENEWAL BY THE HOLY SPIRIT.

Titus 3:5

TITUS

1 Paul, a servant of God and an apostle of Jesus Christ to further the faith of God's elect and their knowledge of the truth that leads to godliness— [2]in the hope of eternal life, which God, who does not lie, promised before the beginning of time, [3]and which now at his appointed season he has brought to light through the preaching entrusted to me by the command of God our Savior,

[4]To Titus, my true son in our common faith:

Grace and peace from God the Father and Christ Jesus our Savior.

Appointing Elders Who Love What Is Good

[5]The reason I left you in Crete was that you might put in order what was left unfinished and appoint[a] elders in every town, as I directed you. [6]An elder must be blameless, faithful to his wife, a man whose children believe[b] and are not open to the charge of being wild and disobedient. [7]Since an overseer manages God's household, he must be blameless—not overbearing, not quick-tempered, not given to drunkenness, not violent, not pursuing dishonest gain. [8]Rather, he must be hospitable, one who loves what is good, who is self-controlled, upright, holy and disciplined. [9]He must hold firmly to the trustworthy message as it has been taught, so that he can encourage others by sound doctrine and refute those who oppose it.

Rebuking Those Who Fail to Do Good

[10]For there are many rebellious people, full of meaningless talk and deception, especially those of the circumcision group. [11]They must be silenced, because they are disrupting whole households by teaching things they ought not to teach—and that for the sake of dishonest gain. [12]One of Crete's own prophets has said it: "Cretans are always liars, evil brutes, lazy gluttons."[c] [13]This saying is true. Therefore rebuke them sharply, so that they will be sound in the faith [14]and will pay no attention to Jewish myths or to the merely human commands of those who reject the truth. [15]To the pure, all things are pure, but to those who are corrupted and do not believe, nothing is pure. In fact, both their minds and consciences are corrupted. [16]They claim to know God, but by their actions they deny him. They are detestable, disobedient and unfit for doing anything good.

Doing Good for the Sake of the Gospel

2 You, however, must teach what is appropriate to sound doctrine. [2]Teach the older men to be temperate, worthy of respect, self-controlled, and sound in faith, in love and in endurance.

[3]Likewise, teach the older women to be reverent in the way they live, not to be slanderers or addicted to much wine, but to teach what is good. [4]Then they can urge the younger women to love their husbands and children, [5]to be self-controlled and pure, to be busy at home, to be kind, and to be subject to their husbands, so that no one will malign the word of God.

[6]Similarly, encourage the young men to be self-controlled. [7]In everything set them an example by doing what is good. In your teaching show integrity, seriousness [8]and soundness of speech that cannot be condemned, so that those who oppose you may be ashamed because they have nothing bad to say about us.

[9]Teach slaves to be subject to their masters in everything, to try to please them, not to talk back to them, [10]and not to steal from them, but to show that

[a] *5* Or *ordain* [b] *6* Or *children are trustworthy* [c] *12* From the Cretan philosopher Epimenides

TITUS 2:2–3

MULTIGENERATIONAL MINISTRY

Too often, generations struggle to understand and appreciate one another. In a church context, such conflict can result in a weakened church or even a church split. The biblical vision of community, however, has always been multigenerational. Some of the earliest biblical instruction to parents is about passing on God's Word to their children (Dt 6:4–9). Multigenerational ministry is championed in Psalm 145:4: "One generation commends your works to another; they tell of your mighty acts."

In Titus, Paul commended multigenerational ministry because he knew how it could strengthen the church and advance its mission. He knew younger generations need to see examples of older godly men and women that they can emulate. By looking to their elders, young people can find a wealth of wisdom and experience, such as how to honor God in their marriages and vocations. This kind of multigenerational ministry requires the younger generation to display humility and a teachable attitude.

Jesus modeled humility when he visited the temple as a 12-year-old boy to learn and ask questions from those who were older and wiser (Lk 2:46). Christians today should follow Jesus' example. They should remain teachable and open to mentoring by older, mature believers. If they do this, the church will experience the blessing of increased unity and will grow stronger and healthier.

THE GOSPEL TO ALL PEOPLE

Titus was part of a band of early Christians who were gripped with a passion to spread the gospel of Jesus Christ to unreached peoples. He did not end up in Crete randomly. He was sent by Paul to make disciples of all nations, following God's desire from the beginning for all nations to know and worship him. In Genesis 12:1 – 3, God promised Abram that all of the peoples of the earth would be blessed through him. After his resurrection, Jesus commissioned his followers to make disciples of all nations (Mt 28:18 – 20), and John wrote in Revelation 7:9 – 12 about a vision of the future that God gave him. This future included people from every nation, tribe and language around the throne worshiping Jesus. Titus' very presence in Crete is evidence that his passion for Jesus translated into action for Jesus. That is also what is needed from the church today: passion wedded to action.

Today there are multiple thousands of unreached people groups around the world. A "people group" is an *ethnolinguistic group* (a group with a common culture and language) with a common self-identity. A people group is considered to be unreached when evangelical Christians make up less than two percent of the population. Jesus is calling his followers today to leverage their lives to spread the gospel to unreached people groups. In order to reach these people, the church needs people like Paul and Titus — those who will give of their lives to take the gospel into unchartered territory and those who will build on the work God has started in these infant churches and labor to build them in a healthy, God-honoring, manner (Titus 1:5).

Yet the challenge of spreading the gospel to unreached people groups is sobering. New languages, new cultures and new contexts await those who answer the call. Throughout history, believers have made innumerable sacrifices to get the gospel to unreached people groups. Many Christians make financial sacrifices, fast and pray for these efforts. Some people work to translate Scripture into new languages. Many have lost their lives spreading the gospel.

Despite the challenges, the church must get the gospel to unreached people groups. A passion for God's glory naturally propels the church around the world to reach the nations. The church should be discontent with a world where God is not receiving the worship of which he is worthy. Titus' presence in Crete should encourage every believer that reaching unreached people is possible. May the Spirit give his church compassion, and may he motivate his church to spread the gospel to all nations.

TITUS 3:3–7

THE KINDNESS OF GOD OUR SAVIOR

God's love is not blind. He knows the depths and details of every person's sin. Here in the third chapter of Titus, he describes humanity as being "foolish, disobedient, deceived and enslaved" and continues by describing how people envy and hate one another. Yet, God loves sinners. He is kind and showed great mercy by sending a Savior for sinful people who can never save themselves. This Savior is Jesus Christ.

When Jesus came to this earth, he arrived as the clearest picture of God's kindness and love. Jesus is described as "the radiance of God's glory and the exact representation of his being" (Heb 1:3). Jesus befriended sinners and showed compassion to the outcasts of society. In love, Jesus sacrificially laid down his life for sinners. God's love and kindness are plain for all to see in the person of Jesus Christ.

All of God's people can find freedom in not trying to hide their sin and brokenness. Instead, people can fall freely on the mercy of God and experience his kindness and love through the forgiveness that Jesus provides. God gives the gift of the Holy Spirit to dwell inside everyone who turns to him in faith. God's children need not doubt the lovingkindness of the Father—they can receive his love by faith and find joy through the knowledge that their sins have been forgiven.

they can be fully trusted, so that in every way they will make the teaching about
God our Savior attractive.
11For the grace of God has appeared that offers salvation to all people. 12It
teaches us to say "No" to ungodliness and worldly passions, and to live self-controlled, upright and godly lives in this present age, 13while we wait for the blessed
hope—the appearing of the glory of our great God and Savior, Jesus Christ,
14who gave himself for us to redeem us from all wickedness and to purify for
himself a people that are his very own, eager to do what is good.
15These, then, are the things you should teach. Encourage and rebuke with all
authority. Do not let anyone despise you.

Saved in Order to Do Good

3 Remind the people to be subject to rulers and authorities, to be obedient,
to be ready to do whatever is good, 2to slander no one, to be peaceable and
considerate, and always to be gentle toward everyone.
3At one time we too were foolish, disobedient, deceived and enslaved by
all kinds of passions and pleasures. We lived in malice and envy, being hated
and hating one another. 4But when the kindness and love of God our Savior appeared, 5he saved us, not because of righteous things we had done, but because
of his mercy. He saved us through the washing of rebirth and renewal by the
Holy Spirit, 6whom he poured out on us generously through Jesus Christ our Savior, 7so that, having been justified by his grace, we might become heirs having
the hope of eternal life. 8This is a trustworthy saying. And I want you to stress
these things, so that those who have trusted in God may be careful to devote
themselves to doing what is good. These things are excellent and profitable for
everyone.
9But avoid foolish controversies and genealogies and arguments and quarrels about the law, because these are unprofitable and useless. 10Warn a divisive
person once, and then warn them a second time. After that, have nothing to do
with them. 11You may be sure that such people are warped and sinful; they are
self-condemned.

Final Remarks

12As soon as I send Artemas or Tychicus to you, do your best to come to me at
Nicopolis, because I have decided to winter there. 13Do everything you can to
help Zenas the lawyer and Apollos on their way and see that they have everything they need. 14Our people must learn to devote themselves to doing what is
good, in order to provide for urgent needs and not live unproductive lives.
15Everyone with me sends you greetings. Greet those who love us in the faith.
Grace be with you all.

JESUS: OUR SOURCE OF RECONCILIATION

PHILEMON

PHILEMON

PAUL'S EXTENDED STAY IN EPHESUS	PAUL IMPRISONED, WRITES PHILEMON	PAUL MARTYRED IN ROME
c. AD 54 – 56	*c. AD 60 – 62*	*c. AD 67 – 68*

The gospel radically affects a person's relationship with God and all people, since they have been created in his image. In his letter to Philemon, Paul invites his brother in Christ to demonstrate a love, mercy and grace that could only be possible because of the work of Jesus.

Philemon, like many in his day, was a slave owner, but he had come to faith during Paul's missionary travels. A resident of Colossae, Philemon owned a slave named Onesimus, who had apparently run away from his master and took some of his possessions in the process. In God's providence, Onesimus fled to Rome, met Paul and came to faith in Christ. Following his conversion, Onesimus served Paul while he was in prison. However, the two men agreed that full restitution and restoration were needed between Onesimus and his former master, Philemon. Paul wrote this brief letter and sent it with the letter to the church at Colossae. In it, he asked Philemon to demonstrate Christian love toward Onesimus and receive him back, not as a slave, but as a beloved brother (vv. 16 – 17).

It was a life-threatening risk for Onesimus to seek to be restored to a right relationship with Philemon. Typically, a rebellious, treacherous slave would be subject to death should he be caught. For Onesimus to willingly pursue Philemon was unheard of. Philemon, however, was given a monumental opportunity to demonstrate the change that faith in Jesus could produce. Jesus provided the model of one who sought out his enemy and willingly laid down his life in order to bring his people into right relationship with God. Reconciliation with God was only possible because of Jesus, who can make God's enemies his friends. As a loving master, he can restore sinful humans into a right relationship with himself out of the sheer abundance of his grace. Now Philemon was given a chance to model this type of love. Their relationship could demonstrate the reality that, in Christ, all dividing walls that separate humanity are rendered obsolete. Only in Christ can masters and slaves be brothers. God's people, reborn into his family, can follow Paul's encouragement and demonstrate the unity that comes to all people regardless of gender, race, class or life history.

YOUR LOVE HAS GIVEN ME GREAT JOY AND ENCOURAGEMENT, BECAUSE YOU, BROTHER, HAVE REFRESHED THE HEARTS OF THE LORD'S PEOPLE.

Philemon 7

PHILEMON

[1]Paul, a prisoner of Christ Jesus, and Timothy our brother,

To Philemon our dear friend and fellow worker— [2]also to Apphia our sister and Archippus our fellow soldier—and to the church that meets in your home:

[3]Grace and peace to you[a] from God our Father and the Lord Jesus Christ.

Thanksgiving and Prayer

[4]I always thank my God as I remember you in my prayers, [5]because I hear about your love for all his holy people and your faith in the Lord Jesus. [6]I pray that your partnership with us in the faith may be effective in deepening your understanding of every good thing we share for the sake of Christ. [7]Your love has given me great joy and encouragement, because you, brother, have refreshed the hearts of the Lord's people.

Paul's Plea for Onesimus

[8]Therefore, although in Christ I could be bold and order you to do what you ought to do, [9]yet I prefer to appeal to you on the basis of love. It is as none other than Paul—an old man and now also a prisoner of Christ Jesus— [10]that I appeal to you for my son Onesimus,[b] who became my son while I was in chains. [11]Formerly he was useless to you, but now he has become useful both to you and to me.

[12]I am sending him—who is my very heart—back to you. [13]I would have liked to keep him with me so that he could take your place in helping me while I am in chains for the gospel. [14]But I did not want to do anything without your consent, so that any favor you do would not seem forced but would be voluntary. [15]Perhaps the reason he was separated from you for a little while was that you might have him back forever— [16]no longer as a slave, but better than a slave, as a dear brother. He is very dear to me but even dearer to you, both as a fellow man and as a brother in the Lord.

[17]So if you consider me a partner, welcome him as you would welcome me. [18]If he has done you any wrong or owes you anything, charge it to me. [19]I, Paul, am writing this with my own hand. I will pay it back—not to mention that you owe me your very self. [20]I do wish, brother, that I may have some benefit from you in the Lord; refresh my heart in Christ. [21]Confident of your obedience, I write to you, knowing that you will do even more than I ask.

[22]And one thing more: Prepare a guest room for me, because I hope to be restored to you in answer to your prayers.

[23]Epaphras, my fellow prisoner in Christ Jesus, sends you greetings. [24]And so do Mark, Aristarchus, Demas and Luke, my fellow workers.

[25]The grace of the Lord Jesus Christ be with your spirit.

---

[a] *3* The Greek is plural; also in verses 22 and 25; elsewhere in this letter "you" is singular.
[b] *10* *Onesimus* means *useful.*

THE SLAVE IS OUR BROTHER

The issue of slavery was very real and present under the rule of the Roman Empire. Paul wrote to slaves: "Obey your earthly masters with respect and fear, and with sincerity of heart, just as you would obey Christ" (Eph 6:5). He also commanded the masters of slaves to treat their slaves well (Eph 6:9). While he did not advocate for the outright abolition of slavery as an institution, he instead argued for the gospel truth to be infused into every layer of the socioeconomic system.

In Philemon, Paul addressed the idea of slavery and introduced a new, revolutionary perspective. This book is a personal letter from Paul to Philemon about a runaway slave named Onesimus. Paul had crossed paths with Onesimus in Rome and led him to become a believer in Jesus. Paul, respecting Philemon's legal right to Onesimus, sent him back to Colossae. In Philemon 10 – 16, Paul referred to Onesimus as his son and asked Philemon to regard Onesimus as his brother. Because slaves were considered property, this request was very countercultural. Paul advocated that Onesimus be treated the same way he himself would be treated.

The essence of the gospel is freedom. Jesus was anointed by the Holy Spirit to "bind up the brokenhearted, to proclaim freedom for the captives and release from darkness for the prisoners" (Isa 61:1). Jesus came to bring the dead to life. This gospel transcends any socioeconomic status. Without Christ, everyone is lost and enslaved to sin (Ro 6:17 – 18). No one can earn or attain their freedom. Everyone needs Jesus and to embrace his finished work on the cross. Because of the cross, the slave can be set free.

The power of the gospel can exist in every context and at every human level. Paul's words to Philemon help the church understand that in Christ there is a new value system. People are no longer defined by who they once were but rather by their status as children of God. When the church sees people the way that God sees them, it is empowered and emboldened to stand for slaves' freedom. Humans are not property and should never be devalued in any way. Because every person bears the image of God, the church is called to be a voice for those who do not have a voice.

JESUS: OUR GREATER SACRIFICE

HEBREWS

HEBREWS

JESUS' MINISTRY, DEATH, RESURRECTION *c. AD 27 – 30*	HEBREWS WRITTEN *c. AD 68*	JERUSALEM AND THE TEMPLE DESTROYED *c. AD 70*

All of the Old Testament is fulfilled in the person of Christ. To a modern reader, this claim may seem clear. Yet, to the early converts of the Christian faith, the relationship between Jesus and the Old Testament law, sacrificial system and priesthood required careful explanation.

Some of the first Christians were Jewish and understood that Jesus was the one who embodied the ceremonies, sacrifices and laws they held dear. Others were Gentiles who may not have been familiar with the significance of the Jewish faith for the coming of the Christ. The author of Hebrews wrote to connect the Christian faith with all that God had done to reveal himself and his promises throughout the Old Testament.

This task was vital because many of the recipients of the book of Hebrews were questioning their faith in Christ and considering returning to their former way of life in Judaism. Though the author of the book is unknown, he wrote to exhort these believers not to fall away, but to persevere in Christ.

He systematically considers various facets of life for the Old Testament people of God and shows that Jesus is their fulfillment. He wrote to show that Jesus is greater than everything that came before him. He is greater than the towering figures of the Old Testament — men like the inimitable Moses (3:1 – 6). He is a greater Sabbath-rest because he can truly provide long-term rest for his people (3:7 – 19). He is a better priest than those who mediated between the people and God in the Old Testament (4:14 – 16). He is greater than the tabernacle because God does not dwell in a temple built with human hands (8:1 — 9:11). He is a better sacrifice because his substitutionary death was a once-and-for-all offering to God that does not have to be repeated year after year (9:11 – 28). He offers a better covenant between God and mankind, one established on the basis of Christ's blood (8:1 – 13).

Because Jesus is greater, the people would be foolish to neglect such a great salvation and return to lesser forms of worship. The author gives five dire warnings throughout the book on the implications of neglecting the salvation provided in Christ (2:1 – 4; 4:12 – 13; 6:4 – 8; 10:26 – 31; 12:25 – 29). These warnings, combined with the author's testimony to the greatness of Christ, were meant to protect these first Christians from apostasy and to foster their passionate worship of the One who is greater.

WE HAVE BEEN MADE HOLY THROUGH
THE SACRIFICE OF THE BODY
OF JESUS CHRIST ONCE FOR ALL.

Hebrews 10:10

HEBREWS

God's Final Word: His Son

1 In the past God spoke to our ancestors through the prophets at many times and
in various ways, [2]but in these last days he has spoken to us by his Son, whom he
appointed heir of all things, and through whom also he made the universe. [3]The
Son is the radiance of God's glory and the exact representation of his being, sustaining all things by his powerful word. After he had provided purification for sins,
he sat down at the right hand of the Majesty in heaven. [4]So he became as much
superior to the angels as the name he has inherited is superior to theirs.

The Son Superior to Angels

[5]For to which of the angels did God ever say,

"You are my Son;
today I have become your Father"[a]?

Or again,

"I will be his Father,
and he will be my Son"[b]?

[6]And again, when God brings his firstborn into the world, he says,

"Let all God's angels worship him."[c]

[7]In speaking of the angels he says,

"He makes his angels spirits,
and his servants flames of fire."[d]

[8]But about the Son he says,

"Your throne, O God, will last for ever and ever;
a scepter of justice will be the scepter of your kingdom.
[9]You have loved righteousness and hated wickedness;
therefore God, your God, has set you above your companions
by anointing you with the oil of joy."[e]

[10]He also says,

"In the beginning, Lord, you laid the foundations of the earth,
and the heavens are the work of your hands.
[11]They will perish, but you remain;
they will all wear out like a garment.
[12]You will roll them up like a robe;
like a garment they will be changed.
But you remain the same,
and your years will never end."[f]

[13]To which of the angels did God ever say,

"Sit at my right hand
until I make your enemies
a footstool for your feet"[g]?

[14]Are not all angels ministering spirits sent to serve those who will inherit salvation?

---

[a] *5* Psalm 2:7 [b] *5* 2 Samuel 7:14; 1 Chron. 17:13 [c] *6* Deut. 32:43 (see Dead Sea Scrolls and Septuagint) [d] *7* Psalm 104:4 [e] *9* Psalm 45:6,7 [f] *12* Psalm 102:25-27 [g] *13* Psalm 110:1

JESUS IS GREATER

Jesus is greater. This is one of the major themes in the book of Hebrews. Jesus is greater than every person, practice, policy and procedure in the Old Testament. The fact that Jesus is unquestionably greater than the people and practices in the Old Testament is not just an abstract idea with little bearing on life today. Rather, it demonstrates the fact that God's plan to redeem his people has moved forward in the person and work of Jesus. The author of Hebrews drives home the greatness of Jesus by comparing him to a number of people and events from the Old Testament.

Jesus is greater than every person in the Old Testament. Jesus is the Son of God who represents the Father perfectly (v. 3). As a result, Jesus is greater than the angels, and he is greater than Moses (Heb 3:3). Further, Jesus is the ultimate "apostle" and leader of God's people (Heb 3:1). He is the ultimate High Priest whom all the other high priests merely foreshadowed (Heb 4:14). Because of all these things, Jesus and Jesus alone is the only person who can serve as an "anchor for the soul" (Heb 6:19). No one in the Old Testament comes close to Jesus in terms of importance; he is greater than all of them.

Jesus is greater than every event in the Old Testament. Animal sacrifices in the Old Testament were never intended to be an end in themselves; the covering they provided was only temporary. Instead, God designed the entire sacrificial system as a means of pointing people to the ultimate sacrifice for sins: Jesus' work on the cross. Jesus' death established a permanent path by which sinful people could have a relationship with the holy God (Heb 7:24). God promised a day when he would give his people the ability to obey him, a day when he would live in harmony with his people. With this in view, Jesus made a "new covenant" between people and God (Heb 9:15).

Finally, Jesus is the "pioneer and perfecter of faith," which means that he is where people first encounter God and keep encountering God (Heb 12:1 – 2). Jesus never changes, unlike so many patterns and seasons of life (Heb 13:8). To encounter God, people simply need to go to Jesus and trust in his sacrificial work to cover their sins.

Warning to Pay Attention

2 We must pay the most careful attention, therefore, to what we have heard, so that we do not drift away. [2]For since the message spoken through angels was binding, and every violation and disobedience received its just punishment, [3]how shall we escape if we ignore so great a salvation? This salvation, which was first announced by the Lord, was confirmed to us by those who heard him. [4]God also testified to it by signs, wonders and various miracles, and by gifts of the Holy Spirit distributed according to his will.

Jesus Made Fully Human

[5]It is not to angels that he has subjected the world to come, about which we are speaking. [6]But there is a place where someone has testified:

"What is mankind that you are mindful of them,
a son of man that you care for him?
[7]You made them a little[a] lower than the angels;
you crowned them with glory and honor
8 and put everything under their feet."[b,c]

In putting everything under them,[d] God left nothing that is not subject to them.[d] Yet at present we do not see everything subject to them.[d] [9]But we do see Jesus, who was made lower than the angels for a little while, now crowned with glory and honor because he suffered death, so that by the grace of God he might taste death for everyone.

[10]In bringing many sons and daughters to glory, it was fitting that God, for whom and through whom everything exists, should make the pioneer of their salvation perfect through what he suffered. [11]Both the one who makes people holy and those who are made holy are of the same family. So Jesus is not ashamed to call them brothers and sisters.[e] [12]He says,

"I will declare your name to my brothers and sisters;
in the assembly I will sing your praises."[f]

[13]And again,

"I will put my trust in him."[g]

And again he says,

"Here am I, and the children God has given me."[h]

[14]Since the children have flesh and blood, he too shared in their humanity so that by his death he might break the power of him who holds the power of death— that is, the devil— [15]and free those who all their lives were held in slavery by their fear of death. [16]For surely it is not angels he helps, but Abraham's descendants. [17]For this reason he had to be made like them,[i] fully human in every way, in order that he might become a merciful and faithful high priest in service to God, and that he might make atonement for the sins of the people. [18]Because he himself suffered when he was tempted, he is able to help those who are being tempted.

Jesus Greater Than Moses

3 Therefore, holy brothers and sisters, who share in the heavenly calling, fix your thoughts on Jesus, whom we acknowledge as our apostle and high priest. [2]He was faithful to the one who appointed him, just as Moses was faithful in all God's house. [3]Jesus has been found worthy of greater honor than Moses, just as the builder of a house has greater honor than the house itself. [4]For

HEBREWS 3:1–4

APOSTLE AND HIGH PRIEST

In the Old Testament, the office of high priest was critical to the religious life of the Jewish people. The high priest had the important role of representing God to the people and making sacrifices for sin on their behalf to God (Nu 18:1–7). In the New Testament, the office of apostle was critical to the early Christian church. God sent apostles to declare his message of salvation from sin.

Hebrews points out that Jesus is both the greatest high priest and the greatest apostle who ever lived. No one is greater than Jesus, and no one holds a more significant office than he, for he holds the highest position in both the Old and New Testaments. Once and for all, Jesus made the sacrifice for sin that is sufficient for all who would trust him in faith (Heb 10:1–4). Jesus was sent from the Father (Mt 10:40; Mk 9:37), and he sends his church to preach the gospel to the whole world (Jn 20:21).

[a] 7 Or *them for a little while* [b] 6-8 Psalm 8:4-6 [c] 7,8 Or [7]*You made him a little lower than the angels;/ you crowned him with glory and honor/* [8]*and put everything under his feet."*
[d] 8 Or *him* [e] 11 The Greek word for *brothers and sisters* (*adelphoi*) refers here to believers, both men and women, as part of God's family; also in verse 12; and in 3:1, 12; 10:19; 13:22.
[f] 12 Psalm 22:22 [g] 13 Isaiah 8:17 [h] 13 Isaiah 8:18 [i] 17 Or *like his brothers*

every house is built by someone, but God is the builder of everything. 5 "Moses
was faithful as a servant in all God's house,"[a] bearing witness to what would be
spoken by God in the future. 6 But Christ is faithful as the Son over God's house.
And we are his house, if indeed we hold firmly to our confidence and the hope
in which we glory.

Warning Against Unbelief

7 So, as the Holy Spirit says:

"Today, if you hear his voice,
8 do not harden your hearts
as you did in the rebellion,
during the time of testing in the wilderness,
9 where your ancestors tested and tried me,
though for forty years they saw what I did.
10 That is why I was angry with that generation;
I said, 'Their hearts are always going astray,
and they have not known my ways.'
11 So I declared on oath in my anger,
'They shall never enter my rest.' "[b]

12 See to it, brothers and sisters, that none of you has a sinful, unbelieving
heart that turns away from the living God. 13 But encourage one another daily,
as long as it is called "Today," so that none of you may be hardened by sin's deceitfulness. 14 We have come to share in Christ, if indeed we hold our original
conviction firmly to the very end. 15 As has just been said:

"Today, if you hear his voice,
do not harden your hearts
as you did in the rebellion."[c]

16 Who were they who heard and rebelled? Were they not all those Moses led
out of Egypt? 17 And with whom was he angry for forty years? Was it not with those
who sinned, whose bodies perished in the wilderness? 18 And to whom did God
swear that they would never enter his rest if not to those who disobeyed? 19 So we
see that they were not able to enter, because of their unbelief.

A Sabbath-Rest for the People of God

4 Therefore, since the promise of entering his rest still stands, let us be careful
that none of you be found to have fallen short of it. 2 For we also have had the
good news proclaimed to us, just as they did; but the message they heard was
of no value to them, because they did not share the faith of those who obeyed.[d]
3 Now we who have believed enter that rest, just as God has said,

"So I declared on oath in my anger,
'They shall never enter my rest.' "[e]

And yet his works have been finished since the creation of the world. 4 For somewhere he has spoken about the seventh day in these words: "On the seventh day
God rested from all his works."[f] 5 And again in the passage above he says, "They
shall never enter my rest."

6 Therefore since it still remains for some to enter that rest, and since those
who formerly had the good news proclaimed to them did not go in because of
their disobedience, 7 God again set a certain day, calling it "Today." This he did
when a long time later he spoke through David, as in the passage already quoted:

"Today, if you hear his voice,
do not harden your hearts."[c]

---

[a] *5* Num. 12:7 [b] *11* Psalm 95:7-11 [c] *15,7* Psalm 95:7,8 [d] *2* Some manuscripts *because those who heard did not combine it with faith* [e] *3* Psalm 95:11; also in verse 5 [f] *4* Gen. 2:2

HEBREWS 5:1 – 10

COMPASSIONATE HIGH PRIEST

Old Testament priests had many rules to follow. God was not one to be approached flippantly; the priests had to go through certain steps in order to prepare themselves to encounter God (Lev 16; Heb 5:1 – 3). Only on specific occasions could the high priest enter the Most Holy Place to intercede between God and his people.

Jesus is superior to every high priest in the Old Testament priesthood (Heb 4:14 — 7:28). He came to be both the sin sacrifice and the high priest who presided over the atonement. Jesus is fully human — he is able to empathize with the people for whom he makes atonement. And Jesus is fully God — he is able to atone for the sins of people fully and completely. Jesus is also the only high priest who can usher believers directly into the presence of the Father. When he died on the cross for the sins of his people, the curtain of the temple was torn in two from top to bottom (Mk 15:38). This signified that God was no longer unapproachable and that people now have direct access to God through Jesus instead of having to go through an intermediary (Heb 4:16).

Most major religions of the world teach that God dwells at a great distance from people and that he can only be approached with great apprehension. Christianity teaches that Jesus has made a way for God to be with his people.

[8]For if Joshua had given them rest, God would not have spoken later about another day. [9]There remains, then, a Sabbath-rest for the people of God; [10]for anyone
who enters God's rest also rests from their works,[a] just as God did from his. [11]Let
us, therefore, make every effort to enter that rest, so that no one will perish by
following their example of disobedience.

[12]For the word of God is alive and active. Sharper than any double-edged
sword, it penetrates even to dividing soul and spirit, joints and marrow; it judges the thoughts and attitudes of the heart. [13]Nothing in all creation is hidden
from God's sight. Everything is uncovered and laid bare before the eyes of him
to whom we must give account.

Jesus the Great High Priest

[14]Therefore, since we have a great high priest who has ascended into heaven,[b]
Jesus the Son of God, let us hold firmly to the faith we profess. [15]For we do not
have a high priest who is unable to empathize with our weaknesses, but we have
one who has been tempted in every way, just as we are — yet he did not sin. [16]Let
us then approach God's throne of grace with confidence, so that we may receive
mercy and find grace to help us in our time of need.

5 Every high priest is selected from among the people and is appointed to represent the people in matters related to God, to offer gifts and sacrifices for
sins. [2]He is able to deal gently with those who are ignorant and are going astray,
since he himself is subject to weakness. [3]This is why he has to offer sacrifices for
his own sins, as well as for the sins of the people. [4]And no one takes this honor on
himself, but he receives it when called by God, just as Aaron was.

[5]In the same way, Christ did not take on himself the glory of becoming a high
priest. But God said to him,

"You are my Son;
today I have become your Father."[c]

[6]And he says in another place,

"You are a priest forever,
in the order of Melchizedek."[d]

[7]During the days of Jesus' life on earth, he offered up prayers and petitions
with fervent cries and tears to the one who could save him from death, and he
was heard because of his reverent submission. [8]Son though he was, he learned
obedience from what he suffered [9]and, once made perfect, he became the source
of eternal salvation for all who obey him [10]and was designated by God to be high
priest in the order of Melchizedek.

Warning Against Falling Away

[11]We have much to say about this, but it is hard to make it clear to you because
you no longer try to understand. [12]In fact, though by this time you ought to be
teachers, you need someone to teach you the elementary truths of God's word
all over again. You need milk, not solid food! [13]Anyone who lives on milk, being
still an infant, is not acquainted with the teaching about righteousness. [14]But
solid food is for the mature, who by constant use have trained themselves to
distinguish good from evil.

6 Therefore let us move beyond the elementary teachings about Christ and
be taken forward to maturity, not laying again the foundation of repentance
from acts that lead to death,[e] and of faith in God, [2]instruction about cleansing
rites,[f] the laying on of hands, the resurrection of the dead, and eternal judgment.
[3]And God permitting, we will do so.

[4]It is impossible for those who have once been enlightened, who have tasted the heavenly gift, who have shared in the Holy Spirit, [5]who have tasted the

[a] *10* Or *labor* [b] *14* Greek *has gone through the heavens* [c] *5* Psalm 2:7 [d] *6* Psalm 110:4
[e] *1* Or *from useless rituals* [f] *2* Or *about baptisms*

HEBREWS 4:16

THE MAJESTY OF CHRIST

"Christology" is simply the study of who Jesus is and what that implies for the lives of those who believe in him for their salvation. The book of Hebrews provides an especially robust Christology, describing who Jesus is, detailing his many roles in relation to Old Testament Scriptures and outlining what all of this means for each Christian.

Jesus is heir of all things (1:2), which means that as God's "firstborn" Son, Christ will inherit infinite glory and honor.

He is the One through whom God made the world (1:2), the creative agent behind the universe and the One who still stewards his creation.

He is the radiance of God's glory and the exact representation of God's person (1:3), the One who perfectly reflects the majesty of God and is himself God in the flesh.

Jesus sustains the world by his power and sits at the right hand of God (1:3). He is the living, ruling Savior who provides for his creation on a daily basis and who also superintends the universe.

Because he is one with God, Jesus is better than the angels (1:4) — no matter how glorious and awe-inspiring they are — and is also better than Moses (3:3) and all the prophets.

He is the pioneer of our salvation (2:10), the founder of the effort to bring "many sons and daughters to glory."

He is the destroyer of the devil (2:14), overcoming death and Satan through his resurrection.

As a merciful high priest (2:17), Jesus presented his own blood as the perfect sacrifice for human sin.

Also as believers' high priest, he can sympathize with our weaknesses (4:15) because he experienced life as a human on earth.

As an eternal priest, Jesus always makes intercession before God for his people (7:25).

Jesus is the mediator of a better covenant (8:6), superseding the old covenant with its earthly tabernacle and need for animal sacrifices.

He is our model for enduring hostility from sinful people (12:2 – 3). When we are discouraged, we can find great strength and inspiration in Christ's willingness to persevere under persecution.

Jesus is the great Shepherd of the sheep (13:20), the One who cares for us and who will ultimately lead us to our eternal home.

goodness of the word of God and the powers of the coming age 6and who have fallen[a] away, to be brought back to repentance. To their loss they are crucifying the Son of God all over again and subjecting him to public disgrace. 7Land that drinks in the rain often falling on it and that produces a crop useful to those for whom it is farmed receives the blessing of God. 8But land that produces thorns and thistles is worthless and is in danger of being cursed. In the end it will be burned.

9Even though we speak like this, dear friends, we are convinced of better things in your case — the things that have to do with salvation. 10God is not unjust; he will not forget your work and the love you have shown him as you have helped his people and continue to help them. 11We want each of you to show this same diligence to the very end, so that what you hope for may be fully realized. 12We do not want you to become lazy, but to imitate those who through faith and patience inherit what has been promised.

The Certainty of God's Promise

13When God made his promise to Abraham, since there was no one greater for him to swear by, he swore by himself, 14saying, "I will surely bless you and give you many descendants."[b] 15And so after waiting patiently, Abraham received what was promised.

16People swear by someone greater than themselves, and the oath confirms what is said and puts an end to all argument. 17Because God wanted to make the unchanging nature of his purpose very clear to the heirs of what was promised, he confirmed it with an oath. 18God did this so that, by two unchangeable things in which it is impossible for God to lie, we who have fled to take hold of the hope set before us may be greatly encouraged. 19We have this hope as an anchor for the soul, firm and secure. It enters the inner sanctuary behind the curtain, 20where our forerunner, Jesus, has entered on our behalf. He has become a high priest forever, in the order of Melchizedek.

Melchizedek the Priest

7 This Melchizedek was king of Salem and priest of God Most High. He met Abraham returning from the defeat of the kings and blessed him, 2and Abraham gave him a tenth of everything. First, the name Melchizedek means "king of righteousness"; then also, "king of Salem" means "king of peace." 3Without father or mother, without genealogy, without beginning of days or end of life, resembling the Son of God, he remains a priest forever.

4Just think how great he was: Even the patriarch Abraham gave him a tenth of the plunder! 5Now the law requires the descendants of Levi who become priests to collect a tenth from the people — that is, from their fellow Israelites — even though they also are descended from Abraham. 6This man, however, did not trace his descent from Levi, yet he collected a tenth from Abraham and blessed him who had the promises. 7And without doubt the lesser is blessed by the greater. 8In the one case, the tenth is collected by people who die; but in the other case, by him who is declared to be living. 9One might even say that Levi, who collects the tenth, paid the tenth through Abraham, 10because when Melchizedek met Abraham, Levi was still in the body of his ancestor.

Jesus Like Melchizedek

11If perfection could have been attained through the Levitical priesthood — and indeed the law given to the people established that priesthood — why was there still need for another priest to come, one in the order of Melchizedek, not in the order of Aaron? 12For when the priesthood is changed, the law must be changed also. 13He of whom these things are said belonged to a different tribe, and no one from that tribe has ever served at the altar. 14For it is clear that our

HEBREWS 6:1

MATURITY

Having faith in Jesus is all it takes to be made right with God. However, this first step alone is not enough to grow into all of the good things that God desires for his people. The author of Hebrews encouraged his readers to grow in their faith until they reached maturity. To illustrate what this was going to require, the author appealed to the way physical growth relies on nourishment acquired through right eating.

Growth cannot be dependent on "milk" alone — the "elementary teachings about Christ." Instead, growth takes place through "solid food" — the study of God's Word and the daily pursuit of holy living. All of this is possible only by depending on Jesus. Therefore, the writer of Hebrews instructs people in how to strengthen their faith and live a morally acceptable life before God.

The Christian life is a life of progress. It begins with simply trusting in Jesus, and it ends with an eternity of coming to know more about God as one continually grows in both knowledge about God and experiences with God. The life of a Christian is a life that seeks these heavenly realities here and now by growing to maturity by grace, through faith, in Christ.

---

[a] *6* Or *age, 6if they fall* [b] *14* Gen. 22:17

Lord descended from Judah, and in regard to that tribe Moses said nothing
about priests. 15And what we have said is even more clear if another priest like
Melchizedek appears, 16one who has become a priest not on the basis of a regulation as to his ancestry but on the basis of the power of an indestructible life.
17For it is declared:

"You are a priest forever,
in the order of Melchizedek."[a]

18The former regulation is set aside because it was weak and useless 19(for the
law made nothing perfect), and a better hope is introduced, by which we draw
near to God.
20And it was not without an oath! Others became priests without any oath,
21but he became a priest with an oath when God said to him:

"The Lord has sworn
and will not change his mind:
'You are a priest forever.' "[a]

22Because of this oath, Jesus has become the guarantor of a better covenant.
23Now there have been many of those priests, since death prevented them
from continuing in office; 24but because Jesus lives forever, he has a permanent
priesthood. 25Therefore he is able to save completely[b] those who come to God
through him, because he always lives to intercede for them.
26Such a high priest truly meets our need — one who is holy, blameless, pure,
set apart from sinners, exalted above the heavens. 27Unlike the other high
priests, he does not need to offer sacrifices day after day, first for his own sins,
and then for the sins of the people. He sacrificed for their sins once for all when
he offered himself. 28For the law appoints as high priests men in all their weakness; but the oath, which came after the law, appointed the Son, who has been
made perfect forever.

The High Priest of a New Covenant

8 Now the main point of what we are saying is this: We do have such a high
priest, who sat down at the right hand of the throne of the Majesty in heaven,
2and who serves in the sanctuary, the true tabernacle set up by the Lord, not by
a mere human being.
3Every high priest is appointed to offer both gifts and sacrifices, and so it was
necessary for this one also to have something to offer. 4If he were on earth, he
would not be a priest, for there are already priests who offer the gifts prescribed
by the law. 5They serve at a sanctuary that is a copy and shadow of what is in
heaven. This is why Moses was warned when he was about to build the tabernacle: "See to it that you make everything according to the pattern shown you
on the mountain."[c] 6But in fact the ministry Jesus has received is as superior to
theirs as the covenant of which he is mediator is superior to the old one, since the
new covenant is established on better promises.
7For if there had been nothing wrong with that first covenant, no place would
have been sought for another. 8But God found fault with the people and said[d]:

"The days are coming, declares the Lord,
when I will make a new covenant
with the people of Israel
and with the people of Judah.
9It will not be like the covenant
I made with their ancestors
when I took them by the hand
to lead them out of Egypt,

[a] *17,21* Psalm 110:4 [b] *25* Or *forever* [c] *5* Exodus 25:40 [d] *8* Some manuscripts may be translated *fault and said to the people.*

HEBREWS 8:1 – 2

OLD TESTAMENT CONNECTION

People broke the relationship with God that he had established. The creation and the Creator were once tethered together by a life-giving relationship, and humanity broke the bond by sinning against their Creator. Since that moment, life has been filled with pain and frustration because it has not had the life-giving power of God flowing through it. But God loves people too much to leave them in this condition, so he made a series of promises to bring his people out of it.

The Bible speaks of a "new covenant" that God makes with his people. This covenant does not depend on people's ability to fulfill it by loving and being faithful to God. Instead, this covenant depends on God. In this covenant, God promises to help his people obey his law (Jer 31:31 – 34). God also promises to bring his people from death to life and to care for them forever (Eze 37:24 – 26). The author of Hebrews declared that God has fulfilled and accomplished that covenant through Jesus. The sacrifice of the great high priest Jesus supersedes all Old Testament rituals. Jesus, therefore, fulfilled the Old Testament laws. He fulfilled the terms of the covenant by being the priest who presides over the covenant. He is the priest who brings his people into the presence of God (Heb 10:19).

THE SUPERIORITY OF JESUS

The book of Hebrews was written to a group of people in the midst of a great struggle. The original audience was a group of Jewish Christians. Life was difficult as followers of Jesus. These believers faced persecution and hardship. They had their doubts about the gospel and whether their salvation depended only on Jesus. Some were even tempted to give up and turn away from the faith. To these people God sent a clear message: look to Jesus.

More than a prophet, Jesus is God in the flesh (1:2 – 3). More than a man, Jesus is the Creator and Sustainer of all that exists (1:3,10 – 12). More than a high priest who works on behalf of God, Jesus is the Great High Priest who is God and serves people as God (2:10 – 11).

Many Christians look at their circumstances and settle for superficial spirituality. They look for religious practices to improve their lives without truly turning to Jesus to provide what they really need. They major on minor points and don't take Jesus' offer of a better life seriously. Many other Christians are tempted to be overwhelmed by the weight and worry of life and give up on asking Jesus for help. These kinds of Christians suffer in a different way as they allow negativity and difficulty to dominate their lives. For both types of people, God sends the message of Hebrews, which is the message of the gospel: Jesus Christ comes to people and gives his life to them. For every situation that followers of Jesus face, the message of the book is to simply look to Jesus, who is better than any person or experience they have ever encountered before. Jesus is the perfect example of perseverance and is also the One who actively provides for and cares for his people.

Jesus has provided forgiveness of sins. This means that people can go to him and find eternal life. Eternal life is not just about where we go when we die (though that is certainly important); it is also about the fullness of life. Life with Jesus is about having a full and rich experience of life now; this is God's word of hope to people who struggle with their circumstances. When people look to Jesus, they receive from God the assurance that they do not need to look anywhere else or settle for anything less (13:20 – 21).

because they did not remain faithful to my covenant,
and I turned away from them,
declares the Lord.
10 This is the covenant I will establish with the people of Israel
after that time, declares the Lord.
I will put my laws in their minds
and write them on their hearts.
I will be their God,
and they will be my people.
11 No longer will they teach their neighbor,
or say to one another, 'Know the Lord,'
because they will all know me,
from the least of them to the greatest.
12 For I will forgive their wickedness
and will remember their sins no more."[a]

13 By calling this covenant "new," he has made the first one obsolete; and what
is obsolete and outdated will soon disappear.

Worship in the Earthly Tabernacle

9 Now the first covenant had regulations for worship and also an earthly
sanctuary. 2 A tabernacle was set up. In its first room were the lampstand
and the table with its consecrated bread; this was called the Holy Place. 3 Behind the second curtain was a room called the Most Holy Place, 4 which had the
golden altar of incense and the gold-covered ark of the covenant. This ark contained the gold jar of manna, Aaron's staff that had budded, and the stone tablets of the covenant. 5 Above the ark were the cherubim of the Glory, overshadowing the atonement cover. But we cannot discuss these things in detail now.
6 When everything had been arranged like this, the priests entered regularly
into the outer room to carry on their ministry. 7 But only the high priest entered
the inner room, and that only once a year, and never without blood, which he offered for himself and for the sins the people had committed in ignorance. 8 The
Holy Spirit was showing by this that the way into the Most Holy Place had not
yet been disclosed as long as the first tabernacle was still functioning. 9 This is
an illustration for the present time, indicating that the gifts and sacrifices being
offered were not able to clear the conscience of the worshiper. 10 They are only a
matter of food and drink and various ceremonial washings — external regulations applying until the time of the new order.

The Blood of Christ

11 But when Christ came as high priest of the good things that are now already
here,[b] he went through the greater and more perfect tabernacle that is not made
with human hands, that is to say, is not a part of this creation. 12 He did not enter
by means of the blood of goats and calves; but he entered the Most Holy Place
once for all by his own blood, thus obtaining[c] eternal redemption. 13 The blood
of goats and bulls and the ashes of a heifer sprinkled on those who are ceremonially unclean sanctify them so that they are outwardly clean. 14 How much more,
then, will the blood of Christ, who through the eternal Spirit offered himself
unblemished to God, cleanse our consciences from acts that lead to death,[d] so
that we may serve the living God!
15 For this reason Christ is the mediator of a new covenant, that those who
are called may receive the promised eternal inheritance — now that he has
died as a ransom to set them free from the sins committed under the first covenant.
16 In the case of a will,[e] it is necessary to prove the death of the one who made

[a] *12* Jer. 31:31-34 [b] *11* Some early manuscripts *are to come* [c] *12* Or *blood, having obtained* [d] *14* Or *from useless rituals* [e] *16* Same Greek word as *covenant*; also in verse 17

HEBREWS 9:11–15

THE BLOOD THAT CLEANSES

Some things can easily be removed or fixed with minor adjustments. Sin is not one of those things. Sin separates people from God because God is holy (1Pe 1:16). From creation, God has spoken clearly about the fact that sin leads to death (Ge 2:17). Therefore, sin will always lead to the shedding of blood. Sin is costly.

God set up a temporary sacrificial system to provide relief and cover the sins of people — sin-payment from the blood of animals (Lev 4; 16). This system was only temporary because the blood of animals cannot cover the sins of people forever (Heb 9:12,14). The animals functioned as substitutes for people, and they died so that the people could live.

In dramatic fashion, God sent Jesus to be the sacrificial Lamb who would die for the sins of the world. Jesus was "unblemished," meaning that his relationship with God was not broken because of sin. This means that Jesus did not deserve to die, but chose to die for sinners as their substitute. Therefore, Jesus' blood cleanses people from their sins. Unlike Old Testament priests who entered into a man-made temple, God admitted Jesus into his very presence (9:24). When Jesus returns to earth, it will not be "to bear sin, but to bring salvation to those who are waiting for him" (9:28). His offer of forgiveness must be accepted in faith (1Pe 1:18–21).

it, [17]because a will is in force only when somebody has died; it never takes effect
while the one who made it is living. [18]This is why even the first covenant was not
put into effect without blood. [19]When Moses had proclaimed every command of
the law to all the people, he took the blood of calves, together with water, scarlet wool and branches of hyssop, and sprinkled the scroll and all the people.
[20]He said, "This is the blood of the covenant, which God has commanded you
to keep."[a] [21]In the same way, he sprinkled with the blood both the tabernacle
and everything used in its ceremonies. [22]In fact, the law requires that nearly
everything be cleansed with blood, and without the shedding of blood there is
no forgiveness.

[23]It was necessary, then, for the copies of the heavenly things to be purified
with these sacrifices, but the heavenly things themselves with better sacrifices
than these. [24]For Christ did not enter a sanctuary made with human hands that
was only a copy of the true one; he entered heaven itself, now to appear for us in
God's presence. [25]Nor did he enter heaven to offer himself again and again, the
way the high priest enters the Most Holy Place every year with blood that is not
his own. [26]Otherwise Christ would have had to suffer many times since the creation of the world. But he has appeared once for all at the culmination of the ages
to do away with sin by the sacrifice of himself. [27]Just as people are destined to
die once, and after that to face judgment, [28]so Christ was sacrificed once to take
away the sins of many; and he will appear a second time, not to bear sin, but to
bring salvation to those who are waiting for him.

Christ's Sacrifice Once for All

10 The law is only a shadow of the good things that are coming — not the
realities themselves. For this reason it can never, by the same sacrifices
repeated endlessly year after year, make perfect those who draw near to worship. [2]Otherwise, would they not have stopped being offered? For the worshipers
would have been cleansed once for all, and would no longer have felt guilty for
their sins. [3]But those sacrifices are an annual reminder of sins. [4]It is impossible
for the blood of bulls and goats to take away sins.

[5]Therefore, when Christ came into the world, he said:

"Sacrifice and offering you did not desire,
but a body you prepared for me;
[6]with burnt offerings and sin offerings
you were not pleased.
[7]Then I said, 'Here I am — it is written about me in the scroll —
I have come to do your will, my God.'"[b]

[8]First he said, "Sacrifices and offerings, burnt offerings and sin offerings you
did not desire, nor were you pleased with them" — though they were offered in
accordance with the law. [9]Then he said, "Here I am, I have come to do your will."
He sets aside the first to establish the second. [10]And by that will, we have been
made holy through the sacrifice of the body of Jesus Christ once for all.

[11]Day after day every priest stands and performs his religious duties; again
and again he offers the same sacrifices, which can never take away sins. [12]But
when this priest had offered for all time one sacrifice for sins, he sat down at the
right hand of God, [13]and since that time he waits for his enemies to be made his
footstool. [14]For by one sacrifice he has made perfect forever those who are being
made holy.

[15]The Holy Spirit also testifies to us about this. First he says:

[16]"This is the covenant I will make with them
after that time, says the Lord.
I will put my laws in their hearts,
and I will write them on their minds."[c]

---

[a] *20* Exodus 24:8 [b] *7* Psalm 40:6-8 (see Septuagint) [c] *16* Jer. 31:33

[17]Then he adds:

"Their sins and lawless acts
I will remember no more."[a]

[18]And where these have been forgiven, sacrifice for sin is no longer necessary.

A Call to Persevere in Faith

[19]Therefore, brothers and sisters, since we have confidence to enter the Most
Holy Place by the blood of Jesus, [20]by a new and living way opened for us through
the curtain, that is, his body, [21]and since we have a great priest over the house
of God, [22]let us draw near to God with a sincere heart and with the full assurance that faith brings, having our hearts sprinkled to cleanse us from a guilty
conscience and having our bodies washed with pure water. [23]Let us hold unswervingly to the hope we profess, for he who promised is faithful. [24]And let us
consider how we may spur one another on toward love and good deeds, [25]not
giving up meeting together, as some are in the habit of doing, but encouraging
one another—and all the more as you see the Day approaching.

[26]If we deliberately keep on sinning after we have received the knowledge of the
truth, no sacrifice for sins is left, [27]but only a fearful expectation of judgment and of
raging fire that will consume the enemies of God. [28]Anyone who rejected the law of
Moses died without mercy on the testimony of two or three witnesses. [29]How much
more severely do you think someone deserves to be punished who has trampled
the Son of God underfoot, who has treated as an unholy thing the blood of the
covenant that sanctified them, and who has insulted the Spirit of grace? [30]For we
know him who said, "It is mine to avenge; I will repay,"[b] and again, "The Lord will
judge his people."[c] [31]It is a dreadful thing to fall into the hands of the living God.

[32]Remember those earlier days after you had received the light, when you
endured in a great conflict full of suffering. [33]Sometimes you were publicly exposed to insult and persecution; at other times you stood side by side with those
who were so treated. [34]You suffered along with those in prison and joyfully accepted the confiscation of your property, because you knew that you yourselves
had better and lasting possessions. [35]So do not throw away your confidence; it
will be richly rewarded.

[36]You need to persevere so that when you have done the will of God, you will
receive what he has promised. [37]For,

"In just a little while,
he who is coming will come
and will not delay."[d]

[38]And,

"But my righteous[e] one will live by faith.
And I take no pleasure
in the one who shrinks back."[f]

[39]But we do not belong to those who shrink back and are destroyed, but to those
who have faith and are saved.

Faith in Action

11 Now faith is confidence in what we hope for and assurance about what we
do not see. [2]This is what the ancients were commended for.

[3]By faith we understand that the universe was formed at God's command, so
that what is seen was not made out of what was visible.

[4]By faith Abel brought God a better offering than Cain did. By faith he was
commended as righteous, when God spoke well of his offerings. And by faith
Abel still speaks, even though he is dead.

[a] *17* Jer. 31:34 [b] *30* Deut. 32:35 [c] *30* Deut. 32:36; Psalm 135:14 [d] *37* Isaiah 26:20; Hab. 2:3 [e] *38* Some early manuscripts *But the righteous* [f] *38* Hab. 2:4 (see Septuagint)

HEBREWS 10:35–39

PERSEVERANCE

Newton's third law states that "For every action, there is an equal and opposite reaction." When an object is pushed, there will always be movement of some sort. In a similar way, the Christian life is full of pressures that God allows to happen in order to push his people into deeper dependence on him.

One of the reasons that God gave his church the book of Hebrews is to encourage his people to endure in the midst of persecution. The Christian life will have moments, perhaps even seasons, of opposition. This should not surprise followers of Christ. Jesus himself even warned his disciples that they would experience hardships (Mt 24:9–10). Yet, this warning is followed by an encouragement: some people will continue to believe, all people will have an opportunity to believe and Jesus will come back to save his people (Mt 24:11–14).

The author of Hebrews twice told his audience to hang on and endure, and in between those exhortations he highlights Jesus as the hope for people who are in the midst of difficult situations. When the pressure increases, Christians are encouraged to remember those who endured faithfully. Among those who lived lives worthy of imitation, Jesus is the greatest example. Jesus won victory through suffering and lives to give strength in every moment.

5By faith Enoch was taken from this life, so that he did not experience death:
"He could not be found, because God had taken him away."[a] For before he was
taken, he was commended as one who pleased God. 6And without faith it is impossible to please God, because anyone who comes to him must believe that he
exists and that he rewards those who earnestly seek him.

7By faith Noah, when warned about things not yet seen, in holy fear built an
ark to save his family. By his faith he condemned the world and became heir of
the righteousness that is in keeping with faith.

8By faith Abraham, when called to go to a place he would later receive as his
inheritance, obeyed and went, even though he did not know where he was going. 9By faith he made his home in the promised land like a stranger in a foreign
country; he lived in tents, as did Isaac and Jacob, who were heirs with him of
the same promise. 10For he was looking forward to the city with foundations,
whose architect and builder is God. 11And by faith even Sarah, who was past
childbearing age, was enabled to bear children because she[b] considered him
faithful who had made the promise. 12And so from this one man, and he as good
as dead, came descendants as numerous as the stars in the sky and as countless
as the sand on the seashore.

13All these people were still living by faith when they died. They did not receive the things promised; they only saw them and welcomed them from a distance, admitting that they were foreigners and strangers on earth. 14People who
say such things show that they are looking for a country of their own. 15If they had
been thinking of the country they had left, they would have had opportunity to
return. 16Instead, they were longing for a better country — a heavenly one. Therefore God is not ashamed to be called their God, for he has prepared a city for them.

17By faith Abraham, when God tested him, offered Isaac as a sacrifice. He who
had embraced the promises was about to sacrifice his one and only son, 18even
though God had said to him, "It is through Isaac that your offspring will be reckoned."[c] 19Abraham reasoned that God could even raise the dead, and so in a
manner of speaking he did receive Isaac back from death.

20By faith Isaac blessed Jacob and Esau in regard to their future.

21By faith Jacob, when he was dying, blessed each of Joseph's sons, and worshiped as he leaned on the top of his staff.

22By faith Joseph, when his end was near, spoke about the exodus of the Israelites from Egypt and gave instructions concerning the burial of his bones.

23By faith Moses' parents hid him for three months after he was born, because
they saw he was no ordinary child, and they were not afraid of the king's edict.

24By faith Moses, when he had grown up, refused to be known as the son of
Pharaoh's daughter. 25He chose to be mistreated along with the people of God
rather than to enjoy the fleeting pleasures of sin. 26He regarded disgrace for the
sake of Christ as of greater value than the treasures of Egypt, because he was
looking ahead to his reward. 27By faith he left Egypt, not fearing the king's anger;
he persevered because he saw him who is invisible. 28By faith he kept the Passover and the application of blood, so that the destroyer of the firstborn would not
touch the firstborn of Israel.

29By faith the people passed through the Red Sea as on dry land; but when the
Egyptians tried to do so, they were drowned.

30By faith the walls of Jericho fell, after the army had marched around them
for seven days.

31By faith the prostitute Rahab, because she welcomed the spies, was not
killed with those who were disobedient.[d]

32And what more shall I say? I do not have time to tell about Gideon, Barak, Samson and Jephthah, about David and Samuel and the prophets, 33who
through faith conquered kingdoms, administered justice, and gained what was

---

[a] *5* Gen. 5:24 [b] *11* Or *By faith Abraham, even though he was too old to have children — and Sarah herself was not able to conceive — was enabled to become a father because he*
[c] *18* Gen. 21:12 [d] *31* Or *unbelieving*

HEBREWS 11:1 – 40

FAITH

Faith is an intense form of trust, and people's relationship with God has always operated on the basis of faith. Time and time again, all throughout the Bible, salvation is found in the same way: trusting God's promises by faith, and then following God's commands. Hebrews 11 looks at faith through the lens of the stories of people who lived their lives by faith in God. Faith is "confidence in what we hope for and assurance about what we do not see" (v. 1), and these biblical characters were commended for having such faith, understanding that faith was necessary to please God (v. 6). In faith, Abel offered a costly sacrifice (v. 4); Enoch lived in a way that pleased God (v. 5); Noah obeyed divine warnings and built a giant ark (v. 7), having never seen a drop of rain; Abraham left his hometown of Ur and went out, not knowing where God was leading (v. 8); Sarah bore Isaac in her old age (v. 11), and the stories continue.

The writer of Hebrews makes the point that many Old Testament people of faith trusted God for power and victory, and they refused to compromise their faith in God, even in the midst of life-threatening circumstances (vv. 32 – 38). Some of these faithful people died without having received what God had promised (v. 13); some had to find consolation in the fact that they would not realize the full blessings of God until they entered heaven (vv. 14 – 16). Other people powerfully experienced God's strength and deliverance (vv. 33 – 35) and their testimony of deliverance still stands. But many others, despite their implicit trust in God, experienced torture, mocking, beatings, imprisonment, stoning, destitution and affliction (vv. 35 – 38). These are the people of whom the world was not worthy (v. 38).

Because of the example of these faithful ones, we should be motivated to lay aside every weight that threatens to slow us down in our pursuit of God's kingdom. When we do, we'll be much better able to "run with perseverance the race marked out for us" (12:1), looking to Jesus as our ultimate example of determination and faithfulness.

All of God's promises are kept in Jesus. Every promise that God made to these people in the Old Testament looked ahead to Jesus. By believing the promise, these people were made right with God. Every promise God makes to people in the New Testament also looks to Jesus, whose work enables the blessings of God to come to people. In every case, God's promises are kept in Jesus, the "pioneer and perfecter of faith" (12:2).

promised; who shut the mouths of lions, [34]quenched the fury of the flames, and escaped the edge of the sword; whose weakness was turned to strength; and who became powerful in battle and routed foreign armies. [35]Women received back their dead, raised to life again. There were others who were tortured, refusing to be released so that they might gain an even better resurrection. [36]Some faced jeers and flogging, and even chains and imprisonment. [37]They were put to death by stoning;[a] they were sawed in two; they were killed by the sword. They went about in sheepskins and goatskins, destitute, persecuted and mistreated — [38]the world was not worthy of them. They wandered in deserts and mountains, living in caves and in holes in the ground.

[39]These were all commended for their faith, yet none of them received what had been promised, [40]since God had planned something better for us so that only together with us would they be made perfect.

12 Therefore, since we are surrounded by such a great cloud of witnesses, let us throw off everything that hinders and the sin that so easily entangles. And let us run with perseverance the race marked out for us, [2]fixing our eyes on Jesus, the pioneer and perfecter of faith. For the joy set before him he endured the cross, scorning its shame, and sat down at the right hand of the throne of God. [3]Consider him who endured such opposition from sinners, so that you will not grow weary and lose heart.

HEBREWS 12:1 – 3

FIXING OUR EYES ON JESUS

Perception is a powerful thing. The author of Hebrews encouraged Christians to stare obsessively at Jesus in the face of their circumstances. While remembering Jesus in everything is a wonderful idea, it is difficult actually to do. Life is full of needs and demands, and people can easily become distracted by things that are inconsequential; they become burdened by things that are beyond their ability to control.

Despite the problems of life, God wants people to look to Jesus. When people get a glimpse of who God really is, they then see themselves for what they really are, and life comes into focus. God tells people to look to Jesus because doing so actually has a transformative effect on life. Paul spoke of this as well when writing to encourage the church to be faithful to Jesus. He told them that as they beheld God's glory, God would transform them and change their lives (2Co 3:18). Put simply, people become what they behold.

God Disciplines His Children

[4]In your struggle against sin, you have not yet resisted to the point of shedding your blood. [5]And have you completely forgotten this word of encouragement that addresses you as a father addresses his son? It says,

"My son, do not make light of the Lord's discipline,
and do not lose heart when he rebukes you,
[6]because the Lord disciplines the one he loves,
and he chastens everyone he accepts as his son."[b]

[7]Endure hardship as discipline; God is treating you as his children. For what children are not disciplined by their father? [8]If you are not disciplined — and everyone undergoes discipline — then you are not legitimate, not true sons and daughters at all. [9]Moreover, we have all had human fathers who disciplined us and we respected them for it. How much more should we submit to the Father of spirits and live! [10]They disciplined us for a little while as they thought best; but God disciplines us for our good, in order that we may share in his holiness. [11]No discipline seems pleasant at the time, but painful. Later on, however, it produces a harvest of righteousness and peace for those who have been trained by it.

[12]Therefore, strengthen your feeble arms and weak knees. [13]"Make level paths for your feet,"[c] so that the lame may not be disabled, but rather healed.

Warning and Encouragement

[14]Make every effort to live in peace with everyone and to be holy; without holiness no one will see the Lord. [15]See to it that no one falls short of the grace of God and that no bitter root grows up to cause trouble and defile many. [16]See that no one is sexually immoral, or is godless like Esau, who for a single meal sold his inheritance rights as the oldest son. [17]Afterward, as you know, when he wanted to inherit this blessing, he was rejected. Even though he sought the blessing with tears, he could not change what he had done.

The Mountain of Fear and the Mountain of Joy

[18]You have not come to a mountain that can be touched and that is burning with fire; to darkness, gloom and storm; [19]to a trumpet blast or to such a voice

[a] *37* Some early manuscripts *stoning; they were put to the test;* [b] *5,6* Prov. 3:11,12 (see Septuagint) [c] *13* Prov. 4:26

speaking words that those who heard it begged that no further word be spoken to
them, [20]because they could not bear what was commanded: "If even an animal
touches the mountain, it must be stoned to death."[a] [21]The sight was so terrifying
that Moses said, "I am trembling with fear."[b]

[22]But you have come to Mount Zion, to the city of the living God, the heavenly
Jerusalem. You have come to thousands upon thousands of angels in joyful assembly, [23]to the church of the firstborn, whose names are written in heaven. You
have come to God, the Judge of all, to the spirits of the righteous made perfect,
[24]to Jesus the mediator of a new covenant, and to the sprinkled blood that speaks
a better word than the blood of Abel.

[25]See to it that you do not refuse him who speaks. If they did not escape when
they refused him who warned them on earth, how much less will we, if we turn
away from him who warns us from heaven? [26]At that time his voice shook the
earth, but now he has promised, "Once more I will shake not only the earth but
also the heavens."[c] [27]The words "once more" indicate the removing of what can
be shaken — that is, created things — so that what cannot be shaken may remain.

[28]Therefore, since we are receiving a kingdom that cannot be shaken, let us
be thankful, and so worship God acceptably with reverence and awe, [29]for our
"God is a consuming fire."[d]

Concluding Exhortations

13 Keep on loving one another as brothers and sisters. [2]Do not forget to show
hospitality to strangers, for by so doing some people have shown hospitality to angels without knowing it. [3]Continue to remember those in prison as if
you were together with them in prison, and those who are mistreated as if you
yourselves were suffering.

[4]Marriage should be honored by all, and the marriage bed kept pure, for God
will judge the adulterer and all the sexually immoral. [5]Keep your lives free from
the love of money and be content with what you have, because God has said,

> "Never will I leave you;
> never will I forsake you."[e]

[6]So we say with confidence,

> "The Lord is my helper; I will not be afraid.
> What can mere mortals do to me?"[f]

[7]Remember your leaders, who spoke the word of God to you. Consider the
outcome of their way of life and imitate their faith. [8]Jesus Christ is the same yesterday and today and forever.

[9]Do not be carried away by all kinds of strange teachings. It is good for our
hearts to be strengthened by grace, not by eating ceremonial foods, which is of
no benefit to those who do so. [10]We have an altar from which those who minister
at the tabernacle have no right to eat.

[11]The high priest carries the blood of animals into the Most Holy Place as a
sin offering, but the bodies are burned outside the camp. [12]And so Jesus also suffered outside the city gate to make the people holy through his own blood. [13]Let
us, then, go to him outside the camp, bearing the disgrace he bore. [14]For here
we do not have an enduring city, but we are looking for the city that is to come.

[15]Through Jesus, therefore, let us continually offer to God a sacrifice of
praise — the fruit of lips that openly profess his name. [16]And do not forget to do
good and to share with others, for with such sacrifices God is pleased.

[17]Have confidence in your leaders and submit to their authority, because they
keep watch over you as those who must give an account. Do this so that their
work will be a joy, not a burden, for that would be of no benefit to you.

[18]Pray for us. We are sure that we have a clear conscience and desire to live

---

[a] *20* Exodus 19:12,13 [b] *21* See Deut. 9:19. [c] *26* Haggai 2:6 [d] *29* Deut. 4:24
[e] *5* Deut. 31:6 [f] *6* Psalm 118:6,7

honorably in every way. [19]I particularly urge you to pray so that I may be restored
to you soon.

Benediction and Final Greetings

[20]Now may the God of peace, who through the blood of the eternal covenant
brought back from the dead our Lord Jesus, that great Shepherd of the sheep,
[21]equip you with everything good for doing his will, and may he work in us what
is pleasing to him, through Jesus Christ, to whom be glory for ever and ever.
Amen.

[22]Brothers and sisters, I urge you to bear with my word of exhortation, for in
fact I have written to you quite briefly.
[23]I want you to know that our brother Timothy has been released. If he arrives
soon, I will come with him to see you.
[24]Greet all your leaders and all the Lord's people. Those from Italy send you
their greetings.
[25]Grace be with you all.

JESUS: OUR PERFECT EXAMPLE

JAMES

JAMES

JAMES WRITES HIS LETTER *c. AD 46 – 61*	JAMES LEADS JERUSALEM COUNCIL *c. AD 50*	JAMES MARTYRED IN JERUSALEM *c. AD 62 – 69*

Jesus transforms every aspect of life. All of the New Testament letters describe the transformation that the good news brings to those who embrace it by faith. The book of James is unique in its singular focus on this theme. James, the half brother of Jesus, is thought to be the author of this book bearing his name. He wrote to the believers scattered abroad who were undoubtedly facing persecution for their faith in Christ (1:1).

James begins his letter by challenging believers to find joy in the midst of their suffering. They can find comfort in the knowledge that God is using these trials to make his people holy (1:2 – 4). Though they were a scattered, persecuted minority living among idolatrous nations, believers could have hope that God was at work.

Christians today also can seek wisdom from the Lord and find guidance for faithful living (1:5 – 7). God provides wisdom to his people through his Spirit and his Word, and believers honor God when they listen to the voice of God and obey what he says (1:19 – 27). James connects one's faith in God with their obedience to his commands. He wrote that one who professes faith in Christ but lives in rebellion to his commands is a liar (2:14 – 26). The connection between faith and obedience, according to James, should be seen in the way a Christian loves and serves others (2:1 – 13), guards their speech from sin (3:1 – 12) and rejects worldly forms of wickedness and rebellion from God (4:1 – 10). James bookends his letter with another reminder of patient suffering in light of the coming return of Christ (5:7 – 11). Endurance under this kind of intense suffering requires Christian community — other believers who are given by God to pray, love and serve one another, as they together seek to obey God.

Though James does not speak at great length about Jesus, it is clear that the principles he outlines in his letter follow the model set forth by Jesus during his earthly ministry. As the perfect Son of God, he patiently suffered with an awareness that he was fulfilling the Father's perfect plan. All the while, he modeled virtues that James calls the church to embody. By fixing their gaze and affections on Christ, they could be doers of the Word and not merely hearers only.

CONSIDER IT PURE JOY,
MY BROTHERS AND SISTERS,
WHENEVER YOU FACE TRIALS
OF MANY KINDS.

James 1:2

JAMES

1 James, a servant of God and of the Lord Jesus Christ,

To the twelve tribes scattered among the nations:

Greetings.

Trials and Temptations

[2]Consider it pure joy, my brothers and sisters,[a] whenever you face trials of many kinds, [3]because you know that the testing of your faith produces perseverance. [4]Let perseverance finish its work so that you may be mature and complete, not lacking anything. [5]If any of you lacks wisdom, you should ask God, who gives generously to all without finding fault, and it will be given to you. [6]But when you ask, you must believe and not doubt, because the one who doubts is like a wave of the sea, blown and tossed by the wind. [7]That person should not expect to receive anything from the Lord. [8]Such a person is double-minded and unstable in all they do.

[9]Believers in humble circumstances ought to take pride in their high position. [10]But the rich should take pride in their humiliation — since they will pass away like a wild flower. [11]For the sun rises with scorching heat and withers the plant; its blossom falls and its beauty is destroyed. In the same way, the rich will fade away even while they go about their business.

[12]Blessed is the one who perseveres under trial because, having stood the test, that person will receive the crown of life that the Lord has promised to those who love him.

[13]When tempted, no one should say, "God is tempting me." For God cannot be tempted by evil, nor does he tempt anyone; [14]but each person is tempted when they are dragged away by their own evil desire and enticed. [15]Then, after desire has conceived, it gives birth to sin; and sin, when it is full-grown, gives birth to death.

[16]Don't be deceived, my dear brothers and sisters. [17]Every good and perfect gift is from above, coming down from the Father of the heavenly lights, who does not change like shifting shadows. [18]He chose to give us birth through the word of truth, that we might be a kind of firstfruits of all he created.

Listening and Doing

[19]My dear brothers and sisters, take note of this: Everyone should be quick to listen, slow to speak and slow to become angry, [20]because human anger does not produce the righteousness that God desires. [21]Therefore, get rid of all moral filth and the evil that is so prevalent and humbly accept the word planted in you, which can save you.

[22]Do not merely listen to the word, and so deceive yourselves. Do what it says. [23]Anyone who listens to the word but does not do what it says is like someone who looks at his face in a mirror [24]and, after looking at himself, goes away and immediately forgets what he looks like. [25]But whoever looks intently into the perfect law that gives freedom, and continues in it — not forgetting what they have heard, but doing it — they will be blessed in what they do.

[26]Those who consider themselves religious and yet do not keep a tight rein on their tongues deceive themselves, and their religion is worthless. [27]Religion that

[a] *2* The Greek word for *brothers and sisters* (*adelphoi*) refers here to believers, both men and women, as part of God's family; also in verses 16 and 19; and in 2:1, 5, 14; 3:10, 12; 4:11; 5:7, 9, 10, 12, 19.

JAMES 1:19 – 27

LIVING FOR JESUS

The book of James is filled with practical commands for authentic Christian living. In his letter, James, the brother of Jesus, instructed Christians to control their tongues, be slow to anger and fight selfish ambition. But James was not interested in simply sharing a list of things Christians *should not* do — he also included a number of positive commands for believers.

Just as Jesus spent much of his ministry among those neglected by society, followers of Jesus are commanded to care for and show concern for people who are orphans and widows, the underprivileged, and for sinning brothers and sisters. James placed a specific emphasis on believers emulating the everyday ministry of Jesus within their own lives by showing compassion toward the brokenhearted and poor and by avoiding sin.

The disciples of Jesus should not merely listen to the words of Jesus; they should actively seek opportunities to engage the world with his life-changing message. Just as with Jesus, a believer's relationships with others — be it family, friends, coworkers or a person who is begging on the street — should be defined by love, mercy, patience and grace.

God our Father accepts as pure and faultless is this: to look after orphans and widows in their distress and to keep oneself from being polluted by the world.

Favoritism Forbidden

2 My brothers and sisters, believers in our glorious Lord Jesus Christ must not show favoritism. 2Suppose a man comes into your meeting wearing a gold ring and fine clothes, and a poor man in filthy old clothes also comes in. 3If you show special attention to the man wearing fine clothes and say, "Here's a good seat for you," but say to the poor man, "You stand there" or "Sit on the floor by my feet," 4have you not discriminated among yourselves and become judges with evil thoughts?

5Listen, my dear brothers and sisters: Has not God chosen those who are poor in the eyes of the world to be rich in faith and to inherit the kingdom he promised those who love him? 6But you have dishonored the poor. Is it not the rich who are exploiting you? Are they not the ones who are dragging you into court? 7Are they not the ones who are blaspheming the noble name of him to whom you belong?

8If you really keep the royal law found in Scripture, "Love your neighbor as yourself,"[a] you are doing right. 9But if you show favoritism, you sin and are convicted by the law as lawbreakers. 10For whoever keeps the whole law and yet stumbles at just one point is guilty of breaking all of it. 11For he who said, "You shall not commit adultery,"[b] also said, "You shall not murder."[c] If you do not commit adultery but do commit murder, you have become a lawbreaker.

12Speak and act as those who are going to be judged by the law that gives freedom, 13because judgment without mercy will be shown to anyone who has not been merciful. Mercy triumphs over judgment.

Faith and Deeds

14What good is it, my brothers and sisters, if someone claims to have faith but has no deeds? Can such faith save them? 15Suppose a brother or a sister is without clothes and daily food. 16If one of you says to them, "Go in peace; keep warm and well fed," but does nothing about their physical needs, what good is it? 17In the same way, faith by itself, if it is not accompanied by action, is dead.

18But someone will say, "You have faith; I have deeds."

Show me your faith without deeds, and I will show you my faith by my deeds. 19You believe that there is one God. Good! Even the demons believe that—and shudder.

20You foolish person, do you want evidence that faith without deeds is useless[d]? 21Was not our father Abraham considered righteous for what he did when he offered his son Isaac on the altar? 22You see that his faith and his actions were working together, and his faith was made complete by what he did. 23And the scripture was fulfilled that says, "Abraham believed God, and it was credited to him as righteousness,"[e] and he was called God's friend. 24You see that a person is considered righteous by what they do and not by faith alone.

25In the same way, was not even Rahab the prostitute considered righteous for what she did when she gave lodging to the spies and sent them off in a different direction? 26As the body without the spirit is dead, so faith without deeds is dead.

Taming the Tongue

3 Not many of you should become teachers, my fellow believers, because you know that we who teach will be judged more strictly. 2We all stumble in many ways. Anyone who is never at fault in what they say is perfect, able to keep their whole body in check.

3When we put bits into the mouths of horses to make them obey us, we can turn the whole animal. 4Or take ships as an example. Although they are so large and are driven by strong winds, they are steered by a very small rudder wherever the pilot

---

[a] *8* Lev. 19:18 [b] *11* Exodus 20:14; Deut. 5:18 [c] *11* Exodus 20:13; Deut. 5:17 [d] *20* Some early manuscripts *dead* [e] *23* Gen. 15:6

JAMES 2:14–26

FAITH AND WORKS

At first glance, James's statements concerning justification seem to contradict the message of the apostle Paul. In 2:24, James declared that "a person is considered righteous by what they do and not by faith alone." But in Romans 3:28, Paul wrote that "a person is justified by faith apart from the works of the law." This raises a critical question: Are Christians saved by faith in Jesus alone or by faith combined with their own efforts? It is important to note that these men were not as far apart as the above quotes seem. James and Paul knew each other. They were both major contributors at the first church council in Jerusalem, which assembled specifically to address the relationship between faith and works. As recorded in Acts 15, they arrived at a consensus.

Paul preached that a person is declared to be in a right relationship with God by grace alone, through faith alone in the finished work of Jesus, with no basis whatsoever in works (Ro 3:28; Gal 2:16; Eph 2:8–9). At the moment of conversion, God sends his Spirit into the new believer (Gal 3:26; 4:6). Paul describes this as a new birth. The Spirit then works within the Christian to manifest good works. Paul said that true saving faith expresses itself through love (Gal 5:6). Loving deeds display outwardly the inward change that has occurred by grace through faith.

James also declared that a person enters a right relationship with God by the grace of God alone. Like Jesus (Jn 3:3–8), James used birth imagery to describe conversion. James stated that God "chose to give us birth through the word of truth" and then planted that word in the souls of believers (Jas 1:18,21). James then went to great lengths to explain that this kind of faith manifests itself in loving acts toward those in need (Jas 1:27). According to James, acts of love toward God and others display the inward faith of the believer. This stands in complete agreement with Paul.

Tensions in the verses quoted at the outset are resolved when one understands that Paul and James used the word "justification" in different ways. The word can mean "declared to be in right standing" or "displayed to be right standing." Paul used the first sense. God declares an individual to be in right standing with him upon the basis of faith alone, as occurred with Abraham in Genesis 15:6. James used the second sense. A person's faith is shown to be legitimate when their outward works display the inward change that has taken place as a result of their conversion. Faith alone saves, but the faith that saves is never alone.

wants to go. 5Likewise, the tongue is a small part of the body, but it makes great
boasts. Consider what a great forest is set on fire by a small spark. 6The tongue also
is a fire, a world of evil among the parts of the body. It corrupts the whole body, sets
the whole course of one's life on fire, and is itself set on fire by hell.
7All kinds of animals, birds, reptiles and sea creatures are being tamed and
have been tamed by mankind, 8but no human being can tame the tongue. It is a
restless evil, full of deadly poison.
9With the tongue we praise our Lord and Father, and with it we curse human
beings, who have been made in God's likeness. 10Out of the same mouth come
praise and cursing. My brothers and sisters, this should not be. 11Can both fresh
water and salt water flow from the same spring? 12My brothers and sisters, can
a fig tree bear olives, or a grapevine bear figs? Neither can a salt spring produce
fresh water.

Two Kinds of Wisdom

13Who is wise and understanding among you? Let them show it by their good
life, by deeds done in the humility that comes from wisdom. 14But if you harbor
bitter envy and selfish ambition in your hearts, do not boast about it or deny the
truth. 15Such "wisdom" does not come down from heaven but is earthly, unspiritual, demonic. 16For where you have envy and selfish ambition, there you find
disorder and every evil practice.
17But the wisdom that comes from heaven is first of all pure; then peace-loving,
considerate, submissive, full of mercy and good fruit, impartial and sincere.
18Peacemakers who sow in peace reap a harvest of righteousness.

Submit Yourselves to God

4 What causes fights and quarrels among you? Don't they come from your desires that battle within you? 2You desire but do not have, so you kill. You covet but you cannot get what you want, so you quarrel and fight. You do not have
because you do not ask God. 3When you ask, you do not receive, because you ask
with wrong motives, that you may spend what you get on your pleasures.
4You adulterous people,[a] don't you know that friendship with the world
means enmity against God? Therefore, anyone who chooses to be a friend of the
world becomes an enemy of God. 5Or do you think Scripture says without reason
that he jealously longs for the spirit he has caused to dwell in us[b]? 6But he gives
us more grace. That is why Scripture says:

"God opposes the proud
  but shows favor to the humble."[c]

7Submit yourselves, then, to God. Resist the devil, and he will flee from you.
8Come near to God and he will come near to you. Wash your hands, you sinners,
and purify your hearts, you double-minded. 9Grieve, mourn and wail. Change
your laughter to mourning and your joy to gloom. 10Humble yourselves before
the Lord, and he will lift you up.
11Brothers and sisters, do not slander one another. Anyone who speaks
against a brother or sister[d] or judges them speaks against the law and judges
it. When you judge the law, you are not keeping it, but sitting in judgment on it.
12There is only one Lawgiver and Judge, the one who is able to save and destroy.
But you—who are you to judge your neighbor?

Boasting About Tomorrow

13Now listen, you who say, "Today or tomorrow we will go to this or that city,
spend a year there, carry on business and make money." 14Why, you do not even

[a] *4* An allusion to covenant unfaithfulness; see Hosea 3:1. [b] *5* Or *that the spirit he caused to dwell in us envies intensely;* or *that the Spirit he caused to dwell in us longs jealously*
[c] *6* Prov. 3:34 [d] *11* The Greek word for *brother or sister* (*adelphos*) refers here to a believer, whether man or woman, as part of God's family.

JAMES 3:9–12

HYPOCRISY

James demanded that believers display a changed life. His letter seems to pack more commands per square inch than any other book in the Bible. Yet James does not call Christians to alter their behavior in order to earn God's approval. Rather, he calls for consistency.

According to James, God "chose to give us birth through the word of truth" (1:18). An individual becomes a child of God entirely by the grace of God. But when the gospel of Jesus Christ renovates a person's heart, changes in activity should naturally result. New identity results in new activity. James called his audience to evaluate the way they deal with hardship, handle money, use words and plan for the future in light of their allegiance to the Lord. James confronted the inconsistency of claiming to belong to Jesus, yet making decisions that are incompatible with that confession—in other words, saying one thing and doing another. James did not advocate throwing a garment of religious activity over an unconverted heart. Rather, he called for the Christian to live a consistent life. Everything in the world produces something according to its own nature. Fig trees produce figs. Grapevines produce grapes. In the same way, James asserted that Christian people should naturally produce Christ-honoring activity. In doing so, he simply restated Jesus' illustration from Matthew 7:15–20: As a good tree produces good fruit, so a Christian produces a life that honors Christ.

JAMES 4:13 – 17

GOD'S WILL

The will of God has two meanings in the Bible—first, God's law, or the way he wants us to live; second, the events God allows in history, including pain and suffering. It appears James used both meanings in his instruction on how Christians should view and approach their lives. James was not encouraging an apathetic attitude toward events that may appear outside of humanity's control. To the contrary, James was actually pointing Christians toward the example set by Jesus.

Jesus is the only person in history who perfectly fulfilled the will of God. Not only did Jesus live a perfect life by following God's law, but he also accepted God's will for his life—the unimaginable suffering of crucifixion and separation from God that paid for human sin. It is because of Jesus' example that the Christian can joyfully submit to God's will in this life.

The Son of God is a not a far-off deity who sits idly and toys with humanity's fate. He is intimately present as his people struggle to obey his commands, and he walks with believers through the painful suffering of life's darkest valleys. This is the Lord who guides a Christian's future—a God who empathizes with, relates to and loves his people. Accepting the will of God is not a burden. Instead, it should be regarded with all the reverence and joy that comes with following in the footsteps of God himself.

know what will happen tomorrow. What is your life? You are a mist that appears for a little while and then vanishes. 15Instead, you ought to say, "If it is the
Lord's will, we will live and do this or that." 16As it is, you boast in your arrogant
schemes. All such boasting is evil. 17If anyone, then, knows the good they ought
to do and doesn't do it, it is sin for them.

Warning to Rich Oppressors

5 Now listen, you rich people, weep and wail because of the misery that is
coming on you. 2Your wealth has rotted, and moths have eaten your clothes.
3Your gold and silver are corroded. Their corrosion will testify against you and
eat your flesh like fire. You have hoarded wealth in the last days. 4Look! The wages you failed to pay the workers who mowed your fields are crying out against
you. The cries of the harvesters have reached the ears of the Lord Almighty. 5You
have lived on earth in luxury and self-indulgence. You have fattened yourselves
in the day of slaughter.[a] 6You have condemned and murdered the innocent one,
who was not opposing you.

Patience in Suffering

7Be patient, then, brothers and sisters, until the Lord's coming. See how the
farmer waits for the land to yield its valuable crop, patiently waiting for the autumn and spring rains. 8You too, be patient and stand firm, because the Lord's
coming is near. 9Don't grumble against one another, brothers and sisters, or you
will be judged. The Judge is standing at the door!
10Brothers and sisters, as an example of patience in the face of suffering, take
the prophets who spoke in the name of the Lord. 11As you know, we count as
blessed those who have persevered. You have heard of Job's perseverance and
have seen what the Lord finally brought about. The Lord is full of compassion
and mercy.
12Above all, my brothers and sisters, do not swear—not by heaven or by earth
or by anything else. All you need to say is a simple "Yes" or "No." Otherwise you
will be condemned.

The Prayer of Faith

13Is anyone among you in trouble? Let them pray. Is anyone happy? Let them
sing songs of praise. 14Is anyone among you sick? Let them call the elders of the
church to pray over them and anoint them with oil in the name of the Lord. 15And
the prayer offered in faith will make the sick person well; the Lord will raise them
up. If they have sinned, they will be forgiven. 16Therefore confess your sins to
each other and pray for each other so that you may be healed. The prayer of a
righteous person is powerful and effective.
17Elijah was a human being, even as we are. He prayed earnestly that it would
not rain, and it did not rain on the land for three and a half years. 18Again he
prayed, and the heavens gave rain, and the earth produced its crops.
19My brothers and sisters, if one of you should wander from the truth and
someone should bring that person back, 20remember this: Whoever turns a sinner from the error of their way will save them from death and cover over a multitude of sins.

[a] 5 Or *yourselves as in a day of feasting*

JESUS: OUR ETERNAL REWARD

1 PETER

1 PETER

PETER LEADS THE CHURCH AFTER PENTECOST	PETER WRITES FIRST LETTER	PETER MARTYRED IN ROME
c. AD 30	*c. AD 62 – 64*	*c. AD 67 – 68*

Suffering is a vital part of the Christian life. The recipients of Peter's letter knew this reality firsthand. Asia Minor was a difficult place to live in obedience to Christ's commands and to proclaim the gospel. Christians were often persecuted by their pagan neighbors and by the governing authorities of the day. Most likely, Peter wrote his first letter during the sporadic persecutions that occurred before the severe, official persecutions under kings Nero, Domitian and Trajan at the end of the first century and the beginning of the second.

Peter wrote to prepare the church for the ongoing reality of suffering. He did not want them to lose heart or think that God had abandoned them during these trials. God was using their sufferings, first and foremost, to shape their character and conform them to the image of Christ (1:6 – 7; 3:14; 4:12 – 14). Suffering is a primary tool that God uses to refine his people. Peter also reminded the church that God was with them in their suffering and would, by the power of his Spirit, empower them to live holy lives (1:13 – 16). Though it can be tempting, believers must not return evil for evil but entrust themselves to God in the face of hostility from others. God sees the plight of believers, knows their burdens and will reward his people for their faithfulness (2:29; 3:16 – 17; 4:15 – 19). Life in a fallen world brings great trouble, but Christians can trust that they will receive their eternal reward that will far surpass temporary pain.

Persecuted believers must pursue harmonious relationships with other people in order to suffer well (2:13 – 19). The church community is the God-given context where Christ is worshiped, believers are reminded of the truths of the gospel and people are encouraged to persevere (4:7 – 11; 5:1 – 7). The fires of persecution purify the church from hypocrisy and false converts, leaving true believers to band together in faithfulness and holiness. Peter concluded with the hope that awaits all true believers: “The God of all grace, who called you to his eternal glory in Christ, after you have suffered a little while, will himself restore you and make you strong, firm and steadfast” (5:10).

THESE HAVE COME SO THAT THE PROVEN GENUINENESS OF YOUR FAITH — OF GREATER WORTH THAN GOLD, WHICH PERISHES EVEN THOUGH REFINED BY FIRE — MAY RESULT IN PRAISE, GLORY AND HONOR WHEN JESUS CHRIST IS REVEALED.

---

1 Peter 1:7

1 PETER

1 Peter, an apostle of Jesus Christ,

To God's elect, exiles scattered throughout the provinces of Pontus, Galatia, Cappadocia, Asia and Bithynia, [2]who have been chosen according to the foreknowledge of God the Father, through the sanctifying work of the Spirit, to be obedient to Jesus Christ and sprinkled with his blood:

Grace and peace be yours in abundance.

Praise to God for a Living Hope

[3]Praise be to the God and Father of our Lord Jesus Christ! In his great mercy he has given us new birth into a living hope through the resurrection of Jesus Christ from the dead, [4]and into an inheritance that can never perish, spoil or fade. This inheritance is kept in heaven for you, [5]who through faith are shielded by God's power until the coming of the salvation that is ready to be revealed in the last time. [6]In all this you greatly rejoice, though now for a little while you may have had to suffer grief in all kinds of trials. [7]These have come so that the proven genuineness of your faith — of greater worth than gold, which perishes even though refined by fire — may result in praise, glory and honor when Jesus Christ is revealed. [8]Though you have not seen him, you love him; and even though you do not see him now, you believe in him and are filled with an inexpressible and glorious joy, [9]for you are receiving the end result of your faith, the salvation of your souls.

[10]Concerning this salvation, the prophets, who spoke of the grace that was to come to you, searched intently and with the greatest care, [11]trying to find out the time and circumstances to which the Spirit of Christ in them was pointing when he predicted the sufferings of the Messiah and the glories that would follow. [12]It was revealed to them that they were not serving themselves but you, when they spoke of the things that have now been told you by those who have preached the gospel to you by the Holy Spirit sent from heaven. Even angels long to look into these things.

Be Holy

[13]Therefore, with minds that are alert and fully sober, set your hope on the grace to be brought to you when Jesus Christ is revealed at his coming. [14]As obedient children, do not conform to the evil desires you had when you lived in ignorance. [15]But just as he who called you is holy, so be holy in all you do; [16]for it is written: "Be holy, because I am holy."[a]

[17]Since you call on a Father who judges each person's work impartially, live out your time as foreigners here in reverent fear. [18]For you know that it was not with perishable things such as silver or gold that you were redeemed from the empty way of life handed down to you from your ancestors, [19]but with the precious blood of Christ, a lamb without blemish or defect. [20]He was chosen before the creation of the world, but was revealed in these last times for your sake. [21]Through him you believe in God, who raised him from the dead and glorified him, and so your faith and hope are in God.

[22]Now that you have purified yourselves by obeying the truth so that you have sincere love for each other, love one another deeply, from the heart.[b] [23]For you have been born again, not of perishable seed, but of imperishable, through the living and enduring word of God. [24]For,

---

[a] *16* Lev. 11:44,45; 19:2   [b] *22* Some early manuscripts *from a pure heart*

HOLINESS

People who believe in Christ Jesus have been made holy through faith — set apart and dedicated strictly to God (Heb 10:10). Therefore, believers live as claimed and purchased people (1Co 6:20). Christians do not live in purity in order to become holy — they live this way because they *are* holy. Peter affirmed this reality with a call to a lifestyle of holiness. God expects Christians to live distinctive lives among people who do not know Jesus. By observing Christians' lives, the culture learns how God cares for those he loves and how believers care for each other. The abundant Christian life dedicated to the teachings of Scripture shows the world a contrast to an empty life spent in the service of sin.

Holiness requires a separation from certain parts of culture in order to pursue purity and obedience out of reverence for God. This separation refers to choices that honor God's Word — not a separation that prohibits engaging with and showing love to those who need to give their lives to Christ. Pleasing God while remaining winsome to the culture is a challenge for all Christians. When one is fully satisfied in Christ — with no need for the sinful pleasures of earth — he or she becomes a light in the darkness. This is in keeping with what Jesus desires for those who love and follow him: "Let your light shine before others, that they may see your good deeds and glorify your Father in heaven" (Mt 5:16).

Believers who read Peter's letter can clearly understand that there is a cost associated with the choice to live a godly life. Internally, they experience the tug-of-war between the Spirit and their flesh. Holiness requires discipline and self-denial. Externally, Christ-followers risk persecution and rejection from the people around them. Choosing to honor God rather than adopt the unholy practices of the culture will most often result in persecution (2Ti 3:12).

A relationship with Jesus brings overflowing joy and lasting satisfaction (Jn 17:3). Following him in discipleship leads to an abundant life (Jn 10:10). Every day Jesus' presence, provision and plan for a believer are sufficient. He is *enough*. Holiness for Christians is evidence that satisfaction in life does not require the fleeting and empty pleasures of sin.

"All people are like grass,
and all their glory is like the flowers of the field;
the grass withers and the flowers fall,
25 but the word of the Lord endures forever."[a]

And this is the word that was preached to you.

2 Therefore, rid yourselves of all malice and all deceit, hypocrisy, envy, and
slander of every kind. [2]Like newborn babies, crave pure spiritual milk, so
that by it you may grow up in your salvation, [3]now that you have tasted that the
Lord is good.

The Living Stone and a Chosen People

[4]As you come to him, the living Stone — rejected by humans but chosen by
God and precious to him — [5]you also, like living stones, are being built into a
spiritual house[b] to be a holy priesthood, offering spiritual sacrifices acceptable
to God through Jesus Christ. [6]For in Scripture it says:

"See, I lay a stone in Zion,
a chosen and precious cornerstone,
and the one who trusts in him
will never be put to shame."[c]

[7]Now to you who believe, this stone is precious. But to those who do not believe,

"The stone the builders rejected
has become the cornerstone,"[d]

[8]and,

"A stone that causes people to stumble
and a rock that makes them fall."[e]

They stumble because they disobey the message — which is also what they were
destined for.

[9]But you are a chosen people, a royal priesthood, a holy nation, God's special possession, that you may declare the praises of him who called you out of
darkness into his wonderful light. [10]Once you were not a people, but now you
are the people of God; once you had not received mercy, but now you have received mercy.

Living Godly Lives in a Pagan Society

[11]Dear friends, I urge you, as foreigners and exiles, to abstain from sinful desires, which wage war against your soul. [12]Live such good lives among the pagans that, though they accuse you of doing wrong, they may see your good deeds
and glorify God on the day he visits us.

[13]Submit yourselves for the Lord's sake to every human authority: whether to
the emperor, as the supreme authority, [14]or to governors, who are sent by him to
punish those who do wrong and to commend those who do right. [15]For it is God's
will that by doing good you should silence the ignorant talk of foolish people.
[16]Live as free people, but do not use your freedom as a cover-up for evil; live as
God's slaves. [17]Show proper respect to everyone, love the family of believers, fear
God, honor the emperor.

[18]Slaves, in reverent fear of God submit yourselves to your masters, not only
to those who are good and considerate, but also to those who are harsh. [19]For it
is commendable if someone bears up under the pain of unjust suffering because
they are conscious of God. [20]But how is it to your credit if you receive a beating
for doing wrong and endure it? But if you suffer for doing good and you endure
it, this is commendable before God. [21]To this you were called, because Christ
suffered for you, leaving you an example, that you should follow in his steps.

[a] *25* Isaiah 40:6-8 (see Septuagint) [b] *5* Or *into a temple of the Spirit* [c] *6* Isaiah 28:16
[d] *7* Psalm 118:22 [e] *8* Isaiah 8:14

---

1 PETER 2:4–7

LIVING TEMPLE

Peter, whose name means "rock" (Jn 1:42), reminded his readers that God sent Jesus to build a spiritual temple. During the reigns of King David and his heir Solomon, God arranged for a physical structure to be built where his presence would dwell. Now, because of Jesus and the indwelling of the Holy Spirit, all believers comprise God's temple. His presence lives in people all over the world, not just in one building made of stone.

The ancient temple was spectacular in design and detail. The church — the community of believers in Jesus — is equally beautiful. Men and women who are alive in Christ gather to worship God, to proclaim and practice his Word, mobilizing to carry the gospel to those who do not yet believe in Jesus.

In ancient construction, the first stone set in place was called the cornerstone, and all subsequent work was built upon this key foundational element. Jesus is the cornerstone of the church, precious to those who believe. He is first in importance and the source of the church's power, direction and purpose. He is a strong foundation — those who build their lives on the rock of Christ will endure (Mt 7:24 – 29).

22 "He committed no sin,
and no deceit was found in his mouth."[a]

23 When they hurled their insults at him, he did not retaliate; when he suffered,
he made no threats. Instead, he entrusted himself to him who judges justly.
24 "He himself bore our sins" in his body on the cross, so that we might die to sins
and live for righteousness; "by his wounds you have been healed." 25 For "you
were like sheep going astray,"[b] but now you have returned to the Shepherd and
Overseer of your souls.

3 Wives, in the same way submit yourselves to your own husbands so that, if
any of them do not believe the word, they may be won over without words
by the behavior of their wives, 2 when they see the purity and reverence of your
lives. 3 Your beauty should not come from outward adornment, such as elaborate hairstyles and the wearing of gold jewelry or fine clothes. 4 Rather, it should
be that of your inner self, the unfading beauty of a gentle and quiet spirit, which
is of great worth in God's sight. 5 For this is the way the holy women of the past
who put their hope in God used to adorn themselves. They submitted themselves to their own husbands, 6 like Sarah, who obeyed Abraham and called
him her lord. You are her daughters if you do what is right and do not give way
to fear.

7 Husbands, in the same way be considerate as you live with your wives, and
treat them with respect as the weaker partner and as heirs with you of the gracious gift of life, so that nothing will hinder your prayers.

Suffering for Doing Good

8 Finally, all of you, be like-minded, be sympathetic, love one another, be compassionate and humble. 9 Do not repay evil with evil or insult with insult. On the
contrary, repay evil with blessing, because to this you were called so that you
may inherit a blessing. 10 For,

"Whoever would love life
and see good days
must keep their tongue from evil
and their lips from deceitful speech.
11 They must turn from evil and do good;
they must seek peace and pursue it.
12 For the eyes of the Lord are on the righteous
and his ears are attentive to their prayer,
but the face of the Lord is against those who do evil."[c]

13 Who is going to harm you if you are eager to do good? 14 But even if you
should suffer for what is right, you are blessed. "Do not fear their threats[d]; do not
be frightened."[e] 15 But in your hearts revere Christ as Lord. Always be prepared
to give an answer to everyone who asks you to give the reason for the hope that
you have. But do this with gentleness and respect, 16 keeping a clear conscience,
so that those who speak maliciously against your good behavior in Christ may
be ashamed of their slander. 17 For it is better, if it is God's will, to suffer for doing
good than for doing evil. 18 For Christ also suffered once for sins, the righteous for
the unrighteous, to bring you to God. He was put to death in the body but made
alive in the Spirit. 19 After being made alive,[f] he went and made proclamation to
the imprisoned spirits— 20 to those who were disobedient long ago when God
waited patiently in the days of Noah while the ark was being built. In it only a
few people, eight in all, were saved through water, 21 and this water symbolizes
baptism that now saves you also — not the removal of dirt from the body but the
pledge of a clear conscience toward God.[g] It saves you by the resurrection of

[a] *22* Isaiah 53:9 [b] *24,25* Isaiah 53:4,5,6 (see Septuagint) [c] *12* Psalm 34:12-16
[d] *14* Or *fear what they fear* [e] *14* Isaiah 8:12 [f] *18,19* Or *but made alive in the spirit,* 19*in which also* [g] *21* Or *but an appeal to God for a clear conscience*

1 PETER 3:18–22

WATER

Water was featured prominently at various times in God's relationship with his people. In the time of Noah, God used water to flood the earth as an act of judgment, yet preserved a faithful man and his family (Ge 6:13–18). Water ceremonially cleansed the one made unclean by sin or contamination (Lev 14:8). God demonstrated love, protection and power by parting the waters of the Red Sea (Ex 14:21), destroying those who pursued the Israelites and performing a miracle to be forever remembered. Water satisfies thirst, and God graciously provided water after desperate days in the desert (Dt 8:15).

In the New Testament, the water of baptism symbolizes spiritual cleansing through the blood of Jesus Christ that washes away sin (1Pe 3:21). The Holy Spirit is living water for all who believe (Jn 4:10–14). He is capable of satisfying the deepest thirsts of the soul and the simplest needs of daily life.

Jesus Christ, [22]who has gone into heaven and is at God's right hand—with angels, authorities and powers in submission to him.

Living for God

4 Therefore, since Christ suffered in his body, arm yourselves also with the
same attitude, because whoever suffers in the body is done with sin. [2]As a
result, they do not live the rest of their earthly lives for evil human desires, but
rather for the will of God. [3]For you have spent enough time in the past doing what
pagans choose to do—living in debauchery, lust, drunkenness, orgies, carousing and detestable idolatry. [4]They are surprised that you do not join them in their
reckless, wild living, and they heap abuse on you. [5]But they will have to give account to him who is ready to judge the living and the dead. [6]For this is the reason
the gospel was preached even to those who are now dead, so that they might be
judged according to human standards in regard to the body, but live according
to God in regard to the spirit.

[7]The end of all things is near. Therefore be alert and of sober mind so that you
may pray. [8]Above all, love each other deeply, because love covers over a multitude of sins. [9]Offer hospitality to one another without grumbling. [10]Each of you
should use whatever gift you have received to serve others, as faithful stewards
of God's grace in its various forms. [11]If anyone speaks, they should do so as one
who speaks the very words of God. If anyone serves, they should do so with the
strength God provides, so that in all things God may be praised through Jesus
Christ. To him be the glory and the power for ever and ever. Amen.

Suffering for Being a Christian

[12]Dear friends, do not be surprised at the fiery ordeal that has come on you to
test you, as though something strange were happening to you. [13]But rejoice inasmuch as you participate in the sufferings of Christ, so that you may be overjoyed
when his glory is revealed. [14]If you are insulted because of the name of Christ,
you are blessed, for the Spirit of glory and of God rests on you. [15]If you suffer, it
should not be as a murderer or thief or any other kind of criminal, or even as a
meddler. [16]However, if you suffer as a Christian, do not be ashamed, but praise
God that you bear that name. [17]For it is time for judgment to begin with God's
household; and if it begins with us, what will the outcome be for those who do
not obey the gospel of God? [18]And,

> "If it is hard for the righteous to be saved,
> what will become of the ungodly and the sinner?"[a]

[19]So then, those who suffer according to God's will should commit themselves
to their faithful Creator and continue to do good.

To the Elders and the Flock

5 To the elders among you, I appeal as a fellow elder and a witness of Christ's
sufferings who also will share in the glory to be revealed: [2]Be shepherds of
God's flock that is under your care, watching over them—not because you must,
but because you are willing, as God wants you to be; not pursuing dishonest
gain, but eager to serve; [3]not lording it over those entrusted to you, but being
examples to the flock. [4]And when the Chief Shepherd appears, you will receive
the crown of glory that will never fade away.

[5]In the same way, you who are younger, submit yourselves to your elders. All
of you, clothe yourselves with humility toward one another, because,

> "God opposes the proud
> but shows favor to the humble."[b]

[6]Humble yourselves, therefore, under God's mighty hand, that he may lift you up
in due time. [7]Cast all your anxiety on him because he cares for you.

---

[a] *18* Prov. 11:31 (see Septuagint) [b] *5* Prov. 3:34

CHURCH LEADERS

Peter concluded his first letter with an exhortation for church leaders to be "shepherds of God's flock" (v. 2). This image of leadership assumes both vigilance and tenderness. Shepherds cannot become passive, for if they do, the sheep suffer. And God desires his leaders to exercise gentle guidance rather than kingly rule. The fact that the people are *God's flock* reminds leaders that the foundation of their role is caretaking — their primary responsibility is to lead them as God would.

Those who are called to lead God's people must meet a higher standard — they hold positions of authority over willing followers, and they will eventually give an account to God (Jas 3:1). The Greek word *presbuteros* means *elder, bishop* or *overseer* (1Pe 5:2 – 4; 1Ti 3:1 – 7; 5:17 – 18, Titus 1:6 – 9;). Overseers are responsible for leading, guiding and nurturing a local church. They administrate governance, teach and preach, represent the church, and pray for the sick. These are the qualifications listed in the book of 1 Timothy for the office of elder: he must be above reproach, faithful to his wife, temperate, self-controlled, respectable, hospitable, able to teach, not given to drunkenness, not violent but gentle, not quarrelsome, not a lover of money, a good manager of his family, not a recent convert and he must have a good reputation with outsiders. The book of Titus adds that an elder must be self-controlled, upright, holy, disciplined, and one who loves what is good and holds firmly to the gospel.

Likewise, the Greek word *diakonos* means *servant* (Ac 6:1 – 6; 1Ti 3:8 – 13). Servants are responsible for tending to physical needs among the believers so that overseers are released to minister through teaching and prayer. These are the qualifications for deacons, as listed in the book of 1 Timothy: they must be worthy of respect, sincere, not indulging in much wine, not pursuing dishonest gain, holding doctrine with a clear conscience and tested for approval. And they must be faithful spouses and parents, managing their households well.

Leaders in the church represent God to all those who come together to worship, but also to all those they meet in their everyday lives. That's why the New Testament is careful to outline these stringent guidelines.

[8]Be alert and of sober mind. Your enemy the devil prowls around like a roaring lion looking for someone to devour. [9]Resist him, standing firm in the faith,
because you know that the family of believers throughout the world is undergoing the same kind of sufferings.
[10]And the God of all grace, who called you to his eternal glory in Christ, after
you have suffered a little while, will himself restore you and make you strong,
firm and steadfast. [11]To him be the power for ever and ever. Amen.

Final Greetings

[12]With the help of Silas,[a] whom I regard as a faithful brother, I have written
to you briefly, encouraging you and testifying that this is the true grace of God.
Stand fast in it.
[13]She who is in Babylon, chosen together with you, sends you her greetings,
and so does my son Mark. [14]Greet one another with a kiss of love.

Peace to all of you who are in Christ.

[a] 12 Greek *Silvanus*, a variant of *Silas*

JESUS: OUR LORD OF SALVATION

2 PETER

2 PETER

PETER SPEAKS AT JERUSALEM COUNCIL *c. AD 50*	NERO BEGINS REIGN IN ROME *c. AD 54*	PETER WRITES SECOND LETTER, THEN MARTYRED *c. AD 64 – 68*

The enemy seeks to destroy God's people. From the beginning of the book of Genesis, Satan has been bent on distorting God's Word and leading people away from God to their sure and certain death. Satan's plan does not change throughout the Bible — he is still at work, bringing great harm to God's people and his church.

Peter's second letter addressed believers facing a steady onslaught of attacks from the enemy. As he warned in his first letter, Satan is prowling around like a roaring lion seeking to devour as many people as he can (1Pe 5:8). Without constant vigilance, the church could have been deceived and destroyed. By the time of the writing of 2 Peter, the believers scattered throughout Asia Minor needed encouragement to continue to fight — and fight hard against Satan's advances.

Peter knew that this life was soon coming to a close (1:12 – 15). He, like Paul, proclaimed the gospel message and fulfilled the mission that God had given him. He wrote to those he had been given to serve. He had a desire that they not stumble and fall away once he was gone.

Foremost in Peter's mind was the deceptive nature of false teaching that continually oppresses the church (2:1 – 3). False teaching is one of the primary ways Satan breeds destruction in the church, and Peter knew that believers scattered among the pagan nations must be on their guard against distorting the gospel message. He reminded believers that false teachers are doomed to destruction (2:4 – 22) and that God will see to it that they face the just consequences of their deception (3:1 – 9).

God's church must resist the devil and false teachers and hold fast to the gospel message Peter proclaimed. The day of the Lord's return will come, as Jesus had promised, and the earth will be purified from all ungodliness (3:10 – 13). Christians should focus not on Satan and his advances, but on the future coming of the Lord Jesus Christ when all wrongs will be made right and righteousness will reign upon the earth forever. Jesus has given salvation to his people, and those who have received this gift should see to it that they remain steadfast in the face of great suffering. His church can take heart that he has already defeated Satan on the cross, and one day this truth will be seen clearly by all of the world.

BUT IN KEEPING WITH HIS PROMISE WE ARE LOOKING FORWARD TO A NEW HEAVEN AND A NEW EARTH, WHERE RIGHTEOUSNESS DWELLS. SO THEN, DEAR FRIENDS, SINCE YOU ARE LOOKING FORWARD TO THIS, MAKE EVERY EFFORT TO BE FOUND SPOTLESS, BLAMELESS AND AT PEACE WITH HIM. BEAR IN MIND THAT OUR LORD'S PATIENCE MEANS SALVATION, JUST AS OUR DEAR BROTHER PAUL ALSO WROTE YOU WITH THE WISDOM THAT GOD GAVE HIM.

---

2 Peter 3:13 – 15

2 PETER

2 PETER 1:1–8

KNOWING GOD

In the Old Testament, the people of Israel were continually reminded of their separation from God due to sin. The people knew the Most Holy Place in the temple of the Lord was forbidden to everyone except the high priest who himself only entered it once a year (Lev 16). They were taught the story of the unapproachable smoking mountain of God (Ex 19:16–25) and were told of the tragedy of Uzzah, who was struck dead after irreverently reaching out to steady the ark of God (2Sa 6:6–8). They had learned that God was unapproachable in his holiness. Only a complex system of sacrifices and priestly mediators allowed the people to relate to God.

But when Jesus came to earth, God reached down and made himself available to his people in a previously unimaginable way. While God will always remain holy and does not excuse or ignore sin, Jesus' work as the ultimate and final mediator allows his followers to draw near to the Father in freedom and intimacy. And as God in the flesh, Jesus assures his followers that "anyone who has seen me has seen the Father" (Jn 14:9). So to know the Father essentially means knowing Christ; in fact, no one can bypass Jesus and truly know God at all. Jesus came to show the world what his Father was like, but more importantly, his sacrifice on the cross established the one and only path to fellowship with him (Jn 14:6).

1 Simon Peter, a servant and apostle of Jesus Christ,

To those who through the righteousness of our God and Savior Jesus Christ have received a faith as precious as ours:

[2]Grace and peace be yours in abundance through the knowledge of God and of Jesus our Lord.

Confirming One's Calling and Election

[3]His divine power has given us everything we need for a godly life through
our knowledge of him who called us by his own glory and goodness. [4]Through
these he has given us his very great and precious promises, so that through them
you may participate in the divine nature, having escaped the corruption in the
world caused by evil desires.
[5]For this very reason, make every effort to add to your faith goodness; and to
goodness, knowledge; [6]and to knowledge, self-control; and to self-control, perseverance; and to perseverance, godliness; [7]and to godliness, mutual affection;
and to mutual affection, love. [8]For if you possess these qualities in increasing
measure, they will keep you from being ineffective and unproductive in your
knowledge of our Lord Jesus Christ. [9]But whoever does not have them is near-
sighted and blind, forgetting that they have been cleansed from their past sins.
[10]Therefore, my brothers and sisters,[a] make every effort to confirm your calling
and election. For if you do these things, you will never stumble, [11]and you will receive a rich welcome into the eternal kingdom of our Lord and Savior Jesus Christ.

Prophecy of Scripture

[12]So I will always remind you of these things, even though you know them
and are firmly established in the truth you now have. [13]I think it is right to refresh your memory as long as I live in the tent of this body, [14]because I know that
I will soon put it aside, as our Lord Jesus Christ has made clear to me. [15]And I
will make every effort to see that after my departure you will always be able to
remember these things.
[16]For we did not follow cleverly devised stories when we told you about the
coming of our Lord Jesus Christ in power, but we were eyewitnesses of his majesty. [17]He received honor and glory from God the Father when the voice came
to him from the Majestic Glory, saying, "This is my Son, whom I love; with him I
am well pleased."[b] [18]We ourselves heard this voice that came from heaven when
we were with him on the sacred mountain.
[19]We also have the prophetic message as something completely reliable, and
you will do well to pay attention to it, as to a light shining in a dark place, until the
day dawns and the morning star rises in your hearts. [20]Above all, you must understand that no prophecy of Scripture came about by the prophet's own interpretation of things. [21]For prophecy never had its origin in the human will, but prophets, though human, spoke from God as they were carried along by the Holy Spirit.

False Teachers and Their Destruction

2 But there were also false prophets among the people, just as there will be false teachers among you. They will secretly introduce destructive heresies, even denying the sovereign Lord who bought them — bringing swift destruction

[a] *10* The Greek word for *brothers and sisters* (*adelphoi*) refers here to believers, both men and women, as part of God's family. [b] *17* Matt. 17:5; Mark 9:7; Luke 9:35

TRUSTWORTHY AND TRUE

History records many religious figures who have claimed exclusive spiritual knowledge. From Egyptian pharaohs who were once hailed as divine to modern-day advisors who present themselves as spokespersons for God, leaders such as these attempt to exert control over their followers by proclaiming their words infallible. So when Scripture is held up as the only reliable source of truth, how can one be sure that this claim is authoritative against the backdrop of so many other voices? The apostle Paul wrote the definitive statement on the veracity of Scripture, reminding readers that the verses penned by its authors are more than ordinary literature or historical accounts. They are "God-breathed" (2Ti 3:16). The Lord himself took an active role in birthing these manuscripts, and through them equips people with an unparalleled foundation for right thinking and living. The approximately 40 writers of the 66 books that form the biblical text composed their contributions in three languages in a variety of literary genres (poetry, history, narrative, correspondence, exposition, parable and apocalyptic) over the span of many hundreds of years. And yet, remarkably, they contain a unified story of creation, revolt, redemption and restoration. Compelling evidence for the reliability of Scripture lies also in its many incidences of fulfilled prophecy. For example, centuries before the event itself, the prophet Ezekiel accurately predicted the cataclysmic fate of the city of Tyre (Eze 26); the book of Psalms described crucifixion as a capital punishment more than 400 years before it was used (Ps 22); and, as one of hundreds of Messianic prophecies, Micah identified Bethlehem (Mic 5:2) as the birthplace of the Christ 600 years before Jesus arrived on earth in that exact spot.

In addition to Scripture's internal consistencies, archaeology continues to provide convincing evidence that supports Scripture. Findings pointing to biblical people groups, places and customs greatly increase textual credibility. Most significantly, the Dead Sea Scrolls — discovered in caves outside Jerusalem in the 1940s and 50s — contain over 800 ancient Jewish documents that include at least fragments of every book of the Old Testament except Esther. These scrolls, estimated to have been written between 150 BC and AD 70, clearly establish the high degree of fidelity between the modern texts and the original source material and serve as strong evidence of the authenticity and trustworthiness of the entire scriptural record. The more that readers examine the evidence for the accuracy of God's Word, the more they can be assured that "his divine power has given us everything we need for a godly life through our knowledge of him who called us by his own glory and goodness" (2Pe 1:3).

on themselves. [2]Many will follow their depraved conduct and will bring the way of truth into disrepute. [3]In their greed these teachers will exploit you with fabricated stories. Their condemnation has long been hanging over them, and their destruction has not been sleeping.

[4]For if God did not spare angels when they sinned, but sent them to hell,[a] putting them in chains of darkness[b] to be held for judgment; [5]if he did not spare the ancient world when he brought the flood on its ungodly people, but protected Noah, a preacher of righteousness, and seven others; [6]if he condemned the cities of Sodom and Gomorrah by burning them to ashes, and made them an example of what is going to happen to the ungodly; [7]and if he rescued Lot, a righteous man, who was distressed by the depraved conduct of the lawless [8](for that righteous man, living among them day after day, was tormented in his righteous soul by the lawless deeds he saw and heard)— [9]if this is so, then the Lord knows how to rescue the godly from trials and to hold the unrighteous for punishment on the day of judgment. [10]This is especially true of those who follow the corrupt desire of the flesh[c] and despise authority.

Bold and arrogant, they are not afraid to heap abuse on celestial beings; [11]yet even angels, although they are stronger and more powerful, do not heap abuse on such beings when bringing judgment on them from[d] the Lord. [12]But these people blaspheme in matters they do not understand. They are like unreasoning animals, creatures of instinct, born only to be caught and destroyed, and like animals they too will perish.

[13]They will be paid back with harm for the harm they have done. Their idea of pleasure is to carouse in broad daylight. They are blots and blemishes, reveling in their pleasures while they feast with you.[e] [14]With eyes full of adultery, they never stop sinning; they seduce the unstable; they are experts in greed—an accursed brood! [15]They have left the straight way and wandered off to follow the way of Balaam son of Bezer,[f] who loved the wages of wickedness. [16]But he was rebuked for his wrongdoing by a donkey—an animal without speech—who spoke with a human voice and restrained the prophet's madness.

[17]These people are springs without water and mists driven by a storm. Blackest darkness is reserved for them. [18]For they mouth empty, boastful words and, by appealing to the lustful desires of the flesh, they entice people who are just escaping from those who live in error. [19]They promise them freedom, while they themselves are slaves of depravity—for "people are slaves to whatever has mastered them." [20]If they have escaped the corruption of the world by knowing our Lord and Savior Jesus Christ and are again entangled in it and are overcome, they are worse off at the end than they were at the beginning. [21]It would have been better for them not to have known the way of righteousness, than to have known it and then to turn their backs on the sacred command that was passed on to them. [22]Of them the proverbs are true: "A dog returns to its vomit,"[g] and, "A sow that is washed returns to her wallowing in the mud."

The Day of the Lord

3 Dear friends, this is now my second letter to you. I have written both of them as reminders to stimulate you to wholesome thinking. [2]I want you to recall the words spoken in the past by the holy prophets and the command given by our Lord and Savior through your apostles.

[3]Above all, you must understand that in the last days scoffers will come, scoffing and following their own evil desires. [4]They will say, "Where is this 'coming' he promised? Ever since our ancestors died, everything goes on as it has since the beginning of creation." [5]But they deliberately forget that long ago by God's

[a] *4* Greek *Tartarus* [b] *4* Some manuscripts *in gloomy dungeons* [c] *10* In contexts like this, the Greek word for *flesh* (*sarx*) refers to the sinful state of human beings, often presented as a power in opposition to the Spirit; also in verse 18. [d] *11* Many manuscripts *beings in the presence of* [e] *13* Some manuscripts *in their love feasts* [f] *15* Greek *Bosor*
[g] *22* Prov. 26:11

DEMONIC ACTIVITY

Demons. These unseen wicked forces are common subjects of popular movies, fantasy games and literature. While those depictions are largely the stuff of imagination, one cannot accept the Word of God as authentic without acknowledging the existence of a spiritual dimension populated with malicious adversaries. Scripture is not abundantly clear on demonic origins, but it does suggest they were once servants of the Most High God but who engaged in a doomed rebellion and were cast from his presence.

In the book of Revelation, John used bold imagery and symbolic language to describe Satan's ill-fated revolt, and he attested to the outcome of the "war" that "broke out in heaven" (Rev 12:7): "The great dragon ... called the devil, or Satan ... was hurled to the earth, and his angels with him" (Rev 12:9). At present, it appears that not all of these fallen angels have free reign upon the earth. The New Testament refers to some of these beings as kept in darkness and bound with everlasting chains until their final judgment (2Pe 2:4; Jude 6). But whatever their current state, Jesus assured his followers that these evil entities are destined for unending torment of "eternal fire" in a "lake of burning sulfur" (Mt 25:41; Rev 20:10). However, until their judgment is meted out, the devil and his cohorts continue to lead a calculated effort to thwart God, deceive humanity and lead "the whole world astray" (Rev 12:9). Their tactics include temptation to sin (Ge 3:1 – 6; Mt 4:1 – 4; Lk 4:1 – 2; Eph 2:1 – 2), physical ailments (Job 2:7; Mt 12:22; Mk 9:25; Lk 13:11; Ac 10:37 – 38; 2Co 12:7), deceitful miraculous signs (Rev 16:14), manipulation of the environment (Job 1:16 – 19), mental/emotional distress (Mt 8:28; Eph 4:26 – 27), spiritual possession/oppression (Mt 12:22 – 28; 17:18; Lk 4:33 – 35), confusion and false teaching (Lk 22:31; 1Ti 4:1; 1Jn 4:1 – 3) and issues of self-control and moral compromise (1Co 7:4 – 5; Rev 2:20).

Although the devil is called "the ruler of the kingdom of the air" (Eph 2:2) and, along with his legions, seems to have much influence, believers have no reason to fear. Demonic activity is sovereignly limited by God's power. Colossians 2:15 points to the certain victory over these spiritual enemies already achieved by Christ: "Having disarmed the powers and authorities, he made a public spectacle of them, triumphing over them by the cross."

WHAT KIND OF PEOPLE OUGHT YOU BE?

A right relationship with God begins by accepting Christ's forgiveness of sins by grace through faith (Eph 2:8 – 9). But that is only the launching point of a journey that should be marked by ongoing spiritual development. Peter's second letter challenged new believers to make a lifelong investment in growing "in the grace and knowledge of our Lord and Savior Jesus Christ" (2Pe 3:18). With a strong emphasis on correct doctrine, he stressed the importance of a deep commitment to Christ that should result in holy living. Instead of recommending outward actions to effect inward change, Peter pointed to the urgent need for believers to root their relationship with Jesus deeply in the Scriptures. God's "great and precious promises" and union with Christ serve as the foundation for a life of godliness and as protection from the corrupting influence of an ungodly world system with its perverse and selfish desires (1:2 – 4). Since God has made such a vast supply of divine resources available, believers must participate actively in applying them. Resting on the solid underpinning of faith, disciplines such as goodness, knowledge, self-control, perseverance, godliness, mutual affection and love ought to be evident and obvious in the lives of those who claim Jesus as their Savior (1:5 – 7).

In addition, diligent study and application of the truth form a solid shield against "destructive heresies" that are continually introduced into Christian fellowships by false teachers (2:1). Often approving of lustful indulgences, aberrant philosophies can appear persuasive, but their empty promises (ironically, championed by those who are themselves enslaved to fleshly passions) provide no real freedom or stability (2:18 – 19). Warnings against false prophets appear first in the Law of Moses (Dt 13:1 – 4; 18:20 – 22) and are reiterated throughout the New Testament (2Pe 2:1 – 22; Ro 16:17 – 18; 2Co 11:13 – 15; Gal 1:6 – 9; 1Jn 4:1 – 6; Jude 3 – 4). Jesus warned that a proliferation of these teachers would be a sign of the end of the age and of his eventual return (Mt 24:5,11).

While the fate of those who lead others astray is fixed (2Pe 2:1 – 22), Christians must vigilantly guard against their infiltration into the church. Though scoffers, mockers and those who twist the truth will always exist (3:3), Peter encouraged his audience to remain resolutely rooted in the promises of God, knowing that the Lord has set a firm date at which time he will bring about cleansing and final justice (3:10). In the meantime, he was also clear about a believer's personal responsibility: "You ought to live holy and godly lives as you look forward to the day of God and speed its coming" (3:11 – 12).

word the heavens came into being and the earth was formed out of water and by water. [6]By these waters also the world of that time was deluged and destroyed. [7]By the same word the present heavens and earth are reserved for fire, being kept for the day of judgment and destruction of the ungodly.

[8]But do not forget this one thing, dear friends: With the Lord a day is like a thousand years, and a thousand years are like a day. [9]The Lord is not slow in keeping his promise, as some understand slowness. Instead he is patient with you, not wanting anyone to perish, but everyone to come to repentance.

[10]But the day of the Lord will come like a thief. The heavens will disappear with a roar; the elements will be destroyed by fire, and the earth and everything done in it will be laid bare.[a]

[11]Since everything will be destroyed in this way, what kind of people ought you to be? You ought to live holy and godly lives [12]as you look forward to the day of God and speed its coming.[b] That day will bring about the destruction of the heavens by fire, and the elements will melt in the heat. [13]But in keeping with his promise we are looking forward to a new heaven and a new earth, where righteousness dwells.

[14]So then, dear friends, since you are looking forward to this, make every effort to be found spotless, blameless and at peace with him. [15]Bear in mind that our Lord's patience means salvation, just as our dear brother Paul also wrote you with the wisdom that God gave him. [16]He writes the same way in all his letters, speaking in them of these matters. His letters contain some things that are hard to understand, which ignorant and unstable people distort, as they do the other Scriptures, to their own destruction.

[17]Therefore, dear friends, since you have been forewarned, be on your guard so that you may not be carried away by the error of the lawless and fall from your secure position. [18]But grow in the grace and knowledge of our Lord and Savior Jesus Christ. To him be glory both now and forever! Amen.

---

[a] *10* Some manuscripts *be burned up* [b] *12* Or *as you wait eagerly for the day of God to come*

JESUS: OUR WORD OF LIFE AND LOVE

1 JOHN

1 JOHN

JESUS CALLS JOHN *c. AD 27*	TEMPLE DESTROYED, CHURCH SCATTERS *c. AD 70*	JOHN WRITES HIS GOSPEL AND LETTERS *c. AD 90*

A restored relationship with God produces a right relationship with others. The two cannot be separated. When asked about the greatest commandments, Jesus made this point clearly. He said, " 'Love the Lord your God with all your heart and with all your soul and with all your mind.' This is the first and greatest commandment. And the second is like it: 'Love your neighbor as yourself' " (Mt 22:37 – 39). A true Christian cannot profess to love God without pursuing authentic and enduring relationships with others.

John knew that the fellowship of the church was vital for the perseverance of Christians living near the end of the first century. But the love of Christians for one another does not merely serve a practical purpose of accountability and support. The love of the church models the love of God. The trinitarian God — Father, Son and Holy Spirit — exists in loving harmony. The nature of the Godhead serves as a model for the communal nature of God's people (1Jn 1:5; 2:29; 4:7 – 8). They are to love one another in a way that models the love of the Trinity. Genuine love is an indication of the authenticity of their relationship with God (4:7 – 16; 4:20 — 5:5) and provides believers with assurance that their salvation is indeed genuine (4:17 – 19). Love also has a missionary purpose — others see mature, self-sacrificial love between God's people and have a picture of the way that God loves his people.

Those who do not truly know Christ will not fulfill this law of love. False teachers were continuing to deceive the church — failing to model the love of God for his people. Their teaching consisted of an early form of Gnosticism that falsely divided one's spiritual life from their physical existence. Many false teachers went so far as to teach the heresy that Jesus was a spiritual being but lacked a physical body. John countered this claim, arguing that Jesus Christ was a physical being who, in his body, accomplished the plan of God (1:1 – 4). Those who follow the Word made flesh should live out the gospel message in real, tangible and concrete ways that can be observed by all people — primarily through their love and service to one another. Love, not mystical experiences, is meant to be the defining mark of God's people.

THIS IS HOW WE KNOW WHAT LOVE IS:
JESUS CHRIST LAID DOWN HIS LIFE FOR US.
AND WE OUGHT TO LAY DOWN OUR LIVES
FOR OUR BROTHERS AND SISTERS.

---

1 John 3:16

1 JOHN

1 JOHN 1:1–3

LOGOS: THE WORD

John's reference to Jesus as "the Word" (Greek *logos*, v. 1) carried great significance to his Jewish readers. They clearly understood the power and authority that was present when the Lord spoke: to create the world (Ge 1:1 — 2:25; Ps 33:6), to enter into his covenant with Abraham (Ge 15:1–8) and to deliver his Law to Moses on Mount Sinai (Ex 24:1–18; Dt 9:9–10). Greek readers also acknowledged the concept of "logos" as the fundamental commanding force that gave order and form to the universe. So when John ascribed this designation to Jesus (Jn 1:1–2; 1Jn 1:1; Rev 19:13), he clearly pointed to Christ as the embodiment of God's creative, sustaining power and as the final word to humanity. His eyewitness account went beyond simply recording that a mere mortal named Jesus lived, but that this man whom he had "heard," "seen" and "touched" (v. 1) was none other than the author of eternal life (v. 2). Christ's entrance into the world replaced the concept of God as distant with a clarified one showing him as personal and involved, as a God who, through faith in the death and resurrection of his Son, believers can know and love (v. 3).

The Incarnation of the Word of Life

1 That which was from the beginning, which we have heard, which we have seen with our eyes, which we have looked at and our hands have touched — this we proclaim concerning the Word of life. 2 The life appeared; we have seen it and testify to it, and we proclaim to you the eternal life, which was with the Father and has appeared to us. 3 We proclaim to you what we have seen and heard, so that you also may have fellowship with us. And our fellowship is with the Father and with his Son, Jesus Christ. 4 We write this to make our[a] joy complete.

Light and Darkness, Sin and Forgiveness

5 This is the message we have heard from him and declare to you: God is light; in him there is no darkness at all. 6 If we claim to have fellowship with him and yet walk in the darkness, we lie and do not live out the truth. 7 But if we walk in the light, as he is in the light, we have fellowship with one another, and the blood of Jesus, his Son, purifies us from all[b] sin.

8 If we claim to be without sin, we deceive ourselves and the truth is not in us. 9 If we confess our sins, he is faithful and just and will forgive us our sins and purify us from all unrighteousness. 10 If we claim we have not sinned, we make him out to be a liar and his word is not in us.

2 My dear children, I write this to you so that you will not sin. But if anybody does sin, we have an advocate with the Father — Jesus Christ, the Righteous One. 2 He is the atoning sacrifice for our sins, and not only for ours but also for the sins of the whole world.

Love and Hatred for Fellow Believers

3 We know that we have come to know him if we keep his commands. 4 Whoever says, "I know him," but does not do what he commands is a liar, and the truth is not in that person. 5 But if anyone obeys his word, love for God[c] is truly made complete in them. This is how we know we are in him: 6 Whoever claims to live in him must live as Jesus did.

7 Dear friends, I am not writing you a new command but an old one, which you have had since the beginning. This old command is the message you have heard. 8 Yet I am writing you a new command; its truth is seen in him and in you, because the darkness is passing and the true light is already shining.

9 Anyone who claims to be in the light but hates a brother or sister[d] is still in the darkness. 10 Anyone who loves their brother and sister[e] lives in the light, and there is nothing in them to make them stumble. 11 But anyone who hates a brother or sister is in the darkness and walks around in the darkness. They do not know where they are going, because the darkness has blinded them.

Reasons for Writing

12 I am writing to you, dear children,
 because your sins have been forgiven on account of his name.
13 I am writing to you, fathers,
 because you know him who is from the beginning.

---

[a] 4 Some manuscripts *your* [b] 7 Or *every* [c] 5 Or *word, God's love* [d] 9 The Greek word for *brother or sister* (*adelphos*) refers here to a believer, whether man or woman, as part of God's family; also in verse 11; and in 3:15, 17; 4:20; 5:16. [e] 10 The Greek word for *brother and sister* (*adelphos*) refers here to a believer, whether man or woman, as part of God's family; also in 3:10; 4:20, 21.

FATHER, SON AND HOLY SPIRIT

A time-honored hymn entitled "Holy, Holy, Holy" declares, "God in three persons, blessed Trinity." "Trinity" is a term coined between the second and fourth centuries to describe a fundamental doctrine of the Christian faith. This doctrine states that simultaneously and individually, the Father, Son and Holy Spirit are wholly God. While the word itself does not occur in Scripture, there is ample evidence to support God's triune nature throughout the Bible (Ge 1:26; 3:22; Isa 48:16; 61:1; Mt 3:13 – 17; 22:43 – 46; 28:19; 2Co 13:14; 1Pe 1:2). However, it is in the writings of John that Christians find the most nuanced view of the divine relationship.

In a very straightforward way, John opened by proclaiming the most important thing his readers needed to know: Jesus is God. Jesus has always existed, from the beginning, and he is not a subservient being as the heavenly hosts are. Rather Jesus was, is and will always be of the same nature as the Father (Jn 1:1 – 4). Jesus himself attested to this unique relationship when he laid claim to the revered name of God revealed to Moses at the burning bush (Jn 8:58; cf. Ex 3:14) and later reiterated this truth by stating "I and the Father are one" (Jn 10:30).

John also delivered key insight into the special unity Jesus shares with the Holy Spirit. While the word "advocate" (Greek *parakletos*) appears other places in Scripture, the form of the word used to describe a person appears only twice in the New Testament writings and uniquely in John's letters. He once used *parakletos* to identify the "advocate with the Father" to be "Jesus Christ, the Righteous One" (1Jn 2:1). And in Christ's last discourse with his disciples, John's Gospel recorded Jesus' words that gave this same designation to the promised Holy Spirit, calling him another "advocate" (Jn 14:16,26; 15:26; 16:7). John also taught that the Spirit and Christ interchangeably serve as companion (Jn 14:26 – 28), teacher (Jn 14:26; 2Jn 9), judge (Jn 5:22 – 23; 16:8), guide (Jn 10:3 – 4; 16:13) and truth (Jn 14:6; 1Jn 5:6 – 8).

Throughout his letters, John encourages all believers to be confident in the certainty of their salvation that is initiated, completed and secured by the harmonious work of the Father, Son and Spirit. "This is how we know that we live in him and he in us: He has given us of his Spirit. And we have seen and testify that the Father has sent his Son to be the Savior of the world" (1Jn 4:13 – 14).

1 JOHN 2:18–27

SPIRIT OF ANTICHRIST

The word *antichrist* is often associated only with the powerful and influential leader who will come into the spotlight to deceive the masses during the world's last days. While the Bible certainly does refer to this "man of lawlessness" who will emerge in the future (2Th 2:3), John's letter alerted believers to the danger of false teachers in the church and warned them to be aware that "the spirit of the antichrist" exists now (1Jn 2:18; 4:3). As the simple definition of the term indicates, this force encompasses any attitude or action that is generally "anti" (or against) Christ, and it especially includes any viewpoint that opposes belief in Jesus as fully God and the promised Messiah (2:22; 4:2–3).

Those who know scriptural truth but neglect to apply it to their lives easily fall prey to corrupt teachings that sound attractive but, in reality, are only myths that appeal to fleshly desires and satisfy "itching ears" (2Ti 4:3). Christians are not powerless against these deceptions. John reminded readers that God has equipped them with two key defenses against those who attempt to distort the gospel: first, a commitment to consistent study and application of the Word of truth (2Ti 2:15; 1Jn 2:24–25) and second, the indwelling guidance given by the Spirit of truth (Jn 16:13; 1Jn 2:27; 4:6). Both of these teach discernment and form a solid shield of protection against any falsehood.

I am writing to you, young men,
because you have overcome the evil one.

14 I write to you, dear children,
because you know the Father.
I write to you, fathers,
because you know him who is from the beginning.
I write to you, young men,
because you are strong,
and the word of God lives in you,
and you have overcome the evil one.

On Not Loving the World

15 Do not love the world or anything in the world. If anyone loves the world,
love for the Father[a] is not in them. 16 For everything in the world — the lust of the
flesh, the lust of the eyes, and the pride of life — comes not from the Father but
from the world. 17 The world and its desires pass away, but whoever does the will
of God lives forever.

Warnings Against Denying the Son

18 Dear children, this is the last hour; and as you have heard that the antichrist
is coming, even now many antichrists have come. This is how we know it is the
last hour. 19 They went out from us, but they did not really belong to us. For if they
had belonged to us, they would have remained with us; but their going showed
that none of them belonged to us.

20 But you have an anointing from the Holy One, and all of you know the truth.[b]
21 I do not write to you because you do not know the truth, but because you do
know it and because no lie comes from the truth. 22 Who is the liar? It is whoever
denies that Jesus is the Christ. Such a person is the antichrist — denying the Father and the Son. 23 No one who denies the Son has the Father; whoever acknowledges the Son has the Father also.

24 As for you, see that what you have heard from the beginning remains in you.
If it does, you also will remain in the Son and in the Father. 25 And this is what he
promised us — eternal life.

26 I am writing these things to you about those who are trying to lead you
astray. 27 As for you, the anointing you received from him remains in you, and
you do not need anyone to teach you. But as his anointing teaches you about all
things and as that anointing is real, not counterfeit — just as it has taught you,
remain in him.

God's Children and Sin

28 And now, dear children, continue in him, so that when he appears we may
be confident and unashamed before him at his coming.

29 If you know that he is righteous, you know that everyone who does what is
right has been born of him.

3 See what great love the Father has lavished on us, that we should be called
children of God! And that is what we are! The reason the world does not know
us is that it did not know him. 2 Dear friends, now we are children of God, and
what we will be has not yet been made known. But we know that when Christ
appears,[c] we shall be like him, for we shall see him as he is. 3 All who have this
hope in him purify themselves, just as he is pure.

4 Everyone who sins breaks the law; in fact, sin is lawlessness. 5 But you know
that he appeared so that he might take away our sins. And in him is no sin. 6 No
one who lives in him keeps on sinning. No one who continues to sin has either
seen him or known him.

[a] 15 Or *world, the Father's love* [b] 20 Some manuscripts *and you know all things*
[c] 2 Or *when it is made known*

7Dear children, do not let anyone lead you astray. The one who does what is right is righteous, just as he is righteous. 8The one who does what is sinful is of the devil, because the devil has been sinning from the beginning. The reason the Son of God appeared was to destroy the devil's work. 9No one who is born of God will continue to sin, because God's seed remains in them; they cannot go on sinning, because they have been born of God. 10This is how we know who the children of God are and who the children of the devil are: Anyone who does not do what is right is not God's child, nor is anyone who does not love their brother and sister.

More on Love and Hatred

11For this is the message you heard from the beginning: We should love one another. 12Do not be like Cain, who belonged to the evil one and murdered his brother. And why did he murder him? Because his own actions were evil and his brother's were righteous. 13Do not be surprised, my brothers and sisters,[a] if the world hates you. 14We know that we have passed from death to life, because we love each other. Anyone who does not love remains in death. 15Anyone who hates a brother or sister is a murderer, and you know that no murderer has eternal life residing in him.

16This is how we know what love is: Jesus Christ laid down his life for us. And we ought to lay down our lives for our brothers and sisters. 17If anyone has material possessions and sees a brother or sister in need but has no pity on them, how can the love of God be in that person? 18Dear children, let us not love with words or speech but with actions and in truth.

19This is how we know that we belong to the truth and how we set our hearts at rest in his presence: 20If our hearts condemn us, we know that God is greater than our hearts, and he knows everything. 21Dear friends, if our hearts do not condemn us, we have confidence before God 22and receive from him anything we ask, because we keep his commands and do what pleases him. 23And this is his command: to believe in the name of his Son, Jesus Christ, and to love one another as he commanded us. 24The one who keeps God's commands lives in him, and he in them. And this is how we know that he lives in us: We know it by the Spirit he gave us.

On Denying the Incarnation

4 Dear friends, do not believe every spirit, but test the spirits to see whether they are from God, because many false prophets have gone out into the world. 2This is how you can recognize the Spirit of God: Every spirit that acknowledges that Jesus Christ has come in the flesh is from God, 3but every spirit that does not acknowledge Jesus is not from God. This is the spirit of the antichrist, which you have heard is coming and even now is already in the world.

4You, dear children, are from God and have overcome them, because the one who is in you is greater than the one who is in the world. 5They are from the world and therefore speak from the viewpoint of the world, and the world listens to them. 6We are from God, and whoever knows God listens to us; but whoever is not from God does not listen to us. This is how we recognize the Spirit[b] of truth and the spirit of falsehood.

God's Love and Ours

7Dear friends, let us love one another, for love comes from God. Everyone who loves has been born of God and knows God. 8Whoever does not love does not know God, because God is love. 9This is how God showed his love among us: He sent his one and only Son into the world that we might live through him. 10This is love: not that we loved God, but that he loved us and sent his Son as an atoning sacrifice for our sins. 11Dear friends, since God so loved us, we also ought to love

---

[a] *13* The Greek word for *brothers and sisters* (*adelphoi*) refers here to believers, both men and women, as part of God's family; also in verse 16. [b] *6* Or *spirit*

one another. 12No one has ever seen God; but if we love one another, God lives in us and his love is made complete in us.

13This is how we know that we live in him and he in us: He has given us of his Spirit. 14And we have seen and testify that the Father has sent his Son to be the Savior of the world. 15If anyone acknowledges that Jesus is the Son of God, God lives in them and they in God. 16And so we know and rely on the love God has for us.

God is love. Whoever lives in love lives in God, and God in them. 17This is how love is made complete among us so that we will have confidence on the day of judgment: In this world we are like Jesus. 18There is no fear in love. But perfect love drives out fear, because fear has to do with punishment. The one who fears is not made perfect in love.

19We love because he first loved us. 20Whoever claims to love God yet hates a brother or sister is a liar. For whoever does not love their brother and sister, whom they have seen, cannot love God, whom they have not seen. 21And he has given us this command: Anyone who loves God must also love their brother and sister.

Faith in the Incarnate Son of God

5 Everyone who believes that Jesus is the Christ is born of God, and everyone who loves the father loves his child as well. 2This is how we know that we love the children of God: by loving God and carrying out his commands. 3In fact, this is love for God: to keep his commands. And his commands are not burdensome, 4for everyone born of God overcomes the world. This is the victory that has overcome the world, even our faith. 5Who is it that overcomes the world? Only the one who believes that Jesus is the Son of God.

6This is the one who came by water and blood — Jesus Christ. He did not come by water only, but by water and blood. And it is the Spirit who testifies, because the Spirit is the truth. 7For there are three that testify: 8the[a] Spirit, the water and the blood; and the three are in agreement. 9We accept human testimony, but God's testimony is greater because it is the testimony of God, which he has given about his Son. 10Whoever believes in the Son of God accepts this testimony. Whoever does not believe God has made him out to be a liar, because they have not believed the testimony God has given about his Son. 11And this is the testimony: God has given us eternal life, and this life is in his Son. 12Whoever has the Son has life; whoever does not have the Son of God does not have life.

Concluding Affirmations

13I write these things to you who believe in the name of the Son of God so that you may know that you have eternal life. 14This is the confidence we have in approaching God: that if we ask anything according to his will, he hears us. 15And if we know that he hears us — whatever we ask — we know that we have what we asked of him.

16If you see any brother or sister commit a sin that does not lead to death, you should pray and God will give them life. I refer to those whose sin does not lead to death. There is a sin that leads to death. I am not saying that you should pray about that. 17All wrongdoing is sin, and there is sin that does not lead to death.

18We know that anyone born of God does not continue to sin; the One who was born of God keeps them safe, and the evil one cannot harm them. 19We know that we are children of God, and that the whole world is under the control of the evil one. 20We know also that the Son of God has come and has given us understanding, so that we may know him who is true. And we are in him who is true by being in his Son Jesus Christ. He is the true God and eternal life.

21Dear children, keep yourselves from idols.

---

[a] 7,8 Late manuscripts of the Vulgate *testify in heaven: the Father, the Word and the Holy Spirit, and these three are one. 8And there are three that testify on earth: the* (not found in any Greek manuscript before the fourteenth century)

JESUS: OUR GOD IN THE FLESH

2 JOHN

2 JOHN

JOHN LEADS IN THE EARLY CHURCH	TEMPLE DESTROYED, CHURCH SCATTERS	JOHN WRITES HIS GOSPEL AND LETTERS
c. AD 30	*c. AD 70*	*c. AD 90*

Followers of Jesus must be on their guard against deception. The recurring themes of false teaching is pervasive throughout the New Testament epistles and is the central focus of John's second letter. Little is known about the recipient of John's letter: "to the lady chosen by God and to her children," though it is clear that the apostle John has deep love for those to whom he writes (v. 1).

This love is seen most clearly in his desire to protect them from harmful false teaching. An abundance of false views regarding God's nature and his work through Jesus had infiltrated God's people. One such view, Docetism, taught that Jesus had not come in the flesh. False teachers deceived many with the notion that Jesus did not have a physical body but only appeared to have one. Thus, his death on the cross and resurrection were not physical realities.

John warns true believers to beware of such heresy. The physical life, actual death and bodily resurrection of Jesus are vital components of the Christian faith. Someone had to actually live the perfect life that God desired in order to give God's people the gift of a righteous standing before God. Someone had to die a physical death and endure the spiritual weight of humanity's sin in order to satisfy the wrath of God for that sin. Someone had to overcome death in a physical body in order to demonstrate that Satan, sin and death had been defeated.

For this reason, John wrote that the false teachers were not peddling a minor distortion to the truth. They were teaching rank heresy and had to be silenced. The same law of love he established in his first letter motivated John's challenge to the church. False teachers must be silenced out of love and protection for God's people. Elders and church members alike must see to it that they protect one another from the harm that Satan brings through false teaching. Together, they must hold to the truth of the gospel, which was handed down by God to the apostles and protected by the careful leadership of the church. Throughout all generations, though the nature of the false teaching may change, churches must fight for the truth of the gospel.

AND THIS IS LOVE: THAT WE WALK IN OBEDIENCE TO HIS COMMANDS. AS YOU HAVE HEARD FROM THE BEGINNING, HIS COMMAND IS THAT YOU WALK IN LOVE.

---

2 John 6

2 JOHN

2 JOHN 6

TRUTH AND LOVE

In the latter half of the first century, the young church faced many new problems. At the command of Emperor Nero, the Roman government launched a structured campaign to persecute Christians that included some of the most atrocious forms of torture and execution ever devised. Historians believe that both Peter, Christ's boldest disciple and preacher at Pentecost; and Paul, the greatest church planter and missionary of the first century, were martyred under Nero's brutal reign. And while attacks from outside the church escalated, deceptive philosophies from false teachers proliferated and began to erode it from the inside. This confusion caused many ungrounded believers to embrace aberrant ideas about the person and work of Christ.

Into this troubling atmosphere, John ("the elder" [v. 1] and the last of Jesus' twelve disciples to survive) wrote this short letter to remind the early church of the importance of holding fast to the truth of the gospel (as recorded in the pages of Scripture) and of walking in love. Instead of defining love in situational or emotional terms, he gave believers a clear understanding of the meaning of genuine love: to walk according to Jesus' commands (v. 6). And that love is exhibited most genuinely by a life lived in consistency with the teachings of Christ.

1 The elder,

To the lady chosen by God and to her children, whom I love in the truth—and
not I only, but also all who know the truth— 2 because of the truth, which lives in
us and will be with us forever:

3 Grace, mercy and peace from God the Father and from Jesus Christ, the Father's Son, will be with us in truth and love.

4 It has given me great joy to find some of your children walking in the truth,
just as the Father commanded us. 5 And now, dear lady, I am not writing you a
new command but one we have had from the beginning. I ask that we love one
another. 6 And this is love: that we walk in obedience to his commands. As you
have heard from the beginning, his command is that you walk in love.
7 I say this because many deceivers, who do not acknowledge Jesus Christ as
coming in the flesh, have gone out into the world. Any such person is the deceiver and the antichrist. 8 Watch out that you do not lose what we[a] have worked
for, but that you may be rewarded fully. 9 Anyone who runs ahead and does not
continue in the teaching of Christ does not have God; whoever continues in the
teaching has both the Father and the Son. 10 If anyone comes to you and does not
bring this teaching, do not take them into your house or welcome them. 11 Anyone who welcomes them shares in their wicked work.
12 I have much to write to you, but I do not want to use paper and ink. Instead,
I hope to visit you and talk with you face to face, so that our joy may be complete.

13 The children of your sister, who is chosen by God, send their greetings.

[a] *8* Some manuscripts *you*

JESUS: OUR BOND OF FELLOWSHIP

3 JOHN

3 JOHN

JOHN RESIDES IN EPHESUS	TEMPLE DESTROYED, CHURCH SCATTERS	JOHN WRITES HIS GOSPEL AND LETTERS
c. AD 67	*c. AD 70*	*c. AD 90*

Internal conflict is divisive for the church of Jesus Christ. In his first two letters, John warned the church against false teachers who were deceiving the church from the outside. Their heresy was leading many astray and contaminating their understanding of the truthfulness of the gospel. In 3 John, the church is facing another destructive influence. Diotrephes, a church leader, was exerting control over his congregation by barring other ministers from serving his congregation. Even worse, Diotrephes was disassociating from members of the congregation who demonstrated kindness to these ministers. In so doing, he was violating John's challenge for the church to model the love of Christ in their relationships with all believers.

Diotrephes's arrogance was harming the church, and it needed to be stopped. John was planning a visit to the church to address this issue, but in the meantime he wrote to challenge this moral failure of its leader.

John's letter is addressed to a member of the church, Gaius, who had the resources to show care to these itinerant ministers. John encouraged Gaius in his support of these fellow workers "for the truth" (v. 8). They were fellow ministers of the gospel, doing faithful ministry among the Gentiles. The church, according to John, had a responsibility to support, encourage and equip these gospel workers. Diotrephes's actions were hindering the good work these laborers were doing. Apparently, John felt that Gaius had the confidence, strength and ability to counter Diotrephes's actions and continue to lead the church to support and send workers.

The sending of missionaries and ministers of the gospel should mark the church. Established churches, founded on the truth claims of Jesus Christ, must see to it that they invest time, effort and energy in the advancement of the gospel around the world. Missionaries such as Paul, Barnabas, John Mark and others throughout the book of Acts are examples of the faithfulness of God's church in sending gospel ministers and the way God uses these leaders to build up his church around the world. Faithful leaders should follow John's exhortation in this brief letter and empower their churches to love, serve and send those taking the name of Jesus around the world.

IT GAVE ME GREAT JOY WHEN SOME BELIEVERS CAME AND TESTIFIED ABOUT YOUR FAITHFULNESS TO THE TRUTH, TELLING HOW YOU CONTINUE TO WALK IN IT.

---

3 John 3

3 JOHN

1 The elder,

To my dear friend Gaius, whom I love in the truth.

2 Dear friend, I pray that you may enjoy good health and that all may go well
with you, even as your soul is getting along well. 3 It gave me great joy when some
believers came and testified about your faithfulness to the truth, telling how you
continue to walk in it. 4 I have no greater joy than to hear that my children are
walking in the truth.

5 Dear friend, you are faithful in what you are doing for the brothers and sisters,[a] even though they are strangers to you. 6 They have told the church about
your love. Please send them on their way in a manner that honors God. 7 It was
for the sake of the Name that they went out, receiving no help from the pagans.
8 We ought therefore to show hospitality to such people so that we may work together for the truth.

9 I wrote to the church, but Diotrephes, who loves to be first, will not welcome
us. 10 So when I come, I will call attention to what he is doing, spreading malicious nonsense about us. Not satisfied with that, he even refuses to welcome
other believers. He also stops those who want to do so and puts them out of the
church.

11 Dear friend, do not imitate what is evil but what is good. Anyone who does
what is good is from God. Anyone who does what is evil has not seen God. 12 Demetrius is well spoken of by everyone—and even by the truth itself. We also
speak well of him, and you know that our testimony is true.

13 I have much to write you, but I do not want to do so with pen and ink. 14 I hope
to see you soon, and we will talk face to face.

Peace to you. The friends here send their greetings. Greet the friends there by name.

[a] 5 The Greek word for *brothers and sisters* (*adelphoi*) refers here to believers, both men and women, as part of God's family.

3 JOHN 2

HAVE OR HAVE NOT

In John's greeting to Gaius, he prayed that his friend would find balance between the spiritual and physical world (v. 2). While much is written in the Bible about material possessions, there is little written to indicate that either worldly prosperity or poverty are reliable indicators of God's approval or disapproval. Scripture records that some of God's key servants possessed significant material means, including Abraham (Ge 13:2), Isaac (Ge 26:12–14), Jacob (Ge 36:6–7), David (1Ch 28:1), Solomon (2Ch 9:22), Jehoshaphat (2Ch 17:5) and Joseph of Arimathea (Mt 27:57). Conversely, the lives of others such as Elijah (1Ki 17:1–14), Naomi (Ru 1:1–21), Jeremiah (Jer 37:1–21), John the Baptist (Mt 3:4; Lk 1:80) and Paul (Ac 16:16–36; 28:16–31; Php 1:12–14) bear witness that others had to endure want, imprisonment and unjust punishment. Though there's no indication that Jesus lacked for food or clothing, it is likely that he accumulated very little, if anything, in the way of material belongings during his time on earth (Mt 8:20).

Living as Jesus' disciples today does not guarantee health and financial success nor lead necessarily to a life of poverty. It does, however, promise believers the opportunity to flourish spiritually and be assured of God's enduring prosperity that will not fail when they are careful to set their eyes and hearts on things above rather than earthly things (Col 3:1–2) and are vigilant to lay up "treasures in heaven" that will not wear out (Mt 6:20).

JESUS: OUR SUSTAINING GRACE

JUDE

JUDE

REIGN OF NERO *c. AD 54 – 68*	JUDE WRITES HIS LETTER *c. AD 60 – 64*	TEMPLE DESTROYED, CHURCH SCATTERS *c. AD 70*

God will judge and punish all evil. From cover to cover, the Bible testifies to this fact. At times, however, it may appear that evil prospers and wickedness prevails. Evildoers include the false teachers who were embattling the church during the first century of its existence.

Jude earnestly wrote to the church "to contend for the faith that was once for all entrusted to God's holy people" (v. 3). The gospel message is irrevocable and true. God, in his kindness, gave his Word to the apostles, which testified to the nature of God and his work through Jesus Christ. False teachers undermined this message — distorting its meaning and leading the church astray.

Jude reminds the church that God will judge these deceivers. God has already demonstrated his judgment in the condemnation of the devil — the chief deceiver himself. Since God has judged Satan, he will also pour out his wrath on all those who deceived God's people (vv. 5 – 11).

The church, however, should not be surprised when these false teachers continue to harm the church. And, they should expect that some will be led astray (vv. 12 – 19). They will follow after their own passions, rebel from God's Word and bring upon themselves the condemnation of God.

In contrast, God's church will be sustained by the grace of God. Believers should build one another up in Christ and keep themselves in the love of God (vv. 20 – 21). The mercy of God protects those who truly know Christ and sustains them in the gospel message and faithful obedience in the face of outward hostility (v. 21). Jesus keeps his people from stumbling and will present them faultless one day (v. 24).

Jude's message is an encouragement that truth will prevail. The deception of false teachers will be exposed, and they will be judged — in God's time and in God's way. The hypocrisy of false converts will also be exposed. They will leave the church and prove they were never truly converted. And, the true church will be sustained by the grace of God. Those who truly have been saved by his might will be kept by his power until the time when the earth is purified from all falsehood forever.

TO HIM WHO IS ABLE TO KEEP YOU FROM STUMBLING AND TO PRESENT YOU BEFORE HIS GLORIOUS PRESENCE WITHOUT FAULT AND WITH GREAT JOY — TO THE ONLY GOD OUR SAVIOR BE GLORY, MAJESTY, POWER AND AUTHORITY, THROUGH JESUS CHRIST OUR LORD, BEFORE ALL AGES, NOW AND FOREVERMORE! AMEN.

Jude 24 – 25

JUDE

1 Jude, a servant of Jesus Christ and a brother of James,

To those who have been called, who are loved in God the Father and kept for[a]
Jesus Christ:

2 Mercy, peace and love be yours in abundance.

The Sin and Doom of Ungodly People

3 Dear friends, although I was very eager to write to you about the salvation
we share, I felt compelled to write and urge you to contend for the faith that
was once for all entrusted to God's holy people. 4 For certain individuals whose
condemnation was written about[b] long ago have secretly slipped in among you.
They are ungodly people, who pervert the grace of our God into a license for immorality and deny Jesus Christ our only Sovereign and Lord.

5 Though you already know all this, I want to remind you that the Lord[c] at
one time delivered his people out of Egypt, but later destroyed those who did
not believe. 6 And the angels who did not keep their positions of authority but
abandoned their proper dwelling — these he has kept in darkness, bound with
everlasting chains for judgment on the great Day. 7 In a similar way, Sodom and
Gomorrah and the surrounding towns gave themselves up to sexual immorality
and perversion. They serve as an example of those who suffer the punishment
of eternal fire.

8 In the very same way, on the strength of their dreams these ungodly people
pollute their own bodies, reject authority and heap abuse on celestial beings.
9 But even the archangel Michael, when he was disputing with the devil about the
body of Moses, did not himself dare to condemn him for slander but said, "The
Lord rebuke you!"[d] 10 Yet these people slander whatever they do not understand,
and the very things they do understand by instinct — as irrational animals do —
will destroy them.

11 Woe to them! They have taken the way of Cain; they have rushed for profit
into Balaam's error; they have been destroyed in Korah's rebellion.

12 These people are blemishes at your love feasts, eating with you without the
slightest qualm — shepherds who feed only themselves. They are clouds without
rain, blown along by the wind; autumn trees, without fruit and uprooted — twice
dead. 13 They are wild waves of the sea, foaming up their shame; wandering stars,
for whom blackest darkness has been reserved forever.

14 Enoch, the seventh from Adam, prophesied about them: "See, the Lord is
coming with thousands upon thousands of his holy ones 15 to judge everyone,
and to convict all of them of all the ungodly acts they have committed in their
ungodliness, and of all the defiant words ungodly sinners have spoken against
him."[e] 16 These people are grumblers and faultfinders; they follow their own evil
desires; they boast about themselves and flatter others for their own advantage.

A Call to Persevere

17 But, dear friends, remember what the apostles of our Lord Jesus Christ foretold. 18 They said to you, "In the last times there will be scoffers who will follow
their own ungodly desires." 19 These are the people who divide you, who follow
mere natural instincts and do not have the Spirit.

---

[a] *1* Or *by*; or *in*   [b] *4* Or *individuals who were marked out for condemnation*   [c] *5* Some early manuscripts *Jesus*   [d] *9* Jude is alluding to the Jewish *Testament of Moses* (approximately the first century A.D.).   [e] *14,15* From the Jewish *First Book of Enoch* (approximately the first century B.C.)

[20]But you, dear friends, by building yourselves up in your most holy faith and
praying in the Holy Spirit, [21]keep yourselves in God's love as you wait for the
mercy of our Lord Jesus Christ to bring you to eternal life.
[22]Be merciful to those who doubt; [23]save others by snatching them from the
fire; to others show mercy, mixed with fear—hating even the clothing stained
by corrupted flesh.[a]

Doxology

[24]To him who is able to keep you from stumbling and to present you before his
glorious presence without fault and with great joy— [25]to the only God our Savior
be glory, majesty, power and authority, through Jesus Christ our Lord, before all
ages, now and forevermore! Amen.

[a] *22,23* The Greek manuscripts of these verses vary at several points.

JUDE 24–25

TO HIM

Jude concluded his book with a beautiful doxology, inviting readers throughout history to join him in ascribing glory to God. In this passage, Jude took human weakness into account as something God can easily overcome. He also reaffirmed human destiny, that one day all people will stand before the Lord.

These verses read like a song that grows into a shout of triumphant praise—all for God our Savior (v. 25). God arranged for believers to be saved through faith in Jesus (Jn 3:16). He showed mercy to those who deserved to be crushed. God sacrificed his own Son to purchase pardon for the whole world—for all who will believe the gospel (1Jn 2:2).

Jesus' work makes it possible for believers to know and praise their holy God. Jesus gives believers hope and assurance that they will someday stand before God in righteousness, without blame (Php 3:9) and with great joy. Jesus is the difference-maker for all mankind: He is the Lamb (Rev 5:6), the Branch (Isa 4:2; 11:1), the Redeemer (Isa 44:24), the Savior (1Jn 4:14), the gate (Jn 10:9), the way (Jn 14:6), the living water (Jn 4:10), the light of the world (Jn 9:5), and the bread of life (Jn 6:35). He offers salvation to all who will accept it, and he is worthy of resounding praise forever!

JESUS: OUR WORSHIP FOREVER

REVELATION

REVELATION

JOHN WRITES HIS GOSPEL AND LETTERS *c. AD 90*	JOHN EXILED TO ISLAND OF PATMOS *c. AD 93*	JOHN WRITES REVELATION *c. AD 95*

Christ's promised return was the hope of the church. In the first century, the church faced ongoing persecution, spiritual warfare, internal divisions and heretical doctrine. These factors caused the faithful believers to look forward to the second coming of Christ with great anticipation, though they were still filled with questions regarding the timing and nature of his return.

John wrote to encourage the church with the hope of the coming of Christ and to challenge them to ongoing faithfulness in the meantime. While exiled on the island of Patmos, John was given a vision of the return of Christ, and he recorded this vision for the churches of his day — particularly the seven churches in Asia Minor.

John's vision is vivid and beautiful. The reigning king, the lion of Judah, the worthy Lamb of God would return and reign as the victorious king (5:8 – 13; 12:5). Through symbolic imagery, John captured the climatic stages of God's redemptive plan to restore his kingdom on earth and rule and reign with his chosen people forever. His return will mark the final destruction of all wickedness — both those who failed to repent and place their faith in Christ and all forms of brokenness and destruction that have plagued the earth since the fall. Believers will be saved from the coming destruction and given the glorious privilege of dwelling with God, worshiping him as king and serving him in a new, purified world (21:1 – 8). John seemingly grasps for words to describe the glorious splendor of the coming kingdom and the beauty of the spotless Lamb of God who sits on the throne. In light of these sure promises, the church should not cower in the midst of persecution. Should they falter, God will remove his presence from them (2:1 — 3:22).

Though many questions remain about the exact nature of John's prophecy concerning the second coming, one thing is sure — God wins, and Jesus reigns. Worship today is a mere shadow of the magnificent scenes of worship around the throne of God (4:1 – 11; 5:8 – 14). There, believers of every tribe, tongue and nation will gather together to proclaim the glory of Jesus Christ. Throughout the generations, the church has longed and continues to long for that day, begging God to hasten his coming (22:20 – 21).

HE WILL WIPE EVERY TEAR FROM THEIR EYES. THERE WILL BE NO MORE DEATH OR MOURNING OR CRYING OR PAIN, FOR THE OLD ORDER OF THINGS HAS PASSED AWAY.

Revelation 21:4

REVELATION

Prologue

1 The revelation from Jesus Christ, which God gave him to show his servants what must soon take place. He made it known by sending his angel to his servant John, [2]who testifies to everything he saw — that is, the word of God and the testimony of Jesus Christ. [3]Blessed is the one who reads aloud the words of this prophecy, and blessed are those who hear it and take to heart what is written in it, because the time is near.

Greetings and Doxology

[4]John,

To the seven churches in the province of Asia:

Grace and peace to you from him who is, and who was, and who is to come, and from the seven spirits[a] before his throne, [5]and from Jesus Christ, who is the faithful witness, the firstborn from the dead, and the ruler of the kings of the earth.

To him who loves us and has freed us from our sins by his blood, [6]and has made us to be a kingdom and priests to serve his God and Father — to him be glory and power for ever and ever! Amen.

[7] "Look, he is coming with the clouds,"[b]
  and "every eye will see him,
even those who pierced him";
  and all peoples on earth "will mourn because of him."[c]
So shall it be! Amen.

[8]"I am the Alpha and the Omega," says the Lord God, "who is, and who was, and who is to come, the Almighty."

John's Vision of Christ

[9]I, John, your brother and companion in the suffering and kingdom and patient endurance that are ours in Jesus, was on the island of Patmos because of the word of God and the testimony of Jesus. [10]On the Lord's Day I was in the Spirit, and I heard behind me a loud voice like a trumpet, [11]which said: "Write on a scroll what you see and send it to the seven churches: to Ephesus, Smyrna, Pergamum, Thyatira, Sardis, Philadelphia and Laodicea."

[12]I turned around to see the voice that was speaking to me. And when I turned I saw seven golden lampstands, [13]and among the lampstands was someone like a son of man,[d] dressed in a robe reaching down to his feet and with a golden sash around his chest. [14]The hair on his head was white like wool, as white as snow, and his eyes were like blazing fire. [15]His feet were like bronze glowing in a furnace, and his voice was like the sound of rushing waters. [16]In his right hand he held seven stars, and coming out of his mouth was a sharp, double-edged sword. His face was like the sun shining in all its brilliance.

[17]When I saw him, I fell at his feet as though dead. Then he placed his right hand on me and said: "Do not be afraid. I am the First and the Last. [18]I am the Living One; I was dead, and now look, I am alive for ever and ever! And I hold the keys of death and Hades.

[19]"Write, therefore, what you have seen, what is now and what will take place later. [20]The mystery of the seven stars that you saw in my right hand and of the

---

[a] *4* That is, the sevenfold Spirit [b] *7* Daniel 7:13 [c] *7* Zech. 12:10 [d] *13* See Daniel 7:13.

A PICTURE OF JESUS

The first chapter of Revelation provides an introduction to the rest of the book, and it also provides three critical depictions of Jesus.

In verse 5, John wrote that Jesus is "the faithful witness," which is to say that he is a prophet who came to earth as a witness to the truth. Not only did Jesus remain faithful to God's message throughout his life, but also he remained steadfast to God's truth, even to the point of death (Lk 22:42). He encouraged believers to do the same (Rev 2:10). John also referred to Jesus as "the firstborn from the dead" (1:5) because in his resurrection, Jesus was the first one to overcome death by his own power (Jn 2:19). He is the only person to die, to physically rise from the dead and continue to live forever (Ro 8:34; 6:9 – 11). Lastly, John called Jesus "the ruler of the kings of the earth" (Rev 1:5) because Jesus is the one to whom God gave the throne of David forever, as the angel attested when he announced his upcoming birth to Mary (Lk 1:31 – 33).

Between these three descriptions, John confirmed Jesus' threefold office as prophet (Dt 18:18 – 19), priest (Ps 110:1 – 4) and king (Ps 2:4 – 9). Because Jesus filled each of these roles on earth, he was qualified to be the "anointed one" (Ac 4:26; see Lk 4:18), and John's vision reaffirms each of these positions that Jesus fulfilled to further confirm that he is the Son of God.

After establishing Jesus' elevated position, John wrote a vivid description of the exalted Jesus. John observed that the one "like a son of man" wears a robe and sash (Rev 1:13), which is similar to what a priest would typically wear (Ex 28:4). His hair is "white like wool, as white as snow" (Rev 1:14), which is a symbol of wisdom and dignity (Lev 19:32; Pr 16:31). John described Jesus' voice as "like the sound of rushing waters" (Rev 1:15), which is a description that is also used to describe what God sounds like (Eze 43:2). Also, John depicts a "sharp, double-edged sword" (Rev 1:16) coming out of his mouth, which is to show both how precise Jesus' Word is (Heb 4:12) and that what he says is meant for judgment (Mt 10:34).

John's description of Jesus in the first chapter of Revelation is incredibly vivid, and it is meant to set the scene for the rest of the book. John started by confirming that Jesus is who he claimed to be during his earthy ministry (Rev 1:5), and also confirmed that, when Jesus returns, it will be clear to all people that he is the Son of God (v. 7).

seven golden lampstands is this: The seven stars are the angels[a] of the seven
churches, and the seven lampstands are the seven churches.

To the Church in Ephesus

2 "To the angel[b] of the church in Ephesus write:

These are the words of him who holds the seven stars in his right hand
and walks among the seven golden lampstands. [2]I know your deeds, your
hard work and your perseverance. I know that you cannot tolerate wicked
people, that you have tested those who claim to be apostles but are not, and
have found them false. [3]You have persevered and have endured hardships
for my name, and have not grown weary.
[4]Yet I hold this against you: You have forsaken the love you had at first.
[5]Consider how far you have fallen! Repent and do the things you did at first.
If you do not repent, I will come to you and remove your lampstand from
its place. [6]But you have this in your favor: You hate the practices of the Nicolaitans, which I also hate.
[7]Whoever has ears, let them hear what the Spirit says to the churches.
To the one who is victorious, I will give the right to eat from the tree of life,
which is in the paradise of God.

To the Church in Smyrna

[8]"To the angel of the church in Smyrna write:

These are the words of him who is the First and the Last, who died and
came to life again. [9]I know your afflictions and your poverty—yet you are
rich! I know about the slander of those who say they are Jews and are not,
but are a synagogue of Satan. [10]Do not be afraid of what you are about to
suffer. I tell you, the devil will put some of you in prison to test you, and you
will suffer persecution for ten days. Be faithful, even to the point of death,
and I will give you life as your victor's crown.
[11]Whoever has ears, let them hear what the Spirit says to the churches.
The one who is victorious will not be hurt at all by the second death.

To the Church in Pergamum

[12]"To the angel of the church in Pergamum write:

These are the words of him who has the sharp, double-edged sword. [13]I
know where you live—where Satan has his throne. Yet you remain true to my
name. You did not renounce your faith in me, not even in the days of Antipas,
my faithful witness, who was put to death in your city—where Satan lives.
[14]Nevertheless, I have a few things against you: There are some among
you who hold to the teaching of Balaam, who taught Balak to entice the
Israelites to sin so that they ate food sacrificed to idols and committed sexual immorality. [15]Likewise, you also have those who hold to the teaching
of the Nicolaitans. [16]Repent therefore! Otherwise, I will soon come to you
and will fight against them with the sword of my mouth.
[17]Whoever has ears, let them hear what the Spirit says to the churches.
To the one who is victorious, I will give some of the hidden manna. I will
also give that person a white stone with a new name written on it, known
only to the one who receives it.

To the Church in Thyatira

[18]"To the angel of the church in Thyatira write:

These are the words of the Son of God, whose eyes are like blazing fire
and whose feet are like burnished bronze. [19]I know your deeds, your love

REVELATION 2:7

HE WHO HAS EARS, LET HIM HEAR

In the first chapters of Revelation, Jesus ended each of his addresses to the seven churches with the phrase, "Whoever has ears, let them hear" (vv. 7,11,17,29; 3:6,13,22). Jesus used this same phrase in Matthew 11:15 prior to his message of warning to unrepentant cities. In Revelation, Jesus gives one final warning to each of the seven major churches, telling them that it is important for them to heed what he is saying while there is still time.

Isaiah 6:10 described how the ears of the people would be closed when Jesus came, and this prophecy was fulfilled by the many people who did not understand his teachings and in the actions of the Jewish leaders who openly opposed him. However, Isaiah 32:3 also promises that the eyes and ears of the people will one day be opened, and that many will accept the words of Jesus.

Believers and nonbelievers alike have the choice to be the people described in Isaiah 6 or the people described in Isaiah 32. Revelation 2–3 begins Jesus' last appeal for people to follow Isaiah 32—to listen to and heed his words. These chapters are also a warning that one day it will be too late; that those who chose to hear and repent will be saved and those who chose to keep their ears and hearts closed to the gospel will be subject to judgment.

[a] *20* Or *messengers* [b] *1* Or *messenger*; also in verses 8, 12 and 18

and faith, your service and perseverance, and that you are now doing more
than you did at first.
20Nevertheless, I have this against you: You tolerate that woman Jezebel, who calls herself a prophet. By her teaching she misleads my servants
into sexual immorality and the eating of food sacrificed to idols. 21I have
given her time to repent of her immorality, but she is unwilling. 22So I will
cast her on a bed of suffering, and I will make those who commit adultery
with her suffer intensely, unless they repent of her ways. 23I will strike her
children dead. Then all the churches will know that I am he who searches
hearts and minds, and I will repay each of you according to your deeds.
24Now I say to the rest of you in Thyatira, to you who do not hold to her
teaching and have not learned Satan's so-called deep secrets, 'I will not
impose any other burden on you, 25except to hold on to what you have until I come.'
26To the one who is victorious and does my will to the end, I will give authority over the nations — 27that one 'will rule them with an iron scepter
and will dash them to pieces like pottery'[a] — just as I have received authority from my Father. 28I will also give that one the morning star. 29Whoever
has ears, let them hear what the Spirit says to the churches.

To the Church in Sardis

3 "To the angel[b] of the church in Sardis write:

These are the words of him who holds the seven spirits[c] of God and the
seven stars. I know your deeds; you have a reputation of being alive, but
you are dead. 2Wake up! Strengthen what remains and is about to die, for
I have found your deeds unfinished in the sight of my God. 3Remember,
therefore, what you have received and heard; hold it fast, and repent. But if
you do not wake up, I will come like a thief, and you will not know at what
time I will come to you.
4Yet you have a few people in Sardis who have not soiled their clothes.
They will walk with me, dressed in white, for they are worthy. 5The one who
is victorious will, like them, be dressed in white. I will never blot out the
name of that person from the book of life, but will acknowledge that name
before my Father and his angels. 6Whoever has ears, let them hear what the
Spirit says to the churches.

To the Church in Philadelphia

7"To the angel of the church in Philadelphia write:

These are the words of him who is holy and true, who holds the key of
David. What he opens no one can shut, and what he shuts no one can open.
8I know your deeds. See, I have placed before you an open door that no one
can shut. I know that you have little strength, yet you have kept my word
and have not denied my name. 9I will make those who are of the synagogue
of Satan, who claim to be Jews though they are not, but are liars — I will
make them come and fall down at your feet and acknowledge that I have
loved you. 10Since you have kept my command to endure patiently, I will
also keep you from the hour of trial that is going to come on the whole world
to test the inhabitants of the earth.
11I am coming soon. Hold on to what you have, so that no one will take
your crown. 12The one who is victorious I will make a pillar in the temple of
my God. Never again will they leave it. I will write on them the name of my
God and the name of the city of my God, the new Jerusalem, which is coming down out of heaven from my God; and I will also write on them my new
name. 13Whoever has ears, let them hear what the Spirit says to the churches.

[a] *27* Psalm 2:9 [b] *1* Or *messenger*; also in verses 7 and 14 [c] *1* That is, the sevenfold Spirit

REVELATION 3:1 – 6

SPIRITUAL DEATH

John recorded Jesus' address to the church in Sardis in which he admonishes the church for having a reputation for being alive, yet being dead all the while (v. 1). Jesus implores the people of Sardis to wake up and reinvigorate their deeds, which are incomplete before God.

John's writing is reminiscent of James 2:14 – 26, in which James challenges believers by saying that "faith by itself, if it is not accompanied by action, is dead." The church in Sardis is an example of a group of Christians who had deeds without faith. They were going through the motions and doing what they thought was right, but Jesus warned them that God had seen their works and found them to be lacking. In the same way that faith without works is dead, works without faith are also dead.

Believers today can take note: faith and works should go hand in hand. The relationship between faith and works is natural, and neither one should be overemphasized at the expense of the other. Jesus taught that God clearly sees into the hearts of people (Lk 16:15), and this is exactly what he demonstrated in Revelation 3:1 – 6. The church of Sardis was spiritually dead, but Jesus reminded them that it was not too late for them to change their hearts — nor is it too late for those who are alive today.

To the Church in Laodicea

[14]"To the angel of the church in Laodicea write:

These are the words of the Amen, the faithful and true witness, the ruler
of God's creation. [15]I know your deeds, that you are neither cold nor hot. I
wish you were either one or the other! [16]So, because you are lukewarm—
neither hot nor cold—I am about to spit you out of my mouth. [17]You say, 'I
am rich; I have acquired wealth and do not need a thing.' But you do not realize that you are wretched, pitiful, poor, blind and naked. [18]I counsel you
to buy from me gold refined in the fire, so you can become rich; and white
clothes to wear, so you can cover your shameful nakedness; and salve to
put on your eyes, so you can see.

[19]Those whom I love I rebuke and discipline. So be earnest and repent.
[20]Here I am! I stand at the door and knock. If anyone hears my voice and
opens the door, I will come in and eat with that person, and they with me.

[21]To the one who is victorious, I will give the right to sit with me on my
throne, just as I was victorious and sat down with my Father on his throne.
[22]Whoever has ears, let them hear what the Spirit says to the churches."

The Throne in Heaven

4 After this I looked, and there before me was a door standing open in heaven.
And the voice I had first heard speaking to me like a trumpet said, "Come up
here, and I will show you what must take place after this." [2]At once I was in the
Spirit, and there before me was a throne in heaven with someone sitting on it.
[3]And the one who sat there had the appearance of jasper and ruby. A rainbow
that shone like an emerald encircled the throne. [4]Surrounding the throne were
twenty-four other thrones, and seated on them were twenty-four elders. They
were dressed in white and had crowns of gold on their heads. [5]From the throne
came flashes of lightning, rumblings and peals of thunder. In front of the throne,
seven lamps were blazing. These are the seven spirits[a] of God. [6]Also in front of
the throne there was what looked like a sea of glass, clear as crystal.

In the center, around the throne, were four living creatures, and they were
covered with eyes, in front and in back. [7]The first living creature was like a lion,
the second was like an ox, the third had a face like a man, the fourth was like a
flying eagle. [8]Each of the four living creatures had six wings and was covered
with eyes all around, even under its wings. Day and night they never stop saying:

"'Holy, holy, holy
is the Lord God Almighty,'[b]
who was, and is, and is to come."

[9]Whenever the living creatures give glory, honor and thanks to him who sits on
the throne and who lives for ever and ever, [10]the twenty-four elders fall down
before him who sits on the throne and worship him who lives for ever and ever.
They lay their crowns before the throne and say:

[11]"You are worthy, our Lord and God,
to receive glory and honor and power,
for you created all things,
and by your will they were created
and have their being."

The Scroll and the Lamb

5 Then I saw in the right hand of him who sat on the throne a scroll with writing on both sides and sealed with seven seals. [2]And I saw a mighty angel proclaiming in a loud voice, "Who is worthy to break the seals and open the scroll?"

[a] *5* That is, the sevenfold Spirit [b] *8* Isaiah 6:3

NAMES AND TITLES OF JESUS IN REVELATION

John described God as "him who is, and who was, and who is to come" (Rev 1:4; cf. 4:8). His vision of heaven includes an image of four creatures who worship God day and night, and they also refer to God as him "who was, and is, and is to come" (v. 8). This phrase echoes Exodus 3:14 – 15, where God spoke of himself as "I AM" as he revealed his name to Moses. Jesus also referred to himself as "I am" (Jn 8:58) and thereby declared himself to be God. John reinforces this reality by declaring that not only is God who he says he is now, but he is also the same God he was throughout history, and he will continue to be the same God in the future. With this eternal consistency in mind, let's look at the names for Jesus revealed throughout John's book.

Jesus is the Christ (Rev 1:1; 20:4); the faithful witness, the firstborn from the dead, the ruler of the kings of the earth (1:5); the Alpha and Omega (1:8 – 13); the son of man (1:13) who holds the sharp, double-edged sword (1:16); the First and the Last (1:17); the Living One who lives and was dead (1:18; 2:8); the one who holds the keys of death and Hades (1:18); the one who holds the seven stars and who walks among the seven golden lampstands (2:1); the Son of God (2:18); the one who searches hearts and minds (2:23); the one who holds the seven spirits of God and the seven stars (3:1); the one who is holy and true and who has the key of David (3:7); the Amen, the faithful and true witness, the ruler of God's creation (3:14); the Lord, who is worthy to receive glory and honor and power (4:11); the Lion of the tribe of Judah and the Root of David (5:5); the Lamb that has been slain (5:6 – 7); the Lamb who lives (5:8 – 9); the Lord of lords and King of kings (17:14; 19:16); the just Judge who is Faithful and True and the warrior on the white horse (19:11); the Word of God (19:13 – 16); the Lord, the God who inspires the prophets (22:6); the Beginning and the End (22:13); and the bright and Morning Star (22:16).

This list may be a little overwhelming, but this quick look presents Jesus as the promised Messiah, the one who died and was raised to life again to defeat death, and the eternally consistent and powerful ruler who loves his people — yesterday, today and forever.

3But no one in heaven or on earth or under the earth could open the scroll or
even look inside it. 4I wept and wept because no one was found who was worthy
to open the scroll or look inside. 5Then one of the elders said to me, "Do not weep!
See, the Lion of the tribe of Judah, the Root of David, has triumphed. He is able to
open the scroll and its seven seals."

6Then I saw a Lamb, looking as if it had been slain, standing at the center of
the throne, encircled by the four living creatures and the elders. The Lamb had
seven horns and seven eyes, which are the seven spirits[a] of God sent out into all
the earth. 7He went and took the scroll from the right hand of him who sat on the
throne. 8And when he had taken it, the four living creatures and the twenty-four
elders fell down before the Lamb. Each one had a harp and they were holding
golden bowls full of incense, which are the prayers of God's people. 9And they
sang a new song, saying:

"You are worthy to take the scroll
and to open its seals,
because you were slain,
and with your blood you purchased for God
persons from every tribe and language and people and nation.
10You have made them to be a kingdom and priests to serve our God,
and they will reign[b] on the earth."

11Then I looked and heard the voice of many angels, numbering thousands
upon thousands, and ten thousand times ten thousand. They encircled the
throne and the living creatures and the elders. 12In a loud voice they were saying:

"Worthy is the Lamb, who was slain,
to receive power and wealth and wisdom and strength
and honor and glory and praise!"

13Then I heard every creature in heaven and on earth and under the earth and
on the sea, and all that is in them, saying:

"To him who sits on the throne and to the Lamb
be praise and honor and glory and power,
for ever and ever!"

14The four living creatures said, "Amen," and the elders fell down and worshiped.

The Seals

6 I watched as the Lamb opened the first of the seven seals. Then I heard one
of the four living creatures say in a voice like thunder, "Come!" 2I looked, and
there before me was a white horse! Its rider held a bow, and he was given a crown,
and he rode out as a conqueror bent on conquest.

3When the Lamb opened the second seal, I heard the second living creature
say, "Come!" 4Then another horse came out, a fiery red one. Its rider was given
power to take peace from the earth and to make people kill each other. To him
was given a large sword.

5When the Lamb opened the third seal, I heard the third living creature say,
"Come!" I looked, and there before me was a black horse! Its rider was holding
a pair of scales in his hand. 6Then I heard what sounded like a voice among the
four living creatures, saying, "Two pounds[c] of wheat for a day's wages,[d] and six
pounds[e] of barley for a day's wages,[d] and do not damage the oil and the wine!"

7When the Lamb opened the fourth seal, I heard the voice of the fourth living
creature say, "Come!" 8I looked, and there before me was a pale horse! Its rider
was named Death, and Hades was following close behind him. They were given
power over a fourth of the earth to kill by sword, famine and plague, and by the
wild beasts of the earth.

[a] *6* That is, the sevenfold Spirit [b] *10* Some manuscripts *they reign* [c] *6* Or about 1 kilogram [d] *6* Greek *a denarius* [e] *6* Or about 3 kilograms

REVELATION 5:11–12

WORTHY OF ALL

The second half of Revelation 5 vividly portrays the worship in heaven as the heavenly throng gathers around the throne on which the King of kings sits. In verse 6, John describes the Lamb as slain yet standing between the throne and the elders. The Lamb pictured here is Jesus, the one who overcame death. Jesus sacrificed himself for the sins of humankind, so that believers can stand before the throne of God and accept for themselves Jesus' sacrifice, which takes away the wrath that they deserve.

Verse 9 says that the Lamb is worthy of praise because he has "purchased for God persons from every tribe and language and people and nation" with his blood. Jesus' sacrifice makes it possible for humans to be made right with God, and this verse refers to what Jesus' blood purchased. The praise continues in verse 12, which lists seven things that the Lamb is worthy of: power, wealth, wisdom, strength, honor, glory and praise. Jesus deserves all these things and more by virtue of what he accomplished on the cross and through the empty tomb. The Lamb who is worthy of all praise gives the angels, and his people, a reason to sing.

9When he opened the fifth seal, I saw under the altar the souls of those who
had been slain because of the word of God and the testimony they had maintained. 10They called out in a loud voice, "How long, Sovereign Lord, holy and
true, until you judge the inhabitants of the earth and avenge our blood?" 11Then
each of them was given a white robe, and they were told to wait a little longer,
until the full number of their fellow servants, their brothers and sisters,[a] were
killed just as they had been.

12I watched as he opened the sixth seal. There was a great earthquake. The
sun turned black like sackcloth made of goat hair, the whole moon turned blood
red, 13and the stars in the sky fell to earth, as figs drop from a fig tree when shak-
en by a strong wind. 14The heavens receded like a scroll being rolled up, and
every mountain and island was removed from its place.

15Then the kings of the earth, the princes, the generals, the rich, the mighty,
and everyone else, both slave and free, hid in caves and among the rocks of the
mountains. 16They called to the mountains and the rocks, "Fall on us and hide
us[b] from the face of him who sits on the throne and from the wrath of the Lamb!
17For the great day of their[c] wrath has come, and who can withstand it?"

144,000 Sealed

7 After this I saw four angels standing at the four corners of the earth, holding
back the four winds of the earth to prevent any wind from blowing on the land or
on the sea or on any tree. 2Then I saw another angel coming up from the east, having
the seal of the living God. He called out in a loud voice to the four angels who had
been given power to harm the land and the sea: 3"Do not harm the land or the sea
or the trees until we put a seal on the foreheads of the servants of our God." 4Then
I heard the number of those who were sealed: 144,000 from all the tribes of Israel.

5 From the tribe of Judah 12,000 were sealed,
from the tribe of Reuben 12,000,
from the tribe of Gad 12,000,
6 from the tribe of Asher 12,000,
from the tribe of Naphtali 12,000,
from the tribe of Manasseh 12,000,
7 from the tribe of Simeon 12,000,
from the tribe of Levi 12,000,
from the tribe of Issachar 12,000,
8 from the tribe of Zebulun 12,000,
from the tribe of Joseph 12,000,
from the tribe of Benjamin 12,000.

The Great Multitude in White Robes

9After this I looked, and there before me was a great multitude that no one
could count, from every nation, tribe, people and language, standing before the
throne and before the Lamb. They were wearing white robes and were holding
palm branches in their hands. 10And they cried out in a loud voice:

"Salvation belongs to our God,
who sits on the throne,
and to the Lamb."

11All the angels were standing around the throne and around the elders and the
four living creatures. They fell down on their faces before the throne and worshiped God, 12saying:

"Amen!
Praise and glory

---

a 11 The Greek word for *brothers and sisters* (*adelphoi*) refers here to believers, both men and women, as part of God's family; also in 12:10; 19:10. *b* 16 See Hosea 10:8. *c* 17 Some manuscripts *his*

REVELATION 7:17

THE LAMB AS SHEPHERD

In Luke 15:1–7 Jesus told the parable of the lost sheep, recounting the joy that a shepherd experiences when he finds one lost sheep. Revelation 7 infinitely multiplies this as it depicts all of God's lost sheep being found, and Jesus is shown as both Lamb and shepherd. John describes great worship and praise in verses 10 and 12, which recalls the rejoicing that Jesus described in Luke 15:6–7.

Furthermore, John wrote here that this Lamb will shepherd his people "to springs of living water." Jesus promised this living water in John 4:14, where he declared that anyone who follows him will be given water that leads to eternal life. It is this exact water to which the Lamb is leading the great multitude of people in Revelation 7. No longer will there be sadness or tears (v. 17), but there will only be cause for rejoicing as the Lamb leads his sheep into eternal refreshment and rejoicing.

REVELATION 8:2

TRUMPETS AND TIMING

In Old Testament times, trumpets were used to signify important events, to give signals during war and to warn people of something that was coming (Eze 33:4–5). In Revelation 8:6, the angels prepare to sound the trumpets to warn people of the coming judgment—these are the same trumpets that Jesus described in Matthew 24:31.

(continued on next page)

and wisdom and thanks and honor
and power and strength
be to our God for ever and ever.
Amen!"

13Then one of the elders asked me, "These in white robes—who are they, and
where did they come from?"
14I answered, "Sir, you know."
And he said, "These are they who have come out of the great tribulation;
they have washed their robes and made them white in the blood of the Lamb.
15Therefore,

"they are before the throne of God
and serve him day and night in his temple;
and he who sits on the throne
will shelter them with his presence.
16'Never again will they hunger;
never again will they thirst.
The sun will not beat down on them,'[a]
nor any scorching heat.
17For the Lamb at the center of the throne
will be their shepherd;
'he will lead them to springs of living water.'[a]
'And God will wipe away every tear from their eyes.'[b]"

The Seventh Seal and the Golden Censer

8 When he opened the seventh seal, there was silence in heaven for about half
an hour.
2And I saw the seven angels who stand before God, and seven trumpets were
given to them.
3Another angel, who had a golden censer, came and stood at the altar. He was
given much incense to offer, with the prayers of all God's people, on the golden
altar in front of the throne. 4The smoke of the incense, together with the prayers
of God's people, went up before God from the angel's hand. 5Then the angel took
the censer, filled it with fire from the altar, and hurled it on the earth; and there
came peals of thunder, rumblings, flashes of lightning and an earthquake.

The Trumpets

6Then the seven angels who had the seven trumpets prepared to sound them.
7The first angel sounded his trumpet, and there came hail and fire mixed with
blood, and it was hurled down on the earth. A third of the earth was burned up, a
third of the trees were burned up, and all the green grass was burned up.
8The second angel sounded his trumpet, and something like a huge mountain, all ablaze, was thrown into the sea. A third of the sea turned into blood,
9a third of the living creatures in the sea died, and a third of the ships were destroyed.
10The third angel sounded his trumpet, and a great star, blazing like a torch,
fell from the sky on a third of the rivers and on the springs of water— 11the name
of the star is Wormwood.[c] A third of the waters turned bitter, and many people
died from the waters that had become bitter.
12The fourth angel sounded his trumpet, and a third of the sun was struck, a
third of the moon, and a third of the stars, so that a third of them turned dark. A
third of the day was without light, and also a third of the night.
13As I watched, I heard an eagle that was flying in midair call out in a loud
voice: "Woe! Woe! Woe to the inhabitants of the earth, because of the trumpet
blasts about to be sounded by the other three angels!"

[a] *16,17* Isaiah 49:10 [b] *17* Isaiah 25:8 [c] *11* Wormwood is a bitter substance.

9 The fifth angel sounded his trumpet, and I saw a star that had fallen from the
sky to the earth. The star was given the key to the shaft of the Abyss. 2When
he opened the Abyss, smoke rose from it like the smoke from a gigantic furnace.
The sun and sky were darkened by the smoke from the Abyss. 3And out of the
smoke locusts came down on the earth and were given power like that of scorpions of the earth. 4They were told not to harm the grass of the earth or any plant or
tree, but only those people who did not have the seal of God on their foreheads.
5They were not allowed to kill them but only to torture them for five months. And
the agony they suffered was like that of the sting of a scorpion when it strikes.
6During those days people will seek death but will not find it; they will long to
die, but death will elude them.

7The locusts looked like horses prepared for battle. On their heads they wore
something like crowns of gold, and their faces resembled human faces. 8Their
hair was like women's hair, and their teeth were like lions' teeth. 9They had
breastplates like breastplates of iron, and the sound of their wings was like the
thundering of many horses and chariots rushing into battle. 10They had tails
with stingers, like scorpions, and in their tails they had power to torment people for five months. 11They had as king over them the angel of the Abyss, whose
name in Hebrew is Abaddon and in Greek is Apollyon (that is, Destroyer).

12The first woe is past; two other woes are yet to come.

13The sixth angel sounded his trumpet, and I heard a voice coming from the
four horns of the golden altar that is before God. 14It said to the sixth angel who
had the trumpet, "Release the four angels who are bound at the great river Euphrates." 15And the four angels who had been kept ready for this very hour and
day and month and year were released to kill a third of mankind. 16The number
of the mounted troops was twice ten thousand times ten thousand. I heard their
number.

17The horses and riders I saw in my vision looked like this: Their breastplates
were fiery red, dark blue, and yellow as sulfur. The heads of the horses resembled
the heads of lions, and out of their mouths came fire, smoke and sulfur. 18A third
of mankind was killed by the three plagues of fire, smoke and sulfur that came
out of their mouths. 19The power of the horses was in their mouths and in their
tails; for their tails were like snakes, having heads with which they inflict injury.

20The rest of mankind who were not killed by these plagues still did not repent of the work of their hands; they did not stop worshiping demons, and idols
of gold, silver, bronze, stone and wood — idols that cannot see or hear or walk.
21Nor did they repent of their murders, their magic arts, their sexual immorality
or their thefts.

The Angel and the Little Scroll

10 Then I saw another mighty angel coming down from heaven. He was
robed in a cloud, with a rainbow above his head; his face was like the sun,
and his legs were like fiery pillars. 2He was holding a little scroll, which lay open
in his hand. He planted his right foot on the sea and his left foot on the land,
3and he gave a loud shout like the roar of a lion. When he shouted, the voices of
the seven thunders spoke. 4And when the seven thunders spoke, I was about to
write; but I heard a voice from heaven say, "Seal up what the seven thunders have
said and do not write it down."

5Then the angel I had seen standing on the sea and on the land raised his right
hand to heaven. 6And he swore by him who lives for ever and ever, who created
the heavens and all that is in them, the earth and all that is in it, and the sea and
all that is in it, and said, "There will be no more delay! 7But in the days when the
seventh angel is about to sound his trumpet, the mystery of God will be accomplished, just as he announced to his servants the prophets."

8Then the voice that I had heard from heaven spoke to me once more: "Go,
take the scroll that lies open in the hand of the angel who is standing on the sea
and on the land."

(Trumpets and Timing, continued)

Furthermore, the seven trumpets are reminiscent of the seven trumpets that Israel's priests sounded when God defeated Jericho (Jos 6). In Joshua, God called the people to march around the city once a day for six days, while the priests blew their trumpets. Then on the seventh day, they marched around the city seven times, but this time when the priests blew the trumpets the people gave a war cry, and God pulled down the walls of that great city.

The sound of the trumpets served not only to announce the coming of the Lord in Joshua's victory, but also here in Revelation. As God toppled those walls, so he will also topple those people and institutions and other entities that stand in rebellion to him and refuse to heed the good news of the gospel. Once the angels sound the trumpets, the judgment of the Lord is coming. His judgment, and his timing, will be perfect.

HUMAN STUBBORNNESS

This chapter represents God's judgment as swift, severe and just, with an intensity that no human would want to confront. John's vision of the end times includes multiple beasts released by angels to wreak havoc on the earth in response to human sin. The devastation that he describes is shocking. However, these verses record that some people who will not be killed by the plagues will fail to repent and will continue living in their sin (Rev 9:20–21). How incredible that, even though God will continue to offer people the opportunity to repent throughout the entire period of judgment, there will still be people who choose their own sinful ways over God's way!

These verses serve as a warning concerning the sure judgment that is to come, and a reminder of the ultimate depravity of humanity and its need for a Savior. The people who will remain in their rebellion shock us, but Jesus came to die for these same people. In fact, they're representative of all people who become believers (Ro 5:8). Jesus' sacrifice was not merely for some of the sin that exists in the world; it was for *all* of the sin — past, present and future. People who refuse to recognize their own sin and accept Jesus' free gift of salvation scorn Christ's work and run swiftly to their own demise.

It is easy for believers to compare themselves to those described in these verses and think, "Well, that's not me," but the truth is that, apart from Christ, every human is rebellious at their core and is therefore capable of being that far away from God. The most devout saint was once a sinner destined for hell until God awakened their spirit to new life. The message here is that it is important for Christians to continually surrender their lives and their circumstances to God so that they can be found to be walking in humility with the Lord (Mic 6:8) when he comes again.

Also, these verses are a challenge to believers to tell others about the good news so that there are fewer people who will choose to remain stubborn in the face of God's judgment. Believers live in a broken world filled with broken people, but God's redemptive power is enough to overcome all of the evil that has infiltrated this world. Those who accept Jesus' saving work on their behalf, in gratitude for the grace that they have received, should do everything in their power to share that grace with others so that the number of those who remain stubbornly rebellious in their sin may be few.

9So I went to the angel and asked him to give me the little scroll. He said to
me, "Take it and eat it. It will turn your stomach sour, but 'in your mouth it will
be as sweet as honey.'[a]" 10I took the little scroll from the angel's hand and ate it.
It tasted as sweet as honey in my mouth, but when I had eaten it, my stomach
turned sour. 11Then I was told, "You must prophesy again about many peoples,
nations, languages and kings."

The Two Witnesses

11 I was given a reed like a measuring rod and was told, "Go and measure the
temple of God and the altar, with its worshipers. 2But exclude the outer
court; do not measure it, because it has been given to the Gentiles. They will
trample on the holy city for 42 months. 3And I will appoint my two witnesses, and
they will prophesy for 1,260 days, clothed in sackcloth." 4They are "the two olive
trees" and the two lampstands, and "they stand before the Lord of the earth."[b] 5If
anyone tries to harm them, fire comes from their mouths and devours their enemies. This is how anyone who wants to harm them must die. 6They have power
to shut up the heavens so that it will not rain during the time they are prophesying; and they have power to turn the waters into blood and to strike the earth
with every kind of plague as often as they want.

7Now when they have finished their testimony, the beast that comes up from
the Abyss will attack them, and overpower and kill them. 8Their bodies will lie
in the public square of the great city — which is figuratively called Sodom and
Egypt — where also their Lord was crucified. 9For three and a half days some
from every people, tribe, language and nation will gaze on their bodies and refuse them burial. 10The inhabitants of the earth will gloat over them and will
celebrate by sending each other gifts, because these two prophets had tormented those who live on the earth.

11But after the three and a half days the breath[c] of life from God entered them,
and they stood on their feet, and terror struck those who saw them. 12Then they
heard a loud voice from heaven saying to them, "Come up here." And they went
up to heaven in a cloud, while their enemies looked on.

13At that very hour there was a severe earthquake and a tenth of the city collapsed. Seven thousand people were killed in the earthquake, and the survivors
were terrified and gave glory to the God of heaven.

14The second woe has passed; the third woe is coming soon.

The Seventh Trumpet

15The seventh angel sounded his trumpet, and there were loud voices in heav-
en, which said:

"The kingdom of the world has become
 the kingdom of our Lord and of his Messiah,
 and he will reign for ever and ever."

16And the twenty-four elders, who were seated on their thrones before God, fell
on their faces and worshiped God, 17saying:

"We give thanks to you, Lord God Almighty,
 the One who is and who was,
because you have taken your great power
 and have begun to reign.
18The nations were angry,
 and your wrath has come.
The time has come for judging the dead,
 and for rewarding your servants the prophets
and your people who revere your name,
 both great and small —
and for destroying those who destroy the earth."

[a] 9 Ezek. 3:3 [b] 4 See Zech. 4:3,11,14. [c] 11 Or *Spirit* (see Ezek. 37:5,14)

REVELATION 10:11

THE WHOLE WORLD

It is important to note that the book of Revelation is written for the entire world. The book does not prophesy to one people, nation, language or king, but rather to all of them. John's writing makes clear that judgment is not coming only to parts of our planet, but it is coming to the entire world. When Satan is mentioned, John said that he "leads the whole world astray" (12:9). John said that "all inhabitants of the earth" who have not followed the gospel will worship the beast out of the sea (13:8), and the actions of the beast out of the earth will affect "all people, great and small, rich and poor, free and slave" (13:16). The multiple tribulations foretold in Revelation involve everybody on earth, and this serves as a reminder of the universal scope of God's judgment.

However, not only does judgment come to all parts of the earth, but redemption will also come to all parts of the world as well, as people "from every nation, tribe, people and language" turn to him in faith (7:9). When the seventh trumpet is sounded, the angels declare, "The kingdom of the world has become the kingdom of our Lord and of his Messiah" (11:15). When Jesus returns, he will return with justice and salvation for those who follow him and will establish his kingdom, both throughout the world and for eternity.

REVELATION 11:15

JESUS' VICTORY

This verse marks the declaration of Christ's complete victory over the

(continued on page 1983)

THE CHALLENGE OF INTERPRETING REVELATION

Scholars generally espouse one of four main views on how to interpret the book of Revelation:

The preterist view says that most of what is depicted in Revelation happened during John's lifetime while the Roman Empire was in power.

The historicist view believes that most of the prophecies in Revelation have been fulfilled throughout history and are continuing to be fulfilled today.

The futurist view believes that everything after chapter 3 of Revelation is going to happen sometime in the future.

The spiritual (or symbolic) view argues that Revelation is a symbolic interpretation of the ongoing cosmic conflict, which has had, and will continue to have, many fulfillments throughout history.

While these views have their differences, it is important for Christians not to get distracted in continuous debates over which view is more accurate. No matter what view one takes on the book of Revelation, the dominant idea is that Christ will return sometime in the future and that his return will be a welcome sight to his people. Regardless of when, where and how God's judgment occurs, Jesus promised he would one day return (Jn 14:3), and it is this promise to which believers should hold fast, repeating John's closing prayer: "Come, Lord Jesus" (Rev 22:20).

Also, no matter how one interprets Revelation, the book is intended to be a reminder and warning that when Jesus comes, he will be coming for those who trust in him for salvation. Many people in the world do not believe that Jesus is who he said he is, and the future of those people is tragic. Believers who have a secure future in Christ should be challenged by Revelation to tell as many people as they can about Jesus, so that more people can share in the joy that believers will experience at the return of Christ.

19Then God's temple in heaven was opened, and within his temple was seen
the ark of his covenant. And there came flashes of lightning, rumblings, peals of
thunder, an earthquake and a severe hailstorm.

The Woman and the Dragon

12 A great sign appeared in heaven: a woman clothed with the sun, with the
moon under her feet and a crown of twelve stars on her head. 2She was
pregnant and cried out in pain as she was about to give birth. 3Then another sign
appeared in heaven: an enormous red dragon with seven heads and ten horns
and seven crowns on its heads. 4Its tail swept a third of the stars out of the sky
and flung them to the earth. The dragon stood in front of the woman who was
about to give birth, so that it might devour her child the moment he was born.
5She gave birth to a son, a male child, who "will rule all the nations with an iron
scepter."[a] And her child was snatched up to God and to his throne. 6The woman
fled into the wilderness to a place prepared for her by God, where she might be
taken care of for 1,260 days.

7Then war broke out in heaven. Michael and his angels fought against the
dragon, and the dragon and his angels fought back. 8But he was not strong
enough, and they lost their place in heaven. 9The great dragon was hurled
down — that ancient serpent called the devil, or Satan, who leads the whole
world astray. He was hurled to the earth, and his angels with him.

10Then I heard a loud voice in heaven say:

"Now have come the salvation and the power
and the kingdom of our God,
and the authority of his Messiah.
For the accuser of our brothers and sisters,
who accuses them before our God day and night,
has been hurled down.
11They triumphed over him
by the blood of the Lamb
and by the word of their testimony;
they did not love their lives so much
as to shrink from death.
12Therefore rejoice, you heavens
and you who dwell in them!
But woe to the earth and the sea,
because the devil has gone down to you!
He is filled with fury,
because he knows that his time is short."

13When the dragon saw that he had been hurled to the earth, he pursued the
woman who had given birth to the male child. 14The woman was given the two
wings of a great eagle, so that she might fly to the place prepared for her in the
wilderness, where she would be taken care of for a time, times and half a time,
out of the serpent's reach. 15Then from his mouth the serpent spewed water like
a river, to overtake the woman and sweep her away with the torrent. 16But the
earth helped the woman by opening its mouth and swallowing the river that
the dragon had spewed out of his mouth. 17Then the dragon was enraged at the
woman and went off to wage war against the rest of her offspring — those who
keep God's commands and hold fast their testimony about Jesus.

The Beast out of the Sea

13 The dragon[b] stood on the shore of the sea. And I saw a beast coming out
of the sea. It had ten horns and seven heads, with ten crowns on its horns,
and on each head a blasphemous name. 2The beast I saw resembled a leopard, but

[a] 5 Psalm 2:9 [b] 1 Some manuscripts *And I*

(Jesus' Victory, continued)

kingdom of the world. Jesus foretold this event in John 12:31 – 32, and in Revelation his promise is manifested. After Jesus' victory was declared, the 24 elders "fell on their faces and worshiped God" (Rev 11:16). Five times in the book of Revelation the elders similarly demonstrate with their bodies the posture of their hearts (5:8,14; 7:11; 11:26; 19:4).

This absolute victory should cause those who rebel against Christ to shudder. Their doom is promised and assured. They will face the tribulation and punishment described in John's vision. Yet, Jesus' ultimate victory is a great hope for his followers. Though the world is in chaos, believers can be assured that Jesus has already won the victory over sin and death, and that the whole earth will soon see this victory. The kingdom of God will fully and finally come on earth as it has been in heaven (Mt 6:9 – 13). At the end of time, God's promise from Genesis 3:15 will come true as the offspring of the woman will crush the serpent's head forever.

REVELATION 12:11

OVERCOMING THE ENEMY

The first half of chapter 12 describes the battle that takes place between Satan and the angels in heaven, which ends with Satan being thrown down to earth in utter defeat. John said that this victory comes by virtue of the blood of the Lamb, and that, while Michael and his angels fight in the heavenly realm, the people also triumph over their accuser by the word of their testimony and their willingness to obey to the point of death.

(continued on next page)

(Overcoming the Enemy, continued)

The blood of Jesus is the means by which God's people are spared the wrath of God and kept from the hand of the enemy. They testify to the truth that God is who he says he is and that Jesus accomplished what he said he would, and they have accepted his gift by faith. Finally, these individuals do not "love their lives so much as to shrink from death" (Rev 12:11). God sustains his children, even in the face of great suffering, thus proving that they are in fact his.

REVELATION 14:1–20

PERFECT AND COMPLETE

Chapter 14 of Revelation is divided into seven parts: the Lamb with his glorious company (vv. 1–5), the angel proclaims the eternal gospel (vv. 6–7), another angel declares the fall of Babylon (v. 8), the threat against worshiping the beast (vv. 9–12), the blessing for those who die in the Lord (v. 13), the harvest (vv. 14–16) and the gathering of grapes into the winepress (vv. 17–20).

The number seven, thought to be the number of perfection, appears thirty-six times in Revelation to symbolize the finality and brilliance of God's saving work. John writes of seven messages to seven churches, seven seals, seven trumpets and seven bowls of God's wrath. Furthermore, Jesus is represented with multiple sets of seven to show his perfection and completion under God. In Chapter 1, Jesus has seven stars in his right hand, which show his com-

(continued on next page)

had feet like those of a bear and a mouth like that of a lion. The dragon gave the
beast his power and his throne and great authority. [3]One of the heads of the beast
seemed to have had a fatal wound, but the fatal wound had been healed. The
whole world was filled with wonder and followed the beast. [4]People worshiped
the dragon because he had given authority to the beast, and they also worshiped
the beast and asked, "Who is like the beast? Who can wage war against it?"

[5]The beast was given a mouth to utter proud words and blasphemies and to
exercise its authority for forty-two months. [6]It opened its mouth to blaspheme
God, and to slander his name and his dwelling place and those who live in heav-
en. [7]It was given power to wage war against God's holy people and to conquer
them. And it was given authority over every tribe, people, language and nation.
[8]All inhabitants of the earth will worship the beast—all whose names have not
been written in the Lamb's book of life, the Lamb who was slain from the creation of the world.[a]

[9]Whoever has ears, let them hear.

[10]"If anyone is to go into captivity,
into captivity they will go.
If anyone is to be killed[b] with the sword,
with the sword they will be killed."[c]

This calls for patient endurance and faithfulness on the part of God's people.

The Beast out of the Earth

[11]Then I saw a second beast, coming out of the earth. It had two horns like a
lamb, but it spoke like a dragon. [12]It exercised all the authority of the first beast
on its behalf, and made the earth and its inhabitants worship the first beast,
whose fatal wound had been healed. [13]And it performed great signs, even causing fire to come down from heaven to the earth in full view of the people. [14]Be-
cause of the signs it was given power to perform on behalf of the first beast, it
deceived the inhabitants of the earth. It ordered them to set up an image in hon-
or of the beast who was wounded by the sword and yet lived. [15]The second beast
was given power to give breath to the image of the first beast, so that the image
could speak and cause all who refused to worship the image to be killed. [16]It also
forced all people, great and small, rich and poor, free and slave, to receive a mark
on their right hands or on their foreheads, [17]so that they could not buy or sell unless they had the mark, which is the name of the beast or the number of its name.

[18]This calls for wisdom. Let the person who has insight calculate the number
of the beast, for it is the number of a man.[d] That number is 666.

The Lamb and the 144,000

14 Then I looked, and there before me was the Lamb, standing on Mount Zion,
and with him 144,000 who had his name and his Father's name written on
their foreheads. [2]And I heard a sound from heaven like the roar of rushing waters
and like a loud peal of thunder. The sound I heard was like that of harpists playing
their harps. [3]And they sang a new song before the throne and before the four living creatures and the elders. No one could learn the song except the 144,000 who
had been redeemed from the earth. [4]These are those who did not defile themselves with women, for they remained virgins. They follow the Lamb wherever he
goes. They were purchased from among mankind and offered as firstfruits to God
and the Lamb. [5]No lie was found in their mouths; they are blameless.

The Three Angels

[6]Then I saw another angel flying in midair, and he had the eternal gospel to
proclaim to those who live on the earth—to every nation, tribe, language and
people. [7]He said in a loud voice, "Fear God and give him glory, because the hour

[a] 8 Or *written from the creation of the world in the book of life belonging to the Lamb who was slain* [b] 10 Some manuscripts *anyone kills* [c] 10 Jer. 15:2 [d] 18 Or *is humanity's number*

of his judgment has come. Worship him who made the heavens, the earth, the
sea and the springs of water."
8A second angel followed and said, "'Fallen! Fallen is Babylon the Great,'[a]
which made all the nations drink the maddening wine of her adulteries."
9A third angel followed them and said in a loud voice: "If anyone worships
the beast and its image and receives its mark on their forehead or on their hand,
10they, too, will drink the wine of God's fury, which has been poured full strength
into the cup of his wrath. They will be tormented with burning sulfur in the presence of the holy angels and of the Lamb. 11And the smoke of their torment will
rise for ever and ever. There will be no rest day or night for those who worship
the beast and its image, or for anyone who receives the mark of its name." 12This
calls for patient endurance on the part of the people of God who keep his commands and remain faithful to Jesus.
13Then I heard a voice from heaven say, "Write this: Blessed are the dead who
die in the Lord from now on."

"Yes," says the Spirit, "they will rest from their labor, for their deeds will follow them."

Harvesting the Earth and Trampling the Winepress

14I looked, and there before me was a white cloud, and seated on the cloud was
one like a son of man[b] with a crown of gold on his head and a sharp sickle in his
hand. 15Then another angel came out of the temple and called in a loud voice to
him who was sitting on the cloud, "Take your sickle and reap, because the time
to reap has come, for the harvest of the earth is ripe." 16So he who was seated on
the cloud swung his sickle over the earth, and the earth was harvested.
17Another angel came out of the temple in heaven, and he too had a sharp
sickle. 18Still another angel, who had charge of the fire, came from the altar and
called in a loud voice to him who had the sharp sickle, "Take your sharp sickle
and gather the clusters of grapes from the earth's vine, because its grapes are
ripe." 19The angel swung his sickle on the earth, gathered its grapes and threw
them into the great winepress of God's wrath. 20They were trampled in the winepress outside the city, and blood flowed out of the press, rising as high as the
horses' bridles for a distance of 1,600 stadia.[c]

Seven Angels With Seven Plagues

15 I saw in heaven another great and marvelous sign: seven angels with the
seven last plagues—last, because with them God's wrath is completed.
2And I saw what looked like a sea of glass glowing with fire and, standing beside
the sea, those who had been victorious over the beast and its image and over the
number of its name. They held harps given them by God 3and sang the song of
God's servant Moses and of the Lamb:

"Great and marvelous are your deeds,
 Lord God Almighty.
Just and true are your ways,
 King of the nations.[d]
4Who will not fear you, Lord,
 and bring glory to your name?
For you alone are holy.
All nations will come
 and worship before you,
for your righteous acts have been revealed."[e]

5After this I looked, and I saw in heaven the temple—that is, the tabernacle of
the covenant law—and it was opened. 6Out of the temple came the seven angels

[a] *8* Isaiah 21:9 [b] *14* See Daniel 7:13. [c] *20* That is, about 180 miles or about 300 kilometers [d] *3* Some manuscripts *ages* [e] *3,4* Phrases in this song are drawn from Psalm 111:2,3; Deut. 32:4; Jer. 10:7; Psalms 86:9; 98:2.

(Perfect and Complete, continued)

plete authority over the church (1:16) represented by seven lampstands (1:16). In chapter 5, the Lamb has seven horns and seven eyes, which show its power and omniscience (5:6). And the many other mentions of this symbolic number in Revelation make it clear that, at the end of creation, God's plan and his judgment will be perfectly and completely realized.

REVELATION 15:1–4

THE LAST EXODUS

This portion of Revelation is reminiscent of God freeing the Israelites from Egypt (Ex 1–14). Just as God used plagues against Egypt, he will also use plagues against those who stand against him during the tribulation.

In the first exodus the people of God sang a song of deliverance, praising God for his faithfulness in leading them out of Egypt (Ex 15:1–21). Now, in the second exodus, God's people will also sing praises to God because they have been spared from his judgment. While the Israelites sang to God after they had witnessed the plagues and had been delivered from the Egyptian army, the singing in Revelation precedes the seven plagues because God's people have already been saved and know they are spared from God's wrath as described in chapter 16.

In both cases, there is great singing and shouts of praise to God because of his faithfulness in saving his people. Throughout history, God's salvation has caused his people to sing, and they will continue to do so for all eternity.

with the seven plagues. They were dressed in clean, shining linen and wore golden sashes around their chests. 7Then one of the four living creatures gave to the seven angels seven golden bowls filled with the wrath of God, who lives for ever and ever. 8And the temple was filled with smoke from the glory of God and from his power, and no one could enter the temple until the seven plagues of the seven angels were completed.

The Seven Bowls of God's Wrath

16 Then I heard a loud voice from the temple saying to the seven angels, "Go, pour out the seven bowls of God's wrath on the earth."

2The first angel went and poured out his bowl on the land, and ugly, festering sores broke out on the people who had the mark of the beast and worshiped its image.

3The second angel poured out his bowl on the sea, and it turned into blood like that of a dead person, and every living thing in the sea died.

4The third angel poured out his bowl on the rivers and springs of water, and they became blood. 5Then I heard the angel in charge of the waters say:

"You are just in these judgments, O Holy One,
  you who are and who were;
6for they have shed the blood of your holy people and your prophets,
  and you have given them blood to drink as they deserve."

7And I heard the altar respond:

"Yes, Lord God Almighty,
  true and just are your judgments."

8The fourth angel poured out his bowl on the sun, and the sun was allowed to scorch people with fire. 9They were seared by the intense heat and they cursed the name of God, who had control over these plagues, but they refused to repent and glorify him.

10The fifth angel poured out his bowl on the throne of the beast, and its kingdom was plunged into darkness. People gnawed their tongues in agony 11and cursed the God of heaven because of their pains and their sores, but they refused to repent of what they had done.

12The sixth angel poured out his bowl on the great river Euphrates, and its water was dried up to prepare the way for the kings from the East. 13Then I saw three impure spirits that looked like frogs; they came out of the mouth of the dragon, out of the mouth of the beast and out of the mouth of the false prophet. 14They are demonic spirits that perform signs, and they go out to the kings of the whole world, to gather them for the battle on the great day of God Almighty.

15"Look, I come like a thief! Blessed is the one who stays awake and remains clothed, so as not to go naked and be shamefully exposed."

16Then they gathered the kings together to the place that in Hebrew is called Armageddon.

17The seventh angel poured out his bowl into the air, and out of the temple came a loud voice from the throne, saying, "It is done!" 18Then there came flashes of lightning, rumblings, peals of thunder and a severe earthquake. No earthquake like it has ever occurred since mankind has been on earth, so tremendous was the quake. 19The great city split into three parts, and the cities of the nations collapsed. God remembered Babylon the Great and gave her the cup filled with the wine of the fury of his wrath. 20Every island fled away and the mountains could not be found. 21From the sky huge hailstones, each weighing about a hundred pounds,[a] fell on people. And they cursed God on account of the plague of hail, because the plague was so terrible.

---

[a] *21* Or about 45 kilograms

JESUS IN JUDGMENT

The first time Jesus came to earth he came to seek and to save the lost (Lk 19:10). He came in peace with the intention of redeeming and saving God's people. The second time will be much different from the first. While he once rode into Jerusalem on a colt as a sign of peace (Mt 21:7), he will ride on a white horse as a sign of war during his second coming (Rev 19:11). Jesus is the same yesterday, today and forever. He will not change between his first and second coming, but his purpose in coming will. He first came to save; he will one day come again to judge.

The mercy and justice of God may seem like two incompatible characteristics. On the one hand, God will bring righteous judgment and pour out his wrath on those who refuse to trust in his saving grace. On the other hand, he is merciful and compassionate toward humanity, not wanting any to be lost (2Pe 3:9). God is unique in that his mercy is shown through his justice. Because of sin, humans deserve death and eternal separation from God (Ro 6:23). However, Jesus died on the cross and his perfect sacrifice was both an act of justice against the sin in the world and an act of mercy toward mankind. The cross is the symbol of the perfect integration of God's justice and mercy.

Standing as we are between Jesus' first and second coming, the world is now living in a state of peace and mercy. God's compassion and patience are extended to everyone on earth, and his mercies are new every morning (La 3:22–23). However, soon the justice of God will come, and Jesus will be the judge of all mankind. In Revelation 16, the angels praise God for exacting justice in the wrath that he pours out. The reason the angels are able to praise God is that justice is finally coming for every sin ever committed. God is glorified in his judgment because he is perfectly just. But he is also merciful. He poured out his wrath on Christ so that any who believe in him could be forgiven, once and for all. But sin is always punished — either at Calvary or in eternity — because God is a righteous judge.

Babylon, the Prostitute on the Beast

17 One of the seven angels who had the seven bowls came and said to me,
"Come, I will show you the punishment of the great prostitute, who sits by
many waters. 2With her the kings of the earth committed adultery, and the inhabitants of the earth were intoxicated with the wine of her adulteries."

3Then the angel carried me away in the Spirit into a wilderness. There I saw a
woman sitting on a scarlet beast that was covered with blasphemous names and
had seven heads and ten horns. 4The woman was dressed in purple and scarlet,
and was glittering with gold, precious stones and pearls. She held a golden cup
in her hand, filled with abominable things and the filth of her adulteries. 5The
name written on her forehead was a mystery:

BABYLON THE GREAT
THE MOTHER OF PROSTITUTES
AND OF THE ABOMINATIONS OF THE EARTH.

6I saw that the woman was drunk with the blood of God's holy people, the blood
of those who bore testimony to Jesus.

When I saw her, I was greatly astonished. 7Then the angel said to me: "Why
are you astonished? I will explain to you the mystery of the woman and of the
beast she rides, which has the seven heads and ten horns. 8The beast, which you
saw, once was, now is not, and yet will come up out of the Abyss and go to its destruction. The inhabitants of the earth whose names have not been written in
the book of life from the creation of the world will be astonished when they see
the beast, because it once was, now is not, and yet will come.

9"This calls for a mind with wisdom. The seven heads are seven hills on which
the woman sits. 10They are also seven kings. Five have fallen, one is, the other
has not yet come; but when he does come, he must remain for only a little while.
11The beast who once was, and now is not, is an eighth king. He belongs to the
seven and is going to his destruction.

12"The ten horns you saw are ten kings who have not yet received a kingdom,
but who for one hour will receive authority as kings along with the beast. 13They
have one purpose and will give their power and authority to the beast. 14They
will wage war against the Lamb, but the Lamb will triumph over them because
he is Lord of lords and King of kings — and with him will be his called, chosen
and faithful followers."

15Then the angel said to me, "The waters you saw, where the prostitute sits,
are peoples, multitudes, nations and languages. 16The beast and the ten horns
you saw will hate the prostitute. They will bring her to ruin and leave her naked;
they will eat her flesh and burn her with fire. 17For God has put it into their hearts
to accomplish his purpose by agreeing to hand over to the beast their royal authority, until God's words are fulfilled. 18The woman you saw is the great city that
rules over the kings of the earth."

Lament Over Fallen Babylon

18 After this I saw another angel coming down from heaven. He had great
authority, and the earth was illuminated by his splendor. 2With a mighty
voice he shouted:

" 'Fallen! Fallen is Babylon the Great!'[a]
She has become a dwelling for demons
and a haunt for every impure spirit,
a haunt for every unclean bird,
a haunt for every unclean and detestable animal.
3For all the nations have drunk
the maddening wine of her adulteries.

[a] 2 Isaiah 21:9

REVELATION 18:2

GOD'S GUARANTEE

The repetition of the word "fallen" in verse two points to the fact that God has already predicted the destruction of Babylon, and his promise is coming true (Isa 21:9; Jer 51:8; Rev 14:8). The prophecies made long ago by Ezekiel and Daniel have now come true (Eze 38 – 39; Da 7; 11). Babylon, a vivid picture of a world system broken by sin, is now destroyed forever. Through God's eternal power, sin and death are destroyed, including all the broken systems and structures that define this sinful world.

As with Jesus' first coming, his second coming will usher in the fulfillment of the prophecies that involve his final work. Though no one knows the timing of Jesus' return, God uses John's words to continually remind this people that they have nothing to fear. Sin will not run amok forever. God will defeat it and destroy Babylon the Great and all it represents, once and for all time.

The kings of the earth committed adultery with her,
and the merchants of the earth grew rich from her excessive luxuries."

Warning to Escape Babylon's Judgment

4 Then I heard another voice from heaven say:

" 'Come out of her, my people,'[a]
so that you will not share in her sins,
so that you will not receive any of her plagues;
5 for her sins are piled up to heaven,
and God has remembered her crimes.
6 Give back to her as she has given;
pay her back double for what she has done.
Pour her a double portion from her own cup.
7 Give her as much torment and grief
as the glory and luxury she gave herself.
In her heart she boasts,
'I sit enthroned as queen.
I am not a widow;[b]
I will never mourn.'
8 Therefore in one day her plagues will overtake her:
death, mourning and famine.
She will be consumed by fire,
for mighty is the Lord God who judges her.

Threefold Woe Over Babylon's Fall

9 "When the kings of the earth who committed adultery with her and shared
her luxury see the smoke of her burning, they will weep and mourn over her.
10 Terrified at her torment, they will stand far off and cry:

" 'Woe! Woe to you, great city,
you mighty city of Babylon!
In one hour your doom has come!'

11 "The merchants of the earth will weep and mourn over her because no one
buys their cargoes anymore— 12 cargoes of gold, silver, precious stones and
pearls; fine linen, purple, silk and scarlet cloth; every sort of citron wood, and
articles of every kind made of ivory, costly wood, bronze, iron and marble; 13 cargoes of cinnamon and spice, of incense, myrrh and frankincense, of wine and
olive oil, of fine flour and wheat; cattle and sheep; horses and carriages; and
human beings sold as slaves.

14 "They will say, 'The fruit you longed for is gone from you. All your luxury
and splendor have vanished, never to be recovered.' 15 The merchants who sold
these things and gained their wealth from her will stand far off, terrified at her
torment. They will weep and mourn 16 and cry out:

" 'Woe! Woe to you, great city,
dressed in fine linen, purple and scarlet,
and glittering with gold, precious stones and pearls!
17 In one hour such great wealth has been brought to ruin!'

"Every sea captain, and all who travel by ship, the sailors, and all who earn
their living from the sea, will stand far off. 18 When they see the smoke of her
burning, they will exclaim, 'Was there ever a city like this great city?' 19 They will
throw dust on their heads, and with weeping and mourning cry out:

" 'Woe! Woe to you, great city,
where all who had ships on the sea
became rich through her wealth!
In one hour she has been brought to ruin!'

---

[a] 4 Jer. 51:45 [b] 7 See Isaiah 47:7,8.

20 "Rejoice over her, you heavens!
Rejoice, you people of God!
Rejoice, apostles and prophets!
For God has judged her
with the judgment she imposed on you."

The Finality of Babylon's Doom

21 Then a mighty angel picked up a boulder the size of a large millstone and threw it into the sea, and said:

"With such violence
the great city of Babylon will be thrown down,
never to be found again.
22 The music of harpists and musicians, pipers and trumpeters,
will never be heard in you again.
No worker of any trade
will ever be found in you again.
The sound of a millstone
will never be heard in you again.
23 The light of a lamp
will never shine in you again.
The voice of bridegroom and bride
will never be heard in you again.
Your merchants were the world's important people.
By your magic spell all the nations were led
astray.
24 In her was found the blood of prophets and of God's
holy people,
of all who have been slaughtered on the earth."

Threefold Hallelujah Over Babylon's Fall

19 After this I heard what sounded like the roar of a great multitude in heav-
en shouting:

"Hallelujah!
Salvation and glory and power belong to our God,
2 for true and just are his judgments.
He has condemned the great prostitute
who corrupted the earth by her adulteries.
He has avenged on her the blood of his servants."

3 And again they shouted:

"Hallelujah!
The smoke from her goes up for ever and ever."

4 The twenty-four elders and the four living creatures fell down and worshiped God, who was seated on the throne. And they cried:

"Amen, Hallelujah!"

5 Then a voice came from the throne, saying:

"Praise our God,
all you his servants,
you who fear him,
both great and small!"

6 Then I heard what sounded like a great multitude, like the roar of rushing waters and like loud peals of thunder, shouting:

"Hallelujah!
For our Lord God Almighty reigns.

7 Let us rejoice and be glad
and give him glory!
For the wedding of the Lamb has come,
and his bride has made herself ready.
8 Fine linen, bright and clean,
was given her to wear."
(Fine linen stands for the righteous acts of God's holy people.)

9 Then the angel said to me, "Write this: Blessed are those who are invited to
the wedding supper of the Lamb!" And he added, "These are the true words of
God."
10 At this I fell at his feet to worship him. But he said to me, "Don't do that! I
am a fellow servant with you and with your brothers and sisters who hold to the
testimony of Jesus. Worship God! For it is the Spirit of prophecy who bears testimony to Jesus."

The Heavenly Warrior Defeats the Beast

11 I saw heaven standing open and there before me was a white horse, whose
rider is called Faithful and True. With justice he judges and wages war. 12 His eyes
are like blazing fire, and on his head are many crowns. He has a name written
on him that no one knows but he himself. 13 He is dressed in a robe dipped in
blood, and his name is the Word of God. 14 The armies of heaven were following
him, riding on white horses and dressed in fine linen, white and clean. 15 Coming out of his mouth is a sharp sword with which to strike down the nations. "He
will rule them with an iron scepter."[a] He treads the winepress of the fury of the
wrath of God Almighty. 16 On his robe and on his thigh he has this name written:

KING OF KINGS AND LORD OF LORDS.

17 And I saw an angel standing in the sun, who cried in a loud voice to all the
birds flying in midair, "Come, gather together for the great supper of God, 18 so
that you may eat the flesh of kings, generals, and the mighty, of horses and their
riders, and the flesh of all people, free and slave, great and small."
19 Then I saw the beast and the kings of the earth and their armies gathered
together to wage war against the rider on the horse and his army. 20 But the beast
was captured, and with it the false prophet who had performed the signs on its
behalf. With these signs he had deluded those who had received the mark of
the beast and worshiped its image. The two of them were thrown alive into the
fiery lake of burning sulfur. 21 The rest were killed with the sword coming out
of the mouth of the rider on the horse, and all the birds gorged themselves on
their flesh.

The Thousand Years

20 And I saw an angel coming down out of heaven, having the key to the
Abyss and holding in his hand a great chain. 2 He seized the dragon, that
ancient serpent, who is the devil, or Satan, and bound him for a thousand years.
3 He threw him into the Abyss, and locked and sealed it over him, to keep him
from deceiving the nations anymore until the thousand years were ended. After
that, he must be set free for a short time.
4 I saw thrones on which were seated those who had been given authority to
judge. And I saw the souls of those who had been beheaded because of their testimony about Jesus and because of the word of God. They[b] had not worshiped
the beast or its image and had not received its mark on their foreheads or their
hands. They came to life and reigned with Christ a thousand years. 5 (The rest of
the dead did not come to life until the thousand years were ended.) This is the
first resurrection. 6 Blessed and holy are those who share in the first resurrection.

[a] 15 Psalm 2:9 [b] 4 Or *God; I also saw those who*

REVELATION 19:11

JESUS AND HIS WHITE HORSE

In the era when Rome was the dominant world power, a Roman general riding on a white horse after a battle was symbolic of victory in that battle; it showed that the captives and spoils of war belonged to Rome. In ancient cultures the white horse was considered a symbol of dominant rule and royalty, and that's the image in this passage as well.

John recorded Jesus riding a white horse *into* battle (v. 11), demonstrating that he has already won the war. What might have been considered an arrogant gesture in ancient culture is, for Jesus, a symbol that this battle is over before it even begins. He will not come to earth to struggle against the enemy; he will come to destroy the enemy. The captives and the spoils of war already belong to Jesus: He is superior, and the victory is already won.

The second death has no power over them, but they will be priests of God and of Christ and will reign with him for a thousand years.

The Judgment of Satan

7When the thousand years are over, Satan will be released from his prison 8and will go out to deceive the nations in the four corners of the earth—Gog and Magog—and to gather them for battle. In number they are like the sand on the seashore. 9They marched across the breadth of the earth and surrounded the camp of God's people, the city he loves. But fire came down from heaven and devoured them. 10And the devil, who deceived them, was thrown into the lake of burning sulfur, where the beast and the false prophet had been thrown. They will be tormented day and night for ever and ever.

The Judgment of the Dead

11Then I saw a great white throne and him who was seated on it. The earth and the heavens fled from his presence, and there was no place for them. 12And I saw the dead, great and small, standing before the throne, and books were opened. Another book was opened, which is the book of life. The dead were judged according to what they had done as recorded in the books. 13The sea gave up the dead that were in it, and death and Hades gave up the dead that were in them, and each person was judged according to what they had done. 14Then death and Hades were thrown into the lake of fire. The lake of fire is the second death. 15Anyone whose name was not found written in the book of life was thrown into the lake of fire.

A New Heaven and a New Earth

21 Then I saw "a new heaven and a new earth,"[a] for the first heaven and the first earth had passed away, and there was no longer any sea. 2I saw the Holy City, the new Jerusalem, coming down out of heaven from God, prepared as a bride beautifully dressed for her husband. 3And I heard a loud voice from the throne saying, "Look! God's dwelling place is now among the people, and he will dwell with them. They will be his people, and God himself will be with them and be their God. 4'He will wipe every tear from their eyes. There will be no more death'[b] or mourning or crying or pain, for the old order of things has passed away."

5He who was seated on the throne said, "I am making everything new!" Then he said, "Write this down, for these words are trustworthy and true."

6He said to me: "It is done. I am the Alpha and the Omega, the Beginning and the End. To the thirsty I will give water without cost from the spring of the water of life. 7Those who are victorious will inherit all this, and I will be their God and they will be my children. 8But the cowardly, the unbelieving, the vile, the murderers, the sexually immoral, those who practice magic arts, the idolaters and all liars—they will be consigned to the fiery lake of burning sulfur. This is the second death."

The New Jerusalem, the Bride of the Lamb

9One of the seven angels who had the seven bowls full of the seven last plagues came and said to me, "Come, I will show you the bride, the wife of the Lamb." 10And he carried me away in the Spirit to a mountain great and high, and showed me the Holy City, Jerusalem, coming down out of heaven from God. 11It shone with the glory of God, and its brilliance was like that of a very precious jewel, like a jasper, clear as crystal. 12It had a great, high wall with twelve gates, and with twelve angels at the gates. On the gates were written the names of the twelve tribes of Israel. 13There were three gates on the east, three on the north, three on the south and three on the west. 14The wall of the city had twelve foundations, and on them were the names of the twelve apostles of the Lamb.

[a] *1* Isaiah 65:17 [b] *4* Isaiah 25:8

GOD AND THE PROBLEM OF EVIL

The presence of evil in the world makes many people doubt the existence or the goodness of God. Critics have argued that if God were perfect and loving, then he would not allow the presence of evil in the world. However, this argument does not account for the multiple ways God has worked to deal with evil and sin.

The first and most basic way that God brings justice to evil is through natural consequences. In this imperfect world, all people experience the natural consequences of their sin. On a larger scale, the story of the cities of Sodom and Gomorrah provide us with an example of God's judgment coming about as a consequence of people's rebellion (Ge 19). In a similar way, the book of Revelation as a whole shows the consequences that will come as a result of the world's sin.

Second, God dealt with sin on the cross. Jesus' death, though it did not eliminate evil from the world, dealt a deathblow to its permanent presence in the world. While the world today is obviously still plagued with evil, Jesus' sacrifice and resurrection made it possible for the world to one day be free from evil. By giving Jesus over to be crucified and raising him from the dead, God defeated death and made it possible for his children to be made right with him. Jesus served as a perfect sacrifice for the evil of mankind; the judgment of sin was carried out against him as he hung on the cross in humanity's place.

Third, Revelation depicts God's ultimate elimination of evil from the world. The judgment day is his final act of justice and retribution against the evil that humans have brought upon themselves. God is perfect and therefore cannot be associated with anything that is evil or sinful, and so he will one day completely eliminate the existence of evil from the world when his kingdom is perfectly realized in the new earth (Isa 65:17; Rev 21:1 – 4).

While it may look to us as if sin goes unchecked, God will surely right all wrongs in his time. The consequences of sin, Jesus' death on the cross and the final judgment day are three parts of God's plan to ultimately defeat evil and to fully establish his kingdom plans. While people may wonder why God does things the way he does, it is important to remember that his plan is perfect; it has been and will continue to be fulfilled, and it will lead to a good and perfect kingdom that believers will share with him.

THE ALPHA AND OMEGA

Alpha and *Omega* are the first and last letters of the Greek alphabet, and together they also comprise one of the names for God. The name "the first and the last" appears in multiple places in the Old Testament as a representation for God's eternal existence (see Isa 41:4; 44:6; 48:12). God is the Alpha and the Omega because he is responsible for both the beginning and end of everything that has ever existed. Jesus had no beginning; he was present for the creation of the world (Jn 1:3), and he will be present for the end of the world (Rev 21:6), after which he will reign over the universe for eternity.

Jesus is the beginning and the end in many ways. Hebrews 12:2 says that he is the "pioneer and perfecter" of faith, which signifies that he initiated faith and he will bring it to completion. He is the summation of and the actual Word of God (Jn 1:1,14); he is the fulfillment of the Law (Mt 5:17); and he is the beginning of the gospel of grace through faith, not works (Eph 2:8 – 9).

Jesus is there in the first verse of Genesis and the last verse of Revelation, and he is present in every Bible verse, story and teaching in between. To say that Jesus is the Alpha and the Omega is to say that he is God, a declaration that is reinforced as true in the Gospels and throughout the entire New Testament. The book of Revelation never wavers from proclaiming that Jesus and God are one, and that together they bring about the creation and culmination of everything.

The Bible paints an astonishing picture of how everything began and how everything will end. And the best part about the beginning, the end and everything in between is that Jesus is the backbone, the central thread, the main theme and the summation of all of it. Not a single second in history has or will escape God's watchful eye; there is no part of the story where Jesus was not, is not or will not be present and perfectly sovereign. That's the hopeful message of God's Word, his revelation to all who will believe.

Believers can be confident that the God they trust in is fully in control of everything that was, everything that is and everything that will be. The name "the Alpha and the Omega" succinctly defines who God is and what he has done. From the beginning and to the end, God is eternal, God is in control, God is gracious and loving, God is just and GOD WINS.

[15]The angel who talked with me had a measuring rod of gold to measure the city, its gates and its walls. [16]The city was laid out like a square, as long as it was wide. He measured the city with the rod and found it to be 12,000 stadia[a] in length, and as wide and high as it is long. [17]The angel measured the wall using human measurement, and it was 144 cubits[b] thick.[c] [18]The wall was made of jasper, and the city of pure gold, as pure as glass. [19]The foundations of the city walls were decorated with every kind of precious stone. The first foundation was jasper, the second sapphire, the third agate, the fourth emerald, [20]the fifth onyx, the sixth ruby, the seventh chrysolite, the eighth beryl, the ninth topaz, the tenth turquoise, the eleventh jacinth, and the twelfth amethyst.[d] [21]The twelve gates were twelve pearls, each gate made of a single pearl. The great street of the city was of gold, as pure as transparent glass.

[22]I did not see a temple in the city, because the Lord God Almighty and the Lamb are its temple. [23]The city does not need the sun or the moon to shine on it, for the glory of God gives it light, and the Lamb is its lamp. [24]The nations will walk by its light, and the kings of the earth will bring their splendor into it. [25]On no day will its gates ever be shut, for there will be no night there. [26]The glory and honor of the nations will be brought into it. [27]Nothing impure will ever enter it, nor will anyone who does what is shameful or deceitful, but only those whose names are written in the Lamb's book of life.

Eden Restored

22 Then the angel showed me the river of the water of life, as clear as crystal, flowing from the throne of God and of the Lamb [2]down the middle of the great street of the city. On each side of the river stood the tree of life, bearing twelve crops of fruit, yielding its fruit every month. And the leaves of the tree are for the healing of the nations. [3]No longer will there be any curse. The throne of God and of the Lamb will be in the city, and his servants will serve him. [4]They will see his face, and his name will be on their foreheads. [5]There will be no more night. They will not need the light of a lamp or the light of the sun, for the Lord God will give them light. And they will reign for ever and ever.

John and the Angel

[6]The angel said to me, "These words are trustworthy and true. The Lord, the God who inspires the prophets, sent his angel to show his servants the things that must soon take place."

[7]"Look, I am coming soon! Blessed is the one who keeps the words of the prophecy written in this scroll."

[8]I, John, am the one who heard and saw these things. And when I had heard and seen them, I fell down to worship at the feet of the angel who had been showing them to me. [9]But he said to me, "Don't do that! I am a fellow servant with you and with your fellow prophets and with all who keep the words of this scroll. Worship God!"

[10]Then he told me, "Do not seal up the words of the prophecy of this scroll, because the time is near. [11]Let the one who does wrong continue to do wrong; let the vile person continue to be vile; let the one who does right continue to do right; and let the holy person continue to be holy."

Epilogue: Invitation and Warning

[12]"Look, I am coming soon! My reward is with me, and I will give to each person according to what they have done. [13]I am the Alpha and the Omega, the First and the Last, the Beginning and the End.

[14]"Blessed are those who wash their robes, that they may have the right to the

[a] *16* That is, about 1,400 miles or about 2,200 kilometers [b] *17* That is, about 200 feet or about 65 meters [c] *17* Or *high* [d] *20* The precise identification of some of these precious stones is uncertain.

REVELATION 22:1–2

PARADISE REGAINED

The river and tree pictured here are reminiscent of the Garden of Eden, and rightly so (Ge 2:8–10; 3:22–24). In the garden, people could have perfect fellowship with God, though they chose to rebel against him and broke that fellowship. In heaven, the relationship between God and his people will be free of sin; therefore, it will embody God's created design.

The great hope of believers is that they will one day be able to worship God and find joy in his presence forever. John must have grappled for words to describe the glory of heaven: All that sin has destroyed will be no more. The relationship between God and his people will be made right, as will the entire world. Since his ascension, Jesus, the Creator of the world, has been preparing this paradise for all of his people who will dwell with him and revel in his glory forever (Jn 14:3). In fact, after all of these events come to pass, all of God's creation will proclaim his glory, which will fill the earth as the waters cover the sea (Hab 2:14).

FOREVER

MADE FOR A DIFFERENT PLACE

— RANDY ALCORN

REVELATION 21 – 22

We were made for a person and a place. Jesus is the person. Heaven is the place.

God promises that all his children — whoever places their faith in Jesus to rescue them from sin and eternal death — will live *forever* with him in heaven (Lk 24:23 – 24; Jn 1:12; 3:16; 1Th 5:10).

But what exactly will eternal life with Jesus in heaven be like?

Heaven is God's central dwelling place. God is everywhere-present, yet heaven is the special location from which he rules the universe; it's where his throne is (1Ki 22:19).

When God's children die, we immediately go to heaven to be with Christ (Lk 23:43). But when we carefully read Scripture, we find that one day God will permanently relocate the present heaven to the newly transformed earth, which then will become the "forever heaven."

We normally think death ushers us into heaven to live with God in his place. That's in fact what happens when Christ-followers die (2Co 5:8). But the ultimate promise is that *God will come down to live with us in our place.* He says of the new earth, "Look! God's dwelling place is now among the people, and he will dwell with them. They will be his people, and God himself will be with them and be their God" (Rev 21:3). Three times in this one verse God says he will live "with" or "among" us! So the ultimate heaven, on the new earth, will not be "us with God" but "God with us."

While the throne of God is now in the present heaven, when God descends to live on the new earth, "The throne of God and of the Lamb will be in the city" (Rev 22:3). Where God's throne is, that is heaven, his central dwelling place. So the new earth will literally be "heaven on earth."

A WHOLE NEW WORLD!

God created the entire physical universe for his glory and our good. But humanity rebelled and the universe fell under the weight of our sin. Yet Adam and Eve's seduction by the serpent didn't catch God off guard. He had a plan in place for humanity's redemption — and the restoration of creation, forever rescuing it from sin, corruption and death. Just as he promises to make humankind new, he promises to renew earth itself.

> "See, I will create new heavens and a new earth" (Isa 65:17).
>
> " 'As the new heavens and the new earth that I make will endure before me,' declares the LORD, 'so will your name and descendants endure' " (Isa 66:22).

> "In keeping with his promise we are looking forward to a new heaven and a new earth, where righteousness dwells" (2Pe 3:13).
>
> "Then I saw 'a new heaven and a new earth,' for the first heaven and the first earth had passed away" (Rev 21:1).

Imagine how delighted Jesus' disciples were when he said to them, "At *the renewal of all things,* when the Son of Man sits on his glorious throne, you who have followed me will also sit on twelve thrones, judging the twelve tribes of Israel" (Mt 19:28, italics added).

Christ didn't speak of the *destruction* or *abandonment* of all things but "the renewal of all things." God designed humans to live on earth to his glory. Christ's incarnation, life, death and resurrection secured the new earth's eternal future, where life will be lived in complete fulfillment and without sin, the way God always intended.

So never think Satan beat God and thwarted his plans by tempting Adam and Eve in Eden. Rather, unwittingly his attempts to sabotage God's plans were used by the sovereign Creator as a part of his redemptive story that includes the incarnation, life, death, resurrection and return of Jesus, as well as the devil's final destruction (Ge 3:15; Rev 20:10).

Similarly, Peter preached that Christ must remain in heaven "until the time comes for God *to restore everything,* as he promised long ago through his holy prophets" (Ac 3:21, italics added).

This cosmic restoration will not consist of God bringing disembodied angel-like people to fellowship with him in a spirit realm. Rather, God will bring humankind to something greater than even his original design in Eden. The entire physical universe won't go back to its pre-fall glory but forward to something still more magnificent.

THE FUTURE HEAVEN, WHERE WE'LL LIVE FOREVER

The exact location of the present heaven is unknown. It seems likely that it's not in our physical universe, but it exists in another dimension that we can't see. But we do know it is a wonderful place to live between the time the followers of Jesus die and our future resurrection.

Life in the present heaven (which theologians call the "intermediate" heaven) "is better by far" than living here on earth under the curse (Php 1:23). But it's not our final destination.

Many understand Revelation 20:1 – 10 to teach that after we're raised, we will live on the original

FOREVER

(CONTINUED)

REVELATION 21 – 22

earth for a thousand years. After that will come the final judgment and end of the old earth, followed by its resurrection in the form of the new earth, where we will live with God and each other forever.

When the New Jerusalem comes down out of heaven from God, it will descend to the new earth. From that time on, God's dwelling place will be with his redeemed people on *earth*. This means the new earth will literally be heaven on earth!

Jesus says of those who would be his disciple, "My Father will love them, and we will come to them and make our home with them" (Jn 14:23). This is a picture of God's ultimate plan. Think about this: God could have taken Adam and Eve up to heaven to visit with him — but he didn't. Instead, he walked with them here in their own world (Ge 3:8). And that's what he will do with us forever!

The idea of the new earth as a physical place isn't an invention of shortsighted human imagination. It's the invention of our infinitely resourceful Creator, who made physical human beings to live on a physical earth, *and* who chose to become a man himself on that same earth. He wanted to redeem mankind *and* earth. Why? In order to glorify himself and enjoy forever the company of men and women in a world he's made for us.

JESUS: THE PRIME EXAMPLE OF OUR RESURRECTED LIVES

When Jesus Christ came to earth, one of his names was Immanuel, which means "God with us" (Mt 1:23). Jesus' ascension to heaven in his resurrected body demonstrated the permanence of the incarnation. This has great bearing on where God chooses for us to dwell together. The new earth will be heaven incarnate, just as Jesus Christ is God incarnate. It will not be strange for Jesus to live on the new earth, since like all of us, he first lived on the original earth!

In the forty days between Christ's resurrection and ascension, he walked, talked, ate and drank with his disciples. They saw a preview of the resurrected life reminding us that we will be both spiritual *and* physical beings forever.

It's fascinating to compare the first three and last three chapters of the Bible. In both we see the "tree of life," a great river or rivers, a bride and a bridegroom. In Genesis, paradise is lost; in Revelation, paradise is regained. In Genesis, Satan wins his first victory; in Revelation, he experiences his final defeat. In Genesis, God hides his face from sinful man; in Revelation, it's said of God's children "they will see his face" (Rev 22:4).

In Genesis, the curse is pronounced; in Revelation, it's removed. In Genesis, the gates of paradise are shut; in Revelation, the heavenly city's gates are open. In Genesis, death appears; in Revelation, death is finally destroyed. It's the Lamb of God, Jesus Christ, the second Adam, who is given full credit for his sweeping victory over sin and death and his dramatic rescue of his people. By his incredible grace, those who believe in him will live forever in heaven rather than in hell.

UNITING HEAVEN AND EARTH

"The holy people of the Most High will receive the kingdom and will possess it forever" (Da 7:18). What is "the kingdom"? Earth. God's people will reign over it not just for a thousand years but forever. God never abandoned his original plan for righteous humans to rule the earth — and through Jesus he will yet fulfill that plan in glorious ways. Earth is unique. It's the one planet — perhaps among billions — where God chose to act out the unfolding drama of redemption and reveal the wonders of his grace.

If the new Jerusalem will be capital city of the new earth, the new earth will be capital planet of the new universe. There God will establish an eternal kingdom where he will "bring unity to all things in heaven and on earth under Christ" (Eph 1:10). "All things" is inclusive — neither animals nor trees nor flowers nor mountains nor valleys will be left out. This verse corresponds precisely to the culmination of history we see enacted in Revelation 21, the merging together of previously separate realms of heaven and earth, fully under Christ's lordship.

As God and humankind are reconciled and united in Jesus, so too the dwellings of God and humankind — heaven and earth — will be reconciled and united in Jesus. The prayer of the ages, "your will be done, on earth as it is in heaven" (Mt 6:10) will at last be fully answered!

Heaven is God's home. Earth is our home. Jesus Christ, as the God-man, forever links God and humankind, and thereby forever links heaven and earth. As Ephesians 1:10 demonstrates, this idea of earth and heaven becoming one is explicitly biblical. Just as the veil that separated God from humankind was torn in two at Christ's death (Mt 27:51), so the veil that separates heaven and earth will be forever split. The gulf between the spiritual and physical worlds will be removed. No divided realms or divided loyalties to different homelands. Just one cosmos, one universe united under one Lord — forever. This is the unstoppable plan of God. This is history's destination, the culmination of the greatest story ever told, a Jesus-centered story with a happy ending that will never end.

When God walked with Adam and Eve in the Garden of Eden, earth was heaven's backyard.

FOREVER

(CONTINUED)

REVELATION 21–22

The new earth will be heaven itself. And those who know Jesus will have the privilege of living there.

OUR FOREVER HOME

God paints a compelling picture of the coming world: "'See, I will create new heavens and a new earth … But be glad and rejoice forever in what I will create, for I will create Jerusalem to be a delight and its people a joy. I will rejoice over Jerusalem and take delight in my people; the sound of weeping and of crying will be heard in it no more … They will build houses and dwell in them; they will plant vineyards and eat their fruit … The wolf and the lamb will feed together, and the lion will eat straw like the ox, and dust will be the serpent's food. They will neither harm nor destroy on all my holy mountain,' says the LORD" (Isa 65:17–19,21,25).

Although Isaiah 60 doesn't contain the term *new earth* (as do nearby chapters 65 and 66), we know much of the chapter describes that place, since John applied the prophet's words directly to the new earth in Revelation 21–22.

This will be a time of unprecedented rejoicing: "Then you will look and be radiant, your heart will throb and swell with joy." On the renewed earth, the nations will bring their greatest treasures into this glorified city: "The wealth on the seas will be brought to you, to you the riches of the nations will come" (Isa 60:5).

There will be animals from various nations on the new earth: "Herds of camels will cover your land, young camels of Midian and Ephah" (Isa 60:6). Redeemed people will travel from far places to the glorified Jerusalem: "All from Sheba will come, bearing gold and incense and proclaiming the praise of the LORD" (v. 6). People who dwell on islands will worship God, and ships will come from "Tarshish, bringing your children from afar, with their silver and gold, to the honor of the LORD your God, the Holy One of Israel, for he has endowed you with splendor" (v. 9).

Most of us are unaccustomed to thinking of nations, rulers, civilizations and culture (as well as animals) in heaven, but Isaiah 60 is one of many passages demonstrating the new earth's true earthiness.

THE WONDERS OF THE HOLY CITY

John applied Isaiah 60:11 directly to the New Jerusalem: "The nations will walk by its light, and the kings of the earth will bring their splendor into it. On no day will its gates ever be shut, for there will be no night there. The glory and honor of the nations will be brought into it" (Rev 21:24–26).

The references to splendor of kings and glory of nations give us biblical basis to suppose that the best history, culture, art, music, and the languages of the old earth will be redeemed, purified, and restored to the new earth. Even now in heaven there are people "from every tribe and language and people and nation" (Rev 5:9). It appears God's people will forever be multicultural!

God promises something that has never yet been true of the present Jerusalem: "I will make peace your governor and well-being your ruler. No longer will violence be heard in your land, nor ruin or destruction within your borders, but you will call your walls Salvation and your gates Praise" (Isa 60:17 – 18).

Isaiah then describes another scene that John connects directly to the new earth in Revelation 21:23; 22:5: "The sun will no more be your light by day, nor will the brightness of the moon shine on you, for the LORD will be your everlasting light, and your God will be your glory. Your sun will never set again, and your moon will wane no more; the LORD will be your everlasting light, and your days of sorrow will end" (Isa 60:19 – 20).

Of the new Jerusalem, we're told, "Nothing impure will ever enter it, nor will anyone who does what is shameful or deceitful, but only those whose names are written in the Lamb's book of life" (Rev 21:27). Likewise, Isaiah uses inclusive language that could not apply to the old earth under the curse: "Then all your people will be righteous" (Isa 60:21). Verse 21 continues, "They will possess the land [in the Hebrew, literally *earth*] forever." The earth will be theirs — not for a glorious decade or century or millennium, but *forever*.

ANYTHING BUT BORING!

A pastor once told me he dreaded heaven. Why? "I can't stand the thought of endless tedium. To float around in the clouds with nothing to do but strum a harp . . . it's all so terribly boring. Heaven doesn't sound much better than hell. I'd rather be annihilated than spend eternity in a place like that."

Jesus said of the devil, "When he lies, he speaks his native language, for he is a liar and the father of lies" (Jn 8:44). Our enemy slanders three things: God's person, God's people and God's place — namely, heaven. Satan need not convince us that heaven doesn't exist, only that heaven is a place of boring, unearthly existence. What an insult to the infinitely fascinating Maker of the universe, whose creative wonders will never cease!

Believing Satan's lies robs us of our joy and anticipation. We set our minds on this life — not the

FOREVER

(CONTINUED)

REVELATION 21 – 22

next — and lose motivation to share our faith. Why should we share the "good news" that people can spend eternity in a boring, ghostly place that *even we* don't look forward to?

The new Jerusalem will be a new Eden, a huge garden city of startling beauty. Heaven won't be filled with hammocks — with nothing to do but rest (though some rest will be great for a while). We'll honor God by enjoying him through enjoying his creation. We'll always get to do what we want to do, and we'll always want to do what brings joy to God and to us.

On the new earth, we're told "his servants will serve him" (Rev 22:3). Servants of a King — especially his children who are royalty themselves — have important things to do, places to go, people to see. It's said of God's children "they will reign for ever and ever" (Rev 22:5). Servants work and rulers work. But on the new earth, with a totally righteous and loving Father, our work will be a privilege — refreshing work without the curse — similar to work done by Adam and Eve in the Garden of Eden.

ANTICIPATING LIFE ON THE NEW EARTH

The Westminster Shorter Catechism, completed in 1647, begins, "Man's chief end is to glorify God and to enjoy him forever." What will we do forever? Enjoy God! Will we use the arts to praise God? Since the new earth will supersede and surpass the present earth, then surely the greatest books, dramas and poems have yet to be written. Just as we can use our voices and musical instruments to worship God, we can also dance to honor him.

What about sports? Picture yourself enjoying your favorite sport (which may be a new one you haven't yet played) when you live on the new earth with a perfectly healthy body. Olympic champion Eric Liddell said, "God made me fast. And when I run I feel his pleasure."

After our resurrection, Matthew 8:11 and several other Scriptures say we'll enjoy feasts with Jesus "in the kingdom of heaven." But that heavenly kingdom is depicted in a very tangible earthly way. What do people do at a feast? Eat and drink, tell stories, celebrate and laugh. God will be the host and Christ the guest of honor, and all stories and laughter will honor him.

We'll never know everything — we're not God. But as resurrected beings, we'll certainly be capable of learning and growing, discovering and exploring. God tells us "in the coming ages" he'll "show the immeasurable riches of his grace, expressed in his kindness to us in Christ Jesus" (Eph 2:6 – 7). We may learn exactly how God fulfilled his promise to work all things, even the hardest things in our lives, together for our good (Ro 8:28).

THE OLD EARTH MADE NEW AND FAR BETTER

The whole creation groans and, implicitly, awaits with us the redemption of our bodies in the resurrection (Ro 8:22 – 23). This suggests that animals, which experience suffering due to our sin will likewise experience new life on the new earth. The creation that fell on our coattails will rise on our coattails. Perhaps God will bring even extinct animals back to life. Since he's a kind Father and the giver of all good gifts, if having your pets on the new earth would please you, God might well bring them back.

Though the splendor of creation that remains testifies to God's greatness (Ro 1:20), the curse removed much of the world's beauty. But Revelation 22:3 says "no longer will there be any curse." God will make all his children beautiful and whole and happy.

When God brings heaven down to the new earth, "he will wipe every tear from their eyes" (Rev 21:4). What an intimate picture — God's hands will touch the face of each individual child, removing every tear. The same verse says, "There will be no more death or mourning or crying or pain." As Thomas Moore put it, "Earth has no sorrow that heaven cannot heal."

There'll be no diseases, no disabilities, no tragic accidents. No hospitals. No cemeteries. No sin. No evil. No fear. No abuse, rape, murder, drugs, drunkenness, bombs, shootings or terrorism.

The disabled, liberated from ravaged bodies and minds, and the sick and elderly, free from pains and restrictions, will deeply appreciate heaven. They'll walk and run and see and hear, some for the first time. Hymn writer Fanny Crosby said, "Don't pity me for my blindness, for the first face I ever see will be the face of my Lord Jesus."

The promise of the resurrection means that none of God's children will pass our peak in this life. We won't have to look back with regret, pining away for an earlier time when we were at our best. The resurrection means not simply taking us back to the best we once were, but moving us forward to a new best, beyond our wildest dreams! Our peaks are yet to come, and we will never pass them!

OUR BEST RELATIONSHIPS ARE AHEAD OF US

Crowds followed Jesus because they loved him and wanted to be near him. The best part of heaven will be spending time with Jesus.

FOREVER

(CONTINUED)

REVELATION 21 – 22

While Jesus will be our best friend, God understands our need and desire for friendships to continue in heaven. He made us that way. In heaven we'll have our old friends who know Jesus and many new friends as well. Every time we sit together at feasts we will meet new people and hear new stories!

Married couples needn't fear the words of Jesus concerning human marriage discontinuing in heaven (Mt 22:30). Scripture does *not* teach there will be no marriage in heaven. Instead there'll be *one* marriage, between Christ and his bride — and we'll all be part of it. Our marriage to Christ will be so completely satisfying that even the most wonderful earthly marriage couldn't compete.

But Christ never suggested an end to deep relationships between couples. I fully expect my wife, Nanci, and I will be closer friends than ever. We'll remember fondly the lives we forged together on the old earth, our children and grandchildren and friends. All of us together will be part of the same unbreakable marriage to Jesus.

The most ordinary moment in heaven will far surpass the best moments of this life. In that day we'll all agree with the apostle Paul: "Our present sufferings are not worth comparing with the glory that will be revealed in us" (Ro 8:18).

GET A HEAD START ON KINGDOM LIVING

"Set your hearts on things above, where Christ is, seated at the right hand of God. Set your minds on things above, not on earthly things" (Col 3:1 – 2). If we understand what "a new heaven and a new earth" means, we'll look forward to and focus on our forever home.

Knowing where we're going and what rewards we'll receive for serving Christ directly affects how we live today. Our choices make an indelible mark on eternity — including our choices of personal holiness and how we act toward others. After saying "we are looking forward to a new heaven and a new earth, where righteousness dwells," Peter immediately adds, "So then, dear friends . . . make every effort to be found spotless, blameless and at peace with him" (2Pe 3:13 – 14).

When this is true of us, we can face death with an eternal perspective. Calvin Miller, in the *Divine Symphony* prayed,

> I once scorned ev'ry fearful thought of death,
> When it was but the end of pulse and breath,
> But now my eyes have seen that past the pain
> There is a world that's waiting to be claimed.
> Earthmaker, Holy, let me now depart,
> For living's such a temporary art.
> And dying is but getting dressed for God,
> Our graves are merely doorways cut in sod.

C. S. Lewis said, "I must keep alive in myself the desire for my true country, which I shall not find till after death; I must never let it get snowed under or turned aside; I must make it the main object of life to press on to that other country and to help others to do the same."

If you know Jesus, we'll live together on that resurrected world. With the Lord we love and with friends we cherish, we'll embark together on the ultimate adventure, in a spectacular new universe. Jesus will be the center of all things, and joy will be the air we breathe. And we really will live "happily ever after."

And right when we think, "It can't get any better than this" ... it will!

BEGINNINGS	REVOLT	PEOPLE	INTERTESTAMENTAL PERIOD	SAVIOR	CHURCH	FOREVER
GENESIS 1–2 (pg. 8)	GENESIS 3–11 (pg. 24)	GENESIS 12 to MALACHI (pg. 266)	(pg. 1508)	GOSPELS to ACTS 1 (pg. 1560)	ACTS 2 to REVELATION 20 (pg. 1736)	REVELATION 21–22 (pg. 1996)

tree of life and may go through the gates into the city. [15]Outside are the dogs,
those who practice magic arts, the sexually immoral, the murderers, the idolaters and everyone who loves and practices falsehood.
[16]"I, Jesus, have sent my angel to give you[a] this testimony for the churches. I
am the Root and the Offspring of David, and the bright Morning Star."

[17]The Spirit and the bride say, "Come!" And let the one who hears say, "Come!"
Let the one who is thirsty come; and let the one who wishes take the free gift of
the water of life.

[18]I warn everyone who hears the words of the prophecy of this scroll: If anyone
adds anything to them, God will add to that person the plagues described in
this scroll. [19]And if anyone takes words away from this scroll of prophecy, God
will take away from that person any share in the tree of life and in the Holy City,
which are described in this scroll.
[20]He who testifies to these things says, "Yes, I am coming soon."
Amen. Come, Lord Jesus.
[21]The grace of the Lord Jesus be with God's people. Amen.

[a] *16* The Greek is plural.

TABLE OF WEIGHTS AND MEASURES

	Biblical Unit	Approximate American Equivalent	Approximate Metric Equivalent
Weights	talent (60 minas)	75 pounds	34 kilograms
	mina (50 shekels)	1 1/4 pounds	560 grams
	shekel (2 bekas)	2/5 ounce	11.5 grams
	pim (2/3 shekel)	1/4 ounce	7.8 grams
	beka (10 gerahs)	1/5 ounce	5.7 grams
	gerah	1/50 ounce	0.6 gram
	daric	1/3 ounce	8.4 grams
Length	cubit	18 inches	45 centimeters
	span	9 inches	23 centimeters
	handbreadth	3 inches	7.5 centimeters
	stadion (pl. stadia)	600 feet	183 meters
Capacity			
Dry Measure	cor [homer] (10 ephahs)	6 bushels	220 liters
	lethek (5 ephahs)	3 bushels	110 liters
	ephah (10 omers)	3/5 bushel	22 liters
	seah (1/3 ephah)	7 quarts	7.5 liters
	omer (1/10 ephah)	2 quarts	2 liters
	cab (1/18 ephah)	1 quart	1 liter
Liquid Measure	bath (1 ephah)	6 gallons	22 liters
	hin (1/6 bath)	1 gallon	3.8 liters
	log (1/72 bath)	1/3 quart	0.3 liter

The figures of the table are calculated on the basis of a shekel equaling 11.5 grams, a cubit equaling 18 inches and an ephah equaling 22 liters. The quart referred to is either a dry quart (slightly larger than a liter) or a liquid quart (slightly smaller than a liter), whichever is applicable. The ton referred to in the footnotes is the American ton of 2,000 pounds. These weights are calculated relative to the particular commodity involved. Accordingly, the same measure of capacity in the text may be converted into different weights in the footnotes.

This table is based upon the best available information, but it is not intended to be mathematically precise; like the measurement equivalents in the footnotes, it merely gives approximate amounts and distances. Weights and measures differed somewhat at various times and places in the ancient world. There is uncertainty particularly about the ephah and the bath; further discoveries may shed more light on these units of capacity.

DICTIONARY-CONCORDANCE

A

Aaron—the brother of Moses; he served as Moses' spokesman before Pharaoh (Ex 4:14–16, 27–31; 7:1–2); he was Israel's first high priest (Ex 28:1; Nu 17; Heb 5:1–4).

abandon—to leave completely; to desert.

Abba—the word for *father* in Aramaic, one of the three languages Jesus spoke.

Ro 8:15 And by him we cry, "*A*, Father."
Gal 4:6 the Spirit who calls out, "*A*, Father."

Abel—the second son of Adam (Ge 4:2); he offered a pleasing sacrifice to God (Ge 4:4; Heb 11:4) but was murdered by his brother Cain (Ge 4:8; Mt 23:35; 1Jn 3:12).

abhor—to hate or to turn away from.

Ps 26:5 I *a* the assembly of evildoers
Am 6:8 "I *a* the pride of Jacob

Abigail—the wife of Nabal; she helped save David's life (1Sa 25:14–35) and later became his wife (1Sa 25:36–42).

abolish—to destroy completely; to put an end to.

abomination—a thing to be hated.

abound—to be more than enough; to overflow.

Ex 34:6 slow to anger, *a* in love
Php 1:9 that your love may *a* more

Abraham—the father of the Jewish nation and of all believers. God promised that he would make a mighty nation of Abraham's children and would give them the land of Canaan (Ge 15; 17; 22; Ro 4; Heb 6:13–15). As a test, God told him to offer his son Isaac as a sacrifice (Ge 22; Heb 11:17–19) but withdrew this command when Abraham showed that he would trust God and obey him.

Absalom—a son of David (2Sa 3:3); he plotted to take David's throne. He died when his long hair became tangled in an oak tree and Joab, David's commander, plunged javelins into his heart (2Sa 14—18).

abstain—to keep from doing something.

abundance, **abundant**—having plenty; more than enough.

Jude 2 Mercy, peace and love be yours in *a*.

Abyss—the place of the dead; the place where evil spirits live.

Achan—an Israelite who kept spoil from the conquest of Jericho for himself; as a result of Achan's stealing what belonged to God, the Israelites were defeated at Ai and he and his family were stoned to death (Jos 7; 22:20).

acknowledge—to know and to say that something is true; to recognize.

Mt 10:32 I will also *a* before my Father in heaven.
1Jn 4:3 spirit that does not *a* Jesus is not from God.

acts—deeds.

Ps 150:2 Praise him for his *a* of power
Isa 64:6 all our righteous *a* are like filthy rags

Adam—the first person God created (Ge 1:26–2:25); he sinned by disobeying God (Ge 3) and in that way brought all people under the curse of sin (Ro 5:12–21).

admonish—to give warning or advice in a caring way.

adorn—to make more beautiful.

adultery—having sexual relations with someone other than one's husband or wife. Spiritual adultery means being unfaithful to God (Jer 3).

Ex 20:14 You shall not commit *a*.
Mt 5:28 lustfully has already committed *a*

adversary—enemy; opponent.

advice—an opinion given about a decision to be made.

1Ki 12:14 he followed the *a* of the young men
Pr 20:18 Plans are established by seeking *a*;

advocate—1. *(v.)* to speak in favor of; 2. *(n.)* someone who speaks in another person's defense; 3. *(n.)* another name for the Holy Spirit.

Jn 14:16 he will give you another *a* to help you
Jn 14:26 But the *A*, the Holy Spirit,
Jn 15:26 "When the *A* comes, whom I will

affliction—trouble or pain that lasts a long time.

Ro 12:12 patient in *a*, faithful in prayer.

agony—extreme pain of mind or body.

Ahab—a wicked king of Israel; the husband of Jezebel (1Ki 16:31). He caused Israel to worship Baal rather than God (1Ki 16:31–33) and was opposed by God's prophet Elijah (1Ki 17:1; 18; 21).

alabaster—a hard marble like material that can be made into jars, vases or sculptures.

alienate—to make unfriendly; to turn a person's interest or affection away from another person or thing.

allot—to divide and give away in parts. In Old Testament times the land of Canaan was allotted to the twelve tribes of Israel.

Almighty—a name used to show how strong and powerful God is.

Ge 17:1 "I am God *A*; walk before me
Isa 6:3 "Holy, holy, holy is the LORD *A*;

altar—a raised platform made of stones, metal, dirt or wood, on which sacrifices were made.

ambush—the act of hiding in order to attack by surprise.

Amen—Hebrew word that means "so be it" or "let it become true."

Amos—a prophet of Israel who lived about the same time as Hosea and Jonah; he spoke about God's justice and righteousness.

Ananias—1. the husband of Sapphira; he was struck dead for lying to God (Ac 5:1–11); 2. the disciple who baptized Saul (Ac 9:10–19); 3. the high priest before whom Paul was tried in Jerusalem (Ac 22:30–24:1).

ancestor—a person from whom someone is descended.

Ps 78:5 commanded our *a* to teach their children,

ancient—very old.

Andrew—one of the twelve apostles; the brother of Peter (Mt 4:18; 10:2; Ac 1:13).

angel—a heavenly being.

Ps 34:7	The *a* of the LORD encamps
Heb 1:14	Are not all *a* ministering spirits
Heb 2:7	made them a little lower than the *a*;
1Pe 1:12	Even *a* long to look

anger—a strong feeling of displeasure; rage; fury.

Ps 103:8	slow to *a*, abounding in love.
Jas 1:20	human *a* does not produce the righteousness

anguish—extreme pain or distress of mind or body.

Jer 49:24	*a* and pain have seized her;

annihilate—to destroy completely.

anoint—to pour oil on a person's head, either for a physical benefit (Jas 5:14) or to set someone apart for service to God (Ex 28:41).

antichrist—a person who is against Christ.

1Jn 2:18	you have heard that the *a* is coming,
1Jn 2:22	Such a person is the *a*

anxiety—worry.

1Pe 5:7	Cast all your *a* on him

Apollos—a Christian from Alexandria who knew the Scriptures well (Ac 18:24–28) and helped Paul to minister in Corinth (Ac 19:1; 1Co 1:12).

apostle—1. any of the twelve men Jesus chose to work with him during his earthly ministry; after being equipped by the Holy Spirit, they were sent out to preach about Jesus; 2. later, someone who had been with Jesus, had seen his miracles and then taught others about him.

Mt10:2	These are the names of the twelve *a*:
1Co 12:28	God has placed in the church first of all *a*,
1Co 15:9	For I am the least of the *a*

appalled—overcome with shock or horror.

appeal—to make an earnest request.

1Pe 5:1	I *a* as a fellow elder

appoint—to assign someone officially to a job or position.

Aquila—the husband of Priscilla; Aquila and Priscilla were co-workers with Paul in Corinth (Ac 18; Ro 16:3).

Aramaic—the language that was commonly spoken in the countries east of the Mediterranean Sea during Jesus' earthly ministry.

ark of the covenant law—also called the ark of the covenant; a large gold-covered box, which contained the Ten Commandments (tablets of the covenant law), a jar of manna and Aaron's staff, and was kept inside the Most Holy Place in the tabernacle (tent of meeting). It was a reminder to the Israelites of God's presence with them.

armor—protective clothing worn in battle, usually made of metal.

Eph 6:11	Put on the full *a* of God

aroma—an odor or smell, usually pleasant.

arouse—to excite; to stir to action.

arrest—to officially or lawfully make a prisoner of someone.

arrogant—proud; conceited.

arrow—See bow.

ascend—to go up. Jesus ascended to heaven to return to God the Father.

ascribe—to think of as caused by, coming from or belonging to.

1Ch 16:28	*a* to the LORD glory and strength,

Ashera poles—wooden poles honoring Ashera, the Canaanite goddess of love and war.

Dt 12:3	burn their *A* in the fire;

assemble—to bring a group of people together; to meet together.

Assyria—one of the powerful nations of Biblical times; it often attacked the Israelites; its capital was Nineveh.

astray—mistaken; not on the right path; lost.

Isa 53:6	We all, like sheep, have gone *a*,

atone—to make right, by paying the penalty, the relationship between God and humans that was broken through sin. In the Old Testament people atoned symbolically for their sins by offering sacrifices to God. In the New Testament Jesus corrected the relationship between God and people once and for all by dying to take away sins.

atonement—the payment that corrects the relationship between God and humans that was broken through sin.

Lev 17:11	it is the blood that makes *a*
Lev 23:27	this seventh month is the Day of *A*.
Ro 3:25	God presented Christ as a sacrifice of *a*,
Heb 2:17	that he might make *a* for the sins

attack—to set upon with force, as in a battle.

authority—the right and power to give orders.

Mt 9:6	the Son of Man has *a* on earth
Mt 28:18	"All *a* in heaven and on earth has
Ro 13:1	for there is no *a* except that which
Heb 13:17	your leaders and submit to their *a*,

avenge—to get back at or punish someone who has done wrong.

Dt 32:35	It is mine to *a*; I will repay.

avoid—to keep away from.

Pr 20:19	*a* anyone who talks too much.

awe—respect and wonder; a holy fear of God because of his great power.

Ps 65:8	earth is filled with *a* at your wonders;

B

Baal—the name of many false gods in Canaan.

1Ki 18:25	Elijah said to the prophets of *B*,

Babel—a tower built soon after the flood; the builders were attempting to reach up to God, but God confused their language so that the building was stopped.

Babylon—the beautiful capital of Babylonia; it was a powerful and influential city in the Near East from the eighteenth to the sixth centuries B.C. In the New Testament, Babylon represents the godless city.

Ps 137:1	By the rivers of *B* we sat and wept
Rev 14:8	Fallen is *B* the Great,

Balaam—a seer who tried to curse Israel during their journey to the promised land, but God would not allow it (Nu 22—24).

balm—a skin cream used to heal sores and relieve pain.

Jer 8:22	Is there no *b* in Gilead?

banish—to force a person away from a place.

banquet—a formal meal, usually for a large group of people.

baptize—a religious ceremony in which water is used as a symbol of cleansing from sin. Churches today baptize by sprinkling or pouring or immersing in water. Baptism is a sign that sin is washed away.

Mk 1:9 and was *b* by John in the Jordan.
Ac 1:5 but in a few days you will be *b*
Ac 2:38 "Repent and be *b*, every one of you,

Barabbas—the Jews chose this criminal, rather than Jesus, to be released by Pilate (Mt 27:26).

Barnabas—an apostle; he was a co-worker with Paul on his first missionary journey (Ac 9:27; Ac 13—15).

barren—1. unable to have children; 2. unable to produce crops.

Bartholomew—one of the twelve apostles (Mt 10:3; Ac 1:13). He was also probably known as Nathanael (Jn 1:45–49; 21:2).

Bathsheba—the wife of Uriah; she committed adultery with David and later became his wife (2Sa 11); she was the mother of Solomon (2Sa 12:24).

Beelzebul—the prince of demons; Satan.

Lk 11:19 if I drive out demons by *B*,

Beersheba—an important town that marked the southern boundary of Judah.

believe—to accept as true; to trust; to have faith.

Mk 1:15 Repent and *b* the good news!"
Mk 9:24 "I do *b*; help me overcome my
Jn 1:7 that through him all might *b*.
Jn 3:18 does not *b* stands condemned
Jn 20:27 Stop doubting and *b*."
Ac 16:31 They replied, "*B* in the Lord Jesus,
Ro 3:22 faith in Jesus Christ to all who *b*.
1Th 4:14 we *b* that Jesus died and rose again

Benjamin—the twelfth son of Jacob. Rachel was his mother, and he was the younger brother of Joseph (Ge 35:16–24; Ge 42—45).

besiege—to surround a city or town completely with an army, so that nothing can go in or out.

bestow—to give.

Bethlehem—the city in Judea where Jesus was born (Mt 2:1).

betray—to turn a friend over to his or her enemies; to be unfaithful to.

Mt 27:3 When Judas, who had *b* him,
1Co 11:23 on the night he was *b*, took bread,

betroth—to promise to marry.

bewildered—confused; puzzled.

bind—1. to tie with a rope or string; 2. to make tight or firm.

Dt 6:8 and *b* them on your foreheads.
Mt 16:19 whatever you *b* on earth will be

birthright—the special rights of the firstborn son. In the Old Testament, after the father died, the oldest son received the father's power and right to make decisions for the entire family. He also got twice as much money and property as each of his brothers.

bitter—having harsh or hateful feelings.

Eph 4:31 Get rid of all *b*, rage
Heb 12:15 and that no *b* root grows up

blameless—without fault.

Ge 17:1 walk before me faithfully and be *b*.
1Co 1:8 so that you will be *b* on the day

blaspheme—to speak carelessly, falsely or insultingly about God or holy things.

Mk 3:29 whoever *b* against the Holy Spirit

blemish—a spot or mark that makes something imperfect.

1Pe 1:19 a lamb without *b* or defect.

bless—1. to make holy; 2. to show favor to; 3. to ask God to show favor to.

Ge 2:3 Then God *b* the seventh day
Ge 12:3 I will *b* those who *b* you,
Mt 5:3 "*B* are the poor in spirit
Ro 12:14 *b* those who persecute you; *b*

blight—a disease in plants that makes them shrivel up and die.

blind—unable to see. Spiritual blindness is an inability to understand the things of God.

Mt 11:5 The *b* receive sight, the lame walk,
Jn 9:25 I was *b* but now I see!"

blood—as the life-giving fluid in the body, it represents life itself. In the Old Testament, the blood of sacrifices symbolized the giving of life for life. Through the blood of Jesus on the cross, believers are saved from death for their sins.

Ex 12:13 and when I see the *b*, I will pass
Lev 17:11 For the life of a creature is in the *b*,
Mt 26:28 This is my *b* of the covenant,
Eph 1:7 we have redemption through his *b*,
Heb 9:12 once for all by his own *b*,

blot—to erase or get rid of.

Ex 32:32 then *b* me out of the book you have
Ps 51:1 *b* out my transgressions.

boast—to brag; to call attention to.

Ps 44:8 In God we make our *b*
Gal 6:14 May I never *b* except in the cross

Boaz—a wealthy man who lived in Bethlehem in the days of the judges; he married Ruth (Ru 2; 4).

body—1. physical part of a person; 2. a group working as a unit.

Pr 3:8 This will bring health to your *b*
Ro 12:1 to offer your *b* as a living sacrifice,
1Co 6:19 not know that your *b* are temples
Eph 5:30 for we are members of his *b*.

bondage—slavery.

Ezr 9:9 God has not forsaken us in our *b*.

born again—refers to the experience of salvation; entering God's family through faith in Christ.

Jn 3:3 no one can see the kingdom of God unless they are *b*.
1Pe 1:23 For you have been *b*,

bow—a weapon made of a strip of flexible material with a cord connecting the two ends and holding the strip bent; used to shoot arrows.

branch—an extension of another body or system.

Jer 33:15 I will make a righteous *B* sprout
Jn 15:5 "I am the vine; you are the *b*.

bread—in Bible times the most important food in the diet.

Dt 8:3 that man does not live on *b* alone
Mt 6:11 Give us today our daily *b*.
Jn 6:35 Jesus declared, "I am the *b* of life.

breastpiece—a decorated square of linen cloth worn by the high priest when he entered the Holy Place.

breastplate—a chest-covering made of metal or leather, worn by soldiers for protection.

bribe—money or favor given to influence judgment or conduct.

Ex 23:8 "Do not accept a *b*,

bride—a woman who is about to get married. The church is called Jesus' bride.

bridegroom—a man who is about to get married. Christ is called the church's bridegroom.

bronze—a metal, the combination of copper and tin, used to make tools, weapons and ornamental articles.

brother—a male who has the same parents as another person.

Ge 4:9 "Am I my *b* keeper?"
Mt 18:15 "If your *b* or sister sins,
2Co 13:11 Finally, *b* and sisters, rejoice!

burden—a heavy load.

Mt 11:30 my yoke is easy and my *b* is light.
Gal 6:2 Carry each other's *b*,

burnt offering—in the Old Testament a sacrifice to the Lord that expressed devotion and complete surrender (Ge 8:20; Ex 29:18).

C

Caesar—the title of many Roman emperors.

Lk 2:1 In those days *C* Augustus
Mt 22:21 "Give back to *C* what is Caesar's,

Cain—Adam and Eve's firstborn son; he murdered his brother Abel (Ge 4:1–16).

calamity—a disaster, usually causing great loss and suffering.

Caleb—one of the twelve men who was sent to spy on Canaan. He came back with a positive report and encouraged the Israelites to take possession of Canaan (Nu 13:6–14:38; Dt 1:36).

call—1. (*v.*) to ask to come; 2. to give a name to; 3. (*n.*) a summons for a particular purpose or job.

2Ch 7:14 if my people, who are *c*
Ps 145:18 near to all who *c* on him,
Mt 9:13 not come to *c* the righteous,
Ro 8:30 And those he predestined, he also *c*;
Ro 11:29 gifts and his *c* are irrevocable.
1Pe 2:9 of him who *c* you out of darkness

camel—a large animal, able to travel long distances and used for transportation of people and goods.

Canaan—1. the land God promised to the nation of Israel; 2. the promised land.

capstone—the stone that holds two walls together; the stone that finishes a wall.

1Pe 2:7 has become the *c*,"

care—to show concern for.

Ps 8:4 human beings that you *c* for them?
1 Pe 5:7 on him because he *c* for you.

cavalry—a group of soldiers riding horses.

censer—a bowl or dish used for carrying hot coals or for burning incense.

census—a count of the population of a group of people.

centurion—a Roman army officer in charge of one hundred soldiers.

chaff—the seed covering of a grain such as wheat. In Bible times, the grain and chaff were separated by tossing the grain into the air so the wind could blow the chaff away.

Ps 1:4 They are like *c*
Mt 3:12 up the *c* with unquenchable fire."

chariot—a two-wheeled vehicle pulled by horses.

2Ki 6:17 and *c* of fire all around Elisha.

cheerful—full of joy; pleasant.

Pr 15:13 A happy heart makes the face *c*,
2Co 9:7 for God loves a *c* giver.

cherub (pl. cherubim)—an angel, with an appearance something like a human being.

children—sons and daughters.

Mt 19:14 "Let the little *c* come to me,
Eph 6:1 *C*, obey your parents in the Lord,
1Jn 3:1 that we should be called *c* of God!

choose (chosen)—to select.

Jos 24:15 then *c* for yourselves this day
Mt 22:14 "For many are invited, but few are *c*."
Jn 15:16 You did not *c* me,
Eph 1:4 he *c* us in him before the creation
1Pe 2:9 But you are a *c* people, a royal

Christ—the official title of Jesus, meaning "the Anointed One." It is a Greek word, and it means the same as the Hebrew word *Messiah*.

Jn 1:17 grace and truth came through Jesus *C*.
Ac 3:6 name of Jesus *C* of Nazareth, walk."
Ro 5:8 While we were still sinners, *C* died
Eph 5:23 as *C* is the head of the church,
Php 1:21 to live is *C* and to die is gain.

Christian—a believer in or follower of Christ.

Ac 11:26 The disciples were called *C* first
1Pe 4:16 as a *C*, do not be ashamed,

chronicles—a history of events in the order in which they took place.

church—the entire group of people who believe in Christ.

Mt 16:18 and on this rock I will build my *c*,
Eph 5:23 as Christ is the head of the *c*,
Col 1:24 the sake of his body, which is the *c*.

circumcision—the cutting off of the loose fold of skin at the end of the penis; it symbolized the agreement God made with the Israelites, and they came to be known as "the circumcision" (Eph 2:11).

Ge 17:10 Every male among you shall be *c*.

cistern—a pit dug into the ground for storing rainwater.

citadel—a tower or building, especially in a city, equipped for war.

city of refuge—one of six cities set aside by Moses and Joshua for those who had accidentally killed someone. Such people would be safe there until a fair trial could be held (Nu 35:9–15).

clan—a group of people belonging to the same extended family.

Ge 24:38 to my father's family and to my own *c*,
Zec 12:12 The land will mourn, each *c* by itself,

clean animals—animals God allowed the Israelites to sacrifice and eat.

cleanse—to make clean; to wash.

cloak—a loose-fitting coat without sleeves.

comfort—to relieve from distress; to console.

Ps 23:4 rod and your staff, they *c* me.
2Co 1:4 so that we can *c* those

commandment—an order given by God. God gave the Ten Commandments to the Israelites while they were encamped in the area of Mount Sinai.

Ex 20:6 who love me and keep my *c*.
Ecc 12:13 Fear God and keep his *c*,
Mt 22:38 This is the first and greatest *c*.

commend—1. to praise; 2. to hand over to someone for safekeeping.

Ps 145:4 One generation *c* your works

companion—one who is a friend or associate or helper.

compassion (compassionate)—sympathy; pity.

Ne 9:17 gracious and *c*, slow to anger
Ps 103:4 and crowns you with love and *c*,
Mt 9:36 When he saw the crowds, he had *c*
Ro 9:15 and I will have *c* on whom I have *c*."
Col 3:12 clothe yourselves with *c*, kindness,

conceive—1. to become pregnant; 2. to think up or imagine.

Mt 1:20 what is *c* in her is from the Holy
1Co 2:9 no human mind has *c*

concubine—in Bible times, a woman who belonged to a man but did not have the rights of a wife. She was often one of the spoils of war, and her primary purpose was to bear children for the man.

condemn (condemnation)—to punish; to pronounce guilty.

Jn 3:17 Son into the world to *c* the world,
Ro 8:1 there is now no *c* for those who are

confess—1. to say what you believe; 2. to tell your sins to someone.

2Ti 2:19 "Everyone who *c* the name of the Lord
1Jn 1:9 If we *c* our sins, he is faithful

conform—to agree with and try to be like someone; to do what others say to do.

Ro 8:29 predestined to be *c* to the image
1Pe 1:14 do not *c* to the evil desires you had

conscience—the sense of knowing if something is good or bad; a sense of right and wrong.

Ro 2:15 their *c* also bearing witness,
Tit 1:15 their minds and *c* are corrupted.
Heb 9:14 cleanse our *c* from acts that lead

consecrate—to set aside or dedicate for God's use.

Ex 13:2 "*C* to me every firstborn male.
Lev 20:7 "*C* yourselves and be holy,

consider—to think about carefully.

Ps 8:3 When I *c* your heavens,

console—to comfort.

conspire—to plan together to do wrong.

consult—to ask the advice or opinion of someone.

consume—1. to use up or eat up; 2. to destroy completely.

Jn 2:17 "Zeal for your house will *c* me."
Heb 12:29 for our "God is a *c* fire."

contempt—lack of respect; looking down on someone or something as being worthless.

Pr 14:31 Whoever oppresses the poor shows *c*
1Th 5:20 Do not treat prophecies with *c*

contend—to struggle, as in a contest or against difficulties.

content—satisfied.

Php 4:11 to be *c* whatever the circumstances.
Heb 13:5 and be *c* with what you have,

contrite—to feel sorry for one's sins; to feel repentant.

Ps 51:17 a broken and *c* heart,
Isa 66:2 those who are humble and *c* in spirit,

convert—a person who has changed from one belief to another.

1Ti 3:6 He must not be a recent *c*,

convict—1. to prove one guilty; 2. to make a person feel sorrow.

Jas 2:9 and are *c* by the law as lawbreakers.

copper—a common metal, easy to work with; often used to make coins.

Cornelius—a Roman to whom Peter preached the gospel; he became the first Gentile Christian (Ac 10).

cornerstone—the first or most important stone laid when constructing a building.

Eph 2:20 with Christ Jesus himself as the chief *c*.

corrupt—1. (*v.*) to change something from good to bad; 2. (*adj.*) wicked.

Ge 6:11 Now the earth was *c* in God's sight
1Co 15:33 "Bad company *c* good character."

counsel—to give advice to.

Pr 15:22 Plans fail for lack of *c*,

covenant—1. an agreement between two people or two groups of people, in which both usually make specific promises; 2. the promises of God for salvation.

Ge 9:9 "I now establish my *c* with you
Ex 19:5 if you obey me fully and keep my *c*,
Jer 31:31 "when I will make a new *c*
1Co 11:25 "This cup is the new *c* in my blood;
Heb 9:15 Christ is the mediator of a new *c*,

covet—to want for oneself something that belongs to another person.

Ex 20:17 "You shall not *c* your neighbor's

crafty—sly, clever.

Ge 3:1 Now the serpent was more *c*

crave—to desire strongly; to feel a deep need for.

1Pe 2:2 newborn babies, *c* pure spiritual

create—to make; to bring into being.

Ge 1:1	In the beginning God *c* the heavens
Ps 51:10	*C* in me a pure heart, O God,
Col 1:16	For in him all things were *c*:
Rev 10:6	who *c* the heavens and all that is

crime—an unlawful act.

criminal—someone who commits an unlawful act.

Lk 23:32	Two other men, both *c*,

cripple—a disabled person or animal.

cross—a tall beam with a crossbar on which a criminal was hung or tied to die.

Mt 10:38	Whoever does not take up their *c*
Gal 6:14	in the *c* of our Lord Jesus Christ,
Php 2:8	even death on a *c!*
Col 2:14	taken it away, nailing it to the *c*.
Heb 12:2	set before him he endured the *c*,

crown—a headpiece worn to symbolize glory, honor and victory.

1Co 9:25	it to get a *c* that will last forever.
2Ti 4:8	store for me the *c* of righteousness,
Rev 2:10	life as your victor's crown.

crucify—to put to death by nailing or tying a person's body to a cross.

Mt 27:22	They all answered, "*C* him!"
1Co 1:23	but we preach Christ *c*: a stumbling
Gal 2:20	I have been *c* with Christ

cruel—causing envy, grief or pain.

cubit—a measure of length in Bible times; about 18 inches.

cupbearer—an officer of considerable responsibility who tasted the king's food and wine before serving them to him (Ne 1:11).

curse—1. (*v.*) to ask God to bring evil or injury to; 2. (*n.*) a prayer or desire that evil or injury come upon someone.

Lev 20:9	"Anyone who *c* their father or mother
Lk 6:28	bless those who *c* you, pray
Gal 3:13	"*C* is everyone who is hung on a pole."

custom—a practice common to a particular place or group of people.

Mk 15:6	Now it was the *c* at the festival
Ac 17:2	As was his *c*, Paul went into the synagogue

cymbals—a musical instrument; round metal disks either struck with a stick or struck together to produce a clanging sound.

cypress—an evergreen tree of the pine family.

D

Daniel—a young Jewish exile; he lived in Babylon during the reign of several kings, including Nebuchadnezzar. He prayed to God rather than obey an order to pray only to the king and was thrown into a lion's den (Da 1–6).

daughter—a female descendant.

Job 1:2	He had seven sons and three *d*,

David—the son of Jesse; anointed by Samuel to become king of Israel (1Sa 16:1–13); killed the giant Goliath (1Sa 17); during his reign Israel's place in the land of Canaan was made secure.

day—1. the period of time between dawn and darkness; 2. a specified time.

Ge 1:5	God called the light "*d*,"
Ecc 12:1	Creator in the *d* of your youth,
Joel 2:31	and dreadful *d* of the LORD.
Mic 4:1	In the last *d*
Lk 11:3	Give us each *d* our daily bread.
Lk 18:33	On the third *d* he will rise
Heb 1:2	in these last *d* he has spoken to us
2Pe 3:8	With the Lord a *d* is like

deacon—a church officer whose qualifications are given in 1 Ti 3:8–13.

death—the end of physical life; also the penalty for sin (Ro 6:23).

Ecc 7:2	for *d* is the destiny of everyone;
Isa 25:8	he will swallow up *d* forever.
1Co 15:21	For since *d* came through a man,
1Co 15:55	Where, O *d*, is your sting?"
Rev 21:4	There will be no more *d*

debauchery—living an immoral life or a life without religion; living to please only oneself.

Deborah—a prophetess who led Israel to victory over the Canaanites (Jdg 4—5).

debt—something that one person owes another.

Mt 6:12	And forgive us our *d*,

deceive—to fool or trick; to lie.

Ge 3:13	"The serpent *d* me, and I ate."
Gal 6:7	Do not be *d*: God cannot be
1Jn 1:8	we *d* ourselves and the truth is not

declare—to make known formally; to state forcefully.

Ps 19:1	The heavens *d* the glory of God;
Eph 6:20	Pray that I may *d* it fearlessly,

decree—1. (*v.*) to order or command; 2. (*n.*) an order or law given by someone with power and authority.

dedicate—to set apart for a special purpose, often for God's use.

defect—imperfection; fault.

defile—to make something that is good and pure into something impure or unclean.

defraud—to cheat someone by trickery.

Deity—God.

Col 2:9	of the *D* lives in bodily form,

delight—something that gives great pleasure.

Ps 119:47	for I *d* in your commands
Mt 12:18	the one I love, in whom I *d*;

deliver—to rescue; to set free.

demon—evil spirit. A demon-possessed person is one who is controlled by evil spirits.

Mk 5:15	possessed by the legion of *d*,
Jas 2:19	Good! Even the *d* believe that

denarius—a small Roman coin made of silver. During Jesus' earthly ministry, one denarius was the payment for about one day's work.

denounce—to say a person or thing is evil.

deposit—something pledged or given as part of the payment.

Eph 1:14	who is a *d* guaranteeing our

depraved (depravity)—evil or sinful.

2Ti 3:8 They are men of *d* minds,
2Pe 2:19 they themselves are slaves of *d*

deprive—to take something away from.

Am 5:12 and *d* the poor of justice

depths—the deepest part of a thing.

Ps 130:1 Out of the *d* I cry
La 3:55 from the *d* of the pit.

descendant—a member of a particular family line.

desecrate—to treat without respect or reverence.

desolate—not lived in; lonely; deserted.

despise—to look down on with contempt.

Pr 1:7 but fools *d* wisdom
Tit 2:15 Do not let anyone *d* you.

destiny—a predetermined course of events.

Php 3:19 Their *d* is destruction,

destitute—not having necessary things such as money and food.

destroy—to ruin completely.

detest—to hate.

devastate—to bring to ruin by violent action.

Jer 19:8 I will *d* this city

devil—the great enemy of God and tempter of people.

Lk 4:2 forty days he was tempted by the *d*.
Eph 6:11 stand against the *d* schemes.
2Ti 2:26 and escape from the trap of the *d*,
Jas 4:7 Resist the *d*, and he will flee
1Pe 5:8 Your enemy the *d* prowls

devote—to set apart for a special person or for a special reason; to set apart for God's use.

devour—1. to eat up greedily; 2. to destroy.

1Pe 5:8 looking for someone to *d*.

devout—religious; giving much time to prayer and worship.

die—1. to lose life; 2. to become insensitive to, as to die to the law (Gal 2:19).

Ge 2:17 when you eat from it you will certainly *d*."
Ecc 3:2 a time to be born and a time to *d*,
Eze 18:4 one who sins is the one who will *d*.
Jn 11:26 by believing in me will never *d*.
1Co 15:22 in Adam all *d*, so in Christ all will
Php 1:21 to live is Christ and to *d* is gain.

diligence (diligent)—characterized by hard work or earnest effort.

disaster—a sudden event bringing great damage, loss or destruction.

Dt 31:29 *d* will fall on you

discern—to understand; to come to know the difference between two or more things.

Php 1:10 you may be able to *d* what is best

disciple—a follower or student, especially one who believes what the leader teaches. Anyone who believes in Jesus is his disciple.

Lk 14:27 and follow me cannot be my *d*.
Jn 13:35 everyone will know that you are my *d*,

discipline—1. (*v.*) to correct; to teach what is right; 2. (*n.*) training that corrects, molds or perfects moral character.

Pr 29:17 *D* your children, and they will give you
Heb 12:6 the Lord *d* the one he loves,
Rev 3:19 Those whom I love I rebuke and *d*.

disgrace—to bring shame to.

disobey (disobedient)—to fail to obey.

1Pe 2:8 because they *d* the message

disown—to reject someone or something so completely that it no longer belongs to you.

Mt 26:34 you will *d* me three times."
2Ti 2:12 If we *d* him,

disperse—to scatter; to spread around.

dispute—to argue irritably.

dissension—disagreement; quarreling.

distress—suffering, misery, agony.

Ps 57:6 I was bowed down in *d*.
Ro 2:9 There will be trouble and *d*

divination—seeing into the future by magic.

Lev 19:26 "Do not practice *d* or seek omens.

divine—given by God; belonging to God.

Ro 1:20 his eternal power and *d* nature

divorce—to legally dissolve a marriage.

Mal 2:16 who hates and *d* his wife,"
Mt 19:3 for a man to *d* his wife for any
1Co 7:11 And a husband must not *d* his wife.

doctrine—teachings or beliefs about God.

1Ti 4:16 Watch your life and *d* closely.
Tit 2:1 what is appropriate to sound *d*.

dominion—power; rule.

Ps 22:28 for *d* belongs to the LORD
Eph 1:21 far above all rule and authority, power and *d*,

doom—1. (*v.*) to make certain something will fail or be destroyed; 2. (*n.*) fate; condemnation; ruin.

Rev 18:10 In one hour your *d* has come!'

door—a barrier that can be opened and closed; Christians open the doors of their hearts to Jesus.

Mt 7:7 and the *d* will be opened to you.
Rev 3:20 I stand at the *d* and knock.

doubt—uncertainty.

Mt 21:21 if you have faith and do not *d*,
Mk 11:23 and does not *d* in their heart
Jas 1:6 you must believe and not *d*,

dread—great fear.

dream—thoughts, images or emotion occurring during sleep; God sometimes spoke to his people through dreams.

Da 2:4 Tell your servants the *d*,

dross—the impure scum that floats on the surface of molten metals; sometimes used as a picture of the wicked.

Ps 119:119 you discard like *d*;

drought—a long period of time without rain.

drunkard—a person who is often or usually drunk.

Pr 23:21 for *d* and gluttons become poor,

dwelling—place in which people live; house; in Scripture usually refers to the place where God lives.

1Ki 8:30 Hear from heaven, your *d* place,
Ps 84:1 How lovely is your *d* place,

E

earth—the place that God created for human beings to live.

Ge 1:1 God created the heavens and the *e*.
Ps 24:1 *e* is the LORD's, and everything
Mt 6:10 done, on *e* as it is in heaven.
Mt 24:35 Heaven and *e* will pass away,
Lk 2:14 on *e* peace to those
Php 2:10 in heaven and on *e* and under the *e*,
2Pe 3:13 to a new heaven and a new *e*,

Eden—the location of the beautiful garden God created for Adam and Eve.

edict—an order or law made by a person who has the power to enforce it.

Est 2:8 the king's order and *e*

edify—to teach someone to live a godly life, or to help someone to live in such a way.

1Co 14:4 but the one who prophesies *e* the church.

Egypt—one of the most powerful nations of ancient times, located in the northeast corner of Africa; the Israelites were captives in Egypt at the beginning of the book of Exodus.

elders—1. the older men of a town or nation; they were the leaders of their community and made all the important decisions; 2. the leaders of the church.

1Ti 5:17 The *e* who direct the affairs
Tit 1:5 and appoint *e* in every town,

election—the choosing of Christians by God, as people who belong to him. Christians are called "the elect" (2Ti 2:10).

Ro 9:11 God's purpose in *e* might stand:
2Pe 1:10 to confirm your calling and *e*.

Eli—the high priest with whom Samuel spent the early years of his life (1Sa 2:11–26).

Elijah—a prophet of the Lord who predicted a famine in Israel (1Ki 17:1) and defeated the prophets of Baal in the test of whose God would set fire to the altar (1Ki 18:16–46).

Elisha—the prophet who succeeded Elijah. He was present when God took Elijah to heaven, and he took his place as prophet to Israel (2Ki 2:1–18).

Elizabeth—the mother of John the Baptist. Mary went to visit her when she found out she, too, was pregnant (Lk 1:5–58).

enchanter—a magician or snake charmer.

encourage—to inspire with courage or hope.

2Sa 19:7 Now go out and *e* your men.
1Th 4:18 Therefore *e* one another with these words.

endure—to continue; to keep on going; to bear something that is difficult or painful.

Ps 136:1 His love *e* forever.
Mal 3:2 who can *e* the day of his coming?
1Co 10:13 so that you can *e* it.

enemy—a person who opposes another person or a cause.

Mt 5:44 Love your *e* and pray
Php 3:18 many live as *e* of the cross of Christ.

enjoy—to take pleasure in.

Jdg 19:9 Stay and *e* yourself.
Jer 33:6 and will let them *e* abundant peace
3Jn 2 I pray that you may *e* good health

enmity—a feeling of antagonism, hostility or hatred.

Ge 3:15 put *e* between you and the woman,

Enoch—a man who "walked with God." Later in life, God "took him away" (Ge 5:18–24).

entice—to tempt or lure.

envoy—a person who represents one government in its dealings with another.

envy—to want for oneself something that belongs to another person.

1Co 13:4 It does not *e*, it does not boast,

ephod—a linen apron worn by a priest over his robe. It was decorated with gold, blue, purple and scarlet yarns.

Ephraim—1. one of Joseph's sons; 2. the tribe of Israel whose members were descendants of Ephraim; 3. a name for the northern kingdom of Israel after the ten tribes of Israel and the two tribes of Judah separated from each other.

Esau—the firstborn son of Isaac and twin of Jacob (Ge 25:21–26). He sold his birthright to Jacob for a pot of stew (Ge 25:29–34) and was tricked out of his blessing by this same brother (Ge 27).

esteem—1. (*v.*) to value; to consider important; 2. (*n.*) high regard or respect.

Pr 22:1 to be *e* is better than silver or gold.
Isa 53:3 and we held him in low *e*.

Esther—a Jewish woman who lived in Persia (Est 2:7) and became queen (Est 2:8–18). Upon being told of a plot to kill the Jews, she went to the king and pleaded for the Jewish people and thus saved them (Est 3—4; 7—9).

eternal—without beginning or end; forever; timeless.

Dt 33:27 The *e* God is your refuge,
Jn 3:16 him shall not perish but have *e* life.
Ro 6:23 but the gift of God is *e* life
1Jn 5:13 you may know that you have *e* life.

eunuch—a man whose sex organs have been removed so that he cannot produce children. Often in Bible times these men were important officials in royal palaces.

Eve—the first woman God created (Ge 2:20–24). Her name means "mother of all the living" (Ge 3:20).

everlasting—forever; without end.

Ps 90:2 from *e* to *e* you are God.
Isa 9:6 *E* Father, Prince of Peace.
Isa 55:3 I will make an *e* covenant with you,
2Th 1:9 punished with *e* destruction

evil—wicked; doing things against God's will.

Ge 2:9 of the knowledge of good and *e*.
Ps 23:4 I will fear no *e*,

Mt 6:13 but deliver us from the *e* one.
Ro 12:9 Hate what is *e*; cling
Ro 12:17 Do not repay anyone *e* for *e*.
Eph 6:16 all the flaming arrows of the *e* one.

exalt—to praise; to raise to an important position.

Ps 118:28 you are my God, and I will *e* you.
Ps 148:13 for his name alone is *e*;
Pr 14:34 Righteousness *e* a nation,
Mt 23:12 For those who *e* themselves

examine—to look over carefully; to test.

1Co 11:28 Everyone ought to *e* themselves

exclaim—to cry out or speak in sudden or strong emotion.

Lk 1:42 In a loud voice she *e*: "Blessed

exclude—to leave out.

execute—to put to death, especially as punishment for an illegal act.

Lk 23:32 were also led out with him to be *e*.

exile—1. (*v.*) to force someone to leave his or her country or home; 2. (*n.*) forced removal from one's country or home.

Ezr 6:19 the *e* celebrated the Passover.
1Pe 1:1 To God's elect, *e* scattered

exodus—the departure of a large group of people from one place to go to another. The book of Exodus is the story of the Israelites' journey from Egypt to Canaan.

exploit—to take unfair advantage of.

Pr 22:22 Do not *e* the poor

extol—to praise.

Ps 34:1 I will *e* the LORD at all times;
Ps 95:2 and *e* him with music and song.

extortion—something gotten from a person by force or by using other illegal means.

Ezekiel—a priest who was called to be a prophet to the Jewish people when they were in exile in Babylon (Eze 1—3). He had many visions from the Lord (Eze 37; 40).

Ezra—a priest and teacher of the Law; he led a group of Jewish exiles back to Israel and helped them reestablish the temple of God and restore proper worship (Ezr 7—8).

F

fail—to be unsuccessful.

Ecc 6:6 but *f* to enjoy his prosperity.
1Co 13:8 Love never *f*.

faint—1. (*adj.*) lacking courage; 2. (*v.*) to lose courage.

Ps 142:3 When my spirit grows *f* within me,
Lk 21:26 People will *f* from terror,

faith—belief and trust in God; knowing that God is real, even though one can't see him.

Mt 17:20 if you have *f* as small as a mustard
Lk 7:9 I have not found such great *f*
Ro 1:17 "The righteous will live by *f*."
Ro 3:22 given through *f* in Jesus Christ
1Co 13:2 and if I have a *f* that can move
2Co 5:7 we live by *f*, not by sight.
Eph 6:16 to all this, take up the shield of *f*,
1Ti 6:12 Fight the good fight of the *f*.
Heb 11:1 *f* is confidence in what we hope for
Heb 11:8 By *f* Abraham, when called to go
Heb 12:2 the pioneer and perfecter of *f*
Jas 2:26 so *f* without deeds is dead.

faithful (faithfulness)—trustworthy; loyal.

Ps 145:13 and *f* in all he does.
La 3:23 great is your *f*.
Mt 25:21 'Well done, good and *f* servant!
Ro 12:12 patient in affliction, *f* in prayer.
1Co 10:13 And God is *f*; he will not let you
1Jn 1:9 he is *f* and just and will forgive us
Rev 1:5 who is the *f* witness, the firstborn

false (falsehood)—a lie.

Ex 20:16 "You shall not give *f* testimony

family—a group of people who are related to each other.

Ps 68:6 God sets the lonely in *f*,
Lk 9:61 go back and say goodbye to my *f*."
1Ti 3:4 He must manage his own *f* well

famine—1. a time when there is not enough food; 2. any severe shortage.

Am 8:11 but a *f* of hearing the words
Mt 24:7 There will be *f* and earthquakes

fast—1. (*adj.*) firmly fixed; not movable; 2. (*v.*) to go without food for a period of time.

Ps 139:10 your right hand will hold me *f*.
Mt 6:16 "When you *f*, do not look somber

father—a male parent; God is also known as one's father.

Ge 2:24 why a man leaves his *f*
Ge 17:4 You will be the *f* of many nations.
Ex 20:12 "Honor your *f* and your mother,
Mt 6:9 " 'Our *F* in heaven,
Lk 11:11 "Which of you *f*, if your son asks
Jn 10:30 I and the *F* are one."
Jn 14:6 No one comes to the *F*

favor—goodwill; a positive attitude toward another person.

1Sa 20:3 I have found *f* in your eyes,

fear—(*v.*) 1. to respect highly; to feel reverence and awe for; 2. to be afraid of; (*n.*) 1. profound reverence toward God; 2. anticipation or awareness of danger.

Dt 6:13 *F* the LORD your God, serve him
Ps 91:5 You will not *f* the terror of night,
Ps 111:10 *f* of the LORD is the beginning
Isa 41:10 So do not *f*, for I am with you;
Php 2:12 to work out your salvation with *f*

fellowship—companionship or friendship.

1Jn 1:6 claim to have *f* with him yet walk
1Jn 1:7 we have *f* with one another,

fertile—producing fruit in great quantities; productive.

Nu 13:20 How is the soil? Is it *f* or poor?

festival—a religious celebration.

Nu 29:12 Celebrate a *f* to the LORD

Ezr 6:22 with joy the *F* of Unleavened Bread,
Jn 4:45 in Jerusalem at the Passover *F*,

fig—1. a brownish pear-shaped fruit that grows in countries near the Mediterranean Sea; 2. the tree that grows this fruit.

Joel 2:22 the *f* tree and the vine yield their riches.

firstborn—a family's first child. The firstborn son in an Israelite family became the head of the family when his father died, and he received twice as much money and property as each of his brothers.

Ex 11:5 Every *f* son in Egypt will die,

firstfruits—the first vegetables, fruits and grains harvested from the field.

Ex 23:19 "Bring the best of the *f* of your soil

flesh—1. the soft parts of the bodies of humans and animals; 2. the believer's sinful nature.

Job 6:12 Is my *f* bronze?
Php 3:3 put no confidence in the *f*
Ro 8:13 live according to the *f*, you will die;
Ro 13:14 gratify the desires of the *f*.

flock—a collection of sheep under the care of a shepherd.

Ps 65:13 The meadows are covered with *f*
Isa 40:11 He tends his *f* like a shepherd:

flog—to beat with a stick or a whip.

flood—a large amount of water that covers the ground, as in the time of Noah (Ge 6—8).

foe—an enemy.

Ps 61:3 a strong tower against the *f*.

folly—foolishness; the lack of wisdom.

Pr 26:5 Answer a fool according to his *f*,
2Ti 3:9 their *f* will be clear to everyone.

fool—a person who is not wise.

Ps 14:1 The *f* says in his heart,
Lk 12:20 "But God said to him, 'You *f*!

forbearance—patient endurance; self-control; not enforcing a right.

Gal 5:22 love, joy, peace, *f*, kindness,

forefather—a male ancestor.

forever—for a limitless time.

Dt 32:40 As surely as I live *f*,
Ps 136:1 His love endures *f*.

forgive—to pardon or excuse; to no longer blame or be angry with someone who has done you wrong.

Mt 6:14 For if you *f* other people
Lk 23:34 Jesus said, "Father, *f* them,
Col 3:13 *F* as the Lord forgave you.
1Jn 1:9 and just and will *f* us our sins

forsake—to leave another completely alone; to abandon

Jos 1:5 I will never leave you nor *f* you.
Isa 55:7 Let the wicked *f* their ways
Mt 27:46 my God, why have you *f* me?"

fortified—to make strong, such as a town with a wall.

fortress—a city that is fortified.

fragrance (fragrant)—a sweet or pleasant odor.

SS 4:10 the *f* of your perfume
Php 4:18 They are a *f* offering,

free (freedom)—not bound; liberated.

Jn 8:32 and the truth will set you *f*."
Ro 6:18 You have been set *f* from sin
2Co 3:17 the Spirit of the Lord is, there is *f*.

friend—a person who loves and respects another person.

Pr 18:24 there is a *f* who sticks closer
Jn 15:13 to lay down one's life for one's *f*.
Jas 4:4 Anyone who chooses to be a *f*

fruitful—productive; yielding much fruit.

Ge 1:22 "Be *f* and increase in number
Jn 15:2 prunes so that it will be even more *f*.

fulfill (fulfillment)—to complete a promise or project.

Ps 116:14 I will *f* my vows to the LORD
Mk 14:49 But the Scriptures must be *f*."
Ro 13:10 Therefore love is the *f* of the law.

fury—intense anger.

Pr 6:34 jealousy arouses a husband's *f*,

G

Gabriel—the angel who announced the births of John the Baptist and Jesus (Lk 1:11–20, 26–38).

Galilee—the northern part of Palestine. Jesus grew up, preached and did most of his miracles there. Today this area is in northern Israel.

gall—1. a plant with an extremely bitter-tasting fruit; 2. the liquid made by the liver.

Mt 27:34 mixed with *g*; but after tasting it,

genealogy—a list of a person's ancestors or descendants; a family tree.

generation—the entire number of people born and living at about the same time. Grandparents, parents and children are three different generations.

Ps 102:12 your renown endures through all *g*.
Lk 1:48 now on all *g* will call me blessed,

Gentile—anyone who is not a Jew.

Ro 3:9 and *G* alike are all under
Ro 11:13 as I am the apostle to the *G*,

Gideon—a judge who freed Israel from the rule and terror of the Midianites (Jdg 6—8). He asked for a sign from God, and God showed him his will by means of dew and a fleece (Jdg 6:36–40).

gift—1. a present; 2. a talent or ability.

Ro 6:23 but the *g* of God is eternal life
1Co 12:4 There are different kinds of *g*,
2Co 9:15 be to God for his indescribable *g*!

glean—to pick up the grain or fruit left behind after harvesting; usually a way for the poor to get food.

Ruth 2:8 Don't go and *g* in another field

gloat—to look at or think about something or someone with malicious satisfaction.

Mic 7:8 Do not *g* over me, my enemy!

glorify—to praise and honor in worship.

Ps 34:3 *G* the LORD with me;
Jn 17:1 *G* your Son, that your Son may

glory—1. honor; praise; 2. a source of pride or worthiness.

Ps 8:5 and crowned them with *g* and honor.
Ps 19:1 The heavens declare the *g* of God;
Lk 2:14 "*G* to God in the highest heaven,
Jn 1:14 We have seen his *g*, the *g* of the one
1Co 10:31 whatever you do, do it all for the *g*
Rev 4:11 to receive *g* and honor and power,

glutton—a person who eats too much.

Dt 21:20 He is a *g* and a drunkard."

gnash—to grind (one's teeth) together.

Mt 8:12 there will be weeping and *g* of teeth."

goat—an animal raised for its meat and milk; sometimes used in religious sacrifices.

God—the supreme creator and the powerful force of the universe; the one who is to be worshiped.

Ge 1:1 In the beginning *G* created
Ex 20:5 the LORD your *G*, am a jealous *G*,
Nu 23:19 *G* is not human, that he should lie,
Dt 6:4 LORD our *G*, the LORD is one.
Dt 6:5 Love the LORD your *G*
Ps 46:1 *G* is our refuge and strength,
Jn 1:18 ever seen *G*, but the one
Jn 3:16 For *G* so loved the world that he
Jn 4:24 *G* is spirit, and his worshipers must
1Jn 4:16 *G* is love.
Rev 4:8 holy is the Lord *G* Almighty,

godly—to be devoted and loving toward God, wanting to do his will.

1Ti 4:7 train yourself to be *g*.
2Pe 3:11 live holy and *g* lives

Golgotha—the hill outside Jerusalem where Jesus was hung on a cross.

Goliath—the Philistine giant who was killed by David (1Sa 17; 21:9).

gospel—1. the good news that Jesus died for sins and rose again; 2. any of the first four books of the New Testament.

Ro 1:16 I am not ashamed of the *g*,
1Co 9:16 Woe to me if I do not preach the *g!*
1Co 15:2 By this *g* you are saved,

gossip—to talk too much about others, especially in a way that is hurtful.

2Co 12:20 slander, *g*, arrogance and disorder.

grace—an undeserved favor or gift; the undeserved forgiveness, kindness and mercy that God gives us.

Ro 3:24 all are justified freely by his *g*
Ro 5:20 where sin increased, *g* increased all
2Co 12:9 "My *g* is sufficient for you,
Eph 2:5 it is by *g* you have been saved.
Tit 3:7 having been justified by his *g*,

greed—selfish desire for more money or possessions than one needs.

Lk 12:15 on your guard against all kinds of *g*;
Col 3:5 evil desires and *g*, which is idolatry.

grieve—to cause someone pain or sorrow.

Jn 16:20 You will *g*, but your grief will turn
Eph 4:30 do not *g* the Holy Spirit of God,

guarantee—a pledge that something will take place.

Eph 1:14 who is a deposit *g* our inheritance

guardian-redeemer—in Old Testament times a close male relative who had the responsibility to marry a widow and buy her husband's property (Dt 25:5–6).

Ruth 3:9 since you are a *g* of our family.

guide—to direct or point out the way.

Ps 23:3 He *g* me along the right paths

guilty—deserving punishment for having broken a law or commandment.

Ex 34:7 does not leave the *g* unpunished;
Heb 10:22 to cleanse us from a *g* conscience
Jas 2:10 at just one point is *g* of breaking all

H

Hades—hell; the place where the spirits of the dead live.

Mt 16:18 the gates of *H* will not overcome it.

Hagar—a slave of Sarah and one of Abraham's wives; the mother of Ishmael (Ge 16:1–6; 25:12).

Haggai—a prophet who encouraged the Israelites returning from exile in Babylon to rebuild the temple (Ezr 5:1; Hag 1—2).

hallelujah—praise the Lord; a song of praise.

Rev 19:1 "*H!* Salvation and glory and power

hallowed—holy; sacred.

Mt 6:9 *h* be your name,

Ham—the youngest of Noah's three sons (Ge 5:32).

Hannah—she prayed for a son, and God gave her Samuel. She dedicated him to God; he lived in the temple as a boy and became a prophet and judge (1Sa 1—2).

harp—a musical instrument with twelve strings for strumming; frequently used in religious ceremonies.

Ps 71:22 I will praise you with the *h*

harvest—the season for gathering in crops.

Ge 8:22 "As long as the earth endures, seedtime and *h*,

hate—to detest, to have extreme dislike for.

Ps 5:5 You *h* all who do wrong;
Mk 13:13 Everyone will *h* you because of me,

haughty—proud.

Pr 16:18 a *h* spirit before a fall.

heal—to make well again.

Lk 8:43 but no one could *h* her.
Ac 28:27 and I would *h* them.'

heart—the center of a person's life, including the mind, the will and the emotions.

Dt 6:5 LORD your God with all your *h*
1Sa 16:7 but the LORD looks at the *h*."
Ps 51:10 Create in me a pure *h*, O God,
Ps 119:11 I have hidden your word in my *h*
Ps 139:23 Search me, O God, and know my *h*;

Eze 36:26 I will give you a new *h*
Mt 5:8 Blessed are the pure in *h*,

heaven—1. the place where God lives; 2. the sky.

Ge 14:19 Creator of *h* and earth.
Mt 19:23 to enter the kingdom of *h*.
Lk 24:51 and was taken up into *h*.
Php 3:20 But our citizenship is in *h*.
Rev 21:1 Then I saw "a new *h* and a new earth,"

Hebrew—1. another name for an Israelite; a descendant of Abraham; 2. the language spoken by the Jews. The Old Testament was written in Hebrew.

heir—someone who receives the property or blessings of a person who has died.

Ro 8:17 then we are *h*—*h* of God
Eph 3:6 gospel the Gentiles are *h* together

herd—a large number of animals of one kind kept together in a group.

Herod—the family name of five kings who ruled Palestine under the Roman emperor: Herod the Great (Mt 2:16); Herod Antipas (Mk 6:14–29); Herod Philip (Mt 14:3; Mk 6:17); Herod Agrippa I (Ac 12:1–4,19–23); Herod Agrippa II (Ac 23:35; 25:13–26:32).

Herodias—the wife of Herod Antipas; she persuaded her daughter to ask Antipas for the head of John the Baptist (Mk 6:17).

Hezekiah—a king of Judah; he restored the temple, reinstituted proper worship and sought the Lord's help against the Assyrians.

high priest—the chief religious official in the Jewish religion. In the Old Testament he offered the most important sacrifices to God in behalf of the people.

Heb 4:14 a great high *p* who has ascended
Heb 7:26 a high *p* truly meets our need

hinder—to hold back; to prevent; to delay.

Mt 19:14 come to me, and do not *h* them,

holy—set apart for God; belonging to God; pure; godly.

Ex 20:8 the Sabbath day by keeping it *h*.
Lev 11:44 and be *h*, because I am *h*.
Isa 6:3 "*H*, *h*, *h* is the LORD Almighty;
Ro 12:1 as a living sacrifice, *h* and pleasing
Rev 4:8 "*H*, *h*, *h* is the Lord God Almighty,

Holy Spirit—the third person of the Trinity; he lives and works in the hearts and minds of believers; he came at Pentecost in a powerful way (Ac 2). Other names are: the Spirit, Counselor and Comforter.

Ps 51:11 or take your *H* from me.
Jn 14:26 But the Advocate, the *H*,
Jn 20:22 and said, "Receive the *H*.
Ac 2:4 of them were filled with the *H*
Gal 5:22 But the fruit of the *S* is love, joy,

honor—to show respect to; to give credit to.

Ex 20:12 "*H* your father and your mother,
Ps 8:5 and crowned them with glory and *h*.

hope—the anticipation of something good.

Ps 42:5 Put your *h* in God,
Isa 40:31 but those who *h* in the LORD
Ro 8:24 But *h* that is seen is no *h* at all.
1Co 15:19 for this life we have *h* in Christ,
Heb 11:1 faith is confidence in what we *h* for

hordes—a loosely organized or disorderly crowd of people; usually committing harmful acts.

Hab 1:9 Their *h* advance like a desert wind

horror—strong and painful fear or dread.

Jer 8:21 I mourn, and *h* grips me.

hosanna—a Hebrew word of praise meaning "save."

Mt 21:9 "*H* in the highest heaven!"

hospitality—welcoming people into one's home; sharing one's home and food with others.

Ro 12:13 Practice *h*.
1Pe 4:9 Offer *h* to one another

hostile—like an enemy; unfriendly.

human—like people rather than animals, in actions or thoughts or appearance.

humble—1. (*v.*) to make lower; 2. (*adj.*) not proud; not pretending to be important.

Ps 147:6 The LORD sustains the *h*
Mt 23:12 who exalt themselves will be *h*,
Jas 4:10 *H* yourselves before the Lord,

humiliate—to make humble; to reduce to a lower position; to make ashamed.

1Co 11:22 by *h* those who have nothing?

humility—the absence of pride.

Php 2:3 but in *h* value others above
1Pe 5:5 clothe yourselves with *h*

hymn—a song of praise to God.

Eph 5:19 with psalms, *h*, and songs

hypocrite—a person who pretends to be better than he or she is.

Mt 6:5 when you pray, do not be like the *h*,
Mt 7:5 You *h*, first take the plank out

hyssop—a plant used to sprinkle water or blood for religious cleansing.

Ps 51:7 with *h*, and I will be clean;

I

idle—1. lacking worth or basis; 2. lazy.

Dt 32:47 They are not just *i* words
1Th 5:14 warn those who are *i*

idol—a statue made by people and worshiped as if it had the power of a god; anything that takes the place of God in a person's life. Worshiping idols is called idolatry.

1Co 8:4 We know that "An *i* is nothing at all
Col 3:5 evil desires and greed, which is *i*.

image—likeness.

Ge 1:27 God created mankind in his own *i*,
Da 3:12 nor worship the *i* of gold you have set up."

Immanuel—a name for Jesus meaning "God with us."

Mt 1:23 and they will call him *I*"

immoral (immorality)—wicked; not living by right standards.

1Co 6:18 Flee from sexual *i*.
Eph 5:5 No *i*, impure or greedy person

immortal (immortality)—free from death; not able to die.

1Co 15:53 and the mortal with *i.*
1Ti 1:17 Now to the King eternal, *i,*

imperishable—not able to die or to be destroyed.

1Pe 1:23 not of perishable seed, but of *i,*

impure—not pure; not clean.

Ac 10:15 not call anything *i* that God has
1Th 4:7 For God did not call us to be *i,*

incense—1. spices burned to make a sweet-smelling smoke, as a way of worshiping God; 2. the sweet smell or the smoke of burning spices.

Ps 141:2 my prayer be set before you like *i;*
Rev 8:3 He was given much *i* to offer,

indignation—anger.

Na 1:6 Who can withstand his *i?*

infirmity—physical weakness; disease.

Lk 13:12 set free from your *i.*"

inflict—to cause to be endured.

Eze 5:8 I will *i* punishment on you
2Co 2:6 The punishment *i* on him by

inhabitant—one who lives in a particular place.

Nu 33:55 drive out all the *i* of the land
Rev 6:10 the *i* of the earth and avenge

inherit—to receive money, property or keepsakes from a person after his or her death.

Mt 5:5 for they will *i* the earth.
Mk 10:17 "what must I do to *i* eternal life?"

inheritance—money, property or keepsakes received from a person after his or her death.

Dt 4:20 to be the people of his *i,*
1Pe 1:4 and into an *i* that can never perish,

iniquity—sin; wickedness.

Ps 51:2 Wash away all my *i*
Ps 103:10 or repay us according to our *i.*
Isa 53:6 the *i* of us all.

injustice—unfairness.

Pr 22:8 Whoever sows *i* reaps calamity,

inscription—1. the writing on a coin; 2. a written title or message.

instruct—to give knowledge or information; to teach.

Pr 9:9 *I* the wise and they will be wiser
1Th 4:1 we *i* you how to live

instruction—the action of a teacher; a lesson.

Ac 1:2 after giving *i* through the Holy Spirit
2Ti 4:2 with great patience and careful *i*

insult—1. (*v.*) to treat with contempt by word or action; to offend; 2. (*n.*) an act or speech of contempt.

Ps 69:9 the *i* of those who *i* you fall on me
Mt 5:11 "Blessed are you when people *i* you,

insurrection—revolt or rebellion against a government.

integrity—complete honesty.

Ps 25:21 May *i* and uprightness protect me,

intercede—to beg or plead for another person.

Ro 8:26 but the Spirit himself *i* for us

intercession—the plea made on behalf of another person.

Isa 53:12 and made *i* for the transgressors.

intermarry—to marry someone from a different race or religion.

Dt 7:3 Do not *i* with them.

interpret—to explain the meaning of.

Mt 16:3 you cannot *i* the signs of the times.
1Co 12:30 Do all speak in tongues? Do all *i?*

invoke—to call for help or support.

Ac 19:13 to *i* the name of the Lord Jesus

Isaac—the promised son of Abraham and Sarah (Ge 17:19; 21:1–7); offered as a sacrifice by Abraham (Ge 22); married Rebekah (Ge 24) and was the father of Esau and Jacob (Ge 25).

Isaiah—a prophet called by God (Isa 6) to prophesy to Judah (Isa 1:1). Some of his prophesies were about the coming Messiah (Isa 53).

Ishmael—the son of Abraham and Hagar (Ge 16); he was not to be the son of the covenant (Ge 17:18–21).

Israel—1. the new name God gave to Jacob (Ge 32:28); 2. the nation made up of descendants of the twelve sons of Jacob; 3. the northern ten tribes after they separated from Judah and Benjamin.

Ge 37:3 Now *I* loved Joseph more than
Dt 6:4 Hear, O *I*: The LORD our God,
Lk 22:30 judging the twelve tribes of *I.*
Eph 3:6 Gentiles are heirs together with *I,*

Israelites—the people of Israel.

Ex 14:22 and the *I* went through the sea
Ro 9:27 the number of the *I* be like the sand

J

Jacob—the son of Isaac and Rebekah; he was the twin brother of Esau (Ge 25:21–26); he bought Esau's birthright for a pot of stew (Ge 25:29–34); he wrestled with God, and his name was changed to Israel (Ge 32:22–32); the descendants of his twelve sons became the nation of Israel.

James—1. one of the twelve apostles; the brother of John (Mt 4:21–22); 2. one of the twelve apostles; the son of Alphaeus (Mt 10:3); 3. the brother of Jesus (Mk 6:3); the author of the letter of James (Jas 1:1).

Japheth—one of the sons of Noah (Ge 5:32); he was blessed because he covered his father's nakedness (Ge 9:18–28).

jealous (jealousy)—1. afraid of losing someone's love or affection; 2. angry or unhappy because of what someone else has; 3. careful to guard or keep what one has.

Joel 2:18 Then the LORD was *j* for his land
2Co 11:2 I am *j* for you with a godly *j.*
Gal 5:20 hatred, discord, *j,* fits of rage,

Jeremiah—a prophet called by God to prophesy to Judah (Jer 1:1–3). He is often referred to as the prophet of gloom, because he prophesied about the destruction of Judah.

Jericho—the ancient city destroyed by Joshua when the Hebrews entered Canaan (Jos 6).

Jeroboam—an official in Solomon's court; he rebelled and became the first king of the northern ten tribes of Israel (1Ki 11:26–40; 12:1–20).

Jerusalem—the political and religious center of the Jews; it was the site of many important events in the Bible; also called "Zion" and "the City of David."

2Ki 23:27	and I will reject *J*, the city I chose,
Ne 2:17	Come, let us rebuild the wall of *J*,
Ps 137:5	If I forget you, O *J*,
Jn 4:20	where we must worship is in *J*."
Rev 21:2	I saw the Holy City, the new *J*,

Jesse—the father of David, king of Israel (1Sa 16:10–13).

Jesus—The Son of God; the Savior of the world; the Messiah, through whom people can be saved.

Mt 1:21	you are to give him the name *J*,
Mk 11:22	"Have faith in God," *J* answered.
Php 2:10	name of *J* every knee should bow,

Jew—an Israelite; one of the chosen people of God; a descendant of Abraham through Jacob.

Mt 2:2	who has been born king of the *J*?
Ro 3:29	Or is God the God of *J* only?
Gal 3:28	There is neither *J* nor Gentile,

Jezebel—the wife of King Ahab (1Ki 16:31). She promoted Baal worship in Israel (1Ki 16:32–33), had many prophets of God killed (1Ki 18:4,13) and opposed the prophet Elijah (1Ki 19:1–2).

Joab—the commander of the armies of King David.

Joash—the boy-king of Judah; he repaired the temple (2Ki 12).

Job—a wealthy man from the land of Uz who feared God (Job 1:1–5). His righteousness was tested by disaster (Job 1:6–22) and personal affliction (Job 2), but in the end God restored wealth and honor to him (Job 42).

John—1. the Baptist (Mk 1:2–8); the son of Zechariah and Elizabeth (Lk 1). He preached in the desert, preparing the people for Jesus (Mt 3:11–12); baptized Jesus in the Jordan River (Mt 3:13–17); executed by Herod (Mk 6:14–29); 2. one of the twelve apostles; brother of the apostle James (Lk 5:1–10); wrote the Gospel of John, the letters of John (2Jn 1; 3Jn 1) and the book of Revelation (Rev 1:1; 22:8).

John Mark (see Mark, John).

Jonah—a prophet who was called to preach to Nineveh but instead fled to Tarshish (Jnh 1:1–3). While at sea a great storm arose because of his disobedience; he was thrown into the sea and was swallowed by a large fish (Jnh 1:4–17). He then repented and went to Nineveh and preached, telling the people to repent (Jnh 3).

Jonathan—a son of King Saul (1Sa 13:16) who had a close friendship with David (1Sa 18:1–4; 19—20; 23:16–18). When he was killed (1Sa 31) David mourned greatly for him (2Sa 1).

Joppa—an ancient walled town on the coast of Palestine.

Jordan—a river in Palestine that flows between the Sea of Galilee and the Dead Sea.

Jos 4:22	'Israel crossed the *J* on dry ground.'
Mt 3:6	baptized by him in the *J* River.

Joseph—1. the son of Jacob and Rachel (Ge 30:24), who was favored by his father but hated by his brothers (Ge 37:3–4). He was sold into slavery (Ge 37:12–36), taken to Egypt and eventually given a high position under Pharaoh (Ge 41:41–57); 2. the husband of Mary and childhood father of Jesus (Mt 1:16–24; 2:13–19); 3. a disciple of Jesus from Arimathea; he gave his tomb for Jesus' burial (Mt 27:57–61); 4. the original name of Barnabas (Ac 4:36).

Joshua—1. the son of Nun (Nu 13:8); Moses' aide and later his successor (Dt 31:1–18); he led the Israelites across the Jordan River into Canaan (Jos 3—4); was the commander in the conquest of Jericho (Jos 6), Ai (Jos 7—8), and a large part of Canaan (Jos 10—12); oversaw the dividing up of the promised land among the twelve tribes of Israel (Jos 13—22); 2. the high priest in Israel during the rebuilding of both the temple (Hag 1—2) and the altar (Ezr 3:2,8); also called Jeshua.

Josiah—godly king of Judah for thirty-one years shortly before the destruction of Jerusalem.

Judah—1. Jacob's fourth son; 2. the tribe of Israel whose members were descendants of Judah; 3. a name for the southern kingdom after Judah and Benjamin separated from the northern ten tribes.

Ge 29:35	So she named him *J*.
Zec 10:4	From *J* will come the cornerstone,
Mt 2:6	Bethlehem, in the land of *J*,
Rev 5:5	See, the Lion of the tribe of *J*,

Judaism—the teachings of the Jewish religion.

Judas—1. one of the twelve apostles (Lk 6:16; Ac 1:13); was probably also called Thaddaeus (Mt 10:3); 2. one of the brothers of Jesus (Mt 13:55); author of the last letter in the New Testament (Jude 1); 3. one of the twelve apostles, also called Iscariot; he betrayed Jesus (Mk 3:19; 14:10–50) and then hung himself (Mt 27:3–5).

Judea—the area of Palestine where the tribe of Judah lived after the exile.

Mk 10:1	into the region of *J* and across the Jordan.
Gal 1:22	to the churches of *J* that are in Christ.

judge—to decide if something is good or bad; to condemn.

Ps 9:8	and *j* the peoples with equity.
Mt 7:1	"Do not *j*, or you too will be judged.
2Ti 4:1	who will *j* the living and the dead,

judgment—1. a decision or opinion; 2. a decision of guilt or innocence made by a judge in a court of law; punishment decided on by a court; 3. a decision from God, especially the final judgment when God will reward those who believe in him and condemn all others to hell.

Dt 1:17	of anyone, for *j* belongs to God.
Ps 119:66	Teach me knowledge and good *j*,
Isa 66:16	the LORD will execute *j*
Mt 5:21	who murders will be subject to *j*.'
Mt 12:36	have to give account on the day of *j*
Jn 5:22	but has entrusted all *j* to the Son,
Ro 14:10	stand before God's *j* seat.
2Co 5:10	appear before the *j* seat of Christ,

just—righteous, legally correct.

Ps 111:7	The works of his hands are faithful and *j*;
Rev 16:7	true and *j* are your judgments."

justice—fairness.

Isa 30:18	For the LORD is a God of *j*.
Isa 61:8	"For I, the LORD, love *j*;
Zec 7:9	'Administer true *j*; show mercy
Lk 11:42	you neglect *j* and the love of God.

justify (justification)—to erase someone's sins; to declare righteous.

Ac 13:39 a *j* you were not able to obtain
Ro 3:24 and all are *j* freely by his grace
Ro 4:25 and was raised to life for our *j*.
Ro 5:1 since we have been *j* through faith,
Gal 3:24 Christ came that we might be *j* by faith.

K

kind—considerate, loving.

Eph 4:32 Be *k* and compassionate

king—ruler over a country or kingdom; Christ is often referred to as the King of kings.

1Ki 22:3 The *k* of Israel had said
1 Ti 6:15 the *K* of *k* and Lord of lords,

kingdom—an area or group of people headed by a king; God's kingdom, or the kingdom of heaven, is made up of all believers.

Ex 19:6 you will be for me a *k* of priests
Mt 3:2 "Repent, for the *k* of heaven has come
Mt 5:3 for theirs is the *k* of heaven.
Mt 6:33 But seek first his *k* and his
Mt 16:19 the keys of the *k* of heaven;
Jn 18:36 "My *k* is not of this world.
1Co 15:24 hands over the *k* to God the Father
Rev 11:15 "The *k* of the world has become the *k*

Kish—the father of King Saul, the first king of Israel.

knowledge—possessing the facts, understanding.

Pr 1:7 of the LORD is the beginning of *k*,
Hos 4:6 are destroyed from lack of *k*.
1Co 8:1 *k* puffs up while love builds up.

L

Laban—the brother of Rebekah (Ge 24:29–51) and father of Rachel and Leah (Ge 29—31).

labor—1. (*v.*) to work; 2. (*n.*) a task; 3. (*n.*) the time just before giving birth.

Ge 5:29 the *l* and painful toil of our hands
Ex 20:9 Six days you shall *l* and do all your work,
Jer 13:21 like that of a woman in *l*?

lack—1. (*v.*) to stand in need of; 2. (*n.*) the state of being in need of something.

Ps 34:9 those who fear him *l* nothing.

lamb—a principal sacrificial animal in the Old Testament; since Jesus is the supreme sacrifice of God, he is called the "Lamb of God."

Isa 53:7 he was led like a *l* to the slaughter,
Jn 1:29 *L* of God, who takes away the sin
1Co 5:7 our Passover *l*, has been sacrificed.
Rev 5:6 Then I saw a *L*, looking

lament, lamentation—a cry of grief.

Ps 5:1 LORD, consider my *l*.

law—1. God's rules, which help his people know what is right and wrong (the Ten Commandments are part of God's law); 2. (cap.) the first five books of the Bible, written by Moses.

Ps 1:2 and who meditates on his *l*
Ps 19:7 The *l* of the LORD is perfect,
Ps 119:97 Oh, how I love your *l*!
Mt 22:40 All the *L* and the Prophets hang
Ro 8:3 For what the *l* was powerless to do
Ro 13:10 love is the fulfillment of the *l*.
Gal 3:24 So the *l* was our guardian

Lazarus—1. the poor man in one of Jesus' parables (Lk 16:19–31); 2. the brother of Mary and Martha; Jesus raised him from the dead (Jn 11:1–12:19).

Leah—the wife of Jacob; she had six sons and one daughter (Ge 29:16–30:21).

leprosy—a word used in the Bible for many different skin diseases and infections.

Mk 1:42 Immediately the *l* left him

Levite—a member of the tribe of Levi. The Levites took care of the temple. Only Levites could become priests, but not all Levites were priests.

lewd—indecent; wicked.

life—the total substance of a person's existence; can refer to both physical and spiritual existence.

Ge 2:7 into his nostrils the breath of *l*,
Jn 3:16 shall not perish but have eternal *l*.
Jn 11:25 "I am the resurrection and the *l*.
Jn 14:6 am the way and the truth and the *l*.
Ro 6:23 but the gift of God is eternal *l*

light—the form of energy that allows a person to see; in the Old Testament it symbolized life and blessing.

Ge 1:3 "Let there be *l*," and there was *l*.
Ps 27:1 The LORD is my *l* and my salvation
Ps 119:105 a *l* on my path.
Isa 9:2 have seen a great *l*;
Mt 5:16 let your *l* shine before others,
Jn 8:12 he said, "I am the *l* of the world.
1Jn 1:5 God is *l*; in him there is no

linen—cloth made from the fiber of flax plants.

live—to be alive; may refer to both physical and spiritual existence.

Ex 20:12 so that you may *l* long
Ro 1:17 "The righteous will *l* by faith."
2Co 5:7 For we *l* by faith, not by sight.
Php 1:21 to *l* is Christ and to die is gain.

loathe—to feel disgust or hatred.

Job 10:1 "I *l* my very life;

locusts—a type of grasshopper. When they settle in a grain field, orchard or other cultivated area, they can destroy the crop.

Lord—refers to God as the master. (See also LORD.)

Mt 3:3 'Prepare the way for the *L*,
Lk 2:9 glory of the *L* shone around them,
Ac 16:31 replied, "Believe in the *L* Jesus,
Ro 10:13 on the name of the *L* will be saved."
Php 2:11 acknowledge that Jesus Christ is *L*,
2Pe 1:16 the coming of our *L* Jesus Christ,

Rev 17:14 he is *L* of lords and King of kings
Rev 22:20 Come, *L* Jesus.

Lord (Yahweh)—the intimate and personal name of God; it emphasizes his role as Israel's Redeemer and covenant Lord. (See also Lord.)

Ge 2:4 when the *L* God made the earth
Ex 20:2 "I am the *L* your God, who
Ps 23:1 The *L* is my shepherd, I lack
Ps 103:1 Praise the *L*, my soul;
Pr 1:7 The fear of the *L* is the beginning
Isa 6:3 "Holy, holy, holy is the *L* Almighty;
Isa 55:6 Seek the *L* while he may be found;

Lot—the nephew of Abraham (Ge 12:5). He chose to live in Sodom (Ge 13); Abraham pleaded with God for Lot's life when God was about to destroy Sodom (Ge 19:1–29).

lot—one of the ways used in Bible times to find out God's will about something. It is somewhat like drawing straws.

Mt 27:35 divided up his clothes by casting *l*.
Ac 1:26 Then they cast *l*, and the *l* fell

love—wanting good to come to another person; being concerned and willing to work for another person's benefit.

Ex 20:6 showing *l* to a thousand generations
Ps 23:6 Surely your goodness and *l* will follow
Ps 136:1–26 His *l* endures forever.
Mt 3:17 "This is my Son, whom I *l*;
Mt 5:44 *l* your enemies and pray
Mt 19:19 and '*l* your neighbor as yourself.'"
Jn 13:34 I give you: *L* one another.
Jn 15:13 Greater *l* has no one than this:
Ro 13:10 Therefore *l* is the fulfillment
Gal 5:22 But the fruit of the Spirit is *l*, joy,
Eph 1:4–5 In *l* he predestined us
1Jn 3:10 anyone who does not *l* their brother.
1Jn 3:16 This is how we know what *l* is:
1Jn 4:7 for *l* comes from God.
1Jn 4:10 This is *l*: not that we loved God,
1Jn 4:16 God is *l*.

Luke—a co-worker with Paul; he wrote the books of Luke and Acts (Col 4:14).

lust—a strong desire for something wrong.

Pr 6:25 Do not *l* in your heart
Ro 1:26 God gave them over to shameful *l*.

lyre—a small lap harp with three to twelve strings.

1Sa 18:10 David was playing the *l*,

M

Macedonia—a Roman province; the first part of Europe to receive Christianity.

Magi—men of Arabia and Persia who studied the stars. People thought they had the power to tell the meaning of dreams.

Mt 2:1 *M* from the east came to Jerusalem

maimed—crippled; having lost a part of one's body, such as an arm or leg.

majestic (majesty)—great and powerful.

Ex 15:6 was *m* in power.
Ps 8:1 how *m* is your name in all the earth!
Ps 111:3 Glorious and *m* are his deeds,

malice—hatred; wishing harm on someone else.

1Pe 2:1 rid yourselves of all *m*

Manasseh—1. the older son of Joseph and the tribe descended from him (Ge 41:51; Nu 1:34); 2. one of the kings of Judah (2Ki 21:1).

manger—a feed box for cows or other animals.

Lk 2:7 placed him in a *m*, because there

maniac—an insane person; an overly enthusiastic person.

2Ki 9:20 he drives like a *m*."

manna—the special food God gave daily to the Israelites until they reached the promised land.

Ex 16:31 people of Israel called the bread *m*.
Jn 6:49 Your ancestors ate the *m*

Mark, John—the cousin of Barnabas (Col 4:10); a helper to Paul and Barnabas (Ac 13:5); later a co-worker with Barnabas (Ac 15:39) and then Paul (Phm 24); author of the second Gospel, according to early church tradition.

marriage—the joining together before God and other people of a man and a woman to form a new family.

Ge 29:26 younger daughter in *m* before the older
Mt 22:30 neither marry nor be given in *m*;
Heb 13:4 by all, and the *m* bed kept pure,

Martha—the sister of Mary and Lazarus, the man whom Jesus raised from the dead (Jn 11; 12:2).

marvelous—something that surprises, that fills one with wonder.

Ps 118:23 and it is *m* in our eyes.
Rev 15:3 "Great and *m* are your deeds,

Mary—1. the mother of Jesus (Mt 1:16–25); 2. Mary Magdalene—a woman whom Jesus freed from demons (Lk 8:2), who was present at the cross (Mk 15:40) and who came on Easter morning to the tomb (Mt 27:61); 3. the sister of Martha and Lazarus; she washed Jesus' feet with expensive perfume (Jn 12:1–8).

master—one who rules over others.

Mt 6:24 "No one can serve two *m*.
Jn 13:16 no servant is greater than his *m*,

Matthew—a tax collector who became one of the twelve apostles (Mt 9:9–13); also called Levi (Mk 2:14–17).

mediator—one who makes peace between two people or two groups who are displeased and/or angry with each other. Jesus is the mediator between us and God.

1Ti 2:5 and one *m* between God and mankind,
Heb 9:15 For this reason Christ is the *m*

meditate—to think seriously and carefully.

Ps 1:2 who *m* on his law day and night.
Ps 119:15 I *m* on your precepts

medium—a person who can supposedly talk with the spirits of people who have died.

1Sa 28:7 "Find me a woman who is a *m*,

meek—patient; mild; gentle.

Ps 37:11 But the *m* will inherit the land
Mt 5:5 Blessed are the *m*,

Melchizedek—a priest and king of early Salem (Jerusalem); Jesus was said to be a priest like Melchizedek (Heb 5:6).

Mephibosheth—son of Jonathan and grandson of Saul; he lived out his life under King David's protection (2Sa 9:11).

mercy—kindness and forgiveness, especially when given to a person who doesn't deserve it.

Mic 6:8	To act justly and to love *m*
Ro 9:15	"I will have *m* on whom I have *m*,
1Pe 1:3	In his great *m* he has given us new

Messiah—the "Anointed One"; Christ; the one the Jews expected to come and be their king.

Lk 9:20	Peter answered, "God's *M*."
Jn 1:41	"We have found the *M*"

Methuselah—a man in early Bible times who lived 969 years (Ge 5:27).

Michal—daughter of Saul, wife of David, both of whom were kings of Israel.

midwives—women who helped with the birth of a baby.

Ex 1:17	The *m*, however, feared God

millstone—one of a pair of stones used to crush grain for flour.

Lk 17:2	sea with a *m* tied around their neck

minister—1. (*v.*) to serve; to give care or attention to; 2. (*n.*) one who serves others as God directs.

2Co 3:6	as *m* of a new covenant
1Ti 4:6	you will be a good *m*

miracle—an unusual event, one that goes against the normal laws of nature. Miracles are done by the power of God.

Ps 77:14	You are the God who performs *m*;
Mk 6:2	What are these remarkable *m* he is
Ac 2:22	accredited by God to you by *m*,
Heb 2:4	it by signs, wonders and various *m*,

Miriam—the sister of Moses and Aaron (Nu 26:59); led the Israelites in praising God in dance and song after he had parted the waters of the Red Sea (Ex 15:20–21); later temporarily struck with leprosy because she criticized Moses (Nu 12).

Moab—1. a son of Lot whose descendants became bitter enemies of the Israelites; 2. the land occupied by the Moabites, to the east of the Dead Sea.

money—a medium of exchange.

Ecc 5:10	Whoever loves *m* never has
Mt 6:24	You cannot serve both God and *m*.
1Co 16:2	set aside a sum of *m* in keeping
1Ti 6:10	For the love of *m* is a root

Mordecai—cousin of Esther, queen of Persia; he and Esther saved the Jews from a plot to put them all to death.

mortal—human; able to die.

Ps 9:20	the nations know they are only *m*.
Ps 103:15	The life of *m* is like grass,
1Co 15:53	and the *m* with immortality,

Moses—the leader of Israel in the exodus out of Egypt, ending in their passing through the Red Sea (Ex 12—14). He received the law of God at Sinai (Ex 19—23) and gave it to the people of Israel. Moses was allowed to view the land of Canaan from the top of Mount Nebo, but he died without entering it (Nu 20:1–13; Dt 34:5–12).

mother—the female parent.

Ge 2:24	and *m* and is united to his wife,
Dt 5:16	"Honor your father and your *m*,

mourn—to feel deep sorrow; to grieve.

Mt 5:4	Blessed are those who *m*,

murder—to kill someone illegally.

Ex 20:13	"You shall not *m*.

muster—to gather together, especially to gather soldiers for war.

mute—unable to speak.

Mt 9:33	the man who had been *m* spoke.

myrrh—the sweet-smelling sap of the myrrh bush. It was used to make the sacred anointing oil.

Mt 2:11	gifts of gold, frankincense and *m*.

N

Nabal—a rich sheepherder in Judah who insulted David; when David planned to take revenge, Nabal's wife Abigail brought gifts to calm David; Nabal died shortly afterwards, and Abigail married David (1Sa 25:1–42).

Naboth—owner of a vineyard that King Ahab wanted and gained by having Naboth accused of blasphemy and stoned (1Ki 21:1–29).

Naomi—the mother-in-law of Ruth (Ru 1); she advised Ruth to seek marriage with Boaz (Ru 2—4).

Naphtali—a son of Jacob and father of the tribe of Naphtali (Nu 1:42–43).

nard—an expensive, pleasant-smelling oil from the spikenard, a plant that grew in India.

Mk 14:3	perfume, made of pure *n*.

Nathan—the prophet of God who exposed David's sin with Bathsheba, causing David to repent (2Sa 12:1–25).

Nathanael—one of the twelve apostles (Jn 1:45–49); was probably also called Bartholomew (Mt 10:3).

Nazarene—a person who lived in or came from the town of Nazareth in Galilee.

Mk 16:6	looking for Jesus the *N*,

Nazirite—a person who separated himself or herself by taking a vow to do special work for God. This included a promise not to cut one's hair and not to drink wine.

Jdg 16:17	I have been a *N* dedicated to God

Nebuchadnezzar—king of Babylon who took Judah into captivity.

Negev—the desert region south of Judea.

Ge 24:62	for he was living in the *N*.

Nehemiah—the Jewish cupbearer of King Artaxerxes of Persia (Ne 2:1); while in Jerusalem rebuilt the walls of the city (Ne 2—6) and with Ezra reestablished the worship of God there after the exile in Babylon (Ne 8).

neighbor—1. someone who lives nearby; 2. any fellow human being.

Lev 19:18	but love your *n* as yourself.
Lk 10:36	of these three do you think was a *n*

Nicodemus—a Pharisee who visited Jesus at night (Jn 3) and learned about being born again.

Nile—the primary river in Egypt.

Nineveh—the city to which Jonah was sent to preach (Jnh 1:2); the ancient capital of Assyria.

Noah—"a righteous man" in early Bible times; he built an ark, as God commanded him (Ge 6—8). God made a covenant with him never again to cover the entire earth with a flood (Ge 9).

nullify—to make of no value; to make unimportant.

Mk 7:13 Thus you *n* the word of God

O

oath—a promise in which one asks God to witness that something is true.

Dt 10:20 take your *o* in his name.

obey (obedience)—to do as asked; to follow someone's commands or wishes.

Dt 6:3 careful to *o* so that it may go well
1Sa 15:22 To *o* is better than sacrifice,
Jn 14:23 who loves me will *o* my teaching.
Ac 5:29 "We must *o* God rather than human
Eph 6:1 *o* your parents in the Lord,

offense—an act that makes someone angry by what was done.

offering—1. something given to God as an act of worship; 2. the sacrifice of an animal to make the relationship between God and human beings right again. In the Old Testament, animals and grains were regularly used as offerings in an attempt to bring the people closer to God.

Ge 22:8 provide the lamb for the burnt *o*,
Isa 53:10 the LORD makes his life an *o*
Mk 12:33 is more important than all burnt *o*
Eph 5:2 as a fragrant *o* and sacrifice to God.

offspring—children.

Ge 3:15 and between your *o* and hers;
Ge 12:7 "To your *o* I will give this land."

oil—almost always refers to olive oil; used to anoint someone for a physical benefit or to set someone apart for service.

2Ki 9:6 prophet poured the *o* on Jehu's head
Lk 7:46 You did not put *o* on my head,

olive—a tree whose fruit gives olive oil, which was used for varied purposes.

oppress—to control people unfairly and cruelly by the use of one's power.

Isa 53:7 He was *o* and afflicted,
Zec 7:10 Do not *o* the widow

oracle—1. a saying or answer; 2. the word of the Lord.

ordain—1. to set apart for a specific office or duty; 2. to order or command.

Ps 111:9 he *o* his covenant forever

ordinance—1. an official law; 2. a law made or commanded by God.

1Sa 30:25 a statute and *o* for Israel

ornate—elaborately decorated or adorned.

Ge 37:3 he made an *o* robe for him.

overseer—one of the terms used for leaders in the early church.

Ac 20:28 the Holy Spirit has made you *o*.
1Ti 3:2 Now the *o* is to be above reproach,

oxen—strong animals that were used in various ways in farming communities.

P

pagan—a person who does not worship God, especially someone who worships idols.

1Pe 2:12 such good lives among the *p* that,

papyrus—1. a large water plant, similar to the reed, which grows in marshes and lakes. Moses' mother put him in a basket made from papyrus (Ex 2:3); 2. a paper made from this plant.

parable—a story that tells a special lesson or truth. Jesus told many parables.

paralyzed—unable to move certain parts of one's body.

Mk 2:3 bringing to him a *p* man,

parents—fathers and mothers.

Pr 17:6 and *p* are the pride of their children.
Eph 6:1 Children, obey your *p* in the Lord,
Col 3:20 obey your *p* in everything,

Passover—an annual holiday that still today reminds the Jewish people of how God freed them from slavery in Egypt. The Lord "passed over" the homes marked with the blood of a lamb on their doorframes, but he killed all the other firstborn in Egypt.

Ex 12:11 Eat it in haste; it is the LORD's *P*.

Passover lamb—the lamb killed on the Passover as a sacrifice. Jesus is our Passover lamb, because he was sacrificed for our deliverance from sin, in the same way a lamb was sacrificed when the Israelites were delivered from Egypt.

1Co 5:7 our *P* lamb, has been sacrificed.

pasture—a plot or section of grassy land used for grazing cattle.

patient (patience)—able to put up with problems or pain without complaining or becoming angry.

Ro 12:12 Be joyful in hope, *p* in affliction,
1Co 13:4 Love is *p*, love is kind.
Col 3:12 kindness, humility, gentleness and *p*.

patriarch—the father and ruler of a family; the head of a tribe.

Paul—a Pharisee from Tarsus (Ac 9:11); named Saul at birth (Ac 13:9). Jesus appeared to him on the road to Damascus (Ac 9:4–9), and he became a powerful apostle (Gal 1). His writings make up a large part of the New Testament, ranging from intricate theology to passionate letters to struggling churches.

peace—freedom from disturbance; calm.

Isa 9:6 Everlasting Father, Prince of *P*.
Lk 2:14 on earth *p* to those on whom his
Jn 14:27 *P* I leave with you; my *p*
Ro 5:1 we have *p* with God
Gal 5:22 joy, *p*, forbearance, kindness,

Pentecost—a Jewish feast celebrated fifty days after the Passover. Today the Christian church celebrates Pentecost because it was the day the Holy Spirit came to dwell with Christ's followers (Ac 2:1–4).

people—a collective group.

2Ch 7:14 if my *p*, who are called by my name,
1Pe 2:9 you are a chosen *p*,

perfect—flawless; without defect.

Mt 5:48 Be *p*, therefore, as your heavenly

perish—to spoil; to be destroyed.

Ps 102:26 They will *p*, but you remain;

persecute (persecution)—to continually treat someone cruelly and unfairly, even though that person has done nothing wrong. The early Christians were persecuted for believing in Jesus as the Son of God.

Jn 15:20 they *p* me, they will *p* you
Ac 26:14 'Saul, Saul, why do you *p* me?
Ro 12:14 Bless those who *p* you; bless

persevere (perseverance)—to refuse to give up; to keep on trying; to continue in one's actions or beliefs in spite of problems.

Ro 5:3 we know that suffering produces *p*;
Heb 10:36 You need to *p* so that
Heb 12:1 let us run with *p* the race

Persia—ancient geographical area and kingdom located north of the Persian Gulf.

pervert—to use wrongly; to turn from what is right.

pestilence—a plague; a disease that spreads quickly and kills many people.

Ps 91:3 snare and from the deadly *p*.

Peter—one of the twelve apostles; the brother of Andrew; also called Simon (Lk 6:14) and Cephas (Jn 1:42); he denied Jesus three times (Mk 14:66–72) but became a bold evangelist. He wrote the books of 1 and 2 Peter.

petition—to make a formal request.

pharaoh—the title given to the ruler of Egypt.

Pharisees—a group of Jews who obeyed very strictly both God's laws and all their own rules about God's laws.

Mt 5:20 surpasses that of the *P*

Philip—1. one of the twelve apostles (Mt 10:3); 2. a deacon (Ac 6:1–7) and evangelist in Samaria; he witnessed to an Ethiopian (Ac 8:4–40).

Philistines—enemies of the Israelites throughout much of Old Testament history; they were especially powerful during the reigns of Saul and David.

Pilate—the governor of Judea who questioned Jesus (Lk 22:66–23:25) and then sent him to Herod (Lk 23:6–12). Pilate finally consented to Jesus' crucifixion when the crowds chose Barabbas rather than Jesus to be released (Lk 23:13–25).

pity—a sympathy or sorrow for the suffering of another.

Mk 9:22 take *p* on us and help us."

plague—1. a disease that kills many people, such as the plague of boils; 2. an event that causes much suffering or loss, such as the plague of locusts.

plead—to appeal earnestly; to beg.

Job 16:21 he *p* with God as one *p* for a friend.

pledge—a binding promise or agreement.

1Ti 5:12 they have broken their first *p*.

plot—to plan, usually secretly; to scheme.

Ps 83:5 With one mind they *p* together;

plowshare—the pointed part of the plow; it cuts into the soil to make rows.

Mic 4:3 will beat their swords into *p*

plunder—1. (*v.*) to loot or rob during a war; 2. (*n.*) property taken by plundering.

pomegranate—a reddish fruit about the size of an orange. It has many seeds and a juicy pulp.

poor—those who have little money.

Dt 15:4 there need be no *p* people
Isa 61:1 me to proclaim good news to the *p*.
Mt 26:11 The *p* you will always have
1Co 13:3 If I give all I possess to the *p*
2Co 8:9 yet for your sake he became *p*,

portico—a porch, usually at the front of a building.

2Ch 3:4 The *p* at the front of the temple

praise—1. (*v.*) to glorify; to say good things about someone or something; 2. (*n.*) approval; worship.

Ex 15:2 He is my God, and I will *p* him,
Ps 119:175 Let me live that I may *p* you,
Eph 1:12 might be for the *p* of his glory.

pray—to talk with God.

2Ch 7:14 will humble themselves and *p*
Mt 6:5 "And when you *p*, do not be like
Ro 8:26 do not know what we ought to *p*
1Th 5:16–17 Rejoice always, *p* continually,

preach—to tell the message of the gospel in public; to deliver a sermon.

Mt 11:1 and *p* in the towns of Galilee.
Ro 10:15 how can they *p* unless they are sent?

precept—command; law; rule.

Ps 19:8 The *p* of the LORD are right,
Ps 119:69 I keep your *p* with all my heart.

precious—valuable; of great worth.

Ps 139:17 How *p* to me are your thoughts,

predestine—to decide or decree ahead of time.

Ro 8:30 And those he *p*, he also called;
Eph 1:5 he *p* us for adoption

pregnant—carrying an unborn child within a woman's body.

Lk 1:24 his wife Elizabeth became *p*

prevail—to triumph or succeed.

pride—1. (negative) the attitude that one is better than others; 2. (positive) a healthy self-respect or sense of satisfaction.

Pr 16:18 *P* goes before destruction,
Gal 6:4 they can take *p* in themselves

priest (priesthood)—a Levite who offered sacrifices and prayers to God for the people.

1Pe 2:9 you are a chosen people, a royal *p*,

prince—a male member of a royal family.

prison—a building where people are held, usually for committing a crime.

proclaim—to announce or declare.

1Ch 16:23 *p* his salvation day after day.
Ps 19:1 the skies *p* the work of his hands.

Isa 61:1 to *p* good news to the poor.
1Co 11:26 you *p* the Lord's death

profane—to make a holy thing impure by treating it with disrespect or irreverence.

Lev 22:32 Do not *p* my holy name,

prophecy—a message from God that a prophet brings to the people.

1Co 13:8 where there are *p*, they will cease;
2Pe 1:20 you must understand that no *p*

prophesy—to give the message of God to the people.

Joel 2:28 Your sons and daughters will *p*,
1Co 14:39 brothers and sisters, be eager to *p*,

prophet—a person who receives messages from God to tell to his people. A prophet is called by God to speak for him.

Dt 18:18 up for them a *p* like you
Lk 24:25 believe all that the *p* have spoken!
Ac 10:43 All the *p* testify about him that
Heb 1:1 through the *p* at many times

prosper—to succeed; achieve economic success.

Pr 11:25 A generous person will *p*;

prostitute—a person who lets someone use his or her body for sexual relations in exchange for money.

Jos 2:1 house of a *p* named Rahab

prostrate—lying facedown on the ground.

proud—to have pride.

Ro 12:16 Do not be *p*, but be willing
Jas 4:6 "God opposes the *p*

proverbs—1. wise sayings; 2. (Proverbs) a book of the Bible that contains many wise sayings.

1Ki 4:32 He spoke three thousand *p*

provoke—to make angry; to cause trouble.

prudent—wise.

Pr 19:14 a *p* wife is from the LORD.

psalms—1. poetry written to praise God; 2. (Psalms) a book of the Bible that contains many psalms.

Eph 5:19 speaking to one another with *p*,

punish (punishment)—to cause someone to suffer for doing wrong.

Ge 4:13 "My *p* is more than I can bear.
Ex 20:5 jealous God, *p* the children for the sin

pure—perfectly free from fault or blemish.

Ps 51:10 Create in me a *p* heart, O God,

purify—to make pure or clean.

1Jn 1:7 of Jesus, his Son, *p* us from all sin.
1Jn 1:9 and *p* us from all unrighteousness.

Purim—an annual Jewish holiday celebrating Queen Esther's rescue of the Jews when Haman plotted to destroy them.

pursue—1. to follow in order to overtake; to chase; 2. to seek a goal.

Lev 26:7 You will *p* your enemies,
1Ti 6:11 and *p* righteousness, godliness,

Q

quail—a small spotted bird similar to the partridge; God provided quail and manna to the Israelites when they wandered in the wilderness.

Nu 11:32 people went out and gathered *q*.

quake—1. (*v.*) to shake or tremble; 2. (*n.*) an earthquake.

Ps 75:3 the earth and all its people *q*,
Rev 16:18 so tremendous was the *q*.

queen—1. the female ruler of a country; 2. the wife of a king.

R

Rabbi—a teacher of Jewish law.

Rachel—the daughter of Laban (Ge 29:16); she became Jacob's wife (Ge 29:28) and bore him two sons, Joseph and Benjamin (Ge 30:22–24; 35:16–24).

rage—a fit of anger.

Eph 4:31 Get rid of all bitterness, *r*

ram—a male sheep.

ransom—the price paid to get back a person who is held as a slave. Because people are slaves of sin, a ransom had to be paid, which was the death of the sinless one, Jesus.

Mt 20:28 and to give his life as a *r* for many."
Heb 9:15 as a *r* to set them free

reap—1. to cut down grain at harvest time; to gather a crop together; 2. to get as a result or reward.

Gal 6:7 A man *r* what he sows.

Rebekah—Isaac's wife (Ge 24); the mother of Esau and Jacob (Ge 25:19–26). With her encouragement, Jacob tricked his father into giving him the blessing that belonged to Esau (Ge 27:1–17).

rebel—1. (*v.*) to disobey and turn against those in authority; 2. (*n.*) a person who disobeys and flaunts authority.

Ro 13:2 whoever *r* against the authority

rebuke—to scold sharply.

2Ti 4:2 correct, *r* and encourage
Rev 3:19 Those whom I love I *r*

reconcile (reconciliation)—to return to friendship after a quarrel; human beings are "reconciled" to God through Christ.

Mt 5:24 First go and be *r* to them;
Ro 5:10 we were *r* to him through the death
2Co 5:18 and gave us the ministry of *r*:

redeem (redemption)—1. to free from evil by paying a price (Gal 3:13); 2. to buy back.

Ex 21:30 the owner may *r* his life
Gal 3:13 Christ *r* us from the curse
Eph 1:7 In him we have *r* through his blood,
Col 1:14 in whom we have *r*, the forgiveness

Red Sea—the body of water the Israelites crossed in a miraculous way when they were escaping from slavery in Egypt.

refuge—a place of shelter and safety.

Ps 46:1 God is our *r* and strength,

regard—to pay attention to.

Ps 41:1 Blessed are those who have *r* for the weak;

regulations—rules dealing with procedure or ceremony.

Rehoboam—the son of Solomon; he became king after his father's death (1Ki 11:43). Because of his harsh treatment of the people, Israel was divided into two kingdoms (1Ki 12:1–24; 14:21–31).

reign—the time during which a king or other official rules.

rejoice—to express joy or gladness.

Ps 118:24 let us *r* today be glad.
Lk 1:47 and my spirit *r* in God my Savior,
Php 4:4 *R* in the Lord always.

remnant—a small part remaining; a small surviving group.

Isa 10:21 A *r* will return,

repent (repentance)—to turn away from sin; to be sorry for what one has done and to promise not to do it again.

Mt 4:17 "*R*, for the kingdom of heaven
Lk 3:8 Produce fruit in keeping with *r*.
Ac 2:38 Peter replied, "*R* and be baptized,

reproach—1. (*v.*) to blame or accuse; 2. (*n.*) something for which one can be blamed or criticized.

Job 27:6 my conscience will not *r* me

require (requirement)—to demand as necessary.

1Ki 8:31 is *r* to take an oath
Zec 3:7 obedience to me and keep my *r*,

rescue—to save or deliver.

Ps 140:1 *R* me, LORD from evildoers;

respect—to look up to or hold in high esteem.

1Pe 2:17 Show proper *r* to everyone,

restitution—to restore or pay back for damage, loss or injury.

Nu 5:7 must make full *r* for the wrong

restore—to bring back; to return something to its former condition.

Ps 51:12 *R* to me the joy of your salvation
Ac 3:21 time comes for God to *r* everything,

resurrection—the act of coming back to life after being dead.

Jn 11:25 Jesus said to her, "I am the *r*
Ro 1:4 in power by his *r* from the dead:
1Co 15:12 some of you say that there is no *r*

retribution—punishment for doing wrong.

Jer 51:56 For the LORD is a God of *r*;

Reuben—oldest son of Jacob and founder of the tribe of the same name.

revelation—the act of making known or telling about.

Gal 1:12 I received it by *r* from Jesus Christ.
Rev 1:1 *r* from Jesus Christ, which God gave

revenge—to hurt or punish a person who has wronged you; to get back at someone who has hurt you.

Lev 19:18 " 'Do not seek *r* or bear a grudge
Ro 12:19 Do not take *r*, my dear friends,

reverence (revere)—a deep respect, honor and awe.

Ps 5:7 in *r* I bow down
Col 3:22 of heart and *r* for the Lord.

reward—1. (*v.*) to repay with good for something someone has done; 2. (*n.*) the gift one receives for good behavior or character.

Ps 127:3 offspring a *r* from him.
Jer 17:10 to *r* each person according to
Mt 5:12 because great is your *r* in heaven,
Mt 6:5 they have received their *r* in full.

righteous (righteousness)—being in a right relationship to God; not guilty before God.

Isa 64:6 and all our *r* acts are like filthy rags;
Ro 3:10 "There is no one *r*, not even one;

Rome—1. the empire that controlled much of the known world at the time of Christ; 2. the capital city of the Roman Empire, located in Italy.

royal—of or belonging to the ruler of a country and his family.

Ruth—a Moabite widow who went with her mother-in-law Naomi to Bethlehem (Ru 1). There she gathered the gleanings from the field of Boaz (Ru 2), whom she later married (Ru 3—4:12). She was an ancestor of David (Ru 4:13–22) and of Jesus (Mt 1:5).

ruthless—merciless; cruel.

Ps 54:3 *r* people are trying to kill me
Hab 1:6 that *r* and impetuous people,

S

Sabbath—the seventh day of the week; the Jewish day of rest and worship. It extended from Friday sunset until Saturday sunset.

Ex 20:8 "Remember the *S* day

sackcloth—a rough cloth, usually woven from goats' hair. Clothing made of sackcloth was worn as a sign of mourning for the dead or as a sign that a person was sorry for his or her sins.

sacred—holy; set apart for God in a special way.

1Co 3:17 God's temple is *s*,

sacrifice—1. (*v.*) to offer something as a gift to God; 2. (*n.*) an offering given to God. In the Old Testament God commanded the people to pay for their sins by sacrificing the blood of cattle, lambs, goats, doves or pigeons. These sacrifices were pictures of Jesus' coming as a once-for-all sacrifice for sinners.

Ex 12:27 'It is the Passover *s* to the LORD,
1Sa 15:22 To obey is better than *s*,
Ro 12:1 to offer your bodies as a living *s*,
Heb 9:28 so Christ was *s* once
1Jn 2:2 He is the atoning *s* for our sins,

Sadducees—a group of Jewish leaders, many of them priests. Unlike the Pharisees, the Sadducees did not believe in a resurrection of the dead, but they agreed with the Pharisees in their hatred of Jesus.

Mk 12:18 *S*, who say there is no resurrection,

salvation—deliverance from the guilt and power of sin. By his death and resurrection, Jesus brings salvation to people who believe in him.

Ps 27:1 The LORD is my light and my *s*
Lk 2:30 For my eyes have seen your *s*,
Ac 4:12 *S* is found in no one else,
2Co 7:10 brings repentance that leads to *s*
Php 2:12 to work out your *s* with fear
Heb 2:3 escape if we ignore so great a *s*?

Samaritan—a person who lived in or came from Samaria. Because the Samaritans were only partly Jewish and worshiped God differently from the Jews, Jews from Judea and Galilee hated the Samaritans. They would go out of their way to travel around Samaria (Lk 10:30–37).

Samson — an Israelite judge who was known for his great strength. He was betrayed by Delilah but in the end was used by God to punish the Philistines (Jdg 16).

Samuel — often called the last of Israel's judges and the first of Israel's prophets (see also Heb 11:32). His birth was earnestly prayed for by his mother Hannah (1Sa 1:10–18), and when he was old enough, she brought him to the temple and he was dedicated to the Lord (1Sa 1:21–28). There he was raised by Eli (1Sa 2:11; 18—26) and was called to be a prophet (1Sa 3).

sanctify (sanctification) — to make holy; sanctification is the ongoing work of the Holy Spirit in the hearts of believers.

Ro 15:16 to God, *s* by the Holy Spirit.
1Th 5:23 *s* you through and through.
2Th 2:13 through the *s* work of the Spirit

sanctuary — a place where God is worshiped; a holy place.

Ps 150:1 Praise God in his *s*;

Sanhedrin — the ruling council of the Jews in Jesus' time. It was made up of seventy men, and the leader was the high priest. The Sanhedrin could decide whether someone was innocent or guilty of breaking a Jewish law, but it could not put anyone to death without the permission of the Roman governor.

Mk 14:55 the whole *S* were looking for evidence

Sarah — the wife of Abraham and mother of Isaac; first called Sarai (Ge 11:29–31). God promised her that, though she had been barren throughout her life, she would give birth to a son in her old age (Ge 17:15–21; 18:10–15).

Satan — the devil; the leader of the fallen spirits; the most powerful enemy of God and humans.

Mk 4:15 *S* comes and takes away the word
2Co 11:14 for *S* himself masquerades
Rev 12:9 serpent called the devil, or *S*,

satisfy — 1. to please, to make happy; 2. to fulfill a condition.

Ps 103:5 who *s* your desires with good things

satrap — the governor of a province in ancient Persia.

Saul — 1. the first king of Israel (1Sa 9—10). He was anointed by Samuel but was later rejected by God because of disobedience; David was chosen to be his successor; 2. see Paul.

saved — 1. (*v.*) rescued from danger; 2. (*n.*) people who acknowledge that by Jesus' death they have been rescued from the punishment of death that their sins deserve.

Ro 10:13 on the name of the Lord will be *s*."
Eph 2:8 For it is by grace you have been *s*,

Savior — a name for Jesus that means he saves his people from sin.

Lk 1:47 and my spirit rejoices in God my *S*,
1Ti 4:10 who is the *S* of all people,
1Jn 4:14 Son to be the *S* of the world.

scarlet — the color bright red.

scepter — a rod or stick held by a king or queen as a sign of royal power and authority.

Ge 49:10 The *s* will not depart from Judah,

scoff — to mock or sneer at.

Ps 2:4 the Lord *s* at them.

scorn — to despise, to reject with anger or contempt.

Ps 69:20 *S* has broken my heart

scorpion — a spider-like animal with a poisonous stinger at the end of its tail.

scoundrel — a mean, worthless person; a villain.

Pr 16:27 A *s* plots evil,

scourge — to whip.

2Ch 10:11 My father *s* you with whips;

scribe — a person with the important task of copying letters, books and legal papers.

Scripture — all or part of the Bible. When the Bible uses this word it means the Old Testament, since the New Testament had not yet been written. Today we call the Old and New Testaments the Bible or Scripture.

Jn 10:35 and *S* cannot be set aside
2Ti 3:16 All *S* is God-breathed
2Pe 1:20 that no prophecy of *S* came about

scroll — a book made of a long piece of leather or paper that was rolled around a stick at both ends.

Jos 18:9 They wrote its description on a *s*,

seal — 1. a tool with a design raised on it or cut into it; 2. the mark made by pressing this tool onto wax, paper or other soft material. A seal was used to close a letter or legal paper or to prove the authority of the paper.

2Co 1:22 set his *s* of ownership on us,
Rev 5:2 "Who is worthy to break the *s*

sect — a group of people who hold one or more beliefs in common; especially, a small religious group that has separated from a larger group.

seer — a prophet; a person who, with God's help, can see what will happen in the future.

1Sa 9:19 "I am the *s*," Samuel replied.

self-control — the ability to control one's own actions and feelings.

Gal 5:23 gentleness and *s*.
2Pe 1:6 and to knowledge, *s*; and to *s*,

selfish — centered on oneself; not interested in others.

Php 2:3 Do nothing out of *s* ambition

Sennacherib — an Assyrian king who raided Judah during the time of Hezekiah.

sexual immorality — using sex in ways God says are wrong.

1Co 6:13 body, however, is not meant for *s*,
1Th 4:3 that you should avoid *s*;

shame — a painful emotion caused by an awareness of guilt or shortcoming.

Pr 19:26 a child who brings *s* and disgrace.
1Co 15:34 I say this to your *s*.

sheep — the animal most often mentioned in Scripture, probably because it was the animal most often raised in Bible times; used for meat, for cloth, and for religious sacrifice.

Isa 53:6 We all, like *s*, have gone astray,

shekel — a specific weight of silver, used as money.

Shem — one of the three sons of Noah (Ge 5:32). He, along with his brother Japheth, covered his father when he was naked (Ge 9:21–31). Abraham was one of his descendants (Ge 11:10–32).

shepherd—someone who takes care of a flock of sheep. It is often used in the Bible as a figure of speech for anyone who cares for a group of people.

Ps 23:1	The LORD is my *s*, I lack nothing.
Jer 31:10	will watch over his flock like a *s*.'
Jn 10:11	The good *s* lays down his life
Ac 20:28	Be *s* of the church of God,

shield—a piece of defensive armor, usually carried on the arm; often a figure of speech in the Bible used to describe God's protection of his people.

Ps 7:10	My *s* is God Most High,

shrine—a dwelling for a god.

sickle—a tool with a long, curved blade and a short handle, used for cutting grain.

siege—see besiege.

signet—a ring with a design on it. The design was stamped in wax to seal a letter or legal paper. Signet rings were usually worn by people in authority.

Silas—a member of the church in Jerusalem; he traveled with Paul.

Simon—1. see Peter; 2. one of the twelve apostles; also called the Zealot (Mt 10:4; Ac 1:13); 3. a sorcerer in Samaria who had great influence on the Samaritan people during the early days of the church; he was severely rebuked by Peter (Ac 8:9–24) for attempting to buy the power of the Holy Spirit.

sin—1. (*v.*) to break the law of God; 2. (*n.*) the act of not doing what God wants.

Nu 32:23	be sure that your *s* will find you
Ps 51:2	and cleanse me from my *s*.
Ps 119:11	that I might not *s* against you.
Isa 1:18	"Though your *s* are like scarlet,
Mt 1:21	he will save his people from their *s*."
Lk 11:4	Forgive us our *s*,
Jn 1:29	who takes away the *s* of the world!
Ro 3:23	for all have *s* and fall short
Ro 6:23	For the wages of *s* is death,
2Co 5:21	God made him who had no *s* to be *s*
1Jn 1:9	If we confess our *s*, he is faithful

Sinai, Mount—the mountain where Moses received the Ten Commandments (Ex 19—20).

sinner—a person who breaks the law of God.

Ps 1:1	or stand in the way that *s* take
Mt 9:13	come to call the righteous, but *s*."
Lk 15:7	in heaven over one *s* who repents
Lk 18:13	'God, have mercy on me, a *s*.'
Ro 5:8	While we were still *s*, Christ died

slander—1. (*v.*) saying untrue things about another person in order to hurt him or her; 2. (*n.*) false charges or misrepresentations about another person.

Lev 19:16	" 'Do not go about spreading *s*
Titus 3:2	to *s* no one, to be peaceable

slaughter—1. the butchering of livestock for food; 2. the killing of great numbers of human beings, as in a battle.

slave—1. a person who is owned by another; 2. a person who is dominated or controlled by an outside force.

Ro 7:14	I am unspiritual, sold as a *s* to sin.
Gal 3:28	*s* nor free, male nor female,

slay, slain—to kill violently or in great numbers.

sluggard—a lazy person.

Pr 19:24	A *s* buries his hand in the dish;

slumber—to sleep.

snare—a trap; something risky that tempts or endangers a person.

snatch—to grab suddenly, often without permission or right.

Sodom and Gomorrah—the two cities destroyed by God because the people were so wicked.

Ge 19:24	rained down burning sulfur on *S*

Solomon—the son of David and Bathsheba (2Sa 12:24). He became king of Israel after David died (1Ki 1). He asked God for wisdom and was given it (1Ki 3), and he built the temple (1Ki 5—7). His many foreign wives turned his heart away from God (1Ki 11:1–13).

son—a male descendant.

Pr 10:1	A wise *s* brings joy to his father,
Joel 2:28	Your *s* and daughters will prophesy,
2Co 6:18	you will be my *s* and daughters,
Heb 2:10	many *s* and daughters to glory,
1Jn 4:9	only *S* into the world that we might

Son of Man—a title Jesus used for himself to show his humanity as distinct from his divinity. It was also a reference to the Messiah prophesied about in Daniel 7:13.

Mt 20:18	and the *S* will be delivered
Mk 14:62	you will see the *S* sitting
Lk 19:10	For the *S* came to seek
Jn 3:14	so the *S* must be lifted up,

sorcery—the use of magic and supernatural powers that are evil; witchcraft.

Dt 18:10	practices divination or *s*,

soul—the spiritual part of a person; the part of a person that does not die.

Dt 6:5	with all your *s* and with all your
Ps 23:3	he refreshes my *s*.
Mt 10:28	kill the body but cannot kill the *s*.
Mt 11:29	and you will find rest for your *s*.
Mt 16:26	yet forfeit their *s*? Or what can
Mt 22:37	with all your *s* and with all your

sovereign—having authority over everything; often used in Scripture as a descriptive title for God, "Sovereign LORD."

sow—to plant seeds. In Jesus' time seeds were sown by scattering them by hand over the ground.

Job 4:8	and those who *s* trouble reap it.
Mk 4:3	A farmer went out to *s* his seed.
Gal 6:7	A man reaps what he *s*.

spear—a weapon with a long handle and a sharp point, usually thrown.

spirit—1. the part of a person that is not the body; the soul; 2. a being who does not have a body; 3. (cap.) see Holy Spirit.

Ps 31:5	Into your hands I commit my *s*;
Eze 36:26	you a new heart and put a new *s*

Mt 5:3 "Blessed are the poor in *s*,
Mt 26:41 *s* is willing, but the flesh is weak."
1Jn 4:1 Dear friends, do not believe every *s*,

splendor—something magnificent or splendid.

spoils—booty or plunder taken from an enemy in war.

springs—a source of water coming up from the ground.
Dt 8:7 streams, and deep *s* gushing out
Rev 7:17 lead them to *s* of living water.

staff—a stick used to lean on; a rod used by a shepherd.
Ps 23:4 your rod and your *s*,

starry hosts—the stars and other heavenly bodies.
2Ki 21:3 He bowed down to all the *s*

statutes—established rules or laws.
Ps 19:7 *s* of the LORD are trustworthy,

steadfast—settled; not changing or wavering.
Ps 51:10 and renew a *s* spirit within me.

steal—to rob; to take what belongs to someone else.
Ex 20:15 "You shall not *s*.
Eph 4:28 must *s* no longer,

stench—a terrible smell.

Stephen—one of the first seven men to serve the Jerusalem church (Ac 6:5); he became the first Christian martyr (Ac 7:60).

stiff-necked—stubborn.
Ac 7:51 "You *s* people!

stone—to kill or to try to kill someone by throwing rocks or stones.

strength—power; forcefulness.
Ex 15:2 "The LORD is my *s* and my defense;
Dt 6:5 all your soul and with all your *s*.
Ps 46:1 God is our refuge and *s*,
Isa 40:31 will renew their *s*.
Php 4:13 through him who gives me *s*.

strife—bitter and sometimes violent conflict.
Pr 30:33 stirring up anger produces *s*."

stronghold—a fortified place; a place of security.
1Sa 24:22 David and his men went up to the *s*.
Ps 27:1 The LORD is the *s* of my life

subdue—to bring under control; to conquer.
Ps 81:14 how quickly I would *s* their enemies

submission—humbleness; obedience.
1Co 14:34 but must be in *s*, as the law says.
1Ti 2:11 learn in quietness and full *s*.

submit—to willingly yield to another.
Pr 3:6 in all your ways *s* to him,
Eph 5:21 *S* to one another out of reverence
Col 3:18 Wives, *s* yourselves to your husbands,
Jas 4:7 *S* yourselves, then, to God.

succeed—1. to turn out well; 2. to follow another as heir or successor of a title or rank.

suffer—to bear or endure something painful.
Mk 8:31 the Son of Man must *s* many things
Lk 24:26 the Messiah have to *s* these things
1Co 12:26 If one part *s*, every part *s* with it;

suffering—the experience of enduring pain.
Isa 53:3 of *s*, and familiar with *pain*.
Ac 5:41 worthy of *s* disgrace for the Name.
Ro 8:17 share in his *s* in order that we may
2Ti 1:8 Rather, join with me in *s* for the gospel,

summon—to issue a call to come together; to send for.
Isa 43:1 I have *s* you by name; you are mine.

sustain—to give support; to help; to comfort.
Ps 18:35 and your right hand *s* me;
Ps 146:9 and *s* the fatherless and the widow,

swear—to promise forcefully or earnestly.
1Sa 30:15 "*S* to me before God that you will

swindler—someone who cheats another person out of money or other possessions.
1Co 6:10 nor *s* will inherit the kingdom

sword—a weapon with a long blade for cutting or thrusting.

symbol—an object or action that stands for or suggests something else. The cross is a symbol of Jesus' death.

synagogue—the Jewish place of worship and religious teaching.
Lk 4:16 the Sabbath day he went into the *s*,
Ac 17:2 his custom, Paul went into the *s*,

T

tabernacle—the tent used by the Israelites for meeting with God; the place where God chose to show his presence. The tabernacle was made by God's command and according to his plans. It is described in detail in Exodus 26. Also call the tent of meeting.
Ex 40:34 the glory of the LORD filled the *t*.

talent—a large amount of silver or gold, worth very much money.
Ex 25:39 A *t* of pure gold is to be used

tax—money a government requires its citizens to pay.
Mt 22:19 the coin used for paying the *t*."

teach—to instruct; to help someone learn.
Ex 33:13 *t* me your ways so I may know you
Ps 90:12 *T* us to number our days,
Lk 11:1 said to him, "Lord, *t* us to pray,
Jn 14:26 will *t* you all things and will remind

tempest—a violent storm.

temple—1. the place where the Jewish people worshiped and sacrificed in Jerusalem; the first temple was built by King Solomon as a house for God; 2. any place of worship. In this sense, the human body is referred to as a temple (1Co 6:19).
1Ki 8:27 How much less this *t* I have built!
Ac 17:24 not live in *t* built by human hands.
2Co 6:16 For we are the *t* of the living God.

tempt (temptation)—trying to get someone to do wrong.
Mt 4:1 the wilderness to be *t* by the devil.
1Co 10:13 No *t* has overtaken you except

tenant—one who rents land or a house from a landlord.

testimony—a statement made by a witness to prove that something is true.
Lk 18:20 not give false *t*, honor your father

tetrarch—a ruler over one-fourth of a kingdom.

Thaddaeus—one of the twelve apostles (Mk 3:18); son of James and probably also known as Judas (Lk 6:16; Ac 1:13).

thanks—the expression of gratitude.

1Ch 16:34	Give *t* to the LORD, for
Ps 100:4	give *t* to him and praise his name.
1Co 15:57	*t* be to God! He gives us the victory
2Co 9:15	*T* be to God for his indescribable
1Th 5:18	give *t* in all circumstances;

thanksgiving—recognizing and thanking the one who has provided a gift.

Ps 100:4	Enter his gates with *t*
Php 4:6	by prayer and petition, with *t*,

Thomas—one of the twelve apostles (Lk 6:15; Ac 1:13); at first he doubted Jesus' resurrection, but when he saw Jesus, he believed (Jn 20:24–28).

thrive—to grow vigorously.

Thummim—see Urim.

threshing floor—the place where grain was trampled by oxen or beaten with a stick to separate it from the stalk.

Ru 3:6	So she went down to the *t*

Timothy—fellow-traveler and official representative of the apostle Paul. He joined Paul on his second missionary journey (Ac 16—20), and at one point in this journey Paul sent him to minister to the church at Corinth (1Co 4:17; 16:10). He was the leader of the church at Ephesus (1Ti 1:3) and a co-writer with Paul (1Th 1:1; 2Th 1:1; Phm 1).

tithe—the giving to God of one-tenth of what one earns.

Lev 27:30	" 'A *t* of everything from the land,
Mal 3:10	the whole *t* into the storehouse,

Titus—a Gentile co-worker with Paul (Gal 2:1–3; 2Ti 4:10). Paul sent him to Corinth to help solve some of the problems there (2Co 2:13; 7—8; 12:18).

toil—1. (*n.*) strenuous and tiring work; 2. (*v.*) to work long and hard.

Ecc 3:9	What do workers gain from their *t?*

tomb—a burial place. In Bible times, a tomb was often either a cave or a cavity dug into a stone cliff, with a large stone rolled in front to close it.

Mt 27:65	make the *t* as secure as you know
Lk 24:2	the stone rolled away from the *t*,
Jn 11:17	been in the *t* for four days.

tongue—1. the organ of speech in the mouth; 2. a language.

Ps 39:1	and keep my *t* from sin;
Ac 2:4	and began to speak in other *t*
Php 2:11	every *t* acknowledge that Jesus
Jas 1:26	do not keep a tight rein on their *t*

torment—extreme pain or anguish; agony.

2Co 12:7	a messenger of Satan, to *t* me.

tradition—the handing down of information and beliefs from one generation to another.

Mt 15:2	break the *t* of the elders?

trample—to walk heavily causing injury or damage.

Ps 60:12	he will *t* down our enemies.

transfigure—to change the appearance of; to make bright and glorious.

Mt 17:2	There he was *t* before them.

transgression—sin; disobeying the law of God.

Ps 32:1	whose *t* are forgiven,
Isa 53:5	But he was pierced for our *t*,
Eph 2:1	you were dead in your *t* and sins,

treacherous—untrustworthy, unreliable, faithless.

tread—to step or walk on or over.

Job 24:11	they *t* the winepresses,

treasure—1. (*n.*) wealth that is stored up or hidden away; 2. (*v.*) to hold or keep something precious, something of value; to cherish.

Mt 6:21	your *t* is, there your heart will be also.

treaty—an agreement between two people or groups or nations.

Ex 34:12	Be careful not to make a *t*

trespass—sin; wrongdoing.

Ro 5:17	For if, by the *t* of the one man,

tribe—a social group made up of a particular branch of a family.

tribute—payment by one ruler or nation to another as an act of submission or in order to guarantee protection.

Isa 16:1	Send lambs as *t* to the ruler

triumph—a victory; a notable success.

Pr 28:12	the righteous *t*, there is great elation;

true—certain; exactly right.

Ps 119:160	All your words are *t*;
Jn 17:3	the only *t* God, and Jesus Christ,
Ro 3:4	Let God be *t*, and every human
Php 4:8	whatever is *t*, whatever is noble,

trust—firm belief or faith in another.

Ps 37:3	*T* in the LORD and do good;
Pr 3:5	*T* in the LORD with all your heart
Isa 26:3	because they *t* in you.
Isa 30:15	in quietness and *t* is your strength,
1Co 4:2	been given a *t* must prove faithful.

trustworthy—deserving of trust; reliable.

Ps 19:7	The statutes of the LORD are *t*,
1Ti 1:15	Here is a *t* saying that deserves full

truth—that which conforms to the facts.

Ps 145:18	to all who call on him in *t*.
Zec 8:16	are to do: Speak the *t* to each other,
Jn 8:32	know the *t*, and the *t*
Jn 14:6	I am the way and the *t* and the life.
Ro 1:25	They exchanged the *t* about God
1Co 13:6	in evil but rejoices with the *t*.
Eph 4:15	Instead, speaking the *t* in love,
Heb 10:26	received the knowledge of the *t*,
1Jn 1:6	we lie and do not live out the *t*.
1Jn 1:8	deceive ourselves and the *t* is not

tunic—a long shirt worn by men in Bible times.

Ezr 9:3	When I heard this, I tore my *t*

turban—a head-covering made by winding a cloth around the head.

U

unbelief—doubt.

Mk 9:24 help me overcome my *u!*"

unbeliever—one who does not believe in Jesus.

2Co 6:14 Do not be yoked together with *u*.

unclean—morally or spiritually impure; unclean animals were those which the Israelites were not allowed to sacrifice or to eat.

unity—being one.

Ps 133:1 God's people live together in *u!*
Col 3:14 them all together in perfect *u*.

unleavened bread—bread made without yeast. It is usually flat, like a pancake or cracker.

Ex 12:17 "Celebrate the Festival of *U*,

uphold—to give support to.

Ps 37:17 the LORD *u* the righteous.

upright—honest; doing what is right and good.

Urim and Thummim—objects that were placed on the vest of the high priest; used to determine God's will for the nation of Israel.

utter—to pronounce, to speak.

Ps 78:2 I will *u* hidden things,
Jer 15:19 if you *u* worthy, not worthless, words,

utterly—completely, totally.

V

vain—worthless; unsuccessful; foolish. "In vain" means without success or result.

valiant—courageous.

vast—very great in size or amount; huge.

vault—the atmosphere or sky as seen from the earth.

Ge 1:8 God called the *v* "sky."

vengeance—hurt or punishment done to another person who has done something wrong against another.

Isa 34:8 For the LORD has a day of *v*,

vigor—strength and health in the body and its growth.

Job 20:11 The youthful *v* that fills his bones

vile—disgusting, evil.

Rev 22:11 let the *v* person continue to be *v*;

vindicate—to defend; to provide justice for; to set free.

Ps 135:4 For the LORD will *v* his people

violate—1. to rape; 2. to make something unholy; 3. to fail to obey.

viper—1. a venomous snake; 2. a treacherous or vicious person.

virgin—a woman or girl who has never had sexual intercourse.

Isa 7:14 The *v* will conceive
Mt 1:23 "The *v* will conceive

vision—a dream from God.

Nu 12:6 reveal myself to them in *v*,
Joel 2:28 your young men will see *v*.
Ac 26:19 disobedient to the *v* from heaven.

vow—a solemn promise made before God or to God.

Jdg 11:30 Jephthah made a *v* to the LORD:
Ps 116:14 I will fulfill my *v* to the LORD

W

wages—payment received for work completed.

Ro 6:23 For the *w* of sin is death,

wail—to cry loudly.

walk—to follow a certain course.

Ps 1:1 who does not *w* in step
Isa 2:5 let us *w* in the light of the LORD.
Mic 6:8 and to *w* humbly with your God.
2Jn 6 his command is that you *w* in love.

wander—to move about without a fixed course.

Nu 32:13 he made them *w* in the wilderness
Jas 5:19 if one of you should *w* from the truth

warn—to give notice beforehand of danger or evil.

warrior—a soldier.

Isa 9:3 as *w* rejoice when dividing

wash—to clean.

Ps 51:7 *w* me, and I will be whiter
Ac 22:16 be baptized and *w* your sins away,

watch—to be on the lookout for someone or something.

Jer 31:10 will *w* over his flock like a shepherd.'
Mt 26:41 "*W* and pray so that you will not fall

way—the means of getting somewhere; the path.

2Sa 22:31 "As for God, his *w* is perfect:
Ps 1:1 or stand in the *w* that sinners
Ps 37:5 Commit your *w* to the LORD;
Isa 53:6 each of us has turned to our own *w*;
Jn 14:6 "I am the *w* and the truth
1Co 12:31 will show you the most excellent *w*.

wean—to help a child or animal begin to eat solid food rather than his or her mother's milk.

weapon—an object used for fighting.

weary—1. tired; 2. having one's patience or tolerance exhausted.

Dt 25:18 When you were *w* and worn out,
Zec 11:8 and I grew *w* of them

weep, wept—to cry.

Jn 11:35 Jesus *w*.

welcome—1. to greet a person pleasantly; 2. to make a person feel at home.

Jdg 19:20 "You are *w* at my house,"

wholehearted—sincere; devoted without holding anything back.

wicked—sinful.

Ps 1:1 walk in step with the *w*
Isa 55:7 Let the *w* forsake their ways

widow—a woman whose husband has died.

will—desire; seeking God's will means looking for what God wants to be done.

Ps 143:10 Teach me to do your *w*,
Isa 53:10 Yet it was the LORD's *w*

Mt 6:10 your *w* be done,
Mt 26:39 Yet not as I *w*, but as you *w*."
Ro 12:2 and approve what God's *w* is
Eph 5:17 understand what the Lord's *w* is.
1Jn 5:14 we ask anything according to his *w*,
Rev 4:11 and by your *w* they were created

winepress — a vat or tub in which the juice of grapes is pressed out. Used in the Bible as a symbol for the anger of God against wickedness.

Rev 14:19 into the great *w* of God's wrath.

wisdom — the understanding that comes from God.

Lk 2:52 And Jesus grew in *w* and stature,
Jas 1:5 of you lacks *w*, you should ask God,

witchcraft — practices using evil spirits, magic, or sorcery.

Mic 5:12 I will destroy your *w*

wither — to dry or shrivel up, usually from a lack of moisture.

witness — one who personally sees an event take place.

Ac 22:15 You will be his *w* to all people

woe — great misery; distress.

Isa 6:5 "*W* to me!" I cried.
Lk 11:42 "*W* to you Pharisees, because you

womb — the organ within a woman's body where a child grows before birth.

Lk 1:44 the baby in my *w* leaped for joy.

word — 1. the means of expressing oneself through language; 2. the Bible, as God's written message to people; 3. (cap.) Jesus is the Word sent from God because his life on earth told the message of God.

Jn 1:14 The *W* became flesh and made his
Heb 4:12 For the *w* of God is alive

work — 1. (*n.*) employment; duty; 2. (*v.*) to bring about; to try to achieve a goal.

Ex 23:12 "Six days do your *w*,
Jn 9:4 we must do the *w* of him who sent
Php 2:12 continue to *w* out your salvation
2Ti 3:17 equipped for every good *w*.

world — 1. the earth and those who live in it; 2. the secular, as opposed to the spiritual or religious.

Mt 5:14 "You are the light of the *w*.
Jn 1:29 who takes away the sin of the *w*!
Jn 3:16 so loved the *w* that he gave his one
Jn 8:12 he said, "I am the light of the *w*.
Ro 12:2 Do not conform to the pattern of this *w*,
1Jn 2:15 not love the *w* or anything in the *w*.

worldly — loving the things of the world more than the things of God.

Tit 2:12 to ungodliness and *w* passions,

worry — to feel anxious and uneasy.

Mt 6:25 I tell you, do not *w* about your life,

worship — 1. (*v.*) to give praise, honor and respect to God; 2. (*n.*) reverence given to God.

Ps 95:6 Come, let us bow down in *w*,
Jn 4:24 his worshipers must *w* in the Spirit

worthy — having value; honorable; deserving.

1Ch 16:25 For great is the LORD and most *w*
Eph 4:1 to live a life *w* of the calling you
Rev 5:2 "Who is *w* to break the seals

wrath — great anger; the strong anger of God.

Pr 15:1 A gentle answer turns away *w*,
Ro 5:9 saved from God's *w* through him!

X

Xerxes — king of Persia; he made Esther, a young Jewess, his queen (Est 2:15–18).

Y

yearn — to long for; to want very much.

yeast — the ingredient that makes dough rise; sometimes a figure of speech for the influence someone has over others.

Mt 16:6 guard against the *y* of the Pharisees
Gal 5:9 little *y* works through the whole

yield — 1. to submit; 2. to grow or produce fruit.

Ps 67:6 The land *y* its harvest;
Isa 48:11 I will not *y* my glory to another.

yoke — 1. (*v.*) to join together; 2. (*n.*) a wooden bar that goes over the necks of two animals, usually oxen. The yoke holds the animals together as they pull an object, such as a plow or a cart.

Mt 11:29 Take my *y* upon you and learn
2Co 6:14 Do not be *y* together

youth — the time when a person is young.

Ecc 12:1 Creator in the days of your *y*,

Z

Zacchaeus — a tax collector who climbed a tree in order to see Jesus.

zeal — eagerness; strong desire.

Ro 12:11 Never be lacking in *z*,

Zealot — a member of the Jewish group that wanted to fight against and overthrow the Roman government.

Zechariah — a prophet and priest who returned to Jerusalem from the Babylonian captivity; he encouraged the Jews to rebuild the temple (Ezr 5:1; 6:14; Zec 1:1).

Zerubbabel — a descendant of David (1Ch 3:19); he led the return of the Jews from the Babylonian captivity (Ezr 1—3; Ne 7:7; Hag 1—2; Zec 4).

Zion — 1. the hill on which the city of Jerusalem first stood; David's royal palace and the temple were both built on Mount Zion; 2. the entire city of Jerusalem.

Jer 50:5 They will ask the way to *Z*
Ro 11:26 "The deliverer will come from *Z*;